1869 — Francis Galton, Charles Darwin's cousin, publishes *Hereditary Genius*, in which he claims that intelligence is inherited. In **1876** he coins the expression "nature and nurture" to correspond with "heredity and environment."

1874 — Carl Wernicke, a German neurologist and psychiatrist, shows that damage to a specific area in the left temporal lobe (now called Wernicke's area) disrupts ability to comprehend or produce spoken or written language.

1878 — G. Stanley Hall receives from Harvard University's Department of Philosophy the first U.S. Ph.D. degree based on psychological research.

1879 — Wilhelm Wundt establishes at the University of Leipzig, Germany, the first psychology laboratory, which becomes a mecca for psychology students from all over the world.

1883 — G. Stanley Hall, student of Wilhelm Wundt, establishes the first formal U.S. psychology laboratory at Johns Hopkins University.

1885 — Hermann Ebbinghaus publishes *On Memory*, summarizing his extensive research on learning and memory, including the "forgetting curve."

1886 — Joseph Jastrow receives from Johns Hopkins University the first Ph.D. degree in psychology awarded by a Department of Psychology in the United States.

1889 — Alfred Binet and Henri Beaunis establish the first psychology laboratory in France at the Sorbonne, and the first International Congress of Psychology meets in Paris.

1890 — William James, Harvard University philosopher and psychologist, publishes *The Principles of Psychology*, describing psychology as "the science of mental life."

1891 — James Mark Baldwin establishes the first psychology laboratory in the British Commonwealth at the University of Toronto.

1892 — G. Stanley Hall spearheads the founding of the American Psychological Association (APA) and becomes its first president.

1893 — Mary Whiton Calkins and Christine Ladd-Franklin are the first women elected to membership in the APA.

1894 — Margaret Floy Washburn is the first woman to receive a Ph.D. degree in psychology (Cornell University).

Harvard University denies Mary Whiton Calkins admission to doctoral candidacy because of her gender, despite Hugo Münsterberg's claim that she was the best student he had ever had there.

1896 — John Dewey publishes "The Reflex Arc Concept in Psychology," helping to formalize the school of psychology called functionalism.

1898 — In *Animal Intelligence*, Edward L. Thorndike, Columbia University, describes h s learning experiments with cats in "puzzle boxes." In **1905**, he proposes the "law of effect."

1900 — Sigmund Freud publishes *The Interpretation of Dreams*, his major theoretical work on psychoanalysis.

1933 — Inez Beverly Prosser becomes the first African-American woman to receive a doctoral degree in psychology from a U.S. institution (Ph.D., University of Cincinnati).

1935 — Christiana Morgan and Henry Murray introduce the Thematic Apperception Test to elicit fantasies from people undergoing psychoanalysis.

1936 — Egas Moniz, a Portuguese physician, publishes work on the first frontal lobotomies performed on humans.

1938 — B. F. Skinner publishes *The Behavior of Organisms*, which describes operant conditioning of animals.

In *Primary Mental Abilities*, Louis L. Thurstone proposes seven such abilities.

Ugo Cerletti and Lucio Bini use electroshock treatment with a human patient.

1939 — David Wechsler publishes the Wechsler–Bellevue intelligence test, forerunner of the Wechsler Intelligence Scale for Children (WISC) and the Wechsler Adult Intelligence Scale (WAIS).

Mamie Phipps Clark receives a master's degree from Howard University. In collaboration with Kenneth B. Clark, she later extends her thesis, "The Development of Consciousness of Self in Negro Preschool Children," providing joint research cited in the U.S. Supreme Court's **1954** decision to end racial segregation in public schools.

Edward Alexander Bott helps found the Canadian Psychological Association. He becomes its first president in **1940**.

World War II provides many opportunities for psychologists to enhance the popularity and influence of psychology, especially in applied areas.

1943 — Psychologist Starke Hathaway and physician J. Charnley McKinley publish the Minnesota Multiphasic Personality Inventory (MMPI).

1945 — Karen Horney, who criticized Freud's theory of female sexual development, publishes *Our Inner Conflicts*.

1946 — Benjamin Spock's first edition of *The Commonsense Book of Baby and Child Care* appears; the book will influence child raising in North America for several decades.

1948 — Alfred Kinsey and his colleagues publish *Sexual Behavior in the Human Male*, and they publish *Sexual Behavior in the Human Female* in **1953**.

B. F. Skinner's novel, *Walden Two*, describes a Utopian community based on positive reinforcement, which becomes a clarion call for applying psychological principles in everyday living, especially communal living.

Ernest R. Hilgard publishes *Theories of Learning*, which was required reading for several generations of psychology students in North America.

1949 — Raymond B. Cattell publishes the Sixteen Personality Factor Questionnaire (16PF).

Continued on inside back cover

PSYCHOLOGY

ELEVENTH EDITION

IN MODULES

PSYCHOLOGY

ELEVENTH EDITION

IN MODULES

DAVID G. MYERS

Hope College
Holland, Michigan

C. NATHAN DEWALL

University of Kentucky
Lexington, Kentucky

WORTH
PUBLISHERS

A Macmillan Education Imprint
New York

Publisher, Psychology and Sociology: Rachel Losh
Executive Marketing Manager: Katherine Nurre
Development Editors: Christine Brune, Nancy Fleming,
    Trish Morgan
Assistant Editor: Nadina Persaud
Editorial Assistant: Katie Pachnos
Director of Editing, Design, and Media Production:
    Tracey Kuehn
Media Editor: Lauren Samuelson
Supplements Editor: Betty Probert
Photo Editor: Robin Fadool
Photo Researcher: Lisa Passmore
Art Director: Diana Blume
Cover Designer and Interior Designer: Charles Yuen
Layout Designer: Lee Ann McKevitt
Managing Editor: Lisa Kinne
Project Editor: Robert Errera
Art Manager: Matthew McAdams
Illustrations: TSI Graphics, Keith Kasnot, Todd Buck
Production Manager: Sarah Segal
Composition: TSI Graphics
Printing and Binding: RR Donnelley

Library of Congress Control Number: 2014957352

ISBN-13: 978-1-4641-6752-2
ISBN-10: 1-4641-6752-4

David Myers' royalties from the sale of this book are
assigned to the David and Carol Myers Foundation, which
exists to receive and distribute funds to other charitable
organizations.

Worth Publishers
41 Madison Avenue
New York, NY 10010
www.macmillanhighered.com

For Danielle Baker, in celebration of your becoming part of our family

To Charles K. DeWall,
tireless educator, delightful dad, and consummate artist

ABOUT THE AUTHORS

David Myers received his psychology Ph.D. from the University of Iowa. He has spent his career at Hope College in Michigan, where he has taught dozens of introductory psychology sections. Hope College students have invited him to be their commencement speaker and voted him "outstanding professor."

His research and writings have been recognized by the Gordon Allport Intergroup Relations Prize, by a 2010 Honored Scientist award from the Federation of Associations in Behavioral & Brain Sciences, by a 2010 Award for Service on Behalf of Personality and Social Psychology, by a 2013 Presidential Citation from APA Division 2, and by three honorary doctorates.

With support from National Science Foundation grants, Myers' scientific articles have appeared in three dozen scientific periodicals, including *Science, American Scientist, Psychological Science,* and the *American Psychologist.* In addition to his scholarly writing and his textbooks for introductory and social psychology, he also digests psychological science for the general public. His writings have appeared in four dozen magazines, from *Today's Education* to *Scientific American.* He also has authored five general audience books, including *The Pursuit of Happiness* and *Intuition: Its Powers and Perils.*

David Myers has chaired his city's Human Relations Commission, helped found a thriving assistance center for families in poverty, and spoken to hundreds of college and community groups. Drawing on his experience, he also has written articles and a book (*A Quiet World*) about hearing loss, and he is advocating a transformation in American assistive listening technology (see www.hearingloop.org). For his leadership, he received an American Academy of Audiology Presidential Award in 2011, and the Hearing Loss Association of America Walter T. Ridder Award in 2012.

He bikes to work year-round and plays regular pickup basketball. David and Carol Myers have raised two sons and a daughter, and have one granddaughter.

Brian Connors Manke

Nathan DeWall is professor of psychology and director of the Social Psychology Lab at the University of Kentucky. He received his bachelor's degree from St. Olaf College, a master's degree in social science from the University of Chicago, and a master's degree and Ph.D. in social psychology from Florida State University. DeWall received the 2011 College of Arts and Sciences Outstanding Teaching Award, which recognizes excellence in undergraduate and graduate teaching. In 2011, the Association for Psychological Science identified DeWall as a "Rising Star" for "making significant contributions to the field of psychological science."

DeWall conducts research on close relationships, self-control, and aggression. With funding from the National Institutes of Health and the National Science Foundation, he has published over 140 scientific articles and chapters. DeWall's research awards include the SAGE Young Scholars Award from the Foundation for Personality and Social Psychology, the Young Investigator Award from the International Society for Research on Aggression, and the Early Career Award from the International Society for Self and Identity. His research has been covered by numerous media outlets, including *Good Morning America, Wall Street Journal, Newsweek, Atlantic Monthly, New York Times, Los Angeles Times, Harvard Business Review, USA Today,* and National Public Radio. DeWall blogs for *Psychology Today.* He has lectured nationally and internationally, including in Hong Kong, China, the Netherlands, England, Greece, Hungary, Sweden, and Australia.

Nathan is happily married to Alice DeWall. He enjoys playing with his two golden retrievers, Finnegan and Atticus. In his spare time, he writes novels, watches sports, and runs and runs and runs—including in 2014 two 50-kilometer ultramarathons, one 60-kilometer ultramarathon, a 75-mile run through the Mojave Desert, and three 100-mile ultramarathons.

BRIEF CONTENTS

CONTENTS

THE STORY OF PSYCHOLOGY   1

THINKING CRITICALLY WITH PSYCHOLOGICAL SCIENCE   19

THE BIOLOGY OF MIND   51

CONSCIOUSNESS AND THE TWO-TRACK MIND 91

NATURE, NURTURE, AND HUMAN DIVERSITY 133

DEVELOPING THROUGH THE LIFE SPAN 177

PREFACE

In the thirty-two years since Worth Publishers invited me (David Myers) to write this book, so much has changed in the world, in psychology, and within the covers of this book across its eleven editions. With this edition, I continue as lead author while beginning a gradual, decade-long process of welcoming a successor author, the award-winning teacher-scholar-writer, Nathan DeWall.

Yet across these three decades of *Psychology* there has also been a stability of purpose: *to merge rigorous science with a broad human perspective that engages both mind and heart.* We aim to offer a state-of-the-art introduction to psychological science that speaks to students' needs and interests. We aspire to help students understand and appreciate the wonders of their everyday lives. And we seek to convey the inquisitive spirit with which psychologists *do* psychology.

We are enthusiastic about psychology and its applicability to our lives. Psychological science has the potential to expand our minds and enlarge our hearts. By studying and applying its tools, ideas, and insights, we can supplement our intuition with critical thinking, restrain our judgmentalism with compassion, and replace our illusions with understanding. By the time students complete this guided tour of psychology, they will also, we hope, have a deeper understanding of our moods and memories, about the reach of our unconscious, about how we flourish and struggle, about how we perceive our physical and social worlds, and about how our biology and culture in turn shape us. (See **TABLES** 1 and 2.)

Believing with Thoreau that "anything living is easily and naturally expressed in popular language," we seek to communicate psychology's scholarship with crisp narrative and

▼ TABLE 1
Evolutionary Psychology and Behavior Genetics

In addition to the coverage found in Module 12, the **evolutionary perspective** is covered on the following pages:		In addition to the coverage found in Module 11, **behavior genetics** is covered on the following pages:	
Aging, p. 215	Hunger and taste preference, p. 428	Abuse, intergenerational transmission of, p. 311	Obesity and weight control, pp. 430–432
Anxiety disorders, pp. 626–627	Instincts, p. 420	Adaptability, p. 74	Parenting styles, p. 202
Biological predispositions:	Intelligence, pp. 386, 393, 409–413	Aggression, pp. 545–550	Perception, pp. 254–255
in learning, pp. 300–306	Language, pp. 370–371, 373–375	intergenerational transmission of, p. 311	Personality, p. lv
in operant conditioning, pp. 303–306	Love, pp. 220–221	Autism spectrum disorder, pp. 192–195	Personality traits, pp. 587–594
Brainstem, pp. 69–70	Math and spatial ability, p. 410	Behavior genetics perspective, p. 10	Psychological disorders and:
Consciousness, p. 92	Mating preferences, pp. 148–149	Biological perspective, pp. 52–53	ADHD, p. 615
Darwin, Charles, pp. 6, 144–146	Menopause, p. 214	Brain plasticity, pp. 81–82	anxiety disorders, pp. 625–627
Depression and light exposure therapy, p. 678	Need to belong, p. 448	Continuity and stages, p. 178	biopsychosocial approach, pp. 612–613
Emotion, effects of facial expressions and, p. 474	Obesity, p. 430	Deprivation of attachment, pp. 199–201	bipolar disorder and depressive disorders, pp. 631–634
Emotional expression, pp. 472–473	Overconfidence, pp. 360–361	Depth perception, p. 249	depression, pp. 628, 631–634
Evolutionary perspective, defined, pp. 9–10	Perceptual adaptation, pp. 254–255	Development, pp. 181–182	personality disorders, pp. 649–651
Exercise, pp. 507–508	Puberty, onset of, p. 204	Drives and incentives, pp. 420–421	posttraumatic stress disorder, pp. 623–627
Fear, pp. 362–363	Sensation, p. 230	Drug dependence, p. 128	schizophrenia, pp. 641–645
Feature detection, pp. 244–245	Sensory adaptation, pp. 234–235	Drug use, pp. 127–128	violent behavior, p. 616
Hearing, p. 256	Sexual orientation, pp. 443–446	Eating disorders, p. 652	Reward deficiency syndrome, p. 73
	Sexuality, pp. 147–150, 433	Epigenetics, pp. 182, 612, 634, 644	Romantic love, p. 220
	Sleep, p. 105	Happiness, pp. 479–481, 483–486	Sexual disorders, pp. 435–436
	Smell, pp. 266–267	Hunger and taste preference, pp. 428–429	Sexual orientation, pp. 443–446
	Taste, p. 266	Intelligence:	Sexuality, pp. 433–434
		Down syndrome, p. 403	Sleep patterns, p. 104
		genetic and environmental influences, pp. 405–415	Smell, pp. 266–268
		Learning, pp. 300–303	Stress, personality, and illness, pp. 496–499
		Motor development, p. 185	benefits of exercise, pp. 507–509
		Nature-nurture, p. 6	Traits, pp. 394, 409
		twins, p. 7	

▼ TABLE 2
Neuroscience

In addition to the coverage found in Modules 5–7, **neuroscience** can be found on the following pages:

Aggression, pp. 545–546

Aging: physical exercise and the brain, p. 216

Animal language, pp. 367–368

Antisocial personality disorder, pp. 649–651

Arousal, pp. 437–438

Attention deficit/hyperactivity disorder (ADHD) and the brain, p. 615

Autism spectrum disorder, pp. 192–195

Automatic prejudice: amygdala, pp. 539–540

Biofeedback, p. 509

Biopsychosocial approach, p. 9
 aggression, p. 547
 aging, pp. 224, 339
 dementia and Alzheimer's, pp. 218–219, 333
 development, pp. 170–172
 dreams, pp. 112–116
 drug use, pp. 128–129
 emotion, pp. 204–205, 331–332, 461–467, 470–471
 learning, pp. 300–305
 pain, pp. 262–263
 personality, pp. 594–596
 psychological disorders, p. 612
 sleep, pp. 100–105
 therapeutic lifestyle change, pp. 688–689

Brain development:
 adolescence, pp. 204–205
 experience and, pp. 152–153
 infancy and childhood, pp. 184–185
 sexual differentiation in utero, p. 165

Brain stimulation therapies, pp. 685–687

Cognitive neuroscience, pp. 5, 93

Drug dependence, pp. 128–129

Dual-processing, pp. 93–94

Emotion and cognition, pp. 460–464

Fear-learning, p. 626

Fetal alcohol syndrome and brain abnormalities, p. 182

Hallucinations, pp. 124–126
 and near-death experiences, p. 124
 and schizophrenia, pp. 640, 642
 and sleep, p. 102

Hormones and:
 abuse, pp. 200–201
 appetite, pp. 426–427
 development, p. 165
  in adolescents, pp. 167, 140–141, 205–205
  of sexual characteristics, pp. 167, 204–205
 emotion, pp. 464–465
 gender, pp. 165–167
 sex, pp. 165–167, 433–434
 sexual behavior, pp. 433–434
 stress, pp. 464–465, 491–494, 506
 weight control, pp. 426–427

Hunger, pp. 424–427

Insight, pp. 357–358

Intelligence, pp. 386–388
 creativity, pp. 365–367
 twins, pp. 406–407

Language, pp. 370, 376–377
 and deafness, pp. 374–376
 and thinking in images, pp. 381–382

Light-exposure therapy: brain scans, p. 678

Meditation, pp. 509–511

Memory:
 emotional memories, pp. 331–332
 explicit memories, pp. 329–330
 implicit memories, p. 330
 physical storage of, pp. 328–333
 and sleep, p. 106
 and synaptic changes, pp. 332–333

Mirror neurons, pp. 307–309

Neuroscience perspective, defined, pp. 9–10

Neurotransmitters and:
 anxiety disorders, pp. 626, 682–683
 biomedical therapy:
  depression, pp. 633–634
  ECT, pp. 685–686
  schizophrenia, pp. 642, 682
 child abuse, p. 200
 cognitive-behavioral therapy: obsessive-compulsive disorder, pp. 669–670
 depression, pp. 633–634, 683–684
 drugs, pp. 119, 122–123
 exercise, p. 509
 narcolepsy, pp. 110–111
 schizophrenia, pp. 642–645

Observational learning and brain imaging, p. 306

Optimum arousal: brain mechanisms for rewards, pp. 421–422

Orgasm, pp. 435, 438

Pain, pp. 261–263
 experienced and imagined pain, p. 309
 phantom limb pain, p. 262
 virtual reality, p. 264

Parallel vs. serial processing, pp. 246–247

Perception:
 brain damage and, p. 246
 color vision, pp. 243–244
 feature detection, pp. 244–245
 transduction, p. 230
 visual information processing, pp. 241–246

Perceptual organization, pp. 247–250

Personality and brain-imaging, p. 587

Posttraumatic stress disorder (PTSD) and the limbic system, pp. 623–624

Psychosurgery: lobotomy, pp. 687–688

Schizophrenia and brain abnormalities, pp. 642–645

Sensation:
 body position and movement, p. 269
 deafness, pp. 257–259
 hearing, pp. 256–259
 sensory adaptation, pp. 234–235
 smell, pp. 266–268
 taste, p. 266
 touch, p. 261
 vision, pp. 239–255

Sexual orientation, pp. 443–445

Sleep:
 cognitive development and, pp. 114–115
 memory and, p. 106
 recuperation during, p. 105

Smell and emotion, pp. 268–269

Unconscious mind, pp. 580–581

vivid storytelling. We hope to tell psychology's story in a way that is warmly personal as well as rigorously scientific. We love to reflect on connections between psychology and other realms, such as literature, philosophy, history, sports, religion, politics, and popular culture. And we love to provoke thought, to play with words, and to laugh. For his pioneering 1890 *Principles of Psychology*, William James sought "humor and pathos." And so do we.

We are grateful for the privilege of assisting with the teaching of this mind-expanding discipline to so many students, in so many countries, through so many different languages. To be entrusted with discerning and communicating psychology's insights is both an exciting honor and a great responsibility.

Creating this book is a team sport. Like so many human achievements, it reflects a collective intelligence. Woodrow Wilson spoke for us: "I not only use all the brains I have, but all I can borrow." The thousands of instructors and millions of students across the globe who have taught or studied with this book have contributed immensely to its development. Much of this contribution has occurred spontaneously, through correspondence and conversations. And we look forward to continuing feedback as we strive, over future editions, to create an ever better book and teaching package.

New Co-Author

For this new edition I [DM] welcome my new co-author, University of Kentucky professor Nathan DeWall. (For more information and videos that introduce Nathan DeWall and our collaboration, see www.macmillanhighered.com/dewallvideos.) Nathan is not only one of psychology's "rising stars" (as the Association for Psychological Science rightly said in 2011), he also is an award-winning teacher and someone who shares my passion for writing—and for communicating psychological science through writing. Although I continue as lead author, Nathan's fresh insights and contributions are already enriching this book, especially for this eleventh edition, through his leading the revision of Modules 11–13, 37–41, 46–48, and 49–53. But my fingerprints are also on those modules' revisions, even as his are on the other modules. With support from our wonderful editors, this is a team project. In addition to our work together on the textbook, Nathan and I enjoy co-authoring the monthly Teaching Current Directions in Psychological Science column in the *APS Observer*, and we blog at www.talkpsych.com, where we share exciting new findings, everyday applications, and observations on all things psychology.

www.TalkPsych.com

Why a Modular Book?

This 56-module text has been a wish come true for me [DM]. It breaks out of the box by restructuring the material into a buffet of (a) short, digestible chapters (called modules) that (b) can be selected and assigned in any order.

Have we not all heard the familiar student complaint: "The chapters are too long!" A text's typical 30- to 50-page chapters cannot be read in a single sitting before the eyes grow weary and the mind wanders. So, why not parse the material into readable units? Ask your students whether they would prefer a 700-page book to be organized as fourteen 50-page chapters or as fifty 14-page chapters. You may be surprised at their overwhelming support for shorter chapters. Indeed, students digest material better when they process it in smaller chunks—as spaced rather than massed practice.

I have equally often heard from instructors bemoaning the fact that they "just can't get to everything" in the book. Sometimes instructors want to cover certain sections in a traditional, long chapter but not others. For example, in the typical Consciousness chapter, someone may want to cover Sleep and Dreams but not Drugs. In *Psychology, Eleventh Edition in Modules*, instructors could easily choose to cover Module 9, Sleep and Dreams, but not Module 10, Drugs and Consciousness.

How Is This Different From *Psychology*, Eleventh Edition?

The primary differences between this book and *Psychology*, eleventh edition, are organization and module independence.

Organization

This book really IS *Psychology*, eleventh edition—just in a different format. So, this modular version contains all the updated research and innovative new coverage from *Psychology*, eleventh edition. This version offers the same content from *Psychology*, eleventh edition's 16 chapters parsed instead into 56 modules.

The Modules Are Independent

Each module in this book is self-standing rather than dependent upon the others for understanding. Cross-references to other parts of the book have been replaced with brief explanations. In some cases, illustrations or key terms are repeated to avoid possible confusion. No assumptions are made about what students have read prior to each module. This independence gives instructors ultimate flexibility in deciding which modules to use, and in what order. Connections among psychology's subfields and findings are still made—they are just made in a way that does not assume knowledge of other parts of the book.

What Else Is New Since *Psychology, Tenth Edition in Modules?*

This eleventh edition is the most carefully reworked and extensively updated of all the revisions to date. This new edition features improvements to the organization and presentation, especially to our system of supporting student learning and remembering. And we offer the exciting new **How Would You Know?** feature in LaunchPad, engaging students in the scientific process.

"How Would You Know?" Research Activities

These online activities engage students in the scientific process, showing them how psychological research begins with a question, and how key decision points can alter the meaning and value of a psychological study. In a fun, interactive environment, students learn about important aspects of research design and interpretation. I [ND] have enjoyed taking the lead on this project and sharing my research experience and enthusiasm with students.

EXPANDED Study System Follows Best Practices From Learning and Memory Research

The improved learning system harnesses the *testing effect*, which documents the benefits of actively retrieving information through self-testing (**FIGURE 1**). Thus, each module offers several Retrieval Practice questions interspersed throughout. Creating these *desirable difficulties* for students along the way optimizes the testing effect, as does *immediate feedback* (via an inverted answer beneath each question).

In addition, each section of text begins with numbered questions that establish *learning objectives* and direct student reading. A *Review* section follows each module, providing students an opportunity to practice rehearsing what they've just learned. The Review offers self-testing through repeated learning objective questions (with answers for checking in the Complete Module Reviews Appendix), along with a page-referenced list of key terms. At the end of each unit of modules, new *Test Yourself* questions in multiple formats promote optimal retention.

▼ FIGURE 1
How to learn and remember
For a 5-minute animated guide
to more effective study, visit
www.tinyurl.com/HowToRemember.

Over 1200 New Research Citations

Our ongoing scrutiny of dozens of scientific periodicals and science news sources, enhanced by commissioned reviews and countless e-mails from instructors and students, enables integrating our field's most important, thought-provoking, and

▼ TABLE 3
Positive Psychology

Coverage of **positive psychology** topics can be found in the following modules:

Topic	Module
Altruism/Compassion	16, 29, 45, 47, 55
Coping	41
Courage	43, 45
Creativity	27, 29, 47
Emotional intelligence	29, 45
Empathy	15, 23, 38, 43, 54, 55
Flow	Appendix A
Gratitude	41, 45
Happiness/Life Satisfaction	17, 33, 36, 39, 41
Humility	2
Humor	41, 43
Justice	43
Leadership	45, 47, 48, Appendix A
Love	12, 15, 17, 33, 36, 39, 45, 47, 54
Morality	14, 16
Optimism	41, 48
Personal control	41
Resilience	17, 39, 43, 56
Self-discipline	16, 36, 47
Self-efficacy	39, 48
Self-esteem	33, 36, 39, 48
Spirituality	41, 43
Toughness (grit)	29, 36
Wisdom	8, 15, 27, 45, 47

▼ FIGURE 2
Sample LaunchPad callout from Module 5.

student-relevant new discoveries. Part of the pleasure that sustains this work is learning something new every day! See p. xxxvi for a list of significant **Content Changes** to this edition.

Reorganized Modules

In addition to the new study aids and updated coverage, we've introduced the following organizational changes:

- Module 1, What Is Psychology?, now has a clearer organization and greater emphasis on modern approaches, including Cross-Cultural and Gender Psychology, and new coverage of Positive Psychology (see also **TABLE 3**).

- Module 3, Research Strategies, now offers greater emphasis on Psychology's Research Ethics.

- Hypnosis is now covered in the Pain discussion in Module 20, The Nonvisual Senses (moved from the Consciousness modules).

- The Motivation and Work modules have been re-titled What Drives Us: Hunger, Sex, Friendship, and Achievement, with the Psychology at Work discussion moving to its own Appendix.

- The Social Psychology modules now follow the Personality modules.

Dedicated Versions of Next-Generation Media

This eleventh edition is accompanied by the new **LaunchPad,** with carefully crafted, prebuilt assignments, **LearningCurve** formative assessment activities, **How Would You Know?** activities, and **Assess Your Strengths** projects. This system also incorporates the full range of Worth's psychology media products. (For details, see p. xxvi and www.macmillanhighered.com/launchpad/myers11einmodules.)

For this new edition, you will see that we've offered callouts from the text pages to especially pertinent, helpful resources from LaunchPad. (See **FIGURE 2** for a sample.)

🅐 LaunchPad For an animated explanation of this process, visit LaunchPad's *Concept Practice: Action Potentials.*

What Continues?
Eight Guiding Principles

Despite all the exciting changes, this new edition retains its predecessors' voice, as well as much of the content and organization. It also retains the goals—the guiding principles—that have animated the previous ten editions:

Facilitating the Learning Experience

1. **To teach critical thinking** By presenting research as intellectual detective work, we illustrate an inquiring, analytical mind-set. Whether students are studying development, cognition, or social behavior, they will become involved in, and see

the rewards of, critical reasoning. Moreover, they will discover how an empirical approach can help them evaluate competing ideas and claims for highly publicized phenomena—ranging from ESP and alternative therapies to group differences in intelligence and repressed and recovered memories.

2. **To integrate principles and applications** Throughout—by means of anecdotes, case histories, and the posing of hypothetical situations—we relate the findings of basic research to their applications and implications. Where psychology can illuminate pressing human issues—be they racism and sexism, health and happiness, or violence and war—we have not hesitated to shine its light.

3. **To reinforce learning at every step** Everyday examples and rhetorical questions encourage students to process the material actively. Concepts presented earlier are frequently applied, and reinforced. For instance, in Module 2, students learn that much of our information processing occurs outside of our conscious awareness. Ensuing modules drive home this concept. Numbered Learning Objective Questions at the beginning of main sections, Retrieval Practice self-tests throughout each module, Reviews at the end of each module, a marginal glossary, and Test Yourself questions at the end of each unit of modules help students learn and retain important concepts and terminology.

Demonstrating the Science of Psychology

4. **To exemplify the process of inquiry** We strive to show students not just the outcome of research, but how the research process works. Throughout, the book tries to excite the reader's curiosity. It invites readers to imagine themselves as participants in classic experiments. Several modules introduce research stories as mysteries that progressively unravel as one clue after another falls into place. Our new "How Would You Know?" activities in LaunchPad encourage students to think about research questions and how they may be studied effectively.

5. **To be as up to date as possible** Few things dampen students' interest as quickly as the sense that they are reading stale news. While retaining psychology's classic studies and concepts, we also present the discipline's most important recent developments. In this edition, 867 references are dated 2012–2014. Likewise, new photos and everyday examples are drawn from today's world.

6. **To put facts in the service of concepts** Our intention is not to fill students' intellectual file drawers with facts, but to reveal psychology's major concepts—to teach students how to think, and to offer psychological ideas worth thinking about. In each module, we place emphasis on those concepts we hope students will carry with them long after they complete the course. Always, we try to follow Albert Einstein's purported dictum that "everything should be made as simple as possible, but not simpler." Learning Objective Questions and Retrieval Practice questions throughout each module help students learn and retain the key concepts.

Promoting Big Ideas and Broadened Horizons

7. **To enhance comprehension by providing continuity** We often present concepts with a significant issue or theme that links subtopics, forming a thread that ties ideas together. For Learning, we convey the idea that bold thinkers can serve as intellectual pioneers. For Thinking and Language, we raise the issue of human rationality and irrationality. In Psychological Disorders, we convey empathy for, and understanding of, troubled lives. Other threads, such as cognitive neuroscience, dual processing, and cultural and gender diversity, weave throughout the whole book, and students hear a consistent voice.

8. **To convey respect for human unity and diversity** Throughout the book, readers will see evidence of our human kinship—our shared biological heritage, our common mechanisms of seeing and learning, hungering and feeling, loving and hating. They will also better understand the dimensions of our diversity—our individual diversity in development and aptitudes, temperament and personality, and disorder and health; and our cultural diversity in attitudes and expressive styles, child raising and care for the elderly, and life priorities.

Continually Improving Cultural and Gender Diversity Coverage

Discussion of the relevance of cultural and gender diversity begins on the first page and continues throughout the text.

This edition presents an even more thoroughly cross-cultural perspective on psychology (**TABLE 4**)—reflected in research findings and in text and photo examples. Cross-cultural and gender psychology are now given greater visibility with enhanced coverage

▼ TABLE 4
Culture and Multicultural Experience

Coverage of culture and multicultural experience can be found on the following pages:

Aggression, pp. 546–550
  and video games, pp. 312-313, 549
Aging population, pp. 214–215
AIDS, p. 495
Anger, pp. 477–478
Animal research ethics, p. 40
Attraction: love and marriage,
  pp. 557–558
Attractiveness, pp. 147–149,
  551–552, 554–555
Attribution: political effects of, p. 519
Behavioral effects of culture,
  pp. 7, 141
Body ideal, p. 652
Body image, p. 652
Categorization, p. 356
Conformity, p. 527
Corporal punishment practices,
  pp. 295–296
Culture:
  context effects, p. 237
  definition, pp. 155–156
  variation over time, pp. 156–157
Cultural norms, pp. 156, 171–172
Culture and the self, pp. 157–160
Culture shock, p. 156
Deaf culture, pp. 81, 85, 372–375
Development:
  adolescence, pp. 203–204
  attachment, pp. 199–200
  child raising, pp. 160–161
  cognitive development, p. 192
  moral development, pp. 206–208
  parenting styles, p. 202
  social development, pp. 197–199

Drug use, pp. 128–129
Emotion:
  emotion-detecting ability,
    pp. 468–469
  expressing, pp. 468–475
Enemy perceptions, pp. 563–564
Fear, p. 363
Flow, p. A-1
Fundamental attribution error,
  pp. 518–519
Gender:
  cultural norms, p. 161, 167–168
  roles, pp. 167–168
  social power, pp. 162–163
Grief, expressing, p. 225
Happiness, pp. 480, 482, 484–486
Hindsight bias, pp. 20–21
History of psychology, pp. 2–9
Homosexuality, views on, p. 440
Human diversity/kinship, pp. 40,
  155–161
Identity: forming social, pp. 209–210
Individualism/collectivism, p. 159
Intelligence, pp. 386, 410–413
  and nutrition, pp. 408–409, 412
  bias, pp. 413–414
  Down syndrome, pp. 403–404
Language, pp. 155, 371–372, 379–381
  critical periods, p. 374
  monolingual/bilingual, pp. 379–381
  universal grammar, pp. 373–374
Leaving the nest, p. 212
Life satisfaction, pp. 480, 482–486
Life span and well-being, p. 223
Management styles, p. A-13

Marriage, pp. 220–221
Memory, encoding, pp. 324–325
Menopause, p. 214
Mental illness rate, pp. 617–618
Motivating achievement, p. A-8
Motivation: hierarchy of needs,
  pp. 422–423
Need to belong, pp. 448–450
Neurotransmitters: curare, p. 59
Obesity, pp. 430–432
Observational learning: television
  and aggression, pp. 312–313
Organ donation, pp. 362–363
Pace of life, pp. 30, 156
Pain: perception of, p. 263
Parent and peer relationships,
  pp. 210–211
Participative management,
  p. A-12-A-13
Peacemaking:
  conciliation, p. 567
  contact, pp. 564–565
  cooperation, pp. 565–566
Peer influence, pp. 154–155
Personal control: democracies,
  p. 502
Power of individuals, p. 536
Prejudice, pp. 37, 41, 538–545
  "missing women," p. 540
Prejudice prototypes, p. 356
Psychological disorders:
  cultural norms, pp. 610–611
  dissociative identity disorder,
    p. 648
  eating disorders, pp. 612, 652

schizophrenia, pp. 612, 641–644
suicide, pp. 637–638
susto, p. 612
taijin-kyofusho, p. 612
Psychotherapy:
  culture and values in, p. 680
  EMDR training, p. 677
Puberty and adult independence,
  p. 212
Self-esteem, p. 485
Self-serving bias, pp. 602–603
Sex drive, p. 147
Sexual orientation, pp. 440–441
Similarities, pp. 145–146
Sleep patterns, p. 104
Social clock, p. 220
Social loafing, p. 533
Social networking, pp. 451–453
Social-cultural perspective,
  pp. 9–10
Spirituality: Israeli kibbutz
  communities, pp. 512–513
Stress:
  adjusting to a new culture, p. 490
  health consequences, pp. 490–491,
    495, 497–498
  racism and, p. 490
Taste preferences, p. 428
Teen sexuality, pp. 438–439
Testing bias, pp. 414–415
Weight control, p. 429

See also Modules 42–45: Social
Thinking, Social Influence,
Antisocial Relations, and Prosocial
Relations.

moved to Module 1. There is focused coverage of culture and the psychology of women and men in Module 13, Culture, Gender, and Other Environmental Influences, with thoroughly integrated coverage throughout the text (see **TABLE 5**). In addition, we are working to offer a world-based psychology for our worldwide student readership. We continually search the world for research findings and text and photo examples, conscious that readers may be in Sydney, Seattle, or Singapore. Although we reside in the United States, we travel abroad regularly and maintain contact with colleagues in Canada, Britain, China, and many other places; and subscribe to European periodicals. Thus, each new edition offers a broad, world-based perspective, and includes research from around the world. We are all citizens of a shrinking world, so American students, too, benefit from information and examples that internationalize their world-consciousness. And if psychology seeks to explain *human* behavior (not just American or Canadian or Australian behavior), the broader the scope of studies presented, the more accurate is our picture of this world's people. Our aim is to expose all students to the world beyond their own culture, and we continue to welcome input and suggestions from all readers.

▼ TABLE 5
The Psychology of Men and Women

Coverage of the **psychology of men and women** can be found on the following pages:

Absolute thresholds, pp. 231–232
ADHD, p. 615
Adulthood: physical changes, pp. 214–215
Aggression, pp. 545–546
 father absence, p. 548
 pornography, pp. 548–549
 rape, pp. 548–549
Alcohol:
 and addiction, p. 120
 and sexual aggression, p. 119
 use, pp. 119–120
Altruism, p. 560
Androgyny, p. 169
Antisocial personality disorder, pp. 650–651
Attraction, pp. 551–556
Autism spectrum disorder, pp. 193–194
Biological predispositions in color perceptions, pp. 302–303
Biological sex/gender, pp. 165–167
Bipolar disorder, pp. 629–630
Body image, p. 652
Color vision, p. 243
Conformity/obedience, p. 528
Dating, pp. 552–553
Depression, pp. 631–632
 learned helplessness, p. 635
Dream content, p. 112
Drug use:
 biological influences, p. 127
 psychological/social-cultural influences, pp. 128–129
Eating disorders, pp. 651–653

Emotion-detecting ability, pp. 470–471
Empty nest, p. 222
Father care, p. 198
Father presence, p. 439
Freud's views:
 evaluating, p. 579
 identification/gender identity, p. 575
 Oedipus/Electra complexes, pp. 574–575
 penis envy, pp. 576–577
Fundamental attribution error, pp. 518–519
Gender:
 and anxiety, p. 620
 and child raising, pp. 168–169
 definition, p. 161
 development, pp. 165–167
 prejudice, pp. 538–540
 "missing women," p. 540
 roles, pp. 167–171
 similarities/differences, pp. 161–164
Gendered brain, pp. 165–166, 438, 443–445
Generic pronoun "he," p. 380
Grief, p. 225
Group polarization, p. 534
Happiness, pp. 484–485
Hearing loss, pp. 257, 375
Hormones and:
 aggression, p. 546
 sexual behavior, pp. 433–434
 sexual development, pp. 165–167, 204–205
 testosterone-replacement therapy, p. 434

Intelligence, pp. 410–411
 bias, p. 413
 stereotype threat, pp. 414–415
Leadership: transformational, p. A-12
Life expectancy, pp. 214–215
Losing weight, pp. 430–432
Love, pp. 220–222, 556–558
Marriage, pp. 220–221, 505–506
Maturation, pp. 204–205
Menarche, p. 204
Menopause, p. 214
Midlife crisis, p. 220
Obesity:
 genetic factors, pp. 430–431
 health risks, p. 430
 weight discrimination, p. 429
Observational learning:
 sexually violent media, p. 312
 TV's influence, p. 311
Pain sensitivity, p. 261
Paraphilias, pp. 435–436
Pornography, pp. 437–438
Prejudice, p. 356
Psychological disorders, rates of, p. 618
PTSD: development of, pp. 623–624
Rape, p. 544
Religiosity and life expectancy, pp. 511–513
REM sleep, arousal in, p. 103
Romantic love, pp. 556–557
Savant syndrome, p. 387
Schizophrenia, p. 641

Self-injury, p. 639
Sense of smell, pp. 267–268
Sex reassignment, p. 167
Sex: definition, p. 161
Sexual abuse, p. 442
Sexual attraction, pp. 148–149, 554
Sexual dysfunctions, pp. 433–439
Sexual fantasies, p. 438
Sexual orientation, pp. 440–446
Sexuality, p. 433
 adolescent, pp. 438–439
 evolutionary explanation, pp. 147–149
 external stimuli, pp. 437–438
 imagined stimuli, p. 438
Sexualization of girls, p. 439
Sexually transmitted infections, pp. 436–437
Stereotyping, p. 236
Stress and:
 AIDS, p. 495
 depression, p. 498
 health, and sexual abuse, pp. 506–507
 heart disease, p. 497
 immune system, p. 493
 response to, p. 492
Suicide, p. 637
Teratogens: alcohol consumption, p. 182
Transgender, pp. 169–170
Women in psychology's history, pp. 3–4

Strong Critical Thinking Coverage

We love to write in a way that gets students thinking and keeps them active as they read, and we aim to introduce students to critical thinking throughout the book. Revised and more plentiful Learning Objective Questions at the beginning of text sections, and even more regular Retrieval Practice questions encourage critical reading to glean an understanding of important concepts. This eleventh edition also includes the following opportunities for students to learn or practice their critical thinking skills.

- The ***Thinking Critically With Psychological Science*** unit of modules introduces students to psychology's research methods, emphasizing the fallacies of our everyday intuition and common sense and, thus, the need for psychological science. *Critical thinking* is introduced as a key term on page 24. Module 4, Statistical Reasoning in Everyday Life, encourages students to "focus on thinking smarter by applying simple statistical principles to everyday reasoning" (pp. 36–40).

- ***"Thinking Critically About . . ." boxes*** are found throughout the book, modeling for students a critical approach to some key issues in psychology. For example, see "Thinking Critically About: Prenatal Testing to Predict Future Traits" (Module 11), or "Thinking Critically About: The Stigma of Introversion" (Module 48).

- ***Detective-style stories*** throughout the narrative get students thinking critically about psychology's key research questions. For example, in Module 52, we present the causes of schizophrenia piece by piece, showing students how researchers put the puzzle together.

- ***"Apply this"*** and ***"Think about it"*** style discussions keep students active in their study. In Module 43, for example, students take the perspective of participants in a Solomon Asch conformity experiment, and later in one of Stanley Milgram's obedience experiments. We've also asked students to join the fun by taking part in activities they can try along the way. For example, in Module 18, they try out a quick sensory adaptation activity. In Module 38, they try matching expressions to faces and test the effects of different facial expressions on themselves.

- ***Critical examinations of pop psychology*** spark interest and provide important lessons in thinking critically about everyday topics. For example, Module 22 offers an examination of ESP claims, and Module 26 examines claims of the repression of painful memories.

See **TABLE 6** for a complete list of this text's coverage of critical thinking topics and Thinking Critically About boxes.

APA Assessment Tools

In 2011, the American Psychological Association (APA) approved the **Principles for Quality Undergraduate Education in Psychology.** These broad-based principles and their associated recommendations were designed to "produce psychologically literate citizens who apply the principles of psychological science at work and at home." (See www.apa.org/education/undergrad/principles.aspx.)

APA's more specific **2013 Learning Goals and Outcomes,** from their *Guidelines for the Undergraduate Psychology Major,* Version 2.0, were designed to gauge progress in students graduating with psychology majors. (See www.apa.org/ed/precollege/about/psymajor-guidelines.pdf.) Many psychology departments use

▼ TABLE 6
Critical Thinking and Research Emphasis

Critical thinking coverage and in-depth stories of psychology's **scientific research** process, can be found on the following pages:

Thinking Critically About . . . boxes:

Handedness, p. 86

Addiction, p. 118

Prenatal Testing to Predict Future Traits, p. 143

Subliminal Persuasion, p. 233

Hypnosis and Pain Relief, p. 265

ESP—Perception Without Sensation?, pp. 272–274

Does Viewing Media Violence Trigger Violent Behavior?, pp. 312–313

Repressed or Constructed Memories of Abuse?, pp. 348–349

The Fear Factor—Why We Fear the Wrong Things, pp. 362–363

Lie Detection, pp. 466–467

The Stigma of Introversion, p. 588

ADHD—Normal High Energy or Disordered Behavior?, p. 615

Are People With Psychological Disorders Dangerous?, p. 616

Critical Examinations of Pop Psychology:

The need for psychological science, pp. 20–25

Perceiving order in random events, p. 22

Do we use only 10 percent of our brains?, p. 79

Has the concept of "addiction" been stretched too far?, p. 118

Near-death experiences, p. 124

Critiquing the evolutionary perspective, pp. 149–150

How much credit or blame do parents deserve?, pp. 153–154

Sensory restriction, p. 254

Can hypnosis be therapeutic? Alleviate pain?, p. 265

Is there extrasensory perception?, pp. 272–273

Do other species exhibit language?, pp. 377–379

Do video games teach or release violence?, p. 549

How valid is the Rorschach test?, pp. 578–579

Is Freud credible?, pp. 579–582

Is repression a myth?, p. 580

Is psychotherapy effective?, pp. 673–675

Evaluating alternative therapies, pp. 677–678

Thinking Critically With Psychological Science:

The limits of intuition and common sense, pp. 20–21

The scientific attitude, pp. 23–25

"Critical thinking" introduced as a key term, p. 24

The scientific method, pp. 26–27

Regression toward the mean, pp. 33–34

Correlation and causation, pp. 34–35

Exploring cause and effect, p. 35

Random assignment, p. 35

Independent and dependent variables, pp. 37–38

Statistical reasoning, pp. 42–48

Describing data, pp. 43–46

Making inferences, pp. 46–47

The evolutionary perspective on human sexuality, pp. 147–151

Scientific Detective Stories:

Is breast milk better than formula?, pp. 35–36

Our divided brains, pp. 82–86

Why do we sleep?, pp. 105–106

Why we dream, pp. 113–116

Twin and adoption studies, pp. 135–140

How a child's mind develops, pp. 184–192

How do we see in color?, pp. 243–244

Parallel processing, p. 246

Is hypnosis an extension of normal consciousness or an altered state?, p. 265

How are memories constructed?, pp. 321–328

How do we store memories in our brains?, pp. 328–334

Do other species exhibit language?, pp. 377–379

Aging and intelligence, pp. 399–401

Why do we feel hunger?, pp. 425–427

What determines sexual orientation?, pp. 442–446

The pursuit of happiness: Who is happy, and why?, pp. 479–487

Why—and in whom—does stress contribute to heart disease?, pp. 496–499

How and why is social support linked with health?, pp. 505–507

Why do people fail to help in emergencies?, pp. 559–560

Self-esteem versus self-serving bias, pp. 601–605

What causes depressive disorders and bipolar disorder?, pp. 631–637

Do prenatal viral infections increase the risk of schizophrenia?, pp. 642–643

Is psychotherapy effective?, pp. 673–675

---

these goals and outcomes to help establish their own benchmarks for departmental assessment purposes.

Some instructors are eager to know whether a given text for the introductory course helps students get a good start at achieving these APA benchmarks. **TABLE 7** on the next page outlines the way *Psychology, Eleventh Edition in Modules,* could help you to address the 2013 APA Learning Goals and Outcomes in your department.

In addition, an APA working group in 2013 drafted guidelines for **Strengthening the Common Core of the Introductory Psychology Course** (http://tinyurl.com/14dsdx5). Their goals are to "strike a nuanced balance providing flexibility yet guidance." The group noted that "a mature science should be able to agree upon and communicate its unifying core while embracing diversity."

MCAT Now Includes Psychology

Starting in 2015, the Medical College Admission Test (MCAT) is devoting 25 percent of its questions to the "Psychological, Social, and Biological Foundations of Behavior," with most of those questions coming from the psychological science taught in introductory psychology courses. From 1977 to 2014, the MCAT focused on biology, chemistry, and physics.

▼ TABLE 7
Psychology, Eleventh Edition in Modules, Corresponds to 2013 APA Learning Goals

Relevant Feature from *Psychology, Eleventh Edition in Modules*	APA Learning Goals				
	Knowledge Base in Psychology	Scientific Inquiry and Critical Thinking	Ethical and Social Responsibility in a Diverse World	Communication	Professional Development
Text content	•	•	•	•	•
Thinking Critically boxes	•	•	•		•
Learning Objective Questions previewing text sections	•	•		•	
Retrieval Practice self-tests throughout text	•	•		•	
Module Reviews	•	•		•	
"Try this"-style activities integrated throughout	•	•		•	•
Unit Tests	•	•		•	
Psychology at Work appendix	•	•	•		•
Subfields of Psychology appendix, with Careers in Psychology in LaunchPad	•		•		•
LaunchPad with LearningCurve formative quizzing	•	•	•	•	•
"How Would You Know?" activities in LaunchPad	•	•	•	•	•
Assess Your Strengths feature in LaunchPad	•	•	•	•	•

Hereafter, reported the *Preview Guide for MCAT 2015*, the exam will also recognize "the importance of socio-cultural and behavioral determinants of health and health outcomes." The exam's new psychology section covers the breadth of topics in this text. For example, see **TABLE 8,** which outlines the precise correlation between the topics in this text's Sensation and Perception modules and the corresponding portion of the MCAT exam. For a complete pairing of the new MCAT psychology topics with this book's contents, see www.macmillanhighered.com/Catalog/product/psychologyinmodules-eleventhedition-myers.

Next-Generation Multimedia

Psychology, Eleventh Edition in Modules boasts impressive multimedia options. For more information about any of these choices, visit Worth Publishers' online catalog at www.macmillanhighered.com/Catalog/product/psychologyinmodules-eleventhedition-myers.

LaunchPad With LearningCurve Quizzing and "How Would You Know?" Activities

LaunchPad (www.macmillanhighered.com/launchpad/myers11einmodules) offers a set of prebuilt assignments, carefully crafted by a group of instructional designers and instructors with an abundance of teaching experience as well as deep familiarity with Worth content. Each LaunchPad unit contains videos, activities, and formative assessment pieces to build student understanding for each topic, culminating with a randomized summative quiz to hold students accountable for the unit. Assign units

▼ TABLE 8
Sample MCAT Correlation With *Psychology, Eleventh Edition in Modules*

MCAT 2015	*Psychology, Eleventh Edition in Modules* Correlations	
Sample Content Category 6A: Sensing the environment		Page Number
Sensory Processing	**Sensation and Perception**	228–277
Sensation	Basic Concepts of Sensation and Perception	230–238
Thresholds	Thresholds	231–233
	Difference Thresholds	232–233
Weber's Law	*Weber's law* (key term)	232–233
Signal detection theory	*Signal detection theory* (key term)	231
Sensory adaptation	Sensory Adaptation	234–235
Sensory receptors	Transduction	230
Sensory pathways	Vision: Sensory and Perceptual Processing	239–255
	Hearing	256–260
	Pain	261–265
	Taste	266
	Smell	266–269
	Body Position and Movement	269
Types of sensory receptors	The Eye	240–242
	Color Processing	243–244
	Hearing	256–260
	Understanding Pain	261–263
	Taste	266
	Smell	266–269
	Body Position and Movement	269
	Table 20.2, Summarizing the Senses	271
Vision	Vision: Sensory and Perceptual Processing	239–255
Structure and function of the eye	The Eye	240–242
Visual processing	Information Processing in the Eye and Brain	241–247
Visual pathways in the brain	*Figure 19.6, Pathway from the eyes to the visual cortex*	242
Parallel processing	*Parallel Processing*	246
Feature detection	*Feature Detection*	244–245
Hearing	Hearing	256–260
Auditory processing	Hearing	256–260
Auditory pathways in the brain	The Ear	257–259
	Pitch (key term)	256
	Figure 20.1, The physical properties of waves	256
	Locating Sounds	260
Sensory reception by hair cells	*The Ear*	257–259
	Table 20.2, Summarizing the Senses	271
Other Senses	Touch, Taste, Smell, Body Position and Movement	260–271
Somatosensation	Touch	261–264
	Sensory Functions (of the cortex)	78
	Somatosensory cortex (key term)	78–79
	Table 20.2, Summarizing the Senses	271

(continued)

▼ TABLE 8
Sample MCAT Correlation With *Psychology, Eleventh Edition in Modules* *(continued)*

MCAT 2015	*Psychology, Eleventh Edition in Modules* Correlations	
Sample Content Category 6A: Sensing the environment		Page Number
Pain perception	Pain	261–265
	Understanding Pain	261–263
	Controlling Pain	263–265
	Hypnosis and Pain Relief	265
Taste	Taste	266
Taste buds/chemoreceptors that detect specific chemicals	Taste	266
	Table 20.2, Summarizing the Senses	271
	Figure 20.11, Taste, Smell, and Memory	268
Smell	Smell	266–269
Olfactory cells/chemoreceptors that detect specific chemicals	Smell	266–269
	Table 20.2, Summarizing the Senses	271
Pheromones	*Smell of sex-related hormones*	443, 445
Olfactory pathways in the brain	*Figure 20.11, Taste, Smell, and Memory*	268
	Sensory Interaction	269–271
Kinesthetic sense	Body Position and Movement	269
Vestibular sense	Body Position and Movement	269
Perception	Sensation and Perception	228–277
Perception	Basic Concepts of Sensation and Perception	230–238
Bottom-up/Top-down processing	Basic Concepts of Sensation and Perception: *bottom-up* and *top-down processing* (key terms)	230
Perceptual organization (e.g., depth, form, motion, constancy)	*Perceptual Organization: Form Perception, Depth Perception, Motion Perception, and Perceptual Constancy*	247–253
	Figure 19.11, Parallel processing (of motion, form, depth, color)	246
Gestalt principles	Perceptual Organization: Form Perception—*gestalt* (key term)	246–248

▼ FIGURE 3
Sample from LaunchPad

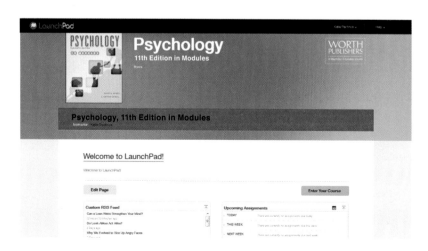

in just a few clicks, and find scores in your gradebook upon submission. Customize units as you wish, adding and dropping content to fit your course. (See **FIGURE 3**.)

- **LearningCurve** combines adaptive question selection, personalized study plans, immediate and valuable feedback, and state-of-the-art question analysis reports. Based on the latest findings from learning and memory research, LearningCurve's game-like nature keeps students engaged while helping them learn and *remember* key concepts.

- New **How Would You Know?** activities offer a fun, interactive environment for learning about important aspects of research design and interpretation. Topics include "How Would You Know If Having Children Relates to Being Happier?", "If a Cup of Coffee Can Warm Up Relationships?", and "If People Can Learn to Reduce Anxiety?" Students work through the process of setting up an effective research design and interpreting results, and see first-hand how decisions at each step affect outcomes.

- With **Assess Your Strengths** activities, students may take inventories and questionnaires developed by researchers across psychological science. These self-assessments allow students to apply psychology's principles to their own lives and experiences. After taking each self-assessment, students will find additional information about the strength being tested (for example, personal growth initiative, sleep quality, empathizing/systemizing, intrinsic/extrinsic motivation, mindfulness, self-control, and hope), as well as tips for nurturing that strength more effectively in their own lives.

- An **Interactive eBook** allows students to highlight, bookmark, and make their own notes, just as they would with a printed textbook.

- **Concept Practice,** created by award-winning multimedia author Thomas Ludwig (Hope College), helps students solidify their understanding of key concepts. With these in-depth tutorials, students explore a variety of important topics, often in an experimental context in the role of either researcher or participant. Tutorials combine animations, video, illustrations, and self-assessment.

- **PsychSim 6.0** Thoroughly re-imagined and retooled for the mobile web, the new release of PsychSim by Thomas Ludwig uses interactive videos, charts, and simulations to immerse students in the world of psychological research, placing them in the role of scientist or participant in activities that highlight important concepts, processes, and experimental approaches.

- **Video Activities** include more than 100 engaging video modules that instructors can easily assign and customize for student assessment. Videos cover classic experiments, current news footage, and cutting-edge research, all of which are sure to spark discussion and encourage critical thinking.

- **Labs** offer an interactive experience that fortifies the most important concepts and content of introductory psychology. In these activities, students participate in classic and contemporary experiments, generating real data and reviewing the broader implications of those findings. A virtual host makes this a truly interactive experience.

- The **Scientific American Newsfeed** delivers weekly articles, podcasts, and news briefs on the very latest developments in psychology from the first name in popular science journalism.

- **Deep integration** is available between LaunchPad products and Blackboard, Brightspace by D2L, Canvas, and Moodle. These deep integrations offer educators single sign-on and gradebook sync now with auto-refresh. Also, these best-in-class integrations offer deep linking to all Macmillan digital content at the unit and asset level, giving professors ultimate flexibility and customization capability within their LMS.

Faculty Support and Student Resources

- **Instructor's Resources** available in LaunchPad
- **Lecture Guides** available in LaunchPad
- **Faculty Lounge**—http://psych.facultylounge.worthpublishers.com—(see **FIGURE 4,** next page) is an online gathering place to find and share favorite teaching ideas and materials, including videos, animations, images, PowerPoint

▼ FIGURE 4
Sample from our Faculty Lounge
site (http://psych.facultylounge.
worthpublishers.com)

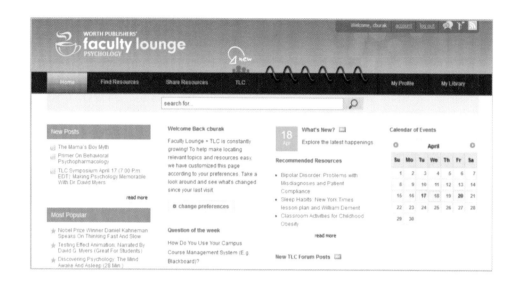

slides and lectures, news stories, articles, web links, and lecture activities. Includes publisher- as well as peer-provided resources—all faculty-reviewed for accuracy and quality.

- **Instructor's Media Guide for Introductory Psychology**

- Enhanced Course Management Solutions (including course cartridges)

- e-Book in various available formats

Video and Presentation

- **The Video Collection for Introductory Psychology** is a complete collection, all in one place, of all of our video clips. The set is accompanied by its own Faculty Guide.

- **Interactive Presentation Slides for Introductory Psychology** is an extraordinary series of PowerPoint lectures. This is a dynamic, yet easy-to-use way to engage students during classroom presentations of core psychology topics. This collection provides opportunities for discussion and interaction, and includes an unprecedented number of embedded video clips and animations.

Assessment

- **LearningCurve** quizzing

- Diploma Test Banks, downloadable from LaunchPad and on our online catalog

- Unit Quizzes in LaunchPad

- Clicker Question Presentation Slides now in PowerPoint

Print

- Study Guide

- *Pursuing Human Strengths: A Positive Psychology Guide*

- *Critical Thinking Companion,* Second Edition

- *Psychology and the Real World: Essays Illustrating Fundamental Contributions to Society,* second edition. This project of the FABBS Foundation brought together a virtual "Who's Who" of contemporary psychological scientists to describe—in clear, captivating ways—the research they have passionately pursued and what it means to the "real world." Each contribution is an original essay written for this project.

In Appreciation

If it is true that "whoever walks with the wise becomes wise" then we are wiser for all the wisdom and advice received from colleagues. Aided by thousands of consultants and reviewers over the last two decades, this has become a better, more effective, more accurate book than two authors alone (these two authors, at least) could write. All of us together are smarter than any one of us.

Our indebtedness continues to each of the teacher-scholars whose influence was acknowledged in the ten previous editions, to the innumerable researchers who have been so willing to share their time and talent to help us accurately report their research, and to the 500 instructors who took the time to offer feedback over the phone, in a survey or review, or at one of our face-to-face focus groups.

Our gratitude extends to the colleagues who contributed criticism, corrections, and creative ideas related to the content, pedagogy, and format of this new edition and its teaching package. For their expertise and encouragement, and the gifts of their time to the teaching of psychology, we thank the reviewers and consultants listed here.

Aneeq Ahmad
Henderson State University

Dana Alston
South Suburban College

Nancy Armbruster
Mott Community College

Melanie Arpaio
Sussex County Community College

Kristen Begosh
University of Delaware

Barney Beins
Ithaca College

Susanne Biehle
DePauw University

Mark Brewer
Tacoma Community College

Lauren Brown
Mott Community College

Carolyn Burns
Washtenaw Community College

David Bush
Villanova University

Allison Butler
Bryant University

Shawn Charlton
University of Central Arkansas

Joy Crawford
Green River Community College

Pamela Danker
Blackburn College

Cheryl DeLeon
Purdue University North Central

Casey Dexter
Berry College

Mary Dolan
California State University, San Bernardino

Victor Duarte
North Idaho College

Robert DuBois
Waukesha County Technical College

Guadalupe Espinoza
California State University, Fullerton

Kristin Flora
Franklin College

Anastasia Ford
University of Florida

Alisha Francis
Northwest Missouri State University

Amber Garcia
The College of Wooster

Parastoo Ghazi
Suffolk University

Kimberly Glackin
Metropolitan Community College

Ethan Gologor
Medgar Evers College - The City University of New York

Nicholas Greco
Columbia College - Lake County

Donnell Griffin
Davidson County Community College

Regan A. R. Gurung
University of Wisconsin - Green Bay

Robert Hoff
Mercyhurst University

Mia Holland
Bridgewater State College

Amy Holmes
Davidson County Community College

Lynn Ingram
University of North Carolina, Wilmington

Alisha Janowsky
University of Central Florida

Katherine Judge
Cleveland State University

Tracy Juliao
University of Michigan, Flint

Georgia Klamon-Miller
Northeastern University

Kristina Klassen
North Idaho College

Reza Kormi-Nouri
Örebro University, Sweden

Frederick Kosinski, Jr.
Andrews University

Kenneth Leising
Texas Christian University

Fabio Leite
The Ohio State University

Stine Linden-Andersen
Bishop's University

Mark Robert Ludorf
Stephen F. Austin State University

Mark Mach
Dodge City Community College

Constance Manos-Andrea
Inver Hills Community College

Patsy McCall
Angelo State University

Megan McIlreavy
Coastal Carolina University

John McNeeley
Daytona State College

Antoinette Miller
Clayton State University

Deborah Moore
Central New Mexico Community College

Robin Morgan
Indiana University Southeast

Brenda Mueller
Otero Junior College

Morrie Mullins
Xavier University

Sara Neeves
Davidson County Community College

Marion Perlmutter
University of Michigan

Kathleen Peters
Eastern Florida State College

Mark Rittman
Cuyahoga Community College

Rebecca Roberts
Franklin College

Jeff Rudski
Muhlenberg College

Beth Schwartz
Randolph College

Rachel Schwartz
Valparaiso University

Zachary Shipstead
Arizona State University

Emily Stark
Minnesota State University, Mankato

Michael Stroud
Merrimack College

Jennifer Sumner
University of California, San Diego

Casey Trainor
Augustana College

Eugenia Valentine
Delgado Community College

Catherine Wehlburg
Texas Christian University

Nancie Wilson
Southwestern Community College

Linda Woolf
Webster University

Ivan Wu
Michigan State University

Robert Zimmerman
DePaul University

We were pleased to be supported by a 2012/2013 Content Advisory Board, which helped guide the development of this new edition of *Psychology, Eleventh Edition in Modules*, as well as our other introductory psychology titles. For their helpful input and support, we thank

Barbara Angleberger, *Frederick Community College*

Chip (Charles) Barker, *Olympic College*

Mimi Dumville, *Raritan Valley Community College*

Paula Frioli-Peters, *Truckee Meadows Community College*

Deborah Garfin, *Georgia State University*

Karla Gingerich, *Colorado State University*

Toni Henderson, *Langara College*

Bernadette Jacobs, *Santa Fe Community College*

Mary Livingston, *Louisiana Tech University*

Molly Lynch, *Northern Virginia Community College*

Shelly Metz, *Central New Mexico Community College*

Jake Musgrove, *Broward College - Central Campus*

Robin Musselman, *Lehigh Carbon Community College*

Dana Narter, *The University of Arizona*

Lee Osterhout, *University of Washington*

Nicholas Schmitt, *Heartland Community College*

Christine Shea-Hunt, *Kirkwood Community College*

Brenda Shook, *National University*

Starlette Sinclair, *Columbus State University*

David Williams, *Spartanburg Community College*

Melissa (Liz) Wright, *Northwest Vista College*

We also involved students in a survey to determine level of difficulty of key concepts. We are grateful to the 277 students from the following schools who participated:

Brevard Community College

Community College of Baltimore County

Florida International University

Millsaps College

Salt Lake Community College

And we appreciate the helpful guidance offered by the dozens of instructors who reviewed our new "How Would You Know?" feature in LaunchPad. (See www.macmillanhighered.com/launchpad/myers11einmodules for details.)

At Worth Publishers a host of people played key roles in creating this eleventh edition.

Although the information gathering is never ending, the formal planning began as the author-publisher team gathered for a two-day retreat. This happy and creative gathering included John Brink, Thomas Ludwig, Richard Straub, Nathan, and Dave from the author team, along with assistants Kathryn Brownson and Sara Neevel. We were joined by Worth Publishers executives Tom Scotty, Joan Feinberg, Craig Bleyer, Doug Bolton, Catherine Woods, Kevin Feyen, and Elizabeth Widdicombe; editors Christine Brune, Nancy Fleming, Tracey Kuehn, Betty Probert, Trish Morgan, and Dora Figueiredo; sales and marketing colleagues Kate Nurre, Carlise Stembridge, Tom Kling, Lindsay Johnson, Mike Krotine, Kelli Goldenberg, Jen Cawsey, and Janie Pierce-Bratcher; media specialists Rachel Comerford, Gayle Yamazaki, Andrea Messineo, and Pepper Williams; and special guest Jennifer Peluso (Florida Atlantic University). The input and brainstorming during this meeting of minds gave birth, among other things, to LaunchPad's new "How Would You Know?" activities and the text's improved and expanded system of study aids.

Publishers Kevin Feyen and Rachel Losh have been valued team leaders, thanks to their dedication, creativity, and sensitivity. Kevin, now, Digital Product Development, has supported us in so many ways, including helping to envision the new interactive LaunchPad. Rachel, Worth's Publisher for Psychology and Sociology, has overseen, encouraged, and guided our author-editor team. Catherine Woods, Vice President, Editing, Design, and Media, helped construct and execute the plan for this text and its supplements. Lauren Samuelson helped envision our new "How Would You Know?" activities and expertly directed all the details of their production. Lauren and Nadina Persaud coordinated production of the huge media and print supplements package for this edition. Betty Probert efficiently edited and produced the supplements and, in the process, also helped fine-tune the whole book. Nadina and Katie Pachnos also provided invaluable support in commissioning and organizing the multitude of reviews, sending information to professors, and handling numerous other daily tasks related to the book's development and production. Lee McKevitt did a splendid job of laying out each page. Robin Fadool and Lisa Passmore worked together to locate the myriad photos.

Tracey Kuehn, Director of Editing, Design, and Media Production, displayed tireless tenacity, commitment, and impressive organization in leading Worth's gifted artistic production team and coordinating editorial input throughout the production process. Project Editor Robert Errera and Production Manager Sarah Segal masterfully kept the book to its tight schedule, and Art Director Diana Blume skillfully directed creation of the beautiful new design and art program. Production Manager Stacey Alexander, along with Supplements Production Editor Julio Espin, did their usual excellent work of producing the supplements.

Christine Brune, chief editor for the last nine editions, is a wonder worker. She offers just the right mix of encouragement, gentle admonition, attention to detail, and passion for excellence. An author could not ask for more. Development Editor Nancy Fleming is one of those rare editors who is gifted both at "thinking big" about a module—and with a kindred spirit to our own—while also applying her sensitive, graceful, line-by-line touches. Development Editor Trish Morgan amazed us with her meticulous eye, impressive knowledge, and deft editing. And Deborah Heimann did an excellent job with the copyediting.

To achieve our goal of supporting the teaching of psychology, this teaching package not only must be authored, reviewed, edited, and produced, but also made available to teachers of psychology. For their exceptional success in doing that, our author team is grateful to Worth Publishers' professional sales and marketing team. We are especially grateful to Executive Marketing Manager Kate Nurre, Marketing Manager Lindsay Johnson, and National Psychology and Economics Consultant emeritus Tom Kling, both for their tireless efforts to inform our teaching colleagues of our efforts to assist their teaching, and for the joy of working with them.

At Hope College, the supporting team members for this edition included Kathryn Brownson, who researched countless bits of information and proofed hundreds of pages. Kathryn has become a knowledgeable and sensitive adviser on many matters, and Sara Neevel has become our high-tech manuscript developer, par excellence. At the University of Kentucky, we've been happy to welcome our sharp new assistant, Lorie Hailey, to our team.

Again, I [DM] gratefully acknowledge the editing assistance and mentoring of my writing coach, poet Jack Ridl, whose influence resides in the voice you will be hearing in the pages that follow. He, more than anyone, cultivated my delight in dancing with the language, and taught me to approach writing as a craft that shades into art. Likewise, I [ND] am grateful to my intellectual hero and mentor, Roy Baumeister, who taught me how to hone my writing and embrace the writing life.

After hearing countless dozens of people say that this book's supplements have taken their teaching to a new level, we reflect on how fortunate we are to be a part of a team in which everyone has produced on-time work marked by the highest professional standards. For their remarkable talents, their long-term dedication, and their friendship, we thank John Brink, Thomas Ludwig, and Richard Straub. With this new edition, we also welcome and thank Sue Frantz for her gift of instructors' resources.

Finally, our gratitude extends to the many students and instructors who have written to offer suggestions, or just an encouraging word. It is for them, and those about to begin their study of psychology, that we have done our best to introduce the field we love.

*   *   *

The day this book went to press was the day we started gathering information and ideas for the next edition. Your input will influence how this book continues to evolve. So, please, do share your thoughts.

Hope College
Holland, Michigan 49422-9000 USA
www.davidmyers.org

University of Kentucky
Lexington, Kentucky 40506-0044 USA
www.NathanDeWall.com

CONTENT CHANGES

Psychology, Eleventh Edition in Modules includes 1200 new research citations, an expanded study system that reflects the latest in cognitive psychology research on retention, new research activities in LaunchPad, a lightly revised unit organization, a fresh new design, and many fun new photos and cartoons. In addition, you will find the following significant content changes in this new eleventh edition.

The Story of Psychology

- New art richly illustrates the discussion of psychology's roots, where new subsections help organize the presentation.
- *Structuralism* and *functionalism,* are now key terms.
- Contemporary Psychology section substantially updated, with expanded coverage of *evolutionary psychology* and *behavior genetics,* cross-cultural and gender psychology, and *positive psychology.*
- Updated coverage of women in psychology.
- New art illustrates cultural diversity.
- New illustration with figure introduces the *biopsychosocial approach* more effectively.
- Updated table of current perspectives.
- Now introduces *health psychologists*; and new *forensic psychology* example and photo.
- Updated discussion on how to Improve Your Retention— And Your Grades details the *testing effect,* and how to apply it effectively to learning with this text.

Thinking Critically With Psychological Science

- Unit organization lightly modified and improved. (For example, naturalistic observation is now covered before surveys, and the section on frequently asked questions about psychological research has been reorganized, with new section on Psychology's Research Ethics.)
- *Intuition* now defined in this unit, with new illustration (as well as in Thinking and Language). New current event examples incorporated.
- New research support for *hindsight bias* in people of all ages from across the world.

- Critical thinking strategies discussion enriched with new art illustrating that the study of psychology prepares people for varied occupations.
- Improved sleep deprivation example illustrates how theories are developed through the scientific method.
- Importance of research replication given increased emphasis.
- New research with figure on Twitter message moods, and on international Facebook friendships, illustrates discussion of "big data" methods in naturalistic observation.
- New photo illustrates naturalistic observation, and new survey data examples.
- Coverage of *regression toward the mean* has moved here (from Therapy in the tenth edition).
- Includes new research examples of correlations that may seem to be simple cause and effect.
- New research explores parenting and happiness.
- Updated research for breast-feeding versus bottle-feeding experimentation example.
- New research examples of the placebo effect in athletes and others.
- Expanded discussion of psychology's research ethics, with subsections on studying and protecting participants and on values in research.
- Expanded discussion of descriptive and inferential statistics.
- New research demonstrates the dangers of statistical illiteracy.
- Updated discussion of our love of big, round numbers, but also new research on how precise numbers can sometimes seem more credible.
- Table on computing standard deviation now appears here, rather than in Appendix B as in the previous edition.

The Biology of Mind

- *Refractory period* and *all-or-none response* are now key terms.
- Improved coverage of *agonists* and *antagonists,* which are now key terms, along with improved figure.
- Sensory neurons are now identified as *afferent* (inward), and motor neurons as *efferent* (outward).

- Expanded illustration of the functional divisions of the nervous system.
- Additional research on the vast number of neurons and synapses.
- Updated research on *oxytocin's* effects on physical and social responses.
- New research on how the endocrine system enables the persistence of emotions even without conscious awareness of their cause.
- New illustration of a living human brain demonstrates neuroscientists studying the brain at work.
- Now includes information on how much energy our brain consumes in relation to its size.
- New commentary and research on the sometimes overblown claims about neuroimaging often found in the media and in advertising.
- Updated information on the massive funding of the Human Brain Project and the Human Connectome Project.
- Improved figure showing the brainstem and thalamus.
- *Hippocampus* now defined here as well as in the Memory unit.
- New research example of woman with damaged amygdala experiencing no fear, even when threatened with a gun.
- New research demonstrates the role of dopamine in pleasant experiences and memories, such as the "chills" response to a favorite piece of music.
- New photos show examples of neural prosthetics in action.
- Now discusses research funding by the U.S. Army to build a helmet that might read and transmit soldiers' thoughts.
- Coverage of the *somatosensory cortex* (previously referred to as the "sensory cortex") has been fully updated.
- Improved figure showing the visual cortex and auditory cortex.
- New research on how complex tasks integrate many parts of the brain.
- Updated research on the damage to the neurons in Phineas Gage's left frontal lobe, but also to a portion of its axons that connect the frontal lobes with the rest of the brain.
- New high-resolution diffusion spectrum image reveals brain neural networks within the two hemispheres and the corpus callosum neural bridge between them.
- New research on brain plasticity in those who cannot see or hear.

- Updated research on brain plasticity in young children.
- New research on evidence of neurogenesis discovered by the carbon-dating of neurons in the hippocampus (made possible by the release of radioactive carbon isotopes during Cold War nuclear tests).

Consciousness and the Two-Track Mind

- Expanded coverage of conscious awareness, with several new research examples.
- Research update to studies of communication in comatose patients.
- New example illustrates connection between conscious and unconscious processing.
- *Parallel processing* is now also defined in this unit (rather than only in Sensation and Perception, as in the previous edition).
- Increased coverage of the question of consciousness and free will.
- *Selective attention* discussion expanded, with updated research and new examples.
- New art illustrates *inattentional blindness* in two new examples.
- Change blindness is illustrated with new art, there is new research on change deafness, and a new photo series depicts choice blindness.
- Updates to research on sleep pattern variations.
- *Suprachiasmatic nucleus* is now a key term, identified in an improved figure.
- New research supports idea that ample sleep aids skill learning and high performance.
- Updated research on why we sleep and on the effects of sleep deprivation.
- New research on how sleep-deprived students have more conflicts in friendships and romantic relationships.
- Updated figure shows physiological effects of sleep deprivation (in the brain, immune system, and stomach, and reflected in blood pressure and weight).
- Updated table on natural sleep aids.
- New research on sleep apnea, and new photo of a CPAP machine being used for treatment.
- Research updates to What We Dream section, including cases of those unable to see or walk from birth having these abilities in their dreams.

- New research on our ability to learn to associate a particular sound with an odor while asleep.
- New art illustrates how learning is consolidated into long-term memory during sleep, supporting the cognitive development theory of why we dream.
- Added research support for increased activity in the emotion-related amygdala during emotional dreams.
- Updated table compares dream theories.
- Coverage of hypnosis now appears in a Thinking Critically box on pain control in the Sensation and Perception unit.
- Drugs and Consciousness discussion fully updated for DSM-5.
- *Substance use disorder* and *alcohol use disorder* are new key terms, and includes updated definitions, such as for *addiction* and *withdrawal.*
- New table outlines When Is Drug Use a Disorder?
- Updated Thinking Critically About box on addiction now includes discussion of DSM-5's inclusion of behavior addictions such as gambling disorder, and its proposal for further study of "Internet gaming disorder."
- New research on alcohol "intervention studies" that have lowered college students' positive expectations about alcohol and reduced their consumption.
- New illustration demonstrates tragic effects of drinking and driving.
- Updates on the lethal effects of smoking, including a life expectancy at least 10 years shorter.
- New research on smokers' relapse rates and on success of smoking cessation attempts.
- New photos illustrate the effects of a methamphetamine addiction over the course of 18 months.
- Updated research on negative health effects of Ecstasy.
- New research on the drop in IQ scores among persistent teen marijuana users.
- Updates to the Guide to Selective Psychoactive Drugs table.
- High school trends in drug use chart updated with latest data.
- New photo illustrates media models of smoking that influence teens.
- New research on the biological influences on drug use.
- Updates on the cultural, social, and cognitive influences on drug use.

Nature, Nurture, and Human Diversity

- New co-author Nathan DeWall led the revision of this unit for the eleventh edition.
- New example opens the discussion of *behavior genetics.*
- Updated research on similarities as well as variation among identical and fraternal twins.
- New research on how genes influence personality traits and even specific behaviors.
- New photos throughout the unit of identical twins, siblings, and those adopted highlight gene-environment interaction.
- Updated research on the stability of temperament, and the greater temperament similarity among identical twins.
- New key term, *molecular behavior genetics.*
- Research updates on epigenetic influences, and on epigenetic marks left by trauma.
- New Thinking Critically About box on prenatal testing to predict future traits.
- New evolutionary psychology photo example.
- New research updates An Evolutionary Explanation of Human Sexuality; new table illustrates typical male-female differences in sexual attitudes.
- New research on the *sexual overperception bias,* which may occur when men misperceive a woman's friendliness.
- New research on Experience and Brain Development shows that premature babies given skin-on-skin contact are better off even 10 years later.
- New photo illustrates cultural differences in parenting.
- New research on greater reward activation influencing risk-taking among teens when with peers.
- Updates to discussion of collectivism and individualism, including new neuroscience research on distress in others resulting in greater emotional pain to collectivists.
- Sex and gender now more clearly differentiated, with *sex* a new key term.
- *Social script* now defined here as well as in the Social Psychology unit.
- New research on gender differences in aggression, with *relational aggression* now a key term illustrated with new photo.
- New research on gender and social power, and gender and social connectedness.
- The Nature of Gender now includes coverage of adolescent sexual development (moved here from Developing Across the Life Span unit in previous edition).

- New research updates discussion of earlier puberty and average age at onset.
- New photo illustrates height differences in adolescence; includes new key term, *spermarche*.
- New coverage of variations in sexual development, with *disorder of sexual development* a new key term.
- The Nurture of Gender section updated and reorganized with subsections. How Do We Learn Gender? subsection discusses gender identity and expression, with new coverage of *transgender* and *androgynous* gender identity.
- Updated discussion of nature, nurture, and their interaction concludes the unit.

Developing Through the Life Span

- Unit headings and organization lightly modified and improved. (For example, complete coverage of the three main developmental issues now appears at the start of the unit, rather than at the ends of major chronological periods.)
- Research updates support the stability of temperament.
- Updated research on newborns' recognition of the familiar sounds of their mothers' language.
- New research on prenatal effects of mothers experiencing extreme stress.
- New research on how infants learn to walk, and discussion of research on when infants become consciously aware.
- Updated research demonstrates babies' rudimentary understanding of statistics.
- New photo shows egocentrism in action.
- Autism spectrum disorder discussion significantly revised to match DSM-5 update and with new research and a new photo.
- Expanded discussion of the value of Harlow experiments.
- New table, Dual Parenting Facts.
- New research on how an avoidant attachment style increases conflict and decreases commitment.
- Updated research on childhood trauma and its lasting effects that suggests in some cases it may boost *resilience*.
- Parenting Styles expanded with new cross-cultural research.
- Coverage of puberty has moved to the Nature, Nurture, and Human Diversity unit.
- New research with new figure on teen impulse control lagging reward seeking, which peaks in the mid-teens.

- Updated coverage of moral judgments and automatic moral responses, with new photo illustrating moral reasoning.
- Expanded discussion of moral action and the ability to delay gratification.
- New research on adolescent identity development, and on decline of self-esteem in the early to mid-teen years and rebound in late adolescence.
- Updated social networking research in peer relationship discussion, and new research on parents' and teens' shared self-disclosure on social media.
- Emerging Adulthood discussion includes updated figure on the lengthening transition to adulthood.
- Global data on life expectancy for women and men updated.
- Includes new research on childhood bullying leading to biological scars, in the discussion of *telomeres*.
- Updated research on older drivers and on speech patterns slowing with age.
- Neuroscience research on the aging brain's plasticity, evident with activity in both right and left frontal lobes in memory tasks.
- In Adulthood, the Cognitive Development section has been reorganized and expanded, with the aging and memory discussion followed by coverage of *neurocognitive disorders* and *Alzheimer's disease*, now both key terms.
- New commentary and research on "brain fitness" programs.
- New figure in Adulthood's Commitments illustrates changing ways Americans meet their partners.
- Updated figure illustrates stability of life satisfaction over the life span.
- New research, with new graph, suggests well-being relates to social time for all ages.
- Updated research on bereavement.

Sensation and Perception

- Unit introduction now notes unusual condition of "voice blindness" in addition to face blindness.
- New neuroscience research on how priming can evoke brain activity without conscious awareness.
- New coverage of the adaptation of emotion perception, with "try this" photo example.
- New illustrations demonstrate perceptual set.
- Updated research and new pair of photos illustrate context effects.

- New research on how emotions and motives color our social perceptions.
- New research on how the iris dilates or constricts even when imagining different light conditions.
- Baseball pitch example now illustrates the astonishing speed of visual information processing.
- Expanded discussion of classic research on feature detectors.
- New art illustrates the visual cliff experiments.
- Research update on children's difficulty in accurately perceiving motion, and their resulting increased risk for pedestrian accidents.
- New research on cataract surgery in children supports doing so at as young an age as possible.
- New coverage of the speed of audition.
- Updated coverage of the experience of hearing loss, including global statistics as well as *cochlear implants,* with new art.
- New research on hearing loss among teens.
- New research illustrates how our responses to touch are influenced by cognition.
- Updated research on women's greater sensitivity to pain.
- Two new sports examples of the powerful effect of distraction on the experience of pain.
- New research support for maximizing pain relief with placebos, distraction, and hypnosis.
- Hypnosis now covered in a new Thinking Critically About Hypnosis and Pain Relief box.
- Updated cognitive neuroscience research helps explain smell-cognition connection.
- New research on the vast number of odors we could potentially discriminate, given that they trigger combinations of receptors.
- New research updates the interaction of taste and touch, and other types of sensory interaction.
- Expanded discussion with new research on *synesthesia.*
- New example of psychic predictions about missing person cases in the Thinking Critically About ESP box.

Learning

- Compelling new unit introduction.
- New example supports subtle effect of learned associations.

- New research on process of learning habits, and on how we tend to fall back on old habits when our willpower is low.
- New figure illustrates Pavlov's device for recording salivation.
- Research update supports finding that we generalize our like or dislike based on learned facial features.
- New information on what happened to "Little Albert."
- New art with figure illustrates Thorndike's law of effect, and a new photo illustrates shaping.
- Punishment section now includes research on children's compliance after a reprimand and a time out.
- Improved table compares Ways to Decrease Behavior.
- Updated research on physical punishment and increased aggressiveness, as well as global figures on legal protections for children.
- New research supports idea that punishment should focus on prohibitions rather than positive obligations.
- New discussion in Skinner's Legacy of how his work anticipated some of today's positive psychology.
- New research on how adaptive learning software supports individualized learning.
- Updated summary on how to best reinforce desired behaviors.
- Taste aversion illustrated with new photo.
- Updated research on biologically predisposed, learned association between the color red and sex.
- New photo illustrates how animals can most easily learn and retain behaviors that draw on their biological predispositions.
- New research on how a focus on intrinsic rewards in schooling and career may lead to extrinsic rewards as well.
- New research supports vicarious reinforcement, with even learned fears being extinguished when we observe others safely navigating the feared situation.
- Updated research on how the brain might support empathy and imitation, and how we may act even when a vicarious prompt is a fictional story.
- Expanded coverage, with new photos, of social learning among other animals.
- New research on how prosocial media boosts helping behaviors, and new photo illustrates prosocial modeling.
- New research examples update media violence viewing/ violent behavior discussion.
- Research update supports finding that observing risk-taking increases real-life risk-taking.

Memory

- New photo example from a worldwide memory competition.
- New music and face recognition research examples, and new research on face recognition among sheep.
- New photo illustrates measures of retention.
- *Parallel processing* is now defined in this set of modules.
- New research shows we remember less when we know information will be available online.
- Memory subsystems clarified and simplified as automatic vs. effortful, with implicit/explicit differences presented within that simpler organization; details provided about brain areas for these differing memory functions.
- Updated research on how those with a large working memory capacity tend to retain more information after sleep and to be creative problem solvers.
- Figure illustrating the effects of *chunking* on memory updated with new examples.
- New research supports the *testing effect* and updates other study tips. New link to author's Testing Effect YouTube animation.
- Memory storage discussion updated with new research on memory components that are distributed across a network, with some of those brain cells activating again upon memory retrieval.
- New art illustrates the hippocampus, and *memory consolidation* has become a key term.
- New research on flashbulb memory and tunnel vision memory.
- Research update on how experience and learning increase synaptic number as well as efficiency.
- New personal story from author illustrates example of insufficient time for memory consolidation.
- Research updates how priming can influence behaviors.
- New examples illustrate context-dependent memory, with *encoding specificity principle* a new key term.
- New photo accompanies graph illustrating the serial position effect.
- New research on enlarged brain areas in "super memory" people.
- New research on Henry Molaison's nondeclarative memory abilities.
- Includes new research on wide belief in repression of traumatic memories.
- *Reconsolidation* is a new key term.
- Memory construction now demonstrated with author's personal experience at Loftus presentation.
- Discussion of memories of abuse includes new research and has become a Thinking Critically box.

Thinking and Language

- New photo demonstrates *prototype*.
- New research on how *insight* improves when electrical stimulation disrupts assumptions created by past experiences.
- New photo illustrates heuristic thinking strategy.
- Updated research on the effectiveness of cigarette package warnings and graphic photos in risk assessment.
- New research explains the planning fallacy.
- Updated discussion of why we fear the wrong things.
- Research updates on unconsciously learned associations in newlyweds and others.
- Includes new research on the value of employing intuition for complex decisions; new examples relate to attitudes and decision-making.
- Discussion of *creativity* moved here from the Intelligence unit, with new key terms *convergent* and *divergent* thinking.
- New photo and research on the development of creative traits in girls.
- New research on animal consciousness and cognitive feats.
- New research updates discussion of babies' language comprehension and productive language development.
- Discussion of language development in the brain updated with new neuroscience research.
- Revised figure illustrates brain activity when speaking and hearing words.
- Includes new research on animal cognition, as well as neuroscience research on a gene unique to humans that helps enable speech.
- *Linguistic determinism* discussion updated with new research on unsymbolized thoughts and new cross-cultural research.
- Other new cross-cultural research outlines advantages of bilingualism.

Intelligence

- New photo example illustrates how cultural understandings of intelligence are socially constructed.
- New research on distinct brain networks enabling distinct abilities updates discussion of *g* factor.

- Now includes Gardner's ninth possible intelligence, existential intelligence, in Theories of Multiple Intelligences.
- New photo illustrates savant syndrome.
- New research suggests mastery (e.g., of chess) requires 3000–11,000 practice hours.
- Table comparing theories of intelligence now includes emotional intelligence.
- Improved organization of section on the history of intelligence testing.
- New photo illustrates testing with block design puzzles.
- New research updates continuing global rise in intelligence test scores, illustrated in updated figure, and possible reasons for this phenomenon.
- Grade inflation effects now included, with new research.
- Updated research supports strength of intelligence stability over time.
- Updated research suggests those with higher intelligence live healthier and longer.
- New example demonstrates legal connotations of low IQ scores.
- New photo example illustrates the high extreme of intelligence.
- New neuroscience and other research updates and clarifies discussion of the heritability of intelligence.
- Updated research on the benefits of enrichment programs for disadvantaged children and on how poverty-related stresses impede cognitive performance.
- Updated research supports importance of establishing a *growth mind-set* for academic success.
- New research supports impact of cultural and other expectations on academic flourishing.
- Updated discussion outlines interaction of schooling, intelligence, and motivation.
- New photo example of Shakuntala Devi, "the human computer."
- Updated cross-cultural research that supports impact of gender expectations on academic flourishing.
- New research shows that as gender equity has increased, the gap between boys and girls with very high math SAT scores has narrowed.
- Updated discussion of intelligence variation due to racial, ethnic, and socioeconomic differences.
- New research supports the effect of expectations on test performance and suggests ways to boost school achievement among stereotyped minorities.

What Drives Us: Hunger, Sex, Friendship, and Achievement

- The new unit title reflects the meaningful ways in which motivation directs our behavior.
- Powerful new unit introduction.
- Coverage of industrial-organizational psychology has moved to Appendix A: Psychology at Work.
- The *Yerkes-Dodson law* is now included in the discussion of optimum arousal.
- *Hunger Games* example now illustrates Maslow's hierarchy.
- New research updates biological and cultural influences on taste preferences, and situational influences on eating.
- Discussion of obesity and weight control streamlined with improved organization, and updated with global statistics and a new photo.
- New research on negative social, health, and memory effects of obesity.
- Updates on our changing workplace, with most modern jobs not requiring physical activity.
- Sexual Motivation section extensively updated with improved organization.
- New research expands discussion of The Physiology of Sex, with *asexuality* a new key term.
- New section on Sexual Dysfunctions and Paraphilias with DSM-5 updates; includes enhanced discussion of sexual disorders in women.
- Updated statistics on sexually transmitted infections.
- Psychology of Sex updated with new research and improved organization.
- New photo illustrates hypersexuality in video games.
- New research and statistics on sexual orientation, including increased coverage of lesbian and bisexual orientations.
- Origins of Sexual Orientation updated with new research.
- New research enhances coverage of Sex and Human Values.
- Affiliation and Achievement section updated, with *affiliation need* now a key term.
- New research on attachment bonds and our physiological responses to them updates The Benefits of Belonging discussion.
- New research updates in The Pain of Ostracism, with *ostracism* a new key term.
- New example with photo of first African-American West Point graduate.
- Connecting and Social Networking section fully updated.

Emotions, Stress, and Health

- New co-author Nathan DeWall led the revision of this unit for the eleventh edition.

- Restructured opening to Introduction to Emotion more clearly outlines the bodily arousal, expressive behaviors, and conscious experiences in emotion and the resulting puzzle for psychologists of how these pieces fit together.

- New research on how emotional experience is subjective and yet real.

- Improved figure showing the brain's pathways to emotions.

- Updates to table summarizing emotion theories.

- Includes new research on speedy first impressions.

- Update on accurate lie detection by police professionals, and on how the unconscious mind can outperform the conscious mind in lie detection.

- New research on how humans excel at detecting nonverbal threats.

- Updated discussion of gender differences in emotional experience, and the importance of context for accurate detection of facial expressions.

- The *facial feedback effect* research on Botox and depression has been updated, and *behavior feedback effect* is a new key term.

- Discussion of anger has been updated, including research on *catharsis* (with new photo), tips for managing our anger, and a new study on forgiveness.

- Updates on the benefits of happiness and ways to increase happiness, including buying shared experiences rather than material goods.

- Coverage of positive psychology has moved here from the Personality unit.

- New research on how economic inequality has increased, how specific genes influence our sense of well-being, and how nations may assess citizens' overall satisfaction.

- New research on how some stress early in life can build resilience, but can also lead to greater adult stress responses and disease risk.

- Updated research on the health-depleting effects of depression, anxiety, and stress, and the connection between social threats and inflammation.

- Stress and Vulnerability to Disease section updated with new research and examples.

- Stress and Heart Disease subsection revised and updated; now includes *Type D* personality (as well as *Type A* and *Type B*).

- Reorganized/improved new Health and Coping section.

- Personal Control section revised and expanded with new research.

- Coverage of *learned helplessness, external locus of control,* and *internal locus of control* moved here (from the Personality unit). New key term *self-control* and new photo examples.

- Revised and expanded discussion of optimism and health; new research on how to become more optimistic and reduce levels of depression.

- Social Support revised and updated with new research and new examples, including a study of people in low-conflict marriages living longer, healthier lives.

- New research supports effects of exercise on preventing or reducing depression and anxiety, and new cross-cultural research supports exercise/life satisfaction link.

- Now includes information about the 150-minutes-per-week exercise target shown to have highest effect on well-being.

- Relaxation and Meditation section revised and updated with new research and examples, including research showing link between meditation and a decrease in depression and anxiety, and improvement in decision-making.

- Support for the longevity/religiosity link updated, with new research about possible contributions of healthy lifestyle choices among those who are religiously active.

Social Psychology

- This unit now appears before the Personality unit.

- New research and examples show power of priming in how attitudes affect actions.

- New photo illustrates attitudes following behavior.

- New research expands group pressure and conformity discussion, including new example of lasting changes in personality due to career choices.

- New research on brain regions that become active when people experience cognitive conflict and negative arousal also becoming active when experiencing *cognitive dissonance*.

- Coverage of persuasion includes updates using climate change as central example.

- New research expands discussion of social synchrony and mimicry being spread through our social networks.
- New photo illustrates how some appear to conform to non-conformity.
- New study with figure on how "I voted" message influenced others on social media.
- Milgram discussion includes updated coverage of replications of his research with different groups.
- Table showing home advantage in team sports updated with new data and additional team sports.
- New photo illustrates social loafing.
- New table helps students distinguish among *social facilitation*, *social loafing*, and *deindividuation*.
- Updates on the Internet as social amplifier, with new examples that demonstrate *group polarization* online.
- Updated figure illustrates increased acceptance of interracial dating among Americans.
- Significantly updated and reorganized prejudice discussion now covers ethnicity, gender, and sexual orientation separately.
- New research and examples of persisting subtle prejudice, including *implicit prejudice*.
- New research examples of *ingroup bias*, including the finding that ingroup discrimination sometimes results from networking and mutual support rather than hostility.
- New coverage of the MAOA gene in The Biology of Aggression.
- Research updates on women's perception of men with higher facial width-to-height ratios as more dominant.
- Psychological and Social-Cultural Factors in Aggression updated, including new research on media models and video games.
- Updated research on contributors to aggression, and updates to the biopsychosocial understanding of aggression figure.
- New photos illustrate the *mere exposure effect*.
- Updated discussion of modern matchmaking, including new graph of heterosexual and same-sex couples that met online.
- New research and examples update discussion of physical attraction.
- New research on increased personal happiness in people from both rich and poor countries if they had donated to a charity in the past month.
- Updated research on people who had been generously treated later being more likely to be generous themselves.

- New photo illustrates altruism during the Rwandan genocide.
- Research updates to The Norms for Helping discussion.
- New example illustrates *mirror-image perceptions*.

Personality

- New co-author Nathan DeWall led the revision of this unit for the eleventh edition.
- This unit now appears immediately before the Psychological Disorders unit.
- Compelling new unit introduction.
- Improved coverage of modern-day psychodynamic approaches, now more clearly distinguished from historical Freudian roots.
- Assessing Unconscious Processes discussion now includes the *Thematic Apperception Test (TAT)*.
- New research expands discussion of the *modern unconscious mind*, and how modern theorists have continued to study irrationality, sexuality, and other areas of interest to Freud.
- New research and examples support value of humanistic psychology's positive regard and focus on listening with empathy.
- New photo illustrates extraversion.
- New Thinking Critically box, The Stigma of Introversion.
- Updated section on Biology and Personality covers personality-related brain activity variation, and personality differences in animals.
- Big Five discussion updated with new research, including cultural changes over time, relation to brain structure/function, and actual prediction of behavior.
- New research on how personality tendencies taken to either extreme may become maladaptive, and updates on how music preferences, personal spaces, online spaces, and written communications relate to personality traits, with new photo.
- Social-Cognitive Theories revised and updated, and expanded to include *heredity-environment interaction*.
- New photo illustrates *reciprocal determinism*.
- Personal Control and Positive Psychology sections moved to the Emotions, Stress, and Health unit.
- Exploring the Self section updated; *self-efficacy* now a key term.
- Updates to the table comparing the major personality theories.
- New research and discussion outlines importance of positive goal-setting in considering *possible selves*.

- New research on the perils of excessive optimism, blindness to one's own incompetence, and self-serving bias, but with some value placed on self-serving bias helping us replace despair with confidence.
- Discussion of *narcissism* updated.

Psychological Disorders

- New co-author Nathan DeWall led the revision of this unit for the eleventh edition.
- Reorganized and thoroughly updated to reflect changes to psychiatry's latest edition of its diagnostic manual—the **DSM-5.** Includes integration of psychiatric diagnoses into mainstream medical practice, redefinition of disorders, new disorder categories, changes in labels, and updated definition of *psychological disorder.*
- The biopsychosocial approach enriched with discussion of *epigenetics,* with associated updates throughout the unit.
- New mentions of controversial changes in the DSM-5 throughout these modules, including the new disruptive mood dysregulation disorder, removal of the bereavement exception for depression, and loosened criteria for adult ADHD.
- New, careful explanation of how care providers use DSM-5 criteria and codes for diagnosis and treatment, using insomnia disorder as illustrative example.
- New results of *field trials* on clinician agreement with DSM-5 for certain categories of disorder.
- Updated Thinking Critically box on ADHD, including controversies about diagnosis and concerns about those seeking the "good-grade pills."
- Thinking Critically About Insanity box significantly revised, with new focus and title—Are People With Psychological Disorders Dangerous?
- New photo example of media portrayals of psychological disorders.
- More research on gender differences in generalized anxiety disorder.
- New photo example illustrates discussion of *panic disorder.*
- New research on misperceiving panic symptoms as a heart attack or other illness, with new example.
- New example and research updates discussion of *obsessive-compulsive disorder,* and new research updates *PTSD* statistics.
- New photo example illustrates how we are biologically prepared to fear some things more than others.

- New research and examples in Understanding Anxiety Disorders, OCD, and PTSD on learned fears and stimulus generalization, as well as neural, hormonal, and genetic influences.
- Updated table on Diagnosing Major Depressive Disorder.
- New research updates discussion of depression, including updated statistics and new research on gender differences and on cultural influences.
- New research on the possible factors that put women at greater risk for depression.
- New data on incidence of bipolar disorder, particularly its diagnosis among Americans and among those in creative professions.
- New coverage of *dysthymia,* and updated discussion of a *seasonal pattern* for depression and bipolar disorder.
- Suicide rates discussion updated, including with more research on ethnic differences, and updates to the nonsuicidal self-injury research.
- Updated research on the dangers of relentless, self-focused *rumination.*
- Understanding Depressive Disorders and Bipolar Disorder updated with new research studies exploring genetic, biochemical, cognitive, and behavioral predictors.
- New research updates discussion of cognitive symptoms of schizophrenia, including an impaired theory of mind.
- *Chronic* and *acute schizophrenia* are new key terms.
- New neuroscience and genetic research updates Understanding Schizophrenia.
- Includes new schizophrenia risk factors—childhood physical, sexual, and emotional abuse.
- New research on how abnormal brain anatomy may accompany dissociative identity disorder.
- New research on how those with antisocial personality disorder may show lower emotional intelligence.
- Understanding Antisocial Personality Disorder updated and improved with new genetics research, and discussion of adaptive aspects of some symptoms of psychopathy, such as fearlessness and dominance.
- New examples and other research update Eating Disorders.
- New research on a gene that reduces available serotonin, increasing risk for developing anorexia or bulimia.

Therapy

- Introduction to Therapy and the Psychological Therapies reorganized/improved; now distinguishes psychotherapy and biomedical therapy more clearly.
- New explanations and research updates Psychoanalysis and Psychodynamic Therapy.
- New photo illustrates face-to-face therapy.
- Helpful new examples of people overcoming fears in Exposure Therapies discussion.
- New photos illustrates virtual reality exposure therapy.
- Cognitive-Behavioral Therapy discussion updated with new research and information, including how positive self-talk is helpful even for those without depression.
- New information on how psychotherapy can be more accessible and affordable through web- and phone-based interventions, work setting treatments, and self-help efforts facilitated by groups, books, and smart-phone apps.
- Improved and updated table compares psychotherapies.
- Updated research on effectiveness of certain psychotherapies for specific disorders.
- New research with new photo supports the importance of the *therapeutic alliance*.
- Updated discussion of cultural influences in successful therapy.
- Reorganized section on Finding a Mental Health Professional.
- Updated explanation of how primary care providers prescribe most psychiatric drugs, followed by psychiatrists (and psychologists in some U.S. states).
- New research on the placebo effect in drug therapy showing that even mere exposure to advertising about a drug's effectiveness can increase its effect.
- Clarified and updated explanation of *antidepressants*, and about the preference for the term *SSRIs*, given their multiple treatment uses (not just for depression).
- New research on the possibility of quicker-acting antidepressants.
- Revised explanation more explicitly differentiates today's gentler ECT from its harsher form when first introduced in 1938, and updated research on its effectiveness for severe depression and "treatment-resistant" patients.
- New neuroscience research on how ECT may weaken connections in a "hyperconnected" neural hub in the left frontal lobe.
- New research on the effectiveness of rTMS neurostimulation therapy to treat depression.

- Research updates on deep brain stimulation treatment of depression.
- Therapeutic Lifestyle Change updated with new research supporting value of healthy lifestyle choices, including time spent in natural environments.
- New table compares psychotherapies and biomedical therapies.
- Reorganized/expanded final sections on Preventing Psychological Disorders and Building Resilience.
- Updated research supports concept of higher *resilience* in certain groups.
- Coverage of *posttraumatic growth* now appears here, in reference to struggles with challenging crises.
- Updated research suggests importance of *finding meaning* to foster posttraumatic growth after tragedy, and as a preventive mental health strategy.

Appendix A: Psychology at Work

- This new appendix, part of the Motivation and Work unit in the previous edition, offers a focused look at industrial-organizational psychology.
- New section on Matching Interests to Work in discussion of personnel psychology.
- New information on career planning in Discovering Your Strengths.
- New research suggests busier, focused people are happier.
- New research on the interviewer illusion updates Do Interviews Predict Performance?
- Updated research on worker satisfaction and engagement, and on the success/morale relationship in employees, supports the finding that successful managers consider employee well-being.
- Updated research on leadership styles, with a new photo illustrating the power of positive leadership.
- Expanded discussion of successful goal-setting from effective leaders introduces value of *collective intelligence*.

Appendix B: Subfields of Psychology

- This appendix focuses on educational requirements, type of work, and likely places to work for each of psychology's main subfields.
- New photo examples illustrate community psychology, forensic psychology, and sport psychology.

Appendix C: Complete Module Reviews

- In an effort to encourage students to self-test, the Reviews at the end of each module include only a list of the learning objective questions—repeated from within that module. Answers to those questions form these complete module reviews, which students may use to check their answers or review the material.

Appendix D: Answers to *Test Yourself* Questions

- Students may check their answers here for the new multiple-format questions found in a self-test at the end of each unit.

TIME MANAGEMENT

Or, How to Be a Great Student and Still Have a Life

—Richard O. Straub University of Michigan, Dearborn

 How Are You Using Your Time Now?

 Design a Better Schedule

Plan the Term

Plan Your Week

 Make Every Minute of Your Study Time Count

Take Useful Class Notes

Create a Study Space That Helps You Learn

Set Specific, Realistic Daily Goals

Use SQ3R to Help You Master This Text

Don't Forget About Rewards!

 Do You Need to Revise Your New Schedule?

Are You Doing Well in Some Courses But Not in Others?

Have You Received a Poor Grade on a Test?

Are You Trying to Study Regularly for the First Time and Feeling Overwhelmed?

© Desislava Draganova / Alamy

We all face challenges in our schedules. If you are making the transition from high school to college, you may be delighting in new freedoms, but also struggling to balance your many new responsibilities. Or you may be a student returning to school after spending a few years at work. You may be balancing work and family along with your classes.

How can you balance all of your life's demands and be successful? Time management. Manage the time you have so that you can find the time you need.

In this section, I will outline a simple, four-step process for improving the way you make use of your time.

1. Keep a time-use diary to understand how you are using your time. You may be surprised at how much time you're wasting.

2. Design a new schedule for using your time more effectively.

MGP/Photodisc/Getty Images

3. Make the most of your study time so that your new schedule will work for you.

4. If necessary, refine your new schedule, based on what you've learned.

How Are You Using Your Time Now?

Although everyone gets 24 hours in the day and seven days in the week, we fill those hours and days with different obligations and interests. If you are like most people, you probably use your time wisely in some ways, and not so wisely in others. Answering the questions in **TABLE 1** can help you find trouble spots—and hopefully more time for the things that matter most to you.

The next thing you need to know is how you actually spend your time. To find out, record your activities in a time-use diary for one week. Be realistic. Take notes on how much time you spend attending class, studying, working, commuting, meeting personal and family needs, fixing and eating meals, socializing (don't forget texting, gaming, and social networking), exercising, and anything else that occupies your time, including life's small practical tasks, which can take up plenty of your 24/7. As you record your activities, take notes on how you are feeling at various times of the day. When does your energy slump, and when do you feel most energetic?

Design a Better Schedule

Take a good look at your time-use diary. Where do you think you may be wasting time? Do you spend a lot of time commuting, for example? If so, could you use that time more productively? If you take public transportation, commuting is a great time to read and test yourself for review.

Did you remember to include time for meals, personal care, work schedules, family commitments, and other fixed activities?

How much time do you sleep? In the battle to meet all of life's daily commitments and interests, we tend to treat sleep as optional. Do your best to manage your life so that you can get enough sleep to feel rested. You will feel better and be healthier, and you will also do better academically and in relationships with your family and friends. (You will read more about this in Module 9.)

Are you dedicating enough time for focused study? Take a last look at your notes to see if any other patterns pop out. Now it's time to create a new and more efficient schedule.

Plan the Term

Before you draw up your new schedule, think ahead. Use your phone's calendar feature, or buy a portable calendar that covers the entire school term, with a writing space for each day. Using the course outlines provided by your instructors, enter the dates of all exams, term-paper deadlines, and other important assignments. Also be sure to enter your own long-range personal plans (work and family commitments, etc.). Keep your calendar up to date, refer to it often, and change it as needed. Through this process, you will develop a regular schedule that will help you achieve success.

Plan Your Week

To pass those exams, meet those deadlines, and keep up with your life outside of class, you will need to convert your long-term goals into a daily schedule. Be realistic—you

▼ TABLE 1
Study Habits Survey

Answer the following questions, writing *Yes* or *No* for each line.

1. Do you usually set up a schedule to budget your time for studying, work, recreation, and other activities?

   _____

2. Do you often put off studying until time pressures force you to cram?

   _____

3. Do other students seem to study less than you do, but get better grades? _____

4. Do you usually spend hours at a time studying one subject, rather than dividing that time among several subjects? _____

5. Do you often have trouble remembering what you have just read in your course work? _____

6. Before reading a module, do you skim through it and read the section headings? _____

7. Do you try to predict test questions from your class notes and reading?

   _____

8. Do you usually try to summarize in your own words what you have just finished reading? _____

9. Do you find it difficult to concentrate for very long when you study?

   _____

10. Do you often feel that you studied the wrong material for a test?

    _____

Thousands of students have participated in similar surveys. Students who are fully realizing their academic potential usually respond as follows: (1) yes, (2) no, (3) no, (4) no, (5) no, (6) yes, (7) yes, (8) yes, (9) no, (10) no.

Do your responses fit that pattern? If not, you could benefit from improving your time management and study habits.

will be living with this routine for the entire school term. Here are some more things to add to your calendar.

1. Enter your class times, work hours, and any other fixed obligations. Be thorough. Allow plenty of time for such things as commuting, meals, and laundry.

2. Set up a study schedule for each course. Remember what you learned about yourself in the study habits survey (Table 1) and your time-use diary. **TABLE 2**, More Tips for Effective Scheduling, offers some detailed guidance drawn from psychology's research.

3. After you have budgeted time for studying, fill in slots for other obligations, exercise, fun, and relaxation.

Make Every Minute of Your Study Time Count

How do you study from a textbook? Many students simply read and reread in a passive manner. As a result, they remember the wrong things—the catchy stories but not the main points that show up later in test questions. To make things worse, many

▼ TABLE 2
More Tips for Effective Scheduling

There are a few other things you will want to keep in mind when you set up your schedule.

Spaced study is more effective than massed study. If you need 3 hours to study one subject, for example, it's best to divide that into shorter periods spaced over several days.

Alternate subjects, but avoid interference. Alternating the subjects you study in any given session will keep you fresh and will, surprisingly, increase your ability to remember what you're learning in each different area. Studying similar topics back-to-back, however, such as two different foreign languages, could lead to interference in your learning. (You will hear more about this in Module 26).

Be smart about your smart phone. Texting, snapchatting, browsing, and e-mail can be real distractions. When your concentration is interrupted, it takes extra time and energy to regain the focus you need to make study time count. Consider scheduling a time for checking the phone—perhaps once per hour on the hour—and ignore it during the rest of your study time. (Module 36 has more tips for maintaining balance and focus in your social networking.)

Determine the amount of study time you need to do well in each course. The time you need depends on the difficulty of your courses and the effectiveness of your study methods. Ideally, you would spend at least 1 to 2 hours studying for each hour spent in class. Increase your study time slowly by setting weekly goals that will gradually bring you up to the desired level.

Create a schedule that makes sense. Tailor your schedule to meet the demands of each course. For the course that emphasizes lecture notes, plan a daily review of your notes soon after each class. If you are evaluated for class participation (for example, in a language course), allow time for a review just before the class meets. Schedule study time for your most difficult (or least motivating) courses during hours when you are the most alert and distractions are fewest.

Schedule open study time. Life can be unpredictable. Emergencies and new obligations can throw off your schedule. Or you may simply need some extra time for a project or for review in one of your courses. Try to allow for some flexibility in your schedule each week.

Following these guidelines will help you find a schedule that works for you!

© Hero Images/Corbis

students take poor notes during class. Here are some tips that will help you get the most from your class and your text.

Take Useful Class Notes

Good notes will boost your understanding and retention. Are yours thorough? Do they form a sensible outline of each lecture? If not, you may need to make some changes.

Keep Each Course's Notes Separate and Organized

Keeping all your notes for a course in one location will allow you to flip back and forth easily to find answers to questions. Three options are (1) separate notebooks for each course, (2) clearly marked sections in a shared ring binder, or (3) carefully organized folders if you opt to take notes electronically. For the print options, removable pages will allow you to add new information and weed out past mistakes. Choosing notebook pages with lots of space, or using mark-up options in electronic files, will allow you to add comments when you review and revise your notes after class.

Use an Outline Format

Use roman numerals for major points, letters for supporting arguments, and so on. (See **FIGURE 1** for a sample.) In some courses, taking notes will be easy, but some instructors may be less organized, and you will have to work harder to form your outline.

Clean Up Your Notes After Class

Try to reorganize your notes soon after class. Expand or clarify your comments and clean up any hard-to-read scribbles while the material is fresh in your mind. Write

▼ FIGURE 1
Sample class notes in outline form Here is a sample from a student's notes taken in outline form from a lecture on sleep.

Sleep (Module 9)

When is my daily peak in circadian arousal? Study hardest subject then!

I. Biological Rhythms

　A. Circadian Rhythm (circa-about; diem-day)—24-hour cycle.

　　1. Ups and downs throughout day/night.
　　　Dip in afternoon (siesta time).
　　2. Melatonin—hormone that makes us sleepy. Produced by pineal gland in brain. Bright light shuts down production of melatonin. (Dim the lights at night to get sleepy.)

　B. FOUR Sleep Stages, cycle through every 90 minutes all night! Aserinsky discovered—his son—REM sleep (dreams, rapid eye movement, muscles paralyzed but brain super active). EEG measurements showed sleep stages.

　　1. NREM-1 (non-Rapid Eye Movement sleep; brief, images like hallucinations; hypnagogic jerks)
　　2. NREM-2 (harder to waken, sleep spindles)
　　3. NREM-3 (DEEP sleep—hard to wake up! Long slow waves on EEG; bedwetting, night terrors, sleepwalking occurs here; asleep but not dead—can still hear, smell, etc. Will wake up for baby.)
　　4. REM Sleep (Dreams…)

important questions in the margin, or by using an electronic markup feature, next to notes that answer them. (For example: "What are the sleep stages?") This will help you when you review your notes before a test.

Create a Study Space That Helps You Learn

It's easier to study effectively if your work area is well designed.

Organize Your Space

Work at a desk or table, not on your bed or in a comfy chair that will tempt you to nap.

Minimize Distractions

Turn the TV off, put away your phone, and close distracting windows on your computer. If you must listen to music to mask outside noise, play soft instrumentals, not vocal selections that will draw your mind to the lyrics.

Ask Others to Honor Your Quiet Time

Tell roommates, family, and friends about your new schedule. Try to find a study place where you are least likely to be disturbed.

Set Specific, Realistic Daily Goals

The simple note "7–8 P.M.: Study Psychology" is too broad to be useful. Instead, break your studying into manageable tasks. For example, you will want to subdivide large reading assignments. If you aren't used to studying for long periods, start with relatively short periods of concentrated study, with breaks in between. In this text, for example, you might decide to read one major section before each break. Limit your breaks to 5 or 10 minutes to stretch or move around a bit.

Your attention span is a good indicator of whether you are pacing yourself successfully. At this early stage, it's important to remember that you're in training. If your attention begins to wander, get up immediately and take a short break. It is better to study effectively for 15 minutes and then take a break than to fritter away 45 minutes out of your study hour. As your endurance develops, you can increase the length of study periods.

Use SQ3R to Help You Master This Text

You will hear more about SQ3R in Module 1.

David Myers and Nathan DeWall organized this text by using a system called SQ3R (Survey, Question, Read, Retrieve, Review). Using SQ3R can help you to understand what you read, and to retain that information longer.

Applying SQ3R may feel at first as though it's taking more time and effort to "read" a module, but with practice, these steps will become automatic.

Survey

Before you read a module, survey its key parts. Scan the outline. Note that text sections have numbered Learning Objective Questions to help you focus. Pay attention to headings, which indicate important subtopics, and to words set in bold type.

Surveying gives you the big picture of a module's content and organization. Understanding the module's logical sections will help you break your work into manageable pieces in your study sessions.

Question

As you survey, don't limit yourself to the numbered Learning Objective Questions that appear throughout the module. Jotting down additional questions of your own will cause you to look at the material in a new way. (You might, for example, scan this section's headings and ask "What does 'SQ3R' mean?") Information becomes easier to remember when you make it personally meaningful. Trying to answer your questions while reading will keep you in an active learning mode.

Read

As you read, keep your questions in mind and actively search for the answers. If you come to material that seems to answer an important question that you haven't jotted down, stop and write down that new question.

Be sure to read everything. Don't skip photo or art captions, graphs, boxes, tables, or quotes. An idea that seems vague when you read about it may become clear when you see it in a graph or table. Keep in mind that instructors sometimes base their test questions on figures and tables.

Retrieve

When you have found the answer to one of your questions, close your eyes and mentally recite the question and its answer. Then write the answer next to the question in your own words. Trying to explain something in your own words will help you figure out where there are gaps in your understanding. These kinds of opportunities to practice *retrieving* develop the skills you will need when you are taking exams. If you study without ever putting your book and notes aside, you may develop false confidence about what you know. With the material available, you may be able to recognize the correct answer to your questions. But will you be able to recall it later, when you take an exam without having your mental props in sight?

Test your understanding as often as you can. Testing yourself is part of successful learning, because the act of testing forces your brain to work at remembering, thus establishing the memory more permanently (so you can find it later for the exam!). Use the self-testing opportunities throughout each module, including the periodic Retrieval Practice items. Also take advantage of the self-testing that is available through LaunchPad.

Review

After working your way through the module, read over your questions and your written answers. Take an extra few minutes to create a brief written summary covering all of your questions and answers. At the end of each main text section, you should take advantage of two important opportunities for self-testing and review—a list of that module's Learning Objective Questions for you to try answering before checking Appendix C (Complete Module Reviews), and a list of that module's key terms for you to try to define before checking the referenced page. At the end of each unit of modules, be sure to try answering the Test Yourself questions, which cover all of the key concepts (with answers in Appendix D).

Don't Forget About Rewards!

If you have trouble studying regularly, giving yourself a reward may help. What kind of reward works best? That depends on what you enjoy. You might start by making a list of 5 or 10 things that put a smile on your face. Spending time with a loved one, taking a walk or going for a bike ride, relaxing with a magazine or novel, or watching a favorite show can provide immediate rewards for achieving short-term study goals.

To motivate yourself when you're having trouble sticking to your schedule, allow yourself an immediate reward for completing a specific task. If running makes you smile, change your shoes, grab a friend, and head out the door! You deserve a reward for a job well done.

Do You Need to Revise Your New Schedule?

What if you've lived with your schedule for a few weeks, but you aren't making progress toward your academic and personal goals? What if your studying hasn't paid off in better grades? Don't despair and abandon your program, but do take a little time to figure out what's gone wrong.

Are You Doing Well in Some Courses But Not in Others?

Perhaps you need to shift your priorities a bit. You may need to allow more study time for chemistry, for example, and less time for some other course.

Have You Received a Poor Grade on a Test?

Did your grade fail to reflect the effort you spent preparing for the test? This can happen to even the hardest-working student, often on a first test with a new instructor. This common experience can be upsetting. "What do I have to do to get an A?" "The test was unfair!" "I studied the wrong material!"

Try to figure out what went wrong. Analyze the questions you missed, dividing them into two categories: class-based questions and text-based questions. How many questions did you miss in each category? If you find far more errors in one category than in the other, you'll have some clues to help you revise your schedule. Depending on the pattern you've found, you can add extra study time to review of class notes, or to studying the text.

Are You Trying to Study Regularly for the First Time and Feeling Overwhelmed?

Perhaps you've set your initial goals too high. Remember, the point of time management is to identify a regular schedule that will help you achieve success. Like any skill, time management takes practice. Accept your limitations and revise your schedule to work slowly up to where you know you need to be—perhaps adding 15 minutes of study time per day.

* * *

I hope that these suggestions help make you more successful academically, and that they enhance the quality of your life in general. Having the necessary skills makes any job a lot easier and more pleasant. Let me repeat my warning not to attempt to make too drastic a change in your lifestyle immediately. Good habits require time and self-discipline to develop. Once established, they can last a lifetime.

1. How Are You Using Your Time Now?

- Identify your areas of weakness.
- Keep a time-use diary.
- Record the time you actually spend on activities.
- Record your energy levels to find your most productive times.

2. Design a Better Schedule

- Decide on your goals for the term and for each week.
- Enter class times, work times, social times (for family and friends), and time needed for other obligations and for practical activities.
- Tailor study times to avoid interference and to meet each course's needs.

3. Make Every Minute of Your Study Time Count

- Take careful class notes (in outline form) that will help you recall and rehearse material covered in lectures.
- Try to eliminate distractions to your study time, and ask friends and family to help you focus on your work.
- Set specific, realistic daily goals to help you focus on each day's tasks.
- Use the SQ3R system (survey, question, read, retrieve, review) to master material covered in your text.
- When you achieve your daily goals, reward yourself with something that you value.

4. Do You Need to Revise Your New Schedule?

- Allocate extra study time for courses that are more difficult, and a little less time for courses that are easy for you.
- Study your test results to help determine a more effective balance in your schedule.
- Make sure your schedule is not too ambitious. Gradually establish a schedule that will be effective for the long term.

THE STORY OF PSYCHOLOGY

· · · · · · · · · · · ·

Harvard astronomer Owen Gingerich (2006) reported that there are more than 100 billion galaxies. One of these, our own relative speck of a galaxy, has a few hundred billion stars, many of which, like our Sun-star, are circled by planets. On the scale of outer space, we are less than a single grain of sand on all the oceans' beaches, and our lifetime but a relative nanosecond.

Yet there is nothing more awe inspiring and absorbing than our own inner space. Our brain, adds Gingerich, "is by far the most complex physical object known to us in the entire cosmos" (p. 29). Our consciousness—our mind somehow arising from matter—remains a profound mystery. Our thinking, emotions, and actions (and their interplay with others' thinking, emotions, and actions) fascinate us. Outer space staggers us with its enormity. But inner space enthralls us. Enter psychological science.

For people whose exposure to psychology comes from the news and popular media, psychologists seem to analyze personality, offer counseling, dispense child-raising advice, examine crime scenes, and testify in court. Do they? Yes, and much more. Consider some of psychology's questions that you may wonder about:

- Have you ever found yourself reacting to something as one of your biological parents would—perhaps in a way you vowed you never would—and then wondered how much of your personality you inherited? *To what extent do genes predispose our person-to-person differences in personality? To what extent do home and community environments shape us?*

- Have you ever worried about how to act among people of a different culture, race, gender, or sexual orientation? *In what ways are we alike as members of the human family? How do we differ?*

- Have you ever awakened from a nightmare and wondered why you had such a crazy dream? *Why do we dream?*

- Have you ever played peekaboo with a 6-month-old and wondered why the baby finds the game so delightful? The infant reacts as though, when you momentarily move behind a door, you actually disappear—only to reappear out of thin air. *What do babies actually perceive and think?*

- Have you ever wondered what fosters school and work success? *Are some people just born smarter? Does sheer intelligence explain why some people get richer, think more creatively, or relate more sensitively?*

- Have you ever wondered how the Internet, video games, and electronic social networks affect people? *How do today's electronic media influence what we think and how we relate?*

- Have you ever become depressed or anxious and wondered whether you'll ever feel "normal"? *What triggers our bad moods—and our good ones? What's the line between a normal mood swing and a psychological disorder for which someone should seek help?*

As we will see in Module 1, psychology is a science that seeks to answer such questions about us all—how and why we think, feel, and act as we do.

A smile is a smile the world around Throughout this book, you will see examples not only of our cultural and gender diversity but also of the similarities that define our shared human nature. People in different cultures vary in when and how often they smile, but a naturally happy smile *means* the same thing anywhere in the world.

Roy Toft/National Geographic/Getty Images

Antonia Brune

1 What Is Psychology?

ONCE UPON A TIME, ON a planet in this neighborhood of the universe, there came to be people. Soon thereafter, these creatures became intensely interested in themselves and in one another: "Who are we? What produces our thoughts? Our feelings? Our actions? And how are we to understand and manage those around us?"

Psychological Science Is Born

1-1 What were some important milestones in psychology's early development?

To assist your active learning of psychology, numbered Learning Objectives, framed as questions, appear at the beginning of major sections. You can test your understanding by trying to answer the question before, and then again after, you read the section.

To be human is to be curious about ourselves and the world around us. Before 300 B.C.E., the Greek naturalist and philosopher Aristotle theorized about learning and memory, motivation and emotion, perception and personality. Today we chuckle at some of his guesses, like his suggestion that a meal makes us sleepy by causing gas and heat to collect around the source of our personality, the heart. But credit Aristotle with asking the right questions.

Psychology's First Laboratory Philosophers' thinking about thinking continued until the birth of psychology as we know it, on a December day in 1879, in a small, third-floor room at Germany's University of Leipzig. There, two young men were helping an austere, middle-aged professor, Wilhelm Wundt, create an experimental apparatus. Their machine measured the time lag between people's hearing a ball hit a platform and their pressing a telegraph key (Hunt, 1993). Curiously, people responded in about one-tenth of a second when asked to press the key as soon as the sound occurred—and in about two-tenths of a second when asked to press the key as soon as they were consciously aware of perceiving the sound. (To be aware of one's awareness takes a little longer.) Wundt was seeking to measure "atoms of the mind"—the fastest and simplest mental processes. So began the first psychological laboratory, staffed by Wundt and by psychology's first graduate students.

Information sources are cited in parentheses, with name and date. Every citation can be found in the end-of-book References, with complete documentation that follows American Psychological Association (APA) style.

Throughout the text, important concepts are **boldfaced.** As you study, you can find these terms with their definitions in a nearby margin and in the Glossary at the end of the book.

Structuralism and Functionalism Before long, this new science of psychology became organized into different branches, or schools of thought, each promoted by pioneering thinkers. Two early schools were **structuralism** and **functionalism.**

Wilhelm Wundt Wundt established the first psychology laboratory at the University of Leipzig, Germany.

Edward Bradford Titchener Titchener used introspection to search for the mind's structural elements.

STRUCTURALISM As physicists and chemists discerned the structure of matter, so Edward Bradford Titchener aimed to discover the mind's structure. He engaged people in self-reflective *introspection* (looking inward), training them to report elements of their experience as they looked at a rose, listened to a metronome, smelled a scent, or tasted a substance. What were their immediate sensations, their images, their feelings? And how did these relate to one another? Alas, introspection proved somewhat unreliable. It required smart, verbal people, and its results varied from person to person and experience to experience. As introspection waned, so did structuralism.

FUNCTIONALISM Hoping to assemble the mind's structure from simple elements was rather like trying to understand a car by examining its disconnected parts. Philosopher-psychologist William James thought it would be more fruitful to consider the evolved functions of our thoughts and feelings. Smelling is what the nose does; thinking is what the brain does. But *why* do the nose and brain do these things? Under the influence of evolutionary theorist Charles Darwin, James assumed that thinking, like smelling, developed because it was *adaptive*—it contributed to our ancestors' survival. Consciousness serves a function. It enables us to consider our past, adjust to our present, and plan our future. James encouraged explorations of the functions of emotions, memories, willpower, habits, and moment-to-moment streams of consciousness.

James' writings moved the publisher Henry Holt to offer James a contract for a textbook of the new science of psychology. James agreed and began work in 1878, with an apology for requesting two years to finish his writing. The text proved an unexpected chore and actually took him 12 years. (Why am I not surprised?) More than a century later, people still read the resulting *Principles of Psychology* (1890) and marvel at the brilliance and elegance with which James introduced psychology to the educated public.

First Women in Psychology James' legacy stems partly from his Harvard mentoring and his writing. In 1890, over the objections of Harvard's president, he admitted Mary Whiton Calkins into his graduate seminar (Scarborough & Furumoto, 1987). (In those years women lacked even the right to vote.) When Calkins joined, the other students (all men) dropped out. So James tutored her alone. Later, she finished all of Harvard's Ph.D. requirements, outscoring all the male students on the qualifying exams. Alas, Harvard denied her the degree she had earned, offering her instead a degree from Radcliffe College, its undergraduate "sister" school for women. Calkins resisted the unequal treatment

> **structuralism** early school of thought promoted by Wundt and Titchener; used introspection to reveal the structure of the human mind.
>
> **functionalism** early school of thought promoted by James and influenced by Darwin; explored how mental and behavioral processes function—how they enable the organism to adapt, survive, and flourish.

William James and Mary Whiton Calkins James was a legendary teacher-writer who authored an important 1890 psychology text. He mentored Calkins, who became a pioneering memory researcher and the first woman to be president of the American Psychological Association.

Margaret Floy Washburn The first woman to receive a psychology Ph.D., Washburn synthesized animal behavior research in *The Animal Mind* (1908).

and refused the degree. She nevertheless went on to become a distinguished memory researcher and the American Psychological Association's (APA's) first female president in 1905.

The honor of being the first female psychology Ph.D. later fell to Margaret Floy Washburn, who also wrote an influential book, *The Animal Mind,* and became the second female APA president in 1921. But Washburn's gender barred doors for her, too. Although her thesis was the first foreign study Wundt published in his psychology journal, she could not join the all-male organization of experimental psychologists founded by Titchener, her own graduate adviser (Johnson, 1997). (What a different world from the recent past—1996 to 2014—when women were 10 of the 19 elected presidents of the science-oriented Association for Psychological Science. In the United States, Canada, and Europe, most psychology doctorates are now earned by women.)

Study Tip: Memory research reveals a *testing effect:* We retain information much better if we actively retrieve it by self-testing and rehearsing. (More on this at the end of this module.) To bolster your learning and memory, take advantage of the *Retrieval Practice* opportunities you'll find throughout this text.

RETRIEVAL PRACTICE

- What event defined the start of scientific psychology?

ANSWER: Scientific psychology began in Germany in 1879 when Wilhelm Wundt opened the first psychology laboratory.

- Why did introspection fail as a method for understanding how the mind works?

ANSWER: People's self-reports varied, depending on the experience and the person's intelligence and verbal ability.

- _____ used introspection to define the mind's makeup; _____ focused on how mental processes enable us to adapt, survive, and flourish.

ANSWER: Structuralism; functionalism

Psychological Science Develops

1-2 How did psychology continue to develop from the 1920s through today?

Behaviorism In the field's early days, many psychologists shared with the English essayist C. S. Lewis the view that "there is one thing, and only one in the whole universe which we know more about than we could learn from external observation." That one thing, Lewis said, is ourselves. "We have, so to speak, inside information" (1960, pp. 18–19). Wundt and Titchener focused on inner sensations, images, and feelings. James also engaged in introspective examination of the stream of consciousness and of emotion. For these and other early pioneers, *psychology* was defined as "the science of mental life."

That definition continued until the 1920s, when the first of two provocative American psychologists appeared on the scene. John B. Watson, and later B. F. Skinner, dismissed introspection and redefined *psychology* as "the scientific study of observable behavior." After all, they said, science is rooted in observation: What you cannot observe and measure, you cannot scientifically study. You cannot observe a sensation, a feeling, or a thought, but you *can* observe and record people's *behavior* as they respond to and learn in different situations. Many agreed, and the **behaviorists** became one of two major forces in psychology well into the 1960s.

John B. Watson and Rosalie Rayner Working with Rayner, Watson championed psychology as the scientific study of behavior. He and Rayner showed that fear could be learned, in experiments on a baby who became famous as "Little Albert."

Freudian Psychology The other major force was *Freudian psychology,* which emphasized the ways our unconscious thought processes and our emotional responses to childhood experiences affect our behavior. (In modules to come, we'll

B. F. Skinner This leading behaviorist rejected introspection and studied how consequences shape behavior.

Sigmund Freud The controversial ideas of this famed personality theorist and therapist have influenced humanity's self-understanding.

look more closely at Sigmund Freud's teachings, including his theory of personality, and his views on unconscious sexual conflicts and the mind's defenses against its own wishes and impulses.)

Humanistic Psychology As the behaviorists had rejected the early 1900's definition of *psychology*, two other groups rejected the behaviorist definition in the 1960s. The first, the **humanistic psychologists,** led by Carl Rogers and Abraham Maslow, found both Freudian psychology and behaviorism too limiting. Rather than focusing on the meaning of early childhood memories or the learning of conditioned responses, the humanistic psychologists drew attention to ways that current environmental influences can nurture or limit our growth potential, and to the importance of having our needs for love and acceptance satisfied.

Cognitive Revolution In the 1960s, the *cognitive revolution* led the field back to its early interest in mental processes, such as the importance of how our mind processes and retains information. *Cognitive psychology* scientifically explores the ways we perceive, process, and remember information. The cognitive approach has given us new ways to understand ourselves and to treat disorders such as depression. **Cognitive neuroscience** was birthed by the marriage of cognitive psychology (the science of mind) and neuroscience (the science of brain). This interdisciplinary field studies the brain activity underlying mental activity.

Modern Definition of Psychology To encompass psychology's concern with observable behavior *and* with inner thoughts and feelings, today we define **psychology** as the *science of behavior and mental processes.* Let's unpack this definition. *Behavior* is anything an organism *does*—any action we can observe and record. Yelling, smiling, blinking, sweating, talking, and questionnaire marking are all observable behaviors. *Mental processes* are the internal, subjective experiences we infer from behavior—sensations, perceptions, dreams, thoughts, beliefs, and feelings.

The key word in psychology's definition is *science.* Psychology is less a set of findings than a way of asking and answering questions. Our aim, then, is not merely to report results but also to show you how psychologists play their game. You will see how researchers evaluate conflicting opinions and ideas. And you will learn how all of us, whether scientists or simply curious people, can think smarter when experiencing and explaining the events of our lives.

behaviorism the view that psychology (1) should be an objective science that (2) studies behavior without reference to mental processes. Most psychologists today agree with (1) but not with (2).

humanistic psychology historically significant perspective that emphasized human growth potential.

cognitive neuroscience the interdisciplinary study of the brain activity linked with cognition (including perception, thinking, memory, and language).

psychology the science of behavior and mental processes.

nature–nurture issue the longstanding controversy over the relative contributions that genes and experience make to the development of psychological traits and behaviors. Today's science sees traits and behaviors arising from the interaction of nature and nurture.

natural selection the principle that, among the range of inherited trait variations, those contributing to reproduction and survival will most likely be passed on to succeeding generations.

- From the 1920s through the 1960s, the two major forces in psychology were _____ and _____ psychology.

ANSWERS: behaviorism; Freudian

- How did the cognitive revolution affect the field of psychology?

ANSWER: It recaptured the field's early interest in mental processes and made them legitimate topics for scientific study.

Contemporary Psychology

1-3 How has our understanding of biology and experience, culture and gender, and human flourishing shaped contemporary psychology?

The young science of psychology developed from the more established fields of philosophy and biology. Wundt was both a philosopher and a physiologist. James was an American philosopher. Freud was an Austrian physician. Ivan Pavlov, who pioneered the study of learning, was a Russian physiologist. Jean Piaget, the last century's most influential observer of children, was a Swiss biologist. These "Magellans of the mind," as Morton Hunt (1993) has called them, illustrate psychology's origins in many disciplines and many countries.

Like those pioneers, today's psychologists are citizens of many lands. The International Union of Psychological Science has 182 member nations, from Albania to Zimbabwe. In China, the first university psychology department began in 1978; by 2008 there were nearly 200 (Han, 2008; Tversky, 2008). Moreover, thanks to international publications, joint meetings, and the Internet, collaboration and communication now cross borders. Psychology is *growing* and it is *globalizing*. The story of psychology—the subject of this book—continues to develop in many places, at many levels, with interests ranging from the study of nerve cell activity to the study of international conflicts.

Evolutionary Psychology and Behavior Genetics

Are our human traits present at birth, or do they develop through experience? This has been psychology's biggest and most persistent issue. But the debate over the **nature–nurture issue** is ancient. The Greek philosopher Plato (428–348 B.C.E.) assumed that we inherit character and intelligence and that certain ideas are inborn. Aristotle (384–322 B.C.E.) countered that there is nothing in the mind that does not first come in from the external world through the senses.

In the 1600s, European philosophers rekindled the debate. John Locke argued that the mind is a blank slate on which experience writes. René Descartes disagreed, believing that some ideas are innate. Descartes' views gained support from a curious naturalist two centuries later. In 1831, an indifferent student but ardent collector of beetles, mollusks, and shells set sail on a historic round-the-world journey. The 22-year-old voyager, Charles Darwin, pondered the incredible species variation he encountered, including tortoises on one island that differed from those on nearby islands. Darwin's 1859 *On the Origin of Species* explained this diversity by proposing the evolutionary process of **natural selection:** From among chance variations, nature selects traits that best enable an organism to survive and reproduce in a particular environment. Darwin's principle of natural selection—what philosopher Daniel Dennett (1996) has called "the single best idea anyone has ever had"—is still with us 150+ years later as biology's organizing principle. Evolution also has become an important principle for twenty-first-century psychology. This would surely have pleased Darwin, who believed his theory explained not only animal structures (such as a polar bear's white coat) but also animal behaviors (such as the emotional expressions associated with human lust and rage).

The nature–nurture issue recurs throughout this text as today's psychologists explore the relative contributions of biology and experience. They ask, for example, how are we humans alike because of our common biology and evolutionary history?

Charles Darwin Darwin argued that natural selection shapes behaviors as well as bodies.

That's the focus of **evolutionary psychology.** And how are we diverse because of our differing genes and environments? That's the focus of **behavior genetics.** Are gender differences biologically predisposed or socially constructed? Is children's grammar mostly innate or formed by experience? How are intelligence and personality differences influenced

(left) © Rubberball/Getty Images; (right) Tony Freemont/PhotoEdit

by heredity and by environment? Are sexual behaviors more "pushed" by inner biology or "pulled" by external incentives? Should we treat psychological disorders—depression, for example—as disorders of the brain, disorders of thought, or both?

Such debates continue. Yet over and over again we will see that in contemporary science the nature–nurture tension dissolves: *Nurture works on what nature endows.* Our species is biologically endowed with an enormous capacity to learn and adapt. Moreover, every psychological event (every thought, every emotion) is simultaneously a biological event. Thus, depression can be both a brain disorder and a thought disorder.

A nature-made nature–nurture experiment Because identical twins have the same genes, they are ideal participants in studies designed to shed light on hereditary and environmental influences on intelligence, personality, and other traits. Studies of identical and fraternal twins provide a rich array of findings—described in other modules—that underscore the importance of both nature and nurture.

RETRIEVAL PRACTICE

- What is natural selection?

ANSWER: This is the process by which nature selects from chance variations the traits that best enable an organism to survive and reproduce in a particular environment.

- What is contemporary psychology's position on the nature–nurture debate?

ANSWER: Psychological events often stem from the interaction of nature and nurture, rather than from either of them acting alone.

Cross-Cultural and Gender Psychology

What can we learn about people in general from psychological studies done in one time and place—often with people from what Joseph Henrich, Steven Heine, and Ara Norenzayan (2010) call the WEIRD cultures (Western, Educated, Industrialized, Rich, and Democratic)? As we will see time and again, **culture**—shared ideas and behaviors that one generation passes on to the next—matters. Our culture shapes our behavior. It influences our standards of promptness and frankness, our attitudes toward premarital sex and varying body shapes, our tendency to be casual or formal, our willingness to make eye contact, our conversational distance, and much, much more. Being aware of such differences, we can restrain our assumptions that others will think and act as we do.

It is also true, however, that our shared biological heritage unites us as a universal human family. The same underlying processes guide people everywhere:

- People diagnosed with specific learning disorder (formerly called dyslexia) exhibit the same brain malfunction whether they are Italian, French, or British (Paulesu et al., 2001).

- Variation in languages may impede communication across cultures. Yet all languages share deep principles of grammar, and people from opposite hemispheres can communicate with a smile or a frown.

- People in different cultures vary in feelings of loneliness. But across cultures, loneliness is magnified by shyness, low self-esteem, and being unmarried (Jones et al., 1985; Rokach et al., 2002).

We are each in certain respects like all others, like some others, and like no other. Studying people of all races and cultures helps us discern our similarities and our differences, our human kinship and our diversity.

"All people are the same; only their habits differ."

Confucius, 551–479 B.C.E

evolutionary psychology the study of the evolution of behavior and the mind, using principles of natural selection.

behavior genetics the study of the relative power and limits of genetic and environmental influences on behavior.

culture the enduring behaviors, ideas, attitudes, values, and traditions shared by a group of people and transmitted from one generation to the next.

Culture and kissing Kissing crosses cultures. Yet how we do it varies. Imagine yourself kissing someone on the lips. Do you tilt your head right or left? In Western cultures, in which people read from left to right, about two-thirds of couples kiss right, as in William and Kate's famous kiss, and in Auguste Rodin's sculpture, *The Kiss*. In one study, 77 percent of Hebrew- and Arabic-language right-to-left readers kissed tilting left (Shaki, 2013).

(left) Mark Cuthbert/UK Press Getty Images; (right) © Hemis/Alamy

 LaunchPad is a research-based online learning tool that will help you excel in this course. Visit LaunchPad to take advantage of self-tests, interactive simulations, and **HOW WOULD YOU KNOW?** activities. For a 1-minute introduction to LaunchPad, including how to get in and use its helpful resources, go to http://tinyurl.com/LaunchPadIntro. In LaunchPad, you will find resources collected by module groups. Additional resources may be found by clicking on the "Resources" star in the left column.

You will see throughout this book that *gender* matters, too. Researchers report gender differences in what we dream, in how we express and detect emotions, and in our risk for alcohol use disorder, depression, and eating disorders. Gender differences fascinate us, and studying them is potentially beneficial. For example, many researchers have observed that women carry on conversations more readily to build relationships, while men talk more to give information and advice (Tannen, 2001). Knowing this difference can help us prevent conflicts and misunderstandings in everyday relationships.

But again, psychologically as well as biologically, women and men are overwhelmingly similar. Whether female or male, we learn to walk at about the same age. We experience the same sensations of light and sound. We feel the same pangs of hunger, desire, and fear. We exhibit similar overall intelligence and well-being.

The point to remember: Even when specific attitudes and behaviors vary by gender or across cultures, as they often do, the underlying causes are much the same.

Positive Psychology

Psychology's first hundred years focused on understanding and treating troubles, such as abuse and anxiety, depression and disease, prejudice and poverty. Much of today's psychology continues the exploration of such challenges. Without slighting the need

LaunchPad For an excellent tour of psychology's roots, view the 9.5-minute *Video: The History of Psychology.*

to repair damage and cure disease, Martin Seligman and others (2002, 2005, 2011) have called for more research on *human flourishing.* These psychologists call their approach **positive psychology.** They believe that happiness is a by-product of a pleasant, engaged, and meaningful life. Thus, positive psychology uses scientific methods to explore the building of a "good life" that engages our skills, and a "meaningful life" that points beyond ourselves.

Psychology's Three Main Levels of Analysis

1-4 What are psychology's levels of analysis and related perspectives?

Each of us is a complex system that is part of a larger social system. But each of us is also composed of smaller systems, such as our nervous system and body organs, which are composed of still smaller systems—cells, molecules, and atoms.

These tiered systems suggest different **levels of analysis,** which offer complementary outlooks. It's like explaining horrific school shootings. Is it because the shooters have brain disorders or genetic tendencies that cause them to be violent? Because they have been rewarded for violent behavior? Because we live in a gun-promoting society that accepts violence? Such perspectives are complementary because "everything is related to everything else" (Brewer, 1996). Together, different levels of analysis form an integrated **biopsychosocial approach,** which considers the influences of biological, psychological, and social-cultural factors (**FIGURE 1-1**).

Each level provides a valuable playing card in psychology's explanatory deck. It's a vantage point for looking at a behavior or mental process, yet each by itself is incomplete. Like different academic disciplines, psychology's varied perspectives ask different questions and have their own limits. One perspective may stress the biological, psychological, or social-cultural level more than another, but the different perspectives described in **TABLE 1-1** on the next page complement one another. Consider, for example, how they shed light on anger:

- Someone working from a *neuroscience perspective* might study brain circuits that cause us to be red in the face and "hot under the collar."

- Someone working from the *evolutionary perspective* might analyze how anger facilitated the survival of our ancestors' genes.

- Someone working from the *behavior genetics perspective* might study how heredity and experience influence our individual differences in temperament.

Biological influences:
- genetic predispositions (genetically influenced traits)
- genetic mutations
- natural selection of adaptive traits and behaviors passed down through generations
- genes responding to the environment

Psychological influences:
- learned fears and other learned expectations
- emotional responses
- cognitive processing and perceptual interpretations

Social-cultural influences:
- presence of others
- cultural, societal, and family expectations
- peer and other group influences
- compelling models (such as in the media)

▼ FIGURE 1-1
Biopsychosocial approach This integrated viewpoint incorporates various levels of analysis and offers a more complete picture of any given behavior or mental process.

JUERGEN SCHWARZ/AFP/Getty Images

positive psychology the scientific study of human functioning, with the goals of discovering and promoting strengths and virtues that help individuals and communities to thrive.

levels of analysis the differing complementary views, from biological to psychological to social-cultural, for analyzing any given phenomenon.

biopsychosocial approach an integrated approach that incorporates biological, psychological, and social-cultural levels of analysis.

▼ TABLE 1-1
Psychology's Current Perspectives

Perspective	Focus	Sample Questions	Examples of Subfields Using This Perspective
Neuroscience	How the body and brain enable emotions, memories, and sensory experiences	How do pain messages travel from the hand to the brain? How is blood chemistry linked with moods and motives?	Biological; cognitive; clinical
Evolutionary	How the natural selection of traits has promoted the survival of genes	How does evolution influence behavior tendencies?	Biological; developmental; social
Behavior genetics	How our genes and our environment influence our individual differences	To what extent are psychological traits such as intelligence, personality, sexual orientation, and vulnerability to depression products of our genes? Of our environment?	Personality; developmental; legal/forensic
Psychodynamic	How behavior springs from unconscious drives and conflicts	How can someone's personality traits and disorders be explained by unfulfilled wishes and childhood traumas?	Clinical; counseling; personality
Behavioral	How we learn observable responses	How do we learn to fear particular objects or situations? What is the most effective way to alter our behavior, say, to lose weight or stop smoking?	Clinical; counseling; industrial-organizational
Cognitive	How we encode, process, store, and retrieve information	How do we use information in remembering? Reasoning? Solving problems?	Cognitive neuroscience; clinical; counseling; industrial-organizational
Social-cultural	How behavior and thinking vary across situations and cultures	How are we alike as members of one human family? How do we differ as products of our environment?	Developmental; social; clinical; counseling

- Someone working from the *psychodynamic perspective* might view an outburst as an outlet for unconscious hostility.

- Someone working from the *behavioral perspective* might attempt to determine which external stimuli trigger angry responses or aggressive acts.

- Someone working from the *cognitive perspective* might study how our interpretation of a situation affects our anger and how our anger affects our thinking.

- Someone working from the *social-cultural perspective* might explore how expressions of anger vary across cultural contexts.

The point to remember: Like two-dimensional views of a three-dimensional object, each of psychology's perspectives is helpful. But each by itself fails to reveal the whole picture.

━━━━━━━━━━━━━ **RETRIEVAL PRACTICE** ━━━━━━━━━━━━━

- What advantage do we gain by using the biopsychosocial approach in studying psychological events?

ANSWER: By incorporating different levels of analysis, the biopsychosocial approach can provide a more complete view than any one perspective could offer.

- The _____ perspective in psychology focuses on how behavior and thought differ from situation to situation and from culture to culture, while the _____ perspective emphasizes observation of how we respond to and learn in different situations.

ANSWERS: social-cultural; behavioral

Psychology's Subfields

1-5 What are psychology's main subfields?

Picturing a chemist at work, you may envision a white-coated scientist surrounded by test tubes and high-tech equipment. Picture a psychologist at work and you would be right to envision

- a white-coated scientist probing a rat's brain.

- an intelligence researcher measuring how quickly an infant shows boredom by looking away from a familiar picture.

- an executive evaluating a new "healthy lifestyles" training program for employees.

- someone at a computer analyzing data on whether adopted teens' temperaments more closely resemble those of their adoptive parents or their biological parents.

- a therapist listening carefully to a depressed client's thoughts.

- a traveler visiting another culture and collecting data on variations in human values and behaviors.

- a teacher or writer sharing the joy of psychology with others.

The cluster of subfields we call psychology is a meeting ground for different disciplines. "Psychology is a hub scientific discipline," said Association for Psychological Science president John Cacioppo (2007). Thus, it's a perfect home for those with wide-ranging interests. In its diverse activities, from biological experimentation to cultural comparisons, the tribe of psychology is united by a common quest: *describing and explaining behavior and the mind underlying it.*

Some psychologists conduct **basic research** that builds psychology's knowledge base. We will meet a wide variety of such researchers, including *biological psychologists* exploring the links between brain and mind; *developmental psychologists* studying our changing abilities from womb to tomb; *cognitive psychologists* experimenting with how we perceive, think, and solve problems; *personality psychologists* investigating our persistent traits; and *social psychologists* exploring how we view and affect one another.

"I'm a social scientist, Michael. That means I can't explain electricity or anything like that, but if you ever want to know about people I'm your man."

basic research pure science that aims to increase the scientific knowledge base.

Psychology in court Forensic psychologists apply psychology's principles and methods in the criminal justice system. They may assess witness credibility, or testify in court on a defendant's state of mind and future risk.

Image Source/Punchstock

Psychology: A science and a profession Psychologists experiment with, observe, test, and treat behavior. Here we see psychologists testing a child, measuring emotion-related physiology, and doing face-to-face therapy.

applied research scientific study that aims to solve practical problems.

counseling psychology a branch of psychology that assists people with problems in living (often related to school, work, or marriage) and in achieving greater well-being.

clinical psychology a branch of psychology that studies, assesses, and treats people with psychological disorders.

psychiatry a branch of medicine dealing with psychological disorders; practiced by physicians who sometimes provide medical (for example, drug) treatments as well as psychological therapy.

community psychology a branch of psychology that studies how people interact with their social environments and how social institutions affect individuals and groups.

🎮 **LaunchPad** Want to learn more? See Appendix B, Subfields of Psychology, at the end of this book, and go to LaunchPad's regularly updated *Careers in Psychology* resource to learn about the many interesting options available to those with bachelor's, master's, and doctoral degrees in psychology.

These and other psychologists also may conduct **applied research,** tackling practical problems. *Industrial-organizational psychologists,* for example, use psychology's concepts and methods in the workplace to help organizations and companies select and train employees, boost morale and productivity, design products, and implement systems.

Although most psychology textbooks focus on psychological science, psychology is also a helping profession devoted to such practical issues as how to have a happy marriage, how to overcome anxiety or depression, and how to raise thriving children. As a science, psychology at its best bases such interventions on *evidence of effectiveness.* **Counseling psychologists** help people to cope with challenges and crises (including academic, vocational, and marital issues) and to improve their personal and social functioning. **Clinical psychologists** assess and treat people with mental, emotional, and behavior disorders. Both counseling and clinical psychologists administer and interpret tests, provide counseling and therapy, and sometimes conduct basic and applied research. By contrast, **psychiatrists,** who also may provide psychotherapy, are medical doctors licensed to prescribe drugs and otherwise treat physical causes of psychological disorders.

Rather than seeking to change people to fit their environment, **community psychologists** work to create social and physical environments that are healthy for all (Bradshaw et al., 2009; Trickett, 2009). For example, if school bullying is a problem, some psychologists will seek to change the bullies. Knowing that many students struggle with the transition from elementary to middle school, they might train individual kids how to cope. Community psychologists instead seek ways to adapt the school experience to early adolescent needs. To prevent bullying, they might study how the school and neighborhood foster bullying and how to increase bystander intervention (Polanin et al., 2012).

With perspectives ranging from the biological to the social, and with settings from the laboratory to the clinic, psychology relates to many fields. Psychologists teach in medical schools, law schools, and theological seminaries, and they work in hospitals, factories, and corporate offices. They engage in interdisciplinary studies, such as psychohistory (the psychological analysis of historical characters), psycholinguistics (the study of language and thinking), and psychoceramics (the study of crackpots).[1]

Psychology also influences modern culture. Knowledge transforms us. Learning about the solar system and the germ theory of disease alters the way people think and act. Learning about psychology's findings also changes people: They less often judge psychological disorders as moral failings, treatable by punishment and ostracism.

---

1. Confession: I [DM] wrote the last part of this sentence on April Fools' Day.

They less often regard and treat women as men's mental inferiors. They less often view and raise children as ignorant, willful beasts in need of taming. "In each case," noted Morton Hunt (1990, p. 206), "knowledge has modified attitudes, and, through them, behavior." Once aware of psychology's well-researched ideas—about how body and mind connect, how a child's mind grows, how we construct our perceptions, how we remember (and misremember) our experiences, how people across the world differ (and are alike)—your mind may never again be quite the same.

But bear in mind psychology's limits. Don't expect it to answer the ultimate questions, such as those posed by Russian novelist Leo Tolstoy (1904): "Why should I live? Why should I do anything? Is there in life any purpose which the inevitable death that awaits me does not undo and destroy?"

Although many of life's significant questions are beyond psychology, some very important ones are illuminated by even a first psychology course. Through painstaking research, psychologists have gained insights into brain and mind, dreams and memories, depression and joy. Even the unanswered questions can renew our sense of mystery about things we do not yet understand. Moreover, your study of psychology can help teach you how to ask and answer important questions—how to think critically as you evaluate competing ideas and claims.

Psychology deepens our appreciation for how we humans perceive, think, feel, and act. By so doing it can indeed enrich our lives and enlarge our vision. Through this book we hope to help guide you toward that end. As educator Charles Eliot said a century ago: "Books are the quietest and most constant of friends, and the most patient of teachers."

> "Once expanded to the dimensions of a larger idea, [the mind] never returns to its original size."
>
> Oliver Wendell Holmes, 1809–1894

> "I have uttered what I did not understand, things too wonderful for me."
>
> Job 42:3

RETRIEVAL PRACTICE

- Match the specialty on the left with the description on the right.

1. Clinical psychology
2. Psychiatry
3. Community psychology

a. Works to create social and physical environments that are healthy for all.

b. Studies, assesses, and treats people with psychological disorders but usually does not provide medical therapy.

c. Branch of medicine dealing with psychological disorders.

ANSWERS: 1. b, 2. c, 3. a

Improve Your Retention—and Your Grades

1-6 How can psychological principles help you learn and remember?

Do you, like most students, assume that the way to cement your new learning is to reread? What helps even more—and what this book therefore encourages—is repeated self-testing and rehearsal of previously studied material. Memory researchers Henry Roediger and Jeffrey Karpicke (2006) call this phenomenon the **testing effect.** (It is also sometimes called the *retrieval practice effect* or *test-enhanced learning*.) They note that "testing is a powerful means of improving learning, not just assessing it." In one of their studies, students recalled the meaning of 40 previously learned Swahili words much better if tested repeatedly than if they spent the same time restudying the words (Karpicke & Roediger, 2008).

As you will see in other modules, to master information you must *actively process it*. Your mind is not like your stomach, something to be filled passively; it is more like a muscle that grows stronger with exercise. Countless experiments reveal that people learn and remember best when they put material in their own words, rehearse it, and then retrieve and review it again.

testing effect enhanced memory after retrieving, rather than simply rereading, information. Also sometimes referred to as a *retrieval practice effect* or *test-enhanced learning*.

SQ3R a study method incorporating five steps: *Survey, Question, Read, Retrieve, Review.*

The **SQ3R** study method incorporates these principles (McDaniel et al., 2009; Robinson, 1970). SQ3R is an acronym for its five steps: Survey, Question, Read, Retrieve,[2] Review.

To study a module, first *survey,* taking a bird's-eye view. Scan the headings, and notice how the module is organized.

Before you read each main section, try to answer its numbered Learning Objective *Question* (for this section: "How can psychological principles help you learn and remember?"). Roediger and Bridgid Finn (2009) have found that "trying and failing to retrieve the answer is actually helpful to learning." Those who test their understanding *before* reading, and discover what they don't yet know, will learn and remember better.

Then *read,* actively searching for the answer to the question. At each sitting, read only as much of the module (usually a single main section) as you can absorb without tiring. Read actively and critically. Ask questions. Take notes. Make the ideas your own: How does what you've read relate to your own life? Does it support or challenge your assumptions? How convincing is the evidence?

Having read a section, *retrieve* its main ideas. "Active retrieval promotes meaningful learning," says Karpicke (2012). So *test yourself.* This will not only help you figure out what you know, the testing itself will help you learn and retain the information more effectively. Even better, test yourself repeatedly. To facilitate this, we offer periodic *Retrieval Practice* opportunities throughout each module (see, for example, the questions in this module). After answering these questions for yourself, you can check the answers provided, and reread as needed.

"It pays better to wait and recollect by an effort from within, than to look at the book again."

William James, *Principles of Psychology,* 1890

Finally, *review:* Read over any notes you have taken, again with an eye on the module's organization, and quickly review the whole module. Write or say what a concept is before rereading to check your understanding.

Survey, question, read, retrieve, review. I have organized this book's modules to facilitate your use of the SQ3R study system. Each module begins with an outline that aids your *survey.* Headings and Learning Objective *Questions* suggest issues and concepts you should consider as you *read.* The material is organized into sections of

---

2. Also sometimes called "Recite."

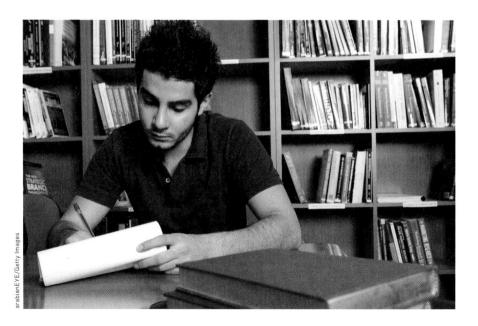

arabianEYE/Getty Images

readable length. The Retrieval Practice questions will challenge you to *retrieve* what you have learned, and thus better remember it. The end-of-module *Review* includes the collected Learning Objective Questions and key terms for self-testing. Complete Module Reviews can be found in Appendix C. Additional self-test questions in a variety of formats appear together, organized by section, at the end of each module, with answers appearing in Appendix D. Survey, question, read . . .

Four additional study tips may further boost your learning:

Distribute your study time. One of psychology's oldest findings is that *spaced practice* promotes better retention than *massed practice*. You'll remember material better if you space your time over several study periods—perhaps one hour a day, six days a week—rather than cram it into one long study blitz. For example, rather than trying to read an entire module in a single sitting, read just one main section and then turn to something else. *Interleaving* your study of psychology with your study of other subjects boosts long-term retention and protects against overconfidence (Kornell & Bjork, 2008; Taylor & Rohrer, 2010).

Spacing your study sessions requires a disciplined approach to managing your time. (Richard O. Straub explains time management in a helpful preface at the beginning of this text.)

Learn to think critically. Whether you are reading or in class, note people's assumptions and values. What perspective or bias underlies an argument? Evaluate evidence. Is it anecdotal? Or is it based on informative experiments? Assess conclusions. Are there alternative explanations?

Process class information actively. Listen for the main ideas and sub-ideas of a lecture. *Write them down.* Ask questions during and after class. In class, as in your private study, process the information actively and you will understand and retain it better. As psychologist William James urged a century ago, "*No reception without reaction, no impression without . . . expression.*" Make the information your own. Take notes in your own words. (Handwritten notes typically engage more active processing into your own words, and thus better memory, than does verbatim note-taking on laptops [Mueller & Oppenheimer, 2014]). Relate what you read to what you already know. Tell someone else about it. (As any teacher will confirm, to teach is to remember.)

Overlearn. Psychology tells us that overlearning improves retention. We are prone to overestimating how much we know. You may understand a module as you read it, but that feeling of familiarity can be deceptively comforting. Using the Retrieval Practice questions as well as LaunchPad's varied opportunities, devote extra study time to testing your knowledge and exploring psychology.

Memory experts Elizabeth Bjork and Robert Bjork (2011) offer the bottom line for how to improve your retention and your grades:

> Spend less time on the input side and more time on the output side, such as summarizing what you have read from memory or getting together with friends and asking each other questions. Any activities that involve testing yourself—that is, activities that require you to retrieve or generate information, rather than just representing information to yourself—will make your learning both more durable and flexible. (p. 63)

More learning tips To learn more about the testing effect and the SQ3R method, view the 5-minute animation, Make Things Memorable, at tinyurl.com/HowToRemember.

RETRIEVAL PRACTICE

• The _____ _____ describes the enhanced memory that results from repeated retrieval (as in self-testing) rather than from simple rereading of new information.

ANSWER: testing effect

• What does the acronym SQ3R stand for?

ANSWER: Survey, Question, Read, Retrieve, and Review

MODULE 1 REVIEW What is Psychology?

LEARNING OBJECTIVES

RETRIEVAL PRACTICE Take a moment to answer each of these Learning Objective Questions (repeated here from within this module). Then turn to Appendix C, Complete Module Reviews, to check your answers. Research suggests that trying to answer these questions on your own will improve your long-term retention (McDaniel et al., 2009).

1-1 What were some important milestones in psychology's early development?

1-2 How did psychology continue to develop from the 1920s through today?

1-3 How has our understanding of biology and experience, culture and gender, and human flourishing shaped contemporary psychology?

1-4 What are psychology's levels of analysis and related perspectives?

1-5 What are psychology's main subfields?

1-6 How can psychological principles help you learn and remember?

TERMS AND CONCEPTS TO REMEMBER

RETRIEVAL PRACTICE Test yourself on these terms by trying to write down the definition before flipping back to check your answers.

structuralism, p. 3
functionalism, p. 3
behaviorism, p. 5
humanistic psychology, p. 5
cognitive neuroscience, p. 5
psychology, p. 5
nature–nurture issue, p. 6
natural selection, p. 6
evolutionary psychology, p. 7
behavior genetics, p. 7
culture, p. 7
positive psychology, p. 9
levels of analysis, p. 9
biopsychosocial approach, p. 9
basic research, p. 11
applied research, p. 12
counseling psychology, p. 12
clinical psychology, p. 12
psychiatry, p. 12
community psychology, p. 12
testing effect, p. 13
SQ3R, p. 14

Use **LearningCurve** to create your personalized study plan, which will direct you to the resources that will help you most in **LaunchPad**.

TEST YOUR-SELF   THE STORY OF PSYCHOLOGY

Test yourself repeatedly throughout your studies. This will not only help you figure out what you know and don't know; the testing itself will help you learn and remember the information more effectively thanks to the *testing effect*.

MODULE 1   What Is Psychology?

1. In 1879, in psychology's first experiment, _____ and his students measured the time lag between hearing a ball hit a platform and pressing a key.

2. William James would be considered a(n) _____ . Wilhelm Wundt and Edward Titchener would be considered _____ .

   a. functionalist; structuralists
   b. structuralist; functionalists
   c. evolutionary theorist; structuralists
   d. functionalist; evolutionary theorists

3. In the early twentieth century, _____ redefined psychology as "the science of observable behavior."

   a. John B. Watson
   b. Abraham Maslow
   c. William James
   d. Sigmund Freud

4. Nature is to nurture as

   a. personality is to intelligence.
   b. biology is to experience.
   c. intelligence is to biology.
   d. psychological traits are to behaviors.

5. "Nurture works on what nature endows." Describe what this means, using your own words.

6. A psychologist treating emotionally troubled adolescents at a local mental health agency is most likely to be a(n)

   a. research psychologist.

   b. psychiatrist.

   c. industrial-organizational psychologist.

   d. clinical psychologist.

7. A mental health professional with a medical degree who can prescribe medication is a _____ .

8. A psychologist conducting basic research to expand psychology's knowledge base would be most likely to

   a. design a computer screen with limited glare and assess the effect on computer operators' eyes after a day's work.

   b. treat older people who are overcome by depression.

   c. observe 3- and 6-year-olds solving puzzles and analyze differences in their abilities.

   d. interview children with behavioral problems and suggest treatments.

Find answers to these questions in Appendix D, in the back of the book.

Holger Hill/© I Stop/Alamy

THINKING CRITICALLY WITH PSYCHOLOGICAL SCIENCE

· · · · · · · · · · · · ·

Hoping to satisfy their curiosity and remedy their woes, millions turn to "psychology." They listen to talk-radio counseling, read articles on psychic powers, attend stop-smoking hypnosis seminars, and immerse themselves in self-help—on the meaning of dreams, the path to ecstatic love, and the roots of personal happiness.

Others, intrigued by claims of psychological truth, wonder: How does parenting shape children's personalities? Are first-born children more driven? Do dreams have deep meaning? Does psychotherapy heal?

In working with such questions, how can we separate uninformed opinions from examined conclusions? *How can we best use psychology to understand why people think, feel, and act as they do?* In Modules 2 through 4 we explore how psychological science can help you think critically and consider psychology's research methods and ways of interpreting data.

MODULE 2 The Need for Psychological Science

2-1 How does our everyday thinking sometimes lead us to a wrong conclusion?

SOME PEOPLE SUPPOSE THAT PSYCHOLOGY merely documents and dresses in jargon what people already know: "You get paid for using fancy methods to prove what my grandmother knows?" Others place their faith in human **intuition**: "Buried deep within each and every one of us, there is an instinctive, heart-felt awareness that provides—if we allow it to—the most reliable guide," offered Prince Charles (2000).

Prince Charles has much company, judging from the long list of pop psychology books on "intuitive managing," "intuitive trading," and "intuitive healing." Today's psychological science does document a vast intuitive mind. As we will see, our thinking, memory, and attitudes operate on two levels—conscious and unconscious—with the larger part operating automatically, offscreen. Like jumbo jets, we fly mostly on autopilot.

So, are we smart to listen to the whispers of our inner wisdom, to simply trust "the force within"? Or should we more often be subjecting our intuitive hunches to skeptical scrutiny?

This much seems certain: We often underestimate intuition's perils. My [DM] geographical intuition tells me that Reno is east of Los Angeles, that Rome is south of New York, that Atlanta is east of Detroit. But I am wrong, wrong, and wrong.

Studies show that people greatly overestimate their lie detection accuracy, their eyewitness recollections, their interviewee assessments, their risk predictions, and their stock-picking talents. As a Nobel Prize–winning physicist explained, "The first principle is that you must not fool yourself—and you are the easiest person to fool" (Feynman, 1997).

Indeed, observed novelist Madeleine L'Engle, "The naked intellect is an extraordinarily inaccurate instrument" (1973). Three phenomena—*hindsight bias, overconfidence,* and our *tendency to perceive patterns in random events*—illustrate why we cannot rely solely on intuition and common sense.

Jose Luis Pelaez Inc./Blend Images/Getty Images

The limits of intuition Personnel interviewers tend to be overconfident of their gut feelings about job applicants. Their confidence stems partly from their recalling cases where their favorable impression proved right, and partly from their ignorance about rejected applicants who succeeded elsewhere.

"Those who trust in their own wits are fools."

Proverbs 28:26

"Life is lived forwards, but understood backwards."

Philosopher Søren Kierkegaard, 1813–1855

"Anything seems commonplace, once explained."

Dr. Watson to Sherlock Holmes

intuition an effortless, immediate, automatic feeling or thought, as contrasted with explicit, conscious reasoning.

hindsight bias the tendency to believe, after learning an outcome, that one would have foreseen it. (Also known as the *I-knew-it-all-along phenomenon.*)

Did We Know It All Along? Hindsight Bias

Consider how easy it is to draw the bull's eye *after* the arrow strikes. After the stock market drops, people say it was "due for a correction." After the football game, we credit the coach if a "gutsy play" wins the game, and fault the coach for the "stupid play" if it doesn't. After a war or an election, its outcome usually seems obvious. Although history may therefore seem like a series of inevitable events, the actual future is seldom foreseen. No one's diary recorded, "Today the Hundred Years War began."

This **hindsight bias** (also known as the *I-knew-it-all-along phenomenon*) is easy to demonstrate: Give half the members of a group some purported psychological finding, and give the other half an opposite result. Tell the first group, "Psychologists have found that separation weakens romantic attraction. As the saying goes, "Out of sight, out of mind." Ask them to imagine why this might be true. Most people can, and nearly all will then view this true finding as unsurprising.

Tell the second group the opposite, "Psychologists have found that separation strengthens romantic attraction. As the saying goes, "Absence makes the heart grow fonder." People given this untrue result can also easily imagine it, and most will also see it as unsurprising. When opposite findings both seem like common sense, there is a problem.

Such errors in our recollections and explanations show why we need psychological research. Just asking people how and why they felt or acted as they did can sometimes be misleading—not because common sense is usually wrong, but because common sense more easily describes what *has* happened than what *will* happen. As physicist Niels Bohr reportedly jested, "Prediction is very difficult, especially about the future."

More than 800 scholarly papers have shown hindsight bias in people young and old from across the world (Roese & Vohs, 2012). Nevertheless, Grandma's intuition is often right. As baseball great Yogi Berra once said, "You can observe a lot by watching." (We have Berra to thank for other gems, such as "Nobody ever comes here—it's too crowded," and "If the people don't want to come out to the ballpark, nobody's gonna stop 'em.") Because we're all behavior watchers, it would be surprising if many of psychology's findings had *not* been foreseen. Many people believe that love breeds happiness, and they are right (we have what researchers identify as a deep "need to belong").

REUTERS/U.S. Coast Guard/Handout

Hindsight bias When drilling its Deepwater Horizon oil well in 2010, BP employees took shortcuts and ignored warning signs, without intending to harm the environment or their company's reputation. *After* the resulting Gulf oil spill, with the benefit of 20/20 hindsight, the foolishness of those judgments became obvious.

Indeed, noted Daniel Gilbert, Brett Pelham, and Douglas Krull (2003), "good ideas in psychology usually have an oddly familiar quality, and the moment we encounter them we feel certain that we once came close to thinking the same thing ourselves and simply failed to write it down." Good ideas are like good inventions: Once created, they seem obvious. (Why did it take so long for someone to invent suitcases on wheels and Post-it Notes?)

But sometimes Grandma's intuition, informed by countless casual observations, is wrong. In other modules, we will see how research has overturned popular ideas—that familiarity breeds contempt, that dreams predict the future, and that most of us use only 10 percent of our brain. We will also see how it has surprised us with discoveries about how the brain's chemical messengers control our moods and memories, about other animals' abilities, and about the effects of stress on our capacity to fight disease.

Overconfidence

We humans tend to think we know more than we do. Asked how sure we are of our answers to factual questions (*Is Boston north or south of Paris?*), we tend to be more confident than correct.[1] Or consider these three anagrams, which Richard Goranson (1978) asked people to unscramble:

WREAT → WATER

ETRYN → ENTRY

GRABE → BARGE

About how many seconds do you think it would have taken you to unscramble each of these? Did hindsight influence you? Knowing the answers tends to make us overconfident. (Surely the solution would take only 10 seconds or so.) In reality, the average problem solver spends 3 minutes, as you also might, given a similar anagram without the solution: OCHSA.[2]

Are we any better at predicting social behavior? University of Pennsylvania psychologist Philip Tetlock (1998, 2005) collected more than 27,000 expert predictions of world events, such as the future of South Africa or whether Quebec would separate from Canada.

Fun anagram solutions from Wordsmith (www.wordsmith.org):
Snooze alarms = Alas! No more z's
Dormitory = dirty room
Slot machines = cash lost in 'em

---

1. Boston is south of Paris.

2. The anagram solution: CHAOS.

Overconfidence in history:

"We don't like their sound. Groups of guitars are on their way out."

Decca Records, in turning down a recording contract with the Beatles in 1962

"Computers in the future may weigh no more than 1.5 tons."

Popular Mechanics, 1949

"They couldn't hit an elephant at this distance."

General John Sedgwick just before being killed during a U.S. Civil War battle, 1864

"The telephone may be appropriate for our American cousins, but not here, because we have an adequate supply of messenger boys."

British expert group evaluating the invention of the telephone

LaunchPad

HOW WOULD YOU KNOW?

Consider how scientific inquiry can help you think smarter about hot streaks in sports with LaunchPad's *How Would You Know If There Is a Hot Hand in Basketball?*

LaunchPad is a research-based online learning tool that will help you excel in this course. Visit LaunchPad to take advantage of self-tests, interactive simulations, and **HOW WOULD YOU KNOW?** activities. For a 1-minute introduction to LaunchPad, including how to get in and use its helpful resources, go to http://tinyurl.com/LaunchPadIntro. In LaunchPad, you will find resources collected by module groups. Additional resources may be found by clicking on the "Resources" star in the left column.

His repeated finding: These predictions, which experts made with 80 percent confidence on average, were right less than 40 percent of the time. Nevertheless, even those who erred maintained their confidence by noting they were "almost right." "The Québécois separatists *almost* won the secessionist referendum."

─────────────── **RETRIEVAL PRACTICE** ───────────────

• Why, after friends start dating, do we often feel that we *knew* they were meant to be together?

ANSWER: We often suffer from hindsight bias—after we've learned a situation's outcome, that outcome seems familiar and therefore obvious.

Bizarre-looking, perhaps. But actually no more unlikely than any other number sequence.

Perceiving Order in Random Events

In our natural eagerness to make sense of our world, we perceive patterns. People see a face on the Moon, hear Satanic messages in music, perceive the Virgin Mary's image on a grilled cheese sandwich. Even in random data, we often find order, because— here's a curious fact of life—*random sequences often don't look random* (Falk et al., 2009; Nickerson, 2002, 2005). Flip a coin 50 times and you may be surprised at the streaks of heads and tails. In actual random sequences, patterns and streaks (such as repeating digits) occur more often than people expect (Oskarsson et al., 2009).

However, some happenings, such as winning a lottery twice, seem so extraordinary that we struggle to conceive an ordinary, chance-related explanation. "But with a large enough sample, any outrageous thing is likely to happen," note statisticians Persi Diaconis and Frederick Mosteller (1989). An event that happens to but 1 in 1 billion people every day occurs about 7 times a day, 2500 times a year.

The point to remember: Hindsight bias, overconfidence, and our tendency to perceive patterns in random events often lead us to overestimate our intuition. But scientific inquiry can help us sift reality from illusion.

Given enough random events, some weird-seeming streaks will occur During the 2010 World Cup, a German octopus—Paul, "the oracle of Oberhausen"— was offered two boxes, each with mussels and with a national flag on one side. Paul selected the correct box eight out of eight times in predicting the outcome of Germany's seven matches and Spain's triumph in the final.

The Scientific Attitude: Curious, Skeptical, and Humble

2-2 How do the scientific attitude's three main components relate to critical thinking?

Underlying all science is, first, a hard-headed *curiosity*, a passion to explore and understand without misleading or being misled. Some questions (*Is there life after death?*) are beyond science. Answering them in any way requires a leap of faith. With many other ideas (*Can some people demonstrate ESP?*), the proof is in the pudding. Let the facts speak for themselves.

Magician James Randi has used this *empirical approach* when testing those claiming to see glowing auras around people's bodies:

> *Randi:* Do you see an aura around my head?
>
> *Aura seer:* Yes, indeed.
>
> *Randi:* Can you still see the aura if I put this magazine in front of my face?
>
> *Aura seer:* Of course.
>
> *Randi:* Then if I were to step behind a wall barely taller than I am, you could determine my location from the aura visible above my head, right?

Randi once told me that no aura seer has agreed to take this simple test.

No matter how sensible-seeming or wild an idea, the smart thinker asks: *Does it work?* When put to the test, can its predictions be confirmed? Subjected to such scrutiny, crazy-sounding ideas sometimes find support. During the 1700s, scientists scoffed at the notion that meteorites had extraterrestrial origins. When two Yale scientists challenged the conventional opinion, Thomas Jefferson reportedly jeered, "Gentlemen, I would rather believe that those two Yankee professors would lie than to believe that stones fell from Heaven." Sometimes scientific inquiry turns jeers into cheers.

More often, science becomes society's garbage disposal, sending crazy-sounding ideas to the waste heap, atop previous claims of perpetual motion machines, miracle cancer cures, and out-of-body travels into centuries past. To sift reality from fantasy, sense from nonsense, therefore requires a scientific attitude: being skeptical but not cynical, open but not gullible.

"To believe with certainty," says a Polish proverb, "we must begin by doubting." As scientists, psychologists approach the world of behavior with a *curious skepticism*, persistently asking two questions: *What do you mean? How do you know?*

When ideas compete, skeptical testing can reveal which ones best match the facts. Do parental behaviors determine children's sexual orientation? Can astrologers predict your future based on the position of the planets at your birth? Is electroconvulsive therapy (delivering an electric shock to the brain) an effective treatment for severe depression? As we will see, putting such claims to the test has led psychological scientists to answer *No* to the first two questions and *Yes* to the third.

Putting a scientific attitude into practice requires not only curiosity and skepticism but also *humility*—an awareness of our own vulnerability to error and an openness to surprises and new perspectives. In the last analysis, what matters is not my opinion or yours, but the truths nature reveals in response to our questioning. If people or other animals don't behave as our ideas predict, then so much the worse for our ideas. This humble attitude was expressed in one of psychology's early mottos: "The rat is always right."

"The really unusual day would be one where nothing unusual happens."

Statistician Persi Diaconis (2002)

AP Photo/Alan Diaz

The Amazing Randi The magician James Randi exemplifies skepticism. He has tested and debunked supposed psychic phenomena.

Non Sequitur

THE IRRESISTIBLE FORCE MEETS THE IMMOVABLE OBJECT

THE FACTS AS THEY ARE

THE TRUTH AS I SEE IT

WILEY 5-16

Sidney Harris/American Scientist magazine, 1990.
Reprinted by permission of Universal Press Syndicate.
© 1997 Wiley.

Historians of science tell us that these three attitudes—curiosity, skepticism, and humility—helped make modern science possible. Some deeply religious people today may view science, including psychological science, as a threat. Yet, many of the leaders of the scientific revolution, including Copernicus and Newton, were deeply religious people acting on the idea that "in order to love and honor God, it is necessary to fully appreciate the wonders of his handiwork" (Stark, 2003a,b).

Of course, scientists, like anyone else, can have big egos and may cling to their preconceptions. Nevertheless, the ideal of curious, skeptical, humble scrutiny of competing ideas unifies psychologists as a community as they check and recheck one another's findings and conclusions.

Critical Thinking

The scientific attitude prepares us to think smarter. Smart thinking, called **critical thinking,** examines assumptions, appraises the source, discerns hidden values, evaluates evidence, and assesses conclusions. Whether reading online commentary or listening to a conversation, critical thinkers ask questions: *How do they know that? What is this person's agenda? Is the conclusion based on anecdote and gut feelings, or on evidence? Does the evidence justify a cause–effect conclusion? What alternative explanations are possible?*

Critical thinking, informed by science, helps clear the colored lenses of our biases. Consider: Does climate change threaten our future, and, if so, is it human-caused? In 2009, climate-action advocates interpreted an Australian heat wave and dust storms as evidence of climate change. In 2010, climate-change skeptics perceived North American bitter cold and East Coast blizzards as discounting global warming. Rather than having their understanding of climate change swayed by today's weather, or by their own political views, critical thinkers say, "Show me the evidence." Over time, is the Earth actually warming? Are the polar ice caps melting? Are vegetation patterns changing? And is human activity spewing gases that would lead us to expect such changes? When contemplating such issues, critical thinkers will consider the credibility of sources. They will look at the evidence (*Do the facts support them, or are they just makin' stuff up?*). They will recognize multiple perspectives. And they will expose themselves to news sources that challenge their preconceived ideas.

Has psychology's critical inquiry been open to surprising findings? The answer, as ensuing modules illustrate, is plainly *Yes*. Some examples: Massive losses of brain tissue early in life may actually have minimal long-term effects. Within days, newborns can recognize their mother by her odor. After brain damage, a person may be able to learn new skills yet be completely unaware of such learning. Diverse groups—men and women, old and young, rich and middle class, those with disabilities and those without—report roughly comparable levels of personal happiness.

"My deeply held belief is that if a god anything like the traditional sort exists, our curiosity and intelligence are provided by such a god. We would be unappreciative of those gifts . . . if we suppressed our passion to explore the universe and ourselves."

Carl Sagan, *Broca's Brain,* 1979

From a Twitter feed:

"The problem with quotes on the Internet is that you never know if they're true." —Abraham Lincoln

"The real purpose of the scientific method is to make sure Nature hasn't misled you into thinking you know something you don't actually know."

Robert M. Pirsig, *Zen and the Art of Motorcycle Maintenance,* 1974

critical thinking thinking that does not blindly accept arguments and conclusions. Rather, it examines assumptions, appraises the source, discerns hidden values, evaluates evidence, and assesses conclusions.

And has critical inquiry convincingly debunked popular presumptions? The answer, as ensuing modules also illustrate, is again *Yes*. Research shows that sleep-walkers are *not* acting out their dreams. Our past experiences are *not* all recorded verbatim in our brains; with brain stimulation or hypnosis, one *cannot* simply "hit the replay button" and relive long-buried or repressed memories. Most people do *not* suffer from low self-esteem, and high self-esteem is not all good. Opposites do *not* generally attract. In each of these instances and more, what scientists have learned is not what is widely believed.

Psychological science can also identify effective policies. To deter crime, should we invest money in lengthening prison sentences or increase the likelihood of arrest? To help people recover from a trauma, should counselors help them relive it, or not? To increase voting, should we tell people about the low turnout problem, or emphasize that their peers are voting? When put to critical thinking's test—and contrary to common practice—the second option in each case wins (Shafir, 2013).

Life after studying psychology The study of psychology, and its critical thinking strategies, have helped prepare people for varied occupations, as illustrated by Facebook founder Mark Zuckerburg (who studied psychology and computer science while at Harvard) and satirist Jon Stewart (a psych major at William and Mary).

RETRIEVAL PRACTICE

- "For a lot of bad ideas, science is society's garbage disposal." Describe what this tells us about the scientific attitude and what's involved in critical thinking.

ANSWER: The scientific attitude combines (1) *curiosity* about the world around us, (2) *skepticism* about unproven claims and ideas, and (3) *humility* about one's own understanding. Evaluating evidence, assessing conclusions, and examining our own assumptions are essential parts of critical thinking.

MODULE 2 REVIEW   The Need for Psychological Science

LEARNING OBJECTIVES

RETRIEVAL PRACTICE Take a moment to answer each of these Learning Objective Questions (repeated here from within this module). Then turn to Appendix C, Complete Module Reviews, to check your answers. Research suggests that trying to answer these questions on your own will improve your long-term retention (McDaniel et al., 2009).

2-1 How does our everyday thinking sometimes lead us to a wrong conclusion?

2-2 How do the scientific attitude's three main components relate to critical thinking?

TERMS AND CONCEPTS TO REMEMBER

RETRIEVAL PRACTICE Test yourself on these terms by trying to write down the definition before flipping back to check your answers.

intuition, p. 20

hindsight bias, p. 20

critical thinking, p. 24

Use 🔵 LearningCurve to create your personalized study plan, which will direct you to the resources that will help you most in 🔵 LaunchPad.

MODULE 3 Research Strategies: How Psychologists Ask and Answer Questions

PSYCHOLOGISTS ARM THEIR SCIENTIFIC ATTITUDE with the *scientific method*—a self-correcting process for evaluating ideas with observation and analysis. In its attempt to describe and explain human nature, psychological science welcomes hunches and plausible-sounding theories. And it puts them to the test. If a theory works—if the data support its predictions—so much the better for that theory. If the predictions fail, the theory will be revised or rejected.

The Scientific Method

3-1 How do theories advance psychological science?

In everyday conversation, we often use *theory* to mean "mere hunch." Someone might, for example, discount evolution as "only a theory"—as if it were mere speculation. In science, a **theory** *explains* behaviors or events by offering ideas that *organize* what we have observed. By organizing isolated facts, a theory simplifies. By linking facts with deeper principles, a theory offers a useful summary. As we connect the observed dots, a coherent picture emerges.

A theory about the effects of sleep on memory, for example, helps us organize countless sleep-related observations into a short list of principles. Imagine that we observe over and over that people with good sleep habits tend to answer questions correctly in class, and they do well at test time. We might therefore theorize that sleep improves memory. So far so good: Our principle neatly summarizes a list of facts about the effects of a good night's sleep on memory.

Yet no matter how reasonable a theory may sound—and it does seem reasonable to suggest that sleep could improve memory—we must put it to the test. A good theory produces testable *predictions*, called **hypotheses.** Such predictions specify what results (what behaviors or events) would support the theory and what results would disconfirm it. To test our theory about the effects of sleep on memory, our hypothesis might be that when sleep deprived, people will remember less from the day before. To test that hypothesis, we might assess how well people remember course materials they studied before a good night's sleep, or before a shortened night's sleep (**FIGURE 3.1**). The results will either confirm our theory or lead us to revise or reject it.

Our theories can bias our observations. Having theorized that better memory springs from more sleep, we may see what we expect: We may perceive sleepy people's comments as less insightful. The urge to see what we expect is ever-present, both inside and outside the laboratory. According to the bipartisan U.S. Senate Select Committee on Intelligence (2004), preconceived expectations that Iraq had weapons of mass destruction led intelligence analysts to wrongly interpret ambiguous observations as confirming that theory (much as people's views of climate change may influence their interpretation of local weather events). This theory-driven conclusion then led to the preemptive U.S. invasion of Iraq.

To avoid biases, psychologists report their research with precise **operational definitions** of procedures and concepts. *Sleep deprived,* for example, may be defined as "X hours less" than the person's natural sleep. Using these carefully worded statements, others can **replicate** (repeat) the original observations with different participants, materials, and circumstances. The first study of hindsight bias (the tendency to believe, after learning an outcome, that one would have foreseen it) aroused psychologists' curiosity.

theory an explanation using an integrated set of principles that organizes observations and predicts behaviors or events.

hypothesis a testable prediction, often implied by a theory.

operational definition a carefully worded statement of the exact procedures (operations) used in a research study. For example, *human intelligence* may be operationally defined as what an intelligence test measures.

replication repeating the essence of a research study, usually with different participants in different situations, to see whether the basic finding extends to other participants and circumstances.

Theories
Example: Sleep boosts memory.

confirm, reject, or revise

lead to

Research and observations
Example: Give study material to people before (a) an ample night's sleep, or (b) a shortened night's sleep, then test memory.

lead to

Hypotheses
Example: When sleep deprived, people remember less from the day before.

▼ FIGURE 3.1
The scientific method A self-correcting process for asking questions and observing nature's answers.

Now, after many successful replications with differing people and questions, we feel sure of the phenomenon's power. Although a "mere replication" of someone else's research seldom makes headline news, recent instances of fraudulent or hard-to-believe findings have sparked calls for more replications (Asendorff et al., 2013). Replication is confirmation. Replication enables scientific self-correction. One Association for Psychological Science journal now devotes a section to replications and 72 researchers are collaborating on a "reproducibility project" that aims to replicate a host of recent findings (Open Science Collaboration, 2012). So, replications are increasing, and so far, most "report similar findings to their original studies" (Makel et al., 2012).

In the end, our theory will be useful if it (1) *organizes* a range of self-reports and observations, and (2) implies *predictions* that anyone can use to check the theory or to derive practical applications. (Does people's sleep predict their retention?) Eventually, our research may (3) stimulate further research that leads to a revised theory that better organizes and predicts what we know.

As we will see next, we can test our hypotheses and refine our theories using *descriptive* methods (which describe behaviors, often through case studies, surveys, or naturalistic observations), *correlational* methods (which associate different factors), and *experimental* methods (which manipulate factors to discover their effects). To think critically about popular psychology claims, we need to understand these methods and know what conclusions they allow.

───────────────── **RETRIEVAL PRACTICE** ─────────────────

• What does a good theory do?

ANSWER: 1. It *organizes* observed facts. 2. It implies hypotheses that offer testable *predictions* and, sometimes, practical applications. 3. It often stimulates further research.

• Why is replication important?

ANSWER: Psychologists watch eagerly for new findings, but they also proceed with caution—by awaiting other investigators' repeating the experiment to see if the finding can be confirmed (the result replicated).

Description

3-2 How do psychologists use case studies, naturalistic observations, and surveys to observe and describe behavior, and why is random sampling important?

The starting point of any science is description. In everyday life, we all observe and describe people, often drawing conclusions about why they act as they do.

case study a descriptive technique in which one individual or group is studied in depth in the hope of revealing universal principles.

"'Well my dear,' said Miss Marple, 'human nature is very much the same everywhere, and of course, one has opportunities of observing it at closer quarters in a village'."

Agatha Christie,
The Tuesday Club Murders, 1933

Skye Hohmann/Alamy

Freud and Little Hans Sigmund Freud's case study of 5-year-old Hans' extreme fear of horses led Freud to his theory of childhood sexuality. He conjectured that Hans felt unconscious desire for his mother, feared castration by his rival father, and then transferred this fear into his phobia about being bitten by a horse. Today's psychological science discounts Freud's theory of childhood sexuality but acknowledges that much of the human mind operates outside our conscious awareness.

naturalistic observation a descriptive technique of observing and recording behavior in naturally occurring situations without trying to manipulate and control the situation.

Professional psychologists do much the same, though more objectively and systematically, through

- *case studies* (in-depth analyses of individuals or groups).
- *naturalistic observations* (watching and recording the natural behavior of many individuals).
- *surveys* and interviews (asking people questions).

The Case Study

Among the oldest research methods, the **case study** examines one individual or group in depth in the hope of revealing things true of us all. Some examples: Much of our early knowledge about the brain came from case studies of individuals who suffered a particular impairment after damage to a certain brain region. Jean Piaget taught us about children's thinking after carefully observing and questioning only a few children. Studies of only a few chimpanzees have revealed their capacity for understanding and language. Intensive case studies are sometimes very revealing. They show us what *can* happen, and they often suggest directions for further study.

But atypical individual cases may mislead us. Unrepresentative information can lead to mistaken judgments and false conclusions. Indeed, anytime a researcher mentions a finding (*Smokers die younger: 95 percent of men over 85 are nonsmokers*) someone is sure to offer a contradictory anecdote (*Well, I have an uncle who smoked two packs a day and lived to be 89*). Dramatic stories and personal experiences (even psychological case examples) command our attention and are easily remembered. Journalists understand that, and often begin their articles with personal stories. Stories move us. But stories can mislead. Which of the following do you find more memorable? (1) "In one study of 1300 dream reports concerning a kidnapped child, only 5 percent correctly envisioned the child as dead" (Murray & Wheeler, 1937). (2) "I know a man who dreamed his sister was in a car accident, and two days later she died in a head-on collision!" Numbers can be numbing, *but the plural of anecdote is not evidence.* As psychologist Gordon Allport (1954, p. 9) said, "Given a thimbleful of [dramatic] facts we rush to make generalizations as large as a tub."

The point to remember: Individual cases can suggest fruitful ideas. What's true of all of us can be glimpsed in any one of us. But to discern the general truths that cover individual cases, we must answer questions with other research methods.

RETRIEVAL PRACTICE

- We cannot assume that case studies always reveal general principles that apply to all of us. Why not?

ANSWER: Case studies involve only one individual or group, so we can't know for sure whether the principles observed would apply to a larger population.

Naturalistic Observation

A second descriptive method records behavior in natural environments. These **naturalistic observations** range from watching chimpanzee societies in the jungle, to videotaping and analyzing parent-child interactions in different cultures, to recording racial differences in students' self-seating patterns in a school lunchroom.

Naturalistic observation has mostly been "small science"—science that can be done with pen and paper rather than fancy equipment and a big budget (Provine, 2012). But new technologies are enabling "big data" observations. New smart-phone apps and body-worn sensors are expanding naturalistic observation. Using such tools, researchers can track willing volunteers—their location, activities, and opinions—without interference. The billions of people on Facebook, Twitter, and Google, for example, have created a huge new opportunity for big-data naturalistic observation. One research team

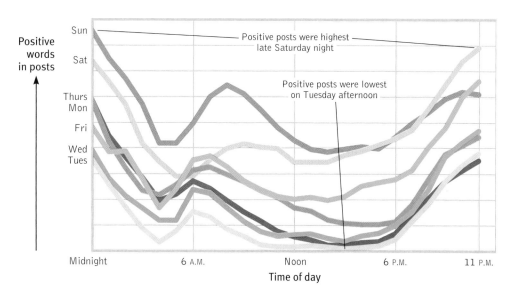

▼ FIGURE 3.2
Twitter message moods, by time and by day This illustrates how, without knowing anyone's identity, big data enable researchers to study human behavior on a massive scale. It now is also possible to associate people's moods with, for example, their locations or with the weather, and to study the spread of ideas through social networks. (Data from Golder & Macy, 2011.)

analyzed all 30.5 billion international Facebook friendships formed over four years, and found that people tended to "friend up." Those from countries with lower economic status were more likely to solicit friendship with those in higher-status countries than vice versa (Landis et al., 2014).

Another research team studied the ups and downs of human moods by counting positive and negative words in 504 million Twitter messages from 84 countries (Golder & Macy, 2011). As **FIGURE 3.2** shows, people seem happier on weekends, shortly after arising, and in the evenings. (Are late Saturday evenings often a happy time for you, too?)

Like the case study, naturalistic observation does not explain behavior. It *describes* it. Nevertheless, descriptions can be revealing. We once thought, for example, that only humans use tools. Then naturalistic observation revealed that chimpanzees sometimes insert a stick in a termite mound and withdraw it, eating the stick's load of termites. Such unobtrusive naturalistic observations paved the way for later studies of animal thinking, language, and emotion, which further expanded our understanding of our fellow animals. "Observations, made in the natural habitat, helped to show that the societies and behavior of animals are far more complex than previously supposed," chimpanzee observer Jane Goodall noted (1998). Thanks to researchers' observations, we know that chimpanzees and baboons use deception: Psychologists repeatedly saw one young baboon pretending to have been attacked by another as a tactic to get its mother to drive the other baboon away from its food (Whiten & Byrne, 1988).

Naturalistic observations also illuminate human behavior. Here are four findings you might enjoy:

- A *funny finding.* We humans laugh 30 times more often in social situations than in solitary situations. (Have you noticed how seldom you laugh when alone?) As we laugh, 17 muscles contort our mouth and squeeze our eyes, and we emit a series of 75-millisecond vowel-like sounds, spaced about one-fifth of a second apart (Provine, 2001).

- *Sounding out students.* What, really, are introductory psychology students saying and doing during their everyday lives? To find out, Matthias Mehl and James Pennebaker (2003) equipped 52 such students from the University of Texas with electronic recorders. For up to four days, the recorders captured 30 seconds of the students' waking hours every 12.5 minutes, thus enabling the researchers to eavesdrop on more than

A natural observer Chimpanzee researcher Frans de Waal (2005) reported, "I am a born observer. . . . When picking a seat in a restaurant I want to face as many tables as possible. I enjoy following the social dynamics—love, tension, boredom, antipathy—around me based on body language, which I consider more informative than the spoken word. Since keeping track of others is something I do automatically, becoming a fly on the wall of an ape colony came naturally to me."

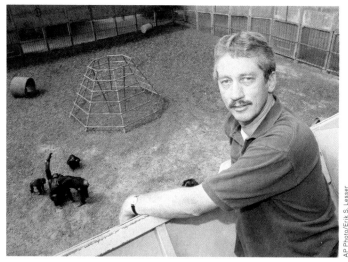

AP Photo/Erik S. Lesser

An EAR for naturalistic observation
Psychologists Matthias Mehl and James Pennebaker have used electronically activated recorders (EARs) to sample naturally occurring slices of daily life.

Courtesy of Matthias Mehl

- What are the advantages and disadvantages of naturalistic observation, such as Mehl and Pennebaker used in this study?

ANSWER: The researchers were able to carefully observe and record naturally occurring behaviors outside the artificiality of the lab. However, outside the lab they were not able to control for all the factors that may have influenced the everyday interactions they were recording.

10,000 half-minute life slices by the end of the study. On what percentage of the slices do you suppose they found the students talking with someone? What percentage captured the students at a computer? The answers: 28 and 9 percent. (What percentage of *your* waking hours are spent in these activities?)

- *What's on your mind?* To find out what was on the minds of their University of Nevada, Las Vegas, students, Christopher Heavey and Russell Hurlburt (2008) gave them beepers. On a half-dozen occasions, a beep interrupted students' daily activities, signaling them to pull out a notebook and record their inner experience at that moment. When the researchers later coded the reports in categories, they found five common forms of inner experience (**TABLE 3.1**).

- *Culture, climate, and the pace of life.* Naturalistic observation also enabled Robert Levine and Ara Norenzayan (1999) to compare the pace of life in 31 countries. (Their operational definition of *pace of life* included walking speed, the speed with which postal clerks completed a simple request, and the accuracy of public clocks.) Their conclusion: Life is fastest paced in Japan and Western Europe, and slower paced in economically less-developed countries. People in colder climates also tend to live at a faster pace (and are more prone to die from heart disease).

Naturalistic observation offers interesting snapshots of everyday life, but it does so without controlling for all the factors that may influence behavior. It's one thing to observe the pace of life in various places, but another to understand what makes some people walk faster than others.

▼ TABLE 3.1
A Penny for Your Thoughts:
The Inner Experience of University Students*

Inner Experience	Example	Frequency
Inner speech	Susan was saying to herself, "I've got to get to class."	26%
Inner seeing	Paul was imagining the face of a best friend, including her neck and head.	34%
Unsymbolized thinking	Alphonse was wondering whether the workers would drop the bricks.	22%
Feeling	Courtney was experiencing anger and its physical symptoms.	26%
Sensory awareness	Fiona was feeling the cold breeze on her cheek and her hair moving.	22%

* More than one experience could occur at once.

The Survey

A **survey** looks at many cases in less depth. A survey asks people to report their behavior or opinions. Questions about everything from sexual practices to political opinions are put to the public. In recent surveys:

- Saturdays and Sundays have been the week's happiest days (confirming what the Twitter researchers found) (Stone et al., 2012).

- 1 in 5 people across 22 countries report believing that alien beings have come to Earth and now walk among us disguised as humans (Ipsos, 2010b).

- 68 percent of all humans—some 4.6 billion people—say that religion is important in their daily lives (from Gallup World Poll data analyzed by Diener et al., 2011).

But asking questions is tricky, and the answers often depend on how questions are worded and respondents are chosen.

survey a descriptive technique for obtaining the self-reported attitudes or behaviors of a particular group, usually by questioning a representative, *random sample* of the group.

Wording Effects Even subtle changes in the order or wording of questions can have major effects. People are much more approving of "aid to the needy" than of "welfare," of "affirmative action" than of "preferential treatment," of "not allowing" televised cigarette ads and pornography than of "censoring" them, and of "revenue enhancers" than of "taxes." In another survey, adults estimated a 55 percent chance "that I will live to be 85 years old or older," while comparable other adults estimated a 68 percent chance "that I will die at 85 years old or younger" (Payne et al., 2013). Because wording is such a delicate matter, critical thinkers will reflect on how the phrasing of a question might affect people's expressed opinions.

Random Sampling In everyday thinking, we tend to generalize from samples we observe, especially vivid cases. Given (a) a statistical summary of a professor's student evaluations and (b) the vivid comments of a biased sample (two irate students), an administrator's impression of the professor may be influenced as much by the two unhappy students as by the many favorable evaluations in the statistical summary. The temptation to ignore the *sampling bias* and to generalize from a few vivid but unrepresentative cases is nearly irresistible.

So how do you obtain a *representative sample* of, say, the students at your college or university? It's not always possible to survey the whole group you want to study and describe. How could you choose a group that would represent the total student **population?** Typically, you would seek a **random sample,** in which every person in the entire group has an equal chance of participating. You might number the names in the general student listing and then use a random number generator to pick your survey participants. (Sending each student a questionnaire wouldn't work because the conscientious people who returned it would not be a random sample.) Large representative samples are better than small ones, but a small representative sample of 100 is better than an unrepresentative sample of 500.

Political pollsters sample voters in national election surveys just this way. Using some 1500 randomly sampled people, drawn from all areas of a country, they can provide a remarkably accurate snapshot of the nation's opinions. Without random sampling, large samples—including call-in phone samples and TV or website polls—often merely give misleading results.

The point to remember: Before accepting survey findings, think critically. Consider the sample. The best basis for generalizing is from a representative sample. You cannot compensate for an unrepresentative sample by simply adding more people.

With very large samples, estimates become quite reliable. *E* is estimated to represent 12.7 percent of the letters in written English. *E*, in fact, is 12.3 percent of the 925,141 letters in Melville's *Moby-Dick*, 12.4 percent of the 586,747 letters in Dickens' *A Tale of Two Cities*, and 12.1 percent of the 3,901,021 letters in 12 of Mark Twain's works (*Chance News*, 1997).

RETRIEVAL PRACTICE

- What is an unrepresentative sample, and how do researchers avoid it?

ANSWER: An unrepresentative sample is a survey group that does not represent the population being studied. *Random sampling* helps researchers form a representative sample, because each member of the population has an equal chance of being included.

Correlation

3-3 What does it mean when we say two things are correlated, and what are positive and negative correlations?

Describing behavior is a first step toward predicting it. Naturalistic observations and surveys often show us that one trait or behavior is related to another. In such cases, we say the two **correlate.** A statistical measure (the **correlation coefficient**) helps us figure how closely two things vary together, and thus how well either one *predicts* the other. Knowing how much aptitude test scores *correlate* with school success tells us how well the scores *predict* school success.

Throughout this book, we will often ask how strongly two things are related: For example, how closely related are the personality scores of identical twins? How well do intelligence test scores predict career achievement? How closely is stress related to disease? In such cases, **scatterplots** can be very revealing.

population all those in a group being studied, from which samples may be drawn. (*Note:* Except for national studies, this does *not* refer to a country's whole population.)

random sample a sample that fairly represents a population because each member has an equal chance of inclusion.

correlation a measure of the extent to which two factors vary together, and thus of how well either factor predicts the other.

correlation coefficient a statistical index of the relationship between two things (from –1.00 to +1.00).

scatterplot a graphed cluster of dots, each of which represents the values of two variables. The slope of the points suggests the direction of the relationship between the two variables. The amount of scatter suggests the strength of the correlation (little scatter indicates high correlation).

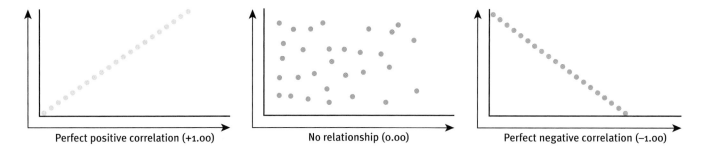

Perfect positive correlation (+1.00)   No relationship (0.00)   Perfect negative correlation (–1.00)

▼ FIGURE 3.3
Scatterplots, showing patterns of correlation Correlations can range from +1.00 (scores on one measure increase in direct proportion to scores on another), to 0.00 (no relationship), to –1.00 (scores on one measure decrease precisely as scores rise on the other).

Each dot in a scatterplot represents the values of two variables. The three scatterplots in **FIGURE 3.3** illustrate the range of possible correlations from a perfect positive to a perfect negative. (Perfect correlations rarely occur in the real world.) A correlation is positive if two sets of scores, such as height and weight, tend to rise or fall together.

Saying that a correlation is "negative" says nothing about its strength. A correlation is negative if two sets of scores relate inversely, one set going up as the other goes down. The study of University of Nevada students discussed earlier found their reports of inner speech correlated negatively (–.36) with their reported psychological distress. Those who reported more inner speech tended to report somewhat *less* psychological distress.

Statistics can help us see what the naked eye sometimes misses. To demonstrate this for yourself, try an imaginary project. You wonder if tall men are more or less easygoing, so you collect two sets of scores: men's heights and men's temperaments. You measure the heights of 20 men, and you have someone else independently assess their temperaments from 0 (*extremely calm*) to 100 (*highly reactive*).

With all the relevant data right in front of you (**TABLE 3.2**), can you tell whether the correlation between height and reactive temperament is positive, negative, or close to zero?

▼ TABLE 3.2
Height and Temperamental Reactivity of 20 Men

Person	Height in Inches	Temperament	Person	Height in Inches	Temperament
1	80	75	11	64	48
2	63	66	12	76	69
3	61	60	13	71	72
4	79	90	14	66	57
5	74	60	15	73	63
6	69	42	16	70	75
7	62	42	17	63	30
8	75	60	18	71	57
9	77	81	19	68	84
10	60	39	20	70	39

Comparing the columns in Table 3.2, most people detect very little relationship between height and temperament. In fact, the correlation in this imaginary example is positive, +.63, as we can see if we display the data as a scatterplot (**FIGURE 3.4**).

If we fail to see a relationship when data are presented as systematically as in Table 3.2, how much less likely are we to notice them in everyday life? To see what is right in front of us, we sometimes need statistical illumination. We can easily see evidence of gender discrimination when given statistically summarized information about job level, seniority, performance, gender, and salary. But we often see no discrimination when the same information dribbles in, case by case (Twiss et al., 1989).

The point to remember: A correlation coefficient helps us see the world more clearly by revealing the extent to which two things relate.

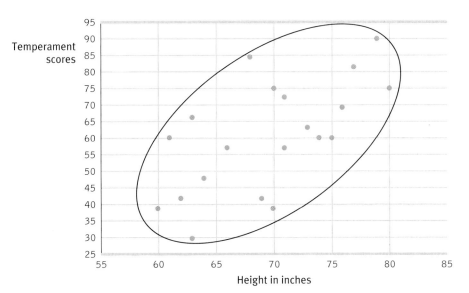

▼ FIGURE 3.4
Scatterplot for height and reactive temperament This display of data from 20 imagined people (each represented by a data point) reveals an upward slope, indicating a positive correlation. The considerable scatter of the data indicates the correlation is much lower than +1.00.

RETRIEVAL PRACTICE

- Indicate whether each association is a positive correlation or a negative correlation.
1. The more children and youth used various media, the less happy they were with their lives (Kaiser, 2010). _____
2. The less sexual content teens saw on TV, the less likely they were to have sex (Collins et al., 2004). _____
3. The longer children were breast-fed, the greater their later academic achievement (Horwood & Ferguson, 1998). _____
4. The more income rose among a sample of poor families, the fewer psychiatric symptoms their children experienced (Costello et al., 2003). _____

ANSWERS: 1. negative, 2. negative, 3. positive, 4. negative

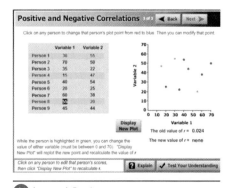

LaunchPad For an animated tutorial on correlations, visit LaunchPad's *Concept Practice: Positive and Negative Correlations.*

Regression Toward the Mean

3-4 What is regression toward the mean?

Correlations not only make visible the relationships we might otherwise miss, they also restrain our "seeing" nonexistent relationships. When we believe there is a relationship between two things, we are likely to notice and recall instances that confirm our belief. If we believe that dreams are forecasts of actual events, we may notice and recall confirming instances more than disconfirming instances. The result is an *illusory correlation.*

Illusory correlations feed an illusion of control—that chance events are subject to our personal control. Gamblers, remembering their lucky rolls, may come to believe they can influence the roll of the dice by again throwing gently for low numbers and hard for high numbers. The illusion that uncontrollable events correlate with our actions is also fed by a statistical phenomenon called **regression toward the mean.** Average results are more typical than extreme results. Thus, after an unusual event, things tend to return toward their average level; extraordinary happenings tend to be followed by more ordinary ones.

The point may seem obvious, yet we regularly miss it: We sometimes attribute what may be a normal regression (the expected return to normal) to something we have done. Consider two examples:

- Students who score much lower or higher on an exam than they usually do are likely, when retested, to return to their average.

regression toward the mean the tendency for extreme or unusual scores or events to fall back (regress) toward the average.

- Unusual ESP subjects who defy chance when first tested nearly always lose their "psychic powers" when retested (a phenomenon parapsychologists have called the *decline effect*).

Failure to recognize regression is the source of many superstitions and of some ineffective practices as well. When day-to-day behavior has a large element of chance fluctuation, we may notice that others' behavior improves (regresses toward average) after we criticize them for very bad performance, and that it worsens (regresses toward average) after we warmly praise them for an exceptionally fine performance. Ironically, then, regression toward the average can mislead us into feeling rewarded for having criticized others and into feeling punished for having praised them (Tversky & Kahneman, 1974).

The point to remember: When a fluctuating behavior returns to normal, there is no need to invent fancy explanations for why it does so. Regression toward the mean is probably at work.

> "Once you become sensitized to it, you see regression everywhere."
>
> Psychologist Daniel Kahneman (1985)

RETRIEVAL PRACTICE

- You hear the school basketball coach telling her friend that she rescued her team's winning streak by yelling at the players after an unusually bad first half. What is another explanation of why the team's performance improved?

ANSWER: The team's poor performance was not their typical behavior. Their return to their normal—their winning streak—may just have been a case of regression toward the mean.

Correlation and Causation

3-5 Why do correlations enable prediction but not cause-effect explanation?

Consider some recent newsworthy correlations:

- "Study finds that increased parental support for college results in lower grades" (Jaschik, 2013).
- People with mental illness more likely to be smokers, study finds" (Belluck, 2013).
- "Teens who play mature-rated, risk-glorifying video games [tend] to become reckless drivers" (Bowen, 2012).

What shall we make of these correlations? Do they indicate that students would achieve more if their parents would support them less? That stopping smoking would improve mental health? That abstaining from video games would make reckless teen drivers more responsible?

No, because such correlations do not come with built-in cause-effect arrows. But correlations do help us *predict*. An example: Parenthood is associated with happiness (Nelson et al., 2013, 2014). So, does having children make people happier? Not so fast, say researchers: Parents also are more likely to be married, and married people tend to be happier than the unmarried (Bhargava et al., 2014). Thus, the correlation between parenthood and happiness needn't mean that parenting increases happiness.

Another example: Self-esteem correlates negatively with (and therefore predicts) depression. (The lower people's self-esteem, the more they are at risk for depression.) So, does low self-esteem *cause* depression? If, based on the correlational evidence, you assume that it does, you have much company. A nearly irresistible thinking error is assuming that an association, sometimes presented as a correlation coefficient, proves causation. But no matter how strong the relationship, it does not. As **FIGURE 3.5** indicates, we'd get the same negative correlation between self-esteem and depression if depression caused people to be down on themselves, or if some third factor—such as heredity or brain chemistry—caused both low self-esteem and depression.

This point is so important—so basic to thinking smarter with psychology—that it merits one more example. A survey of over 12,000 adolescents found that the more teens feel loved by their parents, the less likely they are to behave in unhealthy

---

RETRIEVAL PRACTICE

Correlation need not mean causation

- Length of marriage positively correlates with hair loss in men. Does this mean that marriage causes men to lose their hair (or that balding men make better husbands)?

ANSWER: In this case, as in many others, a third factor can explain the correlation: Golden anniversaries and baldness both accompany aging.

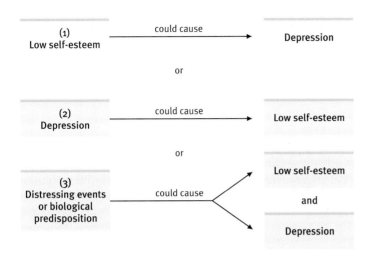

▼ FIGURE 3.5
Three possible cause-effect relationships People low in self-esteem are more likely to report depression than are those high in self-esteem. One possible explanation of this negative correlation is that a bad self-image causes depressed feelings. But, as the diagram indicates, other cause-effect relationships are possible.

ways—having early sex, smoking, abusing alcohol and drugs, exhibiting violence (Resnick et al., 1997). "Adults have a powerful effect on their children's behavior right through the high school years," gushed an Associated Press (AP) story reporting the finding. But again, correlations come with no built-in cause-effect arrow. The AP could as well have reported, "Well-behaved teens feel their parents' love and approval; out-of-

The point to remember (turn the volume up here): *Correlation does not prove causation.*[1] Correlation indicates the *possibility* of a *cause-effect relationship but does not prove such.* Remember this principle and you will be wiser as you read and hear news of scientific studies.

Experimentation

3-6 What are the characteristics of experimentation that make it possible to isolate cause and effect?

Happy are they, remarked the Roman poet Virgil, "who have been able to perceive the causes of things." How might psychologists perceive causes in correlational studies, such as the correlation between breast feeding and intelligence?

Researchers have found that the intelligence scores of children who were breast-fed as infants are somewhat higher than the scores of children who were bottle-fed (Angelsen et al., 2001; Mortensen et al., 2002; Quinn et al., 2001). Moreover, the longer they breast-feed, the higher their later IQ scores (Jedrychowski et al., 2012).

What do such findings mean? Do smarter mothers have smarter children? (Breast-fed children tend to be healthier and higher achieving than other children. But their bottle-fed siblings, born and raised in the same families, tend to be similarly healthy and higher achieving [Colen & Ramey, 2014].) Or, as some researchers believe, do the nutrients of mother's milk also contribute to brain development? To find answers to such questions—to isolate cause and effect—researchers can **experiment.** Experiments enable researchers to isolate the effects of one or more factors by (1) *manipulating the factors of interest* and (2) *holding constant ("controlling") other factors.* To do so, they often create an **experimental group,** in which people receive the treatment, and a contrasting **control group** that does not receive the treatment. To minimize any preexisting differences between the two groups, researchers **randomly assign** people to the two conditions. Random assignment—whether with a random numbers

experiment a research method in which an investigator manipulates one or more factors (independent variables) to observe the effect on some behavior or mental process (the dependent variable). By *random assignment* of participants, the experimenter aims to control other relevant factors.

experimental group in an experiment, the group exposed to the treatment, that is, to one version of the independent variable.

control group in an experiment, the group *not* exposed to the treatment; contrasts with the experimental group and serves as a comparison for evaluating the effect of the treatment.

random assignment assigning participants to experimental and control groups by chance, thus minimizing preexisting differences between the different groups.

Lane Oatey /Getty Images

---

1. This maxim is true not only of correlations, but also of associations verified by other nonexperimental statistics. So we could also say, association does not prove causation.

Recall that in a well-done survey, *random sampling* is important. In an experiment, *random assignment* is equally important.

table or flip of the coin—effectively equalizes the two groups. If one-third of the volunteers for an experiment can wiggle their ears, then about one-third of the people in each group will be ear wigglers. So, too, with ages, attitudes, and other characteristics, which will be similar in the experimental and control groups. Thus, if the groups differ at the experiment's end, we can surmise that the treatment had an effect.

To experiment with breast feeding, one research team randomly assigned some 17,000 Belarus newborns and their mothers either to a control group given normal pediatric care, or an experimental group that promoted breast-feeding, thus increasing expectant mothers' breast intentions (Kramer et al., 2008). At three months of age, 43 percent of the infants in the experimental group were being exclusively breast-fed, as were 6 percent in the control group. At age 6, when nearly 14,000 of the children were restudied, those who had been in the breast-feeding promotion group had intelligence test scores averaging six points higher than their control condition counterparts.

With parental permission, one British research team directly experimented with breast milk. They randomly assigned 424 hospitalized premature infants either to formula feedings or to breast-milk feedings (Lucas et al., 1992). Their finding: For premature infants' developing intelligence, breast was best. On intelligence tests taken at age 8, those nourished with breast milk scored significantly higher than those who were formula-fed. Breast was best.

No single experiment is conclusive, of course. But randomly assigning participants to one feeding group or the other effectively eliminated all factors except nutrition. This supported the conclusion that for developing intelligence, breast is indeed best. If test performance changes when we vary infant nutrition, then we infer that nutrition matters.

The point to remember: Unlike correlational studies, which uncover naturally occurring relationships, an experiment manipulates a factor to determine its effect.

Consider, then, how we might assess therapeutic interventions. Our tendency to seek new remedies when we are ill or emotionally down can produce misleading testimonies. If three days into a cold we start taking vitamin C tablets and find our cold symptoms lessening, we may credit the pills rather than the cold naturally subsiding. In the 1700s, bloodletting *seemed* effective. People sometimes improved after the treatment; when they didn't, the practitioner inferred the disease was too advanced to be reversed. So, whether or not a remedy is truly effective, enthusiastic users will probably endorse it. To determine its effect, we must control for other factors.

And that is precisely how investigators evaluate new drug treatments and new methods of psychological therapy. They randomly assign participants in these studies to research groups. One group receives a treatment (such as a medication). The other group receives a pseudotreatment—an inert *placebo* (perhaps a pill with no drug in it). The participants are often *blind* (uninformed) about what treatment, if any, they are receiving. If the study is using a **double-blind procedure,** neither the participants nor those who administer the drug and collect the data will know which group is receiving the treatment.

In double-blind studies, researchers check a treatment's actual effects apart from the participants' and the staff's belief in its healing powers. Just *thinking* you are getting a treatment can boost your spirits, relax your body, and relieve your symptoms. This **placebo effect** is well documented in reducing pain, depression, and anxiety (Kirsch, 2010). Athletes have run faster when given a supposed performance-enhancing drug (McClung & Collins, 2007). Drinking decaf coffee has boosted vigor and alertness—for those who thought it had caffeine in it (Dawkins et al., 2011). People have felt better after receiving a phony mood-enhancing drug (Michael et al., 2012). And the more expensive the placebo, the more "real" it seems to us—a fake pill that costs $2.50 works better than one costing 10 cents (Waber et al., 2008). To know how effective a therapy really is, researchers must control for a possible placebo effect.

double-blind procedure an experimental procedure in which both the research participants and the research staff are ignorant (blind) about whether the research participants have received the treatment or a placebo. Commonly used in drug-evaluation studies.

placebo [pluh-SEE-bo; Latin for "I shall please"] effect experimental results caused by expectations alone; any effect on behavior caused by the administration of an inert substance or condition, which the recipient assumes is an active agent.

• What measures do researchers use to prevent the *placebo effect* from confusing their results?

ANSWER: Research designed to prevent the placebo effect randomly assigns participants to an experimental group (which receives the real treatment) or to a *control group* (which receives a placebo). A comparison of the results will demonstrate whether the real treatment produces better results than *belief* in that treatment.

> **independent variable** in an experiment, the factor that is manipulated; the variable whose effect is being studied.
>
> **confounding variable** in an experiment, a factor other than the independent variable that might produce an effect.
>
> **dependent variable** in an experiment, the outcome that is measured; the variable that may change when the independent variable is manipulated.

Independent and Dependent Variables

Here is an even more potent example: The drug Viagra was approved for use after 21 clinical experiments. One trial was an experiment in which researchers randomly assigned 329 men with erectile disorder to either an experimental group (Viagra takers) or a control group (placebo takers given an identical-looking pill). The procedure was double-blind—neither the men nor the person giving them the pills knew what they were receiving. The result: At peak doses, 69 percent of Viagra-assisted attempts at intercourse were successful, compared with 22 percent for men receiving the placebo (Goldstein et al., 1998). For many, Viagra worked.

This simple experiment manipulated just one factor: the drug dosage (none versus peak dose). We call this experimental factor the **independent variable** because we can vary it *independently* of other factors, such as the men's age, weight, and personality. Other factors, which can potentially influence the results of the experiment, are called **confounding variables.** Random assignment controls for possible confounding variables.

Experiments examine the effect of one or more independent variables on some measurable behavior, called the **dependent variable** because it can vary *depending* on what takes place during the experiment. Both variables are given precise *operational definitions*, which specify the procedures that manipulate the independent variable (the precise drug dosage and timing in this study) or measure the dependent variable (the questions that assessed the men's responses). These definitions provide a level of precision that enables others to repeat the study. (See **FIGURE** 3.6 for the British breast milk experiment's design.)

Let's pause to check your understanding using a simple psychology experiment: To test the effect of perceived ethnicity on the availability of a rental house, Adrian Carpusor and William Loges (2006) sent identically worded e-mail inquiries to 1115 Los Angeles–area landlords. The researchers varied the ethnic connotation of the sender's name and tracked the percentage of positive replies (invitations to view the apartment in person). "Patrick McDougall," "Said Al-Rahman," and "Tyrell Jackson" received, respectively, 89 percent, 66 percent, and 56 percent invitations.

Experiments can also help us evaluate social programs. Do early childhood education programs boost impoverished children's chances for success? What are the effects of different antismoking campaigns? Do school sex-education programs reduce teen pregnancies? To answer such questions, we can experiment: If an intervention is welcomed but resources are scarce, we could use a lottery to randomly assign some people

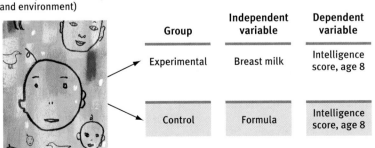

Random assignment (controlling for other variables such as parental intelligence and environment)

Group	Independent variable	Dependent variable
Experimental	Breast milk	Intelligence score, age 8
Control	Formula	Intelligence score, age 8

▼ FIGURE 3.6
Experimentation To discern causation, psychologists may randomly assign some participants to an experimental group, others to a control group. Measuring the dependent variable (intelligence score in later childhood) will determine the effect of the independent variable (type of milk).

▼ TABLE 3.3
Comparing Research Methods

Research Method	Basic Purpose	How Conducted	What Is Manipulated	Weaknesses
Descriptive	To observe and record behavior	Do case studies, naturalistic observations, or surveys	Nothing	No control of variables; single cases may be misleading
Correlational	To detect naturally occurring relationships; to assess how well one variable predicts another	Collect data on two or more variables; no manipulation	Nothing	Cannot specify cause and effect
Experimental	To explore cause and effect	Manipulate one or more factors; use random assignment	The independent variable(s)	Sometimes not feasible; results may not generalize to other contexts; not ethical to manipulate certain variables

LaunchPad To review and test your understanding of experimental methods and concepts, visit LaunchPad's *Concept Practice: The Language of Experiments,* and the interactive *PsychSim 6: Understanding Psychological Research.*

"If I don't think it's going to work, will it still work?"

(or regions) to experience the new program and others to a control condition. If later the two groups differ, the intervention's effect will be supported (Passell, 1993).

Let's recap. A *variable* is anything that can vary (infant nutrition, intelligence, TV exposure—anything within the bounds of what is feasible and ethical). Experiments aim to *manipulate* an *independent* variable, *measure* a *dependent* variable, and control *confounding* variables. An experiment has at least two different conditions: an *experimental condition* and a *comparison* or *control condition. Random assignment* works to minimize preexisting differences between the groups before any treatment effects occur. In this way, an experiment tests the effect of at least one independent variable (what we manipulate) on at least one dependent variable (the outcome we measure). **TABLE 3.3** compares the features of psychology's research methods.

RETRIEVAL PRACTICE

- In the rental housing experiment, what was the independent variable? The dependent variable?

ANSWER: The independent variable, which the researchers manipulated, was the set of ethnically distinct names. The dependent variable, which they measured, was the positive response rate.

- By using *random assignment,* researchers are able to control for _____ _____, which are other factors besides the independent variable(s) that may influence research results.

ANSWER: confounding variables

- Match the term on the left with the description on the right.

  1. double-blind procedure
  2. random sampling
  3. random assignment

  a. helps researchers generalize from a small set of survey responses to a larger population
  b. helps minimize preexisting differences between experimental and control groups
  c. controls for the placebo effect; neither researchers nor participants know who receives the real treatment

ANSWERS: 1. c, 2. a, 3. b

- Why, when testing a new drug to control blood pressure, would we learn more about its effectiveness from giving it to half of the participants in a group of 1000 than to all 1000 participants?

ANSWER: We learn more about the drug's effectiveness when we can compare the results of those who took the drug (the experimental group) with the results of those who did not (the control group). If we gave the drug to all 1000 participants, we would have no way of knowing whether the drug is serving as a placebo or is actually medically effective.

Predicting Real Behavior

3-7 Can laboratory experiments illuminate everyday life?

When you see or hear about psychological research, do you ever wonder whether people's behavior in the lab will predict their behavior in real life? Does detecting the blink of a faint red light in a dark room say anything useful about flying a plane at night? After viewing a violent, sexually explicit film, does an aroused man's increased willingness to push buttons that he thinks will electrically shock a woman really say anything about whether violent pornography makes a man more likely to abuse a woman?

Before you answer, consider: The experimenter *intends* the laboratory environment to be a simplified reality—one that simulates and controls important features of everyday life. Just as a wind tunnel lets airplane designers re-create airflow forces under controlled conditions, a laboratory experiment lets psychologists re-create psychological forces under controlled conditions.

An experiment's purpose is not to re-create the exact behaviors of everyday life but to test *theoretical principles* (Mook, 1983). In aggression studies, deciding whether to push a button that delivers a shock may not be the same as slapping someone in the face, but the principle is the same. *It is the resulting principles—not the specific findings—that help explain everyday behaviors.*

When psychologists apply laboratory research on aggression to actual violence, they are applying theoretical principles of aggressive behavior, principles they have refined through many experiments. Similarly, it is the principles of the visual system, developed from experiments in artificial settings (such as looking at red lights in the dark), that researchers apply to more complex behaviors such as night flying. And many investigations show that principles derived in the laboratory do typically generalize to the everyday world (Anderson et al., 1999).

The point to remember: Psychological science focuses less on particular behaviors than on seeking general principles that help explain many behaviors.

Psychology's Research Ethics

3-8 Why do psychologists study animals, and what ethical guidelines safeguard human and animal research participants? How do human values influence psychology?

We have reflected on how the scientific method can restrain biases. We have seen how case studies, naturalistic observations, and surveys help us describe behavior. We have also noted that correlational studies assess the association between two factors, which indicates how well one thing predicts another. We have examined the logic that underlies experiments, which use control conditions and random assignment of participants to isolate the effects of an independent variable on a dependent variable.

Yet, even knowing this much, you may still be approaching psychology with a mixture of curiosity and apprehension. So before we plunge in, let's entertain some common questions about psychology's ethics and values.

Protecting Research Participants

Studying and protecting animals. Many psychologists study animals because they find them fascinating. They want to understand how different species learn, think, and behave. Psychologists also study animals to learn about people. We humans are not *like* animals; we *are* animals, sharing a common biology. Animal experiments have therefore led to treatments for human diseases—insulin for diabetes, vaccines to prevent polio and rabies, transplants to replace defective organs.

Humans are complex. But the same processes by which we learn are present in rats, monkeys, and even sea slugs. The simplicity of the sea slug's nervous system is precisely what makes it so revealing of the neural mechanisms of learning.

"Rats are very similar to humans except that they are not stupid enough to purchase lottery tickets."

Dave Barry, July 2, 2002

Please do not forget those of us who suffer from incurable diseases or disabilities who hope for a cure through research that requires the use of animals."

Psychologist Dennis Feeney (1987)

"The greatness of a nation can be judged by the way its animals are treated."

Mahatma Gandhi, 1869–1948

Animal research benefiting animals Psychologists have helped zoos enrich animal environments (Weir, 2013). Thanks partly to research on the benefits of novelty, control, and stimulation, these gorillas are enjoying an improved quality of life in New York's Bronx Zoo.

Mary Altaffer/AP Photo

Sharing such similarities, should we not respect our animal relatives? The animal protection movement protests the use of animals in psychological, biological, and medical research. "We cannot defend our scientific work with animals on the basis of the similarities between them and ourselves and then defend it morally on the basis of differences," noted Roger Ulrich (1991).

Out of this heated debate, two issues emerge. The basic one is whether it is right to place the well-being of humans above that of other animals. In experiments on stress and cancer, is it right that mice get tumors in the hope that people might not? Should some monkeys be exposed to an HIV-like virus in the search for an AIDS vaccine? Is our use and consumption of other animals as natural as the behavior of carnivorous hawks, cats, and whales? The answers to such questions vary by culture. In Gallup surveys in Canada and the United States, about 60 percent of adults have deemed medical testing on animals "morally acceptable." In Britain, only 37 percent have agreed (Mason, 2003).

If we give human life first priority, what safeguards should protect the well-being of animals in research? One survey of animal researchers gave an answer. Some 98 percent supported government regulations protecting primates, dogs, and cats, and 74 percent supported regulations providing for the humane care of rats and mice (Plous & Herzog, 2000). Many professional associations and funding agencies already have such guidelines. Most universities screen research proposals, often through Institutional Review Board ethics committees, and laboratories are regulated and inspected. British Psychological Society (BPS) guidelines call for housing animals under reasonably natural living conditions, with companions for social animals (Lea, 2000). American Psychological Association (APA) guidelines state that researchers must ensure the "comfort, health, and humane treatment" of animals and minimize "infection, illness, and pain" (APA, 2002). The European Parliament mandates standards for animal care and housing (Vogel, 2010).

Animals have themselves benefited from animal research. One Ohio team of research psychologists measured stress hormone levels in samples of millions of dogs brought each year to animal shelters. They devised handling and stroking methods to reduce stress and ease the dogs' transition to adoptive homes (Tuber et al., 1999). Other studies have helped improve care and management in animals' natural habitats. By revealing our behavioral kinship with animals and the remarkable intelligence of chimpanzees, gorillas, and other animals, experiments have also led to increased empathy and protection for them. At its best, a psychology concerned for humans and sensitive to animals serves the welfare of both.

Studying and protecting humans. What about human participants? Does the image of white-coated scientists delivering electric shocks trouble you? Actually, most psychological studies are free of such stress. With people, blinking lights, flashing words, and pleasant social interactions are more common. Moreover, psychology's experiments are mild compared with the stress and humiliation often inflicted by reality TV shows. In one episode of *The Bachelor*, a man dumped his new fiancée—on camera, at the producers' request—for the woman who earlier had finished second (Collins, 2009).

Occasionally, though, researchers do temporarily stress or deceive people, but only when they believe it is essential to a justifiable end, such as understanding and controlling violent behavior or studying mood swings. Some experiments won't work if participants know everything beforehand. (Wanting to be helpful, the participants might try to confirm the researcher's predictions.)

The ethics codes of the APA and Britain's BPS urge researchers to (1) obtain potential participants' **informed consent** before the experiment,

(2) protect them from harm and discomfort, (3) keep information about individual participants confidential, and (4) fully **debrief** people (explain the research afterward). University ethics committees use these guidelines to screen research proposals and safeguard participants' well-being.

Values in Research

Psychology is not value free. Values affect what we study, how we study it, and how we interpret results. Researchers' values influence what they deem worthy of investigation. Should we study worker productivity or worker morale? Sex discrimination or gender differences? Conformity or independence? Values can also color "the facts." Our preconceptions can bias our observations and interpretations; sometimes we see what we want or expect to see (**FIGURE 3.7**).

informed consent giving potential participants enough information about a study to enable them to choose whether they wish to participate.

debriefing the postexperimental explanation of a study, including its purpose and any deceptions, to its participants.

Mike Kemp/Getty Images

▼ FIGURE 3.7
What do you see? Our expectations influence what we perceive. Did you see a duck or a rabbit? Show some friends this image with the rabbit photo covered up and see if they are more likely to perceive a duck instead. (Inspired by Shepard, 1990.)

Even the words we use to describe something can reflect our values. Are the sex acts we do not practice *perversions* or *sexual variations?* In psychology and in everyday speech, labels describe and labels evaluate: One person's *rigidity* is another's *consistency.* One person's *faith* is another's *fanaticism.* One country's *enhanced interrogation techniques,* such as cold-water immersion, become *torture* when practiced by its enemies. Our labeling someone as *firm* or *stubborn, careful* or *picky, discreet* or *secretive* reveals our own attitudes.

Popular applications of psychology also contain hidden values. If you defer to "professional" guidance about how to live—how to raise children, how to achieve self-fulfillment, what to do with sexual feelings, how to get ahead at work—you are accepting value-laden advice. A science of behavior and mental processes can help us reach our goals. But it cannot decide what those goals should be.

Some people see psychology as merely common sense. But others have a different concern—that it is becoming dangerously powerful. Is it an accident that astronomy is the oldest science and psychology the youngest? To some, exploring the external universe seems far safer than exploring our own inner universe. Might psychology, they ask, be used to manipulate people?

Knowledge, like all power, can be used for good or evil. Nuclear power has been used to light up cities—and to demolish them. Persuasive power has been used to educate people—and to deceive them. Although psychology does have the power to deceive, its purpose is to enlighten. Every day, psychologists are exploring ways to enhance learning, creativity, and compassion. Psychology speaks to many of our world's great problems—war, overpopulation, prejudice, family crises, crime—all of which involve attitudes and behaviors. Psychology also speaks to our deepest longings—for nourishment, for love, for happiness. Psychology cannot address all of life's great questions, but it speaks to some mighty important ones.

Psychology speaks In making its historic 1954 school desegregation decision, the U.S. Supreme Court cited the expert testimony and research of psychologists Kenneth Clark and Mamie Phipps Clark (1947). The Clarks reported that, when given a choice between Black and White dolls, most African-American children chose the White doll, which seemingly indicated internalized anti-Black prejudice.

Office of Public Affairs at Columbia University, publication permission granted by Columbia University Archives, Columbia Library

• How are animal and human research participants protected?

ANSWER: Animal protection legislation, laboratory regulation and inspection, and local ethics committees serve to protect animal and human welfare. At universities, Institutional Review Boards screen research proposals. Ethical principles developed by international psychological organizations urge researchers using human participants to obtain *informed consent*, to protect them from harm and discomfort, to treat their personal information confidentially, and to fully *debrief* all participants.

MODULE 3   REVIEW   Research Strategies: How Psychologists Ask and Answer Questions

LEARNING OBJECTIVES

RETRIEVAL PRACTICE Take a moment to answer each of these Learning Objective Questions (repeated here from within this module). Then turn to Appendix C, Complete Module Reviews, to check your answers. Research suggests that trying to answer these questions on your own will improve your long-term retention (McDaniel et al., 2009).

3-1 How do theories advance psychological science?

3-2 How do psychologists use case studies, naturalistic observations, and surveys to observe and describe behavior, and why is random sampling important?

3-3 What does it mean when we say two things are correlated, and what are positive and negative correlations?

3-4 What is regression toward the mean?

3-5 Why do correlations enable prediction but not cause–effect explanation?

3-6 What are the characteristics of experimentation that make it possible to isolate cause and effect?

3-7 Can laboratory experiments illuminate everyday life?

3-8 Why do psychologists study animals, and what ethical guidelines safeguard human and animal research participants? How do human values influence psychology?

TERMS AND CONCEPTS TO REMEMBER

RETRIEVAL PRACTICE Test yourself on these terms by trying to write down the definition before flipping back to the page number referenced to check your answer.

theory, p. 26

hypothesis, p. 26

operational definition, p. 26

replication, p. 26

case study, p. 28

naturalistic observation, p. 28

survey, p. 30

population, p. 31

random sample, p. 31

correlation, p. 31

correlation coefficient, p. 31

scatterplot, p. 32

regression toward the mean, p. 33

experiment, p. 35

experimental group, p. 35

control group, p. 35

random assignment, p. 35

double-blind procedure, p. 36

placebo [pluh-SEE-bo] effect, p. 36

independent variable, p. 37

confounding variable, p. 37

dependent variable, p. 37

informed consent, p. 40

debriefing, p. 41

Use 🔄 LearningCurve to create your personalized study plan, which will direct you to the resources that will help you most in 🔄 LaunchPad.

MODULE 4 Statistical Reasoning in Everyday Life

Asked about the *ideal* wealth distribution in America, Democrats and Republicans were surprisingly similar. In the Democrats' ideal world, the richest 20 percent would possess 30 percent of the wealth. Republicans preferred a similar 35 percent (Norton & Ariely, 2011).

IN DESCRIPTIVE, CORRELATIONAL, AND EXPERIMENTAL research, statistics are tools that help us see and interpret what the unaided eye might miss. Sometimes the unaided eye misses badly. Researchers Michael Norton and Dan Ariely (2011) invited 5522 Americans to estimate the percent of wealth possessed by the richest 20 percent in their country. The average person's guess—58 percent—"dramatically underestimated" the actual wealth inequality. (The wealthiest 20 percent, they reported, possessed 84 percent of the wealth.)

Accurate statistical understanding benefits everyone. To be an educated person today is to be able to apply simple statistical principles to everyday reasoning. One needn't memorize complicated formulas to think more clearly and critically about data.

Off-the-top-of-the-head estimates often misread reality and then mislead the public. Someone throws out a big, round number. Others echo it, and before long the big, round number becomes public misinformation. A few examples:

- *Ten percent of people are homosexual.* Or is it 2 to 4 percent, as suggested by various national surveys?

- *We ordinarily use only 10 percent of our brain.* Or is it closer to 100 percent?

- *The human brain has 100 billion nerve cells.* Or is it more like 40 billion, as suggested by extrapolation from sample counts?

The point to remember: Doubt big, round, undocumented numbers. That's actually a lesson we intuitively appreciate, by finding precise numbers more credible (Oppenheimer et al., 2014). When U.S. Secretary of State John Kerry sought to rally American support in 2013 for a military response to Syria's apparent use of chemical weapons, his argument gained credibility from its precision: "The United States government now knows that at least 1429 Syrians were killed in this attack, including at least 426 children."

Statistical illiteracy also feeds needless health scares (Gigerenzer et al., 2008, 2009, 2010). In the 1990s, the British press reported a study showing that women taking a particular contraceptive pill had a 100 percent increased risk of blood clots that could produce strokes. This caused thousands of women to stop taking the pill, leading to a wave of unwanted pregnancies and an estimated 13,000 additional abortions (which also are associated with increased blood-clot risk). And what did the study find? A 100 percent increased risk, indeed—but only from 1 in 7000 to 2 in 7000. Such false alarms underscore the need to teach statistical reasoning and to present statistical information more transparently.

When setting goals, we love big round numbers. We're far more likely to want to lose 20 pounds than 19 or 21 pounds. We're far more likely to retake the SAT if our verbal plus math score is just short of a big round number, such as 1200. By modifying their behavior, batters are nearly four times more likely to finish the season with a .300 average than with a .299 average (Pope & Simonsohn, 2011).

"Figures can be misleading—so I've written a song which I think expresses the real story of the firm's performance this quarter."

Describing Data

4-1 How do we describe data using three measures of central tendency, and what is the relative usefulness of the two measures of variation?

Once researchers have gathered their data, they may use *descriptive statistics* to organize that data meaningfully. One way to do this is to convert the data into a simple *bar graph,* as in **FIGURE 4.1** on the next page, which displays a distribution of different brands of trucks still on the road after a decade. When reading statistical graphs such as this, take care. It's easy to design a graph to make a difference look big (Figure 4.1a) or small (Figure 4.1b). The secret lies in how you label the vertical scale (the *y-axis*).

The point to remember: Think smart. When viewing graphs, read the scale labels and note their range.

Measures of Central Tendency

The next step is to summarize the data using some *measure of central tendency,* a single score that represents a whole set of scores. The simplest measure is the **mode,** the most frequently occurring score or scores. The most familiar is the **mean,** or arithmetic average—the total sum of all the scores divided by the number of scores. The midpoint—the 50th percentile—is the **median.** On a divided highway, the median is the middle. So, too, with data: If you arrange all the scores in order from the highest to the lowest, half will be above the median and half will be below it.

Measures of central tendency neatly summarize data. But consider what happens to the mean when a distribution is lopsided, when it's *skewed* by a few way-out scores.

mode the most frequently occurring score(s) in a distribution.

mean the arithmetic average of a distribution, obtained by adding the scores and then dividing by the number of scores.

median the middle score in a distribution; half the scores are above it and half are below it.

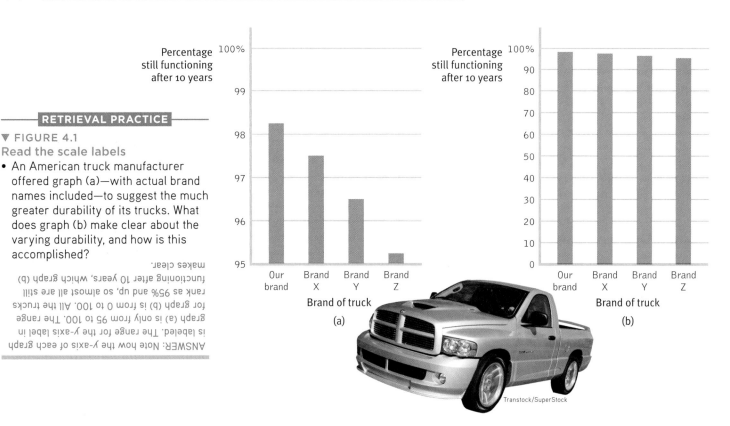

▼ FIGURE 4.1
Read the scale labels
• An American truck manufacturer offered graph (a)—with actual brand names included—to suggest the much greater durability of its trucks. What does graph (b) make clear about the varying durability, and how is this accomplished?

ANSWER: Note how the y-axis of each graph is labeled. The range for the y-axis label in graph (a) is only from 95 to 100. The range for graph (b) is from 0 to 100. All the trucks rank as 95% and up, so almost all are still functioning after 10 years, which graph (b) makes clear.

The average person has one ovary and one testicle.

▼ FIGURE 4.2
A skewed distribution This graphic representation of the distribution of a village's incomes illustrates the three measures of central tendency—mode, median, and mean. Note how just a few high incomes make the mean—the fulcrum point that balances the incomes above and below—deceptively high.

With income data, for example, the mode, median, and mean often tell very different stories (**FIGURE 4.2**). This happens because the mean is biased by a few extreme scores. When Microsoft co-founder Bill Gates sits down in an intimate café, its average (mean) customer instantly becomes a billionaire. But the customers' median wealth remains unchanged. Understanding this, you can see how a British newspaper could accurately run the headline "Income for 62% Is Below Average" (Waterhouse, 1993). Because the bottom *half* of British income earners receive only a *quarter* of the national income cake, most British people, like most people everywhere, make less than the mean. Mean and median tell different true stories.

The point to remember: Always note which measure of central tendency is reported. If it is a mean, consider whether a few atypical scores could be distorting it.

Measures of Variation

Knowing the value of an appropriate measure of central tendency can tell us a great deal. But the single number omits other information. It helps to know something about the amount of *variation* in the data—how similar or diverse the scores are. Averages derived from scores with low variability are more reliable than averages based on scores with high variability. Consider a basketball player who scored between 13 and 17 points in each of the season's first 10 games. Knowing this, we would be more confident that she would score near 15 points in her next game than if her scores had varied from 5 to 25 points.

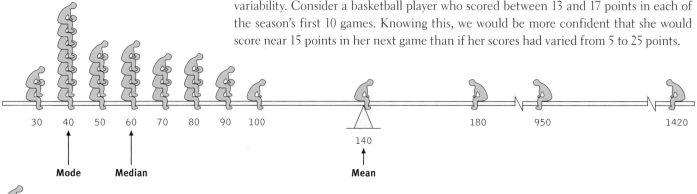

| 30 | 40 | 50 | 60 | 70 | 80 | 90 | 100 | | 180 | 950 | | 1420 |

140

Mode   **Median**   **Mean**

One family   Income per family in thousands of dollars

▼ TABLE 4.1
Standard Deviation Is Much More Informative Than Mean Alone

Note that the test scores in Class A and Class B have the same mean (80), but very different standard deviations, which tell us more about how the students in each class are really faring.

Test Scores in Class A			Test Scores in Class B		
Score	Deviation From the Mean	Squared Deviation	Score	Deviation From the Mean	Squared Deviation
72	−8	64	60	−20	400
74	−6	36	60	−20	400
77	−3	9	70	−10	100
79	−1	1	70	−10	100
82	+2	4	90	+10	100
84	+4	16	90	+10	100
85	+5	25	100	+20	400
87	+7	49	100	+20	400

Total = 640   Sum of (deviations)² = 204

Mean = 640 ÷ 8 = 80

Standard deviation =

$$\sqrt{\frac{\text{Sum of (deviations)}^2}{\text{Number of scores}}} = \sqrt{\frac{204}{8}} = 5.0$$

Total = 640   Sum of (deviations)² = 2000

Mean = 640 ÷ 8 = 80

Standard deviation =

$$\sqrt{\frac{\text{Sum of (deviations)}^2}{\text{Number of scores}}} = \sqrt{\frac{2000}{8}} = 15.8$$

The **range** of scores—the gap between the lowest and highest—provides only a crude estimate of variation. A couple of extreme scores in an otherwise uniform group, such as the $950,000 and $1,420,000 incomes in Figure 4.2, will create a deceptively large range.

The more useful standard for measuring how much scores deviate from one another is the **standard deviation.** It better gauges whether scores are packed together or dispersed, because it uses information from each score. The computation (see **TABLE 4.1** for an example) assembles information about how much individual scores differ from the mean. If your college or university attracts students of a certain ability level, their intelligence scores will have a relatively small standard deviation compared with the more diverse community population outside your school.

You can grasp the meaning of the standard deviation if you consider how scores tend to be distributed in nature. Large numbers of data—heights, weights, intelligence scores, grades (though not incomes)—often form a symmetrical, *bell-shaped* distribution. Most cases fall near the mean, and fewer cases fall near either extreme. This bell-shaped distribution is so typical that we call the curve it forms the **normal curve.**

As **FIGURE 4.3** shows, a useful property of the normal curve is that roughly 68 percent of the cases fall within one standard deviation on either side of the mean.

range the difference between the highest and lowest scores in a distribution.

standard deviation a computed measure of how much scores vary around the mean score.

normal curve *(normal distribution)* a symmetrical, bell-shaped curve that describes the distribution of many types of data; most scores fall near the mean (about 68 percent fall within one standard deviation of it) and fewer and fewer near the extremes.

Number of scores

About 68 percent of people score within 15 points above or below 100

About 95 percent of all people fall within 30 points of 100

68%

95%

0.1%   2%   13.5%   34%   34%   13.5%   2%   0.1%

55   70   85   100   115   130   145

Wechsler intelligence score

▼ FIGURE 4.3
The normal curve Scores on aptitude tests tend to form a normal, or bell-shaped, curve. For example, the most commonly used intelligence test, the Wechsler Adult Intelligence Scale, calls the average score 100.

About 95 percent of cases fall within two standard deviations. Thus, about 68 percent of any group of people taking an intelligence test will score within ±15 points of 100. About 95 percent will score within ±30 points.

LaunchPad For an interactive tutorial on these statistical concepts, visit LaunchPad's *PsychSim 6: Descriptive Statistics.*

RETRIEVAL PRACTICE

- The average of a distribution of scores is the _____. The score that shows up most often is the _____. The score right in the middle of a distribution (half the scores above it; half below) is the _____. We determine how much scores vary around the average in a way that includes information about the _____ of scores (difference between highest and lowest) by using the _____ _____ formula.

ANSWERS: mean; mode; median; range; standard deviation

Significant Differences

4-2 How do we know whether an observed difference can be generalized to other populations?

Data are "noisy." The average score in one group (children who were breast-fed as babies, for example) could conceivably differ from that in another group (children who were bottle-fed as babies) not because of any real difference but merely because of chance fluctuations in the people sampled. How confidently, then, can we infer that an observed difference is not just a fluke—a chance result from the research sample? For guidance, we can ask how reliable and significant the differences are. These *inferential statistics* help us determine if results can be generalized to a larger population.

When Is an Observed Difference Reliable?

In deciding when it is safe to generalize from a sample, we should keep three principles in mind:

1. *Representative samples are better than biased samples.* The best basis for generalizing is not from the exceptional and memorable cases one finds at the extremes but from a representative sample of cases. Research never randomly samples the whole human population. Thus, it pays to keep in mind what population a study has sampled.

2. *Less-variable observations are more reliable than those that are more variable.* As we noted earlier in the example of the basketball player whose game-to-game points were consistent, an average is more reliable when it comes from scores with low variability.

3. *More cases are better than fewer.* An eager prospective student visits two university campuses, each for a day. At the first, the student randomly attends two classes and discovers both instructors to be witty and engaging. At the next campus, the two sampled instructors seem dull and uninspiring. Returning home, the student (discounting the small sample size of only two teachers at each institution) tells friends about the "great teachers" at the first school, and the "bores" at the second. Again, we know it but we ignore it: *Averages based on many cases are more reliable* (less variable) than averages based on only a few cases.

The point to remember: Smart thinkers are not overly impressed by a few anecdotes. Generalizations based on a few unrepresentative cases are unreliable.

"The poor are getting poorer, but with the rich getting richer it all averages out in the long run."

When Is an Observed Difference Significant?

Perhaps you've compared men's and women's scores on a laboratory test of aggression, and found a gender difference. But individuals differ. How likely is it that the difference you observed was just a fluke? Statistical testing can estimate that.

Here is the underlying logic: When averages from two samples are each reliable measures of their respective populations (as when each is based on many observations that have small variability), then their *difference* is likely to be reliable as well. (Example: The less the variability in women's and in men's aggression scores, the more confidence we would have that any observed gender difference is reliable.) And when the difference between the sample averages is *large*, we have even more confidence that the difference between them reflects a real difference in their populations.

In short, when sample averages are reliable, and when the difference between them is relatively large, we say the difference has **statistical significance.** This means that the observed difference is probably not due to chance variation between the samples.

In judging statistical significance, psychologists are conservative. They are like juries who must presume innocence until guilt is proven. For most psychologists, proof beyond a reasonable doubt means not making much of a finding unless the odds of its occurring by chance, if no real effect exists, are less than 5 percent.

> **statistical significance** a statistical statement of how likely it is that an obtained result occurred by chance.

When reading about research, you should remember that, given large enough or homogeneous enough samples, a difference between them may be "statistically significant" yet have little practical significance. For example, comparisons of intelligence test scores among hundreds of thousands of firstborn and later-born individuals indicate a highly significant tendency for first-born individuals to have higher average scores than their later-born siblings (Kristensen & Bjerkedal, 2007; Zajonc & Markus, 1975). But because the scores differ by only one to three points, the difference has little practical importance.

PEANUTS

Reprinted by permission of United Features Syndicate, Inc.

The point to remember: Statistical significance indicates the *likelihood* that a result will happen by chance. But this does not say anything about the *importance* of the result.

RETRIEVAL PRACTICE

- Can you solve this puzzle?
  The registrar's office at the University of Michigan has found that usually about 100 students in Arts and Sciences have perfect marks at the end of their first term at the University. However, only about 10 to 15 students graduate with perfect marks. What do you think is the most likely explanation for the fact that there are more perfect marks after one term than at graduation (Jepson et al., 1983)?

  ANSWER: Averages based on fewer courses are more variable, which guarantees a greater number of extremely low and high marks at the end of the first term.

- _____ statistics summarize data, while _____ statistics determine if data can be generalized to other populations.

  ANSWERS: Descriptive; inferential

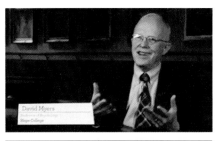

LaunchPad For a 9.5-minute video synopsis of psychology's scientific research strategies, visit LaunchPad's *Video: Research Methods.*

MODULE
4   REVIEW Statistical Reasoning in Everyday Life

LEARNING OBJECTIVES

RETRIEVAL PRACTICE Take a moment to answer each of these Learning Objective Questions (repeated here from within this module). Then turn to Appendix C, Complete Module Reviews, to check your answers. Research suggests that trying to answer these questions on your own will improve your long-term retention (McDaniel et al., 2009).

4-1 How do we describe data using three measures of central tendency, and what is the relative usefulness of the two measures of variation?

4-2 How do we know whether an observed difference can be generalized to other populations?

TERMS AND CONCEPTS TO REMEMBER

RETRIEVAL PRACTICE Test yourself on these terms by trying to write down the definition before flipping back to check your answers.

mode, p. 43

mean, p. 43

median, p. 43

range, p. 45

standard deviation, p. 45

normal curve, p. 45

statistical significance, p. 47

Use 🅜 LearningCurve to create your personalized study plan, which will direct you to the resources that will help you most in 🅜 LaunchPad.

TEST
YOUR-
SELF   THINKING CRITICALLY WITH PSYCHOLOGICAL SCIENCE

Test yourself repeatedly throughout your studies. This will not only help you figure out what you know and don't know; the testing itself will help you learn and remember the information more effectively thanks to the *testing effect*.

MODULE
2   The Need for Psychological Science

1. _____ _____ refers to our tendency to perceive events as obvious or inevitable after the fact.

2. As scientists, psychologists
   a. approach research with negative cynicism.
   b. assume that an article published in a leading scientific journal must be true.
   c. believe that every important human question can be studied scientifically.
   d. are willing to ask questions and to reject claims that cannot be verified by research.

3. How can critical thinking help you evaluate claims in the media, even if you're not a scientific expert on the issue?

MODULE
3   Research Strategies: How Psychologists Ask and Answer Questions

4. Theory-based predictions are called _____ .

5. Which of the following is NOT one of the descriptive methods psychologists use to observe and describe behavior?
   a. A case study
   b. Naturalistic observation
   c. Correlational research
   d. A phone survey

6. You wish to survey a group of people who truly represent the country's adult population. Therefore, you need to ensure that you question a _____ sample of the population.

7. A study finds that the more childbirth training classes women attend, the less pain medication they require during childbirth. This finding can be stated as a _____ (positive/negative) correlation.

8. A _____ provides a visual representation of the direction and the strength of a relationship between two variables.

9. In a _____ correlation, the scores rise and fall together; in a _____ correlation, one score falls as the other rises.
   a. positive; negative
   b. positive; illusory
   c. negative; weak
   d. strong; weak

10. What is regression toward the mean, and how can it influence our interpretation of events?

11. Knowing that two events are correlated provides
   a. a basis for prediction.
   b. an explanation of why the events are related.
   c. proof that as one increases, the other also increases.
   d. an indication that an underlying third factor is at work.

12. Here are some recently reported correlations, with interpretations drawn by journalists. Knowing just these correlations, can you come up with other possible explanations for each of these?

    a. Alcohol use is associated with violence. (One interpretation: Drinking triggers or unleashes aggressive behavior.)

    b. Educated people live longer, on average, than less-educated people. (One interpretation: Education lengthens life and enhances health.)

    c. Teens engaged in team sports are less likely to use drugs, smoke, have sex, carry weapons, and eat junk food than are teens who do not engage in team sports. (One interpretation: Team sports encourage healthy living.)

    d. Adolescents who frequently see smoking in movies are more likely to smoke. (One interpretation: Movie stars' behavior influences impressionable teens.)

13. To explain behaviors and clarify cause and effect, psychologists use _____ .

14. To test the effect of a new drug on depression, we randomly assign people to control and experimental groups. Those in the control group take a pill that contains no medication. This is a _____ .

15. In a double-blind procedure,

    a. only the participants know whether they are in the control group or the experimental group.

    b. experimental and control group members will be carefully matched for age, sex, income, and education level.

    c. neither the participants nor the researchers know who is in the experimental group or control group.

    d. someone separate from the researcher will ask people to volunteer for the experimental group or the control group.

16. A researcher wants to determine whether noise level affects workers' blood pressure. In one group, she varies the level of noise in the environment and records participants' blood pressure. In this experiment, the level of noise is the _____ _____ .

17. The laboratory environment is designed to

    a. exactly re-create the events of everyday life.

    b. re-create psychological forces under controlled conditions.

    c. provide a safe place.

    d. minimize the use of animals and humans in psychological research.

18. In defending their experimental research with animals, psychologists have noted that

    a. animals' physiology and behavior can tell us much about our own.

    b. animal experimentation sometimes helps animals as well as humans.

    c. advancing the well-being of humans justifies animal experimentation.

    d. all of these statements are correct.

MODULE 4 | Statistical Reasoning in Everyday Life

19. Which of the three measures of central tendency is most easily distorted by a few very large or very small scores?

    a. The mode

    b. The mean

    c. The median

    d. They are all equally vulnerable to distortion from atypical scores.

20. The standard deviation is the most useful measure of variation in a set of data because it tells us

    a. the difference between the highest and lowest scores in the set.

    b. the extent to which the sample being used deviates from the bigger population it represents.

    c. how much individual scores differ from the mode.

    d. how much individual scores differ from the mean.

21. Another name for a bell-shaped distribution, in which most scores fall near the middle and fewer scores fall at each extreme, is a _____ _____ .

22. When sample averages are _____ and the difference between them is _____ , we can say the difference has statistical significance.

    a. reliable; large

    b. reliable; small

    c. due to chance; large

    d. due to chance; small

Find answers to these questions in Appendix D, in the back of the book.

© Gregg Vignal/Alamy

THE BIOLOGY OF MIND

· · · · · · · · · · · · ·

In 2000, a Virginia teacher began collecting sex magazines, visiting child pornography websites, and then making subtle advances on his young step-daughter. When his wife called the police, he was arrested and later convicted of child molestation. Though put into a sexual addiction rehabilitation program, he still felt overwhelmed by his sexual urges. The day before being sentenced to prison, he went to his local emergency room complaining of a headache and thoughts of suicide. He was also distraught over his uncontrollable impulses, which led him to proposition nurses.

A brain scan located the problem—in his mind's biology. Behind his right temple there was an egg-sized brain tumor. After surgeons removed the tumor, his lewd impulses faded and he returned home to his wife and stepdaughter. Alas, a year later the tumor partially grew back, and with it the sexual urges. A second tumor removal again lessened the urges (Burns & Swerdlow, 2003).

This case illustrates what you likely believe: that you reside in your head. If surgeons transplanted all your organs below your neck, and even your skin and limbs, you would (*Yes?*) still be you. An acquaintance received a new heart from a woman who, in a rare operation, received a matched heart-lung transplant. When the two chanced to meet in their hospital ward, she introduced herself: "I think you have my heart." But only her heart. Her self, she assumed, still resided inside her skull. We rightly presume that our brain enables our mind. Indeed, no principle is more central to today's psychology, or to this book, than this: *Everything psychological is simultaneously biological.*

Throughout this book you will find examples of this interplay. In the next three modules, we start small and build from the bottom up—from nerve cells up to the brain. (Other modules in the text explore environmental influences, where we will work from the top down to consider how our thinking and emotions influence our brain and our health.)

"Then it's agreed—you can't have a mind without a brain, but you can have a brain without a mind."

MODULE 5 Neural and Hormonal Systems

Biology, Behavior, and Mind

5-1 Why are psychologists concerned with human biology?

YOUR EVERY IDEA, EVERY MOOD, every urge is a biological happening. You love, laugh, and cry with your body. Without your body—your genes, your brain, your appearance—you would, indeed, be nobody. Although we find it convenient to talk separately of biological and psychological influences on behavior, we need to remember: To think, feel, or act without a body would be like running without legs.

Our understanding of how the brain gives birth to the mind has come a long way. The ancient Greek philosopher Plato correctly located the mind in the spherical head—his idea of the perfect form. His student, Aristotle, believed the mind was in the heart, which pumps warmth and vitality to the body. The heart remains our symbol for love, but science has long since overtaken philosophy on this issue: It's your brain, not your heart, that falls in love.

In the early 1800s, German physician Franz Gall proposed that *phrenology*, studying bumps on the skull, could reveal a person's mental abilities and character traits (**FIGURE 5.1**). At one point, Britain had 29 phrenological societies, and phrenologists traveled North America giving skull readings (Dean, 2012; Hunt, 1993). Using a false name, humorist Mark Twain put one famous phrenologist to the test. "He found a cavity [and] startled me by saying that that cavity represented the total absence of the sense of humor!" Three months later, Twain sat for a second reading, this time identifying himself. Now "the cavity was gone, and in its place was . . . the loftiest bump of humor he had ever encountered in his life-long experience!" (Lopez, 2002). The "science" of phrenology remains known today as a reminder of our need for critical thinking and scientific analysis. Although its initial popularity faded, phrenology succeeded in focusing attention on the *localization of function*—the idea that various brain regions have particular functions.

You and I are living in a time Gall could only dream about. By studying the links between biological activity and psychological events, those working from the **biological perspective** are announcing discoveries about the interplay of our biology and our

▼ FIGURE 5.1
A wrongheaded theory
Despite initial acceptance of Franz Gall's speculations (right), bumps on the skull tell us nothing about the brain's underlying functions. Nevertheless, some of his assumptions have held true. Though they are not the functions Gall proposed, different parts of the brain do control different aspects of behavior (far right, from *The Human Brain Book*).

behavior and mind at an exhilarating pace. Within little more than the past century, researchers seeking to understand the biology of the mind have discovered that

- among the body's cells are nerve cells that conduct electricity and "talk" to one another by sending chemical messages across a tiny gap that separates them.
- specific brain systems serve specific functions (though not the functions Gall supposed).
- we integrate information processed in these different brain systems to construct our experience of sights and sounds, meanings and memories, pain and passion.
- our adaptive brain is wired by our experience.

We have also realized that we are each a system composed of subsystems that are in turn composed of even smaller subsystems. Tiny cells organize to form body organs. These organs form larger systems for digestion, circulation, and information processing. And those systems are part of an even larger system—the individual, who in turn is a part of a family, culture, and community. Thus, we are *biopsychosocial* systems. To understand our behavior, we need to study how these biological, psychological, and social systems work and interact.

RETRIEVAL PRACTICE

- What do phrenology and psychology's biological perspective have in common?

ANSWER: They share a focus on the links between the brain and behavior. Phrenology faded because it had no scientific basis—skull bumps don't reveal mental traits and abilities.

Neural Communication

For scientists, it is a happy fact of nature that the information systems of humans and other animals operate similarly—so similarly that you could not distinguish between small samples of brain tissue from a human and a monkey. This similarity allows researchers to study relatively simple animals, such as squids and sea slugs, to discover how our neural systems operate. It allows them to study other mammals' brains to understand the organization of our own. Cars differ, but all have engines, accelerators, steering wheels, and brakes. A space alien could study any one of them and grasp the operating principles. Likewise, animals differ, yet their nervous systems operate similarly. Though the human brain is more complex than a rat's, both follow the same principles.

Neurons

5-2 What are neurons, and how do they transmit information?

Our body's neural information system is complexity built from simplicity. Its building blocks are **neurons,** or nerve cells. To fathom our thoughts and actions, our memories and moods, we must first understand how neurons work and communicate.

Neurons differ, but all are variations on the same theme (**FIGURE 5.2** on the next page). Each consists of a *cell body* and its branching fibers. The bushy **dendrite** fibers receive information and conduct it toward the cell body. From there, the cell's single lengthy **axon** fiber passes the message through its terminal branches to other neurons or to muscles or glands. Dendrites listen. Axons speak.

Unlike the short dendrites, axons may be very long, projecting several feet through the body. A human neuron carrying orders to a leg muscle, for example, has a cell body and axon roughly on the scale of a basketball attached to a 4-mile-long rope. Much as home electrical wire is insulated, some axons are encased in a **myelin sheath,** a layer of fatty tissue that insulates them and speeds their impulses. As myelin is laid down up to about age 25, neural efficiency, judgment, and self-control grow (Fields, 2008). If the myelin sheath degenerates, *multiple sclerosis* results: Communication to muscles slows, with eventual loss of muscle control.

biological perspective concerned with the links between biology and behavior. Includes psychologists working in neuroscience, behavior genetics, and evolutionary psychology. These researchers may call themselves *behavioral neuroscientists, neuropsychologists, behavior geneticists, physiological psychologists,* or *biopsychologists.*

neuron a nerve cell; the basic building block of the nervous system.

dendrites a neuron's bushy, branching extensions that receive messages and conduct impulses toward the cell body.

axon the neuron extension that passes messages through its branches to other neurons or to muscles or glands.

myelin [MY-uh-lin] **sheath** a fatty tissue layer segmentally encasing the axons of some neurons; enables vastly greater transmission speed as neural impulses hop from one node to the next.

▼ FIGURE 5.2
A motor neuron

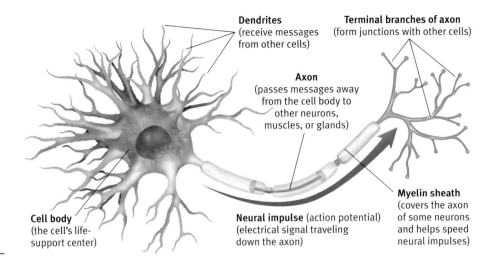

Dendrites
(receive messages
from other cells)

Terminal branches of axon
(form junctions with other cells)

Axon
(passes messages away
from the cell body to
other neurons,
muscles, or glands)

Cell body
(the cell's life-
support center)

Neural impulse (action potential)
(electrical signal traveling
down the axon)

Myelin sheath
(covers the axon
of some neurons
and helps speed
neural impulses)

🅜 LaunchPad To review and assess
your understanding of neurons,
visit LaunchPad's *Concept Practice:
Structure of a Motor Neuron.*

Neuron by sculptor Roxy Paine

"I sing the body electric."

Walt Whitman, "Children of Adam" (1855)

glial cells (glia) cells in the nervous
system that support, nourish, and protect
neurons; they may also play a role in
learning, thinking, and memory.

action potential a neural impulse; a
brief electrical charge that travels down
an axon.

Supporting these billions of nerve cells are spidery **glial cells** ("glue cells"). Neurons are like queen bees; on their own they cannot feed or sheathe themselves. Glial cells are worker bees. They provide nutrients and insulating myelin, guide neural connections, and mop up ions and neurotransmitters. Glia also play a role in learning and thinking. By "chatting" with neurons they participate in information transmission and memory (Fields, 2011, 2013; Miller, 2005).

In more complex animal brains, the proportion of glia to neurons increases. A postmortem analysis of Einstein's brain did not find more or larger-than-usual neurons, but it did reveal a much greater concentration of glial cells than found in an average Albert's head (Fields, 2004).

The Neural Impulse

Neurons transmit messages when stimulated by signals from our senses or when triggered by chemical signals from neighboring neurons. In response, a neuron fires an impulse, called the **action potential**—a brief electrical charge that travels down its axon.

Depending on the type of fiber, a neural impulse travels at speeds ranging from a sluggish 2 miles per hour to more than 200 miles per hour. But even its top speed is 3 million times slower than that of electricity through a wire. We measure brain activity in milliseconds (thousandths of a second) and computer activity in nanoseconds (billionths of a second). Thus, unlike the nearly instantaneous reactions of a computer, your reaction to a sudden event, such as a child darting in front of your car, may take a quarter-second or more. Your brain is vastly more complex than a computer, but slower at executing simple responses. And if you were an elephant—whose round-trip message travel time from a yank on the tail to the brain and back to the tail is 100 times longer than that of a tiny shrew—your reflexes would be slower yet (More et al., 2010).

Like batteries, neurons generate electricity from chemical events. In the neuron's chemistry-to-electricity process, *ions* (electrically charged atoms) are exchanged. The fluid outside an axon's membrane has mostly positively charged sodium ions; a resting axon's fluid interior has mostly negatively charged potassium ions. This positive-outside/negative-inside state is called the *resting potential*. Like a tightly guarded facility, the axon's surface is very selective about what it allows through its gates. We say the axon's surface is *selectively permeable*.

When a neuron fires, however, the security parameters change: The first section of the axon opens its gates, rather like sewer covers flipping open, and positively charged sodium ions flood in through the cell membrane (**FIGURE** 5.3). The loss of the inside/outside charge difference, called *depolarization,* causes the next axon channel to open, and then the next, like a line of falling dominos, each tripping the next.

During a resting pause called the **refractory period,** the neuron pumps the positively charged sodium ions back outside. Then it can fire again. (In myelinated neurons, as in Figure 5.2, the action potential speeds up by hopping from the end of one myelin "sausage" to the next.) The mind boggles when imagining this electrochemical process repeating up to 100 or even 1000 times a second. But this is just the first of many astonishments.

Each neuron is itself a miniature decision-making device performing complex calculations as it receives signals from hundreds, even thousands, of other neurons. Most signals are *excitatory,* somewhat like pushing a neuron's accelerator. Some are *inhibitory,* more like pushing its brake. If excitatory signals exceed the inhibitory signals by a minimum intensity, or **threshold,** the combined signals trigger an action potential. (Think of it this way: If the excitatory party animals outvote the inhibitory party poopers, the party's on.) The action potential then travels down the axon, which branches into junctions with hundreds or thousands of other neurons or with the body's muscles and glands.

Increasing the level of stimulation above the threshold will not increase the neural impulse's intensity. The neuron's reaction is an **all-or-none response:** Like guns, neurons either fire or they don't. How, then, do we detect the intensity of a stimulus? How do we distinguish a gentle touch from a big hug? A strong stimulus can trigger *more* neurons to fire, and to fire more often. But it does not affect the action potential's strength or speed. Squeezing a trigger harder won't make a bullet go faster.

refractory period a period of inactivity after a neuron has fired.

threshold the level of stimulation required to trigger a neural impulse.

all-or-none response a neuron's reaction of either firing (with a full-strength response) or not firing.

 LaunchPad For an animated explanation of this process, visit LaunchPad's *Concept Practice: Action Potentials.*

"What one neuron tells another neuron is simply how much it is excited."

Francis Crick, *The Astonishing Hypothesis,* 1994

▼ FIGURE 5.3
Action potential

Cell body end of axon

1. Neuron stimulation causes a brief change in electrical charge. If strong enough, this produces depolarization and an action potential.

2. This depolarization produces another action potential a little farther along the axon. Gates in this neighboring area now open, and charged sodium atoms rush in. A pump in the cell membrane (the sodium/potassium pump) transports the sodium ions back out of the cell.

3. As the action potential continues speedily down the axon, the first section has now completely recharged.

Direction of action potential: toward axon terminals

synapse [SIN-aps] the junction between the axon tip of the sending neuron and the dendrite or cell body of the receiving neuron. The tiny gap at this junction is called the *synaptic gap* or *synaptic cleft*.

neurotransmitters chemical messengers that cross the synaptic gaps between neurons. When released by the sending neuron, neurotransmitters travel across the synapse and bind to receptor sites on the receiving neuron, thereby influencing whether that neuron will generate a neural impulse.

reuptake a neurotransmitter's reabsorption by the sending neuron.

"All information processing in the brain involves neurons 'talking to' each other at synapses."

Neuroscientist Solomon H. Snyder (1984)

"When it comes to the brain, if you want to see the action, follow the neurotransmitters."

Neuroscientist Floyd Bloom (1993)

• When a neuron fires an action potential, the information travels through the axon, the dendrites, and the cell body, but not in that order. Place these three structures in the correct order.

ANSWER: dendrites, cell body, axon

• How does our nervous system allow us to experience the difference between a slap and a tap on the back?

ANSWER: Stronger stimuli (the slap) cause more neurons to fire and to fire more frequently than happens with weaker stimuli (the tap).

How Neurons Communicate

5-3 How do nerve cells communicate with other nerve cells?

Neurons interweave so intricately that even with a microscope you would have trouble seeing where one neuron ends and another begins. Scientists once believed that the axon of one cell fused with the dendrites of another in an uninterrupted fabric. Then British physiologist Sir Charles Sherrington (1857–1952) noticed that neural impulses were taking an unexpectedly long time to travel a neural pathway. Inferring that there must be a brief interruption in the transmission, Sherrington called the meeting point between neurons a **synapse.**

We now know that the axon terminal of one neuron is in fact separated from the receiving neuron by a *synaptic gap* (or *synaptic cleft*) less than a millionth of an inch wide. Spanish anatomist Santiago Ramón y Cajal (1852–1934) marveled at these near-unions of neurons, calling them "protoplasmic kisses." "Like elegant ladies air-kissing so as not to muss their makeup, dendrites and axons don't quite touch," noted poet Diane Ackerman (2004, p. 37). How do the neurons execute this protoplasmic kiss, sending information across the tiny synaptic gap? The answer is one of the important scientific discoveries of our age.

When an action potential reaches the knob-like terminals at an axon's end, it triggers the release of chemical messengers, called **neurotransmitters** (**FIGURE 5.4**). Within 1/10,000th of a second, the neurotransmitter molecules cross the synaptic gap and bind to receptor sites on the receiving neuron—as precisely as a key fits a lock. For an instant, the neurotransmitter unlocks tiny channels at the receiving site, and electrically charged atoms flow in, exciting or inhibiting the receiving neuron's readiness to fire. The excess neurotransmitters then drift away, are broken down by enzymes, or are reabsorbed by the sending neuron—a process called **reuptake.**

• What happens in the *synaptic gap*?

ANSWER: Neurons send neurotransmitters (chemical messengers) across this tiny space between one neuron's terminal branch and the next neuron's dendrite or cell body.

• What is *reuptake*? What two other things can happen to excess neurotransmitters after a neuron reacts?

ANSWER: Reuptake occurs when excess neurotransmitters are reabsorbed by the sending neuron. (They can also drift away or be broken down by enzymes.)

How Neurotransmitters Influence Us

5-4 How do neurotransmitters influence behavior, and how do drugs and other chemicals affect neurotransmission?

In their quest to understand neural communication, researchers have discovered several dozen neurotransmitters and as many new questions: Are certain neurotransmitters found only in specific places? How do they affect our moods, memories, and mental abilities? Can we boost or diminish these effects through drugs or diet?

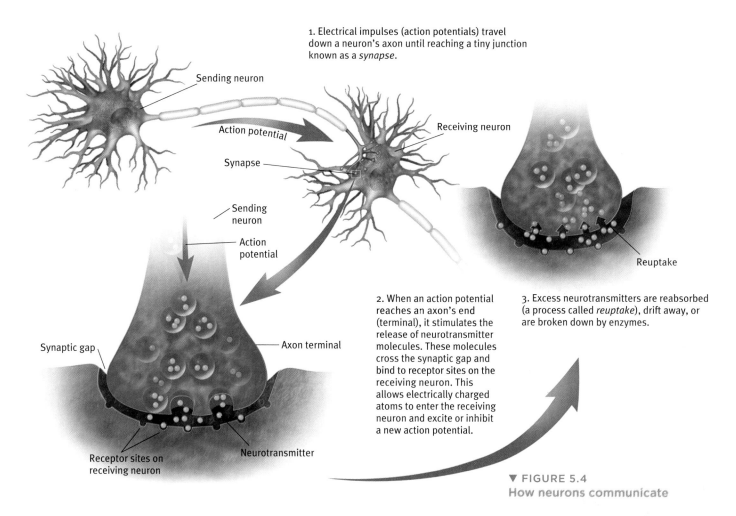

1. Electrical impulses (action potentials) travel down a neuron's axon until reaching a tiny junction known as a *synapse*.

Sending neuron

Action potential

Synapse

Receiving neuron

Sending neuron

Action potential

Reuptake

Synaptic gap

Axon terminal

Receptor sites on receiving neuron

Neurotransmitter

2. When an action potential reaches an axon's end (terminal), it stimulates the release of neurotransmitter molecules. These molecules cross the synaptic gap and bind to receptor sites on the receiving neuron. This allows electrically charged atoms to enter the receiving neuron and excite or inhibit a new action potential.

3. Excess neurotransmitters are reabsorbed (a process called *reuptake*), drift away, or are broken down by enzymes.

▼ FIGURE 5.4
How neurons communicate

Other modules explore neurotransmitter influences on hunger and thinking, depression and euphoria, addictions and therapy. For now, let's glimpse how neurotransmitters influence our motions and our emotions. A particular brain pathway may use only one or two neurotransmitters (**FIGURE 5.5**), and particular neurotransmitters may affect specific behaviors and emotions (**TABLE 5.1** on the next page). But neurotransmitter systems don't operate in isolation; they interact, and their effects vary with the receptors they stimulate. *Acetylcholine* (*ACh*), which is one of the best-understood neurotransmitters, plays a role in learning and memory. In addition, it is the messenger at

LaunchPad For an animated explanation, visit LaunchPad's *Concept Practice* activities: *Structure of a Synapse* and *Neural Communication*.

Serotonin pathways

Dopamine pathways

Both photos from Mapping the Mind, Rita Carter, 1989 Moonrunner Ltd.

▼ FIGURE 5.5
Neurotransmitter pathways Each of the brain's differing chemical messengers has designated pathways where it operates, as shown here for serotonin and dopamine (Carter, 1998).

LiquidLibrary/Jupiterimages

▼ TABLE 5.1
Some Neurotransmitters and Their Functions

Neurotransmitter	Function	Examples of Malfunctions
Acetylcholine (ACh)	Enables muscle action, learning, and memory	With Alzheimer's disease, ACh-producing neurons deteriorate.
Dopamine	Influences movement, learning, attention, and emotion	Oversupply linked to schizophrenia. Undersupply linked to tremors and loss of motor control in Parkinson's disease.
Serotonin	Affects mood, hunger, sleep, and arousal	Undersupply linked to depression. Some drugs that raise serotonin levels are used to treat depression.
Norepinephrine	Helps control alertness and arousal	Undersupply can depress mood.
GABA (gamma-aminobutyric acid)	A major inhibitory neurotransmitter	Undersupply linked to seizures, tremors, and insomnia.
Glutamate	A major excitatory neurotransmitter; involved in memory	Oversupply can overstimulate the brain, producing migraines or seizures (which is why some people avoid MSG, monosodium glutamate, in food).

Physician Lewis Thomas, on the endorphins: "There it is, a biologically universal act of mercy. I cannot explain it, except to say that I would have put it in had I been around at the very beginning, sitting as a member of a planning committee."

The Youngest Science, 1983

every junction between motor neurons (which carry information from the brain and spinal cord to the body's tissues) and skeletal muscles. When ACh is released to our muscle cell receptors, the muscle contracts. If ACh transmission is blocked, as happens during some kinds of anesthesia and with some poisons, the muscles cannot contract and we are paralyzed.

Candace Pert and Solomon Snyder (1973) made an exciting discovery about neurotransmitters when they attached a radioactive tracer to morphine, showing where it was taken up in an animal's brain. The morphine, an opiate drug that elevates mood and eases pain, bound to receptors in areas linked with mood and pain sensations. But why would the brain have these "opiate receptors"? Why would it have a chemical lock, unless it also had a natural key to open it?

Researchers soon confirmed that the brain does indeed produce its own naturally occurring opiates. Our body releases several types of neurotransmitter molecules similar to morphine in response to pain and vigorous exercise. These **endorphins** (short for *endogenous* [produced within] m*orphine*) help explain good feelings such as the "runner's high," the painkilling effects of acupuncture, and the indifference to pain in some severely injured people. But once again, new knowledge led to new questions.

─────────── RETRIEVAL PRACTICE ───────────

• Serotonin, dopamine, and endorphins are all chemical messengers called
_____ .

ANSWER: neurotransmitters

How Drugs and Other Chemicals Alter Neurotransmission If indeed the endorphins lessen pain and boost mood, why not flood the brain with artificial opiates, thereby intensifying the brain's own "feel-good" chemistry? But there is a problem: When flooded with opiate drugs such as heroin and morphine, the brain, to maintain its chemical balance, may stop producing its own natural opiates. When the drug is

endorphins [en-DOR-fins] "morphine within"—natural, opiate-like neurotransmitters linked to pain control and to pleasure.

withdrawn, the brain may then be deprived of any form of opiate, causing intense discomfort. For suppressing the body's own neurotransmitter production, nature charges a price.

Drugs and other chemicals affect brain chemistry, often by either exciting or inhibiting neurons' firing. **Agonist** molecules *increase* a neurotransmitter's action. Agonists may increase the production or release of neurotransmitters, or block reuptake in the synapse. Other agonists may be similar enough to a neurotransmitter to bind to its receptor and mimic its excitatory or inhibitory effects. Some opiate drugs are agonists and produce a temporary "high" by amplifying normal sensations of arousal or pleasure.

Antagonists *decrease* a neurotransmitter's action by blocking production or release. Botulin, a poison that can form in improperly canned food, causes paralysis by blocking ACh release. (Small injections of botulin—Botox—smooth wrinkles by paralyzing the underlying facial muscles.) These antagonists are enough like the natural neurotransmitter to occupy its receptor site and block its effect, as in **FIGURE 5.6**, but are not similar enough to stimulate the receptor (rather like foreign coins that fit into, but won't operate, a candy machine). Curare, a poison some South American Indians have applied to hunting-dart tips, occupies and blocks ACh receptor sites on muscles, producing paralysis in their prey.

🎓 **LaunchPad** For an illustrated review of neural communication, visit Launch-Pad's *PsychSim 6: Neural Messages.*

> **agonist** a molecule that increases a neurotransmitter's action.
>
> **antagonist** a molecule that inhibits or blocks a neurotransmitter's action.

RETRIEVAL PRACTICE

▼ FIGURE 5.6
Agonists and antagonists
• Curare poisoning paralyzes its victims by blocking ACh receptors involved in muscle movements. Morphine mimics endorphin actions. Which is an agonist, and which is an antagonist?

ANSWER: Morphine is an agonist; curare is an antagonist.

Sending neuron

Vesicles containing neurotransmitters

Action potential

Synaptic gap

Neurotransmitter molecule

Receptor sites

Receiving neuron

Neurotransmitters carry a message from a sending neuron across a synapse to receptor sites on a receiving neuron.

Receptor site on receiving neuron

Neurotransmitter opens the receptor site.

Agonist drug mimics neurotransmitter, opening receptor site.

Antagonist drug blocks neurotransmitter from opening receptor site.

Neurotransmitter

Closed   Open   Open   Closed

nervous system the body's speedy, electrochemical communication network, consisting of all the nerve cells of the peripheral and central nervous systems.

central nervous system (CNS) the brain and spinal cord.

peripheral nervous system (PNS) the sensory and motor neurons that connect the central nervous system (CNS) to the rest of the body.

nerves bundled axons that form neural cables connecting the central nervous system with muscles, glands, and sense organs.

sensory (afferent) neurons neurons that carry incoming information from the sensory receptors to the brain and spinal cord.

motor (efferent) neurons neurons that carry outgoing information from the brain and spinal cord to the muscles and glands.

interneurons neurons within the brain and spinal cord; communicate internally and process information between the sensory inputs and motor outputs.

somatic nervous system the division of the peripheral nervous system that controls the body's skeletal muscles. Also called the *skeletal nervous system.*

autonomic [aw-tuh-NAHM-ik] nervous system (ANS) the part of the peripheral nervous system that controls the glands and the muscles of the internal organs (such as the heart). Its sympathetic division arouses; its parasympathetic division calms.

The Nervous System

5-5 What are the functions of the nervous system's main divisions, and what are the three main types of neurons?

To live is to take in information from the world and the body's tissues, to make decisions, and to send back information and orders to the body's tissues. All this happens thanks to our body's **nervous system** (**FIGURE 5.7**). A quick overview: The brain and spinal cord form the **central nervous system (CNS),** the body's decision maker. The **peripheral nervous system (PNS)** is responsible for gathering information and for transmitting CNS decisions to other body parts. **Nerves,** electrical cables formed of bundles of axons, link the CNS with the body's sensory receptors, muscles, and glands. The optic nerve, for example, bundles a million axons into a single cable carrying the messages each eye sends to the brain (Mason & Kandel, 1991).

Information travels in the nervous system through three types of neurons. **Sensory neurons** carry messages from the body's tissues and sensory receptors inward (thus, they are *afferent*) to the brain and spinal cord for processing. **Motor neurons** (which are *efferent*) carry instructions from the central nervous system out to the body's muscles and glands. Between the sensory input and motor output, information is processed via the brain's **interneurons.** Our complexity resides mostly in these interneurons. Our nervous system has a few million sensory neurons, a few million motor neurons, and billions and billions of interneurons.

The Peripheral Nervous System

Our peripheral nervous system has two components—somatic and autonomic. Our **somatic nervous system** enables voluntary control of our skeletal muscles. As you reach the end of this page, your somatic nervous system will report to your brain the current state of your skeletal muscles and carry instructions back, triggering a response from your hand so you can read on.

Our **autonomic nervous system (ANS)** controls our glands and our internal organ muscles, thus influencing glandular activity, heartbeat, and digestion. (*Autonomic* means "self-regulating.") Like an automatic pilot, this system may be consciously overridden, but usually operates on its own (autonomously).

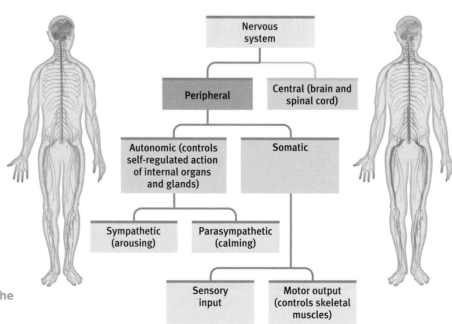

▼ FIGURE 5.7
The functional divisions of the human nervous system

SYMPATHETIC NERVOUS SYSTEM (arousing)

Brain

PARASYMPATHETIC NERVOUS SYSTEM (calming)

Dilates pupils

Contracts pupils

Heart

Accelerates heartbeat

Slows heartbeat

Spinal cord

Stomach

Inhibits digestion

Stimulates digestion

Pancreas

Liver

Stimulates glucose release by liver

Stimulates gallbladder

Adrenal gland

Kidney

Stimulates secretion of epinephrine, norepinephrine

Contracts bladder

Relaxes bladder

Stimulates ejaculation in male

Allows bloodflow to sex organs

▼ FIGURE 5.8
The dual functions of the autonomic nervous system The autonomic nervous system controls the more autonomous (or self-regulating) internal functions. Its sympathetic division arouses and expends energy. Its parasympathetic division calms and conserves energy, allowing routine maintenance activity. For example, sympathetic stimulation accelerates heartbeat, whereas parasympathetic stimulation slows it.

The autonomic nervous system serves two important functions (**FIGURE 5.8**). The **sympathetic nervous system** arouses and expends energy. If something alarms or challenges you (such as a longed-for job interview), your sympathetic nervous system will accelerate your heartbeat, raise your blood pressure, slow your digestion, raise your blood sugar, and cool you with perspiration, making you alert and ready for action. When the stress subsides (the interview is over), your **parasympathetic nervous system** will produce the opposite effects, conserving energy as it calms you. The sympathetic and parasympathetic nervous systems work together to keep us in a steady internal state called *homeostasis.*

I [DM] recently experienced my ANS in action. Before sending me into an MRI machine for a routine shoulder scan, the technician asked if I had issues with claustrophobia. "No, I'm fine," I assured her, with perhaps a hint of macho swagger. Moments later, as I found myself on my back, stuck deep inside a coffin-sized box and unable to move, my sympathetic nervous system had a different idea. As claustrophobia overtook me, my heart began pounding and I felt a desperate urge to escape. Just as I was about to cry out for release, I felt my calming parasympathetic nervous system kick in. My heart rate slowed and my body relaxed, though my arousal surged again before the 20-minute confinement ended. "You did well!" the technician said, unaware of my ANS roller-coaster ride.

sympathetic nervous system the division of the autonomic nervous system that arouses the body, mobilizing its energy.

parasympathetic nervous system the division of the autonomic nervous system that calms the body, conserving its energy.

• Match the type of neuron to its description.

Type	Description
1. Motor neurons	a. carry incoming messages from sensory receptors to the CNS.
2. Sensory neurons	b. communicate within the CNS and process information between incoming and outgoing messages.
3. Interneurons	c. carry outgoing messages from the CNS to muscles and glands.

ANSWERS: 1. c, 2. a, 3. b

• What bodily changes does your ANS direct before and after you give an important speech?

ANSWER: Responding to this challenge, your ANS *sympathetic* division will arouse you. It accelerates your heartbeat, raises your blood pressure and blood sugar, slows your digestion, and cools you with perspiration. After you give the speech, your ANS *parasympathetic* division will reverse these effects.

© Tom Swick/Cartoon Stock

"The body is made up of millions and millions of crumbs."

The Central Nervous System

From neurons "talking" to other neurons arises the complexity of the central nervous system's brain and spinal cord.

It is the brain that enables our humanity—our thinking, feeling, and acting. Tens of billions of neurons, each communicating with thousands of other neurons, yield an ever-changing wiring diagram. By one estimate—projecting from neuron counts in small brain samples—our brains have some 40 billion neurons, each connecting with roughly 10,000 other neurons (de Courten-Myers, 2005). This implies some 400 trillion synapses—places where neurons meet and greet their neighbors. (A different research team projected 86 billion brain neurons [Azevedo et al., 2009]. The moral: Distrust big round numbers, such as the familiar but undocumented claim that the human brain has 100 billion neurons.)

The brain's neurons cluster into work groups called *neural networks.* To understand why, Stephen Kosslyn and Olivier Koenig (1992, p. 12) have invited us to "think about why cities exist; why don't people distribute themselves more evenly across the countryside?" Like people networking with people, neurons network with nearby neurons with which they can have short, fast connections. As in **FIGURE 5.9**, each layer's cells connect with various cells in the neural network's next layer. Learning—to play the violin, speak a foreign language, or solve a math problem—occurs as experience strengthens connections. Neurons that fire together wire together.

The other part of the CNS, the *spinal cord,* is a two-way information highway connecting the peripheral nervous system and the brain. Ascending neural fibers send up

Bluemoon Stock/Jupiterimages

▼ FIGURE 5.9
A simplified neural network
Neurons network with nearby neurons. Encoded in these networks is your own enduring identity (as a musician, an athlete, a devoted friend)—your sense of self that extends across the years. How neural networks organize themselves into complex circuits capable of learning, feeling, and thinking remains one of the great scientific mysteries. How does biology give birth to mind?

Neurons in the brain connect with one another to form networks

Inputs
(lessons, practice, master classes, music camps, time spent with musical friends)

Outputs
(beautiful music!)

The brain learns by modifying certain connections in response to feedback (specific skills develop)

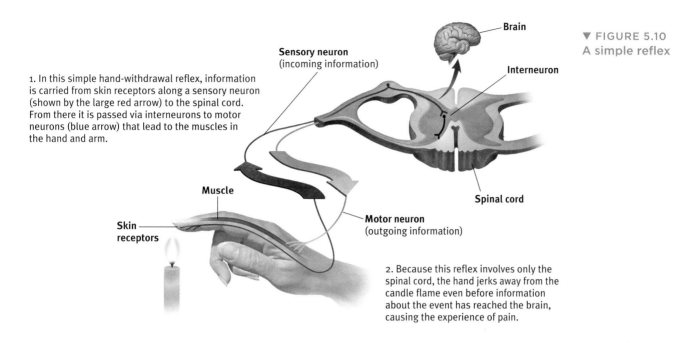

▼ FIGURE 5.10
A simple reflex

1. In this simple hand-withdrawal reflex, information is carried from skin receptors along a sensory neuron (shown by the large red arrow) to the spinal cord. From there it is passed via interneurons to motor neurons (blue arrow) that lead to the muscles in the hand and arm.

Brain

Sensory neuron (incoming information)

Interneuron

Spinal cord

Muscle

Skin receptors

Motor neuron (outgoing information)

2. Because this reflex involves only the spinal cord, the hand jerks away from the candle flame even before information about the event has reached the brain, causing the experience of pain.

sensory information, and descending fibers send back motor-control information. The neural pathways governing our **reflexes,** our automatic responses to stimuli, illustrate the spinal cord's work. A simple spinal reflex pathway is composed of a single sensory neuron and a single motor neuron. These often communicate through an interneuron. The knee-jerk response, for example, involves one such simple pathway. A headless warm body could do it.

Another neural circuit enables the pain reflex (**FIGURE 5.10**). When your finger touches a flame, neural activity (excited by the heat) travels via sensory neurons to interneurons in your spinal cord. These interneurons respond by activating motor neurons leading to the muscles in your arm. Because the simple pain-reflex pathway runs through the spinal cord and right back out, your hand jerks away from the candle's flame *before* your brain receives and responds to the information that causes you to feel pain. That's why it feels as if your hand jerks away not by your choice, but on its own.

Information travels to and from the brain by way of the spinal cord. Were the top of your spinal cord severed, you would not feel pain from your paralyzed body below. Nor would you feel pleasure. With your brain literally out of touch with your body, you would lose all sensation and voluntary movement in body regions with sensory and motor connections to the spinal cord below its point of injury. You would exhibit the knee-jerk response without feeling the tap. Men paralyzed below the waist may be capable of an erection (a simple reflex) if their genitals are stimulated (Goldstein, 2000). Women similarly paralyzed may respond with vaginal lubrication. But, depending on where and how completely the spinal cord is severed, both may be genitally unresponsive to erotic images and have no genital feeling (Kennedy & Over, 1990; Sipski & Alexander, 1999). To produce bodily pain or pleasure, the sensory information must reach the brain.

The Endocrine System

5-6 How does the endocrine system transmit information and interact with the nervous system?

So far we have focused on the body's speedy electrochemical information system. Interconnected with your nervous system is a second communication system, the **endocrine system** (**FIGURE 5.11** on the next page). The endocrine system's glands secrete another form of chemical messengers, **hormones,** which travel through the bloodstream and

reflex a simple, automatic response to a sensory stimulus, such as the knee-jerk response.

endocrine [EN-duh-krin] **system** the body's "slow" chemical communication system; a set of glands that secrete hormones into the bloodstream.

hormones chemical messengers that are manufactured by the endocrine glands, travel through the bloodstream, and affect other tissues.

"If the nervous system be cut off between the brain and other parts, the experiences of those other parts are nonexistent for the mind. The eye is blind, the ear deaf, the hand insensible and motionless."

William James, *Principles of Psychology,* 1890

▼ FIGURE 5.11
The endocrine system

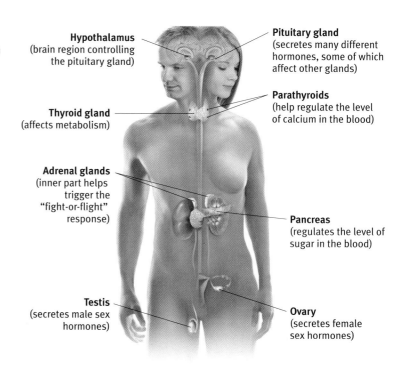

Hypothalamus
(brain region controlling
the pituitary gland)

Pituitary gland
(secretes many different
hormones, some of which
affect other glands)

Parathyroids
(help regulate the level
of calcium in the blood)

Thyroid gland
(affects metabolism)

Adrenal glands
(inner part helps
trigger the
"fight-or-flight"
response)

Pancreas
(regulates the level of
sugar in the blood)

Testis
(secretes male sex
hormones)

Ovary
(secretes female
sex hormones)

affect other tissues, including the brain. When hormones act on the brain, they influence our interest in sex, food, and aggression.

Some hormones are chemically identical to neurotransmitters (the chemical messengers that diffuse across a synapse and excite or inhibit an adjacent neuron). The endocrine system and nervous system are therefore close relatives: Both produce molecules that act on receptors elsewhere. Like many relatives, they also differ. The speedy nervous system zips messages from eyes to brain to hand in a fraction of a second. Endocrine messages trudge along in the bloodstream, taking several seconds or more to travel from the gland to the target tissue. If the nervous system transmits information with text-message speed, the endocrine system delivers an old-fashioned letter.

But slow and steady sometimes wins the race. Endocrine messages tend to outlast the effects of neural messages. Upset feelings may linger beyond our awareness of the reason, and it takes time for us to "simmer down." The persistence of emotions—without conscious awareness of what caused them—was dramatically evident in one ingenious experiment. Brain-damaged patients unable to form new conscious memories watched a sad film and later a happy film. After each viewing, they did not consciously recall the films, but the sad or happy emotion persisted (Feinstein et al., 2010).

In a moment of danger, the ANS orders the **adrenal glands** on top of the kidneys to release *epinephrine* and *norepinephrine* (also called *adrenaline* and *noradrenaline*). These hormones increase heart rate, blood pressure, and blood sugar, providing a surge of energy. When the emergency passes, the hormones—and the feelings—linger a while.

The most influential endocrine gland is the **pituitary gland,** a pea-sized structure located in the core of the brain, where it is controlled by an adjacent brain area, the *hypothalamus.* Among the hormones released by the pituitary is a growth hormone that stimulates physical development. Another is *oxytocin,* which enables contractions associated with birthing, milk flow during nursing, and orgasm. Oxytocin also promotes pair bonding, group cohesion, and social trust (De Dreu et al., 2010; Zak, 2012). During a laboratory game, those given a nasal squirt of oxytocin rather than a placebo were more likely to trust strangers with their money (Kosfeld et al., 2005).

Pituitary secretions also direct other endocrine glands to release their hormones. The pituitary, then, is a master gland (whose own master is the hypothalamus).

adrenal [ah-DREEN-el] glands a pair of endocrine glands that sit just above the kidneys and secrete hormones (epinephrine and norepinephrine) that help arouse the body in times of stress.

pituitary gland the endocrine system's most influential gland. Under the influence of the hypothalamus, the pituitary regulates growth and controls other endocrine glands.

For example, under the brain's influence, the pituitary triggers your sex glands to release sex hormones. These in turn influence your brain and behavior. So, too, with stress. A stressful event triggers your hypothalamus to instruct your pituitary to release a hormone that causes your adrenal glands to flood your body with cortisol, a stress hormone that increases blood sugar.

This feedback system (brain → pituitary → other glands → hormones → body and brain) reveals the intimate connection of the nervous and endocrine systems. The nervous system directs endocrine secretions, which then affect the nervous system. Conducting and coordinating this whole electrochemical orchestra is that maestro we call the brain.

RETRIEVAL PRACTICE

• Why is the pituitary gland called the "master gland"?

ANSWER: Responding to signals from the hypothalamus, the pituitary releases hormones that trigger other endocrine glands to secrete hormones, which in turn influence brain and behavior.

• How are the nervous and endocrine systems alike, and how do they differ?

ANSWER: Both of these communication systems produce chemical molecules that act on the body's receptors to influence our behavior and emotions. The endocrine system, which secretes hormones into the bloodstream, delivers its messages much more slowly than the speedy nervous system, and the effects of the endocrine system's messages tend to linger much longer than those of the nervous system.

MODULE 5 REVIEW Neural and Hormonal Systems

LEARNING OBJECTIVES

RETRIEVAL PRACTICE Take a moment to answer each of these Learning Objective Questions (repeated here from within this module). Then turn to Appendix C, Complete Module Reviews, to check your answers. Research suggests that trying to answer these questions on your own will improve your long-term retention (McDaniel et al., 2009).

5-1 Why are psychologists concerned with human biology?

5-2 What are neurons, and how do they transmit information?

5-3 How do nerve cells communicate with other nerve cells?

5-4 How do neurotransmitters influence behavior, and how do drugs and other chemicals affect neurotransmission?

5-5 What are the functions of the nervous system's main divisions, and what are the three main types of neurons?

5-6 How does the endocrine system transmit information and interact with the nervous system?

TERMS AND CONCEPTS TO REMEMBER

RETRIEVAL PRACTICE Test yourself on these terms by trying to write down the definition before flipping back to check your answers.

biological perspective, p. 52
neuron, p. 53
dendrites, p. 53
axon, p. 53
myelin [MY-uh-lin] sheath, p. 53
glial cells (glia), p. 54
action potential, p. 54

refractory period, p. 55
threshold, p. 55
all-or-none response, p. 55
synapse [SIN-aps], p. 56
neurotransmitters, p. 56
reuptake, p. 56
endorphins [en-DOR-fins], p. 58
agonist, p. 59
antagonist, p. 59
nervous system, p. 60
central nervous system (CNS), p. 60
peripheral nervous system (PNS), p. 60
nerves, p. 60
sensory (afferent) neurons, p. 60
motor (efferent) neurons, p. 60
interneurons, p. 60
somatic nervous system, p. 60
autonomic [aw-tuh-NAHM-ik] nervous system (ANS), p. 60
sympathetic nervous system, p. 61
parasympathetic nervous system, p. 61
reflex, p. 63
endocrine [EN-duh-krin] system, p. 63
hormones, p. 63
adrenal [ah-DREEN-el] glands, p. 64
pituitary gland, p. 64

Use LearningCurve to create your personalized study plan, which will direct you to the resources that will help you most in LaunchPad.

"You're certainly a lot less fun since the operation."

"I am a brain, Watson. The rest of me is a mere appendix."

Sherlock Holmes, in Arthur Conan Doyle's "The Adventure of the Mazarin Stone"

A living human brain exposed
Today's neuroscience tools enable us to "look under the hood" and glimpse the brain at work, enabling the mind.

MODULE 6 Tools of Discovery and Older Brain Structures

IN A JAR ON A display shelf in Cornell University's psychology department resides the well-preserved brain of Edward Bradford Titchener, a late-nineteenth-century experimental psychologist and proponent of the study of consciousness. Imagine yourself gazing at that wrinkled mass of grayish tissue, wondering if in any sense Titchener is still in there.[1]

You might answer that, without the living whir of electrochemical activity, there could be nothing of Titchener in his preserved brain. Consider, then, an experiment about which the inquisitive Titchener himself might have daydreamed. Imagine that just moments before his death, someone had removed Titchener's brain and kept it alive by feeding it enriched blood. Would Titchener still be in there? Further imagine that someone then transplanted the still-living brain into the body of a person whose own brain had been severely damaged. To whose home should the recovered patient return?

That we can imagine such questions illustrates how convinced we are that we live "somewhere north of the neck" (Fodor, 1999). And for good reason: The brain enables the mind—seeing, hearing, smelling, feeling, remembering, thinking, speaking, dreaming. Moreover, it is the brain that self-reflectively analyzes the brain. When we're thinking *about* our brain, we're thinking *with* our brain—by firing across millions of synapses and releasing billions of neurotransmitter molecules. The effect of hormones on experiences such as love reminds us that we would not be of the same mind if we were a bodiless brain. Brain + body = mind. Nevertheless, say neuroscientists, the *mind is what the brain does*. Brain, behavior, and cognition are an integrated whole. But precisely where and how are the mind's functions tied to the brain? Let's first see how scientists explore such questions.

The Tools of Discovery: Having Our Head Examined

6-1 How do neuroscientists study the brain's connections to behavior and mind?

A century ago, scientists had no tools high powered yet gentle enough to explore the living human brain. Early case studies helped localize some brain functions. Damage to one side of the brain often caused numbness or paralysis on the body's opposite side, suggesting that the body's right side is wired to the brain's left side, and vice versa. Damage to the back of the brain disrupted vision, and to the left-front part of the brain produced speech difficulties. Gradually, these early explorers were mapping the brain.

Now, within a lifetime, a new generation of neural cartographers is probing and mapping the known universe's most amazing organ. Scientists can selectively **lesion** (destroy) tiny clusters of brain cells, leaving the surrounding tissue unharmed. In the laboratory, such studies have revealed, for example, that damage to one area of the hypothalamus in a rat's brain reduces eating, to the point of starvation, whereas damage in another area produces overeating.

Today's neuroscientists can also *stimulate* various brain parts—electrically, chemically, or magnetically—and note the effect. Depending on the stimulated brain part, people may—to name a few examples—giggle, hear voices, turn their head, feel themselves falling, or have an out-of-body experience (Selimbeyoglu & Parvizi, 2010). Scientists can even snoop on the messages of individual neurons. With tips small enough

---

1. Carl Sagan's *Broca's Brain* (1979) inspired this question.

to detect the electrical pulse in a single neuron, modern microelectrodes can, for example, now detect exactly where the information goes in a cat's brain when someone strokes its whisker. Researchers can also eavesdrop on the chatter of billions of neurons and can see color representations of the brain's energy-consuming activity.

Right now, your mental activity is emitting telltale electrical, metabolic, and magnetic signals that would enable neuroscientists to observe your brain at work. Electrical activity in your brain's billions of neurons sweeps in regular waves across its surface. An **electroencephalogram (EEG)** is an amplified readout of such waves. Researchers record the brain waves through a shower-cap-like hat that is filled with electrodes covered with a conductive gel. Studying an EEG of the brain's activity is like studying a car engine by listening to its hum. With no direct access to the brain, researchers present a stimulus repeatedly and have a computer filter out brain activity unrelated to the stimulus. What remains is the electrical wave evoked by the stimulus (**FIGURE 6.1**).

"You must look into people, as well as at them," advised Lord Chesterfield in a 1746 letter to his son. Unlike EEGs, newer neuroimaging techniques give us that Superman-like ability to see inside the living brain. One such tool, the **PET (positron emission tomography) scan** (**FIGURE 6.2**), depicts brain activity by showing each brain area's consumption of its chemical fuel, the sugar glucose. Active neurons are glucose hogs. Our brains, though only about 2 percent of our body weight, consume 20 percent of our calorie intake. After a person receives temporarily radioactive glucose, the PET scan can track the gamma rays released by this "food for thought" as a task is performed. Rather like weather radar showing rain activity, PET-scan "hot spots" show the most active brain areas as the person does mathematical calculations, looks at images of faces, or daydreams.

In **MRI (magnetic resonance imaging)** brain scans, the person's head is put in a strong magnetic field, which aligns the spinning atoms of brain molecules. Then, a radio-wave pulse momentarily disorients the atoms. When the atoms return to their normal spin, they emit signals that provide a detailed picture of soft tissues, including the brain. MRI scans have revealed a larger-than-average neural area in the left hemisphere of musicians who display perfect pitch (Schlaug et al., 1995). They have also revealed enlarged *ventricles*—fluid-filled brain areas (marked by the red arrows in **FIGURE 6.3** on the next page)—in some patients who have schizophrenia, a disabling psychological disorder.

AJPhoto/Science Source

▼ FIGURE 6.1
Brain hacking An electroencephalograph provides amplified tracings of waves of electrical activity in the brain.

lesion [LEE-zhuhn] tissue destruction. A brain lesion is a naturally or experimentally caused destruction of brain tissue.

electroencephalogram (EEG) an amplified recording of the waves of electrical activity sweeping across the brain's surface. These waves are measured by electrodes placed on the scalp.

PET (positron emission tomography) scan a visual display of brain activity that detects where a radioactive form of glucose goes while the brain performs a given task.

MRI (magnetic resonance imaging) a technique that uses magnetic fields and radio waves to produce computer-generated images of soft tissue. MRI scans show brain anatomy.

Mark Harmel/The Image Bank/Getty Images

▼ FIGURE 6.2
The PET scan To obtain a PET scan, researchers inject volunteers with a low and harmless dose of a short-lived radioactive sugar. Detectors around the person's head pick up the release of gamma rays from the sugar, which has concentrated in active brain areas. A computer then processes and translates these signals into a map of the brain at work.

From Daniel Weinberger, M.D., CBDB, NIMH

▼ FIGURE 6.3
MRI scan of a healthy individual (left) and a person with schizophrenia (right) Note the enlarged ventricle, the fluid-filled brain region at the tip of the arrow in the image on the right.

A special application of MRI—fMRI (functional MRI)—can reveal the brain's functioning as well as its structure. Where the brain is especially active, blood goes. By comparing successive MRI scans, researchers can watch as specific brain areas activate, showing increased oxygen-laden bloodflow. As the person looks at a scene, for example, the fMRI machine detects blood rushing to the back of the brain, which processes visual information.

Such snapshots of the brain's changing activity are providing new insights into how the brain divides its labor. A mountain of recent fMRI studies suggests which brain areas are most active when people feel pain or rejection, listen to angry voices, think about scary things, feel happy, or become sexually excited. The technology enables a very crude sort of mind reading. One neuroscience team scanned 129 people's brains as they did eight different mental tasks (such as reading, gambling, or rhyming). Later, they were able, with 80 percent accuracy, to predict which of these mental activities a person was doing (Poldrack et al., 2009). Other studies have explored brain activity associated with religious experience, though without settling the question of whether the brain is producing or perceiving God (Fingelkurts & Fingelkurts, 2009; Inzlicht et al., 2009; Kapogiannis et al., 2009).

You've seen the pictures—of colorful brains with accompanying headlines, such as "your brain on music." Hot brains make hot news. But "neuroskeptics" caution against overblown claims about any ability to predict customer preferences, detect lies, and foretell crime (Satel & Lilienfeld, 2013; Vul et al., 2009a,b). Neuromarketing, neurolaw, neuropolitics, and neurotheology are often neurohype. We can credit brain imaging with illuminating the brain's structure and activity, and with sometimes helping us test different theories of behavior (Mather et al., 2013). But given that all human experience is brain-based, it's no surprise that different brain areas become active when one listens to a lecture or lusts for a lover.

* * *

Today's techniques for peering into the thinking, feeling brain are doing for psychology what the microscope did for biology and the telescope did for astronomy. From them we have learned more about the brain in the last 30 years than in the previous 30,000. And the next decade will reveal much more, as each year massive funding goes into brain research. Europe's Human Brain Project promises $1 billion for brain computer modeling and the $40 million Human Connectome Project (2013; Gorman, 2014) seeks "neural pathways [that] will reveal much about what makes us uniquely human and what makes every person different from all others." A new super-powerful *diffusion spectrum imaging* machine, built as part of the Human Connectome Project, can even map long-distance brain connections.

To be learning about the neurosciences now is like studying world geography while Magellan was exploring the seas. The whole brain mapping effort now underway has been likened to last century's Apollo program that landed humans on the Moon, and to the Human Genome Project's mapping our DNA. This truly is the golden age of brain science.

RETRIEVAL PRACTICE

• Match the scanning technique with the correct description.

Technique

1. fMRI scan
2. PET scan
3. MRI scan

Description

a. tracks radioactive glucose to reveal brain activity.

b. tracks successive images of brain tissue to show brain function.

c. uses magnetic fields and radio waves to show brain anatomy.

fMRI (functional MRI) a technique for revealing bloodflow and, therefore, brain activity by comparing successive MRI scans. fMRI scans show brain function as well as structure.

Older Brain Structures

6-2 What structures make up the brainstem, and what are the functions of the brainstem, thalamus, reticular formation, and cerebellum?

An animal's capacities come from its brain structures. In primitive animals, such as sharks, a not-so-complex brain primarily regulates basic survival functions: breathing, resting, and feeding. In lower mammals, such as rodents, a more complex brain enables emotion and greater memory. In advanced mammals, such as humans, a brain that processes more information enables increased foresight as well.

This increasing complexity arises from new brain systems built on top of the old, much as the Earth's landscape covers the old with the new. Digging down, one discovers the fossil remnants of the past—brainstem components performing for us much as they did for our distant ancestors. Let's start with the brain's basement.

LaunchPad For an introductory 12.5-minute overview of the brain, visit LaunchPad's *Video: The Central Nervous System—Spotlight on the Brain.*

The Brainstem

The brain's oldest and innermost region is the **brainstem.** It begins where the spinal cord swells slightly after entering the skull. This slight swelling is the **medulla** (**FIGURE 6.4**). Here lie the controls for your heartbeat and breathing. As some brain-damaged patients in a vegetative state illustrate, we need no higher brain or conscious mind to orchestrate our heart's pumping and lungs' breathing. The brainstem handles those tasks. Just above the medulla sits the *pons,* which helps coordinate movements and control sleep.

If a cat's brainstem is severed from the rest of the brain above it, the animal will still breathe and live—and even run, climb, and groom (Klemm, 1990). But cut off from the brain's higher regions, it won't *purposefully* run or climb to get food.

The brainstem is a crossover point, where most nerves to and from each side of the brain connect with the body's opposite side (**FIGURE 6.5** on the next page). This peculiar cross-wiring is but one of the brain's many surprises.

> **brainstem** the oldest part and central core of the brain, beginning where the spinal cord swells as it enters the skull; the brainstem is responsible for automatic survival functions.
>
> **medulla** [muh-DUL-uh] the base of the brainstem; controls heartbeat and breathing.

▼ FIGURE 6.4
The brainstem and thalamus The brainstem, including the pons and medulla, is an extension of the spinal cord. The thalamus is attached to the top of the brainstem. The reticular formation passes through both structures.

▼ FIGURE 6.5
The body's wiring
• Nerves from the left side of the brain are mostly linked to the _____ side of the body, and vice versa.

ANSWER: right

The Thalamus

Sitting atop the brainstem is the **thalamus,** a pair of egg-shaped structures that act as the brain's sensory control center (Figure 6.4). The thalamus receives information from all the senses except smell and routes it to the higher brain regions that deal with seeing, hearing, tasting, and touching. The thalamus also receives some of the higher brain's replies, which it then directs to the medulla and to the cerebellum (see below). Think of the thalamus as being to sensory information what London is to England's trains: a hub through which traffic passes en route to various destinations.

The Reticular Formation

Inside the brainstem, between your ears, lies the **reticular** ("net-like") **formation,** a neuron network extending from the spinal cord right up through the thalamus. As the spinal cord's sensory input flows up to the thalamus, some of it travels through the reticular formation, which filters incoming stimuli, relays important information to other brain areas, and controls arousal.

Andrew Swift

In 1949, Giuseppe Moruzzi and Horace Magoun discovered that electrically stimulating a sleeping cat's reticular formation almost instantly produced an awake, alert animal. When Magoun *severed* a cat's reticular formation without damaging nearby sensory pathways, the effect was equally dramatic: The cat lapsed into a coma from which it never awakened. The conclusion? The reticular formation enables arousal.

The Cerebellum

Sergio Torres/AP

Extending from the rear of the brainstem is the baseball-sized **cerebellum,** meaning "little brain," which is what its two wrinkled halves resemble (**FIGURE 6.6**). The cerebellum (along with the *basal ganglia,* deep brain structures involved in motor movement) enables nonverbal learning and skill memory. It also helps us judge time, modulate our emotions, and discriminate sounds and textures (Bower & Parsons, 2003). And (with assistance from the pons) it coordinates voluntary movement. When a soccer player masterfully controls the ball, give his cerebellum some credit. Under alcohol's influence, coordination suffers. And if you injured your cerebellum, you would have difficulty walking, keeping your balance, or shaking hands. Your movements would be jerky and exaggerated. Gone would be any dreams of being a dancer or guitarist.

* * *

Note: These older brain functions all occur without any conscious effort. This illustrates another of our recurring themes: *Our brain processes most information outside of our awareness.* We are aware of the *results* of our brain's labor (say, our current visual experience) but not of the *how.* Likewise, whether we are asleep or awake, our brainstem manages its life-sustaining functions, freeing our newer brain regions to think, talk, dream, or savor a memory.

 LaunchPad To review and check your understanding, visit LaunchPad's *Concept Practice: Lower Brain Structures.*

Cerebellum

Spinal cord

▼ FIGURE 6.6
The brain's organ of agility Hanging at the back of the brain, the cerebellum coordinates our voluntary movements.

• In what brain region would damage be most likely to (1) disrupt your ability to skip rope? (2) disrupt your ability to hear and taste? (3) perhaps leave you in a coma? (4) cut off the very breath and heartbeat of life?

ANSWER: 1. cerebellum, 2. thalamus, 3. reticular formation, 4. medulla

The Limbic System

6-3 What are the limbic system's structures and functions?

We've now considered the brain's oldest parts. Its newest and highest regions are the *cerebral hemispheres* (the two halves of the brain). Between the oldest and newest brain areas lies the **limbic system** (*limbus* means "border"). This system contains the *amygdala*, the *hypothalamus*, and the *hippocampus* (**FIGURE 6.7**). The **hippocampus** process conscious, explicit memories. Animals or humans who lose their hippocampus to surgery or injury also lose their ability to form new memories of facts and events. Other modules explain how our two-track mind uses the hippocampus to process our memories. For now, let's look at the limbic system's links to emotions such as fear and anger, and to basic motives such as those for food and sex.

The Amygdala Research has linked the **amygdala,** two lima-bean-sized neural clusters, to aggression and fear. In 1939, psychologist Heinrich Klüver and neurosurgeon Paul Bucy surgically removed a rhesus monkey's amygdala, turning the normally ill-tempered animal into the most mellow of creatures. In studies with other wild animals, including the lynx, wolverine, and wild rat, researchers noted the same effect. So, too, with human patients. Those with amygdala lesions often display reduced arousal to fear- and anger-arousing stimuli (Berntson et al., 2011). One such woman, patient S. M., has been called "the woman with no fear," even of being threatened with a gun (Feinstein et al., 2013).

What then might happen if we electrically stimulated the amygdala of a placid domestic animal, such as a cat? Do so in one spot and the cat prepares to attack, hissing with its back arched, its pupils dilated, its hair on end. Move the electrode only slightly within the amygdala, cage the cat with a small mouse, and now it cowers in terror.

These and other experiments have confirmed the amygdala's role in fear and rage. One study found math anxiety associated with hyperactivity in the right amygdala (Young et al., 2012). Other studies have shown people angry and happy faces: The amygdala activates in response to the angry ones (Mende-Siedlecki et al., 2013). But we must be careful. The brain is not neatly organized into structures that correspond to our behavior categories. When we feel or act in aggressive or fearful ways, there is neural activity in many areas of our brain. If you destroy a car's dead battery, you can't start the engine. Yet the battery is merely one link in an integrated system.

Jane Burton/Dorling Kindersley/Gettyimages

RETRIEVAL PRACTICE

• Electrical stimulation of a cat's amygdala provokes angry reactions. Which *autonomic nervous system* division is activated by such stimulation?

ANSWER: The sympathetic nervous system

The Hypothalamus Just below (*hypo*) the thalamus is the **hypothalamus** (**FIGURE 6.8** on the next page), an important link in the command chain governing bodily maintenance. Some neural clusters in the hypothalamus influence hunger; others regulate thirst, body temperature, and sexual behavior. Together, they help maintain a steady (*homeostatic*) internal state.

As the hypothalamus monitors the state of your body, it tunes into your blood chemistry and any incoming orders from other brain parts. For example, picking up signals from your brain's cerebral cortex that you are thinking about sex, your hypothalamus will secrete hormones. These hormones will in turn trigger the adjacent "master gland" of the endocrine system, your pituitary (see Figure 6.7), to influence your sex glands

Hypothalamus

Pituitary gland

Amygdala   **Hippocampus**

▼ FIGURE 6.7
The limbic system This neural system sits between the brain's older parts and its cerebral hemispheres. The limbic system's hypothalamus controls the nearby pituitary gland.

thalamus [THAL-uh-muss] the brain's sensory control center, located on top of the brainstem; it directs messages to the sensory receiving areas in the cortex and transmits replies to the cerebellum and medulla.

reticular formation a nerve network that travels through the brainstem into the thalamus and plays an important role in controlling arousal.

cerebellum [sehr-uh-BELL-um] the "little brain" at the rear of the brainstem; functions include processing sensory input, coordinating movement output and balance, and enabling nonverbal learning and memory.

limbic system neural system (including the *hippocampus, amygdala,* and *hypothalamus*) located below the cerebral hemispheres; associated with emotions and drives.

hippocampus a neural center located in the limbic system; helps process explicit memories for storage.

amygdala [uh-MIG-duh-la] two lima-bean-sized neural clusters in the limbic system; linked to emotion.

hypothalamus [hi-po-THAL-uh-muss] a neural structure lying below (*hypo*) the thalamus; it directs several maintenance activities (eating, drinking, body temperature), helps govern the endocrine system via the pituitary gland, and is linked to emotion and reward.

ISM/Phototake

▼ FIGURE 6.8
The hypothalamus This small but important structure, colored yellow/orange in this MRI-scan photograph, helps keep the body's internal environment in a steady state.

▼ FIGURE 6.9
Rat with an implanted electrode With an electrode implanted in a reward center of its hypothalamus, the rat readily crosses an electrified grid, accepting the painful shocks, to press a pedal that sends electrical impulses to that center.

to release their hormones. These will intensify the thoughts of sex in your cerebral cortex. (Note the interplay between the nervous and endocrine systems: The brain influences the endocrine system, which in turn influences the brain.)

A remarkable discovery about the hypothalamus illustrates how progress in science often occurs—when curious, open-minded investigators make an unexpected observation. Two young McGill University neuropsychologists, James Olds and Peter Milner (1954), were trying to implant an electrode in a rat's reticular formation when they made a magnificent mistake: They placed the electrode incorrectly (Olds, 1975). Curiously, as if seeking more stimulation, the rat kept returning to the location where it had been stimulated by this misplaced electrode. On discovering that they had actually placed the device in a region of the hypothalamus, Olds and Milner realized they had stumbled upon a brain center that provides pleasurable rewards (Olds, 1975).

In a meticulous series of experiments, Olds (1958) went on to locate other "pleasure centers," as he called them. (What the rats actually experience only they know, and they aren't telling. Rather than attribute human feelings to rats, today's scientists refer to *reward centers*, not "pleasure centers.") When allowed to press pedals to trigger their own stimulation, rats would sometimes do so more than 1000 times per hour. Moreover, they would even cross an electrified floor that a starving rat would not cross to reach food (**FIGURE 6.9**).

Stimulation pedal   Electrified grid

In other species, including dolphins and monkeys, researchers later discovered other limbic system reward centers, such as the *nucleus accumbens* in front of the hypothalamus. Animal research has also revealed both a general dopamine-related reward system and specific centers associated with the pleasures of eating, drinking, and sex. Animals, it seems, come equipped with built-in systems that reward activities essential to survival.

Researchers are experimenting with new ways of using brain stimulation to control animals' actions in search-and-rescue operations. By rewarding rats for turning left or right, one research team trained previously caged rats to navigate natural environments (Talwar et al., 2002; **FIGURE 6.10**). By pressing buttons on a laptop, the researchers were then able to direct the rat—which carried a receiver, power source, and video camera on a backpack—to turn on cue, climb trees, scurry along branches, and return.

Do humans have limbic centers for pleasure? To calm violent patients, one neurosurgeon implanted electrodes in such areas. Stimulated patients reported mild pleasure;

▼ FIGURE 6.10
Ratbot on a pleasure cruise Researchers used a remote control brain stimulator to guide rats across a field and even up a tree.

unlike Olds' rats, however, they were not driven to a frenzy (Deutsch, 1972; Hooper & Teresi, 1986). Moreover, newer research reveals that stimulating the brain's "hedonic hotspots" (its reward circuits) produces more *desire* than pure enjoyment (Kringelbach & Berridge, 2012). Experiments have also revealed the effects of a dopamine-related reward system in people. For example, dopamine release produces our pleasurable "chills" response to a favorite piece of music (Zatorre & Salimpoor, 2013).

Some researchers believe that addictive disorders, such as substance use disorders and binge eating, may stem from malfunctions in natural brain systems for pleasure and well-being. People genetically predisposed to this *reward deficiency syndrome* may crave whatever provides that missing pleasure or relieves negative feelings (Blum et al., 1996).

* * *

FIGURE 6.11 locates the brain areas we've discussed, as well as the next module's focus, the *cerebral cortex*.

🏫 **LaunchPad** To review and assess your understanding, visit LaunchPad's *Concept Practice: The Limbic System.*

RETRIEVAL PRACTICE

• What are the three key structures of the limbic system, and what functions do they serve?

ANSWER: (1) The *amygdala* is involved in aggression and fear responses. (2) The *hypothalamus* is involved in bodily maintenance, pleasurable rewards, and control of the hormonal systems. (3) The *hippocampus* processes conscious memory.

> "If you were designing a robot vehicle to walk into the future and survive, . . . you'd wire it up so that behavior that ensured the survival of the self or the species—like sex and eating—would be naturally reinforcing."
>
> Candace Pert (1986)

▼ FIGURE 6.11
Brain structures and their functions

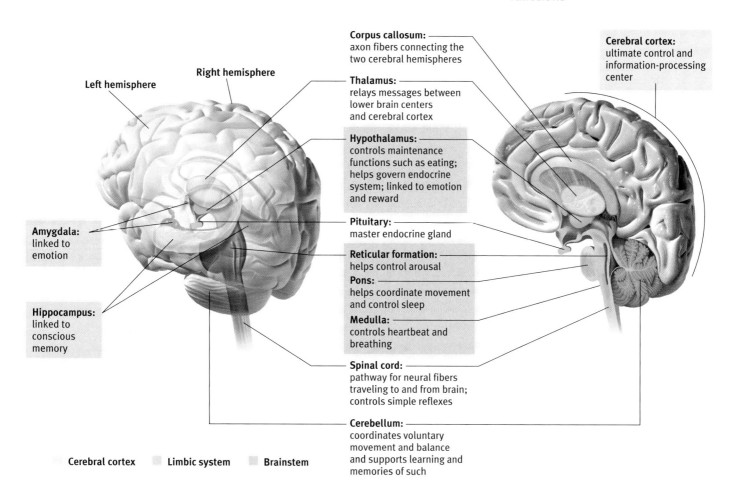

Corpus callosum: axon fibers connecting the two cerebral hemispheres

Thalamus: relays messages between lower brain centers and cerebral cortex

Hypothalamus: controls maintenance functions such as eating; helps govern endocrine system; linked to emotion and reward

Pituitary: master endocrine gland

Reticular formation: helps control arousal

Pons: helps coordinate movement and control sleep

Medulla: controls heartbeat and breathing

Spinal cord: pathway for neural fibers traveling to and from brain; controls simple reflexes

Cerebellum: coordinates voluntary movement and balance and supports learning and memories of such

Cerebral cortex: ultimate control and information-processing center

Left hemisphere   **Right hemisphere**

Amygdala: linked to emotion

Hippocampus: linked to conscious memory

Cerebral cortex   Limbic system   Brainstem

MODULE 6 REVIEW   Tools of Discovery and Older Brain Structures

LEARNING OBJECTIVES

RETRIEVAL PRACTICE Take a moment to answer each of these Learning Objective Questions (repeated here from within this module). Then turn to Appendix C, Complete Module Reviews, to check your answers. Research suggests that trying to answer these questions on your own will improve your long-term retention (McDaniel et al., 2009).

6-1 How do neuroscientists study the brain's connections to behavior and mind?

6-2 What structures make up the brainstem, and what are the functions of the brainstem, thalamus, reticular formation, and cerebellum?

6-3 What are the limbic system's structures and functions?

TERMS AND CONCEPTS TO REMEMBER

RETRIEVAL PRACTICE Test yourself on these terms by trying to write down the definition before flipping back to check your answers.

lesion [LEE-zhuhn], p. 66

electroencephalogram (EEG), p. 67

PET (positron emission tomography) scan, p. 67

MRI (magnetic resonance imaging), p. 67

fMRI (functional MRI), p. 68

brainstem, p. 69

medulla [muh-DUL-uh], p. 69

thalamus [THAL-uh-muss], p. 70

reticular formation, p. 70

cerebellum [sehr-uh-BELL-um], p. 70

limbic system, p. 71

hippocampus, p. 71

amygdala [uh-MIG-duh-la], p. 71

hypothalamus [hi-po-THAL-uh-muss], p. 71

Use 🌀 LearningCurve to create your personalized study plan, which will direct you to the resources that will help you most in 🌀 LaunchPad.

MODULE 7 The Cerebral Cortex and Our Divided Brain

The Cerebral Cortex

7-1 What are the functions of the various cerebral cortex regions?

OLDER BRAIN NETWORKS SUSTAIN BASIC life functions and enable memory, emotions, and basic drives. Newer neural networks within the *cerebrum*—the two cerebral hemispheres contributing 85 percent of the brain's weight—form specialized work teams that enable our perceiving, thinking, and speaking. Like other structures above the brainstem (including the thalamus, hippocampus, and amygdala), the cerebral hemispheres come as a pair. Covering those hemispheres, like bark on a tree, is the **cerebral cortex,** a thin surface layer of interconnected neural cells. It is your brain's thinking crown, your body's ultimate control and information-processing center.

As we move up the ladder of animal life, the cerebral cortex expands, tight genetic controls relax, and the organism's adaptability increases. Frogs and other small-cortex amphibians operate extensively on preprogrammed genetic instructions. The larger cortex of mammals offers increased capacities for learning and thinking, enabling them to be more adaptable. What makes us distinctively human mostly arises from the complex functions of our cerebral cortex.

The people who first dissected and labeled the brain used the language of scholars—Latin and Greek. Their words are actually attempts at graphic description: For example, *cortex* means "bark," *cerebellum* is "little brain," and *thalamus* is "inner chamber."

cerebral [seh-REE-bruhl] **cortex** the intricate fabric of interconnected neural cells covering the cerebral hemispheres; the body's ultimate control and information-processing center.

RETRIEVAL PRACTICE

• Which area of the human brain is most similar to that of less complex animals? Which part of the human brain distinguishes us most from less complex animals?

ANSWERS: The brainstem; the cerebral cortex

Structure of the Cortex

If you opened a human skull, exposing the brain, you would see a wrinkled organ, shaped somewhat like the meat of an oversized walnut. Without these wrinkles, a flattened cerebral cortex would require triple the area—roughly that of a large pizza. The brain's left and right hemispheres are filled mainly with axons connecting the cortex to the brain's other regions. The cerebral cortex—that thin surface layer—contains some 20 to 23 billion of the brain's nerve cells and 300 trillion synaptic connections (de Courten-Myers, 2005). Being human takes a lot of nerve.

Each hemisphere's cortex is subdivided into four *lobes*, separated by prominent *fissures*, or folds (**FIGURE 7.1**). Starting at the front of your brain and moving over the top, there are the **frontal lobes** (behind your forehead), the **parietal lobes** (at the top and to the rear), and the **occipital lobes** (at the back of your head). Reversing direction and moving forward, just above your ears, you find the **temporal lobes.** Each of the four lobes carries out many functions, and many functions require the interplay of several lobes.

Functions of the Cortex

More than a century ago, surgeons found damaged cortical areas during autopsies of people who had been partially paralyzed or speechless. This rather crude evidence did not prove that specific parts of the cortex control complex functions like movement or speech. After all, if the entire cortex controlled speech and movement, damage to almost any area might produce the same effect. A TV with its power cord cut would go dead, but we would be fooling ourselves if we thought we had "localized" the picture in the cord.

Motor Functions Scientists had better luck in localizing simpler brain functions. For example, in 1870, German physicians Gustav Fritsch and Eduard Hitzig made an important discovery: Mild electrical stimulation to parts of an animal's cortex made parts of its body move. The effects were selective: Stimulation caused movement only when applied to an arch-shaped region at the back of the frontal lobe, running roughly ear-to-ear across the top of the brain. Moreover, stimulating parts of this region in the left or right hemisphere caused movements of specific body parts on the *opposite* side of the body. Fritsch and Hitzig had discovered what is now called the **motor cortex.**

MAPPING THE MOTOR CORTEX Lucky for brain surgeons and their patients, the brain has no sensory receptors. Knowing this, Otfrid Foerster and Wilder Penfield

frontal lobes portion of the cerebral cortex lying just behind the forehead; involved in speaking and muscle movements and in making plans and judgments.

parietal [puh-RYE-uh-tuhl] **lobes** portion of the cerebral cortex lying at the top of the head and toward the rear; receives sensory input for touch and body position.

occipital [ahk-SIP-uh-tuhl] **lobes** portion of the cerebral cortex lying at the back of the head; includes areas that receive information from the visual fields.

temporal lobes portion of the cerebral cortex lying roughly above the ears; includes the auditory areas, each receiving information primarily from the opposite ear.

motor cortex an area at the rear of the frontal lobes that controls voluntary movements.

The brain has left and right hemispheres

Frontal lobe
Parietal lobe
Temporal lobe
Occipital lobe

▼ FIGURE 7.1
The cortex and its basic subdivisions

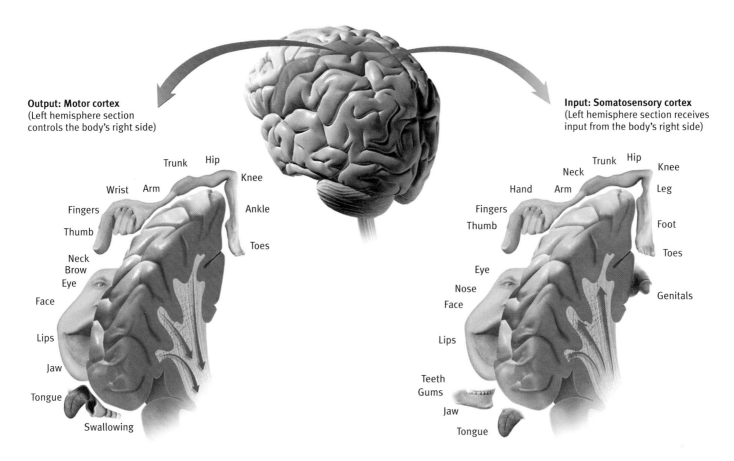

Output: Motor cortex
(Left hemisphere section controls the body's right side)

Trunk   Hip
Wrist   Arm   Knee
Fingers   Ankle
Thumb
   Toes
Neck
Brow
Eye
Face
Lips
Jaw
Tongue
   Swallowing

Input: Somatosensory cortex
(Left hemisphere section receives input from the body's right side)

Trunk   Hip
Neck   Knee
Hand   Arm   Leg
Fingers
Thumb   Foot
   Toes
Eye
Nose   Genitals
Face
Lips
Teeth
Gums
Jaw
Tongue

▼ FIGURE 7.2

Left hemisphere tissue devoted to each body part in the motor cortex and the somatosensory cortex As you can see from this classic though inexact representation, the amount of cortex devoted to a body part in the motor cortex (in the frontal lobes) or in the somatosensory cortex (in the parietal lobes) is not proportional to that body part's size. Rather, the brain devotes more tissue to sensitive areas and to areas requiring precise control. Thus, the fingers have a greater representation in the cortex than does the upper arm.

were able to map the motor cortex in hundreds of wide-awake patients by stimulating different cortical areas and observing responses. They discovered that body areas requiring precise control, such as the fingers and mouth, occupy the greatest amount of cortical space (**FIGURE 7.2**). In one of his many demonstrations of motor behavior mechanics, Spanish neuroscientist José Delgado stimulated a spot on a patient's left motor cortex, triggering the right hand to make a fist. Asked to keep the fingers open during the next stimulation, the patient, whose fingers closed despite his best efforts, remarked, "I guess, Doctor, that your electricity is stronger than my will" (Delgado, 1969, p. 114).

─────────── RETRIEVAL PRACTICE ───────────

• Try moving your right hand in a circular motion, as if cleaning a table. Then start your right foot doing the same motion, synchronized with your hand. Now reverse the right foot's motion, but not the hand's. Finally, try moving the *left* foot opposite to the right hand.

   1. Why is reversing the right foot's motion so hard?

   2. Why is it easier to move the left foot opposite to the right hand?

ANSWERS: 1. The right limbs' opposed activities interfere with each other because both are controlled by the same (left) side of your brain. 2. Opposite sides of your brain control your left and right limbs, so the reversed motion causes less interference.

More recently, scientists were able to predict a monkey's arm motion a tenth of a second *before* it moved—by repeatedly measuring motor cortex activity preceding specific arm movements (Gibbs, 1996). Such findings have opened the door to research on brain-controlled computers.

BRAIN–COMPUTER INTERFACES By eavesdropping on the brain, could we enable a paralyzed person to move a robotic limb? Could a brain–computer interface command a cursor to write an e-mail or do an online search? To find out, Brown University brain researchers implanted 100 tiny recording electrodes in the motor cortexes of three monkeys (Nicolelis, 2011; Serruya et al., 2002). As the monkeys gained rewards by using a joystick to follow a moving red target, the researchers matched the brain signals with the arm movements. Then they programmed a computer to monitor the signals and operate the joystick. When a monkey merely thought about a move, the mind-reading computer moved the cursor with nearly the same proficiency as had the reward-seeking monkey. In follow-up experiments, both monkeys and humans have learned to control a robot arm that could grasp and deliver food (Collinger et al., 2013; Hochberg et al., 2012; Velliste et al., 2008; see **FIGURE** 7.3).

Research has also recorded messages not from the arm-controlling motor neurons, but from a brain area involved in planning and intention (Leuthardt et al., 2009; Musallam et al., 2004). In one study, a monkey seeking a juice reward awaited a cue telling it to reach toward a spot flashed on a screen in one of up to eight locations. A computer program captured the monkey's thinking by recording the associated activity. By matching this neural activity to the monkey's subsequent pointing, the mind-reading researchers could program a cursor to move in response to the monkey's thoughts. Monkey think, computer do.

If this technique works, why not use it to capture the words a person can think but cannot say (for example, after a stroke)? Cal Tech neuroscientist Richard Andersen (2004, 2005) has speculated that researchers could implant electrodes in speech areas, then "ask a patient to think of different words and observe how the cells fire in different ways. So you build up your database, and then when the patient thinks of the word, you compare the signals with your database, and you can predict the words they're thinking. Then you take this output and connect it to a speech synthesizer. This would be identical to what we're doing for motor control." With this goal in mind, the U.S. Army is investing $6.3 million in neuroscientists' efforts to build a helmet that might read and transmit soldiers' thoughts (Piore, 2011).

Clinical trials of such *cognitive neural prosthetics* are now under way with people who have suffered paralysis or amputation (Andersen et al., 2010; Nurmikko et al., 2010). The first patient, a paralyzed 25-year-old man, was able to mentally control a TV, draw shapes on a computer screen, and play video games—all thanks to an aspirin-sized chip with 100 microelectrodes recording activity in his motor cortex (Hochberg et al., 2006).

▼ FIGURE 7.3
Mind over matter Strokes caused Cathy's (left) complete paralysis, as did a neurodegenerative disease for Jan (right). Yet, thanks to a tiny, 96-electrode implant in each woman's motor cortex, both have learned to direct a robotic arm with their thoughts (Collinger et al., 2013; Hochberg et al., 2012).

Nature. Hochberg, L.R. et al. Reach and grasp by people with tetraplegia using a neurally controlled robotic arm. *Nature* 485, 372–375 (2012).

UPMC

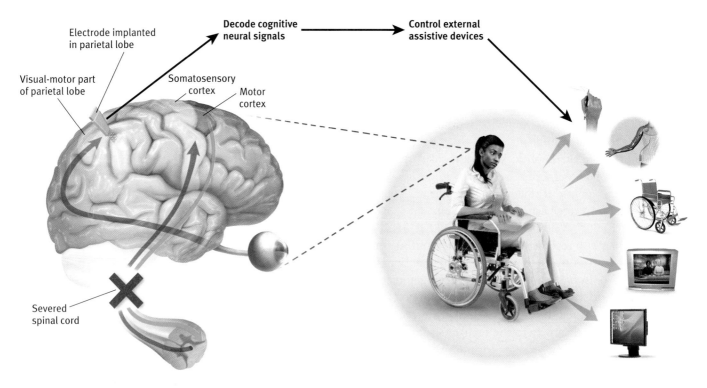

Decode cognitive neural signals ⟶ **Control external assistive devices**

Electrode implanted in parietal lobe

Visual-motor part of parietal lobe

Somatosensory cortex

Motor cortex

Severed spinal cord

▼ **FIGURE 7.4**
Brain–computer interaction
A patient with a severed spinal cord has electrodes planted in a parietal lobe region involved with planning to reach out one's arm. The resulting signal can enable the patient's thoughts to move a robotic limb, stimulate muscles that activate a paralyzed limb, navigate a wheelchair, control a TV, and use the Internet. (Graphic adapted from Andersen et al., 2010.)

▼ **FIGURE 7.5**
The brain in action This fMRI (functional MRI) scan shows the visual cortex in the occipital lobes activated (color represents increased bloodflow) as a research participant looks at a photo. When the person stops looking, the region instantly calms down.

NeuroImage, Vol. 4, V.P. Clark, K. Keill, J. Ma, Maisog, S. Courtney, L. G. Ungerleider, and J. V. Haxby, Functional Magnetic Resonance Imaging of Human

If everything psychological is also biological—if, for example, every thought is also a neural event—then perhaps microelectrodes could detect thoughts well enough to enable people to control their environment with ever-greater precision (see **FIGURE 7.4**).

Sensory Functions If the motor cortex sends messages out to the body, where does the cortex receive incoming messages? Penfield identified a cortical area—at the front of the parietal lobes, parallel to and just behind the motor cortex—that specializes in receiving information from the skin senses and from the movement of body parts. We now call this area the **somatosensory cortex** (Figure 7.2). Stimulate a point on the top of this band of tissue and a person may report being touched on the shoulder; stimulate some point on the side and the person may feel something on the face.

The more sensitive the body region, the larger the somatosensory cortex area devoted to it (Figure 7.2). Your supersensitive lips project to a larger brain area than do your toes, which is one reason we kiss with our lips rather than touch toes. Rats have a large area of the brain devoted to their whisker sensations, and owls to their hearing sensations.

Scientists have identified additional areas where the cortex receives input from senses other than touch. Any visual information you are receiving now is going to the visual cortex in your occipital lobes, at the back of your brain (**FIGURES 7.5** and **7.6**). Stimulated in the occipital lobes, you might see flashes of light or dashes of color. (In a sense, we *do* have eyes in the back of our head!) Having lost much of his right occipital lobe to a tumor removal, a friend was blind to the left half of his field of vision. Visual information travels from the occipital lobes to other areas that specialize in tasks such as identifying words, detecting emotions, and recognizing faces.

Any sound you now hear is processed by your auditory cortex in your temporal lobes (just above your ears; see Figure 7.6). Most of this auditory information travels a circuitous route from one ear to the auditory receiving area above your opposite ear. If stimulated in your auditory cortex, you might hear a sound. MRI scans of people with schizophrenia have revealed active auditory areas in the temporal lobes during the false sensory experience of auditory *hallucinations* (Lennox et al., 1999). Even the phantom ringing sound experienced by people with hearing loss is—if heard in one ear—associated with activity in the temporal lobe on the brain's opposite side (Muhlnickel, 1998).

▼ FIGURE 7.6
The visual cortex and auditory cortex The visual cortex in the occipital lobes at the rear of your brain receives input from your eyes. The auditory cortex, in your temporal lobes—above your ears—receives information from your ears.

Auditory cortex

Visual cortex

RETRIEVAL PRACTICE

- Our brain's _____ cortex registers and processes body touch and movement sensations. The _____ cortex controls our voluntary movements.

ANSWERS: somatosensory; motor

Association Areas So far, we have pointed out small cortical areas that either receive sensory input or direct muscular output. Together, these occupy about one-fourth of the human brain's thin, wrinkled cover. What, then, goes on in the remaining vast regions of the cortex? In these **association areas** (the peach-colored areas in **FIGURE** 7.7), neurons are busy with higher mental functions—many of the tasks that make us human.

Electrically probing an association area won't trigger any observable response. So, unlike the somatosensory and motor areas, association area functions cannot be neatly mapped. Their silence has led to what Donald McBurney (1996, p. 44) called "one of the hardiest weeds in the garden of psychology": the claim that we ordinarily use only 10 percent of our brain. (If true, wouldn't this imply a 90 percent chance that a bullet to your brain would strike an unused area?) Surgically lesioned animals and brain-damaged humans bear witness that association areas are not dormant. Rather, these areas interpret, integrate, and act on sensory information and link it with stored memories—a very important part of thinking. Simple tasks often increase activity in small brain patches, far less than 10 percent. Yet complex tasks integrate many islands of brain activity: some of which take in information and perform automatic tasks; others of which require conscious control (Chein & Schneider, 2012). The brain is an integrated system, with no dead spot for a stray bullet.

somatosensory cortex area at the front of the parietal lobes that registers and processes body touch and movement sensations.

association areas areas of the cerebral cortex that are not involved in primary motor or sensory functions; rather, they are involved in higher mental functions such as learning, remembering, thinking, and speaking.

Rat

Cat

Chimpanzee

Human

■ Motor areas
▨ Sensory areas
▨ Association areas

▼ FIGURE 7.7
Areas of the cortex in four mammals More intelligent animals have increased "uncommitted" or association areas of the cortex. These vast areas of the brain are responsible for interpreting, integrating, and acting on sensory information and linking it with stored memories.

plasticity the brain's ability to change, especially during childhood, by reorganizing after damage or by building new pathways based on experience.

Association areas are found in all four lobes. The *prefrontal cortex* in the forward part of the frontal lobes enables judgment, planning, and processing of new memories. People with damaged frontal lobes may have intact memories, high scores on intelligence tests, and great cake-baking skills. Yet they would not be able to plan ahead to *begin* baking a cake for a birthday party (Huey et al., 2006).

Frontal lobe damage also can alter personality and remove a person's inhibitions. Consider the classic case of railroad worker Phineas Gage. One afternoon in 1848, Gage, then 25 years old, was using a tamping iron to pack gunpowder into a rock. A spark ignited the gunpowder, shooting the rod up through his left cheek and out the top of his skull, leaving his frontal lobes damaged (**FIGURE** 7.8). The rod not only damaged some of Gage's left frontal lobe's neurons, but also about 11 percent of its axons that connect the frontal lobes with the rest of the brain (Van Horn et al., 2012). To everyone's amazement, he was immediately able to sit up and speak, and after the wound healed he returned to work. But having lost some of the neural tracts that enabled his frontal lobes to control his emotions, the affable, soft-spoken man was now irritable, profane, and dishonest. This person, said his friends, was "no longer Gage." His mental abilities and memories were intact, but his personality was not. (Although Gage lost his railroad job, he did, over time, adapt to his injury and find work as a stagecoach driver [Macmillan & Lena, 2010].)

Studies of others with damaged frontal lobes have revealed similar impairments. Not only may they become less inhibited (without the frontal lobe brakes on their impulses), but their moral judgments may seem unrestrained by normal emotions. Would you advocate pushing one person in front of a runaway trolley to save five others? Most people do not, but those with damage to a brain area behind the eyes often do (Koenigs et al., 2007). With their frontal lobes ruptured, people's moral compass seems to disconnect from their behavior.

Association areas also perform other mental functions. The parietal lobes, parts of which were large and unusually shaped in Einstein's normal-weight brain, enable mathematical and spatial reasoning (Witelson et al., 1999). Stimulation of one parietal lobe area in brain-surgery patients produced a feeling of wanting to move an upper limb, the lips, or the tongue without any actual movement. With increased stimulation, patients falsely believed they *had* moved. Curiously, when surgeons stimulated a different association area near the motor cortex in the frontal lobes, the patients did move but had no awareness of doing so (Desmurget et al., 2009). These head-scratching findings suggest that our perception of moving flows not from the movement itself, but rather from our intention and the results we expected.

▼ FIGURE 7.8

A blast from the past (a) Phineas Gage's skull was kept as a medical record. Using measurements and modern neuroimaging techniques, researchers have reconstructed the probable path of the rod through Gage's brain (Van Horn et al., 2012). (b) This photo shows Gage after his accident. (The image has been reversed to show the features correctly. Early photos, including this one, were actually mirror images.)

Collection of Jack and Beverly Wilgus

(a)   (b)

On the underside of the right temporal lobe, another association area enables us to recognize faces. If a stroke or head injury destroyed this area of your brain, you would still be able to describe facial features and to recognize someone's gender and approximate age, yet be strangely unable to identify the person as, say, your grandmother.

Nevertheless, as noted elsewhere, we should be wary of using pictures of brain "hot spots" to create a new phrenology that locates complex functions in precise brain areas (Beck, 2010; Shimamura, 2010; Uttal, 2001). Complex mental functions don't reside in any one place. There is no one spot in a rat's small association cortex that, when damaged, will obliterate its ability to learn or remember a maze. Your memory, language, and attention result from the synchronized activity among distinct brain areas and neural networks (Knight, 2007). Ditto for religious experience. More than 40 distinct brain regions become active in different religious states, such as prayer and meditation, indicating that there is no simple "God spot" (Fingelkurts & Fingelkurts, 2009). *The point to remember:* Our mental experiences arise from coordinated brain activity.

RETRIEVAL PRACTICE

- Why are association areas important?

ANSWER: Association areas are involved in higher mental functions—interpreting, integrating, and acting on information processed in other areas.

The Brain's Plasticity

7-2 To what extent can a damaged brain reorganize itself, and what is neurogenesis?

Our brains are sculpted not only by our genes but also by our experiences. MRI scans show that well-practiced pianists have a larger-than-usual auditory cortex area that encodes piano sounds (Bavelier et al., 2000; Pantev et al., 1998). In other modules, we focus on how experience molds the brain. For now, let's turn to another aspect of the brain's **plasticity:** its ability to modify itself after damage.

Some brain-damage effects can be traced to two hard facts: (1) Severed brain and spinal cord neurons, unlike cut skin, usually do not regenerate. (If your spinal cord were severed, you would probably be permanently paralyzed.) And (2) some brain functions seem preassigned to specific areas. One newborn who suffered damage to temporal lobe facial recognition areas later remained unable to recognize faces (Farah et al., 2000). But there is good news: Some neural tissue can *reorganize* in response to damage. Under the surface of our awareness, the brain is constantly changing, building new pathways as it adjusts to little mishaps and new experiences.

Plasticity may also occur after serious damage, especially in young children (Kolb, 1989; see also **FIGURE 7.9**). *Constraint-induced therapy* aims to rewire brains and improve the dexterity of a brain-damaged child or even an adult stroke victim (Taub, 2004). By restraining a fully functioning limb, therapists force patients to use the "bad" hand or leg, gradually reprogramming the brain. One stroke victim, a surgeon in his fifties, was put to work cleaning tables, with his good arm and hand restrained. Slowly, the bad arm recovered its skills. As damaged-brain functions migrated to other brain regions, he gradually learned to write again and even to play tennis (Doidge, 2007).

The brain's plasticity is good news for those blind or deaf. Blindness or deafness makes their unused brain areas available for other uses (Amedi et al., 2005). If a blind person uses one finger to read Braille, the brain area dedicated to that finger expands as the sense of touch invades the visual cortex that normally helps people see (Barinaga, 1992a; Sadato et al., 1996). Plasticity also helps explain why some studies have found that deaf people have enhanced peripheral and motion-detection vision (Bosworth & Dobkins, 1999; Shiell et al., 2014). In deaf people whose native language is sign, the temporal lobe area normally dedicated to hearing waits in vain for stimulation. Finally, it looks for other signals to process, such as those from the visual system.

▼ FIGURE 7.9
Brain plasticity This 6-year-old had surgery to end her life-threatening seizures. Although most of her right hemisphere was removed (see MRI of hemispherectomy above), her remaining hemisphere compensated by putting other areas to work. One Johns Hopkins medical team reflected on the child hemispherectomies they had performed. Although use of the opposite arm was compromised, the team reported being "awed" by how well the children had retained their memory, personality, and humor (Vining et al., 1997). The younger the child, the greater the chance that the remaining hemisphere can take over the functions of the one that was surgically removed (Choi, 2008; Danelli et al., 2013).

neurogenesis the formation of new neurons.

corpus callosum [KOR-pus kah-LOW-sum] the large band of neural fibers connecting the two brain hemispheres and carrying messages between them.

split brain a condition resulting from surgery that isolates the brain's two hemispheres by cutting the fibers (mainly those of the corpus callosum) connecting them.

Similar reassignment may occur when disease or damage frees up other brain areas normally dedicated to specific functions. If a slow-growing left hemisphere tumor disrupts language (which resides mostly in the left hemisphere), the right hemisphere may compensate (Thiel et al., 2006). If a finger is amputated, the somatosensory cortex that received its input will begin to receive input from the adjacent fingers, which then become more sensitive (Fox, 1984). So what do you suppose was the sexual intercourse experience of one patient whose lower leg had been amputated? "I actually experience my orgasm in my [phantom] foot. [Note that in Figure 7.2, the toes region is adjacent to the genitals.] And there it's much bigger than it used to be because it's no longer just confined to my genitals" (Ramachandran & Blakeslee, 1998, p. 36).

Although the brain often attempts self-repair by reorganizing existing tissue, it sometimes attempts to mend itself by producing new brain cells. This process, known as **neurogenesis,** has been found in adult mice, birds, monkeys, and humans (Jessberger et al., 2008). These baby neurons originate deep in the brain and may then migrate elsewhere and form connections with neighboring neurons (Aimone et al., 2010; Gould, 2007).

Cold War nuclear tests between 1945 and 1963 oddly later enabled scientists to confirm the birth of new brain neurons. The blasts released radioactive carbon isotopes, which carbon-dated neurons in the hippocampus, a brain center crucial to memory formation. By detecting neurons birthed since then, researchers discovered that 700 new hippocampus neurons are born daily, making nearly a 2 percent annual turnover rate (Kempermann, 2013; Spalding, 2013). Our bombs have taught us something about our brains.

Master stem cells that can develop into any type of brain cell have also been discovered in the human embryo. If mass-produced in a lab and injected into a damaged brain, might neural stem cells turn themselves into replacements for lost brain cells? Might surgeons someday be able to rebuild damaged brains, much as we reseed damaged lawns? Stay tuned. Today's biotech companies are hard at work on such possibilities. In the meantime, we can all benefit from natural promoters of neurogenesis, such as exercise, sleep, and nonstressful but stimulating environments (Iso et al., 2007; Pereira et al., 2007; Stranahan et al., 2006).

Our Divided Brain

7-3 What do split brains reveal about the functions of our two brain hemispheres?

Our brain's look-alike left and right hemispheres serve differing functions. This *lateralization* is apparent after brain damage. Research spanning more than a century has shown that left hemisphere accidents, strokes, and tumors can impair reading, writing, speaking, arithmetic reasoning, and understanding. Similar right hemisphere damage has effects that are less visibly dramatic. Does this mean that the right hemisphere is just along for the ride? Many believed this was the case until the 1960s, when a fascinating chapter in psychology's history began to unfold: Researchers found that the "minor" right hemisphere was not so limited after all.

Splitting the Brain

In 1961, Los Angeles neurosurgeons Philip Vogel and Joseph Bogen speculated that major epileptic seizures were caused by an amplification of abnormal brain activity bouncing back and forth between the two cerebral hemispheres, which work together as a whole system. If so, they wondered, could they put an end to this biological tennis match by severing the **corpus callosum,** the wide band of axon fibers connecting the two hemispheres and carrying messages between them (see **FIGURE 7.10**)? Vogel and

▼ FIGURE 7.10
The corpus callosum This large band of neural fibers connects the two brain hemispheres. To photograph the half brain at left, a surgeon separated the hemispheres by cutting through the corpus callosum and lower brain regions. The high-resolution diffusion spectrum image on the right, showing a top view, reveals brain neural networks within the two hemispheres, and the corpus callosum neural bridge between them.

Bogen knew that psychologists Roger Sperry, Ronald Myers, and Michael Gazzaniga had divided cats' and monkeys' brains in this manner, with no serious ill effects.

So the surgeons operated. The result? The seizures all but disappeared. The patients with these **split brains** were surprisingly normal, their personality and intellect hardly affected. Waking from surgery, one even joked that he had a "splitting headache" (Gazzaniga, 1967). By sharing their experiences, these patients have greatly expanded our understanding of interactions between the intact brain's two hemispheres.

To appreciate these findings, we need to focus for a minute on the peculiar nature of our visual wiring, illustrated in **FIGURE 7.11**. Note that each eye receives sensory information from the entire visual field. But in each eye, information from the left half of your field of vision goes to your right hemisphere, and information from the right half of your visual field goes to your left hemisphere, which usually controls speech. Data received by either hemisphere are quickly transmitted to the other across the corpus callosum. In a person with a severed corpus callosum, this information-sharing does not take place.

Knowing these facts, Sperry and Gazzaniga could send information to a patient's left or right hemisphere. As the person stared at a spot, they flashed a stimulus to its right or left. They could do this with you, too, but in your intact brain, the hemisphere receiving the information would instantly pass the news to the other side. Because the split-brain surgery had cut the communication lines between the hemispheres, the researchers could, with these patients, quiz each hemisphere separately.

In an early experiment, Gazzaniga (1967) asked these people to stare at a dot as he flashed HE·ART on a screen (**FIGURE 7.12** on the next page). Thus, HE appeared in their left visual field (which transmits to the right hemisphere) and ART in the right field (which transmits to the left hemisphere). When he then asked them to *say* what they had seen, the patients reported that they had seen ART. But when asked to *point* to the word they had seen, they were startled when their left hand (controlled by the right

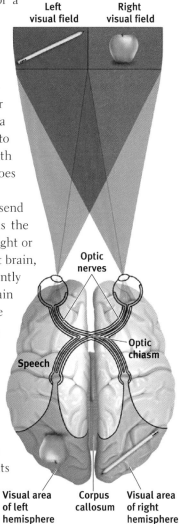

▼ FIGURE 7.11
The information highway from eye to brain

▼ FIGURE 7.12
One skull, two minds When an experimenter flashes the word HEART across the visual field, a woman with a split brain verbally reports seeing the portion of the word transmitted to her left hemisphere. However, if asked to indicate with her left hand what she saw, she points to the portion of the word transmitted to her right hemisphere. (From Gazzaniga, 1983.)

"Look at the dot."

(a)

Two words separated by a dot are momentarily projected.

(b)

"What word did you see?"   or   "Point with your left hand to the word you saw."

(c)

"Do not let your left hand know what your right hand is doing."

Matthew 6:3

▼ FIGURE 7.13
Try this! People who have had split-brain surgery can simultaneously draw two different shapes.

hemisphere) pointed to HE. Given an opportunity to express itself, each hemisphere indicated what it had seen. The right hemisphere (controlling the left hand) intuitively knew what it could not verbally report.

When a picture of a spoon was flashed to their right hemisphere, the patients could not *say* what they had viewed. But when asked to *identify* what they had viewed by feeling an assortment of hidden objects with their left hand, they readily selected the spoon. If the experimenter said, "Correct!" the patient might reply, "What? Correct? How could I possibly pick out the correct object when I don't know what I saw?" It is, of course, the left hemisphere doing the talking here, bewildered by what the nonverbal right hemisphere knows.

A few people who have had split-brain surgery have been for a time bothered by the unruly independence of their left hand, which might unbutton a shirt while the right hand buttoned it, or put grocery store items back on the shelf after the right hand put them in the cart. It was as if each hemisphere was thinking "I've half a mind to wear my green (blue) shirt today." Indeed, said Sperry (1964), split-brain surgery leaves people "with two separate minds." With a split brain, both hemispheres can comprehend and follow an instruction to copy—*simultaneously*—different figures with the left and right hands (Franz et al., 2000; see also **FIGURE 7.13**). (Reading these reports, I [DM] fantasize a patient enjoying a solitary game of "rock, paper, scissors"—left versus right hand.)

When the "two minds" are at odds, the left hemisphere does mental gymnastics to rationalize reactions it does not understand. If a patient follows an order ("Walk") sent to the right hemisphere, a strange thing happens. The unaware left hemisphere doesn't know why the patient begins walking. If asked, the patient doesn't reply, "I don't know." Instead, the left hemisphere improvises—"I'm going into the house to get a Coke." Gazzaniga (1988), who considers these patients "the most fascinating people on earth," concluded that the conscious left hemisphere is an "interpreter" that instantly constructs explanations. The brain, he concludes, often runs on autopilot; it acts first and then explains itself.

LaunchPad **HOW WOULD YOU KNOW?** Have you ever been asked if you are "left-brained" or "right-brained?" Consider this popular misconception with LaunchPad's *How Would You Know If People Can be "Left-Brained" or "Right-Brained"?*

RETRIEVAL PRACTICE

- (1) If we flash a red light to the right hemisphere of a person with a split brain, and flash a green light to the left hemisphere, will each observe its own color? (2) Will the person be aware that the colors differ? (3) What will the person verbally report seeing?

ANSWERS: 1. yes, 2. no, 3. green

Right–Left Differences in the Intact Brain

So, what about the 99.99+ percent of us with undivided brains? Does each of *our* hemispheres also perform distinct functions? Several different types of studies indicate they do. When a person performs a *perceptual* task, for example, brain waves, bloodflow, and glucose consumption reveal increased activity in the *right* hemisphere. When the person speaks or calculates, activity usually increases in the *left* hemisphere.

A dramatic demonstration of hemispheric specialization happens before some types of brain surgery. To locate the patient's language centers, the surgeon injects a sedative into the neck artery feeding blood to the left hemisphere, which usually controls speech. Before the injection, the patient is lying down, arms in the air, chatting with the doctor. Can you predict what probably happens when the drug puts the left hemisphere to sleep? Within seconds, the person's right arm falls limp. If the left hemisphere is controlling language, the patient will be speechless until the drug wears off. If the drug is injected into the artery to the right hemisphere, the *left* arm will fall limp, but the person will still be able to speak.

To the brain, language is language, whether spoken or signed. Just as hearing people usually use the left hemisphere to process spoken language, deaf people use the left hemisphere to process sign language (Corina et al., 1992; Hickok et al., 2001). Thus, a left hemisphere stroke disrupts a deaf person's signing, much as it would disrupt a hearing person's speaking (Corina, 1998).

Although the left hemisphere is adept at making quick, literal interpretations of language, the right hemisphere

- *excels in making inferences* (Beeman & Chiarello, 1998; Bowden & Beeman, 1998; Mason & Just, 2004). Primed with the flashed word *foot*, the left hemisphere will be especially quick to recognize the closely associated word *heel*. But if given an insight-like problem—"What word goes with *boot, summer,* and *ground*?"—the right hemisphere more quickly recognizes the solution: *camp*. As one patient explained after a right hemisphere stroke, "I understand words, but I'm missing the subtleties." The right side of the brain is also better than the left at copying drawings, recognizing faces, noticing differences, perceiving emotion, and expressing emotion through the more expressive left side of the face. Right hemisphere damage can greatly disrupt these abilities.

- *helps us modulate our speech* to make meaning clear—as when we ask "What's that in the road ahead?" instead of "What's that in the road, a head?" (Heller, 1990).

- *helps orchestrate our self-awareness.* People who suffer partial paralysis will sometimes obstinately deny their impairment—strangely claiming they can move a paralyzed limb—if the damage is to the right hemisphere (Berti et al., 2005).

Simply looking at the two hemispheres, so alike to the naked eye, who would suppose they contribute uniquely to the harmony of the whole? Yet a variety of observations—of people with split brains, of people with normal brains, and even of other species' brains—converge beautifully, leaving little doubt that we have unified brains with specialized parts (Hopkins & Cantalupo 2008; MacNeilage et al., 2009; and see Thinking Critically About: Handedness).

💿 **LaunchPad** For a helpful animated review of this research, see LaunchPad's *PsychSim 6: Hemispheric Specialization.*

Handedness

7-4 What does research tell us about being left-handed? Is it advantageous to be right-handed?

Nearly 90 percent of us are primarily right-handed (Leask & Beaton, 2007; Medland et al., 2004; Peters et al., 2006). Most people also kick with their right foot and look through a microscope with their right eye. Some 10 percent of us (somewhat more among males, somewhat less among females) are left-handed. (A few people write with their right hand and throw a ball with their left, or vice versa.) Almost all right-handers (96 percent) process speech primarily in the left hemisphere, which tends to be the slightly larger hemisphere (Bishop, 2013). Left-handers are more diverse. Seven in ten process speech in the left hemisphere, as right-handers do. The rest either process language in the right hemisphere or use both hemispheres.

Is Handedness Inherited?

Judging from prehistoric human cave drawings, tools, and hand and arm bones, this veer to the right occurred long ago (Corballis, 1989; MacNeilage et al., 2009). Right-handedness prevails in all human cultures, and even in chimpanzees (Hopkins, 2013). Moreover, it appears prior to culture's impact: More than 9 in 10 fetuses suck the right hand's thumb (Hepper et al., 1990, 2004). Twin studies indicate only a small genetic influence on individual handedness (Vuoksimaa et al., 2009). But the universal prevalence of right-handers in humans and other primates suggests that either genes or some prenatal factors influence handedness.

So, Is It All Right to Be Left-Handed?

Judging by our everyday conversation, left-handedness is not all right. To be "coming out of left field" is hardly better than to be "gauche" (derived from the French word for "left"). On the other hand, right-handedness is "right on," which any "righteous," "right-hand man" "in his right mind" usually is.

Left-handers are more numerous than usual among those with reading disabilities, allergies, and migraine headaches (Geschwind & Behan, 1984). But in Iran, where students report which hand they write with when taking the university entrance exam, lefties have outperformed righties in all subjects (Noroozian et al., 2003). Left-handedness is also more common among musicians, mathematicians, professional baseball and cricket players, architects, and artists, including such luminaries as Michelangelo, Leonardo da Vinci, and Picasso.[1] Although left-

Nati Harnik/AP Photo   Nati Harnik/AP Photo

The rarest of baseball players: an ambidextrous pitcher Using a glove with two thumbs, Creighton University pitcher Pat Venditte, shown here in a 2008 game, pitched to right-handed batters with his right hand, then switched to face left-handed batters with his left hand. After one switch-hitter switched sides of the plate, Venditte switched pitching arms, which triggered the batter to switch again, and so on. The umpires ultimately ended the comedy routine by applying a little-known rule: A pitcher must declare which arm he will use before throwing his first pitch to a batter (Schwarz, 2007).

handers must tolerate elbow jostling at the dinner table, right-handed desks, and awkward scissors, the pros and cons of being a lefty seem roughly equal.

RETRIEVAL PRACTICE

• Almost all right-handers process speech in the _____ hemisphere; most left-handers process speech in the _____ hemisphere.

ANSWER: left; left—the other 30 percent vary, processing speech in the right hemisphere or in both hemispheres

1. Strategic factors explain the higher-than-normal percentage of lefties in sports. For example, it helps a soccer team to have left-footed players on the left side of the field (Wood & Aggleton, 1989). In golf, however, no left-hander won the Masters tournament until Canadian Mike Weir did so in 2003.

* * *

We have glimpsed an overriding principle: Everything psychological is simultaneously biological. We have focused on how our thoughts, feelings, and actions arise from our specialized yet integrated brain. Elsewhere in this text, we further explore the significance of the biological revolution in psychology.

From nineteenth-century phrenology to today's neuroscience, we have come a long way. Yet what is unknown still dwarfs what is known. We can describe the brain. We can learn the functions of its parts. We can study how the parts communicate. But how do we get mind out of meat? How does the electrochemical whir in a hunk of tissue the size of a head of lettuce give rise to elation, a creative idea, or that memory of Grandmother?

Much as gas and air can give rise to something different—fire—so also, believed Roger Sperry, does the complex human brain give rise to something different: *consciousness.* The mind, he argued, emerges from the brain's dance of ions, yet is not reducible to it. As neuroscientist Donald MacKay (1978) observed, "[My brain activity] reflects what I am thinking, as [computer] activity reflects the equation it is solving." The mind and brain activities are yoked (no brain, no mind), he noted, but are complementary and conceptually distinct.

Cells cannot be fully explained by the actions of atoms, nor minds by the activity of cells. Psychology is rooted in biology, which is rooted in chemistry, which is rooted in physics. Yet psychology is more than applied physics. As Jerome Kagan (1998) reminded us, the meaning of the Gettysburg Address is not reducible to neural activity. Sexual love is more than blood flooding to the genitals. Morality and responsibility become possible when we understand the mind as a "holistic system," said Sperry (1992) (**FIGURE** 7.14). We are not mere jabbering robots. Brains make thoughts. And thoughts change brains.

> "All psychological phenomena are caused by the brain, but many are better understood at the level of the mind."
>
> Tweet from psychologist Steven Pinker, June 10, 2013

> "'Was the cause psychological or biological?' is the wrong question when assigning responsibility for an action. All psychological states are also biological ones."
>
> Psychologists John Monterosso and Barry Schwartz, "Did Your Brain Make You Do It?" 2012

▼ FIGURE 7.14
Mind and brain as holistic system In Roger Sperry's view, the brain creates and controls the emergent mind, which in turn influences the brain. (Think vividly about biting into a lemon and you may salivate.)

The mind seeking to understand the brain—that is indeed among the ultimate scientific challenges. And so it will always be. To paraphrase cosmologist John Barrow, a brain simple enough to be understood is too simple to produce a mind able to understand it.

MODULE 7 REVIEW The Cerebral Cortex and Our Divided Brain

LEARNING OBJECTIVES

RETRIEVAL PRACTICE Take a moment to answer each of these Learning Objective Questions (repeated here from within this module). Then turn to Appendix C, Complete Module Reviews, to check your answers. Research suggests that trying to answer these questions on your own will improve your long-term retention (McDaniel et al., 2009).

7-1 What are the functions of the various cerebral cortex regions?

7-2 To what extent can a damaged brain reorganize itself, and what is neurogenesis?

7-3 What do split brains reveal about the functions of our two brain hemispheres?

7-4 What does research tell us about being left-handed? Is it advantageous to be right-handed?

TERMS AND CONCEPTS TO REMEMBER

RETRIEVAL PRACTICE Test yourself on these terms by trying to write down the definition before flipping back to check your answers.

cerebral [seh-REE-bruhl] cortex, p. 74

frontal lobes, p. 75

parietal [puh-RYE-uh-tuhl] lobes, p. 75

occipital [ahk-SIP-uh-tuhl] lobes, p. 75

temporal lobes, p. 75

motor cortex, p. 75

somatosensory cortex, p. 78

association areas, p. 79

plasticity, p. 81

neurogenesis, p. 82

corpus callosum [KOR-pus kah-LOW-sum], p. 82

split brain, p. 83

Use 🔘 LearningCurve to create your personalized study plan, which will direct you to the resources that will help you most in 🔘 LaunchPad.

TEST YOUR-SELF THE BIOLOGY OF MIND

Test yourself repeatedly throughout your studies. This will not only help you figure out what you know and don't know; the testing itself will help you learn and remember the information more effectively thanks to the testing effect.

MODULE 5 Neural and Hormonal Systems

1. The neuron fiber that passes messages through its branches to other neurons or to muscles and glands is the _____ .

2. The tiny space between the axon of one neuron and the dendrite or cell body of another is called the
   a. axon terminal.
   b. branching fiber.
   c. synaptic gap.
   d. threshold.

3. Regarding a neuron's response to stimulation, the intensity of the stimulus determines
   a. whether or not an impulse is generated.
   b. how fast an impulse is transmitted.
   c. how intense an impulse will be.
   d. whether reuptake will occur.

4. In a sending neuron, when an action potential reaches an axon terminal, the impulse triggers the release of chemical messengers called _____ .

5. Endorphins are released in the brain in response to
   a. morphine or heroin.
   b. pain or vigorous exercise.
   c. the all-or-none response.
   d. all of the above.

6. The autonomic nervous system controls internal functions, such as heart rate and glandular activity. The word *autonomic* means
   a. calming.
   b. voluntary.
   c. self-regulating.
   d. arousing.

7. The sympathetic nervous system arouses us for action and the parasympathetic nervous system calms us down. Together, the two systems make up the _____ nervous system.

8. The neurons of the spinal cord are part of the _____ nervous system.

9. The most influential endocrine gland, known as the master gland, is the
   a. pituitary.
   b. hypothalamus.
   c. thyroid.
   d. pancreas.

10. The _____ _____ secrete(s) epinephrine and norepinephrine, helping to arouse the body during times of stress.

MODULE 6 Tools of Discovery and Older Brain Structures

11. The part of the brainstem that controls heartbeat and breathing is the
    a. cerebellum.
    b. medulla.
    c. cortex.
    d. thalamus.

12. The thalamus functions as a
    a. memory bank.
    b. balance center.
    c. breathing regulator.
    d. sensory control center.

13. The lower brain structure that governs arousal is the
    a. spinal cord.
    b. cerebellum.
    c. reticular formation.
    d. medulla.

14. The part of the brain that coordinates voluntary movement and enables nonverbal learning and memory is the _____ .

15. Two parts of the limbic system are the amygdala and the
    a. cerebral hemispheres.
    b. hippocampus.
    c. thalamus.
    d. pituitary.

16. A cat's ferocious response to electrical brain stimulation would lead you to suppose the electrode had touched the _____ .

17. The neural structure that most directly regulates eating, drinking, and body temperature is the
    a. endocrine system.
    b. hypothalamus.
    c. hippocampus.
    d. amygdala.

18. The initial reward center discovered by Olds and Milner was located in the _____ .

MODULE 7 The Cerebral Cortex and Our Divided Brain

19. If a neurosurgeon stimulated your right motor cortex, you would most likely
    a. see light.
    b. hear a sound.
    c. feel a touch on the right arm.
    d. move your left leg.

20. How do different neural networks communicate with one another to let you respond when a friend greets you at a party?

21. Which of the following body regions has the greatest representation in the somatosensory cortex?
    a. Upper arm
    b. Toes
    c. Lips
    d. All regions are equally represented.

22. Judging and planning are enabled by the _____ lobes.

23. What would it be like to talk on the phone if you didn't have temporal lobe association areas? What would you hear? What would you understand?

24. The "uncommitted" areas that make up about three-fourths of the cerebral cortex are called _____ _____ .

25. Plasticity is especially evident in the brains of
    a. split-brain patients.
    b. young adults.
    c. young children.
    d. right-handed people.

26. An experimenter flashes the word HERON across the visual field of a man whose corpus callosum has been severed. HER is transmitted to his right hemisphere and ON to his left hemisphere. When asked to indicate what he saw, the man says he saw _____ but points to _____ .

27. Studies of people with split brains and brain scans of those with undivided brains indicate that the left hemisphere excels in
    a. processing language.
    b. visual perceptions.
    c. making inferences.
    d. neurogenesis.

28. Damage to the brain's right hemisphere is most likely to reduce a person's ability to
    a. recite the alphabet rapidly.
    b. make inferences.
    c. understand verbal instructions.
    d. solve arithmetic problems.

Find answers to these questions in Appendix D, in the back of the book.

Robert Churchill/E+/Getty Images

Brain States and Consciousness

Sleep and Dreams

Drugs and Consciousness

CONSCIOUSNESS AND THE TWO-TRACK MIND

....

Consciousness can be a funny thing. It offers us weird experiences, as when entering sleep or leaving a dream, and sometimes it leaves us wondering who is really in control. After zoning me [DM] out with nitrous oxide, my dentist tells me to turn my head to the left. My conscious mind resists: "*No way,*" I silently say. "*You can't boss me around!*" Whereupon my robotic head, ignoring my conscious mind, turns obligingly under the dentist's control.

During my noontime pickup basketball games, I am sometimes mildly irritated as my body passes the ball while my conscious mind is saying, "*No, stop! Sarah is going to intercept!*" Alas, my body completes the pass. Other times, as psychologist Daniel Wegner (2002) noted in *The Illusion of Conscious Will*, people believe their consciousness is controlling their actions when it isn't. In one experiment, two people jointly controlled a computer mouse. Even when their partner (who was actually the experimenter's accomplice) caused the mouse to stop on a predetermined square, the participants perceived that *they* had caused it to stop there.

Then there are those times when consciousness seems to split. Reading *Green Eggs and Ham* to one of my preschoolers for the umpteenth time, my obliging mouth could say the words while my mind wandered elsewhere. And if someone drops by my office while I'm typing a sentence, it's not a problem. My fingers can complete it as I strike up a conversation.

What do such experiences reveal? Does the mind going elsewhere while reading or typing reveal a split in consciousness? During sleep, when do those weird dream experiences occur, and why? Before considering these questions and more, let's ask a fundamental question: What is *consciousness* (Module 8)? We'll then look at sleep and dreams (Module 9), and follow that with an exploration of psychoactive drugs (Module 10).

consciousness our awareness of ourselves and our environment.

MODULE 8 Brain States and Consciousness

EVERY SCIENCE HAS CONCEPTS SO fundamental they are nearly impossible to define. Biologists agree on what is alive but not on precisely what life is. In physics, *matter* and *energy* elude simple definition. To psychologists, consciousness is similarly a fundamental yet slippery concept.

Defining Consciousness

8-1 What is the place of consciousness in psychology's history?

At its beginning, *psychology* was "the description and explanation of states of consciousness" (Ladd, 1887). But during the first half of the twentieth century, the difficulty of scientifically studying consciousness led many psychologists—including those in the emerging school of *behaviorism*—to turn to direct observations of behavior. By the 1960s, psychology had nearly lost consciousness and was defining itself as "the science of behavior." Consciousness was likened to a car's speedometer: "It doesn't make the car go, it just reflects what's happening" (Seligman, 1991, p. 24).

After 1960, mental concepts reemerged. Neuroscience advances linked brain activity to sleeping, dreaming, and other mental states. Researchers began studying consciousness altered by hypnosis, drugs, and meditation. Psychologists of all persuasions were affirming the importance of *cognition*, or mental processes. Psychology was regaining consciousness.

Most psychologists now define **consciousness** as our awareness of ourselves and our environment. This awareness allows us to assemble information from many sources as we reflect on our past and plan for our future. And it focuses our attention when we learn a complex concept or behavior. When learning to drive, we focus on the car and the traffic. With practice, driving becomes semiautomatic, freeing us to focus our attention on other things. Over time, we flit between different *states of consciousness*, including normal waking awareness and various altered states (**FIGURE 8.1**).

Today's science explores the biology of consciousness. Evolutionary psychologists presume that consciousness offers a reproductive advantage (Barash, 2006; Murdik et al., 2011). Consciousness helps us cope with novel situations and act in our long-term interests, rather than merely seeking short-term pleasure and avoiding pain. Consciousness also promotes our survival by anticipating how we seem to others and helping us read their minds: "He looks really angry! I'd better run!"

Such explanations still leave us with the "hard problem": How do brain cells jabbering to one another create our awareness of the taste of a taco, the idea of infinity, the feeling of fright? The question of how consciousness arises from the material brain is, for many scientists, one of life's deepest mysteries.

"Psychology must discard all reference to consciousness."

Behaviorist John B. Watson (1913)

For coverage of hypnosis, see the Module 20 discussion of pain. For more on meditation, see Module 41.

INSADCO Photography/Alamy

▼ **FIGURE 8.1**
Altered states of consciousness
In addition to normal, waking awareness, consciousness comes to us in altered states, including daydreaming, drug-induced hallucinating, and meditating.

Some states occur spontaneously	Daydreaming	Drowsiness	Dreaming
Some are physiologically induced	Hallucinations	Orgasm	Food or oxygen starvation
Some are psychologically induced	Sensory deprivation	Hypnosis	Meditation

The Biology of Consciousness

8-2 What is the "dual processing" being revealed by today's cognitive neuroscience?

Cognitive Neuroscience

Scientists assume, in the words of neuroscientist Marvin Minsky (1986, p. 287), that "the mind is what the brain does." We just don't know *how* it does it. Even with all the world's technology, we still don't have a clue *how* to make a conscious robot. Yet today's **cognitive neuroscience**—the interdisciplinary study of the brain activity linked with our mental processes—is relating specific brain states to conscious experiences.

A stunning demonstration of consciousness appeared in brain scans of a noncommunicative patient—a 23-year-old woman who had been in a car accident and showed no outward signs of conscious awareness (Owen, 2014; Owen et al., 2006). When researchers asked her to *imagine* playing tennis, fMRI scans revealed activity in a brain area that normally controls arm and leg movements (**FIGURE 8.2**). Even in a motionless body, the researchers concluded, the brain—and the mind—may still be active. A follow-up analysis of 42 behaviorally unresponsive patients revealed 13 more who also showed meaningful, though less than normal, brain responses to questions (Stender et al., 2014). But reanalysis of some of these EEG data found the positive results to be mere muscle twitches (Goldfine et al., 2013). So this research is an unfinished story.

Many cognitive neuroscientists are exploring and mapping the conscious functions of the cortex. Based on your cortical activation patterns, they can now, in limited ways, read your mind (Bor, 2010). They could, for example, tell which of 10 similar objects (hammer, drill, and so forth) you were viewing (Shinkareva et al., 2008).

Some neuroscientists believe that conscious experience arises from synchronized activity across the brain (Gaillard et al., 2009; Koch & Greenfield, 2007; Schurger et al., 2010). If a stimulus activates enough brain-wide coordinated neural activity—with strong signals in one brain area triggering activity elsewhere—it crosses a threshold for consciousness. A weaker stimulus—perhaps a word flashed too briefly to consciously perceive—may trigger localized visual cortex activity that quickly fades. A stronger stimulus will engage other brain areas, such as those involved with language, attention, and memory. Such reverberating activity (detected by brain scans) is a telltale sign of conscious awareness (Boly et al., 2011). How the synchronized activity produces awareness—how matter makes mind—remains a mystery.

Patient

Healthy Volunteers

Tennis Imagery   Spatial Navigation Imagery

Courtesy of Adrian M. Owen, the Brain and Mind Institute, Western University

▼ **FIGURE 8.2**
Evidence of awareness? When asked to imagine playing tennis or navigating her home, a vegetative patient's brain (top) exhibited activity similar to a healthy person's brain (bottom). Researchers wonder if such fMRI scans might enable a "conversation" with some unresponsive patients, by instructing them, for example, to answer *yes* to a question by imagining playing tennis (top and bottom left), and *no* by imagining walking around their home (top and bottom right).

RETRIEVAL PRACTICE

- Those working in the interdisciplinary field called _____ _____ study the brain activity associated with perception, thinking, memory, and language.

ANSWER: cognitive neuroscience

Dual Processing: The Two-Track Mind

Many cognitive neuroscience discoveries tell us of a particular brain region that becomes active with a particular conscious experience. Such findings strike many people as interesting but not mind blowing. (If everything psychological is simultaneously biological, then our ideas, emotions, and spirituality must all, somehow, be embodied.) What *is* mind blowing to many of us is the growing evidence that we have, so to speak, two minds, each supported by its own neural equipment.

At any moment, you and I are aware of little more than what's on the screen of our consciousness. But beneath the surface, unconscious information processing occurs

cognitive neuroscience the interdisciplinary study of the brain activity linked with cognition (including perception, thinking, memory, and language).

> **dual processing** the principle that information is often simultaneously processed on separate conscious and unconscious tracks.
>
> **blindsight** a condition in which a person can respond to a visual stimulus without consciously experiencing it.

simultaneously on many parallel tracks. When we look at a bird flying, we are consciously aware of the result of our cognitive processing ("It's a hummingbird!") but not of our subprocessing of the bird's color, form, movement, and distance. One of the grand ideas of recent cognitive neuroscience is that much of our brain work occurs off stage, out of sight. Perception, memory, thinking, language, and attitudes all operate on two levels—a conscious, deliberate "high road" and an unconscious, automatic "low road." The high road is reflective, the low road is intuitive (Evans & Stanovich, 2013; Kahneman, 2011). Today's researchers call this **dual processing.** We know more than we know we know.

If you are a driver, consider how you move to the right lane. Drivers know this unconsciously but cannot accurately explain it (Eagleman, 2011). Most say they would bank to the right, then straighten out—a procedure that would actually steer them off the road. In reality, an experienced driver, after moving right, automatically reverses the steering wheel just as far to the left of center, and only then returns to the center position. The lesson: The human brain is a device for converting conscious into unconscious knowledge.

Or consider this story, which illustrates how science can be stranger than science fiction. During my sojourns at Scotland's University of St. Andrews, I [DM] came to know cognitive neuroscientists David Milner and Melvyn Goodale (2008). A local woman, whom they call D.F., suffered brain damage when overcome by carbon monoxide, leaving her unable to recognize and discriminate objects visually. Consciously, D.F. could see nothing. Yet she exhibited **blindsight**—she acted as though she could see. Asked to slip a postcard into a vertical or horizontal mail slot, she could do so without error. Asked the width of a block in front of her, she was at a loss, but she could grasp it with just the right finger–thumb distance. Likewise, if your right and left eyes view different scenes, you will only be consciously aware of one at a time. Yet you will display some blindsight awareness of the other (Baker & Cass, 2013).

How could this be? Don't we have one visual system? Goodale and Milner knew from animal research that the eye sends information simultaneously to different brain areas, which support different tasks (Weiskrantz, 2009, 2010). Sure enough, a scan of D.F.'s brain activity revealed normal activity in the area concerned with reaching for, grasping, and navigating objects, but damage in the area concerned with consciously recognizing objects.[1] (See another example in **FIGURE** 8.3.)

How strangely intricate is this thing we call vision, conclude Goodale and Milner in their aptly titled book, *Sight Unseen.* We may think of our vision as a single system that controls our visually guided actions. Actually, it is a dual-processing system. A *visual perception track* enables us "to think about the world"—to recognize things and to plan future actions. A *visual action track* guides our moment-to-moment movements. Some scientists have questioned whether blindsight patients are utterly without conscious vision (Himmelbach et al., 2012; Overgaard, 2012). But the big idea—that human perceptions, memories, thinking, language, and attitudes operate on both conscious and unconscious levels—stands as one of the great insights of today's cognitive neuroscience.

The dual-track mind also appears in a patient who lost all of his left visual cortex, leaving him blind to objects and faces presented on the right side of his field of vision. He nevertheless can sense the emotion expressed in faces, which he does not consciously perceive (De Gelder, 2010). The same is true of normally sighted people whose visual cortex has been disabled with magnetic stimulation. Such findings suggest that brain areas below the cortex are processing emotion-related information.

People often have trouble accepting that much of our everyday thinking, feeling, and acting operates outside our conscious awareness (Bargh & Chartrand, 1999). We

▼ FIGURE 8.3

When the blind can "see" In this compelling demonstration of blindsight and the two-track mind, researcher Lawrence Weiskrantz trailed a blindsight patient down a cluttered hallway. Although told the hallway was empty, the patient meandered around all the obstacles without any awareness of them.

---

1. So, would the reverse damage lead to the opposite symptoms? Indeed, there are a few such patients—who can see and recognize objects but have difficulty pointing toward or grasping them.

are understandably biased to believe that our intentions and deliberate choices rule our lives. But consciousness, though enabling us to exert voluntary control and to communicate our mental states to others, is but the tip of the information-processing iceberg. Being intensely focused on an activity (such as reading this module, we'd love to think) increases your total brain activity no more than 5 percent above its baseline rate. And even when you rest, "hubs of dark energy" are whirling inside your head (Raichle, 2010).

Here's another weird (and provocative) finding: Experiments show that when you move your wrist at will, you consciously experience the decision to move it about 0.2 seconds before the actual movement (Libet, 1985, 2004). No surprise there. But your brain waves jump about 0.35 seconds before you consciously perceive your decision to move (**FIGURE 8.4**)! The startling conclusion: Consciousness sometimes arrives late to the decision-making party.

That inference has triggered more research and much debate. Does our brain really make decisions before we know about them? If so, is free will an illusion? Using fMRI scans, EEG recordings, or implanted electrodes, some studies seem to confirm that brain activity precedes—and helps predict—people's decisions to press a button or to choose a card in a simplified poker game (Carter et al., 2012; Fried et al., 2011; Soon et al., 2008). However, other studies indicate that brain activity continuously ebbs and flows, including during the experiments' predecision phase—regardless of whether the decision is made and executed (Schurger et al., 2012). The actual decision to move occurs when the brain activity crosses a threshold, which happens to coincide with the average "time of awareness of intention to move" (about 0.15 second before the movement). This view sees the mind's decision and the brain's activity, like a computer's problem solving and its electronic activity, as simultaneous and parallel.

▼ FIGURE 8.4
Is the brain ahead of the mind?
In this study, volunteers watched a computer clock sweep through a full revolution every 2.56 seconds. They noted the time at which they decided to move their wrist. About one-third of a second before that decision, their brain-wave activity jumped, indicating a *readiness potential* to move. Watching a slow-motion replay, the researchers were able to predict when a person was about to decide to move (following which, the wrist did move) (Libet, 1985, 2004). Other researchers, however, question the clock measurement procedure (Miller et al., 2011).

🅜 **LaunchPad** To think further about the implications of these provocative findings for our understanding of free will and decision making, visit LaunchPad's *PsychSim 6: Who's in Charge?*

Running on automatic pilot allows our consciousness—our mind's CEO—to monitor the whole system and deal with new challenges, while neural assistants automatically take care of routine business. A skilled tennis player's brain and body respond automatically to an oncoming serve before becoming consciously aware of the ball's trajectory (which takes about three-tenths of a second). Ditto for other skilled athletes, for whom action precedes awareness. *The bottom line:* In everyday life, we mostly function like an automatic camera, but with a manual (conscious) override.

Great myths often engage simple pairs: good Cinderella and the evil stepmother, the slow Tortoise and fast Hare, the logical Sherlock Holmes and emotional Dr. Watson. The myths have enduring power because they express our human reality. Dualities are us.

RETRIEVAL PRACTICE

• What are the mind's two tracks, and what is "dual processing"?

ANSWER: Our mind has separate conscious and unconscious tracks that perform dual processing—organizing and interpreting information simultaneously.

Selective Attention

8-3 How does selective attention direct our perceptions?

Unconscious parallel processing is faster than sequential conscious processing, but both are essential. **Parallel processing** enables your mind to take care of routine business. Sequential processing is best for solving new problems, which requires our focused attention. Try this: If you are right-handed, move your right foot in a smooth counterclockwise circle and write the number 3 repeatedly with your right hand—at the same time. Try something equally difficult: Tap a steady three times with your

parallel processing the processing of many aspects of a problem simultaneously; the brain's natural mode of information processing for many functions.

selective attention the focusing of conscious awareness on a particular stimulus.

inattentional blindness failing to see visible objects when our attention is directed elsewhere.

left hand while tapping four times with your right hand. Both tasks require conscious attention, which can be in only one place at a time. If time is nature's way of keeping everything from happening at once, then consciousness is nature's way of keeping us from thinking and doing everything at once.

Through **selective attention,** your awareness focuses, like a flashlight beam, on a minute aspect of all that you experience. By one estimate, your five senses take in 11,000,000 bits of information per second, of which you consciously process about 40 (Wilson, 2002). Yet your mind's unconscious track intuitively makes great use of the other 10,999,960 bits. Until reading this sentence, for example, you have been unaware of the chair pressing against your bottom or that your nose is in your line of vision. Now, suddenly, your attentional spotlight shifts. Your feel the chair, your nose stubbornly intrudes on the words before you. While focusing on these words, you've also been blocking other parts of your environment from awareness, though your peripheral vision would let you see them easily. You can change that. As you stare at the X below, notice what surrounds these sentences.

X

A classic example of selective attention is the *cocktail party effect*—your ability to attend to only one voice among many. Let another voice speak your name and your cognitive radar, operating on your mind's other track, will instantly bring that unattended voice into consciousness. This effect might have prevented an embarrassing and dangerous situation in 2009, when two Northwest Airlines pilots "lost track of time." Focused on their laptops and in conversation, they ignored alarmed air traffic controllers' attempts to reach them and overflew their Minneapolis destination by 150 miles. If only the controllers had known and spoken the pilots' names.

Selective Attention and Accidents

Talk or text while driving, or attend to music selection or route planning, and your selective attention will shift back and forth between the road and its electronic competition. Indeed, it shifts more often than we realize. One study left people in a room free to surf the Internet and to control and watch a TV. On average, they guessed their attention switched 14.8 times during the 27.5 minute session. But they were not even close. Eye-tracking revealed eight times that many attentional switches—120 in all (Brasel & Gips, 2011). Such "rapid toggling" between activities is today's great enemy of sustained, focused attention.

We pay a toll for switching attentional gears, especially when we shift to complex tasks, like noticing and avoiding cars around us. The toll is a slight and sometimes fatal delay in coping (Rubenstein et al., 2001). About 28 percent of traffic accidents occur when people are chatting or texting on cell phones (National Safety Council, 2010). One study tracked long-haul truck drivers for 18 months. The video cameras mounted in their cabs showed they were at 23 times greater risk of a collision while texting (VTTI, 2009). Mindful of such findings, the United States in 2010 banned truckers and bus drivers from texting while driving (Halsey, 2010).

It's not just truck drivers who are at risk. One in four drivers admit to texting while driving (Pew, 2011). Multitasking comes at a cost: fMRI scans offer a biological account of how multitasking distracts from brain resources allocated to driving. In areas vital to driving, brain activity decreases an average 37 percent when a driver is attending to conversation (Just et al., 2008). To demonstrate the impossibility of simultaneous multitasking, try mentally multiplying 18 × 42 while passing a truck in busy traffic. (Actually, don't try this.)

Even hands-free cell-phone talking is more distracting than chatting with passengers, who can see the driving demands, pause the conversation, and alert the driver to risks:

"I wasn't texting. I was building this ship in a bottle."

- University of Sydney researchers analyzed phone records for the moments before a car crash. Cell-phone users (even those with hands-free sets) were, like the average drunk driver, four times more at risk (McEvoy et al., 2005, 2007). Having a passenger increased risk only 1.6 times.

- When another research team installed cameras, GPS systems, and various sensors to the cars of teen drivers, they found that crashes and near-crashes increased sevenfold when dialing or reaching for a phone, and fourfold when sending or receiving a text message (Klauer et al., 2014).

- This risk difference also appeared when drivers were asked to pull off at a freeway rest stop 8 miles ahead. Of drivers conversing with a passenger, 88 percent did so. Of those talking on a cell phone, 50 percent drove on by (Strayer & Drews, 2007). And the increased risks are equal for handheld and hands-free phones, indicating that the distraction effect is mostly cognitive rather than visual (Strayer & Watson, 2012).

Most European countries and some American states now ban hand-held cell phones while driving (Rosenthal, 2009). Engineers are also devising ways to monitor drivers' gaze and to direct their attention back to the road (Lee, 2009).

Selective Inattention

At the level of conscious awareness, we are "blind" to all but a tiny sliver of visual stimuli. Ulric Neisser (1979) and Robert Becklen and Daniel Cervone (1983) demonstrated this **inattentional blindness** dramatically by showing people a one-minute video in which images of three black-shirted men tossing a basketball were superimposed over the images of three white-shirted players. The viewers' supposed task was to press a key every time a black-shirted player passed the ball. Most focused their attention so completely on the game that they failed to notice a young woman carrying an umbrella saunter across the screen midway through the video (**FIGURE 8.5**). Seeing a replay of the video, viewers were astonished to see her (Mack & Rock, 2000). This inattentional blindness is a by-product of what we are really good at: focusing attention on some part of our environment.

In a repeat of the experiment, smart-aleck researchers sent a gorilla-suited assistant through the swirl of players (Simons & Chabris, 1999). During its 5- to 9-second cameo appearance, the gorilla paused to thump its chest. Still, half the conscientious pass-counting viewers failed to see it. Psychologists have continued to have fun with invisible gorillas. One study of "inattentional deafness" delivered, separately to each ear, a

LaunchPad Visit LaunchPad to watch the thought-provoking *Video—Automatic Skills: Disrupting a Pilot's Performance.*

Reprinted with permission of Bill Whitehead

Driven to distraction In driving-simulation experiments, people whose attention is diverted by texting and cell-phone conversation make more driving errors.

▼ **FIGURE 8.5**
Selective inattention Viewers who were attending to basketball tosses among the black-shirted players usually failed to notice the umbrella-toting woman sauntering across the screen (Neisser, 1979).

▼ FIGURE 8.6
The invisible gorilla strikes again When exposed to the gorilla in the upper right several times, and even when looking at it, radiologists, searching for much tinier cancer nodules, usually failed to see it (Drew et al., 2013).

Trafton Drew, Melissa L.-H. V6, Jeremy M. Wolfe Psychological Science, © 2013. Reprinted by Permission of SAGE

"Has a generation of texters, surfers, and twitterers evolved the enviable ability to process multiple streams of novel information in parallel? Most cognitive psychologists doubt it."

Steven Pinker, "Not at All," 2010

LaunchPad With this forewarning, are you still vulnerable to change blindness? To find out, watch the 3-minute Video: Visual Attention, and prepare to be stunned.

▼ FIGURE 8.7
Change blindness While a man (in red) provides directions to a construction worker, two experimenters rudely pass between them carrying a door. During this interruption, the original worker switches places with another person wearing different-colored clothing. Most people, focused on their direction giving, do not notice the switch (Simons & Levin, 1998).

recording of men talking and of women talking. When volunteers were assigned to pay attention to the women, 70 percent failed to hear one of the men saying, over and over for 19 seconds, "I'm a gorilla" (Dalton & Fraenkel, 2012). And when 24 radiologists were looking for cancer nodules in lung scans, 20 of them missed the gorilla superimposed in the upper right **FIGURE** 8.6—though, to their credit, they were able to see what they were looking for, the much tinier cancer tissue (Drew et al., 2013). The serious point to this psychological mischief: Attention is powerfully selective. Your conscious mind is in one place at a time.

Given that most people miss someone in a gorilla suit while their attention is riveted elsewhere, imagine the fun that magicians can have by manipulating our selective attention. Misdirect people's attention and they will miss the hand slipping into the pocket. "Every time you perform a magic trick, you're engaging in experimental psychology," says magician Teller, a master of mind-messing methods (2009). One Swedish psychologist was surprised in Stockholm by a woman exposing herself, only later realizing that he had been pickpocketed (Gallace, 2012).

In other experiments, people exhibited a form of inattentional blindness called **change blindness.** In laboratory experiments, viewers didn't notice that, after a brief visual interruption, a big Coke bottle had disappeared, a railing had risen, or clothing color had changed (Chabris & Simons, 2010; Resnick et al., 1997). Focused on giving directions to a construction worker, two out of three people also failed to notice when he was replaced by another worker during a staged interruption (**FIGURE** 8.7). Out of sight, out of mind.

A Swedish research team discovered that people's blindness extends to their own choices. Petter Johansson and his colleagues (2005, 2014) showed 120 volunteers two female faces and asked which face was more attractive. After putting both photos face down, they handed viewers the one chosen and invited them to explain why they preferred it. But on 3 of 15 occasions, the researchers used sleight-of-hand to switch the photos—showing viewers the face they had *not* chosen (**FIGURE** 8.8). People noticed the switch only 13 percent of the time, and readily explained why they preferred the face they had actually rejected. "I chose her because she smiled," said one person (after

▼ FIGURE 8.8
Choice blindness Pranksters Petter Johansson, Lars Hall, and others (2005) invited people to choose pre-ferred faces. On occasion, they asked people to explain their preference for the *unchosen* photo. Most—failing to notice the switch—readily did so.

picking the solemn-faced one). Asked later whether they would notice such a switch in a "hypothetical experiment," 84 percent insisted they would.

Change deafness can also occur. In one experiment, 40 percent of people focused on repeating a list of words that someone spoke failed to notice a change in the person speaking (Vitevitch, 2003). In two follow-up phone interview experiments, only 2 of 40 people noticed that the female interviewer changed after the third question (a change that was noticeable if people were forewarned of a possible interviewer change) (Fenn et al., 2011). Some stimuli, however, are so powerful, so strikingly distinct, that we experience *popout*, as with the only smiling face in **FIGURE 8.9** We don't choose to attend to these stimuli; they draw our eye and demand our attention. Likewise, when the female phone interviewer changed to a male interviewer, virtually everyone noticed.

The dual-track mind is active even during sleep, as the next module reveals.

▼ FIGURE 8.9
The popout phenomenon

RETRIEVAL PRACTICE

• Explain three attentional principles that magicians may use to fool us.

ANSWER: Our *selective attention* allows us to focus on only a limited portion of our surroundings. *Inattentional blindness* explains why we don't perceive some things when we are distracted by others. And *change blindness* happens when we fail to notice a relatively unimportant change in our environment. All these principles help magicians fool us, as they direct our attention elsewhere to perform their tricks.

> **change blindness** failing to notice changes in the environment.

MODULE 8 REVIEW Brain States and Consciousness

LEARNING OBJECTIVES

RETRIEVAL PRACTICE Take a moment to answer each of these Learning Objective Questions (repeated here from within this module). Then turn to Appendix C, Complete Module Reviews, to check your answers. Research suggests that trying to answer these questions on your own will improve your long-term retention (McDaniel et al., 2009).

8-1 What is the place of consciousness in psychology's history?

8-2 What is the "dual processing" being revealed by today's cognitive neuroscience?

8-3 How does selective attention direct our perceptions?

TERMS AND CONCEPTS TO REMEMBER

RETRIEVAL PRACTICE Test yourself on these terms by trying to write down the definition before flipping back to check your answers.

consciousness, p. 92

cognitive neuroscience, p. 93

dual processing, p. 94

blindsight, p. 94

parallel processing, p. 95

selective attention, p. 96

inattentional blindness, p. 97

change blindness, p. 98

Use **LearningCurve** to create your personalized study plan, which will direct you to the resources that will help you most in **LaunchPad**.

sleep periodic, natural loss of consciousness—as distinct from unconsciousness resulting from a coma, general anesthesia, or hibernation. (Adapted from Dement, 1999.)

circadian [ser-KAY-dee-an] **rhythm** the biological clock; regular bodily rhythms (for example, of temperature and wakefulness) that occur on a 24-hour cycle.

Sleep and Dreams

9-1 What is sleep?

SLEEP—THE IRRESISTIBLE TEMPTER TO whom we inevitably succumb. Sleep—the equalizer of presidents and peasants. Sleep—sweet, renewing, mysterious sleep. While sleeping, you may feel "dead to the world," but you are not. Even when you are deeply asleep, your perceptual window is open a crack. You move around on your bed, but you manage not to fall out. The occasional roar of passing vehicles may leave your deep sleep undisturbed, but a baby's cry interrupts it. So does the sound of your name. EEG recordings confirm that the brain's auditory cortex responds to sound stimuli even during sleep (Kutas, 1990). And when you sleep, as when awake, you process most information outside your conscious awareness.

Many of sleep's mysteries are being solved as some people sleep, attached to recording devices, while others observe. By recording brain waves and muscle movements, and by observing and occasionally waking sleepers, researchers are glimpsing things that a thousand years of common sense never told us. Perhaps you can anticipate some of their discoveries. Are the following statements true or false?

1. When people dream of performing some activity, their limbs often move in concert with the dream.

2. Older adults sleep more than young adults.

3. Sleepwalkers are acting out their dreams.

4. Sleep experts recommend treating insomnia with an occasional sleeping pill.

5. Some people dream every night; others seldom dream.

All these statements (adapted from Palladino & Carducci, 1983) are *false*. To see why, read on.

"I love to sleep. Do you? Isn't it great? It really is the best of both worlds. You get to be alive and unconscious."

Comedian Rita Rudner, 1993

Biological Rhythms and Sleep

Like the ocean, life has its rhythmic tides. Over varying time periods, our bodies fluctuate, and with them, our minds. Let's look more closely at two of those biological rhythms—our 24-hour biological clock and our 90-minute sleep cycle.

Circadian Rhythm

9-2 How do our biological rhythms influence our daily functioning?

The rhythm of the day parallels the rhythm of life—from our waking at a new day's birth to our nightly return to what Shakespeare called "death's counterfeit." Our bodies roughly synchronize with the 24-hour cycle of day and night thanks to an internal biological clock called the **circadian rhythm** (from the Latin *circa,* "about," and

Some students sleep like the fellow who stayed up all night to see where the Sun went. (Then it dawned on him.)

diem, "day"). As morning approaches, body temperature rises, then peaks during the day, dips for a time in early afternoon (when many people take siestas), and begins to drop again in the evening. Thinking is sharpest and memory most accurate when we are at our daily peak in circadian arousal. Try pulling an all-nighter or working an occasional night shift. You'll feel groggiest in the middle of the night but may gain new energy when your normal wake-up time arrives.

Age and experience can alter our circadian rhythm. Most 20-year-olds are evening-energized "owls," with performance improving across the day (May & Hasher, 1998). Most older

Eric Isselée/Shutterstock

Peter Chadwick/Science Source

adults are morning-loving "larks," with performance declining as the day wears on. By mid-evening, when the night has hardly begun for many young adults, retirement homes are typically quiet. After about age 20 (slightly earlier for women), we begin to shift from being owls to being larks (Roenneberg et al., 2004). Women become more morning oriented as they have children and also as they transition to menopause (Leonhard & Randler, 2009; Randler & Bausback, 2010). Night owls tend to be smart and creative (Giampietro & Cavallera, 2007). Morning types tend to do better in school, to take more initiative, and to be less vulnerable to depression (Randler, 2008, 2009; Preckel et al., 2013).

Sleep Stages

9-3 What is the biological rhythm of our sleeping and dreaming stages?

Sooner or later, sleep overtakes us and consciousness fades as different parts of our brain's cortex stop communicating (Massimini et al., 2005). Yet the sleeping brain remains active and has its own biological rhythm.

About every 90 minutes, we cycle through four distinct sleep stages. This simple fact apparently was unknown until 8-year-old Armond Aserinsky went to bed one night in 1952. His father, Eugene, a University of Chicago graduate student, needed to test an electroencephalograph he had repaired that day (Aserinsky, 1988; Seligman & Yellen, 1987). Placing electrodes near Armond's eyes to record the rolling eye movements then believed to occur during sleep, Aserinsky watched the machine go wild, tracing deep zigzags on the graph paper. Could the machine still be broken? As the night proceeded and the activity recurred, Aserinsky realized that the periods of fast, jerky eye movements were accompanied by energetic brain activity. Awakened during one such episode, Armond reported having a dream. Aserinsky had discovered what we now know as **REM sleep** (rapid *eye m*ovement sleep).

Similar procedures used with thousands of volunteers showed the cycles were a normal part of sleep (Kleitman, 1960). To appreciate these studies, imagine yourself as a participant. As the hour grows late, you feel sleepy and yawn in response to reduced brain metabolism. (Yawning, which can be socially contagious, stretches your neck muscles and increases your heart rate, which increases your alertness [Moorcroft, 2003].) When you are ready for bed, a researcher comes in and tapes electrodes to your scalp (to detect your brain waves), on your chin (to detect muscle tension), and just outside the corners of your eyes (to detect eye movement; **FIGURE 9.1**). Other devices will record your heart rate, respiration rate, and genital arousal.

> **REM sleep** rapid eye movement sleep; a recurring sleep stage during which vivid dreams commonly occur. Also known as *paradoxical sleep,* because the muscles are relaxed (except for minor twitches) but other body systems are active.

Dolphins, porpoises, and whales sleep with one side of their brain at a time (Miller et al., 2008).

Hank Morgan/Science Source

Left eye movements

Right eye movements

EMG (muscle tension)

EEG (brain waves)

▼ **FIGURE 9.1**
Measuring sleep activity Sleep researchers measure brain-wave activity, eye movements, and muscle tension with electrodes that pick up weak electrical signals from the brain, eyes, and facial muscles. (From Dement, 1978.)

"My problem has always been an overabundance of alpha waves."

▼ FIGURE 9.2
Brain waves and sleep stages
The beta waves of an alert, waking state and the regular alpha waves of an awake, relaxed state differ from the slower, larger delta waves of deep NREM-3 sleep. Although the rapid REM sleep waves resemble the near-waking NREM-1 sleep waves, the body is more aroused during REM sleep than during NREM sleep.

To catch your own hypnagogic experiences, you might use your alarm's snooze function.

When you are in bed with your eyes closed, the researcher in the next room sees on the EEG the relatively slow **alpha waves** of your awake but relaxed state (**FIGURE 9.2**). As you adapt to all this equipment, you grow tired and, in an unremembered moment, slip into sleep (**FIGURE 9.3**). The transition is marked by the slowed breathing and the irregular brain waves of non-REM stage 1 sleep. Using the American Academy of Sleep Medicine classification of sleep stages, this is called *NREM-1* (Silber et al., 2008).

In one of his 15,000 research participants, William Dement (1999) observed the moment the brain's perceptual window to the outside world slammed shut. Dement asked a sleep-deprived young man with eyelids taped open to press a button every time a strobe light flashed in his eyes (about every 6 seconds). After a few minutes the young man missed one. Asked why, he said, "Because there was no flash." But there was a flash. He missed it because (as his brain activity revealed) he had fallen asleep for 2 seconds, missing not only the flash 6 inches from his nose but also the awareness of the abrupt moment of entry into sleep.

During this brief NREM-1 sleep you may experience fantastic images resembling **hallucinations**—sensory experiences that occur without a sensory stimulus. You may have a sensation of falling (at which moment your body may suddenly jerk) or of floating weightlessly. These *hypnagogic* sensations may later be incorporated into your memories. People who claim to have been abducted by aliens—often shortly after getting into bed—commonly recall being floated off of or pinned down on their beds (Clancy, 2005; McNally, 2012).

▼ FIGURE 9.3
The moment of sleep We seem unaware of the moment we fall into sleep, but someone watching our brain waves could tell (Dement, 1999).

Sleep

1 second

LaunchPad To better understand EEG readings and their relation to consciousness and sleep and dreams, experience the tutorial and simulation at LaunchPad's *PsychSim 6: EEG and Sleep Stages.*

You then relax more deeply and begin about 20 minutes of *NREM-2* sleep, with its periodic *sleep spindles*—bursts of rapid, rhythmic brain-wave activity. Although you could still be awakened without too much difficulty, you are now clearly asleep.

Then you transition to the deep sleep of *NREM-3*. During this slow-wave sleep, which lasts for about 30 minutes, your brain emits large, slow **delta waves** and you are hard to awaken. (It is at the end of the deep, slow-wave NREM-3 sleep that children may wet the bed.)

REM Sleep

About an hour after you first fall asleep, a strange thing happens. Rather than continuing in deep slumber, you ascend from your initial sleep dive. Returning through NREM-2 (where you spend about half your night), you enter the most intriguing sleep

REM increases as night progresses

▼ FIGURE 9.4
The stages in a typical night's sleep People pass through a multistage sleep cycle several times each night, with the periods of deep sleep diminishing and REM sleep periods increasing in duration. As people age, sleep becomes more fragile, with awakenings common among older adults (Kamel & Gammack, 2006; Neubauer, 1999).

phase—REM sleep (**FIGURE 9.4**). For about 10 minutes, your brain waves become rapid and saw-toothed, more like those of the nearly awake NREM-1 sleep. But unlike NREM-1, during REM sleep your heart rate rises, your breathing becomes rapid and irregular, and every half-minute or so your closed eyes dart around in momentary bursts of activity. These eye movements announce the beginning of a dream—often emotional, usually story-like, and richly hallucinatory. Because anyone watching a sleeper's eyes can notice these REM bursts, it is amazing that science was ignorant of REM sleep until 1952.

Except during very scary dreams, your genitals become aroused during REM sleep. You have an erection or increased vaginal lubrication and clitoral engorgement, regardless of whether the dream's content is sexual (Karacan et al., 1966). Men's common "morning erection" stems from the night's last REM period, often just before waking. In young men, sleep-related erections outlast REM periods, lasting 30 to 45 minutes on average (Karacan et al., 1983; Schiavi & Schreiner-Engel, 1988). A typical 25-year-old man therefore has an erection during nearly half his night's sleep, a 65-year-old man for one-quarter. Many men troubled by *erectile disorder* (impotence) have sleep-related erections, suggesting the problem is not between their legs.

Your brain's motor cortex is active during REM sleep, but your brainstem blocks its messages. This leaves your muscles relaxed, so much so that, except for an occasional finger, toe, or facial twitch, you are essentially paralyzed. Moreover, you cannot easily be awakened. (This immobility may occasionally linger as you awaken from REM sleep, producing a disturbing experience of *sleep paralysis* [Santomauro & French, 2009].) REM sleep is thus sometimes called *paradoxical* sleep: The body is internally aroused, with waking-like brain activity, yet asleep and externally calm.

The sleep cycle repeats itself about every 90 minutes for younger adults (somewhat more frequently for older adults). As the night wears on, deep NREM-3 sleep grows shorter and disappears. The REM and NREM-2 sleep periods get longer (see Figure 9.4). By morning, we have spent 20 to 25 percent of an average night's

alpha waves the relatively slow brain waves of a relaxed, awake state.

hallucinations false sensory experiences, such as seeing something in the absence of an external visual stimulus.

delta waves the large, slow brain waves associated with deep sleep.

RETRIEVAL PRACTICE

Safety in numbers?

Uriel Sinai/Getty Images

• Why would communal sleeping provide added protection for those whose safety depends upon vigilance, such as these soldiers?

ANSWER: With each soldier cycling through the sleep stages independently, it is very likely that at any given time at least one of them will be awake or easily wakened in the event of a threat.

Horses, which spend 92 percent of each day standing and can sleep standing, must lie down for REM sleep (Morrison, 2003).

sleep—some 100 minutes—in REM sleep. Thirty-seven percent of people report rarely or never having dreams "that you can remember the next morning" (Moore, 2004). Yet even they will, more than 80 percent of the time, recall a dream after being awakened during REM sleep. We spend about 600 hours a year experiencing some 1500 dreams, or more than 100,000 dreams over a typical lifetime—dreams swallowed by the night but not acted out, thanks to REM's protective paralysis.

RETRIEVAL PRACTICE

• What are the four sleep stages, and in what order do we normally travel through those stages?

ANSWERS: REM, NREM-1, NREM-2, NREM-3; normally we move through NREM-1, then NREM-2, then NREM-3, then back up through NREM-2 before we experience REM sleep.

• Can you match the cognitive experience with the sleep stage?

1. NREM-1   a. story-like dream
2. NREM-3   b. fleeting images
3. REM   c. minimal awareness

ANSWERS: 1. b, 2. c, 3. a

What Affects Our Sleep Patterns?

9-4 How do biology and environment interact in our sleep patterns?

The idea that "everyone needs 8 hours of sleep" is untrue. Newborns often sleep two-thirds of their day, most adults no more than one-third (with some thriving on fewer than 6 hours nightly, others racking up 9 or more). There is more to our sleep differences than age. Some are awake between nighttime "first sleep" and "second sleep" periods (Randall, 2012). And some find that a 15-minute midday nap equals another hour of nighttime sleep (Horne, 2011).

People rarely snore during dreams. When REM starts, snoring stops.

Sleep patterns are genetically influenced (Hor & Tafti, 2009). In studies of fraternal and identical twins, only the identical twins had strikingly similar sleep patterns and durations (Webb & Campbell, 1983). Researchers are discovering the genes that regulate sleep in humans and animals (Donlea et al., 2009; He et al., 2009). Sleep patterns are also culturally influenced. In the United States and Canada, adults average 7 to 8 hours per night (Hurst, 2008; National Sleep Foundation [NSF], 2010; Robinson & Martin, 2009). The weeknight sleep of many students and workers falls short of this average, however (NSF, 2008). And thanks to modern lighting, shift work, and social media diversions, many who would have gone to bed at 9:00 P.M. a century ago are now up until 11:00 P.M. or later. With sleep, as with waking behavior, biology and environment interact.

suprachiasmatic nucleus (SCN) a pair of cell clusters in the hypothalamus that controls circadian rhythm. In response to light, the SCN causes the pineal gland to adjust melatonin production, thus modifying our feelings of sleepiness.

Bright morning light tweaks the circadian clock by activating light-sensitive retinal proteins. These proteins control the circadian clock by triggering signals to the brain's **suprachiasmatic nucleus (SCN)**—a pair of grain-of-rice-sized, 10,000-cell clusters in the hypothalamus (Wirz-Justice, 2009). The SCN does its job partly by causing the brain's pineal gland to decrease its production of the sleep-inducing hormone *melatonin* in the morning and to increase it in the evening (**FIGURE 9.5**).

A circadian disadvantage: One study of a decade's 24,121 Major League Baseball games found that teams who had crossed three time zones before playing a multiday series had nearly a 60 percent chance of losing their first game (Winter et al., 2009).

Being bathed in (or deprived of) light disrupts our 24-hour biological clock (Czeisler et al., 1999; Dement, 1999). Curiously—given that our ancestors' body clocks were attuned to the rising and setting Sun of the 24-hour day—many of today's young adults adopt something closer to a 25-hour day, by staying up too late to get 8 hours of sleep. For this, we can thank (or blame) Thomas Edison, inventor of the light bulb. This helps explain why, until our later years, we must discipline ourselves to go to bed and force ourselves to get up. Most animals, too, when placed under unnatural constant illumination will exceed a 24-hour day. Artificial light delays sleep.

Sleep often eludes those who stay up late and sleep in on weekends, and then go to bed earlier on Sunday evening in preparation for the new workweek (Oren & Terman,

Melatonin produced

- Suprachiasmatic nucleus
- Pineal gland
- Melatonin
- Blood vessel

Melatonin production suppressed

Light

- Suprachiasmatic nucleus
- Pineal gland
- No melatonin
- Blood vessel

1998). Like New Yorkers whose biology is on California time, they experience "social jet lag." For North Americans who fly to Europe and need to be up when their circadian rhythm cries "*SLEEP*," bright light (spending the next day outdoors) helps reset the biological clock (Czeisler et al., 1986, 1989; Eastman et al., 1995).

RETRIEVAL PRACTICE

- The _____ nucleus helps monitor the brain's release of melatonin, which affects our _____ rhythm.

ANSWERS: suprachiasmatic, circadian

▼ **FIGURE 9.5**
The biological clock Light striking the retina signals the suprachiasmatic nucleus (SCN) to suppress the pineal gland's production of the sleep hormone melatonin. At night, the SCN quiets down, allowing the pineal gland to release melatonin into the bloodstream.

Why Do We Sleep?

9-5 What are sleep's functions?

So, our sleep patterns differ from person to person. But why do we have this need for sleep?

Psychologists believe sleep may exist for five reasons.

1. ***Sleep protects.*** When darkness shut down the day's hunting, food gathering, and travel, our distant ancestors were better off asleep in a cave, out of harm's way. Those who didn't try to navigate around dark cliffs were more likely to leave descendants. This fits a broader principle: A species' sleep pattern tends to suit its ecological niche (Siegel, 2009). Animals with the greatest need to graze and the least ability to hide tend to sleep less. Animals also sleep less, with no ill effects, during times of mating and migration (Siegel, 2012). (For a sampling of animal sleep times, see **FIGURE 9.6**.)

2. ***Sleep helps us recuperate.*** It helps restore the immune system and repair brain tissue. Bats and other animals with high waking metabolism burn a lot of calories, producing a lot of *free radicals*, molecules that are toxic to neurons. Sleeping a lot gives resting neurons time to repair themselves, while pruning or weakening unused connections (Gilestro et al., 2009; Tononi & Cirelli, 2013). Sleep also enables house cleaning. Studies of mice show that sleep sweeps the brain of toxic metabolic waste products (Xie et al., 2013). Think of it this way: When consciousness leaves your house, workers come in for a makeover, saying "Good night. Sleep tidy."

"Sleep faster, we need the pillows."
Yiddish proverb

"Corduroy pillows make headlines."
Anonymous

▼ **FIGURE 9.6**
Animal sleep time Would you rather be a brown bat and sleep 20 hours a day or a giraffe and sleep 2 hours a day? (Data from NIH, 2010.)

Kruglov Orda/Shutterstock; Courtesy of Andrew D. Myers; © Anna63/Dreamstime.com; Steffen Foerster Photography/Shutterstock; The Agency Collection/Punchstock; Eric Isselée/Shutterstock; pandapaw/Shutterstock

20 hours
Kruglov Orda/Shutterstock

16 hours
Courtesy of Andrew D. Myers

12 hours
Utekhina Anna/Shutterstock

10 hours
Steffen Foerster Photography/Shutterstock

8 hours
Rubberball/Vetta/Getty Images

4 hours
Eric Isselée/Shutterstock

2 hours
pandapa/Shutterstock

3. *Sleep helps restore and rebuild our fading memories of the day's experiences.* Sleep consolidates our memories. It reactivates recent experiences stored in the hippocampus and shifts them for permanent storage elsewhere in the cortex (Diekelmann & Born, 2010; Racsmány et al., 2010). Adults and children trained to perform tasks therefore recall them better after a night's sleep, or even after a short nap, than after several hours awake (Kurdziel et al., 2013; Stickgold & Ellenbogen, 2008). Among older adults, more frequently disrupted sleep also disrupts memory consolidation (Pace-Shott & Spencer, 2011). After sleeping well, older people remember more of recently learned material (Drummond, 2010). Sleep, it seems, strengthens memories in a way that being awake does not.

4. *Sleep feeds creative thinking.* Dreams can inspire noteworthy artistic and scientific achievements, such as the dreams that clued chemist August Kekulé to the structure of benzene (Ross, 2006) and medical researcher Carl Alving (2011) to invent the vaccine patch. More commonplace is the boost that a complete night's sleep gives to our thinking and learning. After working on a task, then sleeping on it, people solve difficult problems more insightfully than do those who stay awake (Barrett, 2011; Sio et al., 2013). They also are better at spotting connections among novel pieces of information (Ellenbogen et al., 2007). To think smart and see connections, it often pays to ponder a problem just before bed and then sleep on it.

5. *Sleep supports growth.* During deep sleep, the pituitary gland releases a growth hormone that is necessary for muscle development. As we age, we release less of this hormone and spend less time in deep sleep (Pekkanen, 1982).

A regular full night's sleep can also "*dramatically* improve your athletic ability," report James Maas and Rebecca Robbins (2010). Well-rested athletes have faster reaction times, more energy, and greater endurance, and teams that build 8 to 10 hours of daily sleep into their training show improved performance. One study observed Stanford University men's basketball players' performance for about three weeks. During an ensuing five to seven weeks of extended sleep—aiming for 10 hours in bed—their average sleep increased 110 minutes per night, their sprint times decreased, and their free throw and 3-point shooting percentages both increased 9 percent (Mah et al., 2011). Top violinists also report sleeping 8.5 hours a day on average, and rate practice and sleep as the two most important improvement-fostering activities (Ericsson et al., 1993).

Slow-wave sleep, which occurs mostly in the first half of a night's sleep, produces the human growth hormone necessary for muscle development. REM sleep and NREM-2 sleep, which occur mostly in the final hours of a long night's sleep, help strengthen the neural connections that build enduring memories, including the "muscle memories" learned while practicing tennis or shooting baskets.

The optimal exercise time is late afternoon or early evening, Maas and Robbins advise, when the body's natural cooling is most efficient. Early morning workouts are ill-advised, because they increase the risk of injury and rob athletes of valuable sleep. Heavy workouts within three hours of bedtime should also be avoided because the arousal disrupts falling asleep. Precision muscle training, such as shooting free throws or piano playing, benefits when practiced shortly before sleep (Holz et al., 2012; Tamaki et al., 2013).

Maas has been a sleep consultant for college and professional athletes and teams. On his advice, basketball's Orlando Magic cut early morning practices. He also advised one young woman, Sarah Hughes, who felt stymied in her efforts to excel in figure-skating competition. "Cut the early morning practice," he instructed, as part of the recommended sleep regimen. Soon thereafter, Hughes' performance scores increased, ultimately culminating in her 2002 Olympic gold medal. Given all the benefits of sleep, it's no wonder that sleep loss hits us so hard.

Ample sleep supports skill learning and high performance This was the experience of Olympic gold medalist Sarah Hughes.

Timothy A. Clary/AFP/Getty Images

• What are five proposed reasons for our need for sleep?

ANSWERS: (1) Sleep has survival value. (2) Sleep helps us restore and repair brain tissue. (3) During sleep we consolidate memories. (4) Sleep fuels creativity. (5) Sleep plays a role in the growth process.

Sleep Deprivation and Sleep Disorders

9-6 How does sleep loss affect us, and what are the major sleep disorders?

When our body yearns for sleep but does not get it, we begin to feel terrible. Trying to stay awake, we will eventually lose. In the tiredness battle, sleep always wins.

Effects of Sleep Loss

Today, more than ever, our sleep patterns leave us not only sleepy but drained of energy and feelings of well-being. After a succession of 5-hour nights, we accumulate a sleep debt that need not be entirely repaid but cannot be satisfied by one long sleep. "The brain keeps an accurate count of sleep debt for at least two weeks," reported sleep researcher William Dement (1999, p. 64).

Obviously, then, we need sleep. Sleep commands roughly one-third of our lives—some 25 years, on average. Allowed to sleep unhindered, most adults will sleep at least 9 hours a night (Coren, 1996). With that much sleep, we awake refreshed, sustain better moods, and perform more efficient and accurate work. The U.S. Navy and the National Institutes of Health have demonstrated the benefits of unrestricted sleep in experiments in which volunteers spent 14 hours daily in bed for at least a week. For the first few days, the volunteers averaged 12 hours of sleep a day or more, apparently paying off a sleep debt that averaged 25 to 30 hours. That accomplished, they then settled back to 7.5 to 9 hours nightly and felt energized and happier (Dement, 1999). In one Gallup survey (Mason, 2005), 63 percent of adults who reported getting the sleep they needed also reported being "very satisfied" with their personal life (as did only 36 percent of those needing more sleep). And when 909 working women reported on their daily moods, the researchers were struck by what mattered little (such as money, so long as the person was not battling poverty), and what mattered a lot: less time pressure at work and a good night's sleep (Kahneman et al., 2004).

College and university students are especially sleep deprived; 69 percent in one national survey reported "feeling tired" or "having little energy" on several or more days in the last two weeks (AP, 2009). For students, less sleep also predicts more conflicts in friendships and romantic relationships (Gordon & Chen, 2014; Tavernier & Willoughby, 2014). Tired triggers crabby. In another survey, 28 percent of high school students acknowledged falling asleep in class at least once a week (National Sleep Foundation, 2006). The going needn't get boring before students start snoring.

LaunchPad To see whether you are one of the many sleep-deprived students, visit LaunchPad's *Assess Your Strengths self-assessment quiz, Sleep Deprivation.*

Sleep loss is also a predictor of depression. Researchers who studied 15,500 12- to 18-year-olds found that those who slept 5 or fewer hours a night had a 71 percent higher risk of depression than their peers who slept 8 hours or more (Gangwisch et al., 2010). This link does not appear to reflect depression-causing sleep difficulties. When children and youth are followed through time, sleep loss predicts depression rather than vice versa (Gregory et al., 2009). Moreover, REM sleep's processing of emotional experiences helps protect against depression (Walker & van der Helm, 2009). After a good night's sleep, we often do feel better the next day. And that may help to explain why parentally enforced bedtimes predict less depression, and why pushing back school start times leads to improved adolescent sleep, alertness, and mood (Gregory et al., 2009; Owens et al., 2010; Perkinson-Gloor et al., 2013).

In 1989, Michael Doucette was named America's Safest Driving Teen. In 1990, while driving home from college, he fell asleep at the wheel and collided with an oncoming car, killing both himself and the other driver. Michael's driving instructor later acknowledged never having mentioned sleep deprivation and drowsy driving (Dement, 1999).

"Maybe 'Bring Your Pillow To Work Day' wasn't such a good idea."

In a 2013 Gallup poll, 40 percent of Americans reported getting 6 hours or less sleep a night (Jones, 2013).

"You wake up in the middle of the night and grab your smartphone to check the time—it's 3 A.M.—and see an alert. Before you know it, you fall down a rabbit hole of email and Twitter. Sleep? Forget it."

Nick Bilton, "Disruptions: For a Restful Night, Make Your Smartphone Sleep on the Couch," 2014

"Remember to sleep because you have to sleep to remember."

James B. Maas and Rebecca S. Robbins,
Sleep for Success, 2010

Sleep-deprived students often function below their peak. And they know it: Four in five teens and three in five 18- to 29-year-olds wish they could get more sleep on weekdays (Mason, 2003, 2005). Yet that teen who staggers glumly out of bed in response to an unwelcome alarm, yawns through morning classes, and feels half-depressed much of the day may be energized at 11:00 P.M. and mindless of the next day's looming sleepiness (Carskadon, 2002). "Sleep deprivation has consequences—difficulty studying, diminished productivity, tendency to make mistakes, irritability, fatigue," noted Dement (1999, p. 231). A large sleep debt "makes you stupid."

It can also make you gain weight. Sleep deprivation

- increases *ghrelin*, a hunger-arousing hormone, and decreases its hunger-suppressing partner, *leptin* (Shilsky et al., 2012).

- decreases metabolic rate, a gauge of energy use (Buxton et al., 2012).

- increases *cortisol*, a stress hormone that stimulates the body to make fat.

- enhances limbic brain responses to the mere sight of food and decreases cortical inhibition (Benedict et al., 2012; Greer et al., 2013; St-Onge et al., 2012).

Thus, children and adults who sleep less are fatter than average, and in recent decades people have been sleeping less and weighing more (Shiromani et al., 2012). Moreover, experimental sleep deprivation of adults increases appetite and eating (Nixon et al., 2008; Patel et al., 2006; Spiegel et al., 2004; Van Cauter et al., 2007). So, sleep loss helps explain the common weight gain among sleep-deprived students (Hull et al., 2007).

Sleep also affects our physical health. When infections do set in, we typically sleep more, boosting our immune cells. Sleep deprivation can suppress immune cells that battle viral infections and cancer (Möller-Levet et al., 2013; Motivala & Irwin, 2007). One experiment exposed volunteers to a cold virus. Those who had been averaging less then 7 hours' sleep a night were three times more likely to develop a cold than were those sleeping 8 or more hours a night (Cohen et al., 2009). Sleep's protective effect may help explain why people who sleep 7 to 8 hours a night tend to outlive those who are chronically sleep deprived, and why older adults who have no difficulty falling or staying asleep tend to live longer than their sleep-deprived agemates (Dement, 1999; Dew et al., 2003).

"So shut your eyes
Kiss me goodbye
And sleep
Just sleep."

Song by My Chemical Romance

Sleep deprivation slows reactions and increases errors on visual attention tasks similar to those involved in screening airport baggage, performing surgery, and reading X-rays (Caldwell, 2012; Lim & Dinges, 2010). Slow responses can also spell disaster for those operating equipment, piloting, or driving. Driver fatigue has contributed to an estimated 20 percent of American traffic accidents (Brody, 2002) and to some 30 percent of Australian highway deaths (Maas, 1999). One two-year study examined the driving accidents of more than 20,000 Virginia 16- to 18-year-olds in two major cities. In one city, the high schools started 75 to 80 minutes later than in the other. The late starters had about 25 percent fewer crashes (Vorona et al., 2011). When sleepy frontal lobes confront an unexpected situation, misfortune often results.

Stanley Coren capitalized on what is, for many North Americans, a semi-annual sleep-manipulation experiment—the "spring forward" to daylight saving time and "fall backward" to standard time. Searching millions of records, Coren found that in both Canada and the United States, accidents increased immediately after the time change that shortens sleep (**FIGURE 9.7**). Less sleep = more accidents.

Tired people have trouble concentrating, which leads to more "cyberloafing"—frittering away time online. On the Monday after daylight saving time begins, entertainment-related Google searches have been 3.1 percent higher than on the preceding Monday, and 6.4 higher than on the following Monday (Wagner et al., 2012).

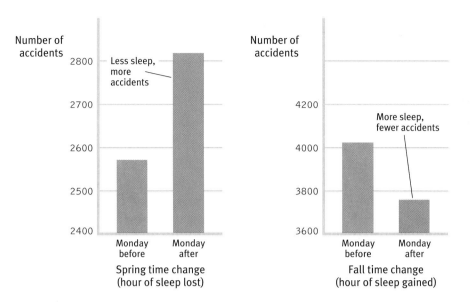

▼ FIGURE 9.7
Canadian traffic accidents On the Monday after the spring time change, when people lose one hour of sleep, accidents increased, as compared with the Monday before. In the fall, traffic accidents normally increase because of greater snow, ice, and darkness, but they diminished after the time change. (Data from Coren, 1996.)

Another study showed sleep-deprived students (compared to well-rested students) spending more time cyberloafing during a 42-minute video lecture.

FIGURE 9.8 summarizes the effects of sleep deprivation. But there is good news! Psychologists have discovered a treatment that strengthens memory, increases concentration, boosts mood, moderates hunger, reduces obesity, fortifies the disease-fighting immune system, and lessens the risk of fatal accidents. Even better news: The treatment feels good, it can be self-administered, the supplies are limitless, and it's free! If you are a typical university-age student, often going to bed near 2:00 A.M. and dragged out of bed six hours later by the dreaded alarm, the treatment is simple: Each night just add 15 minutes to your sleep.

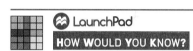

HOW WOULD YOU KNOW?
Consider how researchers have addressed these issues in Launch-Pad's *How Would You Know if Sleep Deprivation Affects Academic Performance?*

▼ FIGURE 9.8
How sleep deprivation affects us

off the mark.com   by Mark Parisi

WHEN CATS EXPERIENCE INSOMNIA

"The lion and the lamb shall lie down together, but the lamb will not be very sleepy."

Woody Allen, in the movie *Love and Death*, 1975

"Sleep is like love or happiness. If you pursue it too ardently it will elude you."

Wilse Webb, *Sleep: The Gentle Tyrant*, 1992

Imagine observing a person with narcolepsy in medieval times. Might such symptoms (especially the instant dreams from dropping into REM sleep) have seemed like demon possession?

Major Sleep Disorders

No matter what their normal need for sleep, 1 in 10 adults, and 1 in 4 older adults, complain of **insomnia**—persistent problems in either falling or staying asleep (Irwin et al., 2006). The result is tiredness and increased risk of depression (Baglioni et al., 2011). All of us, when anxious or excited, may have trouble sleeping. (And smart phones under the pillow and used as alarm clocks increase the likelihood of disrupted sleep.) From middle age on, awakening occasionally during the night becomes the norm, not something to fret over or treat with medication (Vitiello, 2009). Ironically, insomnia is worsened by fretting about it. In laboratory studies, insomnia complainers do sleep less than others. But they typically overestimate how long it takes them to fall asleep and underestimate how long they actually have slept (Harvey & Tang, 2012). Even if we have been awake only an hour or two, we may *think* we have had very little sleep because it's the waking part we remember.

The most common quick fixes for true insomnia—sleeping pills and alcohol—can aggravate the problem, reducing REM sleep and leaving the person with next-day blahs. Such aids can also lead to *tolerance*—a state in which increasing doses are needed to produce an effect. An ideal sleep aid would mimic the natural chemicals abundant during sleep, reliably producing sound sleep without side effects. Until scientists can supply this magic pill, sleep experts have offered some tips for getting better quality sleep (**TABLE 9.1**).

Falling asleep is not the problem for people with **narcolepsy** (from *narco*, "numbness," and *lepsy*, "seizure"), who have sudden attacks of overwhelming sleepiness, usually lasting less than 5 minutes. Narcolepsy attacks can occur at the most inopportune times, perhaps just after taking a terrific swing at a softball or when laughing loudly, shouting angrily, or having sex (Dement, 1978, 1999). In severe cases, the person collapses directly into a brief period of REM sleep, with loss of muscular tension. People with narcolepsy—1 in 2000 of us, estimated the Stanford University Center for Narcolepsy (2002)—must therefore live with extra caution. As a traffic menace, "snoozing is second only to boozing," says the American Sleep Disorders Association, and those with narcolepsy are especially at risk (Aldrich, 1989).

Researchers have discovered genes that cause narcolepsy in dogs and humans, such as by producing an immune system attack on brain cells that enable alertness (De la Herrán-Arita et al., 2013; Miyagawa et al., 2008). Genes help sculpt the brain, and neuroscientists are searching the brain for narcolepsy-linked abnormalities. One team discovered a relative absence of a hypothalamic neural center that produces *orexin* (also called *hypocretin*), an alertness-related neurotransmitter (Taheri et al., 2002; Thannickal et al., 2000). (That discovery has led to the clinical testing of a new sleeping pill that works by blocking orexin's arousing activity.) Narcolepsy, it is now clear, is a

▼ TABLE 9.1
Some Natural Sleep Aids

- Exercise regularly but not in the late evening. (Late afternoon is best.)
- Avoid caffeine after early afternoon, and avoid food and drink near bedtime. The exception would be a glass of milk, which provides raw materials for the manufacture of serotonin, a neurotransmitter that facilitates sleep.
- Relax before bedtime, using dimmer light.
- Sleep on a regular schedule (rise at the same time even after a restless night) and avoid long naps.
- Hide the time so you aren't tempted to check repeatedly.
- Reassure yourself that temporary sleep loss causes no great harm.
- Focus your mind on nonarousing, engaging thoughts, such as song lyrics, TV programs, or vacation travel (Gellis et al., 2013).
- If all else fails, settle for less sleep, either going to bed later or getting up earlier.

brain disease; it is not just "in your mind." And this gives hope that narcolepsy might be effectively relieved by a drug that mimics the missing orexin and can sneak through the blood-brain barrier (Fujiki et al., 2003; Siegel, 2000). In the meantime, physicians are prescribing other drugs to relieve narcolepsy's sleepiness in humans.

Although 1 in 20 of us have **sleep apnea,** it was unknown before modern sleep research. *Apnea* means "with no breath," and people with this condition intermittently stop breathing during sleep. After an airless minute or so, decreased blood oxygen arouses them enough to snort in air for a few seconds, in a process that repeats hundreds of times each night, depriving them of slow-wave sleep. Apnea sufferers don't recall these episodes the next day. So, despite feeling fatigued and depressed—and hearing their mate's complaints about their loud "snoring"—many are unaware of their disorder (Peppard et al., 2006).

Sleep apnea is associated with obesity, and as the number of obese Americans has increased, so has this disorder, particularly among overweight men (Keller, 2007). Apnea-related sleep loss also contributes to obesity. In addition to loud snoring, other warning signs are daytime sleepiness, irritability, and (possibly) high blood pressure, which increases the risk of a stroke or heart attack (Dement, 1999). If one doesn't mind looking a little goofy in the dark (imagine a snorkeler at a slumber party), the treatment—a masklike device with an air pump that keeps the sleeper's airway open—can effectively relieve apnea symptoms. By so doing, it can also alleviate the depression symptoms that often accompany sleep apnea (Levine, 2012; Wheaton et al., 2012).

Unlike sleep apnea, **night terrors** target mostly children, who may sit up or walk around, talk incoherently, experience doubled heart and breathing rates, and appear terrified (Hartmann, 1981). They seldom wake up fully during an episode and recall little or nothing the next morning—at most, a fleeting, frightening image. Night terrors are not nightmares (which, like other dreams, typically occur during early morning REM sleep); night terrors usually occur during the first few hours of NREM-3.

Sleepwalking—another NREM-3 sleep disorder—and *sleeptalking* are usually childhood disorders and, like narcolepsy, they run in families. (Sleeptalking—usually garbled or nonsensical—can occur during any sleep stage [Mahowald & Ettinger, 1990].) Occasional childhood sleepwalking occurs for about one-third of those with a sleepwalking fraternal twin and half of those with a sleepwalking identical twin. The same is true for sleeptalking (Hublin et al., 1997, 1998). Sleepwalking is usually harmless. After returning to bed on their own or with the help of a family member, few sleepwalkers recall their trip the next morning. About 20 percent of 3- to 12-year-olds have at least one episode of sleepwalking, usually lasting 2 to 10 minutes; some 5 percent have repeated episodes (Giles et al., 1994). Young children, who have the deepest and lengthiest NREM-3 sleep, are the most likely to experience both night terrors and sleepwalking. As we grow older and deep NREM-3 sleep diminishes, so do night terrors and sleepwalking.

Now I lay me down to sleep For many with sleep apnea, a continuous positive airway pressure (CPAP) machine makes for sounder sleeping and better quality of life.

insomnia recurring problems in falling or staying asleep.

narcolepsy a sleep disorder characterized by uncontrollable sleep attacks. The sufferer may lapse directly into REM sleep, often at inopportune times.

sleep apnea a sleep disorder characterized by temporary cessations of breathing during sleep and repeated momentary awakenings.

night terrors a sleep disorder characterized by high arousal and an appearance of being terrified; unlike nightmares, night terrors occur during NREM-3 sleep, within two or three hours of falling asleep, and are seldom remembered.

Did Brahms need his own lullabies? Cranky, overweight, and nap-prone, classical composer Johannes Brahms exhibited common symptoms of sleep apnea (Margolis, 2000).

A dreamy take on dreamland
The 2010 movie *Inception* creatively played off our interest in finding meaning in our dreams, and in understanding the layers of our consciousness. It further explored the idea of creating false memories through the power of suggestion.

"I do not believe that I am now dreaming, but I cannot prove that I am not."

Philosopher Bertrand Russell (1872–1970)

"For what one has dwelt on by day, these things are seen in visions of the night."

Menander of Athens (342–292 b.c.e.), *Fragments*

Dreams

Now playing at an inner theater near you: the premiere showing of a sleeping person's vivid dream. This never-before-seen mental movie features captivating characters wrapped in a plot so original and unlikely, yet so intricate and so seemingly real, that the viewer later marvels at its creation.

Waking from a troubling dream (you were late to something and your legs weren't working), who among us has not wondered about this weird state of consciousness? How can our brain so creatively, colorfully, and completely construct this alternative world? In the shadowland between our dreaming and waking consciousness, we may even wonder for a moment which is real.

Discovering the link between REM sleep and dreaming opened a new era in dream research. Instead of relying on someone's hazy recall hours or days after having a dream, researchers could catch dreams as they happened. They could awaken people during or within 3 minutes after a REM sleep period and hear a vivid account.

What We Dream

9-7 What do we dream?

Daydreams tend to involve the familiar details of our life—perhaps picturing ourselves explaining to an instructor why a paper will be late, or replaying in our minds personal encounters we relish or regret. REM **dreams** are vivid, emotional, and often bizarre—so vivid we may confuse them with reality. Awakening from a nightmare, a 4-year-old may be sure there is a bear in the house.

We spend six years of our life in dreams, many of which are anything but sweet. For both women and men, 8 in 10 dreams are marked by at least one negative event or emotion (Domhoff, 2007). Common themes are repeatedly failing in an attempt to do something; being attacked, pursued, or rejected; or experiencing misfortune (Hall et al., 1982). Dreams with sexual imagery occur less often than you might think. In one study, only 1 in 10 dreams among young men and 1 in 30 among young women had sexual content (Domhoff, 1996).

More commonly, a dream's story line incorporates traces of previous days' nonsexual experiences and preoccupations (De Koninck, 2000):

• After suffering a trauma, people commonly report nightmares, which help extinguish daytime fears (Levin & Nielsen, 2007, 2009). One sample of Americans recording their dreams during September 2001 reported an increase in threatening dreams following the 9/11 terrorist attacks (Propper et al., 2007).

• Compared with city dwellers, people in hunter-gatherer societies more often dream of animals (Mestel, 1997). Compared with nonmusicians, musicians report twice as many dreams of music (Uga et al., 2006).

• Studies in four countries have found blind people (even those blind from birth) dreaming of using their nonvisual senses (Buquet, 1988; Taha, 1972; Vekassy, 1977). But natively blind people may also "see" in their dreams (Bértolo, 2005). Likewise, people born paralyzed below the waist sometimes dream of walking, standing, running, or cycling (Saurat et al., 2011; Voss et al., 2011).

Our two-track mind continues to monitor our environment while we sleep. Sensory stimuli—a particular odor or a phone's ringing—may be instantly and ingeniously woven into the dream story. In a classic experiment, researchers lightly sprayed cold water on dreamers' faces (Dement & Wolpert, 1958). Compared with sleepers who did not get the cold-water treatment, these people were more likely to dream about a waterfall, a leaky roof, or even about being sprayed by someone.

So, could we learn a foreign language by hearing it played while we sleep? If only. While sleeping we can learn to associate a sound with a mild electric shock (and to react to the sound accordingly). We can also learn to associate a particular sound with a pleasant or unpleasant odor (Arzi et al., 2012). But we do not remember recorded information played while we are soundly asleep (Eich, 1990; Wyatt & Bootzin, 1994). In fact, anything that happens during the 5 minutes just before we fall asleep is typically lost from memory (Roth et al., 1988). This explains why sleep apnea patients, who repeatedly awaken with a gasp and then immediately fall back to sleep, do not recall the episodes. Ditto someone who awakens momentarily, sends a text message, but the next day can't remembering doing so. It also explains why dreams that momentarily awaken us are mostly forgotten by morning. To remember a dream, get up and stay awake for a few minutes.

Why We Dream

9-8 What functions have theorists proposed for dreams?

Dream theorists have proposed several explanations of why we dream, including these:

To satisfy our own wishes. In 1900, in his landmark book *The Interpretation of Dreams*, Sigmund Freud offered what he thought was "the most valuable of all the discoveries it has been my good fortune to make." He proposed that dreams provide a psychic safety valve that discharges otherwise unacceptable feelings. He viewed a dream's **manifest content** (the apparent and remembered story line) as a censored, symbolic version of its **latent content,** the unconscious drives and wishes that would be threatening if expressed directly. Although most dreams have no overt sexual imagery, Freud nevertheless believed that most adult dreams could be "traced back by analysis to erotic wishes." Thus, a gun might be a disguised representation of a penis.

Freud considered dreams the key to understanding our inner conflicts. However, his critics say it is time to wake up from Freud's dream theory, which is a scientific nightmare. Based on the accumulated science, "there is no reason to believe any of Freud's specific claims about dreams and their purposes," observed dream researcher William Domhoff (2003). Some contend that even if dreams are symbolic, they could be interpreted any way one wished. Others maintain that dreams hide nothing. A dream about a gun is a dream about a gun. Legend has it that even Freud, who loved to smoke cigars, acknowledged that "sometimes, a cigar is just a cigar." Freud's wish-fulfillment theory of dreams has in large part given way to other theories.

To file away memories. The *information-processing* perspective proposes that dreams may help sift, sort, and fix the day's experiences in our memory. Some studies support this view. When tested the day after learning a task, those who had been deprived of both slow-wave and REM sleep did not do as well as those who had slept undisturbed (Stickgold, 2012). In other studies, people who heard unusual phrases or learned to find hidden visual images before bedtime remembered less the next morning if they had been awakened every time they began REM sleep than if awakened during other sleep stages (Empson & Clarke, 1970; Karni & Sagi, 1994).

Brain scans confirm the link between REM sleep and memory. The brain regions that buzzed as rats learned to navigate a maze, or as people learned to perform a visual-discrimination task, buzzed again during later REM sleep (Louie & Wilson, 2001; Maquet, 2001). So precise were these activity patterns that scientists could tell where in the maze the rat would be if awake. Some researchers dispute the dreaming-strengthens-memory idea, noting that REM sleep may support memory for reasons

A popular sleep myth: If you dream you are falling and hit the ground (or if you dream of dying), you die. (Unfortunately, those who could confirm these ideas are not around to do so. Many people, however, have had such dreams and are alive to report them.)

"Follow your dreams, except for that one where you're naked at work."

Attributed to comedian Henny Youngman

"When people interpret [a dream] as if it were meaningful and then sell those interpretations, it's quackery."

Sleep researcher J. Allan Hobson (1995)

dream a sequence of images, emotions, and thoughts passing through a sleeping person's mind. Dreams are notable for their hallucinatory imagery, discontinuities and incongruities, and for the dreamer's delusional acceptance of the content and later difficulties remembering it.

manifest content according to Freud, the remembered story line of a dream (as distinct from its latent, or hidden, content).

latent content according to Freud, the underlying meaning of a dream (as distinct from its manifest content).

Rapid eye movements also stir the liquid behind the cornea; this delivers fresh oxygen to corneal cells, preventing their suffocation.

Question: Does eating spicy foods cause us to dream more?

Answer: Any food that causes you to awaken more increases your chance of recalling a dream (Moorcroft, 2003).

▼ FIGURE 9.9
A sleeping brain is a working brain

unrelated to dreaming. Also, memory consolidation may occur during non-REM sleep (Diekelmann & Born, 2010). This much seems true: A night of solid sleep (and dreaming) has an important place in our lives. To sleep, perchance to remember.

This is important news for students, many of whom, observed researcher Robert Stickgold (2000), suffer from a kind of sleep bulimia—binge sleeping on the weekend. "If you don't get good sleep and enough sleep after you learn new stuff, you won't integrate it effectively into your memories," he warned. That helps explain why high school students with high grades have averaged 25 minutes more sleep a night than their lower-achieving classmates (Wolfson & Carskadon, 1998; see **FIGURE 9.9**). Sacrificing sleep time to study actually *worsens* academic performance, by making it harder the next day to understand class material or do well on a test (Gillen-O'Neel et al., 2013).

To develop and preserve neural pathways. Perhaps dreams, or the brain activity associated with REM sleep, serve a *physiological* function, providing the sleeping brain with periodic stimulation. This theory makes sense from a developmental point of view. Stimulating experiences preserve and expand the brain's neural pathways. Infants, whose neural networks are fast developing, spend much of their abundant sleep time in REM sleep (**FIGURE 9.10**).

To make sense of neural static. Other theories propose that dreams erupt from neural activation spreading upward from the brainstem (Antrobus, 1991; Hobson, 2003, 2004, 2009). According to "activation–synthesis theory," dreams are the brain's attempt to synthesize random neural activity. Much as a neurosurgeon can produce hallucinations by stimulating different parts of a patient's cortex, so can stimulation originating within the brain. These internal stimuli activate brain areas that process visual images, but not the visual cortex area, which receives raw input from the eyes. As Freud might have expected, PET scans of sleeping people also reveal increased activity in the emotion-related limbic system (in the amygdala) during emotional dreams (Schwartz, 2012). In contrast, frontal lobe regions responsible for inhibition and logical thinking seem to idle, which may explain why our dreams are less inhibited than we are when awake (Maquet et al., 1996). Add the limbic system's emotional tone to the brain's visual bursts and—Voila!—we dream. Damage either the limbic system or the visual centers active during dreaming, and dreaming itself may be impaired (Domhoff, 2003).

To reflect cognitive development. Some dream researchers dispute both the Freudian and neural activation theories, preferring instead to see dreams as part of brain maturation and cognitive development (Domhoff, 2010, 2011; Foulkes, 1999). For example, prior to age 9, children's dreams seem more like a slide show and less

(a) Learning

(b) Sleep consolidates our learning into long-term memory.

(c) Learning is retained.

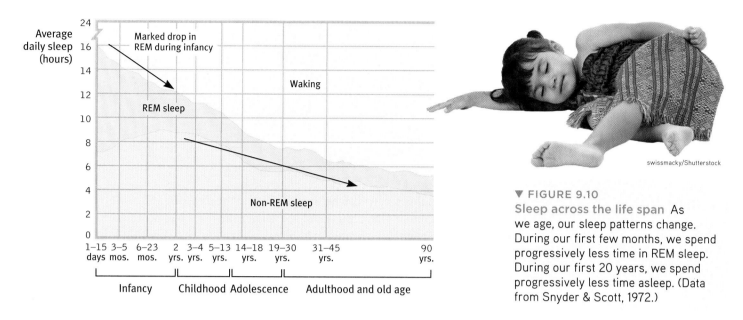

swissmacky/Shutterstock

▼ **FIGURE 9.10**
Sleep across the life span As
we age, our sleep patterns change.
During our first few months, we spend
progressively less time in REM sleep.
During our first 20 years, we spend
progressively less time asleep. (Data
from Snyder & Scott, 1972.)

like an active story in which the dreamer is an actor. Dreams overlap with waking
cognition and feature coherent speech. They *simulate reality* by drawing on our concepts and knowledge. They engage brain networks that also are active during daydreaming—and so may be viewed as intensified mind wandering, enhanced by visual
imagery (Fox et al., 2013).

Unlike the idea that dreams arise from bottom-up brain activation, the cognitive
perspective emphasizes our mind's top-down control of our dream content (Nir &
Tononi, 2010). Dreams, says G. William Domhoff (2014), "dramatize our wishes, fears,
concerns, and interests in striking scenarios that we experience as real events." Given
a healthy, mature brain, such mental simulations happen whenever there is (1) a loss of
conscious attention, (2) an absence of external stimuli, and (3) sufficient brain activation, such as during REM sleep.

TABLE 9.2 compares these major dream theories. Although today's sleep researchers debate dreams' function—and some are skeptical that dreams serve any function—

▼ TABLE 9.2
Dream Theories

Theory	Explanation	Critical Considerations
Freud's wish-fulfillment	Dreams preserve sleep and provide a "psychic safety valve"—expressing otherwise unacceptable feelings; contain manifest (remembered) content and a deeper layer of latent content (a hidden meaning).	Lacks any scientific support; dreams may be inter-preted in many different ways.
Information-processing	Dreams help us sort out the day's events and con-solidate our memories.	But why do we sometimes dream about things we have not experienced and about past events?
Physiological function	Regular brain stimulation from REM sleep may help develop and preserve neural pathways.	This does not explain why we experience *meaningful* dreams.
Neural activation	REM sleep triggers neural activity that evokes ran-dom visual memories, which our sleeping brain weaves into stories.	The individual's brain is weaving the stories, which still tells us something about the dreamer.
Cognitive development	Dream content reflects dreamers' level of cognitive development—their knowledge and understanding. Dreams simulate our lives, including worst-case scenarios.	Does not propose an adaptive function of dreams.

> **REM rebound** the tendency for REM sleep to increase following REM sleep deprivation (created by repeated awakenings during REM sleep).

there is one thing they agree on: We need REM sleep. Deprived of it by repeatedly being awakened, people return more and more quickly to the REM stage after falling back to sleep. When finally allowed to sleep undisturbed, they literally sleep like babies—with increased REM sleep, a phenomenon called **REM rebound.** Withdrawing REM-suppressing sleeping medications also increases REM sleep, but with accompanying nightmares. Most other mammals also experience REM rebound, suggesting that the causes and functions of REM sleep are deeply biological. (That REM sleep occurs in mammals—and not in animals such as fish, whose behavior is less influenced by learning—fits the information-processing theory of dreams.)

So does this mean that because dreams serve physiological functions and extend normal cognition, they are psychologically meaningless? Not necessarily. Every psychologically meaningful experience involves an active brain. We are once again reminded of a basic principle: *Biological and psychological explanations of behavior are partners, not competitors.*

Dreams are a fascinating altered state of consciousness. But they are not the only altered states. As we will see next, drugs also alter conscious awareness.

RETRIEVAL PRACTICE

• What five theories propose explanations for why we dream?

ANSWERS: (1) Freud's wish-fulfillment (dreams as a psychic safety valve), (2) information-processing (dreams sort the day's events and form memories), (3) physiological function (dreams pave neural pathways), (4) neural activation (REM sleep triggers random neural activity that the mind weaves into stories), (5) cognitive development (dreams reflect the dreamer's developmental stage)

---

9 REVIEW Sleep and Dreams

LEARNING OBJECTIVES

RETRIEVAL PRACTICE Take a moment to answer each of these Learning Objective Questions (repeated here from within this module). Then turn to Appendix C, Complete Module Reviews, to check your answers. Research suggests that trying to answer these questions on your own will improve your long-term retention (McDaniel et al., 2009).

9-1 What is sleep?

9-2 How do our biological rhythms influence our daily functioning?

9-3 What is the biological rhythm of our sleeping and dreaming stages?

9-4 How do biology and environment interact in our sleep patterns?

9-5 What are sleep's functions?

9-6 How does sleep loss affect us, and what are the major sleep disorders?

9-7 What do we dream?

9-8 What functions have theorists proposed for dreams?

TERMS AND CONCEPTS TO REMEMBER

RETRIEVAL PRACTICE Test yourself on these terms by trying to write down the definition before flipping back to check your answers.

sleep, p. 100

circadian [ser-KAY-dee-an] rhythm, p. 100

REM sleep, p. 101

alpha waves, p. 102

hallucinations, p. 102

delta waves, p. 102

suprachiasmatic nucleus (SCN), p. 104

insomnia, p. 110

narcolepsy, p. 110

sleep apnea, p. 111

night terrors, p. 111

dream, p. 112

manifest content, p. 113

latent content, p. 113

REM rebound, p. 116

Use **LearningCurve** to create your personalized study plan, which will direct you to the resources that will help you most in **LaunchPad**.

MODULE 10 Drugs and Consciousness

LET'S IMAGINE A DAY IN the life of a legal drug user. It begins with a wake-up latte. By midday, several cigarettes have calmed frazzled nerves before an appointment at the plastic surgeon's office for wrinkle-smoothing Botox injections. A diet pill before dinner helps stem the appetite, and its stimulating effects can later be partially offset with a glass of wine or two Advil PMs. And if performance needs enhancing, there are beta blockers for onstage performers, Viagra for middle-aged men, hormone-delivering "libido patches" for middle-aged women, and Adderall for students hoping to focus their concentration.

Tolerance and Addiction

10-1 What are substance use disorders, and what roles do tolerance, withdrawal, and addiction play in these disorders?

Most of us manage to use some nonprescription drugs in moderation and without disrupting our lives. But some of us develop a self-harming **substance use disorder (TABLE 10.1).** Such substances are **psychoactive drugs,** chemicals that change perceptions and moods. A drug's overall effect depends not only on its biological effects but also on the user's expectations, which vary with social and cultural contexts (Ward, 1994). If one culture assumes that a particular drug produces euphoria (or aggression or sexual arousal) and another does not, each culture may find its expectations fulfilled. We'll take a closer look at these interacting forces in the use and potential abuse of particular psychoactive drugs. But first, let's consider how our bodies react to the ongoing use of psychoactive drugs.

The odds of getting hooked after using various drugs:

Tobacco	32%
Heroin	23%
Alcohol	15%
Marijuana	9%

Source: National Academy of Science, Institute of Medicine (Brody, 2003).

▼ TABLE 10.1
When Is Drug Use a Disorder?

According to the American Psychiatric Association, a person may be diagnosed with *substance use disorder* when drug use continues despite significant life disruption. Resulting brain changes may persist after quitting use of the substance (thus leading to strong cravings when exposed to people and situations that trigger memories of drug use). The severity of substance use disorder varies from *mild* (two to three of these indicators) to *moderate* (four to five indicators) to *severe* (six or more indicators). (Source: American Psychiatric Association, 2013.)

Diminished Control

1. Uses more substance, or for longer, than intended.

2. Tries unsuccessfully to regulate use of substance.

3. Spends much time acquiring, using, or recovering from effects of substance.

4. Craves the substance.

Diminished Social Functioning

5. Use disrupts commitments at work, school, or home.

6. Continues use despite social problems.

7. Causes reduced social, recreational, and work activities.

Hazardous Use

8. Continues use despite hazards.

9. Continues use despite worsening physical or psychological problems.

Drug Action

10. Experiences tolerance (needing more substance for the desired effect).

11. Experiences withdrawal when attempting to end use.

substance use disorder continued substance craving and use despite significant life disruption and/or physical risk.

psychoactive drug a chemical substance that alters perceptions and moods.

▼ FIGURE 10.1
Drug tolerance

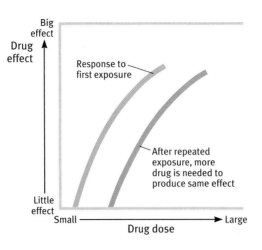

Why might a person who rarely drinks alcohol get buzzed on one can of beer while a long-term drinker shows few effects until the second six-pack? The answer is **tolerance.** With continued use of alcohol and some other drugs (not marijuana), the user's brain chemistry adapts to offset the drug effect (a process called *neuroadaptation*). To experience the same effect, the user requires larger and larger doses (**FIGURE 10.1**). Ever-increasing doses of most psychoactive drugs may lead to **addiction:** The person craves and uses the substance despite its adverse consequences. (See Thinking Critically About: Addiction.)

The World Health Organization (2008) has reported that, worldwide, 90 million people suffer from such problems related to alcohol and other drugs. Regular users often try to fight their addiction, but abruptly stopping the drug may lead to the undesirable side effects of **withdrawal.**

THINKING CRITICALLY ABOUT

Addiction

10-2 How has the concept of addiction changed?

In recent years, the concept of addiction has been extended to cover many behaviors formerly considered bad habits or even sins. Psychologists debate whether the concept has been stretched too far, and whether addictions are really as irresistible as commonly believed. For example, "even for a very addictive drug like cocaine, only 15 to 16 percent of people become addicted within 10 years of first use," observed Terry Robinson and Kent Berridge (2003).

Addictions can be powerful, and many addicts do benefit from therapy or group support. Alcoholics Anonymous has supported millions in overcoming alcohol addiction. But viewing addiction as an uncontrollable disease can undermine people's self-confidence and their belief that they can change. And that, critics say, would be unfortunate, for many people do voluntarily stop using addictive drugs, without any treatment. Most ex-smokers, for example, have kicked the habit on their own (Newport, 2013).

The addiction-as-disease-needing-treatment idea has been offered for a host of driven, excessive behaviors—eating, gambling, work, sex, and accumulating wealth. However, critics suggest that "addiction" can become an all-purpose excuse when used not as a metaphor ("I'm a science fiction addict") but as reality. Moreover, they note that labeling a behavior doesn't explain it. Attributing serial adultery to a "sex addiction" does not *explain* the sexual impulsiveness (Radford, 2010).

Sometimes, though, behaviors such as gambling, video gaming, or online surfing do become compulsive and dysfunctional, much like abusive drug taking (Gentile, 2009; Griffiths, 2001; Hoeft et al., 2008). Thus, psychiatry's manual of disorders

A social networking addiction?

now includes behavior addictions such as "gambling disorder" and proposes "Internet gaming disorder" for further study (American Psychiatric Association, 2013). Studies in Asia, Europe, and North America estimate gaming addiction rates of from 3 to 12 percent of players (Anderson et al., 2012; Ferguson et al., 2011). Some Internet users display an apparent inability to resist logging on, and staying on, even when this excessive use impairs their work and relationships (Ko et al., 2005). But there is hope. One research review found both psychological and drug therapies for Internet addiction "highly effective" (Winkler et al., 2013).

• What is the process that leads to drug tolerance?

ANSWER: With repeated exposure to a psychoactive drug, the drug's effect lessens. Thus, it takes bigger doses to get the desired effect.

Types of Psychoactive Drugs

The three major categories of psychoactive drugs are *depressants*, *stimulants*, and *hallucinogens*. All do their work at the brain's synapses, stimulating, inhibiting, or mimicking the activity of the brain's own chemical messengers, the neurotransmitters.

Depressants

10-3 What are depressants, and what are their effects?

Depressants are drugs such as alcohol, barbiturates (tranquilizers), and opiates that calm neural activity and slow body functions.

Alcohol True or false? In small amounts, alcohol is a stimulant. *False.* Low doses of alcohol may, indeed, enliven a drinker, but they do so by acting as a *disinhibitor*—they slow brain activity that controls judgment and inhibitions. Alcohol is an equal-opportunity drug: It increases (disinhibits) helpful tendencies—as when tipsy restaurant patrons leave extravagant tips and social drinkers bond in groups (Hirsch et al., 2011; Lynn, 1988; Sayette et al., 2012). And it increases harmful tendencies, as when sexually aroused men become more disposed to sexual aggression. One University of Illinois campus survey showed that before sexual assaults, 80 percent of the male assailants and 70 percent of the female victims had been drinking (Camper, 1990). Another survey of 89,874 American collegians found alcohol or drugs involved in 79 percent of unwanted sexual intercourse experiences (Presley et al., 1997). When drinking, both men and women are more disposed to casual sex (Garcia et al., 2012; Rehm et al., 2012). "Beauty is in the eyes of the beer holder." *The bottom line:* The urges you would feel if sober are the ones you will more likely act upon when intoxicated.

SLOWED NEURAL PROCESSING Low doses of alcohol relax the drinker by slowing sympathetic nervous system activity. Larger doses cause reactions to slow, speech to slur, and skilled performance to deteriorate. Paired with sleep deprivation, alcohol is a potent sedative. Add these physical effects to lowered inhibitions, and the result can be deadly. Worldwide, several hundred thousand lives are lost each year in alcohol-related accidents and violent crime. As blood-alcohol levels rise and judgment falters, people's qualms about drinking and driving lessen. In experiments, virtually all drinkers who had insisted when sober that they would not drive under the influence later decided to drive home from a bar, even if given a breathalyzer test and told they were intoxicated (Denton & Krebs, 1990; MacDonald et al., 1995). Alcohol can be life threatening when heavy drinking follows an earlier period of moderate drinking, which depresses the vomiting response. People may poison themselves with an overdose that their bodies would normally throw up.

MEMORY DISRUPTION Alcohol can disrupt memory formation, and heavy drinking can also have long-term effects on the brain and cognition. In rats, at a developmental period corresponding to human adolescence, binge drinking contributes to nerve cell death and reduces the birth of new nerve cells. It also impairs the growth of

tolerance the diminishing effect with regular use of the same dose of a drug, requiring the user to take larger and larger doses before experiencing the drug's effect.

addiction compulsive craving of drugs or certain behaviors (such as gambling) despite known adverse consequences.

withdrawal the discomfort and distress that follow discontinuing an addictive drug or behavior.

depressants drugs (such as alcohol, barbiturates, and opiates) that reduce neural activity and slow body functions.

Drinking disaster demo Firefighters reenacted the trauma of an alcohol-related car accident, providing a memorable demonstration for these high school students. Alcohol consumption leads to feelings of invincibility, which become especially dangerous behind the wheel of a car.

Scan of woman with   Scan of woman without
alcohol use disorder   alcohol use disorder

▼ **FIGURE 10.2**
Disordered drinking shrinks the brain MRI scans show brain shrinkage in women with alcohol use disorder (left) compared with women in a control group (right).

---

alcohol use disorder (popularly known as *alcoholism*) alcohol use marked by tolerance, withdrawal, and a drive to continue problematic use.

barbiturates drugs that depress central nervous system activity, reducing anxiety but impairing memory and judgment.

opiates opium and its derivatives, such as morphine and heroin; depress neural activity, temporarily lessening pain and anxiety.

stimulants drugs (such as caffeine, nicotine, and the more powerful amphetamines, cocaine, Ecstasy, and methamphetamine) that excite neural activity and speed up body functions.

amphetamines drugs that stimulate neural activity, causing speeded-up body functions and associated energy and mood changes.

nicotine a stimulating and highly addictive psychoactive drug in tobacco.

---

synaptic connections (Crews et al., 2006, 2007). In humans, heavy drinking may lead to blackouts, in which drinkers are unable to recall people they met the night before or what they said or did while intoxicated. These blackouts result partly from the way alcohol suppresses REM sleep, which helps fix the day's experiences into permanent memories.

The prolonged and excessive drinking that characterizes **alcohol use disorder** can shrink the brain (**FIGURE 10.2**). Women, who have less of a stomach enzyme that digests alcohol, are especially vulnerable (Wuethrich, 2001). Girls and young women can become addicted to alcohol more quickly than boys and young men do, and they are at risk for lung, brain, and liver damage at lower consumption levels (CASA, 2003).

REDUCED SELF-AWARENESS AND SELF-CONTROL In one experiment, those who consumed alcohol (rather than a placebo beverage) were doubly likely to be caught mind wandering during a reading task, yet were *less* likely to notice that they zoned out (Sayette et al., 2009). Alcohol not only reduces self-awareness, it also produces a sort of "myopia" by focusing attention on an arousing situation (say, provocation) and distracting it from normal inhibitions and future consequences (Giancola et al., 2010; Steele & Josephs, 1990).

Reduced self-awareness may help explain why people who want to suppress their awareness of failures or shortcomings are more likely to drink than are those who feel good about themselves. Losing a business deal, a game, or a romantic partner sometimes elicits a drinking binge.

EXPECTANCY EFFECTS As with other psychoactive drugs, expectations influence behavior. When people *believe* that alcohol affects social behavior in certain ways, and *believe* they have been drinking alcohol, they will behave accordingly (Moss & Albery, 2009). In a now-classic experiment, researchers gave Rutgers University men (who had volunteered for a study on "alcohol and sexual stimulation") either an alcoholic or a nonalcoholic drink (Abrams & Wilson, 1983). (Both had strong tastes that masked any alcohol.) In each group, half the participants thought they were drinking alcohol and half thought they were not. After watching an erotic movie clip, the men who *thought* they had consumed alcohol were more likely to report having strong sexual fantasies and feeling guilt free. Being able to *attribute* their sexual responses to alcohol released their inhibitions—whether or not they had actually consumed any alcohol.

So, alcohol's effect lies partly in that powerful sex organ, the mind. Fourteen "intervention studies" have educated college drinkers about that very point (Scott-Sheldon, et al., 2014). Most participants have come away with lower positive expectations of alcohol and have reduced their drinking the ensuing month.

Barbiturates Like alcohol, the **barbiturate** drugs, or *tranquilizers*, depress nervous system activity. Barbiturates such as Nembutal, Seconal, and Amytal are sometimes prescribed to induce sleep or reduce anxiety. In larger doses, they can impair memory and judgment. If combined with alcohol—as sometimes happens when people take a sleeping pill after an evening of heavy drinking—the total depressive effect on body functions can be lethal.

Opiates The **opiates**—opium and its derivatives—also depress neural functioning. When using the opiates, which include *heroin*, pupils constrict, breathing slows, and lethargy sets in as blissful pleasure replaces pain and anxiety. For this short-term pleasure, opiate users may pay a long-term price: a gnawing craving for another fix, a need for progressively larger doses (as tolerance develops), and the extreme discomfort of withdrawal. When repeatedly flooded with an artificial opiate, the brain eventually stops producing *endorphins*, its own opiates. If the artificial opiate is then withdrawn, the brain lacks the normal level of these painkilling neurotransmitters. Those who cannot or choose not to tolerate this state may pay an ultimate price—death by overdose. Opiates include the *narcotics*, such as codeine and morphine (and the synthetic *methadone*, a heroin substitute), which physicians may prescribe for pain relief and which can also lead to addiction.

RETRIEVAL PRACTICE

- How is a "shopping addiction" different from the psychological definition of addiction?

ANSWER: Being strongly interested in something in a way that is not compulsive and dysfunctional is not an addiction. It does not involve obsessive craving in spite of known negative consequences.

- Alcohol, barbiturates, and opiates are all in a class of drugs called _____.

ANSWER: depressants

Stimulants

10-4 What are stimulants, and what are their effects?

A **stimulant** excites neural activity and speeds up body functions. Pupils dilate, heart and breathing rates increase, and blood sugar levels rise, causing a drop in appetite. Energy and self-confidence also rise.

Stimulants include caffeine, nicotine, the **amphetamines**, cocaine, methamphetamine ("speed"), and Ecstasy. People use stimulants to feel alert, lose weight, or boost mood or athletic performance. Unfortunately, stimulants can be addictive, as you may know if you are one of the many who use caffeine daily in your coffee, tea, soda, or energy drinks. Cut off from your usual dose, you may crash into fatigue, headaches, irritability, and depression (Silverman et al., 1992). A mild dose of caffeine typically lasts three or four hours, which—if taken in the evening—may be long enough to impair sleep.

Vasca/Shutterstock

Nicotine Cigarettes and other tobacco products deliver highly addictive **nicotine**. Imagine that cigarettes were harmless—except, once in every 25,000 packs, an occasional innocent-looking one is filled with dynamite instead of tobacco. Not such a bad risk of having your head blown off. But with 250 million packs a day consumed worldwide, we could expect more than 10,000 gruesome daily deaths (more than three times the 9/11 fatalities each and every day)—surely enough to have cigarettes banned everywhere.[1]

The lost lives from these dynamite-loaded cigarettes approximate those from today's actual cigarettes. A teen-to-the-grave smoker has a 50 percent chance of dying from the habit, and each year, tobacco kills nearly 5.4 million of its 1.3 billion customers worldwide. (Imagine the outrage if terrorists took down an equivalent of 25 loaded jumbo jets today, let alone tomorrow and every day thereafter.) By 2030, annual deaths are expected to increase to 8 million. That means that *1 billion* twenty-first-century people may be killed by tobacco (WHO, 2012).

Smoke a cigarette and nature will charge you 12 minutes—ironically, just about the length of time you spend smoking it (*Discover*, 1996). Compared with nonsmokers, smokers' life expectancy is "at least 10 years shorter" (CDC, 2013). Eliminating smoking would increase life expectancy more than any other preventive measure. Why, then, do so many people smoke?

Those drawn to nicotine find it very hard to quit, because tobacco products are powerfully and quickly addictive. Attempts to quit even within the first weeks of smoking often fail (DiFranza, 2008). As with other addictions, smokers develop *tolerance*, and quitting causes withdrawal symptoms, including craving, insomnia, anxiety, irritability, and distractibility. Nicotine-deprived smokers trying to focus on a task experience a tripled rate of mind wandering (Sayette et al., 2010). When not craving a cigarette, they tend to underestimate the power of such cravings (Sayette et al., 2008).

"There is an overwhelming medical and scientific consensus that cigarette smoking causes lung cancer, heart disease, emphysema, and other serious diseases in smokers. Smokers are far more likely to develop serious diseases, like lung cancer, than nonsmokers."

Philip Morris Companies Inc., 1999

For HIV patients who smoke, the virus is now much less lethal than the smoking (Helleberg et al., 2013).

"Smoking cures weight problems . . . eventually."

Comedian-writer Steven Wright

"To cease smoking is the easiest thing I ever did; I ought to know because I've done it a thousand times."

Mark Twain (1835–1910)

---

[1] This analogy, adapted here with world-based numbers, was suggested by mathematician Sam Saunders, as reported by K. C. Cole (1998).

▼ FIGURE 10.3
Where there's smoke . . . : The physiological effects of nicotine Nicotine reaches the brain within 7 seconds, twice as fast as intravenous heroin. Within minutes, the amount in the blood soars.

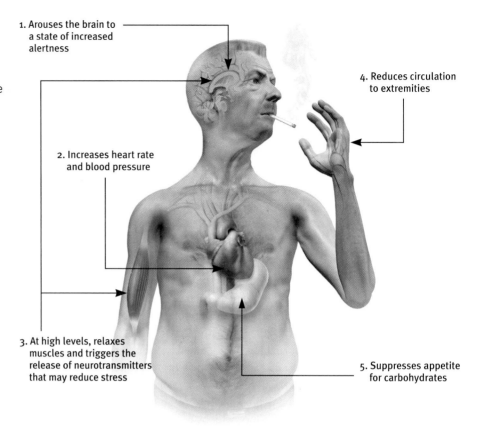

1. Arouses the brain to a state of increased alertness

4. Reduces circulation to extremities

2. Increases heart rate and blood pressure

3. At high levels, relaxes muscles and triggers the release of neurotransmitters that may reduce stress

5. Suppresses appetite for carbohydrates

cocaine a powerful and addictive stimulant derived from the coca plant; produces temporarily increased alertness and euphoria.

methamphetamine a powerfully addictive drug that stimulates the central nervous system, with speeded-up body functions and associated energy and mood changes; over time, appears to reduce baseline dopamine levels.

Humorist Dave Barry (1995) recalling why he smoked his first cigarette the summer he turned 15: "Arguments against smoking: 'It's a repulsive addiction that slowly but surely turns you into a gasping, gray-skinned, tumor-ridden invalid, hacking up brownish gobs of toxic waste from your one remaining lung.' Arguments for smoking: 'Other teenagers are doing it.' Case closed! Let's light up!"

All it takes to relieve this aversive state is a single puff on a cigarette. Within 7 seconds, a rush of nicotine signals the central nervous system to release a flood of neurotransmitters (**FIGURE 10.3**). Epinephrine and norepinephrine diminish appetite and boost alertness and mental efficiency. Dopamine and opioids temporarily calm anxiety and reduce sensitivity to pain (Ditre et al., 2011; Scott et al., 2004). Thus, ex-smokers will sometimes, under stress, return to smoking—as did some 1 million Americans after the 9/11 terrorist attacks (Pesko, 2014).

These rewards keep people smoking, even among the 3 in 4 smokers who wish they could stop (Newport, 2013). Each year, fewer than 1 in 7 smokers who want to quit will be able to resist. Even those who know they are committing slow-motion suicide may be unable to stop (Saad, 2002).

Nevertheless, repeated attempts seem to pay off. Half of all Americans who have ever smoked have quit, sometimes aided by a nicotine replacement drug and with encouragement from a counselor or support group. Success is equally likely whether smokers quit abruptly or gradually (Fiore et al., 2008; Lichtenstein et al., 2010; Lindson et al., 2010). For those who endure, the acute craving and withdrawal symptoms gradually dissipate over the ensuing six months (Ward et al., 1997). After a year's abstinence, only 10 percent will relapse in the next year (Hughes, 2010). These nonsmokers may live not only healthier but also happier lives. Smoking correlates with higher rates of depression, chronic disabilities, and divorce (Doherty & Doherty, 1998; Edwards & Kendler, 2012; Vita et al., 1998). Healthy living seems to add both years to life and life to years.

──────────────── **RETRIEVAL PRACTICE** ────────────────

• What withdrawal symptoms should your friend expect when she finally decides to quit smoking?

ANSWER: Your friend will likely experience strong craving, insomnia, anxiety, irritability, and distractibility. She'll probably find it harder to concentrate. However, if she sticks with it, the craving and withdrawal symptoms will gradually dissipate over about six months.

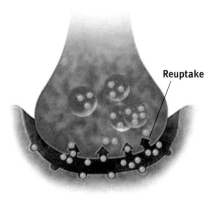

Sending neuron

Action potential

Synaptic gap

Receiving neuron

Neurotransmitter molecule

Receptor sites

(a)

Neurotransmitters carry a message from a sending neuron across a synapse to receptor sites on a receiving neuron.

Reuptake

(b)

The sending neuron normally reabsorbs excess neurotransmitter molecules, a process called *reuptake*.

Cocaine

(c)

By binding to the sites that normally reabsorb neurotransmitter molecules, cocaine blocks reuptake of dopamine, norepinephrine, and serotonin (Ray & Ksir, 1990). The extra neurotransmitter molecules therefore remain in the synapse, intensifying their normal mood-altering effects and producing a euphoric rush. When the cocaine level drops, the absence of these neurotransmitters produces a crash.

▼ FIGURE 10.4
Cocaine euphoria and crash

"Cocaine makes you a new man. And the first thing that new man wants is more cocaine."

Comedian George Carlin (1937–2008)

Cocaine Cocaine use offers a fast track from euphoria to crash. The recipe for Coca-Cola originally included an extract of the coca plant, creating a cocaine tonic for tired elderly people. Between 1896 and 1905, Coke was indeed "the real thing." But no longer. Cocaine is now snorted, injected, or smoked. It enters the bloodstream quickly, producing a rush of euphoria that depletes the brain's supply of the neurotransmitters dopamine, serotonin, and norepinephrine (**FIGURE 10.4**). Within the hour, a crash of agitated depression follows as the drug's effect wears off.

In situations that trigger aggression, ingesting cocaine may heighten reactions. Caged rats fight when given foot shocks, and they fight even more when given cocaine *and* foot shocks. Likewise, humans who voluntarily ingest high doses of cocaine in laboratory experiments impose higher shock levels on a presumed opponent than do those receiving a placebo (Licata et al., 1993). Cocaine use may also lead to emotional disturbances, suspiciousness, convulsions, cardiac arrest, or respiratory failure.

In national surveys, 3 percent of U.S. high school seniors and 6 percent of British 18- to 24-year-olds reported having tried cocaine during the past year (ACMD, 2009; Johnston et al., 2014). Nearly half had smoked *crack*, a faster-working crystallized form of cocaine that produces a briefer but more intense high, followed by a more intense crash. After several hours, the craving for more wanes, only to return several days later (Gawin, 1991).

Cocaine's psychological effects depend in part on the dosage and form consumed, but the situation and the user's expectations and personality also play a role. Given a placebo, cocaine users who *thought* they were taking cocaine often had a cocaine-like experience (Van Dyke & Byck, 1982).

Methamphetamine **Methamphetamine** is chemically related to its parent drug, *amphetamine* (NIDA, 2002, 2005) but has greater effects. Methamphetamine triggers the release of the neurotransmitter dopamine, which stimulates brain cells that enhance energy and mood, leading to eight hours or so of heightened energy and euphoria. Its aftereffects may include irritability, insomnia, hypertension, seizures, social isolation, depression, and occasional violent outbursts (Homer et al., 2008). Over time, methamphetamine may reduce baseline dopamine levels, leaving the user with continuing depressed functioning.

Dramatic drug-induced decline
In the 18 months between these two mug shots, this woman's methamphetamine addiction led to obvious physical changes.

1.5 Years Later

Multnomah County Sheriff's Office

The hug drug MDMA, known as Ecstasy, produces a euphoric high and feelings of intimacy. But repeated use can destroy serotonin-producing neurons, impair memory, and may permanently deflate mood.

Ecstasy Ecstasy, a street name for **MDMA** (methylenedioxymethamphetamine, also known in its powder form as "Molly"), is both a stimulant and a mild hallucinogen. As an amphetamine derivative, Ecstasy triggers dopamine release, but its major effect is releasing stored serotonin and blocking its reuptake, thus prolonging serotonin's feel-good flood (Braun, 2001). Users feel the effect about a half-hour after taking an Ecstasy pill. For three or four hours, they experience high energy, emotional elevation, and (given a social context) connectedness with those around them ("I love everyone").

During the 1990s, Ecstasy's popularity soared as a "club drug" taken at nightclubs and all-night dance parties (Landry, 2002). The drug's popularity crosses national borders, with an estimated 60 million tablets consumed annually in Britain (ACMD, 2009). There are, however, reasons not to be ecstatic about Ecstasy. One is its dehydrating effect, which—when combined with prolonged dancing—can lead to severe overheating, increased blood pressure, and death. Another is that long-term, repeated leaching of brain serotonin can damage serotonin-producing neurons, leading to decreased output and increased risk of permanently depressed mood (Croft et al., 2001; McCann et al., 2001; Roiser et al., 2005). Ecstasy also suppresses the disease-fighting immune system, impairs memory, slows thought, and disrupts sleep by interfering with serotonin's control of the circadian clock (Laws & Kokkalis, 2007; Schilt et al., 2007; Wagner et al., 2012). Ecstasy delights for the night but dispirits the morrow.

Hallucinogens

10-5 What are hallucinogens, and what are their effects?

Hallucinogens distort perceptions and evoke sensory images in the absence of sensory input (which is why these drugs are also called *psychedelics,* meaning "mind-manifesting"). Some, such as LSD and MDMA (Ecstasy), are synthetic. Others, including the mild hallucinogen marijuana, are natural substances.

Whether provoked to hallucinate by drugs, loss of oxygen, or extreme sensory deprivation, the brain hallucinates in basically the same way (Siegel, 1982). The experience typically begins with simple geometric forms, such as a lattice, cobweb, or spiral. The next phase consists of more meaningful images; some may be superimposed on a tunnel or funnel, others may be replays of past emotional experiences. As the hallucination peaks, people frequently feel separated from their body and experience dreamlike scenes so real that they may become panic-stricken or harm themselves.

These sensations are strikingly similar to the **near-death experience,** an altered state of consciousness reported by about 10 to 15 percent of patients revived from cardiac arrest (Agrillo, 2011; Greyson, 2010; Parnia et al., 2013). Many describe visions of tunnels (**FIGURE 10.5**), bright lights or beings of light, a replay of old memories, and out-of-body sensations (Siegel, 1980). Given that oxygen deprivation and other insults to the brain are known to produce hallucinations, it is difficult to resist wondering whether a brain under stress manufactures the near-death experience. During epilepsy seizures and migraines, patients may experience similar hallucinations of geometric patterns (Billock & Tsou, 2012). So have solitary sailors and polar explorers while enduring monotony, isolation, and cold (Suedfeld & Mocellin, 1987). Such experiences represent "neural funny business," surmises philosopher-neuroscientist Patricia Churchland (2013, p. 70; Zuger, 2013).

▼ **FIGURE 10.5**
Near-death vision or hallucination? Psychologist Ronald Siegel (1977) reported that people under the influence of hallucinogenic drugs often see "a bright light in the center of the field of vision. . . . The location of this point of light create[s] a tunnel-like perspective." This is very similar to others' near-death experiences.

LSD Albert Hofmann, a chemist, created—and on one Friday afternoon in April 1943 accidentally ingested—**LSD** (lysergic acid diethylamide). The result—"an uninterrupted stream of fantastic pictures, extraordinary shapes with intense, kaleidoscopic play of colors"—reminded him of a childhood mystical experience that had left him longing for another glimpse of "a miraculous, powerful, unfathomable reality" (Siegel, 1984; Smith, 2006). The user's current mood and expectations color the emotional experience, which may vary from euphoria to detachment to panic.

Marijuana Marijuana leaves and flowers contain **THC** (delta-9-tetrahydrocannabinol). Whether smoked (getting to the brain in about 7 seconds) or eaten (causing its peak concentration to be reached at a slower, unpredictable rate), THC produces a mix of effects. Synthetic marijuana ("K2," also called "Spice") mimics THC. Its harmful side effects, which can include agitation and hallucinations, led to its ingredient becoming illegal under the U.S. Synthetic Drug Abuse Prevention Act of 2012.

Marijuana is a mild hallucinogen, amplifying sensitivity to colors, sounds, tastes, and smells. But like alcohol, marijuana relaxes, disinhibits, and may produce a euphoric high. Both alcohol and marijuana impair the motor coordination, perceptual skills, and reaction time necessary for safely operating an automobile or other machine. "THC causes animals to misjudge events," reported Ronald Siegel (1990, p. 163). "Pigeons wait too long to respond to buzzers or lights that tell them food is available for brief periods; and rats turn the wrong way in mazes."

Marijuana and alcohol also differ. The body eliminates alcohol within hours. THC and its by-products linger in the body for more than a week, which means that regular users experience less abrupt withdrawal and may achieve a high with smaller than usual drug amounts. This is unlike typical tolerance, in which repeat users need to take larger doses to feel the same effect.

A marijuana user's experience can vary with the situation. If the person feels anxious or depressed, marijuana may intensify the feelings. The more often the person uses marijuana, especially during adolescence, the greater the risk of anxiety, depression, or addiction (Bambico et al., 2010; Hurd et al., 2013; Murray et al., 2007).

Marijuana also disrupts memory formation and interferes with immediate recall of information learned only a few minutes before (Bossong et al., 2012). Such cognitive effects outlast the period of smoking (Messinis et al., 2006). Heavy adult use for over 20 years is associated with a shrinkage of brain areas that process memories and emotions (Yücel et al., 2008). One study, which has tracked more than 1000 New Zealanders from birth, found that the IQ scores of persistent teen marijuana users dropped eight points from age 13 to 38 (Meier et al., 2012). (This mental decline was seen only in those who started regular use before age 18, while their brains were still rapidly developing.) Prenatal exposure through maternal marijuana use impairs brain development (Berghuis et al., 2007; Huizink & Mulder, 2006).

To free up resources to fight crime, some states and countries have passed laws legalizing the possession of small quantities of marijuana. In some cases, legal *medical marijuana* use has been granted to relieve the pain and nausea associated with diseases such as AIDS and cancer (Munsey, 2010; Watson et al., 2000). In such cases, the Institute of Medicine recommends delivering the THC with medical inhalers. Marijuana smoke, like cigarette smoke, is toxic and can cause cancer, lung damage, and pregnancy complications (BLF, 2012).

* * *

Despite their differences, the psychoactive drugs summarized in **TABLE 10.2** on the next page share a common feature: They trigger negative aftereffects that offset their immediate positive effects and grow stronger with repetition. And that helps explain both tolerance and withdrawal. As the opposing, negative aftereffects grow stronger, it takes larger and larger doses to produce the desired high (*tolerance*), causing the after-effects to worsen in the drug's absence (*withdrawal*). This in turn creates a need to switch off the withdrawal symptoms by taking yet more of the drug.

Ecstasy (MDMA) a synthetic stimulant and mild hallucinogen. Produces euphoria and social intimacy, but with short-term health risks and longer-term harm to serotonin-producing neurons and to mood and cognition.

hallucinogens psychedelic ("mind-manifesting") drugs, such as LSD, that distort perceptions and evoke sensory images in the absence of sensory input.

near-death experience an altered state of consciousness reported after a close brush with death (such as through cardiac arrest); often similar to drug-induced hallucinations.

LSD a powerful hallucinogenic drug; also known as acid (*lysergic acid diethylamide*).

THC the major active ingredient in marijuana; triggers a variety of effects, including mild hallucinations.

LaunchPad To review the basic psychoactive drugs and their actions, and to play the role of experimenter as you administer drugs and observe their effects, visit LaunchPad's *PsychSim 6: Your Mind on Drugs.*

▼ TABLE 10.2
A Guide to Selected Psychoactive Drugs

Drug	Type	Pleasurable Effects	Negative Aftereffects
Alcohol	Depressant	Initial high followed by relaxation and disinhibition	Depression, memory loss, organ damage, impaired reactions
Heroin	Depressant	Rush of euphoria, relief from pain	Depressed physiology, agonizing withdrawal
Caffeine	Stimulant	Increased alertness and wakefulness	Anxiety, restlessness, and insomnia in high doses; uncomfortable withdrawal
Nicotine	Stimulant	Arousal and relaxation, sense of well-being	Heart disease, cancer
Cocaine	Stimulant	Rush of euphoria, confidence, energy	Cardiovascular stress, suspiciousness, depressive crash
Methamphet-amine	Stimulant	Euphoria, alertness, energy	Irritability, insomnia, hypertension, seizures
Ecstasy (MDMA)	Stimulant; mild hallucinogen	Emotional elevation, disinhibition	Dehydration, overheating, depressed mood, impaired cognitive and immune functioning
LSD	Hallucinogen	Visual "trip"	Risk of panic
Marijuana (THC)	Mild hallucinogen	Enhanced sensation, relief of pain, distortion of time, relaxation	Impaired learning and memory, increased risk of psychological disorders, lung damage from smoke

---

RETRIEVAL PRACTICE

"How strange would appear to be this thing that men call pleasure! And how curiously it is related to what is thought to be its opposite, pain! . . . Wherever the one is found, the other follows up behind."

Plato, *Phaedo,* fourth century b.c.e.

• How does this pleasure-pain description apply to the repeated use of psychoactive drugs?

ANSWER: Psychoactive drugs create pleasure by altering brain chemistry. With repeated use of the drug, the brain develops tolerance and needs more of the drug to achieve the desired effect. (Marijuana is an exception.) Discontinuing use of the substance then produces painful or psychologically unpleasant withdrawal symptoms.

Influences on Drug Use

10-6 Why do some people become regular users of consciousness-altering drugs?

Drug use by North American youth increased during the 1970s. Then, with increased drug education and a more realistic and deglamorized media depiction of taking drugs, drug use declined sharply (except for a small rise in the mid-1980s). After the early 1990s, the cultural antidrug voice softened, and some drugs for a time were again glamorized in music and films. Consider, for example, historical trends in the use of marijuana:

• In the University of Michigan's annual survey of 15,000 U.S. high school seniors, the proportion who said there is "great risk" in regular marijuana use rose from 35 percent in 1978 to 79 percent in 1991, then retreated to 40 percent in 2013 (Johnston et al., 2014).

• After peaking in 1978, marijuana use by U.S. high school seniors declined through 1992, then rose, but has recently been holding steady (see **FIGURE** 10.6). Among Canadian 15- to 24-year-olds, 23 percent report using marijuana monthly, weekly, or daily (Health Canada, 2012).

For some adolescents, occasional drug use represents thrill seeking. Why, though, do others become regular drug users? In search of answers, researchers have engaged biological, psychological, and social-cultural levels of analysis.

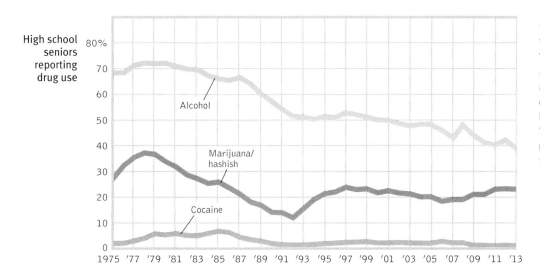

FIGURE 10.6
Trends in drug use
The percentage of U.S. high school seniors who report having used alcohol, marijuana, or cocaine during the past 30 days largely declined from the late 1970s to 1992, when it partially rebounded for a few years. (Data from Johnston et al., 2014.)

Biological Influences

Some people may be biologically vulnerable to particular drugs. For example, evidence accumulates that heredity influences some aspects of substance use problems, especially those appearing by early adulthood (Crabbe, 2002):

- Adopted individuals are more susceptible to alcohol use disorder if there is a history of it in one or both biological parents.

- Having an identical rather than fraternal twin with alcohol use disorder puts one at increased risk for alcohol problems (Kendler et al., 2002). In marijuana use also, identical twins more closely resemble each other than do fraternal twins.

- Boys who at age 6 are excitable, impulsive, and fearless (genetically influenced traits) are more likely as teens to smoke, drink, and use other drugs (Masse & Tremblay, 1997).

- Researchers have bred rats and mice that prefer alcoholic drinks to water. One such strain has reduced levels of the brain chemical NPY. Mice engineered to *overproduce* NPY are very sensitive to alcohol's sedating effect and drink little (Thiele et al., 1998).

- Researchers have identified genes that are more common among people and animals predisposed to alcohol use disorder, and they are seeking genes that contribute to tobacco addiction (Stacey et al., 2012). These culprit genes seemingly produce deficiencies in the brain's natural dopamine reward system: While triggering temporary dopamine-produced pleasure, the addictive drugs disrupt normal dopamine balance. Studies of how drugs reprogram the brain's reward systems raise hopes for anti-addiction drugs that might block or blunt the effects of alcohol and other drugs (Miller, 2008; Wilson & Kuhn, 2005).

Biological influences on drug use extend to other drugs as well. One study tracked 18,115 Swedish adoptees. Those with drug-abusing biological parents were at doubled risk of drug abuse, indicating a genetic influence. But then those with drug-abusing adoptive siblings also had a doubled risk of drug abuse, indicating an environmental influence (Kendler et al., 2012). Let's next see what those environmental influences might be.

Psychological and Social-Cultural Influences

Throughout this text, we see that biological, psychological, and social-cultural factors interact to produce behavior. So, too, with disordered drug use (**FIGURE 10.7** on the next page). One psychological factor that has appeared in studies of youth and young adults is the feeling that life is meaningless and directionless (Newcomb & Harlow, 1986).

Warning signs of alcohol use disorder

- Drinking binges
- Craving alcohol
- Use results in unfulfilled work, school, or home tasks
- Failing to honor a resolve to drink less
- Continued use despite health risk
- Avoiding family or friends when drinking

▼ FIGURE 10.7
Levels of analysis for disordered drug use The biopsychosocial approach enables researchers to investigate disordered drug use from complementary perspectives.

Biological influences:
• genetic predispositions
• variations in neurotransmitter systems

Psychological influences:
• lacking sense of purpose
• significant stress
• psychological disorders, such as depression

Disordered drug use

Social-cultural influences:
• difficult environment
• cultural acceptance of drug use
• negative peer influences

Nic-A-Teen Virtually nobody starts smoking past the vulnerable teen years. Eager to hook customers whose addiction will give them business for years to come, cigarette companies target teens. Portrayals of smoking by popular actors, such as Emma Stone in *Gangster Squad,* entice teens to imitate.

This feeling is common among school dropouts who subsist without job skills, without privilege, and with little hope.

Sometimes the psychological influence is obvious. Many heavy users of alcohol, marijuana, and cocaine have experienced significant stress or failure and are depressed. Girls with a history of depression, eating disorders, or sexual or physical abuse are at risk for substance addiction. So are youth undergoing school or neighborhood transitions (CASA, 2003; Logan et al., 2002). Collegians who have not yet achieved a clear identity are also at greater risk (Bishop et al., 2005). By temporarily dulling the pain of self-awareness, psychoactive drugs may offer a way to avoid coping with depression, anger, anxiety, or insomnia. (As other modules explain, behavior is often controlled more by its immediate consequences than by its later ones.)

Smoking usually begins during early adolescence. (If you are in college or university, and the cigarette manufacturers haven't yet made you their devoted customer, they almost surely never will.) Adolescents, self-conscious and often thinking the world is watching their every move, are vulnerable to smoking's allure. They may first light up to imitate glamorous celebrities, to project a mature image, to handle stress, or to get the social reward of being accepted by other smokers (Cin et al., 2007; Tickle et al., 2006). Mindful of these tendencies, cigarette companies have effectively modeled smoking with themes that appeal to youths: attractiveness, independence, adventurousness, social approval (Surgeon General, 2012). Typically, teens who start smoking also have friends who smoke, who suggest its pleasures and offer them cigarettes (Rose et al., 1999). Among teens whose parents and best friends are nonsmokers, the smoking rate is close to zero (Moss et al., 1992; also see **FIGURE 10.8**). Most teen drinking is also done for social reasons, not as a way to cope with problems (Kuntsche et al., 2005).

Rates of drug use also vary across cultural and ethnic groups. One survey of 100,000 teens in 35 European countries found that marijuana use in the prior 30 days ranged

▼ FIGURE 10.8
Peer influence Kids don't smoke if their friends don't (Philip Morris, 2003). A correlation-causation question: Does the close link between teen smoking and friends' smoking reflect peer influence? Teens seeking similar friends? Or both?

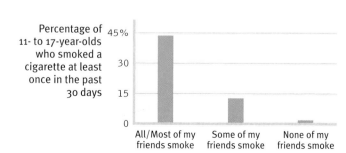

Percentage of 11- to 17-year-olds who smoked a cigarette at least once in the past 30 days

45%
30
15
0

All/Most of my friends smoke   Some of my friends smoke   None of my friends smoke from zero to 1 percent in Romania and Sweden to 20 to 22 percent in Britain, Switzerland, and France (ESPAD, 2003). Independent U.S. government studies of drug use in households nationwide and among high schoolers in all regions reveal that African-American teens have sharply lower rates of drinking, smoking, and cocaine use (Johnston et al., 2007). Alcohol and other drug addiction rates have also been low among actively religious people, with extremely low rates among Orthodox Jews, Mormons, Mennonites, and the Amish (Salas-Wright et al., 2012; Vaughn et al., 2011; Yeung et al., 2009).

Whether in cities or rural areas, peers influence attitudes about drugs. They also throw the parties and provide (or don't provide) the drugs. If an adolescent's friends use drugs, the odds are that he or she will, too. If the friends do not, the opportunity may not even arise. Teens who come from happy families, who do not begin drinking before age 15, and who do well in school tend not to use drugs, largely because they rarely associate with those who do (Bachman et al., 2007; Hingson et al., 2006; Odgers et al., 2008).

Peer influence is more than what friends do or say. Adolescents' expectations—what they *believe* friends are doing and favoring—influence their behavior (Vitória et al., 2009). One study surveyed sixth graders in 22 U.S. states. How many believed their friends had smoked marijuana? About 14 percent. How many of those friends acknowledged doing so? Only 4 percent (Wren, 1999). University students are not immune to such misperceptions: Drinking dominates social occasions partly because students overestimate their fellow students' enthusiasm for alcohol and underestimate their views of its risks (Prentice & Miller, 1993; Self, 1994) (**TABLE 10.3**). When students' overestimates of peer drinking are corrected, alcohol use often subsides (Moreira et al., 2009).

People whose beginning use of drugs was influenced by their peers are more likely to stop using when friends stop or their social network changes (Kandel & Raveis, 1989). One study that followed 12,000 adults over 32 years found that smokers tend to quit in clusters (Christakis & Fowler, 2008). Within a social network, the odds of a person quitting increased when a spouse, friend, or co-worker stopped smoking. Similarly, most soldiers who became drug addicted while in Vietnam ceased their drug use after returning home (Robins et al., 1974).

As always with correlations, the traffic between friends' drug use and our own may be two-way: Our friends influence us. Social networks matter. But we also select as friends those who share our likes and dislikes.

What do the findings on drug use suggest for drug prevention and treatment programs? Three channels of influence seem possible:

- Educate young people about the long-term costs of a drug's temporary pleasures.

- Help young people find other ways to boost their self-esteem and purpose in life.

- Attempt to modify peer associations or to "inoculate" youths against peer pressures by training them in refusal skills.

SNAPSHOTS

Once upon a time, peer pressure caused Bob to start smoking.

Twenty years later, it forces him to quit.

©Jason Love

▼ TABLE 10.3
Facts About "Higher" Education

- College and university students drink more alcohol than their nonstudent peers and exhibit 2.5 times the general population's rate of substance abuse.

- Fraternity and sorority members report nearly twice the binge-drinking rate of nonmembers.

- Since 1993, campus smoking rates have declined, alcohol use has been steady, and abuse of prescription opioids, stimulants, tranquilizers, and sedatives has increased, as has marijuana use.

Source: NCASA, 2007.

People rarely abuse drugs if they understand the physical and psychological costs, feel good about themselves and the direction their lives are taking, and are in a peer group that disapproves of using drugs. These educational, psychological, and social-cultural factors may help explain why 26 percent of U.S. high school dropouts, but only 6 percent of those with a postgraduate education, report smoking (CDC, 2011).

RETRIEVAL PRACTICE

- Why do tobacco companies try so hard to get customers hooked as teens?

ANSWER: Nicotine is powerfully addictive, expensive, and deadly. Those who start paving the neural pathways when young may find it very hard to stop using nicotine. As a result, tobacco companies may have lifelong customers.

- Studies have found that people who begin drinking in their early teens are much more likely to develop alcohol use disorder than those who begin at age 21 or after. What possible explanations might there be for this correlation?

ANSWER: Possible explanations include (a) a biological predisposition to both early use and later abuse; (b) brain changes and taste preferences triggered by early use; and (c) enduring habits, attitudes, activities, or peer relationships that foster alcohol misuse.

MODULE 10 REVIEW   Drugs and Consciousness

LEARNING OBJECTIVES

RETRIEVAL PRACTICE Take a moment to answer each of these Learning Objective Questions (repeated here from within this module). Then turn to Appendix C, Complete Module Reviews, to check your answers. Research suggests that trying to answer these questions on your own will improve your long-term retention (McDaniel et al., 2009).

10-1 What are substance use disorders, and what roles do tolerance, withdrawal, and addiction play in these disorders?

10-2 How has the concept of addiction changed?

10-3 What are depressants, and what are their effects?

10-4 What are stimulants, and what are their effects?

10-5 What are hallucinogens, and what are their effects?

10-6 Why do some people become regular users of consciousness-altering drugs?

TERMS AND CONCEPTS TO REMEMBER

RETRIEVAL PRACTICE Test yourself on these terms by trying to write down the definition before flipping back to check your answers.

substance use disorder, p. 117

psychoactive drug, p. 117

tolerance, p. 118

addiction, p. 118

withdrawal, p. 118

depressants, p. 119

alcohol use disorder, p. 120

barbiturates, p. 120

opiates, p. 120

stimulants, p. 121

amphetamines, p. 121

nicotine, p. 121

cocaine, p. 123

methamphetamine, p. 123

Ecstasy (MDMA), p. 124

hallucinogens, p. 124

near-death experience, p. 124

LSD, p. 124

THC, p. 125

Use 🐾 **LearningCurve** to create your personalized study plan, which will direct you to the resources that will help you most in 🐾 **LaunchPad**.

CONSCIOUSNESS AND THE TWO-TRACK MIND

Test yourself repeatedly throughout your studies. This will not only help you figure out what you know and don't know; the testing itself will help you learn and remember the information more effectively thanks to the *testing effect.*

MODULE 8 Brain States and Consciousness

1. Failure to see visible objects because our attention is occupied elsewhere is called _____ _____ .

2. We register and react to stimuli outside of our awareness by means of _____ processing. When we devote deliberate attention to stimuli, we use _____ processing.

3. _____ blindness and change blindness are forms of selective attention.

MODULE 9 Sleep and Dreams

4. Our body temperature tends to rise and fall in sync with a biological clock, which is referred to as _____ _____ .

5. During the NREM-1 sleep stage, a person is most likely to experience
   a. sleep spindles.
   b. hallucinations.
   c. night terrors or nightmares.
   d. rapid eye movements.

6. The brain emits large, slow delta waves during _____ sleep.

7. As the night progresses, what happens to the REM stage of sleep?

8. Which of the following is NOT one of the reasons that have been proposed to explain why we need sleep?
   a. Sleep has survival value.
   b. Sleep helps us recuperate.
   c. Sleep rests the eyes.
   d. Sleep plays a role in the growth process.

9. What is the difference between narcolepsy and sleep apnea?

10. In interpreting dreams, Freud was most interested in their
   a. information-processing function.
   b. physiological function.
   c. manifest content, or story line.
   d. latent content, or hidden meaning.

11. What is the *neural activation* theory of dreaming?

12. "For what one has dwelt on by day, these things are seen in visions of the night" (Menander of Athens, *Fragments*). How might the information-processing perspective on dreaming interpret this ancient Greek quote?

13. The tendency for REM sleep to increase following REM sleep deprivation is referred to as _____ _____ .

MODULE 10 Drugs and Consciousness

14. After continued use of a psychoactive drug, the drug user needs to take larger doses to get the desired effect. This is referred to as _____ .

15. The depressants include alcohol, barbiturates,
   a. and opiates.
   b. cocaine, and morphine.
   c. caffeine, nicotine, and marijuana.
   d. and amphetamines.

16. Why might alcohol make a person more helpful *or* more aggressive?

17. Long-term use of Ecstasy can
   a. depress sympathetic nervous system activity.
   b. deplete the brain's supply of epinephrine.
   c. deplete the brain's supply of dopamine.
   d. damage serotonin-producing neurons.

18. Near-death experiences are strikingly similar to the hallucinations evoked by _____ .

19. Use of marijuana
   a. impairs motor coordination, perception, reaction time, and memory.
   b. inhibits people's emotions.
   c. leads to dehydration and overheating.
   d. stimulates brain cell development.

20. An important psychological contributor to drug use is
   a. inflated self-esteem.
   b. the feeling that life is meaningless and directionless.
   c. genetic predispositions.
   d. overprotective parents.

Find answers to these questions in Appendix D, in the back of the book.

Emily Shur/The Image Bank/Getty Images

NATURE, NURTURE, AND HUMAN DIVERSITY

· · · · · · · · · · · · ·

What makes you you? In important ways, we are each unique. We look different. We sound different. We have varying personalities, interests, and cultural and family backgrounds.

We are also the leaves of one tree. Our human family shares not only a common biological heritage—cut us and we bleed—but also common behavioral tendencies. Our shared brain architecture predisposes us to sense the world, develop language, and feel hunger through identical mechanisms. Whether we live in the Arctic or the tropics, we prefer sweet tastes to sour. We divide the color spectrum into similar colors. And we feel drawn to behaviors that produce and protect offspring.

Our kinship appears in our social behaviors as well. Whether named Gonzales, Nkomo, Smith, or Wong, we start fearing strangers at about eight months, and as adults we prefer the company of those with attitudes and attributes similar to our own. Coming from different parts of the globe, we know how to read one another's smiles and frowns. As members of one species, we affiliate, conform, return favors, punish offenses, organize hierarchies of status, and grieve a child's death. A visitor from outer space could drop in anywhere and find humans dancing and feasting, singing and worshiping, playing sports and games, laughing and crying, living in families and forming groups. Taken together, such universal behaviors define our human nature.

What causes our striking diversity, and also our shared human nature? How much are human differences shaped by our differing genes? And how much by our *environment*—by every external influence, from maternal nutrition while in the womb to social support while nearing the tomb? To what extent are we formed by our upbringing? By our culture? By our current circumstances? By people's reactions to our genetic dispositions? Modules 11, 12, and 13 tell the scientific story of how our genes (nature) and environments (nurture) define us.

The nurture of nature Parents everywhere wonder: Will my baby grow up to be peaceful or aggressive? Homely or attractive? Successful or struggling at every step? What comes built in, and what is nurtured—and how? Research reveals that nature and nurture together shape our development—every step of the way.

"Thanks for almost everything, Dad."

behavior genetics the study of the relative power and limits of genetic and environmental influences on behavior.

environment every nongenetic influence, from prenatal nutrition to the people and things around us.

chromosomes threadlike structures made of DNA molecules that contain the genes.

DNA (deoxyribonucleic acid) a complex molecule containing the genetic information that makes up the chromosomes.

genes the biochemical units of heredity that make up the chromosomes; segments of DNA capable of synthesizing proteins.

Behavior Genetics: Predicting Individual Differences

11-1 What are *chromosomes, DNA, genes,* and the human *genome*? How do behavior geneticists explain our individual differences?

If Chelsea Clinton, daughter of former President Bill Clinton and former Secretary of State Hillary Rodham Clinton, becomes a politician, should we attribute her superior political talent to her "White House genes"? To growing up in a politically savvy environment? To high expectations? Such questions intrigue **behavior geneticists,** who study our differences and weigh the effects and the interplay of heredity and **environment**.

Genes: Our Codes for Life

Behind the story of our body and of our brain—surely the most awesome thing on our little planet—is the heredity that interacts with our experience to create both our universal nature and our individual and social diversity. Barely more than a century ago, few would have guessed that every cell nucleus in your body contains the genetic master code for your entire body. It's as if every room in Dubai's Burj Khalifa (the world's tallest building) contained a book detailing the architect's plans for the entire structure. The plans for your own book of life run to 46 chapters—23 donated by your mother's egg and 23 by your father's sperm. Each of these 46 chapters, called a **chromosome,** is composed of a coiled chain of the molecule **DNA** (*deoxyribonucleic acid*). **Genes,** small segments of the giant DNA molecules, form the words of those chapters (**FIGURE 11.1**). All told, you have 20,000 to 25,000 genes, which are either active (*expressed*) or inactive. Environmental events "turn on" genes, rather like hot water enabling a tea bag to express its flavor. When turned on, genes provide the code for creating *protein molecules*, our body's building blocks.

▼ **FIGURE 11.1**
The life code The nucleus of every human cell contains chromosomes, each of which is made up of two strands of DNA connected in a double helix. Genes are DNA segments that, when expressed (turned on) direct the development of proteins that influence a person's individual development.

Chromosome

Cell

Gene

Nucleus

DNA

Genetically speaking, every other human is nearly your identical twin. Human **genome** researchers have discovered the common sequence within human DNA. This shared genetic profile makes us humans, rather than tulips, bananas, or chimpanzees.

We aren't all that different from our chimpanzee cousins. At a genetic level, humans and chimpanzees are 96 percent identical (Mikkelsen et al., 2005). At "functionally important" DNA sites, this number reaches 99.4 percent (Wildman et al., 2003)! Yet that wee 0.6 percent difference matters. Shakespeare intricately wove 17,677 words into his literary masterpieces. Despite some remarkable abilities, chimpanzees do not compose sonnets.

Small differences matter among other species, too. Common chimpanzees and bonobos resemble each other in many ways. They should—their genomes differ by much less than 1 percent. But they display markedly differing behaviors. Chimpanzees are aggressive and male dominated. Bonobos are peaceable and female led.

The occasional variations found at particular gene sites in human DNA fascinate geneticists and psychologists. Slight person-to-person variations from the common pattern give clues to our uniqueness—why one person has a disease that another does not, why one person is short and another tall, why one is anxious and another calm.

Most of our traits have complex genetic roots. How tall you are, for example, reflects the size of your face, vertebrae, leg bones, and so forth—each of which may be influenced by different genes interacting with your specific environment. Traits such as intelligence, happiness, and aggressiveness are similarly influenced by groups of genes. Thus, our genes help explain both our shared human nature and our human diversity. But knowing our heredity tells only part of our story. To form us, environmental influences interact with our genetic predispositions.

> "We share half our genes with the banana."
>
> Evolutionary biologist Robert May, president of Britain's Royal Society, 2001

> "Your DNA and mine are 99.9 percent the same. . . . At the DNA level, we are clearly all part of one big world-wide family."
>
> Francis Collins, Human Genome Project director, 2007

RETRIEVAL PRACTICE

- Put the following cell structures in order from smallest to largest: nucleus, gene, chromosome

ANSWER: gene, chromosome, nucleus

- When the mother's egg and the father's sperm unite, each contributes 23 _____.

ANSWER: chromosomes

> **genome** the complete instructions for making an organism, consisting of all the genetic material in that organism's chromosomes.
>
> **identical twins (monozygotic twins)** develop from a single fertilized egg that splits in two, creating two genetically identical organisms.

Twin and Adoption Studies

11-2 How do twin and adoption studies help us understand the effects and interactions of nature and nurture?

To scientifically tease apart the influences of heredity and environment, behavior geneticists could wish for two types of experiments. The first would control heredity while varying the home environment. The second would control the home environment while varying heredity. Although such experiments with human infants would be unethical, nature has done this work for us.

Identical Versus Fraternal Twins

Identical (*monozygotic*) **twins** develop from a single fertilized egg that splits in two. Thus they are *genetically* identical—nature's own human

David Yellen

Canadian real estate twins Identical twins Drew and Jonathan Scott share matching DNA and run the same real estate renovation business, but they have different interests. Drew finds the best deals. Jonathan, a contractor, transforms the properties.

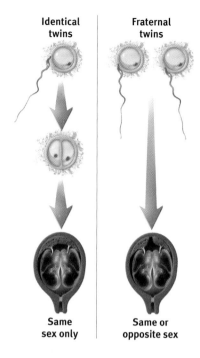

Identical twins

Fraternal twins

Same sex only

Same or opposite sex

▼ **FIGURE 11.2**
Same fertilized egg, same genes; different eggs, different genes
Identical twins develop from a single fertilized egg, fraternal twins from two.

More twins Curiously, twin rates vary by race. The rate among Caucasians is roughly twice that of Asians and half that of Africans. In Africa and Asia, most twins are identical. In Western countries, most twins are fraternal, and fraternal twins have increased with the use of fertility drugs (Hall, 2003; Steinhauer, 1999).

clones (**FIGURE 11.2**). Indeed, they are clones who share not only the same genes but the same conception and uterus, and usually the same birth date and cultural history. Two slight qualifications:

- Although identical twins have the same genes, they don't always have the same *number of copies* of those genes. That variation helps explain why one twin may have a greater risk for certain illnesses and disorders, including schizophrenia (Maiti et al., 2011).

- Most identical twins share a placenta during prenatal development, but one of every three sets has separate placentas. One twin's placenta may provide slightly better nourishment, which may contribute to identical twin differences (Davis et al., 1995b; Phelps et al., 1997; Sokol et al., 1995).

Fraternal (*dizygotic*) **twins** develop from two separate fertilized eggs. As womb-mates, they share a prenatal environment, but they are genetically no more similar than ordinary brothers and sisters.

Shared genes can translate into shared experiences. A person whose identical twin has autism spectrum disorder, for example, has about a 3 in 4 risk of being similarly diagnosed. If the affected twin is fraternal, the co-twin has about a 1 in 3 risk (Ronald & Hoekstra, 2011). To study the effects of genes and environments, hundreds of researchers have studied some 800,000 identical and fraternal twin pairs (Johnson et al., 2009).

Are identical twins also *behaviorally* more similar than fraternal twins? Studies of thousands of twin pairs in Germany, Australia, and the United States have found that on the personality traits of *extraversion* (outgoingness) and *neuroticism* (emotional instability) identical twins report much greater similarity than do fraternal twins (Kandler et al., 2011; Laceulle et al., 2011; Loehlin, 2012). Genes also influence many specific behaviors. For example, compared with rates for fraternal twins, drinking and driving convictions are 12 times greater among those who have an identical twin with such a conviction (Beaver & Barnes, 2012). As twins grow older, their behaviors remain similar (McGue & Christensen, 2013).

Identical twins, more than fraternal twins, also report being treated alike. So, do their experiences rather than their genes account for their similarities? *No.* Studies have shown that identical twins whose parents treated them alike (for example, dressing them identically) were not psychologically more alike than identical twins who were treated less similarly (Kendler et al., 1994; Loehlin & Nichols, 1976). In explaining individual differences, genes matter.

Separated Twins

Imagine the following science fiction experiment: A mad scientist decides to separate identical twins at birth, then raise them in differing environments. Better yet, consider a *true* story:

On a chilly February morning in 1979, some time after divorcing his first wife, Linda, Jim Lewis awoke in his modest home next to his second wife, Betty. Determined that this marriage would work, Jim made a habit of leaving love notes to Betty around the house. As he lay in bed he thought about others he had loved, including his son, James Alan, and his faithful dog, Toy.

Jim looked forward to spending part of the day in his basement woodworking shop, where he enjoyed building furniture, picture frames, and other items, including a white bench now circling a tree in his front yard. Jim also liked to spend free time driving his Chevy, watching stock-car racing, and drinking Miller Lite beer.

Jim was basically healthy, except for occasional half-day migraine headaches and blood pressure that was a little high, perhaps related to his chain-smoking habit. He had become overweight a while back but had shed some of the pounds. Having undergone a vasectomy, he was done having children.

What was extraordinary about Jim Lewis, however, was that at that same moment (we are not making this up) there existed another man—also named Jim—for whom all these things (right down to the dog's name) were also true.[1] This other Jim—Jim Springer—just happened, 38 years earlier, to have been his fetal partner. Thirty-seven days after their birth, these genetically identical twins were separated, adopted by blue-collar families, and raised with no contact or knowledge of each other's whereabouts until the day Jim Lewis received a call from his genetic clone (who, having been told he had a twin, set out to find him).

One month later, the brothers became the first of many separated twin pairs tested by University of Minnesota psychologist Thomas Bouchard and his colleagues (Miller, 2012). The brothers' voice intonations and inflections were so similar that, hearing a playback of an earlier interview, Jim Springer guessed "That's me." Wrong—it was Jim Lewis. Given tests measuring their personality, intelligence, heart rate, and brain waves, the Jim twins—despite 38 years of separation—were virtually as alike as the same person tested twice. Both married women named Dorothy Jane Scheckelburger. Okay, the last item is a joke. But as Judith Rich Harris (2006) has noted, it is hardly weirder than some other reported similarities.

Aided by publicity in magazine and newspaper stories, Bouchard (2009) and his colleagues located and studied 74 pairs of identical twins raised apart. They continued to find similarities not only of tastes and physical attributes but also of personality (characteristic patterns of thinking, feeling, and acting), abilities, attitudes, interests, and even fears.

---

1. Actually, this description of the two Jims errs in one respect: Jim Lewis named his son James Alan. Jim Springer named his James Allan.

Twins Lorraine and Levinia Christmas, driving to deliver Christmas presents to each other near Flitcham, England, collided (Shepherd, 1997).

In 2009, thieves broke into a Berlin store and stole jewelry worth $6.8 million. One thief left a drop of sweat—a link to his genetic signature. Police analyzed the DNA and encountered two matches: The DNA belonged to identical twin brothers. The court ruled that "at least one of the brothers took part in the crime, but it has not been possible to determine which one." Birds of a feather can rob together.

Video material is provided by BBC Worldwide Learning and CBS New Archives, and produced by Princeton Academic Resources.

LaunchPad For a 2-minute synopsis of twin similarity, visit LaunchPad's *Video—Nature Versus Nurture: Growing Up Apart.*

Beth Eberth, St. Bonaventure University, St. Bonaventure, N.Y.

True brothers The identical friars Julian and Adrian Reister—two "quiet, gentle souls"—both died of heart failure, at age 92, on the same day in 2011.

fraternal twins (dizygotic twins) develop from separate fertilized eggs. They are genetically no closer than ordinary brothers and sisters, but they share a prenatal environment.

Bouchard's famous twin research was, appropriately enough, conducted in Minneapolis, the "Twin City" (with St. Paul) and home to the Minnesota Twins baseball team.

Coincidences are not unique to twins. Patricia Kern of Colorado was born March 13, 1941, and named Patricia Ann Campbell. Patricia DiBiasi of Oregon also was born March 13, 1941, and named Patricia Ann Campbell. Both had fathers named Robert, worked as bookkeepers, and at the time of this comparison had children ages 21 and 19. Both studied cosmetology, enjoyed oil painting as a hobby, and married military men, within 11 days of each other. They are not genetically related. (From an AP report, May 2, 1983.)

"Mom may be holding a full house while Dad has a straight flush, yet when Junior gets a random half of each of their cards his poker hand may be a loser."

David Lykken (2001)

In Sweden, researchers identified 99 separated identical twin pairs and more than 200 separated fraternal twin pairs (Pedersen et al., 1988). Compared with equivalent samples of identical twins raised together, the separated identical twins had somewhat less identical personalities. Still, separated twins were more alike if genetically identical than if fraternal. And separation shortly after birth (rather than, say, at age 8) did not amplify their personality differences.

Stories of startling twin similarities have not impressed critics, who remind us that "The plural of *anecdote* is not *data*." They have noted that if any two strangers were to spend hours comparing their behaviors and life histories, they would probably discover many coincidental similarities. If researchers created a control group of biologically unrelated pairs of the same age, sex, and ethnicity, who had not grown up together but who were as similar to one another in economic and cultural background as are many of the separated twin pairs, wouldn't these pairs also exhibit striking similarities (Joseph, 2001)? Twin researchers have replied that separated fraternal twins do not exhibit similarities comparable to those of separated identical twins.

Even the impressive data from personality assessments are clouded by the reunion of many of the separated twins some years before they were tested. Moreover, identical twins share an appearance, and the responses it evokes. Adoption agencies also tend to place separated twins in similar homes. Despite these criticisms, the striking twin-study results helped shift scientific thinking toward a greater appreciation of genetic influences.

Biological Versus Adoptive Relatives

For behavior geneticists, nature's second real-life experiment—adoption—creates two groups: *genetic relatives* (biological parents and siblings) and *environmental relatives* (adoptive parents and siblings). For personality or any other given trait, we can therefore ask whether adopted children are more like their biological parents, who contributed their genes, or their adoptive parents, who contribute a home environment. While sharing that home environment, do adopted siblings also come to share traits?

The stunning finding from studies of hundreds of adoptive families is that people who grow up together, whether biologically related or not, do not much resemble one another in personality (McGue & Bouchard, 1998; Plomin, 2011; Rowe, 1990). In personality traits such as extraversion and agreeableness, people who have been adopted are more similar to their biological parents than to their caregiving adoptive parents.

The finding is important enough to bear repeating: *The environment shared by a family's children has virtually no discernible impact on their personalities.* Two adopted children raised in the same home are no more likely to share personality traits with each other than with the child down the block. Heredity shapes other primates' personalities, too. Macaque monkeys raised by foster mothers exhibited social behaviors that resemble their biological, rather than foster, mothers (Maestripieri, 2003). Add in the similarity of identical twins, whether they grow up together or apart, and the effect of a shared raising environment seems shockingly modest.

What we have here is perhaps "the most important puzzle in the history of psychology," contended Steven Pinker (2002): *Why are children in the same family so different?* Why does shared family environment have so little effect on children's personalities? Is it because each sibling experiences unique peer influences and life events? Because sibling relationships ricochet off each other, amplifying their differences? Because siblings—despite sharing half their genes—have very different combinations of genes and may evoke very different kinds of parenting? Such questions fuel behavior geneticists' curiosity.

The genetic leash may limit the family environment's influence on personality, but it does not mean that adoptive parenting is a fruitless venture. Parents do influence

Nature or nurture or both? When talent runs in families, as with Wynton Marsalis, Branford Marsalis, and Delfeayo Marsalis, how do heredity and environment together do their work?

their children's attitudes, values, manners, politics, and faith (Reifman & Cleveland, 2007). Religious involvement is genetically influenced (Steger et al., 2011). But a pair of adopted children or identical twins *will*, especially during adolescence, have more similar religious beliefs if raised together (Koenig et al., 2005). Parenting matters!

Moreover, in adoptive homes, child neglect and abuse and even parental divorce are rare. (Adoptive parents are carefully screened; natural parents are not.) So it is not surprising that studies have shown that, despite a somewhat greater risk of psychological disorder, most adopted children thrive, especially when adopted as infants (Loehlin et al., 2007; van IJzendoorn & Juffer, 2006; Wierzbicki, 1993). Seven in eight adopted children have reported feeling strongly attached to one or both adoptive parents. As children of self-giving parents, they have grown up to be more self-giving and altruistic than average (Sharma et al., 1998). Many scored higher than their biological parents on intelligence tests, and most grew into happier and more stable adults. In one Swedish study, children adopted as infants grew up with fewer problems than were experienced by children whose biological mothers initially registered them for adoption but then decided to raise the children themselves (Bohman & Sigvardsson, 1990). Regardless of personality differences between adoptive family members, most adopted children benefit from adoption.

"Do you, Ashley, take Nesbitt and his genome to be your husband?"

Adoption matters As country music singer Faith Hill and late Apple founder Steve Jobs experienced, children benefit from one of the biggest gifts of love: adoption.

• How do researchers use twin and adoption studies to learn about psychological principles?

ANSWER: Researchers use twin and adoption studies to understand how much variation among individuals is due to genetic makeup and how much to environmental factors. Some studies compare the traits and behaviors of identical twins (same genes) and fraternal twins (different genes), as in any two siblings). They also compare adopted children with their adoptive and biological parents. Some studies compare traits and behaviors of twins raised together or separately.

Temperament and Heredity

11-3 What have psychologists learned about temperament?

As most parents will tell you after having their second child, babies differ even before gulping their first breath. One aspect of personality—**temperament** (emotional reactivity and excitability) is quickly apparent, and it is genetically influenced (Kandler et al., 2013; Rothbart, 2007). From their first weeks of life, some infants are noticeably *difficult*—irritable, intense, fidgety, and unpredictable. Others are *easy*—cheerful and relaxed, feeding and sleeping on predictable schedules. Still others tend to be *slow to warm up*, resisting or withdrawing from new people and situations (Chess & Thomas, 1987; Thomas & Chess, 1977).

Temperament differences typically persist. Consider:

• The most emotionally reactive newborns tended also to be the most reactive 9-month-olds (Wilson & Matheny, 1986; Worobey & Blajda, 1989).

• Exceptionally shy 6-month-olds often were still shy as 13-year-olds; over 4 in 10 children rated as consistently shy developed anxiety problems in adolescence (Prior et al., 2000).

• The most emotionally intense preschoolers tended to be relatively intense young adults (Larsen & Diener, 1987). In one study of more than 900 New Zealanders, emotionally reactive and impulsive 3-year-olds developed into somewhat more impulsive, aggressive, and conflict-prone 21-year-olds (Caspi, 2000).

• Identical twins, more than fraternal twins, often have similar temperaments (Fraley & Tancredy, 2012; Kandler et al., 2013).

The genetic effect appears in physiological differences. Anxious, inhibited infants have high and variable heart rates and a reactive nervous system. When facing new or strange situations, they become more physiologically aroused (Kagan & Snidman, 2004; Roque et al., 2012). One form of a gene that regulates the neurotransmitter serotonin predisposes a fearful temperament and, in combination with unsupportive caregiving, an emotionally reactive child (Raby et al., 2012).

Heritability

11-4 What is *heritability*, and how does it relate to individuals and groups?

So our biology helps form our personality. Yet asking whether our personality is more a product of our genes or our environment is like asking whether a flat-screen TV's size is more the result of its length or its width. We could, however, ask whether the different TV sizes are more the result of differences in their length or differences in their width. Similarly, we can ask whether person-to-person personality differences are influenced more by nature or by nurture.

Using twin and adoption studies, behavior geneticists can mathematically estimate the **heritability** of a trait—the extent to which variation among individuals can be

"Oh, he's cute, all right, but he's got the temperament of a car alarm."

HOW WOULD YOU KNOW?

Consider how researchers have studied these issues with LaunchPad's *How Would You Know If Personality Runs in the Genes?*

temperament a person's characteristic emotional reactivity and intensity.

heritability the proportion of variation among individuals that we can attribute to genes. The heritability of a trait may vary, depending on the range of populations and environments studied.

attributed to their differing genes. By one estimate, the heritability of general intelligence is 66 percent (Haworth et al., 2010). This does *not* mean that *your* intelligence is 66 percent genetic. (The heritability of height is 90 percent, but this does not mean that a 60-inch-tall woman can credit her genes for 54 inches and her environment for the other 6 inches.) Rather, it means that genetic influence explains about 66 percent of the observed *variation among people*. This point is so often misunderstood that we repeat: We can never say what percentage of an *individual's* personality or intelligence is inherited. It makes no sense to say that your personality is due *x* percent to your heredity and *y* percent to your environment. Heritability refers instead to the extent to which *differences among people* are due to genes.

Even this conclusion must be qualified, because heritability can vary from study to study. Consider humorist Mark Twain's (1835–1910) fictional idea of raising boys in barrels to age 12, feeding them through a hole. If we were to follow his suggestion, the boys would all emerge with lower-than-normal intelligence scores at age 12. Yet, given their equal environments, their test score differences could be explained only by their heredity. With the same environment, heritability—differences due to genes—would be near 100 percent.

As environments become more similar, heredity becomes the primary source of differences. If all schools were of uniform quality, all families equally loving, and all neighborhoods equally healthy, then heritability would *increase* (because differences due to environment would *decrease*). But consider the other extreme: If all people had similar heredities but were raised in drastically different environments (some in barrels, some in luxury homes), heritability would be much lower.

If genetic influences help explain variations in traits among individuals in a group, can the same be said of trait differences *between* groups? Not necessarily. As we have seen, height is 90 percent heritable, yet nutrition (an environmental factor) rather than genetic influences explains why, as a group, today's adults are taller than those of a century ago. More available food has caused Americans to grow to greater heights (Floud et al., 2011). In 1850, the average American male stood 5 feet 7 inches; in the 1980s, his counterpart stood three inches taller. The two groups differ, but not because human genes have changed in a mere century's eyeblink of time. And today's South Koreans, with their better diets, average six inches taller than today's North Koreans, who come from the same genetic stock (Johnson et al., 2009). Genes matter, but so does environment.

"*The title of my science project is 'My Little Brother: Nature or Nurture.'*"

As with height and weight, so with personality and intelligence scores: Heritable individual differences need not imply heritable group differences. If some *individuals* are genetically disposed to be more aggressive than others, that needn't explain why some *groups* are more aggressive than others. Putting people in a new social context can change their aggressiveness. Today's peaceful Scandinavians carry many genes inherited from their Viking warrior ancestors.

 LaunchPad For a 7-minute explanation of genes and environment, visit LaunchPad's *Video: Behavior Genetics.*

RETRIEVAL PRACTICE

• Those studying the *heritability* of a trait try to determine how much of the person-to-person variation in that trait among members of a specific group is due to their differing _____.

ANSWER: genes

Gene–Environment Interaction

"Men's natures are alike; it is their habits that carry them far apart."

Confucius, *Analects,* 500 B.C.E.

"Heredity deals the cards; environment plays the hand."

Psychologist Charles L. Brewer (1990)

Among our similarities, the most important—the behavioral hallmark of our species—is our enormous adaptive capacity. Some human traits, such as having two eyes, develop the same in virtually every environment. But other traits are expressed only in particular environments. Go barefoot for a summer and you will develop toughened, callused feet—a biological adaptation to friction. Meanwhile, your shod neighbor will remain a tenderfoot. The difference between the two of you is an effect of environment. But it is also the product of a biological mechanism—adaptation. Our shared biology enables our developed diversity (Buss, 1991). Thus, to say that genes and experience are *both* important is true. But more precisely, they **interact.** Just *how* our genes and our experiences interact to form us as unique individuals is one of the hottest topics in psychology today.

The New Frontier: Molecular Behavior Genetics

11-5 How is molecular genetics research changing our understanding of the effects of nature and nurture?

Behavior geneticists have progressed beyond asking "Do genes influence behavior?" The new frontier of behavior-genetic research draws on "bottom-up" **molecular genetics,** which studies the molecular structure and function of genes.

Searching for Specific Genes Influencing Behavior Most human traits are influenced by teams of genes. For example, twin and adoption studies tell us that heredity influences body weight, but there is no single "obesity gene." More likely, some genes influence how quickly the stomach tells the brain, "I'm full." Others might dictate how much fuel the muscles need, how many calories are burned off by fidgeting, and how efficiently the body converts extra calories into fat (Vogel, 1999). Genes typically are not solo players. So, one goal of **molecular behavior genetics** is to find some of the many genes that together orchestrate complex traits such as body weight, sexual orientation, and impulsivity (Derringer et al., 2010; Holden, 2008; Tsankova et al., 2007).

Genetic tests can now reveal at-risk populations for dozens of diseases, and the search continues. (For another aspect of genetic testing, see Thinking Critically About: Prenatal Testing to Predict Future Traits.)

Searching for Triggers That Switch Genes On and Off Genes can be either active (expressed, as hot water activates the tea bag) or inactive. **Epigenetics** (meaning "in addition to" or "above and beyond" genetics), studies the molecular mechanisms by which environments can trigger or block genetic expression. Genes are *self-regulating.* Rather than acting as blueprints that lead to the same result no matter the context, genes react. An African butterfly that is green in summer turns brown in fall, thanks to a temperature-controlled genetic switch. The same genes that produced green in one situation will produce brown in another.

Our experiences also lay down *epigenetic marks,* which are often organic methyl molecules attached to part of a DNA strand (**FIGURE 11.3**). If a mark instructs the cell to

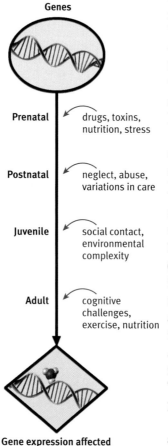

▼ FIGURE 11.3
Epigenetics influences gene expression Life experiences beginning in the womb lay down *epigenetic marks*—often organic methyl molecules—that can affect the expression of any gene in the associated DNA segment. (Inspired by Champagne, 2010.)

Prenatal Testing to Predict Future Traits

11-6 What are some benefits and risks of prenatal genetic testing?

In labs worldwide, molecular geneticists are teaming with psychologists to pinpoint genes that put people at risk for genetically influenced disorders. One worldwide research effort is sleuthing the genes that make people vulnerable to the emotional swings of bipolar disorder, formerly known as manic-depressive disorder. Other searches are targeting conditions such as specific learning disorder, depression, schizophrenia, and alcohol use disorder. But identifying specific culprit genes is often difficult (Hewitt, 2012). The challenge stems from a single gene's typically small effect, and from the sheer number of genes in our human genome (Peikoff, 2013).

Even so, aided by inexpensive DNA-scanning techniques, medical personnel can now give would-be parents a readout on how their fetus' genes differ from normal and help them understand what this might mean. Assuming it were possible, should prospective parents take their eggs and sperm to a genetics lab for screening before combining them to produce an embryo? Should screening of fertilized eggs be limited to health factors? Should we encourage would-be parents to have their genes inspected for rare brain diseases, allowing them to know what they might pass on to their future children (Andersson et al., 2012)? Would prenatal testing be acceptable for traits that predict brains or beauty? Prenatal screening poses ethical dilemmas. In China and India, where boys are highly valued, testing for an offspring's sex has enabled selective abortions resulting in millions—yes, millions—of "missing women."

Progress is a double-edged sword, raising both hopeful possibilities and difficult problems. By selecting out certain traits, such as a vulnerability to a psychological disorder, we may deprive ourselves of future Handels and van Goghs, Churchills and Lincolns, Tolstoys and Dickinsons—troubled people all.

---

ignore any gene present in that DNA segment, those genes will be "turned off"—they will prevent the DNA from producing the proteins normally coded by that gene. As one geneticist said, "Things written in pen you can't change. That's DNA. Things written in pencil you can. That's epigenetics" (Reed, 2012).

Environmental factors such as diet, drugs, and stress can affect the epigenetic molecules that regulate gene expression. Mother rats normally lick their infants. Deprived of this licking, infant rats in one experiment had more epigenetic molecules blocking access to their brain's "on" switch for developing stress hormone receptors. When stressed, those animals had above-average levels of free-floating stress hormones and were more stressed out (Champagne et al., 2003; Champagne & Mashoodh, 2009).

Researchers now wonder if epigenetics might help solve some scientific mysteries, such as why only one member of an identical twin pair may develop a genetically influenced mental disorder, and how childhood abuse leaves its fingerprints in a person's brain (Spector, 2012). Epigenetics can also help explain why identical twins may look slightly different. Researchers studying mice have found that in utero exposure to certain chemicals can cause genetically identical twins to have different-colored fur (Dolinoy et al., 2007). These discoveries will be made easier by efforts such as the National Institute of Health-funded Roadmap Epigenetics Project, a massive undertaking aimed at making epigenetic data publicly available.

RETRIEVAL PRACTICE

- Match the following terms to the correct explanation.

  1. Epigenetics

  2. Molecular behavior genetics

  3. Behavior genetics

  a. Study of the relative effects of our genes and our environment on our behavior.

  b. Study of how the structure and function of specific genes interact with our environment to influence behavior.

  c. Study of environmental factors that affect how our genes are *expressed*.

ANSWERS: 1. c, 2. b, 3. a

---

interaction the interplay that occurs when the effect of one factor (such as environment) depends on another factor (such as heredity).

molecular genetics the subfield of biology that studies the molecular structure and function of genes.

molecular behavior genetics the study of how the structure and function of genes interact with our environment to influence behavior.

epigenetics the study of environmental influences on gene expression that occur without a DNA change.

MODULE 11 **REVIEW** Behavior Genetics: Predicting Individual Differences

LEARNING OBJECTIVES

RETRIEVAL PRACTICE Take a moment to answer each of these Learning Objective Questions (repeated here from within this module). Then turn to Appendix C, Complete Module Reviews, to check your answers. Research suggests that trying to answer these questions on your own will improve your long-term retention (McDaniel et al., 2009).

11-1 What are *chromosomes, DNA, genes,* and the human *genome?* How do behavior geneticists explain our individual differences?

11-2 How do twin and adoption studies help us understand the effects and interactions of nature and nurture?

11-3 What have psychologists learned about temperament?

11-4 What is *heritability,* and how does it relate to individuals and groups?

11-5 How is molecular genetics research changing our understanding of the effects of nature and nurture?

11-6 What are some benefits and risks of prenatal genetic testing?

TERMS AND CONCEPTS TO REMEMBER

RETRIEVAL PRACTICE Test yourself on these terms by trying to write down the definition before flipping back to the page number referenced to check your answer.

behavior genetics, p. 134

environment, p. 134

chromosomes, p. 134

DNA (deoxyribonucleic acid), p. 134

genes, p. 134

genome, p. 135

identical twins (monozygotic twins), p. 135

fraternal twins (dizygotic twins), p. 136

temperament, p. 140

heritability, p. 140

interaction, p. 142

molecular genetics, p. 142

molecular behavior genetics, p. 142

epigenetics, p. 142

Use 🔁 **LearningCurve** to create your personalized study plan, which will direct you to the resources that will help you most in 🔁 **LaunchPad**.

MODULE 12 Evolutionary Psychology: Understanding Human Nature

12-1 How do evolutionary psychologists use natural selection to explain behavior tendencies?

Behavior geneticists explore the genetic and environmental roots of human differences. **Evolutionary psychologists** instead focus mostly on what makes us so much alike as humans. They use Charles Darwin's principle of **natural selection**—"arguably the most momentous idea ever to occur to a human mind," said Richard Dawkins (2007)—to understand the roots of behavior and mental processes. The idea, simplified, is this:

- Organisms' varied offspring compete for survival.

- Certain biological and behavioral variations increase organisms' reproductive and survival chances in their particular environment.

- Offspring that survive are more likely to pass their genes to ensuing generations.

- Thus, over time, population characteristics may change.

To see these principles at work, let's consider a straightforward example in foxes.

Natural Selection and Adaptation

A fox is a wild and wary animal. If you capture a fox and try to befriend it, be careful. Stick your hand in the cage and, if the timid fox cannot flee, it may snack on your fingers. Russian scientist Dmitry Belyaev wondered how our human ancestors had domesticated dogs from their equally wild wolf forebears. Might he, within a comparatively short stretch of time, accomplish a similar feat by transforming the fearful fox into a friendly fox?

evolutionary psychology the study of the evolution of behavior and the mind, using principles of natural selection.

natural selection the principle that, among the range of inherited trait variations, those contributing to reproduction and survival will most likely be passed on to succeeding generations.

mutation a random error in gene replication that leads to a change.

To find out, Belyaev set to work with 30 male and 100 female foxes. From their offspring he selected and mated the tamest 5 percent of males and 20 percent of females. (He measured tameness by the foxes' responses to attempts to feed, handle, and stroke them.) Over more than 30 generations of foxes, Belyaev and his successor, Lyudmila Trut, repeated that simple procedure. Forty years and 45,000 foxes later, they had a new breed of foxes that, in Trut's (1999) words, were "docile, eager to please, and unmistakably domesticated. . . . Before our eyes, 'the Beast' has turned into 'beauty,' as the aggressive behavior of our herd's wild [ancestors] entirely disappeared." So friendly and eager for human contact were these animals, so inclined to whimper to attract attention and to lick people like affectionate dogs, that the cash-strapped institute seized on a way to raise funds—marketing its foxes as house pets.

Eric Isselée/Shutterstock

Over time, traits that give an individual or a species a reproductive advantage are *selected* and will prevail. Animal breeding experiments manipulate genetic selection. Dog breeders have given us sheepdogs that herd, retrievers that retrieve, trackers that track, and pointers that point (Plomin et al., 1997). Psychologists, too, have bred animals to be serene or reactive, quick learners or slow ones.

Does the same process work with naturally occurring selection? Does natural selection explain our human tendencies? Nature has indeed selected advantageous variations from the new gene combinations produced at each human conception plus the **mutations** (random errors in gene replication) that sometimes result. But the tight genetic leash that predisposes a dog's retrieving, a cat's pouncing, or a bird's nesting is looser on humans. The genes selected during our ancestral history provide more than a long leash; they give us a great capacity to learn and therefore to *adapt* to life in varied environments, from the tundra to the jungle. Genes and experience together wire the brain. Our adaptive flexibility in responding to different environments contributes to our *fitness*—our ability to survive and reproduce.

RETRIEVAL PRACTICE

- How are Belyaev and Trut's breeding practices similar to, and how do they differ from, the way natural selection normally occurs?

ANSWER: Over multiple generations, Belyaev and Trut selected and bred foxes that exhibited a trait they desired: tameness. This process is similar to naturally occurring selection, but it differs in that natural selection normally favors traits (including those arising from mutations) that contribute to reproduction and survival.

- Would the heritability of aggressiveness be greater in Belyaev and Trut's foxes, or in a wild population of foxes?

ANSWER: Heritability of aggressiveness would be greater in the wild population, with its greater genetic variation in aggressiveness.

Evolutionary Success Helps Explain Similarities

Human differences grab our attention. The Guinness World Records entertains us with the height of the tallest-ever human, the oldest living person, and the person with the most tattoos. But our deep similarities also demand explanation. In the big picture, our lives are remarkably alike. Visit the international arrivals area at Amsterdam's Schiphol Airport, a world hub where arriving passengers meet their excited loved ones. There you will see the same delighted joy in the faces of Indonesian grandmothers, Chinese children, and homecoming Dutch. Evolutionary psychologist Steven Pinker (2002, p. 73) has noted that it is no wonder our emotions, drives, and reasoning "have a common logic across cultures": Our shared human traits "were shaped by natural selection acting over the course of human evolution."

Differences grab attention, but our similarities run deep Lucky Diamond Rich, born Gregory Paul Mclaren, is a New Zealand performance artist. He has held the world record for the most tattoos. But he also shares a common human concern for disadvantaged children.

Gareth McConnell/eyevine/Redux

Our Genetic Legacy

Our behavioral and biological similarities arise from our shared human *genome,* our common genetic profile. No more than 5 percent of the genetic differences among humans arise from population group differences. Some 95 percent of genetic variation exists *within* populations (Rosenberg et al., 2002). The typical genetic difference between two Icelandic villagers or between two Kenyans is much greater than the *average* difference between the two groups. Thus, if after a worldwide catastrophe only Icelanders or Kenyans survived, the human species would suffer only "a trivial reduction" in its genetic diversity (Lewontin, 1982).

And how did we develop this shared human genome? At the dawn of human history, our ancestors faced certain questions: Who is my ally, who is my foe? With whom should I mate? What food should I eat? Some individuals answered those questions more successfully than others. For example, women who experienced nausea in the critical first three months of pregnancy were genetically predisposed to avoid certain bitter, strongly flavored, and novel foods. Avoiding such foods has survival value, since they are the very foods most often toxic to prenatal development (Profet, 1992; Schmitt & Pilcher, 2004). Early humans disposed to eat nourishing rather than poisonous foods survived to contribute their genes to later generations. Those who deemed leopards "nice to pet" often did not.

Similarly successful were those whose mating helped them produce and nurture offspring. Over generations, the genes of individuals not so disposed tended to be lost from the human gene pool. As success-enhancing genes continued to be selected, behavioral tendencies and thinking and learning capacities emerged that prepared our Stone Age ancestors to survive, reproduce, and send their genes into the future, and into you.

Across our cultural differences, we even share a "universal moral grammar" (Mikhail, 2007). Men and women, young and old, liberal and conservative, living in Sydney or Seoul, all respond negatively when asked, "If a lethal gas is leaking into a vent and is headed toward a room with seven people, is it okay to push someone into the vent—saving the seven but killing the one?" And they all respond more approvingly when asked if it's okay to allow someone to fall into the vent, again sacrificing one life but saving seven. Our shared moral instincts survive from a distant past where we lived in small groups in which direct harm-doing was punished. For all such universal human tendencies, from our intense need to give parental care, to our shared fears and lusts, evolutionary theory proposes a one-stop-shopping explanation (Schloss, 2009).

As inheritors of this prehistoric legacy, we are genetically predisposed to behave in ways that promoted our ancestors' surviving and reproducing. But in some ways, we are biologically prepared for a world that no longer exists. We love the taste of sweets and fats, nutrients that prepared our physically active ancestors to survive food shortages. But few of us now hunt and gather our food. Too often, we search for sweets and fats in fast-food outlets and vending machines. Our natural dispositions, rooted deep in history, are mismatched with today's junk-food and often inactive lifestyle.

Evolutionary Psychology Today

Darwin's theory of evolution has become one of biology's organizing principles. "Virtually no contemporary scientists believe that Darwin was basically wrong," noted Jared Diamond (2001). Today, Darwin's theory lives on in the *second Darwinian revolution,* the application of evolutionary principles to psychology. In concluding *On the Origin of Species,* Darwin (1859, p. 346) anticipated this, foreseeing "open fields for far more important researches. Psychology will be based on a new foundation."

Despite high infant mortality and rampant disease in past millennia, not one of your countless ancestors died childless.

Those who are troubled by an apparent conflict between scientific and religious accounts of human origins may find it helpful to consider that different perspectives of life can be complementary. For example, the scientific account attempts to tell us *when* and *how*; religious creation stories usually aim to tell about an ultimate *who* and *why*. As Galileo explained to the Grand Duchess Christina, "The Bible teaches how to go to heaven, not how the heavens go."

Jacob Hamblin/Shutterstock

Elsewhere in this text, we address questions that intrigue evolutionary psychologists: Why do infants start to fear strangers about the time they become mobile? Why are biological fathers so much less likely than unrelated boyfriends to abuse and murder the children with whom they share a home? Why do so many more people have phobias about spiders, snakes, and heights than about more dangerous threats, such as guns and electricity? And why do we fear air travel so much more than driving?

To see how evolutionary psychologists think and reason, let's pause to explore their answers to two questions: How are males and females alike? How and why does their sexuality differ?

An Evolutionary Explanation of Human Sexuality

12-2 How might an evolutionary psychologist explain male-female differences in sexuality and mating preferences?

Having faced many similar challenges throughout history, males and females have adapted in similar ways: We eat the same foods, avoid the same predators, and perceive, learn, and remember similarly. It is only in those domains where we have faced differing adaptive challenges—most obviously in behaviors related to reproduction—that we differ, say evolutionary psychologists.

Male-Female Differences in Sexuality

And differ we do. Consider sex drives. Both men and women are sexually motivated, some women more so than many men. Yet, on average, who thinks more about sex? Masturbates more often? Initiates more sex? Views more pornography? The answers worldwide: *men, men, men,* and *men* (Baumeister et al., 2001; Lippa, 2009; Petersen & Hyde, 2010). No surprise, then, that in one BBC survey of more than 200,000 people in 53 nations, men everywhere more strongly agreed that "I have a strong sex drive" and "It doesn't take much to get me sexually excited" (Lippa, 2008).

Indeed, "with few exceptions anywhere in the world," reported cross-cultural psychologist Marshall Segall and his colleagues (1990, p. 244), "males are more likely than females to initiate sexual activity." This is the largest sexuality difference between males and females, but there are others (Hyde, 2005; Petersen & Hyde, 2010; Regan & Atkins, 2007). To see if you can predict some of these differences, take the quiz in **TABLE 12.1** on the next page.

Compared with lesbians, gay men (like straight men) have reported more interest in uncommitted sex, more responsiveness to visual sexual stimuli, and more concern with their partner's physical attractiveness (Bailey et al., 1994; Doyle, 2005; Schmitt, 2007; Sprecher et al., 2013). Gay male couples report having sex more often than do

"Not tonight, hon, I have a concussion."

"It's not that gay men are oversexed; they are simply men whose male desires bounce off other male desires rather than off female desires."

Steven Pinker, *How the Mind Works*, 1997

What evolutionary psychologists study Each word's size in this "word cloud" shows how frequently it has appeared in evolutionary psychology article titles. (Derived by Gregory Webster, Peter Jonason, and Tatiana Schember [2009] from all articles published in *Evolution and Human Behavior* between 1997 and 2008.)

Webster, G. D., Jonason, P. K., & Schember, T. O. (2009). Hot topics and popular papers in evolutionary psychology: Analyses of title words and citation counts in *Evolution and Human Behavior*, 1979–2008. *Evolutionary Psychology*, 7, 348–362.

▼ TABLE 12.1
Predict the Responses

Researchers asked samples of U.S. adults whether they agreed or disagreed with the following statements. For each item below, give your best guess about the percentage who agreed with the statement.

Statement	Percentage of males who agreed	Percentage of females who agreed
1. If two people really like each other, it's all right for them to have sex even if they've known each other for a very short time.	_____	_____
2. I can imagine myself being comfortable and enjoying "casual" sex with different partners.	_____	_____
3. Affection was the reason I first had intercourse.	_____	_____
4. I think about sex every day, or several times a day.	_____	_____

Answers: (1) males, 58 percent; females, 34 percent; (2) males, 48 percent; females, 12 percent; (3) males, 25 percent; females, 48 percent; (4) males, 54 percent; females, 19 percent.

Sources: (1) Pryor et al., 2005; (2) Bailey et al., 2000; (3 and 4) Adapted from Laumann et al., 1994.

lesbian couples (Peplau & Fingerhut, 2007). And in the first year of Vermont's same-sex civil unions, and among the first 12,000 Massachusetts same-sex marriages, a striking fact emerged. Although men are roughly two-thirds of the gay population, they were only about one-third of those electing legal partnership (Crary, 2009; Rothblum, 2007).

Heterosexual men often misperceive a woman's friendliness as a sexual come-on (Abbey, 1987). In one speed-dating study, men believed their dating partners expressed more sexual interest than the partners reported actually expressing (Perilloux et al., 2012). This *sexual overperception bias* is strongest among men who require little emotional closeness before intercourse (Howell et al., 2012; Perilloux et al., 2012).

🌊 LaunchPad To listen to experts discuss evolutionary psychology and sex differences, visit LaunchPad's *Video: Evolutionary Psychology and Sex Differences.*

Natural Selection and Mating Preferences

The principle of natural selection proposes that nature selects traits and appetites that contribute to survival and reproduction. Evolutionary psychologists use this principle to explain how men and women differ more in the bedroom than in the boardroom. Our natural yearnings, they say, are our genes' way of reproducing themselves. "Humans are living fossils—collections of mechanisms produced by prior selection pressures" (Buss, 1995).

Why do women tend to be choosier than men when selecting sexual partners? Women have more at stake. To send her genes into the future, a woman must—at a minimum—conceive and protect a fetus growing inside her body for up to nine months. And unlike men, women are limited in how many children they can have between puberty and menopause. No surprise then, that heterosexual women prefer partners who will offer their joint offspring support and protection. They prefer stick-around dads over likely cads. Heterosexual women are attracted to tall men with slim waists and broad shoulders—all signs of reproductive success (Mautz et al., 2012). And

"I had a nice time, Steve. Would you like to come in, settle down, and raise a family?"

they prefer men who appear mature, dominant, bold, and affluent (Asendorpf et al., 2011; Gangestad & Simpson, 2000; Singh, 1995). One study of hundreds of Welsh pedestrians asked people to rate a driver pictured at the wheel of a humble Ford Fiesta or a swanky Bentley. Men said a female driver was equally attractive in both cars. Women, however, found a male driver more attractive if he was in the luxury car (Dunn & Searle, 2010). When put in a mating mindset, men buy more showy items, express more aggressive intentions, and take more risks (Baker & Maner, 2009; Griskevicius et al., 2009; Shan et al., 2012; Sundie et al., 2011).

The data are in, say evolutionists: Men pair widely; women pair wisely. And what traits do straight men find desirable? Some, such as a woman's smooth skin and youthful shape, cross place and time, and they convey health and fertility (Buss, 1994). Mating with such women might give a man a better chance of sending his genes into the future. And sure enough, men feel most attracted to women whose waists (thanks to their genes or their surgeons) are roughly a third narrower than their hips—a sign of future fertility (Perilloux et al., 2010). Even blind men show this preference for women with a low waist-to-hip ratio (Karremans et al., 2010). Men are most attracted to women whose ages in the ancestral past (when ovulation began later than today) would be associated with peak fertility (Kenrick et al., 2009). Thus, teen boys are most excited by a woman several years older than themselves, mid-twenties men prefer women around their own age, and older men prefer younger women. This pattern consistently appears across European singles ads, Indian marital ads, and marriage records from North and South America, Africa, and the Philippines (Singh, 1993; Singh & Randall, 2007).

There is a principle at work here, say evolutionary psychologists: Nature selects behaviors that increase the likelihood of sending one's genes into the future. As mobile gene machines, we are designed to prefer whatever worked for our ancestors in their environments. They were genetically predisposed to act in ways that would leave grandchildren. Had they not been, we wouldn't be here. As carriers of their genetic legacy, we are similarly predisposed.

MGP/Photodisc/Getty Images

"She's beautiful, and therefore to be woo'd."

William Shakespeare, *King Henry IV*

🔵 **LaunchPad** To experience a demonstration and explanation of evolutionary psychology and mating preferences, visit LaunchPad's *PsychSim 6: Dating and Mating.*

Critiquing the Evolutionary Perspective

12-3 What are the key criticisms of evolutionary explanations of human sexuality, and how do evolutionary psychologists respond?

Most psychologists agree that natural selection prepares us for survival and reproduction. But critics say there is a weakness in the reasoning evolutionary psychologists use to explain our mating preferences. Let's consider how an evolutionary psychologist might explain the findings in a startling study (Clark & Hatfield, 1989), and how a critic might object.

Participants were approached by a "stranger" of the other sex (someone working for the experimenter). The stranger remarked "I have been noticing you around campus. I find you to be very attractive," and then asked one of three questions:

1. Would you go out with me tonight?

2. Would you come over to my apartment tonight?

3. Would you go to bed with me tonight?

social script culturally modeled guide for how to act in various situations.

"It is dangerous to show a man too clearly how much he resembles the beast, without at the same time showing him his greatness. It is also dangerous to allow him too clear a vision of his greatness without his baseness. It is even more dangerous to leave him in ignorance of both."

Blaise Pascal, *Pensées,* 1659

What percentage of men and women do you think agreed to each offer? The evolutionary explanation of sexuality predicts that women will be choosier than men in selecting their sexual partners and will be less willing to hop in bed with a complete stranger. In fact, not a single woman—but 70 percent of men—agreed to question 3. A recent repeat of this study produced a similar result in France (Gueguen, 2011). The research seemed to support an evolutionary explanation.

Or did it? Critics note that evolutionary psychologists start with an effect—in this case, the survey result showing that men were more likely to accept casual sex offers—and work backward to explain what happened. What if research showed the opposite effect? If men refused an offer for casual sex, might we not reason that men who partner with one woman for life make better fathers, whose children more often survive?

Other critics ask why we should try to explain today's behavior based on decisions our distant ancestors made thousands of years ago. They believe social learning theory offers a better, more immediate explanation for these results. Perhaps women learn **social scripts**—their culture's guide to how people should act in certain situations. By watching and imitating others in their culture, they may learn that sexual encounters with strangers are dangerous, and that men who ask for casual sex will not offer women much sexual pleasure (Conley, 2011). This alternative explanation of the study's effects proposes that women react to sexual encounters in ways that their modern culture teaches them.

A third criticism focuses on the social consequences of accepting an evolutionary explanation. Are heterosexual men truly hard-wired to have sex with any woman who approaches them? If so, does it mean that men have no moral responsibility to remain faithful to their partners? Does this explanation excuse men's sexual aggression—"boys will be boys"—because of our evolutionary history?

Evolutionary psychologists agree that much of who we are is *not* hard-wired. "Evolution forcefully rejects a genetic determinism," insisted one research team (Confer et al., 2010). And evolutionary psychologists remind us that men and women, having faced similar adaptive problems, are far more alike than different. Natural selection has prepared us to be flexible. We humans have a great capacity for learning and social progress. We adjust and respond to varied environments. We adapt and survive, whether we live in the Arctic or the desert.

Evolutionary psychologists also agree with their critics that some traits and behaviors, such as suicide, are hard to explain in terms of natural selection (Barash, 2012; Confer et al., 2010). But they ask us to remember evolutionary psychology's scientific goal: to explain behaviors and mental traits by offering testable predictions using principles of natural selection. We can, for example, scientifically test hypotheses such as: Do we tend to favor others to the extent that they share our genes or can later return our favors? (The answer is *Yes.*) They also remind us that studying how we *came to be* need not dictate how we *ought to be.* Understanding our tendencies can help us overcome them.

RETRIEVAL PRACTICE

- How do evolutionary psychologists explain sex differences in sexuality?

ANSWER: Evolutionary psychologists theorize that females have inherited their ancestors' tendencies to be more cautious, sexually, because of the challenges associated with incubating and nurturing offspring. Males have inherited an inclination to be more casual about sex, because their act of fathering requires a smaller investment.

- What are the three main criticisms of the evolutionary explanation of human sexuality?

ANSWER: (1) It starts with an effect and works backward to propose an explanation. (2) Unethical and immoral men could use such explanations to rationalize their behavior toward women. (3) This explanation may overlook the effects of cultural expectations and socialization.

MODULE 12 REVIEW Evolutionary Psychology: Understanding Human Nature

LEARNING OBJECTIVES

RETRIEVAL PRACTICE Take a moment to answer each of these Learning Objective Questions (repeated here from within this module). Then turn to Appendix C, Complete Module Reviews, to check your answers. Research suggests that trying to answer these questions on your own will improve your long-term retention (McDaniel et al., 2009).

12-1 How do evolutionary psychologists use natural selection to explain behavior tendencies?

12-2 How might an evolutionary psychologist explain male-female differences in sexuality and mating preferences?

12-3 What are the key criticisms of evolutionary explanations of human sexuality, and how do evolutionary psychologists respond?

TERMS AND CONCEPTS TO REMEMBER

RETRIEVAL PRACTICE Test yourself on these terms by trying to write down the definition before flipping back to the page number referenced to check your answer.

evolutionary psychology, p. 144

natural selection, p. 144

mutation, p. 145

social script, p. 150

Use 🔵 **LearningCurve** to create your personalized study plan, which will direct you to the resources that will help you most in 🔵 **LaunchPad**.

MODULE 13 Culture, Gender, and Other Environmental Influences

From conception onward, we are the product of a cascade of interactions between our genetic predispositions and our surrounding environments (McGue, 2010). Our genes affect how people react to and influence us. Forget nature *versus* nurture; think nature *via* nurture.

Imagine two babies, one genetically predisposed to be attractive, sociable, and easygoing, the other less so. Assume further that the first baby attracts more affectionate and stimulating care and so develops into a warmer and more outgoing person. As the two children grow older, the more naturally outgoing child may seek more activities and friends that encourage further social confidence.

What has caused their resulting personality differences? Neither heredity nor experience acts alone. Environments trigger gene activity. And our genetically influenced traits *evoke* significant responses in others. Thus, a child's impulsivity and aggression may evoke an angry response from a parent or teacher, who reacts warmly to model children in the family or classroom. In such cases, the child's nature and the parents' nurture interact. Gene and scene dance together.

Gene-environment interaction
Biological appearances have social consequences. People respond differently to recording artist Nicki Minaj and concert violinist Hilary Hahn.

Identical twins not only share the same genetic predispositions, they also seek and create similar experiences that express their shared genes (Kandler et al., 2012). Evocative interactions may help explain why identical twins raised in different families recall their parents' warmth as remarkably similar—almost as similar as if they had been raised by the same parents (Plomin et al., 1988, 1991, 1994). Fraternal twins have more differing recollections of their early family life—even if raised in the same family! "Children experience us as different parents, depending on their own qualities," noted Sandra Scarr (1990). Moreover, a selection effect may be at work. As we grow older, we select environments well suited to our natures. Talkative children may become salespeople. Shy children may become laboratory technicians.

How Does Experience Influence Development?

Our genes, when expressed in specific environments, influence our developmental differences. We are not "blank slates" (Kenrick et al., 2009). We are more like coloring books, with certain lines predisposed and experience filling in the full picture. We are formed by nature *and* nurture. But what are the most influential components of our nurture? How do our early experiences, our family and peer relationships, and all our other experiences guide our development and contribute to our diversity?

The formative nurture that conspires with nature begins at conception, with the prenatal environment in the womb, where embryos receive differing nutrition and varying levels of exposure to toxic agents. Nurture then continues outside the womb, where our early experiences foster brain development.

Experience and Brain Development

13-1 How do early experiences modify the brain?

Our genes dictate our overall brain architecture, but experience fills in the details. Developing neural connections prepare our brain for thought, language, and other later experiences. So how do early experiences leave their "fingerprints" in the brain? Mark Rosenzweig, David Krech, and their colleagues (1962) opened a window on that process when they raised some young rats in solitary confinement and others in a communal playground. When they later analyzed the rats' brains, those who died with the most toys had won. The rats living in the enriched environment, which simulated a natural environment, usually developed a heavier and thicker brain cortex (**FIGURE 13.1**).

Rosenzweig was so surprised by this discovery that he repeated the experiment several times before publishing his findings (Renner & Rosenzweig, 1987; Rosenzweig, 1984). So great are the effects that, shown brief video clips of rats, you could tell from their activity and curiosity whether their environment had been impoverished or enriched (Renner & Renner, 1993). After 60 days in the enriched environment, the rats' brain weights increased 7 to 10 percent and the number of synapses mushroomed by about 20 percent (Kolb & Whishaw, 1998).

Courtesy of C. Brune

Stringing the circuits young String musicians who started playing before age 12 have larger and more complex neural circuits controlling the note-making left-hand fingers than do string musicians whose training started later (Elbert et al., 1995).

▼ FIGURE 13.1
Experience affects brain development Mark Rosenzweig, David Krech, and their colleagues (1962) raised rats either alone in an environment without playthings, or with other rats in an environment enriched with playthings changed daily. In 14 of 16 repetitions of this basic experiment, rats in the enriched environment developed significantly more cerebral cortex (relative to the rest of the brain's tissue) than did those in the impoverished environment.

Impoverished environment   **Impoverished rat brain cell**   **Enriched environment**   **Enriched rat brain cell**

Such results have motivated improvements in environments for laboratory, farm, and zoo animals—and for children in institutions. Stimulation by touch or massage also benefits infant rats and premature babies (Field et al., 2007). "Handled" infants of both species develop faster neurologically and gain weight more rapidly. Preemies who have had skin-to-skin contact with their mothers sleep better, experience less stress, and show better cognitive development 10 years later (Feldman et al., 2014).

Nature and nurture interact to sculpt our synapses. Brain maturation provides us with an abundance of neural connections. Experiences trigger sights and smells, touches and tugs, and activate and strengthen connections. Unused neural pathways weaken. Like forest pathways, popular tracks are broadened and less-traveled ones gradually disappear. By puberty, this *pruning process* results in a massive loss of unemployed connections.

Here at the juncture of nurture and nature is the biological reality of early childhood learning. During early childhood—while excess connections are still on call—youngsters can most easily master such skills as the grammar and accent of another language. Lacking any exposure to language before adolescence, a person will never master any language. Likewise, lacking visual experience during the early years, a person whose vision is later restored by cataract removal will never achieve normal perceptions (Gregory, 1978; Wiesel, 1982). Without that early visual stimulation, the brain cells normally assigned to vision will die or be diverted to other uses. The maturing brain's rule: Use it or lose it.

Although normal stimulation during the early years is critical, the brain's development does not end with childhood. Thanks to the brain's amazing *plasticity*, our neural tissue is ever changing and reorganizing in response to new experiences. New neurons are also born. If a monkey pushes a lever with the same finger many times a day, brain tissue controlling that finger will change to reflect the experience (**FIGURE 13.2**). Human brains work similarly. Whether learning to keyboard, skateboard, or navigate London's streets, we perform with increasing skill as our brain incorporates the learning (Ambrose, 2010; Maguire et al., 2000).

> "Genes and experiences are just two ways of doing the same thing—wiring synapses."
>
> Joseph LeDoux, *The Synaptic Self,* 2002

Courtesy of Avi Karni & Leslie Ungerleider, National Institute of Mental Health

▼ FIGURE 13.2
A trained brain A well-learned finger-tapping task activates more motor cortex neurons (orange area, right) than were active in this monkey's brain before training (left). (From Karni et al., 1998.)

How Much Credit or Blame Do Parents Deserve?

13-2 In what ways do parents and peers shape children's development?

In procreation, a woman and a man shuffle their gene decks and deal a life-forming hand to their child-to-be, who is then subjected to countless influences beyond their control. Parents, nonetheless, feel enormous satisfaction in their children's successes or guilt and shame over their failures. They beam over the child who wins trophies and titles. They wonder where they went wrong with the child who is repeatedly in trouble. Freudian psychiatry and psychology encouraged such ideas by blaming problems from asthma to schizophrenia on "bad mothering." Society has reinforced such parent blaming: Believing that parents shape their offspring as a potter molds clay, people readily

"*To be frank, officer, my parents never set boundaries.*"

"So I blame you for everything—whose fault is that?"

A controlling mom Amy Chua, law professor and author of *Battle Hymn of the Tiger Mother* (2011), sparked controversy by comparing strict "Chinese" and more permissive "Western" parenting styles. In raising her two daughters, Chua came to appreciate the benefits and the costs of the more externally controlled traditional Chinese parenting.

"Men resemble the times more than they resemble their fathers."

Ancient Arab proverb

praise parents for their children's virtues and blame them for their children's vices. Popular culture endlessly proclaims the psychological harm toxic parents inflict on their fragile children. No wonder having and raising children can seem so risky.

But do parents really produce future adults with an inner wounded child by being (take your pick from the toxic-parenting lists) overbearing—or uninvolved? Pushy—or indecisive? Overprotective—or distant? Are children really so easily wounded? If so, should we then blame our parents for our failings, and ourselves for our children's failings? Or does talk of wounding fragile children through normal parental mistakes trivialize the brutality of real abuse?

Parents do matter. But parenting wields its largest effects at the extremes: the abused children who become abusive, the neglected who become neglectful, the loved but firmly handled who become self-confident and socially competent. The power of the family environment also appears in the remarkable academic and vocational successes of children of people who fled war-torn Vietnam and Cambodia—successes attributed to close-knit, supportive, even demanding families (Caplan et al., 1992). Asian Americans and European Americans differ in their expectations for mothering. An Asian-American mother may push (or "nag," as one study called it) her children to do well, but that pressure likely won't strain their relationship (Fu & Markus, 2014). Having a supportive "Tiger Mother"—one who pushes them to do well and works alongside them (versus forcing them to work alone)—motivates Asian-American children to work harder. European Americans might view that kind of parenting as "smothering-mothering," believing that it undermines children's motivation (Deal, 2011).

Yet in personality measures, shared environmental influences from the womb onward typically account for less than 10 percent of children's differences. In the words of behavior geneticists Robert Plomin and Denise Daniels (1987; Plomin, 2011), "Two children in the same family are [apart from their shared genes] as different from one another as are pairs of children selected randomly from the population." To developmental psychologist Sandra Scarr (1993), this implied that "parents should be given less credit for kids who turn out great and blamed less for kids who don't." Knowing children are not easily sculpted by parental nurture, perhaps parents can relax a bit more and love their children for who they are.

Peer Influence

As children mature, what other experiences do the work of nurturing? At all ages, but especially during childhood and adolescence, we seek to fit in with our groups (Harris, 1998, 2000):

- Preschoolers who disdain a certain food often will eat that food if put at a table with a group of children who like it.

- Children who hear English spoken with one accent at home and another in the neighborhood and at school will invariably adopt the accent of their peers, not their parents. Accents (and slang) reflect culture, "and children get their culture from their peers," as Judith Rich Harris (2007), has noted.

- Teens who start smoking typically have friends who model smoking, suggest its pleasures, and offer cigarettes (J. S. Rose et al., 1999; R. J. Rose et al., 2003). Part of this peer similarity may result from *a selection effect,* as kids seek out peers with similar attitudes and interests. Those who smoke (or don't) may select as friends those who also smoke (or don't).

- Put two teens together and their brains become hypersensitive to reward (Albert et al., 2013). This increased activation helps explain why teens take more driving risks when with friends than they do when alone (Chein et al., 2011).

Howard Gardner (1998) has concluded that parents and peers are complementary:

> Parents are more important when it comes to education, discipline, responsibility, orderliness, charitableness, and ways of interacting with authority figures. Peers are more important for learning cooperation, for finding the road to popularity, for inventing styles of interaction among people of the same age. Youngsters may find their peers more interesting, but they will look to their parents when contemplating their own futures. Moreover, parents [often] choose the neighborhoods and schools that supply the peers.

This power to select a child's neighborhood and schools gives parents an ability to influence the culture that shapes the child's peer group. And because neighborhood influences matter, parents may want to become involved in intervention programs that aim at a whole school or neighborhood. If the vapors of a toxic climate are seeping into a child's life, that climate—not just the child—needs reforming. Even so, peers are but one medium of cultural influence. As an African proverb declares, "It takes a village to raise a child."

RETRIEVAL PRACTICE

- What is the *selection effect,* and how might it affect a teen's decision to drink alcohol?

ANSWER: Adolescents tend to *select* out similar others and sort themselves into like-minded groups. This could lead a teen who wants to experiment with drinking alcohol to seek out others who already drink alcohol.

Peer power As we develop, we play, mate, and partner with peers. No wonder children and youths are so sensitive and responsive to peer influences.

Cultural Influences

13-3 How does culture affect our behavior?

Compared with the narrow path taken by flies, fish, and foxes, the road along which environment drives us is wider. The mark of our species—nature's great gift to us—is our ability to learn and adapt. We come equipped with a huge cerebral hard drive ready to receive cultural software.

Culture is the behaviors, ideas, attitudes, values, and traditions shared by a group of people and transmitted from one generation to the next (Brislin, 1988; Cohen, 2009). Human nature, noted Roy Baumeister (2005), seems designed for culture. We are social animals, but more. Wolves are social animals; they live and hunt in packs. Ants are incessantly social, never alone. But "culture is a better way of being social," noted Baumeister. Wolves function pretty much as they did 10,000 years ago. You and I enjoy things unknown to most of our century-ago ancestors, including electricity, indoor plumbing, antibiotics, and the Internet. Culture works.

Other animals exhibit smaller kernels of culture. Primates have local customs of tool use, grooming, and courtship. Chimpanzees sometimes invent customs using leaves to clean their bodies, slapping branches to get attention, and doing a "rain dance" by slowly displaying themselves at the start of rain and pass them on to their peers and offspring (Whiten et al., 1999). Culture supports a species' survival and reproduction by transmitting learned behaviors that give a group an edge. But human culture does more.

Thanks to our mastery of language, we humans enjoy the *preservation of innovation.* Within the span of this day, we have used Google, laser printers, digital hearing technology [DM], and a GPS running watch [ND]. On a grander scale, we have culture's accumulated knowledge to thank for the last century's 30-year extension of the average

culture the enduring behaviors, ideas, attitudes, values, and traditions shared by a group of people and transmitted from one generation to the next.

norm an understood rule for accepted and expected behavior. Norms prescribe "proper" behavior.

human life expectancy in most countries where this book is being read. Moreover, culture enables an efficient *division of labor*. Although two lucky people get their name on this book's cover, the product actually results from the coordination and commitment of a gifted team of people, no one of whom could produce it alone.

Across cultures, we differ in our language, our monetary systems, our sports, even which side of the road we drive on. But beneath these differences is our great similarity—our capacity for culture. Culture works. It transmits the customs and beliefs that enable us to communicate, to exchange money for things, to play, to eat, and to drive with agreed-upon rules and without crashing into one another.

Variation Across Cultures

We see our adaptability in cultural variations among our beliefs and our values, in how we nurture our children and bury our dead, and in what we wear (or whether we wear anything at all). We are ever mindful that the readers of this book are culturally diverse. You and your ancestors reach from Australia to Africa and from Singapore to Sweden.

Riding along with a unified culture is like running with the wind: As it carries us along, we hardly notice it is there. When we try running *against* the wind we feel its force. Face to face with a different culture, we become aware of the cultural winds. Visiting Europe, most North Americans notice the smaller cars, the left-handed use of the fork, the uninhibited attire on the beaches. Stationed in Iraq, Afghanistan, and Kuwait, American and European soldiers alike realized how liberal their home cultures were. Arriving in North America, visitors from Japan and India struggle to understand why so many people wear their dirty *street* shoes in the house.

But humans in varied cultures nevertheless share some basic moral ideas. Even before they can walk, babies prefer helpful people over naughty ones (Hamlin et al., 2011). Yet each cultural group also evolves its own **norms**—rules for accepted and expected behavior. The British have a norm for orderly waiting in line. Many South Asians use only the right hand's fingers for eating. Sometimes social expectations seem oppressive: "Why should it matter how I dress?" Yet, norms grease the social machinery and free us from self-preoccupation.

When cultures collide, their differing norms often befuddle. Should we greet people by shaking hands, bowing, or kissing each cheek? Knowing what sorts of gestures and compliments are culturally appropriate, we can relax and enjoy one another without fear of embarrassment or insult.

When we don't understand what's expected or accepted, we may experience *culture shock*. People from Mediterranean cultures have perceived northern Europeans as efficient but cold and preoccupied with punctuality (Triandis, 1981). People from time-conscious Japan—where bank clocks keep exact time, pedestrians walk briskly, and postal clerks fill requests speedily—have found themselves growing impatient when visiting Indonesia, where clocks keep less accurate time and the pace of life is more leisurely (Levine & Norenzayan, 1999). Someone from the European community, which requires 20 paid vacation days each year, may also experience culture shock when working in the United States, which does not guarantee workers any paid vacation (Ray et al., 2013).

Variation Over Time

Like biological creatures, cultures vary and compete for resources, and thus evolve over time (Mesoudi, 2009). Consider how rapidly cultures may change. English poet Geoffrey Chaucer (1342–1400) is separated from a modern Briton by only 20 generations, but the two would have great difficulty speaking. In the thin slice of history since 1960, most Western cultures have changed with remarkable speed. Middle-class people fly to places they once only read about. They enjoy the convenience of air-conditioned housing, online shopping, anywhere-anytime electronic communication, and—enriched by doubled per-person real income—eating out more than twice as often as did their grandparents back in the culture of 1960. Many minority groups enjoy expanded human rights. And, with greater economic independence, today's women more often marry for love and less often endure abusive relationships.

But some changes seem not so wonderfully positive. Had you fallen asleep in the United States in 1960 and awakened today, you would open your eyes to a culture with more divorce and depression. You would also find North Americans—like their counterparts in Britain, Australia, and New Zealand—spending more hours at work, fewer hours with friends and family, and fewer hours asleep (BLS, 2011; Putnam, 2000).

Whether we love or loathe these changes, we cannot fail to be impressed by their breathtaking speed. And we cannot explain them by changes in the human gene pool, which evolves far too slowly to account for high-speed cultural transformations. Cultures vary. Cultures change. And cultures shape our lives.

Culture and the Self

13-4 How do individualist and collectivist cultures differ in their values and goals?

Imagine that someone ripped away your social connections, making you a solitary refugee in a foreign land. How much of your identity would remain intact?

If you are an **individualist,** a great deal of your identity would remain intact. You would have an independent sense of "me," and an awareness of your unique personal convictions and values. Individualists give higher priority to personal goals. They define their identity mostly in terms of personal traits. They strive for personal control and individual achievement.

Individualism is valued in most areas of North America, Western Europe, Australia, and New Zealand. The United States is mostly an individualist culture. Founded by settlers who wanted to differentiate themselves from others, Americans have cherished the "pioneer" spirit (Kitayama et al., 2010). Some 85 percent of Americans say it is possible "to pretty much be who you want to be" (Sampson, 2000).

Individualists share the human need to belong. They join groups. But they are less focused on group harmony and doing their duty to the group (Brewer & Chen, 2007). Being more self-contained, individualists move in and out of social groups more easily. They feel relatively free to switch places of worship, switch jobs, or even leave their extended families and migrate to a new place. Marriage is often for as long as they both shall love.

Although individuals within cultures vary, different cultures emphasize either individualism or collectivism. If set adrift in a foreign land as a **collectivist,** you might experience a greater loss of identity. Cut off from family, groups, and loyal friends, you would lose the connections that have defined who you are. *Group identifications* provide a sense of belonging, a set of values, and an assurance of security in collectivist cultures. In return, collectivists have deeper, more stable attachments to their groups—their family, clan, or company. Elders receive great respect. In some collectivist cultures, disrespecting family elders violates the law. The *Law of the People's Republic of China on Protection of the Rights and Interests of the Elderly* states that parents aged 60 or above can sue their sons and daughters if they fail to provide "for the elderly, taking care of them and comforting them, and cater[ing] to their special needs."

Collectivists are like athletes who take more pleasure in their team's victory than in their own performance. They find satisfaction in advancing their groups' interests, even at the expense of personal needs. Preserving group spirit and avoiding social embarrassment are important goals. Collectivists therefore avoid direct confrontation, blunt honesty, and uncomfortable topics. They value humility, not self-importance (Bond et al., 2012). Instead of dominating conversations, collectivists hold back and

individualism giving priority to one's own goals over group goals and defining one's identity in terms of personal attributes rather than group identifications.

collectivism giving priority to the goals of one's group (often one's extended family or work group) and defining one's identity accordingly.

The New Yorker Collection, 2000. From cartoonbank.com

"One needs to cultivate the spirit of sacrificing the *little me* to achieve the benefits of the *big me*."

Chinese saying

Considerate collectivists Japan's collectivist values, including duty to others and social harmony, were on display after the devastating 2011 earthquake and tsunami. Virtually no looting was reported, and residents remained calm and orderly, as shown here while waiting for drinking water.

Kyodo/Reuters/Landov

display shyness when meeting strangers (Cheek & Melchior, 1990). When the priority is "we," not "me," that individualized latte—"decaf, single shot, skinny, extra hot"—that feels so good in a North American coffee shop might sound like a selfish demand in Seoul (Kim & Markus, 1999).

To be sure, there is diversity within cultures. Within many countries, there are also distinct subcultures related to one's religion, economic status, and region (Cohen, 2009). In China, greater collectivist thinking occurs in provinces that produce large amounts of rice, a difficult-to-grow crop that often involves cooperation between groups of people (Talhelm et al., 2014). In collectivist Japan, a spirit of individualism marks the "northern frontier" island of Hokkaido (Kitayama et al., 2006). And even in the most individualist countries, some people have collectivist values. But in general, people (especially men) in competitive, individualist cultures have more personal freedom, are less geographically bound to their families, enjoy more privacy, and take more pride in personal achievements (**TABLE 13.1**).

Individualists even prefer unusual names, as psychologist Jean Twenge noticed while seeking a name for her first child. Over time, the most common American names listed by year on the U.S. Social Security baby names website were becoming less desirable. When she and her colleagues (2010) analyzed the first names of 325 million American babies born between 1880 and 2007, they confirmed this trend. As **FIGURE 13.3** illustrates, the percentage of boys and girls given one of the 10 most common names for their birth year has plunged, especially in recent years. Even

▼ TABLE 13.1
Value Contrasts Between Individualism and Collectivism

Concept	Individualism	Collectivism
Self	Independent (identity from individual traits)	Interdependent (identity from belonging)
Life task	Discover and express one's uniqueness	Maintain connections, fit in, perform role
What matters	Me—personal achievement and fulfillment; rights and liberties; self-esteem	Us—group goals and solidarity; social responsibilities and relationships; family duty
Coping method	Change reality	Accommodate to reality
Morality	Defined by individuals (self-based)	Defined by social networks (duty-based)
Relationships	Many, often temporary or casual; confrontation acceptable	Few, close and enduring; harmony valued
Attributing behavior	Behavior reflects one's personality and attitudes	Behavior reflects social norms and roles

Sources: Adapted from Thomas Schoeneman (1994) and Harry Triandis (1994).

within the United States, parents from more recently settled states (for example, Utah and Arizona) give their children more distinct names compared with parents who live in more established states (for example, New York and Massachusetts) (Varnum & Kitayama, 2011).

The individualist–collectivist divide appeared in reactions to medals received during the 2000 and 2002 Olympic games. U.S. gold medal winners and the U.S. media covering them attributed the achievements mostly to the athletes themselves (Markus et al., 2006). "I think I just stayed focused," explained swimming gold medalist Misty Hyman. "It was time to show the world what I could do. I am just glad I was able to do it." Japan's gold medalist in the women's marathon, Naoko Takahashi, had a different explanation: "Here is the best coach in the world, the best manager in the world, and all of the people who support me—all of these things were getting together and became a gold medal." Even when describing friends, Westerners tend to use trait-describing adjectives ("*she is helpful*"), whereas East Asians more often use verbs that describe behaviors in context ("*she helps her friends*") (Heine & Buchtel, 2009; Maass et al., 2006).

There has been more loneliness, divorce, homicide, and stress-related disease in individualist cultures (Popenoe, 1993; Triandis et al., 1988). Demands for more romance and personal fulfillment in marriage can subject relationships to more pressure (Dion & Dion, 1993). In one survey, "keeping romance alive" was rated as important to a good marriage by 78 percent of U.S. women but only 29 percent of Japanese women (*American Enterprise*, 1992). In China, love songs have often expressed enduring commitment and friendship (Rothbaum & Tsang, 1998): "We will be together from now on. . . . I will never change from now to forever."

As cultures evolve, some trends weaken and others grow stronger. In Western cultures, individualism increased strikingly over the last century. This trend reached a new high in 2012, when U.S. high school and college students reported the greatest-ever interest in obtaining benefits for themselves and the lowest-ever concern for others (Twenge et al., 2012).

What predicts changes in one culture over time, or between differing cultures? Social history matters. In Western cultures, individualism and independence have been fostered by voluntary migration, a capitalist economy, and a sparsely populated, challenging environment (Kitayama et al., 2009, 2010; Varnum et al., 2010). Might biology also play a role? In search of biological underpinnings to such cultural differences—remembering that everything psychological is also biological—a new subfield, *cultural neuroscience,* is studying how neurobiology and cultural traits influence each other (Chiao et al., 2013). One study compared collectivists' and individualists' brain

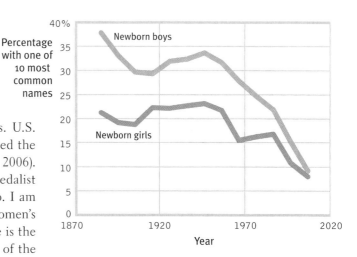

▼ FIGURE 13.3
A child like no other Americans' individualist tendencies are reflected in their choice of names for their babies. In recent years, the percentage of American babies receiving one of that year's 10 most common names has plunged. (Data from Twenge et al., 2010.)

Collectivist culture Although the United States is largely individualist, many cultural subgroups remain collectivist. This is true for Alaska Natives, who demonstrate respect for tribal elders, and whose identity springs largely from their group affiliations.

activity when viewing other people in distress. The brain scans suggested that collectivists experienced greater emotional pain when exposed to others' distress (Cheon et al., 2011). As we will see over and again, biological, psychological, and social-cultural perspectives intersect. We are biopsychosocial creatures.

Culture and Child Raising

Child-raising practices reflect not only individual values, but also cultural values that vary across time and place. Should children be independent or obedient? If you live in a Westernized culture, you likely prefer independence. "You are responsible for yourself," Western families and schools tell their children. "Follow your conscience. Be true to yourself. Discover your gifts. Think through your personal needs." A half-century ago and more, Western cultural values placed greater priority on obedience, respect, and sensitivity to others (Alwin, 1990; Remley, 1988). "Be true to your traditions," parents then taught their children. "Be loyal to your heritage and country. Show respect toward your parents and other superiors." Cultures can change.

Cultures vary Parents everywhere care about their children, but raise and protect them differently depending on the surrounding culture. In metropolitan centers, such as New York City, parents keep children close. In smaller, close-knit communities, such as Scotland's Orkney Islands' town of Stromness, social trust has enabled parents to park their toddlers outside shops.

Children across place and time have thrived under various child-raising systems. Many Americans now give children their own bedrooms and entrust them to day care. Upper-class British parents traditionally handed off routine caregiving to nannies, then sent their 10-year-olds away to boarding school. These children generally grew up to be pillars of British society.

Many Asians and Africans live in cultures that value emotional closeness. Infants and toddlers may sleep with their mothers and spend their days close to a family member (Morelli et al., 1992; Whiting & Edwards, 1988). These cultures encourage a strong sense of *family self*—a feeling that what shames the child shames the family, and what brings honor to the family brings honor to the self.

Parental involvement promotes development Parents in every culture help their children discover the world, but cultures differ in what they deem important. Many Asian cultures place more emphasis on school and hard work than do North American cultures. This may help explain why Japanese and Taiwanese children get higher scores on mathematics achievement tests.

In the African Gusii society, babies nurse freely but spend most of the day on their mother's back—with lots of body contact but little face-to-face and language interaction. When the mother becomes pregnant again, the toddler is weaned and handed over to someone else, often an older sibling. Westerners may wonder about the negative effects of this lack of verbal interaction, but then the African Gusii may in turn wonder about Western mothers pushing their babies around in strollers and leaving them in playpens (Small, 1997). Such diversity in child raising cautions us against presuming that our culture's way is the only way to raise children successfully.

Developmental Similarities Across Groups

Mindful of how others differ from us, we often fail to notice the similarities predisposed by our shared biology. One 49-country study revealed smaller than expected nation-to-nation differences in personality traits, such as conscientiousness and extraversion (Terracciano et al., 2006). National stereotypes exaggerate differences that, although real, are modest: Australians see themselves as outgoing, German-speaking Swiss see themselves as conscientious, and Canadians see themselves as agreeable.

Actually, compared with the person-to-person differences within groups, between-group differences are small. Regardless of our culture, we humans are more alike than different. We share the same life cycle. We speak to our infants in similar ways and respond similarly to their coos and cries (Bornstein et al., 1992a,b). All over the world, the children of warm and supportive parents feel better about themselves and are less hostile than are the children of punitive and rejecting parents (Rohner, 1986; Scott et al., 1991).

Even differences *within* a culture, such as those sometimes attributed to race, are often easily explained by an interaction between our biology and our culture. David Rowe and his colleagues (1994, 1995) illustrated this with an analogy: Black men tend to have higher blood pressure than White men. Suppose that (1) in both groups, salt consumption correlates with blood pressure, and (2) salt consumption is higher among Black men than among White men. The blood pressure "race difference" might then actually be, at least partly, a *diet* difference—a cultural preference for certain foods.

And that, said Rowe and his colleagues, parallels psychological findings. Although Latino, Asian, Black, White, and Native Americans differ in school achievement and delinquency, the differences are "no more than skin deep." To the extent that family structure, peer influences, and parental education predict behavior in one of these ethnic groups, they do so for the others as well.

So as members of different ethnic and cultural groups, we may differ in surface ways. But as members of one species we seem subject to the same psychological forces. Our languages vary, yet they reflect universal principles of grammar. Our tastes vary, yet they reflect common principles of hunger. Our social behaviors vary, yet they reflect pervasive principles of human influence. Cross-cultural research helps us appreciate both our cultural diversity *and* our human similarity.

sex in psychology, the biologically influenced characteristics by which people define *males* and *females*.

gender in psychology, the socially influenced characteristics by which people define *men* and *women*.

"When [someone] has discovered why men in Bond Street wear black hats he will at the same moment have discovered why men in Timbuctoo wear red feathers."

G. K. Chesterton, *Heretics*, 1905

RETRIEVAL PRACTICE

- How do individualist and collectivist cultures differ?

ANSWER: Individualists give priority to personal goals over group goals and tend to define their identity in terms of their own personal attributes. Collectivists give priority to group goals over individual goals and tend to define their identity in terms of group identifications.

Gender Development

13-5 How does the meaning of *gender* differ from the meaning of *sex*?

We humans share an irresistible urge to organize our worlds into simple categories. Among the ways we classify people—as tall or short, younger or older, smart or dull—one stands out. Immediately after your birth (or perhaps even before), everyone wanted to know, "Boy or girl?" Your parents may have offered clues with pink or blue clothing. The simple answer described your **sex**, your biological status, defined by your chromosomes and anatomy. For most people, those biological traits help define their **gender**, their culture's expectations about what it means to be male or female.

Our gender is the product of the interplay among our biological dispositions, our developmental experiences, and our current situations (Eagly & Wood, 2013). Before we consider that interplay in more detail, let's take a closer look at some ways that males and females are both similar and different.

Similarities and Differences

13-6 What are some ways in which males and females tend to be alike and to differ?

Whether male or female, each of us receives 23 chromosomes from our mother and 23 from our father. Of those 46 chromosomes, 45 are unisex. Our similar biology helped our evolutionary ancestors face similar adaptive challenges. Both men and women needed to

Pink and blue baby outfits illustrate how cultural norms vary and change. "The generally accepted rule is pink for the boy and blue for the girl," declared the *Earnshaw's Infants' Department* in June of 1918 (Frassanito & Pettorini, 2008). "The reason is that pink being a more decided and stronger color is more suitable for the boy, while blue, which is more delicate and dainty, is prettier for the girls."

Number of people

Females
Males

Lower scores ——————→ Higher scores
Self-esteem scores

▼ FIGURE 13.4
Much ado about a small difference in self-esteem These two normal distributions differ by the approximate magnitude (0.21 standard deviation) of the sex difference in self-esteem, averaged over all available samples (Hyde, 2005). Moreover, such comparisons illustrate differences between the *average* female and male. The variation among individual females greatly exceeds this difference, as it also does among individual males.

Deadly relational aggression Sladjana Vidovic was a high school student who committed suicide after suffering constant relational aggression by bullies.

Amy Sancetta/AP Photo

survive, reproduce, and avoid predators, and so today we are in most ways alike. Tell me whether you are male or female and you give me no clues to your vocabulary, happiness, or ability to see, hear, learn, and remember. Women and men, on average, have comparable creativity and intelligence and feel the same emotions and longings. Our "opposite" sex is, in reality, our very similar sex.

But in some areas, males and females do differ, and differences command attention. Some much talked-about differences (like the difference in self-esteem shown in **FIGURE 13.4**) are actually quite modest. Other differences are more striking. The average woman enters puberty about a year earlier than the average man, and her life span is 5 years longer. She expresses emotions more freely, can detect fainter odors, and receives offers of help more often. She also has twice the risk of developing depression and anxiety and 10 times the risk of developing an eating disorder. Yet the average man is 4 times more likely to die by suicide or to develop an alcohol use disorder. His "more likely" list includes autism spectrum disorder, color-blindness, and attention-deficit/hyperactivity disorder (ADHD). And as an adult, he is more at risk for antisocial personality disorder. Male or female, each has its own share of risks.

Let's take a closer look at three areas—aggression, social power, and social connectedness—in which the average male and female differ.

Aggression To a psychologist, **aggression** is any physical or verbal behavior intended to hurt someone physically or emotionally. Think of some aggressive people you have heard about. Are most of them men? Men generally admit to more aggression. They also commit more extreme physical violence (Bushman & Huesmann, 2010). In romantic relationships between men and women, minor acts of physical aggression, such as slaps, are roughly equal—but extremely violent acts are mostly committed by men (Archer, 2000; Johnson, 2008).

Laboratory experiments have demonstrated gender differences in aggression. Men have been more willing to blast people with what they believed was intense and prolonged noise (Bushman et al., 2007). And outside the laboratory, men—worldwide—commit more violent crime (Antonaccio et al., 2011; Caddick & Porter, 2012; Frisell et al., 2012). They also take the lead in hunting, fighting, warring, and supporting war (Liddle et al., 2012; Wood & Eagly, 2002, 2007).

Here's another question: Think of examples of people harming others by passing along hurtful gossip, or by shutting someone out of a social group or situation. Were most of those people men? Perhaps not. Those behaviors are acts of **relational aggression,** and women are slightly more likely than men to commit them (Archer, 2004, 2007, 2009).

Social Power Imagine walking into a job interview. You sit down and peer across the table at your two interviewers. The unsmiling person on the left oozes self-confidence and independence and maintains steady eye contact with you. The person on the right gives you a warm, welcoming smile but makes less eye contact and seems to expect the other interviewer to take the lead.

Which interviewer is male?

If you said the person on the left, you're not alone. Around the world, from Nigeria to New Zealand, people have perceived gender differences in power (Williams & Best, 1990). Indeed, in most societies men do place more importance on power and achievement and *are* socially dominant (Schwartz & Rubel-Lifschitz, 2009):

- When groups form, whether as juries or companies, leadership tends to go to males (Colarelli et al., 2006). And when salaries are paid, those in traditionally male occupations receive more.

- When people run for election, women who appear hungry for political power more than their equally power-hungry male counterparts experience less success (Okimoto & Brescoll, 2010). And when elected, political leaders usually are men, who held 78 percent of the seats in the world's governing parliaments in 2014 (IPU, 2014).

Men and women also lead differently. Men tend to be more *directive*, telling people what they want and how to achieve it. Women tend to be more *democratic*, more welcoming of others' input in decision making (Eagly & Carli, 2007; van Engen & Willemsen, 2004). When interacting, men have been more likely to offer opinions, women to express support (Aries, 1987; Wood, 1987). In everyday behavior, men tend to act as powerful people often do: talking assertively, interrupting, initiating touches, and staring. And they smile and apologize less (Leaper & Ayres, 2007; Major et al., 1990; Schumann & Ross, 2010). Such behaviors help sustain men's greater social power.

Social Connectedness Whether male or female, we all have a need to belong, though we may satisfy this need in different ways (Baumeister, 2010). Males tend to be *independent*. Even as children, males typically form large play groups. Boys' games brim with activity and competition, with little intimate discussion (Rose & Rudolph, 2006). As adults, men enjoy doing activities side by side, and they tend to use conversation to communicate solutions (Tannen, 1990; Wright, 1989). When asked a difficult question—"Do you have any idea why the sky is blue?—men are more likely than women to hazard answers than to admit they don't know, a phenomenon researchers have called the *male answer syndrome* (Giuliano et al., 1998).

Females tend to be more *interdependent*. In childhood, girls usually play in small groups, often with one friend. They compete less and imitate social relationships more (Maccoby, 1990; Roberts, 1991). Teen girls spend more time with friends and less time alone (Wong & Csikszentmihalyi, 1991). In late adolescence, they spend more time on social-networking Internet sites (Pryor et al., 2007, 2011). As adults, women take more pleasure in talking face to face, and they tend to use conversation more to explore relationships.

Brain scans suggest that women's brains are better wired to improve social relationships, and men's brains to connect perception with action (Ingalhalikar et al., 2013). The communication style gender difference is apparent even in electronic communication. In one New Zealand study of student e-mails, people correctly guessed two-thirds of the time whether the author was male or female (Thomson & Murachver, 2001). The gap appears in phone-based communications, too. How many texts does an American teen send and receive each day? Girls average 100, boys only 50 (Lenhart, 2012). In France, women have made 63 percent of phone calls and, when talking to a woman, stayed connected longer (7.2 minutes) than men did when talking to other men (4.6 minutes) (Smoreda & Licoppe, 2000).

Do such findings mean that women are just more talkative? *No.* In another study, researchers counted the number of words 396 college students spoke in an average day (Mehl et al., 2007). Not surprisingly, the participants' talkativeness varied enormously—by 45,000 words between the most and least talkative. (How many words would you guess you speak a day?) Contrary to stereotypes of wordy women, both men and women averaged about 16,000 words daily.

The words we use may not peg women or men as more talkative, but those words do open windows on our interests. Worldwide, women's interests and vocations tilt more toward people and less toward things (Eagly, 2009; Lippa, 2005, 2006, 2008). In one analysis of over 700 million words collected from Facebook messages, women used more family-related words, whereas men used more work-related words (Schwartz et al., 2013). More than a half-million people's responses to various interest inventories

aggression any physical or verbal behavior intended to harm someone physically or emotionally.

relational aggression an act of aggression (physical or verbal) intended to harm a person's relationship or social standing.

Women's 2011 representations in national parliaments ranged from 13 percent in the Pacific region to 42 percent in Scandinavia (IPU, 2014).

Question: Why does it take 200 million sperm to fertilize one egg? *Answer:* Because they won't stop for directions.

reveal that "men prefer working with things and women prefer working with people" (Su et al., 2009). On entering American colleges, men are seven times more likely than women to express interest in computer science (Pryor et al., 2011).

In the workplace, women are less often driven by money and status and more apt to opt for reduced work hours (Pinker, 2008). In the home, they are five times more likely than men to claim primary responsibility for taking care of children (*Time*, 2009). Women's emphasis on caring helps explain another interesting finding: Although 69 percent of people have said they have a close relationship with their father, 90 percent said they feel close to their mother (Hugick, 1989). When searching for understanding from someone who will share their worries and hurts, people usually turn to women. Both men and women have reported their friendships with women as more intimate, enjoyable, and nurturing (Kuttler et al., 1999; Rubin, 1985; Sapadin, 1988).

Bonds and feelings of support are even stronger among women than among men (Rossi & Rossi, 1993). Women's ties—as mothers, daughters, sisters, aunts, and grand-mothers—bind families together. As friends, women talk more often and more openly (Berndt, 1992; Dindia & Allen, 1992). "Perhaps because of [women's] greater desire for intimacy," reported Joyce Benenson and colleagues (2009), first-year college and univer-sity women are twice as likely as men to change roommates. How do they cope with their own stress? Compared with men, women are more likely to turn to others for sup-port. They are said to *tend and befriend* (Tamres et al., 2002; Taylor, 2002).

As empowered people generally do, men value freedom and self-reliance, which may help explain why men of all ages, worldwide, are less religious and pray less (Benson, 1992; Stark, 2002). Men also dominate the ranks of professional skeptics. All 10 win-ners and 14 runners-up on the *Skeptical Inquirer* list of outstanding twentieth-century rationalist skeptics were men. In one Skeptics Society survey, nearly 4 in 5 respondents were men (Shermer, 1999). And in the Science and the Paranormal section of the 2010 Prometheus Books catalog (from the leading publisher of skepticism), one could find 98 male and 4 female authors. (Women are far more likely to author books on spirituality.)

The gender gap in both social connectedness and power peaks in late adolescence and early adulthood—the prime years for dating and mating. Teenage girls become less asser-tive and more flirtatious, and boys appear more dominant and less expressive. Gender differences in attitudes and behavior often peak after the birth of a first child. Mothers especially may become more traditional (Ferriman et al., 2009; Katz-Wise et al., 2010). By age 50, most parent-related gender differences subside. Men become less domineer-ing and more empathic, and women—especially those with paid employment—become more assertive and self-confident (Kasen et al., 2006; Maccoby, 1998).

So, although women and men are more alike than different, there are some behav-ior differences between the average woman and man. Are such differences dictated by our biology? Shaped by our cultures and other experiences? Do we vary in the extent to which we are male or female? Read on.

"In the long years liker must they grow; The man be more of woman, she of man."

Alfred Lord Tennyson, *The Princess*, 1847

Every man for himself, or tend and befriend? Sex differences in the way we interact with others be-gin to appear at a very young age.

The Nature of Gender: Our Biological Sex

13-7 How do sex hormones influence prenatal and adolescent sexual development, and what is a disorder of sexual development?

Men and women employ similar solutions when faced with challenges: sweating to cool down, guzzling an energy drink or coffee to get going in the morning, or finding darkness and quiet to sleep. When looking for a mate, men and women also prize many of the same traits. They prefer having a mate who is "kind," "honest," and "intelligent." But according to evolutionary psychologists, in mating-related domains, guys act like guys whether they're chimpanzees or elephants, rural peasants or corporate presidents (Geary, 2010).

Biology does not *dictate* gender, but it can influence it in two ways:

- *Genetically*—males and females have differing *sex chromosomes*.
- *Physiologically*—males and females have differing concentrations of *sex hormones*, which trigger other anatomical differences.

These two sets of influences began to form you long before you were born, when your tiny body started developing in ways that determined your sex.

Prenatal Sexual Development Six weeks after you were conceived, you and someone of the other sex looked much the same. Then, as your genes kicked in, your biological sex—determined by your twenty-third pair of chromosomes (the two sex chromosomes)—became more apparent. Whether you are male or female, your mother's contribution to that chromosome pair was an **X chromosome.** From your father, you received the one chromosome out of 46 that is not unisex—either another X chromosome, making you female, or a **Y chromosome,** making you male.

About seven weeks after conception, a single gene on the Y chromosome throws a master switch, which triggers the testes to develop and to produce **testosterone,** the principal male hormone that promotes development of male sex organs. (Females also have testosterone, but less of it.) The male's greater testosterone output starts the development of external male sex organs at about the seventh week.

Later, during the fourth and fifth prenatal months, sex hormones bathe the fetal brain and influence its wiring. Different patterns for males and females develop under the influence of the male's greater testosterone and the female's ovarian hormones (Hines, 2004; Udry, 2000). Male-female differences emerge in brain areas with abundant sex hormone receptors (Cahill, 2005).

Adolescent Sexual Development A flood of hormones triggers another period of dramatic physical change during adolescence, when boys and girls enter **puberty.** In this two-year period of rapid sexual maturation, pronounced male-female differences occur. A variety of changes begin at about age 11 in girls and at about age 12 in boys, though the subtle beginnings of puberty, such as enlarging testes, appear earlier (Herman-Giddens et al., 2012). A year or two before the physical changes are visible, girls and boys often feel the first stirrings of attraction toward someone of the other or their own sex (McClintock & Herdt, 1996).

Girls' slightly earlier entry into puberty can at first propel them to greater height than boys of the same age (**FIGURE 13.5** on the next page). But boys catch up when they begin puberty, and by age 14, they are usually taller than girls. During these growth spurts, the **primary sex characteristics**—the reproductive organs and external genitalia—develop dramatically. So do the **secondary sex characteristics.** Girls develop breasts and larger hips. Boys' facial hair begins growing and their voices deepen. Pubic and underarm hair emerges in both girls and boys (**FIGURE 13.6** on the next page).

X chromosome the sex chromosome found in both men and women. Females have two X chromosomes; males have one. An X chromosome from each parent produces a female child.

Y chromosome the sex chromosome found only in males. When paired with an X chromosome from the mother, it produces a male child.

testosterone the most important of the male sex hormones. Both males and females have it, but the additional testosterone in males stimulates the growth of the male sex organs during the fetal period, and the development of the male sex characteristics during puberty.

puberty the period of sexual maturation, when a person becomes capable of reproducing.

primary sex characteristics the body structures (ovaries, testes, and external genitalia) that make sexual reproduction possible.

secondary sex characteristics non-reproductive sexual traits, such as female breasts and hips, male voice quality, and body hair.

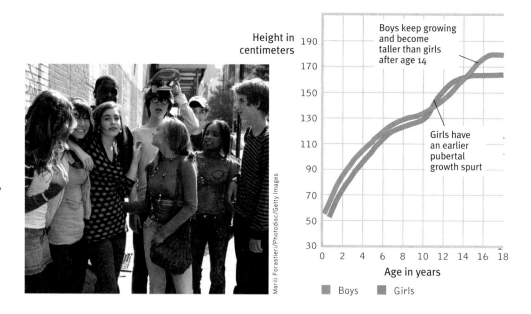

▼ FIGURE 13.5
Height differences Throughout childhood, boys and girls are similar in height. At puberty, girls surge ahead briefly, but then boys typically overtake them at about age 14. (Data from Tanner, 1978.) Studies suggest that sexual development and growth spurts are now beginning somewhat earlier than was the case a half-century ago (Herman-Giddens et al., 2001).

Pubertal boys may not at first like their sparse beard. (But then it grows on them.)

For boys, puberty's landmark is the first ejaculation, which often occurs first during sleep (as a "wet dream"). This event, called **spermarche** (sper-MAR-key), usually happens by about age 14.

In girls, the landmark is the first menstrual period (**menarche**—meh-NAR-key), usually within a year of age 12½ (Anderson et al., 2003). Early menarche is more likely following stresses related to father absence, sexual abuse, insecure attachments, or a history of a mother's smoking during pregnancy (DelPriore & Hill, 2013; Rickard et al., 2014; Shrestha et al., 2011). In various countries, girls are developing breasts earlier (sometimes before age 10) and reaching puberty earlier than in the past. Suspected triggers include increased body fat, diets filled with hormone-mimicking chemicals, and possibly greater stress due to family disruption (Biro et al., 2010, 2012; Herman-Giddens, 2012).

▼ FIGURE 13.6
Body changes at puberty At about age 11 in girls and age 12 in boys, a surge of hormones triggers a variety of visible physical changes.

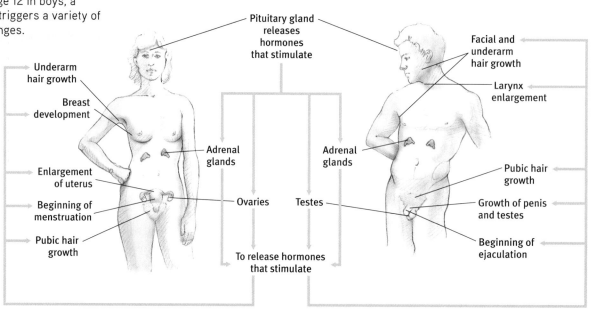

Girls prepared for menarche usually experience it positively (Chang et al., 2009). Most women recall their first menstrual period with mixed emotions—pride, excitement, embarrassment, and apprehension (Greif & Ulman, 1982; Woods et al., 1983). Men report mostly positive emotional reactions to spermarche (Fuller & Downs, 1990).

spermarche [sper-MAR-key] first ejaculation.

menarche [meh-NAR-key] the first menstrual period.

disorder of sexual development an inherited condition that involves unusual development of sex chromosomes and anatomy.

role a set of expectations (norms) about a social position, defining how those in the position ought to behave.

gender role a set of expected behaviors, attitudes, and traits for males or for females.

RETRIEVAL PRACTICE

- Adolescence is marked by the onset of _____ .

ANSWER: puberty

LaunchPad For a 7-minute discussion of our sexual development, visit Launch-Pad's *Video: Gender Development.*

Sexual Development Variations Sometimes nature blurs the biological line between males and females. When a fetus is exposed to unusual levels of sex hormones, or is especially sensitive to those hormones, the individual may develop a **disorder of sexual development,** with chromosomes or anatomy not typically male or female. A genetic male may be born with normal male hormones and testes but no penis or a very small one.

In the past, medical professionals often recommended *sex-reassignment surgery* to create an unambiguous identity for some children with this condition. One study reviewed 14 cases of boys who had undergone early surgery and been raised as girls. Of those cases, 6 had later declared themselves male, 5 were living as females, and 3 reported an unclear male or female identity (Reiner & Gearhart, 2004).

Sex-reassignment surgery can create confusion and distress among those not born with a disorder of sexual development. In one famous case, a little boy lost his penis during a botched circumcision. His parents followed a psychiatrist's advice to raise him as a girl rather than as a damaged boy. Alas, "Brenda" Reimer was not like most other girls. "She" didn't like dolls. She tore her dresses with rough-and-tumble play. At puberty she wanted no part of kissing boys. Finally, Brenda's parents explained what had happened, whereupon "Brenda" immediately rejected the assigned female identity. He cut his hair and chose a male name, David. He eventually married a woman and became a stepfather. And, sadly, he later committed suicide (Colapinto, 2000).

The bottom line: "Sex matters," concluded the National Academy of Sciences (2001). Sex-related genes and physiology "result in behavioral and cognitive differences between males and females." Yet environmental factors matter too, as we will see next. Nature and nurture work together.

"I am who I am." Dramatic improvements in South African track star Caster Semenya's race times prompted the International Association of Athletics Federations to undertake sex testing in 2009. Semenya was reported to have a disorder of sexual development, with physical characteristics not typically male or female. She was officially cleared to continue competing as a woman. Semenya declared, "God made me the way I am and I accept myself. I am who I am" (YOU, 2009).

Michael Dalder/Reuters

The Nurture of Gender: Our Culture and Experiences

13-8 How do gender roles and gender identity differ?

For many people, biological sex and gender coexist in harmony. Biology draws the outline, and culture paints the details. The physical traits that define us as biological males or females are the same worldwide. But the gender traits that define how men (or boys) and women (or girls) *should* act, interact, or feel about themselves may differ from one place to another (APA, 2009).

Gender Roles Cultures shape our behaviors by defining how we ought to behave in a particular social position, or **role.** We can see this shaping power in **gender roles**—the social expectations that guide our behavior as men or as women. Gender roles shift

New Yorker Collection, 2001, Barbara Smaller from cartoonbank.com.

"Sex brought us together, but gender drove us apart."

The gendered tsunami In Sri Lanka, Indonesia, and India, the gendered division of labor helps explain the excess of female deaths from the 2004 tsunami. In some villages, 80 percent of those killed were women, who were mostly at home while the men were more likely to be at sea fishing or doing out-of-the-home chores (Oxfam, 2005).

over time. A century ago, North American women could not vote in national elections, serve in the military, or divorce a husband without cause. And if a woman worked for pay outside the home, she would more likely have been a midwife or a seamstress, rather than a surgeon or a fashion designer.

Gender roles can change dramatically in a thin slice of history. At the beginning of the twentieth century, only one country in the world—New Zealand—granted women the right to vote (Briscoe, 1997). Today, worldwide, only Saudi Arabia *denies* women the right to vote. Even there, the culture shows signs of shifting toward women's voting rights (Alsharif, 2011). More U.S. women than men now graduate from college, and nearly half the work force is female (Fry & Cohn, 2010). The modern economy has produced jobs that rely not on brute strength but on social intelligence, open communication, and the ability to sit still and focus (Rosin, 2010). What changes might the next hundred years bring?

Gender roles also vary from one place to another. Nomadic societies of food-gathering people have had little division of labor by sex. Boys and girls receive much the same upbringing. In agricultural societies, where women work in the nearby fields and men roam while herding livestock, cultures have shaped children to assume more distinct gender roles (Segall et al., 1990; Van Leeuwen, 1978).

Take a minute to check your own gender expectations. Would you agree that "When jobs are scarce, men should have more rights to a job"? In the United States, Britain, and Spain, barely over 12 percent of adults agree. In Nigeria, Pakistan, and India, about 80 percent of adults agree (Pew, 2010). We're all human, but my how our views differ. Australia and the Scandinavian countries offer the greatest gender equity, Middle Eastern and North African countries the least (Social Watch, 2006).

How Do We Learn Gender? A *gender role* describes how others expect us to think, feel, and act. Our **gender identity** is our personal sense of being male, female, or a combination of the two. How do we develop that personal viewpoint?

Social learning theory assumes that we acquire our gender identity in childhood, by observing and imitating others' gender-linked behaviors and by being rewarded or punished for acting in certain ways. ("Tatiana, you're such a good mommy to your dolls"; "Big boys don't cry, Armand.") Some critics think there's more to gender identity than imitating parents and being repeatedly rewarded for certain responses. They point out that **gender typing**—taking on the traditional male or female role—varies from child to child (Tobin et al., 2010). No matter how much parents encourage or discourage traditional gender behavior, children may drift toward what feels right to them.

gender identity our sense of being male, female, or a combination of the two.

social learning theory the theory that we learn social behavior by observing and imitating and by being rewarded or punished.

gender typing the acquisition of a traditional masculine or feminine role.

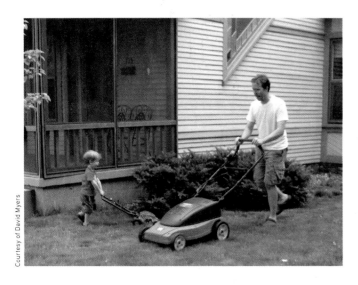

The social learning of gender Children observe and imitate parental models.

Some organize themselves into "boy worlds" and "girl worlds," each guided by rules. Others seem to prefer **androgyny:** A blend of male and female roles feels right to them. Androgyny has benefits. Androgynous people are more adaptable. They show greater flexibility in behavior and career choices (Bem, 1993). They tend to be more resilient and self-accepting, and they experience less depression (Lam & McBride-Chang, 2007; Mosher & Danoff-Burg, 2008; Ward, 2000).

How we feel matters, but so does how we think. Early in life, we form *schemas*, or concepts that help us make sense of our world. Our *gender schemas* organized our experiences of male-female characteristics and helped us think about our gender identity, about who we are (Bem, 1987, 1993; Martin et al., 2002). Our parents help to transmit their culture's views on gender. In one analysis of 43 studies, parents with traditional gender schemas were more likely to have gender-typed children who shared their culture's expectations about how males and females should act (Tenenbaum & Leaper, 2002).

As a young child, you (like other children) were a "gender detective" (Martin & Ruble, 2004). Before your first birthday, you knew the difference between a male and female voice or face (Martin et al., 2002). After you turned 2, language forced you to label the world in terms of gender. If you are an English speaker, you learned to classify people as *he* and *she*. If you are a French speaker, you learned also to classify objects as masculine ("*le* train") or feminine ("*la* table").

Once children grasp that two sorts of people exist—and that they are of one sort—they search for clues about gender. In every culture, people communicate their gender in many ways. Their *gender expression* drops hints not only in their language but also in their clothing, interests, and possessions. Having divided the human world in half, 3-year-olds will then like their own kind better and seek them out for play. "Girls," they may decide, are the ones who watch *Dora the Explorer* and have long hair. "Boys" watch battles from *Kung Fu Panda* and don't wear dresses. Armed with their newly collected "proof," they then adjust their behaviors to fit their concept of gender. These rigid stereotypes peak at about age 5 or 6. If the new neighbor is a boy, a 6-year-old girl may assume that she cannot share his interests. For young children, gender looms large.

For a **transgender** person, comparing one's personal gender identity with cultural concepts of gender roles produces feelings of confusion and discord. A transgender person's gender identity differs from the behaviors or traits considered typical for that person's birth sex (APA, 2010; Bockting, 2014). A person who was born a female may feel he is a man living in a woman's body, or a person born male may feel she

androgyny displaying both traditional masculine and feminine psychological characteristics.

transgender an umbrella term describing people whose gender identity or expression differs from that associated with their birth sex.

Transgender contestant
In 2012, Jenna Talackova became the first transgender contestant to compete for the title of Miss Universe Canada. Talackova, a male-to-female transsexual, had sex-reassignment surgery in her late teens.

Vincent Elkaim/The Canadian Press, Aaron/AP Photo

"The more I was treated as a woman, the more woman I became."

Writer Jan Morris, male-to-female transsexual

is a woman living in a man's body. Some transgender people are also *transsexual:* They prefer to live as members of the other birth sex. Some transsexual people (about three times as many men as women) may seek medical treatment (including sex-reassignment surgery) to achieve their preferred gender identity (Van Kesteren et al., 1997).

Note that *gender identity* is distinct from *sexual orientation* (the direction of one's sexual attraction). Transgender people may be sexually attracted to people of the opposite birth sex (*heterosexual*), the same birth sex (*homosexual*), both sexes (*bisexual*), or to no one at all (*asexual*).

Transgender people may express their gender identity by dressing as a person of the other biological sex typically would. Most who dress this way are biological males who are attracted to women (APA, 2010).

RETRIEVAL PRACTICE

• What are gender roles, and what do their variations tell us about our human capacity for learning and adaptation?

ANSWER: *Gender roles* are social rules or norms for accepted and expected behavior for females and males. The norms associated with various roles, including gender roles, vary widely in different cultural contexts, which is proof that we are very capable of learning and adapting to the social demands of different environments.

Reflections on Nature, Nurture, and Their Interaction

13-9 What is included in the biopsychosocial approach to development?

"There are trivial truths and great truths," reflected the physicist Niels Bohr on the paradoxes of science. "The opposite of a trivial truth is plainly false. The opposite of a great truth is also true." Our ancestral history helped form us as a species. Where there is variation, natural selection, and heredity, there will be evolution. The unique gene combination created when our mother's egg engulfed our father's sperm predisposed both our shared humanity and our individual differences. Our genes form us. This is a great truth about human nature.

But our experiences also shape us. Our families and peer relationships teach us how to think and act. Differences initiated by our nature may be amplified by our nurture. If their genes and hormones predispose males to be more physically aggressive than females, culture can amplify this gender difference through norms that shower benefits on macho men and gentle women. If men are encouraged toward roles that demand physical power, and women toward more nurturing roles, each may act accordingly. Roles remake their players. Presidents in time become more presidential, servants more servile. Gender roles similarly shape us.

In many modern cultures, gender roles are merging. Brute strength is becoming increasingly less important for power and status (think Mark Zuckerberg and Hillary Clinton). From 1960 into the next century, women soared from 6 percent to nearly 50 percent of U.S. medical school graduates (AAMC, 2012). In the mid-1960s, U.S. married women devoted seven times as many hours to housework as did their husbands; by 2003 this gap had shrunk to twice as many (Bianchi et al., 2000, 2006). Such swift changes signal that biology does not fix gender roles.

Culture matters As this exhibit at San Diego's Museum of Man illustrates, children learn their culture. A baby's foot can step into any culture.

San Diego Museum of Man, photograph by Rose Tyson

* * *

If nature and nurture jointly form us, are we "nothing but" the product of nature and nurture? Are we rigidly determined?

We *are* the product of nature and nurture, but we are also an open system (**FIGURE 13.7** on the next page). Genes are all-pervasive but not all-powerful. People may reject their evolutionary role as transmitters of genes and choose not to reproduce. Culture, too, is all-pervasive but not all-powerful. People may defy peer pressures and do the opposite of the expected.

We can't excuse our failings by blaming them solely on bad genes or bad influences. In reality, we are both the creatures and the creators of our worlds. So many things about us—including our gender identities and our mating behaviors—are the products of our genes and environments. Yet the future-shaping stream of causation runs through our present choices. Our decisions today design our environments tomorrow. The human environment is not like the weather—something that just

▼ FIGURE 13.7
The biopsychosocial approach
to development

Biological influences:
• Shared human genome
• Individual genetic variations
• Prenatal environment
• Sex-related genes, hormones, and physiology

Psychological influences:
• Gene-environment interaction
• Neurological effect of early experiences
• Responses evoked by our own temperament, gender, etc.
• Beliefs, feelings, and expectations

Individual development

Social-cultural influences:
• Parental influences
• Peer influences
• Cultural individualism or collectivism
• Cultural gender norms

happens randomly. We are its architects. Our hopes, goals, and expectations influence our future. And that is what enables cultures to vary and to change. Mind matters.

RETRIEVAL PRACTICE

• How does the biopsychosocial approach explain our individual development?

ANSWER: The biopsychosocial approach considers all the factors that influence our individual development: biological factors (including evolution and our genes, hormones, and brain), psychological factors (including our experiences, beliefs, feelings, and expectations), and social-cultural factors (including parental and peer influences, cultural individualism or collectivism, and gender norms).

* * *

"Let's hope that it's not true; but if it is true, let's hope that it doesn't become widely known."

Lady Ashley, commenting on Darwin's theory

"Is it not stirring to understand how the world actually works—that white light is made of colors, that color measures light waves, that transparent air reflects light . . . ? It does no harm to the romance of the sunset to know a little about it."

Carl Sagan, *Skies of Other Worlds,* 1988

We know from our correspondence and from surveys that some readers feel troubled by the naturalism and evolutionism of contemporary science. (Readers from other nations bear with us, but in the United States there is a wide gulf between scientific and lay thinking about evolution.) "The idea that human minds are the product of evolution is . . . unassailable fact," declared a 2007 editorial in *Nature,* a leading science journal. That sentiment concurs with a 2006 statement of "evidence-based facts" about evolution jointly issued by the national science academies of 66 nations (IAP, 2006). In *The Language of God,* Human Genome Project director Francis Collins (2006, pp. 141, 146), a self-described evangelical Christian, compiled the "utterly compelling" evidence that led him to conclude that Darwin's big idea is "unquestionably correct." Yet Gallup pollsters have reported that half of U.S. adults do not believe in evolution's role in "how human beings came to exist on Earth" (Newport, 2007). Many of those who dispute the scientific story worry that a science of behavior (and evolutionary science in particular) will destroy our sense of the beauty, mystery, and spiritual significance of the human creature. For those concerned, we offer some reassuring thoughts.

When Isaac Newton explained the rainbow in terms of light of differing wavelengths, the British poet John Keats feared that Newton had destroyed the rainbow's mysterious beauty. Yet, as Richard Dawkins (1998) noted in *Unweaving the Rainbow,* Newton's analysis led to an even deeper mystery—Einstein's theory of special relativity. Moreover, nothing about Newton's optics need diminish our appreciation for the dramatic elegance of a rainbow arching across a brightening sky.

When Galileo assembled evidence that the Earth revolved around the Sun, not vice versa, he did not offer irrefutable proof for his theory. Rather, he offered a coherent explanation for a variety of observations, such as the changing shadows cast by the Moon's mountains. His explanation eventually won the day because it described and explained things in a way that made sense, that hung together. Darwin's theory of evolution likewise is a coherent view of natural history. It offers an organizing principle that unifies various observations.

Collins is not the only person of faith to find the scientific idea of human origins congenial with his spirituality. In the fifth century, St. Augustine (quoted by Wilford, 1999) wrote, "The universe was brought into being in a less than fully formed state, but was gifted with the capacity to transform itself from unformed matter into a truly marvelous array of structures and life forms." Some 1600 years later, Pope John Paul II in 1996 welcomed a science-religion dialogue, finding it noteworthy that evolutionary theory "has been progressively accepted by researchers, following a series of discoveries in various fields of knowledge."

Meanwhile, many people of science are awestruck at the emerging understanding of the universe and the human creature. It boggles the mind—the entire universe popping out of a point some 14 billion years ago, and instantly inflating to cosmological size. Had the energy of this Big Bang been the tiniest bit less, the universe would have collapsed back on itself. Had it been the tiniest bit more, the result would have been a soup too thin to support life. Astronomer Sir Martin Rees has described *Just Six Numbers* (1999), any one of which, if changed ever so slightly, would produce a cosmos in which life could not exist. Had gravity been a tad stronger or weaker, or had the weight of a carbon proton been a wee bit different, our universe just wouldn't have worked.

What caused this almost-too-good-to-be-true, finely tuned universe? Why is there something rather than nothing? How did it come to be, in the words of Harvard-Smithsonian astrophysicist Owen Gingerich (1999), "so extraordinarily right, that it seemed the universe had been expressly designed to produce intelligent, sentient beings"? Is there a benevolent superintelligence behind it all? Have there instead been an infinite number of universes born and we just happen to be the lucky inhabitants of one that, by chance, was exquisitely fine-tuned to give birth to us? Or does that idea violate *Occam's razor*, the principle that we should prefer the simplest of competing explanations? On such matters, a humble, awed, scientific silence is appropriate, suggested philosopher Ludwig Wittgenstein: "Whereof one cannot speak, thereof one must be silent" (1922, p. 189).

Rather than fearing science, we can welcome its enlarging our understanding and awakening our sense of awe. In *The Fragile Species*, Lewis Thomas (1992) described his utter amazement that the Earth in time gave rise to bacteria and eventually to Bach's Mass in B Minor. In a short 4 billion years, life on Earth has come from nothing to structures as complex as a 6-billion-unit strand of DNA and the incomprehensible intricacy of the human brain. Atoms no different from those in a rock somehow formed dynamic entities that became conscious. Nature, said cosmologist Paul Davies (2007), seems cunningly and ingeniously devised to produce extraordinary, self-replicating, information-processing systems—us. Although we appear to have been created from dust, over eons of time, the end result is a priceless creature, one rich with potential beyond our imagining.

"The causes of life's history [cannot] resolve the riddle of life's meaning."

Stephen Jay Gould, *Rocks of Ages: Science and Religion in the Fullness of Life*, 1999

MODULE 13 REVIEW Culture, Gender, and Other Environmental Influences

LEARNING OBJECTIVES

RETRIEVAL PRACTICE Take a moment to answer each of these Learning Objective Questions (repeated here from within this module). Then turn to Appendix C, Complete Module Reviews, to check your answers. Research suggests that trying to answer these questions on your own will improve your long-term retention (McDaniel et al., 2009).

13-1 How do early experiences modify the brain?

13-2 In what ways do parents and peers shape children's development?

13-3 How does culture affect our behavior?

13-4 How do individualist and collectivist cultures differ in their values and goals?

13-5 How does the meaning of *gender* differ from the meaning of *sex*?

13-6 What are some ways in which males and females tend to be alike and to differ?

13-7 How do sex hormones influence prenatal and adolescent sexual development, and what is a disorder of sexual development?

13-8 How do gender roles and gender identity differ?

13-9 What is included in the biopsychosocial approach to development?

TERMS AND CONCEPTS TO REMEMBER

RETRIEVAL PRACTICE Test yourself on these terms by trying to write down the definition before flipping back to check your answers.

culture, p. 155
norm, p. 156
individualism, p. 157
collectivism, p. 157
sex, p. 161
gender, p. 161
aggression, p. 162
relational aggression, p. 162
X chromosome, p. 165
Y chromosome, p. 165
testosterone, p. 165
puberty, p. 165
primary sex characteristics, p. 165
secondary sex characteristics, p. 165
spermarche [sper-MAR-key], p. 166
menarche [meh-NAR-key], p. 166
disorder of sexual development, p. 167
role, p. 167
gender role, p. 167
gender identity, p. 168
social learning theory, p. 168
gender typing, p. 168
androgyny, p. 169
transgender, p. 169

Use **LearningCurve** to create your personalized study plan, which will direct you to the resources that will help you most in **LaunchPad**.

TEST YOURSELF NATURE, NURTURE, AND HUMAN DIVERSITY

Test yourself repeatedly throughout your studies. This will not only help you figure out what you know and don't know; the testing itself will help you learn and remember the information more effectively thanks to the *testing effect*.

MODULE 11 Behavior Genetics: Predicting Individual Differences

1. The threadlike structures made largely of DNA molecules are called _____ .

2. A small segment of DNA that codes for particular proteins is referred to as a _____ .

3. When the mother's egg and the father's sperm unite, each contributes
   a. one chromosome pair.
   b. 23 chromosomes.
   c. 23 chromosome pairs.
   d. 25,000 chromosomes.

4. Fraternal twins result when
   a. a single egg is fertilized by a single sperm and then splits.
   b. a single egg is fertilized by two sperm and then splits.
   c. two eggs are fertilized by two sperm.
   d. two eggs are fertilized by a single sperm.

5. _____ twins share the same DNA.

6. Adoption studies seek to understand genetic influences on personality. They do this mainly by
   a. comparing adopted children with nonadopted children.
   b. evaluating whether adopted children's personalities more closely resemble those of their adoptive parents or their biological parents.
   c. studying the effect of prior neglect on adopted children.
   d. studying the effect of children's age at adoption.

7. From the very first weeks of life, infants differ in their characteristic emotional reactions, with some infants being intense and anxious, while others are easygoing and relaxed. These differences are usually explained as differences in _____ .

8. _____ is the proportion of variation among individuals that we can attribute to genes.

9. Epigenetics is the study of the molecular mechanisms by which _____ trigger or block genetic expression.

MODULE 12 Evolutionary Psychology: Understanding Human Nature

10. Behavior geneticists are most interested in exploring _____ (commonalities/differences) in our behaviors. Evolutionary psychologists are most interested in exploring _____ (commonalities/differences).

11. Evolutionary psychologists are most likely to focus on
    a. how individuals differ from one another.
    b. the social consequences of sexual behaviors.
    c. natural selection of the fittest adaptations.
    d. twin and adoption studies.

MODULE 13 Culture, Gender, and Other Environmental Influences

12. Individualist cultures tend to value _____ ; collectivist cultures tend to value _____ .
    a. interdependence; independence
    b. independence; interdependence
    c. group solidarity; uniqueness
    d. duty to family; personal fulfillment

13. Psychologists define _____ as the biologically influenced characteristics by which people define males and females. The socially influenced characteristics by which people define men and women is _____ .

14. Females and males are very similar to each other. But one way they differ is that
    a. females are more physically aggressive than males.
    b. males are more democratic than females in their leadership roles.
    c. girls tend to play in small groups, while boys tend to play in large groups.
    d. females are more likely to commit suicide.

15. A fertilized egg will develop into a boy if it receives a/n _____ chromosome from its father.

16. Primary sex characteristics relate to _____ ; secondary sex characteristics refer to _____ .
    a. ejaculation; menarche
    b. breasts and facial hair; ovaries and testes
    c. emotional maturity; hormone surges
    d. reproductive organs; nonreproductive traits

17. On average, girls begin puberty at about the age of _____ , boys at about the age of _____ .

18. An individual who is born with sexual anatomy that differs from typical male or female anatomy has a _____ _____ _____ .

19. *Gender role* refers to our
    a. personal sense of being male or female.
    b. culture's expectations about the "right" way for males and females to behave.
    c. birth sex—our chomosomes and anatomy.
    d. unisex characteristics.

20. When children have developed a _____ _____ , they have a sense of being male, female, or a combination of the two.

Find answers to these questions in Appendix D, in the back of the book.

DEVELOPING THROUGH THE LIFE SPAN

ife is a journey, from womb to tomb. So it is for me [DM], and so it will be for you. My story, and yours, began when a man and a woman together contributed 20,000+ genes to an egg that became a unique person. Those genes coded the protein building blocks that, with astonishing precision, formed our bodies and predisposed our traits. My grandmother bequeathed to my mother a rare hearing loss pattern, which she, in turn, gave to me (the least of her gifts). My father was an amiable extravert, and sometimes I forget to stop talking. As a child, my talking was impeded by painful stuttering, for which Seattle Public Schools provided speech therapy.

Along with my parents' nature, I also received their nurture. Like you, I was born into a particular family and culture, with its own way of viewing the world. My values have been shaped by a family culture filled with talking and laughter, by a religious culture that speaks of love and justice, and by an academic culture that encourages critical thinking (asking, *What do you mean? How do you know?*).

We are formed by our genes, and by our contexts, so our stories will differ. But in many ways we are each like nearly everyone else on Earth. Being human, you and I have a need to belong. My mental video library, which began after age 4, is filled with scenes of social attachment. Over time, my attachments to parents loosened as peer friendships grew. After lacking confidence to date in high school, I fell in love with a college classmate and married at age 20. Natural selection predisposes us to survive and perpetuate our genes. Sure enough, two years later a child entered our lives and I experienced a new form of love that surprised me with its intensity.

But life is marked by change. That child now lives 2000 miles away, and one of his two siblings has found her calling in South Africa. The tight rubber bands linking parent and child have loosened, as yours likely have as well.

Change also marks most vocational lives, which for me transitioned from a teen working in the family insurance agency, to a premed chemistry major and hospital aide, to (after discarding my half-completed medical school applications) a psychology professor and author. I predict that in 10 years you, too, will be doing things you do not currently anticipate.

Stability also marks our development: We experience a continuous self. When I look in the mirror, I do not see the person I once was, but I feel like the person I have always been. I am the same person who, as a late teen, played basketball and discovered love. A half-century later, I still play basketball and still love (with less passion but more security) the life partner with whom I have shared life's griefs and joys.

Continuity morphs through stages—growing up, raising children, enjoying a career, and, eventually, life's final stage, which will demand my presence. As I wend my way through this cycle of life and death, I am mindful that life is a journey, a continuing process of development, seeded by nature and shaped by nurture, animated by love and focused by work, begun with wide-eyed curiosity and completed, for those blessed to live to a good old age, with peace and never-ending hope.

Across the life span, we grow from newborn to toddler, from toddler to teenager, and from teen to mature adult. At each stage of life there are physical, cognitive, and social milestones. Let's begin with prenatal development and the newborn (Module 14), then turn to infancy and childhood (Module 15), adolescence (Module 16), and adulthood (Module 17).

developmental psychology a branch of psychology that studies physical, cognitive, and social change throughout the life span.

MODULE 14 Developmental Issues, Prenatal Development, and the Newborn

Developmental Psychology's Major Issues

14-1 What three issues have engaged developmental psychologists?

DEVELOPMENTAL PSYCHOLOGY EXAMINES OUR PHYSICAL, cognitive, and social development across the life span, with a focus on three major issues:

1. **Nature and nurture:** How does our genetic inheritance (our *nature*) interact with our experiences (our *nurture*) to influence our development? (This is our focus in other modules.)

2. **Continuity and stages:** What parts of development are gradual and continuous, like riding an escalator? What parts change abruptly in separate stages, like climbing rungs on a ladder?

3. **Stability and change:** Which of our traits persist through life? How do we change as we age?

"Nature is all that a man brings with him into the world; nurture is every influence that affects him after his birth."

Francis Galton, *English Men of Science*, 1874

Continuity and Stages

Do adults differ from infants as a giant redwood differs from its seedling—a difference created by gradual, cumulative growth? Or do they differ as a butterfly differs from a caterpillar—a difference of distinct stages?

Generally speaking, researchers who emphasize experience and learning see development as a slow, continuous shaping process. Those who emphasize biological maturation tend to see development as a sequence of genetically predisposed stages or steps: Although progress through the various stages may be quick or slow, everyone passes through the stages in the same order.

Are there clear-cut stages of psychological development, as there are physical stages such as walking before running? The stage theories we will consider—of Jean Piaget on cognitive development, Lawrence Kohlberg on moral development, and Erik Erikson on psychosocial development—propose developmental stages (summarized in **FIGURE 14.1**). But as we will also see, some research casts doubt on the idea that life proceeds through neatly defined age-linked stages. Young children have some abilities Piaget attributed to later stages. Kohlberg's work reflected an individualist worldview and emphasized thinking over acting. And adult life does not progress through a fixed, predictable series of steps. Chance events can influence us in ways we would never have predicted.

Nevertheless, the *stage* concept remains useful. The human brain does experience growth spurts during childhood and puberty that correspond roughly to Piaget's stages (Thatcher et al., 1987). And stage theories contribute a developmental perspective on the whole life span, by suggesting how people of one age think and act differently when they arrive at a later age.

TOO MUCH COFFEE MAN BY SHANNON WHEELER

LIFE:

PLAY, SCHOOL, PLAY, SCHOOL, PLAY, SCHOOL, PLAY, SCHOOL, FIRST LOVE, BRIEF HAPPINESS, BREAK UP, REGRET, SCHOOL, SCHOOL, SCHOOL, SCHOOL, SCHOOL, SCHOOL, SCHOOL, SCHOOL, SCHOOL, SCHOOL, SCHOOL, SCHOOL, SCHOOL, SCHOOL, PLAY, WORK, PLAY, WORK, PLAY, WORK, PLAY, WORK, IDEALISM, EFFORT, REJECTION, FAILURE, WORK, EFFORT, FAILURE, COMPROMISE, WORK, WORK, WORK, WORK, WORK, WORK, PLAY, COMMITMENT, WORK, WORK, WORK, WORK, WORK, WORK, PLAY, WORK, WORK, WORK, WORK, WORK, WORK, WORK, WORK, PLAY, WORK, WORK, WORK, WORK, WORK, WORK, WORK, WORK, PLAY, WORK, WORK, WORK, WORK, WORK, WORK, WORK, WORK, PLAY, WORK, WORK, WORK, WORK, WORK, WORK, WORK, WORK, PLAY, WORK, WORK, WORK, WORK, WORK, WORK, WORK, WORK, PLAY, WORK, WORK, WORK, WORK, WORK, WORK, WORK, WORK, PLAY, WORK, WORK, WORK, WORK, WORK, WORK, WORK, WORK, PLAY, WORK, WORK, WORK, WORK, WORK, WORK, WORK, WORK, PLAY, WORK, WORK, WORK, WORK, WORK, WORK, WORK, WORK, PLAY, WORK, WORK, WORK, WORK, WORK, WORK, WORK, WORK, PLAY, WORK, WORK, WORK, WORK, WORK, WORK, WORK, WORK, PLAY, WORK, WORK, WORK, WORK, WORK, WORK, WORK, WORK, PLAY, RETIRE, PLAY, DIE.

Shannon Wheeler

Stages of the life cycle

Lawrence Kohlberg

| Preconventional morality | Conventional morality | Postconventional morality for some |

Erik Erikson

| Basic Trust | Autonomy | Initiative | Competence | Identity | Intimacy | Genera-tivity | Integrity |

Jean Piaget

| Sensorimotor | Preoperational | Concrete operational | Formal operational |

Birth 1 2 3 4 5 6 7 8 9 10 11 12 13 14 Death

Age (years)

Stability and Change

As we follow lives through time, do we find more evidence for stability or change? If reunited with a long-lost grade-school friend, do we instantly realize that "it's the same old Andy"? Or do people we befriend during one period of life seem like strangers at a later period? (At least one acquaintance of mine [DM] would choose the second option. He failed to recognize a former classmate at his 40-year college reunion. The aghast classmate eventually pointed out that she was his long-ago first wife.)

Research reveals that we experience both stability and change. Some of our characteristics, such as *temperament,* are very stable:

- One research team that studied 1000 people from ages 3 to 38 was struck by the consistency of temperament and emotionality across time (Moffitt et al., 2013; Slutske et al., 2012). Out-of-control 3-year-olds were the most likely to become teen smokers or adult criminals or out-of-control gamblers.

- Other studies have found that hyperactive, inattentive 5-year-olds required more teacher effort at age 12 (Houts et al., 2010); that 6-year-old Canadian boys with conduct problems were four times more likely than other boys to be convicted of a violent crime by age 24 (Hodgins et al., 2013); and that extraversion among British 16-year-olds predicts their future happiness as 60-year-olds (Gale et al., 2013).

- Another research team interviewed adults who, 40 years earlier, had their talkativeness, impulsiveness, and humility rated by their elementary schoolteachers (Nave et al., 2010). To a striking extent, their traits persisted.

"As at 7, so at 70," says a Jewish proverb. The widest smilers in childhood and college photos are, years later, the ones most likely to enjoy enduring marriages (Hertenstein et al., 2009). While 1 in 4 of the weakest college smilers eventually divorced, only 1 in 20 of the widest smilers did so. As people grow older, personality gradually stabilizes (Ferguson, 2010; Hopwood et al., 2011; Kandler et al., 2010). The struggles of the present may be laying a foundation for a happier tomorrow.

▼ FIGURE 14.1
Comparing the stage theories (With thanks to Dr. Sandra Gibbs, Muskegon Community College, for inspiring this illustration.)

"At 70, I would say the advantage is that you take life more calmly. You know that 'this, too, shall pass'!"

Eleanor Roosevelt, 1954

Smiles predict marital stability In one study of 306 college alums, 1 in 4 with yearbook expressions like the one on the left later divorced, as did only 1 in 20 with smiles like the one on the right (Hertenstein et al., 2009).

As adults grow older, there is continuity of self.

We cannot, however, predict all of our eventual traits based on our early years of life (Kagan et al., 1978, 1998). Some traits, such as social attitudes, are much less stable than temperament (Moss & Susman, 1980). Older children and adolescents learn new ways of coping. Although delinquent children have elevated rates of later problems, many confused and troubled children blossom into mature, successful adults (Moffitt et al., 2002; Roberts et al., 2013; Thomas & Chess, 1986). Life is a process of becoming.

In some ways, we *all* change with age. Most shy, fearful toddlers begin opening up by age 4, and most people become more conscientious, stable, agreeable, and self-confident in the years after adolescence (Lucas & Donnellan, 2009; Roberts & Mroczek, 2008; Shaw et al., 2010). Many irresponsible 18-year-olds have matured into 40-year-old business or cultural leaders. (If you are the former, you aren't done yet.) Openness, self-esteem, and agreeableness often peak in midlife (Lucas & Donnellan, 2011; Orth et al., 2012; Specht et al., 2011). Such changes can occur without changing a person's position *relative to others* of the same age. The hard-driving young adult may mellow by later life, yet still be a relatively driven senior citizen.

Life requires *both* stability and change. Stability provides our identity. It enables us to depend on others and be concerned about children's healthy development. Our potential for change gives us our hope for a brighter future. It motivates our concerns about present influences and lets us adapt and grow with experience.

RETRIEVAL PRACTICE

- Developmental researchers who emphasize learning and experience are supporting _____; those who emphasize biological maturation are supporting _____.

ANSWERS: continuity; stages

- What findings in psychology support (1) the stage theory of development and (2) the idea of stability in personality across the life span? What findings challenge these ideas?

ANSWER: (1) Stage theory is supported by the work of Piaget (cognitive development), Kohlberg (moral development), and Erikson (psychosocial development), but it is challenged by findings that change is more gradual and less culturally universal than these theorists supposed. (2) Some traits, such as temperament, do exhibit remarkable stability across many years. But we do change in other ways, such as in our social attitudes.

Prenatal Development and the Newborn

14-2 What is the course of prenatal development, and how do teratogens affect that development?

Conception

Nothing is more natural than a species reproducing itself. And nothing is more wondrous. For you, the process started inside your *grandmother*—as an egg formed inside a developing female inside of her. Your mother was born with all the immature eggs she would ever have. Your father, in contrast, began producing sperm cells nonstop at puberty—in the beginning at a rate of more than 1000 sperm during the second it takes to read this phrase.

Some time after puberty, your mother's ovary released a mature egg—a cell roughly the size of the period that ends this sentence. Like space voyagers approaching a huge planet, some 250 million deposited sperm began their race upstream, approaching a cell 85,000 times their own size. Those reaching the egg released digestive enzymes that ate away its protective coating (**FIGURE 14.2a**). As soon as one sperm penetrated the coating and was welcomed in (Figure 14.2b), the egg's surface blocked out the others. Before half a day elapsed, the egg nucleus and the sperm nucleus fused: The two became one.

zygote the fertilized egg; it enters a 2-week period of rapid cell division and develops into an embryo.

embryo the developing human organism from about 2 weeks after fertilization through the second month.

fetus the developing human organism from 9 weeks after conception to birth.

(a)   (b)

Meckes/Ottawa/Eye of Science/Science Source

David M. Phillips/Science Source

▼ FIGURE 14.2
Life is sexually transmitted
(a) Sperm cells surround an egg. (b) As one sperm penetrates the egg's jelly-like outer coating, a series of chemical events begins that will cause sperm and egg to fuse into a single cell. If all goes well, that cell will subdivide again and again to emerge 9 months later as a 100-trillion-cell human being.

Consider it your most fortunate of moments. Among 250 million sperm, the one needed to make you, in combination with that one particular egg, won the race. And so it was for innumerable generations before us. If any one of our ancestors had been conceived with a different sperm or egg, or died before conceiving, or not chanced to meet their partner or . . . . The mind boggles at the improbable, unbroken chain of events that produced us.

Prenatal Development

Fewer than half of all fertilized eggs, called **zygotes,** survive beyond the first 2 weeks (Grobstein, 1979; Hall, 2004). But for us, good fortune prevailed. One cell became 2, then 4—each just like the first—until this cell division had produced some 100 identical cells within the first week. Then the cells began to differentiate— to specialize in structure and function. How identical cells do this—as if one decides "I'll become a brain, you become intestines!"—is a puzzle that scientists are just beginning to solve.

About 10 days after conception, the zygote attaches to the mother's uterine wall, beginning approximately 37 weeks of the closest human relationship. The zygote's inner cells become the **embryo** (**FIGURE 14.3a**). Many of its outer cells become the *placenta,* the life-link that transfers nutrients and oxygen from mother to embryo. Over the next 6 weeks, the embryo's organs begin to form and function. The heart begins to beat.

By 9 weeks after conception, an embryo looks unmistakably human (Figure 14.3b). It is now a **fetus** (Latin for "offspring" or "young one"). During the sixth month, organs such as the stomach have developed enough to give the fetus a good chance of survival if born prematurely.

(a)   (b)   (c)

Lennart Nilsson/Albert Bonniers Publishing Company

▼ FIGURE 14.3
Prenatal development
(a) The embryo grows and develops rapidly. At 40 days, the spine is visible and the arms and legs are beginning to grow. (b) By the end of the second month, when the fetal period begins, facial features, hands, and feet have formed. (c) As the fetus enters the fourth month, its 3 ounces could fit in the palm of your hand.

teratogens (literally, "monster maker") agents, such as chemicals and viruses, that can reach the embryo or fetus during prenatal development and cause harm.

fetal alcohol syndrome (FAS) physical and cognitive abnormalities in children caused by a pregnant woman's heavy drinking. In severe cases, signs include a small, out-of-proportion head and abnormal facial features.

Prenatal development
Zygote: Conception to 2 weeks
Embryo: 2 to 9 weeks
Fetus: 9 weeks to birth

"You shall conceive and bear a son. So then drink no wine or strong drink."

Judges 13:7

moodboard/JupiterImages

At each prenatal stage, genetic and environmental factors affect our development. By the sixth month, microphone readings taken inside the uterus reveal that the fetus is responsive to sound and is exposed to the sound of its mother's muffled voice (Ecklund-Flores, Hepper, 2005). Immediately after emerging from their underwater world, newborns prefer her voice to another woman's, or to their father's (Busnel et al., 1992; DeCasper et al., 1984, 1986, 1994).

They also prefer hearing their mother's language. At about 30 hours old, American and Swedish newborns pause more in their pacifier sucking when listening to familiar vowels from their mother's language (Moon et al., 2013). After repeatedly hearing a fake word (*tatata*) in the womb, Finnish newborns' brain waves display recognition when hearing the word after birth (Partanen et al., 2013). If their mother spoke two languages during pregnancy, they display interest in both (Byers-Heinlein et al., 2010). And just after birth, babies born to French-speaking mothers tend to cry with the rising intonation of French; babies born to German-speaking mothers cry with the falling tones of German (Mampe et al., 2009). Would you have guessed? The learning of language begins in the womb.

In the two months before birth, fetuses demonstrate learning in other ways, as when they adapt to a vibrating, honking device placed on their mother's abdomen (Dirix et al., 2009). Like people who adapt to the sound of trains in their neighborhood, fetuses get used to the honking. Moreover, four weeks later, they recall the sound (as evidenced by their blasé response, compared with the reactions of those not previously exposed).

Sounds are not the only stimuli fetuses are exposed to in the womb. In addition to transferring nutrients and oxygen from mother to fetus, the placenta screens out many harmful substances. But some slip by. **Teratogens,** agents such as viruses and drugs, can damage an embryo or fetus. This is one reason pregnant women are advised not to drink alcoholic beverages. A pregnant woman never drinks alone. As alcohol enters her bloodstream, and her fetus', it depresses activity in both their central nervous systems. Alcohol use during pregnancy may prime the woman's offspring to like alcohol and may put them at risk for heavy drinking and alcohol use disorder during their teen years. In experiments, when pregnant rats drank alcohol, their young offspring later displayed a liking for alcohol's taste and odor (Youngentob et al., 2007, 2009).

Even light drinking or occasional binge drinking can affect the fetal brain (Braun, 1996; Ikonomidou et al., 2000; Sayal et al., 2009). Persistent heavy drinking puts the fetus at risk for birth defects and for future behavior problems, hyperactivity, and lower intelligence. For 1 in about 800 infants, the effects are visible as **fetal alcohol syndrome (FAS),** marked by lifelong physical and mental abnormalities (May & Gossage, 2001). The fetal damage may occur because alcohol has an *epigenetic effect:* It leaves chemical marks on DNA that switch genes abnormally on or off (Liu et al., 2009).

If a pregnant woman experiences extreme stress, the stress hormones flooding her body may indicate a survival threat to the fetus and produce an earlier delivery (Glynn & Sandman, 2011). Some stress early in life prepares us to cope with later adversity in life. But substantial prenatal stress exposure puts a child at increased risk for health problems such as hypertension, heart disease, obesity, and psychiatric disorders.

 LaunchPad For an interactive review of prenatal development, see Launch-Pad's *PsychSim 6: Conception to Birth.* LaunchPad also offers the 8-minute *Video: Prenatal Development.*

RETRIEVAL PRACTICE

• The first two weeks of prenatal development is the period of the _____. The period of the _____ lasts from 9 weeks after conception until birth. The time between those two prenatal periods is considered the period of the _____.

ANSWERS: zygote; fetus; embryo

The Competent Newborn

14-3 What are some newborn abilities, and how do researchers explore infants' mental abilities?

Babies come with software preloaded on their neural hard drives. Having survived prenatal hazards, we as newborns came equipped with automatic reflex responses ideally suited for our survival. We withdrew our limbs to escape pain. If a cloth over our face interfered with our breathing, we turned our head from side to side and swiped at it.

New parents are often in awe of the coordinated sequence of reflexes by which their baby gets food. When something touches their cheek, babies turn toward that touch, open their mouth, and vigorously *root* for a nipple. Finding one, they automatically close on it and begin *sucking*—which itself requires a coordinated sequence of reflexive *tonguing, swallowing,* and *breathing.* Failing to find satisfaction, the hungry baby may *cry*—a behavior parents find highly unpleasant and very rewarding to relieve.

The pioneering American psychologist William James presumed that the newborn experiences a "blooming, buzzing confusion," an assumption few people challenged until the 1960s. But then scientists discovered that babies can tell you a lot—if you know how to ask. To ask, you must capitalize on what babies can do—gaze, suck, turn their heads. So, equipped with eye-tracking machines and pacifiers wired to electronic gear, researchers set out to answer parents' age-old questions: What can my baby see, hear, smell, and think?

Consider how researchers exploit **habituation**—a decrease in responding with repeated stimulation. We saw this earlier when fetuses adapted to a vibrating, honking device placed on their mother's abdomen. The novel stimulus gets attention when first presented. With repetition, the response weakens. This seeming boredom with familiar stimuli gives us a way to ask infants what they see and remember.

Even as newborns, we prefer sights and sounds that facilitate social responsiveness. We turn our heads in the direction of human voices. We gaze longer at a drawing of a face-like image (**FIGURE 14.4**). We prefer to look at objects 8 to 12 inches away. Wonder of wonders, that just happens to be the approximate distance between a nursing infant's eyes and its mother's (Maurer & Maurer, 1988).

Within days after birth, our brain's neural networks were stamped with the smell of our mother's body. Week-old nursing babies, placed between a gauze pad from their mother's bra and one from another nursing mother, have usually turned toward the smell of their own mother's pad (MacFarlane, 1978). What's more, that smell preference lasts. One experiment capitalized on the fact that some nursing mothers in a French maternity ward used a chamomile-scented balm to prevent nipple soreness (Delaunay-El Allam et al., 2010). Twenty-one months later, their toddlers preferred playing with chamomile-scented toys! Their peers who had not sniffed the scent while breast feeding showed no such preference. (This makes one wonder: Will adults, who as babies associated chamomile scent with their mother's breast, become devoted chamomile tea drinkers?) Such studies reveal the remarkable abilities we come with as we enter our world.

habituation decreasing responsiveness with repeated stimulation. As infants gain familiarity with repeated exposure to a stimulus, their interest wanes and they look away sooner.

"I felt like a man trapped in a woman's body. Then I was born."

Comedian Chris Bliss

▼ FIGURE 14.4
Newborns' preference for faces When shown these two stimuli with the same elements, Italian newborns spent nearly twice as many seconds looking at the face-like image (Johnson & Morton, 1991). Canadian newborns—average age 53 minutes in one study—displayed the same apparently inborn preference to look toward faces (Mondloch et al., 1999).

Prepared to feed and eat Animals are predisposed to respond to their offsprings' cries for nourishment.

REVIEW Developmental Issues, Prenatal Development, and the Newborn

LEARNING OBJECTIVES

RETRIEVAL PRACTICE Take a moment to answer each of these Learning Objective Questions (repeated here from within this module). Then turn to Appendix C, Complete Module Reviews, to check your answers. Research suggests that trying to answer these questions on your own will improve your long-term retention (McDaniel et al., 2009).

14-1 What three issues have engaged developmental psychologists?

14-2 What is the course of prenatal development, and how do teratogens affect that development?

14-3 What are some newborn abilities, and how do researchers explore infants' mental abilities?

TERMS AND CONCEPTS TO REMEMBER

RETRIEVAL PRACTICE Test yourself on these terms by trying to write down the definition before flipping back to check your answers.

developmental psychology, p. 178

zygote, p. 181

embryo, p. 181

fetus, p. 181

teratogens, p. 182

fetal alcohol syndrome (FAS), p. 182

habituation, p. 183

Use 🔵 LearningCurve to create your personalized study plan, which will direct you to the resources that will help you most in 🔵 LaunchPad.

---

15 Infancy and Childhood

> "It is a rare privilege to watch the birth, growth, and first feeble struggles of a living human mind."
>
> Annie Sullivan, in Helen Keller's *The Story of My Life*, 1903

AS A FLOWER UNFOLDS IN accord with its genetic instructions, so do we. **Maturation**— the orderly sequence of biological growth—decrees many of our commonalities. We stand before walking. We use nouns before adjectives. Severe deprivation or abuse can slow development. Yet the genetic growth tendencies are inborn. Maturation (nature) sets the basic course of development; experience (nurture) adjusts it. Genes and scenes interact.

Physical Development

15-1 During infancy and childhood, how do the brain and motor skills develop?

Brain Development

In your mother's womb, your developing brain formed nerve cells at the explosive rate of nearly one-quarter million per minute. The developing brain cortex actually overproduces neurons, with the number peaking at 28 weeks (Rabinowicz et al., 1996, 1999).

From infancy on, brain and mind—neural hardware and cognitive software— develop together. On the day you were born, you had most of the brain cells you would ever have. However, your nervous system was immature: After birth, the branching neural networks that eventually enabled you to walk, talk, and remember had a wild growth spurt (**FIGURE 15.1**). From ages 3 to 6, the most rapid growth was in your frontal lobes, which enable rational planning. This explains why preschoolers display a rapidly developing ability to control their attention and behavior (Garon et al., 2008).

maturation biological growth processes that enable orderly changes in behavior, relatively uninfluenced by experience.

The brain's association areas—those linked with thinking, memory, and language—are the last cortical areas to develop. As they do, mental abilities surge (Chugani & Phelps, 1986; Thatcher et al., 1987). Fiber pathways supporting agility, language, and self-control proliferate into puberty. Under the influence of adrenal hormones, tens of billions of synapses form and organize, while a use-it-or-lose-it *pruning* process shuts down unused links (Paus et al., 1999; Thompson et al., 2000).

Newborn · 3 months · 15 months

▼ FIGURE 15.1
Drawings of human cerebral cortex sections In humans, the brain is immature at birth. As the child matures, the neural networks grow increasingly more complex.

Motor Development

The developing brain enables physical coordination. As an infant exercises its maturing muscles and nervous system, skills emerge. With occasional exceptions, the sequence of physical (motor) development is universal. Babies roll over before they sit unsupported, and they usually crawl on all fours before they walk. These behaviors reflect not imitation but a maturing nervous system; blind children, too, crawl before they walk.

And how do infants learn to walk? With a great deal of practice. Karen Adolph and her colleagues (2012, 2014) documented that effort by observing 20 experienced crawlers and 20 novice walkers—all 12 months of age. In an average hour, the novice walkers fell 32 times. Still, walking beats crawling for getting someplace: Walkers took about 1500 steps per hour. They traveled three times the distance as crawlers. And they saw the whole room (unlike crawlers, who looked mostly at the floor).

In the United States, 25 percent of all babies walk by 11 months of age, 50 percent within a week after their first birthday, and 90 percent by age 15 months (Frankenburg et al., 1992). The recommended infant *back to sleep position* (putting babies to sleep on their backs to reduce the risk of a smothering crib death) has been associated with somewhat later crawling but not with later walking (Davis et al., 1998; Lipsitt, 2003).

Genes guide motor development. Identical twins typically begin walking on nearly the same day (Wilson, 1979). Maturation—including the rapid development of the cerebellum at the back of the brain—creates our readiness to learn walking at about age 1. The same is true for other physical skills, including bowel and bladder control. Before necessary muscular and neural maturation, neither pleading nor punishment will produce successful toilet training.

Physical development Sit, crawl, walk, run—the sequence of these motor development milestones is the same the world around, though babies reach them at varying ages.

In the eight years following the 1994 launch of a U.S. Back to Sleep educational campaign, the number of infants sleeping on their stomach dropped from 70 to 11 percent—and sudden unexpected infant deaths fell significantly (Braiker, 2005).

RETRIEVAL PRACTICE

- The biological growth process, called _____, explains why most children begin walking by about 12 to 15 months.

ANSWER: maturation

Brain Maturation and Infant Memory

Can you recall your first day of preschool or your third birthday party? In one study, three-year-olds displayed recognition of someone they met at age one (Kingo et al., 2014). But our earliest *conscious* memories seldom predate our third birthday. We see this *infantile amnesia* in the memories of some preschoolers who experienced an emergency fire evacuation caused by a burning popcorn maker. Seven years later, they were able to recall the alarm and what caused it—*if* they were 4 to 5 years old at the time. Those experiencing the event as 3-year-olds could not remember the cause and usually misrecalled being already outside when the alarm sounded (Pillemer, 1995). Other

"*Someday we'll look back at this time in our lives and be unable to remember it.*"

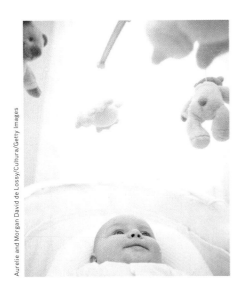

Aurelie and Morgan David de Lossy/Cultura/Getty Images

▼ FIGURE 15.2

Infant at work Babies only 3 months old can learn that kicking moves a mobile, and they can retain that learning for a month. (From Rovee-Collier, 1989, 1997.)

cognition all the mental activities associated with thinking, knowing, remembering, and communicating.

© Bill Anderson/Science Source

Jean Piaget (1896–1980) "If we examine the intellectual development of the individual or of the whole of humanity, we shall find that the human spirit goes through a certain number of stages, each different from the other" (1930).

studies have confirmed that our average age of earliest conscious memory is 3.5 years (Bauer, 2002, 2007). But as children mature, by age 7 or so, childhood amnesia wanes, and they become increasingly capable of remembering experiences, even for a year or more (Bauer & Larkina, 2013; Morris et al., 2010). The brain areas underlying memory, such as the hippocampus and frontal lobes, continue to mature into adolescence (Bauer, 2007).

Apart from constructed memories based on photos and family stories, we *consciously* recall little from our early years, yet our brain was processing and storing information. While finishing her doctoral work in psychology, Carolyn Rovee-Collier observed nonverbal infant memory in action. Her colicky 2-month-old, Benjamin, could be calmed by moving a crib mobile. Weary of hitting the mobile, she strung a cloth ribbon connecting the mobile to Benjamin's foot. Soon, he was kicking his foot to move the mobile. Thinking about her unintended home experiment, Rovee-Collier realized that, contrary to popular opinion in the 1960s, babies are capable of learning. To know for sure that her son wasn't just a whiz kid, she repeated the experiment with other infants (Rovee-Collier, 1989, 1999). Sure enough, they, too, soon kicked more when hitched to a mobile, both on the day of the experiment and the day after. If, however, she hitched them to a different mobile the next day, the infants showed no learning, indicating that they remembered the original mobile and recognized the difference. Moreover, when tethered to the familiar mobile a month later, they remembered the association and again began kicking (**FIGURE 15.2**).

Traces of forgotten childhood languages may also persist. One study tested English-speaking British adults who had no conscious memory of the Hindi or Zulu they had spoken as children. Yet, up to age 40, they could relearn subtle sound contrasts in these languages that other people could *not* learn (Bowers et al., 2009). What the conscious mind does not know and cannot express in words, the nervous system and our two-track mind somehow remember.

Cognitive Development

15-2 From the perspectives of Piaget, Vygotsky, and today's researchers, how does a child's mind develop?

Somewhere on your precarious journey "from egghood to personhood" (Broks, 2007), you became conscious. When was that? In search of the conscious thoughts of an infant—or, rather, a neural signal that marks early conscious awareness—one French research team flashed faces on a screen. At first, the faces appeared so briefly that even adults could not consciously perceive them. Gradually, the presentation slowed until an adult brain-wave response signaled conscious awareness, about 300 milliseconds after an image appeared. With more exposure time while looking at the faces, 5-month-old infants displayed the same brain signature of visual awareness (Dehaene, 2014; Kouider et al., 2013).

If you, too, were consciously aware then, how did your mind unfold from there? Developmental psychologist Jean Piaget [pee-ah-ZHAY] spent his life searching for the answers to such questions. He studied children's **cognitive** development—all the mental activities associated with thinking, knowing, remembering, and communicating. His interest began in 1920, when he was in Paris developing questions for children's intelligence tests. While administering the tests, Piaget became intrigued by children's wrong answers, which were often strikingly similar among same-age children. Where others saw childish mistakes, Piaget saw intelligence at work.

A half-century spent with children convinced Piaget that a child's mind is not a miniature model of an adult's. Thanks partly to his work, we now understand that children reason *differently* than adults, in "wildly illogical ways about problems whose solutions are self-evident to adults" (Brainerd, 1996).

Courtesy of Judy DeLoache

▼ FIGURE 15.3
Scale errors Psychologists Judy DeLoache, David Uttal, and Karl Rosengren (2004) report that 18- to 30-month-old children may fail to take the size of an object into account when trying to perform impossible actions with it. At left, a 21-month-old attempts to slide down a miniature slide. At right, a 24-month-old opens the door to a miniature car and tries to step inside.

Piaget's studies led him to believe that a child's mind develops through a series of stages, in an upward march from the newborn's simple reflexes to the adult's abstract reasoning power. Thus, an 8-year-old can comprehend things a toddler cannot, such as the analogy that "getting an idea is like having a light turn on in your head," or that a miniature slide is too small for sliding, and a miniature car is much too small to get into (**FIGURE 15.3**).

Piaget's core idea was that our intellectual progression reflects an unceasing struggle to make sense of our experiences. To this end, the maturing brain builds **schemas,** concepts or mental molds into which we pour our experiences (**FIGURE 15.4**). By adulthood we have built countless schemas, ranging from *cats* and *dogs* to our concept of *love*.

To explain how we use and adjust our schemas, Piaget proposed two more concepts. First, we **assimilate** new experiences—we interpret them in terms of our current understandings (schemas). Having a simple schema for *dog*, for example, a toddler may call all four-legged animals *dogs*. But as we interact with the world, we also adjust, or **accommodate,** our schemas to incorporate information provided by new experiences. Thus, the child soon learns that the original *dog* schema is too broad and accommodates by refining the category (**FIGURE 15.5**). Many people whose schema of *marriage* was a man-woman union have now accommodated same-sex marriages, with a broadened marriage concept.

Piaget's Theory and Current Thinking

Piaget believed that children construct their understanding of the world while interacting with it. Their minds experience spurts of change, followed by greater stability as they move from one cognitive plateau to the next, each with distinctive characteristics that permit specific kinds of thinking. In Piaget's view, cognitive development consisted of four major stages—*sensorimotor, preoperational, concrete operational,* and *formal operational.*

▼ FIGURE 15.4
An impossible object Look carefully at the "devil's tuning fork." Now look away—no, better first study it some more—and then look away and draw it. . . . Not so easy, is it? Because this tuning fork is an impossible object, you have no schema for such an image.

schema a concept or framework that organizes and interprets information.

assimilation interpreting our new experiences in terms of our existing schemas.

accommodation adapting our current understandings (schemas) to incorporate new information.

(a) Two-year-old Alexandra has learned the schema for *doggy* from her picture books.

(b) Alexandra sees a cat and calls it a *doggy*. She is trying to assimilate this new animal into an existing schema. Her mother tells her, "No, it's a *cat*."

(c) Alexandra accommodates her schema for furry four-legged animals, distinguishing dogs from cats. Over time her schemas become more sophisticated as she learns to distinguish the pets of family and friends by name.

▼ FIGURE 15.5
Pouring experience into mental molds We use our existing schemas to *assimilate* new experiences. But sometimes we need to *accommodate* (adjust) our schemas to include new experiences.

sensorimotor stage in Piaget's theory, the stage (from birth to nearly 2 years of age) during which infants know the world mostly in terms of their sensory impressions and motor activities.

object permanence the awareness that things continue to exist even when not perceived.

preoperational stage in Piaget's theory, the stage (from about 2 to about 6 or 7 years of age) during which a child learns to use language but does not yet comprehend the mental operations of concrete logic.

conservation the principle (which Piaget believed to be a part of concrete operational reasoning) that properties such as mass, volume, and number remain the same despite changes in the forms of objects.

egocentrism in Piaget's theory, the preoperational child's difficulty taking another's point of view.

Sensorimotor Stage In the **sensorimotor stage,** from birth to nearly age 2, babies take in the world through their senses and actions—through looking, hearing, touching, mouthing, and grasping. As their hands and limbs begin to move, they learn to make things happen.

Very young babies seem to live in the present: Out of sight is out of mind. In one test, Piaget showed an infant an appealing toy and then flopped his beret over it. Before the age of 6 months, the infant acted as if the toy ceased to exist. Young infants lack **object permanence**—the awareness that objects continue to exist even when not perceived. By 8 months, infants begin exhibiting memory for things no longer seen. If you hide a toy, the infant will momentarily look for it (**FIGURE 15.6**). Within another month or two, the infant will look for it even after being restrained for several seconds.

So does object permanence in fact blossom suddenly at 8 months, much as tulips blossom in spring? Today's researchers believe object permanence unfolds gradually, and they see development as more continuous than Piaget did. Even young infants will at least momentarily look for a toy where they saw it hidden a second before (Wang et al., 2004).

Researchers also believe Piaget and his followers underestimated young children's competence. Preschoolers think like little scientists. They test ideas, make causal inferences, and learn from statistical patterns (Gopnik, 2012). Consider these simple experiments:

- *Baby physics*: Like adults staring in disbelief at a magic trick (the *"Whoa!"* look), infants look longer at an unexpected and unfamiliar scene of a car seeming to pass through a solid object, a ball stopping in midair, or an object violating object permanence by magically disappearing (Baillargeon, 1995, 2008; Wellman & Gelman, 1992).

- *Baby math*: Karen Wynn (1992, 2000, 2008) showed 5-month-olds one or two objects (**FIGURE 15.7a**). Then she hid the objects behind a screen, and visibly removed or added one (Figure 15.7d). When she lifted the screen, the infants sometimes did a double take, staring longer when shown a wrong number of objects (Figure 15.7f). But were they just responding to a greater or smaller *mass* of objects, rather than a change in *number* (Feigenson et al., 2002)? Later experiments showed that babies' number sense extends to larger numbers, to ratios, and to such things as drumbeats and motions (Libertus & Brannon, 2009; McCrink & Wynn, 2004; Spelke et al., 2013). If accustomed to a Daffy Duck puppet jumping three times on stage, they showed surprise if it jumped only twice.

Clearly, infants are smarter than Piaget appreciated. Even as babies, we had a lot on our minds.

▼ FIGURE 15.6

Object permanence Infants younger than 6 months seldom understand that things continue to exist when they are out of sight. But for this older infant, out of sight is definitely not out of mind.

© Doug Goodman/Science Source

Then either: possible outcome

(e) Screen drops revealing 1 object

(a) Objects placed in case

(b) Screen comes up

(c) Empty hand enters

(d) One object removed

or: impossible outcome

(f) Screen drops revealing 2 objects

Preoperational Stage Piaget believed that until about age 6 or 7, children are in a **preoperational stage**—able to represent things with words and images but too young to perform *mental operations* (such as imagining an action and mentally reversing it). For a 5-year-old, the milk that seems "too much" in a tall, narrow glass may become an acceptable amount if poured into a short, wide glass. Focusing only on the height dimension, this child cannot perform the operation of mentally pouring the milk back. Before about age 6, said Piaget, children lack the concept of **conservation**—the principle that quantity remains the same despite changes in shape (**FIGURE 15.8**).

Piaget did not view the stage transitions as abrupt. Even so, symbolic thinking, and with it *pretend play*, appear at an earlier age than he supposed. Judy DeLoache (1987) discovered this when she showed children a model of a room and hid a miniature stuffed dog behind its miniature couch. The 2½-year-olds easily remembered where to find the miniature toy, but they could not use the model to locate an actual stuffed dog behind a couch in a real room. Three-year-olds—only 6 months older—usually went right to the actual stuffed animal in the real room, showing they *could* think of the model as a symbol for the room. Piaget probably would have been surprised.

EGOCENTRISM Piaget contended that preschool children are **egocentric:** They have difficulty perceiving things from another's point of view. Asked to "show Mommy your picture," 2-year-old Gabriella holds the picture up facing her own eyes. Three-year-old Gray makes himself "invisible" by putting his hands over his eyes, assuming that if he can't see his grandparents, they can't see him. Children's conversations also reveal their egocentrism, as one young boy demonstrated (Phillips, 1969, p. 61):

> *"Do you have a brother?"*
> *"Yes."*
> *"What's his name?"*
> *"Jim."*
> *"Does Jim have a brother?"*
> *"No."*

▼ FIGURE 15.7
Baby math Shown a numerically impossible outcome, 5-month-old infants stare longer. (From Wynn, 1992.)

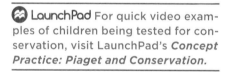 **LaunchPad** For quick video examples of children being tested for conservation, visit LaunchPad's *Concept Practice: Piaget and Conservation.*

▼ FIGURE 15.8
Piaget's test of conservation This visually focused preoperational child does not yet understand the principle of conservation. When the milk is poured into a tall, narrow glass, it suddenly seems like "more" than when it was in the shorter, wider glass. In another year or so, she will understand that the amount stays the same.

Bianca Moscatelli/Worth Publishers

Egocentrism in action "Look grand-daddy, a match!" So says my [DM] 4-year-old granddaughter, Allie, when showing me two memory game cards with matching faces—that face her.

▼ FIGURE 15.9
Testing children's theory of mind This simple problem illustrates how researchers explore children's presumptions about others' mental states. (Inspired by Baron-Cohen et al., 1985.)

This is Sally.   This is Anne.

Sally puts her ball in the red cupboard.

Sally goes away.

Anne moves the ball to the blue cupboard.

Where will Sally look for her ball?

Like Gabriella, TV-watching preschoolers who block your view of the TV assume that you see what they see. They simply have not yet developed the ability to take another's viewpoint. Even we adults may overestimate the extent to which others share our opinions and perspectives, a trait known as the *curse of knowledge*. We assume that something will be clear to others if it is clear to us, or that email recipients will "hear" our "just kidding" intent (Epley et al., 2004; Kruger et al., 2005). Perhaps you can recall asking someone to guess a simple tune such as "Happy Birthday" as you clapped or tapped it out. With the tune in your head, it seemed so obvious! But you suffered the egocentric curse of knowledge, by assuming that what was in your head was also in someone else's.

THEORY OF MIND When Little Red Riding Hood realized her "grandmother" was really a wolf, she swiftly revised her ideas about the creature's intentions and raced away. Preschoolers, although still egocentric, develop this ability to infer others' mental states when they begin forming a **theory of mind** (Premack & Woodruff, 1978).

Infants as young as 7 months show some knowledge of others' beliefs (Kovács et al., 2010). With time, the ability to take another's perspective develops. They come to understand what made a playmate angry, when a sibling will share, and what might make a parent buy a toy. And they begin to tease, empathize, and persuade.

Between about 3 and 4½, children worldwide come to realize that others may hold false beliefs (Callaghan et al., 2005; Rubio-Fernandez & Geurtz, 2013; Sabbagh et al., 2006). Jennifer Jenkins and Janet Astington (1996) showed Toronto children a Band-Aid box and asked them what was inside. Expecting Band-Aids, the children were surprised to discover that the box actually contained pencils. Asked what a child who had never seen the box would think was inside, 3-year-olds typically answered "pencils." By age 4 to 5, the children's theory of mind had leapt forward, and they anticipated their friends' false belief that the box would hold Band-Aids.

In a follow-up experiment, children viewed a doll named Sally leaving her ball in a red cupboard (**FIGURE 15.9**). Another doll, Anne, then moved the ball to a blue cupboard. Researchers then posed a question: When Sally returns, where will she look for the ball? Children with *autism spectrum disorder* had difficulty understanding that Sally's state of mind differed from their own—that Sally, not knowing the ball had been moved, would return to the red cupboard. They also have difficulty reflecting on their own mental states. They are, for example, less likely to use the personal pronouns *I* and *me*. Deaf children with hearing parents and minimal communication opportunities have had similar difficulty inferring others' states of mind (Peterson & Siegal, 1999).

Concrete Operational Stage By about age 7, said Piaget, children enter the **concrete operational stage.** Given concrete (physical) materials, they begin to grasp conservation. Understanding that change in form does not mean change in quantity, they can mentally pour milk back and forth between glasses of different shapes. They also enjoy jokes that use this new understanding:

Mr. Jones went into a restaurant and ordered a whole pizza for his dinner. When the waiter asked if he wanted it cut into 6 or 8 pieces, Mr. Jones said, "Oh, you'd better make it 6, I could never eat 8 pieces!" (McGhee, 1976)

Piaget believed that during the concrete operational stage, children become able to comprehend mathematical transformations and conservation. When my [DM] daughter, Laura, was 6, I was astonished at her inability to reverse simple arithmetic. Asked, "What is 8 plus 4?" she required 5 seconds to compute "12," and another 5 seconds to then compute 12 minus 4. By age 8, she could answer a reversed question instantly.

▼ TABLE 15.1
Piaget's Stages of Cognitive Development

Typical Age Range	Description of Stage	Developmental Phenomena
Birth to nearly 2 years	*Sensorimotor* Experiencing the world through senses and actions (looking, hearing, touching, mouthing, and grasping)	• Object permanence • Stranger anxiety
About 2 to about 6 or 7 years	*Preoperational* Representing things with words and images; using intuitive rather than logical reasoning	• Pretend play • Egocentrism
About 7 to 11 years	*Concrete operational* Thinking logically about concrete events; grasping concrete analogies and performing arithmetical operations	• Conservation • Mathematical transformations
About 12 through adulthood	*Formal operational* Abstract reasoning	• Abstract logic • Potential for mature moral reasoning

Pretend play

theory of mind people's ideas about their own and others' mental states—about their feelings, perceptions, and thoughts, and the behaviors these might predict.

concrete operational stage in Piaget's theory, the stage of cognitive development (from about 7 to 11 years of age) during which children gain the mental operations that enable them to think logically about concrete events.

formal operational stage in Piaget's theory, the stage of cognitive development (normally beginning about age 12) during which people begin to think logically about abstract concepts.

Formal Operational Stage   By age 12, our reasoning expands from the purely concrete (involving actual experience) to encompass abstract thinking (involving imagined realities and symbols). As children approach adolescence, said Piaget, they can ponder hypothetical propositions and deduce consequences: *If* this, *then* that. Systematic reasoning, what Piaget called **formal operational** thinking, is now within their grasp.

Although full-blown logic and reasoning await adolescence, the rudiments of formal operational thinking begin earlier than Piaget realized. Consider this simple problem:

If John is in school, then Mary is in school. John is in school. What can you say about Mary?

Formal operational thinkers have no trouble answering correctly. But neither do most 7-year-olds (Suppes, 1982). **TABLE 15.1** summarizes the four stages in Piaget's theory.

An Alternative Viewpoint: Lev Vygotsky and the Social Child

As Piaget was forming his theory of cognitive development, Russian psychologist Lev Vygotsky was also studying how children think and learn. He noted that by age 7, they increasingly think in words and use words to solve problems. They do this, he said, by internalizing their culture's language and relying on inner speech (Fernyhough, 2008). Parents who say "*No, no!*" when pulling a child's hand away from a cake are giving the child a self-control tool. When the child later needs to resist temptation, he may likewise say "*No, no!*" Second graders who muttered to themselves while doing math problems grasped third-grade math better the following year (Berk, 1994). Whether out loud or inaudibly, talking to themselves helps children control their behavior and emotions and master new skills.

Where Piaget emphasized how the child's mind grows through interaction with the physical environment, Vygotsky emphasized how the child's mind grows through interaction with the *social* environment. If Piaget's child was a young scientist, Vygotsky's was a young apprentice. By mentoring children and giving them new words, parents and others provide a temporary *scaffold* from which children can step to higher levels of thinking (Renninger & Granott, 2005). Language, an important ingredient of social mentoring, provides the building blocks for thinking, noted Vygotsky (who was born the same year as Piaget, but died prematurely of tuberculosis).

Lev Vygotsky (1896–1934)
Vygotsky, pictured here with his daughter, was a Russian developmental psychologist. He studied how a child's mind feeds on the language of social interaction.

Family Circus ® Bil Keane

Bill Keane, Inc. Reprinted with permission of King Features Syndicate

"Don't you remember, Grandma? You were in it with me."

"Assessing the impact of Piaget on developmental psychology is like assessing the impact of Shakespeare on English literature."

Developmental psychologist Harry Beilin (1992)

"Childhood has its own way of seeing, thinking, and feeling, and there is nothing more foolish than the attempt to put ours in its place."

Philosopher Jean-Jacques Rousseau, 1798

---

autism spectrum disorder (ASD) a disorder that appears in childhood and is marked by significant deficiencies in communication and social interaction, and by rigidly fixated interests and repetitive behaviors.

RETRIEVAL PRACTICE

- Object permanence, pretend play, conservation, and abstract logic are developmental milestones for which of Piaget's stages, respectively?

  ANSWER: Object permanence for the sensorimotor stage, pretend play for the preoperational stage, conservation for the concrete operational stage, and abstract logic for the formal operational stage.

- Match the correct cognitive developmental stage (a–d) to each developmental phenomenon (1–6).

  a. Sensorimotor   b. Preoperational   c. Concrete operational   d. Formal operational

  1. Thinking about abstract concepts, such as "freedom."

  2. Enjoying imaginary play (such as dress-up).

  3. Understanding that physical properties stay the same even when objects change form.

  4. Having the ability to reverse math operations.

  5. Understanding that something is not gone for good when it disappears from sight, as when Mom "disappears" behind the shower curtain.

  6. Having difficulty taking another's point of view (as when blocking someone's view of the TV).

  ANSWERS: 1. d, 2. b, 3. c, 4. c, 5. a, 6. b

Reflecting on Piaget's Theory

What remains of Piaget's ideas about the child's mind? Plenty—enough to merit his being singled out by *Time* magazine as one of the twentieth century's 20 most influential scientists and thinkers, and to his being rated in a survey of British psychologists as the last century's greatest psychologist (*Psychologist*, 2003). Piaget identified significant cognitive milestones and stimulated worldwide interest in how the mind develops. His emphasis was less on the ages at which children typically reach specific milestones than on their sequence. Studies around the globe, from aboriginal Australia to Algeria to North America, have confirmed that human cognition unfolds basically in the sequence Piaget described (Lourenco & Machado, 1996; Segall et al., 1990).

However, today's researchers see development as more continuous than did Piaget. By detecting the beginnings of each type of thinking at earlier ages, they have revealed conceptual abilities Piaget missed. Moreover, they see formal logic as a smaller part of cognition than he did. Piaget would not be surprised that today, as part of our own cognitive development, we are adapting his ideas to accommodate new findings.

Implications for Parents and Teachers   Future parents and teachers remember: Young children are incapable of adult logic. Preschoolers who block one's view of the TV simply have not learned to take another's viewpoint. What seems simple and obvious to us—getting off a teeter-totter will cause a friend on the other end to crash—may be incomprehensible to a 3-year-old. Also remember that children are not passive receptacles waiting to be filled with knowledge. Better to build on what they already know, engaging them in concrete demonstrations and stimulating them to think for themselves. And, finally, accept children's cognitive immaturity as adaptive. It is nature's strategy for keeping children close to protective adults and providing time for learning and socialization (Bjorklund & Green, 1992).

LaunchPad For a 7-minute synopsis of Piaget's concepts, see LaunchPad's *Video: Cognitive Development.*

Autism Spectrum Disorder

15-3 What is autism spectrum disorder?

Diagnoses of **autism spectrum disorder (ASD),** a disorder marked by social deficiencies and repetitive behaviors, have been increasing. Once believed to affect 1 in 2500 children (and referred to simply as *autism*), ASD now gets diagnosed in 1 in 68 American children at age 8. But the reported rates vary by place, with New Jersey having four times the reported prevalence of Alabama, while Britain's children have a 1 in 100 rate, and South Korea's 1 in 38 (CDC, 2014; Kim et al., 2011; NAS, 2011). The increase in ASD diagnoses has been offset by a decrease in the number of children with a "cognitive disability" or "learning disability," which suggests a relabeling of children's disorders (Gernsbacher et al., 2005; Grinker, 2007; Shattuck, 2006). A massive $6.7 billion National Children's Study now under way has enrolled some 100,000 pregnant women to follow their babies until they turn 21—partly in hopes of explaining the rising rates of ASD, as well as premature births, childhood obesity, and asthma (Belluck, 2010; Murphy, 2008).

The underlying source of ASD's symptoms seems to be poor communication among brain regions that normally work together to let us take another's viewpoint. From age 2 months on, as other children spend more and more time looking into others' eyes, those who later develop ASD do so less and less (Jones & Klin, 2013). People with ASD are said to have an *impaired theory of mind* (Rajendran & Mitchell, 2007; Senju et al., 2009). Mind reading that most of us find intuitive (*Is that face conveying a smirk or a sneer?*) is difficult for those with ASD. They have difficulty inferring and remembering others' thoughts and feelings, learning that twinkling eyes mean happiness or mischief, and appreciating that playmates and parents might view things differently (Boucher et al., 2012; Frith & Frith, 2001). Partly for such reasons, a national survey of parents and school staff reported that 46 percent of adolescents with ASD had suffered the taunts and torments of bullying—four times the 11 percent rate for other children (Sterzing et al., 2012). In hopes of a cure, desperate parents have sometimes subjected children to dubious therapies (Shute, 2010).

ASD has differing levels of severity. Some (those diagnosed with what used to be called *Asperger syndrome*) generally function at a high level. They have normal intelligence, often accompanied by exceptional skill or talent in a specific area, but deficient social and communication skills and a tendency to become distracted by irrelevant stimuli (Remington et al., 2009).

Biological factors, including genetic influences and abnormal brain development, contribute to ASD (State & Šestan, 2012). Studies suggest that the prenatal environment matters, especially when altered by maternal infection and inflammation, psychiatric drug use, or stress hormones (NIH, 2013; Wang, 2014). Childhood MMR vaccinations do not (Demicheli et al., 2012; DeStefano et al., 2013). Based on a fraudulent 1998 study— "the most damaging medical hoax of the last 100 years" (Flaherty, 2011)—some parents were misled into thinking that the childhood MMR vaccine increased risk of ASD. The unfortunate result was a drop in vaccination rates and an increase in cases of measles and mumps. Some unvaccinated children suffered long-term harm or even death.

ASD afflicts about four boys for every girl. Children for whom amniotic fluid analyses indicated high prenatal testosterone develop more masculine and ASD-related traits (Auyeung et al., 2009). Psychologist Simon Baron-Cohen (2008, 2009) argues that ASD represents an "extreme male brain." Girls are naturally predisposed to be "empathizers," he contends. They tend to be better at reading facial expressions and gestures, though less so if given testosterone (van Honk et al., 2011). And, although the sexes overlap, he believes boys are more often "systemizers"—better at understanding things according to rules or laws, as in mathematical and mechanical systems.

If two tech-minded systemizers mate, then does that increase both the rate of this type of cognitive talent—and also ASD—among their offspring? Indeed, Baron-Cohen (2012) reports, ASD rates are higher not only among elite math students, but also among the children and grandchildren of engineers and MIT graduates. Eindhoven— the engineering and computing hub city of the Netherlands—has triple the rate of schoolchildren with ASD as that in other Dutch cities (Roelfsema et al., 2012).

Twin and sibling studies verify biology's influence. If one identical twin is diagnosed with ASD, the chances are 50 to 70 percent that the co-twin will be as well (Lichtenstein et al., 2010; Sebat et al., 2007). A younger sibling of a child with ASD also is at a heightened risk (Sutcliffe, 2008). No one "autism gene" accounts for the disorder.

Autism spectrum disorder This speech-language pathologist is helping a boy with ASD learn to form sounds and words. ASD is marked by deficient social communication and difficulty grasping others' states of mind.

"Autism" case number 1 In 1943, Donald Gray Triplett, an "odd" child with unusual gifts and social deficits, was the first person to receive the diagnosis of "autism." (After a 2013 change in the diagnosis manual, his condition is now called autism spectrum disorder.) In 2010, at age 77, Triplett was still living in his native home and Mississippi town, where he often played golf (Donvan & Zucker, 2010).

Lisa Wiltse/Corbis

Sharing more than appearance
Twins Johanna and Eva share a
genetically influenced mild ASD.

Rather, many genes—with more than 200 identified so far—appear to contribute (Heil & Schaaf, 2013). Random genetic mutations in sperm-producing cells may also play a role. As men age, these mutations become more frequent, which may help explain why an over-40 man has a much higher risk of fathering a child with ASD than does a man under 30 (Reichenberg et al., 2007).

Researchers are also sleuthing ASD's telltale signs in the brain's structure. Several studies have revealed "underconnectivity"—fewer than normal fiber tracts connecting the front of the brain to the back (Ecker et al., 2012; Just et al., 2012; Wolff et al., 2012). With underconnectivity, there is less of the whole-brain synchrony that, for example, integrates visual and emotional information.

Biology's role in ASD also appears in the brain's functioning. People without ASD often yawn after seeing others yawn. And as they view and imitate another's smiling or frowning, they feel something of what the other is feeling. Not so among those with ASD, who are less imitative and show much less activity in brain areas involved in mirroring others' actions (Dapretto et al., 2006; Perra et al., 2008; Senju et al., 2007). When people with ASD watch another person's hand movements, for example, their brain displays less than normal mirroring activity (Oberman & Ramachandran, 2007; Théoret et al., 2005). Scientists are exploring and debating this idea that the brains of people with ASD have "broken mirrors" (Gallese et al., 2011). And they are exploring whether treatment with oxytocin, the hormone that promotes social bonding, might improve social behavior in those with ASD (Gordon et al., 2013; Lange & McDougle, 2013).

Seeking to "systemize empathy," Baron-Cohen and his Cambridge University colleagues (2007; Golan et al., 2010) collaborated with Britain's National Autistic Society and a film production company. Knowing that television shows with vehicles have been popular among kids with ASD, they created animations with toy vehicle characters in a pretend boy's bedroom, grafting emotion-conveying faces onto toy trams, trains, and tractors (**FIGURE 15.10**). After the boy leaves for school, the characters come to life and have experiences that lead them to display various emotions (see

▼ FIGURE 15.10
Transported into a world of emotion (a) A research team at Cambridge University's Autism Research Centre introduced children with ASD to emotions experienced and displayed by toy vehicles. (b) After four weeks of viewing animations, the children displayed a markedly increased ability to recognize emotions not only in the toy faces but also in humans.

Point to the face that shows how Louise is feeling.

© moodboard/Corbis

"The neighbor's dog has bitten people before. He is barking at Louise."

Three photos iStockphoto/Thinkstock/Getty Images

(b) Children matched the correct face with the story.
(The graph below shows data for two trials.)

Simon Baron-Cohen, Crown Copyright MMVI.
www.thetransporters.com courtesy Changing Media Development

(a) Emotion-conveying faces were grafted onto toy trains.

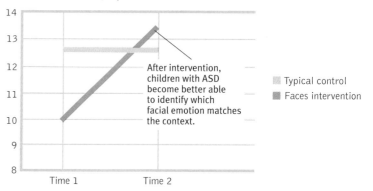

After intervention, children with ASD become better able to identify which facial emotion matches the context.

▪ Typical control
▪ Faces intervention

www.thetransporters.com). The children were surprisingly able to generalize what they had learned to a new, real context. By the intervention's end, their previously deficient ability to recognize emotions on real faces now equaled that of children without ASD.

RETRIEVAL PRACTICE

• What does *theory of mind* have to do with autism spectrum disorder?

ANSWER: Theory of mind focuses on our ability to understand our own and others' mental states. Those with autism spectrum disorder struggle with this ability.

stranger anxiety the fear of strangers that infants commonly display, beginning by about 8 months of age.

attachment an emotional tie with another person; shown in young children by their seeking closeness to the caregiver and showing distress on separation.

Social Development

15-4 How do parent-infant attachment bonds form?

From birth, babies are social creatures, developing an intense bond with their caregivers. Infants come to prefer familiar faces and voices, then to coo and gurgle when given a parent's attention. After about 8 months, soon after object permanence emerges and children become mobile, a curious thing happens: They develop **stranger anxiety.** They may greet strangers by crying and reaching for familiar caregivers. "No! Don't leave me!" their distress seems to say. Children this age have schemas for familiar faces; when they cannot assimilate the new face into these remembered schemas, they become distressed (Kagan, 1984). Once again, we see an important principle: *The brain, mind, and social-emotional behavior develop together.*

Human Bonding

One-year-olds typically cling tightly to a parent when they are frightened or expect separation. Reunited after being apart, they shower the parent with smiles and hugs. This **attachment** bond is a powerful survival impulse that keeps infants close to their caregivers. Infants become attached to those—typically their parents—who are comfortable and familiar. For many years, psychologists reasoned that infants became attached to those who satisfied their need for nourishment. But an accidental finding overturned this explanation.

Body Contact During the 1950s, University of Wisconsin psychologists Harry Harlow and Margaret Harlow bred monkeys for their learning studies. To equalize experiences and to isolate any disease, they separated the infant monkeys from their mothers shortly after birth and raised them in sanitary individual cages, which included a cheesecloth baby blanket (Harlow et al., 1971). Then came a surprise: When their soft blankets were taken to be laundered, the monkeys became distressed.

The Harlows recognized that this intense attachment to the blanket contradicted the idea that attachment derives from an association with nourishment. But how could they show this more convincingly? To pit the drawing power of a food source against the contact comfort of the blanket, they created two artificial mothers. One was a bare wire cylinder with a wooden head and an attached feeding bottle, the other a cylinder wrapped with terry cloth.

When raised with both, the monkeys overwhelmingly preferred the comfy cloth mother (**FIGURE 15.11** on the next page). Like other infants clinging to their live mothers, the monkey babies would cling to their cloth mothers when anxious. When exploring their environment, they used her as a *secure base,* as if attached to her by an invisible elastic band that stretched only so far before pulling them back. Researchers soon learned that other qualities—rocking, warmth, and feeding—made the cloth mother even more appealing.

Human infants, too, become attached to parents who are soft and warm and who rock, feed, and pat. Much parent-infant emotional communication occurs via soothing

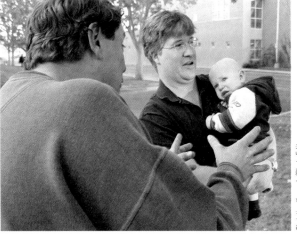

Christina Kennedy/Photo Edit

Stranger anxiety A newly emerging ability to evaluate people as unfamiliar and possibly threatening helps protect babies 8 months and older.

For some people a perceived relationship with God functions as do other attachments, by providing a secure base for exploration and a safe haven when threatened (Granqvist et al., 2010; Kirkpatrick, 1999).

▼ FIGURE 15.11
The Harlows' monkey mothers Psychologists Harry Harlow and Margaret Harlow raised monkeys with two artificial mothers—one a bare wire cylinder with a wooden head and an attached feeding bottle, the other a cylinder with no bottle but covered with foam rubber and wrapped with terry cloth. The Harlows' discovery surprised many psychologists: The infants much preferred contact with the comfortable cloth mother, even while feeding from the nourishing mother.

Harlow Primate Laboratory

critical period an optimal period early in the life of an organism when exposure to certain stimuli or experiences produces normal development.

imprinting the process by which certain animals form strong attachments during early life.

Imprinting Whooping cranes normally learn to migrate by following their parents. These cranes, hand-raised from eggs, have imprinted on a crane-costumed ultralight pilot, who then guided them to winter nesting grounds (Mooallem, 2009).

Mark Peterson/Redux

or arousing touch (Hertenstein et al., 2006). Human attachment also consists of one person providing another with a secure base from which to explore and a safe haven when distressed. As we mature, our secure base and safe haven shift—from parents to peers and partners (Cassidy & Shaver, 1999). But at all ages we are social creatures. We gain strength when someone offers, by words and actions, a safe haven: "I will be here. I am interested in you. Come what may, I will support you" (Crowell & Waters, 1994).

Familiarity Contact is one key to attachment. Another is familiarity. In many animals, attachments based on familiarity form during a **critical period**—an optimal period when certain events must take place to facilitate proper development (Bornstein, 1989). For goslings, ducklings, or chicks, that period falls in the hours shortly after hatching, when the first moving object they see is normally their mother. From then on, the young fowl follow her, and her alone.

Konrad Lorenz (1937) explored this rigid attachment process, called **imprinting.** He wondered: What would ducklings do if he was the first moving creature they observed? What they did was follow him around: Everywhere that Konrad went, the ducks were sure to go. Although baby birds imprint best to their own species, they also will imprint to a variety of moving objects—an animal of another species, a box on wheels, a bouncing ball (Colombo, 1982; Johnson, 1992). Once formed, this attachment is difficult to reverse.

Children—unlike ducklings—do not imprint. However, they do become attached to what they've known. *Mere exposure* to people and things fosters fondness. Children like to reread the same books, rewatch the same movies, reenact family traditions. They prefer to eat familiar foods, live in the same familiar neighborhood, attend school with the same old friends. Familiarity is a safety signal. Familiarity breeds content.

• What distinguishes imprinting from attachment?

ANSWER: Attachment is the normal process by which we form emotional ties with important others. Imprinting occurs only in certain animals that have a critical period very early in their development during which they must form their attachments, and they do so in an inflexible manner.

Attachment Differences

15-5 How have psychologists studied attachment differences, and what have they learned?

What accounts for children's attachment differences? To answer this question, Mary Ainsworth (1979) designed the *strange situation* experiment. She observed mother–infant pairs at home during their first six months. Later she observed the 1-year-old infants in a strange situation (usually a laboratory playroom). Such research has shown that about 60 percent of infants display *secure attachment.* In their mother's presence they play comfortably, happily exploring their new environment. When she leaves, they become distressed; when she returns, they seek contact with her.

Other infants avoid attachment or show *insecure attachment,* marked either by anxiety or avoidance of trusting relationships. They are less likely to explore their surroundings; they may even cling to their mother. When she leaves, they either cry loudly and remain upset or seem indifferent to her departure and return (Ainsworth, 1973, 1989; Kagan, 1995; van IJzendoorn & Kroonenberg, 1988).

Ainsworth and others found that sensitive, responsive mothers—those who noticed what their babies were doing and responded appropriately—had infants who exhibited secure attachment (De Wolff & van IJzendoorn, 1997). Insensitive, unresponsive mothers—mothers who attended to their babies when they felt like doing so but ignored them at other times—often had infants who were insecurely attached. The Harlows' monkey studies, with unresponsive artificial mothers, produced even more striking effects. When put in strange situations without their artificial mothers, the deprived infants were terrified (**FIGURE 15.12**).

Although remembered by some as the researcher who tortured helpless monkeys, Harry Harlow defended his methods: "Remember, for every mistreated monkey there exist a million untreated children," he said, expressing the hope that his research would sensitize people to child abuse and neglect. "No one who knows Harry's work could ever argue that babies do fine without companionship, that a caring mother doesn't matter," noted Harlow biographer Deborah Blum (2010, pp. 292, 307). "And since we . . . didn't fully believe that before Harry Harlow came along, then perhaps we needed—just once—to be smacked really hard with that truth so that we could never again doubt."

So, caring parents matter. But is attachment style the *result* of parenting? Or is attachment style the result of genetically influenced *temperament*—a person's characteristic emotional reactivity and intensity? Twin and developmental studies reveal that heredity matters, too (Picardi et al., 2011; Raby et al., 2012). Shortly after birth, some babies are noticeably *difficult*—irritable, intense, and unpredictable. Others are *easy*—cheerful, relaxed, and feeding and sleeping on predictable schedules (Chess & Thomas, 1987). By neglecting such inborn differences, the parenting studies, noted Judith Harris (1998), are like "comparing foxhounds reared in kennels with poodles reared in apartments." So to separate nature and nurture, we would need to vary parenting while controlling temperament. (Pause and think: If you were the researcher, how might you have done this?)

Dutch researcher Dymphna van den Boom's solution was to randomly assign 100 temperamentally difficult 6- to 9-month-olds to either an experimental group, in which mothers received personal training in sensitive responding, or to a control group, in which they did not. At 12 months of age, 68 percent of the infants in the experimental group were rated securely attached, as were only 28 percent of the control group infants.

Harlow Primate laboratory

▼ FIGURE 15.12
Social deprivation and fear In the Harlows' experiments, monkeys raised with inanimate surrogate mothers were overwhelmed when placed in strange situations without that source of emotional security. (Today there is greater oversight and concern for animal welfare, which would regulate this type of study.)

"Harry Harlow, whose name has become synonymous with cruel monkey experiments, actually helped put an end to cruel child-rearing practices."

Primatologist Frans de Waal (2011)

Full-time dad Financial analyst Walter Cranford, shown here with his baby twins, is one of a growing number of stay-at-home dads. Cranford says the experience has made him appreciate how difficult the work can be: "Sometimes at work you can just unplug, but with this you've got to be going all the time."

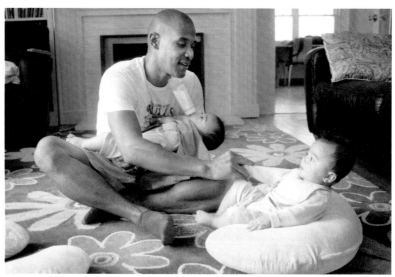

Other studies have confirmed that intervention programs can increase parental sensitivity and, to a lesser extent, infant attachment security (Bakermans-Kranenburg et al., 2003; Van Zeijl et al., 2006).

As these examples indicate, researchers have more often studied mother care than father care. Infants who lack a caring mother are said to suffer "maternal deprivation"; those lacking a father's care merely experience "father absence." This reflects a wider attitude in which "fathering a child" has meant impregnating, and "mothering" has meant nurturing. But fathers are more than just mobile sperm banks. Across nearly 100 studies worldwide, a father's love and acceptance have been comparable to a mother's love in predicting their offspring's health and well-being (Rohner & Veneziano, 2001; see also **TABLE 15.2**). In one mammoth British study following 7259 children from birth to adulthood, those whose fathers were most involved in parenting (through outings, reading to them, and taking an interest in their education) tended to achieve more in school, even after controlling for other factors such as parental education and family wealth (Flouri & Buchanan, 2004).

Children's anxiety over separation from parents peaks at around 13 months, then gradually declines (**FIGURE 15.13**). This happens whether they live with one parent or two, are cared for at home or in a day-care center, live in North America, Guatemala,

▼ TABLE 15.2
Dual Parenting Facts

Some hard facts about declining father care:	Some encouraging findings:
• *Increased father separation.* From 1960 to 2010, the number of children in the United States living apart from their fathers more than doubled (Livingston & Parker, 2011).	• *Active dads are caregiving more.* Today's co-parenting fathers are more engaged, with a doubling in the weekly hours spent with their children, compared with 1965 fathers (Livingston & Parker, 2011).
• *Increased father absence.* Only one in five absent fathers say they visit their children more than once a week, and 27 percent say they have not seen their children in the last year (Livingston & Parker, 2011).	• *Couples that share housework and child care are happier in their relationships and less divorce prone* (Wilcox & Marquardt, 2011).
• *Nonmarital births predict father separation.* Increased father absence accompanies increased nonmarital births. Even among couples cohabiting when a first child is born, the 39 percent odds of their relationship ending during the child's first years are triple the 13 percent odds of parental breakup among those who are married when their first baby is born (Hymowitz et al., 2013).	• *Dual parenting supports children, regardless of parent gender.* The American Academy of Pediatrics (2013) reports that what matters is competent, secure, nurturing parents, regardless of their gender and sexual orientation. The American Sociological Association (2013) concurs: Decades of research confirm that parental stability and resources matter. "Whether a child is raised by same-sex or opposite-sex parents has no bearing on a child's well-being."

or the Kalahari Desert. Does this mean our need for and love of others also fades away? Hardly. Our capacity for love grows, and our pleasure in touching and holding those we love never ceases.

Attachment Styles and Later Relationships Developmental theorist Erik Erikson (1902–1994), working with his wife, Joan Erikson (1902–1997), believed that securely attached children approach life with a sense of **basic trust**—a sense that the world is predictable and reliable. He attributed basic trust not to environment or inborn temperament, but to early parenting. He theorized that infants blessed with sensitive, loving caregivers form a lifelong attitude of trust rather than fear.

Many researchers now believe that our early attachments form the foundation for our adult relationships and our comfort with affection and intimacy (Birnbaum et al., 2006; Fraley et al., 2013). People who report secure relationships with their parents tend to enjoy secure friendships (Gorrese & Ruggieri, 2012). When leaving home to attend college—another kind of "strange situation"—those closely attached to parents tend to adjust well (Mattanah et al., 2011).

Our adult styles of romantic love tend to exhibit (1) secure, trusting attachment; (2) insecure, anxious attachment; or (3) the avoidance of attachment (Feeney & Noller, 1990; Rholes & Simpson, 2004; Shaver & Mikulincer, 2007). Feeling insecurely attached to others may take either of these two main forms (Fraley et al., 2011). In the one, *anxiety*, people constantly crave acceptance but remain vigilant to signs of possible rejection. (Being sensitive to threat, anxiously attached people also tend to be skilled lie detectors and poker players [Ein-Dor & Perry, 2012, 2013].) In the other, *avoidance*, people experience discomfort getting close to others and use avoidant strategies to maintain distance from others. In romantic relationships, an anxious attachment style diminishes social connections and support. An avoidant style decreases commitment, increases openness to infidelity, and increases conflict (DeWall et al., 2011; Li & Chan, 2012).

Adult attachment styles can also affect relationships with one's own children. But say this for those (nearly half of all humans) who exhibit insecure attachments: Anxious or avoidant tendencies have helped our groups detect or escape dangers (Ein-Dor et al., 2010).

Deprivation of Attachment

15-6 How does childhood neglect or abuse affect children's attachments?

If secure attachment nurtures social competence, what happens when circumstances prevent a child's forming attachments? In all of psychology, there is no sadder research literature. Babies locked away at home under conditions of abuse or extreme neglect are often withdrawn, frightened, even speechless. The same is true of those raised in institutions without the stimulation and attention of a regular caregiver, as was tragically illustrated during the 1970s and 1980s in Romania. Having decided that economic growth for his impoverished country required more human capital, Nicolae Ceaușescu, Romania's Communist dictator, outlawed contraception, forbade abortion, and taxed families with fewer than five children. The birthrate skyrocketed. But unable to afford the children they had been coerced into having, many families abandoned them to government-run orphanages with untrained and overworked staff. Child-to-caregiver ratios often were 15 to 1, so the children were deprived of healthy attachments with at least one adult. When tested after Ceaușescu was assassinated in 1989, these children had lower intelligence scores and double the 20 percent rate of anxiety symptoms found in children assigned to quality foster care settings (Nelson et al., 2009, 2014). Dozens of other studies across 19 countries have confirmed that orphaned children tend to fare better on later intelligence tests if raised in family homes. This is especially so for those placed at an early age (van IJzendoorn et al., 2008).

Percentage of infants who cried when their mothers left

Jouke van Keulen/ Shutterstock

▼ FIGURE 15.13
Infants' distress over separation from parents In an experiment, groups of infants were left by their mothers in an unfamiliar room. In both groups, the percentage who cried when the mother left peaked at about 13 months. Whether the infant had experienced day care made little difference. (From Kagan, 1976.)

"Out of the conflict between trust and mistrust, the infant develops hope, which is the earliest form of what gradually becomes faith in adults."

Erik Erikson (1983)

"What is learned in the cradle, lasts to the grave."

French proverb

basic trust according to Erik Erikson, a sense that the world is predictable and trustworthy; said to be formed during infancy by appropriate experiences with responsive caregivers.

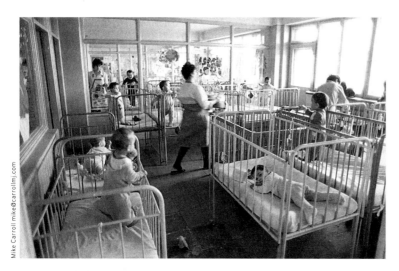

Mike Carroll mike@carrollmj.com

The deprivation of attachment In this Romanian orphanage, the 250 children between ages one and five outnumbered caregivers 15 to 1.

"Stress can set off a ripple of hormonal changes that permanently wire a child's brain to cope with a malevolent world."

Abuse researcher Martin Teicher (2002)

Most children growing up under adversity (as did the surviving children of the Holocaust) are *resilient*; they withstand the trauma and become normal adults (Helmreich, 1992; Masten, 2001). So do most victims of childhood sexual abuse, noted Harvard researcher Susan Clancy (2010), while emphasizing that using children for sex is revolting and never the victim's fault. Indeed, hardship short of trauma often boosts mental toughness (Seery, 2011). And though growing up poor puts children at risk for some social pathologies, growing up rich puts them at risk for other pathologies. Affluent children are at elevated risk for substance abuse, eating disorders, anxiety, and depression (Lund & Dearing, 2012; Luthar et al., 2013). So when you face adversity, consider the possible silver lining.

But those who experience no sharp break from their abusive past don't bounce back so readily. The Harlows' monkeys raised in total isolation, without even an artificial mother, bore lifelong scars. As adults, when placed with other monkeys their age, they either cowered in fright or lashed out in aggression. When they reached sexual maturity, most were incapable of mating. If artificially impregnated, females often were neglectful, abusive, even murderous toward their first-born. Another primate experiment confirmed the abuse-breeds-abuse phenomenon: 9 of 16 female monkeys who had been abused by their mothers became abusive parents, as did *no* female raised by a nonabusive mother (Maestripieri, 2005).

In humans, too, the unloved may become the unloving. Most abusive parents—and many condemned murderers—have reported being neglected or battered as children (Kempe & Kempe, 1978; Lewis et al., 1988). Some 30 percent of people who have been abused later abuse their children—a rate lower than that found in the primate study, but four times the U.S. national rate of child abuse (Dumont et al., 2007; Kaufman & Zigler, 1987).

Although most abused children do *not* later become violent criminals or abusive parents, extreme early trauma may nevertheless leave footprints on the brain. Like battle-stressed soldiers, their brains respond to angry faces with heightened activity in threat-detecting areas (McCrory et al., 2011). In conflict-plagued homes, even sleeping infants' brains show heightened reactivity to hearing angry speech (Graham et al., 2013). As adults, they exhibit stronger startle responses (Jovanovic et al., 2009). If repeatedly threatened and attacked while young, normally placid golden hamsters grow up to be cowards when caged with same-sized hamsters, or bullies when caged with weaker ones (Ferris, 1996). Such animals show changes in the brain chemical serotonin, which calms aggressive impulses. A similarly sluggish serotonin response has been found in abused children who become aggressive teens and adults. By sensitizing the stress response system, early stress can permanently heighten reactions to later stress (van Zuiden et al., 2012; Wei et al., 2012). In another module, we note that child abuse also leaves *epigenetic* marks—chemical tags—that can alter normal gene expression.

Such findings help explain why young children who have survived severe or prolonged physical abuse, childhood sexual abuse, bullying, or wartime atrocities are at increased risk for health problems, psychological disorders, substance abuse, and criminality (Nanni et al., 2012; Trickett et al., 2011; Wolke et al., 2013; Whitelock et al., 2013). In one national study of 43,093 adults, 8 percent reported experiencing physical abuse at least fairly often before age 18 (Sugaya et al., 2012). Among these, 84 percent had experienced at least one psychiatric disorder. Moreover, the greater the abuse, the greater the odds of anxiety, depression, and substance use disorder, and of attempted suicide. Abuse victims are at considerable risk for depression *if* they carry a gene variation that spurs stress-hormone production (Bradley et al., 2008). As we will see again and again, behavior and emotion arise from a particular environment interacting with particular genes.

We adults also suffer when our attachment bonds are severed. Whether through death or separation, a break produces a predictable sequence. Agitated preoccupation with the lost partner is followed by deep sadness and, eventually, the beginnings of emotional detachment and a return to normal living (Hazan & Shaver, 1994). Newly separated couples who have long ago ceased feeling affection are sometimes surprised at their desire to be near the former partner. Detaching is a process, not an event.

> **self-concept** all our thoughts and feelings about ourselves, in answer to the question, "Who am I?"

Self-Concept

15-7 How do children's self-concepts develop?

Infancy's major social achievement is attachment. *Childhood's* major social achievement is a positive sense of self. By the end of childhood, at about age 12, most children have developed a **self-concept**—an understanding and assessment of who they are. Parents often wonder when and how this sense of self develops. "Is my baby girl aware of herself—does she know she is a person distinct from everyone else?"

Of course we cannot ask the baby directly, but we can capitalize on what she can do—letting her *behavior* provide clues to the beginnings of her self-awareness. In 1877, biologist Charles Darwin offered one idea: Self-awareness begins when we recognize ourselves in a mirror. To see whether a child recognizes that the girl in the mirror is indeed herself, researchers sneakily dabbed color on her nose. At about 6 months, children reach out to touch their mirror image as if it were another child (Courage & Howe, 2002; Damon & Hart, 1982, 1988, 1992). By 15 to 18 months, they begin to touch their own noses when they see the colored spot in the mirror (Butterworth, 1992; Gallup & Suarez, 1986). Apparently, 18-month-olds have a schema of how their face should look, and they wonder, "What is that spot doing on *my* face?"

Self-awareness Mirror images fascinate infants from the age of about 6 months. Only at about 18 months, however, does the child recognize that the image in the mirror is "me."

By school age, children's self-concept has blossomed into more detailed descriptions that include their gender, group memberships, psychological traits, and similarities and differences compared with other children (Newman & Ruble, 1988; Stipek, 1992). They come to see themselves as good and skillful in some ways but not others. They form a concept of which traits, ideally, they would like to have. By age 8 or 10, their self-image is quite stable.

Children's views of themselves affect their actions. Children who form a positive self-concept are more confident, independent, optimistic, assertive, and sociable (Maccoby, 1980). So how can parents encourage a positive yet realistic self-concept?

Self-aware animals After prolonged exposure to mirrors, several species—chimpanzees, orangutans, gorillas, dolphins, elephants, and magpies—have similarly demonstrated self-recognition of their mirror image (Gallup, 1970; Prior et al., 2008; Reis & Marino, 2001). In an experiment by Joshua Plotnik and colleagues (2006), Happy, an Asian elephant, when facing a mirror, repeatedly used her trunk to touch an "X" painted above her eye (but not a similar mark above the other eye that was visible only under black light). As one report said, "She's Happy and she knows it!"

Parenting Styles

15-8 What are three parenting styles, and how do children's traits relate to them?

Some parents spank, some reason. Some are strict, some are lax. Some show little affection, some liberally hug and kiss. Do such differences in parenting styles affect children?

The most heavily researched aspect of parenting has been how, and to what extent, parents seek to control their children. Investigators have identified three parenting styles:

1. *Authoritarian* parents are *coercive*. They impose rules and expect obedience: "Don't interrupt." "Keep your room clean." "Don't stay out late or you'll be grounded." "Why? Because I said so."

2. *Permissive* parents are *unrestraining*. They make few demands and use little punishment. They may be indifferent, unresponsive, or unwilling to set limits.

3. *Authoritative* parents are *confrontive*. They are both demanding and responsive. They exert control by setting rules, but, especially with older children, they encourage open discussion and allow exceptions.

Too hard, too soft, and just right, these styles have been called, especially by pioneering researcher Diana Baumrind and her followers. Research indicates that children with the highest self-esteem, self-reliance, and social competence usually have warm, concerned, *authoritative* parents (Baumrind, 1996, 2013; Buri et al., 1988; Coopersmith, 1967). Those with authoritarian parents tend to have less social skill and self-esteem, and those with permissive parents tend to be more aggressive and immature. The participants in most studies have been middle-class White families, and some critics suggest that effective parenting may vary by culture. Yet studies with families in more than 200 cultures worldwide have confirmed the social and academic correlates of loving and authoritative parenting (Rohner & Veneziano, 2001; Sorkhabi, 2005; Steinberg & Morris, 2001). For example, two studies of thousands living in Germany found that those whose parents had maintained a curfew exhibited better adjustment and greater achievements in young adulthood than did those with permissive parents (Haase et al., 2008). And the effects are stronger when children are embedded in *authoritative communities* with connected adults who model a good life (Commission on Children at Risk, 2003).

A *word of caution:* The association between certain parenting styles (being firm but open) and certain childhood outcomes (social competence) is correlational. *Correlation is not causation.* Here are two possible alternative explanations for this parenting-competence link:

- Children's traits may influence parenting. Parental warmth and control vary somewhat from child to child, even in the same family (Holden & Miller, 1999; Klahr & Burt, 2014). Perhaps socially mature, agreeable, easygoing children *evoke* greater trust and warmth from their parents. Twin studies have supported this possibility (Kendler, 1996).

- Some underlying third factor may be at work. Perhaps, for example, competent parents and their competent children share genes that predispose social competence. Twin studies have also supported this possibility (South et al., 2008).

Parents who struggle with conflicting advice should remember that *all advice reflects the advice-giver's values*. For parents who prize unquestioning obedience, or whose children live in dangerous environments, an authoritarian style may have the desired effect. For those who value children's sociability and self-reliance, authoritative firm-but-open parenting is advisable.

The investment in raising a child buys many years not only of joy and love but of worry and irritation. Yet for most people who become parents, a child is one's biological and social legacy—one's personal investment in the human future. To paraphrase psychiatrist Carl Jung, we reach backward into our parents and forward into our children, and through their children into a future we will never see, but about which we must therefore care.

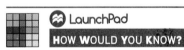

HOW WOULD YOU KNOW?

Have you ever wondered about the effects of children on their parents' well-being? Try LaunchPad's *How Would You Know If Having Children Relates to Being Happier?*

"You are the bows from which your children as living arrows are sent forth."

Kahlil Gibran, *The Prophet*, 1923

RETRIEVAL PRACTICE

- The three parenting styles have been called "too hard, too soft, and just right." Which one is "too hard," which one "too soft," and which one "just right," and why?

ANSWER: The authoritarian style would be too hard, the permissive style too soft, and the authoritative style just right. Parents using the authoritative style tend to have children with high self-esteem, self-reliance, and social competence.

| MODULE 15 | REVIEW | Infancy and Childhood |

LEARNING OBJECTIVES

RETRIEVAL PRACTICE Take a moment to answer each of these Learning Objective Questions (repeated here from within this module). Then turn to Appendix C, Complete Module Reviews, to check your answers. Research suggests that trying to answer these questions on your own will improve your long-term retention (McDaniel et al., 2009).

15-1 During infancy and childhood, how do the brain and motor skills develop?

15-2 From the perspectives of Piaget, Vygotsky, and today's researchers, how does a child's mind develop?

15-3 What is autism spectrum disorder?

15-4 How do parent-infant attachment bonds form?

15-5 How have psychologists studied attachment differences, and what have they learned?

15-6 How does childhood neglect or abuse affect children's attachments?

15-7 How do children's self-concepts develop?

15-8 What are three parenting styles, and how do children's traits relate to them?

TERMS AND CONCEPTS TO REMEMBER

RETRIEVAL PRACTICE Test yourself on these terms by trying to write down the definition before flipping back to check your answers.

maturation, p. 184

cognition, p. 186

schema, p. 187

assimilation, p. 187

accommodation, p. 187

sensorimotor stage, p. 188

object permanence, p. 188

preoperational stage, p. 189

conservation, p. 189

egocentrism, p. 189

theory of mind, p. 190

concrete operational stage, p. 190

formal operational stage, p. 191

autism spectrum disorder (ASD), p. 192

stranger anxiety, p. 195

attachment, p. 195

critical period, p. 196

imprinting, p. 196

basic trust, p. 199

self-concept, p. 201

Use 🔵 LearningCurve to create your personalized study plan, which will direct you to the resources that will help you most in 🔵 LaunchPad.

MODULE 16 Adolescence

16-1 How is *adolescence* defined, and how do physical changes affect developing teens?

MANY PSYCHOLOGISTS ONCE BELIEVED THAT childhood sets our traits. Today's developmental psychologists see development as lifelong. As this *life-span perspective* emerged, psychologists began to look at how maturation and experience shape us not only in infancy and childhood, but also in adolescence and beyond. **Adolescence**—the years spent morphing from child to adult—starts with the physical beginnings of sexual maturity and ends with the social achievement of independent adult status (which means that in some cultures, where teens are self-supporting, adolescence hardly exists).

> **adolescence** the transition period from childhood to adulthood, extending from puberty to independence.

At a five-year high school reunion, former best friends may be surprised at their divergence; a decade later, they may have trouble sustaining a conversation.

How will you look back on your life 10 years from now? Are you making choices that someday you will recollect with satisfaction?

puberty the period of sexual maturation, during which a person becomes capable of reproducing.

In industrialized countries, what are the teen years like? In Leo Tolstoy's *Anna Karenina*, the teen years were "that blissful time when childhood is just coming to an end, and out of that vast circle, happy and gay, a path takes shape." But another teenager, Anne Frank, writing in her diary while hiding from the Nazis, described tumultuous teen emotions:

> My treatment varies so much. One day Anne is so sensible and is allowed to know everything; and the next day I hear that Anne is just a silly little goat who doesn't know anything at all and imagines that she's learned a wonderful lot from books. . . . Oh, so many things bubble up inside me as I lie in bed, having to put up with people I'm fed up with, who always misinterpret my intentions.

G. Stanley Hall (1904), one of the first psychologists to describe adolescence, believed that this tension between biological maturity and social dependence creates a period of "storm and stress." Indeed, after age 30, many who grow up in independence-fostering Western cultures look back on their teenage years as a time they would not want to relive, a time when their peers' social approval was imperative, their sense of direction in life was in flux, and their feeling of alienation from their parents was deepest (Arnett, 1999; Macfarlane, 1964).

But for many, adolescence is a time of vitality without the cares of adulthood, a time of rewarding friendships, heightened idealism, and a growing sense of life's exciting possibilities.

Physical Development

Adolescence begins with **puberty,** the time when we mature sexually. Puberty follows a surge of hormones, which may intensify moods and which trigger the bodily changes discussed in another module.

Early versus late maturing. Just as in the earlier life stages, the *sequence* of physical changes in puberty (for example, breast buds and visible pubic hair before *menarche*—the first menstrual period) is far more predictable than their *timing*. Some girls start their growth spurt at 9, some boys as late as age 16. Though such variations have little effect on height at maturity, they may have psychological consequences. It is not only when we mature that counts, but how people react to our physical development.

For boys, early maturation has mixed effects. Boys who are stronger and more athletic during their early teen years tend to be more popular, self-assured, and independent, though also more at risk for alcohol use, delinquency, and premature sexual activity (Conley & Rudolph, 2009; Copeland et al., 2010; Lynne et al., 2007). For girls, early maturation can be a challenge (Mendle et al., 2007). If a young girl's body and hormone-fed feelings are out of sync with her emotional maturity and her friends' physical development and experiences, she may begin associating with older adolescents or may suffer teasing or sexual harassment (Ge & Natsuaki, 2009). She may also be somewhat more vulnerable to an anxiety disorder (Weingarden & Renshaw, 2012).

Girls in various countries are developing breasts and reaching puberty earlier today than in the past, a phenomenon variously attributed to increased body fat, increased hormone-mimicking chemicals in the diet, and increased stress related to family disruption (Biro et al., 2010, 2012; Ellis et al., 2012; Herman-Giddens, 2013). Researchers wonder: If early puberty is disadvantageous for girls, are today's girls paying a price? Remember: *Nature and nurture interact.*

The teenage brain. An adolescent's brain is also a work in progress. Until puberty, brain cells increase their connections, like trees growing more roots and branches. Then, during adolescence, comes a selective *pruning* of unused neurons and connections (Blakemore, 2008). What we don't use, we lose. It's rather like traffic engineers

"Young man, go to your room and stay there until your cerebral cortex matures."

reducing congestion by eliminating certain streets and constructing new beltways that move traffic more efficiently.

As teens mature, their frontal lobes also continue to develop. The growth of *myelin*, the fatty tissue that forms around axons and speeds neurotransmission, enables better communication with other brain regions (Kuhn, 2006; Silveri et al., 2006). These developments bring improved judgment, impulse control, and long-term planning.

Frontal lobe maturation nevertheless lags behind that of the emotional limbic system. Puberty's hormonal surge and limbic system development help explain teens' occasional impulsiveness, risky behaviors, and emotional storms—slamming doors and turning up the music (Casey et al., 2008, 2013). No wonder younger teens (whose unfinished frontal lobes aren't yet fully equipped for making long-term plans and curbing impulses) may succumb to the tobacco corporations, which most adult smokers could tell them they will later regret. Teens actually don't underestimate the risks of smoking—or fast driving or unprotected sex. They just, when reasoning from their gut, weigh the benefits more heavily (Reyna & Farley, 2006; Steinberg, 2007, 2010). Teens find rewards more exciting than adults do. So they seek thrills and rewards, without a fully developed brake pedal controlling their impulses (**FIGURE 16.1**).

So, when Junior drives recklessly and academically self-destructs, should his parents reassure themselves that "he can't help it; his frontal cortex isn't yet fully grown"? They can at least take hope: Brain changes underlie teens' new self-consciousness about what others are thinking and their valuing of risky rewards (Barkley-Levenson & Galván, 2014; Somerville et al., 2013). And the brain with which Junior begins his teens differs from the brain with which he will end his teens. Unless he slows his brain development with heavy drinking—leaving him prone to impulsivity and addiction—his frontal lobes will continue maturing until about age 25 (Beckman, 2004; Crews et al., 2007). They will also become better connected with the limbic system, enabling better emotion regulation (Steinberg, 2012).

In 2004, the American Psychological Association (APA) joined seven other medical and mental health associations in filing U.S. Supreme Court briefs, arguing against the death penalty for 16- and 17-year-olds. The briefs documented the teen brain's immaturity "in areas that bear upon adolescent decision making." Brain scans of young teens reveal that frontal lobe immaturity is most evident among juvenile offenders and drug users (Shannon et al., 2011; Whelan et al., 2012). Thus, teens are "less guilty by reason of adolescence," suggested psychologist Laurence Steinberg and law professor Elizabeth Scott (2003; Steinberg et al., 2009). In 2005, by a 5-to-4 margin, the Court concurred, declaring juvenile death penalties unconstitutional. In 2012, the APA offered similar arguments against sentencing juveniles to life without parole (Banville, 2012; Steinberg, 2013). Once again, the court, by a narrow 5-to-4 vote, concurred.

Cognitive Development

16-2 How did Piaget, Kohlberg, and later researchers describe adolescent cognitive and moral development?

During the early teen years, reasoning is often self-focused. Adolescents may think their private experiences are unique, something parents just could not understand: "But, Mom, *you* don't really know how it feels to be in love" (Elkind, 1978). Capable of thinking about their own thinking, and about other people's thinking, they also begin imagining what others are thinking about *them*. (They might worry less if they understood their peers' similar self-absorption.) Gradually, though, most begin to reason more abstractly.

Compared with adults, teens listen more to music and prefer more intense music (Bonneville-Roussy et al., 2013).

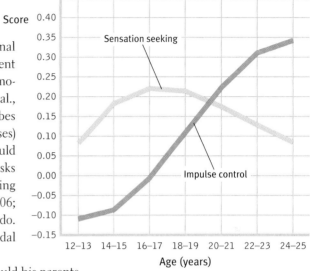

▼ FIGURE 16.1
Impulse control lags reward seeking National surveys of more than 7000 American 12- to 24-year-olds reveal that sensation seeking peaks in the mid-teens, with impulse control developing more slowly as frontal lobes mature. (National Longitudinal Study of Youth and Children and Young Adults survey data presented by Steinberg, 2013.)

"Be afraid to try new things!"

"When the pilot told us to brace and grab our ankles, the first thing that went through my mind was that we must all look pretty stupid."

Jeremiah Rawlings, age 12, after a 1989 DC-10 crash in Sioux City, Iowa

"Ben is in his first year of high school, and he's questioning all the right things."

Developing Reasoning Power

When adolescents achieve the intellectual summit that Jean Piaget called *formal operations*, they apply their new abstract reasoning tools to the world around them. They may think about what is ideally possible and compare that with the imperfect reality of their society, their parents, and themselves. They may debate human nature, good and evil, truth and justice. Their sense of what's fair changes from simple equality to equity—to what's proportional to merit (Almås et al., 2010). Having left behind the concrete images of early childhood, they may now seek a deeper conception of God and existence (Boyatzis, 2012; Elkind, 1970). Reasoning hypothetically and deducing consequences also enables adolescents to detect inconsistencies and spot hypocrisy in others' reasoning. This can lead to heated debates with parents and silent vows never to lose sight of their own ideals (Peterson et al., 1986).

Demonstrating their reasoning ability Although on opposite sides of the immigration policy debate, these teens are all demonstrating their ability to think logically about abstract topics. According to Piaget, they are in the final cognitive stage, formal operations.

Developing Morality

Two crucial tasks of childhood and adolescence are discerning right from wrong and developing character—the psychological muscles for controlling impulses. To be a moral person is to *think* morally and *act* accordingly. Jean Piaget and Lawrence Kohlberg proposed that moral reasoning guides moral actions. A newer view builds on psychology's game-changing recognition that much of our functioning occurs not on the "high road" of deliberate, conscious thinking but on the "low road," unconscious and automatic.

Moral Reasoning Piaget (1932) believed that children's moral judgments build on their cognitive development. Agreeing with Piaget, Lawrence Kohlberg (1981, 1984) sought to describe the development of *moral reasoning*, the thinking that occurs as we consider right and wrong. Kohlberg posed moral dilemmas (for example, whether a person should steal medicine to save a loved one's life) and asked children, adolescents, and adults whether the action was right or wrong. His analysis of their answers led him to propose three basic levels of moral thinking: preconventional, conventional, and postconventional (**TABLE 16.1**). Kohlberg claimed these levels form a moral ladder. As with all stage theories, the sequence is unvarying. We begin on the bottom rung. Preschoolers, typically identifying with their cultural group, conform to and enforce its moral norms (Schmidt & Tomasello, 2012). Later, we ascend to varying heights. Kohlberg's critics have noted that his postconventional stage is culturally limited, appearing mostly among people who prize individualism (Eckensberger, 1994; Miller & Bersoff, 1995).

Moral Intuition Psychologist Jonathan Haidt (2002, 2012) believes that much of our morality is rooted in *moral intuitions*—"quick gut feelings, or affectively laden intuitions." According to this intuitionist view, the mind makes moral judgments as it makes aesthetic judgments—quickly and automatically. We feel disgust when seeing people engaged in degrading or subhuman acts. Even a disgusting taste in the mouth heightens people's disgust over various moral digressions (Eskine et al., 2011). We feel

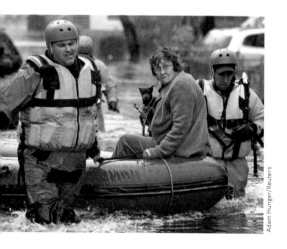

Moral reasoning Some Staten Island, New York, residents faced a moral dilemma in 2012 when Superstorm Sandy caused disastrous flooding. Should they risk their lives to try to rescue family, friends, and neighbors in dangerously flooded areas? Their reasoning likely reflected different levels of moral thinking, even if they behaved similarly.

▼ TABLE 16.1
Kohlberg's Levels of Moral Thinking

Level (approximate age)	Focus	Example
Preconventional morality (before age 9)	Self-interest; obey rules to avoid punishment or gain concrete rewards.	"If you save your dying wife, you'll be a hero."
Conventional morality (early adolescence)	Uphold laws and rules to gain social approval or maintain social order.	"If you steal the drug for her, everyone will think you're a criminal."
Postconventional morality (adolescence and beyond)	Actions reflect belief in basic rights and self-defined ethical principles.	"People have a right to live."

elevation—a tingly, warm, glowing feeling in the chest—when seeing people display exceptional generosity, compassion, or courage. These feelings in turn trigger moral reasoning, says Haidt.

One woman recalled driving through her snowy neighborhood with three young men as they passed "an elderly woman with a shovel in her driveway. I did not think much of it, when one of the guys in the back asked the driver to let him off there. . . . When I saw him jump out of the back seat and approach the lady, my mouth dropped in shock as I realized that he was offering to shovel her walk for her." Witnessing this unexpected goodness triggered elevation: "I felt like jumping out of the car and hugging this guy. I felt like singing and running, or skipping and laughing. I felt like saying nice things about people" (Haidt, 2000).

"Could human morality really be run by the moral emotions," Haidt wonders, "while moral reasoning struts about pretending to be in control?" Consider the desire to punish. Laboratory games reveal that the desire to punish wrongdoings is mostly driven not by reason (such as an objective calculation that punishment deters crime) but rather by emotional reactions, such as moral outrage (Darley, 2009). After the emotional fact, moral reasoning—our mind's press secretary—aims to convince us and others of the logic of what we have intuitively felt.

This intuitionist perspective on morality finds support in a study of moral paradoxes. Imagine seeing a runaway trolley headed for five people. All will certainly be killed unless you throw a switch that diverts the trolley onto another track, where it will kill one person. Should you throw the switch? Most say *Yes*. Kill one, save five.

Now imagine the same dilemma, except that your opportunity to save the five requires you to push a large stranger onto the tracks, where he will die as his body stops the trolley. The logic is the same—kill one, save five?—but most say *No*. Seeking to understand why, a Princeton research team led by Joshua Greene (2001) used brain imaging to spy on people's neural responses as they contemplated such dilemmas. Only when given the body-pushing type of moral dilemma did their brain's emotion areas activate. Thus, our moral judgments provide another example of the two-track mind—of dual processing (Feinberg et al., 2012). Moral reasoning, centered in one brain area, says throw the switch. Our intuitive moral emotions, rooted in other brain areas, override reason when saying *don't* push the man.

While the new research illustrates the many ways moral intuitions trump moral reasoning, other research reaffirms the importance of moral reasoning. The religious and moral reasoning of the Amish, for example, shapes their practices of forgiveness, communal life, and modesty (Narvaez, 2010). Joshua Greene (2010) likens our moral cognition to a camera. Usually, we rely on the automatic point-and-shoot. But sometimes we use reason to manually override the camera's automatic impulse.

"This might not be ethical. Is that a problem for anybody?"

identity our sense of self; according to Erikson, the adolescent's task is to solidify a sense of self by testing and integrating various roles.

social identity the "we" aspect of our self-concept; the part of our answer to "Who am I?" that comes from our group memberships.

"It is a delightful harmony when doing and saying go together."

Michel Eyquem de Montaigne (1533–1592)

"Somewhere between the ages of 10 and 13 (depending on how hormone-enhanced their beef was), children entered adolescence, a.k.a. 'the de-cutening.'"

Jon Stewart et al., *Earth (The Book),* 2010

Moral Action Our moral thinking and feeling surely affect our moral talk. But sometimes talk is cheap and emotions are fleeting. Morality involves *doing* the right thing, and what we do also depends on social influences. As political theorist Hannah Arendt (1963) observed, many Nazi concentration camp guards during World War II were ordinary "moral" people who were corrupted by a powerfully evil situation.

Today's character education programs tend to focus on the whole moral package—thinking, feeling, and *doing* the right thing. In service-learning programs, teens have tutored, cleaned up their neighborhoods, and assisted older adults. The result? The teens' sense of competence and desire to serve has increased, and their school absenteeism and dropout rates have diminished (Andersen, 1998; Piliavin, 2003). Moral action feeds moral attitudes.

A big part of moral development is the self-discipline needed to restrain one's own impulses—to delay small gratifications now to enable bigger rewards later. In one of psychology's best-known experiments, Walter Mischel (1988, 1989) gave Stanford nursery school 4-year-olds a choice between a marshmallow now, or two marshmallows when he returned a few minutes later. The children who had the willpower to delay gratification went on to have higher college completion rates and incomes, and less often suffered addiction problems. Moreover, when a sample of Mischel's marshmallow alums were retested on a new willpower test 40 years later, their differences persisted (Casey et al., 2011).

Our capacity to *delay gratification*—to pass on small rewards now for bigger rewards later—is basic to our future academic, vocational, and social success. Teachers and parents rate children who delay gratification on a marshmallow-like test as more self-controlled (Duckworth et al., 2013). A preference for large-later rather than small-now rewards minimizes one's risk of problem gambling, smoking, and delinquency (Callan et al., 2011; Ert et al., 2013; van Gelder et al., 2013). The moral of the story: Delaying gratification—living with one eye on the future—fosters flourishing.

RETRIEVAL PRACTICE

- According to Kohlberg, _____ morality focuses on self-interest, _____ morality focuses on self-defined ethical principles, and _____ morality focuses on upholding laws and social rules.

ANSWERS: preconventional; postconventional; conventional

Social Development

16-3 What are the social tasks and challenges of adolescence?

Theorist Erik Erikson (1963) contended that each stage of life has its own *psychosocial* task, a crisis that needs resolution. Young children wrestle with issues of *trust,* then *autonomy* (independence), then *initiative.* School-age children strive for *competence,* feeling able and productive. The adolescent's task is to synthesize past, present, and future possibilities into a clearer sense of self (**TABLE 16.2**). Adolescents wonder, "Who am I as an individual? What do I want to do with my life? What values should I live by? What do I believe in?" Erikson called this quest the adolescent's *search for identity.*

As sometimes happens in psychology, Erikson's interests were bred by his own life experience. As the son of a Jewish mother and a Danish Gentile father, Erikson was "doubly an outsider," reported Morton Hunt (1993, p. 391). He was "scorned as a Jew in school but mocked as a Gentile in the synagogue because of his blond hair and blue eyes." Such episodes fueled his interest in the adolescent struggle for identity.

▼ TABLE 16.2
Erikson's Stages of Psychosocial Development

Stage (approximate age)	Issue	Description of Task
Infancy (to 1 year)	Trust vs. mistrust	If needs are dependably met, infants develop a sense of basic trust.
Toddlerhood (1 to 3 years)	Autonomy vs. shame and doubt	Toddlers learn to exercise their will and do things for themselves, or they doubt their abilities.
Preschool (3 to 6 years)	Initiative vs. guilt	Preschoolers learn to initiate tasks and carry out plans, or they feel guilty about their efforts to be independent.
Elementary school (6 years to puberty)	Competence vs. inferiority	Children learn the pleasure of applying themselves to tasks, or they feel inferior.
Adolescence (teen years into 20s)	Identity vs. role confusion	Teenagers work at refining a sense of self by testing roles and then integrating them to form a single identity, or they become confused about who they are.
Young adulthood (20s to early 40s)	Intimacy vs. isolation	Young adults struggle to form close relationships and to gain the capacity for intimate love, or they feel socially isolated.
Middle adulthood (40s to 60s)	Generativity vs. stagnation	In middle age, people discover a sense of contributing to the world, usually through family and work, or they may feel a lack of purpose.
Late adulthood (late 60s and up)	Integrity vs. despair	Reflecting on his or her life, an older adult may feel a sense of satisfaction or failure.

Competence vs. inferiority

Intimacy vs. isolation

Forming an Identity

To refine their sense of identity, adolescents in individualist cultures usually try out different "selves" in different situations. They may act out one self at home, another with friends, and still another at school or online. If two situations overlap—as when a teenager brings friends home—the discomfort can be considerable. The teen asks, "Which self should I be? Which is the real me?" The resolution is a self-definition that unifies the various selves into a consistent and comfortable sense of who one is—an **identity.**

For both adolescents and adults, group identities are often formed by how we differ from those around us. When living in Britain, I [DM] become conscious of my Americanness. When spending time with my daughter in Africa, I become conscious of my minority White race. When surrounded by women, I am mindful of my gender identity. For international students, for those of a minority ethnic group or sexual orientation, or for people with a disability, a **social identity** often forms around their distinctiveness.

Erikson noticed that some adolescents forge their identity early, simply by adopting their parents' values and expectations. (Traditional, less individualist cultures teach adolescents who they are, rather than encouraging them to decide on their own.) Other adolescents may adopt the identity of a particular peer group—jocks, preps, geeks, band kids, debaters.

Most young people develop a sense of contentment with their lives. A question: Which statement best describes you? "I would choose my life the way it is right now" or, "I wish I were somebody else"? When American teens answered, 81 percent picked the first, and 19 percent the second (Lyons, 2004). Reflecting on their existence, 75 percent of

"Self-consciousness, the recognition of a creature by itself as a 'self,' [cannot] exist except in contrast with an 'other,' a something which is not the self."

C. S. Lewis, *The Problem of Pain*, 1940

Nine times out of ten, it's all about peer pressure.

Who shall I be today? By varying the way they look, adolescents try out different "selves." Although we eventually form a consistent and stable sense of identity, the self we present may change with the situation.

🌐 **LaunchPad** For an interactive self-assessment of your own identity, see LaunchPad's *PsychSim 6: Who Am I?*

---

intimacy in Erikson's theory, the ability to form close, loving relationships; a primary developmental task in young adulthood.

"She says she's someone from your past who gave birth to you, and raised you, and sacrificed everything so you could have whatever you wanted."

"I love u guys."

Emily Keyes' final text message to her parents before dying in a Colorado school shooting, 2006

American collegians say they "discuss religion/spirituality" with friends, "pray," and agree that "we are all spiritual beings" and "search for meaning/purpose in life" (Astin et al., 2004; Bryant & Astin, 2008). This would not surprise Stanford psychologist William Damon and his colleagues (2003), who have contended that a key task of adolescence is to achieve a purpose—a desire to accomplish something personally meaningful that makes a difference to the world beyond oneself.

Several nationwide studies indicate that young Americans' self-esteem falls during the early to mid-teen years, and, for girls, depression scores often increase. But then self-image rebounds during the late teens and twenties (Chung et al., 2014; Erol & Orth, 2011; Wagner et al., 2013). Late adolescence is also a time when agreeableness and emotional stability scores increase (Klimstra et al., 2009).

These are the years when many people in industrialized countries begin exploring new opportunities by attending college or working full time. Many college seniors have achieved a clearer identity and a more positive self-concept than they had as first-year students (Waterman, 1988). Collegians who have achieved a clear sense of identity are less prone to alcohol misuse (Bishop et al., 2005).

Erikson contended that adolescent identity formation (which continues into adulthood) is followed in young adulthood by a developing capacity for **intimacy,** the ability to form emotionally close relationships. Romantic relationships, which tend to be emotionally intense, are reported by some two in three North American 17-year-olds, but fewer among those in collectivist countries such as China (Collins et al., 2009; Li et al., 2010). Those who enjoy high-quality (intimate, supportive) relationships with family and friends tend also to enjoy similarly high-quality romantic relationships in adolescence, which set the stage for healthy adult relationships. Such relationships are, for most of us, a source of great pleasure. When Mihaly Csikszentmihalyi [chick-SENT-me-hi] and Jeremy Hunter (2003) used a beeper to sample the daily experiences of American teens, they found them unhappiest when alone and happiest when with friends. As Aristotle long ago recognized, we humans are "the social animal." Relationships matter.

Parent and Peer Relationships

16-4 How do parents and peers influence adolescents?

As adolescents in Western cultures seek to form their own identities, they begin to pull away from their parents (Shanahan et al., 2007). The preschooler who can't be close enough to her mother, who loves to touch and cling to her, becomes the 14-year-old who wouldn't be caught dead holding hands with Mom. The transition occurs gradually (**FIGURE** 16.2). By adolescence, parent-child arguments occur more often, usually over mundane things—household chores, bedtime, homework (Tesser et al., 1989). Conflict during the transition to adolescence tends to be greater with first-born than with second-born children, and greater with mothers than with fathers (Burk et al., 2009; Shanahan et al., 2007).

For a minority of parents and their adolescents, differences lead to real splits and great stress (Steinberg & Morris, 2001). But most disagreements are at the level of harmless bickering. With sons, the issues often are behavior problems, such as acting out or hygiene, while for daughters, the issues commonly involve relationships, such as dating and friendships (Schlomer et al., 2011). Most adolescents—6000 of them surveyed in 10 countries, from Australia to Bangladesh to Turkey—have said they like their parents (Offer et al., 1988). "We usually get along but . . . ," adolescents often reported (Galambos, 1992; Steinberg, 1987).

Positive parent-teen relations and positive peer relations often go hand in hand. High school girls who had the most affectionate relationships with their mothers tended also to enjoy the most intimate friendships with girlfriends (Gold & Yanof, 1985). And teens who felt close to their parents have tended to be healthy and happy and to do well in school (Resnick et al., 1997). Of course, we can state this correlation the other way: Misbehaving teens are more likely to have tense relationships with parents and other adults.

Adolescence is typically a time of diminishing parental influence and growing peer influence. Asked in a survey if they had "ever had a serious talk" with their child about illegal drugs, 85 percent of American parents answered *Yes*. But if the parents had indeed given this earnest advice, many teens had apparently tuned it out: Only 45 percent could recall such a talk (Morin & Brossard, 1997).

As we note in other modules, heredity does much of the heavy lifting in forming individual temperament and personality differences, and peer influences do much of the rest. When with peers, teens discount the future and focus more on immediate rewards (O'Brien et al., 2011). Most teens are herd animals. They talk, dress, and act more like their peers than their parents. What their friends are, they often become, and what "everybody's doing," they often do.

Part of what everybody's doing is networking—a lot. Teens rapidly adopt social media. U.S. teens typically send 60 text messages daily and average 300 Facebook friends (Pew, 2012, 2013). Online communication stimulates intimate self-disclosure—both for better (support groups) and for worse (online predators and extremist groups) (Subrahmanyam & Greenfield, 2008; Valkenburg & Peter, 2009; Wilson et al., 2012). Facebook, from a study of all its English-language users, reports this: Among parents and children, 371 days elapse, on average, before they include each other in their circle of self-disclosure (Burke et al., 2013).

Both online and in real life, for those who feel excluded by their peers, the pain is acute. "The social atmosphere in most high schools is poisonously clique-driven and exclusionary," observed social psychologist Elliot Aronson (2001). Most excluded "students suffer in silence. . . . A small number act out in violent ways against their classmates." Those who withdraw are vulnerable to loneliness, low self-esteem, and depression (Steinberg & Morris, 2001). Peer approval matters.

Teens have tended to see their parents as having more influence in other areas—for example, in shaping their religious faith and in thinking about college and career choices (*Emerging Trends*, 1997). A Gallup Youth Survey revealed that most shared their parents' political views (Lyons, 2005).

"It's you who don't understand me—I've been fifteen, but you have never been forty-eight."

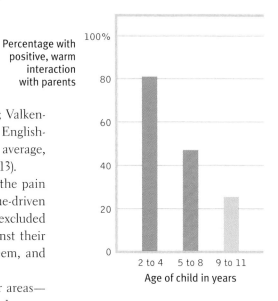

Percentage with positive, warm interaction with parents

▼ FIGURE 16.2
The changing parent-child relationship In a large national study of Canadian families, interviews revealed that the typically close, warm relationships between parents and preschoolers loosened as children became older. (Data from Statistics Canada, 1999.)

"First, I did things for my parents' approval, then I did things for my parents' disapproval, and now I don't know why I do things."

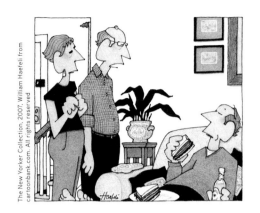

"When I was your age, I was an adult."

Emerging Adulthood

16-5 What is emerging adulthood?

In the Western world, adolescence now roughly corresponds to the teen years. At earlier times, and in other parts of the world today, this slice of life has been much smaller (Baumeister & Tice, 1986). Shortly after sexual maturity, young people would assume adult responsibilities and status. The event might be celebrated with an elaborate initiation—a public rite of passage. The new adult would then work, marry, and have children.

When schooling became compulsory in many Western countries, independence was put on hold until after graduation. From Europe to Australia, adolescents now take more time to establish themselves as adults. In the United States, for example, the average age at first marriage has increased more than 5 years since 1960, to 29 for men, and 27 for women. In 1960, three in four women and two in three men had, by age 30, finished school, left home, become financially independent, married, and had a child. Today, fewer than half of 30-year-old women and one-third of men have met these five milestones (Henig, 2010).

Together, later independence and earlier sexual maturity have widened the once-brief interlude between biological maturity and social independence (**FIGURE 16.3**). In prosperous communities, the time from 18 to the mid-twenties is an increasingly not-yet-settled phase of life, now often called **emerging adulthood** (Arnett, 2006, 2007; Reitzle, 2006). No longer adolescents, these emerging adults, having not yet assumed full adult responsibilities and independence, feel "in between." After high school, those who enter the job market or go to college may be managing their own time and priorities more than ever before. Yet they may be doing so from their parents' home—unable to afford their own place and perhaps still emotionally dependent as well. Recognizing today's more gradually emerging adulthood, the U.S. government now allows dependent children up to age 26 to remain on their parents' health insurance (Cohen, 2010).

> **emerging adulthood** a period from about age 18 to the mid-twenties, when many in Western cultures are no longer adolescents but have not yet achieved full independence as adults.

▼ **FIGURE 16.3**
The transition to adulthood is being stretched from both ends In the 1890s, the average interval between a woman's first menstrual period and marriage, which typically marked a transition to adulthood, was about 7 years; a century later in industrialized countries it was about 14 years (Finer & Philbin, 2014; Guttmacher, 1994). Although many adults are unmarried, later marriage combines with prolonged education and earlier menarche to help stretch out the transition to adulthood.

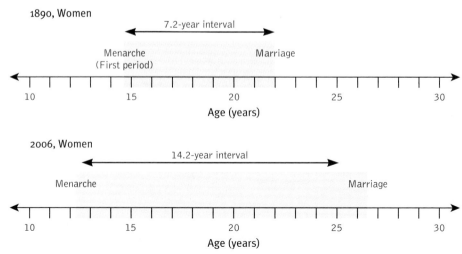

RETRIEVAL PRACTICE

• Match the psychosocial development stage below (1–8) with the issue that Erikson believed we wrestle with at that stage (a–h).

1. Infancy   4. Elementary school   7. Middle adulthood

2. Toddlerhood   5. Adolescence   8. Late adulthood

3. Preschool   6. Young adulthood

   a. Generativity vs. stagnation   e. Identity vs. role confusion

   b. Integrity vs. despair   f. Competence vs. inferiority

   c. Initiative vs. guilt   g. Trust vs. mistrust

   d. Intimacy vs. isolation   h. Autonomy vs. shame and doubt

ANSWERS: 1. g, 2. h, 3. c, 4. f, 5. e, 6. d, 7. a, 8. b

"I just don't know what to do with myself in that long stretch after college but before social security."

LEARNING OBJECTIVES

RETRIEVAL PRACTICE Take a moment to answer each of these Learning Objective Questions (repeated here from within this module). Then turn to Appendix C, Complete Module Reviews, to check your answers. Research suggests that trying to answer these questions on your own will improve your long-term retention (McDaniel et al., 2009).

16-1 How is *adolescence* defined, and how do physical changes affect developing teens?

16-2 How did Piaget, Kohlberg, and later researchers describe adolescent cognitive and moral development?

16-3 What are the social tasks and challenges of adolescence?

16-4 How do parents and peers influence adolescents?

16-5 What is emerging adulthood?

Use 🔿 **LearningCurve** to create your personalized study plan, which will direct you to the resources that will help you most in 🔿 **LaunchPad**.

TERMS AND CONCEPTS TO REMEMBER

RETRIEVAL PRACTICE Test yourself on these terms by trying to write down the definition before flipping back to check your answers.

adolescence, p. 203

puberty, p. 204

identity, p. 209

social identity, p. 209

intimacy, p. 210

emerging adulthood, p. 212

MODULE **17** Adulthood

THE UNFOLDING OF PEOPLE'S ADULT lives continues across the life span. It is, however, more difficult to generalize about adulthood stages than about life's early years. If you know that James is a 1-year-old and Jamal is a 10-year-old, you could say a great deal about each child. Not so with adults who differ by a similar number of years. The boss may be 30 or 60; the marathon runner may be 20 or 50; the 19-year-old may be a parent who supports a child or a child who receives an allowance. Yet our life courses are in some ways similar. Physically, cognitively, and especially socially, we differ at age 50 from our 25-year-old selves. In the discussion that follows, we recognize these differences and use three terms: *early adulthood* (roughly twenties and thirties), *middle adulthood* (to age 65), and *late adulthood* (the years after 65). Within each of these stages, people will vary widely in physical, psychological, and social development.

How old does a person have to be before you think of him or her as old? Depends on who you ask. For 18- to 29-year-olds, 67 was old. For those 60 and over, old was 76 (Yankelovich, 1995).

"I am still learning."

Michelangelo, 1560, at age 85

Rick Doyle/CORBIS

Adult abilities vary widely In 2012, George Blair maintained his place in the record books as the world's oldest barefoot water skier. He is shown here in 2002 when he first set the record, at age 87. (He died in 2013 at age 98.)

The New Yorker Collection, 1999. From cartoonbank.com

"Happy fortieth. I'll take the muscle tone in your upper arms, the girlish timbre of your voice, your amazing tolerance for caffeine, and your ability to digest french fries. The rest of you can stay."

> menopause the time of natural cessation of menstruation; also refers to the biological changes a woman experiences as her ability to reproduce declines.

"I intend to live forever—so far, so good."

Comedian Steven Wright

Physical Development

17-1 What physical changes occur during middle and late adulthood?

Like the declining daylight after the summer solstice, our physical abilities—muscular strength, reaction time, sensory keenness, and cardiac output—all begin an almost imperceptible decline in our mid-twenties. Athletes are often the first to notice. World-class sprinters and swimmers peak by their early twenties. Baseball players peak at about age 27—with 60 percent of Most Valuable Player awardees since 1985 coming ±2 years of that (Silver, 2012). Women—who mature earlier than men—peak earlier. But most of us—especially those of us whose daily lives do not require top physical performance—hardly perceive the early signs of decline.

Physical Changes in Middle Adulthood

Post-40 athletes know all too well that physical decline gradually accelerates. As a lifelong basketball player, I [DM] have found myself increasingly not racing for that loose ball. But even diminished vigor is sufficient for normal activities. Moreover, during early and middle adulthood, physical vigor has less to do with age than with a person's health and exercise habits. Many of today's physically fit 50-year-olds run four miles with ease, while sedentary 25-year-olds find themselves huffing and puffing up two flights of stairs.

Aging also brings a gradual decline in fertility, especially for women. For a 35- to 39-year-old woman, the chance of getting pregnant after a single act of intercourse is only half that of a woman 19 to 26 (Dunson et al., 2002). Men experience a gradual decline in sperm count, testosterone level, and speed of erection and ejaculation. Women experience **menopause,** as menstrual cycles end, usually within a few years of age 50. Expectations and attitudes influence the emotional impact of this event. Is it a sign of lost femininity and growing old, or liberation from menstrual periods and fears of pregnancy? For men, too, expectations influence perceptions. Some experience distress related to a perception of declining virility and physical capacities, but most age without such problems.

With age, sexual activity lessens. Nearly 9 in 10 Americans in their late twenties reported having had vaginal intercourse in the past year, compared with 22 percent of women and 43 percent of men who were over 70 (Herbenick et al., 2010; Reece et al., 2010). Nevertheless, most men and women remain capable of satisfying sexual activity, and most express satisfaction with their sex life. This was true of 70 percent of Canadians surveyed (ages 40 to 64) and 75 percent of Finns (ages 65 to 74) (Kontula & Haavio-Mannila, 2009; Wright, 2006). In one survey, 75 percent of respondents reported being sexually active into their 80s (Schick et al., 2010). And in an American Association of Retired Persons sexuality survey, it was not until age 75 or older that most women and nearly half of men reported little sexual desire (DeLamater, 2012; DeLamater & Sill, 2005). Given good health and a willing partner, the flames of desire, though simmered down, live on. As Alex Comfort (1992, p. 240) jested, "The things that stop you having sex with age are exactly the same as those that stop you riding a bicycle (bad health, thinking it looks silly, no bicycle)."

Physical Changes in Late Adulthood

Is old age "more to be feared than death" (Juvenal, *Satires*)? Or is life "most delightful when it is on the downward slope" (Seneca, *Epistulae ad Lucilium*)? What is it like to grow old?

Life Expectancy From 1950 to 2011, life expectancy at birth increased worldwide from 46.5 years to 70 years—and to 80 and beyond in some developed countries (WHO, 2014a,b). What a gift—two decades more of life! In China, the United States, Britain, Canada, and Australia (to name some countries where students read this book), life expectancy has risen to 76, 79, 80, 82, and 82 respectively (WHO, 2014). This increasing

This increasing life expectancy (humanity's greatest achievement, say some) combines with decreasing birthrates: Older adults are a bigger and bigger population segment, creating an increasing demand for hearing aids, retirement villages, and nursing homes. Today, 1 in 10 people worldwide are 60 or older. The United Nations (2001, 2010) projects that number will double to 2 in 10 by 2050 (and to nearly 4 in 10 in Europe).

Throughout the life span, males are more prone to dying. Although 126 male embryos begin life for every 100 females, the sex ratio is down to 105 males for every 100 females at birth (Strickland, 1992). During the first year, male infants' death rates exceed females' by one-fourth. Worldwide, women outlive men by 4.6 years (WHO, 2014b). (Rather than marrying a man older than themselves, 20-year-old women who want a husband who shares their life expectancy should wait for the 16-year-old boys to mature.) By age 100, women outnumber men 5 to 1.

World record for longevity? French woman Jeanne Calment, the oldest human in history with authenticated age, died in 1998 at age 122. At age 100, she was still riding a bike. At age 114, she became the oldest film actor ever, by portraying herself in *Vincent and Me.*

Both photos Pascal Parrot/Sygma/Corbis

But few of us live to 100. Disease strikes. The body ages. Its cells stop reproducing. It becomes frail and vulnerable to tiny insults—hot weather, a fall, a mild infection—that at age 20 would have been trivial. Tips of chromosomes, called *telomeres*, wear down, much as the tip of a shoelace frays. This wear is accelerated by smoking, obesity, or stress. Children who suffer frequent abuse or bullying exhibit shortened telomeres as biological scars (Shalev et al., 2013). As telomeres shorten, aging cells may die without being replaced with perfect genetic replicas (Epel, 2009).

Low stress and good health habits enable longevity, as does a positive spirit. Chronic anger and depression increase our risk of premature death. Researchers have even observed an intriguing *death-deferral* phenomenon (Shimizu & Pelham, 2008). Across one 15-year-period, the 82,000 deaths on Christmas Day rose to 85,000 on December 26 and 27. The death rate also increases when people reach their birthdays, and when they survive until after other milestones, like the first day of the new millennium.

Sensory Abilities, Strength, and Stamina Although physical decline begins in early adulthood, we are not usually acutely aware of it until later life, when the stairs get steeper, the print gets smaller, and other people seem to mumble more. Visual sharpness diminishes, and distance perception and adaptation to light-level changes are less acute. Muscle strength, reaction time, and stamina also diminish, as do the senses of smell and hearing. In Wales, teens' loitering around a convenience store has been discouraged by a device that emits an aversive high-pitched sound that almost no one over 30 can hear (Lyall, 2005).

With age, the eye's pupil shrinks and its lens becomes less transparent, reducing the amount of light reaching the retina. A 65-year-old retina receives only about one-third as much light as its 20-year-old counterpart (Kline & Schieber, 1985). Thus, to see as well as a 20-year-old when reading or driving, a 65-year-old needs three times as much light—a reason for buying cars with untinted windshields. This also explains why older people sometimes ask younger people, "Don't you need better light for reading?"

Health As people age, they care less about what their bodies look like and more about how they function. For those growing older, there is both bad and good news about health. The bad news: The body's disease-fighting immune system weakens, making older adults more susceptible to life-threatening ailments such as cancer and pneumonia. The good news: Thanks partly to a lifetime's accumulation of antibodies, people over 65 suffer fewer short-term ailments, such as common flu and cold viruses. One study found they were half as likely as 20-year-olds and one-fifth as likely as preschoolers to suffer upper respiratory flu each year (National Center for Health Statistics, 1990).

Shoot, we'd better hurry up and figure this out.

Aging researchers

Betsy Streeter/CartoonStock

"For some reason, possibly to save ink, the restaurants had started printing their menus in letters the height of bacteria."

Dave Barry, *Dave Barry Turns Fifty,* 1998

Most stairway falls taken by older people occur on the top step, precisely where the person typically descends from a window-lit hallway into the darker stairwell (Fozard & Popkin, 1978). Our knowledge of aging could be used to design environments that would reduce such accidents (National Research Council, 1990).

The Aging Brain Up to the teen years, we process information with greater and greater speed (Fry & Hale, 1996; Kail, 1991). But compared with teens and young adults, older people take a bit more time to react, to solve perceptual puzzles, even to remember names (Bashore et al., 1997; Verhaeghen & Salthouse, 1997). The neural processing lag is greatest on complex tasks (Cerella, 1985; Poon, 1987). At video games, most 70-year-olds are no match for a 20-year-old. And, as **FIGURE** 17.1 indicates, fatal accident rates per mile driven increase sharply after age 75. By age 85, they exceed the 16-year-old level. Older drivers appear to focus well on the road ahead, but attend less to other vehicles approaching from the side (Pollatsek et al., 2012). Nevertheless, because older people drive less, they account for fewer than 10 percent of crashes (Coughlin et al., 2004).

Even speech slows (Jacewicz et al. 2009). One research team compared speeches of the renowned psychologist, B. F. Skinner, and observed his speaking rate at ages 58, 73, and 90 as 148, 137, and 106 words per minute, respectively (Epstein, 2012).

Brain regions important to memory begin to atrophy during aging (Schacter, 1996). No wonder older adults, after taking a memory test, feel older: "aging 5 years in 5 minutes," jested one research report (Hughes et al., 2013). In early adulthood, a small, gradual net loss of brain cells begins, contributing by age 80 to a brain-weight reduction of 5 percent or so. In adolescence, late-maturing frontal lobes help account for teen impulsivity. Late in life, atrophy of the inhibition-controlling frontal lobes seemingly explains older people's occasional blunt questions and comments ("Have you put on weight?") (von Hippel, 2007). But good news: The aging brain is plastic, and partly compensates for what it loses by recruiting and reorganizing neural networks (Park & McDonough, 2013). During memory tasks, for example, the left frontal lobes are especially active in young adult brains, while older adult brains use both left and right frontal lobes.

EXERCISE AND AGING And more good news: Exercise slows aging. Active older adults tend to be mentally quick older adults. Physical exercise not only enhances muscles, bones, and energy and helps prevent obesity and heart disease, it maintains the telomeres that protect the chromosome ends (Leslie, 2011).

Exercise also stimulates brain cell development and neural connections, thanks perhaps to increased oxygen and nutrient flow (Erickson et al., 2013; Pereira et al., 2007). Sedentary older adults randomly assigned to aerobic exercise programs exhibit enhanced memory, sharpened judgment, and reduced risk of significant cognitive decline (DeFina et al., 2013; Liang et al., 2010; Nagamatsu et al., 2013). In aging brains, exercise reduces brain shrinkage (Gow et al., 2012). It promotes neurogenesis (the birth of new nerve cells) in the hippocampus, a brain region important for memory (Cherkas et al., 2008; Erickson, 2009; Pereira et al., 2007). And it increases the cellular mitochondria that help power both muscles and brain cells (Steiner et al., 2011). We are more likely to rust from disuse than to wear out from overuse. Fit bodies support fit minds.

▼ FIGURE 17.1

Age and driver fatalities
Slowing reactions contribute to increased accident risks among those 75 and older, and their greater fragility increases their risk of death when accidents happen (NHTSA, 2000). Would you favor driver exams based on performance, not age, to screen out those whose slow reactions or sensory impairments indicate accident risk?

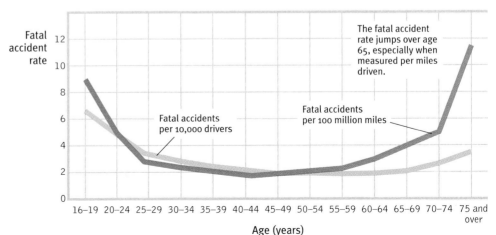

Cognitive Development

Aging and Memory

17-2 How does memory change with age?

Among the most intriguing developmental psychology questions is whether adult cognitive abilities, such as memory, intelligence, and creativity, parallel the gradually accelerating decline of physical abilities.

As we age, we remember some things well. Looking back in later life, adults asked to recall the one or two most important events over the last half-century tend to name events from their teens or twenties (Conway et al., 2005; Rubin et al., 1998). They also display this "reminiscence bump" when asked to name their all-time favorite music, movies, and athletes (Janssen et al., 2011). Whatever people experience around this time—World War II, the 9/11 terrorist attacks, the election of the first U.S. Black president—becomes pivotal (Pillemer, 1998; Schuman & Scott, 1989). In our teens and twenties are so many memorable "firsts"—first kiss, first job, first day at college or university, first meeting in-laws.

Early adulthood is indeed a peak time for some types of learning and remembering. In one test of recall, people watched video clips as 14 strangers said their names, using a common format: "Hi, I'm Larry" (Crook & West, 1990). Then those strangers reappeared and gave additional details. For example, they said, "I'm from Philadelphia," providing more visual *and* voice cues for remembering the person's name. As **FIGURE 17.2** shows, after a second and third replay of the introductions, everyone remembered more names, but younger adults consistently surpassed older adults.

Perhaps it is not surprising, then, that nearly two-thirds of people over age 40 have said their memory is worse than it was 10 years ago (KRC, 2001). In fact, how well older people remember depends on the task. In another experiment, when asked to *recognize* 24 words they had earlier tried to memorize, people showed only a minimal decline in memory. When asked to *recall* that information without clues, the decline was greater (**FIGURE 17.3**).

Teens and young adults surpass both young children and 70-year-olds at *prospective memory* ("Remember to . . .") (Zimmerman & Meier, 2006). But older people's prospective memory remains strong when events help trigger a memory (as when walking by a convenience store triggers "Pick up milk!"). Time-based tasks ("Client meeting at 3:00 P.M.") and especially habitual tasks ("Take medications at 9:00 A.M., 2:00 P.M., and 6:00 P.M.") can be challenging (Einstein et al., 1990, 1995, 1998). To minimize such problems, older adults rely more on time management and reminder cues, such as notes to themselves (Henry et al., 2004). This might have helped John Basinger, who, at age 76, was to be interviewed by a local paper regarding a psychology journal article on his late-life memorization of all 12 volumes of John Milton's epic poem *Paradise Lost* (Seamon et al., 2010; Weir, 2010). He forgot a scheduled meeting with the reporter. When calling to apologize, he noted the irony of forgetting his interview about memory.

In our capacity to learn and remember, as in other areas of development, we differ. Younger adults vary in their abilities to learn and remember, but 70-year-olds vary much more. "Differences between the most and least able 70-year-olds become much greater than between the most and least able 50-year-olds," reported Oxford researcher Patrick Rabbitt (2006). Some 70-year-olds perform below nearly all 20-year-olds; other 70-year-olds match or outdo the average 20-year-old.

No matter how quick or slow we are, remembering seems also to depend on the type of information we are trying to retrieve. If the information is meaningless—nonsense syllables or unimportant events—then the older we are, the more errors we are likely to make. If the information is *meaningful*, as was *Paradise Lost* for John Basinger, older people's rich web of existing knowledge will help them to hold it. But they may take longer than

Percentage of names recalled

After three introductions

Older age groups have poorer performance

After two introductions

After one introduction

Age (years)

▼ FIGURE 17.2
Tests of recall Recalling new names introduced once, twice, or three times is easier for younger adults than for older ones. (Data from Crook & West, 1990.)

▼ FIGURE 17.3
Recall and recognition in adulthood In this experiment, the ability to *recall* new information declined during early and middle adulthood, but the ability to *recognize* new information did not. (Data from Schonfield & Robertson, 1966.)

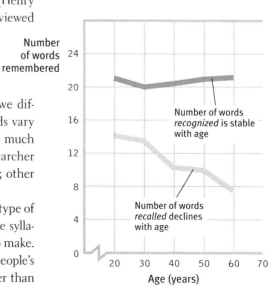

Number of words remembered

Number of words *recognized* is stable with age

Number of words *recalled* declines with age

Age (years)

cross-sectional study a study in which people of different ages are compared with one another.

longitudinal study research in which the same people are restudied and retested over a long period.

neurocognitive disorders (NCDs) acquired (not lifelong) disorders marked by cognitive deficits; often related to Alzheimer's disease, brain injury or disease, or substance abuse. In older adults neurocognitive disorders were formerly called *dementia*.

Alzheimer's disease a neurocognitive disorder marked by neural plaques, often with an onset after age 80, and entailing a progressive decline in memory and other cognitive abilities.

If you are within five years of 20, what experiences from the past year will you likely never forget? (This is the time of your life you may best remember when you are 50.)

younger adults to *produce* the words and things they know. Older adults also more often experience memories on the tip-of-the-tongue (Ossher et al., 2012). Quick-thinking game show winners have usually been young or middle-aged adults (Burke & Shafto, 2004).

Psychologists who study the aging mind have been debating whether "brain fitness" computer training programs can build mental muscles and stave off cognitive decline. Given what we know about the brain's plasticity, can exercising our brains on a "cognitive treadmill"—with memory, visual tracking, and problem-solving exercises—avert losing our minds? "At every point in life, the brain's natural plasticity gives us the ability to improve . . . function," said one neuroscientist-entrepreneur (Merzenich, 2007). One five-year study of nearly 3000 people found that 10 one-hour cognitive training sessions, with follow-up booster sessions a year (and more later), led to improved cognitive scores on tests related to their training (Boron et al., 2007; Willis et al., 2006). Other studies with children and adults also found that brain training that exercises *working memory* can sharpen the mind (Anguera et al., 2013; Jonides et al., 2012).

Based on such findings, some computer game makers are marketing daily brain-exercise programs for older adults. But other researchers, after reviewing all the available studies, advise caution (Melby-Lervåg & Hulme, 2013; Redick et al., 2013; Salthouse, 2010; Shipstead et al., 2012a,b). The available evidence, they argue, suggests that brain training can produce short-term gains, but only on the trained tasks (Berkman et al., 2014; Harrison et al., 2013). A British study of 11,430 people, who either completed brain training activities over six weeks or a control task, confirmed the limited benefits. Although the training improved the practiced skills, it did not boost overall cognitive fitness (Owen et al., 2010).

Other modules explore another dimension of cognitive development: intelligence. There we discuss how **cross-sectional studies** (comparing people of different ages) and **longitudinal studies** (restudying people over time) have identified mental abilities that do and do not change as people age. Age is less a predictor of memory and intelligence than is proximity to death. Tell me whether someone is 8 months or 8 years from a natural death and, regardless of age, you've given me a clue to that person's mental ability. In the last three or four years of life and especially as death approaches, cognitive decline typically accelerates and negative feelings increase (Vogel et al., 2013; Wilson et al., 2007). Researchers call this near-death drop *terminal decline* (Backman & MacDonald, 2006).

Neurocognitive Disorders and Alzheimer's Disease

17-3 How do neurocognitive disorders and Alzheimer's disease affect cognitive ability?

Most people who live into their nineties do so with clear minds. Some, unfortunately, suffer a substantial loss of brain cells in a process that is *not* normal aging. A series of small strokes, a brain tumor, or alcohol use disorder can progressively damage the brain, causing that mental erosion we call a **neurocognitive disorder** (**NCD,** formerly called *dementia*). Heavy midlife smoking more than doubles later risk of the disorder (Rusanen et al., 2011). The feared brain ailment **Alzheimer's disease** strikes 3 percent of the world's population by age 75. Up to age 95, the incidence of mental disintegration doubles roughly every 5 years (**FIGURE 17.4**).

Alzheimer's destroys even the brightest of minds. First memory deteriorates, then reasoning. (Occasionally forgetting where you laid the car keys is no cause for alarm; forgetting how to get home may suggest Alzheimer's.) Robert Sayre (1979) recalled his father shouting at his afflicted mother to "think harder," while his mother, confused, embarrassed, on the verge of tears, randomly searched the house for lost objects. As the disease runs its course, after 5 to 20 years, the person becomes emotionally flat, then disoriented and disinhibited, then incontinent, and finally mentally vacant—a sort of living death, a mere body stripped of its humanity.

"We're keeping people alive so they can live long enough to get Alzheimer's disease."

Steve McConnell, Alzheimer's Association
Vice President, 2007

▼ FIGURE 17.4
Incidence of neurocognitive disorders (NCDs) by age
The risk of mental disintegration due to Alzheimer's disease, strokes, or other brain disease increases with age (Brookmeyer et al., 2011). Still, most people who live into their nineties do so with clear minds.

Underlying the symptoms of Alzheimer's are a loss of brain cells and a deterioration of neurons that produce the neurotransmitter acetylcholine, which is vital to memory and thinking. An autopsy reveals two telltale abnormalities in these acetylcholine-producing neurons: shriveled protein filaments in the cell body, and clumps of a free-floating protein fragment that accumulate as plaque at neuron tips where synaptic communication normally occurs. Long before its symptoms occur, new technologies can now test for the Alzheimer's susceptibility gene or check spinal fluid for the culprit protein fragments (De Meyer et al., 2010; Luciano et al., 2009). Such discoveries have stimulated a race to invent and test drugs that may forestall the disease, such as by reducing the activity of a memory inhibiting neurotransmitter, called GABA (Chen et al., 2014). The recent discovery of 21 associated genes may help (Lambert et al., 2013).

A diminishing sense of smell and slowed or wobbly walking may foretell Alzheimer's (Belluck, 2012; Wilson et al., 2007). Among older adults, hearing loss, and its associated social isolation, predicts risk of depression and accelerated mental decline (Li et al., 2014; Lin et al., 2011a,b, 2013). Compared with people with good hearing, those with hearing loss show declines in memory, attention, and learning about three years earlier. In people at risk for Alzheimer's, brain scans (**FIGURE 17.5**) have also revealed—before symptoms appear—the degeneration of critical brain cells and diminished activity in Alzheimer's-related brain areas (Apostolova et al., 2006; Johnson et al., 2006; Wu & Small, 2006). When people memorized words, scans also showed diffuse brain activity, as if more exertion was required to achieve the same performance (Bookheimer et al., 2000).

Alzheimer's is somewhat less common among those who exercise their minds as well as their bodies (Agrigoroaei & Lachman, 2011). As with muscles, so with the brain: Those who use it less often lose it.

Social Development

17-4 What themes and influences mark our social journey from early adulthood to death?

Many differences between younger and older adults are created by significant life events. A new job means new relationships, new expectations, and new demands. Marriage brings the joy of intimacy and the stress of merging two lives. The three years surrounding the birth of a child bring increased life satisfaction for most parents (Dyrdal & Lucas, 2011). The death of a loved one creates an irreplaceable loss. Do these adult life events shape a sequence of life changes?

▼ FIGURE 17.5
Predicting Alzheimer's disease
During a memory test, MRI scans of the brains of people at risk for Alzheimer's (top) revealed more intense activity (yellow, followed by orange and red) when compared with normal brains (bottom). As brain scans and genetic tests make it possible to identify those likely to suffer Alzheimer's, would you want to be tested? At what age?

social clock   the culturally preferred timing of social events such as marriage, parenthood, and retirement.

Adulthood's Ages and Stages

As people enter their forties, they undergo a transition to middle adulthood, a time when they realize that life will soon be mostly behind instead of ahead of them. Some psychologists have argued that for many the *midlife transition* is a crisis, a time of great struggle, regret, or even feeling struck down by life. The popular image of the midlife crisis is an early-forties man who forsakes his family for a younger girlfriend and a hot sports car. But the fact—reported by large samples of people—is that unhappiness, job dissatisfaction, marital dissatisfaction, divorce, anxiety, and suicide do *not* surge during the early forties (Hunter & Sundel, 1989; Mroczek & Kolarz, 1998). Divorce, for example, is most common among those in their twenties, suicide among those in their seventies and eighties. One study of emotional instability in nearly 10,000 men and women found "not the slightest evidence" that distress peaks anywhere in the midlife age range (McCrae & Costa, 1990).

For the 1 in 4 adults who report experiencing a life crisis, the trigger is not age, but a major event, such as illness, divorce, or job loss (Lachman, 2004). Some middle-aged adults describe themselves as a "sandwich generation," simultaneously supporting their aging parents and their emerging adult children or grandchildren (Riley & Bowen, 2005).

Life events trigger transitions to new life stages at varying ages. The **social clock**—the definition of "the right time" to leave home, get a job, marry, have children, and retire—varies from era to era and culture to culture. The once-rigid sequence has loosened; the social clock still ticks, but people feel freer about being out of sync with it.

Even *chance events* can have lasting significance, by deflecting us down one road rather than another. Albert Bandura (1982, 2005) recalls the ironic true story of a book editor who came to one of Bandura's lectures on the "Psychology of Chance Encounters and Life Paths"—and ended up marrying the woman who happened to sit next to him. The sequence that led to my [DM] authoring this book (which was not my idea) began with my being seated near, and getting to know, a distinguished colleague at an international conference. Chance events can change our lives.

"The important events of a person's life are the products of chains of highly improbable occurrences."

Joseph Traub, "Traub's Law," 2003

Adulthood's Commitments

Two basic aspects of our lives dominate adulthood. Erik Erikson called them *intimacy* (forming close relationships) and *generativity* (being productive and supporting future generations). Researchers have chosen various terms—*affiliation* and *achievement, attachment* and *productivity, connectedness* and *competence*. Sigmund Freud (1935) put it most simply: The healthy adult, he said, is one who can *love* and *work*.

Love   We typically flirt, fall in love, and commit—one person at a time. "Pair-bonding is a trademark of the human animal," observed anthropologist Helen Fisher (1993). From an evolutionary perspective, relatively monogamous pairing makes sense: Parents who cooperated to nurture their children to maturity were more likely to have their genes passed along to posterity than were parents who didn't.

Adult bonds of love are most satisfying and enduring when marked by a similarity of interests and values, a sharing of emotional and material support, and intimate self-disclosure. There also appears to be "vow power." Straight and gay couples who seal their love with commitment—via marriage or other public vows—more often endure (Balsam et al., 2008; Rosenfeld, in press). Such bonds are especially likely to last when couples marry after age 20 and are well educated. Compared with their counterparts of 50 years ago, people in Western countries *are* better educated and marrying later. Yet, ironically, they are nearly twice as likely to divorce. (Both Canada and the United

States now have about one divorce for every two marriages, and in Europe, divorce is only slightly less common.) The divorce rate partly reflects women's lessened economic dependence and men and women's rising expectations. We now hope not only for an enduring bond, but also for a mate who is a wage earner, caregiver, intimate friend, and warm and responsive lover.

Love Intimacy, attachment, commitment—love by whatever name—is central to healthy and happy adulthood.

Historically, couples have met at school, on the job, through family, or, especially, through friends. Since the advent of the Internet, such matchmaking has been supplemented by a striking rise in couples who meet online—as have nearly a quarter of heterosexual couples and some two-thirds of same-sex couples in one recent national survey (**FIGURE** 17.6).

Might test-driving life together in a "trial marriage" minimize divorce risk? In Europe, Canada, and the

Andersen Ross/Blend Images/Alamy

United States, those who cohabit before marriage have had *higher* rates of divorce and marital dysfunction than those who did not cohabit (Jose et al., 2010). In recent data, however, those who cohabited only after engagement and only with their future spouse did not have an increased divorce risk (Goodwin et al., 2010; Jose et al., 2010; Manning & Cohen, 2011; Stanley et al., 2010). American children born to cohabiting parents have been four to five times more likely to experience their parents' separation than children born to married parents (Osborne et al., 2007; Smock & Manning, 2004). Two factors contribute. First, cohabiters tend to be initially less committed to the ideal of enduring marriage. Second, they may become even less marriage supporting while cohabiting.

Although there is more variety in relationships today, the institution of marriage endures. In Western countries, people marry for love. What counts as a "very important" reason to marry? Among Americans, 31 percent say financial stability, and 93 percent say love (Cohn, 2013). And marriage is a predictor of happiness, sexual satisfaction, income, and physical and mental health (Scott et al., 2010). National Opinion Research Center surveys of more than 50,000 Americans since 1972 reveal that 40 percent of married adults, though only 23 percent of unmarried adults, have reported being "very happy." Lesbian couples, too, have reported greater well-being than those single (Peplau & Fingerhut, 2007; Wayment & Peplau, 1995). Moreover, neighborhoods with high marriage rates typically have low rates of social pathologies such as crime, delinquency, and emotional disorders among children (Myers & Scanzoni, 2005).

What do you think? Does marriage correlate with happiness because marital support and intimacy breed happiness, because happy people more often marry and stay married, or both?

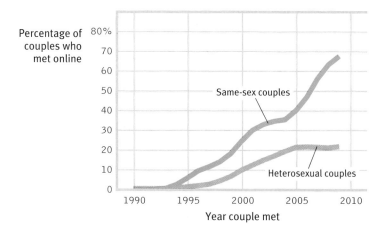

▼ FIGURE 17.6
The changing way Americans meet their partners A national survey of 2452 straight couples and 462 gay and lesbian couples reveals the increasing role of the Internet. (Data from Rosenfeld, 2013; Rosenfeld & Thomas, 2012.)

"Our love for children is so unlike any other human emotion. I fell in love with my babies so quickly and profoundly, almost completely independently of their particular qualities. And yet 20 years later I was (more or less) happy to see them go—I had to be happy to see them go. We are totally devoted to them when they are little and yet the most we can expect in return when they grow up is that they regard us with bemused and tolerant affection."

Developmental psychologist Alison Gopnik, "The Supreme Infant," 2010

"To understand your parents' love, bear your own children."

Chinese proverb

For more on work, including discovering your own strengths, see Appendix A: Psychology at Work.

Relationships that last are not always devoid of conflict. Some couples fight but also shower each other with affection. Other couples never raise their voices yet also seldom praise each other or nuzzle. Both styles can last. After observing the interactions of 2000 couples, John Gottman (1994) reported one indicator of marital success: at least a five-to-one ratio of positive to negative interactions. Stable marriages provide five times more instances of smiling, touching, complimenting, and laughing than of sarcasm, criticism, and insults. So, if you want to predict which couples will stay together, don't pay attention to how passionately they are in love. The pairs who make it are more often those who refrain from putting down their partners. To prevent a cancerous negativity, successful couples learn to fight fair (to state feelings without insulting) and to steer conflict away from chaos with comments like "I know it's not your fault" or "I'll just be quiet for a moment and listen."

Often, love bears children. For most people, this most enduring of life changes is a happy event—one that adds meaning and joy (Nelson et al., 2013). "I feel an overwhelming love for my children unlike anything I feel for anyone else," said 93 percent of American mothers in a national survey (Erickson & Aird, 2005). Many fathers feel the same. A few weeks after the birth of my first child I was suddenly struck by a realization: "So *this* is how my parents felt about me!"

When children begin to absorb time, money, and emotional energy, satisfaction with the relationship itself may decline (Doss et al., 2009). This is especially likely among employed women who, more than they expected, may carry the traditional burden of doing the chores at home. Putting effort into creating an equitable relationship can thus pay double dividends: greater satisfaction, which breeds better parent–child relations (Erel & Burman, 1995).

Although love bears children, children eventually leave home. This departure is a significant and sometimes difficult event. For most people, however, an empty nest is a happy place (Adelmann et al., 1989; Gorchoff et al., 2008). Many parents experience a "postlaunch honeymoon," especially if they maintain close relationships with their children (White & Edwards, 1990). As Daniel Gilbert (2006) has said, "The only known symptom of 'empty nest syndrome' is increased smiling."

Work For many adults, the answer to "Who are you?" depends a great deal on the answer to "What do you do?" For women and men, choosing a career path is difficult, especially during bad economic times. Even in the best of times, few students in their first two years of college or university can predict their later careers.

In the end, happiness is about having work that fits your interests and provides you with a sense of competence and accomplishment. It is having a close, supportive companion who cheers your accomplishments (Gable et al., 2006). And for some, it includes having children who love you and whom you love and feel proud of.

Job satisfaction and life satisfaction Work can provide us with a sense of identity and competence and opportunities for accomplishment. Perhaps this is why challenging and interesting occupations enhance people's happiness.

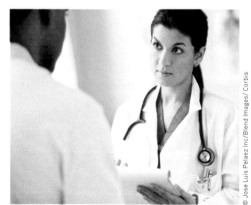

Well-Being Across the Life Span

17-5 How does our well-being change across the life span?

To live is to grow older. This moment marks the oldest you have ever been and the youngest you will henceforth be. That means we all can look back with satisfaction or regret, and forward with hope or dread. When asked what they would have done differently if they could relive their lives, people's most common answer has been "taken my education more seriously and worked harder at it" (Kinnier & Metha, 1989; Roese & Summerville, 2005). Other regrets—"I should have told my father I loved him," "I regret that I never went to Europe"—have also focused less on mistakes made than on the things one *failed* to do (Gilovich & Medvec, 1995).

From the teens to midlife, people typically experience a strengthening sense of identity, confidence, and self-esteem (Huang, 2010; Robins & Trzesniewski, 2005). In later life, challenges arise: Income shrinks, work is often taken away, the body deteriorates, recall fades, energy wanes, family members and friends die or move away, and the great enemy, death, looms ever closer. And for those in the terminal decline phase, life satisfaction does decline as death approaches (Gerstorf et al., 2008).

Small wonder that most presume that happiness declines in later life (Lacey et al., 2006). But worldwide, as Gallup researchers discovered, most find that the over-65 years are not notably unhappy (**FIGURE 17.7**). Self-esteem remains stable (Wagner et al., 2013). If anything, positive feelings, supported by enhanced emotional control, grow after midlife and negative feelings subside (Stone et al., 2010; Urry & Gross, 2010). Older adults increasingly use words that convey positive emotions (Pennebaker & Stone, 2003), and they attend less and less to negative information. Compared with younger adults, for example, they are slower to perceive negative faces and more attentive to positive news (Isaacowitz, 2012; Scheibe & Carstensen, 2010).

Compared with teens and young adults, older adults also have a smaller social network, with fewer friendships (Wrzus et al., 2012). Like people of all ages, older adults are, however, happiest when not alone (**FIGURE 17.8** on the next page). They also experience fewer problems in their relationships—less attachment anxiety, stress, and anger (Chopik et al., 2013; Fingerman & Charles, 2010; Stone et al., 2010). With age, we become more stable and more accepting (Carstensen et al., 2011; Shallcross et al., 2013).

"When you were born, you cried and the world rejoiced. Live your life in a manner so that when you die the world cries and you rejoice."

Native American proverb

"Hope I die before I get old."

Pete Townshend, of the Who (written at age 20)

"Still married after all these years?
No mystery.
We are each other's habit,
And each other's history."

Judith Viorst,
"The Secret of Staying Married," 2007

▼ FIGURE 17.7
Nelson Mandela embodied stable life satisfaction The Gallup Organization asked 658,038 people worldwide to rate their lives on a ladder from 0 ("the worst possible life") to 10 ("the best possible life"). Age gave no clue to life satisfaction. (Data from Morrison et al., 2014.)

Life ratings (Best life 10 — Worst life 0)

| Age (years) |
| 15–20, 21–30, 31–40, 41–50, 51–60, 61–70, 71–80, 81–90, 91+ |

Media24/Gallo Images/Getty Images

▼ FIGURE 17.8
Humans are social creatures Both younger and older adults report greater happiness when spending time with others. (Note, this correlation could also reflect happier people being more social.) (Gallup survey data reported by Crabtree, 2011.)

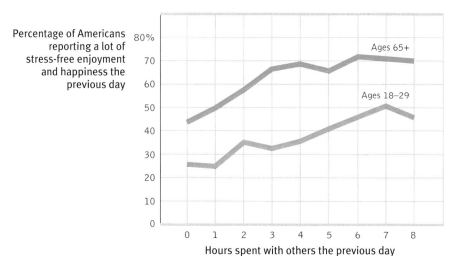

Percentage of Americans reporting a lot of stress-free enjoyment and happiness the previous day

Ages 65+

Ages 18–29

Hours spent with others the previous day

"At 20 we worry about what others think of us. At 40 we don't care what others think of us. At 60 we discover they haven't been thinking about us at all."

Anonymous

"The best thing about being 100 is *no peer pressure.*"

Lewis W. Kuester, 2005, on turning 100

The aging brain may help nurture these positive feelings. Brain scans of older adults show that the amygdala, a neural processing center for emotions, responds less actively to negative events (but not to positive events) (Mather et al., 2004). Brain-wave reactions to negative images also diminish with age (Kisley et al., 2007).

Moreover, at all ages, the bad feelings we associate with negative events fade faster than do the good feelings we associate with positive events (Walker et al., 2003). This contributes to most older people's sense that life, on balance, has been mostly good. Given that growing older is an outcome of living (an outcome most prefer to early dying), the positivity of later life is comforting. Thanks to biological, psychological, and social-cultural influences, more and more people flourish into later life (**FIGURE 17.9**).

The resilience of well-being across the life span obscures some interesting age-related emotional differences. Psychologists Mihaly Csikszentmihalyi [chick-SENT-me-hi] and Reed Larson (1984) mapped people's emotional terrain by periodically signaling them with electronic beepers to report their current activities and feelings. They found that teenagers typically come down from elation or up from gloom in less than an hour, but adult moods are less extreme and more enduring. As the years go by, feelings mellow (Costa et al., 1987; Diener et al., 1986). Highs become less high, lows less low. Compliments provoke less elation and criticisms less despair, as both become merely additional feedback atop a mountain of accumulated praise and blame. As we age, life therefore becomes less of an emotional roller coaster.

Biological influences:
• no genetic predisposition to early cognitive or physical decline
• appropriate nutrition

Psychological influences:
• optimistic outlook
• physically and mentally active lifestyle

Successful aging

Social-cultural influences:
• support from family and friends
• cultural respect for aging
• safe living conditions

▼ FIGURE 17.9
Biopsychosocial influences on successful aging

- What are some of the most significant challenges and rewards of growing old?

ANSWERS: Challenges: decline of muscular strength, reaction times, stamina, sensory keenness, cardiac output, and immune system functioning. Risk of cognitive decline increases. Rewards: positive feelings tend to grow, negative emotions are less intense, and anger, stress, worry, and social-relationship problems decrease.

Death and Dying

17-6 A loved one's death triggers what range of reactions?

Warning: If you begin reading the next paragraph, you will die.

But of course, if you hadn't read this, you would still die in due time. "Time is a great teacher," noted the nineteenth-century composer Hector Berlioz, "but unfortunately it kills all its pupils." Death is our inevitable end. We enter the world with a wail, and usually leave it in silence.

Most of us will also suffer and cope with the deaths of relatives and friends. Usually, the most difficult separation is from one's partner—a loss suffered by five times more women than men. Grief is especially severe when a loved one's death comes suddenly and before its expected time on the social clock. The sudden illness or accident claiming a 45-year-old life partner or a child may trigger a year or more of memory-laden mourning that eventually subsides to a mild depression (Lehman et al., 1987).

For some, however, the loss is unbearable. One Danish long-term study of more than 1 million people found that about 17,000 of them had suffered the death of a child under 18. In the five years following that death, 3 percent of them had a first psychiatric hospitalization, a 67 percent higher rate than among other parents (Li et al., 2005).

Even so, reactions to a loved one's death range more widely than most suppose. Some cultures encourage public weeping and wailing; others hide grief. Within any culture, individuals differ. Given similar losses, some people grieve hard and long, others less so (Ott et al., 2007). Contrary to popular misconceptions, however,

- terminally ill and bereaved people do not go through identical predictable stages, such as denial before anger (Friedman & James, 2008; Nolen-Hoeksema & Larson, 1999).

- those who express the strongest grief immediately do not purge their grief more quickly (Bonanno & Kaltman, 1999; Wortman & Silver, 1989). On the other hand, grieving parents who try to protect their partner by "staying strong" and not discussing their child's death may actually prolong the grieving (Stroebe et al., 2013).

- bereavement therapy and self-help groups offer support, but there is similar healing power in the passing of time, the support of friends, and the act of giving support and help to others (Baddeley & Singer, 2009; Brown et al., 2008; Neimeyer & Currier, 2009). Grieving spouses who talk often with others or receive grief counseling adjust about as well as those who grieve more privately (Bonanno, 2004; Stroebe et al., 2005).

Facing death with dignity and openness helps people complete the life cycle with a sense of life's meaningfulness and unity—the sense that their existence has been good and that life and death are parts of an ongoing cycle. Although death may be unwelcome, life itself can be affirmed even at death. This is especially so for people who review their lives not with despair but with what Erik Erikson called a sense of *integrity*—a feeling that one's life has been meaningful and worthwhile.

"Love—why, I'll tell you what love is: It's you at 75 and her at 71, each of you listening for the other's step in the next room, each afraid that a sudden silence, a sudden cry, could mean a lifetime's talk is over."

Brian Moore, *The Luck of Ginger Coffey*, 1960

"Consider, friend, as you pass by, as you are now, so once was I. As I am now, you too shall be. Prepare, therefore, to follow me."

Scottish tombstone epitaph

MODULE 17 REVIEW Adulthood

LEARNING OBJECTIVES

RETRIEVAL PRACTICE Take a moment to answer each of these Learning Objective Questions (repeated here from within this module). Then turn to Appendix C, Complete Module Reviews, to check your answers. Research suggests that trying to answer these questions on your own will improve your long-term retention (McDaniel et al., 2009).

17-1 What physical changes occur during middle and late adulthood?

17-2 How does memory change with age?

17-3 How do neurocognitive disorders and Alzheimer's disease affect cognitive ability?

17-4 What themes and influences mark our social journey from early adulthood to death?

17-5 How does our well-being change across the life span?

17-6 A loved one's death triggers what range of reactions?

TERMS AND CONCEPTS TO REMEMBER

RETRIEVAL PRACTICE Test yourself on these terms by trying to write down the definition before flipping back to check your answers.

menopause, p. 214

cross-sectional study, p. 218

longitudinal study, p. 218

neurocognitive disorders (NCDs), p. 218

Alzheimer's disease, p. 218

social clock, p. 220

Use ⊘ LearningCurve to create your personalized study plan, which will direct you to the resources that will help you most in ⊘ LaunchPad.

TEST YOUR-SELF DEVELOPING THROUGH THE LIFE SPAN

Test yourself repeatedly throughout your studies. This will not only help you figure out what you know and don't know; the testing itself will help you learn and remember the information more effectively thanks to the *testing effect.*

MODULE 14 Developmental Issues, Prenatal Development, and the Newborn

1. The three major issues that interest developmental psychologists are nature/nurture, stability/change, and _____ / _____ .

2. Although development is lifelong, there is stability of personality over time. For example,

   a. most personality traits emerge in infancy and persist throughout life.

   b. temperament tends to remain stable throughout life.

   c. few people change significantly after adolescence.

   d. people tend to undergo greater personality changes as they age.

3. Body organs first begin to form and function during the period of the _____ ; within 6 months, during the period of the _____ , the organs are sufficiently functional to allow a good chance of survival.

   a. zygote; embryo

   b. zygote; fetus

   c. embryo; fetus

   d. placenta; fetus

4. Chemicals that pass through the placenta's screen and may harm an embryo or fetus are called _____ .

MODULE 15 Infancy and Childhood

5. Stroke a newborn's cheek and the infant will root for a nipple. This illustrates

   a. a reflex.

   b. nurture.

   c. differentiation.

   d. continuity.

6. Between ages 3 and 6, the human brain experiences the greatest growth in the _____ lobes, which enable rational planning and aid memory.

7. Which of the following is true of motor-skill development?

   a. It is determined solely by genetic factors.

   b. The sequence, but not the timing, is universal.

   c. The timing, but not the sequence, is universal.

   d. It is determined solely by environmental factors.

8. Why can't we consciously recall how we learned to walk when we were infants?

9. Use Piaget's first three stages of cognitive development to explain why young children are not just miniature adults in the way they think.

10. Although Piaget's stage theory continues to inform our understanding of children's thinking, many researchers believe that
    a. Piaget's stages begin earlier and development is more continuous than he realized.
    b. children do not progress as rapidly as Piaget predicted.
    c. few children progress to the concrete operational stage.
    d. there is no way of testing much of Piaget's theoretical work.

11. An 8-month-old infant who reacts to a new babysitter by crying and clinging to his father's shoulder is showing _____ _____ .

12. In a series of experiments, the Harlows found that monkeys raised with artificial mothers tended, when afraid, to cling to their cloth mother, rather than to a wire mother holding the feeding bottle. Why was this finding important?

 Adolescence

13. Adolescence is marked by the onset of
    a. an identity crisis.
    b. puberty.
    c. separation anxiety.
    d. parent-child conflict.

14. According to Piaget, a person who can think logically about abstractions is in the _____ _____ stage.

15. In Erikson's stages, the primary task during adolescence is
    a. attaining formal operations.
    b. forging an identity.
    c. developing a sense of intimacy with another person.
    d. living independent of parents.

16. Some developmental psychologists now refer to the period that occurs in some Western cultures from age 18 to the mid-twenties and beyond (up to the time of full adult independence) as _____ _____ .

MODULE 17 Adulthood

17. By age 65, a person would be most likely to experience a cognitive decline in the ability to
    a. recall and list all the important terms and concepts in a module.
    b. select the correct definition in a multiple-choice question.
    c. recall their own birth date.
    d. practice a well-learned skill, such as knitting.

18. How do cross-sectional and longitudinal studies differ?

19. Freud defined the healthy adult as one who is able to love and work. Erikson agreed, observing that the adult struggles to attain intimacy and _____ .

20. Contrary to what many people assume,
    a. older people are much happier than adolescents.
    b. men in their forties express much greater dissatisfaction with life than do women of the same age.
    c. people of all ages report similar levels of happiness.
    d. those whose children have recently left home—the empty nesters—have the lowest level of happiness of all groups.

Find answers to these questions in Appendix D, in the back of the book.

SENSATION AND PERCEPTION

. . . .

have perfect vision," explains acclaimed writer and teacher Heather Sellers. Her vision may be fine, but there is a problem with her perception. She cannot recognize faces. In her memoir, *You Don't Look Like Anyone I Know,* Sellers (2010) tells of awkward moments resulting from her lifelong *prosopagnosia*—face blindness.

> In college, on a date at the Spaghetti Station, I returned from the bathroom and plunked myself down in the wrong booth, facing the wrong man. I remained unaware he was not my date even as my date (a stranger to me) accosted Wrong Booth Guy, and then stormed out of the Station. . . . I do not recognize myself in photos or videos. I can't recognize my step-sons in the soccer pick-up line; I failed to determine which husband was mine at a party, in the mall, at the market.

"Voice blind" people with *phonagnosia*—an inability to recognize familiar voices—may make similar mistakes. One man flirted on the phone with someone he presumed was his wife, not realizing it was a different woman (Siegel, 2010).

To avoid being perceived as snobby or aloof, Sellers sometimes fakes recognition. She often smiles at people she passes, in case she knows them. Or she pretends to know the person with whom she is talking. (Similarly, those of us with hearing loss may fake hearing or shy away from busy social situations.) But, Sellers points out, there is an upside: When encountering someone who previously irritated her, she typically feels no ill will, because she doesn't recognize the person.

Unlike Sellers, most of us have a functioning area on the underside of our brain's right hemisphere that helps us recognize a familiar human face as soon as we detect it—in only one-seventh of a second (Jacques & Rossion, 2006; Rossion & Boremanse, 2011). This remarkable ability illustrates a broader principle. *Nature's sensory gifts enable each animal to obtain essential information.* Some examples:

- Frogs, which feed on flying insects, have cells in their eyes that fire only in response to small, dark, moving objects. A frog could starve to death knee-deep in motionless flies. But let one zoom by and the frog's "bug detector" cells snap awake. (As Kermit the Frog said, "Time's fun when you're having flies.")

- Male silkworm moths' odor receptors can detect one-billionth of an ounce of sex attractant per second released by a female one mile away. That is why there continue to be silkworms.

- Human ears are most sensitive to sound *frequencies* that include human voices, especially a baby's cry.

In these modules, we'll look at what psychologists have learned about how we sense and perceive our world. Module 18 begins by considering some basic principles that apply to all our senses. In Module 19, we take a close look at sensory and perceptual processes in vision. Finally, Module 20 reviews our nonvisual senses.

▼ FIGURE 18.1

What's going on here? Our sensory and perceptual processes work together to help us sort out the complex images, including the hidden couple in Sandro Del-Prete's drawing, *The Flowering of Love.*

Basic Concepts of Sensation and Perception

18-1 What are *sensation* and *perception*? What do we mean by *bottom-up processing* and *top-down processing*?

HEATHER SELLERS' CURIOUS MIX OF "perfect vision" and face blindness illustrates the distinction between *sensation* and *perception*. When she looks at a friend, her **sensation** is normal: Her sensory receptors detect the same information yours would, and her nervous system transmits that information to her brain. Her **perception**—the processes by which her brain organizes and interprets sensory input—is *almost* normal. Thus, she may recognize people from their hair, gait, voice, or particular physique, just not their face. Her experience is much like the struggle you or I would have trying to recognize a specific penguin.

In our everyday experiences, sensation and perception blend into one continuous process.

- Our **bottom-up processing** starts at the sensory receptors and works up to higher levels of processing.
- Our **top-down processing** constructs perceptions from the sensory input by drawing on our experience and expectations.

As our brain absorbs the information in **FIGURE 18.1**, bottom-up processing enables our sensory systems to detect the lines, angles, and colors that form the flower and leaves. Using top-down processing we interpret what our senses detect.

But *how* do we do it? How do we create meaning from the blizzard of sensory stimuli that bombards our bodies 24 hours a day? Meanwhile, in a silent, cushioned, inner world, our brain floats in utter darkness. By itself, it sees nothing. It hears nothing. It feels nothing. *So, how does the world out there get in?* To phrase the question scientifically: How do we construct our representations of the external world? How do a campfire's flicker, crackle, and smoky scent activate neural connections? And how, from this living neurochemistry, do we create our conscious experience of the fire's motion and temperature, its aroma and beauty? In search of answers, let's look at some processes that cut across all our sensory systems.

Transduction

18-2 What three steps are basic to all our sensory systems?

Every second of every day, our sensory systems perform an amazing feat: They convert one form of energy into another. Vision processes light energy. Hearing processes sound waves. All our senses

- *receive* sensory stimulation, often using specialized receptor cells.
- *transform* that stimulation into neural impulses.
- *deliver* the neural information to our brain.

The process of converting one form of energy into another that our brain can use is called **transduction.** How do we see? Hear? Taste? Smell? Feel pain? Keep our balance? In each case, one of our sensory systems receives, transforms, and delivers the information to our brain. The field of **psychophysics** studies the relationships between the physical energy we can detect and its effects on our psychological experiences.

Let's explore some strengths and weaknesses in our ability to detect and interpret stimuli in the vast sea of energy around us.

---

sensation the process by which our sensory receptors and nervous system receive and represent stimulus energies from our environment.

perception the process of organizing and interpreting sensory information, enabling us to recognize meaningful objects and events.

bottom-up processing analysis that begins with the sensory receptors and works up to the brain's integration of sensory information.

top-down processing information processing guided by higher-level mental processes, as when we construct perceptions drawing on our experience and expectations.

transduction conversion of one form of energy into another. In sensation, the transforming of stimulus energies, such as sights, sounds, and smells, into neural impulses our brain can interpret.

psychophysics the study of relationships between the physical characteristics of stimuli, such as their intensity, and our psychological experience of them.

• What is the rough distinction between sensation and perception?

ANSWER: *Sensation* is the bottom-up process by which our sensory receptors and our nervous system receive and represent stimuli. *Perception* is the top-down process in which our brain creates meaning by organizing and interpreting what our senses detect.

Thresholds

18-3 How do *absolute thresholds* and *difference thresholds* differ, and what effect, if any, do stimuli below the absolute threshold have on us?

At this moment, we are being struck by X-rays and radio waves, ultraviolet and infrared light, and sound waves of very high and very low frequencies. To all of these we are blind and deaf. Other animals with differing needs detect a world that lies beyond our experience. Migrating birds stay on course aided by an internal magnetic compass. Bats and dolphins locate prey using sonar, bouncing echoing sound off objects. Bees navigate on cloudy days by detecting invisible (to us) polarized light.

The shades on our own senses are open just a crack, allowing us a restricted awareness of this vast sea of energy. But for our needs, this is enough.

Absolute Thresholds

To some kinds of stimuli we are exquisitely sensitive. Standing atop a mountain on an utterly dark, clear night, most of us could see a candle flame atop another mountain 30 miles away. We could feel the wing of a bee falling on our cheek. We could smell a single drop of perfume in a three-room apartment (Galanter, 1962).

German scientist and philosopher Gustav Fechner (1801–1887) studied our awareness of these faint stimuli and called them our **absolute thresholds**—the minimum stimulation necessary to detect a particular light, sound, pressure, taste, or odor 50 percent of the time. To test your absolute threshold for sounds, a hearing specialist would expose each of your ears to varying sound levels (**FIGURE 18.2** on the next page). For each tone, the test would define where half the time you could detect the sound and half the time you could not. That 50-50 point would define your absolute threshold.

Detecting a weak stimulus, or signal (such as a hearing-test tone), depends not only on its strength but also on our psychological state—our experience, expectations, motivation, and alertness. **Signal detection theory** predicts when we will detect weak signals (measured as our ratio of "hits" to "false alarms"). Lonely, anxious people at speed-dating events tend to respond with a low threshold, and thus can be unselective in reaching out to potential dates (McClure et al., 2010). Signal detection theorists seek to understand why people respond differently to the same stimuli, and why the same person's reactions vary as circumstances change.

Stimuli you cannot detect 50 percent of the time are **subliminal**—below your absolute threshold (see Figure 18.2). Under certain conditions, you can be affected by stimuli so weak that you don't consciously notice them. An unnoticed image or word can reach your visual cortex and briefly **prime** your response to a later question. In a typical experiment, the image or word is quickly flashed, then replaced by a *masking stimulus* that interrupts the brain's processing before conscious perception (Herring et al., 2013; Van den Bussche et al., 2009). In one such experiment, researchers monitored brain activity as they primed people with either unperceived action words (such as *go* and *start*) or inaction words (such as *still* or *stop*). Without any conscious awareness, the inaction words automatically evoked brain activity associated with inhibiting behavior (Hepler & Albarracin, 2013).

Another priming experiment illustrated the deep reality of sexual orientation. As people gazed at the center of a screen, a photo of a nude person was flashed on one side and a scrambled version of the photo on the other side (Jiang et al., 2006). Because the nude images were immediately masked by a colored checkerboard, viewers saw

---

absolute threshold the minimum stimulus energy needed to detect a particular stimulus 50 percent of the time.

signal detection theory a theory predicting how and when we detect the presence of a faint stimulus (*signal*) amid background stimulation (*noise*). Assumes there is no single absolute threshold and that detection depends partly on a person's experience, expectations, motivation, and alertness.

subliminal below one's absolute threshold for conscious awareness.

priming the activation, often unconsciously, of certain associations, thus predisposing one's perception, memory, or response.

Try out this old riddle on a couple of friends. "You're driving a bus with 12 passengers. At your first stop, 6 passengers get off. At the second stop, 3 get off. At the third stop, 2 more get off but 3 new people get on. What color are the bus driver's eyes?" Do your friends detect the signal—who is the bus driver?—amid the accompanying noise?

"The heart has its reasons which reason does not know."

Pascal, *Pensées*, 1670

▼ FIGURE 18.2
Absolute threshold Can I detect this sound? An *absolute threshold* is the intensity at which a person can detect a stimulus half the time. Hearing tests locate these thresholds for various frequencies.

▼ FIGURE 18.3
The hidden mind After an image of a nude man or woman was flashed to one side or another, then masked before being perceived, people's attention was unconsciously drawn to images in a way that reflected their sexual orientation (Jiang et al., 2006).

difference threshold the minimum difference between two stimuli required for detection 50 percent of the time. We experience the difference threshold as a *just noticeable difference* (or *jnd*).

Weber's law the principle that, to be perceived as different, two stimuli must differ by a constant minimum percentage (rather than a constant amount).

nothing but flashes of color and were unable to state on which side the nude had appeared. To test whether this unseen image unconsciously attracted their attention, the experimenters then flashed a geometric figure to one side or the other. This, too, was quickly followed by a masking stimulus. When asked to give the figure's angle, straight men guessed more accurately when it appeared where a nude *woman* had been a moment earlier (**FIGURE 18.3**). *Gay* men (and straight women) guessed more accurately when the geometric figure replaced a nude *man*. As other experiments confirm, we can evaluate a stimulus even when we are not aware of it—and even when we are unaware of our evaluation (Ferguson & Zayas, 2009).

How can we feel or respond to what we do not know and cannot describe? An imperceptibly brief stimulus often triggers a weak response that *can* be detected by brain scanning (Blankenburg et al., 2003; Haynes & Rees, 2005, 2006). The stimulus may reach consciousness only when it triggers synchronized activity in multiple brain areas (Dehaene, 2009, 2014). Such experiments reveal the dual-track mind at work: *Much of our information processing occurs automatically, out of sight, off the radar screen of our conscious mind.* Our conscious minds are upstairs executives who delegate routine tasks to downstairs mental butlers.

So can we be controlled by subliminal messages? For more on that question, see Thinking Critically About: Subliminal Persuasion.

Difference Thresholds

To function effectively, we need absolute thresholds low enough to allow us to detect important sights, sounds, textures, tastes, and smells. We also need to detect small differences among stimuli. A musician must detect minute discrepancies when tuning an instrument. Parents must detect the sound of their own child's voice amid other children's voices. While living two years in Scotland, I [DM] noticed that sheep *baa's* all sound alike to my ears. But not to those of ewes, who, after shearing, will streak directly to the *baa* of *their* lamb amid the chorus of other distressed lambs.

The **difference threshold** (or the *just noticeable difference* [*jnd*]) is the minimum difference a person can detect between any two stimuli half the time. That difference threshold increases with the size of the stimulus. If we listen to our music at 40 decibels, we might detect an added 5 decibels. But if we increase the volume to 110 decibels, we probably won't detect a 5 decibel change.

Subliminal Persuasion

18-4 Does subliminal sensation enable subliminal persuasion?

Hoping to penetrate our unconscious, entrepreneurs offer audio and video programs to help us lose weight, stop smoking, or improve our memories. Soothing ocean sounds may mask messages we cannot consciously hear: "I am thin"; "Smoke tastes bad"; or "I do well on tests—I have total recall of information." Such claims make two assumptions: (1) We can unconsciously sense subliminal (literally, "below threshold") stimuli. (2) Without our awareness, these stimuli have extraordinary suggestive powers. Can we? Do they?

As we have seen, subliminal *sensation* is a fact. Remember that an "absolute" threshold is merely the point at which we can detect a stimulus *half the time.* At or slightly below this threshold, we will still detect the stimulus some of the time.

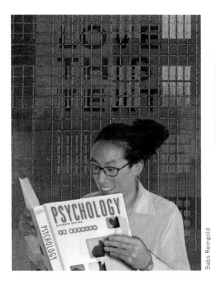

Babs Reingold

Subliminal persuasion? Although subliminally presented stimuli *can* subtly influence people, experiments discount attempts at subliminal advertising and self-improvement. (The playful message here is not actually subliminal— because you can easily perceive it.)

But does this mean that claims of subliminal *persuasion* are also facts? The near-consensus among researchers is *No.* The laboratory research reveals a *subtle, fleeting* effect. Priming thirsty people with the subliminal word *thirst* might therefore, for a moment, make a thirst-quenching beverage ad more persuasive (Strahan et al., 2002). Likewise, priming thirsty people with Lipton Iced Tea may increase their choosing the primed brand (Karremans et al., 2006; Veltkamp et al., 2011; Verwijmeren et al., 2011a,b). But the subliminal-message hucksters claim something different: a *powerful, enduring* effect on behavior.

To test whether subliminal recordings have this enduring effect, Anthony Greenwald and his colleagues (1991, 1992) randomly assigned university students to listen daily for five weeks to commercial subliminal messages claiming to improve either self-esteem or memory. But the researchers played a practical joke and switched half the labels. Some students who thought they were receiving affirmations of self-esteem were actually hearing the memory-enhancement message. Others got the self-esteem message but thought their memory was being recharged.

Were the recordings effective? Students' test scores for self-esteem and memory, taken before and after the five weeks, revealed no changes. Yet the students *perceived* themselves receiving the benefits they *expected.* Those who *thought* they had heard a memory recording *believed* their memories had improved. Those who thought they had heard a self-esteem recording believed their self-esteem had grown. (Reading this research, one hears echoes of the testimonies that ooze from ads for such products. Some customers, having bought what is not supposed to be heard (and having indeed not heard it!) offer testimonials like, "I really know that your recordings were invaluable in reprogramming my mind.")

Over a decade, Greenwald conducted 16 double-blind experiments evaluating subliminal self-help recordings. His results were uniform: No recording helped more than a placebo, which works only because of our belief in it (Greenwald, 1992).

In the late 1800s, Ernst Weber noted something so simple and so widely applicable that we still refer to it as **Weber's law.** This law states that for an average person to perceive a difference, two stimuli must differ by a constant minimum *percentage* (not a constant *amount*). The exact proportion varies, depending on the stimulus. Two lights, for example, must differ in intensity by 8 percent. Two objects must differ in weight by 2 percent. And two tones must differ in frequency by only 0.3 percent (Teghtsoonian, 1971).

The LORD is my shepherd;
    I shall not want.
He maketh me to lie down
        in green pastures:
    he leadeth me
        beside the still waters.
He restoreth my soul:
    he leadeth me
        in the paths of righteousness
        for his name's sake.
Yea, though I walk through the valley
        of the shadow of death,
    I will fear no evil:
for thou art with me;
        thy rod and thy staff
        they comfort me.
Thou preparest a table before me
        in the presence of mine enemies:
    thou anointest my head with oil,
        my cup runneth over.
Surely goodness and mercy
        shall follow me
        all the days of my life:
and I will dwell
        in the house of the LORD
        for ever.

The difference threshold In this computer-generated copy of the Twenty-third Psalm, each line of the typeface increases slightly. How many lines are required for you to experience a just noticeable difference?

sensory adaptation diminished sensitivity as a consequence of constant stimulation.

perceptual set a mental predisposition to perceive one thing and not another.

RETRIEVAL PRACTICE

• Using sound as your example, explain how these concepts differ: *absolute threshold*, *subliminal stimulation*, and *difference threshold*.

ANSWER: *Absolute threshold* is the minimum stimulation needed to detect a particular sound (such as an approaching bike on the sidewalk behind us) 50 percent of the time. *Subliminal stimulation* happens when, without our awareness, our sensory system processes the sound of the approaching bike (when it is below our absolute threshold). A *difference threshold* is the minimum difference needed to distinguish between two sounds (such as the familiar hum of a friend's bike and the unfamiliar sound of another bike).

"We need above all to know about changes; no one wants or needs to be reminded 16 hours a day that his shoes are on."

Neuroscientist David Hubel (1979)

Sensory Adaptation

18-5 What is the function of sensory adaptation?

Entering your neighbors' living room, you smell a musty odor. You wonder how they endure it, but within minutes you no longer notice it. **Sensory adaptation** has come to your rescue. When we are constantly exposed to an unchanging stimulus, we become less aware of it because our nerve cells fire less frequently. (To experience sensory adaptation, move your watch up your wrist an inch: You will feel it—but only for a few moments.)

Why, then, if we stare at an object without flinching, does it *not* vanish from sight? Because, unnoticed by us, our eyes are always moving. This continual flitting from one spot to another ensures that stimulation on the eyes' receptors continually changes (**FIGURE 18.4**).

What if we actually could stop our eyes from moving? Would sights seem to vanish, as odors do? To find out, psychologists have devised ingenious instruments that maintain a constant image on the eye's inner surface. Imagine that we have fitted a volunteer, Mary, with one of these instruments—a miniature projector mounted on a contact lens (**FIGURE 18.5a**). When Mary's eye moves, the image from the projector moves as well. So everywhere that Mary looks, the scene is sure to go.

If we project images through this instrument, what will Mary see? At first, she will see the complete image. But within a few seconds, as her sensory system begins to fatigue, things get weird. Bit by bit, the image vanishes, only to reappear and then disappear—often in fragments (**FIGURE 18.5a**).

Although sensory adaptation reduces our sensitivity, it offers an important benefit: freedom to focus on *informative* changes in our environment without being distracted by background chatter. Stinky or heavily perfumed people don't notice their odor because, like you and me, they adapt to what's constant and detect only change. Our sensory receptors are alert to novelty; bore them with repetition and they free our attention for more important things. The point to remember: *We perceive the world not exactly as it is, but as it is useful for us to perceive it.*

Our sensitivity to changing stimulation helps explain television's attention-grabbing power. Cuts, edits, zooms, pans, sudden noises—all demand attention. The phenomenon is irresistible even to TV researchers. One noted that during conversations, "I cannot for the life of me stop from periodically glancing over to the screen" (Tannenbaum, 2002).

Sensory adaptation even influences how we perceive emotions. By creating a 50-50 morphed blend of an angry face and a scared face, researchers showed that our visual system adapts to a static facial expression by becoming less responsive to it (Butler et al., 2008; **FIGURE 18.6**). The effect is created by

▼ FIGURE 18.4

The jumpy eye Our gaze jumps from one spot to another every third of a second or so, as eye-tracking equipment illustrated as a person looked at this photograph of Edinburgh's Princes Street Gardens (Henderson, 2007). The circles represent visual fixations, and the numbers indicate the time of fixation in milliseconds (300 milliseconds = 3/10ths of a second).

John M. Henderson

(a)

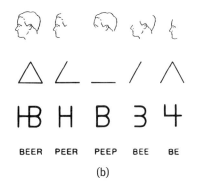

BEER PEER PEEP BEE BE

(b)

▼ FIGURE 18.5
Sensory adaptation: now you see it, now you don't! (a) A projector mounted on a contact lens makes the projected image move with the eye. (b) Initially, the person sees the stabilized image, but soon she sees fragments fading and reappearing. (From "Stabilized images on the retina," by R. M. Pritchard. Copyright © 1961 Scientific American, Inc. All rights reserved.)

our brain, not our retinas. We know this because the illusion also works when we view either side image with one eye, and the center image with the other eye.

Sensory adaptation and sensory thresholds are important ingredients in our perceptions of the world around us. Much of what we perceive comes not just from what's "out there" but also from what's behind our eyes and between our ears.

▼ FIGURE 18.6
Emotion adaptation Gaze at the angry face on the left for 20 to 30 seconds, then look at the center face (looks scared, yes?). Then gaze at the scared face on the right for 20 to 30 seconds, before returning to the center face (now looks angry, yes?). (From Butler et al., 2008.)

RETRIEVAL PRACTICE

• Why is it that after wearing shoes for a while, you cease to notice them (until questions like this draw your attention back to them)?

ANSWER: The shoes provide constant stimulation. *Sensory adaptation* allows us to focus on changing stimuli.

Perceptual Set

18-6 How do our expectations, contexts, motivation, and emotions influence our perceptions?

To see is to believe. As we less fully appreciate, to believe is to see. Through experience, we come to expect certain results. Those expectations may give us a **perceptual set,** a set of mental tendencies and assumptions that affects (top-down) what we hear, taste, feel, and see.

Consider: Is the center image in **FIGURE** 18.7 on the next page an old or young woman? What we see in such a drawing can be influenced by first looking at either of the two unambiguous versions (Boring, 1930).

Everyday examples of perceptual set—of "mind over mind"—abound. In 1972, a British newspaper published unretouched photographs of a "monster" in Scotland's Loch Ness—"the most amazing pictures ever taken," stated the paper. If this information creates in you the same expectations it did in most of the paper's readers, you, too,

IT'S AMAZING HOW PEOPLE SLOW DOWN WHEN YOU POINT A HAIR DRYER AT THEM.

▼ **FIGURE 18.7**
Perceptual set Show a friend either the left or right image. Then show the center image and ask, "What do you see?" Whether your friend reports seeing an old woman's face or young woman's profile may depend on which of the other two drawings was viewed first. In each of those images, the meaning is clear, and it will establish perceptual expectations.

W.E. Hill, 1915

There
Are Two
Errors in The
The Title Of
This Book

Book by Robert M. Martin, 2011

Did you perceive what you expected in this title—and miss the errors? If you are still puzzled, see explanation upside down below.

ɘno ʎlno ƨi ɘɿɘʜɈ nɘʜw ,ƨɿoɿɿɘ
-ƨim ƨɈi ƨi ɿoɿɿɘ bnoɔɘƨ ɔino ƨɈI ".ɘʜɈ"
bɘɈɒɘqɘɿ ƨi ɿoɿɿɘ Ɉƨɿᴉᴵ ƨ'ɘlɈiɈ ɘʜT

"We hear and apprehend only what we already half know."

Henry David Thoreau, *Journal,* 1860

will see the monster in a similar photo in **FIGURE 18.8**. But when a skeptical researcher approached the original photos with different expectations, he saw a curved tree limb—as had others the day that photo was shot (Campbell, 1986). With this different perceptual set, you may now notice that the object is floating motionless, with ripples outward in all directions—hardly what we would expect of a swimming monster.

Perceptual set can also affect what we hear. Consider the kindly airline pilot who, on a takeoff run, looked over at his sad co-pilot and said, "Cheer up." Expecting to hear the usual "Gear up," the co-pilot promptly raised the wheels—before they left the ground (Reason & Mycielska, 1982).

Perceptual set similarly affects taste. One experiment invited bar patrons to sample free beer (Lee et al., 2006). When researchers added a few drops of vinegar to a brand-name beer, the tasters preferred it—unless they had been told they were drinking vinegar-laced beer. Then they expected, and usually experienced, a worse taste. In another experiment, preschool children, by a 6-to-1 margin, thought french fries tasted better when served in a McDonald's bag rather than a plain white bag (Robinson et al., 2007).

What determines our perceptual set? Through experience we form concepts, or *schemas,* that organize and interpret unfamiliar information. Our preexisting schemas for monsters and tree trunks influence how we apply top-down processing to interpret ambiguous sensations.

In everyday life, stereotypes about gender (another instance of perceptual set) can color perception. Without the obvious cues of pink or blue, people will struggle over whether to call the new baby "he" or "she." But told an infant is "David," people (especially children) have perceived "him" as bigger and stronger than if the same infant was called "Diana" (Stern & Karraker, 1989). Some differences, it seems, exist merely in the eyes of their beholders.

▼ **FIGURE 18.8**
Believing is seeing What do you perceive? Is this Nessie, the Loch Ness monster, or a log?

Keystone/Stringer/Getty Images

▼ FIGURE 18.9
Culture and context effects What is above the woman's head? In one study, nearly all the East Africans who were questioned said the woman was balancing a metal box or can on her head and that the family was sitting under a tree. Westerners, for whom corners and box-like architecture were more common, were more likely to perceive the family as being indoors, with the woman sitting under a window. (Adapted from Gregory & Gombrich, 1973.)

Context Effects

A given stimulus may trigger radically different perceptions, partly because of our differing perceptual set (**FIGURE 18.9**), but also because of the immediate context. Some examples:

- When holding a gun, people become more likely to perceive another person as gun-toting—a phenomenon that has led to the shooting of some unarmed people who were actually holding their phone or wallet (Witt & Brockmole, 2012).

- Imagine hearing a noise interrupted by the words "eel is on the wagon." Likely, you would actually perceive the first word as *wheel*. Given "eel is on the orange," you would more likely hear *peel*. This curious phenomenon suggests that the brain can work backward in time to allow a later stimulus to determine how we perceive an earlier one. The context creates an expectation that, top-down, influences our perception (Grossberg, 1995).

- How is the woman in **FIGURE 18.10** feeling?

Julian Finney/Getty Images

▼ FIGURE 18.10
What emotion is this? (See Figure 20.11 on the next page.)

RETRIEVAL PRACTICE

- Does *perceptual set* involve bottom-up or top-down processing? Why?

ANSWER: It involves top-down processing. Our perceptual set influences our interpretation of stimuli based on our experiences, assumptions, and expectations.

Motivation and Emotion

Perceptions are influenced, top-down, not only by our expectations and by the context, but also by our emotions and motivation.

Hearing sad rather than happy music can predispose people to perceive a sad meaning in spoken homophonic words—*mourning* rather than *morning, die* rather than *dye, pain* rather than *pane* (Halberstadt et al., 1995). When angry, people more often perceive neutral objects as guns (Baumann & Steno, 2010). After listening to irritating (and anger-cuing) music, they also perceive a harmful action such as robbery as more serious (Seidel & Prinz, 2013).

Dennis Proffitt (2006a,b; Schnall et al., 2008) and others have demonstrated the power of emotions with other clever experiments showing that

- walking destinations look farther away to those who have been fatigued by prior exercise.

- a hill looks steeper to those who are wearing a heavy backpack or have just been exposed to sad, heavy classical music rather than light, bouncy music. As with so many of life's challenges, a hill also seems less steep to those with a friend beside them.

▼ FIGURE 18.11
Context makes
clearer Serena Williams is
celebrating! (Example from
Barrett et al., 2011.)

Julian Finney/Getty Images

"When you're hitting
the ball, it comes at you
looking like a grapefruit.
When you're not, it looks
like a blackeyed pea."

Former major league baseball
player George Scott

• a target seems farther away to those throwing a heavy rather than a light object at it.

• even a softball appears bigger when you are hitting well, observed Jessica Witt and Proffitt (2005), after asking players to choose a circle the size of the ball they had just hit well or poorly. (There's also a reciprocal phenomenon: Seeing a target as bigger—as happens when athletes focus directly on a target—improves performance [Witt et al., 2012].)

Motives also matter. Desired objects, such as a water bottle when thirsty, seem closer (Balcetis & Dunning, 2010). This perceptual bias energizes our going for it. Our motives also direct our perception of ambiguous images.

Emotions and motives color our *social* perceptions, too. People more often perceive solitary confinement, sleep deprivation, and cold temperatures as "torture" when experiencing a small dose of such themselves (Nordgren et al., 2011). Spouses who feel loved and appreciated perceive less threat in stressful marital events— "He's just having a bad day" (Murray et al., 2003). Professional referees, if told a soccer team has a history of aggressive behavior, will assign more penalty cards after watching videotaped fouls (Jones et al., 2002). The moral of these stories: To believe is, indeed, to see.

MODULE 18 REVIEW Basic Concepts of Sensation and Perception

LEARNING OBJECTIVES

RETRIEVAL PRACTICE Take a moment to answer each of these Learning Objective Questions (repeated here from within this module). Then turn to Appendix C, Complete Module Reviews, to check your answers. Research suggests that trying to answer these questions on your own will improve your long-term retention (McDaniel et al., 2009).

18-1 What are *sensation* and *perception?* What do we mean by *bottom-up processing* and *top-down processing?*

18-2 What three steps are basic to all our sensory systems?

18-3 How do *absolute thresholds* and *difference thresholds* differ, and what effect, if any, do stimuli below the absolute threshold have on us?

18-4 Does subliminal sensation enable subliminal persuasion?

18-5 What is the function of sensory adaptation?

18-6 How do our expectations, contexts, motivation, and emotions influence our perceptions?

TERMS AND CONCEPTS TO REMEMBER

RETRIEVAL PRACTICE Test yourself on these terms by trying to write down the definition before flipping back to check your answers.

sensation, p. 230

perception, p. 230

bottom-up processing, p. 230

top-down processing, p. 230

transduction, p. 230

psychophysics, p. 230

absolute threshold, p. 231

signal detection theory, p. 231

subliminal, p. 231

priming, p. 231

difference threshold, p. 232

Weber's law, p. 233

sensory adaptation, p. 234

perceptual set, p. 235

Use 🔵 LearningCurve to create your personalized study plan, which will direct you to the resources that will help you most in 🔵 LaunchPad.

\blacksquare 19 Vision: Sensory and Perceptual Processing

Light Energy and Eye Structures

19-1 What are the characteristics of the energy that we see as visible light? What structures in the eye help focus that energy?

OUR EYES RECEIVE LIGHT ENERGY and *transduce* (transform) it into neural messages that our brain then processes into what we consciously see. How does such a taken-for-granted yet extraordinary thing happen?

The Stimulus Input: Light Energy

When you look at a bright red tulip, the stimuli striking your eyes are not particles of the color red but pulses of electromagnetic energy that your visual system *perceives* as red. What we see as visible light is but a thin slice of the whole spectrum of electromagnetic energy, ranging from imperceptibly short gamma waves to the long waves of radio transmission (**FIGURE 19.1**). Other organisms are sensitive to differing portions of the spectrum. Bees, for instance, cannot see what we perceive as red but can see ultraviolet light.

Two physical characteristics of light help determine our sensory experience. Light's **wavelength**—the distance from one wave peak to the next (**FIGURE 19.2a** on the next page)—determines its **hue** (the color we experience, such as the tulip's red petals or green leaves). **Intensity**—the amount of energy in light waves (determined by a wave's *amplitude*, or height)—influences brightness (**FIGURE 19.2b**). To understand *how* we transform physical energy into color and meaning, consider the eye.

> **wavelength** the distance from the peak of one light or sound wave to the peak of the next. Electromagnetic wavelengths vary from the short blips of cosmic rays to the long pulses of radio transmission.
>
> **hue** the dimension of color that is determined by the wavelength of light; what we know as the color names *blue, green,* and so forth.
>
> **intensity** the amount of energy in a light wave or sound wave, which influences what we perceive as brightness or loudness. Intensity is determined by the wave's amplitude (height).

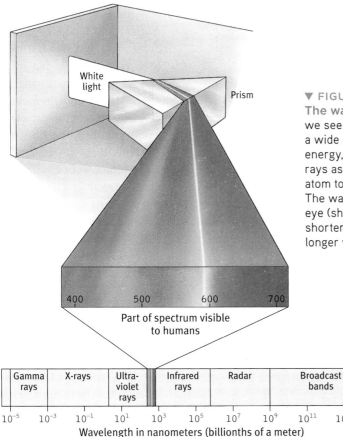

White light

Prism

400   500   600   700

Part of spectrum visible to humans

Gamma rays	X-rays	Ultra-violet rays	Infrared rays	Radar	Broadcast bands

10^{-5} 10^{-3} 10^{-1} 10^{1} 10^{3} 10^{5} 10^{7} 10^{9} 10^{11} 10^{13}

Wavelength in nanometers (billionths of a meter)

▼ **FIGURE 19.1**
The wavelengths we see What we see as light is only a tiny slice of a wide spectrum of electromagnetic energy, which ranges from gamma rays as short as the diameter of an atom to radio waves over a mile long. The wavelengths visible to the human eye (shown enlarged) extend from the shorter waves of blue-violet light to the longer waves of red light.

▼ FIGURE 19.2

The physical properties of waves (a) Waves vary in *wavelength* (the distance between successive peaks). *Frequency,* the number of complete wavelengths that can pass a point in a given time, depends on the wavelength. The shorter the wavelength, the higher the frequency. Wavelength determines the perceived color of light. (b) Waves also vary in *amplitude* (the height from peak to trough). Wave amplitude influences the perceived *brightness* of colors.

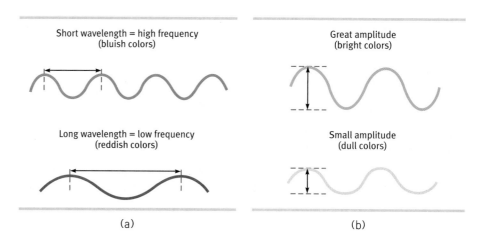

(a)   (b)

The Eye

Light enters the eye through the *cornea*, which bends light to help provide focus (**FIGURE 19.3**). The light then passes through the **pupil,** a small adjustable opening. Surrounding the pupil and controlling its size is the **iris,** a colored muscle that dilates or constricts in response to light intensity—or even to imagining a sunny sky or a dark room (Laeng & Sulutvedt, 2014). The iris also responds to our cognitive and emotional states. When you feel disgust or you are about to answer *No* to a question, your pupils constrict (de Gee et al., 2014; Goldinger & Papesh, 2012). When you're feeling amorous, your telltale dilated pupils and dark eyes subtly signal your interest. Each iris is so distinctive that an iris-scanning machine can confirm your identity.

Behind the pupil is a transparent **lens** that focuses incoming light rays into an image on the **retina,** a multilayered tissue on the eyeball's sensitive inner surface. The lens focuses the rays by changing its curvature and thickness in a process called **accommodation.**

For centuries, scientists knew that when an image of a candle passes through a small opening, it casts an inverted mirror image on a dark wall behind. If the image passing through the pupil casts this sort of upside-down image on the retina, as in Figure 19.3, how can we see the world right side up? The ever-curious Leonardo da Vinci had an idea: Perhaps the eye's watery fluids bend the light rays, reinverting the image to an upright position as it reaches the retina. Unfortunately for da Vinci, that idea was disproved in 1604, when the astronomer and optics expert Johannes Kepler showed that the retina *does* receive upside-down images of the world (Crombie, 1964). So how could we understand such a world? "I leave it," said the befuddled Kepler, "to natural philosophers."

Today's answer: The retina doesn't "see" a whole image. Rather, its millions of receptor cells convert particles of light energy into neural impulses and forward those to the brain. *There,* the impulses are reassembled into a perceived, upright-seeming image. And along the way, visual information processing percolates through progressively more abstract levels. All this happens with astonishing speed. As a baseball pitcher's fastball approaches home plate, the light signals work their way from the batter's retina to the visual cortex, which then informs the motor cortex, which then sends out orders to contract the muscles—all in the 4/10ths of a second that the ball is in flight.

Pascal Goetgheluck/Science Source

▼ FIGURE 19.3

The eye Light rays reflected from a candle pass through the cornea, pupil, and lens. The curvature and thickness of the lens change to bring nearby or distant objects into focus on the retina. Rays from the top of the candle strike the bottom of the retina, and those from the left side of the candle strike the right side of the retina. The candle's image on the retina thus appears upside down and reversed.

---

pupil the adjustable opening in the center of the eye through which light enters.

iris a ring of muscle tissue that forms the colored portion of the eye around the pupil and controls the size of the pupil opening.

1. Light entering eye triggers chemical reaction in rods and cones at back of retina.

Light

2. Chemical reaction in turn activates bipolar cells.

Cone

Rod

Ganglion cell

Bipolar cell

Neural impulse

Light

Cross section of retina

Optic nerve

To the brain's visual cortex via the thalamus

3. Bipolar cells then activate the ganglion cells, whose combined axons form the optic nerve. This nerve transmits information (via the thalamus) to the brain.

▼ FIGURE 19.4
The retina's reaction to light

lens the transparent structure behind the pupil that changes shape to help focus images on the retina.

retina the light-sensitive inner surface of the eye, containing the receptor rods and cones plus layers of neurons that begin the processing of visual information.

accommodation the process by which the eye's lens changes shape to focus near or far objects on the retina.

rods retinal receptors that detect black, white, and gray; necessary for peripheral and twilight vision, when cones don't respond.

cones retinal receptor cells that are concentrated near the center of the retina and that function in daylight or in well-lit conditions. The cones detect fine detail and give rise to color sensations.

optic nerve the nerve that carries neural impulses from the eye to the brain.

blind spot the point at which the optic nerve leaves the eye, creating a "blind" spot because no receptor cells are located there.

Information Processing in the Eye and Brain

Retinal Processing

19-2 How do the rods and cones process information, and what is the path information travels from the eye to the brain?

Imagine that you could follow behind a single light-energy particle after it entered your eye. First, you would thread your way through the retina's sparse outer layer of cells. Then, reaching the back of the eye, you would encounter its buried receptor cells, the **rods** and **cones** (**FIGURE 19.4**). There, you would see the light energy trigger chemical changes. That chemical reaction would spark neural signals, activating nearby *bipolar cells*. The bipolar cells in turn would activate the neighboring *ganglion cells*, whose axons twine together like the strands of a rope to form the **optic nerve.** The optic nerve is an information highway to your brain, where your thalamus stands ready to distribute the information it receives from your eyes. The optic nerve can send nearly 1 million messages at once through its nearly 1 million ganglion fibers. (The auditory nerve, which enables hearing, carries much less information through its mere 30,000 fibers.) We pay a small price for this eye-to-brain highway. Where the optic nerve leaves the eye, there are no receptor cells—creating a **blind spot** (**FIGURE 19.5**). Close one eye and you won't see a black hole, however. Without seeking your approval, your brain fills in the hole.

RETRIEVAL PRACTICE

▼ FIGURE 19.5
The blind spot

• There are no receptor cells where the optic nerve leaves the eye. This creates a blind spot in your vision. To demonstrate, first close your left eye, look at the spot above, and move your face away to a distance at which one of the cars disappears. (Which one do you predict it will be?) Repeat with your right eye closed—and note that now the other car disappears. Can you explain why?

ANSWER: Your blind spot is on the nose side of each retina, which means that objects to your right may fall onto the right eye's blind spot. Objects to your left may fall on the left eye's blind spot. The blind spot does not normally impair your vision, because your eyes are moving and because one eye catches what the other misses.

▼ TABLE 19.1
Receptors in the Human Eye: Rod-Shaped
Rods and Cone-Shaped Cones

	Cones	Rods
Number	6 million	120 million
Location in retina	Center	Periphery
Sensitivity in dim light	Low	High
Color sensitivity	High	Low
Detail sensitivity	High	Low

Omikron/Science Source

▼ FIGURE 19.6
Pathway from the eyes to the visual cortex Ganglion axons forming the optic nerve run to the thalamus, where they synapse with neurons that run to the visual cortex.

Rods and cones differ in where they're found and in what they do (**TABLE** 19.1). *Cones* cluster in and around the **fovea,** the retina's area of central focus (see Figure 19.3). Many cones have their own hotline to the brain: Each cone transmits its message to a single bipolar cell. That cell helps relay the cone's individual message to the visual cortex, which devotes a large area to input from the fovea. These direct connections preserve the cones' precise information, making them better able to detect fine detail.

Rods don't have dedicated hotlines. Rods share bipolar cells which send combined messages. To experience this rod-cone difference in sensitivity to details, pick a word in this sentence and stare directly at it, focusing its image on the cones in your fovea. Notice that words a few inches off to the side appear blurred? Their image strikes the outer regions of your retina, where rods predominate. Thus, when driving or biking, you can detect a car in your peripheral vision well before you perceive its details.

Cones also enable you to perceive color. In dim light they become ineffectual, so you see no colors. Rods, which enable black-and-white vision, remain sensitive in dim light. Several rods will funnel their faint energy output onto a single bipolar cell. Thus, cones and rods each provide a special sensitivity—cones to detail and color, and rods to faint light.

When you enter a darkened theater or turn off the light at night, your eyes adapt. Your pupils dilate to allow more light to reach your retina, but it typically takes 20 minutes or more before your eyes fully adapt. You can demonstrate dark adaptation by closing or covering one eye for up to 20 minutes. Then make the light in the room not quite bright enough to read this book with your open eye. Now open the dark-adapted eye and read (easily). This period of dark adaptation matches the average natural twilight transition between the Sun's setting and darkness. How wonderfully made we are.

To summarize: The retina's neural layers don't just pass along electrical impulses. They also help to encode and analyze sensory information. (The third neural layer in a frog's eye, for example, contains the "bug detector" cells that fire only in response to moving fly-like stimuli.) In human eyes, information follows this pathway:

- After processing by your retina's nearly 130 million receptor rods and cones, information travels forward again, to your bipolar cells.

- From there, it moves to your eye's million or so ganglion cells, and through their axons making up the optic nerve to your brain.

- After a momentary stop-off in the thalamus, the information travels to your visual cortex. Any given retinal area relays its information to a corresponding location in your visual cortex, in the occipital lobe at the back of your brain (**FIGURE** 19.6).

The same sensitivity that enables retinal cells to fire messages can lead them to misfire, as you can demonstrate. Turn your eyes to the left, close them, and then gently rub the right side of your right eyelid with your fingertip. Note the patch of light to the left, moving as your finger moves.

Why do you see light? Why at the left? This happens because your retinal cells are so responsive that even pressure triggers them. But your brain interprets their firing as light. Moreover, it interprets the light as coming from the left—the normal direction of light that activates the right side of the retina.

Visual area
of the thalamus

Optic
nerve

Retina

Visual
cortex

- Some nocturnal animals, such as toads, mice, rats, and bats, have impressive night vision thanks to having many more _____ (rods/cones) than _____ (rods/cones) in their retinas. These creatures probably have very poor _____ (color/black-and-white) vision.

ANSWERS: rods; cones; color

- Cats are able to open their _____ much wider than we can, which allows more light into their eyes so they can see better at night.

ANSWER: pupils

Kruglov Orda/Shutterstock

Color Processing

19-3 How do we perceive color in the world around us?

One of vision's most basic and intriguing mysteries is how we see the world in color. In everyday conversation, we talk as though objects possess color: "A tomato is red." Recall the old question, "If a tree falls in the forest and no one hears it, does it make a sound?" We can ask the same of color: If no one sees the tomato, is it red?

The answer is *No*. First, the tomato is everything *but* red, because it *rejects* (reflects) the long wavelengths of red. Second, the tomato's color is our mental construction. As Isaac Newton (1704) noted, "The [light] rays are not colored." Like all aspects of vision, our perception of color resides not in the object itself but in the theater of our brains, as evidenced by our dreaming in color.

How, from the light energy striking the retina, does our brain construct our experience of color—and of such a multitude of colors? Our difference threshold for colors is so low that we can discriminate more than 1 million different color variations (Neitz et al., 2001). At least most of us can. For about 1 person in 50, vision is color deficient—and that person is usually male, because the defect is genetically sex linked.

Modern detective work on the mystery of color vision began in the nineteenth century, when Hermann von Helmholtz built on the insights of an English physicist, Thomas Young. Any color can be created by combinations of different amounts of light waves of three primary colors—red, green, and blue. Knowing this, Young and von Helmholtz formed a hypothesis: The eye must have three corresponding types of color receptors. The **Young-Helmholtz trichromatic (three-color) theory** thus implies that the eye's receptors do their color magic in teams of three. Years later, researchers measured the response of various cones to different color stimuli and confirmed that the retina does have three types of color receptors, each especially sensitive to one of three colors. And those colors are, in fact, red, green, and blue. When we stimulate combinations of these cones, we see other colors. We see yellow when light stimulates both red-sensitive and green-sensitive cones.

Most people with color-deficient vision are not actually "color-blind." They simply lack functioning red- or green-sensitive cones, or sometimes both. Their vision—perhaps unknown to them, because their lifelong vision *seems* normal—is monochromatic (one-color) or dichromatic (two-color) instead of trichromatic, making it impossible to distinguish the red and green in **FIGURE** 19.7 (Boynton, 1979). Dogs, too, lack receptors for the wavelengths of red, giving them only limited, dichromatic color vision (Neitz et al., 1989).

But why do people blind to red and green often still see yellow? And why does yellow appear to be a pure color and not a mixture of red and green, the way purple is of red and blue? Trichromatic theory left some parts of the color vision mystery unsolved, and this sparked researcher Ewald Hering's curiosity.

"Only mind has sight and hearing; all things else are deaf and blind."

Epicharmus, *Fragments*, 550 B.C.E.

fovea the central focal point in the retina, around which the eye's cones cluster.

Young-Helmholtz trichromatic (three-color) theory the theory that the retina contains three different color receptors—one most sensitive to red, one to green, one to blue—which, when stimulated in combination, can produce the perception of any color.

▼ **FIGURE 19.7 Color-deficient vision** People who suffer red–green deficiency have trouble perceiving the number within the design.

Garo/Phanie/Science Source

▼ FIGURE 19.8
Afterimage effect Stare at the center of the flag for a minute and then shift your eyes to the dot in the white space beside it. What do you see? (After tiring your neural response to black, green, and yellow, you should see their opponent colors.) Stare at a white wall and note how the size of the flag grows with the projection distance.

Hering, a physiologist, found a clue in *afterimages*. Stare at a green square for a while and then look at a white sheet of paper, and you will see red, green's *opponent color*. Stare at a yellow square and its opponent color, blue, will appear on the white paper. (To experience this, try the flag demonstration in **FIGURE 19.8**.) Hering formed another hypothesis: There must be two *additional* color processes, one responsible for red-versus-green perception, and one for blue-versus-yellow perception.

Indeed, a century later, researchers also confirmed Hering's **opponent-process theory.** Three sets of opponent retinal processes—*red-green, yellow-blue,* and *white-black*—enable color vision. Recall that the thalamus relays visual information from the retina to the visual cortex. In both the retina and the thalamus, some neurons are turned "on" by red but turned "off" by green. Others are turned on by green but off by red (DeValois & DeValois, 1975). Like red and green marbles sent down a narrow tube, "red" and "green" messages cannot both travel at once. Red and green are thus opponents, so we do not experience a reddish green. But red and blue travel in separate channels, so we *can* see a reddish-blue magenta.

So how do we explain afterimages, such as in the flag demonstration? By staring at green, we tire our green response. When we then stare at white (which contains all colors, including red), only the red part of the green-red pairing will fire normally.

The present solution to the mystery of color vision is therefore roughly this: Color processing occurs in two stages.

1. The retina's red, green, and blue cones respond in varying degrees to different color stimuli, as the Young-Helmholtz trichromatic theory suggested.

2. The cones' responses are then processed by opponent-process cells, as Hering's theory proposed.

LaunchPad For an interactive review and demonstration of these color vision principles, visit LaunchPad's *PsychSim 6: Colorful World.*

-------------------------------- **RETRIEVAL PRACTICE** --------------------------------

• What are two key theories of color vision? Are they contradictory or complementary? Explain.

ANSWER: The *Young-Helmholtz trichromatic theory* shows that the retina contains color receptors for red, green, and blue. The *opponent-process theory* shows that we have opponent-process cells in the retina for red-green, yellow-blue, and white-black. These theories are complementary and outline the two stages of color vision: (1) The retina's receptors for red, green, and blue respond to different color stimuli. (2) The receptors' signals are then processed by the opponent-process cells on their way to the visual cortex in the brain.

opponent-process theory the theory that opposing retinal processes (red-green, yellow-blue, white-black) enable color vision. For example, some cells are stimulated by green and inhibited by red; others are stimulated by red and inhibited by green.

feature detectors nerve cells in the brain that respond to specific features of the stimulus, such as shape, angle, or movement.

Feature Detection

19-4 Where are feature detectors located, and what do they do?

Once upon a time, scientists believed that the brain was like a movie screen, on which the eye projected images. But then along came David Hubel and Torsten Wiesel (1979), who showed that our brain's computing system deconstructs visual images and then reassembles them. Hubel and Wiesel received a Nobel Prize for their work on **feature detectors,** nerve cells in the brain that respond to a scene's specific features—to particular edges, lines, angles, and movements.

Using microelectrodes, they had discovered that some neurons fired actively when cats were shown lines at one angle, while other neurons responded to lines at a different angle. They surmised that these specialized neurons in the occipital lobe's visual cortex—now known as feature detectors—receive information from individual ganglion cells in the retina. Feature detectors pass this specific information to other cortical areas, where teams of cells (*supercell clusters*) respond to more complex patterns.

One temporal lobe area by your right ear (**FIGURE 19.9**) enables you to perceive faces and, thanks to a specialized neural network, to recognize them from varied viewpoints (Connor, 2010). If stimulated in this area, you might spontaneously see faces. If this region were damaged, you might recognize other forms and objects, but not familiar faces.

Researchers can temporarily disrupt the brain's face-processing areas with magnetic pulses. When this happens, people cannot recognize faces, but they can recognize houses, because the brain's face-perception occurs separately from its object-perception (McKone et al., 2007; Pitcher et al., 2007). Thus, functional MRI (fMRI) scans have shown different brain areas activating when people viewed varied objects (Downing et al., 2001). Brain activity is so specific (**FIGURE 19.10**) that, with the help of brain scans, "we can tell if a person is looking at a shoe, a chair, or a face, based on the pattern of their brain activity," noted one researcher (Haxby, 2001).

For biologically important objects and events, monkey brains (and surely ours as well) have a "vast visual encyclopedia" distributed as specialized cells (Perrett et al., 1988, 1992, 1994). These cells respond to one type of stimulus, such as a specific gaze, head angle, posture, or body movement. Other supercell clusters integrate this information and fire only when the cues collectively indicate the direction of someone's attention and approach. This instant analysis, which aided our ancestors' survival, also helps a soccer player anticipate where to strike the ball, and a driver anticipate a pedestrian's next movement.

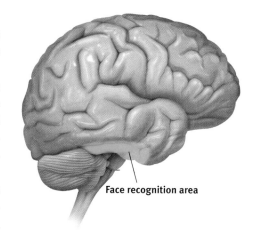

Face recognition area

▼ FIGURE 19.9
Face recognition processing In social animals such as humans, a large right temporal lobe area (shown here in a right-facing brain) is dedicated to the crucial task of face recognition.

■ Faces   ■ Chairs
□ Houses   □ Houses and chairs

▼ FIGURE 19.10
The telltale brain Looking at faces, houses, and chairs activates different brain areas in this right-facing brain.

Well-developed supercells In this 2011 World Cup match, USA's Abby Wambach instantly processed visual information about the positions and movements of Brazil's defenders and goalkeeper and somehow managed to get the ball around them all and into the net.

FIFA via Getty Images

parallel processing the processing of many aspects of a problem simultaneously; the brain's natural mode of information processing for many functions, including vision.

gestalt an organized whole. Gestalt psychologists emphasized our tendency to integrate pieces of information into meaningful wholes.

"I am . . . wonderfully made."

King David, Psalm 139:14

▼ FIGURE 19.11
Parallel processing Studies of patients with brain damage suggest that the brain delegates the work of processing motion, form, depth, and color to different areas. After taking a scene apart, the brain integrates these subdimensions into the perceived image. How does the brain do this? The answer to this question is the Holy Grail of vision research.

Parallel Processing

19-5 How does the brain use parallel processing to construct visual perceptions?

Our brain achieves these and other remarkable feats by **parallel processing:** doing many things at once. To analyze a visual scene, the brain divides it into subdimensions—motion, form, depth, color—and works on each aspect simultaneously (Livingstone & Hubel, 1988). We then construct our perceptions by integrating the separate but parallel work of these different visual teams (**FIGURE 19.11**).

To recognize a face, your brain integrates information projected by your retinas to several visual cortex areas, compares it to stored information, and enables you to recognize the face: *Grandmother!* Scientists have debated whether this stored information is contained in a single cell or, more likely, distributed over a vast network of cells. Some supercells—*grandmother cells*—do appear to respond very selectively to 1 or 2 faces in 100 (Bowers, 2009; Quiroga et al., 2013). The whole facial recognition process requires tremendous brain power: 30 percent of the cortex (10 times the brain area devoted to hearing).

Destroy or disable a neural workstation for a visual subtask, and something peculiar results, as happened to "Mrs. M." (Hoffman, 1998). Since a stroke damaged areas near the rear of both sides of her brain, she has been unable to perceive movement. People in a room seem "suddenly here or there but I have not seen them moving." Pouring tea into a cup is a challenge because the fluid appears frozen—she cannot perceive it rising in the cup.

After stroke or surgery has damaged the brain's visual cortex, others have experienced *blindsight.* Shown a series of sticks, they report seeing nothing. Yet when asked to guess whether the sticks are vertical or horizontal, their visual intuition typically offers the correct response. When told, "You got them all right," they are astounded. There is, it seems, a second "mind"—a parallel processing system—operating unseen. These separate visual systems for perception and action illustrate once again the astonishing dual processing of our two-track mind.

🅜 **LaunchPad** For a 4-minute depiction of a blindsight patient, visit the LaunchPad *Video—Blindsight: Seeing Without Awareness.*

* * *

Think about the wonders of visual processing. As you read this page, the letters are transmitted by reflected light rays onto your retina, which triggers a process that sends formless nerve impulses to several areas of your brain, which integrates the information and decodes meaning, thus completing the transfer of information across time and space from my mind to your mind (**FIGURE 19.12**). That all of this happens instantly, effortlessly, and continuously is indeed awesome. As Roger Sperry (1985) observed, the "insights of science give added, not lessened, reasons for awe, respect, and reverence."

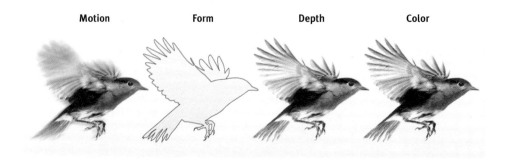

| Motion | Form | Depth | Color |

| Scene | → | Retinal processing:
Receptor rods and
cones ⟶ bipolar cells
⟶ ganglion cells | → | Feature detection:
Brain's detector cells
respond to specific
features—edges, lines,
and angles | → | Parallel processing:
Brain cell teams
process combined
information about
color, movement,
form, and depth | → | Recognition:
Brain interprets the
constructed image
based on information
from stored images |

Tom Walker/Photographer's Choice/Getty Images

RETRIEVAL PRACTICE

- What is the rapid sequence of events that occurs when you see and recognize a friend?

ANSWER: Light waves reflect off the person and travel into your eye, where the receptor cells in your retina convert the light waves' energy into neural impulses sent to your brain. Your brain processes the subdimensions of this visual input—including depth, movement, form, and color—separately but simultaneously. It interprets this information based on previously stored information and your expectations into a conscious perception of your friend.

▼ FIGURE 19.12
A simplified summary of visual information processing

Perceptual Organization

19-6 How did the Gestalt psychologists understand perceptual organization, and how do figure-ground and grouping principles contribute to our perceptions?

It's one thing to understand how we see colors and shapes. But how do we organize and interpret those sights so that they become *meaningful* perceptions—a rose in bloom, a familiar face, a sunset?

Early in the twentieth century, a group of German psychologists noticed that when given a cluster of sensations, people tend to organize them into a **gestalt,** a German word meaning a "form" or a "whole." As we look straight ahead, we cannot separate the perceived scene into our left and right fields of view. It is, at every moment, one whole, seamless scene. Our conscious perception is an integrated whole.

Consider **FIGURE 19.13:** The individual elements of this figure, called a *Necker cube,* are really nothing but eight blue circles, each containing three converging white lines. When we view these elements all together, however, we see a cube that sometimes reverses direction. This phenomenon nicely illustrates a favorite saying of Gestalt psychologists: In perception, the whole may exceed the sum of its parts, rather as water differs from its hydrogen and oxygen parts.

Over the years, the Gestalt psychologists demonstrated many principles we use to organize our sensations into perceptions (Wagemans et al., 2012a,b). Underlying all of them is a fundamental truth: *Our brain does more than register information about the world.* Perception is not just opening a shutter and letting a picture print itself on the brain. We filter incoming information and *construct* perceptions. Mind matters.

Form Perception

Imagine designing a video-computer system that, like your eye-brain system, can recognize faces at a glance. What abilities would it need?

Figure and Ground To start with, the video-computer system would need to separate faces from their backgrounds. Likewise, in our eye-brain system, our first perceptual task is to perceive any object (the *figure*) as distinct from its surroundings (the

▼ FIGURE 19.13
A Necker cube What do you see: circles with white lines, or a cube? If you stare at the cube, you may notice that it reverses location, moving the tiny X in the center from the front edge to the back. At times, the cube may seem to float forward, with circles behind it. At other times, the circles may become holes through which the cube appears, as though it were floating behind them. There is far more to perception than meets the eye. (From Bradley et al., 1976.)

▼ FIGURE 19.14
Reversible figure and ground

Proximity

Continuity

Closure

figure-ground the organization of the visual field into objects (the *figures*) that stand out from their surroundings (the *ground*).

grouping the perceptual tendency to organize stimuli into coherent groups.

depth perception the ability to see objects in three dimensions although the images that strike the retina are two-dimensional; allows us to judge distance.

visual cliff a laboratory device for testing depth perception in infants and young animals.

binocular cues depth cues, such as retinal disparity, that depend on the use of two eyes.

ground). Among the voices you hear at a party, the one you attend to becomes the figure; all others are part of the ground. As you read, the words are the figure; the white space is the ground. Sometimes the same stimulus can trigger more than one perception. In **FIGURE 19.14**, the **figure-ground** relationship continually reverses—but always we organize the stimulus into a figure seen against a ground.

Grouping   Having discriminated figure from ground, we (and our video-computer system) must also organize the figure into a *meaningful* form. Some basic features of a scene—such as color, movement, and light-dark contrast—we process instantly and automatically (Treisman, 1987). Our minds bring order and form to stimuli by following certain rules for **grouping**, also identified by the Gestalt psychologists. These rules, which we apply even as infants and even in our touch perceptions, illustrate how the perceived whole differs from the sum of its parts (Gallace & Spence, 2011; Quinn et al., 2002; Rock & Palmer, 1990). Three examples:

Proximity We group nearby figures together. We see not six separate lines, but three sets of two lines.

Continuity We perceive smooth, continuous patterns rather than discontinuous ones. This pattern could be a series of alternating semicircles, but we perceive it as two continuous lines—one wavy, one straight.

Closure We fill in gaps to create a complete, whole object. Thus we assume that the circles on the left are complete but partially blocked by the (illusory) triangle. Add nothing more than little line segments to close off the circles and your brain stops constructing a triangle.

Such principles usually help us construct reality. Sometimes, however, they lead us astray, as when we look at the doghouse in **FIGURE 19.15**.

▼ FIGURE 19.15
Grouping principles What's the secret to this impossible doghouse? You probably perceive this doghouse as a gestalt—a whole (though impossible) structure. Actually, your brain imposes this sense of wholeness on the picture. As Figure 19.19 shows, Gestalt grouping principles such as closure and continuity are at work here.

Photo by Walter Wick. Reprinted from *GAMES* Magazine. © 1983 PCS Games Limited Partnership.

━━━━━━━━━━━ **RETRIEVAL PRACTICE** ━━━━━━━━━━━

• In terms of perception, a band's lead singer would be considered _____ (figure/ground), and the other musicians would be considered _____ (figure/ground).

ANSWERS: figure; ground

• What do we mean when we say that, in perception, the whole may exceed the sum of its parts?

ANSWER: Gestalt psychologists used this saying to describe our perceptual tendency to organize clusters of sensations into meaningful forms or coherent groups.

Depth Perception

19-7 How do we use binocular and monocular cues to perceive the world in three dimensions, and how do we perceive motion?

From the two-dimensional images falling on our retinas, we somehow organize three-dimensional perceptions. **Depth perception** enables us to estimate an object's distance from us. At a glance, we can estimate the distance of an oncoming car or the height of a house. Depth perception is partly innate, as Eleanor Gibson and Richard Walk (1960) discovered using a model of a cliff with a drop-off area (which was covered by sturdy glass). Gibson's inspiration for these **visual cliff** experiments occurred while she was picnicking on the rim of the Grand Canyon. She wondered: Would a toddler peering over the rim perceive the dangerous drop-off and draw back?

Back in their Cornell University laboratory, Gibson and Walk placed 6- to 14-month-old infants on the edge of a safe canyon and had the infants' mothers coax them to crawl out onto the glass (**FIGURE 19.16**). Most infants refused to do so, indicating that they could perceive depth.

Had they *learned* to perceive depth? Learning seems to be part of the answer because crawling, no matter when it begins, seems to increase infants' wariness of heights (Campos et al., 1992). As infants become mobile, their experience leads them to fear heights (Adolph et al., 2014).

How do we do it? *How* do we transform two differing two-dimensional retinal images into a single three-dimensional perception?

Binocular Cues Try this: With both eyes open, hold two pens or pencils in front of you and touch their tips together. Now do so with one eye closed. With one eye, the task becomes noticeably more difficult, demonstrating the importance of **binocular cues** in judging the distance of nearby objects. Two eyes are better than one.

Because your eyes are about 2½ inches apart, your retinas receive slightly different images of the world. By comparing these two images, your brain can judge how close an object is to you. The greater the **retinal disparity,** or difference between the two images, the closer the object. Try it. Hold your two index fingers, with the tips about half an inch apart, directly in front of your nose, and your retinas will receive quite different views. If you close one eye and then the other, you can see the difference. (Bring your fingers close and you can create a finger sausage, as in **FIGURE 19.17**.) At a greater distance—say, when you hold your fingers at arm's length—the disparity is smaller.

▼ FIGURE 19.16
Visual cliff Eleanor Gibson and Richard Walk devised this miniature cliff with a glass-covered drop-off to determine whether crawling infants and newborn animals can perceive depth. Even when coaxed, infants are reluctant to venture onto the glass over the cliff.

retinal disparity a binocular cue for perceiving depth: By comparing images from the retinas in the two eyes, the brain computes distance—the greater the disparity (difference) between the two images, the closer the object.

▼ FIGURE 19.17
The floating finger sausage Hold your two index fingers about 5 inches in front of your eyes, with their tips half an inch apart. Now look beyond them and note the weird result. Move your fingers out farther and the retinal disparity—and the finger sausage—will shrink.

"*I can't go on living with such lousy depth perception!*"

Carnivorous animals, including humans, have eyes that enable forward focus on prey and offer binocular vision-enhanced depth perception. Grazing herbivores, such as horses and sheep, typically have eyes on the sides of their skull. Although lacking binocular depth perception, they have sweeping peripheral vision.

We could easily build this feature into our video-computer system. Moviemakers can simulate or exaggerate retinal disparity by filming a scene with two cameras placed a few inches apart. Viewers then wear glasses that allow the left eye to see only the image from the left camera, and the right eye to see only the image from the right camera. The resulting effect, as 3-D movie fans know, mimics or exaggerates normal retinal disparity. Similarly, twin cameras in airplanes can take photos of terrain for integration into 3-D maps.

Monocular Cues How do we judge whether a person is 10 or 100 meters away? Retinal disparity won't help us here, because there won't be much difference between the images cast on our right and left retinas. At such distances, we depend on **monocular cues** (depth cues available to each eye separately). See **FIGURE 19.18** for some examples.

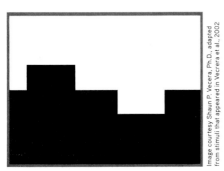

Image courtesy Shaun P. Vecera, Ph.D.; adapted from stimuli that appeared in Vecera et al., 2002

Relative height We perceive objects higher in our field of vision as farther away. Because we assume the lower part of a figure-ground illustration is closer, we perceive it as figure (Vecera et al., 2002). Invert this illustration and the black will become ground, like a night sky.

Relative motion As we move, objects that are actually stable may appear to move. If while riding on a bus you fix your gaze on some point—say, a house—the objects beyond the fixation point will appear to move with you. Objects in front of the point will appear to move backward. The farther an object is from the fixation point, the faster it will seem to move.

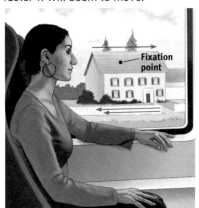

Direction of passenger's motion ⟶

Dan Piraro Bizarro.com

Relative size If we assume two objects are similar in size, *most* people perceive the one that casts the smaller retinal image as farther away.

Linear perspective Parallel lines appear to meet in the distance. The sharper the angle of convergence, the greater the perceived distance.

©The New Yorker Collection, 2002, Jack Ziegler from cartoonbank.com. All Rights Reserved.

THE FREIGHT ELEVATOR FOR THE MAN WHO HAS EVERYTHING

Interposition If one object partially blocks our view of another, we perceive it as closer.

Philip Mugridge/Alamy

Light and shadow Shading produces a sense of depth consistent with our assumption that light comes from above. If you invert this illustration, the hollow will become a hill.

© George V. Kelvin

▼ FIGURE 19.18
Monocular depth cues

🅜 LaunchPad For animated demonstrations and explanations of these cues, visit LaunchPad's *Concept Practice: Depth Cues.*

• How do we normally perceive depth?

ANSWER: We are normally able to perceive depth thanks to (1) binocular cues (which are based on our retinal disparity), and (2) monocular cues (which include relative height, relative size, interposition, linear perspective, light and shadow, and relative motion).

Motion Perception

Imagine that you could perceive the world as having color, form, and depth but that you could not see motion. Not only would you be unable to bike or drive, you would have trouble writing, eating, and walking.

Normally your brain computes motion based partly on its assumption that shrinking objects are retreating (not getting smaller) and enlarging objects are approaching. But you are imperfect at motion perception. In young children, this ability to correctly perceive approaching (and enlarging) vehicles is not yet fully developed, which puts them at risk for pedestrian accidents (Wann et al., 2011). But it's not just children who have occasional difficulties with motion perception. Our adult brains are sometimes tricked into believing what they are not seeing. When large and small objects move at the same speed, the large objects appear to move more slowly. Thus, trains seem to move slower than cars, and jumbo jets seem to land more slowly than little jets.

Our brain also perceives a rapid series of slightly varying images as continuous movement (a phenomenon called *stroboscopic movement*). As film animators know well, a superfast slide show of 24 still pictures a second will create an illusion of movement. We construct that motion in our heads, just as we construct movement in blinking marquees and holiday lights. We perceive two adjacent stationary lights blinking on and off in quick succession as one single light moving back and forth. Lighted signs exploit this **phi phenomenon** with a succession of lights that creates the impression of, say, a moving arrow.

Perceptual Constancy

19-8 How do perceptual constancies help us construct meaningful perceptions?

So far, we have noted that our video-computer system must perceive objects as we do—as having a distinct form, location, and perhaps motion. Its next task is to recognize objects without being deceived by changes in their color, brightness, shape, or size—a *top-down* process called **perceptual constancy.** Regardless of the viewing angle, distance, and illumination, we can identify people and things in less time than it takes to draw a breath, a feat that challenges even advanced computers and has intrigued researchers for decades. This would be a monumental challenge for a video-computer system.

Color and Brightness Constancies Our experience of color depends on an object's *context.* This would be clear if you viewed an isolated tomato through a paper tube over the course of a day. The tomato's color would seem to change as the light—and thus the wavelengths reflected from its surface—changed. But if you viewed that tomato as one item in a salad bowl, its color would remain roughly constant as the lighting shifts. This perception of consistent color is known as **color constancy.**

Though we take color constancy for granted, this ability is truly remarkable. A blue poker chip under indoor lighting reflects wavelengths that match those reflected by a sunlit gold chip (Jameson, 1985). Yet bring a bluebird indoors and it won't look like a goldfinch. The color is not in the bird's feathers. You and I see color thanks to our brain's computations of the light reflected by an object *relative to the objects surrounding it.*

FIGURE 19.20 on the next page dramatically illustrates the ability of a blue object to appear very different in three different contexts. Yet we have no trouble seeing these disks as blue. Nor does knowing the truth—that these disks are identically colored—diminish our perception that they are quite different. Because we construct our perceptions, we can simultaneously accept alternative objective and subjective realities.

Brightness constancy (also called *lightness constancy*) similarly depends on context. We perceive an object as having a constant brightness even while its illumination varies. This perception of constancy depends on *relative luminance*—the amount of light

monocular cues depth cues, such as interposition and linear perspective, available to either eye alone.

phi phenomenon an illusion of movement created when two or more adjacent lights blink on and off in quick succession.

perceptual constancy perceiving objects as unchanging (having consistent color, brightness, shape, and size) even as illumination and retinal images change.

color constancy perceiving familiar objects as having consistent color, even if changing illumination alters the wavelengths reflected by the objects.

"From there to here, from here to there, funny things are everywhere."

Dr. Seuss,
One Fish, Two Fish, Red Fish, Blue Fish, 1960

"Sometimes I wonder: Why is that Frisbee getting bigger? And then it hits me."

Anonymous

▼ FIGURE 19.19
The solution Another view of the impossible doghouse in Figure 19.15 reveals the secrets of this illusion. From the photo angle in Figure 19.15, the grouping principle of closure leads us to perceive the boards as continuous.

Photo by Walter Wick. Reprinted from GAMES Magazine. © 1983 PCS Games Limited Partnership.

▼ FIGURE 19.20
Color depends on context (a) Believe it or not, these three blue disks are identical in color. (b) Remove the surrounding context and see what results.

(a)   (b)

R. Beau Lotto/Lottolab

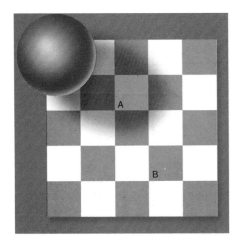

▼ FIGURE 19.21
Relative luminance Because of its surrounding context, we perceive Square B as lighter than Square A. But believe it or not, they are identical. To channel comedian Richard Pryor, "Who you gonna believe: me, or your lying eyes?" If you believe your lying eyes—actually, your lying brain—you can photocopy (or screen-capture and print) the illustration, then cut out the squares and compare them.

an object reflects *relative to its surroundings* (**FIGURE** 19.21). White paper reflects 90 percent of the light falling on it; black paper, only 10 percent. Although a black paper viewed in sunlight may reflect 100 times more light than does a white paper viewed indoors, it will still look black (McBurney & Collings, 1984). But if you view sunlit black paper through a narrow tube so nothing else is visible, it may look gray, because in bright sunshine it reflects a fair amount of light. View it without the tube and it is again black, because it reflects much less light than the objects around it.

This principle—that we perceive objects not in isolation but in their environmental context—matters to artists, interior decorators, and clothing designers. Our perception of the color and brightness of a wall or of a streak of paint on a canvas is determined not just by the paint in the can but by the surrounding colors. The take-home lesson: *Comparisons govern our perceptions.*

Shape and Size Constancies Sometimes an object whose actual shape cannot change *seems* to change shape with the angle of our view (**FIGURE** 19.22). More often, thanks to *shape constancy*, we perceive the form of familiar objects, such as the door in **FIGURE** 19.23, as constant even while our retinas receive changing images of them. Our brain manages this feat thanks to visual cortex neurons that rapidly learn to associate different views of an object (Li & DiCarlo, 2008).

Thanks to *size constancy*, we perceive objects as having a constant size, even while our distance from them varies. We assume a car is large enough to carry people, even when we see its tiny image from two blocks away. This assumption also illustrates the close connection between perceived *distance* and perceived *size*. Perceiving an object's distance gives us cues to its size. Likewise, knowing its general size—that the object is a car—provides us with cues to its distance.

Even in size-distance judgments, however, we consider an object's context. This interplay between perceived size and perceived distance helps explain several well-known illusions, including the *Moon illusion:* The Moon looks up to 50 percent larger when near the horizon than when high in the sky. Can you imagine why?

▼ FIGURE 19.22
Perceiving shape Do the tops of these tables have different dimensions? They appear to. But—believe it or not—they are identical. (Measure and see.) With both tables, we adjust our perceptions relative to our viewing angle.

▼ FIGURE 19.23
Shape constancy A door casts an increasingly trapezoidal image on our retinas as it opens. Yet we still perceive it as rectangular.

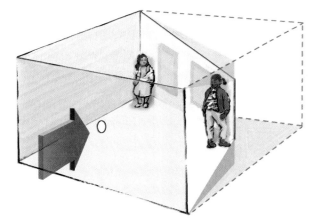

For at least 22 centuries, scholars have wondered (Hershenson, 1989). One reason is that monocular cues to objects' distances make the horizon Moon seem farther away. If it's farther away, our brain assumes, it must be larger than the Moon high in the night sky (Kaufman & Kaufman, 2000). Take away the distance cue, by looking at the horizon Moon through a paper tube, and the object will immediately shrink.

Size-distance relationships also explain why in **FIGURE** 19.24 the two same-age girls seem so different in size. As the diagram reveals, the girls are actually about the same size, but the room is distorted. Viewed with one eye through a peephole, the Ames room's trapezoidal walls produce the same images you would see in a normal rectangular room viewed with both eyes. Presented with the camera's one-eyed view, your brain makes the reasonable assumption that the room *is* normal and each girl is therefore the same distance from you. Given the different sizes of the girls' images on your retinas, your brain ends up calculating that the girls must be very different in size.

Perceptual illusions reinforce a fundamental lesson: Perception is not merely a projection of the world onto our brain. Rather, our sensations are disassembled into information bits that our brain then reassembles into its own functional model of the external world. During this reassembly process, our assumptions—such as the usual relationship between distance and size—can lead us astray. *Our brain constructs our perceptions.*

LaunchPad To experience more visual illusions, and to understand what they reveal about how you perceive the world, visit LaunchPad's *PsychSim 6: Visual Illusions.*

* * *

Form perception, depth perception, motion perception, and perceptual constancies illuminate how we organize our visual experiences. Perceptual organization applies to our other senses, too. Listening to an unfamiliar language, we have trouble hearing where one word stops and the next one begins. Listening to our own language, we automatically hear distinct words. This, too, reflects perceptual organization. But it is more, for we even organize a string of letters—THEDOGATEMEAT—into words that make an intelligible phrase, more likely "The dog ate meat" than "The do gate me at" (McBurney & Collings, 1984). This process involves not only the organization we've been discussing, but also interpretation—discerning meaning in what we perceive.

Perceptual Interpretation

Philosophers have debated whether our perceptual abilities should be credited to our nature or our nurture. To what extent do we *learn* to perceive? German philosopher Immanuel Kant (1724–1804) maintained that knowledge comes from our *inborn* ways of organizing sensory experiences. Indeed, we come equipped to process sensory information. But British philosopher John Locke (1632–1704) argued that through our experiences we also *learn* to perceive the world. Indeed, we learn to link an object's distance with its size. So, just how important is experience? How radically does it shape our perceptual interpretations?

▼ **FIGURE 19.24**
The illusion of the shrinking and growing girls This distorted room, designed by Adelbert Ames, appears to have a normal rectangular shape when viewed through a peephole with one eye. The girl in the right corner appears disproportionately large because we judge her size based on the false assumption that she is the same distance away as the girl in the far corner.

"Let us then suppose the mind to be, as we say, white paper void of all characters, without any ideas: How comes it to be furnished? . . . To this I answer, in one word, from EXPERIENCE."

John Locke, *An Essay Concerning Human Understanding,* 1690

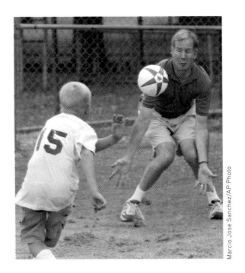

Learning to see: At age 3, Mike May lost his vision in an explosion. Decades later, after a new cornea restored vision to his right eye, he got his first look at his wife and children. Alas, although signals were now reaching his visual cortex, it lacked the experience to interpret them. May could not recognize expressions, or faces, apart from features such as hair. Yet he can see an object in motion and has learned to navigate his world and to marvel at such things as dust floating in sunlight (Abrams, 2002; Gorlick, 2010).

Perceptual adaptation "Oops, missed," thought researcher Hubert Dolezal as he viewed the world through inverting goggles. Yet, believe it or not, kittens, monkeys, and humans can adapt to an inverted world.

📌 **LaunchPad** For both classic and modern video on people experiencing an inverted world, and for tests of your own visual blind spot, visit LaunchPad's *Lab: Psychology of Vision.*

Experience and Visual Perception

19-9 What does research on restored vision, sensory restriction, and perceptual adaptation reveal about the effects of experience on perception?

Restored Vision and Sensory Restriction Writing to John Locke, William Molyneux wondered whether "a man *born* blind, and now adult, taught by his *touch* to distinguish between a cube and a sphere" could, if made to see, visually distinguish the two. Locke's answer was *No*, because the man would never have *learned* to see the difference.

Molyneux's hypothetical case has since been put to the test with a few dozen adults who, though blind from birth, later gained sight (Gregory, 1978; von Senden, 1932). Most were born with cataracts—clouded lenses that allowed them to see only diffused light, rather as you might see a foggy image through a Ping-Pong ball sliced in half. After cataract surgery, the patients could distinguish figure from ground and could sense colors—suggesting that these aspects of perception are innate. But much as Locke supposed, they often could not visually recognize objects that were familiar by touch.

Seeking to gain more control than is provided by clinical cases, researchers have outfitted infant kittens and monkeys with goggles through which they could see only diffuse, unpatterned light (Wiesel, 1982). After infancy, when the goggles were removed, these animals exhibited perceptual limitations much like those of humans born with cataracts. They could distinguish color and brightness, but not the form of a circle from that of a square. Their eyes had not degenerated; their retinas still relayed signals to their visual cortex. But lacking stimulation, the cortical cells had not developed normal connections. Thus, the animals remained functionally blind to shape. Experience guides, sustains, and maintains the brain neural organization that enables our perceptions.

In both humans and animals, similar sensory restrictions later in life do no permanent harm. When researchers cover the eye of an adult animal for several months, its vision will be unaffected after the eye patch is removed. When surgeons remove cataracts that develop during late adulthood, most people are thrilled at the return to normal vision.

The effect of sensory restriction on infant cats, monkeys, and humans suggests that for normal sensory and perceptual development, there is a *critical period*—an optimal period when exposure to certain stimuli or experiences is required. Surgery on blind children in India reveals that children blind from birth can benefit from removal of cataracts. But the younger they are, the more they will benefit, and their visual acuity (sharpness) may never be normal (Sinha, 2013). Early nurture sculpts what nature has endowed. In less dramatic ways, it continues to do so throughout our lives. Our visual experience matters. For example, despite concerns about their social costs, playing action video games sharpens spatial skills such as visual attention, eye-hand coordination and speed, and tracking multiple objects (Jeon et al., 2012; Spence & Feng, 2010).

Experiments on the perceptual limitations and advantages produced by early sensory deprivation provide a partial answer to the enduring question about experience: Does the effect of early experience last a lifetime? For some aspects of perception, the answer is clearly *Yes*: "Use it *soon* or lose it." We retain the imprint of some early sensory experiences far into the future.

Perceptual Adaptation Given a new pair of glasses, we may feel slightly disoriented, even dizzy. Within a day or two, we adjust. Our **perceptual adaptation** to changed visual input makes the world seem normal again. But imagine a far more dramatic new pair of glasses—one that shifts the apparent location of objects 40 degrees to the left. When you first put them on and toss a ball to a friend, it sails off to the left. Walking forward to shake hands with the person, you veer to the left.

Could you adapt to this distorted world? Baby chicks cannot. When fitted with such lenses, they continue to peck where food grains *seem* to be (Hess, 1956; Rossi, 1968). But we humans adapt to distorting lenses quickly. Within a few minutes your throws would again be accurate, your stride on target. Remove the lenses and you would experience an aftereffect: At first your throws would err in the *opposite* direction, sailing off to the right; but again, within minutes you would readapt.

Indeed, given an even more radical pair of glasses—one that literally turns the world upside down—you could still adapt. Psychologist George Stratton (1896) experienced this. He invented, and for eight days wore, optical headgear that flipped left to right *and* up to down, making him the first person to experience a right-side-up retinal image while standing upright. The ground was up, the sky was down.

At first, when Stratton wanted to walk, he found himself searching for his feet, which were now "up." Eating was nearly impossible. He became nauseated and depressed. But he persisted, and by the eighth day he could comfortably reach for an object in the right direction and walk without bumping into things. When Stratton finally removed the headgear, he readapted quickly.

In later experiments, people wearing the optical gear have even been able to ride a motorcycle, ski the Alps, and fly an airplane (Dolezal, 1982; Kohler, 1962). The world around them still seemed above their heads or on the wrong side. But by actively moving about in these topsy-turvy worlds, they adapted to the context and learned to coordinate their movements.

perceptual adaptation in vision, the ability to adjust to an artificially displaced or even inverted visual field.

MODULE 19 REVIEW Vision: Sensory and Perceptual Processing

LEARNING OBJECTIVES

RETRIEVAL PRACTICE Take a moment to answer each of these Learning Objective Questions (repeated here from within this module). Then turn to Appendix C, Complete Module Reviews, to check your answers. Research suggests that trying to answer these questions on your own will improve your long-term retention (McDaniel et al., 2009).

19-1 What are the characteristics of the energy that we see as visible light? What structures in the eye help focus that energy?

19-2 How do the rods and cones process information, and what is the path information travels from the eye to the brain?

19-3 How do we perceive color in the world around us?

19-4 Where are feature detectors located, and what do they do?

19-5 How does the brain use parallel processing to construct visual perceptions?

19-6 How did the Gestalt psychologists understand perceptual organization, and how do figure-ground and grouping principles contribute to our perceptions?

19-7 How do we use binocular and monocular cues to perceive the world in three dimensions, and how do we perceive motion?

19-8 How do perceptual constancies help us construct meaningful perceptions?

19-9 What does research on restored vision, sensory restriction, and perceptual adaptation reveal about the effects of experience on perception?

TERMS AND CONCEPTS TO REMEMBER

RETRIEVAL PRACTICE Test yourself on these terms by trying to write down the definition before flipping back to check your answers.

wavelength, p. 239

hue, p. 239

intensity, p. 239

pupil, p. 240

iris, p. 240

lens, p. 240

retina, p. 240

accommodation, p. 240

rods, p. 241

cones, p. 241

optic nerve, p. 241

blind spot, p. 241

fovea, p. 242

Young-Helmholtz trichromatic (three-color) theory, p. 243

opponent-process theory, p. 244

feature detectors, p. 245

parallel processing, p. 246

gestalt, p. 247

figure-ground, p. 248

grouping, p. 248

depth perception, p. 249

visual cliff, p. 249

binocular cues, p. 249

retinal disparity, p. 249

monocular cues, p. 250

phi phenomenon, p. 251

perceptual constancy, p. 251

color constancy, p. 251

perceptual adaptation, p. 254

Use **LearningCurve** to create your personalized study plan, which will direct you to the resources that will help you most in **LaunchPad**.

audition the sense or act of hearing.

frequency the number of complete wavelengths that pass a point in a given time (for example, per second).

pitch a tone's experienced highness or lowness; depends on frequency.

MODULE 20 The Nonvisual Senses

Hearing

LIKE OUR OTHER SENSES, OUR **audition,** or hearing, helps us adapt and survive. For those of us who communicate invisibly—by shooting unseen air waves across space and receiving back the same—hearing provides information and enables relationships. Hearing loss is therefore an invisible disability. To not catch someone's name, to not grasp what someone is asking, and to miss the hilarious joke is to be deprived of what others know, and sometimes to feel excluded. (As a person with hearing loss, I [DM] know the feeling.)

Most of us, however, can hear a wide range of sounds, and the ones we hear best are those in the range of the human voice. With normal hearing, we are remarkably sensitive to faint sounds, such as a child's whimper. (If our ears were much more sensitive, we would hear a constant hiss from the movement of air molecules.) Our distant ancestors' survival depended on this keen hearing when hunting or being hunted.

We are also remarkably attuned to sound variations. Among thousands of possible human voices, we easily recognize a friend on the phone, from the moment she says "Hi." Moreover, hearing is fast. "It might take you a full second to notice something out of the corner of your eye, turn your head toward it, recognize it, and respond to it," notes auditory neuroscientist Seth Horowitz (2012). "The same reaction to a new or sudden sound happens at least 10 times as fast." A fraction of a second after such events stimulate the ear's receptors, millions of neurons have simultaneously coordinated in extracting the essential features, comparing them with past experience, and identifying the stimulus (Freeman, 1991). For hearing as for our other senses, we wonder: How do we do it?

The sounds of music A violin's short, fast waves create a high pitch. The longer, slower waves of a cello or bass create a lower pitch. Differences in the waves' height, or amplitude, also create differing degrees of loudness.

Zdorov Kirill Vladimirovich/Shutterstock

sbarabu/Shutterstock

The Stimulus Input: Sound Waves

20-1 What are the characteristics of air pressure waves that we hear as sound?

Draw a bow across a violin, and you will unleash the energy of sound waves. Jostling molecules of air, each bumping into the next, create waves of compressed and expanded air, like the ripples on a pond circling out from a tossed stone. As we swim in our ocean of moving air molecules, our ears detect these brief air pressure changes.

Like light waves, sound waves vary in shape (**FIGURE 20.1**). The *amplitude* of sound waves determines their *loudness*. Their length, or **frequency,** determines the **pitch** we experience. Long waves have low frequency—and low pitch. Short waves have high frequency—and high pitch. Sound waves produced by a violin are much shorter and faster than those produced by a cello or a bass guitar.

▼ FIGURE 20.1
The physical properties of waves
(a) Waves vary in *wavelength* (the distance between successive peaks). *Frequency,* the number of complete wavelengths that can pass a point in a given time, depends on the wavelength. The shorter the wavelength, the higher the frequency. Wavelength determines the *pitch* of sound. (b) Waves also vary in *amplitude* (the height from peak to trough). Wave amplitude influences sound intensity.

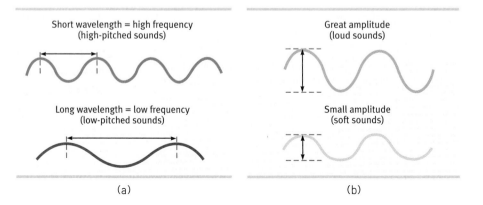

(a)   (b)

We measure sounds in *decibels*, with zero decibels representing the absolute threshold for hearing. Every 10 decibels correspond to a tenfold increase in sound intensity. Thus, normal conversation (60 decibels) is 10,000 times more intense than a 20-decibel whisper. And a temporarily tolerable 100-decibel passing subway train is 10 billion times more intense than the faintest detectable sound.

The Ear

20-2 How does the ear transform sound energy into neural messages?

The intricate process that transforms vibrating air into nerve impulses, which our brain decodes as sounds, begins when sound waves enter the *outer ear.* An intricate mechanical chain reaction begins as the visible outer ear channels the waves through the *auditory canal* to the *eardrum,* a tight membrane, causing it to vibrate (**FIGURE** 20.2 on the next page). In the **middle ear,** a piston made of three tiny bones (the *hammer, anvil,* and *stirrup*) picks up the vibrations and transmits them to the **cochlea,** a snail-shaped tube in the **inner ear.** The incoming vibrations cause the cochlea's membrane (the *oval window*) to vibrate, jostling the fluid that fills the tube. This motion causes ripples in the *basilar membrane,* bending the *hair cells* lining its surface, not unlike the wind bending a wheat field. Hair cell movement triggers impulses in the adjacent nerve cells. Axons of those cells converge to form the *auditory nerve,* which sends neural messages (via the thalamus) to the *auditory cortex* in the brain's temporal lobe. From vibrating air to moving piston to fluid waves to electrical impulses to the brain: Voila! We hear.

Perhaps the most intriguing part of the hearing process is the hair cells—"quivering bundles that let us hear" thanks to their "extreme sensitivity and extreme speed" (Goldberg, 2007). A cochlea has 16,000 of them, which sounds like a lot until we compare that with an eye's 130 million or so photoreceptors. But consider their responsiveness. Deflect the tiny bundles of *cilia* on the tip of a hair cell by the width of an atom—the equivalent of displacing the top of the Eiffel Tower by half an inch—and the alert hair cell, thanks to a special protein at its tip, triggers a neural response (Corey et al., 2004).

Across the world, 360 million people are challenged by hearing loss (WHO, 2012). Damage to the cochlea's hair cell receptors or their associated nerves can cause **sensorineural hearing loss** (or nerve deafness). Occasionally, disease damages these receptors, but more often the culprits are biological changes linked with heredity, aging, and prolonged exposure to ear-splitting noise or music. Sensorineural hearing loss is more common than **conduction hearing loss,** which is caused by damage to the mechanical system that conducts sound waves to the cochlea.

The cochlea's hair cells have been likened to carpet fibers. Walk around on them and they will spring back with a quick vacuuming. But leave a heavy piece of furniture on them for a long time and they may never rebound. As a general rule, if we cannot talk over a noise, it is potentially harmful, especially if prolonged and repeated (Roesser, 1998). Such experiences are common when sound exceeds 100 decibels, as happens in venues from frenzied sports arenas to personal music systems playing near maximum volume (**FIGURE** 20.3 on the next page). Ringing in the ears after exposure to loud sounds indicates that we have been bad to our unhappy hair cells. One study of teen rock concert attendees found that after three hours of sound averaging 99 decibels, 54 percent reported not hearing as well, and 1 in 4 had ringing in their ears. As pain alerts us to possible bodily harm, ringing of the ears alerts us to possible hearing damage. It is hearing's equivalent of bleeding.

The rate of teen hearing loss, now 1 in 5, has risen by a third since the early 1990s (Shargorodsky et al., 2010). Teen boys more than teen girls or adults blast themselves with loud volumes for long periods (Zogby, 2006). Males' greater noise exposure may help explain why men's hearing tends to be less acute than women's. But male or female, those who spend many hours in a loud nightclub, behind a power mower, or above a

middle ear the chamber between the eardrum and cochlea containing three tiny bones (hammer, anvil, and stirrup) that concentrate the vibrations of the eardrum on the cochlea's oval window.

cochlea [KOHK-lee-uh] a coiled, bony, fluid-filled tube in the inner ear; sound waves traveling through the cochlear fluid trigger nerve impulses.

inner ear the innermost part of the ear, containing the cochlea, semicircular canals, and vestibular sacs.

sensorineural hearing loss the most common form of hearing loss, also called *nerve deafness;* caused by damage to the cochlea's receptor cells or to the auditory nerves.

conduction hearing loss less common form of hearing loss caused by damage to the mechanical system that conducts sound waves to the cochlea.

Mark J. Terrill/AP Photo

That Baylen may hear When Super Bowl-winning quarterback Drew Brees celebrated New Orleans' 2010 victory amid pandemonium, he used ear muffs to protect the vulnerable hair cells of his son, Baylen.

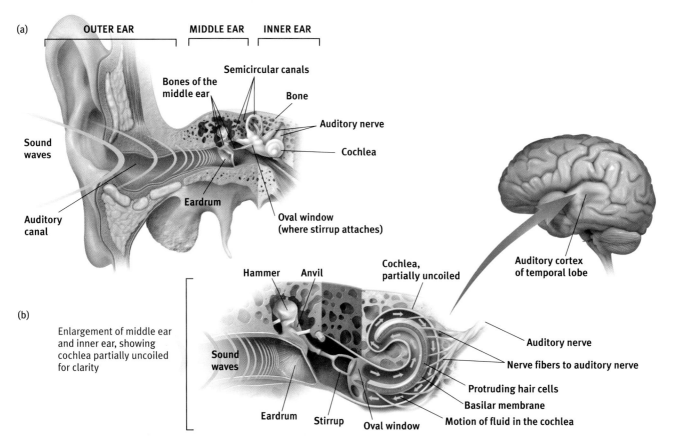

(a)

OUTER EAR   MIDDLE EAR   INNER EAR

Semicircular canals

Bones of the middle ear

Bone

Auditory nerve

Cochlea

Sound waves

Oval window (where stirrup attaches)

Eardrum

Auditory canal

Auditory cortex of temporal lobe

(b)

Enlargement of middle ear and inner ear, showing cochlea partially uncoiled for clarity

Hammer   Anvil   Cochlea, partially uncoiled

Sound waves

Auditory nerve

Nerve fibers to auditory nerve

Protruding hair cells

Basilar membrane

Eardrum   Stirrup   Oval window   Motion of fluid in the cochlea

▼ FIGURE 20.2
Hear here: How we transform sound waves into nerve impulses that our brain interprets (a) The outer ear funnels sound waves to the eardrum. The bones of the middle ear (hammer, anvil, and stirrup) amplify and relay the eardrum's vibrations through the oval window into the fluid-filled cochlea. (b) As shown in this detail of the middle and inner ear, the resulting pressure changes in the cochlear fluid cause the basilar membrane to ripple, bending the hair cells on its surface. Hair cell movements trigger impulses at the base of the nerve cells, whose fibers converge to form the auditory nerve. That nerve sends neural messages to the thalamus and on to the auditory cortex.

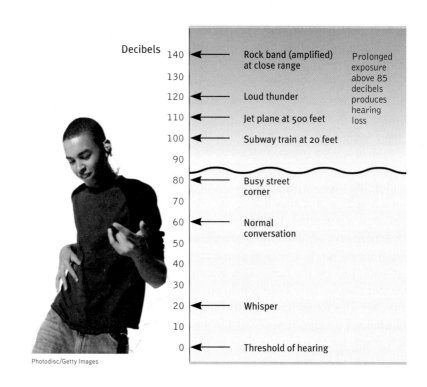

Decibels   140   Rock band (amplified) at close range   Prolonged exposure above 85 decibels produces hearing loss
            130
            120   Loud thunder
            110   Jet plane at 500 feet
            100   Subway train at 20 feet
            90
            80   Busy street corner
            70
            60   Normal conversation
            50
            40
            30
            20   Whisper
            10
            0   Threshold of hearing

Photodisc/Getty Images

▼ FIGURE 20.3
The intensity of some common sounds

jackhammer should wear earplugs. "Condoms or, safer yet, abstinence," say sex educators. "Earplugs or walk away," say hearing educators.

For now, the only way to restore hearing for people with nerve deafness is a sort of bionic ear—a **cochlear implant**, which, by 2011, had been given to 219,000 people worldwide (NIDCD, 2013). This electronic device translates sounds into electrical signals that, wired into the cochlea's nerves, convey information about sound to the brain. Cochlear implants given to deaf kittens and human infants have seemed to trigger an "awakening" of the pertinent brain area (Klinke et al., 1999; Sireteanu, 1999). These devices can help children become proficient in oral communication (especially if they receive them as preschoolers or even before age 1) (Dettman et al., 2007; Schorr et al., 2005). Cochlear implants can help restore hearing for most adults, but only if their brain learned to process sound during childhood.

Transmitter

Receiver/Stimulator

Electrode

Speech processor

Hardware for hearing Cochlear implants work by translating sounds into electrical signals that are transmitted to the cochlea and, via the auditory nerve, on to the brain.

RETRIEVAL PRACTICE

• What are the basic steps in transforming sound waves into perceived sound?

ANSWER: The *outer ear* collects sound waves, which are translated into mechanical waves by the *middle ear* and turned into fluid waves in the *inner ear*. The *auditory nerve* then translates the energy into electrical waves and sends them to the brain, which perceives and interprets the sound.

• The amplitude of a sound wave determines our perception of _____ (loudness/pitch).

ANSWER: loudness

• The longer the sound waves are, the _____ (lower/higher) their frequency is and the _____ (higher/lower) their pitch.

ANSWERS: lower; lower

Perceiving Loudness, Pitch, and Location

20-3 How do we detect loudness, discriminate pitch, and locate sounds?

Responding to Loud and Soft Sounds How do we detect loudness? If you guessed that it's related to the intensity of a hair cell's response, you'd be wrong. Rather, a soft, pure tone activates only the few hair cells attuned to its frequency. Given louder sounds, neighboring hair cells also respond. Thus, your brain interprets loudness from the *number* of activated hair cells.

If a hair cell loses sensitivity to soft sounds, it may still respond to loud sounds. This helps explain another surprise: Really loud sounds may seem loud to people with or without normal hearing. As a person with hearing loss, I [DM] used to wonder what really loud music must sound like to people with normal hearing. Now I realize it sounds much the same; where we differ is in our perception of soft sounds. This is why we hard-of-hearing people do not want *all* sounds (loud and soft) amplified. We like sound *compressed*, which means harder-to-hear sounds are amplified more than loud sounds (a feature of today's digital hearing aids).

Hearing Different Pitches How do we know whether a sound is the high-frequency, high-pitched chirp of a bird or the low-frequency, low-pitched roar of a truck? Current thinking on how we discriminate pitch combines two theories.

• Hermann von Helmholtz's **place theory** presumes that we hear different pitches because different sound waves trigger activity at different places along the cochlea's basilar membrane. Thus, the brain determines a sound's pitch by recognizing the specific place (on the membrane) that is generating the neural signal. When Nobel

Experiments are also under way to restore vision—with a bionic retina (a 2-millimeter-diameter microchip with photoreceptors that simulate the damaged retinal cells), and with a video camera and computer that simulate the visual cortex. In test trials, both devices have enabled blind people to gain partial sight (Boahen, 2005; Steenhuysen, 2002).

cochlear implant a device for converting sounds into electrical signals and stimulating the auditory nerve through electrodes threaded into the cochlea.

place theory in hearing, the theory that links the pitch we hear with the place where the cochlea's membrane is stimulated.

frequency theory in hearing, the theory that the rate of nerve impulses traveling up the auditory nerve matches the frequency of a tone, thus enabling us to sense its pitch. (Also called *temporal theory*.)

LaunchPad For an interactive review of how we perceive sound, visit LaunchPad's *PsychSim 6: The Auditory System.* For an animated explanation, visit LaunchPad's *Concept Practice: The Auditory Pathway.*

▼ FIGURE 20.4
How we locate sounds Sound waves strike one ear sooner and more intensely than the other. From this information, our nimble brain can compute the sound's location. As you might therefore expect, people who lose all hearing in one ear often have difficulty locating sounds.

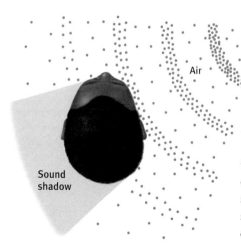

laureate-to-be Georg von Békésy (1957) cut holes in the cochleas of guinea pigs and human cadavers and looked inside with a microscope, he discovered that the cochlea vibrated, rather like a shaken bedsheet, in response to sound. High frequencies produced large vibrations near the beginning of the cochlea's membrane. Low frequencies vibrated more of the membrane. But a problem remains: Place theory can explain how we hear high-pitched sounds but not low-pitched sounds. The neural signals generated by low-pitched sounds are not so neatly localized on the basilar membrane.

- **Frequency theory** (also called *temporal theory*) suggests an alternative: The brain reads pitch by monitoring the frequency of neural impulses traveling up the auditory nerve. The whole basilar membrane vibrates with the incoming sound wave, triggering neural impulses to the brain at the same rate as the sound wave. If the sound wave has a frequency of 100 waves per second, then 100 pulses per second travel up the auditory nerve. But again, a problem remains: An individual neuron cannot fire faster than 1000 times per second. How, then, can we sense sounds with frequencies above 1000 waves per second (roughly the upper third of a piano keyboard)?

- Enter the *volley principle*: Like soldiers who alternate firing so that some can shoot while others reload, neural cells can alternate firing. By firing in rapid succession, they can achieve a *combined frequency* above 1000 waves per second. Thus,

1. Place theory best explains how we sense *high pitches*.

2. Frequency theory best explains how we sense *low pitches*.

3. Some combination of place and frequency theories seems to handle the *pitches in the intermediate range*.

RETRIEVAL PRACTICE

- Which theory of pitch perception would best explain a symphony audience's enjoyment of a high-pitched piccolo? How about a low-pitched cello?

ANSWERS: place theory; frequency theory

Locating Sounds Why don't we have one big ear—perhaps above our one nose? "The better to hear you," as the wolf said to Red Riding Hood. Thanks to the placement of our two ears, we enjoy stereophonic ("three-dimensional") hearing. Two ears are better than one for at least two reasons (**FIGURE 20.4**). If a car to your right honks, your right ear will receive a more *intense* sound, and it will receive the sound slightly *sooner* than your left ear.

Because sound travels 750 miles per hour and human ears are but 6 inches apart, the intensity difference and the time lag are extremely small. A just noticeable difference in the direction of two sound sources corresponds to a time difference of just 0.000027 second! Lucky for us, our supersensitive auditory system can detect such minute differences (Brown & Deffenbacher, 1979; Middlebrooks & Green, 1991).

The Other Senses

Our brain gives seeing and hearing priority in the allocation of cortical tissue. But extraordinary happenings also occur within our other senses. Sharks and dogs rely on their outstanding sense of smell, aided by large brain areas devoted to this system. Without our senses of touch, taste, smell, and body position and movement, we humans would be seriously handicapped, and our capacities for enjoying the world would be greatly diminished.

Touch

20-4 How do we sense touch?

Touch is vital. Right from the start, touch aids our development. Infant rats deprived of their mother's grooming produce less growth hormone and have a lower metabolic rate—a good way to keep alive until the mother returns, but a reaction that stunts growth if prolonged. Infant monkeys allowed to see, hear, and smell—but not touch—their mother become desperately unhappy; those separated by a screen with holes that allow touching are much less miserable. Premature human babies gain weight faster and go home sooner if they are stimulated by hand massage (Field et al., 2006). As adults, we still yearn to touch—to kiss, to stroke, to snuggle. In experiments, strangers separated by a curtain, using their hands to touch only each other's forearms, have been able to communicate anger, fear, disgust, love, gratitude, and sympathy at levels well above chance (Hertenstein et al., 2006).

Humorist Dave Barry was perhaps right to jest that your skin "keeps people from seeing the inside of your body, which is repulsive, and it prevents your organs from falling onto the ground." But skin does much more. Touching various spots on the skin with a soft hair, a warm or cool wire, and the point of a pin reveals that some spots are especially sensitive to *pressure*, others to *warmth*, others to *cold*, still others to *pain*. Our "sense of touch" is actually a mix of these four basic and distinct skin senses, and our other skin sensations are variations of pressure, warmth, cold, and pain: Some examples:

- Stroking adjacent pressure spots creates a tickle.

- Repeated gentle stroking of a pain spot creates an itching sensation.

- Touching adjacent cold and pressure spots triggers a sense of wetness, which you can experience by touching dry, cold metal.

- Stimulating nearby cold and warm spots produces the sensation of hot (**FIGURE** 20.5).

Touch sensations involve more than tactile stimulation, however. A self-administered tickle produces less somatosensory cortex activation than does the same tickle from something or someone else (Blakemore et al., 1998). Likewise, a sensual leg caress evokes a different somatosensory cortex response when a heterosexual man believes it comes from an attractive woman rather than a man (Gazzola et al., 2012). Our responses to tickles and caresses reveal how quickly cognition influences our brain's sensory response.

Pain

20-5 What biological, psychological, and social-cultural influences affect our experience of pain? How do placebos, distraction, and hypnosis help control pain?

Be thankful for occasional pain. Pain is your body's way of telling you something has gone wrong. By drawing your attention to a burn, a break, or a sprain, pain orders you to change your behavior—"Stay off that turned ankle!" The rare people born without the ability to feel pain may experience severe injury or even death before early adulthood. Without the discomfort that makes us occasionally shift position, their joints fail from excess strain. Without the warnings of pain, the effects of unchecked infections and injuries accumulate (Neese, 1991).

More numerous are those who live with chronic pain, which is rather like an alarm that won't shut off. The suffering of such people, and of those with persistent or recurring backaches, arthritis, headaches, and cancer-related pain, prompts two questions: What is pain? How might we control it?

Understanding Pain Our pain experiences vary widely. Women are more sensitive to pain than men are (their senses of hearing and smell also tend to be more sensitive) (Ruau et al., 2011; Wickelgren, 2009). Our individual pain sensitivity varies,

The precious sense of touch As William James wrote in his *Principles of Psychology* (1890), "Touch is both the alpha and omega of affection."

▼ FIGURE 20.5
Warm + cold = hot When ice-cold water passes through one coil and comfortably warm water through another, we perceive the combined sensation as burning hot.

Cold water ——— Warm water

HOT!

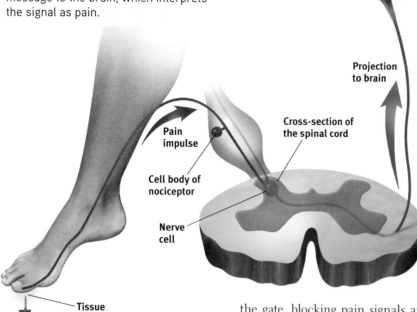

The pain circuit Sensory receptors (*nociceptors*) respond to potentially damaging stimuli by sending an impulse to the spinal cord, which passes the message to the brain, which interprets the signal as pain.

Projection to brain

Pain impulse

Cross-section of the spinal cord

Cell body of nociceptor

Nerve cell

Tissue injury

nociceptors sensory receptors that enable the perception of pain in response to potentially harmful stimuli.

gate-control theory the theory that the spinal cord contains a neurological "gate" that blocks pain signals or allows them to pass on to the brain. The "gate" is opened by the activity of pain signals traveling up small nerve fibers and is closed by activity in larger fibers or by information coming from the brain.

"Pain is a gift." So said a doctor studying Ashlyn Blocker, who has a rare genetic mutation that prevents her from feeling pain. At birth, she didn't cry. As a child, she ran around for two days on a broken ankle. She has put her hands on a hot machine and burned the flesh off. And she has reached into boiling water to retrieve a dropped spoon. "Everyone in my class asks me about it, and I say, 'I can feel pressure, but I can't feel pain.' *Pain!* I cannot feel it!"

Jeff Riedel/Contour/Getty Images

too, depending on genes, physiology, experience, attention, and surrounding culture (Gatchel et al., 2007; Reimann et al., 2010). Thus, our experience of pain reflects both *bottom-up* sensations and *top-down* cognition.

BIOLOGICAL INFLUENCES There is no one type of stimulus that triggers pain (as light triggers vision). Instead, there are different **nociceptors**—sensory receptors in our skin, muscles, and organs that detect hurtful temperatures, pressure, or chemicals (**FIGURE 20.6**).

Although no theory of pain explains all available findings, psychologist Ronald Melzack and biologist Patrick Wall's (1965, 1983; Melzack & Katz, 2013) classic **gate-control theory** provides a useful model. The spinal cord contains small nerve fibers that conduct most pain signals, and larger fibers that conduct most other sensory signals. Melzack and Wall theorized that the spinal cord contains a neurological "gate." When tissue is injured, the small fibers activate and open the gate, and you feel pain. Large-fiber activity closes the gate, blocking pain signals and preventing them from reaching the brain. Thus, one way to treat chronic pain is to stimulate (by massage, electric stimulation, or acupuncture) "gate-closing" activity in the large neural fibers (Wall, 2000).

But pain is not merely a physical phenomenon of injured nerves sending impulses to a definable brain area—like pulling on a rope to ring a bell. Melzack and Wall noted that brain-to-spinal-cord messages can also close the gate.

The brain can also create pain, as it does in people's experiences of *phantom limb sensations*, after a limb has been amputated. Their brain may misinterpret the spontaneous central nervous system (CNS) activity that occurs in the absence of normal sensory input. As the dreamer may see with eyes closed, so 7 in 10 such people may feel pain or movement in nonexistent limbs (Melzack, 1992, 2005). (Some may also try to step off a bed onto a phantom limb or to lift a cup with a phantom hand.) Even those born without a limb sometimes perceive sensations from the absent arm or leg. The brain, Melzack (1998) has surmised, comes prepared to anticipate "that it will be getting information from a body that has limbs."

Phantoms may haunt other senses too, as the brain, responding to the absence of sensory signals, amplifies irrelevant neural activity. People with hearing loss often experience the sound of silence: *tinnitus*, the phantom sound of ringing in the ears. Those who lose vision to glaucoma, cataracts, diabetes, or macular degeneration may experience phantom sights—nonthreatening hallucinations (Ramachandran & Blakeslee, 1998). Others who have nerve damage in the systems for tasting and smelling have experienced phantom tastes or smells, such as ice water that seems sickeningly sweet or fresh air that reeks of rotten food (Goode, 1999). The point to remember: *We feel, see, hear, taste, and smell with our brain, which can sense even without functioning senses.*

PSYCHOLOGICAL INFLUENCES One powerful influence on our perception of pain is the attention we focus on it. Athletes, focused on winning, may play through the pain. Halfway through his lap of the 2012 Olympics 1600 meter relay, Manteo Mitchell broke one of his leg bones—and kept running.

We also seem to edit our *memories* of pain, which often differ from the pain we actually experienced. In experiments, and after medical procedures, people overlook a pain's duration. Their memory snapshots instead record two factors: their pain's *peak* moment (which can lead them to recall variable pain, with peaks, as worse [Stone et al., 2005]), and how much pain they felt at the *end*. In one experiment, researchers asked people to immerse one hand in painfully cold water for 60 seconds, and then the other hand in the same painfully cold water for 60 seconds followed by a slightly less painful 30 seconds more (Kahneman et al., 1993). Which experience would you expect to recall as most painful?

Curiously, when asked which trial they would prefer to repeat, most preferred the 90- second trial, with more net pain—but less pain at the end. Physicians have used this principle with patients undergoing colon exams—lengthening the discomfort by a minute, but lessening its intensity (Kahneman, 1999). Although the extended milder discomfort added to their net pain experience, patients experiencing this taper-down treatment later recalled the exam as less painful than did those whose pain ended abruptly. (If, at the end of a painful root canal, the oral surgeon asks if you'd like to go home or to have a few more minutes of milder discomfort, there's a case to be made for prolonging your hurt.)

The end of an experience can color our memory of pleasures, too. In one simple experiment, some people, on receiving a fifth and last piece of chocolate, were told it was their "next" one. Others, told it was their "last" piece, liked it better and also rated the whole experiment as being more enjoyable (O'Brien & Ellsworth, 2012). Endings matter.

SOCIAL-CULTURAL INFLUENCES Our perception of pain varies with our social situation and our cultural traditions. We tend to perceive more pain when others seem to be experiencing pain (Symbaluk et al., 1997). This may help explain other apparent social aspects of pain, as when pockets of Australian keyboard operators during the mid-1980s suffered outbreaks of severe pain while typing or performing other repetitive work—without any discernible physical abnormalities (Gawande, 1998). Sometimes the pain in sprain is mainly in the brain—literally. When people felt empathy for another's pain, their own brain activity partly mirrored the activity in the actual brain in pain (Singer et al, 2004).

Thus, our perception of pain is a biopsychosocial phenomenon (Hadjistavropoulos et al., 2011). Viewing pain from many perspectives can help us better understand how to cope with it and treat it (**FIGURE 20.7**).

Controlling Pain If pain is where body meets mind—if it is both a physical and a psychological phenomenon—then it should be treatable both physically and psychologically. Depending on the patient's symptoms, pain control clinics select one or more therapies from a list that includes drugs, surgery, acupuncture, electrical stimulation, massage, exercise, hypnosis, relaxation training, and thought distraction.

That explains some striking influences on pain. When we are distracted from pain (a psychological influence) and soothed by the release of our naturally painkilling *endorphins* (a biological influence), our experience of pain diminishes. Sports injuries may go unnoticed until the

Distracted from the pain After a tackle in the first half of a competitive game, BK Hacken soccer player Mohammed Ali Khan (in white) said he "had a bit of pain" but thought it was "just a bruise." With his attention focused on the game, he played on. In the second half he was surprised to learn from an attending doctor that the leg was broken.

Reinhold Matay/AP Photo

Biological influences:
• activity in spinal cord's large and small fibers
• genetic differences in endorphin production
• the brain's interpretation of CNS activity

Barros & Barros/Getty Images

Psychological influences:
• attention to pain
• learning based on experience
• expectations

Halfpoint/Shutterstock

Social-cultural influences:
• presence of others
• empathy for others' pain
• cultural expectations

Robert Nickelsberg/Hulton Archive Getty Images

Personal experience of pain

▼ FIGURE 20.7
Biopsychosocial approach to pain Our experience of pain is much more than the neural messages sent to our brain.

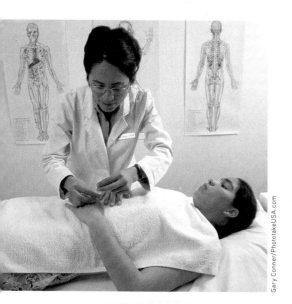

Acupuncture: A jab well done This acupuncturist is attempting to help this woman gain relief from back pain by using needles on points of the patient's hand.

"When belly with bad pains doth swell, It matters naught what else goes well."

Sadi, *The Gulistan*, 1258

"Pain is increased by attending to it."

Charles Darwin, *Expression of Emotions in Man and Animals*, 1872

after-game shower. People who carry a gene that boosts the availability of endorphins are less bothered by pain, and their brain is less responsive to pain (Zubieta et al., 2003). Others, who carry a mutated gene that disrupts pain circuit neurotransmission, may be unable to experience pain (Cox et al., 2006). Such discoveries could point the way toward new pain medications that mimic these genetic effects.

PLACEBOS Even an inert placebo can help, by dampening the central nervous system's attention and responses to painful experiences—mimicking analgesic drugs (Eippert et al., 2009; Wager & Atlas, 2013). After being injected in the jaw with a stinging saltwater solution, men in one experiment received a placebo said to relieve pain, and they immediately felt better. Being given fake painkilling chemicals caused the brain to dispense real ones, as indicated by activity in an area that releases natural painkilling opiates (Scott et al., 2007; Zubieta et al., 2005). "Believing becomes reality," noted one commentator (Thernstrom, 2006), as "the mind unites with the body."

Another experiment pitted two placebos—fake pills and pretend acupuncture—against each other (Kaptchuk et al., 2006). People with persistent arm pain received either sham acupuncture (with trick needles that retracted without puncturing the skin) or blue cornstarch pills that looked like a medication often prescribed for strain injury. A fourth of those receiving the nonexistent needle pricks and 31 percent of those receiving the fake pills complained of side effects, such as painful skin or dry mouth and fatigue. After two months, both groups were reporting less pain, with the fake acupuncture group reporting the greater pain drop.

DISTRACTION Distracting people with pleasant images (*"Think of a warm, comfortable environment"*) or drawing their attention away from the painful stimulation (*"Count backward by 3's"*) is an effective way to activate pain-inhibiting circuits and to increase pain tolerance (Edwards et al., 2009). A well-trained nurse may distract needle-shy patients by chatting with them and asking them to look away when inserting the needle. Burn victims receiving excruciating wound care can benefit from an even more effective distraction: immersion in a computer-generated 3-D world, like the snow scene in **FIGURE 20.8**. Functional MRI (fMRI) scans have revealed that playing in the virtual reality reduces the brain's pain-related activity (Hoffman, 2004). Because pain is in the brain, diverting the brain's attention may bring relief. Better yet, research suggests, maximize pain relief by combining a placebo with distraction (Buhle et al., 2012), and amplify their effects with hypnosis. Hypnosis can also divert attention (see Thinking Critically About: Hypnosis and Pain Relief).

▼ **FIGURE 20.8**
Virtual-reality pain control For burn victims undergoing painful skin repair, an escape into virtual reality can powerfully distract attention, thus reducing pain and the brain's response to painful stimulation. fMRI scans have illustrated a lowered pain response when the patient is distracted.

Hypnosis and Pain Relief

Imagine you are about to be hypnotized. The hypnotist invites you to sit back, fix your gaze on a spot high on the wall, and relax. In a quiet, low voice the hypnotist suggests, "Your eyes are growing tired. . . . Your eyelids are becoming heavy . . . now heavier and heavier. . . . They are beginning to close. . . . You are becoming more deeply relaxed. . . . Your breathing is now deep and regular. . . . Your muscles are becoming more and more relaxed. Your whole body is beginning to feel like lead."

After a few minutes of this *hypnotic induction,* you may experience **hypnosis**. Hypnotists have no magical mind-control power; they merely focus people on certain images or behaviors. To some extent, we are all open to suggestion. But highly hypnotizable people—such as the 20 percent who can carry out a suggestion not to smell or react to an open bottle of ammonia held under their nose—are especially suggestible and imaginative (Barnier & McConkey, 2004; Silva & Kirsch, 1992).

Can hypnosis relieve pain? *Yes.* When unhypnotized people put their arms in an ice bath, they felt intense pain within 25 seconds (Elkins et al., 2012; Jensen, 2008). When hypnotized people did the same after being given suggestions to feel no pain, they indeed reported feeling little pain. As some dentists know, light hypnosis can reduce fear, thus reducing hypersensitivity to pain.

Hypnosis inhibits pain-related brain activity. In surgical experiments, hypnotized patients have required less medication, recovered sooner, and left the hospital earlier than unhypnotized control patients (Askay & Patterson, 2007; Hammond, 2008; Spiegel, 2007). Nearly 10 percent of us can become so deeply hypnotized that even major surgery can be performed without anesthesia. Half of us can gain at least some pain relief from hypnosis. The surgical use of hypnosis has flourished in Europe, where one Belgian medical team has performed more than 5000 surgeries with a combination of hypnosis, local anesthesia, and a mild sedative (Song, 2006).

Psychologists have proposed two explanations for how hypnosis works. One theory proposes that hypnosis is a form of normal *social influence* (Lynn et al., 1990; Spanos & Coe, 1992). In this view, hypnosis is a by-product of normal social and mental processes. Like actors caught up in their roles, people begin to feel and behave in ways appropriate for "good hypnotic subjects." They may allow the hypnotist to direct their attention and fantasies away from pain.

Another theory views hypnosis as a special dual-processing state of **dissociation**—a split between different levels of consciousness. Dissociation theory offers an explanation for why people hypnotized for pain relief may show brain activity in areas that receive sensory information, but not in areas that normally process pain-related information. It also seeks to explain why, when no one is watching, hypnotized people may carry out **posthypnotic suggestions**

Courtesy of Elizabeth Jecker

Dissociation or social influence? This hypnotized woman being tested by famous researcher Ernest Hilgard showed no pain when her arm was placed in an ice bath. But asked to press a key if some part of her felt the pain, she did so. To Hilgard (1986, 1992), this was evidence of dissociation, or divided consciousness. The social influence perspective, however, maintains that people responding this way are caught up in playing the role of "good subject."

(which are made during hypnosis but carried out after the person is no longer hypnotized) (Perugini et al., 1998).

Another form of dual processing—*selective attention*—may also play a role in hypnotic pain relief. Brain scans show that hypnosis increases activity in frontal lobe attention systems (Oakley & Halligan, 2013). And it reduces brain activity in a region that processes painful stimuli, but not in the somatosensory cortex, which receives the raw sensory input (Rainville et al., 1997). So, hypnosis does not block sensory input, but it may block our attention to those stimuli. This helps explain why an injured athlete, caught up in the competition, may feel little or no pain until the game ends.

hypnosis a social interaction in which one person (the hypnotist) suggests to another (the subject) that certain perceptions, feelings, thoughts, or behaviors will spontaneously occur.

dissociation a split in consciousness, which allows some thoughts and behaviors to occur simultaneously with others.

posthypnotic suggestion a suggestion, made during a hypnosis session, to be carried out after the subject is no longer hypnotized; used by some clinicians to help control undesired symptoms and behaviors.

RETRIEVAL PRACTICE

• Which of the following options has NOT been proven to reduce pain?

a. Distraction b. Hypnotic suggestion c. Phantom limb sensations d. Endorphins

ANSWER: c.

Lauren Burke/Digital Vision/Getty Images

▼ TABLE 20.1
The Survival Functions of Basic Tastes

Taste	Indicates
Sweet	Energy source
Salty	Sodium essential to physiological processes
Sour	Potentially toxic acid
Bitter	Potential poisons
Umami	Proteins to grow and repair tissue

(Adapted from Cowart, 2005.)

"Life is not measured by the number of breaths we take, but by the moments that take our breath away."

Author unknown

Impress your friends with your new word for the day: People unable to see are said to experience blindness. People unable to hear experience deafness. People unable to smell experience *anosmia*. The 1 in 7500 people born with anosmia not only have trouble cooking and eating, but also are somewhat more prone to depression, accidents, and relationship insecurity (Croy et al., 2012, 2013).

Taste

20-6 In what ways are our senses of taste and smell similar, and how do they differ?

Like touch, our sense of taste involves several basic sensations. Taste's sensations were once thought to be sweet, sour, salty, and bitter, with all others stemming from mixtures of these four (McBurney & Gent, 1979). Then, as investigators searched for specialized nerve fibers for the four taste sensations, they encountered a receptor for what we now know is a fifth—the savory meaty taste of *umami*, best experienced as the flavor enhancer monosodium glutamate (MSG).

Tastes exist for more than our pleasure (see **TABLE 20.1**). Pleasureful tastes attracted our ancestors to energy- or protein-rich foods that enabled their survival. Aversive tastes deterred them from new foods that might be toxic. We see the inheritance of this biological wisdom in today's 2- to 6-year-olds, who are typically fussy eaters, especially when offered new meats or bitter-tasting vegetables, such as spinach and brussels sprouts (Cooke et al., 2003). Meat and plant toxins were both potentially dangerous sources of food poisoning for our ancestors, especially for children. Given repeated small tastes of disliked new foods, however, most children begin to accept them (Wardle et al., 2003). We come to like what we eat. Compared with breast-fed babies, German babies bottle fed vanilla-flavored milk grew up to be adults with a striking preference for vanilla flavoring (Haller et al., 1999).

Taste is a chemical sense. Inside each little bump on the top and sides of your tongue are 200 or more taste buds, each containing a pore that catches food chemicals. In each taste bud pore, 50 to 100 taste receptor cells project antenna-like hairs that sense food molecules. Some receptors respond mostly to sweet-tasting molecules, others to salty-, sour-, umami-, or bitter-tasting ones. It doesn't take much to trigger a response that alerts your brain's temporal lobe. If a stream of water is pumped across your tongue, the addition of a concentrated salty or sweet taste for but one-tenth of a second will get your attention (Kelling & Halpern, 1983). When a friend asks for "just a taste" of your soft drink, you can squeeze off the straw after a mere instant.

Taste receptors reproduce themselves every week or two, so if you burn your tongue with hot food it hardly matters. However, as you grow older, the number of taste buds decreases, as does taste sensitivity (Cowart, 1981). (No wonder adults enjoy strong-tasting foods that children resist.) Smoking and alcohol use accelerate these declines. Those who have lost their sense of taste have reported that food tastes like "straw" and is hard to swallow (Cowart, 2005).

Essential as taste buds are, there's more to taste than meets the tongue. Expectations can influence taste. When told a sausage roll was "vegetarian," people in one experiment found it decidedly inferior to its identical partner labeled "meat" (Allen et al., 2008). In another experiment, being told that a wine cost $90 rather than its real $10 price made it taste better and triggered more activity in a brain area that responds to pleasant experiences (Plassmann et al., 2008).

Smell

Life begins with an inhale and ends with an exhale. Between birth and death, you will daily inhale and exhale nearly 20,000 breaths of life-sustaining air, bathing your nostrils in a stream of scent-laden molecules. The resulting experiences of smell (*olfaction*) are strikingly intimate: You inhale something of whatever or whoever it is you smell.

Like taste, smell is a chemical sense. We smell something when molecules of a substance carried in the air reach a tiny cluster of 20 million receptor cells at the top of each nasal cavity (**FIGURE 20.9**). These olfactory receptor cells, waving like sea anemones on a reef, respond selectively—to the aroma of a cake baking, to a wisp of smoke, to a friend's fragrance. Instantly, they alert the brain through their axon fibers. Being part of an old, primitive sense, olfactory neurons bypass the brain's sensory control center, the thalamus.

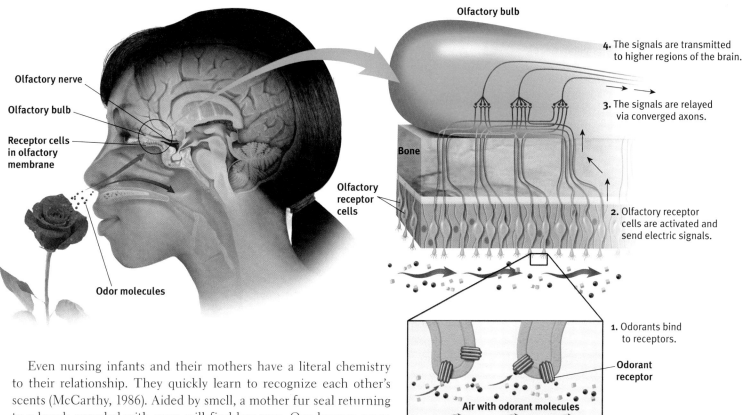

Olfactory bulb

4. The signals are transmitted to higher regions of the brain.

3. The signals are relayed via converged axons.

Olfactory nerve

Olfactory bulb

Receptor cells in olfactory membrane

Bone

Olfactory receptor cells

2. Olfactory receptor cells are activated and send electric signals.

Odor molecules

1. Odorants bind to receptors.

Odorant receptor

Air with odorant molecules

Even nursing infants and their mothers have a literal chemistry to their relationship. They quickly learn to recognize each other's scents (McCarthy, 1986). Aided by smell, a mother fur seal returning to a beach crowded with pups will find her own. Our human sense of smell is less acute than our senses of seeing and hearing. Looking out across a garden, we see its forms and colors in exquisite detail and hear a variety of birds singing, yet we smell little of it without sticking our nose into the blossoms.

Odor molecules come in many shapes and sizes—so many, in fact, that it takes many different receptors to detect them. A large family of genes designs the 350 or so receptor proteins that recognize particular odor molecules (Miller, 2004). Linda Buck and Richard Axel (1991) discovered (in work for which they received a 2004 Nobel Prize) that these receptor proteins are embedded on the surface of nasal cavity neurons. As a key slips into a lock, so odor molecules slip into these receptors. Yet we don't seem to have a distinct receptor for each detectable odor. Odors trigger combinations of receptors, in patterns that are interpreted by the olfactory cortex. As the English alphabet's 26 letters can combine to form many words, so odor molecules bind to different receptor arrays, producing at least 1 trillion odors that we could potentially discriminate (Bushdid et al., 2014). It is the combinations of olfactory receptors, which activate different neuron patterns, that allow us to distinguish between the aromas of fresh-brewed and hours-old coffee (Zou et al., 2005).

Gender and age influence our ability to identify scents. Women and young adults have the best sense of smell (Wickelgren, 2009; Wysocki & Gilbert, 1989). Physical condition also matters. Smokers and people with Alzheimer's disease, Parkinson's disease, or alcohol use disorder typically have a diminished sense of smell (Doty, 2001). For all of us, however, the sense of smell tends to peak in early adulthood and gradually declines thereafter (**FIGURE 20.10** on the next page).

Despite our skill at discriminating scents, we aren't very good at describing them. Try it: Which is easier, describing the *sound* of coffee brewing, or the *aroma* of coffee? For most people, it's the sound. Compared with how we experience and remember sights and sounds, smells are primitive and harder to describe and recall (Richardson & Zucco, 1989; Zucco, 2003).

As any dog or cat with a good nose could tell us, we each have our own identifiable chemical signature. (One noteworthy exception: A dog will follow the tracks of one

▼ FIGURE 20.9

The sense of smell If you are to smell a flower, airborne molecules of its fragrance must reach receptors at the top of your nose. Sniffing swirls air up to the receptors, enhancing the aroma. The receptor cells send messages to the brain's olfactory bulb, and then onward to the temporal lobe's primary smell cortex and to the parts of the limbic system involved in memory and emotion.

LaunchPad For an animated explanation of how we smell, visit LaunchPad's *Concept Practice: Sense of Smell.*

"There could be a stack of truck tires burning in the living room, and I wouldn't necessarily smell it. Whereas my wife can detect a lone spoiled grape two houses away."

Dave Barry, 2005

▼ **FIGURE 20.10**
Age, sex, and sense of smell Among the 1.2 million people who responded to a *National Geographic* scratch-and-sniff survey, women and younger adults most successfully identified six sample odors. (Data from Wysocki & Gilbert, 1989.)

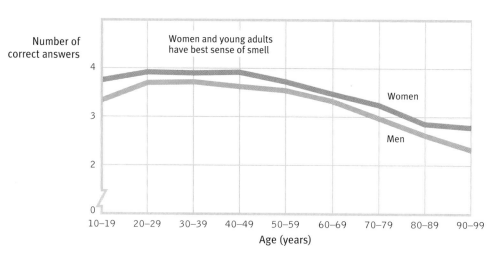

The nose knows Humans have some 20 million olfactory receptors. A bloodhound has 220 million (Herz, 2007).

Layne Bailey/The Charlotte Observer/AP Photo

identical twin as though they had been made by the other [Thomas, 1974].) Animals that have many times more olfactory receptors than we do also use their sense of smell to communicate and to navigate. Long before a shark can see its prey, or a moth its mate, olfactory cues direct their way, as they also do for migrating salmon returning to their home stream. After being exposed in a hatchery to one of two odorant chemicals, salmon have, when returning two years later, sought whichever stream near their release site was spiked with the familiar smell (Barinaga, 1999).

For humans, too, the attractiveness of smells depends on learned associations (Herz, 2001). As babies nurse, their preference for the smell of their mother's breast builds. So, too, with other associations. As good experiences are linked with a particular scent, people come to like that scent. This helps explain why people in the United States tend to like the smell of wintergreen (which they associate with candy and gum) more than do those in Great Britain (where it often is associated with medicine). In another example of odors evoking unpleasant emotions, researchers frustrated Brown University students with a rigged computer game in a scented room (Herz et al., 2004). Later, if exposed to the same odor while working on a verbal task, the students' frustration was rekindled and they gave up sooner than others exposed to a different odor or no odor.

Though it's difficult to recall odors by name, we may recognize long-forgotten odors and their associated memories (Engen, 1987; Schab, 1991). The smell of the sea, the scent of a perfume, or an aroma of a favorite relative's kitchen can bring to mind a happy time. It's a phenomenon the British travel agent chain Lunn Poly understood well. To evoke memories of relaxing on sunny, warm beaches, the company once piped the aroma of coconut suntan oil into its shops (Fracassini, 2000).

Our brain's circuitry helps explain an odor's power to evoke feelings and memories (**FIGURE 20.11**). A hotline runs between the brain area receiving information from the nose and the brain's ancient limbic centers associated with memory and emotion. Thus, when put in a foul-smelling room, people expressed harsher judgments of immoral acts (such as lying or keeping a found wallet) and more negative attitudes toward gay men (Inbar et al., 2011; Schnall et al., 2008). Exposed to a fishy smell during a trust game, people become more suspicious (Lee & Schwarz, 2012). And when riding on a train car with the citrus scent of a cleaning product, people have left behind less trash (de Lange et al., 2012).

Smell is indeed primitive. Eons before the elaborate analytical areas of our cerebral cortex had fully evolved, our mammalian ancestors

▼ **FIGURE 20.11**
Taste, smell, and memory Information from the taste buds (yellow arrow) travels to an area between the frontal and temporal lobes of the brain. It registers in an area not far from where the brain receives information from our sense of smell, which interacts with taste. The brain's circuitry for smell (red area) also connects with areas involved in memory storage, which helps explain why a smell can trigger a memory.

Processes taste

Processes smell (near memory area)

sniffed for food—and for predators. When running in the Republican primary to select a candidate in the next election of a governor of New York, Carl Paladino understood that primitive, disgusting smells can affect judgments. He mailed a flyer that smelled of rotting garbage with a message attacking his opponent—whom he then defeated 62 to 38 percent (Liberman & Pizarro, 2010).

RETRIEVAL PRACTICE

• How does our system for sensing smell differ from our sensory systems for touch and taste?

ANSWER: We have four basic touch senses and five basic taste sensations. But we have no basic smell receptors. Instead, different combinations of odor receptors send messages to the brain, enabling us to recognize some 10,000 different smells.

Body Position and Movement

20-7 How do we sense our body's position and movement?

Important sensors in your joints, tendons, and muscles enable your **kinesthesia**—your sense of the position and movement of your body parts. By closing your eyes or plugging your ears you can momentarily imagine being without sight or sound. But what would it be like to live without touch or kinesthesia—without, therefore, being able to sense the positions of your limbs when you wake during the night? Ian Waterman of Hampshire, England, knows. In 1972, at age 19, Waterman contracted a rare viral infection that destroyed the nerves enabling his sense of light touch and of body position and movement. People with this condition report feeling disembodied, as though their body is dead, not real, not theirs (Sacks, 1985). With prolonged practice, Waterman learned to walk and eat—by visually focusing on his limbs and directing them accordingly. But if the lights go out, he crumples to the floor (Azar, 1998). Even for the rest of us, vision interacts with kinesthesia. Stand with your right heel in front of your left toes. Easy. Now close your eyes and you will probably wobble.

A companion **vestibular sense** monitors your head's (and thus your body's) position and movement. The biological gyroscopes for this sense of equilibrium are two structures in your inner ear. The first, your *semicircular canals*, look like a three-dimensional pretzel (see Figure 20.2a). The second, connecting those canals with the cochlea, is the pair of *vestibular sacs*, which contain fluid that moves when your head rotates or tilts. When this movement stimulates hair-like receptors, sending messages to the cerebellum at the back of your brain, you sense your body position and maintain your balance.

If you twirl around and then come to an abrupt halt, neither the fluid in your semicircular canals nor your kinesthetic receptors will immediately return to their neutral state. The dizzy aftereffect fools your brain with the sensation that you're still spinning. This illustrates a principle that underlies perceptual illusions: *Mechanisms that normally give us an accurate experience of the world can, under special conditions, fool us.* Understanding how we get fooled provides clues to how our perceptual system works.

RETRIEVAL PRACTICE

• Where are the kinesthetic receptors and the vestibular sense receptors located?

ANSWER: Kinesthetic receptors are located in our joints, tendons, and muscles. Vestibular sense receptors are located in our inner ear.

Sensory Interaction

20-8 How does *sensory interaction* influence our perceptions, and what is *embodied cognition*?

Our senses—seeing, hearing, tasting, smelling, touching—eavesdrop on one another (Rosenblum, 2013). In interpreting the world, our brain blends their inputs. Consider what happens to your sense of taste if you hold your nose, close your eyes, and have

© Robert Kanavel

Bodies in space These high school competitive cheer team members can thank their inner ears for the information that enables their brains to monitor their bodies' position so expertly.

---

kinesthesia [kin-ehs-THEE-zhuh] the system for sensing the position and movement of individual body parts.

vestibular sense the sense of body movement and position, including the sense of balance.

Courtesy of Action Hearing Loss

▼ FIGURE 20.12

Sensory interaction When a hard-of-hearing listener sees an animated face forming the words being spoken at the other end of a phone line, the words become easier to understand (Knight, 2004).

someone feed you various foods. A slice of apple may be indistinguishable from a chunk of raw potato. A piece of steak may taste like cardboard. Without their smells, a cup of cold coffee may be hard to distinguish from a glass of red wine. Our sense of smell sticks its nose into the business of taste.

Thus, to savor a taste, we normally breathe the aroma through our nose—which is why eating is not much fun when you have a bad cold. Smell can also change our perception of taste: A drink's strawberry odor enhances our perception of its sweetness. Depending on its texture, a potato chip "tastes" fresh or stale (Smith, 2011). This is **sensory interaction** at work—the principle that one sense may influence another. Smell + texture + taste = flavor. Yet, despite the nose's contribution of smell, flavor feels located in the mouth (Stevenson, 2014).

Vision and hearing may similarly interact. A weak flicker of light that we have trouble perceiving becomes more visible when accompanied by a short burst of sound (Kayser, 2007). And a sound may be easier to hear with a visual cue. If I [DM], as a person with hearing loss, watch a video with simultaneous captioning, I have no trouble hearing the words I am seeing. I may therefore think I don't need the captioning, but if I then turn off the captioning, I suddenly realize I do need it. The eyes guide the ears (**FIGURE 20.12**).

But what do you suppose happens if the eyes and the ears disagree? What if we *see* a speaker saying one syllable while we *hear* another? Surprise: We may perceive a third syllable that blends both inputs. Seeing the mouth movements for *ga* while hearing *ba* we may perceive *da*. This phenomenon is known as the *McGurk effect,* after its discoverers, Scottish psychologist Harry McGurk and his assistant John MacDonald (1976). For all of us, lip reading is part of hearing.

Touch also interacts with our other senses. In detecting events, the brain can combine simultaneous touch and visual signals, thanks to neurons projecting from the somatosensory cortex back to the visual cortex (Macaluso et al., 2000). Touch even interacts with hearing. One experiment blew a puff of air (such as our mouths produce when saying *pa* and *ta*) on the neck or hands as people heard either these sounds or the more airless sounds *ba* or *da*. The result? People more often misheard *ba* or *da* as *pa* or *ta* when played with the faint puff (Gick & Derrick, 2009). Thanks to sensory interaction, they heard with their skin.

Our brain even blends our tactile and social judgments, as demonstrated in these playful experiments:

- After holding a warm drink rather than a cold one, people were more likely to rate someone more warmly, feel closer to them, and behave more generously (IJzerman & Semin, 2009; Williams & Bargh, 2008). Physical warmth promotes social warmth.

- After being given the cold shoulder by others in an experiment, people judge the room as colder than do those treated warmly (Zhong & Leonardelli, 2008). Social exclusion literally feels cold.

- Sitting at a wobbly desk and chair makes others' relationships seem less stable (Kille et al., 2013).

- When leaning to the left—by sitting in a left- rather than right-leaning chair, or squeezing a handgrip with their left hand, or using a mouse with their left hand—people lean more left in their expressed political attitudes (Oppenheimer & Trail, 2010). When holding a soft ball, American students become more likely to categorize a face as a Democrat rather than a Republican, and vice versa when holding a hard ball (Slepian et al., 2012).

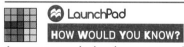

HOW WOULD YOU KNOW?

Are you wondering how researchers test these kinds of questions? Try LaunchPad's *How Would You Know If a Cup of Coffee Can Warm Up Relationships?*

These examples of **embodied cognition** illustrate how brain circuits processing bodily sensations connect with brain circuits responsible for cognition. We think from within a body.

So, the senses interact: As we attempt to decipher our world, our brain blends inputs from multiple channels. For many people, an odor, perhaps of mint or chocolate, can evoke a sensation of taste (Stevenson & Tomiczek, 2007). But in a few select individuals, the senses become joined in a phenomenon called *synesthesia*, where one sort of sensation (such as hearing sound) involuntarily produces another (such as seeing color). Early in life, "exuberant neural connectivity" produces some arbitrary associations among the senses, which later are normally—but not always—pruned (Wagner & Dobkins, 2011). Thus, hearing music may activate color-sensitive cortex regions and trigger a sensation of color (Brang et al., 2008; Hubbard et al., 2005). Seeing the number 3 may evoke a taste sensation (Ward, 2003). Those who experience such sensory shifts are known as *synesthetes*.

* * *

For a summary of our sensory systems, see **TABLE 20.2**. The river of perception is fed by sensation, cognition, and emotion. And that is why we need biological, psychological, and social-cultural levels of analysis (**FIGURE 20.13**).

> **sensory interaction** the principle that one sense may influence another, as when the smell of food influences its taste.
>
> **embodied cognition** in psychological science, the influence of bodily sensations, gestures, and other states on cognitive preferences and judgments.

▼ TABLE 20.2
Summarizing the Senses

Sensory System	Source	Receptors
Vision	Light waves striking the eye	Rods and cones in the retina
Hearing	Sound waves striking the outer ear	Cochlear hair cells in the inner ear
Touch	Pressure, warmth, cold on the skin	Skin receptors detect pressure, warmth, cold, and pain
Taste	Chemical molecules in the mouth	Basic tongue receptors for sweet, sour, salty, bitter, and umami
Smell	Chemical molecules breathed in through the nose	Millions of receptors at top of nasal cavity
Body position— kinesthesia	Any change in position of a body part, interacting with vision	Kinesthetic sensors in joints, tendons, and muscles.
Body movement— vestibular sense	Movement of fluids in the inner ear caused by head/body movement	Hairlike receptors in the semicircular canals and vestibular sacs

If perception is the product of these three sources, what can we say about extrasensory perception, which claims that perception can occur apart from sensory input? For more on that question, see Thinking Critically About: ESP—Perception Without Sensation?

* * *

To feel awe, mystery, and a deep reverence for life, we need look no further than our own perceptual system and its capacity for organizing formless nerve impulses into colorful sights, vivid sounds, and evocative smells. As Shakespeare's Hamlet recognized, "There are more things in Heaven and Earth, Horatio, than are dreamt of in your philosophy." Within our ordinary sensory and perceptual experiences lies much that is truly extraordinary—surely much more than has so far been dreamt of in our psychology.

Biological influences:
• sensory analysis
• unlearned visual phenomena
• critical period for sensory development

Psychological influences:
• selective attention
• learned schemas
• Gestalt principles
• context effects
• perceptual set

Perception: Our version of reality

Social-cultural influences:
• cultural assumptions and expectations

▼ FIGURE 20.13
Perception is a biopsychosocial phenomenon Psychologists study how we perceive with different levels of analysis, from the biological to the social-cultural.

ESP—Perception Without Sensation?

20-9 What are the claims of ESP, and what have most research psychologists concluded after putting these claims to the test?

Without sensory input, are we capable of **extrasensory perception (ESP)**? Are there indeed people—any people—who can read minds, see through walls, or foretell the future? Nearly half of Americans have agreed there are (AP, 2007; Moore, 2005).

The most testable and, for this discussion, most relevant ESP claims are

- *telepathy:* mind-to-mind communication.
- *clairvoyance:* perceiving remote events, such as a house on fire in another state.
- *precognition:* perceiving future events, such as an unexpected death in the next month.

Closely linked is *psychokinesis,* or "mind over matter," such as levitating a table or influencing the roll of a die. (The claim is illustrated by the wry request, "Will all those who believe in psychokinesis please raise my hand?")

If ESP is real, we would need to overturn the scientific understanding that we are creatures whose minds are tied to our physical brains and whose perceptual experiences of the world are built of sensations. Sometimes new evidence does overturn our scientific preconceptions. Science, as we will see throughout this book, offers us surprises—about the extent of the unconscious mind, about the effects of emotions on health, about what heals and what doesn't, and much more.

Most research psychologists and scientists are skeptical that paranormal phenomena exist. But reputable universities in Great Britain, the Netherlands, and Australia, have added faculty chairs or research units in **parapsychology** (Storm, 2010a,b; Turpin,

2005). These researchers perform scientific experiments searching for possible ESP and other paranormal phenomena. Before seeing how parapsychologists do research on ESP, let's consider some popular beliefs.

Premonitions or Pretensions?

Can psychics see into the future? Although one might wish for a psychic stock forecaster, the tallied forecasts of "leading psychics" reveal meager accuracy. During the 1990s, the tabloid psychics were all wrong in predicting surprising events. (Madonna did not become a gospel singer, the Statue of Liberty did not lose both its arms in a terrorist blast, Queen Elizabeth did not abdicate her throne to enter a convent.) And the psychics have missed recent big-news events. Where were the psychics on 9/10 when we needed them? Why, despite a $50 million reward offered, could none of them help locate Osama bin Laden after 9/11, or step forward to predict the impending stock crashes in 2008? In 2010, when a mine collapse trapped 33 miners, the Chilean government reportedly consulted four psychics. Their verdict? "They're all dead" (Kraul, 2010). But 69 days later, all 33 were rescued.

After Amanda Berry went missing in Cleveland in 2003, her distraught and desperate mother turned to a famed psychic on a national television show for answers. "She's not alive, honey," the psychic told the devastated mom, who died without living to see her daughter rescued in 2013 (Radford, 2013). According to one analysis, this result brought that psychic's record on 116 missing person and death cases to 83 unknown outcomes, 33 incorrect, and zero mostly correct. To researcher Ryan Shaffer (2013), that's the record of a "psychic defective."

The psychic visions offered to police departments have been no more accurate than guesses made by others (Nickell, 1994, 2005; Radford, 2010; Reiser, 1982). But their sheer volume does increase the odds of an occasional correct guess, which psychics can then report to the media. Police departments are wise to all this. When researchers asked the police departments of America's 50 largest cities whether they ever had used psychics, 65 percent said *No* (Sweat & Durm, 1993). Of those that had, not one had found them helpful.

Psychics' vague predictions sometimes sound correct when later interpreted ("retrofitted") to match events that provide a perceptual set for "understanding" them. Nostradamus, a sixteenth-century French psychic, explained in an unguarded

Will you marry me, live happily for 3 years, become bored, pretend to be taking a pottery class but actually be having an affair, then agree to go to marriage counseling to stay together for the sake of our hyperactive son, Derrick?

WHEN PSYCHICS PROPOSE

© Dan Piraro, Bizarro.

---

extrasensory perception (ESP) the controversial claim that perception can occur apart from sensory input; includes telepathy, clairvoyance, and precognition.

parapsychology the study of paranormal phenomena, including ESP and psychokinesis.

MODULE 20: THE NONVISUAL SENSES 273

moment that his ambiguous prophecies "could not possibly be understood till they were interpreted after the event and by it."

Are the spontaneous "visions" of everyday people any more accurate? Do dreams, for example, foretell the future, as people from both Eastern and Western cultures tend to believe—making some people more reluctant to fly after dreaming of a plane crash (Morewedge & Norton, 2009)? Or do they only seem to do so when we recall or reconstruct them in light of what has already happened? Two Harvard psychologists tested the prophetic power of dreams after superhero aviator Charles Lindbergh's baby son was kidnapped and murdered in 1932 (Murray & Wheeler, 1937). Before the body was discovered, they invited people to report their dreams about the child and 1300 visionaries submitted dream reports. How many accurately envisioned the child dead? Five percent. And how many also correctly anticipated the body's location—buried among trees? Only 4 of the 1300. Although this number was surely no better than chance, to those 4 dreamers the accuracy of their apparent precognitions must have seemed uncanny.

Given the billions of events in the world each day, and given enough days, some stunning coincidences are sure to occur. By one careful estimate, chance alone would predict that more than a thousand times a day someone on Earth will think of another person and then within the next five minutes will learn of that person's death (Charpak & Broch, 2004). Thus, when explaining an astonishing event, we should "give chance a chance" (Lilienfeld, 2009). With enough time and people, the improbable becomes inevitable.

Putting ESP to Experimental Test

When faced with claims of mind reading or out-of-body travel or communication with the dead, how can we separate bizarre ideas from those that sound strange but are true? At the heart of science is a simple answer: *Test them to see if they work.* If they do, so much the better for the ideas. If they don't, so much the better for our skepticism.

This scientific attitude has led both believers and skeptics to agree that what parapsychology needs is a reproducible phenomenon and a theory to explain it. Parapsychologist Rhea White (1998) spoke for many in saying that "the image of parapsychology that comes to my mind, based on nearly 44 years in the field,

is that of a small airplane [that] has been perpetually taxiing down the runway of the Empirical Science Airport since 1882 . . . its movement punctuated occasionally by lifting a few feet off the ground only to bump back down on the tarmac once again. It has never taken off for any sustained flight."

How might we test ESP claims in a controlled, reproducible experiment? An experiment differs from a staged demonstration. In the laboratory, the experimenter controls what the "psychic" sees and hears. On stage, the psychic controls what the audience sees and hears.

The search for a valid and reliable test of ESP has resulted in thousands of experiments. After digesting data from 30 such studies, parapsychologist Lance Storm and his colleagues (2010a,b; 2013) concluded that, given participants with experience or belief in ESP, there is "consistent and reliable" parapsychological evidence. Psychologist Ray Hyman (2010), who has been scrutinizing parapsychological research since 1957, replied that if this is the best evidence, it fails to impress: "Parapsychology will achieve scientific acceptability only when it provides a positive theory with . . . independently replicable evidence. This is something it has yet to achieve after more than a century."

Daryl Bem (2011), a respected social psychologist, has been a skeptic of stage psychics; he once quipped that "a psychic is an actor playing the role of a psychic" (1984). Yet he reignited hopes for replicable evidence with nine experiments that seemed to show people anticipating future events. In one, when an erotic scene was about to appear on a screen in one of two randomly selected positions, Cornell University participants guessed right 53.1 percent of the time (beating 50 percent by a small but statistically significant margin). In another, people viewed a set of words, took a recall test of those words, and then rehearsed a randomly selected subset of those words. People better remembered the rehearsed words—even when the rehearsal took place *after* the recall test. The upcoming rehearsal—a future event—apparently affected their ability to recall words, he suggested.

Bem wonders if his "anomalous" findings reflect an evolutionary advantage to those who can precognitively anticipate future dangers. Critics scoff. "If any of his claims were true," wrote cognitive scientist Douglas Hofstadter (2011), "then all of the bases underlying contemporary science would be toppled, and

"To be sure of hitting the target, shoot first and call whatever you hit the target."

Writer-artist Ashleigh Brilliant

"A person who talks a lot is sometimes right."

Spanish proverb

"At the heart of science is an essential tension between two seemingly contradictory attitudes—an openness to new ideas, no matter how bizarre or counterintuitive they may be, and the most ruthless skeptical scrutiny of all ideas, old and new."

Carl Sagan (1987)

(Continued on next page)

Courtesy of Claire Cole

Testing psychic powers in the British population Psychologists created a "mind machine" to see if people could influence or predict a coin toss (Wiseman & Greening, 2002). Using a touch-sensitive screen, visitors to British festivals were given four attempts to call heads or tails, playing against a computer that kept score. By the time the experiment ended, nearly 28,000 people had predicted 110,959 tosses—with 49.8 percent correct.

Despite the paper having survived critical reviews by a top-tier journal, other critics found the methods "badly flawed" (Alcock, 2011) or the statistical analyses "biased" (Wagenmakers et al., 2011). "A result—especially one of this importance—must recur several times in tests by independent and skeptical researchers to gain scientific credibility," observed astronomer David Helfand (2011). "I have little doubt that Professor Bem's experiments will fail this test."

Anticipating such skepticism, Bem has made his computer materials available to anyone who wishes to replicate his studies. Multiple attempts have since been made, without success (Galak et al., 2012; Ritchie et al., 2012). Regardless, science is doing its work. It has been open to a finding that challenges its own assumptions. And then, through follow-up research, it has assessed its validity. And that is how science sifts crazy-sounding ideas, leaving most on the historical waste heap while occasionally surprising us.

One skeptic, magician James Randi, has had a longstanding offer of $1 million to be given "to anyone who proves a genuine psychic power under proper observing conditions" (Randi, 1999; Thompson, 2010). French, Australian, and Indian groups have made similar offers of up to 200,000 euros (CFI, 2003). Large as these sums are, the scientific seal of approval would be worth far more. To refute those who say there is no ESP, one need only produce a single person who can demonstrate a single, reproducible ESP event. (To refute those who say pigs can't talk would take but one talking pig.) So far, no such person has emerged.

we would have to rethink everything about the nature of the universe." Moreover, if future events retroactively affect present feelings, then why can't people intuitively predict casino outcomes or stock market futures?

RETRIEVAL PRACTICE

- If an ESP event occurred under controlled conditions, what would be the next best step to confirm that ESP really exists?

ANSWER: The ESP event would need to be reproduced in other scientific studies.

20 REVIEW The Nonvisual Senses

LEARNING OBJECTIVES

RETRIEVAL PRACTICE Take a moment to answer each of these Learning Objective Questions (repeated here from within this module). Then turn to Appendix C, Complete Module Reviews, to check your answers. Research suggests that trying to answer these questions on your own will improve your long-term retention (McDaniel et al., 2009).

20-1 What are the characteristics of air pressure waves that we hear as sound?

20-2 How does the ear transform sound energy into neural messages?

20-3 How do we detect loudness, discriminate pitch, and locate sounds?

20-4 How do we sense touch?

20-5 What biological, psychological, and social-cultural influences affect our experience of pain? How do placebos, distraction, and hypnosis help control pain?

20-6 In what ways are our senses of taste and smell similar, and how do they differ?

20-7 How do we sense our body's position and movement?

20-8 How does *sensory interaction* influence our perceptions, and what is *embodied cognition*?

20-9 What are the claims of ESP, and what have most research psychologists concluded after putting these claims to the test?

TERMS AND CONCEPTS TO REMEMBER

RETRIEVAL PRACTICE Test yourself on these terms by trying to write down the definition before flipping back to check your answers.

audition, p. 256

frequency, p. 256

pitch, p. 256

middle ear, p. 257

cochlea [KOHK-lee-uh], p. 257

inner ear, p. 257

sensorineural hearing loss, p. 257

conduction hearing loss, p. 257

cochlear implant, p. 259

place theory, p. 259

frequency theory, p. 260

nociceptors, p. 262

gate-control theory, p. 262

hypnosis, p. 265

dissociation, p. 265

posthypnotic suggestion, p. 265

kinesthesia [kin-ehs-THEE-zhuh], p. 269

vestibular sense, p. 269

sensory interaction, p. 270

embodied cognition, p. 271

extrasensory perception (ESP), p. 272

parapsychology, p. 272

Use LearningCurve to create your personalized study plan, which will direct you to the resources that will help you most in LaunchPad.

TEST YOUR-SELF — SENSATION AND PERCEPTION

Test yourself repeatedly throughout your studies. This will not only help you figure out what you know and don't know; the testing itself will help you learn and remember the information more effectively thanks to the *testing effect*.

18 Basic Concepts of Sensation and Perception

1. Sensation is to _____ as perception is to _____ .
   a. absolute threshold; difference threshold
   b. bottom-up processing; top-down processing
   c. interpretation; detection
   d. grouping; priming

2. The process by which we organize and interpret sensory information is called _____ .

3. Subliminal stimuli are
   a. too weak to be processed by the brain in any way.
   b. consciously perceived more than 50 percent of the time.
   c. always strong enough to affect our behavior.
   d. below our absolute threshold for conscious awareness.

4. Another term for difference threshold is the _____
   _____ _____ .

5. Weber's law states that for a difference to be perceived, two stimuli must differ by
   a. a fixed or constant energy amount.
   b. a constant minimum percentage.
   c. a constantly changing amount.
   d. more than 7 percent.

6. Sensory adaptation helps us focus on
   a. visual stimuli.
   b. auditory stimuli.
   c. constant features of the environment.
   d. important changes in the environment.

7. Our perceptual set influences what we perceive. This mental tendency reflects our
   a. experiences, assumptions, and expectations.
   b. perceptual adaptation.
   c. priming ability.
   d. difference thresholds.

MODULE 19 Vision: Sensory and Perceptual Processing

8. The characteristic of light that determines the color we experience, such as blue or green, is _____ .

9. The amplitude of a light wave determines our perception of _____ .
   a. brightness.
   b. color.
   c. meaning.
   d. distance.

10. The blind spot in your retina is located where
    a. there are rods but no cones.
    b. there are cones but no rods.
    c. the optic nerve leaves the eye.
    d. the bipolar cells meet the ganglion cells.

11. Cones are the eye's receptor cells that are especially sensitive to _____ light and are responsible for our _____ vision.
    a. bright; black-and-white
    b. dim; color
    c. bright; color
    d. dim; black-and-white

12. Two theories together account for color vision. The Young-Helmholtz trichromatic theory shows that the eye contains _____ , and the opponent-process theory accounts for the nervous system's having _____ .
    a. opposing retinal processes; three pairs of color receptors
    b. opponent-process cells; three types of color receptors
    c. three pairs of color receptors; opposing retinal processes
    d. three types of color receptors; opponent-process cells

13. What mental processes allow you to perceive a lemon as yellow?

14. The cells in the visual cortex that respond to certain lines, edges, and angles are called _____ _____ .

15. The brain's ability to process many aspects of an object or a problem simultaneously is called _____ _____ .

16. Our tendencies to fill in the gaps and to perceive a pattern as continuous are two different examples of the organizing principle called
    a. interposition.
    b. depth perception.
    c. shape constancy.
    d. grouping.

17. In listening to a concert, you attend to the solo instrument and perceive the orchestra as accompaniment. This illustrates the organizing principle of
    a. figure-ground.
    b. shape constancy.
    c. grouping.
    d. depth perception.

18. The visual cliff experiments suggest that
    a. infants have not yet developed depth perception.
    b. crawling human infants and very young animals perceive depth.
    c. we have no way of knowing whether infants can perceive depth.
    d. unlike other species, humans are able to perceive depth in infancy.

19. Depth perception underlies our ability to
    a. group similar items in a gestalt.
    b. perceive objects as having a constant shape or form.
    c. judge distances.
    d. fill in the gaps in a figure.

20. Two examples of _____ depth cues are interposition and linear perspective.

21. Perceiving a tomato as consistently red, despite lighting shifts, is an example of
    a. shape constancy.
    b. perceptual constancy.
    c. a binocular cue.
    d. continuity.

22. After surgery to restore vision, patients who had been blind from birth had difficulty
    a. recognizing objects by touch.
    b. recognizing objects by sight.
    c. distinguishing figure from ground.
    d. distinguishing between bright and dim light.

23. In experiments, people have worn glasses that turned their visual fields upside down. After a period of adjustment, they learned to function quite well. This ability is called _____ _____ .

MODULE 20 The Nonvisual Senses

24. The snail-shaped tube in the inner ear, where sound waves are converted into neural activity, is called the _____ .

25. What are the basic steps in transforming sound waves into perceived sound?

26. _____ theory explains how we hear high-pitched sounds, and _____ theory explains how we hear low-pitched sounds.

27. The gate-control theory of pain proposes that

    a. special pain receptors send signals directly to the brain.

    b. pain is a property of the senses, not of the brain.

    c. small spinal cord nerve fibers conduct most pain signals, but large-fiber activity can close access to those pain signals.

    d. the stimuli that produce pain are unrelated to other sensations.

28. How does the biopsychosocial approach explain our experience of pain? Provide examples.

29. We have specialized nerve receptors for detecting which five tastes? How did this ability aid our ancestors?

30. _____ is your sense of body position and movement. Your _____ _____ specifically monitors your head's movement, with sensors in the inner ear.

31. Why do you feel a little dizzy immediately after a roller-coaster ride?

32. A food's aroma can greatly enhance its taste. This is an example of

    a. sensory adaptation.

    b. chemical sensation.

    c. kinesthesia.

    d. sensory interaction.

33. Which of the following ESP phenomena is supported by solid, replicable scientific evidence?

    a. Telepathy

    b. Clairvoyance

    c. Precognition

    d. None of these answers

Find answers to these questions in Appendix D, in the back of the book.

Rara Faure/Getty Images

LEARNING

. . . .

In the early 1940s, University of Minnesota graduate students Marian Breland and Keller Breland witnessed the power of a new learning technology. Their mentor, B. F. Skinner, would become famous for *shaping* rat and pigeon behaviors by delivering well-timed rewards as the animals inched closer and closer to a desired behavior. Impressed by Skinner's results, the Brelands began shaping the behavior of cats, chickens, parakeets, turkeys, pigs, ducks, and hamsters (Bailey & Gillaspy, 2005). The rest is history. They eventually formed Animal Behavior Enterprises and spent the next half-century training more than 15,000 animals from 140 species for movies, traveling shows, amusement parks, corporations, and the government. The Brelands also trained trainers, including Sea World's first training director.

While writing a book about animal trainers, journalist Amy Sutherland wondered if shaping had uses closer to home (2006a,b). If baboons could be trained to skateboard and elephants to paint, might "the same techniques . . . work on that stubborn but lovable species, the American husband"? Step by step, she "began thanking Scott if he threw one dirty shirt into the hamper. If he threw in two, I'd kiss him [and] as he basked in my appreciation, the piles became smaller." After two years of "thinking of my husband as an exotic animal species," she reports, "my marriage is far smoother, my husband much easier to love."

Like husbands and other animals, much of what we do we learn from experience. Indeed, nature's most important gift may be our *adaptability*—our capacity to learn new behaviors that help us cope with our changing world. We can learn how to build grass huts or snow shelters, submarines or space stations, and thereby adapt to almost any environment.

Learning breeds hope. What is learnable we can potentially teach—a fact that encourages parents, educators, coaches, and animal trainers. What has been learned we can potentially change by new learning—an assumption that underlies counselling, psychotherapy, and rehabilitation programs. No matter how unhappy, or unsuccessful, or unloved we are, that need not be the end of our story.

No topic is closer to the heart of psychology than *learning*. Psychologists study infants' learning, and the learning of visual perceptions, of a drug's expected effect, and of gender roles. They also consider how learning shapes our thought and language, our motivations and emotions, our personalities and attitudes. In other modules we see how the brain stores and retrieves learning. Here, in Modules 21 through 23, we examine classical conditioning, operant conditioning, the effects of biology and cognition on learning, and learning by observation.

MODULE 21   Basic Learning Concepts and Classical Conditioning

How Do We Learn?

21-1 What is *learning*, and what are some basic forms of learning?

Psychologists define **learning** as the process of acquiring new and relatively enduring information or behaviors. By learning, we humans are able to adapt to our environments. We learn to expect and prepare for significant events such as food or pain (*classical conditioning*). We typically learn to repeat acts that bring rewards and avoid acts that bring unwanted results (*operant conditioning*). We learn new behaviors by observing events and watching others, and through language, we learn things we have neither experienced nor observed (*cognitive learning*). But *how* do we learn?

More than 200 years ago, philosophers John Locke and David Hume echoed Aristotle's conclusion from 2000 years earlier: We learn by *association*. Our minds naturally connect events that occur in sequence. Suppose you see and smell freshly baked bread, eat some, and find it satisfying. The next time you see and smell fresh bread, you will expect that eating it will again be satisfying. So, too, with sounds. If you associate a sound with a frightening consequence, hearing the sound alone may trigger your fear. As one 4-year-old exclaimed after watching a TV character get mugged, "If I had heard that music, I wouldn't have gone around the corner!" (Wells, 1981).

Learned associations often operate subtly:

- Give people a red pen (associated with error marking) rather than a black pen and, when correcting essays, they will spot more errors and give lower grades (Rutchick et al., 2010).

- When voting, people are more likely to support taxes to aid education if their assigned voting place is in a school (Berger et al., 2008). In the conservative American South, voters are more likely to support a same-sex marriage ban when voting in a church (Rutchick, 2010).

- After handling dirty paper money, people (market vendors, students in laboratory games) become more selfish and exploitative; after handling fresh, clean money they become more unselfish and fair (Yang et al., 2013).

Learned associations also feed our habitual behaviors (Wood et al., 2014). As we repeat behaviors in a given context—sleeping in a certain posture in bed, walking certain routes on campus, eating popcorn in a movie theater—the behaviors become associated with the contexts. Our next experience of the context then evokes our habitual response. Especially in times when our willpower is depleted, such as when we're mentally fatigued, we tend to fall back on our habits (Neal et al., 2013). That's true of both good habits (eating fruit) or bad (overindulging in alcohol), all of which get embodied in brain circuits (Graybiel & Smith, 2014).

How long does it take to form such habits? To find out, one British research team asked 96 university students to choose some healthy behavior (such as running before dinner or eating fruit with lunch), to do it daily for 84 days, and to record whether the behavior felt automatic (something they did without thinking and would find it hard not to do). On average, behaviors became habitual after about 66 days (Lally et al., 2010). Is there something you'd like to make a routine part of your life? Just do it every day for two months, or a bit longer for exercise, and you likely will find yourself with a new habit.

Other animals also learn by association. Disturbed by a squirt of water, the sea slug *Aplysia* protectively withdraws its gill. If the squirts continue, as happens naturally in choppy water, the withdrawal response diminishes. But if the sea slug repeatedly

---

learning the process of acquiring through experience new information or behaviors.

associative learning learning that certain events occur together. The events may be two stimuli (as in classical conditioning) or a response and its consequences (as in operant conditioning).

stimulus any event or situation that evokes a response.

respondent behavior behavior that occurs as an automatic response to some stimulus.

operant behavior behavior that operates on the environment, producing consequences.

Two related events:

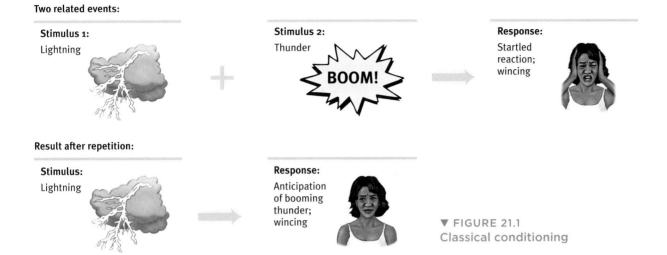

Stimulus 1:
Lightning

+

Stimulus 2:
Thunder

BOOM!

→

Response:
Startled
reaction;
wincing

Result after repetition:

Stimulus:
Lightning

→

Response:
Anticipation
of booming
thunder;
wincing

▼ FIGURE 21.1
Classical conditioning

receives an electric shock just after being squirted, its response to the squirt instead grows stronger. The animal has associated the squirt with the impending shock.

Complex animals can learn to associate their own behavior with its outcomes. An aquarium seal will repeat behaviors, such as slapping and barking, that prompt people to toss it a herring.

By linking two events that occur close together, both animals are exhibiting **associative learning.** The sea slug associates the squirt with an impending shock; the seal associates slapping and barking with a herring treat. Each animal has learned something important to its survival: anticipating the immediate future.

This process of learning associations is *conditioning.* It takes two main forms:

- In *classical conditioning,* we learn to associate two stimuli and thus to anticipate events. (A **stimulus** is any event or situation that evokes a response.) We learn that a flash of lightning signals an impending crack of thunder; when lightning flashes nearby, we start to brace ourselves (**FIGURE 21.1**). We associate stimuli that we do not control, and we respond automatically, which is called **respondent behavior.**

- In *operant conditioning,* we learn to associate a response (our behavior) and its consequence. Thus we (and other animals) learn to repeat acts followed by good results (**FIGURE 21.2**) and avoid acts followed by bad results. These associations produce **operant behaviors.**

To simplify, we will explore these two types of associative learning separately. Often, though, they occur together, as on one Japanese cattle ranch, where the clever rancher outfits his herd with electronic pagers which he calls from his cell phone. After a week of training, the animals learn to associate two stimuli—the beep on their pager and the arrival of food (classical conditioning). But they also learn to associate their hustling to the food trough with the pleasure of eating (operant conditioning), which simplifies the rancher's work.

Most of us would be unable to name the order of the songs on our favorite album or playlist. Yet, hearing the end of one piece cues (by association) an anticipation of the next. Likewise, when singing your national anthem, you associate the end of each line with the beginning of the next. (Pick a line out of the middle and notice how much harder it is to recall the *previous* line.)

(a) Response: Being polite   (b) Consequence: Getting a treat   (c) Behavior strengthened

▼ FIGURE 21.2
Operant conditioning

cognitive learning the acquisition of mental information, whether by observing events, by watching others, or through language.

classical conditioning a type of learning in which one learns to link two or more stimuli and anticipate events.

behaviorism the view that psychology (1) should be an objective science that (2) studies behavior without reference to mental processes. Most research psychologists today agree with (1) but not with (2).

neutral stimulus (NS) in classical conditioning, a stimulus that elicits no response before conditioning.

unconditioned response (UR) in classical conditioning, an unlearned, naturally occurring response (such as salivation) to an unconditioned stimulus (US) (such as food in the mouth).

unconditioned stimulus (US) in classical conditioning, a stimulus that unconditionally—naturally and automatically—triggers an unconditioned response (UR).

Conditioning is not the only form of learning. Through **cognitive learning,** we acquire mental information that guides our behavior. *Observational learning,* one form of cognitive learning, lets us learn from others' experiences. Chimpanzees, for example, sometimes learn behaviors merely by watching others perform them. If one animal sees another solve a puzzle and gain a food reward, the observer may perform the trick more quickly. So, too, in humans: We look and we learn.

Let's look more closely now at classical conditioning.

• Why are habits, such as having something sweet with that cup of coffee, so hard to break?

ANSWER: Habits form when we repeat behaviors in a given context and, as a result, learn associations—often without our awareness. For example, we may have eaten a sweet pastry with a cup of coffee often enough to associate the flavor of the coffee with the treat, so that the cup of coffee alone just doesn't seem right anymore!

Classical Conditioning

21-2 What was behaviorism's view of learning?

For many people, the name Ivan Pavlov (1849–1936) rings a bell. His early twentieth-century experiments—now psychology's most famous research—are classics, and the phenomenon he explored we justly call **classical conditioning.**

Pavlov's work laid the foundation for many of psychologist John B. Watson's ideas. In searching for laws underlying learning, Watson (1913) urged his colleagues to discard reference to inner thoughts, feelings, and motives. The science of psychology should instead study how organisms respond to stimuli in their environments, said Watson: "Its theoretical goal is the prediction and control of behavior. Introspection forms no essential part of its methods." Simply said, psychology should be an objective science based on observable behavior.

This view, which Watson called **behaviorism,** influenced North American psychology during the first half of the twentieth century. Pavlov and Watson shared both a disdain for "mentalistic" concepts (such as consciousness) and a belief that the basic laws of learning were the same for all animals—whether sea slugs or dogs or humans. Few researchers today propose that psychology should ignore mental processes, but most now agree that classical conditioning is a basic form of learning by which all organisms adapt to their environment.

Pavlov's Experiments

21-3 Who was Pavlov, and what are the basic components of classical conditioning?

Pavlov was driven by a lifelong passion for research. After setting aside his initial plan to follow his father into the Russian Orthodox priesthood, Pavlov received a medical degree at age 33 and spent the next two decades studying the digestive system. This work earned him Russia's first Nobel Prize in 1904. But his novel experiments on learning, which consumed the last three decades of his life, earned this feisty scientist his place in history.

Pavlov's new direction came when his creative mind seized on an incidental observation. Without fail, putting food in a dog's mouth caused the animal to salivate. Moreover, the dog began salivating not only at the taste of the food, but also at the mere sight of the food, or the food dish, or the person delivering the food, or even at the sound of that person's approaching footsteps. At first, Pavlov considered these "psychic secretions" an annoyance—until he realized they pointed to a simple but fundamental form of learning.

Pavlov and his assistants tried to imagine what the dog was thinking and feeling as it drooled in anticipation of the food. This only led them into fruitless debates. So, to explore the phenomenon more objectively, they experimented. To eliminate other possible influences, they isolated the dog in a small room, secured it in a harness, and attached a device to divert its saliva to a measuring instrument (**FIGURE 21.3**). From the

Ivan Pavlov "Experimental investigation . . . should lay a solid foundation for a future true science of psychology" (1927).

▼ FIGURE 21.3
Pavlov's device for recording salivation A tube in the dog's cheek collects saliva, which is measured in a cylinder outside the chamber.

next room, they presented food—first by sliding in a food bowl, later by blowing meat powder into the dog's mouth at a precise moment. They then paired various **neutral stimuli (NS)**—events the dog could see or hear but didn't associate with food—with food in the dog's mouth. If a sight or sound regularly signaled the arrival of food, would the dog learn the link? If so, would it begin salivating in anticipation of the food?

The answers proved to be *Yes* and *Yes*. Just before placing food in the dog's mouth to produce salivation, Pavlov sounded a tone. After several pairings of tone and food, the dog, now anticipating the meat powder, began salivating to the tone alone. In later experiments, a buzzer[1], a light, a touch on the leg, even the sight of a circle set off the drooling. (This procedure works with people, too. When hungry young Londoners viewed abstract figures before smelling peanut butter or vanilla, their brain soon responded in anticipation to the abstract images alone [Gottfried et al., 2003].)

A dog does not learn to salivate in response to food in its mouth. Rather, food in the mouth automatically, *unconditionally,* triggers a dog's salivary reflex (**FIGURE 21.4**). Thus, Pavlov called the drooling an **unconditioned response (UR)**. And he called the food an **unconditioned stimulus (US)**.

---

1. The "buzzer" (English translation) was perhaps a small electric bell (Tully, 2003).

▼ FIGURE 21.4
Pavlov's classic experiment Pavlov presented a neutral stimulus (a tone) just before an unconditioned stimulus (food in mouth). The neutral stimulus then became a conditioned stimulus, producing a conditioned response.

BEFORE CONDITIONING

US (food in mouth)
UR (salivation)

NS (tone)
No salivation

An unconditioned stimulus (US) produces an unconditioned response (UR).

A neutral stimulus (NS) produces no salivation response.

DURING CONDITIONING

NS (tone) + US (food in mouth)
UR (salivation)

The US is repeatedly presented just after the NS. The US continues to produce a UR.

AFTER CONDITIONING

CS (tone)
CR (salivation)

The previously neutral stimulus alone now produces a conditioned response (CR), thereby becoming a conditioned stimulus (CS).

PEANUTS

Peanuts reprinted with permission of United Features Syndicate

conditioned response (CR) in classical conditioning, a learned response to a previously neutral (but now conditioned) stimulus (CS).

conditioned stimulus (CS) in classical conditioning, an originally irrelevant stimulus that, after association with an unconditioned stimulus (US), comes to trigger a conditioned response (CR).

acquisition in classical conditioning, the initial stage, when one links a neutral stimulus and an unconditioned stimulus so that the neutral stimulus begins triggering the conditioned response. In operant conditioning, the strengthening of a reinforced response.

higher-order conditioning a procedure in which the conditioned stimulus in one conditioning experience is paired with a new neutral stimulus, creating a second (often weaker) conditioned stimulus. For example, an animal that has learned that a tone predicts food might then learn that a light predicts the tone and begin responding to the light alone. (Also called *second-order conditioning*.)

extinction the diminishing of a conditioned response; occurs in classical conditioning when an unconditioned stimulus (US) does not follow a conditioned stimulus (CS); occurs in operant conditioning when a response is no longer reinforced.

spontaneous recovery the reappearance, after a pause, of an extinguished conditioned response.

Salivation in response to the tone, however, is learned. It is *conditional* upon the dog's associating the tone with the food. Thus, we call this response the **conditioned response (CR)**. The stimulus that used to be neutral (in this case, a previously meaningless tone that now triggers salivation) is the **conditioned stimulus (CS)**. Distinguishing these two kinds of stimuli and responses is easy: Conditioned = learned; *un*conditioned = *un*learned.

If Pavlov's demonstration of associative learning was so simple, what did he do for the next three decades? What discoveries did his research factory publish in his 532 papers on salivary conditioning (Windholz, 1997)? He and his associates explored five major conditioning processes: *acquisition, extinction, spontaneous recovery, generalization,* and *discrimination.*

RETRIEVAL PRACTICE

- An experimenter sounds a tone just before delivering an air puff to your blinking eye. After several repetitions, you blink to the tone alone. What is the NS? The US? The UR? The CS? The CR?

ANSWER: NS = tone before conditioning; US = air puff; UR = blink to air puff; CS = tone after conditioning; CR = blink to tone.

Acquisition

21-4 In classical conditioning, what are the processes of acquisition, extinction, spontaneous recovery, generalization, and discrimination?

To understand the **acquisition,** or initial learning, of the stimulus-response relationship, Pavlov and his associates wondered: How much time should elapse between presenting the NS (the tone, the light, the touch) and the US (the food)? In most cases, not much—half a second usually works well.

What do you suppose would happen if the food (US) appeared before the tone (NS) rather than after? Would conditioning occur? Not likely. With but a few exceptions, conditioning doesn't happen when the NS follows the US. *Remember, classical conditioning is biologically adaptive because it helps humans and other animals prepare for good or bad events.* To Pavlov's dogs, the originally neutral tone became a CS after signaling an important biological event—the arrival of food (US). To deer in the forest, the snapping of a twig (CS) may signal a predator's approach (US).

More recent research on male Japanese quail shows how a CS can signal another important biological event (Domjan, 1992, 1994, 2005). Just before presenting a sexually approachable female quail, the researchers turned on a red light. Over time, as the red light continued to herald the female's arrival, the light caused the male quail to become excited. They developed a preference for their cage's red-light district, and when a female appeared, they mated with her more quickly and released more semen and sperm (Matthews et al., 2007). This capacity for classical conditioning gives the quail a reproductive edge.

Eric Isselée/Shutterstock

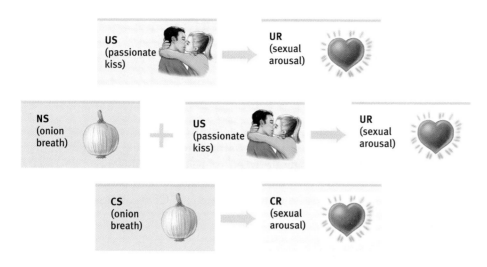

▼ FIGURE 21.5
An unexpected CS Psychologist Michael Tirrell (1990) recalled: "My first girlfriend loved onions, so I came to associate onion breath with kissing. Before long, onion breath sent tingles up and down my spine. Oh what a feeling!"

In humans, too, objects, smells, and sights associated with sexual pleasure—even a geometric figure in one experiment—can become conditioned stimuli for sexual arousal (Byrne, 1982; Hoffman, 2012). Onion breath does not usually produce sexual arousal. But when repeatedly paired with a passionate kiss, it can become a CS and do just that (**FIGURE 21.5**). The larger lesson: *Conditioning helps an animal survive and reproduce—by responding to cues that help it gain food, avoid dangers, locate mates, and produce offspring* (Hollis, 1997). Learning makes for yearning.

Through **higher-order conditioning**, a new NS can become a new CS without the presence of a US. All that's required is for it to become associated with a previously conditioned stimulus. If a tone regularly signals food and produces salivation, then a light that becomes associated with the tone may also begin to trigger salivation. Although this higher-order conditioning (also called *second-order conditioning*) tends to be weaker than first-order conditioning, it influences our everyday lives. Imagine that something makes us very afraid (perhaps a guard dog associated with a previous dog bite). If something else, such as the sound of a barking dog, brings to mind that guard dog, the bark alone may make us feel a little afraid.

Remember:
NS = Neutral Stimulus
US = Unconditioned Stimulus
UR = Unconditioned Response
CS = Conditioned Stimulus
CR = Conditioned Response

RETRIEVAL PRACTICE

• If the aroma of a baking cake sets your mouth to watering, what is the US? The CS? The CR?

ANSWER: The cake (and its taste) are the US. The associated aroma is the CS. Salivation to the aroma is the CR.

Extinction and Spontaneous Recovery What would happen, Pavlov wondered, if after conditioning, the CS occurred repeatedly without the US? If the tone sounded again and again, but no food appeared, would the tone still trigger salivation? The answer was mixed. The dogs salivated less and less, a reaction known as **extinction,** which is the diminished response that occurs when the CS (tone) no longer signals an impending US (food). But a different picture emerged when Pavlov allowed several hours to elapse before sounding the tone again. After the delay, the dogs would again begin salivating to the tone (**FIGURE 21.6**). This **spontaneous recovery**—the reappearance of a (weakened) CR after a pause— suggested to Pavlov that extinction was suppressing the CR rather than eliminating it.

▼ FIGURE 21.6
Idealized curve of acquisition, extinction, and spontaneous recovery The rising curve shows the CR rapidly growing stronger as the NS becomes a CS due to repeated pairing with the US (*acquisition*). The CR then weakens rapidly as the CS is presented alone (*extinction*). After a pause, the (weakened) CR reappears (*spontaneous recovery*).

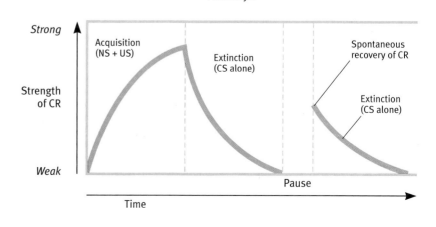

generalization the tendency, once a response has been conditioned, for stimuli similar to the conditioned stimulus to elicit similar responses.

Generalization Pavlov and his students noticed that a dog conditioned to the sound of one tone also responded somewhat to the sound of a new and different tone. Likewise, a dog conditioned to salivate when rubbed would also drool a bit when scratched (Windholz, 1989) or when touched on a different body part (**FIGURE 21.7**). This tendency to respond likewise to stimuli similar to the CS is called **generalization.**

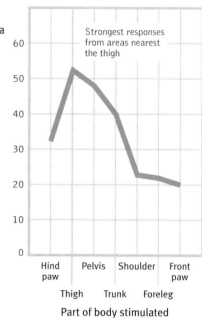

▼ FIGURE 21.7
Generalization Pavlov demonstrated generalization by attaching miniature vibrators to various parts of a dog's body. After conditioning salivation to stimulation of the thigh, he stimulated other areas. The closer a stimulated spot was to the dog's thigh, the stronger the conditioned response. (Data from Pavlov, 1927.)

Generalization can be adaptive, as when toddlers taught to fear moving cars also become afraid of moving trucks and motorcycles. And generalized fears can linger. One Argentine writer who underwent torture still recoils with fear when he sees black shoes—his first glimpse of his torturers as they approached his cell. Generalized anxiety reactions have been demonstrated in laboratory studies comparing abused with nonabused children (**FIGURE 21.8**). When an angry face appears on a computer screen, abused children's brain-wave responses are dramatically stronger and longer lasting (Pollak et al., 1998). And when a face that we've been conditioned to like (or dislike) is morphed into another face, we also have some tendency to like (or dislike) the vaguely similar morphed face (Gawronski & Quinn, 2013).

Stimuli similar to naturally disgusting objects will, by association, also evoke some disgust, as otherwise desirable fudge does when shaped to resemble dog feces (Rozin et al., 1986). In each of these human examples, people's emotional reactions to one stimulus have generalized to similar stimuli.

▼ FIGURE 21.8
Child abuse leaves tracks in the brain Abused children's sensitized brains react more strongly to angry faces (Pollak et al., 1998). This generalized anxiety response may help explain their greater risk of psychological disorder.

- What conditioning principle is influencing the snail's affections?

"I don't care if she's a tape dispenser. I love her."

ANSWER: Generalization

Discrimination Pavlov's dogs also learned to respond to the sound of a particular tone and *not* to other tones. This learned ability to *distinguish* between a conditioned stimulus (which predicts the US) and other irrelevant stimuli is called **discrimination.** Being able to recognize differences is adaptive. Slightly different stimuli can be followed by vastly different consequences. Confronted by a guard dog, your heart may race; confronted by a guide dog, it probably will not.

Pavlov's Legacy

21-5 Why does Pavlov's work remain so important?

What remains today of Pavlov's ideas? A great deal. Most psychologists now agree that classical conditioning is a basic form of learning. Judged with today's knowledge of the interplay of our biology, psychology, and social-cultural environment, Pavlov's ideas were incomplete. But if we see further than Pavlov did, it is because we stand on his shoulders.

Why does Pavlov's work remain so important? If he had merely taught us that old dogs can learn new tricks, his experiments would long ago have been forgotten. Why should we care that dogs can be conditioned to salivate at the sound of a tone? The importance lies, first, in the finding that *many other responses to many other stimuli can be classically conditioned in many other organisms*—in fact, in every species tested, from earthworms to fish to dogs to monkeys to people (Schwartz, 1984). Thus, classical conditioning is one way that virtually all organisms learn to adapt to their environment.

Second, *Pavlov showed us how a process such as learning can be studied objectively.* He was proud that his methods involved virtually no subjective judgments or guesses about what went on in a dog's mind. The salivary response is a behavior measurable in cubic centimeters of saliva. Pavlov's success therefore suggested a scientific model for how the young discipline of psychology might proceed—by isolating the basic building blocks of complex behaviors and studying them with objective laboratory procedures.

LaunchPad To review Pavlov's classic work and to play the role of experimenter in classical conditioning research, visit LaunchPad's *PsychSim 6: Classical Conditioning.* See also a 3-minute re-creation of Pavlov's lab in the *Video: Pavlov's Discovery of Classical Conditioning.*

- In slasher movies, sexually arousing images of women are sometimes paired with violence against women. Based on classical conditioning principles, what might be an effect of this pairing?

ANSWER: If viewing an attractive nude or seminude woman (a US) elicits sexual arousal (a UR), then pairing the US with a new stimulus (violence) could turn the violence into a conditioned stimulus (CS) that also becomes sexually arousing, a conditioned response (CR).

discrimination in classical conditioning, the learned ability to distinguish between a conditioned stimulus and stimuli that do not signal an unconditioned stimulus.

Applications of Classical Conditioning

21-6 What have been some applications of Pavlov's work to human health and well-being? How did Watson apply Pavlov's principles to learned fears?

In countless areas of psychology, including consciousness, motivation, emotion, health, psychological disorders, and therapy, Pavlov's principles are now being used to influence human health and well-being.

- Former drug users often feel a craving when they are again in the drug-using context—with people or in places they associate with previous highs. Thus, drug counselors advise addicts to steer clear of people and settings that may trigger these cravings (Siegel, 2005).

- Classical conditioning even works on the body's disease-fighting immune system. When a particular taste accompanies a drug that influences immune responses, the taste by itself may come to produce an immune response (Ader & Cohen, 1985).

Pavlov's work also provided a basis for Watson's (1913) idea that human emotions and behaviors, though biologically influenced, are mainly a bundle of conditioned responses. Working with an 11-month-old, Watson and Rosalie Rayner (1920; Harris, 1979) showed how specific fears might be conditioned. Like most infants, "Little Albert" feared loud noises but not white rats. Watson and Rayner presented a white rat and, as Little Albert reached to touch it, struck a hammer against a steel bar just behind his head. After seven repeats of seeing the rat and hearing the frightening noise, Albert burst into tears at the mere sight of the rat. Five days later, he had generalized this startled fear reaction to the sight of a rabbit, a dog, and a sealskin coat, but not to dissimilar objects, such as toys.

For years, people wondered what became of Little Albert. Sleuthing by Russell Powell and his colleagues (2014) found a well-matched child of one of the hospital's wet nurses. The child, William Albert Barger, went by Albert B.—precisely the name used by Watson and Rayner. This Albert lived to 2007. He was an easygoing person, though, perhaps coincidentally, he had an aversion to dogs. Albert died without ever knowing of his early life in a hospital residence or his role in psychology's history.

People also wondered what became of Watson. After losing his Johns Hopkins professorship over an affair with Raynor (his graduate student, whom he later married), he joined an advertising agency as the company's resident psychologist. There, he used his knowledge of associative learning to conceive many successful advertising campaigns, including one for Maxwell House that helped make the "coffee break" an American custom (Hunt, 1993).

The treatment of Little Albert would be unacceptable by today's ethical standards. Also, some psychologists had difficulty repeating Watson and Rayner's findings with other children. Nevertheless, Little Albert's learned fears led many psychologists to wonder whether each of us might be a walking repository of conditioned emotions. If so, might extinction procedures or even new conditioning help us change our unwanted responses to emotion-arousing stimuli?

One patient, who for 30 years had feared entering an elevator alone, did just that. Following his therapist's advice, he forced himself to enter 20 elevators a day. Within 10 days, his fear had nearly vanished (Ellis & Becker, 1982). With support from airline AirTran, comedian-writer Mark Malkoff likewise extinguished his fear of flying. He lived on an airplane for 30 days, taking 135 flights that had him in the air 14 hours a day (NPR, 2009). After a week and a half, his fears had faded and he began playing games with fellow passengers. (His favorite antic was

John B. Watson Watson (1924) admitted to "going beyond my facts" when offering his famous boast: "Give me a dozen healthy infants, well-formed, and my own specified world to bring them up in and I'll guarantee to take any one at random and train him to become any type of specialist I might select—doctor, lawyer, artist, merchant-chief, and, yes, even beggar-man and thief, regardless of his talents, penchants, tendencies, abilities, vocations, and race of his ancestors."

the "toilet paper experiment": He'd put one end of a roll in the toilet, unroll the rest down the aisle, and flush. The entire roll would be sucked down in three seconds.)

RETRIEVAL PRACTICE

- In Watson and Rayner's experiments, "Little Albert" learned to fear a white rat after repeatedly experiencing a loud noise as the rat was presented. In this experiment, what was the US? The UR? The NS? The CS? The CR?

ANSWERS: The US was the loud noise; the UR was the fear response to the noise; the NS was the rat before it was paired with the noise; the CS was the rat after pairing; the CR was fear of the rat.

MODULE 21 REVIEW Basic Learning Concepts and Classical Conditioning

LEARNING OBJECTIVES

RETRIEVAL PRACTICE Take a moment to answer each of these Learning Objective Questions (repeated here from within this module). Then turn to Appendix C, Complete Module Reviews, to check your answers. Research suggests that trying to answer these questions on your own will improve your long-term retention (McDaniel et al., 2009).

21-1 What is *learning,* and what are some basic forms of learning?

21-2 What was behaviorism's view of learning?

21-3 Who was Pavlov, and what are the basic components of classical conditioning?

21-4 In classical conditioning, what are the processes of acquisition, extinction, spontaneous recovery, generalization, and discrimination?

21-5 Why does Pavlov's work remain so important?

21-6 What have been some applications of Pavlov's work to human health and well-being? How did Watson apply these principles to learned fears?

TERMS AND CONCEPTS TO REMEMBER

RETRIEVAL PRACTICE Test yourself on these terms by trying to write down the definition before flipping back to the page number referenced to check your answer.

learning, p. 280

associative learning, p. 281

stimulus, p. 281

respondent behavior, p. 281

operant behavior, p. 281

cognitive learning, p. 282

classical conditioning, p. 282

behaviorism, p. 282

neutral stimulus (NS), p. 283

unconditioned response (UR), p. 283

unconditioned stimulus (US), p. 283

conditioned response (CR), p. 284

conditioned stimulus (CS), p. 284

acquisition, p. 284

higher-order conditioning, p. 285

extinction, p. 285

spontaneous recovery, p. 285

generalization, p. 286

discrimination, p. 287

Use 🔁 LearningCurve to create your personalized study plan, which will direct you to the resources that will help you most in 🔁 LaunchPad.

learning the process of acquiring through experience new information or behaviors.

associative learning learning that certain events occur together. The events may be two stimuli (as in classical conditioning) or a response and its consequence (as in operant conditioning).

stimulus any event or situation that evokes a response.

respondent behavior behavior that occurs as an automatic response to some stimulus.

operant conditioning a type of learning in which behavior is strengthened if followed by a reinforcer or diminished if followed by a punisher.

operant behavior behavior that operates on the environment, producing consequences.

law of effect Thorndike's principle that behaviors followed by favorable consequences become more likely, and that behaviors followed by unfavorable consequences become less likely.

operant chamber in operant conditioning research, a chamber (also known as a *Skinner box*) containing a bar or key that an animal can manipulate to obtain a food or water reinforcer; attached devices record the animal's rate of bar pressing or key pecking.

reinforcement in operant conditioning, any event that *strengthens* the behavior it follows.

shaping an operant conditioning procedure in which reinforcers guide behavior toward closer and closer approximations of the desired behavior.

▼ **FIGURE 22.1**

Cat in a puzzle box Thorndike used a fish reward to entice cats to find their way out of a puzzle box (left) through a series of maneuvers. The cats' performance tended to improve with successive trials (right), illustrating Thorndike's *law of effect*. (Adapted from Thorndike, 1898.)

MODULE 22 Operant Conditioning

22-1 What is operant conditioning?

It's one thing to classically condition a dog to salivate at the sound of a tone, or a child to fear moving cars. To teach an elephant to **learn** to walk on its hind legs or a child to say *please*, we turn to operant conditioning.

Classical conditioning and operant conditioning are both forms of **associative learning,** yet their differences are straightforward:

- *Classical conditioning* forms associations between **stimuli** (a *conditioned stimulus*, or CS, and the *unconditioned stimulus*, or US, it signals). It also involves **respondent behavior**—actions that are automatic responses to a stimulus (such as salivating in response to meat powder and later in response to a tone).

- In **operant conditioning,** organisms associate their own actions with consequences. Actions followed by reinforcers increase; those followed by punishments often decrease. Behavior that *operates* on the environment to produce rewarding or punishing stimuli is called **operant behavior.**

RETRIEVAL PRACTICE

- With _____ conditioning, we learn associations between events we do not control. With _____ conditioning, we learn associations between our behavior and resulting events.

ANSWERS: classical; operant

Skinner's Experiments

22-2 Who was Skinner, and how is operant behavior reinforced and shaped?

B. F. Skinner (1904–1990) was a college English major and aspiring writer who, seeking a new direction, entered psychology graduate school. He went on to become modern behaviorism's most influential and controversial figure. Skinner's work elaborated on what psychologist Edward L. Thorndike (1874–1949) called the **law of effect:** Rewarded behavior is likely to recur (**FIGURE 22.1**), and punished behavior is less likely to recur. Using Thorndike's law of effect as a starting point, Skinner developed a behavioral technology that revealed principles of *behavior control*. By shaping pigeons' natural walking and pecking behaviors, for example, Skinner was able to teach them such unpigeon-like behaviors as walking in a figure 8, playing Ping-Pong, and keeping a missile on course by pecking at a screen target.

For his pioneering studies, Skinner designed an **operant chamber,** popularly known as a *Skinner box* (**FIGURE 22.2**). The box has a bar (a lever) that an animal presses—or a

Time required to escape (seconds)

Successive trials in the puzzle box

key (a disc) the animal pecks—to release a reward of food or water. It also has a device that records these responses. This design creates a stage on which rats and other animals act out Skinner's concept of **reinforcement:** any event that strengthens (increases the frequency of) a preceding response. What is reinforcing depends on the animal and the conditions. For people, it may be praise, attention, or a paycheck. For hungry and thirsty rats, food and water work well. Skinner's experiments have done far more than teach us how to pull habits out of a rat. They have explored the precise conditions that foster efficient and enduring learning.

▼ FIGURE 22.2
A Skinner box Inside the box, the rat presses a bar for a food reward. Outside, a measuring device (not shown here) records the animal's accumulated responses.

Shaping Behavior

Imagine that you wanted to condition a hungry rat to press a bar. Like Skinner, you could tease out this action with **shaping,** gradually guiding the rat's actions toward the desired behavior. First, you would watch how the animal naturally behaves, so that you could build on its existing behaviors. You might give the rat a bit of food each time it approaches the bar. Once the rat is approaching regularly, you would give the food only when it moves close to the bar, then closer still. Finally, you would require it to touch the bar to get food. With this method of *successive approximations,* you reward responses that are ever closer to the final desired behavior, and you ignore all other responses. By making rewards contingent on desired behaviors, researchers and animal trainers gradually shape complex behaviors.

Shaping can also help us understand what nonverbal organisms perceive. Can a dog distinguish red and green? Can a baby hear the difference between lower- and higher-pitched tones? If we can shape them to respond to one stimulus and not to another, then we know they can perceive the difference. Such experiments have even shown that some animals can form concepts. When experimenters reinforced pigeons for pecking after seeing a human face, but not after seeing other images, the pigeon's behavior showed that it could recognize human faces (Herrnstein & Loveland, 1964). In this experiment, the human face was a *discriminative stimulus.* Like a green traffic light, discriminative stimuli signal that a response will be reinforced. After being trained to discriminate among classes of events or objects— flowers, people, cars, chairs—pigeons can usually identify the category in which a new pictured object belongs (Bhatt et al., 1988; Wasserman, 1993). They have even been trained to discriminate between the music of Bach and Stravinsky (Porter & Neuringer, 1984).

Skinner noted that we continually reinforce and shape others' everyday behaviors, though we may not mean to do so. Billy's whining annoys his parents, for example, but consider how they typically respond:

Reinforcers vary with circumstances What is reinforcing (a heat lamp) to one animal (a cold meerkat) may not be to another (an overheated child). What is reinforcing in one situation (a cold snap at the Taronga Zoo in Sydney) may not be in another (a sweltering summer day).

> *Billy:* Could you tie my shoes?
>
> *Father:* (Continues reading paper.)
>
> *Billy:* Dad, I need my shoes tied.
>
> *Father:* Uh, yeah, just a minute.
>
> *Billy:* DAAAAD! TIE MY SHOES!
>
> *Father:* How many times have I told you not to whine? Now, which shoe do we do first?

Billy's whining is reinforced, because he gets something desirable—his dad's attention. Dad's response is reinforced because it gets rid of something aversive—Billy's whining.

Shaping a dog to play the piano Using a method of successive approximations, with a food reward for each small step—hopping up on the piano bench, putting her paws on the keys, actually making sounds—this dog was taught to "play" the piano, and now does so frequently!

Or consider a teacher who pastes gold stars on a wall chart beside the names of children scoring 100 percent on spelling tests. As everyone can then see, some children consistently do perfect work. The others, who may have worked harder than the academic all-stars, get no rewards. The teacher would be better advised to apply the principles of operant conditioning—to reinforce all spellers for gradual improvements (successive approximations toward perfect spelling of words they find challenging).

Types of Reinforcers

22-3 How do positive and negative reinforcement differ, and what are the basic types of reinforcers?

Until now, we've mainly been discussing **positive reinforcement,** which strengthens responding by *presenting* a typically pleasurable stimulus after a response. But, as we saw in the whining Billy story, there are *two* basic kinds of reinforcement (**TABLE 22.1**). **Negative reinforcement** strengthens a response by *reducing or removing* something negative. Billy's whining was *positively* reinforced, because Billy got something desirable—his father's attention. His dad's response to the whining (tying Billy's shoes) was *negatively* reinforced, because it ended an aversive event—Billy's whining. Similarly, taking aspirin may relieve your headache, and hitting snooze will silence your annoying alarm. These welcome results provide negative reinforcement and increase the odds that you will repeat these behaviors. For drug addicts, the negative reinforcement of ending withdrawal pangs can be a compelling reason to resume using (Baker et al., 2004). Note that *negative reinforcement is not punishment.* (Some friendly advice: Repeat the italicized words in your mind.) Rather, negative reinforcement—psychology's most misunderstood concept—*removes* a punishing (aversive) event. Think of negative reinforcement as something that provides relief—from that whining child, bad headache, or annoying alarm.

▼ **TABLE 22.1**
Ways to Increase Behavior

Operant Conditioning Term	Description	Examples
Positive reinforcement	Add a desirable stimulus	Pet a dog that comes when you call it; pay the person who paints your house.
Negative reinforcement	Remove an aversive stimulus	Take painkillers to end pain; fasten seatbelt to end loud beeping.

RETRIEVAL PRACTICE

• How is operant conditioning at work in this cartoon?

ANSWER: The baby negatively reinforces her parents when she stops crying once they grant her wish. Her parents positively reinforce her cries by letting her sleep with them.

Sometimes negative and positive reinforcement coincide. Imagine a worried student who, after goofing off and getting a bad exam grade, studies harder for the next exam. This increased effort may be *negatively* reinforced by reduced anxiety, and *positively* reinforced by a better grade. We reap the rewards of escaping the aversive stimulus, which increases the chances that we will repeat our behavior. The point to remember: Whether it works by reducing something aversive, or by providing something desirable, *reinforcement is any consequence that strengthens behavior.*

Primary and Conditioned Reinforcers Getting food when hungry or having a painful headache go away is innately satisfying. These **primary reinforcers** are unlearned. **Conditioned reinforcers,** also called *secondary reinforcers*, get their power

positive reinforcement increasing behaviors by presenting positive reinforcers. A positive reinforcer is any stimulus that, when *presented* after a response, strengthens the response.

negative reinforcement increasing behaviors by stopping or reducing negative stimuli. A negative reinforcer is any stimulus that, when *removed* after a response, strengthens the response. (*Note:* Negative reinforcement is not punishment.)

primary reinforcer an innately reinforcing stimulus, such as one that satisfies a biological need.

conditioned reinforcer a stimulus that gains its reinforcing power through its association with a primary reinforcer; also known as a *secondary reinforcer.*

through learned association with primary reinforcers. If a rat in a Skinner box learns that a light reliably signals a food delivery, the rat will work to turn on the light (see Figure 22.2). The light has become a conditioned reinforcer. Our lives are filled with conditioned reinforcers—money, good grades, a pleasant tone of voice—each of which has been linked with more basic rewards. If money is a conditioned reinforcer—if people's desire for money is derived from their desire for food—then hunger should also make people more money hungry, reasoned one European research team (Briers et al., 2006). Indeed, in their experiments, people were less likely to donate to charity when food deprived, and less likely to share money with fellow participants when in a room with hunger-arousing aromas.

Immediate and Delayed Reinforcers Let's return to the imaginary shaping experiment in which you were conditioning a rat to press a bar. Before performing this "wanted" behavior, the hungry rat will engage in a sequence of "unwanted" behaviors—scratching, sniffing, and moving around. If you present food immediately after any one of these behaviors, the rat will likely repeat that rewarded behavior. But what if the rat presses the bar while you are distracted, and you delay giving the reinforcer? If the delay lasts longer than about 30 seconds, the rat will not learn to press the bar. It will have moved on to other incidental behaviors, such as scratching, sniffing, and moving, and one of these behaviors will instead get reinforced.

Unlike rats, humans do respond to delayed reinforcers: the paycheck at the end of the week, the good grade at the end of the semester, the trophy at the end of the season. Indeed, to function effectively we must learn to delay gratification. In laboratory testing, some 4-year-olds show this ability. In choosing a candy, they prefer having a big one tomorrow to munching on a small one right now. Learning to control our impulses in order to achieve more valued rewards is a big step toward maturity (Logue, 1998a,b). No wonder children who delay gratification have tended to become socially competent and high-achieving adults (Mischel et al., 1989).

To our detriment, small but immediate consequences (the enjoyment of watching late-night TV, for example) are sometimes more alluring than big but delayed consequences (feeling alert tomorrow). For many teens, the immediate gratification of risky, unprotected sex in passionate moments prevails over the delayed gratifications of safe sex or saved sex. And for many people, the immediate rewards of today's gas-guzzling vehicles, air travel, and air conditioning prevail over the bigger future consequences of global climate change, rising seas, and extreme weather.

"Oh, not bad. The light comes on, I press the bar, they write me a check. How about you?"

Reinforcement Schedules

22-4 How do different reinforcement schedules affect behavior?

In most of our examples, the desired response has been reinforced every time it occurs. But **reinforcement schedules** vary. With **continuous reinforcement,** learning occurs rapidly, which makes this the best choice for mastering a behavior. But extinction also occurs rapidly. When reinforcement stops—when we stop delivering food after the rat presses the bar—the behavior soon stops. If a normally dependable candy machine fails to deliver a chocolate bar twice in a row, we stop putting money into it (although a week later we may exhibit spontaneous recovery by trying again).

Real life rarely provides continuous reinforcement. Salespeople do not make a sale with every pitch. But they persist because their efforts are occasionally rewarded. This persistence is typical with **partial (intermittent) reinforcement schedules,** in which responses are sometimes reinforced, sometimes not. Learning is slower to appear, but *resistance to extinction* is greater than with continuous reinforcement. Imagine a pigeon that has learned to peck a key to obtain food. If you gradually phase out the food delivery until it occurs only rarely, in no predictable pattern, the pigeon may peck 150,000 times without a reward (Skinner, 1953). Slot machines reward gamblers in much the

reinforcement schedule a pattern that defines how often a desired response will be reinforced.

continuous reinforcement schedule reinforcing the desired response every time it occurs.

partial (intermittent) reinforcement schedule reinforcing a response only part of the time; results in slower acquisition of a response but much greater resistance to extinction than does continuous reinforcement.

same way—occasionally and unpredictably. And like pigeons, slot players keep trying, time and time again. With intermittent reinforcement, hope springs eternal.

Lesson for parents: Partial reinforcement also works with children. *Occasionally* giving in to children's tantrums for the sake of peace and quiet intermittently reinforces the tantrums. This is the very best procedure for making a behavior persist.

Skinner (1961) and his collaborators compared four schedules of partial reinforcement. Some are rigidly fixed, some unpredictably variable.

Fixed-ratio schedules reinforce behavior after a set number of responses. Coffee shops may reward us with a free drink after every 10 purchased. Once conditioned, rats may be reinforced on a fixed ratio of, say, one food pellet for every 30 responses. Once conditioned, animals will pause only briefly after a reinforcer before returning to a high rate of responding (**FIGURE 22.3**).

Variable-ratio schedules provide reinforcers after a seemingly unpredictable number of responses. This unpredictable reinforcement is what slot-machine players and fly fishers experience, and it's what makes gambling and fly fishing so hard to extinguish even when they don't produce the desired results. Because reinforcers increase as the number of responses increases, variable-ratio schedules produce high rates of responding.

Fixed-interval schedules reinforce the first response after a fixed time period. Animals on this type of schedule tend to respond more frequently as the anticipated time for reward draws near. People check more frequently for the mail as the delivery time approaches. A hungry child jiggles the Jell-O more often to see if it has set. Pigeons peck keys more rapidly as the time for reinforcement draws nearer. This produces a choppy stop-start pattern rather than a steady rate of response (see Figure 22.3).

Variable-interval schedules reinforce the first response after *varying* time intervals. Like the longed-for message that finally rewards persistence in rechecking e-mail or Facebook, variable-interval schedules tend to produce slow, steady responding. This makes sense, because there is no knowing when the waiting will be over (**TABLE 22.2**).

In general, response rates are higher when reinforcement is linked to the number of responses (a ratio schedule) rather than to time (an interval schedule). But responding is more consistent when reinforcement is unpredictable (a variable schedule) than when it is predictable (a fixed schedule). Animal behaviors differ, yet Skinner (1956) contended that the reinforcement principles of operant conditioning are universal. It matters

"The charm of fishing is that it is the pursuit of what is elusive but attainable, a perpetual series of occasions for hope."

Scottish author John Buchan (1875–1940)

Vitaly Titov & Maria Sidelnikova/Shutterstock

▼ FIGURE 22.3
Intermittent reinforcement schedules Skinner's (1961) laboratory pigeons produced these response patterns to each of four reinforcement schedules. (Reinforcers are indicated by diagonal marks.) For people, as for pigeons, reinforcement linked to number of responses (a *ratio schedule*) produces a higher response rate than reinforcement linked to amount of time elapsed (an *interval schedule*). But the predictability of the reward also matters. An unpredictable *(variable)* schedule produces more consistent responding than does a predictable *(fixed)* schedule.

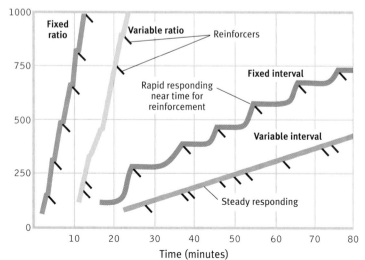

▼ TABLE 22.2
Schedules of Reinforcement

	Fixed	Variable
Ratio	*Every so many:* reinforcement after every *nth* behavior, such as buy 10 coffees, get 1 free, or pay workers per product unit produced	*After an unpredictable number:* reinforcement after a random number of behaviors, as when playing slot machines or fly fishing
Interval	*Every so often:* reinforcement for behavior after a fixed time, such as Tuesday discount prices	*Unpredictably often:* reinforcement for behavior after a random amount of time, as when checking for a Facebook response

little, he said, what response, what reinforcer, or what species you use. The effect of a given reinforcement schedule is pretty much the same: "Pigeon, rat, monkey, which is which? It doesn't matter. . . . Behavior shows astonishingly similar properties."

──────── **RETRIEVAL PRACTICE** ────────

- Telemarketers are reinforced by which schedule? People checking the oven to see if the cookies are done are on which schedule? Airline frequent-flyer programs that offer a free flight after every 25,000 miles of travel are using which reinforcement schedule?

ANSWERS: Telemarketers are reinforced on a variable-ratio schedule (after a varying number of calls). Cookie checkers are reinforced on a fixed-interval schedule. Frequent-flyer programs use a fixed-ratio schedule.

Punishment

22-5 How does punishment differ from negative reinforcement, and how does punishment affect behavior?

Reinforcement increases a behavior; **punishment** does the opposite. A *punisher* is any consequence that *decreases* the frequency of a preceding behavior (**TABLE 22.3**). Swift and sure punishers can powerfully restrain unwanted behavior. The rat that is shocked after touching a forbidden object and the child who is burned by touching a hot stove will learn not to repeat those behaviors. A dog that has learned to come running at the sound of an electric can opener will stop coming if its owner runs the machine to attract the dog and then banish it to the basement. Children's compliance often increases after a reprimand and a "time out" punishment (Owen et al., 2012).

Criminal behavior, much of it impulsive, is also influenced more by swift and sure punishers than by the threat of severe sentences (Darley & Alter, 2012). Thus, when Arizona introduced an exceptionally harsh sentence for first-time drunk drivers, the drunk-driving rate changed very little. But when Kansas City police started patrolling a high crime area to increase the sureness and swiftness of punishment, that city's crime rate dropped dramatically.

fixed-ratio schedule in operant conditioning, a reinforcement schedule that reinforces a response only after a specified number of responses.

variable-ratio schedule in operant conditioning, a reinforcement schedule that reinforces a response after an unpredictable number of responses.

fixed-interval schedule in operant conditioning, a reinforcement schedule that reinforces a response only after a specified time has elapsed.

variable-interval schedule in operant conditioning, a reinforcement schedule that reinforces a response at unpredictable time intervals.

punishment an event that tends to *decrease* the behavior that it follows.

▼ TABLE 22.3
Ways to Decrease Behavior

Type of Punisher	Description	Examples
Positive punishment	Administer something that's undesired.	Spray water on a barking dog; give a traffic ticket for speeding.
Negative punishment	End something that's desired.	Take away a misbehaving teen's driving privileges; revoke a library card for nonpayment of fines.

How should we interpret the punishment studies in relation to parenting practices? Many psychologists and supporters of nonviolent parenting note four major drawbacks of physical punishment (Gershoff, 2002; Marshall, 2002).

1. *Punished behavior is suppressed, not forgotten. This temporary state may (negatively) reinforce parents' punishing behavior.* The child swears, the parent swats, the parent hears no more swearing and feels the punishment successfully stopped the behavior. No wonder spanking is a hit with so many U.S. parents of 3- and 4-year-olds—more than 9 in 10 of whom acknowledged spanking their children (Kazdin & Benjet, 2003).

2. *Punishment teaches discrimination among situations.* In operant conditioning, *discrimination* occurs when an organism learns that certain responses, but not others, will be reinforced. Did the punishment effectively end the child's swearing? Or did the child simply learn that while it's not okay to swear around the house, it's okay to swear elsewhere?

3. *Punishment can teach fear.* In operant conditioning, *generalization* occurs when an organism's response to similar stimuli is also reinforced. A punished child may associate fear not only with the undesirable behavior but also with the person who delivered the punishment or where it occurred. Thus, children may learn to fear a punishing teacher and try to avoid school, or may become more anxious (Gershoff et al., 2010). For such reasons, most European countries and most U.S. states now ban hitting children in schools and child-care institutions (stophitting.com). Thirty-three countries, including those in Scandinavia, further outlaw hitting by parents, providing children the same legal protection given to spouses.

4. *Physical punishment may increase aggression by modeling aggression as a way to cope with problems.* Studies find that spanked children are at increased risk for aggression (MacKenzie et al., 2013). We know, for example, that many aggressive delinquents and abusive parents come from abusive families (Straus & Gelles, 1980; Straus et al., 1997).

Some researchers note a problem. Well, yes, they say, physically punished children may be more aggressive, for the same reason that people who have undergone psychotherapy are more likely to suffer depression—because they had preexisting problems that triggered the treatments (Ferguson, 2013; Larzelere, 2000, 2004). Which is the chicken and which is the egg? Correlations don't hand us an answer.

If one adjusts for preexisting antisocial behavior, then an occasional single swat or two to misbehaving 2- to 6-year-olds looks more effective (Baumrind et al., 2002; Larzelere & Kuhn, 2005). That is especially so if two other conditions are met:

1. The swat is used only as a backup when milder disciplinary tactics, such as a time-out (removing children from reinforcing surroundings) fail.

2. The swat is combined with a generous dose of reasoning and reinforcing.

Other researchers remain unconvinced. After controlling for prior misbehavior, they report that more frequent spankings of young children predict future aggressiveness (Grogan-Kaylor, 2004; Taylor et al., 2010).

Parents of delinquent youths are often unaware of how to achieve desirable behaviors without screaming, hitting, or threatening their children with punishment (Patterson et al., 1982). Training programs can help transform dire threats ("You clean up your room this minute or no dinner!") into positive incentives ("You're welcome at the dinner table after you get your room cleaned up"). Stop and think about it. Aren't many threats of punishment just as forceful, and perhaps more effective, when rephrased positively? Thus, "If you don't get your homework done, there'll be no car" would better be phrased as . . . .

In classrooms, too, teachers can give feedback on papers by saying, "No, but try this . . ." and "Yes, that's it!" Such responses reduce unwanted behavior while reinforcing more desirable alternatives. Remember: *Punishment tells you what not to do; reinforcement tells you what to do.* Thus, punishment trains a particular sort of morality—one focused on prohibition (what *not* to do) rather than positive obligations (Sheikh & Janoff-Bultman, 2013).

What punishment often teaches, said Skinner, is how to avoid it. Most psychologists now favor an emphasis on reinforcement: *Notice people doing something right and affirm them for it.*

RETRIEVAL PRACTICE

- Fill in the three blanks below with one of the following terms: positive reinforcement (PR), negative reinforcement (NR), positive punishment (PP), and negative punishment (NP). We have provided the first answer (PR) for you.

Type of Stimulus	Give It	Take It Away
Desired (for example, a teen's use of the car)	1. PR	2.
Undesired/aversive (for example, an insult)	3.	4.

ANSWERS: 1. PR (positive reinforcement); 2. NP (negative punishment); 3. PP (positive punishment); 4. NR (negative reinforcement)

Skinner's Legacy

22-6 Why did Skinner's ideas provoke controversy, and how might his operant conditioning principles be applied at school, in sports, at work, and at home?

B. F. Skinner stirred a hornet's nest with his outspoken beliefs. He repeatedly insisted that external influences, not internal thoughts and feelings, shape behavior. And he urged people to use operant principles to influence others' behavior at school, work, and home. Knowing that behavior is shaped by its results, he argued that we should use rewards to evoke more desirable behavior.

Skinner's critics objected, saying that he dehumanized people by neglecting their personal freedom and by seeking to control their actions. Skinner's reply: External consequences already haphazardly control people's behavior. Why not administer those consequences toward human betterment? Wouldn't reinforcers be more humane than the punishments used in homes, schools, and prisons? And if it is humbling to think that our history has shaped us, doesn't this very idea also give us hope that we can shape our future? In such ways, and through his ideas for positively reinforcing character strengths, Skinner actually anticipated some of today's positive psychology (Adams, 2012).

🎧 **LaunchPad** To review and experience simulations of operant conditioning, visit LaunchPad's *PsychSim 6: Operant Conditioning* and also *Shaping.*

Applications of Operant Conditioning

Psychologists are applying operant conditioning principles to help people with a variety of challenges, from moderating high blood pressure to gaining social skills. Reinforcement technologies are also at work in schools, sports, workplaces, and homes, and these principles can support our self-improvement as well (Flora, 2004).

At School A generation ago, Skinner envisioned a day when teaching machines and textbooks would shape learning in small steps, immediately reinforcing correct responses. He believed such machines and texts would revolutionize education and free teachers to focus on each student's special needs.

B. F. Skinner "I am sometimes asked, 'Do you think of yourself as you think of the organisms you study?' The answer is yes. So far as I know, my behavior at any given moment has been nothing more than the product of my genetic endowment, my personal history, and the current setting" (1983).

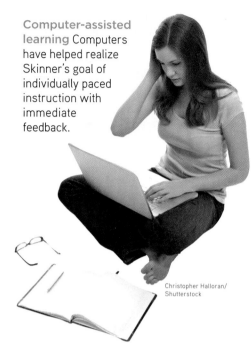

Computer-assisted learning Computers have helped realize Skinner's goal of individually paced instruction with immediate feedback.

Christopher Halloran/ Shutterstock

Stand in Skinner's shoes for a moment and imagine two math teachers, each with a class of students ranging from whiz kids to slow learners. Teacher A gives the whole class the same lesson, knowing that some kids will breeze through the math concepts, while others will be frustrated and fail. Teacher B, faced with a similar class, paces the material according to each student's rate of learning and provides prompt feedback, with positive reinforcement, to both the slow and the fast learners. Thinking as Skinner did, how might you achieve the individualized instruction of Teacher B?

Computers were Skinner's final hope. "Good instruction demands two things," he said. "Students must be told immediately whether what they do is right or wrong and, when right, they must be directed to the step to be taken next." Thus, the computer could be Teacher B—pacing math drills to the student's rate of learning, quizzing the student to find gaps in understanding, giving immediate feedback, and keeping flawless records. To the end of his life, Skinner (1986, 1988, 1989) believed his ideal was achievable. The predicted education revolution has not occurred, partly because the early teaching machines often trained rote learning, not deep processing. Today's interactive student software, web-based learning, and online testing bring us closer to achieving Skinner's ideal. As an alternative to one-size-fits-all teaching, *adaptive learning* software assesses each student's thinking and learning, and continually adjusts what it presents and tests (Fletcher, 2013).

In Sports The key to shaping behavior in athletic performance, as elsewhere, is first reinforcing small successes and then gradually increasing the challenge. Golf students can learn putting by starting with very short putts, and then, as they build mastery, stepping back farther and farther. Novice batters can begin with half swings at an oversized ball pitched from 10 feet away, giving them the immediate pleasure of smacking the ball. As the hitters' confidence builds with their success and they achieve mastery at each level, the pitcher gradually moves back—to 15, then 22, 30, and 40.5 feet—and eventually introduces a standard baseball. Compared with children taught by conventional methods, those trained by this behavioral method have shown faster skill improvement (Simek & O'Brien, 1981, 1988).

OH! THAT WAS A WONDERFUL REPORT, BOB. A WONDERFUL, WONDERFUL REPORT.

THE VICE-PRESIDENT IN CHARGE OF SINCERITY

At Work Knowing that reinforcers influence productivity, many organizations have invited employees to share the risks and rewards of company ownership. Others focus on reinforcing a job well done. Rewards are most likely to increase productivity if the desired performance has been well defined and is achievable. The message for managers? *Reward specific, achievable behaviors, not vaguely defined "merit."*

Operant conditioning also reminds us that reinforcement should be *immediate*. IBM legend Thomas Watson understood this. When he observed an achievement, he wrote the employee a check on the spot (Peters & Waterman, 1982). But rewards need not be material, or lavish. An effective manager may simply walk the floor and sincerely affirm people for good work, or write notes of appreciation for a completed project. As Skinner said, "How much richer would the whole world be if the reinforcers in daily life were more effectively contingent on productive work?"

At Home As we have seen, parents can learn from operant conditioning practices. Parent-training researchers remind us that by saying, "Get ready for bed" and then caving in to protests or defiance, parents reinforce such whining and arguing (Wierson & Forehand, 1994). Exasperated, they may then yell or gesture menacingly. When the child, now frightened, obeys, that reinforces the parents' angry behavior. Over time, a destructive parent-child relationship develops.

To disrupt this cycle, parents should remember that basic rule of shaping: *Notice people doing something right and affirm them for it.* Give children attention and other reinforcers when they are behaving *well*. Target a specific behavior, reward it, and watch it increase. When children misbehave or are defiant, don't yell at them or hit them. Simply explain the misbehavior and give them a time-out.

Finally, we can use operant conditioning in our own lives. To reinforce your own desired behaviors (perhaps to improve your study habits) and extinguish the undesired ones (to stop smoking, for example), psychologists suggest taking these steps:

1. *State a realistic goal in measurable terms.* You might, for example, aim to boost your study time by an hour a day.

2. *Decide how, when, and where you will work toward your goal.* Take time to plan. Those who specify how they will implement goals more often fulfill them (Gollwitzer & Oettingen, 2012).

3. *Monitor how often you engage in your desired behavior.* You might log your current study time, noting under what conditions you do and don't study. (When I [DM] began writing textbooks, I logged how I spent my time each day and was amazed to discover how much time I was wasting. I [ND] experienced a similar rude awakening when I started tracking my daily writing hours.)

4. *Reinforce the desired behavior.* To increase your study time, give yourself a reward (a snack or some activity you enjoy) only after you finish your extra hour of study. Agree with your friends that you will join them for weekend activities only if you have met your realistic weekly studying goal.

5. *Reduce the rewards gradually.* As your new behaviors become more habitual, give yourself a mental pat on the back instead of a cookie.

"I wrote another five hundred words. Can I have another cookie?"

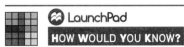

HOW WOULD YOU KNOW?

Conditioning principles may also be applied in clinical settings. Explore some of these applications in LaunchPad's *How Would You Know If People Can Learn to Reduce Anxiety?*

Contrasting Classical and Operant Conditioning

22-7 How does operant conditioning differ from classical conditioning?

Both classical and operant conditioning are forms of *associative learning*. Both involve *acquisition, extinction, spontaneous recovery, generalization,* and *discrimination*. But these two forms of learning also differ. Through classical (Pavlovian) conditioning, we associate different stimuli we do not control, and we respond automatically (*respondent behaviors*) (**TABLE 22.4**). Through operant conditioning, we associate our own behaviors—which act on our environment to produce rewarding or punishing stimuli (*operant behaviors*)—with their consequences.

"O! This learning, what a thing it is."

William Shakespeare,
The Taming of the Shrew, 1597

▼ TABLE 22.4
Comparison of Classical and Operant Conditioning

	Classical Conditioning	Operant Conditioning
Basic idea	Organism associates events.	Organism associates behavior and resulting events.
Response	Involuntary, automatic.	Voluntary, operates on environment.
Acquisition	Associating events; NS is paired with US and becomes CS.	Associating response with a consequence (reinforcer or punisher).
Extinction	CR decreases when CS is repeatedly presented alone.	Responding decreases when reinforcement stops.
Spontaneous recovery	The reappearance, after a rest period, of an extinguished CR.	The reappearance, after a rest period, of an extinguished response.
Generalization	The tendency to respond to stimuli similar to the CS.	Organism's response to similar stimuli is also reinforced.
Discrimination	The learned ability to distinguish between a CS and other stimuli that do not signal a US.	Organism learns that certain responses, but not others, will be reinforced.

• Salivating in response to a tone paired with food is a(n) _____ behavior; pressing a bar to obtain food is a(n) _____ behavior.

ANSWERS: respondent; operant

MODULE 22 REVIEW Operant Conditioning

LEARNING OBJECTIVES

RETRIEVAL PRACTICE Take a moment to answer each of these Learning Objective Questions (repeated here from within this module). Then turn to Appendix C, Complete Module Reviews, to check your answers. Research suggests that trying to answer these questions on your own will improve your long-term retention (McDaniel et al., 2009).

22-1 What is operant conditioning?

22-2 Who was Skinner, and how is operant behavior reinforced and shaped?

22-3 How do positive and negative reinforcement differ, and what are the basic types of reinforcers?

22-4 How do different reinforcement schedules affect behavior?

22-5 How does punishment differ from negative reinforcement, and how does punishment affect behavior?

22-6 Why did Skinner's ideas provoke controversy, and how might his operant conditioning principles be applied at school, in sports, at work, and at home?

22-7 How does operant conditioning differ from classical conditioning?

TERMS AND CONCEPTS TO REMEMBER

RETRIEVAL PRACTICE Test yourself on these terms by trying to write down the definition before flipping back to the page number referenced to check your answer.

learning, p. 290
associative learning, p. 290
stimulus, p. 290
respondent behavior, p. 290
operant conditioning, p. 290
operant behavior, p. 290
law of effect, p. 290
operant chamber, p. 290
reinforcement, p. 291
shaping, p. 291
positive reinforcement, p. 292
negative reinforcement, p. 292
primary reinforcer, p. 292
conditioned reinforcer, p. 292
reinforcement schedule, p. 293
continuous reinforcement schedule, p. 293
partial (intermittent) reinforcement schedule, p. 293
fixed-ratio schedule, p. 294
variable-ratio schedule, p. 294
fixed-interval schedule, p. 294
variable-interval schedule, p. 294
punishment, p. 295

Use 🅜 LearningCurve to create your personalized study plan, which will direct you to the resources that will help you most in 🅜 LaunchPad.

MODULE 23 Biology, Cognition, and Learning

FROM DROOLING DOGS, RUNNING RATS, and pecking pigeons, we have learned much about the basic processes of **learning** through *classical* and *operant conditioning*. But conditioning principles don't tell us the whole story. Today's learning theorists recognize that learning is the product of the interaction of biological, psychological, and social-cultural influences (**FIGURE 23.1**).

Biological Constraints on Conditioning

23-1 How do biological constraints affect classical and operant conditioning?

Ever since Charles Darwin, scientists have assumed that all animals share a common evolutionary history and thus share commonalities in their makeup and functioning. Ivan Pavlov and John D. Watson, for example, believed the basic laws of learning were essentially similar in all animals. So it should make little difference whether one studied pigeons or people. Moreover, it seemed that any natural response could be conditioned to any *neutral stimulus*.

learning the process of acquiring through experience new information or behaviors.

Biological influences:
• genetic
  predispositions
• unconditioned
  responses
• adaptive responses

Psychological influences:
• previous experiences
• predictability of
  associations
• generalization
• discrimination

Learning

Social-cultural influences:
• culturally learned
  preferences
• motivation, affected by
  presence of others

▼ FIGURE 23.1
Biopsychosocial influences on learning Our learning results not only from environmental experiences, but also from cognitive and biological influences.

Limits on Classical Conditioning

In 1956, learning researcher Gregory Kimble proclaimed, "Just about any activity of which the organism is capable can be conditioned and . . . these responses can be conditioned to any stimulus that the organism can perceive" (p. 195). Twenty-five years later, he humbly acknowledged that "half a thousand" scientific reports had proven him wrong (Kimble, 1981). More than the early behaviorists realized, an animal's capacity for conditioning is constrained by its biology. Each species' predispositions prepare it to learn the associations that enhance its survival. Environments are not the whole story.

John Garcia was among those who challenged the prevailing idea that all associations can be learned equally well. While researching the effects of radiation on laboratory animals, Garcia and Robert Koelling (1966) noticed that rats began to avoid drinking water from the plastic bottles in radiation chambers. Could classical conditioning be the culprit? Might the rats have linked the plastic-tasting water (a *conditioned stimulus*, or CS) to the sickness (*unconditioned response*, or UR) triggered by the radiation (*unconditioned stimulus*, or US)?

To test their hunch, Garcia and Koelling exposed the rats to a particular taste, sight, or sound (CS) and later also to radiation or drugs (US) that led to nausea and vomiting (UR). Two startling findings emerged: First, even if sickened as late as several hours after tasting a particular novel flavor, the rats thereafter avoided that flavor. This appeared to violate the Pavlovian notion that for conditioning to occur, the US must immediately follow the CS.

Second, the sickened rats developed aversions to tastes but not to sights or sounds. This contradicted the behaviorists' idea that any perceivable stimulus could serve as a CS. But it made adaptive sense. For rats, the easiest way to identify tainted food is to taste it; if sickened after sampling a new food, they thereafter avoid it. This response, called *taste aversion*, makes it difficult to eradicate a population of "bait-shy" rats by poisoning.

Humans, too, seem biologically prepared to learn some associations rather than others. If you become violently ill four hours after eating contaminated mussels, you will probably develop an aversion to the taste of mussels but usually not to the sight of the associated

John Garcia As the laboring son of California farmworkers, Garcia attended school only in the off-season during his early childhood years. After entering junior college in his late twenties, and earning his Ph.D. in his late forties, he received the American Psychological Association's Distinguished Scientific Contribution Award "for his highly original, pioneering research in conditioning and learning." He was also elected to the National Academy of Sciences.

Taste aversion If you became violently ill after eating oysters, you would probably have a hard time eating them again. Their smell and taste would have become a CS for nausea. This learning occurs readily because our biology prepares us to learn taste aversions to toxic foods.

BSIP SA/Alamy

restaurant, its plates, the people you were with, or the music you heard there. (In contrast, birds, which hunt by sight, appear biologically primed to develop aversions to the *sight* of tainted food [Nicolaus et al., 1983].)

Garcia's early findings on taste aversion were met with an onslaught of criticism. As the German philosopher Arthur Schopenhauer (1788–1860) once said, important ideas are first ridiculed, then attacked, and finally taken for granted. Leading journals refused to publish Garcia's work: The findings are impossible, said some critics. But, as often happens in science, Garcia and Koelling's taste-aversion research is now basic textbook material.

It is also a good example of experiments that begin with the discomfort of some laboratory animals and end by enhancing the welfare of many others. In one conditioned taste-aversion study, coyotes and wolves were tempted into eating sheep carcasses laced with a sickening poison. Thereafter, they developed an aversion to sheep meat; two wolves later penned with a live sheep seemed actually to fear it (Gustavson et al., 1974, 1976). These studies not only saved the sheep from their predators, but also saved the sheep-shunning coyotes and wolves from angry ranchers and farmers who had wanted to destroy them. Similar applications have prevented baboons from raiding African gardens, raccoons from attacking chickens, ravens and crows from feeding on crane eggs. In all these cases, research helped preserve both the prey and their predators, all of whom occupy an important ecological niche (Dingfelder, 2010; Garcia & Gustavson, 1997).

Such research supports Darwin's principle that natural selection favors traits that aid survival. Our ancestors who readily learned taste aversions were unlikely to eat the same toxic food again and were more likely to survive and leave descendants. Nausea, like anxiety, pain, and other bad feelings, serves a good purpose. Like a low-oil warning on a car dashboard, each alerts the body to a threat (Neese, 1991).

In an example illustrating how a CS can signal an important biological event, Japanese quail were conditioned to get sexually excited by a red light that signaled a receptive female's arrival. Michael Domjan and his colleagues (2004) report that such conditioning is even speedier, stronger, and more durable when the CS is *ecologically relevant*— something similar to stimuli associated with sexual activity in the natural environment, such as the stuffed head of a female quail. In the real world, observes Domjan (2005), conditioned stimuli have a natural association with the unconditioned stimuli they predict.

The tendency to learn behaviors favored by natural selection may help explain why we humans seem naturally disposed to learn associations between the color red and sexuality. Female primates display red when nearing ovulation. In human females, enhanced bloodflow produces the red blush of flirtation and sexual excitation. Does the frequent pairing of red and sex—with Valentine's hearts, red-light districts, and red lipstick—naturally enhance men's attraction to women? Experiments (**FIGURE 23.2**) suggest that, without men's awareness, it does (Elliot & Niesta, 2008). In follow-up studies,

- men tipped waitresses in red more generously than waitresses in any other color, and on a dating website, men were most likely to contact a woman wearing red (Guéguen & Jacob, 2013, 2014).

> "All animals are on a voyage through time, navigating toward futures that promote their survival and away from futures that threaten it. Pleasure and pain are the stars by which they steer."
>
> Psychologists Daniel T. Gilbert and Timothy D. Wilson, "Prospection: Experiencing the Future," 2007

Animal taste aversion As an alternative to killing wolves and coyotes that preyed on sheep, some ranchers have sickened the animals with lamb laced with a drug.

▼ FIGURE 23.2

Romantic red In a series of experiments that controlled for other factors (such as the brightness of the image), men found women more attractive and sexually desirable when framed in red (Elliot & Niesta, 2008). The phenomenon has been found not only in North America and Europe, but also in the West African nation of Burkina Faso (Elliot et al., 2013).

- women became more likely to select a red rather than a green shirt to wear when expecting to converse with an attractive rather than an unattractive man (Elliot et al., 2013).
- when at peak fertility, women are more likely to wear red or pink (Beall & Tracy, 2013). The red effect enhances men's attraction only to younger, fertile (not menopausal) women (Schwarz & Singer, 2013).
- and it's not just men: Women tend to perceive men as more attractive when seen in photos on a red background or in red clothing (Elliot et al., 2010; Roberts et al., 2010).

A genetic predisposition to associate a CS with a US that follows predictably and immediately is adaptive. Causes often immediately precede effects, so we may associate an effect with the event that preceded it. As we saw in the taste-aversion findings, however, these predispositions can trick us. When chemotherapy triggers nausea and vomiting more than an hour following treatment, cancer patients may over time develop classically conditioned nausea (and sometimes anxiety) to the sights, sounds, and smells associated with the clinic (**FIGURE 23.3**) (Hall, 1997). Merely returning to the clinic's waiting room or seeing the nurses can provoke these conditioned feelings (Burish & Carey, 1986; Davey, 1992). Under normal circumstances, such revulsion to sickening stimuli would be adaptive.

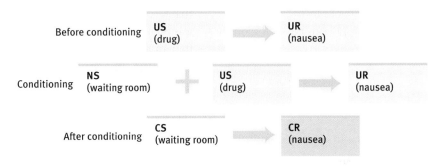

▼ FIGURE 23.3
Nausea conditioning in cancer patients

Limits on Operant Conditioning

As with classical conditioning, nature sets limits on each species' capacity for operant conditioning. Science fiction writer Robert Heinlein (1907–1988) said it well: "Never try to teach a pig to sing; it wastes your time and annoys the pig."

We most easily learn and retain behaviors that reflect our biological predispositions. Thus, using food as a reinforcer, you could easily condition a hamster to dig or to rear up, because these are among the animal's natural food-searching behaviors. But you won't be so successful if you use food as a reinforcer to shape face washing and other hamster behaviors that aren't normally associated with food or hunger (Shettleworth, 1973). Similarly, you could easily teach pigeons to flap their wings to avoid being shocked, and to peck to obtain food: Fleeing with their wings and eating with their beaks are natural pigeon behaviors. However, pigeons would have a hard time learning to peck to avoid a shock, or to flap their wings to obtain food (Foree & LoLordo, 1973). The principle: *Biological constraints predispose organisms to learn associations that are naturally adaptive.*

In their early days of training animals, psychologists Marian and Keller Breland presumed that operant principles would work on almost any response an animal could make. But along the way, they too learned about biological constraints. In one act, pigs trained to pick up large wooden "dollars" and deposit them in a piggy bank began to drift back to their natural ways. They dropped the coin, pushed it with their snouts as pigs are prone to do, picked it up again, and then repeated the sequence—delaying their food reinforcer. This *instinctive drift* occurred as the animals reverted to their biologically predisposed patterns.

"Once bitten, twice shy."

G. F. Northall, *Folk-Phrases*, 1894

Natural athletes Animals can most easily learn and retain behaviors that draw on their biological predispositions, such as horses' inborn ability to move around obstacles with speed and agility.

cognitive learning the acquisition of mental information, whether by observing events, by watching others, or through language.

For more information on animal behavior, see books by (we are not making this up) Robin Fox and Lionel Tiger.

"All brains are, in essence, anticipation machines."

Daniel C. Dennett,
Consciousness Explained, 1991

Cognition's Influence on Conditioning

23-2 How do cognitive processes affect classical and operant conditioning?

Cognitive Processes and Classical Conditioning

In their dismissal of "mentalistic" concepts such as consciousness, Pavlov and Watson underestimated the importance of not only biological constraints, but also the effects of cognitive processes (thoughts, perceptions, expectations). Through **cognitive learning** we acquire mental information that guides our behavior. The early behaviorists believed that rats' and dogs' learned behaviors could be reduced to mindless mechanisms, so there was no need to consider cognition. But Robert Rescorla and Allan Wagner (1972) showed that an animal can learn the *predictability* of an event. If a shock always is preceded by a tone, and then may also be preceded by a light that accompanies the tone, a rat will react with fear to the tone but not to the light. Although the light is always followed by the shock, it adds no new information; the tone is a better predictor. The more predictable the association, the stronger the conditioned response. It's as if the animal learns an *expectancy,* an awareness of how likely it is that the US will occur.

Associations can influence attitudes (Hofmann et al., 2010). When British children viewed novel cartoon characters alongside either ice cream (*Yum!*) or brussels sprouts (*Yuk!*), they came to like best the ice-cream-associated characters (Field, 2006). Other researchers have classically conditioned adults' attitudes, using little-known Pokémon characters (Olson & Fazio, 2001). The participants, playing the role of a security guard monitoring a video screen, viewed a stream of words, images, and Pokémon characters. Their task, they were told, was to respond to one target Pokémon character by pressing a button. Unnoticed by the participants, when two other Pokémon characters appeared on the screen, one was consistently associated with various positive words and images (such as *awesome* or a hot fudge sundae); the other appeared with negative words and images (such as *awful* or a cockroach). Later, they evaluated the extra Pokémon characters. Without any conscious memory of the pairings, the participants formed more gut-level liking for the characters associated with the positive stimuli.

Follow-up studies indicate that conditioned likes and dislikes are even stronger when people notice and are aware of the associations they have learned (Shanks, 2010). Cognition matters.

Such experiments help explain why classical conditioning treatments that ignore cognition often have limited success. For example, people receiving therapy for alcohol use disorder may be given alcohol spiked with a nauseating drug. Will they then associate alcohol with sickness? If classical conditioning were merely a matter of "stamping in" stimulus associations, we might hope so, and to some extent this does occur. However, one's awareness that the nausea is induced by the drug, not the alcohol, often weakens the association between drinking alcohol and feeling sick. So, even in classical conditioning, it is—especially with humans—not simply the CS-US association, but also the thought that counts.

Cognitive Processes and Operant Conditioning

B. F. Skinner acknowledged the biological underpinnings of behavior and the existence of private thought processes. Nevertheless, many psychologists criticized him for discounting cognition's importance.

A mere eight days before dying of leukemia in 1990, Skinner stood before the American Psychological Association convention. In this final address, he again resisted the growing belief that cognitive processes (thoughts, perceptions, expectations) have a necessary place in the science of psychology and even in our understanding of conditioning. He viewed "cognitive science" as a throwback to early twentieth-century

"Bathroom? Sure, it's just down the hall to the left, jog right, left, another left, straight past two more lefts, then right, and it's at the end of the third corridor on your right."

introspectionism. For Skinner, thoughts and emotions were behaviors that follow the same laws as other behaviors.

Nevertheless, the evidence of cognitive processes cannot be ignored. For example, animals on a *fixed-interval reinforcement schedule* respond more and more frequently as the time approaches when a response will produce a reinforcer. Although a strict behaviorist would object to talk of "expectations," the animals behave as if they expected that repeating the response would soon produce the reward.

Evidence of cognitive processes has also come from studying rats in mazes. Rats exploring a maze, given no obvious rewards, seem to develop a **cognitive map,** a mental representation of the maze. When an experimenter then places food in the maze's goal box, these rats run the maze as quickly and efficiently as other rats that were previously reinforced with food for this result. Like people sightseeing in a new town, the exploring rats seemingly experienced **latent learning** during their earlier tours. That learning became apparent only when there was some incentive to demonstrate it. Children, too, may learn from watching a parent but demonstrate the learning only much later, as needed. The point to remember: *There is more to learning than associating a response with a consequence; there is also cognition.* We will encounter more striking evidence of animals' cognitive abilities in solving problems and in using aspects of language.

The cognitive perspective has also shown us the limits of rewards: Promising people a reward for a task they already enjoy can backfire. Excessive rewards can destroy **intrinsic motivation**—the desire to perform a behavior effectively and for its own sake. In experiments, children have been promised a payoff for playing with an interesting puzzle or toy. Later, they played with the toy *less* than unpaid children (Deci et al., 1999; Tang & Hall, 1995). Likewise, rewarding children with toys or candy for reading diminishes the time they spend reading (Marinak & Gambrell, 2008). It is as if they think, "If I have to be bribed into doing this, it must not be worth doing for its own sake."

To sense the difference between intrinsic motivation and **extrinsic motivation** (behaving in certain ways to gain external rewards or avoid threatened punishment), think about your experience in this course. Are you feeling pressured to finish this reading before a deadline? Worried about your grade? Eager for the credits that will count toward graduation? If *Yes*, then you are extrinsically motivated (as, to some extent, almost all students must be). Are you also finding the material interesting? Does learning it make you feel more competent? If there were no grade at stake, might you be curious enough to want to learn the material for its own sake? If *Yes*, intrinsic motivation also fuels your efforts.

Youth sports coaches who aim to promote enduring interest in an activity, not just to pressure players into winning, should focus on the intrinsic joys of playing and reaching one's potential (Deci & Ryan, 1985, 2009). Doing so may also ultimately lead to greater rewards. Students who focus on learning (intrinsic reward) often get good grades and graduate (extrinsic rewards). Doctors who focus on healing (intrinsic) may make a good living (extrinsic). Indeed, research suggests that people who focus on their work's meaning and significance not only do better work but ultimately enjoy more extrinsic rewards (Wrzesniewski et al., 2014). Giving people choices also enhances their intrinsic motivation (Patall et al., 2008).

Nevertheless, extrinsic rewards used to signal a job well done (rather than to bribe or control someone) can be effective (Boggiano et al., 1985). "Most improved player" awards, for example, can boost feelings of competence and increase enjoyment of a sport. Rightly administered, rewards can improve performance and spark creativity (Eisenberger & Aselage, 2009; Henderlong & Lepper, 2002). And the rewards that often follow academic achievement, such as scholarships and jobs, are here to stay.

TABLE 23.1 on the next page compares the biological and cognitive influences on classical and operant conditioning.

Latent learning Animals, like people, can learn from experience, with or without reinforcement. After exploring a maze for 10 days, rats received a food reward at the end of the maze. They quickly demonstrated their prior learning of the maze—by immediately completing it as quickly as (and even faster than) rats that had been reinforced for running the maze (Tolman & Honzik, 1930).

cognitive map a mental representation of the layout of one's environment. For example, after exploring a maze, rats act as if they have learned a cognitive map of it.

latent learning learning that occurs but is not apparent until there is an incentive to demonstrate it.

intrinsic motivation a desire to perform a behavior effectively for its own sake.

extrinsic motivation a desire to perform a behavior to receive promised rewards or avoid threatened punishment.

▼ TABLE 23.1
Biological and Cognitive Influences on Conditioning

	Classical Conditioning	Operant Conditioning
Cognitive processes	Organisms develop expectation that CS signals the arrival of US.	Organisms develop expectation that a response will be reinforced or punished; they also exhibit latent learning, without reinforcement.
Biological predispositions	Natural predispositions constrain what stimuli and responses can easily be associated.	Organisms most easily learn behaviors similar to their natural behaviors; unnatural behaviors instinctively drift back toward natural ones.

Learning by Observation

23-3 How does observational learning differ from associative learning? How may observational learning be enabled by mirror neurons?

Cognition is certainly a factor in **observational learning,** in which higher animals, especially humans, learn without direct experience, by watching and imitating others. A child who sees his sister burn her fingers on a hot stove learns not to touch it. We learn our native languages and various other specific behaviors by observing and imitating others, a process called **modeling.**

Picture this scene from an experiment by Albert Bandura, the pioneering researcher of observational learning (Bandura et al., 1961): A preschool child works on a drawing. An adult in another part of the room builds with Tinkertoys. As the child watches, the adult gets up and for nearly 10 minutes pounds, kicks, and throws around the room a large inflated Bobo doll, yelling, "Sock him in the nose. . . . Hit him down. . . . Kick him."

The child is then taken to another room filled with appealing toys. Soon the experimenter returns and tells the child she has decided to save these good toys "for the other children." She takes the now-frustrated child to a third room containing a few toys, including a Bobo doll. Left alone, what does the child do?

Compared with children not exposed to the adult model, those who viewed the model's actions were more likely to lash out at the doll. Observing the aggressive outburst apparently lowered their inhibitions. But *something more* was also at work, for the children imitated the very acts they had observed and used the very words they had heard (**FIGURE 23.4**).

⏯ **LaunchPad** For three minutes of classic footage, see LaunchPad's *Video: Bandura's Bobo Doll Experiment.*

That "something more," Bandura suggests, was this: By watching a model, we experience *vicarious reinforcement* or *vicarious punishment,* and we learn to anticipate a behavior's consequences in situations like those we are observing. We are especially likely to learn from people we perceive as similar to ourselves, as successful, or as admirable. fMRI scans show that when people observe someone winning a reward (and especially when it's someone likable and similar to themselves), their own brain reward systems activate, much as if they themselves had won the reward (Mobbs et al., 2009). When we identify with someone, we experience their outcomes vicariously. Even our learned fears may extinguish as we observe another safely navigating the feared situation (Golkar et al., 2013). Lord Chesterfield (1694–1773) had the idea: "We are, in truth, more than half what we are by imitation."

Albert Bandura
"The Bobo doll follows me wherever I go. The photographs are published in every introductory psychology text and virtually every undergraduate takes introductory psychology. I recently checked into a Washington hotel. The clerk at the desk asked, 'Aren't you the psychologist who did the Bobo doll experiment?' I answered, 'I am afraid that will be my legacy.' He replied, 'That deserves an upgrade. I will put you in a suite in the quiet part of the hotel'" (2005). A recent analysis of citations, awards, and textbook coverage identified Bandura as the world's most eminent psychologist (Diener et al., 2014).

observational learning learning by observing others.

modeling the process of observing and imitating a specific behavior.

Courtesy of Albert Bandura, Stanford University

▼ FIGURE 23.4
The famous Bobo doll experiment
Notice how the children's actions directly imitate the adult's.

Mirrors and Imitation in the Brain

On a 1991 hot summer day in Parma, Italy, a lab monkey awaited its researchers' return from lunch. The researchers had implanted wires next to its motor cortex, in a frontal lobe brain region that enabled the monkey to plan and enact movements. The monitoring device would alert the researchers to activity in that region of the monkey's brain. When the monkey moved a peanut into its mouth, for example, the device would buzz. That day, as one of the researchers reentered the lab, ice cream cone in hand, the monkey stared at him. As the researcher raised the cone to lick it, the monkey's monitor buzzed—as if the motionless monkey had itself moved (Blakeslee, 2006; Iacoboni, 2008, 2009).

The same buzzing had been heard earlier, when the monkey watched humans or other monkeys move peanuts to their mouths. The flabbergasted researchers, led by Giacomo Rizzolatti (2002, 2006), had, they believed, stumbled onto a previously unknown type of neuron. These presumed **mirror neurons** may provide a neural basis for everyday imitation and observational learning. When a monkey grasps, holds, or tears something, these neurons fire. And they likewise fire when the monkey observes another doing so. When one monkey sees, its neurons mirror what another monkey does. (For a debate regarding the importance of mirror neurons, which are sometimes overblown in the popular press, see Gallese et al., 2011; Hickok, 2014.)

Imitation is widespread in other species. In one experiment, a monkey watching another selecting certain pictures to gain treats learned to imitate the order of choices (**FIGURE 23.5** on the next page). In other research, rhesus macaque monkeys rarely made up quickly after a fight—unless they grew up with forgiving older macaques. Then, more often than not, their fights, too, were quickly followed by reconciliation (de Waal & Johanowicz, 1993). Rats, pigeons, crows, and gorillas all observe others and learn (Byrne et al., 2011; Dugatkin, 2002).

Chimpanzees observe and imitate all sorts of novel foraging and tool use behaviors, which are then transmitted from generation to generation within their local culture (Hopper et al., 2008; Whiten et al., 2007). In one 27-year analysis of 73,790 humpback whale observations, a single whale in 1980 whacked the water to drive prey fish into a clump. In the years since, this "lobtail" technique spread among other whales (Allen et al., 2013). Humpback see, humpback do.

Mirror neurons at work?

SIPRESS

David Sipress

"Your back is killing me!"

> **mirror neurons** frontal lobe neurons that some scientists believe fire when performing certain actions or when observing another doing so. The brain's mirroring of another's action may enable imitation and empathy.

Copyright Herb Terrace, Columbia University

Monkey A's screen   Monkey B's screen

▼ FIGURE 23.5
Cognitive imitation Monkey A (left) watched Monkey B touch four pictures on a display screen in a certain order to gain a banana. Monkey A learned to imitate that order, even when shown the same pictures in a different configuration (Subiaul et al., 2004).

So, too, with monkeys. Erica van de Waal and her co-researchers (2013) trained groups of vervet monkeys to prefer either blue or pink corn by soaking one color in a disgusting-tasting solution. Four to six months later, after a new generation of monkeys was born, the adults stuck with whatever color they had learned to prefer—and, on observing them, so did all but one of 27 infant monkeys. Moreover, when blue- (or pink-) preferring males migrated to the other group, they switched preferences and began eating as the other group did. Monkey see, monkey do.

In humans, imitation is pervasive. Our catchphrases, fashions, ceremonies, foods, traditions, morals, and fads all spread by one person copying another. Imitation shapes even very young humans' behavior (Bates & Byrne, 2010). Shortly after birth, babies may imitate adults who stick out their tongue. By 8 to 16 months, infants imitate various novel gestures (Jones, 2007). By age 12 months (**FIGURE 23.6**), they look where an adult is looking (Meltzoff et al., 2009). And by age 14 months, children imitate acts modeled on TV (Meltzoff, 1988; Meltzoff & Moore, 1989, 1997). Even as 2½-year-olds, when many of their mental abilities are near those of adult chimpanzees, young humans surpass chimps at social tasks such as imitating another's solution to a problem (Herrmann et al., 2007). Children see, children do.

So strong is the human predisposition to learn from watching adults that 2- to 5-year-old children *overimitate*. Whether living in urban Australia or rural Africa, they copy even irrelevant adult actions. Before reaching for a toy in a plastic jar, they will first stroke the jar with a feather if that's what they have observed (Lyons et al., 2007). Or, imitating an adult, they will wave a stick over a box and then use the stick to push on a

▼ FIGURE 23.6
Imitation This 12-month-old infant sees an adult look left, and immediately follows her gaze. (From Meltzoff et al., 2009.)

Meltzoff, A. N., Kuhl, P. K., Movellan, J. & Sejnowski, T. J. (2009). Foundations for a new science of learning. *Science, 325,* 284–288.

knob that opens the box—when all they needed to do to open the box was to push on the knob (Nielsen & Tomaselli, 2010).

Humans, like monkeys, have brains that support empathy and imitation. Researchers cannot insert experimental electrodes in human brains, but they can use fMRI scans to see brain activity associated with performing and with observing actions. So, is the human capacity to simulate another's action and to share in another's experience due to specialized mirror neurons? Or is it due to distributed brain networks? That issue is currently being debated (Gallese et al. 2011; Iacoboni, 2008, 2009; Mukamel et al., 2010; Spaulding, 2013). Regardless, children's brains do enable their empathy and their ability to infer another's mental state, an ability known as *theory of mind*.

The brain's response to observing others makes emotions contagious. Through its neurological echo, our brain simulates and vicariously experiences what we observe. So real are these mental instant replays that we may misremember an action we have observed as an action we have performed (Lindner et al., 2010). But through these reenactments, we grasp others' states of mind. Observing others' postures, faces, voices, and writing styles, we unconsciously synchronize our own to theirs—which helps us feel what they are feeling (Bernieri et al., 1994; Ireland & Pennebaker, 2010). We find ourselves yawning when they yawn, laughing when they laugh.

When observing movie characters smoking, smokers' brains spontaneously simulate smoking, which helps explain their cravings (Wagner et al., 2011). Seeing a loved one's pain, our faces mirror the other's emotion. But as **FIGURE 23.7** shows, so do our brains.

Animal social learning Whacking the water to boost feeding has spread among humpback whales through social learning (Allen et al., 2013). Likewise, monkeys learn to prefer whatever color corn they observe other monkeys eating.

"Children need models more than they need critics."

Joseph Joubert, *Pensées*, 1842

Pain   Empathy

▼ FIGURE 23.7
Experienced and imagined pain in the brain Brain activity related to actual pain (left) is mirrored in the brain of an observing loved one (right). Empathy in the brain shows up in emotional brain areas, but not in the somatosensory cortex, which receives the physical pain input.

prosocial behavior positive, constructive, helpful behavior. The opposite of antisocial behavior.

In this fMRI scan, the pain imagined by an empathic romantic partner has triggered some of the same brain activity experienced by the loved one actually having the pain (Singer et al., 2004). Even fiction reading may trigger such activity, as we mentally simulate (and vicariously experience) the experiences described (Mar & Oatley, 2008; Speer et al., 2009). In one experiment, university students read (and vicariously experienced) a fictional fellow student's description of overcoming obstacles to vote. A week later, those who read the first-person account were more likely to vote in a presidential primary election (Kaufman & Libby, 2012).

Applications of Observational Learning

So the big news from Bandura's studies and the mirror-neuron research is that we look, we mentally imitate, and we learn. Models—in our family or neighborhood, or on TV—may have effects, good and bad.

Prosocial Effects

23-4 What is the impact of prosocial modeling and of antisocial modeling?

The good news is that **prosocial** (positive, helpful) models can have prosocial effects. Many business organizations effectively use *behavior modeling* to help new employees learn communications, sales, and customer service skills (Taylor et al., 2005). Trainees gain these skills faster when they are able to observe the skills being modeled effectively by experienced workers (or actors simulating them).

People who exemplify nonviolent, helpful behavior can also prompt similar behavior in others. India's Mahatma Gandhi and America's Martin Luther King, Jr. both drew on the power of modeling, making nonviolent action a powerful force for social change in both countries. The media offer models. One research team found that across seven countries, viewing prosocial media boosted later helping behavior (Prot et al., 2013).

Parents are also powerful models. European Christians who risked their lives to rescue Jews from the Nazis usually had a close relationship with at least one parent who modeled a strong moral or humanitarian concern; this was also true for U.S. civil rights activists in the 1960s (London, 1970; Oliner & Oliner, 1988). The observational learning of morality begins early. Socially responsive toddlers who readily imitate their parents tend to become preschoolers with a strong internalized conscience (Forman et al., 2004).

A model caregiver This girl is learning orphan-nursing skills, as well as compassion, by observing her mentor in this Humane Society program. As the sixteenth-century proverb states, "Example is better than precept."

Models are most effective when their actions and words are consistent. Sometimes, however, models say one thing and do another. To encourage children to read, read to them and surround them with books and people who read. To increase the odds that your children will practice your religion, worship and attend religious activities with them. Many parents seem to operate according to the principle "Do as I *say*, not as I *do*." Experiments suggest that children learn to do both (Rice & Grusec, 1975; Rushton, 1975). Exposed to a hypocrite, they tend to imitate the hypocrisy—by doing what the model did and saying what the model said.

Antisocial Effects   The bad news is that observational learning may have *antisocial effects*. This helps us understand why abusive parents might have aggressive children, and why many men who beat their wives had wife-battering fathers (Stith et al., 2000). Critics note that aggressiveness could be genetic. But with monkeys, we know it can be environmental. In study after study, young monkeys separated from their mothers and subjected to high levels of aggression grew up to be aggressive themselves (Chamove, 1980). The lessons we learn as children are not easily replaced as adults, and they are sometimes visited on future generations.

TV shows and Internet videos are powerful sources of observational learning. While watching TV and videos, children may "learn" that bullying is an effective way to control others, that free and easy sex brings pleasure without later misery or disease, or that men should be tough and women gentle. And they have ample time to learn such lessons. During their first 18 years, most children in developed countries spend more time watching TV than they spend in school. The average teen watches more than 4 hours a day; the average adult, 3 hours (Robinson & Martin, 2009; Strasburger et al., 2010).

"The problem with television is that the people must sit and keep their eyes glued to a screen: The average American family hasn't time for it. Therefore the showmen are convinced that . . . television will never be a serious competitor of [radio] broadcasting."

New York Times, 1939

Children see, children do? Children who often experience physical punishment tend to display more aggression.

TV viewers are learning about life from a rather peculiar storyteller, one that reflects the culture's mythology but not its reality. Between 1998 and 2006, prime-time violence reportedly increased 75 percent (PTC, 2007). If we include cable programming and video rentals, the violence numbers escalate. An analysis of more than 3000 network and cable programs aired during one closely studied year revealed that nearly 6 in 10 featured violence, that 74 percent of the violence went unpunished, that 58 percent did not show the victims' pain, that nearly half the incidents involved "justified" violence, and that nearly half involved an attractive perpetrator. These conditions define the recipe for the *violence-viewing effect* described in many studies (Donnerstein, 1998, 2011). To read more about this effect, see Thinking Critically About: Does Viewing Media Violence Trigger Violent Behavior? on the next page.

Screen time's greatest effect may stem from what it displaces. Children and adults who spend several hours a day in front of a screen spend that many fewer hours in other pursuits—talking, studying, playing, reading, or socializing face-to-face with friends. What would you have done with your extra time if you had spent even half as many hours in front of a screen? How might you be different as a result?

Does Viewing Media Violence Trigger Violent Behavior?

Was the judge who in 1993 tried two British 10-year-olds for their murder of a 2-year-old right to suspect that the pair had been influenced by "violent video films"? Were the American media right to wonder if Adam Lanza, the 2012 mass killer of young children and their teachers at Connecticut's Sandy Hook Elementary School, was influenced by the violent video games found stockpiled in his home? To understand whether violence viewing leads to violent behavior, researchers have done both correlational and experimental studies (Groves et al., in press).

Correlational studies do support this link:

- In the United States and Canada, homicide rates doubled between 1957 and 1974, just when TV was introduced and spreading. Moreover, census regions with later dates for TV service also had homicide rates that jumped later (Centerwall, 1989).

- White South Africans were first introduced to TV in 1975. A similar near-doubling of the homicide rate began after 1975 (Centerwall, 1989).

- Elementary schoolchildren with heavy exposure to media violence (via TV, videos, and video games) tend to get into more fights (**FIGURE 23.8**). As teens, they are at greater risk for violent behavior (Boxer et al., 2009).

But remember, correlation need not mean causation. So these studies do not prove that viewing violence causes aggression (Ferguson, 2009; Freedman, 1988; McGuire, 1986). Maybe aggressive children prefer violent programs. Maybe abused or neglected children are both more aggressive and more often left in front of the TV or computer. Maybe violent programs reflect, rather than affect, violent trends.

To pin down causation, psychologists experimented. They randomly assigned some viewers to observe violence and others to watch entertaining nonviolence. Does viewing cruelty prepare people, when irritated, to react more cruelly? To some extent, it does. This is especially so when an attractive person commits seemingly justified, realistic violence that goes unpunished and causes no visible pain or harm (Donnerstein, 1998, 2011).

The violence-viewing effect seems to stem from at least two factors. One is *imitation*. More than 100 studies confirm that people sometimes imitate what they've viewed. Watching risk-glorifying behaviors (dangerous driving, extreme sports, unprotected sex) increases viewers' real-life risk-taking (Fischer et al., 2011; Geen & Thomas, 1986). Children as young as 14 months will imitate acts they observe on TV (Meltzoff & Moore, 1989, 1997). As they watch, their brains simulate the behavior, and after this inner rehearsal they become more likely to act it out. Thus, in one experiment, violent play increased sevenfold immediately after children viewed *Power Rangers* episodes (Boyatzis et al., 1995). As happened in the Bobo doll experiment, children often precisely imitated the models' violent acts—in this case, flying karate kicks. Another large experiment randomly assigned some preschoolers to a media diet. With their exposure to violence-laden programs limited, and their exposure to educational programs increased, their aggressive behavior diminished (Christakis et al., 2013).

Prolonged exposure to violence also *desensitizes* viewers. They become more indifferent to it when later viewing a brawl, whether on TV or in real life (Fanti et al., 2009; Rule & Ferguson, 1986). Adult males who spent three evenings watching sexually violent movies became progressively less bothered by the rapes and slashings. Compared with those in a control group, the film watchers later expressed less sympathy for domestic violence victims, and they rated the victims' injuries as less severe (Mullin & Linz, 1995). Likewise, moviegoers were less likely to help an injured woman pick up her crutches if they had just watched a violent rather than a nonviolent movie (Bushman & Anderson, 2009).

RETRIEVAL PRACTICE

- Jason's parents and older friends all smoke, but they advise him not to. Juan's parents and friends don't smoke, but they say nothing to deter him from doing so. Will Jason or Juan be more likely to start smoking?

ANSWER: Jason may be more likely to smoke, because observational learning studies suggest that children tend to do as others do and say what they say.

＊ ＊ ＊

Bandura's work—like that of Ivan Pavlov, John Watson, B. F. Skinner, and thousands of others who advanced our knowledge of learning principles—illustrates the impact that can result from single-minded devotion to a few well-defined problems and ideas. These researchers defined the issues and impressed on us the importance of learning. As their legacy demonstrates, intellectual history is often made by people who risk going to extremes in pushing ideas to their limits (Simonton, 2000).

Drawing on such findings, the International Society for Research on Aggression's Media Violence Commission (2012) concluded that violent media are not the primary cause of school shootings, but that "exposure to media violence is one risk factor for increased aggression." And the American Academy of Pediatrics (2009) has advised pediatricians that "media violence can contribute to aggressive behavior, desensitization to violence, nightmares, and fear of being harmed." Indeed, an evil psychologist could hardly imagine a better way to make people indifferent to brutality than to expose them to a graded series of scenes, from fights to killings to the mutilations in slasher movies (Donnerstein et al., 1987). Watching cruelty fosters indifference.

"Thirty seconds worth of glorification of a soap bar sells soap. Twenty-five minutes worth of glorification of violence sells violence."

U.S. Senator Paul Simon,
Remarks to the Communitarian Network, 1993

▼ FIGURE 23.8
Heavy exposure to media violence predicts future aggressive behavior Researchers studied more than 400 third- to fifth-graders. After controlling for existing differences in hostility and aggression, the researchers reported increased aggression in those heavily exposed to violent TV, videos, and video games (Gentile et al., 2011; Gentile & Bushman, 2012).

Percentage of students involved in fights at time 2 (vertical axis: 0 to 90%)
Media violence exposure at time 1 (Low, Medium, High)
■ Girls ■ Boys

RETRIEVAL PRACTICE

Match the examples (1-5) to the appropriate underlying learning principle (a-e):

a. Classical conditioning   d. Observational learning
b. Operant conditioning   e. Biological predispositions
c. Latent learning

1. Knowing the way from your bed to the bathroom in the dark
2. Your little brother getting in a fight after watching a violent action movie
3. Salivating when you smell brownies in the oven
4. Disliking the taste of chili after becoming violently sick a few hours after eating chili
5. Your dog racing to greet you on your arrival home

ANSWERS: 1. c, 2. d, 3. a, 4. e, 5. b

MODULE 23 REVIEW Biology, Cognition, and Learning

LEARNING OBJECTIVES

RETRIEVAL PRACTICE Take a moment to answer each of these Learning Objective Questions (repeated here from within this module). Then turn to Appendix C, Complete Module Reviews, to check your answers. Research suggests that trying to answer these questions on your own will improve your long-term retention (McDaniel et al., 2009).

23-1 How do biological constraints affect classical and operant conditioning?

23-2 How do cognitive processes affect classical and operant conditioning?

23-3 How does observational learning differ from associative learning? How may observational learning be enabled by mirror neurons?

23-4 What is the impact of prosocial modeling and of antisocial modeling?

TERMS AND CONCEPTS TO REMEMBER

RETRIEVAL PRACTICE Test yourself on these terms by trying to write down the definition before flipping back to check your answers.

learning, p. 300

cognitive learning, p. 304

cognitive map, p. 305

latent learning, p. 305

intrinsic motivation, p. 305

extrinsic motivation, p. 305

observational learning, p. 306

modeling, p. 306

mirror neurons, p. 307

prosocial behavior, p. 310

Use 🔵 **LearningCurve** to create your personalized study plan, which will direct you to the resources that will help you most in 🔵 **LaunchPad**.

TEST YOUR-SELF LEARNING

Test yourself repeatedly throughout your studies. This will not only help you figure out what you know and don't know; the testing itself will help you learn and remember the information more effectively thanks to the *testing effect*.

MODULE 21 Basic Learning Concepts and Classical Conditioning

1. Learning is defined as "the process of acquiring through experience new and relatively enduring _____ or _____ ."

2. Two forms of associative learning are classical conditioning, in which the organism associates _____ , and operant conditioning, in which the organism associates _____ .

   a. two or more responses; a response and consequence

   b. two or more stimuli; two or more responses

   c. two or more stimuli; a response and consequence

   d. two or more responses; two or more stimuli

3. In Pavlov's experiments, the tone started as a neutral stimulus, and then became a(n) _____ stimulus.

4. Dogs have been taught to salivate to a circle but not to a square. This process is an example of _____ .

5. After Watson and Rayner classically conditioned Little Albert to fear a white rat, the child later showed fear in response to a rabbit, a dog, and a sealskin coat. This illustrates

   a. extinction.

   b. generalization.

   c. spontaneous recovery.

   d. discrimination between two stimuli.

6. "Sex sells!" is a common saying in advertising. Using classical conditioning terms, explain how sexual images in advertisements can condition your response to a product.

MODULE 22 Operant Conditioning

7. Thorndike's law of effect was the basis for _____ work on operant conditioning and behavior control.

8. One way to change behavior is to reward natural behaviors in small steps, as the organism gets closer and closer to a desired behavior. This process is called _____ .

9. Your dog is barking so loudly that it's making your ears ring. You clap your hands, the dog stops barking, your ears stop ringing, and you think to yourself, "I'll have to do that when he barks again." The end of the barking was for you a

   a. positive reinforcer.

   b. negative reinforcer.

   c. positive punishment.

   d. negative punishment.

10. How could your psychology instructor use negative reinforcement to encourage your attentive behavior during class?

11. Reinforcing a desired response only some of the times it occurs is called _____ reinforcement.

12. A restaurant is running a special deal. After you buy four meals at full price, your fifth meal will be free. This is an example of a _____ schedule of reinforcement.
    a. fixed-ratio
    b. variable-ratio
    c. fixed-interval
    d. variable-interval

13. The partial reinforcement schedule that reinforces a response after unpredictable time periods is a _____-_____ schedule.

14. A medieval proverb notes that "a burnt child dreads the fire." In operant conditioning, the burning would be an example of a
    a. primary reinforcer.
    b. negative reinforcer.
    c. punisher.
    d. positive reinforcer.

MODULE 23 Biology, Cognition, and Learning

15. Garcia and Koelling's _____ - _____ studies showed that conditioning can occur even when the unconditioned stimulus (US) does not immediately follow the neutral stimulus (NS).

16. Taste-aversion research has shown that some animals develop aversions to certain tastes but not to sights or sounds. What evolutionary psychology finding does this support?

17. Evidence that cognitive processes play an important role in learning comes in part from studies in which rats
    a. spontaneously recover previously learned behavior.
    b. develop cognitive maps.
    c. exhibit respondent behavior.
    d. generalize responses.

18. Rats that explored a maze without any reward were later able to run the maze as well as other rats that had received food rewards for running the maze. The rats that had learned without reinforcement demonstrated _____ _____ .

19. Children learn many social behaviors by imitating parents and other models. This type of learning is called _____ .

20. According to Bandura, we learn by watching models because we experience _____ reinforcement or _____ punishment.

21. Parents are most effective in getting their children to imitate them if
    a. their words and actions are consistent.
    b. they have outgoing personalities.
    c. one parent works and the other stays home to care for the children.
    d. they carefully explain why a behavior is acceptable in adults but not in children.

22. Some scientists believe that the brain has _____ neurons that enable empathy and imitation.

23. Most experts agree that repeated viewing of media violence
    a. makes all viewers significantly more aggressive.
    b. has little effect on viewers.
    c. dulls viewers' sensitivity to violence.
    d. makes viewers angry and frustrated.

Find answers to these questions in Appendix D, in the back of the book.

Dimitri Otis/Photographer's Choice RF/Getty Images

MEMORY[1]

. . . .

Be thankful for memory. We take it for granted, except when it malfunctions. But it is our memory that accounts for time and defines our life. It is our memory that enables us to recognize family, speak our language, find our way home, and locate food and water. It is our memory that enables us to enjoy an experience and then mentally replay and enjoy it again. Our shared memories help bind us together as Irish or Aussies, as Serbs or Albanians. And it is our memory that occasionally pits us against those whose offenses we cannot forget.

In large part, we are what we remember. Without memory—our storehouse of accumulated learning—there would be no savoring of past joys, no guilt or anger over painful recollections. We would instead live in an enduring present, each moment fresh. But each person would be a stranger, every language foreign, every task—dressing, cooking, biking—a new challenge. You would even be a stranger to yourself, lacking that continuous sense of self that extends from your distant past to your momentary present.

Researchers study memory from many perspectives. Module 24 introduces the measuring, modeling, and encoding of memories. Module 25 examines how memories are stored and retrieved. Module 26 explores what happens when our memories fail us, and offers some tips for improving memory.

1. The Memory modules benefit from our collaboration with Janie Wilson, Georgia Southern University, in the previous edition.

317

memory the persistence of learning over time through the encoding, storage, and retrieval of information.

MODULE 24 # Studying and Encoding Memories

Studying Memory

24-1 What is memory, and how is it measured?

MEMORY IS LEARNING THAT PERSISTS over time; it is information that has been acquired and stored and can be retrieved. Research on memory's extremes has helped us understand how memory works. At age 92, my [DM] father suffered a small stroke that had but one peculiar effect. He was as mobile as before. His genial personality was intact. He knew us and enjoyed poring over family photo albums and reminiscing about his past. But he had lost most of his ability to lay down new memories of conversations and everyday episodes. He could not tell me what day of the week it was, or what he'd had for lunch. Told repeatedly of his brother-in-law's death, he was surprised and saddened each time he heard the news.

Memory Olympians Participants in a worldwide memory competition view and then reproduce long strings of numbers, words, and cards. The competitors have an unusual capacity for focused attention, which they can enhance by blocking out distractions.

Sandy Huffaker/The New York Times/Redux

At the other extreme are people who would be gold medal winners in a memory Olympics. Russian journalist Solomon Shereshevskii, or S, had merely to listen while other reporters scribbled notes (Luria, 1968). You and I could parrot back a string of about 7—maybe even 9—digits. S could repeat up to 70, if they were read about 3 seconds apart in an otherwise silent room. Moreover, he could recall digits or words backward as easily as forward. His accuracy was unerring, even when recalling a list 15 years later. "Yes, yes," he might recall. "This was a series you gave me once when we were in your apartment. . . . You were sitting at the table and I in the rocking chair. . . . You were wearing a gray suit. . . ."

Amazing? Yes, but consider your own impressive memory. You remember countless faces, places, and happenings; tastes, smells, and textures; voices, sounds, and songs. In one study, students listened to snippets—a mere four-tenths of a second—from popular songs. How often did they recognize the artist and song? More than 25 percent of the time (Krumhansl, 2010). We often recognize songs as quickly as we recognize someone's voice.

So, too, with faces and places. Imagine viewing more than 2500 slides of faces and places for 10 seconds each. Later, you see 280 of these slides, paired with others you've never seen. Actual participants in this experiment recognized 90 percent of the slides they had viewed in the first round (Haber, 1970). In a follow-up experiment, people exposed to 2800 images for only 3 seconds each spotted the repeats with 82 percent accuracy (Konkle et al., 2010). Some "super-recognizers" display an extraordinary ability to recognize faces. Eighteen months after viewing a video of an armed robbery, one such police officer spotted and arrested the robber walking on a busy street (Davis et al., 2013). And it's not just humans who have shown remarkable memory for faces (**FIGURE 24.1**).

How do we accomplish such memory feats? How does our brain pluck information out of the world around us and tuck that information away for later use? How can we remember things we have not thought about for years, yet forget the name of someone we met a minute ago? How are memories stored in our brains? Why will you be likely, later in this module, to misrecall this sentence: "*The angry rioter threw the rock at the window*"? Here and in the coming modules, we consider these fascinating questions and more, including tips on how we can improve our own memories.

Kendrick's "Sheep Don't Forget a Face," in Nature, 414, November, 2001, p. 165]

▼ **FIGURE 24.1**
Other animals also display face smarts After repeatedly experiencing food rewards associated with some sheep faces, but not with others, sheep remember those faces for two years (Kendrick & Feng, 2011).

Measuring Retention

To a psychologist, evidence that learning persists includes these three *measures of retention*:

- **recall**—retrieving information that is not currently in your conscious awareness but that was learned at an earlier time. A fill-in-the-blank question tests your recall.

- **recognition**—identifying items previously learned. A multiple-choice question tests your recognition.

- **relearning**—learning something more quickly when you learn it a second or later time. When you study for a final exam or engage a language used in early childhood, you will relearn the material more easily than you did initially.

Long after you cannot recall most of the people in your high school graduating class, you may still be able to recognize their yearbook pictures from a photographic lineup and pick their names from a list of names. In one experiment, people who had graduated 25 years earlier could not recall many of their old classmates. But they could *recognize* 90 percent of their pictures and names (Bahrick et al., 1975). If you are like most students, you, too, could probably recognize more names of Snow White's seven dwarfs than you could recall (Miserandino, 1991).

Our recognition memory is impressively quick and vast. "Is your friend wearing a new or old outfit?" "Old." "Is this five-second movie clip from a film you've ever seen?" "Yes." "Have you ever seen this person before—this minor variation on the same old human features (two eyes, one nose, and so on)?" "No." Before the mouth can form our answer to any of millions of such questions, the mind knows, and knows that it knows.

Our speed at *relearning* also reveals memory. Pioneering memory researcher Hermann Ebbinghaus (1850–1909) showed this more than a century ago, using nonsense syllables. He randomly selected a sample of syllables, practiced them, and tested himself. To get a feel for his experiments, rapidly read aloud, eight times over, the following list (from Baddeley, 1982), then look away and try to recall the items:

JIH, BAZ, FUB, YOX, SUJ, XIR, DAX, LEQ, VUM, PID, KEL, WAV, TUV, ZOF, GEK, HIW.

The day after learning such a list, Ebbinghaus could recall few of the syllables. But they weren't entirely forgotten. As **FIGURE 24.2** portrays, the more frequently he repeated the list aloud on Day 1, the less time he required to *relearn* the list on Day 2. Additional rehearsal (*overlearning*) of verbal information increases retention, especially when practice is distributed over time. For students, this means that it helps to rehearse course material even after you know it.

The point to remember: Tests of recognition and of time spent relearning demonstrate that *we remember more than we can recall.*

recall a measure of memory in which the person must retrieve information learned earlier, as on a fill-in-the-blank test.

recognition a measure of memory in which the person need only identify items previously learned, as on a multiple-choice test.

relearning a measure of memory that assesses the amount of time saved when learning material again.

Remembering things past Even if Taylor Swift and Leonardo DiCaprio had not become famous, their high school classmates would most likely still recognize them in these photos.

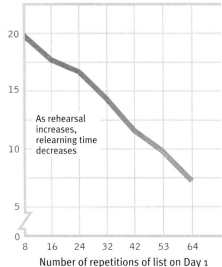

As rehearsal increases, relearning time decreases

Time in minutes taken to relearn list on Day 2

Number of repetitions of list on Day 1

▼ **FIGURE 24.2**
Ebbinghaus' retention curve
Ebbinghaus found that the more times he practiced a list of nonsense syllables on Day 1, the less time he required to relearn it on Day 2. Speed of relearning is one measure of memory retention. (From Baddeley, 1982.)

encoding the processing of information into the memory system—for example, by extracting meaning.

storage the process of retaining encoded information over time.

retrieval the process of getting information out of memory storage.

parallel processing the processing of many aspects of a problem simultaneously; the brain's natural mode of information processing for many functions.

sensory memory the immediate, very brief recording of sensory information in the memory system.

short-term memory activated memory that holds a few items briefly, such as the seven digits of a phone number while calling, before the information is stored or forgotten.

long-term memory the relatively permanent and limitless storehouse of the memory system. Includes knowledge, skills, and experiences.

▼ **FIGURE 24.3**

A modified three-stage processing model of memory Atkinson and Shiffrin's classic three-step model helps us to think about how memories are processed, but today's researchers recognize other ways long-term memories form. For example, some information slips into long-term memory via a "back door," without our consciously attending to it *(automatic processing)*. And so much active processing occurs in the short-term memory stage that many now prefer the term *working memory*.

— RETRIEVAL PRACTICE —

• Multiple-choice questions test our _____. Fill-in-the-blank questions test our _____.

ANSWERS: recognition; recall

• If you want to be sure to remember what you're learning for an upcoming test, would it be better to use *recall* or *recognition* to check your memory? Why?

ANSWER: It would be better to test your memory with *recall* (such as with short-answer or fill-in-the-blank self-test questions) rather than *recognition* (such as with multiple-choice questions). Recalling information is harder than recognizing it. So if you can recall it, that means your retention of the material is better than if you could only recognize it. Your chances of test success are therefore greater.

Memory Models

24-2 How do psychologists describe the human memory system?

Architects make miniature house models to help clients imagine their future homes. Similarly, psychologists create memory models to help us think about how our brain forms and retrieves memories. An *information-processing model* likens human memory to computer operations. Thus, to remember any event, we must

• *get information into our brain*, a process called **encoding.**

• *retain that information*, a process called **storage.**

• later *get the information back out*, a process called **retrieval.**

Like all analogies, computer models have their limits. Our memories are less literal and more fragile than a computer's. Moreover, most computers process information sequentially, even while alternating between tasks. Our agile brain processes many things simultaneously (some of them unconsciously) by means of **parallel processing.** To focus on this multitrack processing, one information-processing model, *connectionism,* views memories as products of interconnected neural networks. Specific memories arise from particular activation patterns within these networks. Every time you learn something new, your brain's neural connections change, forming and strengthening pathways that allow you to interact with and learn from your constantly changing environment.

To explain our memory-forming process, Richard Atkinson and Richard Shiffrin (1968) proposed a three-stage model:

1. We first record to-be-remembered information as a fleeting **sensory memory.**

2. From there, we process information into **short-term memory,** where we encode it through *rehearsal.*

3. Finally, information moves into **long-term memory** for later retrieval.

Other psychologists have updated this model (**FIGURE 24.3**) with important newer concepts, including *working memory* and *automatic processing.*

Working Memory Alan Baddeley and others (Baddeley, 2001, 2002; Barrouillet et al., 2011; Engle, 2002) extended Atkinson and Shiffrin's view of short-term memory as a small, brief storage space for recent thoughts and experiences. This stage is not just a temporary shelf for holding incoming information. It's an active desktop where your brain processes information by making sense of new input and linking it with long-term

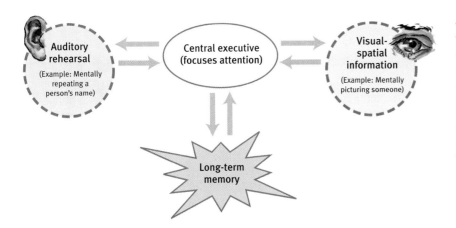

▼ FIGURE 24.4
Working memory Alan Baddeley's (2002) model of working memory, simplified here, includes *visual* and *auditory rehearsal* of new information. A hypothetical *central executive* (manager) focuses attention and pulls information from long-term memory to help make sense of new information.

memories. Whether we hear *eye-screem* as "ice cream" or "I scream" will depend on how the context and our experience guide our interpreting and encoding the sounds. To focus on the active processing that takes place in this middle stage, psychologists use the term **working memory.** Right now, you are using your working memory to link the information you're reading with your previously stored information (Cowan, 2010; Kail & Hall, 2001).

For most of you, what you are reading enters working memory through vision. You might also repeat the information using auditory rehearsal. As you integrate these memory inputs with your existing long-term memory, your attention is focused. Baddeley (1998, 2002) suggested a *central executive* handles this focused processing (**FIGURE 24.4**).

Without focused attention, information often fades. If you think you can look something up later, you attend to it less and forget it more quickly. In one experiment, people read and typed new bits of trivia they would later need, such as "An ostrich's eye is bigger than its brain." If they knew the information would be available online they invested less energy and remembered it less well (Sparrow et al., 2011; Wegner & Ward, 2013). Sometimes Google replaces rehearsal.

RETRIEVAL PRACTICE

• What two new concepts update the classic Atkinson-Shiffrin three-stage information-processing model?

ANSWER: (1) We form some memories through automatic processing, without our awareness. The Atkinson-Shiffrin model focused only on conscious memories. (2) The newer concept of a *working memory* emphasizes the active processing that we now know takes place in Atkinson-Shiffrin's short-term memory stage.

• What are two basic functions of *working memory?*

ANSWER: (1) Active processing of incoming visual-spatial and auditory information, and (2) focusing our spotlight of attention.

Encoding Memories

Dual-Track Memory: Effortful Versus Automatic Processing

24-3 How do explicit and implicit memories differ?

Atkinson and Shiffrin's model focused on how we process our **explicit memories**—the facts and experiences that we can consciously know and declare (thus, also called *declarative memories*). But our mind has a second, unconscious track. We encode explicit memories through conscious **effortful processing.** Behind the scenes, other information skips the conscious encoding track and barges directly into storage. This **automatic processing,** which happens without our awareness, produces **implicit memories** (also called *nondeclarative memories*).

---

working memory a newer understanding of short-term memory that focuses on conscious, active processing of incoming auditory and visual-spatial information, and of information retrieved from long-term memory.

explicit memory memory of facts and experiences that one can consciously know and "declare." (Also called *declarative memory*.)

effortful processing encoding that requires attention and conscious effort.

automatic processing unconscious encoding of incidental information, such as space, time, and frequency, and of well-learned information, such as word meanings.

implicit memory retention of learned skills or classically conditioned associations independent of conscious recollection. (Also called *nondeclarative memory*.)

🎧 **LaunchPad** For a 14-minute explanation and demonstration of our memory systems, visit LaunchPad's *Video: Models of Memory.*

Automatic Processing and Implicit Memories

24-4 What information do we process automatically?

Our implicit memories include *procedural* memory for automatic skills (such as how to ride a bike) and classically conditioned *associations* among stimuli. If attacked by a dog in childhood, years later you may, without recalling the conditioned association, automatically tense up as a dog approaches.

Without conscious effort you also automatically process information about

- *space.* While studying, you often encode the place on a page where certain material appears; later, when you want to retrieve the information, you may visualize its location on the page.
- *time.* While going about your day, you unintentionally note the sequence of its events. Later, realizing you've left your coat somewhere, the event sequence your brain automatically encoded will enable you to retrace your steps.
- *frequency.* You effortlessly keep track of how many times things happen, as when you realize, "This is the third time I've run into her today."

Our two-track mind engages in impressively efficient information processing. As one track automatically tucks away many routine details, the other track is free to focus on conscious, effortful processing. Mental feats such as vision, thinking, and memory may seem to be single abilities, but they are not. Rather, we split information into different components for separate and simultaneous parallel processing.

Effortful Processing and Explicit Memories

Automatic processing happens effortlessly. When you see words in your native language, perhaps on the side of a delivery truck, you can't help but read them and register their meaning. *Learning* to read wasn't automatic. You may recall working hard to pick out letters and connect them to certain sounds. But with experience and practice, your reading became automatic. Imagine now learning to read reversed sentences like this:

.citamotua emoceb nac gnissecorp luftroffE

At first, this requires effort, but after enough practice, you would also perform this task much more automatically. We develop many skills in this way: driving, texting, and speaking a new language.

Sensory Memory

24-5 How does sensory memory work?

Sensory memory (recall Figure 24.3) feeds our active working memory, recording momentary images of scenes or echoes of sounds. How much of this page could you sense and recall with less exposure than a lightning flash? In one experiment, people viewed three rows of three letters each, for only one-twentieth of a second (**FIGURE 24.5**). After the nine letters disappeared, they could recall only about half of them.

▼ FIGURE 24.5
Total recall—briefly When George Sperling (1960) flashed a group of letters similar to this for one-twentieth of a second, people could recall only about half the letters. But when signaled to recall a particular row immediately after the letters had disappeared, they could do so with near-perfect accuracy.

```
K    Z    R

Q    B    T

S    G    N
```

Was it because they had insufficient time to glimpse them? *No.* George Sperling cleverly demonstrated that people actually *could* see and recall all the letters, but only momentarily. Rather than ask them to recall all nine letters at once, he sounded a high, medium, or low tone immediately *after* flashing the nine letters. This tone directed participants to report only the letters of the top, middle, or bottom row, respectively. Now they rarely missed a letter, showing that all nine letters were momentarily available for recall.

Sperling's experiment demonstrated **iconic memory,** a fleeting sensory memory of visual stimuli. For a few tenths of a second, our eyes register a photographic or picture-image memory of a scene, and we can recall any part of it in amazing detail. But if Sperling delayed the tone signal by more than half a second, the image faded and participants again recalled only about half the letters. Our visual screen clears quickly, as new images are superimposed over old ones.

We also have an impeccable, though fleeting, memory for auditory stimuli, called **echoic memory** (Cowan, 1988; Lu et al., 1992). Picture yourself in conversation, as your attention veers to your smartphone screen. If your mildly irked companion tests you by asking, "What did I just say?" you can recover the last few words from your mind's echo chamber. Auditory echoes tend to linger for 3 or 4 seconds.

Capacity of Short-Term and Working Memory

24-6 What is the capacity of our short-term and working memory?

Recall that working memory is an active stage, where our brains make sense of incoming information and link it with stored memories. What are the limits of what we can hold in this middle stage?

George Miller (1956) proposed that we can store about seven bits of information (give or take two) in short-term memory. Miller's magical number seven is psychology's contribution to the list of magical sevens—the seven wonders of the world, the seven seas, the seven deadly sins, the seven primary colors, the seven musical scale notes, the seven days of the week—seven magical sevens.

Other researchers have confirmed that we can, if nothing distracts us, recall about seven digits, or about six letters or five words (Baddeley et al., 1975). How quickly do our short-term memories disappear? To find out, Lloyd Peterson and Margaret Peterson (1959) asked people to remember three-consonant groups, such as *CHJ*. To prevent rehearsal, the researchers asked them, for example, to start at 100 and count aloud backward by threes. After 3 seconds, people recalled the letters only about half the time; after 12 seconds, they seldom recalled them at all (**FIGURE 24.6**). Without the active processing that we now understand to be a part of our working memory, short-term memories have a limited life.

Working memory capacity varies, depending on age and other factors. Compared with children and older adults, young adults have more working memory capacity, so they can use their mental workspace more efficiently. This means their ability to

iconic memory a momentary sensory memory of visual stimuli; a photographic or picture-image memory lasting no more than a few tenths of a second.

echoic memory a momentary sensory memory of auditory stimuli; if attention is elsewhere, sounds and words can still be recalled within 3 or 4 seconds.

After Miller's 2012 death, his daughter recalled his best moment of golf: "He made the one and only hole-in-one of his life at the age of 77, on the seventh green . . . with a seven iron. He loved that" (quoted by Vitello, 2012).

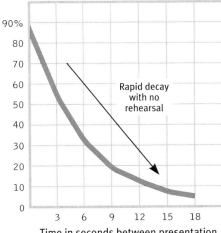

Percentage who recalled consonants (vertical axis: 0 to 90%)

Time in seconds between presentation of consonants and recall request (no rehearsal allowed) (horizontal axis: 3, 6, 9, 12, 15, 18)

Rapid decay with no rehearsal

▼ FIGURE 24.6
Short-term memory decay Unless rehearsed, verbal information may be quickly forgotten. (Data from Peterson & Peterson, 1959; see also Brown, 1958.)

multitask is relatively greater. But whatever our age, we do better and more efficient work when focused, without distractions, on one task at a time. *The bottom line:* It's probably a bad idea to try to watch TV, text your friends, and write a psychology paper all at the same time (Willingham, 2010)!

Unlike short-term memory capacity, working memory capacity appears to reflect intelligence level (Cowan, 2008; Shelton et al., 2010). Imagine seeing a letter of the alphabet, then a simple question, then another letter, followed by another question, and so on. In such experiments, those who could juggle the most mental balls—who could remember the most letters despite the interruptions—tended in everyday life to exhibit high intelligence and an ability to maintain their focus (Kane et al., 2007; Unsworth & Engle, 2007). When beeped to report in at various times, they were less likely than others to report that their mind was wandering. Those with a large working memory capacity—whose minds can juggle multiple items while processing information—tend also to retain more information after sleep and to be creative problem solvers (De Dreu et al., 2012; Fenn & Hambrick, 2012; Wiley & Jarosz, 2012).

LaunchPad For a review of memory stages and a test of your own short-term memory capacity, visit LaunchPad's *PsychSim 6: Short-Term Memory.*

RETRIEVAL PRACTICE

- What is the difference between *automatic* and *effortful* processing, and what are some examples of each?

ANSWER: *Automatic* processing occurs unconsciously (automatically) for such things as the sequence and frequency of a day's events, and reading and comprehending words in our own language. *Effortful* processing requires attention and awareness and happens, for example, when we work hard to learn new material in class, or new lines for a play.

- At which of Atkinson-Shiffrin's three memory stages would *iconic* and *echoic* memory occur?

ANSWER: sensory memory

---

1. M G V S R M T
2. W G V S R M T

3. VRESLI UEGBN GSORNW CDOUL LWLE NTOD WTO
4. SILVER BEGUN WRONGS CLOUD WELL DONT TWO

5. SILVER BEGUN WRONGS CLOUD DONT TWO
   HALF MAKE WELL HAS A
   EVERY IS RIGHT A DONE LINING

6. WELL BEGUN IS HALF DONE
   EVERY CLOUD HAS A SILVER LINING
   TWO WRONGS DONT MAKE A RIGHT

▼ FIGURE 24.7
Effects of chunking on memory
When Doug Hintzman (1978) showed people information similar to this, they recalled it more easily when it was organized into meaningful units, such as letters, words, and phrases.

Effortful Processing Strategies

24-7 What are some effortful processing strategies that can help us remember new information?

Several effortful processing strategies can boost our ability to form new memories. Later, when we try to retrieve a memory, these strategies can make the difference between success and failure.

CHUNKING Glance for a few seconds at the first set of letters in **FIGURE 24.7**, then look away and try to reproduce what you saw. Impossible, yes? But you can easily reproduce set 2, which is no less complex. Similarly, you will probably remember sets 4 and 6 more easily than the same elements in sets 3 and 5. As this demonstrates, **chunking** information—organizing items into familiar, manageable units—enables us to recall it more easily. Try remembering 43 individual numbers and letters. It would be impossible, unless chunked into, say, seven meaningful chunks, such as "Try remembering 43 individual numbers and letters." ☺

Chunking usually occurs so naturally that we take it for granted. If you are a native English speaker, you can reproduce perfectly the 150 or so line segments that make up the words in the three phrases of set 6 in Figure 24.7. It would astonish someone unfamiliar with the language. I am similarly awed at a Chinese reader's ability to glance at **FIGURE 24.8** and then reproduce all the strokes; or of a varsity basketball player's recall of the positions of the players after a 4-second glance at a basketball play (Allard & Burnett, 1985). We all remember information best when we can organize it into personally meaningful arrangements.

MNEMONICS To help them encode lengthy passages and speeches, ancient Greek scholars and orators developed **mnemonics.** Many of these memory aids use vivid imagery, because we are particularly good at remembering mental pictures. We more easily remember concrete, visualizable words than we do abstract words. (When we quiz you later, which three of these words—*bicycle, void, cigarette, inherent, fire, process*—will you most likely recall?) If you still recall the rock-throwing rioter sentence, it is probably not only because of the meaning you encoded but also because the sentence painted a mental image.

The *peg-word system* harnesses our superior visual imagery skill. This mnemonic requires you to memorize a jingle: *"One is a bun; two is a shoe; three is a tree; four is a door; five is a hive; six is sticks; seven is heaven; eight is a gate; nine is swine; ten is a hen."* Without much effort, you will soon be able to count by peg words instead of numbers: *bun, shoe, tree* . . . and then to visually associate the peg words with to-be-remembered items. Now you are ready to challenge anyone to give you a grocery list to remember. Carrots? Stick them into the imaginary bun. Milk? Fill the shoe with it. Paper towels? Drape them over the tree branch. Think *bun, shoe, tree* and you see their associated images: carrots, milk, paper towels. With few errors, you will be able to recall the items in any order and to name any given item (Bugelski et al., 1968). Memory whizzes understand the power of such systems. A study of star performers in the World Memory Championships showed them not to have exceptional intelligence, but rather to be superior at using mnemonic strategies (Maguire et al., 2003).

When combined, chunking and mnemonic techniques can be great memory aids for unfamiliar material. Want to remember the colors of the rainbow in order of wavelength? Think of the mnemonic ROY G. BIV (red, orange, yellow, green, blue, indigo, violet). Need to recall the names of North America's five Great Lakes? Just remember HOMES (Huron, Ontario, Michigan, Erie, Superior). In each case, we chunk information into a more familiar form by creating a word (called an *acronym*) from the first letters of the to-be-remembered items.

HIERARCHIES When people develop expertise in an area, they process information not only in chunks but also in *hierarchies* composed of a few broad concepts divided and subdivided into narrower concepts and facts. (Figure 25.4 in the next module provides a hierarchy of our automatic and effortful memory processing systems.) Organizing knowledge in hierarchies helps us retrieve information efficiently, as Gordon Bower and his colleagues (1969) demonstrated by presenting words either randomly or grouped into categories. When the words were grouped, recall was two to three times better. Such results show the benefits of organizing what you study—of giving special attention to module headings, numbered Learning Objective questions, Retrieval Practice questions, module reviews, and the Test Yourself questions. Taking lecture and text notes in outline format—a type of hierarchical organization—may also prove helpful.

Distributed Practice We retain information better when our encoding is distributed over time. More than 300 experiments over the past century have consistently revealed the benefits of this **spacing effect** (Cepeda et al., 2006). *Massed practice* (cramming) can produce speedy short-term learning and a feeling of confidence. But to paraphrase early memory researcher Hermann Ebbinghaus (1885), those who learn quickly also forget quickly. *Distributed practice* produces better long-term recall. After you've studied long enough to master the material, further study at that time becomes inefficient. Better to spend that extra reviewing time later—a day later if you need to remember something 10 days hence, or a month later if you need to remember something 6 months hence (Cepeda et al., 2008). The spacing effect is one of psychology's

春
夏
秋
冬

▼ FIGURE 24.8
An example of chunking—for those who read Chinese After looking at these characters, can you reproduce them exactly? If so, you are literate in Chinese.

chunking organizing items into familiar, manageable units; often occurs automatically.

mnemonics [nih-MON-iks] memory aids, especially those techniques that use vivid imagery and organizational devices.

spacing effect the tendency for distributed study or practice to yield better long-term retention than is achieved through massed study or practice.

Making things memorable
For suggestions on how to apply the testing effect to your own learning, watch this 5-minute animation: tinyurl.com/HowToRemember.

🅜 **LaunchPad** For a 14-minute tutorial and then a demonstration of how memory works, visit LaunchPad's *Lab: Levels of Processing.*

most reliable findings, and it extends to motor skills and online game performance, too (Stafford & Dewar, 2014). Memory researcher Henry Roediger (2013) sums it up: "Hundreds of studies have shown that distributed practice leads to more durable learning."

Distributing your learning over several months, rather than over a shorter term, can even help you retain information for a lifetime. In a 9-year experiment, Harry Bahrick and three family members (1993) practiced foreign language word translations for a given number of times, at intervals ranging from 14 to 56 days. Their consistent finding: The longer the space between practice sessions, the better their retention up to 5 years later.

One effective way to distribute practice is *repeated* self-testing, a phenomenon that researchers Roediger and Jeffrey Karpicke (2006) have called the **testing effect.** Testing does more than assess learning: It improves it (Karpicke, 2012; McDaniel, 2012). In this text, for example, the Retrieval Practice and Test Yourself questions offer such an opportunity. Better to practice retrieval (as any exam will demand) than merely to reread material (which may lull you into a false sense of mastery). Roediger (2013) explains, "Two techniques that students frequently report using for studying—highlighting (or underlining) text and rereading text—[have been found] ineffective." Happily, "retrieval practice (or testing) is [a] powerful and general strategy for learning." As another memory expert explained, "What we recall becomes more recallable" (Bjork, 2011).

The point to remember: Spaced study and self-assessment beat cramming and rereading. Practice may not make perfect, but smart practice—occasional rehearsal with self-testing—makes for lasting memories.

Levels of Processing

24-8 What are the levels of processing, and how do they affect encoding?

Memory researchers have discovered that we process verbal information at different levels, and that depth of processing affects our long-term retention. **Shallow processing** encodes on a very basic level, such as a word's letters or, at a more intermediate level, a word's sound. **Deep processing** encodes *semantically,* based on the meaning of the words. The deeper (more meaningful) the processing, the better our retention.

In one classic experiment, researchers Fergus Craik and Endel Tulving (1975) flashed words at people. Then they asked questions that would elicit different levels of processing. To experience the task yourself, rapidly answer the following sample questions:

Sample Questions to Elicit Different Levels of Processing	Word Flashed	Yes	No
Most shallow: Is the word in capital letters?	CHAIR	_____	_____
Shallow: Does the word rhyme with train?	brain	_____	_____
Deep: Would the word fit in this sentence? The girl put the _____ on the table.	doll	_____	_____

Which type of processing would best prepare you to recognize the words at a later time? In Craik and Tulving's experiment, the deeper, semantic processing triggered by the third question yielded a much better memory than did the shallower processing elicited by the second question or the very shallow processing elicited by the first question (which was especially ineffective).

Making Material Personally Meaningful If new information is not meaningful or related to our experience, we have trouble processing it. Put yourself in the place of the students who were asked to remember the following recorded passage:

> The procedure is actually quite simple. First you arrange things into different groups. Of course, one pile may be sufficient depending on how much there is to do. . . . After the procedure is completed, one arranges the materials into different groups again. Then they can be put into their appropriate places. Eventually they will be used once more and the whole cycle will then have to be repeated. However, that is part of life.

When the students heard the paragraph you have just read, without a meaningful context, they remembered little of it (Bransford & Johnson, 1972). When told the paragraph described washing clothes (something meaningful), they remembered much more of it—as you probably could now after rereading it.

Can you repeat the sentence about the rioter that we gave you at this module's beginning? ("The angry rioter threw . . .")?

Perhaps, like those in an experiment by William Brewer (1977), you recalled the sentence by the meaning you encoded when you read it (for example, "The angry rioter threw the rock *through* the window") and not as it was written ("The angry rioter threw the rock *at* the window"). Referring to such mental mismatches, some researchers have likened our minds to theater directors who, given a raw script, imagine the finished stage production (Bower & Morrow, 1990). Asked later what we heard or read, we recall not the literal text but *what we encoded.* Thus, studying for an exam, you may remember your lecture notes rather than the lecture itself.

We can avoid some of these mismatches by rephrasing information into meaningful terms. From his experiments on himself, Ebbinghaus estimated that, compared with learning nonsense material, learning meaningful material required one-tenth the effort. As memory researcher Wayne Wickelgren (1977, p. 346) noted, "The time you spend thinking about material you are reading and relating it to previously stored material is about the most useful thing you can do in learning any new subject matter."

Psychologist-actor team Helga Noice and Tony Noice (2006) have described how actors inject meaning into the daunting task of learning "all those lines." They do it by first coming to understand the flow of meaning: "One actor divided a half-page of dialogue into three [intentions]: 'to flatter,' 'to draw him out,' and 'to allay his fears'." With this meaningful sequence in mind, the actor more easily remembers the lines.

We have especially good recall for information we can meaningfully relate to ourselves. Asked how well certain adjectives describe someone else, we often forget them; asked how well the adjectives describe us, we remember the words well. This tendency, called the *self-reference effect,* is especially strong in members of individualist Western cultures (Symons & Johnson, 1997; Wagar & Cohen, 2003). Information deemed "relevant to me" is processed more deeply and remains more accessible. Knowing this, you can profit from taking time to find personal meaning in what you are studying.

The point to remember: The amount remembered depends both on the time spent learning and on your making it meaningful for deep processing.

testing effect enhanced memory after retrieving, rather than simply rereading, information. Also sometimes referred to as a *retrieval practice effect* or *test-enhanced learning.*

shallow processing encoding on a basic level based on the structure or appearance of words.

deep processing encoding semantically, based on the meaning of the words; tends to yield the best retention.

In the discussion of mnemonics, we gave you six words and told you we would quiz you about them later. How many of these words can you now recall? Of these, how many are high-imagery words? How many are low-imagery? (You can check your list against the six inverted words below.)

process
Bicycle, void, cigarette, inherent, fire,

RETRIEVAL PRACTICE

- Which strategies are better for long-term retention: cramming and rereading material, or spreading out learning over time and repeatedly testing yourself?

ANSWER: Although cramming may lead to short-term gains in knowledge, distributed practice and repeated self-testing will result in the greatest long-term retention.

- If you try to make the material you are learning personally meaningful, are you processing at a shallow or a deep level? Which level leads to greater retention?

ANSWER: Making material personally meaningful involves processing at a deep level, because you are processing *semantically*—based on the meaning of the words. Deep processing leads to greater retention.

MODULE 24 REVIEW Studying and Encoding Memories

LEARNING OBJECTIVES

RETRIEVAL PRACTICE Take a moment to answer each of these Learning Objective Questions (repeated here from within this module). Then turn to Appendix C, Complete Module Reviews, to check your answers. Research suggests that trying to answer these questions on your own will improve your long-term retention (McDaniel et al., 2009).

24-1 What is memory, and how is it measured?

24-2 How do psychologists describe the human memory system?

24-3 How do explicit and implicit memories differ?

24-4 What information do we process automatically?

24-5 How does sensory memory work?

24-6 What is the capacity of our short-term and working memory?

24-7 What are some effortful processing strategies that can help us remember new information?

24-8 What are the levels of processing, and how do they affect encoding?

TERMS AND CONCEPTS TO REMEMBER

RETRIEVAL PRACTICE Test yourself on these terms by trying to write down the definition before flipping back to the page number referenced to check your answer.

memory, p. 318

recall, p. 319

recognition, p. 319

relearning, p. 319

encoding, p. 320

storage, p. 320

retrieval, p. 320

parallel processing, p. 320

sensory memory, p. 320

short-term memory, p. 320

long-term memory, p. 320

working memory, 321

explicit memory, p. 321

effortful processing, p. 321

automatic processing, p. 321

implicit memory, p. 321

iconic memory, p. 323

echoic memory, p. 323

chunking, p. 324

mnemonics [nih-MON-iks], p. 325

spacing effect, p. 325

testing effect, p. 326

shallow processing, p. 326

deep processing, p. 326

Use **LearningCurve** to create your personalized study plan, which will direct you to the resources that will help you most in **LaunchPad**.

MODULE 25 Storing and Retrieving Memories

Memory Storage

25-1 What is the capacity of long-term memory? Are our long-term memories processed and stored in specific locations?

IN ARTHUR CONAN DOYLE'S *A Study in Scarlet*, Sherlock Holmes offers a popular theory of memory capacity:

> I consider that a man's brain originally is like a little empty attic, and you have to stock it with such furniture as you choose. . . . It is a mistake to think that that little room has elastic walls and can distend to any extent. Depend upon it, there comes a time when for every addition of knowledge you forget something that you knew before.

Contrary to Holmes' "memory model," our capacity for storing *long-term memories* is essentially limitless. Our brains are *not* like attics, which once filled can store more items only if we discard old ones.

Retaining Information in the Brain

I [DM] marveled at my aging mother-in-law, a retired pianist and organist. At age 88, her blind eyes could no longer read music. But let her sit at a keyboard and she would flawlessly play any of hundreds of hymns, including ones she had not thought of for 20 years. Where did her brain store those thousands of sequenced notes?

For a time, some surgeons and memory researchers recorded patients' seemingly vivid memories triggered by brain stimulation during surgery. Did this prove that our whole past, not just well-practiced music, is "in there," in complete detail, just waiting to be relived? On closer analysis, the seeming flashbacks appeared to have been invented, not a vivid reliving of long-forgotten experiences (Loftus & Loftus, 1980). In a further demonstration that memories do not reside in single, specific spots, psychologist Karl Lashley (1950) trained rats to find their way out of a maze, then surgically removed pieces of their brain's cortex and retested their memory. No matter which small brain section he removed, the rats retained at least a partial memory of how to navigate the maze. Memories *are* brain-based, but the brain distributes the components of a memory across a network of locations. These specific locations include some of the circuitry involved in the original experience: Some brain cells that fire when we experience something fire again when we recall it (G. Miller, 2012; J. F. Miller et al., 2013).

The point to remember: Despite the brain's vast **storage** capacity, we do not store information as libraries store their books, in single, precise locations. Instead, brain networks *encode*, store, and **retrieve** the information that forms our complex memories.

Explicit Memory System: The Frontal Lobes and Hippocampus

25-2 What are the roles of the frontal lobes and hippocampus in memory processing?

The network that processes and stores your **explicit memories** for facts and episodes includes your frontal lobes and hippocampus. When you summon up a mental encore of a past experience, many brain regions send input to your frontal lobes for *working memory* processing (Fink et al., 1996; Gabrieli et al., 1996; Markowitsch, 1995). The left and right frontal lobes process different types of memories. Recalling a password and holding it in working memory, for example, would activate the left frontal lobe. Calling up a visual party scene would more likely activate the right frontal lobe.

Cognitive neuroscientists have found that the **hippocampus,** a temporal-lobe-neural center located in the limbic system, is the brain's equivalent of a "save" button for explicit memories (**FIGURE 25.1**). The hippocampus and nearby brain networks are active as people form explicit memories of names, images, and events (Squire & Wixted, 2011).

Damage to this structure therefore disrupts recall of explicit memories. Chickadees and other birds can store food in hundreds of places and return to these unmarked caches months later—but not if their hippocampus has been removed (Kamil & Cheng, 2001; Sherry & Vaccarino, 1989). With left-hippocampus damage, people have trouble remembering verbal information, but they have no trouble recalling visual designs and locations. With right-hippocampus damage, the problem is reversed (Schacter, 1996).

Subregions of the hippocampus also serve different functions. One part is active as people learn to associate names with faces (Zeineh et al., 2003). Another part is active as memory champions engage in spatial *mnemonics* (Maguire et al., 2003b). The rear area, which processes spatial memory, grows bigger the longer a London cabbie has navigated the maze of streets (Woolett & Maguire, 2011).

Memories are not permanently stored in the hippocampus. Instead, this structure seems to act as a loading dock where the brain registers and temporarily holds the elements of a remembered episode—its smell, feel, sound, and location. Then, like older files shifted to a basement storeroom, memories migrate for storage elsewhere.

storage the process of retaining encoded information over time.

retrieval the process of getting information out of memory storage.

explicit memory memory of facts and experiences that one can consciously know and "declare." (Also called *declarative memory.*)

hippocampus a neural center located in the limbic system; helps process explicit memories for storage.

"Our memories are flexible and superimposable, a panoramic blackboard with an endless supply of chalk and erasers."

Elizabeth Loftus and Katherine Ketcham, *The Myth of Repressed Memory,* 1994

▼ FIGURE 25.1

The hippocampus Explicit memories for facts and episodes are processed in the hippocampus (orange structure) and fed to other brain regions for storage.

Roger Harris/Science Source

Hippocampus hero Among animals, one contender for champion memorist would be a mere birdbrain—the Clark's Nutcracker—which during winter and spring can locate up to 6000 caches of pine seed it had previously buried (Shettleworth, 1993).

off the mark.com   by Mark Parisi

THE BAD NEWS IS WE LEFT A CLAMP IN YOUR TEMPORAL LOBE... THE GOOD NEWS IS THAT YOU WON'T REMEMBER WHAT I JUST SAID...

Tim Zurowski/All Canada Photos/Corbis

This storage process is called **memory consolidation.** Removing a rat's hippocampus 3 hours after it learns the location of some tasty new food disrupts this process and prevents long-term memory formation; removal 48 hours later does not (Tse et al., 2007).

Sleep supports memory consolidation. During deep sleep, the hippocampus processes memories for later retrieval. After a training experience, the greater the hippocampus activity during sleep, the better the next day's memory will be (Peigneux et al., 2004). Researchers have watched the hippocampus and brain cortex displaying simultaneous activity rhythms during sleep, as if they were having a dialogue (Euston et al., 2007; Mehta, 2007). They suspect that the brain is replaying the day's experiences as it transfers them to the cortex for long-term storage. Cortex areas surrounding the hippocampus support the processing and storing of explicit memories (Squire & Zola-Morgan, 1991).

Implicit Memory System: The Cerebellum and Basal Ganglia

25-3 What roles do the cerebellum and basal ganglia play in memory processing?

Your hippocampus and frontal lobes are processing sites for your *explicit* memories. But you could lose those areas and still, thanks to *automatic* (not *effortful*) *processing,* lay down **implicit memories** for skills and newly conditioned associations. Joseph LeDoux (1996) recounted the story of a brain-damaged patient whose amnesia left her unable to recognize her physician as, each day, he shook her hand and introduced himself. One day, she yanked her hand back, for the physician had pricked her with a tack in his palm. The next time he returned, she refused to shake his hand but couldn't explain why. Having been *classically conditioned,* she just wouldn't do it. Intuitively (implicitly) she felt what she could not explain.

The *cerebellum* plays a key role in forming and storing the implicit memories created by classical conditioning. With a damaged cerebellum, people cannot develop certain conditioned reflexes, such as associating a tone with an impending puff of air—and thus do not blink in anticipation of the puff (Daum & Schugens, 1996; Green & Woodruff-Pak, 2000). When researchers surgically disrupted the function of different pathways in the cerebellum of rabbits, the rabbits became unable to learn a conditioned eyeblink response (Krupa et al., 1993; Steinmetz, 1999). Implicit memory formation needs the cerebellum.

The *basal ganglia,* deep brain structures involved in motor movement, facilitate formation of our procedural memories for skills (Mishkin, 1982; Mishkin et al., 1997). The basal ganglia receive input from the cortex but do not return the favor of sending information back to the cortex for conscious awareness of procedural learning. If you have learned how to ride a bike, thank your basal ganglia.

Our implicit memory system, enabled by the cerebellum and basal ganglia, helps explain why the reactions and skills we learned during infancy reach far into our future. Yet as adults, our *conscious* memory of our first three years is blank, an experience called *infantile amnesia.* In one study, events children experienced and discussed with their mothers at age 3 were 60 percent remembered at age 7 but only 34 percent remembered at age 9 (Bauer et al., 2007). Two influences contribute to infantile amnesia: First, we index much of our explicit memory using words that nonspeaking children have not learned. Second, the hippocampus is one of the last brain structures to mature, and as it does, more gets retained (Akers et al., 2014).

memory consolidation the neural storage of a long-term memory.

implicit memory retention of learned skills or classically conditioned associations independent of conscious recollection. (Also called *nondeclarative memory.*)

RETRIEVAL PRACTICE

- Which parts of the brain are important for *implicit* memory processing, and which parts play a key role in *explicit* memory processing?

ANSWER: The cerebellum and basal ganglia are important for *implicit* memory processing and the frontal lobes and hippocampus are key to *explicit* memory formation.

- Your friend has experienced brain damage in an accident. He can remember how to tie his shoes but has a hard time remembering anything told to him during a conversation. What's going on here?

ANSWER: Our *explicit* conscious memories of facts and episodes differ from our *implicit* memories of skills (such as shoe tying) and classically conditioned responses. Our implicit memories are processed by more ancient brain areas, which apparently escaped damage during the accident.

The Amygdala, Emotions, and Memory

25-4 How do emotions affect our memory processing?

Our emotions trigger stress hormones that influence memory formation. When we are excited or stressed, these hormones make more glucose energy available to fuel brain activity, signaling the brain that something important has happened. Moreover, stress hormones focus memory. Stress provokes the *amygdala* (two limbic system, emotion-processing clusters) to initiate a memory trace in the frontal lobes and basal ganglia and to boost activity in the brain's memory-forming areas (Buchanan, 2007; Kensinger, 2007) (**FIGURE 25.2**). The result? Emotional arousal can sear certain events into the brain, while disrupting memory for neutral events (Birnbaum et al., 2004; Brewin et al., 2007).

Emotions often persist without our conscious awareness of what caused them. In one ingenious experiment, patients with hippocampal damage (which left them unable to form new explicit memories) watched a sad film and later a happy film. After the viewing, they did not consciously recall the films, but the sad or happy emotion persisted (Feinstein et al., 2010).

Significantly stressful events can form almost indelible memories. After traumatic experiences—a school shooting, a house fire, a rape—vivid recollections of the horrific event may intrude again and again. It is as if they were burned in: "Stronger emotional experiences make for stronger, more reliable memories," noted James McGaugh (1994, 2003). This makes adaptive sense. Memory serves to predict the future and to alert us to potential dangers. Emotional events produce tunnel vision memory. They focus our attention and recall on high priority information, and reduce our recall of irrelevant details (Mather & Sutherland, 2012). Whatever rivets our attention gets well recalled, at the expense of the surrounding context.

Emotion-triggered hormonal changes help explain why we long remember exciting or shocking events, such as our first kiss or our whereabouts when learning of a loved one's death. In a 2006 Pew survey, 95 percent of American adults said they could recall exactly where they were or what they were doing when they first heard the news of the 9/11 terrorist attacks. This perceived clarity of memories of surprising, significant events leads some psychologists to call them **flashbulb memories.** It's as if the brain commands, "Capture this!"

The people who experienced a 1989 San Francisco earthquake did just that. A year and a half later, they had perfect recall of where they had been and what they were doing (verified by their recorded thoughts within a day or two of the quake). Others' memories for the circumstances under which they merely *heard* about the quake were more prone to errors (Neisser et al., 1991; Palmer et al., 1991).

Our flashbulb memories are noteworthy for their vividness and our confidence in them. But as we relive, rehearse, and discuss them, these memories may come to err. With time, some errors crept into people's 9/11 recollections (compared with their earlier reports taken

▼ FIGURE 25.2
Review key memory structures in the brain
Frontal lobes and *hippocampus:* explicit memory formation
Cerebellum and *basal ganglia:* implicit memory formation
Amygdala: emotion-related memory formation

Which is more important—your experiences or your memories of them?

---

flashbulb memory a clear memory of an emotionally significant moment or event.

right after 9/11). Mostly, however, people's memories of 9/11 remained consistent over the next two to three years (Conway et al., 2009; Hirst et al., 2009; Kvavilashvili et al., 2009).

Dramatic experiences remain bright and clear in our memory in part because we rehearse them. We think about them and describe them to others. Memories of our best experiences, which we enjoy recalling and recounting, also endure (Storm & Jobe, 2012; Talarico & Moore, 2012). One study invited 1563 Boston Red Sox and New York Yankees fans to recall the baseball championship games between their two teams in 2003 (Yankees won) and 2004 (Red Sox won). Fans recalled much better the game their team won (Breslin & Safer, 2011).

Synaptic Changes

25-5 How do changes at the synapse level affect our memory processing?

As you read this module and think and learn about memory, your brain is changing. Given increased activity in particular pathways, neural interconnections are forming and strengthening.

The quest to understand the physical basis of memory—how information becomes embedded in brain matter—has sparked study of the synaptic meeting places where neurons communicate with one another via their neurotransmitter messengers. Eric Kandel and James Schwartz (1982) observed synaptic changes during learning in the neurons of the California sea slug, *Aplysia*, a simple animal with a mere 20,000 or so unusually large and accessible nerve cells. Other modules describe how the sea slug can be classically conditioned (with electric shock) to reflexively withdraw its gills when squirted with water, much as a battle-weary soldier jumps at the sound of a snapping twig. When learning occurs, Kandel and Schwartz discovered, the slug releases more of the neurotransmitter *serotonin* into certain neurons. These synapses then become more efficient at transmitting signals. Experience and learning can increase—even double—the number of synapses, even in slugs (Kandel, 2012).

In experiments with people, rapidly stimulating certain memory-circuit connections has increased their sensitivity for hours or even weeks to come. The sending neuron now needs less prompting to release its neurotransmitter, and more connections exist between neurons. This increased efficiency of potential neural firing, called **long-term potentiation (LTP)**, provides a neural basis for learning and remembering associations (Lynch, 2002; Whitlock et al., 2006) (**FIGURE 25.3**). Several lines of evidence confirm that LTP is a physical basis for memory:

- Drugs that block LTP interfere with learning (Lynch & Staubli, 1991).

- Mutant mice engineered to lack an enzyme needed for LTP couldn't learn their way out of a maze (Silva et al., 1992).

- Rats given a drug that enhanced LTP learned a maze with half the usual number of mistakes (Service, 1994).

After long-term potentiation has occurred, passing an electric current through the brain won't disrupt old memories. But the current will wipe out very recent memories. Such is the experience both of laboratory animals and of severely depressed people given *electroconvulsive therapy (ECT)*. A blow to the head can do the same. Football players and boxers momentarily knocked unconscious typically have no memory of events just before the knockout (Yarnell & Lynch, 1970). Their working memory had no time to consolidate the information into long-term memory before the lights went out.

Aplysia The California sea slug, which neuroscientist Eric Kandel studied for 45 years, has increased our understanding of the neural basis of learning.

▼ FIGURE 25.3

Doubled receptor sites An electron microscope image (a) shows just one receptor site (gray) reaching toward a sending neuron before long-term potentiation. Image (b) shows that, after LTP, the receptor sites have doubled. This means the receiving neuron has increased sensitivity for detecting the presence of the neurotransmitter molecules that may be released by the sending neuron. (From Toni et al., 1999.)

(a)

(b)

Recently, I [DM] did a little test of memory consolidation. While on an operating table for a basketball-related tendon repair, I was given a face mask and soon could smell the anesthesia gas. "So how much longer will I be with you?" I asked the anesthesiologist. My last moment of memory was her answer: "About 10 seconds." My brain spent that 10 seconds consolidating a memory for her words, but could not tuck any further memory away before I was out cold.

Some memory-biology explorers have helped found companies that are competing to develop memory-altering drugs. The target market for memory-boosting drugs includes millions of people with Alzheimer's disease, millions more with *mild cognitive impairment* that often becomes Alzheimer's, and countless millions who would love to turn back the clock on age-related memory decline. From expanding memories perhaps will come bulging profits.

One approach to improving memory focuses on drugs that boost the LTP-enhancing neurotransmitter *glutamate* (Lynch et al., 2011). Another approach involves developing drugs that boost production of CREB, a protein that also enhances the LTP process (Fields, 2005). Boosting CREB production might trigger increased production of other proteins that help reshape synapses and transfer short-term memories into long-term memories. Sea slugs, mice, and fruit flies with enhanced CREB production have displayed enhanced learning.

Other people wish for memory-blocking drugs. Among them are those who would welcome a drug that, when taken after a traumatic experience, might blunt intrusive memories (Adler, 2012; Kearns et al., 2012). In one experiment, victims of car accidents, rapes, and other traumas received, for 10 days following their horrific event, either one such drug, propranolol, or a placebo. When tested three months later, half the placebo group but none of the drug-treated group showed signs of stress disorder (Pitman et al., 2002, 2005).

In your lifetime, will you have access to safe and legal drugs that boost your fading memory without nasty side effects and without cluttering your mind with trivia best forgotten? That question has yet to be answered. But in the meantime, one effective, safe, and free memory enhancer is already available on your college campus: effective study techniques followed by adequate *sleep!*

FIGURE 25.4 summarizes the brain's two-track memory processing and storage system for implicit (automatic) and explicit (effortful) memories. *The bottom line:* Learn something and you change your brain a little.

> **long-term potentiation (LTP)** an increase in a cell's firing potential after brief, rapid stimulation. Believed to be a neural basis for learning and memory.

▼ FIGURE 25.4
Our two memory systems

Memory processing

Automatic → Implicit memories (Nondeclarative) Without conscious recall → Processed in cerebellum and basal ganglia → Space, time, frequency (where you ate dinner yesterday) | Motor and cognitive skills (riding a bike) | Classical conditioning (reaction to dentist's office)

Effortful → Explicit memories (Declarative) With conscious recall → Processed in hippocampus and frontal lobes → Facts and general knowledge (this module's concepts) | Personally experienced events (family holidays)

Memory Retrieval

After the magic of brain encoding and storage, we still have the daunting task of retrieving the information. What triggers retrieval?

Retrieval Cues

25-6 How do external cues, internal emotions, and order of appearance influence memory retrieval?

Imagine a spider suspended in the middle of her web, held up by the many strands extending outward from her in all directions to different points. If you were to trace a pathway to the spider, you would first need to create a path from one of these anchor points and then follow the strand down into the web.

The process of retrieving a memory follows a similar principle, because memories are held in storage by a web of associations, each piece of information interconnected with others. When you encode into memory a target piece of information, such as the name of the person sitting next to you in class, you associate with it other bits of information about your surroundings, mood, seating position, and so on. These bits can serve as *retrieval cues* that you can later use to access the information. The more retrieval cues you have, the better your chances of finding a route to the suspended memory.

The best retrieval cues come from associations we form at the time we encode a memory—smells, tastes, and sights that can evoke our memory of the associated person or event. To call up visual cues when trying to recall something, we may mentally place ourselves in the original context. After losing his sight, British scholar John Hull (1990, p. 174) described his difficulty recalling such details:

> I knew I had been somewhere, and had done particular things with certain people, but where? I could not put the conversations . . . into a context. There was no background, no features against which to identify the place. Normally, the memories of people you have spoken to during the day are stored in frames which include the background.

───────────────────────────────────

🎬 **LaunchPad** For an 8-minute synopsis of how we access what's stored in our brain, visit LaunchPad's *Video: Memory Retrieval.*

───────────────────────────────────

Priming Often our associations are activated without our awareness. Philosopher-psychologist William James referred to this process, which we call **priming**, as the "wakening of associations." Seeing or hearing the word *rabbit* primes associations with *hare*, even though we may not recall having seen or heard *rabbit* (**FIGURE 25.5**).

Priming is often "memoryless memory"—invisible memory, without your conscious awareness. If, walking down a hallway, you see a poster of a missing child, you will then unconsciously be primed to interpret an ambiguous adult-child interaction as a possible kidnapping (James, 1986). Although you no longer have the poster in mind, it predisposes your interpretation. Meeting someone who reminds us of a person we've previously met can awaken our associated feelings about that earlier person, which may transfer into the new context (Andersen & Saribay, 2005; Lewicki, 1985).

"Memory is not like a container that gradually fills up; it is more like a tree growing hooks onto which memories are hung."

Peter Russell, *The Brain Book,* 1979

Ask a friend two rapid-fire questions: (a) How do you pronounce the word spelled by the letters *s-h-o-p*? (b) What do you do when you come to a green light? If your friend answers "stop" to the second question, you have demonstrated priming.

▼ FIGURE 25.5
Priming—awakening associations
After seeing or hearing *rabbit,* we are later more likely to spell the spoken word as *h-a-r-e* (Bower, 1986). Associations unconsciously activate related associations. This process is called priming.

Priming can influence behaviors as well (Herring et al., 2013). In one study, participants primed with money-related words were less likely to help another person when asked (Vohs et al., 2006). In another, people primed with money words or images expressed more support for free-market capitalism and social inequality (Caruso et al., 2013). In such cases, money may prime our materialism and self-interest rather than the social norms that encourage us to help (Ariely, 2009).

Context-Dependent Memory Have you noticed? Putting yourself back in the context where you experienced something, such as in a childhood home or neighborhood, can prime your memory retrieval. As **FIGURE 25.6** illustrates, when scuba divers listened to a word list in two different settings (either 10 feet underwater or sitting on the beach), they recalled more words if retested in the same place (Godden & Baddeley, 1975).

By contrast, experiencing something outside the usual setting can be confusing. Have you ever run into your doctor in an unusual place, such as at the store or park? You knew the person but struggled to figure out who it was and how you were acquainted? The **encoding specificity principle** helps us understand how cues *specific* to an event or person will most effectively trigger that memory. In new settings, you may not have the memory cues needed for speedy face recognition. Our memories depend on *context,* and on the cues we have associated with that context.

> **priming** the activation, often unconsciously, of particular associations in memory.
>
> **encoding specificity principle** the idea that cues and contexts specific to a particular memory will be most effective in helping us recall it.

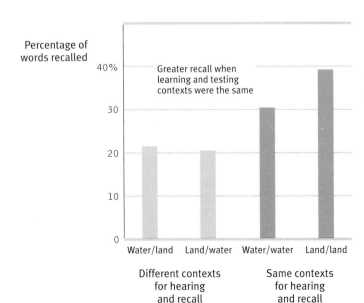

Greater recall when learning and testing contexts were the same

Percentage of words recalled

Different contexts for hearing and recall — Water/land, Land/water

Same contexts for hearing and recall — Water/water, Land/land

Alexis Rosenfeld/Science Source

▼ FIGURE 25.6
The effects of context on memory Words heard underwater were best recalled underwater; words heard on land were best recalled on land. (Data from Godden & Baddeley, 1975.)

In several experiments, Carolyn Rovee-Collier (1993) found that a familiar context could activate memories even in 3-month-olds. After infants learned that kicking a crib mobile would make it move (via a connecting ribbon from the ankle), the infants kicked more when tested again in the same crib with the same bumper than when in a different context.

State-Dependent Memory Closely related to context-dependent memory is *state-dependent memory.* What we learn in one state—be it drunk or sober—may be more easily recalled when we are again in that state. What people learn when drunk they don't recall well in any state (alcohol disrupts storage). But they recall it slightly better when again drunk. Someone who hides money when drunk may forget the location until drunk again.

Our mood states provide an example of memory's state dependence. Emotions that accompany good or bad events become retrieval cues (Fiedler et al., 2001). Thus, our memories are somewhat **mood congruent**. If you've had a bad evening—your date never showed, your Toledo Mud Hens hat disappeared, your TV went out 10 minutes before the end of a show—your gloomy mood may facilitate recalling other bad times. Being depressed sours memories by priming negative associations, which we then use to explain our current mood. In many experiments, people put in a buoyant mood—whether under hypnosis or just by the day's events (a World Cup soccer victory for German participants in one study)—have recalled the world through rose-colored glasses (DeSteno et al., 2000; Forgas et al., 1984; Schwarz et al., 1987). They judged themselves competent and effective, other people benevolent, happy events more likely.

Knowing this mood-memory connection, we should not be surprised that in some studies *currently* depressed people have recalled their parents as rejecting, punitive, and guilt promoting, whereas *formerly* depressed people's recollections more closely resembled the more positive descriptions given by those who never suffered depression (Lewinsohn & Rosenbaum, 1987; Lewis, 1992). Similarly, adolescents' ratings of parental warmth in one week gave little clue to how they would rate their parents six weeks later (Bornstein et al., 1991). When teens were down, their parents seemed inhuman; as their mood brightened, their parents morphed from devils into angels. We may nod our heads knowingly. Yet, in a good or bad mood, we persist in attributing to reality our own changing judgments, memories, and interpretations. In a bad mood, we may read someone's look as a glare and feel even worse. In a good mood, we may encode the same look as interest and feel even better. Passions exaggerate.

Mood effects on retrieval help explain why our moods persist. When happy, we recall happy events and therefore see the world as a happy place, which helps prolong our good mood. When depressed, we recall sad events, which darkens our interpretations of current events. For those of us with a predisposition to depression, this process can help maintain a vicious, dark cycle.

Serial Position Effect Another memory-retrieval quirk, the **serial position effect,** explains why we may have large holes in our memory of a list of recent events. Imagine it's your first day in a new job, and your manager is introducing co-workers. As you meet each person, you silently repeat everyone's name, starting from the beginning. As the last person smiles and turns away, you feel confident you'll be able to greet your new co-workers by name the next day.

Don't count on it. Because you have spent more time rehearsing the earlier names than the later ones, those are the names you'll probably recall more easily the next day. In experiments, when people viewed a list of items (words, names, dates, even odors) and immediately tried to recall them in any order, they fell prey to the serial position

"I can't remember what we're arguing about, either. Let's keep yelling, and maybe it will come back to us."

"When a feeling was there, they felt as if it would never go; when it was gone, they felt as if it had never been; when it returned, they felt as if it had never gone."

George MacDonald, *What's Mine's Mine,* 1886

mood-congruent memory the tendency to recall experiences that are consistent with one's current good or bad mood.

serial position effect our tendency to recall best the last (a *recency effect*) and first (a *primacy effect*) items in a list.

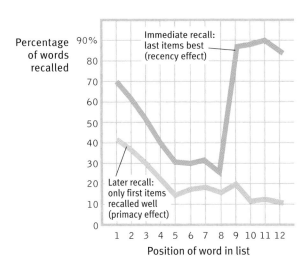

Percentage of words recalled

Immediate recall: last items best (recency effect)

Later recall: only first items recalled well (primacy effect)

Position of word in list

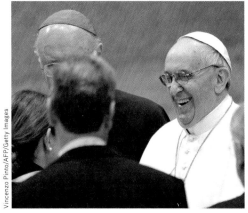

Vincenzo Pinto/AFP/Getty Images

▼ FIGURE 25.7
The serial position effect Immediately after Pope Francis made his way through this receiving line of special guests, he would probably have recalled the names of the last few people best *(recency effect).* But later he may have been able to recall the first few people best *(primacy effect).*

effect (Reed, 2000). They briefly recalled the last items especially quickly and well (a *recency effect*), perhaps because those last items were still in working memory. But after a delay, when their attention was elsewhere, their recall was best for the first items (a *primacy effect*; see **FIGURE** 25.7).

RETRIEVAL PRACTICE

• What is priming?

ANSWER: *Priming* is the activation (often without our awareness) of associations. Seeing a gun, for example, might temporarily predispose someone to interpret an ambiguous face as threatening or to recall a boss as nasty.

• When we are tested immediately after viewing a list of words, we tend to recall the first and last items best, which is known as the _____ _____ effect.

ANSWER: serial position

MODULE 25 REVIEW Storing and Retrieving Memories

LEARNING OBJECTIVES

RETRIEVAL PRACTICE Take a moment to answer each of these Learning Objective Questions (repeated here from within this module). Then turn to Appendix C, Complete Module Reviews, to check your answers. Research suggests that trying to answer these questions on your own will improve your long-term retention (McDaniel et al., 2009).

25-1 What is the capacity of long-term memory? Are our long-term memories processed and stored in specific locations?

25-2 What are the roles of the frontal lobes and hippocampus in memory processing?

25-3 What roles do the cerebellum and basal ganglia play in memory processing?

25-4 How do emotions affect our memory processing?

25-5 How do changes at the synapse level affect our memory processing?

25-6 How do external cues, internal emotions, and order of appearance influence memory retrieval?

TERMS AND CONCEPTS TO REMEMBER

RETRIEVAL PRACTICE Test yourself on these terms by trying to write down the definition before flipping back to the page number referenced to check your answer.

storage, p. 329

retrieval, p. 329

explicit memory, p. 329

hippocampus, p. 329

memory consolidation, p. 330

implicit memory, p. 330

flashbulb memory, p. 331

long-term potentiation (LTP), p. 332

priming, p. 334

encoding specificity principle, p. 335

mood-congruent memory, p. 336

serial position effect, p. 336

Use 🍄 LearningCurve to create your personalized study plan, which will direct you to the resources that will help you most in 🍄 LaunchPad.

"Oh, is that today?"

Later in this module we will ask you to recall this sentence: *The fish attacked the swimmer.*

The woman who can't forget "A. J." in real life is Jill Price, who, with writer Bart Davis, told her story in a 2008 published memoir. Price remembers every day of her life since age 14 with detailed clarity, including both the joys and the hurts. Researchers have identified enlarged brain areas in such "super memory" people (Ally et al., 2013; LePort et al., 2012).

Forgetting, Memory Construction, and Improving Memory

Forgetting

26-1 Why do we forget?

AMID ALL THE APPLAUSE FOR memory—all the efforts to understand it, all the books on how to improve it—have any voices been heard in praise of forgetting? William James (1890, p. 680) was such a voice: "If we remembered everything, we should on most occasions be as ill off as if we remembered nothing." To discard the clutter of useless or out-of-date information—where we parked the car yesterday, our old phone number, restaurant orders already cooked and served—is surely a blessing. The Russian memory whiz Solomon Shereshevskii (or S, as he was known), was haunted by his junk heap of memories. They dominated his consciousness. He had difficulty thinking abstractly—generalizing, organizing, evaluating. After reading a story, he could recite it but would struggle to summarize its gist.

A more recent case of a life overtaken by memory is "A. J.," whose experience has been studied and verified by a University of California at Irvine research team, along with several dozen other "highly superior autobiographical memory" cases (McGaugh & LePort, 2014; Parker et al., 2006). A. J., who has identified herself as Jill Price, compares her memory to "a running movie that never stops. It's like a split screen. I'll be talking to someone and seeing something else. . . . Whenever I see a date flash on the television (or anywhere for that matter) I automatically go back to that day and remember where I was, what I was doing, what day it fell on, and on and on and on and on. It is nonstop, uncontrollable, and totally exhausting." A good memory is helpful, but so is the ability to forget. If a memory-enhancing pill ever becomes available, it had better not be *too* effective.

More often, however, our unpredictable memory dismays and frustrates us. Memories are quirky. My [DM] own memory can easily call up such episodes as that wonderful first kiss with the woman I love, or trivial facts like the air mileage from London to Detroit. Then it abandons me when I discover I have failed to *encode, store,* or *retrieve* a student's name or where I left my sunglasses.

Forgetting and the Two-Track Mind

For some, memory loss is severe and permanent. Consider Henry Molaison (known as "H. M.," 1926–2008). For 55 years after the removal of much of his hippocampus to stop severe seizures, Molaison was unable to form new conscious memories. He was, as before his surgery, intelligent and did daily crossword puzzles. Yet, reported neuroscientist Suzanne Corkin (2005, 2013), "I've known H. M. since 1962, and he still doesn't know who I am." For about half a minute he could keep something in mind, enough to carry on a conversation. When distracted, he would lose what was just said or what had just occurred. Without the neural tissue for turning new information into long-term memories, he never could name the current president of the United States (Ogden, 2012).

Molaison suffered from **anterograde amnesia**—he could recall his past, but he could not form new memories. (Those who cannot recall their past—the old information stored in long-term memory—suffer from **retrograde amnesia**.)

Neurologist Oliver Sacks (1985, pp. 26–27) described another patient, Jimmie, who had anterograde amnesia resulting from brain damage. Jimmie had no memories—thus, no sense of elapsed time—beyond his injury in 1945.

When Jimmie gave his age as 19, Sacks set a mirror before him: "Look in the mirror and tell me what you see. Is that a 19-year-old looking out from the mirror?"

Jimmie turned ashen, gripped the chair, cursed, then became frantic: "What's going on? What's happened to me? Is this a nightmare? Am I crazy? Is this a joke?" When his attention was diverted to some children playing baseball, his panic ended, the dreadful mirror forgotten.

Sacks showed Jimmie a photo from *National Geographic*. "What is this?" he asked. "It's the Moon," Jimmie replied.

"No, it's not," Sacks answered. "It's a picture of the Earth taken from the Moon."

"Doc, you're kidding! Someone would've had to get a camera up there!"

"Naturally."

"Hell! You're joking—how the hell would you do that?" Jimmie's wonder was that of a bright young man from 40 years previous reacting with amazement to his travel back to the future.

Careful testing of these unique people reveals something even stranger: Although incapable of recalling new facts or anything they have done recently, Molaison, Jimmie, and others with similar conditions can learn nonverbal tasks. Shown hard-to-find figures in pictures (in the *Where's Waldo?* series), they can quickly spot them again later. They can find their way to the bathroom, though without being able to tell you where it is. They can learn to read mirror-image writing or do a jigsaw puzzle, and they have even been taught complicated job skills (Schacter, 1992, 1996; Xu & Corkin, 2001). They can be classically conditioned. However, *they do all these things with no awareness of having learned them.* "Well, this is strange," Molaison said, after demonstrating his nondeclarative memory of skillful mirror tracing. "I thought that would be difficult. But it seems as though I've done it quite well" (Shapin, 2013).

Molaison and Jimmie lost their ability to form new explicit memories, but their automatic processing ability remained intact. Like Alzheimer's patients, whose *explicit* memories for new people and events are lost, they could form new *implicit* memories (Lustig & Buckner, 2004). These patients can learn *how* to do something, but they will have no conscious recall of learning their new skill. Such sad cases confirm that we have two distinct memory systems, controlled by different parts of the brain.

For most of us, forgetting is a less drastic process. Let's consider some of the reasons we forget.

Encoding Failure

Much of what we sense we never notice, and what we fail to encode, we will never remember (**FIGURE 26.1** on the next page). The English novelist and critic C. S. Lewis (1967, p. 107) described the enormity of what we never encode:

> Each of us finds that in [our] own life every moment of time is completely filled. [We are] bombarded every second by sensations, emotions, thoughts . . . nine-tenths of which [we] must simply ignore. The past [is] a roaring cataract of billions upon billions of such moments: Any one of them too complex to grasp in its entirety, and the aggregate beyond all imagination. . . . At every tick of the clock, in every inhabited part of the world, an unimaginable richness and variety of 'history' falls off the world into total oblivion.

Age can affect encoding efficiency. The brain areas that jump into action when young adults encode new information are less responsive in older adults. This slower encoding helps explain age-related memory decline (Grady et al., 1995).

But no matter how young we are, we selectively attend to few of the myriad sights and sounds continually bombarding us. Consider this example: If you live in the United States, you have looked at thousands of pennies in your lifetime. You can surely recall their color and size, but can you recall what the side with the head looks like? If not, let's make the memory test easier: If you are familiar with U.S. coins, can you, in

"*Waiter, I'd like to order, unless I've eaten, in which case bring me the check.*"

anterograde amnesia an inability to form new memories.

retrograde amnesia an inability to retrieve information from one's past.

Henry Molaison In an effort to reduce his severe seizures, surgeons removed part of Molaison's hippocampus, along with some nearby tissue. This resulted "in severe disconnection of the remaining hippocampus" from the rest of the brain (Annese et al., 2014).

🔵 **LaunchPad** For a 6-minute example of another dramatic case—of an accomplished musician who has lost the ability to form new memories—visit LaunchPad's *Video—Clive Wearing: Living Without Memory.*

▼ FIGURE 26.1
Forgetting as encoding failure
We cannot remember what we
have not encoded.

▼ FIGURE 26.2
Test your memory Which of these
U.S. pennies is the real thing? (If you
live outside the United States, try drawing one of your own country's coins.)
(From Nickerson & Adams, 1979.) See
answer below.

The first penny (a) is the real penny.

FIGURE 26.2, just *recognize* the real thing? Most people cannot (Nickerson & Adams, 1979). Likewise, few British people can draw from memory the details of a one-pence coin (Richardson, 1993). The details of these coins are not very meaningful, nor are they essential for distinguishing them from other coins. Without encoding effort, many potential memories never form.

Storage Decay

Even after encoding something well, we sometimes later forget it. To study the durability of stored memories, Hermann Ebbinghaus (1885) learned lists of nonsense syllables and measured how much he retained when relearning each list, from 20 minutes to 30 days later. The result, confirmed by later experiments, was his famous forgetting curve: *The course of forgetting is initially rapid, then levels off with time* (FIGURE 26.3; Wixted & Ebbesen, 1991). Harry Bahrick (1984) found a similar forgetting curve for Spanish vocabulary learned in school. Compared with those just completing a high school or college Spanish course, people 3 years out of school had forgotten much of what they had learned (FIGURE 26.4). However, what people remembered then, they still remembered 25 and more years later. Their forgetting had leveled off.

▼ FIGURE 26.3
Ebbinghaus' forgetting curve
After learning lists of nonsense
syllables, such as YOX and JIH,
Ebbinghaus studied how much he
retained up to 30 days later. He
found that memory for novel information fades quickly, then levels
out. (Data from Ebbinghaus, 1885.)

One explanation for these forgetting curves is a gradual fading of the physical memory trace. Cognitive neuroscientists are getting closer to solving the mystery of the physical storage of memory and are increasing our understanding of how memory storage could decay. Like books you can't find in your campus library, memories may be inaccessible for many reasons. Some were never acquired (not encoded). Others were discarded (stored memories decay). And others are out of reach because we can't retrieve them.

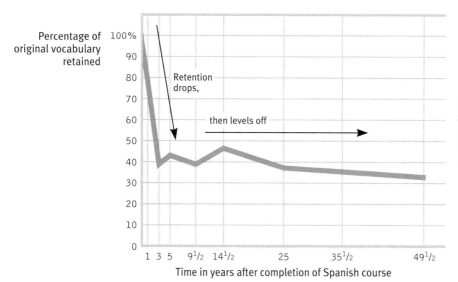

Percentage of original vocabulary retained

Time in years after completion of Spanish course

▼ FIGURE 26.4
The forgetting curve for Spanish learned in school Compared with people just completing a Spanish course, those 3 years out of the course remembered much less (on a vocabulary recognition test). Compared with the 3-year group, however, those who studied Spanish even longer ago did not forget much more. (Data from Bahrick, 1984.)

Retrieval Failure

Often, forgetting is not memories faded but memories unretrieved. We store in long-term memory what's important to us or what we've rehearsed. But sometimes important events defy our attempts to access them (**FIGURE 26.5**). How frustrating when a name lies poised on the tip of our tongue, just beyond reach. Given retrieval cues (*"It begins with an M"*), we may easily retrieve the elusive memory. Retrieval problems contribute to the occasional memory failures of older adults, who more frequently are frustrated by tip-of-the-tongue forgetting (Abrams, 2008; Salthouse & Mandell, 2013).

Do you recall the gist of the sentence we asked you to remember? If not, does the word *shark* serve as a retrieval cue? Experiments show that *shark* (likely what you visualized) more readily retrieves the image you stored than does the sentence's actual word, *fish* (Anderson et al., 1976). (The sentence was *"The fish attacked the swimmer."*)

But retrieval problems occasionally stem from interference and, perhaps, from motivated forgetting.

Deaf persons fluent in sign language experience a parallel "tip of the fingers" phenomenon (Thompson et al., 2005).

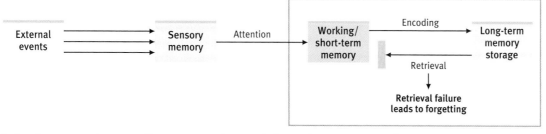

▼ FIGURE 26.5
Retrieval failure Sometimes even stored information cannot be accessed, which leads to forgetting.

Interference As you collect more and more information, your mental attic never fills, but it surely gets cluttered. An ability to tune out clutter helps people to focus, and focusing helps us recall information. Sometimes, however, clutter wins, and new learning and old collide. **Proactive** *(forward-acting)* **interference** occurs when prior learning disrupts your recall of new information. If you buy a new combination lock, your well-rehearsed old combination may interfere with your retrieval of the new one.

Retroactive *(backward-acting)* **interference** occurs when new learning disrupts recall of old information. If someone sings new lyrics to the tune of an old song, you may have trouble remembering the original words. It is rather like a second stone tossed in a pond, disrupting the waves rippling out from the first.

proactive interference the forward-acting disruptive effect of prior learning on the recall of new information.

retroactive interference the backward-acting disruptive effect of new learning on the recall of old information.

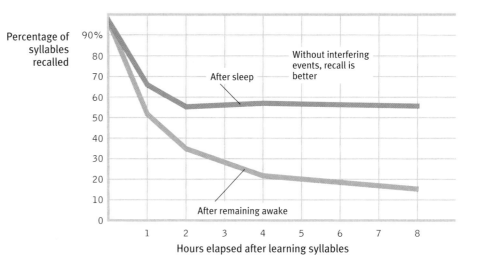

▼ FIGURE 26.6
Retroactive interference More forgetting occurred when a person stayed awake and experienced other new material. (Data from Jenkins & Dallenbach, 1924.)

repression in psychoanalytic theory, the basic defense mechanism that banishes from consciousness anxiety-arousing thoughts, feelings, and memories.

reconsolidation a process in which previously stored memories, when retrieved, are potentially altered before being stored again.

🎮 **LaunchPad** To experience a demonstration and explanation of interference effects on memory, visit LaunchPad's *PsychSim 6: Forgetting.*

Information presented in the hour before sleep is protected from retroactive interference because the opportunity for interfering events is minimized (Diekelmann & Born, 2010; Nesca & Koulack, 1994). Researchers John Jenkins and Karl Dallenbach (1924) first discovered this in a now-classic experiment. Day after day, two people each learned some nonsense syllables, then tried to recall them after up to eight hours of being awake or asleep at night. As **FIGURE 26.6** shows, forgetting occurred more rapidly after being awake and involved with other activities. The investigators surmised that "forgetting is not so much a matter of the decay of old impressions and associations as it is a matter of interference, inhibition, or obliteration of the old by the new" (1924, p. 612).

The hour before sleep is a good time to commit information to memory (Scullin & McDaniel, 2010), though information presented in the *seconds* just before sleep is seldom remembered (Wyatt & Bootzin, 1994). If you're considering learning *while* sleeping, forget it. We have little memory for information played aloud in the room during sleep, although the ears do register it (Wood et al., 1992).

Old and new learning do not always compete with each other, of course. Previously learned information (Latin) often facilitates our learning of new information (French). This phenomenon is called *positive transfer*.

Motivated Forgetting   To remember our past is often to revise it. Years ago, the huge cookie jar in my [DM] kitchen was jammed with freshly baked chocolate chip cookies. Still more were cooling across racks on the counter. Twenty-four hours later, not a crumb was left. Who had taken them? During that time, my wife, three children, and I were the only people in the house. So while memories were still fresh, I conducted a little memory test. Andy admitted wolfing down as many as 20. Peter thought he had eaten 15. Laura guessed she had stuffed her then-6-year-old body with 15 cookies. My wife, Carol, recalled eating 6, and I remembered consuming 15 and taking 18 more to the office. We sheepishly accepted responsibility for 89 cookies. Still, we had not come close; there had been 160.

Why do our memories fail us? This happens in part because memory is an "unreliable, self-serving historian" (Tavris & Aronson, 2007, p. 6). Consider one study, in which researchers told some participants about the benefits of frequent toothbrushing. Those individuals then recalled (more than others did) having frequently brushed their teeth in the preceding two weeks (Ross et al., 1981).

FIGURE 26.7 reminds us that as we process information we filter, alter, or lose much of it. So why were my family and I so far off in our estimates of the cookies we had eaten? Was it an *encoding* problem? (Did we just not notice what we had eaten?) Was it a storage problem? (Might our memories of cookies, like Ebbinghaus' memory of nonsense syllables, have melted away almost as fast as the cookies themselves?) Or was the information still intact but not *retrievable* because it would be embarrassing to remember?[1]

Sigmund Freud might have argued that our memory systems self-censored this information. He proposed that we **repress** painful or unacceptable memories to protect our self-concept and to minimize anxiety. But the repressed memory lingers, he believed, and can be retrieved by some later cue or during therapy. Repression was central to Freud's psychoanalytic theory of personality and was a popular idea in mid-twentieth century psychology and beyond. One Norwegian study found that educated people tend to believe in repressed memories more than do those with less formal education (Magnussen et al., 2006). In an American study, 81 percent of university students, and 60 to 90 percent of therapists (depending on their perspective), agreed that "traumatic memories are often repressed" (Patihis et al., 2014). Today, however, increasing numbers of memory researchers think repression rarely, if ever, occurs. People succeed in forgetting unwanted neutral information (yesterday's parking place), but it's harder to forget emotional events (Payne & Corrigan, 2007). Thus, we may have intrusive memories of the very traumatic experiences we would most like to forget.

Information bits

Sensory memory
The senses momentarily register amazing detail.

Working/short-term memory
A few items are both noticed and encoded.

Long-term storage
Some items are altered or lost.

Retrieval from long-term memory
Depending on interference, retrieval cues, moods, and motives, some things get retrieved, some don't.

─────── **RETRIEVAL PRACTICE** ───────

- What are three ways we forget, and how does each of these happen?

ANSWER: (1) *Encoding failure:* Unattended information never entered our memory system. (2) *Storage decay:* Information fades from our memory. (3) *Retrieval failure:* We cannot access stored information accurately, sometimes due to interference or motivated forgetting.

▼ **FIGURE 26.7**
When do we forget? Forgetting can occur at any memory stage. As we process information, we filter, alter, or lose much of it.

Memory Construction Errors

26-2 How do misinformation, imagination, and source amnesia influence our memory construction? How do we decide whether a memory is real or false?

Memory is not precise. Like scientists who infer a dinosaur's appearance from its remains, we infer our past from stored information plus what we later imagined, expected, saw, and heard. We don't just retrieve memories, we reweave them. Like Wikipedia pages, memories can be continuously revised. When we "replay" a memory, we often replace the original with a slightly modified version (Hardt et al., 2010). (Memory researchers call this **reconsolidation.**) So, in a sense, said Joseph LeDoux (2009), "your memory is only as good as your last memory. The fewer times you use it, the more pristine it is." This means that, to some degree, "all memory is false" (Bernstein & Loftus, 2009).

Despite knowing all this, I [DM] recently rewrote my own past. It happened at an international conference, where memory researcher Elizabeth Loftus (2012) was demonstrating how memory works. Loftus showed us a handful of individual faces that we were later to identify, as if in a police lineup. Later, she showed us some pairs of faces, one face we had seen earlier and one we had not, and asked us to identify the one we had seen. But one pair she had slipped in included *two* new faces, one of which was rather *like* a face we had seen earlier. Most of us understandably but wrongly identified this face as one we had previously seen. To climax the demonstration, when she showed us the originally seen face and the previously chosen wrong face, most of us picked the wrong face!

This is one of those beautiful summer days when I'm flooded with memories of things that never happened to me.

SiPRESS

Sipress, 1988

─────────────

1. One of my cookie-scarfing sons, on reading this in his father's textbook years later, confessed he had fibbed "a little."

misinformation effect when misleading information has corrupted one's memory of an event.

As a result of our memory reconsolidation, we—an audience of psychologists who should have known better—had replaced the original memory with a false memory.

Clinical researchers are experimenting with people's memory reconsolidation. They have people recall a traumatic or negative experience, then disrupt the reconsolidation of that memory with a drug or brief, painless electroconvulsive shock (Kroes et al., 2014; Lonergan, 2013). If, indeed, it becomes possible to erase your memory for a specific traumatic experience—by reactivating your memory and then disrupting its storage—would you wish for this? If brutally assaulted, would you welcome having your memory of the attack and its associated fears deleted?

Misinformation and Imagination Effects

In more than 200 experiments involving more than 20,000 people, Loftus has shown how eyewitnesses reconstruct their memories after a crime or an accident. In one experiment, two groups of people watched a film clip of a traffic accident and then answered questions about what they had seen (Loftus & Palmer, 1974). Those asked, "About how fast were the cars going when they *smashed* into each other?" gave higher speed estimates than those asked, "About how fast were the cars going when they *hit* each other?" A week later, when asked whether they recalled seeing any broken glass, people who had heard *smashed* were more than twice as likely to report seeing glass fragments (**FIGURE 26.8**). In fact, the clip showed no broken glass.

In many follow-up experiments around the world, others have witnessed an event, received or not received misleading information about it, and then taken a memory test. The repeated result is a **misinformation effect:** Exposed to misleading information, we often, though feeling confident, misremember. A yield sign becomes a stop sign, hammers become screwdrivers, Coke cans become peanut cans, breakfast cereal becomes eggs, and a clean-shaven man morphs into a man with a mustache (Loftus et al., 1992).

So powerful is the misinformation effect that it can influence later attitudes and behaviors (Bernstein & Loftus, 2009). One experiment falsely suggested to some Dutch university students that, as children, they became ill after eating spoiled egg salad (Geraerts et al., 2008). After absorbing that suggestion, they were less likely to eat egg salad sandwiches, both immediately and four months later.

Because the misinformation effect happens outside our awareness, it is nearly impossible to sift the suggested ideas out of the larger pool of real memories (Schooler et al., 1986). Perhaps you can recall describing a childhood experience to a friend and filling in memory gaps with reasonable guesses and assumptions. We all do it, and after more retellings, those guessed details—now absorbed into our memories—may feel as real as if we had actually experienced them (Roediger et al., 1993). False memories, like fake diamonds, seem real.

Even repeatedly *imagining* nonexistent actions and events can create false memories. American and British university students were asked to imagine certain childhood events, such as breaking a window with their hand or having a skin sample removed from a finger. One in four of them later recalled the imagined event as something that had really happened (Garry et al., 1996; Mazzoni & Memon, 2003).

"Memory is insubstantial. Things keep replacing it. Your batch of snapshots will both fix and ruin your memory. . . . You can't remember anything from your trip except the wretched collection of snapshots."

Annie Dillard, "To Fashion a Text," 1988

▼ FIGURE 26.8
Memory construction In this experiment, people viewed a film clip of a car accident (left). Those who later were asked a leading question recalled a more serious accident than they had witnessed (Loftus & Palmer, 1974).

Leading question:
"About how fast were the cars going when they smashed into each other?"

Image of actual accident   **Memory construction**

False memories More than 5000 *Slate* magazine readers were asked whether they remembered various world events—three real, and one of five randomly selected false events (Frenda et al., 2013). For example, when asked if they recalled Barack Obama's shaking hands with Iran's former president, Mahmoud Ahmadinejad, 26 percent recalled the event—despite it never having happened. (Ahmadinejad's head was put into another photo.)

Digitally altered photos have also produced this *imagination inflation*. In experiments, researchers have altered photos from a family album to show some family members taking a hot air balloon ride. After viewing these photos (rather than photos showing just the balloon), children reported more false memories and indicated high confidence in those memories. When interviewed several days later, they reported even richer details of their false memories (Strange et al., 2008; Wade et al., 2002).

Misinformation and imagination effects occur partly because visualizing something and actually perceiving it activate similar brain areas (Gonsalves et al., 2004). Imagined events also later seem more familiar, and familiar things seem more real. The more vividly we can imagine things, the more likely they are to become memories (Loftus, 2001; Porter et al., 2000).

In British and Canadian university surveys, nearly one-fourth of students have reported autobiographical memories that they later realized were not accurate (Mazzoni et al., 2010). I [DM] empathize. For decades, my cherished earliest memory was of my parents getting off the bus and walking to our house, bringing my baby brother home from the hospital. When, in middle age, I shared that memory with my father, he assured me they did *not* bring their newborn home on the Seattle Transit System. The human mind, it seems, comes with built-in Photoshopping software.

"It isn't so astonishing, the number of things I can remember, as the number of things I can remember that aren't so."

Author Mark Twain (1835–1910)

DOONESBURY

source amnesia attributing to the wrong source an event we have experienced, heard about, read about, or imagined. (Also called *source misattribution*.) Source amnesia, along with the misinformation effect, is at the heart of many false memories.

déjà vu that eerie sense that "I've experienced this before." Cues from the current situation may unconsciously trigger retrieval of an earlier experience.

"Do you ever get that strange feeling of vujà dé? Not déjà vu; vujà dé. It's the distinct sense that, somehow, something just happened that has never happened before. Nothing seems familiar. And then suddenly the feeling is gone. Vujà dé."

Comedian George Carlin (1937–2008), in *Funny Times*, December 2001

Source Amnesia

Among the frailest parts of a memory is its source. We may recognize someone but have no idea where we have seen the person. We may dream an event and later be unsure whether it really happened. We may misrecall how we learned about something (Henkel et al., 2000). Psychologists are not immune to the process. Famed child psychologist Jean Piaget was startled as an adult to learn that a vivid, detailed memory from his childhood—a nursemaid's thwarting his kidnapping—was utterly false. He apparently constructed the memory from repeatedly hearing the story (which his nursemaid, after undergoing a religious conversion, later confessed had never happened). In attributing his "memory" to his own experiences, rather than to his nursemaid's stories, Piaget exhibited **source amnesia** (also called *source misattribution*). Misattribution is at the heart of many false memories. Authors and songwriters sometimes suffer from it. They think an idea came from their own creative imagination, when in fact they are unintentionally plagiarizing something they earlier read or heard.

Debra Poole and Stephen Lindsay (1995, 2001, 2002) demonstrated source amnesia among preschoolers. They had the children interact with "Mr. Science," who engaged them in activities such as blowing up a balloon with baking soda and vinegar. Three months later, on three successive days, their parents read them a story describing some things the children had experienced with Mr. Science and some they had not. When a new interviewer asked what Mr. Science had done with them—"Did Mr. Science have a machine with ropes to pull?"—4 in 10 children spontaneously recalled him doing things that had happened only in the story.

Source amnesia also helps explain **déjà vu** (French for "already seen"). Two-thirds of us have experienced this fleeting, eerie sense that "I've been in this exact situation before." It happens most commonly to well-educated, imaginative young adults, especially when tired or stressed (Brown, 2003, 2004a,b; McAneny, 1996). Some wonder, "How could I recognize a situation I'm experiencing for the first time?" Others may think of reincarnation ("I must have experienced this in a previous life") or precognition ("I viewed this scene in my mind before experiencing it").

Alan Brown and Elizabeth Marsh (2009) devised an intriguing way to induce déjà vu in the laboratory. They invited participants to view symbols on a computer screen and to report whether they had ever seen them before. What the viewers didn't know was that these symbols had earlier been subliminally flashed on the screen, too briefly for conscious awareness. The result? Half the participants reported experiencing déjà vu—a sense of familiarity without awareness of why. Brown and Marsh suggest that real-life experiences may include glancing very briefly at a visual scene, looking away without consciously processing it, then looking again—only to feel the uncanny sense of having seen it before.

The key to déjà vu seems to be familiarity with a stimulus without a clear idea of where we encountered it before (Cleary, 2008). Normally, we experience a feeling of *familiarity* (thanks to temporal lobe processing) before we consciously remember details (thanks to hippocampus and frontal lobe processing). When these functions (and brain regions) are out of sync, we may experience a feeling of familiarity without conscious recall. Our amazing brains try to make sense of such an improbable situation, and we get an eerie feeling that we're reliving some earlier part of our life. After all, the situation is familiar, even though we have no idea why. Our source amnesia forces us to do our best to make sense of an odd moment.

Discerning True and False Memories

Because memory is reconstruction as well as reproduction, we can't be sure whether a memory is real by how real it feels. Much as perceptual illusions may seem like real perceptions, unreal memories *feel* like real memories.

False memories can be persistent. Imagine that we were to read aloud a list of words such as *candy, sugar, honey,* and *taste.* Later, we ask you to recognize the presented words from a larger list. If you are at all like the people tested by Henry Roediger and Kathleen McDermott (1995), you would err three out of four times—by falsely remembering a nonpresented similar word, such as *sweet.* We more easily remember the gist than the words themselves.

Memory construction helps explain why about 75 percent of 301 convicts exonerated by later DNA testing had been misjudged based on faulty eyewitness identification (Lilienfeld & Byron, 2013). It explains why "hypnotically refreshed" memories of crimes so easily incorporate errors, some of which originate with the hypnotist's leading questions (*"Did you hear loud noises?"*). It explains why dating partners who fell in love have *over*estimated their first impressions of one another (*"It was love at first sight"*), while those who broke up *under*estimated their earlier liking (*"We never really clicked"*) (McFarland & Ross, 1987). And it explains why people asked how they felt 10 years ago about marijuana or gender issues recalled attitudes closer to their current views than to the views they had actually reported a decade earlier (Markus, 1986). How people feel today tends to be how they recall they have always felt (Mazzoni & Vannucci, 2007).

One research team interviewed 73 ninth-grade boys and then reinterviewed them 35 years later. When asked to recall how they had reported their attitudes, activities, and experiences, most men recalled their ninth-grade statements at a rate no better than chance. Only 1 in 3 now remembered receiving physical punishment, though as ninth-graders 82 percent had said they had (Offer et al., 2000). As George Vaillant (1977, p. 197) noted after following adult lives through time, "It is all too common for caterpillars to become butterflies and then to maintain that in their youth they had been little butterflies. Maturation makes liars of us all."

🎧 **LaunchPad** To participate in a simulated experiment on false memory formation, and to review related research, visit LaunchPad's *PsychSim 6: Can You Trust Your Memory?*

🎧 **LaunchPad** For a 5-minute demonstration and explanation of a false memory experiment, visit LaunchPad's *Video—Creating False Memories: A Laboratory Study.*

Children's Eyewitness Recall

26-3 How reliable are young children's eyewitness descriptions?

If memories can be sincere, yet sincerely wrong, might children's recollections of sexual abuse be prone to error? "It would be truly awful to ever lose sight of the enormity of child abuse," observed Stephen Ceci (1993). Yet Ceci and Maggie Bruck's (1993, 1995) studies of children's memories have made them aware of how easily children's memories can be molded. For example, they asked 3-year-olds to show on anatomically correct dolls where a pediatrician had touched them. Of the children who had not received genital examinations, 55 percent pointed to either genital or anal areas.

In other experiments, the researchers studied the effect of suggestive interviewing techniques (Bruck & Ceci, 1999, 2004). In one study, children chose a card from a deck of possible happenings, and an adult then read the card to them. For example, "Think real hard, and tell me if this ever happened to you. Can you remember going to the hospital with a mousetrap on your finger?" In interviews, the same adult repeatedly asked children to think about several real and fictitious events. After 10 weeks of this, a new adult asked the same question. The stunning result: 58 percent of preschoolers produced false (often vivid) stories regarding one or more events they had never experienced (Ceci et al., 1994). Here's one:

My brother Colin was trying to get Blowtorch [an action figure] from me, and I wouldn't let him take it from me, so he pushed me into the wood pile where the mousetrap was. And then my finger got caught in it. And then we went to the hospital, and my mommy, daddy, and Colin drove me there, to the hospital in our van, because it was far away. And the doctor put a bandage on this finger.

© Darren Matthews/Alamy

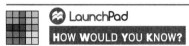

HOW WOULD YOU KNOW?

Consider how researchers have studied these issues with LaunchPad's *How Would You Know If People's Memories Are Accurate?*

Given such detailed stories, professional psychologists who specialize in interviewing children could not reliably separate the real memories from the false ones. Nor could the children themselves. The above child, reminded that his parents had told him several times that the mousetrap incident never happened—that he had imagined it—protested, "But it really did happen. I remember it!" In another experiment, preschoolers merely overheard an erroneous remark that a magician's missing rabbit had gotten loose in their classroom. Later, when the children were suggestively questioned, 78 percent of them recalled actually seeing the rabbit (Principe et al., 2006). "[The] research leads me to worry about the possibility of false allegations. It is not a tribute to one's scientific integrity to walk down the middle of the road if the data are more to

---

THINKING CRITICALLY ABOUT

Repressed or Constructed Memories of Abuse?

26-4 Why are reports of repressed and recovered memories so hotly debated?

There are two tragedies related to adult recollections of child abuse. One happens when people don't believe abuse survivors who tell their secret. The other happens when innocent people are falsely accused. What, then, shall we say about clinicians who have guided people in "recovering" childhood abuse memories? Were these well-intentioned therapists triggering false memories that damaged innocent adults? Or were they uncovering the truth?

The research on source amnesia and the misinformation effect raises concerns about therapist-guided recovered memories. Some have reasoned with patients that "people who've been abused often have your symptoms, so you probably were abused. Let's see if, aided by hypnosis or drugs, or helped to dig back and visualize your trauma, you can recover it." Patients exposed to such techniques may then form an image of a threatening person. With further visualization, the image grows more vivid. The patient ends up stunned, angry, and ready to confront or sue the remembered abuser. The accused person (often a parent or relative) is equally stunned and devastated, and vigorously denies the accusation.

Critics are not questioning the professionalism of most therapists. Nor are they questioning the accusers' sincerity; even if false, their memories are heartfelt. Critics' charges are specifically directed against clinicians who have used "memory work" techniques, such as "guided imagery," hypnosis, and dream analysis. "Thousands of families were cruelly ripped apart," with "previously loving adult daughters" suddenly accusing fathers (Gardner, 2006). Irate clinicians countered that those who argue that recovered memories of abuse never happen are adding to abused people's trauma and playing into the hands of child molesters.

Is there a sensible common ground that might resolve psychology's "memory war"—which exposed researcher and expert witness Elizabeth Loftus (2011) to "relentless vitriol and harrassment"? Professional organizations (the American Medical, American Psychological, and American Psychiatric Associations; the

Australian Psychological Society; the British Psychological Society; and the Canadian Psychiatric Association) have convened study panels and issued public statements, and greater agreement is emerging (Patihis et al., 2014). Those committed to protecting abused children and those committed to protecting wrongly accused adults have agreed on the following:

- *Sexual abuse happens.* And it happens more often than we once supposed. Although sexual abuse can leave its victims at risk for problems ranging from sexual dysfunction to depression (Freyd et al., 2007), there is no characteristic "survivor syndrome"—no group of symptoms that lets us spot victims of sexual abuse (Kendall-Tackett et al., 1993).

- *Injustice happens.* Some innocent people have been falsely convicted. And some guilty people have evaded responsibility by casting doubt on their truth-telling accusers.

- *Forgetting happens.* Many of those actually abused were either very young when abused or may not have understood the meaning of their experience—circumstances under which forgetting is common. Forgetting isolated past events, both negative and positive, is an ordinary part of everyday life.

- *Recovered memories are commonplace.* Cued by a remark or an experience, we all recover memories of long-forgotten events, both pleasant and unpleasant. What psychologists debate is twofold: Does the unconscious mind sometimes *forcibly repress* painful experiences? If so, can these experiences be retrieved by certain therapist-aided techniques? (Memories that surface naturally are more likely to be verified [Geraerts et al., 2007].)

- *Memories of events before the age of 3 are unreliable.* We cannot reliably recall happenings from our first three years. This *infantile amnesia* happens because our brain pathways have not yet developed enough to form the kinds of memories we will form later in life. Most psychologists—including most clinical and counseling psychologists—therefore doubt "recovered" memories of abuse during infancy one side," said Ceci (1993). (See Thinking Critically About: Repressed or Constructed Memories of Abuse?)

Children can, however, be accurate eyewitnesses. When questioned about their experiences in neutral words they understood, children often accurately recalled what happened and who did it (Goodman, 2006; Howe, 1997; Pipe, 1996). When interviewers used less suggestive, more effective techniques, even 4- to 5-year-old children produced more accurate recall (Holliday & Albon, 2004; Pipe et al., 2004). Children were especially accurate when they had not talked with involved adults prior to the interview and when their disclosure was made in a first interview with a neutral person who asked nonleading questions.

Like children (whose frontal lobes have not fully matured), older adults—especially those whose frontal lobe functioning has declined—are more susceptible than young adults to false memories. This makes older adults more vulnerable to scams, as when a repair person overcharges by falsely claiming, "I told you it would cost x, and you agreed to pay" (Jacoby et al., 2005; Jacoby & Rhodes, 2006; Roediger & Geraci, 2007; Roediger & McDaniel, 2007).

(Gore-Felton et al., 2000; Knapp & VandeCreek, 2000). The older a child was when suffering sexual abuse, and the more severe the abuse, the more likely it is to be remembered (Goodman et al., 2003).

- *Memories "recovered" under hypnosis or the influence of drugs are especially unreliable.* Under hypnosis, people will incorporate all kinds of suggestions into their memories, even memories of "past lives."

- *Memories, whether real or false, can be emotionally upsetting.* Both the accuser and the accused may suffer when what was born of mere suggestion becomes, like an actual trauma, a stinging memory that drives bodily stress (McNally, 2003, 2007). Some people knocked unconscious in unremembered accidents know this all too well. They have later developed stress disorders after being haunted by memories they constructed from photos, news reports, and friends' accounts (Bryant, 2001).

The debate over repression and childhood sexual abuse, like many other scientific debates, has stimulated new research and new theories. Richard McNally and Elke Geraerts (2009; McNally, 2012) contend that victims of most childhood sexual abuse do not repress their abuse; rather, they simply stop devoting thought and emotion to it. McNally and Geraerts believe this letting go of the memory is most likely when

- the experience, when it occurred, was strange, uncomfortable, and confusing, rather than severely traumatic.

- the abuse happened once or only a few times.

"When memories are 'recovered' after long periods of amnesia, particularly when extraordinary means were used to secure the recovery of memory, there is a high probability that the memories are false."

Royal College of Psychiatrists Working Group on Reported Recovered Memories of Child Sexual Abuse (Brandon et al., 1998)

- victims have not spent time thinking about the abuse, either because of their own resilience or because no reminders are available.

McNally and Geraerts agree that victims do sometimes accurately and spontaneously recall memories of childhood abuse. But these memories usually occur outside of therapy. Moreover, people who recall abuse spontaneously rarely form false memories when in a lab setting. Conversely, those who form memories of abuse during suggestive therapy tend to have vivid imaginations and score high on false-memory tests in the lab (Clancy et al., 2000; McNally, 2003).

So, does *repression* of threatening memories ever occur? Or is this concept—the cornerstone of Freud's theory and of so much popular psychology—misleading? Other modules discuss this hotly debated issue. But this much appears certain: The most common response to a traumatic experience (witnessing a loved one's murder, being terrorized by a hijacker or a rapist, losing everything in a natural disaster) is not banishment of the experience into the unconscious. Rather, such experiences are typically etched on the mind as vivid, persistent, haunting memories (Porter & Peace, 2007). As Robert Kraft (2002) said of the experience of those trapped in the Nazi death camps, "Horror sears memory, leaving . . . the consuming memories of atrocity."

RETRIEVAL PRACTICE

- Imagine being a jury member in a trial for a parent accused of sexual abuse based on a recovered memory. What insights from memory research should you offer the jury?

ANSWER: It will be important to remember the key points agreed upon by most researchers and professional associations: Sexual abuse, injustice, forgetting, and memory construction all happen; recovered memories are common; memories from before age 3 are unreliable; memories claimed to be recovered through hypnosis or drug influence are especially unreliable; and memories, whether real or false, can be emotionally upsetting.

- What—given the commonality of source amnesia—might life be like if we remembered all our waking experiences and all our dreams?

ANSWER: Real experiences would be confused with those we dreamed. When meeting someone, we might therefore be unsure whether we were reacting to something they previously did or to something we dreamed they did.

Improving Memory

26-5 How can you use memory research findings to do better in this and other courses?

Biology's findings benefit medicine. Botany's findings benefit agriculture. So, too, can psychology's research on memory benefit education. Here, for easy reference, is a summary of some research-based suggestions that could help you remember information when you need it. The SQ3R—Survey, Question, Read, Retrieve, Review—study technique used in this book incorporates several of these strategies.

> *Rehearse repeatedly.* To master material, use distributed (spaced) practice. To learn a concept, give yourself many separate study sessions. Take advantage of life's little intervals—riding a bus, walking across campus, waiting for class to start. New memories are weak; exercise them and they will strengthen. To memorize specific facts or figures, Thomas Landauer (2001) has advised, "rehearse the name or number you are trying to memorize, wait a few seconds, rehearse again, wait a little longer, rehearse again, then wait longer still and rehearse yet again. The waits should be as long as possible without losing the information." Reading complex material with minimal rehearsal yields little retention. Rehearsal and critical reflection help more. As the *testing effect* has shown, it pays to study actively. Taking lecture notes in longhand, which requires summarizing material in your own words, leads to better retention than does verbatim laptop note taking. "The pen is mightier than the keyboard," note researchers Pam Mueller and Daniel Oppenheimer (2014).
>
> *Make the material meaningful.* You can build a network of retrieval cues by taking text and class notes in your own words. Apply the concepts to your own life.

Thinking and memory Actively thinking as we read, by rehearsing and relating ideas, and by making the material personally meaningful, yields the best retention.

© Sigrid Olsson/PhotoAlto/Corbis

Form images. Understand and organize information. Relate the material to what you already know or have experienced. As William James (1890) suggested, "Knit each new thing on to some acquisition already there." Restate concepts in your own words. Mindlessly repeating someone else's words won't supply many retrieval cues. On an exam, you may find yourself stuck when a question uses phrasing different from the words you memorized.

Activate retrieval cues. Mentally re-create the situation and the mood in which your original learning occurred. Jog your memory by allowing one thought to cue the next.

Use mnemonic devices. Associate items with peg words to harness visual imagery skills to illustrate in your mind's eye what is to be remembered *("one is a bun, two is a shoe")*. Make up a story that incorporates vivid images of the items. Chunk information into acronyms. Create rhythmic rhymes ("i *before* e, *except after* c").

Minimize interference. Study before sleep. Do not schedule back-to-back study times for topics that are likely to interfere with each other, such as Spanish and French.

Sleep more. During sleep, the brain reorganizes and consolidates information for long-term memory. Sleep deprivation disrupts this process. Even 10 minutes of waking rest enhances memory of what we have read (Dewar et al., 2012). So, after a period of hard study, perhaps just sit or lie down for a few minutes before tackling the next subject.

Test your own knowledge, both to rehearse it and to find out what you don't yet know. Don't be lulled into overconfidence by your ability to recognize information. Test your recall using the periodic Retrieval Practice items, the numbered Learning Objective questions in the Review sections, and the self-test questions at the end of each set of modules. Outline sections using a blank page. Define the terms and concepts listed at each module's end before turning back to their definitions. Take practice tests; the websites and study guides that accompany many texts, including this one, are a good source for such tests.

RETRIEVAL PRACTICE

- What are the recommended memory strategies you just read about?

ANSWER: Rehearse repeatedly to boost long-term recall. Schedule spaced (not crammed) study times. Spend more time rehearsing or actively thinking about the material. Make the material personally meaningful, with well-organized and vivid associations. Refresh your memory by returning to contexts and moods to activate retrieval cues. Use mnemonic devices. Minimize interference. Plan for a complete night's sleep. Test yourself repeatedly—retrieval practice is a proven retention strategy.

26 **REVIEW** Forgetting, Memory Construction, and Improving Memory

LEARNING OBJECTIVES

RETRIEVAL PRACTICE Take a moment to answer each of these Learning Objective Questions (repeated here from within this module). Then turn to Appendix C, Complete Module Reviews, to check your answers. Research suggests that trying to answer these questions on your own will improve your long-term retention (McDaniel et al., 2009).

26-1 Why do we forget?

26-2 How do misinformation, imagination, and source amnesia influence our memory construction? How do we decide whether a memory is real or false?

26-3 How reliable are young children's eyewitness descriptions?

26-4 Why are reports of repressed and recovered memories so hotly debated?

26-5 How can you use memory research findings to do better in this and other courses?

TERMS AND CONCEPTS TO REMEMBER

RETRIEVAL PRACTICE Test yourself on these terms by trying to write down the definition before flipping back to check your answers.

anterograde amnesia, p. 338

retrograde amnesia, p. 338

proactive interference, p. 341

retroactive interference, p. 341

repression, p. 343

reconsolidation, p. 343

misinformation effect, p. 344

source amnesia, p. 346

déjà vu, p. 346

Use 🅛 LearningCurve to create your personalized study plan, which will direct you to the resources that will help you most in 🅛 LaunchPad.

TEST YOUR-SELF MEMORY

Test yourself repeatedly throughout your studies. This will not only help you figure out what you know and don't know; the testing itself will help you learn and remember the information more effectively thanks to the *testing effect.*

24 Studying and Encoding Memories

1. A psychologist who asks you to write down as many objects as you can remember having seen a few minutes earlier is testing your _____ .

2. The psychological terms for taking in information, retaining it, and later getting it back out are _____ , _____ , and _____ .

3. The concept of working memory

   a. clarifies the idea of short-term memory by focusing on the active processing that occurs in this stage.

   b. splits short-term memory into two substages—sensory memory and working memory.

   c. splits short-term memory into two areas—working (retrievable) memory and inaccessible memory.

   d. clarifies the idea of short-term memory by focusing on space, time, and frequency.

4. Sensory memory may be visual (_____ memory) or auditory (_____ memory).

5. Our short-term memory for new information is limited to about _____ items.

6. Memory aids that use visual imagery (such as peg words) or other organizational devices (such as acronyms) are called _____ .

25 Storing and Retrieving Memories

7. The hippocampus seems to function as a

   a. temporary processing site for explicit memories.

   b. temporary processing site for implicit memories.

   c. permanent storage area for emotion-based memories.

   d. permanent storage area for iconic and echoic memories.

8. Amnesia following hippocampus damage typically leaves people unable to learn new facts or recall recent events. However, they may be able to learn new skills, such as riding a bicycle, which is an _____ (explicit/implicit) memory.

9. Long-term potentiation (LTP) refers to

   a. emotion-triggered hormonal changes.

   b. the role of the hippocampus in processing explicit memories.

   c. an increase in a cell's firing potential after brief, rapid stimulation.

   d. aging people's potential for learning.

10. Specific odors, visual images, emotions, or other associations that help us access a memory are examples of _____ _____ .

11. When you feel sad, why might it help to look at pictures that reawaken some of your best memories?

12. When tested immediately after viewing a list of words, people tend to recall the first and last items more readily than those in the middle. When retested after a delay, they are most likely to recall

    a. the first items on the list.

    b. the first and last items on the list.

    c. a few items at random.

    d. the last items on the list.

MODULE 26 Forgetting, Memory Construction, and Improving Memory

13. When forgetting is due to encoding failure, meaningless information has not been transferred from

    a. the environment into sensory memory.

    b. sensory memory into long-term memory.

    c. long-term memory into short-term memory.

    d. short-term memory into long-term memory.

14. Ebbinghaus' "forgetting curve" shows that after an initial decline, memory for novel information tends to

    a. increase slightly.

    b. decrease noticeably.

    c. decrease greatly.

    d. level out.

15. The hour before sleep is a good time to memorize information, because going to sleep after learning new material minimizes _____ interference.

16. Freud proposed that painful or unacceptable memories are blocked from consciousness through a mechanism called _____ .

17. One reason false memories form is our tendency to fill in memory gaps with our reasonable guesses and assumptions, sometimes based on misleading information. This tendency is an example of

    a. proactive interference.

    b. the misinformation effect.

    c. retroactive interference.

    d. the forgetting curve.

18. Eliza's family loves to tell the story of how she "stole the show" as a 2-year-old, dancing at her aunt's wedding reception. Even though she was so young, Eliza can recall the event clearly. How is this possible?

19. We may recognize a face at a social gathering but be unable to remember how we know that person. This is an example of _____ _____ .

20. When a situation triggers the feeling that "I've been here before," you are experiencing _____ _____ .

21. Children can be accurate eyewitnesses if

    a. interviewers give the children hints about what really happened.

    b. a neutral person asks nonleading questions soon after the event, in words the children can understand.

    c. the children have a chance to talk with involved adults before the interview.

    d. interviewers use precise technical and medical terms.

22. Psychologists involved in the study of memories of abuse tend to DISAGREE about which of the following statements?

    a. Memories of events that happened before age 3 are not reliable.

    b. We tend to repress extremely upsetting memories.

    c. Memories can be emotionally upsetting.

    d. Sexual abuse happens.

Find answers to these questions in Appendix D, in the back of the book.

THINKING AND LANGUAGE

Throughout history, we humans have both celebrated our wisdom and bemoaned our foolishness. The poet T. S. Eliot was struck by "the hollow men . . . Headpiece filled with straw." But Shakespeare's Hamlet extolled the human species as "noble in reason! . . . infinite in faculties! . . . in apprehension how like a god!" Throughout this text, we likewise marvel at both our abilities and our errors.

We study the human brain—three pounds of wet tissue the size of a small cabbage, yet containing staggeringly complex circuitry. We appreciate the amazing abilities of newborns. We marvel at our visual system, which converts physical stimuli into nerve impulses, distributes them for parallel processing, and reassembles them into colorful perceptions. We ponder our memory's enormous capacity, and the ease with which our two-track mind processes information, with and without our awareness. Little wonder that our species has had the collective genius to invent the camera, the car, and the computer; to unlock the atom and crack the genetic code; to travel out to space and into our brain's depths.

Yet we also see that in some other ways we are either simple or error prone. Our species is kin to the other animals, influenced by the same principles that produce learning in rats and pigeons. We note that we not-so-wise humans are easily deceived by perceptual illusions, pseudopsychic claims, and false memories.

In Modules 27 and 28, we encounter further instances of these two images of the human condition—the rational and the irrational. We will consider how we use and misuse the information we receive, perceive, store, and retrieve. We will look at our gift for language and consider how and why it develops. And we will reflect on how deserving we are of our species name, *Homo sapiens*—wise human.

27 Thinking

Concepts

27-1 What is cognition, and what are the functions of concepts?

PSYCHOLOGISTS WHO STUDY **COGNITION** FOCUS on the mental activities associated with thinking, knowing, remembering, and communicating information. One of these activities is forming **concepts**—mental groupings of similar objects, events, ideas, or people. The concept *chair* includes many items—a baby's high chair, a reclining chair, a dentist's chair—all for sitting. Concepts simplify our thinking. Imagine life without them. We would need a different name for every person, event, object, and idea. We could not ask a child to "throw the ball" because there would be no concept of *throw* or *ball*. Instead of saying, "They were angry," we would have to describe expressions, intensities, and words. Concepts such as *ball* and *anger* give us much information with little cognitive effort.

We often form our concepts by developing **prototypes**—a mental image or best example of a category (Rosch, 1978). People more quickly agree that "a robin is a bird" than that "a penguin is a bird." For most of us, the robin is the birdier bird; it more closely resembles our *bird* prototype. Similarly, for people in modern multiethnic Germany, Caucasian Germans are more prototypically German (Kessler et al., 2010). And the more closely something matches our prototype of a concept—such as a bird or a German—the more readily we recognize it as an example of the concept (**FIGURE 27.1**).

Once we place an item in a category, our memory of it later shifts toward the category prototype, as it did for Belgian students who viewed ethnically blended faces. For example, when viewing a blended face in which 70 percent of the features were Caucasian and 30 percent were Asian, the students categorized the face as Caucasian (**FIGURE 27.2**). Later, as their memory shifted toward the Caucasian prototype, they were more likely to remember an 80 percent Caucasian face than the 70 percent Caucasian they had actually seen (Corneille et al., 2004). Likewise, if shown a 70 percent Asian face, they later remembered a more prototypically Asian face. So, too, with gender: People who viewed 70 percent male faces categorized them as male (no surprise there) and then later misremembered them as even more prototypically male (Huart et al., 2005).

Move away from our prototypes, and category boundaries may blur. Is a tomato a fruit? Is a 17-year-old female a girl or a woman? Is a whale a fish or a mammal? Because a whale fails to match our *mammal* prototype, we are slower to recognize it as a mammal. Similarly, when symptoms don't fit one of our disease prototypes, we are slow to perceive an illness (Bishop, 1991). People whose heart attack symptoms (shortness of breath, exhaustion, a dull weight in the chest) don't match their *heart attack* prototype (sharp chest pain) may not seek help. And when behaviors don't fit our *discrimination* prototypes—of White against Black, male against female, young against old—we often fail to notice prejudice. People more easily detect male prejudice against females than female against males or female against females (Inman & Baron, 1996; Marti et al., 2000). Although concepts speed and guide our thinking, they don't always make us wise.

"Attention, everyone! I'd like to introduce the newest member of our family."

Eduardo Ramirez Sanchez/Shutterstock

▼ FIGURE 27.1
Tasty fungus? Botanically, a mushroom is a fungus. But it doesn't fit most people's *fungus* prototype.

▼ FIGURE 27.2
Categorizing faces influences recollection Shown a face that was 70 percent Caucasian, people tended to classify the person as Caucasian and to recollect the face as more Caucasian than it was. (Recreation of experiment courtesy of Olivier Corneille.)

FaceGen TM

90% CA   80% CA   70% CA   60% CA   50%/50%   60% AS   70% AS   80% AS   90% AS

Problem Solving: Strategies and Obstacles

27-2 What cognitive strategies assist our problem solving, and what obstacles hinder it?

One tribute to our rationality is our problem-solving skill. What's the best route around this traffic jam? How shall we handle a friend's criticism? How can we get in the house without our keys?

Some problems we solve through *trial and error*. Thomas Edison tried thousands of light bulb filaments before stumbling upon one that worked. For other problems, we use **algorithms,** step-by-step procedures that guarantee a solution. But step-by-step algorithms can be laborious and exasperating. To find a word using the 10 letters in *SPLOYOCHYG*, for example, you could try each letter in each of the 10 positions—907,200 permutations in all. Rather than give you a computing brain the size of a beach ball, nature resorts to **heuristics,** simpler thinking strategies. Thus, you might reduce the number of options in the *SPLOYOCHYG* example by grouping letters that often appear together (*CH* and *GY*) and excluding rare letter combinations (such as two *Y*'s together). By using heuristics and then applying trial and error, you may hit on the answer. Have you guessed it?[1]

Sometimes we puzzle over a problem and the pieces suddenly fall together in a flash of **insight**—an abrupt, true-seeming, and often satisfying solution (Topolinski & Reber, 2010). Ten-year-old Johnny Appleton's insight solved a problem that had stumped construction workers: how to rescue a young robin from a narrow 30-inch-deep hole in a cement-block wall. Johnny's solution: Slowly pour in sand, giving the bird enough time to keep its feet on top of the constantly rising pile (Ruchlis, 1990).

Teams of researchers have identified brain activity associated with sudden flashes of insight (Kounios & Beeman, 2009; Sandkühler & Bhattacharya, 2008). They gave people a problem: Think of a word that will form a compound word or phrase with each of three other words in a set (such as *pine, crab,* and *sauce*), and press a button to sound a bell when you know the answer. (If you need a hint: The word is a fruit.[2]) EEGs or fMRIs (functional MRIs) revealed the problem solver's brain activity. In the first experiment, about half the solutions were by a sudden Aha! insight. Before the Aha! moment, the problem solvers' frontal lobes (which are involved in focusing attention) were active, and there was a burst of activity in the right temporal lobe, just above the ear (**FIGURE 27.3** on the next page). In another experiment, researchers used electrical stimulation to decrease left hemisphere activity and increase right hemisphere activity. The result was improved insight, less restrained by the assumptions created by past experience (Chi & Snyder, 2011).

Insight strikes suddenly, with no prior sense of "getting warmer" or feeling close to a solution (Knoblich & Oellinger, 2006; Metcalfe, 1986). When the answer pops into mind (*apple!*), we feel a happy sense of satisfaction. The joy of a joke may similarly lie in our sudden comprehension of an unexpected ending or a double meaning: "You don't need a parachute to skydive. You only need a parachute to skydive twice." Comedian Groucho Marx was a master at this: "I once shot an elephant in my pajamas. How he got in my pajamas I'll never know."

Inventive as we are, other cognitive tendencies may lead us astray. For example, we more eagerly seek out and favor evidence that supports our ideas than evidence that refutes them (Klayman & Ha, 1987; Skov & Sherman, 1986). Peter Wason (1960) demonstrated this tendency, known as **confirmation bias,** by giving British university students the three-number sequence *2-4-6* and asking them to guess the rule he had

cognition all the mental activities associated with thinking, knowing, remembering, and communicating.

concept a mental grouping of similar objects, events, ideas, or people.

prototype a mental image or best example of a category. Matching new items to a prototype provides a quick and easy method for sorting items into categories (as when comparing feathered creatures to a prototypical bird, such as a robin).

algorithm a methodical, logical rule or procedure that guarantees solving a particular problem. Contrasts with the usually speedier—but also more error-prone—use of *heuristics*.

heuristic a simple thinking strategy that often allows us to make judgments and solve problems efficiently; usually speedier but also more error-prone than *algorithms*.

insight a sudden realization of a problem's solution; contrasts with strategy-based solutions.

confirmation bias a tendency to search for information that supports our preconceptions and to ignore or distort contradictory evidence.

Heuristic searching To find guava juice, you could search every supermarket aisle (an algorithm), or check the bottled beverage, natural foods, and produce sections (heuristics). The heuristics approach is often speedier, but an algorithmic search guarantees you will find it eventually.

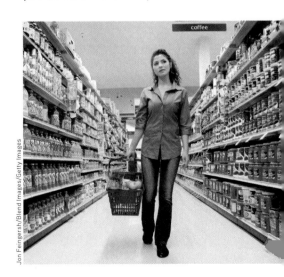

---

1. Answer to SPLOYOCHYG anagram: PSYCHOLOGY.

2. The word is *apple*: pineapple, crabapple, applesauce.

mental set a tendency to approach a problem in one particular way, often a way that has been successful in the past.

▼ FIGURE 27.3
The Aha! moment A burst of right temporal lobe activity accompanied insight solutions to word problems (Jung-Beeman et al., 2004). The red dots designate EEG electrodes. The light gray lines show the distribution of high-frequency activity accompanying insight. The insight-related activity is centered in the right temporal lobe (yellow area).

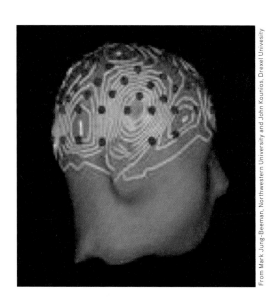

"The human understanding, when any proposition has been once laid down . . . forces everything else to add fresh support and confirmation."

Francis Bacon, *Novum Organum*, 1620

▼ FIGURE 27.4
The matchstick problem How would you arrange six matches to form four equilateral triangles?

used to devise the series. (The rule was simple: any three ascending numbers.) Before submitting answers, students generated their own three-number sets and Wason told them whether their sets conformed to his rule. Once *certain* they had the rule, they could announce it. The result? Seldom right but never in doubt. Most students formed a wrong idea (*"Maybe it's counting by twos"*) and then searched only for confirming evidence (by testing *6-8-10, 100-102-104,* and so forth).

"Ordinary people," said Wason (1981), "evade facts, become inconsistent, or systematically defend themselves against the threat of new information relevant to the issue." Thus, once people form a belief—that vaccines cause (or do not cause) autism spectrum disorder, that people can (or cannot) change their sexual orientation, that gun control does (or does not) save lives—they prefer belief-confirming information. The results can be momentous. The U.S. war against Iraq was launched on the belief that dictator Saddam Hussein possessed weapons of mass destruction (WMD) that posed an immediate threat. When that assumption turned out to be false, the bipartisan U.S. Senate Select Committee on Intelligence (2004) laid blame on confirmation bias: Administration analysts "had a tendency to accept information which supported [their presumptions] . . . more readily than information which contradicted" them. Sources denying such weapons were deemed "either lying or not knowledgeable about Iraq's problems," while those sources who reported ongoing WMD activities were seen as "having provided valuable information."

Once we incorrectly represent a problem, it's hard to restructure how we approach it. If the solution to the matchstick problem in **FIGURE** 27.4 eludes you, you may be experiencing *fixation*—an inability to see a problem from a fresh perspective. (For the solution, see **FIGURE** 27.5.)

A prime example of fixation is **mental set,** our tendency to approach a problem with the mind-set of what has worked for us previously. Indeed, solutions that worked in the past often do work on new problems. Consider:

Given the sequence *O-T-T-F-?-?-?,* what are the final three letters?

Most people have difficulty recognizing that the three final letters are *F*(ive), *S*(ix), and *S*(even). But solving this problem may make the next one easier:

Given the sequence *J-F-M-A-?-?-?,* what are the final three letters? (If you don't get this one, ask yourself what month it is.)

As a *perceptual set* predisposes what we perceive, a mental set predisposes how we think; sometimes this can be an obstacle to problem solving, as when our mental set from our past experiences with matchsticks predisposes us to arrange them in two dimensions.

Forming Good and Bad Decisions and Judgments

27-3 What is intuition, and how can the availability heuristic, overconfidence, belief perseverance, and framing influence our decisions and judgments?

When making each day's hundreds of judgments and decisions (*Is it worth the bother to take a jacket? Can I trust this person? Should I shoot the basketball or pass to the player who's hot?*), we seldom take the time and effort to reason systematically. We just follow our **intuition,** our fast, automatic, unreasoned feelings and thoughts. After interviewing policy makers in government, business, and education, social psychologist Irving Janis (1986) concluded that they "often do not use a reflective problem-solving approach. How do they usually arrive at their decisions? If you ask, they are likely to tell you . . . they do it mostly by *the seat of their pants.*"

The Availability Heuristic

When we need to act quickly, the mental shortcuts we call *heuristics* enable snap judgments. Thanks to our mind's automatic information processing, intuitive judgments are instantaneous. They also are usually effective (Gigerenzer & Sturm, 2012). However, research by cognitive psychologists Amos Tversky and Daniel Kahneman (1974) showed how these generally helpful shortcuts can lead even the smartest people into dumb decisions.[3] The **availability heuristic** operates when we estimate the likelihood of events based on how mentally available they are—how easily they come to mind. Casinos entice us to gamble by signaling even small wins with bells and lights—making them mentally vivid—while keeping big losses invisible.

The availability heuristic can distort our judgments of other people, too. Anything that makes information pop into mind—its vividness, recency, or distinctiveness—can make it seem commonplace. If someone from a particular ethnic or religious group commits a terrorist act, as happened on September 11, 2001, our readily available memory of the dramatic event may shape our impression of the whole group.

---

3. Tversky and Kahneman's joint work on decision making received a 2002 Nobel Prize; sadly, only Kahneman was alive to receive the honor.

"The problem is I can't tell the difference between a deeply wise, intuitive nudge from the Universe and one of my own bone-headed ideas!"

"Kahneman and his colleagues and students have changed the way we think about the way people think."

American Psychological Association
President Sharon Brehm, 2007

"In creating these problems, we didn't set out to fool people. All our problems fooled us, too."
Amos Tversky (1985)

"Intuitive thinking [is] fine most of the time. . . . But sometimes that habit of mind gets us in trouble."
Daniel Kahneman (2005)

intuition an effortless, immediate, automatic feeling or thought, as contrasted with explicit, conscious reasoning.

availability heuristic estimating the likelihood of events based on their availability in memory; if instances come readily to mind (perhaps because of their vividness), we presume such events are common.

Even during that horrific year, terrorist acts claimed comparatively few lives. Yet when the statistical reality of greater dangers (see **FIGURE 27.6**) was pitted against the 9/11 terror, the memorable case won: Emotion-laden images of terror exacerbated our fears (Sunstein, 2007).

We often fear the wrong things (Turn the page to see Thinking Critically About: The Fear Factor). We fear flying because we visualize air disasters. We fear letting our sons and daughters walk to school because we see mental snapshots of abducted and brutalized children. We fear swimming in ocean waters because we replay *Jaws* with ourselves as victims. Even just passing by a person who sneezes and coughs heightens our perceptions of various health risks (Lee et al., 2010). And so, thanks to such readily available images, we come to fear extremely rare events.

Meanwhile, the lack of comparably available images of global climate change—which some scientists regard as a future "Armageddon in slow motion"—has left many people little concerned (Pew, 2014). What's more cognitively available than slow climate change is our recently experienced local weather, which tells us nothing about long-term planetary trends (Egan & Mullin, 2012; Zaval et al., 2014). Unusually hot local weather increases people's worry about global climate warming, while a recent cold day reduces their concern and overwhelms less memorable scientific data (Li et al., 2011). After Hurricane Sandy devastated New Jersey, its residents' vivid experience of extreme weather increased their environmentalism (Rudman et al., 2013).

Dramatic outcomes make us gasp; probabilities we hardly grasp. As of 2013, some 40 nations—including Canada, many in Europe, and the United States—have, however, sought to harness the positive power of vivid, memorable images by putting eye-catching warnings and graphic photos on cigarette packages (Riordan, 2013). This campaign has worked (Huang et al., 2013). As psychologist Paul Slovic (2007) points out, we reason emotionally and neglect probabilities. We overfeel and underthink. In one experiment, donations to a starving 7-year-old were greater when her image was *not* accompanied by statistical information about the millions of needy African children like her (Small et al., 2007). "The more who die, the less we care," noted Slovic (2010).

Overconfidence

Sometimes our judgments and decisions go awry simply because we are more confident than correct. Across various tasks, people overestimate their performance (Metcalfe, 1998). If 60 percent of people correctly answer a factual question, such as "Is absinthe a liqueur or a precious stone?," they will typically average 75 percent confidence

To offer a vivid depiction of climate change, Cal Tech scientists created an interactive map of global temperatures over the past 120 years (see www.tinyurl.com/TempChange).

▼ FIGURE 27.5
Solution to the matchstick problem
To solve this problem, you must view it from a new perspective, breaking the fixation of limiting solutions to two dimensions.

▼ FIGURE 27.6
Risk of death from various causes in the United States, 2001 (Data assembled from various government sources by Randall Marshall et al., 2007.)

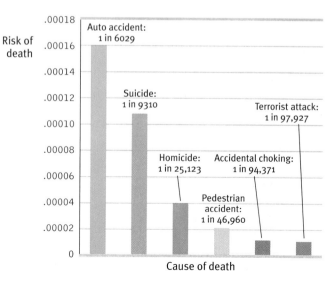

(Fischhoff et al., 1977). (It's a licorice-flavored liqueur.) This tendency to overestimate the accuracy of our knowledge and judgments is **overconfidence**.

It was an overconfident BP that, before its exploded drilling platform spewed oil into the Gulf of Mexico, downplayed safety concerns, and then downplayed the spill's magnitude (Mohr et al., 2010; Urbina, 2010). It is overconfidence that drives stockbrokers and investment managers to market their ability to outperform stock market averages (Malkiel, 2012). A purchase of stock X, recommended by a broker who judges this to be the time to buy, is usually balanced by a sale made by someone who judges this to be the time to sell. Despite their confidence, buyer and seller cannot both be right.

Overconfidence can also feed extreme political views. People with a superficial understanding of proposals for cap-and-trade carbon emissions or a national flat tax often express strong pro or con views. Asking them to explain the details of these policies exposes them to their own ignorance, which in turn leads them to express more moderate views (Fernbach et al., 2013). Sometimes the less people know, the more immoderate they are.

Classrooms are full of overconfident students who expect to finish assignments and write papers ahead of schedule (Buehler et al., 1994, 2002). In fact, the projects generally take about twice the number of days predicted. We also overestimate our future leisure time (Zauberman & Lynch, 2005). Anticipating how much more we will accomplish next month, we happily accept invitations and assignments, only to discover we're just as busy when the day rolls around. The same "planning fallacy" (underestimating time and money) appears everywhere. Boston's mega-construction "Big Dig" was projected to take 10 years and actually took 20. And the average kitchen remodeling project ends up costing about double what homeowners expect (Kahneman, 2011).

Overconfidence can have adaptive value. People who err on the side of overconfidence live more happily. They seem more competent than others (Anderson et al., 2012). Moreover, given prompt and clear feedback, as weather forecasters receive after each day's predictions, we can learn to be more realistic about the accuracy of our judgments (Fischhoff, 1982). The wisdom to know when we know a thing and when we do not is born of experience.

Belief Perseverance

Our overconfidence is startling; equally so is our **belief perseverance**—our tendency to cling to our beliefs in the face of contrary evidence. One study of belief perseverence engaged people with opposing views of capital punishment (Lord et al., 1979). After studying two supposedly new research findings, one supporting and the other refuting the claim that the death penalty deters crime, each side was more impressed by the study supporting its own beliefs. And each readily disputed the other study. Thus, showing the pro- and anti-capital-punishment groups the *same* mixed evidence actually *increased* their disagreement.

To rein in belief perseverance, a simple remedy exists: *Consider the opposite.* When the same researchers repeated the capital-punishment study, they asked some participants to be "as *objective* and *unbiased* as possible" (Lord et al., 1984). The plea did nothing to reduce biased evaluations of evidence. They also asked another group to consider "whether you would have made the same high or low evaluations had exactly the same study produced results on the *other* side of the issue." Having imagined and pondered *opposite* findings, these people became much less biased.

The more we come to appreciate why our beliefs might be true, the more tightly we cling to them. Once we have explained to ourselves why we believe a child is "gifted" or has a "specific learning disorder," we tend to ignore evidence undermining our belief. Once beliefs form and get justified, it takes more compelling evidence to change them than it did to create them. Prejudice persists. Beliefs often persevere.

Bianca Moscatelli/Worth Publishers

Predict your own behavior When will you finish reading this module?

Hofstadter's Law: It always takes longer than you expect, even when you take into account Hofstadter's Law.

Douglas Hofstadter, *Gödel, Escher, Bach: The Eternal Golden Braid*, 1979

"When you know a thing, to hold that you know it; and when you do not know a thing, to allow that you do not know it; this is knowledge."

Confucius (551–479 B.C.E.), *Analects*

overconfidence the tendency to be more confident than correct—to overestimate the accuracy of our beliefs and judgments.

belief perseverance clinging to one's initial conceptions after the basis on which they were formed has been discredited.

THINKING CRITICALLY ABOUT

The Fear Factor—Why We Fear the Wrong Things

27-4 What factors contribute to our fear of unlikely events?

After the 9/11 attacks, many people feared flying more than driving. In a 2006 Gallup survey, only 40 percent of Americans reported being "not afraid at all" to fly. Yet from 2009 to 2011 Americans were—mile for mile—170 times more likely to die in a vehicle accident than on a scheduled flight (National Safety Council, 2014). In 2011, 21,221 people died in U.S. car or light truck accidents, while *zero* (as in 2010) died on scheduled airline flights. When flying, the most dangerous part of the trip is the drive to the airport.

In a late 2001 essay, I [DM] calculated that if—because of 9/11—we flew 20 percent less and instead drove half those unflown miles, about 800 more people would die in the year after the 9/11 attacks (Myers, 2001). German psychologist Gerd Gigerenzer (2004, 2006; Gaissmaier & Gigerenzer, 2012) later checked my estimate against actual accident data. (Why didn't I think to do that?) U.S. traffic deaths did indeed increase significantly in the last three months of 2001 (**FIGURE 27.7**). By the end of 2002, Gigerenzer estimated, 1600 Americans had "lost their lives on the road by trying to avoid the risk of flying."

Why do we in so many ways fear the wrong things? Why do so many American parents fear school shootings, when their child is more likely to be killed by lightning (Ripley, 2013)? Psychologists have identified four influences that feed fear and cause us to ignore higher risks.

1. *We fear what our ancestral history has prepared us to fear.* Human emotions were road tested in the Stone Age. Our old brain prepares us to fear yesterday's risks: snakes, lizards, and spiders (which combined now kill a tiny fraction of the number killed by modern-day threats, such as cars and cigarettes). Yesterday's risks also prepare us to fear confinement and heights, and therefore flying.

Lars Christensen/Shutterstock

© Transtock/Corbis

Number of U.S. traffic deaths

Oct.–Dec. 2001: 353 excess deaths

Number of traffic deaths, 2001

Average number of traffic deaths, 1996–2000

▼ FIGURE 27.7
Scared onto deadly highways Images of 9/11 etched a sharper image in American minds than did the millions of fatality-free flights on U.S. airlines during 2002 and after. Dramatic events are readily available to memory, and they shape our perceptions of risk. In the three months after 9/11, those faulty perceptions led more Americans to travel, and some to die, by car. (Data from Gigerenzer, 2004.)

"I'm happy to say that my final judgment of a case is almost always consistent with my prejudgment of the case."

The Effects of Framing

Framing—the way we present an issue—sways our decisions and judgments. Imagine two surgeons explaining a surgery risk. One tells patients that 10 percent of people die during this surgery. The other says that 90 percent survive. Although the information is the same, the effect is not. Both patients and physicians perceive greater risk when they hear that 10 percent *die* (Marteau, 1989; McNeil et al., 1988; Rothman & Salovey, 1997).

Similarly, 9 in 10 college students rated a condom as effective if told it had a supposed "95 percent success rate" in stopping the HIV virus. Only 4 in 10 judged it effective when told it had a "5 percent failure rate" (Linville et al., 1992). To scare people even more, frame risks as numbers, not percentages. People told that a chemical exposure was projected to kill 10 of every 10 million people (imagine 10 dead people!)

2. *We fear what we cannot control.* Driving we control; flying we do not.

3. We fear what is immediate. The dangers of flying are mostly telescoped into the moments of takeoff and landing. The dangers of driving are diffused across many moments to come, each trivially dangerous.

4. *Thanks to the availability heuristic, we fear what is most readily available in memory.* Vivid images, like that of United Flight 175 slicing into the World Trade Center, feed our judgments of risk. Thousands of safe car trips have extinguished our anxieties about driving. Shark attacks kill about one American per

Ian Berry/Magnum Photos

Dramatic deaths in bunches breed concern and fear The memorable 2010 Haitian earthquake that killed some 250,000 people stirred an outpouring of justified concern. Meanwhile, according to the World Health Organization, a silent earthquake of poverty-related malaria was killing about that many people, mostly in Africa, *every four months.*

year, while heart disease kills 800,000—but it's much easier to visualize a shark bite, and thus many people fear sharks more than cigarettes (Daley, 2011). Similarly, we remember (and fear) widespread disasters (hurricanes, tornadoes, earthquakes) that kill people dramatically, in bunches. But we fear too little the less dramatic threats that claim lives quietly, one by one, continuing into the distant future. Horrified citizens and commentators renewed calls for U.S. gun control in 2012, after 20 children and 6 adults were slain in a Connecticut elementary school—although even more Americans are murdered by guns daily, though less dramatically, one by one. Philanthropist Bill Gates has noted that each year a half-million children worldwide die from rotavirus. This is the equivalent of four 747s full of children dying every day, and we hear nothing of it (Glass, 2004).

The news, and our own memorable experiences, can make us disproportionately fearful of infinitesimal risks. As one risk analyst explained, "If it's in the news, don't worry about it. The very definition of *news* is 'something that hardly ever happens'" (Schneier, 2007).

> "Fearful people are more dependent, more easily manipulated and controlled, more susceptible to deceptively simple, strong, tough measures and hard-line postures."
>
> Media researcher George Gerbner to U.S. Congressional Subcommittee on Communications, 1981

RETRIEVAL PRACTICE

- Why can news be described as "something that hardly ever happens"? How does knowing this help us assess our fears?

ANSWER: If a tragic event such as a plane crash makes the news, it is noteworthy and unusual, unlike much more common bad events, such as traffic accidents. Knowing this, we can worry less about unlikely events and think more about improving the safety of our everyday activities. (For example, we can wear a seat belt when in a vehicle and use the crosswalk when walking.)

felt more frightened than did those told the fatality risk was an infinitesimal .000001 (Kraus et al., 1992).

Framing can be a powerful persuasion tool. Carefully posed options can nudge people toward decisions that could benefit them or society as a whole (Benartzi & Thaler, 2013; Thaler & Sunstein, 2008):

- *Why choosing to be an organ donor depends on where you live.* In many European countries as well as the United States, those renewing their driver's license can decide whether they want to be organ donors. In some countries, the default option is *Yes*, but people can opt out. Nearly 100 percent of the people in opt-out countries have agreed to be donors. In the United States, Britain, and Germany, the default option is *No*, but people can "opt in." There, less than half have agreed to be donors (Hajhosseini et al., 2013; Johnson & Goldstein, 2003).

framing the way an issue is posed; how an issue is framed can significantly affect decisions and judgments.

- *How to help employees decide to save for their retirement.* A 2006 U.S. pension law recognized the framing effect. Before that law, employees who wanted to contribute to a 401(k) retirement plan typically had to choose a lower take-home pay, which few people will do. Companies can now automatically enroll their employees in the plan but allow them to opt out (which would raise the employees' take-home pay). In both plans, the decision to contribute is the employee's. But under the new "opt-out" arrangement, enrollments in one analysis of 3.4 million workers soared from 59 to 86 percent (Rosenberg, 2010).

- *How to help save the planet.* Although a "carbon tax" may be the most effective way to curb greenhouse gases, many people oppose new taxes. But they are more supportive of funding clean energy development with a "carbon offset" fee (Hardisty et al., 2010).

  The point to remember: Those who understand the power of framing can use it to nudge our decisions.

The Perils and Powers of Intuition

27-5 How do smart thinkers use intuition?

The perils of intuition—irrational fears, cloudy judgments, illogical reasoning—feed gut fears and prejudices. Irrational thinking can persist even when people are offered extra pay for thinking smart, even when they are asked to justify their answers, and even when they are expert physicians or clinicians (Shafir & LeBoeuf, 2002). Highly intelligent people (including U.S. federal intelligence agents in one study) are similarly vulnerable to them (Reyna et al., 2013; Stanovich et al., 2013). Even very smart people can make not-so-smart judgments.

So, are our heads indeed filled with straw? Good news: Cognitive scientists are also revealing intuition's powers. Here is a summary of some of the high points:

- *Intuition is analysis "frozen into habit"* (Simon, 2001). It is implicit knowledge—what we've learned and recorded in our brains but can't fully explain (Chassy & Gobet, 2011; Gore & Sadler-Smith, 2011). Chess masters display this tacit expertise in "blitz chess," where, after barely more than a glance, they intuitively know the right move (Burns, 2004). We see this expertise in the smart and quick judgments of experienced nurses, firefighters, art critics, car mechanics, and musicians. Skilled athletes can react *without thinking.* Indeed, conscious thinking may disrupt well-practiced movements such as batting or shooting free throws. For all of us who have developed some special skill, what feels like instant intuition is an acquired ability to perceive and react in an eyeblink.

- *Intuition is usually adaptive, enabling quick reactions.* Our fast and frugal heuristics let us intuitively assume that fuzzy looking objects are far away—which they usually are, except on foggy mornings. If a stranger looks like someone who previously harmed or threatened us, we may—without consciously recalling the earlier experience—react warily. People's automatic, unconscious associations with a political position can even predict their future decisions *before* they consciously make up their minds (Galdi et al., 2008). Newlyweds' automatic associations—their gut reactions—to their new spouses likewise predict their future marital happiness (McNulty et al., 2013). Our learned associations surface as gut feelings, the intuitions of our two-track mind.

- *Intuition is huge.* Today's cognitive science offers many examples of unconscious, automatic influences on our judgments (Custers & Aarts, 2010). Consider: Most people guess that the more complex the choice, the smarter it is to make decisions rationally rather than intuitively (Inbar et al., 2010). Actually, Dutch psychologists have shown that in making complex decisions, we benefit by letting our brain work on a problem without thinking about it (Strick et al., 2010, 2011). In one series of experiments, three groups of people read complex information (about apartments or roommates or art posters or soccer football matches). One group stated their preference immediately after reading information about each of four options. The second group, given several minutes to analyze the information, made slightly smarter decisions. But wisest of all, in study after study, was the third group, whose attention was distracted for a time, enabling their minds to engage in automatic, unconscious processing of the complex information. The practical lesson: Letting a problem "incubate" while we attend to other things can pay dividends (Sio & Ormerod, 2009). Facing a difficult decision involving lots of facts, we're wise to gather all the information we can, and then say, "Give me some time *not* to think about this." By taking time to sleep on it, we let our unconscious mental machinery work. Thanks to our active brain, nonconscious thinking (reasoning, problem solving, decision making, planning) is surprisingly astute (Creswell et al., 2013; Hassin, 2013).

Critics of this research remind us that deliberate, conscious thought also furthers smart thinking (Lassiter et al., 2009; Payne et al., 2008). In challenging situations, superior decision makers, including chess players, take time to think (Moxley et al., 2012). And with many sorts of problems, deliberative thinkers are aware of the intuitive option, but know when to override it (Mata et al., 2013). Consider:

Hmm . . . male or female? When acquired expertise becomes an automatic habit, as it is for experienced chicken sexers, it feels like intuition. At a glance, they just know, yet cannot easily tell you how they know.

> A bat and a ball together cost 110 cents.
> The bat costs 100 cents more than the ball.
> How much does the ball cost?

Most people's intuitive response—10 cents—is wrong, and a few moments of deliberate thinking reveals why.[4]

The bottom line: Our two-track mind makes sweet harmony as smart, critical thinking listens to the creative whispers of our vast unseen mind, and then evaluates evidence, tests conclusions, and plans for the future.

Thinking Creatively

27-6 What is creativity, and what fosters it?

Creativity is the ability to produce ideas that are both novel and valuable (Hennessey & Amabile, 2010). Consider Princeton mathematician Andrew Wiles' incredible, creative moment. Pierre de Fermat, a seventeenth-century mischievous genius, had challenged mathematicians of his day to match his solutions to various number theory problems. His most famous challenge—*Fermat's last theorem*—baffled the greatest mathematical minds, even after a $2 million prize (in today's dollars) was offered in 1908 to whoever first created a proof.

Wiles had pondered Fermat's theorem for more than 30 years and had come to the brink of a solution. One morning, out of the blue, the final "incredible revelation" struck him. "It was so indescribably beautiful; it was so simple and so elegant. I couldn't understand how I'd missed it. . . . It was the most important moment of my working life" (Singh, 1997, p. 25).

Creativity like Wiles' is supported by a certain level of *aptitude* (ability to learn). Those who score exceptionally high in quantitative aptitude as 13-year-olds, for example, are more likely to obtain graduate science and math degrees and create published or patented work (Park et al., 2008; Robertson et al., 2010). And the more intelligence and *working memory,* the better (Arneson et al., 2011; Hambrick & Meinz, 2011). Yet, there is more to creativity than aptitude, or what intelligence tests reveal. Indeed, brain activity

creativity the ability to produce new and valuable ideas.

4. The answer is 5 cents. The bat would then cost $1.05, for a $1.10 total.

Industrious creativity Researcher Sally Reis (2001) found that notably creative women were typically "intelligent, hard working, imaginative, and strong willed" as girls, noting examples such as Nobel Prize–winning geneticist Barbara McClintock. In her acceptance speech for the 2013 Nobel Prize for Literature, author Alice Munro, shown here, also spoke about creativity as hard work. "Stories are so important in the world. . . . [The part that's hardest is] when you go over the story and realize how bad it is. You know, the first part, excitement, the second, pretty good, but then you pick it up one morning and you think, 'what nonsense,' and that is when you really have to get to work on it. And for me, it always seemed the right thing to do."

A creative environment

associated with intelligence differs from that associated with creativity (Jung & Haier, 2013). Intelligence tests, which are intended to assess aptitude and typically demand a single correct answer, require **convergent thinking.** Injury to the left parietal lobe damages this ability. Creativity tests (*How many uses can you think of for a brick?*) require **divergent thinking.** Injury to certain areas of the frontal lobes can leave reading, writing, and arithmetic skills intact but destroy imagination (Kolb & Whishaw, 2006).

Although there is no agreed-upon creativity measure—there is no creativity quotient (CQ) score corresponding to an intelligence quotient (IQ) score—Robert Sternberg and his colleagues believe creativity has five components (Sternberg, 1988, 2003; Sternberg & Lubart, 1991, 1992):

1. *Expertise*—well-developed knowledge—furnishes the ideas, images, and phrases we use as mental building blocks. "Chance favors only the prepared mind," observed Louis Pasteur. The more blocks we have, the more chances we have to combine them in novel ways. Wiles' well-developed knowledge put the needed theorems and methods at his disposal.

2. *Imaginative thinking skills* provide the ability to see things in novel ways, to recognize patterns, and to make connections. Having mastered a problem's basic elements, we redefine or explore it in a new way. Copernicus first developed expertise regarding the solar system and its planets, and then creatively defined the system as revolving around the Sun, not the Earth. Wiles' imaginative solution combined two partial solutions.

3. A *venturesome personality* seeks new experiences, tolerates ambiguity and risk, and perseveres in overcoming obstacles. Wiles said he labored in near-isolation from the mathematics community partly to stay focused and avoid distraction. Such determination is an enduring trait.

4. *Intrinsic motivation* is being driven more by interest, satisfaction, and challenge than by external pressures (Amabile & Hennessey, 1992). Creative people focus less on extrinsic motivators—meeting deadlines, impressing people, or making money—than on the pleasure and stimulation of the work itself. Asked how he solved such difficult scientific problems, Isaac Newton reportedly answered, "By thinking about them all the time." Wiles concurred: "I was so obsessed by this problem that . . . I was thinking about it all the time—[from] when I woke up in the morning to when I went to sleep at night" (Singh & Riber, 1997).

5. A *creative environment* sparks, supports, and refines creative ideas. Wiles stood on the shoulders of others and collaborated with a former student. After studying the careers of 2026 prominent scientists and inventors, Dean Keith Simonton (1992) noted that the most eminent were mentored, challenged, and supported by their colleagues. Creativity-fostering environments support innovation, team building, and communication (Hülsheger et al., 2009). They also minimize anxiety and foster contemplation (Byron & Khazanchi, 2011). After Jonas Salk solved a problem that led to the polio vaccine while in a monastery, he designed the Salk Institute to provide contemplative spaces where scientists could work without interruption (Sternberg, 2006).

For those seeking to boost the creative process, research offers some ideas:

- *Develop your expertise.* Ask yourself what you care about and most enjoy. Follow your passion and become an expert at something.

- *Allow time for incubation.* Given sufficient knowledge available for novel connections, a period of inattention to a problem ("sleeping on it") allows for automatic processing to form associations (Zhong et al., 2008). So think hard on a problem, then set it aside and come back to it later.

- *Set aside time for the mind to roam freely.* Take time away from attention-absorbing distractions. Creativity springs from "defocused attention" (Simonton, 2012a,b). So jog, go for a long walk, or meditate. Serenity seeds spontaneity.

- *Experience other cultures and ways of thinking.* Living abroad sets the creative juices flowing. Even after controlling for other variables, students who have spent time abroad and embraced their host culture are more adept at working out creative solutions to problems (Lee et al., 2012; Tadmor et al., 2012). Multicultural experiences expose us to multiple perspectives and facilitate flexible thinking, and may also trigger another stimulus for creativity—a sense of difference from others (Kim et al., 2013; Ritter et al., 2012).

Imaginative thinking Cartoonists often display creativity as they see things in new ways or make unusual connections.

RETRIEVAL PRACTICE

- Match the process or strategy listed below (1–10) with its description (a–j).

    1. Algorithm
    2. Intuition
    3. Insight
    4. Heuristics
    5. Fixation
    6. Confirmation bias
    7. Overconfidence
    8. Creativity
    9. Framing
    10. Belief perseverance

    a. Inability to view problems from a new angle; focuses thinking but hinders creative problem solving.

    b. Methodological rule or procedure that guarantees a solution but requires time and effort.

    c. Fast, automatic, effortless feelings and thoughts based on our experience; huge and adaptive but can lead us to overfeel and underthink.

    d. Simple thinking shortcuts that allow us to act quickly and efficiently, but put us at risk for errors.

    e. Sudden Aha! reaction that provides instant realization of the solution.

    f. Tendency to search for support for our own views and ignore contradictory evidence.

    g. Ignoring evidence that proves our beliefs are wrong; closes our mind to new ideas.

    h. Overestimating the accuracy of our beliefs and judgments; allows us to be happy and to make decisions easily, but puts us at risk for errors.

    i. Wording a question or statement so that it evokes a desired response; can influence others' decisions and produce a misleading result.

    j. The ability to produce novel and valuable ideas.

ANSWERS: 1. b, 2. c, 3. e, 4. d, 5. a, 6. f, 7. h, 8. j, 9. i, 10. g

---

"For the love of God, is there a doctor in the house?"

Do Other Species Share Our Cognitive Skills?

27-7 What do we know about thinking in other animals?

Other animals are smarter than we often realize. In her 1908 book, *The Animal Mind*, pioneering psychologist Margaret Floy Washburn argued that animal consciousness and intelligence can be inferred from their behavior. In 2012, neuroscientists convening at the University of Cambridge added that animal consciousness can also be inferred from their brains: "Nonhuman animals, including all mammals and birds," possess the neural networks "that generate consciousness" (Low et al., 2012). Consider, then, what animal brains can do.

Using Concepts and Numbers

Even pigeons—mere birdbrains—can sort objects (pictures of cars, cats, chairs, flowers) into categories, or concepts. Shown a picture of a never-before-seen chair, pigeons have reliably pecked a key that represents *chairs* (Wasserman, 1995). By touching screens in quest of a food reward, black bears have learned to sort pictures into animal and nonanimal categories (Vonk et al., 2012). The great apes also form concepts, such as *cat* and *dog*. After monkeys learned these concepts, certain frontal lobe neurons in their brains fired in response to new "catlike" images, others to new "doglike" images (Freedman et al., 2001).

convergent thinking narrowing the available problem solutions to determine the single best solution.

divergent thinking expanding the number of possible problem solutions; creative thinking that diverges in different directions.

Life on white/Alamy

Until his death in 2007, Alex, an African Grey parrot, categorized and named objects (Pepperberg, 2009, 2012, 2013). Among his jaw-dropping numerical skills was the ability to comprehend numbers up to 8. He could speak the number of objects. He could add two small clusters of objects and announce the sum. He could indicate which of two numbers was greater. And he gave correct answers when shown various groups of objects. Asked, for example, "What color four?" (meaning "What's the color of the objects of which there are four?"), he could speak the answer.

Displaying Insight

Psychologist Wolfgang Köhler (1925) showed that we are not the only creatures to display insight. He placed a piece of fruit and a long stick outside the cage of a chimpanzee named Sultan, beyond his reach. Inside the cage, he placed a short stick, which Sultan grabbed, using it to try to reach the fruit. After several failed attempts, he dropped the stick and seemed to survey the situation. Then suddenly (as if thinking "Aha!"), Sultan jumped up and seized the short stick again. This time, he used it to pull in the longer stick—which he then used to reach the fruit. Apes have even exhibited foresight by storing a tool they could use to retrieve food the next day (Mulcahy & Call, 2006).

Birds, too, have displayed insight. One experiment, by (yes) Christopher Bird and Nathan Emery (2009), has brought to life an Aesop fable in which a thirsty crow was unable to reach the water in a partly filled pitcher. See its solution in **FIGURE 27.8a**.

Using Tools and Transmitting Culture

Like humans, many other species invent behaviors and transmit cultural patterns to their peers and offspring (Boesch-Achermann & Boesch, 1993). Forest-dwelling chimpanzees select different tools for different purposes—a heavy stick for making holes, a light, flexible stick for fishing for termites (Sanz et al., 2004). They break off the reed or stick, strip off any leaves, carry it to a termite mound, twist it just so, and carefully remove it. Termites for lunch! (This is very reinforcing for a chimpanzee.) One anthropologist, trying to mimic the animal's deft fishing moves, failed miserably.

Researchers have found at least 39 local customs related to chimpanzee tool use, grooming, and courtship (Claidière & Whiten, 2012; Whiten & Boesch, 2001). One

▼ FIGURE 27.8
Animal talents (a) Crows studied by Christopher Bird and Nathan Emery (2009) quickly learned to raise the water level in a tube and nab a floating worm by dropping in stones. Other crows have used twigs to probe for insects, and bent strips of metal to reach food. (b) Capuchin monkeys have learned not only to use heavy rocks to crack open palm nuts, but also to test stone hammers and select a sturdier, less crumbly one (Visalberghi et al., 2009). (c) One male chimpanzee in Sweden's Furuvik Zoo was observed every morning collecting stones into a neat little pile, which later in the day he used as ammunition to pelt visitors (Osvath & Karvonen, 2012). (d) Dolphins form coalitions, cooperatively hunt, and learn tool use from one another (Bearzi & Stanford, 2010). This bottlenose dolphin in Shark Bay, Western Australia, belongs to a small group that uses marine sponges as protective nose guards when probing the sea floor for fish (Krützen et al., 2005).

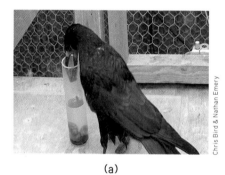

Chris Bird & Nathan Emery

(a)

Ben Cranke/The Image Bank/Getty Images

(b)

Neurology/PA/AP Photo

(c)

Copyright Amanda K. Coakes

(d)

group may slurp termites directly from a stick, another group may pluck them off individually. One group may break nuts with a stone hammer, their neighbors with a wooden hammer. These group differences, along with differing communication and hunting styles, are the chimpanzee version of cultural diversity. Several experiments have brought chimpanzee cultural transmission into the laboratory (Horner et al., 2006). If Chimpanzee A obtains food either by sliding or by lifting a door, Chimpanzee B will then typically do the same to get food. And so will Chimpanzee C after observing Chimpanzee B. Across a chain of six animals, chimpanzees see, and chimpanzees do.

Other Cognitive Skills

A baboon knows everyone's voice within its 80-member troop (Jolly, 2007). Great apes and dolphins have demonstrated self-awareness by recognizing themselves in a mirror. So have elephants, which in tests also display their abilities to learn, remember, discriminate smells, empathize, cooperate, teach, and spontaneously use tools (Byrne et al., 2009). As social creatures, chimpanzees have shown altruism, cooperation, and group aggression. Like humans, they will kill their neighbor to gain land, and they grieve over dead relatives (Anderson et al., 2010; Biro et al., 2010; Mitani et al., 2010).

There is no question that other species display many remarkable cognitive skills. But one big question remains: Do they, like humans, exhibit language? In the next module, we'll first consider what language is and how it develops.

* * *

Returning to our debate about how deserving we humans are of our name *Homo sapiens*, let's pause to issue an interim report card. On decision making and risk assessment, our error-prone species might rate a C+. On problem solving and creativity, where humans are inventive yet vulnerable to fixation, we would probably receive a better mark, perhaps a B. And when it comes to cognitive efficiency, our fallible but quick heuristics and divergent thinking would surely earn us an A.

Johan Swanepoel/Alamy

What time is it now? When we asked you (in the section on overconfidence) to estimate how quickly you would finish this module, did you underestimate or overestimate?

MODULE 27 REVIEW   Thinking

LEARNING OBJECTIVES

RETRIEVAL PRACTICE Take a moment to answer each of these Learning Objective Questions (repeated here from within this module). Then turn to Appendix C, Complete Module Reviews, to check your answers. Research suggests that trying to answer these questions on your own will improve your long-term retention (McDaniel et al., 2009).

27-1 What is cognition, and what are the functions of concepts?

27-2 What cognitive strategies assist our problem solving, and what obstacles hinder it?

27-3 What is intuition, and how can the availability heuristic, overconfidence, belief perseverance, and framing influence our decisions and judgments?

27-4 What factors contribute to our fear of unlikely events?

27-5 How do smart thinkers use intuition?

27-6 What is creativity, and what fosters it?

27-7 What do we know about thinking in other animals?

TERMS AND CONCEPTS TO REMEMBER

RETRIEVAL PRACTICE Test yourself on these terms by trying to write down the definition before flipping back to the page number referenced to check your answer.

cognition, p. 356	intuition, p. 359
concept, p. 356	availability heuristic, p. 359
prototype, p. 356	overconfidence, p. 361
algorithm, p. 357	belief perseverance, p. 361
heuristic, p. 357	framing, p. 362
insight, p. 357	creativity, p. 365
confirmation bias, p. 357	convergent thinking, p. 366
mental set, p. 358	divergent thinking, p. 366

Use 🔵 LearningCurve to create your personalized study plan, which will direct you to the resources that will help you most in 🔵 LaunchPad.

Language and Thought

IMAGINE AN ALIEN SPECIES THAT could pass thoughts from one head to another merely by pulsating air molecules in the space between them. Perhaps these weird creatures could inhabit a future science fiction movie?

Actually, we are those creatures. When we speak, our brain and voice apparatus conjure up air pressure waves that we send banging against another's eardrum—enabling us to transfer thoughts from our brain into theirs. As cognitive scientist Steven Pinker (1998) has noted, we sometimes sit for hours "listening to other people make noise as they exhale, because those hisses and squeaks contain *information*." And thanks to all those funny sounds created in our heads from the air pressure waves, we get people's attention. We get them to do things. We maintain relationships (Guerin, 2003). Depending on how you vibrate the air after opening your mouth, you may get a scowl or a kiss.

But **language** is more than vibrating air. As I [DM] create this paragraph, my fingers on a keyboard generate electronic binary numbers that are translated into the squiggles in front of you. When transmitted by reflected light rays into your retina, those squiggles trigger formless nerve impulses that project to several areas of your brain, which integrate the information, compare it to stored information, and decode meaning. Thanks to language, information is moving from my mind to yours. Monkeys mostly know what they see. Thanks to language (spoken, written, or signed), we comprehend much that we've never seen and that our distant ancestors never knew. Today, notes Daniel Gilbert (2006), the average taxi driver in Pittsburgh "knows more about the universe than did Galileo, Aristotle, Leonardo, or any of those other guys who were so smart they only needed one name."

To Pinker (1990), language is "the jewel in the crown of cognition." If you were able to retain only one cognitive ability, make it language, suggests researcher Lera Boroditsky (2009). Without sight or hearing, you could still have friends, family, and a job. But without language, could you have these things? "Language is so fundamental to our experience, so deeply a part of being human, that it's hard to imagine life without it."

Language transmits knowledge Whether spoken, written, or signed, language—the original wireless communication—enables mind-to-mind information transfer, and with it the transmission of civilization's accumulated knowledge across generations.

M. Spencer Green/AP Photo

Language Structure

28-1 What are the structural components of a language?

Consider how we might go about inventing a language. For a spoken language, we would need three building blocks:

- **Phonemes** are the smallest distinctive sound units in a language. To say *bat*, English speakers utter the phonemes *b*, *a*, and *t*. (Phonemes aren't the same as letters. *That* also has three phonemes—*th*, *a*, and *t*.) Linguists surveying nearly 500 languages have identified 869 different phonemes in human speech, but no language uses all of them (Holt, 2002; Maddieson, 1984). English uses about 40; other languages use anywhere from half to more than twice that many. As a general rule, consonant phonemes carry more information than do vowel phonemes. *The treth ef thes stetement shed be evedent frem thes bref demenstretien.*

- **Morphemes** are the smallest language units that carry meaning. In English, a few morphemes are also phonemes—the article *a*, for instance. But most morphemes combine two or more phonemes. Some, like *bat* or *gentle* are words. Others—like the prefix *pre-* in *preview* or the suffix *-ed* in *adapted*—are parts of words.

language our spoken, written, or signed words and the ways we combine them to communicate meaning.

phoneme in a language, the smallest distinctive sound unit.

morpheme in a language, the smallest unit that carries meaning; may be a word or a part of a word (such as a prefix).

grammar in a language, a system of rules that enables us to communicate with and understand others. In a given language, *semantics* is the set of rules for deriving meaning from sounds, and *syntax* is the set of rules for combining words into grammatically sensible sentences.

- **Grammar** is the system of rules that enables us to communicate with one another. Grammatical rules guide us in deriving meaning from sounds (*semantics*) and in ordering words into sentences (*syntax*).

Like life constructed from the genetic code's simple alphabet, language is complexity built of simplicity. In English, for example, 40 or so phonemes can be combined to form more than 100,000 morphemes, which alone or in combination produce the 616,500 word forms in the *Oxford English Dictionary*. Using those words, we can then create an infinite number of sentences, most of which (like this one) are original. I know that you can know why I worry that you think this sentence is starting to get too complex, but that complexity—and our capacity to communicate and comprehend it—is what distinguishes our human language capacity (Hauser et al., 2002; Premack, 2007).

"Eye dew."

RETRIEVAL PRACTICE

- How many morphemes are in the word *cats*? How many phonemes?

ANSWERS: Two morphemes—*cat* and *s*, and four phonemes—*c, a, t,* and *s*

Language Development

28-2 What are the milestones in language development, and how do we acquire language?

Make a quick guess: How many words of your native language did you learn between your first birthday and your high school graduation? Although you use only 150 words for about half of what you say, you probably learned about 60,000 words (Bloom, 2000; McMurray, 2007). That averages (after age 2) to nearly 3500 words each year, or nearly 10 each day! How you did it—how those 3500 words could so far outnumber the roughly 200 words your schoolteachers consciously taught you each year—is one of the great human wonders.

Could you even state your language's rules of syntax (the correct way to string words together to form sentences)? Most of us cannot. Yet before you were able to add 2 + 2, you were creating your own original and grammatically appropriate sentences. As a preschooler, you comprehended and spoke with a facility that puts to shame college students struggling to learn a foreign language.

We humans have an astonishing facility for language. With remarkable efficiency, we sample tens of thousands of words in our memory, effortlessly assemble them with near-perfect syntax, and spew them out, three words a second (Vigliocco & Hartsuiker, 2002). Seldom do we form sentences in our minds before speaking them. Rather we organize them on the fly as we speak. And while doing all this, we also adapt our utterances to our social and cultural context, following rules for speaking (How *far apart should we stand?*) and listening (*Is it OK to interrupt?*). Given how many ways there are to mess up, it's amazing that we master this social dance. When and how does it happen?

When Do We Learn Language?

Receptive Language Children's language development moves from simplicity to complexity. Infants start without language (*in fantis* means "not speaking"). Yet by 4 months of age, babies can recognize differences in speech sounds (Stager & Werker, 1997). They can also read lips: They prefer to look at a face that matches a sound, so we know they can recognize that *ah* comes from wide open lips and *ee* from a mouth with corners pulled back (Kuhl & Meltzoff, 1982). This marks the beginning of the development of babies' *receptive language*, their ability to understand what is said to and about them. Infants' language comprehension greatly outpaces their language production.

Jaimie Duplass/Shutterstock

babbling stage beginning at about 4 months, the stage of speech development in which the infant spontaneously utters various sounds at first unrelated to the household language.

one-word stage the stage in speech development, from about age 1 to 2, during which a child speaks mostly in single words.

two-word stage beginning about age 2, the stage in speech development during which a child speaks mostly in two-word statements.

telegraphic speech early speech stage in which a child speaks like a telegram—"go car"—using mostly nouns and verbs.

"*Got idea. Talk better. Combine words. Make sentences.*"

▼ TABLE 28.1
Summary of Language Development

Month (approximate)	Stage
4	Babbles many speech sounds ("ah-goo")
10	Babbling resembles household language ("ma-ma")
12	One-word stage ("Kitty!")
24	Two-word speech ("Get ball.")
24+	Rapid development into complete sentences

Even at six months, long before speaking, many infants recognize object names (Bergelson & Swingley, 2012, 2013). At 7 months and beyond, babies grow in their power to do what you and I find difficult when listening to an unfamiliar language: to segment spoken sounds into individual words.

Productive Language Long after the beginnings of receptive language, babies' *productive language,* their ability to produce words, matures. They recognize noun–verb differences—as shown by their responses to a misplaced noun or verb—earlier than they utter sentences with nouns and verbs (Bernal et al., 2010).

Before nurture molds babies' speech, nature enables a wide range of possible sounds in the **babbling stage,** beginning at around 4 months. Many of these spontaneously uttered sounds are consonant-vowel pairs formed by simply bunching the tongue in the front of the mouth (*da-da, na-na, ta-ta*) or by opening and closing the lips (*ma-ma*), both of which babies do naturally for feeding (MacNeilage & Davis, 2000). Babbling does not imitate the adult speech babies hear—it includes sounds from various languages. From this early babbling, a listener could not identify an infant as being, say, French, Korean, or Ethiopian. Deaf infants who observe their deaf parents signing begin to babble more with their hands. (Petitto & Marentette, 1991)

By about 10 months old, infants' babbling has changed so that a trained ear can identify the household language (de Boysson-Bardies et al., 1989). Without exposure to other languages, babies lose their ability to hear and produce sounds and tones found outside their native language (Meltzoff et al., 2009; Pallier et al., 2001). Thus, by adulthood, those who speak only English cannot discriminate certain sounds in Japanese speech. Nor can Japanese adults with no training in English hear the difference between the English *r* and *l*. For a Japanese-speaking adult, *la-la-ra-ra* may sound like the same syllable repeated. A Japanese-speaking person told that the train station is "just after the next light" may wonder, "The next what? After the street veering right, or farther down, after the light?"

Around their first birthday, most children enter the **one-word stage.** They have already learned that sounds carry meanings, and if repeatedly trained to associate, say, *fish* with a picture of a fish, 1-year-olds will look at a fish when a researcher says, "Fish, fish! Look at the fish!" (Schafer, 2005). They now begin to use sounds—usually only one barely recognizable syllable, such as *ma* or *da*—to communicate meaning. But family members learn to understand, and gradually the infant's language conforms more to the family's language. Across the world, baby's first words are often nouns that label objects or people (Tardif et al., 2008). At this one-word stage, a single inflected word ("*Doggy!*") may equal a sentence ("*Look at the dog out there!*").

At about 18 months, children's word learning explodes from about a word per week to a word per day. By their second birthday, most have entered the **two-word stage** (TABLE 28.1). They start uttering two-word sentences in **telegraphic speech.** Like yesterday's telegrams that charged by the word (TERMS ACCEPTED. SEND MONEY), a 2-year-old's speech contains mostly nouns and verbs ("*Want juice*"). Also like telegrams, it follows rules of syntax, arranging words in a sensible order. English-speaking children typically place adjectives before nouns—*white house* rather than *house white.* Spanish reverses this order, as in *casa blanca.*

Moving out of the two-word stage, children quickly begin uttering longer phrases (Fromkin & Rodman, 1983). If they get a late start on learning a particular language, such as after receiving a cochlear implant or being adopted by a family in another country, their language development still proceeds through the same sequence, although usually at a faster pace (Ertmer et al., 2007; Snedeker et al., 2007). By early elementary school, children understand complex sentences and begin to enjoy the humor conveyed by double meanings: "You never starve in the desert because of all the sand-which-is there."

RETRIEVAL PRACTICE

- What is the difference between *receptive* and *productive* language, and when do children normally hit these milestones in language development?

ANSWER: Infants normally start developing *receptive language* skills (ability to understand what is said to and about them) around 4 months of age. Then, starting with babbling at 4 months and beyond, infants normally start building *productive language* skills (ability to produce sounds and eventually words).

Explaining Language Development

The world's 6000+ or so languages are structurally very diverse (Evans & Levinson, 2009). Linguist Noam Chomsky has argued that all languages nonetheless share some basic elements, which he calls *universal grammar*. All human languages, for example, have nouns, verbs, and adjectives as grammatical building blocks. Moreover, said Chomsky, we humans are born with a built-in predisposition to learn grammar rules, which helps explain why preschoolers pick up language so readily and use grammar so well. It happens so naturally—as naturally as birds learn to fly—that training hardly helps.

We are not born with a built-in *specific* language, and languages are much more diverse than the universal grammar idea implies (Bergen, 2014; Ibbotson, 2012). Europeans and Native Australia–New Zealand populations, though geographically separated for 50,000 years, can readily learn each others' languages (Chater et al., 2009). And whatever language we experience as children, whether spoken or signed, we all readily learn its specific grammar and vocabulary (Bavelier et al., 2003). Yet no matter what language we learn, we start speaking it mostly in nouns (*kitty*, *da-da*) rather than in verbs and adjectives (Bornstein et al., 2004). Biology and experience work together.

Statistical Learning When adults listen to an unfamiliar language, the syllables all run together. A young Sudanese couple new to North America and unfamiliar with English might, for example, hear *United Nations* as "Uneye Tednay Shuns." Their 7-month-old daughter would not have this problem. Human infants display a remarkable ability to learn statistical aspects of human speech (Aslin & Newport, 2012; Werker et al., 2012). Their brains not only discern word breaks, they statistically analyze which syllables, as in "hap-py-ba-by," most often go together. After just two minutes of exposure to a computer voice speaking an unbroken, monotone string of nonsense syllables (*bidakupadotigolabubidaku* . . .), 8-month-old infants were able to recognize (as indicated by their attention) three-syllable sequences that appeared repeatedly (Saffran et al., 1996, 2009).

Purestock/Agefotostock

In further testimony to infants' surprising knack for soaking up language, research shows that 7-month-olds can learn simple sentence structures. After repeatedly hearing syllable sequences that follow one rule (an ABA pattern, such as *ga-ti-ga* and *li-na-li*), infants listened longer to syllables in a different sequence (an ABB pattern, such as *wo-fe-fe*, rather than *wo-fe-wo*). Their detecting the difference between the two patterns supports the idea that babies come with a built-in readiness to learn grammatical rules (Marcus et al., 1999).

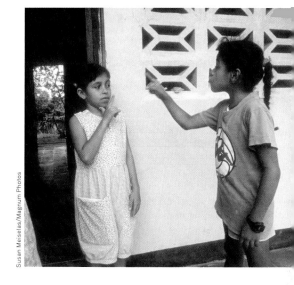
Susan Meiselas/Magnum Photos

Creating a language Brought together as if on a desert island (actually a school), Nicaragua's young deaf children over time drew upon sign gestures from home to create their own Nicaraguan Sign Language, complete with words and intricate grammar. Our biological predisposition for language does not create language in a vacuum. But activated by a social context, nature and nurture work creatively together (Osborne, 1999; Sandler et al., 2005; Senghas & Coppola, 2001).

A natural talent Human infants come with a remarkable capacity to soak up language. But the particular language they learn will reflect their unique interactions with others.

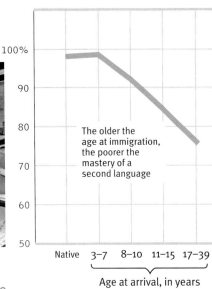

Percentage correct on grammar test

The older the age at immigration, the poorer the mastery of a second language

Age at arrival, in years

▼ **FIGURE 28.1**
Our ability to learn a new language diminishes with age Ten years after coming to the United States, Asian immigrants took an English grammar test. Although there is no sharply defined critical period for second language learning, those who arrived before age 8 understood American English grammar as well as native speakers did. Those who arrived later did not. (Data from Johnson & Newport, 1991.)

"Childhood is the time for language, no doubt about it. Young children, the younger the better, are good at it; it is child's play. It is a onetime gift to the species."

Lewis Thomas, *The Fragile Species*, 1992

"Children can learn multiple languages without an accent and with good grammar, if they are exposed to the language before puberty. But after puberty, it's very difficult to learn a second language so well. Similarly, when I first went to Japan, I was told not even to bother trying to bow, that there were something like a dozen different bows and I was always going to 'bow with an accent.'"

Psychologist Stephen M. Kosslyn, "The World in the Brain," 2008

Critical Periods Could we train adults to perform this same feat of statistical analysis later in the human life span? Many researchers believe not. Childhood seems to represent a *critical* (or "sensitive") *period* for mastering certain aspects of language before the language-learning window closes (Hernandez & Li, 2007). People who learn a second language as adults usually speak it with the accent of their native language, and they also have difficulty mastering the new grammar. In one experiment, Korean and Chinese immigrants considered 276 English sentences (*"Yesterday the hunter shoots a deer"*) and decided whether they were grammatically correct or incorrect (Johnson & Newport, 1991). All had been in the United States for approximately 10 years: Some had arrived in early childhood, others as adults. As **FIGURE 28.1** reveals, those who learned their second language early learned it best. The older one is when moving to a new country, the harder it will be to learn its language and to absorb its culture (Cheung et al., 2011; Hakuta et al., 2003).

The window on language learning closes gradually in early childhood. Later-than-usual exposure to language (at age 2 or 3) unleashes the idle language capacity of a child's brain, producing a rush of language. But by about age 7, those who have not been exposed to either a spoken or a signed language gradually lose their ability to master *any* language.

Deafness and Language Development

The impact of early experiences is evident in language learning in prelingually (before learning language) deaf[1] children born to hearing-nonsigning parents. These children typically do not experience language during their early years. Natively deaf children who learn sign language after age 9 never learn it as well as those who lose their hearing at age 9 after learning a spoken language such as English. They also never learn English as well as other natively deaf children who learned sign in infancy (Mayberry et al., 2002). Those who learn to sign as teens or adults are like immigrants who learn English after childhood: They can master basic words and learn to order them, but they never become as fluent as native signers in producing and comprehending subtle grammatical differences (Newport, 1990). Moreover, the late learners show less right hemisphere brain activity in regions that are active as native signers read sign language (Newman et al., 2002). As a flower's growth will be stunted without nourishment, so, too, children will typically become linguistically stunted if isolated from language during the critical period for its acquisition.

More than 90 percent of all deaf children are born to hearing parents. Most of these parents want their children to experience their world of sound and talk. Cochlear implants enable this by converting sounds into electrical signals and stimulating the auditory nerve by means of electrodes threaded into the child's cochlea. But if an implant is to help children become proficient in oral communication, parents cannot delay the surgery until their child reaches the age of consent. Giving cochlear implants to children is hotly debated. Deaf culture advocates object to giving implants to children who were

---
1. Deaf culture advocates prefer capitalizing "Deaf" when referring to those self-identified with Deaf culture.

deaf prelingually. The National Association of the Deaf, for example, argues that deafness is *not* a disability because native signers are not linguistically disabled. More than five decades ago, Gallaudet University linguist William Stokoe (1960) showed that sign is a complete language with its own grammar, syntax, and meanings.

Deaf culture advocates sometimes further contend that deafness could as well be considered "vision enhancement" as "hearing impairment." Close your eyes and immediately you, too, will notice your attention being drawn to your other senses. In one experiment, people who had spent 90 minutes sitting quietly blindfolded became more accurate in their location of sounds (Lewald, 2007). When kissing, lovers minimize distraction and increase sensitivity by closing their eyes.

People who lose one channel of sensation compensate with a slight enhancement of their other sensory abilities (Backman & Dixon, 1992; Levy & Langer, 1992). Blind musicians are more likely than sighted ones to develop perfect pitch (Hamilton, 2000). Blind people are also more accurate than sighted people at locating a sound source with one ear plugged (Gougoux et al., 2005; Lessard et al., 1998). And when reading Braille—requiring sensitive touch perception—the unused processing power of the visual cortex gets used (Amedi et al., 2003).

In deaf cats, brain areas normally used for hearing donate themselves to the visual system (Lomber et al., 2010). So, too, in people who have been deaf from birth: They exhibit enhanced attention to their peripheral vision (Bavelier et al., 2006). Their auditory cortex, starved for sensory input, remains largely intact but becomes responsive to touch and to visual input (Karns et al., 2012). Once repurposed, the auditory cortex becomes less available for hearing—which helps explain why cochlear implants are most effective when given before age 2 (Geers & Nicholas, 2013; Niparko et al., 2010).

Living in a Silent World Worldwide, 360 million people live with disabling hearing loss (WHO, 2013). Some are profoundly deaf; others (more men than women) have hearing loss (Agrawal et al., 2008). Some were deaf prelingually; others have known the hearing world. Some sign and identify with the language-based Deaf culture. Others, especially those who lost their hearing after speaking a language, are "oral" and converse with the hearing world by reading lips or reading written notes. Still others move between the two cultures.

The challenges of life without hearing may be greatest for children. Unable to communicate in customary ways, signing playmates may struggle to coordinate their play with speaking playmates. School achievement may also suffer; academic subjects are rooted in *spoken* languages. Adolescents may feel socially excluded, with a resulting low self-confidence. Children who grow up around other deaf people more often identify with Deaf culture and feel positive self-esteem. If raised in a signing household, whether by deaf or hearing parents, they also express higher self-esteem and feel more accepted (Bat-Chava, 1993, 1994).

Adults whose hearing becomes impaired later in life also face challenges. When older people with hearing loss must expend effort to hear words, they have less remaining cognitive capacity available to remember and comprehend them (Wingfield et al., 2005). In several studies, people with hearing loss, especially those not wearing hearing aids, have reported feeling sadder, being less socially engaged, and more often experiencing others' irritation (Chisolm et al., 2007; Fellinger et al., 2007; Kashubeck-West & Meyer, 2008; National Council on Aging, 1999). They also may experience a sort of shyness: "It's almost universal among the deaf to want to cause hearing people as little fuss as possible," observed Henry Kisor (1990, p. 244), a Chicago newspaper editor and columnist who lost his hearing at age 3. "We can be self-effacing and diffident to the point of invisibility. Sometimes this tendency can be crippling. I must fight it all the time." Helen Keller, both blind and deaf, noted that "Blindness cuts people off from things. Deafness cuts people off from people."

Don't means *Don't*—no matter how you say it! Deaf children of deaf-signing parents and hearing children of hearing parents have much in common. They develop language skills at about the same rate, and they are equally effective at opposing parental wishes and demanding their way.

Hearing improved

aphasia impairment of language, usually caused by left hemisphere damage either to Broca's area (impairing speaking) or to Wernicke's area (impairing understanding).

Broca's area controls language expression—an area of the frontal lobe, usually in the left hemisphere, that directs the muscle movements involved in speech.

Wernicke's area controls language reception—a brain area involved in language comprehension and expression; usually in the left temporal lobe.

I [DM] understand. My mother, with whom we communicated by writing notes on an erasable "magic pad," spent her last dozen years in an utterly silent world, largely withdrawn from the stress and strain of trying to interact with people outside a small circle of family and old friends. With my own hearing declining on a trajectory toward hers, I find myself sitting front and center at plays and meetings, seeking quiet corners in restaurants, and asking my wife to make necessary calls to friends whose accents differ from ours. I do benefit from cool technology (see www.hearingloop.org) that, at the press of a button, can transform my hearing aids into in-the-ear loudspeakers for the broadcast of phone, TV, and public address system sound. Yet I still experience frustration when, with or without hearing aids, I can't hear the joke everyone else is guffawing over; when, after repeated tries, I just can't catch that exasperated person's question and can't fake my way around it; when family members give up and say, "Oh, never mind" after trying three times to tell me something unimportant.

As she aged, my mother came to feel that seeking social interaction was simply not worth the effort. I share newspaper columnist Kisor's belief that communication is worth the effort (p. 246): "So, . . . I will grit my teeth and plunge ahead." To reach out, to connect, to communicate with others, even across a chasm of silence, is to affirm our humanity as social creatures.

RETRIEVAL PRACTICE

• What was the premise of researcher Noam Chomsky's work in language development?

ANSWER: Chomsky maintained that all languages share a universal grammar, and humans are biologically predisposed to learn the grammar rules of language.

• Why is it so difficult to learn a new language in adulthood?

ANSWER: Our brain's *critical period* for language learning is in childhood, when we can absorb language structure almost effortlessly. As we move past that stage in our brain's development, our ability to learn a new language diminishes dramatically.

The Brain and Language

28-3 What brain areas are involved in language processing and speech?

We think of speaking and reading, or writing and reading, or singing and speaking as merely different examples of the same general ability—language. But consider this curious finding: **Aphasia,** an impairment of language, can result from damage to any of several cortical areas. Even more curious, some people with aphasia can speak fluently but cannot read (despite good vision), while others can comprehend what they read but cannot speak. Still others can write but not read, read but not write, read numbers but not letters, or sing but not speak. These cases suggest that language is complex, and that different brain areas must serve different language functions.

Indeed, in 1865, French physician Paul Broca reported that after damage to an area of the left frontal lobe (later called **Broca's area**) a person would struggle to *speak* words while still being able to sing familiar songs and comprehend speech.

In 1874, German investigator Carl Wernicke discovered that after damage to an area of the left temporal lobe (**Wernicke's area**) people could speak only meaningless words. Asked to describe a picture that showed two boys stealing cookies behind a woman's back, one patient responded: "Mother is away her working her work to get her better, but when she's looking the two boys looking the other part. She's working another time" (Geschwind, 1979). Damage to Wernicke's area also disrupts understanding.

Today's neuroscience has confirmed brain activity in Broca's and Wernicke's areas during language processing (**FIGURE 28.2**). But language functions are distributed across other brain areas as well. Functional MRI scans show that different neural networks are activated by nouns and verbs (or objects and actions); by different vowels; and by reading stories of visual versus motor experiences (Shapiro et al., 2006; Speer et al., 2009). Different neural networks also enable one's native language and a second language (Perani & Abutalebi, 2005).

LaunchPad To review research on left and right hemisphere language processing—and to test your own speed in processing words presented to your left and right hemispheres—visit LaunchPad's *PsychSim 6: Dueling Hemispheres.*

"It is the way systems interact and have a dynamic interdependence that is—unless one has lost all sense of wonder—quite awe-inspiring."

Simon Conway Morris,
"The Boyle Lecture," 2005

(a)
Speaking words
(Broca's area and
the motor cortex)

(b)
Hearing words
(auditory cortex and
Wernicke's area)

▼ FIGURE 28.2
Brain activity when speaking and
hearing words

The big point to remember: In processing language, as in other forms of information processing, the brain operates by dividing its mental functions—speaking, perceiving, thinking, remembering—into subfunctions. Your conscious experience of reading this page *seems* indivisible, but you are engaging many different neural networks in your brain to compute each word's form, sound, and meaning (Posner & Carr, 1992). Different brain areas also process information about *who* spoke and *what* was said (Perrachione et al., 2011). We can also see this distributed processing in our visual system, for which the brain engages specialized subtasks, such as discerning color, depth, movement, and form. And in vision as in language, a localized trauma that destroys one of these neural work teams may cause people to lose just one aspect of processing. In visual processing, a stroke may destroy the ability to perceive movement but not color. In language processing, a stroke may impair the ability to speak distinctly without harming the ability to read. What we experience as a continuous, unified stream of experience is actually but the visible tip of a subdivided information-processing iceberg. *E pluribus unum:* Out of many, one.

RETRIEVAL PRACTICE

- _____ _____ is the part of the brain that, if damaged, might impair your ability to *speak* words. Damage to _____ _____ might impair your ability to understand language.

ANSWERS: Broca's area; Wernicke's area

Do Other Species Have Language?

28-4 What do we know about other animals' capacity for language?

Humans have long and proudly proclaimed that language sets us above all other animals. "When we study human language," asserted linguist Noam Chomsky (1972), "we are approaching what some might call the 'human essence,' the qualities of mind that are, so far as we know, unique [to humans]." Let's see if research on animal language supports claims that humans, alone, have language.

Animals display impressive comprehension and communication. Vervet monkeys sound different alarm cries for different predators: a barking call for a leopard, a cough for an eagle, and a chuttering for a snake. Hearing the leopard alarm, other vervets climb the nearest tree. Hearing the eagle alarm, they rush into the bushes. Hearing the snake chutter, they stand up and scan the ground (Byrne, 1991). To indicate such things as a type of threat—an eagle, leopard, falling tree, or neighboring group—monkeys will combine 6 different calls into a 25-call sequence (Balter, 2010). But is this language? This question launched many studies with chimpanzees.

In the late 1960s, psychologists Allen Gardner and Beatrix Gardner (1969) built on chimpanzees' natural tendencies for gestured communication by teaching sign

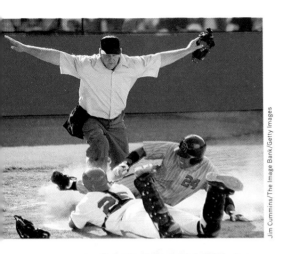

Talking hands Human language appears to have evolved from gestured communications (Corballis, 2002, 2003; Pollick & de Waal, 2007). Even today, gestures are naturally associated with spontaneous speech, especially speech that has spatial content. Both gesture and speech communicate, and when they convey the same rather than different information (as they do in baseball's sign language), we humans understand faster and more accurately (Hostetter, 2011; Kelly et al., 2010). Outfielder William Hoy, the first deaf player to join the major leagues (1892), reportedly helped invent hand signals for "Strike!" "Safe!" (shown here) and "Yerr out!" (Pollard, 1992). Referees in all sports now use invented signs, and fans are fluent in sports sign language.

language to a young chimpanzee named Washoe. After four years, Washoe could use 132 signs; by her life's end in 2007, she was using more than 245 signs (Metzler, 2011; Sanz et al., 1998). Washoe, for example, signed "You me go out, please." Some word combinations seemed creative—saying *water bird* for "swan" or *apple-which-is-orange* for "orange" (Patterson, 1978; Rumbaugh, 1977). But some psychologists grew skeptical. Were the chimps language champs or were the researchers chumps? Consider, said the skeptics:

- Ape vocabularies and sentences are simple, rather like those of a 2-year-old child. And unlike speaking or signing children, apes gain their limited vocabularies only with great difficulty (Wynne, 2004, 2008). Saying that apes can learn language because they can sign words is like saying humans can fly because they can jump.

- Chimpanzees can make signs or push buttons in sequence to get a reward. But pigeons, too, can peck a sequence of keys to get grain (Straub et al., 1979). The apes' signing might be nothing more than aping their trainers' signs and learning that certain arm movements produce rewards (Terrace, 1979).

- Studies of *perceptual set* (described in another module) show that when information is unclear, we tend to see what we want or expect to see. Interpreting chimpanzee signs as language may be little more than the trainers' wishful thinking (Terrace, 1979). When Washoe signed *water bird*, she may have been separately naming *water* and *bird*.

- "Give orange me give eat orange me eat orange . . ." is a far cry from the exquisite syntax of a 3-year-old (Anderson, 2004; Pinker, 1995). To the child, "You tickle" and "Tickle you" communicate different ideas. A chimpanzee, lacking human syntax, might use the same sequence of signs for both phrases.

Controversy can stimulate progress, and in this case, it triggered more evidence of chimpanzees' abilities to think and communicate. One surprising finding was that Washoe trained her adopted son Loulis to use the signs she had learned. After her second infant died, Washoe became withdrawn when told, "Baby dead, baby gone, baby finished." Two weeks later, researcher-caretaker Roger Fouts (1992, 1997) signed better news: "I have baby for you." Washoe reacted with instant excitement. Hair on end, she swaggered and panted while signing over and again, "Baby, my baby." It took several hours for the foster mom and infant to warm to each other, but then Washoe broke the ice by signing, "Come baby" and cuddling Loulis. Without human assistance, Loulis eventually picked up 68 signs, simply by observing Washoe and three other language-trained chimps signing together.

Even more stunning was a report that Kanzi, a bonobo with a reported 384-word vocabulary, could understand syntax (rules of word order) in spoken English (Savage-Rumbaugh et al., 1993, 2009). Kanzi, who appears to have the receptive language ability of a human 2-year-old, has responded appropriately when asked, "Can you show me the light?" and "Can you bring me the [flash]light?" and "Can you turn the light on?" Given stuffed animals and asked—for the first time—to "make the dog bite the snake," he put the snake to the dog's mouth.

So, how should we interpret these studies? Are humans the only language-using species? If by *language* we mean verbal or signed expression of complex grammar, most psychologists would now agree that humans alone possess

Comprehending canine Border collie Rico had a vocabulary of 200 human words. If asked to retrieve a toy with a name he had never heard, Rico would pick out a new toy from a group of familiar items (Kaminski et al., 2004). Hearing that name for the second time four weeks later, Rico more often than not would retrieve the same toy. Another border collie, Chaser, has set an animal record by learning 1022 object names (Pilley & Reid, 2011). Like a 3-year-old child, she can also categorize them by function and shape. She can "fetch a ball" or "fetch a doll."

language. If we mean, more simply, an ability to communicate through a meaningful sequence of symbols, then apes are indeed capable of language.

One thing is certain: Studies of animal language and thinking have moved psychologists toward a greater appreciation of other species, not only for our common traits but also for their own remarkable abilities. In the past, many psychologists doubted that other species could plan, form concepts, count, use tools, show compassion, or use language (Thorpe, 1974). Today, thanks to animal researchers, we know better. It's true that humans alone are capable of complex sentences. Moreover, 2½-year-old children display some cognitive abilities, such as following an actor's gaze to a target, that are unmatched even by chimpanzees (Herrmann et al., 2010). Humans, alone, also have a version of a gene (*FOXP2*) that helps enable the lip, tongue, and vocal cord movements of human speech (Lieberman, 2013). Humans with a mutated form of this gene have difficulty speaking words.

Nevertheless, other species do exhibit insight, show family loyalty, communicate with one another, care for one another, and transmit cultural patterns across generations. Working out what this means for the moral rights of other animals is an unfinished task.

LaunchPad For examples of intelligent communication and problem solving among orangutans, elephants, and killer whales, watch LaunchPad's 6-minute *Video: How Intelligent Are Animals?*

Paul Fusco/Magnum Photos

But is this language?
Chimpanzees' ability to express themselves in American Sign Language (ASL) raises questions about the very nature of language. Here, the trainer is asking, "What is this?" The sign in response is "Baby." Does the response constitute language?

RETRIEVAL PRACTICE

- If your dog barks at a stranger at the front door, does this qualify as language? What if the dog yips in a telltale way to let you know she needs to go out?

ANSWER: These are definitely communications. But if language consists of words and the grammatical rules we use to combine them to communicate meaning, few scientists would label a dog's barking and yipping as language.

Thinking and Language

28-5 What is the relationship between thinking and language, and what is the value of thinking in images?

Thinking and language intricately intertwine. Asking which comes first is one of psychology's chicken-and-egg questions. Do our ideas come first and then the words to name them? Or are our thoughts conceived in words and unthinkable without them?

Language Influences Thinking

Linguist Benjamin Lee Whorf (1956) contended that "language itself shapes a [person's] basic ideas." The Hopi, who have no past tense for their verbs, could not readily *think* about the past, said Whorf.

Whorf's **linguistic determinism** hypothesis is too extreme. We all think about things for which we have no words. (Can you think of a shade of blue you cannot name?) And we routinely have *unsymbolized* (wordless, imageless) thoughts, as when someone, while watching two men carry a load of bricks, wondered whether the men would drop them (Heavey & Hurlburt, 2008; Hurlburt et al., 2013).

Nevertheless, to those who speak two dissimilar languages, such as English and Japanese, it seems obvious that a person may think differently in different languages (Brown, 1986). Unlike English, which has a rich vocabulary for self-focused emotions such as anger, Japanese has more words for interpersonal emotions such as sympathy (Markus & Kitayama, 1991). Many bilingual individuals report that they have different senses of self, depending on which language they are using (Matsumoto, 1994). In one series of studies with bilingual Israeli Arabs (who spoke both Arabic and Hebrew), participants thought differently about their social world, with differing automatic associations with Arabs and Jews, depending on which language the testing session used (Danziger & Ward, 2010).

linguistic determinism Whorf's hypothesis that language determines the way we think.

Culture and color In Papua New Guinea, Berinmo children have words for different shades of "yellow," which might enable them to spot and recall yellow variations more quickly. Here and everywhere, "the languages we speak profoundly shape the way we think, the way we see the world, the way we live our lives," notes psychologist Lera Boroditsky (2009).

▼ FIGURE 28.3
Language and perception When people view blocks of equally different colors, they perceive those with different names as more different. Thus the "green" and "blue" in contrast A may appear to differ more than the two equally different blues in contrast B (Özgen, 2004).

Depending on which emotion they want to express, bilingual parents will often switch languages. "When my mom gets angry at me, she'll speak in Mandarin," explained one Chinese-American student. "If she's really mad, she'll switch to Cantonese" (Chen et al., 2012). Bilingual individuals may even reveal different personality profiles when taking the same test in two languages, with their differing cultural associations (Chen & Bond, 2010; Dinges & Hull, 1992). This happened when China-born, bilingual University of Waterloo students were asked to describe themselves in English or Chinese (Ross et al., 2002). The English-language self-descriptions fit typical Canadian profiles, expressing mostly positive self-statements and moods. Responding in Chinese, the same students gave typically Chinese self-descriptions, reporting more agreement with Chinese values and roughly equal positive and negative self-statements and moods. Similar personality changes have been shown when bicultural, bilingual Americans and Mexicans shifted between the cultural frames associated with English and Spanish (Ramírez-Esparza et al., 2006). "Learn a new language and get a new soul," says a Czech proverb.

So our words may not *determine* what we think, but they do *influence* our thinking (Boroditsky, 2011). We use our language in forming categories. In Brazil, the isolated Piraha people have words for the numbers 1 and 2, but numbers above that are simply "many." Thus, if shown 7 nuts in a row, they find it difficult to lay out the same number from their own pile (Gordon, 2004).

Words also influence our thinking about colors. Whether we live in New Mexico, New South Wales, or New Guinea, we *see* colors much the same, but we use our native language to *classify* and *remember* them (Davidoff, 2004; Roberson et al., 2004, 2005). Imagine viewing three colors and calling two of them "yellow" and one of them "blue." Later you would likely see and recall the yellows as being more similar. But if you speak the language of Papua New Guinea's Berinmo tribe, which has words for two different shades of yellow, you would more speedily perceive and better recall the variations between the two yellows. And if your language is Russian, which has distinct names for various shades of blue, such as *goluboy* and *siniy*, you might recall the yellows as more similar and remember the blues better. Words matter.

Perceived differences grow as we assign different names. On the color spectrum, blue blends into green—until we draw a dividing line between the portions we call "blue" and "green." Although equally different on the color spectrum, two different items that share the same color name (as the two "blues" do in **FIGURE 28.3**, contrast B) are harder to distinguish than two items with different names ("blue" and "green," as in Figure 28.3, contrast A) (Özgen, 2004). Likewise, two places seem closer and more vulnerable to the same natural disaster if labeled as in the same state rather than at an equal distance in adjacent states (Burris & Branscombe, 2005; Mishra & Mishra, 2010). Tornadoes don't know about state lines, but people do.

Given words' subtle influence on thinking, we do well to choose our words carefully. Is "A child learns language as *he* interacts with *his* caregivers" any different from "Children learn language as *they* interact with *their* caregivers"? Many studies have found that it is. When hearing the generic *he* (as in "the artist and his work") people are more likely to picture a male (Henley, 1989; Ng, 1990). If *he* and *his* were truly gender free, we shouldn't skip a beat when hearing that "man, like other mammals, nurses his young."

To expand language is to expand the ability to think. Children's thinking develops hand in hand with their language (Gopnik & Meltzoff, 1986). Indeed, it is very difficult to think about or conceptualize certain abstract ideas (*commitment, freedom,* or *rhyming*) without language! And what is true for preschoolers is true for everyone: *It pays to increase your word power.* That's why most textbooks, including this one, introduce new words—to teach new ideas and new ways of thinking. And that's also why psychologist Steven Pinker (2007) titled his book on language *The Stuff of Thought*.

Increased word power helps explain what McGill University researcher Wallace Lambert (1992; Lambert et al., 1993) has called the *bilingual advantage*. Bilingual people are skilled at inhibiting one language while using the other. And thanks to their well-practiced "executive control" over language, they also are better at inhibiting their attention to irrelevant information (Kroll & Bialystok, 2013). This superior attentional control is evident from 7 months of age into adulthood and even helps protect against cognitive decline in later life (Bak et al., 2014; Bialystok et al., 2012; Kroll et al., 2014).

Lambert helped devise a Canadian program that immerses English-speaking children in French. (The number of non-Quebec children enrolled rose from 65,000 in 1981 to over 328,000 in 2010 [Statistics Canada, 2013].) Not surprisingly, the children attain a natural French fluency unrivaled by other methods of language teaching. Moreover, compared with similarly capable children in control groups, they do so without detriment to their English fluency, and with increased aptitude scores, creativity, and appreciation for French-Canadian culture (Genesee & Gándara, 1999; Lazaruk, 2007).

Whether we are in the linguistic minority or majority, language links us to one another. Language also connects us to the past and the future. "To destroy a people, destroy their language," observed poet Joy Harjo.

> "All words are pegs to hang ideas on."
>
> Henry Ward Beecher,
> *Proverbs from Plymouth Pulpit*, 1887

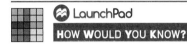

HOW WOULD YOU KNOW?

To consider how researchers have learned about the benefits of learning more than one language, visit LaunchPad's *How Would You Know If There is a Bilingual Advantage?*

RETRIEVAL PRACTICE

- Benjamin Lee Whorf's controversial hypothesis, called _____ _____ , suggested that we cannot think about things unless we have words for those concepts or ideas.

ANSWER: linguistic determinism

Thinking in Images

When you are alone, do you talk to yourself? Is "thinking" simply conversing with yourself? Without a doubt, words convey ideas. But sometimes ideas precede words. To turn on the cold water in your bathroom, in which direction do you turn the handle? To answer, you probably thought not in words but with *implicit* (nondeclarative, procedural) memory—a mental picture of how you do it.

Indeed, we often think in images. Artists think in images. So do composers, poets, mathematicians, athletes, and scientists. Albert Einstein reported that he achieved some of his greatest insights through visual images and later put them into words. Pianist Liu Chi Kung harnessed the power of thinking in images. One year after placing second in the 1958 Tschaikovsky piano competition, Liu was imprisoned during China's cultural revolution. Soon after his release, after seven years without touching a piano, he was back on tour. Critics judged Liu's musicianship as better than ever. How did he continue to develop without practice? "I did practice," said Liu, "every day. I rehearsed every piece I had ever played, note by note, in my mind" (Garfield, 1986).

For someone who has learned a skill, such as ballet dancing, even *watching* the activity will activate the brain's internal simulation of it, reported one British research team after collecting fMRIs as people watched videos (Calvo-Merino et al., 2004). So, too, will imagining a physical experience, which activates some of the same neural networks that are active during the actual experience (Grèzes & Decety, 2001). Small wonder, then, that mental practice has become a standard part of training for Olympic athletes (Suinn, 1997; Ungerleider, 2005).

One experiment on mental practice and basketball free-throw shooting tracked the University of Tennessee women's team over 35 games (Savoy & Beitel, 1996). During that time, the team's free-throw accuracy increased from approximately 52 percent in games following standard physical practice to some 65 percent after mental practice. Players had repeatedly imagined making free throws under various conditions, including being

> "When we see a person walking down the street talking to himself, we generally assume that he is mentally ill. But we all talk to ourselves continuously—we just have the good sense of keeping our mouths shut. . . . It's as though we are having a conversation with an imaginary friend possessed of infinite patience. Who are we talking to?"
>
> Sam Harris, "We Are Lost in Thought," 2011

Blend Images/Jupiterimages

"trash-talked" by their opposition. In a dramatic conclusion, Tennessee won the national championship game in overtime, thanks in part to their free-throw shooting.

Mental rehearsal can also help you achieve an academic goal, as researchers demonstrated with two groups of introductory psychology students facing a midterm exam one week later (Taylor et al., 1998). (Scores of other students, not engaging in any mental simulation, formed a control group.) The first group spent five minutes each day visualizing themselves scanning the posted grade list, seeing their A, beaming with joy, and feeling proud. This *outcome simulation* had little effect, adding only 2 points to their exam-score average. Another group spent five minutes each day visualizing themselves effectively studying—reading the textbook, going over notes, eliminating distractions, declining an offer to go out. This *process simulation* paid off: This second group began studying sooner, spent more time at it, and beat the others' average by 8 points. *The point to remember:* It's better to spend your fantasy time planning *how* to get somewhere than to dwell on the imagined destination.

LaunchPad To experience your own thinking as (a) manipulating words and (b) manipulating images, visit LaunchPad's *PsychSim 6: My Head Is Spinning!*

* * *

What, then, should we say about the relationship between thinking and language? As we have seen, language influences our thinking. But if thinking did not also affect language, there would never be any new words. And new words and new combinations of old words express new ideas. The basketball term *slam dunk* was coined after the act itself had become fairly common. *Blogs* became part of our language after web logs appeared. So, let us say that *thinking affects our language, which then affects our thought* (**FIGURE** 28.4).

▼ FIGURE 28.4
The interplay of thought and language The traffic runs both ways between thinking and language. Thinking affects our language, which affects our thought.

Thinking / Language

Psychological research on thinking and language mirrors the mixed impressions of our species by those in fields such as literature and religion. The human mind is simultaneously capable of striking intellectual failures and of striking intellectual power. Misjudgments are common and can have disastrous consequences. So we do well to appreciate our capacity for error. Yet our efficient heuristics—our snap judgment strategies—often serve us well. Moreover, our ingenuity at problem solving and our extraordinary power of language mark humankind as almost "infinite in faculties."

RETRIEVAL PRACTICE

• What is mental practice, and how can it help you to prepare for an upcoming event?

ANSWER: Mental practice uses visual imagery to mentally rehearse future behaviors, activating some of the same brain areas used during the actual behaviors. Visualizing the details of the process is more effective than visualizing only your end goal.

28 REVIEW Language and Thought

LEARNING OBJECTIVES

RETRIEVAL PRACTICE Take a moment to answer each of these Learning Objective Questions (repeated here from within this section). Then turn to Appendix C, Complete Chapter Reviews, to check your answers. Research suggests that trying to answer these questions on your own will improve your long-term retention (McDaniel et al., 2009).

28-1 What are the structural components of a language?

28-2 What are the milestones in language development, and how do we acqiure language?

28-3 What brain areas are involved in language processing and speech?

28-4 What do we know about other animals' capacity for language?

28-5 What is the relationship between thinking and language, and what is the value of thinking in images?

TERMS AND CONCEPTS TO REMEMBER

RETRIEVAL PRACTICE Test yourself on these terms by trying to write down the definition before flipping back to the page number referenced to check your answer.

language, p. 370

phoneme, p. 370

morpheme, p. 370

grammar, p. 371

babbling stage, p. 372

one-word stage, p. 372

two-word stage, p. 372

telegraphic speech, p. 372

aphasia, p. 376

Broca's area, p. 376

Wernicke's area, p. 376

linguistic determinism, p. 379

Use **LearningCurve** to create your personalized study plan, which will direct you to the resources that will help you most in **LaunchPad**.

TEST YOUR-SELF THINKING AND LANGUAGE

Test yourself repeatedly throughout your studies. This will not only help you figure out what you know and don't know; the testing itself will help you learn and remember the information more effectively thanks to the *testing effect.*

MODULE 27 Thinking

1. A mental grouping of similar things is called a _____ .

2. The most systematic procedure for solving a problem is a(n) _____ .

3. Oscar describes his political beliefs as "strongly liberal," but he has decided to explore opposing viewpoints. How might he be affected by *confirmation bias* and *belief perseverance* in this effort?

4. A major obstacle to problem solving is fixation, which is a(n)
   a. tendency to base our judgments on vivid memories.
   b. tendency to wait for insight to occur.
   c. inability to view a problem from a new perspective.
   d. rule of thumb for judging the likelihood of an event in terms of our mental image of it.

5. Widely reported terrorist attacks, such as on 9/11 in the United States, led some observers to initially assume in 2014 that the missing Malaysian Airlines Flight 370 was probably also the work of terrorists. This assumption illustrates the _____ heuristic.

6. When consumers respond more positively to ground beef described as "75 percent lean" than to the same product labeled "25 percent fat," they have been influenced by _____ .

7. Which of the following is NOT a characteristic of a creative person?
   a. Expertise
   b. Extrinsic motivation
   c. A venturesome personality
   d. Imaginative thinking skills

MODULE 28 Language and Thought

8. Children reach the one-word stage of speech development at about
   a. 4 months.
   b. 6 months.
   c. 1 year.
   d. 2 years.

9. The three basic building blocks of language are _____ , _____ , and _____ .

10. When young children speak in short phrases using mostly verbs and nouns, this is referred to as _____ .

11. According to Chomsky, all languages share a(n) _____ .

12. Most researchers agree that apes can
    a. communicate through symbols.
    b. reproduce most human speech sounds.
    c. master language in adulthood.
    d. surpass a human 3-year-old in language skills.

Find answers to these questions in Appendix D, in the back of the book.

INTELLIGENCE
· · · · · · · · · · · ·

Three huge controversies have sparked recent debate in and beyond psychology. First is the "memory war," over whether traumatic experiences are repressed and can later be recovered, with therapeutic benefit. The second great controversy is the "gender war," over the extent to which nature and nurture shape our behaviors as men and women. In these modules, we meet the "intelligence war": Does each of us have an inborn general mental capacity (intelligence)? And can we quantify this capacity as a meaningful number?

School boards, courts, and scientists debate the use and fairness of tests that assess people's mental abilities and assign them a score. Is intelligence testing a constructive way to guide people toward suitable opportunities? Or is it a potent, discriminatory weapon camouflaged as science? First, some basic questions:

- What is intelligence?
- How can we best assess intelligence?
- How do heredity and experience together weave the intelligence fabric?
- What do test score differences among individuals and groups really mean? Should we use such differences to rank people? To admit them to colleges or universities? To hire them?

Modules 29 through 32 offer answers, by identifying a variety of mental gifts and concluding that the recipe for high achievement blends talent and grit.

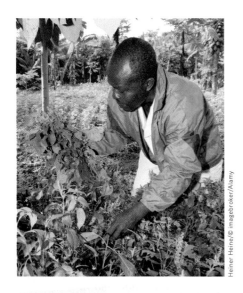

Hands-on healing The socially constructed concept of intelligence varies from culture to culture. This natural healer in Cameroon displays intelligence in his knowledge about medicinal plants and his understanding of the needs of the people he is helping.

" *g* is one of the most reliable and valid measures in the behavioral domain . . . and it predicts important social outcomes such as educational and occupational levels far better than any other trait."

Behavior geneticist Robert Plomin (1999)

What Is Intelligence?

29-1 How do psychologists define *intelligence,* and what are the arguments for *g?*

In many studies, *intelligence* has been defined as whatever *intelligence tests* measure, which has tended to be school smarts. But intelligence is not a quality like height or weight, which has the same meaning to everyone worldwide. People assign the term *intelligence* to the qualities that enable success in their own time and culture (Sternberg & Kaufman, 1998). In Cameroon's equatorial forest, *intelligence* may be understanding the medicinal qualities of local plants. In a North American high school, it may be mastering difficult concepts in tough courses. In both places, **intelligence** is the mental potential to learn from experience, solve problems, and use knowledge to adapt to new situations.

You probably know some people with talents in science, others who excel in the humanities, and still others gifted in athletics, art, music, or dance. You may also know a talented artist who is stumped by the simplest math problem, or a brilliant math student who struggles when discussing literature. Are all these people intelligent? Could you rate their intelligence on a single scale? Or would you need several different scales?

Spearman's General Intelligence Factor and Thurstone's Response

Charles Spearman (1863–1945) believed we have one **general intelligence** (often shortened to *g*) that is at the heart of all our intelligent behavior, from navigating the sea to excelling in school. He granted that people often have special, outstanding abilities. But he noted that those who score high in one area, such as verbal intelligence, typically score higher than average in other areas, such as spatial or reasoning ability. Spearman's belief stemmed in part from his work with *factor analysis,* a statistical procedure that identifies clusters of related items.

This idea of a general mental capacity expressed by a single intelligence score was controversial in Spearman's day, and so it remains. One of Spearman's early opponents was L. L. Thurstone (1887–1955). Thurstone gave 56 different tests to people and mathematically identified seven clusters of primary mental abilities (word fluency, verbal comprehension, spatial ability, perceptual speed, numerical ability, inductive reasoning, and memory). Thurstone did not rank people on a single scale of general aptitude. But when other investigators studied these profiles, they detected a persistent tendency: Those who excelled in one of the seven clusters generally scored well on the others. So, the investigators concluded, there was still some evidence of a *g* factor.

We might, then, liken mental abilities to physical abilities: The ability to run fast is distinct from the eye-hand coordination required to throw a ball on target. Yet there remains some tendency for good things to come packaged together—for running speed and throwing accuracy to correlate. So, too, with intelligence. Several distinct abilities tend to cluster together and to correlate enough to define a general intelligence factor. Distinct brain networks enable distinct abilities, with *g* explained by their coordinated activity (Hampshire et al., 2012).

Satoshi Kanazawa (2004, 2010) argues that general intelligence evolved as a form of intelligence that helps people solve *novel* (unfamiliar) problems—how to stop a fire from spreading, how to find food during a drought, how to reunite with one's tribe on the other side of a flooded river. More common problems—such as how to mate or how to read a stranger's face or how to find your way back to camp—require a different sort of intelligence. Kanazawa asserts that general intelligence scores *do* correlate with the ability to solve various novel problems (like those found in academic and many vocational situations) but do *not* correlate much with individuals' skills in *evolutionarily familiar* situations—such as marrying and parenting, forming close friendships, and navigating without maps.

Jonathan Larsen/Diadem Images/Alamy

Theories of Multiple Intelligences

29-2 How do Gardner's and Sternberg's theories of multiple intelligences differ, and what criticisms have they faced?

Other psychologists, particularly since the mid-1980s, have sought to extend the definition of *intelligence* beyond the idea of academic smarts.

Gardner's Multiple Intelligences

Howard Gardner has identified eight *relatively independent intelligences*, including the verbal and mathematical aptitudes assessed by standard tests (**FIGURE 29.1**). Thus, the computer programmer, the poet, the street-smart adolescent who becomes a crafty executive, and the basketball team's play-making point guard exhibit different kinds of intelligence (Gardner, 1998). Gardner (1999) has also proposed a ninth possible intelligence—*existential intelligence*—the ability "to ponder large questions about life, death, existence."

Gardner (1983, 2006; 2011; Davis et al., 2011) views these intelligence domains as multiple abilities that come in different packages. Brain damage, for example, may destroy one ability but leave others intact. And consider people with **savant syndrome.** Despite their island of brilliance, these people often score low on intelligence tests and may have limited or no language ability (Treffert & Wallace, 2002). Some can compute complicated calculations quickly and accurately, or identify the day of the week corresponding to any given historical date, or render incredible works of art or musical performance (Miller, 1999).

About 4 in 5 people with savant syndrome are males, and many also have *autism spectrum disorder (ASD)*, a developmental disorder. The late memory whiz Kim Peek

intelligence the mental potential to learn from experience, solve problems, and use knowledge to adapt to new situations.

general intelligence (*g*) a general intelligence factor that, according to Spearman and others, underlies specific mental abilities and is therefore measured by every task on an intelligence test.

savant syndrome a condition in which a person otherwise limited in mental ability has an exceptional specific skill, such as in computation or drawing.

▼ FIGURE 29.1
Gardner's eight intelligences Gardner has also proposed a ninth possible intelligence—existential intelligence—the ability to ponder deep questions about life.

Islands of genius: Savant syndrome
After a brief helicopter ride over Singapore followed by five days of drawing, British savant artist Stephen Wiltshire accurately reproduced an aerial view of the city from memory.

(who did not have ASD) inspired the movie *Rain Man*. In 8 to 10 seconds, he could read and remember a page. During his lifetime, he memorized 9000 books, including Shakespeare's works and the Bible. He could provide GPS-like travel directions within any major U.S. city, yet he could not button his clothes. And he had little capacity for abstract concepts. Asked by his father at a restaurant to lower his voice, he slid lower in his chair to lower his voice box. Asked for Lincoln's Gettysburg Address, he responded, "227 North West Front Street. But he only stayed there one night—he gave the speech the next day" (Treffert & Christensen, 2005).

Sternberg's Three Intelligences

Robert Sternberg (1985, 2011) agrees with Gardner that there is more to success than traditional intelligence and that we have multiple intelligences. But his *triarchic theory* proposes three, not eight or nine, intelligences:

- *Analytical (academic problem-solving) intelligence* is assessed by intelligence tests, which present well-defined problems having a single right answer. Such tests predict school grades reasonably well and vocational success more modestly.

- *Creative intelligence* is demonstrated in innovative smarts: the ability to generate novel ideas.

"You have to be careful, if you're good at something, to make sure you don't think you're good at other things that you aren't necessarily so good at. . . . Because I've been very successful at [software development] people come in and expect that I have wisdom about topics that I don't."

Philanthropist Bill Gates (1998)

"You're wise, but you lack tree smarts."

- *Practical intelligence* is required for everyday tasks that are not well-defined, and that may have many possible solutions. Managerial success, for example, depends less on academic problem-solving skills than on a shrewd ability to manage oneself, one's tasks, and other people. Sternberg and Richard Wagner (1993, 1995; Wagner, 2011) offer a test of practical managerial intelligence that measures skill at writing effective memos, motivating people, delegating tasks and responsibilities, reading people, and promoting one's own career. Business executives who score relatively high on this test tend to earn high salaries and receive high performance ratings.

With support from the U.S. College Board (which administers the widely used SAT Reasoning Test to U.S. college and university applicants), Sternberg (2006, 2007, 2010) and a team of collaborators have developed new measures of creativity (such as thinking up a caption for an untitled cartoon) and practical thinking (such as figuring out how to move a large bed up a winding staircase). These more comprehensive assessments improve prediction of American students' first-year college grades, and they do so with reduced ethnic-group differences.

Gardner and Sternberg differ on specific points, but they agree on two important

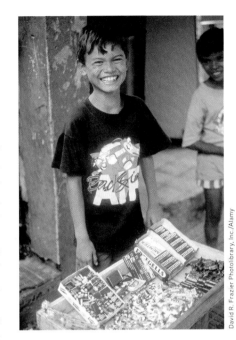

Street smarts This child selling candy on the streets of Manaus, Brazil, is developing practical intelligence at a very young age.

David R. Frazier Photolibrary, Inc./Alamy

points: Multiple abilities can contribute to life success, and differing varieties of giftedness add spice to life and challenges for education. Under their influence, many teachers have been trained to appreciate such variety and to apply multiple intelligence theories in their classrooms.

Criticisms of Multiple Intelligence Theories

Wouldn't it be nice if the world were so just that a weakness in one area would be compensated by genius in another? Alas, say critics, the world is not just (Ferguson, 2009; Scarr, 1989). Research using factor analysis confirms that there *is* a general intelligence factor (Johnson et al., 2008): *g* matters. It predicts performance on various complex tasks and in various jobs (Gottfredson, 2002a,b, 2003a,b; see also **FIGURE 29.2**). Much as jumping ability is not a predictor of jumping performance when the bar is set a foot off the ground—but becomes a predictor when the bar is set higher—so extremely high cognitive ability scores predict exceptional attainments, such as doctoral degrees and publications (Kuncel & Hezlett, 2010).

▼ FIGURE 29.2
Smart and rich? Jay Zagorsky (2007) tracked 7403 participants in the U.S. National Longitudinal Survey of Youth across 25 years. As shown in this scatterplot, their intelligence scores correlated +.30, a moderate positive correlation, with their later income. Each dot indicates a given youth's intelligence score and later adult income.

Spatial intelligence genius In 1998, World Checkers Champion Ron "Suki" King of Barbados set a new record by simultaneously playing 385 players in 3 hours and 44 minutes. Thus, while his opponents often had hours to plot their game moves, King could only devote about 35 seconds to each game. Yet he still managed to win all 385 games!

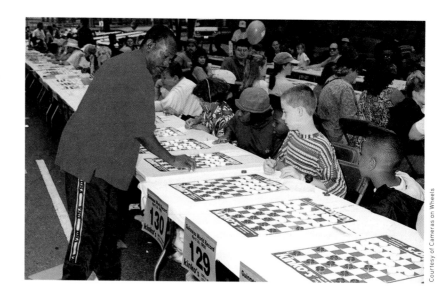

Courtesy of Cameras on Wheels

Even so, "success" is not a one-ingredient recipe. High intelligence may help you get into a profession (via the schools and training programs that take you there), but it won't make you successful once there. Success is a combination of talent with *grit*: Those who become highly successful tend also to be conscientious, well-connected, and doggedly energetic. K. Anders Ericsson (2002, 2007; Ericsson et al., 2007) reports a *10-year rule*: A common ingredient of expert performance in chess, dancing, sports, computer programming, music, and medicine is "about 10 years of intense, daily practice" (Ericsson, 2002, 2007; Simon & Chase, 1973). Becoming a professional musician requires a certain cognitive ability. But it also requires practice—about 11,000 hours on average, and a *minimum* of 3000 hours (Campitelli & Gobet, 2011). The recipe for success is a gift of nature plus a whole lot of nurture.

RETRIEVAL PRACTICE

• How does the existence of savant syndrome support Gardner's theory of multiple intelligences?

ANSWER: People with savant syndrome have limited overall but possess one or more exceptional skills, which, according to Howard Gardner, suggests that our abilities come in separate packages rather than being fully expressed by one general intelligence that encompasses all of our talents.

Emotional Intelligence

29-3 What are the four components of emotional intelligence?

Is being in tune with yourself and others also a sign of intelligence, distinct from academic intelligence? Some researchers say *Yes*. They define *social intelligence* as the know-how involved in social situations and managing yourself successfully (Cantor & Kihlstrom, 1987). People with high social intelligence can read social situations the way a skilled soccer player reads the defense or a meterologist reads the weather. The concept was first proposed in 1920 by psychologist Edward Thorndike, who noted, "The best mechanic in a factory may fail as a foreman for lack of social intelligence" (Goleman, 2006, p. 83).

One line of research has explored a specific aspect of social intelligence called **emotional intelligence,** consisting of four abilities (Mayer et al., 2002, 2011, 2012):

• *Perceiving* emotions (recognizing them in faces, music, and stories)

• *Understanding* emotions (predicting them and how they may change and blend)

emotional intelligence the ability to perceive, understand, manage, and use emotions.

- *Managing* emotions (knowing how to express them in varied situations)
- *Using* emotions to enable adaptive or creative thinking

Emotionally intelligent people are both socially aware and self-aware. Those who score high on managing emotions enjoy higher-quality interactions with friends (Lopes et al., 2004). They avoid being hijacked by overwhelming depression, anxiety, or anger. They can read others' emotional cues and know what to say to soothe a grieving friend, encourage a workmate, and manage a conflict.

These emotional intelligence high scorers also perform modestly better on the job (O'Boyle et al., 2011). On and off the job, they can delay gratification in pursuit of long-range rewards, rather than being overtaken by immediate impulses. Simply said, they are emotionally smart. Thus, they often succeed in career, marriage, and parenting situations where academically smarter (but emotionally less intelligent) people might fail (Cherniss, 2010a,b; Ciarrochi et al., 2006).

Some scholars, however, are concerned that emotional intelligence stretches the intelligence concept too far (Visser et al., 2006). Howard Gardner (1999) includes interpersonal and intrapersonal intelligences as two of his eight forms of multiple intelligences. But let us also, he acknowledges, respect emotional sensitivity, creativity, and motivation as important but different. Stretch *intelligence* to include everything we prize and the word will lose its meaning.

The procrastinator's motto: "Hard works pays off later; laziness pays off now."

* * *

For a summary of these theories of intelligence, see **TABLE 29.1**.

▼ TABLE 29.1
Comparing Theories of Intelligence

Theory	Summary	Strengths	Other Considerations
Spearman's general intelligence (g)	A basic intelligence predicts our abilities in varied academic areas.	Different abilities, such as verbal and spatial, do have some tendency to correlate.	Human abilities are too diverse to be encapsulated by a single general intelligence factor.
Thurstone's primary mental abilities	Our intelligence may be broken down into seven factors: word fluency, verbal comprehension, spatial ability, perceptual speed, numerical ability, inductive reasoning, and memory.	A single *g* score is not as informative as scores for seven primary mental abilities.	Even Thurstone's seven mental abilities show a tendency to cluster, suggesting an underlying *g* factor.
Gardner's multiple intelligences	Our abilities are best classified into eight or nine independent intelligences, which include a broad range of skills beyond traditional school smarts.	Intelligence is more than just verbal and mathematical skills. Other abilities are equally important to our human adaptability.	Should all of our abilities be considered *intelligences?* Shouldn't some be called less vital *talents?*
Sternberg's triarchic theory	Our intelligence is best classified into three areas that predict real-world success: analytical, creative, and practical.	These three domains can be reliably measured.	1. These three domains may be less independent than Sternberg thought and may actually share an underlying *g* factor. 2. Additional testing is needed to determine whether these domains can reliably predict success.
Emotional intelligence	Social intelligence is an important indicator of life success. Emotional intelligence is a key aspect, consisting of perceiving, understanding, managing, and using emotions.	The four components that predict social success.	Does this stretch the concept of intelligence too far?

MODULE 29   REVIEW   What Is Intelligence?

LEARNING OBJECTIVES

RETRIEVAL PRACTICE Take a moment to answer each of these Learning Objective Questions (repeated here from within this module). Then turn to Appendix C, Complete Module Reviews, to check your answers. Research suggests that trying to answer these questions on your own will improve your long-term retention (McDaniel et al., 2009).

29-1 How do psychologists define *intelligence,* and what are the arguments for *g?*

29-2 How do Gardner's and Sternberg's theories of multiple intelligences differ, and what criticisms have they faced?

29-3 What are the four components of emotional intelligence?

TERMS AND CONCEPTS TO REMEMBER

RETRIEVAL PRACTICE Test yourself on these terms by trying to write down the definition before flipping back to the page number referenced to check your answer.

intelligence, p. 387

general intelligence (*g*), p. 387

savant syndrome, p. 387

emotional intelligence, p. 390

Use 🐝 **LearningCurve** to create your personalized study plan, which will direct you to the resources that will help you most in 🐝 **LaunchPad**.

---

intelligence test a method for assessing an individual's mental aptitudes and comparing them with those of others, using numerical scores.

achievement test a test designed to assess what a person has learned.

aptitude test a test designed to predict a person's future performance; *aptitude* is the capacity to learn.

MODULE 30   Assessing Intelligence

30-1 What is an intelligence test, and what is the difference between achievement and aptitude tests?

An **intelligence test** assesses people's mental abilities and compares them with others, using numerical scores. How do we design such tests, and what makes them credible? Consider why psychologists created tests of mental abilities and how they have used them.

By this point in your life, you've faced dozens of ability tests: school tests of basic reading and math skills, course exams, intelligence tests, driver's license exams. Psychologists classify such tests as either **achievement tests,** intended to *reflect* what you have learned, or **aptitude tests,** intended to *predict* your ability to learn a new skill. Exams covering what you have learned in this course are achievement tests. A college entrance exam, which seeks to predict your ability to do college work, is an aptitude test—a "thinly disguised intelligence test," says Howard Gardner (1999). Indeed, report Meredith Frey and Douglas Detterman (2004), total scores on the U.S. SAT have correlated +.82 with *general intelligence* scores in a national sample of 14- to 21-year-olds (**FIGURE 30.1**).

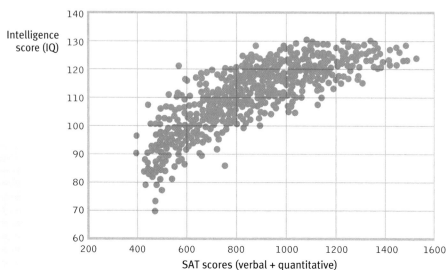

▼ FIGURE 30.1
Close cousins: Aptitude and intelligence scores A scatterplot shows the close correlation that has existed between intelligence scores and verbal and quantitative SAT scores. (Data from Frey and Detterman, 2004.)

Early and Modern Tests of Mental Abilities

30-2 When and why were intelligence tests created, and how do today's tests differ from early intelligence tests?

Some societies concern themselves with promoting the collective welfare of the family, community, and society. Other societies emphasize individual opportunity. Plato, a pioneer of the individualist tradition, wrote more than 2000 years ago in *The Republic* that "no two persons are born exactly alike; but each differs from the other in natural endowments, one being suited for one occupation and the other for another." As heirs to Plato's individualism, people in Western societies have pondered how and why individuals differ in mental ability.

Francis Galton: Belief in Hereditary Genius

Western attempts to assess such differences began in earnest with English scientist Francis Galton (1822–1911), who was fascinated with measuring human traits. When his cousin Charles Darwin proposed that nature selects successful traits through the survival of the fittest, Galton wondered if it might be possible to measure "natural ability" and to encourage those of high ability to mate with one another. At the 1884 London Health Exhibition, more than 10,000 visitors received his assessment of their "intellectual strengths" based on such things as reaction time, sensory acuity, muscular power, and body proportions. But alas, on these measures, well-regarded adults and students did not outscore others. Nor did the measures correlate with each other.

Although Galton's quest for a simple intelligence measure failed, he gave us some statistical techniques that we still use (as well as the phrase *nature and nurture*). And his persistent belief in the inheritance of genius—reflected in his book, *Hereditary Genius*—illustrates an important lesson from both the history of intelligence research and the history of science: Although science itself strives for objectivity, individual scientists are affected by their own assumptions and attitudes.

Alfred Binet: Predicting School Achievement

Modern intelligence testing traces its birth to early twentieth-century France, where a new law required all children to attend school. French officials knew that some children, including many newcomers to Paris, would struggle and need special classes. But how could the schools make fair judgments about children's learning potential? Teachers might assess children who had little prior education as slow learners. Or they might sort children into classes on the basis of their social backgrounds. To minimize such bias, France's minister of public education gave Alfred Binet and others, including Théodore Simon, the task of studying this problem.

In 1905, Binet and Simon first presented their work under the archaic title, "New Methods for Diagnosing the Idiot, the Imbecile, and the Moron" (Nicolas & Levine, 2012). They began by assuming that all children follow the same course of intellectual development but that some develop more rapidly. On tests, therefore, a "dull" child should score much like a typical younger child, and a "bright" child like a typical older child. Thus, their goal became measuring each child's **mental age,** the level of performance typically associated with a certain chronological age. The average 9-year-old, then, has a mental age of 9. Children with below-average mental ages, such as 9-year-olds who perform at the level of typical 7-year-olds, would struggle with age-appropriate schoolwork. A 9-year-old who performs at the level of typical 11-year-olds should find schoolwork easy.

To measure mental age, Binet and Simon theorized that mental aptitude, like athletic aptitude, is a general capacity that shows up in various ways. They tested a variety of reasoning and problem-solving questions on Binet's two daughters, and then on "bright" and "backward" Parisian schoolchildren. The items they developed eventually predicted how well French children would handle their schoolwork.

Alfred Binet (1857–1911) "Some recent philosophers have given their moral approval to the deplorable verdict that an individual's intelligence is a fixed quantity, one which cannot be augmented. We must protest and act against this brutal pessimism" (Binet, 1909, p. 141).

---

mental age a measure of intelligence test performance devised by Binet; the chronological age that most typically corresponds to a given level of performance. Thus, a child who does as well as an average 8-year-old is said to have a mental age of 8.

"The IQ test was invented to predict academic performance, nothing else. If we wanted something that would predict life success, we'd have to invent another test completely."

Social psychologist Robert Zajonc (1984b)

Binet and Simon made no assumptions concerning *why* a particular child was slow, average, or precocious. Binet personally leaned toward an environmental explanation. To raise the capacities of low-scoring children, he recommended "mental orthopedics" that would help develop their attention span and self-discipline. He believed his intelligence test did not measure inborn intelligence as a scale measures weight. Rather, it had a single practical purpose: to identify French schoolchildren needing special attention. Binet hoped his test would be used to improve children's education, but he also feared it would be used to label children and limit their opportunities (Gould, 1981).

RETRIEVAL PRACTICE

• What did Binet hope to achieve by establishing a child's *mental age?*

ANSWER: Binet hoped that the child's *mental age* (the age that typically corresponds to the child's level of performance), would help identify appropriate school placements of children.

Stanford-Binet the widely used American revision (by Terman at Stanford University) of Binet's original intelligence test.

intelligence quotient (IQ) defined originally as the ratio of mental age (*ma*) to chronological age (*ca*) multiplied by 100 (thus, IQ = *ma/ca* × 100). On contemporary intelligence tests, the average performance for a given age is assigned a score of 100.

Lewis Terman: The Innate IQ

Binet's fears were realized soon after his death in 1911, when others adapted his tests for use as a numerical measure of inherited intelligence. This began when Stanford University professor Lewis Terman (1877–1956) found that the Paris-developed questions and age norms worked poorly with California schoolchildren. Adapting some of Binet's original items, adding others, and establishing new age norms, Terman extended the upper end of the test's range from teenagers to "superior adults." He also gave his revision the name it retains today—the **Stanford-Binet.**

From such tests, German psychologist William Stern derived the famous **intelligence quotient,** or **IQ.** The IQ is simply a person's mental age divided by chronological age and multiplied by 100 to get rid of the decimal point:

$$IQ = \frac{\text{mental age}}{\text{chronological age}} \times 100$$

Thus, an average child, whose mental and chronological ages are the same, has an IQ of 100. But an 8-year-old who answers questions as would a typical 10-year-old has an IQ of 125.

The original IQ formula worked fairly well for children but not for adults. (Should a 40-year-old who does as well on the test as an average 20-year-old be assigned an IQ of only 50?) Most current intelligence tests, including the Stanford-Binet, no longer compute an IQ in this manner (though the term *IQ* still lingers as a shorthand expression for "intelligence test score"). Instead, they represent the test-taker's performance *relative to the average performance of others the same age.* This average performance is arbitrarily assigned a score of 100, and about two-thirds of all test-takers fall between 85 and 115.

Terman (1916, p. 4) promoted the widespread use of intelligence testing to "take account of the inequalities of children in original endowment" by assessing their "vocational fitness." In sympathy with Francis Galton's *eugenics*—the much-criticized nineteenth-century movement that proposed measuring human traits and using the results to encourage only smart and fit people to reproduce—Terman envisioned that the use of intelligence tests would "ultimately result in curtailing the reproduction of feeble-mindedness and in the elimination of an enormous amount of crime, pauperism, and industrial inefficiency" (p. 7).

With Terman's help, the U.S. government developed new tests to evaluate both newly arriving immigrants and World War I army recruits—the world's first mass administration of an intelligence test. To some psychologists, the results indicated the inferiority of people not sharing their Anglo-Saxon heritage. Such findings were part of the cultural climate that led to a 1924 immigration law that reduced Southern and Eastern European immigration quotas to less than a fifth of those for Northern and Western Europe.

THAT'S MY BOY, MARK... HE'S 39, BUT HE'S ALREADY READING AT A 42-YEAR-OLD LEVEL...

Mrs. Randolph takes mother's pride too far.

Binet probably would have been horrified that his test had been adapted and used to draw such conclusions. Indeed, such sweeping judgments became an embarrassment to most of those who championed testing. Even Terman came to appreciate that test scores reflected not only people's innate mental abilities but also their education, native language, and familiarity with the culture assumed by the test. Abuses of the early intelligence tests serve to remind us that science can be value-laden. Behind a screen of scientific objectivity, ideology sometimes lurks.

> **Wechsler Adult Intelligence Scale (WAIS)** the WAIS and its companion versions for children are the most widely used intelligence tests; contain verbal and performance (nonverbal) subtests.

RETRIEVAL PRACTICE

• What is the IQ of a 4-year-old with a mental age of 5?

ANSWER: 125 (5 ÷ 4 × 100 = 125)

David Wechsler: Separate Scores for Separate Skills

Psychologist David Wechsler created what is now the most widely used individual intelligence test, the **Wechsler Adult Intelligence Scale (WAIS),** together with a version for school-age children (the *Wechsler Intelligence Scale for Children [WISC]*), and another for preschool children (Evers et al., 2012). The latest (2008) edition of the WAIS consists of 15 subtests, including these:

• *Similarities*—Reasoning the commonality of two objects or concepts, such as "In what way are wool and cotton alike?"

• *Vocabulary*—Naming pictured objects, or defining words ("What is a guitar?")

• *Block Design*—Visual abstract processing, such as "Using the four blocks, make one just like this."

• *Letter-Number Sequencing*—On hearing a series of numbers and letters, repeat the numbers in ascending order, and then the letters in alphabetical order: "R-2-C-1-M-3."

The WAIS yields not only an overall intelligence score, as does the Stanford-Binet, but also separate scores for verbal comprehension, perceptual organization, working memory, and processing speed. Striking differences among these scores can provide clues to cognitive strengths or weaknesses. For example, a low verbal comprehension score combined with high scores on other subtests could indicate a reading or language disability. Other comparisons can help a psychologist or psychiatrist establish a rehabilitation plan for a stroke patient. In such ways, these tests help realize Binet's aim: to identify opportunities for improvement and strengths that teachers and others can build upon. Such uses are possible, of course, only when we can trust the test results.

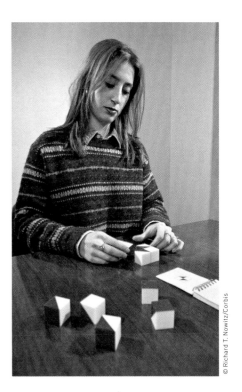

Matching patterns Block design puzzles test visual abstract processing ability. Wechsler's individually administered intelligence test comes in forms suited for adults and children.

RETRIEVAL PRACTICE

• An employer with a pool of applicants for a single available position is interested in testing each applicant's potential. To help her decide whom she should hire, she should use an _____ (achievement/aptitude) test. That same employer wishing to test the effectiveness of a new, on-the-job training program would be wise to use an _____ (achievement/aptitude) test.

ANSWERS: aptitude; achievement

Principles of Test Construction

30-3 What is a normal curve, and what does it mean to say that a test has been standardized and is reliable and valid?

To be widely accepted, a psychological test must meet three criteria: It must be *standardized, reliable,* and *valid.* The Stanford-Binet and Wechsler tests meet these requirements.

standardization defining uniform testing procedures and meaningful scores by comparison with the performance of a pretested group.

normal curve the bell-shaped curve that describes the distribution of many physical and psychological attributes. Most scores fall near the average, and fewer and fewer scores lie near the extremes.

Standardization

The number of questions you answer correctly on an intelligence test would reveal almost nothing. To know how well you performed, you would need some basis for comparison. That's why test-makers give new tests to a representative sample of people. The scores from this pretested group become the basis for future comparisons. If you later take the test following the same procedures, your score will be meaningful when compared with others. This process is called **standardization.**

If we construct a graph of test-takers' scores, the scores typically form a bell-shaped pattern called the **normal curve.** No matter what attributes we measure—height, weight, or mental aptitude—people's scores tend to form a *bell curve*. The highest point is the midpoint, or the average score. On an intelligence test, we give this average score a value of 100 (**FIGURE 30.2**). Moving out from the average, toward either extreme, we find fewer and fewer people. For both the Stanford-Binet and Wechsler tests, a person's score indicates whether that person's performance fell above or below the average. A performance higher than all but 2 percent of all scores earns an intelligence score of 130. A performance lower than 98 percent of all scores earns an intelligence score of 70.

To keep the average score near 100, the Stanford-Binet and Wechsler scales are periodically restandardized. If you took the WAIS, Fourth Edition, recently, your performance was compared with a standardization sample who took the test during 2007, not to David Wechsler's initial 1930s sample. If you compared the performance of the most recent standardization sample with that of the 1930s sample, do you suppose you would find rising or declining test performance? Amazingly—given that college entrance aptitude scores have sometimes dropped, such as during the 1960s and 1970s—intelligence test performance has improved. This worldwide phenomenon is called the *Flynn effect*, in honor of New Zealand researcher James Flynn (1987, 2012), who first calculated its magnitude. As **FIGURE 30.3** indicates, the average person's intelligence test score in 1920 was—by today's standard—only a 76! Such rising performance has been observed in 29 countries, from Canada to rural Australia (Ceci & Kanaya, 2010). Although there have been some regional reversals, the historic increase is now widely accepted as an important phenomenon (Lynn, 2009; Teasdale & Owen, 2005, 2008).

The Flynn effect's cause has been a psychological mystery. Did it result from greater test sophistication? But the gains began before testing was widespread and have even been observed among preschoolers. Better nutrition? As the nutrition explanation would predict, people have gotten not only smarter but taller. But in postwar Britain, notes Flynn (2009), the lower-class children gained the most from improved nutrition but the intelligence performance gains were greater among upper-class children.

▼ **FIGURE 30.2**
The normal curve Scores on aptitude tests tend to form a normal, or bell-shaped, curve around an average score. For the Wechsler scale, for example, the average score is 100.

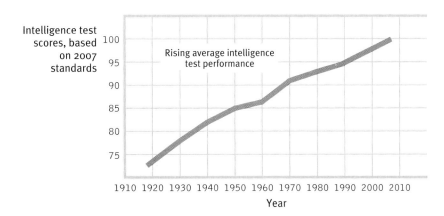

Intelligence test scores, based on 2007 standards

Rising average intelligence test performance

▼ FIGURE 30.3
Getting smarter? In every country studied, intelligence test performance rose during the twentieth century, as shown here with American Wechsler and Stanford-Binet test performance between 1918 and 2007. In Britain, test scores have risen 27 points since 1942. (Data from Horgan, 1995, updated with Flynn, 2012, 2014.)

Or did the Flynn effect stem from more education? More stimulating environments? Less childhood disease? Smaller families and more parental investment (Sundet et al., 2008)? Flynn (2012) attributes the performance increase to our need to develop new mental skills to cope with modern environments. But others argue that it may be accounted for by changes in the tests (Kaufman et al., 2013). Regardless of what combination of factors explains the rise in intelligence test scores, the phenomenon counters one concern of some hereditarians—that the higher twentieth-century birthrates among those with lower scores would shove human intelligence scores downward (Lynn & Harvey, 2008).

Reliability

Knowing where you stand in comparison to a standardization group still won't say much about your intelligence unless the test has **reliability.** A reliable test gives consistent scores, no matter who takes the test or when they take it. To check a test's reliability, researchers test people many times. They may retest using the same test or they may split the test in half to see whether odd-question scores and even-question scores agree. If the two scores generally agree, or *correlate,* the test is reliable. The higher the correlation between the *test–retest* or the *split-half* scores, the higher the test's reliability. The tests we have considered so far—the Stanford-Binet, the WAIS, and the WISC—are very reliable (about +.9). When retested, people's scores generally match their first score closely.

Validity

High reliability does not ensure a test's **validity**—the extent to which the test actually measures or predicts what it promises. Imagine using a miscalibrated tape measure to measure people's heights. Your results would be very reliable. No matter how many times you measured, people's heights would be the same. But your results would not be valid—you would not be giving the information you promised—real height.

Tests that tap the pertinent behavior, or *criterion,* have **content validity.** The road test for a driver's license has content validity because it samples the tasks a driver routinely faces. Course exams have content validity if they assess one's mastery of a representative sample of course material. But we expect intelligence tests to have **predictive validity:** They should predict the criterion of future performance, and to some extent they do.

Are general aptitude tests as predictive as they are reliable? As critics are fond of noting, the answer is plainly No. The predictive power of aptitude tests is fairly strong in the early school years, but later it weakens. Academic aptitude test scores are reasonably good predictors of achievement for children ages 6 to 12, where the correlation between intelligence score and school performance is about +.6 (Jensen, 1980). Intelligence scores correlate even more closely with scores on *achievement tests:* +.81 in one comparison of 70,000 English children's intelligence scores at age 11 with their

reliability the extent to which a test yields consistent results, as assessed by the consistency of scores on two halves of the test, on alternative forms of the test, or on retesting.

validity the extent to which a test measures or predicts what it is supposed to. (See also *content validity* and *predictive validity.*)

content validity the extent to which a test samples the behavior that is of interest.

predictive validity the success with which a test predicts the behavior it is designed to predict; it is assessed by computing the correlation between test scores and the criterion behavior. (Also called *criterion-related validity.*)

academic achievement in national exams at age 16 (Deary et al., 2007, 2009). The SAT, used in the United States as a college entrance exam, has been less successful in predicting first-year college grades. (The correlation, less than +.5, has been, however, a bit higher when adjusting for high scorers electing tougher courses [Berry & Sackett, 2009; Willingham et al., 1990].) By the time we get to the Graduate Record Examination (GRE; an aptitude test similar to the SAT but for those applying to graduate school), the correlation with graduate school performance is an even more modest but still significant +.4 (Kuncel & Hezlett, 2007).

Why does the predictive power of aptitude scores diminish as students move up the educational ladder? Consider a parallel situation: Among all American and Canadian football linemen, body weight correlates with success. A 300-pound player tends to overwhelm a 200-pound opponent. But within the narrow 280- to 320-pound range typically found at the professional level, the correlation between weight and success becomes negligible (**FIGURE 30.4**). The narrower the *range* of weights, the lower the predictive power of body weight becomes. If an elite university takes only those students who have very high aptitude scores, and then gives them a restricted range of high grades, those scores cannot possibly predict much. This will be true even if the test has excellent predictive validity with a more diverse sample of students. Likewise, modern grade inflation has produced less diverse high school grades. With their diminished range, high school grades now predict college grades no better than have SAT scores (Sackett et al., 2012). So, when we validate a measure using a wide range of scores but then use it with a restricted range of scores, it loses much of its predictive validity.

▼ FIGURE 30.4
Diminishing predictive power Let's imagine a correlation between football linemen's body weight and their success on the field. Note how insignificant the relationship becomes when we narrow the range of weight to 280 to 320 pounds. As the range of data under consideration narrows, its predictive power diminishes.

RETRIEVAL PRACTICE

• What are the three criteria that a psychological test must meet in order to be widely accepted? Explain.

ANSWER: A psychological test must be *standardized* (pretested on a similar group of people), *reliable* (yielding consistent results), and *valid* (measuring what it is supposed to measure).

• Corelation coefficients were used in this module. Here's a quick review: Correlations do not indicate cause-effect, but they do tell us whether two things are associated in some way. A correlation of –1.0 represents perfect _____ (agreement/disagreement) between two sets of scores: As one score goes up, the other score goes _____ (up/down). A correlation of _____ represents no association. The highest correlation, +1.0, represents perfect _____ (agreement/disagreement): As the first score goes up, the other score goes _____ (up/down).

ANSWERS: disagreement; down; zero; agreement; up

LEARNING OBJECTIVES

RETRIEVAL PRACTICE Take a moment to answer each of these Learning Objective Questions (repeated here from within this module). Then turn to Appendix C, Complete Module Reviews, to check your answers. Research suggests that trying to answer these questions on your own will improve your long-term retention (McDaniel et al., 2009).

30-1 What is an intelligence test, and what is the difference between achievement and aptitude tests?

30-2 When and why were intelligence tests created, and how do today's tests differ from early intelligence tests?

30-3 What is a normal curve, and what does it mean to say that a test has been standardized and is reliable and valid?

TERMS AND CONCEPTS TO REMEMBER

RETRIEVAL PRACTICE Test yourself on these terms by trying to write down the definition before flipping back to the page number referenced to check your answer.

intelligence test, p. 392

achievement test, p. 392

aptitude test, p. 392

mental age, p. 393

Stanford-Binet, p. 394

intelligence quotient (IQ), p. 394

Wechsler Adult Intelligence Scale (WAIS), p. 395

standardization, p. 396

normal curve, p. p. 396

reliability, p. 397

validity, p. 397

content validity, p. 397

predictive validity, p. 397

Use 🅜 LearningCurve to create your personalized study plan, which will direct you to the resources that will help you most in 🅜 LaunchPad.

MODULE
31 The Dynamics of Intelligence

Researchers are exploring some age-old questions about human intelligence. You know it: You are smarter than some people and not as smart as others. So what in that heart of smarts—the brain—creates this difference? Is it our brain's relative *size?* (Was Einstein big-brained?) Our amounts of certain brain *tissue?* Our brain networks' *speed?* These are among the possibilities that researchers have identified.

Here we will focus on two other questions: How stable is intelligence over the life span? (Will the precocious 5-year-old likely mature into a talented collegian and a brilliant senior citizen?) And what are the traits and talents of those at the low and high extremes of intelligence?

Stability or Change?

31-1 How stable are intelligence scores over the life span, and how does aging affect crystallized and fluid intelligence?

If we retested people periodically throughout their lives, would their *intelligence test* scores be stable? Let's first explore the stability of mental abilities in later life.

Aging and Intelligence

What happens to our intellectual muscles as we age? Do they gradually decline, as does our body strength? Or do they remain constant? The quest for answers to these questions illustrates psychology's self-correcting process. This research developed in phases.

Phase I: Cross-Sectional Evidence for Intellectual Decline In *cross-sectional studies*, researchers at one point in time test and compare people of different ages. In such studies, older adults give fewer correct answers on intelligence tests than do younger adults. WAIS-creator David Wechsler (1972) therefore concluded that "the decline of mental ability with age is part of the general [aging] process of the organism as a whole."

For a long time, this rather dismal view went unchallenged. Many corporations established mandatory retirement policies, assuming the companies would benefit by replacing aging workers with younger, more capable, employees. As "everyone knows," you can't teach an old dog new tricks.

Phase II: Longitudinal Evidence for Intellectual Stability After colleges in the 1920s began giving intelligence tests to entering students, several psychologists saw their chance to study intelligence *longitudinally*. They retested the same **cohort—** the same group of people—over a period of years (Schaie & Geiwitz, 1982). What they found was a surprise: Until late in life, intelligence remained stable (**FIGURE 31.1**). On some tests, it even increased.

How then are we to account for the cross-sectional findings? In retrospect, researchers saw the problem. When older cross-sectional studies compared 70-year-olds and 30-year-olds, they compared people not only of two different ages but of two different eras. It compared generally less-educated people (born, say, in the early 1900s) with better-educated people (born after 1950), people raised in large families with people raised in smaller families, people growing up in less affluent families with people raised in more affluent families.

With the more optimistic results from longitudinal studies, the myth that intelligence sharply declines with age was laid to rest. Famed painter Anna Mary Robertson Moses ("Grandma Moses") took up painting in her seventies, and at age 88 a popular magazine named her "Young Woman of the Year." At age 89, architect Frank Lloyd Wright designed New York City's Guggenheim Museum. As "everyone knows," given good health, you're never too old to learn.

Phase III: It All Depends With "everyone knowing" two different and opposing facts about age and intelligence, something was wrong. As it turns out, longitudinal studies have their own pitfalls. Those who survive to the end of such studies may be bright, healthy people whose intelligence is least likely to decline. (Perhaps people who died younger and were removed from the study had declining intelligence.) Adjusting for the loss of participants, as did a study following more than 2000 people over age 75 in Cambridge, England, revealed a steeper intelligence decline, especially after 85 (Brayne et al., 1999).

Research is further complicated by the finding that intelligence is not a single trait, but rather several distinct abilities. Intelligence tests that assess speed of thinking may place older adults at a disadvantage because of their slower neural processing. Meeting old friends on the street, names rise to the mind's surface more slowly—"like air bubbles in molasses," said David Lykken (1999). But slower processing need not mean less intelligence. In four studies in which players were given 15 minutes to complete *New York Times* crossword puzzles, the highest average performance was achieved by adults in their fifties, sixties, and seventies (Salthouse, 2004). "Wisdom" tests—which assess "expert knowledge about life in general and good judgment and advice about how to conduct oneself in the face of complex, uncertain circumstances"—also suggested that older adults more than hold their own (Baltes et al., 1993, 1994, 1999).

So the answers to our age-and-intelligence questions depend on what we assess and how we assess it. **Crystallized intelligence**—our accumulated knowledge as reflected in vocabulary and analogies tests—*increases* up to old age. **Fluid intelligence**—our

Reasoning ability score

Cross-sectional method suggests decline

Longitudinal method suggests more stability

Age in years

■ Cross-sectional method
□ Longitudinal method

▼ FIGURE 31.1
Cross-sectional versus longitudinal testing of intelligence at various ages In this test of one type of verbal intelligence (inductive reasoning), the cross-sectional method showed declining scores with age. The longitudinal method (in which the same people were retested over a period of years) showed a slight rise in scores well into adulthood. (Data from Schaie, 1994.)

"Knowledge is knowing a tomato is a fruit; wisdom is not putting it in a fruit salad."

Anonymous

Relative performance above or below the mean (in "z-score" standard deviations)

Vocabulary knowledge
Reasoning
Spatial visualization
Memory
Processing speed

Age (in years)

▼ FIGURE 31.2
With age, we lose and we win. Studies reveal that word power grows with age, while fluid intelligence dimensions decline. (Data from Salthouse, 2010.)

Ann Baldwin/Shutterstock

ability to reason speedily and abstractly, as when solving novel logic problems—*decreases* beginning in the twenties and thirties, slowly up to age 75 or so, then more rapidly, especially after age 85 (Cattell, 1963; Horn, 1982; Salthouse, 2009, 2013). With age we lose and we win. We lose recall memory and processing speed, but we gain vocabulary knowledge (**FIGURE 31.2**). Our decisions also become less distorted by negative emotions such as anxiety, depression, and anger (Blanchard-Fields, 2007; Carstensen & Mikels, 2005). And despite their lesser fluid intelligence, older people also display greater wisdom in seeing multiple perspectives, allowing for compromise, and recognizing the limits of what they know (Grossman et al., 2010, 2012).

Age-related cognitive differences help explain why older adults are less likely to embrace new technologies (Charness & Boot, 2009). These cognitive differences also help explain why mathematicians and scientists produce much of their most creative work during their thirties, when fluid intelligence is at its peak (Jones et al., 2014). In contrast, authors, historians, and philosophers tend to produce their best work in their forties, fifties, and beyond—after accumulating more knowledge (Simonton, 1988, 1990). Poets, for example, who depend on fluid intelligence, reach their peak output earlier than prose authors, who need the deeper knowledge reservoir that accumulates with age. This finding holds in every major literary tradition, for both living and dead languages.

cohort a group of people sharing a common characteristic, such as from a given time period.

crystallized intelligence our accumulated knowledge and verbal skills; tends to increase with age.

fluid intelligence our ability to reason speedily and abstractly; tends to decrease during late adulthood.

"In youth we learn, in age we understand."

Marie Von Ebner-Eschenbach,
Aphorisms, 1883

RETRIEVAL PRACTICE

- Researcher A is well-funded to learn about how intelligence changes over the life span. Researcher B wants to study the intelligence of people who are now at various life stages. Which researcher should use the cross-sectional method, and which the longitudinal method?

ANSWER: Researcher A should develop a *longitudinal study* to examine how intelligence changes in the same people over the life span. Researcher B should develop a *cross-sectional study* to examine the intelligence of people now at various life stages.

Stability Over the Life Span

Now what about the stability of intelligence scores early in life? Infants' and toddlers' attention, processing speed, and learning give some clue to their intelligence score in later childhood and early adulthood (Fagan, 2011; Rose et al., 2012). For extremely impaired or very precocious children, those early indications can be very predictive. Yet for most children, casual observation and intelligence tests before age 3 only modestly predict their future aptitudes (Humphreys & Davey, 1988; Tasbihsazan et al., 2003). Even Albert Einstein was once thought "slow"—as he was in learning to talk (Quasha, 1980).

"My dear Adele, I am 4 years old and I can read any English book. I can say all the Latin substantives and adjectives and active verbs besides 52 lines of Latin poetry."

Francis Galton, letter to his sister, 1827

Ironically, SAT and GRE scores have correlated better with each other than either has with its intended criterion, school achievement. Thus, their reliability has far exceeded their predictive validity. If either test was much affected by coaching, luck, or how one feels on the test day (as so many people believe), such reliability would be impossible.

By age 4, however, children's performance on intelligence tests begins to predict their adolescent and adult scores. The consistency of scores over time increases with the age of the child. The remarkable stability of aptitude scores by late adolescence is seen in a U.S. Educational Testing Service study of 23,000 students who took the SAT and then later took the GRE (Angoff, 1988). On either test, verbal scores correlated only modestly with math scores—revealing that these two aptitudes are distinct. Yet scores on the SAT verbal test correlated +.86 with the scores on the GRE verbal tests taken four to five years later. An equally astonishing +.86 correlation occurred between the two math tests. Given the time lapse and differing educational experiences of these 23,000 students, the stability of their aptitude scores is remarkable.

Ian Deary and his colleagues (2004, 2009, 2013) set the record for long-term follow-up. Their amazing longitudinal studies have been enabled by their country, Scotland, doing something that no nation has done before or since. On June 1, 1932, essentially every child in the country born in 1921—87,498 children around age 11—took an intelligence test. The aim was to identify working-class children who would benefit from further education. Sixty-five years later to the day, Patricia Whalley, the wife of Deary's co-worker, Lawrence Whalley, discovered the test results on dusty storeroom shelves at the Scottish Council for Research in Education, not far from Deary's Edinburgh University office. "This will change our lives," Deary replied when Whalley told him the news.

And so it has, with dozens of studies of the stability and the predictive capacity of these early test results. For example, when the intelligence test administered to 11-year-old Scots in 1932 was readministered to 542 survivors as turn-of-the-millennium 80-year-olds, the correlation between the two sets of scores—after nearly 70 years of varied life experiences—was striking (**FIGURE 31.3**). Ditto when 106 survivors were retested at age 90 (Deary et al., 2013). Another study that followed Scots born in 1936 from ages 11 to 70 confirmed the remarkable stability of intelligence, independent of life circumstance (Johnson et al., 2010).

High-scoring 11-year-olds also were more likely to be living independently as 77-year-olds and were less likely to have suffered *Alzheimer's disease* (Starr et al., 2000; Whalley et al., 2000). Among girls scoring in the highest 25 percent, 70 percent were still alive at age 76—as were only 45 percent of those scoring in the lowest 25 percent (**FIGURE 31.4**). (World War II prematurely ended the lives of many of the male test-takers.) Follow-up studies with other large samples confirm the phenomenon: More intelligent children and adults live healthier and longer (Calvin et al., 2011; Deary et al., 2008, 2010; Johnson et al., 2011). One study that followed 93 nuns found that those exhibiting less verbal ability in essays written when entering convents in their teens were more at risk for Alzheimer's disease after age 75 (Snowdon et al., 1996).

"Whether you live to collect your old-age pension depends in part on your IQ at age 11."

Ian Deary,
"Intelligence, Health, and Death," 2005

▼ FIGURE 31.3
Intelligence endures When Ian Deary and his colleagues (2004) retested 80-year-old Scots, using an intelligence test they had taken as 11-year-olds, their scores across seven decades correlated +.66, as shown here. (Data from Deary et al., 2004.) When 207 survivors were again retested at age 90, the correlation with their age 11 scores was +.54 (Deary et al., 2013).

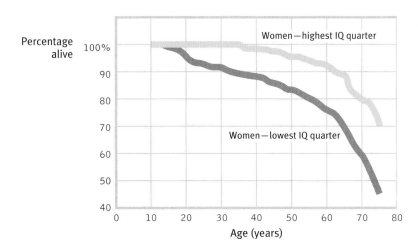

▼ FIGURE 31.4
Living smart Women scoring in the highest 25 percent on the Scottish national intelligence test at age 11 tended to live longer than those who scored in the lowest 25 percent. (Data from Whalley & Deary, 2001.)

Pause a moment: Have you any idea why more intelligent people might live longer? Deary (2008) reports four possible explanations:

1. Intelligence facilitates more education, better jobs, and a healthier environment.

2. Intelligence encourages healthy living: less smoking, better diet, more exercise.

3. Prenatal events or early childhood illnesses might have influenced both intelligence and health.

4. A "well-wired body," as evidenced by fast reaction speeds, perhaps fosters both intelligence and longevity.

Extremes of Intelligence

31-2 What are the traits of those at the low and high intelligence extremes?

One way to glimpse the *validity* and significance of any test is to compare people who score at the two extremes of the *normal curve*. The two groups should differ noticeably, and they do.

The Low Extreme

At one extreme of the intelligence test normal curve are those with unusually low scores. To be diagnosed with an **intellectual disability** (formerly referred to as *mental retardation*), a person must meet two criteria. The first is a low test score. American Association on Intellectual and Developmental Disabilities guidelines specify performance that is approximately two standard deviations below average (Schalock et al., 2010). For an intelligence test with 100 as average and a standard deviation of 15, that means (allowing for some variation in one's test score) an intelligence score of approximately 70 or below. The second criterion is that the person must have difficulty adapting to the normal demands of independent living, as expressed in three areas:

• *conceptual skills,* such as language, literacy, and concepts of money, time, and number.

• *social skills,* such as interpersonal skills, social responsibility, and the ability to follow basic rules and laws and avoid being victimized.

• *practical skills,* such as daily personal care, occupational skill, travel, and health care.

Intellectual disability is a developmental condition that is apparent before age 18, sometimes with a known physical cause. **Down syndrome,** for example, is a disorder of varying severity caused by an extra copy of chromosome 21 in the person's genetic makeup.

Consider one reason why people diagnosed with a mild intellectual disability—those just below the 70 score—might be better able to live independently today than many

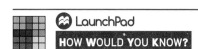

Explore how researchers have studied these issues with LaunchPad's *How Would You Know If Intelligence Changes With Age?*

---

intellectual disability a condition of limited mental ability, indicated by an intelligence test score of 70 or below and difficulty adapting to the demands of life. (Formerly referred to as *mental retardation.*)

Down syndrome a condition of mild to severe intellectual disability and associated physical disorders caused by an extra copy of chromosome 21.

decades ago, when they were institutionalized. Over the years, thanks to the *Flynn effect*, the tests have been periodically restandardized. As that happened, individuals who scored near 70 on earlier tests have suddenly lost about 6 test-score points. Two people with the same ability level could thus be classified differently, depending on when they were tested (Kanaya et al., 2003; Reynolds et al., 2010). As the intellectual disability boundary has shifted, more people have become eligible for special education and for Social Security payments.

And in the United States (one of only a few industrialized countries with the death penalty), fewer people are now eligible for execution: The U.S. Supreme Court ruled in 2002 that the execution of people with an intellectual disability is "cruel and unusual punishment." For people near the cutoff score of 70, intelligence testing can be a high-stakes competition. And so it was for Teresa Lewis, a "dependent personality" with limited intellect, who was executed by the state of Virginia in 2010. Lewis, whose reported test score was 72, allegedly agreed to a plot in which two men killed her husband and stepson in exchange for a split of a life insurance payout (Eckholm, 2010). If only she had scored 69.

In 2014, the U.S. Supreme Court recognized the imprecision and arbitrariness of a fixed cutoff score of 70, and required states with death row inmates who have scored just above 70 to consider other evidence. Thus, Ted Herring, who had scored 72 and 74 on intelligence tests—but without knowing that summer follows spring or how to transfer between buses—could be taken off Florida's death row (Alvarez & Schwartz, 2014).

RETRIEVAL PRACTICE

- Why do psychologists NOT diagnose an intellectual disability based solely on the person's intelligence test score?

ANSWER: IQ score is only one measure of a person's ability to function. Other important factors to consider in an overall assessment include conceptual skills, social skills, and practical skills.

The High Extreme

In one famous project begun in 1921, Lewis Terman studied more than 1500 California schoolchildren with IQ scores over 135. Contrary to the popular notion that intellectually gifted children are frequently maladjusted, Terman's high-scoring children (the "Termites"), like those in later studies, were healthy, well-adjusted, and unusually successful academically (Friedman & Martin, 2012; Koenen et al., 2009; Lubinski, 2009a). When restudied over the next seven decades, most people in Terman's group had attained high levels of education (Austin et al., 2002; Holahan & Sears, 1995). Many were doctors, lawyers, professors, scientists, and writers, though no Nobel Prize winners.

A more recent study of precocious youths who had aced the math SAT at age 13—by scoring in the top quarter of 1 percent of their age group—found them at age 33 twice as likely to have patents as were those in the bottom quarter of the top 1 percent (Wai et al., 2005). Compared with the math aces, 13-year-olds scoring high on verbal aptitude were, by age 38, more likely to have become humanities professors or written a novel (Kell et al., 2013). About 1 percent of Americans earn doctorates. But among those scoring in the top 1 in 10,000—on the SAT at age 12 or 13—63 percent had done so.

One of psychology's whiz kids was Jean Piaget, who by age 15 was publishing scientific articles on mollusks and who went on to become the twentieth century's most famous developmental psychologist (Hunt, 1993). Children with extraordinary academic gifts are sometimes more isolated, shy, and in their own worlds (Winner, 2000). But most thrive.

There are critics who question many of the assumptions of "gifted child" programs, such as the belief that only 3 to 5 percent of children are gifted and that it pays to

Terman did test two future Nobel laureates in physics, but they failed to score above his gifted sample cutoff (Hulbert, 2005).

identify and "track" these special few—segregating them in special classes and giving them academic enrichment not available to their peers. Critics note that tracking by aptitude sometimes creates a self-fulfilling prophecy: Those implicitly labeled "ungifted" may be influenced to become so (Lipsey & Wilson, 1993; Slavin & Braddock, 1993). Denying lower-ability students opportunities for enriched education can widen the achievement gap between ability groups and increase their social isolation from one another (Carnegie, 1989; Stevenson & Lee, 1990). Because minority and low-income youth are more often placed in lower academic groups, tracking can also promote segregation and prejudice—hardly, note critics, a healthy preparation for working and living in a multicultural society.

Critics and proponents of gifted education do, however, agree on this: Children have differing gifts, whether at math, verbal reasoning, art, or social leadership. Some children exhibit exceptional potential or talent in a given domain. Educating children as if all were alike is as naive as assuming that giftedness is something, like blue eyes, that you either have or do not have. One need not hang labels on children to affirm their special talents and to challenge them all at the frontiers of their own ability and understanding. By providing *appropriate placement* suited to each child's talents (as when allowing a math whiz to study math at a higher level), we can promote both equity and excellence for all (Subotnik et al., 2011).

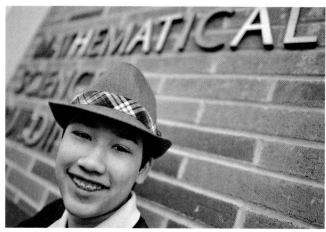

Joe Klamar/AFP/Getty Images

The extremes of intelligence Moshe Kai Cavalin completed his third college degree at age 14, graduating with a UCLA math degree. According to his mother, he started reading at age 2.

MODULE 31 REVIEW The Dynamics of Intelligence

LEARNING OBJECTIVES

RETRIEVAL PRACTICE Take a moment to answer each of these Learning Objective Questions (repeated here from within this module). Then turn to Appendix C, Complete Module Reviews, to check your answers. Research suggests that trying to answer these questions on your own will improve your long-term retention (McDaniel et al., 2009).

31-1 How stable are intelligence scores over the life span, and how does aging affect crystallized and fluid intelligence?

31-2 What are the traits of those at the low and high intelligence extremes?

TERMS AND CONCEPTS TO REMEMBER

RETRIEVAL PRACTICE Test yourself on these terms by trying to write down the definition before flipping back to the page number referenced to check your answer.

cohort, p. 400

crystallized intelligence, p. 400

fluid intelligence, p. 400

intellectual disability, p. 403

Down syndrome, p. 403

Use ⊕ LearningCurve to create your personalized study plan, which will direct you to the resources that will help you most in ⊕ LaunchPad.

MODULE 32 Genetic and Environmental Influences on Intelligence

Intelligence runs in families. But why? Are our intellectual abilities mostly inherited? Or are they molded by our environment?

Few issues arouse such passion or have such serious political implications. Consider: If we mainly inherit our differing mental abilities, and if success reflects those abilities, then people's socioeconomic standing will correspond to their inborn differences. This could lead to those on top believing their intellectual birthright justifies their social position.

"I told my parents that if grades were so important they should have paid for a smarter egg donor."

But if mental abilities are primarily nurtured by our environments, then children from disadvantaged environments can expect to lead disadvantaged lives. In this case, people's standing will result from their unequal opportunities.

For now, as best we can, let's set aside such political implications and examine some of the evidence.

Twin and Adoption Studies

32-1 What evidence points to a genetic influence on intelligence, and what is heritability?

Do people who share the same genes also share mental abilities? As you can see from **FIGURE 32.1**, which summarizes many studies, the answer is clearly *Yes*. Consider:

- The *intelligence test* scores of identical twins raised together are nearly as similar as those of the same person taking the same test twice (Haworth et al., 2009; Lykken, 2006). (The scores of fraternal twins, who share only about half their genes, differ more.) Estimates of the **heritability** of intelligence—the extent to which intelligence test score variation can be attributed to genetic variation—range from 50 to 80 percent (Calvin et al., 2012; Johnson et al., 2009; Neisser et al., 1996). Identical twins also exhibit substantial similarity (and heritability) in specific talents, such as music, math, and sports, with heredity even accounting for more than half the variation in the national math and science exam scores of British 16-year-olds (Shakeshaft et al., 2013; Vinkhuyzen et al., 2009).

- Scans reveal that identical twins' brains have similar gray- and white-matter volume, and the areas associated with verbal and spatial intelligence are virtually the same (Deary et al., 2009; Thompson et al., 2001). Their brains also show similar activity while doing mental tasks (Koten et al., 2009).

- Are there known genes for genius? Today's researchers have identified chromosomal regions important to intelligence, and they have pinpointed specific genes that seemingly influence variations in intelligence and learning disorders (Davies et al., 2011; Plomin et al., 2013). But efforts to isolate specific intelligence-influencing genes have not found any one mighty gene (Chabris et al., 2012). One worldwide team of more than 200 researchers pooled their data on the DNA and schooling of 126,559 people (Rietveld et al., 2013). No single DNA segment was more than a minuscule predictor of years of schooling, and together all the genetic variations they examined accounted for only about 2 percent of the schooling differences. After examining 21,151 people's brain scans, the researchers were able to identify a gene variation that predicted a slightly bigger brain, which is a modest predictor of intelligence (Stein et al., 2012). The gene sleuthing continues, but this much seems clear: Intelligence is *polygenetic*, involving many genes. Wendy Johnson (2010) likens it to height: 54 specific gene variations together have accounted for 5 percent of our individual differences in height, leaving the rest yet to be discovered. For height as for intelligence, what matters is the combination of many genes.

Other evidence points to environment effects:

- Where environments vary widely, as they do among children of less-educated parents, environmental differences are more predictive of intelligence scores (Rowe et al., 1999; Tucker-Drob et al., 2011; Turkheimer et al., 2003).

- Studies also show that adoption enhances the intelligence scores of mistreated or neglected children (van IJzendoorn & Juffer, 2005, 2006). So does adoption from poverty into middle-class homes (Nisbett et al., 2012).

- The intelligence scores of "virtual twins"—same-age, unrelated siblings adopted as infants and raised together—correlate +.28 (Segal et al., 2012). This suggests a modest influence of their shared environment.

heritability the proportion of variation among individuals that we can attribute to genes. The heritability of a trait may vary, depending on the range of populations and environments studied.

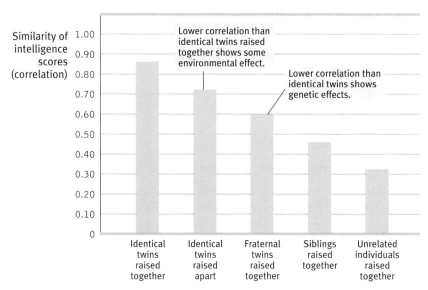

Similarity of intelligence scores (correlation)

Lower correlation than identical twins raised together shows some environmental effect.

Lower correlation than identical twins shows genetic effects.

Identical twins raised together / Identical twins raised apart / Fraternal twins raised together / Siblings raised together / Unrelated individuals raised together

▼ FIGURE 32.1
Intelligence: Nature and nurture
The most genetically similar people have the most similar intelligence scores. Remember: 1.0 indicates a perfect correlation; zero indicates no correlation at all. (Data from McGue et al., 1993.)

Seeking to disentangle genes and environment, researchers have also compared the intelligence test scores of adopted children with those of (a) their *biological parents* (the providers of their genes) and (b) their *adoptive parents* (the providers of their home environment). Over time, adopted children accumulate experience in their differing adoptive families. So would you expect the family-environment effect to grow with age and the genetic-legacy effect to shrink?

If you would, behavior geneticists have a stunning surprise for you. Mental similarities between adopted children and their adoptive families wane with age, until the correlation approaches zero by adulthood (McGue et al., 1993). Genetic influences—not environmental ones—become more apparent as we accumulate life experience. Identical twins' similarities, for example, continue or increase into their eighties. Thus, report Ian Deary and his colleagues (2009, 2012), the heritability of general intelligence increases from "about 30 percent" in early childhood to "well over 50 percent in adulthood." In one massive study of 11,000 twin pairs in four countries, the heritability of *general intelligence (g)* increased from 41 percent in middle childhood to 55 percent in adolescence to 66 percent in young adulthood (Haworth et al., 2010). Similarly, adopted children's verbal ability scores over time become more like those of their biological parents (**FIGURE 32.2**). Who would have guessed?

"Selective breeding has given me an aptitude for the law, but I still love fetching a dead duck out of freezing water."

Child-parent correlation in verbal ability scores

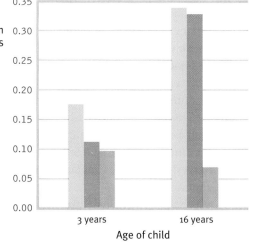

Children and their birth parents

Adopted children and their birth parents

Adopted children and their adoptive parents

Age of child

▼ FIGURE 32.2
In verbal ability, who do adopted children resemble? As the years went by in their adoptive families, children's verbal ability scores became more like their *biological* parents' scores. (Data from Plomin & DeFries, 1998.)

- A check on your understanding of heritability: If environments become more equal, the heritability of intelligence would
  a. increase.   b. decrease.   c. be unchanged.

ANSWER: a. (Heritability—variation explained by genetic influences—will increase as environmental variation decreases.)

Environmental Influences

32-2 What does evidence reveal about environmental influences on intelligence?

Genes make a difference. Even if we were all raised in the same intellectually stimulating environment, we would have differing aptitudes. But life experiences also matter. Human environments are rarely as impoverished as the dark and barren cages inhabited by deprived rats that develop thinner-than-normal brain cortexes (Rosenzweig, 1984). Yet severe deprivation also leaves footprints on the human brain.

Early Environmental Influences

Nowhere is the intertwining of biology and experience more apparent than in the most hopeless human environments, such as J. McVicker Hunt (1982) observed in a destitute

Devastating neglect Some Romanian orphans, such as this child in the Leaganul Pentru Copii orphanage in 1990, had minimal interaction with caregivers, and suffered delayed development.

Iranian orphanage. The typical child Hunt observed there could not sit up unassisted at age 2 or walk at age 4. The little care the infants received was not in response to their crying, cooing, or other behaviors, so the children developed little sense of personal control over their environment. They were instead becoming passive "glum lumps." Extreme deprivation was bludgeoning native intelligence—a finding confirmed by studies of children raised in poorly run orphanages in Romania and elsewhere (Nelson et al., 2009, 2013; van IJzendoorn et al., 2008).

Aware of both the dramatic effects of early experiences and the impact of early intervention, Hunt began a training program of *tutored human enrichment* for the Iranian caregivers, teaching them to play language-fostering games with 11 infants. They imitated the babies' babbling, engaged them in vocal follow-the-leader, and, finally, they taught the infants sounds from the Persian language. The results were dramatic. By 22 months of age, the infants could name more than 50 objects and body parts, and so charmed visitors that most were adopted—an unprecedented success for the orphanage.

Hunt's findings are an extreme case of a more general finding: Poor environmental conditions can depress cognitive development. Schools with many poverty-level children often have less-qualified teachers, as one study of 1450 Virginia schools found, which has predicted lower achievement scores (Tuerk, 2005).

Poverty-related stresses also impede cognitive *performance*. Like a computer that slows when running multiple operations, impoverished people's worries and distractions consume cognitive bandwidth and can diminish their thinking capacity. For example, on tests of cognitive functioning, sugar cane farmers in India scored better after being paid for their harvest, when their money worries dropped (Mani et al., 2013). Poverty can deplete cognitive capacity.

Malnutrition also plays a role. Relieve infant malnutrition with nutritional supplements, and poverty's effect on physical and cognitive development lessens (Brown & Pollitt, 1996).

So, extreme conditions—malnutrition, sensory deprivation, and social isolation—can retard normal brain development. Is the reverse also true? Will an "enriched" environment give children a superior intellect? Most experts are doubtful (Bruer, 1999; DeLoache et al., 2010; Reichert et al., 2010). There is no environmental recipe for fast-forwarding a normal infant into a genius. All babies should have normal exposure to sights, sounds, and speech. Although preschool experiences matter, Sandra Scarr's (1984) verdict still is widely shared: "Parents who are very concerned about providing special educational lessons for their babies are wasting their time."

Schooling and Intelligence

Later in childhood, schooling is one intervention that pays intelligence score dividends. Schooling and intelligence interact, and both enhance later income (Ceci & Williams, 1997, 2009). Hunt was a strong believer in the ability of education to boost children's chances for success by developing their cognitive and social skills. Indeed, his 1961 book, *Intelligence and Experience*, helped launch Project Head Start in 1965, a U.S. government-funded preschool program that has served more than 30 million children, most of whom come from families below the poverty level (Head Start, 2013). Does it succeed? Studies suggest that Head Start increases school readiness and gives a modest boost to later health and high school completion rate (Deming, 2009; Mervis, 2011a; Pianta et al., 2009). Generally, however, aptitude benefits fade out over time (reminding us that life experiences *after* Head Start matter, too).

Encouraging results come from intensive, high-quality preschool programs (Mervis, 2011a; Tucker-Drob, 2012). Across a number of experiments, intelligence scores also rise with nutritional supplements to pregnant mothers and newborns (3.5 points), with quality preschool experiences (4 points), and with interactive reading programs (6 points) (Protzko et al., 2013).

Genes and experience together weave the fabric of intelligence. (*Epigenetics* is one field that studies this nature–nurture meeting place.) But what we accomplish with our intelligence depends also on our own beliefs and motivation. One analysis of 72,431 collegians found that study motivation and study skills rivaled aptitude and previous grades as predictors of academic achievement (Credé & Kuncel, 2008). Motivation can even affect intelligence test performance. Four dozen studies show that, when promised money for doing well, adolescents score higher on such tests (Duckworth et al., 2011).

These observations lend support to research by psychologist Carol Dweck (2006, 2012a,b). She reports that believing intelligence is changeable, not fixed, can foster a *growth mind-set*, which focuses on learning and growing. As collegians, these believers also tend to happily flourish (Howell, 2009). Dweck has developed interventions that effectively teach young teens that the brain is like a muscle; it grows stronger with use as neuron connections grow. Praising children's *effort* rather than their ability encourages their growth mind-set and their attributing success to hard work (Gunderson et al., 2013). Fostering a growth mind-set also makes teens more resilient when others frustrate them (Yeager et al., 2013, 2014). Indeed, superior achievements in fields from sports to science to music arise from the combination of ability, opportunity, and disciplined effort (Ericsson et al., 2007; Subotnik et al., 2011).

Real world studies confirm that ability + opportunity + motivation = success. High school students' math proficiency and college students' grades reflect their aptitude but also their self-discipline, their belief in the power of effort, and a curious, "hungry mind" (Murayama et al., 2013; Richardson et al., 2012; von Stumm et al., 2011). Indian-Americans won all seven national spelling bee contests between 2008 and 2014, an achievement likely influenced by a cultural belief that strong effort will meet with success (Rattan et al., 2012).

"It is our choices . . . that show what we truly are, far more than our abilities."

Professor Dumbledore to Harry Potter in J. K. Rowling's *Harry Potter and the Chamber of Secrets*, 1999

Group Differences in Intelligence Test Scores

If there were no group differences in *aptitude test* scores, psychologists could politely debate hereditary and environmental influences in their ivory towers. But there are group differences. What are they? And what shall we make of them?

Gender Similarities and Differences

32-3 How and why do the genders differ in mental ability scores?

In science, as in everyday life, differences, not similarities, excite interest. Compared with the anatomical and physiological similarities between men and women, our differences are minor. In a 1932 testing of all Scottish 11-year-olds, for example, girls' average intelligence score was 100.6 and boys' was 100.5 (Deary et al., 2003). So far as *g* is concerned, boys and girls, men and women, are the same species.

Yet, most people find differences more newsworthy. Girls outpace boys in spelling, verbal fluency, locating objects, detecting emotions, and sensitivity to touch, taste, and color (Halpern et al., 2007). Boys outperform girls in tests of spatial ability and complex math problems, though in math computation and overall math performance, boys and girls hardly differ (Else-Quest et al., 2010; Hyde & Mertz, 2009; Lindberg et al., 2010). Males' mental ability scores also vary more than females'. Thus, boys worldwide outnumber girls at both the low extreme and the high extreme (Brunner et al., 2013). Boys, for example, are more often found in special education classes, but also among those scoring very high on the SAT math test.

The most reliable male edge appears in spatial ability tests like the one shown in **FIGURE 32.3** (Maeda & Yoon, 2013; Wei et al., 2012). The solution requires speedily rotating three-dimensional objects in one's mind. Today, such skills help when fitting suitcases into a car trunk, playing chess, or doing certain types of geometry problems. From an evolutionary perspective, those same skills would have helped our ancestral fathers track prey and make their way home (Geary, 1995, 1996; Halpern et al., 2007). The survival of our ancestral mothers may have benefited more from a keen memory for the location of edible plants—a legacy that lives today in women's superior memory for objects and their location. But experience matters. One experiment found that playing action video games boosts spatial abilities, generally a male more than female pursuit (Eagan et al, 2013; Feng et al., 2007). Evolutionary psychologist Steven Pinker (2005) has argued that biology affects gender differences in life priorities (women's greater interest in people versus men's in money and things), in risk-taking (with men more reckless), and in math reasoning and spatial abilities. Such differences are, he noted, observed across cultures, stable over time, influenced by prenatal hormones, and observed in genetic boys raised as girls. But social influences also construct gender. Stephen Ceci and Wendy Williams (2010, 2011) note that culturally

Alexey Lebedev/Shutterstock

▼ **FIGURE 32.3**
The mental rotation test This is a test of spatial abilities. (From Vandenberg & Kuse, 1978.) See inverted answer below.

ANSWER: The first and fourth alternatives.

Which two circles contain a configuration of blocks identical to the one in the circle at the left?

Standard

Responses

Republished with permission of Perceptual and Motor Skills, from Mental Rotations, A Group Test Of Three-Dimensional Spatial Visualization, *Steven G. Vandenberg And Allan R. Kuse, Volume 47, Issue 2, October 1978: pp. 599-604* (doi: 10.2466/pms.1978.47.2.599); permission Mental Rotations, A Group Test Of Three-Dimensional Spatial Visualization Steven G. Vandenberg, And Allan R. Kuse influenced preferences help explain women selecting people- rather than math-intensive vocations.

Other researchers remind us that social expectations and divergent opportunities shape boys' and girls' interests and abilities (Crawford et al., 1995; Eccles et al., 1990). In Asia and Russia, teen girls have outperformed boys in an international science exam; in North America and Britain, boys have scored higher (Fairfield, 2012). More gender-equal cultures, such as Sweden and Iceland, exhibit little of the gender math gap found in gender-unequal cultures, such as Turkey and Korea (Guiso et al., 2008; Kane & Mertz, 2012). Since the 1970s, as gender equity has increased in the United States, the boy-to-girl ratio among 12- to 14-year-olds with very high SAT math scores (above 700) has declined from 13 to 1 to 3 to 1 (Nisbett et al., 2012).

Racial and Ethnic Similarities and Differences

32-4 How and why do racial and ethnic groups differ in mental ability scores?

Fueling the group-differences debate are two other disturbing but agreed-upon facts:

- Racial and ethnic groups differ in their average intelligence test scores.
- High-scoring people (and groups) are more likely to attain high levels of education and income.

There are many group differences in average intelligence test scores. New Zealanders of European descent outscore native Maori New Zealanders. Israeli Jews outscore Israeli Arabs. Most Japanese outscore most Burakumin, a stigmatized Japanese minority. Those who can hear have outscored those born deaf (Braden, 1994; Steele, 1990; Zeidner, 1990). And White Americans have outscored Black Americans. This Black-White difference has diminished somewhat in recent years, especially among children (Dickens & Flynn, 2006; Nisbett et al., 2012). Such *group* differences provide little basis for judging individuals. Worldwide, women outlive men by four years, but knowing only that you are male or female won't tell us how long you will live.

We have seen that heredity contributes to *individual* differences in intelligence. But group differences in a heritable trait may be entirely environmental. Consider one of nature's experiments: Allow some children to grow up hearing their culture's dominant language, while others, born deaf, do not. Then give both groups an intelligence test rooted in the dominant language, and (no surprise) those with expertise in that language will score higher. Although individual performance differences may be substantially genetic, the group difference is not (**FIGURE 32.4** on the next page).

"The human computer" Indian math wizard Shakuntala Devi made it into the 1982 *Guinness Book of World Records* when she multiplied two randomly selected 13-digit numbers (7,686,369,774,870 × 2,465,099,745,779) to give, within seconds, the 26-digit solution: 18,947,668,177,995,426,462,773,730 (Pandya, 2013).

▼ FIGURE 32.4
Group differences and environmental impact Even if the variation between members within a group reflects genetic differences, the average difference between groups may be wholly due to the environment. Imagine that seeds from the same mixture are sown in different soils. Although height differences *within* each window box of flowers will be genetic, the height difference *between* the two groups will be environmental. (Inspired by Lewontin, 1976.)

© David Turnley/Corbis; © Rob Howard/Corbis; © Barbara Bannister/Gallo Images/Corbis; © Dave Bartruff/Corbis; © Haruyoshi Yamaguchi/Corbis; © Richard T. Nowitz/Corbis; © Owen Franken/Corbis; © Sean De Burca/Corbis

Nature's own morphing Nature draws no sharp boundaries between races, which blend gradually one into the next around the Earth. But the human urge to classify causes people to socially define themselves in racial categories, which become catchall labels for physical features, social identity, and nationality.

Might the racial gap be similarly environmental? Consider:

Genetics research reveals that under the skin, the races are remarkably alike. The average genetic difference between two Icelandic villagers or between two Kenyans greatly exceeds the group difference between Icelanders and Kenyans (Cavalli-Sforza et al., 1994; Rosenberg et al., 2002). Moreover, looks can deceive. Light-skinned Europeans and dark-skinned Africans are genetically closer than are dark-skinned Africans and dark-skinned Aboriginal Australians.

Race is not a neatly defined biological category. Many social scientists see race primarily as a social construction without well-defined physical boundaries, as each race blends seamlessly into the race of its geographical neighbors (Helms et al., 2005; Smedley & Smedley, 2005). Moreover, with increasingly mixed ancestries, more and more people defy neat racial categorization and self-identify as multiracial (Pauker et al., 2009).

The intelligence test performance of today's better-fed, better-educated, and more test-prepared population exceeds that of the 1930s population—by a greater margin than the intelligence test score of the average White today exceeds that of the average Black. One research review noted that the average intelligence test performance of today's sub-Saharan Africans is the same as British adults in 1948, with the possibility of more gains to come, given improved nutrition, economic development, and education (Wicherts et al., 2010).

When Blacks and Whites have or receive the same pertinent knowledge, they exhibit similar information-processing skill. "The data support the view that cultural differences in the provision of information may account for racial differences in [intelligence test performance]," reported researchers Joseph Fagan and Cynthia Holland (2007).

Schools and culture matter. Countries whose economies create a large wealth gap between rich and poor tend also to have a large rich-versus-poor intelligence test score gap (Nisbet, 2009). Moreover, educational policies such as kindergarten attendance, school discipline, and instructional time per year predict national differences in intelligence and knowledge tests (Rindermann & Ceci, 2009). Math achievement and aptitude test differences may reflect conscientiousness more than competence. Asian students who have outperformed North American students on such tests have also spent 30 percent more time in school and much more time in and out of school studying math (Geary et al., 1996; Larson & Verma, 1999; Stevenson, 1992).

In different eras, different ethnic groups have experienced golden ages—periods of remarkable achievement. Twenty-five-hundred years ago, it was the Greeks and the Egyptians, then the Romans. In the eighth and ninth centuries, genius seemed to reside in the Arab world. Five hundred years ago, the Aztec Indians and the peoples of

Northern Europe were the superachievers. Today, many people notice Asian technological genius and Jewish cultural success. Cultures rise and fall over centuries; genes do not. That fact makes it difficult to attribute a natural superiority to any race.

"Do not obtain your slaves from Britain, because they are so stupid and so utterly incapable of being taught."

Cicero, 106–43 B.C.E.

RETRIEVAL PRACTICE

- In prosperous country X, everyone eats all they want. In country Y, the rich are well fed, but the semistarved poor are often thin. In which country will the heritability of body weight be greater?

ANSWER: The heritability (differences due to genes) of body weight will be greater in country X, where environmental differences in available nutrition are minimal.

The Question of Bias

32-5 Are intelligence tests inappropriately biased?

If one assumes that *race* is a meaningful concept, the debate over racial differences in intelligence divides into three camps (Hunt & Carlson, 2007):

- There are genetically disposed racial differences in intelligence.
- There are socially influenced racial differences in intelligence.
- There are racial differences in test scores, but the tests are inappropriate or biased.

We have considered group difference from the first and second perspectives. Let's turn now to the third: Are intelligence tests biased? The answer depends on which of two very different definitions of *bias* we use.

Two Meanings of Bias

The *scientific* meaning of *bias* hinges on a test's validity—on whether it predicts future behavior only for some groups of test-takers. For example, if the SAT accurately predicted the college achievement of women but not that of men, then the test would be biased. In this statistical meaning of the term, the near-consensus among psychologists (as summarized by the U.S. National Research Council's Committee on Ability Testing and the American Psychological Association's Task Force on Intelligence) has been that the major U.S. aptitude tests are *not* biased (Hunt & Carlson, 2007; Neisser et al., 1996; Wigdor & Garner, 1982). The tests' predictive validity is roughly the same for women and men, for various races, and for rich and poor. If an intelligence test score of 95 predicts slightly below-average grades, that rough prediction usually applies equally to all.

But we can also consider a test biased if it detects not only innate differences in intelligence but also performance differences caused by cultural experiences. This in fact happened to Eastern European immigrants in the early 1900s. Lacking the experience to answer questions about their new culture, many were classified as "feeble-minded." In this popular sense, intelligence tests are biased. They measure your developed abilities, which reflect, in part, your education and experiences.

You may have read examples of intelligence test items that make assumptions (for example, that a cup goes with a saucer). Such items bias the test against those who do not use saucers. Could such questions explain cultural differences in test performance? In such cases, tests can be a vehicle for discrimination, consigning potentially capable children (some of whom may have a different native language) to dead-end classes and jobs. Thus, some intelligence researchers recommend creating culture-neutral questions—such as assessing people's ability to learn novel words, sayings, and analogies—to enable culture-fair aptitude tests (Fagan & Holland, 2007, 2009).

Defenders of the existing aptitude tests have noted that racial group differences persist on nonverbal items, such as counting digits backward (Jensen, 1983, 1998). Moreover, they add, blaming the test for a group's lower scores is like blaming a messenger for bad news. Why blame the tests for exposing unequal experiences and opportunities? If, because of malnutrition, people were to suffer stunted growth, would you blame the measuring stick that reveals it? If unequal past experiences predict unequal future achievements, a valid aptitude test will detect such inequalities.

So, test-makers' expectations can introduce bias in an intelligence test. This is consistent with an observation we have seen throughout this text: Our expectations and attitudes can influence our perceptions and behaviors. This is also true for the person taking the test.

RETRIEVAL PRACTICE

- What is the difference between a test that is biased culturally and a test that is biased in terms of its validity?

ANSWER: A test may be *culturally* biased if higher scores are achieved by those with certain cultural experiences. That same test may not be biased in terms of *validity* if it predicts what it is supposed to predict. For example, the SAT may be culturally biased in favor of those with experience in the U.S. school system, but it does still accurately predict U.S. college success.

Test-Takers' Expectations

When Steven Spencer and his colleagues (1997) gave a difficult math test to equally capable men and women, women did not do as well—except when they had been led to expect that women usually do as well as men on the test. Otherwise, something affected their performance. And with Claude Steele and Joshua Aronson, Spencer (2002) again observed this self-fulfilling **stereotype threat** when Black students were reminded of their race just before taking verbal aptitude tests and performed worse. Follow-up experiments have confirmed that negatively stereotyped minorities and women may have unrealized academic potential (Nguyen & Ryan, 2008; Walton & Spencer, 2009). If, when taking an intelligence test or an exam, you are worried that your group or "type" often doesn't do well, your self-doubts and self-monitoring may hijack your *working memory* and impair your performance (Schmader, 2010). Such thoughts, and worries about what others are thinking about you, can be distracting. For such reasons, stereotype threat may impair attention, performance, and learning (Inzlicht & Kang, 2010; Rydell, 2010). Remove the threat—by labeling the assessment as a "warm-up" exercise rather than a "test"—and stereotyped minorities often perform better (Taylor & Walton, 2011).

Critics argue that stereotype threat does not fully account for Black-White aptitude score differences or the gender gap in high-level math achievements (Sackett et al., 2004, 2008; Stoet & Geary, 2012). But it does help explain why Blacks have scored higher when tested by Blacks than when tested by Whites (Danso & Esses, 2001; Inzlicht & Ben-Zeev, 2000). It gives us insight into why women have scored higher on math tests with no male test-takers present, and why women's online chess play drops sharply when they *think* they are playing a male opponent (Maass et al., 2008). It also explains "the Obama effect"—the finding that African-American adults performed better if they took a verbal aptitude test immediately after watching then-candidate Barack Obama's stereotype-defying nomination acceptance speech or just after his 2008 presidential victory (Marx et al., 2009).

Steele (1995, 2010) concludes that telling students they probably won't succeed (as is sometimes implied

"Math class is tough!"

"Teen talk" talking Barbie doll (introduced July 1992, recalled October 1992)

Stereotype threat Academic success can be hampered by self-doubt and self-monitoring during exams, which may impair attention, memory, and performance.

by remedial "minority support" programs) functions as a stereotype that can erode performance. Over time, such students may detach their self-esteem from academics and look for recognition elsewhere. Indeed, as African-American male students progress from eighth to twelfth grade, a growing disconnect appears between their grades and their self-esteem, and they tend to underachieve (Osborne, 1997).

One experiment randomly assigned some African-American seventh graders to write for 15 minutes about their most important values (Cohen et al., 2006, 2009). That simple exercise in self-affirmation had the apparent effect of boosting their semester grade point average by 0.26 in a first experiment and 0.34 in a replication. Can a brief confidence-boosting exercise actually increase school achievement? "It was hard for us to believe," reported Geoffrey Cohen (2013), "but we've replicated it since," including among women in college physics. Other research teams also have reproduced the benefits of the self-affirmation exercise (Bowen et al., 2012; Harackiewicz et al., 2013; Miyake et al., 2010; Sherman et al., 2013). Minority students in university programs that have challenged them to believe in their potential, or to focus on the idea that intelligence is malleable and not fixed, have likewise produced markedly higher grades and had lower dropout rates (Wilson, 2006).

* * *

What, then, can we realistically conclude about aptitude tests and bias? The tests are not biased in the scientific sense of failing to make valid statistical predictions for different groups. But they are indeed biased (appropriately so, some would say) in one sense—sensitivity to performance differences caused by cultural experience. Are the tests discriminatory? Again, the answer can be *Yes* or *No*. In one sense, *Yes*, their purpose is to discriminate—to distinguish among individuals. In another sense, *No*, their purpose is to reduce discrimination by decreasing reliance on subjective criteria for school and job placement—who you know, how you dress, or whether you are the "right kind of person." Civil service aptitude tests, for example, were devised to discriminate more fairly and objectively by reducing the political, racial, ethnic, and gender discrimination that preceded their use. Banning aptitude tests would lead those who decide on jobs and admissions to rely more on other considerations, such as personal opinion.

Perhaps, then, our goals for tests of mental abilities should be threefold. First, we should realize the benefits that intelligence testing pioneer Alfred Binet foresaw—to enable schools to recognize who might profit most from early intervention. Second, we must remain alert to Binet's fear that intelligence test scores may be misinterpreted as literal measures of a person's worth and potential. Third, we must remember that the competence that general intelligence tests sample is important; it helps enable success in some life paths. But it reflects only one aspect of personal competence, while missing the irrational thoughts and other kinds of thinking common to us all (Stanovich et al., 2013, 2014). Our *practical intelligence* and *emotional intelligence* matter, too, as do other forms of creativity, talent, and character.

The point to remember: There are many ways of being successful; our differences are variations of human adaptability. Life's great achievements result not only from "can do" abilities (and fair opportunity) but also from "will do" motivation. Competence + Diligence → Accomplishment.

> **stereotype threat** a self-confirming concern that one will be evaluated based on a negative stereotype.

> "Almost all the joyful things of life are outside the measure of IQ tests."
>
> Madeleine L'Engle, *A Circle of Quiet*, 1972

> "[Einstein] showed that genius equals brains plus tenacity squared."
>
> Walter Isaacson, "Einstein's Final Quest," 2009

RETRIEVAL PRACTICE

- What psychological principle helps explain why women tend to perform more poorly when they believe their online chess opponent is male?

ANSWER: stereotype threat

MODULE 32 REVIEW Genetic and Environmental Influences on Intelligence

LEARNING OBJECTIVES

RETRIEVAL PRACTICE Take a moment to answer each of these Learning Objective Questions (repeated here from within this module). Then turn to Appendix C, Complete Module Reviews, to check your answers. Research suggests that trying to answer these questions on your own will improve your long-term retention (McDaniel et al., 2009).

32-1 What evidence points to a genetic influence on intelligence, and what is heritability?

32-2 What does evidence reveal about environmental influences on intelligence?

32-3 How and why do the genders differ in mental ability scores?

32-4 How and why do racial and ethnic groups differ in mental ability scores?

32-5 Are intelligence tests inappropriately biased?

Use **LearningCurve** to create your personalized study plan, which will direct you to the resources that will help you most in **LaunchPad**.

TERMS AND CONCEPTS TO REMEMBER

RETRIEVAL PRACTICE Test yourself on these terms by trying to write down the definition before flipping back to the page number referenced to check your answer.

heritability, p. 406

stereotype threat, p. 414

TEST YOURSELF INTELLIGENCE

Test yourself repeatedly throughout your studies. This will not only help you figure out what you know and don't know; the testing itself will help you learn and remember the information more effectively thanks to the testing effect.

MODULE 29 What Is Intelligence?

1. Charles Spearman suggested we have one _____ _____ underlying success across a variety of intellectual abilities.

2. The existence of savant syndrome seems to support
   a. Sternberg's distinction among three types of intelligence.
   b. criticism of multiple intelligence theories.
   c. Gardner's theory of multiple intelligences.
   d. Thorndike's view of social intelligence.

3. Sternberg's three types of intelligence are _____, _____, and _____.

4. Emotionally intelligent people tend to
   a. seek immediate gratification.
   b. understand their own emotions but not those of others.
   c. understand others' emotions but not their own.
   d. succeed in their careers.

MODULE 30 Assessing Intelligence

5. The IQ of a 6-year-old with a measured mental age of 9 would be
   a. 67.
   b. 133.
   c. 86.
   d. 150.

6. The Wechsler Adult Intelligence Scale (WAIS) is best able to tell us
   a. what part of an individual's intelligence is determined by genetic inheritance.
   b. whether the test-taker will succeed in a job.
   c. how the test-taker compares with other adults in vocabulary and arithmetic reasoning.
   d. whether the test-taker has specific skills for music and the performing arts.

7. The Stanford-Binet, the Wechsler Adult Intelligence Scale, and the Wechsler Intelligence Scale for Children yield consistent results, for example on retesting. In other words, these tests have high _____.

31 The Dynamics of Intelligence

8. Use the concepts of crystallized and fluid intelligence to explain why writers tend to produce their most creative work later in life, and scientists may hit their peak much earlier.

9. More intelligent children and adults tend to live healthier and longer lives. Which of the following is NOT a possible reason for this phenomenon?

   a. Intelligence facilitates more education, better jobs, and a healthier environment.

   b. Intelligence encourages healthy living: less smoking, better diet, more exercise.

   c. Intelligent people have slower reaction times, making it less likely that they will put themselves at risk.

   d. A "well-wired body," as evidenced by fast reaction speeds, perhaps fosters both intelligence and longevity.

32 Genetic and Environmental Influences on Intelligence

10. The strongest support for heredity's influence on intelligence is the finding that

    a. identical twins, but not other siblings, have nearly identical intelligence test scores.

    b. the correlation between intelligence test scores of fraternal twins is not higher than that for other siblings.

    c. mental similarities between adopted siblings increase with age.

    d. children in impoverished families have similar intelligence scores.

11. To say that the heritability of intelligence is about 50 percent means that 50 percent of

    a. an individual's intelligence is due to genetic factors.

    b. the similarities between two groups of people are attributable to genes.

    c. the variation in intelligence within a group of people is attributable to genetic factors.

    d. intelligence is due to the mother's genes and the rest is due to the father's genes.

12. The environmental influence that has the clearest, most profound effect on intellectual development is

    a. exposing normal infants to enrichment programs before age 1.

    b. growing up in an economically disadvantaged home or neighborhood.

    c. being raised in conditions of extreme deprivation.

    d. being an identical twin.

13. _____ _____ can lead to poor performance on tests by undermining test-takers' belief that they can do well on the test.

Find answers to these questions in Appendix D, in the back of the book.

Erik Snyder/Getty Images

What Drives Us: Hunger, Sex, Friendship, and Achievement

· · · · · · · · · · · · ·

How well I [DM] remember the response to my first discussion question in a new introductory psychology class. Several hands rose, along with one left foot. The foot belonged to Chris Klein, who was the unlikeliest person to have made it to that class. At birth, Chris suffered oxygen deprivation that required 40 minutes of CPR. "One doctor wanted to let him go," recalls his mother.

The result was severe cerebral palsy. With damage to the brain area that controls muscle movement, Chris is unable to control his constantly moving hands (on which he wears protective padded gloves). He cannot feed, dress, or care for himself. And he cannot speak. But what Chris does have is a keen mind and a mobile left foot. With that blessed foot he controls the joystick on his motorized wheelchair. Using his big toe, he can type sentences, which his communication system can store, e-mail, or speak. And Chris has motivation, lots of motivation.

When Chris was a high school student in suburban Chicago, three teachers doubted he would be able to leave home for college. Yet he persisted, and, with lots of support, he ventured out to my college called Hope. Five years later, as his left foot drove him across the stage to receive his diploma, his admiring classmates honored his achievement with a spontaneous standing ovation.

Today, Chris is an inspirational speaker for schools, churches, and community events, giving "a voice to those that have none, and a helping hand to those with disabilities." He is president of the United States Society of Augmentative Alternative Communication. He is writing a book, *Lessons from the Big Toe*. And he has found love and married.

Although few of us face Chris Klein's challenges, we all seek to direct our energy in ways that will produce satisfaction and success. We are pushed by biological motives, such as hunger and sex (Modules 34 and 35). And we are pulled by social motives, such as affiliation and achievement (Module 36). Chris Klein's brute will to live, learn, and love highlight the essence of our own *motivations*, which energize and direct our lives.

Module 33 examines how psychologists have approached the study of motivation.

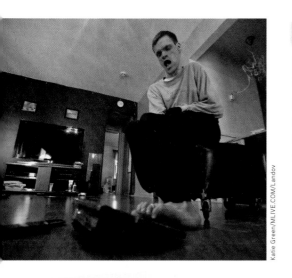

A motivated man: Chris Klein To see and hear Chris presenting his story, visit tinyurl.com/ChrisPsychStudent.

MODULE 33 Basic Motivational Concepts

33-1 How do psychologists define *motivation?* From what perspectives do they view motivated behavior?

Psychologists define **motivation** as a need or desire that energizes and directs behavior. Our motivations arise from the interplay between nature (the bodily "push") and nurture (the "pulls" from our thought processes and culture). Consider four perspectives for viewing motivated behaviors:

- *Instinct theory* (now replaced by the *evolutionary perspective*) focuses on genetically predisposed behaviors.
- *Drive-reduction theory* focuses on how we respond to our inner pushes.
- *Arousal theory* focuses on finding the right level of stimulation.
- And Abraham Maslow's *hierarchy of needs* focuses on the priority of some needs over others.

Instincts and Evolutionary Psychology

Early in the twentieth century, as Charles Darwin's influence grew, it became fashionable to classify all sorts of behaviors as instincts. If people criticized themselves, it was because of their "self-abasement instinct." If they boasted, it reflected their "self-assertion instinct." After scanning 500 books, one sociologist compiled a list of 5759 supposed human instincts! Before long, this instinct-naming fad collapsed under its own weight. Rather than *explaining* human behaviors, the early instinct theorists were simply *naming* them. It was like "explaining" a bright child's low grades by labeling the child an "underachiever." To name a behavior is *not* to explain it.

To qualify as an **instinct,** a complex behavior must have a fixed pattern throughout a species and be unlearned (Tinbergen, 1951). Such behaviors are common in other species (think of imprinting in birds and the return of salmon to their birthplace). Some human behaviors, such as infants' innate reflexes for rooting and sucking, also exhibit unlearned fixed patterns, but many more are directed by both physiological needs and psychological wants.

Instinct theory failed to explain most human motives, but its underlying assumption continues in evolutionary psychology: Genes do predispose some species-typical behavior. Psychologists might apply this perspective, for example, to explain our human similarities, animals' biological predispositions, and the influence of evolution on our phobias, our helping behaviors, and our romantic attractions.

motivation a need or desire that energizes and directs behavior.

instinct a complex behavior that is rigidly patterned throughout a species and is unlearned.

Same motive, different wiring The more complex the nervous system, the more adaptable the organism. Both humans and weaverbirds satisfy their need for shelter in ways that reflect their inherited capacities. Human behavior is flexible; we can learn whatever skills we need to build a house. The bird's behavior pattern is fixed; it can build only this kind of nest.

Drives and Incentives

When the original instinct theory of motivation collapsed, it was replaced by **drive-reduction theory**—the idea that a physiological need (such as for food or water) creates an aroused state that drives the organism to reduce the need. With few exceptions, when a physiological need increases, so does a psychological *drive*—an aroused, motivated state.

The physiological aim of drive reduction is **homeostasis**—the maintenance of a steady internal state. An example of homeostasis (literally "staying the same") is the body's temperature-regulation system, which works like a room's thermostat. Both systems operate through feedback loops: Sensors feed room temperature to a control device. If the room's temperature cools, the control device switches on the furnace. Likewise, if our body's temperature cools, our blood vessels constrict to conserve warmth, and we feel driven to put on more clothes or seek a warmer environment (**FIGURE 33.1**).

| Need
(food, water) | → | Drive
(hunger, thirst) | → | Drive-reducing
behaviors
(eating, drinking) |

▼ FIGURE 33.1
Drive-reduction theory Drive-reduction motivation arises from *homeostasis*—an organism's natural tendency to maintain a steady internal state. Thus, if we are water deprived, our thirst drives us to drink and to restore the body's normal state.

Not only are we *pushed* by our need to reduce drives, we also are *pulled* by **incentives**—positive or negative environmental stimuli that lure or repel us. This is one way our individual learning histories influence our motives. Depending on our learning, the aroma of good food, whether fresh roasted peanuts or toasted ants, can motivate our behavior. So can the sight of those we find attractive or threatening.

When there is both a need and an incentive, we feel strongly driven. The food-deprived person who smells pizza baking feels a strong hunger drive and the baking pizza becomes a compelling incentive. For each motive, we can therefore ask, "How is it pushed by our inborn physiological needs and pulled by incentives in the environment?"

drive-reduction theory the idea that a physiological need creates an aroused tension state (a drive) that motivates an organism to satisfy the need.

homeostasis a tendency to maintain a balanced or constant internal state; the regulation of any aspect of body chemistry, such as blood glucose, around a particular level.

incentive a positive or negative environmental stimulus that motivates behavior.

Optimum Arousal

We are much more than homeostatic systems, however. Some motivated behaviors actually *increase* arousal. Well-fed animals will leave their shelter to explore and gain information, seemingly in the absence of any need-based drive. Curiosity drives monkeys to monkey around trying to figure out how to unlock a latch that opens nothing or how to open a window that allows them to see outside their room (Butler, 1954). It drives the 9-month-old infant to investigate every accessible corner of the house. It drives the scientists whose work this text discusses. And it drives explorers and adventurers such as George Mallory. Asked why he wanted to climb Mount Everest, the *New York Times* reported that Mallory answered, "Because it is there." Those who, like Mallory, enjoy

Driven by curiosity Young monkeys and children are fascinated by the unfamiliar. Their drive to explore maintains an optimum level of arousal and is one of several motives that do not fill any immediate physiological need.

Yerkes-Dodson law the principle that performance increases with arousal only up to a point, beyond which performance decreases.

hierarchy of needs Maslow's pyramid of human needs, beginning at the base with physiological needs that must first be satisfied before higher-level safety needs and then psychological needs become active.

high arousal are most likely to seek out intense music, novel foods, and risky behaviors and careers (Roberti et al., 2004; Zuckerman, 1979, 2009). Although they have been called "sensation-seekers," many risk takers (such as mountaineers) also are motivated in other ways, such as by a drive to master their emotions and actions (Barlow et al., 2013).

So, human motivation aims not to eliminate arousal but to seek optimum levels of arousal. Having all our biological needs satisfied, we feel driven to experience stimulation and we hunger for information. Lacking stimulation, we feel bored and look for a way to increase arousal to some optimum level. However, with too much stimulation comes stress, and we then look for a way to decrease arousal.

Two early-twentieth-century psychologists studied the relationship of arousal to performance and identified the **Yerkes-Dodson law,** suggesting that moderate arousal would lead to optimal performance (Yerkes & Dodson, 1908). When taking an exam, for example, it pays to be moderately aroused—alert but not trembling with nervousness. Between depressed low arousal and anxious hyperarousal lies a flourishing life. But optimal arousal levels depend upon the task as well, with more difficult tasks requiring lower arousal for best performance (Hembree, 1988) (**FIGURE 33.2**). When anxious, it's better not to become further aroused with a caffeinated energy drink.

▼ **FIGURE 33.2**
Arousal and performance

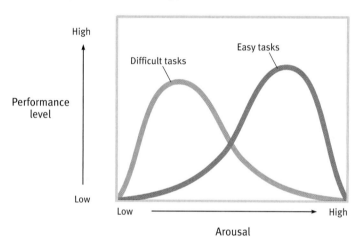

RETRIEVAL PRACTICE

• Performance peaks at lower levels of arousal for difficult tasks, and at higher levels for easy or well-learned tasks. (1) How might this phenomenon affect runners? (2) How might this phenomenon affect anxious test-takers facing a difficult exam? (3) How might the performance of anxious students be affected by relaxation training?

ANSWER: (1) Runners tend to excel when aroused by competition. (2) High anxiety in test-takers may disrupt their performance. (3) Teaching anxious students how to relax before an exam can enable them to perform better (Hembree, 1988).

"Hunger is the most urgent form of poverty."

Alliance to End Hunger, 2002

Small psychological world: Abraham Maslow was the first graduate student of the famed monkey attachment researcher, Harry Harlow. (Harlow, in turn, had been mentored at Stanford by the famed intelligence researcher, Lewis Terman.)

A Hierarchy of Motives

Some needs take priority. At this moment, with your needs for air and water hopefully satisfied, other motives—such as your desire to achieve—are energizing and directing your behavior. Let your need for water go unsatisfied and your thirst will preoccupy you. Deprived of air, your thirst would disappear.

Abraham Maslow (1970) described these priorities as a **hierarchy of needs** (**FIGURE 33.3**). At the base of this pyramid are our physiological needs, such as those for food and water. Only if these needs are met are we prompted to meet our need for safety, and then to satisfy our human needs to give and receive love and to enjoy self-esteem. Beyond this, said Maslow (1971), lies the need to actualize one's full potential.

Near the end of his life, Maslow proposed that some people also reach a level of *self-transcendence*. At the self-actualization level, people seek to realize their own potential.

Self-transcendence needs
Need to find meaning and identity beyond the self

Self-actualization needs
Need to live up to our fullest and unique potential

Esteem needs
Need for self-esteem, achievement, competence, and independence; need for recognition and respect from others

Belongingness and love needs
Need to love and be loved, to belong and be accepted; need to avoid loneliness and separation

Safety needs
Need to feel that the world is organized and predictable; need to feel safe, secure, and stable

Physiological needs
Need to satisfy hunger and thirst

▼ FIGURE 33.3
Maslow's hierarchy of needs Reduced to near-starvation by their rulers, inhabitants of Suzanne Collins' fictional nation, Panem, hunger for food and survival. *Hunger Games* heroine Katniss Everdeen expresses higher-level needs for actualization and transcendence, and in the process inspires the nation.

At the self-transcendence level, people strive for meaning, purpose, and communion that are transpersonal, beyond the self (Koltko-Rivera, 2006).

Maslow's hierarchy is somewhat arbitrary; the order of such needs is not universally fixed. People have starved themselves to make a political statement. Culture also matters: Self-esteem matters most in individualist nations, whose citizens tend to focus more on personal achievements than on family and community identity (Oishi et al., 1999). And, while agreeing with Maslow's basic levels of need, today's evolutionary psychologists note that gaining and retaining mates and parenting offspring are also universal human motives (Kenrick et al., 2010).

Nevertheless, the simple idea that some motives are more compelling than others provides a framework for thinking about motivation. Worldwide life-satisfaction surveys support this basic idea (Oishi et al., 1999; Tay & Diener, 2011). In poorer nations that lack easy access to money and the food and shelter it buys, financial satisfaction more strongly predicts feelings of well-being. In wealthy nations, where most are able to meet basic needs, home-life satisfaction is a better predictor.

Let's now consider four representative motives, beginning at the physiological level with hunger and working up through sexual motivation to the higher-level needs to belong and to achieve. At each level, we shall see how experience interacts with biology.

RETRIEVAL PRACTICE

- How do instinct theory, drive-reduction theory, and arousal theory contribute to our understanding of motivated behavior?

ANSWER: Instincts and evolutionary psychology help explain the genetic basis for our unlearned, species-typical behaviors. From drive-reduction theory, we know that our physiological needs (such as hunger) create an aroused state that drives us to reduce the need (for example, by eating). Arousal theory suggests we need to maintain an optimal level of arousal, which helps explain our motivation toward behaviors that meet no physiological need.

- After hours of driving alone in an unfamiliar city, you finally see a diner. Although it looks deserted and a little creepy, you stop because you are *really* hungry. How would Maslow's hierarchy of needs explain your behavior?

ANSWER: According to Maslow, our drive to meet the physiological needs of hunger and thirst take priority over safety needs, prompting us to take risks at times in order to eat.

MODULE 33 REVIEW Basic Motivational Concepts

LEARNING OBJECTIVES

RETRIEVAL PRACTICE Take a moment to answer each of these Learning Objective Questions (repeated here from within this module). Then turn to Appendix C, Complete Module Reviews, to check your answers. Research suggests that trying to answer these questions on your own will improve your long-term retention (McDaniel et al., 2009).

33-1 How do psychologists define *motivation?* From what perspectives do they view motivated behavior?

TERMS AND CONCEPTS TO REMEMBER

RETRIEVAL PRACTICE Test yourself on these terms by trying to write down the definition before flipping back to the page number referenced to check your answer.

motivation, p. 420

instinct, p. 420

drive-reduction theory, p. 421

homeostasis, p. 421

incentive, p. 421

Yerkes-Dodson law, p. 422

hierarchy of needs, p. 422

Use 🔁 LearningCurve to create your personalized study plan, which will direct you to the resources that will help you most in 🔁 LaunchPad.

MODULE 34 Hunger

A vivid demonstration of the supremacy of physiological needs came when Ancel Keys and his research team (1950) studied semistarvation among wartime conscientious objectors. After three months of normal eating, they cut in half the food intake of 36 men selected from 200 volunteers. The semistarved men became listless and apathetic as their bodies conserved energy. Eventually, their body weights stabilized at about 25 percent below their starting weights.

More dramatic were the psychological effects. Consistent with Abraham Maslow's idea of a *hierarchy of needs,* the men became food obsessed. They talked food. They daydreamed food. They collected recipes, read cookbooks, and feasted their eyes on delectable forbidden foods. Preoccupied with their unfulfilled basic need, they lost interest in sex and social activities. As one participant reported, "If we see a show, the most interesting part of it is contained in scenes where people are eating. I couldn't laugh at the funniest picture in the world, and love scenes are completely dull."

The semistarved men's preoccupations illustrate how powerful motives can hijack our consciousness. When you are hungry, thirsty, fatigued, or sexually aroused, little else may seem to matter. When you're not, food, water, sleep, or sex just don't seem like such big things in your life, now or ever.

"Nobody wants to kiss when they are hungry."

Journalist Dorothy Dix (1861-1951)

"Nature often equips life's essentials—sex, eating, nursing—with built-in gratification."

Frans de Waal, "Morals Without God?," 2010

In University of Amsterdam studies, Loran Nordgren and his colleagues (2006, 2007) found that people in a motivational "hot" state (from fatigue, hunger, or sexual arousal) easily recalled such feelings in their own past and perceived them as driving forces in others' behavior. (Interestingly, there is a parallel effect of our current good or bad mood on our memories.) In another experiment, people were given $4 cash they could keep or draw from to bid for foods. Hungry people overbid for a snack they would eat later when sated, and sated people underbid for a snack they would eat later when hungry (Fisher & Rangel, 2014). Likewise, when sexually motivated, men more often perceive a smile as flirtation rather than simple friendliness (Howell et al., 2012). Grocery shop with an empty stomach and you are more likely to see those jelly-filled doughnuts as just what you've always loved and will be wanting tomorrow. *Motives matter mightily.*

"The full person does not understand the needs of the hungry."

Irish proverb

The Physiology of Hunger

34-1 What physiological factors produce hunger?

Keys' semistarved volunteers felt their hunger because of a *homeostatic* system designed to maintain normal body weight and an adequate nutrient supply. But what precisely triggers hunger? Is it the pangs of an empty stomach? So it seemed to A. L. Washburn. Working with Walter Cannon (Cannon & Washburn, 1912), Washburn agreed to swallow a balloon attached to a recording device (**FIGURE 34.1**). When inflated to fill his stomach, the balloon transmitted his stomach contractions. Washburn supplied information about his *feelings* of hunger by pressing a key each time he felt a hunger pang. The discovery: Washburn was indeed having stomach contractions whenever he felt hungry.

Can hunger exist without stomach pangs? To answer that question, researchers removed some rats' stomachs, creating a direct path to their small intestines (Tsang, 1938). Did the rats continue to eat? Indeed they did. Some hunger similarly persists in humans whose ulcerated or cancerous stomachs have been removed.

If the pangs of an empty stomach are not the only source of hunger, what else matters?

Body Chemistry and the Brain

People and other animals automatically regulate their caloric intake to prevent energy deficits and maintain a stable body weight. This suggests that somehow, somewhere, the body is keeping tabs on its available resources. One such resource is the blood

Washburn swallows balloon, which measures stomach contractions.

Washburn presses key each time he feels hungry.

Stomach contractions

Hunger pangs

0 1 2 3 4 5 6 7 8 9 10
Time in minutes

▼ FIGURE 34.1
Monitoring stomach contractions
Using this procedure, Washburn showed that stomach contractions (transmitted by the stomach balloon) accompany our feelings of hunger (indicated by a key press). (From Cannon, 1929.)

▼ FIGURE 34.2
The hypothalamus The hypothalamus (colored orange) performs various
body maintenance functions, including control of hunger. Blood vessels
supply the hypothalamus, enabling it to
respond to our current blood chemistry
as well as to incoming neural information about the body's state.

glucose the form of sugar that circulates in the blood and provides the major
source of energy for body tissues. When
its level is low, we feel hunger.

set point the point at which your "weight
thermostat" is supposedly set. When your
body falls below this weight, increased
hunger and a lowered metabolic rate may
combine to restore the lost weight.

basal metabolic rate the body's resting rate of energy expenditure.

▼ FIGURE 34.3
The appetite hormones
• *Ghrelin:* Hormone secreted by
  empty stomach; sends "I'm
  hungry" signals to the brain.
• *Insulin:* Hormone secreted by
  pancreas; controls blood glucose.
• *Leptin:* Protein hormone secreted
  by fat cells; when abundant,
  causes brain to increase metabolism and decrease hunger.
• *Orexin:* Hunger-triggering
  hormone secreted by
  hypothalamus.
• *PYY:* Digestive tract hormone;
  sends "I'm *not* hungry" signals to
  the brain.

sugar **glucose.** Increases in the hormone *insulin* (secreted by the pancreas) diminish blood glucose, partly by converting it to stored fat. If your blood glucose level drops, you won't consciously feel the lower blood sugar. But your brain, which is automatically monitoring your blood chemistry and your body's internal state, will trigger hunger. Signals from your stomach, intestines, and liver (indicating whether glucose is being deposited or withdrawn) all signal your brain to motivate eating or not.

How does the brain integrate these messages and sound the alarm? The work is done by several neural areas, some housed deep in the brain within the hypothalamus, a neural traffic intersection (**FIGURE 34.2**). For example, one neural arc (called the *arcuate nucleus*) has a center that secretes appetite-stimulating hormones. When stimulated electrically, well-fed animals begin to eat. If the area is destroyed, even starving animals have no interest in food. Another neural center secretes appetite-suppressing hormones. When electrically stimulated, animals will stop eating. Destroy this area and animals will eat and eat, and become extremely fat (Duggan & Booth, 1986; Hoebel & Teitelbaum, 1966).

Blood vessels connect the hypothalamus to the rest of the body, so it can respond to our current blood chemistry and other incoming information. One of its tasks is monitoring levels of appetite hormones, such as *ghrelin*, a hunger-arousing hormone secreted by an empty stomach. During bypass surgery for severe obesity, surgeons seal off or remove part of the stomach. The remaining stomach then produces much less ghrelin, and the person's appetite lessens (Ammori, 2013; Lemonick, 2002). Besides insulin and ghrelin, other appetite hormones include *leptin, orexin,* and *PYY*; **FIGURE 34.3** describes how they influence our feelings of hunger.

Experimental manipulation of appetite hormones has raised hopes for an appetite-reducing medication. Such a nose spray or skin patch might counteract the body's hunger-producing chemicals or mimic (or even increase) the levels of hunger-dampening chemicals.

The complex interaction of appetite hormones and brain activity may help explain the body's apparent predisposition to maintain itself at a particular weight. When semistarved rats fall below their normal weight, their "weight thermostat" signals the body to restore the lost weight. Fat cells cry out (so to speak) "Feed me!" and grab glucose from the bloodstream (Ludwig & Friedman, 2014). Thus, hunger increases and energy expenditure decreases. This stable weight toward which semistarved rats return is their **set point** (Keesey & Corbett, 1983). In rats and humans, heredity influences body type and approximate set point.

Voisin/Phanie/Science Source

Evidence for the brain's control of eating The fat mouse on the left has nonfunctioning receptors in the appetite-suppressing part of the hypothalamus.

🌀 **LaunchPad** For an interactive and visual tutorial on the brain and eating, visit LaunchPad's *PsychSim 6: Hunger and the Fat Rat.*

Our bodies regulate weight through the control of food intake, energy output, and **basal metabolic rate**—the rate of energy expenditure for maintaining basic body functions when at rest. By the end of their 6 months of semistarvation, the men who participated in Keys' experiment had stabilized at three-quarters of their normal weight, while taking in *half* of their previous calories. How did their bodies achieve this dieter's nightmare? They reduced their energy expenditure, partly through inactivity but partly because of a 29 percent drop in their basal metabolic rate.

Some researchers, however, doubt that our bodies have a preset tendency to maintain optimum weight (Assanand et al., 1998). They point out that slow, sustained changes in body weight can alter one's set point, and that psychological factors also sometimes drive our feelings of hunger. Given unlimited access to a wide variety of tasty foods, people and other animals tend to overeat and gain weight (Raynor & Epstein, 2001). For these reasons, some researchers have abandoned the idea of a biologically fixed *set point*. They prefer the term *settling point* to indicate the level at which a person's weight settles in response to caloric intake and expenditure (which are influenced by environment as well as biology).

Over the next 40 years you will eat about 20 tons of food. If, during those years, you increase your daily intake by just .01 ounce more than required for your energy needs, you will gain an estimated 24 pounds (Martin et al., 1991).

RETRIEVAL PRACTICE

- Hunger occurs in response to _____ (low/high) blood glucose and _____ (low/high) levels of ghrelin.

ANSWERS: low; high

The Psychology of Hunger

34-2 What cultural and situational factors influence hunger?

Our internal hunger games are indeed pushed by our physiological state—our body chemistry and hypothalamic activity. Yet there is more to hunger than meets the stomach. This was strikingly apparent when Paul Rozin and his trickster colleagues (1998) tested two patients with amnesia who had no memory for events occurring more than a minute ago. If, 20 minutes after eating a normal lunch, the patients were offered another, both readily consumed it . . . and usually a third meal offered 20 minutes after the second was finished. This suggests that part of knowing when to eat is our memory of our last meal. As time passes since we last ate, we anticipate eating again and start feeling hungry.

The New Yorker Collection, 2002, Alex Gregory from cartoonbank.com. All Rights Reserved.

"Never get a tattoo when you're drunk and hungry."

RICHARD OLSENIUS/NGS Image Collection

© Mark Bowler/Alamy

An acquired taste People everywhere learn to enjoy the fatty, bitter, or spicy foods common in their culture. For these Alaska Natives (left), but not for most other North Americans, whale blubber is a tasty treat. For Peruvians (right), roasted guinea pig is similarly delicious.

Taste Preferences: Biology and Culture

Body chemistry and environmental factors together influence not only the when of hunger, but also the what—our taste preferences. When feeling tense or depressed, do you crave starchy, carbohydrate-laden foods? Are you like ardent football fans who, after a big loss, tend to take solace in high-calorie foods (Cornil & Chandon, 2013)? Carbohydrates boost the neurotransmitter serotonin, which has calming effects. When stressed, both rats and many humans find it extra rewarding to scarf Oreos (Artiga et al., 2007; Sproesser et al., 2014).

Our preferences for sweet and salty tastes are genetic and universal. Other taste preferences are conditioned, as when people given highly salted foods develop a liking for excess salt (Beauchamp, 1987), or when people who have been sickened by a food develop an aversion to it. (The frequency of children's illnesses provides many chances for them to learn food aversions.)

Culture affects taste, too. Bedouins enjoy eating the eye of a camel, which most North Americans would find repulsive. Many Japanese people enjoy nattó, a fermented soybean dish that "smells like the marriage of ammonia and a tire fire," reports smell expert Rachel Herz (2012). Although many Westerners find this disgusting, Asians, she adds, are often repulsed by what Westerners love—"the rotted bodily fluid of an ungulate" (a.k.a. cheese, some varieties of which have the same bacteria and odor as stinky feet). Most North Americans and Europeans shun horse, dog, and rat meat, all of which are prized elsewhere.

Rats tend to avoid unfamiliar foods (Sclafani, 1995). So do we, especially animal-based foods. Such *neophobia* (dislike of things unfamiliar) surely was adaptive for our ancestors, protecting them from potentially toxic substances. Disgust works. Nevertheless, in experiments, people who repeatedly sample an initially novel fruit drink or unfamiliar food typically experience increasing appreciation for the new taste. Moreover, exposure to one set of novel foods increases our willingness to try another (Pliner, 1982, Pliner et al., 1993).

Other taste preferences also are adaptive. For example, the spices most commonly used in hot-climate recipes—where food, especially meat, is at risk of spoiling more quickly—inhibit bacteria growth (**FIGURE 34.4**). Pregnancy-related nausea and food aversions peak about the tenth week, when the developing embryo is most vulnerable to toxins. So there is biological wisdom to our taste preferences.

▼ FIGURE 34.4
Hot cultures like hot spices
Countries with hot climates, in which food historically spoiled more quickly, feature recipes with more bacteria-inhibiting spices (Sherman & Flaxman, 2001). India averages nearly 10 spices per meat recipe; Finland, 2 spices.

Spices per recipe

The hotter the climate, the more spices used.

Mean annual temperature (degrees Celsius)

Situational Influences on Eating

To a surprising extent, situations also control our eating—a phenomenon psychologists have called the *ecology of eating*. Here are three situations you may have noticed but underestimated:

- Do you eat more when eating with others? Most of us do (Herman et al., 2003; Hetherington et al., 2006). After a party, you may realize you've overeaten. This happens because the presence of others tends to amplify our natural behavior tendencies. (We explore this *social facilitation* in the Social Psychology modules.)

- *Unit bias* occurs with similar mindlessness. At France's National Center for Scientific Research, Andrew Geier and his colleagues (2006) wondered why French waistlines are smaller than American waistlines. From soda drinks to yogurt sizes, the French offer foods in smaller portion sizes. Does it matter? (One could as well order two small sandwiches as one large one.) To find out, the investigators offered people varieties of free snacks. For example, in the lobby of an apartment house, they laid out either full or half pretzels, big or little Tootsie Rolls, or a big bowl of M&M's with either a small or large serving scoop. Their consistent result: Offered a supersized standard portion, people put away more calories. In another study, people offered pasta ate more when given a big plate (Van Ittersum & Wansink, 2012). Children also eat more when using adult-sized (rather than child-sized) dishware (DiSantis et al., 2013). Even nutrition experts helped themselves to 31 percent more ice cream when given a big bowl rather than a small one, and 15 percent more when scooping with a big rather than a small scoop (Wansink, 2006, 2007). People pour more into and drink more from short, wide than tall, narrow glasses. And they take more of easier-to-reach food on buffet lines (Marteau et al., 2012). Portion size matters.

- *Food variety* also stimulates eating. Offered a dessert buffet, we eat more than we do when choosing a portion from one favorite dessert. For our early ancestors, variety was healthy. When foods were abundant and varied, eating more provided a wide range of vitamins and minerals and produced fat that protected them during winter cold or famine. When a bounty of varied foods was unavailable, eating less extended the food supply until winter or famine ended (Polivy et al., 2008; Remick et al., 2009).

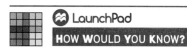

LaunchPad
HOW WOULD YOU KNOW?
Consider how researchers test some of these ideas with LaunchPad's *How Would You Know If Larger Dinner Plates Make People Fat?*

LaunchPad For a 7-minute video review of hunger, see LaunchPad's *Video: Hunger and Eating.*

RETRIEVAL PRACTICE

- After an eight-hour hike without food, your long-awaited favorite dish is placed in front of you, and your mouth waters in anticipation. Why?

ANSWER: You have learned to respond to the sight and aroma that signal the food about to enter your mouth. Both *physiological* cues (low blood sugar) and *psychological* cues (anticipation of the tasty meal) heighten your experienced hunger.

Obesity and Weight Control

34-3 What factors predispose some people to become and remain obese?

Obesity can be socially toxic, by affecting both how you are treated and how you feel about yourself. Obesity has been associated with lower psychological well-being, especially among women, and increased depression (de Wit et al., 2010; Luppino et al., 2010; Riffkin, 2014). Obese 6- to 9-year-olds are 60 percent more likely to suffer bullying (Lumeng et al., 2010). And obesity has physical health risks. Yet few overweight people win the battle of the bulge. Why? And why do some people gain weight while others eat the same amount and seldom add a pound?

Weight woes New Jersey Governor Chris Christie (on Nightline, July 3, 2012, before undergoing stomach lap-band surgery): "I think there's a fundamental misunderstanding among people regarding weight. I think folks say—yeah, well he must just not be disciplined, you know, or he must not have willpower . . . If it were easy, I'd already have it fixed."

"American men, on average, say they weigh 196 pounds and women say they weigh 160 pounds. Both figures are nearly 20 pounds heavier than in 1990."

Elizabeth Mendes, www.gallup.com, 2011

"*Remember when we used to have to fatten the kids up first?*"

The Physiology of Obesity

Our bodies store fat for good reason. Fat is an ideal form of stored energy—a high-calorie fuel reserve to carry the body through periods when food is scarce—a common occurrence in our prehistoric ancestors' world. No wonder people in developing societies have often found heavier bodies attractive: Obesity signals affluence and social status (Furnham & Baguma, 1994; Swami et al., 2011).

In parts of the world where food and sweets are now abundantly available, the rule that once served our hungry distant ancestors—*When you find energy-rich fat or sugar, eat it!*—has become dysfunctional. Pretty much everywhere this book is being read, people have a growing problem. A worldwide study of 188 countries (Ng et al., 2014) revealed that

- between 1980 and 2013 the proportion of overweight adults increased from 29 to 37 percent among the world's men, and from 30 to 38 percent among women.
- over the last 33 years, *no* country has reduced its obesity rate. Not one.
- national variations are huge, with the percentage overweight ranging from 85 percent in Tonga to 3 percent in Timor-Leste.

According to the World Health Organization (WHO), an overweight person has a *body mass index* (BMI) of 25 or more; someone obese has a BMI of 30 or more. (See www.tinyurl.com/GiveMyBMI to calculate your BMI and to see where you are in relation to others in your country and in the world.) In the United States, the adult obesity rate has more than doubled in the last 40 years, reaching 36 percent, and child-teen obesity has quadrupled (Flegal et al., 2010, 2012). In 1990, no U.S. state had an obesity rate greater than 15 percent. By 2010, no state had an obesity rate of *less* than 20 percent (CDC, 2012).

In one digest of 97 studies of 2.9 million people, being simply overweight was not a health risk, while being obese was (Flegal et al., 2013). Fitness matters more than being a little overweight. But significant obesity increases the risk of diabetes, high blood pressure, heart disease, gallstones, arthritis, and certain types of cancer, thus increasing health care costs and shortening life expectancy (de Gonzales et al., 2010; Jarrett et al., 2010; Sun et al., 2009). Extreme obesity increases risk of suicidal behaviors (Wagner et al., 2013). Research also has linked women's obesity to their risk of late-life cognitive decline, including Alzheimer's disease and brain tissue loss (Bruce-Keller et al., 2009; Whitmer et al., 2008). One experiment found improved memory performance 12 weeks after severely obese people had weight-loss surgery and lost significant weight. Those not having the surgery showed some further cognitive decline (Gunstad et al., 2011).

Set Point and Metabolism Research on the physiology of obesity challenges the stereotype of severely overweight people being weak-willed gluttons. Once we become fat, we require less food to maintain our weight than we did to attain it. Fat has a lower metabolic rate than does muscle—it takes less food energy to maintain. When an overweight person's body drops below its previous set (or settling) point, the brain triggers increased hunger and decreased metabolism. The body adapts to starvation by burning off fewer calories and seeking to restore lost weight. Blame your brain for weight regain (Cornier, 2011).

Lean people also seem naturally disposed to move about. They burn more calories than do energy-conserving overweight people, who tend to sit still longer (Levine et al., 2005). These individual differences in resting metabolism help explain why two people of the same height, age, and activity level can maintain the same weight, even if one of them eats much less than does the other.

The Genetic Factor Do our genes predispose us to eat more or less? To burn more calories by fidgeting or fewer by sitting still? Studies confirm a genetic influence on body weight. Consider two examples:

- Despite shared family meals, adoptive siblings' body weights are uncorrelated with one another or with those of their adoptive parents. Rather, people's weights resemble those of their biological parents (Grilo & Pogue-Geile, 1991).

- Identical twins have closely similar weights, even when raised apart (Hjelmborg et al., 2008; Plomin et al., 1997). Across studies, their weight correlates +.74. The much lower +.32 correlation among fraternal twins suggests that genes explain two-thirds of our varying body mass (Maes et al., 1997).

The Food and Activity Factors Genes tell an important part of the obesity story. But environmental factors are mighty important, too.

Studies in Europe, Japan, and the United States show that children and adults who suffer from *sleep loss* are more vulnerable to obesity (Keith et al., 2006; Nedeltcheva et al., 2010; Taheri, 2004a,b). With sleep deprivation, the levels of leptin (which reports body fat to the brain) fall, and ghrelin (the appetite-stimulating stomach hormone) rise.

Social influence is another factor. One 32-year study of 12,067 people found them most likely to become obese when a friend became obese (Christakis & Fowler, 2007). If the obese friend was a close one, the odds of likewise becoming obese almost tripled. Moreover, the correlation among friends' weights was not simply a matter of seeking out similar people as friends. Friends matter.

The strongest evidence that environment influences weight comes from *our fattening world* (**FIGURE 34.5**). What explains this growing problem? Changing *food consumption* and *activity levels* are at work. We are eating more and moving less, with lifestyles sometimes approaching those of animal feedlots (where farmers fatten inactive animals). In the United States, jobs requiring moderate physical activity declined from about 50 percent in 1960 to 20 percent in 2011 (Church et al., 2011). Worldwide, 31 percent of adults (including 43 percent of Americans and 25 percent of Europeans) are now sedentary, which means they average less than 20 minutes per day of moderate activity such as walking (Hallal et al., 2012). Sedentary occupations increase the chance of being overweight, as 86 percent of U.S. truck drivers reportedly are (Jacobson et al., 2007).

The "bottom" line: New stadiums, theaters, and subway cars—but not airplanes—are widening seats to accommodate the girth growth (Hampson, 2000; Kim & Tong, 2010).

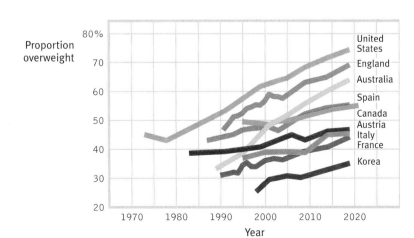

▼ FIGURE 34.5
Past and projected overweight rates, by the Organization for Economic Cooperation and Development

Washington State Ferries abandoned a 50-year-old standard: "Eighteen-inch butts are a thing of the past" (Shepherd, 1999). New York City, facing a large problem with Big Apple bottoms, has mostly replaced 17.5-inch bucket-style subway seats with bucketless seats (Hampson, 2000). In the end, today's people need more room.

These findings reinforce an important finding from psychology's study of intelligence: There can be high levels of heritability (genetic influence on individual differences) without heredity explaining group differences. Genes mostly determine why one person today is heavier than another. Environment mostly determines why people today are heavier than their counterparts 50 years ago. Our eating behavior also demonstrates the now-familiar interaction among biological, psychological, and social-cultural factors. For tips on shedding unwanted pounds, see **TABLE 34.1**.

> "We put fast food on every corner, we put junk food in our schools, we got rid of [physical education classes], we put candy and soda at the checkout stand of every retail outlet you can think of. The results are in. It worked."
>
> Harold Goldstein, Executive Director of the California Center for Public Health Advocacy, 2009, when imagining a vast U.S. national experiment to encourage weight gain

▼ TABLE 34.1
Waist Management

People struggling with obesity are well advised to seek medical evaluation and guidance. For others who wish to take off a few pounds, researchers have offered these tips:

- *Begin only if you feel motivated and self-disciplined.* For most people, permanent weight loss requires a lifelong change in eating habits combined with increased exercise.

- *Exercise and get enough sleep.* Inactive people are often overweight. Especially when supported by 7 to 8 hours of sleep a night, exercise empties fat cells, builds muscle, speeds up metabolism, helps lower your settling point, and reduces stress and stress-induced craving for carbohydrate-rich comfort foods (Bennett, 1995; Kolata, 1987; Thompson et al., 1982).

- *Minimize exposure to tempting food cues.* Food shop on a full stomach. Keep tempting foods out of the house, and store other appealing foods out of sight.

- *Limit variety and eat healthy foods.* Given more variety, people consume more. So eat simple meals with whole grains, fruits, and vegetables. Water-rich foods such as veggies and broth soups can fill the stomach with few calories. Healthy fats, such as those found in olive oil and fish, help regulate appetite and artery-clogging cholesterol (Taubes, 2001, 2002). Better crispy greens than Krispy Kremes.

- *Reduce portion sizes.* Serve food with smaller bowls, plates, and utensils.

- **Don't starve all day and eat one big meal at night.** This eating pattern, common among overweight people, slows metabolism. Moreover, those who eat a balanced breakfast are, by late morning, more alert and less fatigued (Spring et al., 1992).

- *Beware of the binge.* Especially for men, eating slowly can lead to eating less (Martin et al., 2007). Among people who do consciously restrain their eating, drinking alcohol or feeling anxious or depressed can unleash the urge to eat (Herman & Polivy, 1980).

- *Before eating with others, decide how much you want to eat.* Eating with friends can distract us from monitoring our own eating (Ward & Mann, 2000).

- *Remember, most people occasionally lapse.* A lapse need not become a full collapse.

- *Connect to a support group.* Join with others, either face-to-face or online, with whom you can share your goals and progress (Freedman, 2011).

American idle: Couch potatoes beware—TV watching correlates with obesity Over time, lifestyles have become more sedentary and TV watching and other screen time has increased, and so has the percentage of overweight people in Britain, Canada, and the United States (Pagani et al., 2010). As televisions have become flatter, people have become fatter.

RETRIEVAL PRACTICE

- Why can two people of the same height, age, and activity level maintain the same weight, even if one of them eats much less than the other does?

ANSWER: Individuals have very different set points and genetically influenced metabolism levels, causing them to burn calories differently.

MODULE 34 REVIEW Hunger

LEARNING OBJECTIVES

RETRIEVAL PRACTICE Take a moment to answer each of these Learning Objective Questions (repeated here from within this module). Then turn to Appendix C, Complete Module Reviews, to check your answers. Research suggests that trying to answer these questions on your own will improve your long-term retention (McDaniel et al., 2009).

34-1 What physiological factors produce hunger?

34-2 What cultural and situational factors influence hunger?

34-3 What factors predispose some people to become and remain obese?

TERMS AND CONCEPTS TO REMEMBER

RETRIEVAL PRACTICE Test yourself on these terms by trying to write down the definition before flipping back to the page number referenced to check your answer.

glucose, p. 426

set point, p. 427

basal metabolic rate, p. 427

Use 🔯 LearningCurve to create your personalized study plan, which will direct you to the resources that will help you most in 🔯 LaunchPad.

Sexual Motivation
MODULE 35

Sex is a part of life. For all but the tiny fraction of us considered **asexual,** dating and mating become a high priority from puberty on. Physiological and psychological influences affect our sexual feelings and behaviors.

The Physiology of Sex

Sex is not like hunger, because it is not an actual *need.* (Without it, we may feel like dying, but we will not.) Yet sex motivates. Had this not been so for all your ancestors, you would not be reading this book. Sexual motivation is nature's clever way of making people procreate, thus enabling our species' survival. When two people feel an attraction, they hardly stop to think of themselves as guided by their ancestral genes. As the pleasure we take in eating is nature's method of getting our body nourishment, so the desires and pleasures of sex are our genes' way of preserving and spreading themselves. Life is sexually transmitted.

"It is a near-universal experience, the invisible clause on one's birth certificate stipulating that one will, upon reaching maturity, feel the urge to engage in activities often associated with the issuance of more birth certificates."

Science writer Natalie Angier, 2007

Hormones and Sexual Behavior

35-1 How do hormones influence human sexual motivation?

Among the forces driving sexual behavior are the *sex hormones.* The main male sex hormone is **testosterone.** The main female sex hormones are the **estrogens,** such as estradiol. Sex hormones influence us at many points in the life span:

• During the prenatal period, they direct our development as males or females.

• During puberty, a sex hormone surge ushers us into adolescence.

• After puberty and well into the late adult years, sex hormones activate sexual behavior.

In most mammals, nature neatly synchronizes sex with fertility. Females become sexually receptive (in other animals, "in heat") when their estrogens peak at ovulation. In experiments, researchers can cause female animals to become receptive by injecting them with estrogens. Male hormone levels are more constant, and hormone injection does not so easily manipulate the sexual behavior of male animals (Feder, 1984). Nevertheless, male rats that have had their testes (which manufacture testosterone) surgically removed will gradually lose much of their interest in receptive females. They slowly regain it if injected with testosterone.

asexual having no sexual attraction to others.

testosterone the most important of the male sex hormones. Both males and females have it, but the additional testosterone in males stimulates the growth of the male sex organs during the fetal period, and the development of the male sex characteristics during puberty.

estrogens sex hormones, such as estradiol, secreted in greater amounts by females than by males and contributing to female sex characteristics. In nonhuman female mammals, estrogen levels peak during ovulation, promoting sexual receptivity.

Hormones do influence human sexual behavior, but in a looser way. Among women with mates, sexual desire rises slightly at ovulation, when there is a surge of estrogens and a smaller surge of testosterone, a change that men can sometimes detect in women's behaviors and voices (Haselton & Gildersleeve, 2011). One study invited partnered women to keep a diary of their sexual activity. On the days around ovulation, intercourse was 24 percent more frequent (Wilcox et al., 2004).

Women have much less testosterone than men. And more than other mammalian females, women are responsive to their testosterone level (van Anders, 2012). If a woman's natural testosterone level drops, as happens with removal of the ovaries or adrenal glands, her sexual interest may wane. But as controlled experiments with hundreds of surgically or naturally menopausal women have demonstrated, testosterone-replacement therapy can often restore diminished sexual activity, arousal, and desire (Braunstein et al., 2005; Buster et al., 2005; Petersen & Hyde, 2011).

In human males with abnormally low testosterone levels, testosterone-replacement therapy often increases sexual desire and also energy and vitality (Yates, 2000). But normal fluctuations in testosterone levels, from man to man and hour to hour, have little effect on sexual drive (Byrne, 1982). Indeed, male hormones sometimes vary in *response* to sexual stimulation (Escasa et al., 2011). In one study, Australian skateboarders' testosterone surged in the presence of an attractive female, contributing to riskier moves and more crash landings (Ronay & von Hippel, 2010). Thus, sexual arousal can be a *cause* as well as a consequence of increased testosterone levels. At the other end of the mating spectrum, international studies have found that married fathers tend to have lower testosterone levels than do bachelors and married men without children (Gettler et al., 2013; Gray et al., 2006).

Large hormonal surges or declines affect men and women's desire in shifts that tend to occur at two predictable points in the life span, and sometimes at an unpredictable third point:

1. *The pubertal surge in sex hormones triggers the development of sex characteristics and sexual interest.* If the hormonal surge is precluded—as it was during the 1600s and 1700s for prepubertal boys who were castrated to preserve their soprano voices for Italian opera—sex characteristics and sexual desire do not develop normally (Peschel & Peschel, 1987).

2. *In later life, estrogen levels fall, and women experience menopause (the cessation of menstruation).* As sex hormone levels decline, sex remains a part of life, but the frequency of sexual fantasies and intercourse subsides (Leitenberg & Henning, 1995).

3. *For some, surgery or drugs may cause hormonal shifts.* When adult men were castrated, sex drive typically fell as testosterone levels declined sharply (Hucker & Bain, 1990). Male sex offenders who take Depo-Provera, a drug that reduces testosterone levels to that of a prepubertal boy, have similarly lost much of their sexual urge (Bilefsky, 2009; Money et al., 1983).

To summarize: We might compare human sex hormones, especially testosterone, to the fuel in a car. Without fuel, a car will not run. But if the fuel level is minimally adequate, adding more fuel to the gas tank won't change how the car runs. The analogy is imperfect, because hormones and sexual motivation interact. However, it correctly suggests that biology is a necessary but not sufficient explanation of human sexual behavior. The hormonal fuel is essential, but so are the psychological stimuli that turn on the engine, keep it running, and shift it into high gear.

RETRIEVAL PRACTICE

• The primary male sex hormone is _____. The primary female sex hormones are the _____.

ANSWERS: testosterone; estrogens

The Sexual Response Cycle

35-2 What is the human sexual response cycle, and how do sexual dysfunctions and paraphilias differ?

In the 1960s, gynecologist-obstetrician William Masters and his collaborator Virginia Johnson (1966) made headlines by recording the physiological responses of volunteers who came to their lab to masturbate or have intercourse. With the help of 382 female and 312 male volunteers—a somewhat atypical sample, consisting only of people able and willing to display arousal and orgasm while scientists observed—Masters and Johnson reported observing more than 10,000 sexual "cycles." Their description of the **sexual response cycle** identified four stages:

1. *Excitement:* The genital areas become engorged with blood, causing a woman's clitoris and a man's penis to swell. A woman's vagina expands and secretes lubricant; her breasts and nipples may enlarge.

2. *Plateau:* Excitement peaks as breathing, pulse, and blood pressure rates continue to increase. A man's penis becomes fully engorged—to an average length of 5.6 inches, among 1661 men who measured themselves for condom fitting (Herbenick, 2014). Some fluid—frequently containing enough live sperm to enable conception—may appear at its tip. A woman's vaginal secretion continues to increase, and her clitoris retracts. Orgasm feels imminent.

3. *Orgasm:* Muscle contractions appear all over the body and are accompanied by further increases in breathing, pulse, and blood pressure rates. A woman's arousal and orgasm facilitate conception: They help propel semen from the penis, position the uterus to receive sperm, and draw the sperm further inward, increasing retention of deposited sperm (Furlow & Thornhill, 1996). The pleasurable feeling of sexual release apparently is much the same for both sexes. One panel of experts could not reliably distinguish between descriptions of orgasm written by men and those written by women (Vance & Wagner, 1976). In another study, PET scans showed that the same subcortical brain regions were active in men and women during orgasm (Holstege et al., 2003a,b).

4. *Resolution:* The body gradually returns to its unaroused state as the genital blood vessels release their accumulated blood. This happens relatively quickly if orgasm has occurred, relatively slowly otherwise. (It's like the nasal tickle that goes away rapidly if you have sneezed, slowly otherwise.) Men then enter a **refractory period** that lasts from a few minutes to a day or more, during which they are incapable of another orgasm. A woman's much shorter refractory period may enable her, if restimulated during or soon after resolution, to have more orgasms.

A nonsmoking 50-year-old male has about a 1-in-a-million chance of a heart attack during any hour. This increases to merely 2-in-a-million in the two hours during and following sex (with no increase for those who exercise regularly). Compared with risks associated with heavy exertion or anger, this risk seems not worth losing sleep (or sex) over (Jackson, 2009; Muller et al., 1996).

Sexual Dysfunctions and Paraphilias

Masters and Johnson sought not only to describe the human sexual response cycle but also to understand and treat the inability to complete it. **Sexual dysfunctions** are problems that consistently impair sexual arousal or functioning. Some involve sexual motivation, especially lack of sexual energy and arousability. For men, others include **erectile disorder** (inability to have or maintain an erection) and *premature ejaculation*. For women, the problem may be pain or **female orgasmic disorder** (distress over infrequently or never experiencing orgasm). In separate surveys of some 3000 Boston women and 32,000 other American women, about 4 in 10 reported a sexual problem, such as orgasmic disorder or low desire, but only about 1 in 8 reported that this caused personal distress (Lutfey et al., 2009; Shifren et al., 2008). Most women who have experienced sexual distress have related it to their emotional relationship with the partner during sex (Bancroft et al., 2003).

sexual response cycle the four stages of sexual responding described by Masters and Johnson—excitement, plateau, orgasm, and resolution.

refractory period a resting period after orgasm, during which a man cannot achieve another orgasm.

sexual dysfunction a problem that consistently impairs sexual arousal or functioning.

erectile disorder inability to develop or maintain an erection due to insufficient bloodflow to the penis.

female orgasmic disorder distress due to infrequently or never experiencing orgasm.

paraphilias sexual arousal from fantasies, behaviors, or urges involving nonhuman objects, the suffering of self or others, and/or nonconsenting persons.

AIDS (acquired immune deficiency syndrome) a life-threatening, sexually transmitted infection caused by the *human immunodeficiency virus* (HIV). AIDS depletes the immune system, leaving the person vulnerable to infections.

Therapy can help men and women with sexual dysfunctions (Frühauf et al., 2013). In behaviorally oriented therapy, for example, men learn ways to control their urge to ejaculate, and women are trained to bring themselves to orgasm. Starting with the introduction of Viagra in 1998, erectile disorder has been routinely treated by taking a pill. Equally effective drug treatments for *female sexual interest/arousal disorder* are not yet available.

Sexual dysfunction involves problems with arousal or sexual functioning. People with **paraphilias** do experience sexual desire, but they direct it in unusual ways. The American Psychiatric Association (2013) only classifies such behavior as disordered if

- a person experiences distress from an unusual sexual interest *or*

- it entails harm or risk of harm to others.

The serial killer Jeffrey Dahmer had *necrophilia*, a sexual attraction to corpses. Those with *exhibitionism* derive pleasure from exposing themselves sexually to others, without consent. People with the paraphilic disorder *pedophilia* experience sexual arousal toward children who haven't entered puberty.

Sexually Transmitted Infections

35-3 How can sexually transmitted infections be prevented?

Worldwide, more than 1 million people acquire a *sexually transmitted infection* (STI; also called *STD* for *sexually transmitted disease*) every day (WHO, 2013). Teenage girls, because of their not yet fully mature biological development and lower levels of protective antibodies, are especially vulnerable (Dehne & Riedner, 2005; Guttmacher, 1994). A Centers for Disease Control and Prevention study of sexually experienced 14- to 19-year-old U.S. females found 39.5 percent had STIs (Forhan et al., 2008).

To comprehend the mathematics of infection transmission, imagine this scenario. Over the course of a year, Pat has sex with 9 people, each of whom over the same period has sex with 9 other people, who in turn have sex with 9 others. How many "phantom" sex partners (past partners of partners) will Pat have? The actual number—511—is more than five times the estimate given by the average student (Brannon & Brock, 1993).

Condoms offer only limited protection against certain skin-to-skin STIs, such as herpes, but they do reduce other risks (Medical Institute, 1994; NIH, 2001). The effects were clear when Thailand promoted 100 percent condom use by commercial sex workers. Over a four-year period, as condom use soared from 14 to 94 percent, the annual number of bacterial STIs plummeted from 410,406 to 27,362 (WHO, 2000).

Across the available studies, condoms also have been 80 percent effective in preventing transmission of *HIV* (*human immunodeficiency virus*—the virus that causes **AIDS**) from an infected partner (Weller & Davis-Beaty, 2002; WHO, 2003). Although AIDS can be transmitted by other means, such as needle sharing during drug use, its sexual transmission is most common. Women's AIDS rates are increasing fastest, partly because the virus is passed from man to woman much more often than from woman to man. A man's semen can carry more of the virus than can a woman's vaginal and cervical secretions. The HIV-infected semen can also linger for days in a woman's vagina and cervix, increasing the time of exposure (Allen & Setlow, 1991; WHO, 2004).

Most Americans with AIDS have been in midlife and younger—ages 25 to 44 (U.S. Centers for Disease Control and Prevention, 2011). Given AIDS' long incubation period, this means that many of these young people were infected as teens. In 2012, the death of 1.6 million people with AIDS worldwide left behind countless grief-stricken partners and millions of orphaned children (UNAIDS, 2013). Sub-Saharan Africa is home to two-thirds of those infected with HIV, and medical treatment that extends life and care for the dying are sapping the region's social resources.

Many people assume that oral sex falls in the category of "safe sex," but recent studies show a significant link between oral sex and transmission of STIs, such as the *human papilloma virus (HPV)*. Risks rise with the number of sexual partners (Gillison et al., 2012). Most HPV infections can now be prevented with a vaccination administered before sexual contact.

RETRIEVAL PRACTICE

- The inability to complete the sexual response cycle may be considered a _____ _____. Exhibitionism would be considered a _____.

ANSWERS: sexual dysfunction; paraphilia

- From a biological perspective, AIDS is passed more readily from women to men than from men to women. True or false?

ANSWER: False. AIDS is transmitted more easily and more often from men to women.

The Psychology of Sex

35-4 How do external and imagined stimuli contribute to sexual arousal?

Biological factors powerfully influence our sexual motivation and behavior. Yet the wide variations over time, across place, and among individuals document the great influence of psychological factors as well (**FIGURE 35.1**). Thus, despite the shared biology that underlies sexual motivation, 281 expressed reasons for having sex ranged widely—from "to get closer to God" to "to get my boyfriend to shut up" (Buss, 2008; Meston & Buss, 2007).

Biological influences:
- sexual maturity
- sex hormones, especially testosterone

Psychological influences:
- exposure to stimulating conditions
- sexual fantasies

Sexual motivation

Social-cultural influences:
- family and society values
- religious and personal values
- cultural expectations
- media

Petrenko Andriy/Shutterstock

▼ FIGURE 35.1
Levels of analysis for sexual motivation Compared with our motivation for eating, our sexual motivation is less influenced by biological factors. Psychological and social-cultural factors play a bigger role.

External Stimuli

Men and women become aroused when they see, hear, or read erotic material (Heiman, 1975; Stockton & Murnen, 1992). In 132 experiments, men's feelings of sexual arousal have much more closely mirrored their (more obvious) genital response than have women's (Chivers et al., 2010).

People may find sexual arousal either pleasing or disturbing. (Those who wish to control their arousal often limit their exposure to such materials, just as those wishing to control hunger limit their exposure to tempting cues.) With repeated exposure, the emotional response to any erotic stimulus often lessens, or *habituates*. During the 1920s, when Western women's rising hemlines first reached the knee, an exposed leg was a mildly erotic stimulus.

Can exposure to sexually explicit material have adverse effects? Research indicates that it can:

- *Rape acceptance.* Depictions of women being sexually coerced—and liking it—have increased viewers' belief in the false idea that women enjoy rape, and have increased male viewers' willingness to hurt women (Malamuth & Check, 1981; Zillmann, 1989).

- *Devaluing partner.* Viewing images of sexually attractive women and men may also lead people to devalue their own partners and relationships. After male collegians viewed TV or magazine depictions of sexually attractive women, they often found an average woman, or their own girlfriend or wife, less attractive (Kenrick & Gutierres, 1980; Kenrick et al., 1989; Weaver et al., 1984).

- *Diminished satisfaction.* Viewing X-rated sex films has similarly tended to reduce people's satisfaction with their own sexual partner (Zillmann, 1989). Reading or watching erotica's unlikely scenarios may create expectations that few men and women can fulfill.

Imagined Stimuli

The brain, it has been said, is our most significant sex organ. The stimuli inside our heads—our imagination—can influence sexual arousal and desire. Lacking genital sensation because of a spinal-cord injury, people can still feel sexual desire (Willmuth, 1987).

Wide-awake people become sexually aroused not only by memories of prior sexual activities but also by fantasies, which in a few women can produce orgasms (Komisaruk & Whipple, 2011). About 95 percent of both men and women have said they have sexual fantasies. Men (whether gay or straight) fantasize about sex more often, more physically, and less romantically (Schmitt et al., 2012). They also prefer less personal and faster-paced sexual content in books and videos (Leitenberg & Henning, 1995). Fantasizing about sex does *not* indicate a sexual problem or dissatisfaction. If anything, sexually active people have more sexual fantasies.

©The New Yorker Collection, Robert Mankoff from cartoonbank.com. All Rights Reserved.

"Condoms should be used on every conceivable occasion."

Anonymous

RETRIEVAL PRACTICE

- What factors influence our sexual motivation and behavior?

ANSWER: Influences include biological factors such as sexual maturity and sex hormones; psychological factors such as environmental stimuli and fantasies; and social-cultural factors such as the values and expectations absorbed from family and the surrounding culture.

Teen Pregnancy

35-5 What factors influence teenagers' sexual behaviors and use of contraceptives?

Sexual attitudes and behaviors vary dramatically across cultures. "Sex between unmarried adults" is "morally unacceptable," agree 97 percent of Indonesians, 58 percent of Chinese, 30 percent of Americans, and 6 percent of Germans (Pew, 2014). We are all one species, but in some ways how differently we think. Compared with European teens, today's American teens have a higher pregnancy rate—but a lower rate than their parents' generation (CDC, 2011, 2012).

So, what produces these variations in teen sexuality and pregnancy? Twin studies show that genes influence teen sexual behavior—by influencing pubertal development and hormone levels, and also by influencing teen exposure to environments that stimulate sexual activity (Harden, 2014). Other influences include:

Minimal communication about birth control Many teenagers are uncomfortable discussing contraception with their parents, partners, and peers. Teens who talk freely with parents, and who are in an exclusive relationship with a partner with whom they communicate openly, are more likely to use contraceptives (Aspy et al., 2007; Milan & Kilmann, 1987).

Guilt related to sexual activity In another survey, 72 percent of sexually active 12- to 17-year-old American girls said they regretted having had sex (Reuters, 2000). Sexual inhibitions or ambivalence can restrain sexual activity, but also reduce planning for birth control (Gerrard & Luus, 1995; MacDonald & Hynie, 2008).

Alcohol use Most sexual hook-ups occur among people who are mildly to very intoxicated (Fielder et al., 2013; Garcia et al., 2013). Those who use alcohol prior to sex are less likely to use condoms (Kotchick et al., 2001). By depressing the brain centers that control judgment, inhibition, and self-awareness, alcohol disarms normal restraints—a phenomenon well known to sexually coercive males.

Mass media norms of unprotected promiscuity Media help write the "social scripts" that affect our perceptions and actions. So what sexual scripts do today's media write on our minds? Sexual content appears in approximately 85 percent of movies, 82 percent of television programs, 59 percent of music videos, and 37 percent of music lyrics (Ward et al., 2014). And sexual partners on TV shows rarely have communicated any concern for birth control or STIs (Brown et al., 2002; Kunkel, 2001; Sapolski & Tabarlet, 1991). The more sexual content adolescents and young adults view or read (even when controlling for other predictors of early sexual activity), the more likely they are to perceive their peers as sexually active, to develop sexually permissive attitudes, and to experience early intercourse (Escobar-Chaves et al., 2005; Kim & Ward, 2012; Parkes et al., 2014).

Media influences can either increase or decrease sexual risk taking. One study asked more than a thousand 12- to 14-year-olds what movies they had seen, and then after age 18 asked them about their teen sexual experiences (O'Hara et al., 2012). After controlling for various adolescent and family characteristics, the more the adolescents viewed movies with high sexual content, the greater was their sexual risk taking—with earlier debut, more partners, and inconsistent condom use. Another study analyzed the effect of MTV's series *16 and Pregnant*, which portrayed the consequences of unprotected sex and the challenges of having a child. By analyzing viewership and pregnancy rates over time in specific areas, the researchers concluded that the program led to a 6 percent reduction in the national teen pregnancy rate (Kearney & Levine, 2014).

Later sex may pay emotional dividends. One national study followed participants to about age 30. Even after controlling for several other factors, those who had later first sex reported greater relationship satisfaction in their marriages and partnerships (Harden, 2012). Several other factors also predict sexual restraint:

- *High intelligence* Teens with high rather than average intelligence test scores more often delayed sex, partly because they appreciated possible negative consequences and were more focused on future achievement than on here-and-now pleasures (Halpern et al., 2000).

- *Religious engagement* Actively religious teens have more often reserved sexual activity for adulthood (Hull et al., 2011; Lucero et al., 2008).

- *Father presence* In studies that followed hundreds of New Zealand and U.S. girls from age 5 to 18, a father's absence was linked to sexual activity before age 16 and to teen pregnancy (Ellis et al., 2003). These associations held even after adjusting for other adverse influences, such as poverty. Close family attachments—families that eat together and where parents know their teens' activities and friends—also predicted later sexual initiation (Coley et al., 2008).

- *Participation in service learning programs* Several experiments have found that teens volunteering as tutors or teachers' aides, or participating in community projects, had lower pregnancy rates than were found among comparable teens randomly assigned to control conditions (Kirby, 2002; O'Donnell et al., 2002). Researchers are unsure why. Does service learning promote a sense of personal competence, control, and responsibility? Does it encourage more future-oriented thinking? Or does it simply reduce opportunities for unprotected sex?

Keeping abreast of hypersexuality An analysis of the 60 top-selling video games found 489 characters, 86 percent of whom were males (like most of the game players). The female characters were much more likely than the male characters to be "hypersexualized"—partially nude or revealingly clothed, with large breasts and tiny waists (Downs & Smith, 2010). Such depictions can lead to unrealistic expectations about sexuality and contribute to the early sexualization of girls. The American Psychological Association suggests countering this by teaching girls to "value themselves for who they are rather than how they look" (APA, 2007).

In one British survey, of the 18,876 people contacted, 1 percent were asexual, having "never felt sexually attracted to anyone at all" (Bogaert, 2004, 2006b; 2012). People identifying as asexual are, however, nearly as likely as others to report masturbating, noting that it feels good, reduces anxiety, or "cleans out the plumbing."

Sexual Orientation

35-6 What has research taught us about sexual orientation?

To motivate is to energize and direct behavior. So far, we have considered the energizing of sexual motivation but not its direction, which is our **sexual orientation**—our enduring sexual attraction toward members of our own sex (*homosexual orientation*), the other sex (*heterosexual orientation*), or both sexes (*bisexual orientation*). We experience this attraction in our interests, thoughts, and fantasies (who's that person in your imagination?). Cultures vary in their attitudes toward same-sex attractions. "Should society accept homosexuality?" *Yes*, say 88 percent of Spaniards, 80 percent of Canadians, 60 percent of Americans, 39 percent of South Koreans, 21 percent of Chinese, and 1 percent of Nigerians, with women everywhere being more accepting than men (Pew, 2013). Yet whether a culture condemns or accepts same-sex unions, heterosexuality prevails.

Sexual Orientation: The Numbers

How many people are exclusively homosexual? About 10 percent, as the popular press has often assumed? Or 20 percent, as the average American estimated in a 2013 survey (Jones et al., 2014)? According to more than a dozen national surveys that have explored sexual orientation in Europe and the United States, a better estimate is about 3 or 4 percent of men and 2 percent of women (Chandra et al., 2011; Herbenick et al., 2010a; Savin-Williams et al., 2012). When Gallup asked 121,290 Americans about their sexual identity—"Do you, personally, identify as lesbian, gay, bisexual, or transgender?"—3.4 percent answered *Yes* (Gates & Newport, 2012). When the National Center for Health Statistics asked 34,557 Americans about their sexual identity, they found essentially the same result: All but 3.4 percent answered "straight," with 1.6 percent answering "gay" or "lesbian" and 0.7 percent saying "bisexual" (Ward et al., 2014).

Survey methods that absolutely guarantee people's anonymity reveal another percent or two of gay people (Coffman et al., 2013). Moreover, people in less tolerant places are more likely to hide their sexual orientation. About 3 percent of California men express a same-sex preference on Facebook, for example, as do only about 1 percent in Mississippi. Yet about 5 percent of Google pornography searches in both states are for gay porn. And Craigslist ads for males seeking "casual encounters" with other men tend to be at least as large in less tolerant states, where there are also more Google searches for "Is my husband gay?" (Stephens-Davidowitz, 2013).

Fewer than 1 percent of people—for example, only 12 people out of 7076 Dutch adults in one survey (Sandfort et al., 2001)—reported being actively bisexual. A larger number of adults—13 percent of women and 5 percent of men in a U.S. National Center for Health Statistics survey—report some same-sex sexual contact during their lives (Chandra et al., 2011). And still more have had an occasional homosexual fantasy. In laboratory assessments, some self-identified bisexual men show a homosexual arousal pattern by responding with genital arousal mostly to male erotic images. Others exhibit increased viewing time and genital arousal to both male and female images (Cerny & Janssen, 2011; Lippa, 2013; Rieger et al., 2013; Rosenthal et al., 2012).

sexual orientation an enduring sexual attraction toward members of one's own sex (homosexual orientation), the other sex (heterosexual orientation), or both sexes (bisexual orientation).

What does it feel like to be homosexual in a heterosexual culture? If you are heterosexual, one way to understand is to imagine how you would feel if you were socially isolated for openly admitting or displaying your feelings toward someone of the other sex. How would you react if you overheard people making crude jokes about heterosexual people, or if most movies, TV shows, and advertisements portrayed (or implied) homosexuality? And how would you answer if your family members were pleading with you to change your heterosexual lifestyle and to enter into a homosexual marriage?

Facing such reactions, some individuals struggle with their sexual attractions, especially during adolescence and if feeling rejected by parents or harassed by peers. If lacking social support, the result may be lower self-esteem and higher anxiety and depression (Jager & Davis-Kean, 2011; Kwon, 2013; Oswalt & Wyatt, 2011), as well as an increased risk of contemplating suicide (Plöderl et al., 2013; Ryan et al., 2009; Wang et al., 2012). They may at first try to ignore or deny their desires, hoping they will go away. But they don't. Then they may try to change, through psychotherapy, willpower, or prayer. But the feelings typically persist, as do those of heterosexual people—who are similarly incapable of becoming homosexual (Haldeman, 1994, 2002; Myers & Scanzoni, 2005). Moreover, people's sexual orientation is so basic to who they are that it operates unconsciously, as seen in experiments that draw their attention toward particular flashed nude images not consciously perceived.

Today's psychologists therefore view sexual orientation as neither willfully chosen nor willfully changed. "Efforts to change sexual orientation are unlikely to be successful and involve some risk of harm," declared a 2009 American Psychological Association report. Sexual orientation in some ways is like handedness: Most people are one way, some the other. A very few are truly ambidextrous. Regardless, the way one is endures.

This conclusion is most strongly established for men. Women's sexual orientation tends to be less strongly felt and potentially more fluid and changing (Chivers, 2005; Diamond, 2008; Dickson et al., 2013). In general, men are sexually simpler. Their lesser sexual variability is apparent in many ways, notes Roy Baumeister (2000). Across time, across cultures, across situations, and across differing levels of education, religious observance, and peer influence, adult women's sexual drive and interests are more flexible and varying than are adult men's. Women, for example, more often prefer to alternate periods of high sexual activity with periods of almost none (Mosher et al., 2005). In their pupil dilation and genital responses to erotic videos, and in their implicit attitudes, heterosexual women exhibit more bisexual attraction than do men (Rieger & Savin-Williams, 2012; Snowden & Gray, 2013). Baumeister calls women's more varying sexuality a difference in *erotic plasticity*.

In men, a high sex drive is associated with increased attraction to women (if heterosexual), or men (if homosexual). In women, a high sex drive is generally associated with increased attraction to both men and women (Lippa, 2006, 2007a; Lippa et al., 2010). When shown sexually explicit film clips, men's genital and subjective sexual arousal is mostly to preferred sexual stimuli (for heterosexual viewers, depictions of women). Women respond more nonspecifically to depictions of sexual activity involving males or females (Chivers et al., 2007).

Is there truth to the homosexual-as-child-molester stereotype? No. Measuring men's genital response to various sexual images indicates that sexual orientation is unrelated to pedophilia (Blanchard et al., 2009; Herek, 2014). A Canadian research team led by Ray Blanchard (2012; Dreger, 2011) outfitted 2278 men (mostly sex offenders) with a device that measured their "phallometric response" to viewing nude photos of adults and children of both sexes, accompanied by sexual audio stories. Most of the men responded not to children, but to adult men (if gay) or to adult women (if straight). Some of the men exhibited pedophilia, by instead responding mostly to young boys or girls, and much less to adults.

Stan Honda/AFP/Getty Images

Driven to suicide In 2010, Rutgers University student Tyler Clementi jumped off this bridge after his intimate encounter with another man reportedly became known. Reports then surfaced of other gay teens who had reacted in a similarly tragic fashion after being taunted. Since 2010, Americans—especially those under 30—have been increasingly supportive of those with same-sex orientations.

Personal values affect sexual orientation less than they affect other forms of sexual behavior Compared with people who rarely attend religious services, for example, those who attend regularly are one-third as likely to have lived together before marriage, and they report having had many fewer sex partners. But (if male) they are just as likely to be homosexual (Smith, 1998).

Stephen J. Carrerra/AP Photo

Note that the scientific question is not "What causes homosexuality?" (or "What causes heterosexuality?") but "What causes differing sexual orientations?" In pursuit of answers, psychological science compares the backgrounds and physiology of people whose sexual orientations *differ*.

Origins of Sexual Orientation

So, our sexual orientation is something we do not choose and (especially for males) cannot change. Where, then, do these preferences come from? See if you can anticipate the conclusions that have emerged from hundreds of research studies by responding *Yes* or *No* to the following questions:

1. Is homosexuality linked with problems in a child's relationships with parents, such as with a domineering mother and an ineffectual father, or a possessive mother and a hostile father?

2. Does homosexuality involve a fear or hatred of people of the other sex, leading individuals to direct their desires toward members of their own sex?

3. Is sexual orientation linked with levels of sex hormones currently in the blood?

4. As children, were most homosexuals molested, seduced, or otherwise sexually victimized by an adult homosexual?

The answer to all these questions has been *No* (Storms, 1983). In a search for possible environmental influences on sexual orientation, Kinsey Institute investigators interviewed nearly 1000 homosexuals and 500 heterosexuals. They assessed nearly every imaginable psychological cause of homosexuality—parental relationships, childhood sexual experiences, peer relationships, dating experiences (Bell et al., 1981; Hammersmith, 1982). Their findings: Homosexuals are no more likely than heterosexuals to have been smothered by maternal love or neglected by their father. In one national survey of nearly 35,000 adults, those with a same-sex attraction were somewhat more likely to report having experienced child sexual abuse. But 86 percent of the men and 75 percent of the women with same-sex attraction reported no such abuse (Roberts et al., 2013).

And consider this: If "distant fathers" were more likely to produce homosexual sons, then shouldn't boys growing up in father-absent homes more often be gay? (They are not.) And shouldn't the rising number of such homes have led to a noticeable increase in the gay population? (It has not.) Most children raised by gay or lesbian parents grow up straight and well-adjusted (Gartrell & Bos, 2010).

So, what else might influence sexual orientation? One theory has proposed that people develop same-sex erotic attachments if segregated by sex at the time their sex drive matures (Storms, 1981). Indeed, gay men tend to recall going through puberty somewhat earlier, when peers are more likely to be all males (Bogaert et al., 2002). But even in tribal cultures in which homosexual behavior is expected of all boys before marriage, heterosexuality prevails (Hammack, 2005; Money, 1987). (As this illustrates, homosexual *behavior* does not always indicate a homosexual *orientation*.) Moreover, though peer network attitudes predict teens' sexual attitudes and behavior, they do not predict same-sex attraction. "Peer influence has little or no effect" on sexual orientation (Brakefield et al., 2014).

The bottom line from a half-century's theory and research: If there are environmental factors that influence sexual orientation, we do not yet know what they are. This reality has motivated researchers to explore same-sex behaviors in animals and to consider gay-straight brain differences, genetics, and prenatal influences.

Same-Sex Attraction in Other Species In Boston's Public Gardens, caretakers solved the mystery of why a much-loved swan couple's eggs never hatched. Both swans were female. In New York City's Central Park Zoo, penguins Silo and Roy spent several years as devoted same-sex partners. Same-sex sexual behaviors

Juliet and Juliet Boston's beloved swan couple, "Romeo and Juliet," were discovered actually to be, as are many other animal partners, a same-sex pair.

John Tlumacki/The Boston Globe/Getty Images

have also been observed in several hundred other species, including grizzlies, gorillas, monkeys, flamingos, and owls (Bagemihl, 1999). Among rams, for example, some 7 to 10 percent display same-sex attraction by shunning ewes and seeking to mount other males (Perkins & Fitzgerald, 1997). Homosexual behavior seems a natural part of the animal world.

Gay-Straight Brain Differences Researcher Simon LeVay (1991) studied sections of the hypothalamus taken from deceased heterosexual and homosexual people. As a gay scientist, LeVay wanted to do "something connected with my gay identity." To avoid biasing the results, he did a *blind study*, not knowing which donors were gay. For nine months he peered through his microscope at a cell cluster he thought might be important. Then, one morning, he broke the code: One cell cluster was reliably larger in heterosexual men than in women and homosexual men. "I was almost in a state of shock," LeVay said (1994). "I took a walk by myself on the cliffs over the ocean. I sat for half an hour just thinking what this might mean."

It should not surprise us that in other ways, too, brains differ with sexual orientation (Bao & Swaab, 2011; Savic & Lindström, 2008). Remember our maxim: *Everything psychological is simultaneously biological.* But when do such brain differences begin? At conception? In the womb? During childhood or adolescence? Does experience produce these differences? Or is it genes or prenatal hormones (or genes via prenatal hormones)?

LeVay does not view the hypothalamus as a sexual orientation center; rather, he sees it as an important part of the neural pathway engaged in sexual behavior. He acknowledges that sexual behavior patterns may influence the brain's anatomy. In fish, birds, rats, and humans, brain structures vary with experience—including sexual experience, reports sex researcher Marc Breedlove (1997). But LeVay believes it more likely that brain anatomy influences sexual orientation. His hunch seems confirmed by the discovery of a similar hypothalamic difference between the male sheep that do and don't display same-sex attraction (Larkin et al., 2002; Roselli et al., 2002, 2004). Moreover, report University of London psychologists Qazi Rahman and Glenn Wilson (2003), "the neuroanatomical correlates of male homosexuality differentiate very early postnatally, if not prenatally."

Responses to hormone-derived sexual scents also point to a brain difference (Savic et al., 2005). When straight women were given a whiff of a scent derived from men's sweat, their hypothalamus activated in an area governing sexual arousal. Gay men's brains responded similarly to the men's scent. But straight men's brains showed the arousal response only to a female hormone derivative. Other studies of brain responses to sex-related sweat odors and to pictures of male and female faces have found similar gay-straight differences, including differing responses between lesbians and straight women (Kranz & Ishai, 2006; Martins et al., 2005).

Genetic Influences Evidence indicates a genetic influence on sexual orientation. "First, homosexuality does appear to run in families," noted Brian Mustanski and Michael Bailey (2003). "Second, twin studies have established that genes play a substantial role in explaining individual differences in sexual orientation." Identical twins are somewhat more likely than fraternal twins to share a homosexual orientation (Alanko et al., 2010; Lángström et al., 2008, 2010). (Because sexual orientations differ in many identical twin pairs, especially female twins, we know that other factors besides genes are also at work.)

By genetic manipulations, experimenters have created female fruit flies that during courtship act like males (pursuing other females) and males that act like females (Demir & Dickson, 2005). "We have shown that a single gene in the fruit fly is sufficient to determine all aspects of the flies' sexual orientation and behavior," explained

"Gay men simply don't have the brain cells to be attracted to women."

Simon LeVay, *The Sexual Brain*, 1993

Barry Dickson (2005). With humans, it's likely that multiple genes, possibly in interaction with other influences, shape sexual orientation. A genome-wide study of 409 pairs of gay brothers identified sexual orientation links with areas of two chromosomes, one maternally transmitted (Sanders et al., 2014). And molecules attached to genes may affect their expression. Some scientists speculate that, by affecting sensitivity to testosterone, such epigenetic influences might also cause the masculinization of females in the womb, or the feminization of males (Rice et al., 2012).

Researchers have speculated about possible reasons why "gay genes" might exist in the human gene pool, given that same-sex couples cannot naturally reproduce. One possible answer is kin selection. It is important to note the evolutionary psychology reminder that many of our genes also reside in our biological relatives. Perhaps, then, gay people's genes live on through their supporting the survival and reproductive success of their nieces, nephews, and other relatives (who also carry many of the same genes). Gay men make generous uncles, suggests one study of Samoans (Vasey & VanderLaan, 2010).

A *fertile females theory* offers further support for the idea that maternal genetics may be at work (Bocklandt et al., 2006). Recent Italian studies confirm what others have found—that homosexual men tend to have more homosexual relatives on their mother's side than on their father's (Camperio-Ciani et al., 2004, 2009, 2012; Vander-Laan et al., 2011, 2012). And the relatives on the mother's side also produce more offspring than do the maternal relatives of heterosexual men. Perhaps the genes that dispose women to be strongly attracted (or attractive) to men, and therefore to have more children, also dispose some men to be attracted to men (LeVay, 2011). Thus, the decreased reproduction by gay men appears offset by the increased reproduction by their maternal extended family.

Prenatal Influences   Elevated rates of homosexual orientation in identical *and* fraternal twins suggest the influence not only of shared genes but also a shared prenatal environment. In animals and some human cases, prenatal hormone conditions have altered a fetus' sexual orientation. German researcher Gunter Dorner (1976, 1988) pioneered research on the influence of prenatal hormones by manipulating a fetal rat's exposure to male hormones, thereby "inverting" its sexual orientation. In other studies, when pregnant sheep were injected with testosterone during a critical period of fetal development, their female offspring later showed homosexual behavior (Money, 1987).

A critical period for the human brain's neural-hormonal control system may exist between the middle of the second and fifth months after conception (Ellis & Ames, 1987; Gladue, 1990; Meyer-Bahlburg, 1995). Exposure to the hormone levels typically experienced by female fetuses during this time appears to predispose the person (whether female or male) to be attracted to males in later life. "Prenatal sex hormones control the sexual differentiation of brain centers involved in sexual behaviors," notes Simon LeVay (2011, p. 216). Thus, female fetuses most exposed to testosterone, and male fetuses least exposed to testosterone, appear most likely later to exhibit gender-atypical traits and to experience same-sex desires.

The mother's immune system may also play a role in the development of sexual orientation. Men who have older brothers are somewhat more likely to be gay, report Ray Blanchard (2004, 2008a,b, 2014) and Anthony Bogaert (2003)—about one-third more likely for each additional older brother. If the odds of homosexuality are roughly 2 percent among first sons, they would rise to nearly 3 percent among second sons, 4 percent for third sons, and so on for each additional older brother (see **FIGURE 35.2**). The reason for this curious phenomenon—the *older brother* or *fraternal birth-order effect*—is unclear. Blanchard suspects a defensive maternal immune response to foreign substances produced by male fetuses. With each pregnancy with a male fetus, the maternal antibodies may become stronger and may

"Modern scientific research indicates that sexual orientation is . . . partly determined by genetics, but more specifically by hormonal activity in the womb."

Glenn Wilson and Qazi Rahman, *Born Gay: The Psychobiology of Sex Orientation*, 2005 prevent the fetus' brain from developing in a male-typical pattern. Consistent with this biological explanation, the fraternal birth-order effect occurs only in men with older brothers born to the same mother (whether raised together or not). Sexual orientation is unaffected by adoptive brothers (Bogaert, 2006b). The birth-order effect on sexual orientation is not found among women with older sisters, women who were womb-mates of twin brothers, and men who are not right-handed (Rose et al., 2002).

Gay-Straight Trait Differences

On several traits, gays and lesbians appear to fall midway between straight females and males (**TABLE 35.1**; see also LeVay, 2011; Rahman & Koerting, 2008). For example, lesbians' cochlea and hearing systems develop in a way that is intermediate between those of heterosexual females and heterosexual males, which seems attributable to prenatal hormonal influence (McFadden, 2002). Gay men tend to be shorter and lighter, even at birth, than straight men, while women in same-sex marriages were mostly heavier than average at birth (Bogaert, 2010; Frisch & Zdravkovic, 2010). Fingerprint ridge counts may also differ: Although most people have more fingerprint ridges on their right hand than on their left, some studies find a greater right-left difference in heterosexual males than in females and gay males (Hall & Kimura, 1994; Mustanski et al., 2002; Sanders et al., 2002). Given that fingerprint ridges are complete by the sixteenth fetal week, this difference may be due to prenatal hormones.

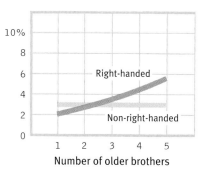

▼ FIGURE 35.2
The fraternal birth-order effect
Researcher Ray Blanchard (2008a) offers these approximate curves depicting a man's likelihood of homosexuality as a function of his number of older brothers. This correlation has been found in several studies, but only among right-handed men (as about 9 in 10 men are).

▼ TABLE 35.1
Biological Correlates of Sexual Orientation

Gay-straight trait differences

Sexual orientation is part of a package of traits. Studies—some in need of replication—indicate that homosexuals and heterosexuals differ in the following biological and behavioral traits.

- spatial abilities
- fingerprint ridge counts
- auditory system development
- handedness
- occupational preferences
- relative finger lengths
- gender nonconformity
- age of onset of puberty in males
- birth size and weight
- sleep length
- physical aggression
- walking style

On average (the evidence is strongest for males), results for gays and lesbians fall between those of straight men and straight women. Three biological influences—brain, genetic, and prenatal—may contribute to these differences.

Brain differences

- One hypothalamic cell cluster is smaller in women and gay men than in straight men.
- Gay men's hypothalamus reacts as do straight women's to the smell of sex-related hormones.

Genetic influences

- Shared sexual orientation is higher among identical twins than among fraternal twins.
- Sexual attraction in fruit flies can be genetically manipulated.
- Male homosexuality often appears to be transmitted from the mother's side of the family.

Prenatal influences

- Altered prenatal hormone exposure may lead to homosexuality in humans and other animals.
- Men with several older biological brothers are more likely to be gay, possibly due to a maternal immune-system reaction.

LaunchPad For an 8-minute overview of the biology of sexual orientation, see LaunchPad's *Video: Homosexuality and the Nature-Nurture Debate.*

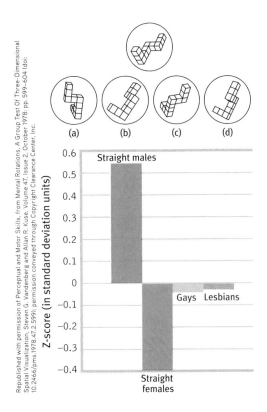

Republished with permission of Perceptual and Motor Skills, from Mental Rotations, A Group Test Of Three-Dimensional Spatial Visualization, Steven G. Vandenberg and Allan R. Kuse, Volume 47, Issue 2, October 1978; pp. 599–604 (doi: 10.2466/pms.1978.47.2.599); permission conveyed through Copyright Clearance Center, Inc.

▼ FIGURE 35.3

Spatial abilities and sexual orientation Which of the four figures can be rotated to match the target figure at the top? Straight males tend to find this an easier task than do straight females, with gays and lesbians intermediate. (From Rahman et al., 2003, with 60 people tested in each group.)

Answer: Figures a and d.

"There is no sound scientific evidence that sexual orientation can be changed."

UK Royal College of Psychiatrists, 2009

Another you-never-would-have-guessed-it gay-straight difference appears in studies showing that gay men's spatial abilities resemble those typical of straight women (Cohen, 2002; Gladue, 1994; McCormick & Witelson, 1991; Sanders & Wright, 1997). On mental rotation tasks such as the one illustrated in **FIGURE 35.3**, straight men tend to outscore straight women. (So do women who were womb-mates of a male co-twin [Vuoksimaa et al., 2010].) Studies by Qazi Rahman and colleagues (2004, 2008) find that, as on a number of other measures, the scores of gays and lesbians fall between those of heterosexual males and females. But straight women and gays both outperform straight men at remembering objects' spatial locations in tasks like those found in memory games (Hassan & Rahman, 2007).

* * *

The consistency of the brain, genetic, and prenatal findings has swung the pendulum toward a biological explanation of sexual orientation (Rahman & Wilson, 2003; Rahman & Koerting, 2008). Still, some people wonder: Should the cause of sexual orientation matter? Perhaps it shouldn't, but people's assumptions matter. To justify his signing a 2014 bill that made some homosexual acts punishable by life in prison, the president of Uganda, Yoweri Museveni, declared that homosexuality is not inborn but rather is a matter of "choice" (Balter, 2014; Landau et al., 2014).

However, the new biological research is a double-edged sword (Diamond, 1993; Roan, 2010). If sexual orientation, like skin color and sex, is genetically influenced, that offers a further rationale for civil rights protection. At the same time, this research raises the troubling possibility that genetic markers of sexual orientation could someday be identified through fetal testing, that a fetus could be aborted simply for being predisposed to an unwanted orientation, or that hormonal treatment in the womb might engineer a desired orientation.

RETRIEVAL PRACTICE

- Which THREE of the following five factors have researchers found to have an effect on sexual orientation?

    a. A domineering mother

    b. Size of certain cell clusters in the hypothalamus

    c. Prenatal hormone exposure

    d. A distant or ineffectual father

    e. For men, having multiple older biological brothers

ANSWERS: b., c., e.

Sex and Human Values

35-7 Is scientific research on sexual motivation value free?

Recognizing that values are both personal and cultural, most sex researchers and educators strive to keep their writings value free. But the very words we use to describe behavior can reflect our personal values. Whether we label certain sexual behaviors as "perversions" or as an "alternative sexual lifestyle" depends on our attitude toward the behaviors. Labels describe, but they also evaluate.

Scientific research on sexual motivation does not aim to define the personal meaning of sex in our own lives. You could know every available fact about sex—that the initial spasms of male and female orgasm come at 0.8-second intervals, that the female nipples expand 10 millimeters at the peak of sexual arousal, that systolic blood pressure rises some 60 points and the respiration rate to 40 breaths per minute—but fail to understand the human significance of sexual intimacy.

Surely one significance of such intimacy is its expression of our profoundly social nature. One recent study asked 2035 married people when they started having sex (while controlling for education, religious engagement, and relationship length). Those whose relationship first developed to a deep commitment, such as marriage, not only reported greater relationship satisfaction and stability but also better sex (Busby et al., 2010; Galinsky & Sonenstein, 2013). For both men and women, but especially for women, orgasm occurs more often (and with less morning-after regret) when sex happens in a committed relationship rather than a sexual hook-up (Garcia et al., 2012, 2013). Partners who share regular meals are more likely than one-night dinner guests to have educated one another about what seasoning touches suit their food tastes; so likewise with the touches of loyal partners who share a bed.

The benefits of commitment—of "vow power"—apply regardless of sexual orientation. Gay and straight couples experience almost identical stability in their relationships, *if* they have married or entered into a civil union—and almost identical instability, if they have not (Rosenfeld, 2014). Thus, as the opportunity for straight and gay people to marry becomes more equal, we can expect the stability of their relationships to become more similar.

Sex is a socially significant act. Men and women can achieve orgasm alone, yet most people find greater satisfaction—and experience a much greater surge in the *prolactin* hormone associated with sexual satisfaction and satiety—after intercourse and orgasm with their loved one (Brody & Tillmann, 2006). Thanks to their overlapping brain reward areas, sexual desire and love feed each other (Cacioppo et al., 2012). Sex at its human best is life uniting and love renewing.

A sharing of love For most adults, a sexual relationship fulfills not only a biological motive but also a social need for intimacy.

Yuri Arcurs/Shutterstock

MODULE 35 REVIEW Sexual Motivation

LEARNING OBJECTIVES

RETRIEVAL PRACTICE Take a moment to answer each of these Learning Objective Questions (repeated here from within this module). Then turn to Appendix C, Complete Module Reviews, to check your answers. Research suggests that trying to answer these questions on your own will improve your long-term retention (McDaniel et al., 2009).

35-1 How do hormones influence human sexual motivation?

35-2 What is the human sexual response cycle, and how do sexual dysfunctions and paraphilias differ?

35-3 How can sexually transmitted infections be prevented?

35-4 How do external and imagined stimuli contribute to sexual arousal?

35-5 What factors influence teenagers' sexual behaviors and use of contraceptives?

35-6 What has research taught us about sexual orientation?

35-7 Is scientific research on sexual motivation value free?

TERMS AND CONCEPTS TO REMEMBER

RETRIEVAL PRACTICE Test yourself on these terms by trying to write down the definition before flipping back to the page number referenced to check your answer.

asexual, p. 433

testosterone, p. 433

estrogens, p. 433

sexual response cycle, p. 435

refractory period, p. 435

sexual dysfunction, p. 435

erectile disorder, p. 435

female orgasmic disorder, p. 435

paraphilias, p. 436

AIDS (acquired immune deficiency syndrome), p. 436

sexual orientation, p. 440

Use 🔵 LearningCurve to create your personalized study plan, which will direct you to the resources that will help you most in 🔵 LaunchPad.

36 Affiliation and Achievement

The Need to Belong

36-1 What evidence points to our human affiliation need—our need to belong?

affiliation need the need to build relationships and to feel part of a group.

Separated from friends or family—alone in prison or at a new school or in a foreign land—most people feel keenly their lost connections with important others. We are what Greek philosopher Aristotle called *the social animal.* "Without friends," wrote Aristotle in his *Nichomachean Ethics,* "no one would choose to live, though he had all other goods." This deep *need to belong*—our **affiliation need**—seems to be a basic human motivation (Baumeister & Leary, 1995). Although people vary in their wish for privacy and solitude, most of us seek to affiliate with others, even to become strongly attached to certain others in enduring, close relationships. Human beings, contended personality theorist Alfred Adler, have an "urge to community" (Ferguson, 1989, 2001, 2010). Our psychological needs drive our adaptive behaviors and, when satisfied, enhance our psychological well-being (Sheldon, 2011).

Mauricio Anton/Science Source

"We must love one another or die."

W. H. Auden, "September 1, 1939"

The Benefits of Belonging

Social bonds boosted our early ancestors' chances of survival. Adults who formed attachments were more likely to reproduce and to co-nurture their offspring to maturity. Attachment bonds motivated caregivers to keep children close, calming them and protecting them from threats (Esposito et al., 2013). Indeed, to be "wretched" literally means, in its Middle English origin *(wrecche),* to be without kin nearby.

Cooperation also enhanced survival. In solo combat, our ancestors were not the toughest predators. But as hunters, they learned that six hands were better than two. As food gatherers, they gained protection from two-footed and four-footed enemies by traveling in groups. Those who felt a need to belong survived and reproduced most successfully, and their genes now predominate. We are innately social creatures. Our need to belong drives us to befriend people who cooperate and avoid those who exploit (Feinberg et al., 2014). People in every society on Earth belong to groups and prefer and favor "us" over "them."

Do you have close friends—people with whom you freely disclose your ups and downs? Having someone who rejoices with us over good news helps us feel even better about the good news, as well as about the friendship (Reis et al., 2010). Close friends can literally make us feel warm, as if we are holding a soothing cup of warm tea (Inagaki & Eisenberger, 2013). The need to belong runs deeper, it seems, than any need to be rich. One study found that *very* happy university students were distinguished not by their money but by their "rich and satisfying close relationships" (Diener & Seligman, 2002).

The need to belong colors our thoughts and emotions. We spend a great deal of time thinking about actual and hoped-for relationships. When relationships form, we often feel joy. Falling in mutual love, people have been known to feel their cheeks ache from their irrepressible grins. Asked, "What is necessary for your happiness?" or "What is it that makes your life meaningful?" most people have mentioned—before anything else—close, satisfying relationships with family, friends, or romantic partners (Berscheid, 1985). Happiness hits close to home.

Consider: What was your most satisfying moment in the past week? Researchers asked that question of American and South Korean collegians, then asked them to rate how much that moment had satisfied various needs (Sheldon et al., 2001). In both countries, the peak moment had contributed most to satisfaction of self-esteem and relatedness-belonging needs. When our need for relatedness is satisfied in balance with two other basic psychological needs—*autonomy* (a sense of personal control) and *competence*—we experience a deep sense of well-being, and our self-esteem rides high (Deci & Ryan, 2002, 2009; Milyavskaya et al., 2009). Indeed, *self-esteem* is a gauge of how valued and accepted we feel (Leary, 2012).

Is it surprising, then, that so much of our social behavior aims to increase our feelings of belonging? To gain acceptance, we generally conform to group standards. We wait in lines, obey laws, and help group members. We monitor our behavior, hoping to make a good impression. We spend billions on clothes, cosmetics, and diet and fitness aids—all motivated by our search for love and acceptance.

By drawing a sharp circle around "us," the need to belong feeds both deep attachments and menacing threats. Out of our need to define a "we" come loving families, faithful friendships, and team spirit, but also teen gangs, ethnic rivalries, and fanatic nationalism.

For good or for bad, we work hard to build and maintain our relationships. Familiarity breeds liking, not contempt. Thrown together in groups at school, at work, in a tornado shelter, we behave like magnets, moving closer, forming bonds. Parting, we feel distress. We promise to call, to write, to return for reunions.

This happens in part because feelings of love activate brain reward and safety systems. In one experiment involving exposure to heat, deeply-in-love university students felt markedly less pain when looking at their beloved's picture (rather than viewing someone else's photo or being distracted by a word task) (Younger et al., 2010). Pictures of our loved ones also activate a brain region associated with safety—the prefrontal cortex—that dampens feelings of physical pain (Eisenberger et al., 2011). Love is a natural painkiller.

Even when bad relationships break, people suffer. In one 16-nation survey, and in repeated U.S. surveys, separated and divorced people have been half as likely as married people to say they were "very happy" (Inglehart, 1990; NORC, 2010). Divorce also predicts earlier mortality. Studies that have followed 6.5 million people in 11 countries reveal that, compared with married people, separated and divorced people are at greater risk for early death (Sbarra et al., 2011).

Children who move through a series of foster homes or through repeated family relocations know the fear of being alone. After repeated disruption of budding attachments, they may have difficulty forming deep attachments (Oishi & Schimmack, 2010). The evidence is clearest at the extremes—the children who grow up in institutions without a sense of belonging to anyone, or who are locked away at home and severely neglected. Too many become withdrawn, frightened, speechless.

No matter how secure our early years were, we all experience anxiety, loneliness, jealousy, or guilt when something threatens or dissolves our social ties. Much as life's best moments occur when close relationships begin—making a new friend, falling in love, having a baby—life's worst moments happen when close relationships end (Jaremka et al., 2011). Bereaved, we may feel life is empty, pointless. Even the first weeks of living on a college campus can be distressing. But our need to belong pushes us to form a new web of social connections (Oishi et al., 2013).

The need to connect Six days a week, women from the Philippines work as "domestic helpers" in 154,000 Hong Kong households. On Sundays, they throng to the central business district to picnic, dance, sing, talk, and laugh. "Humanity could stage no greater display of happiness," reported one observer (*Economist*, 2001).

Vincent Yu/AP Photo

For immigrants and refugees moving alone to new places, the stress and loneliness can be depressing. After years of placing individual families in isolated communities, U.S. immigration policies began to encourage *chain migration* (Pipher, 2002). The second refugee Sudanese family settling in a town generally has an easier adjustment than the first.

Social isolation can put us at risk for mental decline and ill health (Cacioppo & Hawkley, 2009). But if feelings of acceptance and connection increase, so will self-esteem, positive feelings, and physical health (Blackhart et al., 2009; Holt-Lunstad et al., 2010; Smart Richman & Leary, 2009). A socially connected life is often a happy and healthy life.

The Pain of Being Shut Out

Can you recall feeling excluded or ignored or shunned? Perhaps you received the silent treatment. Perhaps people avoided you or averted their eyes in your presence or even mocked you behind your back. If you are like others, even being in a group speaking a different language may have left you feeling excluded, a linguistic outsider (Dotan-Elias et al., 2009). In one mock-interview study, women felt more excluded if interviewers used gender-exclusive language (*he, his, him*) rather than inclusive (*his* or *her*) or neutral (*their*) language (Stout & Dasgupta, 2011).

All these experiences are instances of **ostracism**—of social exclusion (Williams, 2007, 2009). Worldwide, humans use many forms of ostracism—exile, imprisonment, solitary confinement—to punish, and therefore control, social behavior. For children, even a brief time-out in isolation can be punishing. Asked to describe personal episodes that made them feel especially *bad* about themselves, people will—about four times in five—describe a relationship difficulty (Pillemer et al., 2007). Feelings of loneliness can also spread through a social network—like a disease—as people complain of loneliness (Cacioppo et al., 2009).

Being shunned—given the cold shoulder or the silent treatment, with others' eyes avoiding yours—threatens one's need to belong (Wirth et al., 2010). "It's the meanest thing you can do to someone, especially if you know they can't fight back. I never should have been born," said Lea, a lifelong victim of the silent treatment by her mother and grandmother. Like Lea, people often respond to ostracism with initial efforts to restore their acceptance, depressed moods, and then withdrawal. William Blake has spent more than 25 years incarcerated in solitary confinement. "I cannot fathom how dying any death could be harder and more terrible than living through all that I have been forced to endure," he said (Blake, 2012). To him, social exclusion is a sentence worse than death.

To experience ostracism is to experience real pain, as social psychologists Kipling Williams and his colleagues were surprised to discover in their studies of exclusion on social media (Gonsalkorale & Williams, 2006). (Perhaps you can recall the feeling of being unfriended or having few followers on a social networking site, being ignored in a chat room, or having a text message or e-mail go unanswered.) Such ostracism, they discovered, takes a toll: It elicits increased activity in brain areas, such as the *anterior cingulate cortex,* that also activate in response to physical pain (Eisenberger, 2012; Kross et al., 2011). When viewing pictures of romantic partners who caused our hearts to break, our brains and bodies begin to ache (Wager et al., 2013). That helps explain another surprising finding: The pain-reliever acetaminophen (as in Tylenol and Anacin) lessens *social* as well as physical pain (DeWall et al., 2010). Across cultures, people use the same words (for example, *hurt, crushed*) for social pain and physical pain (MacDonald & Leary, 2005). Psychologically, we seem to experience social pain with the same emotional unpleasantness that marks physical pain.

Enduring the pain of ostracism Caucasian cadets at the United States Military Academy at West Point ostracized Henry Flipper for years, hoping he would drop out. He somehow resisted their cruelty and in 1877 became the first African-American West Point graduate.

ostracism deliberate social exclusion of individuals or groups.

Social acceptance and rejection Successful participants on the reality TV show *Survivor* form alliances and gain acceptance among their peers. The rest receive the ultimate social punishment as they are "voted off the island."

Pain, whatever its source, focuses our attention and motivates corrective action. Rejected and unable to remedy the situation, people may relieve stress by seeking new friends, eating comforting but calorie-laden foods (such as ice cream), or strengthening their religious faith (Aydin et al., 2010; Maner et al., 2007; Sproesser et al., 2014). Or they may turn nasty. In a series of experiments, researchers told some students (who had taken a personality test) that they were "the type likely to end up alone later in life," or that people they had met didn't want them in a group that was forming (Baumeister et al., 2002; Gaertner et al., 2008; Twenge et al., 2001, 2002, 2007). They told other students that they would have "rewarding relationships throughout life," or that "everyone chose you as someone they'd like to work with." Those who were excluded became much more likely to engage in self-defeating behaviors and to underperform on aptitude tests. The rejection also interfered with their empathy for others and made them more likely to act in disparaging or aggressive ways against those who had excluded them (blasting them with noise, for example). "If intelligent, well-adjusted, successful . . . students can turn aggressive in response to a small laboratory experience of social exclusion," noted the research team, "it is disturbing to imagine the aggressive tendencies that might arise from . . . chronic exclusion from desired groups in actual social life." Indeed, as Williams (2007) has observed, ostracism "weaves through case after case of school violence."

Note: The researchers later *debriefed* and reassured the participants.

"If no one turned around when we entered, answered when we spoke, or minded that we did, but if every person we met 'cut us dead,' and acted as if we were non-existing things, a kind of rage and impotent despair would ere long well up in us."

William James, *Principles of Psychology,* 1890/1950, pp. 293–294

RETRIEVAL PRACTICE

- How have students reacted in studies where they were made to feel rejected and unwanted? What helps explain these results?

ANSWER: These students' basic *need to belong* seems to have been disrupted. They engaged in more self-defeating behaviors, underperformed on aptitude tests, and displayed less empathy and more aggression.

Connecting and Social Networking

36-2 How does social networking influence us?

As social creatures, we live for connection. Researcher George Vaillant (2013) was asked what he had learned from studying 238 Harvard University men from the 1930s to the end of their lives. He replied, "Happiness is love." A South African Zulu saying captures the idea: *Umuntu ngumuntu ngabantu*—"a person is a person through other persons."

Mobile Networks and Social Media Look around and see humans connecting: talking, tweeting, texting, posting, chatting, social gaming, e-mailing. The changes in how we connect have been fast and vast.

"There's no question in my mind about what stands at the heart of the communication revolution—the human desire to connect."

Skype President Josh Silverman, 2009

- At the end of 2013, the world had 7.1 billion people and 6.8 billion mobile cell-phone subscriptions (ITU, 2013). But phone talking now accounts for less than half of U.S. mobile network traffic (Wortham, 2010). In Canada and elsewhere, e-mailing is being displaced by texting, social media sites, and other messaging technology (IPSOS, 2010a). Speedy texting is not really writing, said one observer (McWhorter, 2012), but rather a new form of conversation—"fingered speech."

- Three in four U.S. teens text. Half (mostly females) send 60 or more texts daily (Lenhart, 2012). For many, it's as though friends, for better or worse, are always present.

- How many of us are using social networking sites, such as Facebook or Twitter? Among 2010's entering American collegians, 94 percent were (Pryor et al., 2011). With so many of your friends on a social network, its lure becomes hard to resist. Such is our need to belong. Check in or miss out.

The Net Result: Social Effects of Social Networking By connecting like-minded people, the Internet serves as a social amplifier. In times of social crisis or personal stress, it provides information and supportive connections. It also functions as an online dating matchmaker. (I [ND] can attest to this. I met my wife online.) As electronic communication has become an integral part of life, researchers have explored how it has affected our relationships.

HAVE SOCIAL NETWORKING SITES MADE US MORE, OR LESS, SOCIALLY ISOLATED? Online communication in chat rooms and during social games used to be mostly between strangers. In that period, the adolescents and adults who spent more time online thus spent less time with friends; as a result, their offline relationships suffered (Kraut et al., 1998; Mesch, 2001; Nie, 2001). Even in more recent times, lonely people have tended to spend greater-than-average time online, while social butterflies have gravitated toward face-to-face interactions (Bonetti et al., 2010; Pea et al., 2012; Stepanikova et al., 2010). Social networkers have been less likely to know their real-world neighbors and "64 percent less likely than non-Internet users to rely on neighbors for help in caring for themselves or a family member" (Pew, 2009).

But the Internet has also diversified our social networks. (I [DM] am now connected to other hearing-technology advocates across the world.) And despite the decrease in neighborliness, social networking is mostly strengthening our connections with the variety of people we already know (DiSalvo, 2010; Ugander et al., 2012; Valkenburg & Peter, 2009). If your social networking helps you connect with friends, stay in touch with extended family, or find support when facing challenges, then you are not alone (Rainie et al., 2011). Social networks connect us. But they can also, as you've surely noticed, become gigantic time- and attention-sucking distractions that interfere with sleep, exercise, and face-to-face relationships. If you are like most other students, two days without social networking access would be followed by a glut of online time, much as a two-day food fast would be followed by a period of feasting (Sheldon et al., 2011). The net result is an imbalance between face-to-face and online social connection.

DOES ELECTRONIC COMMUNICATION STIMULATE HEALTHY SELF-DISCLOSURE? *Self-disclosure* is sharing ourselves—our joys, worries, and weaknesses—with others. Confiding can be a healthy way of coping with day-to-day challenges. When communicating electronically rather than face to face, we often are less focused on others' reactions. We are less self-conscious and thus less inhibited. Sometimes this is taken to an extreme, as when teens send photos of themselves they later regret, or bullies hound a victim, or hate groups post messages promoting bigotry or crimes. More often, however, the increased self-disclosure serves to deepen friendships (Valkenburg & Peter, 2009).

Although electronic networking pays dividends, nature has designed us for face-to-face communication, which appears to be a better predictor of life satisfaction (Killingsworth & Gilbert, 2010; Lee et al., 2011). Texting, tweeting, and e-mailing are rewarding, but eye-to-eye conversation is even more so.

DO SOCIAL NETWORKING PROFILES AND POSTS REFLECT PEOPLE'S ACTUAL PERSONALITIES? We've all heard stories of online predators hiding behind false personalities, values, and motives. Generally, however, social networks reveal a person's real personality. In one study, participants completed a personality test twice. In one test, they described their "actual personality"; in the other, they described their "ideal self." Other volunteers then used the participants' Facebook profiles to create an independent set of personality ratings. The Facebook-profile ratings were much closer to the participants' actual personalities than to their ideal personalities (Back et al., 2010). In another study, people who seemed most likable on their Facebook page also seemed most likable in face-to-face meetings (Weisbuch et al., 2009). Twitter posts similarly reveal people's actual friendliness (Qiu et al., 2012). Your online profiles and tweets may indeed reflect the real you!

DOES SOCIAL NETWORKING PROMOTE NARCISSISM? Narcissism is self-esteem gone wild. Narcissistic people are self-important, self-focused, and self-promoting. Some personality tests assess narcissism with items such as "I like to be the center of attention." People with high narcissism test scores are especially active on social networking sites. They collect more superficial "friends." They offer more staged, glamorous photos. They retaliate more when people post negative comments. And, not surprisingly, they *seem* more narcissistic to strangers (Buffardi & Campbell, 2008; Carpenter, 2012).

For narcissists, social networking sites are more than a gathering place; they are a feeding trough. In one study, college students were randomly assigned either to edit and explain their online profiles for 15 minutes, or to use that time to study and explain a Google Maps routing (Freeman & Twenge, 2010). After completing their tasks, all were tested. Who then scored higher on a narcissism measure? Those who had spent the time focused on themselves.

Maintaining Balance and Focus In both Taiwan and the United States, excessive online socializing and gaming have been associated with lower grades (Chen & Fu, 2008; Kaiser Family Foundation, 2010; Walsh et al., 2013). In one U.S. survey, 47 percent of the heaviest users of the Internet and other media were receiving mostly C grades or lower, as were just 23 percent of the lightest users (Kaiser Family Foundation, 2010).

In today's world, each of us is challenged to maintain a healthy balance between our real-world and online time. Experts offer some practical suggestions for balancing online connecting and real-world responsibilities.

- *Monitor your time.* Keep a log of how you use your time. Then ask yourself, "Does my time use reflect my priorities? Am I spending more or less time online than I intended? Is my time online interfering with school or work performance? Have family or friends commented on this?"

- *Monitor your feelings.* Ask yourself, "Am I emotionally distracted by my online interests? When I disconnect and move to another activity, how do I feel?"

"The women on these dating sites don't seem to believe I'm a prince."

narcissism excessive self-love and self-absorption.

"It keeps me from looking at my phone every two seconds."

- *"Hide" your more distracting online friends.* And in your own postings, practice the golden rule. Before you post, ask yourself, "Is this something I'd care about reading if someone else posted it?"

- *Try turning off your mobile devices or leaving them elsewhere.* Selective attention—the flashlight of your mind—can be in only one place at a time. When we try to do two things at once, we don't do either one of them very well (Willingham, 2010). If you want to study or work productively, resist the temptation to check for updates. Disable sound alerts and pop-ups, which can hijack your attention just when you've managed to get focused. (I [DM] am proofing and editing this module in a coffee shop, where I escape the distractions of the office.)

- *Try a social networking fast* (give it up for an hour, a day, or a week) *or a time-controlled social media diet* (check in only after homework is done, or only during a lunch break). Take notes on what you're losing and gaining on your new "diet."

- *Refocus by taking a nature walk.* People learn better after a peaceful walk in the woods, which—unlike a walk on a busy street—refreshes our capacity for focused attention (Berman et al., 2008). Connecting with nature boosts our spirits and sharpens our minds (Zelenski & Nisbet, 2014).

As psychologist Steven Pinker (2010) said, "The solution is not to bemoan technology but to develop strategies of self-control, as we do with every other temptation in life."

RETRIEVAL PRACTICE

- Social networking tends to _____ (strengthen/weaken) your relationships with people you already know, _____ (increase/decrease) your self-disclosure, and _____ (reveal/hide) your true personality.

ANSWERS: strengthen; increase; reveal

Achievement Motivation

36-3 What is achievement motivation?

The biological perspective on motivation—the idea that physiological needs drive us to satisfy those needs—provides only a partial explanation of what energizes and directs our behavior. Some motives, such as hunger and the need to belong, have social as well as biological components. Moreover, there are motives that seem to have little obvious survival value. Billionaires may be motivated to make ever more money, movie stars to become ever more famous, politicians to achieve ever more power, daredevils to seek ever greater thrills. Such motives seem not to diminish when they are fed. The more we achieve, the more we may need to achieve.

Think of someone you know who strives to succeed by excelling at any task where evaluation is possible. Now think of someone who is less driven. Psychologist Henry Murray (1938) defined the first person's **achievement motivation** as a desire for significant accomplishment, for mastering skills or ideas, for control, and for attaining a high standard.

Thanks to their persistence and eagerness for challenge, people with high achievement motivation do achieve more. One study followed the lives of 1528 California children whose intelligence test scores were in the top 1 percent. Forty years later, when researchers compared those who were most and least successful professionally, they found a motivational difference. Those most successful were more ambitious, energetic, and persistent. As children, they had more active hobbies. As adults, they participated in more groups and sports (Goleman, 1980). Gifted children are able learners. Accomplished adults are tenacious doers. Most of us are energetic doers when starting and

"Genius is 1% inspiration and 99% perspiration."

Thomas Edison (1847–1931)

when finishing a project. It's easiest—have you noticed?—to get stuck in the middle. That's when high achievers keep going (Bonezzi et al., 2011).

In other studies of both secondary school and university students, self-discipline has surpassed intelligence test scores to better predict school performance, attendance, and graduation honors. When combined with a positive enthusiasm, sustained, gritty effort predicts success for teachers, too—with their students making good academic progress (Duckworth et al., 2009). "Discipline outdoes talent," concluded researchers Angela Duckworth and Martin Seligman (2005, 2006).

Discipline refines talent. By their early twenties, top violinists have accu-

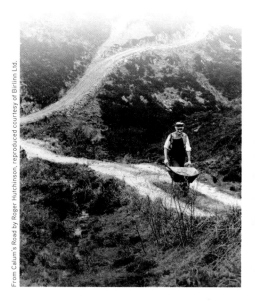

From Calum's Road by Roger Hutchinson, reproduced courtesy of Birlinn Ltd.

mulated thousands of lifetime practice hours—in fact, double the practice time of other violin students aiming to be teachers (Ericsson 2001, 2006, 2007). A study of outstanding scholars, athletes, and artists found that all were highly motivated and self-disciplined, willing to dedicate hours every day to the pursuit of their goals (Bloom, 1985). As child prodigies illustrate (think young Mozart composing at age 8), native talent matters, too (Hambrick & Meinz, 2011; Ruthsatz & Urbach, 2012). In sports, music, and chess, for example, people's practice time differences account for a third or less of their performance differences (Hambrick et al., 2014a,b; Macnamara et al., 2014). Superstar achievers are, it seems, distinguished both by their extraordinary daily discipline and by their extraordinary natural talent.

Duckworth and Seligman have a name for this passionate dedication to an ambitious, long-term goal: **grit.** "If you want to look good in front of thousands," the saying goes, "you have to outwork thousands in front of nobody."

Although intelligence is distributed like a bell curve, achievements are not. That tells us that achievement involves much more than raw ability. That is why organizational psychologists seek ways to engage and motivate ordinary people doing ordinary jobs (see Appendix A: Psychology at Work). And that is why training students in "hardiness"—resilience under stress—leads to better grades (Maddi et al., 2009).

Calum's road: What grit can accomplish Having spent his life on the Scottish island of Raasay, farming a small patch of land, tending its lighthouse, and fishing, Malcolm ("Calum") MacLeod (1911–1988) felt anguished. His local government repeatedly refused to build a road that would enable vehicles to reach his north end of the island. With the once-flourishing population there having dwindled to two—MacLeod and his wife—he responded with heroic determination. One spring morning in 1964, MacLeod, then in his fifties, gathered an ax, a chopper, a shovel, and a wheelbarrow. By hand, he began to transform the existing footpath into a 1.75-mile road (Miers, 2009).

"With a road," a former neighbor explained, "he hoped new generations of people would return to the north end of Raasay," restoring its culture (Hutchinson, 2006). Day after day he worked through rough hillsides, along hazardous cliff faces, and over peat bogs. Finally, 10 years later, he completed his supreme achievement. The road, which the government has since surfaced, remains a visible example of what vision plus determined grit can accomplish. It bids us each to ponder: What "roads"—what achievements—might we, with sustained effort, build in the years before us?

RETRIEVAL PRACTICE

• What have researchers found an even better predictor of school performance than intelligence test scores?

ANSWER: self-discipline

---

achievement motivation a desire for significant accomplishment; for mastery of skills or ideas; for control; and for attaining a high standard.

grit in psychology, passion and perseverance in the pursuit of long-term goals.

MODULE 36 REVIEW Affiliation and Achievement

LEARNING OBJECTIVES

RETRIEVAL PRACTICE Take a moment to answer each of these Learning Objective Questions (repeated here from within this module). Then turn to Appendix C, Complete Module Reviews, to check your answers. Research suggests that trying to answer these questions on your own will improve your long-term retention (McDaniel et al., 2009).

36-1 What evidence points to our human affiliation need—our need to belong?

36-2 How does social networking influence us?

36-3 What is achievement motivation?

TERMS AND CONCEPTS TO REMEMBER

RETRIEVAL PRACTICE Test yourself on these terms by trying to write down the definition before flipping back to check your answers.

affiliation need, p. 448

ostracism, p. 450

narcissism, p. 453

achievement motivation, p. 454

grit, p. 455

Use **LearningCurve** to create your personalized study plan, which will direct you to the resources that will help you most in **LaunchPad**.

TEST YOUR-SELF WHAT DRIVES US: HUNGER, SEX, FRIENDSHIP, AND ACHIEVEMENT

Test yourself repeatedly throughout your studies. This will not only help you figure out what you know and don't know; the testing itself will help you learn and remember the information more effectively thanks to the *testing effect*.

MODULE 33 Basic Motivational Concepts

1. Today's evolutionary psychology shares an idea that was an underlying assumption of instinct theory. That idea is that
   a. physiological needs arouse psychological states.
   b. genes predispose species-typical behavior.
   c. physiological needs increase arousal.
   d. external needs energize and direct behavior.

2. An example of a physiological need is _____ . An example of a psychological drive is _____ .
   a. hunger; a "push" to find food
   b. a "push" to find food; hunger
   c. curiosity; a "push" to reduce arousal
   d. a "push" to reduce arousal; curiosity

3. Jan walks into a friend's kitchen, smells bread baking, and begins to feel very hungry. The smell of baking bread is a(n) _____ (incentive/drive).

4. _____ theory attempts to explain behaviors that do NOT reduce physiological needs.

5. With a challenging task, such as taking a difficult exam, performance is likely to peak when arousal is
   a. very high.
   b. moderate.
   c. very low.
   d. absent.

6. According to Maslow's hierarchy of needs, our most basic needs are physiological, including the need for food and water; just above these are _____ needs.
   a. safety
   b. self-esteem
   c. belongingness
   d. self-transcendence

MODULE 34 Hunger

7. Journalist Dorothy Dix (1861-1951) once remarked, "Nobody wants to kiss when they are hungry." How does Maslow's hierarchy of needs support her statement?

8. According to the concept of set point, our body maintains itself at a particular weight level. This "weight thermostat" is an example of _____ .

9. Which of the following is a genetically predisposed response to food?
   a. An aversion to eating cats and dogs
   b. An interest in novel foods
   c. A preference for sweet and salty foods
   d. An aversion to carbohydrates

10. The blood sugar _____ provides the body with energy. When it is _____ (low/high), we feel hungry.

11. The rate at which your body expends energy while at rest is referred to as the _____ _____ rate.

12. Obese people find it very difficult to lose weight permanently. This is due to several factors, including the fact that
    a. dieting triggers neophobia.
    b. the set point of obese people is lower than average.
    c. with dieting, metabolism increases.
    d. there is a genetic influence on body weight.

13. Sanjay recently adopted the typical college diet high in fat and sugar. He knows he may gain weight, but he figures it's no big deal because he can lose the extra pounds in the future. How would you evaluate Sanjay's plan?

MODULE 35 Sexual Motivation

14. A striking effect of hormonal changes on human sexual behavior is the

    a. end of sexual desire in men over 60.

    b. sharp rise in sexual interest at puberty.

    c. decrease in women's sexual desire at the time of ovulation.

    d. increase in testosterone levels in castrated males.

15. In describing the sexual response cycle, Masters and Johnson noted that

    a. a plateau phase follows orgasm.

    b. men experience a refractory period during which they cannot experience orgasm.

    c. the feeling that accompanies orgasm is stronger in men than in women.

    d. testosterone is released equally in women and men.

16. What is the difference between sexual dysfunctions and paraphilias?

17. The use of condoms during sex _____ (does/doesn't) reduce the risk of getting HIV and _____ (does/doesn't) fully protect against skin-to-skin STIs.

18. An example of an external stimulus that might influence sexual behavior is

    a. blood level of testosterone.

    b. the onset of puberty.

    c. a sexually explicit film.

    d. an erotic fantasy or dream.

19. Which factors have researchers thus far found to be *unrelated* to the development of our sexual orientation?

MODULE 36 Affiliation and Achievement

20. Which of the following is NOT part of the evidence presented to support the view that humans are strongly motivated by a need to belong?

    a. Students who rated themselves as "very happy" also tended to have satisfying close relationships.

    b. Social exclusion—such as exile or solitary confinement— is considered a severe form of punishment.

    c. As adults, adopted children tend to resemble their biological parents and to yearn for an affiliation with them.

    d. Children who are extremely neglected become withdrawn, frightened, and speechless.

21. What are some ways to manage our social networking time successfully?

Find answers to these questions in Appendix D, in the back of the book.

Zia Soleil/Getty Images

EMOTIONS, STRESS, AND HEALTH

. . . .

No one needs to tell you that feelings add color to your life, or that in times of stress they can disrupt your life, or save it. Fear, anger, sadness, joy, and love are psychological states that also entail physical reactions. Nervous about an important encounter, we feel stomach butterflies. Anxious over public speaking, we frequent the bathroom. Smoldering over a family conflict, we get a splitting headache.

You can surely recall a time when emotion overwhelmed you. I [DM] retain a flashbulb memory of the day I went to a huge store to drop off film and brought along Peter, my toddler first-born child. As I set Peter down on his feet and prepared to complete the paperwork, a passerby warned, "You'd better be careful or you'll lose that boy!" Not more than a few breaths later, after dropping the film in the slot, I turned and found no Peter beside me.

With mild anxiety, I peered around one end of the counter. No Peter in sight. With slightly more anxiety, I peered around the other end. No Peter there, either. Now, with my heart accelerating, I circled the neighboring counters. Still no Peter anywhere. As anxiety turned to panic, I began racing up and down the store aisles. He was nowhere to be found. Apprised of my alarm, the store manager used the public-address system to ask customers to assist in looking for a missing child. Soon after, I passed the customer who had warned me. "I told you that you were going to lose him!" he now scorned. With visions of kidnapping (strangers routinely adored that beautiful child), I braced for the possibility that my negligence had caused me to lose what I loved above all else, and that I might have to return home and face my wife without our only child.

But then, as I passed the customer service counter yet again, there he was, having been found and returned by some obliging customer. In an instant, the arousal of terror spilled into ecstasy. Clutching my son, with tears suddenly flowing, I found myself unable to speak my thanks and stumbled out of the store awash in grateful joy.

Emotions are subjective. You can't pick them up, throw them, or order them at your favorite restaurant. But emotions are real, says researcher Lisa Feldman Barrett (2012, 2013): "My experience of anger is not an illusion. When I'm angry, I feel angry. That's real." Where do our emotions come from? Why do we have them? What are they made of?

Emotions are our body's adaptive response. They support our survival. When we face challenges, emotions focus our attention and energize our actions (Cyders & Smith, 2008). Our heart races. Our pace quickens. All our senses go on high alert. Receiving unexpected good news, we may find our eyes tearing up. We raise our hands triumphantly. We feel exuberance and a newfound confidence. Yet negative and prolonged emotions can harm our health.

In Modules 37, 38, and 39, we explore how psychologists think about and study our emotional expression and experiences. In Modules 40 and 41, we take a close look at the challenges of stress and some ways of coping that help us meet those challenges.

Introduction to Emotion

Emotion: Arousal, Behavior, and Cognition

37-1 How do arousal, expressive behavior, and cognition interact in emotion?

AS MY [DM'S] PANICKED SEARCH for Peter illustrates, **emotions** are a mix of

- *bodily arousal* (heart pounding).
- *expressive behaviors* (quickened pace).
- *conscious experience*, including thoughts (*"Is this a kidnapping?"*) and feelings (panic, fear, joy).

The puzzle for psychologists is figuring out how these three pieces fit together. To do that, we need answers to two big questions:

1. A chicken-and-egg debate: Does your bodily arousal come *before* or *after* your emotional feelings? (Did I first notice my racing heart and faster step, and then feel terror about losing Peter? Or did my sense of fear come first, stirring my heart and legs to respond?)

2. How do *thinking* (cognition) and *feeling* interact? Does cognition always come before emotion? (Did I think about a kidnapping threat before I reacted emotionally?)

Courtesy of David Myers

Historical emotion theories, as well as current research, have sought to answer these questions.

Historical Emotion Theories

James-Lange Theory: Arousal Comes Before Emotion Common sense tells most of us that we cry because we are sad, lash out because we are angry, tremble because we are afraid. First comes conscious awareness, then the feeling. But to pioneering psychologist William James, this commonsense view of emotion had things backward. Rather, "We feel sorry because we cry, angry because we strike, afraid because we tremble" (1890, p. 1066). James' idea was also proposed by Danish physiologist Carl Lange, and so is called the **James-Lange theory.** James and Lange would have guessed that I noticed my racing heart and then, shaking with fright, felt the whoosh of emotion—that my feeling of fear *followed* my body's response.

Cannon-Bard Theory: Arousal and Emotion Occur Simultaneously Physiologist Walter Cannon (1871–1945) disagreed with James and Lange. Does a racing heart signal fear or anger or love? The body's responses—heart rate, perspiration, and body temperature—are too similar, and they change too slowly, to *cause* the different emotions, said Cannon. He, and later another physiologist, Philip Bard, concluded that our bodily responses and experienced emotions occur separately but simultaneously. So, according to the **Cannon-Bard theory,** my heart began pounding *as* I experienced fear. The emotion-triggering stimulus traveled to my sympathetic nervous system, causing my body's arousal. *At the same time,* it traveled to my brain's cortex, causing my awareness of my emotion. My pounding heart did not cause my feeling of fear, nor did my feeling of fear cause my pounding heart.

If our bodily responses and emotional experiences occur simultaneously and one does *not* affect the other, as Cannon and Bard believed, then people who suffer spinal cord injuries should not notice a difference in their experience of emotion after the injury. But there *are* differences, according to one study of 25 World War II soldiers

Not only emotion, but most psychological phenomena (vision, sleep, memory, sex, and so forth) can be approached these three ways—physiologically, behaviorally, and cognitively.

Joy expressed According to the James-Lange theory, we don't just smile because we share our teammates' joy. We also share the joy because we are smiling with them.

Matt Sullivan/Reuters/Landov

(Hohmann, 1966). Those with *lower-spine injuries,* who had lost sensation only in their legs, reported little change in their emotions' intensity. Those with *high spinal cord injury,* who could feel nothing below the neck, did report changes. Some reactions were much less intense than before the injuries. Anger, one high spinal cord-injured man confessed, "just doesn't have the heat to it that it used to. It's a mental kind of anger." Other emotions, those expressed mostly in body areas above the neck, were felt *more* intensely. These men reported increases in weeping, lumps in the throat, and getting choked up when saying good-bye, worshiping, or watching a touching movie. Our bodily responses seemingly feed our experienced emotions.

But most researchers now agree that our emotions also involve cognition (Averill, 1993; Barrett, 2006). Whether we fear the man behind us on the dark street depends entirely on whether we interpret his actions as threatening or friendly.

RETRIEVAL PRACTICE

- According to the Cannon-Bard theory, (a) our *physiological response* to a stimulus (for example, a pounding heart), and (b) the *emotion* we experience (for example, fear) occur _____ (simultaneously/sequentially). According to the James-Lange theory, (a) and (b) occur _____ (simultaneously/sequentially).

ANSWERS: simultaneously; sequentially (first the physiological response, and then the experienced emotion)

Schachter and Singer Two-Factor Theory: Arousal + Label = Emotion

37-2 To experience emotions, must we consciously interpret and label them?

Stanley Schachter and Jerome Singer (1962) believed that an emotional experience requires a conscious interpretation of arousal: Our physical reactions and our thoughts (perceptions, memories, and interpretations) together create emotion. In their **two-factor theory,** emotions therefore have two ingredients: physical arousal and cognitive appraisal.

Consider how arousal spills over from one event to the next. Imagine arriving home after an invigorating run and finding a message that you got a longed-for job. With arousal lingering from the run, would you feel more elated than if you received this news after awakening from a nap?

To explore this *spillover effect,* Schachter and Singer injected college men with the hormone epinephrine, which triggers feelings of arousal. Picture yourself as a participant: After receiving the injection, you go to a waiting room, where you find yourself with another person (actually an accomplice of the experimenters) who is acting either euphoric or irritated. As you observe this person, you begin to feel your heart race, your body flush, and your breathing become more rapid. If you had been told to expect these effects from the injection, what would you feel? The actual volunteers felt little emotion—because they attributed their arousal to the drug. But if you had been told the injection would produce no effects, what would you feel? Perhaps you would react as another group of participants did. They "caught" the apparent emotion of the other person in the waiting room. They became happy if the accomplice was acting euphoric, and testy if the accomplice was acting irritated.

This discovery—that a stirred-up state can be experienced as one emotion or another, depending on how we interpret and label it—has been replicated in dozens of experiments (Reisenzein, 1983; Sinclair et al., 1994; Zillmann, 1986). As researcher Daniel Gilbert (2006) noted, "Feelings that one interprets as fear in the presence of a sheer drop may be interpreted as lust in the presence of a sheer blouse."

The point to remember: Arousal fuels emotion; cognition channels it.

emotion a response of the whole organism, involving (1) physiological arousal, (2) expressive behaviors, and (3) conscious experience.

James-Lange theory the theory that our experience of emotion is our awareness of our physiological responses to emotion-arousing stimuli.

Cannon-Bard theory the theory that an emotion-arousing stimulus simultaneously triggers (1) physiological responses and (2) the subjective experience of emotion.

two-factor theory the Schachter-Singer theory that to experience emotion one must (1) be physically aroused and (2) cognitively label the arousal.

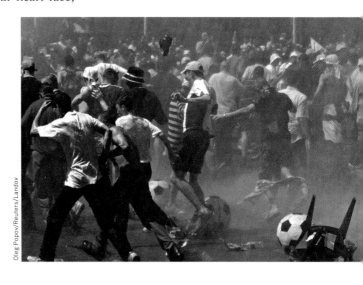

The spillover effect Arousal from a soccer match can fuel anger, which can descend into rioting or other violent confrontations.

Oleg Popow/Reuters/Landov

> **LaunchPad** For a 4-minute demonstration of the relationship between arousal and cognition, visit LaunchPad's *Video: Emotion = Arousal Plus Interpretation.*

RETRIEVAL PRACTICE

- According to Schachter and Singer, two factors lead to our experience of an emotion: (1) physiological arousal and (2) _____ appraisal.

ANSWER: cognitive

Zajonc, LeDoux, and Lazarus: Does Cognition Always Precede Emotion?

But is the heart always subject to the mind? Must we *always* interpret our arousal before we can experience an emotion? Robert Zajonc (1923–2008) (pronounced ZI-yence; 1980, 1984a) contended that we actually have many emotional reactions apart from, or even before, our interpretation of a situation. Perhaps you can recall liking something or someone immediately, without knowing why.

For example, when people repeatedly view stimuli flashed too briefly for them to interpret, they come to prefer those stimuli. Unaware of having previously seen them, they nevertheless like them. We have an acutely sensitive automatic radar for emotionally significant information, such that even a subliminally flashed stimulus can prime us to feel better or worse about a follow-up stimulus (Murphy et al., 1995; Zeelenberg et al., 2006). In experiments, thirsty people were given a fruit-flavored drink after viewing a subliminally flashed (thus unperceived) face. Those exposed to a happy face drank about 50 percent more than those exposed to a neutral face (Berridge & Winkielman, 2003). Those flashed an angry face drank substantially less.

Neuroscientists are charting the neural pathways of emotions (Ochsner et al., 2009). Our emotional responses can follow two different brain pathways. Some emotions (especially more complex feelings like hatred and love) travel a "high road." A stimulus following this path would travel (by way of the thalamus) to the brain's cortex (**FIGURE 37.1a**). There, it would be analyzed and labeled before the response command is sent out, via the amygdala (an emotion-control center).

But sometimes our emotions (especially simple likes, dislikes, and fears) take what Joseph LeDoux (2002) has called the "low road," a neural shortcut that bypasses the

▼ **FIGURE 37.1**
The brain's pathways for emotions In the two-track brain, sensory input may be routed (a) to the cortex (via the thalamus) for analysis and then transmission to the amygdala; or (b) directly to the amygdala (via the thalamus) for an instant emotional reaction.

(a) The thinking high road

(b) The speedy low road

cortex. Following the low road, a fear-provoking stimulus would travel from the eye or ear (again via the thalamus) directly to the amygdala (**FIGURE 37.1B**). This short-cut, bypassing the cortex, enables our greased-lightning emotional response before our intellect intervenes. Like speedy reflexes that also operate apart from the brain's thinking cortex, the amygdala reactions are so fast that we may be unaware of what's transpired (Dimberg et al., 2000).

The amygdala sends more neural projections up to the cortex than it receives back, which makes it easier for our feelings to hijack our thinking than for our thinking to rule our feelings (LeDoux & Armony, 1999). Thus, in the forest, we can jump at the sound of rustling bushes nearby, leaving it to our cortex to decide later whether the sound was made by a snake or by the wind. Such experiences support Zajonc's belief that *some* of our emotional reactions involve no deliberate thinking.

Emotion researcher Richard Lazarus (1991, 1998) conceded that our brain processes vast amounts of information without our conscious awareness, and that some emotional responses do not require *conscious* thinking. Much of our emotional life operates via the automatic, speedy low road. But, he asked, how would we *know* what we are reacting to if we did not in some way appraise the situation? The appraisal may be effortless and we may not be conscious of it, but it is still a mental function. To know whether a stimulus is good or bad, the brain must have some idea of what it is (Storbeck et al., 2006). Thus, said Lazarus, emotions arise when we *appraise* an event as harmless or dangerous, whether we truly *know* it is or not. We appraise the sound of the rustling bushes as the presence of a threat. Later, we realize that it was "just the wind."

So, as Zajonc and LeDoux have demonstrated, some emotional responses—especially simple likes, dislikes, and fears—involve no conscious thinking (**FIGURE 37.2**). We may fear a big spider, even if we "know" it is harmless. Such responses are difficult to alter by changing our thinking. We may automatically like one person more than another. This instant appeal can even influence our political decisions if we vote (as many people do) for a candidate we *like* over the candidate expressing positions closer to our own (Westen, 2007).

But our feelings about politics are also subject to our memories, expectations, and interpretations, as Lazarus, Schachter, and Singer might have predicted. Moreover, highly emotional people are intense partly *because* of their interpretations. They may *personalize* events as being somehow directed at them, and they may *generalize* their experiences by blowing single incidents out of proportion (Larsen & Diener, 1987). Thus, learning to *think* more positively can help people *feel* better. Although the emotional low road functions automatically, the thinking high road allows us to retake some control over our emotional life. Together, automatic emotion and conscious thinking weave the fabric of our emotional lives. (**TABLE 37.1** on the next page summarizes these emotion theories.)

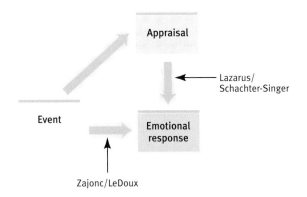

▼ FIGURE 37.2
Two pathways for emotions
Zajonc and LeDoux emphasized that some emotional responses are immediate, before any conscious appraisal. Lazarus, Schachter, and Singer emphasized that our appraisal and labeling of events also determine our emotional responses.

▼ TABLE 37.1
Summary of Emotion Theories

Theory	Explanation of Emotions	Example
James-Lange	Emotions arise from our awareness of our specific bodily responses to emotion-arousing stimuli.	We observe our heart racing after a threat and then feel afraid.
Cannon-Bard	Emotion-arousing stimuli trigger our bodily responses and simultaneous subjective experience.	Our heart races at the same time that we feel afraid.
Schachter-Singer	Our experience of emotion depends on two factors: general arousal and a conscious cognitive label.	We may interpret our arousal as fear or excitement, depending on the context.
Zajonc; LeDoux	Some emotional responses happen instantly, without conscious appraisal.	We automatically feel startled by a sound in the forest before labeling it as a threat.
Lazarus	Cognitive appraisal ("Is it dangerous or not?")—sometimes without our awareness—defines emotion.	The sound is "just the wind."

RETRIEVAL PRACTICE

• Emotion researchers have disagreed about whether emotional responses occur in the absence of cognitive processing. How would you characterize the approach of each of the following researchers: Zajonc, LeDoux, Lazarus, Schachter, and Singer?

ANSWERS: Zajonc and LeDoux suggested that we experience some emotions without any conscious, cognitive appraisal. Lazarus, Schachter, and Singer emphasized the importance of appraisal and cognitive labeling in our experience of emotion.

Embodied Emotion

Whether you are falling in love or grieving a death, you need little convincing that emotions involve the body. Feeling without a body is like breathing without lungs. Some physical responses are easy to notice. Other emotional responses we experience without awareness.

Emotions and the Autonomic Nervous System

37-3 What is the link between emotional arousal and the autonomic nervous system? How does arousal affect performance?

In a crisis, the *sympathetic division* of your *autonomic nervous system (ANS)* mobilizes your body for action (**FIGURE 37.3**). It directs your adrenal glands to release the stress hormones epinephrine (adrenaline) and norepinephrine (noradrenaline). To provide energy, your liver pours extra sugar into your bloodstream. To help burn the sugar, your respiration increases to supply needed oxygen. Your heart rate and blood pressure increase. Your digestion slows, diverting blood from your internal organs to your muscles. With blood sugar driven into the large muscles, running becomes easier. Your pupils dilate, letting in more light. To cool your stirred-up body, you perspire. If wounded, your blood would clot more quickly.

According to the *Yerkes-Dodson law*, arousal affects performance in different ways, depending on the task, with moderate arousal leading to optimal performance (Yerkes & Dodson, 1908). When taking an exam, it pays to be somewhat aroused—alert but not trembling with nervousness. Too little arousal (as when sleepy) can be disruptive. And, as we'll see, prolonged high arousal can tax the body.

"Fear lends wings to his feet."

Virgil, *Aeneid*, 19 b.c.e.

Autonomic Nervous System Controls Physiological Arousal

Sympathetic division (arousing)		Parasympathetic division (calming)
Pupils dilate	EYES	Pupils contract
Decreases	SALIVATION	Increases
Perspires	SKIN	Dries
Increases	RESPIRATION	Decreases
Accelerates	HEART	Slows
Inhibits	DIGESTION	Activates
Secrete stress hormones	ADRENAL GLANDS	Decrease secretion of stress hormones
Reduced	IMMUNE SYSTEM FUNCTIONING	Enhanced

When the crisis passes, the *parasympathetic division* of your ANS gradually calms your body, as stress hormones slowly leave your bloodstream. After your next crisis, think of this: Without any conscious effort, your body's response to danger is wonderfully coordinated and adaptive—preparing you to *fight* or *flee*. So, do the different emotions have distinct arousal fingerprints?

▼ **FIGURE 37.3**
Emotional arousal Like a crisis control center, the autonomic nervous system arouses the body in a crisis and calms it when danger passes.

The Physiology of Emotions

37-4 Do different emotions activate different physiological and brain-pattern responses?

Imagine conducting an experiment measuring the physiological responses of emotion. In each of four rooms, you have someone watching a movie: In the first, the person is viewing a horror show; in the second, an anger-provoking film; in the third, a sexually arousing film; in the fourth, a boring film. From the control center, you monitor each person's perspiration, breathing, and heart rate. Could you tell who is frightened? Who is angry? Who is sexually aroused? Who is bored?

© Gary Dobner/Alamy

Emotional arousal Elated excitement and panicky fear involve similar physiological arousal. That allows us to flip rapidly between the two emotions.

With training, you could probably pick out the bored viewer. But discerning physiological differences among fear, anger, and sexual arousal is much more difficult (Barrett, 2006). Different emotions can share common biological signatures.

A single brain region can also serve as the seat of seemingly different emotions. Consider the broad emotional portfolio of the *insula*, a neural center deep inside the brain. The insula is activated when we experience various negative social emotions, such as lust, pride, and disgust. In brain scans, it becomes active when people bite into some disgusting food, smell the same disgusting food, think about biting into a disgusting cockroach, or feel moral disgust over a sleazy business exploiting a saintly widow (Sapolsky, 2010). Similar multitasking regions are found in other brains areas.

Yet our emotions—such as sexual arousal, fear, anger, and disgust—*feel* different to us, and they often *look* different to others. We may appear "paralyzed with fear" or "ready to explode." Fear and joy prompt similar increased heart rate, but they stimulate different facial muscles. During fear, your brow muscles tense. During joy, muscles in your cheeks and under your eyes pull into a smile (Witvliet & Vrana, 1995).

Some of our emotions also differ in their brain circuits (Panksepp, 2007). Observers watching fearful faces showed more amygdala activity than did other observers who watched angry faces (Whalen et al., 2001). Brain scans and EEG recordings show that emotions also activate different areas of the brain's cortex. When you experience negative emotions such as disgust, your right prefrontal cortex tends to be more

> "No one ever told me that grief felt so much like fear. I am not afraid, but the sensation is like being afraid. The same fluttering in the stomach, the same restlessness, the yawning. I keep on swallowing."
>
> C. S. Lewis, *A Grief Observed*, 1961

Lie Detection

37-5 How effective are polygraphs in using body states to detect lies?

Can a *lie detector*—a **polygraph**—reveal lies? Polygraphs don't literally detect lies. Instead, they measure emotion-linked changes in breathing, cardiovascular activity, and perspiration. If you were taking this test, an examiner would monitor these responses as you answered questions. She might ask, "In the last 20 years, have you ever taken something that didn't belong to you?" This is a control question, aimed at making everyone a little nervous. If you lied and said *"No!"* (as many people do) the polygraph would detect arousal. This response will establish a baseline, a useful comparison for your responses to *critical questions* ("Did you ever steal anything from your previous employer?"). If your responses to critical questions are weaker than to control questions, the examiner will infer you are telling the truth.

Critics point out two problems: First, our physiological arousal is much the same from one emotion to another. Anxiety, irritation, and guilt all prompt similar physiological reactivity. Second, many innocent people respond with heightened tension to the accusations implied by the critical questions (**FIGURE 37.4**). Many rape victims, for example, have "failed" these tests when reacting emotionally but truthfully (Lykken, 1991).

A 2002 U.S. National Academy of Sciences report noted that "no spy has ever been caught [by] using the polygraph." It is not for lack of trying. The FBI, CIA, and U.S. Departments of Defense and Energy have tested tens of thousands of employees, and

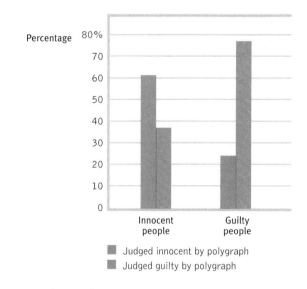

▼ **FIGURE 37.4**

How often do lie detection tests lie? In one study, polygraph experts interpreted the polygraph data of 100 people who had been suspects in theft crimes (Kleinmuntz & Szucko, 1984). Half the suspects were guilty and had confessed; the other half had been proven innocent. Had the polygraph experts been the judges, more than one-third of the innocent would have been declared guilty, and one-fourth of the guilty would have been declared innocent.

active than the left. Depression-prone people, and those with generally negative personalities, have also shown more right frontal lobe activity (Harmon-Jones et al., 2002).

Positive moods tend to trigger more left frontal lobe activity. People with positive personalities—exuberant infants and alert, enthusiastic, energized, and persistently goal-directed adults—have also shown more activity in the left frontal lobe than in the right (Davidson, 2000, 2003; Urry et al., 2004). Indeed, the more a person's baseline frontal lobe activity tilts left—or is made to tilt left by perceptual activity—the more upbeat the person typically is (Drake & Myers, 2006).

To sum up, we can't easily see differences in emotions from tracking heart rate, breathing, and perspiration. But facial expressions and brain activity can vary with the emotion. So, do we, like Pinocchio, give off telltale signs when we lie? For more on that question, see Thinking Critically About: Lie Detection.

RETRIEVAL PRACTICE

- How do the two divisions of the autonomic nervous system affect our emotional responses?

ANSWER: The *sympathetic division* of the ANS arouses us for more intense experiences of emotion, pumping out the stress hormones epinephrine and norepinephrine to prepare our body for fight or flight. The *parasympathetic division* of the ANS takes over when a crisis passes, restoring our body to a calm physiological and emotional state.

---

polygraph use in Europe has also increased (Meijer & Verschuere, 2010). Yet Aldrich Ames, a Russian spy within the CIA, went undetected. Ames took many "polygraph tests and passed them all," noted Robert Park (1999). "Nobody thought to investigate the source of his sudden wealth—after all, he was passing the lie detector tests."

A more effective lie detection approach uses a *guilty knowledge test,* which assesses a suspect's physiological responses to crime-scene details known only to the police and the guilty person (Ben-Shakhar & Elaad, 2003). If a camera and computer had been stolen, for example, only a guilty person should react strongly to the brand names of the stolen items. Given enough such specific probes, an innocent person will seldom be wrongly accused.

Research teams are now exploring new ways to nab liars. "Forensic neuroscience" researchers are going straight to the seat of deceit—the brain. fMRI scans have shown liars' brains activating in places that honest people's brains do not (Langleben et al., 2002, 2006, 2008; Lui & Rosenfeld, 2009). The Pinocchio-like giveaway signal of lying may be not the length of our nose, but rather the telltale activity in our brain. fMRI scans have shown that brain areas such as the left frontal lobe and anterior cingulate cortex become active when the brain inhibits truth-telling (**FIGURE 37.5**). A U.S. $10 million Law and Neuroscience Project, led by psychologist Michael Gazzaniga, aims to assess appropriate uses of the new technology in identifying terrorists, convicting criminals, and protecting the innocent. In 2010, a U.S. federal court declared that fMRI lie detection is not yet ready for courtroom use (Miller, 2010).

▼ FIGURE 37.5

Liar, liar, brain's on fire An fMRI scan identified two brain areas that became especially active when a participant lied about holding a five of clubs. (fMRI scan from Langleben et al., 2002.)

Many neuroscientists concur (Gazzaniga, 2011; Wagner, 2010). Others argue that jurors' and judges' seat-of-the-pants judgments "are worse than the science that is excluded" (Schauer, 2010).

polygraph a machine, commonly used in attempts to detect lies, that measures several of the physiological responses (such as perspiration and cardiovascular and breathing changes) accompanying emotion.

LEARNING OBJECTIVES

RETRIEVAL PRACTICE Take a moment to answer each of these Learning Objective Questions (repeated here from within this module). Then turn to Appendix C, Complete Module Reviews, to check your answers. Research suggests that trying to answer these questions on your own will improve your long-term retention (McDaniel et al., 2009).

37-1 How do arousal, expressive behavior, and cognition interact in emotion?

37-2 To experience emotions, must we consciously interpret and label them?

37-3 What is the link between emotional arousal and the autonomic nervous system? How does arousal affect performance?

37-4 Do different emotions activate different physiological and brain-pattern responses?

37-5 How effective are polygraphs in using body states to detect lies?

TERMS AND CONCEPTS TO REMEMBER

RETRIEVAL PRACTICE Test yourself on these terms by trying to write down the definition before flipping back to the page number referenced to check your answer.

emotion, p. 460

James-Lange theory, p. 460

Cannon-Bard theory, p. 460

two-factor theory, p. 461

polygraph, p. 467

Use 🔁 **LearningCurve** to create your personalized study plan, which will direct you to the resources that will help you most in 🔁 **LaunchPad**.

MODULE
38 Expressing Emotion

EXPRESSIVE BEHAVIOR IMPLIES EMOTION. DOLPHINS, with smiles seemingly plastered on their faces, appear happy. To decipher people's emotions we read their bodies, listen to their voice tones, and study their faces. Does nonverbal language vary with culture—or is it universal? And do our expressions influence our experienced emotions?

"Your face, my thane, is a book where men may read strange matters."

Lady Macbeth to her husband,
in William Shakespeare's *Macbeth*

Detecting Emotion in Others

38-1 How do we communicate nonverbally?

To Westerners, a firm handshake conveys an outgoing, expressive personality (Chaplin et al., 2000). A gaze, an averted glance, or a stare communicates intimacy, submission, or dominance (Kleinke, 1986). Darting eyes and swiveled heads signal anxiety (Perkins et al., 2012). When two people are passionately in love, they typically spend time— quite a bit of time—gazing into each other's eyes (Rubin, 1970). Would such gazes stir these feelings between strangers? To find out, researchers have asked unacquainted male-female pairs to gaze intently for 2 minutes either at each other's hands or into each other's eyes. After separating, the eye gazers reported feeling a tingle of attraction and affection (Kellerman et al., 1989).

Most of us read nonverbal cues well. Shown 10 seconds of video from the end of a speed-dating interaction, people can often detect whether one person is attracted to another (Place et al., 2009). We also excel at detecting nonverbal threat. We readily sense subliminally presented negative words (*snake* or *bomb*; Dijksterhuis & Aarts, 2003). In a crowd, angry faces will "pop out" faster than happy ones (Hansen & Hansen, 1988; Pinkham et al., 2010). Signs of status are also easy to spot. When shown an

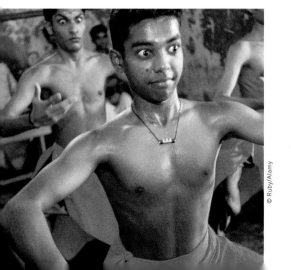

A silent language of emotion Hindu classic dance uses the face and body to effectively convey 10 different emotions (Hejmadi et al., 2000).

▼ FIGURE 38.1
Experience influences how we perceive emotions Viewing the morphed middle face, evenly mixing fear with anger, physically abused children were more likely than nonabused children to perceive the face as angry (Pollak & Kistler, 2002; Pollak & Tolley-Schell, 2003).

image of a person with arms raised, chest expanded, and a slight smile, people—from Canadian undergraduates to Fijian villagers—perceive the person as experiencing the emotion pride and having high status (Tracy et al., 2013).

Experience can sensitize us to particular emotions, as shown by experiments using a series of faces (like those in **FIGURE** 38.1) that morph from anger to fear (or sadness). Viewing such faces, physically abused children are much quicker than other children to spot the signals of anger. Shown a face that is 50 percent fear and 50 percent anger, they are more likely to perceive anger than fear. Their perceptions become sensitively attuned to glimmers of danger that nonabused children miss.

Hard-to-control facial muscles may reveal emotions you may be trying to conceal. Lifting just the inner part of your eyebrows, which few people do consciously, reveals distress or worry. Eyebrows raised and pulled together signal fear. Activated muscles under the eyes and raised cheeks suggest a natural smile. A feigned smile, such as one we make for a photographer, is often frozen in place for several seconds, then suddenly switched off. Genuine happy smiles tend to be briefer and to fade less abruptly (Bugental, 1986).

Our brain is an amazing detector of subtle expressions. When researchers filmed teachers talking to unseen schoolchildren, a mere 10-second clip of the teacher's voice or face provided enough clues for both young and old viewers to determine whether the teacher liked and admired a child (Babad et al., 1991). In other experiments, even glimpsing a face for one-tenth of a second enabled people to judge people's attractiveness or trustworthiness or to rate politicians' competence and predict their voter support (Willis & Todorov, 2006). "First impressions . . . occur with astonishing speed," note Christopher Olivola and Alexander Todorov (2010).

Despite our brain's emotion-detecting skill, we find it difficult to detect deceiving expressions (Porter & ten Brinke, 2008). The behavioral differences between liars and truth tellers are too minute for most people to detect (Hartwig & Bond, 2011). In one digest of 206 studies of discerning truth from lies, people were just 54 percent accurate—barely better than a coin toss (Bond & DePaulo, 2006). Moreover, the available research indicates that virtually no one—save perhaps police professionals in high-stakes situations—beats chance by much (Bond & DePaulo, 2008; O'Sullivan et al., 2009). Might the unconscious mind see what the conscious mind does not? Perhaps. Distracting people, rather than encouraging them to think deeply, increases their lie-detection accuracy (Reinhard et al., 2013). If you want to catch the person who stole your mutt, go with your gut.

Some of us are more sensitive than others to physical cues to various emotions. In one study, hundreds of people were asked to name the emotion displayed in brief film clips. The clips showed portions of a person's emotionally expressive face or body, sometimes accompanied by a garbled voice (Rosenthal et al., 1979). For example, after a 2-second scene revealing only the face of an upset woman, the researchers would ask whether the woman was criticizing someone for being late or was talking about her divorce. Given such "thin slices," some people were much better emotion detectors than others. Introverts tend to excel at reading others' emotions, while extraverts are generally easier to read (Ambady et al., 1995).

Which of researcher Paul Ekman's smiles is feigned, which natural? The smile on the right engages the facial muscles of a natural smile.

Gestures, facial expressions, and voice tones, which are absent in written communication, convey important information. The difference was clear in one study. In one group, participants heard 30-second recordings of people describing their marital separations. In the other group, participants read a script of the recording. Those who *heard* the recording were better able to predict the people's current and future adjustment (Mason et al., 2010).

The absence of expressive emotion can make for ambiguous emotion in electronic communications. To partly remedy that, we sometimes embed visual cues to emotion (ROFL!) in our texts, e-mails, and online posts. Without the vocal nuances that signal whether our statement is serious, kidding, or sarcastic, we are in danger of what Piaget called *egocentrism,* by failing to perceive how others interpret our "just kidding" message (Kruger et al., 2005).

Gender, Emotion, and Nonverbal Behavior

38-2 Do the genders differ in their ability to communicate nonverbally?

Is women's intuition, as so many believe, superior to men's? After analyzing 125 studies of sensitivity to nonverbal cues, Judith Hall (1984, 1987) concluded that women generally do surpass men at reading people's emotional cues when given thin slices of behavior. The female advantage emerges early in development. In one analysis of 107 study findings, female infants, children, and adolescents outperformed males (McClure, 2000).

Women's nonverbal sensitivity helps explain their greater emotional literacy. When invited to describe how they would feel in certain situations, men described simpler emotional reactions (Barrett et al., 2000). You might like to try this yourself: Ask some people how they might feel when saying good-bye to friends after graduation. Research suggests men are more likely to say, simply, "I'll feel bad," and women to express more complex emotions: "It will be bittersweet; I'll feel both happy and sad."

Women's skill at decoding others' emotions may also contribute to their greater emotional responsiveness (Vigil, 2009). In studies of 23,000 people from 26 cultures, women more than men reported themselves open to feelings (Costa et al., 2001). Children show the same gender difference: Girls express stronger emotions than boys do (Chaplin & Aldao, 2013). That helps explain the extremely strong perception that emotionality is "more true of women"—a perception expressed by nearly 100 percent of 18- to 29-year-old Americans (Newport, 2001).

One exception: Quickly—imagine an angry face. What gender is the person? If you're like 3 in 4 Arizona State University students, you imagined a male (Becker et al., 2007). And when a gender-neutral face was made to look angry, most people perceived it as male. If the face was smiling, they were more likely to perceive it as female (**FIGURE 38.2**). Anger strikes most people as a more masculine emotion.

"*Now, that wasn't so hard, was it?*"

▼ FIGURE 38.2
Male or female? Researchers manipulated a gender-neutral face. People were more likely to see it as a male when it wore an angry expression, and as a female when it wore a smile (Becker et al., 2007).

The perception of women's emotionality also feeds—and is fed by—people's attributing women's emotionality to their disposition and men's to their circumstances: "She's emotional. He's having a bad day" (Barrett & Bliss-Moreau, 2009). Many factors influence our attributions, including cultural norms (Mason & Morris, 2010). Nevertheless, there are some gender differences in descriptions of emotional experiences. When surveyed, women are also far more likely than men to describe themselves as empathic. If you have *empathy,* you identify with others and imagine what it must be like to walk in their shoes. You rejoice with those who rejoice and weep with those who weep. Fiction readers, who immerse themselves in the lives of their favorite characters, report higher empathy levels (Mar et al., 2009). This may help explain why, compared with men, women read more fiction (Tepper, 2000). Physiological measures, such as heart rate while seeing another's distress, confirm the empathic gender gap, though a smaller one than indicated in survey self-reports (Eisenberg & Lennon, 1983; Rueckert et al., 2010).

Females are also more likely to *express* empathy—to cry and to report distress when observing someone in distress. As **FIGURE** 38.3 shows, this gender difference was clear in videotapes of male and female students watching film clips that were sad (children with a dying parent), happy (slapstick comedy), or frightening (a man nearly falling off the ledge of a tall building) (Kring & Gordon, 1998). Women also tend to experience emotional events, such as viewing pictures of mutilation, more deeply and with more brain activation in areas sensitive to emotion. And they better remember the scenes three weeks later (Canli et al., 2002).

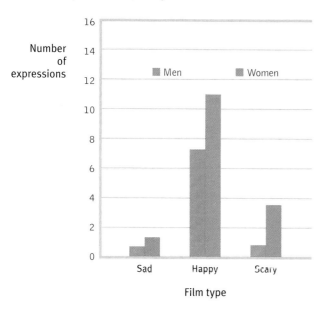

▼ FIGURE 38.3
Gender and expressiveness Male and female film viewers did not differ dramatically in self-reported emotions or physiological responses. But the women's faces *showed* much more emotion. (Data from Kring & Gordon, 1998.)

RETRIEVAL PRACTICE

• _____ (Women/Men) report experiencing emotions more deeply, and they tend to be more adept at reading nonverbal behavior.

ANSWER: Women

Culture and Emotional Expression

38-3 Do gestures and facial expressions mean the same thing in all cultures?

The meaning of *gestures* varies with the culture. U.S. President Richard Nixon learned this after making the North American "A-OK" sign before a welcoming crowd of Brazilians, not realizing it was a crude insult in that country. The importance of cultural definitions of gestures was again demonstrated in 1968, when North Korea publicized photos of supposedly happy officers from a captured U.S. Navy spy ship. In the photo,

▼ FIGURE 38.4
Culture-specific or culturally universal expressions?
As people of differing cultures and races, do our faces speak differing languages? Which face expresses disgust? Anger? Fear? Happiness? Sadness? Surprise? (From Matsumoto & Ekman, 1989.) See inverted answers below.

From left to right, top to bottom: happiness, surprise, fear, sadness, anger, disgust.

three men had raised their middle finger, telling their captors it was a "Hawaiian good luck sign" (Fleming & Scott, 1991).

Do *facial expressions* also have different meanings in different cultures? To find out, two investigative teams showed photographs of various facial expressions to people in different parts of the world and asked them to guess the emotion (Ekman et al., 1975, 1987, 1994; Izard, 1977, 1994). You can try this matching task yourself by pairing the six emotions with the six faces in **FIGURE 38.4**.

Regardless of your cultural background, you probably did pretty well. A smile's a smile the world around. Ditto for sadness, and to a lesser extent the other basic expressions (Jack et al., 2012). (There is no culture where people frown when they are happy.)

Facial expressions do convey some nonverbal accents that provide clues to one's culture (Marsh et al., 2003). Thus, data from 182 studies have shown slightly enhanced accuracy when people judged emotions from their own culture (Elfenbein & Ambady, 2002, 2003a,b). Still, the telltale signs of emotion generally cross cultures. The world over, children cry when distressed, shake their heads when defiant, and smile when they are happy. So, too, with blind children who have never seen a face (Eibl-Eibesfeldt, 1971). People blind from birth spontaneously exhibit the common facial expressions associated with such emotions as joy, sadness, fear, and anger (Galati et al., 1997).

Musical expressions of emotion also cross cultures. Happy and sad music feels happy and sad around the world. Whether you live in an African village or a European city, fast-paced music seems happy, and slow-paced music seems sadder (Fritz et al., 2009).

Do these shared emotional categories reflect shared *cultural* experiences, such as movies and TV broadcasts seen around the world? Apparently not. Paul Ekman and his

Universal emotions No matter where on Earth you live, you have no trouble knowing which photo depicts Michael Owen and his fans feeling distraught (after missing a goal) and triumphant (after scoring it).

team asked isolated people in New Guinea to respond to such statements as, "Pretend your child has died." When North American collegians viewed the taped responses, they easily read the New Guineans' facial reactions.

So we can say that facial muscles speak a universal language. This discovery would not have surprised Charles Darwin (1809–1882) who argued that in prehistoric times, before our ancestors communicated in words, they communicated threats, greetings, and submission with facial expressions. Their shared expressions helped them survive (Hess & Thibault, 2009). In confrontations, for example, a human sneer retains elements of an animal baring its teeth in a snarl. Emotional expressions may enhance our survival in other ways, too. Surprise raises the eyebrows and widens the eyes, enabling us to take in more information. Disgust wrinkles the nose, closing it from foul odors.

Smiles are social as well as emotional events. Euphoric Olympic gold-medal winners typically don't smile when they are awaiting their ceremony. But they wear broad grins when interacting with officials and facing the crowd and cameras (Fernández-Dols & Ruiz-Belda, 1995). Thus, a glimpse at competitors' spontaneous expressions following an Olympic judo competition gives a very good clue to who won, no matter their country (Matsumoto & Willingham, 2006, 2009a). Even natively blind athletes, who have never observed smiles, display the same social smiles in such situations (Matsumoto et al., 2009b).

> 🌀 **LaunchPad** For a 4-minute demonstration of our universal facial language, visit LaunchPad's *Video: Emotions and Facial Expression*.

Although we share a universal facial language, it has been adaptive for us to interpret faces in particular contexts (**FIGURE 38.5**). People judge an angry face set in a frightening situation as afraid. They judge a fearful face set in a painful situation as pained (Carroll & Russell, 1996). Movie directors harness this phenomenon by creating contexts and soundtracks that amplify our perceptions of particular emotions.

Although cultures share a universal facial language for some basic emotions, they differ in how *much* emotion they express. Those that encourage individuality, as in Western Europe, Australia, New Zealand, and North America, display mostly visible emotions (van Hemert et al., 2007). Those that encourage people to adjust to others, as in China, tend to have less visible displays of personal emotions (Matsumoto et al.,

"For news of the heart, ask the face."
Guinean proverb

While weightless, astronauts' internal bodily fluids move toward their upper body and their faces become puffy. This makes nonverbal communication more difficult, especially among multi-national crews (Gelman, 1989).

▼ FIGURE 38.5
We read faces in context
Whether we perceive the man in the top row as disgusted or angry depends on which body his face appears on (Aviezer et al., 2008). In the second row, tears on a face make its expression seem sadder (Provine et al., 2009).

facial feedback effect the tendency of facial muscle states to trigger corresponding feelings such as fear, anger, or happiness.

behavior feedback effect the tendency of behavior to influence our own and others' thoughts, feelings, and actions.

"Whenever I feel afraid
I hold my head erect
And whistle a happy tune."

Richard Rodgers and Oscar Hammerstein,
The King and I, 1958

A request from your authors: Smile often as you read this book.

2009b; Tsai et al., 2007). In Japan, people infer emotion more from the surrounding context. Moreover, the mouth, which is so expressive in North Americans, conveys less emotion than do the telltale eyes (Masuda et al., 2008; Yuki et al., 2007).

Cultural differences also exist *within* nations. The Irish and their Irish-American descendants have tended to be more expressive than the Scandinavians and their Scandinavian-American descendants (Tsai & Chentsova-Dutton, 2003). And that reminds us of a familiar lesson: Like most psychological events, emotion is best understood not only as a biological and cognitive phenomenon, but also as a social-cultural phenomenon.

RETRIEVAL PRACTICE

- Are people in different cultures more likely to differ in their interpretations of facial expressions or of gestures?

ANSWER: gestures

The Effects of Facial Expressions

38-4 How do our facial expressions influence our feelings?

As William James (1890) struggled with feelings of depression and grief, he came to believe that we can control emotions by going "through the outward movements" of any emotion we want to experience. "To feel cheerful," he advised, "sit up cheerfully, look around cheerfully, and act as if cheerfulness were already there."

Studies of emotional effects of facial expressions reveal precisely what James might have predicted. Expressions not only communicate emotion, they also amplify and regulate it. In *The Expression of the Emotions in Man and Animals*, Charles Darwin (1872) contended that "the free expression by outward signs of an emotion intensifies it. . . . He who gives way to violent gestures will increase his rage."

Was Darwin right? You can test his hypothesis: Fake a big grin. Now scowl. Can you feel the "smile therapy" difference? Participants in dozens of experiments have felt a difference. James Laird and his colleagues (1974, 1984, 1989) subtly induced students to make a frowning expression by asking them to "contract these muscles" and "pull your brows together" (supposedly to help the researchers attach facial electrodes). The results? The students reported feeling a little angry, and they similarly adopted other basic emotions. For example, people reported feeling more fear than anger, disgust, or sadness when made to construct a fearful expression: "Raise your eyebrows. And open your eyes wide. Move your whole head back, so that your chin is tucked in a little bit, and let your mouth relax and hang open a little" (Duclos et al., 1989).

This **facial feedback effect** has been found many times, in many places, for many basic emotions (**FIGURE 38.6**). Just activating one of the smiling muscles by holding a pen in the teeth (rather than gently in the mouth, which produces a neutral expression) makes stressful situations less upsetting (Kraft & Pressman, 2012). A heartier smile—made not just with the mouth but with raised cheeks that crinkle the eyes—enhances positive feelings even more when you are reacting to something pleasant or funny (Soussignan, 2001). Smile warmly on the outside and you feel better on the inside. When smiling, you will even more quickly understand sentences that describe pleasant events (Havas et al., 2007). Scowl and the whole world seems to scowl back.

So your face is more than a billboard that displays your feelings; it also feeds your feelings. No wonder people feel less depressed after Botox injections that paralyze the frowning muscles (Wollmer et al., 2012). Four months after treatment, people continued to report lower depression levels. Follow-up studies have found that Botox paralysis of the frowning muscles slowed people's reading of sadness- or anger-related sentences, and it slowed activity in emotion-related brain circuits (Havas et al., 2010; Hennenlotter et al., 2008). In such ways, Botox smooths life's emotional wrinkles.

Other researchers have observed a similar **behavior feedback effect** (Flack, 2006; Snodgrass et al., 1986). You can duplicate the participants' experience: Walk for a few

A chain of rubber bands

Adhesive bandages

A chain of rubber bands

▼ FIGURE 38.6
How to make people smile without telling them to smile Do as Kazuo Mori and Hideko Mori (2009) did with students in Japan: Attach rubber bands to the sides of the face with adhesive bandages, and then run them either over the head or under the chin. (1) Based on the *facial feedback effect,* how might students report feeling when the rubber bands raise their cheeks as though in a smile? (2) How might students report feeling when the rubber bands pull their cheeks downward?

ANSWERS: (1) Most students report feeling more happy than sad when their cheeks are raised upward. (2) Most students report feeling more sad than happy when their cheeks are pulled downward.

minutes with short, shuffling steps, keeping your eyes downcast. Now walk around taking long strides, with your arms swinging and your eyes looking straight ahead. Can you feel your mood shift? Going through the motions awakens the emotions.

Likewise, people perceive ambiguous behaviors differently depending on which finger they move up and down while reading a story. (This was said to be a study of the effect of using finger muscles "located near the reading muscles on the motor cortex.") If participants read the story while moving an extended middle finger, the story behaviors seemed more hostile. If read with a thumb up, they seemed more positive. Hostile gestures prime hostile perceptions (Chandler & Schwarz, 2009; Goldin-Meadow & Beilock, 2010).

You can use your understanding of feedback effects to become more empathic: Let your own face mimic another person's expression. Acting as another acts helps us feel what another feels (Vaughn & Lanzetta, 1981). Indeed, natural mimicry of others' emotions helps explain why emotions are contagious (Dimberg et al., 2000; Neumann & Strack, 2000). Positive, upbeat Facebook posts create a ripple effect, leading Facebook friends to also express more positive emotions (Kramer, 2012). Primates also ape one another, and their synchronized expressions help bond them (and us) together (de Waal, 2009). Losing this ability to mimic others can leave us struggling to make emotional connections, as one social worker with Moebius syndrome, a rare facial paralysis disorder, discovered while working with Hurricane Katrina refugees: When people made a sad expression, "I wasn't able to return it. I tried to do so with words and tone of voice, but it was no use. Stripped of the facial expression, the emotion just dies there, unshared" (Carey, 2010).

MODULE 38 REVIEW Expressing Emotion

LEARNING OBJECTIVES

RETRIEVAL PRACTICE Take a moment to answer each of these Learning Objective Questions (repeated here from within this module). Then turn to Appendix C, Complete Module Reviews, to check your answers. Research suggests that trying to answer these questions on your own will improve your long-term retention (McDaniel et al., 2009).

38-1 How do we communicate nonverbally?

38-2 Do the genders differ in their ability to communicate nonverbally?

38-3 Do gestures and facial expressions mean the same thing in all cultures?

38-4 How do our facial expressions influence our feelings?

TERMS AND CONCEPTS TO REMEMBER

RETRIEVAL PRACTICE Test yourself on these terms by trying to write down the definition before flipping back to the page number referenced to check your answer.

facial feedback effect, p. 474

behavior feedback effect, p. 474

Use 🅜 LearningCurve to create your personalized study plan, which will direct you to the resources that will help you most in 🅜 LaunchPad.

39 Experiencing Emotion

39-1 What are some basic emotions, and what two dimensions help differentiate them?

HOW MANY DISTINCT EMOTIONS ARE there? Carroll Izard (1977) isolated 10 basic emotions (joy, interest-excitement, surprise, sadness, anger, disgust, contempt, fear, shame, and guilt), most present in infancy (**FIGURE 39.1**). Others (Tracy & Robins, 2004) believe that pride is also a distinct emotion, signaled by a small smile, head slightly tilted back, and an open posture. Love, too, may be a basic emotion (Shaver et al., 1996). But Izard has argued that other emotions are combinations of these 10, with love, for example, being a mixture of joy and interest-excitement.

▼ FIGURE 39.1
Infants' naturally occurring emotions
To identify the emotions present from birth, Carroll Izard analyzed the facial expressions of infants.

(a) Joy (mouth forming smile, cheeks lifted, twinkle in eye)

(b) Anger (brows drawn together and downward, eyes fixed, mouth squarish)

(c) Interest (brows raised or knitted, mouth softly rounded, lips may be pursed)

(d) Disgust (nose wrinkled, upper lip raised, tongue pushed outward)

(e) Surprise (brows raised, eyes widened, mouth rounded in oval shape)

(f) Sadness (brow's inner corners raised, mouth corners drawn down)

(g) Fear (brows level, drawn in and up, eyelids lifted, mouth corners retracted)

▼ FIGURE 39.2
Two dimensions of emotion James Russell, David Watson, Auke Tellegen, and others have described emotions as variations on two dimensions—*arousal* (low versus high) and *valence* (pleasant versus unpleasant feeling).

Pleasant/Positive

relaxed   elated enthusiastic

Low arousal   High arousal

sluggish sad   fearful angry

Unpleasant/Negative

The ingredients of emotion include not only physiology and expressive behavior but also our conscious experience. Across the world, people place emotional experience along the two dimensions illustrated in **FIGURE 39.2**—positive-versus-negative *valence*, and low-versus-high *arousal* (Russell et al., 1989, 1999a,b, 2009; Watson et al., 1999). Any emotion is some combination of feeling good versus bad, and of being aroused and energized or not. On the valence and arousal dimensions, *terrified* is more frightened (more unpleasant and aroused) than *afraid*, *enraged* is angrier than *angry*, *delighted* is happier than *happy*.

Let's take a closer look at anger and happiness. What functions do they serve? What influences our experience of each?

Anger

39-2 What are the causes and consequences of anger?

Anger, the sages have said, is "a short madness" (Horace, 65–8 B.C.E.) that "carries the mind away" (Virgil, 70–19 B.C.E.) and can be "many times more hurtful than the injury that caused it" (Thomas Fuller, 1654–1734). But they have also said that "noble anger" (William Shakespeare, 1564–1616) "makes any coward brave" (Cato, 234–149 B.C.E.) and "brings back . . . strength" (Virgil).

When we face a threat or challenge, fear triggers flight but anger triggers fight—each at times an adaptive behavior. What makes us angry? Sometimes anger is a response to someone's perceived misdeeds, especially when the person's act seems willful, unjustified, and avoidable (Averill, 1983). But small hassles and blameless annoyances—foul odors, high temperatures, a traffic jam, aches and pains—also have the power to make us angry (Berkowitz, 1990).

Anger can harm us: Chronic hostility is linked to heart disease. Anger boosts our heart rate, causes our skin to drip with sweat, and raises our testosterone levels (Herrero et al., 2010; Kubo et al., 2012; Peterson & Harmon-Jones, 2012). Anger also triggers blood flow to our brain's "alarm system," causing us to reflect on why we are angry (Denson et al., 2009). How, then, can we rid ourselves of our anger? In a Gallup teen survey, boys more than girls reported walking away from the situation or working it off with exercise; girls more often reported talking with a friend, listening to music, or writing (Ray, 2005). Popular books and articles sometimes advise that releasing angry feelings can be better than internalizing them. When irritated, should we lash out at the offender? Are advice columnists right in urging us to teach children to vent their anger? Are "recovery" therapists right in encouraging us to rage at our dead parents, imaginatively curse the boss, or confront our childhood abuser?

Individualist cultures encourage people to vent their rage. Such advice is seldom heard in cultures where people's identity is centered more on the group. People who keenly sense their *inter*dependence see anger as a threat to group harmony (Markus & Kitayama, 1991). In Tahiti, for instance, people learn to be considerate and gentle. In Japan, from infancy on, angry expressions are less common than in Western cultures, where in recent politics, anger seems all the rage.

The Western vent-your-anger advice presumes that we can achieve emotional release, or **catharsis**, through aggressive action or fantasy. Experimenters report that *sometimes* when people retaliate against a provoker, they may indeed calm down (Geen & Quanty, 1977; Hokanson & Edelman, 1966; Verona & Sullivan, 2008). But this tends to be true only *if*

- they direct their counterattack toward the provoker.
- their retaliation seems justifiable.
- their target is not intimidating.

In short, expressing anger can be *temporarily* calming *if* it does not leave us feeling guilty or anxious. But despite this temporary afterglow, catharsis usually fails to cleanse our rage. More often, expressing anger breeds more anger. For one thing, it may provoke further retaliation, causing a minor conflict to escalate into a major confrontation. For another, expressing anger can magnify anger. As *behavior feedback* research demonstrates, *acting* angry can make us *feel* angrier (Flack, 2006; Snodgrass et al., 1986). Anger's backfire potential appeared in a study of 100 frustrated engineers and technicians just laid off by an aerospace company (Ebbesen et al., 1975). Researchers asked some workers questions that released hostility, such as, "What instances can you think of where the company has not been fair with you?" After expressing their anger, the workers later filled out a questionnaire that assessed their attitudes toward the company. Had the opportunity to "drain off" their hostility reduced it? Quite the contrary. These people expressed *more* hostility than those who had discussed neutral topics.

catharsis emotional release. In psychology, the catharsis hypothesis maintains that "releasing" aggressive energy (through action or fantasy) relieves aggressive urges.

Blowing off steam My [DM] daughter, a resident of South Africa, experienced a temporary catharsis while cheering on her new country in a World Cup soccer match. "Every time I got angry at Uruguay, blowing that vuvuzela and joining the chorus of dissent released something in me."

Mike Hutchings/Reuters/Landov

SIX CHIX

Isabella Bannerman. Distributed by King Features Syndicate

The catharsis idea: Is it true?

"Anger will never disappear so long as thoughts of resentment are cherished in the mind."

The Buddha, 500 b.c.e.

In another study, people who had been provoked were asked to wallop a punching bag while ruminating about the person who had angered them. Later, when given a chance for revenge, they became even more aggressive. "Venting to reduce anger is like using gasoline to put out a fire," concluded the researcher (Bushman, 2002).

When anger fuels physically or verbally aggressive acts we later regret, it becomes maladaptive. Anger primes prejudice. After the 9/11 terrorist attacks, Americans who responded with anger more than fear displayed intolerance for immigrants and Muslims (DeSteno et al., 2004; Skitka et al., 2004). Angry outbursts that temporarily calm us are dangerous in another way: They may be reinforcing and therefore habit forming. If stressed managers find they can drain off some of their tension by berating an employee, then the next time they feel irritated and tense they may be more likely to explode again. Think about it: The next time you are angry you are likely to repeat whatever relieved (and reinforced) your anger in the past.

What is the best way to manage your anger? Experts offer three suggestions:

- *Wait.* You can reduce the level of physiological arousal of anger by waiting. "It is true of the body as of arrows," noted Carol Tavris (1982), "what goes up must come down. Any emotional arousal will simmer down if you just wait long enough."

- *Find a healthy distraction or support.* Calm yourself by exercising, playing an instrument, or talking things through with a friend. Brain scans show that ruminating inwardly about why you are angry serves only to increase amygdala blood flow (Fabiansson et al., 2012).

- *Distance yourself.* Try to move away from the situation mentally, as if you are watching it unfold from a distance. Self-distancing reduces rumination, anger, and aggression (Kross & Ayduk, 2011; Mischkowski et al., 2012).

Anger is not always wrong. Used wisely, it can communicate strength and competence (Tiedens, 2001). Anger also motivates people to take action and achieve goals (Aarts et al., 2010). Controlled expressions of anger are more adaptive than either hostile outbursts or pent-up angry feelings. When James Averill (1983) asked people to recall or keep careful records of their experiences with anger, they often recalled reacting assertively rather than hurtfully. Their anger frequently led them to talk things over with the offender, thereby lessening the aggravation. Civility means not only keeping silent about trivial irritations but also communicating important ones clearly and assertively. A nonaccusing statement of feeling—perhaps letting one's housemate know that "I get irritated when the dirty dishes are left for me to clean up"—can help resolve conflicts. Anger that expresses a grievance in ways that promote reconciliation rather than retaliation can benefit a relationship.

What if someone's behavior really hurts you, and you cannot resolve the conflict? Research commends the age-old response of forgiveness. Without letting the offender off the hook or inviting further harm, forgiveness releases anger and calms the body. To explore the neural effects of forgiveness, German students had their brain scanned while someone thwarted their opportunity to earn money (Strang et al., 2014). Next, the students were asked whether or not they forgave the wrongdoer. Forgiveness increased blood flow to brain regions that help people understand their own emotions and make socially appropriate decisions.

RETRIEVAL PRACTICE

- Which one of the following is an effective strategy for reducing angry feelings?

  a. Retaliate verbally or physically.   c. Express anger in action or fantasy.

  b. Wait or "simmer down."   d. Review the grievance silently.

ANSWER: b

Happiness

39-3 What is the *feel-good, do-good phenomenon*, and what is the focus of positive psychology research?

People aspire to, and wish one another, health and happiness. And for good reason. Our state of happiness or unhappiness colors everything. Happy people perceive the world as safer and feel more confident. They are more decisive and cooperate more easily. They rate job applicants more favorably, savor their positive past experiences without dwelling on the negative, and are more socially connected. They live healthier and more energized and satisfied lives (DeNeve et al., 2013; Mauss et al., 2011). When your mood is gloomy, life as a whole seems depressing and meaningless—and you think more skeptically and attend more critically to your surroundings. Let your mood brighten, and your thinking broadens and becomes more playful and creative (Baas et al., 2008; Forgas, 2008b; Fredrickson, 2013).

This helps explain why college students' happiness helps predict their life course. One study showed that the happiest 20-year-olds were more likely to marry and less likely to divorce (Stutzer & Frey, 2006). In another study, which surveyed thousands of U.S. college students in 1976 and restudied them at age 37, happy students had gone on to earn significantly more money than their less-happy-than-average peers (Diener et al., 2002). When we are happy, our relationships, self-image, and hopes for the future also seem more promising.

Moreover—and this is one of psychology's most consistent findings—happiness doesn't just feel good, it *does* good. In study after study, a mood-boosting experience (finding money, succeeding on a challenging task, recalling a happy event) has made people more likely to give money, pick up someone's dropped papers, volunteer time, and do other good deeds. Psychologists call it the **feel-good, do-good phenomenon** (Salovey, 1990).

The reverse is also true: Doing good also promotes good feeling. Feeling good, for example, increases people's willingness to donate kidneys. And kidney donation leaves donors feeling good (Brethel-Haurwitz & Marsh, 2014). One survey of more than 200,000 people in 136 countries found that, nearly everywhere, people report feeling happier after spending money on others rather than on themselves (Aknin et al., 2013). Some happiness coaches harness the *do-good, feel-good phenonemon* as they assign people to perform a daily "random act of kindness" and to record the results.

Positive Psychology

William James was writing about the importance of happiness ("the secret motive for all [we] do") as early as 1902. By the 1960s, the *humanistic psychologists* were interested in advancing human fulfillment. In the twenty-first century, under the leadership of American Psychological Association past-president Martin Seligman, **positive psychology** is using scientific methods to study human flourishing. This young subfield includes studies of **subjective well-being**—our feelings of happiness (sometimes defined as a high ratio of positive to negative feelings) or sense of satisfaction with life. For example, researchers are exploring:

- *positive emotions* by assessing exercises and interventions aimed at increasing happiness (Schueller, 2010; Sin & Lyubomirsky, 2009).

- *positive health* by studying how positive emotions enhance and sustain physical well-being (Seligman, 2008; Seligman et al., 2011).

- *positive neuroscience* by examining the biological foundations of positive emotions, resilience, and social behavior (www.posneuroscience.org).

- *positive education* by evaluating educational efforts to increase students' engagement, resilience, character strengths, optimism, and sense of meaning (Seligman et al., 2009).

feel-good, do-good phenomenon people's tendency to be helpful when already in a good mood.

positive psychology the scientific study of human flourishing, with the goals of discovering and promoting strengths and virtues that help individuals and communities to thrive.

subjective well-being self-perceived happiness or satisfaction with life. Used along with measures of objective well-being (for example, physical and economic indicators) to evaluate people's quality of life.

Martin E. P. Seligman "The main purpose of a positive psychology is to measure, understand, and then build the human strengths and the civic virtues."

Courtesy of Martin Seligman

Taken together, satisfaction with the past, happiness with the present, and optimism about the future define the positive psychology movement's first pillar: *positive well-being.* Seligman views happiness as a by-product of a pleasant, engaged, and meaningful life.

Positive psychology is about building not just a pleasant life, says Seligman, but also a good life that engages one's skills, and a meaningful life that points beyond oneself. Thus, the second pillar, *positive character,* focuses on exploring and enhancing creativity, courage, compassion, integrity, self-control, leadership, wisdom, and spirituality.

The third pillar, *positive groups, communities,* and *cultures,* seeks to foster a positive social ecology. This includes healthy families, communal neighborhoods, effective schools, socially responsible media, and civil dialogue.

"Positive psychology," Seligman and colleagues have said (2005), "is an umbrella term for the study of positive emotions, positive character traits, and enabling institutions." Its focus differs from psychology's traditional interests during its first century, when attention was directed toward understanding and alleviating negative states—abuse and anxiety, depression and disease, prejudice and poverty. Indeed, articles on selected negative emotions since 1887 have outnumbered those on positive emotions by 17 to 1.

In ages past, times of relative peace and prosperity have enabled cultures to turn their attention from repairing weakness and damage to promoting what Seligman (2002) has called "the highest qualities of life." Prosperous fifth-century Athens nurtured philosophy and democracy. Flourishing fifteenth-century Florence nurtured great art. Victorian England, flush with the bounty of the British Empire, nurtured honor, discipline, and duty. In this millennium, Seligman believes, thriving Western cultures have a parallel opportunity to create, as a "humane, scientific monument," a more positive psychology, concerned not only with weakness and damage but also with strength and virtue. Thanks to his leadership, the movement has gained strength, with supporters in 77 countries from Croatia to China (IPPA, 2009, 2010; Seligman, 2004, 2011). Their research on human flourishing has given us insights into many aspects of our well-being, including studies of the predictors of happiness.

Will psychology have a more positive mission in this century? Without slighting the need to repair damage and cure disease, positive psychology's proponents hope so. With *American Psychologist* and *British Psychologist* special issues devoted to positive psychology; with many new books; with networked scientists working in worldwide research groups; and with prizes, research awards, summer institutes, and a graduate program promoting positive psychology scholarship, these psychologists have reason to be positive. Cultivating a more positive psychology mission may help Seligman achieve his most ambitious goal: By the year 2051, 51 percent of the world will be "flourishing." "It's in our hands not only to witness this," he says, "but to take part in making this happen" (Seligman, 2011).

The Short Life of Emotional Ups and Downs

39-4 How do time, wealth, adaptation, and comparison affect our happiness levels?

Are some days of the week happier than others? In what is likely psychology's biggest-ever data sample, social psychologist Adam Kramer (at my [DM's] request and in cooperation with Facebook) did a naturalistic observation of emotion words in "billions" of status updates. After eliminating exceptional days, such as holidays, he tracked the frequency of positive and negative emotion words by day of the week. The most positive moods days? Friday and Saturday (**FIGURE 39.3**). A similar analysis of emotion-related words in 59 million Twitter messages found Friday to Sunday the week's happiest days (Golder & Macy, 2011). For you, too?

Over the long run, our emotional ups and downs tend to balance out. This is true even over the course of the day (**FIGURE 39.4**). Positive emotion rises over the early to middle part of most days and then drops off (Kahneman et al., 2004; Watson, 2000). A stressful event—an argument, a sick child, a car problem—can trigger a bad mood. No

"No happiness lasts for long."

Seneca, *Agamemnon,* c.e. 60

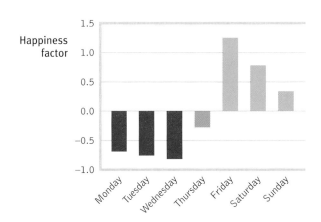

▼ FIGURE 39.3
Using Web science to track happy days Adam Kramer (personal correspondence, 2010) tracked positive and negative emotion words in many "billions" (the exact number is proprietary information) of status updates of U.S. users of Facebook between September 7, 2007, and November 17, 2010.

surprise there. But by the next day, the gloom nearly always lifts (Affleck et al., 1994; Bolger et al., 1989; Stone & Neale, 1984). Our overall judgments of our lives often show lingering effects of good or bad events, but our moods typically rebound (Luhmann et al., 2012). If anything, people tend to bounce back from a bad day to a *better*-than-usual good mood the following day.

Even when negative events drag us down for longer periods, our bad mood usually ends. A romantic breakup feels devastating, but eventually the wound heals. In one study, faculty members up for tenure expected their lives would be deflated by a negative decision. Actually, 5 to 10 years later, their happiness level was about the same as for those who received tenure (Gilbert et al., 1998).

Grief over the loss of a loved one or anxiety after a severe trauma (such as child abuse, rape, or the terrors of war) can linger. But usually, even tragedy is not permanently depressing. People who become blind or paralyzed may not completely recover their previous well-being, but those with an agreeable personality usually recover near-normal levels of day-to-day happiness (Boyce & Wood, 2011). So do those who must go on kidney dialysis or have permanent colostomies (Riis et al., 2005; Smith et al., 2009). Even if you lose the use of all four limbs, explained psychologist Daniel Kahneman (2005), "you will gradually start thinking of other things, and the more time you spend thinking of other things the less miserable you are going to be." Contrary to what many people believe, most patients "locked-in" a motionless body do not indicate they want to die (Bruno et al., 2008, 2011; Nizzi et al., 2012; Smith & Delargy, 2005).

The surprising reality: *We overestimate the duration of our emotions and underestimate our resiliency and capacity to adapt.* (As one who inherited hearing loss with a trajectory toward that of my mother, who spent the last 13 years of her life completely deaf, I [DM] take heart from these findings.)

Human resilience Seven weeks after her 1994 wedding, Anna Putt of South Midlands, England, shown here with her husband, Des, suffered a brainstem stroke that left her "locked-in." For months after, she recalled, "I was paralyzed from the neck down and was unable to communicate. These were VERY frightening times. But with encouragement from family, friends, faith, and medical staff, I tried to keep positive." In the ensuing three years, she became able to "talk" (by nodding at letters), to steer an electric wheelchair with her head, and to use a computer (with head movements that guide a cursor). Despite her paralysis, she has reported that "I enjoy going out in the fresh air. My motto is 'Don't look back, move forward.' God would not want me to stop trying and I have no intention of doing so. Life is what you make of it!"

"Weeping may tarry for the night, but joy comes with the morning."

Psalm 30:5

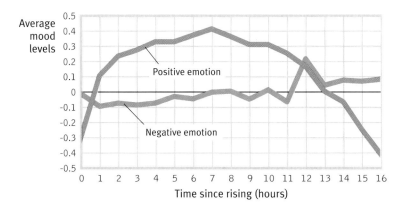

▼ FIGURE 39.4
Moods across the day When psychologist David Watson (2000) sampled nearly 4500 mood reports from 150 people, he found this pattern of variation from the average levels of positive and negative emotions.

"Money won't make you happy, Waldron. So instead of a raise, I'm giving a Prozac."

"But on the positive side, money can't buy happiness—so who cares?"

"Australians are three times richer than their parents and grandparents were in the 1950s, but they are not happier."

A Manifesto for Well-Being, 2005

Wealth and Well-Being

"Do you think you would be happier if you made more money?" *Yes,* replied 73 percent of Americans in a 2006 Gallup poll. How important is "Being very well off financially?" *Very important,* say 82 percent of entering U.S. collegians (**FIGURE 39.5**).

And to a point, wealth does correlate with well-being. Consider:

- In most countries, and especially in poor countries, individuals with lots of money are typically happier than those who struggle to afford life's basic needs (Diener & Biswas-Diener, 2009; Howell & Howell, 2008; Lucas & Schimmack, 2009). And, as we will see, they often enjoy better health than those stressed by poverty and lack of control over their lives.

- People in rich countries also experience greater well-being than those in poor countries (Diener et al., 2009; Inglehart, 2008 ; Tay & Diener, 2011). The same is true for those in higher-income American states (Oswald & Wu, 2010).

So, it seems that having enough money to buy your way out of hunger and to have a sense of control over your life does buy some happiness (Fischer & Boer, 2011). As Australian data confirm, the power of more money to increase happiness is significant at low incomes and diminishes as income rises (Cummins, 2006). A $1000 annual wage increase does a lot more for the average person in Malawi than for the average person in Switzerland. This implies that raising low incomes will do more to increase happiness than raising high incomes.

Once one has enough money for comfort and security, piling up more and more matters less and less. Experiencing luxury diminishes our savoring of life's simpler pleasures (Quoidbach et al., 2010). If you've skied the Alps, your neighborhood sledding hill pales.

And consider this: During the last half-century, the average U.S. citizen's buying power almost tripled. Did this greater wealth—enabling twice as many cars per person, not to mention iPads, smartphones, and HDTVs—also buy more happiness? As **FIGURE 39.6** shows, the average American, though certainly richer, is not a bit happier. In 1957, some 35 percent said they were "very happy," as did slightly fewer—33 percent—in 2012. Much the same has been true of Europe, Australia, and Japan, where increasing real incomes have *not* produced increasing happiness (Australian Unity, 2008; Diener & Biswas-Diener, 2002, 2009; Di Tella & MacCulloch, 2010). Ditto China, where living standards have risen but life satisfaction has not (Davey & Rato, 2012; Easterlin et al., 2012). These findings lob a bombshell at modern materialism: *Economic growth in affluent countries has provided no apparent boost to morale or social well-being.*

Ironically, in every culture, those who strive hardest for wealth have tended to live with lower well-being, especially when they seek money to prove themselves, gain power, or show off rather than support their families (Niemiec et al., 2009; Ryan, 1999; Srivastava et al., 2001). Those who instead strive for intimacy, personal growth, and community contribution experience a higher quality of life (Kasser, 2002, 2011).

▼ FIGURE 39.5
The changing materialism of entering collegians Surveys of more than 200,000 entering U.S. collegians per year have revealed an increasing desire for wealth after 1970. (Data from *The American Freshman* surveys, UCLA, 1966 to 2013.)

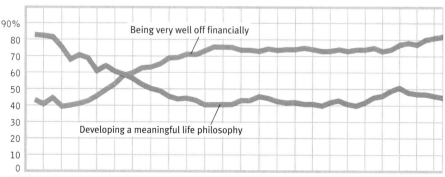

Percentage rating goal as very important or essential

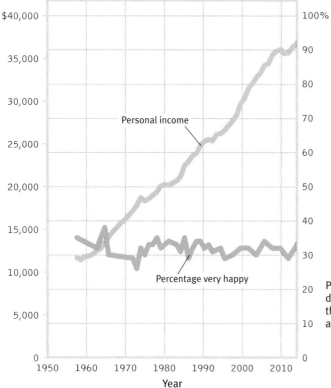

Two Psychological Phenomena: Adaptation and Comparison

Two psychological principles explain why, for those who are not poor, more money buys little more than a temporary surge of happiness and why our emotions seem attached to elastic bands that pull us back from highs or lows. In its own way, each principle suggests that happiness is relative.

Happiness Is Relative to Our Own Experience The **adaptation-level phenomenon** describes our tendency to judge various stimuli in comparison with our past experiences. As psychologist Harry Helson (1898–1977) explained, we adjust our *neutral* levels—the points at which sounds seem neither loud nor soft, temperatures neither hot nor cold, events neither pleasant nor unpleasant—based on our experience. We then notice and react to variations up or down from these levels. Thus, after an initial surge of pleasure, improvements become our "new normal," and we then require something even better to give us another surge of happiness. Yesterday's marvelous becomes today's mundane.

So, could we ever create a permanent social paradise? Probably not (Campbell, 1975; Di Tella et al., 2010). People who have experienced a recent windfall—from a lottery, an inheritance, or a surging economy—typically feel elated (Diener & Oishi, 2000; Gardner & Oswald, 2007). So would you, if you woke up tomorrow to your utopia—perhaps a world with no bills, no ills, perfect scores, and someone who loves you unreservedly. But after a time, you would gradually recalibrate your adaptation level, and you would adjust your new neutral level to include these new experiences. Before long, you would again sometimes feel gratified (when events exceed your expectations) and sometimes feel deprived (when they fall below), and sometimes feel neutral. *The point to remember:* Feelings of satisfaction and dissatisfaction, success and failure are judgments we make based partly on our prior experience. Satisfaction, as Richard Ryan (1999) said, "has a short half life." Ditto disappointment, which means that you may bounce back from a setback sooner than you expect.

> adaptation-level phenomenon our tendency to form judgments (of sounds, of lights, of income) relative to a neutral level defined by our prior experience.

> "Continued pleasures wear off. . . . Pleasure is always contingent upon change and disappears with continuous satisfaction."
>
> Dutch psychologist Nico Frijda (1988)

> "I have a 'fortune cookie maxim' that I'm very proud of: Nothing in life is quite as important as you think it is while you are thinking about it. So, nothing will ever make you as happy as you think it will."
>
> Nobel laureate psychologist Daniel Kahneman, Gallup interview, "What Were They Thinking?" 2005

relative deprivation the perception that one is worse off relative to those with whom one compares oneself.

The effect of comparison with others helps explain why students of a given level of academic ability tended to have a higher academic self-concept if they attended a school where most other students were not exceptionally able (Marsh & Parker, 1984). If you were near the top of your graduating class, you might feel inferior upon entering a college or university where all students were near the top of their class.

"Comparison is the thief of joy."

Attributed to Theodore Roosevelt

"*Researchers say I'm not happier for being richer, but do you know how much researchers make?*"

Happiness Is Relative to Others' Success We are always comparing ourselves with others. And whether we feel good or bad depends on who those others are (Lyubomirsky, 2001). We are slow-witted or clumsy only when others are smarter or more agile. When we sense that we are worse off than others with whom we compare ourselves, we are experiencing **relative deprivation.** Thus, when Miguel Cabrera achieved an 8-year, $248 million baseball contract, his deal surely made him temporarily happy, but it likely also diminished other star players' satisfaction with their lesser, multimillion-dollar contracts. Likewise, the economic surge that has made some urban Chinese newly affluent appears to have fueled among other Chinese a sense of relative deprivation (Davey & Rato, 2012: Easterlin et al., 2012). Seeing others succeed may inflate our own expectations, and when expectations soar above attainments, the result is disappointment.

Satisfaction stems less from our income than from our income rank (Boyce et al., 2010). Better to make $50,000 when others make $25,000 than to make $100,000 when friends, neighbors, and co-workers make $200,000 (Solnick & Hemenway, 1998, 2009). Likewise, a raise will make you happier if it's greater than the raise received by others around you (Graham, 2011).

Such comparisons help us understand why the middle- and upper-income people in a given country, who can compare themselves with the relatively poor, tend to have greater life satisfaction than their less fortunate compatriots. Nevertheless, once people reach a moderate income level, further increases buy little more happiness. Why? Because as people climb the ladder of success they mostly compare themselves with local peers who are at or above their current level (Gruder, 1977; Suls & Tesch, 1978; Zell & Alicke, 2010). "Beggars do not envy millionaires, though of course they will envy other beggars who are more successful," noted British philosopher Bertrand Russell (1930, p. 90). Thus, "Napoleon envied Caesar, Caesar envied Alexander, and Alexander, I daresay, envied Hercules, who never existed. You cannot, therefore, get away from envy by means of success alone, for there will always be in history or legend some person even more successful than you are" (pp. 68–69).

Over the last half century, inequality in Western countries has increased. The rising economic tide shown in Figure 39.6 has lifted the yachts faster than the rowboats. Does it matter? Places with great inequality have higher crime rates, obesity, anxiety, and drug use, and lower life expectancy (Kawachi et al., 1999; Ratcliff, 2013; Wilkinson & Pickett, 2009). Times and places with greater income inequality also tend to be less happy—a result that people's social comparisons help explain (Hagerty, 2000; Helliwell et al., 2013; Oishi et al., 2011).

Just as comparing ourselves with those who are better off creates envy, so counting our blessings as we compare ourselves with those worse off boosts our contentment. In one study, University of Wisconsin-Milwaukee women considered others' deprivation and suffering (Dermer et al., 1979). They viewed vivid depictions of how grim life was in Milwaukee in 1900. They imagined and then wrote about various personal tragedies, such as being burned and disfigured. Later, the women expressed greater satisfaction with their own lives. Similarly, when mildly depressed people have read about someone who was even more depressed, they felt somewhat better (Gibbons, 1986). "I cried because I had no shoes," states a Persian saying, "until I met a man who had no feet."

What Predicts Our Happiness Levels?

39-5 What are some predictors of happiness?

Happy people share many characteristics (**TABLE 39.1**). But why are some people normally so joyful and others so somber? Here, as in so many other areas, the answer is found in the interplay between nature and nurture.

▼ TABLE 39.1
Happiness Is . . .

Researchers Have Found That Happy People Tend to	However, Happiness Seems Not Much Related to Other Factors, Such as
Have high self-esteem (in individualist countries).	Age.
Be optimistic, outgoing, and agreeable.	Gender (women are more often depressed, but also more often joyful).
Have close friendships or a satisfying marriage.	Physical attractiveness.
Have work and leisure that engage their skills.	
Have an active religious faith (especially in more religious cultures).	
Sleep well and exercise.	

* *Sources:* Summarized from DeNeve & Cooper (1998); Diener et al. (2003, 2011); Headey et al. (2010); Lucas et al. (2004); Myers (1993, 2000); Myers & Diener (1995, 1996); and Steel et al. (2008). Veenhoven (2014) offers a database of 13,000+ correlates of happiness at worlddatabaseofhappiness.eur.nl.

Genes matter. In one study of hundreds of identical and fraternal twins, about 50 percent of the difference among people's happiness ratings was heritable (Gigantesco et al., 2011; Lykken & Tellegen, 1996). Other twin studies report similar or slightly less heritability (Bartels & Boomsma, 2009; Lucas, 2008; Nes et al., 2010). Identical twins raised apart are often similarly happy. Moreover, researchers are now drilling down to identify how specific genes influence our happiness (De Neve et al., 2012; Fredrickson et al., 2013).

But our personal history and our culture matter, too. On the personal level, as we have seen, our emotions tend to balance around a level defined by our experience. On the cultural level, groups vary in the traits they value. Self-esteem and achievement matter more to Westerners, who value individualism. Social acceptance and harmony matter more to those in communal cultures such as Japan, which stress family and community (Diener et al., 2003; Fulmer et al., 2010; Uchida & Kitayama, 2009).

Depending on our genes, our outlook, and our recent experiences, our happiness seems to fluctuate around our "happiness set point," which disposes some people to be ever upbeat and others more negative. Even so, after following thousands of lives over two decades, researchers have determined that our satisfaction with life is not fixed (Lucas & Donnellan, 2007). Happiness rises and falls, and can be influenced by factors that are under our control. A striking example: In a long-term German study, married partners were as similarly satisfied with their lives as were identical twins (Schimmack & Lucas, 2007). Relationship quality matters.

If we can enhance our happiness on an *individual* level, could we use happiness research to refocus our *national* priorities more on the pursuit of happiness? Many psychologists believe we could. Ed Diener (2006, 2009, 2013), supported by 52 colleagues, has proposed ways in which nations might measure national well-being. "Policymakers should be interested in subjective well-being not only because of its inherent value to citizens, but also because individuals' subjective well-being can have positive spillover benefits for the society as a whole."

Happiness research offers new ways to assess the impacts of various public policies, argue Diener and his colleagues. Happy societies are not only prosperous, but also places where people trust one another, feel free, and enjoy close relationships (Helliwell et al., 2013; Oishi & Schimmack, 2010). Thus, in debates about the minimum wage, economic inequality, tax rates, divorce laws, health care, and city planning, people's psychological well-being should be a prime consideration—a point affirmed by 41 nations that have added well-being measures to their national

"*I could cry when I think of the years I wasted accumulating money, only to learn that my cheerful disposition is genetic.*"

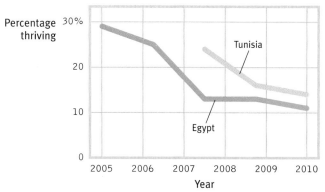

▼ FIGURE 39.7
Declining well-being in Egypt and Tunisia prior to popular revolts In Gallup surveys, the percentage of people who were "thriving" (rating their life satisfaction 7 or higher and projecting their next five years at 8 or higher on a 10-step scale) declined in advance of 2011 demonstrations that led to a change of government. (Data from Clifton & Morales, 2011.)

agendas (Diener, 2013). Britain's Annual Population Survey, for example, asks its citizens how satisfied they are with their lives, how worthwhile they judge their lives, and how happy and how anxious they felt yesterday (BLS, 2012). The Organisation for Economic Co-operation and Development (2013) has offered guidelines to its 34 member nations for how to assess citizen's well-being using such questions. The predictive power of national well-being assessments was apparent in 2011, as the governments of Egypt and Tunisia succumbed to popular uprisings in the aftermath of declining life satisfaction (**FIGURE** 39.7).

Evidence-Based Suggestions For a Happier Life[1]

Your happiness, like your cholesterol level, is genetically influenced. Yet as cholesterol is also influenced by diet and exercise, so happiness is partly under your control (Layous & Lyubomirsky, 2014; Nes, 2010). Here are 11 research-based suggestions for improving your mood and increasing your satisfaction with life.

1. *Realize that enduring happiness may not come from financial success.* We adapt to change by adjusting our expectations. Neither wealth, nor any other circumstance we long for, will guarantee happiness.

2. *Take control of your time.* Happy people feel in control of their lives. To master your use of time, set goals and break them into daily aims. This may be frustrating at first because we all tend to overestimate how much we will accomplish in any given day. The good news is that we generally *underestimate* how much we can accomplish in a year, given just a little progress every day.

3. *Act happy.* Research shows that people who are manipulated into a smiling expression feel better. So put on a happy face. Talk *as if* you feel positive self-esteem, are optimistic, and are outgoing. We can often act our way into a happier state of mind.

4. *Seek work and leisure that engage your skills.* Happy people often are in a zone called *flow*—absorbed in tasks that challenge but don't overwhelm them. The most expensive forms of leisure (sitting on a yacht) often provide less flow experience than simpler forms, such as gardening, socializing, or craft work.

5. *Buy shared experiences rather than things.* Compared with money spent on stuff, money buys more happiness when spent on experiences that you look forward to, enjoy, remember, and talk about (Carter & Gilovich, 2010; Kumar & Gilovich, 2013). This is especially so for socially shared experiences (Caprariello & Reis, 2012). The shared experience of a college education may cost a lot, but, as pundit Art Buchwald said, "The best things in life aren't things."

6. *Join the "movement" movement.* Aerobic exercise can relieve mild depression and anxiety as it promotes health and energy. Sound minds reside in sound bodies. Off your duffs, couch potatoes!

---

1. Digested from David G. Myers, *The Pursuit of Happiness* (Harper).

RubberBall Selects/Alamy

7. *Give your body the sleep it wants.* Happy people live active lives yet reserve time for renewing sleep and solitude. Many people suffer from sleep debt, with resulting fatigue, diminished alertness, and gloomy moods.

8. *Give priority to close relationships.* Intimate friendships can help you weather difficult times. Confiding is good for soul and body. Compared with unhappy people, happy people engage in less superficial small talk and more meaningful conversations (Mehl et al., 2010). So resolve to nurture your closest relationships by *not* taking your loved ones for granted. This means displaying to them the sort of kindness you display to others, affirming them, playing together, and sharing together.

9. *Focus beyond self.* Reach out to those in need. Perform acts of kindness. Happiness increases helpfulness (those who feel good do good). But doing good also makes us feel good.

10. *Count your blessings and record your gratitude.* Keeping a gratitude journal heightens well-being (Emmons, 2007; Seligman et al., 2005). When something good happens, such as an achievement, take time to appreciate and savor the experience (Sheldon & Lyubomirsky, 2012). Record positive events and why they occurred. Express your gratitude to others.

11. *Nurture your spiritual self.* For many people, faith provides a support community, a reason to focus beyond self, and a sense of purpose and hope. That helps explain why people active in faith communities report greater-than-average happiness and often cope well with crises.

RETRIEVAL PRACTICE

- Which of the following factors do NOT predict self-reported happiness? Which factors are better predictors?

  a. Age   d. Gender

  b. Personality traits   e. Sleep and exercise

  c. Close relationships   f. Religious faith

ANSWERS: Age and gender (a. and d.) do NOT effectively predict happiness levels. Better predictors are personality traits, close relationships, sleep and exercise, and religious faith (b., c., e., and f.).

---

39 REVIEW Experiencing Emotion

LEARNING OBJECTIVES

RETRIEVAL PRACTICE Take a moment to answer each of these Learning Objective Questions (repeated here from within this module). Then turn to Appendix C, Complete Module Reviews, to check your answers. Research suggests that trying to answer these questions on your own will improve your long-term retention (McDaniel et al., 2009).

39-1 What are some basic emotions, and what two dimensions help differentiate them?

39-2 What are the causes and consequences of anger?

39-3 What is the *feel-good, do-good phenomenon,* and what is the focus of positive psychology research?

39-4 How do time, wealth, adaptation, and comparison affect our happiness levels?

39-5 What are some predictors of happiness?

TERMS AND CONCEPTS TO REMEMBER

RETRIEVAL PRACTICE Test yourself on these terms by trying to write down the definition before flipping back to the page number referenced to check your answer.

catharsis, p. 477

feel-good, do-good phenomenon, p. 479

positive psychology, p. 479

subjective well-being, p. 479

adaptation-level phenomenon, p. 483

relative deprivation, p. 484

Use 🔄 LearningCurve to create your personalized study plan, which will direct you to the resources that will help you most in 🔄 LaunchPad.

40 Stress and Illness

Extreme stress From the audio recording of a 911 caller reporting Ben Carpenter's distress: "You are not going to believe this. There is a semitruck pushing a guy in a wheelchair on Red Arrow highway!"

HOW OFTEN DO YOU EXPERIENCE stress in your daily life? Never? Rarely? Sometimes? Or frequently? When pollsters put a similar question to other collegians, some 85 percent recalled experiencing stress during the last three months—and most said it had disrupted their schoolwork at least once (Associated Press, 2009). On entering college or university, 18 percent of men and 39 percent of women reported having been "frequently overwhelmed" by all they had to do during the past year (Pryor et al., 2011).

Stress often strikes without warning. Imagine being 21-year-old Ben Carpenter, who experienced the world's wildest and fastest wheelchair ride. As he crossed a street, his wheelchair handles got stuck in a semi-truck's grille. The driver, unaware of the mishap, took off down the highway, pushing the wheelchair at 50 miles per hour! "It was very scary," said Ben, who has muscular dystrophy.

In this section, we take a closer look at stress—what it is and how it affects our health and well-being. Let's begin with some basic terms.

Stress: Some Basic Concepts

40-1 What events provoke stress responses, and how do we respond and adapt to stress?

Stress is a slippery concept. We sometimes use the word informally to describe threats or challenges ("Ben was under a lot of stress"), and at other times our responses ("Ben experienced acute stress"). To a psychologist, the dangerous truck ride was a *stressor*. Ben's physical and emotional responses were a *stress reaction*. And the process by which he related to the threat was *stress*. Thus, **stress is the process of appraising and responding to a threatening or challenging event** (**FIGURE 40.1**). Stress arises less from events themselves than from how we appraise them (Lazarus, 1998). One person, alone in a house, ignores its creaking sounds and experiences no stress; someone else suspects an intruder and becomes alarmed. One person regards a new job as a welcome challenge; someone else appraises it as risking failure.

▼ FIGURE 40.1

Stress appraisal The events of our lives flow through a psychological filter. How we appraise an event influences how much stress we experience and how effectively we respond.

Stressful event
(tough math test)

Appraisal

| Threat ("Yikes! This is beyond me!") | Challenge ("I've got to apply all I know.") |

Response

| Stressed to distraction | Aroused, focused |

When short-lived, or when perceived as challenges, stressors can have positive effects. A momentary stress can mobilize the immune system for fending off infections and healing wounds (Segerstrom, 2007). Stress also arouses and motivates us to conquer problems. In a Gallup World Poll, those who were stressed but not depressed reported being energized and satisfied with their lives. This is the opposite of the lethargy reported by those who were depressed but not stressed (Ng et al., 2009). Championship athletes, successful entertainers, and great teachers and leaders all thrive and excel when aroused by a challenge (Blascovich & Mendes, 2010). Compared with nonleaders, military and business leaders produce lower-than-average levels of stress hormones and report lower anxiety levels (Sherman et al., 2012). Having conquered a major stressor, some people emerge with stronger self-esteem and a deepened spirituality and sense of purpose. Indeed, experiencing some stress early in life builds resilience (Seery, 2011). Adversity can beget growth.

But extreme or prolonged stress can harm us. Demanding jobs that mentally exhaust workers also damage their physical health (Huang et al., 2010). Pregnant women with overactive stress systems tend to have shorter pregnancies, which pose health risks for their infants (Entringer et al., 2011).

So there is an interplay between our heads and our health. That isn't surprising. *Behavioral medicine* research provides a reminder of one of contemporary psychology's overriding themes: *Mind and body interact; everything psychological is simultaneously physiological.* Before exploring that interplay, let's look more closely at stressors and stress reactions.

Stressors—Things That Push Our Buttons

Stressors fall into three main types: catastrophes, significant life changes, and daily hassles. All can be toxic.

Catastrophes Catastrophes are unpredictable large-scale events, such as earthquakes, floods, wildfires, and storms. After such events, damage to emotional and physical health can be significant. In the four months after Hurricane Katrina, New Orleans' suicide rate reportedly tripled (Saulny, 2006). And in surveys taken in the three weeks after the 9/11 terrorist attacks, 58 percent of Americans said they were experiencing greater-than-average arousal and anxiety (Silver et al., 2002). In the New York area, people were especially likely to report such symptoms, and sleeping pill prescriptions rose by a reported 28 percent (HMHL, 2002; NSF, 2001). Extensively watching 9/11 terrorist attack television footage predicted worse health outcomes two to three years later (Silver et al., 2013).

> **stress** the process by which we perceive and respond to certain events, called *stressors*, that we appraise as threatening or challenging.

> "Too many parents make life hard for their children by trying, too zealously, to make it easy for them".
>
> Johann Wolfgang von Goethe (1749–1832), German author

Toxic stress Unpredictable large-scale events, such as the severe earthquake that devastated Haiti in 2010, trigger significant levels of stress-related ills. When an earthquake struck Los Angeles in 1994, sudden-death heart attacks increased fivefold. Most occurred in the first two hours after the quake and near its center and were unrelated to physical exertion (Muller & Verrier, 1996).

© Julien Tack

For those who respond to catastrophes by relocating to another country, the stress may be twofold if the trauma of uprooting and family separation combine with the challenges of adjusting to a new culture's language, ethnicity, climate, and social norms (Pipher, 2002; Williams & Berry, 1991). In the first half-year, before their morale begins to rebound, newcomers often experience culture shock and deteriorating well-being (Markovizky & Samid, 2008). In years to come, such relocations may become increasingly common due to climate change.

Significant Life Changes Life transitions—leaving home, becoming divorced, losing a job, having a loved one die—are often keenly felt. Even happy events, such as getting married, can be stressful. Many of these changes happen during young adulthood. One survey, in which 15,000 Canadian adults were asked whether "You are trying to take on too many things at once," found the highest stress levels among young adults (Statistics Canada, 1999). Young adult stress appeared again when 650,000 Americans were asked if they had experienced a lot of stress "yesterday" (**FIGURE 40.2**).

Some psychologists study the health effects of life changes by following people over time. Others compare the life changes recalled by those who have or have not suffered a specific health problem, such as a heart attack. In such studies, those recently widowed, fired, or divorced have been more vulnerable to disease (Dohrenwend et al., 1982; Strully, 2009). One Finnish study of 96,000 widowed people found that the survivor's risk of death doubled in the week following a partner's death (Kaprio et al., 1987). A cluster of crises—losing a job, home, and partner—puts one even more at risk.

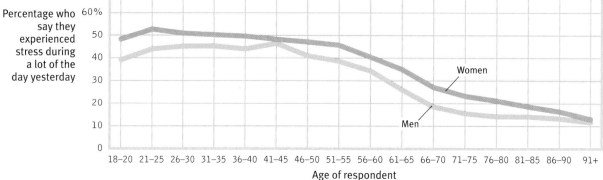

▼ **FIGURE 40.2**
Age and stress A Gallup-Healthways survey of more than 650,000 Americans during 2008 and 2009 found daily stress highest among younger adults. (Data from Newport & Pelham, 2009.)

Daily Hassles Events don't have to remake our lives to cause stress. Stress also comes from *daily hassles*—spotty phone connections, aggravating housemates, long lines at the store, too many things to do, e-mail and text spam, and loud talkers behind us (Lazarus, 1990; Pascoe & Richman, 2009; Ruffin, 1993). Some people shrug off such hassles. For others, the everyday annoyances add up and take a toll on health and well-being.

Many people face more significant daily hassles. As the Great Recession of 2008–2009 bottomed out, Americans' most oft-cited stressors related to money (76 percent), work (70 percent), and the economy (65 percent) (APA, 2010). In impoverished areas—where many people routinely face inadequate income, unemployment, solo parenting, and overcrowding—such stressors are part of daily life.

Daily economic pressures may be compounded by anti-gay prejudice or racism, which—like other stressors—can have both psychological and physical consequences (Lick et al., 2013; Pascoe & Richman, 2009; Schetter et al., 2013). Thinking that some of the people you encounter each day will dislike you, distrust you, or doubt your abilities makes daily life stressful. When prolonged, such stress takes a toll on our health, especially our cardiovascular system. For many African-Americans, stress helps drive up blood pressure levels (Mays et al., 2007; Ong et al., 2009).

The Stress Response System

Medical interest in stress dates back to Hippocrates (460–377 B.C.E.). In the 1920s, Walter Cannon (1929) confirmed that the stress response is part of a unified mind-body system. He observed that extreme cold, lack of oxygen, and emotion-arousing events all trigger an outpouring of the stress hormones epinephrine and norepinephrine from the core of the adrenal glands. When alerted by any of a number of brain pathways, the sympathetic nervous system arouses us, preparing the body for the wonderfully adaptive response that Cannon called *fight or flight*. It increases heart rate and respiration, diverts blood from digestion to the skeletal muscles, dulls feelings of pain, and releases sugar and fat from the body's stores.

Since Cannon's time, physiologists have identified an additional stress response system. On orders from the cerebral cortex (via the hypothalamus and pituitary gland), the outer part of the adrenal glands secrete *glucocorticoid* stress hormones such as *cortisol*. The two systems work at different speeds, explained biologist Robert Sapolsky (2003): "In a fight-or-flight scenario, epinephrine is the one handing out guns; glucocorticoids are the ones drawing up blueprints for new aircraft carriers needed for the war effort." The epinephrine guns were firing at high speed during an experiment inadvertently conducted on a British Airways San Francisco to London flight. Three hours after takeoff, a mistakenly played message told passengers the plane was about to crash into the sea. Although the flight crew immediately recognized the error and tried to calm the terrified passengers, several required medical assistance (Associated Press, 1999).

Canadian scientist Hans Selye's (1936, 1976) 40 years of research on stress extended Cannon's findings. His studies of animals' reactions to various stressors, such as electric shock and surgery, helped make stress a major concept in both psychology and medicine. Selye proposed that the body's adaptive response to stress is so general that, like a single burglar alarm, it sounds, no matter what intrudes. He named this response the **general adaptation syndrome (GAS),** and he saw it as a three-phase process (**FIGURE 40.3**). Let's say you suffer a physical or an emotional trauma.

general adaptation syndrome (GAS) Selye's concept of the body's adaptive response to stress in three phases—alarm, resistance, exhaustion.

▼ FIGURE 40.3
Selye's general adaptation syndrome When a gold and copper mine in Chile collapsed in 2010, family and friends rushed to the scene, fearing the worst. Many of those holding vigil outside the mine were nearly exhausted with the stress of waiting and worrying when, after 18 days, they received news that all 33 of the miners inside were alive and well.

- In *Phase 1*, you have an *alarm reaction*, as your sympathetic nervous system is suddenly activated. Your heart rate zooms. Blood is diverted to your skeletal muscles. You feel the faintness of shock. With your resources mobilized, you are now ready to fight back.

- During *Phase 2, resistance,* your temperature, blood pressure, and respiration remain high. Your adrenal glands pump hormones into your bloodstream. You are fully engaged, summoning all your resources to meet the challenge. As time passes, with no relief from stress, your body's reserves begin to dwindle.

- You have reached *Phase 3, exhaustion.* With exhaustion, you become more vulnerable to illness or even, in extreme cases, collapse and death.

Selye's basic point: Although the human body copes well with temporary stress, prolonged stress can damage it. Childhood stress gets under the skin, leading to greater adult stress responses and disease risk (Miller et al., 2011). The brain's production of new neurons also slows and some neural circuits degenerate (Dias-Ferreira et al., 2009; Mirescu & Gould, 2006). One study found shortening of *telomeres* (DNA pieces at the ends of chromosomes) in women who suffered enduring stress as caregivers for children with serious disorders (Epel et al., 2004). Telomere shortening is a normal part of the aging process; when telomeres get too short, the cell can no longer divide and it ultimately dies. The most stressed women had cells that looked a decade older than their chronological age, which helps explain why severe stress seems to age people. Even fearful, easily stressed rats have been found to die sooner (after about 600 days) than their more confident siblings, which average 700-day life spans (Cavigelli & McClintock, 2003).

There are other ways to deal with stress. One option is a common response to a loved one's death: Withdraw. Pull back. Conserve energy. Faced with an extreme disaster, such as a ship sinking, some people become paralyzed by fear. Another option (found often among women) is to give and seek support (Taylor et al., 2000, 2006). This **tend-and-befriend** response is demonstrated in the outpouring of help after natural disasters.

Facing stress, men more often than women tend to withdraw socially, turn to alcohol, or become aggressive. Women more often respond to stress by nurturing and banding together. This may in part be due to *oxytocin,* a stress-moderating hormone associated with pair bonding in animals and released by cuddling, massage, and breast feeding in humans (Campbell, 2010; Taylor, 2006). Brain scans reflect such stress-response differences: In women, areas important for face processing and empathy become more active; in men, these areas become less active (Mather et al., 2010).

It often pays to spend our resources in fighting or fleeing an external threat. But we do so at a cost. When stress is momentary, the cost is small. When stress persists, the cost may be much higher, in the form of lowered resistance to infections and other threats to mental and physical well-being.

"You may be suffering from what's known as full-nest syndrome."

RETRIEVAL PRACTICE

- The stress response system: When alerted to a negative, uncontrollable event, our _____ nervous system arouses us. Heart rate and respiration _____ (increase/decrease). Blood is diverted from digestion to the skeletal _____. The body releases sugar and fat. All this prepares the body for the _____ - _____ - _____ response.

ANSWERS: sympathetic; increase; muscles; fight-or-flight

---

tend and befriend under stress, people (especially women) often provide support to others (tend) and bond with and seek support from others (befriend).

health psychology a subfield of psychology that provides psychology's contribution to behavioral medicine.

psychoneuroimmunology the study of how psychological, neural, and endocrine processes together affect the immune system and resulting health.

Stress and Vulnerability to Disease

40-2 How does stress make us more vulnerable to disease?

To study how stress, and healthy and unhealthy behaviors influence health and illness, psychologists and physicians have created the interdisciplinary field of *behavioral medicine,* integrating behavioral and medical knowledge. **Health psychology** provides psychology's contribution to behavioral medicine. The subfield of **psychoneuroimmunology,** focuses on mind-body interactions (Kiecolt-Glaser, 2009). This awkward name makes sense when said slowly: Your thoughts and feelings *(psycho)* influence your brain *(neuro),* which influences the endocrine hormones that affect your disease-fighting immune system. And this subfield is the study of *(ology)* those interactions.

If you've ever had a stress headache, or felt your blood pressure rise with anger, you don't need to be convinced that our psychological states have physiological effects. Stress can even leave you less able to fight off disease because your nervous and endocrine systems influence your immune system (Sternberg, 2009). You can think of the immune system as a complex surveillance system. When it functions properly, it keeps you healthy by isolating and destroying bacteria, viruses, and other invaders. Four types of cells are active in these search-and-destroy missions (**FIGURE 40.4**).

- *B lymphocytes* (white blood cells) mature in the *b*one marrow and release antibodies that fight bacterial infections.

- *T lymphocytes* (white blood cells) mature in the *t*hymus and other lymphatic tissue and attack cancer cells, viruses, and foreign substances.

- *Macrophages* ("big eaters") identify, pursue, and ingest harmful invaders and worn-out cells.

- *Natural killer cells* (NK cells) pursue diseased cells (such as those infected by viruses or cancer).

Your age, nutrition, genetics, body temperature, and stress all influence your immune system's activity. When your immune system doesn't function properly, it can err in two directions:

1. Responding too strongly, it may attack the body's own tissues, causing an allergic reaction or a self-attacking disease, such as lupus, multiple sclerosis, or some forms of arthritis. Women, who are immunologically stronger than men, are more susceptible to self-attacking diseases (Nussinovitch & Schoenfeld, 2012; Schwartzman-Morris & Putterman, 2012).

2. Underreacting, the immune system may allow a bacterial infection to flare, a dormant virus to erupt, or cancer cells to multiply. To protect transplanted organs, which the recipient's system would view as a foreign body, surgeons may deliberately suppress the patient's immune system.

▼ FIGURE 40.4
A simplified view of immune responses

Stress can also trigger immune suppression by reducing the release of disease-fighting lymphocytes. This has been observed when animals were stressed by physical restraints, unavoidable electric shocks, noise, crowding, cold water, social defeat, or separation from their mothers (Maier et al., 1994). One study monitored immune responses in 43 monkeys over six months (Cohen et al., 1992). Half were left in stable groups. The rest were stressed by being housed with new roommates—3 or 4 new monkeys each month. By the end of the experiment, the socially disrupted monkeys had weaker immune systems.

Human immune systems react similarly. Some examples:

- *Surgical wounds heal more slowly in stressed people.* In one experiment, dental students received punch wounds (precise small holes punched in the skin). Compared with wounds placed during summer vacation, those placed three days before a major exam healed 40 percent more slowly (Kiecolt-Glaser et al., 1998). In other studies, marriage conflict has also slowed punch-wound healing (Kiecolt-Glaser et al., 2005).

- *Stressed people are more vulnerable to colds.* Major life stress increases the risk of a respiratory infection (Pedersen et al., 2010). When researchers dropped a cold virus into the noses of stressed and relatively unstressed people, 47 percent of those living stress-filled lives developed colds (**FIGURE 40.5**). Among those living relatively free of stress, only 27 percent did. In follow-up research, the happiest and most relaxed people were likewise markedly less vulnerable to an experimentally delivered cold virus (Cohen et al., 2003; Cohen & Pressman, 2006).

© D. Hurst/Alamy

- *Low stress may increase the effectiveness of vaccinations.* Nurses gave older adults a flu vaccine and then measured how well their bodies fought off bacteria and viruses. The vaccine was most effective among older adults who experienced low stress (Segerstrom et al., 2012).

The stress effect on immunity makes physiological sense. It takes energy to track down invaders, produce swelling, and maintain fevers. Thus, when diseased, your body reduces its muscular energy output by decreasing activity and increasing sleep. Stress does the opposite. It creates a competing energy need. During an aroused fight-or-flight reaction, your stress responses divert energy from your disease-fighting immune system and send it to your muscles and brain. This renders you more vulnerable to illness. *The point to remember:* Stress does not make us sick, but it does alter our immune functioning, which leaves us less able to resist infection.

▼ FIGURE 40.5
Stress and colds In an experiment by Sheldon Cohen and colleagues (1991), people with the highest life stress scores were also most vulnerable when exposed to an experimentally delivered cold virus. (Data from Cohen et al., 1991.)

Laurent/Yakou/Science Source

Percentage with colds

50%
45
40
35
30
25
0

3–4   5–6   7–8   9–10   11–12
Psychological stress index

- The field of _____ studies mind-body interactions, including the effects of psychological, neural, and endocrine functioning on the immune system and overall health.

ANSWER: psychoneuroimmunology

- What general effect does stress have on our overall health?

ANSWER: Stress tends to reduce our immune system's ability to function properly, so that higher stress generally leads to greater incidence of physical illness.

Stress and AIDS

We know that stress suppresses immune system functioning. What does this mean for people with *AIDS (acquired immune deficiency syndrome)*? As its name tells us, AIDS is an immune disorder, caused by the *human immunodeficiency virus (HIV)*. Although AIDS-related deaths have decreased 29 percent since 2001, AIDS remains the world's sixth leading cause of death and Africa's number one killer (UNAIDS, 2013; WHO, 2013).

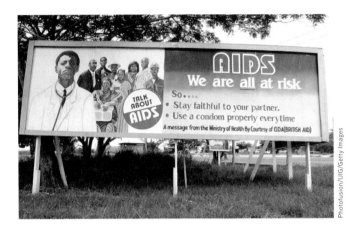

Photofusion/UIG/Getty Images

Ironically, if a disease is spread by human contact (as AIDS is, through the exchange of bodily fluids, primarily semen and blood), and if it kills slowly (as AIDS does), it can be lethal to more people. Those who acquire HIV often spread it in the highly contagious first few weeks before they know they are infected. Worldwide, some 2.3 million people—slightly more than half of them women— became infected with HIV in 2012, often without their awareness (UNAIDS, 2013). Years after the initial infection, when AIDS appears, people have difficulty fighting off other diseases, such as pneumonia.

Africa is ground zero for AIDS In Lesotho, Uganda, and elsewhere, prevention efforts have included the "ABC" Campaign—Abstinence, *Be* faithful, and use *Condoms*.

Stress cannot give people AIDS. But could stress and negative emotions speed the transition from HIV infection to AIDS? And might stress predict a faster decline in those with AIDS? An analysis of 33,252 participants from around the world suggest the answer to both questions is *Yes* (Chida & Vedhata, 2009). The greater the stress that HIV-infected people experience, the faster their disease progresses.

Would efforts to reduce stress help control the disease? Again, the answer appears to be *Yes*. Educational initiatives, bereavement support groups, cognitive therapy, relaxation training, and exercise programs that reduce distress have all had positive consequences for HIV-positive people (Baum & Posluszny, 1999; McCain et al., 2008; Schneiderman, 1999). But compared with available drug treatments, the benefits have been small.

Although AIDS is now more treatable than ever before, preventing HIV infection is a far better option. This is the focus of many educational programs, such as the ABC (Abstinence, *Be* faithful, *Condom* use) program that has been used with seeming success in Uganda (Altman, 2004; UNAIDS, 2005). In addition to such programs that seek to influence sexual norms and behaviors, today's *combination prevention* programs also include medical strategies (such as drugs and male circumcision that reduce HIV transmission) and efforts to reduce social inequalities that increase HIV risk (UNAIDS, 2010).

Stress and Cancer

Stress does not create cancer cells. But in a healthy, functioning immune system, lymphocytes, macrophages, and NK cells search out and destroy cancer cells and cancer-damaged cells. If stress weakens the immune system, might this weaken a person's ability to fight off cancer? To explore a possible connection between stress and cancer, experimenters have implanted tumor cells in rodents or given them *carcinogens* (cancer-producing substances). They then exposed some rodents to uncontrollable stress, such as inescapable shocks, which weakened their immune systems (Sklar & Anisman, 1981). Stressed rodents, compared with their unstressed counterparts, developed cancer more often, experienced tumor growth sooner, and grew larger tumors.

Does this stress-cancer link also hold with humans? The results are mixed. Some studies find that people are at increased risk for cancer within a year after experiencing depression, helplessness, or bereavement (Chida et al., 2008; Steptoe et al., 2010). In one large Swedish study, the risk of colon cancer was 5.5 times greater among people with a history of workplace stress than among those who reported no such problems. This difference was not due to group differences in age, smoking, drinking, or physical characteristics (Courtney et al., 1993). Other studies, however, have found no link between stress and human cancer (Coyne et al., 2010; Petticrew et al., 1999, 2002). Concentration camp survivors and former prisoners of war, for example, do not have elevated cancer rates.

One danger in hyping reports on emotions and cancer is that some patients may then blame themselves for their illness: "If only I had been more expressive, relaxed, and hopeful." A corollary danger is a "wellness macho" among the healthy, who take credit for their "healthy character" and lay a guilt trip on the ill: "She has cancer? That's what you get for holding your feelings in and being so nice." Dying thus becomes the ultimate failure.

It's important enough to repeat: *Stress does not create cancer cells.* At worst, it may affect their growth by weakening the body's natural defenses against multiplying malignant cells (Antoni & Lutgendorf, 2007). Although a relaxed, hopeful state may enhance these defenses, we should be aware of the thin line that divides science from wishful thinking. The powerful biological processes at work in advanced cancer or AIDS are not likely to be completely derailed by avoiding stress or maintaining a relaxed but determined spirit (Anderson, 2002; Kessler et al., 1991). And that explains why research has consistently indicated that psychotherapy does not extend cancer patients' survival (Coyne et al., 2007, 2009; Coyne & Tennen, 2010).

> "I didn't give myself cancer."
>
> Mayor Barbara Boggs Sigmund (1939–1990), Princeton, New Jersey

When organic causes of illness are unknown, it is tempting to invent psychological explanations. Before the germ that causes tuberculosis was discovered, personality explanations of TB were popular (Sontag, 1978).

🅜 **LaunchPad** For a 7-minute demonstration of the links between stress, cancer, and the immune system, visit LaunchPad's *Video—Fighting Cancer: Mobilizing the Immune System.*

Stress and Heart Disease

40-3 Why are some of us more prone than others to coronary heart disease?

Depart from reality for a moment. In this new world, you wake up each day, eat your breakfast, and check the news. Political coverage buzzes, local events snap up airtime, and your favorite sports team occasionally wins. But there is a fourth story: Four 747 jumbo jet airlines crashed yesterday and all 1642 passengers died. You finish your breakfast, grab your books, and head to class. It's just an average day.

Replace airline crashes with **coronary heart disease,** the United States' leading cause of death, and you have re-entered reality. About 600,000 Americans die annually from heart disease (CDC, 2013). Heart disease occurs when the blood vessels that nourish the heart muscle gradually close. High blood pressure and a family history of the disease increase the risk. So do smoking, obesity, a high-fat diet, physical inactivity, and a high cholesterol level.

Stress and personality also play a big role in heart disease. The more psychological trauma people experience, the more their bodies generate *inflammation,* which is associated with heart and other health problems (O'Donovan et al., 2012). Plucking a hair and measuring its level of cortisol (a stress hormone) can help predict whether a person will have a future heart attack (Pereg et al., 2011).

coronary heart disease the clogging of the vessels that nourish the heart muscle; the leading cause of death in many developed countries.

Type A Friedman and Rosenman's term for competitive, hard-driving, impatient, verbally aggressive, and anger-prone people.

Type B Friedman and Rosenman's term for easygoing, relaxed people.

Type A Personality In a now-classic study, Meyer Friedman, Ray Rosenman, and their colleagues tested the idea that stress increases vulnerability to heart disease by measuring the blood cholesterol level and clotting speed of 40 U.S. male tax accountants at different times of year (Friedman & Ulmer, 1984). From January through March, the test results were completely normal. Then, as the accountants began scrambling to finish their clients' tax returns before the April 15 filing deadline, their cholesterol and clotting measures rose to dangerous levels. In May and June, with the deadline past, the measures returned to normal. For these men, stress predicted heart attack risk. Blood pressure also rises as students approach everyday academic stressors (Conley & Lehman, 2012).

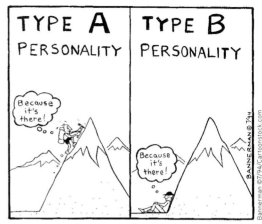

So, are some of us at high risk of stress-related coronary heart disease? To answer this question, the researchers who studied the tax accountants launched a nine-year study of more than 3000 healthy men, aged 35 to 59. The researchers first interviewed each man for 15 minutes, noting his work and eating habits, manner of talking, and other behavior patterns. Those who seemed the most reactive, competitive, hard-driving, impatient, time-conscious, supermotivated, verbally aggressive, and easily angered they called **Type A.** The roughly equal number who were more easygoing they called **Type B.** Which group do you suppose turned out to be the most prone to coronary heart disease?

Nine years later, 257 men had suffered heart attacks, and 69 percent of them were Type A. Moreover, not one of the "pure" Type Bs—the most mellow and laid back of their group—had suffered a heart attack.

As often happens in science, this exciting discovery provoked enormous public interest. After that initial honeymoon period, researchers wanted to know more. Was the finding reliable? If so, what was the toxic component of the Type A profile: Time-consciousness? Competitiveness? Anger?

More than 700 studies have now explored possible psychological correlates or predictors of cardiovascular health (Chida & Hamer, 2008; Chida & Steptoe, 2009). These reveal that Type A's toxic core is negative emotions—especially the anger associated with an aggressively reactive temperament. When we are harassed or challenged, our active sympathetic nervous system redistributes bloodflow to our muscles, pulling it away from our internal organs. One of those organs, the liver, which normally removes cholesterol and fat from the blood, can't do its job. Type A individuals are more often "combat ready." Thus, excess cholesterol and fat may continue to circulate in their blood and later get deposited around the heart. Further stress—sometimes conflicts brought on by their own abrasiveness—may trigger altered heart rhythms. In people with weakened hearts, this altered pattern can cause sudden death (Kamarck & Jennings, 1991). Hostility also correlates with other risk factors, such as smoking, drinking, and obesity (Bunde & Suls, 2006). In important ways, people's minds and hearts interact.

Hundreds of other studies of young and middle-aged men and women have confirmed the finding that people who react with anger over little things are the most coronary-prone. Suppressing negative emotions only heightens the risk (Kupper & Denollet, 2007). One study followed 13,000 middle-aged people for 5 years. Among those with normal blood pressure, people who had scored high on anger were three times more likely to have had heart attacks, even after researchers controlled for smoking and weight (Williams et al., 2000). Another study followed 1055 male medical students over an average of 36 years. Those who had reported being hot tempered were five times more likely to have had a heart attack by age 55 (Chang et al., 2002). Rage "seems to lash back and strike us in the heart muscle" (Spielberger & London, 1982).

In both India and America, Type A bus drivers are literally hard-driving: They brake, pass, and honk their horns more often than their more easygoing Type B colleagues (Evans et al., 1987).

"The fire you kindle for your enemy often burns you more than him."

Chinese proverb

© PhotoSpin, Inc/Alamy

▼ FIGURE 40.6
Pessimism and heart disease
A Harvard School of Public Health team found pessimistic men at doubled risk of developing heart disease over a 10-year period. (Data from Kubzansky et al., 2001.)

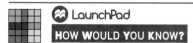

"A cheerful heart is a good medicine, but a downcast spirit dries up the bones."

Proverbs 17:22

LaunchPad

HOW WOULD YOU KNOW?

To consider how researchers have studied these issues, visit Launch-Pad's *How Would You Know If Stress Increases Risk of Disease?*

Type D Personality   In recent years, another personality type has interested stress and heart disease researchers. Type A individuals direct their negative emotion toward dominating others. People with another personality type—Type D—suppress their negative emotion to avoid social disapproval. The negative emotion these *Type D* individuals experience during social interactions is mainly *distress* (Denollet, 2005; Denollet et al., 1996). In one analysis of 12 studies, having a Type D personality significantly increased risk for mortality and nonfatal heart attack (Grande et al., 2012).

Effects of Pessimism and Depression   Pessimism seems to be similarly toxic. Laura Kubzansky and her colleagues (2001) studied 1306 initially healthy men who a decade earlier had scored as optimists, pessimists, or neither. Even after other risk factors such as smoking had been ruled out, pessimists were more than twice as likely as optimists to develop heart disease (**FIGURE 40.6**).

Depression, too, can be lethal. Happy people tend to be healthier and to outlive their unhappy peers (Diener & Chan, 2011; Siahpush et al., 2008). Even a big, happy smile predicts longevity, as researchers discovered when they examined the photographs of 150 Major League Baseball players who had appeared in the 1952 *Baseball Register* and had died by 2009 (Abel & Kruger, 2010). On average, the nonsmilers had died at 73, compared with an average 80 years for those with a broad, genuine smile. People with broad smiles tend to have extensive social networks, which predict longer life (Hertenstein, 2009).

The accumulated evidence suggests that "depression substantially increases the risk of death, especially death by unnatural causes and cardiovascular disease" (Wulsin et al., 1999). After following 63,469 women over a dozen years, researchers found more than a doubled rate of heart attack death among those who initially scored as depressed (Whang et al., 2009). In the years following a heart attack, people with high scores for depression were four times more likely than their low-scoring counterparts to develop further heart problems (Frasure-Smith & Lesperance, 2005). Depression is disheartening.

Stress and Inflammation   Depressed people tend to smoke more and exercise less (Whooley et al., 2008), but stress itself is also disheartening:

- When following 17,415 middle-aged American women, researchers found an 88 percent increased risk of heart attacks among those facing significant work stress (Slopen et al., 2010).

- In Denmark, a study of 12,116 female nurses found that those reporting "much too high" work pressures had a 40 percent increased risk of heart disease (Allesøe et al., 2010).

- In the United States, a 10-year study of middle-aged workers found that involuntary job loss more than doubled their risk of a heart attack (Gallo et al., 2006). A 14-year study of 1059 women found that those with five or more trauma-related stress symptoms had three times the normal risk of heart disease (Kubzansky et al., 2009).

As **FIGURE 40.7** illustrates, both heart disease and depression may result when chronic stress triggers persistent inflammation (Matthews, 2005; Miller & Blackwell, 2006). After a heart attack, stress and anxiety increase the risk of death or of another attack (Roest et al., 2010). As we have seen, stress disrupts the body's disease-fighting immune system, enabling the body to focus its energies on fleeing or fighting the threat. Yet stress hormones enhance one immune response, the production of proteins that contribute

© Sean Locke Photography/Shutterstock

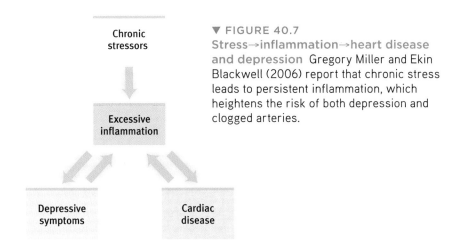

▼ FIGURE 40.7
Stress→inflammation→heart disease and depression Gregory Miller and Ekin Blackwell (2006) report that chronic stress leads to persistent inflammation, which heightens the risk of both depression and clogged arteries.

to inflammation. Thus, people who experience social threats, including children raised in harsh families, are more prone to inflammation responses (Dickerson et al., 2009; Miller & Chen, 2010). Inflammation fights infections; if you cut yourself, inflammation recruits infection-fighting cells. But persistent inflammation can produce problems such as asthma or clogged arteries, and worsen depression. Researchers are now uncovering the molecular mechanisms by which stress, in some people, activates genes that control inflammation (Cole et al., 2010).

We can view the stress effect on our disease resistance as a price we pay for the benefits of stress (**FIGURE 40.8**). Stress invigorates our lives by arousing and motivating us. An unstressed life would hardly be challenging or productive.

* * *

Psychological states are physiological events that influence other parts of our physiological system. Just pausing to *think* about biting into an orange section—the sweet, tangy juice from the pulpy fruit flooding across your tongue—can trigger salivation. As the Indian sage Santi Parva recognized more than 4000 years ago, "Mental disorders arise from physical causes, and likewise physical disorders arise from mental causes." There is an interplay between our heads and our health. We are biopsychosocial systems.

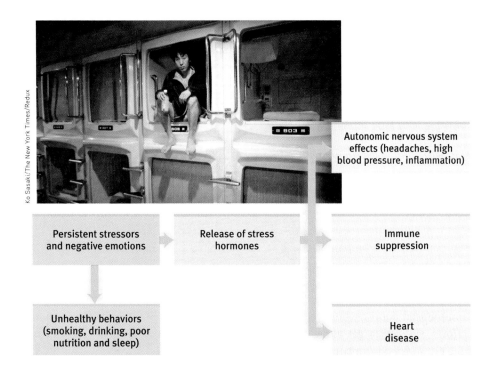

▼ FIGURE 40.8
Stress can have a variety of health-related consequences This is especially so when stress is experienced by angry, depressed, or anxious people. Job and income loss caused by the recent economic recession has created stress for many people, such as this jobless Japanese man living in a Tokyo "capsule hotel."

RETRIEVAL PRACTICE

- Which component of the Type A personality has been linked most closely to coronary heart disease?

  ANSWERS: Feeling angry and negative much of the time.

- How does Type D personality differ from Type A?

  ANSWER: Type D individuals experience distress rather than anger, and they tend to suppress their negative emotions to avoid social disapproval.

MODULE 40 REVIEW Stress and Illness

LEARNING OBJECTIVES

RETRIEVAL PRACTICE Take a moment to answer each of these Learning Objective Questions (repeated here from within this module). Then turn to Appendix C, Complete Module Reviews, to check your answers. Research suggests that trying to answer these questions on your own will improve your long-term retention (McDaniel et al., 2009).

40-1 What events provoke stress responses, and how do we respond and adapt to stress?

40-2 How does stress make us more vulnerable to disease?

40-3 Why are some of us more prone than others to coronary heart disease?

TERMS AND CONCEPTS TO REMEMBER

RETRIEVAL PRACTICE Test yourself on these terms by trying to write down the definition before flipping back to the page number referenced to check your answer.

stress, p. 489

general adaptation syndrome (GAS), p. 491

tend and befriend, p. 492

health psychology, p. 492

psychoneuroimmunology, p. 492

coronary heart disease, p. 496

Type A, p. 497

Type B, p. 497

Use 🔁 **LearningCurve** to create your personalized study plan, which will direct you to the resources that will help you most in 🔁 **LaunchPad**.

MODULE 41 Health and Coping

PROMOTING HEALTH BEGINS WITH IMPLEMENTING strategies that prevent illness and enhance wellness. Traditionally, people have thought about their health only when something goes wrong—visiting a physician for diagnosis and treatment. That, say health psychologists, is like ignoring a car's maintenance and going to a mechanic only when the car breaks down. Health maintenance includes alleviating stress, preventing illness, and promoting well-being.

Coping With Stress

41-1 In what two ways do people try to alleviate stress?

Stressors are unavoidable. This fact, coupled with the fact that persistent stress correlates with heart disease, depression, and lowered immunity, gives us a clear message. We need to learn to **cope** with the stress in our lives, alleviating it with emotional, cognitive, or behavioral methods. We address some stressors directly, with **problem-focused coping**. If our impatience leads to a family fight, we may go directly to that family member to work things out. We tend to use problem-focused strategies when we feel a sense of control over a situation and think we can change the circumstances, or at least change ourselves to deal with the circumstances more capably. We turn to **emotion-focused coping** when we *believe* we cannot change a situation. If, despite our best efforts, we cannot get along with that family member, we may relieve stress by reaching out to friends for support and comfort.

coping alleviating stress using emotional, cognitive, or behavioral methods.

problem-focused coping attempting to alleviate stress directly—by changing the stressor or the way we interact with that stressor.

emotion-focused coping attempting to alleviate stress by avoiding or ignoring a stressor and attending to emotional needs related to our stress reaction.

learned helplessness the hopelessness and passive resignation an animal or human learns when unable to avoid repeated aversive events.

When challenged, some of us tend to respond with cool problem-focused coping, others with emotion-focused coping (Connor-Smith & Flachsbart, 2007). Our feelings of personal control, our explanatory style, and our supportive connections all influence our ability to cope successfully.

Personal Control

41-2 How does a perceived lack of control affect health?

Picture the scene: Two rats receive simultaneous shocks. One can turn a wheel to stop the shocks (as illustrated in **FIGURE 41.1**). The helpless rat, but not the wheel turner, becomes more susceptible to ulcers and lowered immunity to disease (Laudenslager & Reite, 1984). In humans, too, uncontrollable threats trigger the strongest stress responses (Dickerson & Kemeny, 2004).

At times, we all feel helpless, hopeless, and depressed after experiencing a series of bad events beyond our control. Martin Seligman and his colleagues have shown that for some animals and people, a series of uncontrollable events creates a state of **learned helplessness,** with feelings of passive resignation (**FIGURE 41.2**). In one series of experiments, dogs were strapped in a harness and given repeated shocks, with no opportunity to avoid them (Seligman & Maier, 1967). Later, when placed in another situation where they could escape the punishment by simply leaping a hurdle, the dogs cowered as if without hope. Other dogs that had been able to escape the first shocks reacted differently. They had learned they were in control and easily escaped the shocks in the new situation (Seligman & Maier, 1967). In other experiments, people have shown similar patterns of learned helplessness (Abramson et al., 1978, 1989; Seligman, 1975).

Perceiving a loss of control, we become more vulnerable to ill health. A famous study of elderly nursing home residents with little perceived control over their activities found that they declined faster and died sooner than those given more control (Rodin, 1986). Workers able to adjust office furnishings and control interruptions and distractions in their work environment have also experienced less stress (O'Neill, 1993). Such findings help explain why British civil service workers at the executive grades have tended to outlive those at clerical or laboring grades, and why Finnish workers with low job stress have been less than half as likely to die of strokes or heart disease as were those with a demanding job and little control. The more control workers have, the longer they live (Bosma et al., 1997, 1998; Kivimaki et al., 2002; Marmot et al., 1997).

Control also helps explain a link between economic status and longevity (Jokela et al., 2009). In one study of 843 grave markers in an old graveyard in Glasgow, Scotland, those with the costliest, highest pillars (indicating the most affluence) tended to have lived the longest (Carroll et al., 1994). Likewise, those living in Scottish regions with the least overcrowding and unemployment have the greatest longevity. There and elsewhere, high economic status predicts a lower risk of heart and respiratory diseases (Sapolsky, 2005). Wealth predicts better health among children, too (Chen, 2004).

"Executive" rat   "Subordinate" rat   Control rat

To shock control   To shock source   No connection to shock source

▼ FIGURE 41.1
Health consequences of a loss of control The "executive" rat at the left can switch off the tail shock by turning the wheel. Because it has control over the shock, it is no more likely to develop ulcers than is the unshocked control rat on the right. The "subordinate" rat in the center receives the same shocks as the executive rat, but with no control over the shocks. It is, therefore, more likely to develop ulcers. (Adapted from Weiss, 1977.)

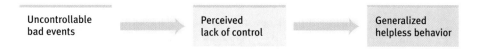

Uncontrollable bad events → Perceived lack of control → Generalized helpless behavior

▼ FIGURE 41.2
Learned helplessness When animals and people experience no control over repeated bad events, they often learn helplessness.

With higher economic status come reduced risks of low birth weight, infant mortality, smoking, and violence. Even among other primates, those at the bottom of the social pecking order have been more likely than their higher-status companions to become sick when exposed to a cold-like virus (Cohen et al., 1997). But for those high-status baboons and monkeys who frequently have to physically defend their dominant position, high status also entails stress (Sapolsky, 2005).

Why does perceived loss of control predict health problems? Because losing control provokes an outpouring of stress hormones. When rats cannot control shock or when primates or humans feel unable to control their environment, stress hormone levels rise, blood pressure increases, and immune responses drop (Rodin, 1986; Sapolsky, 2005). One study found these effects among nurses, who reported their workload and their level of personal control on the job. The greater their workload, the higher their cortisol level and blood pressure—but only among nurses who reported little control over their environment (Fox et al., 1993). Another study found that captive animals experienced more stress and were more vulnerable to disease than their wild counterparts (Roberts, 1988). The crowding that occurs in high-density neighborhoods, prisons, and college and university dorms is another source of diminished feelings of control—and of elevated levels of stress hormones and blood pressure (Fleming et al., 1987; Ostfeld et al., 1987). By boosting feelings of control, people often lead happier and healthier lives (Ng et al., 2012).

Increasing control—allowing prisoners to move chairs and to control room lights and the TV; having workers participate in decision making; allowing people to personalize their work space—has noticeably improved health and morale (Humphrey et al., 2007; Krueger & Killham, 2006; Ruback et al., 1986; Warburton et al., 2006).

In the case of nursing home patients, 93 percent of those who were encouraged to exert more control became more alert, active, and happy (Rodin, 1986). As researcher Ellen Langer concluded, "Perceived control is basic to human functioning" (1983, p. 291). "For the young and old alike," she suggested, environments should enhance people's sense of control over their world. No wonder mobile devices and DVRs, which enhance our control of the content and timing of our entertainment, are so popular.

Google incorporates these principles effectively. Each week, Google employees can spend 20 percent of their working time on projects they find personally interesting. This Innovation Time Off program increases employees' personal control over their work environment, and it has paid off. Gmail was developed this way.

People thrive when they live in conditions of personal freedom and empowerment. At the national level, citizens of stable democracies report higher levels of happiness (Inglehart et al., 2008).

Happy to have control After working on the building—alongside Habitat for Humanity volunteers—for several months, this family is finally experiencing the joy of having their own new home.

So, some freedom and control are better than none. But does ever-increasing choice breed ever-happier lives? Some researchers have suggested that today's Western cultures offer an "excess of freedom"—too many choices. The result can be decreased life satisfaction, increased depression, or even behavior paralysis (Schwartz, 2000, 2004). In one study, people offered a choice of one of 30 brands of jam or chocolate were less satisfied with their decision than were others who had chosen from only 6 options (Iyengar & Lepper, 2000). This *tyranny of choice* brings information overload and a greater likelihood that we will feel regret over some of the things we left behind. (Do you, too, ever waste time agonizing over too many choices?)

Internal Versus External Locus of Control If experiencing a loss of control can be stressful and unhealthy, do people who generally feel in control of their lives enjoy better health? Consider your own feelings of control. Do you believe that your life is beyond your control? That the world is run by a few powerful people? That getting a good job depends mainly on being in the right place at the right time? Or do you more strongly believe that you control your own fate? That each of us can influence our government's decisions? That being a success is a matter of hard work?

Hundreds of studies have compared people who differ in their perceptions of control. On the one side are those who have what Julian Rotter called an **external locus of control,** the perception that chance or outside forces control their fate. On the other side are those who perceive an **internal locus of control,** who believe they control their own destiny. In study after study, the "internals" have achieved more in school and work, acted more independently, enjoyed better health, and felt less depressed than did the "externals" (Lefcourt, 1982; Ng et al., 2006). In one long-term study of more than 7500 people, those who had expressed a more internal locus of control at age 10 exhibited less obesity, lower blood pressure, and less distress at age 30 (Gale et al., 2008).

Another way to say that we believe we are in control of our own life is to say we have *free will,* or that we can control our own willpower. Studies show that people who believe in their freedom learn better, perform better at work, behave more helpfully, and have a stronger desire to punish rule breakers (Clark et al., 2014; Job et al., 2010; Stillman et al., 2010).

Compared with their parents' generation, more young Americans now endorse an external locus of control (Twenge et al., 2004). This shift may help explain an associated increase in rates of depression and other psychological disorders in young people (Twenge et al., 2010).

external locus of control the perception that chance or outside forces beyond our personal control determine our fate.

internal locus of control the perception that we control our own fate.

self-control the ability to control impulses and delay short-term gratification for greater long-term rewards.

RETRIEVAL PRACTICE

- To cope with stress, we tend to use _____ -focused (emotion/problem) strategies when we feel in control of our world, and _____ -focused (emotion/problem) strategies when we believe we cannot change a situation.

ANSWERS: problem; emotion

Depleting and Strengthening Self-Control

41-3 How can our self-control be depleted, and why is it important to build this strength?

Self-control is the ability to control impulses and delay short-term gratification for longer-term rewards. In studies, self-control predicts good health, higher income, and better grades (Kuhnle et al., 2012; Moffitt et al., 2011). In one study that followed eighth-graders over a school year, better self-control was more than twice as important as intelligence score in predicting academic success (Duckworth & Seligman, 2005).

Self-control is constantly changing—from day to day, hour to hour, and even minute to minute. Like a muscle, self-control weakens after use, recovers after rest, and grows stronger with exercise (Baumeister & Tierney, 2011; Hagger et al., 2010; Vohs & Baumeister, 2011). Exercising willpower temporarily depletes the mental energy needed for self-control on other tasks (Vohs et al., 2012). In one experiment, hungry people who had resisted the temptation to eat chocolate chip cookies abandoned a tedious task sooner than those who had not resisted the cookies. And after expending willpower on laboratory tasks, such as stifling prejudice or ignoring flashing words on a computer screen, people were less restrained in their aggressive responses to provocation and in their sexuality (Finkel et al., 2012; Gaillot & Baumeister, 2007). Similar self-control weakening happens when people flex their self-control muscle outside the laboratory, such as when people try to control their alcohol use (Hofmann et al., 2012).

Exercising willpower decreases neural activation in regions associated with mental control (Wagner et al., 2013). Might sugar provide a sweet solution to self-control fatigue? Sugar not only makes us feel good, it also increases neural activation in mental control regions (Chambers et al., 2009). In several studies, giving sugar (in a naturally rather than an artificially sweetened lemonade) had a sweet effect: It strengthened

Extreme self-control Our ability to exert self-control increases with practice, and some of us have practiced more than others! Magician David Blaine (top) endured standing in a block of ice (in which a small space had been carved out for him) for nearly 62 hours for a stunt in New York's Times Square. A number of performing artists make their living as very convincing human statues, as does this actress (bottom) performing on The Royal Mile in Edinburgh, Scotland.

people's effortful thinking and reduced their financial impulsiveness (Masicampo & Baumeister, 2008; Wang & Dvorak, 2010). Even dogs can experience self-control depletion and rejuvenation with sugar (Miller et al., 2010).

Researchers do not encourage candy bar diets to improve self-control. Simply rinsing your mouth with sugary liquid can give you the mental energy you need (Hagger & Chatzisarantis, 2013; Sanders et al., 2012). You will get the boost in self-control without the bulge in your waistline.

Decreased mental energy after exercising self-control is a short-term effect. The long-term effect of exercising self-control is increased self-control, much as a hard physical workout leaves you temporarily tired out, but stronger in the long term. Strengthened self-control improves people's performance on laboratory tasks and improves their self-management of eating, drinking, anger, and household chores (Denson et al., 2011; Oaten & Cheng, 2006a,b).

The point to remember: Develop self-discipline in one area of your life, and your strengthened self-control may spill over into other areas as well, making for a healthier, happier, and more successful life.

Explanatory Style: Optimism Versus Pessimism

41-4 How does an optimistic outlook affect health and longevity?

In *The How of Happiness,* psychologist Sonja Lyubomirsky (2008) tells the true story of Randy. By any measure, Randy lived a hard life. His dad and best friend died by suicide. Growing up, his mother's boyfriend treated him poorly. Randy's own first marriage was troubled. His wife was unfaithful, and they divorced. Despite these setbacks, Randy is a happy person whose presence can light up a room. He remarried and enjoys his role as stepfather to three boys. He also finds his work life to be rewarding. Randy says he survived his life challenges by seeing the "silver lining in the cloud."

Randy's story illustrates how our outlook—what we expect from the world—influences how we cope with stress. *Pessimists* expect things to go badly (Aspinwall & Tedeschi, 2010; Carver et al., 2010; Rasmussen et al., 2009). When bad things happen, pessimists knew it all along. They attribute their poor performance to a basic lack of ability ("I can't do this") or to situations enduringly beyond their control ("There is nothing I can do about it"). *Optimists,* such as Randy, expect to have more control, to cope better with stressful events, and to enjoy better health (Aspinwall & Tedeschi, 2010; Boehm & Kubzansky, 2012; Carver et al., 2010). During a semester's last month, students previously identified as optimistic reported less fatigue and fewer coughs, aches, and pains. And during the stressful first few weeks of law school, those who were optimistic ("It's unlikely that I will fail") enjoyed better moods and stronger immune systems (Segerstrom et al., 1998). Optimists also respond to stress with smaller increases in blood pressure, and they recover more quickly from heart bypass surgery.

Optimistic students have also tended to get better grades because they often respond to setbacks with the hopeful attitude that effort, good study habits, and self-discipline make a difference (Noel et al., 1987; Peterson & Barrett, 1987). When dating couples wrestle with conflicts, optimists and their partners see each other as engaging constructively, and they then tend to feel more supported and satisfied with the resolution and with their relationship (Srivastava et al., 2006). Optimism also relates to well-being and success in China and Japan (Qin & Piao, 2011). Realistic positive expectations fuel motivation and success (Oettingen & Mayer, 2002).

Consider the consistency and startling magnitude of the optimism and positive emotions factor in several other studies:

- One research team followed 941 Dutch people, ages 65 to 85, for nearly a decade (Giltay et al., 2004, 2007). Among those in the lowest optimism quartile, 57 percent died, as did only 30 percent of the top optimism quartile.

- When Finnish researchers followed 2428 men for up to a decade, the number of deaths among those with a bleak, hopeless outlook was more than double that found among their optimistic counterparts (Everson et al., 1996). American researchers found the same when following 4256 Vietnam-era veterans (Phillips et al., 2009).

- A now-famous study followed up on 180 Catholic nuns who had written brief autobiographies at about 22 years of age and had thereafter lived similar lifestyles. Those who had expressed happiness, love, and other positive feelings in their autobiographies lived an average 7 years longer than their more dour counterparts (Danner et al., 2001). By age 80, some 54 percent of those expressing few positive emotions had died, as had only 24 percent of the most positive spirited.

Optimism runs in families, so some people truly are born with a sunny, hopeful outlook. With identical twins, if one is optimistic, the other often will be as well (Mosing et al., 2009). One genetic marker of optimism is a gene that enhances the social-bonding hormone *oxytocin* (Saphire-Bernstein et al., 2011).

The good news is that all of us, even the most pessimistic, can learn to become more optimistic. Compared with pessimists who simply kept diaries of their daily activities, those who became skilled at seeing the bright side of difficult situations and viewing their goals as achievable reported lower levels of depression (Sergeant & Mongrain, 2014). Optimism is the light bulb that can brighten anyone's mood.

Social Support

41-5 How does social support promote good health?

Social support—feeling liked and encouraged by intimate friends and family—promotes both happiness and health. In massive investigations, some following thousands of people for several years, close relationships have predicted health. People are less likely to die early if supported by close relationships (Uchino, 2009). When Brigham Young University researchers combined data from 148 studies totaling more than 300,000 people worldwide, they confirmed a striking effect of social support (Holt-Lunstad et al., 2010). Those with ample social connections had survival rates about 50 percent greater than those with meager connections. The impact of meager connections appeared roughly equal to the effect of smoking 15 cigarettes a day or having an alcohol use disorder, and double the effect of not exercising or being obese. A small taste of acceptance, such as through small talk, can lengthen life expectancy (Steptoe et al., 2013). People aren't the only creatures to benefit from friends. Among baboons, strong social bonds with relatives and friends similarly predict longevity (Silk et al., 2010).

People need people. Some fill this need by connecting with friends, family, co-workers, members of a faith community, or other support groups. The need to belong is so strong that people will sometimes risk their health to gain social acceptance (Rawn & Vohs, 2011). Others connect in positive, happy, supportive marriages. In one analysis of more than 72,000 individuals, people in low-conflict marriages lived longer, healthier lives than the unmarried (Robles et al., 2014). One seven-decade-long study found that at age 50, healthy aging was better predicted by a good marriage than by a low cholesterol level (Vaillant, 2002). On the flip side, divorce predicts poor health. In one analysis of 32 studies involving more than 6.5 million people, divorced people were 23 percent more likely to die early (Sbarra et al., 2011).

What explains the link between social support and health? Are middle-aged and older adults who live alone more likely to smoke, be obese, and have high cholesterol—and therefore to have a doubled risk of heart attacks (Nielsen et al., 2006)? Or are healthy people more supportive and marriage-prone? Possibly. But research indicates some other possibilities.

Positive expectations often motivate eventual success.

The New Yorker Collection, 1995. From cartoonbank.com

"*We just haven't been flapping them hard enough.*"

"The optimist proclaims we live in the best of all possible worlds, and the pessimist fears this is true."

James Branch Cabell, *The Silver Stallion*, 1926

Laughter among friends
is good medicine Laughter
arouses us, massages muscles,
and then leaves us feeling relaxed
(Robinson, 1983). Humor (though
not hostile sarcasm) may defuse
stress, ease pain, and strengthen
immune activity (Ayan, 2009; Berk
et al., 2001; Dunbar et al., 2011;
Kimata, 2001). People who laugh a
lot have also tended to have lower
rates of heart disease (Clark et al.,
2001).

Mark Andersen/Rubberball/Getty Images

Social support calms us and reduces blood pressure and stress hormones. Numerous studies support this finding (Hostinar et al., 2014; Uchino et al., 1996, 1999). To see if social support might calm people's response to threats, one research team subjected happily married women, while lying in an fMRI machine, to the threat of electric shock to an ankle (Coan et al., 2006). During the experiment, some women held their husband's hand. Others held the hand of an unknown person or no hand at all. While awaiting the occasional shocks, women holding their husband's hand showed less activity in threat-responsive areas. This soothing benefit was greatest for those reporting the highest-quality marriages. Supportive family and friends—human and nonhuman—help buffer threats. After stressful events, Medicare patients who have a dog or other companionable pet are less likely to visit their doctor (Siegel, 1990).

Social support fosters stronger immune functioning. Volunteers in studies of resistance to cold viruses showed this effect (Cohen et al., 1997, 2004). Healthy volunteers inhaled nasal drops laden with a cold virus and were quarantined and observed for five days. (In these experiments, more than 600 volunteers received $800 each to endure this experience.) Age, race, sex, smoking, and other health habits being equal, those with the most social ties were least likely to catch a cold. If they did catch one, they produced less mucus. More sociability meant less susceptibility. The cold fact is that the effect of social ties is nothing to sneeze at!

Close relationships give us an opportunity for "open heart therapy," a chance to confide painful feelings (Frattaroli, 2006). Talking about a stressful event can temporarily arouse us, but in the long run it calms us, by calming limbic system activity (Lieberman et al., 2007; Mendolia & Kleck, 1993). In one study, 33 Holocaust survivors spent two hours recalling their experiences, many in intimate detail never before disclosed (Pennebaker et al., 1989). In the weeks following, most watched a tape of their recollections and showed it to family and friends. Those who were most self-disclosing had the most improved health 14 months later. Confiding is good for the body and the soul. In another study of surviving spouses of people who had committed suicide or died in car accidents, those who bore their grief alone had more health problems than those who could express it openly (Pennebaker & O'Heeron, 1984).

Suppressing emotions can be detrimental to physical health. When health psychologist James Pennebaker (1985) surveyed more than 700 undergraduate women, about 1 in 12 of them reported a traumatic sexual experience in childhood. The sexually abused women—especially those who had kept their secret to themselves—reported more headaches and stomach ailments than did other women who had experienced

"Woe to one who is alone and falls and does not have another to help."

Ecclesiastes 4:10

nonsexual traumas, such as parental death or divorce. Another study, of 437 Australian ambulance drivers, confirmed the ill effects of suppressing one's emotions after witnessing traumas (Wastell, 2002).

Even writing about personal traumas in a diary can help (Burton & King, 2008; Hemenover, 2003; Lyubomirsky et al., 2006). In an analysis of 633 trauma victims, writing therapy was as effective as psychotherapy in reducing psychological trauma (van Emmerik et al., 2013). In another experiment, volunteers who wrote trauma diaries had fewer health problems during the ensuing four to six months (Pennebaker, 1990). As one participant explained, "Although I have not talked with anyone about what I wrote, I was finally able to deal with it, work through the pain instead of trying to block it out. Now it doesn't hurt to think about it."

If we are aiming to exercise more, drink less, quit smoking, or be a healthy weight, our social ties can tug us away from or toward our goal. If you are trying to achieve some goal, think about whether your social network can help or hinder you. That social net covers not only the people you know but friends of your friends, and friends of their friends. That's three degrees of separation between you and the most remote people. Within that network, others can influence your thoughts, feelings, and actions without your awareness (Christakis & Fowler, 2009). Obesity, for example, spreads within networks in ways that seem not merely to reflect people's seeking out similar others.

Reducing Stress

Having a sense of control, developing more optimistic thinking, and building social support can help us *experience* less stress and thus improve our health. Moreover, these factors interrelate: People who have been upbeat about themselves and their future have tended also to enjoy health-promoting social ties (Stinson et al., 2008). But sometimes we cannot alleviate stress and simply need to *manage* our stress. Aerobic exercise, relaxation, meditation, and spiritual communities may help us gather inner strength and lessen stress effects.

"Is there anyone here who specializes in stress management?"

Aerobic Exercise

41-6 How effective is aerobic exercise as a way to manage stress and improve well-being?

Aerobic exercise is sustained, oxygen-consuming, exercise—such as jogging, swimming, or biking—that increases heart and lung fitness. It's hard to find bad things to say about exercise. By one estimate, moderate exercise adds not only to your quantity of life—two additional years, on average—but also to your quality of life, with more energy and better mood (Seligman, 1994; Wang et al., 2011).

Exercise helps fight heart disease by strengthening the heart, increasing bloodflow, keeping blood vessels open, and lowering both blood pressure and the blood pressure reaction to stress (Ford, 2002; Manson, 2002). Compared with inactive adults, people who exercise suffer half as many heart attacks (Powell et al., 1987; Visich & Fletcher, 2009). Exercise makes the muscles hungry for the fats that, if not used by the muscles, contribute to clogged arteries (Barinaga, 1997). In one study of over 650,000 American adults, walking 150 minutes per week predicted living seven more years (Moore et al., 2012). People who avoid sedentary activities, such as watching television, also tend to live longer lives (Veerman et al., 2012; Wilmot et al., 2012).

The genes passed down to us from our distant ancestors were those that enabled the physical activity essential to hunting, foraging, and farming (Raichlen & Polk, 2013). In muscle cells, those genes, when activated by exercise, respond by producing proteins.

aerobic exercise sustained exercise that increases heart and lung fitness; may also alleviate depression and anxiety.

In the modern inactive person, these genes produce lower quantities of proteins and leave us susceptible to more than 20 chronic diseases, such as type 2 diabetes, coronary heart disease, stroke, Alzheimer's disease, and cancer (Booth & Neufer, 2005). Inactivity is thus potentially toxic. But physical activity can weaken the influence of some genetic risk factors. In one analysis of 45 studies, the risk of obesity fell by 27 percent (Kilpeläinen et al., 2012).

Does exercise also boost the spirit? Many studies reveal that aerobic exercise can reduce stress, depression, and anxiety. Americans, Canadians, and Britons who do aerobic exercise at least three times a week manage stress better, exhibit more self-confidence, feel more vigor, and feel less depressed and fatigued than their inactive peers (McMurray, 2004; Mead et al., 2010; Puetz et al., 2006; Smits et al., 2011). Going from active exerciser to couch potato can increase the likelihood of depression—by 51 percent in two years for the women in one study (Wang et al., 2011). And in a 21-country survey of university students, physical exercise was a "strong" and consistent predictor of life satisfaction (Grant et al., 2009).

But we could state this observation another way: Stressed and depressed people exercise less. These findings are correlations, and cause and effect are unclear. To sort out cause and effect, researchers experiment. They randomly assign stressed, depressed, or anxious people either to an aerobic exercise group or to a control group. Next, they measure whether aerobic exercise (compared with a control activity) produces a change in stress, depression, anxiety, or some other health-related outcome. One classic experiment randomly assigned mildly depressed female college students to three groups. One-third participated in a program of aerobic exercise. Another third took part in a program of relaxation exercises. The remaining third (the control group) formed a no-treatment group (McCann & Holmes, 1984). As **FIGURE 41.3** shows, 10 weeks later, the women in the aerobic exercise program reported the greatest decrease in depression. Many had, quite literally, run away from their troubles.

Dozens of other experiments confirm that exercise prevents or reduces depression and anxiety (Conn, 2010; Rethorst et al., 2009; Windle et al., 2010). Moreover, exercise is not only as effective as drugs, it may better prevent symptom recurrence (Babyak et al., 2000; Salmon, 2001). When experimenters randomly assigned depressed people

▼ FIGURE 41.3
Aerobic exercise and depression Mildly depressed college women who participated in an aerobic exercise program showed markedly reduced depression, compared with those who did relaxation exercises or received no treatment. (Data from McCann & Holmes, 1984.)

to an exercise group, an antidepressant group, or a placebo pill group, exercise diminished depression levels as effectively as antidepressants—and with longer-lasting effects (Hoffman et al., 2011).

Vigorous exercise provides a substantial and immediate mood boost (Watson, 2000). Even a 10-minute walk stimulates 2 hours of increased well-being by raising energy levels and lowering tension (Thayer, 1987, 1993). How does exercise work its magic? In some ways, exercise works like an antidepressant drug. It increases arousal, thus counteracting depression's low arousal state. It often leads to muscle relaxation and sounder sleep. It also orders up mood-boosting chemicals from our body's internal pharmacy—neurotransmitters such as norepinephrine, serotonin, and the endorphins (Jacobs, 1994; Salmon, 2001). And it may foster *neurogenesis*. In mice, exercise causes the brain to produce a molecule that stimulates the production of new, stress-resistant neurons (Hunsberger et al., 2007; Reynolds, 2009; van Praag, 2009).

On a simpler level, the sense of accomplishment and improved physique and body image that often accompany a successful exercise routine may enhance one's self-image, leading to a better emotional state. Exercise (at least a half-hour on five or more days of the week) is like a drug that prevents and treats disease, increases energy, calms anxiety, and boosts mood—a drug we would all take, if available. Yet few people (only 1 in 4 in the United States) take advantage of it (Mendes, 2010).

The mood boost When energy or spirits are sagging, few things reboot the day better than exercising, as I [DM] can confirm from my noontime basketball, and as I [ND] can confirm from my running.

Relaxation and Meditation

41-7 In what ways might relaxation and meditation influence stress and health?

Knowing the damaging effects of stress, could we learn to counteract our stress responses by altering our thinking and lifestyle? In the late 1960s, some respected psychologists began experimenting with *biofeedback,* a system of recording, amplifying, and feeding back information about subtle physiological responses, many controlled by the autonomic nervous system. Biofeedback instruments mirror the results of a person's own efforts, enabling the person to learn which techniques do (or do not) control a particular physiological response. After a decade of study, however, the initial claims for biofeedback seemed overblown and oversold (Miller, 1985). In 1995, a National Institutes of Health panel declared that biofeedback works best on tension headaches.

Simple methods of relaxation, which require no expensive equipment, produce many of the results biofeedback once promised. Figure 41.3 pointed out that aerobic exercise reduces depression. But did you notice in that figure that depression also decreased among women in the relaxation treatment group? More than 60 studies have found that relaxation procedures can also help alleviate headaches, hypertension, anxiety, and insomnia (Nestoriuc et al., 2008; Stetter & Kupper, 2002).

Such findings would not surprise Meyer Friedman and his colleagues. They tested relaxation in a program designed to help *Type* A heart attack survivors (who are more prone to heart attacks than their *Type* B peers) reduce their risk of future attacks. They randomly assigned hundreds of middle-aged men to one of two groups. The first group received standard advice from cardiologists about medications, diet, and exercise habits. The second group received similar advice, but they also were taught ways of modifying their lifestyles. They learned to slow

Furry friends for finals week Some schools bring cuddly critters on campus for finals week as a way to help students relax and bring disruptive stress levels down. This student at Emory University is relaxing with dogs and puppies. Other schools offer petting zoos or encourage instructors to bring in their own pets that week.

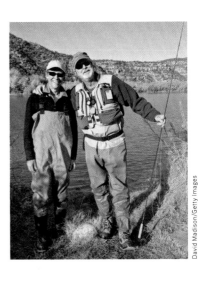

David Madison/Getty Images

▼ FIGURE 41.4
Recurrent heart attacks and lifestyle modification The San Francisco Recurrent Coronary Prevention Project offered counseling from a cardiologist to survivors of heart attacks. Those who were also guided in modifying their Type A lifestyle suffered fewer repeat heart attacks. (Data from Friedman & Ulmer, 1984.)

"Sit down alone and in silence. Lower your head, shut your eyes, breathe out gently, and imagine yourself looking into your own heart. . . . As you breathe out, say 'Lord Jesus Christ, have mercy on me.' . . . Try to put all other thoughts aside. Be calm, be patient, and repeat the process very frequently."

Gregory of Sinai, died 1346

down and relax by walking, talking, and eating more slowly. They learned to smile at others and laugh at themselves. They learned to admit their mistakes; to take time to enjoy life; and to renew their religious faith. The training paid off (**FIGURE 41.4**). During the next three years, those who learned to modify their lifestyle had half as many repeat heart attacks as did the first group. This, wrote the exuberant Friedman, was an unprecedented, spectacular reduction in heart attack recurrence. A smaller-scale British study similarly divided heart-attack–prone people into control and lifestyle modification groups (Eysenck & Grossarth-Maticek, 1991). During the next 13 years, that study also showed a 50 percent reduction in death rate among people trained to alter their thinking and lifestyle. After suffering a heart attack at age 55, Friedman started taking his own behavioral medicine—and lived to age 90 (Wargo, 2007).

Time may heal all wounds, but relaxation can help speed that process. In one study, surgery patients were randomly assigned to two groups. Both groups received standard treatment, but the second group also experienced a 45-minute relaxation exercise and received relaxation recordings to use before and after surgery. A week after surgery, patients in the relaxation group reported lower stress and showed better wound healing (Broadbent el al., 2012).

Meditation is a modern practice with a long history. In many of the world's great religions, meditation has been used to reduce suffering and improve awareness, insight, and compassion. Numerous studies have confirmed the psychological benefits of meditation (Goyal et al., 2014; Sedlmeier et al., 2012). Today, it has found a new home in stress management programs, such as *mindfulness meditation*. If you were taught this practice, you would relax and silently attend to your inner state, without judging it (Kabat-Zinn, 2001). You would sit down, close your eyes, and mentally scan your body from head to toe. Zooming your focus on certain body parts and responses, you would remain aware and accepting. You would also pay attention to your breathing, attending to each breath as if it were a material object.

Practicing mindfulness may improve many health measures. In one study of 1140 people, some received mindfulness-based therapy for several weeks. Others did not. Levels of anxiety and depression were lower among those who received the therapy (Hofmann et al., 2010). In another study, mindfulness training improved immune system functioning and coping in a group of women newly diagnosed with early-stage breast cancer (Witek-Janusek et al., 2008). Mindfulness practices have also been linked with reductions in sleep problems, cigarette use, binge eating, and alcohol and other substance use disorders (Bowen et al., 2006; Brewer et al., 2011; Cincotta et al., 2011;

de Dios et al., 2012; Kristeller et al., 2006). Just 15 minutes of daily mindfulness meditation is enough to improve decision-making performance (Hafenbrack et al., 2014).

So, what's going on in the brain as we practice mindfulness? Correlational and experimental studies offer three explanations. Mindfulness

- *strengthens connections among regions in our brain.* The affected regions are those associated with focusing our attention, processing what we see and hear, and being reflective and aware (Ives-Deliperi et al., 2011; Kilpatrick et al., 2011).

- *activates brain regions associated with more reflective awareness* (Davidson et al., 2003; Way et al., 2010). When labeling emotions, "mindful people" show less activation in the amygdala, a brain region associated with fear, and more activation in the prefrontal cortex, which aids emotion regulation (Creswell et al., 2007).

- *calms brain activation in emotional situations.* This lower activation was clear in one study in which participants watched two movies—one sad, one neutral. Those in the control group, who were not trained in mindfulness, showed strong differences in brain activation when watching the two movies. Those who had received mindfulness training showed little change in brain response to the two movies (Farb et al., 2010). Emotionally unpleasant images also trigger weaker electrical brain responses in mindful people than in their less mindful counterparts (Brown et al., 2013). A mindful brain is strong, reflective, and calm.

Dean Mitchell/Shutterstock

And then there are the mystics who seek to use the mind's power to enable novocaine-free cavity repair. Their aim: transcend dental medication.

Exercise and meditation are not the only routes to healthy relaxation. Massage helps relax both premature infants and those suffering pain. An analysis of 17 experiments revealed another benefit: Massage therapy relaxes muscles and helps reduce depression (Hou et al., 2010).

Faith Communities and Health

41-8 What is the faith factor, and what are some possible explanations for the link between faith and health?

A wealth of studies—some 1800 of them in the twenty-first century's first decade alone—has revealed another curious correlation, called the *faith factor* (Koenig et al., 2011). Religiously active people tend to live longer than those who are not religiously active.

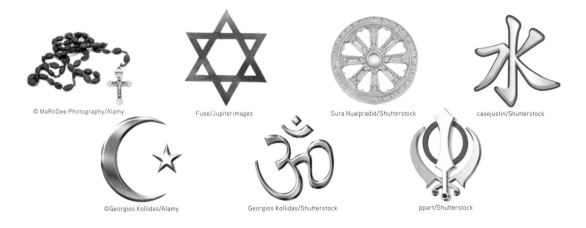

© MaRoDee Photography/Alamy   Fuse/Jupiterimages   Sura Nualpradid/Shutterstock   casejustin/Shutterstock

©Georgios Kollidas/Alamy   Georgios Kollidas/Shutterstock   ppart/Shutterstock

One such study compared the death rates for 3900 people living in two Israeli communities. The first community contained 11 religiously orthodox collective settlements; the second contained 11 matched, nonreligious collective settlements (Kark et al., 1996). Over a 16-year period, "belonging to a religious collective was associated with a strong protective effect" not explained by age or economic differences. In every age group, religious community members were about half as likely to have died as were their nonreligious counterparts. This difference is roughly comparable to the gender difference in mortality.

How should we interpret such findings? Correlations are not cause-effect statements, and they leave many factors uncontrolled (Sloan et al., 1999, 2000, 2002, 2005). Here is another possible interpretation: Women are more religiously active than men, and women outlive men. Might religious involvement merely reflect this gender-longevity link? Apparently not. One 8-year National Institutes of Health study followed 92,395 women, ages 50 to 79. After controlling for many factors, researchers found that women attending religious services weekly (or more) experienced an approximately 20 percent reduced risk of death during the study period (Schnall et al., 2010). Moreover, the association between religious involvement and life expectancy is also found among men (Benjamins et al., 2010; McCullough et al., 2000, 2005, 2009). A 28-year study that followed 5286 Californians found that, after controlling for age, gender, ethnicity, and education, frequent religious attenders were 36 percent less likely to have died in any year (**FIGURE 41.5**). In another 8-year controlled study of more than 20,000 people (Hummer et al., 1999), this effect translated into a life expectancy at age 20 of 83 years for frequent attenders at religious services and 75 years for nonattendees.

▼ FIGURE 41.5

Predictors of longer life: Not smoking, frequent exercise, and regular religious attendance Epidemiologist William Strawbridge and his co-workers (1997, 1999; Oman et al., 2002) followed 5286 Alameda, California, adults over 28 years. After adjusting for age and education, the researchers found that not smoking, regular exercise, and religious attendance all predicted a lowered risk of death in any given year. Women attending weekly religious services, for example, were only 54 percent as likely to die in a typical study year as were nonattendees.

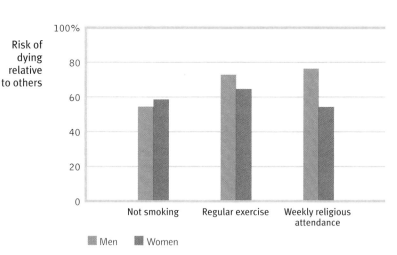

These correlational findings do not indicate that nonattenders can suddenly add 8 years to their life if they start attending services and change nothing. Nevertheless, the findings do indicate that religious involvement, like nonsmoking and exercise, is a *predictor* of health and longevity. Can you imagine what intervening variables might account for the correlation? Research points to three possible sets of influences (**FIGURE 41.6**):

* *Healthy behaviors:* Religion promotes *self-control* (McCullough & Willoughby, 2009), and religiously active people tend to smoke and drink much less and to have healthier lifestyles (Islam & Johnson, 2003; Koenig & Vaillant, 2009; Masters & Hooker, 2013; Park, 2007). In one Gallup survey of 550,000 Americans, 15 percent of the very religious were smokers, as were 28 percent of those nonreligious

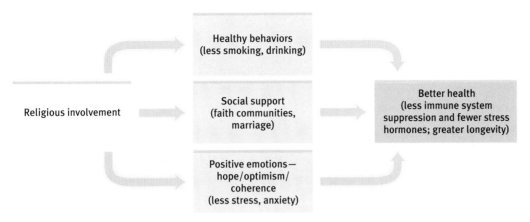

▼ FIGURE 41.6
Possible explanations for the correlation between religious involvement and health/longevity

(Newport et al., 2010). But such lifestyle differences are not great enough to explain the dramatically reduced mortality in the Israeli religious settlements. In American studies, too, about 75 percent of the longevity difference remained when researchers controlled for unhealthy behaviors, such as inactivity and smoking (Musick et al., 1999).

- *Social support:* Could social support explain the faith factor (Ai et al., 2007; Kim-Yeary et al., 2012)? In Judaic, Christian, and Islamic religions, faith is a communal experience. To belong to one of these faith communities is to have access to a support network. Religiously active people are there for one another when misfortune strikes. Moreover, religion encourages marriage, another predictor of health and longevity. In the Israeli religious settlements, for example, divorce has been almost nonexistent.

- *Positive emotions:* Even after controlling for social support, gender, unhealthy behaviors, preexisting health problems, and social support, the mortality studies have found that religiously engaged people tend to live longer (Chida et al., 2009). Researchers therefore speculate that religiously active people may benefit from a stable, coherent worldview, a sense of hope for the long-term future, feelings of ultimate acceptance, and the relaxed meditation of prayer or Sabbath observance. These intervening variables may also help to explain why the religiously active have had healthier immune functioning, fewer hospital admissions, and, for AIDS patients, fewer stress hormones and longer survival (Ironson et al., 2002; Koenig & Larson, 1998; Lutgendorf et al., 2004).

RETRIEVAL PRACTICE

- What are some of the tactics we can use to manage successfully the stress we cannot avoid?

ANSWER: Aerobic exercise, relaxation procedures, mindfulness meditation, and religious engagement

41 REVIEW Health and Coping

LEARNING OBJECTIVES

RETRIEVAL PRACTICE Take a moment to answer each of these Learning Objective Questions (repeated here from within this module). Then turn to Appendix C, Complete Module Reviews, to check your answers. Research suggests that trying to answer these questions on your own will improve your long-term retention (McDaniel et al., 2009).

41-1 In what two ways do people try to alleviate stress?

41-2 How does a perceived lack of control affect health?

41-3 How can our self-control be depleted, and why is it important to build this strength?

41-4 How does an optimistic outlook affect health and longevity?

41-5 How does social support promote good health?

41-6 How effective is aerobic exercise as a way to manage stress and improve well-being?

41-7 In what ways might relaxation and meditation influence stress and health?

41-8 What is the faith factor, and what are some possible explanations for the link between faith and health?

Use 🔗 LearningCurve to create your personalized study plan, which will direct you to the resources that will help you most in 🔗 LaunchPad.

TERMS AND CONCEPTS TO REMEMBER

RETRIEVAL PRACTICE Test yourself on these terms by trying to write down the definition before flipping back to check your answers.

coping, p. 500

problem-focused coping, p. 500

emotion-focused coping, p. 500

learned helplessness, p. 501

external locus of control, p. 503

internal locus of control, p. 503

self-control, p. 503

aerobic exercise, p. 507

TEST YOUR-SELF EMOTIONS, STRESS, AND HEALTH

Test yourself repeatedly throughout your studies. This will not only help you figure out what you know and don't know; the testing itself will help you learn and remember the information more effectively thanks to the *testing effect*.

37 Introduction to Emotion

1. The _____ - _____ theory of emotion maintains that a physiological response happens BEFORE we know what we are feeling.

2. Assume that after spending an hour on a treadmill, you receive a letter saying that your scholarship request has been approved. The two-factor theory of emotion would predict that your physical arousal will
   a. weaken your happiness.
   b. intensify your happiness.
   c. transform your happiness into relief.
   d. have no particular effect on your happiness.

3. Zajonc and LeDoux maintain that some emotional reactions occur before we have had the chance to label or interpret them. Lazarus disagreed. These psychologists differ about whether emotional responses occur in the absence of
   a. physical arousal.
   b. the hormone epinephrine.
   c. cognitive processing.
   d. learning.

4. What does a polygraph measure and why are its results questionable?

38 Expressing Emotion

5. When people are induced to assume fearful expressions, they often report feeling a little fear. This result is known as the _____ _____ effect.

39 Experiencing Emotion

6. One of the most consistent findings of psychological research is that happy people are also
   a. more likely to express anger.
   b. generally luckier than others.
   c. concentrated in the wealthier nations.
   d. more likely to help others.

7. _____ psychology is a scientific field of study focused on how humans thrive and flourish.

8. After moving to a new apartment, you find the street noise irritatingly loud, but after a while, it no longer bothers you. This reaction illustrates the
   a. relative deprivation principle.
   b. adaptation-level phenomenon.
   c. feel-good, do-good phenomenon.
   d. catharsis principle.

9. A philosopher observed that we cannot escape envy, because there will always be someone more successful, more accomplished, or richer with whom to compare ourselves. In psychology, this observation is embodied in the _____ _____ principle.

40 Stress and Illness

10. Selye's general adaptation syndrome (GAS) consists of an alarm reaction followed by _____ , then _____ .

11. When faced with stress, women are more likely than men to experience the _____-and-_____ response.

12. The number of short-term illnesses and stress-related psychological disorders was higher than usual in the months following an earthquake. Such findings suggest that
   a. daily hassles have adverse health consequences.
   b. experiencing a very stressful event increases a person's vulnerability to illness.
   c. the amount of stress a person feels is directly related to the number of stressors experienced.
   d. small, bad events don't cause stress, but large ones can be toxic.

13. Which of the following is NOT one of the three main types of stressors?
   a. Catastrophes
   b. Significant life changes
   c. Daily hassles
   d. Threatening events that we hear about

14. Research has shown that people are at increased risk for cancer a year or so after experiencing depression, helplessness, or bereavement. In describing this link, researchers are quick to point out that
   a. accumulated stress causes cancer.
   b. anger is the negative emotion most closely linked to cancer.
   c. stress does not create cancer cells, but it weakens the body's natural defenses against them.
   d. feeling optimistic about chances of survival ensures that a cancer patient will get well.

15. A Chinese proverb warns, "The fire you kindle for your enemy often burns you more than him." How is this true of Type A individuals?

16. The components of the Type A personality that have been linked most closely to coronary heart disease are anger and other _____ feelings.

41 Health and Coping

17. When faced with a situation over which you feel you have no sense of control, it is most effective to use _____ (emotion/problem)-focused coping.

18. Seligman's research showed that a dog will respond with learned helplessness if it has received repeated shocks and has had
   a. the opportunity to escape.
   b. no control over the shocks.
   c. pain or discomfort.
   d. no food or water prior to the shocks.

19. When elderly patients take an active part in managing their own care and surroundings, their morale and health tend to improve. Such findings indicate that people do better when they experience an _____ (internal/external) locus of control.

20. People who have close relationships are less likely to die prematurely than those who do not, supporting the idea that
   a. social ties can be a source of stress.
   b. gender influences longevity.
   c. Type A behavior is responsible for many premature deaths.
   d. social support has a beneficial effect on health.

21. Because it triggers the release of mood-boosting neurotransmitters such as norepinephrine, serotonin, and the endorphins, _____ exercise raises energy levels and helps alleviate depression and anxiety.

22. Research on the faith factor has found that
   a. pessimists tend to be healthier than optimists.
   b. our expectations influence our feelings of stress.
   c. religiously active people tend to outlive those who are not religiously active.
   d. religious engagement promotes isolation, repression, and ill health.

Find answers to these questions in Appendix D, in the back of the book.

Kristian Sekulic/E+/Getty Images

SOCIAL PSYCHOLOGY

. . . .

Dirk Willems faced a moment of decision in 1569. Threatened with torture and death as a member of a persecuted religious minority, he escaped from his Asperen, Holland, prison and fled across an ice-covered pond. His stronger and heavier jailer pursued him but fell through the ice and, unable to climb out, pled for help.

With his freedom in front of him, Willems acted with ultimate selflessness. He turned back and rescued his pursuer, who, under orders, took him back to captivity. A few weeks later Willems was condemned to be "executed with fire, until death ensues." For his martyrdom, present-day Asperen has named a street in honor of its folk hero (Toews, 2004).

What drives people to feel contempt for religious minorities such as Dirk Willems, and to act so spitefully? What inspires people, such as his jailer, to carry out unfair orders? And what motivated the selflessness of Willems' response, and of so many who have died trying to save others? Indeed, what motivates any of us when we volunteer kindness and generosity toward others?

As such examples demonstrate, we are social animals. We may assume the best or the worst in others. We may approach them with closed fists or open arms. As the novelist Herman Melville remarked, "We cannot live for ourselves alone. Our lives are connected by a thousand invisible threads." *Social psychologists* explore these connections by scientifically studying how we *think about, influence,* and *relate to* one another. Social Thinking (Module 42) asks, *How do we explain people's behavior? How do we form our beliefs and attitudes? What is the relationship between what we think and what we do?* Social Influence (Module 43) asks, *What invisible threads pull us? How strong are they? How do they operate?* Antisocial Relations (Module 44) asks, *What makes us harm others?* And Prosocial Relations (Module 45) asks: *Why do we fall in love?* and *What can we do to transform the closed fists of aggression into the open arms of compassion?*

Social Thinking

42-1 What do social psychologists study? How do we tend to explain others' behavior and our own?

Personality psychologists focus on the person. They study the personal traits and dynamics that explain why *different people* may act differently *in a given situation*, such as the one Willems faced. (Would you have helped the jailer out of the icy water?)

Social psychologists focus on the situation. They study the social influences that explain why *the same person* will act differently in *different situations*. Might the jailer have acted differently—opting not to march Willems back to jail—under differing circumstances?

Dirk Willemfz. 1569.

An etching of Dirk Willems by Dutch artist Jan Luyken (from *The Martyrs Mirror*, 1685)

The Fundamental Attribution Error

Our social behavior arises from our social cognition. Especially when the unexpected occurs, we want to understand and explain why people act as they do. After studying how people explain others' behavior, Fritz Heider (1958) proposed an **attribution theory:** We can attribute the behavior to the person's stable, enduring traits (a *dispositional attribution*), or we can attribute it to the situation (a *situational attribution*).

For example, in class, we notice that Juliette seldom talks. Over coffee, Jack talks nonstop. That must be the sort of people they are, we decide. Juliette must be shy and Jack outgoing. Such attributions—to their dispositions—can be valid, because people do have enduring personality traits. But sometimes we fall prey to the **fundamental attribution error** (Ross, 1977): We overestimate the influence of personality and underestimate the influence of situations. In class, Jack may be as quiet as Juliette. Catch Juliette at a party and you may hardly recognize your quiet classmate.

David Napolitan and George Goethals (1979) demonstrated the fundamental attribution error in an experiment with Williams College students. They had students talk, one at a time, with a young woman who acted either cold and critical or warm and friendly. Before the conversations, the researchers told half the students that the woman's behavior would be spontaneous. They told the other half the truth—that they had instructed her to *act* friendly (or unfriendly).

Did hearing the truth affect students' impressions of the woman? Not at all! If the woman acted friendly, both groups decided she really was a warm person. If she acted unfriendly, both decided she really was a cold person. They attributed her behavior to her personal disposition *even when told that her behavior was situational*—that she was merely acting that way for the purposes of the experiment.

What Factors Affect Our Attributions?

The fundamental attribution error appears more often in some cultures than in others. Individualist Westerners more often attribute behavior to people's personal traits. People in East Asian cultures are somewhat more sensitive to the power of the situation (Heine & Ruby, 2010; Kitayama et al., 2009). This difference has appeared in experiments that asked people to view scenes, such as a big fish swimming. Americans focused more on the individual fish, and Japanese people more on the whole scene (Chua et al., 2005; Nisbett, 2003).

We all commit the fundamental attribution error. Consider: Is your psychology instructor shy or outgoing?

If you answer "outgoing," remember that you know your instructor from one situation—the classroom, which demands outgoing behavior. Your instructor (who

social psychology the scientific study of how we think about, influence, and relate to one another.

attribution theory the theory that we explain someone's behavior by crediting either the situation or the person's disposition.

fundamental attribution error the tendency for observers, when analyzing others' behavior, to underestimate the impact of the situation and to overestimate the impact of personal disposition.

observes his or her own behavior not only in the classroom, but also with family, in meetings, when traveling) might say, "Me, outgoing? It all depends on the situation. In class or with good friends, yes, I'm outgoing. But at professional meetings I'm really rather shy." Outside their assigned roles, professors seem less professorial, presidents less presidential, managers less managerial.

When we explain *our own* behavior, we are sensitive to how behavior changes with the situation (Idson & Mischel, 2001). (An important exception: We more often attribute our intentional and admirable actions not to situations but to our own good reasons [Malle, 2006; Malle et al., 2007].) We also are sensitive to the power of the situation when we explain the behavior of people we know well and have seen in different contexts. We more often commit the fundamental attribution error when a stranger acts badly. Having only seen that red-faced fan screaming at the referee in the heat of competition, we may assume he is a bad person. But outside the stadium, he may be a good neighbor and a great parent.

As we act, our eyes look outward; we see others' faces, not our own. If we could take an observer's point of view, would we become more aware of our own personal style? To test this idea, researchers have filmed two people interacting with a camera behind each person. Then they showed each person a replay of their interaction—filmed from the other person's perspective. It worked. Seeing their behavior from the other person's perspective, participants better appreciated the power of the situation (Lassiter & Irvine, 1986; Storms, 1973).

What Are the Consequences of Our Attributions?

The way we explain others' actions, attributing them to the person or the situation, can have important real-life effects (Fincham & Bradbury, 1993; Fletcher et al., 1990). A person must decide whether to attribute another's friendliness to romantic or sexual interest. A partner must decide whether a loved one's tart-tongued remark reflects a bad day or a mean disposition. A jury must decide whether a shooting was malicious or in self-defense. In one study, 181 state judges gave lighter sentences to a violent offender who a scientist testified had a gene that altered brain areas related to aggressiveness (Aspinwall et al., 2012).

Finally, consider the social and economic effects of attribution. How do we explain poverty or unemployment? In Britain, India, Australia, and the United States (Furnham, 1982; Pandey et al., 1982; Wagstaff, 1982; Zucker & Weiner, 1993), political conservatives have tended to place the blame on the personal dispositions of the poor and unemployed: "People generally get what they deserve. Those who don't work are freeloaders. Those who take initiative can still get ahead." After inviting people to reflect on the power of choice—by having them recall their own choices or take note of another's choices—people become more likely to think that people get what they deserve (Savani & Rattan, 2012). Political liberals, and those not primed to consider the power of choice, are more likely to blame past and present situations: "If you or I had to live with the same poor education, lack of opportunity, and discrimination, would we be any better off?" To understand and prevent terrorism, they say, consider the situations that breed terrorists. Better to drain the swamps than swat the mosquitoes.

The point to remember: Our attributions—to a person's disposition or to the situation—have real consequences.

Some 7 in 10 college women report having experienced a man misattributing her friendliness as a sexual come-on (Jacques-Tiura et al., 2007).

"Otis, shout at that man to pull himself together."

An attribution question
Whether we attribute poverty and homelessness to social circumstances or to personal dispositions affects and reflects our political views.

LaunchPad For a quick interactive tutorial, visit LaunchPad's *Concept Practice: Making Attributions.*

Attitudes and Actions

42-2 How do attitudes and actions interact?

Attitudes are feelings, often influenced by our beliefs, that predispose our reactions to objects, people, and events. If we *believe* someone is threatening us, we may *feel* fear and anger toward the person and *act* defensively. The traffic between our attitudes and our actions is two-way. Our attitudes affect our actions. And our actions affect our attitudes.

Attitudes Affect Actions

Consider the climate-change debate. On one side are climate-change activists and the Intergovernmental Panel on Climate Change (2014), which warn of accumulating greenhouse gases, melting glaciers, shrinking Arctic ice, rising seas, dying coral reefs, migrating species and vegetation, and extreme and warming weather. On the other side are climate-change skeptics, who include many in the general public. The 31 percent who in 1998 thought "the seriousness of global warming is generally exaggerated" increased to 42 percent in 2014 (Dugan, 2014). And the 34 percent of Americans who in 2014 told Gallup they worry "a great deal" about global warming was essentially the same as in 1989 (Newport, 2014).

Knowing that public attitudes affect public policies, activists on both sides are aiming to persuade. Persuasion efforts generally take two forms:

- **Peripheral route persuasion** doesn't engage systematic thinking, but does produce fast results as people respond to uninformative cues (such as celebrity endorsements) and make snap judgments. A trusted politician may declare climate change a hoax. A perfume ad may lure us with images of beautiful or famous people in love.

- **Central route persuasion** offers evidence and arguments that aim to trigger favorable thoughts. It occurs mostly when people are naturally analytical or involved in the issue. Climate scientists marshal evidence of climate warming. An automotive ad may itemize a car's great features. Because it is more thoughtful and less superficial, it is more durable.

Persuaders try to influence our behavior by changing our attitudes. But other factors, including the situation, also influence our behavior. Strong social pressures, for example, can weaken the attitude-behavior connection (Wallace et al., 2005). In roll-call votes, politicians will sometimes vote what their supporters demand, despite privately disagreeing with those demands (Nagourney, 2002). In such cases, external pressure overrides the attitude-behavior link.

Attitudes are especially likely to affect behavior when external influences are minimal, and when the attitude is stable, specific to the behavior, and easily recalled (Glasman & Albarracín, 2006). One experiment used vivid, easily recalled information to persuade people that sustained tanning put them at risk for future skin cancer. One month later, 72 percent of the participants, and only 16 percent of those in a wait-list control group, had lighter skin (McClendon & Prentice-Dunn, 2001). Persuasion changed attitudes, which changed behavior.

Actions Affect Attitudes

Now consider a more surprising principle: Not only will people stand up for what they believe, they also will more strongly believe in what they have stood up for. Many streams of evidence confirm that *attitudes follow behavior* (**FIGURE 42.1**).

attitude feelings, often influenced by our beliefs, that predispose us to respond in a particular way to objects, people, and events.

peripheral route persuasion occurs when people are influenced by incidental cues, such as a speaker's attractiveness.

central route persuasion occurs when interested people focus on the arguments and respond with favorable thoughts.

Actions

Attitudes

▼ FIGURE 42.1
Attitudes follow behavior
Cooperative actions, such as those performed by people on sports teams (including Germany, shown here celebrating their World Cup 2014 victory), feed mutual liking. Such attitudes, in turn, promote positive behavior.

The Foot-in-the-Door Phenomenon How would you react if someone induced you to act against your beliefs? In many cases, people adjust their attitudes. During the Korean war, many U.S. prisoners of war were held in war camps run by Chinese communists. Without using brutality, the captors secured the prisoners' collaboration in various activities. Some merely ran errands or did simple tasks to gain privileges. Others made radio appeals and false confessions. Still others informed on other prisoners and divulged military information. When the war ended, 21 prisoners chose to stay with the communists. More returned home "brainwashed"—convinced that communism was a good thing for Asia.

How did the Chinese captors achieve these amazing results? A key ingredient was their effective use of the **foot-in-the-door phenomenon:** They knew that people who agreed to a small request would find it easier to comply later with a larger one. The Chinese began with harmless requests, such as copying a trivial statement, but gradually escalated their demands (Schein, 1956). The next statement to be copied might list flaws of capitalism. Then, to gain privileges, the prisoners participated in group discussions, wrote self-criticisms, or uttered public confessions. After doing so, they often adjusted their beliefs to be more consistent with their public acts. The point is simple: To get people to agree to something big, start small and build (Cialdini, 1993). A trivial act makes the next act easier. Succumb to a temptation and you will find the next temptation harder to resist.

In dozens of experiments, researchers have coaxed people into acting against their attitudes or violating their moral standards, with the same result: Doing becomes believing. After giving in to a request to harm an innocent victim—by making nasty comments or delivering electric shocks—people begin to disparage their victim. After speaking or writing on behalf of a position they have qualms about, they begin to believe their own words.

Fortunately, the attitudes-follow-behavior principle works with good deeds as well. The foot-in-the-door tactic has helped boost charitable contributions and blood donations, as well as product sales. In one classic experiment, researchers posing as safe-driving volunteers asked Californians to permit the installation of a large, poorly lettered "Drive Carefully" sign in their front yards. Only 17 percent consented. They approached other home owners with a small request first: Would they display a 3-inch-high "Be a Safe Driver" sign? Nearly all readily agreed. When reapproached two weeks later to allow the large, ugly sign in their front yards, 76 percent consented (Freedman

foot-in-the-door phenomenon the tendency for people who have first agreed to a small request to comply later with a larger request.

"If the King destroys a man, that's proof to the King it must have been a bad man."

Thomas Cromwell, in Robert Bolt's
A Man for All Seasons, 1960

& Fraser, 1966). To secure a big commitment, it often pays to put your foot in the door: Start small and build.

Racial attitudes likewise follow behavior. In the years immediately following the introduction of school desegregation in the United States and the passage of the Civil Rights Act of 1964, White Americans expressed diminishing racial prejudice. And as Americans in different regions came to act more alike—thanks to more uniform national standards against discrimination—they began to think more alike. Experiments confirm the observation: Moral action strengthens moral convictions.

Role Playing Affects Attitudes When you adopt a new **role**—when you become a college student, marry, or begin a new job—you strive to follow the social prescriptions. At first, your behaviors may feel phony, because you are *acting* a role. Soldiers may at first feel they are playing war games. Newlyweds may feel they are "playing house." Before long, however, what began as playacting in the theater of life becomes *you*. Researchers have confirmed this effect by assessing people's attitudes before and after they adopt a new role, sometimes in laboratory situations, sometimes in everyday situations, such as before and after taking a job.

Role playing morphed into real life in one famous and controversial study in which male college students volunteered to spend time in a simulated prison. Stanford psychologist Philip Zimbardo (1972) randomly assigned some volunteers to be guards. He gave them uniforms, clubs, and whistles and instructed them to enforce certain rules. Others became prisoners, locked in barren cells and forced to wear humiliating outfits. For a day or two, the volunteers self-consciously "played" their roles. Then the simulation became real—too real. Most guards developed disparaging attitudes, and some devised cruel and degrading routines. One by one, the prisoners broke down, rebelled, or became passively resigned. After only six days, Zimbardo called off the study.

Critics question the reliability of Zimbardo's results (Griggs, 2014). But this much seems true: Role playing can train torturers (Staub, 1989). In the early 1970s, the Greek military government eased men into their roles. First, a trainee stood guard outside an interrogation cell. After this "foot in the door" step, he stood guard inside. Only then was he ready to become actively involved in the questioning and torture. What we do, we gradually become. In one study of German males, military training toughened their personalities, leaving them less agreeable even five years later after leaving the military (Jackson et al., 2012). And it's true of us all: Every time we act like the people around us we slightly change ourselves to be more like them, and less like who we used to be.

Yet people differ. In Zimbardo's Stanford Prison simulation and in other atrocity-producing situations, some people have succumbed to the situation and others have

"Fake it until you make it."

Alcoholics Anonymous saying

LaunchPad To view Philip Zimbardo's 14-minute illustration and explanation of his famous prison simulation, visit the LaunchPad *Video—The Stanford Prison Study: The Power of the Situation.*

The power of the situation In his 1972 Stanford Prison simulation, Philip Zimbardo created a toxic situation (left). Those assigned to the guard role soon degraded the prisoners. In real life in 2004, some U.S. military guards tormented Iraqi prisoners at the U.S.-run Abu Ghraib prison (right). To Zimbardo (2004, 2007), it was a bad barrel rather than a few bad apples that led to the Abu Ghraib atrocities: "When ordinary people are put in a novel, evil place, such as most prisons, Situations Win, People Lose."

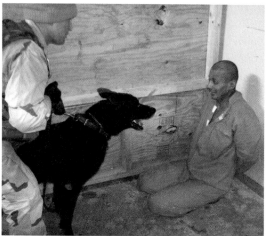

not (Carnahan & McFarland, 2007; Haslam & Reicher, 2007, 2012; Mastroianni & Reed, 2006; Zimbardo, 2007). Person and situation interact. Much as water dissolves salt but not sand, so rotten situations turn some people into bad apples while others resist (Johnson, 2007).

Cognitive Dissonance: Relief From Tension   So far, we have seen that actions can affect attitudes, sometimes turning prisoners into collaborators, doubters into believers, and compliant guards into abusers. But why? One explanation is that when we become aware that our attitudes and actions don't coincide, we experience tension, or *cognitive dissonance*. Indeed, the brain regions that become active when people experience cognitive conflict and negative arousal also become active when people experience cognitive dissonance (Kitayama et al., 2013). To relieve this tension, according to Leon Festinger's (1957) **cognitive dissonance theory,** we often bring our attitudes into line with our actions.

Dozens of experiments have explored this cognitive dissonance phenomenon. Many have made people feel responsible for behavior that clashed with their attitudes and had foreseeable consequences. In one of these experiments, you might agree for a measly $2 to help a researcher by writing an essay that supports something you don't believe in (perhaps a tuition increase). Feeling responsible for the statements (which are inconsistent with your attitudes), you would probably feel dissonance, especially if you thought an administrator would be reading your essay. To reduce the uncomfortable tension you might start believing your phony words. At such times, it's as if we rationalize, "If I chose to do it (or say it), I must believe in it." The less coerced and more responsible we feel for a troubling act, the more dissonance we feel. The more dissonance we feel, the more motivated we are to find consistency, such as changing our attitudes to help justify the act.

The attitudes-follow-behavior principle has a heartening implication: We cannot directly control all our feelings, but we can influence them by altering our behavior. If we are down in the dumps, we can do as cognitive-behavioral therapists advise and talk in more positive, self-accepting ways with fewer self-put-downs. If we are unloving, we can become more loving by behaving as if we were so—by doing thoughtful things, expressing affection, giving affirmation. That helps explain why teens' doing volunteer work promotes a compassionate identity. "Assume a virtue, if you have it not," says Hamlet to his mother. "For use can almost change the stamp of nature." Pretense can become reality. Conduct sculpts character. What we do we become.

The point to remember: Cruel acts shape the self. But so do acts of good will. Act as though you like someone, and you soon may. Changing our behavior can change how we think about others and how we feel about ourselves.

LaunchPad To check your understanding of cognitive dissonance, visit LaunchPad's *Concept Practice: Cognitive Dissonance.*

"Sit all day in a moping posture, sigh, and reply to everything with a dismal voice, and your melancholy lingers. . . . If we wish to conquer undesirable emotional tendencies in ourselves, we must . . . go through the outward movements of those contrary dispositions which we prefer to cultivate."

William James, *Principles of Psychology,* 1890

RETRIEVAL PRACTICE

- Driving to school one snowy day, Marco narrowly misses a car that slides through a red light. "Slow down! What a terrible driver," he thinks to himself. Moments later, Marco himself slips through an intersection and yelps, "Wow! These roads are awful. The city plows need to get out here." What social psychology principle has Marco just demonstrated? Explain.

  ANSWER: By attributing the other person's behavior to the person ("he's a terrible driver") and his own to the situation ("these roads are awful!"), Marco has exhibited the *fundamental attribution error.*

- How do our attitudes and our actions affect each other?

  ANSWER: Our attitudes often influence our actions as we behave in ways consistent with our beliefs. However, our attitudes also follow our actions; we come to believe in what we have done.

- When people act in a way that is not in keeping with their attitudes, and then change their attitudes to match those actions, _____ _____ theory attempts to explain why.

  ANSWER: cognitive dissonance

MODULE
42 REVIEW Social Thinking

LEARNING OBJECTIVES

RETRIEVAL PRACTICE Take a moment to answer each of these Learning Objective Questions (repeated here from within this module). Then turn to Appendix C, Complete Module Reviews, to check your answers. Research suggests that trying to answer these questions on your own will improve your long-term retention (McDaniel et al., 2009).

42-1 What do social psychologists study? How do we tend to explain others' behavior and our own?

42-2 How do attitudes and actions interact?

TERMS AND CONCEPTS TO REMEMBER

RETRIEVAL PRACTICE Test yourself on these terms by trying to write down the definition before flipping back to the page number referenced to check your answer.

social psychology, p. 518

attribution theory, p. 518

fundamental attribution error, p. 518

attitude, p. 520

peripheral route persuasion, p. 520

central route persuasion, p. 520

foot-in-the-door phenomenon, p. 521

role, p. 522

cognitive dissonance theory, p. 523

Use ⊗ LearningCurve to create your personalized study plan, which will direct you to the resources that will help you most in ⊗ LaunchPad.

MODULE
43 Social Influence

Social psychology's great lesson is the enormous power of social influence. This influence can be seen in our conformity, our obedience to authority, and our group behavior. Suicides, bomb threats, airplane hijackings, and UFO sightings all have a curious tendency to come in clusters. On campus, jeans are the dress code; on New York's Wall Street or London's Bond Street, dress suits are the norm. When we know how to act, how to groom, how to talk, life functions smoothly. Armed with social influence principles, advertisers, fundraisers, and campaign workers aim to sway our decisions to buy, to donate, to vote. Isolated with others who share their grievances, dissenters may gradually become rebels, and rebels may become terrorists. Let's examine the pull of these social strings. How strong are they? How do they operate? When do we break them?

"Have you ever noticed how one example—good or bad—can prompt others to follow? How one illegally parked car can give permission for others to do likewise? How one racial joke can fuel another?"

Marian Wright Edelman,
The Measure of Our Success, 1992

Conformity: Complying With Social Pressures

43-1 What is automatic mimicry, and how do conformity experiments reveal the power of social influence?

Automatic Mimicry

Fish swim in schools. Birds fly in flocks. And humans, too, tend to go with their group, to think what it thinks and do what it does. Behavior is contagious. Chimpanzees are more likely to yawn after observing another chimpanzee yawn (Anderson et al., 2004). Ditto for humans. If one of us yawns, laughs, coughs, stares at the sky, or checks a cell phone, others in our group will often do the same. Yawn mimicry can also occur across species: Dogs more often yawn after observing their owners' yawn (Silva et al., 2012). Even just reading about yawning increases people's yawning (Provine, 2012), as perhaps you have noticed?

"Look, I have my misgivings, too, but what choice do we have except stay the course?"

Like the chameleon lizards that take on the color of their surroundings, we humans take on the emotional tones of those around us. Just hearing someone reading a neutral text in either a happy- or sad-sounding voice creates "mood contagion" in listeners (Neumann & Strack, 2000). We are natural mimics, unconsciously imitating others' expressions, postures, and voice tones.

Tanya Chartrand and John Bargh captured this mimicry, which they call the *chameleon effect* (Chartrand & Bargh, 1999). They had students work in a room alongside another person, who was actually a confederate working for the experimenters. Sometimes the confederates rubbed their own face. Sometimes they shook their foot. Sure enough, the students tended to rub their face when with the face-rubbing person and shake their foot when with the foot-shaking person. Other studies have found people synchronizing their grammar to match material they are reading or people they are hearing (Ireland & Pennebaker, 2010).

Dave Coverly/Speedbump

We should not be surprised, then, that intricate studies show that obesity, sleep loss, drug use, loneliness, and happiness spread through social networks (Christakis & Fowler, 2009). We and our friends form a social system. On websites, positive ratings generate more positive ratings—a phenomenon called "positive herding" (Muchnik et al., 2013). In a massive experiment on the 2010 U.S. congressional election day, Facebook showed 61 million people a message that encouraged their voting, with a link to a local voting place and a clickable "I voted" button. Those who also received these messages with pictures of Facebook friends who had already voted became slightly more likely to vote—enough so to have generated an estimated 282,000 additional voters (**FIGURE 43.1**).

© Ted Horowitz Photography, 2014

Automatic mimicry helps us to *empathize*—to feel what others are feeling. This helps explain why we feel happier around happy people than around depressed people. It also helps explain why studies of groups of British workers have revealed *mood linkage*, or the sharing of moods (Totterdell et al., 1998). Empathic people yawn more after seeing others yawn (Morrison, 2007). And empathic mimicking fosters fondness (van Baaren et al., 2003, 2004). Perhaps you've noticed that when someone nods their head as you do and echoes your words, you feel a certain rapport and liking?

Conforming to nonconformity Are these students asserting their individuality or identifying themselves with others of the same microculture?

Suggestibility and mimicry sometimes lead to tragedy. In the eight days following the 1999 shooting rampage at Colorado's Columbine High School, every U.S. state except Vermont experienced threats of copycat violence. Pennsylvania alone recorded 60 such threats (Cooper, 1999). Sociologist David Phillips and his colleagues (1985, 1989) found that suicides, too, sometimes increase following a highly publicized suicide. In the wake of screen idol Marilyn Monroe's suicide on August 5, 1962, for example, the number of suicides in the United States exceeded the usual August count by 200.

"When I see synchrony and mimicry—whether it concerns yawning, laughing, dancing, or aping—I see social connection and bonding."

Primatologist Frans de Waal
"The Empathy Instinct," 2009

Reprinted by permission from Macmillan Publishers Ltd: Nature: Bond, R. M., Fariss, C. J., Jones, J. J., Kramer, A. D. I., Marlow, C., Settle, J. E., & Fowler, J. H. (2012). A 61-million-person experiment in social influence and political mobilization. Nature, 489, 295–298, copyright September 12, 2012.

Informational message

Social message

▼ FIGURE 43.1
Social networking influence On the 2010 U.S. congressional election day, Facebook gave people an *informational message* that encouraged voting. The message had measurably more influence when supplemented with a *social message* that showed friends who had voted (Bond et al., 2012).

NON SEQUITUR   by WILEY

conformity adjusting our behavior or thinking to coincide with a group standard.

normative social influence influence resulting from a person's desire to gain approval or avoid disapproval.

informational social influence influence resulting from one's willingness to accept others' opinions about reality.

What causes behavior clusters? Do people act similarly because of their influence on one another? Or because they are simultaneously exposed to the same events and conditions? Seeking answers to such questions, social psychologists have conducted experiments on group pressure and conformity.

Conformity and Social Norms

Suggestibility and mimicry are subtle types of **conformity**—adjusting our behavior or thinking toward some group standard. To study conformity, Solomon Asch (1955) devised a simple test. Imagine yourself as a participant in what you believe is a study of visual perception. You arrive in time to take a seat at a table with five other people. The experimenter asks the group to state, one by one, which of three comparison lines is identical to a standard line. You see clearly that the answer is Line 2, and you await your turn to say so. Your boredom begins to show when the next set of lines proves equally easy.

Now comes the third trial, and the correct answer seems just as clear-cut (**FIGURE 43.2**). But the first person gives what strikes you as a wrong answer: "Line 3." When the second person and then the third and fourth give the same wrong answer, you sit up straight and squint. When the fifth person agrees with the first four, you feel your heart begin to pound. The experimenter then looks to you for your answer. Torn between the unanimity voiced by the five others and the evidence of your own eyes, you feel tense and suddenly unsure. You hesitate before answering, wondering whether you should suffer the discomfort of being the oddball. What answer do you give?

In Asch's experiments, college students, answering questions alone, erred less than 1 percent of the time. But what about when several others—"confederates" working for the experimenter—answered incorrectly? Although most people told the truth even when others did not, Asch was disturbed by his result: More than one-third of the time, these "intelligent and well-meaning" college students were "willing to call white black" by going along with the group.

▼ FIGURE 43.2
Asch's conformity experiments
Which of the three comparison lines is equal to the standard line? What do you suppose most people would say after hearing five others say, "Line 3"? In this photo from one of Asch's experiments, the student in the center shows the severe discomfort that comes from disagreeing with the responses of other group members (in this case, accomplices of the experimenter).

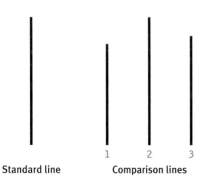

Standard line   Comparison lines

Later investigations have not always found as much conformity as Asch found, but they have revealed that we are more likely to conform when we

- are made to feel incompetent or insecure.
- are in a group with at least three people.
- are in a group in which everyone else agrees. (If just one other person disagrees, the odds of our disagreeing greatly increase.)
- admire the group's status and attractiveness.
- have not made a prior commitment to any response.
- know that others in the group will observe our behavior.
- are from a culture that strongly encourages respect for social standards.

Why do we so often think what others think and do what they do? Why, in college residence halls, do students' *attitudes* become more similar to those living near them (Cullum & Harton, 2007)? Why, when asked controversial questions, are students' answers more diverse when using anonymous electronic clickers than when raising hands (Stowell et al., 2010)? Why do we clap when others clap, eat as others eat, believe what others believe, say what others say, even see what others see?

Frequently, we conform to avoid rejection or to gain social approval. In such cases, we are responding to **normative social influence.** We are sensitive to *social norms*—understood rules for accepted and expected behavior—because the price we pay for being different can be severe. We need to belong.

At other times, we conform because we want to be accurate. Groups provide information, and only an uncommonly stubborn person will never listen to others. "Those who never retract their opinions love themselves more than they love truth," observed Joseph Joubert, an eighteenth-century French essayist. When we accept others' opinions about reality, we are responding to **informational social influence.** As Rebecca Denton demonstrated in 2004, sometimes it pays to assume others are right and to follow their lead. Denton set a record for the farthest distance driven on the wrong side of a British divided highway—30 miles, with only one minor sideswipe, before the motorway ran out and police were able to puncture her tires. Denton, who was intoxicated, later explained that she thought the hundreds of other drivers coming at her were all on the wrong side of the road (Woolcock, 2004).

Is conformity good or bad? The answer depends partly on our culturally influenced values. Western Europeans and people in most English-speaking countries tend to prize individualism. People in many Asian, African, and Latin American countries place a higher value on honoring group standards. In social influence experiments across 17 countries, conformity rates have been lower in individualist cultures (Bond & Smith, 1996). American university students, for example, tend to see themselves, in domains ranging from consumer purchases to political views, as less conforming than others (Pronin et al., 2007). We are, in our own eyes, individuals amid a crowd of sheep.

🅜 **LaunchPad** To review the classic conformity studies and experience a simulated experiment, visit LaunchPad's *PsychSim 6: Everybody's Doing It!*

RETRIEVAL PRACTICE

- Which of the following strengthens conformity to a group?

    a. Finding the group attractive   c. Coming from an individualist culture

    b. Feeling secure   d. Having made a prior commitment

ANSWER: a

Tattoos: Yesterday's noncon-formity, today's conformity? As tattoos become perceived as fashion conformity, their popularity may wane.

"I love the little ways you're identical to everyone else."

Like humans, migrating and herding animals conform for both information-al and normative reasons (Claidière & Whiten, 2012). Following others is informative; compared with solo geese, a flock of geese migrate more accurately. (There is wisdom in the crowd.) But staying with the herd also sustains group membership.

Obedience: Following Orders

43-2 What did Milgram's obedience experiments teach us about the power of social influence?

Social psychologist Stanley Milgram (1963, 1974), a high school classmate of Philip Zimbardo and then a student of Solomon Asch, knew that people often give in to social pressures. But how would they respond to outright commands? To find out, he undertook what became social psychology's most famous and controversial experiments (Benjamin & Simpson, 2009).

Imagine yourself as one of the nearly 1000 people who took part in Milgram's 20 experiments. You respond to an advertisement for participants in a Yale University psychology study of the effect of punishment on learning. Professor Milgram's assistant asks you and another person to draw slips from a hat to see who will be the "teacher" and who will be the "learner." Because (unknown to you) both slips say "teacher," you draw a "teacher" slip and are asked to sit down in front of a machine, which has a series of labeled switches. The supposed learner, a mild and submissive-seeming man, is led to an adjoining room and strapped into a chair. From the chair, wires run through the wall to "your" machine. You are given your task: Teach and then test the learner on a list of word pairs. If the learner gives a wrong answer, you are to flip a switch to deliver a brief electric shock. For the first wrong answer, you will flip the switch labeled "15 Volts—Slight Shock." With each succeeding error, you will move to the next higher voltage. With each flip of a switch, lights flash and electronic switches buzz.

The experiment begins, and you deliver the shocks after the first and second wrong answers. If you continue, you hear the learner grunt when you flick the third, fourth, and fifth switches. After you activate the eighth switch ("120 Volts—Moderate Shock"), the learner cries out that the shocks are painful. After the tenth switch ("150 Volts— Strong Shock"), he begins shouting. "Get me out of here! I won't be in the experiment anymore! I refuse to go on!" You draw back, but the stern experimenter prods you: "Please continue—the experiment requires that you continue." You resist, but the experimenter insists, "It is absolutely essential that you continue," or "You have no other choice, you *must* go on."

If you obey, you hear the learner shriek in apparent agony as you continue to raise the shock level after each new error. After the 330-volt level, the learner refuses to answer and falls silent. Still, the experimenter pushes you toward the final, 450-volt switch. Ask the question, he says, and if no correct answer is given, administer the next shock level.

Would you follow the experimenter's commands to shock someone? At what level would you refuse to obey? Before undertaking the experiments, Milgram asked people what they would do. Most people were sure they would stop soon after the learner first indicated pain, certainly before he shrieked in agony. Forty psychiatrists agreed with that prediction when Milgram asked them. Were the predictions accurate? Not even close. When Milgram conducted the experiment with other men aged 20 to 50, he was astonished. More than 60 percent complied fully—right up to the last switch. When he ran a new study, with 40 new "teachers" and a learner who complained of a "slight heart condition," the results were similar. A full 65 percent of the new teachers obeyed the experimenter right up to 450 volts (**FIGURE 43.3**). In 10 later studies, women obeyed at rates similar to men's (Blass, 1999).

Cultures change over time. Researchers wondered if Milgram's results could be explained by the 1960s American mind-set. To find out, Jerry Burger (2009) replicated Milgram's basic experiment. Seventy percent of the participants obeyed up to the 150-volt point, only a slight reduction from Milgram's result. And in a recent French reality TV show replication, 81 percent of people, egged on by a cheering audience, obeyed and tortured a screaming victim (Beauvois et al., 2012).

Stanley Milgram (1933–1984)
This social psychologist's obedience experiments "belong to the self-understanding of literate people in our age" (Sabini, 1986).

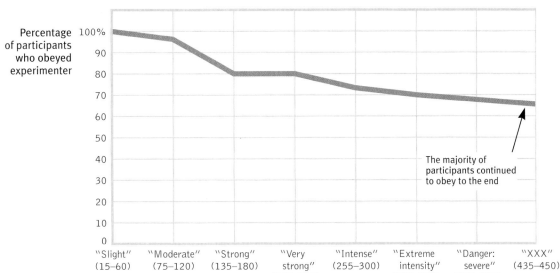

Percentage of participants who obeyed experimenter

The majority of participants continued to obey to the end

"Slight" (15–60)   "Moderate" (75–120)   "Strong" (135–180)   "Very strong" (195–240)   "Intense" (255–300)   "Extreme intensity" (315–360)   "Danger: severe" (375–420)   "XXX" (435–450)

Shock levels in volts

Stanley Milgram, from the film "Obedience." Rights held by Alexandra Milgram

▼ FIGURE 43.3
Milgram's follow-up obedience experiment In a repeat of the earlier experiment, 65 percent of the adult male "teachers" fully obeyed the experimenter's commands to continue. They did so despite the "learner's" earlier mention of a heart condition and despite hearing cries of protest after they administered what they thought were 150 volts and agonized protests after 330 volts. (Data from Milgram, 1974.)

Did Milgram's teachers figure out the hoax—that no real shock was being delivered and the learner was in fact a confederate who was pretending to feel pain? Did they realize the experiment was really testing their willingness to comply with commands to inflict punishment? *No.* The teachers typically displayed genuine distress: They perspired, trembled, laughed nervously, and bit their lips.

Milgram's use of deception and stress triggered a debate over his research ethics. In his own defense, Milgram pointed out that, after the participants learned of the deception and actual research purposes, virtually none regretted taking part (though perhaps by then the participants had reduced their **cognitive dissonance**—the discomfort they felt when their actions conflicted with their attitudes). When 40 of the teachers who had agonized most were later interviewed by a psychiatrist, none appeared to be suffering emotional aftereffects. All in all, said Milgram, the experiments provoked less enduring stress than university students experience when facing and failing big exams (Blass, 1996). Other scholars, however, after delving into Milgram's archives, report that his debriefing was less extensive and his participants' distress greater than what he had suggested (Nicholson, 2011; Perry, 2013).

In later experiments, Milgram discovered some conditions that influence people's behavior. When he varied the situation, the percentage of participants who obeyed fully ranged from 0 to 93 percent. Obedience was highest when

- *the person giving the orders was close at hand and was perceived to be a legitimate authority figure.* Such was the case in 2005 when Temple University's basketball coach sent a 250-pound bench player, Nehemiah Ingram, into a game with instructions to commit "hard fouls." Following orders, Ingram fouled out in four minutes after breaking an opposing player's right arm.

- *the authority figure was supported by a prestigious institution.* Compliance was somewhat lower when Milgram dissociated his experiments from Yale University. People have wondered: Why, during the 1994 Rwandan genocide, did so many Hutu citizens slaughter their Tutsi neighbors? It was partly because they were part of "a culture in which orders from above, even if evil," were understood as having the force of law (Kamatali, 2014).

- *the victim was depersonalized or at a distance, even in another room.* Similarly, many soldiers in combat either have not fired their rifles at an enemy they can see, or

---

cognitive dissonance theory the theory that we act to reduce the discomfort (dissonance) we feel when two of our thoughts (cognitions) are inconsistent. For example, when we become aware that our attitudes and our actions clash, we can reduce the resulting dissonance by changing our attitudes.

Jeff Widener/AP Photo

Standing up for democracy
Some individuals—roughly one in three in Milgram's experiments—resist social coercion, as did this unarmed man in Beijing, by single-handedly challenging an advancing line of tanks the day after the 1989 Tiananmen Square student uprising was suppressed.

The Wreck of HMS Birkenhead off the Cape of Good Hope on 26 Feb. 1852, 1892 (litho) (later colouration), Hemy, Thomas Marie Madawaska (1852–1937)/The Argory, County Armagh, Northern Ireland/Bridgeman

The "Birkenhead drill" To calm and give priority to passengers, soldiers obeyed orders to line up on deck as their ship sank.

have not aimed them properly. Such refusals to kill have been rare among soldiers who were operating long-distance artillery or aircraft weapons (Padgett, 1989). Those who killed from a distance—by operating remotely piloted drones—also have suffered much less posttraumatic stress than have on-the-ground Afghanistan and Iraq War veterans (Miller, 2012).

• *there were no role models for defiance.* "Teachers" did not see any other participant disobey the experimenter.

The power of legitimate, close-at-hand authorities was apparent among those who followed orders to carry out Holocaust atrocities. While obedience alone does not explain the Holocaust, in which anti-Semitic ideology also played a role, it was a significant factor. In the summer of 1942, nearly 500 middle-aged German reserve police officers were dispatched to German-occupied Jozefow, Poland. On July 13, the group's visibly upset commander informed his recruits, mostly family men, of their orders. They were to round up the village's Jews, who were said to be aiding the enemy. Able-bodied men would be sent to work camps, and the rest would be shot on the spot.

The commander gave the recruits a chance to refuse to participate in the executions. Only about a dozen immediately refused. Within 17 hours, the remaining 485 officers killed 1500 helpless women, children, and elderly, shooting them in the back of the head as they lay face down. Hearing the victims' pleas, and seeing the gruesome results, some 20 percent of the officers did eventually dissent, managing either to miss their victims or to wander away and hide until the slaughter was over (Browning, 1992). In real life, as in Milgram's experiments, those who resisted did so early, and they were the minority.

A different story played out in the French village of Le Chambon. There, villagers openly defied orders to cooperate with the "New Order" by sheltering French Jews, who were destined for deportation to Germany. The villagers' Protestant ancestors had themselves been persecuted, and their pastors taught them to "resist whenever our adversaries will demand of us obedience contrary to the orders of the Gospel" (Rochat, 1993). Ordered by police to give a list of sheltered Jews, the head pastor modeled defiance: "I don't know of Jews, I only know of human beings." Without realizing how long and terrible the war would be, or how much punishment and poverty they would suffer, the resisters made an initial commitment to resist. Supported by their beliefs, their role models, their interactions with one another, and their own initial acts, they remained defiant to the war's end.

Lest we presume that obedience is always evil and resistance is always good, consider the obedience of British soldiers who, in 1852, were traveling with civilians aboard the steamship *Birkenhead*. As they neared their South African port, the *Birkenhead* became impaled on a rock. To calm the passengers and permit an orderly exit of civilians on the three available lifeboats, soldiers who were not assisting the passengers or working the pumps lined up at parade rest. "Steady, men!" said their officer as the lifeboats pulled away. Heroically, no one frantically rushed to claim a lifeboat seat. As the boat sank, all were plunged into the sea, most to be drowned or devoured by sharks. For almost a century, noted James Michener (1978), "the Birkenhead drill remained the measure by which heroic behavior at sea was measured."

Lessons From the Obedience Studies

What do the Milgram experiments teach us about ourselves? How does flicking a shock switch relate to everyday social behavior? Psychological experiments aim not to re-create the literal behaviors of everyday life but to capture and explore the underlying processes that shape those behaviors. Participants in Milgram's experiments confronted a dilemma we all face frequently: Do I adhere to my own standards, or do I respond to others?

In Milgram's experiments and their modern replications, participants were torn. Should they respond to the pleas of the victim or the orders of the experimenter? Their moral sense warned them not to harm another, yet it also prompted them to obey the experimenter and to be a good research participant. With kindness and obedience on a collision course, obedience usually won.

These experiments demonstrated that strong social influences can make people conform to falsehoods or capitulate to cruelty. Milgram saw this as the fundamental lesson of this work: "Ordinary people, simply doing their jobs, and without any particular hostility on their part, can become agents in a terrible destructive process" (1974, p. 6).

Focusing on the end point—450 volts, or someone's real-life violence—we can hardly comprehend the inhumanity. But we ignore how they get there, in tiny increments. Milgram did not entrap his teachers by asking them first to zap learners with enough electricity to make their hair stand on end. Rather, he exploited the foot-in-the-door effect, beginning with a little tickle of electricity and escalating step by step. In the minds of those throwing the switches, the small action became justified, making the next act tolerable. In Jozefow and Le Chambon, as in Milgram's experiments, those who resisted usually did so early. After the first acts of compliance or resistance, attitudes began to follow and justify behavior.

So it happens when people succumb, gradually, to evil. In any society, great evils often grow out of people's compliance with lesser evils. The Nazi leaders suspected that most German civil servants would resist shooting or gassing Jews directly, but they found them surprisingly willing to handle the paperwork of the Holocaust (Silver & Geller, 1978). Milgram found a similar reaction in his experiments. When he asked 40 men to administer the learning test while someone else did the shocking, 93 percent complied. Cruelty does not require devilish villains. All it takes is ordinary people corrupted by an evil situation. Ordinary students may follow orders to haze initiates into their group. Ordinary employees may follow orders to produce and market harmful products. Ordinary soldiers may follow orders to punish and then torture prisoners (Lankford, 2009).

"I was only following orders."

Adolf Eichmann, Director of Nazi deportation of Jews to concentration camps

"All evil begins with 15 volts."

Philip Zimbardo, Stanford lecture, 2010

RETRIEVAL PRACTICE

- Psychology's most famous obedience experiments, in which most participants obeyed an authority figure's demands to inflict presumed painful, dangerous shocks on an innocent participant, were conducted by social psychologist _____ _____.

  ANSWER: Stanley Milgram

- What situations have researchers found to be most likely to encourage obedience in participants?

  ANSWER: The Milgram studies showed that people were most likely to follow orders when the experimenter was nearby and was a legitimate authority figure, the victim was not nearby, and there were no models for defiance.

Group Behavior

43-3 How is our behavior affected by the presence of others?

Imagine standing in a room, holding a fishing pole. Your task is to wind the reel as fast as you can. On some occasions you wind in the presence of another participant, who is also winding as fast as possible. Will the other's presence affect your own performance?

Hope College

Social facilitation Skilled athletes often find they are "on" before an audience. What they do well, they do even better when people are watching.

In one of social psychology's first experiments, Norman Triplett (1898) reported that adolescents would wind a fishing reel faster in the presence of someone doing the same thing. Although a modern reanalysis revealed that the difference was modest (Stroebe, 2012), Triplett inspired later social psychologists to study how others' presence affects our behavior. Group influences operate both in simple groups—one person in the presence of another—and in more complex groups.

Social Facilitation

Triplett's claim—of strengthened performance in others' presence—is called **social facilitation.** But on tougher tasks (learning nonsense syllables or solving complex multiplication problems), people perform worse when observers or others working on the same task are present. Further studies revealed that the presence of others sometimes helps and sometimes hinders performance (Guerin, 1986; Zajonc, 1965). Why? Because when others observe us, we become aroused, and this arousal amplifies our other reactions. It strengthens our most *likely* response—the correct one on an easy task, an incorrect one on a difficult task. Thus, expert pool players who made 71 percent of their shots when alone made 80 percent when four people came to watch them (Michaels et al., 1982). Poor shooters, who made 36 percent of their shots when alone, made only 25 percent when watched.

The energizing effect of an enthusiastic audience probably contributes to the home advantage that has shown up in studies of more than a quarter-million college and professional athletic events in various countries (Allen & Jones, 2014; Jamieson, 2010). Home teams win about 6 in 10 games (somewhat fewer for baseball, cricket, and American football, somewhat more for basketball, rugby, and soccer—see **TABLE 43.1**). For most sports, home cooking is best.

Social facilitation also helps explain a funny effect of crowding. Comedians and actors know that a "good house" is a full one. Crowding triggers arousal. Comedy routines that are mildly amusing in an uncrowded room seem funnier in a densely packed room (Aiello et al., 1983; Freedman & Perlick, 1979). In experiments, when seated close to one another, participants like a friendly person even more and an unfriendly person even less (Schiffenbauer & Schiavo, 1976; Storms & Thomas, 1977). So, to ensure an energetic class or event, choose a room or set up seating that will just barely accommodate everyone.

social facilitation improved performance on simple or well-learned tasks in the presence of others.

social loafing the tendency for people in a group to exert less effort when pooling their efforts toward attaining a common goal than when individually accountable.

deindividuation the loss of self-awareness and self-restraint occurring in group situations that foster arousal and anonymity.

▼ TABLE 43.1
Home Advantage in Team Sports

Sport	Years	Home games won
Nippon League Baseball	1998–2009	53.6%
Major League Baseball	1903–2009	53.9%
National Hockey League	1917–2009	55.7%
International Rugby	1871–2009	56.9%
National Football League	1966–2009	57.3%
International Cricket	1877–2009	57.4%
National Basketball Association	1946–2009	60.5%
Women's National Basketball Assoc.	2003-2009	61.7%
English Premier League Soccer	1993–2009	63.0%
NCAA Men's Basketball	1947-2009	68.8%
Major League Soccer	2002-2009	69.1%

Source: Data from Moskowitz & Wertheim, 2011.

The point to remember: What you do well, you are likely to do even better in front of an audience, especially a friendly audience. What you normally find difficult may seem all but impossible when you are being watched.

Social Loafing

Social facilitation experiments test the effect of others' presence on performance of an individual task, such as shooting pool. But what happens when people perform as a group? In a team tug-of-war, would your effort be more than, less than, or the same as the effort you would exert in a one-on-one tug-of-war?

To find out, a University of Massachusetts research team asked blindfolded students "to pull as hard as you can" on a rope. When they fooled the students into believing three others were also pulling behind them, students exerted only 82 percent as much effort as when they knew they were pulling alone (Ingham et al., 1974). And consider what happened when blindfolded people seated in a group clapped or shouted as loudly as they could while hearing (through headphones) other people clapping or shouting loudly (Latané, 1981). When they thought they were part of a group effort, the participants produced about one-third less noise than when clapping or shouting "alone."

Bibb Latané and his colleagues (1981; Jackson & Williams, 1988) described this diminished effort as **social loafing.** Experiments in the United States, India, Thailand, Japan, China, and Taiwan have found social loafing on various tasks, though it was especially common among men in individualist cultures (Karau & Williams, 1993). What causes social loafing? Three things:

- People acting as part of a group feel *less accountable*, and therefore worry less about what others think.

- Group members may view their individual contributions as *dispensable* (Harkins & Szymanski, 1989; Kerr & Bruun, 1983).

- When group members share equally in the benefits, regardless of how much they contribute, some may slack off (as you perhaps have observed on group assignments). Unless highly motivated and strongly identified with the group, people may *free ride* on others' efforts.

Deindividuation

We've seen that the presence of others can arouse people (social facilitation), or it can diminish their feelings of responsibility (social loafing). But sometimes the presence of others does both. The uninhibited behavior that results can range from a food fight to vandalism or rioting. This process of losing self-awareness and self-restraint, called **deindividuation,** often occurs when group participation makes people both *aroused* and *anonymous*. In one experiment, New York University women dressed in depersonalizing Ku Klux Klan–style hoods. Compared with identifiable women in a control group, the hooded women delivered twice as much electric shock to a victim (Zimbardo, 1970). (As in all such experiments, the "victim" did not actually receive the shocks.)

Deindividuation thrives, for better or for worse, in many settings. Tribal warriors who depersonalize themselves with face paints or masks are more likely than those with exposed faces to kill, torture, or mutilate captured enemies (Watson, 1973). On discussion boards, Internet bullies, who would never say "You're so fake" to someone's face, may hide behind anonymity. When we shed self-awareness and self-restraint—whether in a mob, at a rock concert, at a ballgame, or at worship—we become more responsive to the group experience, whether bad or good. For a comparison of social facilitation, social loafing, and deindividuation, see **TABLE 43.2** on the next page.

Working hard, or hardly working? In group projects, such as this Earth Day beach cleanup, social loafing often occurs, as individuals free ride on the efforts of others.

Deindividuation During England's 2011 riots and looting, rioters were disinhibited by social arousal and by the anonymity provided by darkness and their hoods and masks. Later, some of those arrested expressed bewilderment over their own behavior.

▼ TABLE 43.2

Behavior in the Presence of Others: Three Phenomena

Phenomenon	Social context	Psychological effect of others' presence	Behavioral effect
Social facilitation	Individual being observed	Increased arousal	Amplified dominant behavior, such as doing better what one does well (or doing worse what is difficult)
Social loafing	Group projects	Diminished feelings of responsibility when not individually accountable	Decreased effort
Deindividuation	Group setting that fosters arousal and anonymity	Reduced self-awareness	Lowered self-restraint

▼ FIGURE 43.4

Group polarization If a group is like-minded, discussion strengthens its prevailing opinions. Talking over racial issues increased prejudice in a high-prejudice group of high school students and decreased it in a low-prejudice group. (Data from Myers & Bishop, 1970.)

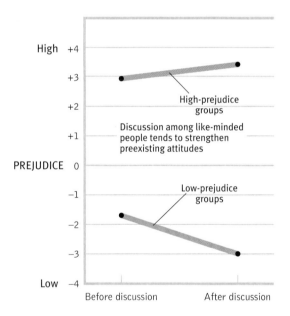

"What explains the rise of fascism in the 1930s? The emergence of student radicalism in the 1960s? The growth of Islamic terrorism in the 1990s?. . . The unifying theme is simple: *When people find themselves in groups of like-minded types, they are especially likely to move to extremes.* [This] is the phenomenon of *group polarization.*"

Cass Sunstein, *Going to Extremes,* 2009

* * *

We have examined the conditions under which the *presence* of others can motivate people to exert themselves or tempt them to free ride on the efforts of others, make easy tasks easier and difficult tasks harder, and enhance humor or fuel mob violence. Research also shows that *interacting* with others can similarly have both bad and good effects.

Group Polarization

43-4 What are *group polarization* and *groupthink,* and how much power do we have as individuals?

Over time, initial differences between groups of college students tend to grow. If the first-year students at College X tend to be artistic, and those at College Y tend to be business-savvy, those differences will probably be even greater by the time they graduate. Similarly, gender differences tend to widen over time, as Eleanor Maccoby (2002) noted from her decades of observing gender development. Girls talk more intimately than boys do and play and fantasize less aggressively; these differences will be amplified as boys and girls interact mostly with their own gender.

In each case, the beliefs and attitudes we bring to a group grow stronger as we discuss them with like-minded others. This process, called **group polarization,** can have beneficial results, as when it amplifies a sought-after spiritual awareness or reinforces the resolve of those in a self-help group. But it can also have dire consequences. George Bishop and I [DM] discovered that when high-prejudice students discussed racial issues, they became *more* prejudiced (**FIGURE 43.4**). Low-prejudice students, alternatively, became even more accepting.

Group polarization can feed extremism and even suicide terrorism. Analyses of terrorist organizations around the world reveal that the terrorist mentality does not erupt suddenly, on a whim (McCauley, 2002; McCauley & Segal, 1987; Merari, 2002). It usually begins slowly, among people who share a grievance. As they interact in isolation (sometimes with other "brothers" and "sisters" in camps) their views grow more and more extreme. Increasingly, they categorize the world as "us" against "them" (Moghaddam, 2005; Qirko, 2004). Given that the self-segregation of the like-minded polarizes people, speculated a 2006 U.S. National Intelligence estimate: "We assess that the operational threat from self-radicalized cells will grow."

When I got my start in social psychology with experiments on group polarization, I never imagined the potential dangers, or the creative possibilities, of polarization in *virtual* groups. Electronic communication and social networking have created virtual town halls where people can isolate themselves from those with different perspectives. By attuning our bookmarks and social media feeds to sites that trash the views we despise, we can retreat into partisan tribes and revel in foregone conclusions. People read blogs that reinforce their views, and those blogs link to kindred blogs (**FIGURE 43.5**). Over time, the resulting political polarization—"loathing across party lines," say some political scientists (Iyengar & Westwood, 2014)—has become much more intense than racial polarization.

As the Internet connects the like-minded and pools their ideas, climate-change skeptics, UFO abductees, and conspiracy theorists find support for their shared ideas and suspicions. White supremacists may become more racist. And militia members may become more terror prone. The longer participants spend in closed "Dark Web" forums, the more violent their messages become (Chen, 2012). Boston Marathon bombers Dzhokhar and Tamerlan Tsarnaev reportedly were "self-radicalized" through their Internet participation (Wilson et al., 2013). In the echo chambers of virtual worlds, as in the real world, separation + conversation = polarization.

But the Internet-as-social-amplifier can also work for good. Social networking sites connect friends and family members sharing common interests or coping with similar challenges. Peacemakers, cancer survivors, and bereaved parents can find strength and solace from kindred spirits. By amplifying shared concerns and ideas, Internet-enhanced communication can also foster social ventures. (I [DM] know this personally from social networking with others with hearing loss in an effort to transform American listening technology.)

The point to remember: By connecting and magnifying the inclinations of like-minded people, the Internet can be very, very bad, but also very, very good.

Groupthink

So, group interaction can influence our personal decisions. Does it ever distort important national decisions? Consider the "Bay of Pigs fiasco." In 1961, President John F. Kennedy and his advisers decided to invade Cuba with 1400 CIA-trained Cuban exiles. When the invaders were easily captured and soon linked to the U.S. government, Kennedy wondered in hindsight, "How could we have been so stupid?"

Social psychologist Irving Janis (1982) studied the decision-making procedures leading to the ill-fated invasion. He discovered that the soaring morale of the recently elected president and his advisers fostered undue confidence. To preserve the good feeling, group members suppressed or self-censored their dissenting views, especially after President Kennedy voiced his enthusiasm for the scheme. Since no one spoke strongly against the idea, everyone assumed the support was unanimous. To describe this harmonious but unrealistic group thinking, Janis coined the term **groupthink.**

Later studies showed that groupthink—fed by overconfidence, conformity, self-justification, and group polarization—contributed to other fiascos as well. Among them were the failure to anticipate the 1941 Japanese attack on Pearl Harbor; the escalation of the Vietnam war; the U.S. Watergate cover-up; the Chernobyl nuclear reactor accident (Reason, 1987); the U.S. space shuttle *Challenger* explosion (Esser & Lindoerfer, 1989); and the Iraq war, launched on the false idea that Iraq had weapons of mass destruction (U.S. Senate Intelligence Committee, 2004).

▼ FIGURE 43.5
Like minds network in the blogosphere Blue liberal blogs link mostly to one another, as do red conservative blogs. (The intervening colors display links across the liberal-conservative boundary.) Each dot represents a blog, and each dot's size reflects the number of other blogs linking to that blog. (From Lazer et al., 2009.)

"*I wonder if we might benefit from socializing more with those who don't harbor anti-government views.*"

"One of the dangers in the White House, based on my reading of history, is that you get wrapped up in groupthink and everybody agrees with everything, and there's no discussion and there are no dissenting views."

Barack Obama, December 1, 2008, press conference

group polarization the enhancement of a group's prevailing inclinations through discussion within the group.

groupthink the mode of thinking that occurs when the desire for harmony in a decision-making group overrides a realistic appraisal of alternatives.

"Truth springs from argument among friends."

Philosopher David Hume, 1711–1776

"If you have an apple and I have an apple and we exchange apples then you and I will still each have one apple. But if you have an idea and I have an idea and we exchange these ideas, then each of us will have two ideas."

Attributed to dramatist
George Bernard Shaw, 1856–1950

Despite the dangers of groupthink, two heads are often better than one. Knowing this, Janis also studied instances in which U.S. presidents and their advisers collectively made good decisions, such as when the Truman administration formulated the Marshall Plan, which offered assistance to Europe after World War II, and when the Kennedy administration successfully prevented the Soviets from installing missiles in Cuba. In such instances—and in the business world, too, Janis believed—groupthink is prevented when a leader welcomes various opinions, invites experts' critiques of developing plans, and assigns people to identify possible problems. Just as the suppression of dissent bends a group toward bad decisions, open debate often shapes good ones. This is especially the case with diverse groups, whose varied perspectives often enable creative or superior outcomes (Nemeth & Ormiston, 2007; Page, 2007). None of us is as smart as all of us.

The Power of Individuals

In affirming the power of social influence, we must not overlook the power of individuals. *Social control* (the power of the situation) and *personal control* (the power of the individual) interact. People aren't billiard balls. When feeling coerced, we may react by doing the opposite of what is expected, thereby reasserting our sense of freedom (Brehm & Brehm, 1981).

Committed individuals can sway the majority and make social history. Were this not so, communism would have remained an obscure theory, Christianity would be a small Middle Eastern sect, and Rosa Parks' refusal to sit at the back of the bus would not have ignited the U.S. civil rights movement. Technological history, too, is often made by innovative minorities who overcome the majority's resistance to change. To many, the railroad was a nonsensical idea; some farmers even feared that train noise would prevent hens from laying eggs. People derided Robert Fulton's steamboat as "Fulton's Folly." As Fulton later said, "Never did a single encouraging remark, a bright hope, a warm wish, cross my path." Much the same reaction greeted the printing press, the telegraph, the incandescent lamp, and the typewriter (Cantril & Bumstead, 1960).

The power of one or two individuals to sway majorities is *minority influence* (Moscovici, 1985). In studies of groups in which one or two individuals consistently express a controversial attitude or an unusual perceptual judgment, one finding repeatedly stands out: When you are the minority, you are far more likely to sway the majority if you hold firmly to your position and don't waffle. This tactic won't make you popular, but it may make you influential, especially if your self-confidence stimulates others to consider *why* you react as you do. Even when a minority's influence is not yet visible, people may privately develop sympathy for the minority position and rethink their views (Wood et al., 1994).

The bottom line: The powers of social influence are enormous, but so are the powers of the committed individual. For classical music, Mozart mattered. For drama, Shakespeare mattered. For world history, Hitler and Mao—and Gandhi and Mandela—mattered. Social forces matter. But individuals matter, too.

Gandhi As the life of Hindu nationalist and spiritual leader Mahatma Gandhi powerfully testifies, a consistent and persistent minority voice can sometimes sway the majority. Gandhi's nonviolent appeals and fasts were instrumental in winning India's independence from Britain in 1947.

RETRIEVAL PRACTICE

- What is social facilitation, and why is it more likely to occur with a well-learned task?

ANSWER: This improved performance in the presence of others is most likely to occur with a well-learned task, because the added arousal caused by an audience tends to strengthen the most likely response. This also predicts poorer performance on a difficult task in others' presence.

- People tend to exert less effort when working with a group than they would alone, which is called _____ _____.

ANSWER: social loafing

- You are organizing a meeting of fiercely competitive political candidates. To add to the fun, friends have suggested handing out masks of the candidates' faces for supporters to wear. What phenomenon might these masks engage?

ANSWER: The anonymity provided by the masks, combined with the arousal of the contentious setting, might create *deindividuation* (lessened self-awareness and self-restraint).

- When like-minded groups discuss a topic, and the result is the strengthening of the prevailing opinion, this is called _____ _____.

ANSWER: group polarization

- When a group's desire for harmony overrides its realistic analysis of other options, _____ has occurred.

ANSWER: groupthink

MODULE 43 REVIEW Social Influence

LEARNING OBJECTIVES

RETRIEVAL PRACTICE Take a moment to answer each of these Learning Objective Questions (repeated here from within this module). Then turn to Appendix C, Complete Module Reviews, to check your answers. Research suggests that trying to answer these questions on your own will improve your long-term retention (McDaniel et al., 2009).

43-1 What is automatic mimicry, and how do conformity experiments reveal the power of social influence?

43-2 What did Milgram's obedience experiments teach us about the power of social influence?

43-3 How is our behavior affected by the presence of others?

43-4 What are *group polarization* and *groupthink,* and how much power do we have as individuals?

TERMS AND CONCEPTS TO REMEMBER

RETRIEVAL PRACTICE Test yourself on these terms by trying to write down the definition before flipping back to the page number referenced to check your answer.

conformity, p. 526

normative social influence, p. 527

informational social influence, p. 527

social facilitation, p. 532

social loafing, p. 533

deindividuation, p. 533

group polarization, p. 534

groupthink, p. 535

Use 🔵 LearningCurve to create your personalized study plan, which will direct you to the resources that will help you most in 🔵 LaunchPad.

MODULE 44 Antisocial Relations

Social psychology studies how we think about and influence one another, and also how we *relate* to one another. What causes us to harm, or to help, or to fall in love? How can we move a destructive conflict toward a just peace? In this section we ponder insights into *antisocial* relations gleaned by researchers who have studied prejudice and aggression.

Prejudice

44-1 What is *prejudice?* What are its social and emotional roots?

Prejudice means "prejudgment." It is an unjustifiable and usually negative attitude toward a group—often a different cultural, ethnic, or gender group. Like all attitudes, prejudice is a three-part mixture of

> **prejudice** an unjustifiable (and usually negative) attitude toward a group and its members. Prejudice generally involves stereotyped beliefs, negative feelings, and a predisposition to discriminatory action.

stereotype a generalized (sometimes accurate but often overgeneralized) belief about a group of people.

discrimination unjustifiable negative behavior toward a group and its members.

- *beliefs* (in this case, called **stereotypes**).
- *emotions* (for example, hostility or fear).
- predispositions to *action* (to discriminate).

Some stereotypes may be at least partly accurate. If you presume that young men tend to drive faster than elderly women, you may be right. People perceive Australians as having a rougher culture than the British, and in one analysis of millions of Facebook status updates, Australians did use more profanity (Kramer & Chung, 2011). But stereotypes can exaggerate—as when liberals and conservatives overestimate the extremity of the other's views (Graham et al., 2012). Stereotypes can also bias behavior. To *believe* that obese people are gluttonous, and to *feel* dislike for an obese person, is to be *prejudiced*; prejudice is a negative *attitude*. To pass over all the obese people on a dating site, or to reject an obese person as a potential job candidate, is to discriminate; **discrimination** is a negative *behavior*.

How Prejudiced Are People?

Prejudice comes as both explicit (overt) and implicit (automatic) attitudes toward people of a particular ethnic group, gender, sexual orientation, or viewpoint. Some examples:

Explicit Ethnic Prejudice Americans' expressed racial attitudes have changed dramatically in the last half-century. For example, support for all forms of racial contact, including interracial dating (**FIGURE 44.1**), has dramatically increased. "It's all right for Blacks and Whites to date each other," agreed 48 percent of Americans in 1987 and 86 percent in 2012 (Pew, 2012). "Marriage between Blacks and Whites" was approved by 4 percent of Americans in 1958 and 87 percent in 2013 (Newport, 2013).

Yet as *overt* prejudice wanes, *subtle* prejudice lingers. Despite increased verbal support for interracial marriage, many people admit that in socially intimate settings (dating, dancing, marrying) they, personally, would feel uncomfortable with someone of another race. And many people who *say* they would feel upset with someone making racist slurs actually, when hearing such racism, respond indifferently (Kawakami et al., 2009). Subtle prejudice may also take the form of "microaggressions," such as race-related traffic stops or people's reluctance to choose a train seat next to someone of a different race (Wang et al., 2011). A slew of recent experiments illustrates that prejudice can be not only subtle but also automatic and unconscious.

Nevertheless, overt prejudice persists. In the aftermath of the 9/11 terrorist attacks and the Iraq and Afghanistan wars, 4 in 10 Americans acknowledged "some feelings of prejudice against Muslims," and about half of non-Muslims in Western Europe and the United States perceived Muslims as "violent" (Saad, 2006; Wike & Grim, 2007). With Americans feeling threatened by Arabs, and as opposition to Islamic mosques and immigration flared in 2010, one observer noted that "Muslims are one of the last

▼ FIGURE 44.1
Prejudice over time Over the last quarter-century, Americans have increasingly approved interracial dating, with each successive generation expressing more approval. (Data from Pew, 2012.)

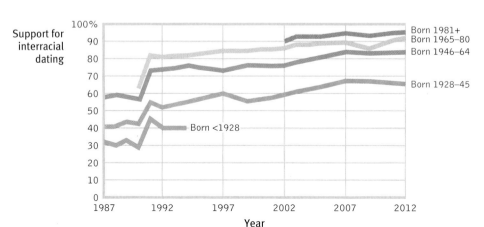

minorities in the United States that it is still possible to demean openly" (Kristof, 2010; Lyons et al., 2010). Muslims worldwide reciprocated the negativity, with most in Jordan, Egypt, Turkey, and Britain seeing Westerners as "greedy" and "immoral."

Implicit Prejudice As we have seen throughout this book, the human mind processes thoughts, memories, and attitudes on two different tracks. Sometimes that processing is *explicit*—on the radar screen of our awareness. To a much greater extent, it is *implicit*—below the radar, leaving us unaware of how our attitudes are influencing our behavior. Modern studies indicate that prejudice is often implicit, an automatic attitude—an unthinking knee-jerk response. Consider these findings:

Implicit racial associations Using Implicit Association Tests, researchers have demonstrated that even people who deny harboring racial prejudice may carry negative associations (Banaji & Greenwald, 2013). (By 2014, about 16 million people had taken the Implicit Association Test, as you can at www.implicit.harvard.edu.) For example, 9 in 10 White respondents took longer to identify pleasant words (such as *peace* and *paradise*) as "good" when presented with Black-sounding names (such as *Latisha* and *Darnell*) rather than with White-sounding names (such as *Katie* and *Ian*). Moreover, people who more quickly associate good things with White names or faces also are the quickest to perceive anger and apparent threat in Black faces (Hugenberg & Bodenhausen, 2003).

Although the test is useful for studying automatic prejudice, critics caution against using it to assess or label individuals (Oswald et al., 2013). Defenders counter that implicit biases predict behaviors ranging from simple acts of friendliness to the evaluation of work quality (Banaji & Greenwald, 2013). In the 2008 U.S. presidential election, implicit as well as explicit prejudice predicted voters' support for candidate Barack Obama, whose election in turn served to reduce implicit prejudice (Bernstein et al., 2010; Payne et al., 2010; Stephens-Davidowitz, 2014).

LaunchPad To take one version of the Implicit Associations Test, visit Launch-Pad's *Lab: Stereotyping.*

Unconscious patronization In one experiment, White university women assessed flawed student essays. When assessing essays supposedly written by White students, the women gave low evaluations, often with harsh comments, but not so when the essays were said to have been written by Black students (Harber, 1998). Did the evaluators calibrate their evaluations to their racial stereotypes, leading to less exacting standards and a patronizing attitude? In real-world evaluations, such low expectations and the resulting "inflated praise and insufficient criticism" could hinder minority student achievement, the researcher noted. (To preclude such bias, many teachers read essays while "blind" to their authors.)

Race-influenced perceptions Our expectations influence our perceptions. In 1999, Amadou Diallo was accosted as he approached his apartment house doorway by police officers looking for a rapist. When he pulled out his wallet, the officers, perceiving a gun, riddled his body with 19 bullets from 41 shots. Curious about this tragic killing of an unarmed, innocent man, two research teams reenacted the situation (Correll et al., 2002, 2007; Greenwald et al., 2003; Sadler et al., 2012). They asked viewers to press buttons quickly to "shoot" or not shoot men who suddenly appeared on screen. Some of the on-screen men held a gun. Others held a harmless object, such as a flashlight or bottle. People (both Blacks and Whites, in one study) more often shot Black men than White men who were holding the harmless objects. Priming people with a flashed Black rather than White face also made them more likely to misperceive a flashed tool as a gun (**FIGURE 44.2**). Fatigue, which diminishes one's conscious control and increases automatic reactions, amplifies racial bias in decisions to shoot (Ma et al., 2013).

Does this automatic racial bias research help us understand the 2013 death of Trayvon Martin? As he walked alone to his father's fiancée's house

> "Unhappily, the world has yet to learn how to live with diversity."
>
> Pope John Paul II, Address to the United Nations, 1995

▼ FIGURE 44.2
Race primes perceptions In experiments by Keith Payne (2006), people viewed (1) a White or Black face, immediately followed by (2) a gun or hand tool, which was then followed by (3) a visual mask. Participants were more likely to misperceive a tool as a gun when it was preceded by a Black rather than White face.

1.　　　　2.　　　　3.

in a gated Florida neighborhood, a suspicious resident started following him, leading to a confrontation and to Martin's being shot dead. Commentators wondered: Had Martin been an unarmed White teen, would he have been perceived and treated the same way?

Reflexive bodily responses Even people who consciously express little prejudice may give off telltale signals as their body responds selectively to another's race. Neuroscientists can detect these signals when people look at White and Black faces. The viewers' implicit prejudice may show up in facial-muscle responses and in the activation of their emotion-processing amygdala (Cunningham et al., 2004; Eberhardt, 2005; Stanley et al., 2008).

If your own gut-check reveals you sometimes have feelings you would rather not have about other people, remember this: It is what we *do* with our feelings that matters. By monitoring our feelings and actions, and by replacing old habits with new ones based on new friendships, we can work to free ourselves from prejudice.

Gender Prejudice Overt gender prejudice has also declined sharply. The one-third of Americans who in 1937 told Gallup pollsters that they would vote for a qualified woman whom their party nominated for president soared to 95 percent in 2012 (Gallup Brain, 2008; Jones, 2012). Nearly everyone now agrees that women and men should receive the same pay for the same job.

But gender prejudice and discrimination persist. Despite equality between the sexes in intelligence scores, people have tended to perceive their fathers as more intelligent than their mothers (Furnham & Wu, 2008). In Saudi Arabia, women have not been allowed to drive. In Western countries, we pay more to those (usually men) who care for our streets than to those (usually women) who care for our children. Worldwide, women are more likely to live in poverty (UN, 2010); they represent nearly two-thirds of illiterate adults (UNESCO, 2013); and 30 percent have experienced intimate partner violence (Devries et al., 2013).

Unwanted female infants are no longer left out on a hillside to die of exposure, as was the practice in ancient Greece. Yet natural female mortality and the normal male-to-female newborn ratio (105-to-100) hardly explain the world's estimated 163 million (say that number slowly) "missing women" (Hvistendahl, 2011). In many places, sons are valued more than daughters. In India, there are 3.5 times more Google searches asking how to conceive a boy than how to conceive a girl (Stephens-Davidowitz, 2014). With testing that enables sex-selective abortions, several Asian countries have experienced a shortfall in female births. Although China has declared that sex-selective abortions—gender genocide—are now a criminal offense, the country's newborn sex ratio has been 111 boys for every 100 girls, similar to India's 112 to 100 ratio (CIA, 2014). Some 95 percent of the children in Chinese orphanages have been girls (Webley, 2009). With under-age-20 males exceeding females by 32 million, many Chinese bachelors will be unable to find mates (Zhu et al., 2009). A shortage of women also contributes to increased crime, violence, prostitution, and trafficking of women (Brooks, 2012).

Studies have shown, however, that most people *feel* more positively about women in general than they do about men (Eagly, 1994; Haddock & Zanna, 1994). Worldwide, people see women as having some traits (such as nurturance, sensitivity, and less aggressiveness) that most people prefer (Glick et al., 2004; Swim, 1994). That may explain why women tend to like women more than men like men (Rudman & Goodwin, 2004). And perhaps that is also why people prefer slightly feminized computer-generated faces—men's and women's—to slightly masculinized faces. Researcher David Perrett and his colleagues (1998) have speculated that a slightly feminized male face connotes kindness, cooperativeness, and other traits of a good father. When the British Broadcasting Corporation invited 18,000 women to guess which of the men in **FIGURE 44.3** was most likely to place a personal ad seeking a "special lady to love and cherish forever," which one do you think they picked?

▼ FIGURE 44.3
(1) Who do you like best?
(2) Which one placed an ad seeking "a special lady to love and cherish forever"? (See answers below.)

Research suggests that subtly feminized features convey a likable image, which people tend to associate more with committed dads than with promiscuous cads. Thus, 66 percent of the women picked computer-generated face (b) in response to both of these questions.

(a)

(b)

Professor Dave Perrett, St. Andrews University

Sexual Orientation Prejudice In most of the world, gay and lesbian people cannot openly and comfortably disclose who they are and whom they love (Katz-Wise & Hyde, 2012; United Nations, 2011). Dozens of countries have laws criminalizing same-sex relationships. But cultural variation is enormous—ranging from the 6 percent in Spain who say that "homosexuality is morally unacceptable" to 98 percent in Ghana (Pew, 2014). Anti-gay prejudice, though rapidly subsiding in Western countries, persists. Consider:

- In national surveys, 40 percent of LGBT Americans said it would be very or somewhat difficult for someone in their community "to live openly as gay or lesbian" (Jones, 2012). Thirty-nine percent reported having "been rejected by a friend or family member" because of their sexual orientation or gender identity. And 58 percent reported being "subject to slurs or jokes" (Pew, 2013).
- In the National School Climate Survey, 8 of 10 LGBT adolescents reported sexual orientation-related harassment in the prior year (GLSEN, 2012).

Do attitudes and practices that label, disparage, and discriminate against gay and lesbian people increase their risk of psychological disorder and ill health? In U.S. states without protections against LGBT hate crime and discrimination, gay and lesbian people experience substantially higher rates for depression and related disorders, even after controlling for income and education differences. In communities where anti-gay prejudice is high, so are gay and lesbian suicide and cardiovascular deaths. In sixteen states that banned same-sex marriage between 2001 and 2005, gays and lesbians (but not heterosexuals) experienced a 37 percent increase in depressive disorder rates, a 42 percent increase in alcohol use disorders, and a 248 percent increase in general anxiety disorders. Meanwhile, gays and lesbians in other states did not experience increased psychiatric disorders (Hatzenbuehler, 2014).

Social Roots of Prejudice

Why does prejudice arise? Social inequalities and divisions are partly responsible.

Social Inequalities When some people have money, power, and prestige and others do not, the "haves" usually develop attitudes that justify things as they are. The **just-world phenomenon** reflects an idea we commonly teach our children—that good is rewarded and evil is punished. From this it is but a short leap to assume that those who succeed must be good and those who suffer must be bad. Such reasoning enables the rich to see both their own wealth and the poor's misfortune as justly deserved. In an extreme case, slave "owners" perceived slaves as innately lazy, ignorant, and irresponsible—as having the very traits that justified enslaving them. Stereotypes rationalize inequalities.

Victims of discrimination may react with either self-blame or anger (Allport, 1954). Either reaction can feed prejudice through the classic *blame-the-victim* dynamic. Do the circumstances of poverty breed a higher crime rate? If so, that higher crime rate can be used to justify discrimination against those who live in poverty.

Us and Them: Ingroup and Outgroup We have inherited our Stone Age ancestors' need to belong, to live and love in groups. There was safety in solidarity (those who didn't band together left fewer descendants). Whether hunting, defending, or attacking, 10 hands were better than 2. Dividing the world into "us" and "them" entails racism and war, but it also provides the benefits of communal solidarity. Thus, we cheer for our groups, kill for them, die for them. Indeed, we define who we are partly in terms of our groups. Through our *social identities* we associate ourselves with certain groups and contrast ourselves with others (Dunham et al., 2013; Hogg, 1996,

just-world phenomenon the tendency for people to believe the world is just and that people therefore get what they deserve and deserve what they get.

The New Yorker Collection, 1981, Robert Mankoff from cartoonbank.com

The ingroup Scotland's famed "Tartan Army" soccer fans, shown here during a match against archrival England, share a social identity that defines "us" (the Scottish ingroup) and "them" (the English outgroup).

> "For if [people were] to choose out of all the customs in the world [they would] end by preferring their own."
>
> Greek historian Herodotus, 440 B.C.E.

> "If the Tiber reaches the walls, if the Nile does not rise to the fields, if the sky doesn't move or the Earth does, if there is famine, if there is plague, the cry is at once: 'The Christians to the lion!'"
>
> Tertullian, *Apologeticus*, 197 C.E.

2006; Turner, 1987, 2007). When Ian identifies himself as a man, an Aussie, a University of Sydney student, a Catholic, and a MacGregor, he knows who he is, and so do we.

Evolution prepared us, when encountering strangers, to make instant judgments: friend or foe? Those from our group, those who look like us, and also those who *sound* like us—with accents like our own—we instantly tend to like, from childhood onward (Gluszek & Dovidio, 2010; Kinzler et al., 2009). Mentally drawing a circle defines "us," the **ingroup**. But the social definition of who you are also states who you are not. People outside that circle are "them," the **outgroup**. An **ingroup bias**—a favoring of our own group—soon follows. Even arbitrarily creating us-them groups by tossing a coin creates this bias. In experiments, people have favored their own group when dividing any rewards (Tajfel, 1982; Wilder, 1981). Much discrimination involves not outgroup hostility but ingroup networking and mutual support, such as hiring a friend's child at the expense of other job candidates (Greenwald & Pettigrew, 2014).

The urge to distinguish enemies from friends predisposes prejudice against strangers (Whitley, 1999). To Greeks of the classical era, all non-Greeks were "barbarians." In our own era, most children believe their school is better than all other schools in town. Many high school students form cliques—jocks, gamers, skaters, gangsters, freaks, geeks—and disparage those outside their own group. Even chimpanzees have been seen to wipe clean the spot where they were touched by a chimpanzee from another group (Goodall, 1986). They also display ingroup empathy by yawning more after seeing ingroup (rather than outgroup) members yawn (Campbell & de Waal, 2011).

Ingroup bias explains the cognitive power of political partisanship (Cooper, 2010; Douthat, 2010). In the United States in the late 1980s, most Democrats believed inflation had risen under Republican president Ronald Reagan (it had dropped). In 2010, most Republicans believed that taxes had increased under Democratic president Barack Obama (for most, they had decreased).

Emotional Roots of Prejudice

Prejudice springs not only from the divisions of society but also from the passions of the heart. **Scapegoat theory** notes that when things go wrong, finding someone to blame can provide a target for anger. Following the 9/11 terrorist attacks, some outraged people lashed out at innocent Arab-Americans. Others called for eliminating Saddam Hussein, the Iraqi leader whom Americans had been grudgingly tolerating. "Fear and anger create aggression, and aggression against citizens of different ethnicity or race creates racism and, in turn, new forms of terrorism," noted Philip Zimbardo (2001). A decade after 9/11, anti-Muslim animosities still flared, with mosque burnings and efforts to block an Islamic community center near Ground Zero.

Evidence for the scapegoat theory of prejudice comes from high prejudice among economically frustrated people. And it comes from experiments in which a temporary frustration intensifies prejudice. Students who experience failure or are made to feel insecure often restore their self-esteem by disparaging a rival school or another person (Cialdini & Richardson, 1980; Crocker et al., 1987). To boost our own sense of status, it helps to denigrate others. That explains why a rival's misfortune sometimes provides a twinge of pleasure. (The German language has a word—*Schadenfreude*—for this secret joy that we sometimes take in another's failure.) By contrast, those made to feel loved and supported become more open to and accepting of others who differ (Mikulincer & Shaver, 2001).

Negative emotions nourish prejudice. When facing death, fearing threats, or experiencing frustration, people cling more tightly to their ingroup and their friends. As terrorism fear heightens patriotism, it also produces loathing and aggression toward "them"—those who threaten our world (Pyszczynski et al., 2002, 2008). The few individuals who lack fear and its associated activity in the emotion-processing amygdala—such as children with the genetic disorder Williams syndrome—also display a notable lack of racial stereotypes and prejudice (Santos et al., 2010).

Cognitive Roots of Prejudice

44-2 What are the cognitive roots of prejudice?

Prejudice springs from a culture's divisions, the heart's passions, and also from the mind's natural workings. Stereotyped beliefs are a by-product of how we cognitively simplify the world.

Forming Categories One way we simplify our world is to categorize. A chemist categorizes molecules as organic and inorganic. Therapists categorize psychological disorders. All of us categorize people by race, with mixed-race people often assigned to their minority identity. Despite his mixed-race background and being raised by a White mother and grandparents, President Barack Obama has been perceived by White Americans as Black. Researchers believe this happens because, after learning the features of a familiar racial group, the observer's selective attention is drawn to the distinctive features of the less-familiar minority. Jamin Halberstadt and his colleagues (2011) illustrated this learned-association effect by showing New Zealanders blended Chinese-Caucasian faces. Compared with participants of Chinese descent, European-descent New Zealanders more readily classified ambiguous faces as Chinese (see **FIGURE 44.4**).

When categorizing people into groups we often stereotype. We recognize how greatly *we* differ from other individuals in *our* groups. But we overestimate the homogeneity of other groups (we perceive *outgroup homogeneity*). "They"—the members of some other group—seem to look and act alike, while "we" are more diverse (Bothwell et al., 1989). To those in one ethnic group, members of another often seem more alike than they really are in attitudes, personality, and appearance. Our greater recognition

> "The misfortunes of others are the taste of honey."
>
> Japanese saying

---

ingroup "us"—people with whom we share a common identity.

outgroup "them"—those perceived as different or apart from our ingroup.

ingroup bias the tendency to favor our own group.

scapegoat theory the theory that prejudice offers an outlet for anger by providing someone to blame.

▼ **FIGURE 44.4**

Categorizing mixed-race people When New Zealanders quickly classified 104 photos by race, those of European descent more often than those of Chinese descent classified the ambiguous middle two as Chinese (Halberstadt et al., 2011).

| 100% Chinese | 80% Chinese 20% Caucasian | 60% Chinese 40% Caucasian | 40% Chinese 60% Caucasian | 20% Chinese 80% Caucasian | 100% Caucasian |

Dr. Jamin Halberstadt

for individual own-race faces—called the **other-race effect** (also called the *cross-race effect* or *own-race bias*)—emerges during infancy, between 3 and 9 months of age (Anzures et al., 2013; Telzer et al., 2013). People's superiority at recognizing faces of their own race is paralleled by an *own-age bias*—better recognition memory for faces of one's own age group (Rhodes & Anastasi, 2012).

With effort and with experience, people get better at recognizing individual faces from another group (Hugenberg et al., 2010; Young et al., 2012). People of European descent, for example, more accurately identify individual African faces if they have watched a great deal of basketball on television, exposing them to many African-heritage faces (Li et al., 1996). And the longer Chinese people have resided in a Western country, the less they exhibit the other-race effect (Hancock & Rhodes, 2008).

Remembering Vivid Cases We often judge the frequency of events by instances that readily come to mind. In a classic experiment, researchers showed two groups of University of Oregon students lists containing information about 50 men (Rothbart et al., 1978). The first group's list included 10 men arrested for *nonviolent* crimes, such as forgery. The second group's list included 10 men arrested for *violent* crimes, such as assault. Later, both groups were asked how many men on their list had committed *any* sort of crime. The second group overestimated the number. Vivid—in this case, violent—cases are more readily available to our memory and feed our stereotypes (**FIGURE 44.5**).

▼ FIGURE 44.5
Vivid cases feed stereotypes The 9/11 Muslim terrorists created, in many minds, an exaggerated stereotype of Muslims as terrorism-prone. Actually, reported a U.S. National Research Council panel on terrorism, when offering this inexact illustration, most terrorists are not Muslim and "the vast majority of Islamic people have no connection with and do not sympathize with terrorism" (Smelser & Mitchell, 2002).

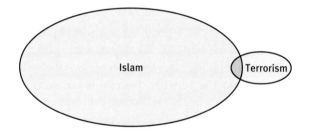

 LaunchPad To review attribution research and experience a simulation of how stereotypes form, visit LaunchPad's *PsychSim 6: Not My Type.* And for a 6.5-minute synopsis of the cognitive and social psychology of prejudice, visit LaunchPad's *Video: Prejudice.*

Believing the World Is Just As we noted earlier, people often justify their prejudices by blaming victims. If the world is just, they assume, people must get what they deserve. As one German civilian is said to have remarked when visiting the Bergen-Belsen concentration camp shortly after World War II, "What terrible criminals these prisoners must have been to receive such treatment."

Hindsight bias is also at work here (Carli & Leonard, 1989). Have you ever heard people say that rape victims, abused spouses, or people with AIDS got what they deserved? In some countries, such as Pakistan, rape victims have been sentenced to severe punishment for violating adultery prohibitions (Mydans, 2002). In one experiment illustrating the blame-the-victim phenomenon, people were given a detailed account of a date that ended with the woman being raped (Janoff-Bulman et al., 1985). They perceived the woman's behavior as at least partly to blame, and in hindsight, they thought, "She should have known better." Others, given the same account with the rape ending deleted, did not perceive the woman's behavior as inviting rape. Hindsight bias promoted a blame-the-victim mentality among members of the first group. Blaming the victim also serves to reassure people that it couldn't happen to them.

other-race effect the tendency to recall faces of one's own race more accurately than faces of other races. Also called the *cross-race effect* and the *own-race bias.*

aggression any act intended to harm someone physically or emotionally.

People also have a basic tendency to justify their culture's social systems (Jost et al., 2009; Kay et al., 2009). We're inclined to see the way things are as the way they ought to be. This natural conservatism makes it difficult to legislate major social changes, such as health care or climate-change policies. Once such policies are in place, our "system justification" tends to preserve them.

RETRIEVAL PRACTICE

- When prejudiced judgment causes us to blame an undeserving person for a problem, that person is called a _____ .

ANSWER: scapegoat

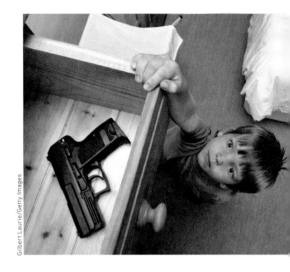

Gilbert Laurie/Getty Images

Aggression

44-3 How does psychology's definition of *aggression* differ from everyday usage? What biological factors make us more prone to hurt one another?

Prejudice hurts, but aggression often hurts more. In psychology, **aggression** is any unwanted behavior intended to harm someone, whether done out of hostility or as a calculated means to an end. The assertive, persistent salesperson is not aggressive. Nor is the dentist who makes you wince with pain. But the person who passes along a vicious rumor about you, the person who bullies you in person or online, and the attacker who mugs you for your money are aggressive.

Aggressive behavior emerges from the interaction of biology and experience. For a gun to fire, the trigger must be pulled; with some people, as with hair-trigger guns, it doesn't take much to trip an explosion. Let's look first at some biological factors that influence our thresholds for aggressive behavior, then at the psychological factors that pull the trigger.

The Biology of Aggression

Aggression varies too widely from culture to culture, era to era, and person to person to be considered an unlearned instinct. But biology does *influence* aggression. We can look for biological influences at three levels—genetic, neural, and biochemical.

Genetic Influences Genes influence aggression. We know this because animals have been bred for aggressiveness—sometimes for sport, sometimes for research. The effect of genes also appears in human twin studies (Miles & Carey, 1997; Rowe et al., 1999). If one identical twin admits to "having a violent temper," the other twin will often independently admit the same. Fraternal twins are much less likely to respond similarly. Researchers continue to search for genetic markers in those who commit violent acts. One is already well known and is carried by half the human race: the Y chromosome. Another such marker is the *monoamine oxidase A (MAOA) gene*, which helps break down neurotransmitters such as dopamine and serotonin. Sometimes called the "warrior gene," people who have low MAOA gene expression tend to behave aggressively when provoked. In one experiment, low (compared with high) MAOA gene carriers gave more unpleasant hot sauce to someone who provoked them (McDermott et al., 2009).

Neural Influences There is no one spot in the brain that controls aggression. Aggression is a complex behavior, and it occurs in particular contexts. But animal and human brains have neural systems that, given provocation, will either inhibit or facilitate aggression (Denson, 2011; Moyer, 1983; Wilkowski et al., 2011). Consider:

- Researchers implanted a radio-controlled electrode in the brain of the domineering leader of a caged monkey colony. The electrode was in an area that, when stimulated, inhibits aggression. When researchers placed the control button for the electrode in the colony's cage, one small monkey learned to push it every time the boss became threatening.

Do guns in the home save or take more lives? In the last 40 years in the United States, well over 1 million people—more than all deaths in all wars in American history—have been killed by firearms in nonwar settings. Compared with people of the same sex, race, age, and neighborhood, those who keep a gun in the home (ironically, often for protection) have been twice as likely to be murdered and three times as likely to commit suicide (Anglemyer et al., 2014; Stroebe, 2013). States and countries with high gun ownership rates also tend to have high gun death rates (VPC, 2013).

"It's a guy thing."

The New Yorker Collection, 1995, D. Reilly from cartoonbank.com

- A neurosurgeon, seeking to diagnose a disorder, implanted an electrode in the amygdala of a mild-mannered woman. Because the brain has no sensory receptors, she was unable to feel the stimulation. But at the flick of a switch she snarled, "Take my blood pressure. Take it now," then stood up and began to strike the doctor.

- Studies of violent criminals have revealed diminished activity in the frontal lobes, which play an important role in controlling impulses. If the frontal lobes are damaged, inactive, disconnected, or not yet fully mature, aggression may be more likely (Amen et al., 1996; Davidson et al., 2000; Raine, 2013).

Biochemical Influences Our genes engineer our individual nervous systems, which operate electrochemically. The hormone testosterone, for example, circulates in the bloodstream and influences the neural systems that control aggression. A raging bull becomes a gentle Ferdinand when castration reduces its testosterone level. Conversely, when injected with testosterone, gentle, castrated mice once again become aggressive.

Humans are less sensitive to hormonal changes. But as men age, their testosterone levels—and their aggressiveness—diminish. Hormonally charged, aggressive 17-year-olds mature into hormonally quieter and gentler 70-year-olds. Men more than women tend to have wide faces, a testosterone-linked trait, rather than roundish or long faces. And men's facial width is a predictor of their aggressiveness and prejudicial attitudes (Carré et al., 2009; Hehman et al., 2013; Stirrat & Perrett, 2010). Women apparently pick up on this by *perceiving* men with higher facial width-to-height ratios as more dominant (Valentine et al., 2014).

High testosterone correlates with irritability, assertiveness, impulsiveness, and low tolerance for frustration—qualities that predispose somewhat more aggressive responses to provocation or competition for status (Dabbs et al., 2001b; McAndrew, 2009; Montoya et al., 2012). Among both teenage boys and adult men, high testosterone levels correlate with delinquency, hard drug use, and aggressive-bullying responses to frustration (Berman et al., 1993; Dabbs & Morris, 1990; Olweus et al., 1988). Drugs that sharply reduce testosterone levels subdue men's aggressive tendencies.

Another drug that sometimes circulates in the bloodstream—alcohol—*unleashes* aggressive responses to frustration. Across police data, prison surveys, and experiments, aggression-prone people are more likely to drink, and to become violent when intoxicated (White et al., 1993). National crime data indicate that 73 percent of Russian homicides and 57 percent of U.S. homicides are alcohol-influenced (Landberg & Norström, 2011). Alcohol effects aggression both biologically and psychologically (Bushman, 1993; Ito et al., 1996; Taylor & Chermack, 1993). Just *thinking* you've imbibed alcohol can increase aggression (Bègue et al., 2009). But so, too, does unknowingly ingesting alcohol slipped into a drink. Unless people are distracted, alcohol tends to focus their attention on a provocation rather than on inhibitory cues (Giancola & Corman, 2007). Alcohol also inclines people to interpret ambiguous acts (such as a bump in a crowd) as provocations (Bègue et al., 2010).

"We could avoid two-thirds of all crime simply by putting all able-bodied young men in cryogenic sleep from the age of 12 through 28."

David T. Lykken,
The Antisocial Personalities, 1995

A lean, mean fighting machine— the testosterone-laden female hyena The hyena's unusual embryology pumps testosterone into female fetuses. The result is revved-up young female hyenas who seem born to fight.

Psychological and Social-Cultural Factors in Aggression

44-4 What psychological and social-cultural factors may trigger aggressive behavior?

Biological factors influence how easily aggression is triggered. But what psychological and social-cultural factors pull the trigger?

Aversive Events Suffering sometimes builds character. In laboratory experiments, however, those made miserable have often made others miserable (Berkowitz, 1983, 1989). This phenomenon is called the **frustration-aggression principle:** Frustration creates anger, which can spark aggression. One analysis of 27,667 hit-by-pitch Major League Baseball incidents between 1960 and 2004 revealed this link (Timmerman, 2007). Pitchers were most likely to hit batters when

- they had been frustrated by the previous batter hitting a home run.
- the current batter had hit a home run the last time at bat.
- a teammate had been hit by a pitch in the previous half inning.

Other aversive stimuli—hot temperatures, physical pain, personal insults, foul odors, cigarette smoke, crowding, and a host of others—can also evoke hostility. In laboratory experiments, when people get overheated, they think, feel, and act more aggressively. Simply thinking about words related to hot temperatures is enough to increase hostile thoughts (DeWall & Bushman, 2009). In baseball games, the number of hit batters rises with the temperature (Reifman et al., 1991; see **FIGURE 44.6**). In the wider world, violent crime and spousal abuse rates have been higher during hotter years, seasons, months, and days (Anderson et al., 1997). Other studies from archaeology, economics, geography, political science, and psychology converge in finding that throughout human history, higher temperatures have predicted increased individual violence, wars, and revolutions (Hsiang et al., 2013). From the available data, Craig Anderson and his colleagues (2000, 2011) have projected that, other things being equal, global warming of 4 degrees Fahrenheit (about 2 degrees Celsius) could induce tens of thousands of additional assaults and murders—and that's before the added violence inducements from climate change-related drought, poverty, food insecurity, and migration.

Reinforcement, Modeling, and Self-Control Aggression may naturally follow aversive events, but learning can alter natural reactions. We learn when our behavior is reinforced, and we learn by watching others.

In situations where experience has taught us that aggression pays, we are likely to act aggressively again. Children whose aggression has successfully intimidated other children may become bullies. Animals that have successfully fought to get food or mates become increasingly ferocious. To foster a kinder, gentler world we had best model and reward sensitivity and cooperation from an early age, perhaps by training parents to discipline without modeling violence.

Parent-training programs often advise parents to avoid modeling violence by screaming and hitting. Instead, parents should reinforce desirable behaviors and frame statements positively. ("When you finish loading the dishwasher you can go play," rather than "If you don't load the dishwasher, there'll be no playing.")

One *aggression-replacement program* worked with juvenile offenders and gang members and their parents. It taught both generations new ways to control anger, and more thoughtful approaches to moral reasoning (Goldstein et al., 1998). The result? The youths' re-arrest rates dropped more than is typical.

Different cultures model, reinforce, and evoke different tendencies toward violence. For example, crime rates are higher and average happiness is lower in times and places

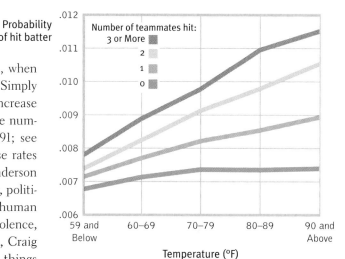

Probability of hit batter

Number of teammates hit:
- 3 or More
- 2
- 1
- 0

Temperature (°F): 59 and Below, 60–69, 70–79, 80–89, 90 and Above

▼ FIGURE 44.6
Temperature and retaliation Richard Larrick and his colleagues (2011) looked for occurrences of batters hit by pitchers during 4,566,468 pitcher-batter matchups across 57,293 Major League Baseball games since 1952. The probability of a hit batter increased if one or more of the pitcher's teammates had been hit, and also with temperature.

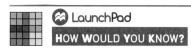 **HOW WOULD YOU KNOW?**

How have researchers studied these concepts? Learn more at LaunchPad's *How Would You Know If Hot Temperatures Cause Aggression?*

> **frustration-aggression principle** the principle that frustration—the blocking of an attempt to achieve some goal—creates anger, which can generate aggression.

marked by a great disparity between rich and poor (Messias et al., 2011; Oishi et al., 2011; Wilkinson & Pickett, 2009). In the United States, cultures and families in which fathers are minimally involved also have high violence rates (Triandis, 1994). Even after controlling for parental education, race, income, and teen motherhood, American male youths from father-absent homes are incarcerated at twice the rate of their peers (Harper & McLanahan, 2004).

Violence can vary by culture within a country. Richard Nisbett and Dov Cohen (1996) analyzed violence among White Americans in southern towns settled by Scots-Irish herders whose tradition emphasized "manly honor," the use of arms to protect one's flock, and a history of coercive slavery. Compared with their White counterparts in New England towns settled by the more traditionally peaceful Puritan, Quaker, and Dutch farmer-artisans, the cultural descendants of those herders have had triple the homicide rates and were more supportive of physically punishing children, of warfare initiatives, and of uncontrolled gun ownership. "Culture-of-honor" states also have higher rates of students bringing weapons to school and of school shootings (Brown et al., 2009).

Media Models for Sexual Violence Parents are hardly the only aggression models. In the United States and elsewhere, TV, films, video games, and the Internet offer supersized portions of violence. Repeatedly viewing on-screen violence tends to make us less sensitive to cruelty (Montag et al., 2012). It also primes us to respond aggressively when provoked. And it teaches us **social scripts**—culturally provided mental files for how to act. When we find ourselves in new situations, uncertain how to behave, we rely on social scripts. After watching so many action films, adolescent boys may acquire a script that plays in their head when they face real-life conflicts. Challenged, they may "act like a man" by intimidating or eliminating the threat. More than 100 studies together confirm that people sometimes imitate what they've viewed. Watching risk-glorifying behaviors (dangerous driving, extreme sports, unprotected sex) increases viewers' real-life risk-taking (Fischer et al., 2011).

Music lyrics also write social scripts. In experiments, German university men who listened to woman-hating song lyrics administered the most hot chili sauce to a woman. They also recalled more negative feelings and beliefs about women. Man-hating song lyrics had a similar effect on the aggressive behavior of women listeners (Fischer & Greitemeyer, 2006).

Sexual scripts depicted in pornographic films are often toxic. Researchers have found that repeatedly watching pornographic films, even nonviolent films, makes sexual aggression seem less serious (Harris, 1994). In one experiment, undergraduates viewed six brief, sexually explicit films each week for six weeks (Zillmann & Bryant, 1984). A control group viewed films with no sexual content during the same six-week period. Three weeks later, both groups read a newspaper report about a man convicted of raping a hitchhiker and were asked to suggest an appropriate prison term. Sentences recommended by those viewing the sexually explicit films were only half as long as the sentences recommended by the control group.

While nonviolent sexual content affects aggression-related sexual attitudes, violent sexual content can also increase men's readiness to actually behave aggressively toward women. A statement by 21 social scientists noted, "Pornography that portrays sexual aggression as pleasurable for the victim increases the acceptance of the use of coercion in sexual relations" (Surgeon General, 1986). Contrary to much popular opinion, viewing such scenes does not provide an outlet for bottled-up impulses. Rather, "in laboratory studies measuring short-term effects, exposure to violent pornography increases punitive behavior toward women."

To a lesser extent, nonviolent pornography can also influence aggression. One set of studies exploring pornography's effects on aggression toward relationship partners found that pornography consumption predicted both self-reported aggression and

social script culturally modeled guide for how to act in various situations.

participants' willingness to administer laboratory noise blasts to their partner (Lambert et al., 2011). Abstaining from one's customary pornography consumption decreased aggression. Abstaining from a favorite food did not.

Do Violent Video Games Teach Social Scripts for Violence?

Experiments in North America, Western Europe, Singapore, and Japan indicate that playing positive games produces positive effects (Greitemeyer & Osswald, 2010, 2011; Prot et al., 2014). For example, playing *Lemmings*, where a goal is to help others, increases real-life helping. So, might a parallel effect occur after playing games that enact violence? Violent video games became an issue for public debate after teenagers in more than a dozen places seemed to mimic the carnage in the shooter games they had so often played (Anderson, 2004a, 2013).

In 2002, three young men in Michigan spent part of a night drinking beer and playing *Grand Theft Auto III*. Using simulated cars, they ran down pedestrians, then beat them with fists, leaving a bloody body behind (Kolker, 2002). These same young men then went out for a real drive. Spotting a 38-year-old man on a bicycle, they ran him down with their car, got out, stomped and punched him, and returned home to play the game some more. (The victim, a father of three, died six days later.)

Such violent mimicry causes some to wonder: What are the effects of actively *role-playing* aggression? Does it cause young people to become less sensitive to violence and more open to violent acts? Nearly 400 studies of 130,000 people offer an answer, report some researchers (Anderson et al., 2010). Video games can prime aggressive thoughts, decrease empathy, and increase aggression. University men who spend the most hours playing violent video games have also tended to be the most physically aggressive (Anderson & Dill, 2000). (For example, they more often acknowledged having hit or attacked someone else.) And people randomly assigned to play a game involving bloody murders with groaning victims (rather than to play nonviolent *Myst*) became more hostile. On a follow-up task, they were more likely to blast intense noise at a fellow student. Studies of young adolescents reveal that those who play a lot of violent video games become more aggressive and see the world as more hostile (Gentile, 2009; Hassin et al., 2013). Compared with nongaming kids, they get into more arguments and fights and earn poorer grades.

Ah, but is this merely because naturally hostile kids are drawn to such games? Apparently not. Comparisons of gamers and nongamers who scored low on hostility measures revealed a difference in the number of fights they reported. Almost 4 in 10 violent-game players had been in fights, compared with only 4 in 100 of the non-gaming kids (Anderson, 2004a). Some researchers believe that, due partly to the more active participation and rewarded violence of game play, violent video games have even greater effects on aggressive behavior and cognition than do violent TV shows and movies (Anderson & Warburton, 2012).

Other researchers are unimpressed by such findings (Ferguson, 2013, 2014). They note that from 1996 to 2006, youth violence declined while video game sales increased, and argue that other factors—depression, family violence, peer influence—better predict aggression. Also, game-playing keeps people off the streets and out of trouble (Engelstätter et al., 2011). Moreover, some point out that avid game players are quick and sharp: They develop speedy reaction times and enhanced visual skills (Dye et al., 2009; Green et al., 2010). The focused fun of game playing can satisfy basic needs for a sense of competence, control, and social connection (Granic et al., 2014).

In 2011, a U.S. Supreme Court decision overturned a California state law that banned violent video game sales to children (modeled after the bans on sales of sexually explicit materials to children). The First Amendment's free speech guarantee protects even offensive games, said the court's majority, which was unpersuaded by the evidence of harm. So, the debate continues.

Andrew Berwick via www.freak.no /Reuters/Landov

Coincidence or cause? In 2011, Norwegian Anders Behring Breivik bombed government buildings in Oslo, and then went to a youth camp where he shot and killed 69 people, mostly teens. As a player of first-person shooter games, Breivik stirred debate when he commented that "I see MW2 *[Modern Warfare 2]* more as a part of my training-simulation than anything else." Did his violent game playing—and that of the 2012 mass murderer of Newtown, Connecticut's first-grade children—contribute to the violence, or was it a merely coincidental association? To explore such questions, psychologists experiment.

Biological influences:
• genetic influences
• biochemical influences, such as testosterone and alcohol
• neural influences, such as a severe head injury

Psychological influences:
• dominating behavior (which boosts testosterone levels in the blood)
• believing that alcohol has been ingested (whether it has or not)
• frustration
• aggressive role models
• rewards for aggressive behavior
• low self-control

Aggressive behavior

Social-cultural influences:
• *deindividuation*, or a loss of self-awareness and self-restraint
• challenging environmental factors, such as crowding, heat, and direct provocations
• parental models of aggression
• minimal father involvement
• rejection from a group
• exposure to violent media

* * *

To sum up, research reveals biological, psychological, and social-cultural influences on aggressive behavior. Complex behaviors, including violence, have many causes, making any single explanation an oversimplification. Asking what causes violence is therefore like asking what causes cancer. Those who study the effects of asbestos exposure on cancer rates may remind us that asbestos is indeed a cancer cause, but it is only one among many. Like so much else, aggression is a biopsychosocial phenomenon (**FIGURE 44.7**).

A happy concluding note: Historical trends suggest that the world is becoming less violent over time (Pinker, 2011). That people vary across time and place reminds us that environments differ. Yesterday's plundering Vikings have become today's peace-promoting Scandinavians. Like all behavior, aggression arises from the interaction of persons and situations.

▼ **FIGURE 44.7**
Biopsychosocial understanding of aggression Because many factors contribute to aggressive behavior, there are many ways to change such behavior, including learning anger management and communication skills, and avoiding violent media and video games.

----------**RETRIEVAL PRACTICE**----------

• What biological, psychological, and social-cultural influences interact to produce aggressive behaviors?

ANSWER: Our biology (our genes, neural systems, and biochemistry—including testosterone and alcohol levels) influences our aggressive tendencies. Psychological factors (such as frustration, previous rewards for aggressive acts, and observation of others' aggression) can trigger any aggressive tendencies we may have. Social influences, such as exposure to violent media or being ostracized from a group, and cultural influences, such as whether we've grown up in a "culture of honor" or a father-absent home, can also affect our aggressive responses.

MODULE 44 REVIEW Antisocial Relations

LEARNING OBJECTIVES

RETRIEVAL PRACTICE Take a moment to answer each of these Learning Objective Questions (repeated here from within this module). Then turn to Appendix C, Complete Module Reviews, to check your answers. Research suggests that trying to answer these questions on your own will improve your long-term retention (McDaniel et al., 2009).

44-1 What is *prejudice*? What are its social and emotional roots?

44-2 What are the cognitive roots of prejudice?

44-3 How does psychology's definition of *aggression* differ from everyday usage? What biological factors make us more prone to hurt one another?

44-4 What psychological and social-cultural factors may trigger aggressive behavior?

TERMS AND CONCEPTS TO REMEMBER

RETRIEVAL PRACTICE Test yourself on these terms by trying to write down the definition before flipping back to the page number referenced to check your answer.

prejudice, p. 537

stereotype, p. 538

discrimination, p. 538

just-world phenomenon, p. 541

ingroup, p. 542

outgroup, p. 542

ingroup bias, p. 542

scapegoat theory, p. 542

other-race effect, p. 544

aggression, p. 545

frustration-aggression principle, p. 547

social script, p. 548

Use 🔗 LearningCurve to create your personalized study plan, which will direct you to the resources that will help you most in 🔗 LaunchPad.

45 Prosocial Relations

Social psychologists focus not only on the dark side of social relationships, but also on the bright side, by studying *prosocial* behavior—behavior that intends to help or benefit someone. Our positive behaviors toward others are evident from explorations of attraction, altruism, and peacemaking.

Attraction

Pause a moment and think about your relationships with two people—a close friend, and someone who has stirred your feelings of romantic love. What psychological chemistry binds us together in these special attachments? Social psychology suggests some answers.

The Psychology of Attraction

45-1 Why do we befriend or fall in love with some people but not others?

We endlessly wonder how we can win others' affection and what makes our own affections flourish or fade. Does familiarity breed contempt, or does it amplify affection? Do birds of a feather flock together, or do opposites attract? Is beauty only skin deep, or does physical attractiveness matter greatly? To explore these questions, let's consider three ingredients of our liking for one another: proximity, attractiveness, and similarity.

Proximity Before friendships become close, they must begin. *Proximity*—geographic nearness—is friendship's most powerful predictor. Proximity provides opportunities for *aggression*, but much more often it breeds liking. Study after study reveals that people are most inclined to like, and even to marry, those who live in the same neighborhood, who sit nearby in class, who work in the same office, who share the same parking lot, who eat in the same dining hall. Look around. Mating starts with meeting.

Proximity breeds liking partly because of the **mere exposure effect.** Repeated exposure to novel stimuli increases our liking for them. This applies to nonsense syllables, musical selections, geometric figures, Chinese characters, human faces, and the letters of our own name (Moreland & Zajonc, 1982; Nuttin, 1987; Zajonc, 2001). We are even somewhat more likely to marry someone whose first or last name resembles our own (Jones et al., 2004).

So, within certain limits, familiarity feeds fondness (Bornstein, 1989, 1999). Researchers demonstrated this by having four equally attractive women silently attend a 200-student class for zero, 5, 10, or 15 class sessions (Moreland & Beach, 1992). At the end of the course, students viewed slides of each woman and rated her attractiveness. The most attractive? The ones they'd seen most often. The phenomenon would come as no surprise to the young Taiwanese man who wrote more than 700 letters to his girlfriend, urging her to marry him. She did marry—the mail carrier (Steinberg, 1993).

mere exposure effect the phenomenon that repeated exposure to novel stimuli increases liking of them.

Familiarity breeds acceptance
When this rare white penguin was born in the Sydney, Australia zoo, his tuxedoed peers ostracized him. Zookeepers thought they would need to dye him black to gain acceptance. But after three weeks of contact, the other penguins came to accept him.

The mere exposure effect The mere exposure effect applies even to ourselves. Because the human face is not perfectly symmetrical, the face we see in the mirror is not the same face our friends see. Most of us prefer the familiar mirror image, while our friends like the reverse (Mita et al., 1977). The person German Chancellor Angela Merkel sees in the mirror each morning is shown at right, and that's the photo she would probably prefer. We might feel more comfortable with the reverse image (left), the one we see.

Voter   George Bush   60:40 Blend

▼ FIGURE 45.1

I like the candidate who looks a bit like dear old me Jeremy Bailenson and his colleagues (2005) incorporated morphed features of voters' faces into the faces of 2004 U.S. presidential candidates George Bush and John Kerry. Without conscious awareness of their own incorporated features, the participants became more likely to favor the candidate whose face incorporated some of their own features.

No face is more familiar than your own. And that helps explain an interesting finding by Lisa DeBruine (2004): We like other people when their faces incorporate some morphed features of our own. When DeBruine (2002) had McMaster University students (both men and women) play a game with a supposed other player, they were more trusting and cooperative when the other person's image had some of their own facial features morphed into it. In me I trust. (See also **FIGURE 45.1**.)

For our ancestors, the mere exposure effect had survival value. What was familiar was generally safe and approachable. What was unfamiliar was more often dangerous and threatening. Evolution may therefore have hard-wired into us the tendency to bond with those who are familiar and to be wary of those who are unfamiliar (Zajonc, 1998). If so, gut-level *prejudice* against those who are culturally different could be a primitive, automatic emotional response (Devine et al., 2012). It's what we do with our knee-jerk prejudice that matters, say researchers. Do we let those feelings control our behavior? Or do we monitor our feelings and act in ways that reflect our conscious valuing of human equality?

Modern Matchmaking Those who have not found a romantic partner in their immediate proximity may cast a wider net by joining an online dating service. Published research on Internet matchmaking effectiveness is sparse. But this much seems well established: Some people, including occasional predators, dishonestly represent their age, attractiveness, occupation, or other details, and thus are not who they seem to be. Nevertheless, Katelyn McKenna and John Bargh and their colleagues have offered a surprising finding: Compared with relationships formed in person, Internet-formed friendships and romantic relationships are, on average, slightly more likely to last and be satisfying (Bargh et al., 2002, 2004; Cacioppo et al., 2013; McKenna et al., 2002). In one of their studies, people disclosed more, with less posturing, to those whom they met online. When conversing online with someone for 20 minutes, they felt more liking for that person than they did for someone they had met and talked with face to face. This was true even when (unknown to them) it was the same person! Internet friendships often feel as real and important to people as in-person relationships. Small wonder that the historic ways couples have met—at school, on the job, through family, or, especially, through friends—have been supplemented by a striking rise in couples who meet over the Internet. In a recent national survey of straight and gay/lesbian couples, nearly a quarter of heterosexual couples and some two-thirds of same-sex couples met online (Rosenfeld & Thomas, 2012; see **FIGURE 45.2**).

Speed dating pushes the search for romance into high gear. In a process pioneered by a matchmaking Jewish rabbi, people meet a succession of prospective partners, either in person or via webcam (Bower, 2009). After a 3- to 8-minute conversation, people move on to the next prospect. (In an in-person meeting, one partner—usually the woman—remains seated and the other circulates.) Those who want to meet again can arrange for future contact. For many participants, 4 minutes is enough time to

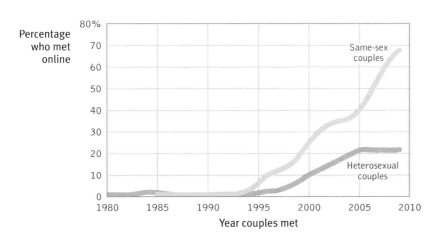

▼ FIGURE 45.2
Percent of heterosexual and
same-sex couples who met online
(Data from Rosenfeld & Thomas, 2012.)

form a feeling about a conversational partner and to register whether the partner likes them (Eastwick & Finkel, 2008a,b).

For researchers, speed dating offers a unique opportunity for studying influences on our first impressions of potential romantic partners. Among recent findings are these:

- Men are more transparent. Observers (male or female) watching videos of speed-dating encounters can read a man's level of romantic interest more accurately than a woman's (Place et al., 2009).

- Given more options, people's choices become more superficial. Meeting lots of potential partners leads people to focus on more easily assessed characteristics, such as height and weight (Lenton & Francesconi, 2010). This was true even when researchers controlled for time spent with each partner.

- Men wish for future contact with more of their speed dates; women tend to be more choosy. But this difference disappears if the conventional roles are reversed, so that men stay seated while women circulate (Finkel & Eastwick, 2009).

Physical Attractiveness Once proximity affords us contact, what most affects our first impressions? The person's sincerity? Intelligence? Personality? Hundreds of experiments reveal that it is something far more superficial: physical appearance. This finding is unnerving for those of us taught that "beauty is only skin deep" and "appearances can be deceiving."

In one early study, researchers randomly matched new University of Minnesota students for a Welcome Week dance (Walster et al., 1966). Before the dance, the researchers gave each student a battery of personality and aptitude tests, and they rated each student's physical attractiveness. During the blind date, the couples danced and talked for more than two hours and then took a brief intermission to rate their dates. What determined whether they liked each other? Only one thing seemed to matter: appearance. Both the men and the women liked good-looking dates best. Women are more likely than men to say that another's looks don't affect them (Lippa, 2007). But studies show that a man's looks do affect women's behavior (Eastwick et al., 2014a,b). Speed-dating experiments confirm that attractiveness influences first impressions for both sexes (Belot & Francesconi, 2006; Finkel & Eastwick, 2008).

Physical attractiveness also predicts how often people date and how popular they feel. It affects initial impressions of people's personalities. We don't assume that attractive people are more compassionate, but research participants perceive them as healthier, happier, more sensitive, more successful, and more socially skilled (Eagly et al., 1991; Feingold, 1992; Hatfield & Sprecher, 1986). Attractive, well-dressed people have been more likely to make a favorable impression on potential employers, and they have

"I'd like to meet the algorithm that thought we'd be a good match."

When Neanderthals fall in love.

Percentage of Men and Women Who "Constantly Think About Their Looks"

	Men	Women
Canada	18%	20%
United States	17	27
Mexico	40	45
Venezuela	47	65

From Roper Starch survey, reported by McCool (1999).

Women have 91 percent of cosmetic procedures (ASPS, 2010). Women also recall others' appearances better than do men (Mast & Hall, 2006).

Estimated length of human nose removed by U.S. plastic surgeons each year: 5469 feet (*Harper's*, 2009).

tended to be more successful in their jobs (Cash & Janda, 1984; Langlois et al., 2000; Solomon, 1987). Income analyses show a penalty for plainness or obesity and a premium for beauty (Engemann & Owyang, 2005).

Even babies have preferred attractive over unattractive faces (Langlois et al., 1987). So do some blind people, as University of Birmingham professor John Hull (1990, p. 23) discovered after going blind. A colleague's remarks on a woman's beauty would strangely affect his feelings. He found this "deplorable. . . . What can it matter to me what sighted men think of women . . . yet I do care what sighted men think, and I do not seem able to throw off this prejudice."

For those who find the importance of looks unfair and unenlightened, two findings may be reassuring. First, people's attractiveness is surprisingly unrelated to their self-esteem and happiness (Diener et al., 1995; Major et al., 1984). Unless we have just compared ourselves with superattractive people, few of us (thanks, perhaps, to the mere exposure effect) view ourselves as unattractive (Thornton & Moore, 1993). Second, strikingly attractive people are sometimes suspicious that praise for their work may simply be a reaction to their looks. Less attractive people have been more likely to accept praise as sincere (Berscheid, 1981).

Beauty is also in the eye of the culture. Hoping to look attractive, people across the globe have pierced and tattooed their bodies, lengthened their necks, bound their feet, and dyed their hair. They have gorged themselves to achieve a full figure or liposuctioned fat to achieve a slim one, applied chemicals hoping to rid themselves of unwanted hair or to regrow wanted hair, strapped on leather garments to make their breasts seem smaller or surgically filled their breasts with silicone and worn Wonderbras to make them look bigger. Cultural ideals change over time. For women in North America, the ultra-thin ideal of the Roaring Twenties gave way to the soft, voluptuous Marilyn Monroe ideal of the 1950s, only to be replaced by today's lean yet busty ideal.

Some aspects of attractiveness, however, do cross place and time (Cunningham et al., 2005; Langlois et al., 2000). By providing reproductive clues, bodies influence sexual attraction. As evolutionary psychologists explain, men in many cultures, from Australia to Zambia, judge women as more attractive if they have a youthful, fertile appearance, suggested by a low waist-to-hip ratio (Karremans et al., 2010; Perilloux et al., 2010; Platek & Singh, 2010). (I [DM] always thought my wife looked cute in her genes.) Women feel attracted to healthy-looking men, but especially—and more so when ovulating—to those who seem mature, dominant, masculine, and affluent (Gallup & Frederick, 2010; Gangestad et al., 2010). But faces matter, too. When people rate opposite-sex faces and bodies separately, the face tends to be the better predictor of overall physical attractiveness (Currie & Little, 2009; Peters et al., 2007).

In the eye of the beholder
Conceptions of attractiveness vary by culture. Yet some adult physical features, such as a healthy appearance, seem attractive everywhere.

People everywhere also seem to prefer physical features—noses, legs, physiques—that are neither unusually large nor small. An averaged face is attractive (**FIGURE 45.3**). In one clever demonstration, researchers digitized the faces of up to 32 college students and used a computer to average them (Langlois & Roggman, 1990). Students judged the averaged, composite faces as more attractive than 96 percent of the individual faces. One reason is that averaged faces are symmetrical, and people with symmetrical faces and bodies are more sexually attractive (Rhodes et al., 1999; Singh, 1995; Thornhill & Gangestad, 1994). Merge either half of your face with its mirror image and your symmetrical new face would boost your attractiveness a notch.

Our feelings also influence our attractiveness judgments. Imagine two people. The first is honest, humorous, and polite. The second is rude, unfair, and abusive. Which one is more attractive? Most people perceive the person with the appealing traits as more physically attractive (Lewandowski et al., 2007). Those we like we find attractive.

▼ FIGURE 45.3
Average is attractive Which of these faces offered by University of St. Andrews psychologist David Perrett (2002, 2010) is most attractive? Most people say it's the face on the right—of a nonexistent person that is the average composite of these 3 plus 57 other actual faces.

Extreme makeover In affluent, beauty-conscious cultures, increasing numbers of people, such as this woman from the former American TV show *Extreme Makeover,* have turned to cosmetic surgery to improve their looks.

In a Rodgers and Hammerstein musical, Prince Charming asks Cinderella, "Do I love you because you're beautiful, or are you beautiful because I love you?" Chances are it's both. As we see our loved ones again and again, their physical imperfections grow less noticeable and their attractiveness grows more apparent (Beaman & Klentz, 1983; Gross & Crofton, 1977). Shakespeare said it in A *Midsummer Night's Dream:* "Love looks not with the eyes, but with the mind." Come to love someone and watch beauty grow.

Similarity So proximity has brought you into contact with someone, and your appearance has made an acceptable first impression. What influences whether you will become friends? As you get to know each other, will the chemistry be better if you are opposites or if you are alike?

It makes a good story—extremely different types liking or loving each other: Rat, Mole, and Badger in *The Wind in the Willows,* Frog and Toad in Arnold Lobel's books, Edward and Bella in the *Twilight* series. The stories delight us by expressing what we seldom experience. In real life, opposites retract (Rosenbaum, 1986; Montoya &

"Play coy if you like, but no one can resist a perfectly symmetrical face."

Beauty grows with mere exposure
Herman Miller, Inc.'s famed Aeron chair initially received high comfort ratings but abysmal beauty ratings. To some it looked like "lawn furniture" or "a giant prehistoric insect" (Gladwell, 2005). But then, with design awards, media visibility, and imitators, the ugly duckling became the company's best-selling chair ever and came to be seen as beautiful. With people, too, beauty lies partly in the beholder's eye and can grow with exposure.

Horton, 2013). Compared with randomly paired people, friends and couples are far more likely to share common attitudes, beliefs, and interests (and, for that matter, age, religion, race, education, intelligence, smoking behavior, and economic status).

Moreover, the more alike people are, the more their liking endures (Byrne, 1971). Journalist Walter Lippmann was right to suppose that love lasts "when the lovers love many things together, and not merely each other." Similarity breeds content. One app therefore matches people with potential dates based on their proximity, and on the similarity of their Facebook profiles.

Proximity, attractiveness, and similarity are not the only determinants of attraction. We also like those who like us. This is especially true when our self-image is low. When we believe someone likes us, we feel good and respond to them warmly, which leads them to like us even more (Curtis & Miller, 1986). To be liked is powerfully rewarding.

Indeed, all the findings we have considered so far can be explained by a simple *reward theory of attraction*: We will like those whose behavior is rewarding to us, including those who are both able and willing to help us achieve our goals (Montoya & Horton, 2014). When people live or work in close proximity to us, it requires less time and effort to develop the friendship and enjoy its benefits. When people are attractive, they are aesthetically pleasing, and associating with them can be socially rewarding. When people share our views, they reward us by validating our beliefs.

RETRIEVAL PRACTICE

• People tend to marry someone who lives or works nearby. This is an example of the _____ _____ _____ in action.

ANSWER: mere exposure effect

• How does being physically attractive influence others' perceptions?

ANSWER: Being physically attractive tends to elicit positive first impressions. People tend to assume that attractive people are healthier, happier, and more socially skilled than others are.

Romantic Love

45-2 How does romantic love typically change as time passes?

Sometimes people move quickly from initial impressions, to friendship, to the more intense, complex, and mysterious state of romantic love. If love endures, temporary *passionate love* will mellow into a lingering *companionate love* (Hatfield, 1988).

Passionate Love A key ingredient of **passionate love** is arousal. The *two-factor theory* of emotion can help us understand this intense positive absorption in another (Hatfield, 1988). That theory assumes that

• emotions have two ingredients—*physical arousal* plus *cognitive appraisal*.

• arousal from any source can enhance one emotion or another, depending on how we interpret and label the arousal.

Arousal can come from within, as we experience the excitement of a new relationship. But in tests of the two-factor theory, college men have been aroused by fright, by running in place, by viewing erotic materials, or by listening to humorous or repulsive monologues. They were then introduced to an attractive woman and asked to rate her (or their girlfriend). Unlike unaroused men, the stirred-up men attributed some of their arousal to the woman or girlfriend, and felt more attracted to her (Carducci et al., 1978; Dermer & Pyszczynski, 1978; White & Kight, 1984).

A sample experiment: Researchers studied people crossing two bridges above British Columbia's rocky Capilano River (Dutton & Aron, 1974, 1989). One, a swaying footbridge, was 230 feet above the rocks; the other was low and solid. The researchers had

Bill looked at Susan, Susan at Bill. Suddenly death didn't seem like an option. This was love at first sight.

an attractive young woman intercept men coming off each bridge, and ask their help in filling out a short questionnaire. She then offered her phone number in case they wanted to hear more about her project. Far more of those who had just crossed the high bridge—which left their hearts pounding—accepted the number and later called the woman. To be revved up and to associate some of that arousal with a desirable person is to feel the pull of passion. Adrenaline makes the heart grow fonder. And when sexual desire is supplemented by a growing attachment, the result is the passion of romantic love (Berscheid, 2010).

Companionate Love Although the desire and attachment of romantic love often endure, the intense absorption in the other, the thrill of the romance, the giddy "floating on a cloud" feelings typically fade. Does this mean the French are correct in saying that "love makes the time pass and time makes love pass"? Or can friendship and commitment keep a relationship going after the passion cools?

As love matures, it typically becomes a steadier **companionate love**—a deep, affectionate attachment (Hatfield, 1988). The flood of passion-facilitating hormones (testosterone, dopamine, adrenaline) subsides and another hormone, *oxytocin*, supports feelings of trust, calmness, and bonding with the mate. In the most satisfying of marriages, attraction and sexual desire endure, minus the obsession of early stage romance (Acevedo & Aron, 2009).

There may be adaptive wisdom to the shift from passion to attachment (Reis & Aron, 2008). Passionate love often produces children, whose survival is aided by the parents' waning obsession with each other. Failure to appreciate passionate love's limited half-life can doom a relationship (Berscheid et al., 1984). Indeed, recognizing the short duration of obsessive passionate love, some societies deem such feelings to be an irrational reason for marrying. Better, they say, to choose (or have someone choose for you) a partner with a compatible background and interests. Non-Western cultures, where people rate love as less important for marriage, do have lower divorce rates (Levine et al., 1995).

One key to a gratifying and enduring relationship is **equity.** When equity exists— when both partners receive in proportion to what they give—their chances for sustained and satisfying companionate love are good (Gray-Little & Burks, 1983; Van Yperen & Buunk, 1990). In one national survey, "sharing household chores" ranked third, after "faithfulness" and a "happy sexual relationship," on a list of nine things people associated with successful marriages. "I like hugs. I like kisses. But what I really love is help with the dishes," summarized the Pew Research Center (2007).

Equity's importance extends beyond marriage. Mutually sharing one's self and possessions, making decisions together, giving and getting emotional support, promoting and caring about each other's welfare—all of these acts are at the core of every type of loving relationship (Sternberg & Grajek, 1984). It's true for lovers, for parent and child, and for close friends.

Another vital ingredient of loving relationships is **self-disclosure,** the revealing of intimate details about ourselves—our likes and dislikes, our dreams and worries, our proud and shameful moments. "When I am with my friend," noted the Roman statesman Seneca, "me thinks I am alone, and as much at liberty to speak anything as to think it." Self-disclosure breeds liking, and liking breeds self-disclosure (Collins & Miller, 1994). As one person reveals a little, the other reciprocates, the first then reveals more, and on and on, as friends or lovers move to deeper levels of intimacy (Baumeister & Bratslavsky, 1999).

One experiment marched student pairs through 45 minutes of increasingly self-disclosing conversation—from "When did you last sing to yourself?" to "When did you last cry in front of another person? By yourself?" Others spent the time with small-talk questions, such as "What was your high school like?" (Aron et al., 1997). By the experiment's end, those experiencing the escalating intimacy felt much closer to their conversation partner than did the small-talkers.

passionate love an aroused state of intense positive absorption in another, usually present at the beginning of a love relationship.

companionate love the deep affectionate attachment we feel for those with whom our lives are intertwined.

equity a condition in which people receive from a relationship in proportion to what they give to it.

self-disclosure the act of revealing intimate aspects of oneself to others.

"When two people are under the influence of the most violent, most insane, most delusive, and most transient of passions, they are required to swear that they will remain in that excited, abnormal, and exhausting condition continuously until death do them part."

George Bernard Shaw, "Getting Married," 1908

HI & LOIS

Love is an ancient thing In 2007, a 5000- to 6000-year-old "Romeo and Juliet" young couple was unearthed locked in embrace, near Rome.

Intimacy can also grow when we pause to ponder and write our feelings. Researchers invited one person from each of 86 dating couples to spend 20 minutes a day over three days either writing their deepest thoughts and feelings about the relationship or writing merely about their daily activities (Slatcher & Pennebaker, 2006). Those who wrote about their feelings expressed more emotion in their instant messages with their partners in the days following, and 77 percent were still dating three months later (compared with 52 percent of those who had written about their activities).

In addition to equity and self-disclosure, a third key to enduring love is *positive support*. While relationship conflicts are inevitable, we can ask ourselves whether our communications more often express sarcasm or support, scorn or sympathy, sneers or smiles. For unhappy couples, disagreements, criticisms, and put downs are routine. For happy couples in enduring relationships, positive interactions (compliments, touches, laughing) outnumber negative interactions (sarcasm, disapproval, insults) by at least 5 to 1 (Gottman, 2007; see also Sullivan et al., 2010).

In the mathematics of love, self-disclosing intimacy + mutually supportive equity = enduring companionate love.

RETRIEVAL PRACTICE

• How does the two-factor theory of emotion help explain *passionate love?*

ANSWER: Emotions consist of (1) physical arousal and (2) our interpretation of that arousal. Researchers have found that any source of arousal (running, fear, laughter) may be interpreted as passion in the presence of a desirable person.

• Two vital components for maintaining companionate love are _____ and _____-_____.

ANSWERS: equity; self-disclosure

Altruism

45-3 When are people most—and least—likely to help?

Altruism is an unselfish concern for the welfare of others. In rescuing his jailer, Dirk Willems exemplified altruism. So also did Carl Wilkens and Paul Rusesabagina in Kigali, Rwanda. Wilkens, a Seventh Day Adventist missionary, was living there in 1994 with his family when militia from the Hutu ethnic group began to slaughter members of a minority ethnic group, the Tutsis. The U.S. government, church leaders, and friends all implored Wilkens to leave. He refused. After evacuating his family, and even after every other American had left Kigali, he alone stayed and contested the 800,000-person genocide. When the militia came to kill him and his Tutsi servants, Wilkens' Hutu neighbors deterred them. Despite repeated death threats, he spent his days running roadblocks to take food and water to orphanages and to negotiate, plead, and bully his way through the bloodshed, saving lives time and again. "It just seemed the right thing to do," he later explained (Kristof, 2004).

altruism unselfish regard for the welfare of others.

Elsewhere in Kigali, Rusesabagina, a Hutu married to a Tutsi and the acting manager of a luxury hotel, was sheltering more than 1200 terrified Tutsis and moderate Hutus. When international peacekeepers abandoned the city and hostile militia threatened his guests in the "Hotel Rwanda" (as it came to be called in a 2004 movie), the courageous Rusesabagina began cashing in past favors. He bribed the militia and telephoned influential people abroad to exert pressure on local authorities, thereby sparing the lives of the hotel's occupants from the surrounding chaos. Both Wilkens and Rusesabagina were displaying altruism, an unselfish regard for the welfare of others.

Altruism became a major concern of social psychologists after an especially vile act. On March 13, 1964, a stalker repeatedly stabbed Kitty Genovese, then raped her as she lay dying outside her Queens, New York, apartment at 3:30 A.M. "Oh, my God, he stabbed me!" Genovese screamed into the early morning stillness. "Please help me!" Windows opened and lights went on as neighbors heard her screams. Her attacker fled and then returned to stab and rape her again. Not until he had fled for good did anyone so much as call the police, at 3:50 A.M.

Bystander Intervention

Reflecting on initial reports of the Genovese murder and other such tragedies, most commentators were outraged by the bystanders' apparent "apathy" and "indifference." Rather than blaming the onlookers, social psychologists John Darley and Bibb Latané (1968b) attributed their inaction to an important situational factor—the presence of others. Given certain circumstances, they suspected, most of us might behave similarly. To paraphrase the French writer Voltaire, we all are guilty of the good we did not do.

After staging emergencies under various conditions, Darley and Latané assembled their findings into a decision scheme: We will help only if the situation enables us first to *notice* the incident, then to *interpret* it as an emergency, and finally to *assume responsibility* for helping (**FIGURE 45.4**). At each step, the presence of others can turn us away from the path that leads to helping.

Darley and Latané reached their conclusions after interpreting the results of a series of experiments. For example, as students in different laboratory rooms talked over an intercom, the experimenters simulated an emergency. Each student was in a separate cubicle, and only the person whose microphone was switched on could be heard. When his turn came, one student (an accomplice of the experimenters) made sounds as though he were having an epileptic seizure, and he called for help (Darley & Latané, 1968a).

How did the others react? As **FIGURE 45.5** on the next page shows, those who believed only they could hear the victim—and therefore thought they alone were

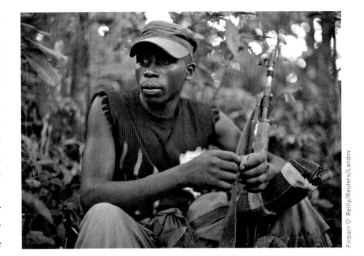

Why do genocides occur?
An estimated 800,000 people died during the Rwandan Genocide of 1994, when Hutu groups carried out mass killings of Tutsis. Social psychology research helps us understand some of the factors motivating genocides. We tend to categorize our world into us and them, and, when threatened, to feel greater animosity toward outside groups.

"Probably no single incident has caused social psychologists to pay as much attention to an aspect of social behavior as Kitty Genovese's murder."

R. Lance Shotland (1984)

▼ FIGURE 45.4
The decision-making process for bystander intervention Before helping, one must first notice an emergency, then correctly interpret it, and then feel responsible. (Adapted from Darley & Latané, 1968b.)

▼ **FIGURE 45.5**
Responses to a simulated physical emergency When people thought they alone heard the calls for help from a person they believed to be having an epileptic seizure, they usually helped. But when they thought four others were also hearing the calls, fewer than a third responded. (Data from Darley & Latané, 1968a.)

LaunchPad For a review of research on emergency helping, visit LaunchPad's *Concept Practice: When Will People Help Others?*

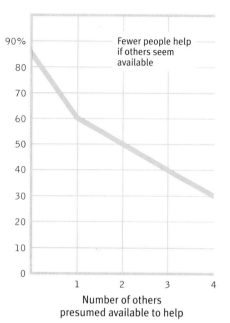

Percentage attempting to help

Fewer people help if others seem available

Number of others presumed available to help

---

bystander effect the tendency for any given bystander to be less likely to give aid if other bystanders are present.

social exchange theory the theory that our social behavior is an exchange process, the aim of which is to maximize benefits and minimize costs.

reciprocity norm an expectation that people will help, not hurt, those who have helped them.

social-responsibility norm an expectation that people will help those needing their help.

PLEASE GIVE TO ALTRUISM RESEARCH

---

responsible for helping him—usually went to his aid. Students who thought others could also hear the victim's cries were more likely to do nothing. When more people shared responsibility for helping—when there was a *diffusion of responsibility*—any single listener was less likely to help.

Hundreds of additional experiments have confirmed this **bystander effect.** For example, researchers and their assistants took 1497 elevator rides in three cities and "accidentally" dropped coins or pencils in front of 4813 fellow passengers (Latané & Dabbs, 1975). When alone with the person in need, 40 percent helped; in the presence of 5 other bystanders, only 20 percent helped.

Observations of behavior in thousands of these situations—relaying an emergency phone call, aiding a stranded motorist, donating blood, picking up dropped books, contributing money, giving time—show that the *best* odds of our helping someone occur when

- the person appears to need and deserve help.
- the person is in some way similar to us.
- the person is a woman.
- we have just observed someone else being helpful.
- we are not in a hurry.
- we are in a small town or rural area.
- we are feeling guilty.
- we are focused on others and not preoccupied.
- we are in a good mood.

This last result, that happy people are helpful people, is one of the most consistent findings in all of psychology. As poet Robert Browning (1868) observed, "Oh, make us happy and you make us good!" It doesn't matter how we are cheered. Whether by being made to feel successful and intelligent, by thinking happy thoughts, by finding money, or even by receiving a posthypnotic suggestion, we become more generous and more eager to help (Carlson et al., 1988). And given a feeling of elevation after witnessing or learning of someone else's self-giving deed, our helping will become even more pronounced (Schnall et al., 2010).

So happiness breeds helpfulness. But it's also true that helpfulness breeds happiness. Making charitable donations activates brain areas associated with reward (Harbaugh et al., 2007). That helps explain a curious finding: People who give money away are happier than those who spend it almost entirely on themselves. In a survey of more than 200,000 people worldwide, people in both rich and poor countries were happier with their lives if they had donated to a charity in the last month (Aknin et al., 2013). Just reflecting on a time when one spent money on others provides most people with a mood boost. And in one experiment, researchers gave people an envelope with cash and instructions either to spend it on themselves or to spend it on others (Dunn et al., 2008, 2013). Which group was happiest at the day's end? It was, indeed, those assigned to the spend-it-on-others condition.

• Why didn't anybody help Kitty Genovese? What social psychology principle did this incident illustrate?

ANSWER: In the presence of others, an individual is less likely to notice a situation, correctly interpret it as an emergency, and take responsibility for offering help. The Kitty Genovese case demonstrated this *bystander effect*, as each witness assumed many others were also aware of the event.

The Norms for Helping

45-4 How do social exchange theory and social norms explain helping behavior?

Why do we help? One widely held view is that self-interest underlies all human interactions, that our constant goal is to maximize rewards and minimize costs. Accountants call it *cost-benefit analysis.* Philosophers call it *utilitarianism.* Social psychologists call it **social exchange theory.** If you are pondering whether to donate blood, you may weigh the costs of doing so (time, discomfort, and anxiety) against the benefits (reduced guilt, social approval, and good feelings). If the rewards exceed the costs, you will help.

Others believe that we help because we have been socialized to do so, through norms that prescribe how we *ought* to behave. Through socialization, we learn the **reciprocity norm:** the expectation that we should return help, not harm, to those who have helped us. In our relations with others of similar status, the reciprocity norm compels us to give (in favors, gifts, or social invitations) about as much as we receive. In one experiment, people who were generously treated also became more likely to be generous to a stranger—to "pay it forward" (Tsvetkova & Macy, 2014).

The reciprocity norm kicked in after Dave Tally, a Tempe, Arizona homeless man, found $3300 in a backpack that an Arizona State University student had misplaced on his way to buy a used car (Lacey, 2010). Instead of using the cash for much-needed bike repairs, food, and shelter, Tally turned the backpack in to the social service agency where he volunteered. To reciprocate Tally's help, the student thanked him with a reward. Hearing about Tally's self-giving deeds, dozens of others also sent him money and job offers.

We also learn a **social-responsibility norm:** that we should help those who need our help—young children and others who cannot give as much as they receive—even if the costs outweigh the benefits. Construction worker Wesley Autrey exemplified the social-responsibility norm on January 2, 2007. He and his 6- and 4-year-old daughters were awaiting a New York City subway train when, before them, a man collapsed in a seizure, got up, then stumbled to the platform's edge and fell onto the tracks. With train headlights approaching, "I had to make a split-second decision," Autrey later recalled (Buckley, 2007). His decision, as his girls looked on in horror, was to leap from the platform, push the man off the tracks and into a foot-deep space between them, and lay atop him. As the train screeched to a halt, five cars traveled just above his head, leaving grease on his knit cap. When Autrey cried out, "I've got two daughters up there. Let them know their father is okay," onlookers erupted into applause.

People who attend weekly religious services often are admonished to practice the social-responsibility norm, and sometimes they do. In American surveys, they have reported twice as many volunteer hours spent helping the poor and infirm, compared with those who rarely or never attend religious services (Hodgkinson & Weitzman, 1992; Independent Sector, 2002). Between 2006 and 2008, Gallup polls sampled more than 300,000 people across 140 countries, comparing the "highly religious" (who said religion was important to them and who had attended a religious service in the prior week) to those less religious. The highly religious, despite being poorer, were about 50 percent more likely to report having "donated money to a charity in the last month" and to have volunteered time to an organization (Pelham & Crabtree, 2008).

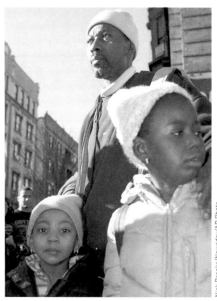

Subway hero Wesley Autrey: "I don't feel like I did something spectacular; I just saw someone who needed help." Five years later, a similar situation occurred when another man was shoved onto subway tracks—and no one helped (Nocera, 2012). Social psychologists have wondered: Under what conditions will people help?

conflict a perceived incompatibility of actions, goals, or ideas.

social trap a situation in which the conflicting parties, by each pursuing their self-interest rather than the good of the group, become caught in mutually destructive behavior.

Peacemaking

We live in surprising times. With astonishing speed, recent democratic movements swept away totalitarian rule in Eastern European and Arab countries, and hopes for a new world order displaced the Cold War chill. And yet, the twenty-first century began with terrorist acts and war. *Every day*, the world has continued to spend almost $5 billion for arms and armies—money that could have been used for housing, nutrition, education, and health care. Knowing that wars begin in human minds, psychologists have wondered: What in the human mind causes destructive conflict? How might the perceived threats of social diversity be replaced by a spirit of cooperation?

Elements of Conflict

45-5 How do social traps and mirror-image perceptions fuel social conflict?

To a social psychologist, a **conflict** is a perceived incompatibility of actions, goals, or ideas. The elements of conflict are much the same, whether we are speaking of nations at war, cultural groups feuding within a society, or partners sparring in a relationship. In each situation, people become enmeshed in potentially destructive processes that can produce unwanted results. Among these processes are social traps and distorted perceptions.

Social Traps In some situations, we support our collective well-being by pursuing our personal interests. As capitalist Adam Smith wrote in *The Wealth of Nations* (1776), "It is not from the benevolence of the butcher, the brewer, or the baker that we expect our dinner, but from their regard to their own interest." In other situations, we harm our collective well-being by pursuing our personal interests. Such situations are **social traps.**

Consider the simple game matrix in **FIGURE 45.6**, which is similar to those used in experiments with thousands of people. Both sides can win or both can lose, depending on the players' individual choices. Pretend you are Person 1, and that you and Person 2 will each receive the amount shown after you separately choose either A or B. (You might invite someone to look at the matrix with you and take the role of Person 2.) Which do you choose—A or B?

You and Person 2 are caught in a dilemma. If you both choose A, you both benefit, making $5 each. Neither of you benefits if you both choose B, for neither of you makes anything. Nevertheless, on any single trial you serve your own interests if you choose B: You can't lose, and you might make $10. But the same is true for the other person. Hence, the social trap: As long as you both pursue your own immediate best interest and choose B, you will both end up with nothing—the typical result—when you could have made $5.

▼ FIGURE 45.6
Social-trap game matrix By pursuing our self-interest and not trusting others, we can end up losers. To illustrate this, imagine playing the game on the right. The light-orange triangles show the outcomes for Person 1, which depend on the choices made by both players. If you were Person 1, would you choose A or B? (This game is called a *non-zero-sum* game because the outcomes need not add up to zero; both sides can win or both can lose.)

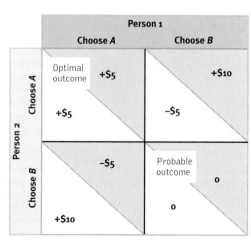

Many real-life situations similarly pit our individual interests against our communal well-being. Individual whalers reasoned that the few whales they took would not threaten the species and that if they didn't take them, others would anyway. The result: Some species of whales became endangered. Ditto for the buffalo hunters of yesterday and the elephant-tusk poachers of today. Individual car owners and home owners reason, "Hybrid and electric cars are more expensive and not as cool as the model I'd like to buy. Besides, the fuel that I burn in my one car doesn't noticeably add to the greenhouse gases." When enough people reason similarly, the collective result threatens disaster—climate change, rising seas, and more extreme weather.

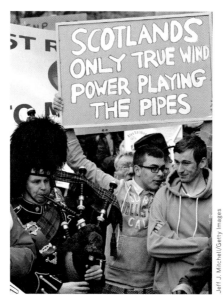

Not in my ocean! Many people support alternative energy sources, including wind turbines. But proposals to construct wind farms in real-world places elicit less support. Potential wind turbines in the Highlands and off the coast of Scotland produced heated debate over the benefits of clean energy versus the costs of altering treasured views.

Social traps challenge us to reconcile our right to pursue our personal well-being with our responsibility for the well-being of all. Psychologists have therefore explored ways to convince people to cooperate for their mutual betterment—through agreed-upon *regulations*, through better *communication*, and through promoting *awareness* of our responsibilities toward community, nation, and the whole of humanity (Dawes, 1980; Linder, 1982; Sato, 1987). Given effective regulations, communication, and awareness, people more often cooperate, whether playing a laboratory game or the real game of life.

Enemy Perceptions Psychologists have noted that those in conflict have a curious tendency to form diabolical images of one another. These distorted images are, ironically, so similar that we call them **mirror-image perceptions:** As we see "them"— as untrustworthy, with evil intentions—so "they" see us. Each demonizes the other.

Mirror-image perceptions can often feed a vicious cycle of hostility. If Juan believes Maria is annoyed with him, he may snub her, causing her to act in ways that justify his perception. As with individuals, so with countries. Perceptions can become **self-fulfilling prophecies.** They may confirm themselves by influencing the other country to react in ways that seem to justify them.

Individuals and nations alike tend to see their own actions as responses to provocation, not as the causes of what happens next. Perceiving themselves as returning tit for tat, they often hit back harder, as University College London volunteers did in one experiment (Shergill et al., 2003). Their task: After feeling pressure on their own finger, they were to use a mechanical device to press on another volunteer's finger. Although told to reciprocate with the same amount of pressure, they typically responded with about 40 percent more force than they had just experienced. Despite seeking only to respond in kind, their touches soon escalated to hard presses, much as when each child after a fight claims that "I just poked him, but he hit me harder."

Mirror-image perceptions feed similar cycles of hostility on the world stage. To most people, torture seems more justified when done by "us" rather than "them" (Tarrant et al., 2012). In American media reports, Muslims who kill have been portrayed as fanatical, hateful terrorists, while an American who allegedly killed 16 Afghans was portrayed as struggling financially, drunk, brain-injured, and stressed out from marriage problems, four tours of duty, and a friend's having had his leg blown off (Greenwald, 2012).

mirror-image perceptions mutual views often held by conflicting people, as when each side sees itself as ethical and peaceful and views the other side as evil and aggressive.

self-fulfilling prophecy a belief that leads to its own fulfillment.

outgroup "them"—those perceived as different or apart from our *ingroup*.

The point is not that truth must lie midway between two such views; one may be more accurate. The point is that enemy perceptions often form mirror images. Moreover, as enemies change, so do perceptions. In American minds and media, the "blood-thirsty, cruel, treacherous" Japanese of World War II later became our "intelligent, hardworking, self-disciplined, resourceful allies" (Gallup, 1972).

Promoting Peace

45-6 How can we transform feelings of prejudice, aggression, and conflict into attitudes that promote peace?

How can we make peace? Can contact, cooperation, communication, and conciliation transform the antagonisms fed by prejudice and conflicts into attitudes that promote peace? Research indicates that, in some cases, they can.

Contact Does it help to put two conflicting parties into close contact? It depends. Negative contact increases *dis*liking (Barlow et al., 2012). But positive contact—especially noncompetitive contact between parties of equal status, such as fellow store clerks—typically helps. Initially prejudiced co-workers of different races have, in such circumstances, usually come to accept one another. This finding is confirmed by a statistical digest of more than 500 studies of face-to-face contact between majority people and **outgroups** (such as ethnic minorities, the elderly, and those with disabilities). Among the quarter-million people studied across 38 nations, contact has been correlated with, or in experimental studies has led to, more positive attitudes (Al Ramiah & Hewstone, 2013; Pettigrew & Tropp, 2011). Some examples:

- With cross-racial contact, South Africans' interracial attitudes have moved "into closer alignment" (Dixon et al., 2007; Finchilescu & Tredoux, 2010). In South Africa, as elsewhere, the contact effect is somewhat less for lower-status ethnic groups' views of higher-status groups (Durrheim & Dixon, 2010; Gibson & Claassen, 2010). Still, cross-group friendships have led to more positive attitudes by South African Coloured teens toward minority White teens (Swart et al., 2011).

- Heterosexuals' attitudes toward gay people are influenced not only by *what* they know but also by *whom* they know (Collier et al., 2012; Smith et al., 2009). In surveys, the reason people most often give for becoming more supportive of same-sex marriage is "having friends, family, or acquaintances who are gay or lesbian" (Pew, 2013).

- Friendly contact, say between Blacks and Whites as roommates, improves attitudes toward others of the different race, and even toward other racial outgroups (Gaither & Sommers, 2013; Tausch et al., 2010).

- Even indirect contact with an outgroup member (via story reading or through a friend who has an outgroup friend) has reduced prejudice (Cameron & Rutland, 2006; Pettigrew et al., 2007).

However, contact is not always enough. In most desegregated schools, ethnic groups resegregate themselves in lunchrooms, in classrooms, and elsewhere on school grounds (Alexander & Tredoux, 2010; Clack et al., 2005; Schofield, 1986). People in each group often think that they would welcome more contact with the other group, but they assume the other group does not reciprocate the wish

(Richeson & Shelton, 2007). "I don't reach out to them, because I don't want to be rebuffed; they don't reach out to me, because they're just not interested." When such mirror-image misperceptions are corrected, friendships may form and prejudices melt.

Cooperation To see if enemies could overcome their differences, researcher Muzafer Sherif (1966) set a conflict in motion. He separated 22 Oklahoma City boys into two separate camp areas. Then he had the two groups compete for prizes in a series of activities. Before long, each group became intensely proud of itself and hostile to the other group's "sneaky," "smart-alecky stinkers." Food wars broke out. Cabins were ransacked. Fistfights had to be broken up by camp counselors. Brought together, the two groups avoided each other, except to taunt and threaten. Little did they know that within a few days, they would be friends.

Sherif accomplished this by giving them **superordinate goals**—shared goals that could be achieved only through cooperation. When he arranged for the camp water supply to "fail," all 22 boys had to work together to restore the water. To rent a movie in those pre-Netflix days, they all had to pool their resources. To move a stalled truck, the boys needed to combine their strength, pulling and pushing together. Having used isolation and competition to make strangers into enemies, Sherif used shared predicaments and goals to turn enemies into friends. What reduced conflict was not mere contact, but *cooperative* contact.

A shared predicament likewise had a powerfully unifying effect in the weeks after the 9/11 attacks. Patriotism soared as Americans felt "we" were under attack. Gallup-surveyed approval of "our President" shot up from 51 percent the week before the attack to a highest-ever 90 percent level 10 days after (Newport, 2002). In chat groups and everyday speech, even the word *we* (relative to *I*) surged in the immediate aftermath (Pennebaker, 2002). Children and youth exposed to war, and minority group members facing rejection or *discrimination*, likewise develop strong **ingroup** identification (Bauer et al., 2014; Ramos et al., 2012).

At such times, cooperation can lead people to define a new, inclusive group that dissolves their former subgroups (Dovidio & Gaertner, 1999). To accomplish this, you might seat members of two groups not on opposite sides, but alternately around a table. Give them a new, shared name. Have them work together. Then watch "us" and "them" become "we." After 9/11, one 18-year-old New Jersey man described this shift in his

"You cannot shake hands with a clenched fist."

Indira Gandhi, 1971

Kofi Annan: "Most of us have over-lapping identities which unite us with very different groups. We *can* love what we are, without hating what—and who—we are *not*. We can thrive in our own tradition, even as we learn from others" (Nobel lecture, 2001).

Shawn Baldwin/file/AP Photo

superordinate goals shared goals that override differences among people and require their cooperation.

ingroup "us"—people with whom we share a common identity.

own social identity: "I just thought of myself as Black. But now I feel like I'm an American, more than ever" (Sengupta, 2001). In a real experiment, White Americans who read a newspaper article about a terrorist threat against all Americans subsequently expressed reduced prejudice against Black Americans (Dovidio et al., 2004).

If cooperative contact between rival group members encourages positive attitudes, might this principle bring people together in multicultural schools? Could interracial friendships replace competitive classroom situations with cooperative ones? Could cooperative learning maintain or even enhance student achievement? Experiments with adolescents from 11 countries confirm that, in each case, the answer is *Yes* (Roseth et al., 2008). In the classroom as in the sports arena, members of interracial groups who work together on projects typically come to feel friendly toward one another. Knowing this, thousands of teachers have made interracial cooperative learning part of their classroom experience.

The power of cooperative activity to make friends of former enemies has led psychologists to urge increased international exchange and cooperation. Some experiments have found that just imagining the shared threat of global climate change reduces international hostilities (Pyszczynski et al., 2012). From adjacent Brazilian tribes to European countries, formerly conflicting groups have managed to build interconnections, interdependence, and a shared social identity as they seek common goals (Fry, 2012). As we engage in mutually beneficial trade, as we work to protect our common destiny on this fragile planet, and as we become more aware that our hopes and fears are shared, we can transform misperceptions that feed conflict into feelings of solidarity based on common interests.

Communication   When real-life conflicts become intense, a third-party mediator—a marriage counselor, labor mediator, diplomat, community volunteer—may facilitate much-needed communication (Rubin et al., 1994). Mediators help each party to voice its viewpoint and to understand the other's needs and goals. If successful, mediators can replace a competitive *win-lose* orientation with a cooperative *win-win* orientation that leads to a mutually beneficial resolution. A classic example: Two friends, after quarreling over an orange, agreed to split it. One squeezed his half for juice. The other used the peel from her half to flavor a cake. If only the two had communicated their motives to one another, they could have hit on the win-win solution of one having all the juice, the other all the peel.

Superordinate goals override differences Cooperative efforts to achieve shared goals are an effective way to break down social barriers.

Conciliation Understanding and cooperative resolution are most needed, yet least likely, in times of anger or crisis (Bodenhausen et al., 1994; Tetlock, 1988). When conflicts intensify, images become more *stereotyped*, judgments more rigid, and communication more difficult, or even impossible. Each party is likely to threaten, coerce, or retaliate. In the weeks before the 1990 Gulf War, the first President George Bush threatened, in the full glare of publicity, to "kick Saddam's ass." Saddam Hussein communicated in kind, threatening to make Americans "swim in their own blood."

Under such conditions, is there an alternative to war or surrender? Social psychologist Charles Osgood (1962, 1980) advocated a strategy of *Graduated and Reciprocated Initiatives in Tension-Reduction*, nicknamed **GRIT.** In applying GRIT, one side first announces its recognition of mutual interests and its intent to reduce tensions. It then initiates one or more small, conciliatory acts. Without weakening one's retaliatory capability, this modest beginning opens the door for reciprocity by the other party. Should the enemy respond with hostility, one reciprocates in kind. But so, too, with any conciliatory response.

In laboratory experiments, small conciliatory gestures—a smile, a touch, a word of apology—have allowed both parties to begin edging down the tension ladder to a safer rung where communication and mutual understanding can begin (Lindskold et al., 1978, 1988). In a real-world international conflict, U.S. President John F. Kennedy's gesture of stopping atmospheric nuclear tests began a series of reciprocated conciliatory acts that culminated in the 1963 atmospheric test-ban treaty.

As working toward shared goals reminds us, we are more alike than different. Civilization advances not by conflict and cultural isolation, but by tapping the knowledge, the skills, and the arts that are each culture's legacy to the whole human race. Thanks to cultural sharing, every modern society is enriched by a cultural mix (Sowell, 1991). We have China to thank for paper and printing and for the magnetic compass that opened the great explorations. We have Egypt to thank for trigonometry. We have the Islamic world and India's Hindus to thank for our Arabic numerals. While celebrating and claiming these diverse cultural legacies, we can also welcome the enrichment of today's social diversity. We can view ourselves as instruments in a human orchestra. And we—including this book's worldwide readers—can therefore each affirm our own culture's heritage while building bridges of communication, understanding, and cooperation across our cultural traditions.

"*To begin with, I would like to express my sincere thanks and deep appreciation for the opportunity to meet with you. While there are still profound differences between us, I think the very fact of my presence here today is a major breakthrough.*"

RETRIEVAL PRACTICE

- What are some ways to reconcile conflicts and promote peace?

ANSWER: Peacemakers should encourage equal-status contact, cooperation to achieve *superordinate goals* (shared goals that override differences), understanding through communication, and reciprocated conciliatory gestures (each side gives a little).

GRIT Graduated and Reciprocated Initiatives in Tension-Reduction—a strategy designed to decrease international tensions.

MODULE 45 REVIEW Prosocial Relations

LEARNING OBJECTIVES

RETRIEVAL PRACTICE Take a moment to answer each of these Learning Objective Questions (repeated here from within this module). Then turn to Appendix C, Complete Module Reviews, to check your answers. Research suggests that trying to answer these questions on your own will improve your long-term retention (McDaniel et al., 2009).

45-1 Why do we befriend or fall in love with some people but not others?

45-2 How does romantic love typically change as time passes?

45-3 When are people most—and least—likely to help?

45-4 How do social exchange theory and social norms explain helping behavior?

45-5 How do social traps and mirror-image perceptions fuel social conflict?

45-6 How can we transform feelings of prejudice, aggression, and conflict into attitudes that promote peace?

TERMS AND CONCEPTS TO REMEMBER

RETRIEVAL PRACTICE Test yourself on these terms by trying to write down the definition before flipping back to check your answers.

mere exposure effect, p. 551

passionate love, p. 556

companionate love, p. 557

equity, p. 557

self-disclosure, p. 557

altruism, p. 558

bystander effect, p. 560

social exchange theory, p. 561

reciprocity norm, p. 561

social-responsibility norm, p. 561

conflict, p. 562

social trap, p. 562

mirror-image perceptions, p. 563

self-fulfilling prophecy, p. 563

outgroup, p. 564

superordinate goals, p. 565

ingroup, p. 565

GRIT, p. 567

Use **LearningCurve** to create your personalized study plan, which will direct you to the resources that will help you most in **LaunchPad**.

TEST YOUR-SELF SOCIAL PSYCHOLOGY

Test yourself repeatedly throughout your studies. This will not only help you figure out what you know and don't know; the testing itself will help you learn and remember the information more effectively thanks to the *testing effect*.

MODULE 42 Social Thinking

1. If we encounter a person who appears to be high on drugs, and we make the fundamental attribution error, we will probably attribute the person's behavior to

   a. moral weakness or an addictive personality.

   b. peer pressure.

   c. the easy availability of drugs on city streets.

   d. society's acceptance of drug use.

2. Celebrity endorsements in advertising often lead consumers to purchase products through _____ (central/peripheral) route persuasion.

3. We tend to agree to a larger request more readily if we have already agreed to a small request. This tendency is called the _____-_____-_____-_____ phenomenon.

4. Jamal's therapist has suggested that Jamal should "act as if" he is confident, even though he feels insecure and shy. Which social psychological theory would best support this suggestion, and what might the therapist be hoping to achieve?

MODULE 43 Social Influence

5. Researchers have found that a person is most likely to conform to a group if

   a. the group members have diverse opinions.

   b. the person feels competent and secure.

   c. the person admires the group's status.

   d. no one else will observe the person's behavior.

6. In Milgram's experiments, the rate of compliance was highest when

   a. the "learner" was at a distance from the "teacher."

   b. the "learner" was close at hand.

   c. other "teachers" refused to go along with the experimenter.

   d. the "teacher" disliked the "learner."

7. Dr. Huang, a popular music professor, delivers fascinating lectures on music history but gets nervous and makes mistakes when describing exam statistics in front of the class. Why does his performance vary by task?

8. In a group situation that fosters arousal and anonymity, a person sometimes loses self-consciousness and self-control. This phenomenon is called _____ .

9. Sharing our opinions with like-minded others tends to strengthen our views, a phenomenon referred to as _____ _____ .

MODULE 44 Antisocial Relations

10. Prejudice toward a group involves negative feelings, a tendency to discriminate, and overly generalized beliefs referred to as _____ .

11. If several well-publicized murders are committed by members of a particular group, we may tend to react with fear and suspicion toward all members of that group. What psychological principle can help explain this reaction?

12. The other-race effect occurs when we assume that other groups are _____ (more/less) homogeneous than our own group.

13. Evidence of a biochemical influence on aggression is the finding that

    a. aggressive behavior varies widely from culture to culture.

    b. animals can be bred for aggressiveness.

    c. stimulation of an area of the brain's limbic system produces aggressive behavior.

    d. a higher-than-average level of the hormone testosterone is associated with violent behavior in males.

14. Studies show that parents of delinquent young people tend to use beatings to enforce discipline. This suggests that aggression can be

    a. learned through direct rewards.

    b. triggered by exposure to violent media.

    c. learned through observation of aggressive models.

    d. caused by hormone changes at puberty.

15. A conference of social scientists studying the effects of pornography unanimously agreed that violent pornography

    a. has little effect on most viewers.

    b. is the primary cause of reported and unreported rapes.

    c. leads viewers to be more accepting of coercion in sexual relations.

    d. has no effect, other than short-term arousal and entertainment.

16. The aspect of pornographic films that most directly influences men's aggression toward women seems to be the

    a. length of the film.

    b. eroticism portrayed.

    c. depictions of sexual violence.

    d. attractiveness of the actors.

MODULE 45 Prosocial Relations

17. The more familiar a stimulus becomes, the more we tend to like it. This exemplifies the _____ _____ effect.

18. A happy couple celebrating their 50th wedding anniversary is likely to experience deep _____ love, even though their _____ love has probably decreased over the years.

19. After vigorous exercise, you meet an attractive person, and you are suddenly seized by romantic feelings for that person. This response supports the two-factor theory of emotion, which assumes that emotions, such as passionate love, consist of physical arousal plus

    a. a reward.

    b. proximity.

    c. companionate love.

    d. our interpretation of that arousal.

20. The bystander effect states that a particular bystander is less likely to give aid if

    a. the victim is similar to the bystander in appearance.

    b. no one else is present.

    c. other people are present.

    d. the incident occurs in a deserted or rural area.

21. Our enemies often have many of the same negative impressions of us as we have of them. This exemplifies the concept of _____ - _____ perceptions.

22. One way of resolving conflicts and fostering cooperation is by giving rival groups shared goals that help them override their differences. These are called _____ goals.

Find answers to these questions in Appendix D, in the back of the book.

© Findlay/Alamy

PERSONALITY

· · · · · · · · · · · · ·

Lady Gaga dazzles millions with her unique musical arrangements, tantalizing outfits, and provocative performance theatrics. In shows around the world, Lady Gaga's most predictable feature is her unpredictability. She has worn a meat dress to an award show, performed in a plastic bubble dress, and caused President Barack Obama to experience her, in her 16-inch heels, as "a little intimidating."

Lady Gaga's fans and critics alike can depend on her openness to new experiences and the energy she gets from the spotlight. But they can also rely on her careful, painstaking dedication to her music and performances. She describes herself in high school as "very dedicated, very studious, and very disciplined." Now, in adulthood, she shows similar self-discipline: "I'm very detailed—every minute of the show has got to be perfect."

Lady Gaga exhibits distinctive and enduring ways of thinking, feeling, and behaving. Other modules focus on the ways we all develop, perceive, learn, remember, think, and feel. These modules emphasize what makes us unique—our *personality*.

Much of this book deals with personality. Across the field, psychologists study biological influences on personality; personality development across the life span; how personality relates to learning, motivation, emotion, and health; social influences on personality; and disorders of personality. These modules focus on personality itself—what it is and how researchers study it.

We begin with two historically important theories of personality: Sigmund Freud's *psychoanalytic theory* and the *humanistic* approach (Module 46 and the first section of Module 47). These laid the foundation for later personality theorists and for what Modules 47 and 48 explore: newer scientific explorations of personality.

Today's personality researchers study the basic dimensions of personality, and the interaction of persons and environments. They also study self-esteem, self-serving bias, and cultural influences on our concept of self—that sense of "Who I am." And they study the unconscious mind—with findings that probably would have surprised even Freud.

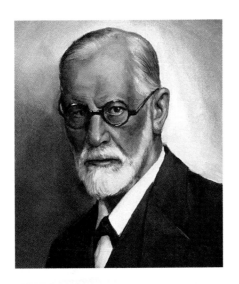

Sigmund Freud (1856–1939) "I was the only worker in a new field."

"The female . . . acknowledges the fact of her castration, and with it, too, the superiority of the male and her own inferiority; but she rebels against this unwelcome state of affairs."

Sigmund Freud, *Female Sexuality*, 1931

Introduction to Personality and Psychodynamic Theories

What Is Personality?

46-1 What historically significant and current theories inform our understanding of personality?

OUR **PERSONALITY** IS OUR CHARACTERISTIC pattern of thinking, feeling, and acting. Two historically significant theories have become part of our cultural legacy. Sigmund Freud's psychoanalytic theory proposed that childhood sexuality and unconscious motivations influence personality. The humanistic approach focused on our inner capacities for growth and self-fulfillment. Later theorists built upon these two broad perspectives. Trait theories, for example, examine characteristic patterns of behavior (*traits*). *Social-cognitive theories* explore the interaction between people's traits (including their thinking) and their social context. Let's begin with psychodynamic theories.

Psychodynamic Theories

Psychodynamic theories of personality view human behavior as a dynamic interaction between the conscious mind and the unconscious mind, including associated motives and conflicts. These theories are descended from Freud's **psychoanalysis**—his theory of personality and the associated treatment techniques. Freud was the first to focus clinical attention on our unconscious mind.

Freud's Psychoanalytic Perspective: Exploring the Unconscious

46-2 How did Sigmund Freud's treatment of psychological disorders lead to his view of the unconscious mind?

Ask 100 people on the street to name a notable deceased psychologist, suggested Keith Stanovich (1996, p. 1), and "Freud would be the winner hands down." In the popular mind, he is to psychology what Elvis Presley is to rock music. Freud's influence not only lingers in psychiatry and clinical psychology, but also in literary and film interpretation. Almost 9 in 10 American college courses that reference psychoanalysis have been outside of psychology departments (Cohen, 2007). His early twentieth-century concepts penetrate our twenty-first-century language. Without realizing their source, we may speak of *ego, repression, projection, complex* (as in "inferiority complex"), *sibling rivalry, Freudian slips,* and *fixation.* So, who was Freud, and what did he teach?

Like all of us, Sigmund Freud was a product of his times. His Victorian era was a time of tremendous discovery and scientific advancement, but it is also known today as a time of sexual repression and male dominance. Men's and women's roles were clearly defined, with male superiority assumed and only male sexuality generally acknowledged (discreetly).

Long before entering the University of Vienna in 1873, young Freud showed signs of independence and brilliance. He so loved reading plays, poetry, and philosophy that he once ran up a bookstore debt beyond his means. As a teen he often took his evening meal in his tiny bedroom in order to lose no time from his studies. After medical school he set up a private practice specializing in nervous disorders. Before long, however, he faced patients whose disorders made no neurological sense. A patient might have lost all feeling in a hand—yet there is no sensory nerve that, if damaged, would numb the entire hand and nothing else. Freud's search for a cause for such disorders set his mind running in a direction destined to change human self-understanding.

Might some neurological disorders have psychological causes? Observing patients led Freud to his "discovery" of the **unconscious.** He speculated that lost feeling in one's hand might be caused by a fear of touching one's genitals; that unexplained blindness or deafness might be caused by not wanting to see or hear something that aroused intense anxiety. After some early unsuccessful trials with hypnosis, Freud turned to **free association,** in which he told the patient to relax and say whatever came to mind, no matter how embarrassing or trivial. He assumed that a line of mental dominoes had fallen from his patients' distant past to their troubled present. Free association, he believed, would allow him to retrace that line, following a chain of thought leading into the patient's unconscious. There, painful unconscious memories, often from childhood, could be retrieved and released.

Basic to Freud's theory was his belief that the mind is mostly hidden (**FIGURE 46.1**). Our *conscious* awareness is like the part of an iceberg that floats above the surface. Beneath our awareness is the larger *unconscious* mind, with its thoughts, wishes, feelings, and memories. Some of these thoughts we store temporarily in a *preconscious* area, from which we can retrieve them into conscious awareness. Of greater interest to Freud was the mass of unacceptable passions and thoughts that he believed we *repress*, or forcibly block from our consciousness because they would be too unsettling to acknowledge. Freud believed that without our awareness, these troublesome feelings and ideas powerfully influence us, sometimes gaining expression in disguised forms— the work we choose, the beliefs we hold, our daily habits, our troubling symptoms.

Personality Structure

46-3 What was Freud's view of personality?

In Freud's view, human personality—including its emotions and strivings—arises from a conflict between impulse and restraint—between our aggressive, pleasure-seeking biological urges and our internalized social controls over these urges. Freud believed personality arises from our efforts to resolve this basic conflict—to express these impulses in ways that bring satisfaction without also bringing guilt or punishment. To understand the mind's dynamics during this conflict, Freud proposed three interacting systems: the *id, ego,* and *superego* (Figure 46.1).

The **id's** unconscious psychic energy constantly strives to satisfy basic drives to survive, reproduce, and aggress. The id operates on the *pleasure principle:* It seeks

unconscious according to Freud, a reservoir of mostly unacceptable thoughts, wishes, feelings, and memories. According to contemporary psychologists, information processing of which we are unaware.

free association in psychoanalysis, a method of exploring the unconscious in which the person relaxes and says whatever comes to mind, no matter how trivial or embarrassing.

id a reservoir of unconscious psychic energy that, according to Freud, strives to satisfy basic sexual and aggressive drives. The id operates on the *pleasure principle,* demanding immediate gratification.

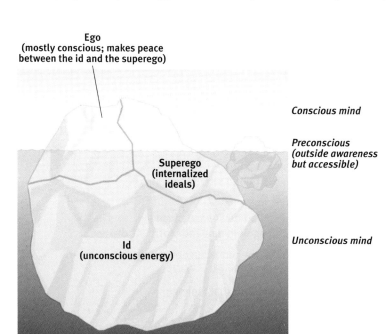

▼ FIGURE 46.1
Freud's idea of the mind's structure Psychologists have used an iceberg image to illustrate Freud's idea that the mind is mostly hidden beneath the conscious surface. Note that the id is totally unconscious, but ego and superego operate both consciously and unconsciously. Unlike the parts of a frozen iceberg, however, the id, ego, and superego interact.

"Fifty is plenty."   "Hundred and fifty."

The ego struggles to reconcile the demands of superego and id, said Freud.

"I heard that as soon as we become aware of our sexual impulses, whatever they are, we'll have to hide them."

ego the largely conscious, "executive" part of personality that, according to Freud, mediates among the demands of the id, superego, and reality. The ego operates on the *reality principle,* satisfying the id's desires in ways that will realistically bring pleasure rather than pain.

superego the part of personality that, according to Freud, represents internalized ideals and provides standards for judgment (the conscience) and for future aspirations.

psychosexual stages the childhood stages of development (oral, anal, phallic, latency, genital) during which, according to Freud, the id's pleasure-seeking energies focus on distinct erogenous zones.

Oedipus [ED-uh-puss] **complex** according to Freud, a boy's sexual desires toward his mother and feelings of jealousy and hatred for the rival father.

immediate gratification. To envision an id-dominated person, think of a newborn infant crying out for satisfaction, caring nothing for the outside world's conditions and demands. Or think of people with a present rather than future time perspective—those who heavily use tobacco, alcohol, and other drugs, and would sooner party now than sacrifice today's pleasure for future success and happiness (Keough et al., 1999).

As the **ego** develops, the young child responds to the real world. The ego, operating on the *reality principle,* seeks to gratify the id's impulses in realistic ways that will bring long-term pleasure. (Imagine what would happen if, lacking an ego, we expressed all our unrestrained sexual or aggressive impulses.) The ego contains our partly conscious perceptions, thoughts, judgments, and memories.

Around age 4 or 5, Freud theorized, a child's ego recognizes the demands of the newly emerging **superego,** the voice of our moral compass (conscience) that forces the ego to consider not only the real but the *ideal.* The superego focuses on how we *ought* to behave. It strives for perfection, judging actions and producing positive feelings of pride or negative feelings of guilt. Someone with an exceptionally strong superego may be virtuous yet guilt ridden; another with a weak superego may be outrageously self-indulgent and remorseless.

Because the superego's demands often oppose the id's, the ego struggles to reconcile the two. It is the personality "executive," mediating among the impulsive demands of the id, the restraining demands of the superego, and the real-life demands of the external world. If chaste Jane feels sexually attracted to John, she may satisfy both id and superego by joining a volunteer organization that John attends regularly.

Personality Development

46-4 What developmental stages did Freud propose?

Analysis of his patients' histories convinced Freud that personality forms during life's first few years. He concluded that children pass through a series of **psychosexual stages,** during which the id's pleasure-seeking energies focus on distinct pleasure-sensitive areas of the body called *erogenous zones* (**TABLE 46.1**). Each stage offers its own challenges, which Freud saw as conflicting tendencies.

Freud believed that during the *phallic stage,* for example, boys seek genital stimulation. They also develop both unconscious sexual desires for their mother and jealousy and hatred for their father, whom they consider a rival. Given these feelings, he thought, boys also experience guilt and a lurking fear of punishment, perhaps by castration, from their father. Freud called this collection of feelings the **Oedipus complex** after the Greek legend of Oedipus, who unknowingly killed his father and married his mother. Some psychoanalysts in Freud's era believed that girls experienced a parallel *Electra complex.*

▼ TABLE 46.1
Freud's Psychosexual Stages

Stage	Focus
Oral (0–18 months)	Pleasure centers on the mouth—sucking, biting, chewing
Anal (18–36 months)	Pleasure focuses on bowel and bladder elimination; coping with demands for control
Phallic (3–6 years)	Pleasure zone is the genitals; coping with incestuous sexual feelings
Latency (6 to puberty)	A phase of dormant sexual feelings
Genital (puberty on)	Maturation of sexual interests

Children eventually cope with the threatening feelings, said Freud, by repressing them and by identifying with (trying to become like) the rival parent. It's as though something inside the child decides, "If you can't beat 'em [the same-sex parent], join 'em." Through this **identification** process, children's superegos gain strength as they incorporate many of their parents' values. Freud believed that identification with the same-sex parent provided what psychologists now call our *gender identity*—our sense of being male, female, or a combination of the two. Freud presumed that our early childhood relations—especially with our parents and caregivers—influence our developing identity, personality, and frailties.

In Freud's view, conflicts unresolved during earlier psychosexual stages could surface as maladaptive behavior in the adult years. At any point in the oral, anal, or phallic stages, strong conflict could lock, or **fixate,** the person's pleasure-seeking energies in that stage. A person who had been either orally overindulged or deprived (perhaps by abrupt, early weaning) might fixate at the oral stage. This orally fixated adult could exhibit either passive dependence (like that of a nursing infant) or an exaggerated denial of this dependence (by acting tough or uttering biting sarcasm). Or the person might continue to seek oral gratification by smoking or excessive eating. In such ways, Freud suggested, the twig of personality is bent at an early age.

Freud's ideas of sexuality were controversial in his own time. "Freud was called a dirty-minded pansexualist and Viennese libertine," noted historian of psychology Morton Hunt (2007, p. 211). Today, Freud's ideas of Oedipal conflict and castration anxiety are disputed even by psychodynamic theorists and therapists (Shedler, 2010b). Yet we still teach them as part of the history of Western ideas.

Defense Mechanisms

46-5 How did Freud think people defended themselves against anxiety?

Anxiety, said Freud, is the price we pay for civilization. As members of social groups, we must control our sexual and aggressive impulses, not act them out. But sometimes the ego fears losing control of this inner id-superego war. The presumed result is a dark cloud of unfocused anxiety that leaves us feeling unsettled but unsure why.

Freud proposed that the ego protects itself with **defense mechanisms**—tactics that reduce or redirect anxiety by distorting reality. For Freud, *all defense mechanisms function indirectly and unconsciously.* Just as the body unconsciously defends itself against disease, so also does the ego unconsciously defend itself against anxiety. For example, **repression** banishes anxiety-arousing wishes and feelings from consciousness. According to Freud, *repression underlies all the other defense mechanisms.* However, because repression is often incomplete, repressed urges may appear as symbols in dreams or as slips of the tongue in casual conversation.

Freud believed he could glimpse the unconscious seeping through when a financially stressed patient, not wanting any large pills, said, "Please do not give me any bills, because I cannot swallow them." (Similarly, sex-related slips of the tongue increased among men sitting next to an attractive young woman rather than a middle-aged man [saying *bare shoulders* instead of *share boulders*; Motley & Baars, 1979].) Freud also viewed jokes as expressions of repressed sexual and aggressive tendencies, and dreams as the "royal road to the unconscious." The remembered content of dreams (their *manifest content*) he believed to be a censored expression of the dreamer's unconscious wishes (the dream's *latent content*). In his dream analyses, Freud searched for patients' inner conflicts.

TABLE 46.2 on the next page describes a sampling of six other well-known defense mechanisms.

"*Oh, for goodness' sake! Smoke!*"

"*Good morning, beheaded—uh, I mean beloved.*"

"I remember your name perfectly but I just can't think of your face."

Oxford professor W. A. Spooner (1844–1930) famous for his linguistic flip-flops *(spoonerisms).* Spooner rebuked one student for "fighting a liar in the quadrangle" and another who "hissed my mystery lecture," adding "You have tasted two worms."

identification the process by which, according to Freud, children incorporate their parents' values into their developing superegos.

fixation according to Freud, a lingering focus of pleasure-seeking energies at an earlier psychosexual stage, in which conflicts were unresolved.

defense mechanisms in psychoanalytic theory, the ego's protective methods of reducing anxiety by unconsciously distorting reality.

repression in psychoanalytic theory, the basic defense mechanism that banishes from consciousness anxiety-arousing thoughts, feelings, and memories.

▼ TABLE 46.2
Six Defense Mechanisms

Freud believed that *repression,* the basic mechanism that banishes anxiety-arousing impulses, enables other defense mechanisms, six of which are listed here.

Defense Mechanism	Unconscious Process Employed to Avoid Anxiety-Arousing Thoughts or Feelings	Example
Regression	Retreating to a more infantile psychosexual stage, where some psychic energy remains fixated.	A little boy reverts to the oral comfort of thumb sucking in the car on the way to his first day of school.
Reaction formation	Switching unacceptable impulses into their opposites.	Repressing angry feelings, a person displays exaggerated friendliness.
Projection	Disguising one's own threatening impulses by attributing them to others.	"The thief thinks everyone else is a thief" (an El Salvadoran saying).
Rationalization	Offering self-justifying explanations in place of the real, more threatening unconscious reasons for one's actions.	A habitual drinker says she drinks with her friends "just to be sociable."
Displacement	Shifting sexual or aggressive impulses toward a more acceptable or less threatening object or person.	A little girl kicks the family dog after her mother sends her to her room.
Denial	Refusing to believe or even perceive painful realities.	A partner denies evidence of his loved one's affair.

Regression Faced with a mild stressor, children and young orangutans seek protection and comfort from their caregivers. Freud might have interpreted these behaviors as regression, a retreat to an earlier developmental stage.

RETRIEVAL PRACTICE

- According to Freud's ideas about the three-part personality structure, the _____ operates on the *reality principle* and tries to balance demands in a way that produces long-term pleasure rather than pain; the _____ operates on the *pleasure principle* and seeks immediate gratification; and the _____ represents the voice of our internalized ideals (our *conscience*).

    ANSWERS: ego; id; superego

- In the psychoanalytic view, conflicts unresolved during one of the psychosexual stages may lead to _____ at that stage.

    ANSWER: fixation

- Freud believed that our defense mechanisms operate _____ (consciously/unconsciously) and defend us against _____ .

    ANSWERS: unconsciously; anxiety

The Neo-Freudian and Later Psychodynamic Theorists

46-6 Which of Freud's ideas did his followers accept or reject?

In a historical period when people never talked about sex, and certainly not unconscious desires for sex with one's parent, Freud's writings prompted considerable debate. "In the Middle Ages, they would have burned me," observed Freud to a friend. "Now they are content with burning my books" (Jones, 1957). Despite the controversy, Freud attracted followers. Several young, ambitious physicians formed an inner circle around their strong-minded leader. These pioneering psychoanalysts, whom we often call *neo-Freudians,* adopted Freud's interviewing technique and accepted Freud's basic ideas: the personality structures of id, ego, and superego; the importance of the unconscious; the childhood roots of personality; and the dynamics of anxiety and the defense mechanisms. But they broke off from Freud in two important ways. First, they placed more emphasis on the conscious mind's role in interpreting experience and in coping with the environment. And second, they doubted that sex and aggression were all-consuming motivations. Instead, they tended to emphasize loftier motives and social interactions.

Alfred Adler and Karen Horney [HORN-eye], for example, agreed with Freud that childhood is important. But they believed that childhood *social,* not sexual, tensions are crucial for personality formation (Ferguson, 2003). Adler (who proposed the still popular idea of the *inferiority complex*) had struggled to overcome childhood illnesses and accidents. He believed that much of our behavior is driven by efforts to conquer childhood inferiority feelings that trigger our strivings for superiority and power. Horney said

Alfred Adler "The individual feels at home in life and feels his existence to be worthwhile just so far as he is useful to others and is overcoming feelings of inferiority" (*Problems of Neurosis*, 1964).

Karen Horney "The view that women are infantile and emotional creatures, and as such, incapable of responsibility and independence is the work of the masculine tendency to lower women's self-respect" (*Feminine Psychology*, 1932).

Carl Jung "From the living fountain of instinct flows everything that is creative; hence the unconscious is the very source of the creative impulse" (*The Structure and Dynamics of the Psyche*, 1960).

childhood anxiety triggers our desire for love and security. She also countered Freud's assumptions, rooted in his conservative culture, that women have weak superegos and suffer "penis envy," and she attempted to balance his masculine bias.

Carl Jung started out a strong follower of Freud, but then he veered off on his own. Jung placed less emphasis on social factors and agreed with Freud that the unconscious exerts a powerful influence. But to Jung [Yoong], the unconscious contains more than our repressed thoughts and feelings. He believed we also have a **collective unconscious,** a common reservoir of images, or *archetypes*, derived from our species' universal experiences. Jung said that the collective unconscious explains why, for many people, spiritual concerns are deeply rooted and why people in different cultures share certain myths and images. Most of today's psychodynamic psychologists and other psychological theorists discount the idea of inherited experiences, but do believe that our shared evolutionary history shaped some universal dispositions. They are also aware that experience can leave *epigenetic* marks.

Freud died in 1939. Since then, some of his ideas have been incorporated into the diversity of perspectives that make up psychodynamic theory. "Most contemporary [psychodynamic] theorists and therapists are not wedded to the idea that sex is the basis of personality," noted Drew Westen (1996). They "do not talk about ids and egos, and do not go around classifying their patients as oral, anal, or phallic characters." What they do assume, with Freud and with much support from today's psychological science, is that much of our mental life is unconscious. With Freud, they also assume that we often struggle with inner conflicts among our wishes, fears, and values, and that childhood shapes our personality and ways of becoming attached to others.

> **collective unconscious** Carl Jung's concept of a shared, inherited reservoir of memory traces from our species' history.

LaunchPad For a helpful, 9-minute overview, visit LaunchPad's *Video: Psychodynamic Theories of Personality.*

Assessing Unconscious Processes

46-7 What are projective tests, how are they used, and what are some criticisms of them?

Personality tests reflect the basic ideas of particular personality theories. Such tools, useful to those who study personality or provide therapy, are tailored to test specific theories. So, what might be the assessment tool of choice for someone working in the Freudian tradition?

"The forward thrust of the antlers shows a determined personality, yet the small sun indicates a lack of self-confidence. . . ."

projective test a personality test, such as the Rorschach, that provides ambiguous stimuli designed to trigger projection of one's inner dynamics.

Thematic Apperception Test (TAT) a projective test in which people express their inner feelings and interests through the stories they make up about ambiguous scenes.

Rorschach inkblot test the most widely used projective test, a set of 10 inkblots, designed by Hermann Rorschach; seeks to identify people's inner feelings by analyzing their interpretations of the blots.

"We don't see things as they are; we see things as we are."

The Talmud

Such a test would need to provide some sort of road into the unconscious, to unearth the residue of early childhood experiences, to move beneath surface pretensions and reveal hidden conflicts and impulses. Objective assessment tools, such as agree-disagree or true-false questionnaires, would be inadequate because they would merely tap the conscious surface.

Projective tests aim to provide this "psychological X-ray," by asking test-takers to describe an ambiguous stimulus or tell a story about it. The clinician may presume that any hopes, desires, and fears that people see in the ambiguous image are projections of their own inner feelings or conflicts.

Henry Murray (1933) demonstrated a possible basis for such a test at a party hosted by his 11-year-old daughter. Murray engaged the children in a frightening game called "Murder." When shown some photographs after the game, the children perceived the photos as more malicious than they had before the game. These children, it seemed to Murray, had *projected* their inner feelings into the pictures.

A few years later, Murray introduced the **Thematic Apperception Test (TAT)**—a test in which people view ambiguous pictures and then make up stories about them. One use of such storytelling has been to assess *achievement motivation* (Schultheiss et al., 2014). Shown a daydreaming boy, those who imagine he is fantasizing about an achievement are presumed to be projecting their own goals. "As a rule," said Murray, "the subject leaves the test happily unaware that he has presented the psychologist with what amounts to an x-ray of his inner self" (quoted by Talbot, 1999).

The most widely used projective test left some blots on the name of Swiss psychiatrist Hermann Rorschach [ROAR-shock; 1884–1922]. He based his famous **Rorschach inkblot test,** in which people describe what they see in a series of inkblots (**FIGURE 46.2**), on a childhood game. He and his friends would drip ink on a paper, fold it, and then say what they saw in the resulting blot (Sdorow, 2005). Do you see predatory animals or weapons? Perhaps you have aggressive tendencies. But is this a reasonable assumption? The answer varies.

Some clinicians cherish the Rorschach, even offering to judges Rorschach-based assessments of criminals' violence potential. Others view the test as a source of suggestive leads, an icebreaker, and a revealing interview technique. The Society for Personality Assessment (2005) commends "its responsible use" (which would *not* include inferring past childhood sexual abuse). And—in response to past criticisms of test scoring and interpretation (Sechrest et al., 1998)—a research-based, computer-aided tool has been designed to improve agreement among raters and enhance the test's validity (Erdberg, 1990; Exner, 2003).

But the evidence is insufficient to its revilers, who insist the Rorschach is no emotional MRI. They argue that only a few of the many Rorschach-derived scores, such as

▼ FIGURE 46.2
The Rorschach test In this projective test, people tell what they see in a series of symmetrical inkblots. Some who use this test are confident that the interpretation of ambiguous stimuli will reveal unconscious aspects of the test-taker's personality.

Spencer Grant/Science Source

ones for hostility and anxiety, have demonstrated validity (Wood, 2006). Moreover, they say, these tests are not reliable. Inkblot assessments diagnose many normal adults as pathological (Mihura et al., 2013; Wood et al., 2003, 2006, 2010). Alternative projective assessment techniques fare little better. "Even seasoned professionals can be fooled by their intuitions and their faith in tools that lack strong evidence of effectiveness," warned Scott Lilienfeld, James Wood, and Howard Garb (2001). "When a substantial body of research demonstrates that old intuitions are wrong, it is time to adopt new ways of thinking."

Evaluating Freud's Psychoanalytic Perspective and Modern Views of the Unconscious

46-8 How do contemporary psychologists view Freud's psychoanalysis?

Modern Research Contradicts Many of Freud's Ideas We critique Freud from a twenty-first-century perspective, a perspective that itself will be subject to revision. Freud did not have access to neurotransmitter or DNA studies, or to all that we have since learned about human development, thinking, and emotion. To criticize his theory by comparing it with today's thinking, some say, is like criticizing Henry Ford's Model T by comparing it with today's hybrid cars. How tempting it always is to judge people in the past from our perspective in the present.

But both Freud's devotees and detractors agree that recent research contradicts many of his specific ideas. Today's developmental psychologists see our development as lifelong, not fixed in childhood. They doubt that infants' neural networks are mature enough to sustain as much emotional trauma as Freud assumed. Some think Freud overestimated parental influence and underestimated peer influence. They also doubt that conscience and gender identity form as the child resolves the Oedipus complex at age 5 or 6. We gain our gender identity earlier, and those who become strongly masculine or feminine do so even without a same-sex parent present. And they note that Freud's ideas about childhood sexuality arose from his skepticism of stories of childhood sexual abuse told by his female patients—stories that some scholars believe he attributed to their own childhood sexual wishes and conflicts (Esterson, 2001; Powell & Boer, 1994). Today, we understand how Freud's questioning might have created false memories of abuse, and we also know that childhood sexual abuse does happen.

New psychological research about why we dream disputes Freud's belief that dreams disguise and fulfill wishes. And slips of the tongue can be explained as competition between similar verbal choices in our memory network. Someone who says "I don't want to do that—it's a lot of brothel" may simply be blending *bother* and *trouble* (Foss & Hakes, 1978). Researchers find little support for Freud's idea that defense mechanisms disguise sexual and aggressive impulses (though our cognitive gymnastics do indeed work to protect our self-esteem). History also has failed to support another of Freud's ideas—that suppressed sexuality causes psychological disorders. From Freud's time to ours, sexual inhibition has diminished; psychological disorders have not.

Psychologists also criticize Freud's theory for its scientific shortcomings. It's important to remember that good scientific theories explain observations and offer testable hypotheses. Freud's theory rests on few objective observations, and parts of it offer few testable hypotheses. For Freud, his own recollections and interpretations of patients' free associations, dreams, and slips were evidence enough.

What is the most serious problem with Freud's theory? It offers after-the-fact explanations of any characteristic (of one person's smoking, another's fear of horses, another's sexual orientation) yet fails to *predict* such behaviors and traits. If

"The Rorschach [Inkblot Test] has the dubious distinction of being, simultaneously, the most cherished and the most reviled of all psychological assessment tools."

John Hunsley and J. Michael Bailey, 1999

"Many aspects of Freudian theory are indeed out of date, and they should be: Freud died in 1939, and he has been slow to undertake further revisions."

Psychologist Drew Westen (1998)

"We are arguing like a man who should say, 'If there were an invisible cat in that chair, the chair would look empty; but the chair does look empty; therefore there is an invisible cat in it'."

C. S. Lewis, *Four Loves*, 1958

"Although [Freud] clearly made a number of mistakes in the formulation of his ideas, his understanding of unconscious mental processes was pretty much on target. In fact, it is very consistent with modern neuroscientists' belief that most mental processes are unconscious."

Nobel Prize–winning neuroscientist Eric Kandel (2012)

"The overall findings . . . seriously challenge the classical psychoanalytic notion of repression."

Psychologist Yacov Rofé, "Does Repression Exist?" 2008

"During the Holocaust, many children . . . were forced to endure the unendurable. For those who continue to suffer [the] pain is still present, many years later, as real as it was on the day it occurred."

Eric Zillmer, Molly Harrower, Barry Ritzler, and Robert Archer, *The Quest for the Nazi Personality*, 1995

you feel angry at your mother's death, you illustrate his theory because "your unresolved childhood dependency needs are threatened." If you do not feel angry, you again illustrate his theory because "you are repressing your anger." That "is like betting on a horse after the race has been run" (Hall & Lindzey, 1978, p. 68). A good theory makes testable predictions.

So, should psychology post an "Allow Natural Death" order on this old theory? Freud's supporters object. To criticize Freudian theory for not making testable predictions is, they say, like criticizing baseball for not being an aerobic exercise, something it was never intended to be. Freud never claimed that psychoanalysis was predictive science. He merely claimed that, looking back, psychoanalysts could find meaning in our state of mind (Rieff, 1979).

Freud's supporters also note that some of his ideas *are* enduring. It was Freud who drew our attention to the unconscious and the irrational, at a time when such ideas were not popular. Today many researchers study our irrationality (Ariely, 2010). Psychologist Daniel Kahneman won the 2002 Nobel Prize in Economics for his studies of our faulty decision making. Freud also drew our attention to the importance of human sexuality, and to the tension between our biological impulses and our social well-being. It was Freud who challenged our self-righteousness, exposed our self-protective defenses, and reminded us of our potential for evil.

Modern Research Challenges the Idea of Repression Psychoanalytic theory presumes that we often *repress* offending wishes, banishing them into the unconscious until they resurface, like long-lost books in a dusty attic. Recover and resolve childhood's conflicted wishes, and emotional healing should follow. Repression became a widely accepted concept, used to explain hypnotic phenomena and psychological disorders. Some psychodynamic followers extended repression to explain apparently lost and recovered memories of childhood traumas (Boag, 2006; Cheit, 1998; Erdelyi, 2006). In one survey, 88 percent of university students believed that painful experiences commonly get pushed out of awareness and into the unconscious (Garry et al., 1994).

Today's researchers agree that we sometimes spare our egos by neglecting threatening information (Green et al., 2008). Yet many contend that repression, if it ever occurs, is a rare mental response to terrible trauma. Even those who witnessed a parent's murder or survived Nazi death camps have retained their unrepressed memories of the horror (Helmreich, 1992, 1994; Malmquist, 1986; Pennebaker, 1990). "Dozens of formal studies have yielded not a single convincing case of repression in the entire literature on trauma," concluded personality researcher John Kihlstrom (2006).

Some researchers do believe that extreme, prolonged stress, such as the stress some severely abused children experience, might disrupt memory by damaging the hippocampus (Schacter, 1996). But the far more common reality is that high stress and associated stress hormones *enhance* memory. Indeed, rape, torture, and other traumatic events haunt survivors, who experience unwanted flashbacks. They are seared onto the soul. "You see the babies," said Holocaust survivor Sally H. (1979). "You see the screaming mothers. You see hanging people. You sit and you see that face there. It's something you don't forget."

The Modern Unconscious Mind

46-9 How has modern research developed our understanding of the unconscious?

Freud was right about a big idea that underlies today's psychodynamic thinking: We indeed have limited access to all that goes on in our minds (Erdelyi, 1985, 1988, 2006; Norman, 2010). Our two-track mind has a vast out-of-sight realm. Some researchers even argue that "most of a person's everyday life is determined by unconscious thought processes" (Bargh & Chartrand, 1999).

Nevertheless, many research psychologists now think of the unconscious not as seething passions and repressive censoring but as cooler information processing that occurs without our awareness. To these researchers, the unconscious also involves

- the *schemas* that automatically control our perceptions and interpretations.

- the *priming* by stimuli to which we have not consciously attended.

- the right-hemisphere activity that enables the *split-brain* patient's left hand to carry out an instruction the patient cannot verbalize.

- the *implicit memories* that operate without conscious recall, even among those with amnesia.

- the *emotions* that activate instantly, before conscious analysis.

- the *stereotypes* that automatically and unconsciously influence how we process information about others.

More than we realize, we fly on autopilot. Our mind wanders, activating the brain's "default network" (Mason et al., 2007). Unconscious processing occurs constantly. Like an enormous ocean, the unconscious mind is huge. This understanding of unconscious information processing is more like the pre-Freudian view of an underground, unattended stream of thought from which spontaneous behavior and creative ideas surface (Bargh & Morsella, 2008).

There is also research support for two of Freud's defense mechanisms. For example, one study demonstrated *reaction formation* (trading unacceptable impulses for their opposite). Men who reported strong anti-gay attitudes, compared with those who did not report such attitudes, experienced greater physiological arousal when watching videos of homosexual men having sex (as measured with an instrument that measures bloodflow to the penis) even though they said the films did not make them sexually aroused (Adams et al., 1996). Likewise, preliminary evidence suggests that people who unconsciously identify as homosexual—but who consciously identify as straight—report more negative attitudes toward gays and less support for pro-gay policies (Weinstein et al., 2012).

Freud's *projection* (attributing our own threatening impulses to others) has also been confirmed. People do tend to see their traits, attitudes, and goals in others (Baumeister et al., 1998; Maner et al., 2005). Today's researchers call this the *false consensus effect*—the tendency to overestimate the extent to which others share our beliefs and behaviors. People who binge-drink or break speed limits tend to think many others do the same. However, defense mechanisms don't work exactly as Freud supposed. They seem motivated less by the sexual and aggressive undercurrents he imagined than by our need to protect our self-image.

Finally, research has supported Freud's idea that we unconsciously defend ourselves against anxiety. Researchers have proposed that one source of anxiety is "the terror resulting from our awareness of vulnerability and death" (Greenberg et al., 1997). Nearly 300 experiments testing **terror-management theory** show that thinking about one's mortality—for example, by writing a short essay on dying and its associated emotions—provokes various terror-management defenses (Burke et al., 2010). For example, death anxiety increases aggression toward rivals and esteem for oneself (Cohen & Solomon, 2011; Koole et al., 2006).

Faced with a threatening world, people act not only to enhance their self-esteem but also to adhere more strongly to worldviews that answer questions about life's meaning. The prospect of death promotes religious sentiments, and deep religious convictions enable people to be less defensive—less likely to rise in defense of their worldview—when reminded of death (Jonas & Fischer, 2006; Norenzayan & Hansen, 2006). Moreover, when contemplating death, people prioritize their close relationships (Cox

terror-management theory a theory of death-related anxiety; explores people's emotional and behavioral responses to reminders of their impending death.

"It says, 'Someday you will die.'"

"I sought the Lord, and he answered me and delivered me out of all my terror."

Psalm 34:4

& Arndt, 2012; Mikulincer et al., 2003). The actual death of loved ones can provoke protective responses as well. For years, I [ND] have studied the way people respond to thoughts about death (Kashdan et al., 2014). It has been fascinating, but not enough to get me off the couch. The shock of my own mother's unexpected death, however, motivated me to start running again, and to live a healthier lifestyle (Hayasaki, 2014). Facing death can inspire us to affirm life.

RETRIEVAL PRACTICE

- What are three big ideas that have survived from Freud's work in psychoanalytic theory? What are three ways in which Freud's work has been criticized?

ANSWER: Freud first drew attention to (1) the importance of childhood experiences, (2) the existence of the unconscious mind, and (3) our self-protective defense mechanisms. Freud's work has been criticized as (1) not scientifically testable and offering after-the-fact explanations, (2) focusing too much on sexual conflicts in childhood, and (3) based on the idea of repression, which has not been supported by modern research.

- Which elements of traditional psychoanalysis have modern-day *psychodynamic* theorists and therapists retained, and which elements have they mostly left behind?

ANSWER: Today's psychodynamic theorists and therapists still rely on the interviewing techniques that Freud used, and they still tend to focus on childhood experiences and attachments, unresolved conflicts, and unconscious influences. However, they are not likely to dwell on fixation at any psychosexual stage, or the idea that resolution of sexual issues is the basis of our personality.

MODULE 46 REVIEW　Introduction to Personality and Psychodynamic Theories

LEARNING OBJECTIVES

RETRIEVAL PRACTICE Take a moment to answer each of these Learning Objective Questions (repeated here from within this module). Then turn to Appendix C, Complete Module Reviews, to check your answers. Research suggests that trying to answer these questions on your own will improve your long-term retention (McDaniel et al., 2009).

46-1 What historically significant and current theories inform our understanding of personality?

46-2 How did Sigmund Freud's treatment of psychological disorders lead to his view of the unconscious mind?

46-3 What was Freud's view of personality?

46-4 What developmental stages did Freud propose?

46-5 How did Freud think people defended themselves against anxiety?

46-6 Which of Freud's ideas did his followers accept or reject?

46-7 What are projective tests, how are they used, and what are some criticisms of them?

46-8 How do contemporary psychologists view Freud's psychoanalysis?

46-9 How has modern research developed our understanding of the unconscious?

TERMS AND CONCEPTS TO REMEMBER

RETRIEVAL PRACTICE Test yourself on these terms by trying to write down the definition before flipping back to the page number referenced to check your answer.

personality, p. 574

psychodynamic theories, p. 574

psychoanalysis, p. 574

unconscious, p. 575

free association, p. 575

id, p. 575

ego, p. 576

superego, p. 576

psychosexual stages, p. 576

Oedipus [ED-uh-puss] complex, p. 576

identification, p. 577

fixation, p. 577

defense mechanisms, p. 577

repression, p. 577

collective unconscious, p. 579

projective test, p. 580

Thematic Apperception Test (TAT), p. 580

Rorschach inkblot test, p. 580

terror-management theory, p. 583

Use 🔵 LearningCurve to create your personalized study plan, which will direct you to the resources that will help you most in 🔵 LaunchPad.

47 Humanistic Theories and Trait Theories

Humanistic Theories

47-1 How did humanistic psychologists view personality, and what was their goal in studying personality?

BY THE 1960s, SOME PERSONALITY psychologists had become discontented with the sometimes bleak focus on drives and conflicts in *psychodynamic theory* and the mechanistic psychology of B. F. Skinner's *behaviorism*. In contrast to Sigmund Freud's emphasis on disorders born out of dark conflicts, these **humanistic theorists** focused on the ways people strive for self-determination and self-realization. In contrast to behaviorism's scientific objectivity, they studied people through their own self-reported experiences and feelings.

Two pioneering theorists—Abraham Maslow (1908–1970) and Carl Rogers (1902–1987)—offered a *third-force perspective* that emphasized human potential.

Abraham Maslow's Self-Actualizing Person

Maslow proposed that we are motivated by a *hierarchy of needs*. If our physiological needs are met, we become concerned with personal safety; if we achieve a sense of security, we then seek to love, to be loved, and to love ourselves; with our love needs satisfied, we seek self-esteem. Having achieved self-esteem, we ultimately seek **self-actualization** (the process of fulfilling our potential) and *self-transcendence* (meaning, purpose, and communion beyond the self).

Maslow (1970) developed his ideas by studying healthy, creative people rather than troubled clinical cases. He based his description of self-actualization on a study of those, such as Abraham Lincoln, who seemed notable for their rich and productive lives. Maslow reported that such people shared certain characteristics: They were self-aware and self-accepting, open and spontaneous, loving and caring, and not paralyzed by others' opinions. Secure in their sense of who they were, their interests were problem-centered rather than self-centered. They focused their energies on a particular task, one they often regarded as their mission in life. Most enjoyed a few deep relationships rather than many superficial ones. Many had been moved by spiritual or personal *peak experiences* that surpassed ordinary consciousness.

These, said Maslow, are mature adult qualities found in those who have learned enough about life to be compassionate, to have outgrown their mixed feelings toward their parents, to have found their calling, to have "acquired enough courage to be unpopular, to be unashamed about being openly virtuous." Maslow's work with college students led him to speculate that those likely to become self-actualizing adults were likable, caring, "privately affectionate to those of their elders who deserve it," and "secretly uneasy about the cruelty, meanness, and mob spirit so often found in young people."

Carl Rogers' Person-Centered Perspective

Fellow humanistic psychologist Carl Rogers agreed with much of Maslow's thinking. Rogers' *person-centered perspective* held that people are basically good and are endowed with self-actualizing tendencies. Unless thwarted by an environment that inhibits growth, each of us is like an acorn, primed for growth and fulfillment. Rogers (1980) believed that a growth-promoting climate required three conditions.

Abraham Maslow "Any theory of motivation that is worthy of attention must deal with the highest capacities of the healthy and strong person as well as with the defensive maneuvers of crippled spirits" (*Motivation and Personality*, 1970, p. 33).

humanistic theories view personality with a focus on the potential for healthy personal growth.

self-actualization according to Maslow, one of the ultimate psychological needs that arises after basic physical and psychological needs are met and self-esteem is achieved; the motivation to fulfill one's potential.

A father *not* offering unconditional positive regard:

P. BYRNES.

"Just remember, son, it doesn't matter whether you win or lose—unless you want Daddy's love."

The picture of empathy Being open and sharing confidences is easier when the listener shows real understanding. Within such relationships we can relax and fully express our true selves. Consider a conversation when you knew someone was waiting for their turn to speak instead of listening to you. Now consider the last time someone heard you with empathy. How did those two experiences differ?

unconditional positive regard according to Rogers, an attitude of total acceptance toward another person.

self-concept all our thoughts and feelings about ourselves, in answer to the question, "Who am I?"

- *Genuineness:* When people are *genuine*, they are open with their own feelings, drop their facades, and are transparent and self-disclosing.
- *Acceptance:* When people are *accepting*, they offer **unconditional positive regard,** an attitude of grace that values us even knowing our failings. It is a profound relief to drop our pretenses, confess our worst feelings, and discover that we are still accepted. In a good marriage, a close family, or an intimate friendship, we are free to be spontaneous without fearing the loss of others' esteem.
- *Empathy:* When people are *empathic*, they share and mirror other's feelings and reflect their meanings. "Rarely do we listen with real understanding, true empathy," said Rogers. "Yet listening, of this very special kind, is one of the most potent forces for change that I know."

Genuineness, acceptance, and empathy are, Rogers believed, the water, sun, and nutrients that enable people to grow like vigorous oak trees. For "as persons are accepted and prized, they tend to develop a more caring attitude toward themselves" (Rogers, 1980, p. 116). As persons are empathically heard, "it becomes possible for them to listen more accurately to the flow of inner experiencings."

Writer Calvin Trillin (2006) recalled an example of parental genuineness and acceptance at a camp for children with severe disorders, where his wife, Alice, worked. L., a "magical child," had genetic diseases that meant she had to be tube-fed and could walk only with difficulty. Alice recalled,

One day, when we were playing duck-duck-goose, I was sitting behind her and she asked me to hold her mail for her while she took her turn to be chased around the circle. It took her a while to make the circuit, and I had time to see that on top of the pile [of mail] was a note from her mom. Then I did something truly awful. . . . I simply had to know what this child's parents could have done to make her so spectacular, to make her the most optimistic, most enthusiastic, most hopeful human being I had ever encountered. I snuck a quick look at the note, and my eyes fell on this sentence: "If God had given us all of the children in the world to choose from, L., we would only have chosen you." Before L. got back to her place in the circle, I showed the note to Bud, who was sitting next to me. "Quick. Read this," I whispered. "It's the secret of life."

Maslow and Rogers would have smiled knowingly. For them, a central feature of personality is one's **self-concept**—all the thoughts and feelings we have in response to the question, "Who am I?" If our self-concept is positive, we tend to act and perceive the world positively. If it is negative—if in our own eyes we fall far short of our *ideal self*—said Rogers, we feel dissatisfied and unhappy. A worthwhile goal for therapists, parents, teachers, and friends is therefore, he said, to help others know, accept, and be true to themselves.

Assessing the Self

47-2 How did humanistic psychologists assess a person's sense of self?

Humanistic psychologists sometimes assessed personality by asking people to fill out questionnaires that would evaluate their self-concept. One questionnaire, inspired by Carl Rogers, asked people to describe themselves both as they would *ideally* like to be and as they *actually* are. When the ideal and the actual self are nearly alike, said Rogers, the self-concept is positive. Assessing his clients' personal growth during therapy, he looked for successively closer ratings of actual and ideal selves.

Some humanistic psychologists believed that any standardized assessment of personality, even a questionnaire, is depersonalizing. Rather than forcing the person to respond to narrow categories, these humanistic psychologists presumed that interviews and intimate conversation would provide a better understanding of each person's unique experiences.

Evaluating Humanistic Theories

47-3 How have humanistic theories influenced psychology? What criticisms have they faced?

As with Freud's psychoanalytic theory, the impact of humanistic psychology has been pervasive. Maslow's and Rogers' ideas have influenced counseling, education, child raising, and management. And they laid the groundwork for today's scientific *positive psychology.*

They have also influenced—sometimes in unintended ways—much of today's popular psychology. Is a positive self-concept the key to happiness and success? Do acceptance and empathy nurture positive feelings about oneself? Are people basically good and capable of self-improvement? Many people answer *Yes, Yes,* and *Yes.* In 2006, U.S. high school students reported notably higher self-esteem and greater expectations of future career success than did students living in 1975 (Twenge & Campbell, 2008). Given a choice, today's North American collegians mostly say they'd rather get a self-esteem boost, such as a compliment or good grade on a paper, than enjoy a favorite food or sexual activity (Bushman et al., 2011). Humanistic psychology's message has been heard.

The prominence of the humanistic perspective set off a backlash of criticism. First, said the critics, its concepts are vague and *subjective.* Consider Maslow's description of self-actualizing people as open, spontaneous, loving, self-accepting, and productive. Is this a scientific description? Or is it merely a description of the theorist's own values and ideals? Maslow, noted M. Brewster Smith (1978), offered impressions of his own personal heroes. Imagine another theorist who began with a different set of heroes—perhaps Napoleon, John D. Rockefeller, Sr., and Donald Trump. This theorist would likely describe self-actualizing people as "undeterred by others' needs and opinions," "motivated to achieve," and "comfortable with power."

Critics also objected to the idea that, as Rogers put it, "The only question which matters is, 'Am I living in a way which is deeply satisfying to me, and which truly expresses me?'" (quoted by Wallach & Wallach, 1985). This emphasis on *individualism*—trusting and acting on one's feelings, being true to oneself, fulfilling oneself—could lead to self-indulgence, selfishness, and an erosion of moral restraint (Campbell & Specht, 1985; Wallach & Wallach, 1983). Imagine working on a group project with people who refuse to complete any task that is not deeply satisfying or does not truly express their identity.

Humanistic psychologists reply that a secure, nondefensive self-acceptance is actually the first step toward loving others. Indeed, people who feel intrinsically liked and accepted—for who they are, not just for their achievements—exhibit less defensive attitudes (Schimel et al., 2001). Those feeling liked and accepted by a romantic partner report being happier in their relationships and acting more kindly toward their partner (Gordon & Chen, 2010).

A final accusation leveled against humanistic psychology is that it is *naive,* that it fails to appreciate the reality of our human capacity for evil. Faced with climate change, overpopulation, terrorism, and the spread of nuclear weapons, we may become apathetic from either of two rationalizations. One is a starry-eyed optimism that denies the threat ("People are basically good; everything will work out"). The other is a dark despair ("It's hopeless; why try?"). Action requires enough realism to fuel concern and enough optimism to provide hope. Humanistic psychology, say the critics, encourages the needed hope but not the equally necessary realism about evil.

"We do pretty well when you stop to think that people are basically good."

- How did *humanistic psychology* provide a fresh perspective?

ANSWER: This movement sought to turn psychology's attention away from drives and conflicts and toward our growth potential, with a focus on the way healthy people strive for self-determination and self-realization, which was in contrast to Freudian theory and strict behaviorism.

- What does it mean to be *empathic*? How about *self-actualized*? Which humanistic psychologists used these terms?

ANSWERS: To be *empathic* is to share and mirror another person's feelings. Carl Rogers believed that people nurture growth in others by being empathic. Abraham Maslow proposed that *self-actualization* is the motivation to fulfill one's potential, and one of the ultimate psychological needs (the other is self-transcendence).

Trait Theories

47-4 How do psychologists use traits to describe personality?

Rather than focusing on thwarted growth opportunities, unconditional positive regard, and the self-actualizing person, some researchers attempt to define personality in terms of stable and enduring behavior patterns. This perspective can be traced in part to a remarkable meeting in 1919, when Gordon Allport, a curious 22-year-old psychology student, interviewed Sigmund Freud in Vienna. Allport soon discovered just how preoccupied the founder of psychoanalysis was with finding hidden motives, even in Allport's own behavior during the interview. That experience ultimately led Allport to do what Freud did not do—to describe personality in terms of fundamental **traits**—people's characteristic behaviors and conscious motives (such as the curiosity that actually motivated Allport to see Freud). Meeting Freud, said Allport, "taught me that [psychoanalysis], for all its merits, may plunge too deep, and that psychologists would do well to give full recognition to manifest motives before probing the unconscious." Allport came to define personality in terms of identifiable behavior patterns. He was concerned less with *explaining* individual traits than with *describing* them.

Like Allport, Isabel Briggs Myers (1987) and her mother, Katharine Briggs, wanted to describe important personality differences. They attempted to sort people according to Carl Jung's personality types, based on their responses to 126 questions. The *Myers-Briggs Type Indicator (MBTI)*, available in 30 languages, has been taken by more than 2 million people a year, mostly for counseling, leadership training, and work-team development (CPP, 2008). It offers choices, such as "Do you usually value sentiment more than logic, or value logic more than sentiment?" Then it counts the test-taker's preferences, labels them as indicating, say, a "feeling type" or "thinking type," and feeds them back to the person in complimentary terms. Feeling types, for example, are told they are "sympathetic, appreciative, and tactful"; thinking types are told they are "good at analyzing." (Every type has its strengths, so everyone is affirmed.)

Most people agree with their announced type profile, which mirrors their declared preferences. They may also accept their label as a basis for being matched with work partners and tasks that supposedly suit their temperaments. But growing research suggests that people should not blindly accept the validity of their test results. A National Research Council report noted that despite the test's popularity in business and career counseling, its initial use outran research on its value as a predictor of job performance, and "the popularity of this instrument in the absence of proven scientific worth is troublesome" (Druckman & Bjork, 1991, p. 101; see also Pittenger, 1993). Although research on the MBTI has been accumulating since those cautionary words were expressed, the test remains mostly a counseling and coaching tool, not a research instrument.

trait a characteristic pattern of behavior or a disposition to feel and act, as assessed by self-report inventories and peer reports.

Exploring Traits

Classifying people as one or another distinct personality type fails to capture their full individuality. We are each a unique complex of multiple traits. So how else could we describe our personalities? We might describe an apple by placing it along several trait dimensions—relatively large or small, red or green, sweet or sour. By placing people on several trait dimensions simultaneously, psychologists can describe countless individual personality variations, just as researchers can describe thousands of colors in terms of their variations on just three color dimensions—hue, saturation, and brightness.

What trait dimensions describe personality? If you had an upcoming blind date, what personality traits might give you an accurate sense of the person? Allport and his associate H. S. Odbert (1936) counted all the words in an unabridged dictionary with which one could describe people. There were almost 18,000! How, then, could psychologists condense the list to a manageable number of basic traits?

Factor Analysis One technique is *factor analysis*, a statistical procedure that has also been used to identify clusters (factors) of test items that tap basic components of intelligence (such as spatial ability or verbal skill). Imagine that people who describe themselves as outgoing also tend to say that they like excitement and practical jokes and dislike quiet reading. Such a statistically correlated cluster of behaviors reflects a basic factor, or trait—in this case, *extraversion*.

British psychologists Hans Eysenck and Sybil Eysenck [EYE-zink] believed that we can reduce many of our normal individual variations to two or three dimensions, including *extraversion–introversion* and *emotional stability–instability* (**FIGURE 47.1**). People in 35 countries around the world, from China to Uganda to Russia, have taken the *Eysenck Personality Questionnaire*. When their answers were analyzed, the extraversion and emotionality factors inevitably emerged as basic personality dimensions (Eysenck, 1990, 1992). The Eysencks believed, and research confirms, that these factors are genetically influenced.

Biology and Personality Brain-activity scans of extraverts add to the growing list of traits and mental states now being explored with brain-imaging procedures. Such studies indicate that extraverts seek stimulation because their normal *brain arousal* is relatively low. For example, PET scans show that a frontal lobe area involved in behavior inhibition is less active in extraverts than in introverts (Johnson et al., 1999). Dopamine and dopamine-related neural activity tend to be higher in extraverts (Kim et al., 2008; Wacker et al., 2006).

"Russ is the sort of person who never wants to be alone with his thoughts."

▼ FIGURE 47.1
Two personality dimensions
Mapmakers can tell us a lot by using two axes (north–south and east–west). Two primary personality factors (extraversion–introversion and stability–instability) are similarly useful as axes for describing personality variation. Varying combinations define other, more specific traits. (from Eysenck & Eysenck, 1963). Those who are naturally introverted, such as primatologist Jane Goodall, may be particularly gifted in field studies. Successful politicians, including former U.S. President Bill Clinton, are often natural extraverts.

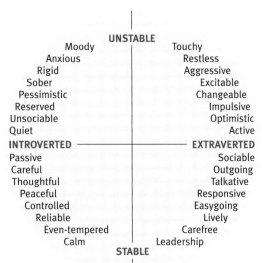

UNSTABLE

Moody	Touchy
Anxious	Restless
Rigid	Aggressive
Sober	Excitable
Pessimistic	Changeable
Reserved	Impulsive
Unsociable	Optimistic
Quiet	Active
INTROVERTED	**EXTRAVERTED**
Passive	Sociable
Careful	Outgoing
Thoughtful	Talkative
Peaceful	Responsive
Controlled	Easygoing
Reliable	Lively
Even-tempered	Carefree
Calm	Leadership

STABLE

Our biology influences our personality in other ways as well. As we know from twin and adoption studies, our genes have much to say about the *temperament* and behavioral style that help define our personality. Jerome Kagan, for example, has attributed differences in children's shyness and inhibition to their autonomic nervous system reactivity (see Thinking Critically About: The Stigma of Introversion). Those with a reactive autonomic nervous system respond to stress with greater anxiety and inhibition. The fearless, curious child may become the rock-climbing or fast-driving adult.

Personality differences among dogs (in energy, affection, reactivity, and curious intelligence) are as evident, and as consistently judged, as personality differences among humans (Gosling et al., 2003; Jones & Gosling, 2005).

Erik Lam /Shutterstock

The Stigma of Introversion

47-5 What are some common misunderstandings about introversion? Does extraversion lead to greater success than introversion?

Psychologists describe personality, but they don't advise which traits people should have. Society does this. Western cultures, for example, prize extraversion. Being introverted may imply that you don't have the "right stuff" (Cain, 2012).

Just look at our superheroes. Extraverted Superman is bold and energetic. His introverted alter ego, Clark Kent, is mild-mannered and bumbling. The message is clear: If you're a superhero, you're an extravert.

TV shows also portray heartthrobs and examples of success as extraverts. Don Draper, the highly successful, attractive advertising executive in the show *Mad Men* is a classic extravert. He is dominant and charismatic. Women clamor for his attention. Again, the point is plain: Extraversion equals success.

Why do we so often celebrate extraversion and belittle introversion? Many people may not understand what introversion really is. People tend to equate introversion with shyness, but the two concepts differ. Introverted people seek low levels of stimulation from their environment because they're sensitive. One classic study suggested that introverted people even have greater taste sensitivity. When given lemon juice, introverted people salivated more than extraverted people (Corcoran, 1964). Shy people, in contrast, remain quiet because they fear others will evaluate them negatively.

People may also believe that introversion acts as a barrier to success. On the contrary, introversion has its benefits; as supervisors, introverts show greater receptiveness when their employees voice their ideas, challenge existing norms, and take charge.

AMC/The Kobal Collection/Art Resource

Under these circumstances, introverted leaders outperform extraverted ones (Grant et al., 2011). In fact, one striking analysis of 35 studies showed no correlation between extraversion and sales performance (Barrick et al., 2001). Perhaps the best example of the misperception that introversion hinders career success lies in the American presidency: The American president who is most consistently ranked number one of all time was introverted. His name was Abraham Lincoln.

So, introversion should not be a sign of weakness. Those who need a quiet break from a loud party are not social rejects or incapable of great things. They simply know how to pick an environment where they can thrive. It's important for extraverts to understand that not everyone needs high levels of stimulation. It's not a crime to unwind.

John Parrot/Stocktrek Images/Getty Images

Monkeys, chimpanzees, orangutans, and even birds also have stable personalities (Weiss et al., 2006). Among the Great Tit (a European relative of the American chickadee), bold birds more quickly inspect new objects and explore trees (Groothuis & Carere, 2005; Verbeek et al., 1994). By selective breeding, researchers can produce bold or shy birds. Both have their place in natural history: In lean years, bold birds are more likely to find food; in abundant years, shy birds feed with less risk.

RETRIEVAL PRACTICE

- Which two primary dimensions did Hans Eysenck and Sybil Eysenck propose for describing personality variation?

ANSWER: introversion–extraversion and emotional stability–instability

Assessing Traits

47-6 What are personality inventories, and what are their strengths and weaknesses as trait-assessment tools?

If stable and enduring traits guide our actions, can we devise valid and reliable tests of them? Several trait assessment techniques exist—some more valid than others. Some provide quick assessments of a single trait, such as extraversion, anxiety, or self-esteem. **Personality inventories**—longer questionnaires covering a wide range of feelings and behaviors—assess several traits at once.

The classic personality inventory is the **Minnesota Multiphasic Personality Inventory (MMPI)**. Although the MMPI was originally developed to identify emotional disorders, it also assesses people's personality traits. One of its creators, Starke Hathaway (1960), compared his effort to that of Alfred Binet. Binet, the founder of modern intelligence testing, developed the first intelligence test by selecting items that identified children who would probably have trouble progressing normally in French schools. Like Binet's items, the MMPI items were **empirically derived.** From a large pool of items, Hathaway and his colleagues selected those on which particular diagnostic groups differed. They then grouped the questions into 10 clinical scales, including scales that assess depressive tendencies, masculinity–femininity, and introversion–extraversion.

Hathaway and others initially gave hundreds of true-false statements ("No one seems to understand me"; "I get all the sympathy I should"; "I like poetry") to groups of psychologically disordered patients and to "normal" people. They retained any statement—no matter how silly it sounded—on which the patient group's answer differed from that of the normal group. "Nothing in the newspaper interests me except the comics" may seem senseless, but it just so happened that depressed people were more likely to answer *True*. Today's MMPI-2 also has scales assessing, for instance, work attitudes, family problems, and anger.

In contrast to the subjectivity of most *projective tests*, personality inventories are scored objectively. (Software can administer and score these tests, and can also provide descriptions of people who previously responded similarly.) Objectivity does not, however, guarantee validity. For example, individuals taking the MMPI for employment purposes can give socially desirable answers to create a good impression. But in so doing they may also score high on a *lie scale* that assesses faking (as when people respond *False* to a universally true statement such as "I get angry sometimes"). The objectivity of the MMPI has contributed to its popularity and to its translation into more than 100 languages.

personality inventory a questionnaire (often with *true-false* or *agree-disagree* items) on which people respond to items designed to gauge a wide range of feelings and behaviors; used to assess selected personality traits.

Minnesota Multiphasic Personality Inventory (MMPI) the most widely researched and clinically used of all personality tests. Originally developed to identify emotional disorders (still considered its most appropriate use), this test is now used for many other screening purposes.

empirically derived test a test (such as the MMPI) developed by testing a pool of items and then selecting those that discriminate between groups.

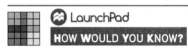
LaunchPad

HOW WOULD YOU KNOW?

Might astrology hold the secret to our personality traits? To consider this question, visit LaunchPad's *How Would You Know If Astrologers Can Describe People's Personality?*

People have had fun spoofing the MMPI with their own mock items: "Weeping brings tears to my eyes," "Frantic screams make me nervous," and "I stay in the bathtub until I look like a raisin" (Frankel et al., 1983).

The Big Five Factors

47-7 Which traits seem to provide the most useful information about personality variation?

Today's trait researchers believe that simple trait factors, such as the Eysencks' introversion-extraversion and stability–instability dimensions, are important, but they do not tell the whole story. A slightly expanded set of factors—dubbed the *Big Five*—does a better job (Costa & McCrae, 2011). If a test specifies where you are on the five dimensions (conscientiousness, agreeableness, neuroticism, openness, and extraversion; see **TABLE** 47.1), it has said much of what there is to say about your personality. Around the world—across 56 nations and 29 languages in one study (Schmitt et al., 2007)—people describe others in terms roughly consistent with this list. The Big Five may not be the last word. Some researchers report it takes only one or two or three factors—such as conscientiousness, agreeableness, and extraversion—to describe the basic personality dimensions (Block, 2010; De Raad et al., 2010; Rushton & Irwing, 2011). But for now, at least, five is the winning number in the personality lottery (Heine & Buchtel, 2009; McCrae, 2009). The Big Five—today's "common currency for personality psychology" (Funder, 2001)—has been the most active personality research topic since the early 1990s and is currently our best approximation of the basic trait dimensions.

Big Five research has explored various questions:

- *How stable are these traits?* One research team analyzed 1.25 million participants ages 10 to 65. They learned that personality continues to develop and change through late childhood and adolescence. By adulthood, our traits have become fairly stable, though conscientiousness, agreeableness, openness, and extraversion continue to increase into middle age, and neuroticism (emotional instability) decreases (Soto et al., 2011).

- *How heritable are they?* Heritability (the extent to which individual differences are attributable to genes) varies with the diversity of people studied, but it generally runs 50 percent or a tad more for each dimension, and genetic influences are similar in different nations (Loehlin et al., 1998; Yamagata et al., 2006). Many genes, each having small effects, combine to influence our traits (McCrae et al., 2010).

Hemera Technologies/ Getty Images

▼ TABLE 47.1
The "Big Five" Personality Factors

Researchers use self-report inventories and peer reports to assess and score the Big Five personality factors.

(Memory tip: Picturing a CANOE will help you recall these.)

Disorganized, careless, impulsive	**C**onscientiousness	Organized, careful, disciplined
Ruthless, suspicious, uncooperative	**A**greeableness	Soft-hearted, trusting, helpful
Calm, secure, self-satisfied	**N**euroticism (emotional stability vs. instability)	Anxious, insecure, self-pitying
Practical, prefers routine, conforming	**O**penness	Imaginative, prefers variety, independent
Retiring, sober, reserved	**E**xtraversion	Sociable, fun-loving, affectionate

Source: Adapted from McCrae & Costa (1986, 2008).

Steve Wisbauer/Getty Images

- *Do these traits reflect differing brain structure?* The size of different brain regions correlates with several Big Five traits (DeYoung et al., 2010). For example, those who score high on conscientiousness tend to have a larger frontal lobe area that aids in planning and controlling behavior. Brain connections also influence the Big Five traits (Adelstein et al., 2011). People high in openness have brains that are wired to experience intense imagination, curiosity, and fantasy.

- *Have these traits changed over time?* Cultures change over time, which can influence shifts in personality. Within the United States and the Netherlands, extraversion and conscientiousness have increased (Mroczek & Spiro, 2003; Smits et al., 2011; Twenge, 2001).

- *How well do these traits apply to various cultures?* The Big Five dimensions describe personality in various cultures reasonably well (Schmitt et al., 2007; Yamagata et al., 2006). "Features of personality traits are common to all human groups," concluded Robert McCrae and 79 co-researchers (2005) from their 50-culture study.

- *Do the Big Five traits predict our actual behaviors?* Yes. If people report being outgoing, conscientious, and agreeable, "they probably are telling the truth," reports Big Five researcher Robert McCrae (2011). For example, introverts more than extraverts prefer communicating by e-mail rather than face-to-face (Hertel et al., 2008). Our traits also appear in our language patterns. In text messaging, extraversion predicts use of personal pronouns. Agreeableness predicts positive-emotion words. Neuroticism (emotional instability) predicts negative-emotion words (Holtgraves, 2011).

By exploring such questions, Big Five research has sustained trait psychology and renewed appreciation for the importance of personality. Traits matter.

🎬 **LaunchPad** For an 8-minute demonstration of trait research, visit LaunchPad's *Video: Trait Theories of Personality.*

RETRIEVAL PRACTICE

- What are the *Big Five* personality factors, and why are they scientifically useful?

ANSWER: The Big Five personality factors are conscientiousness, agreeableness, neuroticism (emotional stability vs. instability), openness, and extraversion (CANOE). These factors may be objectively measured, and research suggests that these factors are relatively stable over the life span and apply to all cultures in which they have been studied.

Evaluating Trait Theories

47-8 Does research support the consistency of personality traits over time and across situations?

Are our personality traits stable and enduring? Or does our behavior depend on where and with whom we find ourselves? In some ways, our personality seems stable. Cheerful, friendly children tend to become cheerful, friendly adults. At a recent college reunion, I [DM] was amazed to find that my jovial former classmates were still jovial, the shy ones still shy, the happy-seeming people still smiling and laughing—50 years later. But it's also true that a fun-loving jokester can suddenly turn serious and respectful at a job interview. The personality traits we express can change from one situation to another.

The Person-Situation Controversy Our behavior is influenced by the interaction of our inner disposition with our environment. Still, the question lingers: Which is more important? When we explore this *person-situation controversy,* we look for genuine personality traits that persist over time *and* across situations. Are some people

"There is as much difference between us and ourselves, as between us and others."

Michel de Montaigne, *Essays,* 1588

Roughly speaking, the temporary, external influences on behavior are the focus of social psychology, and the enduring, inner influences are the focus of personality psychology. In actuality, behavior always depends on the interaction of persons with situations.

Change and consistency can co-exist. If all people were to become somewhat less shy with age, there would be personality change, but also relative stability and predictability.

Trait score correlations over seven years

0.8
0.7
0.6
0.5
0.4
0.3
0.2
0.1
0

Children   Collegians   30-year-olds   50- to 70-year-olds

▼ **FIGURE 47.2**
Personality stability With age, personality traits become more stable, as reflected in the stronger correlation of trait scores with follow-up scores seven years later. (Data from Roberts & DelVecchio, 2000.)

It's not just personality that stablizes with age.

my hair over time

childhood

teens and twenties - experimentation

thirties and up

dependably conscientious and others unreliable, some cheerful and others dour, some friendly and outgoing and others shy? If we are to consider friendliness a trait, friendly people must act friendly at different times and places. Do they?

In considering research that has followed lives through time (in longitudinal studies), some scholars (especially those who study infants) are impressed with personality change; others are struck by personality stability during adulthood. As **FIGURE 47.2** illustrates, data from 152 long-term studies reveal that personality trait scores are positively correlated with scores obtained seven years later, and that as people grow older their personality stabilizes. Interests may change—the avid tropical-fish collector may become an avid gardener. Careers may change—the determined salesperson may become a determined social worker. Relationships may change—the hostile spouse may start over with a new partner. But most people recognize their traits as their own, as Robert McCrae and Paul Costa noted (1994), "and it is well that they do. A person's recognition of the inevitability of his or her one and only personality is . . . the culminating wisdom of a lifetime."

So most people—including most psychologists—would probably presume the stability of personality traits. Moreover, our traits are socially significant. They influence our health, our thinking, and our job choices and performance (Deary & Matthews, 1993; Hogan, 1998; Jackson et al., 2012; Sutin et al., 2011). Studies that follow lives through time show that personality traits rival socioeconomic status and cognitive ability as predictors of mortality, divorce, and occupational attainment (Roberts et al., 2007).

Any of these tendencies, taken to either extreme, become maladaptive. Agreeableness ranges from cynical combativeness at its low extreme to gullible subservience at its high extreme. Conscientiousness ranges from irresponsible negligence to workaholic perfectionism (Widiger & Costa, 2012).

Although our personality *traits* may be both stable and potent, the consistency of our specific *behaviors* from one situation to the next is another matter. As Walter Mischel (1968, 2009) has pointed out, people do not act with predictable consistency. Mischel's studies of college students' conscientiousness revealed but a modest relationship between a student's being conscientious on one occasion (say, showing up for class on time) and being similarly conscientious on another occasion (say, turning in assignments on time). If you've noticed how outgoing you are in some situations and how reserved you are in others, perhaps you're not surprised (though for certain traits, Mischel reports, you may accurately assess yourself as more consistent).

This inconsistency in behaviors also makes personality test scores weak predictors of behaviors. People's scores on an extraversion test, for example, do not neatly predict how sociable they actually will be on any given occasion. If we remember this, says Mischel, we will be more cautious about labeling and pigeonholing individuals. Years in advance, science can tell us the phase of the Moon for any given date. A day in advance, meteorologists can often predict the weather. But we are much further from being able to predict how *you* will feel and act tomorrow.

However, people's *average* outgoingness, happiness, or carelessness over many situations is predictable (Epstein, 1983a,b). People who know someone well, therefore, generally agree when rating that person's shyness or agreeableness (Kenrick & Funder, 1988). By collecting snippets of people's daily experience via body-worn recording devices, Matthias Mehl and his colleagues (2006) confirmed that extraverts really do talk more. A similar extraversion-talkativeness relationship was also found among Bolivian hunter-gathers

(Gurven et al., 2013). (I [DM] have repeatedly vowed to cut back on my jabbering and joking during my noontime pickup basketball games with friends. Alas, moments later, the irrepressible chatterbox inevitably reoccupies my body. And I [ND] have a similar experience each time I try to stay quiet in taxis. Somehow, I always end up chatting with the driver!) As our best friends can verify, we do have genetically influenced personality traits. And those traits even lurk, report Samuel Gosling and his colleagues in a series of studies, in our

- *music preferences.* Your playlist says a lot about your personality. Classical, jazz, blues, and folk music lovers tend to be open to experience and verbally intelligent. Extraverts tend to prefer upbeat and energetic music. Country, pop, and religious music lovers tend to be cheerful, outgoing, and conscientious (Langmeyer et al., 2012; Rentfrow & Gosling, 2003, 2006).

- *bedrooms and offices.* Our personal spaces display our identity and leave a behavioral residue (in our scattered laundry or neat desktop). After just a few minutes' inspection of our living and working spaces, a visitor could give a fairly accurate summary of our conscientiousness, our openness to new experiences, and even our emotional stability (Gosling et al., 2002, 2008).

- *online spaces.* Is a personal website, social media profile, or instant messaging account also a canvas for self-expression? Or is it an opportunity for people to present themselves in false or misleading ways? It's more the former (Back et al., 2010; Gosling et al., 2007; Marcus et al., 2006). Viewers quickly gain important clues to the creator's extraversion, conscientiousness, and openness to experience. Even mere pictures of people, and their associated clothes, expressions, and postures, can give clues to personality (Naumann et al., 2009).

- *written communications.* If you have ever felt you could detect someone's personality from their writing voice, you are right!! (What a cool, exciting finding!!! . . . if you catch our drift.) People's ratings of others' personalities based solely on what they've written correlate with actual personality scores on measures such as extraversion and neuroticism (Gill et al., 2006; Oberlander & Gill, 2006; Pennebaker, 2011; Yarkoni, 2010). Extraverts, for example, use more adjectives.

In unfamiliar, formal situations—perhaps as a guest in the home of a person from another culture—our traits remain hidden as we carefully attend to social cues. In familiar, informal situations—just hanging out with friends—we feel less constrained, allowing our traits to emerge (Buss, 1989). In these informal situations, our expressive styles—our animation, manner of speaking, and gestures—are impressively consistent. Viewing "thin slices" of someone's behavior—such as seeing a photo for a mere fraction of a second or seeing three 2-second video clips of a teacher in action—can tell us a lot about the person's basic personality traits (Ambady, 2010; Rule et al., 2009).

Some people are naturally expressive (and therefore talented at pantomime and charades); others are less expressive (and therefore better poker players). To evaluate people's voluntary control over their expressiveness, Bella DePaulo and her colleagues (1992) asked people to *act* as expressive or inhibited as possible while stating opinions. Their remarkable findings: Inexpressive people, even when feigning expressiveness, were less expressive than expressive people acting naturally. Similarly, expressive people, even when trying to seem inhibited, were less inhibited than inexpressive people acting naturally. It's hard to be someone you're not, or not to be who you are.

To sum up, we can say that at any moment the immediate situation powerfully influences a person's behavior. Social psychologists have learned that this is especially so when a "strong situation" makes clear demands (Cooper & Withey, 2009). We can better predict drivers' behavior at traffic lights from knowing the color of the lights than from knowing the drivers' personalities. Thus, professors may perceive certain

"I'm going to France—I'm a different person in France."

Room with a cue Even at "zero acquaintance," people can catch a glimpse of others' personality from looking at their website, bedroom, or office. So, what's your read on this person's office?

students as subdued (based on their classroom behavior), but friends may perceive them as pretty wild (based on their party behavior). Averaging our behavior across many occasions does, however, reveal distinct personality traits. Traits exist. We differ. And our differences matter.

RETRIEVAL PRACTICE

• How well do personality test scores predict our behavior? Explain.

ANSWER: Our scores on personality tests predict our *average* behavior across many situations much better than they predict our specific behavior in any given situation.

MODULE 47 REVIEW Humanistic Theories and Trait Theories

LEARNING OBJECTIVES

RETRIEVAL PRACTICE Take a moment to answer each of these Learning Objective Questions (repeated here from within this module). Then turn to Appendix C, Complete Module Reviews, to check your answers. Research suggests that trying to answer these questions on your own will improve your long-term retention (McDaniel et al., 2009).

47-1 How did humanistic psychologists view personality, and what was their goal in studying personality?

47-2 How did humanistic psychologists assess a person's sense of self?

47-3 How have humanistic theories influenced psychology? What criticisms have they faced?

47-4 How do psychologists use traits to describe personality?

47-5 What are some common misunderstandings about introversion? Does extraversion lead to greater success than introversion?

47-6 What are personality inventories, and what are their strengths and weaknesses as trait-assessment tools?

47-7 Which traits seem to provide the most useful information about personality variation?

47-8 Does research support the consistency of personality traits over time and across situations?

TERMS AND CONCEPTS TO REMEMBER

RETRIEVAL PRACTICE Test yourself on these terms by trying to write down the definition before flipping back to the page number referenced to check your answer.

humanistic theories, p. 585

self-actualization, p. 585

unconditional positive regard, p. 586

self-concept, p. 586

trait, p. 588

personality inventory, p. 591

Minnesota Multiphasic Personality Inventory (MMPI), p. 591

empirically derived test, p. 591

Use 🐢 LearningCurve to create your personalized study plan, which will direct you to the resources that will help you most in 🐢 LaunchPad.

MODULE 48 Social-Cognitive Theories and the Self

Social-Cognitive Theories

48-1 How do social-cognitive theorists view personality development, and how do they explore behavior?

Today's psychological science views individuals as biopsychosocial organisms. The **social-cognitive perspective** on personality proposed by Albert Bandura (1986, 2006, 2008) emphasizes the interaction of our traits with our situations. Much as nature and nurture always work together, so do individuals and their situations.

> social-cognitive perspective views behavior as influenced by the interaction between people's traits (including their thinking) and their social context.

Social-cognitive theorists believe we learn many of our behaviors either through conditioning or by observing and imitating others. (That's the "social" part.) They also emphasize the importance of mental processes: What we *think* about a situation affects our resulting behavior. (That's the "cognitive" part.) Instead of focusing solely on how our environment *controls* us (behaviorism), social-cognitive theorists focus on how we and our environment *interact:* How do we interpret and respond to external events? How do our schemas, our memories, and our expectations influence our behavior patterns?

> **reciprocal determinism** the interacting influences of behavior, internal cognition, and environment.

Reciprocal Influences

Bandura (1986, 2006) views the person-environment interaction as **reciprocal determinism.** "Behavior, internal personal factors, and environmental influences," he said, "all operate as interlocking determinants of each other" (**FIGURE** 48.1). We can see this interaction in the habits people develop in relationships. For example, Romena's history of romantic relationships (past behavior) influences her attitudes toward relationships in general (internal factor), which changes how she now responds to Ryan (environmental factor).

Consider three specific ways in which individuals and environments interact:

1. *Different people choose different environments.* The schools we attend, the reading we do, the movies we watch, the music we listen to, the friends we associate with—all are part of an environment we have chosen, based partly on our disposition (Funder, 2009; Ickes et al., 1997). We choose our environment and it then shapes us.

2. *Our personalities shape how we interpret and react to events.* Anxious people tend to attend and react strongly to relationship threats (Campbell & Marshall, 2011). If we perceive the world as threatening, we will watch for threats and be prepared to defend ourselves.

3. *Our personalities help create situations to which we react.* How we view and treat people influences how they then treat us. If we expect that others will not like us, our desperate attempts to seek their approval might cause them to reject us. Depressed people often engage in this excessive reassurance seeking, which confirms their negative self-views (Coyne, 1976a,b).

In addition to the interaction of internal personal factors, the environment, and our behaviors, we also experience *gene-environment interaction.* Our genetically influenced traits evoke certain responses from others, which may nudge us in one direction or another. In one classic study, those with the interacting factors of (1) having a specific gene associated with aggression and (2) being raised in a difficult environment were most likely to demonstrate adult antisocial behavior (Caspi et al., 2002).

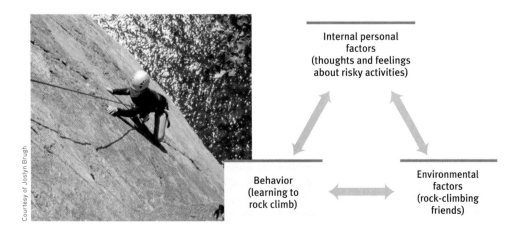

Internal personal factors (thoughts and feelings about risky activities)

Behavior (learning to rock climb)

Environmental factors (rock-climbing friends)

▼ FIGURE 48.1
Reciprocal determinism

Courtesy of Joslyn Brugh

Biological influences:
• genetically determined temperament
• autonomic nervous system reactivity
• brain activity

Psychological influences:
• learned responses
• unconscious thought processes
• expectations and interpretations

Personality

▼ FIGURE 48.2
The biopsychosocial approach to the study of personality
As with other psychological phenomena, personality is fruitfully studied at multiple levels.

Social-cultural influences:
• childhood experiences
• influence of the situation
• cultural expectations
• social support

In such ways, we are both the products and the architects of our environments: *Behavior emerges from the interplay of external and internal influences.* Boiling water turns an egg hard and a potato soft. A threatening environment turns one person into a hero, another into a scoundrel. Extraverts enjoy greater well-being in an extraverted culture than in an introverted one (Fulmer et al., 2010). *At every moment,* our behavior is influenced by our biology, our social and cultural experiences, and our cognition and dispositions (**FIGURE 48.2**).

──────────────── **RETRIEVAL PRACTICE** ────────────────

• Albert Bandura proposed the _____ - _____ perspective on personality, which emphasizes the interaction of people with their environment. To describe the interacting influences of behavior, thoughts, and environment, he used the term _____ _____ .

ANSWERS: social-cognitive; reciprocal determinism

Assessing Behavior in Situations

To predict behavior, social-cognitive psychologists often observe behavior in realistic situations. One ambitious example was the U.S. Army's World War II strategy for assessing candidates for spy missions. Rather than using paper-and-pencil tests, Army psychologists subjected the candidates to simulated undercover conditions. They tested their ability to handle stress, solve problems, maintain leadership, and withstand intense interrogation without blowing their cover. Although time-consuming and expensive, this assessment of behavior in a realistic situation helped predict later success on actual spy missions (OSS Assessment Staff, 1948). Modern studies indicate that assessment center exercises are more revealing of visible dimensions, such as communication ability, than others, such as inner achievement drive (Bowler & Woehr, 2006).

Assessing behavior in situations Reality TV shows, such as Donald Trump's *The Apprentice,* may take "show me" job interviews to the extreme, but they do illustrate a valid point. Seeing how a potential employee behaves in a job-relevant situation helps predict job performance.

Jennifer Szymaszek/AP Photo

Military and educational organizations and many Fortune 500 companies have adopted assessment center strategies (Bray et al., 1991, 1997; Eurich et al., 2009). AT&T has observed prospective managers doing simulated managerial work. Many colleges assess students' potential via internships and student teaching, and assess potential faculty members' teaching abilities by observing them teach. Most American cities with populations of 50,000 or more have used assessment centers in evaluating police officers and firefighters (Lowry, 1997).

These procedures exploit the principle that the best means of predicting future behavior is neither a personality test nor an interviewer's intuition. Rather, it is *the person's past behavior patterns in similar situations* (Lyons et al., 2011; Mischel, 1981; Schmidt & Hunter, 1998). As long as the situation and the person remain much the same, the best predictor of future job performance is past job performance; the best predictor of future grades is past grades; the best predictor of future aggressiveness is past aggressiveness. If you can't check the person's past behavior, the next best thing is to create an assessment situation that simulates the task so you can see how the person handles it (Lievens et al., 2009; Meriac et al., 2008).

"What's past is prologue."

William Shakespeare, *The Tempest*, 1611

Evaluating Social-Cognitive Theories

48-2 What criticisms have social-cognitive theorists faced?

Social-cognitive theories of personality sensitize researchers to how situations affect, and are affected by, individuals. More than other personality theories (see **TABLE 48.1**), they build from psychological research on learning and cognition.

▼ TABLE 48.1
Comparing the Major Personality Theories

Personality Theory	Key Proponents	Assumptions	View of Personality	Personality Assessment Methods
Psychoanalytic	Freud	Emotional disorders spring from unconscious dynamics, such as unresolved sexual and other childhood conflicts, and fixation at various developmental stages. Defense mechanisms fend off anxiety.	Personality consists of pleasure-seeking impulses (the id), a reality-oriented executive (the ego), and an internalized set of ideals (the super-ego).	Free association, projective tests, dream analysis
Psychodynamic	Adler, Horney, Jung	The unconscious and conscious minds interact. Childhood experiences and defense mechanisms are important.	The dynamic interplay of conscious and unconscious motives and conflicts shape our personality.	Projective tests, therapy sessions
Humanistic	Rogers, Maslow	Rather than examining the struggles of sick people, it's better to focus on the ways healthy people strive for self-realization.	If our basic human needs are met, people will strive toward self-actualization. In a climate of unconditional positive regard, we can develop self-awareness and a more realistic and positive self-concept.	Questionnaires, therapy sessions
Trait	Allport, Eysenck, McCrae, Costa	We have certain stable and enduring characteristics, influenced by genetic predispositions.	Scientific study of traits has isolated important dimensions of personality, such as the Big Five traits (conscientiousness, agreeableness, neuroticism, openness, and extraversion).	Personality inventories
Social-Cognitive	Bandura	Our traits and the social context interact to produce our behaviors.	Conditioning and observational learning interact with cognition to create behavior patterns.	Our behavior in one situation is best predicted by considering our past behavior in similar situations.

self in contemporary psychology, assumed to be the center of personality, the organizer of our thoughts, feelings, and actions.

spotlight effect overestimating others' noticing and evaluating our appearance, performance, and blunders (as if we presume a spotlight shines on us).

Critics charge that social-cognitive theories focus so much on the situation that they fail to appreciate the person's inner traits. Where is the person in this view of personality, ask the dissenters, and where are human emotions? True, the situation does guide our behavior. But, say the critics, in many instances our unconscious motives, our emotions, and our pervasive traits shine through. Personality traits have been shown to predict behavior at work, love, and play. Our biologically influenced traits really do matter. Consider Percy Ray Pridgen and Charles Gill. Each faced the same situation: They had jointly won a $90 million lottery jackpot (Harriston, 1993). When Pridgen learned of the winning numbers, he began trembling uncontrollably, huddled with a friend behind a bathroom door while confirming the win, then sobbed. When Gill heard the news, he told his wife and then went to sleep.

RETRIEVAL PRACTICE

- What is the best way to predict a person's future behavior?

ANSWER: Examine the person's past behavior patterns in similar situations.

Exploring the Self

48-3 Why has psychology generated so much research on the self? How important is self-esteem to psychology and to human well-being?

Psychology's concern with people's sense of self dates back at least to William James, who devoted more than 100 pages of his 1890 *Principles of Psychology* to the topic. By 1943, Gordon Allport lamented that the self had become "lost to view." Although humanistic psychology's later emphasis on the self did not instigate much scientific research, it did help renew the concept of self and keep it alive. Now, more than a century after James, the self is one of Western psychology's most vigorously researched topics. Every year, new studies galore appear on self-esteem, self-disclosure, self-awareness, self-schemas, self-monitoring, and so forth. Even neuroscientists have searched for the self, by identifying a central frontal lobe region that activates when people respond to self-reflective questions about their traits and dispositions (Damasio, 2010; Mitchell, 2009; Pauly et al., 2013). Underlying this research is an assumption that the **self,** as organizer of our thoughts, feelings, and actions, is the center of personality.

One example of thinking about self is the concept of *possible selves* put forth by Hazel Markus and her colleagues (Cross & Markus, 1991; Markus & Nurius, 1986). Your possible selves include your visions of the self you dream of becoming—the rich self, the successful self, the loved and admired self. Your possible selves also include the self you fear becoming—the unemployed self, the academically failed self, the lonely and unpopular self. Possible selves motivate us to lay out specific goals that direct our energy effectively and efficiently (Landau et al., 2014). High school students enrolled in a gifted program for math and science were more likely to become scientists if they had a clear vision of themselves as successful scientists (Buday et al., 2012). Dreams do often give birth to achievements.

"The first step to better times is to imagine them."

Chinese fortune cookie

Timothy Large/Shutterstock and © Trinity Mirror/Mirrorpix/Alamy

Our self-focused perspective may motivate us, but it can also lead us to presume too readily that others are noticing and evaluating us. Thomas Gilovich (1996) demonstrated this **spotlight effect** by having individual Cornell University students don Barry Manilow T-shirts before entering a room with other students. Feeling self-conscious, the T-shirt wearers guessed that nearly half their peers would take note of the shirt as they walked in. In reality, only 23 percent did. This absence of attention applies not only to our dorky clothes and bad hair but also to our nervousness, irritation, or attraction: Fewer people notice than we presume (Gilovich & Savitsky, 1999). Others are also less aware than we suppose of the variability—the ups and downs—of our appearance and performance (Gilovich et al., 2002). Even after a blunder (setting off a library alarm, showing up in the wrong clothes), we stick out like a sore thumb less than we imagine (Savitsky et al., 2001). To turn down the brightness of the spotlight, we can use two strategies. The first is simply knowing about the spotlight effect. Public speakers who understand that their natural nervousness is not obvious perform better (Savitsky & Gilovich, 2003). The second is to take the audience's perspective. When we imagine audience members empathizing with our situation, we tend to expect we will not be judged as harshly (Epley et al., 2002).

The Benefits of Self-Esteem

How we feel about ourselves is also important. High **self-esteem**—our feelings of self-worth—pays dividends. So also does **self-efficacy,** our sense of competence on a task. People who feel good about themselves (who strongly agree with self-affirming questionnaire statements such as, "I am fun to be with") have fewer sleepless nights. They succumb less easily to pressures to conform. They make more positive Facebook posts, causing others to like them more (Forest & Wood, 2012). They are more persistent at difficult tasks; they are less shy, anxious, and lonely. And they are just plain happier (Greenberg, 2008; Orth et al., 2008, 2009). If feeling bad, they think they deserve better and thus make more effort to repair their mood (Wood et al., 2009).

But is high self-esteem the horse or the cart? Is it really "the armor that protects kids" from life's problems (McKay, 2000)? Some psychologists have their doubts (Baumeister, 2006; Dawes, 1994; Leary, 1999; Seligman, 1994, 2002). Children's academic self-efficacy—their confidence that they can do well in a subject—predicts school achievement. But general self-image does not (Marsh & Craven, 2006; Swann et al., 2007; Trautwein et al., 2006). Maybe self-esteem simply reflects reality. Maybe it's a side effect of meeting challenges and surmounting difficulties. Maybe self-esteem is a gauge that reads out the state of our relationships with others. If so, isn't pushing the gauge artificially higher with empty compliments much like forcing a car's low fuel gauge to display "full"?

If feeling good *follows* doing well, then giving praise in the absence of good performance may actually harm people. After receiving weekly self-esteem-boosting messages, struggling students earned *lower*-than-expected grades (Forsyth et al., 2007). Other research showed that giving people random rewards hurt their productivity. Martin Seligman reported that "when good things occurred that weren't earned, like nickels coming out of slot machines, it did not increase people's well-being. It produced helplessness. People gave up and became passive."

Experiments do reveal an *effect* of low self-esteem. Temporarily deflate people's self-image (say, by telling them they did poorly on an aptitude test or by disparaging their personality) and they will be more likely to disparage others or to express heightened racial prejudice (vanDellen et al., 2011; Van Dijk et al., 2011; Ybarra, 1999). Self-image threat even increases unconscious racial bias (Allen & Sherman, 2011). Those who are negative about themselves have also tended to be oversensitive and judgmental (Baumgardner et al., 1989; Pelham, 1993). In experiments, people made to feel insecure have often become excessively critical, as if to impress others with their own brilliance (Amabile, 1983). Self-esteem threats also lead people to gravitate toward their online profiles—safe havens in which to rebuild their self-worth (Toma & Hancock, 2013). Such findings are consistent with humanistic psychology's presumption that a healthy self-image is essential. Accept yourself and you'll find it easier to accept others.

self-esteem one's feelings of high or low self-worth.

self-efficacy one's sense of competence and effectiveness.

"When kids increase in self-control, their grades go up later. But when kids increase their self-esteem, there is no effect on their grades."

Angela Duckworth,
In Character interview, 2009

LOW SELF-ESTEEM

Disparage yourself and you will be prone to the floccinaucinihilipilification[1] of others. Said more simply, some "love their neighbors as themselves"; others loathe their neighbors as themselves. People who are down on themselves tend to be down on others.

Costs of Self-Esteem

48-4 How do excessive optimism, blindness to one's own incompetence, and self-serving bias reveal the costs of self-esteem, and how do defensive and secure self-esteem differ?

Excessive Optimism   Positive thinking in the face of adversity can pay dividends, but so, too, can a dash of realism (Schneider, 2001). Realistic anxiety over possible future failures can fuel energetic efforts to avoid the dreaded fate (Goodhart, 1986; Norem, 2001; Showers, 1992). Concerned about failing an upcoming exam, students may study thoroughly and outperform their equally able but more confident peers. Asian-American students have expressed somewhat greater pessimism than their European-American counterparts, which may help explain their often impressive academic achievements (Chang, 2001). Success requires enough optimism to provide hope and enough pessimism to prevent complacency. We want our airline pilots to be mindful of worst-possible outcomes.

Excessive optimism can blind us to real risks. Neil Weinstein (1980, 1982, 1996) has shown how our natural positive thinking bias can promote "an unrealistic optimism about future life events." Most college students perceive themselves as less likely than their average classmate to develop drinking problems, drop out of school, have a heart attack by age 40, or go deeply into debt on their high-interest credit cards (Yang et al., 2006). When people entertain positive fantasies about financial success or travel adventure, they often focus on the rewards and ignore the risks (Kappes & Oettingen, 2012). If overconfident of our ability to control an impulse such as the urge to smoke, we are more likely to expose ourselves to temptations—and to fail (Nordgren et al., 2009). Those who optimistically deny the power and effects of smoking, venture into ill-fated relationships, and outwit themselves in dozens of other ways remind us that blind optimism can be self-defeating.

People also display illusory optimism about their groups. Throughout a National Football League season, fans of all teams correctly guessed that other teams would win about 50 percent of their games. But they incorrectly guessed, on average (across teams and weeks), that their own team stood about a 2 in 3 chance of winning (Massey et al., 2011). This optimistic and illogical bias persisted despite their team's experience and monetary incentives for accuracy.

Our natural positive thinking bias does seem to vanish, however, when we are bracing ourselves for feedback, such as exam results (Carroll et al., 2006). In one analysis of 71 studies, most people shifted their expectations downward shortly before the moment of truth (Sweeny & Krizan, 2013). Positive illusions also vanish after a traumatic personal experience—as they did for victims of a catastrophic California earthquake, who had to give up their illusions of being less vulnerable than others to earthquakes (Helweg-Larsen, 1999).

Blindness to One's Own Incompetence   Ironically, people often are most overconfident when most incompetent. That, say Justin Kruger and David Dunning (1999), is because it often takes competence to recognize competence. They found

---

1. We couldn't resist throwing that in. But don't worry, you won't be tested on floccinaucinihilipilification, which is the act of estimating something as worthless (and was the longest nontechnical word in the first edition of the *Oxford English Dictionary*).

that most students scoring at the low end of grammar and logic tests believed they had scored in the top half. If you do not know what good grammar is, you may be unaware that your grammar is poor. This "ignorance of one's own incompetence" phenomenon has a parallel, as I [DM] can confirm, in hard-of-hearing people's difficulty recognizing their own hearing loss. We're not so much "in denial" as we are simply unaware of what we don't hear. If I fail to hear my friend calling my name, the friend notices my inattention. But for me it's a nonevent. I hear what I hear—which, to me, seems pretty normal.

The difficulty in recognizing one's own incompetence helps explain why so many low-scoring students are dumbfounded after doing badly on an exam. If you don't know all the Scrabble word possibilities you've overlooked, you may feel pretty smart—until they are pointed out. Our ignorance of what we don't know sustains our self-confidence, leading us to make the same mistakes (Williams et al., 2013).

To judge one's competence and predict one's future performance, it pays to invite others' assessments, notes Dunning (2006). Based on studies in which both individuals and their acquaintances predict their future, we can hazard some advice: If you're a junior doctor and want to predict how well you will do on a surgical skills exam, don't rate yourself—ask your peers for their candid prediction. If you're a naval officer and need to assess your leadership ability—don't rate yourself, ask your fellow officers. And if you're in love and want to predict whether it will last, don't listen to your heart—ask your roommate.

Self-Serving Bias Imagine dashing to class, hoping not to miss the first few minutes. But you arrive five minutes late, huffing and puffing. As you sink into your seat, what sorts of thoughts go through your mind? Do you go through a negative door, with thoughts such as, "I hate myself" and "I'm a loser"? Or do you go through a positive door, saying to yourself, "At least I made it to class" and "I really tried to get here on time"?

Personality psychologists have found that most people choose the second door, which leads to positive self-thoughts. We have a good reputation with ourselves. We show a **self-serving bias**—a readiness to perceive ourselves favorably (Myers, 2010). Consider:

People accept more responsibility for good deeds than for bad, and for successes than for failures. Athletes often privately credit their victories to their own prowess, and their losses to bad breaks, lousy officiating, or the other team's exceptional performance.

self-serving bias a readiness to perceive oneself favorably.

Most students who receive poor grades on an exam criticize the exam, not themselves. Drivers filling out insurance forms have explained their accidents in such words as "A pedestrian hit me and went under my car." The question "What have I done to deserve this?" is one we usually ask of our troubles, not our successes. Although a self-serving bias can lead us to avoid uncomfortable truths, it can also motivate us to approach difficult tasks with confidence instead of despair (Tomaka et al., 1992; von Hippel & Trivers, 2011).

Most people see themselves as better than average. Compared with most other people, how nice are you? How easy to get along with? How appealing are you as a friend or romantic partner? Where would you rank yourself from the 1st to the 99th percentile? Most people put themselves well above the 50th percentile. This better-than-average effect appears for nearly any subjectively assessed and socially desirable behavior:

- In national surveys, most business executives say they are more ethical than their average counterpart. In several studies, 90 percent of business managers and more than 90 percent of college professors also rated their performance as superior to that of their average peer.

- In Australia, 86 percent of people rate their job performance as above average, and only 1 percent as below average.

- In the National Survey of Families and Households, 49 percent of men said they provided half or more of the child care, though only 31 percent of their wives or partners saw things that way (Galinsky et al., 2008).

- Brain scans reveal that the more people judge themselves as better than average, the less brain activation they show in regions that aid careful self-reflection (Beer & Hughes, 2010). It seems our brain's default setting is to think we are better than others.

PEANUTS

The phenomenon, which reflects overestimating the self as well as the desire to maintain a positive self-view (Brown, 2012; Epley & Dunning, 2000), is less striking in Asia, where people value modesty (Falk et al., 2009; Heine & Hamamura, 2007). Yet self-serving biases have been observed worldwide: In every one of 53 countries surveyed, people expressed self-esteem above the midpoint of the most widely used scale (Schmitt & Allik, 2005).

Ironically, people even see themselves as more immune than others to self-serving bias (Pronin, 2007). That's right, people believe they are above average at not believing they are above average. (Isn't psychology fun?) The world, it seems, is Garrison Keillor's Lake Wobegon writ large—a place where "all the women are strong, all the men are good-looking, and all the children are above average."

Self-serving bias flies in the face of pop psychology. "All of us have inferiority complexes," wrote John Powell (1989, p. 15). "Those who seem not to have such a complex are only pretending." But additional findings remove any doubts (Guenther & Alicke, 2010; Koudenburg et al., 2011; Myers, 2010):

"If you are like most people, then like most people, you don't know you're like most people. Science has given us a lot of facts about the average person, and one of the most reliable of these facts is the average person doesn't see herself as average."

Daniel Gilbert, *Stumbling on Happiness*, 2006

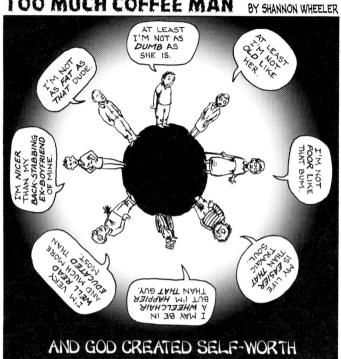

AND GOD CREATED SELF-WORTH

- We remember and justify our past actions in self-enhancing ways, and exhibit an inflated confidence in our beliefs and judgments. We are quicker to believe flattering descriptions of ourselves than unflattering ones, and we are impressed with psychological tests that make us look good.

- In situations where most people behave less than admirably, we overestimate how desirably *we* would act. We shore up our self-image by overestimating the commonality of our foibles and by underestimating the commonality of our strengths.

- We see ourselves making better-than-average contributions to our groups (but so do our teammates, which explains why group members' self-contribution estimates usually total more than 100 percent).

- We exhibit group pride—a tendency to see our group (our school, our country, even our pets) as superior.

Authentic pride that's rooted in actual achievement supports self-confidence and leadership (Tracy et al., 2009; Williams & DeSteno, 2009). Yet self-serving perceptions underlie conflicts ranging from blaming one's spouse for marital discord to arrogantly promoting one's own ethnic superiority. These self-serving tendencies may also explain why people attribute less responsibility for their group's violent actions (Bilali et al., 2012). Finding their self-esteem threatened, people with large egos may react violently. "Aryan pride" fueled Nazi atrocities. "These biases have the effect of making wars more likely to begin and more difficult to end," noted Daniel Kahneman and Jonathan Renshon (2007).

We can see these tendencies even in children, where the recipe for frequent fighting mixes high self-esteem with social rejection. The most aggressive children tend to have high self-regard that gets punctured by other kids' dislike (van Boxtel et al., 2004). Similarly, an adolescent or adult with a swelled head that gets deflated by an insult is potentially dangerous. Brad Bushman and Roy Baumeister (1998; Bushman et al., 2009) experimented with this "dark side of high self-esteem." They had 540 undergraduate volunteers write a brief essay, in response to which another supposed student gave

"The [self-]portraits that we actually believe, when we are given freedom to voice them, are dramatically more positive than reality can sustain."

Shelley Taylor, *Positive Illusions*, 1989

them either praise ("Great essay!") or stinging criticism ("One of the worst essays I have read!"). Then the essay writers played a reaction-time game against the other student. After wins, they could assault their opponent with noise of any intensity for any duration.

Can you anticipate the result? After criticism, those with inflated high self-esteem were "exceptionally aggressive." They delivered three times the auditory torture of those with normal self-esteem. Threatened egotism, more than low self-esteem, it seems, predisposes aggression. "Encouraging people to feel good about themselves when they haven't earned it" poses problems, Baumeister (2001) concluded. "Conceited, self-important individuals turn nasty toward those who puncture their bubbles of self-love."

From 1980 to 2007, popular song lyrics became more self-focused (DeWall et al., 2011). An analysis of 766,513 American books published between 1960 and 2008 showed a similar result: Self-focused words increased (Twenge et al., 2013). On one prominent self-esteem inventory on which 40 is the highest possible self-esteem score, 51 percent of 2008 collegians scored 35 or more (Gentile et al., 2010). Another statistical synopsis—of over 9 million high school seniors and entering college students between 1966 and 2009—also found interest in gaining money, fame, and prestige increasing and concern for others decreasing (Twenge et al., 2012).

After tracking self-importance across the last several decades, psychologist Jean Twenge (2006; Twenge & Foster, 2010) reports that what she calls *Generation Me* expresses more **narcissism** (by agreeing more often with statements such as, "If I ruled the world, it would be a better place," or "I think I am a special person"). Agreement with such narcissistic statements correlates with materialism, the desire to be famous, inflated expectations, more hookups with fewer committed relationships, more gambling, and more cheating, all of which have been on the rise as narcissism has increased. *Narcissistic* people forgive others less, take a game-playing approach to their romantic relationships, and make poor leaders (Campbell et al., 2002; Exline et al., 2004; Nevicka et al., 2011). Hollywood actors and reality television stars—at least those appearing on one national radio show who agreed to take the narcissism test anonymously—are especially narcissistic (Young & Pinsky, 2006). At the collective level, narcissism (sample item: "My group is extraordinary") predicts increased sensitivity to threats and retaliatory aggression (de Zavala et al., 2009; Lyons et al., 2013).

Despite the demonstrated perils of pride, many people object that the idea of self-serving bias overlooks those who feel worthless and unlovable. If self-serving bias prevails, why do so many people disparage themselves? For four reasons: Sometimes self-directed put-downs are *subtly strategic:* They elicit reassuring strokes. Saying "No one likes me" may at least elicit "But not everyone has met you!" Other times, such as before a game or an exam, self-disparaging comments *prepare us for possible failure.* The coach who extols the superior strength of the upcoming opponent makes a loss understandable, a victory noteworthy. A self-disparaging "How could I have been so stupid!" also helps us *learn from our mistakes.* And finally, self-disparagement also frequently *pertains to one's old self.* Asked to remember their really bad behaviors, people recall things from long ago; good behaviors more easily come to mind from their recent past (Escobedo & Adolphs, 2010). People are much more critical of their distant past selves than of their current selves—even when they have not changed (Wilson & Ross, 2001). "At 18, I was a jerk; today I'm more sensitive." In their own eyes, chumps yesterday, champs today.

Even so, it's true: All of us some of the time, and some of us much of the time, do feel inferior—especially when we compare ourselves with those who are a step or two higher on the ladder of status, looks, income, or ability. For example, Olympians who

"The enthusiastic claims of the self-esteem movement mostly range from fantasy to hogwash. The effects of self-esteem are small, limited, and not all good."

Roy Baumeister (1996)

"If you compare yourself with others, you may become vain and bitter; for always there will be greater and lesser persons than yourself."

Max Ehrmann, "Desiderata," 1927

win silver medals, barely missing gold, show greater sadness on the awards podium compared with the bronze medal winners (Medvec et al., 1995). The deeper and more frequently we have such feelings, the more unhappy, even depressed, we are. But for most people, thinking has a naturally positive bias.

While recognizing the dark side of self-serving bias and self-esteem, some researchers prefer isolating the effects of two types of self-esteem—defensive and secure (Kernis, 2003; Lambird & Mann, 2006; Ryan & Deci, 2004). *Defensive self-esteem* is fragile. It focuses on sustaining itself, which makes failure and criticism feel threatening. Such egotism exposes one to perceived threats, which feed anger and feelings of vulnerability, notes Jennifer Crocker (2011).

Secure self-esteem is less fragile, because it is less contingent on external evaluations. To feel accepted for who we are, and not for our looks, wealth, or acclaim, relieves pressures to succeed and enables us to focus beyond ourselves. By losing ourselves in relationships and purposes larger than self, Crocker adds, we may achieve a more secure self-esteem, satisfying relationships, and greater quality of life.

narcissism excessive self-love and self-absorption.

RETRIEVAL PRACTICE

• What are the positive and negative effects of high self-esteem?

ANSWER: People who feel confident in their abilities are often happier, have greater motivation, and are less susceptible to depression. Excessive optimism and very high self-esteem can lead to blindness to one's own incompetence, self-serving bias, and narcissism.

• The tendency to accept responsibility for success and blame circumstances or bad luck for failures is called _____ - _____ _____ .

ANSWER: self-serving bias

• _____ (Secure/Defensive) self-esteem correlates with aggressive and antisocial behavior. _____ (Secure/Defensive) self-esteem is a healthier self-image that allows us to focus beyond ourselves and enjoy a higher quality of life.

ANSWERS: Defensive; Secure

MODULE 48 REVIEW Social-Cognitive Theories and the Self

LEARNING OBJECTIVES

RETRIEVAL PRACTICE Take a moment to answer each of these Learning Objective Questions (repeated here from within this module). Then turn to Appendix C, Complete Module Reviews, to check your answers. Research suggests that trying to answer these questions on your own will improve your long-term retention (McDaniel et al., 2009).

48-1 How do social-cognitive theorists view personality development, and how do they explore behavior?

48-2 What criticisms have social-cognitive theorists faced?

48-3 Why has psychology generated so much research on the self? How important is self-esteem to psychology and to human well-being?

48-4 How do excessive optimism, blindness to one's own incompetence, and self-serving bias reveal the costs of self-esteem, and how do defensive and secure self-esteem differ?

TERMS AND CONCEPTS TO REMEMBER

RETRIEVAL PRACTICE Test yourself on these terms by trying to write down the definition before flipping back to check your answers.

social-cognitive perspective, p. 596

reciprocal determinism, p. 597

self, p. 600

spotlight effect, p. 600

self-esteem, p. 601

self-efficacy, p. 601

self-serving bias, p. 603

narcissism, p. 606

Use **LearningCurve** to create your personalized study plan, which will direct you to the resources that will help you most in **LaunchPad**.

TEST YOUR-SELF PERSONALITY

Test yourself repeatedly throughout your studies. This will not only help you figure out what you know and don't know; the testing itself will help you learn and remember the information more effectively thanks to the *testing effect.*

MODULE 46 Introduction to Personality and Psychodynamic Theories

1. Freud believed that we may block painful or unacceptable thoughts, wishes, feelings, or memories from consciousness through an unconscious process called _____ .

2. According to Freud's view of personality structure, the "executive" system, the _____ , seeks to gratify the impulses of the _____ in more acceptable ways.

   a. id; ego

   b. ego; superego

   c. ego; id

   d. id; superego

3. Freud proposed that the development of the "voice of conscience" is related to the _____ , which internalizes ideals and provides standards for judgments.

4. According to the psychoanalytic view of development, we all pass through a series of psychosexual stages, including the oral, anal, and phallic stages. Conflicts unresolved at any of these stages may lead to

   a. dormant sexual feelings.

   b. fixation at that stage.

   c. preconscious blocking of impulses.

   d. a distorted gender identity.

5. Freud believed that defense mechanisms are unconscious attempts to distort or disguise reality, all in an effort to reduce our _____ .

6. _____ tests ask test-takers to respond to an ambiguous stimulus, for example, by describing it or telling a story about it.

7. In general, neo-Freudians such as Adler and Horney accepted many of Freud's views but placed more emphasis than he did on

   a. development throughout the life span.

   b. the collective unconscious.

   c. the role of the id.

   d. social interactions.

8. Modern-day psychodynamic theorists and therapists agree with Freud about

   a. the existence of unconscious mental processes.

   b. the Oedipus complex.

   c. the predictive value of Freudian theory.

   d. the superego's role as the executive part of personality.

9. Which of the following is NOT part of the contemporary view of the unconscious?

   a. Repressed memories of anxiety-provoking events

   b. Schemas that influence our perceptions and interpretations

   c. Parallel processing that occurs without our conscious knowledge

   d. Instantly activated emotions and implicit memories of learned skills

MODULE 47 Humanistic Theories and Trait Theories

10. Maslow's hierarchy of needs proposes that we must satisfy basic physiological and safety needs before we seek ultimate psychological needs, such as self-actualization. Maslow based his ideas on

    a. Freudian theory.

    b. his experiences with patients.

    c. a series of laboratory experiments.

    d. his study of healthy, creative people.

11. How might Rogers explain how environment influences the development of a criminal?

12. The total acceptance Rogers advocated as part of a growth-promoting environment is called _____ _____ _____ .

13. _____ theories of personality focus on describing characteristic behavior patterns, such as agreeableness or extraversion.

14. One famous personality inventory is the

    a. Extraversion–Introversion Scale.

    b. Person–Situation Inventory.

    c. MMPI.

    d. Rorschach.

15. Which of the following is NOT one of the Big Five personality factors?

    a. Conscientiousness

    b. Anxiety

    c. Extraversion

    d. Agreeableness

16. Our scores on personality tests best predict

    a. our behavior on a specific occasion.

    b. our average behavior across many situations.

    c. behavior involving a single trait, such as conscientiousness.

    d. behavior that depends on the situation or context.

MODULE 48 Social-Cognitive Theories and the Self

17. The social-cognitive perspective proposes our personality is shaped by a process called reciprocal determinism, as personal factors, environmental factors, and behaviors interact. An example of an environmental factor is

    a. the presence of books in a home.

    b. a preference for outdoor play.

    c. the ability to read at a fourth-grade level.

    d. the fear of violent action on television.

18. Critics say that _____ - _____ personality theory is very sensitive to an individual's interactions with particular situations, but that it gives too little attention to the person's enduring traits.

19. Researchers have found that low self-esteem tends to be linked with life problems. How should this link be interpreted?

    a. Life problems cause low self-esteem.

    b. The answer isn't clear because the link is correlational and does not indicate cause and effect.

    c. Low self-esteem leads to life problems.

    d. Because of the self-serving bias, we must assume that external factors cause low self-esteem.

20. A fortune cookie advises, "Love yourself and happiness will follow." Is this good advice?

21. The tendency to overestimate others' attention to and evaluation of our appearance, performance, and blunders is called the _____ _____ .

Find answers to these questions in Appendix D, in the back of the book.

PSYCHOLOGICAL DISORDERS

. . . .

I felt the need to clean my room at home in Indianapolis every Sunday and would spend four to five hours at it. I would take every book out of the bookcase, dust and put it back. At the time I loved doing it. Then I didn't want to do it anymore, but I couldn't stop. The clothes in my closet hung exactly two fingers apart. . . . I made a ritual of touching the wall in my bedroom before I went out because something bad would happen if I didn't do it the right way. I had a constant anxiety about it as a kid, and it made me think for the first time that I might be nuts.

Marc, diagnosed with obsessive-compulsive disorder (from Summers, 1996)

Whenever I get depressed it's because I've lost a sense of self. I can't find reasons to like myself. I think I'm ugly. I think no one likes me. . . . I become grumpy and short-tempered. Nobody wants to be around me. I'm left alone. Being alone confirms that I am ugly and not worth being with. I think I'm responsible for everything that goes wrong.

Greta, diagnosed with depression (from Thorne, 1993, p. 21)

Voices, like the roar of a crowd, came. I felt like Jesus; I was being crucified. It was dark. I just continued to huddle under the blanket, feeling weak, laid bare and defenseless in a cruel world I could no longer understand.

Stuart, diagnosed with schizophrenia (from Emmons et al., 1997)

Now and then, all of us feel, think, or act in ways that may resemble a psychological disorder. We feel anxious, depressed, withdrawn, or suspicious, just less intensely and more briefly. So it's no wonder that we are drawn to try to understand disturbed mental states—we sometimes see ourselves in the psychological disorders we study. "To study the abnormal is the best way of understanding the normal," said William James (1842–1910).

Another reason for our curiosity is that most of us will, at some point, encounter someone with a psychological disorder. Personally or through friends or family, we may experience the bewilderment and pain of unexplained physical symptoms, irrational fears, or a feeling that life is not worth living. In one study of 26 American college campuses, 32 percent of students reported an apparent mental health problem (Eisenberg et al., 2011).

Worldwide, some 450 million people live with mental or behavior disorders (WHO, 2010). Although their rates and symptoms vary by culture, no known society is free of two terrible disorders—major depression and schizophrenia (Baumeister & Härter, 2007; Draguns, 1990a,b, 1997). Modules 49 through 53 examine these disorders and others. Later modules will consider their *treatment*.

MODULE 49 Introduction to Psychological Disorders

Most people would agree that someone who is too depressed to get out of bed for weeks at a time has a psychological disorder. But what about those who, having experienced a loss, are unable to resume their usual social activities? Where should we draw the line between sadness and depression? Between zany creativity and bizarre irrationality? Between normality and abnormality? Let's start with these questions:

- How should we *define* psychological disorders?

- How should we *understand* disorders? How do underlying biological factors contribute to disorder? How do troubling environments influence our well-being? And how do these effects of nature and nurture interact?

- How should we *classify* psychological disorders? And can we do so in a way that allows us to help people without stigmatizing them with *labels*?

- What do we know about *rates* of psychological disorders? How many people have them? Who is vulnerable, and when?

Defining Psychological Disorders

49-1 How should we draw the line between normality and disorder?

psychological disorder a syndrome marked by a clinically significant disturbance in an individual's cognition, emotion regulation, or behavior.

A **psychological disorder** is a syndrome (collection of symptoms) marked by a "clinically significant disturbance in an individual's cognition, emotion regulation, or behavior" (American Psychiatric Association, 2013). Disturbed, or *dysfunctional* thoughts, emotions, or behaviors are *maladaptive*—they interfere with normal day-to-day life. Believing your home must be thoroughly cleaned every weekend is not a disorder. But if cleaning rituals interfere with work and leisure, as Marc's did in this module's opening, they may be signs of a disorder. And occasional sad moods that persist and become disabling may likewise signal a psychological disorder.

Distress often accompanies dysfunctional behaviors. Marc, Greta, and Stuart were all distressed by their behaviors or emotions.

Over time, definitions of what makes for a "significant disturbance" have varied. From 1952 through December 9, 1973, homosexuality was classified as a psychological disorder. By day's end on December 10, it was not. The American Psychiatric Association made this change because more and more of its members no longer viewed same-sex attraction as a psychological problem. Such is the power of shifting societal beliefs. (Later research revealed, however, that the *stigma and stresses* that gay, lesbian, and transsexual people often experience can increase the risk of mental health problems [Hatzenbuehler et al., 2009; Meyer, 2003].) In the twenty-first century, other controversies swirl over new or altered diagnoses (such as *attention-deficit/hyperactivity disorder*) in the most recent classification tool for describing disorders. (You'll hear more about this later.)

Culture and normality Young men of the West African Wodaabe tribe put on elaborate makeup and costumes to attract women. Young American men may buy flashy cars with loud stereos to do the same. Each culture may view the other's behavior as abnormal.

Carol Beckwith

© Image Source/Corbis

• A lawyer is distressed by feeling the need to wash his hands 100 times a day. He has no time left to meet with clients, and his colleagues are wondering about his competence. His behavior would probably be labeled disordered, because it is _____— that is, it interferes with his day-to-day life.

ANSWER: maladaptive

Understanding Psychological Disorders

49-2 How do the medical model and the biopsychosocial approach influence our understanding of psychological disorders?

The way we view a problem influences how we try to solve it. In earlier times, people often viewed strange behaviors as evidence that strange forces—the movements of the stars, godlike powers, or evil spirits—were at work. Had you lived during the Middle Ages, you might have said "The devil made him do it." Believing that, you might have approved of a cure that would drive out the evil demon. Thus, people considered "mad" were sometimes caged or given "therapies" such as genital mutilation, beatings, removal of teeth or lengths of intestines, or transfusions of animal blood (Farina, 1982). Barbaric treatments for mental illness linger even today. In some places, people are chained to a bed, locked in their rooms, or even locked in a room with wild hyenas, in the belief that the animals will see and attack evil spirits (Hooper, 2013). Noting the physical and emotional damage of such restraint, the World Health Organization launched a "chain-free initiative" that aims to reform hospitals "into patient-friendly and humane places with minimum restraints" (WHO, 2014).

Yesterday's "therapy" Through the ages, psychologically disordered people have received brutal treatments, including the trephination evident in this Stone Age skull. Drilling skull holes like these may have been an attempt to release evil spirits and cure those with mental disorders. Did this patient survive the "cure"?

The Medical Model

Brutal treatments may worsen, rather than improve, mental health. Reformers, such as Philippe Pinel (1745–1826) in France, opposed such brutal treatments. Madness is not demon possession, he insisted, but a sickness of the mind caused by severe stress and inhumane conditions. Curing the illness, he said, requires "moral treatment," including boosting patients' morale by unchaining them and talking with them. He and others worked to replace brutality with gentleness, isolation with activity, and filth with clean air and sunshine.

"Moral treatment" Under Philippe Pinel's influence, hospitals sometimes sponsored patient dances, often called "lunatic balls," depicted in this painting by George Bellows (*Dance in a Madhouse*).

medical model the concept that diseases, in this case psychological disorders, have physical causes that can be *diagnosed, treated,* and, in most cases, *cured,* often through treatment in a *hospital.*

epigenetics the study of environmental influences on gene expression that occur without a DNA change.

By the 1800s, the discovery that syphilis infects the brain and distorts the mind drove further gradual reform. Hospitals replaced asylums, and the **medical model** of mental disorders was born. This model is reflected in the terms we still use today. We speak of the mental *health* movement: A mental *illness* (also called a psycho*pathology*) needs to be *diagnosed* on the basis of its *symptoms.* It needs to be *treated* through *therapy,* which may include time in a psychiatric *hospital.*

The medical perspective has gained credibility from recent discoveries that genetically influenced abnormalities in brain structure and biochemistry contribute to many disorders. But as we will see, psychological factors, such as chronic or traumatic stress, also play an important role.

The Biopsychosocial Approach

To call psychological disorders "sicknesses" tilts research heavily toward the influence of biology and away from the influence of our personal histories and social and cultural surroundings. But in the study of disorders, as in so many other areas, we must remember that our behaviors, our thoughts, and our feelings are formed by the interaction of biological, psychological, and social-cultural influences. As individuals, we differ in the amount of stress we experience and in the ways we cope with stressors. Cultures also differ in their sources of stress and in traditional ways of coping.

Some disorders, such as depression and schizophrenia, occur worldwide. From Asia to Africa and across the Americas, schizophrenia's symptoms often include irrationality and incoherent speech. Other disorders tend to be associated with specific cultures. In Malaysia, *amok* describes a sudden outburst of violent behavior (thus the English phrase "run amok"). Latin America lays claim to *susto,* a condition marked by severe anxiety, restlessness, and a fear of black magic. In Japanese culture, people may experience *taijin kyofusho*—social anxiety about their appearance, combined with a readiness to blush and a fear of eye contact. The eating disorders anorexia nervosa and bulimia nervosa occur mostly in food-abundant Western cultures. Such disorders may share an underlying dynamic (such as anxiety) while differing in the symptoms (an eating problem or a type of fear) manifested in a particular culture.

Increasingly, North America's disorders, along with McDonald's and MTV, have spread across the globe (Watters, 2010).

Disorders reflect genetic predispositions and physiological states, inner psychological dynamics, and social and cultural circumstances. The biopsychosocial approach emphasizes that mind and body are inseparable (**FIGURE 49.1**). Negative emotions contribute to physical illness, and physical abnormalities contribute to negative emotions. **Epigenetics,** the study of how nurture shapes nature, also informs our understanding of disorders (Powledge, 2011). Genes and environment are not the whole story, as we've seen in other modules. It turns out our environment can affect whether a gene is *expressed* or not, and thus affect the development of various psychological disorders.

▼ FIGURE 49.1
The biopsychosocial approach to psychological disorders
Today's psychology studies how biological, psychological, and social-cultural factors interact to produce specific psychological disorders.

Biological influences:
• evolution
• individual genes
• brain structure and chemistry

Psychological influences:
• stress
• trauma
• learned helplessness
• mood-related perceptions and memories

Psychological disorder

Social-cultural influences:
• roles
• expectations
• definitions of *normality* and *disorder*

Wavebreakmedia Ltd./Getty Images

For example, even identical twins (with identical genes) do not share the same risks of developing psychological disorders. They are more likely, but not always destined, to develop the same disorders. Their varying environmental factors influence whether certain culprit genes are expressed.

> **DSM-5** the American Psychiatric Association's *Diagnostic and Statistical Manual of Mental Disorders,* Fifth Edition; a widely used system for classifying psychological disorders.

RETRIEVAL PRACTICE

- Are psychological disorders universal, or are they culture-specific? Explain with examples.

ANSWER: Some psychological disorders are culture-specific. For example, anorexia nervosa occurs mostly in North American cultures, and *taijin-kyofusho* appears largely in Japan. Other disorders, such as schizophrenia, are universal—occurring in all cultures.

- What is the biopsychosocial approach, and why is it important in our understanding of psychological disorders?

ANSWER: Biological, psychological, and social-cultural influences combine to produce psychological disorders. This broad perspective helps us understand that our well-being is affected by our genes, brain functioning, inner thoughts and feelings, and the influences of our social and cultural environment.

Classifying Disorders—and Labeling People

49-3 How and why do clinicians classify psychological disorders, and why do some psychologists criticize the use of diagnostic labels?

In biology, classification creates order. To classify an animal as a "mammal" says a great deal—that it is warm-blooded, has hair or fur, and produces milk to nourish its young. In psychiatry and psychology, too, classification orders and describes symptoms. To classify a person's disorder as "schizophrenia" suggests that the person talks incoherently, has bizarre beliefs, shows either little emotion or inappropriate emotion, or is socially withdrawn. "Schizophrenia" is a quick way to describe a complex disorder.

But diagnostic classification gives more than a thumbnail sketch of a person's disordered behavior, thoughts, or feelings. In psychiatry and psychology, classification also aims to

- *predict* the disorder's future course.
- *suggest* appropriate treatment.
- *prompt* research into its causes.

To study a disorder, we must first name and describe it.

The most common tool for describing disorders and estimating how often they occur is the American Psychiatric Association's 2013 *Diagnostic and Statistical Manual of Mental Disorders,* now in its fifth edition (**DSM-5**). Physicians and mental health workers use the detailed "diagnostic criteria and codes" in the DSM-5 to guide medical diagnoses and treatment. For example, a person may be diagnosed with and treated for "insomnia disorder" if he or she meets *all* of the criteria in **TABLE 49.1**.

"*I'm always like this, and my family was wondering if you could prescribe a mild depressant.*"

A book of case illustrations accompanying the previous DSM edition provided several examples for Modules 49 through 53.

▼ TABLE 49.1
Insomnia Disorder

- Feeling unsatisfied with amount or quality of sleep (trouble falling asleep, staying asleep, or returning to sleep)

- Sleep disruption causes distress or diminished everyday functioning

- Happens three or more nights each week

- Occurs during at least three consecutive months

- Happens even with sufficient sleep opportunities

- Independent from other sleep disorders (such as narcolepsy)

- Independent from substance use or abuse

- Independent from other mental disorders or medical conditions

In the DSM-5, some diagnostic labels have changed. The conditions formerly called "autism" and "Asperger's syndrome" have now been combined under the label *autism spectrum disorder*. "Mental retardation" has become *intellectual disability*. New categories, such as *hoarding disorder* and *binge-eating disorder*, have been added.

Some of the new or altered diagnoses are controversial. *Disruptive mood dysregulation disorder* is a new DSM-5 diagnosis for children "who exhibit persistent irritability and frequent episodes of behavior outbursts three or more times a week for more than a year." Will this diagnosis assist parents who struggle with unstable children, or will it "turn temper tantrums into a mental disorder" and lead to overmedication, as the chair of the previous DSM edition has warned (Frances, 2012)?

Real-world tests *(field trials)* have assessed clinician agreement when using the new DSM-5 categories (Freedman et al., 2013). Some diagnoses, such as *adult posttraumatic stress disorder* and *childhood autism spectrum disorder* fared well—with agreement near 70 percent. (If one psychiatrist or psychologist diagnosed someone with one of these disorders, there was a 70 percent chance that another mental health worker would independently give the same diagnosis.) Others, such as *antisocial personality disorder* and *generalized anxiety disorder,* fared poorly.

Critics have long faulted the DSM for casting too wide a net and bringing "almost any kind of behavior within the compass of psychiatry" (Eysenck et al., 1983). Some now worry that the DSM-5's even wider net will extend the pathologizing of everyday life—for example, by turning childish rambunctiousness into ADHD, and bereavement grief into a depressive disorder (Frances, 2013). (See Thinking Critically About: ADHD.) Others respond that hyperactivity and depression, though needing careful definition, are genuine disorders—even when the depression was triggered by a major life stress such as a death when the grief does not go away (Kendler, 2011; Kupfer, 2012).

Other critics register a more basic complaint—that these labels are at best subjective and at worst value judgments masquerading as science. Once we label a person, we view that person differently (Bathje & Pryor, 2011; Farina, 1982; Sadler et al., 2012). Labels can change reality by putting us on alert for evidence that confirms our view. When teachers were told certain students were "gifted," they acted in ways that elicited the behaviors they expected (Snyder, 1984). Someone who was led to think you are nasty may treat you coldly, leading you to respond as a mean-spirited person would. Labels can be self-fulfilling. They create expectations that guide how we perceive and interpret people.

The biasing power of labels was clear in a now-classic study. David Rosenhan (1973) and seven others went to hospital admissions offices, complaining (falsely) of "hearing voices" saying *empty, hollow,* and *thud.* Apart from this complaint and giving false names and occupations, they answered questions truthfully. All eight healthy people were misdiagnosed with disorders.

Should we be surprised? As one psychiatrist noted, if someone swallows blood, goes to an emergency room, and spits it up, should we fault the doctor for diagnosing a bleeding ulcer? Surely not. But what followed the Rosenhan study diagnoses was startling. Until being released an average of 19 days later, those eight "patients" showed no other symptoms. Yet after analyzing their (quite normal) life histories, clinicians were able to "discover" the causes of their disorders, such as having mixed emotions about a parent. Even routine note-taking behavior was misinterpreted as a symptom.

Labels matter. In another study, people watched videotaped interviews. If told the interviewees were job applicants, the viewers perceived them as normal (Langer et al., 1974, 1980).

Struggles and recovery Boston Mayor Martin Walsh spoke openly about his struggles with alcohol. His story of recovery helped him win the closest Boston mayoral election in decades.

Gretchen Ertl/The New York Times/Redux

ADHD—Normal High Energy or Disordered Behavior?

49-4 Why is there controversy over attention-deficit/hyperactivity disorder?

Eight-year-old Todd has always been energetic. At home, he chatters away and darts from one activity to the next, rarely settling down to read a book or focus on a game. At play, he is reckless and overreacts when playmates bump into him or take one of his toys. At school, Todd fidgets, and his exasperated teacher complains that he doesn't listen, follow instructions, or stay in his seat and do his lessons. As Todd matures to adulthood, his hyperactivity likely will subside, but his inattentiveness may persist (Kessler et al., 2010).

If taken for a psychological evaluation, Todd may be diagnosed with **attention-deficit/hyperactivity disorder (ADHD)**. Some 11 percent of American 4- to 17-year-olds receive the diagnosis after displaying its key symptoms (extreme inattention, hyperactivity, and impulsivity) (Schwarz & Cohen, 2013). Studies also find 2.5 percent of adults—though the number diminishes with age—exhibit ADHD symptoms (Simon et al., 2009). The looser criteria for adult ADHD in the DSM-5 has led critics to fear increased diagnosis and overuse of prescription drugs (Frances, 2012).

To skeptics, being distractible, fidgety, and impulsive sounds like a "disorder" caused by a single genetic variation: a Y chromosome (the male sex chromosome). And sure enough, ADHD is diagnosed three times more often in boys than in girls. Children who are "a persistent pain in the neck in school" are often diagnosed with ADHD and given powerful prescription drugs (Gray, 2010). Minority youth less often receive an ADHD diagnosis than do Caucasian youth, but this difference has shrunk as minority ADHD diagnoses have increased (Getahun et al., 2013).

The problem may reside less in the child than in today's abnormal environment that forces children to do what evolution has not prepared them to do—to sit for long hours in chairs. In more natural outdoor environments, these children might seem perfectly healthy.

Rates of medication for presumed ADHD vary by age, sex, and location. Prescription drugs are more often given to teens than to younger children. Boys are nearly three times more likely to receive them than are girls. And location matters. Among 4- to 17-year-olds, prescription rates have varied from 1 percent in Nevada to 9 percent in North Carolina (CDC, 2013). Some students seek out the stimulant drugs—calling them the "good-grade pills." They hope to increase their focus and achievement, but the risks include the development of addiction, depressive disorders, or bipolar disorder (Schwarz, 2012).

Not everyone agrees that ADHD is being overdiagnosed. Some argue that today's more frequent diagnoses reflect increased awareness of the disorder, especially in those areas where rates are highest. They also note that diagnoses can be inconsistent—ADHD is not as clearly defined as a broken arm. Nevertheless, declared the World Federation for Mental Health (2005), "there is strong agreement among the international scientific community that ADHD is a real neurobiological disorder whose existence should no longer be debated." A consensus statement by 75 neuroimaging researchers noted that abnormal brain activity often accompanies ADHD (Barkley et al., 2002).

What, then, is known about ADHD's causes? It is not caused by too much sugar or poor schools. There is mixed evidence suggesting that extensive TV watching and video gaming are associated with reduced cognitive self-regulation and ADHD (Bailey et al., 2011; Courage & Setliff, 2010; Ferguson et al., 2011). ADHD often coexists with a learning disorder or with defiant and temper-prone behavior. ADHD is *heritable,* and research teams are sleuthing the culprit genes and abnormal neural pathways (Lionel et al., 2014; Poelmans et al., 2011; Volkow et al., 2009; Williams et al., 2010). It is treatable with medications such as Ritalin and Adderall, which are considered stimulants but help calm hyperactivity and increase one's ability to sit and focus on a task—and to progress normally in school (Barbaresi et al., 2007). Psychological therapies, such as those focused on shaping classroom and at-home behaviors, also help address the distress of ADHD (Fabiano et al., 2008).

The bottom line: Extreme inattention, hyperactivity, and impulsivity can derail social, academic, and vocational achievements, and these symptoms can be treated with medication and other therapies. But the debate continues over whether normal high energy is too often diagnosed as a psychiatric disorder, and whether there is a cost to the long-term use of stimulant drugs in treating ADHD.

---

attention-deficit/hyperactivity disorder (ADHD) a psychological disorder marked by extreme inattention and/or hyperactivity and impulsivity.

Other viewers who were told they were watching psychiatric or cancer patients perceived the same interviewees as "different from most people." Therapists who thought they were watching an interview of a psychiatric patient perceived him as "frightened of his own aggressive impulses," a "passive, dependent type," and so forth. A label can, as Rosenhan discovered, have "a life and an influence of its own."

Labels also have power outside the laboratory. Getting a job or finding a place to rent can be a challenge for people recently released from a mental hospital.

"My sister suffers from a bipolar disorder and my nephew from schizoaffective disorder. There has, in fact, been a lot of depression and alcoholism in my family and, traditionally, no one ever spoke about it. It just wasn't done. The stigma is toxic."

Actress Glenn Close, "Mental Illness: The Stigma of Silence," 2009

Label someone as "mentally ill" and people may fear them as potentially violent (see Thinking Critically About: Are People With Psychological Disorders Dangerous?) Such negative reactions may fade as people better understand that many psychological disorders involve diseases of the brain, not failures of character (Solomon, 1996). Public figures have helped foster this new understanding by speaking openly about their own struggles with disorders such as depression and substance abuse. The more contact we have with people with disorders, the more accepting our attitudes are (Kolodziej & Johnson, 1996).

THINKING CRITICALLY ABOUT

Are People With Psychological Disorders Dangerous?

49-5 Do psychological disorders predict violent behavior?

September 16, 2013, started like any other Monday at Washington, DC's, Navy Yard, with people arriving early to begin work. Then government contractor Aaron Alexis parked his car, entered the building, and began shooting people. An hour later, 13 people were dead, including Alexis. Reports later confirmed that Alexis had a history of mental illness. Before the shooting, he had stated that an "ultra low frequency attack is what I've been subject to for the last three months. And to be perfectly honest, that is what has driven me to this." This devastating mass shooting, like the one in a Connecticut elementary school in 2012 and many others since then, reinforced public perceptions that people with psychological disorders pose a threat (Jorm et al., 2012). After the 2012 slaughter, New York's governor declared, "People who have mental issues should not have guns" (Kaplan & Hakim, 2013).

Does scientific evidence support the governor's statement? If disorders actually increase the risk of violence, then denying people with psychological disorders the right to bear arms might reduce violent crimes. But real life tells a different story. The vast majority of violent crimes are committed by people with no diagnosed disorder (Fazel & Grann, 2006; Walkup & Rubin, 2013).

People with disorders are more likely to be *victims* than perpetrators of violence (Marley & Bulia, 2001). According to the U.S. Surgeon General's Office (1999, p. 7), "There is very little risk of violence or harm to a stranger from casual contact with an individual who has a mental disorder." People with mental illness commit proportionately little gun violence. *The bottom line:* Focusing gun restrictions only on mentally ill people will likely not reduce gun violence (Friedman, 2012).

If mental illness is not a good predictor of violence, what is? Better predictors are a history of violence, use of alcohol or drugs, and access to a gun. The mass-killing shooters have one more thing in common: They tend to be young males. "We could avoid two-thirds of all crime simply by putting all able-bodied young men in cryogenic sleep from the age of 12 through 28," said one psychologist (Lykken, 1995).

Mental disorders seldom lead to violence, and clinical prediction of violence is unreliable. What, then, are the triggers for the few people with psychological disorders who do commit violent acts? For some, the trigger is substance abuse. For others, like the Navy Yard shooter, it's threatening delusions and hallucinated voices that command them to act (Douglas et al., 2009;

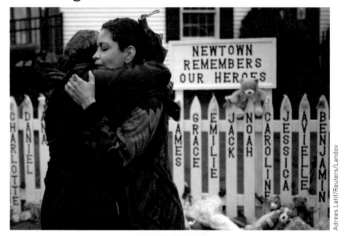

How to prevent mass shootings? Following the Newtown, Connecticut, slaughter of 20 young children and 6 adults, people wondered: Could those at risk for violence be identified in advance by mental health workers and reported to police? Would laws that require such reporting discourage disturbed gun owners from seeking mental health treatment?

Elbogen & Johnson, 2009; Fazel et al., 2009, 2010). Whether people with mental disorders who turn violent should be held responsible for their behavior remains controversial. U.S. President Ronald Reagan's near-assassin, John Hinckley, was sent to a hospital rather than to prison. The public was outraged. "Hinkley insane. Public mad," declared one headline. They were outraged again in 2011, when Jared Lee Loughner killed six people and injured several others, including U.S. Representative Gabrielle Giffords. Loughner was diagnosed with schizophrenia and twice found incompetent to stand trial. He was later judged competent to stand trial, pled guilty to 19 charges of murder and attempted murder, and was sentenced to life in prison without parole.

Which decision was correct? The first two, which blamed Loughner's "madness" for clouding his judgment? Or the final one, which decided that he should be held responsible for the acts he committed? As we come to better understand the biological and environmental bases for all human behavior, from generosity to vandalism, when should we—and should we not—hold people accountable for their actions?

Paramount Pictures/Photofest

Better portrayals Old stereotypes are slowly being replaced in media portrayals of psychological disorders. Recent films offer fairly realistic depictions. *Iron Man 3* (2013) portrayed a main character, shown here, with posttraumatic stress disorder. *Black Swan* (2010) dramatized a lead character suffering a delusional disorder. *A Single Man* (2009) depicted depression.

Despite their risks, diagnostic labels have benefits. Mental health professionals use labels to communicate about their cases, to comprehend the underlying causes, and to discern effective treatment programs. Researchers use labels when discussing work that explores the causes and treatments of disorders. Clients are often relieved to learn that the nature of their suffering has a name, and that they are not alone in experiencing this collection of symptoms.

🅐 LaunchPad To test your ability to form diagnoses, visit LaunchPad's *PsychSim 6: Classifying Disorders.*

"What's the use of their having names," the Gnat said, "if they won't answer to them?"

"No use to *them*," said Alice; "but it's useful to the people that name them, I suppose."

Lewis Carroll, *Through the Looking-Glass*, 1871

RETRIEVAL PRACTICE

• What is the value, and what are the dangers, of labeling individuals with disorders?

ANSWER: Therapists and others use disorder labels to communicate with one another using a common language, and to share concepts during research. Clients may benefit from knowing that they are not the only ones with these symptoms. The dangers of labeling people are that (1) people may begin to act as they have been labeled, and (2) the labels can trigger assumptions that will change our behavior toward those we label.

Rates of Psychological Disorders

49-6 How many people have, or have had, a psychological disorder? Is poverty a risk factor?

Who is most vulnerable to psychological disorders? At what times of life? To answer such questions, various countries have conducted lengthy structured interviews with representative samples of thousands of their citizens. After asking hundreds of questions that probed for symptoms—"Has there ever been a period of two weeks or more when you felt like you wanted to die?"—the researchers have estimated the current, prior-year, and lifetime prevalence of various disorders.

How many people have, or have had, a psychological disorder? More than most of us suppose:

• The U.S. National Institute of Mental Health (2008, based on Kessler et al., 2005) has estimated that just over 1 in 4 adult Americans "suffer from a diagnosable mental disorder in a given year" (**TABLE 49.2**).

• A large-scale World Health Organization (2004a) study—based on 90-minute interviews of 60,463 people—estimated the number of prior-year mental disorders in 20 countries. As **FIGURE 49.2** on the next page displays, the lowest rate of reported mental disorders was in Shanghai, the highest rate in the United States. Moreover, immigrants to the United States from Mexico, Africa, and Asia averaged better mental health than their U.S. counterparts with the same ethnic heritage (Breslau

▼ TABLE 49.2

Percentage of Americans Reporting Selected Psychological Disorders in the Past Year

Psychological Disorder	Percentage
Generalized anxiety disorder	3.1
Social anxiety disorder	6.8
Phobia of specific object or situation	8.7
Depressive disorders or bipolar disorder	9.5
Obsessive-compulsive disorder (OCD)	1.0
Schizophrenia	1.1
Posttraumatic stress disorder (PTSD)	3.5
Attention-deficit/ hyperactivity disorder (ADHD)	4.1

Data from: National Institute of Mental Health, 2008.

▼ FIGURE 49.2
Prior-year prevalence of disorders in selected areas From World Health Organization (WHO, 2004a) interviews in 20 countries.

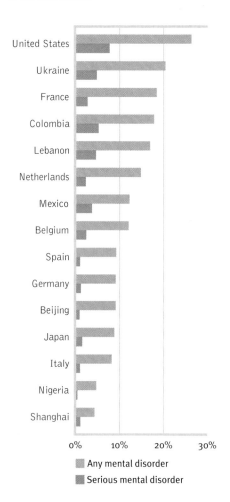

Any mental disorder

Serious mental disorder

et al., 2007; Maldonado-Molina et al., 2011). For example, compared with people who have recently immigrated from Mexico, Mexican-Americans born in the United States are at greater risk of mental disorder—a phenomenon known as the *immigrant paradox* (Schwartz et al., 2010).

What increases vulnerability to mental disorders? As **TABLE 49.3** indicates, there is a wide range of risk and protective factors for mental disorders. But one predictor of mental disorder, poverty, crosses ethnic and gender lines. The incidence of serious psychological disorders has been doubly high among those below the poverty line (CDC, 1992). Like so many other correlations, the poverty-disorder association raises further questions: Does poverty cause disorders? Or do disorders cause poverty? It is both, though the answer varies with the disorder. Schizophrenia understandably leads to poverty. Yet the stresses and demoralization of poverty can also precipitate disorders, especially depression in women and substance abuse in men (Dohrenwend et al., 1992).

▼ TABLE 49.3
Risk and Protective Factors for Mental Disorders

Risk Factors	Protective Factors
Academic failure	Aerobic exercise
Birth complications	Community offering empowerment, opportunity, and security
Caring for those who are chronically ill or who have a neurocognitive disorder	Economic independence
Child abuse and neglect	Effective parenting
Chronic insomnia	Feelings of mastery and control
Chronic pain	Feelings of security
Family disorganization or conflict	Literacy
Low birth weight	Positive attachment and early bonding
Low socioeconomic status	Positive parent-child relationships
Medical illness	Problem-solving skills
Neurochemical imbalance	Resilient coping with stress and adversity
Parental mental illness	Self-esteem
Parental substance abuse	Social and work skills
Personal loss and bereavement	Social support from family and friends
Poor work skills and habits	
Reading disabilities	
Sensory disabilities	
Social incompetence	
Stressful life events	
Substance abuse	
Trauma experiences	

Research from: World Health Organization (WHO, 2004b,c).

In one natural experiment on the poverty-pathology link, researchers tracked rates of behavior problems in North Carolina Native American children as economic development enabled a dramatic reduction in their community's poverty rate. As the study began, children of poverty exhibited more deviant and aggressive behaviors. After four years, children whose families had moved above the poverty line exhibited a 40 percent decrease in the behavior problems. Those who continued in their previous positions below or above the poverty line exhibited no change (Costello et al., 2003).

At what times of life do disorders strike? Usually by early adulthood. "Over 75 percent of our sample with any disorder had experienced [their] first symptoms by age 24," reported Lee Robins and Darrel Regier (1991, p. 331). Among the earliest to appear are the symptoms of antisocial personality disorder (median age 8) and of phobias (median age 10). Alcohol use disorder, obsessive-compulsive disorder, bipolar disorder, and schizophrenia symptoms appear at a median age near 20. Major depressive disorder often hits somewhat later, at a median age of 25.

RETRIEVAL PRACTICE

• What is the relationship between poverty and psychological disorders?

ANSWER: Poverty-related stresses can help trigger disorders, but disabling disorders can also contribute to poverty. Thus, poverty and disorder are often a chicken-and-egg situation, and it's hard to know which came first.

MODULE 49 REVIEW Introduction to Psychological Disorders

LEARNING OBJECTIVES

RETRIEVAL PRACTICE Take a moment to answer each of these Learning Objective Questions (repeated here from within this module). Then turn to Appendix C, Complete Module Reviews, to check your answers. Research suggests that trying to answer these questions on your own will improve your long-term retention (McDaniel et al., 2009).

49-1 How should we draw the line between normality and disorder?

49-2 How do the medical model and the biopsychosocial approach influence our understanding of psychological disorders?

49-3 How and why do clinicians classify psychological disorders, and why do some psychologists criticize the use of diagnostic labels?

49-4 Why is there controversy over attention-deficit/hyperactivity disorder?

49-5 Do psychological disorders predict violent behavior?

49-6 How many people have, or have had a psychological disorder? Is poverty a risk factor?

TERMS AND CONCEPTS TO REMEMBER

RETRIEVAL PRACTICE Test yourself on these terms by trying to write down the definition before flipping back to check your answers.

psychological disorder, p. 610

medical model, p. 612

epigenetics, p. 612

DSM-5, p. 613

attention-deficit/hyperactivity disorder (ADHD), p. 615

Use **LearningCurve** to create your personalized study plan, which will direct you to the resources that will help you most in **LaunchPad**.

Anxiety Disorders, OCD, and PTSD

MODULE 50

Anxiety is part of life. Speaking in front of a class, peering down from a ladder, or waiting to play in a big game, any one of us might feel anxious. Anxiety may even cause us to avoid talking or making eye contact—"shyness," we call it. Fortunately for most of us, our uneasiness is not intense and persistent. Some of us, however, are more prone to notice and remember threats (Mitte, 2008). When the brain's danger-detection system becomes hyperactive, we are at greater risk for an *anxiety disorder*, or for two other disorders that involve anxiety: *obsessive-compulsive disorder* (OCD) or *posttraumatic stress disorder* (PTSD).[1]

---

1. OCD and PTSD were formerly classified as anxiety disorders, but the DSM-5 now classifies them separately.

Anxiety Disorders

50-1 How do generalized anxiety disorder, panic disorder, and phobias differ?

The **anxiety disorders** are marked by distressing, persistent anxiety or dysfunctional anxiety-reducing behaviors. Let's take a closer look at three of them:

- *Generalized anxiety disorder,* in which a person is unexplainably and continually tense and uneasy

- *Panic disorder,* in which a person experiences *panic attacks*—sudden episodes of intense dread—and fears the unpredictable onset of the next episode

- *Phobias,* in which a person is intensely and irrationally afraid of a specific object, activity, or situation

Generalized Anxiety Disorder

For the past two years, Tom, a 27-year-old electrician, has been bothered by dizziness, sweating palms, heart palpitations, and ringing in his ears. He feels on edge and some-times finds himself shaking. With reasonable success, he hides his symptoms from his family and co-workers. But he allows himself few other social contacts, and occasionally he has to leave work. His family doctor and a neurologist can find no physical problem.

Tom's unfocused, out-of-control, agitated feelings suggest a **generalized anxiety disorder,** which is marked by excessive and uncontrollable worry. The symptoms of this disorder are commonplace; their persistence, for six months or more, is not. People with this condition worry continually, and they are often jittery, agitated, and sleep-deprived. Concentration is difficult as attention switches from worry to worry. Their tension and apprehension may leak out through furrowed brows, twitching eyelids, trembling, perspiration, or fidgeting from autonomic nervous system arousal.

The person may not be able to identify, and therefore relieve or avoid, the tension's cause. To use Sigmund Freud's term, the anxiety is *free-floating* (not linked to a specific stressor or threat). Generalized anxiety disorder is often accompanied by depressed mood, but even without depression it tends to be disabling (Hunt et al., 2004; Moffitt et al., 2007b). Moreover, it may lead to physical problems, such as high blood pressure.

Women are twice as likely as men to experience generalized anxiety disorder (McLean & Anderson, 2009). This anxiety gender difference was reflected in a Gallup poll taken eight months after 9/11, when more U.S. women (34 percent) than men (19 percent) said they were still less willing than before 9/11 to go into skyscrapers or fly on planes. And in early 2003, more women (57 percent) than men (36 percent) said they were "somewhat worried" about becoming a terrorist victim (Jones, 2003).

Some people with generalized anxiety disorder were maltreated and inhibited as children (Moffitt et al., 2007a). As time passes, however, emotions tend to mellow, and by age 50, generalized anxiety disorder becomes fairly rare (Rubio & López-Ibor, 2007).

Panic Disorder

For the 1 person in 75 with **panic disorder,** anxiety suddenly escalates into a terrifying panic attack—a minutes-long episode of intense fear that something horrible is about to happen. Physical symptoms, such as irregular heartbeat, chest pains, short-ness of breath, choking, trembling, or dizziness may accompany the panic. One woman recalled suddenly feeling

> hot and as though I couldn't breathe. My heart was racing and I started to sweat and trem-ble and I was sure I was going to faint. Then my fingers started to feel numb and tingly and things seemed unreal. It was so bad I wondered if I was dying and asked my husband to take me to the emergency room. By the time we got there (about 10 minutes) the worst of the attack was over and I just felt washed out (Greist et al., 1986).

anxiety disorders psychological disorders characterized by distressing, persistent anxiety or maladaptive behaviors that reduce anxiety.

generalized anxiety disorder an anxiety disorder in which a person is continually tense, apprehensive, and in a state of autonomic nervous system arousal.

panic disorder an anxiety disorder marked by unpredictable, minutes-long episodes of intense dread in which a person experiences terror and accompanying chest pain, choking, or other frightening sensations. Often followed by worry over a possible next attack.

phobia an anxiety disorder marked by a persistent, irrational fear and avoidance of a specific object, activity, or situation.

MODULE 50: ANXIETY DISORDERS, OCD, AND PTSD **621**

Panicked playing Golfer Charlie Beljan experienced what he later learned were panic attacks during an important tournament. His thumping heartbeat and shortness of breath led him to think he was having a heart attack. But hospital tests revealed that his symptoms, though serious, were not related to a physical illness. He recovered, went on to win $846,000, and has become an inspiration to others.

These anxiety tornados strike suddenly, wreak havoc, and disappear, but they are not forgotten. Ironically, worries about anxiety—perhaps fearing another panic attack, or fearing anxiety-caused sweating in public—can amplify anxiety symptoms (Olatunji & Wolitzky-Taylor, 2009). After several panic attacks, people may avoid situations where the previous panic attacks have struck. If their fear is intense enough, people may develop *agoraphobia*, fear or avoidance of situations in which escape might be difficult when panic strikes. Given such fear, people may avoid being outside the home, in a crowd, on a bus, or in an elevator.

Charles Darwin began suffering panic disorder at age 28, after spending five years sailing the world. Because of the attacks, he moved to the country, avoided social gatherings, and traveled only in his wife's company. But the relative seclusion did free him to focus on developing his evolutionary theory. "Even ill health," he reflected, "has saved me from the distraction of society and its amusements" (quoted in Ma, 1997).

Smokers have at least a doubled risk of panic disorder (Zvolensky & Bernstein, 2005). They also show greater panic symptoms in situations that often produce panic attacks, such as when they hyperventilate (Knuts et al., 2010). Because nicotine is a stimulant, lighting up doesn't lighten up.

Phobias

We all live with some fears. But people with **phobias** are consumed by a persistent, irrational fear and avoidance of some object, activity, or situation. *Specific phobias* may focus on animals, insects, heights, blood, or close spaces (**FIGURE 50.1** on the next page). Many people avoid the triggers, such as high places, that arouse their fear, and they manage to live with their phobia. Others are incapacitated by their efforts to avoid the feared situation. Marilyn, an otherwise healthy and happy 28-year-old, fears thunderstorms so intensely that she feels anxious as soon as a weather forecaster mentions possible storms later in the week. If her husband is away and a storm is forecast, she may stay with a close relative. During a storm, she hides from windows and buries her head to avoid seeing the lightning.

Not all phobias have specific triggers. *Social anxiety disorder* (formerly called "social phobia") is shyness taken to an extreme. People with this disorder have an intense fear of other people's negative judgments. They may avoid potentially embarrassing social situations—such as speaking up, eating out, or going to parties—or they may sweat or tremble when doing so.

▼ FIGURE 50.1

Some common and uncommon specific fears Researchers surveyed Dutch people to identify the most common events or objects they feared. A strong fear becomes a phobia if it provokes a compelling but irrational desire to avoid the dreaded object or situation. (Data from Depla et al., 2008.)

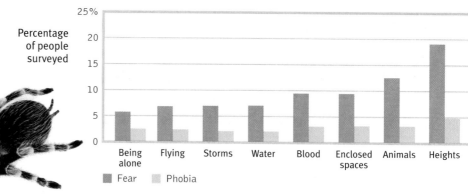

────────── **RETRIEVAL PRACTICE** ──────────

• Unfocused tension, apprehension, and arousal are symptoms of _____ _____ disorder.

ANSWER: generalized anxiety

• Those who experience unpredictable periods of terror and intense dread, accompanied by frightening physical sensations, may be diagnosed with a _____ disorder.

ANSWER: panic

• If a person is focusing anxiety on specific feared objects or situations, that person may have a _____.

ANSWER: phobia

Obsessive-Compulsive Disorder (OCD)

50-2 What is OCD?

"Spin your partner round and round, then spin your partner round again, spin her round six more times, now touch the light switch near the door."

As with the anxiety disorders, we can see aspects of **obsessive-compulsive disorder (OCD)** in our everyday behavior. We all may at times be obsessed with senseless or offensive thoughts that will not go away. Or we may engage in compulsive behaviors, perhaps lining up books and pencils "just so" before studying.

Obsessive thoughts and compulsive behaviors cross the fine line between normality and disorder when they *persistently interfere* with everyday living and cause distress. Checking to see you locked the door is normal; checking 10 times is not. Washing your hands is normal; washing so often that your skin becomes raw is not. (**TABLE 50.1** offers more examples.) At some time during their lives, often during their late teens or twenties, 1 to nearly 3 percent of

obsessive-compulsive disorder (OCD) a disorder characterized by unwanted repetitive thoughts (obsessions), actions (compulsions), or both.

posttraumatic stress disorder (PTSD) a disorder characterized by haunting memories, nightmares, social withdrawal, jumpy anxiety, numbness of feeling, and/or insomnia that lingers for four weeks or more after a traumatic experience.

▼ TABLE 50.1

Common Obsessions and Compulsions Among Children and Adolescents With Obsessive-Compulsive Disorder

Thought or Behavior	Percentage Reporting Symptom
Obsessions (repetitive *thoughts*)	
Concern with dirt, germs, or toxins	40
Something terrible happening (fire, death, illness)	24
Symmetry, order, or exactness	17
Compulsions (repetitive *behaviors*)	
Excessive hand washing, bathing, toothbrushing, or grooming	85
Repeating rituals (in/out of a door, up/down from a chair)	51
Checking doors, locks, appliances, car brakes, homework	46

Source: Data from Rapoport, 1989.

people cross that line from normal preoccupations and fussiness to debilitating disorder (Kessler et al., 2012). An analysis of 14 twin studies showed that OCD has a strong genetic basis (Taylor, 2011). Although the person knows them to be irrational, the anxiety-fueled obsessive thoughts become so haunting, the compulsive rituals so senselessly time-consuming, that effective functioning becomes impossible.

LaunchPad For a 7-minute video illustrating struggles associated with compulsive rituals, visit LaunchPad's Obsessive-Compulsive Disorder: A Young Mother's Struggle.

Former professional basketball player Royce White, who is open about his obsessive-compulsive disorder, said that his wealth allowed him to purchase a large house. What was the most difficult part of his transition to mansion living? "The toughest thing is going around and seeing that dust has collected in a room [I] don't use often. And then I've got to spend 30 minutes dusting that thing" (Wrenn, 2012).

OCD is more common among teens and young adults than among older people (Samuels & Nestadt, 1997). A 40-year follow-up study of 144 Swedish people diagnosed with the disorder found that, for most, the obsessions and compulsions had gradually lessened, though only 1 in 5 had completely recovered (Skoog & Skoog, 1999).

Making everything perfect Soccer star David Beckham has openly discussed his obsessive-compulsive tendencies, which have driven him to line up objects in pairs or to spend hours straightening furniture (Adams, 2011).

Posttraumatic Stress Disorder (PTSD)

50-3 What is PTSD?

As an Iraq war soldier, Jesse "saw the murder of children and women. It was just horrible for anyone to experience." After calling in a helicopter strike on one house where he had seen ammunition crates carried in, he heard the screams of children from within. "I didn't know there were kids there," he recalled. Back home in Texas, he suffered "real bad flashbacks" (Welch, 2005).

Jesse is not alone. In one study of 103,788 veterans returning from Iraq and Afghanistan, 25 percent were diagnosed with a psychological disorder (Seal et al., 2007). Some had *traumatic brain injuries (TBI)*, but the most frequent diagnosis was **posttraumatic stress disorder (PTSD)**. Typical symptoms include recurring haunting memories and nightmares, a numb feeling of social withdrawal, jumpy anxiety, and trouble sleeping (Germain, 2013; Hoge et al., 2004, 2006, 2007; Kessler, 2000). Although many battle-scarred veterans have been diagnosed with PTSD, others also suffer from this disorder. Survivors of accidents, disasters, and violent and sexual assaults (including an estimated two-thirds of prostitutes) have experienced PTSD symptoms (Brewin et al., 1999; Farley et al., 1998; Taylor et al., 1998).

The greater one's emotional distress during a trauma, the higher the risk for post-traumatic symptoms (Ozer et al., 2003). Among American military personnel in Afghanistan, 7.6 percent of combatants and 1.4 percent of noncombatants developed PTSD (McNally, 2012). Among New Yorkers who witnessed or responded to the 9/11 terrorist attacks, most did not experience PTSD (Neria et al., 2011). After experiencing a traumatic life event, about 5 to 10 percent of people develop PTSD (Bonanno et al., 2011). PTSD diagnoses among survivors who had been inside the World Trade Center during the attack were, however, double the rates found among those who were outside (Bonanno et al., 2006).

About half of us will experience at least one traumatic event in our lifetime. Why do some people develop PTSD after a traumatic event, but others don't? Some people may have more sensitive emotion-processing limbic systems that flood their bodies with stress hormones (Kosslyn, 2005; Ozer & Weiss, 2004). PTSD patients have smaller amygdala—that acorn-shaped brain region that governs fear (Morey et al., 2012). Genes and gender also matter. Twins, compared with nontwins, more commonly share PTSD

Bringing the war home Nearly a quarter-million Iraq and Afghanistan war veterans have been diagnosed with PTSD or traumatic brain injury (TBI). Many vets participate in an intensive recovery program using deep breathing, massage, and group and individual discussion techniques to treat their PTSD or TBI.

cognitive risk factors (Gilbertson et al., 2006). And the odds of getting this disorder after a traumatic event are about two times higher for women than for men (Olff et al., 2007; Ozer & Weiss, 2004).

Some psychologists believe that PTSD has been overdiagnosed, due partly to a broadening definition of *trauma* (Dobbs, 2009; McNally, 2003). Too often, say some critics, PTSD gets stretched to include normal bad memories and dreams after a bad experience. In such cases, well-intentioned attempts to have people relive the trauma may amplify their emotions and pathologize normal stress reactions (Wakefield & Spitzer, 2002). For example, survivors may be "debriefed" right after a trauma and asked to revisit the experience and vent emotions. This tactic has been generally ineffective and sometimes harmful (Bonanno et al., 2010).

Most people, male and female, display an impressive *survivor resiliency*, or ability to recover after severe stress (Bonanno et al., 2010). For more on human resilience and on the *posttraumatic growth* that some experience, see Module 54.

RETRIEVAL PRACTICE

- Those who express anxiety through unwanted repetitive thoughts or actions may have a(n) _____-_____ disorder.

ANSWER: obsessive-compulsive

- Those with symptoms of recurring memories and nightmares, social withdrawal, jumpy anxiety, numbness of feeling, and/or insomnia for weeks after a traumatic event may be diagnosed with _____ _____ disorder.

ANSWER: posttraumatic stress

Understanding Anxiety Disorders, OCD, and PTSD

50-4 How do conditioning, cognition, and biology contribute to the feelings and thoughts that mark anxiety disorders, OCD, and PTSD?

Anxiety is both a feeling and a cognition—a doubt-laden appraisal of one's safety or social skill. How do these anxious feelings and cognitions arise? Sigmund Freud's psychoanalytic theory proposed that, beginning in childhood, people *repress* intolerable impulses, ideas, and feelings. This submerged mental energy sometimes, he thought, leaks out in odd symptoms, such as anxious handwashing. Few of today's psychologists share Freud's interpretation of anxiety. Most believe that three modern perspectives—conditioning, cognition, and biology—are more helpful.

Conditioning

Some bad events come with a warning. Your underdog team might lose the big game. You aren't prepared and you may fail your quiz. You're running late and might miss the bus. But when bad events happen unpredictably and uncontrollably, anxiety and other disorders often develop (Field, 2006; Mineka & Oehlberg, 2008). In a classic experiment, an infant called "Little Albert" learned to fear furry objects that were paired with loud noises. In other experiments, researchers have created anxious animals by giving rats unpredictable electric shocks (Schwartz, 1984). The rats, like assault victims who report feeling anxious when returning to the scene of the crime, became uneasy in their lab environment. The lab had become a cue for fear.

Such research helps explain why anxious people are hyperattentive to possible threats, and how panic-prone people come to associate anxiety with certain cues (Bar-Haim et al., 2007; Bouton et al., 2001). In one survey, 58 percent of those with social anxiety disorder experienced their disorder after a traumatic event (Ost & Hugdahl, 1981).

Through conditioning, the short list of naturally painful and frightening events can multiply into a long list of human fears. Can you recall a frightening event that left you fearful for a while? We can. I [DM] was headed home when my car was struck by another when its driver missed a stop sign. For months afterward, I felt a twinge of unease as a car approached from a side street. Likewise, I [ND] remember watching a terrifying movie about spiders, *Arachnophobia*, when a severe thunderstorm struck and the theater lost power. For months, I experienced anxiety at the sight of spiders or harmless cobwebs.

How might conditioning magnify a single painful and frightening event into a full-blown phobia? The answer lies in part in two conditioning processes: *stimulus generalization* and *reinforcement.*

Stimulus generalization occurs when a person experiences a fearful event and later develops a fear of similar events. Each of us [DM and ND] generalized our fears: One of us feared cars approaching from side streets and the other feared spiders. Those fears eventually disappeared, but sometimes fears can linger and grow. Marilyn's thunderstorm phobia may have similarly generalized after a terrifying or painful experience during a thunderstorm.

Once fears and anxieties arise, *reinforcement* helps maintain them. Anything that helps us avoid or escape the feared situation can be reinforcing because it reduces anxiety and gives us a feeling of relief. Fearing a panic attack, we may decide not to leave the house. Reinforced by feeling calmer, we are likely to repeat that maladaptive behavior in the future (Antony et al., 1992). So, too, with compulsive behaviors. If washing our hands relieves our feelings of anxiety, we may wash our hands again when those feelings return.

Cognition

Conditioning influences our feelings of anxiety, but so does cognition—our thoughts, memories, interpretations, and expectations. By observing others, we can learn to fear what they fear. Nearly all monkeys raised in the wild fear snakes, yet lab-raised monkeys do not. Surely, most wild monkeys do not actually suffer snake bites. Do they learn their fear through observation? To find out, Susan Mineka (1985, 2002) experimented with six monkeys raised in the wild (all strongly fearful of snakes) and their lab-raised offspring (virtually none of which feared snakes). After repeatedly observing their parents or peers refusing to reach for food in the presence of a snake, the younger monkeys developed a similar strong fear of snakes. When the monkeys were retested three months later, their learned fear persisted. We humans learn many of our own fears by observing others (Helsen et al., 2011; Olsson et al., 2007).

Our past experiences shape our expectations and influence our interpretations and reactions. Whether we interpret the creaky sound in the old house simply as the wind or as a possible knife-wielding intruder determines whether we panic. People with anxiety disorders tend to be *hypervigilant*. A pounding heart signals a heart attack. A lone spider near the bed becomes a likely infestation. An everyday disagreement with a friend or boss spells possible doom for the relationship. Anxiety is especially common when people cannot switch off such intrusive thoughts and perceive a loss of control and a sense of helplessness (Franklin & Foa, 2011).

Hemera Technologies/PhotoObjects.net/360/Getty Images

Biology

There is, however, more to anxiety disorders, OCD, and PTSD than conditioning and cognitive processes alone. Why will some of us develop lasting phobias or PTSD after suffering traumas? Why do we all learn some fears so readily? Why are some of us more vulnerable? The biological perspective offers insight.

Genes Genes matter. Pair a traumatic event with a sensitive, high-strung temperament and the result may be a new phobia (Belsky & Pluess, 2009). Some of us have genes that make us like orchids—fragile, yet capable of beauty under favorable circumstances. Others of us are like dandelions—hardy, and able to thrive in varied circumstances (Ellis & Boyce, 2008; Pluess & Belsky, 2013).

Among monkeys, fearfulness runs in families. A monkey reacts more strongly to stress if its close biological relatives are anxiously reactive (Suomi, 1986). So, too, with people. If one identical twin has an anxiety disorder, the other is likewise at risk (Hettema et al., 2001; Kendler et al., 2002a,b; Van Houtem et al., 2013). Even when raised separately, identical twins may develop similar phobias (Carey, 1990; Eckert et al., 1981). One pair of 35-year-old female identical twins independently became so afraid of water that each would wade in the ocean backward and only up to the knees.

Given the genetic contribution to anxiety disorders, researchers are now sleuthing the culprit genes. One research team identified 17 gene variations associated with typical anxiety disorder symptoms (Hovatta et al., 2005). Other teams have found genes associated specifically with OCD (Taylor, 2013).

Genes can influence disorders by regulating neurotransmitters. Some studies point to an "anxiety gene" that affects brain levels of *serotonin*, a neurotransmitter that influences sleep, mood, and attention to negative images (Canli, 2008; Pergamin-Hight et al., 2012). Other studies implicate genes that regulate the neurotransmitter *glutamate* (Lafleur et al., 2006; Welch et al., 2007). With too much glutamate, the brain's alarm centers become overactive.

Among PTSD patients, a history of child abuse leaves long-term *epigenetic* marks, increasing the likelihood that a genetic vulnerability to the disorder will be expressed (Mehta et al., 2013). Suicide victims show a similar epigenetic effect (McGowan et al., 2009).

The Brain Our experiences change our brain, paving new pathways. Traumatic fear-learning experiences can leave tracks in the brain, creating fear circuits within the amygdala (Etkin & Wager, 2007; Kolassa & Elbert, 2007; Herringa et al., 2013). These fear pathways create easy inroads for more fear experiences (Armony et al., 1998).

Anxiety-related disorders differ from one another, but they all involve biological events. In OCD, for example, when the disordered brain detects that something is amiss, it generates a mental hiccup of repeating thoughts (obsessions) or actions (compulsions) (Gehring et al., 2000). Brain scans of people with PTSD show higher-than-normal activity in the amygdala when they view traumatic images (Nutt & Malizia, 2004). Brain scans of people with OCD reveal elevated activity in specific brain areas during behaviors such as compulsive hand washing, checking, ordering, or hoarding (Insel, 2010; Mataix-Cols et al., 2004, 2005). These brain areas are not only more active among people with OCD, they are also enlarged (Rotge et al., 2010). As **FIGURE 50.2** shows, the *anterior cingulate cortex*, a brain region that monitors our actions and checks for errors, seems especially likely to be hyperactive (Maltby et al., 2005). When deciding to get rid of one's personal possessions, those with hoarding disorder also show elevated activity in the anterior cingulate cortex (Tolin et al., 2012).

Some antidepressant drugs dampen this fear-circuit activity and its associated obsessive-compulsive behavior. Fears can also be blunted by giving people drugs as they recall and then rerecord ("reconsolidate") a traumatic experience (Kindt et al., 2009; Norberg, et al., 2008). Although they don't forget the experience, the associated emotion is largely erased.

Natural Selection We seem biologically prepared to fear threats faced by our ancestors. Our phobias focus on such specific fears: spiders, snakes, and other animals; enclosed spaces and heights; storms and darkness. (Those fearless about these occasional threats were less likely to survive and leave descendants.) Thus, even in Britain, with only one poisonous snake species, people often fear snakes. It is easy to

▼ FIGURE 50.2
An obsessive-compulsive brain Neuroscientists Nicholas Maltby, David Tolin, and their colleagues (2005) used functional MRI scans to compare the brains of those with and without OCD as they engaged in a challenging cognitive task. The scans of those with OCD showed elevated activity in the anterior cingulate cortex in the brain's frontal area (indicated by the yellow area on the far right).

Reprinted from NeuroImage, 24, Maltby, N., Tolin, D.F., Worhunsky, P., O'Keefe, T. M., & Kiehl, K. A, Dysfunctional action monitoring hyperactivates frontal-striatal circuits in obsessive-compulsive disorder: An event-related fMRI study, 495–503, 2005, with permission from Elsevier.

Fearless The biological perspective helps us understand why most of us have more fear of heights than does Felix Baumgartner, shown here skydiving from 24 miles above the Earth in 2012.

condition and hard to extinguish fears of such "evolutionarily relevant" stimuli (Coelho & Purkis, 2009; Davey, 1995; Öhman, 2009). Some of our modern fears can also have an evolutionary explanation. A fear of flying may be rooted in our biological predisposition to fear confinement and heights.

Compare our easily conditional fears to what we *do not* easily learn to fear. World War II air raids, for example, produced remarkably few lasting phobias. As the air blitzes continued, the British, Japanese, and German populations did not become more and more panicked. Rather, they grew more indifferent to planes outside their immediate neighborhoods (Mineka & Zinbarg, 1996). Evolution has not prepared us to fear bombs dropping from the sky.

Just as our phobias focus on dangers faced by our ancestors, our compulsive acts typically exaggerate behaviors that contributed to our species' survival. Grooming gone wild becomes hair pulling. Washing up becomes ritual hand washing. Checking territorial boundaries becomes rechecking an already locked door (Rapoport, 1989).

RETRIEVAL PRACTICE

• Researchers believe that conditioning and cognitive processes contribute to anxiety disorders, OCD, and PTSD. What *biological* factors also contribute to these disorders?

ANSWER: Biological factors include inherited temperament differences and other gene variations; learned fears that have altered brain pathways; and outdated, inherited responses that had survival value for our distant ancestors.

MODULE 50 REVIEW Anxiety Disorders, OCD, and PTSD

LEARNING OBJECTIVES

RETRIEVAL PRACTICE Take a moment to answer each of these Learning Objective Questions (repeated here from within this module). Then turn to Appendix C, Complete Module Reviews, to check your answers. Research suggests that trying to answer these questions on your own will improve your long-term retention (McDaniel et al., 2009).

50-1 How do generalized anxiety disorder, panic disorder, and phobias differ?

50-2 What is OCD?

50-3 What is PTSD?

50-4 How do conditioning, cognition, and biology contribute to the feelings and thoughts that mark anxiety disorders, OCD, and PTSD?

TERMS AND CONCEPTS TO REMEMBER

RETRIEVAL PRACTICE Test yourself on these terms by trying to write down the definition before flipping back to check your answers.

anxiety disorders, p. 620

generalized anxiety disorder, p. 620

panic disorder, p. 620

phobia, p. 621

obsessive-compulsive disorder (OCD), p. 622

posttraumatic stress disorder (PTSD), p. 623

Use 🔁 LearningCurve to create your personalized study plan, which will direct you to the resources that will help you most in 🔁 LaunchPad.

51 Depressive Disorders and Bipolar Disorder

51-1 How do major depressive disorder, persistent depressive disorder, and bipolar disorder differ?

Most of us will have some direct or indirect experience with depression. If you are like many college students, at some time during this year—more likely the dark months of winter than the bright days of summer—you may experience some of depression's symptoms. You might feel deeply discouraged about the future, dissatisfied with your life, or socially isolated. You may lack the energy to get things done or even to force yourself out of bed; be unable to concentrate, eat, or sleep normally; or even wonder if you would be better off dead. Perhaps academic success came easily to you before, but now you find that disappointing grades jeopardize your goals. Maybe social stress, such as loneliness, feeling you are the target of prejudice, or experiencing a romantic breakup, have plunged you into despair. And per-

Brad Wenner/Moment Select/Getty Images

haps low self-esteem increases your brooding, worsening your self-torment (Sowislo & Orth, 2012). Likely you think you are more alone in having such negative feelings than you really are (Jordan et al., 2011). In one national survey of American collegians, 31 percent said they had at some time in the past year, "felt so depressed that it was difficult to function" (ACHA, 2009). Misery has more company than most suppose.

Joy, contentment, sadness, and despair exist at different points on a continuum, points at which any of us may find ourselves at any given moment. To feel bad in reaction to profoundly sad events is to be in touch with reality. In such times, there is an up side to being down. Sadness is like a car's low-fuel light—a signal that warns us to stop and take appropriate measures. Biologically speaking, life's purpose is not happiness but survival and reproduction. Coughing, vomiting, swelling, and pain protect the body from dangerous toxins. Similarly, depression resembles a sort of psychic hibernation: It slows us down, defuses aggression, helps us let go of unattainable goals, and restrains risk taking (Andrews & Thomson, 2009a,b; Wrosch & Miller, 2009). When we grind temporarily to a halt and reassess our life, as depressed people do, we can redirect our energy in more promising ways (Watkins, 2008). We may also make better decisions. Even mild sadness can improve people's recall, make them more discerning, and help them make complex decisions (Forgas, 2009). It can also help them process and recall faces more accurately (Hills et al., 2011). There is sense to suffering.

But sometimes this response, taken to an extreme, can become seriously maladaptive and signal a disorder. The difference between a blue mood after bad news and a depression-related disorder is like the difference between gasping for breath after a hard run and being chronically short of breath.

In this module, we consider three disorders in which depression impairs daily living:

- *Major depressive disorder*, a persistent state of hopelessness and lethargy
- *Persistent depressive disorder*, in which a person experiences milder depressive feelings
- *Bipolar disorder* (formerly called *manic-depressive disorder*), in which a person alternates between depression and overexcited hyperactivity

"My life had come to a sudden stop. I was able to breathe, to eat, to drink, to sleep. I could not, indeed, help doing so; but there was no real life in me."

Leo Tolstoy, *My Confession*, 1887

"If someone offered you a pill that would make you permanently happy, you would be well advised to run fast and run far. Emotion is a compass that tells us what to do, and a compass that is perpetually stuck on NORTH is worthless."

Daniel Gilbert, "The Science of Happiness," 2006

Major Depressive Disorder

Major depressive disorder occurs when at least five signs of depression last two or more weeks (**TABLE 51.1**). The symptoms must cause near-daily distress or impairment and not be attributable to substance use or another medical or mental illness.

To sense what major depression feels like, suggest some clinicians, imagine combining the anguish of grief with the sluggishness of bad jet lag. If stress-related anxiety is a "crackling, menacing brushfire," noted biologist Robert Sapolsky (2003), "depression is a suffocating heavy blanket thrown on top of it."

▼ TABLE 51.1
Diagnosing Major Depressive Disorder

The DSM-5 classifies major depressive disorder as the presence of at least five of the following symptoms over a two-week period of time (minimally including depressed mood or reduced interest (American Psychiatric Association, 2013).

- Depressed mood most of the time
- Dramatically reduced interest or enjoyment in most activities most of the time
- Significant challenges regulating appetite and weight
- Significant challenges regulating sleep
- Physical agitation or lethargy
- Feeling listless or with much less energy
- Feeling worthless; or feeling unwarranted guilt
- Problems in thinking, concentrating, or making decisions
- Thinking repetitively of death and suicide

Adults diagnosed with persistent depressive disorder (also called *dysthymia*) experience a mildly depressed mood more often than not for two years or more (American Psychiatric Association, 2013). They also display at least two of the following symptoms:

- Difficulty with decision-making and concentration
- Feeling hopeless
- Poor self-esteem
- Reduced energy levels
- Problems regulating sleep
- Problems regulating appetite

Bipolar Disorder

With or without therapy, episodes of major depression usually end, and people temporarily or permanently return to their previous behavior patterns. However, some people rebound to, or sometimes start with, the opposite emotional extreme—the hyperactive, overly talkative, wildly optimistic state of **mania**. If depression is living in slow motion, mania is fast forward. Alternating between depression and mania signals **bipolar disorder.**

Adolescent mood swings, from rage to bubbly, can, when prolonged, lead to a bipolar diagnosis. Between 1994 and 2003, diagnoses of bipolar disorder swelled. U.S. National Center for Health Statistics annual physician surveys revealed an astonishing 40-fold increase in bipolar disorder diagnoses in those 19 and under—from an estimated 20,000 to 800,000 (Carey, 2007; Flora & Bobby, 2008; Moreno et al., 2007). Americans are twice as likely as people of other countries to have ever had a diagnosis of bipolar disorder

major depressive disorder a disorder in which a person experiences, in the absence of drugs or another medical condition, two or more weeks with five or more symptoms, at least one of which must be either (1) depressed mood or (2) loss of interest or pleasure.

mania a hyperactive, wildly optimistic state in which dangerously poor judgment is common.

bipolar disorder a disorder in which a person alternates between the hopelessness and lethargy of depression and the overexcited state of mania. (Formerly called *manic-depressive disorder.*)

Bipolar disorder Artist Abigail Southworth illustrated her experience of bipolar disorder.

Percentage Answering *Yes* When Asked "Have You Cried Today?"

	Percentage who cried	
	Men	Women
August	4%	7%
December	8%	21%

Source: Time/CNN survey, 1994

(Merikangas et al., 2011). The new popularity of the diagnosis, given in two-thirds of the cases to boys, has profited companies whose drugs are prescribed to lessen mood swings. Under the new DSM-5 classifications, the number of child and adolescent bipolar diagnoses will likely decline, because some individuals with emotional volatility will be diagnosed with *disruptive mood dysregulation disorder* (Miller, 2010).

During the manic phase, people with bipolar disorder typically have little need for sleep. They show fewer sexual inhibitions. Their positive emotions persist abnormally (Gruber, 2011; Gruber et al., 2013). Their speech is loud, flighty, and hard to interrupt. They find advice irritating. Yet they need protection from their own poor judgment, which may lead to reckless spending or unsafe sex. Thinking fast feels good, but it also increases risk taking (Chandler & Pronin, 2012; Pronin, 2013).

For some people suffering depressive disorders or bipolar disorder, symptoms may have a *seasonal pattern*. Depression may regularly return each fall or winter, and mania (or a reprieve from depression) may dependably arrive with spring. For many others, winter darkness simply means more blue moods. When asked "Have you cried today?" Americans have agreed more often in the winter (**TABLE 51.2**).

In milder forms, mania's energy and flood of ideas fuel creativity. George Frideric Handel, who may have suffered from a mild form of bipolar disorder, composed his nearly four-hour-long *Messiah* (1742) during three weeks of intense, creative energy (Keynes, 1980). Robert Schumann composed 51 musical works during two years of mania (1840 and 1849) but none during 1844, when he was severely depressed (Slater & Meyer, 1959). Those who rely on precision and logic, such as architects, designers, and journalists, suffer bipolar disorder less often than do those who rely on emotional expression and vivid imagery (Ludwig, 1995). Composers, artists, poets, novelists, and entertainers seem especially prone (Jamison, 1993, 1995; Kaufman & Baer, 2002; Ludwig, 1995). Indeed, one analysis of over a million individuals showed that the only psychiatric condition linked to working in a creative profession was bipolar disorder (Kyaga et al., 2013). As one staff member said of the great leader Winston Churchill, "He's either on the crest of the wave, or in the trough" (Ghaemi, 2011).

It is as true of emotions as of everything else: What goes up comes down. Before long, the elated mood either returns to normal or plunges into a depression. Though bipolar disorder is much less common than major depressive disorder, it is often more dysfunctional, claiming twice as many lost workdays yearly (Kessler et al., 2006). It afflicts adult men and women about equally.

Creativity and bipolar disorder There have been many creative artists, composers, writers, and musical performers with bipolar disorder.

Actor Russell Brand

Writer Virginia Woolf

Humorist Samuel Clemens (Mark Twain)

Understanding Depressive Disorders and Bipolar Disorder

51-2 How can the biological and social-cognitive perspectives help us understand depressive disorders and bipolar disorder?

In thousands of studies, psychologists continue to accumulate evidence to help explain why people have depressive disorders and bipolar disorder and to design more effective ways to treat and prevent them. Here, we focus primarily on depressive disorders. One research group summarized the facts that any theory of depression must explain, including the following (Lewinsohn et al., 1985, 1998, 2003):

- *Many behavioral and cognitive changes accompany depression.* People trapped in a depressed mood become inactive and feel unmotivated. They are sensitive to negative events (Peckham et al., 2010). They more often recall negative information. They expect negative outcomes (my team will lose, my grades will fall, my love will fail). When the depression lifts, these behavioral and cognitive accompaniments disappear. Nearly half the time, people also exhibit symptoms of another disorder, such as anxiety or substance abuse.

- *Depression is widespread.* Worldwide, more than 350 million people suffer depression (WHO, 2012). Although phobias are more common, depression is the number-one reason people seek mental health services. At some point during their lifetime, depression plagues 12 percent of Canadian adults and 17 percent of U.S. adults (Holden, 2010; Patten et al., 2006). Moreover, depression is the leading cause of disability worldwide (Ferrari et al., 2013). Depression's commonality suggests that its causes, too, must be common.

- *Women's risk of major depression is nearly double men's.* In 2009, when Gallup pollsters asked more than a quarter-million Americans if they had ever been diagnosed with depression, 13 percent of men and 22 percent of women said they had (Pelham, 2009). When Gallup asked Americans if they had experienced sadness "during a lot of the day yesterday," 17 percent of men and 28 percent of women answered *Yes* (Mendes & McGeeney, 2012). The depression gender gap has been found worldwide (**FIGURE 51.1**). The trend begins in adolescence; preadolescent girls are not more depression-prone than are boys (Hyde et al., 2008). With adolescence, girls often think and fret more about their bodies.

  The factors that put women at risk for depression (genetic predispositions, child abuse, low self-esteem, marital problems, and so forth) similarly put men at risk (Kendler et al., 2006). Yet women are more vulnerable to disorders involving internalized states, such as depression, anxiety, and inhibited sexual desire. Women experience more situations that may increase their risk for depression, such as receiving less pay for equal work, juggling multiple roles, and caring for children

Life after depression J. K. Rowling, author of the Harry Potter books, reported suffering acute depression—a "dark time," with suicidal thoughts—between ages 25 and 28. It was a "terrible place," she said, but it formed a foundation that allowed her "to come back stronger" (McLaughlin, 2010).

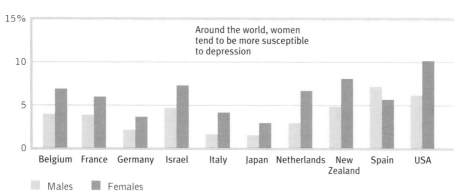

Percentage of adults experiencing major depression in previous 12 months

Around the world, women tend to be more susceptible to depression

Males   Females

Belgium France Germany Israel Italy Japan Netherlands New Zealand Spain USA

▼ **FIGURE 51.1 Gender and major depression** Interviews with 89,037 adults in 18 countries (10 of which are shown here) confirm what many smaller studies have found: Women's risk of major depression is nearly double that of men's. (Data from Bromet et al., 2011.)

and elderly family members (Freeman & Freeman, 2013). Men's disorders tend to be more external—alcohol use disorder, antisocial conduct, lack of impulse control. When women get sad, they often get sadder than men do. When men get mad, they often get madder than women do.

- *Most major depressive episodes self-terminate.* Therapy often helps and tends to speed recovery. But even without professional help, most people recover from major depression and return to normal. The plague of depression comes and, a few weeks or months later, it goes, though for some (about half), it eventually returns (Burcusa & Iacono, 2007; Curry et al., 2011; Hardeveld et al., 2010). Only about 20 percent experience chronic depression (Klein, 2010). On average, a person with major depressive disorder today will spend about three-fourths of the next decade in a normal, nondepressed state (Furukawa et al., 2009). Recovery is more likely to be permanent the later the first episode strikes, the longer the person stays well, the fewer the previous episodes, the less stress experienced, and the more social support received (Belsher & Costello, 1988; Fergusson & Woodward, 2002; Kendler et al., 2001).

- *Stressful events related to work, marriage, and close relationships often precede depression.* As anxiety is a response to the threat of future loss, depression is often a response to past and current loss. About 1 person in 4 diagnosed with depression has been brought down by a significant loss or trauma, such as a loved one's death, a ruptured marriage, a physical assault, or a lost job (Kendler et al., 2008; Monroe & Reid, 2009; Orth et al., 2009; Wakefield et al., 2007). Minor daily stressors can also leave emotional scars. People who overreacted to minor stressors, such as a broken appliance, were more often depressed 10 years later (Charles et al., 2013). Moving to a new culture can also increase depression, especially among younger people who have not yet formed their identities (Zhang et al., 2013). One long-term study (Kendler, 1998) tracked rates of depression in 2000 people. The risk of depression ranged from less than 1 percent among those who had experienced no stressful life event in the preceding month to 24 percent among those who had experienced three such events in that month.

- *With each new generation, depression strikes earlier (now often in the late teens) and affects more people, with the highest rates in developed countries among young adults.* This trend has been reported in Canada, the United States, England, France, Germany, Italy, Lebanon, New Zealand, Puerto Rico, and Taiwan (Collishaw et al., 2007; Cross-National Collaborative Group, 1992; Kessler et al., 2010; Twenge et al., 2008). In one study, 12 percent of Australian adolescents reported symptoms of depression (Sawyer et al., 2000). Most hid it from their parents; almost 90 percent of those parents perceived their depressed teen as *not* suffering depression. In North America, young adults are three times more likely than their grandparents to report having recently—or ever—suffered depression (despite the grandparents' many more years of being at risk). The increase appears partly authentic, but it may also reflect today's young adults' greater willingness to disclose depression.

Armed with these points of understanding, today's researchers propose biological and cognitive explanations of depression, often combined in a biopsychosocial perspective.

The Biological Perspective

Genetic Influences Depressive disorders and bipolar disorder run in families. As one researcher noted, emotions are "postcards from our genes" (Plotkin, 1994). The risk of major depression and bipolar disorder increases if you have a parent or sibling with the disorder (Sullivan et al., 2000). If one identical twin is diagnosed with major depressive disorder, the chances are about 1 in 2 that at some time the other twin will be, too. This effect is even stronger for bipolar disorder: If one identical twin has it, the chances are 7 in 10 that the other twin will at some point be diagnosed similarly—even if the twins were raised apart (DiLalla et al., 1996). Among fraternal twins, the corresponding odds are just under 2 in 10 (Tsuang & Faraone, 1990). Summarizing the major twin studies (see **FIGURE 51.2**), one research team estimated the heritability of major depressive disorder (the extent to which individual differences are attributable to genes) at 37 percent (Bienvenu et al., 2011).

To tease out the genes that put people at risk for depression, some researchers have turned to *linkage analysis*. First, geneticists find families in which the disorder appears across several generations. Next, the researchers examine DNA from affected and unaffected family members, looking for differences. Linkage analysis points them to a chromosome neighborhood; "A house-to-house search is then needed to find the culprit gene" (Plomin & McGuffin, 2003). Such studies reinforce the view that depression is a complex condition. Many genes work together, producing a mosaic of small effects that interact with other factors to put some people at greater risk. If culprit gene variations can be identified—so far, chromosome 3 genes have been implicated in separate British and American studies (Breen et al., 2011; Pergadia et al., 2011)—they may open the door to more effective drug therapy.

The Depressed Brain Scanning devices open a window on the brain's activity during depressed and manic states. One study gave 13 elite Canadian swimmers the wrenching experience of watching a video of the swim in which they failed to make the Olympic team or failed at the Olympic games (Davis et al., 2008). Functional MRI scans showed the disappointed swimmers experiencing brain activity patterns similar to those of patients with depressed moods.

Many studies have found diminished brain activity during slowed-down depressive states, and more activity during periods of mania (**FIGURE 51.3**). The left frontal lobe and an adjacent brain reward center become more active during positive emotions, (Davidson et al., 2002; Heller et al., 2009; Robinson et al., 2012). In studies of depressed people, MRI scans also found their frontal lobes were smaller than normal (Coffey et al., 1993; Ribeiz et al., 2013; Steingard et al., 2002). Other studies show that the *hippocampus*, the memory-processing center linked with the brain's emotional circuitry, is vulnerable to stress-related damage.

Neuroscientists have also discovered altered brain structures in people with bipolar disorder. One analysis discovered decreased white matter and enlarged fluid-filled ventricles (Arnone et al., 2009).

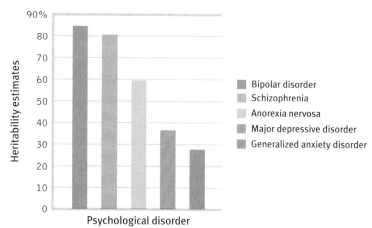

▼ FIGURE 51.2
The heritability of various psychological disorders Researchers Joseph Bienvenu, Dimitry Davydow, and Kenneth Kendler (2011) aggregated data from studies of identical and fraternal twins to estimate the heritability of bipolar disorder, schizophrenia, anorexia nervosa, major depressive disorder, and generalized anxiety disorder.

Depressed state (May 17) **Manic state** (May 18) **Depressed state** (May 27)

▼ FIGURE 51.3
The ups and downs of bipolar disorder These top-facing PET scans show that brain energy consumption rises and falls with the patient's emotional switches. Red areas are where the brain rapidly consumes glucose.

Courtesy of Drs. Lewis Baxter and Michael E. Phelps, UCLA School of Medicine

Neurotransmitter systems also influence depressive disorders and bipolar disorder. *Norepinephrine,* which increases arousal and boosts mood, is scarce during depression and overabundant during mania. (Drugs that decrease mania reduce norepinephrine.) Many people with a history of depression also have a history of habitual smoking (Pasco et al., 2008). Once the urge to smoke is ignited, depression also makes it more difficult to quit (Hitsman et al., 2012). This may indicate an attempt to self-medicate with inhaled nicotine, which can temporarily increase norepinephrine and boost mood (HMHL, 2002).

Researchers are also exploring a second neurotransmitter, *serotonin* (Carver et al., 2008). One well-publicized study of New Zealand young adults found that the recipe for depression combined two necessary ingredients—significant life stress plus a variation of a serotonin-controlling gene (Caspi et al., 2003; Moffitt et al., 2006). Depression arose from the combination of an adverse environment plus a genetic susceptibility, but not from either alone. But stay tuned: The story of gene-environment interactions is still being written, as other researchers debate the reliability of this result (Caspi et al., 2010; Culverhouse et al., 2013; Karg et al., 2011; Munafò et al., 2009; Uher & McGuffin, 2010).

Drugs that relieve depression tend to increase norepinephrine or serotonin supplies by blocking either their reuptake (as Prozac, Zoloft, and Paxil do with serotonin) or their chemical breakdown. Repetitive physical exercise, such as jogging, reduces depression because it increases serotonin, which affects mood and arousal (Airan et al., 2007; Ilardi, 2009; Jacobs, 1994). In one study, running for two hours increased brain activation in regions associated with euphoria (Boecker et al., 2008). To run away from a bad mood, you can use your own two feet.

Nutritional Effects What's good for the heart is also good for the brain and mind. People who eat a heart-healthy "Mediterranean diet" (heavy on vegetables, fish, and olive oil) have a comparatively low risk of developing heart disease, stroke, late-life cognitive decline, and depression—all of which are associated with inflammation (Dowlati et al., 2010; Psaltopoulou et al., 2013; Sánchez-Villegas et al., 2009; Tangney et al., 2011). Excessive alcohol use also correlates with depression—mostly because alcohol misuse leads to depression (Fergusson et al., 2009).

The Social-Cognitive Perspective

Biological influences contribute to depression, but in the nature–nurture dance, our actions also play a part. Diet, drugs, stress, and other life experiences lay down *epigenetic marks,* which are often organic molecules. These molecular tags attach to our chromosomes and turn certain genes on or off. Animal studies suggest that epigenetic influences may play a long-lasting role in depression (Nestler, 2011).

Thinking matters, too. The *social-cognitive perspective* explores how people's assumptions and expectations influence what they perceive. Depressed people view life through the dark glasses of low self-esteem (Kuster et al., 2012; Sowislo & Orth, 2012). Their intensely negative assumptions about themselves, their situation, and their future lead them to magnify bad experiences and minimize good ones (Wenze et al., 2012). Listen to Norman, a Canadian college professor, recalling his depression:

> I [despaired] of ever being human again. I honestly felt subhuman, lower than the lowest vermin. Furthermore, I was self-deprecatory and could not understand why anyone would want to associate with me, let alone love me. . . . I was positive that I was a fraud and a phony and that I didn't deserve my Ph.D. I didn't deserve to have tenure; I didn't deserve to be a Full Professor. . . . I didn't deserve the research grants I had been awarded; I couldn't understand how I had written books and journal articles. . . . I must have conned a lot of people. (Endler, 1982, pp. 45–49)

Expecting the worst, depressed people's *self-defeating beliefs* and their *negative explanatory style* feed depression's vicious cycle.

Negative Thoughts and Negative Moods Interact Self-defeating beliefs may arise from *learned helplessness*, the hopelessness and passive resignation animals and humans learn when they experience uncontrollable painful events. Learned helplessness has been found more often in women than in men, and women may respond more strongly to stress (Hankin & Abramson, 2001; Mazure et al., 2002; Nolen-Hoeksema, 2001, 2003). For example, 38 percent of women and 17 percent of men entering American colleges and universities have reported feeling at least occasionally "overwhelmed by all I have to do" (Pryor et al., 2006). (Men reported spending more time in "light anxiety" activities such as sports, TV watching, and partying, possibly avoiding activities that might make them feel overwhelmed.) This gender difference may help explain why, beginning in their early teens, women have been nearly twice as vulnerable to depression. Susan Nolen-Hoeksema (2003) related women's higher risk of depression to what she described as their tendency to ruminate or *overthink*. **Rumination**—staying focused on a problem (thanks to the continuous firing of a frontal lobe area that sustains attention)—can be adaptive (Altamirano et al., 2010; Andrews & Thomson, 2009a,b). But relentless, self-focused rumination can divert us from thinking about other life tasks, and can increase negative moods (Kuppens et al., 2010; Kuster et al., 2012).

Even so, why do life's unavoidable failures lead only some people to become depressed? The answer lies partly in their *explanatory style*—who or what they blame for their failures. Think of how you might feel if you failed a test. If you can externalize the blame ("What an unfair test!"), you are more likely to feel angry. If you blame yourself, you probably will feel stupid and depressed.

So it is with depressed people, who often explain bad events in terms that are *stable* ("It's going to last forever"), *global* ("It's going to affect everything I do"), and *internal* ("It's all my fault") (**FIGURE 51.4**). Depression-prone people respond to bad events in an especially self-focused, self-blaming way (Mor & Winquist, 2002; Pyszczynski et al., 1991; Wood et al., 1990a,b). When they describe themselves, their brains activate in a region that processes self-relevant information (Sarsam et al., 2013). Their self-esteem is also more plastic—it climbs with praise and plummets with threats (Butler et al., 1994).

Pessimistic, overgeneralized, self-blaming attributions may create a depressing sense of hopelessness (Abramson et al., 1989; Panzarella et al., 2006). As Martin Seligman has

Susan Nolen-Hoeksema (1959–2013) "This epidemic of morbid meditation is a disease that women suffer much more than men. Women can ruminate about anything and everything—our appearance, our families, our career, our health." *(Women Who Think Too Much: How to Break Free of Overthinking and Reclaim Your Life,* 2003)

> **rumination** compulsive fretting; *overthinking* about our problems and their causes.

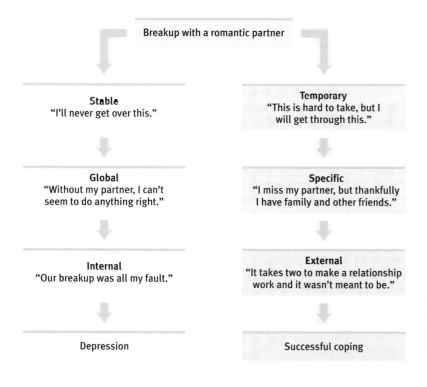

▼ **FIGURE 51.4**
Explanatory style and depression
After a negative experience, a depression-prone person may respond with a negative explanatory style.

"You should never engage in unsupervised introspection."

"Man never reasons so much and becomes so introspective as when he suffers, since he is anxious to get at the cause of his sufferings."

Luigi Pirandello,
Six Characters in Search of an Author, 1922

"Some cause happiness wherever they go; others, whenever they go."

Irish writer Oscar Wilde (1854–1900)

noted, "A recipe for severe depression is preexisting pessimism encountering failure" (1991, p. 78). What then might we expect of new college students who are not depressed but do exhibit a pessimistic explanatory style? In one study, Lauren Alloy and her colleagues (1999) monitored students every 6 weeks for 2.5 years. Among those identified as having a pessimistic thinking style, 17 percent had a first episode of major depression, as did only 1 percent of those who began college with an optimistic thinking style.

Why is depression so common among young Westerners? Seligman (1991, 1995) has pointed to the rise of individualism and the decline of commitment to religion and family, which forces young people to take responsibility for failure or rejection. In non-Western cultures, where close-knit relationships and cooperation are the norm, major depression is less common and less tied to self-blame over personal failure (Ferrari et al., 2013; WHO, 2004a). In Japan, for example, depressed people instead tend to report feeling shame over letting others down (Draguns, 1990a).

Critics note a chicken-and-egg problem nesting in the social-cognitive explanation of depression. Which comes first? The pessimistic explanatory style, or the depressed mood? Certainly, the negative explanations *coincide* with a depressed mood, and they are *indicators* of depression. But do they *cause* depression, any more than a speedometer's reading 70 mph *causes* a car's speed? Before or after being depressed, people's thoughts are less negative. Perhaps a depressed mood triggers negative thoughts. If you temporarily put people in a bad or sad mood, their memories, judgments, and expectations suddenly become more pessimistic. Memory researchers understand this tendency to recall experiences that are consistent with one's current good or bad mood. They call it *state-dependent memory.*

Depression's Vicious Cycle Depression is both a cause and an effect of stressful experiences that disrupt our sense of who we are and why we are worthy human beings. Such disruptions can lead to brooding, which amplifies negative feelings. Being withdrawn, self-focused, and complaining can in turn elicit rejection (Furr & Funder, 1998; Gotlib & Hammen, 1992). One study set up brief phone conversations between participants and people who did or did not have depression. After the conversation, participants could accept or reject the other person. The result? They rejected depression-prone people more often. The participants also noted that they felt more depressed, anxious, and hostile after speaking with depressed people (Coyne, 1976). Indeed, people in the throes of depression are at high risk for divorce, job loss, and other stressful life events. Weary of the person's fatigue, hopeless attitude, and lethargy, a spouse may threaten to leave or a boss may begin to question the person's competence. (This provides another example of genetic-environmental interaction: People genetically predisposed to depression more often experience depressing events.) Rejection and depression feed each other. Misery may love another's company, but company does not love another's misery.

We can now assemble some of the pieces of the depression puzzle (**FIGURE 51.5**): (1) Negative, stressful events interpreted through (2) a ruminating, pessimistic explanatory style create (3) a hopeless, depressed state that (4) hampers the way the person thinks and acts. This, in turn, fuels (1) negative, stressful experiences such as rejection. Depression is a snake that bites its own tail.

None of us are immune to the dejection, diminished self-esteem, and negative thinking brought on by rejection or defeat. Even small losses can temporarily sour our thinking. In one study, researchers studied some avid Indiana University basketball fans who seemed to regard the team as an extension of themselves (Hirt et al., 1992). After the fans watched their team lose or win, the researchers asked them to predict the team's future performance and their own. After a loss, the morose fans offered bleaker assessments not only of the team's future but also of their own likely performance at throwing darts, solving anagrams, and getting a date. When things aren't going our way, it may seem as though they never will.

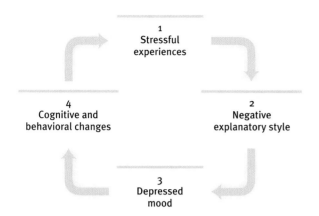

▼ FIGURE 51.5
The vicious cycle of depressed thinking Therapists recognize this cycle, and they work to help depressed people break out of it. Each of the bottom three points offers an exit to work toward: 2. Reverse self-blame and a negative outlook. 3. Turn attention outward. 4. Engage in more pleasant activities and more competent behavior.

It is a cycle we can all recognize. Bad moods feed on themselves: When we feel down, we think negatively and remember bad experiences. Abraham Lincoln was so withdrawn and brooding as a young man that his friends feared he might take his own life (Kline, 1974). Poet Emily Dickinson was so afraid of bursting into tears in public that she spent much of her adult life in seclusion (Patterson, 1951). As their lives remind us, people can and do struggle through depression. Most regain their capacity to love, to work, and even to succeed at the highest levels.

Suicide and Self-Injury

51-3 What factors increase the risk of suicide, and what do we know about nonsuicidal self-injury?

Each year over 800,000 despairing people worldwide will elect a permanent solution to what might have been a temporary problem (WHO, 2014). For those who have been depressed, the risk of suicide is at least five times greater than for the general population (Bostwick & Pankratz, 2000). People seldom commit suicide while in the depths of depression, when energy and initiative are lacking. The risk increases when they begin to rebound and become capable of following through.

Comparing the suicide rates of different groups, researchers have found

- *national differences:* Britain's, Italy's, and Spain's suicide rates are little more than half those of Canada, Australia, and the United States. Austria's and Finland's are about double (WHO, 2011). Within Europe, people in the most suicide-prone country (Belarus) have been 16 times more likely to kill themselves than those in the least (Georgia).

- *racial differences:* Within the United States, Whites and Native Americans kill themselves twice as often as Blacks, Hispanics, and Asians (CDC, 2012).

- *gender differences:* Women are much more likely than men to attempt suicide (WHO, 2011). But men are two to four times more likely (depending on the country) to actually end their lives. Men use more lethal methods, such as firing a bullet into the head, the method of choice in 6 of 10 U.S. suicides.

- *age differences and trends:* In late adulthood, rates increase, peaking in middle age and beyond. In the last half of the twentieth century, the global rate of annual suicide deaths nearly doubled (WHO, 2008).

- *other group differences:* Suicide rates have been much higher among the rich, the nonreligious, and those who were single, widowed, or divorced (Hoyer & Lund, 1993; Okada & Samreth, 2013; Stack, 1992; Stengel, 1981). Witnessing physical pain and trauma can increase the risk of suicide, which may help explain physicians' elevated suicide rates (Bender et al., 2012; Cornette et al., 2009). Gay and lesbian

"But life, being weary of these worldly bars, Never lacks power to dismiss itself."

William Shakespeare, *Julius Caesar*, 1599

youth facing an unsupportive environment, including family or peer rejection, are also at increased risk of attempting suicide (Goldfried, 2001; Haas et al., 2011; Hatzenbuehler, 2011). Among people with alcohol use disorder, 3 percent die by suicide. This rate is roughly 100 times greater than the rate for people without alcohol use disorder (Murphy & Wetzel, 1990; Sher, 2006).

- *day of the week differences:* Negative emotion tends to go up midweek, which can have tragic consequences (Watson, 2000). A surprising 25 percent of U.S. suicides occur on Wednesdays (Kposowa & D'Auria, 2009).

Social suggestion may trigger suicide. Following highly publicized suicides and TV programs featuring suicide, known suicides increase. So do fatal auto and private airplane "accidents." One six-year study tracked suicide cases among all 1.2 million people who lived in metropolitan Stockholm at any time during the 1990s (Hedström et al., 2008). Men exposed to a family suicide were 8 times more likely to commit suicide than were nonexposed men. That phenomenon may be partly attributable to family genes. But shared genetic predispositions cannot explain why men exposed to a co-worker's suicide were 3.5 times more likely to commit suicide, compared with nonexposed men.

Because suicide is so often an impulsive act, environmental barriers (such as jump barriers on high bridges and the unavailability of loaded guns) can save lives (Anderson, 2008). Common sense may suggest that a determined person will simply find another way to complete the act, but such restrictions give time for self-destructive impulses to subside.

Suicide is not necessarily an act of hostility or revenge. People—especially older adults—may choose death as an alternative to current or future suffering, a way to switch off unendurable pain and relieve a perceived burden on family members. Suicidal urges typically arise when people feel disconnected from others and a burden to them, or when they feel defeated and trapped by an inescapable situation (Joiner, 2010; Taylor et al., 2011). Thus, suicide rates increase a bit during economic recessions (Luo et al., 2011). Suicidal thoughts also may increase when people are driven to reach a goal or standard—to become thin or straight or rich—and find it unattainable (Chatard & Selimbegović, 2011).

In hindsight, families and friends may recall signs they believe should have forewarned them—verbal hints, giving possessions away, or withdrawal and preoccupation with death. To judge from surveys of 84,850 people across 17 nations, about 9 percent of people at some point in their lives have thought seriously of suicide. About 3 in 10 of those who think about it will actually attempt suicide (Nock et al., 2008). Only about 1 in 25 Americans die in that attempt (AAS, 2009). Of those who die, one-third had tried to kill themselves previously. Most discussed it beforehand. So, if a friend talks suicide to you, it's important to listen and to direct the person to professional help. Anyone who threatens suicide is at least sending a signal of feeling desperate or despondent.

Nonsuicidal Self-Injury Suicide is not the only way to send a message or deal with distress. Some people, especially adolescents and young adults, may engage in *nonsuicidal self-injury (NSSI)* (**FIGURE 51.6**). These people hurt themselves in various ways. They may cut or burn their skin, hit themselves, insert objects under their nails or skin, or tattoo themselves (Fikke et al., 2011). Though painful, these self-injuries are not fatal. People who engage in NSSI tend to be less able to tolerate emotional distress. They are extremely self-critical and often have poor communication and problem-solving skills (Nock, 2010). Why do they hurt themselves? Through NSSI they may

- find relief from intense negative thoughts through the distraction of pain.

- attract attention and possibly get help.

- relieve guilt by inflicting self-punishment.

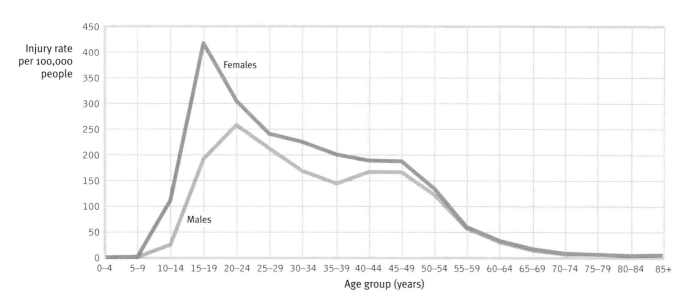

▼ FIGURE 51.6
Rates of nonfatal self-injury in the U.S. Self-injury rates peak higher for females than for males. (Data from CDC, 2009.)

- get others to change their negative behavior (bullying, criticism).

- fit in with a peer group.

Does NSSI lead to suicide? Usually not. Those who engage in NSSI are typically suicide gesturers, not suicide attempters (Nock & Kessler, 2006). Suicide gesturers engage in NSSI as a desperate but non-life-threatening form of communication or when they are feeling overwhelmed. Nevertheless, NSSI is considered a risk factor for future suicide attempts (Wilkinson & Goodyer, 2011). If people do not find help, their nonsuicidal behavior may escalate to suicidal thoughts and, finally, to suicide attempts.

─────────────── **RETRIEVAL PRACTICE** ───────────────

- What does it mean to say that "depression is a whole-body disorder"?

ANSWER: Many factors contribute to depression, including the biological influences of genetics and brain function. Social-cognitive factors also matter, including the interaction of explanatory style, mood, our responses to stressful experiences, and changes in our patterns of thinking and behaving. The whole body is involved.

> "People desire death when two fundamental needs are frustrated to the point of extinction: The need to belong with or connect to others, and the need to feel effective with or to influence others."
>
> Thomas Joiner (2006, p. 47)

---

51 REVIEW Depressive Disorders and Bipolar Disorder

LEARNING OBJECTIVES

RETRIEVAL PRACTICE Take a moment to answer each of these Learning Objective Questions (repeated here from within this module). Then turn to Appendix C, Complete Module Reviews, to check your answers. Research suggests that trying to answer these questions on your own will improve your long-term retention (McDaniel et al., 2009).

51-1 How do major depressive disorder, persistent depressive disorder, and bipolar disorder differ?

51-2 How can the biological and social-cognitive perspectives help us understand depressive disorders and bipolar disorder?

51-3 What factors increase the risk of suicide and what do we know about nonsuicidal self-injury?

TERMS AND CONCEPTS TO REMEMBER

RETRIEVAL PRACTICE Test yourself on these terms by trying to write down the definition before flipping back to check your answers.

major depressive disorder, p. 629

mania, p. 629

bipolar disorder, p. 629

rumination, p. 635

Use 🅰 LearningCurve to create your personalized study plan, which will direct you to the resources that will help you most in 🅰 LaunchPad.

schizophrenia a psychological disorder characterized by delusions, hallucinations, disorganized speech, and/or diminished, inappropriate emotional expression.

delusion a false belief, often of persecution or grandeur, that may accompany psychotic disorders.

"When someone asks me to explain schizophrenia I tell them, you know how sometimes in your dreams you are in them yourself and some of them feel like real nightmares? My schizophrenia was like I was walking through a dream. But everything around me was real. At times, today's world seems so boring and I wonder if I would like to step back into the schizophrenic dream, but then I remember all the scary and horrifying experiences."

Stuart Emmons, with Craig Geiser, Kalman J. Kaplan, and Martin Harrow, *Living With Schizophrenia*, 1997

Art by someone diagnosed with schizophrenia Commenting on the kind of artwork shown here (from Craig Geiser's 2010 art exhibit in Michigan), poet and art critic John Ashbery wrote: "The lure of the work is strong, but so is the terror of the unanswerable riddles it proposes."

© Craig Geiser

MODULE 52 Schizophrenia

During their most severe periods, people with **schizophrenia** live in a private inner world, preoccupied with the strange ideas and images that haunt them. The word itself means "split" *(schizo)* "mind" *(phrenia)*. In this disorder, however, the mind is *not* split into multiple personalities. Rather, the mind has suffered a split from reality that shows itself in disturbed perceptions, disorganized thinking and speech, and diminished, inappropriate emotions. Schizophrenia is the chief example of a *psychosis*, a broad term for a break or split from reality.

Symptoms of Schizophrenia

52-1 What patterns of perceiving, thinking, and feeling characterize schizophrenia?

Schizophrenia comes in varied forms. Schizophrenia patients with *positive symptoms* may experience hallucinations, talk in disorganized and deluded ways, and exhibit inappropriate laughter, tears, or rage. Those with *negative symptoms* may have toneless voices, expressionless faces, or mute and rigid bodies.

Disturbed Perceptions

People with schizophrenia sometimes have *hallucinations*—they see, feel, taste, or smell things that exist only in their minds. Most often, the hallucinations are sounds, frequently voices making insulting remarks or giving orders. The voices may tell the person that she is bad or that she must burn herself with a cigarette lighter. Imagine your own reaction if a dream broke into your waking consciousness, making it hard to separate your experience from your imagination. When the unreal seems real, the resulting perceptions are at best bizarre, at worst terrifying.

Disorganized Thinking and Speech

Hallucinations are false *perceptions*. People with schizophrenia also have disorganized, fragmented thinking, which is often distorted by false *beliefs* called **delusions.** If they have *paranoid* tendencies, they may believe they are being threatened or pursued.

Maxine, a young woman with schizophrenia, believed she was Mary Poppins. Communicating with Maxine was difficult because her thoughts spilled out in no logical order. Her biographer, Susan Sheehan (1982, p. 25), observed her saying aloud to no one in particular, "This morning, when I was at Hillside [Hospital], I was making a movie. I was surrounded by movie stars. . . . Is this room painted blue to get me upset? My grandmother died four weeks after my eighteenth birthday."

Jumbled ideas may make no sense even within sentences, forming what is known as *word salad.* One young man begged for "a little more allegro in the treatment," and suggested that "liberationary movement with a view to the widening of the horizon" will "ergo extort some wit in lectures."

One cause of disorganized thinking may be a breakdown in *selective attention.* Normally, we have a remarkable capacity for giving our undivided attention to one set of sensory stimuli while filtering out others. People with schizophrenia cannot do this. Thus, tiny, irrelevant stimuli, such as the grooves on a brick or the inflections of a voice, may distract their attention from a bigger event or a speaker's meaning. As one former patient recalled, "What had happened to me . . . was a breakdown in the filter, and a hodge-podge of unrelated stimuli were distracting me from things which should have had my undivided attention" (MacDonald, 1960, p. 218). This selective attention difficulty is but one of dozens of cognitive differences associated with schizophrenia (Reichenberg & Harvey, 2007).

Diminished and Inappropriate Emotions

The expressed emotions of schizophrenia are often utterly inappropriate, split off from reality (Kring & Caponigro, 2010). Maxine laughed after recalling her grandmother's death. On other occasions, she cried when others laughed, or became angry for no apparent reason. Others with schizophrenia lapse into an emotionless *flat affect* state of no apparent feeling. Most also have an *impaired theory of mind*—they have difficulty perceiving facial emotions and reading others' states of mind (Green & Horan, 2010; Kohler et al., 2010). These deficiencies occur early in the illness and have a genetic basis (Bora & Pantelis, 2013).

Motor behavior may also be inappropriate. Some perform senseless, compulsive acts, such as continually rocking or rubbing an arm. Others may remain motionless for hours (a condition called *catatonia*) and then become agitated.

As you can imagine, such disturbed perceptions, disorganized thinking, and inappropriate emotions profoundly disrupt social and work relationships. During their most severe periods, people with schizophrenia live in a private inner world, preoccupied with illogical ideas and unreal images. Many have sleep problems, which can increase night eating and obesity (Palmese et al., 2011). Given a supportive environment and medication, over 40 percent of people with schizophrenia will have periods of a year or more of normal life experience (Jobe & Harrow, 2010). Many others remain socially withdrawn and isolated or rejected for much of their lives (Hooley, 2010).

Onset and Development of Schizophrenia

52-2 How do chronic and acute schizophrenia differ?

Nearly 1 in 100 people will experience schizophrenia this year, joining the estimated 24 million worldwide who have this disorder (Abel et al., 2010; WHO, 2011). It typically strikes as young people are maturing into adulthood. It knows no national boundaries, and it affects both males and females. Men tend to be struck earlier, more severely, and slightly more often (Aleman et al., 2003; Eranti et al., 2013; Picchioni & Murray, 2007). The risk of schizophrenia is higher for those who experience childhood abuse: They are three times more likely than their unabused counterparts to develop this disorder (Matheson et al., 2013). Other types of childhood adversity, such as bullying, also increase the risk (Varese et al., 2012).

When schizophrenia is a slow-developing process, called **chronic schizophrenia,** recovery is doubtful (WHO, 1979). This was the case with Maxine's schizophrenia, which took a slow course, emerging from a long history of social inadequacy and poor school performance (MacCabe et al., 2008). Those with chronic schizophrenia often exhibit the persistent and incapacitating negative symptom of social withdrawal (Kirkpatrick et al., 2006). Men, whose schizophrenia develops on average four years earlier than women's, more often exhibit negative symptoms and chronic schizophrenia (Räsänen et al., 2000). In one study that followed people with chronic schizophrenia over 34 years, the majority showed worsened symptoms and functioning (Newman et al., 2012).

When previously well-adjusted people develop schizophrenia rapidly following particular life stresses, this is called **acute schizophrenia,** and recovery is much more likely. They more often have the positive symptoms that are more likely to respond to drug therapy (Fenton & McGlashan, 1991, 1994; Fowles, 1992).

Understanding Schizophrenia

Schizophrenia is a dreaded psychological disorder. It is also one of the most heavily researched. Most studies now link it with abnormal brain tissue and genetic predispositions. Schizophrenia is a disease of the brain manifested in symptoms of the mind.

chronic schizophrenia (also called *process schizophrenia*) a form of schizophrenia in which symptoms usually appear by late adolescence or early adulthood. As people age, psychotic episodes last longer and recovery periods shorten.

acute schizophrenia (also called *reactive schizophrenia*) a form of schizophrenia that can begin at any age, frequently occurs in response to an emotionally traumatic event, and has extended recovery periods.

Most people with schizophrenia smoke, often heavily. Nicotine apparently stimulates certain brain receptors, which helps focus attention (Diaz et al., 2008; Javitt & Coyle, 2004).

Brain Abnormalities

52-3 What brain abnormalities are associated with schizophrenia?

Might chemical imbalances in the brain underlie schizophrenia? Scientists have long known that strange behavior can have strange chemical causes. The saying "mad as a hatter" refers to the psychological deterioration of British hatmakers whose brains, it was later discovered, were slowly poisoned as they moistened the brims of mercury-laden felt hats with their tongue and lips (Smith, 1983). Could schizophrenia symptoms have a similar biochemical key? Scientists continue to track the mechanisms by which chemicals produce hallucinations and other symptoms.

Dopamine Overactivity One possible answer emerged when researchers examined schizophrenia patients' brains after death. They found an excess of receptors for *dopamine*—a sixfold excess for the dopamine receptor D4 (Seeman et al., 1993; Wong et al., 1986). Such a hyper-responsive dopamine system may intensify brain signals in schizophrenia, creating positive symptoms such as hallucinations and paranoia (Grace, 2010). Drugs that block dopamine receptors often lessen these symptoms. Drugs that increase dopamine levels, such as amphetamines and cocaine, sometimes intensify them (Seeman, 2007; Swerdlow & Koob, 1987).

Abnormal Brain Activity and Anatomy Brain scans show that abnormal activity accompanies schizophrenia. Some people diagnosed with schizophrenia have abnormally low brain activity in the frontal lobes, areas that help us reason, plan, and solve problems (Morey et al., 2005; Pettegrew et al., 1993; Resnick, 1992). Brain scans also show a noticeable decline in the brain waves that reflect synchronized neural firing in the frontal lobes (Spencer et al., 2004; Symond et al., 2005). Out-of-sync neurons may disrupt the integrated functioning of neural networks, possibly contributing to schizophrenia symptoms.

One study took PET scans of brain activity while people were hallucinating (Silbersweig et al., 1995). When participants heard a voice or saw something, their brain became vigorously active in several core regions. One was the thalamus, the structure that filters incoming sensory signals and transmits them to the brain's cortex. Another PET scan study of people with paranoia found increased activity in the amygdala, a fear-processing center (Epstein et al., 1998).

Many studies have found enlarged, fluid-filled areas and a corresponding shrinkage and thinning of cerebral tissue in people with schizophrenia (Goldman et al., 2009; Wright et al., 2000). People often inherit these brain differences. If one affected identical twin shows brain abnormalities, the odds are at least 1 in 2 that the other twin will have them (van Haren et al., 2012). Even people who will *later* develop the disorder may show these symptoms (Karlsgodt et al., 2010). The greater the brain shrinkage, the more severe the thought disorder (Collinson et al., 2003; Nelson et al., 1998; Shenton, 1992).

Two smaller-than-normal areas are the cortex and the corpus callosum connecting the brain's two hemispheres (Arnone et al., 2008). Another is the thalamus, which may explain why people with schizophrenia have difficulty filtering sensory input and focusing attention (Andreasen et al., 1994; Ellison-Wright et al., 2008). The bottom line is that schizophrenia involves not one isolated brain abnormality but problems with several brain regions and their interconnections (Andreasen, 1997, 2001).

Prenatal Environment and Risk

52-4 What prenatal events are associated with increased risk of developing schizophrenia?

What causes brain abnormalities in people with schizophrenia? Some scientists point to mishaps during prenatal development or delivery (Fatemi & Folsom, 2009; Walker et al., 2010). Risk factors for schizophrenia include low birth weight, maternal diabetes, older paternal age, and oxygen deprivation during delivery (King et al., 2010). Famine may also increase risks. People conceived during the peak of World War II's Dutch wartime famine later developed schizophrenia at twice the normal rate. Those conceived during the famine of 1959 to 1961 in eastern China also displayed this doubled rate (St. Clair et al., 2005; Susser et al., 1996).

Let's consider another possible culprit. Might a midpregnancy viral infection impair fetal brain development (Brown & Patterson, 2011)? Can you imagine some ways to test this fetal-virus idea? Scientists have asked the following:

- *Are people at increased risk of schizophrenia if, during the middle of their fetal development, their country experienced a flu epidemic?* The repeated answer has been *Yes* (Mednick et al., 1994; Murray et al., 1992; Wright et al., 1995).

- *Are people born in densely populated areas, where viral diseases spread more readily, at greater risk for schizophrenia?* The answer, confirmed in a study of 1.75 million Danes, has again been *Yes* (Jablensky, 1999; Mortensen, 1999).

- *Are those born during the winter and spring months—after the fall-winter flu season—also at increased risk?* Although the increase is small, just 5 to 8 percent, the answer has been *Yes* (Fox, 2010; Schwartz, 2011; Torrey et al., 1997, 2002).

- *In the Southern Hemisphere, where the seasons are the reverse of the Northern Hemisphere, are the months of above-average schizophrenia births similarly reversed?* Again, the answer has been *Yes*, though somewhat less so. In Australia, people born between August and October are at greater risk. But there is an exception: For people born in the Northern Hemisphere, who later moved to Australia, the risk is greater if they were born between January and March (McGrath et al., 1995, 1999).

- *Are mothers who report being sick with influenza during pregnancy more likely to bear children who develop schizophrenia?* In one study of nearly 8000 women, the answer was *Yes*. The schizophrenia risk increased from the customary 1 percent to about 2 percent—but only when infections occurred during the second trimester (Brown et al., 2000). Maternal influenza infection during pregnancy affects brain development in monkeys also (Short et al., 2010).

- *Does blood drawn from pregnant women whose offspring develop schizophrenia show higher-than-normal levels of antibodies that suggest a viral infection?* In one study of 27 women whose children later developed schizophrenia, the answer was *Yes* (Buka et al., 2001). And the answer was again *Yes* in a huge California study, which collected blood samples from some 20,000 pregnant women during the 1950s and 1960s (Brown et al., 2004). Another study found traces of a specific retrovirus (HERV) in nearly half of people with schizophrenia and virtually none in healthy people (Perron et al., 2008).

These converging lines of evidence suggest that fetal-virus infections contribute to the development of schizophrenia. They also strengthen the U.S. government recommendation that "pregnant women need a flu shot" (CDC, 2014).

Why might a second-trimester maternal flu bout put a fetus at risk? Is the virus itself the culprit? The mother's immune response to it? Medications taken (Wyatt et al., 2001)? Does the infection weaken the brain's supportive glial cells, leading to reduced synaptic connections (Moises et al., 2002)? In time, answers may become available.

Genetic Factors

52-5 Do genes influence schizophrenia? What factors may be early warning signs of schizophrenia in children?

Fetal-virus infections may increase the odds that a child will develop schizophrenia. But many women get the flu during their second trimester of pregnancy, and only 2 percent of them bear children who develop schizophrenia. Why are only some children at risk?

▼ FIGURE 52.1

Risk of developing schizophrenia The lifetime risk of developing schizophrenia varies with one's genetic relatedness to someone having this disorder. Across countries, barely more than 1 in 10 fraternal twins, but some 5 in 10 identical twins, share a schizophrenia diagnosis. (Data from Gottesman, 2001.)

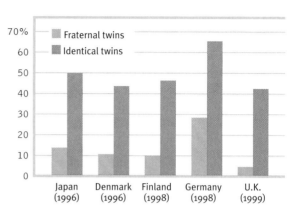

Schizophrenia risk for twins of those diagnosed with schizophrenia

Might some people be more vulnerable because they inherit a predisposition to this disorder? Some people with no family history of schizophrenia develop the disorder (Xu et al., 2011). But the evidence strongly suggests that, *Yes*, some may inherit a predisposition to schizophrenia. The nearly 1-in-100 odds of any person's being diagnosed with schizophrenia become about 1 in 10 among those who have a sibling or parent with the disorder. If the affected sibling is an identical twin, the odds increase to nearly 5 in 10 (**FIGURE 52.1**). Those odds remain the same even when the twins are raised apart (Plomin et al., 1997). (Only about a dozen such cases are on record.)

Remember, though, that identical twins share more than their genes. They also share a prenatal environment. About two-thirds share a placenta and the blood it supplies; the other one-third have separate placentas. Shared placentas matter. If the co-twin of an identical twin with schizophrenia shared the placenta, the chances of developing the disorder are 6 in 10. If the identical twins had separate placentas (as do fraternal twins), the co-twin's chances of developing schizophrenia drop to 1 in 10 (Davis et al., 1995a,b; Phelps et al., 1997). Twins who share a placenta are more likely to share the same prenatal viruses. So perhaps shared germs as well as shared genes produce identical twin similarities.

Adoption studies help untangle genetic and environmental influences. Children adopted by someone who develops schizophrenia seldom "catch" the disorder. Rather, adopted children have an elevated risk if a *biological* parent is diagnosed with schizophrenia (Gottesman, 1991).

The search is on for specific genes that, in some combination, predispose schizophrenia-inducing brain abnormalities (Levinson et al., 2011; Mitchell & Porteous, 2011; Ripke et al., 2011; Vacic et al., 2011). (It is not our genes but our brains that directly control our behavior.) Some of these genes influence the effects of dopamine and other neurotransmitters in the brain. Others affect the production of *myelin*, a fatty substance that coats the axons of nerve cells and lets impulses travel at high speed through neural networks.

Schizophrenia in identical twins When twins differ, only the one afflicted with schizophrenia typically has enlarged, fluid-filled cranial cavities (right) (Suddath et al., 1990). The difference between the twins implies some nongenetic factor, such as a virus, is also at work.

Although genes matter, the genetic formula is not as straightforward as the inheritance of eye color. Genome studies of thousands of individuals with and without schizophrenia indicate that schizophrenia is influenced by many genes, each with very small effects (International Schizophrenia Consortium, 2009; Xu et al., 2012). And, as we have so often seen, nature and nurture interact. *Epigenetic* (literally "in addition to genetic") factors influence whether or not genes will be expressed. Like hot water activating a tea bag, environmental factors such as viral infections, nutritional deprivation, and maternal stress can "turn on" the genes that put some of us at higher risk for schizophrenia. Identical twins' differing histories in the womb and beyond explain why only

No schizophrenia

Schizophrenia

one of them may show differing gene expressions (Dempster et al., 2013; Walker et al., 2010). Our heredity and our life experiences work together. Neither hand claps alone.

Thanks to our expanding understanding of genetic and brain influences on maladies such as schizophrenia, the general public more and more attributes psychiatric disorders to biological factors (Pescosolido et al., 2010). In 2007, one privately funded new research center announced its ambitious aim: "To unambiguously diagnose patients with psychiatric disorders based on their DNA sequence in 10 years' time" (Holden, 2007). In 2010, $120 million in start-up funding launched a bold new effort to study the neuroscience and genetics of schizophrenia and other psychiatric disorders (Kaiser, 2010). So, can scientists develop genetic tests that reveal who is at risk? If so, will people in the future subject their embryos to genetic testing (and gene repair or abortion) if they are at risk for this or some other psychological or physical malady? Might they take their egg and sperm to a genetics lab for screening before combining them to produce an embryo? Or will children be tested for genetic risks and given appropriate preventive treatments? In this brave new twenty-first-century world, such questions await answers.

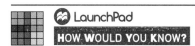

LaunchPad
HOW WOULD YOU KNOW?
Consider how researchers have studied these issues with LaunchPad's *How Would You Know If Schizophrenia is Inherited?*

Environmental Triggers for Schizophrenia

If prenatal viruses and genetic predispositions do not, by themselves, cause schizophrenia, neither do family or social factors alone. It remains true, as Susan Nicol and Irving Gottesman (1983) noted over three decades ago, that "no environmental causes have been discovered that will invariably, or even with moderate probability, produce schizophrenia in persons who are not related to" a person with schizophrenia.

Hoping to identify environmental triggers of schizophrenia, researchers have compared the experiences of high-risk children (for example, those with relatives with schizophrenia) and low-risk children. In one 2.5-year study that followed 163 teens and early-twenties adults who had two relatives with schizophrenia, the 20 percent of participants who developed schizophrenia showed social withdrawal or other abnormal behavior before the onset of the disorder (Johnstone et al., 2005). Researchers (Abel et al., 2010; Freedman et al., 1998; Schiffman et al., 2001; Susser, 1999; Welham et al., 2009) identified these other possible early warning signs:

- A mother whose schizophrenia was severe and long-lasting
- Birth complications, often involving oxygen deprivation and low birth weight
- Separation from parents
- Short attention span and poor muscle coordination
- Disruptive or withdrawn behavior
- Emotional unpredictability
- Poor peer relations and solo play
- Childhood physical, sexual, or emotional abuse

* * *

Few of us can relate to the strange thoughts, perceptions, and behaviors of schizophrenia. Sometimes our thoughts jump around, but we rarely talk nonsensically. Occasionally we feel unjustly suspicious of someone, but we do not fear that the world is plotting against us. Often our perceptions err, but rarely do we see or hear things that are not there. We feel regret after laughing at someone's misfortune, but we rarely giggle in response to bad news. At times we just want to be alone, but we do not live in social isolation. However, millions of people around the world do talk strangely, suffer delusions, hear nonexistent voices, see things that are not there, laugh or cry at inappropriate times, or withdraw into private imaginary worlds. The quest to solve the cruel puzzle of schizophrenia continues, more vigorously than ever.

LaunchPad For an 8-minute description of how clinicians define and treat schizo-phrenia, visit LaunchPad's *Video—Schizophrenia: New Definitions, New Therapies.*

RETRIEVAL PRACTICE

• A person with schizophrenia who has _____ (positive/negative) symptoms may have an expressionless face and toneless voice. These symptoms are most common with _____ (chronic/acute) schizophrenia and are not likely to respond to drug therapy. Those with _____ (positive/negative) symptoms are likely to experi-ence delusions and to be diagnosed with _____ (chronic/acute) schizophrenia, which is much more likely to respond to drug therapy.

ANSWERS: negative; chronic; positive; acute

• What factors contribute to the onset and development of schizophrenia?

ANSWER: Biological factors include abnormalities in brain structure and function, prenatal exposure to a maternal virus, and a genetic predisposition to the disorder. However, a high-risk environment, with many environmental triggers, can increase the odds of developing schizophrenia.

MODULE 52 REVIEW Schizophrenia

LEARNING OBJECTIVES

RETRIEVAL PRACTICE Take a moment to answer each of these Learning Objective Questions (repeated here from within this module). Then turn to Appendix C, Complete Module Re-views, to check your answers. Research suggests that trying to answer these questions on your own will improve your long-term retention (McDaniel et al., 2009).

51-1 What patterns of perceiving, thinking, and feeling characterize schizophrenia?

51-2 How do chronic and acute schizophrenia differ?

51-3 What brain abnormalities are associated with schizophrenia?

51-4 What prenatal events are associated with increased risk of developing schizophrenia?

51-5 Do genes influence schizophrenia? What factors may be early warning signs of schizophrenia in children?

TERMS AND CONCEPTS TO REMEMBER

RETRIEVAL PRACTICE Test yourself on these terms by trying to write down the definition before flipping back to check your answers.

schizophrenia, p. 640

delusion, p. 640

chronic schizophrenia, p. 641

acute schizophrenia, p. 641

Use **LearningCurve** to create your personalized study plan, which will direct you to the resources that will help you most in **LaunchPad**.

MODULE 53 Dissociative, Personality, and Eating Disorders

Dissociative Disorders

53-1 What are dissociative disorders, and why are they controversial?

Among the most bewildering disorders are the rare **dissociative disorders,** in which a person's conscious awareness *dissociates* (separates) from painful memories, thoughts, and feelings. The result may be a *fugue state,* a sudden loss of memory or change in identity, often in response to an overwhelmingly stressful situation. Such was the case for one Vietnam veteran who was haunted by his comrades' deaths, and who had left his World Trade Center office shortly before the 9/11 attack. Later, he disappeared on

dissociative disorders controversial, rare disorders in which conscious awareness becomes separated (dissoci-ated) from previous memories, thoughts, and feelings.

the way to work. Six months later, when he was discovered in a Chicago homeless shelter, he reported no memory of his identity or family (Stone, 2006).

Dissociation itself is not so rare. Any one of us may have a sense of being unreal, of being separated from our body, of watching ourselves as if in a movie. Sometimes we may say, "I was not myself at the time." Perhaps you can recall getting up to go somewhere and ending up at some unintended location while your mind was preoccupied. Or perhaps you can play a well-practiced tune on a guitar or piano while talking to someone. When we face trauma, dissociative detachment may protect us from being overwhelmed by emotion.

Dissociative Identity Disorder

A massive dissociation of self from ordinary consciousness occurs in **dissociative identity disorder (DID),** in which two or more distinct identities—each with its own voice and mannerisms—seem to control a person's behavior at different times. Thus, the person may be prim and proper one moment, loud and flirtatious the next. Typically, the original personality denies any awareness of the other(s).

People diagnosed with DID (formerly called *multiple personality disorder*) are rarely violent. But cases have been reported of dissociations into a "good" and a "bad" (or aggressive) personality—a modest version of the Dr. Jekyll–Mr. Hyde split immortalized in Robert Louis Stevenson's story. One unusual case involved Kenneth Bianchi, accused in the "Hillside Strangler" rapes and murders of 10 California women. During a hypnosis session, Bianchi's psychologist "called forth" a hidden personality: "I've talked a bit to Ken, but I think that perhaps there might be another part of Ken that . . . maybe feels somewhat differently from the part that I've talked to. . . . Would you talk with me, Part, by saying, 'I'm here'?" Bianchi answered "Yes" and then claimed to be "Steve" (Watkins, 1984).

Speaking as Steve, Bianchi stated that he hated Ken because Ken was nice and that he (Steve), aided by a cousin, had murdered women. He also claimed Ken knew nothing about Steve's existence and was innocent of the murders. Was Bianchi's second personality a trick, simply a way of disavowing responsibility for his actions? Indeed, Bianchi—a practiced liar who had read about multiple personality in psychology books—was later convicted.

Understanding Dissociative Identity Disorder

Skeptics have raised serious concerns about DID. First, instead of being a true disorder, could DID be an extension of our normal capacity for personality shifts? Nicholas Spanos (1986, 1994, 1996) asked college students to pretend they were accused murderers being examined by a psychiatrist. Given the same hypnotic treatment Bianchi received, most spontaneously expressed a second personality. This discovery made Spanos wonder: Are dissociative identities simply a more extreme version of our capacity to vary the "selves" we present—as when we display a goofy, loud self while hanging out with friends, and a subdued, respectful self around grandparents? Are clinicians who discover multiple personalities merely triggering role playing by fantasy-prone people? Do these patients, like actors who commonly report "losing themselves" in their roles, then convince themselves of the authenticity of their own role enactments? Spanos was no stranger to this line of thinking. In a related research area, he had also raised these questions about the hypnotic state. Because most DID patients are highly hypnotizable, whatever explains one condition—dissociation or role playing—may help explain the other.

Skeptics also find it suspicious that the disorder has such a short and localized history. Between 1930 and 1960, the number of North American DID diagnoses averaged 2 per decade. By the 1980s, when the American Psychiatric Association's *Diagnostic and Statistical Manual of Mental Disorders* (DSM) contained the first formal code for

Multiple personalities Chris Sizemore's story, told in the book and movie, *The Three Faces of Eve,* gave early visibility to what is now called *dissociative identity disorder.*

The "Hillside Strangler" Kenneth Bianchi is shown here at his trial.

"Pretense may become reality."

Chinese proverb

---

dissociative identity disorder (DID) a rare dissociative disorder in which a person exhibits two or more distinct and alternating personalities. Formerly called *multiple personality disorder.*

Widespread dissociation Shirley Mason was a psychiatric patient diagnosed with dissociative identity disorder. Her life formed the basis of the bestselling book, *Sybil* (Schreiber, 1973), and of two movies. Some argue that the book and movies' popularity fueled the dramatic rise in diagnoses of dissociative identity disorder. Skeptics wonder whether she actually had dissociative identity disorder (Nathan, 2011).

"Though this be madness, yet there is method in 't."

William Shakespeare, *Hamlet*, 1600

"Would it be possible to speak with the personality that pays the bills?"

this disorder, the number exploded to more than 20,000 (McHugh, 1995a). The average number of displayed personalities also mushroomed—from 3 to 12 per patient (Goff & Simms, 1993). This disorder is much less prevalent outside North America, although in other cultures people may be said to be "possessed" by an alien spirit (Aldridge-Morris, 1989; Kluft, 1991). In Britain, DID—which some have considered "a wacky American fad" (Cohen, 1995)—is rare. In India and Japan, it is essentially nonexistent (or at least unreported).

Such findings, skeptics note, point to a cultural phenomenon—a disorder created by therapists in a particular social context (Merskey, 1992). Rather than being provoked by trauma, dissociative symptoms tend to be exhibited by suggestible, fantasy-prone people (Giesbrecht et al., 2008, 2010). Patients do not enter therapy saying "Allow me to introduce myselves." Instead, charge the critics, some therapists go fishing for multiple personalities: *"Have you ever felt like another part of you does things you can't control? Does this part of you have a name? Can I talk to the angry part of you?"* Once patients permit a therapist to talk, by name, "to the part of you that says those angry things," they begin acting out the fantasy. The result may be the experience of another self.

Other researchers and clinicians believe DID is a real disorder. They find support for this view in the distinct body and brain states associated with differing personalities (Putnam, 1991). Handedness sometimes switches with personality (Henninger, 1992). Shifts in visual acuity and eye-muscle balance have been recorded as patients switched personalities, but not as control group members tried to simulate DID behavior (Miller et al., 1991). Abnormal brain anatomy and activity can also accompany DID. Brain scans show shrinkage in areas that aid memory and detection of threat (Vermetten et al., 2006). Heightened activity appears in brain areas associated with the control and inhibition of traumatic memories (Elzinga et al., 2007).

Both the psychodynamic and learning perspectives have interpreted DID symptoms as ways of coping with anxiety. Some psychodynamic theorists see them as defenses against the anxiety caused by the eruption of unacceptable impulses. In this view, a second personality enables the discharge of forbidden impulses. Learning theorists see dissociative disorders as behaviors reinforced by anxiety reduction.

Some clinicians include dissociative disorders under the umbrella of posttraumatic stress disorder—a natural, protective response to traumatic experiences during childhood (Putnam, 1995; Spiegel, 2008). Many DID patients recall being physically, sexually, or emotionally abused as children (Gleaves, 1996; Lilienfeld et al., 1999). In one study of 12 murderers diagnosed with DID, 11 had suffered severe, torturous child abuse (Lewis et al., 1997). One had been set afire by his parents. Another had been used in child pornography and was scarred from being made to sit on a stove burner. Some critics wonder, however, whether vivid imagination or therapist suggestion contributed to such recollections (Kihlstrom, 2005).

So the debate continues. On one side are those who believe multiple personalities are the desperate efforts of people trying to detach from a horrific existence. On the other are the skeptics who think DID is a condition constructed out of the therapist-patient interaction and acted out by fantasy-prone, emotionally vulnerable people. If the skeptics' view wins, predicted psychiatrist Paul McHugh (1995b), "this epidemic will end in the way that the witch craze ended in Salem. The [multiple personality phenomenon] will be seen as manufactured."

RETRIEVAL PRACTICE

- The psychodynamic and learning perspectives agree that dissociative identity disorder symptoms are ways of dealing with anxiety. How do their explanations differ?

ANSWER: The psychodynamic explanation of DID symptoms is that they are defenses against anxiety generated by unacceptable urges. The learning perspective attempts to explain these symptoms as behaviors that have been reinforced by relieving anxiety in the past.

Personality Disorders

53-2 What are the three clusters of personality disorders? What behaviors and brain activity characterize the antisocial personality?

The disruptive, inflexible, and enduring behavior patterns of **personality disorders** interfere with social functioning. These disorders tend to form three clusters, characterized by

- anxiety, such as a fearful sensitivity to rejection that predisposes the withdrawn *avoidant personality disorder.*
- eccentric or odd behaviors, such as the emotionless disengagement of *schizotypal personality disorder.*
- dramatic or impulsive behaviors, such as the attention-getting *borderline personality disorder,* the self-focused and self-inflating *narcissistic personality disorder,* and the callous, and sometimes dangerous, *antisocial personality disorder.*

Antisocial Personality Disorder

A person with **antisocial personality disorder** is typically a male whose lack of conscience becomes plain before age 15, as he begins to lie, steal, fight, or display unrestrained sexual behavior (Cale & Lilienfeld, 2002). About half of such children become antisocial adults—unable to keep a job, irresponsible as a spouse and parent, and assaultive or otherwise criminal (Farrington, 1991). (These people are sometimes called *sociopaths* or *psychopaths.*) They may show lower *emotional intelligence*—the ability to understand, manage, and perceive emotions (Ermer et al., 2012). When the antisocial personality combines a keen intelligence with amorality, the result may be a charming and clever con artist—or even a fearless, focused, ruthless soldier, CEO, or politician (Dutton, 2012).

Despite their remorseless and sometimes criminal behavior, criminality is not an essential component of antisocial behavior (Skeem & Cooke, 2010). Moreover, many criminals do not fit the description of antisocial personality disorder. Why? Because they actually show responsible concern for their friends and family members.

Antisocial personalities behave impulsively, and then feel and fear little (Fowles & Dindo, 2009). Their impulsivity can have violent, horrifying consequences (Camp et al., 2013). Consider the case of Henry Lee Lucas. He killed his first victim when he was 13. He felt little regret then or later. He confessed that, during his 32 years of crime, he had brutally beaten, suffocated, stabbed, shot, or mutilated some 360 women, men, and children. For the last six years of his reign of terror, Lucas teamed with Ottis Elwood Toole, who reportedly slaughtered about 50 people he "didn't think was worth living anyhow" (Darrach & Norris, 1984).

Understanding Antisocial Personality Disorder

Antisocial personality disorder is woven of both biological and psychological strands. Twin and adoption studies reveal that biological relatives of people with antisocial and unemotional tendencies are at increased risk for antisocial behavior (Frisell et al., 2012; Tuvblad et al., 2011). No single gene codes for a complex behavior such as crime. Molecular geneticists have, however, identified some specific genes that are more common in those with antisocial personality disorder (Gunter et al., 2010). The genetic vulnerability of people with antisocial and unemotional tendencies appears as a fearless approach to life. Awaiting aversive events, such as electric shocks or loud noises, they show little autonomic nervous system arousal (Hare, 1975; van Goozen et al., 2007). Long-term studies have shown that their levels of stress hormones were lower than average when

No remorse Dennis Rader, known as the "BTK killer" in Kansas, was convicted in 2005 of killing 10 people over a 30-year span. Rader exhibited the extreme lack of conscience that marks antisocial personality disorder.

"Thursday is out. I have jury duty."

Many criminals, like this one, exhibit a sense of conscience and responsibility in other areas of their life, and thus do not exhibit antisocial personality disorder.

personality disorders inflexible and enduring behavior patterns that impair social functioning.

antisocial personality disorder a personality disorder in which a person (usually a man) exhibits a lack of conscience for wrongdoing, even toward friends and family members; may be aggressive and ruthless or a clever con artist.

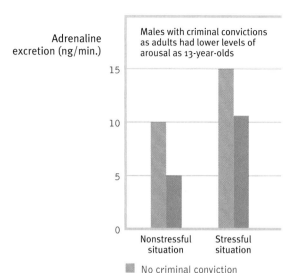

Adrenaline excretion (ng/min.)

Males with criminal convictions as adults had lower levels of arousal as 13-year-olds

No criminal conviction
Criminal conviction

▼ **FIGURE 53.1**
Cold-blooded arousability and risk of crime Levels of the stress hormone adrenaline were measured in two groups of 13-year-old Swedish boys. In both stressful and nonstressful situations, those who would later be convicted of a crime as 18- to 26-year-olds showed relatively low arousal. (Data from Magnusson, 1990.)

Does a full Moon trigger "madness" in some people? James Rotton and I. W. Kelly (1985) examined data from 37 studies that related lunar phase to crime, homicides, crisis calls, and mental hospital admissions. Their conclusion: There is virtually no evidence of "Moon madness." Nor does lunar phase correlate with suicides, assaults, emergency room visits, or traffic disasters (Martin et al., 1992; Raison et al., 1999).

▼ **FIGURE 53.2**
Murderous minds
Researchers have found reduced activation in a murderer's frontal lobes. This brain area (shown in a left-facing brain) helps brake impulsive, aggressive behavior (Raine, 1999).

Frontal lobes

they were youngsters, before committing any crime (**FIGURE 53.1**). Three-year-olds who are slow to develop conditioned fears are later more likely to commit a crime (Gao et al., 2010). Other studies have found that preschool boys who later became aggressive or antisocial adolescents tended to be impulsive, uninhibited, unconcerned with social rewards, and low in anxiety (Caspi et al., 1996; Tremblay et al., 1994).

Traits such as fearlessness and dominance can be adaptive. In fact, some argue that psychopaths and heroes are twigs off the same branch (Smith et al., 2013). If channeled in more productive directions, fearlessness may lead to star-level athleticism, adventurism, or courageous heroism (Poulton & Milne, 2002). One analysis of 42 American presidents showed that they scored higher than the general population on such traits as fearlessness and dominance (Lilienfeld et al., 2012). Consistent with evidence that such traits can run in families, two of the most fearless and dominant presidents were distant cousins with the same last name: Roosevelt. (Two of the least fearless and dominant presidents were a father and son, John Adams and John Quincy Adams.) Lacking a sense of social responsibility, the same disposition may produce a cool con artist or killer (Lykken, 1995).

Genetic influences, often in combination with child abuse, help wire the brain (Dodge, 2009). In people with antisocial criminal tendencies, the emotion-controlling amygdala is smaller (Pardini et al., 2013; Yang et al., 2010). The frontal lobes are also less active, as Adrian Raine (1999, 2005) found when he compared PET scans of 41 murderers' brains with those from people of similar age and sex (**FIGURE 53.2**). This area of the cortex helps control impulses. The reduced activation was especially apparent in those who murdered impulsively. In a follow-up study, Raine and his team (2000) found that violent repeat offenders had 11 percent less frontal lobe tissue than normal. This helps explain why people with antisocial personality disorder exhibit marked deficits in frontal lobe cognitive functions, such as planning, organization, and inhibition (Morgan & Lilienfeld, 2000). Compared with people who feel and display empathy, their brains also respond less to facial displays of others' distress, which may contribute to their lower emotional intelligence (Deeley et al., 2006).

A biologically based fearlessness, as well as early environment, helps explain the reunion of long-separated sisters Joyce Lott, 27, and Mary Jones, 29—in a South Carolina prison where both were sent on drug charges. After a newspaper story about their reunion, their long-lost half-brother Frank Strickland called. He explained it would be a while before he could come see them—because he, too, was in jail, on drug, burglary, and larceny charges (Shepherd et al., 1990). The genes that put people at risk for antisocial behavior also put people at risk for substance use disorders, which may help explain why these disorders often appear in combination (Dick, 2007).

Genetics alone do not tell the whole story of antisocial crime, however. In another Raine-led study (1996), researchers checked criminal records on nearly 400 Danish men at ages 20 to 22. All these men either had experienced biological risk factors at birth (such as premature birth) or came from family backgrounds marked by poverty and family instability. The researchers then compared each of these two groups with a third *biosocial* group (people whose lives were marked by *both* those biological and social risk factors). The biosocial group had double the risk of committing crime (**FIGURE 53.3**). Similar findings emerged from a famous study that followed 1037 children for a quarter-century: Two combined factors—childhood maltreatment and a gene that altered neurotransmitter balance—predicted antisocial problems (Caspi et al., 2002). Neither "bad" genes alone nor a "bad" environment alone predisposed later antisocial behavior. Rather, genes predisposed some children to be more sensitive to maltreatment. Within "genetically vulnerable segments of the population," environmental influences matter—for better or for worse (Belsky et al., 2007; Moffitt, 2005; Pluess & Belsky, 2013).

With antisocial behavior, as with so much else, nature and nurture interact and the biopsychosocial perspective helps us understand the whole story. To explore the neural basis of antisocial personality disorder, neuroscientists are trying to identify brain activity differences in criminals who display symptoms of this disorder. Shown emotionally evocative photographs, such as a man holding a knife to a woman's throat, criminals with antisocial personality disorder display blunted heart rate and perspiration responses, and less activity in brain areas that typically respond to emotional stimuli (Harenski et al., 2010; Kiehl & Buckholtz, 2010). They also have a larger and hyper-reactive dopamine reward system, which predisposes their impulsive drive to do something rewarding despite the consequences (Buckholtz et al., 2010; Glenn et al., 2010). Such data provide another reminder: Everything psychological is also biological.

RETRIEVAL PRACTICE

• How do biological and psychological factors contribute to antisocial personality disorder?

ANSWER: Twin and adoption studies show that biological relatives of people with this disorder are at increased risk for antisocial behavior. Negative environmental factors, such as poverty or childhood abuse, may channel genetic traits such as fearlessness in more dangerous directions—toward aggression and away from social responsibility.

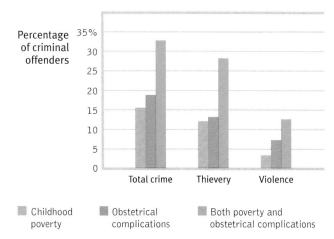

▼ FIGURE 53.3
Biopsychosocial roots of crime Danish male babies whose backgrounds were marked both by obstetrical complications and social stresses associated with poverty were twice as likely to be criminal offenders by ages 20 to 22 as those in either the biological or social risk groups. (Data from Raine et al., 1996.)

Eating Disorders

53-3 What are the three main eating disorders, and how do biological, psychological, and social-cultural influences make people more vulnerable to them?

Our bodies are naturally disposed to maintain a steady weight, including stored energy reserves for times when food becomes unavailable. But sometimes psychological influences overwhelm biological wisdom. This becomes painfully clear in three eating disorders.

• **Anorexia nervosa** typically begins as a weight-loss diet. People with anorexia—usually adolescents and 9 out of 10 times females—drop significantly below normal weight. Yet they feel fat, fear being fat, remain obsessed with losing weight, and sometimes exercise excessively. About half of those with anorexia display a binge-purge-depression cycle.

• **Bulimia nervosa** may also be triggered by a weight-loss diet, broken by gorging on forbidden foods. Binge-purge eaters—mostly women in their late teens or early twenties—eat in spurts, sometimes influenced by negative emotion or by friends who are bingeing (Crandall, 1988; Haedt-Matt & Keel, 2011). In a cycle of repeating episodes, overeating is followed by compensatory purging (through vomiting or laxative use), fasting, or excessive

anorexia nervosa an eating disorder in which a person (usually an adolescent female) maintains a starvation diet despite being significantly underweight; sometimes accompanied by excessive exercise.

bulimia nervosa an eating disorder in which a person alternates binge eating (usually of high-calorie foods) with purging (by vomiting or laxative use) or fasting.

© Nick Holt Photography

Sibling rivalry gone awry Twins Maria and Katy Campbell have anorexia nervosa. As children they competed to see who could be thinner. Now, says Maria, her anorexia nervosa is "like a ball and chain around my ankle that I can't throw off" (Foster, 2011).

binge-eating disorder significant binge-eating episodes, followed by distress, disgust, or guilt, but without the compensatory purging or fasting that marks bulimia nervosa.

A too-fat body image underlies anorexia.

"Why do women have such low self-esteem? There are many complex psychological and societal reasons, by which I mean Barbie."

Dave Barry, 1999

exercise (Wonderlich et al., 2007). Preoccupied with food (craving sweet and high-fat foods), and fearful of becoming overweight, binge-purge eaters experience bouts of depression, guilt, and anxiety during and following binges (Hinz & Williamson, 1987; Johnson et al., 2002). Unlike anorexia, bulimia is marked by weight fluctuations within or above normal ranges, making the condition easy to hide.

- Those with **binge-eating disorder** engage in significant bouts of overeating, followed by remorse. But they do not purge, fast, or exercise excessively and thus may be overweight.

A U.S. National Institute of Mental Health-funded study reported that, at some point during their lifetime, 0.6 percent of the Americans studied had met the criteria for anorexia, 1 percent for bulimia, and 2.8 percent for binge-eating disorder (Hudson et al., 2007). So, how can we explain these disorders?

Understanding Eating Disorders

Eating disorders do *not* provide (as some have speculated) a telltale sign of childhood sexual abuse (Smolak & Murnen, 2002; Stice, 2002). The family environment may provide a fertile ground for the growth of eating disorders in other ways, however.

- Mothers of girls with eating disorders tend to focus on their own weight and on their daughters' weight and appearance (Pike & Rodin, 1991).
- Families of those with bulimia tend to have a higher-than-usual incidence of childhood obesity and negative self-evaluation (Jacobi et al., 2004).
- Families of those with anorexia tend to be competitive, high-achieving, and protective (Berg et al., 2014; Pate et al., 1992; Yates, 1989, 1990).

Those with eating disorders often have low self-evaluations, set perfectionist standards, fret about falling short of expectations, and are intensely concerned with how others perceive them (Brauhardt et al., 2014; Pieters et al., 2007; Polivy & Herman, 2002; Sherry & Hall, 2009). Some of these factors also predict teen boys' pursuit of unrealistic muscularity (Ricciardelli & McCabe, 2004).

Heredity also matters. Identical twins share these disorders more often than fraternal twins do (Culbert et al., 2009; Klump et al., 2009; Root et al., 2010). Scientists are now searching for culprit genes, which may influence the body's available serotonin and estrogen (Klump & Culbert, 2007). In one analysis of 15 studies, having a gene that reduced available serotonin added 30 percent to a person's risk of anorexia or bulimia (Calati et al., 2011).

But these disorders also have cultural and gender components. Ideal shapes vary across culture and time. In impoverished areas of the world, including much of Africa—where plumpness means prosperity and thinness can signal poverty or illness—bigger seems better (Knickmeyer, 2001; Swami et al., 2010). Bigger does not seem better in Western cultures, where, according to 222 studies of 141,000 people, the rise in eating disorders in the last half of the twentieth century coincided with a dramatic increase in women having a poor body image (Feingold & Mazzella, 1998).

Those most vulnerable to eating disorders are also those (usually women or gay men) who most idealize thinness and have the greatest body dissatisfaction (Feldman & Meyer, 2010; Kane, 2010; Stice et al., 2010). Should it surprise us, then, that when women view real and doctored images of unnaturally thin models and celebrities, they often feel ashamed, depressed, and dissatisfied with their own bodies—the very attitudes that predispose eating disorders (Grabe et al., 2008; Myers & Crowther, 2009; Tiggeman & Miller, 2010)? Eric Stice and his colleagues (2001) tested this modeling idea by giving some adolescent girls (but not others) a 15-month subscription to an American teen-fashion magazine. Compared with those who had not received the magazine, vulnerable girls—defined as those who were already dissatisfied, idealizing thinness, and lacking social support—exhibited increased body dissatisfaction and eating disorder tendencies. Even ultra-thin models do not reflect the impossible standard of the classic Barbie doll, who had, when adjusted to a height of 5 feet 7 inches, a 32-16-29 figure (in centimeters, 82-41-73) (Norton et al., 1996).

There is, however, more to body dissatisfaction and anorexia than media effects (Ferguson et al., 2011). Peer influences, such as teasing, also matter. So does affluence, increased marriage age, and especially, competition for available mates.

Nevertheless, the sickness of today's eating disorders stems in part from today's weight-obsessed culture—a culture that says, in countless ways, "Fat is bad," that motivates millions of women to be "always dieting," and that encourages eating binges by pressuring women to live in a constant state of semistarvation. One former model told the story of how her anorexia caused her organs to fail (Caroll, 2013). Starving from not having eaten for days, she walked into a meeting with her modeling agent, who greeted her by saying, "Whatever you are doing, keep doing it."

If cultural learning contributes to eating behavior, then might prevention programs increase acceptance of one's body? Reviews of prevention studies answer *Yes*. They seem especially effective if the programs are interactive and focused on girls over age 15 (Beintner et al., 2012; Stice et al., 2007; Vocks et al., 2010).

* * *

A growing number of people, especially teenagers and young adults are being diagnosed with psychological disorders. Although mindful of their pain, we can also be encouraged by their successes. Many live satisfying lives. Some pursue brilliant careers, as did 18 U.S. presidents, including the periodically depressed Abraham Lincoln, according to one psychiatric analysis of their biographies (Davidson et al., 2006). The bewilderment, fear, and sorrow caused by psychological disorders are real. But, as this text's discussion of therapy shows, hope, too, is real.

Philippe Wojazer/Reuters/Landov

"Thanks, but we don't eat."
©1999 Shannon Burns
www.shannonburns.com/cartoon4.htm

Too thin? Many worry that such super-thin models make self-starvation seem fashionable.

RETRIEVAL PRACTICE

• People with _____ (anorexia nervosa/bulimia nervosa) continue to want to lose weight even when they are underweight. Those with _____ (anorexia nervosa/bulimia nervosa) tend to have weight that fluctuates within or above normal ranges.

ANSWERS: anorexia nervosa; bulimia nervosa

53 **REVIEW** Dissociative, Personality, and Eating Disorders

LEARNING OBJECTIVES

RETRIEVAL PRACTICE Take a moment to answer each of these Learning Objective Questions (repeated here from within this module). Then turn to Appendix C, Complete Module Reviews, to check your answers. Research suggests that trying to answer these questions on your own will improve your long-term retention (McDaniel et al., 2009).

52-1 What are dissociative disorders, and why are they controversial?

52-2 What are the three clusters of personality disorders? What behaviors and brain activity characterize the antisocial personality?

52-3 What are the three main eating disorders, and how do biological, psychological, and social-cultural influences make people more vulnerable to them?

Use 🅐 LearningCurve to create your personalized study plan, which will direct you to the resources that will help you most in 🅐 LaunchPad.

TERMS AND CONCEPTS TO REMEMBER

RETRIEVAL PRACTICE Test yourself on these terms by trying to write down the definition before flipping back to check your answers.

dissociative disorders, p. 646

dissociative identity disorder (DID), p. 647

personality disorders, p. 649

antisocial personality disorder, p. 649

anorexia nervosa, p. 651

bulimia nervosa, p. 651

binge-eating disorder, p. 652

TEST YOUR-SELF PSYCHOLOGICAL DISORDERS

Test yourself repeatedly throughout your studies. This will not only help you figure out what you know and don't know; the testing itself will help you learn and remember the information more effectively thanks to the *testing effect.*

49 Introduction to Psychological Disorders

1. Two disorders are found worldwide. One is schizophrenia, and the other is _____ .

2. Anna is embarrassed that it takes her several minutes to parallel park her car. She usually gets out of the car once or twice to inspect her distance both from the curb and from the nearby cars. Should she worry about having a psychological disorder?

3. What is *susto,* and is this a culture-specific or universal psychological disorder?

4. A therapist says that psychological disorders are sicknesses and people with these disorders should be treated as patients in a hospital. This therapist believes in the _____ model.

5. Many psychologists reject the "disorders-as-illness" view and instead contend that other factors may also be involved—for example, the person's bad habits and poor social skills. This view represents the _____ approach.

   a. medical

   b. evil spirits

   c. biopsychosocial

   d. diagnostic labels

6. Why is the DSM, and the DSM-5 in particular, considered controversial?

7. One predictor of psychiatric disorders that crosses ethnic and gender lines is _____ .

8. The symptoms of _____ appear around age 10; _____ tend[s] to appear later, around age 25.

   a. schizophrenia; bipolar disorder

   b. bipolar disorder; schizophrenia

   c. major depressive disorder; phobias

   d. phobias; major depressive disorder

50 Anxiety Disorders, OCD, and PTSD

9. Anxiety that takes the form of an irrational and maladaptive fear of a specific object, activity, or situation is called a _____ .

10. An episode of intense dread, accompanied by trembling, dizziness, chest pains, or choking sensations and by feelings of terror, is called

    a. a specific phobia.

    b. compulsion.

    c. a panic attack.

    d. an obsessive fear.

11. Marina became consumed with the need to clean the entire house and refused to participate in any other activities. Her family consulted a therapist, who diagnosed her as having _____ - _____ disorder.

12. The learning perspective proposes that phobias are
    a. the result of individual genetic makeup.
    b. a way of repressing unacceptable impulses.
    c. conditioned fears.
    d. a symptom of having been abused as a child.

MODULE 51 Depressive Disorders and Bipolar Disorder

13. The "gender gap" in depression refers to the finding that _____ risk of depression is nearly double that of _____ .

14. Rates of bipolar disorder have risen dramatcally in the twenty-first century, especially among
    a. middle-aged women.
    b. middle-aged men.
    c. females 19 and under.
    d. males 19 and under.

15. Treatment for depression often includes drugs that increase supplies of the neurotransmitters _____ and _____ .

16. Psychologists who emphasize the importance of negative perceptions, beliefs, and thoughts in depression are working within the _____ - _____ perspective.

MODULE 52 Schizophrenia

17. Victor exclaimed, "The weather has been so schizophrenic lately: It's hot one day and freezing the next!" Is this an accurate comparison? Why or why not?

18. A person with positive symptoms of schizophrenia is most likely to experience
    a. catatonia.
    b. delusions.
    c. withdrawal.
    d. flat emotion.

19. People with schizophrenia may hear voices urging self-destruction, an example of a(n) _____ .

20. Chances for recovery from schizophrenia are best when
    a. onset is sudden, in response to stress.
    b. deterioration occurs gradually, during childhood.
    c. no environmental causes can be identified.
    d. there is a detectable brain abnormality.

MODULE 53 Dissociative, Personality, and Eating Disorders

21. Dissociative identity disorder is controversial because
    a. dissociation is actually quite rare.
    b. it was reported frequently in the 1920s but rarely today.
    c. it is almost never reported outside North America.
    d. its symptoms are nearly identical to those of obsessive-compulsive disorder.

22. A personality disorder, such as antisocial personality, is characterized by
    a. depression.
    b. hallucinations.
    c. inflexible and enduring behavior patterns that impair social functioning.
    d. an elevated level of autonomic nervous system arousal.

23. PET scans of murderers' brains have revealed
    a. higher-than-normal activation in the frontal lobes.
    b. lower-than-normal activation in the frontal lobes.
    c. more frontal lobe tissue than normal.
    d. no differences in brain structures or activity.

24. Which of the following statements is true of bulimia nervosa?
    a. People with bulimia continue to want to lose weight even when they are underweight.
    b. Bulimia is marked by weight fluctuations within or above normal ranges.
    c. Bulimia patients often come from middle-class families that are competitive, high-achieving, and protective.
    d. If one twin is diagnosed with bulimia, the chances of the other twin's sharing the disorder are greater if they are fraternal rather than identical twins.

Find answers to these questions in Appendix D, in the back of the book.

THERPY

· · · · · · · · · · · ·

Kay Redfield Jamison, an award-winning clinical psychologist and world expert on the emotional extremes of bipolar disorder, knows her subject firsthand. "For as long as I can remember," she recalled in *An Unquiet Mind,* "I was frighteningly, although often wonderfully, beholden to moods. Intensely emotional as a child, mercurial as a young girl, first severely depressed as an adolescent, and then unrelentingly caught up in the cycles of manic-depressive illness [now known as bipolar disorder] by the time I began my professional life, I became, both by necessity and intellectual inclination, a student of moods" (1995, pp. 4–5). Her life was blessed with times of intense sensitivity and passionate energy. But like her father's, it was also at times plagued by reckless spending, racing conversation, and sleeplessness, alternating with swings into "the blackest caves of the mind."

Then, "in the midst of utter confusion," she made a sane and profoundly helpful decision. Risking professional embarrassment she made an appointment with a therapist, a psychiatrist she would visit weekly for years to come.

> He kept me alive a thousand times over. He saw me through madness, despair, wonderful and terrible love affairs, disillusionments and triumphs, recurrences of illness, an almost fatal suicide attempt, the death of a man I greatly loved, and the enormous pleasures and aggravations of my professional life. . . . He was very tough, as well as very kind, and even though he understood more than anyone how much I felt I was losing—in energy, vivacity, and originality—by taking medication, he never was seduced into losing sight of the overall perspective of how costly, damaging, and life threatening my illness was. . . . Although I went to him to be treated for an illness, he taught me . . . the total beholdenness of brain to mind and mind to brain (pp. 87–88).

"Psychotherapy heals," Jamison reports. "It makes some sense of the confusion, reins in the terrifying thoughts and feelings, returns some control and hope and possibility from it all."

We will begin with *psychotherapies* (Modules 54 and 55), and then focus on *biomedical therapies* (Module 56).

Dorothea Dix "I . . . call your attention to the state of the Insane Persons confined within this Commonwealth, in cages."

MODULE 54 Introduction to Therapy and the Psychological Therapies

THE LONG HISTORY OF EFFORTS to treat psychological disorders has included a bewildering mix of harsh and gentle methods. Well-meaning individuals have cut holes in people's heads and restrained, bled, or "beat the devil" out of them. But they also have given warm baths and massages and placed people in sunny, serene environments. They have administered drugs. And they have talked with their patients about childhood experiences, current feelings, and maladaptive thoughts and behaviors.

Treating Psychological Disorders

54-1 How do *psychotherapy* and the *biomedical therapies* differ?

Reformers Philippe Pinel (1745–1826) and Dorothea Dix (1802–1887) pushed for gentler, more humane treatments and for constructing mental hospitals. Since the 1950s, the introduction of effective drug therapies and community-based treatment programs have emptied most of those hospitals.

Modern Western therapies can be classified into two main categories:

- In **psychotherapy**, a trained therapist uses psychological techniques to assist someone seeking to overcome difficulties or achieve personal growth. The therapist may seek to uncover hidden meaning from a client's early relationships, to encourage the client to adopt new ways of thinking, or to replace old behaviors with new ones.

- **Biomedical therapy** offers medications and other biological treatments. For example, a person with severe depression, as we will see, may receive antidepressants, electroconvulsive shock therapy (ECT), or deep-brain stimulation.

Some psychologists consider psychotherapy to be a biological treatment, because changing the way we think and behave can prompt physical changes in the brain (Kandel, 2013). Effective psychotherapy is a brain-changing experience.

The care provider's training and expertise, as well as the disorder itself, influence the choice of treatment. Psychotherapy and medication are often combined. Kay Redfield Jamison received psychotherapy in her meetings with her psychiatrist, and she took medications to control her wild mood swings.

Let's look first at the psychotherapy options for those treated with "talk therapies." Each is built on one or more of psychology's major theories: psychodynamic, humanistic, behavioral, and cognitive. Most of these techniques can be used one-on-one or in groups. Some therapists combine techniques. And like Jamison, many patients also receive psychotherapy combined with medication. Many psychotherapists describe themselves as taking an **eclectic approach**, using a blend of psychotherapies.

The history of treatment Visitors to eighteenth-century mental hospitals paid to gawk at patients, as though they were viewing zoo animals. William Hogarth's (1697–1764) painting captured one of these visits to London's St. Mary of Bethlehem hospital (commonly called Bedlam).

Psychoanalysis and Psychodynamic Therapies

54-2 What are the goals and techniques of psychoanalysis, and how have they been adapted in psychodynamic therapy?

The first major psychological therapy was Sigmund Freud's **psychoanalysis.** Although few clinicians today practice therapy as Freud did, his work deserves discussion. It helped form the foundation for treating psychological disorders, partly by influencing modern therapists working from the *psychodynamic* perspective.

Goals

Freud believed that in therapy, people could achieve healthier, less anxious living by releasing the energy they had previously devoted to *id-ego-superego* conflicts. Freud assumed that we do not fully know ourselves. There are threatening things that we seem to want not to know—that we disavow or deny. "We can have loving feelings and hateful feelings toward the same person," notes Jonathan Shedler (2009), and "we can desire something and also fear it." Psychoanalysis was Freud's method of helping people to face such unwelcome facts.

Freud's therapy aimed to bring patients' *repressed* or disowned feelings into conscious awareness. By helping them reclaim their unconscious thoughts and feelings, and by giving them *insight* into the origins of their disorders, he aimed to help them reduce growth-impeding inner conflicts.

Techniques

Psychoanalysis is historical reconstruction. Psychoanalytic theory emphasizes the power of childhood experiences to mold the adult. Thus, it aims to unearth one's past in the hope of unmasking the present. After discarding hypnosis as an unreliable excavator, Freud turned to *free association*.

Imagine yourself as a patient using free association. You begin by relaxing, perhaps by lying on a couch. As the psychoanalyst sits out of your line of vision, you say aloud whatever comes to mind. At one moment, you're relating a childhood memory. At another, you're describing a dream or recent experience. It sounds easy, but soon you notice how often you edit your thoughts as you speak. You pause for a second before uttering an embarrassing thought. You omit what seems trivial, irrelevant, or shameful. Sometimes your mind goes blank or you find yourself unable to remember important details. You may joke or change the subject to something less threatening.

To the analyst, these mental blocks indicate **resistance.** They hint that anxiety lurks and you are defending against sensitive material. The analyst will note your resistances and then provide insight into their meaning. If offered at the right moment, this **interpretation**—of, say, your not wanting to talk about your mother—may illuminate the underlying wishes, feelings, and conflicts you are avoiding. The analyst may also offer an explanation of how this resistance fits with other pieces of your psychological puzzle, including those based on analysis of your dream content.

Over many such sessions, your relationship patterns surface in your interaction with your therapist. You may find yourself experiencing strong positive or negative feelings for your analyst. The analyst may suggest you are **transferring** feelings, such as feelings of dependency or mingled love and anger, that you experienced in earlier relationships with family members or other important people. By exposing such feelings, you may gain insight into your current relationships.

Relatively few North American therapists now offer traditional psychoanalysis. Much of its underlying theory is not supported by scientific research. Analysts' interpretations cannot be proven or disproven. And psychoanalysis takes considerable time and money, often years of several sessions per week. Some of these problems have been addressed in the modern psychodynamic perspective that has evolved from psychoanalysis.

RETRIEVAL PRACTICE

- In psychoanalysis, when patients experience strong feelings for their therapist, this is called _____ . Patients are said to demonstrate anxiety when they put up mental blocks around sensitive memories, indicating _____ . The therapist will attempt to provide insight into the underlying anxiety by offering a(n) _____ of the mental blocks.

ANSWERS: transference; resistance; interpretation

---

psychotherapy treatment involving psychological techniques; consists of interactions between a trained therapist and someone seeking to overcome psychological difficulties or achieve personal growth.

biomedical therapy prescribed medications or procedures that act directly on the person's physiology.

eclectic approach an approach to psychotherapy that uses techniques from various forms of therapy.

psychoanalysis Sigmund Freud's therapeutic technique. Freud believed the patient's free associations, resistances, dreams, and transferences—and the therapist's interpretations of them—released previously repressed feelings, allowing the patient to gain self-insight.

resistance in psychoanalysis, the blocking from consciousness of anxiety-laden material.

interpretation in psychoanalysis, the analyst's noting supposed dream meanings, resistances, and other significant behaviors and events in order to promote insight.

transference in psychoanalysis, the patient's transfer to the analyst of emotions linked with other relationships (such as love or hatred for a parent).

"I haven't seen my analyst in 200 years. He was a strict Freudian. If I'd been going all this time, I'd probably almost be cured by now."

Woody Allen, after awakening from suspended animation in the movie *Sleeper*

psychodynamic therapy therapy deriving from the psychoanalytic tradition; views individuals as responding to unconscious forces and childhood experiences, and seeks to enhance self-insight.

Psychodynamic Therapy

Although influenced by Freud's ideas, **psychodynamic therapists** don't talk much about id, ego, and superego. Instead they try to help people understand their current symptoms. They focus on themes across important relationships, including childhood experiences and the therapist relationship. Rather than lying on a couch, out of the therapist's line of vision, patients meet with their therapist face-to-face. These sessions take place once or twice a week (rather than several times per week), and often for only a few weeks or months.

In these sessions, patients gain perspective by exploring defended-against thoughts and feelings. Therapist David Shapiro (1999, p. 8) illustrates this with the case of a young man who had told women that he loved them, when he knew that he didn't. His explanation: They expected it, so he said it. But with his wife, who wishes he would say that he loves her, he finds he "cannot" do that—"I don't know why, but I can't."

> *Therapist*: Do you mean, then, that if you could, you would like to?
>
> *Patient*: Well, I don't know. . . . Maybe I can't say it because I'm not sure it's true. Maybe I don't love her.

Further interactions reveal that he can't express real love because it would feel "mushy" and "soft" and therefore unmanly. He is "in conflict with himself, and he is cut off from the nature of that conflict." Shapiro noted that with such patients, who are estranged from themselves, therapists using psychodynamic techniques "are in a position to introduce them to themselves. We can restore their awareness of their own wishes and feelings, and their awareness, as well, of their reactions against those wishes and feelings."

Psychodynamic therapists may also help reveal past relationship troubles as the origin of current difficulties. Jonathan Shedler (2010a) recalls his patient Jeffrey's complaints of difficulty getting along with his colleagues and wife, who saw him as hypercritical. Jeffrey then "began responding to me as if I were an unpredictable, angry adversary." Shedler seized this opportunity to help Jeffrey recognize the relationship pattern, and its roots in the attacks and humiliation he experienced from his alcohol-abusing father—and to work through and let go of this defensive responding to people.

Interpersonal psychotherapy, a brief (12- to 16-session) variation of psychodynamic therapy, has effectively treated depression (Cuijpers, 2011; Markowitz & Weissman, 2012). Although interpersonal psychotherapy aims to help people gain insight into the roots of their difficulties, its goal is symptom relief in the here and now. Rather than focusing mostly on undoing past hurts and offering interpretations, the therapist concentrates primarily on current relationships and on helping people improve their relationship skills.

Face-to-face therapy In this type of therapy session, the couch has disappeared. But the influence of psychoanalytic theory may not have, especially if the therapist seeks information about the patient's childhood and helps the patient reclaim unconscious feelings.

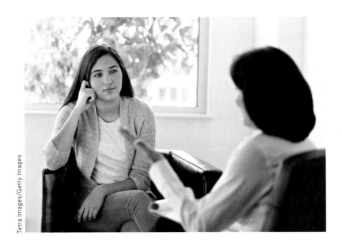

Tetra Images/Getty Images

The case of Anna, a 34-year-old married professional, illustrates these goals. Five months after receiving a promotion, with accompanying increased responsibilities and longer hours, Anna experienced tensions with her husband over his wish for a second child. She began feeling depressed, had trouble sleeping, became irritable, and was gaining weight. A typical psychodynamic therapist might have helped Anna gain insight into her angry impulses and her defenses against anger. An interpersonal therapist would do the same, but would also engage her thinking on more immediate issues—how she could balance work and home, resolve the dispute with her husband, and express her emotions more effectively (Markowitz et al., 1998).

Humanistic Therapies

54-3 What are the basic themes of humanistic therapy? What are the specific goals and techniques of Rogers' client-centered approach?

The *humanistic* perspective emphasizes people's inherent potential for self-fulfillment. Like psychodynamic therapies, humanistic therapies have attempted to reduce growth-impeding inner conflicts by providing clients with new insights. Indeed, the psycho-dynamic and humanistic therapies are often referred to as **insight therapies.** But humanistic therapies differ from psychoanalytic therapies in many other ways:

- *Humanistic therapists aim to boost people's self-fulfillment by helping them grow in self-awareness and self-acceptance.*

- *Promoting this growth, not curing illness, is the therapy focus.* Thus, those in therapy became "clients" or just "persons" rather than "patients" (a change many other therapists have adopted).

- *The path to growth is taking immediate responsibility for one's feelings and actions, rather than uncovering hidden determinants.*

- *Conscious thoughts are more important than the unconscious.*

- *The present and future are more important than the past.* The goal is to explore feelings as they occur, rather than achieve insights into the childhood origins of the feelings.

Carl Rogers (1902–1987) developed the widely used humanistic technique he called **client-centered therapy,** which focuses on the person's conscious self-perceptions. In this *nondirective therapy,* the therapist listens, without judging or interpreting, and seeks to refrain from directing the client toward certain insights.

Believing that most people possess the resources for growth, Rogers (1961, 1980) encouraged therapists to exhibit *genuineness, acceptance,* and *empathy.* When therapists drop their facades and genuinely express their true feelings, when they enable their clients to feel unconditionally accepted, and when they empathically sense and reflect their clients' feelings, the clients may deepen their self-understanding and self-acceptance (Hill & Nakayama, 2000). As Rogers (1980, p. 10) explained,

> Hearing has consequences. When I truly hear a person and the meanings that are important to him at that moment, hearing not simply his words, but him, and when I let him know that I have heard his own private personal meanings, many things happen. There is first of all a grateful look. He feels released. He wants to tell me more about his world. He surges forth in a new sense of freedom. He becomes more open to the process of change.
>
> I have often noticed that the more deeply I hear the meanings of the person, the more there is that happens. Almost always, when a person realizes he has been deeply heard, his eyes moisten. I think in some real sense he is weeping for joy. It is as though he were saying, "Thank God, somebody heard me. Someone knows what it's like to be me."

"Hearing" refers to Rogers' technique of **active listening**—echoing, restating, and seeking clarification of what the person expresses (verbally or nonverbally) and acknowledging the expressed feelings. Active listening is now an accepted part of therapeutic counseling practices in many schools, colleges, and clinics. The counselor listens attentively and interrupts only to restate and confirm feelings, to accept what is being expressed, or to seek clarification. The following brief excerpt between Rogers and a male client illustrates how he sought to provide a psychological mirror that would help clients see themselves more clearly.

> *Rogers:* Feeling that now, hm? That you're just no good to yourself, no good to anybody. Never will be any good to anybody. Just that you're completely worthless, huh?—Those really are lousy feelings. Just feel that you're no good at all, hm?

insight therapies a variety of therapies that aim to improve psychological functioning by increasing a person's awareness of underlying motives and defenses.

client-centered therapy a humanistic therapy, developed by Carl Rogers, in which the therapist uses techniques such as active listening within a genuine, accepting, empathic environment to facilitate clients' growth. (Also called *person-centered therapy.*)

active listening empathic listening in which the listener echoes, restates, and clarifies. A feature of Rogers' client-centered therapy.

"We have two ears and one mouth that we may listen the more and talk the less."

Zeno, 335–263 B.C.E., *Diogenes Laertius*

unconditional positive regard
a caring, accepting, nonjudgmental attitude, which Carl Rogers believed would
help clients develop self-awareness and
self-acceptance.

Client: Yeah. (*Muttering in low, discouraged voice*) That's what this guy I went to town with just the other day told me.

Rogers: This guy that you went to town with really told you that you were no good? Is that what you're saying? Did I get that right?

Client: M-hm.

Rogers: I guess the meaning of that if I get it right is that here's somebody that—meant something to you and what does he think of you? Why, he's told you that he thinks you're no good at all. And that just really knocks the props out from under you. (*Client weeps quietly.*) It just brings the tears. (*Silence of 20 seconds*)

Client: (*Rather defiantly*) I don't care though.

Rogers: You tell yourself you don't care at all, but somehow I guess some part of you cares because some part of you weeps over it.

(*Meador & Rogers, 1984, p. 167*)

Can a therapist be a perfect mirror, without selecting and interpreting what is reflected? Rogers conceded that one cannot be *totally* nondirective. Nevertheless, he believed that the therapist's most important contribution is to accept and understand the client. Given a nonjudgmental, grace-filled environment that provides **unconditional positive regard,** people may accept even their worst traits and feel valued and whole.

If you want to listen more actively in your own relationships, three Rogers-inspired hints may help:

1. *Paraphrase.* Rather than saying "I know how you feel," check your understandings by summarizing the person's words in your own words.

2. *Invite clarification.* "What might be an example of that?" may encourage the person to say more.

3. *Reflect feelings.* "It sounds frustrating" might mirror what you're sensing from the person's body language and intensity.

Active listening Carl Rogers (right) empathized with a client during this group therapy session.

Michael Rougier/The LIFE Picture Collection/Getty Images

Behavior Therapies

54-4 How does the basic assumption of behavior therapy differ from the assumptions of psychodynamic and humanistic therapies? What techniques are used in exposure therapies and aversive conditioning?

The insight therapies assume that many psychological problems diminish as self-awareness grows. Psychodynamic therapists expect problems to subside as people gain insight into their unresolved and unconscious tensions. Humanistic therapists expect problems to diminish as people get in touch with their feelings. Proponents of **behavior therapies**, however, doubt the healing power of self-awareness. (You can become aware of why you are highly anxious during exams and still be anxious.) They assume that problem behaviors *are* the problems, and the application of learning principles can eliminate them. Rather than delving deeply below the surface looking for inner causes, behavior therapists view maladaptive symptoms— such as phobias or sexual dysfunctions—as learned behaviors that can be replaced by constructive behaviors.

Classical Conditioning Techniques

One cluster of behavior therapies derives from principles developed in Ivan Pavlov's early twentieth-century conditioning experiments. As Pavlov and others showed, we learn various behaviors and emotions through *classical conditioning.* Could maladaptive symptoms be examples of conditioned responses? If so, might reconditioning be a solution? Learning theorist O. H. Mowrer thought so and developed a successful conditioning therapy for chronic bed-wetters. The child sleeps on a liquid-sensitive pad connected to an alarm. Moisture on the pad triggers the alarm, waking the child. With sufficient repetition, this association of bladder relaxation with waking up stops the bedwetting. In three out of four cases the treatment is effective, and the success provides a boost to the child's self-image (Christophersen & Edwards, 1992; Houts et al., 1994).

Another example: If a claustrophobic fear of elevators is a learned aversion to being in a confined space, then might one unlearn that association by reconditioning to replace the fear response? **Counterconditioning** pairs the trigger stimulus (in this case, the enclosed space of the elevator) with a new response (relaxation) that is incompatible with fear. Two specific counterconditioning techniques—*exposure therapy* and *aversive conditioning*—have successfully counterconditioned people with such fears.

RETRIEVAL PRACTICE

- What might a psychodynamic therapist say about Mowrer's therapy for bed-wetting? How might a behavior therapist reply?

ANSWER: A psychodynamic therapist might be more interested in helping the child develop insight about the underlying problems that have caused the bed-wetting response. A behavior therapist would be more likely to agree with Mowrer that the bed-wetting symptom *is* the problem, and that counterconditioning the unwanted behavior would indeed bring emotional relief.

Exposure Therapies Picture this scene reported in 1924 by behaviorist psychologist Mary Cover Jones: Three-year-old Peter is petrified of rabbits and other furry objects. Jones plans to replace Peter's fear of rabbits with a conditioned response incompatible with fear. Her strategy is to associate the fear-evoking rabbit with the pleasurable, relaxed response associated with eating.

As Peter begins his midafternoon snack, Jones introduces a caged rabbit on the other side of the huge room. Peter, eagerly munching away on his crackers and drinking his milk, hardly notices. On succeeding days, she gradually moves the rabbit closer and closer. Within two months, Peter is tolerating the rabbit in his lap, even stroking it while he eats. Moreover, his fear of other furry objects subsides as well, having been *countered*, or replaced, by a relaxed state that cannot coexist with fear (Fisher, 1984; Jones, 1924).

Unfortunately for those who might have been helped by her counterconditioning procedures, Jones' story of Peter and the rabbit did not immediately become part of psychology's

Kim Reinick/ Shutterstock
Creativ Studio Heinemann/Getty Images

behavior therapy therapy that applies learning principles to the elimination of unwanted behaviors.

counterconditioning behavior therapy procedures that use classical conditioning to evoke new responses to stimuli that are triggering unwanted behaviors; include *exposure therapies* and *aversive conditioning.*

exposure therapies behavioral techniques, such as *systematic desensitization* and *virtual reality exposure therapy,* that treat anxieties by exposing people (in imagination or actual situations) to the things they fear and avoid.

systematic desensitization a type of exposure therapy that associates a pleasant relaxed state with gradually increasing anxiety-triggering stimuli. Commonly used to treat phobias.

virtual reality exposure therapy an anxiety treatment that progressively exposes people to electronic simulations of their greatest fears, such as airplane flying, spiders, or public speaking.

"The only thing we have to fear is fear itself."

U.S. President Franklin D. Roosevelt First Inaugural Address, 1933

lore. It was more than 30 years later that psychiatrist Joseph Wolpe (1958; Wolpe & Plaud, 1997) refined Jones' technique into what are now the most widely used types of behavior therapies: **exposure therapies,** which expose people to what they normally avoid or escape (behaviors that get reinforced by reduced anxiety). Exposure therapies have them face their fear, and thus overcome their fear of the fear response itself. As people can habituate to the sound of a train passing their new apartment, so, with repeated exposure, can they become less anxiously responsive to things that once petrified them (Barrera et al., 2013; Foa et al., 2013).

One widely used exposure therapy is **systematic desensitization.** Wolpe assumed, as did Jones, that you cannot be simultaneously anxious and relaxed. Therefore, if you can repeatedly relax when facing anxiety-provoking stimuli, you can gradually eliminate your anxiety. The trick is to proceed gradually. Imagine yourself afraid of public speaking. A behavior therapist might first ask for your help in constructing a hierarchy of anxiety-triggering speaking situations. Yours might range from mildly anxiety-provoking situations, perhaps speaking up in a small group of friends, to panic-provoking situations, such as having to address a large audience.

Next, using *progressive relaxation,* the therapist would train you to relax one muscle group after another, until you achieve a blissful state of complete relaxation and comfort. Then the therapist would ask you to imagine, with your eyes closed, a mildly anxiety-arousing situation: You are having coffee with a group of friends and are trying to decide whether to speak up. If imagining the scene causes you to feel any anxiety, you would signal your tension by raising your finger, and the therapist would instruct you to switch off the mental image and go back to deep relaxation. This imagined scene is repeatedly paired with relaxation until you feel no trace of anxiety.

The therapist would progress up the constructed anxiety hierarchy, using the relaxed state to desensitize you to each imagined situation. After several sessions, you move to actual situations and practice what you had only imagined before, beginning with relatively easy tasks and gradually moving to more anxiety-filled ones. Conquering your anxiety in an actual situation, not just in your imagination, raises your self-confidence (Foa & Kozak, 1986; Williams, 1987). Eventually, you may even become a confident public speaker. Often people fear not just a situation, such as public speaking, but also being incapacitated by their own fear response. As their fear subsides, so also does their fear of the fear.

When an anxiety-arousing situation is too expensive, difficult, or embarrassing to re-create, **virtual reality exposure therapy** offers an efficient middle ground. Wearing a head-mounted display unit that projects a three-dimensional virtual world, you would view a lifelike series of scenes that would be tailored to your particular fear and that

Virtual reality exposure therapy Within the confines of a room, virtual reality technology exposes people to vivid simulations of feared stimuli, such as walking across a rickety bridge high off the ground.

shift as your head turns. Experiments led by several research teams have treated many different people with many different fears—flying, heights, particular animals, and public speaking (Parsons & Rizzo, 2008). People who fear flying, for example, can peer out a virtual window of a simulated plane, feel vibrations, and hear the engine roar as the plane taxis down the runway and takes off. In studies comparing control groups with people experiencing virtual reality exposure therapy, the therapy has provided relief from real-life fear (Gonçalves et al., 2012; Opriş et al., 2012).

Aversive Conditioning In systematic desensitization, the goal is substituting a positive (relaxed) response for a negative (fearful) response to a *harmless* stimulus. In **aversive conditioning,** the goal is substituting a negative (aversive) response for a positive response to a *harmful* stimulus (such as alcohol). Thus, aversive conditioning is the reverse of systematic desensitization—it seeks to condition an aversion to something the person *should* avoid.

The procedure is simple: It associates the unwanted behavior with unpleasant feelings. To treat nail biting, one can paint the fingernails with a nasty-tasting nail polish (Baskind, 1997). To treat alcohol use disorder, an aversion therapist offers the client appealing drinks laced with a drug that produces severe nausea. By linking alcohol with violent nausea (many of these taste-aversion experiments were first done with rats and coyotes), the therapist seeks to transform the person's reaction to alcohol from positive to negative (**FIGURE 54.1**).

Does aversive conditioning work? In the short run it may. Arthur Wiens and Carol Menustik (1983) studied 685 hospital patients with alcohol use disorder who completed an aversion therapy program. One year later, after returning for several booster treatments of alcohol-sickness pairings, 63 percent were still successfully abstaining. But after three years, only 33 percent had remained abstinent.

The problem is that in therapy (as in research), cognition influences conditioning. People know that outside the therapist's office they can drink without fear of nausea. Their ability to discriminate between the aversive conditioning situation and all other situations can limit the treatment's effectiveness. Thus, therapists often use aversive conditioning in combination with other treatments.

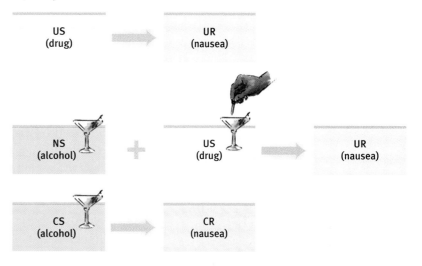

▼ FIGURE 54.1
Aversion therapy for alcohol use disorder After repeatedly imbibing an alcoholic drink mixed with a drug that produces severe nausea, some people with a history of alcohol use disorder develop at least a temporary conditioned aversion to alcohol. (Classical conditioning terms: US is *unconditioned stimulus,* UR is *unconditioned response,* NS is *neutral stimulus,* CS is *conditioned stimulus,* and CR is *conditioned response.*)

Operant Conditioning

54-5 What is the main premise of therapy based on operant conditioning principles, and what are the views of its proponents and critics?

The work of B. F. Skinner and others teaches us a basic principle of *operant conditioning:* Voluntary behaviors are strongly influenced by their consequences. Knowing this, some behavior therapists practice *behavior modification.* They reinforce desired behaviors, and they withhold reinforcement for undesired behaviors. Using operant conditioning to solve specific behavior problems has raised hopes for some otherwise hopeless cases. Children with intellectual disabilities have been taught to care for themselves. Socially withdrawn children with autism spectrum disorder (ASD) have learned to interact. People with schizophrenia have been helped to behave more rationally in their hospital ward. In such cases, therapists use positive reinforcers to shape behavior in a step-by-step manner, rewarding closer and closer approximations of the desired behavior.

In extreme cases, treatment must be intensive. One study worked with 19 withdrawn, uncommunicative 3-year-olds with ASD. Each participated in a 2-year program in which their parents spent 40 hours a week attempting to shape their behavior

aversive conditioning a type of counterconditioning that associates an unpleasant state (such as nausea) with an unwanted behavior (such as drinking alcohol).

token economy an operant conditioning procedure in which people earn a token of some sort for exhibiting a desired behavior and can later exchange their tokens for various privileges or treats.

(Lovaas, 1987). The combination of positively reinforcing desired behaviors, and ignoring or punishing aggressive and self-abusive behaviors, worked wonders for some. By first grade, 9 of the 19 children were functioning successfully in school and exhibiting normal intelligence. In a group of 40 comparable children not undergoing this effortful treatment, only one showed similar improvement. (Ensuing studies focused on the effective aspect—positive reinforcement.)

Rewards used to modify behavior vary. For some people, the reinforcing power of attention or praise is sufficient. Others require concrete rewards, such as food. In institutional settings, therapists may create a **token economy**. When people display appropriate behavior, such as getting out of bed, washing, dressing, eating, talking coherently, cleaning up their rooms, or playing cooperatively, they receive a token or plastic coin as a positive reinforcer. Later, they can exchange their accumulated tokens for various rewards, such as candy, TV time, trips to town, or better living quarters. Token economies have been successfully applied in various settings (homes, classrooms, hospitals, institutions for juvenile offenders) and among members of various populations (including disturbed children and people with schizophrenia and other mental disabilities).

Critics of behavior modification express two concerns. The first is practical: *How durable are the behaviors?* Will people become so dependent on extrinsic rewards that the appropriate behaviors will stop when the reinforcers stop? Proponents of behavior modification believe the behaviors will endure if therapists wean patients from the tokens by shifting them toward other, real-life rewards, such as social approval. They also point out that the appropriate behaviors themselves can be intrinsically rewarding. For example, as a withdrawn person becomes more socially competent, the intrinsic satisfactions of social interaction may help the person maintain the behavior.

The second concern is ethical: *Is it right for one human to control another's behavior?* Those who set up token economies deprive people of something they desire and decide which behaviors to reinforce. To critics, this whole process has an authoritarian taint. Advocates reply that some patients request the therapy. Moreover, control already exists; rewards and punishers are already maintaining destructive behavior patterns. So why not reinforce adaptive behavior instead? Treatment with positive rewards is more humane than being institutionalized or punished, advocates argue, and the right to effective treatment and an improved life justifies temporary deprivation.

RETRIEVAL PRACTICE

- What are the *insight therapies,* and how do they differ from behavior therapies?

  ANSWER: The *insight therapies*—psychodynamic and humanistic therapies—seek to relieve problems by providing an understanding of their origins. Behavior therapies assume the problem behavior *is* the problem and treat it directly, paying less attention to its origins.

- Some maladaptive behaviors are learned. What hope does this fact provide?

  ANSWER: If a behavior can be learned, it can be *unlearned,* and replaced by other more adaptive responses.

- Exposure therapies and aversive conditioning are applications of _____ conditioning. Token economies are an application of _____ conditioning.

  ANSWERS: classical; operant

Cognitive Therapies

54-6 What are the goals and techniques of cognitive therapy and of cognitive-behavioral therapy?

We have seen how behavior therapists treat specific fears and problem behaviors. But how do they deal with depressive disorders? Or with generalized anxiety, in which anxiety has no focus? Behavior therapists treating these less clearly defined psychological problems have had help from the same *cognitive revolution* that has profoundly changed other areas of psychology during the last half-century.

Cognitive therapy for eating disorders aided by journaling Cognitive therapists guide people toward new ways of explaining their good and bad experiences. By recording positive events and how she has enabled them, this woman may become more mindful of her self-control and more optimistic.

The **cognitive therapies** assume that our thinking colors our feelings (**FIGURE 54.2**). Between an event and our response lies the mind. Self-blaming and overgeneralized explanations of bad events are often an integral part of the vicious cycle of depression. The depressed person interprets a suggestion as criticism, disagreement as dislike, praise as flattery, friendliness as pity. Ruminating on such thoughts sustains the negative thinking. If such thinking patterns can be learned, then surely they can be replaced. Cognitive therapies therefore teach people new, more constructive ways of thinking. If people are miserable, they can be helped to change their minds.

"Life does not consist mainly, or even largely, of facts and happenings. It consists mainly of the storm of thoughts that are forever blowing through one's mind."

Mark Twain, 1835–1910

▼ FIGURE 54.2
A cognitive perspective on psychological disorders The person's emotional reactions are produced not directly by the event but by the person's thoughts in response to the event.

Aaron Beck's Therapy for Depression

Cognitive therapist Aaron Beck believes that changing people's thinking can change their functioning. When Beck analyzed depressed people's dreams, he found recurring negative themes of loss, rejection, and abandonment that extended into their waking thoughts. Such negativity even extends into therapy, as clients recall and rehearse their failings and worst impulses (Kelly, 2000). With cognitive therapy, Beck and his colleagues (1979) sought to reverse clients' *catastrophizing* beliefs about themselves, their situations, and their futures. Gentle questioning seeks to reveal irrational thinking, and then to persuade people to remove the dark glasses through which they view life (Beck et al., 1979, pp. 145–146):

> *Client:* I agree with the descriptions of me but I guess I don't agree that the way I think makes me depressed.
>
> *Beck:* How do you understand it?
>
> *Client:* I get depressed when things go wrong. Like when I fail a test.
>
> *Beck:* How can failing a test make you depressed?
>
> *Client:* Well, if I fail I'll never get into law school.

cognitive therapy therapy that teaches people new, more adaptive ways of thinking; based on the assumption that thoughts intervene between events and our emotional reactions.

>
> *Beck:* So failing the test means a lot to you. But if failing a test could drive people into clinical depression, wouldn't you expect everyone who failed the test to have a depression? . . . Did everyone who failed get depressed enough to require treatment?
>
> *Client:* No, but it depends on how important the test was to the person.
>
> *Beck:* Right, and who decides the importance?
>
> *Client:* I do.
>
> *Beck:* And so, what we have to examine is your way of viewing the test (or the way that you think about the test) and how it affects your chances of getting into law school. Do you agree?
>
> *Client:* Right.
>
> *Beck:* Do you agree that the way you interpret the results of the test will affect you? You might feel depressed, you might have trouble sleeping, not feel like eating, and you might even wonder if you should drop out of the course.
>
> *Client:* I have been thinking that I wasn't going to make it. Yes, I agree.
>
> *Beck:* Now what did failing mean?
>
> *Client:* *(tearful)* That I couldn't get into law school.
>
> *Beck:* And what does that mean to you?
>
> *Client:* That I'm just not smart enough.
>
> *Beck:* Anything else?
>
> *Client:* That I can never be happy.
>
> *Beck:* And how do these thoughts make you feel?
>
> *Client:* Very unhappy.
>
> *Beck:* So it is the meaning of failing a test that makes you very unhappy. In fact, believing that you can never be happy is a powerful factor in producing unhappiness. So, you get yourself into a trap—by definition, failure to get into law school equals "I can never be happy."

We often think in words. Therefore, getting people to change what they say to themselves is an effective way to change their thinking. Perhaps you can identify with the anxious students who, before an exam, make matters worse with self-defeating thoughts: "This exam's probably going to be impossible. All these other students seem so relaxed and confident. I wish I were better prepared. Anyhow, I'm so nervous I'll forget everything." To change such negative self-talk, Donald Meichenbaum (1977, 1985) offered *stress inoculation training:* teaching people to restructure their thinking in stressful situations. Sometimes it may be enough simply to say more positive things to oneself: "Relax. The exam may be hard, but it will be hard for everyone else, too. I studied harder than most people. Besides, I don't need a perfect score to get a good grade." After being trained to dispute their negative thoughts, depression-prone children, teens, and college students exhibit a greatly reduced rate of future depression (Reivich et al., 2013; Seligman et al.,

PEANUTS

▼ TABLE 54.1
Selected Cognitive Therapy Techniques

Aim of Technique	Technique	Therapists' Directives
Reveal beliefs	Question your interpretations	Explore your beliefs, revealing faulty assumptions such as "I must be liked by everyone."
	Rank thoughts and emotions	Gain perspective by ranking your thoughts and emotions from mildly to extremely upsetting.
Test beliefs	Examine consequences	Explore difficult situations, assessing possible consequences and challenging faulty reasoning.
	Decatastrophize thinking	Work through the actual worst-case consequences of the situation you face (it is often not as bad as imagined). Then determine how to cope with the real situation you face.
Change beliefs	Take appropriate responsibility	Challenge total self-blame and negative thinking, noting aspects for which you may be truly responsible, as well as aspects that aren't your responsibility.
	Resist extremes	Develop new ways of thinking and feeling to replace maladaptive habits. For example, change from thinking "I am a total failure" to "I got a failing grade on that paper, and I can make these changes to succeed next time."

2009). To a large extent, it *is* the thought that counts. **TABLE 54.1** provides a sampling of techniques commonly used in cognitive therapy.

It's not just depressed people who can benefit from positive self-talk. We all talk to ourselves ("Where did I leave the keys?" "I wish I hadn't said that"). The findings of nearly three dozen sport psychology studies show that self-talk interventions can enhance the learning of athletic skills (Hatzigeorgiadas et al., 2011). For example, novice basketball players may be trained to think "focus" and "follow through," swimmers to think "high elbow," and tennis players to think "look at the ball."

Cognitive-Behavioral Therapy

Cognitive-behavioral therapy (CBT), today's most widely practiced psychotherapy, aims not only to alter the way people think (cognitive therapy), but also to alter the way they act (behavior therapy). It seeks to make people aware of their irrational negative thinking, to replace it with new ways of thinking, and to *practice* the more positive approach in everyday settings. Behavioral change is typically addressed first, followed by sessions on cognitive change; the therapy concludes with a focus on maintaining both and preventing relapses.

Anxiety, depressive disorders, and bipolar disorder share a common problem: emotion regulation (Aldao & Nolen-Hoeksema, 2010). An effective CBT program for these emotional disorders trains people both to replace their catastrophizing thinking with more realistic appraisals, and, as homework, to practice behaviors that are incompatible with their problem (Kazantzis et al., 2010a,b; Moses & Barlow, 2006). A person might, for example, keep a log of daily situations associated with negative and positive emotions, and engage more in activities that lead them to feeling good. Or those who fear social situations might be assigned to practice approaching people.

CBT may also be useful with obsessive-compulsive disorder. In one study, people learned to prevent their compulsive behaviors by relabeling their obsessive thoughts (Schwartz et al., 1996). Feeling the urge to wash their hands again, they would tell themselves, "I'm having a compulsive urge," and attribute it to their brain's abnormal activity, as previously viewed in their PET scans. Instead of giving in to the urge, they would then spend 15 minutes in an enjoyable, alternative behavior, such as practicing an instrument, taking a walk, or gardening. This helped "unstick" the brain by shifting

"The trouble with most therapy is that it helps you to feel better. But you don't get better. You have to back it up with action, action, action."

Therapist Albert Ellis (1913–2007)

cognitive-behavioral therapy (CBT) a popular integrative therapy that combines cognitive therapy (changing self-defeating thinking) with behavior therapy (changing behavior).

attention and engaging other brain areas. For two or three months, the weekly therapy sessions continued, with relabeling and refocusing practice at home. By the study's end, most participants' symptoms had diminished and their PET scans revealed normalized brain activity. Many other studies confirm CBT's effectiveness for treating anxiety, depression, and anorexia or bulimia nervosa (Covin et al., 2008; Zalta, 2011).

Studies have also found that cognitive-behavioral skills can be taught and therapy can be effectively conducted over the Internet (Andersson et al., 2012; Stross, 2011). To make psychological treatment more accessible and affordable, some mental health experts advocate phone-based interventions, web-based skill training, work-setting treatment, and self-help efforts facilitated by groups, books, and even phone apps (Kazdin & Blase, 2011a,b; Merry et al., 2012; Teachman, 2014). Skype therapy may lack eye contact, but it means "the therapist can see you now"—anywhere and anytime.

RETRIEVAL PRACTICE

- How do the humanistic and cognitive therapies differ?

ANSWER: By reflecting clients' feelings in a nondirective setting, the *humanistic therapies* attempt to foster personal growth by helping clients become more self-aware and self-accepting. By making clients aware of self-defeating patterns of thinking, *cognitive therapies* guide people toward more adaptive ways of thinking about themselves and their world.

- An influential cognitive therapy for depression was developed by _____ _____.

ANSWER: Aaron Beck

- What is cognitive-behavioral therapy, and what sorts of problems does this therapy best address?

ANSWER: This integrative therapy helps people change self-defeating thinking and behavior. It has been shown to be effective for those with anxiety disorders, obsessive-compulsive disorder, depressive disorders, bipolar disorder, and eating disorders.

Group and Family Therapies

54-7 What are the aims and benefits of group and family therapies?

Group Therapy

Except for traditional psychoanalysis, most therapies may also occur in small groups. **Group therapy** does not provide the same degree of therapist involvement with each client. However, it offers many benefits:

- *It saves therapists' time and clients' money,* often with no less effectiveness than individual therapy (Fuhriman & Burlingame, 1994).
- *It offers a social laboratory for exploring social behaviors and developing social skills.* Therapists frequently suggest group therapy for people experiencing frequent conflicts or whose behavior distresses others. For up to 90 minutes weekly, the therapist guides people's interactions as they discuss issues and try out new behaviors.
- *It enables people to see that others share their problems.* It can be a relief to discover that you are not alone—to learn that others, despite their composure, experience some of the same troublesome feelings and behaviors.
- *It provides feedback as clients try out new ways of behaving.* Hearing that you look poised, even though you feel anxious and self-conscious, can be very reassuring.

Family Therapy

One special type of group interaction, **family therapy,** assumes that no person is an island: We live and grow in relation to others, especially our families. We struggle to differentiate ourselves from our families, but we also need to connect with them emotionally. Some of our problem behaviors arise from the tension between these two tendencies, which can create family stress.

group therapy therapy conducted with groups rather than individuals, permitting therapeutic benefits from group interaction.

family therapy therapy that treats the family as a system. Views an individual's unwanted behaviors as influenced by, or directed at, other family members.

Unlike most psychotherapy, which focuses on what happens inside the person's own skin, family therapists work with multiple family members to heal relationships and to mobilize family resources. They tend to view the family as a system in which each person's actions trigger reactions from others, and they help family members discover their role within their family's social system. A child's rebellion, for example, affects and is affected by other family tensions. Therapists also attempt—usually with some success, research suggests—to open up communication within the family or to help family members discover new ways of preventing or resolving conflicts (Hazelrigg et al., 1987; Shadish et al., 1993).

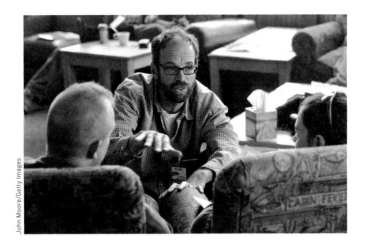

Family therapy This type of therapy often acts as a preventive mental health strategy and may include marriage therapy, as shown here at a retreat for military families. The therapist helps family members understand how their ways of relating to one another create problems. The treatment's emphasis is not on changing the individuals but on changing their relationships and interactions.

Self-Help Groups

Many people also participate in self-help and support groups (Yalom, 1985). One analysis of online support groups and more than 14,000 self-help groups reported that most support groups focus on stigmatized or hard-to-discuss illnesses (Davison et al., 2000). AIDS patients, for example, are 250 times more likely than hypertension patients to be in support groups. Those struggling with anorexia and alcohol use disorder often join groups; those with migraines and ulcers usually do not. People with hearing loss have national organizations with local chapters; people with vision loss more often cope on their own.

The grandparent of support groups, Alcoholics Anonymous (AA), reports having 2.1 million members in 115,000 groups worldwide. Its famous 12-step program, emulated by many other self-help groups, asks members to admit their powerlessness, to seek help from a higher power and from one another, and (the twelfth step) to take the message to others in need of it. In one eight-year, $27 million investigation, AA participants reduced their drinking sharply, although so did those assigned to cognitive-behavioral therapy or to an alternative therapy (Project Match, 1997). Other studies have similarly found that 12-step programs such as AA have helped reduce alcohol use disorder comparably to other treatment interventions (Ferri et al., 2006; Moos & Moos, 2005). Those whose personal stories include a "redemptive narrative"—who see something good as having come from their experience—more often sustain sobriety (Dunlop & Tracy, 2013). Also, the more meetings members attend, the greater their alcohol abstinence (Moos & Moos, 2006). In one study of 2300 veterans who sought treatment for alcohol use disorder, a high level of AA involvement was followed by diminished alcohol problems (McKellar et al., 2003).

With more than 2 million members worldwide, AA is said to be "the largest organization on Earth that nobody wanted to join" (Finlay, 2000).

In an individualistic age, with more and more people living alone or feeling isolated, the popularity of support groups—for the addicted, the bereaved, the divorced, or simply those seeking fellowship and growth—seems to reflect a longing for community and connectedness. More than 100 million Americans belong to small religious, interest, or self-help groups that meet regularly—and 9 in 10 report that group members "support each other emotionally" (Gallup, 1994).

* * *

For a synopsis of the modern forms of psychotherapy we've been discussing, see **TABLE 54.2** on the next page.

Therapy	Presumed Problem	Therapy Aim	Therapy Technique
Psychodynamic	Unconscious conflicts from childhood experiences	Reduce anxiety through self-insight.	Interpret patients' memories and feelings.
Client-centered	Barriers to self-understanding and self-acceptance	Enable growth via unconditional positive regard, genuineness, acceptance, and empathy.	Listen actively and reflect clients' feelings.
Behavior	Dysfunctional behaviors	Learn adaptive behaviors; extinguish problem ones.	Use classical conditioning (via exposure or aversion therapy) or operant conditioning (as in token economies).
Cognitive	Negative, self-defeating thinking	Promote healthier thinking and self-talk.	Train people to dispute negative thoughts and attributions.
Cognitive-behavioral	Self-harmful thoughts and behaviors	Promote healthier thinking and adaptive behaviors.	Train people to counter self-harmful thoughts and to act out their new ways of thinking.
Group and family	Stressful relationships	Heal relationships.	Develop an understanding of family and other social systems, explore roles, and improve communication.

🅐 **LaunchPad** To review the aims and techniques of different psychotherapies, and assess your ability to recognize excerpts from each, visit LaunchPad's *PsychSim 6: Mystery Therapist.*

MODULE 54 REVIEW Introduction to Therapy and the Psychological Therapies

LEARNING OBJECTIVES

RETRIEVAL PRACTICE Take a moment to answer each of these Learning Objective Questions (repeated here from within this module). Then turn to Appendix C, Complete Module Reviews, to check your answers. Research suggests that trying to answer these questions on your own will improve your long-term retention (McDaniel et al., 2009).

54-1 How do *psychotherapy* and the *biomedical therapies* differ?

54-2 What are the goals and techniques of psychoanalysis, and how have they been adapted in psychodynamic therapy?

54-3 What are the basic themes of humanistic therapy? What are the specific goals and techniques of Rogers' client-centered approach?

54-4 How does the basic assumption of behavior therapy differ from the assumptions of psychodynamic and humanistic therapies? What techniques are used in exposure therapies and aversive conditioning?

54-5 What is the main premise of therapy based on operant conditioning principles, and what are the views of its proponents and critics?

54-6 What are the goals and techniques of cognitive therapy and of cognitive-behavioral therapy?

54-7 What are the aims and benefits of group and family therapies?

TERMS AND CONCEPTS TO REMEMBER

RETRIEVAL PRACTICE Test yourself on these terms by trying to write down the definition before flipping back to the page number referenced to check your answer.

psychotherapy, p. 658

biomedical therapy, p. 658

eclectic approach, p. 658

psychoanalysis, p. 658

resistance, p. 659

interpretation, p. 659

transference, p. 659

psychodynamic therapy, p. 660

insight therapies, p. 661

client-centered therapy, p. 661

active listening, p. 661

unconditional positive regard, p. 662

behavior therapy, p. 663

counterconditioning, p. 663

exposure therapies, p. 664

systematic desensitization, p. 664

virtual reality exposure therapy, p. 664

aversive conditioning, p. 665

token economy, p. 666

cognitive therapy, p. 667

cognitive-behavioral therapy (CBT), p. 669

group therapy, p. 670

family therapy, p. 670

Use 🅐 **LearningCurve** to create your personalized study plan, which will direct you to the resources that will help you most in 🅐 **LaunchPad.**

Evaluating Psychotherapies

ADVICE COLUMNISTS FREQUENTLY URGE THEIR troubled letter writers to get professional help: "Seek counseling" or "Ask your mate to find a therapist."

Many Americans share this confidence in **psychotherapy's** effectiveness. Before 1950, psychiatrists were the primary providers of mental health care. Today's providers include clinical and counseling psychologists, clinical social workers, clergy, marital and school counselors, and psychiatric nurses. With such an enormous outlay of time as well as money, effort, and hope, it is important to ask: Are the millions of people worldwide justified in placing their hopes in psychotherapy?

Is Psychotherapy Effective?

55-1 Does psychotherapy work? How can we know?

The question, though simply put, is not simple to answer. Measuring therapy's effectiveness is not like taking your body's temperature after a fever. So how can we assess psychotherapy's effectiveness? By how we feel about our progress? By how our therapist feels about it? By how our friends and family feel about it? By how our behavior has changed?

Clients' Perceptions

If clients' testimonials were the only measuring stick, we could strongly affirm psychotherapy's effectiveness. When 2900 *Consumer Reports* readers (1995; Kotkin et al., 1996; Seligman, 1995) related their experiences with mental health professionals, 89 percent said they were at least "fairly well satisfied." Among those who recalled feeling *fair* or *very poor* when beginning therapy, 9 in 10 now were feeling *very good, good,* or at least *so-so.* We have their word for it—and who should know better?

We should not dismiss these testimonials. But for several reasons, client testimonials do not persuade psychotherapy's skeptics:

- *People often enter therapy in crisis.* When, with the normal ebb and flow of events, the crisis passes, people may attribute their improvement to the therapy. Depressed people often get better no matter what they do.

- *Clients believe that treatment will be effective.* The *placebo effect* is the healing power of positive expectations.

- *Clients want to believe the therapy was worth the effort.* To admit investing time and money in something ineffective is like admitting to having one's car serviced repeatedly by a mechanic who never fixes it. Self-justification is a powerful human motive, which helps explain why all therapies produce appreciative testimonials.

- *Clients generally speak kindly of their therapists.* Even if the problems remain, say the critics, clients "work hard to find something positive to say. The therapist had been very understanding, the client had gained a new perspective, he learned to communicate better, his mind was eased, anything at all so as not to have to say treatment was a failure" (Zilbergeld, 1983, p. 117).

As researchers continue to document, we are prone to selective and biased recall and to making judgments that confirm our beliefs. Consider the testimonials gathered in a massive experiment with over 500 Massachusetts boys, aged 5 to 13 years, many of whom seemed bound for delinquency. By the toss of a coin, half the boys were assigned to a 5-year treatment program. The treated boys were visited by counselors twice a month. They participated in community programs, and they received academic tutoring, medical attention, and family assistance as needed. Some 30 years later, Joan McCord (1978, 1979) located 485 participants, sent them questionnaires, and checked public records from courts, mental hospitals, and other sources. Was the treatment successful?

psychotherapy treatment involving psychological techniques; consists of interaction between a trained therapist and someone seeking to overcome psychological difficulties or achieve personal growth.

Trauma: These women were mourning the tragic loss of lives and homes in the 2010 earthquake in China. Those who suffer through such trauma may benefit from counseling, though many people recover on their own or with the help of supportive relationships with family and friends. "Life itself still remains a very effective therapist," noted psychodynamic therapist Karen Horney (*Our Inner Conflicts,* 1945).

Client testimonials were glowing. Some men noted that, had it not been for their counselors, "I would probably be in jail," "My life would have gone the other way," or "I think I would have ended up in a life of crime." Court records offered apparent support: Even among the "difficult" boys in the treatment group, 66 percent had no official juvenile crime record.

But recall psychology's most powerful tool for sorting reality from wishful thinking: the *control group*. For every boy in the treatment group, there was a similar boy in a control group, receiving no counseling. Of these untreated men, *70 percent* had no juvenile record. On several other measures, such as a record of having committed a second crime, alcohol use disorder, death rate, and job satisfaction, the untreated men exhibited slightly *fewer* problems. The glowing testimonials of those treated had been unintentionally deceiving.

Clinicians' Perceptions

Do clinicians' perceptions give us any more reason to celebrate? Case studies of successful treatment abound. The problem is that clients justify entering psychotherapy by emphasizing their unhappiness and justify leaving by emphasizing their well-being. Therapists treasure compliments from clients as they say good-bye or later express their gratitude, but they hear little from clients who experience only temporary relief and seek out new therapists for their recurring problems. Thus, the same person—with the same recurring anxieties, depression, or marital difficulty—may be a "success" story in several therapists' files.

Because people enter therapy when they are extremely unhappy, and usually leave when they are less unhappy, most therapists, like most clients, testify to therapy's success—regardless of the treatment.

Outcome Research

How, then, can we objectively measure the effectiveness of psychotherapy? How can we determine which people and problems are helped, and by what type of psychotherapy?

In search of answers, psychologists have turned to controlled research studies. Similar research in the 1800s transformed the field of medicine. Physicians, skeptical of many of the fashionable treatments (bleeding, purging, infusions of plant and metal substances), began to realize that many patients got better on their own, without these treatments, and that others died despite them. Sorting fact from superstition required observing patients with and without a particular treatment. Typhoid fever patients, for example, often improved after being bled, convincing most physicians that the treatment worked. Not until a control group was given mere bed rest—and 70 percent were observed to improve after five weeks of fever—did physicians learn, to their shock, that the bleeding was worthless (Thomas, 1992).

In psychology, the opening challenge to the effectiveness of psychotherapy was issued by British psychologist Hans Eysenck (1952). Launching a spirited debate, he summarized studies showing that two-thirds of those receiving psychotherapy for non-psychotic disorders improved markedly. To this day, no one disputes that optimistic estimate.

Why, then, are we still debating psychotherapy's effectiveness? Because Eysenck also reported similar improvement among *untreated* persons, such as those who were on waiting lists. With or without psychotherapy, he said, roughly two-thirds improved noticeably. Time was a great healer.

Later research revealed shortcomings in Eysenck's analyses; his sample was small (only 24 studies of psychotherapy outcomes in 1952). Today, hundreds of studies are available. The best are *randomized clinical trials*, in which researchers randomly assign people on a waiting list to therapy or to no therapy, and later evaluate everyone, using

meta-analysis a procedure for statistically combining the results of many different research studies.

tests and assessments by others who don't know whether therapy was given. The results of many such studies are then digested by means of **meta-analysis,** a statistical procedure that combines the conclusions of a large number of different studies. Simply said, meta-analyses give us the bottom-line result of lots of studies.

Therapists welcomed the first meta-analysis of some 475 psychotherapy outcome studies (Smith et al., 1980). It showed that the average therapy client ends up better off than 80 percent of the untreated individuals on waiting lists (**FIGURE 55.1**). The claim is modest—by definition, about 50 percent of untreated people also are better off than the average untreated person. Nevertheless, Mary Lee Smith and her colleagues exulted that "psychotherapy benefits people of all ages as reliably as schooling educates them, medicine cures them, or business turns a profit" (p. 183).

Dozens of subsequent summaries have now examined psychotherapy's effectiveness. Their verdict echoes the results of the earlier outcome studies: *Those not undergoing therapy often improve, but those undergoing therapy are more likely to improve, and to improve more quickly and with less risk of relapse.* Moreover, between treatment sessions for depression and anxiety, many people experience sudden symptom reductions. Those "sudden gains" bode well for long-term improvement (Aderka et al., 2012).

Is psychotherapy also cost-effective? Again, the answer is *Yes.* Studies show that when people seek psychological treatment, their search for other medical treatment drops—by 16 percent in one digest of 91 studies (Chiles et al., 1999). Given the staggering annual cost of psychological disorders and substance abuse—including crime, accidents, lost work, and treatment—psychotherapy is a good investment, much like money spent on prenatal and well-baby care. Both *reduce* long-term costs. Boosting employees' psychological well-being, for example, can lower medical costs, improve work efficiency, and diminish absenteeism.

But note that the claim—that psychotherapy, *on average*, is somewhat effective—refers to no one therapy in particular. It is like reassuring lung-cancer patients that "on average," medical treatment of health problems is effective. What people want to know is the effectiveness of a *particular* treatment for their specific problems.

Number of persons

Average untreated person

Average psychotherapy client

Poor outcome

Good outcome

80% of untreated people have poorer outcomes than the average treated person.

▼ FIGURE 55.1
Treatment versus no treatment
These two normal distribution curves based on data from 475 studies show the improvement of untreated people and psychotherapy clients. The outcome for the average therapy client surpassed the outcome for 80 percent of the untreated people. (Data from Smith et al., 1980.)

RETRIEVAL PRACTICE

- How might the *placebo effect* bias clients' and clinicians' appraisals of the effectiveness of psychotherapies?

ANSWER: The *placebo effect* is the healing power of *belief* in a treatment. Patients and therapists who expect a treatment to be effective may believe it was.

Which Psychotherapies Work Best?

55-2 Are some psychotherapies more effective than others for specific disorders?

So what can we tell people considering psychotherapy, and those paying for it, about *which* psychotherapy will be most effective for their problem? The statistical summaries and surveys fail to pinpoint any one type of therapy as generally superior (Smith et al., 1977, 1980). Clients seemed equally satisfied, *Consumer Reports* concluded, whether treated by a psychiatrist, psychologist, or social worker; whether seen in a group or individual context; whether the therapist had extensive or relatively limited training and experience (Seligman, 1995). Other studies concur (Barth et al., 2013). There is little if any connection between clinicians' experience, training, supervision, and licensing and their clients' outcomes (Luborsky et al., 2002; Wampold, 2007).

"Whatever differences in treatment efficacy exist, they appear to be extremely small, at best."

Bruce Wampold et al. (1997)

evidence-based practice clinical decision making that integrates the best available research with clinical expertise and patient characteristics and preferences.

"Different sores have different salves."

English proverb

▼ FIGURE 55.2
Evidence-based clinical decision making The ideal clinical decision making is a three-legged stool, upheld by research evidence, clinical expertise, and knowledge of the patient.

Clinical decision making

Patient's values, characteristics, preferences, circumstances

Clinical expertise

Best available research evidence

So, was the dodo bird in *Alice in Wonderland* right: "Everyone has won and all must have prizes"? Not quite. Some forms of therapy get prizes for particular problems, though there is often an overlapping—or *comorbidity*—of disorders. Behavioral conditioning therapies, for example, have achieved especially favorable results with specific behavior problems, such as bed-wetting, phobias, compulsions, marital problems, and sexual dysfunctions (Baker et al., 2008; Hunsley & DiGiulio, 2002; Shadish & Baldwin, 2005). Psychodynamic therapy has helped treat depression and anxiety (Driessen et al., 2010; Leichsenring & Rabung, 2008; Shedler, 2010b). With mild to moderate depression, non-directive (client-centered) counseling often helps (Cuijpers et al., 2013). And new studies confirm cognitive and cognitive-behavioral therapy's effectiveness (some say superiority) in coping with anxiety, posttraumatic stress disorder, and depression (Baker et al., 2008; De Los Reyes & Kazdin, 2009; Stewart & Chambless, 2009; Tolin, 2010).

Moreover, we can say that therapy is most effective when the problem is clear-cut (Singer, 1981; Westen & Morrison, 2001). Those who experience phobias or panic, who are unassertive, or who are frustrated by sexual performance problems can hope for improvement. Those with less-focused problems, such as depression and anxiety, usually benefit in the short term but often relapse later. The more specific the problem, the greater the hope.

But no prizes—and little or no scientific support—go to certain other therapies (Arkowitz & Lilienfeld, 2006). We would all therefore be wise to avoid energy therapies that propose to manipulate people's invisible energy fields, recovered-memory therapies that aim to unearth "repressed memories" of early child abuse, and rebirthing therapies that engage people in reenacting the supposed trauma of their birth.

As with some medical treatments, it's possible for psychological treatments to be not only ineffective but also harmful—by making people worse or preventing their getting better (Barlow, 2010; Castonguay et al., 2010; Dimidjian & Hollon, 2010). The National Science and Technology Council cites the Scared Straight program (seeking to deter children and youth from crime) as an example of well-intentioned programs that have proved ineffective or even harmful.

The evaluation question—which therapies get prizes and which do not?—lies at the heart of what some call psychology's civil war. To what extent should science guide both clinical practice and the willingness of health care providers and insurers to pay for psychotherapy?

On the one side are research psychologists using scientific methods to extend the list of well-defined and validated therapies for various disorders. They decry clinicians who "give more weight to their personal experiences" (Baker et al., 2008). On the other side are non-scientist therapists who view their practice as more art than science, saying that people are too complex and therapy too intuitive to describe in a manual or test in an experiment. Between these two factions stand the science-oriented clinicians, who aim to base practice on evidence and make mental health professionals accountable for effectiveness.

To encourage **evidence-based practice** in psychology, the American Psychological Association and others (2006; Lilienfeld et al., 2013) urge clinicians to integrate the best available research with clinical expertise and with patient preferences and characteristics. Available therapies "should be rigorously evaluated" and then applied by clinicians who are mindful of their skills and of each patient's unique situation (**FIGURE 55.2**). Increasingly, insurer and government support for mental health services requires evidence-based practice.

RETRIEVAL PRACTICE

• Therapy is most likely to be helpful for those with problems that _____ (are/are not) well-defined.

ANSWER: are

Evaluating Alternative Therapies

55-3 How do alternative therapies fare under scientific scrutiny?

The tendency of many abnormal states of mind to return to normal, combined with the placebo effect (the healing power of mere belief in a treatment), creates fertile soil for pseudotherapies. Bolstered by anecdotes, heralded by the media, and broadcast on the Internet, alternative therapies can spread like wildfire. In one national survey, 57 percent of those with a history of anxiety attacks and 54 percent of those with a history of depression had used alternative treatments, such as herbal medicine, massage, and spiritual healing (Kessler et al., 2001).

Testimonials aside, what does the evidence say? This is a tough question, because there is no evidence for or against most of them, though their proponents often feel personal experience is evidence enough. Some, however, have been the subject of controlled research. Let's consider two of these. As we do, remember that sifting sense from nonsense requires the scientific attitude: being skeptical but not cynical, open to surprises but not gullible.

Eye Movement Desensitization and Reprocessing (EMDR)

EMDR (eye movement desensitization and reprocessing) is a therapy adored by thousands and dismissed by thousands more as a sham—"an excellent vehicle for illustrating the differences between scientific and pseudoscientific therapy techniques," suggested James Herbert and seven others (2000). Francine Shapiro (1989, 2007, 2012) developed EMDR while walking in a park and observing that anxious thoughts vanished as her eyes spontaneously darted about. Back in the clinic, she had people imagine traumatic scenes while she triggered eye movements by waving her finger in front of their eyes, supposedly enabling them to unlock and reprocess previously frozen memories. Tens of thousands of mental health professionals from more than 75 countries have since undergone training (EMDR, 2011). Not since the similarly charismatic Franz Anton Mesmer introduced *animal magnetism* (hypnosis) more than two centuries ago (also after feeling inspired by an outdoor experience) has a new therapy attracted so many devotees so quickly.

Does it work? For 84 to 100 percent of single-trauma victims participating in four studies, the answer is *Yes*, reports Shapiro (1999, 2002). Moreover, the treatment need take no more than three 90-minute sessions. The Society of Clinical Psychology task force on empirically validated treatments acknowledges that EMDR is "probably efficacious" for the treatment of nonmilitary posttraumatic stress disorder (Chambless et al., 1997; see also Bisson & Andrew, 2007; Rodenburg et al., 2009; Seidler & Wagner, 2006).

Why, wonder the skeptics, would rapidly moving one's eyes while recalling traumas be therapeutic? Some argue that eye movements serve to relax or distract patients, thus allowing the memory-associated emotions to extinguish (Gunter & Bodner, 2008). Others believe that eye movements in themselves are *not* the therapeutic ingredient (nor is watching high-speed Ping-Pong therapeutic). Trials in which people imagined traumatic scenes and tapped a finger, or just stared straight ahead while the therapist's finger wagged, have also produced therapeutic results (Devilly, 2003). EMDR does work better than doing nothing, acknowledge the skeptics (Lilienfeld & Arkowitz, 2007). But skeptics suspect that what is therapeutic is the combination of exposure therapy—repeatedly calling up traumatic memories and reconsolidating them in a safe and reassuring context—and perhaps some placebo effect. Had Mesmer's pseudotherapy been compared with no treatment at all, it, too (thanks to the healing power of positive belief), might have been found "probably efficacious," observed Richard McNally (1999).

"Studies indicate that EMDR is just as effective with fixed eyes. If that conclusion is right, what's useful in the therapy (chiefly behavioral desensitization) is not new, and what's new is superfluous."

Harvard Mental Health Letter, 2002

Light Exposure Therapy

Have you ever found yourself oversleeping, gaining weight, and feeling lethargic during the dark mornings and overcast days of winter? There likely was a survival advantage to your distant ancestors' slowing down and conserving energy during the dark days of winter. For some people, however, especially women and those living far from the equator, the wintertime blahs constitute a seasonal pattern for major depressive disorder. To counteract these dark spirits, National Institute of Mental Health researchers in the early 1980s had an idea: Give people a timed daily dose of intense light. Sure enough, people reported they felt better.

Was light exposure a bright idea, or another dim-witted example of the placebo effect? Research sheds some light. One study exposed some people with a seasonal pattern in their depression symptoms to 90 minutes of bright light and others to a sham placebo treatment—a hissing "negative ion generator" about which the staff expressed similar enthusiasm (but which was not even turned on). After four weeks, 61 percent of those exposed to morning light had greatly improved, as had 50 percent of those exposed to evening light and 32 percent of those exposed to the placebo (Eastman et al., 1998). Other studies have found that 30 minutes of exposure to 10,000-lux white fluorescent light produced relief for more than half the people receiving morning light therapy (Flory et al., 2010; Terman et al., 1998, 2001). From 20 carefully controlled trials we have a verdict (Golden et al., 2005; Wirz-Justice, 2009): Morning bright light *does* indeed dim depression symptoms for many of those suffering in a seasonal pattern. Moreover, it does so as effectively as taking antidepressant drugs or undergoing cognitive-behavioral therapy (Lam et al., 2006; Rohan et al., 2007). The effects are clear in brain scans; light therapy sparks activity in a brain region that influences the body's arousal and hormones (Ishida et al., 2005).

Light therapy To counteract winter depression, some people spend time each morning exposed to intense light that mimics natural outdoor light. Light boxes are available from health supply and lighting stores.

RETRIEVAL PRACTICE

• What is evidence-based clinical decision making?

ANSWER: Using this approach, therapists make decisions about treatment based on research evidence, clinical expertise, and knowledge of the client.

• Which of the following alternative therapies HAS shown promise as an effective treatment?

    a. light therapy   c. recovered-memory therapies

    b. rebirthing therapies   d. energy therapies

ANSWER: a

How Do Psychotherapies Help People?

55-4 What three elements are shared by all forms of psychotherapy?

Why have studies found little correlation between therapists' training and experience and clients' outcomes? In search of some answers, clinical researchers have studied the common ingredients of various therapies (Frank, 1982; Goldfried & Padawer, 1982; Strupp, 1986; Wampold, 2001, 2007). Their conclusion: They all offer at least three benefits:

- *Hope for demoralized people* People seeking therapy typically feel anxious, depressed, devoid of self-esteem, and incapable of turning things around. What any therapy offers is the expectation that, with commitment from the therapy seeker, things can and will get better. This belief, apart from any therapeutic technique, may function as a placebo, improving morale, creating feelings of self-efficacy, and diminishing symptoms (Prioleau et al., 1983).

- *A new perspective leading to new behaviors* Every therapy also offers people a plausible explanation of their symptoms and an alternative way of looking at themselves or responding to their world. Armed with a believable fresh perspective, they may approach life with a new attitude, open to making changes in their behaviors and their views of themselves.

- *An empathic, trusting, caring relationship* To say that therapy outcome is unrelated to training and experience is not to say all *therapists* are equally effective. No matter what therapeutic technique they use, effective therapists are empathic people who seek to understand another's experience; who communicate their care and concern to the client; and who earn the client's trust through respectful listening, reassurance, and guidance. Marvin Goldfried and his associates (1998) found such qualities in recorded therapy sessions from 36 recognized master therapists. Some took a cognitive-behavioral approach. Others used psychodynamic principles. Regardless, the striking finding was how *similar* they were. At key moments, the empathic therapists of both persuasions would help clients evaluate themselves, link one aspect of their life with another, and gain insight into their interactions with others.

A caring relationship Effective counselors, such as this chaplain working aboard a ship, form a bond of trust with the people they are serving.

The emotional bond between therapist and client—the **therapeutic alliance**—helps explain why some therapists are more effective than others (Klein et al., 2003; Wampold, 2001). One U.S. National Institute of Mental Health depression-treatment study confirmed that the most effective therapists were those who were perceived as most empathic and caring and who established the closest therapeutic bonds with their clients (Blatt et al., 1996). That all therapies offer hope through a fresh perspective offered by a caring person is what also enables paraprofessionals (briefly trained caregivers) to assist so many troubled people so effectively (Christensen & Jacobson, 1994).

These three common elements are also part of what the growing numbers of self-help and support groups offer their members. And they are part of what traditional healers have offered (Jackson, 1992). Healers everywhere—special people to whom others disclose their suffering, whether psychiatrists, witch doctors, or shamans—have listened in order to understand and to empathize, reassure, advise, console, interpret, or explain (Torrey, 1986). Such qualities may explain why people who feel supported by close relationships—who enjoy the fellowship and friendship of caring people—are less likely to need or seek therapy (Frank, 1982; O'Connor & Brown, 1984).

* * *

To recap, people who seek help usually improve. So do many of those who do not undergo psychotherapy, and that is a tribute to our human resourcefulness and our capacity to care for one another. Nevertheless, though the therapist's orientation and experience appear not to matter much, people who receive some psychotherapy usually improve more than those who do not. People with clear-cut, specific problems tend to improve the most.

RETRIEVAL PRACTICE

- Those who undergo psychotherapy are _____ (more/less) likely to show improvement than those who do not undergo psychotherapy.

ANSWER: more

therapeutic alliance a bond of trust and mutual understanding between a therapist and client, who work together constructively to overcome the client's problem.

Culture and Values in Psychotherapy

55-5 How do culture and values influence the therapist-client relationship?

All therapies offer hope, and nearly all therapists attempt to enhance their clients' sensitivity, openness, personal responsibility, and sense of purpose (Jensen & Bergin, 1988). But therapists also differ from one another and may differ from their clients (Delaney et al., 2007; Kelly, 1990).

These differences can become significant when a therapist from one culture meets a client from another. In North America, Europe, and Australia, for example, most therapists reflect their culture's individualism, which often gives priority to personal desires and identity, particularly for men. Clients who are immigrants from Asian countries, where people are mindful of others' expectations, may have trouble relating to therapies that require them to think only of their own well-being. Such differences help explain minority populations' reluctance to use mental health services, and their tendency to prematurely terminate therapy (Chen et al., 2009; Sue, 2006). In one experiment, Asian-American clients matched with counselors who shared their cultural values (rather than mismatched with those who did not) perceived more counselor empathy and felt a stronger alliance with the counselor (Kim et al., 2005). Recognizing that therapists and clients may differ in their values, communication styles, and language, all American Psychological Association–accredited therapy training programs now provide training in cultural sensitivity and welcome members of underrepresented cultural groups.

Another area of potential values-related conflict is religion. Highly religious people may prefer and benefit from religiously similar therapists (Masters, 2010; Smith et al., 2007; Wade et al., 2006). They may have trouble establishing an emotional bond with a therapist who does not share their values. Because clients tend to adopt their therapists' values (Worthington et al., 1996), some psychologists believe therapists should divulge their values. Today's professional training programs also seek to train therapists from diverse backgrounds who can relate, with sensitivity, to diverse clients.

Finding a Mental Health Professional

55-6 What should a person look for when selecting a therapist?

Life for everyone is marked by a mix of serenity and stress, blessing and bereavement, good moods and bad. So, when should we seek a mental health professional's help? The American Psychological Association offers these common trouble signals:

- Feelings of hopelessness
- Deep and lasting depression
- Self-destructive behavior, such as substance abuse
- Disruptive fears
- Sudden mood shifts
- Thoughts of suicide
- Compulsive rituals, such as hand washing
- Sexual difficulties
- Hearing voices or seeing things that others don't experience

In looking for a therapist, you may want to have a preliminary consultation with two or three. College health centers are generally good starting points, and may offer some free services. You can describe your problem and learn each therapist's treatment approach. You can ask questions about the therapist's values, credentials (**TABLE 55.1**), and fees. And you can assess your own feelings about each of them. The emotional bond between therapist and client is perhaps the most important factor in effective therapy.

▼ TABLE 55.1
Therapists and Their Training

Type	Therapy Description
Clinical psychologists	Most are psychologists with a Ph.D. (includes research training) or Psy.D. (focuses on therapy) supplemented by a supervised internship and, often, postdoctoral training. About half work in agencies and institutions, half in private practice.
Psychiatrists	Psychiatrists are physicians who specialize in the treatment of psychological disorders. Not all psychiatrists have had extensive training in psychotherapy, but as M.D.s or D.O.s they can prescribe medications. Thus, they tend to see those with the most serious problems. Many have their own private practice.
Clinical or psychiatric social workers	A two-year master of social work graduate program plus postgraduate supervision prepares some social workers to offer psychotherapy, mostly to people with everyday personal and family problems. About half have earned the National Association of Social Workers' designation of clinical social worker.
Counselors	Marriage and family counselors specialize in problems arising from family relations. Clergy provide counseling to countless people. Abuse counselors work with substance abusers and with spouse and child abusers and their victims. Mental health and other counselors may be required to have a two-year master's degree.

MODULE 55 REVIEW Evaluating Psychotherapies

LEARNING OBJECTIVES

RETRIEVAL PRACTICE Take a moment to answer each of these Learning Objective Questions (repeated here from within this module). Then turn to Appendix C, Complete Module Reviews, to check your answers. Research suggests that trying to answer these questions on your own will improve your long-term retention (McDaniel et al., 2009).

55-1 Does psychotherapy work? How can we know?

55-2 Are some psychotherapies more effective than others for specific disorders?

55-3 How do alternative therapies fare under scientific scrutiny?

55-4 What three elements are shared by all forms of psychotherapy?

55-5 How do culture and values influence the therapist-client relationship?

55-6 What should a person look for when selecting a therapist?

TERMS AND CONCEPTS TO REMEMBER

RETRIEVAL PRACTICE Test yourself on these terms by trying to write down the definition before flipping back to the page number referenced to check your answer.

psychotherapy, p. 673

meta-analysis, p. 675

evidence-based practice, p. 676

therapeutic alliance, p. 679

Use 🔵 LearningCurve to create your personalized study plan, which will direct you to the resources that will help you most in 🔵 LaunchPad.

MODULE 56 Biomedical Therapies and Preventing Psychological Disorders

PSYCHOTHERAPY IS ONE WAY TO treat psychological disorders. The other is **biomedical therapy**—physically changing the brain's functioning by altering its chemistry with drugs; affecting its circuitry with electroconvulsive shock, magnetic impulses, or psychosurgery; or influencing its responses with changes in lifestyle. By far the most widely used biomedical treatments today are the drug therapies. Primary care providers prescribe most drugs for anxiety and depression, followed by psychiatrists and, in some states, psychologists.

> **biomedical therapy** prescribed medications or procedures that act directly on the person's physiology.

Drug Therapies

56-1 What are the drug therapies? How do double-blind studies help researchers evaluate a drug's effectiveness?

Since the 1950s, discoveries in **psychopharmacology** (the study of drug effects on mind and behavior) have revolutionized the treatment of people with severe disorders, liberating hundreds of thousands from hospital confinement. Thanks to drug therapy, along with efforts to replace hospitalization with community mental health programs, today's resident population of mental hospitals is a small fraction of what it was a half-century ago. For some who are unable to care for themselves, however, release from hospitals has meant homelessness, not liberation.

Almost any new treatment, including drug therapy, is greeted by an initial wave of enthusiasm as many people apparently improve. But that enthusiasm often diminishes after researchers subtract the rates of (1) normal recovery among untreated persons and (2) recovery due to the *placebo effect*, which arises from the positive expectations of patients and mental health workers alike. Even mere exposure to advertising about a drug's supposed effectiveness can increase its effect (Kamenica et al., 2013). So, to evaluate the effectiveness of any new drug, researchers give half the patients the drug, and the other half a similar-appearing placebo. Because neither the staff nor the patients know who gets which, this is called a *double-blind procedure.* The good news: In double-blind studies, some drugs have proven useful.

Antipsychotic Drugs

The revolution in drug therapy for psychological disorders began with the accidental discovery that certain drugs, used for other medical purposes, calmed patients with *psychoses* (disorders in which hallucinations or delusions indicate some loss of contact with reality). These first-generation **antipsychotic drugs,** such as chlorpromazine (sold as Thorazine), dampened responsiveness to irrelevant stimuli. Thus, they provided the most help to patients experiencing positive symptoms of schizophrenia, such as auditory hallucinations and paranoia (Lehman et al., 1998; Lenzenweger et al., 1989).

The molecules of most conventional antipsychotic drugs are similar enough to molecules of the neurotransmitter dopamine to occupy its receptor sites and block its activity. This finding reinforces the idea that an overactive dopamine system contributes to schizophrenia.

Antipsychotics also have powerful side effects. Some produce sluggishness, tremors, and twitches similar to those of Parkinson's disease (Kaplan & Saddock, 1989). Long-term use of antipsychotics can produce *tardive dyskinesia,* with involuntary movements of the facial muscles (such as grimacing), tongue, and limbs. Although not more effective in controlling schizophrenia symptoms, many of the newer-generation antipsychotics, such as risperidone (Risperdal) and olanzapine (Zyprexa), have fewer of these effects. These drugs may, however, increase the risk of obesity and diabetes (Buchanan et al., 2010; Tiihonen et al., 2009).

Antipsychotics, combined with life-skills programs and family support, have given new hope to many people with schizophrenia (Guo, 2010). Hundreds of thousands of patients have left the wards of mental hospitals and returned to work and to near-normal lives (Leucht et al., 2003).

Antianxiety Drugs

Like alcohol, **antianxiety drugs,** such as Xanax or Ativan, depress central nervous system activity (and so should not be used in combination with alcohol). Antianxiety drugs are often successfully used in combination with psychological therapy. One antianxiety drug, the antibiotic D-cycloserine, facilitates the extinction of learned fears in

"Our psychopharmacologist is a genius."

Perhaps you can guess an occasional side effect of L-dopa, a drug that raises dopamine levels for Parkinson's patients: hallucinations.

psychopharmacology the study of the effects of drugs on mind and behavior.

antipsychotic drugs drugs used to treat schizophrenia and other forms of severe thought disorder.

antianxiety drugs drugs used to control anxiety and agitation.

combination with behavioral treatments. Experiments indicate that the drug enhances the benefits of exposure therapy and helps relieve the symptoms of posttraumatic stress disorder and obsessive-compulsive disorder (Davis, 2005; Kushner et al., 2007).

A criticism sometimes made of the *behavior therapies*—that they reduce symptoms without resolving underlying problems—is also made of drug therapies. Unlike the behavior therapies, however, these substances may be used as an ongoing treatment. "Popping a Xanax" at the first sign of tension can create a learned response; the immediate relief reinforces a person's tendency to take drugs when anxious. Antianxiety drugs can also be addictive. After heavy use, people who stop taking them may experience increased anxiety, insomnia, and other withdrawal symptoms.

Over the dozen years at the end of the twentieth century, the rate of outpatient treatment for anxiety disorders, obsessive-compulsive disorder, and posttraumatic stress disorder nearly doubled. The proportion of psychiatric patients receiving medication during that time increased from 52 to 70 percent (Olfson et al., 2004). And the new standard drug treatment for anxiety disorders? Antidepressants.

Antidepressant Drugs

The **antidepressants** were named for their ability to lift people up from a state of depression, and this was their main use until recently. The label is a bit of a misnomer now that these drugs are increasingly being used to successfully treat anxiety disorders, obsessive-compulsive disorder, and posttraumatic stress disorder (Wetherell et al., 2013). Many of these drugs work by increasing the availability of neurotransmitters, such as norepinephrine or serotonin, which elevate arousal and mood and appear scarce when a person experiences feelings of depression or anxiety. The most commonly prescribed drugs in this group, including Prozac and its cousins Zoloft and Paxil, work by blocking the reabsorption and removal of serotonin from synapses (**FIGURE 56.1**). Given their use in treating disorders other than depression—from anxiety to strokes—these drugs are most often called *SSRIs—selective serotonin reuptake inhibitors* (rather than antidepressants) (Kramer, 2011). Some of the older antidepressant drugs work by blocking the reabsorption or breakdown of both norepinephrine and serotonin. Though effective, these dual-action drugs have more potential side effects, such as dry mouth, weight gain, hypertension, or dizzy spells (Anderson, 2000; Mulrow, 1999). Administering them by means of a patch, which bypasses the intestines and liver, helps reduce such side effects (Bodkin & Amsterdam, 2002).

> **antidepressant drugs** drugs used to treat depression, anxiety disorders, obsessive-compulsive disorder, and posttraumatic stress disorder. (Several widely used antidepressant drugs are *selective serotonin reuptake inhibitors—SSRIs.*)

© John Greim/Age fotostock

▼ FIGURE 56.1
Biology of antidepressants Shown here is the action of Prozac, which partially blocks the reuptake of serotonin.

Message is sent across synaptic gap.

Message is received; excess serotonin molecules are reabsorbed by sending neuron.

Prozac partially blocks normal reuptake of the neurotransmitter serotonin; excess serotonin in synapse enhances its mood-lifting effect.

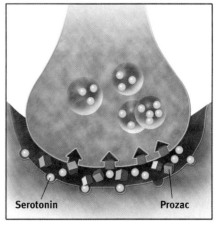

(a)

(b)

(c)

Be advised: Patients with depression who begin taking antidepressants do not wake up the next day singing, "It's a beautiful day!" Although the drugs begin to influence neurotransmission within hours, their full psychological effect often requires four weeks (and may involve a side effect of diminished sexual desire). One possible reason for the delay is that increased serotonin promotes new synapses plus *neurogenesis*—the birth of new brain cells—perhaps reversing stress-induced loss of neurons (Launay et al., 2011). Researchers are also exploring the possibility of quicker-acting antidepressants. One, ketamine, blocks hyperactive receptors for glutamate, a neurotransmitter, and causes a burst of new synapses—but with possible side effects such as hallucinations (Grimm & Scheidegger, 2013; Naughton et al., 2014).

Antidepressant drugs are not the only way to give the body a lift. Aerobic exercise, which calms people who feel anxious and energizes those who feel depressed, does about as much good for most people with mild to moderate depression, and has additional positive side effects. Cognitive therapy, by helping people reverse their habitual negative thinking style, can boost the drug-aided relief from depression and reduce the posttreatment risk of relapse (Hollon et al., 2002; Keller et al., 2000; Vittengl et al., 2007). Better yet, some studies suggest, is to attack depression (and anxiety) from both below and above (Cuijpers et al., 2010; Walkup et al., 2008): Use antidepressant drugs (which work, bottom-up, on the emotion-forming limbic system) in conjunction with cognitive-behavioral therapy (which works, top-down, starting with changed frontal lobe activity).

Researchers generally agree that people with depression often improve after a month on antidepressants. But after allowing for natural recovery and the placebo effect, how big is the drug effect? Not big, report Irving Kirsch and his colleagues (1998, 2002, 2010, 2014). Their analyses of double-blind clinical trials indicate that placebos accounted for about 75 percent of the active drug's effect. In a follow-up review that included unpublished clinical trials, the antidepressant drug effect was again modest (Kirsch et al., 2008). The placebo effect was less for those with severe depression, which made the added benefit of the drug somewhat greater for them. "Given these results, there seems little reason to prescribe antidepressant medication to any but the most severely depressed patients, unless alternative treatments have failed," Kirsch concluded (BBC, 2008). A newer analysis confirms that the antidepressant benefit compared to placebos is "minimal or nonexistent, on average, in patients with mild or moderate symptoms." For those folks, aerobic exercise or psychotherapy is often effective. But among patients with "very severe" depression, the medication advantage becomes "substantial" (Fournier et al., 2010).

LaunchPad **HOW WOULD YOU KNOW?** To better understand how clinical researchers have explored these questions, complete LaunchPad's *How Would You Know How Well Antidepressants Work?*

Mood-Stabilizing Medications

In addition to antipsychotic, antianxiety, and antidepressant drugs, psychiatrists have *mood-stabilizing drugs* in their arsenal. For those suffering the emotional highs and lows of bipolar disorder, the simple salt *lithium* can be an effective mood stabilizer. Australian physician John Cade discovered this in the 1940s when he administered lithium to a patient with severe mania and the patient became well in less than a week (Snyder, 1986). After suffering mood swings for years, about 7 in 10 people with bipolar disorder benefit from a long-term daily dose of this cheap salt, which helps prevent or ease manic episodes and, to a lesser extent, lifts depression (Solomon et al., 1995). Kay Redfield Jamison (1995, pp. 88–89) described the effect:

"If this doesn't help you don't worry, it's a placebo."

"No twisted thought without a twisted molecule."

Attributed to psychologist Ralph Gerard

"First of all I think you should know that last quarter's sales figures are interfering with my mood-stabilizing drugs."

Lithium prevents my seductive but disastrous highs, diminishes my depressions, clears out the wool and webbing from my disordered thinking, slows me down, gentles me out, keeps me from ruining my career and relationships, keeps me out of a hospital, alive, and makes psychotherapy possible.

Lithium reduces bipolar patients' risk of suicide—to about one-sixth of bipolar patients not taking lithium (Oquendo et al., 2011). Naturally occurring lithium in drinking water has also correlated with lower suicide rates (across 18 Japanese cities and towns) and lower crime rates (across 27 Texas counties) (Ohgami et al., 2009; Schrauzer & Shrestha, 1990, 2010; Terao et al., 2010). Although we do not fully understand why, lithium works. And so does Depakote, a drug originally used to treat epilepsy and more recently found effective in the control of manic episodes associated with bipolar disorder.

RETRIEVAL PRACTICE

- How do researchers evaluate the effectiveness of particular drug therapies?

ANSWER: Researchers assign people to treatment and no-treatment conditions to see if those who receive the drug therapy improve more than those who don't. Double-blind controlled studies are most effective. If neither the therapist nor the client knows which participants have received the drug treatment, then any difference between the treated and untreated groups will reflect the drug treatment's actual effect.

- The drugs given most often to treat depression are called _____. Schizophrenia is often treated with _____ drugs.

ANSWERS: antidepressants; antipsychotic

Brain Stimulation

56-2 How are brain stimulation and psychosurgery used in treating specific disorders?

Electroconvulsive Therapy

A more controversial brain manipulation occurs through shock treatment, or **electroconvulsive therapy (ECT)**. When ECT was first introduced in 1938, the wide-awake patient was strapped to a table and jolted with roughly 100 volts of electricity to the brain, producing racking convulsions and brief unconsciousness. ECT therefore gained a barbaric image, one that lingers. Today's ECT is much kinder and gentler. The patient receives a general anesthetic and a muscle relaxant (to prevent injury from convulsions) before a psychiatrist delivers 30 to 60 seconds of electrical current (**FIGURE 56.2**). Within 30 minutes, the patient awakens and remembers nothing of the treatment or of the preceding hours. After three such sessions each week for two to four weeks, 80 percent or more of people receiving ECT improve markedly, showing some memory loss for the treatment period but no discernible brain damage. Study after study confirms that ECT is an effective treatment for severe depression in "treatment-resistant" patients who have not responded to drug therapy (Bailine et al., 2010; Fink, 2009; Lima et al., 2013). An editorial in the *Journal of the American Medical Association* concluded that "the results of ECT in treating severe depression are among the most positive treatment effects in all of medicine" (Glass, 2001).

How does ECT alleviate severe depression? After more than 70 years, no one knows for sure. One recipient likened ECT to the smallpox vaccine, which was saving lives before we knew how it worked. Others think of it as rebooting their cerebral computer. But what makes it therapeutic? Perhaps the shock-induced brain seizures calm neural centers where overactivity produces depression. Some research confirms that ECT works by weakening connections in a "hyperconnected" neural hub in the left frontal lobe (Perrin et al., 2012).

electroconvulsive therapy (ECT) a biomedical therapy for severely depressed patients in which a brief electric current is sent through the brain of an anesthetized patient.

▼ FIGURE 56.2
Electroconvulsive therapy Although controversial, ECT is often an effective treatment for depression that does not respond to drug therapy. ("Electroconvulsive" is no longer accurate, because patients are now given a drug that prevents bodily convulsions.)

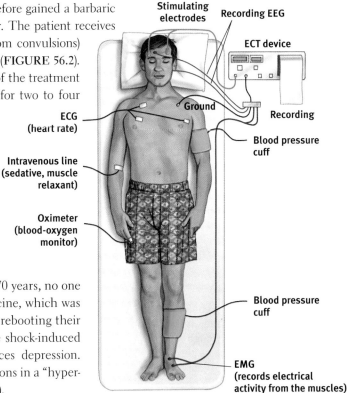

Stimulating electrodes

Recording EEG

ECT device

Ground

Recording

Blood pressure cuff

ECG (heart rate)

Intravenous line (sedative, muscle relaxant)

Oximeter (blood-oxygen monitor)

Blood pressure cuff

EMG (records electrical activity from the muscles)

The medical use of electricity is an ancient practice. Physicians treated the Roman Emperor Claudius (10 B.C.E.–54 C.E.) for headaches by pressing electric eels to his temples.

"I used to . . . be unable to shake the dread even when I was feeling good, because I knew the bad feelings would return. ECT has wiped away that foreboding. It has given me a sense of control, of hope."

Kitty Dukakis (2006)

A meta-analysis of 17 clinical experiments found that one other stimulation procedure alleviates depression: massage therapy (Hou et al., 2010).

ECT is now administered with briefer pulses, sometimes only to the brain's right side and with less memory disruption (HMHL, 2007). Yet no matter how impressive the results, the idea of electrically shocking people still strikes many as barbaric, especially given our ignorance about why ECT works. Moreover, about 4 in 10 ECT-treated patients relapse into depression within six months (Kellner et al., 2006). Nevertheless, in the minds of many psychiatrists and patients, ECT is a lesser evil than severe depression's misery, anguish, and risk of suicide. As research psychologist Norman Endler (1982) reported after ECT alleviated his deep depression, "A miracle had happened in two weeks."

Alternative Neurostimulation Therapies

Two other neural stimulation techniques—magnetic stimulation and deep-brain stimulation—also treat the depressed brain.

Magnetic Stimulation Depressed moods sometimes improve when repeated pulses surge through a magnetic coil held close to a person's skull (**FIGURE 56.3**). The painless procedure—called **repetitive transcranial magnetic stimulation (rTMS)**—is performed on wide-awake patients over several weeks. Unlike ECT, the rTMS procedure produces no brain seizures, memory loss, or other serious side effects aside from possible headaches.

Seven initial studies have found rTMS to be a "promising treatment," with results comparable to antidepressants (Berlim et al., 2013). How it works is unclear. One possible explanation is that the stimulation energizes the brain's left frontal lobe (Helmuth, 2001). Repeated stimulation may cause nerve cells to form new functioning circuits through the process of *long-term potentiation.*

Deep-Brain Stimulation Other patients whose depression has resisted both drugs that flood the body and ECT that jolts at least half the brain have benefited from an experimental treatment pinpointed at a brain depression center. Neuroscientist Helen Mayberg and her colleagues (2005, 2006, 2007, 2009) have been focusing on

repetitive transcranial magnetic stimulation (rTMS) the application of repeated pulses of magnetic energy to the brain; used to stimulate or suppress brain activity.

▼ FIGURE 56.3

Magnets for the mind Repetitive transcranial magnetic stimulation (rTMS) sends a painless magnetic field through the skull to the surface of the cortex. Pulses can be used to alter activity in various cortical areas.

a neural hub that bridges the thinking frontal lobes to the limbic system. This area, which is overactive in the brain of a depressed or temporarily sad person, calms when treated by ECT or antidepressants. To experimentally excite neurons that inhibit this negative emotion-feeding activity, Mayberg drew upon the deep-brain stimulation technology sometimes used to treat Parkinson's tremors. Since 2003, she and others have treated more than 100 depressed patients with deep brain stimulation to the neural "sadness center." About one-third reportedly have responded "extremely well" and another 30 percent have modestly improved (Underwood, 2013). Some felt suddenly more aware and became more talkative and engaged; others improved only slightly if at all. Future research will explore whether Mayberg has discovered a switch that can lift depression. Other researchers are following up on reports that deep-brain stimulation can offer relief to people with obsessive-compulsive disorder and with drug and alcohol addictions (Corse et al., 2013; Luigjes et al., 2012; Rabins et al., 2009).

A depression switch? By comparing the brains of patients with and without depression, researcher Helen Mayberg identified a brain area (highlighted in red) that appears active in people who are depressed or sad, and whose activity may be calmed by deep-brain stimulation.

RETRIEVAL PRACTICE

- Severe depression that has not responded to other therapy may be treated with _____ _____ , which can cause brain seizures and memory loss. More moderate neural stimulation techniques designed to help alleviate depression include _____ _____ magnetic stimulation, and _____ - _____ stimulation.

ANSWERS: electroconvulsive therapy (ECT); repetitive transcranial; deep-brain

Psychosurgery

Because its effects are irreversible, **psychosurgery**—surgery that removes or destroys brain tissue—is the most drastic and least-used biomedical intervention for changing behavior. In the 1930s, Portuguese physician Egas Moniz developed what became the best-known psychosurgical operation: the **lobotomy.** Moniz found that cutting the nerves connecting the frontal lobes with the emotion-controlling centers of the inner brain calmed uncontrollably emotional and violent patients. In what would later

become, in others' hands, a crude but quick and easy procedure, a neurosurgeon would shock the patient into a coma, hammer an icepick-like instrument through each eye socket into the brain, and then wiggle it to sever connections running up to the frontal lobes. Between 1936 and 1954, tens of thousands of severely disturbed people were "lobotomized" (Valenstein, 1986).

Although the intention was simply to disconnect emotion from thought, a lobotomy's effect was often more drastic: It usually decreased the person's misery or tension, but also produced a permanently lethargic, immature, uncreative person. During the 1950s, after some 35,000 people had been lobotomized in the United States alone, calming drugs became available and psychosurgery became scorned, as in the saying sometimes attributed to W. C. Fields that "I'd rather have a bottle in front of me than a frontal lobotomy."

Failed lobotomy This 1940 photo shows Rosemary Kennedy (center) at age 22 with brother (and future U.S. president) John and sister Jean. A year later her father, on medical advice, approved a lobotomy that was promised to control her reportedly violent mood swings. The procedure left her confined to a hospital with an infantile mentality until her death in 2005 at age 86.

Today, lobotomies are history. But more precise, microscale psychosurgery is sometimes used in extreme cases. For example, if a patient suffers uncontrollable seizures, surgeons can deactivate the specific nerve clusters that cause or transmit the convulsions. MRI-guided precision surgery is also occasionally done to cut the circuits involved in severe obsessive-compulsive disorder (Carey, 2009, 2011; Sachdev & Sachdev, 1997). Because these procedures are irreversible, they are controversial and neurosurgeons perform them only as a last resort.

Therapeutic Lifestyle Change

56-3 How, by taking care of themselves with a healthy lifestyle, might people find some relief from depression? How does this reflect our being biopsychosocial systems?

The effectiveness of the biomedical therapies reminds us of a fundamental lesson: We find it convenient to talk of separate psychological and biological influences, but everything psychological is also biological (**FIGURE 56.4**). Every thought and feeling depends on the functioning brain. Every creative idea, every moment of joy or anger, every period of depression emerges from the electrochemical activity of the living brain. The influence is two-way: When psychotherapy relieves obsessive-compulsive behavior, PET scans reveal a calmer brain (Schwartz et al., 1996).

Anxiety disorders, obsessive-compulsive disorder, posttraumatic stress disorder, major depressive disorder, bipolar disorder, and schizophrenia are all biological events. As we have seen over and again, *a human being is an integrated biopsychosocial system.* For years, we have trusted our bodies to physicians and our minds to psychiatrists and psychologists. That neat separation no longer seems valid. Stress affects body chemistry and health. Thus, our lifestyle—our exercise, nutrition, relationships, recreation, relaxation, religious or spiritual engagement, and such—affects our mental health (Walsh, 2011).

That lesson is being applied by Stephen Ilardi (2009) in training seminars promoting *therapeutic lifestyle change.* Human brains and bodies were designed for physical activity and social engagement, he notes. Our ancestors hunted, gathered, and built in groups. Indeed, those whose way of life entails strenuous physical activity, strong community ties, sunlight exposure, and plenty of sleep (think of foraging bands in Papua New Guinea, or Amish farming communities in North America) rarely experience depression. For both children and adults, outdoor activity in natural environments—perhaps a walk in the woods—reduces stress and promotes health (MacKerron & Mourato, 2013; NEEF, 2011; Phillips, 2011). "Simply put: humans were never designed for the sedentary, disengaged, socially isolated, poorly nourished, sleep-deprived pace of twenty-first-century American life."

The Ilardi team was also impressed by research showing that regular aerobic exercise rivals the healing power of antidepressant drugs, and that a complete night's sleep boosts mood and energy. So they invited small groups of people with depression to undergo a 12-week training program with the following goals:

- *Aerobic exercise,* 30 minutes a day, at least 3 times weekly (increasing fitness and vitality, stimulating endorphins)

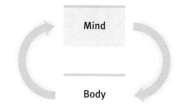

▼ FIGURE 56.4
Mind-body interaction The biomedical therapies assume that mind and body are a unit: Affect one and you will affect the other.

"Forest bathing" In several small studies, Japanese researchers have found that walks in the woods help lower stress hormone and blood pressure levels (Phillips, 2011).

©Randy Faris/Corbis

Nicole Hill/Rubberball/Getty Images

- *Adequate sleep,* with a goal of 7 to 8 hours a night (increasing energy and alertness, boosting immunity)
- *Light exposure,* at least 30 minutes each morning with a light box (amplifying arousal, influencing hormones)
- *Social connection,* with less alone time and at least two meaningful social engagements weekly (satisfying the human need to belong)
- *Anti-rumination,* by identifying and redirecting negative thoughts (enhancing positive thinking)
- *Nutritional supplements,* including a daily fish oil supplement with omega-3 fatty acids (supporting healthy brain functioning)

In one study of 74 people, 77 percent of those who completed the program experienced relief from depressive symptoms, compared with 19 percent in those assigned to a treatment-as-usual control condition. Future research will seek to replicate this striking result of lifestyle change, and also to identify which of the treatment components (additively or in some combination) produce the therapeutic effect. In the meantime, there seems little reason to doubt the truth of the Latin adage, *Mens sana in corpore sano:* "A healthy mind in a healthy body."

TABLE 56.1 summarizes some aspects of the biomedical therapies we've discussed.

▼ TABLE 56.1
Comparing Biomedical Therapies

Therapy	Presumed Problem	Therapy Aim	Therapy Technique
Drug therapies	Neurotransmitter malfunction	Control symptoms of psychological disorders.	Alter brain chemistry through drugs.
Brain stimulation	Severe, "treatment-resistant" depression	Alleviate depression that is unresponsive to drug therapy.	Stimulate brain through electroconvulsive shock, magnetic impulses, or deep-brain stimulation.
Psychosurgery	Brain malfunction	Relieve severe disorders.	Remove or destroy brain tissue.
Therapeutic lifestyle change	Stress and unhealthy lifestyle	Restore healthy biological state.	Alter lifestyle through adequate exercise, sleep, and other changes.

RETRIEVAL PRACTICE

- What are some examples of lifestyle changes we can make to enhance our mental health?

ANSWER: Exercise regularly, get enough sleep, get more exposure to light (get outside and/or use a light box), nurture important relationships, redirect negative thinking, and eat a diet rich in omega-3 fatty acids.

Preventing Psychological Disorders and Building Resilience

56-4 What is the rationale for preventive mental health programs, and why is it important to develop resilience?

Psychotherapies and biomedical therapies tend to locate the cause of psychological disorders within the person. We infer that people who act cruelly must be cruel and that people who act "crazy" must be "sick." We attach labels to such people, thereby distinguishing them from "normal" folks. It follows, then, that we try to treat "abnormal" people by giving them insight into their problems, by changing their thinking, by helping them gain control with drugs.

There is an alternative viewpoint: We could interpret many psychological disorders as understandable responses to a disturbing and stressful society. According to this

THIS ANTI-DEPRESSANT WORKS BEST IF YOU TAKE IT WITH WATER LAPPING NEAR YOUR HAMMOCK ON A CARIBBEAN BEACH.

Dave Coverly/Speed Bump

view, it is not just the person who needs treatment, but also the person's social context. Better to drain the swamps than swat the mosquitoes. Better to prevent a problem by reforming a sick situation and by developing people's coping competencies than to wait for and treat problems.

Preventive Mental Health

A story about the rescue of a drowning person from a rushing river illustrates this viewpoint: Having successfully administered first aid to the first victim, the rescuer spots another struggling person and pulls her out, too. After a half-dozen repetitions, the rescuer suddenly turns and starts running away while the river sweeps yet another floundering person into view. "Aren't you going to rescue that fellow?" asks a bystander. "Heck no," the rescuer replies. "I'm going upstream to find out what's pushing all these people in."

> "It is better to prevent than to cure."
>
> Peruvian folk wisdom

Preventive mental health is upstream work. It seeks to prevent psychological casualties by identifying and alleviating the conditions that cause them. As George Albee (1986; also Yoshikawa et al., 2012) pointed out, there is abundant evidence that poverty, meaningless work, constant criticism, unemployment, racism, and sexism undermine people's sense of competence, personal control, and self-esteem. Such stresses increase their risk of depression, alcohol use disorder, and suicide.

> "Mental disorders arise from physical ones, and likewise physical disorders arise from mental ones."
>
> *The Mahabharata,* 200 B.C.E.

We who care about preventing psychological casualties should, Albee contended, support programs that alleviate these demoralizing situations. We eliminated smallpox not by treating the afflicted but by inoculating the unafflicted. We conquered yellow fever by controlling mosquitoes. Preventing psychological problems means empowering those who have learned an attitude of helplessness and changing environments that breed loneliness. It means renewing fragile family ties and boosting parents' and teachers' skills at nurturing children's achievements and resulting self-concept. "Everything aimed at improving the human condition, at making life more fulfilling and meaningful, may be considered part of primary prevention of mental or emotional disturbance" (Kessler & Albee, 1975, p. 557). Prevention can sometimes provide a double payoff. People with a strong sense of life's meaning are more engaging socially (Stillman et al., 2011). If we can strengthen people's sense of meaning in life, we may also lessen their loneliness as they grow into more engaging companions.

Among the upstream prevention workers are *community psychologists.* Mindful of how people interact with their environment, they focus on creating environments that support psychological health. Through their research and social action, community psychologists aim to empower people and to enhance their competence, health, and well-being.

Building Resilience

We have seen that lifestyle change can help reverse some of the symptoms of psychological disorders. Might such change also prevent some disorders by building individuals' **resilience**—an ability to cope with stress and recover from adversity? Faced with unforeseen trauma, most adults exhibit resilience. This was true of New Yorkers in the aftermath of the September 11 terror attacks, especially those who enjoyed supportive close relationships and who had not recently experienced other stressful events (Bonanno et al., 2007). More than 9 in 10 New Yorkers, although stunned and grief-stricken by 9/11, did *not* have a dysfunctional stress reaction. By the following January, the stress symptoms of those who did were mostly gone (Person et al., 2006). Even most combat-stressed veterans, most political rebels who have survived torture, and most people with spinal cord injuries do not later exhibit posttraumatic stress disorder (Bonanno et al., 2012; Mineka & Zinbarg, 1996).

resilience the personal strength that helps most people cope with stress and recover from adversity and even trauma.

Struggling with challenging crises can even lead to **posttraumatic growth.** Many cancer survivors have reported a greater appreciation for life, more meaningful relationships, increased personal strength, changed priorities, and a richer spiritual life (Tedeschi & Calhoun, 2004). Americans who tried to make sense of the 9/11 terror attacks experienced less distress (Park et al., 2012). Out of even our worst experiences, some good can come. Through preventive efforts, such as community building and personal growth, fewer of us will fall into the rushing river of psychological disorders.

> **posttraumatic growth** positive psychological changes as a result of struggling with extremely challenging circumstances and life crises.

RETRIEVAL PRACTICE

- What is the difference between preventive mental health and psychological or biomedical therapy?

ANSWER: Psychological and biomedical therapies attempt to relieve people's suffering from psychological disorders. Preventive mental health attempts to prevent suffering by identifying and eliminating the conditions that cause disorders.

* * *

If you just finished reading this book, your introduction to psychological science is completed. Our tour of psychological science has taught us much—and you, too?—about our moods and memories, about the reach of our unconscious, about how we flourish and struggle, about how we perceive our physical and social worlds, and about how our biology and culture shape us. Our hope, as your guides on this tour, is that you have shared some of our fascination, grown in your understanding and compassion, and sharpened your critical thinking. And we hope you enjoyed the ride.

With every good wish in your future endeavors,

David G. Myers
www.davidmyers.org

Nathan DeWall
www.NathanDeWall.com

MODULE 56 REVIEW Biomedical Therapies and Preventing Psychological Disorders

LEARNING OBJECTIVES

RETRIEVAL PRACTICE Take a moment to answer each of these Learning Objective Questions (repeated here from within this module). Then turn to Appendix C, Complete Module Reviews, to check your answers. Research suggests that trying to answer these questions on your own will improve your long-term retention (McDaniel et al., 2009).

56-1 What are the drug therapies? How do double-blind studies help researchers evaluate a drug's effectiveness?

56-2 How are brain stimulation and psychosurgery used in treating specific disorders?

56-3 How, by taking care of themselves with a healthy lifestyle, might people find some relief from depression? How does this reflect our being biopsychosocial systems?

56-4 What is the rationale for preventive mental health programs, and why is it important to develop resilience?

TERMS AND CONCEPTS TO REMEMBER

RETRIEVAL PRACTICE Test yourself on these terms by trying to write down the definition before flipping back to check your answers.

biomedical therapy, p. 681

psychopharmacology, p. 682

antipsychotic drugs, p. 682

antianxiety drugs, p. 682

antidepressant drugs, p. 683

electroconvulsive therapy (ECT), p. 685

repetitive transcranial magnetic stimulation (rTMS), p. 686

psychosurgery, p. 687

lobotomy, p. 687

resilience, p. 690

posttraumatic growth, p. 691

Use **(m) LearningCurve** to create your personalized study plan, which will direct you to the resources that will help you most in **(m) LaunchPad**.

TEST YOUR-SELF THERAPY

Test yourself repeatedly throughout your studies. This will not only help you figure out what you know and don't know; the testing itself will help you learn and remember the information more effectively thanks to the *testing effect*.

MODULE 54 Introduction to Therapy and the Psychological Therapies

1. A therapist who helps patients search for the unconscious roots of their problem and offers interpretations of their behaviors, feelings, and dreams, is drawing from

   a. psychoanalysis.

   b. humanistic therapies.

   c. client-centered therapy.

   d. behavior therapy.

2. _____ therapies are designed to help individuals discover the thoughts and feelings that guide their motivation and behavior.

3. Compared with psychoanalysts, humanistic therapists are more likely to emphasize

   a. hidden or repressed feelings.

   b. childhood experiences.

   c. psychological disorders.

   d. self-fulfillment and growth.

4. A therapist who restates and clarifies the client's statements is practicing _____ _____ .

5. The goal of behavior therapy is to

   a. identify and treat the underlying causes of the problem.

   b. improve learning and insight.

   c. eliminate the unwanted behavior.

   d. improve communication and social sensitivity.

6. Behavior therapies often use _____ techniques such as systematic desensitization and aversive conditioning to encourage clients to produce new responses to old stimuli.

7. The technique of _____ _____ teaches people to relax in the presence of progressively more anxiety-provoking stimuli.

8. After a near-fatal car accident, Rico developed such an intense fear of driving on the freeway that he takes lengthy alternative routes to work each day. Which psychological therapy might best help Rico overcome his phobia, and why?

9. At a treatment center, people who display a desired behavior receive coins that they can later exchange for other rewards. This is an example of a(n) _____ _____ .

10. Cognitive therapy has been especially effective in treating

    a. nail biting.

    b. phobias.

    c. alcohol use disorder.

    d. depression.

11. _____ - _____ therapy helps people to change their self-defeating ways of thinking and to act out those changes in their daily behavior.

12. In family therapy, the therapist assumes that

   a. only one family member needs to change.

   b. each person's actions trigger reactions from other family members.

   c. dysfunctional families must improve their interactions or give up their children.

   d. all of the above are true.

MODULE 55 Evaluating Psychotherapies

13. The most enthusiastic or optimistic view of the effectiveness of psychotherapy comes from

   a. outcome research.

   b. randomized clinical trials.

   c. reports of clinicians and clients.

   d. a government study of treatment for depression.

14. Studies show that _____ therapy is the most effective treatment for most psychological disorders.

   a. behavior

   b. humanistic

   c. psychodynamic

   d. no one type of

15. What are the three components of evidence-based practice?

16. How does the placebo effect bias patients' attitudes about the effectiveness of drug therapies?

MODULE 56 Biomedical Therapies and Preventing Psychological Disorders

17. Some antipsychotic drugs, used to calm people with schizophrenia, can have unpleasant side effects, most notably

   a. hyperactivity.

   b. convulsions and momentary memory loss.

   c. sluggishness, tremors, and twitches.

   d. paranoia.

18. Drugs like Xanax and Ativan, which depress central nervous system activity, can become addictive when used as ongoing treatment. These drugs are referred to as _____ drugs.

19. A simple salt that often brings relief to patients suffering the highs and lows of bipolar disorder is _____ .

20. When drug therapies have not been effective, electroconvulsive therapy (ECT) may be used as treatment, largely for people with

   a. severe obsessive-compulsive disorder.

   b. severe depression.

   c. schizophrenia.

   d. anxiety disorders.

21. An approach that seeks to identify and alleviate conditions that put people at high risk for developing psychological disorders is called

   a. deep-brain stimulation.

   b. the mood-stabilizing perspective.

   c. spontaneous recovery.

   d. preventive mental health.

Find answers to these questions in Appendix D, in the back of the book.

APPENDIX A

Psychology at Work

A-1 What is *flow*, and what are the three subfields of industrial-organizational psychology?

For most of us, work is life's biggest single waking activity. To live is to work. Work helps satisfy several levels of need identified in Abraham Maslow's (1970) hierarchy of needs. Work supports us. Work connects us. Work defines us. Meeting someone for the first time, and wondering who they are, we may ask, "So, what do you do?"

Individuals across various occupations vary in their attitudes toward their work. Some view their work as a *job*, an unfulfilling but necessary way to make money. Others view their work as a *career*, an opportunity to advance from one position to a better position. The rest—those who view their work as a *calling*, a fulfilling and socially useful activity—report the highest satisfaction with their work and with their lives (Dik & Duffy, 2012; Wrzesniewski et al., 1997, 2001).

This finding would not surprise Mihaly Csikszentmihalyi [chick-SENT-me-hi] (1990, 1999). He observed that people's quality of life increases when they are purposefully engaged. Between the anxiety of being overwhelmed and stressed, and the apathy of being underwhelmed and bored, lies a zone in which people experience **flow.** Can you recall being in a zoned-out flow state while texting or playing a video game? If so, then perhaps you can sympathize with the two Northwest Airlines pilots who in 2009 were so focused on their laptops that they missed Earth-to-pilot messages from their control tower. The pilots flew 150 miles past their Minneapolis destination—and lost their jobs.

Csikszentmihalyi formulated the flow concept after studying artists who spent hour after hour painting or sculpting with focused concentration. Immersed in a project, they worked as if nothing else mattered, and then, when finished, they promptly forgot about it. The artists seemed driven less by external rewards—money, praise, promotion—than by the intrinsic rewards of creating their art.

Csikszentmihalyi's later observations, of people from varied occupations and countries, and of all ages, confirmed an overriding principle: It's exhilarating to flow with an activity that fully engages our skills. Flow experiences boost our sense of self-esteem, competence, and well-being. Idleness may sound like bliss, but purposeful work enriches our lives. Busy people are happier (Hsee et al., 2010; Robinson & Martin, 2008). One research team interrupted people on about a quarter-million occasions

Sometimes, Gene Weingarten noted (2002), a humor writer knows "when to just get out of the way." Here are some sample job titles from the U.S. Department of Labor *Dictionary of Occupational Titles*: animal impersonator, human projectile, banana ripening-room supervisor, impregnator, impregnator helper, dope sprayer, finger waver, rug scratcher, egg smeller, bottom buffer, cookie breaker, brain picker, hand pouncer, bosom presser, and mother repairer.

Have you ever noticed that when you are immersed in an activity, time flies? And that when you are watching the clock, it seems to move more slowly? French researchers have confirmed that the more we attend to an event's duration, the longer it seems to last (Couli et al., 2004).

> **flow** a completely involved, focused state of consciousness, with diminished awareness of self and time, resulting from optimal engagement of one's skills.

Life disrupted Playing and socializing online are ever-present sources of distraction. It takes energy to resist checking our phones, and time to refocus mental concentration after each disruption. Such regular interruptions disrupt flow, so it's a good idea to instead schedule breaks for checking our handheld devices.

Matthew Palmer/Hill Street Studios/Blend Images/Brand X Pictures/Getty Images

The modern workforce The editorial team that supports the creation of this book and its teaching package works both in-house and from far-flung places. Clockwise from top left are Nancy Fleming in Massachusetts, Rachel Losh in New York, Betty Probert in Florida, Christine Brune in Alaska, Trish Morgan in Alberta, Tracey Kuehn in New York, and Kathryn Brownson in Michigan.

(using a smart-phone app), and found people's minds wandering 47 percent of the time. They were, on average, happier when *not* mind wandering (Killingsworth & Gilbert, 2010).

In many nations work has changed, from farming to manufacturing to *knowledge work*. More and more work is outsourced to temporary employees and consultants or to workers communicating electronically from off-site workplaces. As work has changed, have our attitudes toward our work also changed? Has our satisfaction with work increased or decreased? Has the *psychological contract*—the sense of mutual obligations between workers and employers—become more or less trusting and secure? These are among the questions that fascinate psychologists who study work-related behavior.

Industrial-organizational (I/O) psychology applies psychology's principles to the workplace (**TABLE A.1**). Here we consider three of I/O psychology's subfields:

- **Personnel psychology** applies psychology's methods and principles to selecting and evaluating workers. Personnel psychologists match people with jobs, by identifying and placing well-suited candidates.

- **Organizational psychology** considers how work environments and management styles influence worker motivation, satisfaction, and productivity. Organizational psychologists modify jobs and supervision in ways that boost morale and productivity.

- **Human factors psychology** explores how machines and environments can be optimally designed to fit human abilities. Human factors psychologists study people's natural perceptions and inclinations to create user-friendly machines and work settings.

industrial-organizational (I/O) psychology the application of psychological concepts and methods to optimizing human behavior in workplaces.

personnel psychology an I/O psychology subfield that focuses on employee recruitment, selection, placement, training, appraisal, and development.

organizational psychology an I/O psychology subfield that examines organizational influences on worker satisfaction and productivity and facilitates organizational change.

human factors psychology an I/O psychology subfield that explores how people and machines interact and how machines and physical environments can be made safe and easy to use.

▼ TABLE A.1
I/O Psychology at Work

As scientists, consultants, and management professionals, industrial-organizational (I/O) psychologists are found working in varied areas:

Personnel Psychology	Organizational Psychology
Selecting and placing employees • Developing and validating assessment tools for selecting, placing, and promoting workers • Analyzing job content • Optimizing worker placement	**Developing organizations** • Analyzing organizational structures • Maximizing worker satisfaction and productivity • Facilitating organizational change
Training and developing employees • Identifying needs • Designing training programs • Evaluating training programs	**Enhancing quality of work life** • Expanding individual productivity • Identifying elements of satisfaction • Redesigning jobs
Appraising performance • Developing criteria • Measuring individual performance • Measuring organizational performance	**Human Factors (Engineering) Psychology** • Designing optimum work environments • Optimizing person-machine interactions • Developing systems technologies

Source: Adapted from the Society of Industrial and Organizational Psychology (www.siop.org).

RETRIEVAL PRACTICE

- What is the value of finding flow in our work?

ANSWER: We become more likely to view our work as fulfilling and socially useful.

▓ Personnel Psychology

A-2 How do personnel psychologists help organizations with employee selection, work placement, and performance appraisal?

Psychologists can assist organizations at various stages of selecting and assessing employees. They may help identify needed job skills, decide upon selection methods, recruit and evaluate applicants, introduce and train new employees, and appraise their performance.

Matching Interests to Work

"So what interests you?" we may ask a new acquaintance. When faculty advisers or vocational counselors probe further, we may ask: "What do you love to do? What are you doing when time just flies—and what are you doing when time seems to stand still?" By exploring what someone enjoys, we seek to discern what academic and vocational pursuits might fit the student's interests. Much work is hard or tedious labor that people do solely for self-support. But the best job is one that pays you to do what you love—be it doing things with your hands, thinking of solutions, expressing yourself creatively, assisting people, being in charge, or working with data. Do what you love and you will love what you do.

A career counseling science aims, first, to assess people's differing values, personalities, and, especially, interests, which are remarkably stable (Dik & Rottinghaus, 2013). (Your job may change, but your interests today will likely still be your interests in 10 years.) Second, it aims to alert people to well-matched vocations—vocations with a good *person-environment fit*. One study assessed 400,000 high school students' interests and then followed them over time. The take-home finding: "Interests uniquely predict academic and career success over and above cognitive ability and personality" (Rounds & Su, 2014). The power of well-matched interests to predict income, for example, "greatly exceeded the contributions of ability and personality." Sixty other studies confirm the point both for students in school and workers on the job: Interests predict both performance and persistence (Nye et al., 2012).

Harnessing Strengths

As a new AT&T human resources executive, psychologist Mary Tenopyr (1997) was assigned to solve a problem: Customer-service representatives were failing at a high rate. After concluding that many of the hires were ill-matched to the demands of their new job, Tenopyr developed a new selection instrument:

1. She asked new applicants to respond to various test questions (without as yet making any use of their responses).

2. She followed up later to assess which of the applicants excelled on the job.

3. She identified the earlier test questions that best predicted success.

The happy result of her data-driven work was a new test that enabled AT&T to identify likely-to-succeed representatives. Personnel selection techniques such as this one aim to match people's strengths with work that enables them and their organization to flourish. Marry the strengths of people with the tasks of organizations and the result is often prosperity and profit.

Your strengths are any enduring qualities that can be productively applied. Are you naturally curious? Persuasive? Charming? Persistent? Competitive? Analytical? Empathic? Organized? Articulate? Neat? Mechanical? Any such trait, if matched with suitable work, can function as a strength (Buckingham, 2007).

Alvin Langdon Coburn/George Eastman House/Getty Images

Artistic strengths At age 21, Henri Matisse was a sickly and often depressed lawyer's clerk. When his mother gave him a box of paints to cheer him up one day, he felt the darkness lift and his energy surge. He began to fill his days with painting and drawing and went on to art school and a life as one of the world's great painters. For Matisse, doing art felt like "a comfortable armchair." That is how exercising our strengths often feels.

Gallup researchers Marcus Buckingham and Donald Clifton (2001) have argued that the first step to a stronger organization is instituting a *strengths-based selection system*. Thus, as a manager, you would first identify a group of the most effective people in any role—the ones you would want to hire more of—and compare their strengths with those of a group of the least effective people in that role. In defining these groups, you would try to measure performance as objectively as possible. In one Gallup study of more than 5000 telecommunications customer-service representatives, those evaluated most favorably by their managers were strong in "harmony" and "responsibility," while those actually rated most effective by customers were strong in energy, assertiveness, and eagerness to learn.

An example: If you needed to hire new people in software development, and you had discovered that your best software developers are analytical, disciplined, and eager to learn, you would focus employment ads less on experience than on the identified strengths. Thus "Do you take a logical and systematic approach to problem solving *[analytical]*? Are you a perfectionist who strives for timely completion of your projects *[disciplined]*? Do you want to master Java, C++, and PHP *[eager to learn]*? If you can say *Yes* to these questions, then please call . . ."

Identifying people's strengths and matching those strengths to work is a first step toward workplace effectiveness. To assess applicants' strengths and decide who is best suited to the job, personnel managers use various tools (Sackett & Lievens, 2008), including ability tests, personality tests, and behavioral observations in "assessment centers" that test applicants on tasks that mimic the job they seek.

Discovering Your Strengths

You can use some of the techniques personnel psychologists have developed to identify your own strengths and pinpoint types of work that will likely prove satisfying and successful. Buckingham and Clifton (2001) have suggested asking yourself these questions:

- What activities give me pleasure? Bringing order out of chaos? Playing host? Helping others? Challenging sloppy thinking?

- What activities leave me wondering, "When can I do this again?" rather than, "When will this be over?"

- What sorts of challenges do I relish? And which do I dread?

- What sorts of tasks do I learn easily? And which do I struggle with?

Some people find themselves in flow—their skills engaged and time flying—when teaching or selling or writing or cleaning or consoling or creating or repairing. If an activity feels good, if it comes easily, if you look forward to it, then look deeper and see your strengths at work. For a free (requires registration) assessment of your personal strengths, visit www.authentichappiness.sas.upenn.edu and select the "Brief Strengths Test."

The U.S. Department of Labor also offers a vocational interest questionnaire via its Occupational Information Network (O*NET). At www.mynextmove.org/explore/ip you will need about 10 minutes to respond to 60 items, indicating how much you would like or dislike activities ranging from building kitchen cabinets to playing a musical instrument. You will then receive feedback on how strongly your responses reflect six interest types specified by vocational psychologist John L. Holland (1996): *realistic* (hands-on doers), *investigative* (thinkers), *artistic* (creators), *social* (helpers, teachers), *enterprising* (persuaders, deciders), and *conventional* (organizers). Finally, depending on how much training you indicate being willing to undertake, you will be shown occupations—selected from a national database of 900+ occupations—that are congruent with your interest pattern. A more comprehensive (and fee-based) online service (called VIP) assesses people's values, interests, and personalities; suggests occupations; and connects people to job listings at www.jobzology.com.

Satisfied and successful people devote far less time to correcting their deficiencies than to accentuating their strengths. Top performers are "rarely well rounded," Buckingham and Clifton found (p. 26). Instead, they have sharpened their existing skills. Given the persistence of our traits and temperaments, we should focus not on our deficiencies, but rather on identifying and employing our talents. There may be limits to the benefits of assertiveness training if you are extremely shy, of public speaking courses if you tend to be nervous and soft-spoken, or of drawing classes if you express your artistic side in stick figures.

Identifying your talents can help you recognize the activities you learn quickly and find absorbing. Knowing your strengths, you can develop them further.

Do Interviews Predict Performance?

Most interviewers feel confident of their ability to predict long-term job performance from a get-acquainted interview. What's therefore shocking is how error prone interviewers' predictions are when predicting job or graduate school success. From their review of 85 years of personnel-selection research, I/O psychologists Frank Schmidt and John Hunter (1998; Schmidt, 2002) determined that for all but less-skilled jobs, general mental ability best predicts on-the-job performance. Subjective overall evaluations from informal interviews are more useful than handwriting analysis (which is worthless). But informal interviews are less informative than aptitude tests, work samples, job knowledge tests, and past job performance. If there's a contest between what our gut tells us about someone and what test scores, work samples, and past performance tell us, we should distrust our gut (Highhouse, 2008).

> "Interviews are a terrible predictor of performance."
>
> Laszlo Bock, Google's Vice President, People Operations, 2007

Unstructured Interviews and the Interviewer Illusion

Traditional *unstructured interviews* can provide a sense of someone's personality—their expressiveness, warmth, and verbal ability, for example. But these informal interviews also give interviewees considerable power to control the impression they are making in the interview situation (Barrick et al., 2009). Why, then, do many interviewers have such faith in their ability to discern interviewee's fitness for a job? "I have excellent interviewing skills, so I don't need reference checking as much as someone who doesn't have my ability to read people," I/O consultants often hear. This tendency to overrate their ability to predict people's futures is called the *interviewer illusion* (Dana et al., 2013; Nisbett, 1987). Five factors explain the gap between interviewers' overconfidence and the resulting reality:

- *Interviewers presume that people are what they seem to be in the interview situation.* An unstructured interview may create a false impression of a person's behavior toward others in different situations. As personality psychologists explain, when meeting others, we discount the enormous influence of varying situations and mistakenly presume that what we see is what we will get. But research on everything from chattiness to conscientiousness reveals that how we behave reflects not only our enduring traits, but also the details of the particular situation (such as wanting to impress in a job interview).

- *Interviewers' preconceptions and moods color how they perceive interviewees' responses* (Cable & Gilovich, 1998; Macan & Dipboye, 1994). If interviewers instantly like a person who perhaps is similar to themselves, they may interpret the person's assertiveness as indicating "confidence" rather than "arrogance." If told certain applicants have been prescreened, interviewers are disposed to judge them more favorably.

- *Interviewers judge people relative to those interviewed just before and after them* (Simonsohn & Gino, 2013). If you are being interviewed for business or medical school, hope for a time when the other interviewees have been weak.

- *Interviewers more often follow the successful careers of those they have hired than the successful careers of those they have rejected.* This missing feedback prevents interviewers from getting a reality check on their hiring ability.

- *Interviews disclose the interviewee's good intentions, which are less revealing than habitual behaviors* (Ouellette & Wood, 1998). Intentions matter. People can change. But the best predictor of the person we will be is the person we have been. Compared with work-avoiding university students, those who engage in their tasks are more likely, a decade and more later, to be engaged workers (Salmela-Aro et al., 2009). Educational attainments predict job performance partly because people who have shown up for school each day and done their tasks also tend to show up for work and do their tasks (Ng & Feldman, 2009). Wherever we go, we take ourselves along.

Hoping to improve prediction and selection, personnel psychologists have put people in simulated work situations, sought information on past performance, aggregated evaluations from multiple interviews, administered tests, and developed job-specific interviews.

Structured Interviews

Unlike casual conversation aimed at getting a feel for someone, **structured interviews** offer a disciplined method of collecting information. A personnel psychologist may analyze a job, script questions, and train interviewers. The interviewers then put the same questions, in the same order, to all applicants, and rate each applicant on established scales.

In an unstructured interview, someone might ask, "How organized are you?" "How well do you get along with people?" or "How do you handle stress?" Street-smart applicants know how to score high: "Although I sometimes drive myself too hard, I handle stress by prioritizing and delegating, and by making sure I leave time for sleep and exercise."

By contrast, structured interviews pinpoint strengths (attitudes, behaviors, knowledge, and skills) that distinguish high performers in a particular line of work. The process includes outlining job-specific situations and asking candidates to explain how they would handle them, and how they handled similar situations in their prior employment. "Tell me about a time when you were caught between conflicting demands, without time to accomplish both. How did you handle that?"

To reduce memory distortions and bias, the interviewer takes notes and makes ratings as the interview proceeds and avoids irrelevant and follow-up questions. The structured interview therefore feels less warm, but that can be explained to the applicant: "This conversation won't typify how we relate to each other in this organization."

A review of 150 findings revealed that structured interviews had double the predictive accuracy of unstructured seat-of-the-pants interviews (Schmidt & Hunter, 1998; Wiesner & Cronshaw, 1988). Structured interviews also reduce bias, such as against overweight applicants (Kutcher & Bragger, 2004). Thanks partly to its greater reliability and partly to its job-analysis focus, the predictive power of one structured interview is roughly equal to that of the average judgment from three or four unstructured interviews (Huffcutt et al., 2001; Schmidt & Zimmerman, 2004).

If, instead, we let our intuitions bias the hiring process, noted Malcolm Gladwell (2000, p. 86), then "all we will have done is replace the old-boy network, where you hired your nephew, with the new-boy network, where you hire whoever impressed you

"Between the idea and reality . . . falls the shadow."

T. S. Eliot, *The Hollow Men,* 1925

structured interviews interview process that asks the same job-relevant questions of all applicants, each of whom is rated on established scales.

most when you shook his hand. Social progress, unless we're careful, can merely be the means by which we replace the obviously arbitrary with the not so obviously arbitrary."

To recap, personnel psychologists assist organizations in analyzing jobs, recruiting well-suited applicants, and selecting and placing employees. They also appraise employees' performance (**FIGURE A.1**)—the topic we turn to next.

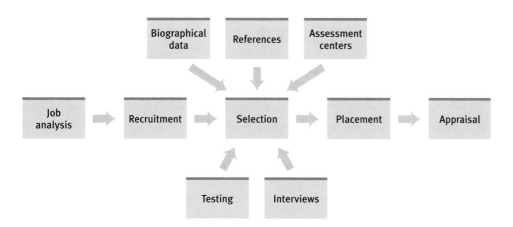

▼ FIGURE A.1
Personnel psychologists' tasks Personnel psychologists consult in human resources activities, from job definition to employee appraisal.

Appraising Performance

Performance appraisal serves organizational purposes: It helps decide who to retain, how to appropriately reward and pay people, and how to better harness employee strengths, sometimes with job shifts or promotions. Performance appraisal also serves individual purposes: Feedback affirms workers' strengths and helps motivate needed improvements.

Performance appraisal methods include

- *checklists* on which supervisors simply check specific behaviors that describe the worker ("always attends to customers' needs," "takes long breaks").

- *graphic rating scales* on which a supervisor checks, perhaps on a five-point scale, how often a worker is dependable, productive, and so forth.

- *behavior rating scales* on which a supervisor checks scaled behaviors that describe a worker's performance. If rating the extent to which a worker "follows procedures," the supervisor might mark the employee somewhere between "often takes short-cuts" and "always follows established procedures" (Levy, 2003).

In some organizations, performance feedback comes not only from supervisors but also from all organizational levels. If you join an organization that practices *360-degree feedback* (**FIGURE A.2**), you will rate yourself, your manager, and your other colleagues, and you will be rated by your manager, other colleagues, and customers (Green, 2002). The net result is often more open communication and more complete appraisal.

Performance appraisal, like other social judgments, is vulnerable to bias (Murphy & Cleveland, 1995). *Halo errors* occur when one's overall evaluation of an employee, or of a personal trait such as their friendliness, biases ratings of their specific work-related behaviors, such as their reliability. *Leniency* and *severity errors* reflect evaluators' tendencies to be either too easy or too harsh on everyone. *Recency errors* occur when raters focus only on easily remembered recent behavior. By using multiple raters and developing objective, job-relevant performance measures, personnel psychologists seek to support their organizations while also helping employees perceive the appraisal process as fair.

▼ FIGURE A.2
360-degree feedback With multi-source 360-degree feedback, our knowledge, skills, and behaviors are rated by ourselves and surrounding others. Professors, for example, may be rated by their department chairs, their students, and their colleagues. After receiving all these ratings, professors discuss the 360-degree feedback with their department chair.

- A human resources director explains to you that "I don't bother with tests or references. It's all about the interview." Based on I/O research, what concerns does this raise?

ANSWER: (1) Interviewers may presume people are what they seem to be in interviews. (2) Interviewers' preconceptions and moods color how they perceive interviewees' responses. (3) Interviewers judge people relative to other recent interviewees. (4) Interviewers tend to track the successful careers of those they hire, not the successful careers of those they reject. (5) Interviews tend to disclose prospective workers' good intentions, not their habitual behaviors.

■ Organizational Psychology

A-3 What is the role of organizational psychologists?

The appraisal of work and the matching of interests and talents to work matter, but so does overall motivation. Organizational psychologists assist with efforts to motivate and engage employees.

Satisfaction and Engagement

Partly because work is such a big part of life, I/O psychologists study employee satisfaction. Satisfaction with work feeds satisfaction with life (Bowling et al., 2010). Moreover, as health psychologists tell us, decreased job stress feeds improved health.

Satisfied employees also contribute to successful organizations. Positive moods at work enhance creativity, persistence, and helpfulness (Ford et al., 2011; Shockley et al., 2012). Are engaged, happy workers also less often absent? Less likely to quit? Less prone to theft? More punctual? More productive? Conclusive evidence of satisfaction's benefits is, some have said, the Holy Grail of I/O psychology. Statistical digests of prior

> "The only place success comes before work is in the dictionary."
>
> Former Green Bay Packers football coach
> Vince Lombardi

Doing well while doing good—"The Great Experiment" At the end of the 1700s, the New Lanark, Scotland, cotton mill had more than 1000 workers. Many were children drawn from Glasgow's poorhouses. They worked 13-hour days and lived in grim conditions.

On a visit to Glasgow, Welsh-born Robert Owen—an idealistic young cotton-mill manager— chanced to meet and marry the mill owner's daughter. Owen and some partners purchased the mill and on the first day of the 1800s began what he said was "the most important experiment for the happiness of the human race that had yet been instituted at any time in any part of the world" (Owen, 1814). The exploitation of child and adult labor was, he observed, producing unhappy and inefficient workers. So he undertook numerous innovations: a nursery for preschool children, education for older

Courtesy of New Lanark Trust

children (with encouragement rather than corporal punishment), Sundays off, health care, paid sick days, unemployment pay for days when the mill could not operate, and a company store selling goods at reduced prices.

He also innovated a goals- and worker-assessment program that included detailed records of daily productivity and costs but with "no beating, no abusive language."

The ensuing commercial success fueled a humanitarian reform movement. By 1816, with decades of profitability still ahead, Owen believed he had demonstrated "that society may be formed so as to exist without crime, without poverty, with health greatly improved, with little if any misery, and with intelligence and happiness increased a hundredfold." Although his Utopian vision has not been fulfilled, Owen's great experiment laid the groundwork for employment practices that have today become accepted in much of the world.

An engaged employee Mohamed Mamow, left, was joined by his employer in saying the Pledge of Allegiance as he became a U.S. citizen. Mamow and his wife met in a Somali refugee camp and now are parents of five children, whom he supports by working as a machine operator. Mindful of his responsibility—"I don't like to lose my job. I have a responsibility for my children and my family"—he arrives for work a half hour early and tends to every detail on his shift. "He is an extremely hard-working employee," noted his employer, and "a reminder to all of us that we are really blessed" (Roelofs, 2010).

research have found a modest positive correlation between individual job satisfaction and performance (Judge et al., 2001; Ng et al., 2009; Parker et al., 2003). In one analysis of 4500 employees at 42 British manufacturing companies, the most productive workers tended to be those in satisfying work environments (Patterson et al., 2004). Happy workers are usually good workers. But does satisfaction *produce* better job performance? The debate continues.

Nevertheless, some organizations do have a knack for cultivating more engaged and productive employees. In the United States, the *Fortune* "100 Best Companies to Work For" have also produced markedly higher-than-average returns for their investors (Fulmer et al., 2003). Other positive data come from the biggest-ever I/O study, an analysis of Gallup data from more than 198,000 employees (**TABLE A.2**) in nearly 8000 business units of 36 large companies (including some 1100 bank branches, 1200 stores, and 4200 teams

▼ TABLE A.2
The Gallup Workplace Audit

Overall satisfaction—On a 5-point scale, where 5 is extremely satisfied and 1 is extremely dissatisfied, how satisfied are you with *(name of company)* as a place to work? _____ On a scale of 1 to 5, where 1 is strongly disagree and 5 is strongly agree, please indicate your agreement with the following items:

1. I know what is expected from me at work.

2. I have the materials and equipment I need to do my work right.

3. At work, I have the opportunity to do what I do best every day.

4. In the last seven days, I have received recognition or praise for doing good work.

5. My supervisor, or someone at work, seems to care about me as a person.

6. There is someone at work who encourages my development.

7. At work, my opinions seem to count.

8. The mission/purpose of my company makes me feel my job is important.

9. My associates (fellow employees) are committed to doing quality work.

10. I have a best friend at work.

11. In the last six months, someone at work has talked to me about my progress.

12. This last year, I have had opportunities at work to learn and grow.

Note: These statements are proprietary and copyrighted by The Gallup Organization. They may not be printed or reproduced in any manner without the written consent of The Gallup Organization. Reprinted here by permission.

▼ TABLE A.3
Three Types of Employees

Engaged: working with passion and feeling a profound connection to their company or organization.

Not engaged: putting in the time but investing little passion or energy into their work.

Actively disengaged: unhappy workers undermining what their colleagues accomplish.

Source: Adapted from Gallup via Crabtree, 2005.

or departments). James Harter, Frank Schmidt, and Theodore Hayes (2002) explored correlations between various measures of organizational success and *employee engagement*—the extent of workers' involvement, enthusiasm, and identification with their organizations (**TABLE A.3**). They found that engaged workers (compared to disengaged workers who are just putting in time) knew what was expected of them, had what they needed to do their work, felt fulfilled in their work, had regular opportunities to do what they do best, perceived that they were part of something significant, and had opportunities to learn and develop. They also found that business units with engaged employees had more loyal customers, lower turnover rates, higher productivity, and greater profits.

But what causal arrows explain this correlation between business success and employee morale and engagement? Does success boost morale, or does high morale boost success? In a follow-up longitudinal study of 142,000 workers, researchers found that, over time, employee attitudes predicted future business success (more than the other way around) (Harter et al., 2010). Another analysis compared companies with top-quartile versus below-average employee engagement levels. Over a three-year period, earnings grew 2.6 times faster for the companies with highly engaged workers (Ott, 2007).

Managing Well

A-4 What are some effective leadership techniques?

Every leader dreams of managing in ways that enhance people's satisfaction, engagement, and productivity and their organization's success. Effective leaders harness job-relevant strengths, set goals, and choose an appropriate leadership style.

Harnessing Job-Relevant Strengths

"The major challenge for CEOs over the next 20 years will be the effective deployment of human assets," observed Marcus Buckingham (2001). That challenge is "about psychology. It's about getting [individuals] to be more productive, more focused, more fulfilled than [they were] yesterday." The first step, he and others have maintained, is selecting the right people, followed by discerning employees' natural talents, adjusting work roles to suit those talents, and developing talents into great strengths (**FIGURE A.3**). Consider the faculty at a given college or university. Should everyone be expected to teach the same course load, advise the same number of students, serve on the same number of committees, and engage in the same amount of research? Or should each job description be tailored to harness a specific person's unique strengths?

Given that our temperament and our traits tend to follow us through our lives, managers would be wise to spend less time trying to instill talents that are not there and more time developing and drawing out those that are there (Tucker, 2002). Managers who excel

- start by helping people identify and measure their talents.
- match tasks to talents and then give people freedom to do what they do best.

▼ FIGURE A.3
On the right path The Gallup Organization offers this path to organizational success. (Adapted from Fleming, 2001.)

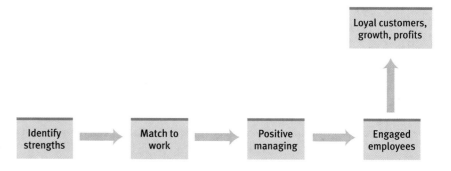

- care how their people feel about their work.
- reinforce positive behaviors through recognition and reward.

Thus, rather than focusing on weaknesses and packing people off to training seminars to fix those problems, effective managers focus training time on educating people about their strengths and building upon them (which means not promoting people into roles ill-suited to their strengths). In Gallup surveys, 77 percent of engaged workers, and only 23 percent of not-engaged workers, strongly agreed that "my supervisor focuses on my strengths or positive characteristics" (Krueger & Killham, 2005).

Celebrating engaged and productive employees in every organizational role builds upon a basic principle of *operant conditioning*: To teach a behavior, catch a person doing something right and reinforce it. It sounds simple, but many managers are like parents who, when a child brings home near-perfect exam scores, focus on the one low score in a troublesome biology class and ignore the rest. "Sixty-five percent of Americans received NO praise or recognition in the workplace last year," reported the Gallup Organization (2004).

The bottom line: In the workplace, great managers support employees' well-being. By caring about their employees and engaging and affirming their strengths, they support happier, more creative, more productive workers with less absenteeism and turnover (Amabile & Kramer, 2011; De Neve et al., 2013). People less often leave bad companies than bad managers (Busteed, 2012). Moreover, the same principles affect college students' satisfaction, retention, and future success (Larkin et al., 2013; Ray & Kafka, 2014). Students who feel supported by caring friends and mentors, and engaged in their campus life, tend to persist and ultimately succeed during and after college.

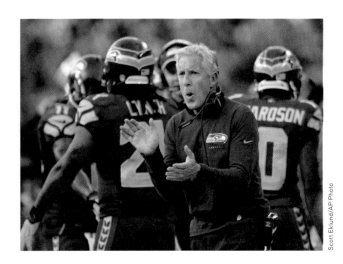

The power of positive coaching
Football coach Pete Carroll, who led the University of Southern California to two national championships and the Seattle Seahawks to a Super Bowl championship, combines positive enthusiasm and fun workouts with "a commitment to a nurturing environment that allows people to be themselves while still being accountable to the team" (Trotter, 2014). "It shows you can win with positivity," notes Seahawks star defensive player Richard Sherman.

Setting Specific, Challenging Goals

Specific, challenging goals motivate achievement, especially when combined with progress reports (Johnson et al., 2006; Latham & Locke, 2007). Specific, measurable objectives, such as "finish gathering the history paper information by Friday," serve to direct attention, promote effort, motivate persistence, and stimulate creative strategies.

When people state goals together with *subgoals* and *implementation intentions*— action plans that specify when, where, and how they will march toward achieving those goals—they become more focused in their work, and on-time completion becomes more likely (Burgess et al., 2004; Fishbach et al., 2006; Koestner et al., 2002). Through a task's ups and downs, people best sustain their mood and motivation when they focus on immediate goals (such as daily study) rather than distant goals (such as a course grade). Better to have one's nose to the grindstone than one's eye on the ultimate prize (Houser-Marko & Sheldon, 2008).

Thus, before beginning each new edition of this book, our author-editor-staff team *manages by objectives*—we agree on target dates for the completion and editing of each draft. If we focus on achieving each of these short-term goals, the prize—an on-time book—takes care of itself. So, to motivate high productivity, effective leaders work with people to define explicit goals, subgoals, and implementation plans, and then provide feedback on progress.

Choosing an Appropriate Leadership Style

Leadership varies from a boss-focused directive style to an empowered-worker democratic style in which people cooperate in setting goals and developing strategies. Which works best depends on the situation and the leader. The best leadership style task leadership goal-oriented leadership that sets standards, organizes work, and focuses attention on goals.

social leadership group-oriented leadership that builds teamwork, mediates conflict, and offers support.

"Good leaders don't ask more than their constituents can give, but they often ask—and get—more than their constituents intended to give or thought it was possible to give."

John W. Gardner, *Excellence*, 1984

for leading a discussion may not be the best style for leading troops on a charge (Fiedler, 1981). Moreover, different leaders are suited to different styles. Some excel at **task leadership**—setting standards, organizing work, and focusing attention on goals. Being goal-oriented, task leaders are good at keeping a group centered on its mission. Typically, they have a directive style, which can work well if the leader is bright enough to give good orders (Fiedler, 1987).

Other managers, many of whom are women, excel at **social leadership**—explaining decisions, mediating conflicts, and building high-achieving teams (Evans & Dion, 1991; Pfaff et al., 2013). Social leaders often have a democratic style: They delegate authority and welcome team members' participation. Many experiments show that social leadership and team-building increases morale and productivity (Shuffler et al., 2011, 2013). Subordinates usually felt more satisfied and motivated, and performed better, when they participated in decision making (Cawley et al., 1998; Pereira & Osburn, 2007). Moreover, when members are sensitive to one another and participate equally, groups solve problems with greater "collective intelligence" (Woolley et al., 2010).

Because effective leadership styles vary with the situation and the person, the once-popular *great person theory of leadership*—that all great leaders share certain traits—now seems overstated (Vroom & Jago, 2007; Wielkiewicz & Stelzner, 2005). The same coach may seem great or inferior depending on the strength of the team and its competition. But a leader's personality does matter (Zaccaro, 2007). Effective leaders tend to be neither extremely assertive (impairing social relationships) or unassertive (limiting task leadership) (Ames, 2008). Effective leaders of laboratory groups, work teams, and large corporations have also been found to exude a *charisma* that blends a goal-based *vision, clear communication,* and *optimism* that inspires others to follow (House & Singh, 1987; Shamir et al., 1993).

In one study of 50 Dutch companies, the firms with highest morale had chief executives who most inspired their colleagues "to transcend their own self-interests for the sake of the collective" (de Hoogh et al., 2004). *Transformational leadership* of this kind motivates others to identify with and commit themselves to the group's mission. Transformational leaders, many of whom are natural extraverts, articulate high standards, inspire people to share their vision, and offer personal attention (Bono & Judge, 2004). The frequent result is more engaged, trusting, and effective workers (Turner et al., 2002). As leaders, women more than men tend to exhibit transformational leadership qualities. Alice Eagly (2007, 2013) believes this helps explain why companies with female top managers have tended to enjoy superior financial results, even after controlling for such variables as company size.

Data compiled from studies in India, Taiwan, and Iran indicating that effective managers—whether in coal mines, banks, or government offices—often exhibit a high degree of *both* task and social leadership (Smith & Tayeb, 1989). As achievement-minded people, effective managers certainly care about how well work is done, yet at the same time they are sensitive to their subordinates' needs. Workers in family-friendly organizations that offer flexible-time hours report feeling greater job satisfaction and loyalty to their employers (Butts et al., 2013; Roehling et al., 2001).

A work environment that satisfies one's need to belong also energizes employees. Employees who enjoy high-quality colleague relationships also engage their work with more vigor (Carmeli et al., 2009). Gallup researchers have asked more than 15 million employees worldwide if they have a "best friend at work." The 30 percent who do "are *seven times* as likely to be engaged in their jobs" as those who don't, report Tom Rath and James Harter (2010). And, as we noted earlier, positive, engaged employees are a mark of thriving organizations.

Increased employee participation in decision making is part of a management style that has spread from Sweden and Japan to many other locations (Naylor, 1990; Sundstrom et al., 1990). Although managers often think better of work they have directly supervised, studies reveal a *voice effect:* Given a chance to voice their opinion and to be part of a decision-making process, people have responded more positively to the decision (van den Bos & Spruijt, 2002). They also feel more empowered, and are likely, therefore, to be more creative and committed (Hennessey & Amabile, 2010; Seibert et al., 2011).

The ultimate in employee participation is the employee-owned company. One such company in my town, the Fleetwood Group, is a 165-employee manufacturer of educational furniture and wireless electronic clickers. When its founder gave 45 percent of the company to his employees, who later bought out other family stockholders, Fleetwood became one of America's first companies with an employee stock ownership plan (ESOP). Today, every employee owns part of the company, and as a group they own 100 percent. The more years employees work, the more they own, yet no one owns more than 5 percent. Like every corporate president, Doug Ruch works for his stockholders—who also just happen to be his employees.

As a company that endorses faith-inspired "servant leadership" and "respect and care for each team member-owner," Fleetwood is free to place people above profits. Thus, when orders lagged during a recession, the employee-owners decided that job security meant more to them than profits. So the company paid otherwise idle workers to do community service—answering phones at nonprofit agencies, building Habitat for Humanity houses, and the like.

Fleetwood employees "act like they own the place," notes Ruch. Employee ownership attracts and retains talented people, "drives dedication," and gives Fleetwood "a sustainable competitive advantage," he contends. With stock growth averaging 17 percent a year, Fleetwood was named the 2006 National ESOP of the year.

* * *

We have considered *personnel psychology* (the I/O subfield that focuses on employee selection, placement, appraisal, and development). And we have considered *organizational psychology* (the I/O subfield that focuses on worker satisfaction and productivity, and on organizational change). Finally, we turn to *human factors psychology*, which explores the human-machine interface.

RETRIEVAL PRACTICE

- What characteristics are important for *transformational leaders?*

ANSWER: *Transformational leaders* are able to inspire others to share a vision and commit themselves to a group's mission. They tend to be naturally extraverted and set high standards.

The Human Factor

A-5 How do human factors psychologists work to create user-friendly machines and work settings?

Designs sometimes neglect the human factor. Psychologist Donald Norman bemoaned the complexity of assembling his new HDTV, related components, and seven remotes into a usable home theater system: "I was VP of Advanced Technology at Apple. I can program dozens of computers in dozens of languages. I understand television, really, I do. . . . It doesn't matter: I am overwhelmed."

How much easier life might be if engineers would routinely test their designs and instructions on real people. *Human factors psychologists* work with designers and engineers to tailor appliances, machines, and work settings to our natural perceptions and inclinations. Bank ATM machines are internally more complex than remote controls ever were, yet, thanks to human factors engineering, ATMs are easier to operate. Digital recorders have solved the TV recording problem with a simple select-and-click menu system ("record that one"). Apple has similarly engineered easy usability with the iPhone and iPad.

Norman (2001) hosts a website (www.jnd.org) that illustrates good designs that fit people (**FIGURE A.4**). Human factors psychologists also help design efficient environments. An ideal kitchen layout, researchers have found, puts needed items close to their usage point and near eye level. It locates work areas to enable doing tasks in order, such as placing the refrigerator, stove, and sink in a triangle. It creates counters that enable hands to work at or slightly below elbow height (Boehm-Davis, 2005).

Understanding human factors can help prevent accidents. By studying the human factor in driving accidents, psychologists seek to devise ways to reduce the distractions, fatigue, and inattention that contribute to 1.3 million annual worldwide traffic fatalities (Lee, 2008). Two-thirds of commercial air accidents have been caused by human error (Nickerson, 1998). After beginning commercial flights in the 1960s, the Boeing 727 was involved in several landing accidents caused by pilot error. Psychologist Conrad Kraft (1978) noted a common setting for these accidents: All took place at night, and all involved landing short of the runway after crossing a dark stretch of water or unilluminated ground. Kraft reasoned that, on rising terrain, city lights beyond the runway would project a larger retinal image, making the ground seem farther away than it was. By re-creating these conditions in flight simulations, Kraft discovered that pilots were deceived into thinking they were flying higher than their actual altitudes

▼ **FIGURE A.4**
Designing products that fit people
Human factors psychologist Donald Norman offers these and other examples of effectively designed products.

The Ride On Carry On foldable chair attachment, "designed by a flight attendant mom," enables a small suitcase to double as a stroller.

The Oxo measuring cup allows the user to see the quantity from above.

(**FIGURE A.5**). Aided by Kraft's finding, the airlines began requiring the co-pilot to monitor the altimeter—calling out altitudes during the descent—and the accidents diminished.

Later Boeing psychologists worked on other human factors problems (Murray, 1998): How should airlines best train and manage mechanics to reduce the maintenance errors that underlie about 50 percent of flight delays and 15 percent of accidents? What illumination and typeface would make on-screen flight data easiest to read? How could warning messages be most effectively worded—as an action statement ("Pull Up") rather than a problem statement ("Ground Proximity")?

Consider, finally, the available *assistive listening* technologies in various theaters, auditoriums, and places of worship. One technology, commonly available in the United States, requires a headset attached to a pocket-sized receiver that detects infrared or FM signals from the room's sound system. The well-meaning people who design, purchase, and install these systems correctly understand that the technology puts sound directly into the user's ears. Alas, few people with hearing loss undergo the hassle and embarrassment of locating, requesting, wearing, and returning a conspicuous headset. Most such units therefore sit in closets. Britain, the Scandinavian countries, and Australia, and now parts of the United States, have instead installed *loop systems* (see www.hearingloop.org) that broadcast customized sound directly through a person's own hearing aid. When suitably equipped, a hearing aid can be transformed by a discrete touch of a switch into an in-the-ear loudspeaker. Offered convenient, inconspicuous, personalized sound, many more people elect to use assistive listening.

Designs that enable safe, easy, and effective interactions between people and technology often seem obvious after the fact. Why, then, aren't they more common? Technology developers sometimes mistakenly assume that others share their expertise—that what's clear to them will similarly be clear to others (Camerer et al., 1989; Nickerson, 1999). When people rap their knuckles on a table to convey a familiar tune (try this with a friend), they often expect their listener to recognize it. But for the listener, this is a near-impossible task (Newton, 1991). When you know a thing, it's hard to mentally simulate what it's like not to know, and that is called the *curse of knowledge*.

The point to remember: Everyone benefits when designers and engineers tailor machines and environments to fit human abilities and behaviors, when they user-test their inventions before production and distribution, and when they remain mindful of the curse of knowledge.

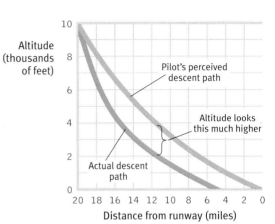

▼ FIGURE A.5
The human factor in accidents
Lacking distance cues when approaching a runway from over a dark surface, pilots simulating a night landing tended to fly too low. (Data from Kraft, 1978.)

RETRIEVAL PRACTICE

• What are the three main divisions within industrial-organizational psychology?

ANSWER: personnel, organizational, human factors

The human factor in safe landings
Advanced cockpit design and rehearsed emergency procedures aided pilot Chesley "Sully" Sullenberger, a U.S. Air Force Academy graduate who studied psychology and human factors. In January 2009, Sullenberger's instantaneous decisions safely guided his disabled airplane onto New York City's Hudson River, where all 155 of the passengers and crew were safely evacuated.

REVIEW Psychology at Work

LEARNING OBJECTIVES

RETRIEVAL PRACTICE Take a moment to answer each of these Learning Objective Questions (repeated here from within this appendix). Then turn to Appendix C to check your answers. Research suggests that trying to answer these questions on your own will improve your long-term retention (McDaniel et al., 2009).

A-1 What is *flow,* and what are the three subfields of industrial-organizational psychology?

A-2 How do personnel psychologists help organizations with employee selection, work placement, and performance appraisal?

A-3 What is the role of organizational psychologists?

A-4 What are some effective leadership techniques?

A-5 How do human factors psychologists work to create user-friendly machines and work settings?

Use 🌐 LearningCurve to create your personalized study plan, which will direct you to the resources that will help you most in 🌐 LaunchPad.

TERMS AND CONCEPTS TO REMEMBER

RETRIEVAL PRACTICE Test yourself on these terms by trying to write down the definition.

flow, p. A-1

industrial-organizational (I/O) psychology, p. A-2

personnel psychology, p. A-2

organizational psychology, p. A-2

human factors psychology, p. A-2

structured interviews, p. A-6

task leadership, p. A-12

social leadership, p. A-12

TEST YOUR-SELF PSYCHOLOGY AT WORK

Test yourself repeatedly throughout your studies. This will not only help you figure out what you know and don't know; the testing itself will help you learn and remember the information more effectively thanks to the *testing effect.*

1. People who view their work as a calling often experience _____ , a focused state of consciousness, with diminished awareness of themselves and of time.

   a. stress

   b. apathy

   c. flow

   d. facilitation

2. _____ psychologists study the recruitment, selection, placement, training, appraisal, and development of employees; _____ _____ psychologists focus on how people and machines interact, and on optimizing devices and work environments.

Personnel Psychology

3. A personnel psychologist scripted a set of questions to ask all applicants for a job opening. She then trained the firm's interviewers to ask only these questions, to take notes, and to rate applicants' responses. This technique is known as a(n)

   a. structured interview.

   b. unstructured interview.

   c. performance appraisal checklist.

   d. behavior rating scale.

4. In your job, you rate your own performance, your manager's, and your peers'. Your manager, your peers, and your customers also rate your performance. Your organization is using a form of performance appraisal called

   a. flow procedure.

   b. graphic feedback.

   c. structured interviews.

   d. 360-degree feedback.

Organizational Psychology

5. What type of goals will best help you stay focused and motivated to do your best work in this class?

6. Research indicates that women are more likely than men to have a _____ leadership style.

7. Effective managers often exhibit

   a. only task leadership.

   b. only social leadership.

   c. both task and social leadership, depending on the situation and the person.

   d. task leadership for building teams and social leadership for setting standards.

The Human Factor

8. To reduce users' frustration and to avoid accidents, human factors psychologists help organizations avoid the curse of knowledge, which is the tendency for

   a. a little bit of knowledge to be dangerous for the user.

   b. users to override machines and resort to familiar habits.

   c. engineers and designers to assume that users are idiots and need overly detailed instructions.

   d. engineers and designers to assume that others will share their knowledge.

Find answers to these questions in Appendix D.

Subfields of Psychology

Jennifer Zwolinski
University of San Diego

What can you do with a degree in psychology? Lots!

As a psychology major, you will graduate with a scientific mind-set and an awareness of basic principles of human behavior (biological mechanisms, development, cognition, psychological disorders, social interaction). This background will prepare you for success in many areas, including business, the helping professions, health services, marketing, law, sales, and teaching. You may even go on to graduate school for specialized training to become a psychology professional. This appendix describes psychology's specialized subfields.[1] I also provide updated information about CAREERS IN PSYCHOLOGY at www.macmillanhighered.com/launchpad/myers11einmodules, where you can learn more about the many interesting options available to those with bachelor's, master's, and doctoral degrees in psychology.

If you are like most psychology students, you may be unaware of the wide variety of specialties and work settings available in psychology (Terre & Stoddart, 2000). To date, the American Psychological Association (APA) has 56 divisions (**TABLE B.1** on the next page). Use social media to learn more about the divisions by visiting www.tinyurl.com/APA-SocialMedia.

The following paragraphs (arranged alphabetically) describe some careers in the main specialty areas of psychology, most of which require a graduate degree in psychology.

Clinical psychologists promote psychological health in individuals, groups, and organizations. Some clinical psychologists specialize in specific psychological disorders. Others treat a range of disorders, from adjustment difficulties to severe psychopathology. Clinical psychologists might engage in research, teaching, assessment, and consultation. Some hold workshops and lectures on psychological issues for other professionals or for the public. Clinical psychologists work in a variety of settings, including private practice, mental health service organizations, schools, universities, industries, legal systems, medical systems, counseling centers, government agencies, and military services.

To become a clinical psychologist, you will need to earn a doctorate from a clinical psychology program. The APA sets the standards for clinical psychology graduate programs, offering accreditation (official recognition) to those who meet their standards. In all U.S. states, clinical psychologists working in independent practice must obtain a license to offer services such as therapy and testing.

Cognitive psychologists study thought processes and focus on such topics as perception, language, attention, problem solving, memory, judgment and decision making, forgetting, and

Cognitive consulting Cognitive psychologists may advise businesses on how to operate more effectively by understanding the human factors involved.

Karen Moskowitz/The Image Bank/Getty Images

1. Although this text covers the world of psychology for students in many countries, this appendix draws primarily from available U.S. data. Its descriptions of psychology's subfields are, however, also applicable in many other countries.

▼ TABLE B.1
APA Divisions by Number and Name

1. Society for General Psychology	29. Society for the Advancement of Psychotherapy
2. Society for the Teaching of Psychology	30. Society of Psychological Hypnosis
3. Experimental Psychology	31. State, Provincial, and Territorial Psychological Association Affairs
4. There is no Division 4.	32. Society for Humanistic Psychology
5. Division for Quantitative and Qualitative Methods	33. Intellectual and Developmental Disabilities
6. Behavioral Neuroscience and Comparative Psychology	34. Society for Environmental, Population, and Conservation Psychology
7. Developmental Psychology	35. Society for the Psychology of Women
8. Society for Personality and Social Psychology	36. Society for the Psychology of Religion and Spirituality
9. Society for the Psychological Study of Social Issues	37. Society for Child and Family Policy and Practice
10. Society for the Psychology of Aesthetics, Creativity, and the Arts	38. Health Psychology
11. There is no Division 11.	39. Psychoanalysis
12. Society of Clinical Psychology	40. Society for Clinical Neuropsychology
13. Society of Consulting Psychology	41. American Psychology-Law Society
14. Society for Industrial and Organizational Psychology	42. Psychologists in Independent Practice
15. Educational Psychology	43. Society for Family Psychology
16. School Psychology	44. Society for the Psychological Study of Lesbian, Gay, Bisexual, and Transgender Issues
17. Society of Counseling Psychology	45. Society for the Psychological Study of Culture, Ethnicity, and Race
18. Psychologists in Public Service	46. Society for Media Psychology and Technology
19. Society for Military Psychology	47. Exercise and Sport Psychology
20. Adult Development and Aging	48. Society for the Study of Peace, Conflict, and Violence: Peace Psychology Division
21. Applied Experimental and Engineering Psychology	49. Society of Group Psychology and Group Psychotherapy
22. Rehabilitation Psychology	50. Society of Addiction Psychology
23. Society for Consumer Psychology	51. Society for the Psychological Study of Men and Masculinity
24. Society for Theoretical and Philosophical Psychology	52. International Psychology
25. Behavior Analysis	53. Society of Clinical Child and Adolescent Psychology
26. Society for the History of Psychology	54. Society of Pediatric Psychology
27. Society for Community Research and Action: Division of Community Psychology	55. American Society for the Advancement of Pharmacotherapy
28. Psychopharmacology and Substance Abuse	56. Trauma Psychology

Source: American Psychological Association. For a chronological history of the 56 divisions including why Divisions 4 and 11 are vacant, please see Appendix VIII at www.tinyurl.com/APA-DivisionHistory.

intelligence. Research interests include designing computer-based models of thought processes and identifying biological correlates of cognition. As a cognitive psychologist, you might work as a professor, industrial consultant, or human factors specialist in an educational or business setting.

Community psychologists move beyond focusing on specific individuals or families and deal with broad problems of mental health in community settings. These psychologists believe that human behavior is powerfully influenced by the interaction between people and their physical, social, political, and economic environments. They seek to promote psychological health by enhancing environmental settings, focusing on preventive measures and crisis intervention, with special attention to the problems of underserved groups and ethnic minorities. Given the shared emphasis on prevention, some community psychologists collaborate with professionals in other areas, such as public health. As a community psychologist, your work settings could include federal, state, and local departments of mental health, corrections, and welfare. You might conduct research or help evaluate research in health service settings, serve as an independent consultant for a private or government agency, or teach and consult as a college or university faculty member.

Counseling psychologists help people adjust to life transitions or make lifestyle changes. Although similar to clinical psychologists, counseling psychologists typically help people with adjustment problems rather than severe psychopathology. Like clinical psychologists, counseling psychologists conduct therapy and provide assessments to individuals and groups. As a counseling psychologist, you would emphasize your clients' strengths, helping them to use their own skills, interests, and abilities to cope during transitions. You might find yourself working in an academic setting as a faculty member or administrator or in a university counseling center, community mental health center, business, or private practice. As with clinical psychology, if you plan to work in independent practice you will need to obtain a state license to provide counseling services to the public.

James Burnett/*Miami Herald*/MCT via Getty Images

Community care This community psychologist (left) helped residents work through the emotional challenges that followed the devastating 2010 earthquake in Haiti.

Developmental psychologists conduct research in age-related behavioral changes and apply their scientific knowledge to educational, child-care, policy, and related settings. As a developmental psychologist, you would investigate change across a broad range of topics, including the biological, psychological, cognitive, and social aspects of development. Developmental psychology informs a number of applied fields, including educational psychology, school psychology, child psychopathology, and gerontology. The field also informs public policy in areas such as education and child-care reform, maternal and child health, and attachment and adoption. You would probably specialize in a specific stage of the life span, such as infancy, childhood, adolescence, or middle or late adulthood. Your work setting could be an educational institution, day-care center, youth group program, or senior center.

Educational psychologists are interested in the psychological processes involved in learning. They study the relationship between learning and the physical and social environments, and they develop strategies for enhancing the learning process. As an educational psychologist, working in a university psychology department or school of education, you might conduct basic research on topics related to learning, or develop innovative methods of teaching to enhance the learning process. You might design effective tests, including measures of aptitude and achievement. You might be employed by a school or government agency or charged with designing and implementing effective employee-training programs in a business setting.

Experimental psychologists are a diverse group of scientists who investigate a variety of basic behavioral processes in humans and other animals. Prominent areas of experimental research include comparative methods of science, motivation, learning, thought, attention, memory, perception, and language. Most experimental psychologists identify with a particular subfield, such as cognitive psychology, depending on their interests and training. It is important to note that experimental research methods are not limited to the field of experimental psychology; many other subfields rely on experimental methodology to conduct studies. As an experimental psychologist, you would most likely work in an academic setting, teaching courses and supervising students' research in addition to conducting your own research. Or you might be employed by a research institution, zoo, business, or government agency.

Forensic psychologists apply psychological principles to legal issues. They conduct research on the interface of law and psychology, help to create public policies related to mental health, help law-enforcement agencies in criminal investigations, or consult on jury selection and deliberation processes. They also provide assessment to assist the legal community. Although most forensic psychologists are clinical psychologists, they might have expertise in other areas of psychology, such as social or cognitive psychology. Some also hold law degrees. As a forensic psychologist, you might work in a university psychology department, law school, research organization, community mental health agency, law-enforcement agency, court, or correctional setting.

Health psychologists are researchers and practitioners concerned with psychology's contribution to promoting health and preventing disease. As applied psychologists or clinicians, they may help individuals lead healthier lives by designing, conducting, and evaluating programs to stop smoking, lose weight, improve sleep, manage pain, prevent the spread of sexually transmitted infections, or treat psychosocial problems associated with chronic and terminal illnesses. As researchers and clinicians, they identify conditions and practices associated with health and illness to help create effective interventions. In public service, health psychologists study and work to improve government policies and health care systems. As a health psychologist, you could be employed in a hospital, medical school, rehabilitation center, public health agency, college or university, or, if you are also a clinical psychologist, in private practice.

Industrial-organizational (I/O) psychologists study the relationship between people and their working environments. They may develop new ways to increase productivity, improve personnel selection, or promote job satisfaction in an organizational setting. Their interests include organizational structure and change, consumer behavior, and personnel selection and training. As an I/O psychologist, you might conduct workplace training or provide organizational analysis and development. You may find yourself working in business, industry, the government, or a college or university. Or you may be self-employed as a consultant or work for a management consulting firm.

Neuropsychologists investigate the relationship between neurological processes (structure and function of the brain) and behavior. As a neuropsychologist you might assess, diagnose, or treat central nervous system disorders, such as Alzheimer's disease or stroke. You might also evaluate individuals for evidence of head injuries; learning and developmental disabilities, such as autism; and other psychiatric disorders, such as attention-deficit hyperactivity disorder (ADHD). If you are a *clinical neuropsychologist*, you might work in a hospital's neurology, neurosurgery, or psychiatric unit. Neuropsychologists also work in academic settings, where they conduct research and teach.

Psychometric and quantitative psychologists study the methods and techniques used to acquire psychological knowledge. A psychometrician may update existing neurocognitive or personality tests or devise new tests for use in clinical and

Criminal investigation Forensic psychologists may be called on to assist police officers investigating a crime scene, as seen here after a shooting in Florida. Most forensic work, however, occurs in the lab and for the judicial system.

school settings or in business and industry. These psychologists also administer, score, and interpret such tests. Quantitative psychologists collaborate with researchers to design, analyze, and interpret the results of research programs. As a psychometric or quantitative psychologist, you will need to be well trained in research methods, statistics, and computer technology. You will most likely be employed by a university or college, testing company, private research firm, or government agency.

Rehabilitation psychologists are researchers and practitioners who work with people who have lost optimal functioning after an accident, illness, or other event. As a rehabilitation psychologist, you would probably work in a medical rehabilitation institution or hospital. You might also work in a medical school, university, state or federal vocational rehabilitation agency, or in private practice serving people with physical disabilities.

School psychologists are involved in the assessment of and intervention for children in educational settings. They diagnose and treat cognitive, social, and emotional problems that may negatively influence children's learning or overall functioning at school. As a school psychologist, you would collaborate with teachers, parents, and administrators, making recommendations to improve student learning. You would work in an academic setting, a federal or state government agency, a child guidance center, or a behavioral research laboratory.

Social psychologists are interested in our interactions with others. Social psychologists study how our beliefs, feelings, and behaviors are affected by and influence other people. They study topics such as attitudes, aggression, prejudice, interpersonal attraction, group behavior, and leadership. As a social psychologist, you would probably be a college or university faculty member. You might also work in organizational consultation, market research, or other applied psychology fields, including social neuroscience. Some social psychologists work for hospitals, federal agencies, or businesses performing applied research.

Sport psychologists study the psychological factors that influence, and are influenced by, participation in sports and other physical activities. Their professional activities include coach education and athlete preparation, as well as research and teaching. Sport psychologists who also have a clinical or counseling degree can apply those skills to working with individuals with psychological problems, such as anxiety or substance abuse, that might interfere with optimal performance. As a sport psychologist, if you were not working in an academic or research setting, you would most likely work as part of a team or an organization or in a private capacity.

* * *

So, the next time someone asks you what you will do with your psychology degree, tell them you have a lot of options. You might use your acquired skills and understanding to get a job and succeed in any number of fields, or you might pursue graduate school and then career opportunities in associated professions. In any case, what you have learned about behavior and mental processes will surely enrich your life (Hammer, 2003).

Class counselor School psychologists, who have their master's degree in psychology, may find themselves working with students individually or in groups, as well as in a consultative role for their school's administrators.

Cricket cures Sport psychologists often work directly with athletes to help them improve their performance. Here a team psychologist consults with Brendon McCullum, a record-breaking athlete who plays international cricket for New Zealand.

Complete Module Reviews

THE STORY OF PSYCHOLOGY

Module 1: What Is Psychology?

1-1 What were some important milestones in psychology's early development?

Wilhelm Wundt established the first psychological laboratory in 1879 in Germany. Two early schools were *structuralism* and *functionalism*.

1-2 How did psychology continue to develop from the 1920s through today?

Early researchers defined *psychology* as "the science of mental life." In the 1920s, under the influence of John B. Watson and the *behaviorists*, the field's focus changed to the "scientific study of observable behavior." In the 1960s, the *humanistic psychologists* and the *cognitive psychologists* revived interest in the study of mental processes. Psychology is now defined as the science of behavior and mental processes.

1-3 How has our understanding of biology and experience, culture and gender, and human flourishing shaped contemporary psychology?

Our growing understanding of biology and experience has fed psychology's most enduring debate. The *nature–nurture issue* centers on the relative contributions of genes and experience, and their interaction in specific environments. Charles Darwin's view that *natural selection* shapes behaviors as well as bodies led to *evolutionary psychology's* study of our similarities because of our common biology and evolutionary history, and *behavior genetics'* focus on the relative power and limits of genetic and environmental influences on behavior.

Cross-cultural and gender studies have diversified psychology's assumptions while also reminding us of our similarities. Attitudes and behaviors may vary somewhat by gender or across *cultures*, but because of our shared human kinship, the underlying processes and principles are more similar than different.

Psychology's traditional focus on understanding and treating troubles has expanded with *positive psychology's* call for more research on human flourishing and its attempt to discover and promote traits that help people to thrive.

1-4 What are psychology's levels of analysis and related perspectives?

The *biopsychosocial approach* integrates information from three differing but complementary *levels of analysis*: the biological, psychological, and social-cultural. This approach offers a more complete understanding than could usually be reached by relying on only one of psychology's current perspectives (neuroscience, evolutionary, behavior genetics, psychodynamic, behavioral, cognitive, and social-cultural).

1-5 What are psychology's main subfields?

Within the science of psychology, researchers may conduct *basic research* to increase the field's knowledge base (often in biological, developmental, cognitive, personality, and social psychology) or *applied research* to solve practical problems (in industrial-organizational psychology and other areas).

Those who engage in psychology as a helping profession may assist people as *counseling psychologists*, helping people with problems in living or achieving greater well-being, or as *clinical psychologists*, studying and assessing people with psychological disorders and treating them with psychotherapy. (*Psychiatrists* also study, assess, and treat people with disorders, but as medical doctors, they may prescribe drugs in addition to psychotherapy.) *Community psychologists* work to create healthy social and physical environments (in schools, for example).

1-6 How can psychological principles help you learn and remember?

The *testing effect* shows that learning and memory are enhanced by actively retrieving, rather than simply rereading, previously studied material. The *SQ3R* study method—survey, question, read, retrieve, and review—applies principles derived from memory research. Four additional tips are (1) distribute your study time; (2) learn to think critically; (3) process class information actively; and (4) overlearn.

THINKING CRITICALLY WITH PSYCHOLOGICAL SCIENCE
Module 2: The Need for Psychological Science

2-1 How does our everyday thinking sometimes lead us to a wrong conclusion?

Our everyday thinking can be perilous because of three phenomena: hindsight bias, overconfidence, and a tendency to perceive patterns in random events. *Hindsight bias* (also called the "I-knew-it-all-along phenomenon") is the tendency to believe, after learning an outcome, that we would have foreseen it. Overconfidence in our judgments results partly from our bias to seek information that confirms them. These tendencies, plus our eagerness to perceive patterns in random events, lead us to overestimate our *intuition*. Although limited by the testable questions it can address, scientific inquiry can help us overcome our intuition's biases and shortcomings.

2-2 How do the scientific attitude's three main components relate to critical thinking?

The scientific attitude equips us to be curious, skeptical, and humble in scrutinizing competing ideas or our own observations. This attitude carries into everyday life as *critical thinking*, which puts ideas to the test by examining assumptions, appraising the source, discerning hidden values, evaluating evidence, and assessing conclusions.

Module 3: Research Strategies: How Psychologists Ask and Answer Questions

3-1 How do theories advance psychological science?

Psychological *theories* are explanations that apply an integrated set of principles to organize observations and generate *hypotheses*—predictions that can be used to check the theory or produce practical applications of it. By testing their hypotheses, researchers can confirm, reject, or revise their theories. To enable other researchers to *replicate* the studies, researchers report them using precise *operational definitions* of their procedures and concepts. If others achieve similar results, confidence in the conclusion will be greater.

3-2 How do psychologists use case studies, naturalistic observations, and surveys to observe and describe behavior, and why is random sampling important?

Descriptive methods, which include *case studies, naturalistic observations,* and *surveys,* show us what can happen, and they may offer ideas for further study. The best basis for generalizing about a *population* is a representative sample; in a *random sample,* every person in the entire population being studied has an equal chance of participating. Descriptive methods cannot show cause and effect because researchers cannot control variables.

3-3 What does it mean when we say two things are correlated, and what are positive and negative correlations?

When we say two things are correlated, we are saying that they accompany each other in their movements. In a positive *correlation*, two factors increase or decrease together. In a negative correlation, one item increases as the other decreases. The strength of their relationship is expressed as a *correlation coefficient*, which ranges from +1.00 (a perfect positive correlation) through 0 (no correlation) to –1.00 (a perfect negative correlation). Their relationship may be displayed in a *scatterplot,* in which each dot represents a value for the two variables.

3-4 What is regression toward the mean?

Regression toward the mean is the tendency for extreme or unusual scores to fall back toward their average.

3-5 Why do correlations enable prediction but not cause-effect explanation?

Correlations enable prediction because they show how two factors move together, either positively or negatively. A correlation can indicate the possibility of a cause-effect relationship, but it does not prove the direction of the influence, or whether an underlying third factor may explain the correlation.

3-6 What are the characteristics of experimentation that make it possible to isolate cause and effect?

To discover cause-effect relationships, psychologists conduct *experiments*, manipulating one or more factors of interest and controlling other factors. Using *random assignment*, they can minimize *confounding variables*, such as preexisting differences between the *experimental group* (exposed to the treatment) and the *control group* (given a placebo or different version of the treatment). The *independent variable* is the factor the experimenter manipulates to study its effect; the *dependent variable* is the factor the experimenter measures to discover any changes occurring in response to the manipulations. Studies may use a *double-blind procedure* to avoid the *placebo effect.*

3-7 Can laboratory experiments illuminate everyday life?

Researchers intentionally create a controlled, artificial environment in the laboratory in order to test general theoretical principles. These general principles help explain everyday behaviors.

3-8 Why do psychologists study animals, and what ethical guidelines safeguard human and animal research participants? How do human values influence psychology?

Some psychologists are primarily interested in animal behavior; others want to better understand the physiological and psychological processes shared by humans and other species. Government agencies have established standards for animal care and housing. Professional associations and funding agencies also establish guidelines for protecting animals' well-being. The APA ethics code outlines standards for safeguarding human participants' well-being, including obtaining their *informed consent* and *debriefing* them later.

Psychologists' values influence their choice of research topics, their theories and observations, their labels for behavior, and their professional advice. Applications of psychology's principles have been used mainly in the service of humanity.

Module 4: Statistical Reasoning in Everyday Life

4-1 How do we describe data using three measures of central tendency, and what is the relative usefulness of the two measures of variation?

A measure of central tendency is a single score that represents a whole set of scores. Three such measures that we use to describe data are the *mode* (the most frequently occurring score), the *mean* (the arithmetic average), and the *median* (the middle score in a group of data).

Measures of variation tell us how diverse data are. Two measures of variation are the *range* (which describes the gap between the highest and lowest scores) and the *standard deviation* (which states how much scores vary around the mean, or average, score). Scores often form a *normal* (or bell-shaped) *curve*.

4-2 How do we know whether an observed difference can be generalized to other populations?

To feel confident about generalizing an observed difference to other populations, we would want to know that the sample studied was representative of the larger population being studied; that the observations, on average, had low variability; that the sample consisted of more than a few cases; and that the observed difference was *statistically significant*.

THE BIOLOGY OF MIND
Module 5: Neural and Hormonal Systems

5-1 Why are psychologists concerned with human biology?

Psychologists working from a *biological* perspective study the links between biology and behavior. We are biopsychosocial systems, in which biological, psychological, and social-cultural factors interact to influence behavior.

5-2 What are neurons, and how do they transmit information?

Neurons are the elementary components of the nervous system, the body's speedy electrochemical information system. A neuron receives signals through its branching *dendrites*, and sends signals through its *axons*. Some axons are encased in a *myelin sheath*, which enables faster transmission. *Glial cells* provide myelin, and they support, nourish, and protect neurons; they may also play a role in learning and thinking.

If the combined signals received by a neuron exceed a minimum *threshold*, the neuron fires, transmitting an electrical impulse (the *action potential*) down its axon by means of a chemistry-to-electricity process. The neuron's reaction is an *all-or-none process*.

5-3 How do nerve cells communicate with other nerve cells?

When action potentials reach the end of an axon (the axon terminals), they stimulate the release of *neurotransmitters*. These chemical messengers carry a message from the sending neuron across a *synapse* to receptor sites on a receiving neuron. The sending neuron, in a process called *reuptake*, then normally reabsorbs the excess neurotransmitter molecules in the synaptic gap. If incoming signals are strong enough, the receiving neuron generates its own action potential and relays the message to other cells.

5-4 How do neurotransmitters influence behavior, and how do drugs and other chemicals affect neurotransmission?

Neurotransmitters travel designated pathways in the brain and may influence specific behaviors and emotions. Acetylcholine (ACh) affects muscle action, learning, and memory. *Endorphins* are natural opiates released in response to pain and exercise.

Drugs and other chemicals affect brain chemistry at synapses. *Agonists* increase a neurotransmitter's action, and may do so in various ways. *Antagonists* decrease a neurotransmitter's action by blocking production or release.

5-5 What are the functions of the nervous system's main divisions, and what are the three main types of neurons?

The *central nervous system (CNS)*—the brain and the spinal cord—is the *nervous system's* decision maker. The *peripheral nervous system (PNS)*, which connects the CNS to the rest of the body by means of *nerves*, gathers information and transmits CNS decisions to the rest of the body. The two main PNS divisions are the *somatic nervous system* (which enables voluntary control of the skeletal muscles) and the *autonomic nervous system* (which controls involuntary muscles and glands by means of its *sympathetic* and *parasympathetic* divisions).

Neurons cluster into working networks. There are three types of neurons: (1) *Sensory (afferent) neurons* carry incoming information from sensory receptors to the brain and spinal cord. (2) *Motor (efferent) neurons* carry information from the brain and spinal cord out to the muscles and glands. (3) *Interneurons* communicate within the brain and spinal cord and between sensory and motor neurons.

5-6 How does the endocrine system transmit information and interact with the nervous system?

The *endocrine system* is a set of glands that secrete *hormones* into the bloodstream, where they travel through the body and affect other tissues, including the brain. The endocrine system's master gland, the *pituitary*, influences hormone release by other glands, including the *adrenal glands*. In an intricate feedback system, the brain's hypothalamus influences the pituitary gland, which influences other glands, which release hormones, which in turn influence the brain.

Module 6: Tools of Discovery and Older Brain Structures

6-1 How do neuroscientists study the brain's connections to behavior and mind?

Clinical observations and *lesioning* reveal the general effects of brain damage. Electrical, chemical, or magnetic stimulation can also reveal aspects of information processing in the brain. *MRI* scans show anatomy. *EEG, PET,* and *fMRI (functional MRI)* recordings reveal brain function.

6-2 What structures make up the brainstem, and what are the functions of the brainstem, thalamus, reticular formation, and cerebellum?

The *brainstem*, the oldest part of the brain, is responsible for automatic survival functions. Its components are the *medulla* (which controls heartbeat and breathing), the pons (which helps coordinate movements), and the *reticular formation* (which affects arousal).

The *thalamus*, sitting above the brainstem, acts as the brain's sensory control center. The *cerebellum*, attached to the rear of the brainstem, coordinates muscle movement and balance and also helps process sensory information.

6-3 What are the limbic system's structures and functions?

The *limbic system* is linked to emotions, memory, and drives. Its neural centers include the *hippocampus* (which processes conscious memories); the *amygdala* (involved in responses of aggression and fear); and the *hypothalamus* (involved in various bodily maintenance functions, pleasurable rewards, and the control of the endocrine system). The hypothalamus controls the pituitary (the "master gland") by stimulating it to trigger the release of hormones.

Module 7: The Cerebral Cortex and Our Divided Brain

7-1 What are the functions of the various cerebral cortex regions?

The *cerebral cortex* has two hemispheres, and each hemisphere has four lobes: the *frontal, parietal, occipital,* and *temporal.* Each lobe performs many functions and interacts with other areas of the cortex.

The *motor cortex*, at the rear of the frontal lobes, controls voluntary movements. The *somatosensory cortex*, at the front of the parietal lobes, registers and processes body touch and movement sensations. Body parts requiring precise control (in the motor cortex) or those that are especially sensitive (in the somatosensory cortex) occupy the greatest amount of space.

Most of the brain's cortex—the major portion of each of the four lobes—is devoted to uncommitted *association areas*, which integrate information involved in learning, remembering, thinking, and other higher-level functions. Our mental experiences arise from coordinated brain activity.

7-2 To what extent can a damaged brain reorganize itself, and what is neurogenesis?

If one hemisphere is damaged early in life, the other will pick up many of its functions by reorganizing or building new pathways. This *plasticity* diminishes later in life. The brain sometimes mends itself by forming new neurons, a process known as *neurogenesis*.

7-3 What do split brains reveal about the functions of our two brain hemispheres?

Split-brain research (experiments on people with a severed *corpus callosum*) has confirmed that in most people, the left hemisphere is the more verbal, and that the right hemisphere excels in visual perception and the recognition of emotion. Studies of healthy people with intact brains confirm that each hemisphere makes unique contributions to the integrated functioning of the brain.

7-4 What does research tell us about being left-handed? Is it advantageous to be right-handed?

Some 10 percent of us (somewhat more among males, somewhat less among females) are left-handed. Handedness appears to be influenced by genetic or prenatal factors. Most left-handers process speech in the left hemisphere, as right-handers do, but some do so in the right hemisphere or use both hemispheres. Left-handers are more likely to be among those with reading disabilities, allergies, and migraine headaches, but sometimes do better academically. Left-handedness is also more common among musicians, mathematicians, architects, artists, and in professional baseball and cricket players. The pros and cons of being left-handed seem roughly equal.

Consciousness and the Two-Track Mind
Module 8: Brain States and Consciousness

8-1 What is the place of consciousness in psychology's history?

Since 1960, under the influence of cognitive psychology, neuroscience, and *cognitive neuroscience*, our awareness of ourselves and our environment—our *consciousness*—has reclaimed its place as an important area of research. After initially claiming consciousness as its area of study in the nineteenth century, psychologists had abandoned it in the first half of the twentieth century, turning instead to the study of observable behavior because they believed consciousness was too difficult to study scientifically.

8-2 What is the "dual processing" being revealed by today's cognitive neuroscience?

Scientists studying the brain mechanisms underlying consciousness and cognition have discovered that the mind processes information on two separate tracks, one operating at an explicit, conscious level (conscious sequential processing) and the other at an implicit, unconscious level (unconscious parallel processing). This *dual processing* affects our perception, memory, attitudes, and other cognitions.

8-3 How does selective attention direct our perceptions?

We *selectively attend* to, and process, a very limited portion of incoming information, blocking out much and often shifting the spotlight of our attention from one thing to another. *Parallel processing* takes care of the routine business, while sequential processing is best for solving new problems that require our attention. Focused intently on one task, we often display *inattentional blindness* to other events and *change blindness* to changes around us.

Module 9: Sleep and Dreams

9-1 What is sleep?

Sleep is the periodic, natural loss of consciousness—as distinct from unconsciousness resulting from a coma, general anesthesia, or hibernation. (Adapted from Dement, 1999.)

9-2 How do our biological rhythms influence our daily functioning?

Our bodies have an internal biological clock, roughly synchronized with the 24-hour cycle of night and day. This *circadian rhythm* appears in our daily patterns of body temperature, arousal, sleeping, and waking. Age and experiences can alter these patterns, resetting our biological clock.

9-3 What is the biological rhythm of our sleeping and dreaming stages?

Younger adults cycle through four distinct sleep stages about every 90 minutes. (The sleep cycle repeats more frequently for older adults.) Leaving the *alpha waves* of the awake, relaxed stage, we descend into the irregular brain waves of non-REM stage 1 (NREM-1) sleep, often with *hallucinations*, such as the sensation of falling or floating. NREM-2 sleep (in which we spend the most time) follows, lasting about 20 minutes, with its characteristic sleep spindles. We then enter NREM-3 sleep, lasting about 30 minutes, with large, slow *delta waves*.

   About an hour after falling asleep, we begin periods of *REM* (rapid eye movement) *sleep*. Most dreaming occurs in this stage (also known as paradoxical sleep) of internal arousal but outward paralysis. During a normal night's sleep, NREM-3 sleep shortens and REM and NREM-2 sleep lengthens.

9-4 How do biology and environment interact in our sleep patterns?

Our biology—our circadian rhythm as well as our age and our body's production of melatonin (influenced by the brain's *suprachiasmatic nucleus*)—interacts with cultural expectations and individual behaviors to determine our sleeping and waking patterns.

9-5 What are sleep's functions?

Sleep may have played a protective role in human evolution by keeping people safe during potentially dangerous periods. Sleep also helps restore and repair damaged neurons. REM and NREM-2 sleep help strengthen neural connections that build enduring memories. Sleep promotes creative problem solving the next day. Finally, during deep sleep, the pituitary gland secretes a growth hormone necessary for muscle development.

9-6 How does sleep loss affect us, and what are the major sleep disorders?

Sleep deprivation causes fatigue and irritability, and it impairs concentration, productivity, and memory consolidation. It can also lead to depression, obesity, joint pain, a suppressed immune system, and slowed performance (with greater vulnerability to accidents).

   Sleep disorders include *insomnia* (recurring wakefulness); *narcolepsy* (sudden uncontrollable sleepiness or lapsing into REM sleep); *sleep apnea* (the stopping of breathing while asleep; associated with obesity, especially in men); *night terrors* (high arousal and the appearance of being terrified; NREM-3 disorder found mainly in children); sleep-walking (NREM-3 disorder also found mainly in children); and sleeptalking.

9-7 What do we dream?

We usually *dream* of ordinary events and everyday experiences, most involving some anxiety or misfortune. Fewer than 10 percent of dreams among men (and less among women) have any sexual content. Most dreams occur during REM sleep.

9-8 What functions have theorists proposed for dreams?

There are five major views of the function of dreams. (1) Freud's wish-fulfillment: Dreams provide a psychic "safety valve," with *manifest content* (story line) acting as a censored version of *latent content* (underlying meaning that gratifies our unconscious wishes). (2) Information-processing: Dreams help us sort out the day's events and consolidate them in memory. (3) Physiological function: Regular brain stimulation may help develop and preserve neural pathways in the brain. (4) Neural activation: The brain attempts to make sense of neural static by weaving it into a story line. (5) Cognitive development: Dreams reflect the dreamer's level of development.

Most sleep theorists agree that REM sleep and its associated dreams serve an important function, as shown by the *REM rebound* that occurs following REM deprivation in humans and other species.

Module 10: Drugs and Consciousness

10-1 What are substance use disorders, and what roles do tolerance, withdrawal, and addiction play in these disorders?

Those with a *substance use disorder* may exhibit impaired control, social disruption, risky behavior, and the physical effects of tolerance and withdrawal. *Psychoactive drugs* alter perceptions and moods. They may produce *tolerance*—requiring larger doses to achieve the desired effect—and *withdrawal*—significant discomfort accompanying attempts to quit. Continued use may lead to *addiction*, which is the compulsive craving of drugs or certain behaviors (such as gambling) despite known adverse consequences.

10-2 How has the concept of addiction changed?

Psychologists debate whether the concept of addiction has been stretched too far, and whether addictions are really as irresistible as commonly believed. Addictions can be powerful, and many with addictions do benefit from therapy or group support. But viewing addiction as an uncontrollable disease can undermine people's self-confidence and their belief that they can change. The addiction-as-disease-needing-treatment idea has been extended to a host of excessive, driven behaviors, but labeling a behavior doesn't explain it. The concept of addiction continues to evolve, as psychiatry's manual of disorders now includes behavior addictions such as "gambling disorder" and proposes "Internet gaming disorder" for further study.

10-3 What are depressants, and what are their effects?

Depressants, such as alcohol, *barbiturates*, and the *opiates*, dampen neural activity and slow body functions. Alcohol tends to disinhibit, increasing the likelihood that we will act on our impulses, whether harmful or helpful. It also impairs judgment, disrupts memory processes by suppressing REM sleep, and reduces self-awareness and self-control. User expectations strongly influence alcohol's behavioral effects.

10-4 What are stimulants, and what are their effects?

Stimulants—including caffeine, *nicotine*, *cocaine*, the *amphetamines*, *methamphetamine*, and *Ecstasy*—excite neural activity and speed up body functions, triggering energy and mood changes. All are highly addictive. Nicotine's effects make smoking a difficult habit to kick, yet the percentage of Americans who smoke has been dramatically decreasing. Cocaine gives users a fast high, followed within an hour by a crash. Its risks include cardiovascular stress and suspiciousness. Use of methamphetamines may permanently reduce dopamine production. Ecstasy (MDMA) is a combined stimulant and mild hallucinogen that produces euphoria and feelings of intimacy. Its users risk immune system suppression, permanent damage to mood and memory, and (if taken during physical activity) dehydration and escalating body temperatures.

10-5 What are hallucinogens, and what are their effects?

Hallucinogens—such as *LSD* and marijuana—distort perceptions and evoke hallucinations—sensory images in the absence of sensory input. The user's mood and expectations influence the effects of LSD, but common experiences are hallucinations and emotions varying from euphoria to panic. Marijuana's main ingredient, *THC*, may trigger feelings of disinhibition, euphoria, relaxation, relief from pain, and intense sensitivity to sensory stimuli. It may also increase feelings of depression or anxiety, impair motor coordination and reaction time, disrupt memory formation, and damage lung tissue (because of the inhaled smoke).

10-6 Why do some people become regular users of consciousness-altering drugs?

Some people may be biologically vulnerable to particular drugs, such as alcohol. Psychological factors (such as stress, depression, and hopelessness) and social factors (such as peer pressure) combine to lead many people to experiment with—and sometimes become addicted to—drugs. Cultural and ethnic groups have differing rates of drug use. Each type of influence—biological, psychological, and social-cultural—offers a possible path for drug misuse prevention and treatment programs.

NATURE, NURTURE, AND HUMAN DIVERSITY

Module 11: Behavior Genetics: Predicting Individual Differences

11-1 What are *chromosomes*, *DNA*, *genes*, and the human *genome*? How do behavior geneticists explain our individual differences?

Genes are the biochemical units of heredity that make up *chromosomes*, the threadlike coils of *DNA*. When genes are "turned on" (expressed), they provide the code for creating the proteins that form our body's building blocks. Most human traits are influenced by many genes acting together. The *human genome* is the shared genetic profile that distinguishes humans from other species, consisting at an individual level of all the genetic material in an organism's chromosomes. *Behavior geneticists* study the relative power and limits of genetic and *environmental* influences on behavior.

11-2 How do twin and adoption studies help us understand the effects and interactions of nature and nurture?

Studies of *identical* (monozygotic) *twins* versus *fraternal* (dizygotic) *twins*, separated twins, and biological versus adoptive relatives allow researchers to tease apart the influences of heredity and environment. Research studies on separated identical twins maintain the same genes while testing the effects of different home environments. Studies of adoptive families let researchers maintain the same home environment while studying the effects of genetic differences. Heritable individual differences (in traits such as height and weight) do not necessarily explain gender or ethnic group differences. Shared family environments have little effect on personality.

11-3 What have psychologists learned about temperament?

The stability of *temperament*, a person's characteristic emotional reactivity and intensity, from the first weeks of life suggests a genetic predisposition. The genetic effect appears in physiological differences such as heart rate and nervous system reactivity.

11-4 What is *heritability,* and how does it relate to individuals and groups?

Heritability describes the extent to which variation among members of a group can be attributed to genes. Heritable individual differences (in traits such as height or intelligence) need not imply heritable group differences. Genes mostly explain why some people are taller than others, but not why people are taller today than they were a century ago.

11-5 How is molecular genetics research changing our understanding of the effects of nature and nurture?

Molecular genetics research on structure and function of genes is building new understandings of how teams of genes influence many human traits. One goal of *molecular behavior genetics*, the study of how the structure and function of genes interact with our environment to influence behavior, is to find some of the many genes that together orchestrate complex traits (such as body weight, sexual orientation, and impulsivity). Environments can trigger or block genetic expression. The field of *epigenetics* studies the influences on gene expression that occur without changes in DNA.

11-6 What are some benefits and risks of prenatal genetic testing?

Genetic tests can now reveal at-risk populations for dozens of diseases, and the search is on to discover the markers of genetically influenced disorders. But prenatal screening poses ethical dilemmas. For example, testing for an offspring's sex has enabled selective abortions, which in some cultures has resulted in millions more male births. And future screening for vulnerability to psychological disorders could deprive the world of great talents. (Handel, van Gogh, Churchill, Lincoln, Tolstoy, and Dickinson were all troubled people, for example.)

Module 12: Evolutionary Psychology: Understanding Human Nature

12-1 How do evolutionary psychologists use natural selection to explain behavior tendencies?

Evolutionary psychologists seek to understand how our traits and behavior tendencies are shaped by *natural selection*, as genetic variations increasing the odds of reproducing and surviving in their particular environment are most likely to be passed on to future generations. Some variations arise from *mutations* (random errors in gene replication), others from new gene combinations at conception. Humans share a genetic legacy and are predisposed to behave in ways that promoted our ancestors' surviving and reproducing. Charles Darwin's theory of evolution is an organizing principle in biology. He anticipated today's application of evolutionary principles in psychology.

12-2 How might an evolutionary psychologist explain male-female differences in sexuality and mating preferences?

Men tend to have a recreational view of sexual activity; women tend to have a relational view. Evolutionary psychologists reason that men's attraction to multiple healthy, fertile-appearing partners increases their chances of spreading their genes widely. Because women incubate and nurse babies, they increase their own and their children's chances of survival by searching for mates with the potential for long-term investment in their joint offspring.

12-3 What are the key criticisms of evolutionary explanations of human sexuality, and how do evolutionary psychologists respond?

Critics argue that evolutionary psychologists start with an effect and work backward to an explanation. They also charge that evolutionary psychologists try to explain today's behavior based on decisions our distant ancestors made thousands of years ago, noting that a better, more immediate explanation takes learned *social scripts* into account. And, the critics wonder, does this kind of explanation absolve people from taking responsibility for their sexual behavior? Evolutionary psychologists respond that understanding our predispositions can help us overcome them. They recognize the importance of social and cultural influences, but they also cite the value of testable predictions based on evolutionary principles.

Module 13: Culture, Gender, and Other Environmental Influences

13-1 How do early experiences modify the brain?

Our genetic predispositions and our specific environments *interact*. Environments can trigger gene activity, and genetically influenced traits can evoke responses from others.

As a child's brain develops, neural connections grow more numerous and complex. Experiences then prompt a pruning process, in which unused connections weaken and heavily used ones strengthen. Early childhood is an important period for shaping the brain, but throughout our lives our brain modifies itself in response to our learning.

13-2 In what ways do parents and peers shape children's development?

Parents influence their children in areas such as manners and political and religious beliefs, but not in other areas, such as personality. As children attempt to fit in with their peers, they tend to adopt their culture—styles, accents, slang, attitudes. By choosing their children's neighborhoods and schools, parents exert some influence over peer group culture.

13-3 How does culture affect our behavior?

A *culture* is an enduring set of behaviors, ideas, attitudes, values, and traditions shared by a group and transmitted from one generation to the next. Cultural *norms* are understood rules that inform members of a culture about accepted and expected behaviors. Cultures differ across time and space.

13-4 How do individualist and collectivist cultures differ in their values and goals?

Within any culture, the degree of individualism or collectivism varies from person to person. Cultures based on self-reliant *individualism*, like those found in North America and Western Europe, tend to value personal independence and individual achievement. They define identity in terms of self-esteem, personal goals and attributes, and personal rights and liberties. Cultures based on socially connected *collectivism*, like those in many parts of Asia and Africa, tend to value interdependence, tradition, and harmony, and they define identity in terms of group goals, commitments, and belonging to one's group.

13-5 How does the meaning of *gender* differ from the meaning of *sex*?

In psychology, *gender* is the socially influenced characteristics by which people define men and women. *Sex* refers to the biologically influenced characteristics by which people define males and females. Our gender is thus the product of the interplay among our biological dispositions, our developmental experiences, and our current situation.

13-6 What are some ways in which males and females tend to be alike and to differ?

We are more alike than different, thanks to our similar genetic makeup—we see, hear, learn, and remember similarly. Males and females do differ in body fat, muscle, height, age of onset of puberty, life expectancy, and vulnerability to certain disorders. Men admit to more *aggression* than women do, and they are more likely to be physically aggressive.

Women's aggression is more likely to be *relational*. In most societies, men have more social power, and their leadership style tends to be directive, whereas women's is more democratic. Women focus more on social connectedness, and they "tend and befriend."

13-7 How do sex hormones influence prenatal and adolescent sexual development, and what is a disorder of sexual development?

Both sex chromosomes and sex hormones influence development. Biological sex is determined by the father's contribution to the twenty-third pair of chromosomes. The mother always contributes an X *chromosome*. The father may also contribute an X chromosome, producing a female, or a Y *chromosome*, producing a male by triggering additional *testosterone* release and the development of male sex organs. During *puberty*, both *primary* and *secondary sex characteristics* develop. Sex-related genes and physiology influence behavioral and cognitive differences between males and females. *Disorders of sexual development* are inherited conditions that involve unusual development of sex chromosomes and anatomy.

13-8 How do gender roles and gender identity differ?

Gender roles, the behaviors a culture expects from its males and females, vary across place and time. *Social learning theory* proposes that we learn *gender identity*—our sense of being male, female, or some combination of the two—as we learn other things: through reinforcement, punishment, and observation. Critics argue that cognition also plays a role because modeling and rewards cannot explain *gender typing*. Some children organize themselves into "boy worlds" and "girl worlds"; others prefer *androgyny*. *Transgender* people's gender identity or expression differs from their birth sex. Their sexual orientation may be heterosexual, homosexual, bisexual, or asexual.

13-9 What is included in the biopsychosocial approach to development?

Individual development results from the interaction of biological, psychological, and social-cultural influences. Biological influences include our shared human genome; individual variations; prenatal environment; and sex-related genes, hormones, and physiology. Psychological influences include gene-environment interactions; the effect of early experiences on neural networks; responses evoked by our own characteristics, such as gender and temperament; and personal beliefs, feelings, and expectations. Social-cultural influences include parental and peer influences; cultural traditions and values; and cultural gender norms.

DEVELOPING THROUGH THE LIFE SPAN

Module 14: Developmental Issues, Prenatal Development, and the Newborn

14-1 What three issues have engaged developmental psychologists?

Developmental psychologists study physical, mental, and social changes throughout the life span. They focus on three issues: nature and nurture (the interaction between our genetic inheritance and our experiences); continuity and stages (whether development is gradual and continuous or a series of relatively abrupt changes); and stability and change (whether our traits endure or change as we age).

14-2 What is the course of prenatal development, and how do teratogens affect that development?

The life cycle begins at conception, when one sperm cell unites with an egg to form a *zygote*. The zygote's inner cells become the *embryo*, and the outer cells become the placenta. In the next 6 weeks, body organs begin to form and function, and by 9 weeks, the *fetus* is recognizably human.

Teratogens are potentially harmful agents that can pass through the placental screen and harm the developing embryo or fetus, as happens with *fetal alcohol syndrome.*

14-3 What are some newborn abilities, and how do researchers explore infants' mental abilities?

Babies are born with sensory equipment and reflexes that facilitate their survival and their social interactions with adults. For example, they quickly learn to discriminate their mother's smell and sound. Researchers use techniques that test *habituation*, such as the novelty-preference procedure, to explore infants' abilities.

Module 15: Infancy and Childhood

15-1 During infancy and childhood, how do the brain and motor skills develop?

The brain's nerve cells are sculpted by heredity and experience. As a child's brain develops, neural connections grow more numerous and complex. Experiences then trigger a pruning process, in which unused connections weaken and heavily used ones strengthen. This process continues until puberty. Early childhood is an important period for shaping the brain, but our brain modifies itself in response to our learning throughout life. In childhood, complex motor skills—sitting, standing, walking—develop in a predictable sequence, though the timing of that sequence is a function of individual *maturation* and culture. We have no conscious memories of events occurring before about age 3½. This infantile amnesia occurs in part because major brain areas have not yet matured.

15-2 From the perspectives of Piaget, Vygotsky, and today's researchers, how does a child's mind develop?

In his theory of *cognitive* development, Jean Piaget proposed that children actively construct and modify their understanding of the world through the processes of *assimilation* and *accommodation.* They form *schemas* that help them organize their experiences. Progressing from the simplicity of the *sensorimotor stage* of the first two years, in which they develop *object permanence*, children move to more complex ways of thinking. In the *preoperational stage* (about age 2 to about 6 or 7), they develop a *theory of mind.* In the preoperational stage, children are *egocentric* and unable to perform simple logical operations. At about age 7, they enter the *concrete operational stage* and are able to comprehend the principle of *conservation.* By about age 12, children enter the *formal operational stage* and can reason systematically.

Research supports the sequence Piaget proposed, but it also shows that young children are more capable, and their development more continuous, than he believed.

Lev Vygotsky's studies of child development focused on the ways a child's mind grows by interacting with the social environment. In his view, parents and caretakers provide temporary scaffolds enabling children to step to higher levels of learning.

15-3 What is autism spectrum disorder?

Autism spectrum disorder (ASD) is a disorder marked by social deficiencies and repetitive behaviors. By age 8, 1 in 68 U.S. children now gets diagnosed with ASD, though the reported rates vary by place. The increase in ASD diagnoses has been offset by a decrease in the number of children with a "cognitive disability" or "learning disability," suggesting a relabeling of children's disorders.

15-4 How do parent-infant attachment bonds form?

At about 8 months, soon after object permanence develops, children separated from their caregivers display *stranger anxiety.* Infants form *attachments* not simply because parents gratify biological needs but, more important, because they are comfortable, familiar, and responsive. Many birds and other animals have a more rigid attachment process, called *imprinting*, that occurs during a *critical period.*

15-5 How have psychologists studied attachment differences, and what have they learned?

Attachment has been studied in strange situation experiments, which show that some children are securely attached and others are insecurely attached. Infants' differing attachment styles reflect both their individual temperament and the responsiveness of their parents and child-care providers. Adult relationships seem to reflect the attachment styles of early childhood, lending support to Erik Erikson's idea that *basic trust* is formed in infancy by our experiences with responsive caregivers.

15-6 How does childhood neglect or abuse affect children's attachments?

Children are very resilient, but those who are severely neglected by their parents, or otherwise prevented from forming attachments at an early age, may be at risk for attachment problems.

15-7 How do children's self-concepts develop?

Self-concept, an understanding and evaluation of who we are, emerges gradually. By 15 to 18 months, children recognize themselves in a mirror. By school age, they can describe many of their own traits, and by age 8 or 10 their self-image is stable.

15-8 What are three parenting styles, and how do children's traits relate to them?

Parenting styles—authoritarian, permissive, and authoritative—reflect varying degrees of control. Children with high self-esteem tend to have authoritative parents and to be self-reliant and socially competent, but the direction of cause and effect in this relationship is not clear. Child-raising practices reflect both individual and cultural values.

Module 16: Adolescence

16-1 How is *adolescence* defined, and how do physical changes affect developing teens?

Adolescence is the transition period from childhood to adulthood, extending from *puberty* to social independence. Boys seem to benefit (though with risks) from "early" maturation, girls from "late" maturation. The brain's frontal lobes mature and myelin growth increases during adolescence and the early twenties, enabling improved judgment, impulse control, and long-term planning.

16-2 How did Piaget, Kohlberg, and later researchers describe adolescent cognitive and moral development?

Piaget theorized that adolescents develop a capacity for formal operations and that this development is the foundation for moral judgment. Lawrence Kohlberg proposed a stage theory of moral reasoning, from a preconventional morality of self-interest, to a conventional morality concerned with upholding laws and social rules, to (in some people) a postconventional morality of universal ethical principles. Other researchers believe that morality lies in moral intuition and moral action as well as thinking. Some critics argue that Kohlberg's postconventional level represents morality from the perspective of individualist, middle-class people.

16-3 What are the social tasks and challenges of adolescence?

Erikson theorized that each life stage has its own psychosocial task, and that a chief task of adolescence is solidifying one's sense of self—one's *identity*. This often means trying out a number of different roles. *Social identity* is the part of the self-concept that comes from a person's group memberships.

16-4 How do parents and peers influence adolescents?

During adolescence, parental influence diminishes and peer influence increases, in part because of the selection effect—the tendency to choose similar others. But adolescents also do adopt their peers' ways of dressing, acting, and communicating. Parents have more influence in religion, politics, and college and career choices.

16-5 What is emerging adulthood?

The transition from adolescence to adulthood is now taking longer. *Emerging adulthood* is the period from age 18 to the mid-twenties, when many young people are not yet fully independent. But observers note that this stage is found mostly in today's Western cultures.

Module 17: Adulthood

17-1 What physical changes occur during middle and late adulthood?

Muscular strength, reaction time, sensory abilities, and cardiac output begin to decline in the late twenties and continue to decline throughout middle adulthood (roughly age 40 to 65) and late adulthood (the years after 65). Women's period of fertility ends with *menopause* around age 50; men have no similar age-related sharp drop in hormone levels or fertility. In late adulthood, the immune system weakens, increasing susceptibility to life-threatening illnesses. Chromosome tips (telomeres) wear down, reducing the chances of normal genetic replication. But for some, longevity-supporting genes, low stress, and good health habits enable better health in later life.

17-2 How does memory change with age?

As the years pass, recall begins to decline, especially for meaningless information, but recognition memory remains strong. Older adults rely more on time management and memory cues to remember time-based and habitual tasks. Developmental researchers study age-related changes such as in memory with *cross-sectional studies* (comparing people of different ages) and *longitudinal studies* (retesting the same people over a period of years). "Terminal decline" describes the cognitive decline in the final few years of life.

17-3 How do neurocognitive disorders and Alzheimer's disease affect cognitive ability?

Neurocognitive disorders (NCDs) are acquired (not lifelong) disorders marked by cognitive deficits, which are often related to Alzheimer's disease, brain injury or disease, or substance abuse. This damage to brain cells results in the erosion of mental abilities that is not typical of normal aging. *Alzheimer's disease* is marked by neural plaques, often with an onset after age 80, entailing a progressive decline in memory and other cognitive abilities.

17-4 What themes and influences mark our social journey from early adulthood to death?

Adults do not progress through an orderly sequence of age-related social stages. Chance events can determine life choices. The *social clock* is a culture's preferred timing for social events, such as marriage, parenthood, and retirement. Adulthood's dominant themes are love and work, which Erikson called intimacy and generativity.

17-5 How does our well-being change across the life span?

Self-confidence tends to strengthen across the life span. Surveys show that life satisfaction is unrelated to age. Positive emotions increase after midlife and negative ones decrease.

17-6 A loved one's death triggers what range of reactions?

People do not grieve in predictable stages, as was once supposed. Strong expressions of emotion do not purge grief, and bereavement therapy is not significantly more effective than grieving without such aid. Erikson viewed the late-adulthood psychosocial task as developing a sense of integrity (versus despair).

SENSATION AND PERCEPTION

Module 18: Basic Concepts of Sensation and Perception

18-1 What are *sensation* and *perception?* What do we mean by *bottom-up processing* and *top-down processing?*

Sensation is the process by which our sensory receptors and nervous system receive and represent stimulus energies from our environment. *Perception* is the process of organizing and interpreting this information, enabling recognition of meaningful events. Sensation and perception are actually parts of one continuous process. *Bottom-up processing* is sensory analysis that begins at the entry level, with information flowing from the sensory receptors to the brain. *Top-down processing* is information processing guided by high-level mental processes, as when we construct perceptions by filtering information through our experience and expectations.

18-2 What three steps are basic to all our sensory systems?

Our senses (1) receive sensory stimulation (often using specialized receptor cells); (2) transform that stimulation into neural impulses; and (3) deliver the neural information to the brain. *Transduction* is the process of converting one form of energy into another. Researchers in *psychophysics* study the relationships between stimuli's physical characteristics and our psychological experience of them.

18-3 How do *absolute thresholds* and *difference thresholds* differ, and what effect, if any, do stimuli below the absolute threshold have on us?

Our *absolute threshold* for any stimulus is the minimum stimulation necessary for us to be consciously aware of it 50 percent of the time. *Signal detection theory* predicts how and when we will detect a faint stimulus amid background noise. Individual absolute thresholds vary, depending on the strength of the signal and also on our experience, expectations, motivation, and alertness. Our *difference threshold* (also called *just noticeable difference,* or *jnd*) is the difference we can discern between two stimuli 50 percent of the time. *Weber's law* states that two stimuli must differ by a constant minimum percentage (not a constant amount) to be perceived as different.

Priming (the often unconscious activation of certain associations that may predispose one's perception, memory, or response) shows that we process some information from stimuli below our absolute threshold for conscious awareness.

18-4 Does subliminal sensation enable subliminal persuasion?

Subliminal stimuli are those that are too weak to detect 50 percent of the time. While subliminal sensation is a fact, such sensations are too fleeting to enable exploitation with subliminal messages: There is no powerful, enduring effect.

18-5 What is the function of sensory adaptation?

Sensory adaptation (our diminished sensitivity to constant or routine odors, sounds, and touches) focuses our attention on informative changes in our environment.

18-6 How do our expectations, contexts, motivation, and emotions influence our perceptions?

Perceptual set is a mental predisposition that functions as a lens through which we perceive the world. Our learned concepts (schemas) prime us to organize and interpret ambiguous stimuli in certain ways. Our physical and emotional context, as well as our motivation, can create expectations and color our interpretation of events and behaviors.

Module 19: Vision: Sensory and Perceptual Processing

19-1 What are the characteristics of the energy that we see as visible light? What structures in the eye help focus that energy?

What we see as light is only a thin slice of the broad spectrum of electromagnetic energy. The portion visible to humans extends from the blue-violet to the red light wavelengths. After entering the eye and being focused by a *lens*, light energy particles strike the eye's inner surface, the *retina*. The *hue* we perceive in a light depends on its *wavelength*, and its brightness depends on its *intensity*.

19-2 How do the rods and cones process information, and what is the path information travels from the eye to the brain?

Light entering the eye triggers chemical reaction in the light-sensitive *rods* and color-sensitive *cones* at the back of the retina, which converts light energy into neural impulses. After processing by bipolar and ganglion cells, neural impulses travel from the retina through the *optic nerve* to the thalamus, and on to the visual cortex.

19-3 How do we perceive color in the world around us?

According to the *Young-Helmholtz trichromatic (three-color) theory*, the retina contains three types of color receptors. Contemporary research has found three types of cones, each most sensitive to the wavelengths of one of the three primary colors of light (red, green, or blue).

Hering's *opponent-process theory* proposed three additional color processes (red-versus-green, blue-versus-yellow, black-versus-white). Research has confirmed that, en route to the brain, neurons in the retina and the thalamus code the color-related information from the cones into pairs of opponent colors.

These two theories, and the research supporting them, show that color processing occurs in two stages.

19-4 Where are feature detectors located, and what do they do?

Feature detectors, located in the visual cortex, respond to specific features of the visual stimulus, such as shape, angle, or movement. Supercell clusters in other critical areas respond to more complex patterns.

19-5 How does the brain use parallel processing to construct visual perceptions?

Through *parallel processing*, the brain handles many aspects of vision (color, movement, form, and depth) simultaneously. Other neural teams integrate the results, comparing them with stored information and enabling perceptions.

19-6 How did the Gestalt psychologists understand perceptual organization, and how do figure-ground and grouping principles contribute to our perceptions?

Gestalt psychologists searched for rules by which the brain organizes fragments of sensory data into *gestalts* (from the German word for "whole"), or meaningful forms. In pointing out that the whole may exceed the sum of its parts, they noted that we filter sensory information and construct our perceptions.

To recognize an object, we must first perceive it (see it as a *figure*) as distinct from its surroundings (the *ground*). We bring order and form to stimuli by organizing them into meaningful *groups*, following such rules as proximity, continuity, and closure.

19-7 How do we use binocular and monocular cues to perceive the world in three dimensions, and how do we perceive motion?

Depth perception is our ability to see objects in three dimensions and judge distance. The *visual cliff* and other research demonstrate that many species perceive the world in three dimensions at, or very soon after, birth. *Binocular cues,* such as *retinal disparity,* are depth cues that rely on information from both eyes. *Monocular cues* (such as relative size, interposition, relative height, relative motion, linear perspective, and light and shadow) let us judge depth using information transmitted by only one eye.

As objects move, we assume that shrinking objects are retreating and enlarging objects are approaching. A quick succession of images on the retina can create an illusion of movement, as in stroboscopic movement or the *phi phenomenon.*

19-8 How do perceptual constancies help us construct meaningful perceptions?

Perceptual constancy enables us to perceive objects as stable despite the changing image they cast on our retinas. *Color constancy* is our ability to perceive consistent color in objects, even though the lighting and wavelengths shift. Brightness (or lightness) constancy is our ability to perceive an object as having a constant lightness even when its illumination—the light cast upon it—changes. Our brain constructs our experience of an object's color or brightness through comparisons with other surrounding objects.

Shape constancy is our ability to perceive familiar objects (such as an opening door) as unchanging in shape. Size constancy is perceiving objects as unchanging in size despite their changing retinal images. Knowing an object's size gives us clues to its distance; knowing its distance gives clues about its size, but we sometimes misread monocular distance cues and reach the wrong conclusions, as in the Moon illusion.

19-9 What does research on restored vision, sensory restriction, and perceptual adaptation reveal about the effects of experience on perception?

Experience guides our perceptual interpretations. People blind from birth who gained sight after surgery lack the experience to visually recognize shapes, forms, and complete faces.

Sensory restriction research indicates that there is a critical period for some aspects of sensory and perceptual development. Without early stimulation, the brain's neural organization does not develop normally.

People given glasses that shift the world slightly to the left or right, or even upside down, experience *perceptual adaptation.* They are initially disoriented, but they manage to adapt to their new context.

Module 20: The Nonvisual Senses

20-1 What are the characteristics of air pressure waves that we hear as sound?

Sound waves are bands of compressed and expanded air. Our ears detect these changes in air pressure and transform them into neural impulses, which the brain decodes as sound. Sound waves vary in amplitude, which we perceive as differing loudness, and in *frequency,* which we experience as differing *pitch.*

20-2 How does the ear transform sound energy into neural messages?

The outer ear is the visible portion of the ear. The *middle ear* is the chamber between the eardrum and *cochlea.* The *inner ear* consists of the cochlea, semicircular canals, and vestibular sacs. Through a mechanical chain of events, sound waves traveling through the auditory canal cause tiny vibrations in the eardrum. The bones of the middle ear amplify the vibrations and relay them to the fluid-filled cochlea. Rippling of the basilar membrane, caused by pressure changes in the cochlear fluid, causes movement of the tiny hair cells, triggering neural messages to be sent (via the thalamus) to the auditory cortex in the brain.

Sensorineural hearing loss (or nerve deafness) results from damage to the cochlea's hair cells or their associated nerves. *Conduction hearing loss* results from damage to the mechanical system that transmits sound waves to the cochlea. *Cochlear implants* can restore hearing for some people.

20-3 How do we detect loudness, discriminate pitch, and locate sounds?

Loudness is not related to the intensity of a hair cell's response. The brain interprets loudness from the number of activated hair cells.

Place theory explains how we hear high-pitched sounds, and *frequency theory* explains how we hear low-pitched sounds. (A combination of the two theories explains how we hear pitches in the middle range.) Place theory proposes that our brain interprets a particular pitch by decoding the place where a sound wave stimulates the cochlea's basilar membrane. *Frequency theory* proposes that the brain deciphers the frequency of the neural impulses traveling up the auditory nerve to the brain.

Sound waves strike one ear sooner and more intensely than the other. To locate sounds, the brain analyzes the minute differences in the sounds received by the two ears and computes the sound's source.

20-4 How do we sense touch?

Our sense of touch is actually several senses—pressure, warmth, cold, and pain—that combine to produce other sensations, such as "hot."

20-5 What biological, psychological, and social-cultural influences affect our experience of pain? How do placebos, distraction, and hypnosis help control pain?

Pain reflects bottom-up sensations (such as input from *nociceptors*, the sensory receptors that detect hurtful temperatures, pressure, or chemicals) and top-down processes (such as experience, attention, and culture). One theory of pain is that a *"gate"* in the spinal cord either opens to permit pain signals traveling up small nerve fibers to reach the brain, or closes to prevent their passage. The biopsychosocial perspective views our perception of pain as the sum of biological, psychological, and social-cultural influences. For example, our experience of pain is influenced by activity in the spinal cord's large and small fibers (a biological influence), attention to pain (a psychological influence), and cultural expectations (a social-cultural influence).

Pain treatments often combine physical and psychological elements. Placebos can help by dampening the central nervous system's attention and response to painful experiences. Distractions draw people's attention away from painful stimulation. *Hypnosis*, which increases our response to suggestions, can also help relieve pain. *Posthypnotic suggestion* is used by some clinicians to control undesired symptoms.

20-6 In what ways are our senses of taste and smell similar, and how do they differ?

Taste and smell are both chemical senses. Taste is a composite of five basic sensations—sweet, sour, salty, bitter, and umami—and of the aromas that interact with information from the taste receptor cells of the taste buds.

There are no basic sensations for smell. We smell something when molecules of a substance carried in the air reach a tiny cluster of 20 million receptor cells at the top of each nasal cavity. Odor molecules trigger combinations of receptors, in patterns that the olfactory cortex interprets. The receptor cells send messages to the brain's olfactory bulb, then to the temporal lobe, and to parts of the limbic system.

20-7 How do we sense our body's position and movement?

Through *kinesthesia*, we sense the position and movement of our body parts. We monitor our head's (and thus our body's) position and movement, and maintain our balance, with our *vestibular sense*.

20-8 How does *sensory interaction* influence our perceptions, and what is *embodied cognition*?

Our senses can influence one another. This *sensory interaction* occurs, for example, when the smell of a favorite food amplifies its taste. *Embodied cognition* is the influence of bodily sensations, gestures, and other states on cognitive preferences and judgments.

20-9 What are the claims of ESP, and what have most research psychologists concluded after putting these claims to the test?

Parapsychology is the study of paranormal phenomena, including *extrasensory perception (ESP)* and psychokinesis. The three most testable forms of ESP are telepathy (mind-to-mind communication), clairvoyance (perceiving remote events), and precognition (perceiving future events).

Skeptics argue that (1) to believe in ESP, you must believe the brain is capable of perceiving without sensory input, and (2) researchers have been unable to replicate ESP phenomena under controlled conditions.

LEARNING

Module 21: Basic Learning Concepts and Classical Conditioning

21-1 What is *learning,* and what are some basic forms of learning?

Learning is the process of acquiring through experience new information or behaviors. In *associative learning*, we learn that certain events occur together. In classical conditioning, we learn to associate two or more stimuli (a *stimulus* is any event or situation that evokes a response). We associate stimuli that we do not control, and we respond automatically. This is called *respondent behavior*. In operant conditioning, we learn to associate a response and its consequences. These associations produce *operant behaviors*. Through *cognitive learning*, we acquire mental information that guides our behavior. For example, in observational learning, we learn new behaviors by observing events and watching others.

21-2 What was behaviorism's view of learning?

Ivan Pavlov's work on classical conditioning laid the foundation for *behaviorism*, the view that psychology should be an objective science that studies behavior without reference to mental processes. The behaviorists believed that the basic laws of learning are the same for all species, including humans.

21-3 Who was Pavlov, and what are the basic components of classical conditioning?

Ivan Pavlov, a Russian physiologist, created novel experiments on learning. His early twentieth-century research over the last three decades of his life demonstrated that classical conditioning is a basic form of learning.

Classical conditioning is a type of learning in which an organism comes to associate stimuli. In classical conditioning, an NS is a stimulus that elicits no response before conditioning. A UR is an event that occurs naturally (such as salivation), in response to some stimulus. A US is something that naturally and automatically (without learning) triggers the unlearned response (as food in the mouth triggers salivation). A CS is a previously neutral stimulus (such as a tone) that, after association with a US (such as food) comes to trigger a CR. A CR is the learned response (salivating) to the originally neutral (but now conditioned) stimulus.

21-4 In classical conditioning, what are the processes of acquisition, extinction, spontaneous recovery, generalization, and discrimination?

In classical conditioning, *acquisition* is associating an NS with the US so that the NS begins triggering the CR. Acquisition occurs most readily when the NS is presented just before (ideally, about a half-second before) a US, preparing the organism for the upcoming event. This finding supports the view that classical conditioning is biologically adaptive. Through higher-order conditioning, a new NS can become a new CS.

Extinction is diminished responding when the CS no longer signals an impending US. *Spontaneous recovery* is the appearance of a formerly extinguished response, following a rest period. *Generalization* is the tendency to respond to stimuli that are similar to a CS. *Discrimination* is the learned ability to distinguish between a CS and other irrelevant stimuli.

21-5 Why does Pavlov's work remain so important?

Pavlov taught us that significant psychological phenomena can be studied objectively, and that classical conditioning is a basic form of learning that applies to all species.

21-6 What have been some applications of Pavlov's work to human health and well-being? How did Watson apply Pavlov's principles to learned fears?

Classical conditioning techniques are used to improve human health and well-being in many areas, including behavioral therapy for some types of psychological disorders. The body's immune system may also respond to classical conditioning.

Pavlov's work also provided a basis for Watson's idea that human emotions and behaviors, though biologically influenced, are mainly a bundle of conditioned responses. Watson applied classical conditioning principles in his studies of "Little Albert" to demonstrate how specific fears might be conditioned.

Module 22: Operant Conditioning

22-1 What is operant conditioning?

In *operant conditioning,* behaviors followed by reinforcers increase; those followed by punishers often decrease.

22-2 Who was Skinner, and how is operant behavior reinforced and shaped?

B. F. Skinner was a college English major and aspiring writer who later entered psychology graduate school. He became modern behaviorism's most influential and controversial figure.

Operant behavior operates on the environment, producing consequences. Expanding on Edward Thorndike's *law of effect,* Skinner and others found that the behavior of rats or pigeons placed in an *operant chamber* (Skinner box) can be *shaped* by using reinforcers to guide closer and closer approximations of the desired behavior.

22-3 How do positive and negative reinforcement differ, and what are the basic types of reinforcers?

Reinforcement is any consequence that strengthens behavior. *Positive reinforcement* adds a desirable stimulus to increase the frequency of a behavior. *Negative reinforcement* removes an aversive stimulus to increase the frequency of a behavior.

Primary reinforcers (such as receiving food when hungry or having nausea end during an illness) are innately satisfying—no learning is required. *Conditioned* (or secondary) *reinforcers* (such as cash) are satisfying because we have learned to associate them with more basic rewards (such as the food or medicine we buy with them). Immediate reinforcers (such as a purchased treat) offer immediate payback; delayed reinforcers (such as a weekly paycheck) require the ability to delay gratification.

22-4 How do different reinforcement schedules affect behavior?

A *reinforcement schedule* defines how often a response will be reinforced. In *continuous reinforcement* (reinforcing desired responses every time they occur), learning is rapid, but so is extinction if rewards cease. In *partial (intermittent) reinforcement* (reinforcing responses only sometimes), initial learning is slower, but the behavior is much more resistant to extinction. *Fixed-ratio schedules* reinforce behaviors after a set number of responses; *variable-ratio schedules,* after an unpredictable number. *Fixed-interval schedules* reinforce behaviors after set time periods; *variable-interval schedules,* after unpredictable time periods.

22-5 How does punishment differ from negative reinforcement, and how does punishment affect behavior?

Punishment administers an undesirable consequence (such as spanking) or withdraws something desirable (such as taking away a favorite toy) in an attempt to decrease the frequency of a behavior (a child's disobedience). Negative reinforcement (taking an aspirin) removes an aversive stimulus (a headache). This desired consequence (freedom from pain) increases the likelihood that the behavior (taking aspirin to end pain) will be repeated.

Punishment can have undesirable side effects, such as suppressing rather than changing unwanted behaviors; teaching aggression; creating fear; encouraging discrimination (so that the undesirable behavior appears when the punisher is not present); and fostering depression and feelings of helplessness.

22-6 Why did Skinner's ideas provoke controversy, and how might his operant conditioning principles be applied at school, in sports, at work, and at home?

Critics of Skinner's principles believed the approach dehumanized people by neglecting their personal freedom and seeking to control their actions. Skinner replied that people's actions are already controlled by external consequences, and that reinforcement is more humane than punishment as a means for controlling behavior.

At school, teachers can use shaping techniques to guide students' behaviors, and they can use interactive software and websites to provide immediate feedback. In sports, coaches can build players' skills and self-confidence by rewarding small improvements. At work, managers can boost productivity and morale by rewarding well-defined and achievable behaviors. At home, parents can reward desired behaviors but not undesirable ones. We can shape our own behaviors by stating our goals, monitoring the frequency of desired behaviors, reinforcing desired behaviors, and gradually reducing rewards as behaviors become habitual.

22-7 How does operant conditioning differ from classical conditioning?

In operant conditioning, an organism learns associations between its own behavior and resulting events; this form of conditioning involves operant behavior (behavior that operates on the environment, producing rewarding or punishing consequences). In classical conditioning, the organism forms associations between stimuli—events it does not control; this form of conditioning involves respondent behavior (automatic responses to some stimulus).

Module 23: Biology, Cognition, and Learning

23-1 How do biological constraints affect classical and operant conditioning?

Classical conditioning principles, we now know, are constrained by biological predispositions, so that learning some associations is easier than learning others. Learning is adaptive: Each species learns behaviors that aid its survival. Biological constraints also place limits on operant conditioning. Training that attempts to override biological constraints will probably not endure because animals will revert to predisposed patterns.

23-2 How do cognitive processes affect classical and operant conditioning?

In classical conditioning, animals may learn when to expect a US and may be aware of the link between stimuli and responses. In operant conditioning, *cognitive mapping* and *latent learning* research demonstrate the importance of cognitive processes in learning. Other research shows that excessive rewards (driving *extrinsic motivation*) can undermine *intrinsic motivation*.

23-3 How does observational learning differ from associative learning? How may observational learning be enabled by mirror neurons?

In *observational learning,* as we observe and imitate others we learn to anticipate a behavior's consequences because we experience vicarious reinforcement or vicarious punishment. In associative learning, we merely learn associations between different events.

Our brain's frontal lobes have a demonstrated ability to mirror the activity of another's brain. Some psychologists believe *mirror neurons* enable this process. The same areas fire when we perform certain actions (such as responding to pain or moving our mouth to form words) as when we observe someone else performing those actions.

23-4 What is the impact of prosocial modeling and of antisocial modeling?

Children tend to imitate what a model does and says, whether the behavior being *modeled* is *prosocial* (positive, constructive, and helpful) or antisocial. If a model's actions and words are inconsistent, children may imitate the hypocrisy they observe.

MEMORY
Module 24: Studying and Encoding Memories

24-1 What is memory, and how is it measured?

Memory is learning that has persisted over time, through the encoding, storage, and retrieval of information. Evidence of memory may be *recalling* information, *recognizing* it, or *relearning* it more easily on a later attempt.

24-2 How do psychologists describe the human memory system?

Psychologists use memory models to think and communicate about memory. Information-processing models involve three processes: *encoding, storage,* and *retrieval.* Our agile brain processes many things simultaneously (some of them unconsciously) by means of *parallel processing.* The connectionism information-processing model focuses on this multitrack processing, viewing memories as products of interconnected neural networks. The three processing stages in the Atkinson-Shiffrin model are *sensory memory, short-term memory,* and *long-term memory.* This model has since been updated to include two important concepts: (1) *working memory,* to stress the active processing occurring in the second memory stage; and (2) automatic processing, to address the processing of information outside of conscious awareness.

24-3 How do explicit and implicit memories differ?

The human brain processes information on dual tracks, consciously and unconsciously. *Explicit* (declarative) *memories*—our conscious memories of facts and experiences—form through *effortful processing,* which requires conscious effort and attention. *Implicit* (nondeclarative) *memories*—of skills and classically conditioned associations—happen without our awareness, through *automatic processing.*

24-4 What information do we process automatically?

In addition to skills and classically conditioned associations, we automatically process incidental information about space, time, and frequency.

24-5 How does sensory memory work?

Sensory memory feeds some information into working memory for active processing there. An *iconic memory* is a very brief (a few tenths of a second) sensory memory of visual stimuli; an *echoic memory* is a three- or four-second sensory memory of auditory stimuli.

24-6 What is the capacity of our short-term and working memory?

Short-term memory capacity is about seven items, plus or minus two, but this information disappears from memory quickly without rehearsal. Working memory capacity varies, depending on age, intelligence level, and other factors.

24-7 What are some effortful processing strategies that can help us remember new information?

Effective effortful processing strategies include *chunking, mnemonics,* hierarchies, and distributed practice sessions. The *testing effect* is enhanced memory after consciously retrieving, rather than simply rereading, information.

24-8 What are the levels of processing, and how do they affect encoding?

Depth of processing affects long-term retention. In *shallow processing,* we encode words based on their structure or appearance. Retention is best when we use *deep processing,* encoding words based on their meaning. We also more easily remember material that is personally meaningful—the self-reference effect.

Module 25: Storing and Retrieving Memories

25-1 What is the capacity of long-term memory? Are our long-term memories processed and stored in specific locations?

Our long-term memory capacity is essentially unlimited. Memories are not stored intact in the brain in single spots. Many parts of the brain interact as we encode, store, and retrieve memories.

25-2 What are the roles of the frontal lobes and hippocampus in memory processing?

Explicit (declarative) *memories*—our conscious memories of facts and experiences—form through effortful processing, which requires conscious effort and attention. The frontal lobes and *hippocampus* are parts of the brain network dedicated to explicit memory formation. Many brain regions send information to the frontal lobes for processing. The hippocampus, with the help of surrounding areas of cortex, registers and temporarily holds elements of explicit memories before moving them to other brain regions for long-term storage. The neural storage of long-term memories is called *memory consolidation.*

25-3 What roles do the cerebellum and basal ganglia play in memory processing?

Implicit (nondeclarative) *memories*—of skills and classically conditioned associations—happen without our awareness, through automatic processing. The cerebellum and basal ganglia are parts of the brain network dedicated to implicit memory formation. The cerebellum is important for storing classically conditioned memories. The basal ganglia are involved in motor movement and help form procedural memories for skills. Many reactions and skills learned during our first three years continue into our adult lives, but we cannot consciously remember learning these associations and skills, a phenomenon psychologists call "infantile amnesia."

25-4 How do emotions affect our memory processing?

Emotional arousal causes an outpouring of stress hormones, which lead to activity in the brain's memory-forming areas. Significantly stressful events can trigger very clear *flashbulb memories.*

25-5 How do changes at the synapse level affect our memory processing?

Long-term potentiation (LTP) appears to be the neural basis of learning. In LTP, neurons become more efficient at releasing and sensing the presence of neurotransmitters, and more connections develop between neurons.

25-6 How do external cues, internal emotions, and order of appearance influence memory retrieval?

External cues activate associations that help us retrieve memories; this process may occur without our awareness, as it does in *priming.* The *encoding specificity principle* is the idea that cues and contexts specific to a particular memory will be most effective in helping us recall it. Returning to the same physical context or emotional state (*mood congruency*) in which we formed a memory can help us retrieve it. The *serial position effect* accounts for our tendency to recall best the last items (which may still be in working memory) and the first items (which we've spent more time rehearsing) in a list.

Module 26: Forgetting, Memory Construction, and Improving Memory

26-1 Why do we forget?

Anterograde amnesia is an inability to form new memories. *Retrograde amnesia* is an inability to retrieve old memories. Normal forgetting can happen because we have never encoded information (encoding failure); because the physical trace has decayed (storage decay); or because we cannot retrieve what we have encoded and stored (retrieval failure). Retrieval problems may result from *proactive* (forward-acting) *interference*, as prior learning interferes with recall of new information, or from *retroactive* (backward-acting) *interference*, as new learning disrupts recall of old information. Some believe that motivated forgetting occurs, but researchers have found little evidence of *repression*.

26-2 How do misinformation, imagination, and source amnesia influence our memory construction? How do we decide whether a memory is real or false?

In experiments demonstrating the *misinformation effect*, people have formed false memories, incorporating misleading details, after receiving wrong information after an event, or after repeatedly imagining and rehearsing something that never happened. When we reassemble a memory during retrieval, we may attribute it to the wrong source (*source amnesia*). Source amnesia may help explain *déjà vu*. False memories feel like real memories and can be persistent but are usually limited to the gist of the event.

26-3 How reliable are young children's eyewitness descriptions?

Children are susceptible to the misinformation effect, but if questioned in neutral words they understand, they can accurately recall events and people involved in them.

26-4 Why are reports of repressed and recovered memories so hotly debated?

The debate (between memory researchers and some well-meaning therapists) focuses on whether most memories of early childhood abuse are repressed and can be recovered during therapy using "memory work" techniques using leading questions or hypnosis. Psychologists now agree that (1) sexual abuse happens; (2) injustice happens; (3) forgetting happens; (4) recovered memories are commonplace; (5) memories of things that happened before age 3 are unreliable; (6) memories "recovered" under hypnosis or the influence of drugs are especially unreliable; and (7) memories, whether real or false, can be emotionally upsetting.

26-5 How can you use memory research findings to do better in this and other courses?

Memory research findings suggest the following strategies for improving memory: Study repeatedly, make material meaningful, activate retrieval cues, use mnemonic devices, minimize interference, sleep more, and test yourself to be sure you can retrieve, as well as recognize, material.

THINKING AND LANGUAGE
Module 27: Thinking

27-1 What is cognition, and what are the functions of concepts?

Cognition refers to all the mental activities associated with thinking, knowing, remembering, and communicating. We use *concepts*, mental groupings of similar objects, events, ideas, or people, to simplify and order the world around us. We form most concepts around *prototypes*, or best examples of a category.

27-2 What cognitive strategies assist our problem solving, and what obstacles hinder it?

An *algorithm* is a methodical, logical rule or procedure (such as a step-by-step description for evacuating a building during a fire) that guarantees a solution to a problem. A *heuristic* is a simpler strategy (such as running for an exit if you smell smoke) that is usually speedier than an algorithm but is also more error prone. *Insight* is not a strategy-based solution, but rather a sudden flash of inspiration that solves a problem.

Obstacles to problem solving include *confirmation bias,* which predisposes us to verify rather than challenge our hypotheses, and fixation, such as *mental set,* which may prevent us from taking the fresh perspective that would lead to a solution.

27-3 What is intuition, and how can the availability heuristic, overconfidence, belief perseverance, and framing influence our decisions and judgments?

Intuition is the effortless, immediate, automatic feelings or thoughts we often use instead of systematic reasoning. Heuristics enable snap judgments. Using the *availability heuristic,* we judge the likelihood of things based on how readily they come to mind, which often leads us to fear the wrong things. *Overconfidence* can lead us to overestimate the accuracy of our beliefs. When a belief we have formed and explained has been discredited, *belief perseverance* may cause us to cling to that belief. A remedy for belief perseverance is to consider how we might have explained an opposite result. *Framing* is the way a question or statement is worded. Subtle wording differences can dramatically alter our responses.

27-4 What factors contribute to our fear of unlikely events?

We tend to be afraid of what our ancestral history has prepared us to fear (thus, snakes instead of cigarettes); what we cannot control (flying instead of driving); what is immediate (the takeoff and landing of flying instead of countless moments of trivial danger while driving); and what is most readily available (vivid images of air disasters instead of countless safe car trips).

27-5 How do smart thinkers use intuition?

As people gain expertise, they grow adept at making quick, shrewd judgments. Smart thinkers welcome their intuitions (which are usually adaptive), but when making complex decisions they gather as much information as possible and then take time to let their two-track mind process all available information.

27-6 What is creativity, and what fosters it?

Creativity, the ability to produce novel and valuable ideas, correlates somewhat with aptitude, but is more than school smarts. Aptitude tests require *convergent thinking,* but creativity requires *divergent thinking.* Robert Sternberg has proposed that creativity has five components: expertise; imaginative thinking skills; a venturesome personality; intrinsic motivation; and a creative environment that sparks, supports, and refines creative ideas.

27-7 What do we know about thinking in other animals?

Researchers make inferences about other species' consciousness and intelligence based on behavior. Evidence from studies of various species shows that other animals use concepts, numbers, and tools and that they transmit learning from one generation to the next (cultural transmission). And, like humans, other species also show insight, self-awareness, altruism, cooperation, and grief.

Module 28: Language and Thought

28-1 What are the structural components of a language?

Phonemes are a *language's* basic units of sound. *Morphemes* are the elementary units of meaning. *Grammar*—the system of rules that enables us to communicate—includes semantics (rules for deriving meaning) and syntax (rules for ordering words into sentences).

28-2 What are the milestones in language development, and how do we acquire language?

Language development's timing varies, but all children follow the same sequence. Receptive language (the ability to understand what is said to or about you) develops before productive language (the ability to produce words). At about 4 months of age, infants *babble*, making sounds found in languages from all over the world. By about 10 months, their babbling contains only the sounds found in their household language. Around 12 months of age, children begin to speak in single words. This *one-word stage* evolves into *two-word (telegraphic)* utterances before their second birthday, after which they begin speaking in full sentences.

Linguist Noam Chomsky has proposed that all human languages share a universal grammar—the basic building blocks of language—and that humans are born with a predisposition to learn language. We acquire a specific language through learning as our biology and experience interact. Childhood is a critical period for learning to speak and/or sign fluently. This is an important consideration for parents of deaf children, who might master oral communication if given a cochlear implant during this critical period. Deaf culture advocates oppose such implants on the grounds that deafness is a difference, not a disability.

28-3 What brain areas are involved in language processing and speech?

Aphasia is an impairment of language, usually caused by left-hemisphere damage. Two important language- and speech-processing areas are *Broca's area*, a region of the frontal lobe that controls language expression, and *Wernicke's area*, a region in the left temporal lobe that controls language reception. Language processing is spread across other brain areas as well, where different neural networks handle specific linguistic subtasks.

28-4 What do we know about other animals' capacity for language?

A number of chimpanzees and bonobos have (1) learned to communicate with humans by signing or by pushing buttons wired to a computer, (2) developed vocabularies of nearly 400 words, (3) communicated by stringing these words together, (4) taught their skills to younger animals, and (5) demonstrated some understanding of syntax. But only humans communicate in complex sentences. Nevertheless, other animals' impressive abilities to think and communicate challenge humans to consider what this means about the moral rights of other species.

28-5 What is the relationship between thinking and language, and what is the value of thinking in images?

Although Benjamin Lee Whorf's *linguistic determinism* hypothesis suggested that language determines thought, it is more accurate to say that language influences thought. Different languages embody different ways of thinking, and immersion in bilingual education can enhance thinking. We often think in images when we use implicit (non-declarative, procedural) memory—our automatic memory system for motor and cognitive skills and classically conditioned associations. Thinking in images can increase our skills when we mentally practice upcoming events.

INTELLIGENCE

Module 29: What Is Intelligence?

29-1 How do psychologists define *intelligence,* and what are the arguments for *g?*

Intelligence is a mental quality consisting of the potential to learn from experience, solve problems, and use knowledge to adapt to new situations. Charles Spearman proposed that we have one *general intelligence (g)* underlying all other specific mental abilities. He helped develop factor analysis, a statistical procedure that identifies clusters of related abilities. L. L. Thurstone disagreed and identified seven different clusters of mental abilities. Yet a tendency remained for high scorers in one cluster to score high in other clusters. Studies indicate that *g* scores are most predictive in novel situations and do not much correlate with skills in evolutionarily familiar situations.

29-2 How do Gardner's and Sternberg's theories of multiple intelligences differ, and what criticisms have they faced?

Savant syndrome seems to support Howard Gardner's view that we have multiple intelligences. He proposed eight independent intelligences: linguistic, logical-mathematical, musical, spatial, bodily-kinesthetic, intrapersonal, interpersonal, and naturalist. (He has also proposed a ninth possible intelligence—existential intelligence—the ability to ponder deep questions about life.) Robert Sternberg's triarchic theory proposes three intelligence areas that predict real-world skills: analytical (academic problem-solving), creative, and practical.

Critics note research that has confirmed a general intelligence factor. But highly successful people also tend to be conscientious, well-connected, and doggedly energetic.

29-3 What are the four components of emotional intelligence?

Emotional intelligence, which is an aspect of social intelligence, is the ability to perceive, understand, manage, and use emotions. Emotionally intelligent people achieve greater personal and professional success. Some critics question whether calling these abilities "intelligence" stretches that concept too far.

Module 30: Assessing Intelligence

30-1 What is an intelligence test, and what is the difference between achievement and aptitude tests?

An *intelligence test* is a method for assessing an individual's mental aptitudes and comparing them with others, using numerical scores. *Aptitude tests* measure the ability to learn, while *achievement tests* measure what we have already learned.

30-2 When and why were intelligence tests created, and how do today's tests differ from early intelligence tests?

In the late 1800s, Francis Galton, who believed that genius was inherited, attempted but failed to construct a simple intelligence test. Alfred Binet, who tended toward an environmental explanation of intelligence differences, started the modern intelligence-testing movement in France in 1904 when he developed questions to help predict children's future progress in the Paris school system. During the early twentieth century, Lewis Terman of Stanford University revised Binet's work for use in the United States. Terman believed intelligence was inherited, and he thought his *Stanford-Binet* could help guide people toward appropriate opportunities. From such tests, William Stern contributed the concept of the *IQ* (intelligence quotient). During this period, intelligence tests were sometimes used to "document" scientists' assumptions about the innate inferiority of certain ethnic and immigrant groups.

The most widely used intelligence tests today are the *Wechsler Adult Intelligence Scale* (WAIS) and Wechsler's tests for children. These tests differ from their predecessors in the way they offer an overall intelligence score as well as scores for various verbal and performance areas.

30-3 What is a normal curve, and what does it mean to say that a test has been standardized and is reliable and valid?

The distribution of test scores often forms a *normal* (bell-shaped) *curve* around the central average score, with fewer and fewer scores at the extremes.

Standardization establishes a basis for meaningful score comparisons by giving a test to a representative sample of future test-takers. *Reliability* is the extent to which a test yields consistent results (on two halves of the test, on alternative forms of the test, or when people are retested). *Validity* is the extent to which a test measures or predicts what it is supposed to. A test has *content validity* if it samples the pertinent behavior (as a driving test measures driving ability). It has *predictive validity* if it predicts a behavior it was designed to predict. (Aptitude tests have predictive ability if they can predict future achievements; their predictive power is best for the early school years.)

Module 31: The Dynamics of Intelligence

31-1 How stable are intelligence test scores over the life span, and how does aging affect crystallized and fluid intelligence?

Cross-sectional studies (comparing people of different ages) and longitudinal studies (retesting the same group over a period of years) have shown that *fluid intelligence* declines in older adults, in part because neural processing slows. However, *crystallized intelligence* tends to increase.

The stability of intelligence test scores increases with age. At age 4, scores fluctuate somewhat but begin to predict adolescent and adult scores. By early adolescence, scores are very stable and predictive.

31-2 What are the traits of those at the low and high intelligence extremes?

At the low extreme are those with unusually low scores. An intelligence test score of or below 70 is one diagnostic criterion for the diagnosis of *intellectual disability*; other criteria are limited conceptual, social, and practical skills. One condition included in this category is *Down syndrome*, a developmental disorder caused by an extra copy of chromosome 21.

People at the high-intelligence extreme tend to be healthy and well-adjusted, as well as unusually successful academically. Schools sometimes "track" such children, separating them from students with lower scores. Such programs can become self-fulfilling prophecies as both groups live up to—or down to—others' perceptions and expectations.

Module 32: Genetic and Environmental Influences on Intelligence

32-1 What evidence points to a genetic influence on intelligence, and what is heritability?

Studies of twins, family members, and adoptees indicate a significant hereditary contribution to intelligence scores. Intelligence seems to be polygenetic, and researchers are searching for genes that exert an influence. *Heritability* is the proportion of variation among individuals that can be attributed to genes.

32-2 What does evidence reveal about environmental influences on intelligence?

Studies of twins, family members, and adoptees also provide evidence of environmental influences. Test scores of identical twins raised apart are slightly less similar (though still very highly correlated) than the scores of identical twins raised together. Studies of children raised in extremely impoverished environments with minimal social interaction indicate that life experiences can significantly influence intelligence test performance. No evidence supports the idea that normal, healthy children can be molded into geniuses by growing up in an exceptionally enriched environment.

32-3 How and why do the genders differ in mental ability scores?

Males and females tend to have the same average intelligence test scores, but they differ in some specific abilities. Girls are better spellers, more verbally fluent, better at locating objects, better at detecting emotions, and more sensitive to touch, taste, and color. Boys outperform girls at spatial ability and related mathematics, though in math computation and overall math performance, boys and girls hardly differ. Boys also outnumber girls at the low and high extremes of mental abilities. Evolutionary and cultural explanations have been proposed for these gender differences.

33-4 How and why do racial and ethnic groups differ in mental ability scores?

Racial and ethnic groups differ in their average intelligence test scores. The evidence suggests that environmental differences are responsible for these group differences.

33-5 Are intelligence tests inappropriately biased?

Aptitude tests aim to predict how well a test-taker will perform in a given situation. So they are necessarily "biased" in the sense that they are sensitive to performance differences caused by cultural experience. By "inappropriately biased," psychologists mean that a test predicts less accurately for one group than for another. In this sense, most experts consider the major aptitude tests unbiased. *Stereotype threat*, a self-confirming concern that one will be evaluated based on a negative stereotype, affects performance on all kinds of tests.

WHAT DRIVES US: HUNGER, SEX, FRIENDSHIP, AND ACHIEVEMENT

Module 33: Basic Motivational Concepts

33-1 How do psychologists define *motivation?* From what perspectives do they view motivated behavior?

Motivation is a need or desire that energizes and directs behavior. The *instinct/ evolutionary* perspective explores genetic influences on complex behaviors. *Drive-reduction theory* explores how physiological needs create aroused tension states (drives) that direct us to satisfy those needs. Environmental *incentives* can intensify drives. Drive-reduction's goal is *homeostasis,* maintaining a steady internal state. Arousal theory proposes that some behaviors (such as those driven by curiosity) do not reduce physiological needs but rather are prompted by a search for an optimum level of arousal. The *Yerkes-Dodson law* states that performance increases with arousal, but only to a certain point, after which it decreases. Performance peaks at lower levels of arousal for difficult tasks, and at higher levels for easy or well-learned tasks. Abraham Maslow's *hierarchy of needs* proposes a pyramid of human needs, from basic needs such as hunger and thirst up to higher-level needs such as self-actualization and self-transcendence.

Module 34: Hunger

34-1 What physiological factors produce hunger?

Hunger pangs correspond to stomach contractions, but hunger also has other causes. Neural areas in the brain, some within the hypothalamus, monitor blood chemistry (including level of *glucose*) and incoming information about the body's state. Appetite hormones include ghrelin (secreted by an empty stomach); insulin (controls blood glucose); leptin (secreted by fat cells); orexin (secreted by the hypothalamus); and PYY (secreted by the digestive tract). *Basal metabolic rate* is the body's resting rate of energy expenditure. The body may have a *set point* (a biologically fixed tendency to maintain an optimum weight) or a looser settling point (also influenced by the environment).

34-2 What cultural and situational factors influence hunger?

Hunger also reflects our memory of when we last ate and our expectation of when we should eat again. Humans as a species prefer certain tastes (such as sweet and salty), but our individual preferences are also influenced by conditioning, culture, and situation. Some taste preferences, such as the avoidance of new foods, or of foods that have made us ill, have survival value.

34-3 What factors predispose some people to become and remain obese?

Genes and environment interact to produce obesity. Obesity correlates with depression, especially among women. Twin and adoption studies indicate that body weight is also genetically influenced. Environmental influences include lack of exercise, an abundance of high-calorie food, and social influence.

Those wishing to lose weight are advised to make a lifelong change in habits: Get enough sleep; boost energy expenditure through exercise; limit variety and minimize exposure to tempting food cues; eat healthy foods and reduce portion sizes; space meals throughout the day; beware of the binge; monitor eating during social events; forgive the occasional lapse; and connect to a support group.

Module 35: Sexual Motivation

35-1 How do hormones influence human sexual motivation?

For all but the tiny fraction of us considered *asexual*, dating and mating become a high priority from puberty on. The female *estrogen* and male *testosterone* hormones influence human sexual behavior less directly than they influence sexual behavior in other species. Women's sexuality is more responsive to testosterone level than to estrogen level. Short-term shifts in testosterone level are normal in men, partly in response to stimulation.

35-2 What is the human sexual response cycle, and how do sexual dysfunctions and paraphilias differ?

William Masters and Virginia Johnson described four stages in the human *sexual response cycle*: excitement, plateau, orgasm (which seems to involve similar feelings and brain activity in males and females), and resolution. During the resolution phase, males experience a *refractory period* in which renewed arousal and orgasm are impossible.

Sexual dysfunctions are problems that consistently impair sexual arousal or functioning. They include *erectile disorder* and *female orgasmic disorder,* and can often be successfully treated by behaviorally oriented therapy or drug therapy. *Paraphilias* are conditions, which may be classified as disorders, in which sexual arousal is related to nonhuman objects, the suffering of self or others, and/or nonconsenting persons.

35-3 How can sexually transmitted infections be prevented?

Safe-sex practices help prevent sexually transmitted infections (STIs). Condoms are especially effective in preventing transmission of HIV, the virus that causes *AIDS*. A vaccination administered before sexual contact can prevent most human papilloma virus infections.

35-4 How do external and imagined stimuli contribute to sexual arousal?

External stimuli can trigger sexual arousal in both men and women. In experiments, depictions of sexual coercion have increased acceptance of rape. Men respond more specifically to sexual depictions involving their preferred sex. Sexually explicit material may lead people to perceive their partners as comparatively less appealing and to devalue their relationships. Imagined stimuli (dreams and fantasies) also influence sexual arousal.

35-5 What factors influence teenagers' sexual behaviors and use of contraceptives?

Rates of teen intercourse vary from culture to culture and era to era. Factors contributing to teen pregnancy include minimal communication about birth control with parents, partners, and peers; guilt related to sexual activity; alcohol use; and mass media norms of unprotected and impulsive sexuality. High intelligence, religious engagement, father presence, and participation in service learning programs have been predictors of teen sexual restraint.

35-6 What has research taught us about sexual orientation?

Sexual orientation is an enduring sexual attraction toward members of one's own sex (homosexual orientation), the other sex (heterosexual orientation), or both sexes (bisexual orientation). About 3 or 4 percent of men and 2 percent of women in Europe and the United States identify as exclusively homosexual, and 3.4 percent of Americans describe themselves as lesbian, gay, bisexual, or transgender. There is no evidence that environmental influences determine sexual orientation. Evidence for biological influences includes the presence of same-sex attraction in many animal species; straight-gay brain differences; higher rates in certain families and in identical twins; exposure to certain hormones during critical periods of prenatal development; and the fraternal birth-order effect.

35-7 Is scientific research on sexual motivation value free?

Scientific research on sexual motivation does not attempt to define the personal meaning of sex in our lives, but sex research and education are not value free.

Module 36: Affiliation and Achievement

36-1 What evidence points to our human affiliation need—our need to belong?

Our *need to affiliate* or belong—to feel connected and identified with others—had survival value for our ancestors, which may explain why humans in every society live in groups. Because of their need to belong, people suffer when socially excluded, and they may engage in self-defeating behaviors (performing below their ability) or in antisocial behaviors. Feeling loved activates brain regions associated with reward and safety systems. *Ostracism* is the deliberate exclusion of individuals or groups. Social isolation can put us at risk mentally and physically.

36-2 How does social networking influence us?

We connect with others through social networking, strengthening our relationships with those we already know. When networking, people tend toward increased self-disclosure. People with high *narcissism* are especially active on social networking sites. Working out strategies for self-control and disciplined usage can help people maintain a healthy balance between social connections and school and work performance.

36-3 What is achievement motivation?

Achievement motivation is a desire for significant accomplishment, for mastery of skills or ideas, for control, and for attaining a high standard. Achievements are more closely related to *grit* (passionate dedication to a long-term goal) than to raw ability.

EMOTIONS, STRESS, AND HEALTH

Module 37: Introduction to Emotion

37-1 How do arousal, expressive behavior, and cognition interact in emotion?

Emotions are psychological responses of the whole organism involving an interplay among physiological arousal, expressive behaviors, and conscious experience.

Theories of emotion generally address two major questions: (1) Does physiological arousal come before or after emotional feelings, and (2) how do feeling and cognition interact? The *James-Lange theory* maintains that emotional feelings follow our body's response to emotion-inducing stimuli. The *Cannon-Bard theory* proposes that our physiological response to an emotion-inducing stimulus occurs at the same time as our subjective feeling of the emotion (one does not cause the other).

37-2 To experience emotions, must we consciously interpret and label them?

The Schachter-Singer *two-factor theory* holds that our emotions have two ingredients, physical arousal and a cognitive label, and the cognitive labels we put on our states of arousal are an essential ingredient of emotion. Lazarus agreed that many important emotions arise from our interpretations or inferences. Zajonc and LeDoux, however, believe that some simple emotional responses occur instantly, not only outside our conscious awareness, but before any cognitive processing occurs. This interplay between emotion and cognition illustrates our dual-track mind.

37-3 What is the link between emotional arousal and the autonomic nervous system? How does arousal affect performance?

The arousal component of emotion is regulated by the autonomic nervous system's sympathetic (arousing) and parasympathetic (calming) divisions. In a crisis, the fight-or-flight response automatically mobilized your body for action.

Arousal affects performance in different ways, depending on the task. Performance peaks at lower levels of arousal for difficult tasks, and at higher levels for easy or well-learned tasks.

37-4 Do different emotions activate different physiological and brain-pattern responses?

Emotions may be similarly arousing, but some subtle physiological responses, such as facial muscle movements, distinguish them. More meaningful differences have been found in activity in some brain pathways and cortical areas.

37-5 How effective are polygraphs in using body states to detect lies?

Polygraphs, which measure several physiological indicators of emotion, are not accurate enough to justify widespread use in business and law enforcement. The use of guilty knowledge questions and new forms of technology may produce better indications of lying.

Module 38: Expressing Emotion

38-1 How do we communicate nonverbally?

Much of our communication is through body movements, facial expressions, and voice tones. Even seconds-long filmed slices of behavior can reveal feelings.

38-2 Do the genders differ in their ability to communicate nonverbally?

Women tend to read emotional cues more easily and to be more empathic. Their faces also express more emotion.

38-3 Do gestures and facial expressions mean the same thing in all cultures?

The meaning of gestures varies with culture, but facial expressions, such as those of happiness and sadness, are common the world over. Cultures also differ in the amount of emotion they express.

38-4 How do our facial expressions influence our feelings?

Research on the *facial feedback effect* shows that our facial expressions can trigger emotional feelings and signal our body to respond accordingly. We also mimic others' expressions, which helps us empathize. A similar *behavior feedback effect* is the tendency of behavior to influence our own and others' thoughts, feelings, and actions.

Module 39: Experiencing Emotion

39-1 What are some basic emotions, and what two dimensions help differentiate them?

Carroll Izard's 10 basic emotions are joy, interest-excitement, surprise, sadness, anger, disgust, contempt, fear, shame, and guilt.

Two dimensions that help differentiate emotions are positive-versus-negative valence and low-versus-high arousal.

39-2 What are the causes and consequences of anger?

Anger is most often evoked by misdeeds that we interpret as willful, unjustified, and avoidable. But smaller frustrations and blameless annoyances can also trigger anger. Chronic hostility is one of the negative emotions linked to heart disease. Emotional *catharsis* may be temporarily calming, but in the long run it does not reduce anger. Expressing anger can make us angrier. Controlled assertions of feelings may resolve conflicts, and forgiveness may rid us of angry feelings.

39-3 What is the *feel-good, do-good phenomenon,* and what is the focus of positive psychology research?

A good mood brightens people's perceptions of the world. *Subjective well-being* is your perception of being happy or satisfied with life. Happy people tend to be healthy, energized, and satisfied with life. They also are more willing to help others (the *feel-good, do-good phenomenon*).

Positive psychologists use scientific methods to study human flourishing, including topics such as positive emotions, positive health, positive neuroscience, and positive education. The three pillars of positive psychology are positive well-being; positive character; and positive groups, communities, and cultures.

39-4 How do time, wealth, adaptation, and comparison affect our happiness levels?

The moods triggered by good or bad events seldom last beyond that day. Even significant good events, such as sudden wealth, seldom increase happiness for long. Happiness is relative to our own experiences (the *adaptation-level phenomenon*) and to others' success (the *relative deprivation* principle).

39-5 What are some predictors of happiness?

Some individuals, because of their genetic predispositions and personal histories, are happier than others. Cultures, which vary in the traits they value and the behaviors they expect and reward, also influence personal levels of happiness. Researchers have found that happy people tend to have high self-esteem (in individualist countries); be optimistic, outgoing, and agreeable; have close friendships or a satisfying marriage; have work and leisure that engage their skills; have an active religious faith (particularly in more religious cultures); and sleep well and exercise.

Module 40: Stress and Illness

40-1 What events provoke stress responses, and how do we respond and adapt to stress?

Stress is the process by which we appraise and respond to stressors (catastrophic events, significant life changes, and daily hassles) that challenge or threaten us. Walter Cannon viewed the stress response as a "fight-or-flight" system. Hans Selye proposed a general three-phase (alarm-resistance-exhaustion) *general adaptation syndrome (GAS)*. Facing stress, women may have a *tend-and-befriend* response; men may withdraw socially, turn to alcohol, or become aggressive.

40-2 How does stress make us more vulnerable to disease?

Health psychology is a subfield of psychology that provides psychology's contribution to behavioral medicine. *Psychoneuroimmunologists* study mind-body interactions, including stress-related physical illnesses, such as hypertension and some headaches. Stress diverts energy from the immune system, inhibiting the activities of its B and T lymphocytes, macrophages, and NK cells. Stress does not cause diseases such as AIDS and cancer, but by altering our immune functioning it may make us more vulnerable to them and influence their progression.

40-3 Why are some of us more prone than others to coronary heart disease?

Coronary heart disease, the United States' number one cause of death, has been linked with the reactive, anger-prone *Type A* personality. Compared with relaxed, easygoing *Type B* personalities, Type A people secrete more stress hormones. Chronic stress also contributes to persistent inflammation, which heightens the risk of clogged arteries and depression.

Module 41: Health and Coping

41-1 In what two ways do people try to alleviate stress?

We use *problem-focused coping* to change the stressor or the way we interact with it. We use *emotion-focused coping* to avoid or ignore stressors and attend to emotional needs related to stress reactions.

41-2 How does a perceived lack of control affect health?

A perceived lack of control provokes an outpouring of hormones that put people's health at risk. Being unable to avoid repeated aversive events can lead to *learned help-lessness*. People who perceive an *internal locus of control* achieve more, enjoy better health, and are happier than those who perceive an *external locus of control*.

41-3 How can our self-control be depleted, and why is it important to build this strength?

Exercising willpower temporarily depletes the mental energy needed for *self-control* on other tasks. Self-control requires attention and energy, but it predicts good adjustment, better grades, and social success.

41-4 How does an optimistic outlook affect health and longevity?

Studies of people with an optimistic outlook show that their immune system is stronger, their blood pressure does not increase as sharply in response to stress, their recovery from heart bypass surgery is faster, and their life expectancy is longer, compared with their pessimistic counterparts.

41-5 How does social support promote good health?

Social support promotes health by calming us, reducing blood pressure and stress hormones, and by fostering stronger immune functioning.

41-6 How effective is aerobic exercise as a way to manage stress and improve well-being?

Aerobic exercise is sustained, oxygen-consuming activity that increases heart and lung fitness. It increases arousal, leads to muscle relaxation and sounder sleep, triggers the production of neurotransmitters, and enhances self-image. It can relieve depression and, in later life, is associated with better cognitive functioning and longer life.

41-7 In what ways might relaxation and meditation influence stress and health?

Relaxation and meditation have been shown to reduce stress by relaxing muscles, lowering blood pressure, improving immune functioning, and lessening anxiety and depression. Massage therapy also relaxes muscles and reduces depression.

41-8 What is the faith factor, and what are some possible explanations for the link between faith and health?

The faith factor is the finding that religiously active people tend to live longer than those who are not religiously active. Possible explanations may include the effect of intervening variables, such as the healthy behaviors, social support, or positive emotions often found among people who regularly attend religious services.

SOCIAL PSYCHOLOGY

Module 42: Social Thinking

42-1 What do social psychologists study? How do we tend to explain others' behavior and our own?

Social psychologists use scientific methods to study how people think about, influence, and relate to one another. They study the social influences that explain why the same person will act differently in different situations. When explaining others' behavior, we may—especially if we come from an individualist Western culture—commit the *fundamental attribution error*, by underestimating the influence of the situation and overestimating the effects of stable, enduring traits. When explaining our own behavior, we more readily attribute it to the influence of the situation.

42-2 How do attitudes and actions interact?

Attitudes are feelings, often influenced by our beliefs, that predispose us to respond in certain ways. *Peripheral route persuasion* uses incidental cues (such as celebrity endorsement) to try to produce fast but relatively thoughtless changes in attitudes. *Central route persuasion* offers evidence and arguments to trigger thoughtful responses. When other influences are minimal, attitudes that are stable, specific, and easily recalled can affect our actions.

Actions can modify attitudes, as in the *foot-in-the-door phenomenon* (complying with a large request after having agreed to a small request) and *role* playing (acting a social part by following guidelines for expected behavior). When our attitudes don't fit with our actions, *cognitive dissonance theory* suggests that we will reduce tension by changing our attitudes to match our actions.

Module 43: Social Influence

43-1 What is automatic mimicry, and how do conformity experiments reveal the power of social influence?

Automatic mimicry (the chameleon effect)—our tendency to unconsciously imitate others' expressions, postures, and voice tones—is a form of *conformity*.

Solomon Asch and others have found that we are most likely to adjust our behavior or thinking to coincide with a group standard when (a) we feel incompetent or insecure, (b) our group has at least three people, (c) everyone else agrees, (d) we admire the group's status and attractiveness, (e) we have not already committed to another response, (f) we know we are being observed, and (g) our culture encourages respect for social standards. We may conform to gain approval (*normative social influence*) or because we are willing to accept others' opinions as new information (*informational social influence*).

43-2 What did Milgram's obedience experiments teach us about the power of social influence?

Stanley Milgram's experiments—in which people obeyed orders even when they thought they were harming another person—demonstrated that strong social influences can make ordinary people conform to falsehoods or give in to cruelty. Obedience was highest when (a) the person giving orders was nearby and was perceived as a legitimate authority figure; (b) the research was supported by a prestigious institution; (c) the victim was depersonalized or at a distance; and (d) there were no role models for defiance.

43-3 How is our behavior affected by the presence of others?

In *social facilitation*, the mere presence of others arouses us, improving our performance on easy or well-learned tasks but decreasing it on difficult ones. In *social loafing*, participating in a group project makes us feel less responsible, and we may free ride on others' efforts. When the presence of others both arouses us and makes us feel anonymous, we may experience *deindividuation*—loss of self-awareness and self-restraint.

43-4 What are *group polarization* and *groupthink,* and how much power do we have as individuals?

In *group polarization,* group discussions with like-minded others strengthen members' prevailing beliefs and attitudes. Internet communication magnifies this effect, for better and for worse. *Groupthink* is driven by a desire for harmony within a decision-making group, overriding realistic appraisal of alternatives.

The power of the individual and the power of the situation interact. A small minority that consistently expresses its views may sway the majority.

Module 44: Antisocial Relations

44-1 What is *prejudice?* What are its social and emotional roots?

Prejudice is an unjustifiable, usually negative, attitude toward a group and its members. Prejudice's three components are beliefs (often *stereotypes*), emotions, and predispositions to action (*discrimination*). Overt prejudice in North America has decreased over time, but implicit prejudice—an automatic, unthinking attitude—continues.

The social roots of prejudice include social inequalities and divisions. Higher-status groups often justify their privileged position with the *just-world phenomenon.* We tend to favor our own group (*ingroup bias*) as we divide ourselves into "us" (the *ingroup*) and "them" (the *outgroup*).

Prejudice can also be a tool for protecting our emotional well-being, as when we focus our anger by blaming events on a *scapegoat.*

44-2 What are the cognitive roots of prejudice?

The cognitive roots of prejudice grow from our natural ways of processing information: forming categories, remembering vivid cases, and believing that the world is just and that our own and our culture's ways of doing things are the right ways.

44-3 How does psychology's definition of *aggression* differ from everyday usage? What biological factors make us more prone to hurt one another?

In psychology's more specific meaning, *aggression* is any act intended to harm someone physically or emotionally. Biology influences our threshold for aggressive behaviors at three levels: genetic (inherited traits), neural (activity in key brain areas), and biochemical (such as alcohol or excess testosterone in the bloodstream). Aggression is a complex behavior resulting from the interaction of biology and experience.

44-4 What psychological and social-cultural factors may trigger aggressive behavior?

Frustration (*frustration-aggression principle*), previous reinforcement for aggressive behavior, observing an aggressive role model, and poor self-control can all contribute to aggression. Media portrayals of violence provide *social scripts* that children learn to follow. Viewing sexual violence contributes to greater aggression toward women. Playing violent video games increases aggressive thoughts, emotions, and behaviors.

Module 45: Prosocial Relations

45-1 Why do we befriend or fall in love with some people but not others?

Proximity (geographical nearness) increases liking, in part because of the *mere exposure effect*—exposure to novel stimuli increases liking of those stimuli. Physical attractiveness increases social opportunities and improves the way we are perceived. Similarity of attitudes and interests greatly increases liking, especially as relationships develop. We also like those who like us.

45-2 How does romantic love typically change as time passes?

Intimate love relationships start with *passionate love*—an intensely aroused state. Over time, the strong affection of *companionate love* may develop, especially if enhanced by an *equitable* relationship and by intimate *self-disclosure.*

45-3 When are people most—and least—likely to help?

Altruism is unselfish regard for the well-being of others. We are most likely to help when we (a) notice an incident, (b) interpret it as an emergency, and (c) assume responsibility for helping. Other factors, including our mood and our similarity to the victim, also affect our willingness to help. We are least likely to help if other bystanders are present (the *bystander effect*).

45-4 How do social exchange theory and social norms explain helping behavior?

Social exchange theory is the view that we help others because it is in our own self-interest; in this view, the goal of social behavior is maximizing personal benefits and minimizing costs. Others believe that helping results from socialization, in which we are taught guidelines for expected behaviors in social situations, such as the *reciprocity norm* and the *social-responsibility norm.*

45-5 How do social traps and mirror-image perceptions fuel social conflict?

A *conflict* is a perceived incompatibility of actions, goals, or ideas. *Social traps* are situations in which people in conflict pursue their own individual self-interest, harming the collective well-being. Individuals and cultures in conflict also tend to form *mirror-image perceptions*: Each party views the opponent as untrustworthy and evil-intentioned, and itself as an ethical, peaceful victim. Perceptions can become *self-fulfilling prophecies.*

45-6 How can we transform feelings of prejudice, aggression, and conflict into attitudes that promote peace?

Peace can result when individuals or groups work together to achieve *superordinate* (shared) *goals.* Research indicates that four processes—contact, cooperation, communication, and conciliation—help promote peace.

Personality

Module 46: Introduction to Personality and Psychodynamic Theories

46-1 What historically significant and current theories inform our understanding of personality?

Personality is an individual's characteristic pattern of thinking, feeling, and acting. *Psychodynamic theories* view personality from the perspective that behavior is a dynamic interaction between the conscious and unconscious mind. These theories trace their origin to Sigmund Freud's theory of *psychoanalysis*. The humanistic approach focused on our inner capacities for growth and self-fulfillment. Trait theories examine characteristic patterns of behavior (traits). Social-cognitive theories explore the interaction between people's traits (including their thinking) and their social context.

46-2 How did Sigmund Freud's treatment of psychological disorders lead to his view of the unconscious mind?

In treating patients whose disorders had no clear physical explanation, Freud concluded that these problems reflected unacceptable thoughts and feelings, hidden away in the *unconscious* mind. To explore this hidden part of a patient's mind, Freud used *free association* and dream analysis.

46-3 What was Freud's view of personality?

Freud believed that personality results from conflict arising from the interaction among the mind's three systems: the *id* (pleasure-seeking impulses), *ego* (reality-oriented executive), and *superego* (internalized set of ideals, or conscience).

46-4 What developmental stages did Freud propose?

He believed children pass through five *psychosexual stages* (oral, anal, phallic, latency, and genital). Unresolved conflicts at any stage can leave a person's pleasure-seeking impulses *fixated* (stalled) at that stage.

46-5 How did Freud think people defended themselves against anxiety?

For Freud, anxiety was the product of tensions between the demands of the id and superego. The ego copes by using unconscious *defense mechanisms,* such as *repression*, which he viewed as the basic mechanism underlying and enabling all the others.

46-6 Which of Freud's ideas did his followers accept or reject?

Freud's early followers, the neo-Freudians, accepted many of his ideas. They differed in placing more emphasis on the conscious mind and in stressing social motives more than sex or aggression. Most contemporary psychodynamic theorists and therapists reject Freud's emphasis on sexual motivation. They stress, with support from modern research findings, the view that much of our mental life is unconscious, and they believe that our childhood experiences influence our adult personality and attachment patterns. Many also believe that our species' shared evolutionary history shaped some universal predispositions.

46-7 What are projective tests, how are they used, and what are some criticisms of them?

Projective tests attempt to assess personality by showing people ambiguous stimuli (open to many possible interpretations) and treating their answers as revelations of unconscious motives. One such test, the *Rorschach inkblot test*, has low reliability and validity except in a few areas, such as hostility and anxiety.

46-8 How do contemporary psychologists view Freud's psychoanalysis?

They give Freud credit for drawing attention to the vast unconscious, to the struggle to cope with our sexuality, to the conflict between biological impulses and social restraints, and for some forms of defense mechanisms (false consensus effect/projection; reaction formation) and unconscious *terror-management* defenses. But his concept of repression, and his view of the unconscious as a collection of repressed and unacceptable thoughts, wishes, feelings, and memories, cannot survive scientific scrutiny. Freud offered after-the-fact explanations, which are hard to test scientifically. Research does not support many of Freud's specific ideas, such as the view that development is fixed in childhood. (We now know it is lifelong.)

46-9 How has modern research developed our understanding of the unconscious?

Current research confirms that we do not have full access to all that goes on in our mind, but the current view of the unconscious is that it is a separate and parallel track of information processing that occurs outside our awareness. This processing includes schemas that control our perceptions; priming; implicit memories of learned skills; instantly activated emotions; and stereotypes that filter our information processing of others' traits and characteristics.

Module 47: Humanistic Theories and Trait Theories

47-1 How did humanistic psychologists view personality, and what was their goal in studying personality?

The *humanistic* psychologists' view of personality focused on the potential for healthy personal growth and people's striving for self-determination and self-realization. Abraham Maslow proposed that human motivations form a hierarchy of needs; if basic needs are fulfilled, people will strive toward *self-actualization* and self-transcendence. Carl Rogers believed that the ingredients of a growth-promoting environment are genuineness, acceptance (including *unconditional positive regard*), and empathy. *Self-concept* was a central feature of personality for both Maslow and Rogers.

47-2 How did humanistic psychologists assess a person's sense of self?

Some rejected any standardized assessments and relied on interviews and conversations. Rogers sometimes used questionnaires in which people described their ideal and actual selves, which he later used to judge progress during therapy.

47-3 How have humanistic theories influenced psychology? What criticisms have they faced?

Humanistic psychology helped renew interest in the concept of self. Critics have said that humanistic psychology's concepts were vague and subjective, its values self-centered, and its assumptions naively optimistic.

47-4 How do psychologists use traits to describe personality?

Trait theorists see personality as a stable and enduring pattern of behavior. They describe our differences rather than trying to explain them. Using factor analysis, they identify clusters of behavior tendencies that occur together. Genetic predispositions influence many traits.

47-5 What are some common misunderstandings about introversion? Does extraversion lead to greater success than introversion?

Introversion is often misunderstood as shyness, but introverted people often simply seek low levels of stimulation from their environment. Introversion is also sometimes thought to be a barrier to success, but in fact introverts often experience great achievement, even in sales, through characteristics such as their superior listening skills.

47-6 What are personality inventories, and what are their strengths and weaknesses as trait-assessment tools?

Personality inventories (such as the *MMPI*) are questionnaires on which people respond to items designed to gauge a wide range of feelings and behaviors. Test items are *empirically derived*, and the tests are objectively scored. But people can fake their answers to create a good impression, and the ease of computerized testing may lead to misuse of the tests.

47-7 Which traits seem to provide the most useful information about personality variation?

The Big Five personality factors—conscientiousness, agreeableness, neuroticism, openness, and extraversion (CANOE)—currently offer the clearest picture of personality. These factors are quite stable and appear to be found in all cultures.

47-8 Does research support the consistency of personality traits over time and across situations?

A person's average traits persist over time and are predictable over many different situations. But traits cannot predict behavior in any one particular situation.

Module 48: Social-Cognitive Theories and the Self

48-1 How do social-cognitive theorists view personality development, and how do they explore behavior?

Albert Bandura first proposed the *social-cognitive perspective*, which emphasizes the interaction of our traits with our situations. Social-cognitive researchers apply principles of learning, cognition, and social behavior to personality. *Reciprocal determinism* is a term describing the interaction and mutual influence of behavior, internal personal factors, and environmental factors.

48-2 What criticisms have social-cognitive theorists faced?

Social-cognitive theorists build on well-established concepts of learning and cognition. They tend to believe that the best way to predict someone's behavior in a given situation is to observe that person's behavior in similar situations. They have been faulted for underemphasizing the importance of unconscious motives, emotions, and biologically influenced traits.

48-3 Why has psychology generated so much research on the self? How important is self-esteem to psychology and to human well-being?

The *self* is the center of personality, organizing our thoughts, feelings, and actions. Considering possible selves helps motivate us toward positive development, but focusing too intensely on ourselves can lead to the *spotlight effect*.

Self-esteem is our feeling of self-worth; *self-efficacy* is our sense of competence on a task. High self-esteem correlates with less pressure to conform, with persistence at difficult tasks, and with happiness. But the direction of the correlation is not clear. Psychologists caution against unrealistically promoting children's feelings of self-worth. It's better to reward their achievements, which leads to feelings of competence.

48-4 How do excessive optimism, blindness to one's own incompetence, and self-serving bias reveal the costs of self-esteem, and how do defensive and secure self-esteem differ?

Excessive optimism can lead to complacency and prevent us from seeing real risks, while blindness to one's own incompetence may lead us to make the same mistakes repeatedly. *Self-serving bias* is our tendency to perceive ourselves favorably, as when viewing ourselves as better than average or when accepting credit for our successes but not blame for our failures. *Narcissism* is excessive self-love and self-absorption. Defensive self-esteem is fragile, focuses on sustaining itself, and views failure or criticism as a threat. Secure self-esteem enables us to feel accepted for who we are.

PSYCHOLOGICAL DISORDERS

Module 49: Introduction to Psychological Disorders

49-1 How should we draw the line between normality and disorder?

According to psychologists and psychiatrists, *psychological disorders* are marked by a clinically significant disturbance in an individual's cognition, emotion regulation, or behavior.

49-2 How do the medical model and the biopsychosocial approach influence our understanding of psychological disorders?

The *medical model* assumes that psychological disorders are mental illnesses with physical causes that can be diagnosed, treated, and, in most cases, cured through therapy, sometimes in a hospital. The biopsychosocial perspective assumes that three sets of influences—biological (evolution, genetics, brain structure and chemistry), psychological (stress, trauma, learned helplessness, mood-related perceptions and memories), and social and cultural circumstances (roles, expectations, definitions of "normality" and "disorder")—interact to produce specific psychological disorders. *Epigenetics* also informs our understanding of disorders.

49-3 How and why do clinicians classify psychological disorders, and why do some psychologists criticize the use of diagnostic labels?

The American Psychiatric Association's DSM-5 (*Diagnostic and Statistical Manual of Mental Disorders*, Fifth Edition) contains diagnostic labels and descriptions that provide a common language and shared concepts for communication and research. Most U.S. health insurance organizations require a DSM diagnosis before paying for treatment.

   Some critics believe the DSM editions have become too detailed and extensive. Others view DSM diagnoses as arbitrary labels that create preconceptions, which bias perceptions of the labeled person's past and present behavior.

49-4 Why is there controversy over attention-deficit/hyperactivity disorder?

A child (or, less commonly, an adult) who displays extreme inattention and/or hyperactivity and impulsivity may be diagnosed with *attention-deficit/hyperactivity disorder (ADHD)* and treated with medication and other therapy. The controversy centers on whether the growing number of ADHD cases reflects overdiagnosis or increased awareness of the disorder. Long-term effects of stimulant-drug treatment for ADHD are not yet known.

49-5 Do psychological disorders predict violent behavior?

Mental disorders seldom lead to violence, but when they do, they raise moral and ethical questions about whether society should hold people with disorders responsible for their violent actions. Most people with disorders are nonviolent and are more likely to be victims than attackers.

49-6 How many people have, or have had, a psychological disorder? Is poverty a risk factor?

Psychological disorder rates vary, depending on the time and place of the survey. In one multinational survey, rates for any disorder ranged from less than 5 percent (Shanghai) to more than 25 percent (the United States). Poverty is a risk factor: Conditions and experiences associated with poverty contribute to the development of psychological disorders. But some disorders, such as schizophrenia, can drive people into poverty.

Module 50: Anxiety Disorders, OCD, and PTSD

50-1 How do generalized anxiety disorder, panic disorder, and phobias differ?

Anxious feelings and behaviors are classified as an *anxiety disorder* only when they form a pattern of distressing, persistent anxiety or maladaptive behaviors that reduce anxiety. People with *generalized anxiety disorder* feel persistently and uncontrollably tense and apprehensive, for no apparent reason. In the more extreme *panic disorder*, anxiety escalates into periodic episodes of intense dread. Those with a *phobia* may be irrationally afraid of a specific object, activity, or situation. Two other disorders (OCD and PTSD) involve anxiety but are classified separately from the anxiety disorders.

50-2 What is OCD?

Persistent and repetitive thoughts (obsessions), actions (compulsions), or both characterize *obsessive-compulsive disorder (OCD)*.

50-3 What is PTSD?

Symptoms of *posttraumatic stress disorder (PTSD)* include four or more weeks of haunting memories, nightmares, social withdrawal, jumpy anxiety, numbness of feeling, and/or sleep problems following some traumatic experience.

50-4 How do conditioning, cognition, and biology contribute to the feelings and thoughts that mark anxiety disorders, OCD, and PTSD?

The learning perspective views anxiety disorders, OCD, and PTSD as products of fear conditioning, stimulus generalization, fearful behavior reinforcement, and observational learning of others' fears and cognitions (interpretations, irrational beliefs, and hypervigilance). The biological perspective considers the role that fears of life-threatening animals, objects, or situations played in natural selection and evolution; genetic predispositions for high levels of emotional reactivity and neurotransmitter production; and abnormal responses in the brain's fear circuits.

Module 51: Depressive Disorders and Bipolar Disorder

51-1 How do major depressive disorder, persistent depressive disorder, and bipolar disorder differ?

A person with *major depressive disorder* experiences two or more weeks with five or more symptoms, at least one of which must be either (1) depressed mood or (2) loss of interest or pleasure. Persistent depressive disorder includes a mildly depressed mood more often than not for at least two years, along with at least two other symptoms. A person with the less common condition of *bipolar disorder* experiences not only depression but also *mania*—episodes of hyperactive and wildly optimistic, impulsive behavior.

51-2 How can the biological and social-cognitive perspectives help us understand depressive disorders and bipolar disorder?

The biological perspective on depressive disorders and bipolar disorder focuses on genetic predispositions and on abnormalities in brain structures and function (including those found in neurotransmitter systems). The social-cognitive perspective views depression as an ongoing cycle of stressful experiences (interpreted through negative beliefs, attributions, and memories) leading to negative moods and actions and fueling new stressful experiences.

51-3 What factors increase the risk of suicide, and what do we know about nonsuicidal self-injury?

Suicide rates differ by nation, race, gender, age group, income, religious involvement, marital status, and (for gay and lesbian youth, for example) social support structure. Those with depression are more at risk for suicide than others are, but social suggestion, health status, and economic and social frustration are also contributing factors. Environmental barriers (such as jump barriers) are effective in preventing suicides. Forewarnings of suicide may include verbal hints, giving away possessions, withdrawal, preoccupation with death, and discussing one's own suicide.

Nonsuicidal self-injury (NSSI) does not usually lead to suicide but may escalate to suicidal thoughts and acts if untreated. People who engage in NSSI do not tolerate stress well and tend to be self-critical, with poor communication and problem-solving skills.

Module 52: Schizophrenia

52-1 What patterns of perceiving, thinking, and feeling characterize schizophrenia?

Symptoms of *schizophrenia* include disturbed perceptions, disorganized thinking and speech, and diminished, inappropriate emotions. *Delusions* are false beliefs;

hallucinations are sensory experiences without sensory stimulation. Schizophrenia symptoms may be positive (the presence of inappropriate behaviors) or negative (the absence of appropriate behaviors).

52-2 How do chronic and acute schizophrenia differ?

Schizophrenia typically strikes during late adolescence, affects men slightly more than women, and seems to occur in all cultures. In *chronic* (or process) schizophrenia, the disorder develops gradually and recovery is doubtful. In *acute* (or reactive) schizophrenia, the onset is sudden, in reaction to stress, and the prospects for recovery are brighter.

52-3 What brain abnormalities are associated with schizophrenia?

People with schizophrenia have increased dopamine receptors, which may intensify brain signals, creating positive symptoms such as hallucinations and paranoia. Brain abnormalities associated with schizophrenia include enlarged, fluid-filled cerebral cavities and corresponding decreases in the cortex. Brain scans reveal abnormal activity in the frontal lobes, thalamus, and amygdala. Interacting malfunctions in multiple brain regions and their connections may produce schizophrenia's symptoms.

52-4 What prenatal events are associated with increased risk of developing schizophrenia?

Possible contributing factors include viral infections or famine conditions during the mother's pregnancy; low weight or oxygen deprivation at birth; and maternal diabetes or older paternal age.

52-5 Do genes influence schizophrenia? What factors may be early warning signs of schizophrenia in children?

Twin and adoption studies indicate that the predisposition to schizophrenia is inherited. Multiple genes probably interact to produce schizophrenia. No environmental causes invariably produce schizophrenia, but environmental events (such as prenatal viruses or maternal stress) may "turn on" genes for this disorder in those who are predisposed to it.

Possible early warning signs of later development of schizophrenia include both biological factors (a mother with severe and long-lasting schizophrenia; oxygen deprivation and low weight at birth; separation from parents; short attention span and poor muscle coordination) and psychological factors (disruptive or withdrawn behavior; emotional unpredictability; poor peer relations and solo play).

Module 53: Dissociative, Personality, and Eating Disorders

53-1 What are dissociative disorders, and why are they controversial?

Dissociative disorders are conditions in which conscious awareness seems to become separated from previous memories, thoughts, and feelings. Skeptics note that *dissociative identity disorder*, formerly known as multiple personality disorder, increased dramatically in the late twentieth century; is rarely found outside North America; and may reflect role playing by people who are vulnerable to therapists' suggestions. Others view this disorder as a manifestation of feelings of anxiety, or as a response learned when behaviors are reinforced by anxiety-reduction.

53-2 What are the three clusters of personality disorders? What behaviors and brain activity characterize the antisocial personality?

Personality disorders are disruptive, inflexible, and enduring behavior patterns that impair social functioning. This disorder forms three clusters, characterized by (1) anxiety, (2) eccentric or odd behaviors, and (3) dramatic or impulsive behaviors.

Antisocial personality disorder (one of those in the third cluster) is characterized by a lack of conscience and, sometimes, by aggressive and fearless behavior. Genetic predispositions may interact with the environment to produce the altered brain activity associated with antisocial personality disorder.

53-3 What are the three main eating disorders, and how do biological, psychological, and social-cultural influences make people more vulnerable to them?

In those with eating disorders (most often women or gay men), psychological factors can overwhelm the body's tendency to maintain a normal weight. Despite being significantly underweight, people with *anorexia nervosa* (usually adolescent females) continue to diet and exercise excessively because they view themselves as fat. Those with *bulimia nervosa* (usually females in their teens and twenties) secretly binge and then compensate by purging, fasting, or excessive exercise. Those with *binge-eating disorder* binge but do not follow with purging, fasting, and exercise. Cultural pressures, low self-esteem, and negative emotions interact with stressful life experiences and genetics to produce eating disorders.

THERAPY

Module 54: Introduction to Therapy and the Psychological Therapies

54-1 How do *psychotherapy* and the *biomedical therapies* differ?

Psychotherapy is treatment involving psychological techniques; it consists of interactions between a trained therapist and someone seeking to overcome psychological difficulties or achieve personal growth. The major psychotherapies derive from psychology's psychodynamic, humanistic, behavioral, and cognitive perspectives. *Biomedical therapy* treats psychological disorders with medications or procedures that act directly on a patient's physiology. An *eclectic approach* combines techniques from various forms of therapy.

54-2 What are the goals and techniques of psychoanalysis, and how have they been adapted in psychodynamic therapy?

Through *psychoanalysis*, Sigmund Freud tried to give people self-insight and relief from their disorders by bringing anxiety-laden feelings and thoughts into conscious awareness. Psychoanalytic techniques included using free association and *interpretation* of instances of *resistance* and *transference*. *Psychodynamic therapy* has been influenced by traditional psychoanalysis but differs from it in many ways, including the lack of belief in id, ego, and superego. This contemporary therapy is briefer, less expensive, and more focused on helping the client find relief from current symptoms. Psychodynamic therapists help clients understand how past relationships create themes that may be acted out in present relationships. Interpersonal therapy is a brief 12- to 16-session form of psychodynamic therapy that has been effective in treating depression.

54-3 What are the basic themes of humanistic therapy? What are the specific goals and techniques of Rogers' client-centered approach?

Both psychoanalytic and humanistic therapists are *insight therapies*—they attempt to improve functioning by increasing clients' awareness of motives and defenses. Humanistic therapy's goals have included helping clients grow in self-awareness and self-acceptance; promoting personal growth rather than curing illness; helping clients take responsibility for their own growth; focusing on conscious thoughts rather than unconscious motivations; and seeing the present and future as more important than the past.

Carl Rogers' *client-centered therapy* proposed that therapists' most important contributions are to function as a psychological mirror through *active listening* and to provide a growth-fostering environment of *unconditional positive regard*, characterized by genuineness, acceptance, and empathy.

54-4 How does the basic assumption of behavior therapy differ from the assumptions of psychodynamic and humanistic therapies? What techniques are used in exposure therapies and aversive conditioning?

Behavior therapies are not insight therapies. Their goal is to apply learning principles to modify problem behaviors.

Classical conditioning techniques, including *exposure therapies* (such as *systematic desensitization* or *virtual reality exposure therapy*) and *aversive conditioning*, attempt to change behaviors through *counterconditioning*—evoking new responses to old stimuli that trigger unwanted behaviors.

54-5 What is the main premise of therapy based on operant conditioning principles, and what are the views of its proponents and critics?

Operant conditioning operates under the premise that voluntary behaviors are strongly influenced by their consequences. Therapy based on operant conditioning principles uses behavior modification techniques to change unwanted behaviors through positively reinforcing desired behaviors and ignoring or punishing undesirable behaviors.

Critics maintain that (1) techniques such as those used in *token economies* may produce behavior changes that disappear when rewards end, and (2) deciding which behaviors should change is authoritarian and unethical. Proponents argue that treatment with positive rewards is more humane than punishing people or institutionalizing them for undesired behaviors.

54-6 What are the goals and techniques of cognitive therapy and of cognitive-behavioral therapy?

The *cognitive therapies*, such as Aaron Beck's cognitive therapy for depression, assume that our thinking influences our feelings, and that the therapist's role is to change clients' self-defeating thinking by training them to view themselves in more positive ways. The widely researched and practiced *cognitive-behavioral therapy* (CBT) combines cognitive therapy and behavior therapy by helping clients regularly act out their new ways of thinking and talking in their everyday life.

54-7 What are the aims and benefits of group and family therapies?

Group therapy sessions can help more people and costs less per person than individual therapy would. Clients may benefit from exploring feelings and developing social skills in a group situation, from learning that others have similar problems, and from getting feedback on new ways of behaving. *Family therapy* views a family as an interactive system and attempts to help members discover the roles they play and to learn to communicate more openly and directly.

Module 55: Evaluating Psychotherapies

55-1 Does psychotherapy work? How can we know?

Clients' and therapists' positive testimonials cannot prove that psychotherapy is actually effective, and the placebo effect makes it difficult to judge whether improvement occurred because of the treatment.

Using *meta-analyses* to statistically combine the results of hundreds of randomized psychotherapy outcome studies, researchers have found that those not undergoing treatment often improve, but those undergoing psychotherapy are more likely to improve more quickly, and with less chance of relapse.

55-2 Are some psychotherapies more effective than others for specific disorders?

No one type of psychotherapy is generally superior to all others. Therapy is most effective for those with clear-cut, specific problems. Some therapies—such as behavior conditioning for treating phobias and compulsions—are more effective for specific disorders. Psychodynamic therapy has been effective for depression and anxiety, and cognitive and cognitive-behavioral therapies have been effective in coping with anxiety, posttraumatic stress disorder, and depression. *Evidence-based practice* integrates the best available research with clinicians' expertise and patients' characteristics, preferences, and circumstances.

55-3 How do alternative therapies fare under scientific scrutiny?

Abnormal states tend to return to normal on their own, and the placebo effect can create the impression that a treatment has been effective. These two tendencies complicate assessments of alternative therapies (nontraditional therapies that claim to cure certain ailments). Eye movement desensitization and reprocessing (EMDR) has shown some effectiveness—not from the eye movement but rather from the exposure therapy nature of the treatments. Light exposure therapy does seem to relieve depression symptoms for those with a seasonal pattern of major depressive disorder by activating a brain region that influences arousal and hormones.

55-4 What three elements are shared by all forms of psychotherapy?

All psychotherapies offer new hope for demoralized people; a fresh perspective; and (if the therapist is effective) an empathic, trusting, and caring relationship. The emotional bond of trust and understanding between therapist and client—the *therapeutic alliance*—is an important element in effective therapy.

55-5 How do culture and values influence the therapist-client relationship?

Therapists differ in the values that influence their goals in therapy and their views of progress. These differences may create problems if therapists and clients differ in their cultural or religious perspectives.

55-6 What should a person look for when selecting a therapist?

A person seeking therapy may want to ask about the therapist's treatment approach, values, credentials, and fees. An important consideration is whether the therapy seeker feels comfortable and able to establish a bond with the therapist.

Module 56: Biomedical Therapies and Preventing Psychological Disorders

56-1 What are the drug therapies? How do double-blind studies help researchers evaluate a drug's effectiveness?

Psychopharmacology, the study of drug effects on mind and behavior, has helped make drug therapy the most widely used *biomedical therapy*. *Antipsychotic drugs*, used in treating schizophrenia, block dopamine activity. Side effects may include tardive dyskinesia (with involuntary movements of facial muscles, tongue, and limbs) or increased risk of obesity and diabetes. *Antianxiety drugs*, which depress central nervous system activity, are used to treat anxiety disorders, obsessive-compulsive disorder, and posttraumatic stress disorder. These drugs can be physically and psychologically addictive. *Antidepressant drugs*, which increase the availability of serotonin and norepinephrine, are used for depression, with modest effectiveness beyond that of placebo drugs. The antidepressants known as selective serotonin reuptake inhibitors (often called SSRI drugs) are now used to treat other disorders, including strokes and anxiety disorders. Lithium and Depakote are mood stabilizers prescribed for those with bipolar disorder. Studies may use a double-blind procedure to avoid the placebo effect and researcher's bias.

56-2 How are brain stimulation and psychosurgery used in treating specific disorders?

Electroconvulsive therapy (ECT), in which a brief electric current is sent through the brain of an anesthetized patient, is an effective, last-resort treatment for severely depressed people who have not responded to other therapy. Newer alternative treatments for depression include *repetitive transcranial magnetic stimulation (rTMS)* and, in preliminary clinical experiments, deep-brain stimulation that calms an overactive brain region linked with negative emotions.

Psychosurgery removes or destroys brain tissue in hopes of modifying behavior. Radical psychosurgical procedures such as *lobotomy* were once popular, but neurosurgeons now rarely perform brain surgery to change behavior or moods. Brain surgery is a last-resort treatment because its effects are irreversible.

56-3 How, by taking care of themselves with a healthy lifestyle, might people find some relief from depression? How does this reflect our being biopsychosocial systems?

Depressed people who undergo a program of aerobic exercise, adequate sleep, light exposure, social engagement, negative thought reduction, and better nutrition often gain some relief. In our integrated biopsychosocial system, stress affects our body chemistry and health; chemical imbalances can produce depression; and social support and other lifestyle changes can lead to relief of symptoms.

56-4 What is the rationale for preventive mental health programs, and why is it important to develop resilience?

Preventive mental health programs are based on the idea that many psychological disorders could be prevented by changing oppressive, esteem-destroying environments into more benevolent, nurturing environments that foster growth, self-confidence, and *resilience*. Struggling with challenges can lead to *posttraumatic growth*. Community psychologists are often active in preventive mental health programs.

APPENDIX A
Psychology at Work

A-1 What is *flow,* and what are the three subfields of industrial-organizational psychology?

Flow is a completely involved, focused state of consciousness with diminished awareness of self and time. It results from fully engaging one's skills. *Industrial-organizational (I/O) psychology's* three subfields are *personnel, organizational,* and *human factors psychology.*

A-2 How do personnel psychologists help organizations with employee selection, work placement, and performance appraisal?

Personnel psychologists work with organizations to devise selection methods for new employees; recruit and evaluate applicants; design and evaluate training programs; identify people's strengths; analyze job content; and appraise individual and organizational performance. Unstructured, subjective interviews foster the interviewer illusion; *structured interviews* pinpoint job-relevant strengths and are better predictors of performance. Checklists, graphic rating scales, and behavior rating scales are useful performance appraisal methods.

A-3 What is the role of organizational psychologists?

Organizational psychologists examine influences on worker satisfaction and productivity and facilitate organizational change. Employee satisfaction and engagement tend to correlate with organizational success.

A-4 What are some effective leadership techniques?

Effective leaders harness job-relevant strengths; set specific challenging goals; and choose an appropriate leadership style. Leadership style may be goal-oriented (*task leadership*), group-oriented (*social leadership*), or some combination of the two.

A-5 How do human factors psychologists work to create user-friendly machines and work settings?

Human factors psychologists contribute to human safety and improved design by encouraging developers and designers to consider human perceptual abilities, to avoid the curse of knowledge, and to test users to reveal perception-based problems.

Answers to *Test Yourself* Questions

THE STORY OF PSYCHOLOGY
Module 1: What Is Psychology?

1. Wilhelm Wundt

2. a

3. a

4. b

5. The environment (nurture) has an influence on us, but that influence is constrained by our biology (nature). Nature and nurture interact. People predisposed to be very tall (nature), for example, are unlikely to become Olympic gymnasts, no matter how hard they work (nurture).

6. d

7. psychiatrist

8. c

THINKING CRITICALLY WITH PSYCHOLOGICAL SCIENCE
Module 2: The Need for Psychological Science

1. Hindsight bias

2. d

3. Critical thinking examines assumptions, appraises the source, discerns hidden values, evaluates evidence, and assesses conclusions. In evaluating a claim in the media, look for any signs of empirical evidence, preferably from several studies. Ask the following questions in your analysis: Are claims based on scientific findings? Have several studies replicated the findings and confirmed them? Are any experts cited? If so, research their background. Are they affiliated with a credible university, college, or institution? Have they conducted or written about scientific research?

Module 3: Research Strategies: How Psychologists Ask and Answer Questions

4. hypotheses

5. c

6. representative

7. negative

8. scatterplot

9. a

10. Regression toward the mean is a statistical phenomenon describing the tendency of extreme scores or outcomes to return to normal after an unusual event. Without knowing this, we may inaccurately decide the return to normal was a result of our own behavior.

11. a

12. (a) *Alcohol use is associated with violence. (One interpretation: Drinking triggers or unleashes aggressive behavior.)* Perhaps anger triggers drinking, or perhaps the same genes or child-raising practices are predisposing both drinking and aggression. (Here researchers have learned that drinking does indeed trigger aggressive behavior.)

(b) *Educated people live longer, on average, than less-educated people. (One interpretation: Education lengthens life and enhances health.)* Perhaps richer people can afford more education and better health care. (Research supports this conclusion.)

(c) *Teens engaged in team sports are less likely to use drugs, smoke, have sex, carry weapons, and eat junk food than are teens who do not engage in team sports. (One interpretation: Team sports encourage healthy living.)* Perhaps some third factor explains this correlation—teens who use drugs, smoke, have sex, carry weapons, and eat junk food may be "loners" who do not enjoy playing on any team.

(d) *Adolescents who frequently see smoking in movies are more likely to smoke. (One interpretation: Movie stars' behavior influences impressionable teens.)* Perhaps adolescents who smoke and attend movies frequently have less parental supervision and more access to spending money than other adolescents.

13. experiments

14. placebo

15. c

16. independent variable

17. b

18. d

Module 4: Statistical Reasoning in Everyday Life

19. b

20. d

21. normal curve

22. a

THE BIOLOGY OF MIND

Module 5: Neural and Hormonal Systems

1. axon

2. c

3. a

4. neurotransmitters

5. b

6. c

7. autonomic

8. central

9. a

10. adrenal glands

Module 6: Tools of Discovery and Older Brain Structures

11. b

12. d

13. c

14. cerebellum

15. b

16. amygdala

17. b

18. hypothalamus

Module 7: The Cerebral Cortex and Our Divided Brain

19. d

20. The visual cortex is a neural network of sensory neurons connected via interneurons to other neural networks, including auditory networks. This allows you to integrate visual and auditory information to respond when a friend you recognize greets you at a party.

21. c

22. frontal

23. You would hear sounds, but without the temporal lobe association areas you would be unable to make sense of what you were hearing.

24. association areas

25. c

26. ON; HER

27. a

28. b

CONSCIOUSNESS AND THE TWO-TRACK MIND

Module 8: Brain States and Consciousness

1. inattentional blindness

2. unconscious; conscious

3. inattentional

Module 9: Sleep and Dreams

4. circadian rhythm

5. b

6. NREM-3

7. It increases in duration.

8. c

9. With narcolepsy, the person periodically falls directly into REM sleep, with no warning; with sleep apnea, the person repeatedly awakens during the night.

10. d

11. The neural activation theory suggests that dreams are the brain's attempt to make sense of random neural activity.

12. The information-processing explanation of dreaming proposes that brain activity during REM sleep enables us to sift through *what one has dwelt on by day.*

13. REM rebound

Module 10: Drugs and Consciousness

14. tolerance

15. a

16. Alcohol is a disinhibitor—it makes us more likely to do what we would have done when sober, whether that is being helpful or being aggressive.

17. d

18. LSD

19. a

20. b

NATURE, NURTURE, AND HUMAN DIVERSITY

Module 11: Behavior Genetics: Predicting Individual Differences

1. chromosomes
2. gene
3. b
4. c
5. Identical
6. b
7. temperament
8. Heritability
9. environments

Module 12: Evolutionary Psychology: Understanding Human Nature

10. differences; commonalities
11. c

Module 13: Culture, Gender, and Other Environmental Influences

12. b
13. sex; gender
14. c
15. Y
16. d
17. 11; 12
18. disorder of sexual development
19. b
20. gender identity

DEVELOPING THROUGH THE LIFE SPAN

Module 14: Developmental Issues, Prenatal Development, and the Newborn

1. continuity/stages
2. b
3. c
4. teratogens

Module 15: Infancy and Childhood

5. a
6. frontal
7. b

8. We have no conscious memories of events occurring before about age 3½, in part because major brain areas have not yet matured.

9. Infants in Piaget's *sensorimotor stage* tend to be focused only on their own perceptions of the world and may, for example, be unaware that objects continue to exist when unseen. A child in the *preoperational stage* is still egocentric and incapable of appreciating simple logic, such as the reversibility of operations. A preteen in the *concrete operational stage* is beginning to think logically about concrete events but not about abstract concepts.

10. a
11. stranger anxiety
12. Before these studies, many psychologists believed that infants became attached to those who nourished them.

Module 16: Adolescence

13. b
14. formal operations
15. b
16. emerging adulthood

Module 17: Adulthood

17. a
18. Cross-sectional studies compare people of different ages. Longitudinal studies restudy and retest the same people over a long period of time.
19. generativity
20. c

SENSATION AND PERCEPTION

Module 18: Basic Concepts of Sensation and Perception

1. b
2. perception
3. d
4. just noticeable difference
5. b
6. d
7. a

Module 19: Vision: Sensory and Perceptual Processing

8. wavelength
9. a
10. c

11. c

12. d

13. Your brain constructs this perception of color in two stages. In the first stage, the lemon reflects light energy into your eyes, where it is transformed into neural messages. Three sets of cones, each sensitive to a different light frequency (red, blue, and green) process color. In this case, the light energy stimulates both red-sensitive and green-sensitive cones. In the second stage, opponent-process cells sensitive to paired opposites of color (red/green, yellow/blue, and black/white) evaluate the incoming neural messages as they pass through your optic nerve to the thalamus and visual cortex. When the yellow-sensitive opponent-process cells are stimulated, you identify the lemon as yellow.

14. feature detectors

15. parallel processing

16. d

17. a

18. b

19. c

20. monocular

21. b

22. b

23. perceptual adaptation

Module 20: The Nonvisual Senses

24. cochlea

25. The *outer ear* collects sound waves, which are translated into mechanical waves by the *middle ear* and turned into fluid waves in the *inner ear*. The *auditory nerve* then translates the energy into electrical waves and sends them to the brain, which perceives and interprets the sound.

26. Place; frequency

27. c

28. Our experience of pain is influenced by biological factors (such as sensory receptors that detect pressure), psychological factors (such as our focused attention), and social-cultural factors (such as social expectations about tolerance and expression of pain).

29. We have specialized receptors for detecting sweet, salty, sour, bitter, and umami tastes. Being able to detect pleasurable tastes enabled our ancestors to seek out energy- and protein-rich foods. Detecting aversive tastes deterred them from eating toxic substances, increasing their chances of survival.

30. Kinesthesia; vestibular sense

31. Your vestibular sense regulates balance and body positioning through kinesthetic receptors triggered by fluid in your inner ear. Wobbly legs and a spinning world are signs that these receptors are still responding to the ride's turbulence. As your vestibular sense adjusts to solid ground, your balance will be restored.

32. d

33. d

LEARNING

Module 21: Basic Learning Concepts and Classical Conditioning

1. information; behaviors

2. c

3. conditioned

4. discrimination

5. b

6. A sexual image is a US that triggers a UR of interest or arousal. Before the advertisement pairs a product with a sexual image, the product is an NS. Over time the product can become a CS that triggers the CR of interest or arousal.

Module 22: Operant Conditioning

7. Skinner's

8. shaping

9. b

10. Your instructor could reinforce your attentive behavior by taking away something you dislike. For example, your instructor could offer to shorten the length of an assigned paper or replace lecture time with an in-class activity. In both cases, the instructor would remove something aversive in order to negatively reinforce your focused attention.

11. partial

12. a

13. variable-interval

14. c

Module 23: Biology, Cognition, and Learning

15. taste-aversion

16. This finding supports Darwin's principle that natural selection favors traits that aid survival.

17. b

18. latent learning

19. observational learning

20. vicarious; vicarious

21. a

22. mirror

23. c

MEMORY

Module 24: Studying and Encoding Memories

1. recall

2. encoding; storage; retrieval

3. a

4. iconic; echoic

5. seven

6. mnemonics

Module 25: Storing and Retrieving Memories

7. a

8. implicit

9. c

10. retrieval cues

11. Memories are stored within a web of many associations, one of which is mood. When you recall happy moments from your past, you deliberately activate these positive links. You may then experience mood-congruent memory and recall other happy moments, which could improve your mood and brighten your interpretation of current events.

12. a

Module 26: Forgetting, Memory Construction, and Improving Memory

13. d

14. d

15. retroactive

16. repression

17. b

18. Eliza's immature hippocampus and lack of verbal skills would have prevented her from encoding an explicit memory of the wedding reception at the age of two. It's more likely that Eliza learned information (from hearing the story repeatedly) that she eventually constructed into a memory that feels very real.

19. source amnesia

20. déjà vu

21. b

22. b

THINKING AND LANGUAGE

Module 27: Thinking

1. concept

2. algorithm

3. Oscar will need to guard against *confirmation bias* (searching for support for his own views and ignoring contradictory evidence) as he seeks out opposing viewpoints. Even if Oscar encounters new information that disproves his beliefs, *belief perseverance* may lead him to cling to these views anyway. It will take more compelling evidence to change his beliefs than it took to create them.

4. c

5. availability

6. framing

7. b

Module 28: Language and Thought

8. c

9. phonemes; morphemes; grammar

10. telegraphic speech

11. universal grammar

12. a

INTELLIGENCE

Module 29: What Is Intelligence?

1. general intelligence (*g*)

2. c

3. academic; practical; creative

4. d

Module 30: Assessing Intelligence

5. d

6. c

7. reliability

Module 31: The Dynamics of Intelligence

8. Writers' work relies more on *crystallized intelligence*, or accumulated knowledge, which increases with age. For top performance, scientists doing research may need more *fluid intelligence* (speedy and abstract reasoning), which tends to decrease with age.

9. c

Module 32: Genetic and Environmental Influences on Intelligence

10. a

11. c

12. c

13. Stereotype threat

WHAT DRIVES US: HUNGER, SEX, FRIENDSHIP, AND ACHIEVEMENT

Module 33: Basic Motivational Concepts

1. b

2. a

3. incentive

4. Arousal

5. b

6. a

Module 34: Hunger

7. Maslow's hierarchy of needs supports this statement because it addresses the primacy of some motives over others. Once our basic physiological needs are met, safety concerns are addressed next, followed by belongingness and love needs (such as the desire to kiss).

8. homeostasis

9. c

10. glucose; low

11. basal metabolic

12. d

13. Sanjay's plan is problematic. After he gains weight, the extra fat will require less energy to maintain than it did to gain in the first place. Sanjay may have a hard time getting rid of it later, when his metabolism slows down in an effort to retain his body weight.

Module 35: Sexual Motivation

14. b

15. b

16. Sexual dysfunctions are problems that men and women may have related to sexual arousal and sexual function. Paraphilias are conditions, which may be classified as psychological disorders, in which sexual arousal is associated with nonhuman objects, the suffering of self or others, and/or nonconsenting persons.

17. does; doesn't

18. c

19. Researchers have found no evidence that any environmental factor (parental relationships, childhood experiences, peer relationships, or dating experiences) influences the development of our sexual orientation.

Module 36: Affiliation and Achievement

20. c

21. Monitor the time spent online, as well as our feelings about that time. Hide distracting online friends. Turn off or put away distracting devices. Consider a social networking fast, and get outside and away from technology regularly.

EMOTIONS, STRESS, AND HEALTH

Module 37: Introduction to Emotion

1. James-Lange

2. b

3. c

4. A polygraph measures physiological changes, such as heart rate and perspiration, that are associated with emotions. Its use as a lie detector is controversial because the measure cannot distinguish between emotions with similar physiology (such as anxiety and guilt).

Module 38: Expressing Emotion

5. facial feedback

Module 39: Experiencing Emotion

6. d

7. Positive

8. b

9. relative deprivation

Module 40: Stress and Illness

10. resistance; exhaustion

11. tend; befriend

12. b

13. d

14. c

15. Type A individuals frequently experience negative emotions (anger, depression), during which the sympathetic nervous system diverts blood away from the liver. This leaves fat and cholesterol circulating in the bloodstream for deposit near the heart and other organs, increasing the risk of heart disease and other health problems. Thus, Type A individuals actually harm themselves by directing anger at others.

16. negative

Module 41: Health and Coping

17. emotion

18. b

19. internal

20. d

21. aerobic

22. c

SOCIAL PSYCHOLOGY
Module 42: Social Thinking

1. a
2. peripheral
3. foot-in-the-door
4. Cognitive dissonance theory best supports this suggestion. If Jamal acts confident, his behavior will contradict his negative self-thoughts, creating cognitive dissonance. To relieve the tension, Jamal may realign his attitudes with his actions by viewing himself as more outgoing and confident.

Module 43: Social Influence

5. c
6. a
7. The presence of a large audience generates arousal and strengthens Dr. Huang's most likely response: enhanced performance on a task he has mastered (teaching music history) and impaired performance on a task he finds difficult (statistics).
8. deindividuation
9. group polarization

Module 44: Antisocial Relations

10. stereotypes
11. This reaction could occur because we tend to overgeneralize from vivid, memorable cases.
12. more
13. d
14. c
15. c
16. c

Module 45: Prosocial Relations

17. mere exposure
18. companionate; passionate
19. d
20. c
21. mirror-image
22. superordinate

PERSONALITY
Module 46: Introduction to Personality and Psychodynamic Theories

1. repression
2. c
3. superego
4. b

5. anxiety
6. Projective
7. d
8. a
9. a

Module 47: Humanistic Theories and Trait Theories

10. d
11. Rogers might assert that the criminal was raised in an environment lacking genuineness, acceptance (unconditional positive regard), and empathy, which inhibited psychological growth and led to a negative self-concept.
12. unconditional positive regard
13. Trait
14. c
15. b
16. b

Module 48: Social-Cognitive Theories and the Self

17. a
18. social-cognitive
19. b
20. Yes, if that self-love is of the *secure* type. Secure self-esteem promotes a focus beyond the self and a higher quality of life. Excessive self-love may promote artificially high or defensive self-esteem, which may lead to unhappiness if negative external feedback triggers anger or aggression.
21. spotlight effect

PSYCHOLOGICAL DISORDERS
Module 49: Introduction to Psychological Disorders

1. depression
2. No. Anna's behavior is unusual, causes her distress, and may make her a few minutes late on occasion, but it does not appear to significantly disrupt her ability to function. Like most of us, Anna demonstrates some unusual behaviors that are not disabling or dysfunctional, and, thus, do not suggest a psychological disorder.
3. *Susto* is a condition marked by severe anxiety, restlessness, and fear of black magic. It is culture-specific to Latin America.
4. medical
5. c

6. Critics have expressed concerns about the negative effects of the DSM's labeling. Recent critics suggest the DSM-5 casts too wide a net on disorders, pathologizing normal behavior.

7. poverty

8. d

Module 50: Anxiety Disorders, OCD, and PTSD

9. phobia

10. c

11. obsessive-compulsive

12. c

Module 51: Depressive Disorders and Bipolar Disorder

13. women's; men's

14. d

15. norepinephrine; serotonin

16. social-cognitive

Module 52: Schizophrenia

17. No. Schizophrenia involves the altered perceptions, emotions, and behaviors of a mind split from reality. It does not involve the rapid changes in mood or identity suggested by this comparison.

18. b

19. hallucination

20. a

Module 53: Dissociative, Personality, and Eating Disorders

21. c

22. c

23. b

24. b

THERAPY

Module 54: Introduction to Therapy and the Psychological Therapies

1. a

2. Insight

3. d

4. active listening

5. c

6. counterconditioning

7. systematic desensitization

8. Behavior therapies are often the best choice for treating phobias. Viewing Rico's fear of the freeway as a learned response, a behavior therapist might help Rico learn to replace his anxious response to freeway driving with a relaxation response.

9. token economy

10. d

11. Cognitive-behavioral

12. b

Module 55: Evaluating Psychotherapies

13. c

14. d

15. research evidence, clinical expertise, and knowledge of the patient

16. The placebo effect is the healing power of belief in a treatment. When patients expect a treatment to be effective, they may believe it was.

Module 56: Biomedical Therapies and Preventing Psychological Disorders

17. c

18. antianxiety

19. lithium

20. b

21. d

APPENDIX A

PSYCHOLOGY AT WORK

1. c

2. Personnel; human factors

3. a

4. d

5. Focusing on specific, short-term goals, such as maintaining a regular study schedule, will be more helpful than focusing on more distant general goals, such as earning a good grade in this class.

6. transformational

7. c

8. d

Glossary

absolute threshold the minimum stimulus energy needed to detect a particular stimulus 50 percent of the time. (p. 231)

accommodation (1) in developmental psychology, adapting our current understandings (schemas) to incorporate new information. (2) in sensation and perception, the process by which the eye's lens changes shape to focus near or far objects on the retina. (p. 187, 240)

achievement motivation a desire for significant accomplishment; for mastery of skills or ideas; for control; and for attaining a high standard. (p. 454)

achievement test a test designed to assess what a person has learned. (p. 392)

acquisition in classical conditioning, the initial stage, when one links a neutral stimulus and an unconditioned stimulus so that the neutral stimulus begins triggering the conditioned response. In operant conditioning, the strengthening of a reinforced response. (p. 284)

action potential a neural impulse; a brief electrical charge that travels down an axon. (p. 54)

active listening empathic listening in which the listener echoes, restates, and clarifies. A feature of Rogers' client-centered therapy. (p. 661)

acute schizophrenia (also called *reactive schizophrenia*) a form of schizophrenia that can begin at any age, frequently occurs in response to an emotionally traumatic event, and has extended recovery periods. (p. 641)

adaptation-level phenomenon our tendency to form judgments (of sounds, of lights, of income) relative to a neutral level defined by our prior experience. (p. 483)

addiction compulsive craving of drugs or certain behaviors (such as gambling) despite known adverse consequences. (p. 118)

adolescence the transition period from childhood to adulthood, extending from puberty to independence. (p. 203)

adrenal [ah-DREEN-el] glands a pair of endocrine glands that sit just above the kidneys and secrete hormones (epinephrine and norepinephrine) that help arouse the body in times of stress. (p. 64)

aerobic exercise sustained exercise that increases heart and lung fitness; may also alleviate depression and anxiety. (p. 508)

affiliation need the need to build relationships and to feel part of a group. (p. 448)

aggression any physical or verbal behavior intended to harm someone physically or emotionally. (pp. 162, 545)

agonist a molecule that increases a neurotransmitter's action. (p. 59)

AIDS (acquired immune deficiency syndrome) a life-threatening, sexually transmitted infection caused by the *human immunodeficiency virus* (HIV). AIDS depletes the immune system, leaving the person vulnerable to infections. (p. 436)

alcohol use disorder (popularly known as *alcoholism*) alcohol use marked by tolerance, withdrawal, and a drive to continue problematic use. (p. 120)

algorithm a methodical, logical rule or procedure that guarantees solving a particular problem. Contrasts with the usually speedier—but also more error-prone—use of *heuristics*. (p. 357)

all-or-none response a neuron's reaction of either firing (with a full-strength response) or not firing. (p. 55)

alpha waves the relatively slow brain waves of a relaxed, awake state. (p. 102)

altruism unselfish regard for the welfare of others. (p. 558)

Alzheimer's disease a neurocognitive disorder marked by neural plaques, often with an onset after age 80, and entailing a progressive decline in memory and other cognitive abilities. (p. 218)

amphetamines drugs that stimulate neural activity, causing speeded-up body functions and associated energy and mood changes. (p. 121)

amygdala [uh-MIG-duh-la] two lima-bean-sized neural clusters in the limbic system; linked to emotion. (p. 71)

androgyny displaying both traditional masculine and feminine psychological characteristics. (p. 169)

anorexia nervosa an eating disorder in which a person (usually an adolescent female) maintains a starvation diet despite being significantly underweight; sometimes accompanied by excessive exercise. (p. 651)

antagonist a molecule that inhibits or blocks a neurotransmitter's action. (p. 59)

anterograde amnesia an inability to form new memories. (p. 338)

antianxiety drugs drugs used to control anxiety and agitation. (p. 682)

antidepressant drugs drugs used to treat depression, anxiety disorders, obsessive-compulsive disorder, and posttraumatic stress disorder. (Several widely used antidepressant drugs are *selective serotonin reuptake inhibitors—SSRIs*.) (p. 683)

antipsychotic drugs drugs used to treat schizophrenia and other forms of severe thought disorder. (p. 682)

antisocial personality disorder a personality disorder in which a person (usually a man) exhibits a lack of conscience for wrongdoing, even toward friends and family members; may be aggressive and ruthless or a clever con artist. (p. 649)

anxiety disorders psychological disorders characterized by distressing, persistent anxiety or maladaptive behaviors that reduce anxiety. (p. 620)

aphasia impairment of language, usually caused by left hemisphere damage either to Broca's area (impairing speaking) or to Wernicke's area (impairing understanding). (p. 376)

applied research scientific study that aims to solve practical problems. (p. 12)

aptitude test a test designed to predict a person's future performance; *aptitude* is the capacity to learn. (p. 392)

asexual having no sexual attraction to others. (p. 433)

assimilation interpreting our new experiences in terms of our existing schemas. (p. 187)

association areas areas of the cerebral cortex that are not involved in primary motor or sensory functions; rather, they are involved in higher mental functions such as learning, remembering, thinking, and speaking. (p. 79)

associative learning learning that certain events occur together. The events may be two stimuli (as in classical conditioning) or a response and its consequences (as in operant conditioning). (pp. 280, 290)

attachment an emotional tie with another person; shown in young children by their seeking closeness to the caregiver and showing distress on separation. (p. 195)

attention-deficit/hyperactivity disorder (ADHD) a psychological disorder marked by extreme inattention and/or hyperactivity and impulsivity. (p. 615)

attitude feelings, often influenced by our beliefs, that predispose us to respond in a particular way to objects, people, and events. (p. 520)

attribution theory the theory that we explain someone's behavior by crediting either the situation or the person's disposition. (p. 518)

audition the sense or act of hearing. (p. 256)

autism spectrum disorder (ASD) a disorder that appears in childhood and is marked by significant deficiencies in communication and social interaction, and by rigidly fixated interests and repetitive behaviors. (p. 192)

automatic processing unconscious encoding of incidental information, such as space, time, and frequency, and of well-learned information, such as word meanings. (p. 321)

autonomic [aw-tuh-NAHM-ik] nervous system (ANS) the part of the peripheral nervous system that controls the glands and the muscles of the internal organs (such as the heart). Its sympathetic division arouses; its parasympathetic division calms. (p. 60)

availability heuristic estimating the likelihood of events based on their availability in memory; if instances come readily to mind (perhaps because of their vividness), we presume such events are common. (p. 359)

aversive conditioning a type of counterconditioning that associates an unpleasant state (such as nausea) with an unwanted behavior (such as drinking alcohol). (p. 665)

axon the neuron extension that passes messages through its branches to other neurons or to muscles or glands. (p. 53)

babbling stage beginning at about 4 months, the stage of speech development in which the infant spontaneously utters various sounds at first unrelated to the household language. (p. 372)

barbiturates drugs that depress central nervous system activity, reducing anxiety but impairing memory and judgment. (p. 120)

basal metabolic rate the body's resting rate of energy expenditure. (p. 427)

basic research pure science that aims to increase the scientific knowledge base. (p. 11)

basic trust according to Erik Erikson, a sense that the world is predictable and trustworthy; said to be formed during infancy by appropriate experiences with responsive caregivers. (p. 199)

behavior feedback effect the tendency of behavior to influence our own and others' thoughts, feelings, and actions. (p. 474)

behavior genetics the study of the relative power and limits of genetic and environmental influences on behavior. (pp. 7, 134)

behavior therapy therapy that applies learning principles to the elimination of unwanted behaviors. (p. 663)

behaviorism the view that psychology (1) should be an objective science that (2) studies behavior without reference to mental processes. Most research psychologists today agree with (1) but not with (2). (pp. 4, 282)

belief perseverance clinging to one's initial conceptions after the basis on which they were formed has been discredited. (p. 361)

binge-eating disorder significant binge-eating episodes, followed by distress, disgust, or guilt, but without the compensatory purging or fasting that marks bulimia nervosa. (p. 652)

binocular cues depth cues, such as retinal disparity, that depend on the use of two eyes. (p. 249)

biological perspective concerned with the links between biology and behavior. Includes psychologists working in neuroscience, behavior genetics, and evolutionary psychology. These researchers may call themselves *behavioral neuroscientists, neuropsychologists, behavior geneticists, physiological psychologists,* or *biopsychologists.* (p. 52)

biomedical therapy prescribed medications or procedures that act directly on the person's physiology. (pp. 658, 681)

biopsychosocial approach an integrated approach that incorporates biological, psychological, and social-cultural levels of analysis. (p. 9)

bipolar disorder a disorder in which a person alternates between the hopelessness and lethargy of depression and the overexcited state of mania. (Formerly called *manic-depressive disorder.*) (p. 629)

blind spot the point at which the optic nerve leaves the eye, creating a "blind" spot because no receptor cells are located there. (p. 241)

blindsight a condition in which a person can respond to a visual stimulus without consciously experiencing it. (p. 94)

bottom-up processing analysis that begins with the sensory receptors and works up to the brain's integration of sensory information. (p. 230)

brainstem the oldest part and central core of the brain, beginning where the spinal cord swells as it enters the skull; the brainstem is responsible for automatic survival functions. (p. 69)

Broca's area controls language expression—an area of the frontal lobe, usually in the left hemisphere, that directs the muscle movements involved in speech. (p. 376)

bulimia nervosa an eating disorder in which a person alternates binge eating (usually of high-calorie foods) with purging (by vomiting or laxative use) or fasting. (p. 651)

bystander effect the tendency for any given bystander to be less likely to give aid if other bystanders are present. (p. 560)

Cannon-Bard theory the theory that an emotion-arousing stimulus simultaneously triggers (1) physiological responses and (2) the subjective experience of emotion. (p. 460)

case study a descriptive technique in which one individual or group is studied in depth in the hope of revealing universal principles. (p. 28)

catharsis emotional release. In psychology, the catharsis hypothesis maintains that "releasing" aggressive energy (through action or fantasy) relieves aggressive urges. (p. 477)

central nervous system (CNS) the brain and spinal cord. (p. 60)

central route persuasion occurs when interested people focus on the arguments and respond with favorable thoughts. (p. 520)

cerebellum [sehr-uh-BELL-um] the "little brain" at the rear of the brainstem; functions include processing sensory input, coordinating movement output and balance, and enabling nonverbal learning and memory. (p. 70)

cerebral [seh-REE-bruhl] cortex the intricate fabric of interconnected neural cells covering the cerebral hemispheres; the body's ultimate control and information-processing center. (p. 74) change blindness failing to notice changes in the environment. (p. 98)

chromosomes threadlike structures made of DNA molecules that contain the genes. (p. 134)

chronic schizophrenia (also called *process schizophrenia*) a form of schizophrenia in which symptoms usually appear by late adolescence or early adulthood. As people age, psychotic episodes last longer and recovery periods shorten. (p. 641)

chunking organizing items into familiar, manageable units; often occurs automatically. (p. 324)

circadian [ser-KAY-dee-an] rhythm the biological clock; regular bodily rhythms (for example, of temperature and wakefulness) that occur on a 24-hour cycle. (p. 100)

classical conditioning a type of learning in which one learns to link two or more stimuli and anticipate events. (p. 282)

client-centered therapy a humanistic therapy, developed by Carl Rogers, in which the therapist uses techniques such as active listening within a genuine, accepting, empathic environment to facilitate clients' growth. (Also called *person-centered therapy*.) (p. 661)

clinical psychology a branch of psychology that studies, assesses, and treats people with psychological disorders. (p. 12)

cocaine a powerful and addictive stimulant derived from the coca plant; produces temporarily increased alertness and euphoria. (p. 123)

cochlea [KOHK-lee-uh] a coiled, bony, fluid-filled tube in the inner ear; sound waves traveling through the cochlear fluid trigger nerve impulses. (p. 257)

cochlear implant a device for converting sounds into electrical signals and stimulating the auditory nerve through electrodes threaded into the cochlea. (p. 259)

cognition all the mental activities associated with thinking, knowing, remembering, and communicating. (pp. 186, 356)

cognitive-behavioral therapy (CBT) a popular integrative therapy that combines cognitive therapy (changing self-defeating thinking) with behavior therapy (changing behavior). (p. 669)

cognitive dissonance theory the theory that we act to reduce the discomfort (dissonance) we feel when two of our thoughts (cognitions) are inconsistent. For example, when we become aware that our attitudes and our actions clash, we can reduce the resulting dissonance by changing our attitudes. (pp. 523, 529)

cognitive learning the acquisition of mental information, whether by observing events, by watching others, or through language. (pp. 282, 304)

cognitive map a mental representation of the layout of one's environment. For example, after exploring a maze, rats act as if they have learned a cognitive map of it. (p. 305)

cognitive neuroscience the interdisciplinary study of the brain activity linked with cognition (including perception, thinking, memory, and language). (pp. 5, 93)

cognitive therapy therapy that teaches people new, more adaptive ways of thinking; based on the assumption that thoughts intervene between events and our emotional reactions. (p. 667)

cohort a group of people sharing a common characteristic, such as from a given time period. (p. 400)

collective unconscious Carl Jung's concept of a shared, inherited reservoir of memory traces from our species' history. (p. 577)

collectivism giving priority to the goals of one's group (often one's extended family or work group) and defining one's identity accordingly. (p. 157)

color constancy perceiving familiar objects as having consistent color, even if changing illumination alters the wavelengths reflected by the objects. (p. 251)

community psychology a branch of psychology that studies how people interact with their social environments and how social institutions affect individuals and groups. (p. 12)

companionate love the deep affectionate attachment we feel for those with whom our lives are intertwined. (p. 557)

concept a mental grouping of similar objects, events, ideas, or people. (p. 356)

concrete operational stage in Piaget's theory, the stage of cognitive development (from about 7 to 11 years of age) during which children gain the mental operations that enable them to think logically about concrete events. (p. 190)

conditioned reinforcer a stimulus that gains its reinforcing power through its association with a primary reinforcer; also known as a *secondary reinforcer*. (p. 292)

conditioned response (CR) in classical conditioning, a learned response to a previously neutral (but now conditioned) stimulus (CS). (p. 284)

conditioned stimulus (CS) in classical conditioning, an originally irrelevant stimulus that, after association with an unconditioned stimulus (US), comes to trigger a conditioned response (CR). (p. 284)

conduction hearing loss less common form of hearing loss caused by damage to the mechanical system that conducts sound waves to the cochlea. (p. 257)

cones retinal receptor cells that are concentrated near the center of the retina and that function in daylight or in well-lit conditions. The cones detect fine detail and give rise to color sensations. (p. 241)

confirmation bias a tendency to search for information that supports our preconceptions and to ignore or distort contradictory evidence. (p. 357)

conflict a perceived incompatibility of actions, goals, or ideas. (p. 562)

conformity adjusting our behavior or thinking to coincide with a group standard. (p. 526)

confounding variable in an experiment, a factor other than the independent variable that might produce an effect. (p. 37)

consciousness our awareness of ourselves and our environment. (p. 92)

conservation the principle (which Piaget believed to be a part of concrete operational reasoning) that properties such as mass, volume, and number remain the same despite changes in the forms of objects. (p. 189)

content validity the extent to which a test samples the behavior that is of interest. (p. 397)

continuous reinforcement schedule reinforcing the desired response every time it occurs. (p. 293)

control group in an experiment, the group *not* exposed to the treatment; contrasts with the experimental group and serves as a comparison for evaluating the effect of the treatment. (p. 35)

convergent thinking narrowing the available problem solutions to determine the single best solution. (p. 366)

coping alleviating stress using emotional, cognitive, or behavioral methods. (p. 500)

coronary heart disease the clogging of the vessels that nourish the heart muscle; the leading cause of death in many developed countries. (p. 496)

corpus callosum [KOR-pus kah-LOW-sum] the large band of neural fibers connecting the two brain hemispheres and carrying messages between them. (p. 82)

correlation a measure of the extent to which two factors vary together, and thus of how well either factor predicts the other. (p. 32)

correlation coefficient a statistical index of the relationship between two things (from –1.00 to +1.00). (p. 32)

counseling psychology a branch of psychology that assists people with problems in living (often related to school, work, or marriage) and in achieving greater well-being. (p. 12)

counterconditioning behavior therapy procedures that use classical conditioning to evoke new responses to stimuli that are triggering unwanted behaviors; include *exposure therapies* and *aversive conditioning*. (p. 663)

creativity the ability to produce new and valuable ideas. (p. 365)

critical period an optimal period early in the life of an organism when exposure to certain stimuli or experiences produces normal development. (p. 196)

critical thinking thinking that does not blindly accept arguments and conclusions. Rather, it examines assumptions, appraises the source, discerns hidden values, evaluates evidence, and assesses conclusions. (p. 24)

cross-sectional study a study in which people of different ages are compared with one another. (p. 218)

crystallized intelligence our accumulated knowledge and verbal skills; tends to increase with age. (p. 400)

culture the enduring behaviors, ideas, attitudes, values, and traditions shared by a group of people and transmitted from one generation to the next. (pp. 7, 155)

debriefing the postexperimental explanation of a study, including its purpose and any deceptions, to its participants. (p. 41)

deep processing encoding semantically, based on the meaning of the words; tends to yield the best retention. (p. 326)

defense mechanisms in psychoanalytic theory, the ego's protective methods of reducing anxiety by unconsciously distorting reality. (p. 575)

deindividuation the loss of self-awareness and self-restraint occurring in group situations that foster arousal and anonymity. (p. 533)

déjà vu that eerie sense that "I've experienced this before." Cues from the current situation may unconsciously trigger retrieval of an earlier experience. (p. 346)

delta waves the large, slow brain waves associated with deep sleep. (p. 102)

delusion a false belief, often of persecution or grandeur, that may accompany psychotic disorders. (p. 640)

dendrites a neuron's bushy, branching extensions that receive messages and conduct impulses toward the cell body. (p. 53)

dependent variable in an experiment, the outcome that is measured; the variable that may change when the independent variable is manipulated. (p. 37)

depressants drugs (such as alcohol, barbiturates, and opiates) that reduce neural activity and slow body functions. (p. 119)

depth perception the ability to see objects in three dimensions although the images that strike the retina are two-dimensional; allows us to judge distance. (p. 249)

developmental psychology a branch of psychology that studies physical, cognitive, and social change throughout the life span. (p. 178)

difference threshold the minimum difference between two stimuli required for detection 50 percent of the time. We experience the difference threshold as a *just noticeable difference* (or *jnd*). (p. 232)

discrimination (1) in classical conditioning, the learned ability to distinguish between a conditioned stimulus and stimuli that do not signal an unconditioned stimulus. (2) in social psychology, unjustifiable negative behavior toward a group and its members. (pp. 267, 538)

disorder of sexual development an inherited condition that involves unusual development of sex chromosomes and anatomy. (p. 167)

dissociation a split in consciousness, which allows some thoughts and behaviors to occur simultaneously with others. (p. 265)

dissociative disorders controversial, rare disorders in which conscious awareness becomes separated (dissociated) from previous memories, thoughts, and feelings. (p. 646)

dissociative identity disorder (DID) a rare dissociative disorder in which a person exhibits two or more distinct and alternating personalities. Formerly called *multiple personality disorder*. (p. 647)

divergent thinking expanding the number of possible problem solutions; creative thinking that diverges in different directions. (p. 366)

DNA (deoxyribonucleic acid) a complex molecule containing the genetic information that makes up the chromosomes. (p. 134)

double-blind procedure an experimental procedure in which both the research participants and the research staff are ignorant (blind) about whether the research participants have received the treatment or a placebo. Commonly used in drug-evaluation studies. (p. 36)

Down syndrome a condition of mild to severe intellectual disability and associated physical disorders caused by an extra copy of chromosome 21. (p. 403)

dream a sequence of images, emotions, and thoughts passing through a sleeping person's mind. Dreams are notable for their hallucinatory imagery, discontinuities and incongruities, and for the dreamer's delusional acceptance of the content and later difficulties remembering it. (p. 112)

drive-reduction theory the idea that a physiological need creates an aroused tension state (a drive) that motivates an organism to satisfy the need. (p. 421)

DSM-5 the American Psychiatric Association's *Diagnostic and Statistical Manual of Mental Disorders*, Fifth Edition; a widely used system for classifying psychological disorders. (p. 613)

dual processing the principle that information is often simultaneously processed on separate conscious and unconscious tracks. (p. 94)

echoic memory a momentary sensory memory of auditory stimuli; if attention is elsewhere, sounds and words can still be recalled within 3 or 4 seconds. (p. 323)

eclectic approach an approach to psychotherapy that uses techniques from various forms of therapy. (p. 658)

Ecstasy (MDMA) a synthetic stimulant and mild hallucinogen. Produces euphoria and social intimacy, but with short-term health risks and longer-term harm to serotonin-producing neurons and to mood and cognition. (p. 124)

effortful processing encoding that requires attention and conscious effort. (p. 321)

ego the largely conscious, "executive" part of personality that, according to Freud, mediates among the demands of the id, superego, and reality. The ego operates on the *reality principle*, satisfying the id's desires in ways that will realistically bring pleasure rather than pain. (p. 574)

egocentrism in Piaget's theory, the preoperational child's difficulty taking another's point of view. (p. 189)

electroconvulsive therapy (ECT) a biomedical therapy for severely depressed patients in which a brief electric current is sent through the brain of an anesthetized patient. (p. 685)

electroencephalogram (EEG) an amplified recording of the waves of electrical activity sweeping across the brain's surface. These waves are measured by electrodes placed on the scalp. (p. 67)

embodied cognition in psychological science, the influence of bodily sensations, gestures, and other states on cognitive preferences and judgments. (p. 271)

embryo the developing human organism from about 2 weeks after fertilization through the second month. (p. 181)

emerging adulthood a period from about age 18 to the mid-twenties, when many in Western cultures are no longer adolescents but have not yet achieved full independence as adults. (p. 212)

emotion a response of the whole organism, involving (1) physiological arousal, (2) expressive behaviors, and (3) conscious experience. (p. 460)

emotion-focused coping attempting to alleviate stress by avoiding or ignoring a stressor and attending to emotional needs related to our stress reaction. (p. 500)

emotional intelligence the ability to perceive, understand, manage, and use emotions. (p. 390)

empirically derived test a test (such as the MMPI) developed by testing a pool of items and then selecting those that discriminate between groups. (p. 589)

encoding the processing of information into the memory system—for example, by extracting meaning. (p. 320)

encoding specificity principle the idea that cues and contexts specific to a particular memory will be most effective in helping us recall it. (p. 335)

endocrine [EN-duh-krin] system the body's "slow" chemical communication system; a set of glands that secrete hormones into the bloodstream. (p. 63)

endorphins [en-DOR-fins] "morphine within"—natural, opiate-like neurotransmitters linked to pain control and to pleasure. (p. 58)

environment every nongenetic influence, from prenatal nutrition to the people and things around us. (p. 134)

epigenetics the study of environmental influences on gene expression that occur without a DNA change. (pp. 143, 612)

equity a condition in which people receive from a relationship in proportion to what they give to it. (p. 557)

erectile disorder inability to develop or maintain an erection due to insufficient bloodflow to the penis. (p. 435)

estrogens sex hormones, such as estradiol, secreted in greater amounts by females than by males and contributing to female sex characteristics. In nonhuman female mammals, estrogen levels peak during ovulation, promoting sexual receptivity. (p. 433)

evidence-based practice clinical decision making that integrates the best available research with clinical expertise and patient characteristics and preferences. (p. 676)

evolutionary psychology the study of the evolution of behavior and the mind, using principles of natural selection. (pp. 7, 144)

experiment a research method in which an investigator manipulates one or more factors (independent variables) to observe the effect on some behavior or mental process (the dependent variable). By *random assignment* of participants, the experimenter aims to control other relevant factors. (p. 35)

experimental group in an experiment, the group exposed to the treatment, that is, to one version of the independent variable. (p. 35)

explicit memory memory of facts and experiences that one can consciously know and "declare." (Also called *declarative memory*.) (pp. 321, 329)

exposure therapies behavioral techniques, such as *systematic desensitization* and *virtual reality exposure therapy*, that treat anxieties by exposing people (in imagination or actual situations) to the things they fear and avoid. (p. 664)

external locus of control the perception that chance or outside forces beyond our personal control determine our fate. (p. 503)

extinction the diminishing of a conditioned response; occurs in classical conditioning when an unconditioned stimulus (US) does not follow a conditioned stimulus (CS); occurs in operant conditioning when a response is no longer reinforced. (p. 285)

extrasensory perception (ESP) the controversial claim that perception can occur apart from sensory input; includes telepathy, clairvoyance, and precognition. (p. 272)

extrinsic motivation a desire to perform a behavior to receive promised rewards or avoid threatened punishment. (p. 305)

facial feedback effect the tendency of facial muscle states to trigger corresponding feelings such as fear, anger, or happiness. (p. 474)

family therapy therapy that treats the family as a system. Views an individual's unwanted behaviors as influenced by, or directed at, other family members. (p. 670)

feature detectors nerve cells in the brain that respond to specific features of the stimulus, such as shape, angle, or movement. (p. 245)

feel-good, do-good phenomenon people's tendency to be helpful when already in a good mood. (p. 479)

female orgasmic disorder distress due to infrequently or never experiencing orgasm. (p. 435)

fetal alcohol syndrome (FAS) physical and cognitive abnormalities in children caused by a pregnant woman's heavy drinking. In severe cases, signs include a small, out-of-proportion head and abnormal facial features. (p. 182)

fetus the developing human organism from 9 weeks after conception to birth. (p. 181)

figure-ground the organization of the visual field into objects (the *figures*) that stand out from their surroundings (the *ground*). (p. 248)

fixation according to Freud, a lingering focus of pleasure-seeking energies at an earlier psychosexual stage, in which conflicts were unresolved. (p. 575)

fixed-interval schedule in operant conditioning, a reinforcement schedule that reinforces a response only after a specified time has elapsed. (p. 294)

fixed-ratio schedule in operant conditioning, a reinforcement schedule that reinforces a response only after a specified number of responses. (p. 294)

flashbulb memory a clear memory of an emotionally significant moment or event. (p. 331)

flow a completely involved, focused state of consciousness, with diminished awareness of self and time, resulting from optimal engagement of one's skills. (p. A-1)

fluid intelligence our ability to reason speedily and abstractly; tends to decrease during late adulthood. (p. 400)

fMRI (functional MRI) a technique for revealing bloodflow and, therefore, brain activity by comparing successive MRI scans. fMRI scans show brain function as well as structure. (p. 68)

foot-in-the-door phenomenon the tendency for people who have first agreed to a small request to comply later with a larger request. (p. 521)

formal operational stage in Piaget's theory, the stage of cognitive development (normally beginning about age 12) during which people begin to think logically about abstract concepts. (p. 191)

fovea the central focal point in the retina, around which the eye's cones cluster. (p. 242)

framing the way an issue is posed; how an issue is framed can significantly affect decisions and judgments. (p. 362)

fraternal twins (dizygotic twins) develop from separate fertilized eggs. They are genetically no closer than ordinary brothers and sisters, but they share a prenatal environment. (p. 136)

free association in psychoanalysis, a method of exploring the unconscious in which the person relaxes and says whatever comes to mind, no matter how trivial or embarrassing. (p. 573)

frequency the number of complete wavelengths that pass a point in a given time (for example, per second). (p. 256)

frequency theory in hearing, the theory that the rate of nerve impulses traveling up the auditory nerve matches the frequency of a tone, thus enabling us to sense its pitch. (Also called *temporal theory*.) (p. 260)

frontal lobes portion of the cerebral cortex lying just behind the forehead; involved in speaking and muscle movements and in making plans and judgments. (p. 75)

frustration-aggression principle the principle that frustration—the blocking of an attempt to achieve some goal—creates anger, which can generate aggression. (p. 547)

functionalism early school of thought promoted by James and influenced by Darwin; explored how mental and behavioral processes function—how they enable the organism to adapt, survive, and flourish. (p. 3)

fundamental attribution error the tendency for observers, when analyzing others' behavior, to underestimate the impact of the situation and to overestimate the impact of personal disposition. (p. 518)

gate-control theory the theory that the spinal cord contains a neurological "gate" that blocks pain signals or allows them to pass on to the brain. The "gate" is opened by the activity of pain signals traveling up small nerve fibers and is closed by activity in larger fibers or by information coming from the brain. (p. 262)

gender in psychology, the socially influenced characteristics by which people define *men* and *women*. (p. 161)

gender identity our sense of being male, female, or a combination of the two. (p. 168)

gender role a set of expected behaviors, attitudes, and traits for males or for females. (p. 167)

gender typing the acquisition of a traditional masculine or feminine role. (p. 168)

general adaptation syndrome (GAS) Selye's concept of the body's adaptive response to stress in three phases—alarm, resistance, exhaustion. (p. 491)

general intelligence (g) a general intelligence factor that, according to Spearman and others, underlies specific mental abilities and is therefore measured by every task on an intelligence test. (p. 386)

generalization the tendency, once a response has been conditioned, for stimuli similar to the conditioned stimulus to elicit similar responses. (p. 286)

generalized anxiety disorder an anxiety disorder in which a person is continually tense, apprehensive, and in a state of autonomic nervous system arousal. (p. 620)

genes the biochemical units of heredity that make up the chromosomes; segments of DNA capable of synthesizing proteins. (p. 134)

genome the complete instructions for making an organism, consisting of all the genetic material in that organism's chromosomes. (p. 135)

gestalt an organized whole. Gestalt psychologists emphasized our tendency to integrate pieces of information into meaningful wholes. (p. 247)

glial cells (glia) cells in the nervous system that support, nourish, and protect neurons; they may also play a role in learning, thinking, and memory. (p. 54)

glucose the form of sugar that circulates in the blood and provides the major source of energy for body tissues. When its level is low, we feel hunger. (p. 426)

grammar in a language, a system of rules that enables us to communicate with and understand others. In a given language, *semantics* is the set of rules for deriving meaning from sounds, and *syntax* is the set of rules for combining words into grammatically sensible sentences. (p. 371)

GRIT Graduated and Reciprocated Initiatives in Tension-Reduction—a strategy designed to decrease international tensions. (p. 567)

grit in psychology, passion and perseverance in the pursuit of long-term goals. (p. 455)

grouping the perceptual tendency to organize stimuli into coherent groups. (p. 248)

group polarization the enhancement of a group's prevailing inclinations through discussion within the group. (p. 534)

group therapy therapy conducted with groups rather than individuals, permitting therapeutic benefits from group interaction. (p. 670)

groupthink the mode of thinking that occurs when the desire for harmony in a decision-making group overrides a realistic appraisal of alternatives. (p. 535)

habituation decreasing responsiveness with repeated stimulation. As infants gain familiarity with repeated exposure to a stimulus, their interest wanes and they look away sooner. (p. 183)

hallucinations false sensory experiences, such as seeing something in the absence of an external visual stimulus. (p. 102)

hallucinogens psychedelic ("mind-manifesting") drugs, such as LSD, that distort perceptions and evoke sensory images in the absence of sensory input. (p. 124)

health psychology a subfield of psychology that provides psychology's contribution to behavioral medicine. (p. 492)

heritability the proportion of variation among individuals that we can attribute to genes. The heritability of a trait may vary, depending on the range of populations and environments studied. (pp. 140, 406)

heuristic a simple thinking strategy that often allows us to make judgments and solve problems efficiently; usually speedier but also more error-prone than *algorithms*. (p. 357)

hierarchy of needs Maslow's pyramid of human needs, beginning at the base with physiological needs that must first be satisfied before higher-level safety needs and then psychological needs become active. (p. 422)

higher-order conditioning a procedure in which the conditioned stimulus in one conditioning experience is paired with a new neutral stimulus, creating a second (often weaker) conditioned stimulus. For example, an animal that has learned that a tone predicts food might then learn that a light predicts the tone and begin responding to the light alone. (Also called *second-order conditioning*.) (p. 285)

hindsight bias the tendency to believe, after learning an outcome, that one would have foreseen it. (Also known as the *I-knew-it-all-along phenomenon*.) (p. 20)

hippocampus a neural center located in the limbic system; helps process explicit memories for storage. (pp. 71, 329)

homeostasis a tendency to maintain a balanced or constant internal state; the regulation of any aspect of body chemistry, such as blood glucose, around a particular level. (p. 421)

hormones chemical messengers that are manufactured by the endocrine glands, travel through the bloodstream, and affect other tissues. (p. 63)

hue the dimension of color that is determined by the wavelength of light; what we know as the color names *blue*, *green*, and so forth. (p. 239)

human factors psychology an I/O psychology subfield that explores how people and machines interact and how machines and physical environments can be made safe and easy to use. (p. A-2)

humanistic psychology historically significant perspective that emphasized human growth potential. (p. 5)

humanistic theories view personality with a focus on the potential for healthy personal growth. (p. 583)

hypnosis a social interaction in which one person (the hypnotist) suggests to another (the subject) that certain perceptions, feelings, thoughts, or behaviors will spontaneously occur. (p. 265)

hypothalamus [hi-po-THAL-uh-muss] a neural structure lying below (*hypo*) the thalamus; it directs several maintenance activities (eating, drinking, body temperature), helps govern the endocrine system via the pituitary gland, and is linked to emotion and reward. (p. 71)

hypothesis a testable prediction, often implied by a theory. (p. 26)

iconic memory a momentary sensory memory of visual stimuli; a photographic or picture-image memory lasting no more than a few tenths of a second. (p. 323)

id a reservoir of unconscious psychic energy that, according to Freud, strives to satisfy basic sexual and aggressive drives. The id operates on the *pleasure principle*, demanding immediate gratification. (p. 573)

identical twins (monozygotic twins) develop from a single fertilized egg that splits in two, creating two genetically identical organisms. (p. 134)

identification the process by which, according to Freud, children incorporate their parents' values into their developing superegos. (p. 575)

identity our sense of self; according to Erikson, the adolescent's task is to solidify a sense of self by testing and integrating various roles. (p. 209)

implicit memory retention of learned skills or classically conditioned associations independent of conscious recollection. (Also called *nondeclarative memory*.) (pp. 321, 330)

imprinting the process by which certain animals form strong attachments during early life. (p. 196)

inattentional blindness failing to see visible objects when our attention is directed elsewhere. (p. 97)

incentive a positive or negative environmental stimulus that motivates behavior. (p. 421)

independent variable in an experiment, the factor that is manipulated; the variable whose effect is being studied. (p. 37)

individualism giving priority to one's own goals over group goals and defining one's identity in terms of personal attributes rather than group identifications. (p. 157)

industrial-organizational (I/O) psychology the application of psychological concepts and methods to optimizing human behavior in workplaces. (p. A-2)

informational social influence influence resulting from one's willingness to accept others' opinions about reality. (p. 527)

informed consent giving potential participants enough information about a study to enable them to choose whether they wish to participate. (p. 41)

ingroup "us"—people with whom we share a common identity. (pp. 543, 565)

ingroup bias the tendency to favor our own group. (p. 542)

inner ear the innermost part of the ear, containing the cochlea, semicircular canals, and vestibular sacs. (p. 257)

insight a sudden realization of a problem's solution; contrasts with strategy-based solutions. (p. 357)

insight therapies a variety of therapies that aim to improve psychological functioning by increasing a person's awareness of underlying motives and defenses. (p. 661)

insomnia recurring problems in falling or staying asleep. (p. 110)

instinct a complex behavior that is rigidly patterned throughout a species and is unlearned. (p. 420)

intellectual disability a condition of limited mental ability, indicated by an intelligence test score of 70 or below and difficulty adapting to the demands of life. (Formerly referred to as *mental retardation*.) (p. 403)

intelligence the mental potential to learn from experience, solve problems, and use knowledge to adapt to new situations. (p. 386)

intelligence quotient (IQ) defined originally as the ratio of mental age (*ma*) to chronological age (*ca*) multiplied by 100 (thus, IQ × *ma/ca* × 100). On contemporary intelligence tests, the average performance for a given age is assigned a score of 100. (p. 394)

intelligence test a method for assessing an individual's mental aptitudes and comparing them with those of others, using numerical scores. (p. 392)

intensity the amount of energy in a light wave or sound wave, which influences what we perceive as brightness or loudness. Intensity is determined by the wave's amplitude (height). (p. 239)

interaction the interplay that occurs when the effect of one factor (such as environment) depends on another factor (such as heredity). (p. 142)

internal locus of control the perception that we control our own fate. (p. 503)

interneurons neurons within the brain and spinal cord; communicate internally and process information between the sensory inputs and motor outputs. (p. 60)

interpretation in psychoanalysis, the analyst's noting supposed dream meanings, resistances, and other significant behaviors and events in order to promote insight. (p. 659)

intimacy in Erikson's theory, the ability to form close, loving relationships; a primary developmental task in young adulthood. (p. 210)

intrinsic motivation a desire to perform a behavior effectively for its own sake. (p. 305)

intuition an effortless, immediate, automatic feeling or thought, as contrasted with explicit, conscious reasoning. (pp. 20, 359)

iris a ring of muscle tissue that forms the colored portion of the eye around the pupil and controls the size of the pupil opening. (p. 240)

James-Lange theory the theory that our experience of emotion is our awareness of our physiological responses to emotion-arousing stimuli. (p. 460)

just-world phenomenon the tendency for people to believe the world is just and that people therefore get what they deserve and deserve what they get. (p. 541)

kinesthesia [kin-ehs-THEE-zhuh] the system for sensing the position and movement of individual body parts. (p. 269)

language our spoken, written, or signed words and the ways we combine them to communicate meaning. (p. 370)

latent content according to Freud, the underlying meaning of a dream (as distinct from its manifest content). (p. 113)

latent learning learning that occurs but is not apparent until there is an incentive to demonstrate it. (p. 305)

law of effect Thorndike's principle that behaviors followed by favorable consequences become more likely, and that behaviors followed by unfavorable consequences become less likely. (p. 290)

learned helplessness the hopelessness and passive resignation an animal or human learns when unable to avoid repeated aversive events. (p. 501)

learning the process of acquiring through experience new information or behaviors. (pp. 280, 290, 300)

lens the transparent structure behind the pupil that changes shape to help focus images on the retina. (p. 240)

lesion [LEE-zhuhn] tissue destruction. A brain lesion is a naturally or experimentally caused destruction of brain tissue. (p. 66)

levels of analysis the differing complementary views, from biological to psychological to social-cultural, for analyzing any given phenomenon. (p. 9)

limbic system neural system (including the *hippocampus, amygdala,* and *hypothalamus*) located below the cerebral hemispheres; associated with emotions and drives. (p. 71)

linguistic determinism Whorf's hypothesis that language determines the way we think. (p. 379)

lobotomy a psychosurgical procedure once used to calm uncontrollably emotional or violent patients. The procedure cut the nerves connecting the frontal lobes to the emotion-controlling centers of the inner brain. (p. 687)

longitudinal study research in which the same people are restudied and retested over a long period. (p. 218)

long-term memory the relatively permanent and limitless storehouse of the memory system. Includes knowledge, skills, and experiences. (p. 320)

long-term potentiation (LTP) an increase in a cell's firing potential after brief, rapid stimulation. Believed to be a neural basis for learning and memory. (p. 332)

LSD a powerful hallucinogenic drug; also known as acid (*lysergic acid diethylamide*). (p. 124)

major depressive disorder a disorder in which a person experiences, in the absence of drugs or another medical condition, two or more weeks with five or more symptoms, at least one of which must be either (1) depressed mood or (2) loss of interest or pleasure. (p. 629)

mania a hyperactive, wildly optimistic state in which dangerously poor judgment is common. (p. 629)

manifest content according to Freud, the remembered story line of a dream (as distinct from its latent, or hidden, content). (p. 113)

maturation biological growth processes that enable orderly changes in behavior, relatively uninfluenced by experience. (p. 184)

mean the arithmetic average of a distribution, obtained by adding the scores and then dividing by the number of scores. (p. 43)

median the middle score in a distribution; half the scores are above it and half are below it. (p. 43)

medical model the concept that diseases, in this case psychological disorders, have physical causes that can be *diagnosed, treated,* and, in most cases, *cured,* often through treatment in a *hospital.* (p. 612)

medulla [muh-DUL-uh] the base of the brainstem; controls heartbeat and breathing. (p. 69)

memory the persistence of learning over time through the encoding, storage, and retrieval of information. (p. 318)

memory consolidation the neural storage of a long-term memory. (p. 330)

menarche [meh-NAR-key] the first menstrual period. (p. 166)

menopause the time of natural cessation of menstruation; also refers to the biological changes a woman experiences as her ability to reproduce declines. (p. 214)

mental age a measure of intelligence test performance devised by Binet; the chronological age that most typically corresponds to a given level of performance. Thus, a child who does as well as an average 8-year-old is said to have a mental age of 8. (p. 393)

mental set a tendency to approach a problem in one particular way, often a way that has been successful in the past. (p. 358)

mere exposure effect the phenomenon that repeated exposure to novel stimuli increases liking of them. (p. 551)

meta-analysis a procedure for statistically combining the results of many different research studies. (p. 675)

methamphetamine a powerfully addictive drug that stimulates the central nervous system, with speeded-up body functions and associated energy and mood changes; over time, appears to reduce baseline dopamine levels. (p. 123)

middle ear the chamber between the eardrum and cochlea containing three tiny bones (hammer, anvil, and stirrup) that concentrate the vibrations of the eardrum on the cochlea's oval window. (p. 257)

Minnesota Multiphasic Personality Inventory (MMPI) the most widely researched and clinically used of all personality tests. Originally developed to identify emotional disorders (still considered its most appropriate use), this test is now used for many other screening purposes. (p. 589)

mirror-image perceptions mutual views often held by conflicting people, as when each side sees itself as ethical and peaceful and views the other side as evil and aggressive. (p. 563)

mirror neurons frontal lobe neurons that some scientists believe fire when performing certain actions or when observing another doing so. The brain's mirroring of another's action may enable imitation and empathy. (p. 307)

misinformation effect when misleading information has corrupted one's memory of an event. (p. 344)

mnemonics [nih-MON-iks] memory aids, especially those techniques that use vivid imagery and organizational devices. (p. 325)

mode the most frequently occurring score(s) in a distribution. (p. 43)

modeling the process of observing and imitating a specific behavior. (p. 306)

molecular behavior genetics the study of how the structure and function of genes interact with our environment to influence behavior. (p. 142)

molecular genetics the subfield of biology that studies the molecular structure and function of genes. (p. 142)

monocular cues depth cues, such as interposition and linear perspective, available to either eye alone. (p. 250)

mood-congruent memory the tendency to recall experiences that are consistent with one's current good or bad mood. (p. 336)

morpheme in a language, the smallest unit that carries meaning; may be a word or a part of a word (such as a prefix). (p. 370)

motivation a need or desire that energizes and directs behavior. (p. 420)

motor cortex an area at the rear of the frontal lobes that controls voluntary movements. (p. 75)

motor (efferent) neurons neurons that carry outgoing information from the brain and spinal cord to the muscles and glands. (p. 60)

MRI (magnetic resonance imaging) a technique that uses magnetic fields and radio waves to produce computer-generated images of soft tissue. MRI scans show brain anatomy. (p. 67)

mutation a random error in gene replication that leads to a change. (p. 145)

myelin [MY-uh-lin] **sheath** a fatty tissue layer segmentally encasing the axons of some neurons; enables vastly greater transmission speed as neural impulses hop from one node to the next. (p. 53)

narcissism excessive self-love and self-absorption. (pp. 453, 604)

narcolepsy a sleep disorder characterized by uncontrollable sleep attacks. The sufferer may lapse directly into REM sleep, often at inopportune times. (p. 110)

naturalistic observation a descriptive technique of observing and recording behavior in naturally occurring situations without trying to manipulate and control the situation. (p. 28)

natural selection the principle that, among the range of inherited trait variations, those contributing to reproduction and survival will most likely be passed on to succeeding generations. (pp. 6, 144)

nature–nurture issue the longstanding controversy over the relative contributions that genes and experience make to the development of psychological traits and behaviors. Today's science sees traits and behaviors arising from the interaction of nature and nurture. (p. 6)

near-death experience an altered state of consciousness reported after a close brush with death (such as through cardiac arrest); often similar to drug-induced hallucinations. (p. 124)

negative reinforcement increasing behaviors by stopping or reducing negative stimuli. A negative reinforcer is any stimulus that, when *removed* after a response, strengthens the response. (*Note:* Negative reinforcement is not punishment.) (p. 292)

nerves bundled axons that form neural cables connecting the central nervous system with muscles, glands, and sense organs. (p. 60)

nervous system the body's speedy, electrochemical communication network, consisting of all the nerve cells of the peripheral and central nervous systems. (p. 60)

neurocognitive disorders (NCDs) acquired (not lifelong) disorders marked by cognitive deficits; often related to Alzheimer's disease, brain injury or disease, or substance abuse. In older adults neurocognitive disorders were formerly called *dementia*. (p. 218)

neurogenesis the formation of new neurons. (p. 82)

neuron a nerve cell; the basic building block of the nervous system. (p. 53)

neurotransmitters chemical messengers that cross the synaptic gaps between neurons. When released by the sending neuron, neurotransmitters travel across the synapse and bind to receptor sites on the receiving neuron, thereby influencing whether that neuron will generate a neural impulse. (p. 56)

neutral stimulus (NS) in classical conditioning, a stimulus that elicits no response before conditioning. (p. 283)

nicotine a stimulating and highly addictive psychoactive drug in tobacco. (p. 121)

night terrors a sleep disorder characterized by high arousal and an appearance of being terrified; unlike nightmares, night terrors occur during NREM-3 sleep, within two or three hours of falling asleep, and are seldom remembered. (p. 111)

nociceptors sensory receptors that enable the perception of pain in response to potentially harmful stimuli. (p. 262)

norm an understood rule for accepted and expected behavior. Norms prescribe "proper" behavior. (p. 156)

normal curve (*normal distribution*) a symmetrical, bell-shaped curve that describes the distribution of many types of data; most scores fall near the mean (about 68 percent fall within one standard deviation of it) and fewer and fewer near the extremes. (pp. 45, 396)

normative social influence influence resulting from a person's desire to gain approval or avoid disapproval. (p. 527)

object permanence the awareness that things continue to exist even when not perceived. (p. 188)

observational learning learning by observing others. (p. 306)

obsessive-compulsive disorder (OCD) a disorder characterized by unwanted repetitive thoughts (obsessions), actions (compulsions), or both. (p. 622)

occipital [ahk-SIP-uh-tuhl] lobes portion of the cerebral cortex lying at the back of the head; includes areas that receive information from the visual fields. (p. 75)

Oedipus [ED-uh-puss] complex according to Freud, a boy's sexual desires toward his mother and feelings of jealousy and hatred for the rival father. (p. 574)

one-word stage the stage in speech development, from about age 1 to 2, during which a child speaks mostly in single words. (p. 372)

operant behavior behavior that operates on the environment, producing consequences. (pp. 281, 290)

operant chamber in operant conditioning research, a chamber (also known as a *Skinner box*) containing a bar or key that an animal can manipulate to obtain a food or water reinforcer; attached devices record the animal's rate of bar pressing or key pecking. (p. 290)

operant conditioning a type of learning in which behavior is strengthened if followed by a reinforcer or diminished if followed by a punisher. (p. 290)

operational definition a carefully worded statement of the exact procedures (operations) used in a research study. For example, *human intelligence* may be operationally defined as what an intelligence test measures. (p. 26)

opiates opium and its derivatives, such as morphine and heroin; depress neural activity, temporarily lessening pain and anxiety. (p. 120)

opponent-process theory the theory that opposing retinal processes (red-green, yellow-blue, white-black) enable color vision. For example, some cells are stimulated by green and inhibited by red; others are stimulated by red and inhibited by green. (p. 244)

optic nerve the nerve that carries neural impulses from the eye to the brain. (p. 241)

organizational psychology an I/O psychology subfield that examines organizational influences on worker satisfaction and productivity and facilitates organizational change. (p. A-2)

ostracism deliberate social exclusion of individuals or groups. (p. 450)

other-race effect the tendency to recall faces of one's own race more accurately than faces of other races. Also called the *cross-race effect* and the *own-race bias*. (p. 544)

outgroup "them"—those perceived as different or apart from our in-group. (pp. 543, 564)

overconfidence the tendency to be more confident than correct—to overestimate the accuracy of our beliefs and judgments. (p. 361)

panic disorder an anxiety disorder marked by unpredictable, minutes-long episodes of intense dread in which a person experiences terror and accompanying chest pain, choking, or other frightening sensations. Often followed by worry over a possible next attack. (p. 620)

parallel processing the processing of many aspects of a problem simultaneously; the brain's natural mode of information processing for many functions. (pp. 96, 246, 320)

paraphilias sexual arousal from fantasies, behaviors, or urges involving nonhuman objects, the suffering of self or others, and/or non-consenting persons. (p. 436)

parapsychology the study of paranormal phenomena, including ESP and psychokinesis. (p. 272)

parasympathetic nervous system the division of the autonomic nervous system that calms the body, conserving its energy. (p. 61)

parietal [puh-RYE-uh-tuhl] lobes portion of the cerebral cortex lying at the top of the head and toward the rear; receives sensory input for touch and body position. (p. 75)

partial (intermittent) reinforcement schedule reinforcing a response only part of the time; results in slower acquisition of a response but much greater resistance to extinction than does continuous reinforcement. (p. 293)

passionate love an aroused state of intense positive absorption in another, usually present at the beginning of a love relationship. (p. 556)

perception the process of organizing and interpreting sensory information, enabling us to recognize meaningful objects and events. (p. 230)

perceptual adaptation in vision, the ability to adjust to an artificially displaced or even inverted visual field. (p. 254)

perceptual constancy perceiving objects as unchanging (having consistent color, brightness, shape, and size) even as illumination and retinal images change. (p. 251)

perceptual set a mental predisposition to perceive one thing and not another. (p. 235)

peripheral nervous system (PNS) the sensory and motor neurons that connect the central nervous system (CNS) to the rest of the body. (p. 60)

peripheral route persuasion occurs when people are influenced by incidental cues, such as a speaker's attractiveness. (p. 520)

personality an individual's characteristic pattern of thinking, feeling, and acting. (p. 572)

personality disorders inflexible and enduring behavior patterns that impair social functioning. (p. 649)

personality inventory a questionnaire (often with *true-false* or *agree-disagree* items) on which people respond to items designed to gauge a wide range of feelings and behaviors; used to assess selected personality traits. (p. 589)

personnel psychology an I/O psychology subfield that focuses on employee recruitment, selection, placement, training, appraisal, and development. (p. A-2)

PET (positron emission tomography) scan a visual display of brain activity that detects where a radioactive form of glucose goes while the brain performs a given task. (p. 67)

phi phenomenon an illusion of movement created when two or more adjacent lights blink on and off in quick succession. (p. 251)

phobia an anxiety disorder marked by a persistent, irrational fear and avoidance of a specific object, activity, or situation. (p. 621)

phoneme in a language, the smallest distinctive sound unit. (p. 370)

pitch a tone's experienced highness or lowness; depends on frequency. (p. 256)

pituitary gland the endocrine system's most influential gland. Under the influence of the hypothalamus, the pituitary regulates growth and controls other endocrine glands. (p. 64)

placebo [pluh-SEE-bo; Latin for "I shall please"] effect experimental results caused by expectations alone; any effect on behavior caused by the administration of an inert substance or condition, which the recipient assumes is an active agent. (p. 36)

place theory in hearing, the theory that links the pitch we hear with the place where the cochlea's membrane is stimulated. (p. 259)

plasticity the brain's ability to change, especially during childhood, by reorganizing after damage or by building new pathways based on experience. (p. 81)

polygraph a machine, commonly used in attempts to detect lies, that measures several of the physiological responses (such as perspiration and cardiovascular and breathing changes) accompanying emotion. (p. 467)

population all those in a group being studied, from which samples may be drawn. (*Note:* Except for national studies, this does *not* refer to a country's whole population.) (p. 32)

positive psychology the scientific study of human flourishing, with the goals of discovering and promoting strengths and virtues that help individuals and communities to thrive. (pp. 9, 479)

positive reinforcement increasing behaviors by presenting positive reinforcers. A positive reinforcer is any stimulus that, when *presented* after a response, strengthens the response. (p. 292)

posthypnotic suggestion a suggestion, made during a hypnosis session, to be carried out after the subject is no longer hypnotized; used by some clinicians to help control undesired symptoms and behaviors. (p. 265)

posttraumatic growth positive psychological changes as a result of struggling with extremely challenging circumstances and life crises. (p. 691)

posttraumatic stress disorder (PTSD) a disorder characterized by haunting memories, nightmares, social withdrawal, jumpy anxiety, numbness of feeling, and/or insomnia that lingers for four weeks or more after a traumatic experience. (p. 623)

predictive validity the success with which a test predicts the behavior it is designed to predict; it is assessed by computing the correlation between test scores and the criterion behavior. (Also called *criterion-related validity*.) (p. 397)

prejudice an unjustifiable (and usually negative) attitude toward a group and its members. Prejudice generally involves stereotyped beliefs, negative feelings, and a predisposition to discriminatory action. (p. 537)

preoperational stage in Piaget's theory, the stage (from about 2 to about 6 or 7 years of age) during which a child learns to use language but does not yet comprehend the mental operations of concrete logic. (p. 189)

primary reinforcer an innately reinforcing stimulus, such as one that satisfies a biological need. (p. 292)

primary sex characteristics the body structures (ovaries, testes, and external genitalia) that make sexual reproduction possible. (p. 165)

priming the activation, often unconsciously, of certain associations, thus predisposing one's perception, memory, or response. (pp. 231, 334)

proactive interference the forward-acting disruptive effect of prior learning on the recall of new information. (p. 341)

problem-focused coping attempting to alleviate stress directly—by changing the stressor or the way we interact with that stressor. (p. 500)

projective test a personality test, such as the Rorschach, that provides ambiguous stimuli designed to trigger projection of one's inner dynamics. (p. 578)

prosocial behavior positive, constructive, helpful behavior. The opposite of antisocial behavior. (p. 310)

prototype a mental image or best example of a category. Matching new items to a prototype provides a quick and easy method for sorting items into categories (as when comparing feathered creatures to a prototypical bird, such as a robin). (p. 356)

psychiatry a branch of medicine dealing with psychological disorders; practiced by physicians who sometimes provide medical (for example, drug) treatments as well as psychological therapy. (p. 12)

psychoactive drug a chemical substance that alters perceptions and moods. (p. 117)

psychoanalysis Sigmund Freud's theory of personality that attributes thoughts and actions to unconscious motives and conflicts. (2) Freud's therapeutic technique used in treating psychological disorders. Freud believed that the patient's free associations, resistances, dreams, and transferences—and the therapist's interpretations of them—released previously repressed feelings, allowing the patient to gain self-insight. (pp. 572, 658)

psychodynamic theories view personality with a focus on the unconscious and the importance of childhood experiences. (p. 572)

psychodynamic therapy therapy deriving from the psychoanalytic tradition; views individuals as responding to unconscious forces and childhood experiences, and seeks to enhance self-insight. (p. 660)

psychological disorder a syndrome marked by a clinically significant disturbance in an individual's cognition, emotion regulation, or behavior. (p. 610)

psychology the science of behavior and mental processes. (p. 5)

psychoneuroimmunology the study of how psychological, neural, and endocrine processes together affect the immune system and resulting health. (p. 492)

psychopharmacology the study of the effects of drugs on mind and behavior. (p. 682)

psychophysics the study of relationships between the physical characteristics of stimuli, such as their intensity, and our psychological experience of them. (p. 230)

psychosexual stages the childhood stages of development (oral, anal, phallic, latency, genital) during which, according to Freud, the id's pleasure-seeking energies focus on distinct erogenous zones. (p. 574)

psychosurgery surgery that removes or destroys brain tissue in an effort to change behavior. (p. 687)

psychotherapy treatment involving psychological techniques; consists of interactions between a trained therapist and someone seeking to overcome psychological difficulties or achieve personal growth. (pp. 658, 673)

puberty the period of sexual maturation, during which a person becomes capable of reproducing. (pp. 165, 204)

punishment an event that tends to *decrease* the behavior that it follows. (p. 295)

pupil the adjustable opening in the center of the eye through which light enters. (p. 240)

random assignment assigning participants to experimental and control groups by chance, thus minimizing preexisting differences between the different groups. (p. 35)

random sample a sample that fairly represents a population because each member has an equal chance of inclusion. (p. 30)

range the difference between the highest and lowest scores in a distribution. (p. 45)

recall a measure of memory in which the person must retrieve information learned earlier, as on a fill-in-the-blank test. (p. 319)

reciprocal determinism the interacting influences of behavior, internal cognition, and environment. (p. 595)

reciprocity norm an expectation that people will help, not hurt, those who have helped them. (p. 561)

recognition a measure of memory in which the person need only identify items previously learned, as on a multiple-choice test. (p. 319)

reconsolidation a process in which previously stored memories, when retrieved, are potentially altered before being stored again. (p. 343)

reflex a simple, automatic response to a sensory stimulus, such as the knee-jerk response. (p. 63)

refractory period (1) a period of inactivity after a neuron has fired. (2) a resting period after orgasm, during which a man cannot achieve another orgasm. (pp. 55, 435)

regression toward the mean the tendency for extreme or unusual scores or events to fall back (regress) toward the average. (p. 33)

reinforcement in operant conditioning, any event that *strengthens* the behavior it follows. (p. 291)

reinforcement schedule a pattern that defines how often a desired response will be reinforced. (p. 293)

relational aggression an act of aggression (physical or verbal) intended to harm a person's relationship or social standing. (p. 162)

relative deprivation the perception that one is worse off relative to those with whom one compares oneself. (p. 484)

relearning a measure of memory that assesses the amount of time saved when learning material again. (p. 319)

reliability the extent to which a test yields consistent results, as assessed by the consistency of scores on two halves of the test, on alternative forms of the test, or on retesting. (p. 397)

REM rebound the tendency for REM sleep to increase following REM sleep deprivation (created by repeated awakenings during REM sleep). (p. 116)

REM sleep rapid eye movement sleep; a recurring sleep stage during which vivid dreams commonly occur. Also known as *paradoxical sleep*, because the muscles are relaxed (except for minor twitches) but other body systems are active. (p. 101)

repetitive transcranial magnetic stimulation (rTMS) the application of repeated pulses of magnetic energy to the brain; used to stimulate or suppress brain activity. (p. 686)

replication repeating the essence of a research study, usually with different participants in different situations, to see whether the basic finding extends to other participants and circumstances. (p. 26)

repression in psychoanalytic theory, the basic defense mechanism that banishes from consciousness anxiety-arousing thoughts, feelings, and memories. (pp. 343, 575)

resilience the personal strength that helps most people cope with stress and recover from adversity and even trauma. (p. 690)

resistance in psychoanalysis, the blocking from consciousness of anxiety-laden material. (p. 659)

respondent behavior behavior that occurs as an automatic response to some stimulus. (pp. 281, 290)

reticular formation a nerve network that travels through the brainstem into the thalamus and plays an important role in controlling arousal. (p. 70)

retina the light-sensitive inner surface of the eye, containing the receptor rods and cones plus layers of neurons that begin the processing of visual information. (p. 240)

retinal disparity a binocular cue for perceiving depth: By comparing images from the retinas in the two eyes, the brain computes distance—the greater the disparity (difference) between the two images, the closer the object. (p. 249)

retrieval the process of getting information out of memory storage. (pp. 320, 329)

retroactive interference the backward-acting disruptive effect of new learning on the recall of old information. (p. 341)

retrograde amnesia an inability to retrieve information from one's past. (p. 338)

reuptake a neurotransmitter's reabsorption by the sending neuron. (p. 56)

rods retinal receptors that detect black, white, and gray; necessary for peripheral and twilight vision, when cones don't respond. (p. 241)

role a set of expectations (norms) about a social position, defining how those in the position ought to behave. (pp. 167, 523)

Rorschach inkblot test the most widely used projective test, a set of 10 inkblots, designed by Hermann Rorschach; seeks to identify people's inner feelings by analyzing their interpretations of the blots. (p. 578)

rumination compulsive fretting; *overthinking* about our problems and their causes. (p. 635)

savant syndrome a condition in which a person otherwise limited in mental ability has an exceptional specific skill, such as in computation or drawing. (p. 387)

scapegoat theory the theory that prejudice offers an outlet for anger by providing someone to blame. (p. 542)

scatterplot a graphed cluster of dots, each of which represents the values of two variables. The slope of the points suggests the direction of the relationship between the two variables. The amount of scatter suggests the strength of the correlation (little scatter indicates high correlation). (p. 32)

schema a concept or framework that organizes and interprets information. (p. 187)

schizophrenia a psychological disorder characterized by delusions, hallucinations, disorganized speech, and/or diminished, inappropriate emotional expression. (p. 640)

secondary sex characteristics nonreproductive sexual traits, such as female breasts and hips, male voice quality, and body hair. (p. 165)

selective attention the focusing of conscious awareness on a particular stimulus. (p. 96)

self in contemporary psychology, assumed to be the center of personality, the organizer of our thoughts, feelings, and actions. (p. 598)

self-actualization according to Maslow, one of the ultimate psychological needs that arises after basic physical and psychological needs are met and self-esteem is achieved; the motivation to fulfill one's potential. (p. 583)

self-concept all our thoughts and feelings about ourselves, in answer to the question, "Who am I?" (pp. 200, 584)

self-control the ability to control impulses and delay short-term gratification for greater long-term rewards. (p. 503)

self-disclosure the act of revealing intimate aspects of oneself to others. (p. 557)

self-efficacy one's sense of competence and effectiveness. (p. 599)

self-esteem one's feelings of high or low self-worth. (p. 599)

self-fulfilling prophecy a belief that leads to its own fulfillment. (p. 563)

self-serving bias a readiness to perceive oneself favorably. (p. 601)

sensation the process by which our sensory receptors and nervous system receive and represent stimulus energies from our environment. (p. 230)

sensorimotor stage in Piaget's theory, the stage (from birth to nearly 2 years of age) during which infants know the world mostly in terms of their sensory impressions and motor activities. (p. 188)

sensorineural hearing loss the most common form of hearing loss, also called *nerve deafness*; caused by damage to the cochlea's receptor cells or to the auditory nerves. (p. 257)

sensory adaptation diminished sensitivity as a consequence of constant stimulation. (p. 234)

sensory (afferent) neurons neurons that carry incoming information from the sensory receptors to the brain and spinal cord. (p. 60)

sensory interaction the principle that one sense may influence another, as when the smell of food influences its taste. (p. 270)

sensory memory the immediate, very brief recording of sensory information in the memory system. (p. 320)

serial position effect our tendency to recall best the last (a *recency effect*) and first (a *primacy effect*) items in a list. (p. 336)

set point the point at which your "weight thermostat" is supposedly set. When your body falls below this weight, increased hunger and a lowered metabolic rate may combine to restore the lost weight. (p. 427)

sex in psychology, the biologically influenced characteristics by which people define *males* and *females*. (p. 161)

sexual dysfunction a problem that consistently impairs sexual arousal or functioning. (p. 435)

sexual orientation an enduring sexual attraction toward members of one's own sex (homosexual orientation), the other sex (heterosexual orientation), or both sexes (bisexual orientation). (p. 440)

sexual response cycle the four stages of sexual responding described by Masters and Johnson—excitement, plateau, orgasm, and resolution. (p. 435)

shallow processing encoding on a basic level based on the structure or appearance of words. (p. 326)

shaping an operant conditioning procedure in which reinforcers guide behavior toward closer and closer approximations of the desired behavior. (p. 291)

short-term memory activated memory that holds a few items briefly, such as the seven digits of a phone number while calling, before the information is stored or forgotten. (p. 320)

signal detection theory a theory predicting how and when we detect the presence of a faint stimulus (*signal*) amid background stimulation (*noise*). Assumes there is no single absolute threshold and that detection depends partly on a person's experience, expectations, motivation, and alertness. (p. 231)

sleep periodic, natural loss of consciousness—as distinct from unconsciousness resulting from a coma, general anesthesia, or hibernation. (Adapted from Dement, 1999.) (p. 100)

sleep apnea a sleep disorder characterized by temporary cessations of breathing during sleep and repeated momentary awakenings. (p. 111)

social clock the culturally preferred timing of social events such as marriage, parenthood, and retirement. (p. 220)

social-cognitive perspective views behavior as influenced by the interaction between people's traits (including their thinking) and their social context. (p. 594)

social exchange theory the theory that our social behavior is an exchange process, the aim of which is to maximize benefits and minimize costs. (p. 561)

social facilitation improved performance on simple or well-learned tasks in the presence of others. (p. 532)

social identity the "we" aspect of our self-concept; the part of our answer to "Who am I?" that comes from our group memberships. (p. 209)

social leadership group-oriented leadership that builds teamwork, mediates conflict, and offers support. (p. A-12)

social learning theory the theory that we learn social behavior by observing and imitating and by being rewarded or punished. (p. 168)

social loafing the tendency for people in a group to exert less effort when pooling their efforts toward attaining a common goal than when individually accountable. (p. 533)

social psychology the scientific study of how we think about, influence, and relate to one another. (p. 418)

social-responsibility norm an expectation that people will help those needing their help. (p. 560)

social script culturally modeled guide for how to act in various situations. (pp. 150, 548)

social trap a situation in which the conflicting parties, by each pursuing their self-interest rather than the good of the group, become caught in mutually destructive behavior. (p. 562)

somatic nervous system the division of the peripheral nervous system that controls the body's skeletal muscles. Also called the *skeletal nervous system*. (p. 60)

somatosensory cortex area at the front of the parietal lobes that registers and processes body touch and movement sensations. (p. 78)

source amnesia attributing to the wrong source an event we have experienced, heard about, read about, or imagined. (Also called *source misattribution*.) Source amnesia, along with the misinformation effect, is at the heart of many false memories. (p. 346)

spacing effect the tendency for distributed study or practice to yield better long-term retention than is achieved through massed study or practice. (p. 325)

spermarche [sper-MAR-key] first ejaculation. (p. 166)

split brain a condition resulting from surgery that isolates the brain's two hemispheres by cutting the fibers (mainly those of the corpus callosum) connecting them. (p. 83)

spontaneous recovery the reappearance, after a pause, of an extinguished conditioned response. (p. 285)

spotlight effect overestimating others' noticing and evaluating our appearance, performance, and blunders (as if we presume a spotlight shines on us). (p. 598)

SQ3R a study method incorporating five steps: Survey, Question, Read, Retrieve, Review. (p. 14)

standard deviation a computed measure of how much scores vary around the mean score. (p. 45)

standardization defining uniform testing procedures and meaningful scores by comparison with the performance of a pretested group. (p. 396)

Stanford-Binet the widely used American revision (by Terman at Stanford University) of Binet's original intelligence test. (p. 394)

statistical significance a statistical statement of how likely it is that an obtained result occurred by chance. (p. 47)

stereotype a generalized (sometimes accurate but often overgeneralized) belief about a group of people. (p. 538)

stereotype threat a self-confirming concern that one will be evaluated based on a negative stereotype. (p. 414)

stimulants drugs (such as caffeine, nicotine, and the more powerful amphetamines, cocaine, Ecstasy, and methamphetamine) that excite neural activity and speed up body functions. (p. 120)

stimulus any event or situation that evokes a response. (pp. 281, 290)

storage the process of retaining encoded information over time. (pp. 320, 329)

stranger anxiety the fear of strangers that infants commonly display, beginning by about 8 months of age. (p. 195)

stress the process by which we perceive and respond to certain events, called *stressors*, that we appraise as threatening or challenging. (p. 488)

structuralism early school of thought promoted by Wundt and Titchener; used introspection to reveal the structure of the human mind. (p. 3)

structured interviews interview process that asks the same job-relevant questions of all applicants, each of whom is rated on established scales. (p. A-6)

subjective well-being self-perceived happiness or satisfaction with life. Used along with measures of objective well-being (for example, physical and economic indicators) to evaluate people's quality of life. (p. 479)

subliminal below one's absolute threshold for conscious awareness. (p. 231)

substance use disorder continued substance craving and use despite significant life disruption and/or physical risk. (p. 117)

superego the part of personality that, according to Freud, represents internalized ideals and provides standards for judgment (the conscience) and for future aspirations. (p. 574)

superordinate goals shared goals that override differences among people and require their cooperation. (p. 565)

suprachiasmatic nucleus (SCN) a pair of cell clusters in the hypothalamus that controls circadian rhythm. In response to light, the SCN causes the pineal gland to adjust melatonin production, thus modifying our feelings of sleepiness. (p. 104)

survey a descriptive technique for obtaining the self-reported attitudes or behaviors of a particular group, usually by questioning a representative, *random sample* of the group. (p. 30)

sympathetic nervous system the division of the autonomic nervous system that arouses the body, mobilizing its energy. (p. 61)

synapse [SIN-aps] the junction between the axon tip of the sending neuron and the dendrite or cell body of the receiving neuron. The tiny gap at this junction is called the *synaptic gap* or *synaptic cleft*. (p. 56)

systematic desensitization a type of exposure therapy that associates a pleasant relaxed state with gradually increasing anxiety-triggering stimuli. Commonly used to treat phobias. (p. 664)

task leadership goal-oriented leadership that sets standards, organizes work, and focuses attention on goals. (p. A-11)

telegraphic speech early speech stage in which a child speaks like a telegram—"go car"—using mostly nouns and verbs. (p. 372)

temperament a person's characteristic emotional reactivity and intensity. (p. 140)

temporal lobes portion of the cerebral cortex lying roughly above the ears; includes the auditory areas, each receiving information primarily from the opposite ear. (p. 75)

tend and befriend under stress, people (especially women) often provide support to others (tend) and bond with and seek support from others (befriend). (p. 492)

teratogens (literally, "monster maker") agents, such as chemicals and viruses, that can reach the embryo or fetus during prenatal development and cause harm. (p. 182)

terror-management theory a theory of death-related anxiety; explores people's emotional and behavioral responses to reminders of their impending death. (p. 581)

testing effect enhanced memory after retrieving, rather than simply rereading, information. Also sometimes referred to as a *retrieval practice effect* or *test-enhanced learning*. (pp. 13, 326)

testosterone the most important of the male sex hormones. Both males and females have it, but the additional testosterone in males stimulates the growth of the male sex organs during the fetal period, and the development of the male sex characteristics during puberty. (pp. 165, 433)

thalamus [THAL-uh-muss] the brain's sensory control center, located on top of the brainstem; it directs messages to the sensory receiving areas in the cortex and transmits replies to the cerebellum and medulla. (p. 70)

THC the major active ingredient in marijuana; triggers a variety of effects, including mild hallucinations. (p. 125)

Thematic Apperception Test (TAT) a projective test in which people express their inner feelings and interests through the stories they make up about ambiguous scenes. (p. 578)

theory an explanation using an integrated set of principles that organizes observations and predicts behaviors or events. (p. 26)

theory of mind people's ideas about their own and others' mental states—about their feelings, perceptions, and thoughts, and the behaviors these might predict. (p. 190)

therapeutic alliance a bond of trust and mutual understanding between a therapist and client, who work together constructively to overcome the client's problem. (p. 679)

threshold the level of stimulation required to trigger a neural impulse. (p. 55)

token economy an operant conditioning procedure in which people earn a token of some sort for exhibiting a desired behavior and can later exchange their tokens for various privileges or treats. (p. 666)

tolerance the diminishing effect with regular use of the same dose of a drug, requiring the user to take larger and larger doses before experiencing the drug's effect. (p. 118)

top-down processing information processing guided by higher-level mental processes, as when we construct perceptions drawing on our experience and expectations. (p. 230)

trait a characteristic pattern of behavior or a disposition to feel and act, as assessed by self-report inventories and peer reports. (p. 586)

transduction conversion of one form of energy into another. In sensation, the transforming of stimulus energies, such as sights, sounds, and smells, into neural impulses our brain can interpret. (p. 230)

transference in psychoanalysis, the patient's transfer to the analyst of emotions linked with other relationships (such as love or hatred for a parent). (p. 659)

transgender an umbrella term describing people whose gender identity or expression differs from that associated with their birth sex. (p. 169)

two-factor theory the Schachter-Singer theory that to experience emotion one must (1) be physically aroused and (2) cognitively label the arousal. (p. 461)

two-word stage beginning about age 2, the stage in speech development during which a child speaks mostly in two-word statements. (p. 372)

Type A Friedman and Rosenman's term for competitive, hard-driving, impatient, verbally aggressive, and anger-prone people. (p. 497)

Type B Friedman and Rosenman's term for easygoing, relaxed people. (p. 497)

unconditional positive regard a caring, accepting, nonjudgmental attitude, which Carl Rogers believed would help clients develop self-awareness and self-acceptance. (pp. 584, 662)

unconditioned response (UR) in classical conditioning, an unlearned, naturally occurring response (such as salivation) to an unconditioned stimulus (US) (such as food in the mouth). (p. 283)

unconditioned stimulus (US) in classical conditioning, a stimulus that unconditionally—naturally and automatically—triggers an unconditioned response (UR). (p. 283)

unconscious according to Freud, a reservoir of mostly unacceptable thoughts, wishes, feelings, and memories. According to contemporary psychologists, information processing of which we are unaware. (p. 573)

validity the extent to which a test measures or predicts what it is supposed to. (See also *content validity* and *predictive validity*.) (p. 397)

variable-interval schedule in operant conditioning, a reinforcement schedule that reinforces a response at unpredictable time intervals. (p. 294)

variable-ratio schedule in operant conditioning, a reinforcement schedule that reinforces a response after an unpredictable number of responses. (p. 294)

vestibular sense the sense of body movement and position, including the sense of balance. (p. 269)

virtual reality exposure therapy an anxiety treatment that progressively exposes people to electronic simulations of their greatest fears, such as airplane flying, spiders, or public speaking. (p. 664)

visual cliff a laboratory device for testing depth perception in infants and young animals. (p. 249)

wavelength the distance from the peak of one light or sound wave to the peak of the next. Electromagnetic wavelengths vary from the short blips of cosmic rays to the long pulses of radio transmission. (p. 239)

Weber's law the principle that, to be perceived as different, two stimuli must differ by a constant minimum percentage (rather than a constant amount). (p. 233)

Wechsler Adult Intelligence Scale (WAIS) the WAIS and its companion versions for children are the most widely used intelligence tests; contain verbal and performance (nonverbal) subtests. (p. 395)

Wernicke's area controls language reception—a brain area involved in language comprehension and expression; usually in the left temporal lobe. (p. 376)

withdrawal the discomfort and distress that follow discontinuing an addictive drug or behavior. (p. 118)

working memory a newer understanding of short-term memory that focuses on conscious, active processing of incoming auditory and visual-spatial information, and of information retrieved from long-term memory. (p. 321)

X chromosome the sex chromosome found in both men and women. Females have two X chromosomes; males have one. An X chromosome from each parent produces a female child. (p. 165)

Y chromosome the sex chromosome found only in males. When paired with an X chromosome from the mother, it produces a male child. (p. 165)

Yerkes-Dodson law the principle that performance increases with arousal only up to a point, beyond which performance decreases. (p. 422)

Young-Helmholtz trichromatic (three-color) theory the theory that the retina contains three different color receptors—one most sensitive to red, one to green, one to blue—which, when stimulated in combination, can produce the perception of any color. (p. 243)

zygote the fertilized egg; it enters a 2-week period of rapid cell division and develops into an embryo. (p. 181)

References

AAMC. (2012). *Diversity in Medical Education: Facts & Figures 2012*. Association of American Medical Colleges, www.aamc.org/publications. (p. 171)

AAS. (2009, April 25). *USA suicide: 2006 final data*. Prepared for the American Association of Suicidology by J. L. McIntosh (www.suicidology.org). (p. 638)

Abbey, A. (1987). Misperceptions of friendly behavior as sexual interest: A survey of naturally occurring incidents. *Psychology of Women Quarterly, 11*, 173–194. (p. 148)

Abel, E. L., & Kruger, M. L. (2010). Smile intensity in photographs predicts longevity. *Psychological Science, 21*, 542–544. (p. 498)

Abel, K. M., Drake, R., & Goldstein, J. M. (2010). Sex differences in schizophrenia. *International Review of Psychiatry, 22*, 417–428. (pp. 641, 645)

Abel, K. M., Wicks, S., Susser, E. S., Dalman, C., Pedersen, M. G., Mortensen, P. B., & Webb, R. T. (2010). Birth weight, schizophrenia, and adult mental disorder: Is risk confined to the smallest babies? *Archives of General Psychiatry, 67*, 923–930. (p. 478)

Abrams, D. B., & Wilson, G. T. (1983). Alcohol, sexual arousal, and self-control. *Journal of Personality and Social Psychology, 45*, 188–198. (p. 120)

Abrams, L. (2008). Tip-of-the-tongue states yield language insights. *American Scientist, 96*, 234–239. (p. 341)

Abrams, M. (2002, June). Sight unseen—Restoring a blind man's vision is now a real possibility through stem-cell surgery. But even perfect eyes cannot see unless the brain has been taught to use them. *Discover, 23*, 54–60. (p. 254)

Abramson, L. Y., Metalsky, G. I., & Alloy, L. B. (1989). Hopelessness depression: A theory-based subtype. *Psychological Review, 96*, 358–372. (pp. 501, 635)

Abramson, L. Y., Seligman, M. E. P., & Teasdale, J. D. (1978). Learned helplessness in humans: Critique and reformulation. *Journal of Abnormal Psychology, 87*, 49–74. (p. 501)

Acevedo, B. P., & Aron, A. (2009). Does a long-term relationship kill romantic love? *Review of General Psychology, 13*, 59–65. (p. 557)

ACHA. (2009). *American College Health Association-National College Health Assessment II: Reference group executive summary Fall 2008*. Baltimore: American College Health Association. (p. 628)

Ackerman, D. (2004). *An alchemy of mind: The marvel and mystery of the brain*. New York: Scribner. (p. 56)

ACMD. (2009). *MDMA ('ecstasy'): A review of its harms and classification under the misuse of drugs act 1971*. London: Home Office; Advisory Council on the Misuse of Drugs. (pp. 123, 124)

Adams, H. E., Wright, L. W., Jr., & Lohr, B. A. (1996). Is homophobia associated with homosexual arousal? *Journal of Abnormal Psychology, 105*, 440–446. (p. 581)

Adams, S. (2011, February 6). OCD: David Beckham has it—as do over a million other Britons. *The Telegraph* (www.telegraph.co.uk). (pp. 297, 623)

Adelmann, P. K., Antonucci, T. C., Crohan, S. F., & Coleman, L. M. (1989). Empty nest, cohort, and employment in the well-being of midlife women. *Sex Roles, 20*, 173–189. (p. 222)

Adelstein, J. S., Shehzad, Z., Mennes, M., DeYoung, C. G., Zuo, X.-N., Kelly, C., . . . Milham, M. P. (2011). Personality is reflected in the brain's intrinsic functional architecture. *PLoS ONE, 6*, e27633. (p. 591)

Ader, R., & Cohen, N. (1985). CNS-immune system interactions: Conditioning phenomena. *Behavioral and Brain Sciences, 8*, 379–394. (p. 288)

Aderka, I. M., Nickerson, A., Bøe, H. J., & Hofmann, S. G. (2012). Sudden gains during psychological treatments of anxiety and depression: A meta-analysis. *Journal of Consulting and Clinical Psychology, 80*, 93–101. (p. 675)

Adler, J. (2012, May). Erasing painful memories. *Scientific American*, pp. 56–61. (p. 333)

Adolph, K. E., Cole, W. G., Kornati, M., Garciaguirre, J. S., Badaly, D., Lingeman, J. M., Chan, G. L. Y., & Sotsky, R. B. (2012). How do you learn to walk? Thousands of steps and dozens of falls per day. *Psychological Science, 23*, 1387–1394. (p. 185)

Adolph, K. E., Kretch, K. S., & LoBue, V. (2014). Fear of heights in infants? *Current Directions in Psychological Science, 23*, 60–66. (pp. 185, 249)

Affleck, G., Tennen, H., Urrows, S., & Higgins, P. (1994). Person and contextual features of daily stress reactivity: Individual differences in relations of undesirable daily events with mood disturbance and chronic pain intensity. *Journal of Personality and Social Psychology, 66*, 329–340. (p. 481)

Agrawal, Y., Platz, E. A., & Niparko, J. K. (2008). Prevalence of hearing loss and differences by demographic characteristics among US adults: Data from the *National Health and Nutrition Examination Survey, 1999–2004. Archives of Internal Medicine, 168*, 1522–1530. (p. 375)

Agrigoroaei, S., & Lachman, M. E. (2011). Cognitive functioning in midlife and old age: Combined effects of psychosocial and behavioral factors. *The Journals of Gerontology. Series B: Psychological Sciences and Social Sciences, 66* (Suppl 1), 1130–1140. (p. 219)

Agrillo, C. (2011). Near-death experience: Out-of-body and out-of-brain? *Review of General Psychology, 15*, 1–10. (p. 124)

Ai, A. L., Park, C. L., Huang, B., Rodgers, W., & Tice, T. N. (2007). Psychosocial mediation of religious coping styles: A study of short-term psychological distress following cardiac surgery. *Personality and Social Psychology Bulletin, 33*, 867–882. (p. 513)

Aiello, J. R., Thompson, D. D., & Brodzinsky, D. M. (1983). How funny is crowding anyway? Effects of room size, group size, and the introduction of humor. *Basic and Applied Social Psychology, 4*, 193–207. (p. 532)

Aimone, J. B., Jessberger, S., & Gage, F. H. (2010, last modified February 5). Adult neurogenesis. *Scholarpedia* (www.scholarpedia.org). (p. 82)

Ainsworth, M. D. S. (1973). The development of infant-mother attachment. In B. Caldwell & H. Ricciuti (Eds.), *Review of child development research* (Vol. 3). Chicago: University of Chicago Press. (p. 197)

Ainsworth, M. D. S. (1979). Infant-mother attachment. *American Psychologist, 34*, 932–937. (p. 197)

Ainsworth, M. D. S. (1989). Attachments beyond infancy. *American Psychologist, 44*, 709–716. (p. 197)

Airan, R. D., Meltzer, L. A., Roy, M., Gong, Y., Chen, H., & Deisseroth, K. (2007). High-speed imaging reveals neurophysiological links to behavior in an animal model of depression. *Science, 317*, 819–823. (p. 634)

Akers, K. G., et al. (2014). Hippocampal neurogenesis regulates forgetting during adulthood and infancy. *Science, 344*, 598–602. (p. 330)

Aknin, L. B., Barrington-Leigh, C., Dunn, E. W., Helliwell, J. F., Burns, J., Biswas-Diener, R., . . . Norton, M. I. (2013). Prosocial spending and well-being: Cross-cultural evidence for a psychological universal. *Journal of Personality and Social Psychology, 104*, 635–652. (pp. 479, 560)

Alanko, K., Santtila, P., Harlaar, N., Witting, K., Varjonen, M., Jern, P., . . . Sandnabba, N. K. (2010). Common genetic effects of gender atypical behavior in childhood and sexual orientation in adulthood: A study of Finnish twins. *Archives of Sexual Behavior, 39*, 81–92. (p. 443)

Albee, G. W. (1986). Toward a just society: Lessons from observations on the primary prevention of psychopathology. *American Psychologist, 41*, 891–898. (p. 690)

Albert, B., Brown, S., & Flanigan, C. M. (Eds.). (2003). *14 and younger: The sexual behavior of young adolescents*. Washington, DC: National Campaign to Prevent Teen Pregnancy. (p. 155)

Alcock, J. E. (2011, March/April). Back from the future: Parapsychology and the Bem affair. *Skeptical Inquirer*, pp. 31–39. (p. 274)

Aldao, A., & Nolen-Hoeksema, S. (2010). Emotion-regulation strategies across psychopathology: A meta-analytic review. *Clinical Psychology Review, 30*, 217–237. (p. 669)

Aldrich, M. S. (1989). Automobile accidents in patients with sleep disorders. *Sleep, 12*, 487–494. (p. 110)

Aldridge-Morris, R. (1989). *Multiple personality: An exercise in deception*. Hillsdale, NJ: Erlbaum. (p. 648)

Aleman, A., Kahn, R. S., & Selten, J-P. (2003). Sex differences in the risk of schizophrenia: Evidence from meta-analysis. *Archives of General Psychiatry, 60*, 565–571. (p. 641)

Alexander, L., & Tredoux, C. (2010). The spaces between us: A spatial analysis of informal segregation. *Journal of Social Issues, 66*, 367–386. (p. 565)

Allard, F., & Burnett, N. (1985). Skill in sport. *Canadian Journal of Psychology, 39*, 294–312. (p. 324)

Allen, J., Weinrich, M., Hoppitt, W., & Rendell, L. (2013). Network-based diffusion analysis reveals cultural transmission of lobtail feeding in humpback whales. *Science, 340*, 485–488. (pp. 307, 309)

Allen, J. R., & Setlow, V. P. (1991). Heterosexual transmission of HIV: A view of the future. *Journal of the American Medical Association, 266,* 1695–1696. (p. 436)

Allen, M. S., & Jones, M. V. (2014). The "home advantage" in athletic competitions. *Current Directions in Psychological Science, 23,* 48–53. (p. 532)

Allen, M. W., Gupta, R., & Monnier, A. (2008). The interactive effect of cultural symbols and human values on taste evaluation. *Journal of Consumer Research, 35,* 294–308. (p. 266)

Allen, T., & Sherman, J. (2011). Ego threat and intergroup bias: A test of motivated-activation versus self-regulatory accounts. *Psychological Science, 22,* 331–333. (p. 599)

Allesøe, K., Hundrup, V. A., Thomsen, J. F., & Osler, M. (2010). Psychosocial work environment and risk of ischaemic heart disease in women: The Danish Nurse Cohort Study. *Occupational and Environmental Medicine, 67,* 318–322. (p. 498)

Alloy, L. B., Abramson, L. Y., Whitehouse, W. G., Hogan, M. E., Tashman, N. A., Steinberg, D. L., Rose, D. T., & Donovan, P. (1999). Depressogenic cognitive styles: Predictive validity, information processing and personality characteristics, and developmental origins. *Behaviour Research and Therapy, 37,* 503–531. (p. 636)

Allport, G. W. (1954). *The nature of prejudice.* New York: Addison-Wesley. (pp. 28, 540)

Allport, G. W., & Odbert, H. S. (1936). Trait-names: A psycho-lexical study. *Psychological Monographs, 47*(1). (p. 587)

Ally, B. A., Hussey, E. P., & Donahue, M. J. (2013). A case of hyperthymesia: Rethinking the role of the amygdala in autobiographical memory. *Neurocase, 19,* 166–181. (p. 338)

Almås, I., Cappelen, A. W., Sørensen, E. Ø., & Tungodden, B. (2010). Fairness and the development of inequality acceptance. *Science, 328,* 1176–1178. (p. 206)

Al Ramiah, A., & Hewstone, M. (2013). Intergroup contact as a tool for reducing, resolving, and preventing intergroup conflict: Evidence, limitations, and potential. *American Psychologist, 68,* 527–542. (p. 564)

Alsharif, A. (2011, September 25). Saudi king gives women right to vote. *Reuters.* (p. 168)

Altamirano, L. J., Miyake, A., & Whitmer, A. J. (2010). When mental inflexibility facilitates executive control: Beneficial side effects of ruminative tendencies on goal maintenance. *Psychological Science, 21,* 1377–1382. (p. 635)

Altman, L. K. (2004, November 24). Female cases of HIV found rising worldwide. *New York Times* (www.nytimes.com). (p. 495)

Alvarez, L., & Schwartz, J. (2014, May 30). On death row with low I.Q., and new hope for a reprieve. *New York Times* (www.nytimes.com). (p. 404)

Alving, C. R. (2011, March 2). "I was swimming in a pool of liposomes." Podcast, *Science* (www.membercentral.aas.org). (p. 106)

Alwin, D. F. (1990). Historical changes in parental orientations to children. In N. Mandell (Ed.), *Sociological studies of child development* (Vol. 3). Greenwich, CT: JAI Press. (p. 160)

Amabile, T. M. (1983). *The social psychology of creativity.* New York: Springer-Verlag. (p. 599)

Amabile, T. M., & Hennessey, B. A. (1992). The motivation for creativity in children. In A. K. Boggiano & T. S. Pittman (Eds.), *Achievement and motivation: A social-developmental perspective.* New York: Cambridge University Press. (p. 366)

Amabile, T. M., &. Kramer, S. J. (2011). *The progress principle: Using small wins to ignite joy, engagement, and creativity at work.* Cambridge, MA: Harvard Business Review Press. (p. A-11)

Ambady, N. (2010). The perils of pondering: Intuition and thin slice judgments. *Psychological Inquiry, 21,* 271–278. (p. 593)

Ambady, N., Hallahan, M., & Rosenthal, R. (1995). On judging and being judged accurately in zero-acquaintance situations. *Journal of Personality and Social Psychology, 69,* 518–529. (p. 469)

Ambrose, C. T. (2010). The widening gyrus. *American Scientist, 98,* 270–274. (p. 153)

Amedi, A., Merabet, L. B., Bermpohl, F., & Pascual-Leone, A. (2005). The occipital cortex in the blind: Lessons about plasticity and vision. *Current Directions in Psychological Science, 14,* 306–311. (p. 81)

Amedi, A., Raz, N., Pianka, P., Malach, R., & Zohary, E. (2003). Early visual cortex activation correlates with superior verbal memory performance in the blind. *Nature Neuroscience, 6,* 758–766. (p. 375)

Amen, D. G., Stubblefield, M., Carmichael, B., & Thisted, R. (1996). Brain SPECT findings and aggressiveness. *Annals of Clinical Psychiatry, 8,* 129–137. (p. 546)

American Academy of Pediatrics. (2009). Policy statement—media violence. *Pediatrics, 124,* 1495–1503. (p. 313)

American Academy of Pediatrics. (2013). Promoting the well-being of children whose parents are gay or lesbian. www.Pediatrics.aapublications.org. (p. 198)

American Enterprise. (1992, January/February). Women, men, marriages & ministers. p. 106. (p. 159)

American Psychiatric Association. (2013). *Diagnostic and statistical manual of mental disorders* (Fifth ed.). Arlington, VA: American Psychiatric Publishing. (pp. 117, 118, 436, 610, 629)

American Psychological Association. (2006). Evidence-based practice in psychology (from APA Presidential Task Force on Evidence-Based Practice). *American Psychologist, 61,* 271–285. (p. 676)

American Sociological Association. (2013, February 28). Brief of *Amicus Curiae* American Sociaological Association in support of respondent Kristin M. Perry and Respondent Edith Schlain Windsor. Supreme Court of the United States, Nos. 12–144, 12–307. (p. 198)

Ames, D. R. (2008). In search of the right touch: Interpersonal assertiveness in organizational life. *Current Directions in Psychological Science, 17,* 381–385. (p. A-12)

Ammori, B. (2013, January 4). Viewpoint: Benefits of bariatric surgery. GP (www.gponline.com). (p. 426)

Andersen, R. A. (2005, October). Dialogue: A locksmith for the mind. *Discover* (www.discovermagazine.com). (p. 77)

Andersen, R. A., Burdick, J. W., Musallam, S., Pesaran, B., & Cham, J. G. (2004). Cognitive neural prosthetics. *Trends in Cognitive Sciences, 8,* 486–493. (p. 77)

Andersen, R. A., Hwang, E. J., & Mulliken, G. H. (2010). Cognitive neural prosthetics. *Annual Review of Psychology, 61,* 169–190. (pp. 77, 78)

Andersen, S. M. (1998). *Service learning: A national strategy for youth development.* A position paper issued by the Task Force on Education Policy. Washington, DC: Institute for Communitarian Policy Studies, George Washington University. (p. 208)

Andersen, S. M., & Saribay, S. A. (2005). The relational self and transference: Evoking motives, self-regulation, and emotions through activation of mental representations of significant others. In M. W. Baldwin (Ed.), *Interpersonal cognition.* New York: Guilford. (p. 334)

Anderson, B. L. (2002). Biobehavioral outcomes following psychological interventions for cancer patients. *Journal of Consulting and Clinical Psychology, 70,* 590–610. (p. 496)

Anderson, C. A. (2004). An update on the effects of playing violent video games. *Journal of Adolescence, 27,* 113–122. (p. 549)

Anderson, C. A. (2013). Guns, games, and mass shootings in the U.S. *The Bulletin of the International Society for Research on Aggression, 35,* 14–19. (p. 549)

Anderson, C. A., Anderson, K. B., Dorr, N., DeNeve, K. M., & Flanagan, M. (2000). Temperature and aggression. In M. P. Zanna (Ed.), *Advances in Experimental Social Psychology.* San Diego: Academic Press. (p. 547)

Anderson, C. A., Brion, S., Moore, D. A., & Kennedy, J. A. (2012). A status-enhancement account of overconfidence. *Journal of Personality and Social Psychology, 103,* 718–735. (p. 361)

Anderson, C. A., Bushman, B. J., & Groom, R. W. (1997). Hot years and serious and deadly assault: Empirical tests of the heat hypothesis. *Journal of Personality and Social Psychology, 73,* 1213–1223. (p. 547)

Anderson, C. A., & Delisi, M. (2011). Implications of global climate change for violence in developed and developing countries. In J. Forgas, A. Kruglanski., & K. Williams (eds.), *The psychology of social conflict and aggression.* New York: Psychology Press. (p. 547)

Anderson, C. A., & Dill, K. E. (2000). Video games and aggressive thoughts, feelings, and behavior in the laboratory and in life. *Journal of Personality and Social Psychology, 78,* 772–790. (p. 549)

Anderson, C. A., Lindsay, J. J., & Bushman, B. J. (1999). Research in the psychological laboratory: Truth or triviality? *Current Directions in Psychological Science, 8,* 3–9. (p. 39)

Anderson, C. A., Shibuya, A., Ihori, N., Swing, E. L., Bushman, B. J., Sakamoto, A., Rothstein, H. R., & Saleem, M. (2010). Violent video game effects on aggression, empathy, and prosocial behavior in Eastern and Western countries: A meta-analytic review. *Psychological Bulletin, 136,* 151–173. (pp. 369, 549)

Anderson, C. A., & Warburton, W. A. (2012). The impact of violent video games: An overview. In W. Warburton & D. Braunstein (Eds.), *Growing up fast and furious.* Annandale, NSW, Australia: The Federation Press. (pp. 118, 549)

Anderson, I. M. (2000). Selective serotonin reuptake inhibitors versus tricyclic antidepressants: A meta-analysis of efficacy and tolerability. *Journal of Affective Disorders, 58,* 19–36. (p. 683)

Anderson, J. R., Myowa-Yamakoshi, M., & Matsuzawa, T. (2004). Contagious yawning in chimpanzees. *Biology Letters, 271,* S468–S470. (p. 524)

Anderson, R. C., Pichert, J. W., Goetz, E. T., Schallert, D. L., Stevens, K. V., & Trollip, S. R. (1976). Instantiation of general terms. *Journal of Verbal Learning and Verbal Behavior, 15,* 667–679. (p. 341)

Anderson, S. (2008, July 6). The urge to end it. *New York Times* (www.nytimes.com). (p. 638)

Anderson, S. E., Dallal, G. E., & Must, A. (2003). Relative weight and race influence average age at menarche: Results from two nationally representative surveys of U.S. girls studied 25 years apart. *Pediatrics, 111,* 844–850. (p. 166)

Anderson, S. R. (2004). *Doctor Dolittle's delusion: Animals and the uniqueness of human language.* New Haven: Yale University Press. (p. 378)

Andersson, P. L., Juth, N., Petersén, Å., Graff, C., & Edberg, A-K. (2012). Ethical aspects of undergoing a predictive genetic testing for Huntington's disease. *Nursing Ethics, 20,* 189–199. (pp. 143, 670)

Andreasen, N. C. (1997). Linking mind and brain in the study of mental illnesses: A project for a scientific psychopathology. *Science, 275,* 1586–1593. (p. 642)

Andreasen, N. C. (2001). *Brave new brain: Conquering mental illness in the era of the genome.* New York: Oxford University Press. (p. 642)

Andreasen, N. C., Arndt, S., Swayze, V., II, Cizadlo, T., & Flaum, M. (1994). Thalamic abnormalities in schizophrenia visualized through magnetic resonance image averaging. *Science, 266,* 294–298. (p. 642)

Andrews, P. W., & Thomson, J. A., Jr. (2009a). The bright side of being blue: Depression as an adaptation for analyzing complex problems. *Psychological Review, 116,* 620–654. (pp. 628, 635)

Andrews, P. W., & Thomson, Jr., J. A. (2009b, January/February). Depression's evolutionary roots. *Scientific American Mind,* pp. 57–61. (pp. 628, 635)

Angelsen, N. K., Vik, T., Jacobsen, G., & Bakketeig, L. S. (2001). Breast feeding and cognitive development at age 1 and 5 years. *Archives of Disease in Childhood, 85,* 183–188. (p. 35)

Anglemyer, A., Horvath, T., & Rutherford, G. (2014). The accessibility of firearms and risk for suicide and homicide victimization among household members. *Annals of Internal Medicine, 160,* 101–112. (p. 545)

Angoff, W. H. (1988, Winter). A philosophical discussion: The issues of test and item bias. *ETS Developments,* pp. 10–11. (p. 402)

Anguera, J. A., Boccanfuso, J., Rintoul, J. L., Al-Hashimi, O., Faraji, F., Janowich, J., . . . Gazzaley, A. (2013). Video game training enhances cognitive control in older adults. *Nature, 501,* 97–101 (p. 218)

Annan, K. A. (2001). *We can love what we are, without hating who—and what—we are not.* Nobel Peace Prize lecture. (p. 565)

Annese, J., Schenker-Ahmed, N. M., Bartsch, H., Maechler, P., Sheh, C., Thomas, N., Kayano, J., . . . Corkin, S. (2014). Postmortem examination of patient H. M.'s brain based on histological sectioning and digital 3D reconstruction. *Nature Communications, 5,* Article Number 3122. (p. 339)

Antonaccio, O., Botchkovar, E. V., & Tittle, C. R. (2011). Attracted to crime: Exploration of criminal motivation among respondents in three European cities. *Criminal Justice and Behavior, 38,* 1200–1221. (p. 162)

Antoni, M. H., & Lutgendorf, S. (2007). Psychosocial factors and disease progression in cancer. *Current Directions in Psychological Science, 16,* 42–46. (p. 496)

Antony, M. M., Brown, T. A., & Barlow, D. H. (1992). Current perspectives on panic and panic disorder. *Current Directions in Psychological Science, 1,* 79–82. (p. 625)

Antrobus, J. (1991). Dreaming: Cognitive processes during cortical activation and high afferent thresholds. *Psychological Review, 98,* 96–121. (p. 114)

Anzures, G., Quinn, P. C., Pascalis, O., Slater, A. M., Tanaka, J. W., & Lee, K. (2013). Developmental origins of the other-race effect. *Current Directions in Psychological Science, 22,* 173–178. (p. 544)

AP. (1999, April 26). Airline passengers mistakenly told plane would crash. *Grand Rapids Press,* p. A3. (p. 491)

AP. (2007). AP-Ipsos poll of 1,013 U.S. adults taken October 16–18, 2007 and distributed via Associated Press. (p. 272)

AP. (2009, May). mtvU/Associated Press survey by Edison Research. Surveys. ap.org. (p. 488)

AP. (2009, May 9). AP-mtvU poll: Financial worries, stress and depression on college campus. www.hosted.ap.org. (p. 107)

APA. (2002). *Ethical principles of psychologists and code of conduct.* Washington, DC: American Psychological Association. (p. 40)

APA. (2007). *Report of the task force on the sexualization of girls.* Washington, DC: American Psychological Association. (p. 439)

APA. (2009). *Report of the American Psychological Association Task Force on Appropriate Therapeutic Responses to Sexual Orientation.* Washington, DC: American Psychological Association (www.apa.org). (p. 167)

APA. (2010, accessed July 31). *Answers to your questions about transgender individuals and gender identity.* Washington, DC: American Psychological Association. (pp. 169, 170)

APA. (2010, November 9). *Stress in America findings.* Washington, DC: American Psychological Association. (p. 490)

Apostolova, L. G., Dutton, R. A., Dinov, I. D., Hayashi, K. M., Toga, A. W., Cummings, J. L., & Thompson, P. M. (2006). Conversion of mild cognitive impairment to Alzheimer disease predicted by hippocampal atrophy maps. *Archives of Neurology, 63,* 693–699. (p. 219)

Archer, J. (2000). Sex differences in aggression between heterosexual partners: A meta-analytic review. *Psychological Bulletin, 126,* 651–680. (p. 162)

Archer, J. (2004). Sex differences in aggression in real-world settings: A meta-analytic review. Review of *General Psychology, 8,* 291–322. (p. 162)

Archer, J. (2007). A cross-cultural perspective on physical aggression between partners. *Issues in Forensic Psychology,* No. 6, 125–131. (p. 162)

Archer, J. (2009). Does sexual selection explain human sex differences in aggression? *Behavioral and Brain Sciences, 32,* 249–311. (p. 162)

Arendt, H. (1963). *Eichmann in Jerusalem: A report on the banality of evil.* New York: Viking Press. (p. 208)

Ariely, D. (2009). *Predictably irrational: The hidden forces that shape our decisions.* New York: HarperCollins. (p. 335)

Ariely, D. (2010). *Predictably irrational: The hidden forces that shape our decisions.* (revised and expanded ed.) New York: Harper Perennial. (p. 580)

Aries, E. (1987). Gender and communication. In P. Shaver & C. Henrick (Eds.), *Review of Personality and Social Psychology, 7,* 149–176. (p. 163)

Arkowitz, H., & Lilienfeld, S. O. (2006, April/May). Psychotherapy on trial. *Scientific American: Mind,* pp. 42–49. (p. 676)

Armony, J. L., Quirk, G. J., & LeDoux, J. E. (1998). Differential effects of amygdala lesions on early and late plastic components of auditory cortex spike trains during fear conditioning. *Journal of Neuroscience, 18,* 2592–2601. (p. 626)

Arneson, J. J., Sackett, P. R., & Beatty, A. S. (2011). Ability-performance relationships in education and employment settings: Critical tests of the more-is-better and the good-enough hypotheses. *Psychological Science, 22,* 1336–1342. (p. 365)

Arnett, J. J. (1999). Adolescent storm and stress, reconsidered. *American Psychologist, 54,* 317–326. (p. 204)

Arnett, J. J. (2006). Emerging adulthood: Understanding the new way of coming of age. In J. J. Arnett & J. L. Tanner (Eds.), *Emerging adults in America: Coming of age in the 21st century.* Washington, DC: American Psychological Association. (p. 212)

Arnett, J. J. (2007). Socialization in emerging adulthood: From the family to the wider world, from socialization to self-socialization. In J. E. Grusec & P. D. Hastings (Eds.), *Handbook of socialization: Theory and research.* New York: Guilford Press. (p. 212)

Arnone, D., Cavanagh, J., Gerber, D., Lawrie, S. M., Ebmeier, K. P., & McIntosh, A. M. (2009). Magnetic resonance imaging studies in bipolar disorder and schizophrenia: Meta-analysis. *British Journal of Psychiatry, 195,* 194–201. (p. 633)

Arnone, D., McIntosh, A. M., Tan, G. M. Y., & Ebmeier, K. P. (2008). Meta-analysis of magnetic resonance imaging studies of the corpus callosum in schizophrenia. *Schizophrenia Research, 101,* 124–132. (p. 642)

Aron, A. P., Melinat, E., Aron, E. N., Vallone, R. D., & Bator, R. J. (1997). The experimental generation of interpersonal closeness: A procedure and some preliminary findings. *Personality and Social Psychology Bulletin, 23,* 363–377. (p. 557)

Aronson, E. (2001, April 13). Newsworthy violence. E-mail to SPSP discussion list, drawing from *Nobody Left to Hate.* New York: Freeman. (p. 211)

Artiga, A. I., Viana, J. B., Maldonado, C. R., Chandler-Laney, P. C., Oswald, K. D., & Boggiano, M. M. (2007). Body composition and endocrine status of long-term stress-induced binge-eating rats. *Physiology and Behavior, 91,* 424–431. (p. 428)

Arzi, A., Shedlesky, L., Ben-Shaul, M., Nasser, K., Oksenberg, A., Hairston I. S., & Sobel, N. (2012). Humans can learn new information during sleep. *Nature Neuroscience, 15,* 1460–1465. (p. 113)

Asch, S. E. (1955). Opinions and social pressure. *Scientific American, 193,* 31–35. (p. 526)

Asendorpf, J. B., Conner, M., De Fruyt, F., De Houwer, J., Denissen, J. J. A., Fiedler, K., . . . Wicherts, J. M. (2013). Recommendations for increasing replicability in psychology. *European Journal of Personality, 27*, 108–119. (p. 27)

Asendorpf, J. B., Penke, L., & Back, M. D. (2011). From dating to mating and relating: Predictors of initial and long-term outcomes of speed-dating in a community sample. *European Journal of Personality, 25*, 16–30. (p. 149)

Aserinsky, E. (1988, January 17). Personal communication. (p. 101)

Askay, S. W., & Patterson, D. R. (2007). Hypnotic analgesia. *Expert Review of Neurotherapeutics, 7*, 1675–1683. (p. 265)

Aslin, R. N., & Newport, E. L. (2012). Statistical learning: From acquiring specific items to forming general rules. *Current Directions in Psychological Science 21*, 170–176. (p. 373)

Aspinwall, L. G., Brown, T. R., & Tabery, J. (2012). The double-edged sword: Does biomechanism increase or decrease judges' sentencing of psychopaths? *Science, 337*, 846–849. (p. 519)

Aspinwall, L. G., & Tedeschi, R. G. (2010). The value of positive psychology for health psychology: Progress and pitfalls in examining the relation of positive phenomena to health. *Annals of Behavioral Medicine, 39*, 4–15. (p. 504)

ASPS. (2010). *2010 report of the 2009 statistics: National Clearinghouse of Plastic Surgery Statistics.* American Society of Plastic Surgeons (www.plasticsurgery.org). (p. 554)

Aspy, C. B., Vesely, S. K., Oman, R. F., Rodine, S., Marshall, L., & McLeroy, K. (2007). Parental communication and youth sexual behaviour. *Journal of Adolescence, 30*, 449–466. (p. 438)

Assanand, S., Pinel, J. P. J., & Lehman, D. R. (1998). Personal theories of hunger and eating. *Journal of Applied Social Psychology, 28*, 998–1015. (p. 427)

Astin, A. W., Astin, H. S., & Lindholm, J. A. (2004). *Spirituality in higher education: A national study of college students' search for meaning and purpose.* Los Angeles: Higher Education Research Institute, UCLA. (p. 210)

Atkinson, R. C., & Shiffrin, R. M. (1968). Human memory: A control system and its control processes. In K. Spence (Ed.), *The psychology of learning and motivation* (Vol. 2). New York: Academic Press. (p. 320)

Austin, E. J., Deary, I. J., Whiteman, M. C., Fowkes, F. G. R., Pedersen, N. L., Rabbitt, P., Bent, N., & McInnes, L. (2002). Relationships between ability and personality: Does intelligence contribute positively to personal and social adjustment? *Personality and Individual Differences, 32*, 1391–1411. (p. 404)

Australian Unity. (2008). *What makes us happy? The Australian Unity Wellbeing Index.* South Melbourne: Australian Unity. (p. 482)

Auyeung, B., Baron-Cohen, S., Ashwin, E., Knickmeyer, R., Taylor, K., Hackett, G., & Hines, M. (2009). Fetal testosterone predicts sexually differentiated childhood behavior in girls and in boys. *Psychological Science, 20*, 144–148. (p. 193)

Averill, J. R. (1983). Studies on anger and aggression: Implications for theories of emotion. *American Psychologist, 38*, 1145–1160. (pp. 477, 478)

Averill, J. R. (1993). William James's other theory of emotion. In M. E. Donnelly (Ed.), *Reinterpreting the legacy of William James.* Washington, DC: American Psychological Association. (p. 461)

Aviezer, H., Hassin, R. R., Ryan, J., Grady, C., Susskind, J., Anderson, A., Moscovitch, M., & Bentin, S. (2008). Angry, disgusted, or afraid? Studies on the malleability of emotion perception. *Psychological Science, 19*, 724–732. (p. 473)

Ayan, S. (2009, April/May). Laughing matters. *Scientific American Mind*, pp. 24–31. (p. 506)

Aydin, N., Fischer, P., & Frey, D. (2010). Turning to God in the face of estracism: Effects of social exclusion on religiousness. *Personality and Social Psychology Bulletin, 36*, 742–753. (p. 451)

Azar, B. (1998, June). Why can't this man feel whether or not he's standing up? *APA Monitor* (www.apa.org/monitor/jun98/touch.html). (p. 269)

Azevedo, F. A., Carvalho, L. R., Grinberg, L. T., Farfel, J. M., Ferretti, R. E., Leite, R. E., . . . Herculano-Houzel, S. (2009). Equal numbers of neuronal and nonneuronal cells make the human brain an isometrically scaled-up primate brain. *Journal of Comparative Neurology, 513*, 532–541. (p. 62)

Baas, M., De Dreu, C. K. W., & Nijstad, B. A. (2008). A meta-analysis of 25 years of mood-creativity research: hedonic tone, activation, or regulatory focus? *Psychological Bulletin, 134*, 779–806. (p. 479)

Babad, E., Bernieri, F., & Rosenthal, R. (1991). Students as judges of teachers' verbal and nonverbal behavior. *American Educational Research Journal, 28*, 211–234. (p. 469)

Babyak, M., Blumenthal, J. A., Herman, S., Khatri, P., Doraiswamy, M., Moore, K., . . . Krishnan, K. R. (2000). Exercise treatment for major depression: Maintenance of therapeutic benefit at ten months. *Psychosomatic Medicine, 62*, 633–638. (p. 508)

Bachman, J., O'Malley, P. M., Schulenberg, J. E., Johnston, L. D., Freedman-Doan, P., & Messersmith, E. E. (2007). *The education-drug use connection: How successes and failures in school relate to adolescent smoking, drinking, drug use, and delinquency.* Mahwah, NJ: Earlbaum. (p. 129)

Back, M. D., Stopfer, J. M., Vazire, S., Gaddis, S., Schmukle, S. C., Egloff, B., & Gosling, S. D. (2010). Facebook profiles reflect actual personality not self-idealization. *Psychological Science, 21*, 372–374. (pp. 453, 593)

Backman, L., & Dixon, R. A. (1992). Psychological compensation: A theoretical framework. *Psychological Bulletin, 112*, 259–283. (p. 375)

Backman, L., & MacDonald, S. W. S. (2006). Death and cognition: Synthesis and outlook. *European Psychologist, 11*, 224–235. (p. 218)

Baddeley, A. D. (1982). *Your memory: A user's guide.* New York: Macmillan. (p. 319)

Baddeley, A. D. (1998). The central executive: A concept and some misconceptions. *Journal of the International Neuropsychological Society, 4*, 523–526. (p. 321)

Baddeley, A. D. (2001). Is working memory still working? *American Psychologist, 56*, 849–864. (p. 320)

Baddeley, A. D. (2002, June). Is working memory still working? *European Psychologist, 7*, 85–97. (pp. 320, 321)

Baddeley, A. D., Thomson, N., & Buchanan, M. (1975). Word length and the structure of short-term memory. *Journal of Verbal Learning and Verbal Behavior, 14*, 575–589. (p. 323)

Baddeley, J. L., & Singer J. A. (2009). A social interactional model of bereavement narrative disclosure. *Review of General Psychology, 13*, 202–218. (p. 225)

Bagemihl, B. (1999). *Biological exuberance: Animal homosexuality and natural diversity.* New York: St. Martins. (p. 443)

Baglioni, C., Battagliese, G., Feige, B., Spiegelhalder, K., Nissen, C., Voderholzer, U., Lombardo, C., & Riemann, D. (2011). Insomnia as a predictor of depression: A meta-analytic evaluation of longitudinal epidemiological studies. *Journal of Affective Disorders, 135*, 10–19. (p. 110)

Bahrick, H. P. (1984). Semantic memory content in permastore: 50 years of memory for Spanish learned in school. *Journal of Experimental Psychology: General, 111*, 1–29. (pp. 340, 341)

Bahrick, H. P., Bahrick, L. E., Bahrick, A. S., & Bahrick, P. E. (1993). Maintenance of foreign language vocabulary and the spacing effect. *Psychological Science, 4*, 316–321. (p. 326)

Bahrick, H. P., Bahrick, P. O., & Wittlinger, R. P. (1975). Fifty years of memory for names and faces: A cross-sectional approach. *Journal of Experimental Psychology: General, 104*, 54–75. (p. 319)

Bailenson, J. N., Iyengar, S., & Yee, N. (2005). *Facial identity capture and presidential candidate preference.* Paper presented at the Annual Conference of the International Communication Association. (p. 552)

Bailey, J. M., Gaulin, S., Agyei, Y., & Gladue, B. A. (1994). Effects of gender and sexual orientation on evolutionary relevant aspects of human mating psychology. *Journal of Personality and Social Psychology, 66*, 1081–1093. (p. 147)

Bailey, J. M., Kirk, K. M., Zhu, G., Dunne, M. P., & Martin, N. G. (2000). Do individual differences in sociosexuality represent genetic or environmentally contingent strategies? Evidence from the Australian twin registry. *Journal of Personality and Social Psychology, 78*, 537–545. (p. 148)

Bailey, K., West, R., & Anderson, C. A. (2011). The influence of video games on social, cognitive, and affective information processing. In J. Decety & J. Cacioppo (eds.), *Handbook of social neuroscience.* New York: Oxford. (p. 615)

Bailey, R. E., & Gillaspy, J. A., Jr. (2005). Operant psychology goes to the fair: Marian and Keller Breland in the popular press, 1947–1966. *The Behavior Analyst, 28*, 143–159. (p. 279)

Bailine, S., Fink, M., Knapp, R., Petrides, G., Husain, M. M., Rasmussen, K., . . . Kellner, C. H. (2010). Electroconvulsive therapy is equally effective in unipolar and bipolar depression. *Acta Psychiatrica Scandinavica, 121*, 431–436. (p. 685)

Baillargeon, R. (1995). A model of physical reasoning in infancy. In C. Rovee-Collier & L. P. Lipsitt (Eds.), *Advances in infancy research* (Vol. 9). Stamford, CT: Ablex. (p. 188)

Baillargeon, R. (2008). Innate ideas revisited: For a principle of persistence in infants' physical reasoning. *Perspectives in Psychological Science, 3*, 2–13. (p. 188)

Bak, T. H., Nissan, J. J., Allerhand, M. M., & Deary, I. J. (2014, June). Does bilingualism influence cognitive aging? *Annals of Neurology, 75*, 959–963. (p. 381)

Baker, D. H., & Cass, J. R. (2013). A dissociation of performance and awareness during binocular rivalry. *Psychological Science, 24*, 2563–2568. (p. 94)

Baker, M. & Maner, J. (2009). Male risk-taking as a context-sensitive signaling device. *Journal of Experimental Social Psychology, 45,* 1136–1139. (p. 149)

Baker, T. B., McFall, R. M., & Shoham, V. (2008). Current status and future prospects of clinical psychology: Toward a scientifically principles approach to mental and behavioral health care. *Psychological Science in the Public Interest, 9,* 67–103. (p. 676)

Baker, T. B., Piper, M. E., McCarthy, D. E., Majeskie, M. R., & Fiore, M. C. (2004). Addiction motivation reformulated: An affective processing model of negative reinforcement. *Psychological Review, 111,* 33–51. (p. 292)

Bakermans-Kranenburg, M. J., van IJzendoorn, M. H., & Juffer, F. (2003). Less is more: Meta-analyses of sensitivity and attachment interventions in early childhood. *Psychological Bulletin, 129,* 195–215. (p. 198)

Balcetis, E., & Dunning, D. (2010). Wishful seeing: More desire objects are seen as closer. *Psychological Science, 21,* 147–152. (p. 238)

Balsam, K. F., Beauchaine, T. P., Rothblum, E. S., & Solomon, S. E. (2008). Three-year follow-up of same-sex couples who had civil unions in Vermont, same-sex couples not in civil unions, and heterosexual married couples. *Developmental Psychology, 44,* 102–116. (p. 220)

Balter, M. (2010). Animal communication helps reveal roots of language. *Science, 328,* 969–970. (p. 377)

Balter, M. (2014). Science misused to justify Ugandan antigay law. *Science, 343,* 956. (p. 446)

Baltes, P. B. (1993). The aging mind: Potential and limits. *The Gerontologist, 33,* 580–594. (p. 400)

Baltes, P. B. (1994). *Life-span developmental psychology: On the overall landscape of human development.* Invited address, American Psychological Association convention. (p. 400)

Baltes, P. B., & Baltes, M. M. (1999, September-October). Harvesting the fruits of age: Growing older, growing wise. *Science and the Spirit,* pp. 11–14. (p. 400)

Bambico, F. R., Nguyen N-T., Katz, N., & Gobbi, G. (2010). Chronic exposure to cannabinoids during adolescence but not during adulthood impairs emotional behaviour and monoaminergic neurotransmission. *Neurobiology of Disease, 37,* 641–655. (p. 125)

Banaji, M. R., & Greenwald, A. G. (2013). *Blindspot: Hidden biases of good people.* New York: Delacorte Press. (p. 539)

Bancroft, J., Loftus, J., & Long, J. S. (2003). Distress about sex: A national survey of women in heterosexual relationships. *Archives of Sexual Behavior, 32,* 193–208. (p. 435)

Bandura, A. (1982). The psychology of chance encounters and life paths. *American Psychologist, 37,* 747–755. (p. 220)

Bandura, A. (1986). *Social foundations of thought and action: A social-cognitive theory.* Englewood Cliffs, NJ: Prentice-Hall. (pp. 594, 595)

Bandura, A. (2005). The evolution of social cognitive theory. In K. G. Smith & M. A. Hitt (Eds.), *Great minds in management: The process of theory development.* Oxford: Oxford University Press. (pp. 220, 306)

Bandura, A. (2006). Toward a psychology of human agency. *Perspectives on Psychological Science, 1,* 164–180. (pp. 594, 595)

Bandura, A. (2008). An agentic perspective on positive psychology. In S. J. Lopez (Ed.), *The science of human flourishing.* Westport, CT: Praeger. (p. 594)

Bandura, A., Ross, D., & Ross, S. A. (1961). Transmission of aggression through imitation of aggressive models. *Journal of Abnormal and Social Psychology, 63,* 575–582. (p. 306)

Banville, J. (2012, April). APA weighs in on the constitutionality of life without parole for juvenile offenders. *Monitor on Psychology,* p. 12. (p. 205)

Bao, A-M., & Swaab, D. F. (2011). Sexual differentiation of the human brain: Relation to gender identity, sexual orientation and neuropsychiatric disorders. *Frontiers in Neuroendocrinology, 32,* 214–226. (p. 443)

Barash, D. P. (2006, July 14). I am, therefore I think. *Chronicle of Higher Education,* pp. B9, B10. (p. 92)

Barash, D. P. (2012). *Homo mysterius: Evolutionary puzzles of human nature.* New York: Oxford University Press. (p. 150)

Barbaresi. W. J., Katusic, S. KI., Colligan, R. C., Weaver, A. L., & Jacobsen, S. J. (2007). Modifiers of long-term school outcomes for children with attention-deficit/hyperactivity disorder: Does treatment with stimulant medication make a difference? Results from a population-based study. *Journal of Developmental and Behavioral Pediatrics, 28,* 274–287. (p. 615)

Bargh, J. A., & Chartrand, T. L. (1999). The unbearable automaticity of being. *American Psychologist, 54,* 462–479. (pp. 94, 580)

Bargh, J. A., & McKenna, K. Y. A. (2004). The Internet and social life. *Annual Review of Psychology, 55,* 573–590. (p. 552)

Bargh, J. A., McKenna, K. Y. A., & Fitzsimons, G. M. (2002). Can you see the real me? Activation and expression of the "true self" on the Internet. *Journal of Social Issues, 58,* 33–48. (p. 552)

Bargh, J. A., & Morsella, E. (2008). The unconscious mind. *Perspectives on Psychological Science, 3,* 73–79. (p. 581)

Bar-Haim, Y., Lamy, D., Pergamin, L., Bakermans-Kranenburg, M. J., & van IJzendoorn, M. H. (2007). Threat-related attentional bias in anxious and nonanxious individuals: A meta-analytic study. *Psychological Bulletin, 133,* 1–24. (p. 624)

Barinaga, M. B. (1992a). The brain remaps its own contours. *Science, 258,* 216–218. (p. 81)

Barinaga, M. B. (1997). How exercise works its magic. *Science, 276,* 1325. (p. 507)

Barinaga, M. B. (1999). Salmon follow watery odors home. *Science, 286,* 705–706. (p. 268)

Barkley, R. A., et al. (2002). International consensus statement (January 2002). *Clinical Child and Family Psychology Review, 5*(2), 89–111. (p. 615)

Barkley-Levenson, E., & Galván, A. (2014). Neural representation of expected value in the adolescent brain. *PNAS, 111,* 1646–1651. (p. 205)

Barlow, D. H. (2010). Negative effects from psychological treatments: A perspective. *American Psychologist, 65,* 13–20. (p. 676)

Barlow, F. K., Paolini, S., Pedersen, A., Hornsey, M. J., Radke, H. R. M., Harwood, J., Rubin, M., & Sibley, C. G. (2012). The contact caveat: Negative contact predicts increased prejudice more than positive contact predicts reduced prejudice. *Personality and Social Psychology Bulletin, 38,* 1629–1643. (p. 564)

Barlow, M., Woodman, T., & Hardy, L. (2013). Great expectations: Different high-risk activities satisfy different motives. *Journal of Personality and Social Psychology, 105,* 458–475. (p. 422)

Barnier, A. J., & McConkey, K. M. (2004). Defining and identifying the highly hypnotizable person. In M. Heap, R. J. Brown, & D. A. Oakley (Eds.), *High hypnotisability: Theoretical, experimental and clinical issues.* London: Brunner-Routledge. (p. 265)

Baron-Cohen, S. (2008). Autism, hypersystemizing, and truth. *Quarterly Journal of Experimental Psychology, 61,* 64–75. (p. 193)

Baron-Cohen, S. (2009). Autism: The empathizing-systemizing (E-S) theory. *The Year in Cognitive Neuroscience, 1156,* 68–80. (p. 193)

Baron-Cohen, S. (2012, November). Autism and the technical mind. *Scientific American,* pp. 72–75. (p. 193)

Baron-Cohen, S., Golan, O., Chapman, E., & Granader, Y. (2007). Transported to a world of emotion. *The Psychologist, 20,* 76–77. (p. 194)

Baron-Cohen, S., Leslie, A. M., & Frith, U. (1985). Does the autistic child have a "theory of mind"? *Cognition, 21,* 37–46. (p. 190)

Barrera, T. L., Mott, J. M., Hofstein, R. F., & Teng, E. J. (2013). A meta-analytic review of exposure in group cognitive behavioral therapy for posttraumatic stress disorder. *Clinical Psychology Review, 33,* 24–32. (p. 664)

Barrett, D. (2011, November/December). Answers in your dreams. *Scientific American Mind,* pp. 27–35. (p. 106)

Barrett, L. F. (2006). Are emotions natural kinds? *Perspectives on Psychological Science, 1,* 28–58. (p. 461, 466)

Barrett, L. F. (2012). Emotions are real. *Emotion, 12,* 413–429. (p. 459)

Barrett, L. F. (2013). Quoted by Fischer, S. About face: Emotional and facial expressions may not be directly related. *Boston Magazine.* (p. 459)

Barrett, L. F., & Bliss-Moreau, E. (2009). She's emotional. He's having a bad day: Attributional explanations for emotion stereotypes. *Emotion, 9,* 649–658. (p. 471)

Barrett, L. F., Lane, R. D., Sechrest, L., & Schwartz, G. E. (2000). Sex differences in emotional awareness. *Personality and Social Psychology Bulletin, 26,* 1027–1035. (p. 470)

Barrick, M. R., Mount, M. K., & Judge, T. A. (2001). Personality and performance at the beginning of the new millennium: What do we know and where do we go next? *International Journal of Selection and Assessment, 9,* 9–30. (p. 588)

Barrick, M. R., Shaffer, J. A., & DeGrassi, S. W. (2009). What you see may not be what you get: Relationships among self-presentation tactics and ratings of interview and job performance. *Journal of Applied Psychology, 94,* 1304–1411. (p. A-5)

Barrouillet, P., Portrat, S., & Camos, V. (2011). On the law relating processing to storage in working memory. *Psychological Review, 118,* 175–192. (p. 320)

Barry, D. (1995, September 17). Teen smokers, too, get cool, toxic, waste-blackened lungs. *Asbury Park Press*, p. D3. (p. 122)

Barry, D. (2002, April 26). *The Dave Barry 2002 Calendar.* Kansas City: Andrews McMeel. (p. 40)

Bartels, M., & Boomsma, D. I. (2009). Born to be happy? The etiology of subjective well-being. *Behavior Genetics*, 39, 605–615. (p. 485)

Barth, J., Munder, T., Gerger, H., Nuesch, E., Trelle, S., Znoj, H., Ju, P., & Cuijpers, P. (2013). Comparative efficacy of seven psychotherapeutic interventions for patients with depression: A network meta-analysis. *PLOS Medicine*, 10, 001454. (p. 675)

Bashore, T. R., Ridderinkhof, K. R., & van der Molen, M. W. (1997). The decline of cognitive processing speed in old age. *Current Directions in Psychological Science*, 6, 163–169. (p. 216)

Baskind, D. E. (1997, December 14). Personal communication, from Delta College. (p. 665)

Bat-Chava, Y. (1993). Antecedents of self-esteem in deaf people: A meta-analytic review. *Rehabilitation Psychology*, 38(4), 221–234. (p. 375)

Bat-Chava, Y. (1994). Group identification and self-esteem of deaf adults. *Personality and Social Psychology Bulletin*, 20, 494–502. (p. 375)

Bates, L. A., & Byrne, R. W. (2010, September/October). Imitation: What animal imitation tells us about animal cognition. *Wiley Interdisciplinary Reviews: Cognitive Science*, 1, 685–695. (p. 308)

Bathje, G. J., & Pryor, J. B. (2011). The relationships of public and self-stigma to seeking mental health services. *Journal of Mental Health Counseling*, 33, 161–177. (p. 614)

Bauer, M., Cassar, A., Chytilová, J., & Henrich, J. (2014). War's enduring effects on the development of egalitarian motivations and in-group biases. *Psychological Science*, 25, 47–57. (p. 565)

Bauer, P. J. (2002). Long-term recall memory: Behavioral and neurodevelopmental changes in the first 2 years of life. *Current Directions in Psychology*, 11, 137–141. (p. 186)

Bauer, P. J. (2007). Recall in infancy: A neurodevelopmental account. *Current Directions in Psychological Science*, 16, 142–146. (p. 186)

Bauer, P. J., Burch, M. M., Scholin, S. E., & Güler, O. E. (2007). Using cue words to investigate the distribution of autobiographical memories in childhood. *Psychological Science*, 18, 910–916. (p. 330)

Bauer, P. J., & Larkina, M. (Published online, 2013, Nov. 18). The onset of childhood amnesia in childhood: A prospective investigation of the course and determinants of forgetting of early-life events. *Memory*. (p. 186)

Baum, A., & Posluszny, D. M. (1999). Health psychology: Mapping biobehavioral contributions to health and illness. *Annual Review of Psychology*, 50, 137–163. (p. 495)

Baumann, J., & DeSteno, D. (2010). Emotion guided threat detection: Expecting guns where there are none. *Journal of Personality and Social Psychology*, 99, 595–610. (p. 237)

Baumeister, H., & Härter, M. (2007). Prevalence of mental disorders based on general population surveys. *Social Psychiatry and Psychiatric Epidemiology*, 42, 537–546. (p. 609)

Baumeister, R. F. (1996). Should schools try to boost self-esteem? Beware the dark side. *American Educator*, 20, 43. (p. 604)

Baumeister, R. F. (2000). Gender differences in erotic plasticity: The female sex drive as socially flexible and responsive. *Psychological Bulletin*, 126, 347–374. (p. 441)

Baumeister, R. F. (2001, April). Violent pride: Do people turn violent because of self-hate, or self-love? *Scientific American*, pp. 96–101. (p. 604)

Baumeister, R. F. (2005). *The cultural animal: Human nature, meaning, and social life.* New York: Oxford University Press. (p. 155)

Baumeister, R. F. (2006, August/September). Violent pride. *Scientific American Mind*, pp. 54–59. (p. 599)

Baumeister, R. F. (2010). *Is there anything good about men?: How cultures flourish by exploiting men.* New York: Oxford. (p. 163)

Baumeister, R. F., & Bratslavsky, E. (1999). Passion, intimacy, and time: Passionate love as a function of change in intimacy. *Personality and Social Psychology Review*, 3, 49–67. (p. 557)

Baumeister, R. F., Catanese, K. R., & Vohs, K. D. (2001). Is there a gender difference in strength of sex drive? Theoretical views, conceptual distinctions, and a review of relevant evidence. *Personality and Social Psychology Review*, 5, 242–273. (p. 147)

Baumeister, R. F., Dale, K., & Sommer, K. L. (1998). Freudian defense mechanisms and empirical findings in modern personality and social psychology: Reaction formation, projection, displacement, undoing, isolation, sublimation, and denial. *Journal of Personality*, 66, 1081–1125. (p. 581)

Baumeister, R. F., & Leary, M. R. (1995). The need to belong: Desire for interpersonal attachments as a fundamental human motivation. *Psychological Bulletin*, 117, 497–529. (p. 448)

Baumeister, R. F., & Tice, D. M. (1986). How adolescence became the struggle for self: A historical transformation of psychological development. In J. Suls & A. G. Greenwald (Eds.), *Psychological perspectives on the self* (Vol. 3). Hillsdale, NJ: Erlbaum. (p. 212)

Baumeister, R. F., & Tierney, J. (2012). *Willpower: Rediscovering the greatest human strength.* New York: Penguin Books. (p. 503)

Baumeister, R. F., Twenge, J. M., & Nuss, C. K. (2002). Effects of social exclusion on cognitive processes: Anticipated aloneness reduces intelligent thought. *Journal of Personality and Social Psychology*, 83, 817–827. (p. 451)

Baumgardner, A. H., Kaufman, C. M., & Levy, P. E. (1989). Regulating affect interpersonally: When low esteem leads to greater enhancement. *Journal of Personality and Social Psychology*, 56, 907–921. (p. 599)

Baumrind, D. (1996). The discipline controversy revisited. *Family Relations*, 45, 405–414. (p. 202)

Baumrind, D. (2013). Is a pejorative view of power assertion in the socialization process justified? *Review of General Psychology*, 17, 420–427. (p. 202)

Baumrind, D., Larzelere, R. E., & Cowan, P. A. (2002). Ordinary physical punishment: Is it harmful? Comment on Gershoff (2002). *Psychological Bulletin*, 128, 602–611. (p. 296)

Bavelier, D., Dye, M. W. G., & Hauser, P. C. (2006). Do deaf individuals see better? *Trends in Cognitive Sciences*, 10, 512–518. (p. 375)

Bavelier, D., Newport, E. L., & Supalla, T. (2003). Children need natural languages, signed or spoken. *Cerebrum*, 5(1), 19–32. (p. 373)

Bavelier, D., Tomann, A., Hutton, C., Mitchell, T., Corina, D., Liu, G., & Neville, H. (2000). Visual attention to the periphery is enhanced in congenitally deaf individuals. *Journal of Neuroscience*, 20, 1–6. (p. 81)

BBC. (2008, February 26). Anti-depressants 'of little use.' *BBC News* (www.news.bbc.co.uk). (p. 684)

Beall, A. T., & Tracy, J. L. (2013, September). Women are more likely to wear red or pink at peak fertility. *Psychological Science*, 24, 1837–1841. (p. 303)

Beaman, A. L., & Klentz, B. (1983). The supposed physical attractiveness bias against supporters of the women's movement: A meta-analysis. *Personality and Social Psychology Bulletin*, 9, 544–550. (p. 555)

Bearzi, M., & Stanford, C. (2010). A bigger, better brain. *American Scientist*, 98, 402–409. (p. 368)

Beauchamp, G. K. (1987). The human preference for excess salt. *American Scientist*, 75, 27–33. (p. 428)

Beauvois, J-L. Courbet, D., & Oberlé, D. (2012). The prescriptive power of the television host: A transposition of Milgram's obedience paradigm to the context of TV game show. *European Review of Applied Psychology/Revue Européenne De Psychologie Appliquée*, 62, 111–119. (p. 528)

Beaver, K. M., & Barnes, J. C. (2012). Genetic and nonshared environmental factors affect the likelihood of being charged with driving under the influence (DUI) and driving while intoxicated (DWI). *Addictive Behaviors*, 37, 1377–1381. (p. 136)

Beck, A. T., Rush, A. J., Shaw, B. F., & Emery, G. (1979). *Cognitive therapy of depression.* New York: Guilford Press. (p. 667)

Beck, D. M. (2010). The appeal of the brain in the popular press. *Perspectives on Psychological Science*, 5, 762–766. (p. 81)

Becker, D. V., Kenrick, D. T., Neuberg, S. L., Blackwell, K. C., & Smith, D. M. (2007). The confounded nature of angry men and happy women. *Journal of Personality and Social Psychology*, 92, 179–190. (p. 470)

Becklen, R., & Cervone, D. (1983). Selective looking and the noticing of unexpected events. *Memory and Cognition*, 11, 601–608. (p. 97)

Beckman, M. (2004). Crime, culpability, and the adolescent brain. *Science*, 305, 596–599. (p. 205)

Beeman, M. J., & Chiarello, C. (1998). Complementary right- and left-hemisphere language comprehension. *Current Directions in Psychological Science*, 7, 2–8. (p. 85)

Beer, J. S., & Hughes, B. L. (2010). Neural systems of social comparison and the "above-average" effect. *NeuroImage*, 49, 2671–2679. (p. 602)

Bègue, L., Bushman, B. J., Giancola, P. R., Subra, B., & Rosset, E. (2010). "There is no such thing as an accident," especially when people are drunk. *Personality and Social Psychology Bulletin*, 36, 1301–1304. (p. 546)

Bègue, L., Subra, B., Arvers, P., Muller, D., Bricout, V., & Zorman, M. (2009). A message in a bottle: Extrapharmacological effects of alcohol on aggression. *Journal of Experimental Social Psychology*, 45, 137–142. (p. 546)

Beilin, H. (1992). Piaget's enduring contribution to developmental psychology. *Developmental Psychology, 28*, 191–204. (p. 192)

Beintner, I., Jacobi, C., & Taylor, C. B. (2012). Effects of an Internet-based prevention programme for eating disorders in the USA and Germany: A meta-analytic review. *European Eating Disorders Review, 20*, 1–8. (p. 653)

Bell, A. P., Weinberg, M. S., & Hammersmith, S. K. (1981). *Sexual preference: Its development in men and women.* Bloomington: Indiana University Press. (p. 442)

Belluck, P. (2010, February 16). Wanted: Volunteers, all pregnant. *New York Times* (www.nytimes.com). (p. 193)

Belluck, P. (2012, July 16). Footprints to cognitive decline and Alzheimer's are seen in gait. *New York Times* (www.nytimes.com). (p. 219)

Belluck, P. (2013, February 5). People with mental illness more likely to be smokers, study finds. *New York Times* (www.nytimes.com). (p. 34)

Belot, M., & Francesconi, M. (2006, November). *Can anyone be 'the one'? Evidence on mate selection from speed dating.* London: Centre for Economic Policy Research (www.cepr.org). (p. 553)

Belsher, G., & Costello, C. G. (1988). Relapse after recovery from unipolar depression: A critical review. *Psychological Bulletin, 104*, 84–96. (p. 632)

Belsky, J., & Pluess, M. (2009). Beyond diathesis stress: Differential susceptibility to environmental influences. *Psychological Bulletin, 135*, 885–908. (p. 626)

Belsky, J., Bakermans-Kranenburg, M. J., & van IJzendoorn, M. H. (2007). For better *and* for worse: Differential susceptibility to environmental influences. *Current Directions in Psychological Science, 16*, 300–304. (p. 651)

Bem, D. J. (1984). Quoted in *The Skeptical Inquirer, 8*, 194. (p. 273)

Bem, D. J. (2011). Feeling the future: Experimental evidence for anomalous retroactive influences on cognition and affect. *Journal of Personality and Social Psychology, 100*, 407–425. (p. 273)

Bem, S. L. (1987). Masculinity and femininity exist only in the mind of the perceiver. In J. M. Reinisch, L. A. Rosenblum, & S. A. Sanders (Eds.), *Masculinity/femininity: Basic perspectives.* New York: Oxford University Press. (p. 169)

Bem, S. L. (1993). *The lenses of gender.* New Haven, CT: Yale University Press. (p. 169)

Benartzi, S., & Thaler, R. H. (2013). Behavioral economics and the retirement savings crisis. *Science, 339*, 1152–1153. (p. 363)

Bender, T. W., Anestis, M. D., Anestis, J. C., Gordon, K. H., & Joiner, T. E. (2012). Affective and behavioral paths toward the acquired capacity for suicide. *Journal of Social and Clinical Psychology, 31*, 81–100. (p. 637)

Benedict, C., Brooks, S. J., O'Daly, O. G., Almen, M. S., Morell, A., Aberg, K., . . . Schiöth, H. B. (2012). Acute sleep deprivation enhances the brain's response to hedonic food stimuli: An fMRI study. *Journal of Clinical Endocrinology and Metabolism, 97*, 2011–2759. (p. 108)

Benenson, J. F., Markovits, H., Fitzgerald, C., Geoffroy, D., Flemming, J., Kahlenberg, S. M., & Wrangham, R. W. (2009). Males' greater tolerance of same-sex peers. *Psychological Science, 20*, 184–190. (p. 164)

Benjamin, L. T., Jr., & Simpson, J. A. (2009). The power of the situation: The impact of Milgram's obedience studies on personality and social psychology. *American Psychologist, 64*, 12–19. (p. 528)

Benjamins, M. R., Ellison, C. G., & Rogers, R. G. (2010). Religious involvement and mortality risk among pre-retirement aged U.S. adults. In C. E. Ellison & R. A. Hummer (Eds.), *Religion, families, and health: Population-based research in the United States.* New Brunswick, NJ: Rutgers University Press. (p. 512)

Bennett, W. I. (1995). Beyond overeating. *New England Journal of Medicine, 332*, 673–674. (p. 432)

Ben-Shakhar, G., & Elaad, E. (2003). The validity of psychophysiological detection of information with the guilt knowledge test: A meta-analytic review. *Journal of Applied Psychology, 88*, 131–151. (p. 467)

Benson, P. L. (1992, Spring). Patterns of religious development in adolescence and adulthood. *PiRI Newsletter*, pp. 2–9. (p. 164)

Berg, J. M., Wall, M., Larson, N., Eisenberg, M. E., Loth, K. A., & Neumark-Sztainer, D. (2014). The unique and additive associations of family functioning and parenting practices with disordered eating behaviors in diverse adolescents. *Journal of Behavioral Medicine, 37*, 205–217. (p. 652)

Bergelson, E., & Swingley, D. (2012). At 6–9 months, human infants know the meanings of many common nouns. *PNAS Proceedings of the National Academy of Sciences of the United States of America, 109*, 3253–3258. (p. 372)

Bergelson, E., & Swingley, D. (2013). The acquisition of abstract words by young infants. *Cognition, 127*, 391–397. (p. 372)

Bergen, B. K. (2014). Universal grammar. Response to 2014 Edge question: What scientific idea is ready for retirement? www.edge.org. (p. 373)

Berger, J., Meredith, M., & Wheeler, S. C. (2008). Does where you vote affect how you vote? The impact of environmental cues on voting behavior. *Proceedings of the National Academy of Sciences, 105*(26), 8846–8849. (p. 280)

Berghuis, P., et al. (2007). Hardwiring the brain: Endocannabinoids shape neuronal connectivity. *Science, 316*, 1212–1216. (p. 125)

Berk, L. E. (1994, November). Why children talk to themselves. *Scientific American*, pp. 78–83. (p. 191)

Berk, L. S., Felten, D. L., Tan, S. A., Bittman, B. B., & Westengard, J. (2001). Modulation of neuroimmune parameters during the eustress of humor-associated mirthful laughter. *Alternative Therapies, 7*, 62–76. (p. 506)

Berkman, E. T., Kahn, L. E., & Merchant, J. S. (2014). Training-induced changes in inhibitory control network activity. *Journal of Neuroscience, 34*, 149–157. (p. 218)

Berkowitz, L. (1983). Aversively stimulated aggression: Some parallels and differences in research with animals and humans. *American Psychologist, 38*, 1135–1144. (p. 547)

Berkowitz, L. (1989). Frustration-aggression hypothesis: Examination and reformulation. *Psychological Bulletin, 106*, 59–73. (p. 547)

Berkowitz, L. (1990). On the formation and regulation of anger and aggression: A cognitive-neoassociationistic analysis. *American Psychologist, 45*, 494–503. (p. 477)

Berlim, M. T., Van den Eynde, F., & Daskalakis, Z. J. (2013). A systematic review and meta-analysis on the efficacy and acceptability of bilateral repetitive transcranial magnetic stimulation (rTMS) for treating major depression. *Psychological Medicine, 43*, 2245–2254. (p. 686)

Berman, M., Gladue, B., & Taylor, S. (1993). The effects of hormones, Type A behavior pattern, and provocation on aggression in men. *Motivation and Emotion, 17*, 125–138. (p. 546)

Berman, M. G., Jonides, J., & Kaplan, S. (2008). The cognitive benefits of interacting with nature. *Psychological Science, 19*, 1207–1212. (p. 454)

Bernal, S., Dehaene-Lambertz, G. Millotte, S. & Christophe, A. (2010). Two-year-olds compute syntactic structure on-line. *Developmental Science, 13*, 69–76. (p. 372)

Berndt, T. J. (1992). Friendship and friends' influence in adolescence. *Current Directions in Psychological Science, 1*, 156–159. (p. 164)

Bernieri, F., Davis, J., Rosenthal, R., & Knee, C. (1994). Interactional synchrony and rapport: Measuring synchrony in displays devoid of sound and facial affect. *Personality and Social Psychology Bulletin, 20*, 303–311. (p. 309)

Bernstein, D. M., & Loftus, E. F. (2009). How to tell if a particular memory is true or false. *Perspectives on Psychological Science, 4*, 370–374. (p. 343)

Bernstein, D. M., & Loftus, E. F. (2009). The consequences of false memories for food preferences and choices. *Perspectives on Psychological Science, 4*, 135–139. (p. 344)

Bernstein, M. J., Young, S. G., & Claypool, H. M. (2010). Is Obama's win a gain for Blacks? Changes in implicit racial prejudice following the 2008 election. *Social Psychology, 41*, 147–151. (p. 539)

Berntson, G. G., Norman, G. J., Bechara, A., Bruss, J., Tranel, D., & Cacioppo, J. T. (2011). The insula and evaluative processes. *Psychological Science, 22*, 80–86. (p. 71)

Berridge, K. C., & Winkielman, P. (2003). What is an unconscious emotion? (The case of unconscious "liking"). *Cognition and Emotion, 17*, 181–211. (p. 462)

Berry, C. M., & Sackett, P. R. (2009). Individual differences in course choice result in underestimation of the validity of college admissions systems. *Psychological Science, 20*, 822–830. (p. 398)

Berscheid, E. (1981). An overview of the psychological effects of physical attractiveness and some comments upon the psychological effects of knowledge of the effects of physical attractiveness. In G. W. Lucker, K. Ribbens, & J. A. McNamara (Eds.), *Psychological aspects of facial form* (Craniofacial growth series). Ann Arbor: Center for Human Growth and Development, University of Michigan. (p. 554)

Berscheid, E. (1985). Interpersonal attraction. In G. Lindzey & E. Aronson (Eds.), *The handbook of social psychology.* New York: Random House. (p. 448)

Berscheid, E. (2010). Love in the fourth dimension. *Annual Review of Psychology, 61*, 1–25. (p. 557)

Berscheid, E., Gangestad, S. W., & Kulakowski, D. (1984). Emotion in close relationships: Implications for relationship counseling. In S. D. Brown & R. W. Lent (Eds.), *Handbook of counseling psychology.* New York: Wiley. (p. 557)

Berti, A., Cottini, G., Gandola, M., Pia, L., Smania, N., Stracciari, A., . . . Paulesu, E. (2005). Shared cortical anatomy for motor awareness and motor control. *Science, 309*, 488–491. (p. 85)

Bértolo, H. (2005). Visual imagery without visual perception? *Psicológica, 26*(1), 173–188. (p. 112)

Bhargava, S., Kassam, K. S., & Loewenstein, G. (2014). A reassessment of the defense of parenthood. *Psychological Science, 25,* 299–302. (p. 34)

Bhatt, R. S., Wasserman, E. A., Reynolds, W. F., Jr., & Knauss, K. S. (1988). Conceptual behavior in pigeons: Categorization of both familiar and novel examples from four classes of natural and artificial stimuli. *Journal of Experimental Psychology: Animal Behavior Processes, 14,* 219–234. (p. 291)

Bialystok, E., Craik, F. I. M., & Luk, G. (2012). Bilingualism: Consequences for mind and brain. *Trends in Cognitive Sciences, 16,* 240–250. (p. 381)

Bianchi, S. M., Milkie, M. A., Sayer, L. C., & Robinson, J. P. (2000). Is anyone doing the housework? Trends in the gender division of household labor. *Social Forces, 79,* 191–228. (p. 171)

Bianchi, S. M., Robinson, J. P., & Milkie, M. A. (2006). *Changing rhythms of American family life.* New York: Russell Sage. (p. 171)

Bienvenu, O. J., Davydow, D. S., & Kendler, K. S. (2011). Psychiatric 'diseases' *versus* behavioral disorders and degree of genetic influence. *Psychological Medicine, 41,* 33–40. (p. 633)

Bilali, R., Tropp, L. R., & Dasgupta, N. (2012). Attributions of responsibility and perceived harm in the aftermath of mass violence. *Peace and Conflict: Journal of Peace Psychology, 18,* 21–39. (p. 603)

Bilefsky, D. (2009, March 11). Europeans debate castration of sex offenders. *New York Times* (www.nytimes.com). (p. 434)

Billock, V. A., & Tsou, B. H. (2012). Elementary visual hallucinations and their relationships to neural pattern-forming mechanisms. *Psychological Bulletin, 138,* 744–774. (p. 124)

Bird, C. D., & Emery, N. J. (2009). Rooks use stones to raise the water level to reach a floating worm. *Current Biology, 19,* 1410–1414. (p. 368)

Birnbaum, G. E., Reis, H. T., Mikulincer, M., Gillath, O., & Orpaz, A. (2006). When sex is more than just sex: Attachment orientations, sexual experience, and relationship quality. *Journal of Personality and Social Psychology, 91,* 929–943. (p. 199)

Birnbaum, S. G., Yuan, P. X., Wang, M., Vijayraghavan, S., Bloom, A. K., Davis, D. J., . . . Arnsten, A. F. T. (2004). Protein kinase C overactivity impairs prefrontal cortical regulation of working memory. *Science, 306,* 882–884. (p. 331)

Biro, D., Humle, T., Koops, K., Sousa, C., Hayashi, M., & Matsuzawa, T. (2010). Chimpanzee mothers at Bossou, Guinea carry the mummified remains of their dead infants. *Current Biology, 20,* R351–R352. (p. 369)

Biro, F. M., et al. (2010). Pubertal assessment method and baseline characteristics in a mixed longitudinal study of girls. *Pediatrics, 126,* e583–e590. (pp. 166, 204)

Biro, F. M., Greenspan, L. C., & Galvez, M. P. (2012). Puberty in girls of the 21st century. *Journal of Pediatric and Adolescent Gynecology, 25,* 289–294. (pp. 166, 204)

Bishop, D. I., Weisgram, E. S., Holleque, K. M., Lund, K. E., & Wheeler, J. R. (2005). Identity development and alcohol consumption: Current and retrospective self-reports by college students. *Journal of Adolescence, 28,* 523–533.(pp. 128, 210)

Bishop, D. V. M. (2013). Cerebral asymmetry and language development: Cause, correlate, or consequence? *Science, 340,* No. 6138. (p. 86)

Bishop, G. D. (1991). Understanding the understanding of illness: Lay disease representations. In J. A. Skelton & R. T. Croyle (Eds.), *Mental representation in health and illness.* New York: Springer-Verlag. (p. 356)

Bisson, J., & Andrew, M. (2007). Psychological treatment of post-traumatic stress disorder (PTSD). *Cochrane Database of Systematic Reviews 2007,* Issue 3. Art. No. CD003388. (p. 677)

Bjork, E. L., & Bjork, R. (2011). Making things hard on yourself, but in a good way: Creating desirable difficulties to enhance learning. In M. A. Gernsbacher, M. A. Pew, L. M. Hough, & J. R. Pomerantz (eds.), *Psychology and the real world.* New York: Worth Publishers. (p. 15)

Bjork, R. (2011, January 20). Quoted by P. Belluck, To really learn, quit studying and take a test. *New York Times* (www.nytimes.com). (p. 326)

Bjorklund, D. F., & Green, B. L. (1992). The adaptive nature of cognitive immaturity. *American Psychologist, 47,* 46–54. (p. 192)

Blackhart, G. C., Nelson, B. C., Knowles, M. L., & Baumeister, R. F. (2009). Rejection elicits emotional reactions but neither causes immediate distress nor lowers self-esteem: A meta-analytic review of 192 studies on social exclusion. *Personality and Social Psychology Bulletin, 13,* 269–309. (p. 450)

Blake, W. (2013, March). Voices from solitary: A sentence worse than death. Essay published at *Solitary Watch, News from a Nation in Lockdown.* www.solitarywatch.com. (p. 450)

Blakemore, S-J. (2008). Development of the social brain during adolescence. *Quarterly Journal of Experimental Psychology, 61,* 40–49. (p. 204)

Blakemore, S-J., Wolpert, D. M., & Frith, C. D. (1998). Central cancellation of self-produced tickle sensation. *Nature Neuroscience, 1,* 635–640. (p. 261)

Blakeslee, S. (2006, January 10). Cells that read minds. *New York Times* (www.nytimes.com). (p. 307)

Blanchard, R. (2004). Quantitative and theoretical analyses of the relation between older brothers and homosexuality in men. *Journal of Theoretical Biology, 230,* 173–187. (p. 444)

Blanchard, R. (2008a). Review and theory of handedness, birth order, and homosexuality in men. *Laterality, 13,* 51–70. (pp. 444, 445)

Blanchard, R. (2008b). Sex ratio of older siblings in heterosexual and homosexual, right-handed and non-right-handed men. *Archives of Sexual Behavior, 37,* 977–981. (p. 444)

Blanchard, R. (2014, July). Detecting and correcting for family size differences in the study of sexual orientation and fraternal birth order. *Archives of Sexual Behavior, 43,* 845–852. (p. 444)

Blanchard, R., Kuban, M. E., Blak, T., Klassen, P. E., Dickey, R., & Cantor, J. M. (2012). Sexual attraction to others: A comparison of two models of alloerotic responding in men. *Archives of Sexual Behavior, 41,* 13–29. (p. 441)

Blanchard, R., Lykins, A. D., Wherrett, D., Kuban, M. E., Cantor, J. M., Blak, T., Dickey, R., & Klassen, P. E. (2009). Pedophilia, hebephilia, and the DSM-V. *Archives of Sexual Behavior, 38,* 335–350. (p. 441)

Blanchard-Fields, F. (2007). Everyday problem solving and emotion: An adult developmental perspective. *Current Directions in Psychological Science, 16,* 26–31. (p. 401)

Blankenburg, F., Taskin, B., Ruben, J., Moosmann, M., Ritter, P., Curio, G., & Villringer, A. (2003). Imperceptive stimuli and sensory processing impediment. *Science, 299,* 1864. (p. 232)

Blascovich, J. & Mendes, W. B. (2010). Social psychophysiology and embodiment. In S. T. Fiske, D. T. Gilbert, & G. Lindzey (Eds.), *The handbook of social psychology, 5th Edition* (pp. 194–227). New York: John Wiley & Sons Inc. (p. 489)

Blass, T. (1996). Stanley Milgram: A life of inventiveness and controversy. In G. A. Kimble, C. A. Boneau, & M. Wertheimer (Eds.), *Portraits of pioneers in psychology* (Vol. II). Washington, DC and Mahwah, NJ: American Psychological Association and Lawrence Erlbaum Publishers. (p. 529)

Blass, T. (1999). The Milgram paradigm after 35 years: Some things we now know about obedience to authority. *Journal of Applied Social Psychology, 29,* 955–978. (p. 528)

Blatt, S. J., Sanislow, C. A., III, Zuroff, D. C., & Pilkonis, P. (1996). Characteristics of effective therapists: Further analyses of data from the National Institute of Mental Health Treatment of Depression Collaborative Research Program. *Journal of Consulting and Clinical Psychology, 64,* 1276–1284. (p. 679)

BLF. (2012). *The impact of cannabis on your lungs.* London: British Lung Foundation (www.blf.org.uk). (p. 125)

Block, J. (2010). The five-factor framing of personality and beyond: Some ruminations. *Psychological Inquiry, 21,* 2–25. (p. 590)

Bloom, B. C. (Ed.). (1985). *Developing talent in young people.* New York: Ballantine. (p. 455)

Bloom, P. (2000). *How children learn the meanings of words.* Cambridge, MA: MIT Press. (p. 371)

BLS. (2011, June 22). *American time use survey summary.* Bureau of Labor Statistics (www.bls.gov). (pp. 157, 486)

Blum, D. (2011). *Love at Goon Park: Harry Harlow and the science of affection.* New York: Perseus. (p. 197)

Blum, K., Cull, J. G., Braverman, E. R., & Comings, D. E. (1996). Reward deficiency syndrome. *American Scientist, 84,* 132–145. (p. 73)

Boag, S. (2006). Freudian repression, the common view, and pathological science. *Review of General Psychology, 10,* 74–86. (p. 580)

Boahen, K. (2005, May). Neuromorphic microchips. *Scientific American,* pp. 56–63. (p. 259)

Bocklandt, S., Horvath, S., Vilain, E., & Hamer, D. H. (2006). Extreme skewing of X chromosome inactivation in mothers of homosexual men. *Human Genetics, 118,* 691–694. (p. 444)

Bockting, W. O. (2014). Transgender identity development. In W. O. Bockting (Ed.), *APA handbook of sexuality and psychology* (Vol. 1, pp. 739–758). Washington, D.C.: American Psychological Association. (p. 169)

Bodenhausen, G. V., Sheppard, L. A., & Kramer, G. P. (1994). Negative affect and social judgment: The differential impact of anger and sadness. *European Journal of Social Psychology, 24,* 45–62. (p. 567)

Bodkin, J. A., & Amsterdam, J. D. (2002). Transdermal selegiline in major depression: A double-blind, placebo-controlled, parallel-group study in outpatients. *American Journal of Psychiatry, 159,* 1869–1875. (p. 683)

Boecker, H., Sprenger, T., Spilker, M. E., et al. (2008). The runner's high: opioidergic mechanisms in the human brain. *Cerebral Cortex, 18,* 2523–2531. (p. 634)

Boehm, J. K., & Kubzansky, L. D. (2012). The heart's content: The association between positive psychological well-being and cardiovascular health. *Psychological Bulletin, 138,* 655–691. (p. 504)

Boehm-Davis, D. A. (2005). Improving product safety and effectiveness in the home. In R. S. Nickerson (Ed.), *Reviews of human factors and ergonomics* (Vol.1, pp. 219–253). Santa Monica, CA: Human Factors and Ergonomics Society. (p. A-14)

Boesch-Achermann, H., & Boesch, C. (1993). Tool use in wild chimpanzees: New light from dark forests. *Current Directions in Psychological Science, 2,* 18–21. (p. 368)

Bogaert, A. F. (2003). Number of older brothers and sexual orientation: New texts and the attraction/behavior distinction in two national probability samples. *Journal of Personality and Social Psychology, 84,* 644–652. (p. 444)

Bogaert, A. F. (2004). Asexuality: Prevalence and associated factors in a national probability sample. *Journal of Sex Research, 41,* 279–287. (p. 440)

Bogaert, A. F. (2006b). Biological versus nonbiological older brothers and men's sexual orientation. *Proceedings of the National Academy of Sciences, 103,* 10771–10774. (pp. 440, 445)

Bogaert, A. F. (2010). Physical development and sexual orientation in men and women: An analysis of NATSAL-2000. *Archives of Sexual Behavior, 39,* 110–116. (p. 445)

Bogaert, A. F. (2012). *Understanding asexuality.* Lanham, MD: Rowman & Littlefield. (p. 440)

Bogaert, A. F., Friesen, C., & Klentrou, P. (2002). Age of puberty and sexual orientation in a national probability sample. *Archives of Sexual Behavior, 31,* 73–81. (p. 442)

Boggiano, A. K., Harackiewicz, J. M., Bessette, M. M., & Main, D. S. (1985). Increasing children's interest through performance-contingent reward. *Social Cognition, 3,* 400–411. (p. 305)

Bohman, M., & Sigvardsson, S. (1990). Outcome in adoption: Lessons from longitudinal studies. In D. Brodzinsky & M. Schechter (Eds.), *The psychology of adoption.* New York: Oxford University Press. (p. 139)

Bolger, N., DeLongis, A., Kessler, R. C., & Schilling, E. A. (1989). Effects of daily stress on negative mood. *Journal of Personality and Social Psychology, 57,* 808–818. (p. 481)

Boly, M., Garrido, M. I., Gosseries, O., Bruno, M-A., Boveroux, P., Schnakers, C., . . . Friston, K. (2011). Preserved feed-forward but impaired top-down processes in the vegetative state. *Science, 332,* 858–862. (p. 93)

Bonanno, G. A. (2004). Loss, trauma, and human resilience: Have we underestimated the human capacity to thrive after extremely aversive events? *American Psychologist, 59,* 20–28. (p. 225)

Bonanno, G. A., Brewin, C. R., Kaniasty, K., & La Greca, A. M. (2010). Weighing the costs of disaster: Consequences, risks, and resilience in individuals, families, and communities. *Psychological Science in the Public Interest, 11,* 1–49. (p. 624)

Bonanno, G. A., Galea, S., Bucciarelli, A., & Vlahov, D. (2006). Psychological resilience after disaster. *Psychological Science, 17,* 181–186. (p. 623)

Bonanno, G. A., Galea, S., Bucciarelli, A., & Vlahov, D. (2007). What predicts psychological resilience after disaster? The role of demographics, resources, and life stress. *Journal of Consulting and Clinical Psychology, 75*(5), 671–682. (p. 690)

Bonanno, G. A., & Kaltman, S. (1999). Toward an integrative perspective on bereavement. *Psychological Bulletin, 125,* 760–777. (p. 225)

Bonanno, G. A., Kennedy, P., Galatzer-Levy, I. R., Lude, P., & Elfström, M. L. (2012). Trajectories of resilience, depression, and anxiety following spinal cord injury. *Rehabilitation Psychology, 57,* 236–247. (p. 690)

Bonanno, G. A., Westphal, M., & Mancini, A. D. (2011). Resilience to loss and potential trauma. *Annual Review of Clinical Psychology, 11,* 511–535. (p. 623)

Bond, C. F., Jr., & DePaulo, B. M. (2006). Accuracy of deception judgments. *Personality and Social Psychology Review, 10,* 214–234. (p. 469)

Bond, C. F., Jr., & DePaulo, B. M. (2008). Individual differences in detecting deception: Accuracy and bias. *Psychological Bulletin, 134,* 477–492. (p. 469)

Bond, M. H., Lun, V. M-C., Chan, J., Chan, W. W-Y., & Wong, D. (2012). Enacting modesty in Chinese culture: The joint contribution of personal characteristics and contextual features. *Asian Journal of Social Psychology, 15,* 14–25. (p. 157)

Bond, R., & Smith, P. B. (1996). Culture and conformity: A meta-analysis of studies using Asch's (1952b, 1956) line judgment task. *Psychological Bulletin, 119,* 111–137. (p. 527)

Bond, R. M., Fariss, C. J., Jones, J. J., Kramer, A. D. I., Marlow, C., Settle, J. E., & Fowler, J. H. (2012). A 61-million-person experiment in social influence and political mobilization. *Nature, 489,* 295–298. (p. 525)

Bonetti, L., Campbell, M. A., & Gilmore, L. (2010). The relationship of loneliness and social anxiety with children's and adolescents' online communication. *Cyberpsychology, Behavior, and Social Networking, 13,* 279–285. (p. 452)

Bonezzi, A., Brendl, C. M., & DeAngelis, M. (2011). Stuck in the middle: The psychophysics of goal pursuit. *Psychological Science, 22,* 607–612. (p. 455)

Bonneville-Roussy, A., Rentfrow, P.J., Xu, K.M. & Potter, J. (2013). Music through the ages: Trends in musical attitudes and preferences from adolescence through middle adulthood. *Journal of Personality and Social Psychology, 105,* 703–717. (p. 205)

Bono, J. E., & Judge, T. A. (2004). Personality and transformational and transactional leadership: A meta-analysis. *Journal of Applied Psychology, 89,* 901–910. (p. A-12)

Bookheimer, S. H., Strojwas, M. H., Cohen, M. S., Saunders, A. M., Pericak-Vance, M. A., Mazziotta, J. C., & Small, G. W. (2000). Patterns of brain activation in people at risk for Alzheimer's disease. *New England Journal of Medicine, 343,* 450–456. (p. 219)

Booth, F. W., & Neufer, P. D. (2005). Exercise controls gene expression. *American Scientist, 93,* 28–35. (p. 508)

Bor, D. (2010, July/August). The mechanics of mind reading. *Scientific American,* pp. 52–57. (p. 93)

Bora, E., & Pantelis, C. (2013). Theory of mind impairments in first-episode psychosis, individuals at ultra-high risk for psychosis and in first-degree relatives of schizophrenia: Systematic review and meta-analysis. *Schizophrenia Research, 144,* 31–36. (p. 641)

Boring, E. G. (1930). A new ambiguous figure. *American Journal of Psychology, 42,* 444–445. (p. 235)

Bornstein, M. H., Cote, L. R., Maital, S., Painter, K., Park, S-Y., Pascual, L., . . . Vyt, A. (2004). Cross-linguistic analysis of vocabulary in young children: Spanish, Dutch, French, Hebrew, Italian, Korean, and American English. *Child Development, 75,* 1115–1139. (p. 373)

Bornstein, M. H., Tal, J., Rahn, C., Galperin, C. Z., Pecheux, M-G., Lamour, M., . . . Tamis-LeMonda, C. S. (1992a). Functional analysis of the contents of maternal speech to infants of 5 and 13 months in four cultures: Argentina, France, Japan, and the United States. *Developmental Psychology, 28,* 593–603. (p. 161)

Bornstein, M. H., Tamis-LeMonda, C. S., Tal, J., Ludemann, P., Toda, S., Rahn, C. W., . . . Vardi, D. (1992b). Maternal responsiveness to infants in three societies: The United States, France, and Japan. *Child Development, 63,* 808–821. (p. 161)

Bornstein, R. F. (1989). Exposure and affect: Overview and meta-analysis of research, 1968–1987. *Psychological Bulletin, 106,* 265–289. (pp. 196, 551)

Bornstein, R. F. (1999). Source amnesia, misattribution, and the power of unconscious perceptions and memories. *Psychoanalytic Psychology, 16,* 155–178. (p. 551)

Bornstein, R. F., Galley, D. J., Leone, D. R., & Kale, A. R. (1991). The temporal stability of ratings of parents: Test-retest reliability and influence of parental contact. *Journal of Social Behavior and Personality, 6,* 641–649. (p. 336)

Boroditsky, L. (2009, June 12). How does our language shape the way we think? www.edge.org. (pp. 370, 380, 381)

Boroditsky, L. (2011, February). How language shapes thought. *Scientific American,* pp. 63–65. (p. 380)

Boron, J. B., Willis, S. L., & Schaie, K. W. (2007). Cognitive training gain as a predictor of mental status. *Journal of Gerontology: Series B: Psychological Sciences and Social Sciences, 62B*(1), 45–52. (p. 218)

Bosma, H., Marmot, M. G., Hemingway, H., Nicolson, A. C., Brunner, E., & Stansfeld, S. A. (1997). Low job control and risk of coronary heart disease in Whitehall II (prospective cohort) study. *British Medical Journal, 314,* 558–565. (p. 501)

Bosma, H., Peter, R., Siegrist, J., & Marmot, M. (1998). Two alternative job stress models and the risk of coronary heart disease. *American Journal of Public Health, 88,* 68–74. (p. 501)

Bossong, M. G., Jansma, J. M., van Hell H. H., Jagerm G., Oudman, E., Saliasi, E., Kahn, R. S., & Ramsey, N. F. (2012). Effects of Δ9-tetrahydrocannabinol in human working memory function. *Biological Psychiatry, 71,* 693–699. (p. 125)

Bostwick, J. M., & Pankratz, V. S. (2000). Affective disorders and suicide risk: A re-examination. *American Journal of Psychiatry, 157,* 1925–1932. (p. 637)

Bosworth, R. G., & Dobkins, K. R. (1999). Left-hemisphere dominance for motion processing in deaf signers. *Psychological Science, 10,* 256–262. (p. 81)

Bothwell, R. K., Brigham, J. C., & Malpass, R. S. (1989). Cross-racial identification. *Personality and Social Psychology Bulletin, 15,* 19–25. (p. 543)

Bouchard, T. J., Jr. (2009). Genetic influences on human intelligence (Spearman's *g*): How much? *Annals of Human Biology, 36,* 527–544. (p. 137)

Boucher, J., Mayes, A., & Bigham, S. (2012). Memory in autistic spectrum disorder. *Psychological Bulletin, 138,* 458–496. (p. 193)

Bouton, M. E., Mineka, S., & Barlow, D. H. (2001). A modern learning theory perspective on the etiology of panic disorder. *Psychological Review, 108,* 4–32. (p. 624)

Bowden, E. M., & Beeman, M. J. (1998). Getting the right idea: Semantic activation in the right hemisphere may help solve insight problems. *Psychological Science, 9,* 435–440. (p. 85)

Bowen, L. (2012, November). Certain video games may lead teens to drive recklessly. *Monitor on Psychology,* p. 15. (p. 34)

Bowen, N. K., Wegmann, K. M., & Webber, K. C. (2013). Enhancing a brief writing intervention to combat stereotype threat among middle-school students. *Journal of Educational Psychology, 105,* 427–435. (p. 415)

Bowen, S., Witkiewitz, K., Dillworth, T. M., Chawla, N., Simpson, T. L., Ostafin, B. D., . . . Marlatt, G. A. (2006). Mindfulness meditation and substance use in an incarcerated population. *Psychology of Addictive Behaviors, 20,* 343–347. (p. 510)

Bower, B. (2009, February 14). The dating go round. *Science News,* pp. 22–25. (p. 552)

Bower, G. H. (1986). Prime time in cognitive psychology. In P. Eelen (Ed.), *Cognitive research and behavior therapy: Beyond the conditioning paradigm.* Amsterdam: North Holland Publishers. (p. 335)

Bower, G. H., Clark, M. C., Lesgold, A. M., & Winzenz, D. (1969). Hierarchical retrieval schemes in recall of categorized word lists. *Journal of Verbal Learning and Verbal Behavior, 8,* 323–343. (p. 325)

Bower, G. H., & Morrow, D. G. (1990). Mental models in narrative comprehension. *Science, 247,* 44–48. (p. 327)

Bower, J. M., & Parsons, L. M. (2003, August). Rethinking the "lesser brain." *Scientific American,* pp. 50–57. (p. 70)

Bowers, J. S. (2009). On the biological plausibility of grandmother cells: implications for neural network theories in psychology and neuroscience. *Psychological Review, 116,* 220–251. (p. 246)

Bowers, J. S., Mattys, S. L., & Gage, S. H. (2009). Preserved implicit knowledge of a forgotten childhood language. *Psychological Science, 20,* 1064–1069. (p. 186)

Bowler, M. C., & Woehr, D. J. (2006). A meta-analytic evaluation of the impact of dimension and exercise factors on assessment center ratings. *Journal of Applied Psychology, 91,* 1114–1124. (p. 596)

Bowling, N. A., Eschleman, K. J., & Wang, Q. (2010). A meta-analytic examination of the relationship between job satisfaction and subjective well-being. *Journal of Occupational and Organizational Psychology, 83,* 915–934. (p. A-8)

Boxer, P., Huesmann, L. R., Bushman, B. J., O'Brien, M., & Moceri, D. (2009). The role of violent media preference in cumulative developmental risk for violence and general aggression. *Journal of Youth and Adolescence, 38,* 417–428. (p. 312)

Boyatzis, C. J. (2012). Development of spirituality in children and adolescents. In L. Miller (Ed.), *Oxford handbook of the psychology of religion and spirituality.* New York: Oxford University Press. (p. 206)

Boyatzis, C. J., Matillo, G. M., & Nesbitt, K. M. (1995). Effects of the "Mighty Morphin Power Rangers" on children's aggression with peers. *Child Study Journal, 25,* 45–55. (p. 312)

Boyce, C. J., Brown, G. D. A., & Moore, S. C. (2010). Money and happiness: Rank of income, not income, affects life satisfaction. *Psychological Science, 21,* 471–475. (p. 484)

Boyce, C. J., & Wood, A. M. (2011). Personality prior to disability determines adaptation: Agreeable individuals recover lost life satisfaction faster and more completely. *Psychological Science, 22,* 1397–1402. (p. 481)

Boynton, R. M. (1979). *Human color vision.* New York: Holt, Rinehart & Winston. (p. 243)

Braden, J. P. (1994). *Deafness, deprivation, and IQ.* New York: Plenum. (p. 411)

Bradley, D. R., Dumais, S. T., & Petry, H. M. (1976). Reply to Cavonius. *Nature, 261,* 78. (p. 247)

Bradley, R. B., et al. (2008). Influence of child abuse on adult depression: Moderation by the corticotropin-releasing hormone receptor gene. *Archives of General Psychiatry, 65,* 190–200. (p. 201)

Bradshaw, C., Sawyer, A., & O'Brennan, L. (2009). A social disorganization perspective on bullying-related attitudes and behaviors: The influence of school context. *American Journal of Community Psychology, 43,* 204–220. (p. 12)

Braiker, B. (2005, October 18). A quiet revolt against the rules on SIDS. *New York Times* (www.nytimes.com). (p. 185)

Brainerd, C. J. (1996). Piaget: A centennial celebration. *Psychological Science, 7,* 191–195. (p. 186)

Brakefield, T. A., Mednick, S. C., Wilson, H. W., De Neve, J., Christakis, N. A., & Fowler, J. H. (2014). Same-sex sexual attraction does not spread in adolescent social networks. *Archives of Sexual Behavior, 43,* 335–344. (p. 442)

Brandon, S., Boakes, J., Glaser, & Green, R. (1998). Recovered memories of childhood sexual abuse: Implications for clinical practice. *British Journal of Psychiatry, 172,* 294–307. (p. 349)

Brang, D., Edwards, L., Ramachandran, V. S., & Coulson, S. (2008). Is the sky 2? Contextual priming in grapheme-color synaesthesia. *Psychological Science, 19,* 421–428. (p. 271)

Brannon, L. A., & Brock, T. C. (1993). Comment on report of HIV infection in rural Florida: Failure of instructions to correct for gross underestimation of phantom sex partners in perception of AIDS risk. *New England Journal of Medicine, 328,* 1351–1352. (p. 436)

Bransford, J. D., & Johnson, M. K. (1972). Contextual prerequisites for understanding: Some investigations of comprehension and recall. *Journal of Verbal Learning and Verbal Behavior, 11,* 717–726. (p. 327)

Brasel, S. A., & Gips, J. (2011). Media multitasking behavior: Concurrent television and computer usage. *Cyberpsychology, Behavior, and Social Networking, 14,* 527–534. (p. 96)

Brauhardt, A., Rudolph, A., & Hilbert, A. (2014). Implicit cognitive processes in binge-eating disorder and obesity. *Journal of Behavioral Therapy and Experimental Psychiatry, 45*(2), 285-290. (p. 652)

Braun, S. (1996). New experiments underscore warnings on maternal drinking. *Science, 273,* 738–739. (p. 182)

Braun, S. (2001, Spring). Seeking insight by prescription. *Cerebrum,* pp. 10–21. (p. 124)

Braunstein, G. D., Sundwall, D. A., Katz, M., Shifren, J. L., Buster, J. E., Simon, J. A., . . . Watts, N. B. (2005). Safety and efficacy of a testosterone patch for the treatment of hypoactive sexual desire disorder in surgically menopausal women: A randomized, placebo-controlled trial. *Archives of Internal Medicine, 165,* 1582–1589. (p. 434)

Bray, D. W., & Byham, W. C. (1991, Winter). Assessment centers and their derivatives. *Journal of Continuing Higher Education,* pp. 8–11. (p. 597)

Bray, D. W., & Byham, W. C., interviewed by Mayes, B. T. (1997). Insights into the history and future of assessment centers: An interview with Dr. Douglas W. Bray and Dr. William Byham. *Journal of Social Behavior and Personality, 12,* 3–12. (p. 597)

Brayne, C., Spiegelhalter, D. J., Dufouil, C., Chi, L-Y., Dening, T. R., Paykel, E. S., . . . Huppert, F.A. (1999). Estimating the true extent of cognitive decline in the old old. *Journal of the American Geriatrics Society, 47,* 1283–1288. (p. 400)

Breedlove, S. M. (1997). Sex on the brain. *Nature, 389,* 801. (p. 443)

Breen, G., et al. (2011, May). A genome-wide significant linkage for severe depression on chromosome 3: The depression network study. *American Journal of Psychiatry, 167,* 949–957. (p. 633)

Brehm, S., & Brehm, J. W. (1981). *Psychological reactance: A theory of freedom and control.* New York: Academic Press. (p. 536)

Breslau, J., Aguilar-Gaxiola, S., Borges, G., Kendler, K. S., Su, M., & Kessler, R. C. (2007). Risk for psychiatric disorder among immigrants and their US-born descendants. *Journal of Nervous and Mental Disease, 195,* 189–195. (pp. 617, 618)

Breslin, C. W. & Safer, M. A. (2011). Effects of event valence on long-term memory for two baseball championship games. *Psychological Science, 22,* 1408–1412. (p. 332)

Brethel-Haurwitz, K. M., & Marsh, A. A. (2014, March). Geographical differences in subjective well-being predict extraordinary altruism. *Psychological Science, 25,* 762–771. (p. 479)

Brewer, C. L. (1990). Personal correspondence. (p. 142)

Brewer, C. L. (1996). Personal communication. (p. 9)

Brewer, J. A., Malik, S., Babuscio, T. A., Nich, C., Johnson, H. E., Deleone, C. M., . . . Rounsaville, B. J. (2011). Mindfulness training for smoking cessation: Results from a randomized controlled trial. *Drug and Alcohol Dependence, 119,* 72–80. (p. 510)

Brewer, M. B., & Chen, Y-R. (2007). Where (who) are collectives in collectivism? Toward conceptual clarification of individualism and collectivism. *Psychological Review, 114,* 133–151. (p. 157)

Brewer, W. F. (1977). Memory for the pragmatic implications of sentences. *Memory & Cognition, 5,* 673–678. (p. 327)

Brewin, C. R., Andrews, B., Rose, S., & Kirk, M. (1999). Acute stress disorder and posttraumatic stress disorder in victims of violent crime. *American Journal of Psychiatry, 156,* 360–366. (p. 623)

Brewin, C. R., Kleiner, J. S., Vasterling J. J., & Field, A. P. (2007). Memory for emotionally neutral information in posttraumatic stress disorder: A meta-analytic investigation. *Journal of Abnormal Psychology, 116,* 448–463. (p. 331)

Briers, B., Pandelaere, M., Dewitte, S., & Warlop, L. (2006). Hungry for money: The desire for caloric resources increases the desire for financial resources and vice versa. *Psychological Science, 17,* 939–943. (p. 293)

Briscoe, D. (1997, February 16). Women lawmakers still not in charge. *Grand Rapids Press,* p. A23. (p. 168)

Brislin, R. W. (1988). Increasing awareness of class, ethnicity, culture, and race by expanding on students' own experiences. In I. Cohen (Ed.), *The G. Stanley Hall Lecture Series.* Washington, DC: American Psychological Association. (p. 155)

Broadbent, E., Kakokehr, A., Booth, R. J., Thomas, J., Windsor, J. A., Buchanan, C. M., . . . Hill, A. G. (2012). A brief relaxation intervention reduces stress and improves surgical wound healing response: A randomized trial. *Brain, Behavior, and Immunity, 26,* 212–217. (p. 510)

Brody, J. E. (2002, November 26). When the eyelids snap shut at 65 miles an hour. *New York Times* (www.nytimes.com). (p. 108)

Brody, J. E. (2003, September). Addiction: A brain ailment, not a moral lapse. *New York Times* (www.nytimes.com). (p. 117)

Brody, S., & Tillmann, H. C. (2006). The post-orgasmic prolactin increase following intercourse is greater than following masturbation and suggests greater satiety. *Biological Psychology, 71,* 312–315. (p. 447)

Broks, P. (2007, April). The mystery of consciousness. *Prospect* (www.prospect-magazine.co.uk). (p. 186)

Bromet, E., Andrade, L. H., Hwang, I., Sampson, N. A., Alonso, J., de Girolamo, G., . . . Kessler, R. C. (2011). Cross-national epidemiology of DSM-IV major depressive episode. *BMC Medicine, 9,* 90. (p. 631)

Brookmeyer, R., Evans, D. A., Hebert, L., Langa, K. M., Heeringa, S. G., Plassman, B. L., & Kukull, W. A. (2011). National estimates of the prevalence of Alzheimer's disease in the United States. *Alzheimer's & Dementia, 7,* 61–73. (p. 219)

Brooks, R. (2012). "Asia's missing women" as a problem in applied evolutionary psychology? *Evolutionary Psychology, 12,* 910–925. (p. 540)

Brown, A. S. (2003). A review of the déjà vu experience. *Psychological Bulletin, 129,* 394–413. (p. 346)

Brown, A. S. (2004a). *The déjà vu experience.* East Sussex, England: Psychology Press. (p. 346)

Brown, A. S. (2004b). Getting to grips with déja vu. *The Psychologist, 17,* 694–696. (p. 346)

Brown, A. S., Begg, M. D., Gravenstein, S., Schaefer, C. A., Wyatt, R. J., Bresnahan, M., Babulas, V. P., & Susser, E. S. (2004). Serologic evidence of prenatal influenza in the etiology of schizophrenia. *Archives of General Psychiatry, 61,* 774–780. (p. 643)

Brown, A. S., & Marsh, E. (2009). Creating illusions of past encounter through brief exposure. *Psychological Science, 20,* 534–538. (p. 346)

Brown, A. S., & Patterson, P. H. (2011). Maternal infection and schizophrenia: Implications for prevention. *Schizophrenia Bulletin, 37,* 284–290. (p. 643)

Brown, A. S., Schaefer, C. A., Wyatt, R. J., Goetz, R., Begg, M. D., Gorman, J. M., & Susser, E. S. (2000). Maternal exposure to respiratory infections and adult schizophrenia spectrum disorders: A prospective birth cohort study. *Schizophrenia Bulletin, 26,* 287–295. (p. 643)

Brown, E. L., & Deffenbacher, K. (1979). *Perception and the senses.* New York: Oxford University Press. (p. 260)

Brown, J. A. (1958). Some tests of the decay theory of immediate memory. *Quarterly Journal of Experimental Psychology, 10,* 12–21. (p. 323)

Brown, J. D. (2012). Understanding the better than average effect: Motives (still) matter. *Personality and Social Psychology Bulletin, 38,* 209–219. (p. 602)

Brown, J. D., Steele, J. R., & Walsh-Childers, K. (2002). *Sexual teens, sexual media: Investigating media's influence on adolescent sexuality.* Mahwah, NJ: Erlbaum. (p. 439)

Brown, J. L., & Pollitt, E. (1996, February). Malnutrition, poverty and intellectual development. *Scientific American,* pp. 38–43. (p. 408)

Brown, K. W., Goodman, R. J., & Inzlicht, M. (2013). Dispositional mindfulness and the attenuation of neural responses to emotional stimuli. *Social Cognitive and Affective Neuroscience, 8,* 93–99. (p. 511)

Brown, R. (1986). Linguistic relativity. In S. H. Hulse & B. F. Green, Jr. (Eds.), *One hundred years of psychological research in America.* Baltimore: Johns Hopkins University Press. (p. 380)

Brown, R. P., Osterman, L. L., & Barnes, C. D. (2009). School violence and the culture of honor. *Psychological Science, 20,* 1400–1405. (p. 548)

Brown, S. L., Brown, R. M., House, J. S., & Smith, D. M. (2008). Coping with spousal loss: Potential buffering effects of self-reported helping behavior. *Personality and Social Psychology Bulletin, 34,* 849–861. (p. 225)

Browning, C. (1992). *Ordinary men: Reserve police battalion 101 and the final solution in Poland.* New York: HarperCollins. (p. 530)

Bruce-Keller, A. J., Keller, J. N., & Morrison, C. D. (2009). Obesity and vulnerability of the CNS. *Biochimica et Biophysica Acta, 1792,* 395–400. (p. 430)

Bruck, M., & Ceci, S. J. (1999). The suggestibility of children's memory. *Annual Review of Psychology, 50,* 419–439. (p. 347)

Bruck, M., & Ceci, S. J. (2004). Forensic developmental psychology: Unveiling four common misconceptions. *Current Directions in Psychological Science, 15,* 229–232. (p. 347)

Bruer, J. T. (1999). *The myth of the first three years: A new understanding of early brain development and lifelong learning.* New York: Free Press. (p. 409)

Brunner, M., Gogol, K. M., Sonnleitner, P., Keller, U., Krauss, S., & Preckel, F. (2013). Gender differences in the mean level, variability, and profile shape of student achievement: Results from 41 countries. *Intelligence, 41,* 378–395. (p. 410)

Bruno, M-A., Bernheim, J. L., Ledoux, D., Pellas, F., Demertzi, A., & Laureys, S. (2011). A survey on self-assessed well-being in a cohort of chronic locked-in syndrome patients: Happy majority, miserable minority. *BMJ Open.* bmjopen.bmj.com/content/early/2011/02/16/bmjopen-2010-000039.short?rss=1.1. (p. 481)

Bruno, M-A., Pellas, F., & Laureys, S. (2008). Quality of life in locked-in syndrome survivors. In J. L. Vincent (ed.), *2008 yearbook of intensive care and emergency medicine.* New York: Springer. (p. 481)

Bryant, A. N., & Astin, H. A. (2008). The correlates of spiritual struggle during the college years. *Journal of Higher Education, 79,* 1–27. (p. 210)

Bryant, R. A. (2001). Posttraumatic stress disorder and traumatic brain injury: Can they co-exist? *Clinical Psychology Review, 21,* 931–948. (p. 349)

Buchanan, R. W., et al. (2010). The 2009 schizophrenia PORT psychopharmacological treatment recommendations and summary statements. *Schizophrenia Bulletin, 36,* 71–93. (p. 682)

Buchanan, T. W. (2007). Retrieval of emotional memories. *Psychological Bulletin, 133,* 761–779. (p 331)

Buck, L. B., & Axel, R. (1991). A novel multigene family may encode odorant receptors: A molecular basis for odor recognition. *Cell, 65,* 175–187. (p. 267)

Buckholtz, J. W., et al. (2010). Mesolimbic dopamine reward system hypersensitivity in individuals with psychopathic traits. *Nature Neuroscience, 13,* 419–421. (p. 651)

Buckingham, M. (2001, August). Quoted by P. LaBarre, "Marcus Buckingham thinks your boss has an attitude problem." *The Magazine* (fastcompany.com/online/49/buckingham.html). (p. A-10)

Buckingham, M. (2007). *Go put your strengths to work: 6 powerful steps to achieve outstanding performance.* New York: Free Press. (p. A-3)

Buckingham, M., & Clifton, D. O. (2001). *Now, discover your strengths.* New York: Free Press. (p. A-4)

Buckley, C. (2007, January 3). Man is rescued by stranger on subway tracks. *New York Times* (www.nytimes.com). (p. 561)

Buday, S. K., Stake, J. E., & Peterson, Z. D. (2012). Gender and the choice of a science career: The impact of social support and possible selves. *Sex Roles, 66,* 197–209. (p. 598)

Buehler, R., Griffin, D., & Ross, M. (1994). Exploring the "planning fallacy": Why people underestimate their task completion times. *Journal of Personality and Social Psychology, 67,* 366–381. (p. 361)

Buehler, R., Griffin, D., & Ross, M. (2002). Inside the planning fallacy: The causes and consequences of optimistic time predictions. In T. Gilovich, D. Griffin, & D. Kahneman (Eds.), *Heuristics and biases: The psychology of intuitive judgment.* Cambridge: Cambridge University Press. (p. 361)

Buffardi, L. E., & Campbell, W. K. (2008). Narcissism and social networking web sites. *Personality and Social Psychology Bulletin, 34,* 1303–1314. (p. 453)

Bugelski, B. R., Kidd, E., & Segmen, J. (1968). Image as a mediator in one-trial paired-associate learning. *Journal of Experimental Psychology, 76,* 69–73. (p. 325)

Bugental, D. B. (1986). Unmasking the "polite smile": Situational and personal determinants of managed affect in adult-child interaction. *Personality and Social Psychology Bulletin, 12,* 7–16. (p. 469)

Buhle, J. T., Stevens, B. L., Friedman, J. J., & Wager, T. D. (2012). Distraction and placebo: Two separate routes to pain control. *Psychological Science, 23,* 246–253. (p. 264)

Buka, S. L., Tsuang, M. T., Torrey, E. F., Klebanoff, M. A., Wagner, R. L., & Yolken, R. H. (2001). Maternal infections and subsequent psychosis among offspring. *Archives of General Psychiatry, 58,* 1032–1037. (p. 643)

Bunde, J., & Suls, J. (2006). A quantitative analysis of the relationship between the Cook-Medley Hostility Scale and traditional coronary artery disease risk factors. *Health Psychology, 25,* 493–500. (p. 497)

Buquet, R. (1988). Le reve et les deficients visuels [Dreams and the visually impaired]. *Psychanalyse-a-l'Universite, 13,* 319–327. (p. 112)

Burger, J. M. (2009). Replicating Milgram: Would people still obey today? *American Psychologist, 64,* 1–11. (p. 528)

Burgess, M., Enzle, M. E., & Schmaltz, R. (2004). Defeating the potentially deleterious effects of externally imposed deadlines: Practitioners' rules-of-thumb. *Personality and Social Psychology Bulletin, 30,* 868–877. (p. A-11)

Buri, J. R., Louiselle, P. A., Misukanis, T. M., & Mueller, R. A. (1988). Effects of parental authoritarianism and authoritativeness on self-esteem. *Personality and Social Psychology Bulletin, 14,* 271–282. (p. 202)

Burish, T. G., & Carey, M. P. (1986). Conditioned aversive responses in cancer chemotherapy patients: Theoretical and developmental analysis. *Journal of Counseling and Clinical Psychology, 54,* 593–600. (p. 303)

Burk, W. J., Denissen, J., Van Doorn, M. D., Branje, S. J. T., & Laursen, B. (2009). The vicissitudes of conflict measurement: Stability and reliability in the frequency of disagreements. *European Psychologist, 14,* 153–159. (p. 210)

Burke, B. L., Martens, A., & Faucher, E. H. (2010). Two decades of terror management theory: A meta-analysis of mortality salience research. *Personality and Social Psychology Review, 14,* 155–195. (p. 581)

Burke, D. M., & Shafto, M. A. (2004). Aging and language production. *Current Directions in Psychological Science, 13,* 21–24. (p. 218)

Burke, M., Adamic, L. A., & Marciniak, K. (2013). *Families on Facebook.* Association for the Advancement of Artificial Intelligence: Seventh International AAAI Conference on Weblogs and Social Media (www.facebook.com/publications). (p. 211)

Burns, B. C. (2004). The effects of speed on skilled chess performance. *Psychological Science, 15,* 442–447. (p. 364)

Burns, J. M., & Swerdlow, R. H. (2003). Right orbitofrontal tumor with pedophilia symptom and constructional apraxia sign. *Archives of Neurology, 60,* 437–440. (p. 51)

Burris, C. T., & Branscombe, N. R. (2005). Distorted distance estimation induced by a self-relevant national boundary. *Journal of Experimental Social Psychology, 41,* 305–312. (p. 381)

Burton, C. M., & King, L. A. (2008). Effects of (very) brief writing on health: The two-minute miracle. *British Journal of Health Psychology, 13,* 9–14. (p. 507)

Busby, D. M., Carroll, J. S., & Willoughby, B. J. (2010). Compatibility or restraint? The effects of sexual timing on marriage relationships. *Journal of Family Psychology, 24,* 766–774. (p. 447)

Bushdid, C., Magnasco, M. O., Vosshall, L. B., & Keller, A. (2014). Humans can discriminate more than 1 trillion olfactory stimuli. *Science, 343,* 1370–1372. (p. 267)

Bushman, B. J. (1993). Human aggression while under the influence of alcohol and other drugs: An integrative research review. *Current Directions in Psychological Science, 2,* 148–152. (p. 546)

Bushman, B. J. (2002). Does venting anger feed or extinguish the flame? Catharsis, rumination, distraction, anger, and aggressive responding. *Personality and Social Psychology Bulletin, 28,* 724–731. (p. 478)

Bushman, B. J., & Anderson, C. A. (2009). Comfortably numb: Desensitizing effects of violent media on helping others. *Psychological Science, 20,* 273–277. (p. 312)

Bushman, B. J., & Baumeister, R. F. (1998). Threatened egotism, narcissism, self-esteem, and direct and displaced aggression: Does self-love or self-hate lead to violence? *Journal of Personality and Social Psychology, 75,* 219–229. (p. 603)

Bushman, B. J., Baumeister, R. F., Thomaes, S., Ryu, E., Begeer, S., & West, S. G. (2009). Looking again, and harder, for a link between low self-esteem and aggression. *Journal of Personality, 77,* 427–446. (p. 603)

Bushman, B. J., & Huesmann, L. R. (2010). Aggression. In S. T. Fiske, D. T. Gilbert, & G. Lindzey (Eds.), *Handbook of social psychology* (5th ed., Ch. 23, pp. 833–863). New York: John Wiley & Sons. (p. 162)

Bushman, B. J., Moeller, S. J., & Crocker, J. (2011). Sweets, sex, or self-esteem? Comparing the value of self-esteem boosts with other pleasant rewards. *Journal of Personality, 79,* 993–1012. (p. 585)

Bushman, B. J., Ridge, R. D., Das, E., Key, C. W., & Busath, G. L. (2007). When God sanctions killing: Effects of scriptural violence on aggression. *Psychological Science, 18,* 204–207. (p. 162)

Busnel, M. C., Granier-Deferre, C., & Lecanuet, J. P. (1992, October). Fetal audition. *New York Academy of Sciences, 662,* 118–134. (p. 182)

Buss, A. H. (1989). Personality as traits. *American Psychologist, 44,* 1378–1388. (p. 593)

Buss, D. M. (1991). Evolutionary personality psychology. *Annual Review of Psychology, 42,* 459–491. (p. 142)

Buss, D. M. (1994). The strategies of human mating: People worldwide are attracted to the same qualities in the opposite sex. *American Scientist, 82,* 238–249. (p. 149)

Buss, D. M. (1995). Evolutionary psychology: A new paradigm for psychological science. *Psychological Inquiry, 6,* 1–30. (p. 148)

Buss, D. M. (2008). Female sexual psychology. World Question Center 2008 (edge.org). (p. 437)

Busteed, B. (2012, August 27). College grads need to interview the job. *Huffington Post* (www.huffingtonpost.com). (p. A-11)

Buster, J. E., Kingsberg, S. A., Aguirre, O., Brown, C., Breaux, J. G., Buch, A., . . . Casson, P. (2005). Testosterone patch for low sexual desire in surgically menopausal women: A randomized trial. *Obstetrics and Gynecology, 105*(5), 944–952. (p. 434)

Butler, A. C., Hokanson, J. E., & Flynn, H. A. (1994). A comparison of self-esteem lability and low trait self-esteem as vulnerability factors for depression. *Journal of Personality and Social Psychology, 66,* 166–177. (p. 635)

Butler, A., Oruc, I., Fox, C. J., & Barton, J. J. S. (2008). Factors contributing to the adaptation aftereffects of facial expression. *Brain Research, 1191,* 116–126. (pp. 234, 235)

Butler, R. A. (1954, February). Curiosity in monkeys. *Scientific American,* pp. 70–75. (p. 421)

Butterworth, G. (1992). Origins of self-perception in infancy. *Psychological Inquiry, 3,* 103–111. (p. 201)

Butts, M. M., Casper, W. J., & Yang, T. S. (2013). How important are work-family support policies? A meta-analytic investigation of their effects on employee outcomes. *Journal of Applied Psychology, 98,* 1–25. (p. A-13)

Buxton, O. M., Cain, S. W., O'Connor, S. P., Porter, J. H., Duffy, J. F., Wang, W., Czeisler, C. A., & Shea, S. A. (2012). Adverse metabolic consequences in humans of prolonged sleep restriction combined with circadian disruption. *Science Translational Medicine, 4,* 129ra143. (p. 108)

Byers-Heinlein, K., Burns, T. C., & Werker, J. F. (2010). The roots of bilingualism in newborns. *Psychological Science, 21,* 343–348. (p. 182)

Byrne, D. (1971). *The attraction paradigm.* New York: Academic Press. (p. 556)

Byrne, D. (1982). Predicting human sexual behavior. In A. G. Kraut (Ed.), *The G. Stanley Hall Lecture Series* (Vol. 2). Washington, DC: American Psychological Association. (p. 285)

Byrne, D. (1982). Predicting human sexual behavior. In A. G. Kraut (Ed.), *The G. Stanley Hall Lecture Series* (Vol. 2). Washington, DC: American Psychological Association. (p. 434)

Byrne, R. W. (1991, May/June). Brute intellect. *The Sciences,* pp. 42–47. (p. 377)

Byrne, R. W., Bates, L. A., & Moss, C. J. (2009). Elephant cognition in primate perspective. *Comparative Cognition & Behavior Reviews, 4,* 1–15. (p. 369)

Byrne, R. W., Hobaiter, C., & Klailova, M. (2011). Local traditions in gorilla manual skill: Evidence for observational learning of behavioral organization. *Animal Cognition,* 1–11. (p. 307)

Byron, K., & Khazanchi, S. (2011). A meta-analytic investigation of the relationship of state and trait anxiety to performance on figural and verbal creative tasks. *Personality and Social Psychology Bulletin, 37,* 269–283. (p. 366)

Cable, D. M., & Gilovich, T. (1998). Looked over or overlooked? Prescreening decisions and post-interview evaluations. *Journal of Personality and Social Psychology, 83,* 501–508. (p. A-5)

Cacioppo, J. T. (2007). Better interdisciplinary research through psychological science. *APS Observer, 20,* 3, 48–49. (p. 11)

Cacioppo, J. T., Cacioppo, S., Gonzaga, G. C., Ogburn, E. L., & VanderWeele, T. J. (2013). Marital satisfaction and break-ups differ across on-line and off-line meeting venues. *PNAS Proceedings of the National Academy of Sciences of the United States of America, 110,* 10135–10140. (p. 552)

Cacioppo, J. T., Fowler, J. H., & Christakis, N. A. (2009). Alone in the crowd: The structure and spread of loneliness in a large social network. *Journal of Personality and Social Psychology, 97*, 977–991. (p. 450)

Cacioppo, J. T., & Hawkley, L. C. (2009). Perceived social isolation and cognition. *Trends in Cognitive Sciences, 13*, 447–454. (p. 450)

Cacioppo, S., Bianchi-Demicheli, F., Frum, C., Pfaus, J. G., & Lewis, J.W. (2012). The common neural bases between sexual desire and love: A multilevel kernel density fMRI analysis. *Journal of Sexual Medicine, 12*,1048–1054. (p. 447)

Caddick, A., & Porter, L. E. (2012). Exploring a model of professionalism in multiple perpetrator violent crime in the UK. *Criminological & Criminal Justice: An International Journal, 12*, 61–82. (p. 162)

Cahill, L. (2005, May). His brain, her brain. *Scientific American*, pp. 40–47. (p. 165)

Cain, S. (2012). *Quiet: The power of introverts in a world that can't stop talking*. New York: Crown. (p. 588)

Calati, R., De Ronchi, D., Bellini, M., & Serretti, A. (2011). The 5-HTTLPR polymorphism and eating disorders: A meta-analysis. *International Journal of Eating Disorders, 44*, 191–199. (p. 652)

Caldwell, J. A. (2012). Crew schedules, sleep deprivation, and aviation performance. *Current Directions in Psychological Science, 21*, 85–89. (p. 108)

Cale, E. M., & Lilienfeld, S. O. (2002). Sex differences in psychopathy and antisocial personality disorder: A review and integration. *Clinical Psychology Review, 22*, 1179–1207. (p. 649)

Callaghan, T., Rochat, P., Lillard, A., Claux, M. L., Odden, H., Itakura, S., Tapanya, S., & Singh, S. (2005). Synchrony in the onset of mental-state reasoning. *Psychological Science, 16*, 378–384. (p. 190)

Callan, M. J., Shead, N. W., & Olson, J. M. (2011). Personal relative deprivation, delay discounting, and gambling. *Journal of Personality and Social Psychology, 101*, 955–973. (p. 208)

Calvin, C. M., Deary, I. J., Fenton, C., Roberts, B. A., Der, G., Leckenby, N., & Batty, G. D. (2011). Intelligence in youth and all-cause-mortality: Systematic review with meta-analysis. *International Journal of Epidemiology, 40*, 626–644. (p. 402)

Calvin, C. M., Deary, I. J., Webbink, D., Smith, P., Fernandes, C., Lee, S. H., Luciano, M., & Visscher, P. M. (2012). Multivariate genetic analyses of cognition and academic achievement from two population samples of 174,000 and 166,000 school children. *Behavior Genetics, 42*, 699–710. (p. 406)

Calvo-Merino, B., Glaser, D. E., Grèzes, J., Passingham, R. E., & Haggard, P. (2004). Action observation and acquired motor skills: An fMRI study with expert dancers. *Cerebral Cortex, 15*, 1243–1249. (p. 382)

Camerer, C. F., Loewenstein, G., & Weber, M. (1989). The curse of knowledge in economic settings: An experimental analysis. *Journal of Political Economy, 97*, 1232–1254. (p. A-15)

Cameron, L., & Rutland, A. (2006). Extended contact through story reading in school: Reducing children's prejudice toward the disabled. *Journal of Social Issues, 62*, 469–488. (p. 564)

Camp, J. P., Skeem, J. L., Barchard, K., Lilienfeld, S. O., & Poythress, N. G. (2013). Psychopathic predators? Getting specific about the relation between psychopathy and violence. *Journal of Consulting and Clinical Psychology, 81*, 467–480. (p. 649)

Campbell, A. (2010). Oxytocin and human social behavior. *Personality and Social Psychology Review, 14*, 281–205. (p. 492)

Campbell, D. T. (1975). On the conflicts between biological and social evolution and between psychology and moral tradition. *American Psychologist, 30*, 1103–1126. (p. 483)

Campbell, D. T., & Specht, J. C. (1985). Altruism: Biology, culture, and religion. *Journal of Social and Clinical Psychology, 3(1)*, 33–42. (p. 585)

Campbell, L., & Marshall, T. (2011). Anxious attachment and relationship processes: An interactionist perspective. *Journal of Personality, 79*, 1219–1249. (p. 595)

Campbell, M. W., & de Waal, F. B. M. (2011). Ingroup-outgroup bias in contagious yawning by chimpanzees supports link to empathy. *PLoS One, 6*, e18283. (p. 542)

Campbell, S. (1986). *The Loch Ness Monster: The evidence*. Willingborough, Northamptonshire, U.K.: Acquarian Press. (p. 236)

Campbell, W. K., Foster, C. A., & Finkel, E. J. (2002). Does self-love lead to love for others?: A story of narcissistic game-playing. *Journal of Personality and Social Psychology, 83*, 340–354. (p. 604)

Camper, J. (1990, February 7). Drop pompom squad, U. of I. rape study says. *Chicago Tribune*, p. 1. (p. 119)

Camperio-Ciani, A., Corna, F., & Capiluppi, C. (2004). Evidence for maternally inherited factors favouring male homosexuality and promoting female fecundity. *Proceedings of the Royal Society of London B, 271*, 2217–2221. (p. 444)

Camperio-Ciani, A., Lemmola, F., & Blecher, S. R. (2009). Genetic factors increase fecundity in female maternal relatives of bisexual men as in homosexuals. *Journal of Sexual Medicine, 6*, 449–455. (p. 444)

Camperio-Ciani, A., & Pellizzari, E. (2012). Fecundity of paternal and maternal non-parental female relatives of homosexual and heterosexual men. *PLoS One, 7*, e51088. (p. 444)

Campitelli, G., & Gobet, F. (2011). Deliberate practice: Necessary but not sufficient. *Current Directions in Psychological Science, 20*, 280–285. (p. 390)

Campos, J. J., Bertenthal, B. I., & Kermoian, R. (1992). Early experience and emotional development: The emergence of wariness and heights. *Psychological Science, 3*, 61–64. (p. 249)

Canli, T. (2008, February/March). The character code. *Scientific American Mind*, pp. 53–57. (p. 626)

Canli, T., Desmond, J. E., Zhao, Z., & Gabrieli, J. D. E. (2002). Sex differences in the neural basis of emotional memories. *Proceedings of the National Academy of Sciences, 99*, 10789–10794. (p. 471)

Cannon, W. B. (1929). *Bodily changes in pain, hunger, fear, and rage*. New York: Branford. (pp. 425, 491)

Cannon, W. B., & Washburn, A. L. (1912). An explanation of hunger. *American Journal of Physiology, 29*, 441–454. (p. 425)

Cantor, N., & Kihlstrom, J. F. (1987). *Personality and social intelligence*. Englewood Cliffs, NJ: Prentice-Hall. (p. 390)

Cantril, H., & Bumstead, C. H. (1960). *Reflections on the human venture*. New York: New York University Press. (p. 536)

Caplan, N., Choy, M. H., & Whitmore, J. K. (1992, February). Indochinese refugee families and academic achievement. *Scientific American*, pp. 36–42. (p. 154)

Caprariello, P. A., & Reis, H. T. (2013). To do, to have, or to share? Valuing experiences over material possessions depends on the involvement of others. *Journal of Personality and Social Psychology, 104*, 199–215. (p. 486)

Carducci, B. J., Cosby, P. C., & Ward, D. D. (1978). Sexual arousal and interpersonal evaluations. *Journal of Experimental Social Psychology, 14*, 449–457. (p. 556)

Carey, B. (2007, September 4). Bipolar illness soars as a diagnosis for the young. *New York Times* (www.nytimes.com). (p. 629)

Carey, B. (2009, November 27). Surgery for mental ills offers both hope and risk. *New York Times* (www.nytimes.com). (p. 688)

Carey, B. (2010). Seeking emotional clues without facial cues. *New York Times* (www.nytimes.com). (p. 475)

Carey, B. (2011, February 14). Wariness on surgery of the mind. *New York Times* (www.nytimes.com). (p. 688)

Carey, G. (1990). Genes, fears, phobias, and phobic disorders. *Journal of Counseling and Development, 68*, 628–632. (p. 626)

Carli, L. L., & Leonard, J. B. (1989). The effect of hindsight on victim derogation. *Journal of Social and Clinical Psychology, 8*, 331–343. (p. 544)

Carlson, M., Charlin, V., & Miller, N. (1988). Positive mood and helping behavior: A test of six hypotheses. *Journal of Personality and Social Psychology, 55*, 211–229. (p. 560)

Carmeli, A., Ben-Hador, B., Waldman, D. A., & Rupp, D. E. (2009). How leaders cultivate social capital and nurture employee vigor: Implications for job performance. *Journal of Applied Psychology, 94*, 1553–1561. (p. A-13)

Carnahan, T., & McFarland, S. (2007). Revisiting the Stanford Prison Experiment: Could participant self-selection have led to the cruelty? *Personality and Social Psychology Bulletin, 33*, 603–614. (p. 523)

Carnegie Council on Adolescent Development. (1989, June). *Turning points: Preparing American youth for the 21st century*. (The report of the Task Force on Education of Young Adolescents.) New York: Carnegie Corporation. (p. 405)

Caroll, H. (2013, October). Teen fashion model Georgina got so thin her organs were failing. But fashion designers still queued up to book her. Now she's telling her story to shame the whole industry. *The Daily Mail*. www.dailymail.co.uk. (p. 653)

Carpenter, C. J. (2012). Narcissism on Facebook: Self-promotional and anti-social behavior. *Personality and Individual Differences, 52*, 482-486. (p. 453)

Carpusor, A., & Loges, W. E. (2006). Rental discrimination and ethnicity in names. *Journal of Applied Social Psychology, 36*, 934–952. (p. 37)

Carré, J. M., McCormick, C. M., & Mondloch, C. J. (2009). Facial structure is a reliable cue of aggressive behavior. *Psychological Science, 20*, 1194–1198. (p. 546)

Carroll, D., Davey Smith, G., & Bennett, P. (1994, March). Health and socioeconomic status. *The Psychologist*, pp. 122–125. (p. 501)

Carroll, J. M., & Russell, J. A. (1996). Do facial expressions signal specific emotions? Judging emotion from the face in context. *Journal of Personality and Social Psychology, 70*, 205–218. (p. 473)

Carroll, P., Sweeny, K., & Shepperd, J. A. (2006). Forsaking optimism. *Review of General Psychology, 10*, 56–73. (p. 600)

Carskadon, M. (2002). *Adolescent sleep patterns: Biological, social, and psychological influences.* New York: Cambridge University Press. (p. 108)

Carstensen, L. L., & Mikels, J. A. (2005). At the intersection of emotion and cognition: Aging and the positivity effect. *Current Directions in Psychological Science, 14*, 117–121. (p. 401)

Carstensen, L. L., Turan, B., Scheibe, S., Ram, N, Ersner-Hershfield, H, Samanez-Larkin, G. R., Brooks, K. P., & Nesselroade, J. R. (2011). Emotional experience improves with age: Evidence based on over 10 years of experience sampling. *Psychology and Aging, 26*, 21–33. (p. 223)

Carter, R. (1998). *Mapping the mind.* Berkeley: University of California Press. (p. 57)

Carter, R. M., Bowling, D. L., Reeck, C., & Huettel, S. A. (2012). A distinct role of the temporal-parietal junction in predicting socially guided decisions. *Science, 337*, 109–111. (p. 95)

Carter, T. J., & Gilovich, T. (2010). The relative relativity of material and experiential purchases. *Journal of Personality and Social Psychology, 98*, 146–159. (p. 486)

Caruso, E. M., Vohs, K. D., Baxter, B., & Waytz, A. (2013). Mere exposure to money increases endorsement of free-market systems and social inequality. *Journal of Experimental Psychology: General, 142*, 301–306. (p. 335)

Carver, C. S., Johnson, S. L., & Joormann, J. (2008). Serotonergic function, two-mode models of self-regulation, and vulnerability to depression: What depression has in common with impulsive aggression. *Psychological Bulletin, 134*, 912–943. (p. 634)

Carver, C. S., Scheier, M. F., & Segerstrom, S. C. (2010). Optimism. *Clinical Psychology Review, 30*, 879–889. (p. 504)

CASA. (2003). *The formative years: Pathways to substance abuse among girls and young women ages 8–22.* New York: National Center on Addiction and Substance Use, Columbia University. (pp. 120, 128)

Casey, B. J., & Caudle, K. (2013). The teenage brain: Self-control. *Current Directions in Psychological Science, 22*, 82–87. (p. 205)

Casey, B. J., Getz, S., & Galvan, A. (2008). The adolescent brain. *Developmental Review, 28*, 62–77. (p. 205)

Casey, B. J., Somerville, L. H., Gotlib, I. H., Ayduk, O., Franklin, N. T., Askren, M. K., . . . Shoda, Y. (2011). Behavioral and neural correlates of delay of gratification 40 years later. *Proceedings of the National Academy of Sciences, 108*, 14998–15003. (p. 208)

Cash, T., & Janda, L. H. (1984, December). The eye of the beholder. *Psychology Today*, pp. 46–52. (p. 554)

Caspi, A. (2000). The child is father of the man: Personality continuities from childhood to adulthood. *Journal of Personality and Social Psychology, 78*, 158–172. (p. 140)

Caspi, A., Hariri, A. R., Holmes, A., Uher, R., & Moffitt, T. E. (2010). Genetic sensitivity to the environment: The case of the serotonin transporter gene and its implications for studying complex diseases and traits. *American Journal of Psychiatry, 167*, 509–527. (p. 634)

Caspi, A., Harrington, H., Milne, B., Amell, J. W., Theodore, R. F., & Moffitt, T. E. (2003). Children's behavioral styles at age 3 are linked to their adult personality traits at age 26. *Journal of Personality, 71*, 496–513. (p. 634)

Caspi, A., McClay, J., Moffitt, T., Mill, J., Martin, J., Craig, I. W., Taylor, A., & Poulton, R. (2002). Role of genotype in the cycle of violence in maltreated children. *Science, 297*, 851–854. (pp. 595, 651)

Caspi, A., Moffitt, T. E., Newman, D. L., & Silva, P. A. (1996). Behavioral observations at age 3 years predict adult psychiatric disorders: Longitudinal evidence from a birth cohort. *Archives of General Psychiatry, 53*, 1033–1039. (p. 650)

Cassidy, J., & Shaver, P. R. (1999). *Handbook of attachment.* New York: Guilford. (p. 196)

Castonguay, L. G., Boswell, J. F., Constantino, M. J., Goldfried, M. R., & Hill, C. E. (2010). Training implications of harmful effects of psychological treatments. *American Psychologist, 65*, 34–49. (p. 676)

Cattell, R. B. (1963). Theory of fluid and crystallized intelligence: A critical experiment. *Journal of Educational Psychology, 54*, 1–22. (p. 401)

Cavalli-Sforza, L., Menozzi, P., & Piazza, A. (1994). *The history and geography of human genes.* Princeton, NJ: Princeton University Press. (p. 412)

Cavigelli, S. A., & McClintock, M. K. (2003). Fear of novelty in infant rats predicts adult corticosterone dynamics and an early death. *Proceedings of the National Academy of Sciences, 100*, 16131–16136. (p. 492)

Cawley, B. D., Keeping, L. M., & Levy, P. E. (1998). Participation in the performance appraisal process and employee reactions: A meta-analytic review of field investigations. *Journal of Applied Psychology, 83*, 615–633. (p. A-12)

CDC. (1992). Serious mental illness and disability in the adult household population: United States, 1989. *Advance Data No. 218 from Vital and Health Statistics*, National Center for Health Statistics. (p. 618)

CDC. (2009). *Self-harm, all injury causes, nonfatal injuries and rates per 100,000.* National Center for Injury Prevention and Control. http://webappa.cdc.gov/cgi-bin/broker.exe. (p. 639)

CDC. (2011, accessed April 20). *Who's at risk? Tobacco use—smoking.* Centers for Disease Control and Prevention (cdc.gov/vitalsigns/TobaccoUse/Smoking/Risk.html). (p. 130)

CDC. (2011, February). *HIV surveillance report, 2009*, vol. 21. Centers for Disease Control and Prevention (www.cdc.gov/hiv/topics/surveillance/basic.htm#hivaidsage). (p. 436)

CDC. (2011, October). Teenagers in the United States: Sexual activity, contraceptive use, and childbearing, 2006–2010 National Survey of Family Growth. *Vital and Health Statistics*, Series 23, Number 31, Table 1, p. 14. (p. 438)

CDC. (2012, April). Birth rates for U.S. teenagers reach historic lows for all age and ethnic groups. NCHS Data Brief, Number 89. Centers for Disease Control and Prevention (www.cdc.gov). (p. 438)

CDC. (2012, May 11). Suicide rates among persons ages 10 years and older, by race/ethnicity and sex, United States, 2005–2009. National Suicide Statistics at a Glance, Centers for Disease Control and Prevention (www.cdc.gov). (p. 637)

CDC. (2012). Obesity trends among U.S. adults between 1985 and 2010. Centers for Disease Control and Prevention: www.cdc.gov/obesity/downloads/obesity_trends_2010.ppt. (p. 430)

CDC. (2013, accessed June 8). Heart disease facts. Centers for Disease Control and Prevention (cdc.gov/heartdisease/facts.htm). (p. 496)

CDC. (2013, accessed November 9). Tobacco-related mortality. Centers for Disease Control and Prevention (www.cdc.gov.). (p. 121)

CDC. (2013). ADHD, data and statistics. U.S. Centers for Disease Control and Prevention (www.cdc.gov/NCBBDDD/adhd/data.html). (p. 615)

CDC. (2014). Pregnant women need a flu shot. U.S. Centers for Disease Control and Prevention.(www.cdc.gov/flu/pdf/freeresources/pregnant/flushot_pregnant_factsheet.pdf) (p. 643)

CDC. (2014, March 28). Prevalence of autism spectrum disorder among children aged 8 years—Autism and developmental disabilities monitoring network, 11 sites. United States, 2010. *Morbidity and Mortality Weekly Report (MMWR), 63*(SS02), 1–21. (p. 193)

Ceci, S. J. (1993). *Cognitive and social factors in children's testimony.* Master lecture presented at the Annual Convention of the American Psychological Association. (pp. 347, 348)

Ceci, S. J., & Bruck, M. (1993). Child witnesses: Translating research into policy. *Social Policy Report* (Society for Research in Child Development), 7(3), 1–30. (p. 347)

Ceci, S. J., & Bruck, M. (1995). *Jeopardy in the courtroom: A scientific analysis of children's testimony.* Washington, DC: American Psychological Association. (p. 347)

Ceci, S. J., Huffman, M. L. C., Smith, E., & Loftus, E. F. (1994). Repeatedly thinking about a non-event: Source misattributions among preschoolers. *Consciousness and Cognition, 3*, 388–407. (p. 347)

Ceci, S. J., & Kanaya, T. (2010). "Apples and oranges are both round": Furthering the discussion on the Flynn effect. *Journal of Psychoeducational Assessment, 28*, 441–447. (p. 396)

Ceci, S. J., & Williams, W. M. (1997). Schooling, intelligence, and income. *American Psychologist, 52*, 1051–1058. (p. 409)

Ceci, S. J., & Williams, W. M. (2009). *The mathematics of sex: How biology and society conspire to limit talented women and girls.* New York: Oxford University Press. (p. 409)

Ceci, S. J., & Williams, W. M. (2010). Sex differences in math-intensive fields. *Current Directions in Psychological Science, 19*, 275–279. (p. 410)

Ceci, S. J., & Williams, W. M. (2011). Understanding current causes of women's underrepresentation in science. *Proceedings of the National Academy of Sciences, 108.* 3157–3162. (p. 410)

Centerwall, B. S. (1989). Exposure to television as a risk factor for violence. *American Journal of Epidemiology, 129*, 643–652. (p. 312)

Cepeda, N. J., Pashler, H., Vul, E., Wixted, J. T., & Rohrer, D. (2006). Distributed practice in verbal recall tasks: A review and quantitative synthesis. *Psychological Bulletin, 132*, 354–380. (p. 325)

Cepeda, N. J., Vul, E., Rohrer, D., Wixed, J. T., & Pashler, H. (2008). Spacing effects in learning: A temporal ridgeline of optimal retention. *Psychological Science, 19*, 1095–1102. (p. 325)

Cerella, J. (1985). Information processing rates in the elderly. *Psychological Bulletin, 98*, 67–83. (p. 216)

Cerny, J. A., & Janssen, E. (2011). Patterns of sexual arousal in homosexual, bisexual, and heterosexual men. *Archives of Sexual Behavior, 40*, 687–697. (p. 440)

CFI. (2003, July). *International developments. Report*. Amherst, NY: Center for Inquiry International. (p. 274)

Chabris, C. F., & Simons, D. (2010). *The invisible gorilla: And other ways our intuitions deceive us*. New York: Crown. (p. 98)

Chabris, C. F., et al. (2012). Most reported genetic associations with general intelligence are probably false positives. *Psychological Science, 23*, 1314–1323. (p. 406)

Chambers, E. S., Bridge, M. W., & Jones, D. A. (2009). Carbohydrate sensing in the human mouth: Effects on exercise performance and brain activity. *Journal of Physiology, 587*, 1779–1794. (p. 503)

Chambless, D. L., Baker, M. J., Baucom, D. H., Beutler, L. E., Calhoun, K. S., Crits-Christoph, P., . . . Woody, S. R. (1997). Update on empirically validated therapies, II. *The Clinical Psychologist, 51*(1), 3–16. (p. 677)

Chamove, A. S. (1980). Nongenetic induction of acquired levels of aggression. *Journal of Abnormal Psychology, 89*, 469–488. (p. 311)

Champagne, F. A. (2010). Early adversity and developmental outcomes: Interaction between genetics, epigenetics, and social experiences across the life span. *Perspectives on Psychological Science, 5*, 564–574. (p. 142)

Champagne, F. A., Francis, D. D., Mar, A, & Meaney, M. J. (2003). Naturally-occurring variations in maternal care in the rat as a mediating influence for the effects of environment on the development of individual differences in stress reactivity. *Physiology & Behavior, 79*, 359–371. (p. 143)

Champagne, F. A., & Mashoodh, R. (2009). Genes in context: Gene-environment interplay and the origins of individual differences in behavior. *Current Directions in Psychological Science, 18*, 127–131. (p. 143)

Chance News. (1997, 25 November). More on the frequency of letters in texts. Dart. Chance@Dartmouth.edu. (p. 31)

Chandler, J. J., & Pronin, E. (2012). Fast thought speed induces risk taking. *Psychological Science, 23*, 370–374. (p. 630)

Chandler, J., & Schwarz, N. (2009). How extending your middle finger affects your perception of others: learned movements influence concept accessibility. *Journal of Experimental Social Psychology, 45*, 123–128. (p. 475)

Chandra, A., Mosher, W. D., & Copen, C. (2011, March). Sexual behavior, sexual attraction, and sexual identity in the United States: Data from the 2006–2008 National Survey of Family Growth. *National Health Statistics Reports*, Number 36 (Centers for Disease Control and Prevention). (p. 440)

Chang, E. C. (2001). Cultural influences on optimism and pessimism: Differences in Western and Eastern construals of the self. In E. C. Chang (Ed.), *Optimism and pessimism*. Washington, DC: APA Books. (p. 600)

Chang, P. P., Ford, D. E., Meoni, L. A., Wang, N-Y., & Klag, M. J. (2002). Anger in young men and subsequent premature cardiovascular disease: The precursors study. *Archives of Internal Medicine, 162*, 901–906. (p. 497)

Chang, Y-T., Chen, Y-C., Hayter, M., & Lin, M-L. (2009). Menstrual and menarche experience among pubescent female students in Taiwan: Implications for health education and promotion service. *Journal of Clinical Nursing, 18*, 2040–2048. (p. 167)

Chaplin, T. M., & Aldao, A. (2013). Gender differences in emotion expression in children: A meta-analytic review. *Psychological Bulletin, 139*, 735–765. (p. 470)

Chaplin, W. F., Phillips, J. B., Brown, J. D., Clanton, N. R., & Stein, J. L. (2000). Handshaking, gender, personality, and first impressions. *Journal of Personality and Social Psychology, 79*, 110–117. (p. 468)

Charles, S. T., Piazza, J. R., Mogle, J., Sliwinski, M. J., & Almeida, D. M. (2013). The wear and tear of daily stressors on mental health. *Psychological Science, 24*, 733–741. (p. 632)

Charness, N., & Boot, W. R. (2009). Aging and information technology use. *Current Directions in Psychological Science, 18*, 253–258. (p. 401)

Charpak, G., & Broch, H. (2004). *Debunked! ESP, telekinesis, and other pseudoscience*. Baltimore, MD: Johns Hopkins University Press. (p. 273)

Chartrand, T. L., & Bargh, J. A. (1999). The chameleon effect: The perception-behavior link and social interaction. *Journal of Personality and Social Psychology, 76*, 893–910. (p. 525)

Chassy, P., & Gobet, F. (2011). A hypothesis about the biological basis of expert intuition. *Review of General Psychology, 15*, 198–212. (p. 364)

Chatard, A., & Selimbegović, L. (2011). When self-destructive thoughts flash through the mind: Failure to meet standards affects the accessibility of suicide-related thoughts. *Journal of Personality and Social Psychology, 100*, 587–605. (p. 638)

Chater, N., Reali, F., & Christiansen, M. H. (2009). Restrictions on biological adaptation in language evolution. *PNAS, 106*, 1015–1020. (p. 373)

Cheek, J. M., & Melchior, L. A. (1990). Shyness, self-esteem, and self-consciousness. In H. Leitenberg (Ed.), *Handbook of social and evaluation anxiety*. New York: Plenum. (p. 158)

Chein, J., Albert, D., O'Brien, L., Uckert, K., & Steinberg, L. (2011). Peers increase adolescent risk taking by enhancing activity in the brain's reward circuitry. *Developmental Science, 14*, F1–F10. (p. 155)

Chein, J. M., & Schneider, W. (2012). The brain's learning and control architecture. *Current Directions in Psychological Science, 21*, 78–84. (p. 79)

Cheit, R. E. (1998). Consider this, skeptics of recovered memory. *Ethics & Behavior, 8*, 141–160. (p. 580)

Chen, A. W., Kazanjian, A., & Wong, H. (2009). Why do Chinese Canadians not consult mental health services: Health status, language or culture? *Transcultural Psychiatry, 46*, 623–640. (p. 680)

Chen, E. (2004). Why socioeconomic status affects the health of children: A psychosocial perspective. *Current Directions in Psychological Science, 13*, 112–115. (p. 501)

Chen, G., Wu, Z., Guo, Z., & Gearing, M. (2014). Tonic inhibition in dentate gyrus impairs long-term potentiation and memory in an Alzheimer's disease model. *Nature Communications, 5*, 4159. (p. 219)

Chen, H. (2012). *Dark web: Exploring and data mining the dark side of the web*. New York; Springer. (p. 535)

Chen, S. H., Kennedy, M., & Zhou, Q. (2012). Parents' expression and discussion of emotion in the multilingual family: Does language matter? *Perspectives on Psychological Science, 7*, 365–383. (p. 380)

Chen, S-Y., & Fu, Y-C. (2008). Internet use and academic achievement: Gender differences in early adolescence. *Adolescence, 44*, 797–812. (p. 453)

Chen, S. X., & Bond, M. H. (2010). Two languages, two personalities? Examining language effects on the expression of personality in a bilingual context. *Personality and Social Psychology Bulletin, 36*, 1514–1528. (p. 380)

Cheon, B. K., Im, D.-M., Harada, T., Kim, J.-S., Mathur, V. A., Scimeca, J. M., . . . Chiao, J. Y. (2013). Cultural modulation of the neural correlates of emotional pain perception: The role of other-focusedness. *Neuropsychologia, 51*, 1177–1186. (p. 160)

Cherkas, L. F., Hunkin, J. L., Kato, B. S., Richards, J. B., Gardner, J. P., Surdulescu, G. L., . . . Aviv, A. (2008). The association between physical activity in leisure time and leukocyte telomere length. *Archives of Internal Medicine, 168*, 154–158. (p. 216)

Cherniss, C. (2010). Emotional intelligence: Toward clarification of a concept. *Industrial and Organizational Psychology, 3*, 110–126. (p. 391)

Chess, S., & Thomas, A. (1987). *Know your child: An authoritative guide for today's parents*. New York: Basic Books. (pp. 140, 197)

Cheung, B. Y., Chudek, M., & Heine, S. J. (2011). Evidence for a sensitive period for acculturation: Younger immigrants report acculturating at a faster rate. *Psychological Science, 22*, 147–152. (p. 374)

Chi, R. P., & Snyder, A. W. (2011). Facilitate insight by non-invasive brain stimulation. *PLoS One, 6*, e16655. (p. 357)

Chiao, J. Y., Cheon, B. K., Pornpattananangkul, N., Mrazek, A. J., & Blizinsky, K. D. (2013). Cultural neuroscience: Progress and promise. *Psychological Inquiry, 24*, 1–19. (p. 159)

Chida, Y., & Hamer, M. (2008). Chronic psychosocial factors and acute physiological responses to laboratory-induced stress in healthy populations: A quantitative review of 30 years of investigations. *Psychological Bulletin, 134*, 829–885. (p. 497)

Chida, Y., Hamer, M., Wardle, J., & Steptoe, A. (2008). Do stress-related psychosocial factors contribute to cancer incidence and survival? *Nature Reviews: Clinical Oncology, 5*, 466–475. (p. 496)

Chida, Y., & Steptoe, A. (2009). The association of anger and hostility with future coronary heart disease: A meta-analytic review of prospective evidence. *Journal of the American College of Cardiology, 17*, 936–946. (p. 497)

Chida, Y., Steptoe, A., & Powell, L. H. (2009). Religiosity/spirituality and mortality. *Psychotherapy and Psychosomatics, 78*, 81–90. (p. 513)

Chida, Y., & Vedhara, K. (2009). Adverse psychosocial factors predict poorer prognosis in HIV disease: A meta-analytic review of prospective investigations. *Brain, Behavior, and Immunity, 23,* 434–445. (p. 495)

Chiles, J. A., Lambert, M. J., & Hatch, A. L. (1999). The impact of psychological interventions on medical cost offset: A meta-analytic review. *Clinical Psychology: Science and Practice, 6,* 204–220. (p. 675)

Chisolm, T. H., Johnson, C. E., Danhauer, J. L., Portz, L. J. P., Abrams, H. B., Lesner, S., McCarthy, P. A., & Newman, C. W. (2007). A systematic review of health-related quality of life and hearing aids: Final report of the American Academy of Audiology Task Force on the Health-Related Quality of Life Benefits of Amplification in Adults. *Journal of the American Academy of Audiology, 18,* 151–183. (p. 375)

Chivers, M. L. (2005). A brief review and discussion of sex differences in the specificity of sexual arousal. *Sexual and Relationship Therapy, 20,* 377–390. (p. 441)

Chivers, M. L., Seto, M. C., & Blanchard, R. (2007). Gender and sexual orientation differences in sexual response to sexual activities versus gender of actors in sexual films. *Journal of Personality and Social Psychology, 93,* 1108–1121. (p. 441)

Chivers, M. L., Seto, M. C., Lalumière, M. L., Laan, E., & Grimbos, T. (2010). Agreement of self-reported and genital measures of sexual arousal in men and women: A meta-analysis. *Archives of Sexual Behavior, 39,* 5–56. (p. 437)

Choi, C. Q. (2008, March). Do you need only half your brain? *Scientific American,* p. 104. (p. 81)

Chomsky, N. (1972). *Language and mind.* New York: Harcourt Brace. (p. 377)

Chopik, W. J., Edelstein, R. S., & Fraley, R. C. (2013). From the cradle to the grave: Age differences in attachment from early adulthood to old age. *Journal of Personality, 81,* 171–183. (p. 223)

Christakis, D. A., Garrison, M. M., Herrenkohl, T., Haggerty, K., Rivara, K. P., Zhou, C., & Liekweg, K. (2013). Modifying media content for preschool children: A randomized control trial. *Pediatrics, 131,* 431–438. (p. 312)

Christakis, N. A., & Fowler, J. H. (2007). The spread of obesity in a large social network over 32 years. *New England Journal of Medicine, 357,* 370–379. (p. 431)

Christakis, N. A., & Fowler, J. H. (2008, May). The collective dynamics of smoking in a large social network. *New England Journal of Medicine, 358(21),* 2249–2258. (p. 129)

Christakis, N. A., & Fowler, J. H. (2009). *Connected: The surprising power of social networks and how they shape our lives.* New York: Little, Brown. (pp. 507, 525)

Christensen, A., & Jacobson, N. S. (1994). Who (or what) can do psychotherapy: The status and challenge of nonprofessional therapies. *Psychological Science, 5,* 8–14. (p. 679)

Christophersen, E. R., & Edwards, K. J. (1992). Treatment of elimination disorders: State of the art 1991. *Applied & Preventive Psychology, 1,* 15–22. (p. 663)

Chua, A. (2011). *Battle hymn of the tiger mother.* New York: Bloomsbury Publishing. (p. 154)

Chua, H. F., Boland, J. E., & Nisbett, R. E. (2005). Cultural variation in eye movements during scene perception. *Proceedings of the National Academy of Sciences, 102,* 12629–12633. (p. 518)

Chugani, H. T., & Phelps, M. E. (1986). Maturational changes in cerebral function in infants determined by 18FDG positron emission tomography. *Science, 231,* 840–843. (p. 185)

Chung, J. M., Robins, R. W., Trzesniewski, K. H., Noftle, E. E., Roberts, B. W., & Widaman, K. F. (2014). Continuity and change in self-esteem during emerging adulthood. *Journal of Personality and Social Psychology, 106,* 469–483. (p. 210)

Church, T. S., Thomas, D. M., Tudor-Locke, C., Katzmarzyk, P. T., Earnest, C. P., Rodarte, R. Q., . . . Bouchard, C. (2011). Trends over 5 decades in U.S. occupation-related physical activity and their associations with obesity. *PLoS ONE, 6(5),* e19657. (p. 431)

Churchland, P.S. (2013). *Touching a nerve: The self as brain.* New York: Norton. (p. 124)

CIA. (2014, accessed April 23). Sex ratio. *The world fact book* (www.cia.gov). (p. 540)

Cialdini, R. B. (1993). *Influence: Science and practice* (3rd ed.). New York: HarperCollins. (p. 521)

Cialdini, R. B., & Richardson, K. D. (1980). Two indirect tactics of image management: Basking and blasting. *Journal of Personality and Social Psychology, 39,* 406–415. (p. 543)

Ciarrochi, J., Forgas, J. P., & Mayer, J. D. (2006). *Emotional intelligence in everyday life* (2nd ed.). New York: Psychology Press. (p. 391)

Cin, S. D., Gibson, B., Zanna, M. P., Shumate, R., & Fong, G. T. (2007). Smoking in movies, implicit associations of smoking with the self, and intentions to smoke. *Psychological Science, 18,* 559–563. (p. 128)

Cincotta, A. L., Gehrman, P., Gooneratne, N. S., & Baime, M. J. (2011). The effects of a mindfulness-based stress reduction programme on pre-sleep cognitive arousal and insomnia symptoms: A pilot study. *Stress and Health, 27,* e299–e305. (p. 510)

Clack, B., Dixon, J., & Tredoux, C. (2005). Eating together apart: Patterns of segregation in a multi-ethnic cafeteria. *Journal of Community and Applied Social Psychology, 15,* 1–16. (p. 565)

Claidière, N., & Whiten, A. (2012). Integrating the study of conformity and culture in humans and nonhuman animals. *Psychological Bulletin, 138,* 126–145. (pp. 368, 527)

Clancy, S. A. (2005). *Abducted: How people come to believe they were kidnapped by aliens.* Cambridge, MA: Harvard University Press. (p. 102)

Clancy, S. A. (2010). *The trauma myth: The truth about the sexual abuse of children—and its aftermath.* New York: Basic Books. (p. 200)

Clancy, S. A., Schacter, D. L., McNally, R. J., & Pitman, R. K. (2000). False recognition in women reporting recovered memories of sexual abuse. *Psychological Science, 11,* 26–31. (p. 349)

Clark, A., Seidler, A., & Miller, M. (2001). Inverse association between sense of humor and coronary heart disease. *International Journal of Cardiology, 80,* 87–88. (p. 506)

Clark, C. J., Luguri, J. B., Ditto, P. H., Knobe, J., Shariff, A. F., & Baumeister, R. F. (2014). Free to punish: A motivated account of free will belief. *Journal of Personality and Social Psychology, 106,* 501–513. (p. 503)

Clark, K. B., & Clark, M. P. (1947). Racial identification and preference in Negro children. In T. M. Newcomb & E. L. Hartley (Eds.), *Readings in social psychology.* New York: Holt. (p. 41)

Clark, R. D., III, & Hatfield, E. (1989). Gender differences in willingness to engage in casual sex. *Journal of Psychology and Human Sexuality, 2,* 39–55. (p. 149)

Cleary, A. M. (2008). Recognition memory, familiarity, and déjà vu experiences. *Current Directions in Psychological Science, 17,* 353–357. (p. 346)

Clifton, J., & Morales, L. (2011, February 2). Egyptians', Tunisians' well-being plummets despite GDP gains. *Gallup* (www.gallup.com). (p. 486)

Coan, J. A., Schaefer, H. S., & Davidson, R. J. (2006). Lending a hand: Social regulation of the neural response to threat. *Psychological Science, 17,* 1032–1039. (p. 506)

Coelho, C. M., & Purkis, H. (2009). The origins of specific phobias: Influential theories and current perspectives. *Review of General Psychology, 13,* 335–348. (p. 627)

Coffey, C. E., Wilkinson, W. E., Weiner, R. D., Parashos, I. A., Djang, W. T., Webb, M. C., Figiel, G. S., & Spritzer, C. E. (1993). Quantitative cerebral anatomy in depression: A controlled magnetic resonance imaging study. *Archives of General Psychiatry, 50,* 7–16. (p. 633)

Coffman, K. B., Coffman, L. C., & Ericson, K. M. M. (2013, October). *The size of the LGBT population and the magnitude of anti-gay sentiment are substantially underestimated.* NBER Working Paper No. 19508, National Bureau of Economic Research. (p. 440)

Cohen, A. B. (2009). Many forms of culture. *American Psychologist, 64,* 194–204. (pp. 155, 158)

Cohen, D. (1995, June 17). Now we are one, or two, or three. *New Scientist,* pp. 14–15. (p. 648)

Cohen, F., & Solomon, S. (2011). The politics of mortal terror. *Current Directions in Psychological Science, 20,* 316–320. (p. 581)

Cohen, G. L. (2013, June). Quoted by E. Yong, Armor against prejudice. *Scientific American,* pp. 76–80. (p. 415)

Cohen, G. L., Garcia, J., Apfel, N., & Master, A. (2006). Reducing the racial achievement gap: A social-psychological intervention. *Science, 313,* 1307–1310. (p. 415)

Cohen, G. L., Garcia, J., Purdie-Vaughns, V., Apfel, N., Brzustoski, P. (2009). Recursive processes in self-affirmation: Intervening to close the minority achievement gap. *Science, 324,* 400–403. (p. 415)

Cohen, K. M. (2002). Relationships among childhood sex-atypical behavior, spatial ability, handedness, and sexual orientation in men. *Archives of Sexual Behavior, 31,* 129–143. (p. 446)

Cohen, P. (2007, November 15). Freud is widely taught at universities, except in the psychology department. *New York Times* (www.nytimes.com). (p. 572)

Cohen, P. (2010, June 11). Long road to adulthood is growing even longer. *New York Times* (www.nytimes.com). (p. 212)

Cohen, S. (2004). Social relationships and health. *American Psychologist, 59,* 676–684. (p. 506)

Cohen, S., Doyle, W. J., Alper, C. M., Janicki-Deverts, D., & Turner, R. B. (2009). Sleep habits and susceptibility to the common cold. *Archives of Internal Medicine, 169,* 62–67. (p. 108)

Cohen, S., Doyle, W. J., Skoner, D. P., Rabin, B. S., & Gwaltney, J. M., Jr. (1997). Social ties and susceptibility to the common cold. *Journal of the American Medical Association, 277,* 1940–1944. (pp. 502, 506)

Cohen, S., Doyle, W. J., Turner, R., Alper, C. M., & Skoner, D. P. (2003). Sociability and susceptibility to the common cold. *Psychological Science, 14,* 389–395. (p. 494)

Cohen, S., Kaplan, J. R., Cunnick, J. E., Manuck, S. B., & Rabin, B. S. (1992). Chronic social stress, affiliation, and cellular immune response in nonhuman primates. *Psychological Science, 3,* 301–304. (p. 494)

Cohen, S., & Pressman, S. D. (2006). Positive affect and health. *Current Directions in Psychological Science, 15,* 122–125. (p. 494)

Cohen, S., Tyrrell, D. A. J., & Smith, A. P. (1991). Psychological stress and susceptibility to the common cold. *New England Journal of Medicine, 325,* 606–612. (p. 494)

Cohn, Y. (2013, February 13). Love and marriage. Pew Research. www.pewsocialtrends.org. (p. 221)

Colapinto, J. (2000). *As nature made him: The boy who was raised as a girl.* New York: HarperCollins. (p. 167)

Colarelli, S. M., Spranger, J. L., & Hechanova, M. R. (2006). Women, power, and sex composition in small groups: An evolutionary perspective. *Journal of Organizational Behavior, 27,* 163–184. (p. 163)

Cole, K. C. (1998). *The universe and the teacup: The mathematics of truth and beauty.* New York: Harcourt Brace. (p. 121)

Cole, S. W., Arevalo, J. M. G., Takahashi, R., Sloan, E. K., Lutgendorf, S. K., Sood, A. K., Sheridan, J. F., & Seeman, T. E. (2010). Computational identification of gene-social envnironment interaction at the human IL6 locus. *PNAS, 107,* 5681–5686. (p. 499)

Colen C. G., & Ramey, D. M. (2014). Is breast truly best? Estimating the effects of breastfeeding on long-term child health and well-being in the United States using sibling comparisons. *Social Science & Medicine, 109,* 55–65. (p. 35)

Coley, R. L., Medeiros, B. L., & Schindler, H. (2008). Using sibling differences to estimate effects of parenting on adolescent sexual risk behaviors. *Journal of Adolescent Health, 43,* 133–140. (p. 439)

Collier, K. L., Bos, H. M. W., & Sandfort, T. G. M. (2012). Intergroup contact, attitudes toward homosexuality, and the role of acceptance of gender non-conformity in young adolescents. *Journal of Adolescence, 35,* 899–907. (p. 564)

Collinger, J. L., Wodlinger, B., Downey, J. E., Wang, W., Tyler-Kabara, E. C., Weber, D. J., . . . Schwartz, A. B. (2013). High-performance neuroprosthetic control by an individual with tetraplegia. *The Lancet, 381,* 557–564. (p. 77)

Collins, F. (2006). *The language of God.* New York: Free Press. (p. 172)

Collins, G. (2009, March 9). The rant list. *New York Times* (nytimes.com). (p. 40)

Collins, N. L., & Miller, L. C. (1994). Self-disclosure and liking: A meta-analytic review. *Psychological Bulletin, 116,* 457–475. (p. 557)

Collins, R. L., Elliott, M. N., Berry, S. H., Danouse, D. E., Kunkel, D., Hunter, S. B., & Miu, A. (2004). Watching sex on television predicts adolescent initiation of sexual behavior. *Pediatrics, 114,* 280–289. (p. 33)

Collins, W. A., Welsh, D. P., & Furman, W. (2009). Adolescent romantic relationships. *Annual Review of Psychology, 60,* 631–652. (p. 210)

Collinson, S. L., MacKay, C. E., James, A. C., Quested, D. J., Phillips, T., Roberts, N., & Crow, T. J. (2003). Brain volume, asymmetry and intellectual impairment in relation to sex in early-onset schizophrenia. *British Journal of Psychiatry, 183,* 114–120. (p. 642)

Collishaw, S., Pickles, A., Natarajan, L., & Maughan, B. (2007, June). *20-year trends in depression and anxiety in England.* Paper presented at the Thirteenth Scientific Meeting on The Brain and the Developing Child, London. (p. 632)

Colombo, J. (1982). The critical period concept: Research, methodology, and theoretical issues. *Psychological Bulletin, 91,* 260–275. (p. 196)

Comfort, A. (1992). *The new joy of sex.* New York: Pocket. (p. 214)

Commission on Children at Risk. (2003). *Hardwired to connect: The new scientific case for authoritative communities.* New York: Institute for American Values. (p. 202)

Confer, J. C., Easton, J. A., Fleischman, D. S., Goetz, C. D., Lewis, D. M. G., Perilloux, C., & Buss, D. M. (2010). Evolutionary psychology: Controversies, questions, prospects, and limitations. *American Psychologist, 65,* 110–126. (p. 150)

Conley, C. S., & Rudolph, K. D. (2009). The emerging sex difference in adolescent depression: Interacting contributions of puberty and peer stress. *Development and Psychopathology, 21,* 593–620. (p. 204)

Conley, K. M. & Lehman, B. J. (2012). Test anxiety and cardiovascular responses to daily academic stressors. *Stress and Health, 28,* 41–50. (p. 497)

Conley, T. D. (2011). Perceived proposer personality characteristics and gender differences in acceptance of casual sex offers. *Journal of Personality and Social Psychology, 100,* 300–329. (p. 150)

Conn, V. S. (2010). Depressive symptom outcomes of physical activity interventions: Meta-analysis findings. *Annals of Behavioral Medicine, 39,* 128–138. (p. 508)

Connor, C. E. (2010). A new viewpoint on faces. *Science, 330,* 764–765. (p. 245)

Connor-Smith, J. K., & Flachsbart, C. (2007). Relations between personality and coping: A meta-analysis. *Journal of Personality and Social Psychology, 93,* 1080–1107. (p. 501)

Consumer Reports. (1995, November). Does therapy help? pp. 734–739. (p. 673)

Conway, A. R. A., Skitka, L. J., Hemmerich, J. A., & Kershaw, T. C. (2009). Flashbulb memory for 11 September 2001. *Applied Cognitive Psychology, 23,* 605–623. (p. 332)

Conway, M. A., Wang, Q., Hanyu, K., & Haque, S. (2005). A cross-cultural investigation of autobiographical memory. On the universality and cultural variation of the reminiscence bump. *Journal of Cross-Cultural Psychology, 36,* 739–749. (p. 217)

Cooke, L. J., Wardle, J., & Gibson, E. L. (2003). Relationship between parental report of food neophobia and everyday food consumption in 2–6-year-old children. *Appetite, 41,* 205–206. (p. 266)

Cooper, K. J. (1999, May 1). This time, copycat wave is broader. *Washington Post* (www.washingtonpost.com). (p. 525)

Cooper, M. (2010, October 18). From Obama, the tax cut nobody heard of. *New York Times* (www.nytimes.com). (p. 542)

Cooper, W. H., & Withey, M. J. (2009). The strong situation hypothesis. *Personality and Social Psychology Review, 13,* 62–72. (p. 593)

Coopersmith, S. (1967). *The antecedents of self-esteem.* San Francisco: Freeman. (p. 202)

Copeland, W., Shanahan, L., Miller, S., Costello, E. J., Angold, A., & Maughan, B. (2010). Outcomes of early pubertal timing in young women: A prospective population-based study. *American Journal of Psychiatry, 167,* 1218–1225. (p. 204)

Corballis, M. C. (1989). Laterality and human evolution. *Psychological Review, 96,* 492–505. (p. 86)

Corballis, M. C. (2002). *From hand to mouth: The origins of language.* Princeton, NJ: Princeton University Press. (p. 378)

Corballis, M. C. (2003). From mouth to hand: Gesture, speech, and the evolution of right-handedness. *Behavioral and Brain Sciences, 26,* 199–260. (p. 378)

Corcoran, D. W. J. (1964). The relation between introversion and salivation. *The American Journal of Psychology, 77,* 298–300. (p. 588)

Coren, S. (1996). *Sleep thieves: An eye-opening exploration into the science and mysteries of sleep.* New York: Free Press. (pp. 107, 109)

Corey, D. P., et al. (2004). TRPA1 is a candidate for the mechanosensitive transduction channel of vertebrate hair cells. *Nature, 432,* 723–730. (p. 257)

Corina, D. P. (1998). The processing of sign language: Evidence from aphasia. In B. Stemmer & H. A. Whittaker (Eds.), *Handbook of neurolinguistics.* San Diego: Academic Press. (p. 85)

Corina, D. P., Vaid, J., & Bellugi, U. (1992). The linguistic basis of left hemisphere specialization. *Science, 255,* 1258–1260. (p. 85)

Corkin, S. (2013). *Permanent present tense: The unforgettable life of the amnesic patient.* New York: Basic Books. (p. 338)

Corkin, S., quoted by R. Adelson (2005, September). Lessons from H. M. *Monitor on Psychology,* p. 59. (p. 338)

Corneille, O., Huart, J., Becquart, E., & Brédart, S. (2004). When memory shifts toward more typical category exemplars: Accentuation effects in the recollection of ethnically ambiguous faces. *Journal of Personality and Social Psychology, 86,* 236–250. (p. 356)

Cornette, M. M., deRoom-Cassini, T. A., Fosco, G. M., Holloway, R. L., Clark, D. C., & Joiner, T. E. (2009). Application of an interpersonal-psychological model of suicidal behavior to physicians and medical trainees. *Archives of Suicide Research, 13,* 1–14. (p. 637)

Cornier, M-A. (2011). Is your brain to blame for weight regain? *Physiology & Behavior, 104,* 608–612. (p. 430)

Cornil, Y., & Chandon, P. (2013). From fan to fat? vicarious losing increases unhealthy eating, but self-affirmation is an effective remedy. *Psychological Science, 24*, 1936–1946. (p. 428)

Correll, J., Park, B., Judd, C. M., & Wittenbrink, B. (2002). The police officer's dilemma: Using ethnicity to disambiguate potentially threatening individuals. *Journal of Personality and Social Psychology, 83*, 1314–1329. (p. 539)

Correll, J., Park, B., Judd, C. M., Wittenbrink, B., Sadler, M. S., & Keesee, T. (2007). Across the thin blue line: Police officers and racial bias in the decision to shoot. *Journal of Personality and Social Psychology, 92*, 1006–1023. (p. 539)

Corse, A. K., Chou, T., Arulpragasm, A. R., Kaur, N., Deckersbach, T., & Cusin, C. (2013). Deep brain stimulation for obsessive-compulsive disorder. *Psychiatric Annals, 43*, 351–357. (p. 687)

Costa, P. T., Jr., & McCrae, R. R. (2011). The five-factor model, five factor theory, and interpersonal psychology. In L. M. Horowitz & S. Strack (Eds.), *Handbook of interpersonal psychology: Theory, research, assessment, and therapeutic interventions* (pp. 91–104). Hoboken, NJ: John Wiley & Sons. (p. 590)

Costa, P. T., Jr., Terracciano, A., & McCrae, R. R. (2001). Gender differences in personality traits across cultures: Robust and surprising findings. *Journal of Personality and Social Psychology, 81*, 322–331. (p. 470)

Costa, P. T., Jr., Zonderman, A. B., McCrae, R. R., Cornoni-Huntley, J., Locke, B. Z., & Barbano, H. E. (1987). Longitudinal analyses of psychological well-being in a national sample: Stability of mean levels. *Journal of Gerontology, 42*, 50–55. (p. 224)

Costello, E. J., Compton, S. N., Keeler, G., & Angold, A. (2003). Relationships between poverty and psychopathology: A natural experiment. *Journal of the American Medical Association, 290*, 2023–2029. (pp. 33, 618)

Coughlin, J. F., Mohyde, M., D'Ambrosio, L. A., & Gilbert, J. (2004). *Who drives older driver decisions?* Cambridge, MA: MIT Age Lab. (p. 216)

Couli, J. T., Vidal, F., Nazarian, B., & Macar, F. (2004). Functional anatomy of the attentional modulation of time estimation. *Science, 303*, 1506–1508. (p. A-1)

Courage, M. L., & Howe, M. L. (2002). From infant to child: The dynamics of cognitive change in the second year of life. *Psychological Bulletin, 128*, 250–277. (p. 201)

Courage, M. L., & Setliff, A. E. (2010). When babies watch television: Attention-getting, attention-holding, and the implications for learning from video material. *Developmental Review, 30*, 220–238. (p. 615)

Courtney, J. G., Longnecker, M. P., Theorell, T., & de Verdier, M. G. (1993). Stressful life events and the risk of colorectal cancer. *Epidemiology, 4*, 407–414. (p. 496)

Covin, R., Ouimet, A. J., Seeds, P. M., & Dozois, D. J. A. (2008). A meta-analysis of CBT for pathological worry among clients with GAD. *Journal of Anxiety Disorders, 22*, 108–116. (p. 670)

Cowan, N. (1988). Evolving conceptions of memory storage, selective attention, and their mutual constraints within the human information-processing system. *Psychological Bulletin, 104*, 163–191. (p. 323)

Cowan, N. (2008). What are the differences between long-term, short-term, and working memory? *Progress in Brain Research, 169*, 323–338. (p. 324)

Cowan, N. (2010). The magical mystery four: How is working memory capacity limited, and why? *Current Directions in Psychological Science, 19*, 51–57. (p. 321)

Cowart, B. J. (1981). Development of taste perception in humans: Sensitivity and preference throughout the life span. *Psychological Bulletin, 90*, 43–73. (p. 266)

Cowart, B. J. (2005). Taste, our body's gustatory gatekeeper. *Cerebrum, 7*(2), 7–22. (p. 266)

Cox, C. R., & Arndt, J. (2012). How sweet it is to be loved by you: The role of perceived regard in the terror management of close relationships. *Journal of Personality and Social Psychology, 102*, 616–632. (pp. 581, 582)

Cox, J. J., et al. (2006). An SCN9A channelopathy causes congenital inability to experience pain. *Nature, 444*, 894–898. (p. 264)

Coyne, J. C. (1976a). Toward an interactional description of depression. *Psychiatry, 39*, 28–40. (p. 595)

Coyne, J. C. (1976b). Depression and the response of others. *Journal of Abnormal Psychology, 85*, 186–193. (pp. 595, 636)

Coyne, J. C., Ranchor, A. V., & Palmer, S. C. (2010). Meta-analysis of stress-related factors in cancer. *Nature Reviews: Clinical Oncology, 7*, doi:10.1038/ncponc1134-c1. (p. 496)

Coyne, J. C., Stefanek, M., & Palmer, S. C. (2007). Psychotherapy and survival in cancer: The conflict between hope and evidence. *Psychological Bulletin, 133*, 367–394. (p. 496)

Coyne, J. C., & Tennen, H. (2010). Positive psychology in cancer care: Bad science, exaggerated claims, and unproven medicine. *Annals of Behavioral Medicine, 39*, 16–26. (p. 496)

Coyne, J. C., Thombs, B. C., Stefanek, M., & Palmer, S. C. (2009). Time to let go of the illusion that psychotherapy extends the survival of cancer patients: Reply to Kraemer, Kuchler, and Spiegel (2009). *Psychological Bulletin, 135*, 179–182. (p. 496)

CPP. (2008). Myers-Briggs Type Indicator® assessment (MBTI®). CPP, Inc. (www.cpp.com). (p. 586)

Crabbe, J. C. (2002). Genetic contributions to addiction. *Annual Review of Psychology, 53*, 435–462. (p. 127)

Crabtree, S. (2005, January 13). Engagement keeps the doctor away. *Gallup Management Journal* (gmj.gallup.com). (p. A-10)

Crabtree, S. (2011, December 12). U.S. seniors maintain happiness highs with less social time. www.gallup.com. (p. 224)

Craik, F. I. M., & Tulving, E. (1975). Depth of processing and the retention of words in episodic memory. *Journal of Experimental Psychology: General, 104*, 268–294. (p. 326)

Crandall, C. S. (1988). Social contagion of binge eating. *Journal of Personality and Social Psychology, 55*, 588–598. (p. 651)

Crary, D. (2009, May 9). 5 years on, gay marriage debate fades in Mass. AP article in *The Guardian* (guardian.co.uk). (p. 148)

Crawford, M., Chaffin, R., & Fitton, L. (1995). Cognition in social context. Learning and Individual Differences, Special Issue: Psychological and psychobiological perspectives on sex differences in cognition: 1. *Theory and Research, 7*, 341–362. (p. 411)

Credé, M., & Kuncel, N. R. (2008). Study habits, skills, and attitudes: The third pillar supporting collegiate academic performance. *Perspectives on Psychological Science, 3*, 425–453. (p. 409)

Cresswell, J. D., Bursley, J. K., & Satpute, A. B. (2013). Neural reactivation links unconscious thought to decision making performance. *Social Cognitive and Affective Neuroscience, 8*, 863–869. (p. 365)

Creswell, J. D., Way, B. M., Eisenberger, N. I., & Lieberman, M. D. (2007). Neural correlates of dispositional mindfulness during affect labeling. *Psychosomatic Medicine, 69*, 560–565. (p. 511)

Crews, F. T., He, J., & Hodge, C. (2007). Adolescent cortical development: A critical period of vulnerability for addiction. *Pharmacology, Biochemistry and Behavior, 86*, 189–199. (pp. 120, 205)

Crews, F. T., Mdzinarishvili, A., Kim, D., He, J., & Nixon, K. (2006). Neurogenesis in adolescent brain is potently inhibited by ethanol. *Neuroscience, 137*, 437–445. (p. 120)

Crocker, J. (2011). Presidential Address: Self-image and compassionate goals and construction of the social self: Implications for social and personality psychology. *Personality and Social Psychology Review, 15*, 394–407. (p. 605)

Crocker, J., Thompson, L. L., McGraw, K. M., & Ingerman, C. (1987). Downward comparison, prejudice, and evaluation of others: Effects of self-esteem and threat. *Journal of Personality and Social Psychology, 52*, 907–916. (p. 543)

Croft, R. J., Klugman, A., Baldeweg, T., & Gruzelier, J. H. (2001). Electrophysiological evidence of serotonergic impairment in long-term MDMA ("Ecstasy") users. *American Journal of Psychiatry, 158*, 1687–1692. (p. 124)

Crombie, A. C. (1964, May). Early concepts of the senses and the mind. *Scientific American*, pp. 108–116. (p. 240)

Crook, T. H., & West, R. L. (1990). Name recall performance across the adult lifespan. *British Journal of Psychology, 81*, 335–340. (p. 217)

Cross, S., & Markus, H. (1991). Possible selves across the life span. *Human Development, 34*, 230–255. (p. 598)

Cross-National Collaborative Group. (1992). The changing rate of major depression. *Journal of the American Medical Association, 268*, 3098–3105. (p. 632)

Crowell, J. A., & Waters, E. (1994). Bowlby's theory grown up: The role of attachment in adult love relationships. *Psychological Inquiry, 5*, 1–22. (p. 196)

Croy, I., Bojanowski, V., & Hummel, T. (2013). Men without a sense of smell exhibit a strongly reduced number of sexual relationships, women exhibit reduced partnership security: A reanalysis of previously published data. *Biological Psychology, 92*, 292–294. (p. 266)

Croy, I., Negoias, S., Novakova, L., Landis, B. N., & Hummel, T. (2012). Learning about the functions of the olfactory system from people without a sense of smell. *PLoS ONE 7*(3): e33365. doi:10.1371/journal.pone.0033365. (p. 266)

Csikszentmihalyi, M. (1990). *Flow: The psychology of optimal experience.* New York: Harper & Row. (p. A-1)

Csikszentmihalyi, M. (1999). If we are so rich, why aren't we happy? *American Psychologist, 54*, 821–827. (p. A-1)

Csikszentmihalyi, M., & Hunter, J. (2003). Happiness in everyday life: The uses of experience sampling. *Journal of Happiness Studies, 4*, 185–199. (p. 210)

Csikszentmihalyi, M., & Larson, R. (1984). *Being adolescent: Conflict and growth in the teenage years.* New York: Basic Books. (p. 224)

Cuijpers, P., Driessen, E., Hollon, S. D., van Oppen, P., Barth, J., & Andersson, G. (2012). The efficacy of non-directive supportive therapy for adult depression: A meta-analysis. *Clinical Psychology Review, 32,* 280–291. (p. 676)

Cuijpers, P., Geraedts, A. S. van Oppen, P., Andersson, G., Markowitz, J. C., & van Straten, A. (2011). Interpersonal psychotherapy for depression: A meta-analysis. *American Journal of Psychiatry, 168,* 581–592. (p. 660)

Cuijpers, P., van Straten, A., Schuurmans, J., van Oppen, P., Hollon, S. D., & Andersson, G. (2010). Psychotherapy for chronic major depression and dysthymia: A meta-analysis. *Clinical Psychology Review, 30,* 51–62. (p. 684)

Culbert, K. M., Burt, S. A., McGue, M., Iacono, W. G., & Klump, K. L. (2009). Puberty and the genetic diathesis of disordered eating attitudes and behaviors. *Journal of Abnormal* Psychology, *118,* 788–796. (p. 652)

Cullum, J., & Harton, H. C. (2007). Cultural evolution: Interpersonal influence, issue importance, and the development of shared attitudes in college residence halls. *Personality and Social Psychology Bulletin, 33,* 1327–1339. (p. 527)

Culverhouse, R. C., Bowes, L., Breslau, N., Nurnberger, J. I., Jr., Burmeister, M., Fergusson, D. M., . . Bierut, L. J. (2013). Protocol for a collaborative meta-analysis of 5-HTTLPR, stress, and depression. *BMC Psychiatry, 13,* 304. (p. 634)

Cummings, R. A. (2006, April 4). *Australian Unity Wellbeing Index: Survey 14.1.* Melbourne: Australian Centre on Quality of Life, Deakin University. (p. 482)

Cunningham, M. R., et al. (2005). "Their ideas of beauty are, on the whole, the same as ours": Consistency and variability in the cross-cultural perception of female physical attractiveness. *Journal of Personality and Social Psychology, 68,* 261–279. (p. 554)

Cunningham, W. A., Johnson, M. K., Raye, C. L., Gatenby, J. C., Gore, J. C., & Banaji, M. R. (2004). Separable neural components in the processing of Black and White faces. *Psychological Science, 15,* 806–813. (p. 540)

Currie, T. E., & Little, A. C. (2009). The relative importance of the face and body in judgments of human physical attractiveness. *Evolution and Human Behavior, 30,* 409–416. (p. 554)

Curtis, R. C., & Miller, K. (1986). Believing another likes or dislikes you: Behaviors making the beliefs come true. *Journal of Personality and Social Psychology, 51,* 284–290. (p. 556)

Custers, R., & Aarts, H. (2010). The unconscious will: How the pursuit of goals operates outside of conscious awareness. *Science, 329,* 47–50. (p. 364)

Cyders, M. A., & Smith, G. T. (2008). Emotion-based dispositions to rash action: Positive and negative urgency. *Psychological Bulletin, 134,* 807–828. (p. 459)

Czeisler, C. A., Allan, J. S., Strogatz, S. H., Ronda, J. M., Sanchez, R., Rios, . . . Kronauer, R. E. (1986). Bright light resets the human circadian pacemaker independent of the timing of the sleep-wake cycle. *Science, 233,* 667–671. (p. 105)

Czeisler, C. A., Duffy, J. F., Shanahan, T. L., Brown, E. N., Mitchell, J. F., Rimmer, . . . Kronauer, R. E. (1999). Stability, precision, and near-24-hour period of the human circadian pacemaker. *Science, 284,* 2177–2181. (p. 104)

Czeisler, C. A., Kronauer, R. E., Allan, J. S., & Duffy, J. F. (1989). Bright light induction of strong (type O) resetting of the human circadian pacemaker. *Science, 244,* 1328–1333. (p. 105)

Dabbs, J. M., Jr., Bernieri, F. J., Strong, R. K., Campo, R., & Milun, R. (2001b). Going on stage: Testosterone in greetings and meetings. *Journal of Research in Personality, 35,* 27–40. (p. 546)

Dabbs, J. M., Jr., & Morris, R. (1990). Testosterone, social class, and antisocial behavior in a sample of 4,462 men. *Psychological Science, 1,* 209–211. (p. 546)

Daley, J. (2011, July/August). What you don't know can kill you. *Discover* (www.discovermagazine.com). (p. 363)

Dalton, P., & Fraenkel, N. (2012). Gorillas we have missed: Sustained inattentional deafness for dynamic events. *Cognition, 124,* 364–367. (p. 98)

Damasio, A. R. (2010). *Self comes to mind: Constructing the conscious brain.* New York: Pantheon. (p. 598)

Damon, W., & Hart, D. (1982). The development of self-understanding from infancy through adolescence. *Child Development, 53,* 841–864. (p. 201)

Damon, W., & Hart, D. (1988). *Self-understanding in childhood and adolescence.* Cambridge: Cambridge University Press. (p. 201)

Damon, W., & Hart, D. (1992). Self-understanding and its role in social and moral development. In M. H. Bornstein & M. E. Lamb (Eds.), *Developmental psychology: An advanced textbook* (3rd ed.). Hillsdale, NJ: Lawrence Erlbaum. (p. 201)

Damon, W., Menon, J., & Bronk, K. (2003). The development of purpose during adolescence. *Applied Developmental Science, 7,* 119–128. (p. 210)

Dana, J., Dawes, R., & Peterson, N. (2013). Belief in the unstructured interview: The persistence of an illusion. *Judgment and Decision Making, 8,* 512–520. (p. A-5)

Danelli, L., Cossu, G., Berlingeri, M., Bottini, G., Sberna, M., & Paulesu, E. (2013). Is a lone right hemisphere enough? Neurolinguistic architecture in a case with a very early left hemispherectomy. *Neurocase, 19,* 209–231. (p. 81)

Danner, D. D., Snowdon, D. A., & Friesen, W. V. (2001). Positive emotions in early life and longevity: Findings from the Nun Study. *Journal of Personality and Social Psychology, 80,* 804–813. (p. 505)

Danso, H., & Esses, V. (2001). Black experimenters and the intellectual test performance of white participants: The tables are turned. *Journal of Experimental Social Psychology, 37,* 158–165. (p. 414)

Danziger, S., & Ward, R. (2010). Language changes implicit associations between ethnic groups and evaluation in bilinguals. *Psychological Science, 21,* 799–800. (p. 380)

Dapretto, M., Davies, M. S., Pfeifer, J. H., Scott, A. A., Sigman, M., Bookheimer, S. Y., & Iacoboni, M. (2006). Understanding emotions in others: Mirror neuron dysfunction in children with autism spectrum disorders. *Nature Neuroscience, 9,* 28–30. (p. 194)

Darley, J. M. (2009). Morality in the law: The psychological foundations of citizens' desires to punish transgressions. *Annual Review of Law and Social Science, 5,* 1–23. (p. 207)

Darley, J. M., & Alter, A. (2012). Behavioral issues of punishment and deterrence. In E. Shafir (Ed.), *The behavioral foundations of policy.* Princeton, NJ: Princeton University Press and the Russell Sage Foundation. (p. 295)

Darley, J. M., & Latané, B. (1968a). Bystander intervention in emergencies: Diffusion of responsibility. *Journal of Personality and Social Psychology, 8,* 377–383. (pp. 559, 560)

Darley, J. M., & Latané, B. (1968b, December). When will people help in a crisis? *Psychology Today,* pp. 54–57, 70–71. (p. 559)

Darrach, B., & Norris, J. (1984, August). An American tragedy. *Life,* pp. 58–74. (p. 649)

Darwin, C. (1859). *On the origin of species by means of natural selection.* London: John Murray. (p. 146)

Darwin, C. (1872). *The expression of the emotions in man and animals.* London: John Murray. (pp. 264, 474)

Daum, I., & Schugens, M. M. (1996). On the cerebellum and classical conditioning. *Psychological Science, 5,* 58–61. (p. 330)

Davey, G., & Rato, R. (2012). Subjective well-being in China: A review. *Journal of Happiness Studies, 13,* 333–346. (pp. 482, 484)

Davey, G. C. L. (1992). Classical conditioning and the acquisition of human fears and phobias: A review and synthesis of the literature. *Advances in Behavior Research and Therapy, 14,* 29–66. (p. 303)

Davey, G. C. L. (1995). Preparedness and phobias: Specific evolved associations or a generalized expectancy bias? *Behavioral and Brain Sciences, 18,* 289–297. (p. 627)

Davidoff, J. (2004). Coloured thinking. *The Psychologist, 17,* 570–572. (p. 380)

Davidson, J. R. T., Connor, K. M., & Swartz, M. (2006). Mental illness in U.S. presidents between 1776 and 1974: A review of biographical sources. *Journal of Nervous and Mental Disease, 194,* 47–51. (p. 653)

Davidson, R. J. (2000). Affective style, psychopathology, and resilience: Brain mechanisms and plasticity. *American Psychologist, 55,* 1196–1209. (pp. 467, 546)

Davidson, R. J. (2003). Affective neuroscience and psychophysiology: Toward a synthesis. *Psychophysiology, 40,* 655–665. (p. 467)

Davidson, R. J., Kabat-Zinn, J., Schumacher, J., Rosenkranz, M., Muller, D., Santorelli, S. F., . . . Sheridan, J. F. (2003). Alterations in brain and immune function produced by mindfulness meditation. *Psychosomatic Medicine, 65,* 564–570. (p. 511)

Davidson, R. J., Pizzagalli, D., Nitschke, J. B., & Putnam, K. (2002). Depression: Perspectives from affective neuroscience. *Annual Review of Psychology, 53,* 545–574. (p. 633)

Davies, G., et al. (2011). Genome-wide association studies establish that human intelligence is highly heritable and polygenic. *Molecular Psychiatry, 16,* 996–1005. (p. 406)

Davies, P. (2007). *Cosmic jackpot: Why our universe is just right for life.* Boston: Houghton Mifflin. (p. 173)

Davis, B. E., Moon, R. Y., Sachs, H. C., & Ottolini, M. C. (1998). Effects of sleep position on infant motor development. *Pediatrics, 102,* 1135–1140. (p. 185)

Davis, H., IV, Liotti, M., Ngan, E. T., Woodward, T. S., Van Sellenberg, J. X., . . . Mayberg, H. S. (2008). FMRI BOLD signal changes in elite swimmers while viewing videos of personal failures. *Brain Imaging and Behavior, 2,* 94–104. (p. 633)

Davis, J. O., & Phelps, J. A. (1995a). Twins with schizophrenia: Genes or germs? *Schizophrenia Bulletin, 21,* 13–18. (p. 644)

Davis, J. O., Phelps, J. A., & Bracha, H. S. (1995b). Prenatal development of monozygotic twins and concordance for schizophrenia. *Schizophrenia Bulletin, 21,* 357–366. (pp. 136, 644)

Davis, J. P., Lander, K., & Jansari, A. (2013). I never forget a face. *The Psychologist, 26,* 726–729. (p. 318)

Davis, K., Christodoulou, J., Seider, S., & Gardner, H. (2011). The theory of multiple intelligences. In R. J. Sternberg & S. B. Kaufman (Eds.), *Cambridge Handbook of Intelligence.* Cambridge, UK; New York: Cambridge University Press. (p. 387)

Davis, M. (2005). Searching for a drug to extinguish fear. *Cerebrum, 7*(3), 47–58. (p. 683)

Davison, K. P., Pennebaker, J. W., & Dickerson, S. S. (2000). Who talks? The social psychology of illness support groups. *American Psychologist, 55,* 205–217. (p. 671)

Dawes, R. M. (1980). Social dilemmas. *Annual Review of Psychology, 31,* 169–193. (p. 563)

Dawes, R. M. (1994). *House of cards: Psychology and psychotherapy built on myth.* New York: Free Press. (p. 599)

Dawkins, L., Shahzad, F-Z., Ahmed, S. S., & Edmonds, C. J. (2011). Expectation of having consumed caffeine can improve performance and moods. *Appetite, 57,* 597–600. (p. 36)

Dawkins, R. (1998). *Unweaving the rainbow.* Boston: Houghton Mifflin. (p. 172)

Dawkins, R. (2007, July 1). Inferior design. *New York Times* (www.nytimes.com). (p. 144)

Deal, G. (2011, January 14). Chinese parenting: Thanks, I'll pass. *Wall Street Journal.* Available from http://blogs.wsj.com. (p. 154)

Dean, G. (2012, November/December). Phrenology and the grand delusion of experience. *Skeptical Inquirer,* pp. 31–38. (p. 52)

Deary, I. J. (2008). Why do intelligent people live longer? *Nature, 456,* 175–176. (p. 403)

Deary, I. J., Batty, G. D., & Gale, C. R. (2008). Bright children become enlightened adults. *Psychological Science, 19,* 1–6. (p. 402)

Deary, I. J., Johnson, W., & Houlihan, L. M. (2009). Genetic foundations of human intelligence. *Human Genetics, 126,* 215–232. (pp. 406, 407)

Deary, I. J., & Matthews, G. (1993). Personality traits are alive and well. *The Psychologist: Bulletin of the British Psychological Society, 6,* 299–311. (p. 592)

Deary, I. J., Pattie, A., & Starr, J. M. (2013). The stability of intelligence from age 11 to age 90 years: The Lothian birth cohort of 1921. *Psychological Science, 24,* 2361–2368. (p. 402)

Deary, I. J., Strand, S., Smith, P., & Fernandes, C. (2007). Intelligence and educational achievement. *Intelligence, 35,* 13–21. (p. 398)

Deary, I. J., Thorpe, G., Wilson, V., Starr, J. M., & Whalley, L. J. (2003). Population sex differences in IQ at age 11: The Scottish mental survey 1932. *Intelligence, 31,* 533–541. (p. 410)

Deary, I. J., Weiss, A., & Batty, G. D. (2010) Intelligence and personality as predictors of illness and death: How researchers in differential psychology and chronic disease epidemiology are collaborating to understand and address health inequalities. *Psychological Science in the Public Interest, 11,* 53–79. (p. 402)

Deary, I. J., Whalley, L. J., & Starr, J. M. (2009). *A lifetime of intelligence: Follow-up studies of the Scottish Mental Surveys of 1932 and 1947.* Washington, DC: American Psychological Association. (pp. 398, 402)

Deary, I. J., Whiteman, M. C., Starr, J. M., Whalley, L. J., & Fox, H. C. (2004). The impact of childhood intelligence on later life: Following up the Scottish mental surveys of 1932 and 1947. *Journal of Personality and Social Psychology, 86,* 130–147. (p. 402)

Deary, I. J., et al. (2012). Genetic contributions to stability and change in intelligence from childhood to old age. *Nature, 481,* 212–215. (p. 407)

de Boysson-Bardies, B., Halle, P., Sagart, L., & Durand, C. (1989). A cross linguistic investigation of vowel formats in babbling. *Journal of Child Language, 16,* 1–17. (p. 372)

DeBruine, L. M. (2002). Facial resemblance enhances trust. *Proceedings of the Royal Society of London, 269,* 1307–1312. (p. 552)

DeBruine, L. M. (2004). Facial resemblance increases the attractiveness of same-sex faces more than other-sex faces. *Proceedings of the Royal Society of London B, 271,* 2085–2090. (p. 552)

DeCasper, A. J., Lecanuet, J-P., Busnel, M-C., et al. (1994). Fetal reactions to recurrent maternal speech. *Infant Behavior and Development, 17,* 159–164. (p. 182)

DeCasper, A. J., & Prescott, P. A. (1984). Human newborns' perception of male voices: Preference, discrimination and reinforcing value. *Developmental Psychobiology, 17,* 481–491. (p. 182)

DeCasper, A. J., & Spence, M. J. (1986). Prenatal maternal speech influences newborns' perception of speech sounds. *Infant Behavior and Development, 9,* 133–150. (p. 182)

Deci, E. L., Koestner, R., & Ryan, R. M. (1999, November). A meta-analytic review of experiments examining the effects of extrinsic rewards on intrinsic motivation. *Psychological Bulletin, 125*(6), 627–668. (p. 305)

Deci, E. L., & Ryan, R. M. (1985). *Intrinsic motivation and self-determination in human behavior.* New York: Plenum Press. (p. 305)

Deci, E. L., & Ryan, R. M. (Eds.). (2002). *Handbook of self-determination research.* Rochester, NY: University of Rochester Press. (p. 449)

Deci, E. L., & Ryan, R. M. (2009). Self-determination theory: A consideration of human motivational universals. In P. J. Corr & G. Matthews (eds.), *The Cambridge Handbook of Personality Psychology.* New York: Cambridge University Press. (pp. 305, 449)

de Courten-Myers, G. M. (2005, February 4). Personal correspondence (estimating total brain neurons, extrapolating from her carefully estimated 20 to 23 billion cortical neurons). (pp. 62, 75)

de Dios, M. A., Herman, D. S., Britton, W. B., Hagerty, C. E., Anderson, B. J., & Stein, M. D. (2012). Motivational and mindfulness intervention for young adult female marijuana users. *Journal of Substance Abuse Treatment, 42,* 56–64. (p. 511)

De Dreu, C. K. W., Greer, L. L., Handgraaf, M. J. J., Shalvi, S., Van Kleef, G. A., Baas, M., . . . Feith, S. W. W. (2010). The neuropeptide oxytocin regulated parochial altruism in intergroup conflict among humans. *Science, 328,* 1409–1411. (p. 64)

De Dreu, C. K. W., Nijstad, B. A., Baas, M., Wolsink, I., & Roskes, M. (2012). Working memory benefits creative insight, musical improvisation, and original ideation through maintained task-focused attention. *Personality and Social Psychology Bulletin, 38,* 656–669. (p. 324)

Deeley, Q., Daly, E., Surguladze, S., Tunstall, N., Mezey, G., Beer, D., . . . Murphy, D. G. (2006). Facial emotion processing in criminal psychopathy. *British Journal of Psychiatry, 189,* 533–539. (p. 650)

DeFina, L. F., Willis, B. L., Radford, N. B., Gao, A., Leonard, D., Haskell, W. L., Weiner, M. F., & Berry, J. D. (2013). The association between midlife cardiorespiratory fitness levels and later-life dementia. *Annals of Internal Medicine, 158,* 162–168. (p. 216)

De Gee, J., Knapen, T., & Donner, T. H. (2014). Decision-related pupil dilation reflects upcoming choice and individual bias. *PNAS, 111,* E618–E625. (p. 240)

De Gelder, B. (2010, May). Uncanny sight in the blind. *Scientific American,* pp. 61–65. (p. 94)

de Gonzales, A. B., et al. (2010). Body-mass index and mortality among 1.46 million white adults. *New England Journal of Medicine, 363,* 2211–2219. (p. 430)

Dehaene, S. (2009, November 24). Signatures of consciousness. *Edge is Paris.* www.Edge.org. (p. 232)

Dehaene, S. (2014). *Consciousness and the brain: Deciphering how the brain codes our thoughts.* New York: Viking. (pp. 186, 232)

Dehne, K. L., & Riedner, G. (2005). *Sexually transmitted infections among adolescents: The need for adequate health services.* Geneva: World Health Organization. (p. 436)

de Hoogh, A. H. B., den Hartog, D. N., Koopman, P. L., Thierry, H., van den Berg, P. T., van der Weide, J. G., & Wilderom, C. P. M. (2004). Charismatic leadership, environmental dynamism, and performance. *European Journal of Work and Organisational Psychology, 13,* 447–471. (p. A-12)

De Koninck, J. (2000). Waking experiences and dreaming. In M. Kryger, T. Roth, & W. Dement (Eds.), *Principles and practice of sleep medicine* (3rd ed.). Philadelphia: Saunders. (p. 112)

De la Herrán-Arita, A. K., Kornum, B. R., Mahlios, J., Jiang, W., Lin, L., Hou, T., . . . Mignot, E. (2013). CD4+ T cell autoimmunity to hypocretin/orexin and cross-reactivity to a 2009 H1N1 influenza A epitope in narcolepsy. *Science Translational Medicine, 5*(216): 216ra176. (p. 110)

DeLamater, J. (2012). Sexual expression in later life: A review and synthesis. *Journal of Sex Research, 49,* 125–141. (p. 214)

DeLamater, J. D., & Sill, M. (2005). Sexual desire in later life. *Journal of Sex Research, 42,* 138–149. (p. 214) de Lange, M., Debets, L., Ruitenberg, K., & Holland, R. (2012). Making less of a mess: Scent exposure as a tool for behavioral change. *Social Influence, 7,* 90–97. (p. 268)

Delaney, H. D., Miller, W. R., & Bisonó, A. M. (2007). Religiosity and spirituality among psychologists: A survey of clinician members of the American Psychological Association. *Professional Psychology: Research and Practice, 38,* 538–546. (p. 680)

Delaunay-El Allam, M., Soussignan, R., Patris, B., Marlier, L., & Schaal, B. (2010). Long-lasting memory for an odor acquired at the mother's breast. *Developmental Science, 13,* 849–863. (p. 183)

Delgado, J. M. R. (1969). *Physical control of the mind: Toward a psychocivilized society.* New York: Harper & Row. (p. 76)

DeLoache, J. S. (1987). Rapid change in the symbolic functioning of very young children. *Science, 238,* 1556–1557. (p. 189)

DeLoache, J. S., Chiong, C., Sherman, K., Islam, N., Vanderborght, M., Troseth, G. L., Strouse, G. A., & O'Doherty, K. (2010). Do babies learn from baby media? *Psychological Science, 21,* 1570–1574. (p. 409)

DeLoache, J. S., Uttal, D. H., & Rosengren, K. S. (2004). Scale errors offer evidence for a perception-action dissociation early in life. *Science, 304,* 1027–1029. (p. 187)

De Los Reyes, A., & Kazdin, A. E. (2009). Identifying evidence-based interventions for children and adolescents using the range of possible changes model: A meta-analytic illustration. *Behavior Modification, 33,* 583–617. (p. 676)

DelPriore, D. J., & Hill, S. E. (2013). The effects of paternal disengagement on women's sexual decision making: An experimental approach. *Journal of Personality and Social Psychology, 105,* 234–246. (p. 166)

Dement, W. C. (1978). *Some must watch while some must sleep.* New York: Norton. (pp. 101, 110)

Dement, W. C. (1999). *The promise of sleep.* New York: Delacorte Press. (pp. 100, 102, 104, 107, 108, 110, 111, C-7)

Dement, W. C., & Wolpert, E. A. (1958). The relation of eye movements, body mobility, and external stimuli to dream content. *Journal of Experimental Psychology, 55,* 543–553. (p. 113)

De Meyer, G., et al. (2010). Diagnosis-independent Alzheimer disease biomarker signature in cognitively normal elderly people. *Archives of Neurology, 67,* 949–956. (p. 219)

Demicheli, V., Rivetti, A., Debalini, M. G., & Di Pietrantonj, C. (2012, February 15). Vaccines for measles, mumps and rubella in children. *Cochrane Database of Systematic Reviews,* Issue 2, CD004407. (p. 193)

Deming, D. (2009). Early childhood intervention and life-cycle skill development: Evidence from Head Start. *American Economic Journal: Applied Economics, 1*(3), 111–134. (p. 409)

Demir, E., & Dickson, B. J. (2005). Fruitless splicing specifies male courtship behavior in Drosophila. *Cell, 121,* 785–794. (p. 443)

Dempster, E., Viana, J., Pidsley, R., & Mill, J. (2013). Epigenetic studies of schizophrenia: Progress, predicaments, and promises for the future. *Schizophrenia Bulletin, 39,* 11–16. (p. 645)

DeNeve, J., Christakis, N. A., Fowler, J. H., & Frey, B. S. (2012). Genes, economics, and happiness. *Journal of Neuroscience, Psychology, and Economics, 5,* 193–211. (p. 485)

De Neve, J-E., Diener, E., Tay, L., & Xuereb, C. (2013). The objective benefits of subjective well-being. In J. F. Helliwell, R. Layard, & J. Sachs (Eds.), *World happiness report 2013.* Volume 2. (pp. 54–79). New York: UN Sustainable Network Development Solutions Network. (pp. 479, A-11)

De Neve, K. M., & Cooper, H. (1998). The happy personality: A meta-analysis of 137 personality traits and subjective well-being. *Psychological Bulletin, 124,* 197–229. (p. 485)

Dennett, D. C. (1991). *Consciousness explained.* Boston: Little, Brown. (p. 304)

Dennett, D. C. (1996, September 9). Quoted by Ian Parker, Richard Dawkins' evolution. *The New Yorker,* pp. 41–45. (p. 6)

Denollet, J. (2005). DS14: Standard assessment of negative affectivity, social inhibition, and Type D personality. *Psychosomatic Medicine, 67,* 89–97. (p. 498)

Denollet, J., Sys, S. U., Stroobant, N., Rombouts, H. Gillebert, T. C., & Brutsaert, D. L. (1996). Personality as independent predictor of long-term mortality in patients with coronary heart disease. *Lancet, 347,* 417–421. (p. 498)

Denson, T. F. (2011). A social neuroscience perspective on the neurobiological bases of aggression. In P. R. Shaver, & M. Mikulincer (Eds.), *Human aggression and violence: Causes, manifestations, and consequences.* Washington, DC: U. S. American Psychological Association. (p. 545)

Denson, T. F., Capper, M. M., Oaten, M., Friese, M., & Schofield, T. P. (2011). Self-control training decreases aggression in response to provocation in aggressive individuals. *Journal of Research in Personality, 45,* 252–256. (pp. 477, 504)

Denton, K., & Krebs, D. (1990). From the scene to the crime: The effect of alcohol and social context on moral judgment. *Journal of Personality and Social Psychology, 59,* 242–248. (p. 119)

DePaulo, B. M., Blank, A. L., Swaim, G. W., & Hairfield, J. G. (1992). Expressiveness and expressive control. *Personality and Social Psychology Bulletin, 18,* 276–285. (p. 593)

Depla, M. F. I. A., ten Have, M. L., van Balkom, A. J. L. M., & de Graaf, R. (2008). Specific fears and phobias in the general population: Results from the Netherlands Mental Health Survey and Incidence Study (NEMESIS). *Social Psychiatry and Psychiatric Epidemiology, 43,* 200–208. (p. 622)

De Raad, B., Barelds, D. P. H., Levert, E., Ostendorf, F., Mlačić, B., Di Blas, L., . . . Katigbak, M. S. (2010). Only three factors of personality description are fully replicable across languages: A comparison of 14 trait taxonomies. *Journal of Personality and Social Psychology, 98,* 160–173. (p. 590)

Dermer, M., Cohen, S. J., Jacobsen, E., & Anderson, E. A. (1979). Evaluative judgments of aspects of life as a function of vicarious exposure to hedonic extremes. *Journal of Personality and Social Psychology, 37,* 247–260. (p. 484)

Dermer, M., & Pyszczynski, T. A. (1978). Effects of erotica upon men's loving and liking responses for women they love. *Journal of Personality and Social Psychology, 36,* 1302–1309. (p. 556)

Derringer, J., Krueger, R. F., Dick, D. M., Saccone, S., Grucza, R. A., Agrawal, A., . . . Bierut, L. J. (2010). Predicting sensation seeking from dopamine genes: A candidate system approach. *Psychological Science, 21,* 1282–1290. (p. 142)

Desmurget, M., Reilly, K. T., Richard, N., Szathmari, A., Mottolese, C., & Sirigu, A. (2009). Movement intention after parietal cortex stimulation in humans. *Science, 324,* 811–813. (p. 80)

DeStefano, F., Price, C. S., & Weintraub, E. S. (2013). Increasing exposure to antibody-stimulating proteins and polysaccharides in vaccines is not associated with risk of autism. *The Journal of Pediatrics, 163,* 561–567. (p. 193)

DeSteno, D., Dasgupta, N., Bartlett, M. Y., & Cajdric, A. (2004). Prejudice from thin air: The effect of emotion on automatic intergroup attitudes. *Psychological Science, 15,* 319–324. (p. 478)

DeSteno, D., Petty, R. E., Wegener, D. T., & Rucker, D. D. (2000). Beyond valence in the perception of likelihood: The role of emotion specificity. *Journal of Personality and Social Psychology, 78,* 397–416. (p. 336)

Dettman, S. J., Pinder, D., Briggs, R. J. S., Dowell, R. C., & Leigh, J. R. (2007). Communication development in children who receive the cochlear implant younger than 12 months: Risk versus benefits. *Ear and Hearing, 28*(2), Supplement 11S–18S. (p. 259)

Deutsch, J. A. (1972, July). Brain reward: ESP and ecstasy. *Psychology Today,* 46–48. (p. 73)

DeValois, R. L., & DeValois, K. K. (1975). Neural coding of color. In E. C. Carterette & M. P. Friedman (Eds.), *Handbook of perception: Vol. V. Seeing.* New York: Academic Press. (p. 244)

Devilly, G. J. (2003). Eye movement desensitization and reprocessing: A chronology of its development and scientific standing. *Scientific Review of Mental Health Practice, 1,* 113–118. (p. 677)

Devine, P. G. (1995). Prejudice and outgroup perception. In A. Tesser (Ed.), *Advanced social psychology.* New York: McGraw-Hill. (p. 552)

Devries, K. M., et al. (2013). The global prevalence of intimate partner violence against women. *Science, 340,* 1527. (p. 540)

Dew, M. A., Hoch, C. C., Buysse, D. J., Monk, T. H., Begley, A. E., Houck, P. R., . . . Reynolds, C. F., III (2003). Healthy older adults' sleep predicts all-cause mortality at 4 to 19 years of follow-up. *Psychosomatic Medicine, 65,* 63–73. (p. 108)

de Waal, F. (2005, September 23). We're all Machiavellians. *Chronicle of Higher Education.* (p. 29)

de Waal, F. B. M. (2009, October). The empathy instinct. *Discover,* pp. 54–57. (pp. 475, 525)

de Waal, F. B. M. (2011). Back cover quote for D. Blum, *Love at Goon Park: Harry Harlow and the science of affection.* New York: Basic Books. (p. 197)

de Waal, F. B. M., & Johanowicz, D. L. (1993). Modification of reconciliation behavior through social experience: An experiment with two macaque species. *Child Development, 64,* 897–908. (p. 307)

DeWall, C. N., & Bushman, B. J. (2009). Hot under the collar in a lukewarm environment: Words associated with hot temperature increase aggressive thoughts and hostile perceptions. *Journal of Experimental Social Psychology, 45*, 1045–1047. (p. 547)

DeWall, C. N., Lambert, N. M., Slotter, E. B., Pond, R. S., Jr., Deckman, T., Finkel, E. J., Luchies, L. B., & Fincham, F. D. (2011). So far away from one's partner, yet so close to romantic alternatives: Avoidant attachment, interest in alternatives, and infidelity. *Journal of Personality and Social Psychology, 101*, 1302–1316. (p. 199)

DeWall, C. N., MacDonald, G., Webster, G. D., Masten, C. L., Baumeister, R. F., Powell, C., . . . Eisenberger, N. I. (2010). Acetaminophen reduces social pain: Behavioral and neural evidence. *Psychological Science, 21*, 931–937. (p. 450)

DeWall, C. N., Pond, R. S., Jr., Campbell, W. K., & Twenge, J. M. (2011). Tuning in to psychological change: Linguistic markers of psychological traits and emotions over time in popular U.S. song lyrics. *Psychology of Aesthetics, Creativity, and the Arts, 5*, 200–207. (p. 604)

Dewar, M., Alber, J., Butler, C., Cowan, N., & Sala, S. D. (2012). Brief wakeful resting boosts new memories over the long term. *Psychological Science, 23*, 955–960. (p. 351)

de Wit, L., Luppino, F., van Straten, A., Penninx, B., Zitman, F., & Cuijpers, P. (2010). Depression and obesity: A meta-analysis of community-based studies. *Psychiatry Research, 178*, 230–235. (p. 429)

De Wolff, M. S., & van IJzendoorn, M. H. (1997). Sensitivity and attachment: A meta-analysis on parental antecedents of infant attachment. *Child Development, 68*, 571–591. (p. 197)

DeYoung, C. G., Hirsch, J. B., Shane, M. S., Papademetris, X., Rajeevan, N., & Gray, J. R. (2010). Testing predictions from personality neuroscience: Brain structure and the Big Five. *Psychological Science, 21*, 820–828. (p. 591)

de Zavala, A. G., Cichocka, A., Eidelson, R., & Jawawickreme, N. (2009). Collective narcissism and its social consequences. *Journal of Personality and Social Psychology, 97*, 1074–1096. (p. 604)

Diaconis, P. (2002, August 11). Quoted by L. Belkin, The odds of that. *New York Times* (www.nytimes.com). (p. 23)

Diaconis, P., & Mosteller, F. (1989). Methods for studying coincidences. *Journal of the American Statistical Association, 84*, 853–861. (p. 22)

Diamond, J. (2001, February). A tale of two reputations: Why we revere Darwin and give Freud a hard time. *Natural History*, pp. 20–24. (p. 146)

Diamond, L. (2008). *Sexual fluidity: Understanding women's love and desire.* Cambridge, MA: Harvard University Press. (p. 441)

Diamond, R. (1993). Genetics and male sexual orientation (letter). *Science, 261*, 1258. (p. 446)

Dias-Ferreira, E., Sousa, J. C., Melo, I., Morgado, P., Mesquita, A. R., Cerqueira, J. J., Costa, R. M., & Sousa, N. (2009). Chronic stress causes frontostriatal reorganization and affects decision-making. *Science, 325*, 621–625. (p. 492)

Diaz, F. J., Velásquex, D. M., Susce, M. T., & de Leon, J. (2008). The association between schizophrenia and smoking: Unexplained by either the illness or the prodromal period. *Schizophrenia Research, 104*, 214–219. (p. 642)

Dick, D. M. (2007). Identification of genes influencing a spectrum of externalizing psychopathology. *Current Directions in Psychological Science, 16*, 331–335. (p. 650)

Dickens, W. T., & Flynn, J. R. (2006). Black Americans reduce the racial IQ gap: Evidence from standardization samples. *Psychological Science, 17*, 913–920. (p. 411)

Dickerson, S. S., Gable, S. L., Irwin, M. R., Aziz, N., & Kemeny, M. E. (2009). Social-evaluative threat and proinflammatory cytokine regulation: An experimental laboratory investigation. *Psychological Science, 20*, 1237–1243. (p. 499)

Dickerson, S. S., & Kemeny, M. E. (2004). Acute stressors and cortisol responses: A theoretical integration and synthesis of laboratory research. *Psychological Bulletin, 130*, 355–391. (p. 501)

Dickson, B. J. (2005, June 3). Quoted in E. Rosenthal, For fruit flies, gene shift tilts sex orientation. *New York Times* (www.nytimes.com). (p. 444)

Dickson, N., van Roode, T., Cameron, C., & Paul, C. (2013). Stability and change in same-sex attraction, experience, and identity by sex and age in a New Zealand birth cohort. *Archives of Sexual Behavior, 42*, 753–763. (p. 441)

Diekelmann, S., & Born, J. (2010). The memory function of sleep. *Nature Neuroscience, 11*, 114–126. (pp. 106, 114, 342)

Diener, E. (2006). Guidelines of national indicators of subjective well-being and ill-being. *Journal of Happiness Studies, 7*, 397–404. (p. 485)

Diener, E. (2013). The remarkable changes in the science of well-being. *Perspectives on Psychological Science, 8*, 663–666. (pp. 485, 486)

Diener, E. (2014). *Happiness and Well-Being:* (Keynote address). Preconference symposium at the Society for Personality and Social Psychology convention, Austin, Texas. (p. 485)

Diener, E., & Biswas-Diener, R. (2002). Will money increase subjective well-being? A literature review and guide to needed research. *Social Indicators Research, 57*, 119–169. (p. 482)

Diener, E., & Biswas-Diener, R. (2009). *Rethinking happiness: The science of psychological wealth.* Malden, MA: Wiley Blackwell. (pp. 482, 485)

Diener, E., & Chan, M. (2011). Happy people live longer: Subjective well-being contributes to health and longevity. *Applied Psychology: Health and Well-Being, 3*, 1–43. (p. 498)

Diener, E., Emmons, R. A., & Sandvik, E. (1986). *The dual nature of happiness: Independence of positive and negative moods.* Unpublished manuscript, University of Illinois. (p. 224)

Diener, E., Ng, W., Harter, J., & Arora, R. (2009). *Wealth and happiness across the world: Material prosperity predicts life evaluation, while psychosocial prosperity predicts positive feeling.* Unpublished manuscript, University of Illinois and the Gallup Organization. (p. 482)

Diener, E., Nickerson, C., Lucas, R. E., & Sandvik, E. (2002). Dispositional affect and job outcomes. *Social Indicators Research, 59*, 229–259. (p. 479)

Diener, E., & Oishi, S. (2000). Money and happiness: Income and subjective well-being across nations. In E. Diener & E. M. Suh (Eds.), *Subjective well-being across cultures.* Cambridge, MA: MIT Press. (p. 483)

Diener, E., Oishi, S., & Lucas, R. E. (2003). Personality, culture, and subjective well-being: Emotional and cognitive evaluations of life. *Annual Review of Psychology, 54*, 403–425. (p. 485)

Diener, E., Oishi, S., & Park, J. Y. (2014). An incomplete list of eminent psychologists of the modern era. *Archives of Scientific Psychology, 21*, 20–31. (p. 306)

Diener, E., & Seligman, M. E. P. (2002). Very happy people. *Psychological Science, 13*, 81–84. (p. 448)

Diener, E., Tay, L., & Myers, D. G. (2011). The religion paradox: If religion makes people happy, why are so many dropping out? *Journal of Personality and Social Psychology, 101*(6), 1278–1290. (pp. 30, 485)

Diener, E., Wolsic, B., & Fujita, F. (1995). Physical attractiveness and subjective well-being. *Journal of Personality and Social Psychology, 69*, 120–129. (p. 554)

DiFranza, J. R. (2008, May). Hooked from the first cigarette. *Scientific American*, pp. 82–87. (p. 121)

Dijksterhuis, A., & Aarts, H. (2003). On wildebeests and humans: The preferential detection of negative stimuli. *Psychological Science, 14*, 14–18. (p. 468)

Dik, B. J., & Duffy, R. D. (2012). *Make your job a calling: How the psychology of vocation can change your life at work.* Conshohocken, PA: Templeton Press. (p. A-1)

Dik, B. J., & Rottinghaus, P. J. (2013). Assessments of interests. In K. F. Geisinger et al. (Eds.). *APA handbook of testing and assessment in psychology, vol. 2.* Washington, DC: APA. (p. A-3)

DiLalla, D. L., Carey, G., Gottesman, I. I., & Bouchard, T. J., Jr. (1996). Heritability of MMPI personality indicators of psychopathology in twins reared apart. *Journal of Abnormal Psychology, 105*, 491–499. (p. 633)

Dimberg, U., Thunberg, M., & Elmehed, K. (2000). Unconscious facial reactions to emotional facial expressions. *Psychological Science, 11*, 86–89. (pp. 463, 475)

Dimidjian, S., & Hollon, S. D. (2010). How would we know if psychotherapy were harmful? *American Psychologist, 65*, 21–33. (p. 676)

Dindia, K., & Allen, M. (1992). Sex differences in self-disclosure: A meta-analysis. *Psychological Bulletin, 112*, 106–124. (p. 164)

Dinges, N. G., & Hull, P. (1992). Personality, culture, and international studies. In D. Lieberman (Ed.), *Revealing the world: An interdisciplinary reader for international studies.* Dubuque, IA: Kendall-Hunt. (p. 380)

Dingfelder, S. F. (2010, November). A second chance for the Mexican wolf. *Monitor on Psychology*, pp. 20–21. (p. 302)

Dion, K. K., & Dion, K. L. (1993). Individualistic and collectivistic perspectives on gender and the cultural context of love and intimacy. *Journal of Social Issues, 49*, 53–69. (p. 159)

Dirix, C. E. H., Nijhuis, J. G., Jongsma, H. W., & Hornstra, G. (2009). Aspects of fetal learning and memory. *Child Development, 80*, 1251–1258. (p. 182)

DiSalvo, D. (2010, January/February). Are social networks messing with your head? *Scientific American Mind*, pp. 48–55. (p. 452)

DiSantis, K. I., Birch, L. L., Davey, A., Serrano, E. L., Zhang, J., Bruton, Y., & Fisher, J. O. (2013). Plate size and children's appetite: Effects of larger dishware on self-served portions and intake. *Pediatrics, 131*, e1451-e1458. (p. 429)

Discover (1996, May). A fistful of risks. Pp. 82–83. (p. 121)

Di Tella, R., & MacCulloch, R. (2010). Happiness adaptation to income beyond "basic needs." In E. Diener, J. Helliwell, & D. Kahneman (eds.), *International Differences in Well-Being*, pp. 217–247. New York: Oxford University Press. (pp. 482, 483)

Ditre, J. W., Brandon, T. H., Zale, E. L., & Meagher, M. M. (2011). Pain, nicotine, and smoking: Research findings and mechanistic considerations. *Psychological Bulletin, 137*, 1065–1093. (p. 122)

Dixon, J., Durrheim, K., & Tredoux, C. (2007). Intergroup contact and attitudes toward the principle and practice of racial equality. *Psychological Science, 18*, 867–872. (p. 564)

Dobbs, D. (2009, April). The post-traumatic stress trap. *Scientific American*, pp. 64–69. (p. 624)

Dobel, C., Diesendruck, G., & Bölte, J. (2007). How writing system and age influence spatial representations of actions: A developments, cross-linguistic study. *Psychological Science, 18*, 487–491. (p. 380)

Dodge, K. A. (2009). Mechanisms of gene-environment interaction effects in the development of conduct disorder. *Perspectives on Psychological Science, 4*, 408–414. (p. 650)

Doherty, E. W., & Doherty, W. J. (1998). Smoke gets in your eyes: Cigarette smoking and divorce in a national sample of American adults. *Families, Systems, and Health, 16*, 393–400. (p. 122)

Dohrenwend, B. P., Levav, I., Shrout, P. E., Schwartz, S., Naveh, G., Link, B. G., Skodol, A. E., & Stueve, A. (1992). Socioeconomic status and psychiatric disorders: The causation-selection issue. *Science, 255*, 946–952. (p. 618)

Dohrenwend, B. P., Pearlin, L., Clayton, P., Hamburg, B., Dohrenwend, B. P., Riley, M., & Rose, R. (1982). Report on stress and life events. In G. R. Elliott & C. Eisdorfer (Eds.), *Stress and human health: Analysis and implications of research* (A study by the Institute of Medicine/National Academy of Sciences). New York: Springer. (p. 490)

Doidge, N. (2007). *The brain that changes itself*. New York: Viking. (p. 81)

Dolezal, H. (1982). *Living in a world transformed*. New York: Academic Press. (p. 255)

Dolinoy, D. C., Huang, D., Jirtle, R. L. (2007). Maternal nutrient supplementation counteracts bisphenol A-induced DNA hypomethylation in early development. *Proceedings of the National Academic of Sciences, 104*, 13056–13061. (p. 143)

Domhoff, G. W. (1996). *Finding meaning in dreams: A quantitative approach*. New York: Plenum. (p. 112)

Domhoff, G. W. (2003). *The scientific study of dreams: Neural networks, cognitive development, and content analysis*. Washington, DC: APA Books. (pp. 113, 114)

Domhoff, G. W. (2007). Realistic simulations and bizarreness in dream content: Past findings and suggestions for future research. In D. Barrett & P. McNamara (Eds.), *The new science of dreaming: Content, recall, and personality characteristics*. Westport, CT: Praeger. (p. 112)

Domhoff, G. W. (2010). *The case for a cognitive theory of dreams*. Unpublished manuscript: University of California at Santa Cruz (dreamresearch.net/Library/domhoff2010.html). (p. 114)

Domhoff, G. W. (2011). The neural substrate for dreaming: Is it a subsystem of the default network? *Consciousness and Cognition, 20*(4), 1163–1174. (p. 114)

Domhoff, G. W. (2014, January 5). Personal communication. (p. 115)

Domjan, M. (1992). Adult learning and mate choice: Possibilities and experimental evidence. *American Zoologist, 32*, 48–61. (p. 284)

Domjan, M. (1994). Formulation of a behavior system for sexual conditioning. *Psychonomic Bulletin & Review, 1*, 421–428. (p. 284)

Domjan, M. (2005). Pavlovian conditioning: A functional perspective. *Annual Review of Psychology, 56*, 179–206. (pp. 284, 302)

Domjan, M., Cusato, B., & Krause, M. (2004). Learning with arbitrary versus ecological conditioned stimuli: Evidence from sexual conditioning. *Psychonomic Bulletin & Review, 11*, 232–246. (p. 302)

Donlea, J. M., Ramanan, N., & Shaw, P. J. (2009). Use-dependent plasticity in clock neurons regulates sleep need in Drosophila. *Science, 324*, 105–108. (p. 104)

Donnerstein, E. (1998). *Why do we have those new ratings on television?* Invited address to the National Institute on the Teaching of Psychology. (pp. 311, 312)

Donnerstein, E. (2011). The media and aggression: From TV to the Internet. In J. Forgas, A. Kruglanski, & K. Williams (eds.), *The psychology of social conflict and aggression*. New York: Psychology Press. (pp. 311, 312)

Donnerstein, E., Linz, D., & Penrod, S. (1987). *The question of pornography*. New York: Free Press. (p. 313)

Donvan, J., & Zucker, C. (2010, October). Autism's first child. *The Atlantic* (www.theatlantic.com). (p. 193)

Dorner, G. (1976). *Hormones and brain differentiation*. Amsterdam: Elsevier Scientific. (p. 444)

Dorner, G. (1988). Neuroendocrine response to estrogen and brain differentiation in heterosexuals, homosexuals, and transsexuals. *Archives of Sexual Behavior, 17*, 57–75. (p. 444)

Doss, B. D., Rhoades, G. K., Stanley, S. M., & Markman, H. J. (2009). The effect of the transition to parenthood on relationship quality: An 8-year prospective study. *Journal of Personality and Social Psychology, 96*, 601–619. (p. 222)

Dotan-Eliaz, O., Sommer, K. L., & Rubin, S. (2009). Multilingual groups: Effects of linguistic ostracism on felt rejection and anger, coworker attraction, perceived team potency, and creative performance. *Basic and Applied Social Psychology, 31*, 363–375. (p. 450)

Doty, R. L. (2001). Olfaction. *Annual Review of Psychology, 52*, 423–452. (p. 267)

Douglas, K. S., Guy, L. S., & Hart, S. D. (2009). Psychosis as a risk factor for violence to others: A meta-analysis. *Psychological Bulletin, 135*, 679–706. (p. 616)

Douthat, R. (2010, November 28). The partisan mind. *New York Times* (www.nytimes.com). (p. 542)

Dovidio, J. F., & Gaertner, S. L. (1999). Reducing prejudice: Combating intergroup biases. *Current Directions in Psychological Science, 8*, 101–105. (p. 565)

Dovidio, J. F., ten Vergert, M., Stewart, T. L., Gaertner, S. L., Johnson, J. D., Esses, V. M., Riek, B. M., & Pearson, A. R. (2004). Perspective and prejudice: Antecedents and mediating mechanisms. *Personality and Social Psychology Bulletin, 30*, 1537–1549. (p. 566)

Dowlati, Y., Herrmann, N., Swardfager, W., Liu, H., Sham, L., Reim, E. K., & Lanctôt, K. (2010). A meta-analysis of cytokines in major depression. *Biological Psychiatry, 67*, 466–457. (p. 634)

Downing, P. E., Jiang, Y., & Shuman, M. (2001). A cortical area selective for visual processing of the human body. *Science, 293*, 2470–2473. (p. 245)

Downs, E., & Smith, S. L. (2010). Keepin abreast of hypersexuality: A video game character content analysis. *Sex Roles, 62*, 721–733. (p. 439)

Doyle, R. (2005, March). Gay and lesbian census. *Scientific American*, p. 28. (p. 147)

Draguns, J. G. (1990a). Normal and abnormal behavior in cross-cultural perspective: Specifying the nature of their relationship. *Nebraska Symposium on Motivation 1989, 37*, 235–277. (pp. 609, 636)

Draguns, J. G. (1990b). Applications of cross-cultural psychology in the field of mental health. In R. W. Brislin (Ed.), *Applied cross-cultural psychology*. Newbury Park, CA: Sage. (p. 609)

Draguns, J. G. (1997). Abnormal behavior patterns across cultures: Implications for counseling and psychotherapy. *International Journal of Intercultural Relations, 21*, 213–248. (p. 609)

Drake, R. A., & Myers, L. R. (2006). Visual attention, emotion, and action tendency: Feeling active or passive. *Cognition and Emotion, 20*, 608–622. (p. 467)

Dreger, A. (2011, February 28). Do gay men have more sexual interest in children than straight men do? www.psychologytoday.com/blog/fetishes-i-dont-get/201102/do-gay-men-have-more-sexual-interest-in-children-straight-men-do. (p. 441)

Drew, T., Võ, M, L.-H., & Wolfe, J. M. (2013). Sustained inattentional blindness in expert observers. *Psychological Science, 24*, 1848–1853. (p. 98)

Driessen, E., Cuijpers, P., de Maat, S. C. M., Abbas, A. A., de Jonghe, F., & Dekker, J. J. M. (2010). The efficacy of short-term psychodynamic psychotherapy for depression: A meta-analysis. *Clinical Psychology Review, 30*, 25–36. (p. 676)

Druckman, D., & Bjork, R. A. (1991). *In the mind's eye: Enhancing human performance*. Washington, DC: National Academy Press. (p. 586)

Drummond, S. (2010). *Relationship between changes in sleep and memory in older adults*. Presentation at AAAS 2010 Annual Meeting, University of California, San Diego, CA. (p. 106)

Duckworth, A. L., Quinn, P. D., & Seligman, M. E. P. (2009). Positive predictors of teacher effectiveness. *Journal of Positive Psychology, 4*, 540–547. (p. 455)

Duckworth, A. L., Quinn, P. D., Lynam, D. R., Loeber, R., & Stouthamer-Loeber, M. (2011). Role of test motivation in intelligence testing. *PNAS, 108*, 7716–7720. (p. 409)

Duckworth, A. L., & Seligman, M. E. P. (2005). Discipline outdoes talent: Self-discipline predicts academic performance in adolescents. *Psychological Science, 12*, 939–944. (pp. 455, 503)

Duckworth, A. L., & Seligman, M. E. P. (2006). Self-discipline gives girls the edge: Gender in self-discipline, grades, and achievement tests. *Journal of Educational Psychology, 98*, 198–208. (p. 455)

Duckworth, A. L., Tsukayama, E., & Kirby, T.A. (2013). Is it really self-control? Examining the predictive power of the delay of gratification task. *Personality and Social Psychology Bulletin, 39,* 843–855. (p. 208)

Duclos, S. E., Laird, J. D., Sexter, M., Stern, L., & Van Lighten, O. (1989). Emotion-specific effects of facial expressions and postures on emotional experience. *Journal of Personality and Social Psychology, 57,* 100–108. (p. 474)

Dugan, A. (2014, March 17). Americans most likely to say global warming is exaggerated. www.gallup.com. (p. 520)

Dugatkin, L. A. (2002, Winter). Watching culture shape even guppy love. *Cerebrum,* pp. 51–66. (p. 307)

Duggan, J. P., & Booth, D. A. (1986). Obesity, overeating, and rapid gastric emptying in rats with ventromedial hypothalamic lesions. *Science, 231,* 609–611. (p. 426)

Dukakis, K. (2006). *Shock: The healing power of electroconvulsive therapy.* New York: Avery Press. (p. 686)

Dumont, K. A., Widom, C. S., & Czaja, S. J. (2007). Predictors of resilience in abused and neglected children grown-up: The role of individual and neighborhood characteristics. *Child Abuse & Neglect, 31,* 255–274. (p. 200)

Dunbar, R. I. M., Baron, R., Frangou, A., Pearce, E., van Leeuwin, E. J. C., Stow, J., . . . van Vugt, M. (2011). Social laughter is correlated with an elevated pain threshold. *Proceedings of the Royal Society B, 279,* 1161–1167. (p. 506)

Dunham, Y., Chen, E. E., & Banaji, M. R. (2013). Two signatures of implicit intergroup attitudes: Developmental invariance and early enculturation. *Psychological Science, 24,* 860–868. (p. 540)

Dunlop, W. L., & Tracy, J. L. (2013). Sobering stories: Narratives of self-redemption predict behavioral change and improved health among recovering alcoholics. *Journal of Personality and Social Psychology, 104,* 576–590. (p. 671)

Dunn, E. W., Aknin, L. B., & Norton, M. I. (2008). Spending money on others promotes happiness. *Science, 319,* 1687–1688. (p. 560)

Dunn, E., & Norton, M. (2013). *Happy money: The science of smarter spending.* New York: Simon & Schuster. (p. 560)

Dunn, M., & Searle, R. (2010). Effect of manipulated prestige-car ownership on both sex attractiveness ratings. *British Journal of Psychology, 101,* 69–80. (p. 149)

Dunning, D. (2006). Strangers to ourselves? *The Psychologist, 19,* 600–603. (p. 601)

Dunson, D. B., Colombo, B., & Baird, D. D. (2002). Changes with age in the level and duration of fertility in the menstrual cycle. *Human Reproduction, 17,* 1399–1403. (p. 214)

Durrheim, K., & Dixon, J. (2010). Racial contact and change in South Africa. *Journal of Social Issues, 66,* 273–288. (p. 564)

Dutton, D. G., & Aron, A. P. (1974). Some evidence for heightened sexual attraction under conditions of high anxiety. *Journal of Personality and Social Psychology, 30,* 510–517. (p. 556)

Dutton, D. G., & Aron, A. P. (1989). Romantic attraction and generalized liking for others who are sources of conflict-based arousal. *Canadian Journal of Behavioural Sciences, 21,* 246–257. (p. 556)

Dutton, K. (2012). *The wisdom of psychopaths: What saints, spies, and serial killers can teach us about success.* New York: Scientific American/Farrar, Straus and Giroux. (p. 649)

Dweck, C. S. (2006). *Mindset: The new psychology of success.* New York: Random House. (p. 409)

Dweck, C. S. (2012a). Implicit theories. In P. A. M. Van Lange, A. Kruglanski, & E. T. Higgins (Eds.), Handbook of theories of social psychology (Vol. 2, pp. 43–61). Thousand Oaks, CA: Sage. (p. 409)

Dweck, C. S. (2012b). Mindsets and human nature: Promoting change in the Middle East, the schoolyard, the racial divide, and willpower. *American Psychologist, 67,* 614–622. (p. 409)

Dye, M. W. G., Green, C. S., & Bavelier, D. (2009). Increasing speed of processing with action video games. *Current Directions in Psychological Science, 18,* 321–326. (p. 549)

Dyrdal, G. M., & Lucas, R. E. (2011). *Reaction and adaptation to the birth of a child: A couple level analysis.* Unpublished manuscript, Michigan State University. (p. 219)

Eagan, K., Lozano, J. B., Hurtado, S., & Case, M. H. (2013). *The American freshman: National norms Fall 2013.* Los Angeles: Higher Education Research Institute, UCLA (www.heri.ucla.ed). (p. 410)

Eagleman, D. (2011, September). Secret life of the mind. *Discover,* pp. 50–53. (p. 94)

Eagly, A. H. (1994). *Are people prejudiced against women?* Donald Campbell Award invited address, American Psychological Association convention. (p. 540)

Eagly, A. H. (2007). Female leadership advantage and disadvantage: Resolving the contradictions. *Psychology of Women Quarterly, 31,* 1–12. (p. A-12)

Eagly, A. H. (2009). The his and hers of prosocial behavior: An examination of the social psychology of gender. *American Psychologist, 64,* 644–658. (p. 163)

Eagly, A. H. (2013, March 20). Hybrid style works, and women are best at it. *New York Times* (www.nytimes.com). (p. A-12)

Eagly, A. H., Ashmore, R. D., Makhijani, M. G., & Kennedy, L. C. (1991). What is beautiful is good, but . . .: A meta-analytic review of research on the physical attractiveness stereotype. *Psychological Bulletin, 110,* 109–128. (p. 553)

Eagly, A. H., & Carli, L. (2007). *Through the labyrinth: The truth about how women become leaders.* Cambridge, MA: Harvard University Press. (p. 163)

Eagly, A. H., & Wood, W. (2013). The nature-nurture debates: 25 years of challenges in understanding the psychology of gender. *Perspectives on Psychological Science, 8,* 340–357. (p. 161)

Easterlin, R. A., Morgan, R., Switek, M., & Wang, F. (2012). China's life satisfaction, 1990–2010. *PNAS, 109,* 9670–9671. (pp. 482, 484)

Eastman, C. L., Boulos, Z., Terman, M., Campbell, S. S., Dijk, D-J., & Lewy, A. J. (1995). Light treatment for sleep disorders: Consensus report. VI. Shift work. *Journal of Biological Rhythms, 10,* 157–164. (p. 105)

Eastman, C. L., Young, M. A., Fogg, L. F., Liu, L., & Meaden, P. M. (1998). Bright light treatment of winter depression: A placebo-controlled trial. *Archives of General Psychiatry, 55,* 883–889. (p. 678)

Eastwick, P. W., & Finkel, E. J. (2008a). Speed-dating as a methodological innovation. *The Psychologist, 21,* 402–403. (p. 553)

Eastwick, P. W., & Finkel, E. J. (2008b). Sex differences in mate preferences revisited: Do people know what they initially desire in a romantic partner? *Journal of Personality and Social Psychology, 94,* 245–264. (p. 553)

Eastwick, P. W., Luchies, L. B., Finkel, E. J., & Hunt, L. L. (2014a). The predictive validity of ideal partner preferences: A review and meta-analysis. *Psychological Bulletin, 140,* 623–665. (p. 553)

Eastwick, P. W., Luchies, L. B., Finkel, E. J., & Hunt, L. L. (2014b). The many voices of Darwin's descendants: Reply to Schmitt (2014). *Psychological Bulletin, 140,* 673–681. (p. 553)

Ebbesen, E. B., Duncan, B., & Konecni, V. J. (1975). Effects of content of verbal aggression on future verbal aggression: A field experiment. *Journal of Experimental Social Psychology, 11,* 192–204. (p. 477)

Ebbinghaus, H. (1885/1964). *Memory: A contribution to experimental psychology* (H. A. Ruger & C. E. Bussenius, Trans.). New York: Dover. (pp. 325, 340)

Eberhardt, J. L. (2005). Imaging race. *American Psychologist, 60,* 181–190. (p. 540)

Eccles, J. S., Jacobs, J. E., & Harold, R. D. (1990). Gender role stereotypes, expectancy effects, and parents' socialization of gender differences. *Journal of Social Issues, 46,* 183–201. (p. 411)

Eckensberger, L. H. (1994). Moral development and its measurement across cultures. In W. J. Lonner & R. Malpass (Eds.), *Psychology and culture.* Boston: Allyn & Bacon. (p. 206)

Ecker, C. et al. (2012). Brain anatomy and its relationship to behavior in adults with autism spectrum disorder: A multicenter magnetic resonance imaging study. *Archives of General Psychiatry, 69,* 195–209. (p. 194)

Eckert, E. D., Heston, L. L., & Bouchard, T. J., Jr. (1981). MZ twins reared apart: Preliminary findings of psychiatric disturbances and traits. In L. Gedda, P. Paris, & W. D. Nance (Eds.), *Twin research: Vol. 3. Pt. B. Intelligence, personality, and development.* New York: Alan Liss. (p. 626)

Eckholm, E. (2010, September 21). Woman on death row runs out of appeals. *New York Times* (www.nytimes.com). (p. 404)

Ecklund-Flores, L. (1992). *The infant as a model for the teaching of introductory psychology.* Paper presented at the American Psychological Association annual convention. (p. 182)

Economist. (2001, December 20). An anthropology of happiness. *The Economist* (www.economist.com/world/asia). (p. 449)

Edwards, A. C., & Kendler, K. S. (2012). A twin study of depression and nicotine dependence: Shared liability or causal relationship? *Journal of Affective Disorders, 142,* 90–97. (p. 122)

Edwards, R. R., Campbell, C., Jamison, R. N., & Wiech, K. (2009). The neurobiological underpinnings of coping with pain. *Current Directions in Psychological Science, 18,* 237–241. (p. 264)

Egan, P. J., & Mullin, M. (2012). Turning personal experience into political attitudes: The effects of local weather on Americans' perceptions about global warming. *Journal of Politics, 74,* 796–809. (p. 360)

Eibl-Eibesfeldt, I. (1971). *Love and hate: The natural history of behavior patterns*. New York: Holt, Rinehart & Winston. (p. 472)

Eich, E. (1990). Learning during sleep. In R. B. Bootzin, J. F. Kihlstrom, & D. L. Schacter (Eds.), *Sleep and cognition*. Washington, DC: American Psychological Association. (p. 113)

Ein-Dor, T., Mikulincer, M., Doron, G., & Shaver, P. R. (2010). The attachment paradox: How can so many of us (the insecure ones) have no adaptive advantages? *Perspectives on Psychological Science, 5*, 123–141. (p. 199)

Ein-Dor, T., & Perry, A. (2012). Scared saviors: Evidence that people high in attachment anxiety are more effective in alerting others to threat. *European Journal of Social Psychology, 42*, 667–671. (p. 199)

Ein-Dor, T., & Perry, A. (2013, April). Full house of fears: Evidence that people high in attachment anxiety are more accurate in detecting deceit. *Journal of Personality, 82*, 83–92. (p. 199)

Einstein, G. O., & McDaniel, M. A. (1990). Normal aging and prospective memory. *Journal of Experimental Psychology: Learning, Memory, and Cognition, 16*, 717–726. (p. 217)

Einstein, G. O., McDaniel, M. A., Richardson, S. L., Guynn, M. J., & Cunfer, A. R. (1995). Aging and prospective memory: Examining the influences of self-initiated retrieval processes. *Journal of Experimental Psychology: Learning, Memory, and Cognition, 21*, 996–1007. (p. 217)

Einstein, G. O., McDaniel, M. A., Smith, R. E., & Shaw, P. (1998). Habitual prospective memory and aging: Remembering intentions and forgetting actions. *Psychological Science, 9*, 284–288. (p. 217)

Eippert, F., Finsterbush, J., Bingel, U., & Büchel, C. (2009). Direct evidence for spinal cord involvement in placebo analgesia. *Science, 326*, 404. (p. 264)

Eisenberg, D., Hunt, Speer, & Zivin, K. (2011). Mental health service utilization among college students in the United States. *The Journal of Nervous and Mental Disease, 199*, 301–308. (p. 609)

Eisenberg, N., & Lennon, R. (1983). Sex differences in empathy and related capacities. *Psychological Bulletin, 94*, 100–131. (p. 471)

Eisenberger, N. I. (2012). Broken hearts and broken bones: A neural perspective on the similarities between social and physical pain. *Current Directions in Psychological Science, 21*, 42–47. (p. 450)

Eisenberger, N. I., Master, S. L., Inagaki, T. K., Taylor, S.E., Shirinyan, D., Lieberman, M. D., & Naliboff, B. D. (2011). Attachment figures activate a safety signal-related neural region and reduce pain experience. *Proceedings of the National Academy of Sciences, 108*, 11721–11726. (p. 449)

Eisenberger, R., & Aselage, J. (2009). Incremental effects of reward on experienced performance pressure: Positive outcomes for intrinsic interest and creativity. *Journal of Organizational Behavior, 30*, 95–117. (p. 305)

Ekman, P. (1994). Strong evidence for universals in facial expressions: A reply to Russell's mistaken critique. *Psychological Bulletin, 115*, 268–287. (p. 472)

Ekman, P., & Friesen, W. V. (1975). *Unmasking the face*. Englewood Cliffs, NJ: Prentice-Hall. (p. 472)

Ekman, P., Friesen, W. V., O'Sullivan, M., Chan, A., Diacoyanni-Tarlatzis, I., Heider, K., . . . Tzavaras, A. (1987). Universals and cultural differences in the judgments of facial expressions of emotion. *Journal of Personality and Social Psychology, 53*, 712–717. (p. 472)

Elbert, T., Pantev, C., Wienbruch, C., Rockstroh, B., & Taub, E. (1995). Increased cortical representation of the fingers of the left hand in string players. *Science, 270*, 305–307. (p. 152)

Elbogen, E. B., & Johnson, S. C. (2009). The intricate link between violence and mental disorder: Results from the National Epidemiologic Survey on Alcohol and Related Conditions. *Archives of General Psychiatry, 66*, 152–161. (p. 616)

Elfenbein, H. A., & Ambady, N. (2002). On the universality and cultural specificity of emotion recognition: A meta-analysis. *Psychological Bulletin, 128*, 203–235. (p. 472)

Elfenbein, H. A., & Ambady, N. (2003a). When familiarity breeds accuracy: Cultural exposure and facial emotion recognition. *Journal of Personality and Social Psychology, 85*, 276–290. (p. 472)

Elfenbein, H. A., & Ambady, N. (2003b). Universals and cultural differences in recognizing emotions. *Current Directions in Psychological Science, 12*, 159–164. (p. 472)

Elkind, D. (1970). The origins of religion in the child. *Review of Religious Research, 12*, 35–42. (p. 206)

Elkind, D. (1978). *The child's reality: Three developmental themes*. Hillsdale, NJ: Erlbaum. (p. 205)

Elkins, G., Johnson, A., & Fisher, W. (2012). Cognitive hypnotherapy for pain management. *American Journal of Clinical Hypnosis, 54*, 294–310. (p. 265)

Ellenbogen, J. M., Hu, P. T., Payne, J. D., Titone, D., & Walker, M. P. (2007). Human relational memory requires time and sleep. *Proceedings of the National Academy of Sciences, 104*, 7723–7728. (p. 106)

Elliot, A. J., Greitemeyer, T., & Pazda, A.D. (2013). Women's use of red clothing as a sexual signal in intersexual interaction. *Journal of Experimental Social Psychology, 49*, 599–602. (p. 303)

Elliot, A. J., Kayser, D. N., Greitemeyer, T., Lichtenfeld, S., Gramzow, R. H., Maier, M. A., & Liu, H. (2010). Red, rank, and romance in women viewing men. *Journal of Experimental Psychology: General, 139*, 399–417. (p. 303)

Elliot, A. J., & Niesta, D. (2008). Romantic red: Red enhances men's attraction to women. *Journal of Personality and Social Psychology, 95*, 1150–1164. (p. 302)

Elliot, A. J., Tracy, J. L., Pazda, A. D., & Beall, A. T. (2013). Red enhances women's attractiveness to men: First evidence suggesting universality. *Journal of Experimental Social Psychology, 49*, 165–168. (p. 302)

Ellis, A., & Becker, I. M. (1982). *A guide to personal happiness*. North Hollywood, CA: Wilshire Book Co. (p. 288)

Ellis, B. J., Bates, J. E., Dodge, K. A., Fergusson, D. M., John, H. L., Pettit, G. S., & Woodward, L. (2003). Does father absence place daughters at special risk for early sexual activity and teenage pregnancy? *Child Development, 74*, 801–821. (p. 439)

Ellis, B. J., & Boyce, W. T. (2008). Biological sensitivity to context. *Current Directions in Psychological Science, 17*, 183–187. (p. 626)

Ellis, B. J., Schlomer, G. L., Tilley, E. H., & Butler, E. A. (2012). Impact of fathers on risky sexual behavior in daughters: A genetically and environmentally controlled sibling study. *Development and Psychopathology, 24*, 317–332. (p. 204)

Ellis, L., & Ames, M. A. (1987). Neurohormonal functioning and sexual orientation: A theory of homosexuality-heterosexuality. *Psychological Bulletin, 101*, 233–258. (p. 444)

Ellison-Wright, I., Glahn, D. C., Laird, A. R., Thelen, S. M., & Bullmore, E. (2008). The anatomy of first-episode and chronic schizophrenia: An anatomical likelihood estimation meta-analysis. *American Journal of Psychiatry, 165*, 1015–1023. (p. 642)

Else-Quest, N. M., Hyde, J. S., & Linn, M. C. (2010). Cross-national patterns of gender differences in mathematics: A meta-analysis. *Psychological Bulletin, 136*, 103–127. (p. 410)

Elzinga, B. M., Ardon, A. M., Heijnis, M. K., De Ruiter, M. B., Van Dyck, R., & Veltman, D. J. (2007). Neural correlates of enhanced working-memory performance in dissociative disorder: A functional MRI study. *Psychological Medicine, 37*, 235–245. (p. 648)

EMDR. (2011, February 18). E-mail correspondence from Robbie Dunton, EMDR Institute (www.emdr.org). (p. 677)

Emerging Trends. (1997, September). *Teens turn more to parents than friends on whether to attend church*. Princeton, NJ: Princeton Religion Research Center. (p. 211)

Emmons, R. A. (2007). *Thanks! How the new science of gratitude can make you happier*. Boston: Houghton Mifflin. (p. 487)

Emmons, S., Geisler, C., Kaplan, K. J., & Harrow, M. (1997). *Living with schizophrenia*. Muncie, IN: Taylor and Francis (Accelerated Development). (pp. 609, 640)

Empson, J. A. C., & Clarke, P. R. F. (1970). Rapid eye movements and remembering. *Nature, 227*, 287–288. (p. 113)

Endler, N. S. (1982). *Holiday of darkness: A psychologist's personal journey out of his depression*. New York: Wiley. (pp. 634, 686)

Engelstätter, B. A., Cunningham, S., & Ward, M. R. (2011). *Understanding the effects of violent video games on violent crime*. ZEW Discussion Paper No. 11–042. (p. 549)

Engemann, K. M., & Owyang, M. T. (2005, April). So much for that merit raise: The link between wages and appearance. *Regional Economist* (www.stlouisfed.org). (p. 554)

Engen, T. (1987). Remembering odors and their names. *American Scientist, 75*, 497–503. (p. 268)

Engle, R. W. (2002). Working memory capacity as executive attention. *Current Directions in Psychological Science, 11*, 19–23. (p. 320)

Entringer, S., Buss, C., Andersen, J., Chicz-DeMet, A., & Wadhwa, P. D. (2011). Ecological momentary assessment of maternal cortisol profiles over a multiple-day period predicts the length of human gestation. *Psychosomatic Medicine, 73*, 469–474. (p. 489)

Epel, E. S. (2009). Telomeres in a life-span perspective: A new "psychobiomarker"? *Current Directions in Psychological Science, 18*, 6–9. (p. 215)

Epel, E. S., Blackburn, E. H., Lin, J., Dhabhar, F. S., Adler, N. E., Morrow, J. D., & Cawthon, R. M. (2004). Accelerated telomere shortening in response to life stress. *Proceedings of the National Academy of Sciences, 101*, 17312–17315. (p. 492)

Epley, N., & Dunning, D. (2000). Feeling "holier than thou": Are self-serving assessments produced by errors in self- or social prediction? *Journal of Personality and Social Psychology, 79*, 861–875. (p. 602)

Epley, N., Keysar, B., Van Boven, L., & Gilovich, T. (2004). Perspective taking as egocentric anchoring and adjustment. *Journal of Personality and Social Psychology, 87*, 327–339. (p. 190)

Epley, N., Savitsky, K., & Gilovich, T. (2002). Empathy neglect: Reconciling the spotlight effect and the correspondence bias. *Journal of Personality and Social Psychology, 83*, 300–312. (p. 599)

Epstein, J., Stern, E., & Silbersweig, D. (1998). Mesolimbic activity associated with psychosis in schizophrenia: Symptom-specific PET studies. In J. F. McGinty (Ed.), *Advancing from the ventral striatum to the extended amygdala: Implications for neuropsychiatry and drug use: In honor of Lennart Heimer. Annals of the New York Academy of Sciences, 877*, 562–574. (p. 642)

Epstein, R. (2012, October). Brutal truths about the aging brain. *Discover*, pp. 48–50, 70. (p. 216)

Epstein, S. (1983a). Aggregation and beyond: Some basic issues on the prediction of behavior. *Journal of Personality, 51*, 360–392. (p. 592)

Epstein, S. (1983b). The stability of behavior across time and situations. In R. Zucker, J. Aronoff, & A. I. Rabin (Eds.), *Personality and the prediction of behavior.* San Diego: Academic Press. (p. 592)

Eranti, S. V., MacCabe, J. H., Bundy, H., & Murray, R. M. (2013). Gender difference in age at onset of schizophrenia: A meta-analysis. *Psychological Medicine, 43*, 155–167. (p. 641)

Erdberg, P. (1990). Rorschach assessment. In G. Goldstein & M. Hersen (Eds.), *Handbook of psychological assessment* (2nd ed.). New York: Pergamon. (p. 578)

Erdelyi, M. H. (1985). *Psychoanalysis: Freud's cognitive psychology.* New York: Freeman. (p. 580)

Erdelyi, M. H. (1988). Repression, reconstruction, and defense: History and integration of the psychoanalytic and experimental frameworks. In J. Singer (Ed.), *Repression: Defense mechanism and cognitive style.* Chicago: University of Chicago Press. (p. 580)

Erdelyi, M. H. (2006). The unified theory of repression. *Behavioral and Brain Sciences, 29*, 499–551. (p. 580)

Erel, O., & Burman, B. (1995). Interrelatedness of marital relations and parent-child relations: A meta-analytic review. *Psychological Bulletin, 118*, 108–132. (p. 222)

Erickson, K. I. (2009). Aerobic fitness is associated with hippocampal volume in elderly humans. *Hippocampus, 19*, 1030–1039. (p. 216)

Erickson, K. I., Banducci, S. E., Weinstein, A. M., MacDonald, Angus W., I., II, Ferrell, R. E., . . . Manuck, S. B. (2013). The brain-derived neurotrophic factor Val66met polymorphism moderates an effect of physical activity on working memory performance. *Psychological Science, 24*, 1770–1779. (p. 216)

Erickson, M. F., & Aird, E. G. (2005). *The motherhood study: Fresh insights on mothers' attitudes and concerns.* New York: The Motherhood Project, Institute for American Values. (p. 222)

Ericsson, K. A. (2001). Attaining excellence through deliberate practice: Insights from the study of expert performance. In M. Ferrari (Ed.), *The pursuit of excellence in education.* Hillsdale, NJ: Erlbaum. (p. 455)

Ericsson, K. A. (2002). Attaining excellence through deliberate practice: Insights from the study of expert performance. In C. Desforges & R. Fox (Eds.), *Teaching and learning: The essential readings.* Malden, MA: Blackwell Publishers. (p. 390)

Ericsson, K. A. (2006). The influence of experience and deliberate practice on the development of superior expert performance. In K. A. Ericsson, N. Charness, P. J. Feltovich, & R. R. Hoffman (Eds.), *The Cambridge handbook of expertise and expert performance.* Cambridge: Cambridge University Press. (p. 455)

Ericsson, K. A. (2007). Deliberate practice and the modifiability of body and mind: Toward a science of the structure and acquisition of expert and elite performance. *International Journal of Sport Psychology, 38*, 4–34. (pp. 390, 409, 455)

Ericsson, K. A., Krampe, R. T., & Tesch-Römer, C. (1993). The role of deliberate practice in the acquisition of expert performance. *Psychological Review, 100*, 363–406. (p. 106)

Ericsson, K. A., Roring, R. W., & Nandagopal, K. (2007). Giftedness and evidence for reproducibly superior performance: An account based on the expert performance framework. *High Ability Studies, 18*, 3–56. (p. 390)

Erikson, E. H. (1963). *Childhood and society.* New York: Norton. (pp. 208, 209)

Erikson, E. H. (1983, June). A conversation with Erikson (by E. Hall). *Psychology Today*, pp. 22–30. (p. 199)

Ermer, E., Kahn, R. E., Salovey, P., & Kiehl, K. A. (2012). Emotional intelligence in incarcerated men with psychopathic traits. *Journal of Personality and Social Psychology, 103*, 194–204. (p. 649)

Erol, R. Y., & Orth, U. (2011). Self-esteem development from age 14 to 30 years: A longitudinal study. *Journal of Personality and Social Psychology, 101*, 607–619. (p. 210)

Ert, E., Yechiam, E., & Arshavsky, O. (2013). Smokers' decision making: More than mere risk taking. PLOS ONE, 8(7), e68064. (p. 208)

Ertmer, D. J., Young, N. M., & Nathani, S. (2007). Profiles of focal development in young cochlear implant recipients. *Journal of Speech, Language, and Hearing Research, 50*, 393–407. (p. 373)

Escasa, M. J., Casey, J. F., & Gray, P. B. (2011). Salivary testosterone levels in men at a U.S. sex club. *Archives of Sexual Behavior, 40*, 921–926. (p. 434)

Escobar-Chaves, S. L., Tortolero, S. R., Markham, C. M., Low, B. J., Eitel, P., & Thickstun, P. (2005). Impact of the media on adolescent sexual attitudes and behaviors. *Pediatrics, 116*, 303–326. (p. 439)

Escobedo, J. R., & Adolphs, R. (2010). Becoming a better person: Temporal remoteness biases autobiographical memories for moral events. *Emotion, 10*, 511–518. (p. 604)

Eskine, K. J., Kacinik, N. A., & Prinz, J. J. (2011). A bad taste in the mouth: Gustatory disgust influences moral judgment. *Psychological Science, 22*, 295–299. (p. 206)

ESPAD. (2003). *Summary of the 2003 findings.* European School Survey Project on Alcohol and Other Drugs. (www.espad.org). (p. 129)

Esposito, G., Yoshida, S., Ohnishi, R., et al. (2013). Infant calming responses during maternal carrying in humans and mice. *Current Biology, 23*, 739–745. (p. 448)

Esser, J. K., & Lindoerfer, J. S. (1989). Groupthink and the space shuttle *Challenger* accident: Toward a quantitative case analysis. *Journal of Behavioral Decision Making, 2*, 167–177. (p. 535)

Esterson, A. (2001). The mythologizing of psychoanalytic history: Deception and self-deception in Freud's accounts of the seduction theory episode. *History of Psychiatry, 12*, 329–352. (p. 579)

Etkin, A., & Wager, T. D. (2007). Functional neuroimaging of anxiety: A meta-analysis of emotional processing in PTSD, social anxiety disorder, and specific phobia. *American Journal of Psychiatry, 164*, 1476–1488. (p. 626)

Eurich, T. L., Krause, D. E., Cigularov, K., & Thornton, G. C., III. (2009). Assessment centers: Current practices in the United States. *Journal of Business Psychology, 24*, 387–407. (p. 597)

Euston, D. R., Tatsuno, M., & McNaughton, B. L. (2007). Fast-forward playback of recent memory sequences in prefrontal cortex during sleep. *Science, 318*, 1147–1150. (p. 330)

Evans, C. R., & Dion, K. L. (1991). Group cohesion and performance: A meta-analysis. *Small Group Research, 22*, 175–186. (p. A-12)

Evans, G. W., Palsane, M. N., & Carrere, S. (1987). Type A behavior and occupational stress: A cross-cultural study of blue-collar workers. *Journal of Personality and Social Psychology, 52*, 1002–1007. (p. 497)

Evans, J. St. B. T. & Stanovich, K. E. (2013). Dual-process theories of higher cognition: Advancing the debate. *Perspectives on Psychological Science, 8*, 223–241. (p. 94)

Evans, N., & Levinson, S. C. (2009). The myth of language universals: Language diversity and its importance for cognitive science. *Behavioral and Brain Sciences, 32*, 429–492. (p. 373)

Evers, A., et al. (2012). Testing practices in the 21st century: Developments and European psychologists' opinions. *European Psychologist, 17*, 300–319. (p. 395)

Everson, S. A., Goldberg, D. E., Kaplan, G. A., Cohen, R. D., Pukkala, E., Tuomilehto, J., & Salonen, J. T. (1996). Hopelessness and risk of mortality and incidence of myocardial infarction and cancer. *Psychosomatic Medicine, 58*, 113–121. (p. 505)

Exline, J. J., Baumeister, R. F., Bushman, B. J., Campbell, W. K., & Finkel, E. J. (2004). Too proud to let go: Narcissistic entitlement as a barrier to forgiveness. *Journal of Personality and Social Psychology, 87*, 894–912. (p. 604)

Exner, J. E. (2003). *The Rorschach: A comprehensive system* (4th ed.). Hoboken, NJ: Wiley. (p. 578)

Eysenck, H. J. (1952). The effects of psychotherapy: An evaluation. *Journal of Consulting Psychology, 16*, 319–324. (p. 674)

Eysenck, H. J. (1990, April 30). An improvement on personality inventory. *Current Contents: Social and Behavioral Sciences, 22*(18), 20. (p. 587)

Eysenck, H. J. (1992). Four ways five factors are *not* basic. *Personality and Individual Differences, 13*, 667–673. (p. 587)

Eysenck, H. J., & Grossarth-Maticek, R. (1991). Creative novation behaviour therapy as a prophylactic treatment for cancer and coronary heart disease: Part II—Effects of treatment. *Behaviour Research and Therapy, 29*, 17–31. (p. 510)

Eysenck, H. J., Wakefield, J. A., Jr., & Friedman, A. F. (1983). Diagnosis and clinical assessment: The DSM-III. *Annual Review of Psychology, 34,* 167–193. (p. 614)

Eysenck, S. B. G., & Eysenck, H. J. (1963). The validity of questionnaire and rating assessments of extraversion and neuroticism, and their factorial stability. *British Journal of Psychology, 54,* 51–62. (p. 587)

Fabiano, G. A., Pelham, W. E., Jr., Coles, E. K., Gnagy, E. M., Chronis-Tuscano, A., & O'Connor, B. C. (2008). A meta-analysis of behavioral treatments for attention-deficit/hyperactivity disorder. *Clinical Psychology Review, 29,* 129–140. (p. 615)

Fabiansson, E. C., Denson, T. F., Moulds, M. L., Grisham, J. R., & Schira, M. M. (2012). Don't look back in anger: Neural correlates of reappraisal, analytical rumination, and angry rumination during a recall of an anger-inducing autobiographical memory. *NeuroImage, 59,* 2974–2981. (p. 478)

Fagan, J. F. (2011). Intelligence in infancy. In R. J. Sternberg & S. B. Kaufman (Eds.), *The Cambridge handbook of intelligence.* New York: Cambridge University Press. (p. 401)

Fagan, J. F., & Holland, C. R. (2007). Equal opportunity and racial differences in IQ. *Intelligence, 30,* 361–387. (p. 412)

Fagan, J. F., & Holland, C. R. (2007). Racial equality in intelligence: Predictions from a theory of intelligence as processing. *Intelligence, 35,* 319–334. (p. 413)

Fagan, J. F., & Holland, C. R. (2009). Culture-fair prediction of academic achievement. *Intelligence, 37,* 62–67. (p. 413)

Fairfield, H. (2012, February 4). Girls lead in science exam, but NOT in the United States. *New York Times* (www.nytimes.com). (p. 411)

Falk, C. F., Heine, S. J., Yuki, M., & Takemura, K. (2009). Why do Westerners self-enhance more than East Asians? *European Journal of Personality, 23,* 183–203. (p. 602)

Falk, R., Falk, R., & Ayton, P. (2009). Subjective patterns of randomness and choice: Some consequences of collective responses. *Journal of Experimental Psychology: Human Perception and Performance, 35,* 203–224. (p. 22)

Fanti, K. A., Vanman, E., Henrich, C. C., & Avraamides, M. N. (2009). Desensitization to media violence over a short period of time. *Aggressive Behavior, 35,* 179–187. (p. 312)

Farah, M. J., Rabinowitz, C., Quinn, G. E., & Liu, G. T. (2000). Early commitment of neural substrates for face recognition. *Cognitive Neuropsychology, 17,* 117–124. (p. 81)

Farb, N. A. S., Anderson, A. K., Mayberg, H., Bean, J., McKeon, D., & Segal, Z. V. (2010). Minding one's emotions: Mindfulness training alters the neural expression of sadness. *Emotion, 10,* 25–33. (p. 511)

Farina, A. (1982). The stigma of mental disorders. In A. G. Miller (Ed.), *In the eye of the beholder.* New York: Praeger. (pp. 611, 614)

Farley, M., Baral, I., Kiremire, M., & Sezgin, U. (1998). Prostitution in five countries: Violence and post-traumatic stress disorder. *Feminism and Psychology, 8,* 405–426. (p. 623)

Farrington, D. P. (1991). Antisocial personality from childhood to adulthood. *The Psychologist: Bulletin of the British Psychological Society, 4,* 389–394. (p. 649)

Fatemi, S. H., & Folsom, T. D. (2009). The neurodevelopmental hypothesis of schizophrenia, revisted. *Schizophrenia Bulletin, 35,* 528–548. (p. 642)

Fazel, S., Langstrom, N., Hjern, A., Grann, M., & Lichtenstein, P. (2009). Schizophrenia, substance abuse, and violent crime. *JAMA, 301,* 2016–2023. (p. 616)

Fazel, S., Lichtenstein, P., Grann, M., Goodwin, G. M., & Långström, N. (2010). Bipolar disorder and violent crime: New evidence from population-based longitudinal studies and systematic review. *Archives of General Psychiatry, 67,* 931–938. (p. 616)

Feder, H. H. (1984). Hormones and sexual behavior. *Annual Review of Psychology, 35,* 165–200. (p. 433)

Feeney, D. M. (1987). Human rights and animal welfare. *American Psychologist, 42,* 593–599. (p. 40)

Feeney, J. A., & Noller, P. (1990). Attachment style as a predictor of adult romantic relationships. *Journal of Personality and Social Psychology, 58,* 281–291. (p. 199)

Feigenson, L., Carey, S., & Spelke, E. (2002). Infants' discrimination of number vs. continuous extent. *Cognitive Psychology, 44,* 33–66. (p. 188)

Feinberg, M., Willer, R., Antonenko, O., & John, O. P. (2012). Liberating reason from the passions: Overriding intuitionist moral judgments through emotion reappraisal. *Psychological Science, 23,* 788–795. (p. 207)

Feinberg, M., Willer, R., & Schultz, M. (2014). Gossip and ostracism promote cooperation in groups. *Psychological Science, 25,* 656–664. (p. 448)

Feingold, A. (1992). Good-looking people are not what we think. *Psychological Bulletin, 111,* 304–341. (p. 553)

Feingold, A., & Mazzella, R. (1998). Gender differences in body image are increasing. *Psychological Science, 9,* 190–195. (p. 652)

Feinstein, J. S., Buzza, C., Hurlemann, R., Follmer, R. L., Dahdaleh, N. S., Coryell, W. H., . . . Wemmie, J. A. (2013). Fear and panic in humans with bilateral amygdala damage. *Nature Neuroscience, 16,* 270–272. (p. 71)

Feinstein, J. S., Duff, M. C., & Tranel, D. (2010, April 27). Sustained experiences of emotion after loss of memory in patients with amnesia. *Proceedings of the National Academy of Sciences, 107,* 7674–7679. (pp. 64, 331)

Feldman, M. B., & Meyer, I. H. (2010). Comorbidity and age of onset of eating disorders in gay men, lesbians, and bisexuals. *Psychiatry research, 180,* 126–131. (p. 652)

Feldman, R., Rosenthal, Z., & Eidelman, A. I. (2014). Maternal-preterm skin-to-skin contact enhances child physiologic organization and cognitive control across the first 10 years of life. *Biological Psychiatry, 75,* 56–64. (p. 153)

Fellinger, J., Holzinger, D., Gerich, J., & Goldberg, D. (2007). Mental distress and quality of life in the hard of hearing. *Acta Psychiatrica Scandinavica, 115,* 243–245. (p. 375)

Feng, J., Spence, I., & Pratt, J. (2007). Playing an action video game reduces gender differences in spatial cognition. *Psychological Science, 18,* 850–855. (p. 410)

Fenn, K. M., & Hambrick, D. Z. (2012). Individual differences in working memory capacity predict sleep-dependent memory consolidation. *Journal of Experimental Psychology: General, 141*(3), 404–410. (p. 324)

Fenn, K. M., Shintel, H., Atkins, A. S., Skipper, J. I., Bond, V. C., & Nusbaum, H. C. (2011). When less is heard than meets the ear: Change deafness in a telephone conversation. *Quarterly Journal of Experimental Psychology, 64,* 1442–1456. (p. 99)

Fenton, W. S., & McGlashan, T. H. (1991). Natural history of schizophrenia subtypes: II. Positive and negative symptoms and long-term course. *Archives of General Psychiatry, 48,* 978–986. (p. 641)

Fenton, W. S., & McGlashan, T. H. (1994). Antecedents, symptom progression, and long-term outcome of the deficit syndrome in schizophrenia. *American Journal of Psychiatry, 151,* 351–356. (p. 641)

Ferguson, C. (2009, June 14). Not every child is secretly a genius. *The Chronicle Review* (http://chronicle.com/article/Not-Every-Child-Is-Secretly/48001). (p. 389)

Ferguson, C. J. (2009). Media violence effects: Confirmed truth or just another X-file? *Journal of Forensic Psychology Practice, 9,* 103–126. (p. 312)

Ferguson, C. J. (2010). A meta-analysis of normal and disordered personality across the life span. *Journal of Personality and Social Psychology, 98,* 659–667. (p. 179)

Ferguson, C. J. (2013). Spanking, corporal punishment and negative long-term outcomes: A meta-analytic review of longitudinal studies. *Clinical Psychology Review, 33,* 196–208. (p. 296)

Ferguson, C. J. (2013). Violent video games and the Supreme Court: Lessons for the scientific community in the wake of Brown v. Entertainment Merchants Association. *American Psychologist, 68,* 57–74. (p. 549)

Ferguson, C. J. (2014). Is video game violence bad? *Psychologist, 27,* 324–327. (p. 549)

Ferguson, C. J., San Miguel, C., Garza, A., & Jerabeck, J. M. (2011). A longitudinal test of video game violence influences on dating and aggression: A 3-year longitudinal study of adolescents. *Journal of Psychiatric Research, 46,* 141–146. (pp. 118, 615)

Ferguson, C. J., Winegard, B., & Winegard, B. M. (2011). Who is the fairest one of all? How evolution guides peer and media influences on female body dissatisfaction. *Review of General Psychology, 15,* 11–28. (p. 653)

Ferguson, E. D. (1989). Adler's motivational theory: An historical perspective on belonging and the fundamental human striving. *Individual Psychology, 45,* 354–361. (p. 448)

Ferguson, E. D. (2001). Adler and Dreikurs: Cognitive-social dynamic innovators. *Journal of Individual Psychology, 57,* 324–341. (p. 448)

Ferguson, E. D. (2003). Social processes, personal goals, and their intertwining: Their importance in Adlerian theory and practice. *Journal of Individual Psychology, 59,* 136–144. (p. 576)

Ferguson, E. D. (2010). Editor's notes: Adler's innovative contributions regarding the need to belong. *Journal of Individual Psychology, 66*(1), 1–7. (p. 448)

Ferguson, M. J., & Zayas, V. (2009). Automatic evaluation. *Current Directions in Psychological Science, 18,* 362–366. (p. 232)

Fergusson, D. M., Boden, J. M., & Horwood, L. J. (2009). Tests of causal links between alcohol abuse or dependence and major depression. *Archives of General Psychiatry, 66,* 260–266. (p. 634)

Fergusson, D. M., & Woodward, L. G. (2002). Mental health, educational, and social role outcomes of adolescents with depression. *Archives of General Psychiatry, 59,* 225–231. (p. 632)

Fernandez-Dols, J-M., & Ruiz-Belda, M-A. (1995). Are smiles a sign of happiness? Gold medal winners at the Olympic Games. *Journal of Personality and Social Psychology, 69,* 1113–1119. (p. 473)

Fernbach, P. M., Rogers, T., Fox, C. R., & Sloman, S. A. (2013). Political extremism is supported by an illusion of understanding. *Psychological Science, 24,* 939–946. (p. 361)

Fernyhough, C. (2008). Getting Vygotskian about theory of mind: Mediation, dialogue, and the development of social understanding. *Developmental Review, 28,* 225–262. (p. 191)

Ferrari, A. J., Charlson, F. J., Norman, R. E., Patten, S. B., Freedman, G., Murray, C. J. L., Vos, T., & Whiteford, H. A. (2013). Burden of depressive disorders by country, sex, age, and year: Findings from the Global Burden of Disease Study 2010. *PLOS Medicine, 10,* e1001547. (pp. 631, 636)

Ferri, M., Amato, L., & Davoli, M. (2006). Alcoholics Anonymous and other 12-step programmes for alcohol dependence. *Cochrane Database of Systematic Reviews,* Issue 3. Art. No. CD005032. (p. 671)

Ferriman, K., Lubinski, D., & Benbow, C. P. (2009). Work preferences, life values, and personal views of top math/science graduate students and the profoundly gifted: Developmental changes and gender differences during emerging adulthood and parenthood. *Journal of Personality and Social Psychology, 97,* 517–522. (p. 164)

Ferris, C. F. (1996, March). The rage of innocents. *The Sciences,* pp. 22–26. (p. 200)

Festinger, L. (1957). *A theory of cognitive dissonance.* Stanford: Stanford University Press. (p. 523)

Feynman, R. (1997). Quoted by E. Hutchings (Ed.), *"Surely you're joking, Mr. Feynman."* New York: Norton. (p. 20)

Fiedler, F. E. (1981). Leadership effectiveness. *American Behavioral Scientist, 24,* 619–632. (p. A-11)

Fiedler, F. E. (1987, September). When to lead, when to stand back. *Psychology Today,* pp. 26–27. (p. A-12)

Fiedler, K., Nickel, S., Muehlfriedel, T., & Unkelbach, C. (2001). Is mood congruency an effect of genuine memory or response bias? *Journal of Experimental Social Psychology, 37,* 201–214. (p. 336)

Field, A. P. (2006). I don't like it because it eats sprouts: Conditioning preferences in children. *Behaviour Research and Therapy, 44,* 439–455. (p. 304)

Field, A. P. (2006). Is conditioning a useful framework for understanding the development and treatment of phobias? *Clinical Psychology Review, 26,* 857–875. (p. 624)

Field, T., Diego, M., & Hernandez-Reif, M. (2007). Massage therapy research. *Developmental Review, 27,* 75–89. (p. 153)

Field, T., Hernandez-Reif, M., Feijo, L., & Freedman, J. (2006). Prenatal, perinatal and neonatal stimulation: A survey of neonatal nurseries. *Infant Behavior & Development, 29,* 24–31. (p. 261)

Fielder, R. L., Walsh, J. L., Carey, K. B., & Carey, M. P. (2013). Predictors of sexual hookups: A theory-based, prospective study of first-year college women. *Archives of Sexual Behavior, 42,* 1425–1441. (p. 439)

Fields, R. D. (2004, April). The other half of the brain. *Scientific American,* pp. 54–61. (p. 54)

Fields, R. D. (2005, February). Making memories stick. *Scientific American,* pp. 75–81. (p. 333)

Fields, R. D. (2008, March). White matter. *Scientific American,* pp. 54–61. (p. 53)

Fields, R. D. (2011, May/June). The hidden brain. *Scientific American,* pp. 53–59. (p. 54)

Fields, R. D. (2013). Neuroscience: Map the other brain. *Nature, 501,* 25–27. (p. 54)

Fikke, L. T., Melinder, A., & Landrø, N. I. (2011). Executive functions are impaired in adolescents engaging in non-suicidal self-injury. *Psychological Medicine, 41,* 601–610. (p. 638)

Fincham, F. D., & Bradbury, T. N. (1993). Marital satisfaction, depression, and attributions: A longitudinal analysis. *Journal of Personality and Social Psychology, 64,* 442–452. (p. 519)

Finchilescu, G., & Tredoux, C. (Eds.). (2010). Intergroup relations in post apartheid South Africa: Change, and obstacles to change. *Journal of Social Issues, 66,* 223–236. (p. 564)

Finer, L. B. & Philbin, J. M. (2014). Trends in ages at key reproductive transitions in the United States, 1951–2010. *Women's Health Issues, 24,* e271–279. (p. 212)

Fingelkurts, A. A., & Fingelkurts, A. A. (2009). Is our brain hardwired to produce God, or is our brain hardwired to perceive God? A systematic review on the role of the brain in mediating religious experience. *Cognitive Processes, 10,* 293–326. (pp. 68, 81)

Fingerman, K. L., & Charles, S. T. (2010). It takes two to tango: Why older people have the best relationships. *Current Directions in Psychological Science, 19,* 172–176. (p. 223)

Fink, G. R., Markowitsch, H. J., Reinkemeier, M., Bruckbauer, T., Kessler, J., & Heiss, W-D. (1996). Cerebral representation of one's own past: Neural networks involved in autobiographical memory. *Journal of Neuroscience, 16,* 4275–4282. (p. 329)

Fink, M. (2009). *Electroconvulsive therapy: A guide for professionals and their patients.* New York: Oxford University Press. (p. 685)

Finkel, E. J., DeWall, C. N., Slotter, E. B., McNulty, J. K., Pond, R. S., Jr., & Atkins, D. C. (2012). Using I^3 theory to clarify when dispositional aggressiveness predicts intimate partner violence perpetration. *Journal of Personality and Social Psychology, 102,* 533–549. (p. 503)

Finkel, E. J., & Eastwick, P. W. (2008). Speed-dating. *Current Directions in Psychological Science, 17,* 193–197. (p. 553)

Finkel, E. J., & Eastwick, P. W. (2009). Arbitrary social norms influence sex differences in romantic selectivity. *Psychological Science 20,* 1290–1295. (p. 553)

Finlay, S. W. (2000). Influence of Carl Jung and William James on the origin of alcoholics anonymous. *Review of General Psychology, 4,* 3–12. (p. 671)

Fiore, M. C., et al. (2008). *Treating tobacco use and dependence: 2008 update. Clinical practice guideline.* Rockville, MD: U.S. Department of Health and Human Services, Public Health Service. (p. 122)

Fischer, P., & Greitemeyer, T. (2006). Music and aggression: The impact of sexual-aggressive song lyrics on aggression-related thoughts, emotions, and behavior toward the same and the opposite sex. *Personality and Social Psychology Bulletin, 32,* 1165–1176. (p. 548)

Fischer, P., Greitemeyer, T., Kastenmüller, A., Vogrincic, C., & Sauer, A. (2011). The effects of risk-glorifying media exposure on risk-positive cognitions, emotions, and behaviors: A meta-analytic review. *Psychological Bulletin, 137,* 367–390. (pp. 312, 548)

Fischer, R., & Boer, D. (2011). What is more important for national well-being: Money or autonomy? A meta-analysis of well-being, burnout, and anxiety across 63 societies. *Journal of Personality and Social Psychology, 101,* 164–184. (p. 482)

Fischhoff, B. (1982). Debiasing. In D. Kahneman, P. Slovic, & A. Tversky (Eds.), *Judgment under uncertainty: Heuristics and biases.* New York: Cambridge University Press. (p. 361)

Fischhoff, B., Slovic, P., & Lichtenstein, S. (1977). Knowing with certainty: The appropriateness of extreme confidence. *Journal of Experimental Psychology: Human Perception and Performance, 3,* 552–564. (p. 361)

Fishbach, A., Dhar, R., & Zhang, Y. (2006). Subgoals as substitutes or complements: The role of goal accessibility. *Journal of Personality and Social Psychology, 91,* 232–242. (p. A-11)

Fisher, G., & Rangel, A. (2014). Symmetry in cold-to-hot and hot-to-cold valuation gaps. *Psychological Science, 25,* 120–127. (p. 425)

Fisher, H. E. (1993, March/April). After all, maybe it's biology. *Psychology Today,* pp. 40–45. (p. 220)

Fisher, H. T. (1984). Little Albert and Little Peter. *Bulletin of the British Psychological Society, 37,* 269. (p. 663)

Flack, W. F. (2006). Peripheral feedback effects of facial expressions, bodily postures, and vocal expressions on emotional feelings. *Cognition and Emotion, 20,* 177–195. (pp. 474, 477)

Flaherty, D. K. (2011). The vaccine-autism connection: A public health crisis caused by unethical medical practices and fraudulent science. *Annals of Pharmacotherapy, 45,* 1302–1304. (p. 193)

Flegal, K. M., Carroll, M. D., Kit, B. K., Ogden, C. L. (2012). Prevalence of obesity and trends in the distribution of body mass index among U.S. adults, 1999–2010. *JAMA, 307,* 491–497. (p. 430)

Flegal, K. M., Carroll, M. D., Ogden, C. L., & Curtin, L. R. (2010). Prevalence and trends in obesity among US adults, 1999–2008. *JAMA, 303,* 235–241. (p. 430)

Flegal, K. M., Kits, B. K., Orpana, H., & Graubard, B. I. (2013). Association of all-cause mortality with overweight and obesity using standard Body Mass Index categories: A systematic review and meta-analysis. *JAMA, 309,* 71–82. (p. 430)

Fleming, I., Baum, A., & Weiss, L. (1987). Social density and perceived control as mediator of crowding stress in high-density residential neighborhoods. *Journal of Personality and Social Psychology, 52,* 899–906. (p. 502)

Fleming, J. H. (2001, Winter/Spring). Introduction to the special issue on linkage analysis. *The Gallup Research Journal,* pp. i-vi. (p. A-10)

Fleming, J. H., & Scott, B. A. (1991). The costs of confession: The Persian Gulf War POW tapes in historical and theoretical perspective. *Contemporary Social Psychology, 15,* 127–138. (p. 472)

Fletcher, G. J. O., Fitness, J., & Blampied, N. M. (1990). The link between attributions and happiness in close relationships: The roles of depression and explanatory style. *Journal of Social and Clinical Psychology, 9,* 243–255. (p. 519)

Fletcher, S. (2013, August). Machine learning. *Scientific American,* pp. 62–68. (p. 298)

Flora, S. R. (2004). *The power of reinforcement.* Albany, NY: SUNY Press. (p. 297)

Flora, S. R., & Bobby, S. E. (2008, September/October). The bipolar bamboozle. *Skeptical Inquirer,* pp. 41–45. (p. 629)

Flory, R., Ametepe, J., & Bowers, B. (2010). A randomized, place-controlled trial of bright light and high-density negative air ions for treatment of Season Affective Disorder. *Psychiatry Research, 177,* 101–108. (p. 678)

Floud, R., Fogel, R. W., Harris, B., & Hong, S. C. (2011). *The changing body: Health, nutrition, and human development in the western world since 1700.* New York: Cambridge University Press. (p. 141)

Flouri, E., & Buchanan, A. (2004). Early father's and mother's involvement and child's later educational outcomes. *British Journal of Educational Psychology, 74,* 141–153. (p. 198)

Flynn, J. R. (1987). Massive IQ gains in 14 nations: What IQ tests really measure. *Psychological Bulletin, 101,* 171–191. (p. 396)

Flynn, J. R. (2009). Requiem for nutrition as the cause of IQ gains: Raven's gains in Britain 1938–2008. *Economics and Human Biology, 7,* 18–27. (p. 396)

Flynn, J. R. (2012). *Are we getting smarter? Rising IQ in the twenty-first century.* Cambridge: Cambridge University Press. (pp. 396, 397)

Flynn, J. R. (2014, May 16, 17, and 22). Personal correspondence from University of Otago, New Zealand. (p. 397)

Foa, E. B., Gillihan, S. J., & Bryant, R. A. (2013). Challenges and successes in dissemination of evidence-based treatments for posttraumatic stress: Lessons learned from prolonged exposure therapy for PTSD. *Psychological Science in the Public Interest, 14,* 65–111. (p. 664)

Foa, E. B., & Kozak, M. J. (1986). Emotional processing of fear: Exposure to corrective information. *Psychological Bulletin, 99,* 20–35. (p. 664)

Fodor, J. D. (1999). Let your brain alone. *London Review of Books, 21* (www.lrb.co.uk). (p. 66)

Ford, E. S. (2002). Does exercise reduce inflammation? Physical activity and B-reactive protein among U.S. adults. *Epidemiology, 13,* 561–569. (p. 507)

Ford, M. T., Cerasoli, C. P., Higgins, J. A., & Deccesare, A. L. (2011). Relationships between psychological, physical, and behavioural health and work performance: A review and meta-analysis. *Work & Stress, 25,* 185–204. (p. A-8)

Foree, D. D., & LoLordo, V. M. (1973). Attention in the pigeon: Differential effects of food-getting versus shock-avoidance procedures. *Journal of Comparative and Physiological Psychology, 85,* 551–558. (p. 303)

Forest, A. & Wood, J. (2012). When social networking is not working: Individuals with low self-esteem recognize but do not reap the benefits of self-disclosure on Facebook. *Psychological Science, 23,* 295–302. (p. 599)

Forgas, J. P. (2008b). Affect and cognition. *Perspectives on Psychological Science, 3,* 94–101. (p. 479)

Forgas, J. P. (2009, November/December). Think negative! *Australian Science,* pp. 14–17. (p. 628)

Forgas, J. P., Bower, G. H., & Krantz, S. E. (1984). The influence of mood on perceptions of social interactions. *Journal of Experimental Social Psychology, 20,* 497–513. (p. 336)

Forhan, S. E., Gottlieb, S. L., Sternberg, M. R., Xu, F., Datta, D., Berman, S., & Markowitz, L. (2008). *Prevalence of sexually transmitted infections and bacterial vaginosis among female adolescents in the United States: Data from the National Health and Nutrition Examination Survey (NHANES) 2003–2004.* Paper presented to the 2008 National STD Prevention Conference, Chicago, Illinois. (p. 436)

Forman, D. R., Aksan, N., & Kochanska, G. (2004). Toddlers' responsive imitation predicts preschool-age conscience. *Psychological Science, 15,* 699–704. (p. 310)

Forsyth, D. R., Lawrence, N. K., Burnette, J. L., & Baumeister, R. F. (2007). Attempting to improve academic performance of struggling college students by bolstering their self-esteem: An intervention that backfired. *Journal of Social and Clinical Psychology, 26,* 447–459. (p. 599)

Foss, D. J., & Hakes, D. T. (1978). *Psycholinguistics: An introduction to the psychology of language.* Englewood Cliffs, NJ: Prentice-Hall. (p. 579)

Foster, J. (2011). *Our deadly anorexic pact.* Retrieved May 5, 2014 from http://www.dailymail.co.uk/femail/article-2004003/Anorexia-pact-Identical-twins-compete-disturbing-way.html. (p. 651)

Foulkes, D. (1999). *Children's dreaming and the development of consciousness.* Cambridge, MA: Harvard University Press. (p. 114)

Fournier, J. C., DeRubeis, R. J., Hollon, S. D., Dimidjian, S., Amsterdam, J. D., Shelton, R. C., & Fawcett, J. (2010). Antidepressant drug effects and depression severity: A patient-level meta-analysis. *Journal of the American Medical Association, 303,* 47–53. (p. 684)

Fouts, R. S. (1992). Transmission of a human gestural language in a chimpanzee mother-infant relationship. *Friends of Washoe, 12/13,* pp. 2–8. (p. 378)

Fouts, R. S. (1997). *Next of kin: What chimpanzees have taught me about who we are.* New York: Morrow. (p. 378)

Fowles, D. C. (1992). Schizophrenia: Diathesis-stress revisited. *Annual Review of Psychology, 43,* 303–336. (p. 641)

Fowles, D. C., & Dindo, L. (2009). Temperament and psychopathy: A dual-pathway model. *Current Directions in Psychological Science, 18,* 179–183. (p. 649)

Fox, D. (2010, June). The insanity virus. *Discover,* pp. 58–64. (p. 643)

Fox, J. L. (1984). The brain's dynamic way of keeping in touch. *Science, 225,* 820–821. (p. 82)

Fox, K. C. R., Nijeboer, S., Solomonova, E., Domhoff, G. W., & Christoff, K. (2013). Dreaming as mind wandering: Evidence from functional neuroimaging and first-person content reports. *Frontiers in Human Neuroscience, 7,* doi:http://dx.doi.org/10.3389/fnhum.2013.00412. (p. 115)

Fox, M. L., Dwyer, D. J., & Ganster, D. C. (1993). Effects of stressful job demands and control on physiological and attitudinal outcomes in a hospital setting. *Academy of Management Journal, 36,* 289–318. (p. 502)

Fozard, J. L., & Popkin, S. J. (1978). Optimizing adult development: Ends and means of an applied psychology of aging. *American Psychologist, 33,* 975–989. (p. 215)

Fracassini, C. (2000, August 27). Holidaymakers led by the nose in sales quest. *Scotland on Sunday.* (p. 268)

Fraley, R. C., Roisman, G. I., Booth-LaForce, C., Owen, M. T., & Holland, A. S. (2013, May). Interpersonal and genetic origins of adult attachment styles: A longitudinal study from infancy to early adulthood. *Journal of Personality and Social Psychology, 104,* 817–838. (p. 199)

Fraley, R. C., & Tancredy, C. M. (2012). Twin and sibling attachment in a nationally representative sample. *Personality and Social Psychology Bulletin, 38,* 308–316. (p. 140)

Fraley, R. C., Vicary, A. M., Brumbaugh, C. C., & Roisman, G. I. (2011). Patterns of stability in adult attachment: An empirical test of two models of continuity and change. *Journal of Personality and Social Psychology, 101,* 974–992. (p. 199)

Frances, A. J. (2012, December 2). DSM-5 is guide, not Bible—Ignore its ten worst changes. www.psychologytoday.com/blog/dsm5-in-distress/201212/dsm-5-is-guide-not-bible-ignore-its-ten-worst-changes. (p. 614)

Frances, A. J. (2013). *Saving normal: An insider's revolt against out-of-control psychiatric diagnosis, DSM-5, big pharma, and the medicalization of ordinary life.* New York: HarperCollins. (pp. 614, 615)

Frank, J. D. (1982). Therapeutic components shared by all psychotherapies. In J. H. Harvey & M. M. Parks (Eds.), *The Master Lecture Series: Vol. 1. Psychotherapy research and behavior change.* Washington, DC: American Psychological Association. (pp. 678, 679)

Frankel, A., Strange, D. R., & Schoonover, R. (1983). CRAP: Consumer rated assessment procedure. In G. H. Scherr & R. Liebmann-Smith (Eds.), *The best of The Journal of Irreproducible Results.* New York: Workman Publishing. (p. 589)

Frankenburg, W., Dodds, J., Archer, P., Shapiro, H., & Bresnick, B. (1992). The Denver II: A major revision and restandardization of the Denver Developmental Screening Test. *Pediatrics, 89,* 91–97. (p. 185)

Franklin, M., & Foa, E. B. (2011). Treatment of obsessive-compulsive disorder. *Annual Review of Clinical Psychology, 7,* 229–243. (p. 625)

Franz, E. A., Waldie, K. E., & Smith, M. J. (2000). The effect of callosotomy on novel versus familiar bimanual actions: A neural dissociation between controlled and automatic processes? *Psychological Science, 11,* 82–85. (p. 84)

Frassanito, P., & Pettorini, B. (2008). Pink and blue: The color of gender. *Child's Nervous System, 24,* 881–882. (p. 161)

Frasure-Smith, N., & Lesperance, F. (2005). Depression and coronary heart disease: Complex synergism of mind, body, and environment. *Current Directions in Psychological Science, 14,* 39–43. (p. 498)

Frattaroli, J. (2006). Experimental disclosure and its moderators: A meta-analysis. *Psychological Bulletin, 132,* 823–865. (p. 506)

Fredrickson, B. L. (2013). Updated thinking on positivity ratios. *American Psychologist, 68,* 814–822. (p. 479)

Fredrickson, B. L., Grewen, K. M., Coffey, K. A., Algoe, S. B., Firestine, A. M., Arevalo, J. M. G., Ma, J., & Cole, S. W. (2013). A functional genomic perspective on human well-being. *PNAS, 110,* 13684–13689. (p. 485)

Freedman, D. H. (2011, February). How to fix the obesity crisis. *Scientific American,* pp. 40–47. (p. 432)

Freedman, D. J., Riesenhuber, M., Poggio, T., & Miller, E. K. (2001). Categorical representation of visual stimuli in the primate prefrontal cortex. *Science, 291,* 312–316. (p. 367)

Freedman, J. L. (1988). Television violence and aggression: What the evidence shows. In S. Oskamp (Ed.), *Television as a social issue.* Newbury Park, CA: Sage. (p. 312)

Freedman, J. L., & Fraser, S. C. (1966). Compliance without pressure: The foot-in-the-door technique. *Journal of Personality and Social Psychology, 4,* 195–202. (pp. 521, 522)

Freedman, J. L., & Perlick, D. (1979). Crowding, contagion, and laughter. *Journal of Experimental Social Psychology, 15,* 295–303. (p. 532)

Freedman, L. R., Rock, D., Roberts, S. A., Cornblatt, B. A., & Erlenmeyer-Kimling, L. (1998). The New York high-risk project: Attention, anhedonia and social outcome. *Schizophrenia Research, 30,* 1–9. (p. 645)

Freedman, R., et al. (2013). The initial field trials of DSM-5: New blooms and old thorns. *American Journal of Psychiatry, 170,* 1–5. (p. 614)

Freeman, D., & Freeman, J. (2013). *The stressed sex: Uncovering the truth about men, women, and mental health.* Oxford, UK: Oxford University Press. (p. 632)

Freeman, E. C., & Twenge, J. M. (2010, January). *Using MySpace increases the endorsement of narcissistic personality traits.* Poster presented at the annual conference of the Society for Personality and Social Psychology, Las Vegas, NV. (p. 453)

Freeman, W. J. (1991, February). The physiology of perception. *Scientific American,* pp. 78–85. (p. 256)

Frenda, S. J., Knowles, E. D., Saletan, W., & Loftus, E. F. (2013). False memories of fabricated political events. *Journal of Experimental Social Psychology, 49,* 280–286. (p. 345)

Freud, S. (1931; reprinted 1961). Female sexuality. In J. Strachey (Trans.), *The standard edition of the complete psychological works of Sigmund Freud.* London: Hogarth Press. (p. 572)

Freud, S. (1935; reprinted 1960). *A general introduction to psychoanalysis.* New York: Washington Square Press. (p. 220)

Frey, M. C., & Detterman, D. K. (2004). Scholastic assessment or *g*? The relationship between the Scholastic Assessment Test and general cognitive ability. *Psychological Science, 15,* 373–378. (p. 392)

Freyd, J. J., DePrince, A. P., & Gleaves, D. H. (2007). The state of betrayal trauma theory: Reply to McNally—Conceptual issues and future directions. *Memory, 15,* 295–311. (p. 348)

Fried, I., Mukramel, R., & Kreiman, G. (2011). Internally generated preactivation of single neurons in human medial frontal cortex predicts volition. *Neuron, 69,* 548–562. (p. 95)

Friedman, H. S., & Martin, L. R. (2012). *The longevity project.* New York: Penguin (Plume). (p. 404)

Friedman, M., & Ulmer, D. (1984). *Treating Type A behavior—and your heart.* New York: Knopf. (pp. 497, 510)

Friedman, R., & James, J. W. (2008). The myth of the sages of dying, death and grief. *Skeptic, 14*(2), 37–41. (p. 225)

Friedman, R. A. (2012, December 17). In gun debate, a misguided focus on mental illness. *New York Times* (www.nytimes.com). (p. 616)

Frijda, N. H. (1988). The laws of emotion. *American Psychologist, 43,* 349–358. (p. 483)

Frisch, M., & Zdravkovic, S. (2010). Body size at birth and same-sex marriage in young adulthood. *Archives of Sexual Behavior, 39,* 117–123. (p. 445)

Frisell, T., Pawitan, Y., Långström, N., & Lichtenstein, P. (2012). Heritability, assortative mating and gender differences in violent crime: Results from a total population sample using twin, adoption, and sibling models. *Behavior Genetics, 42,* 3–18. (pp. 162, 649)

Frith, U., & Frith, C. (2001). The biological basis of social interaction. *Current Directions in Psychological Science, 10,* 151–155. (p. 193)

Fritz, T., Jentschke, S., Gosselin, N., Sammler, D., Peretz, I., Turner, R., Friederici, A., & Koelsch, S. (2009). Universal recognition of three basic emotions in music. *Current Biology, 19,* 573–576. (p. 472)

Fromkin, V., & Rodman, R. (1983). *An introduction to language* (3rd ed.). New York: Holt, Rinehart & Winston. (p. 372)

Frühauf, S., Gerger, H., Schmidt, H. M., Munder, T., & Barth, J. (2013). Efficacy of psychological interventions for sexual dysfunction: A systematic review and meta-analysis. *Archives of Sexual Behavior, 42,* 915–933. (p. 436)

Fry, A. F., & Hale, S. (1996). Processing speed, working memory, and fluid intelligence: Evidence for a developmental cascade. *Psychological Science, 7,* 237–241. (p. 216)

Fry, D. P. (2012). Life without war. *Science, 336,* 879–884. (p. 566)

Fry, R., & Cohn, D. (2010, January 19). *Women, men and the new economics of marriage.* Pew Research Center (pewresearch.org). (p. 168)

Fu, A., & Markus, H. R. (2014). My mother and me: Why tiger mothers motivate Asian Americans but not European Americans. *Personality and Social Psychology Bulletin, 40,* 739–749. (p. 154)

Fuhriman, A., & Burlingame, G. M. (1994). Group psychotherapy: Research and practice. In A. Fuhriman & G. M. Burlingame (Eds.), *Handbook of group psychotherapy.* New York: Wiley. (p. 670)

Fujiki, N., Yoshida, Y., Ripley, B., Mignot, E., & Nishino, S. (2003). Effects of IV and ICV hypocretin-1 (Orexin A) in hypocretin receptor-2 gene mutated narcoleptic dogs and IV hypocretin-1 replacement therapy in a hypocretin-ligand-deficient narcoleptic dog. *Sleep, 26,* 953–959. (p. 111)

Fuller, M. J., & Downs, A. C. (1990). *Spermarche is a salient biological marker in men's development.* Poster presented at the American Psychological Society convention. (p. 167)

Fulmer, C. A., Gelfand, M. J., Kruglanski, A. W., Kim-Prieto, C., Diener, E., Pierro, A., & Higgins, E. T. (2010). On "feeling right" in cultural contexts: How person-culture match affects self-esteem and subjective well-being. *Psychological Science, 21,* 1563–1569. (pp. 485, 596)

Fulmer, I. S., Gerhart, B., & Scott, K. S. (2003). Are the 100 best better? An empirical investigation of the relationship between being a "great place to work" and firm performance. *Personnel Psychology, 56,* 965–993. (p. A-9)

Funder, D. C. (2001). Personality. *Annual Review of Psychology, 52,* 197–221. (p. 590)

Funder, D. C. (2009). Persons, behaviors and situations: An agenda for personality psychology in the postwar era. *Journal of Research in Personality, 43,* 155–162. (p. 595)

Furlow, F. B., & Thornhill, R. (1996, January/February). The orgasm wars. *Psychology Today,* pp. 42–46. (p. 435)

Furnham, A. (1982). Explanations for unemployment in Britain. *European Journal of Social Psychology, 12,* 335–352. (p. 519)

Furnham, A., & Baguma, P. (1994). Cross-cultural differences in the evaluation of male and female body shapes. *International Journal of Eating Disorders, 15,* 81–89. (p. 430)

Furnham, A., & Wu, J. (2008). Gender differences in estimates of one's own and parental intelligence in China. *Individual Differences Research, 6,* 1–12. (p. 540)

Furr, R. M., & Funder, D. C. (1998). A multimodal analysis of personal negativity. *Journal of Personality and Social Psychology, 74,* 1580–1591. (p. 636)

Furukawa, T. A., Yoshimura, R., Harai, H., Imaizumi, T., Takeuchi, H., Kitamua, T., & Takahashi, K. (2009). How many well vs. unwell days can you expect over 10 years, once you become depressed? *Acta Psychiatrica Scandinavica, 119,* 290–297. (p. 632)

Gable, S. L., Gonzaga, G. C., & Strachman, A. (2006). Will you be there for me when things go right? Supportive responses to positive event disclosures. *Journal of Personality and Social Psychology, 91,* 904–917. (p. 222)

Gabrieli, J. D. E., Desmond, J. E., Demb, J. E., Wagner, A. D., Stone, M. V., Vaidya, C. J., & Glover, G. H. (1996). Functional magnetic resonance imaging of semantic memory processes in the frontal lobes. *Psychological Science, 7,* 278–283. (p. 329)

Gaertner, L., Iuzzini, J., & O'Mara, E. M. (2008). When rejection by one fosters aggression against many: Multiple-victim aggression as a consequence of social rejection and perceived groupness. *Journal of Experimental Social Psychology, 44,* 958–970. (p. 451)

Gaillard, R., Dehaene, S., Adam, C., Clémenceau, S., Hasboun, D., Baulac, M., Cohen, L., & Naccache, L. (2009). Converging intracranial markers of conscious access. *PLoS Biology, 7*(e): e1000061. (p. 93)

Gaillot, M. T., & Baumeister, R. F. (2007). Self-regulation and sexual restraint: Dispositionally and temporally poor self-regulatory abilities contribute to failures at restraining sexual behavior. *Personality and Social Psychology Bulletin, 33,* 173–186. (p. 503)

Gaissmaier, W., & Gigerenzer, G. (2012). 9/11, Act II: A fine-grained analysis of regional variations in traffic fatalities in the aftermath of the terrorist attacks. *Psychological Science, 23,* 1449–1454. (p. 362)

Gaither, S. E., & Sommers, S. R. (2013). Living with an other-race roommate shapes whites' behavior in subsequent diverse settings. *Journal of Experimental Social Psychology, 49,* 272–276. (p. 564)

Galak, J., Leboeuf, R. A., Nelson, L. D., & Simmons, J. P. (2012). Correcting the past: Failures to replicate psi. *Journal of Personality and Social Psychology, 103*, 933–948. (p. 274)

Galambos, N. L. (1992). Parent-adolescent relations. *Current Directions in Psychological Science, 1*, 146–149. (p. 210)

Galanter, E. (1962). Contemporary psychophysics. In R. Brown, E. Galanter, E. H. Hess, & G. Mandler (Eds.), *New directions in psychology*. New York: Holt Rinehart & Winston. (p. 231)

Galati, D., Scherer, K. R., & Ricci-Bitti, P. E. (1997). Voluntary facial expression of emotion: Comparing congenitally blind with normally sighted encoders. *Journal of Personality and Social Psychology, 73*, 1363–1379. (p. 472)

Galdi, S., Arcuri, L., & Gawronski, B. (2008). Automatic mental associations predict future choices of undecided decision-makers. *Science, 321*, 1100–1102. (p. 364)

Gale, C. R., Batty, G. D., & Deary, I. J. (2008). Locus of control at age 10 years and health outcomes and behaviors at age 30 years: The 1970 British Cohort Study. *Psychosomatic Medicine, 70*, 397–403. (p. 503)

Gale, C. R., Booth, T., Mõttus, R., Kuh, D., & Deary, I. J. (2013). Neuroticism and extraversion in youth predict mental well-being and life satisfaction 40 years later. *Journal of Research in Personality, 47*, 687–697. (p. 179)

Galinsky, A. M., & Sonenstein, F. L. (2013). Relationship commitment, perceived equity, and sexual enjoyment among young adults in the United States. *Archives of Sexual Behavior, 42*, 93–104. (p. 447)

Galinsky, E., Aumann, K., & Bond, J. T. (2008). *Times are changing: Gender and generation at work and at home*. Work and Families Institute (www.familiesandwork.org). (p. 602)

Gallace, A. (2012). Living with touch. *Psychologist, 25*, 896–899. (p. 98)

Gallace, A., & Spence, C. (2011). To what extent do Gestalt grouping principles influence tactile perception? *Psychological Bulletin, 137*, 538–561. (p. 248)

Gallese, V., Gernsbacher, M. A., Heyes, C., Hickok, G., & Iacoboni, M. (2011). Mirror neuron forum. *Perspectives on Psychological Science, 6*, 369–407. (pp. 194, 307, 309)

Gallo, W. T., Teng, H. M., Falba, T. A., Kasl, S. V., Krumholz, H. M., & Bradley, E. H. (2006). The impact of late career job loss on myocardial infarction and stroke: A 10-year follow up using the health and retirement survey. *Occupational and Environmental Medicine, 63*, 683–687. (p. 498)

Gallup Brain. (2008, accessed February 20). Woman for president: Question qn2f, March, 2007 wave. Brain.Gallup.com. (p. 540)

Gallup Organization. (2004, August 16). 65% of Americans receive NO praise or recognition in the workplace. Personal communication. (p. A-11)

Gallup, G. G., Jr. (1970). Chimpanzees: Self-recognition. *Science, 167*, 86–87. (p. 201)

Gallup, G. G., Jr., & Frederick, D. A. (2010). The science of sex appeal: An evolutionary perspective. *Review of General Psychology, 14*, 240–250. (p. 554)

Gallup, G. G., Jr., & Suarez, S. D. (1986). Self-awareness and the emergence of mind in humans and other primates. In J. Suls & A. G. Greenwald (Eds.), *Psychological perspectives on the self* (Vol. 3.). Hillsdale, NJ: Erlbaum. (p. 201)

Gallup, G. H. (1972). *The Gallup poll: Public opinion 1935–1971* (Vol. 3). New York: Random House. (p. 564)

Gallup, G. H., Jr. (1994, October). Millions finding care and support in small groups. *Emerging Trends*, pp. 2–5. (p. 671)

Gangestad, S. W., & Simpson, J. A. (2000). The evolution of human mating: Trade-offs and strategic pluralism. *Behavioral and Brain Sciences, 23*, 573–587. (p. 149)

Gangestad, S. W., Thornhill, R., & Garver-Apgar, C. E. (2010). Men's facial masculinity predicts changes in their female partners' sexual interests across the ovulatory cycle, whereas men's intelligence does not. *Evolution and Human Behavior, 31*, 412–424. (p. 554)

Gangwisch, J. E., Babiss, L. A., Malaspina, D., Turner, J. B., Zammit, G. K., & Posner, K. (2010). Earlier parental set bedtimes as a protective factor against depression and suicidal ideation. *Sleep, 33*, 97–106. (p. 107)

Gao, Y., Raine, A., Venables, P. H., Dawson, M. E., & Mednick, S. A. (2010). Association of poor child fear conditioning and adult crime. *American Journal of Psychiatry, 167*, 56–60. (p. 650)

Garcia, J., & Gustavson, A. R. (1997, January). Carl R. Gustavson (1946–1996): Pioneering wildlife psychologist. *APS Observer*, pp. 34–35. (p. 302)

Garcia, J., & Koelling, R. A. (1966). Relation of cue to consequence in avoidance learning. *Psychonomic Science, 4*, 123–124. (p. 301)

Garcia, J. R., Massey, S. G., Merriwether, A. M., & Seibold-Simpson, S. M. (2013). *Orgasm experience among emerging adult men and women: Relationship context and attitudes toward uncommitted sex*. Poster presentation at the Association for Psychological Science convention, Washington, D.C. (p. 447)

Garcia, J. R., Reiber, C., Massey, S. G., & Merriwether, A. M. (2012). Sexual hookup culture: A review. *Review of General Psychology, 16*, 161–176. (pp. 119, 447)

Garcia, J. R., Reiber, C., Massey, S. G., & Merriwether, A. M. (2013, February). Sexual hook-up culture. *Monitor on Psychology*, pp. 60–66. (p. 439)

Gardner, H. (1983). *Frames of mind: The theory of multiple intelligences*. New York: Basic Books. (p. 387)

Gardner, H. (1998, March 19). An intelligent way to progress. *The Independent* (London), p. E4. (p. 387)

Gardner, H. (1998, November 5). Do parents count? *New York Review of Books* (www.nybooks.com). (p. 155)

Gardner, H. (1999, February). Who owns intelligence? *Atlantic Monthly*, pp. 67–76. (p. 392)

Gardner, H. (1999). *Multiple views of multiple intelligence*. New York: Basic Books. (pp. 387, 391)

Gardner, H. (2006). *The development and education of the mind: The selected works of Howard Gardner*. New York: Routledge/Taylor & Francis. (p. 387)

Gardner, H. (2011). *The theory of multiple intelligences: As psychology, as education, as social science*. Address on the receipt of an honorary degree from José Cela University in Madrid and the Prince of Asturias Prize for Social Science. (p. 387)

Gardner, J., & Oswald, A. J. (2007). Money and mental well-being: A longitudinal study of medium-sized lottery wins. *Journal of Health Economics, 6*, 49–60. (p. 483)

Gardner, J. W. (1984). *Excellence: Can we be equal and excellent too?* New York: Norton. (p. A-12)

Gardner, M. (2006, January/February). The memory wars, part one. *Skeptical Inquirer, 30*, 28–31. (p. 348)

Gardner, R. A., & Gardner, B. I. (1969). Teaching sign language to a chimpanzee. *Science, 165*, 664–672. (p. 377)

Garfield, C. (1986). *Peak Performers: The new heroes of American Business*. New York: Morrow. (p. 382)

Garon, N., Bryson, S. E., & Smith, I. M. (2008). Executive function in preschoolers: A review using an integrative framework. *Psychological Bulletin, 134*, 31–60. (p. 184)

Garry, M., Loftus, E. F., & Brown, S. W. (1994). Memory: A river runs through it. *Consciousness and Cognition, 3*, 438–451. (p. 580)

Garry, M., Manning, C. G., Loftus, E. F., & Sherman, S. J. (1996). Imagination inflation: Imagining a childhood event inflates confidence that it occurred. *Psychonomic Bulletin & Review, 3*, 208–214. (p. 344)

Gartrell, N., & Bos, H. (2010). U.S. national longitudinal lesbian family study: Psychological adjustment of 17-year-old adolescents. *Pediatrics, 126*, 28–36. (p. 442)

Gatchel, R. J., Peng, Y. B., Peters, M. L., Fuchs, P. N., & Turk, D. C. (2007). The biopsychosocial approach to chronic pain: Scientific advances and future directions. *Psychological Bulletin, 133*, 581–624. (p. 262)

Gates, G. J., & Newport, F. (2012, October 18). Special report: 3.4% of U.S. adults identify as LGBT. www.gallup.com. (p. 440)

Gates, W. (1998, July 20). Charity begins when I'm ready (interview). *Fortune* (www.pathfinder.com/fortune/1998/980720/bil7.html). (p. 388)

Gawande, A. (1998, September 21). The pain perplex. *The New Yorker*, pp. 86–94. (p. 263)

Gawin, F. H. (1991). Cocaine addiction: Psychology and neurophysiology. *Science, 251*, 1580–1586. (p. 123)

Gawronski, B., & Quinn, K. (2013). Guilty by mere similarity: Assimilative effects of facial resemblance on automatic evaluation. *Journal of Experimental Social Psychology, 49*, 120–125. (p. 286)

Gazzaniga, M. S. (1967, August). The split brain in man. *Scientific American*, pp. 24–29. (p. 83)

Gazzaniga, M. S. (1983). Right hemisphere language following brain bisection: A 20-year perspective. *American Psychologist, 38*, 525–537. (p. 84)

Gazzaniga, M. S. (1988). Organization of the human brain. *Science, 245*, 947–952. (p. 84)

Gazzaniga, M. S. (2011, April). Neuroscience in the courtroom. *Scientific American*, pp. 54–59. (p. 467)

Gazzola, V., Spezio, M. L., Etzel, J. A., Catelli, F., Adolphs, R., & Keysers, C. (2012). Primary somatosensory cortex discriminates affective significance in social touch. *PNAS, 109*, E1657–E1666. (p. 261)

Ge, X., & Natsuaki, M. N. (2009). In search of explanations for early pubertal timing effects on developmental psychopathology. *Current Directions in Psychological Science, 18*, 327–441. (p. 204)

Geary, D. C. (1995). Sexual selection and sex differences in spatial cognition. *Learning and Individual Differences, 7*, 289–301. (p. 410)

Geary, D. C. (1996). Sexual selection and sex differences in mathematical abilities. *Behavioral and Brain Sciences, 19,* 229–247. (p. 410)

Geary, D. C. (2010). *Male, female: The evolution of human sex differences* (second edition). Washington, DC: American Psychological Association. (p. 165)

Geary, D. C., Salthouse, T. A., Chen, G-P., & Fan, L. (1996). Are East Asian versus American differences in arithmetical ability a recent phenomenon? *Developmental Psychology, 32,* 254–262. (p. 412)

Geen, R. G., & Quanty, M. B. (1977). The catharsis of aggression: An evaluation of a hypothesis. In L. Berkowitz (Ed.), *Advances in experimental social psychology* (Vol. 10). New York: Academic Press. (p. 477)

Geen, R. G., & Thomas, S. L. (1986). The immediate effects of media violence on behavior. *Journal of Social Issues, 42*(3), 7–28. (p. 312)

Geers, A. E., & Nicholas, J. G. (2013). Enduring advantages of early cochlear implantation for spoken language development. *Journal of Speech, Language, and Hearing Research, 56,* 643–653. (p. 375)

Gehring, W. J., Wimke, J., & Nisenson, L. G. (2000). Action monitoring dysfunction in obsessive-compulsive disorder. *Psychological Science, 11*(1), 1–6. (p. 626)

Geier, A. B., Rozin, P., & Doros, G. (2006). Unit bias: A new heuristic that helps explain the effects of portion size on food intake. *Psychological Science, 17,* 521–525. (p. 429)

Gellis, L. A., Arigo, D., & Elliott, J. C. (2013). Cognitive refocusing treatment for insomnia: A randomized controlled trial in university students. *Behavior Therapy, 44,* 100–110. (p. 110)

Gelman, D. (1989, May 15). Voyages to the unknown. *Newsweek,* pp. 66–69. (p. 473)

Genesee, F., & Gándara, P. (1999). Bilingual education programs: A cross-national perspective. *Journal of Social Issues, 55,* 665–685, (p. 381)

Gentile, B., Twenge, J. M., & Campbell, W. K. (2010). Birth cohort differences in self-esteem, 1988–2008: A cross-temporal meta-analysis. *Review of General Psychology, 14,* 261–268. (p. 604)

Gentile, D. (2009). Pathological video-game use among youth ages 8 to 18: A national study. *Psychological Science, 20,* 594–602. (pp. 118, 549)

Gentile, D. A., & Bushman, B. J. (2012). Reassessing media violence effects using a risk and resilience approach to understanding aggression. *Psychology of Popular Media Culture, 1,* 138–151. (p. 313)

Gentile, D. A., Coyne, S., & Walsh, D. A. (2011). Media violence, physical aggression and relational aggression in school age children: A short-term longitudinal study. *Aggressive Behavior, 37,* 193–206. (p. 313)

Geraerts, E., Bernstein, D. M., Merckelbach, H., Linders, C., Raymaekers, L., & Loftus, E. F. (2008). Lasting false beliefs and their behavioral consequences. *Psychological Science, 19,* 749–753. (p. 344)

Geraerts, E., Schooler, J. W., Merckelbach, H., Jelicic, M., Hauer, B. J. A., & Ambadar, Z. (2007). The reality of recovered memories: Corroborating continuous and discontinuous memories of childhood sexual abuse. *Psychological Science, 18,* 564–568. (p. 348)

Germain, A. (2013). Sleep disturbances as the hallmark of PTSD: Where are we now? *Archives of Journal of Psychiatry, 170,* 372–382. (p. 623)

Gernsbacher, M. A., Dawson, M., & Goldsmith, H. H. (2005). Three reasons not to believe in an autism epidemic. *Current Directions in Psychological Science, 14,* 55–58. (p. 193)

Gerrard, M., & Luus, C. A. E. (1995). Judgments of vulnerability to pregnancy: The role of risk factors and individual differences. *Personality and Social Psychology Bulletin, 21,* 160–171. (p. 439)

Gershoff, E. T. (2002). Parental corporal punishment and associated child behaviors and experiences: A meta-analytic and theoretical review. *Psychological Bulletin, 128,* 539–579. (p. 296)

Gershoff, E. T., Grogan-Kaylor, A., Lansford, J. E., Chang, L., Zelli, A., Deater-Deckard, K., & Dodge, K. A. (2010). Parent discipline practices in an international sample: Associations with child behaviors and moderation by perceived normativeness. *Child Development, 81,* 487–502. (p. 296)

Gerstorf, D., Ram, N., Röcke, C., Lindenberger, U., & Smith, J. (2008). Decline in life satisfaction in old age: Longitudinal evidence for links to distance-to-death. *Psychology and Aging, 23,* 154–168. (p. 223)

Geschwind, N. (1979, September). Specializations of the human brain. *Scientific American, 241,* 180–199. (p. 376)

Geschwind, N., & Behan, P. O. (1984). Laterality, hormones, and immunity. In N. Geschwind & A. M. Galaburda (Eds.), *Cerebral dominance: The biological foundations.* Cambridge, MA: Harvard University Press. (p. 86)

Getahun, D., Jacobsen, S. J., Fassett, M. J., Chen, W., Demissie, K., & Rhoads, G. G. (2013). Recent trends in childhood attention-deficit/hyperactivity disorder. *Journal of the American Medical Association Pediatrics, 167,* 282–288. (p. 615)

Gettler, L. T., McDade, T. W., Agustin, S. S., Feranil, A. B., & Kuzawa, C. W. (2013). Do testosterone declines during the transition to marriage and fatherhood relate to men's sexual behavior? Evidence from the Philippines. *Hormones and Behavior, 64,* 755–763. (p. 434)

Ghaemi, N. (2011). *A first-rate madness: Uncovering the links between leadership and mental illness.* New York: Penguin. (p. 630)

Giampietro, M., & Cavallera, G. M. (2007). Morning and evening types and creative thinking. *Personality and Individual Differences, 42,* 453–463. (p. 101)

Giancola, P. R., & Corman, M. D. (2007). Alcohol and aggression: A test of the attention-allocation model. *Psychological Science, 18,* 649–655. (p. 546)

Giancola, P. R., Josephs, R. A., Parrott, D. J., & Duke, A. A. (2010). Alcohol myopia revisited: Clarifying aggression and other acts of disinhibition through a distorted lens. *Perspectives on Psychological Science, 5,* 265–278. (p. 120)

Gibbons, F. X. (1986). Social comparison and depression: Company's effect on misery. *Journal of Personality and Social Psychology, 51,* 140–148. (p. 484)

Gibbs, W. W. (1996, June). Mind readings. *Scientific American,* pp. 34–36. (p. 76)

Gibson, E. J., & Walk, R. D. (1960, April). The "visual cliff." *Scientific American,* pp. 64–71. (p. 249)

Gibson, J. L., & Claassen, C. (2010). Racial reconciliation in South Africa: Interracial contact. *Journal of Social Issues, 66,* 255–272. (p. 564)

Gick, B., & Derrick, D. (2009). Aero-tactile integration in speech perception. *Nature, 462,* 502–504. (p. 270)

Giesbrecht, T., Lynn, S. J., Lilienfeld, S. O., & Merckelbach, H. (2008). Cognitive processes in dissociation: An analysis of core theoretical assumptions. *Psychological Bulletin, 134,* 617–647. (p. 648)

Giesbrecht, T., Lynn, S. J., Lilienfeld, S. O., & Merckelbach, H. (2010). Cognitive processes, trauma, and dissociation—Misconceptions and misrepresentations: Reply to Bremmer (2010). *Psychological Bulletin, 136,* 7–11. (p. 648)

Gigantesco, A., Stazi, M. A., Alessandri, G., Medda, E., Tarolla, E., & Fagnani, C. (2011). Psychological well-being (PWB): A natural life outlook? An Italian twin study on heritability on PWB in young adults. *Psychological Medicine, 41,* 2637–2649. (p. 485)

Gigerenzer, G. (2004). Dread risk, September 11, and fatal traffic accidents. *Psychological Science, 15,* 286–287. (p. 362)

Gigerenzer, G. (2006). Out of the frying pan into the fire: Behavioral reactions to terrorist attacks. *Risk Analysis, 26,* 347–351. (p. 362)

Gigerenzer, G. (2010). *Rationality for mortals: How people cope with uncertainty.* New York: Oxford University Press. (p. 43)

Gigerenzer, G., Gaissmaier, W., Kurz-Milcke, E., Schwartz, L. M., & Woloshin, S. (2008). Helping doctors and patients make sense of health statistics. *Psychological Science in the Public Interest, 8,* 53–96. (p. 43)

Gigerenzer, G., Gaissmaier, W., Kurz-Milcke, E., Schwartz, L. M., & Woloshin, S. (2009, April/May). Knowing your chances. *Scientific American Mind,* pp. 44–51. (p. 43)

Gigerenzer, G., & Sturm, T. (2012). How (far) can rationality be naturalized? *Synthese, 187,* 243–268. (p. 359)

Gilbert, D. T. (2006). *Stumbling on happiness.* New York: Knopf. (pp. 222, 370, 461, 602)

Gilbert, D. T., Pelham, B. W., & Krull, D. S. (2003). The psychology of good ideas. *Psychological Inquiry, 14,* 258–260. (p. 21)

Gilbert, D. T., Pinel, E. C., Wilson, T. D., Blumberg, S. J., & Wheatley, T. P. (1998). Immune neglect: A source of durability bias in affective forecasting. *Journal of Personality and Social Psychology, 75,* 617–638. (p. 481)

Gilbertson, M. W., Paulus, L. A., Williston, S. K., Gurvits, T. V., Lasko, N. B., Pitman, R. K., & Orr, S. P. (2006). Neurocognitive function in monozygotic twins discordant for combat exposure: Relationship to posttraumatic stress disorder. *Journal of Abnormal Psychology, 115,* 484–495. (p. 624)

Giles, D. E., Dahl, R. E., & Coble, P. A. (1994). Childbearing, developmental, and familial aspects of sleep. In J. M. Oldham & M. B. Riba (Eds.), *Review of psychiatry* (Vol. 13). Washington, DC: American Psychiatric Press. (p. 111)

Gilestro, G. F., Tononi, G., & Cirelli, C. (2009). Widespread changes in synaptic markers as a function of sleep and wakefulness in *Drosophila. Science, 324,* 109–112. (p. 105)

Gill, A. J., Oberlander, J., & Austin, E. (2006). Rating e-mail personality at zero acquaintance. *Personality and Individual Differences, 40,* 497–507. (p. 593)

Gillen-O'Neel, C., Huynh, V. W., & Fuligni, A. J. (2013). To study or to sleep? The academic costs of extra studying at the expense of sleep. *Child Development, 84*, 133–142. (p. 114)

Gillison, M. L., Broutian, T., Pickard, R. K. L., Tong, Z-Y., Xiao, W., Kahle, L., Graubard, B. I., & Chaturvedi, A. K. (2012). Prevalence of oral HPV infection in the United States, 2009–2010. *JAMA, 307*, 693–703. (p. 437)

Gilovich, T. D. (1996). *The spotlight effect: Exaggerated impressions of the self as a social stimulus.* Unpublished manuscript, Cornell University. (p. 598)

Gilovich, T. D., Kruger, J., & Medvec, V. H. (2002). The spotlight effect revisited: Overestimating the manifest variability of our actions and appearance. *Journal of Experimental Social Psychology, 38*, 93–99. (p. 599)

Gilovich, T. D., & Medvec, V. H. (1995). The experience of regret: What, when, and why. *Psychological Review, 102*, 379–395. (p. 223)

Gilovich, T. D., & Savitsky, K. (1999). The spotlight effect and the illusion of transparency: Egocentric assessments of how we are seen by others. *Current Directions in Psychological Science, 8*, 165–168. (p. 599)

Giltay, E. J., Geleijnse, J. M., Zitman, F. G., Buijsse, B., & Kromhout, D. (2007). Lifestyle and dietary correlates of dispositional optimism in men: The Zutphen Elderly Study. *Journal of Psychosomatic Research, 63*, 483–490. (p. 504)

Giltay, E. J., Geleijnse, J. M., Zitman, F. G., Hoekstra, T., & Schouten, E. G. (2004). Dispositional optimism and all-cause and cardiovascular mortality in a prospective cohort of elderly Dutch men and women. *Archives of General Psychiatry, 61*, 1126–1135. (p. 504)

Gingerich, O. (1999, February 6). Is there a role for natural theology today? *The Real Issue* (www.origins.org/real/n9501/natural.html). (p. 173)

Gingerich, O. (2006). *God's universe.* Cambridge, MA: Belknap Press of Harvard University Press. (p. 1)

Giuliano, T. A., Barnes, L. C., Fiala, S. E., & Davis D. M. (1998). *An empirical investigation of male answer syndrome.* Paper presented at the Southwestern Psychological Association convention. (p. 163)

Gladue, B. A. (1990). Hormones and neuroendocrine factors in atypical human sexual behavior. In J. R. Feierman (Ed.), *Pedophilia: Biosocial dimensions.* New York: Springer-Verlag. (p. 444)

Gladue, B. A. (1994). The biopsychology of sexual orientation. *Current Directions in Psychological Science, 3*, 150–154. (p. 446)

Gladwell, M. (2000, May 9). The new-boy network: What do job interviews really tell us? *New Yorker*, pp. 68–86. (p. A-6)

Gladwell, M. (2005). *Blink: The power of thinking without thinking.* New York: Little, Brown. (p. 556)

Glasman, L. R., & Albarracin, D. (2006). Forming attitudes that predict future behavior: A meta-analysis of the attitude-behavior relation. *Psychological Bulletin, 132*, 778–822. (p. 520)

Glass, R. I. (2004). Perceived threats and real killers. *Science, 304*, 927. (p. 363)

Glass, R. M. (2001). Electroconvulsive therapy: Time to bring it out of the shadows. *Journal of the American Medical Association, 285*, 1346–1348. (p. 685)

Gleaves, D. H. (1996). The sociocognitive model of dissociative identity disorder: A reexamination of the evidence. *Psychological Bulletin, 120*, 42–59. (p. 648)

Glenn, A. L., Raine, A., Yaralian, P.S., & Yang, Y. (2010). Increased volume of the striatum in psychopathic individuals. *Biological Psychiatry, 67*, 52–58. (p. 651)

Glick, P., et al. (2004). Bad but bold: Ambivalent attitudes toward men predict gender inequality in 16 nations. *Journal of Personality and Social Psychology, 86*, 713–728. (p. 540)

GLSEN. (2012). The 2011 National School Climate Survey. New York: Gay, Lesbian & Straight Education Network (www.glsen.org). (p. 540)

Gluszek, A., & Dovidio, J. F. (2010). The way *they* speak: A social psychological perspective on the stigma of nonnative accents in communication. *Personality and Social Psychology Review, 14*, 214–237. (p. 542)

Glynn, L. M., & Sandman, C. A. (2011). Prenatal origins of neurological development: A critical period for fetus *and* mothers. *Current Directions in Psychological Science, 20*, 384–389. (p. 182)

Godden, D. R., & Baddeley, A. D. (1975). Context-dependent memory in two natural environments: On land and underwater. *British Journal of Psychology, 66*, 325–331. (p. 335)

Goff, D. C., & Simms, C. A. (1993). Has multiple personality disorder remained consistent over time? *Journal of Nervous and Mental Disease, 181*, 595–600. (p. 648)

Golan, O., Ashwin, E., Granader, Y., McClintock, S., Day, K., Leggett, V., & Baron-Cohen, S. (2010). Enhancing emotion recognition in children with autism spectrum conditions: An intervention using animated vehicles with real emotional faces. *Journal of Autism Development and Disorders, 40*, 269–279. (p. 194)

Gold, M., & Yanof, D. S. (1985). Mothers, daughters, and girlfriends. *Journal of Personality and Social Psychology, 49*, 654–659. (p. 211)

Goldberg, J. (2007, accessed May 31). *Quivering bundles that let us hear.* Howard Hughes Medical Institute (www.hhmi.org/senses/c120.html). (p. 257)

Golden, R. N., Gaynes, B. N., Ekstrom, R. D., Hamer, R. M., Jacobsen, F. M., Suppes, T., Wisner, K. L., & Nemeroff, C. B. (2005). The efficacy of light therapy in the treatment of mood disorders: A review and meta-analysis of the evidence. *American Journal of Psychiatry, 162*, 656–662. (p. 678)

Golder, S. A., & Macy, M. W. (2011). Diurnal and seasonal mood vary with work, sleep, and day-length across diverse cultures. *Science, 333*, 1878–1881. (pp. 29, 480)

Goldfine, A. M., Bardin, J. C., Noirhomme, Q., Fine, J. J., Schiff, N. D., & Victor, J. D. (2013). Reanalysis of "Bedside detection of awareness in the vegetative state: A cohort study." *The Lancet, 381*, 289–291. (p. 93)

Goldfried, M. R. (2001). Integrating gay, lesbian, and bisexual issues into mainstream psychology. *American Psychologist, 56*, 977–988. (p. 638)

Goldfried, M. R., & Padawer, W. (1982). Current status and future directions in psychotherapy. In M. R. Goldfried (Ed.), *Converging themes in psychotherapy: Trends in psychodynamic, humanistic, and behavioral practice.* New York: Springer. (p. 678)

Goldfried, M. R., Raue, P. J., & Castonguay, L. G. (1998). The therapeutic focus in significant sessions of master therapists: A comparison of cognitive-behavioral and psychodynamic-interpersonal interventions. *Journal of Consulting and Clinical Psychology, 66*, 803–810. (p. 679)

Goldin-Meadow, S., & Beilock, S. L. (2010). Action's influence on thought: The case of gesture. *Perspectives on Psychological Science, 5*, 664–674. (p. 475)

Goldinger, S. D., & Papesh, M. H. (2012). Pupil dilation reflects the creation and retrieval of memories. *Current Directions in Psychological Science, 21*, 90–95. (p. 240)

Goldman, A. L., Pezawas, L., Mattay, V. S., Fischl, B., Verchinski, B. A., Chen, Q., Weinberger, D. R., & Meyer-Lindenberg, A. (2009). Widespread reductions of cortical thickness in schizophrenia and spectrum disorders and evidence of heritability. *Archives of General Psychiatry, 66*, 467–477. (p. 642)

Goldstein, A. P., Glick, B., & Gibbs, J. C. (1998). *Aggression replacement training: A comprehensive intervention for aggressive youth* (rev. ed.). Champaign, IL: Research Press. (p. 547)

Goldstein, I. (2000, August). Male sexual circuitry. *Scientific American*, pp. 70–75. (p. 63)

Goldstein, I., Lue, T. F., Padma-Nathan, H., Rosen, R. C., Steers, W. D., & Wicker, P. A. (1998). Oral sildenafil in the treatment of erectile dysfunction. *New England Journal of Medicine, 338*, 1397–1404. (p. 37)

Goleman, D. (1980, February). 1,528 little geniuses and how they grew. *Psychology Today*, pp. 28–53. (p. 454)

Goleman, D. (2006). *Social intelligence.* New York: Bantam Books. (p. 390)

Golkar, A., Selbing, I., Flygare, O., Öhman, A., & Olsson, A. (2013). Other people as means to a safe end: Vicarious extinction blocks the return of learned fear. *Psychological Science, 24*, 2182–2190. (p. 306)

Gollwitzer, P. M., & Oettingen, G. (2012). Goal pursuit. In P. M. Gollwitzer & G. Oettingen (Eds.), *The Oxford handbook of human motivation*, pp. 208–231. New York: Oxford University Press. (p. 299)

Gonçalves, R., Pedrozo, A. L., Coutinho, E. S. F., Figueira, I., & Ventura, P. (2012). Efficacy of virtual reality exposure therapy in the treatment of PTSD: A systematic review. *PLoS ONE, 7*(12), dx.doi.org/10.1371/journal.pone.0048469. (p. 665)

Gonsalkorale, K., & Williams, K. D. (2006). The KKK would not let me play: Ostracism even by a despised outgroup hurts. *European Journal of Social Psychology, 36*, 1–11. (p. 450)

Gonsalves, B., Reber, P. J., Gitelman, D. R., Parrish, T. B., Mesulam, M.-M., & Paller, K. A. (2004). Neural evidence that vivid imagining can lead to false remembering. *Psychological Science, 15*, 655–659. (p. 345)

Goodall, J. (1986). *The chimpanzees of Gombe: Patterns of behavior.* Cambridge, MA: Harvard University Press. (p. 542)

Goodall, J. (1998). Learning from the chimpanzees: A message humans can understand. *Science, 282*, 2184–2185. (p. 29)

Goode, E. (1999, April 13). If things taste bad, 'phantoms' may be at work. *New York Times* (www.nytimes.com). (p. 262)

Goodhart, D. E. (1986). The effects of positive and negative thinking on performance in an achievement situation. *Journal of Personality and Social Psychology, 51*, 117–124. (p. 600)

Goodman, G. S. (2006). Children's eyewitness memory: A modern history and contemporary commentary. *Journal of Social Issues, 62*, 811–832. (p. 349)

Goodman, G. S., Ghetti, S., Quas, J. A., Edelstein, R. S., Alexander, K. W., Redlich, A. D., Cordon, I. M., & Jones, D. P. H. (2003). A prospective study of memory for child sexual abuse: New findings relevant to the repressed-memory controversy. *Psychological Science, 14*, 113–118. (p. 349)

Goodwin, P. Y., Mosher, W. D., & Chandra, A. (2010). Marriage and cohabitation in the United States: A statistical portrait based on Cycle 6 (2002) of the National Survey of Family Growth. National Center for Health Statistics. *Vital Health Statistics, 23*(28). (p. 221)

Gopnik, A. (2012). Scientific thinking in young children: Theoretical advances, empirical research, and policy implications. *Science, 337*, 1623–1627. (p. 188)

Gopnik, A., & Meltzoff, A. N. (1986). Relations between semantic and cognitive development in the one-word stage: The specificity hypothesis. *Child Development, 57*, 1040–1053. (p. 381)

Goranson, R. E. (1978). *The hindsight effect in problem solving.* Unpublished manuscript, cited by G. Wood (1984), Research methodology: A decision-making perspective. In A. M. Rogers & C. J. Scheirer (Eds.), *The G. Stanley Hall Lecture Series* (Vol. 4). Washington, DC. (p. 21)

Gorchoff, S. M., John, O. P., & Helson, R. (2008). Contextualizing change in marital satisfaction during middle age. *Psychological Science, 19*, 1194–1200. (p. 222)

Gordon, A. M., & Chen, S. (2010). When you accept me for me: The relational benefits of intrinsic affirmations from one's relationship partner. *Personality and Social Psychology Bulletin, 36*, 1439–1453. (p. 585)

Gordon, A. M., & Chen, S. (2014). The role of sleep in interpersonal conflict: Do sleepless nights mean worse fights? *Social Psychological and Personality Science, 5*, 168–175. (p. 107)

Gordon, I., Vander Wyk, B. C., Bennett, R. H., Cordeaux, C., Lucas, M. V., Eilbott, J. A., . . . Pelphrey, K. A. (2013). Oxytocin enhances brain function in children with autism. *PNAS, 110*, 20953–20958. (p. 194)

Gordon, P. (2004). Numerical cognition without words: Evidence from Amazonia. *Science, 306*, 496–499. (p. 380)

Gore, J., & Sadler-Smith, E. (2011). Unpacking intuition: A process and outcome framework. *Review of General Psychology, 15*, 304–316. (p. 364)

Gore-Felton, C., Koopman, C., Thoresen, C., Arnow, B., Bridges, E., & Spiegel, D. (2000). Psychologists' beliefs and clinical characteristics: Judging the veracity of childhood sexual abuse memories. *Professional Psychology: Research and Practice, 31*, 372–377. (p. 349)

Gorlick, A. (2010, January 13). Stanford scientists link brain development to chances of recovering vision after blindness. *Stanford Report* (news.stanford.edu). (p. 254)

Gorman, J. (2014, January 6). The brain, in exquisite detail. *New York Times* (www.nytimes.com). (p. 68)

Gorrese, A., & Ruggieri, R. (2012). Peer attachment: A meta-analytic review of gender and age differences and associations with parent attachment. *Journal of Youth and Adolescence, 41*, 650–672. (p. 199)

Gosling, S. D. (2008). *Snoop: what your stuff says about you.* New York: Basic Books. (p. 593)

Gosling, S. D., Gladdis, S., & Vazire, S. (2007). *Personality impressions based on Facebook profiles.* Paper presented to the Society for Personality and Social Psychology meeting. (p. 593)

Gosling, S. D., Ko, S. J., Mannarelli, T., & Morris, M. E. (2002). A room with a cue: Personality judgments based on offices and bedrooms. *Journal of Personality and Social Psychology, 82*, 379–398. (p. 593)

Gosling, S. D., Kwan, V. S. Y., & John, O. P. (2003). A dog's got personality: A cross-species comparative approach to personality judgments in dogs and humans. *Journal of Personality and Social Psychology, 85*, 1161–1169. (p. 588)

Gotlib, I. H., & Hammen, C. L. (1992). *Psychological aspects of depression: Toward a cognitive-interpersonal integration.* New York: Wiley. (p. 636)

Gottesman, I. I. (2001). Psychopathology through a life span—genetic prism. *American Psychologist, 56*, 867–881. (p. 644)

Gottfredson, L. S. (2002a). Where and why g matters: Not a mystery. *Human Performance, 15*, 25–46. (p. 389)

Gottfredson, L. S. (2002b). g: Highly general and highly practical. In R. J. Sternberg & E. L. Grigorenko (Eds.), *The general factor of intelligence: How general is it?* Mahwah, NJ: Erlbaum. (p. 389)

Gottfredson, L. S. (2003a). Dissecting practical intelligence theory: Its claims and evidence. *Intelligence, 31*, 343–397. (p. 389)

Gottfredson, L. S. (2003b). On Sternberg's "Reply to Gottfredson." *Intelligence, 31*, 415–424. (p. 389)

Gottfried, J. A., O'Doherty, J., & Dolan, R. J. (2003). Encoding predictive reward value in human amygdala and orbitofrontal cortex. *Science, 301*, 1104–1108. (p. 283)

Gottman, J. (2007). *Why marriages succeed or fail—2007 publication.* London: Bloomsbury. (p. 558)

Gottman, J., with Silver, N. (1994). *Why marriages succeed or fail.* New York: Simon & Schuster. (p. 222)

Gougoux, F., Zatorre, R., Lassonde, M., Voss, P., & Lepore, F. (2005). A functional neuroimaging study of sound localization: Visual cortex activity predicts performance in early-blind individuals. *PloS Biology, 3*(2), e27. (p. 375)

Gould, E. (2007). How widespread is adult neurogenesis in mammals? *Nature Neuroscience, 8*, 481–488. (p. 82)

Gould, S. J. (1981). *The mismeasure of man.* New York: Norton. (p. 394)

Gow, A. J., Bastin, M. E., Maniega, S. M., Hernández, M. C. V., Morris, Z., Murray, C., . . . Wardlaw, J. M. (2012). Neuroprotective lifestyles and the aging brain: Activity, atrophy, and white matter integrity. *Neurology, 79*, 1802–1808. (p. 216)

Goyal, M., Singh, S., Sibinga, E. S., et al. (2014). Meditation programs for psychological stress and well-being: A systematic review and meta-analysis. *JAMA Internal Medicine, 174*, 357–368. (p. 510)

Grabe, S., Ward, L. M., & Hyde, J. S. (2008). The role of the media in body image concerns among women: A meta-analysis of experimental and correlational studies. *Psychological Bulletin, 134*, 460–476. (p. 652)

Grace, A. A. (2010). Ventral hippocampus, interneurons, and schizophrenia: A new understanding of the pathophysiology of schizophrenia and its implications for treatment and prevention. *Current Directions in Psychological Science, 19*, 232–237. (p. 642)

Grady, C. L., McIntosh, A. R., Horwitz, B., Maisog, J. M., Ungeleider, L. G., Mentis, M. J., . . . Haxby, J. V. (1995). Age-related reductions in human recognition memory due to impaired encoding. *Science, 269*, 218–221. (p. 339)

Graham, A. M., Fisher, P. A., & Pfeifer, J. H. (2013). What sleeping babies hear: a functional MRI study of interparental conflict and infants' emotion processing. *Psychological Science, 24*, 782–789. (p. 200)

Graham, C. (2011). Does more money make you happier? Why so much debate? *Applied Research in Quality Life, 6*, 219–239. (p. 484)

Graham, J., Nosek, B. A., & Haidt, J. (2012, December 12). The moral stereotypes of liberals and conservatives: Exaggeration of differences across the political spectrum. *PLoS ONE 7*(12), e50092. (p. 538)

Grande, G., Romppel, M., & Barth, J. (2012). Association between type D personality and prognosis in patients with cardiovascular diseases: A systematic review and meta-analysis. *Annals of Behavioral Medicine, 43*, 299–310. (p. 498)

Granic, I., Lobel, A., & Engels, R. C. M. E. (2014). The benefits of playing video games. *American Psychologist, 69*, 66–78. (p. 549)

Granqvist, P., Mikulincer, M., & Shaver, P. R. (2010). Religion as attachment: Normative processes and individual differences. *Personality and Social Psychology Review, 14*, 49–59. (p. 195)

Grant, A. M., Gino, F., & Hofmann, D. A. (2011). Reversing the extraverted leadership advantage: The role of employee proactivity. *Academy of Management Journal, 54*, 528–550. (p. 588)

Grant, N., Wardle, J., & Steptoe, A. (2009). The relationship between life satisfaction and health behavior: A cross-cultural analysis of young adults. *International Journal of Behavioral Medicine, 16*, 259–268. (p. 508)

Gray, P. (2010, July 7). ADHD and school: The problem of assessing normalcy in an abnormal environment. *Psychology Today Blog* (www.psychologytoday.com). (p. 615)

Gray, P. B., Yang, C-F. J., & Pope, Jr., H. G. (2006). Fathers have lower salivary testosterone levels than unmarried men and married non-fathers in Beijing, China. *Proceedings of the Royal Society, 273*, 333–339. (p. 434)

Graybiel, A. M., & Smith, K. S. (2014, June). Good habits, bad habits. *Scientific American*, pp. 39–43. (p. 280)

Gray-Little, B., & Burks, N. (1983). Power and satisfaction in marriage: A review and critique. *Psychological Bulletin, 93*, 513–538. (p. 557)

Green, B. (2002). Listening to leaders: Feedback on 360-degree feedback one year later. *Organizational Development Journal, 20*, 8–16. (p. A-7)

Green, C. S., Pouget, A., & Bavelier, D. (2010). Improved probabilistic inference, as a general learning mechanism with action video games. *Current Biology, 20*, 1573–1579. (p. 549)

Green, J. D., Sedikides, C., & Gregg, A. P. (2008). Forgotten but not gone: The recall and recognition of self-threatening memories. *Journal of Experimental Social Psychology, 44*, 547–561. (p. 580)

Green, J. T., & Woodruff-Pak, D. S. (2000). Eyeblink classical conditioning: Hippocampal formation is for neutral stimulus associations as cerebellum is for association-response. *Psychological Bulletin, 126*, 138–158. (p. 330)

Green, M. F., & Horan, W. P. (2010). Social cognition in schizophrenia. *Current Directions in Psychological Science, 19*, 243–248. (p. 641)

Greenberg, J. (2008). Understanding the vital human quest for self-esteem. *Perspectives on Psychological Science, 3*, 48–55. (p. 599)

Greenberg, J., Solomon, S., & Pyszczynski, T. (1997). Terror management theory of self-esteem and cultural worldviews: Empirical assessments and conceptual refinements. *Advances in Social Psychology, 29*, 61–142. (p. 581)

Greene, J. (2010). Remarks to An Edge conference: The new science of morality. www.edge.org. (p. 207)

Greene, J., Sommerville, R. B., Nystrom, L. E., Darley, J. M., & Cohen, J. D. (2001). An fMRI investigation of emotional engagement in moral judgment. *Science, 293*, 2105. (p. 207)

Greenwald, A. G. (1992). *Subliminal semantic activation and subliminal snake oil.* Paper presented to the American Psychological Association Convention, Washington, DC. (p. 233)

Greenwald, A. G., Oakes, M. A., & Hoffman, H. (2003). Targets of discrimination: Effects of race on responses to weapons holders. *Journal of Experimental Social Psychology, 39*, 399. (p. 539)

Greenwald, A. G., & Pettigrew, T. F. (2014, March). With malice toward none and charity for some: Ingroup favoritism enables discrimination. *American Psychologist, 69*, 645–655. (p. 542)

Greenwald, A. G., Spangenberg, E. R., Pratkanis, A. R., & Eskenazi, J. (1991). Double-blind tests of subliminal self-help audiotapes. *Psychological Science, 2*, 119–122. (p. 233)

Greenwald, G. (2012, March 19). Discussing the motives of the Afghan shooter. *Salon* (www.salon.com). (p. 563)

Greer, S. G., Goldstein, A. N., & Walker, M. P. (2013). The impact of sleep deprivation on food desire in the human brain. *Nature Communications 4*, 2259, DOI: 10.1038/ncomms3259. (p. 108)

Gregory, A. M., Rijksdijk, F. V., Lau, J. Y., Dahl, R. E., & Eley, T. C. (2009). The direction of longitudinal associations between sleep problems and depression symptoms: A study of twins aged 8 and 10 years. *Sleep, 32*, 189–199. (p. 107)

Gregory, R. L. (1978). *Eye and brain: The psychology of seeing* (3rd ed.). New York: McGraw-Hill. (pp. 153, 254)

Gregory, R. L., & Gombrich, E. H. (Eds.). (1973). *Illusion in nature and art.* New York: Charles Scribner's Sons. (p. 237)

Greif, E. B., & Ulman, K. J. (1982). The psychological impact of menarche on early adolescent females: A review of the literature. *Child Development, 53*, 1413–1430. (p. 167)

Greist, J. H., Jefferson, J. W., & Marks, I. M. (1986). *Anxiety and its treatment: Help is available.* Washington, DC: American Psychiatric Press. (p. 620)

Greitemeyer, T., & Osswald, S. (2010). Effects of prosocial video games on prosocial behavior. *Journal of Personality and Social Psychology, 98*, 211–221. (p. 549)

Greitemeyer, T., & Osswald, S. (2011). Playing prosocial video games increases the accessibility of prosocial thoughts. *The Journal of Social Psychology, 151*, 121–128. (p. 549)

Greyson, B. (2010). Implications of near-death experiences for a postmaterialist psychology. *Review of Religion and Spirituality, 2*, 37–45. (p. 124)

Grèzes, J., & Decety, J. (2001). Function anatomy of execution, mental simulation, observation, and verb generation of actions: A meta-analysis. *Human Brain Mapping, 12*, 1–19. (p. 382)

Griffiths, M. (2001). Sex on the Internet: Observations and implications for Internet sex addiction. *Journal of Sex Research, 38*, 333–342. (p. 118)

Griggs, R. (2014). Coverage of the Stanford Prison Experiment in introductory psychology textbooks. *Teaching of Psychology, 41*, 195–203. (p. 522)

Grilo, C. M., & Pogue-Geile, M. F. (1991). The nature of environmental influences on weight and obesity: A behavior genetic analysis. *Psychological Bulletin, 110*, 520–537. (p. 431)

Grimm, S., & Scheidegger, M. (2013, May/June). A trip out of depression. *Scientific American Mind*, pp. 67–71. (p. 684)

Grinker, R. R. (2007). *Unstrange minds: Remapping the world of autism.* New York: Basic Books. (p. 193)

Griskevicius, V., Tybur, J. M., Gangestad, S. W., Perea, E. F., Shapiro, J. R., & Kenrick, D. T. (2009). Aggress to impress: Hostility as an evolved context-dependent strategy. *Journal of Personality and Social Psychology, 96*, 980–994. (p. 149)

Grobstein, C. (1979, June). External human fertilization. *Scientific American*, pp. 57–67. (p. 181)

Grogan-Kaylor, A. (2004). The effect of corporal punishment on antisocial behavior in children. *Social Work Research, 28*, 153–162. (p. 296)

Groothuis, T. G. G., & Carere, C. (2005). Avian personalities: Characterization and epigenesis. *Neuroscience and Biobehavioral Reviews, 29*, 137–150. (p. 589)

Gross, A. E., & Crofton, C. (1977). What is good is beautiful. *Sociometry, 40*, 85–90. (p. 555)

Grossberg, S. (1995). The attentive brain. *American Scientist, 83*, 438–449. (p. 237)

Grossmann, I., Karasawa, M., Izumi, S., Na, J., Varnum, M. E. W., Kitayama, S., & Nisbett, R. E. (2012). Aging and wisdom: Culture matters. *Psychological Science, 23*, 1059–1066. (p. 401)

Grossmann, I., Na, J., Varnum, M. E. W., Park, D. C., Kitayama, S., & Nisbett, R. E. (2010). Reasoning about social conflicts improves into old age. *PNAS, 107*, 7246–7250. (p. 401)

Groves, C. L., Prot, S., & Anderson, C. A. (in press). Violent media effects: Theory and evidence. In H. Friedman (Ed.) *Encyclopedia of Mental Health 2nd Edition.* San Diego, CA: Elsevier. (p. 312)

Gruber, J. (2011). Can feeling too good be bad? Positive emotion persistence (PEP) in bipolar disorder. *Current Directions in Psychological Science, 20*, 217–221. (p. 630)

Gruber, J., Gilbert, K. E., Youngstrom, E., Kogos Youngstrom, J., Feeny, N. C., Findling, R. L. (2013). Reward dysregulation and mood symptoms in an adolescent outpatient sample. *Journal of Abnormal Child Psychology, 41*, 1053–1065. (p. 630)

Gruder, C. L. (1977). Choice of comparison persons in evaluating oneself. In J. M. Suls & R. L. Miller (Eds.), *Social comparison processes.* New York: Hemisphere. (p. 484)

Guéguen, N. (2011). Effects of solicitor sex and attractiveness on receptivity to sexual offers: A field study. *Archives of Sexual Behavior, 40*, 915–919. (p. 150)

Guéguen, N., & Jacob, C. (2013). Color and cyber-attractiveness: Red enhances men's attraction to women's Internet personal ads. *Color Research and Application, 38*, 309–312. (p. 302)

Guéguen, N., & Jacob, C. (2014). Clothing color and tipping: Gentlemen patrons give more tips to waitresses with red clothes. *Journal of Hospitality and Tourism Research, 38*, 275–280. (p. 302)

Guenther, C. L., & Alicke, M. D. (2010). Deconstructing the better-than-average effect. *Journal of Personality and Social Psychology, 99*, 755–770. (p. 602)

Guerin, B. (1986). Mere presence effects in humans: A review. *Journal of Personality and Social Psychology, 22*, 38–77. (p. 532)

Guerin, B. (2003). Language use as social strategy: A review and an analytic framework for the social sciences. *Review of General Psychology, 7*, 251–298. (p. 370)

Guiso, L., Monte, F., Sapienza, P., & Zingales, L. (2008). Culture, gender, and math. *Science, 320*, 1164–1165. (p. 411)

Gunderson, E. A., Gripshover, S. J., Romero, C., Dweck, C. S., Goldin-Meadow, S., & Levine, S. C. (2013). Parent praise to 1- to 3-year-olds predicts children's motivational frameworks 5 years later. *Child Development, 84*, 1526–1541. (p. 409)

Gunstad, J., Strain, G., Devlin, M. J., Wing, R., Cohen, R. A., Paul, R. H., Crosby, R. D., & Mitchell, J. E. (2011). Improved memory function 12 weeks after bariatric surgery. *Surgery for Obesity and Related Diseases, 7*, 465–472. (p. 430)

Gunter, R. W., & Bodner, G. E. (2008). How eye movements affect unpleasant memories: Support for a working-memory account. *Behaviour Research and Therapy, 46*, 913–931. (p. 677)

Gunter, T. D., Vaughn, M. G., & Philibert, R. A. (2010). Behavioral genetics in antisocial spectrum disorders and psychopathy: A review of the recent literature. *Behavioral Sciences and the Law, 28*, 148–173. (p. 649)

Guo, X., et al. (2010). Effect of antipsychotic medication alone vs combined with psychosocial intervention on outcomes of early-stage schizophrenia. *Archives of General Psychiatry, 67*, 895–904. (p. 682)

Gurven, M., von Rueden, C., Massenkoff, M., Kaplan, H., & Vie, M. L. (2013). How universal is the big five? Testing the five-factor model of personality variation among forager-farmers in the Bolivian Amazon. *Journal of Personality and Social Psychology, 104*, 354–370. (p. 593)

Gustavson, C. R., Garcia, J., Hankins, W. G., & Rusiniak, K. W. (1974). Coyote predation control by aversive conditioning. *Science, 184*, 581–583. (p. 302)

Gustavson, C. R., Kelly, D. J., & Sweeney, M. (1976). Prey-lithium aversions I: Coyotes and wolves. *Behavioral Biology, 17*, 61–72. (p. 302)

Guttmacher Institute. (1994). *Sex and America's teenagers.* New York: Alan Guttmacher Institute. (pp. 212, 436)

H., Sally. (1979, August). Videotape recording number T-3, Fortunoff Video Archive of Holocaust Testimonies. New Haven, CT: Yale University Library. (p. 580)

Haas, A. P., et al. (2011). Suicide and suicide risk in lesbian, gay, bisexual, and transgender populations: Review and recommendations. *Journal of Homosexuality, 58,* 10–51. (p. 638)

Haase, C. M., Tomasik, M. J. H., & Silbereisen, R. K. (2008). Premature behavioral autonomy: Correlates in late adolescence and young adulthood. *European Psychologist, 13,* 255–266. (p. 202)

Haber, R. N. (1970, May). How we remember what we see. *Scientific American,* pp. 104–112. (p. 318)

Haddock, G., & Zanna, M. P. (1994). Preferring "housewives" to "feminists." *Psychology of Women Quarterly, 18,* 25–52. (p. 540)

Hadjistavropoulos, T., Craig, K. D., Duck, S. Cano, A., Goubert, L., Jackson, P. L., . . . Fitzgerald, T. D. (2011). A biopsychosocial formulation of pain communication. *Psychological Bulletin, 137,* 910–939. (p. 263)

Haedt-Matt, A. A., & Keel, P. K. (2011). Revisiting the affect regulation model of binge eating: A meta-analysis of studies using ecological momentary assessment. *Psychological Bulletin, 137,* 660–681. (p. 651)

Hafenbrack, A. C., Kinias, Z., & Barsade, S. G. (2014). Debiasing the mind through meditation: Mindfulness and the sunk-cost bias. *Psychological Science, 25,* 369–376. (p. 511)

Hagerty, M. R. (2000). Social comparisons of income in one's community: Evidence from national surveys of income and happiness. *Journal of Personality and Social Psychology, 78,* 764–771. (p. 484)

Hagger, M. S., & Chatzisarantis, N. L. D. (2013). The sweet taste of success: The presence of glucose in the oral cavity moderates the depletion of self-control resources. *Personality and Social Psychology Bulletin, 39,* 28–42. (p. 504)

Hagger, M. S., Wood, C., Stiff, C., & Chatzisarantis, N. L. D. (2010). Ego depletion and the strength model of self-control: A meta-analysis. *Psychological Bulletin, 136,* 495–525. (p. 503)

Haidt, J. (2000). The positive emotion of elevation. *Prevention and Treatment, 3,* article 3 (journals.apa.org/prevention/volume3). (p. 207)

Haidt, J. (2002). The moral emotions. In R. J. Davidson, K. Scherer, & H. H. Goldsmith (Eds.), *Handbook of affective sciences.* New York: Oxford University Press. (p. 206)

Haidt, J. (2012). *The righteous mind: Why good people are divided by politics and religion.* New York: Pantheon. (p. 206)

Hajhosseini, B., Stewart, B., Tan, J. C., Busque, S., & Melcher, M. L. (2013). Evaluating deceased donor registries: Identifying predictive factors of donor designation. *American Surgeon, 79,* 235–241. (p. 363)

Hakuta, K., Bialystok, E., & Wiley, E. (2003). Critical evidence: A test of the critical-period hypothesis for second-language acquisition. *Psychological Science, 14,* 31–38. (p. 374)

Halberstadt, J., Sherman, S. J., & Sherman, J. W. (2011). Why Barack Obama is black. *Psychological Science, 22,* 29–33. (p. 543)

Halberstadt, J. B., Niedenthal, P. M., & Kushner, J. (1995). Resolution of lexical ambiguity by emotional state. *Psychological Science, 6,* 278–281. (p. 237)

Haldeman, D. C. (1994). The practice and ethics of sexual orientation conversion therapy. *Journal of Consulting and Clinical Psychology, 62,* 221–227. (p. 441)

Haldeman, D. C. (2002). Gay rights, patient rights: The implications of sexual orientation conversion therapy. *Professional Psychology: Research and Practice, 33,* 260–264. (p. 441)

Hall, C. S., Dornhoff, W., Blick, K. A., & Weesner, K. E. (1982). The dreams of college men and women in 1950 and 1980: A comparison of dream contents and sex differences. *Sleep, 5,* 188–194. (p. 112)

Hall, C. S., & Lindzey, G. (1978). *Theories of personality* (2nd ed.). New York: Wiley. (p. 580)

Hall, G. (1997). Context aversion, Pavlovian conditioning, and the psychological side effects of chemotherapy. *European Psychologist, 2,* 118–124. (p. 303)

Hall, G. S. (1904). *Adolescence: Its psychology and its relations to physiology, anthropology, sex, crime, religion and education* (Vol. I). New York: Appleton-Century-Crofts. (p. 204)

Hall, J. A. (1984). *Nonverbal sex differences: Communication accuracy and expressive style.* Baltimore: Johns Hopkins University Press. (p. 470)

Hall, J. A. (1987). On explaining gender differences: The case of nonverbal communication. In P. Shaver & C. Hendrick (Eds.), *Review of Personality and Social Psychology, 7,* 177–200. (p. 470)

Hall, J. A. Y., & Kimura, D. (1994). Dermatoglyphic assymetry and sexual orientation in men. *Behavioral Neuroscience, 108,* 1203–1206. (p. 445)

Hall, J. G. (2003). Twinning. *Lancet, 362,* 735–743. (p. 136)

Hall, S. S. (2004, May). The good egg. *Discover,* pp. 30–39. (p. 181)

Hallal, P. C., Andersen, L. B., Bull, F. C., Guthold, R., Haskell, W., & Ekelund, U. (2012). Global physical activity levels: Surveillance progress, pitfalls, and prospects. *The Lancet, 380,* 247–257. (p. 431)

Haller, R., Rummel, C., Henneberg, S., Pollmer, U., & Köster, E. P. (1999). The influence of early experience with vanillin on food preference later in life. *Chemical Senses, 24,* 465–467. (p. 266)

Halpern, D. F. (2000). *Sex-related ability differences: Changing perspectives, changing minds.* Mahwah, NJ: Erlbaum. (p. 439)

Halpern, D. F., Benbow, C. P., Geary, D. C., Gur, R. C., Hyde, J. S., & Gernsbacher, M. A. (2007). The science of sex differences in science and mathematics. *Psychological Science in the Public Interest, 8,* 1–51. (p. 410)

Halsey, A., III. (2010, January 26). U.S. bans truckers, bus drivers from texting while driving. *Washington Post* (www.washingtonpost.com). (p. 96)

Hambrick, D. Z., Altmann, E. M., Oswald, F. L., Meinz, E. J., Gobet, F., & Campitelli, G. (2014a). Accounting for expert performance: The devil is in the details. *Intelligence, 45,* 112–114. (p. 455)

Hambrick, D. Z., & Meinz, E. J. (2011). Limits on the predictive power of domain-specific experience and knowledge in skilled performance. *Current Directions in Psychological Science, 20,* 275–279. (pp. 365, 455)

Hambrick, D. Z., Oswald, F. L., Altmann, E. M., Meinz, E. J., Gobet, F., & Campitelli, G. (2014b). Deliberate practice: Is that all it takes to become an expert? *Intelligence, 45,* 34–45. (p. 455)

Hamilton, R. H. (2000, November). *Increased prevalence of absolute pitch in blind musicians* (Abstract 739.13). Society for Neuroscience meeting, New Orleans. (p. 375)

Hamlin, J. K., Wynn, K., Bloom, P., & Mahajan, N. (2011). How infants and toddlers reach to antisocial others. *Proceedings of the National Academy of Sciences, 108,* 19931–19936. (p. 156)

Hammack, P. L., (2005). The life course development of human sexual orientation: An integrative paradigm. *Human Development, 48,* 267–290. (p. 442)

Hammer, E. (2003). How lucky you are to be a psychology major. *Eye on Psi Chi,* 4–5. (p. B-5)

Hammersmith, S. K. (1982, August). *Sexual preference: An empirical study from the Alfred C. Kinsey Institute for Sex Research.* Paper presented at the meeting of the American Psychological Association, Washington, DC. (p. 442)

Hammond, D. C. (2008). Hypnosis as sole anesthesia for major surgeries: Historical and contemporary perspectives. *American Journal of Clinical Hypnosis, 51,* 101–121. (p. 265)

Hampshire, A., Highfield, R. R., Parkin, B. L., & Owen, A. M. (2012). Fractionating human intelligence. *Neuron, 76,* 1225–1237. (p. 386)

Hampson, R. (2000, April 10). In the end, people just need more room. *USA Today,* p. 19A. (pp. 431, 432)

Han, S. (2008, January). Bloom and grow: My view of psychological research in China. *Observer,* pp. 21–22. (p. 6)

Hancock, K. J., & Rhodes, G. (2008). Contact, configural coding and the other-race effect in face recognition. *British Journal of Psychology, 99,* 45–56. (p. 544)

Hankin, B. L., & Abramson, L. Y. (2001). Development of gender differences in depression: An elaborated cognitive vulnerability-transactional stress theory. *Psychological Bulletin, 127,* 773–796. (p. 635)

Hansen, C. H., & Hansen, R. D. (1988). Finding the face-in-the-crowd: An anger superiority effect. *Journal of Personality and Social Psychology, 54,* 917–924. (p. 468)

Harackiewicz, J. M., Canning, E. A., Tibbetts, Y., Giffen, C. J., Blair, S. S., Rouse, D. I., & Hyde, J. S. (2014). Closing the social class achievement gap for first-generation students in undergraduate biology. *Journal of Educational Psychology, 106,* 375–389. (p. 415)

Harbaugh, W. T., Mayr, U., & Burghart, D. R. (2007). Neural responses to taxation and voluntary giving reveal motives for charitable donations. *Science, 316,* 1622–1625. (p. 560)

Harber, K. D. (1998), Feedback to minorities: Evidence of a positive bias. *Journal of Personality and Social Psychology, 74,* 622–628. (p. 539)

Harden, K. P. (2012). True love waits? A sibling-comparison study of age at first sexual intercourse and romantic relationships in young adulthood. *Psychological Science, 23,* 1324–1336. (p. 439)

Harden, K. P. (2014). Genetic influences on adolescent sexual behavior: Why genes matter for environmentally oriented researchers. *Psychological Bulletin, 140*, 434–465. (p. 438)

Hardeveld, H. S., De Graaf, R., Nolen, W. A., & Beckman, A. T. F. (2010). Prevalence and predictors of recurrence of major depressive disorder in the adult population. *Acta Psychiatrica Scandinavia, 122*, 184–191. (p. 632)

Hardisty, D. J., Johnson, E. J., & Weber, E. U. (2010). A dirty word or a dirty world? Attribute framing, political affiliation, and query theory. *Psychological Science, 21*, 86–92. (p. 364)

Hardt, O., Einarsson, E. O., & Nader, K. (2010). A bridge over troubled water: Reconsolidation as a link between cognitive and neuroscientific memory research traditions. *Annual Review of Psychology, 61*, 141–167. (p. 343)

Hare, R. D. (1975). Psychophysiological studies of psychopathy. In D. C. Fowles (Ed.), *Clinical applications of psychophysiology*. New York: Columbia University Press. (p. 649)

Harenski, C. L., Harenski, K. A., Shane, M. W., & Kiehl, K. A. (2010). Aberrant neural processing of moral violations in criminal psychopaths. *Journal of Abnormal Psychology, 119*, 863–874. (p. 651)

Harkins, S. G., & Szymanski, K. (1989). Social loafing and group evaluation. *Journal of Personality and Social Psychology, 56*, 934–941. (p. 533)

Harlow, H. F., Harlow, M. K., & Suomi, S. J. (1971). From thought to therapy: Lessons from a primate laboratory. *American Scientist, 59*, 538–549. (p. 195)

Harmon-Jones, E., Abramson, L. Y., Sigelman, J., Bohlig, A., Hogan, M. E., & Harmon-Jones, C. (2002). Proneness to hypomania/mania symptoms or depression symptoms and asymmetrical frontal cortical responses to an anger-evoking event. *Journal of Personality and Social Psychology, 82*, 610–618. (p. 467)

Harper, C., & McLanahan, S. (2004). Father absence and youth incarceration. *Journal of Research on Adolescence, 14*, 369–397. (p. 548)

Harper's. (2009, November). Harper's index. *Harper's*, p. 13. (p. 554)

Harris, B. (1979). Whatever happened to Little Albert? *American Psychologist, 34*, 151–160. (p. 288)

Harris, J. R. (1998). *The nurture assumption*. New York: Free Press. (pp. 154, 197)

Harris, J. R. (2000). Beyond the nurture assumption: Testing hypotheses about the child's environment. In J. G. Borkowski & S. L. Ramey (Eds.), *Parenting and the child's world: Influences on academic, intellectual, and social-emotional development*. Washington, DC: APA Books. (p. 154)

Harris, J. R. (2006). *No two are alike: Human nature and human individuality*. New York: Norton. (p. 137)

Harris, J. R. (2007, August 8). Do pals matter more than parents? *The Times* (www.timesonline.co.uk). (p. 154)

Harris, R. J. (1994). The impact of sexually explicit media. In J. Brant & D. Zillmann (Eds.), *Media effects: Advances in theory and research*. Hillsdale, NJ: Erlbaum. (p. 548)

Harrison, T. L., Shipstead, Z., Hicks, K. L., Hambrick, D. Z., Redick, T. S., & Engle, R. W. (2013). Working memory training may increase working memory capacity but not fluid intelligence. *Psychological Science, 24*, 2409–2419. (p. 218)

Harriston, K. A. (1993, December 24). 1 shakes, 1 snoozes: Both win $45 million. *Washington Post* release (in *Tacoma News Tribune*, pp. A1, A2). (p. 598)

Harter, J. K., Schmidt, F. L., Asplund, J. W., Killham, E. A., & Agrawal, S. (2010). Causal impact of employee work perceptions on the bottom line of organizations. *Perspectives on Psychological Science, 5*, 378–389. (p. A-10)

Harter, J. K., Schmidt, F. L., & Hayes, T. L. (2002). Business-unit-level relationship between employee satisfaction, employee engagement, and business outcomes: A meta-analysis. *Journal of Applied Psychology, 87*, 268–279. (pp. A-9, A-10)

Hartmann, E. (1981, April). The strangest sleep disorder. *Psychology Today*, pp. 14, 16, 18. (p. 111)

Hartwig, M., & Bond, C. F., Jr. (2011). Why do lie-catchers fail? A lens model meta-analysis of human lie judgments. *Psychological Bulletin, 137*, 643–659. (p. 469)

Harvard Mental Health Letter. (2002, February). EMDR (Eye movement and reprocessing). *Harvard Mental Health Letter, 18*, 4–5. (p. 677)

Harvey, A. G., & Tang, N. K. Y. (2012). (Mis)perception of sleep in insomnia: A puzzle and a resolution. *Psychological Bulletin, 138*, 77–101. (p. 110)

Haselton, M. G., & Gildersleeve, K. (2011). Can men detect ovulation? *Current Directions in Psychological Science, 20*, 87–92. (p. 434)

Haslam, S. A., & Reicher, S. D. (2007). Beyond the banality of evil: Three dynamics of an interactionist social psychology of tyranny. *Personality and Social Psychology Bulletin, 33*, 615–622. (p. 523)

Haslam, S. A., & Reicher, S. D. (2012). Contesting the "nature" of conformity: What Milgram and Zimbardo's studies really show. *PLOS Biology, 10*(11), e1001426. (p. 523)

Hassan, B., & Rahman, Q. (2007). Selective sexual orientation-related differences in object location memory. *Behavioral Neuroscience, 121*, 625–633. (p. 446)

Hassin, R. R. (2013). Yes it can: On the functional abilities of the human unconscious. *Perspectives on Psychological Science, 8*, 195–207. (pp. 365, 549)

Hatfield, E. (1988). Passionate and companionate love. In R. J. Sternberg & M. L. Barnes (Eds.), *The psychology of love*. New Haven, CT: Yale University Press. (pp. 556, 557)

Hatfield, E., & Sprecher, S. (1986). *Mirror, mirror . . . The importance of looks in everyday life*. Albany: State University of New York Press. (p. 553)

Hathaway, S. R. (1960). *An MMPI Handbook* (Vol. 1, Foreword). Minneapolis: University of Minnesota Press (rev. ed. (p. 1972). (p. 589)

Hatzenbuehler, M. L. (2011). The social environment and suicide attempts in lesbian, gay, and bisexual youth. *Pediatrics, 127*, 896–903. (p. 638)

Hatzenbuehler, M. L. (2014). Structural stigma and the health of lesbian, gay, and bisexual populations. *Current Directions in Psychological Science, 23*, 127–132. (p. 540)

Hatzenbuehler, M. L., Nolen-Hoeksema, S., & Dovidio, J. (2009). How does stigma "get under the skin?" The mediating role of emotion regulation. *Psychological Science, 20*, 1282–1289. (p. 610)

Hatzigeorgiadis, A., Zourbanos, N., Galanis, E., & Theodorakis, Y. (2011). Self-talk and sports performance: A meta-analysis. *Perspectives on Psychological Science, 6*, 348–356. (p. 669)

Hauser, M. D., Chomsky, N., & Fitch, W. T. (2002). The faculty of language: What is it, who has it, and how did it evolve? *Science, 298*, 1569–1579. (p. 371)

Havas, D. A., Glenberg, A. M., Gutowski, K. A., Lucarelli, M. J., & Davidson, R. J. (2010). Cosmetic use of Botulinum Toxin-A affects processing of emotional language. *Psychological Science, 21*, 895–900. (p. 474)

Havas, D. A., Glenberg, A. M., & Rink, M. (2007). Emotion simulation during language comprehension. *Psychonomic Bulletin & Review, 14*, 436–441. (p. 474)

Haworth, C. M. A., et al. (2009). A twin study of the genetics of high cognitive ability selected from 11,000 twin pairs in sex studies from four countries. *Behavior Genetics, 39*, 359–370. (p. 406)

Haworth, C. M. A., et al. (2010). The heritability of general cognitive ability increases linearly from childhood to young adulthood. *Molecular Psychiatry, 15*, 1112–1120. (pp. 141, 407)

Haxby, J. V. (2001, July 7). Quoted by B. Bower, Faces of perception. *Science News*, pp. 10–12. See also J. V. Haxby, M. I. Gobbini, M. L. Furey, A. Ishai, J. L. Schouten & P. Pietrini, Distributed and overlapping representations of faces and objects in ventral temporal cortex. *Science, 293*, 2425–2430. (p. 245)

Hayasaki, E. (2014, July). Want to know when you'll die? Big data could tell you. *Newsweek*. www.newsweek.com. (p. 582)

Haynes, J-D., & Rees, G. (2005). Predicting the orientation of invisible stimuli from activity in human primary visual cortex. *Nature Neuroscience, 8*, 686–691. (p. 232)

Haynes, J-D., & Rees, G. (2006). Decoding mental states from brain activity in humans. *Nature Reviews Neuroscience, 7*, 523–534. (p. 232)

Hazan, C., & Shaver, P. R. (1994). Attachment as an organizational framework for research on close relationships. *Psychological Inquiry, 5*, 1–22., 201)

Hazelrigg, M. D., Cooper, H. M., & Borduin, C. M. (1987). Evaluating the effectiveness of family therapies: An integrative review and analysis. *Psychological Bulletin, 101*, 428–442. (p. 671)

He, Y., Jones, C. R., Fujiki, N., Xu, Y., Guo, B., Holder, J. L., Jr., . . . Fu, Y-H. (2009). The transcriptional repressor DEC2 regulates sleep length in mammals. *Science, 325*, 866–810. (p. 104)

Head Start. (2013, accessed December 20). About. Office of Head Start, An Office of the Administration for Families and Children (www.acf.hhs.gov/programs/ohs/about). (p. 409)

Headey, B., Muffels, R., & Wagner, G. G. (2010). Long-running German panel survey shows that personal and economic choices, not just genes, matter for happiness. *PNAS, 107*, 17922–17926. (p. 485)

Health Canada (2012). Major findings from the Canadian Alcohol and Drug Use Monitoring Survey (CADUMS) 2011. Health Canada (www.hc-sc.gc.ca/hc-ps/drugs-drogues/stat/index-eng.php). (p. 126)

Heavey, C. L., & Hurlburt, R. T. (2008). The phenomena of inner experience. *Consciousness and Cognition, 17*, 798–810. (pp. 30, 379)

Hedström, P., Liu, K-Y., & Nordvik, M. K. (2008). Interaction domains and suicides: A population-based panel study of suicides in the Stockholm metropolitan area, 1991–1999. *Social Forces, 2*, 713–740. (p. 638)

Hehman, E., Leitner, J. B., Deegan, M. P., & Gaertner, S. L. (2013). Facial structure is indicative of explicit support for prejudicial beliefs. *Psychological Science, 24*, 289–296. (p. 546)

Heider, F. (1958). *The psychology of interpersonal relations.* New York: Wiley. (p. 518)

Heil, K. M., & Schaaf, C. P. (2013). The genetics of autism spectrum disorders—A guide for clinicians. *Current Psychiatry Reports, 15*(1), 334. (p. 194)

Heiman, J. R. (1975, April). The physiology of erotica: Women's sexual arousal. *Psychology Today*, pp. 90–94. (p. 437)

Heine, S. J., & Buchtel, E. E. (2009). Personality: The universal and the culturally specific. *Annual Review of Psychology, 60*, 369–394. (pp. 159, 590)

Heine, S. J., & Hamamura, T. (2007). In search of East Asian self-enhancement. *Personality and Social Psychology Review, 11*, 4–27. (p. 602)

Heine, S. J., & Ruby, M. B. (2010). Cultural psychology. *Wiley Interdisciplinary Reviews: Cognitive Science, 1*, 254–266. (p. 518)

Hejmadi, A., Davidson, R. J., & Rozin, P. (2000). Exploring Hindu Indian emotion expressions: Evidence for accurate recognition by Americans and Indians. *Psychological Science, 11*, 183–187. (p. 468)

Helfand, D. (2011, January 7). An assault on rationality. *New York Times* (www.nytimes.com). (p. 274)

Helleberg, M., Afzal, S., Kronborg, G., Larsen, C. S., Pedersen, G., Pedersen, C., . . . Obel, N. (2013). Mortality attributable to smoking among HIV-1-infected individuals: A nationwide, population-based cohort study. *Clinical Infectious Diseases, 56*, 727–734. (p. 121)

Heller, A. S., Johnstone, T., Schackman, A. J., Light, S. N., Peterson, M. J., Kolden, G. G., Kalin, N. H., & Davidson, R. J. (2009). Reduced capacity to sustain positive emotion in major depression reflects diminished maintenance of fronto-striatal brain activation. *PNAS, 106*, 22445–22450. (p. 633)

Heller, W. (1990, May/June). Of one mind: Second thoughts about the brain's dual nature. *The Sciences*, pp. 38–44. (p. 85)

Helliwell, J., Layard, R., & Sachs, J. (Eds.) (2013). *World happiness report.* New York: The Earth Institute, Columbia University. (pp. 484, 485)

Helmreich, W. B. (1992). *Against all odds: Holocaust survivors and the successful lives they made in America.* New York: Simon & Schuster. (pp. 200, 580)

Helmreich, W. B. (1994). Personal correspondence. Department of Sociology, City University of New York. (p. 580)

Helms, J. E., Jernigan, M., & Mascher, J. (2005). The meaning of race in psychology and how to change it: A methodological perspective. *American Psychologist, 60*, 27–36. (p. 412)

Helmuth, L. (2001). Boosting brain activity from the outside in. *Science, 292*, 1284–1286. (p. 686)

Helsen, K., Goubert, L., Peters, M. L., & Vlaeyen, J. W. S. (2011). Observational learning and pain-related fear: An experimental study with colored cold pressor tasks. *The Journal of Pain, 12*, 1230–1239. (p. 625)

Helweg-Larsen, M. (1999). (The lack of) optimistic biases in response to the 1994 Northridge earthquake: The role of personal experience. *Basic and Applied Social Psychology, 21*, 119–129. (p. 600)

Hembree, R. (1988). Correlates, causes, effects, and treatment of test anxiety. *Review of Educational Research, 58*, 47–77. (p. 422)

Hemenover, S. H. (2003). The good, the bad, and the healthy: Impacts of emotional disclosure of trauma on resilient self-concept and psychological distress. *Personality and Social Psychology Bulletin, 29*, 1236–1244. (p. 507)

Henderlong, J., & Lepper, M. R. (2002). The effects of praise on children's intrinsic motivation: A review and synthesis. *Psychological Bulletin, 128*, 774–795. (p. 305)

Henderson, J. M. (2007). Regarding scenes. *Current Directions in Psychological Science, 16*, 219–222. (p. 234)

Henig, R. M. (2010, August 18). What is it about 20-somethings? *New York Times* (www.nytimes.com). (p. 212)

Henkel, L. A., Franklin, N., & Johnson, M. K. (2000, March). Cross-modal source monitoring confusions between perceived and imagined events. *Journal of Experimental Psychology: Learning, Memory, & Cognition, 26*, 321–335. (p. 346)

Henley, N. M. (1989). Molehill or mountain? What we know and don't know about sex bias in language. In M. Crawford & M. Gentry (Eds.), *Gender and thought: Psychological perspectives.* New York: Springer-Verlag. (p. 381)

Hennenlotter, A., Dresel, C., Castrop, F., Ceballos Baumann, A., Wohschlager, A., & Haslinger, B. (2008). The link between facial feedback and neural activity within central circuitries of emotion: New insights from Botulinum Toxin-induced denervation of frown muscles. *Cerebral Cortex, 19*, 537–542. (p. 474)

Hennessey, B. A., & Amabile, T. M. (2010). Creativity. *Annual Review of Psychology, 61*, 569–598. (pp. 365, A-13)

Henninger, P. (1992). Conditional handedness: Handedness changes in multiple personality disordered subject reflect shift in hemispheric dominance. *Consciousness and Cognition, 1*, 265–287. (p. 648)

Henrich, J., Heine, S. J., & Norenzayan, A. (2010). The weirdest people in the world? *Behavioral and Brain Sciences, 33*, 61–135. (p. 7)

Henry, J. D., MacLeod, M. S., Phillips, L. H., & Crawford, J. R. (2004). A meta-analytic review of prospective memory and aging. *Psychology and Aging, 19*, 27–39. (p. 217)

Hepler, J., & Albarracin, D. (2013). Complete unconscious control: using (in)action primes to demonstrate completely unconscious activation of inhibitory control mechanisms. *Cognition, 128*, 271–279. (p. 231)

Hepper, P. (2005). Unravelling our beginnings. *The Psychologist, 18*, 474–477. (p. 182)

Hepper, P. G., Shahidullah, S., & White, R. (1990). Origins of fetal handedness. *Nature, 347*, 431. (p. 86)

Hepper, P. G., Wells, D. L., & Lynch, C. (2004). Prenatal thumb sucking is related to postnatal handedness. *Neuropsychologia, 43*, 313–315. (p. 86)

Herbenick, D., Reece, M., Schick, V., & Sanders, S. A. (2014). Erect penile length and circumference dimensions of 1,661 sexually active men in the United States. *Journal of Sexual Medicine, 11*, 93–101. (p. 435)

Herbenick, D., Reece, M., Schick, V., Sanders, S. A., Dodge, B., & Fortenberry, J. D. (2010). Sexual behaviors, relationships, and perceived health among adult women in the United States: Results from a national probability sample. *Journal of Sexual Medicine, 7* (suppl 5), 277–290. (p. 214)

Herbenick, D., Reece, M., Schick, V., Sanders, S. A., Dodge, B., & Fortenberry, J. D. (2010a). Sexual behavior in the United States: Results from a national probability sample of men and women ages 14–94. *Journal of Sexual Medicine, 7*(suppl. 5): 255–265. (p. 440)

Herbert, J. D., Lilienfeld, S. O., Lohr, J. M., Montgomery, R. W., O'Donohue, W. T., Rosen, G. M., & Tolin, D. F. (2000). Science and pseudoscience in the development of eye movement desensitization and reprocessing: Implications for clinical psychology. *Clinical Psychology Review, 20*, 945–971. (p. 677)

Herek, G. (2014, accessed January 27). Facts about homosexuality and child molestation. www.psychology.ucdavis.edu/rainbow/html/facts_molestation.html. (p. 441)

Herman-Giddens, M. E. (2013). The enigmatic pursuit of puberty in girls. *Pediatrics, 132*, 1125–1126. (p. 204)

Herman-Giddens, M. E., Steffes, J., Harris, D., Slora, E., Hussey, M., Dowshen, S. A., et al. (2012). Secondary sexual characteristics in boys: Data from the pediatric research in office settings network. *Pediatrics, 130*(5), 1058–1068. (pp. 165, 166)

Herman-Giddens, M. E., Wang, L., & Koch, G. (2001). Secondary sexual characteristics in boys: Estimates from the National Health and Nutrition Examination Survey III, 1988–1994. *Archives of Pediatrics and Adolescent Medicine, 155*, 1022–1028. (p. 166)

Herman, C. P., & Polivy, J. (1980). Restrained eating. In A. J. Stunkard (Ed.), *Obesity.* Philadelphia: Saunders. (p. 432)

Herman, C. P., Roth, D. A., & Polivy, J. (2003). Effects of the presence of others on food intake: A normative interpretation. *Psychological Bulletin, 129*, 873–886. (p. 429)

Hernandez, A. E., & Li, P. (2007). Age of acquisition: Its neural and computational mechanisms. *Psychological Bulletin, 133*, 638–650. (p. 374)

Herrero, N., Gadea, M., Rodríguez-Alarcón, G., Espert, R., & Salvador, A. (2010). What happens when we get angry? Hormonal, cardiovascular and asymmetrical brain responses. *Hormones and Behavior, 57*, 276–283. (p. 477)

Herring, D. R., White, K. R., Jabeen, L. N., Hinojos, M., & Terrazas, G. (2013). On the automatic activation of attitudes: A quarter century of evaluative priming research. *Psychological Bulletin, 132*, 1062–1089. (pp. 231, 335)

Herringa, R. J., Phillips, M. L., Fournier, J. C., Kronhaus, D. M., & Germain, A. (2013). Childhood and adult trauma both correlate with dorsal anterior cingulate activation to threat in combat veterans. *Psychological Medicine, 43*, 1533–1542. (p. 626)

Herrmann, E., Call, J., Hernández-Lloreda, M. V., Hare, B., & Tomasello, M. (2007). Humans have evolved specialized skills of social cognition: The cultural intelligence hypothesis. *Science, 317*, 1360–1365. (p. 308)

Herrmann, E., Hernández-Lloreda, V., Call, J., Hare, B., & Tomasello, M. (2010). The structure of individual differences in the cognitive abilities of children and chimpanzees. *Psychological Science, 21,* 102–110. (p. 379)

Herrnstein, R. J., & Loveland, D. H. (1964). Complex visual concept in the pigeon. *Science, 146,* 549–551. (p. 291)

Hershenson, M. (1989). *The moon illusion.* Hillsdale, NJ: Erlbaum. (p. 253)

Hertel, G., Schroer, J., Batinic, B., & Naumann, S. (2008). Do shy people prefer to send e-mail: Personality effects on communication media preferences in threatening and nonthreatening situations. *Social Psychology, 39,* 231–243. (p. 591)

Hertenstein, M. (2009). *The tell: The little cues that reveal big truths about who we are.* New York: Basic Books. (p. 498)

Hertenstein, M. J., Hansel, C., Butts, S., Hile, S. (2009). Smile intensity in photographs predicts divorce later in life. *Motivation & Emotion, 33,* 99–105. (p. 179)

Hertenstein, M. J., Keltner, D., App, B. Bulleit, B., & Jaskolka, A. (2006). Touch communicates distinct emotions. *Emotion, 6,* 528–533. (p. 261)

Hertenstein, M. J., Verkamp, J. M., Kerestes, A. M., & Holmes, R. M. (2006). The communicative functions of touch in humans, nonhumans primates, and rats: A review and synthesis of the empirical research. *Genetic, Social, and General Psychology Monographs, 132,* 5–94. (p. 196)

Herz, R. S. (2001). Ah sweet skunk! Why we like or dislike what we smell. *Cerebrum, 3*(4), 31–47. (p. 268)

Herz, R. (2007). *The scent of desire: Discovering our enigmatic sense of smell.* New York: Morrow/HarperCollins. (p. 268)

Herz, R. (2012, January 28). You eat that? *Wall Street Journal* (www.online.wsj.com). (p. 428)

Herz, R. S., Beland, S. L., & Hellerstein, M. (2004). Changing odor hedonic perception through emotional associations in humans. *International Journal of Comparative Psychology, 17,* 315–339. (p. 268)

Hess, E. H. (1956, July). Space perception in the chick. *Scientific American,* pp. 71–80. (p. 254)

Hess, U., & Thibault, P. (2009). Darwin and emotion expression. *American Psychologist, 64,* 120–128. (p. 473)

Hetherington, M. M., Anderson, A. S., Norton, G. N. M., & Newson, L. (2006). Situational effects on meal intake: A comparison of eating alone and eating with others. *Physiology and Behavior, 88,* 498–505. (p. 429)

Hettema, J. M., Neale, M. C., & Kendler, K. S. (2001). A review and meta-analysis of the genetic epidemiology of anxiety disorders. *American Journal of Psychiatry, 158,* 1568–1578. (p. 626)

Hewitt, J. K. (2012). Editorial policy on candidate gene association and candidate gene-by-environment interaction studies of complex traits. *Behavior Genetics, 42,* 1–2. (p. 143)

Hickok, G. (2014). *The myth of mirror neurons: The real neuroscience of communication and cognition.* New York: Norton. (p. 307)

Hickok, G., Bellugi, U., & Klima, E. S. (2001, June). Sign language in the brain. *Scientific American,* pp. 58–65. (p. 85)

Highhouse, S. (2008). Stubborn reliance on intuition and subjectivity in employee selection. *Industrial and Organizational Psychology: Perspectives on Science and Practice, 1,* 333–342. (p. A-5)

Hilgard, E. R. (1986). *Divided consciousness: Multiple controls in human thought and action.* New York: Wiley. (p. 265)

Hilgard, E. R. (1992). Dissociation and theories of hypnosis. In E. Fromm & M. R. Nash (Eds.), *Contemporary hypnosis research.* New York: Guilford. (p. 265)

Hill, C. E., & Nakayama, E. Y. (2000). Client-centered therapy: Where has it been and where is it going? A comment on Hathaway. *Journal of Clinical Psychology, 56,* 961–875. (p. 661)

Hills, P. J., Werno, M. A., & Lewis, M. B. (2011). Sad people are more accurate at face recognition than happy people. *Consciousness and Cognition, 20,* 1502–1517. (p. 628)

Himmelbach, M., Boehme, R., & Karnath, H-O. (2012). 20 years later: A second look on DF's motor behaviour. *Neuropsychologia, 50,* 139–144. (p. 94)

Hines, M. (2004). *Brain gender.* New York: Oxford University Press. (p. 165)

Hingson, R. W., Heeren, T., & Winter, M. R. (2006). Age at drinking onset and alcohol dependence. *Archives of Pediatrics & Adolescent Medicine, 160,* 739–746. (p. 129)

Hintzman, D. L. (1978). *The psychology of learning and memory.* San Francisco: Freeman. (p. 324)

Hinz, L. D., & Williamson, D. A. (1987). Bulimia and depression: A review of the affective variant hypothesis. *Psychological Bulletin, 102,* 150–158. (p. 652)

Hirsh, J. B., Galinsky, A. D., & Zhong, C-B. (2011). Drunk, powerful, and in the dark: How general processes of disinhibition produce both prosocial and antisocial behavior. *Perspectives on Psychological Science, 6,* 415–427. (p. 119)

Hirst, W., et al. (2009). Long-term memory for the terrorist attack of September 11: flashbulb memories, event memories, and the factors that influence their retention. *Journal of Experimental Psychology: General, 138,* 161–176. (p. 332)

Hirt, E. R., Zillmann, D., Erickson, G. A., & Kennedy, C. (1992). Costs and benefits of allegiance: Changes in fans' self-ascribed competencies after team victory versus defeat. *Journal of Personality and Social Psychology, 63,* 724–738. (p. 636)

Hitsman, B., Papandonatos, G. D., McChargue, D. E., DeMott, A., Herrera, M. J., Spring, B., Borrelli, B., & Niaura, R. (2012). Past major depression and smoking cessation outcome: A systematic review and meta-analysis update. *Addiction, 108,* 294–306. (p. 634)

Hjelmborg, J. v. B., Fagnani, C., Silventoinen, K., McGue, M., Korkeila, M., Christensen, K., Rissanen, A., & Kaprio, J. (2008). Genetic influences on growth traits of BMI: A longitudinal study of adult twins. *Obesity, 16,* 847–852. (p. 431)

HMHL. (2002, January). Disaster and trauma. *Harvard Mental Health Letter,* pp. 1–5. (p. 489)

HMHL. (2002, August). Smoking and depression. *Harvard Mental Health Letter,* pp. 6–7. (p. 634)

HMHL. (2007, February). Electroconvulsive therapy. *Harvard Mental Health Letter,* Harvard Medical School, pp. 1–4. (p. 686)

Hobson, J. A. (1995, September). Quoted by C. H. Colt, The power of dreams. *Life,* pp. 36–49. (p. 113)

Hobson, J. A. (2003). *Dreaming: An introduction to the science of sleep.* New York: Oxford. (p. 114)

Hobson, J. A. (2004). *13 dreams Freud never had: The new mind science.* New York: Pi Press. (p. 114)

Hobson, J. A. (2009). REM sleep and dreaming: Towards a theory of protoconsciousness. *Nature Reviews, 10,* 803–814. (p. 114)

Hochberg, L. R., Bacher, D., Jarosiewicz, B., Masse, N. Y., Simeral, J. D., Vogel, J., . . . Donoghue, J. P. (2012). Reach and grasp by people with tetraplegia using a neutrally controlled robotic arm. *Nature, 485,* 375–375. (p. 77)

Hochberg, L. R., Serruya, M. D., Friehs, G. M., Mukand, J. A., Saleh, M., Caplan, A. H., . . . Donoghue, J. P. (2006). Neuronal ensemble control of prosthetic devices by a human with tetraplegia. *Nature, 442,* 164–171. (p. 77)

Hodgins, S., Larm, P., Ellenbogen, M., Vitaro, F., & Tremblay, R. E. (2013). Teachers' ratings of childhood behaviours predict adolescent and adult crime among 3016 males and females. *The Canadian Journal of Psychiatry/La Revue Canadienne De Psychiatrie, 58,* 143–150. (p. 179)

Hodgkinson, V. A., & Weitzman, M. S. (1992). *Giving and volunteering in the United States.* Washington, DC: Independent Sector. (p. 561)

Hoebel, B. G., & Teitelbaum, P. (1966). Effects of forcefeeding and starvation on food intake and body weight in a rat with ventromedial hypothalamic lesions. *Journal of Comparative and Physiological Psychology, 61,* 189–193. (p. 426)

Hoeft, F., Watson, C. L., Kesler, S. R., Bettinger, K. E., & Reiss, A. L. (2008). Gender differences in the mesocorticolimbic system during computer game-play. *Journal of Psychiatric Research, 42,* 253–258. (p. 118)

Hoffman, B. M., Babyak, M. A., Craighead, W. E., Sherwood, A., Doraiswamy, P. M., Coons, M. J., & Blumenthal, J. A. (2011). Exercise and pharmacotherapy in patients with major depression: One-year follow-up of the SMILE study. *Psychosomatic Medicine, 73,* 127–133. (p. 509)

Hoffman, D. D. (1998). *Visual intelligence: How we create what we see.* New York: Norton. (p. 246)

Hoffman, H. (2012). Considering the role of conditioning in sexual orientation. *Archives of Sexual Behavior, 41,* 63–71. (p. 285)

Hoffman, H. G. (2004, August). Virtual-reality therapy. *Scientific American,* pp. 58–65. (p. 264)

Hofmann, S. G., Sawyer, A. T., Witt, A. A., & Oh, D. (2010). The effect of mindfulness-based therapy on anxiety and depression: A meta-analytic review. *Journal of Consulting and Clinical Psychology, 78,* 169–183. (p. 510)

Hofmann, W., De Houwer, J., Perugini, M., Baeyens, F., & Crombez, G. (2010). Evaluative conditioning in humans: A meta-analysis. *Psychological Bulletin, 136,* 390–421. (p. 304)

Hofmann, W., Vohs, K. D. & Baumeister, R. F. (2012). What people desire, feel conflicted about, and try to resist in everyday life. *Psychological Science, 23,* 582–588. (p. 503)

Hofstadter, D. (2011, January 7). A cutoff for craziness. *New York Times* (www.nytimes. com). (p. 273)

Hogan, R. (1998). Reinventing personality. *Journal of Social and Clinical Psychology, 17*, 1–10. (p. 592)

Hoge, C. W., & Castro, C. A. (2006). Post-traumatic stress disorder in UK and U.S. forces deployed to Iraq. *Lancet, 368*, 837. (p. 623)

Hoge, C. W., Castro, C. A., Messer, S. C., McGurk, D., Cotting, D. I., & Koffman, R. L. (2004). Combat duty in Iraq and Afghanistan, mental health problems, and barriers to care. *New England Journal of Medicine, 351*, 13–22. (p. 623)

Hoge, C. W., Terhakopian, A., Castro, C. A., Messer, S. C., & Engel, C. C. (2007). Association of posttraumatic stress disorder with somatic symptoms, health care visits, and absenteeism among Iraq War veterans. *American Journal of Psychiatry, 164*, 150–153. (p. 623)

Hogg, M. A. (1996). Intragroup processes, group structure and social identity. In W. P. Robinson (Ed.), *Social groups and identities: Developing the legacy of Henri Tajfel.* Oxford: Butterworth Heinemann. (p. 540)

Hogg, M. A. (2006). Social identity theory. In P. J. Burke (Ed.), *Contemporary social psychological theories.* Stanford, CA: Stanford University Press. (p. 542)

Hohmann, G. W. (1966). Some effects of spinal cord lesions on experienced emotional feelings. *Psychophysiology, 3*, 143–156. (p. 461)

Hokanson, J. E., & Edelman, R. (1966). Effects of three social responses on vascular processes. *Journal of Personality and Social Psychology, 3*, 442–447. (p. 477)

Holahan, C. K., & Sears, R. R. (1995). *The gifted group in later maturity.* Stanford, CA: Stanford University Press. (p. 404)

Holden, C. (2007). Mental illness: The next frontier. *Science, 317*, 23. (p. 645)

Holden, C. (2008). Parsing the genetics of behavior. *Science, 322*, 892–895. (p. 142)

Holden, C. (2010). Experts map the terrain of mood disorders. *Science, 327*, p. 1068. (p. 631)

Holden, G. W., & Miller, P. C. (1999). Enduring and different: A meta-analysis of the similarity in parents' child rearing. *Psychological Bulletin, 125*, 223–254. (p. 202)

Holland, J. L. (1996). Exploring careers with a typology: What we have learned and some new directions. *American Psychologist, 51*, 397–406. (p. A-4)

Holliday, R. E., & Albon, A. J. (2004). Minimizing misinformation effects in young children with cognitive interview mnemonics. *Applied Cognitive Psychology, 18*, 263–281. (p. 349)

Hollis, K. L. (1997). Contemporary research on Pavlovian conditioning: A "new" functional analysis. *American Psychologist, 52*, 956–965. (p. 285)

Hollon, S. D., Thase, M. E., & Markowitz, J. C. (2002). Treatment and prevention of depression. *Psychological Science in the Public Interest, 3*, 39–77. (p. 684)

Holstege, G., Georgiadis, J. R., Paans, A. M. J., Meiners, L. C., van der Graaf, F. H. C. E., & Reinders, A. A. T. S. (2003a). Brain activation during male ejaculation. *Journal of Neuroscience, 23*, 9185–9193. (p. 435)

Holstege, G., Reinders, A. A. T., Paans, A. M. J., Meiners, L. C., Pruim, J., & Georgiadis, J. R. (2003b). *Brain activation during female sexual orgasm. Program No. 727.7.* Washington, DC: Society for Neuroscience. (p. 435)

Holt, L. (2002, August). Reported in "Sounds of speech," p. 26, and in personal correspondence, July 18, 2002. (p. 370)

Holt-Lunstad, J., Smith, T. B., & Layton, J. B. (2010). Social relationships and mortality risk: A meta-analytic review. *PLoS Medicine, 7* (www.plosmedicine.org: e1000316). (pp. 450, 505)

Holtgraves, T. (2011). Text messaging, personality, and the social context. *Journal of Research in Personality, 45*, 92–99. (p. 591)

Homer, B. D., Solomon, T. M., Moeller, R. W., Mascia, A., DeRaleau, L., & Halkitis, P. N. (2008). Methamphetamine abuse and impairment of social functioning: A review of the underlying neurophysiological causes and behavioral implications. *Psychological Bulletin, 134*, 301–310. (p. 123)

Hooley, J. M. (2010). Social factors in schizophrenia. *Current Directions in Psychological Science, 19*, 238–242. (p. 641)

Hooper, J., & Teresi, D. (1986). *The three-pound universe.* New York: Macmillan. (p. 73)

Hooper, R. (2013, October). Where hyenas are used to treat mental illness. *BBC News Magazine.* www.bbc.com/news/magazine. (p. 611)

Hopkins, E. D., & Cantalupo, C. (2008). Theoretical speculations on the evolutionary origins of hemispheric specialization. *Current Directions in Psychological Science, 17*, 233–237. (p. 86)

Hopkins, W. D. (2013). Neuroanatomical asymmetries and handedness in chimpanzees (*Pan troglodytes*): a case for continuity in the evolution of hemispheric specialization. *Annals of the New York Academy of Sciences, 1288*, 17–35. (p. 86)

Hopper, L. M., Lambeth, S. P., Schapiro, S. J., & Whiten, A. (2008). Observational learning in chimpanzees and children studied through 'ghost' conditions. *Proceedings of the Royal Society, 275*, 835–840. (p. 307)

Hopwood, C. J., Donnellan, M. B., Blonigen, D. M., Krueger, R. F., McGue, M., Iacono, W. G., & Burt, S. A. (2011). Genetic and environmental influences on personality trait stability and growth during the transition to adulthood: A three-wave longitudinal study. *Journal of Personality and Social Psychology, 100*, 545–556. (p. 179)

Hor, H., & Tafti, M. (2009). How much sleep do we need? *Science, 325*, 825–826. (p. 104)

Horgan, J. (1995, November). Get smart, take a test. *Scientific American,* pp. 12, 14. (p. 397)

Horn, J. L. (1982). The aging of human abilities. In J. Wolman (Ed.), *Handbook of developmental psychology.* Englewood Cliffs, NJ: Prentice-Hall. (p. 401)

Horne, J. (2011). The end of sleep: 'Sleep debt' versus biological adaptation of human sleep to waking needs. *Biological Psychology, 87*, 1–14. (p. 104)

Horner, V., Whiten, A., Flynn, E., & de Waal, F. B. M. (2006). Faithful replication of foraging techniques along cultural transmission chains by chimpanzees and children. *Proceedings of the National Academy of Sciences, 103*, 13878–13883. (p. 369)

Horowitz, S. S. (2012). The science and art of listening. *New York Times* (www. nytimes.com). (p. 256)

Horwood, L. J., & Fergusson, D. M. (1998). Breastfeeding and later cognitive and academic outcomes. *Pediatrics, 101*(1). (p. 33)

Hostetter, A. B. (2011). When do gestures communicate? A meta-analysis. *Psychological Bulletin, 137*, 297–315. (p. 378)

Hostinar, C. E., Sullivan, R., & Gunnar, M. R. (2014). Psychobiological mechanisms underlying the social buffering of the hypothalamic-pituitary-adrenocortical axis: A review of animal models and human studies across development. *Psychological Bulletin, 140*, 256–282. (p. 506)

Hou, W-H., Chiang, P-T, Hsu, T-Y, Chiu, S-Y, & Yen, Y-C. (2010). Treatment effects of massage therapy in depressed people: A meta-analysis. *Journal of Clinical Psychiatry, 71*, 894–901. (pp. 511, 686)

House, R. J., & Singh, J. V. (1987). Organizational behavior: Some new directions for I/O psychology. *Annual Review of Psychology, 38*, 669–718. (p. A-12)

Houser-Marko, L., & Sheldon, K. M. (2008). Eyes on the prize or nose to the grindstone? The effects of level of goal evaluation on mood and motivation. *Personality and Social Psychology Bulletin, 34*, 1556–1569. (p. A-11)

Houts, A. C., Berman, J. S., & Abramson, H. (1994). Effectiveness of psychological and pharmacological treatments for nocturnal enuresis. *Journal of Consulting and Clinical Psychology, 62*, 737–745. (p. 663)

Houts, R. M., Caspi, A., Pianta, R. C., Arseneault, L., & Moffitt, T. E. (2010). The challenging pupil in the classroom: The effect of the child on the teacher. *Psychological Science, 21*, 1802–1810. (p. 179)

Hovatta, I., Tennant, R. S., Helton, R., Marr, R. A., Singer, O., Redwine, J. M., . . . Barlow, C. (2005). Glyoxalase 1 and glutathione reductase 1 regulate anxiety in mice. *Nature, 438*, 662–666. (p. 626)

Howe, M. L. (1997). Children's memory for traumatic experiences. *Learning and Individual Differences, 9*, 153–174. (p. 349)

Howell, A. J. (2009). Flourishing: Achievement-related correlates of students' well-being. *Journal of Positive Psychology, 4*, 1–13. (p. 409)

Howell, E. C., Etchells, P. J., & Penton-Voak, I. S. (2012). The sexual overperception bias is associated with sociosexuality. *Personality and Individual Differences, 53*, 1012–1016. (pp. 148, 425)

Howell, R. T., & Howell, C. J. (2008). The relation of economic status to subjective well-being in developing countries: A meta-analysis. *Psychological Bulletin, 134*, 536–560. (p. 482)

Hoyer, G., & Lund, E. (1993). Suicide among women related to number of children in marriage. *Archives of General Psychiatry, 50*, 134–137. (p. 637)

Hsee, C. K., Yang, A. X., & Wang, L. (2010). Idleness aversion and the need for justifiable busyness. *Psychological Science, 21*, 926–930. (p. A-1)

Hsiang, S. M., Burke, M., & Miguel, E. (2013). Quantifying the influence of climate on human conflict. *Science, 341*, 1212. (p. 547)

Huang, C. (2010). Mean-level change in self-esteem from childhood through adulthood meta-analysis of longitudinal studies. *Review of General Psychology, 14*, 251–260. (p. 223)

Huang, J., Chaloupka, F. J., & Fong, G. T. (2013). Cigarette graphic warning labels and smoking prevalence in Canada: A critical examination and reformulation of the FDA regulatory impact analysis. *Tobacco Control*, published online. (p. 360)

Huang, X., Iun, J., Liu, A., & Gong, Y. (2010). Does participative leadership enhance work performance by inducing empowerment or trust? The differential effects on managerial and non-managerial subordinates. *Journal of Organizational Behavior, 31*, 122–143. (p. 489)

Huart, J., Corneille, O., & Becquart, E. (2005). Face-based categorization, context-based categorization, and distortions in the recollection of gender ambiguous faces. *Journal of Experimental Social Psychology, 41*, 598–608. (p. 356)

Hubbard, E. M., Arman, A. C., Ramachandran, V. S., & Boynton, G. M. (2005). Individual differences among grapheme-color synesthetes: Brain-behavior correlations. *Neuron, 45*, 975–985. (p. 271)

Hubel, D. H. (1979, September). The brain. *Scientific American*, pp. 45–53. (p. 234)

Hubel, D. H., & Wiesel, T. N. (1979, September). Brian mechanisms of vision. *Scientific American*, pp. 150–162. (p. 244)

Hublin, C., Kaprio, J., Partinen, M., Heikkila, K., & Koskenvuo, M. (1997). Prevalence and genetics of sleepwalking—A population-based twin study. *Neurology, 48*, 177–181. (p. 111)

Hublin, C., Kaprio, J., Partinen, M., & Koskenvuo, M. (1998). Sleeptalking in twins: Epidemiology and psychiatric comorbidity. *Behavior Genetics, 28*, 289–298. (p. 111)

Hucker, S. J., & Bain, J. (1990). Androgenic hormones and sexual assault. In W. Marshall, R. Law, & H. Barbaree (Eds.), *The handbook on sexual assault*. New York: Plenum. (p. 434)

Hudson, J. I., Hiripi, E., Pope, H. G., & Kessler, R. C. (2007). The prevalence and correlates of eating disorders in the National Comorbidity Survey Replication. *Biological Psychiatry, 61*, 348–358. (p. 652)

Huey, E. D., Krueger, F., & Grafman, J. (2006). Representations in the human prefrontal cortex. *Current Directions in Psychological Science, 15*, 167–171. (p. 80)

Huffcutt, A. I., Conway, J. M., Roth, P. L., & Stone, N. J. (2001). Identification and meta-analytic assessment of psychological constructs measured in employment interviews. *Journal of Applied Psychology, 86*, 897–913. (p. A-6)

Hugenberg, K., & Bodenhausen, G. V. (2003). Facing prejudice: Implicit prejudice and the perception of facial threat. *Psychological Science, 14*, 640–643. (p. 539)

Hugenberg, K., Young, S. G., Bernstein, M. J., & Sacco, D. F. (2010). The categorization-individuation model: An integrative account of the other-race recognition deficit. *Psychological Review, 117*, 1168–1187. (p. 544)

Hughes, J. R. (2010). Craving among long-abstinent smokers: An Internet survey. *Nicotine & Tobacco Research, 12*, 459–462. (p. 122)

Hughes, M. L., Geraci, L., & De Forrest, R. L. (2013). Aging 5 years in 5 minutes: The effect of taking a memory test on older adults' subjective age. *Psychological Science, 24*, 2481–2488. (p. 216)

Hugick, L. (1989, July). Women play the leading role in keeping modern families close. *Gallup Report*, No. 286, p. 27–34. (p. 164)

Huizink, A. C., & Mulder, E. J. (2006). Maternal smoking, drinking or cannabis use during pregnancy and neurobehavioral and cognitive functioning in human offspring. *Neuroscience and Biobehavioral Reviews, 30*, 24–41. (p. 125)

Hulbert, A. (2005, November 20). The prodigy puzzle. *New York Times Magazine* (www.nytimes.com). (p. 404)

Hull, H. R., Morrow, M. L., Dinger, M. K., Han, J. L., & Fields, D. A. (2007, November 20). Characterization of body weight and composition changes during the sophomore year of college. *BMC Women's Health, 7*, 21 (biomedcentral.com). (p. 108)

Hull, J. M. (1990). *Touching the rock: An experience of blindness*. New York: Vintage Books. (pp. 334, 554)

Hull, S. J., Hennessy, M., Bleakley, A., Fishbein, M., & Jordan, A. (2011). Identifying the causal pathways from religiosity to delayed adolescent sexual behavior. *Journal of Sex Research, 48*, 543–553. (p. 439)

Hülsheger, U. R., Anderson, N., & Salgado, J. F. (2009). Team-level predictors of innovation at work: A comprehensive meta-analysis spanning three decades of research. *Journal of Applied Psychology, 94*, 1128–1145. (p. 366)

Human Connectome Project (2013, accessed July 11). The human connectome project. www.humanconnectome.org. (p. 68)

Hummer, R. A., Rogers, R. G., Nam, C. B., & Ellison, C. G. (1999). Religious involvement and U.S. adult mortality. *Demography, 36*, 273–285. (p. 512)

Humphrey, S. E., Nahrgang, J. D., & Morgeson, F. P. (2007). Integrating motivational, social, and contextual work design features: A meta-analytic summary and theoretical extension of the work design literature. *Journal of Applied Psychology, 92*, 1332–1356. (p. 502)

Humphreys, L. G., & Davey, T. C. (1988). Continuity in intellectual growth from 12 months to 9 years. *Intelligence, 12*, 183–197. (p. 401)

Hunsberger, J. G., Newton, S. S., Bennett, A. H., Duman, C. H., Russell, D. S., Salton, S. R., & Duman, R. S. (2007). Antidepressant actions of the exercise-regulated gene VGF. *Nature Medicine, 13*, 1476–1482. (p. 509)

Hunsley, J., & Bailey, J. M. (2001). Whither the Roschach? An analysis of the evidence. *Psychological Assessment, 13*, 472–486. (p. 579)

Hunsley, J., & Di Giulio, G. (2002). Dodo bird, phoenix, or urban legend? The question of psychotherapy equivalence. *Scientific Review of Mental Health Practice, 1*, 11–22. (p. 676)

Hunt, C., Slade, T., & Andrews, G. (2004). Generalized anxiety disorder and major depressive disorder comorbidity in the National Survey of Mental Health and Well-Being. *Depression and Anxiety, 20*, 23–31. (p. 620)

Hunt, E., & Carlson, J. (2007). Considerations relating to the study of group differences in intelligence. *Perspectives on Psychological Science, 2*, 194–213. (p. 413)

Hunt, J. M. (1982). Toward equalizing the developmental opportunities of infants and preschool children. *Journal of Social Issues, 38*(4), 163–191. (p. 408)

Hunt, M. (1990). The compassionate beast: What science is discovering about the humane side of humankind. New York: William Morrow. (p. 13)

Hunt, M. (1993). *The story of psychology*. New York: Doubleday. (pp. 2, 6, 52, 208, 288, 404)

Hunt, M. (2007). *The story of psychology*. New York: Anchor. (p. 575)

Hunter, S., & Sundel, M. (Eds.). (1989). *Midlife myths: Issues, findings, and practice implications*. Newbury Park, CA: Sage. (p. 220)

Hurd, Y. L., Michaelides, M., Miller, M. L., & Jutras-Aswad, D. (2013). Trajectory of adolescent cannabis use on addiction vulnerability. *Neuropharmacology, 76*, 416–424. (p. 125)

Hurlburt, R. T., Heavey, C. L., & Kelsey, J. M. (2013). Toward a phenomenology of inner speaking. *Consciousness and Cognition: An International Journal, 22*, 1477–1494. (p. 379)

Hurst, M. (2008, April 22). Who gets any sleep these days? Sleep patterns of Canadians. *Canadian Social Trends*. Statistics Canada Catalogue No. 11–008. (p. 104)

Hutchinson, R. (2006). *Calum's road*. Edinburgh: Burlinn Limited. (p. 455)

Hvistendahl, M. (2011). China's population growing slowly, changing fast. *Science, 332*, 650–651. (p. 540)

Hyde, J. S. (2005). The gender similarities hypothesis. *American Psychologist, 60*, 581–592. (pp. 147, 162)

Hyde, J. S., & Mertz, J. E. (2009). Gender, culture, and mathematics performance. *Proceedings of the National Academy of Sciences, 106*, 8801–8807. (p. 410)

Hyde, J. S., Mezulis, A. H., & Abramson, L. Y. (2008). The ABCs of depression: Integrating affective, biological, and cognitive models to explain the emergence of the gender difference in depression. *Psychological Review, 115*, 291–313. (p. 631)

Hyman, R. (2010). Meta-analysis that conceals more than it reveals: Comment on Storm et al. (2010). *Psychological Bulletin, 136*, 486–490. (p. 273)

Hymowitz, K., Carroll, J. S., Wilcox, W. B., & Kaye, K. (2013). *Knot yet: The benefits and costs of delayed marriage in America*. Charlottesville, VA: National Marriage Project (University of Virginia). (p. 198)

Iacoboni, M. (2008). *Mirroring people: The new science of how we connect with others*. New York: Farrar, Straus & Giroux. (pp. 307, 309)

Iacoboni, M. (2009). Imitation, empathy, and mirror neurons. *Annual Review of psychology, 60*, 653–670. (pp. 307, 309)

IAP. (2006, June 21). IAP statement on the teaching of evolution. *The Interacademy Panel on International Issues* (www.interacademies.net/iap). (p. 172)

Ibbotson, P. (2012). A new kind of language. *Psychologist, 25*, 122–125. (p. 373)

Ickes, W., Snyder, M., & Garcia, S. (1997). Personality influences on the choice of situations. In R. Hogan, J. Johnson, & S. Briggs (Eds.). *Handbook of personality psychology*. San Diego, CA: Academic Press. (p. 595)

Idson, L. C., & Mischel, W. (2001). The personality of familiar and significant people: The lay perceiver as a social-cognitive theorist. *Journal of Personality and Social Psychology, 80*, 585–596. (p. 519)

IJzerman, H., & Semin, G. R. (2009). The thermometer of social relations: Mapping social proximity on temperature. *Psychological Science, 20*, 1214–1220. (p. 270)

Ikonomidou, C., Bittigau, P., Ishimaru, M. J., Wozniak, D. F., Koch, C., Genz, K., . . . Olney, J. W. (2000). Ethanol-induced apoptotic neurodegeneration and fetal alcohol syndrome. *Science, 287,* 1056–1060. (p. 182)

Ilardi, S. S. (2009). *The depression cure: The six-step program to beat depression without drugs.* Cambridge, MA: De Capo Lifelong Books. (pp. 634, 688)

Inagaki, T., & Eisenberg, N. (2014). Shared neural mechanisms underlying social warmth and physical warmth. *Psychological Science, 24,* 2272–2280. (p. 448)

Inbar, Y., Cone, J., & Gilovich, T. (2010). People's intuitions about intuitive insight and intuitive choice. *Journal of Personality and Social Psychology, 99,* 232–247. (p. 364)

Inbar, Y., Pizarro, D., & Bloom, P. (2011). *Disgusting smells cause decreased liking of gay men.* Unpublished manuscript, Tillburg University. (p. 268)

Independent Sector. (2002). *Faith and philanthropy: The connection between charitable giving behavior and giving to religion.* Washington, DC: Author. (p. 561)

Ingalhalikar, M., Smith, A., Parker, D., Satterthwaite, T. D., Elliott, M. A., Ruparel, K., . . . Verma, R. (2013). Sex differences in the structural connectome of the human brain. *Proceedings of the National Academy of Sciences.* (p. 163)

Ingham, A. G., Levinger, G., Graves, J., & Peckham, V. (1974). The Ringelmann effect: Studies of group size and group performance. *Journal of Experimental Social Psychology, 10,* 371–384. (p. 533)

Inglehart, R. (1990). *Culture shift in advanced industrial society.* Princeton, NJ: Princeton University Press. (p. 449)

Inglehart, R. (2008). Cultural change and democracy in Latin America. In F. Hagopian (Ed.), *Contemporary Catholicism, religious pluralism and democracy in Latin America.* South Bend, IN: Notre Dame University Press, 67–95. (p. 482)

Inglehart, R., Foa, R., Peterson, C., & Welzel, C. (2008). Development, freedom, and rising happiness: A global perspective (1981–2007). *Perspectives on Psychological Science, 3,* 264–285. (p. 502)

Inman, M. L., & Baron, R. S. (1996). Influence of prototypes on perceptions of prejudice. *Journal of Personality and Social Psychology, 70,* 727–739. (p. 356)

Insel, T. R. (2010, April). Faulty circuits. *Scientific American,* pp. 44–51. (p. 626)

Intergovernmental Panel on Climate Change (2014). *Climate change 2014: Mitigation of climate change.* Geneva: www.ipcc.ch. (p. 520)

International Schizophrenia Consortium. (2009). Common polygenic variation contributes to risk of schizophrenia and bipolar disorder. *Nature, 460,* 748–752. (p. 644)

International Society for Research on Aggression (ISRA). (2012). Report of the media violence commission. *Aggressive Behavior, 38,* 335–341. (p. 313)

Inzlicht, M., & Ben-Zeev, T. (2000). A threatening intellectual environment: Why females are susceptible to experiencing problem-solving deficits in the presence of males. *Psychological Science, 11,* 365–371. (p. 414)

Inzlicht, M., & Kang, S. K. (2010). Stereotype threat spillover: How coping with threats to social identity affects aggression, eating, decision making, and attention. *Journal of Personality and Social Psychology, 99,* 467–481. (p. 414)

Inzlicht, M., McGregor, I., Hirsh, J. C., & Nash, K. (2009). Neural markers of religious conviction. *Psychological Science, 20,* 385–392. (p. 68)

IPPA. (2009, January 22). Membership letter. International Positive Psychology Association. (p. 480)

IPPA. (2010, August). International conference on positive psychology and education in China, by S. Choong. *The IPPA Newsletter,* International Positive Psychology Association. (p. 480)

Ipsos. (2010a, June 29). Online Canadians report a large 35% decline in the amount of email received. www.ipsos-na.com. (p. 452)

Ipsos. (2010b, April 8). One in five (20%) global citizens believe that alien beings have come down to earth and walk amongst us in our communities disguised as humans. www.ipsos-na.com. (p. 30)

IPU. (2014, January 1). Women in national parliaments: Situation as of 31 November 2011. International Parliamentary Union (www.ipu.org). (p. 163)

Ireland, M. E., & Pennebaker, J. W. (2010). Language style matching in writing: Synchrony in essays, correspondence, and poetry. *Journal of Personality and Social Psychology, 99,* 549–571. (pp. 309, 525)

Ironson, G., Solomon, G. F., Balbin, E. G., O'Cleirigh, C., George, A., Kumar, M., Larson, D., & Woods, T. E. (2002). The Ironson-Woods spiritual/religiousness index is associated with long survival, health behaviors, less distress, and low cortisol in people with HIV/AIDS. *Annals of Behavioral Medicine, 24,* 34–48. (p. 513)

Irwin, M. R., Cole, J. C., & Nicassio, P. M. (2006). Comparative meta-analysis of behavioral interventions for insomnia and their efficacy in middle-aged adults and in older adults 55+ years of age. *Health Psychology, 25,* 3–14. (p. 110)

Isaacowitz, D. M. (2012). Mood regulation in real time: Age differences in the role of looking. *Current Directions in Psychological Science, 21,* 237–242. (p. 223)

Isaacson, W. (2009, Spring). *Einstein's final quest.* In Character. http://incharacter.org/features/einsteins-final-quest. (p. 415)

Ishida, A., Mutoh, T., Ueyama, T., Brando, H., Masubuchi, S., Nakahara, D., Tsujimoto, G., & Okamura, H. (2005). Light activates the adrenal gland: Timing of gene expression and glucocorticoid release. *Cell Metabolism, 2,* 297–307. (p. 678)

Islam, S. S., & Johnson, C. (2003). Correlates of smoking behavior among Muslim Arab-American adolescents. *Ethnicity & Health, 8,* 319–337. (p. 512)

Iso, H., Simoda, S., & Matsuyama, T. (2007). Environmental change during postnatal development alters behaviour. *Behavioural Brain Research, 179,* 90–98. (p. 82)

Ito, T. A., Miller, N., & Pollock, V. E. (1996). Alcohol and aggression: A meta-analysis on the moderating effects of inhibitory cues, triggering events, and self-focused attention. *Psychological Bulletin, 120,* 60–82. (p. 546)

ITU. (2013) ITC facts and statistics 2014. www.itu.int/en/ITU-D/Statistics. (p. 452)

Ives-Deliperi, V. L., Solms, M., & Meintjes, E. M. (2011). The neural substrates of mindfulness: An fMRI investigation. *Social Neuroscience, 6,* 231–242. (p. 511)

Iyengar, S. S., & Lepper, M. R. (2000). When choice is demotivating: Can one desire too much of a good thing? *Journal of Personality and Social Psychology, 79,* 995–1006. (p. 502)

Iyengar, S., & Westwood, S. J. (2014). Fear and loathing across party lines: New evidence on group polarization. *American Journal of Political Science.* (p. 535)

Izard, C. E. (1977). *Human emotions.* New York: Plenum Press. (pp. 472, 476)

Izard, C. E. (1994). Innate and universal facial expressions: Evidence from developmental and cross-cultural research. *Psychological Bulletin, 114,* 288–299. (p. 472)

Jablensky, A. (1999). Schizophrenia: Epidemiology. *Current Opinion in Psychiatry, 12,* 19–28. (p. 643)

Jacewicz, E., Fox, R. A., & O'Neil, C. (2009). Articulation rate across dialect, age, and gender. *Language Variation and Change, 21,* 233–256. (p. 216)

Jack, R. E., Garrod, O. G. B., Yu, H., Caldara, & Schyns, P. G. (2012). Facial expressions of emotion are not culturally universal. *Proceedings of the National Academy of Sciences, 109,* 7241–7244. (p. 472)

Jackson, G. (2009). Sexual response in cardiovascular disease. *Journal of Sex Research, 46,* 233–236. (p. 435)

Jackson, J. J., Thoemmes, F., Jonkmann, K., Lüdtke, O., & Trautwien, U. (2012). Military training and personality trait development: Does the military make the man, or does the man make the military? *Psychological Science, 23,* 270–277. (pp. 522, 592)

Jackson, J. M., & Williams, K. D. (1988). *Social loafing: A review and theoretical analysis.* Unpublished manuscript, Fordham University. (p. 533)

Jackson, S. W. (1992). The listening healer in the history of psychological healing. *American Journal Psychiatry, 149,* 1623–1632. (p. 679)

Jacobi, C., Hayward, C., deZwaan, M., Kraemer, H. C., & Agras, W. S. (2004). Coming to terms with risk factors for eating disorders: Application of risk terminology and suggestions for a general taxonomy. *Psychological Bulletin, 130,* 19–65. (p. 652)

Jacobs, B. L. (1994). Serotonin, motor activity, and depression-related disorders. *American Scientist, 82,* 456–463. (pp. 509, 634)

Jacobson, P. J. W., Prawitz, A. D., & Lukaszuk, J. M. (2007). Long-haul truck drivers want healthful meal options at truck-stop restaurants. *Journal of the American Dietetic Association, 107,* 2125–2129. (p. 431)

Jacoby, L. L., Bishara, A. J., Hessels, S., & Toth, J. P. (2005). Aging, subjective experience, and cognitive control: Dramatic false remembering by older adults. *Journal of Experimental Psychology: General, 154,* 131–148. (p. 349)

Jacoby, L. L., & Rhodes, M. G. (2006). False remembering in the aged. *Current Directions in Psychological Science, 15,* 49–53. (p. 349)

Jacques, C., & Rossion, B. (2006). The speed of individual face categorization. *Psychological Science, 17,* 485–492. (p. 229)

Jacques-Tiura, A. J., Abbey, A., Parkhill, M. R., & Zawacki, T. (2007). Why do some men misperceive women's sexual intentions more frequently than others do? An application of the confluence model. *Personality and Social Psychology Bulletin, 33,* 1467–1480. (p. 519)

Jager, J., & Davis-Kean, P. (2011). Same-sex sexuality and adolescent psychological well-being: The influence of sexual orientation, early reports of same-sex attraction, and gender. *Self and Identity, 10,* 417–444. (p. 441)

James, K. (1986). Priming and social categorizational factors: Impact on awareness of emergency situations. *Personality and Social Psychology Bulletin, 12,* 462–467. (p. 334)

James, W. (1890). *The principles of psychology* (Vol. 2). New York: Holt. (pp. 3, 14, 63, 261, 338, 351, 451, 460, 474, 523)

Jameson, D. (1985). Opponent-colors theory in light of physiological findings. In D. Ottoson & S. Zeki (Eds.), *Central and peripheral mechanisms of color vision*. New York: Macmillan. (p. 251)

Jamieson, J. P. (2010). The home field advantage in athletics: A meta-analysis. *Journal of Applied Social Psychology, 40*, 1819–1848. (p. 532)

Jamison, K. R. (1993). *Touched with fire: Manic-depressive illness and the artistic temperament.* New York: Free Press. (p. 630)

Jamison, K. R. (1995). *An unquiet mind.* New York: Knopf. (pp. 630, 657, 684)

Janis, I. L. (1982). *Groupthink: Psychological studies of policy decisions and fiascoes.* Boston: Houghton Mifflin. (p. 535)

Janis, I. L. (1986). Problems of international crisis management in the nuclear age. *Journal of Social Issues, 42*(2), 201–220. (p. 359)

Janoff-Bulman, R., Timko, C., & Carli, L. L. (1985). Cognitive biases in blaming the victim. *Journal of Experimental Social Psychology, 21*, 161–177. (p. 544)

Janssen, S. M. J., Rubin, D. C., & Conway, M. A. (2012). The reminiscence bump in the temporal distribution of the best football players of all time: Pelé, Cruijff or Maradona? *The Quarterly Journal of Experimental Psychology, 65*, 165–178. (p. 217)

Jaremka, L. M., Gabriel, S., & Carvallo, M. (2011). What makes us feel the best also makes us feel the worst: The emotional impact of independent and interdependent experiences. *Self and Identity, 10*, 44–63. (p. 449)

Jarrett, B., Bloch, G. J., Bennett, D., Bleazard, B., & Hedges, D. (2010). The influence of body mass index, age and gender on current illness: A cross-sectional study. *International Journal of Obesity, 34*, 429–436. (p. 430)

Jaschik, S. (2013, January 14). Study finds that increased parental support for college results in lower grades. *Inside Higher Education* (www.insidehighered.com). (p. 34)

Javitt, D. C., & Coyle, J. T. (2004, January). Decoding schizophrenia. *Scientific American*, pp. 48–55. (p. 642)

Jedrychowski, W., Perera, F., Jankowski, J., Butscher, M., Mroz, E., Flak, E., . . . Sowa, A. (2012). Effect of exclusive breastfeeding on the development of children's cognitive function in the Krakow prospective birth cohort study. *European Journal of Pediatrics, 171*, 151–158. (p. 35)

Jenkins, J. G., & Dallenbach, K. M. (1924). Obliviscence during sleep and waking. *American Journal of Psychology, 35*, 605–612. (p. 342)

Jenkins, J. M., & Astington, J. W. (1996). Cognitive factors and family structure associated with theory of mind development in young children. *Developmental Psychology, 32*, 70–78. (p. 190)

Jensen, A. R. (1980). *Bias in mental testing.* New York: Free Press. (p. 397)

Jensen, A. R. (1983, August). *The nature of the Black-White difference on various psychometric tests: Spearman's hypothesis.* Paper presented at the meeting of the American Psychological Association, Anaheim, CA. (p. 413)

Jensen, A. R. (1998). *The g factor: The science of mental ability.* Westport, CT: Praeger/Greenwood. (p. 413)

Jensen, J. P., & Bergin, A. E. (1988). Mental health values of professional therapists: A national interdisciplinary survey. *Professional Psychology: Research and Practice, 19*, 290–297. (p. 680)

Jensen, M. P. (2008). The neurophysiology of pain perception and hypnotic analgesia: Implications for clinical practice. *American Journal of Clinical Hypnosis, 51*, 123–147. (p. 265)

Jeon, S. T., Maurer, D., & Lewis, T. L. (2012). The effect of video game training on the vision of adults with bilateral deprivation Amblyopia. *Seeing and Perceiving, 25*, 493–520. (p. 254)

Jepson, C., Krantz, D. H., & Nisbett, R. E. (1983). Inductive reasoning: Competence or skill. *The Behavioral and Brain Sciences, 3*, 494–501. (p. 47)

Jessberger, S., Aimone, J. B., & Gage, F. H. (2008). *Neurogenesis. In learning and memory: A comprehensive reference.* Oxford: Elsevier. (p. 82)

Jiang, Y., Costello, P., Fang, F., Huang, M., & He, S. (2006). A gender- and sexual orientation-dependent spatial attentional effect of invisible things. *Proceedings of the National Academy of Sciences, 103*, 17048–17052. (pp. 231, 232)

Job, V., Dweck, C. S., & Walton, G. M. (2010). Ego depletion–Is it all in your head?: Implicit theories about willpower affect self-regulation. *Psychological Science, 21*. Published online at http://pss.sagepub.com/content/early/2010/09/28/0956797610384745. (p. 503)

Jobe, T. H., & Harrow, M. (2010). Schizophrenia course, long-term outcome, recovery, and prognosis. *Current Directions in Psychological Science, 19*, 220–225. (p. 641)

Johansson, P., Hall, L., Sikström, S., & Olsson, A. (2005). Failure to detect mismatches between intention and outcome in a simple decision task. *Science, 310*, 116–119. (pp. 98, 99)

Johansson, P., Hall, L., Tärning, B., Sikström, S., & Chater, N. (2014). Choice blindness and preference change: You will like this paper better if you (believe you) chose to read it! *Journal of Behavioral Decision Making, 27*, 281–289. (p. 98)

Johnson, D. L., Wiebe, J. S., Gold, S. M., Andreasen, N. C., Hichwa, R. D., Watkins, G. L., & Ponto, L. L. B. (1999). Cerebral blood flow and personality: A positron emission tomography study. *American Journal of Psychiatry, 156*, 252–257. (p. 587)

Johnson, D. F. (1997). Margaret Floy Washburn. *Psychology of Women Newsletter*, pp. 17, 22. (p. 4)

Johnson, E. J., & Goldstein, D. (2003). Do defaults save lives? *Science, 302*, 1338–1339. (p. 363)

Johnson, J. A. (2007, June 26). Not so situational. Commentary on the SPSP listserv (spsp-discuss@stolaf.edu). (p. 523)

Johnson, J. G., Cohen, P., Kotler, L., Kasen, S., & Brook, J. S. (2002). Psychiatric disorders associated with risk for the development of eating disorders during adolescence and early adulthood. *Journal of Consulting and Clinical Psychology, 70*, 1119–1128. (p. 652)

Johnson, J. S., & Newport, E. L. (1991). Critical period affects on universal properties of language: The status of subjacency in the acquisition of a second language. *Cognition, 39*, 215–258. (p. 374)

Johnson, K. (2008, January 29). For many of USA's inmates, crime runs in the family. *USA Today*, pp. 1A, 2A. (p. 162)

Johnson, M. H. (1992). Imprinting and the development of face recognition: From chick to man. *Current Directions in Psychological Science, 1*, 52–55. (p. 196)

Johnson, M. H., & Morton, J. (1991). *Biology and cognitive development: The case of face recognition.* Oxford: Blackwell Publishing. (p. 183)

Johnson, R. E., Chang, C-H., & Lord, R. G. (2006). Moving from cognition to behavior: What the research says. *Psychological Bulletin, 132*, 381–415. (p. A-11)

Johnson, S. C., et al. (2006). Activation of brain regions vulnerable to Alzheimer's disease: The effect of mild cognitive impairment. *Neurobiology of Aging, 27*, 1604–1612. (p. 219)

Johnson, W. (2010). Understanding the genetics of intelligence: Can height help? Can corn oil? *Current Directions in Psychological Science, 19*, 177–182. (p. 406)

Johnson, W., Carothers, A., & Deary, I. J. (2008). Sex differences in variability in general intelligence: A new look at the old question. *Perspectives on Psychological Science, 3*, 518–531. (p. 389)

Johnson, W., Corley, J., Starr, J. M., & Deary, I. J. (2011). Psychological and physical health at age 70 in the Lothian birth cohort 1936: Links with early life IQ, SES, and current cognitive function and neighborhood environment. *Health Psychology, 30*, 1–11. (p. 402)

Johnson, W., Gow, A. J., Corley, J., Starr, J. M., & Deary, I. J. (2010). Location in cognitive and residential space at age 70 reflects a lifelong trait over parental and environmental circumstances: The Lothian Birth Cohort 1936. *Intelligence, 38*, 403–411. (p. 402)

Johnson, W., Turkheimer, E., Gottesman, I. I., & Bouchard, Jr., T. J. (2009). Beyond heritability: Twin studies in behavioral research. *Current Directions in Psychological Science, 18*, 217–220. (pp. 136, 141, 406)

Johnston, L. D., O'Malley, P. M., Bachman, J. G., & Schulenberg, J. E. (2007). *Monitoring the Future national results on adolescent drug use: Overview of key findings, 2006.* Bethesda, MD: National Institute on Drug Abuse. (p. 129)

Johnston, L. D., O'Malley, P. M., Bachman, J. G., & Schulenberg, J. E. (2013, December 18). National press release, "Teen smoking continues to decline in 2013." University of Michigan News Service, Ann Arbor, 27 pp. (pp. 126, 127)

Johnston, L. D., O'Malley, P. M., Bachman, J. G., & Schulenberg, J. E. (2013). *Monitoring the future: National results on drug use: 2012 overview, key findings on adolescent drug use.* Ann Arbor: Institute for Social Research, The University of Michigan. (p. 123)

Johnstone, E. C., Ebmeier, K. P., Miller, P., Owens, D. G. C., & Lawrie, S. M. (2005). Predicting schizophrenia: Findings from the Edinburgh High-Risk Study. *British Journal of Psychiatry, 186*, 18–25. (p. 645)

Joiner, T. E., Jr. (2006). *Why people die by suicide.* Cambridge, MA: Harvard University Press. (p. 639)

Joiner, T. E., Jr. (2010). *Myths about suicide.* Cambridge, MA: Harvard University Press. (p. 638)

Jokela, M., Elovainio, M., Archana, S-M., & Kivimäki, M. (2009). IQ, socioeconomic status, and early death: The US National Longitudinal Survey of Youth. *Psychosomatic Medicine, 71*, 322–328. (p. 501)

Jolly, A. (2007). The social origin of mind. *Science, 317*, 1326. (p. 369)

Jonas, E., & Fischer, P. (2006). Terror management and religion: Evidence that intrinsic religiousness mitigates worldview defense following mortality salience. *Journal of Personality and Social Psychology, 91*, 553–567. (p. 581)

Jones, A. C., & Gosling, S. D. (2005). Temperament and personality in dogs (*Canis familiaris*): A review and evaluation of past research. *Applied Animal Behaviour Science, 95*, 1–53. (p. 588)

Jones, B., Reedy, E. J., & Weinberg, B. A. (2014, January). *Age and scientific genius*. NBER Working Paper Series (www.nber.org/papers/w19866). (p. 401)

Jones, E. (1957). *Sigmund Freud: Life and Work*, vol. 3, pt. 1., ch. 4. New York: Basic Books Publishing. (p. 576)

Jones, J. M. (2003, February 12). Fear of terrorism increases amidst latest warning. *Gallup News Service* (www.gallup.com/releases/pr030212.asp). (p. 620)

Jones, J. M. (2012, June 21). Atheists, Muslims see most bias as presidential candidates. Gallup Poll (www.gallup.com). (p. 540)

Jones, J. M. (2012, December 6). Most in U.S. say gay/lesbian bias is a serious problem. Gallup Poll (www.gallup.com). (p. 540)

Jones, J. M. (2013, December 19). In U.S., 40% get less than recommended amount of sleep. www.gallup.com. (p. 107)

Jones, J. T., Pelham, B. W., Carvallo, M., & Mirenberg, M. C. (2004). How do I love thee? Let me count the Js: Implicit egotism and interpersonal attraction. *Journal of Personality and Social Psychology, 87*, 665–683. (p. 551)

Jones, M. C. (1924). A laboratory study of fear: The case of Peter. *Journal of Genetic Psychology, 31*, 308–315. (p. 663)

Jones, M. V., Paull, G. C., & Erskine, J. (2002). The impact of a team's aggressive reputation on the decisions of association football referees. *Journal of Sports Sciences, 20*, 991–1000. (p. 238)

Jones, R. P., Cox, D., & Navarro-Rivera, J. (2014). A *shifting landscape: A decade of change in American attitudes about same-sex marriage and LGBT issues*. Washington, D.C.: Public Religion Research Institute. (p. 440)

Jones, S. S. (2007). Imitation in infancy: The development of mimicry. *Psychological Science, 18*, 593–599. (p. 308)

Jones, W., & Klin, A. (2013). Attention to eyes is present but in decline in 2–6-month-old infants later diagnosed with autism. *Nature, 504*, 427–431. (p. 193)

Jones, W. H., Carpenter, B. N., & Quintana, D. (1985). Personality and interpersonal predictors of loneliness in two cultures. *Journal of Personality and Social Psychology, 48*, 1503–1511. (p. 7)

Jonides, J., Jaeggi, S. M., Buschkuehl, M., & Shah, P. (2012, September/October). Building better brains. *Scientific American Mind*, pp. 59–63. (p. 218)

Jordan, A. H., Monin, B., Dweck, C. S., Lovett, B. J., John, O. P., & Gross, J. J. (2011). Misery has more company than people think: Underestimating the prevalence of others' negative emotions. *Personality and Social Psychology Bulletin, 37*, 120–135. (p. 628)

Jorm, A. F., Reavley, N. J., & Ross, A. M. (2012). Belief in the dangerousness of people with mental disorders: A review. *Australian and New Zealand Journal of Psychiatry, 46*, 1029–1045. (p. 616)

Jose, A., O'Leary, D., & Moyer, A. (2010). Does premarital cohabitation predict subsequent marital stability and marital quality? A meta-analysis. *Journal of Marriage and Family, 72*, 105–116. (p. 221)

Joseph, J. (2001). Separated twins and the genetics of personality differences: A critique. *American Journal of Psychology, 114*, 1–30. (p. 138)

Jost, J. T., Kay, A. C., & Thorisdottir, H. (Eds.). (2009). *Social and psychological bases of ideology and system justification*. New York: Oxford University Press. (p. 545)

Jovanovic, T., Blanding, N. Q., Norrholm, S. D., Duncan, E., Bradley, B., & Ressler, K. J. (2009). Childhood abuse is associated with increased startle reactivity in adulthood. *Depression and Anxiety, 26*, 1018–1026. (p. 200)

Judge, T. A., Thoresen, C. J., Bono, J. E., & Patton, G. K. (2001). The job satisfaction/job performance relationship: A qualitative and quantitative review. *Psychological Bulletin, 127*, 376–407. (p. A-9)

Jung, R. E., & Haier, R. J. (2013). Creativity and intelligence: Brain networks that link and differentiate the expression of genius. In O. Vartanian, A. S. Bristol, & J. C. Kaufman (Eds.), *Neuroscience of Creativity*. Cambridge, MA: MIT Press. (p. 366)

Jung-Beeman, M., Bowden, E. M., Haberman, J., Frymiare, J. L., Arambel-Liu, S., Greenblatt, R., Reber, P. J., & Kounios, J. (2004). Neural activity when people solve verbal problems with insight. *PloS Biology 2*(4), e111. (p. 358)

Just, M. A., Keller, T. A., & Cynkar, J. (2008). A decrease in brain activation associated with driving when listening to someone speak. *Brain Research, 1205*, 70–80. (p. 96)

Just, M. A., Keller, T. A., Malave, V. L., Kana, R. K., & Varma, S. (2012). Autism as a neural systems disorder: A theory of frontal-posterior underconnectivity. *Neuroscience and Biobehavioral Reviews, 36*, 1292–1313. (p. 194)

Kabat-Zinn, J. (2001). Mindfulness-based interventions in context: Past, present, and future. *Clinical Psychology: Science and Practice, 10*, 144–156. (p. 510)

Kagan, J. (1976). Emergent themes in human development. *American Scientist, 64*, 186–196. (p. 199)

Kagan, J. (1984). *The nature of the child*. New York: Basic Books. (p. 195)

Kagan, J. (1995). On attachment. *Harvard Review of Psychiatry, 3*, 104–106. (p. 197)

Kagan, J. (1998). *Three seductive ideas*. Cambridge, MA: Harvard University Press. (pp. 87, 180)

Kagan, J., Lapidus, D. R., & Moore, M. (December, 1978). Infant antecedents of cognitive functioning: A longitudinal study. *Child Development, 49*(4), 1005–1023. (p. 180)

Kagan, J., & Snidman, N. (2004). *The long shadow of temperament*. Cambridge, MA: Belknap Press. (p. 140)

Kahneman, D. (1985, June). Quoted by K. McKean, Decisions, decisions. *Discover*, pp. 22–31. (p. 34)

Kahneman, D. (1999). Assessments of objective happiness: A bottom-up approach. In D. Kahneman, E. Diener, & N. Schwartz (Eds.), *Understanding well-being: Scientific perspectives on enjoyment and suffering*. New York: Russell Sage Foundation. (p., 263)

Kahneman, D. (2005, January 13). What were they thinking? Q&A with Daniel Kahneman. *Gallup Management Journal* (gmj.gallup.com). (pp. 359, 483)

Kahneman, D. (2005, February 10). Are you happy now? *Gallup Management Journal* interview (www.gmj.gallup.com). (p. 481)

Kahneman, D. (2011). *Thinking, fast and slow*. New York: Farrar, Straus, and Giroux. (pp. 94, 361)

Kahneman, D., Fredrickson, B. L., Schreiber, C. A., & Redelmeier, D. A. (1993). When more pain is preferred to less: Adding a better end. *Psychological Science, 4*, 401–405. (p. 263)

Kahneman, D., Krueger, A. B., Schkade, D. A., Schwarz, N., & Stone, A. A. (2004). A survey method for characterizing daily life experience: The day reconstruction method. *Science, 306*, 1776–1780. (pp. 10, 480)

Kahneman, D., & Renshon, J. (2007, January/February). Why hawks win. *Foreign Policy* (www.foreignpolicy.com). (p. 603)

Kail, R. (1991). Developmental change in speed of processing during childhood and adolescence. *Psychological Bulletin, 109*, 490–501. (p. 216)

Kail, R., & Hall, L. K. (2001). Distinguishing short-term memory from working memory. *Memory & Cognition, 29*, 1–9. (p. 321)

Kaiser. (2010, January). *Generation M²: Media in the lives of 8- to 18-year-olds* (by V. J. Rideout, U. G. Foeher, & D. F. Roberts). Menlo Park, CA: Henry J. Kaiser Family Foundation. (pp. 33, 453, 645)

Kamarck, T., & Jennings, J. R. (1991). Biobehavioral factors in sudden cardiac death. *Psychological Bulletin, 109*, 42–75. (p. 497)

Kamatali, J-M. (2014, April 4). Following orders in Rwanda. *New York Times* (www.nytimes.com). (p. 529)

Kamel, N. S., & Gammack, J. K. (2006). Insomnia in the elderly: Cause, approach, and treatment. *American Journal of Medicine, 119*, 463–469. (p. 103)

Kamenica, E., Naclerio, R., & Malani, A. (2013). Advertisements impact the physiological efficacy of a branded drug. *PNAS, 110*, 12931–12935. (p. 682)

Kamil, A. C., & Cheng, K. (2001). Way-finding and landmarks: The multiple-bearings hypothesis. *Journal of Experimental Biology, 204*, 103–113. (p. 329)

Kaminski, J., Cali, J., & Fischer, J. (2004). Word learning in a domestic dog: Evidence for "fast mapping." *Science, 304*, 1682–1683. (p. 378)

Kanazawa, S. (2004). General intelligence as a domain-specific adaptation. *Psychological Review, 111*, 512–523. (p. 386)

Kanazawa, S. (2010). Evolutionary psychology and intelligence research. *American Psychologist, 65*, 279–289. (p. 386)

Kandel, D. B., & Raveis, V. H. (1989). Cessation of illicit drug use in young adulthood. *Archives of General Psychiatry, 46,* 109–116. (p. 129)

Kandel, E. (2012, March 5). Interview by Claudia Dreifus: A quest to understand how memory works. *New York Times* (www.nytimes.com). (p. 580)

Kandel, E. (2013, September 6). The new science of mind. *New York Times* (www.nytimes.com). (p. 658)

Kandel, E. R. (2012, March 5). Interview by Claudia Dreifus: A quest to understand how memory works. *New York Times* (www.nytimes.com). (p. 332)

Kandel, E. R., & Schwartz, J. H. (1982). Molecular biology of learning: Modulation of transmitter release. *Science, 218,* 433–443. (p. 332)

Kandler, C. (2011). The genetic links between the big five personality traits and general interest domains. *Personality and Social Psychology Bulletin, 37,* 1633–1643. (p. 136)

Kandler, C., Bleidorn, W., Riemann, R., Angleitner, A., & Spinath, F. M. (2012). Life events as environmental states and genetic traits and the role of personality: A longitudinal twin study. *Behavior Genetics, 42,* 57–72. (p. 152)

Kandler, C., Bleidorn, W., Riemann, R., Spinath, F. M., Thiel, W., & Angleitner, A. (2010). Sources of cumulative continuity in personality: A longitudinal multiple-rater twin study. *Journal of Personality and Social Psychology, 98,* 995–1008. (p. 179)

Kandler, C., Riemann, R., & Angleitner, A. (2013). Patterns and sources of continuity and change of energetic and temporal aspects of temperament in adulthood: A longitudinal twin study of self- and peer reports. *Developmental Psychology, 49,* 1739–1753. (p. 140)

Kane, G. D. (2010). Revisiting gay men's body image issues: Exposing the fault lines. *Review of General Psychology, 14,* 311–317. (p. 652)

Kane, J. M., & Mertz, J. E. (2012). Debunking myths about gender and mathematics performance. *Notices of the American Mathematical Society, 59,* 10–21. (p. 411)

Kane, M. J., Brown, L. H., McVay, J. C., Silvia, P. J., Myin-Germeys, I., & Kwapil, T. R. (2007). For whom the mind wanders, and when: An experience-sampling study of working memory and executive control in daily life. *Psychological Science, 18,* 614–621. (p. 324)

Kaplan, H. I., & Saddock, B. J. (Eds.). (1989). *Comprehensive textbook of psychiatry,* V. Baltimore, MD: Williams and Wilkins. (p. 682)

Kaplan, T., & Hakim, D. (2013, January 14). New York has gun deal, with focus on mental ills. *New York Times* (www.nytimes.com). (p. 616)

Kapogiannis, D., Barbey, A. K., Sue, M., Zamboni, G., Krueger, F., & Grafman, J. (2009). Cognitive and neural foundations of religious belief. *PNAS, 106,* 4876–4881. (p. 68)

Kappes, H. B., & Oettingen, G. (2012). Wishful information preference: Positive fantasies mimic the effects of intentions. *Personality and Social Psychology Bulletin, 38,* 870–881. (p. 600)

Kaprio, J., Koskenvuo, M., & Rita, H. (1987). Mortality after bereavement: A prospective study of 95,647 widowed persons. *American Journal of Public Health, 77,* 283–287. (p. 490)

Kaptchuk, T. J., Stason, W. B., Davis, R. B., Legedza, A. R. T., Schnyer, R. N., Kerr, C. E., . . . Goldman, R. H. (2006). Sham device v inert pill: Randomised controlled trial of two placebo treatments. *British Medical Journal, 332,* 391–397. (p. 264)

Karacan, I., Aslan, C., & Hirshkowitz, M. (1983). Erectile mechanisms in man. *Science, 220,* 1080–1082. (p. 103)

Karacan, I., Goodenough, D. R., Shapiro, A., & Starker, S. (1966). Erection cycle during sleep in relation to dream anxiety. *Archives of General Psychiatry, 15,* 183–189. (p. 103)

Karau, S. J., & Williams, K. D. (1993). Social loafing: A meta-analytic review and theoretical integration. *Journal of Personality and Social Psychology, 65,* 681–706. (p. 533)

Karg, K., Burmeister, M., Shedden, K., & Sen, S. (2011). The serotonin transporter promoters variant (5-HTTLPR), stress, and depression meta-analysis revised: Evidence of genetic moderation. *Archives of General Psychiatry, 68,* 444–454. (p. 634)

Kark, J. D., Shemi, G., Friedlander, Y., Martin, O., Manor, O., & Blondheim, S. H. (1996). Does religious observance promote health? Mortality in secular vs. religious kibbutzim in Israel. *American Journal of Public Health, 86,* 341–346. (p. 512)

Karlsgodt, K. H., Sun, D., & Cannon, T. D. (2010). Structural and functional brain abnormalities in schizophrenia. *Current Directions in Psychological Science, 19,* 226–231. (p. 642)

Karni, A., Meyer, G., Rey-Hipolito, C., Jezzard, P., Adams, M. M., Turner, R., & Ungerleider, L. G. (1998). The acquisition of skilled motor performance: Fast and slow experience-driven changes in primary motor cortex. *Proceedings of the National Academy of Sciences, 95,* 861–868. (p. 153)

Karni, A., & Sagi, D. (1994). Dependence on REM sleep for overnight improvement of perceptual skills. *Science, 265,* 679–682. (p. 113)

Karns, C. M., Dow, M. W., & Neville, H. J. (2012). Altered cross-modal processing in the primary auditory cortex of congenitally deaf adults: A visual-somatosensory fMRI study with a double-flash illusion. *The Journal of Neuroscience, 32,* 9626–9638. (p. 375)

Karpicke, J. D. (2012). Retrieval-based learning: Active retrieval promotes meaningful learning. *Current Directions in Psychological Science, 21,* 157–163. (pp. 14, 326)

Karpicke, J. D., & Roediger, H. L., III. (2008). The critical importance of retrieval for learning. *Science, 319,* 966–968. (p. 13)

Karremans, J. C., Frankenhis, W. E., & Arons, S. (2010). Blind men prefer a low waist-to-hip ratio. *Evolution and Human Behavior, 31,* 182–186. (pp. 149, 554)

Karremans, J. C., Stroebe, W., & Claus, J. (2006). Beyond Vicary's fantasies: The impact of subliminal priming and brand choice. *Journal of Experimental Social Psychology, 42,* 792–798. (p. 233)

Kasen, S., Chen, H., Sneed, J., Crawford, T., & Cohen, P. (2006). Social role and birth cohort influences on gender-linked personality traits in women: A 20-year longitudinal analysis. *Journal of Personality and Social Psychology, 91,* 944–958. (p. 164)

Kashdan, T., DeWall, C. N., Schurtz, D., et al. (2014). More than words: Contemplating death enhances positive emotional word use. *Personality and Individual Differences, 71,* 171–175. (p. 582)

Kashubeck-West, S., & Meyer, J. (2008). The well-being of women who are late deafened. *Journal of Counseling Psychology, 55,* 463–472. (p. 375)

Kasser, T. (2002). *The high price of materialism.* Cambridge, MA: MIT Press. (p. 482)

Kasser, T. (2011). Cultural values and the well-being of future generations: A cross-national study. *Journal of Cross-Cultural Psychology, 42, 42,* 206–215. (p. 482)

Katz-Wise, S. L., & Hyde, J. S. (2012). Victimization experiences of lesbian, gay, and bisexual individuals: A meta-analysis. *Journal of Sex Research, 49,* 142–167. (p. 540)

Katz-Wise, S. L., Priess, H. A., & Hyde, J. S. (2010). Gender-role attitudes and behavior across the transition to parenthood. *Developmental Psychology, 46,* 18–28. (p. 164)

Kaufman, A. S., Dillon, T., & Kirsch, J. W. (2013). "A beautiful theory, killed by a nasty, ugly little fact." *PsycCRITIQUES, 58*(19) dx.doi.org/10.1037/a0032830. (p. 397)

Kaufman, G., & Libby, L. K. (2012). Changing beliefs and behavior through experience-taking. *Journal of Personality and Social Psychology, 103,* 1–19. (p. 310)

Kaufman, J., & Zigler, E. (1987). Do abused children become abusive parents? *American Journal of Orthopsychiatry, 57,* 186–192. (p. 200)

Kaufman, J. C., & Baer, J. (2002). I bask in dreams of suicide: Mental illness, poetry, and women. *Review of General Psychology, 6,* 271–286. (p. 630)

Kaufman, L., & Kaufman, J. H. (2000). Explaining the moon illusion. *Proceedings of the National Academy of Sciences, 97,* 500–505. (p. 253)

Kawachi, I., Kennedy, B. P., & Wilkinson, R. G. (1999). Crime: Social disorganization and relative deprivation. *Social Science and Medicine, 48,* 719–731. (p. 484)

Kawakami, K., Dunn, E., Karmali, F., & Dovidio, J. F. (2009). Mispredicting affective and behavioral responses to racism. *Science, 323,* 276–278. (p. 538)

Kay, A. C., Baucher, D., Peach, J. M., Laurin, K., Friesen, J., Zanna, M. P., & Spencer, S. J. (2009). Inequality, discrimination, and the power of the status quo: Direct evidence for a motivation to see the way things are as the way they should be. *Journal of Personality and social Psychology, 97,* 421–434. (p. 545)

Kayser, C. (2007, April/May). Listening with your eyes. *Scientific American Mind,* pp. 24–29. (p. 270)

Kazantzis, N., & Dattilio, F. M. (2010b). Definitions of homework, types of homework and ratings of the importance of homework among psychologists with cognitive behavior therapy and psychoanalytic theoretical orientations. *Journal of Clinical Psychology, 66,* 758–773. (p. 669)

Kazantzis, N., Whittington, C., & Dattilio, F. M. (2010a). Meta-analysis of homework effects in cognitive and behavioral therapy: A replication and extension. *Clinical Psychology: Science and Practice, 17,* 144–156. (p. 669)

Kazdin, A. E., & Benjet, C. (2003). Spanking children: Evidence and issues. *Current Directions in Psychological Science, 12,* 99–103. (p. 296)

Kazdin, A. E., & Blase, S. L. (2011a). Rebooting psychotherapy research and practice to reduce the burden of mental illness. *Perspectives on Psychological Science, 6,* 21–37. (p. 670)

Kazdin, A. E., & Blase, S. L. (2011b). Interventions and models of their delivery to reduce the burden of mental illness: Reply to commentaries. *Perspectives on Psychological Science, 6,* 507–510. (p. 670)

Kearney, M. S., & Levine, P. B. (2014). *Media influences on social outcomes: The impact of MTV's 16 and Pregnant on teen childbearing.* The National Bureau of Economic Research: NBER Working Paper No. 19795. (p. 439)

Kearns, M. C., Ressler, K. J., Zatzick, D., & Rothbaum, B. O. (2012). Early interventions for PTSD: A review. *Depression and Anxiety, 29,* 833–842. (p. 333)

Keesey, R. E., & Corbett, S. W. (1983). Metabolic defense of the body weight set-point. In A. J. Stunkard & E. Stellar (Eds.), *Eating and its disorders.* New York: Raven Press. (p. 427)

Keith, S. W., et al. (2006). Putative contributors to the secular increase in obesity: Exploring the roads less traveled. *International Journal of Obesity, 30,* 1585–1594. (p. 431)

Kell, H. J., Lubinski, D., & Benbow, C. P. (2013). Who rises to the top? Early indicators. *Psychological Science, 24,* 648–659. (p. 404)

Keller, J. (2007, March 9). As football players get bigger, more of them risk a dangerous sleep disorder. *Chronicle of Higher Education,* pp. A43–A44. (p. 111)

Keller, M. B., McCullough, J. P., Klein, D. N., Arnow, B., Dunner, D. L., Gelenberg, A. J., . . . Zajecka J. (2000). A comparison of nefazodone, the cognitive behavioral-analysis system of psychotherapy, and their combination for the treatment of chronic depression. *New England Journal of Medicine, 342,* 1462–1470. (p. 684)

Kellerman, J., Lewis, J., & Laird, J. D. (1989). Looking and loving: The effects of mutual gaze on feelings of romantic love. *Journal of Research in Personality, 23,* 145–161. (p. 468)

Kelling, S. T., & Halpern, B. P. (1983). Taste flashes: Reaction times, intensity, and quality. *Science, 219,* 412–414. (p., 266)

Kellner, C. H., et al. (2006). Continuation electroconvulsive therapy vs. pharmacotherapy for relapse prevention in major depression: A multisite study from the Consortium for Research in Electroconvulsive Therapy (CORE). *Archives of General Psychiatry, 63,* 1337–1344. (p. 686)

Kelly, A. E. (2000). Helping construct desirable identities: A self-presentational view of psychotherapy. *Psychological Bulletin, 126,* 475–494. (p. 667)

Kelly, S. D., Özyürek, A., & Maris, E. (2010). Two sides of the same coin: Speech and gesture mutually interact to enhance comprehension. *Psychological Science, 21,* 260–267. (p. 378)

Kelly, T. A. (1990). The role of values in psychotherapy: A critical review of process and outcome effects. *Clinical Psychology Review, 10,* 171–186. (p. 680)

Kempe, R. S., & Kempe, C. C. (1978). *Child abuse.* Cambridge, MA: Harvard University Press. (p. 200)

Kempermann, G. (2013). What the bomb said about the brain. *Science, 340,* 1180–1181. (p. 82)

Kendall-Tackett, K. A., Williams, L. M., & Finkelhor, D. (1993). Impact of sexual abuse on children: A review and synthesis of recent empirical studies. *Psychological Bulletin, 113,* 164–180. (p. 348)

Kendler, K. S. (1996). Parenting: A genetic-epidemiologic perspective. *The American Journal of Psychiatry, 153,* 11–20. (p. 202)

Kendler, K. S. (1998, January). Major depression and the environment: A psychiatric genetic perspective. *Pharmacopsychiatry, 31*(1), 5–9. (p. 632)

Kendler, K. S. (2011). A statement from Kenneth S. Kendler, M.D., on the proposal to eliminate the grief exclusion criterion from major depression. www.dsm5.org. (p. 614)

Kendler, K. S., Gardner, C. O., & Prescott, C. A. (2006). Toward a comprehensive developmental model for major depression in men. *American Journal of Psychiatry, 163,* 115–124. (p. 631)

Kendler, K. S., Jacobson, K. C., Myers, J., & Prescott, C. A. (2002a). Sex differences in genetic and environmental risk factors for irrational fears and phobias. *Psychological Medicine, 32,* 209–217. (p. 626)

Kendler, K. S., Myers, J., & Prescott, C. A. (2002b). The etiology of phobias: An evaluation of the stress-diathesis model. *Archives of General Psychiatry, 59,* 242–248. (p. 626)

Kendler, K. S., Myers, J., & Zisook, S. (2008). Does bereavement-related major depression differ from major depression associated with other stressful life events? *American Journal of Psychiatry, 165,* 1449–1455. (p. 632)

Kendler, K. S., Neale, M. C., Kessler, R. C., Heath, A. C., & Eaves, L. J. (1994). Parent treatment and the equal environment assumption in twin studies of psychiatric illness. *Psychological Medicine, 24,* 579–590. (p. 136)

Kendler, K. S., Neale, M. C., Thornton, L. M., Aggen, S. H., Gilman, S. E., & Kessler, R. C. (2002). Cannabis use in the last year in a U.S. national sample of twin and sibling pairs. *Psychological Medicine, 32,* 551–554. (p. 127)

Kendler, K. S., Sundquist, K., Ohlsson, H., Palmer, K., Maes, H., Winkleby, M. A., & Sundquist, J. (2012). Genetic and familiar environmental influences on the risk for drug abuse: A Swedish adoption study. *Archives of General Psychiatry, 69,* 690–697. (p. 127)

Kendler, K. S., Thornton, L. M., & Gardner, C. O. (2001). Genetic risk, number of previous depressive episodes, and stressful life events in predicting onset of major depression. *American Journal of Psychiatry, 158,* 582–586. (p. 632)

Kendrick, K. M., & Feng, J. (2011). Neural encoding principles in face perception revealed using non-primate models. In G. Rhodes, A. Calder, M. Johnson, & J. V. Haxby (Eds.), *The Oxford Handbook of Face Perception.* Oxford: Oxford University Press. (p. 318)

Kennedy, S., & Over, R. (1990). Psychophysiological assessment of male sexual arousal following spinal cord injury. *Archives of Sexual Behavior, 19,* 15–27. (p. 63)

Kenrick, D. T., & Funder, D. C. (1988). Profiting from controversy: Lessons from the person-situation debate. *American Psychologist, 43,* 23–34. (p. 592)

Kenrick, D. T., Griskevicious, V., Neuberg, S. L., & Schaller, M. (2010). Renovating the pyramid of needs: Contemporary extensions build upon ancient foundations. *Perspectives on Psychological Science, 5,* 292–314. (p. 423)

Kenrick, D. T., & Gutierres, S. E. (1980). Contrast effects and judgments of physical attractiveness: When beauty becomes a social problem. *Journal of Personality and Social Psychology, 38,* 131–140. (p. 438)

Kenrick, D. T., Gutierres, S. E., & Goldberg, L. L. (1989). Influence of popular erotica on judgments of strangers and mates. *Journal of Experimental Social Psychology, 25,* 159–167. (p. 438)

Kenrick, D. T., Nieuweboer, S., & Buunk, A. P. (2009). Universal mechanisms and cultural diversity: Replacing the blank slate with a coloring book. In M. Schaller, A. Norenzayan, S. Heine, A. Norenzayan, T. Yamagishi, & T. Kameda (eds.), *Evolution, culture, and the human mind.* Mahwah, NJ: Lawrence Erlbaum. (pp. 149, 152)

Kensinger, E. A. (2007). Negative emotion enhances memory accuracy: Behavioral and neuroimaging evidence. *Current Directions in Psychological Science, 16,* 213–218. (p. 331)

Keough, K. A., Zimbardo, P. G., & Boyd, J. N. (1999). Who's smoking, drinking, and using drugs? Time perspective as a predictor of substance use. *Basic and Applied Social Psychology, 2,* 149–164. (p. 574)

Kernis, M. H. (2003). Toward a conceptualization of optimal self-esteem. *Psychological Inquiry, 14,* 1–26. (p. 605)

Kerr, N. L., & Bruun, S. E. (1983). Dispensability of member effort and group motivation losses: Free-rider effects. *Journal of Personality and Social Psychology, 44,* 78–94. (p. 533)

Kessler, M., & Albee, G. (1975). Primary prevention. *Annual Review of Psychology, 26,* 557–591. (p. 690)

Kessler, R. C. (2000). Posttraumatic stress disorder: The burden to the individual and to society. *Journal of Clinical Psychiatry, 61*(suppl. 5), 4–12. (p. 623)

Kessler, R. C., et al. (2010). Structure and diagnosis of adult attention-deficit/hyperactivity disorder: Analysis of expanded symptom criteria from the adult ADHD Clinical Diagnostic Scale. *Archives of General Psychiatry, 67,* 1168–1178. (p. 615)

Kessler, R. C., et al. (2010). Age differences in the prevalence and co-morbidity of DSM-IV major depressive episodes: Results from the WHO World Mental Health Survey Initiative. *Depression and Anxiety, 27,* 351–364. (pp. 356, 632)

Kessler, R. C., Akiskal, H. S., Ames, M., Birnbaum, H., Greenberg, P., Hirschfeld, R. M. A., . . . Wang, P. S. (2006). Prevalence and effects of mood disorders on work performance in a nationally representative sample of U.S. workers. *American Journal of Psychiatry, 163,* 1561–1568. (p. 630)

Kessler, R. C., Berglund, P., Demler, O., Jin, R., Merikangos, K. R., & Walters, E. E. (2005). Lifetime prevalence and age-of-onset distributions of DSM-IV disorders in the National Comorbidity Survey Replication. *Archives of General Psychiatry, 62,* 593–602. (p. 617)

Kessler, R. C., Foster, C., Joseph, J., Ostrow, D., Wortman, C., Phair, J., & Chmiel, J. (1991). Stressful life events and symptom onset in HIV infection. *American Journal of Psychiatry, 148,* 733–738. (p. 496)

Kessler, R. C., Petukhova, M., Sampson, N. A., Zaslavsky, A. M., & Wittchen, H-A. (2012). Twelve-month and lifetime morbid risk of anxiety and mood disorders in the United States. *International Journal of Methods in Psychiatric Research, 21,* 169–184. (p. 623)

Kessler, R. C., Soukup, J., Davis, R. B., Foster, D. F., Wilkey, S. A., Van Rompay, M. I., & Eisenberg, D. M. (2001). The use of complementary and alternative therapies to treat anxiety and depression in the United States. *American Journal of Psychiatry, 158,* 289–294. (p. 677)

Keynes, M. (1980, December 20/27). Handel's illnesses. *Lancet,* pp. 1354–1355. (p. 630)

Keys, A., Brozek, J., Henschel, A., Mickelsen, O., & Taylor, H. L. (1950). *The biology of human starvation*. Minneapolis: University of Minnesota Press. (p. 424)

Kiecolt-Glaser, J. K. (2009). Psychoneuroimmunology: Psychology's gateway to the biomedical future. *Perspectives on Psychological Science, 4*, 367–369. (p. 492)

Kiecolt-Glaser, J. K., Loving, T. J., Stowell, J. R., Malarkey, W. B., Lemeshow, S., Dickinson, S. L., & Glaser, R. (2005). Hostile marital interactions, proinflammatory cytokine production, and wound healing. *Archives of General Psychiatry, 62*, 1377–1384. (p. 494)

Kiecolt-Glaser, J. K., Page, G. G., Marucha, P. T., MacCallum, R. C., & Glaser, R. (1998). Psychological influences on surgical recovery: Perspectives from psychoneuroimmunology. *American Psychologist, 53*, 1209–1218. (p. 494)

Kiehl, K. A., & Buckholtz, J. W. (2010, September/October). Inside the mind of a psychopath. *Scientific American Mind*, pp. 22–29. (p. 651)

Kihlstrom, J. F. (2005). Dissociative disorders. *Annual Review of Clinical Psychology, 1*, 227–253. (p. 648)

Kihlstrom, J. F. (2006). Repression: A unified theory of a will-o'-the-wisp. *Behavioral and Brain Sciences, 29*, 523. (p. 580)

Kille, D. R., Forest, A. L., & Wood, J. V. (2013). Tall, dark, and stable: Embodiment motivates mate selection preferences. *Psychological Science, 24*, 112–114. (p. 270)

Killingsworth, M. A., & Gilbert, D. T. (2010). A wandering mind is an unhappy mind. *Science, 330*, 932. (p. 453, A-2)

Kilpatrick, L. A., Suyenobu, B. Y., Smith, S. R., Bueller, J. A., Goodman, T., Creswell, J. D., . . . Naliboff, B. D. (2011). Impact of mindfulness-based stress reduction training on intrinsic brain activity. *Neuroimage, 56*, 290–298. (p. 511)

Kilpeläinen, T. O., et al. (2012). Physical activity attenuates the influence of *FTO* variants on obesity risk: A meta-analysis of 218,166 adults and 19,268 children. *Plos Medicine*. http://www.plosmedicine.org/article/info%3Adoi%2F10.1371%2Fjournal.pmed.1001116. (p. 508)

Kim, B. S. K., Ng, G. F., & Ahn, A. J. (2005). Effects of client expectation for counseling success, client-counselor worldview match, and client adherence to Asian and European American cultural values on counseling process with Asian Americans. *Journal of Counseling Psychology, 52*, 67–76. (p. 680)

Kim, G., & Tong, A. (2010, February 23). Airline passengers have grown, seats haven't. *Sacramento Bee* (reprinted by *Grand Rapids Press*, pp. B1, B3). (p. 431)

Kim, H., & Markus, H. R. (1999). Deviance or uniqueness, harmony or conformity? A cultural analysis. *Journal of Personality and Social Psychology, 77*, 785–800. (p. 158)

Kim, J. L., & Ward, L. M. (2012). Striving for pleasure without fear: Short-term effects of reading a women's magazine on women's sexual attitudes. *Psychology of Women Quarterly, 36*, 326–336. (p. 439)

Kim, S. H., Hwang, J. H., Park, H. S., & Kim, S. E. (2008). Resting brain metabolic correlates of neuroticism and extraversion in young men. *NeuroReport, 19*, 883–886. (p. 587)

Kim, S. H., Vincent, L. C., & Goncalo, J. A. (2013). Outside advantage: Can social rejection fuel creative thought? *Journal of Experimental Psychology: General, 142*, 605–611. (p. 367)

Kim, Y. S., Leventhal, B. L., Koh, Y., Fombonne, E., Laska, E., Lim, E., . . . Grinker, R. R. (2011). Prevalence of autism spectrum disorders in a total population sample. *The American Journal of Psychiatry, 168*, 904–912. (p. 193)

Kim-Yeary, K. H., Ounpraseuth, S., Moore, P., Bursac, Z., & Greene, P. (2012). Religion, social capital, and health. *Review of Religious Research, 54*, 331–347. (p. 513)

Kimata, H. (2001). Effect of humor on allergen-induced wheal reactions. *Journal of the American Medical Association, 285*, 737. (p. 506)

Kimble, G. A. (1981). *Biological and cognitive constraints on learning*. Washington, DC: American Psychological Association. (p. 301)

Kindt, M., Soeter, M., & Vervliet, B. (2009). Beyond extinction: Erasing human fear responses and preventing the return of fear. *Nature Neuroscience, 12*, 256–258. (p. 626)

King, S., St-Hilaire, A., & Heidkamp, D. (2010). Prenatal factors in schizophrenia. *Current Directions in Psychological Science, 19*, 209–213. (p. 643)

Kinnier, R. T., & Metha, A. T. (1989). Regrets and priorities at three stages of life. *Counseling and Values, 33*, 182–193. (p. 223)

Kinzler, K. D., Shutts, K., Dejesus, J., & Spelke, E. S. (2009). Accent trumps race in guiding children's social preferences. *Social Cognition, 27*, 623–634. (p. 542)

Kirby, D. (2002). Effective approaches to reducing adolescent unprotected sex, pregnancy, and childbearing. *Journal of Sex Research, 39*, 51–57. (p. 439)

Kirkpatrick, B., Fenton, W. S., Carpenter, W. T., Jr., & Marder, S. R. (2006). The NIMH-MATRICS consensus statement on negative symptoms. *Schizophrenia Bulletin, 32*, 214–219. (p. 641)

Kirkpatrick, L. (1999). Attachment and religious representations and behavior. In J. Cassidy & P. R. Shaver (Eds.), *Handbook of attachment*. New York: Guilford. (p. 195)

Kirsch, I. (2010). *The emperor's new drugs: Exploding the antidepressant myth*. New York: Basic Books. (pp. 36, 684)

Kirsch, I., Deacon, B. J., Huedo-Medina, T. B., Scoboria, A., Moore, T. J., & Johnson, B. T. (2008) Initial severity and antidepressant benefits: A meta-analysis of data submitted to the Food and Drug Administration. *Public Library of Science Medicine, 5*, e45. (p. 684)

Kirsch, I., Kong, J., Sadler, P., Spaeth, R., Cook, A., Kaptchuk, T. J., & Gollub, R. (2014). Expectancy and conditioning in placebo analgesia: Separate or connected processes? *Psychology of Consciousness; Theory, Research, and Practice, 1*, 51–59. (p. 684)

Kirsch, I., Moore, T. J., Scoboria, A., & Nicholls, S. S. (2002, July 15). New study finds little difference between effects of antidepressants and placebo. *Prevention and Treatment* (journals.apa.org/prevention). (p. 684)

Kirsch, I., & Sapirstein, G. (1998). Listening to Prozac but hearing placebo: A meta-analysis of antidepressant medication. *Prevention and Treatment, 1*, posted June 26 at (journals.apa.org/prevention/volume1). (p. 684)

Kisley, M. A., Wood, S., & Burrows, C. L. (2007). Looking at the sunny side of life: Age-related change in an event-related potential measure of the negativity bias. *Psychological Science, 18*, 838–843. (p. 224)

Kisor, H. (1990). *What's that pig outdoors*. New York: Hill and Wang. (p. 375)

Kitayama, S., Chua, H. F., Tompson, S., & Han, S. (2013). Neural mechanisms of dissonance: An fMRI investigation of choice justification. *NeuroImage, 69*, 206–212. (p. 523)

Kitayama, S., Conway, III, L. G., Pietromonaci, P. R., Park, H., & Plaut, V. C. (2010). Ethos of independence across regions in the United States: The production-adoption model of cultural change. *American Psychologist, 65*, 559–574. (pp. 157, 159)

Kitayama, S., Ishii, K., Imada, T., Takemura, K., & Ramaswamy, J. (2006). Voluntary settlement and the spirit of independence: Evidence from Japan's "northern frontier." *Journal of Personality and Social Psychology, 91*, 369–384. (p. 158)

Kitayama, S., Park, H., Sevincer, A. T., Karasawa, M., & Uskul, A. K. (2009). A cultural task analysis of implicit independence: Comparing North America, Western Europe, and East Asia. *Journal of Personality and Social Psychology, 97*, 236–255. (pp. 159, 518)

Kivimaki, M., Leino-Arjas, P., Luukkonen, R., Rihimaki, H., & Kirjonen, J. (2002). Work stress and risk of cardiovascular mortality: Prospective cohort study of industrial employees. *British Medical Journal, 325*, 857. (p. 501)

Klahr, A. M., & Burt, S. A. (2014). Elucidating the etiology of individual differences in parenting: A meta-analysis of behavioral genetic research. *Psychological Bulletin, 140*, 544–586. (p. 202)

Klauer, S. G., Feng, G., Simons-Morton, B. G., Ouimet, M. C., Lee, S. E., & Dingus, T. A. (2014). Distracted driving and risk of road crashes among novice and experienced drivers. *New England Journal of Medicine, 370*, 54–59. (p. 97)

Klayman, J., & Ha, Y-W. (1987). Confirmation, disconfirmation, and information in hypothesis testing. *Psychological Review, 94*, 211–228. (p. 357)

Klein, D. N. (2010). Chronic depression: Diagnosis and classification. *Current Directions in Psychological Science, 19*, 96–100. (p. 632)

Klein, D. N., et al. (2003). Therapeutic alliance in depression treatment: Controlling for prior change and patient characteristics. *Journal of Consulting and Clinical Psychology, 71*, 997–1006. (p. 679)

Kleinke, C. L. (1986). Gaze and eye contact: A research review. *Psychological Bulletin, 1000*, 78–100. (p. 468)

Kleinmuntz, B., & Szucko, J. J. (1984). A field study of the fallibility of polygraph lie detection. *Nature, 308*, 449–450. (p. 466)

Kleitman, N. (1960, November). Patterns of dreaming. *Scientific American*, pp. 82–88. (p. 101)

Klemm, W. R. (1990). Historical and introductory perspectives on brainstem-mediated behaviors. In W. R. Klemm & R. P. Vertes (Eds.), *Brainstem mechanisms of behavior*. New York: Wiley. (p. 69)

Klimstra, T. A., Hale, III, W. W., Raaijmakers, Q. A. W., Branje, S. J. T., & Meeus, W. H. J. (2009). Maturation of personality in adolescence. *Journal of Personality and Social Psychology, 96*, 898–912. (p. 210)

Kline, N. S. (1974). *From sad to glad*. New York: Ballantine Books. (p. 637)

Klinke, R., Kral, A., Heid, S., Tillein, J., & Hartmann, R. (1999). Recruitment of the auditory cortex in congenitally deaf cats by long-term cochlear electrostimulation. *Science, 285*, 1729–1733. (p. 259)

Kluft, R. P. (1991). Multiple personality disorder. In A. Tasman & S. M. Goldfinger (Eds.), *Review of Psychiatry* (Vol. 10). Washington, DC: American Psychiatric Press. (p. 648)

Klump, K. L., & Culbert, K. M. (2007). Molecular genetic studies of eating disorders: Current status and future directions. *Current Directions in Psychological Science, 16,* 37–41. (p. 652)

Klump, K. L., Suisman, J. L., Burt, S. A., McGue, M., & Iacono, W. G. (2009). Genetic and environmental influences on disordered eating: An adoption study. *Journal of Abnormal Psychology, 118,* 797–805. (p. 652)

Knapp, S., & VandeCreek, L. (2000, August). Recovered memories of childhood abuse: Is there an underlying professional consensus? *Professional Psychology: Research and Practice, 31,* 365–371. (p. 349)

Knickmeyer, E. (2001, August 7). In Africa, big is definitely better. *Seattle Times,* p. A7. (p. 652)

Knight, R. T. (2007). Neural networks debunk phrenology. *Science, 316,* 1578–1579. (p. 81)

Knight, W. (2004, August 2). Animated face helps deaf with phone chat. NewScientist. com. (p. 270)

Knoblich, G., & Oellinger, M. (2006, October/November). The Eureka moment. *Scientific American Mind,* pp. 38–43. (p. 357)

Knuts, I. J. E., Cosci, F., Esquivel, G., Goossens, L., van Duinen, M., Bareman, M., . . . & Schruers, K. R. J. (2010). Cigarette smoking and 35% CO_2 induced panic in panic disorder patients. *Journal of Affective Disorders, 124,* 215–218. (p. 621)

Ko, C-K., Yen, J-Y., Chen, C-C., Chen, S-H., & Yen, C-F. (2005). Proposed diagnostic criteria of Internet addiction for adolescents. *Journal of Nervous and Mental Disease, 193,* 728–733. (p. 118)

Koch, C., & Greenfield, S. (2007, October). How does consciousness happen? *Scientific American,* pp. 76–83. (p. 93)

Koenen, K. C., Moffitt, T. E., Roberts, A. L., Martin, L. T., Kubzansky, L., Harrington, H., Poulton, R., & Caspi, A. (2009). Childhood IQ and adult mental disorders: A test of the cognitive reserve hypothesis. *American Journal of Psychiatry, 166,* 50–57. (p. 404)

Koenig, H. G., King, D. E., & Carson, V. B. (2011). *Handbook of religion and health.* New York: Oxford University Press. (p. 511)

Koenig, H. G., & Larson, D. B. (1998). Use of hospital services, religious attendance, and religious affiliation. *Southern Medical Journal, 91,* 925–932. (p. 513)

Koenig, L. B., McGue, M., Krueger, R. F., & Bouchard, T. J., Jr. (2005). Genetic and environmental influences on religiousness: Findings for retrospective and current religiousness ratings. *Journal of Personality, 73,* 471–488. (p. 139)

Koenig, L. B., & Vaillant, G. E. (2009). A prospective study of church attendance and health over the lifespan. *Health Psychology, 28,* 117–124. (p. 512)

Koenigs, M., Young, L., Adolphs, R., Tranel, D., Cushman, F., Hauser, M., & Damasio, A. (2007). Damage to the prefrontal cortex increases utilitarian moral judgements. *Nature, 446,* 908–911. (p. 80)

Koestner, R., Lekes, N., Powers, T. A., & Chicoine, E. (2002). Attaining personal goals: Self-concordance plus implementation intentions equals success. *Journal of Personality and Social Psychology, 83,* 231–244. (p. A-11)

Kohlberg, L. (1981). *The philosophy of moral development: Essays on moral development* (Vol. I). San Francisco: Harper & Row. (p. 206)

Kohlberg, L. (1984). *The psychology of moral development: Essays on moral development* (Vol. II). San Francisco: Harper & Row. (p. 206)

Kohler, C. G., Walker, J. B., Martin, E. A., Healey, K. M., & Moberg, P. J. (2010). Facial emotion perception in schizophrenia: A meta-analytic review. *Schizophrenia Bulletin, 36,* 1009–1019. (p. 641)

Kohler, I. (1962, May). Experiments with goggles. *Scientific American,* pp. 62–72. (p. 255)

Köhler, W. (1925; reprinted 1957). *The mentality of apes.* London: Pelican. (p. 368)

Kolassa, I-T., & Elbert, T. (2007). Structural and functional neuroplasticity in relation to traumatic stress. *Current Directions in Psychological Science, 16,* 321–325. (p. 626)

Kolata, G. (1987). Metabolic catch-22 of exercise regimens. *Science, 236,* 146–147. (p. 432)

Kolb, B. (1989). Brain development, plasticity, and behavior. *American Psychologist, 44,* 1203–1212. (p. 81)

Kolb, B., & Whishaw, I. Q. (1998). Brain plasticity and behavior. *Annual Review of Psychology, 49,* 43–64. (p. 152)

Kolb, B., & Whishaw, I. Q. (2006). *An introduction to brain and behavior,* 2nd edition. New York: Worth Publishers. (p. 366)

Kolker, K. (2002, December 8). Video violence disturbs some: Others scoff at influence. *Grand Rapids Press,* pp. A1, A12. (p. 549)

Kolodziej, M. E., & Johnson, B. T. (1996). Interpersonal contact and acceptance of persons with psychiatric disorders: A research synthesis. *Journal of Consulting and Clinical Psychology, 64,* 1387–1396. (p. 616)

Koltko-Rivera, M. E. (2006). Rediscovering the later version of Maslow's hierarchy of needs: Self-transcendence and opportunities for theory, research, and unification. *Review of General Psychology, 10,* 302–317. (p. 423)

Komisaruk, B. R., & Whipple, B. (2011). Non-genital orgasms. *Sexual and Relationship Therapy, 26,* 356–372. (p. 438)

Konkle, T., Brady, T. F., Alvarez, G. A., & Oliva, A. (2010). Conceptual distinctiveness supports detailed visual long-term memory for real-world objects. *Journal of Experimental Psychology: General, 139,* 558–578. (p. 318)

Kontula, O., & Haavio-Mannila, E. (2009). The impact of aging on human sexual activity and sexual desire. *Journal of Sex Research, 46,* 46–56. (p. 214)

Koole, S. L., Greenberg, J., & Pyszczynski, T. (2006). Introducing science to the psychology of the soul. *Current Directions in Psychological Science, 15,* 212–216. (p. 581)

Kornell, N., & Bjork, R. A. (2008). Learning concepts and categories: Is spacing the "enemy of induction?" *Psychological Science, 19,* 585–592. (p. 15)

Kosfeld, M., Heinrichs, M., Zak, P. J., Fischbacher, U., & Fehr, E. (2005). Oxytocin increases trust in humans. *Nature, 435,* 673–676. (p. 64)

Kosslyn, S. M. (2005). Reflective thinking and mental imagery: A perspective on the development of posttraumatic stress disorder. *Development and Psychopathology, 17,* 851–863. (p. 623)

Kosslyn, S. M., & Koenig, O. (1992). *Wet mind: The new cognitive neuroscience.* New York: Free Press. (p. 62)

Kotchick, B. A., Shaffer, A., & Forehand, R. (2001). Adolescent sexual risk behavior: A multi-system perspective. *Clinical Psychology Review, 21,* 493–519. (p. 439)

Koten, J. W., Jr., Wood, G., Hagoort, P., Goebel, R., Propping, P., Willmes, K., & Boomsma, D. I. (2009). Genetic contribution to variation in cognitive function: An fMRI study in twins. *Science, 323,* 1737–1740. (p. 406)

Kotkin, M., Daviet, C., & Gurin, J. (1996). The *Consumer Reports* mental health survey. *American Psychologist, 51,* 1080–1082. (p. 673)

Koudenburg, N., Postmes, T. & Gordijn, E. (2011). If they were to vote, they would vote for us. *Psychological Science, 22,* 1506–1510. (p. 602)

Kouider, S., Stahlhut, C., Gelskov, S. V., Barbosa, L. S., Dutat, M., de Gardelle, V., . . . Dehaene-Lambertz, G. (2013). A neural marker of perceptual consciousness in infants. *Science, 340,* 376–380. (p. 186)

Kounios, J., & Beeman, M. (2009). The *Aha!* moment: The cognitive neuroscience of insight. *Current Directions in Psychological Science, 18,* 210–215. (p. 357)

Kovács, Á. M., Téglás, E., & Endress, A. D. (2010). The social sense: Susceptibility to others' beliefs in human infants and adults. *Science, 330,* 1830–1834. (p. 190)

Kposowa, A. J., & D'Auria, S. (2009). Association of temporal factors and suicides in the United States, 2000–2004. *Social Psychiatry and Psychiatric Epidemiology, 45,* 433–445. (p. 638)

Kraft, C. (1978). A psychophysical approach to air safety: Simulator studies of visual illusions in night approaches. In H. L. Pick, H. W. Leibowitz, J. E. Singer, A. Steinschneider, & H. W. Stevenson (Eds.), *Psychology: From research to practice.* New York: Plenum Press. (pp. A-14, A-15)

Kraft, R. N. (2002). *Memory perceived: Recalling the Holocaust.* Westport, CT: Praeger. (p. 349)

Kraft, T., & Pressman, S. (2012). Grin and bear it: The influence of the manipulated facial expression on the stress response. *Psychological Science, 23,* 137–1378. (p. 474)

Kramer, A. D. I. (2012). The spread of emotion via Facebook. *Proceedings of the SIGCHI Conference on Human Factors in Computing Systems.* ACM (Association for Computing Machinery), New York, 767–770. (p. 475)

Kramer, A. D. I., & Chung, C. K. (2011). Dimensions of self-expression in Facebook status updates. *Proceedings of the Fifth International AAAI Conference on Weblogs and Social Media* (www.aaai.org). (p. 538)

Kramer, M. S., et al. (2008). Breastfeeding and child cognitive development: New evidence from a large randomized trial. *Archives of General Psychiatry, 65,* 578–584. (p. 36)

Kramer, P. D. (2011, July 9). In defense of antidepressants. *New York Times* (www. nytimes.com). (p. 683)

Kranz, F., & Ishai, A. (2006). Face perception is modulated by sexual preference. *Current Biology, 16,* 63–68. (p. 443)

Kraul, C. (2010, October 12). Chief engineer knew it would take a miracle. *Los Angeles Times* (www.latimes.com). (p. 272)

Kraus, N., Malmfors, T., & Slovic, P. (1992). Intuitive toxicology: Expert and lay judgments of chemical risks. *Risk Analysis, 12,* 215–232. (p. 363)

Kraut, R., Patterson, M., Lundmark, V., Kiesler, S., Mukopadhyay, T., & Scherlis, W. (1998). Internet paradox: A social technology that reduces social involvement and psychological well being? *American Psychologist, 53,* 1017–1031. (p. 452)

KRC Research & Consulting. (2001, August 7). Memory isn't quite what it used to be (survey for General Nutrition Centers). *USA Today,* p. D1. (p. 217)

Kring, A. M., & Caponigro, J. M. (2010). Emotion in schizophrenia: Where feeling meets thinking. *Current Directions in Psychological Science, 19,* 255–259. (p. 641)

Kring, A. M., & Gordon, A. H. (1998). Sex differences in emotion: Expression, experience, and physiology. *Journal of Personality and Social Psychology, 74,* 686–703. (p. 471)

Kringelbach, M. L., & Berridge, K. C. (2012, August). The joyful mind. *Scientific American,* pp. 40–45. (p. 73)

Kristeller, J. L., Baer, R. A., & Quillian-Wolever, R. (2006). Mindfulness-based approaches to eating disorders. In R. A. Baer (Ed.), *Mindfulness-based treatment approaches: A clinician's guide to evidence base and applications.* San Diego, CA: Academic Press. (p. 511)

Kristensen, P., & Bjerkedal, T. (2007). Explaining the relation between birth order and intelligence. *Science, 316,* 1717. (p. 47)

Kristof, N. D. (2004, July 21). Saying no to killers. *New York Times* (www.nytimes.com). (p. 558)

Kristof, N. D. (2010, September 18). Message to Muslims: I'm sorry. *New York Times* (www.nytimes.com). (p. 539)

Kroes, M. C. W., Tendolkar, I., van Wingen, G. A., van Waarde, J. A., Strange, B. A., & Fernández, G. (2014). An electroconvulsive therapy procedure impairs reconsolidation of episodic memories in humans. *Nature Neuroscience, 17,* 204–206. (p. 344)

Kroll, J. F., & Bialystok, E. (2013). Understanding the consequences of bilingualism for language processing and cognition. *Journal of Cognitive Psychology, 25,* 497–514. (p. 381)

Kroll, J. F., Bobb, S. C., & Hoshino, N. (2014). Two languages in mind: Bilingualism as a tool to investigate language, cognition, and the brain. *Current Directions in Psychological Science, 23,* 159–163. (p. 381)

Kross, E., & Ayduk, O. (2011). Making meaning out of negative experiences by self-distancing. *Current Directions in Psychological Science, 20,* 187–191. (p. 478)

Kross, E., Berman, M. G., Mischel, W., Smith, E. E., & Wager, T. D. (2011). Social rejection shares somatosensory representations with physical pain. *PNAS, 108,* 6270–6275. (p. 450)

Krueger, J., & Killham, E. (2005, December 8). At work, feeling good matters. *Gallup Management Journal* (www.gmj.gallup.com). (p. A-11)

Krueger, J., & Killham, E. (2006, March 9). Why Dilbert is right. Uncomfortable work environments make for disgruntled employees—just like the cartoon says. *Gallup Management Journal* (www.gmj.gallup.com). (p. 502)

Kruger, J., & Dunning, D. (1999). Unskilled and unaware of it: How difficulties in recognizing one's own incompetence lead to inflated self-assessments. *Journal of Personality and Social Psychology, 77,* 1121–1134. (p. 600)

Kruger, J., Epley, N., Parker, J., & Ng, Z-W. (2005). Egocentrism over e-mail: Can we communicate as well as we think? *Journal of Personality and Social Psychology, 89,* 925–936. (pp. 190, 470)

Krumhansl, C. L. (2010). Plink: "Thin slices" of music. *Music Perception, 27,* 337–354. (p. 318)

Krupa, D. J., Thompson, J. K., & Thompson, R. F. (1993). Localization of a memory trace in the mammalian brain. *Science, 260,* 989–991. (p. 330)

Krützen, M., Mann, J., Heithaus, M. R., Connor, R. C., Bejder, L., & Sherwin, W. B. (2005). Cultural transmission of tool use in bottlenose dolphins. *Proceedings of the National Academy of Sciences, 102,* 8939–8943. (p. 368)

Kubo, K., Okanoya, K., & Kawai, N. (2012). Apology isn't good enough: An apology suppresses an approach motivation but not the physiological and psychological anger. *PLOS One, 7,* e33006. (p. 477)

Kubzansky, L. D., Koenen, K. C., Jones, C., & Eaton, W. W. (2009). A prospective study of posttraumatic stress disorder symptoms and coronary heart disease in women. *Health Psychology, 28,* 125–130. (p. 498)

Kubzansky, L. D., Sparrow, D., Vokanas, P., & Kawachi, I. (2001). Is the glass half empty or half full? A prospective study of optimism and coronary heart disease in the normative aging study. *Psychosomatic Medicine, 63,* 910–916. (p. 498)

Kuhl, P. K., & Meltzoff, A. N. (1982). The bimodal perception of speech in infancy. *Science, 218,* 1138–1141. (p. 371)

Kuhn, D. (2006). Do cognitive changes accompany developments in the adolescent brain? *Perspectives on Psychological Science, 1,* 59–67. (p. 205)

Kuhnle, C., Hofer, M., & Kilian, B. (2012). Self-control as predictor of school grades, life balance, and flow in adolescents. *British Journal of Educational Psychology, 82,* 533–548. (p. 503)

Kumar, A. & Gilovich, T. (2013). *Talking about what you did and what you have: The differential story utility of experiential and material purchases.* Manuscript submitted for publication, Cornell University. (p. 486)

Kuncel, N. R., & Hezlett, S. A. (2007). Standardized tests predict graduate students' success. *Science, 315,* 1080–1081. (p. 398)

Kuncel, N. R., & Hezlett, S. A. (2010). Fact and fiction in cognitive ability testing for admissions and hiring decisions. *Current Directions in Psychological Science, 19,* 339–345. (p. 389)

Kunkel, D. (2001, February 4). *Sex on TV.* Menlo Park, CA: Henry J. Kaiser Family Foundation (www.kff.org). (p. 439)

Kuntsche, E., Knibbe, R., Gmel, G., & Engels, R. (2005). Why do young people drink? A review of drinking motives. *Clinical Psychology Review, 25,* 841–861. (p. 128)

Kupfer, D. J. (2012, June 1). Dr Kupfer defends DSM-5. www.medscape.com/viewarticle/764735. (p. 614)

Kuppens, P., Allen, N. B., & Sheeber, L. B. (2010). Emotional inertia and psychological maladjustment. *Psychological Science, 21,* 984–991. (p. 635)

Kupper, N., & Denollet, J. (2007). Type D personality as a prognostic factor in heart disease: Assessment and mediating mechanisms. *Journal of Personality Assessment, 89,* 265–276. (p. 497)

Kurdziel, L., Duclos, K., & Spencer, R. M. C. (2013). Sleep spindles in midday naps enhance learning in preschool children. *PNAS, 110,* 17267–17272. (p. 106)

Kushner, M. G., Kim, S. W., Conahue, C., Thuras, P., Adson, D., Kotlyar, M., . . . & Foa, E. B. (2007). D-cycloserine augmented exposure therapy for obsessive-compulsive disorder. *Biological Psychiatry, 62,* 835–838. (p. 683)

Kuster, F., Orth, U., & Meier, L. L. (2012). Rumination mediates the prospective effect of low self-esteem on depression: A five-wave longitudinal study. *Personality and Social Psychology Bulletin, 38,* 747–759. (pp. 634, 635)

Kutas, M. (1990). Event-related brain potential (ERP) studies of cognition during sleep: Is it more than a dream? In R. R. Bootzin, J. F. Kihlstrom, & D. Schacter (Eds.), *Sleep and cognition.* Washington, DC: American Psychological Association. (p. 100)

Kutcher, E. J., & Bragger, J. D. (2004). Selection interviews of overweight job applicants: Can structure reduce the bias? *Journal of Applied Social Psychology, 34,* 1993–2022. (p. A-6)

Kuttler, A. F., La Greca, A. M., & Prinstein, M. J. (1999). Friendship qualities and social-emotional functioning of adolescents with close, cross-sex friendships. *Journal of Research on Adolescence, 9,* 339–366. (p. 164)

Kvavilashvili, L., Mirani, J., Schlagman, S., Foley, K. & Kornbrot, D. E. (2009). Consistency of flashbulb memories of September 11 over long delays: Implications for consolidation and wrong time slice hypotheses. *Journal of Memory and Language, 61,* 556–572. (p. 332)

Kwon, P. (2013). Resilience in lesbian, gay, and bisexual individuals. *Personality and Social Psychology Review, 17,* 371–383. (p. 441)

Kyaga, S., Landén, M., Boman, M., Hultman, C. M., Långström, N., Lichtenstein, P. (2013). Mental illness, suicide, and creativity: 40-year prospective total population study. *Journal of Psychiatric Research, 47,* 83–90. (p. 630)

Laceulle, O. M., Ormel, J., Aggen, S. H., Neale, N. C., & Kendler, K. S. (2011), Genetic and environmental influences on the longitudinal structure of neuroticism: A trait-state approach. *Psychological Science, 24,* 1780–1790. (p. 136)

Lacey, H. P., Smith, D. M., & Ubel, P. A. (2006). Hope I die before I get old: Mispredicting happiness across the lifespan. *Journal of Happiness Studies, 7,* 167–182. (p. 223)

Lacey, M. (2010, December 11). He found bag of cash, but did the unexpected. *New York Times* (www.nytimes.com). (p. 561)

Lachman, M. E. (2004). Development in midlife. *Annual Review of Psychology, 55,* 305–331. (p. 220)

Ladd, G. T. (1887). *Elements of physiological psychology.* New York: Scribner's. (p. 92)

Laeng, B., & Sulutvedt, U. (2014). The eye pupil adjusts to imaginary light. *Psychological Science, 25,* 188–197. (p. 240)

Lafleur, D. L., Pittenger, C., Kelmendi, B., Gardner, T., Wasylink, S., Malison, R. T., . . . Coric, V. (2006). N-acetylcysteine augmentation in serotonin reuptake inhibitor refractory obsessive-compulsive disorder. *Psychopharmacology, 184*, 254–256. (p. 626)

Laird, J. D. (1974). Self-attribution of emotion: The effects of expressive behavior on the quality of emotional experience. *Journal of Personality and Social Psychology, 29*, 475–486. (p. 474)

Laird, J. D. (1984). The real role of facial response in the experience of emotion: A reply to Tourangeau and Ellsworth, and others. *Journal of Personality and Social Psychology, 47*, 909–917. (p. 474)

Laird, J. D., Cuniff, M., Sheehan, K., Shulman, D., & Strum, G. (1989). Emotion specific effects of facial expressions on memory for life events. *Journal of Social Behavior and Personality, 4*, 87–98. (p. 474)

Lally, P., Van Jaarsveld, C. H. M., Potts, H. W. W., & Wardle, J. (2010). How are habits formed: Modelling habit formation in the real world. *European Journal of Social Psychology, 40*, 998–1009. (p. 280)

Lam, C. B., & McBride-Chang, C. A. (2007). Resilience in young adulthood: The moderating influences of gender-related personality traits and coping flexibility. *Sex Roles, 56*, 159–172. (p. 169)

Lam, R. W., Levitt, A. J., Levitan, R. D., Enns, M. W., Morehouse, R., Michalak, E. E., & Tam, E. M. (2006). The Can-SAD study: A randomized controlled trial of the effectiveness of light therapy and fluoxetine in patients with winter seasonal affective disorder. *American Journal of Psychiatry, 163*, 805–812. (p. 678)

Lambert, J-C., et al. (2013). Meta-analysis of 74,046 individuals identifies 11 new susceptibility loci for Alzheimer's disease. *Nature Genetics, 45*, 1452–1458. (p. 219)

Lambert, N. M., DeWall, C. N., Bushman, B. J., Tillman, T. F., Fincham, F. D., Pond, Jr., R. S., & Gwinn, A. M. (2011). *Lashing out in lust: Effect of pornography on nonsexual, physical aggression against relationship partners.* Paper presentation at the Society for Personality and Social Psychology convention. (p. 549)

Lambert, W. E. (1992). Challenging established views on social issues: The power and limitations of research. *American Psychologist, 47*, 533–542. (p. 381)

Lambert, W. E., Genesee, F., Holobow, N., & Chartrand, L. (1993). Bilingual education for majority English-speaking children. *European Journal of Psychology of Education, 8*, 3–22. (p. 381)

Lambird, K. H., & Mann, T. (2006). When do ego threats lead to self-regulation failure? Negative consequences of defensive high self-esteem. *Personality and Social Psychology Bulletin, 32*, 1177–1187. (p. 605)

Landau, E., Verjee, Z., & Mortensen, A. (2014, February 24). Uganda president: Homosexuals are 'disgusting.' CNN (www.cnn.com). (p. 446)

Landau, M. J., Oyserman, D., Keefer, L. A., & Smith, G. C. (2014). The college journey and academic engagement: How metaphor use enhances identity-based motivation. *Journal of Personality and Social Psychology, 106*, 679–698. (p. 598)

Landauer, T. (2001, September). Quoted by R. Herbert, You must remember this. *APS Observer*, p. 11. (p. 350)

Landberg, J., & Norström, T. (2011). Alcohol and homicide in Russia and the United States: A comparative analysis. *Journal of Studies on Alcohol and Drugs, 72*, 723–730. (p. 546)

Landry, M. J. (2002). MDMA: A review of epidemiologic data. *Journal of Psychoactive Drugs, 34*, 163–169. (p. 124)

Lange, N., & McDougle, C. J. (2013, October). Help for the child with autism. *Scientific American*, pp. 72–77. (p. 194)

Langer, E. J. (1983). *The psychology of control.* Beverly Hills, CA: Sage. (p. 502)

Langer, E. J., & Abelson, R. P. (1974). A patient by any other name . . .: Clinician group differences in labeling bias. *Journal of Consulting and Clinical Psychology, 42*, 4–9. (p. 614)

Langer, E. J., & Imber, L. (1980). The role of mindlessness in the perception of deviance. *Journal of Personality and Social Psychology, 39*, 360–367. (p. 614)

Langleben, D. D., Dattilio, F. M., & Gutheil, T. G. (2006). True lies: Delusions and lie-detection technology. *Journal of Psychiatry and Law, 34*, 351–370. (p. 467)

Langleben, D. D., Schroeder, L., Maldjian, J. A., Gur, R. C., McDonald, S., Ragland, J. D., O'Brien, C. P., & Childress, A. R. (2002). Brain activity during simulated deception: An event-related functional magnetic resonance study. *NeuroImage, 15*, 727–732. (p. 467)

Langlois, J. H., Kalakanis, L., Rubenstein, A. J., Larson, A., Hallam, M., & Smoot, M. (2000). Maxims or myths of beauty? A meta-analytic and theoretical review. *Psychological Bulletin, 126*, 390–423. (p. 554)

Langlois, J. H., & Roggman, L. A. (1990). Attractive faces are only average. *Psychological Science, 1*, 115–121. (p. 555)

Langlois, J. H., Roggman, L. A., Casey, R. J., Ritter, J. M., Rieser-Danner, L. A., & Jenkins, V. Y. (1987). Infant preferences for attractive faces: Rudiments of a stereotype? *Developmental Psychology, 23*, 363–369. (p. 554)

Langmeyer, A., Guglhör-Rudan, A., & Tarnai, C. (2012). What do music preferences reveal about personality? A cross-cultural replication using self-ratings and ratings of music samples. *Journal of Individual Differences, 33*, 119–130. (p. 593)

Långström, N. H., Rahman, Q., Carlström, E., & Lichtenstein, P. (2010). Genetic and environmental effects on same-sex sexual behavior: A population study of twins in Sweden. *Archives of Sexual Behavior, 39*, 75–80. (p. 443)

Långström, N. H., Rahman, Q., Carlström, E., & Lichtenstein, P. (2008). Genetic and environmental effects on same-sex sexual behavior: A population study of twins in Sweden. *Archives of Sexual Behavior.* (p. 443)

Lankford, A. (2009). Promoting aggression and violence at Abu Ghraib: The U.S. military's transformation of ordinary people into torturers. *Aggression and Violent Behavior, 14*, 388–395. (p. 531)

Larkin, J. E., Brasel, A. M., & Pines, H. A. (2013). Cross-disciplinary applications of I/O psychology concepts: Predicting student retention and employee turnover. *Review of General Psychology, 17*, 82–92. (p. A-11)

Larkin, K., Resko, J. A., Stormshak, F., Stellflug, J. N., & Roselli, C. E. (2002). Neuroanatomical correlates of sex and sexual partner preference in sheep. Paper presented at Society for Neuroscience convention. (p. 443)

Larrick, R. P., Timmerman, T. A., & Carton, A. M., & Abrevaya, J. (2011). Temper, temperature, and temptation: Heat-related retaliation in baseball. *Psychological Science, 22*, 423–428. (p. 547)

Larsen, R. J., & Diener, E. (1987). Affect intensity as an individual difference characteristic: A review. *Journal of Research in Personality, 21*, 1–39. (pp. 140, 463)

Larson, R. W., & Verma, S. (1999). How children and adolescents spend time across the world: Work, play, and developmental opportunities. *Psychological Bulletin, 125*, 701–736. (p. 412)

Larzelere, R. E. (2000). Child outcomes of non-abusive and customary physical punishment by parents: An updated literature review. *Clinical Child and Family Psychology Review, 3*, 199–221. (p. 296)

Larzelere, R. E., & Kuhn, B. R. (2005). Comparing child outcomes of physical punishment and alternative disciplinary tactics: A meta-analysis. *Clinical Child and Family Psychology Review, 8*, 1–37. (p. 296)

Larzelere, R. E., Kuhn, B. R., & Johnson, B. (2004). The intervention selection bias: An underrecognized confound in intervention research. *Psychological Bulletin, 130*, 289–303. (p. 296)

Lashley, K. S. (1950). In search of the engram. In *Symposium of the Society for Experimental Biology* (Vol. 4). New York: Cambridge University Press. (p. 329)

Lassiter, G. D., & Irvine, A. A. (1986). Video-taped confessions: The impact of camera point of view on judgments of coercion. *Journal of Personality and Social Psychology, 16*, 268–276. (p. 519)

Lassiter, G. D., Lindberg, M. JH., Gonzáles-Vallego, C., Bellezza, F. S., & Phillips, N. D. (2009). The deliberation-without-attention effect: Evidence for an artifactual interpretation. *Psychological Science, 20*, 671–675. (p. 365)

Latané, B. (1981). The psychology of social impact. *American Psychologist, 36*, 343–356. (p. 533)

Latané, B., & Dabbs, J. M., Jr. (1975). Sex, group size and helping in three cities. *Sociometry, 38*, 180–194. (p. 560)

Latané, B., & Nida, S. (1981). Ten years of research on group size and helping. *Psychological Bulletin, 89*, 308–324. (p. 533)

Latham, G. P., & Locke, E. A. (2007). New developments in and directions for goal-setting research. *European Psychologist, 12*, 290–300. (p. A-11)

Laudenslager, M. L., & Reite, M. L. (1984). Losses and separations: Immunological consequences and health implications. *Review of Personality and Social Psychology, 5*, 285–312. (p. 501)

Laumann, E. O., Gagnon, J. H., Michael, R. T., & Michaels, S. (1994). *The social organization of sexuality: Sexual practices in the United States.* Chicago: University of Chicago Press. (p. 148)

Launay, J. M., Mouillet-Richard, S., Baudry, A., Pietri, M., & Kellermann, O. (2011). Raphe-mediated signals control the hippocampal response to SRI antidepressants via miR-16. *Translational Psychiatry, 1*(11), e56. (p. 684)

Laws, K. R., & Kokkalis, J. (2007). Ecstasy (MDMA) and memory function: A meta-analytic update. *Human Psychopharmacology: Clinical and Experimental, 22*, 381–388. (p. 124)

Layous, K., & Lyubomirsky, S. (2014). The how, who, what, when, and why of happiness: Mechanisms underlying the success of positive activity interventions. In J. Gruber & J. T. Moskowitz (Eds.), *Positive emotions: Integrating the light and dark sides*. New York: Oxford University Press. (p. 486)

Lazaruk, W. (2007). Linguistic, academic, and cognitive benefits of French immersion. *Canadian Modern Language Review, 63,* 605–628. (p. 381)

Lazarus, R. S. (1990). Theory-based stress measurement. *Psychological Inquiry, 1,* 3–13. (p. 490)

Lazarus, R. S. (1991). Progress on a cognitive-motivational-relational theory of emotion. *American Psychologist, 46,* 352–367. (p. 463)

Lazarus, R. S. (1998). *Fifty years of the research and theory of R. S. Lazarus: An analysis of historical and perennial issues.* Mahwah, NJ: Erlbaum. (pp. 488, 463)

Lazer, D., et al. (2009). Computational social science. *Science, 323,* 721–723. (p. 535)

Lea, S. E. G. (2000). Towards an ethical use of animals. *The Psychologist, 13,* 556–557. (p. 40)

Leaper, C., & Ayres, M. M. (2007). A meta-analytic review of gender variations in adults' language use: Talkativeness, affiliative speech, and assertive speech. *Personality and Social Psychology Review, 11,* 328–363. (p. 163)

Leary, M. R. (1999). The social and psychological importance of self-esteem. In R. M. Kowalski & M. R. Leary (Eds.), *The social psychology of emotional and behavioral problems.* Washington, DC: APA Books. (p. 599)

Leary, M. R. (2012). Sociometer theory. In L. Van Lange, A. W. Kruglanski, & E. T. Higgins (Eds.), *Handbook of theories of social psychology* (Vol. 2, pp. 141-159). Los Angeles: Sage Publications. (p. 449)

Leask, S. J., & Beaton, A. A. (2007). Handedness in Great Britain. *Laterality, 12,* 559–572. (p. 86)

LeDoux, J. (1996). The emotional brain: The mysterious underpinnings of emotional life. New York: Simon & Schuster. (p. 330)

LeDoux, J. (2009, July/August). Quoted by K. McGowan, Out of the past. *Discover,* pp. 28–37. (p. 343)

LeDoux, J. E. (2002). *The synaptic self.* London: Macmillan. (pp. 153, 462)

LeDoux, J. E., & Armony, J. (1999). Can neurobiology tell us anything about human feelings? In D. Kahneman, E. Diener, & N. Schwartz (Eds.), *Well-being: The foundations of hedonic psychology.* New York: Sage. (p. 463)

Lee, C. S., Therriault, D. J., & Linderholm, T. (2012). On the cognitive benefits of cultural experience: Exploring the relationship between studying abroad and creative thinking. *Applied Cognitive Psychology, 26,* 768–778. (p. 367)

Lee, J. D. (2008). Fifty years of driving safety research. *Human Factors, 50,* 521–528. (p. A-14)

Lee, J. D. (2009). Can technology get your eyes back on the road? *Science, 324,* 344–346. (p. 97)

Lee, L., Frederick, S., & Ariely, D. (2006). Try it, you'll like it: The influence of expectation, consumption, and revelation on preferences for beer. *Psychological Science, 17,* 1054–1058. (p. 236)

Lee, P. S. N., Leung, L., Lo, V., Xiong, C., & Wu, T. (2011). Internet communication versus face-to-face interaction in quality of life. *Social Indicators Research, 100,* 375–389. (p. 453)

Lee, S. W. S., & Schwarz, N. (2012). Bidirectionality, mediation, and moderation of metaphorical effects: The embodiment of social suspicious and fishy smells. *Journal of Personality and Social Psychology, 103,* 737–749. (p. 268)

Lee, S. W. S., Schwarz, N., Taubman, D., & Hou, M. (2010). Sneezing in times of a flu pandemic: Public sneezing increases perception of unrelated risks and shifts preferences for federal spending. *Psychological Science, 21,* 375–377. (p. 360)

Lefcourt, H. M. (1982). *Locus of control: Current trends in theory and research.* Hillsdale, NJ: Erlbaum. (p. 503)

Lehman, A. F., Steinwachs, D. M., Dixon, L. B., Goldman, H. H., Osher, F., Postrado, L., . . . Zito, J. (1998). Translating research into practice: The schizophrenic patient outcomes research team (PORT) treatment recommendations. *Schizophrenia Bulletin, 24,* 1–10. (p. 682)

Lehman, D. R., Wortman, C. B., & Williams, A. F. (1987). Long-term effects of losing a spouse or child in a motor vehicle crash. *Journal of Personality and Social Psychology, 52,* 218–231. (p. 225)

Leichsenring, F., & Rabung, S. (2008). Effectiveness of long-term psychodynamic psychotherapy: A meta-analysis. *JAMA, 300,* 1551–1565. (p. 676)

Leitenberg, H., & Henning, K. (1995). Sexual fantasy. *Psychological Bulletin, 117,* 469–496. (pp. 434, 438)

Lemonick, M. D. (2002, June 3). Lean and hungrier. *Time,* p. 54. (p. 426)

L'Engle, M. (1972). *A Circle of Quiet.* New York: HarperCollins. (p. 415)

L'Engle, M. (1973). *A Wind in the Door,* 87. New York: Farrar, Straus and Giroux. (p. 20)

Lenhart, A. (2012, March 19). Teens, smartphones & texting. Pew Internet & American Life Project (www.pewinternet.org). (pp. 163, 452)

Lennox, B. R., Bert, S., Park, G., Jones, P. B., & Morris, P. G. (1999). Spatial and temporal mapping of neural activity associated with auditory hallucinations. *Lancet, 353,* 644. (p. 78)

Lenton, A. P., & Francesconi, M. (2010). How humans cognitively manage an abundance of mate options. *Psychological Science, 21,* 528–533. (p. 553)

Lenzenweger, M. F., Dworkin, R. H., & Wethington, E. (1989). Models of positive and negative symptoms in schizophrenia: An empirical evaluation of latent structures. *Journal of Abnormal Psychology, 98,* 62–70. (p. 682)

Leonhard, C., & Randler, C. (2009). In sync with the family: Children and partners influence the sleep-wake circadian rhythm and social habits of women. *Chronobiology International, 26,* 510–525. (p. 101)

LePort, A. K. R., Mattfeld, A. T., Dickinson-Anson, H., Fallon, J. H., Stark, C. E. L., Kruggel, F., Cahill, L., & McGaugh, J. L. (2012). Behavioral and neuroanatomical investigation of highly superior autobiographical memory (HSAM). *Neurobiology of Learning and Memory, 98,* 78–92. (p. 338)

Leslie, M. (2011). Are telomere tests ready for prime time? *Science, 322,* 414–415. (p. 216)

Lessard, N., Pare, M., Lepore, F., & Lassonde, M. (1998). Early-blind human subjects localize sound sources better than sighted subjects. *Nature, 395,* 278–280. (p. 375)

Leucht, S., Barnes, T. R. E., Kissling, W., Engel, R. R., Correll, C., & Kane, J. M. (2003). Relapse prevention in schizophrenia with new-generation antipsychotics: A systematic review and exploratory meta-analysis of randomized, controlled trials. *American Journal of Psychiatry, 160,* 1209–1222. (p. 682)

Leuthardt, E. C., Schalk, G., Roland, J., Rouse, A., & Moran, D.W. (2009). Evolution of brain-computer interfaces: Going beyond classic motor physiology. *Neurosurgical Focus, 27,* p. E4. (p. 77)

LeVay, S. (1991). A difference in hypothalamic structure between heterosexual and homosexual men. *Science, 253,* 1034–1037. (p. 443)

LeVay, S. (1994, March). Quoted in D. Nimmons, Sex and the brain. *Discover,* p. 64–71. (p. 443)

LeVay, S. (2011). *Gay, straight, and the reason why: The science of sexual orientation.* New York: Oxford University Press. (pp. 444, 445)

Levin, R., & Nielsen, T. A. (2007). Disturbed dreaming, posttraumatic stress disorder, and affect distress: A review and neurocognitive model. *Psychological Bulletin, 133,* 482–528. (p. 112)

Levin, R., & Nielsen, T. A. (2009). Nightmares, bad dreams, and emotion dysregulation. *Current Directions in Psychological Science, 18,* 84–87. (p. 112)

Levine, D. (2012, November 27). Treating sleep improves psychiatric symptoms. *Scientific American* (www.sciam.com). (p. 111)

Levine, J. A., Lanningham-Foster, L. M., McCrady, S. K., Krizan, A. C., Olson, L. R., Kane, P. H., Jensen, M. D., & Clark, M. M. (2005). Interindividual variation in posture allocation: Possible role in human obesity. *Science, 307,* 584–586. (p. 430)

Levine, R., Sato, S., Hashimoto, T., & Verma, J. (1995). Love and marriage in eleven cultures. *Journal of Cross-Cultural Psychology, 26,* 554–571. (p. 557)

Levine, R. V., & Norenzayan, A. (1999). The pace of life in 31 countries. *Journal of Cross-Cultural Psychology, 30,* 178–205. (pp. 30, 156)

Levinson, D. F., et al. (2011). Copy number variants in schizophrenia: Confirmation of five previous findings and new evidence for 3q29 microdeletions and VIPR2 duplications. *American Journal of Psychiatry, 168,* 302–316. (p. 644)

Levy, B., & Langer, E. (1992). *Avoidance of the memory loss stereotype: Enhanced memory among the elderly deaf.* Paper presented at American Psychological Association convention, Washington, DC. (p. 375)

Levy, P. E. (2003). *Industrial/organizational psychology: Understanding the workplace.* Boston: Houghton Mifflin. (p. A-7)

Lewald, J. (2007). More accurate sound localisation induced by short-term light deprivation. *Neuropsychologia, 45,* 1215–1222. (p. 375)

Lewandowski, G. W., Jr., Aron, A., & Gee, J. (2007). Personality goes a long way: The malleability of opposite-sex physical attractiveness. *Personality Relationships, 14,* 571–585. (p. 555)

Lewicki, P. (1985). Nonconscious biasing effects of single instances on subsequent judgments. *Journal of Personality and Social Psychology, 48,* 563–574. (p. 334)

Lewinsohn, P. M., Hoberman, H., Teri, L., & Hautziner, M. (1985). An integrative theory of depression. In S. Reiss & R. Bootzin (Eds.), *Theoretical issues in behavior therapy.* Orlando, FL: Academic Press. (p. 631)

Lewinsohn, P. M., Petit, J., Joiner, T. E., Jr., & Seeley, J. R. (2003). The symptomatic expression of major depressive disorder in adolescents and young adults. *Journal of Abnormal Psychology, 112,* 244–252. (p. 631)

Lewinsohn, P. M., Rohde, P., & Seeley, J. R. (1998). Major depressive disorder in older adolescents: Prevalence, risk factors, and clinical implications. *Clinical Psychology Review, 18,* 765–794. (p. 631)

Lewinsohn, P. M., & Rosenbaum, M. (1987). Recall of parental behavior by acute depressives, remitted depressives, and nondepressives. *Journal of Personality and Social Psychology, 52,* 611–619. (p. 336)

Lewis, C. S. (1960). *Mere Christianity.* New York: Macmillan. (p. 4)

Lewis, C. S. (1967). *Christian reflections.* Grand Rapids, MI: Eerdmans. (p. 339)

Lewis, D. O., Pincus, J. H., Bard, B., Richardson, E., Prichep, L. S., Feldman, M., & Yeager, C. (1988). Neuropsychiatric, psychoeducational, and family characteristics of 14 juveniles condemned to death in the United States. *American Journal of Psychiatry, 145,* 584–589. (p. 200)

Lewis, D. O., Yeager, C. A., Swica, Y., Pincus, J. H., & Lewis, M. (1997). Objective documentation of child abuse and dissociation in 12 murderers with dissociative identity disorder. *American Journal of Psychiatry, 154,* 1703–1710. (p. 648)

Lewis, M. (1992). Commentary. *Human Development, 35,* 44–51. (p. 336)

Lewontin, R. (1976). Race and intelligence. In N. J. Block & G. Dworkin (Eds.), *The IQ controversy: Critical readings.* New York: Pantheon. (p. 412)

Lewontin, R. (1982). *Human diversity.* New York: Scientific American Library. (p. 146)

Li, C-M., Zhang, X., Hoffman, H. J., Cotch, M. F., Themann, C. L., & Wilson, M. R. (2014). Hearing impairment associated with depression in U.S. adults, National health and Nutrition Examination Survey 2005–2010. *JAMA Otolaryngology—Head & Neck Surgery, 140,* 293–302. (p. 219)

Li, J. C., Dunning, D., & Malpass, R. L. (1996). *Cross-racial identification among European-Americans basketball fandom and the contact hypothesis.* Unpublished manuscript, Cornell University. (p. 544)

Li, J., Laursen, T. M., Precht, D. H., Olsen, J., & Mortensen, P. B. (2005). Hospitalization for mental illness among parents after the death of a child. *New England Journal of Medicine, 352,* 1190–1196. (p. 225)

Li, N., & DiCarlo, J. J. (2008). Unsupervised natural experience rapidly alters invariant object representation in visual cortex. *Science, 321,* 1502–1506. (p. 252)

Li, T., & Chan, D. K-S. (2012). How anxious and avoidant attachment affect romantic relationship quality differently: A meta-analytic review. *European Journal of Social Psychology, 42,* 406–419. (p. 199)

Li, Y., Johnson, E. J., & Zaval, L. (2011). Local warming: Daily temperature change influences belief in global warming. *Psychological Science, 22,* 454–459. (p. 360)

Li, Z. H., Jiang, D., Pepler, D., & Craig, W. (2010). Adolescent romantic relationships in China and Canada: A cross-national comparison. *Internal Journal of Behavioral Development, 34,* 113–120. (p. 210)

Liang, K. Y., Mintun, M. A., Fagan, A. M., Goate, A.M., Bugg, J.M., Holtzman, D. M., Morris, J. C., & Head, D. (2010). Exercise and Alzheimer's disease biomarkers in cognitively normal older adults. *Annals of Neurology, 68,* 311–318. (p. 216)

Liberman, P., & Pizarro, D. (2010, October 23). All politics is olfactory. *New York Times* (www.nytimes.com). (p. 269)

Libertus, M. E., & Brannon, E. M. (2009). Behavioral and neural basis of number sense in infancy. *Current Directions in Psychological Science, 18,* 346–351. (p. 188)

Libet, B. (1985). Unconscious cerebral initiative and the role of conscious will in voluntary action. *Behavioral and Brain Sciences, 12,* 181–187. (p. 95)

Libet, B. (2004). *Mind time: The temporal factor in consciousness.* Cambridge, MA: Harvard University Press. (p. 95)

Licata, A., Taylor, S., Berman, M., & Cranston, J. (1993). Effects of cocaine on human aggression. *Pharmacology Biochemistry and Behavior, 45,* 549–552. (p. 123)

Lichtenstein, E., Zhu, S-H., & Tedeschi, G. J. (2010). Smoking cessation quitlines: An underrecognized intervention success story. *American Psychologist, 65,* 252–261. (p. 122)

Lichtenstein, P., Calström, E., Råstam, M., Gillberg, C., & Anckarsäter, H. (2010). The genetics of autism spectrum disorders and related neuropsychiatric disorders in childhood. *American Journal of Psychiatry, 167,* 1357–1363. (p. 193)

Lick, D. J., Durso, L. E., & Johnson, K. L. (2013). Minority stress and physical health among sexual minorities. *Perspectives on Psychological Science, 8,* 521–548. (p. 490)

Liddle, J. R., Shackelford, T. K., & Weekes-Shackelford, V. W. (2012). Why can't we all just get along?: Evolutionary perspectives on violence, homicide, and war. *Review of General Psychology, 16,* 24-36. (p. 162)

Lieberman, M. D., Eisenberger, N. L., Crockett, M. J., Tom, S. M., Pfeifer, J. H., & Way, B. M. (2007). Putting feelings into words: Affect labeling disrupts amygdala activity in response to affective stimuli. *Psychological Science, 18,* 421–428. (p. 506)

Lieberman, P. (2013). Synapses, language, and being human. *Science, 342,* 944–945. (p. 379)

Lievens, F., Dilchert, S., & Ones, D. S. (2009). The importance of exercise and dimension factors in assessment centers: Simultaneous examinations of construct-related and criterion-related validity. *Human Performance, 22,* 375–390. (p. 597)

Lilienfeld, S. O. (2009, Winter). Tips for spotting psychological pseudoscience: A student-friendly guide. *Eye of Psi Chi,* pp. 23–26. (p. 273)

Lilienfeld, S. O., & Arkowitz, H. (2007, December, 2006/January, 2007). Taking a closer look: Can moving your eyes back and forth help to ease anxiety? *Scientific American Mind,* pp. 80–81. (p. 677)

Lilienfeld, S. O., & Byron, R. (2013). Your brain on trial. *Scientific American Mind,* pp. 44–53. (p. 347)

Lilienfeld, S. O., Lynn, S. J., Kirsch, I., Chaves, J. F., Sarbin, T. R., Ganaway, G. K., & Powell, R. A. (1999). Dissociative identity disorder and the sociocognitive model: Recalling the lessons of the past. *Psychological Bulletin, 125,* 507–523. (p. 648)

Lilienfeld, S. O., Ritschel, L. A., Lynn, S. J., Cautin, R. L., & Latzman, R. D. (2013). Why many clinical psychologists are resistant to evidence-based practice: Root causes and constructive remedies. *Clinical Psychology Review, 33,* 883–900. (p. 676)

Lilienfeld, S. O., Waldman, I. D., Landfield, K., Watts, A. L., Rubenzer, S., & Fashingbauer, T. R. (2012). Fearless dominance and the U.S. presidency: Implications of psychopathic personality traits for successful and unsuccessful political leadership. *Journal of Personality and Social Psychology, 103,* 489–505. (p. 650)

Lilienfeld, S. O., Wood, J. M., & Garb, H. N. (2001, May). What's wrong with this picture? *Scientific American,* pp. 81–87. (p. 579)

Lim, J., & Dinges, D. F. (2010). A meta-analysis of the impact of short-term sleep deprivation on cognitive variables. *Psychological Bulletin, 136,* 375–389. (p. 108)

Lima, N., Nascimento, V., Peixoto, J. A. C., Moreira, M. M., Neto, M. L. R., Almeida, J. C., . . . Reis, A. O. A. (2013). Electroconvulsive therapy use in adolescents: A systematic review. *Annals of General Psychiatry, 12,* p. 17. doi: 10.1186/1744-859X-12-17. (p. 685)

Lin, F. R., Ferrucci, L., Metter, E. J., An, Y., Zonderman, A. B., & Resnick, S. M. (2011b). Hearing loss and cognition in the Baltimore longitudinal study of aging. *Neuropsychology, 25,* 763–770. (p. 219)

Lin, F. R., Metter, E. J., O'Brien, R. J., Resnick, S. M., Zonderman, A. B., & Ferrucci, L. (2011a). Hearing loss and incident dementia. *Archives of Neurology, 68,* 214–220. (p. 219)

Lin, F. R., Yaffe, K., Xia, J., Xue, Q-L., Harris, T. B., Purchase-Helzner, E., . . . Simonsick, E. M. (2013). Hearing loss and cognitive decline in older adults. *JAMA, 173,* 293–299. (p. 219)

Lindberg, S. M., Hyde, J. S., Linn, M. C., & Petersen, J. L. (2010). New trends in gender and mathematics performance: A meta-analysis. *Psychological Bulletin, 136,* 1125–1135. (p. 410)

Linder, D. (1982). Social trap analogs: The tragedy of the commons in the laboratory. In V. J. Derlega & J. Grzelak (Eds.), *Cooperative and helping behavior: Theories and research.* New York: Academic Press. (p. 563)

Lindner, I., Echterhoff, G., Davidson, P. S. R., & Brand, M. (2010). Observation inflation: Your actions become mine. *Psychological Science, 21,* 1291–1299. (p. 309)

Lindskold, S. (1978). Trust development, the GRIT proposal, and the effects of conciliatory acts on conflict and cooperation. *Psychological Bulletin, 85,* 772–793. (p. 567)

Lindskold, S., & Han, G. (1988). GRIT as a foundation for integrative bargaining. *Personality and Social Psychology Bulletin, 14,* 335–345. (p. 567)

Lindson, N., Aveyard, P., & Hughes, J. R. (2010). Reduction versus abrupt cessation in smokers who want to quit (review). *Cochrane Collaboration* (Cochrane Library, Issue 3; www.thecochranelibrary.com). (p. 122)

Linville, P. W., Fischer, G. W., & Fischhoff, B. (1992). AIDS risk perceptions and decision biases. In J. B. Pryor & G. D. Reeder (Eds.), *The social psychology of HIV infection.* Hillsdale, NJ: Erlbaum. (p. 362)

Lionel, A. C., Tammimies, K., Vaags, A. K., Rosenfeld, J. A., Ahn, J. W., Merico, D., . . . Scherer, S. W. (2014). Disruption of the ASTN2/TRIM32 locus at 9q33.1 is a risk factor in males for autism spectrum disorders, ADHD and other neurodevelopmental phenotypes. *Human Molecular Genetics, 23,* 2752–2768. (p. 615)

Lippa, R. A. (2005). *Gender, nature, and nurture* (2nd ed.). Mahwah, NJ: Erlbaum. (p. 163)

Lippa, R. A. (2006). Is high sex drive associated with increased sexual attraction to both sexes? It depends on whether you are male or female. *Psychological Science, 17*, 46–52. (pp. 163, 441)

Lippa, R. A. (2007a). The relation between sex drive and sexual attraction to men and women: A cross-national study of heterosexual, bisexual, and homosexual men and women. *Archives of Sexual Behavior, 36*, 209–222. (pp. 441, 447, 553)

Lippa, R. A. (2007b). The preferred traits of mates in a cross-national study of heterosexual and homosexual men and women: An examination of biological and cultural influences. *Archives of Sexual Behavior, 36*, 193–208. (p. 447)

Lippa, R. A. (2008) Sex differences and sexual orientation differences in personality: Findings from the BBC Internet survey. *Archives of Sexual Behavior, Special Issue: Biological research on sex-dimorphic behavior and sexual orientation, 37*(1), 173–187. (pp. 147, 163, 447)

Lippa, R. A. (2009). Sex differences in sex drive, sociosexuality, and height across 53 nations: Testing evolutionary and social structural theories. *Archives of Sexual Behavior, 38*, 631–651. (p. 147)

Lippa, R. A. (2013). Men and women with bisexual identities show bisexual patterns of sexual attraction to male and female "swimsuit models". *Archives of Sexual Behavior, 42*, 187–196. (p. 440)

Lippa, R. A., Patterson, T. M., & Marelich, W. D. (2010). Looking at and longing for male and female "swimsuit models": Men are much more category-specific than women. *Social Psychological and Personality Science, 1*, 238–245. (p. 441)

Lipsey, M. W., & Wilson, D. B. (1993). The efficacy of psychological, educational, and behavioral treatment: Confirmation from meta-analyses. *American Psychologist, 48*, 1181–1209. (p. 405)

Lipsitt, L. P. (2003). Crib death: A biobehavioral phenomenon? *Current Directions in Psychological Science, 12*, 164–170. (p. 185)

Liu, Y., Balaraman, Y., Wang, G., Nephew, K. P., & Zhou, F. C. (2009). Alcohol exposure alters DNA methylation profiles in mouse embryos at early neurulation. *Epigentics, 4*, 500–511. (p. 182)

Livingston, G., & Parker, K. (2011). A tale of two fathers: More are active, but more are absent. Pew Research Center (www.pewresearch.org). (p. 198)

Livingstone, M., & Hubel, D. (1988). Segregation of form, color, movement, and depth: Anatomy, physiology, and perception. *Science, 240*, 740–749. (p. 246)

Loehlin, J. C. (2012). The differential heritability of personality item clusters. *Behavior Genetics, 42*, 500–507. (p. 136)

Loehlin, J. C., Horn, J. M., & Ernst, J. L. (2007). Genetic and environmental influences on adult life outcomes: Evidence from the Texas adoption project. *Behavior Genetics, 37*, 463–476. (p. 139)

Loehlin, J. C., McCrae, R. R., & Costa, P. T., Jr. (1998). Heritabilities of common and measure-specific components of the Big Five personality factors. *Journal of Research in Personality, 32*, 431–453. (p. 590)

Loehlin, J. C., & Nichols, R. C. (1976). *Heredity, environment, and personality.* Austin: University of Texas Press. (p. 136)

Loftus, E. F. (2001, November). Imagining the past. *The Psychologist, 14*, 584–587. (p. 345)

Loftus, E. F. (2011, May/June). We live in perilous times for science. *Skeptical Inquirer*, p. 13. (p. 348)

Loftus, E. F. (2012, July). *Manufacturing memories.* Invited address to the International Congress of Psychology, Cape Town. (p. 343)

Loftus, E. F., & Ketcham, K. (1994). *The myth of repressed memory.* New York: St. Martin's Press. (p. 329)

Loftus, E. F., Levidow, B., & Duensing, S. (1992). Who remembers best? Individual differences in memory for events that occurred in a science museum. *Applied Cognitive Psychology, 6*, 93–107. (p. 344)

Loftus, E. F., & Loftus, G. R. (1980). On the permanence of stored information in the human brain. *American Psychologist, 35*, 409–420. (p. 329)

Loftus, E. F., & Palmer, J. C. (October, 1974). Reconstruction of automobile destruction: An example of the interaction between language and memory. *Journal of Verbal Learning & Verbal Behavior, 13*(5), 585–589. (p. 344)

Logan, T. K., Walker, R., Cole, J., & Leukefeld, C. (2002). Victimization and substance abuse among women: Contributing factors, interventions, and implications. *Review of General Psychology, 6*, 325–397. (p. 128)

Logue, A. W. (1998a). Laboratory research on self-control: Applications to administration. *Review of General Psychology, 2*, 221–238. (p. 293)

Logue, A. W. (1998b). Self-control. In W. T. O'Donohue (Ed.), *Learning and behavior therapy.* Boston, MA: Allyn & Bacon. (p. 293)

Lomber, S. G., Meredith, M. A., & Krai, A. (2010). Cross-modal plasticity in specific auditory cortices underlies visual compensations in the deaf. *Nature Neuroscience, 13*, 1421–1427. (p. 375)

London, P. (1970). The rescuers: Motivational hypotheses about Christians who saved Jews from the Nazis. In J. Macaulay & L. Berkowitz (Eds.), *Altruism and helping behavior.* New York: Academic Press. (p. 310)

Lonergan, M. H., Olivera-Figueroa, L., Pitman, R. K., & Brunet, A. (2013). Propranolol's effects on the consolidation and reconsolidation of long-term emotional memory in healthy participants: A meta-analysis. *Journal of Psychiatry & Neuroscience, 38*, 222–231. (p. 344)

Lopes, P. N., Brackett, M. A., Nezlek, J. B., Schutz, A., Sellin, II, & Salovey, P. (2004). Emotional intelligence and social interaction. *Personality and Social Psychology Bulletin, 30*, 1018–1034. (p. 391)

Lopez, D. J. (2002, January/February). Snaring the fowler: Mark Twain debunks phrenology. *Skeptical Inquirer* (www.csicop.org). (p. 52)

Lord, C. G., Lepper, M. R., & Preston, E. (1984). Considering the opposite: A corrective strategy for social judgment. *Journal of Personality and Social Psychology, 47*, 1231–1247. (p. 361)

Lord, C. G., Ross, L., & Lepper, M. (1979). Biased assimilation and attitude polarization: The effects of prior theories on subsequently considered evidence. *Journal of Personality and Social Psychology, 37*, 2098–2109. (p. 361)

Lorenz, K. (1937). The companion in the bird's world. *Auk, 54*, 245–273. (p. 196)

Louie, K., & Wilson, M. A. (2001). Temporally structured replay of awake hippocampal ensemble activity during rapid eye movement sleep. *Neuron, 29*, 145–156. (p. 113)

Lourenco, O., & Machado, A. (1996). In defense of Piaget's theory: A reply to 10 common criticisms. *Psychological Review, 103*, 143–164. (p. 192)

Lovaas, O. I. (1987). Behavioral treatment and normal educational and intellectual functioning in young autistic children. *Journal of Consulting and Clinical Psychology, 55*, 3–9. (p. 666)

Low, P., et al. (2012). *The Cambridge Declaration on Consciousness.* Publicly proclaimed in Cambridge, UK, on July 7, 2012, at the Francis Crick Memorial Conference on Consciousness in Human and non-Human Animals (www.fcmconference.org/img/CambridgeDeclarationOnConsciousness.pdf). (p. 367)

Lowry, P. E. (1997). The assessment center process: New directions. *Journal of Social Behavior and Personality, 12*, 53–62. (p. 597)

Lu, Z-L., Williamson, S. J., & Kaufman, L. (1992). Behavioral lifetime of human auditory sensory memory predicted by physiological measures. *Science, 258*, 1668–1670. (p. 323)

Lubinski, D. (2009a). Cognitive epidemiology: With emphasis on untangling cognitive ability and socioeconomic status. *Intelligence, 37*, 625–633. (p. 404)

Luborsky, L., Rosenthal, R., Diguer, L., Andrusyna, T. P., Berman, J. S., Levitt, J. T., Seligman, D. A., & Krause, E. D. (2002). The dodo bird verdict is alive and well—mostly. *Clinical Psychology: Science and Practice, 9*, 2–34. (p. 675)

Lucas, A., Morley, R., Cole, T. J., Lister, G., & Leeson-Payne, C. (1992). Breast milk and subsequent intelligence quotient in children born preterm. *Lancet, 339*, 261–264. (p. 36)

Lucas, R. E. (2008). Personality and subjective well-being. In M. Eid & R. Larsen (Eds.), *The science of subjective well-being.* New York: Guilford. (p. 485)

Lucas, R. E., Clark, A. E., Georgellis, Y., & Diener, E. (2004). Unemployment alters the set point for life satisfaction. *Psychological Science, 15*, 8–13. (p. 485)

Lucas, R. E., & Donnellan, M. B. (2007). How stable is happiness? Using the STARTS model to estimate the stability of life satisfaction. *Journal of Research in Personality, 41*, 1091–1098. (p. 485)

Lucas, R. E., & Donnellan, M. B. (2009). Age differences in personality: Evidence from a nationally representative Australian sample. *Developmental Psychology, 45*, 1353–1363. (p. 180)

Lucas, R. E., & Donnellan, M. B. (2011). Personality development across the life span: Longitudinal analyses with a national sample from Germany. *Journal of Personality and Social Psychology, 101*, 847–861. (p. 180)

Lucas, R. E., & Schimmack, U. (2009). Income and well-being: How big is the gap between the rich and the poor? *Journal of Research in Personality, 43*, 75–78. (p. 482)

Lucero, S. M., Kusner, K. G., & Speace, E. A. (2008, May 24). *Religousness and adolescent sexual behavior: A meta-analytic review.* Paper presented at Association for Psychological Science Convention. (p. 439)

Luciano, M., Gow, A. J., Harris, S. E., Hayward, C., Allerhand, M., Starr, J. M., Visscher, P. M., & Deary, I. J. (2009). Cognitive ability at age 11 and 70 years, information processing speed, and APOE variation: The Lothian birth cohort 1936 study. *Psychology and Aging, 24,* 129–138. (p. 219)

Ludwig, A. M. (1995). *The price of greatness: Resolving the creativity and madness controversy.* New York: Guilford Press. (p. 630)

Ludwig, D. S., & Friedman, M. I. (2014). Increasing adiposity: Consequence or cause of overeating? *JAMA, 311,* 2167–2168. (p. 427)

Luhmann, M., Hofmann, W., Eid, M., & Lucas, R. E. (2012). Subjective well-being and adaptation to life events: A meta-analysis. *Journal of Personality and Social Psychology, 102,* 592–615. (p. 481)

Lui, M., & Rosenfeld, J. P. (2009). The application of subliminal priming in lie detection: Scenario for identification of members of a terrorist ring. *Psycholphysiology, 46,* 889–903. (p. 467)

Luigjes, J., van den Brin, W., Feenstra, M., van den Munckhof, P., Schuurman, P. R., Schippers, R., . . . Denys, D. (2012). Deep brain stimulation in addiction: A review of potential brain targets. *Molecular Psychiatry, 17,* 572–583. (p. 687)

Lumeng, J. C., Forrest, P., Appugliese, D. P., Kaciroti, N., Corwyn, R. F., & Bradley, R. H. (2010). Weight status as a predictor of being bullied in third through sixth grades. *Pediatrics, 125,* e1301–7. (p. 429)

Lund, T. J., & Dearing, E. (2012). Is growing up affluent risky for adolescents or is the problem growing up in an affluent neighborhood? *Journal of Research on Adolescence, 23,* 274–282. (p. 200)

Luo, F., Florence, C. S., Quispe-Agnoli, M., Ouyang, L., & Crosby, A. E. (2011). Impact of business cycles on US suicide rates, 1928–2007. *American Journal of Public Health, 101,* 1139–1146. (p. 638)

Luppino, F. S., de Wit, L. M., Bouvy, P. F., Stijnen, T., Cuijpers, P., Penninx, W. J. H., & Zitman, F. G. (2010). Overweight, obesity, and depression. *Archives of General Psychiatry, 67,* 220–229. (p. 429)

Luria, A. M. (1968). In L. Solotaroff (Trans.), *The mind of a mnemonist.* New York: Basic Books. (p. 318)

Lustig, C., & Buckner, R. L. (2004). Preserved neural correlates of priming in old age and dementia. *Neuron, 42,* 865–875. (p. 339)

Lutfey, K. E., Link, C. L., Rosen, R. C., Wiegel, M., & McKinlay, J. B. (2009). Prevalence and correlates of sexual activity and function in women: Results from the Boston Area Community Health (BACH) survey. *Archives of Sexual Behavior, 38,* 514–527. (p. 435)

Lutgendorf, S. K., Russell, D., Ullrich, P., Harris, T. B., & Wallace, R. (2004). Religious participation, interleukin-6, and mortality in older adults. *Health Psychology, 23,* 465–475. (p. 513)

Luthar, S. S., Barkin, S. H., & Crossman, E. J. (2013). "I can, therefore I must": Fragility in the upper-middle classes. *Development and Psychopathology, 25,* 1529–1549. (p. 200)

Lyall, S. (2005, November 29). What's the buzz? Rowdy teenagers don't want to hear it. *New York Times* (www.nytimes.com). (p. 215)

Lykken, D. T. (1991). *Science, lies, and controversy: An epitaph for the polygraph.* Invited address upon receipt of the Senior Career Award for Distinguished Contribution to Psychology in the Public Interest, American Psychological Association convention. (p. 466)

Lykken, D. T. (1995). *The antisocial personalities.* Hillsdale, NJ: Erlbaum. (pp. 546, 616, 650)

Lykken, D. T. (1999). *Happiness: The Nature and Nurture of Joy and Contentment.* New York: Golden Books. (p. 400)

Lykken, D. T. (2001). Happiness—stuck with what you've got? *The Psychologist, 14,* 470–473. (p. 139)

Lykken, D. T. (2006). The mechanism of emergenesis. *Genes, Brain & Behavior, 5,* 306–310. (p. 406)

Lykken, D. T., & Tellegen, A. (1996). Happiness is a stochastic phenomenon. *Psychological Science, 7,* 186–189. (p. 485)

Lynch, G. (2002). Memory enhancement: The search for mechanism-based drugs. *Nature Neuroscience, 5* (suppl.), 1035–1038. (p. 332)

Lynch, G., & Staubli, U. (1991). Possible contributions of long-term potentiation to the encoding and organization of memory. *Brain Research Reviews, 16,* 204–206. (p. 332)

Lynch, G., Palmer, L. C., & Gall, C. M. (2011). The likelihood of cognitive enhancement. *Pharmacology, Biochemistry and Behavior, 99,* 116–129. (p. 333)

Lynn, M. (1988). The effects of alcohol consumption on restaurant tipping. *Personality and Social Psychology Bulletin, 14,* 87–91. (p. 119)

Lynn, R. (2009). What has caused the Flynn effect? Secular increases in the development quotients of infants. *Intelligence, 37,* 16–24. (p. 396)

Lynn, R., & Harvey, J. (2008). The decline of the world's intelligence. *Intelligence, 36,* 112–120. (p. 397)

Lynn, S. J., Rhue, J. W., & Weekes, J. R. (1990). Hypnotic involuntariness: A social cognitive analysis. *Psychological Review, 97,* 169–184. (p. 265)

Lynne, S. D., Graber, J. A., Nichols, T. R., Brooks-Gunn, J., & Botvin, G. J. (2007). Links between pubertal timing, peer influences, and externalizing behaviors among urban students followed through middle school. *Journal of Adolescent Health, 40,* 181.e7–181.e13. (p. 204)

Lyons, B. D., Hoffman, B. J., Michel, J. W., & Williams, K. J. (2011). On the predictive efficiency of past performance and physical ability: The case of the National Football League. *Human Performance, 24,* 158–172. (p. 597)

Lyons, D. E., Young, A. G., Keil, F. C. (2007). The hidden structure of overimitation. *PNAS, 104,* 19751–10756. (p. 308)

Lyons, L. (2004, February 3). Growing up lonely: Examining teen alienation. *Gallup Poll Tuesday Briefing* (www.gallup.com). (p. 209)

Lyons, L. (2005, January 4). Teens stay true to parents' political perspectives. *Gallup Poll News Service* (www.gallup.com). (p. 211)

Lyons, P., Coursey, L. & Kenworthy, J. (2013). National identity and group narcissism as predictors of intergroup attitudes toward undocumented Latino immigrants in the United States. *Hispanic Journal of Behavioral Sciences, 35,* 323–335. (p. 604)

Lyons, P. A., Kenworthy, J. B., & Popan, J. R. (2010). Ingroup identification and group-level narcissism as predictors of U.S. citizens' attitudes and behavior toward Arab immigrants. *Personality and Social Psychology Bulletin, 36,* 1267–1280. (p. 539)

Lyubomirsky, S. (2001). Why are some people happier than others? The role of cognitive and motivational processes in well-being. *American Psychologist, 56,* 239–249. (p. 484)

Lyubomirsky, S. (2008). *The how of happiness: A scientific approach to getting the life you want.* New York: Penguin Press. (p. 488)

Lyubomirsky, S., Sousa, L., & Dickerhoof, R. (2006). The costs and benefits of writing, talking, and thinking about life's triumphs and defeats. *Journal of Personality and Social Psychology, 90*(4), 690–708. (p. 507)

Ma, D. S., Correll, J., Wittenbrink, B., Bar-Anan, Y., Sriram, N., & Nosek, B. A. (2013). When fatigue turns deadly: The association between fatigue and racial bias in the decision to shoot. *Basic and Applied Social Psychology, 35,* 515–524. (p. 539)

Ma, L. (1997, September). On the origin of Darwin's ills. *Discover,* p. 27. (p. 621)

Maas, J. B. (1999). *Power sleep. The revolutionary program that prepares your mind and body for peak performance.* New York: HarperCollins. (p. 108)

Maas, J. B., & Robbins, R. S. (2010). *Sleep for success: Everything you must know about sleep but are too tired to ask.* Bloomington, IN: Author House. (pp. 106, 108)

Maass, A., D'Ettole, C., & Cadinu, M. (2008). Checkmate? The role of gender stereotypes in the ultimate intellectual sport. *European Journal of Social Psychology, 38,* 231–245. (p. 414)

Maass, A., Karasawa, M., Politi, F., & Suga, S. (2006). Do verbs and adjectives play different roles in different cultures? A cross-linguistic analysis of person representation. *Journal of Personality and Social Psychology, 90,* 734–750. (p. 159)

Maass, A., & Russo, A. (2003). Directional bias in the mental representation of spatial events: Nature or culture? *Psychological Science, 14,* 296–301. (p. 380)

Macaluso, E., Frith, C. D., & Driver, J. (2000). Modulation of human visual cortex by crossmodal spatial attention. *Science, 289,* 1206–1208. (p. 270)

Macan, T. H., & Dipboye, R. L. (1994). The effects of the application on processing of information from the employment interview. *Journal of Applied Social Psychology, 24,* 1291. (p. A-5)

MacCabe, J. H., Lambe, M. P., Cnattingius, S., Torrång, A., Björk, C., Sham, P. C., . . . Hultman, C. M. (2008). Scholastic achievement at age 16 and risk of schizophrenia and other psychoses: A national cohort study. *Psychological Medicine, 38,* 1133–1140. (p. 641)

Maccoby, E. (1980). *Social development: Psychological growth and the parent-child relationship.* New York: Harcourt Brace Jovanovich. (p. 201)

Maccoby, E. E. (1990). Gender and relationships: A developmental account. *American Psychologist, 45,* 513–520. (p. 163)

Maccoby, E. E. (1998). *The paradox of gender.* Cambridge, MA: Harvard University Press. (p. 164)

Maccoby, E. E. (2002). Gender and group process: A developmental perspective. *Current Directions in Psychological Science, 11,* 54–58. (p. 534)

MacDonald, G., & Leary, M. R. (2005). Why does social exclusion hurt? The relationship between social and physical pain. *Psychological Bulletin, 131*, 202–223. (p. 450)

MacDonald, N. (1960). Living with schizophrenia. *Canadian Medical Association Journal, 82*, 218–221. (p. 640)

MacDonald, T. K., & Hynie, M. (2008). Ambivalence and unprotected sex: Failure to predict sexual activity and decreased condom use. *Journal of Applied Social Psychology, 38*, 1092–1107. (p. 439)

MacDonald, T. K., Zanna, M. P., & Fong, G. T. (1995). Decision making in altered states: Effects of alcohol on attitudes toward drinking and driving. *Journal of Personality and Social Psychology, 68*, 973–985. (p. 119)

MacFarlane, A. (1978, February). What a baby knows. *Human Nature*, pp. 74–81. (p. 183)

Macfarlane, J. W. (1964). Perspectives on personality consistency and change from the guidance study. *Vita Humana, 7*, 115–126. (p. 204)

Mack, A., & Rock, I. (2000). *Inattentional blindness.* Cambridge, MA: MIT Press. (p. 97)

MacKay, D. M. (1978). Selves and brains. *Neuroscience, 3*, 599–606. (p. 87)

MacKenzie, M. J., Nicklas, E., Waldfogel, J., & Brooks-Gunn, J. (2013). Spanking and child development across the first decade of life. *Pediatrics, 132*(5), e1118–25. (p. 296)

MacKerron, G., & Mourato, S. (2013). Happiness is greater in natural environments. *Global Environmental Change, 23*, 992–1000. (p. 688)

Macmillan, M., & Lena, M. L. (2010). Rehabilitating Phineas Gage. *Neuropsychological Rehabilitation, 17*, 1–18. (p. 80)

Macnamara, B. N., Hambrick, D. Z., & Oswald, F. L. (2014). Deliberate practice and performance in music, games, sports, education, and professions: A meta-analysis. *Psychological Science, 25*, 1608–1618. (p. 455)

MacNeilage, P. F., & Davis, B. L. (2000). On the origin of internal structure of word forms. *Science, 288*, 527–531. (p. 372)

MacNeilage, P. F., Rogers, L. J., & Vallortigara, G. (2009, July). Origins of the left and right brain. *Scientific American*, pp. 60–67. (p. 86)

Maddi, S. R., Harvey, R. H., Khoshaba, D. M., Fazel, M., & Resurreccion, N. (2009). Hardiness training facilitates performance in college. *Journal of Positive Psychology, 4*, 566–577. (p. 455)

Maddieson, I. (1984). *Patterns of sounds.* Cambridge: Cambridge University Press. (p. 370)

Maeda, Y., & Yoon, S. Y. (2013). A meta-analysis on gender differences in mental rotation ability measured by the Purdue spatial visualization tests: Visualization of rotations (PSVT:R). *Educational Psychology Review, 25*, 69–94. (p. 410)

Maes, H. H. M., Neale, M. C., & Eaves, L. J. (1997). Genetic and environmental factors in relative body weight and human adiposity. *Behavior Genetics, 27*, 325–351. (p. 431)

Maestripieri, D. (2003). Similarities in affiliation and aggression between cross-fostered rhesus macaque females and their biological mothers. *Developmental Psychobiology, 43*, 321–327. (p. 138)

Maestripieri, D. (2005). Early experience affects the intergenerational transmission of infant abuse in rhesus monkeys. *Proceedings of the National Academy of Sciences, 102*, 9726–9729. (p. 200)

Magnussen, S., Andersson, J., Cornoldi, C., De Beni, R., Endestad, T., Goodman, G. S., . . . Zimmer, H. (2006). What people believe about memory. *Memory, 4*, 595–613. (p. 343)

Magnusson, D. (1990). Personality research—challenges for the future. *European Journal of Personality, 4*, 1–17. (p. 650)

Maguire, E. A., Gadian, D. G., Johnsrude, I. S., Good, C. D., Ashburner, J., Frackowiak, R. S. J., & Frith, C. D. (2000). Navigation-related structural change in the hippocampi of taxi drivers. *PNAS Proceedings of the National Academy of Sciences, 97*, 4398–4403. (p. 153)

Maguire, E. A., Spiers, H. J., Good, C. D., Hartley, T., Frackowiak, R. S. J., & Burgess, N. (2003b). Navigation expertise and the human hippocampus: A structural brain imaging analysis. *Hippocampus, 13*, 250–259. (p. 329)

Maguire, E. A., Valentine, E. R., Wilding, J. M., & Kapur, N. (2003a). Routes to remembering: The brains behind superior memory. *Nature Neuroscience, 6*, 90–95. (p. 325)

Mah, C. D., Mah, K. E., Kezirian, E. J., & Dement, W. C. (2011). The effects of sleep extension on the athletic performance of collegiate basketball players. *Sleep, 34*, 943–950. (p. 106)

Mahowald, M. W., & Ettinger, M. G. (1990). Things that go bump in the night: The parsomias revisted. *Journal of Clinical Neurophysiology, 7*, 119–143. (p. 111)

Maier, S. F., Watkins, L. R., & Fleshner, M. (1994). Psychoneuroimmunology: The interface between behavior, brain, and immunity. *American Psychologist, 49*, 1004–1017. (p. 494)

Maiti, S., Kumar, K. H. B. G., Castellini, C. A., O'Reilly, R., & Singh, S. M. (2011). Ontonogenetic de novo copy number variations (CNVs) as a source of genetic individuality: Studies on two families with MZD twins for schizophrenia. *PLOS One, 6*, e17125. (p. 136)

Major, B., Carrington, P. I., & Carnevale, P. J. D. (1984). Physical attractiveness and self-esteem: Attribution for praise from an other-sex evaluator. *Personality and Social Psychology Bulletin, 10*, 43–50. (p. 554)

Major, B., Schmidlin, A. M., & Williams, L. (1990). Gender patterns in social touch: The impact of setting and age. *Journal of Personality and Social Psychology, 58*, 634–643. (p. 163)

Makel, M. C., Plucker, J. A., & Hegarty, B. (2012). Replications in psychology research: How often do they really occur? *Perspectives on Psychological Science, 7*, 537–542. (p. 27)

Malamuth, N. M., & Check, J. V. P. (1981). The effects of media exposure on acceptance of violence against women: A field experiment. *Journal of Research in Personality, 15*, 436–446. (p. 438)

Maldonado-Molina, M. M., Reingle, J. M., Jennings, W. G., & Prado, G. (2011). Drinking and driving among immigrant and US-born Hispanic young adults: Results from a longitudinal and nationally representative study. *Addictive Behavior, 36*, 381–388. (p. 618)

Malkiel, B. G. (2012). *A random walk down Wall Street: The time-tested strategy for successful investing* (Tenth Edition). New York: Norton. (p. 361)

Malle, B. F. (2006). The actor-observer asymmetry in attribution: A (surprising) meta-analysis. *Psychological Bulletin, 132*, 895–919. (p. 519)

Malle, B. F., Knobe, J. M., & Nelson, S. E. (2007). Actor-observe asymmetries in explanations of behavior: New answers to an old question. *Journal of Personality and Social Psychology, 93*, 491–514. (p. 519)

Malmquist, C. P. (1986). Children who witness parental murder: Post-traumatic aspects. *Journal of the American Academy of Child Psychiatry, 25*, 320–325. (p. 580)

Maltby, N., Tolin, D. F., Worhunsky, P., O'Keefe, T. M., & Kiehl, K. A. (2005). Dysfunctional action monitoring hyperactivates frontal-striatal circuits in obsessive-compulsive disorder: An event-related fMRI study. *NeuroImage, 24*, 495–503. (p. 626)

Mampe, B., Friederici, A. D., Christophe, A., & Wermke, K. (2009). Newborns' cry melody is shaped by their native language. *Current Biology, 19*, 1–4. (p. 182)

Maner, J. K., DeWall, C. N, Baumeister, R. F., & Schaller, M. (2007). Does social exclusion motivate interpersonal reconnection? Resolving the "porcupine problem." *Journal of Personality and Social Psychology, 92*, 42–55. (p. 451)

Maner, J. K., Kenrick, D. T., Neuberg, S. L., Becker, D. V., Robertson, T., Hofer, B., . . . Schaller, M. (2005). Functional projection: How fundamental social motives can bias interpersonal perception. *Journal of Personality and Social Psychology, 88*, 63–78. (p. 581)

Mani, A., Mullainathan, S., Shafir, E., & Zhao, J. (2013). Poverty impedes cognitive function. *Science, 341*, 976–980. (p. 408)

Manning, W., & Cohen, J. A. (2012). Premarital cohabitation and marital dissolution: An examination of recent marriages. *Journal of Marriage and Family 74*, 377–387. (p. 221)

Manson, J. E. (2002). Walking compared with vigorous exercise for the prevention of cardiovascular events in women. *New England Journal of Medicine, 347*, 716–725. (p. 507)

Maquet, P. (2001). The role of sleep in learning and memory. *Science, 294*, 1048–1052. (p. 113)

Maquet, P., Peters, J-M., Aerts, J., Delfiore, G., Degueldre, C., Luxen, A., & Franck, G. (1996). Functional neuroanatomy of human rapid-eye-movement sleep and dreaming. *Nature, 383*, 163–166. (p. 114)

Mar, R. A., & Oatley, K. (2008). The function of fiction is the abstraction and simulation of social experience. *Perspectives on Psychological Science, 3*, 173–192. (p. 310)

Mar, R. A., Oatley, K., & Peterson, J. B. (2009). Exploring the link between reading fiction and empathy: Ruling out individual differences and examining outcomes. *Communications: The European Journal of Communication, 34*, 407–428. (p. 471)

Marcus, B., Machilek, F., & Schütz, A. (2006). Personality in cyberspace: Personal web sites as media for personality expressions and impressions. *Journal of Personality and Social Psychology, 90*, 1014–1031. (p. 593)

Marcus, G. F., Vijayan, S., Rao, S. B., & Vishton, P. M. (1999). Rule learning by seven-month-old infants. *Science, 283*, 77–80. (p. 373)

Margolis, M. L. (2000). Brahms' lullaby revisited: Did the composer have obstructive sleep apnea? *Chest, 118,* 210–213. (p. 111)

Marinak, B. A., & Gambrell, L. B. (2008). Intrinsic motivation and rewards: What sustains young children's engagement with text? *Literacy Research and Instruction, 47,* 9–26. (p. 305)

Markovizky, G., & Samid, Y. (2008). The process of immigrant adjustment: The role of time in determining psychological adjustment. *Journal of Cross-Cultural Psychology, 39,* 782–798. (p. 490)

Markowitsch, H. J. (1995). Which brain regions are critically involved in the retrieval of old episodic memory? *Brain Research Reviews, 21,* 117–127. (p. 329)

Markowitz, J. C., Svartberg, M., & Swartz, H. A. (1998). Is IPT time-limited psychodynamic psychotherapy? *Journal of Psychotherapy Practice and Research, 7,* 185–195. (p. 660)

Markowitz, J. C., & Weissman, M. M. (2012). Interpersonal psychotherapy: Past, present and future. *Clinical Psychology and Psychiatry, 19,* 99–105. (p. 660)

Markus, G. B. (1986). Stability and change in political attitudes: Observe, recall, and "explain." *Political Behavior, 8,* 21–44. (p. 347)

Markus, H. R., & Kitayama, S. (1991). Culture and the self: Implications for cognition, emotion, and motivation. *Psychological Review, 98,* 224–253. (pp. 380, 477)

Markus, H. R., & Nurius, P. (1986). Possible selves. *American Psychologist, 41,* 954–969. (p. 598)

Markus, H. R., Uchida, Y., Omoregie, H., Townsend, S. S. M., & Kitayama, S. (2006). Going for the gold: Models of agency in Japanese and American contexts. *Psychological Science, 17,* 103–112. (p. 159)

Marley, J., & Bulia, S. (2001). Crimes against people with mental illness: Types, perpetrators and influencing factors. *Social Work, 46,* 115–124. (p. 616)

Marmot, M. G., Bosma, H., Hemingway, H., Brunner, E., & Stansfeld, S. (1997). Contribution to job control and other risk factors to social variations in coronary heart disease incidents. *Lancet, 350,* 235–239. (p. 501)

Marsh, A. A., Elfenbein, H. A., & Ambady, N. (2003). Nonverbal "accents": Cultural differences in facial expressions of emotion. *Psychological Science, 14,* 373–376. (p. 472)

Marsh, H. W., & Craven, R. G. (2006). Reciprocal effects of self-concept and performance from a multidimensional perspective: Beyond seductive pleasure and unidimensional perspectives. *Perspectives on Psychological Science, 1,* 133–163. (p. 599)

Marsh, H. W., & Parker, J. W. (1984). Determinants of student self-concept: Is it better to be a relatively large fish in a small pond even if you don't learn to swim as well? *Journal of Personality and Social Psychology, 47,* 213–231. (p. 484)

Marshall, M. J. (2002). *Why spanking doesn't work.* Springville, UT: Bonneville Books. (p. 296)

Marshall, R. D., Bryant, R. A., Amsel, L., Suh, E. J., Cook, J. M., & Neria, Y. (2007). The psychology of ongoing threat: Relative risk appraisal, the September 11 attacks, and terrorism-related fears. *American Psychologist, 62,* 304–316. (p. 360)

Marteau, T. M. (1989). Framing of information: Its influences upon decisions of doctors and patients. *British Journal of Social Psychology, 28,* 89–94. (p. 362)

Marteau, T. M., Hollands, G. J., & Fletcher, P. C. (2012). Changing human behavior to prevent disease: The importance of targeting automatic processes. *Science, 337,* 1492–1495. (p. 429)

Marti, M. W., Robier, D. M., & Baron, R. S. (2000). Right before our eyes: The failure to recognize non-prototypical forms of prejudice. *Group Processes and Intergroup Relations, 3,* 403–418. 409–416. (p. 356)

Martin, C. K., Anton, S. D., Walden, H., Arnett, C., Greenway, F. L., & Williamson, D. A. (2007). Slower eating rate reduces the food intake of men, but not women: Implications for behavioural weight control. *Behaviour Research and Therapy, 45,* 2349–2359. (p. 432)

Martin, C. L., & Ruble, D. (2004). Children's search for gender cues. *Current Directions in Psychological Science, 13,* 67–70. (p. 169)

Martin, C. L., Ruble, D. N., & Szkrybalo, J. (2002). Cognitive theories of early gender development. *Psychological Bulletin, 128,* 903–933. (p. 169)

Martin, R. J., White, B. D., & Hulsey, M. G. (1991). The regulation of body weight. *American Scientist, 79,* 528–541. (p. 427)

Martin, S. J., Kelly, I. W., & Saklofske, D. H. (1992). Suicide and lunar cycles: A critical review over 28 years. *Psychological Reports, 71,* 787–795. (p. 650)

Martins, Y., Preti, G., Crabtree, C. R., & Wysocki, C. J. (2005). Preference for human body odors is influenced by gender and sexual orientation. *Psychological Science, 16,* 694–701. (p. 443)

Marx, D. M., Ko, S. J., & Friedman, R. A. (2009). The "Obama effect": How a salient role model reduces race-based performance differences. *Journal of Experimental Social Psychology, 45,* 953–956. (p. 414)

Masicampo, E. J., & Baumeister, R. F. (2008). Toward a physiology of dual-process reasoning and judgment: Lemonade, willpower, and the expensive rule-based analysis. *Psychological Science, 19,* 255–260. (p. 504)

Maslow, A. H. (1970). *Motivation and personality* (2nd ed.). New York: Harper & Row. (pp. 422, 583, A-1)

Maslow, A. H. (1971). *The farther reaches of human nature.* New York: Viking Press. (p. 422)

Mason, A. E., Sbarra, D. A., & Mehl, M. R. (2010). Thin-slicing divorce: Thirty seconds of information predict changes in psychological adjustment over 90 days. *Psychological Science, 21,* 1420–1422. (p. 470)

Mason, C., & Kandel, E. R. (1991). Central visual pathways. In E. R. Kandel, J. H. Schwartz, & T. M. Jessell (Eds.), *Principles of neural science* (3rd ed.). New York: Elsevier. (p. 60)

Mason, H. (2003, March 25). Wake up, sleepy teen. *Gallup Poll Tuesday Briefing* (www.gallup.com). (p. 108)

Mason, H. (2003, September 2). Americans, Britons at odds on animal testing. *Gallup Poll News Service* (http: //www.gallup.com). (p. 40)

Mason, H. (2005, January 25). Who dreams, perchance to sleep? *Gallup Poll News Service* (www.gallup.com). (pp. 107, 108)

Mason, M. F., Norton, M. I., Van Horn, J. D., Wegner, D. M., Grafton, S. T., & Macrae, C. N. (2007). Wandering minds: The default network and stimulus-independent thought. *Science, 315,* 393–395. (p. 581)

Mason, R. A., & Just, M. A. (2004). How the brain processes causal inferences in text. *Psychological Science, 15,* 1–7. (p. 85)

Masse, L. C., & Tremblay, R. E. (1997). Behavior of boys in kindergarten and the onset of substance use during adolescence. *Archives of General Psychiatry, 54,* 62–68. (p. 127)

Massey, C., Simmons, J. P., & Armor, D. A. (2011). Hope over experience: Desirability and the persistence of optimism. *Psychological Science, 22,* 274–281. (p. 600)

Massimini, M., Ferrarelli, F., Huber, R., Esser, S. K., Singh, H., & Tononi, G. (2005). Breakdown of cortical effective connectivity during sleep. *Science, 309,* 2228–2232. (p. 101)

Mast, M. S., & Hall, J. A. (2006). Women's advantage at remembering others' appearance: A systematic look at the why and when of a gender difference. *Personality and Social Psychology Bulletin, 32,* 353–364. (p. 554)

Masten, A. S. (2001). Ordinary magic: Resilience processes in development. *American Psychologist, 56,* 227–238. (p. 200)

Masters, K. S. (2010). The role of religion in therapy: Time for psychologists to have a little faith? *Cognitive and Behavioral Practice, 17,* 393–400. (p. 680)

Masters, K. S., & Hooker, S. A. (2013). Religiousness/spirituality, cardiovascular disease, and cancer: Cultural integration for health research and intervention. *Journal of Consulting and Clinical Psychology, 81,* 206–216. (p. 512)

Masters, W. H., & Johnson, V. E. (1966). *Human sexual response.* Boston: Little, Brown. (p. 435)

Mastroianni, G. R. (2002). Milgram and the Holocaust: A reexamination. *Journal of Theoretical and Philosophical Psychology, 22,* 158–173. (p. 530)

Mastroianni, G. R., & Reed, G. (2006). Apples, barrels, and Abu Ghraib. *Sociological Focus, 39,* 239–250. (p. 523)

Masuda, T., Ellsworth, P. C., Mesquita, B., Leu, J., Tanida, S., & Van de Veerdonk, E. (2008). Placing the face in context: Cultural differences in the perception of facial emotion. *Journal of Personality and Social Psychology, 94,* 365–381. (p. 474)

Mata, A., Ferreira, M. B., & Sherman, S. J. (2013). The metacognitive advantage of deliberative thinkers: A dual-process perspective on overconfidence. *Journal of Personality and Social Psychology, 105,* 353–373. (p. 365)

Mataix-Cols, D., Rosario-Campos, M. C., & Leckman, J. F. (2005). A multidimensional model of obsessive-compulsive disorder. *American Journal of Psychiatry, 162,* 228–238. (p. 626)

Mataix-Cols, D., Wooderson, S., Lawrence, N., Brammer, M. J., Speckens, A., & Phillips, M. L. (2004). Distinct neural correlates of washing, checking, and hoarding symptom dimensions in obsessive-compulsive disorder. *Archives of General Psychiatry, 61,* 564–576. (p. 626)

Mather, M., Cacioppo, J. T., & Kanwisher, N. (2013). How fMRI can inform cognitive theories. *Perspectives on Psychological Science, 8,* 108–113. (p. 68)

Mather, M., Canli, T., English, T., Whitfield, S., Wais, P., Ochsner, K., Gabrieli, J. D. E., & Carstensen, L. L. (2004). Amygdala responses to emotionally valenced stimuli in older and younger adults. *Psychological Science, 15,* 259–263. (p. 224)

Mather, M., Lighthall, N. R., Nga, L., & Gorlick, M. A. (2010). Sex differences in how stress affects brain activity during face viewing. *NeuroReport, 21,* 933–937. (p. 492)

Mather, M., & Sutherland, M. (2012, February). The selective effects of emotional arousal on memory. *APA Science Brief* (www.apa.org). (p. 331)

Matheson, S. L., Shepherd, A. M., Pinchbeck, R. M., Laurens, K. R., & Carr, V. J. (2013). Childhood adversity in schizophrenia: A systematic meta-analysis. *Psychological Medicine, 43,* 225–238. (p. 641)

Matsumoto, D. (1994). *People: Psychology from a cultural perspective.* Pacific Grove, CA: Brooks/Cole. (p. 380)

Matsumoto, D., & Ekman, P. (1989). American-Japanese cultural differences in intensity ratings of facial expressions of emotion. *Motivation and Emotion, 13,* 143–157. (p. 472)

Matsumoto, D., & Willingham, B. (2006). The thrill of victory and the agony of defeat: Spontaneous expressions of medal winners of the 2004 Athens Olympic Games. *Journal of Personality and Social Psychology, 91,* 568–581. (p. 473)

Matsumoto, D., & Willingham, B. (2009a). Spontaneous facial expressions of emotion of congenitally and noncongenitally blind individuals. *Journal of Personality and Social Psychology, 96,* 1–10. (p. 473)

Matsumoto, D., Willingham, B., & Olide, A. (2009b). Sequential dynamics of culturally moderated facial expressions of emotion. *Psychological Science, 20,* 1269–1275. (pp. 473, 474)

Mattanah, J. F., Lopez, F. G, & Govern, J. M. (2011). The contributions of parental attachment bonds to college student development and adjustment: A meta-analytic review. *Journal of Counseling Psychology, 58,* 565–596. (p. 199)

Matthews, K. A. (2005). Psychological perspectives on the development of coronary heart disease. *American Psychologist, 60,* 783–796. (p. 498)

Matthews, R. N., Domjan, M., Ramsey, M., & Crews, D. (2007). Learning effects on sperm competition and reproductive fitness. *Psychological Science, 18,* 758–762. (p. 284)

Maurer, D., & Maurer, C. (1988). *The world of the newborn.* New York: Basic Books. (p. 183)

Mauss, I. B., Shallcross, A. J., Troy, A. S., John, O. P., Ferrer, E., Wilhelm, F. H., & Gross, J. J. (2011). Don't hide your happiness! Positive emotion dissociation, social connectedness, and psychological functioning. *Journal of Personality and Social Psychology, 100,* 738–748. (p. 479)

Mautz, B., Wong, B., Peters, R., & Jennions, M. (2013). Penis size interacts with body shape and height to influence male attractiveness. *Proceedings of the National Academy of Sciences, 110,* 6925–6693. (p. 148)

May, C., & Hasher, L. (1998). Synchrony effects in inhibitory control over thought and action. *Journal of Experimental Psychology: Human Perception and Performance, 24,* 363–380. (p. 100)

May, P. A., & Gossage, J. P. (2001). Estimating the prevalence of fetal alcohol syndrome: A summary. *Alcohol Research and Health, 25,* 159–167. (p. 182)

Mayberg, H. S. (2006). Defining neurocircuits in depression: Strategies toward treatment selection based on neuroimaging phenotypes. *Psychiatric Annals, 36,* 259–268. (p. 686)

Mayberg, H. S. (2007). Defining the neural circuitry of depression: Toward a new nosology with therapeutic implications. *Biological Psychiatry, 61,* 729–730. (p. 686)

Mayberg, H. S. (2009). Targeted modulation of neural circuits: A new treatment strategy for depression. *Journal of Clinical Investigation, 119,* 717–25. (p. 686)

Mayberg, H. S., Lozano, A. M., Voon, V., McNeely, H. E., Seminowicz, D., Hamani, C., Schwalb, J. M., & Kennedy, S. H. (2005). Deep brain stimulation for treatment-resistant depression. *Neuron, 45,* 651–660. (p. 686)

Mayberry, R. I., Lock, E., & Kazmi, H. (2002). Linguistic ability and early language exposure. *Nature, 417,* 38. (p. 374)

Mayer, J. D., Salovey, P., & Caruso, D. R. (2002). *The Mayer-Salovey-Caruso emotional intelligence test (MSCEIT).* Toronto: Multi-Health Systems, Inc. (p. 390)

Mayer, J. D., Salovey, P., & Caruso, D. R. (2012). The validity of the MSCEIT: Additional analyses and evidence. *Emotion Review, 4,* 403–408. (p. 390)

Mayer, J. D., Salovey, P., Caruso, D. R., & Cherkasskiy, L. (2011). Emotional intelligence. In R. J. Sternberg & S. B. Kaufman (Eds.), *The Cambridge handbook of intelligence.* New York: Cambridge University Press. (p. 390)

Mays, V. M., Cochran, S. D., & Barnes, N. W. (2007). Race, race-based discrimination, and health outcomes among African Americans. *Annual Review of Psychology, 58,* 201–225. (p. 490)

Mazure, C., Keita, G., & Blehar, M. (2002). *Summit on women and depression: Proceedings and recommendations.* Washington, DC: American Psychological Association (www.apa.org/pi/wpo/women&depression.pdf). (p. 635)

Mazzoni, G., & Memon, A. (2003). Imagination can create false autobiographical memories. *Psychological Science, 14,* 186–188. (p. 344)

Mazzoni, G., Scoboria, A., & Harvey, L. (2010). Nonbelieved memories. *Psychological Science, 21,* 1334–1340. (p. 345)

Mazzoni, G., & Vannucci, M. (2007). Hindsight bias, the misinformation effect, and false autobiographical memories. *Social Cognition, 25,* 203–220. (p. 347)

McAndrew, F. T. (2009). The interacting roles of testosterone and challenges to status in human male aggression. *Aggression and Violent Behavior, 14,* 330–335. (p. 546)

McAneny, L. (1996, September). Large majority think government conceals information about UFO's. *Gallup Poll Monthly,* pp. 23–26. (p. 346)

McBurney, D. H. (1996). *How to think like a psychologist: Critical thinking in psychology.* Upper Saddle River, NJ: Prentice-Hall. (p. 79)

McBurney, D. H., & Collings, V. B. (1984). *Introduction to sensation and perception* (2nd ed.). Englewood Cliffs, NJ: Prentice-Hall. (pp. 252, 253)

McBurney, D. H., & Gent, J. F. (1979). On the nature of taste qualities. *Psychological Bulletin, 86,* 151–167. (p. 266)

McCain, N. L., Gray, D. P., Elswick, R. K., Jr., Robins, J. W., Tuck, I., Walter, J. M., Rausch, S. M., & Ketchum, J. M. (2008). A randomized clinical trial of alternative stress management interventions in persons with HIV infection. *Journal of Consulting and Clinical Psychology, 76,* 431–441. (p. 495)

McCann, I. L., & Holmes, D. S. (1984). Influence of aerobic exercise on depression. *Journal of Personality and Social Psychology, 46,* 1142–1147. (p. 508)

McCann, U. D., Eligulashvili, V., & Ricaurte, G. A. (2001). (+–)3,4–Methylene-dioxymethamphetamine ('Ecstasy')-induced serotonin neurotoxicity: Clinical studies. *Neuropsychobiology, 42,* 11–16. (p. 124)

McCarthy, P. (1986, July). Scent: The tie that binds? *Psychology Today,* pp. 6, 10. (pp. 266, 267)

McCauley, C. R. (2002). Psychological issues in understanding terrorism and the response to terrorism. In C. E. Stout (Ed.), *The psychology of terrorism* (Vol. 3). Westport, CT: Praeger/Greenwood. (p. 534)

McCauley, C. R., & Segal, M. E. (1987). Social psychology of terrorist groups. In C. Hendrick (Ed.), *Group processes and intergroup relations.* Beverly Hills, CA: Sage. (p. 534)

McClendon, B. T., & Prentice-Dunn, S. (2001). Reducing skin cancer risk: An intervention based on protection motivation theory. *Journal of Health Psychology, 6,* 321–328. (p. 520)

McClintock, M. K., & Herdt, G. (1996, December). Rethinking puberty: The development of sexual attraction. *Current Directions in Psychological Science, 5*(6), 178–183. (p. 165)

McClung, M., & Collins, D. (2007). "Because I know it will!": Placebo effects of an ergogenic aid on athletic performance. *Journal of Sport & Exercise Psychology, 29,* 382–394. (p. 36)

McClure, E. B. (2000). A meta-analytic review of sex differences in facial expression processing and their development in infants, children, and adolescents. *Psychological Bulletin, 126,* 424–453. (p. 470)

McClure, M. J., Lydon, J. E., Baccus, J. R., & Baldwin, M. W. (2010). A signal detection analysis of chronic attachment anxiety at speed dating: Being unpopular is only the first part of the problem. *Personality and Social Psychology Bulletin, 36,* 1024–1036. (p. 231)

McCool, G. (1999, October 26). Mirror-gazing Venezuelans top of vanity stakes. *Toronto Star* (via web.lexis-nexis.com). (p. 554)

McCord, J. (1978). A thirty-year follow-up on treatment effects. *American Psychologist, 33,* 284–289. (p. 673)

McCord, J. (1979). Following up on Cambridge-Somerville. *American Psychologist, 34,* 727. (p. 673)

McCormick, C. M., & Witelson, S. F. (1991). A cognitive profile of homosexual men compared to heterosexual men and women. *Psychoneuroendocrinology, 16,* 459–473. (p. 446)

McCrae, R. R. (2009). The five-factor model of personality traits: Consensus and controversy. In P. J. Corr & G. Matthews, Gerald (eds.). *The Cambridge handbook of personality psychology.* New York: Cambridge University Press. (p. 590)

McCrae, R. R. (2011). Personality theories for the 21st century. *Teaching of Psychology, 38,* 209–214. (p. 591)

McCrae, R. R., & Costa, P. T., Jr. (1986). Clinical assessment can benefit from recent advances in personality psychology. *American Psychologist, 41,* 1001–1003. (p. 590)

McCrae, R. R., & Costa, P. T., Jr. (1990). *Personality in adulthood.* New York: Guilford. (p. 220)

McCrae, R. R., & Costa, P. T., Jr. (1994). The stability of personality: Observations and evaluations. *Current Directions in Psychological Science, 3,* 173–175. (p. 592)

McCrae, R. R., & Costa, P. T., Jr. (2008). The Five-Factor Theory of personality. In O. P. John, R. W., Robins, & L. A. Pervin (eds.), *Handbook of personality: Theory and research,* 3rd edition. New York: Guilford. (p. 590)

McCrae, R. R., Scally, M., Terraccioani, A., Abecasis, G. R., & Costa, Jr., P. T. (2010). An alternative to the search for single polymorphisms: Toward molecular personality scales for the Five-Factor Model. *Journal of Personality and Social Psychology, 99,* 1014–1024. (p. 590)

McCrae, R. R., Terracciano, A., et al. (2005). Universal features of personality traits from the observer's perspective: Data from 50 cultures. *Journal of Personality and Social Psychology, 88,* 547–561. (p. 591)

McCrink, K., & Wynn, K. (2004). Large-number addition and subtraction by 9-month-old infants. *Psychological Science, 15,* 776–781. (p. 188)

McCrory, E. J., De Brito, S. A., Sebastian, C. L., Mechelli, A., Bird, G., Kelly, P. A., & Viding, E. (2011). Heightened neural reactivity to threat in child victims of family violence. *Current Biology, 21,* R947–948. (p. 200)

McCullough, M. E., Hoyt, W. T., Larson, D. B., Koenig, H. G., & Thoresen, C. (2000). Religious involvement and mortality: A meta-analytic review. *Health Psychology, 19,* 211–222. (p. 512)

McCullough, M. E., & Laurenceau, J-P. (2005). Religiousness and the trajectory of self-rated health across adulthood. *Personality and Social Psychology Bulletin, 31,* 560–573. (p. 512)

McCullough, M. E., & Willoughby, B. L. B. (2009). Religion, self-regulation, and self-control: Associations, explanations, and implications. *Psychological Bulletin, 135,* 69–93. (p. 512)

McDaniel, M. (2012). Put the SPRINT in knowledge training: Training with Spacing, Retrieval, and INTerleaving. In M. McDaniel (Ed.), *Training cognition: Optimizing efficiency, durability, and generalizability,* pp. 267–286. New York: Psychology Press. (p. 326)

McDaniel, M. A., Howard, D. C., & Einstein, G. O. (2009). The read-recite-review study strategy: Effective and portable. *Psychological Science, 20,* 516–522. (pp. 14, 16, 25, 42,48, 65, 74, 88, 99, 116, 130, 144, 151, 174, 184, 203, 213, 226, 238, 255, 275, 289, 300, 314, 328, 337, 352, 369, 384, 392, 399, 405, 416, 424, 433, 447, 456, 468, 475, 487, 500, 514, 524, 537, 550, 568, 582, 594, 606, 19, 627, 639, 646, 654, 672, 681, 692, A-16)

McDermott, R., Tingley, D., Cowden, J., Frazzetto, G., & Johnson, D. D. P. (2009). Monoamine oxidase A gene (MAOA) predicts behavioral aggression following provocation. *Proceedings of the National Academy of Sciences, 106,* 2118–2123. (p. 545)

McEvoy, S. P., Stevenson, M. R., McCartt, A. T., Woodward, M., Hawroth, C., Palamara, P., & Ceracelli, R. (2005). Role of mobile phones in motor vehicle crashes resulting in hospital attendance: A case-crossover study. *British Medical Journal, 33,* 428. (p. 97)

McEvoy, S. P., Stevenson, M. R., & Woodward, M. (2007). The contribution of passengers versus mobile phone use to motor vehicle crashes resulting in hospital attendance by the driver. *Accident Analysis and Prevention, 39,* 1170–1176. (p. 97)

McFadden, D. (2002). Masculinization effects in the auditory system. *Archives of Sexual Behavior, 31,* 99–111. (p. 445)

McFarland, C., & Ross, M. (1987). The relation between current impressions and memories of self and dating partners. *Psychological Bulletin, 13,* 228–238. (p. 347)

McGaugh, J. L. (1994). Quoted by B. Bower, Stress hormones hike emotional memories. *Science News, 146,* 262. (p. 331)

McGaugh, J. L. (2003). *Memory and emotion: The making of lasting memories.* New York: Columbia University Press. (p. 331)

McGaugh, J. L., & LePort, A. (2014, February). Remembrance of all things past. *Scientific American,* pp. 41–45. (p. 338)

McGhee, P. E. (June, 1976). Children's appreciation of humor: A test of the cognitive congruency principle. *Child Development, 47*(2), 420–426. (p. 190)

McGowan, P. O., Sasaki, A., D'Alessio, A. C., Dymov, S., Labonté, B., Szyl, M., Turecki, G., & Meaney, M. J. (2009). Epigenetic regulation of the glucocorticoid receptor in human brain associates with childhood abuse. *Nature Neuroscience, 12,* 342–348. (p. 626)

McGrath, J. J., & Welham, J. L. (1999). Season of birth and schizophrenia: A systematic review and meta-analysis of data from the Southern hemisphere. *Schizophrenia Research, 35,* 237–242. (p. 643)

McGrath, J. J., Welham, J., & Pemberton, M. (1995). Month of birth, hemisphere of birth and schizophrenia. *British Journal of Psychiatry, 167,* 783–785. (p. 643)

McGue, M. (2010). The end of behavioral genetics? *Behavioral Genetics, 40,* 284–296. (p. 151)

McGue, M., & Bouchard, T. J., Jr. (1998). Genetic and environmental influences on human behavioral differences. *Annual Review of Neuroscience, 21,* 1–24. (p. 138)

McGue, M., Bouchard, T. J., Jr., Iacono, W. G., & Lykken, D. T. (1993). Behavioral genetics of cognitive ability: A life-span perspective. In R. Plomin & G. E. McClearn (Eds.), *Nature, nurture and psychology.* Washington, DC: American Psychological Association. (p. 407)

McGue, M., & Christensen, K. (2013). Growing old but not growing apart: Twin similarity in the latter half of the lifespan. *Behavior Genetics, 43,* 1–12. (p. 136)

McGuire, W. J. (1986). The myth of massive media impact: Savings and salvagings. In G. Comstock (Ed.), *Public communication and behavior.* Orlando, FL: Academic Press. (p. 312)

McGurk, H., & MacDonald, J. (1976). Hearing lips and seeing voices. *Nature, 264,* 746–748. (p. 270)

McHugh, P. R. (1995a). Witches, multiple personalities, and other psychiatric artifacts. *Nature Medicine, 1*(2), 110–114. (p. 648)

McHugh, P. R. (1995b). Resolved: Multiple personality disorder is an individually and socially created artifact. *Journal of the American Academy of Child and Adolescent Psychiatry, 34,* 957–959. (p. 648)

McKay, J. (2000). Building self-esteem in children. In M. McKay & P. Fanning (eds.), *Self-esteem.* New York: New Harbinger/St. Martins. (p. 599)

McKellar, J., Stewart, E., & Humphreys, K. (2003). Alcoholics Anonymous involvement and positive alcohol-related outcomes: Cause, consequence, or just a correlate? A prospective 2-year study of 2,319 alcohol-dependent men. *Journal of Consulting and Clinical Psychology, 71,* 302–308. (p. 671)

McKenna, K. Y. A., Green, A. S., & Gleason, M. E. J. (2002). What's the big attraction? Relationship formation on the Internet. *Journal of Social Issues, 58,* 9–31. (p. 552)

McKone, E., Kanwisher, N., & Duchaine, B. C. (2007). Can generic expertise explain special processing for faces? *Trends in Cognitive Sciences, 11,* 8–15. (p. 245)

McLaughlin, M. (2010, October 2). JK Rowling: Depression, the 'terrible place that allowed me to come back stronger.' *The Scotsman* (www.scotsman.com). (p. 631)

McLean, C. P., & Anderson, E. R. (2009). Brave men and timid women? A review of the gender differences in fear and anxiety. *Clinical Psychology Review, 29,* 496–505. (p. 620)

McMurray, B. (2007). Defusing the childhood vocabulary explosion. *Science, 317,* 631. (p. 371)

McMurray, C. (2004, January 13). U.S., Canada, Britain: Who's getting in shape? *Gallup Poll Tuesday Briefing* (www.gallup.com). (p. 508)

McNally, R. J. (1999). EMDR and Mesmerism: A comparative historical analysis. *Journal of Anxiety Disorders, 13,* 225–236. (p. 677)

McNally, R. J. (2003). *Remembering trauma.* Cambridge, MA: Harvard University Press. (pp. 349, 624)

McNally, R. J. (2007). Betrayal trauma theory: A critical appraisal. *Memory, 15,* 280–294. (p. 349)

McNally, R. J. (2012). Are we winning the war against posttraumatic stress disorder? *Science, 336,* 872–874. (pp. 102, 623)

McNally, R. J. (2012). Searching for repressed memory. *Nebraska Symposium on Motivation, 58,* 121–147. (p. 349)

McNally, R. J., & Geraerts, E. (2009). A new solution to the recovered memory debate. *Perspectives in Psychological Science, 4,* 126–134. (p. 349)

McNeil, B. J., Pauker, S. G., & Tversky, A. (1988). On the framing of medical decisions. In D. E. Bell, H. Raiffa, & A. Tversky (Eds.), *Decision making: Descriptive, normative, and prescriptive interactions.* New York: Cambridge University Press. (p. 362)

McNulty, J. K., Olson, M. A., Meltzer, A. L., & Shaffer, M. J. (2013). Though they may be unaware newlyweds implicitly know whether their marriage will be satisfying. *Science, 342,* 1119–1120. (p. 364)

McWhorter, J. (2012, April 23). Talking with your fingers. *New York Times* (www.nytimes.com). (p. 452)

Mead, G. E., Morley, W., Campbell, P., Greig, C. A., McMurdo, M., & Lawlor, D. A. (2010). Exercise for depression. *Cochrance Database Systematic Reviews,* Issue 3. Art. No. CD004366. (p. 508)

Meador, B. D., & Rogers, C. R. (1984). Person-centered therapy. In R. J. Corsini (Ed.), *Current psychotherapies* (3rd ed.). Itasca, IL: Peacock. (p. 662)

Medical Institute for Sexual Health. (1994, April). Condoms ineffective against human papilloma virus. *Sexual Health Update,* p. 2. (p. 436)

Medland, S. E., Perelle, I., De Monte, V., & Ehrman, L. (2004). Effects of culture, sex, and age on the distribution of handedness: An evaluation of the sensitivity of three measures of handedness. *Laterality: Asymmetries of Body, Brain, and Cognition, 9,* 287–297. (p. 86)

Mednick, S. A., Huttunen, M. O., & Machon, R. A. (1994). Prenatal influenza infections and adult schizophrenia. *Schizophrenia Bulletin, 20,* 263–267. (p. 643)

Medvec, V. H., Madey, S. F., & Gilovich, T. (1995). When less is more: Counterfactual thinking and satisfaction among Olympic medalists. *Journal of Personality and Social Psychology, 69,* 603–610. (p. 605)

Mehl, M., Gosling, S. D., & Pennebaker, J. W. (2006). Personality in its natural habitat: Manifestations and implicit folk theories of personality in daily life. *Journal of Personality and Social Psychology, 90,* 862–877. (p. 592)

Mehl, M. R., & Pennebaker, J. W. (2003). The sounds of social life: A psychometric analysis of students' daily social environments and natural conversations. *Journal of Personality and Social Psychology, 84,* 857–870. (p. 29)

Mehl, M. R., Vazire, S., Holleran, S. E., & Clark, C. S. (2010). Eavesdropping on happiness: Well-being is related to having less small talk and more substantive conversations. *Psychological Science, 21,* 539–541. (p. 487)

Mehl, M. R., Vazire, S., Ramirez-Esparza, N., Slatcher, R. B., & Pennebaker, J. W. (2007). Are women really more talkative than men? *Science, 317,* 82. (p. 163)

Mehta, D., Klengel, T., Conneely, K. N., Smith, A. K., Altmann, A., Pace, T. W., . . . Binder, E. B. (2013). Childhood maltreatment is associated with distinct genomic and epigenetic profiles in posttraumatic stress disorder. *PNAS Proceedings of the National Academy of Sciences of the United States of America, 110,* 8302–8307. (p. 626)

Mehta, M. R. (2007). Cortico-hippocampal interaction during up-down states and memory consolidation. *Nature Neuroscience, 10,* 13–15. (p. 330)

Meichenbaum, D. (1977). *Cognitive-behavior modification: An integrative approach.* New York: Plenum Press. (p. 668)

Meichenbaum, D. (1985). *Stress inoculation training.* New York: Pergamon. (p. 668)

Meier, M. H., Caspi, A., Ambler, A., Harrington, H., Houts, R., Keefe, R. S., . . . Moffitt, T. E. (2012). Persistent cannabis users show neuropsychological decline from childhood to midlife. *PNAS, 109,* E2657–2664. (p. 125)

Meijer, E. H., & Verschuere, B. (2010). The polygraph and the detection of deception. *Journal of Forensic Psychology Practice, 10,* 525–538. (p. 467)

Melby-Lervåg, M., & Hulme, C. (2013). Is working memory training effective? A meta-analytic review. *Developmental Psychology, 49,* 270–291. (p. 218)

Meltzoff, A. N. (1988). Infant imitation after a 1-week delay: Long-term memory for novel acts and multiple stimuli. *Developmental Psychology, 24,* 470–476. (p. 308)

Meltzoff, A. N., Kuhl, P. K., Movellan, J., & Sejnowski, T. J. (2009). Foundations for a new science of learning. *Science, 325,* 284–288. (pp. 308, 372)

Meltzoff, A. N., & Moore, M. K. (1989). Imitation in newborn infants: Exploring the range of gestures imitated and the underlying mechanisms. *Developmental Psychology, 25,* 954–962. (pp. 308, 312)

Meltzoff, A. N., & Moore, M. K. (1997). Explaining facial imitation: A theoretical model. *Early Development and Parenting, 6,* 179–192. (pp. 308, 312)

Melzack, R. (1992, April). Phantom limbs. *Scientific American,* pp. 120–126. (p. 262)

Melzack, R. (1998, February). Quoted in Phantom limbs. *Discover,* p. 20. (p. 262)

Melzack, R. (2005). Evolution of the neuromatrix theory of pain. *Pain Practice, 5,* 85–94. (p. 262)

Melzack, R., & Katz, J. (2013). Pain. *Wiley Interdisciplinary Reviews: Cognitive Science, 4,* 1–15. (p. 262)

Melzack, R., & Wall, P. D. (1965). Pain mechanisms: A new theory. *Science, 150,* 971–979. (p. 262)

Melzack, R., & Wall, P. D. (1983). *The challenge of pain.* New York: Basic Books. (p. 262)

Mendes, E. (2010, June 2). U.S. exercise levels up, but demographic differences remain. www.gallup.com. (p. 509)

Mendes, E., & McGeeney, K. (2012, July 9). Women's health trails men's most in former Soviet Union. Gallup (www.gallup.com). (p. 631)

Mende-Siedlecki, P., Said, C. P., & Todorov, A. (2013). The social evaluation of faces: A meta-analysis of functional neuroimaging studies. *SCAN, 8,* 285–299. (p. 71)

Mendle, J., Turkheimer, E., & Emery, R. E. (2007). Detrimental psychological outcomes associated with early pubertal timing in adolescent girls. *Developmental Review, 27,* 151–171. (p. 204)

Mendolia, M., & Kleck, R. E. (1993). Effects of talking about a stressful event on arousal: Does what we talk about make a difference? *Journal of Personality and Social Psychology, 64,* 283–292. (p. 506)

Merari, A. (2002). *Explaining suicidal terrorism: Theories versus empirical evidence.* Invited address to the American Psychological Association. (p. 533)

Meriac, J. P., Hoffman, B. J., Woehr, D. J., & Fleisher, M. S. (2008). Further evidence for the validity of assessment center dimensions: A meta-analysis of the incremental criterion-related validity of dimension ratings. *Journal of Applied Psychology, 93,* 1042–1052. (p. 597)

Merikangas, K. R., Jin, R., He, J. P., Kessler, R. C., Lee, S., Sampson, N. A., . . . Zarkov, Z. (2011). Prevalence and correlates of bipolar spectrum disorder in the world mental health survey initiative. *Archives of General Psychiatry, 68,* 241–251. (p. 630)

Merry, S. N., Stasiak, K., Shepherd, M., Frampton, C., Fleming, T., & Lucassen, M. F. G. (2012). The effectiveness of SPARX, a computerised self help intervention for adolescents seeking help for depression: Randomised controlled non-inferiority trial. *British Medical Journal, 344,* 1–16. (p. 670)

Merskey, H. (1992). The manufacture of personalities: The production of multiple personality disorder. *British Journal of Psychiatry, 160,* 327–340. (p. 648)

Mervis, J. (2011a). Giving children a Head Start is possible—but it's not easy. *Science, 333,* 956–957. (p. 409)

Merzenich, M. (2007). Quoted at Posit Science Brain Fitness Program (www.positscience.com). (p. 218)

Mesch, G. (2001). Social relationships and Internet use among adolescents in Israel. *Social Science Quarterly, 82,* 329–340. (p. 452)

Mesoudi, A. (2009). How cultural evolutionary theory can inform social psychology and vice versa. *Psychological Review, 116,* 929–952. (p. 156)

Messias, E., Eaton, W. W., Grooms, A. N. (2011). Economic grand rounds: Income inequality and depression prevalence across the United States: An ecological study. *Psychiatric Services, 62,* 710–712. (p. 548)

Messinis, L., Kyprianidou, A., Malefaki, S., & Papathanasopoulos, P. (2006). Neuropsychological deficits in long-term frequent cannabis users. *Neurology, 66,* 737–739. (p. 125)

Mestel, R. (1997, April 26). Get real, Siggi. *New Scientist* (www.newscientist.com/ns/970426/siggi.html). (p. 112)

Meston, C. M., & Buss, D. M. (2007). Why humans have sex. *Archives of Sexual Behavior, 36,* 477–507. (p. 437)

Metcalfe, J. (1986). Premonitions of *insight* predict impending error. *Journal of Experimental Psychology: Learning, Memory, and Cognition, 12,* 623–634. (p. 357)

Metcalfe, J. (1998). Cognitive optimism: Self-deception or memory-based processing heuristics. *Personality and Social Psychology Review, 2,* 100–110. (p. 360)

Metzler, D. (2011, Spring). Vocabulary growth in adult cross-fostered chimpanzees. *Friends of Washoe, 32*(3), 11–13. (p. 378)

Meyer, I. H. (2003). Prejudice, social stress, and mental health in lesbian, gay, and bisexual populations: Conceptual issues and research evidence. *Psychological Bulletin, 129,* 674–697. (p. 610)

Meyer-Bahlburg, H. F. L. (1995). Psychoneuroendocrinology and sexual pleasure: The aspect of sexual orientation. In P. R. Abramson & S. D. Pinkerton (Eds.), *Sexual nature/sexual culture.* Chicago: University of Chicago Press. (p. 444)

Michael, R. B., Garry, M., & Kirsch, I. (2012). Suggestion, cognition, and behavior. *Current Directions in Psychological Science, 21,* 151–156. (p. 36)

Michaels, J. W., Bloomel, J. M., Brocato, R. M., Linkous, R. A., & Rowe, J. S. (1982). Social facilitation and inhibition in a natural setting. *Replications in Social Psychology, 2,* 21–24. (p. 532)

Michener, J. A. (1978, February 3). *External forces and inner voices.* Speech at the Chapel of the Four Chaplains, Philadelphia, PA. (p. 530)

Middlebrooks, J. C., & Green, D. M. (1991). Sound localization by human listeners. *Annual Review of Psychology, 42,* 135–159. (p. 260)

Miers, R. (2009, Spring). Calum's road. *Scottish Life,* pp. 36–39, 75. (p. 455)

Mihura, J. L., Meyer, G. J., Dumitrascu, N., & Bombel, G. (2013). The validity of individual Rorschach variables: Systematic reviews and meta-analyses of the comprehensive system. *Psychological Bulletin, 139,* 548–605. (p. 579)

Mikhail, J. (2007). Universal moral grammar: Theory, evidence and the future. *Trends in Cognitive Sciences, 11,* 143–152. (p. 146)

Mikkelsen, T. S., et al. (2005). Initial sequence of the chimpanzee genome and comparison with the human genome. *Nature, 437,* 69–87. (p. 135)

Mikulincer, M., Florian, V., & Hirschberger, G. (2003). The existential function of close relationships: Introducing death into the science of love. *Personality and Social Psychology Review, 7,* 20–40. (p. 582)

Mikulincer, M., & Shaver, P. R. (2001). Attachment theory and intergroup bias: Evidence that priming the secure base schema attenuates negative reactions to outgroups. *Journal of Personality and Social Psychology, 81,* 97–115. (p. 543)

Milan, R. J., Jr., & Kilmann, P. R. (1987). Interpersonal factors in premarital contraception. *Journal of Sex Research, 23,* 289–321. (p. 438)

Miles, D. R., & Carey, G. (1997). Genetic and environmental architecture of human aggression. *Journal of Personality and Social Psychology, 72,* 207–217. (p. 545)

Milgram, S. (1963). Behavioral study of obedience. *Journal of Abnormal & Social Psychology, 67*(4), 371–378. (p. 528)

Milgram, S. (1974). *Obedience to authority.* New York: Harper & Row. (pp. 528, 529, 531)

Miller, G. (2004). Axel, Buck share award for deciphering how the nose knows. *Science, 306,* 207. (p. 267)

Miller, G. (2005). The dark side of glia. *Science, 308,* 778–781. (p. 54)

Miller, G. (2008). Tackling alcoholism with drugs. *Science, 320,* 168–170. (p. 127)

Miller, G. (2010). Anything but child's play. *Science, 327,* 1192–1193. (p. 630)

Miller, G. (2010). fMRI lie detection fails a legal test. *Science, 328,* 1336–1337. (p. 467)

Miller, G. (2012). Drone wars: Are remotely piloted aircraft changing the nature of war? *Science, 336,* 842–843. (p. 530)

Miller, G. (2012). How are memories retrieved? *Science, 338,* 30–31. (p. 329)

Miller, G. A. (1956). The magical number seven, plus or minus two: Some limits on our capacity for processing information. *Psychological Review, 63,* 81–97. (p. 323)

Miller, G. E., & Blackwell, E. (2006). Turning up the heat: Inflammation as a mechanism linking chronic stress, depression, and heart disease. *Current Directions in Psychological Science, 15,* 269–272. (pp. 498, 499)

Miller, G. E., & Chen, E. (2010). Harsh family climate in early life presages the emergence of a proinflammatory phenotype in adolescence. *Psychological Science, 21,* 848–856. (p. 499)

Miller, G., Chen, E., & Parker, K. (2011). Psychological stress in childhood and susceptibility to the chronic diseases of aging: Moving toward a model of behavioral and biological mechanisms. *Psychological Bulletin, 137,* 959–997. (p. 492)

Miller, H. C., Pattison, K. F., DeWall, C. N., Rayburn-Reeves, R., & Zentall, T. R. (2010). Self-control without a "self"? Common self-control processes in humans and dogs. *Psychological Science, 21,* 534–538. (p. 504)

Miller, J., Shepherdson, P., & Trevena, J. (2011). Effects of clock monitoring on electroencephalographic activity: Is unconscious movement initiation an artifact of the clock? *Psychological Science, 22,* 103–109. (p. 95)

Miller, J. F., Neufang, M., Solway, A., Brandt, A., Trippel, M., Mader, I., Hefft, S., . . . Schulze-Bonhage, A. (2013). Neural activity in human hippocampal formation reveals the spatial context of retrieved memories. *Science, 342,* 1111–1114. (p. 329)

Miller, J. G., & Bersoff, D. M. (1995). Development in the context of everyday family relationships: Culture, interpersonal morality and adaptation. In M. Killen & D. Hart (Eds.), *Morality in everyday life: A developmental perspective.* New York: Cambridge University Press. (p. 206)

Miller, L. K. (1999). The Savant Syndrome: Intellectual impairment and exceptional skill. *Psychological Bulletin, 125,* 31–46. (p. 387)

Miller, N. E. (1985, February). Rx: Biofeedback. *Psychology Today,* pp. 54–59. (p. 509)

Miller, P. (2012, January). A thing or two about twins. *National Geographic,* pp. 38–65. (p. 137)

Miller, P. J. O., Aoki, K., Rendell, L. E., & Amano, M. (2008). Stereotypical resting behavior of the sperm whale. *Current Biology, 18,* R21–R23. (p. 101)

Miller, S. D., Blackburn, T., Scholes, G., White, G. L., & Mamalis, N. (1991). Optical differences in multiple personality disorder: A second look. *Journal of Nervous and Mental Disease, 179,* 132–135. (p. 648)

Milner, A. D., & Goodale, M. A. (2008). Two visual systems re-viewed. *Neuropsychologia, 46,* 774–785. (p. 94)

Milyavskaya, M., Gingras, I., Mageau, G. A., Koestner, R., Gagnon, H., Fang, J., & Bolché, J. (2009). Balance across contexts: Importance of balanced need satisfaction across various life domains. *Personality and Social Psychology Bulletin, 35,* 1031–1045. (p. 449)

Mineka, S. (1985). The frightful complexity of the origins of fears. In F. R. Brush & J. B. Overmier (Eds.), *Affect, conditioning and cognition: Essays on the determinants of behavior.* Hillsdale, NJ: Erlbaum. (p. 625)

Mineka, S. (2002). Animal models of clinical psychology. In N. Smelser & P. Baltes (Eds.), *International encyclopedia of the social and behavioral sciences.* Oxford, England: Elsevier Science. (p. 625)

Mineka, S., & Oehlberg, K. (2008). The relevance of recent developments in classical conditioning to understanding the etiology and maintenance of anxiety disorders. *Acta Psychologica, 127,* 567–580. (p. 624)

Mineka, S., & Zinbarg, R. (1996). Conditioning and ethological models of anxiety disorders: Stress-in-dynamic-context anxiety models. In D. Hope (Ed.), *Perspectives on anxiety, panic, and fear* (Nebraska Symposium on Motivation). Lincoln: University of Nebraska Press. (pp. 627, 690)

Minsky, M. (1986). *The society of mind.* New York: Simon & Schuster. (p. 93)

Mirescu, C., & Gould, E. (2006). Stress and adult neurogenesis. *Hippocampus, 16,* 233–238. (p. 492)

Mischel, W. (1968). *Personality and assessment.* New York: Wiley. (p. 592)

Mischel, W. (1981). Current issues and challenges in personality. In L. T. Benjamin, Jr. (Ed.), *The G. Stanley Hall Lecture Series* (Vol. 1). Washington, DC: American Psychological Association. (p. 597)

Mischel, W. (2009). From *Personality and Assessment* (1968) to personality science. *Journal of Research in Personality, 43,* 282–290. (p. 592)

Mischel, W., Shoda, Y., & Peake, P. K. (1988). The nature of adolescent competencies predicted by preschool delay of gratification. *Journal of Personality and Social Psychology, 54,* 687–696. (p. 208)

Mischel, W., Shoda, Y., & Rodriguez, M. L. (1989). Delay of gratification in children. *Science, 244,* 933–938. (pp. 208, 293)

Mischkowski, D., Kross, E., & Bushman, B. (2012). Flies on the wall are less aggressive: Self-distancing "in the heat of the moment" reduces aggressive thoughts, angry feelings and aggressive behavior. *Journal of Experimental Social Psychology, 48,* 1187–1191. (p. 478)

Miserandino, M. (1991). Memory and the seven dwarfs. *Teaching of Psychology, 18,* 169–171. (p. 319)

Mishkin, M. (1982). A memory system in the monkey. *Philosophical Transactions of the Royal Society of London: Biological Sciences, 298,* 83–95. (p. 330)

Mishkin, M., Suzuki, W. A., Gadian, D. G., & Vargha-Khadem, F. (1997). Hierarchical organization of cognitive memory. *Philosophical Transactions of the Royal Society of London: Biological Sciences, 352,* 1461–1467. (p. 330)

Mishra, A., & Mishra, H. (2010). Border bias: The belief that state borders can protect against disasters. *Psychological Science, 21,* 1582–1586. (p. 381)

Mita, T. H., Dermer, M., & Knight, J. (1977). Reversed facial images and the mere-exposure hypothesis. *Journal of Personality and Social Psychology, 35,* 597–601. (p. 551)

Mitani, J. C., Watts, D. P., & Amsler, S. J. (2010). Lethal intergroup aggression leads to territorial expansion in wild chimpanzees. *Current Biology, 20,* R507–R509. (p. 369)

Mitchell, J. P. (2009). Social psychology as a natural kind. *Cell, 13,* 246–251. (p. 598)

Mitchell, K. J., & Porteous, D. J. (2011). Rethinking the genetic architecture of schizophrenia. *Psychological Medicine, 41,* 19–32. (p. 644)

Mitte, K. (2008). Memory bias for threatening information in anxiety and anxiety disorders: A meta-analytic review. *Psychological Bulletin, 134,* 886–911. (p. 619)

Miyagawa, T., et al. (2008). Variant between *CPT1B* and *CHKB* associated with susceptibility to narcolepsy. *Nature Genetics, 40,* 1324–1328. (p. 110)

Miyake, A., Kost-Smith, L., Finkelstein, N. D., Pollock, S. J., Cohen, G. L., & Ito, T. A. (2010). Reducing the gender achievement gap in college science: A classroom study of values affirmation. *Science, 330,* 1234–1237. (p. 415)

Mobbs, D., Yu, R., Meyer, M., Passamonti, L., Seymour, B., Calder, A. J., . . . Dalgeish, T. (2009). A key role for similarity in vicarious reward. *Science, 324,* 900. (p. 306)

Moffitt, T. E. (2005). The new look of behavioral genetics in developmental psychopathology: Gene-environment interplay in antisocial behaviors. *Psychological Bulletin, 131,* 533–554. (p. 651)

Moffitt, T. E., Arsenault, L., Belsky, D., Dickson, N., Hancox, R. J., Harrington, H., . . . Caspi, A. (2011). A gradient of childhood self-control predicts health, wealth, and public safety. *Proceedings of the National Academy of Sciences, 108,* 2693–2698. (p. 503)

Moffitt, T. E., Caspi, A., Harrington, H., & Milne, B. J. (2002). Males on the life-course-persistent and adolescence-limited antisocial pathways: Follow-up at age 26 years. *Development and Psychopathology, 14,* 179–207. (p. 180)

Moffitt, T. E., Caspi, A., Harrington, H., Milne, B. J., Melchior, M., Goldberg, D., & Poulton, R. (2007a). Generalized anxiety disorder and depression: Childhood risk factors in a birth cohort followed to age 32. *Psychological Medicine, 37,* 441–452. (p. 620)

Moffitt, T. E., Caspi, A., & Rutter, M. (2006). Measured gene-environment interactions in psychopathology: Concepts, research strategies, and implications for research, intervention, and public understanding of genetics. *Perspectives on Psychological Science, 1,* 5–27. (p. 634)

Moffitt, T. E., Harrington, H., Caspi, A., Kim-Cohen, J., Goldberg, D., Gregory, A. M., & Poulton, R. (2007b). Depression and generalized anxiety disorder: Cumulative and sequential comorbidity in a birth cohort followed prospectively to age 32 years. *Archives of General Psychiatry, 64*, 651–660. (p. 620)

Moffitt, T. E., Poulton, R., & Caspi, A. (2013). Lifelong impact of early self-control. *American Scientist, 101*, 352–359. (p. 179)

Moghaddam, F. M. (2005). The staircase to terrorism: A psychological exploration. *American Psychologist, 60*, 161–169. (p. 534)

Mohr, H., Pritchard, J., & Lush, T. (2010, May 29). BP has been good at downplaying disaster. *Associated Press*. (p. 361)

Moises, H. W., Zoega, T., & Gottesman, I. I. (2002, July 3). The glial growth factors deficiency and synaptic destabilization hypothesis of schizophrenia. *BMC Psychiatry, 2*(8) (www.biomedcentral.com/1471-244X/2/8). (p. 643)

Möller-Levet, C. S., et al. (2013). Effects of insufficient sleep on circadian rhythmicity and expression amplitude of the human blood transcriptome. *PNAS, 110*, E1132–E1141. (p. 108)

Mondloch, C. J., Lewis, T. L., Budreau, D. R., Maurer, D., Dannemiller, J. L., Stephens, B. R., & Kleiner-Gathercoal, K. A. (1999). Face perception during early infancy. *Psychological Science, 10*, 419–422. (p. 183)

Money, J. (1987). Sin, sickness, or status? Homosexual gender identity and psychoneuroendocrinology. *American Psychologist, 42*, 384–399. (pp. 442, 444)

Money, J., Berlin, F. S., Falck, A., & Stein, M. (1983). *Antiandrogenic and counseling treatment of sex offenders*. Baltimore: Department of Psychiatry and Behavioral Sciences, The Johns Hopkins University School of Medicine. (p. 434)

Monroe, S. M., & Reid, M. W. (2009). Life stress and major depression. *Current Directions in Psychological Science, 18*, 68–72. (p. 632)

Montag, C., Weber, B., Trautner, P., Newport, B., Markett, S., Walter, N. T., Felten, A., & Reuter, M. (2012). Does excessive play of violent first-person-shooter-video-games dampen brain activity in response to emotional stimuli? *Biological Psychology, 89*, 107–111. (p. 548)

Montoya, E. R., Terburg, D., Box, P. A., & van Honk, J. (2012). Testosterone, cortisol, and serotonin as key regulators of social aggression: A review and theoretical perspective. *Motivation and Emotion, 36*, 65–73. (p. 546)

Montoya, R. M., & Horton, R. S. (2013). A meta-analytic investigation of the processes underlying the similarity-attraction effect. *Journal of Social and Personal Relationships, 30*, 64–94. (pp. 555, 556)

Montoya, R. M., & Horton, R. S. (2014). A two-dimensional model for the study of interpersonal attraction. *Personality and Social Psychology Review, 18*, 59–86. (p. 556)

Mooallem, J. (2009, February 19). Rescue flight. *New York Times Magazine* (www.nytimes.com). (p. 196)

Mook, D. G. (1983). In defense of external invalidity. *American Psychologist, 38*, 379–387. (p. 39)

Moon, C., Lagercrantz, H., & Kuhl, P. K. (2013). Language experienced in utero affects vowel perception after birth: A two-country study. *Acta Paediatrica, 102*, 156–160. (p. 182)

Moorcroft, W. H. (2003). *Understanding sleep and dreaming*. New York: Kluwer/Plenum. (pp. 101, 114)

Moore, D. W. (2004, December 17). Sweet dreams go with a good night's sleep. *Gallup News Service* (www.gallup.com). (p. 104)

Moore, D. W. (2005, June 16). Three in four Americans believe in paranormal. *Gallup New Service* (www.gallup.com). (p. 272)

Moore, S. C., Patel, A. V., Matthews, C. E., Berrington de Gonzalez, A., Park, Y., et al. (2012). Leisure time physical activity of moderate to vigorous intensity and mortality: A large pooled cohort analysis. *PLoS Medicine, 9*, e1001335. (p. 507)

Moos, R. H., & Moos, B. S. (2005). Sixteen-year changes and stable remission among treated and untreated individuals with alcohol use disorders. *Drug and Alcohol Dependence, 80*, 337–347. (p. 671)

Moos, R. H., & Moos, B. S. (2006). Participation in treatment and Alcoholics Anonymous: A 16-year follow-up of initially untreated individuals. *Journal of Clinical Psychology, 62*, 735–750. (p. 671)

Mor, N., & Winquist, J. (2002). Self-focused attention and negative affect: A meta-analysis. *Psychological Bulletin, 128*, 638–662. (p. 635)

More, H. L., Hutchinson, J. R., Collins, D. F., Weber, D. J., Aung, S. K. H., & Donelan, J. M. (2010). Scaling of sensorimotor control in terrestrial mammals. *Proceedings of the Royal Society B, 277*, 3563–3568. (p. 54)

Moreira, M. T., Smith, L. A., & Foxcroft, D. (2009). Social norms interventions to reduce alcohol misuse in university or college students. *Cochrane Database of Systematic Reviews*. 2009, Issue 3., Art. No. CD006748. (p. 129)

Moreland, R. L., & Beach, S. R. (1992). Exposure effects in the classroom: The development of affinity among students. *Journal of Experimental Social Psychology, 28*, 255–276. (p. 551)

Moreland, R. L., & Zajonc, R. B. (1982). Exposure effects in person perception: Familiarity, similarity, and attraction. *Journal of Experimental Social Psychology, 18*, 395–415. (p. 551)

Morelli, G. A., Rogoff, B., Oppenheim, D., & Goldsmith, D. (1992). Cultural variation in infants' sleeping arrangements: Questions of independence. *Developmental Psychology, 26*, 604–613. (p. 160)

Moreno, C., Laje, G., Blanco, C., Jiang, H., Schmidt, A. B., & Olfson, M. (2007). National trends in the outpatient diagnosis and treatment of bipolar disorder in youth. *Archives of General Psychiatry, 64*, 1032–1039. (p. 629)

Morewedge, C. K., & Norton, M. I. (2009). When dreaming is believing. The (motivated) interpretation of dreams. *Journal of Personality and Social Psychology, 96*, 249–264. (p. 273)

Morey, R. A., Gold, A. L., LaBar, K. S., et al. (2012). Amygdala volume changes in posttraumatic stress disorder in a large case-controlled veterans group. *Archives of General Psychiatry, 69*, 1169–1178. (p. 623)

Morey, R. A., Inan, S., Mitchell, T. V., Perkins, D. O., Lieberman, J. A., & Belger, A. (2005). Imaging frontostriatal function in ultra-high-risk, early, and chronic schizophrenia during executive processing. *Archives of General Psychiatry, 62*, 254–262. (p. 642)

Morgan, A. B., & Lilienfeld, S. O. (2000). A meta-analytic review of the relation between antisocial behavior and neuropsychological measures of executive function. *Clinical Psychology Review, 20*, 113–136. (p. 650)

Mori, K., & Mori, H. (2009). Another test of the passive facial feedback hypothesis: When you face smiles, you feel happy. *Perceptual and Motor Skills, 109*, 1–3. (p. 475)

Morin, R., & Brossard, M. A. (1997, March 4). Communication breakdown on drugs. *Washington Post*, pp. A1, A6. (p. 211)

Morris, G., Baker-Ward, L., & Bauer, P. J. (2010). What remains of that day: The survival of children's autobiographical memories across time. *Applied Cognitive Psychology, 24*, 527–544. (p. 186)

Morrison, A. R. (2003). The brain on night shift. *Cerebrum, 5*(3), 23–36. (p. 104)

Morrison, C. (2007). *What does contagious yawning tell us about the mind?* Unpublished manuscript, University of Leeds. (p. 525)

Morrison, M., Tay, L., & Diener, E. (2014). *Subjective well-being across the lifespan worldwide*. Paper presented at the Society for Personality and Social Psychology convention, Austin, Texas. (p. 223)

Mortensen, E. L., Michaelsen, K. F., Sanders, S. A., & Reinisch, J. M. (2002). The association between duration of breastfeeding and adult intelligence. *Journal of the American Medical Association, 287*, 2365–2371. (p. 35)

Mortensen, P. B. (1999). Effects of family history and place and season of birth on the risk of schizophrenia. *New England Journal of Medicine, 340*, 603–608. (p. 643)

Moscovici, S. (1985). Social influence and conformity. In G. Lindzey & E. Aronson (Eds.), *The handbook of social psychology* (3rd ed). Hillsdale, N.J.: Erlbaum. (p. 536)

Moses, E. B., & Barlow, D. H. (2006). A new unified treatment approach for emotional disorders based on emotion science. *Current Directions in Psychological Science, 15*, 146–150. (p. 669)

Mosher, C. E., & Danoff-Burg, S. (2008). Agentic and communal personality traits: Relations to disordered eating behavior, body shape concern, and depressive symptoms. *Eating Behaviors, 9*, 497–500. (p. 169)

Mosher, W. D., Chandra, A., & Jones, J. (2005, September 15). Sexual behavior and selected health measures: Men and women 15–44 years of age, United States, 2002. *Advance Data from Vital and Health Statistics*, No. 362, National Center for Health Statistics, Centers for Disease Control and Prevention, U.S. Department of Health and Human Services. (p. 441)

Mosing, M. A., Zietsch, B. P., Shekar, S. N., Wright, M. J., & Martin, N. G. (2009). Genetic and environmental influences on optimism and its relationship to mental and self-rated health: A study of aging twins. *Behavior Genetics, 39*, 597–604. (p. 505)

Moskowitz, T. J., & Wertheim, L. J. (2011). *Scorecasting: The hidden influences behind how sports are played and games are won*. New York: Crown Archetype. (p. 532)

Moss, A. C., & Albery, I. P. (2009). A dual-process model of the alcohol-behavior link for social drinking. *Psychological Bulletin, 135*, 516–530. (p. 120)

Moss, A. J., Allen, K. F., Giovino, G. A., & Mills, S. L. (1992, December 2). Recent trends in adolescent smoking, smoking-update correlates, and expectations about the future. *Advance Data No. 221* (from Vital and Health Statistics of the Centers for Disease Control and Prevention). (p. 128)

Moss, H. A., & Susman, E. J. (1980). Longitudinal study of personality development. In O. G. Brim, Jr., & J. Kagan (Eds.), *Constancy and change in human development.* Cambridge, MA: Harvard University Press. (p. 180)

Motivala, S. J., & Irwin, M. R. (2007). Sleep and immunity: Cytokine pathways linking sleep and health outcomes. *Current Directions in Psychological Science, 16,* 21–25. (p. 108)

Motley, M. T., & Baars, B. J. (1979). Effects of cognitive set upon laboratory induced verbal (Freudian) slips. *Journal of Speech and Hearing Research, 22,* 421–432. (p. 575)

Moxley, J. H., Ericsson, K. A., Charness, N., & Krampe, R. T. (2012). The role of intuition and deliberative thinking in experts' superior tactical decision-making. *Cognition, 124,* 72–78. (p. 365)

Moyer, K. E. (1983). The physiology of motivation: Aggression as a model. In C. J. Scheier & A. M. Rogers (Eds.), *G. Stanley Hall Lecture Series* (Vol. 3). Washington, DC: American Psychological Association. (p. 545)

Mroczek, D. K., & Kolarz, D. M. (1998). The effect of age on positive and negative affect: A developmental perspective on happiness. *Journal of Personality and Social Psychology, 75,* 1333–1349. (p. 220)

Mroczek, D. K., & Spiro, A., III. (2003). Modeling intra-individual change in personality traits: Findings from the Normative Aging Study. *Journals of Gerontology: Series B. Psychological Sciences and Social Sciences, 58,* P153–P165. (p. 591)

Muchnik, L., Aral, S., Taylor, S. J. (2013). Social influence bias: A randomized experiment. *Science, 341,* 647–651. (p. 525)

Mueller, P. A., & Oppenheimer, D. M. (2014). The pen is mightier than the keyboard: Advantages of longhand over laptop note-taking. *Psychological Science, 25,* 1159–1168. (pp. 15, 350)

Muhlnickel, W. (1998). Reorganization of auditory cortex in tinnitus. *Proceedings of the National Academy of Sciences, 95,* 10340–10343. (p. 78)

Mukamel, R., Ekstrom, A. D., Kaplan, J., Iacoboni, M., & Fried, I. (2010). Single-neuron responses in humans during execution and observation of actions. *Current Biology, 20,* 750–756. (p. 309)

Mulcahy, N. J., & Call, J. (2006). Apes save tools for future use. *Science, 312,* 1038–1040. (p. 368)

Muller, J. E., Mittleman, M. A., Maclure, M., Sherwood, J. B., & Tofler, G. H. (1996). Triggering myocardial infarction by sexual activity. *Journal of the American Medical Association, 275,* 1405–1409. (p. 435)

Muller, J. E., & Verrier, R. L. (1996). Triggering of sudden death—Lessons from an earthquake. *New England Journal of Medicine, 334,* 461. (p. 489)

Mullin, C. R., & Linz, D. (1995). Desensitization and resensitization to violence against women: Effects of exposure to sexually violent films on judgments of domestic violence victims. *Journal of Personality and Social Psychology, 69,* 449–459. (p. 312)

Mulrow, C. D. (1999, March). Treatment of depression—newer pharmacotherapies, summary. *Evidence Report/Technology Assessment, 7.* Agency for Health Care Policy and Research, Rockville, MD. (http://www.ahrq.gov/clinic/deprsumm.htm). (p. 683)

Munafò, M. R., Durrant, C., Lewis, G., & Flint, J. (2009). Gene × environment interactions at the serotonin transporter locus. *Biological Psychiatry, 65,* 211–219. (p. 634)

Munsey, C. (2010, June). Medicine or menace? Psychologists' research can inform the growing debate over legalizing marijuana. *Monitor on Psychology,* pp. 50–55. (p. 125)

Murayama, K., Pekrun, R., Lichtenfeld, S., & vom Hofe, R. (2013). Predicting long-term growth in students' mathematics achievement: The unique contributions of motivation and cognitive strategies. *Child Development, 84,* 1475–1490. (p. 409)

Murdik, L., Breska, A., Lamy, D., & Deouell, L. Y. (2011). Integration without awareness: Expanding the limits of unconscious processing. *Psychological Science, 22,* 764–770. (p. 92)

Murphy, G. E., & Wetzel, R. D. (1990). The lifetime risk of suicide in alcoholism. *Archives of General Psychiatry, 47,* 383–392. (p. 638)

Murphy, K. (2008, October 28). 21-year study of children set to begin. *New York Times* (www.nytimes.com). (p. 193)

Murphy, K. R., & Cleveland, J. N. (1995). *Understanding performance appraisal: Social, organizational, and goal-based perspectives.* Thousand Oaks, CA: Sage. (p. A-7)

Murphy, S. T., Monahan, J. L., & Zajonc, R. B. (1995). Additivity of nonconscious affect: Combined effects of priming and exposure. *Journal of Personality and Social Psychology, 69,* 589–602. (p. 462)

Murray, B. (1998, May). Psychology is key to airline safety at Boeing. *The APA Monitor,* p. 36. (p. A-15)

Murray, H. (1938). *Explorations in personality.* New York: Oxford University Press. (p. 454)

Murray, H. A. (1933). The effect of fear upon estimates of the maliciousness of other personalities. *Journal of Social Psychology, 4,* 310–329. (p. 578)

Murray, H. A., & Wheeler, D. R. (1937). A note on the possible clairvoyance of dreams. *Journal of Psychology, 3,* 309–313. (pp. 28, 273)

Murray, R., Jones, P., O'Callaghan, E., Takei, N., & Sham, P. (1992). Genes, viruses, and neurodevelopmental schizophrenia. *Journal of Psychiatric Research, 26,* 225–235. (p. 643)

Murray, R. M., Morrison, P. D., Henquet, C., & Di Forti, M. (2007). Cannabis, the mind and society: The hash realities. *Nature Reviews: Neuroscience, 8,* 885–895. (p. 125)

Murray, S. L., Bellavia, G. M., Rose, P., & Griffin, D. W. (2003). Once hurt, twice hurtful: How perceived regard regulates daily marital interactions. *Journal of Personality and Social Psychology, 84,* 126–147. (p. 238)

Musallam, S., Corneil, B. D., Greger, B., Scherberger, H., & Andersen, R. A. (2004). Cognitive control signals for neural prosthetics. *Science, 305,* 258–262. (p. 77)

Musick, M. A., Herzog, A. R., & House, J. S. (1999). Volunteering and mortality among older adults: Findings from a national sample. *Journals of Gerontology, 54B,* 173–180. (p. 513)

Mustanski, B. S., & Bailey, J. M. (2003). A therapist's guide to the genetics of human sexual orientation, *Sexual and Relationship Therapy, 18,* 1468–1479. (p. 443)

Mustanski, B. S., Bailey, J. M., & Kaspar, S. (2002). Dermatoglyphics, handedness, sex, and sexual orientation. *Archives of Sexual Behavior, 31,* 113–122. (p. 445)

Mydans, S. (2002, May 17). In Pakistan, rape victims are the 'criminals.' *New York Times* (www.nytimes.com). (p. 544)

Myers, D. G. (1993). *The pursuit of happiness.* New York: Harper. (pp. 485, 486)

Myers, D. G. (2000). *The American paradox: Spiritual hunger in an age of plenty.* New Haven, CT: Yale University Press. (p. 485)

Myers, D. G. (2001, December). Do we fear the right things? *American Psychological Society Observer,* p. 3. (p. 362)

Myers, D. G. (2010). *Social psychology,* 10th edition. New York: McGraw-Hill. (pp. 601, 602)

Myers, D. G., & Bishop, G. D. (1970). Discussion effects on racial attitudes. *Science, 169,* 78–779. (p. 534)

Myers, D. G., & Diener, E. (1995). Who is happy? *Psychological Science, 6,* 10–19. (p. 485)

Myers, D. G., & Diener, E. (1996, May). The pursuit of happiness. *Scientific American.* (p. 485)

Myers, D. G., & Scanzoni, L. D. (2005). *What God has joined together?* San Francisco: Harper. (pp. 221, 441)

Myers, I. B. (1987). *Introduction to type: A description of the theory and applications of the Myers-Briggs Type Indicator.* Palo Alto, CA: Consulting Psychologists Press. (p. 586)

Myers, T. A., & Crowther, J. H. (2009). Social comparison as a predictor of body dissatisfaction: A meta-analytic review. *Journal of Abnormal Psychology, 118,* 683–698. (p. 652)

Nagamatsu, L. S., Chan, A., Davis, J. C., Beattie, B. L., Graf, P., Voss, M. W., Sharma, D., Liu-Ambrose, T. (2013). Physical activity improves verbal and spatial memory in older adults with probable mild cognitive impairment: A 6-month randomized controlled trial. *Journal of Aging Research, 2013,* Article ID 861893, 10 pages. (p. 216)

Nagourney, A. (2002, September 25). For remarks on Iraq, Gore gets praise and scorn. *New York Times* (www.nytimes.com). (p. 520)

Nanni, V., Uher, R., & Danese, A. (2012). Childhood maltreatment predicts unfavorable course of illness and treatment outcome in depression: A meta-analysis. *American Journal of Psychiatry, 169,* 141–151. (p. 200)

Napolitan, D. A., & Goethals, G. R. (1979). The attribution of friendliness. *Journal of Experimental Social Psychology, 15,* 105–113. (p. 518)

Narvaez, D. (2010). Moral complexity: The fatal attraction of truthiness and the importance of mature moral functioning. *Perspectives on Psychological Science, 5,* 163–181. (p. 207)

NAS (National Autistic Society). (2011, accessed May 11). *Statistics: How many people have autistic spectrum disorders.* www.autism.org.uk. (p. 193)

Nathan, D. (2011). *Sybil exposed: The extraordinary story behind the famous multiple personality case.* New York: Simon and Schuster. (p. 648)

National Academy of Sciences. (2001). *Exploring the biological contributions to human health: Does sex matter?* Washington, DC: Institute of Medicine, National Academy Press. (p. 167)

National Center for Health Statistics. (1990). *Health, United States, 1989.* Washington, DC: U.S. Department of Health and Human Services. (p. 215)

National Council on Aging. (1999). *The consequences of untreated hearing loss in older persons.* Washington, DC: Author. (www.ncoa.org). (p. 375)

National Institute of Mental Health (2008). *The numbers count: Mental disorders in America.* (nimh.nih.gov). (p. 617)

National Research Council. (1990). *Human factors research needs for an aging population.* Washington, DC: National Academy Press. (p. 215)

National Safety Council. (2010). Transportation mode comparison in *Injury facts 2010 edition.* www.nsc.org. (p. 96)

National Safety Council. (2014). Transportation mode comparison in *Injury Facts* (www.nsc.org). (p. 362)

National Sleep Foundation (NSF). (2006). The ABC's of back-to-school sleep schedules: The consequences of insufficient sleep. National Sleep Foundation (press release) (www.sleepfoundation.org). (p. 107)

National Sleep Foundation (NSF). (2008). *2008 sleep in America poll.* National Sleep Foundation (sleepfoundation.org). (p. 104)

National Sleep Foundation (NSF). (2010, March 8). *2010 sleep in America poll.* www.sleepfoundation.org. (p. 104)

Naughton, M., Clarke, G., O'Leary, O. F, Cryan, J. F., & Dinan, T. G. (2014). A review of ketamine in affective disorders: Current evidence of clinical efficacy, limitations of use and pre-clinical evidence on proposed mechanisms of action. *Journal of Affective Disorders, 156,* 24–35. (p. 684)

Naumann, L. P., Vazire, S., Rentfrow, P. J., & Gosling, S. D. (2009). Personality judgments based on physical appearance. *Personality and Social Psychology Bulletin, 35,* 1661–1671. (p. 593)

Nave, C. S., Sherman, R. A., Funder, D.C., Hampson, S. E., & Goldberg, L. R. (2010). On the contextual independence of personality: Teachers' assessments predict directly observed behavior after four decades. *Social Psychological and Personality Science, 3,* 1–9. (p. 179)

Naylor, T. H. (1990). Redefining corporate motivation, Swedish style. *Christian Century, 107,* 566–570. (p. A-13)

NCASA. (2007). *Wasting the best and the brightest: Substance abuse at America's colleges and universities.* New York: National Center on Addiction and Drug Abuse, Columbia University. (p. 129)

Neal, D. T., Wood, W., & Drolet, A. (2013). How do people adhere to goals when willpower is low? The profits (and pitfalls) of strong habits. *Journal of Personality and Social Psychology, 104,* 959–975. (p. 280)

Nedeltcheva, A. V., Kilkus, J. M., Imperial, J., Schoeller, D. A., & Penev, P. D. (2010). Insufficient sleep undermines dietary efforts to reduce adiposity. *Annals of Internal Medicine, 153,* 435–441. (p. 431)

NEEF. (2011; undated, accessed 17 June 2011). *Fact sheet: children's health and nature.* National Environmental Education Foundation (www.neefusa.org). (p. 688)

Neese, R. M. (1991, November/December). What good is feeling bad? The evolutionary benefits of psychic pain. *The Sciences,* pp. 30–37. (pp. 261, 302)

Neimeyer, R. A., & Currier, J. M. (2009). Grief therapy: Evidence of efficacy and emerging directions. *Current Directions in Psychological Science, 18,* 352–356. (p. 225)

Neisser, U. (1979). The control of information pickup in selective looking. In A. D. Pick (Ed.), *Perception and its development: A tribute to Eleanor J. Gibson.* Hillsdale, NJ: Erlbaum. (p. 97)

Neisser, U., Boodoo, G., Bouchard, T. J., Jr., Boykin, A. W., Brody, N., Ceci, S. J., . . . Urbina, S. (1996). Intelligence: Knowns and unknowns. *American Psychologist, 51,* 77–101. (pp. 406, 413)

Neisser, U., Winograd, E., & Weldon, M. S. (1991). *Remembering the earthquake: "What I experienced" vs. "How I heard the news."* Paper presented to the Psychonomic Society convention. (p. 331)

Neitz, J., Carroll, J., & Neitz, M. (2001). Color vision: Almost reason enough for having eyes. *Optics & Photonics News 12,* 26–33. (p. 243)

Neitz, J., Geist, T., & Jacobs, G. H. (1989). Color vision in the dog. *Visual Neuroscience, 3,* 119–125. (p. 243)

Nelson, C. A., III, Fox, N. A., & Zeanah, C. H., Jr. (2013, April). Anguish of the abandoned child. *Scientific American,* pp. 62–67. (pp. 222, 408)

Nelson, C. A., III, Fox, N. A., & Zeanah, C. H., Jr. (2014). *Romania's abandoned children.* Cambridge, MA: Harvard University Press. (p. 199)

Nelson, C. A., III, Furtado, E. Z., Fox, N. A., & Zeanah, C. H., Jr. (2009). The deprived human brain. *American Scientist, 97,* 222–229. (pp. 199, 408)

Nelson, M. D., Saykin, A. J., Flashman, L. A., & Riordan, H. J. (1998). Hippocampal volume reduction in schizophrenia as assessed by magnetic resonance imaging. *Archives of General Psychiatry, 55,* 433–440. (p. 642)

Nelson, S. K., Kushlev, K., English, T., Dunn, E. W., & Lyubomirsky, S. (2013). In defense of parenthood: Children are associated with more joy than misery. *Psychological Science, 24,* 3–10. (p. 34)

Nemeth, C. J., & Ormiston, M. (2007). Creative idea generation: Harmony versus stimulation. *European Journal of Social Psychology, 37,* 524–535. (p. 536)

Neria, Y., DiGrande, L., & Adams, B. G. (2011). Posttraumatic stress disorder following the September 11, 2001, terrorist attacks: A review of the literature among highly exposed populations. *American Psychologist, 66,* 429–446. (p. 623)

Nes, R. B. (2010). Happiness in behaviour genetics: Findings and implications. *Journal of Happiness Studies, 11,* 369–381. (p. 486)

Nes, R. B., Czajkowski, N., & Tambs, K. (2010). Family matters: Happiness in nuclear families and twins. *Behavior Genetics, 40,* 577–590. (p. 485)

Nesca, M., & Koulack, D. (1994). Recognition memory, sleep and circadian rhythms. *Canadian Journal of Experimental Psychology, 48,* 359–379. (p. 342)

Nestler, E. J. (2011, December). Hidden switches in the mind. *Scientific American,* pp. 77–83. (p. 634)

Nestoriuc, Y., Rief, W., & Martin, A. (2008). Meta-analysis of biofeedback for tension-type headache: Efficacy, specificity, and treatment moderators. *Journal of Consulting and Clinical Psychology, 76,* 379–396. (p. 509)

Neubauer, D. N. (1999). Sleep problems in the elderly. *American Family Physician, 59,* 2551–2558. (p. 103)

Neumann, R., & Strack, F. (2000). "Mood contagion": The automatic transfer of mood between persons. *Journal of Personality and Social Psychology, 79,* 211–223. (pp. 475, 525)

Nevicka, B., Ten Velden, F. S., De Hoogh, A. H. B., & Van Vianen, A. E. M. (2011). Reality at odds with perceptions: Narcissistic leaders and group performance. *Psychological Science, 22,* 1259–1264. (p. 604)

Newcomb, M. D., & Harlow, L. L. (1986). Life events and substance use among adolescents: Mediating effects of perceived loss of control and meaninglessness in life. *Journal of Personality and Social Psychology, 51,* 564–577. (p. 127)

Newman, A. J., Bavelier, D., Corina, D., Jezzard, P., & Neville, H. J. (2002). A critical period for right hemisphere recruitment in American Sign Language processing. *Nature Neuroscience, 5,* 76–80. (p. 374)

Newman, L. S., & Ruble, D. N. (1988). Stability and change in self-understanding: The early elementary school years. *Early Child Development and Care, 40,* 77–99. (p. 201)

Newman, S. C., Bland, R. C., & Thompson, A. H. (2012). Long-term course and outcome in schizophrenia: A 34-year follow-up study in Alberta, Canada. *Psychological Medicine, 42,* 2137–2143. (p. 641)

Newport, E. L. (1990). Maturational constraints on language learning. *Cognitive Science, 14,* 11–28. (p. 374)

Newport, F. (2001, February). Americans see women as emotional and affectionate, men as more aggressive. *The Gallup Poll Monthly,* pp. 34–38. (p. 470)

Newport, F. (2002, July 29). Bush job approval update. *Gallup News Service* (www.gallup.com/poll/releases/pr020729.asp). (p. 565)

Newport, F. (2007, June 11). Majority of Republicans doubt theory of evolution. *Gallup Poll* (www.galluppoll.com). (p. 172)

Newport, F. (2013, July 25). In U.S. 87% approve of Black-White marriage, vs. 4% in 1958. Gallup Poll (2www.gallup.com). (p. 538)

Newport, F. (2013, July 31). Former smokers say best way to quit is just to stop "cold turkey." Gallup Poll (www.gallup.com). (pp. 118, 122)

Newport, F. (2014, April 4). Americans show low levels of concern on global warming. www.gallup.com. (p. 520)

Newport, F., Argrawal, S., & Witters, D. (2010, December 23). Very religious Americans lead healthier lives. *Gallup* (www.gallup.com). (p. 513)

Newport, F., & Pelham, B. (2009, December 14). Don't worry, be 80: Worry and stress decline with age. *Gallup* (www.gallup.com). (p. 490)

Newton, E. L. (1991). The rocky road from actions to intentions. *Dissertation Abstracts International, 51*(8–B), 4105. (p. A-15)

Ng, J. Y. Y., Ntoumanis, N., Thøgersen-Ntoumani, C., Deci, E. L., Ryan, R. M., Duda, J. L., & Williams, G. C. (2012). Self-determination theory applied to health contexts: A meta-analysis. *Perspectives on Psychological Science, 7,* 325–340. (p. 502)

Ng, M. (2014, May 29). Global, regional, and national prevalence of overweight and obesity in children and adults during 1980–2013: A systematic analysis for the Global Burden of Disease Study 2013. *The Lancet*. Early online publication. Doi: 10.1016/S0141-6736(14)60460-8. (p. 430)

Ng, S. H. (1990). Androcentric coding of *man* and *his* in memory by language users. *Journal of Experimental Social Psychology, 26*, 455–464. (p. 381)

Ng, T. W. H., & Feldman, D. C. (2009). How broadly does education contribute to job performance. *Personnel Psychology, 62*, 89–134. (p. A-6)

Ng, T. W. H., Sorensen, K. L., & Yim, F. H. K. (2009). Does the job satisfaction—job performance relationship vary across cultures? *Journal of Cross-Cultural Psychology, 40*, 761–796. (p. A-9)

Ng, W., Diener, E., Aurora, R., & Harter, J. (2009). Affluence, feelings of stress, and well-being. *Social Indicators Research, 94*, 257–271. (p. 489)

Ng, W. W. H., Sorensen, K. L., & Eby, L. T. (2006). Locus of control at work: A meta-analysis. *Journal of Organizational Behavior, 27*, 1057–1087. (p. 503)

Nguyen, H-H. D., & Ryan, A. M. (2008). Does stereotype threat affect test performance of minorities and women? A meta-analysis of experimental evidence. *Journal of Applied Psychology, 93*, 1314–1334. (p. 414)

NHTSA. (2000). *Traffic safety facts 1999: Older population*. Washington, DC: National Highway Traffic Safety Administration (National Transportation Library: www.ntl.bts.gov). (p. 216)

Nicholson, I. (2011). "Torture at Yale": Experimental subjects, laboratory torment and the "rehabilitation" of Milgram's "Obedience to Authority." *Theory and Psychology, 21*, 737–761. (p. 529)

Nickell, J. (Ed.). (1994). *Psychic sleuths: ESP and sensational cases*. Buffalo, NY: Prometheus Books. (p. 272)

Nickell, J. (2005, July/August). The case of the psychic detectives. *Skeptical Inquirer* (skeptically.org/skepticism/id10.html). (p. 272)

Nickerson, R. S. (1998). Applied experimental psychology. *Applied Psychology: An International Review, 47*, 155–173. (p. A-14)

Nickerson, R. S. (1999). How we know—and sometimes misjudge—what others know: Imputing one's own knowledge to others. *Psychological Bulletin, 125*, 737–759. (p. A-15)

Nickerson, R. S. (2002). The production and perception of randomness. *Psychological Review, 109*, 330–357. (p. 22)

Nickerson, R. S. (2005). Bertrand's chord, Buffon's needles, and the concept of randomness. *Thinking & Reasoning, 11*, 67–96. (p. 22)

Nickerson, R. S., & Adams, M. J. (1979). Long-term memory for a common object. *Cognitive Psychology, 11*, 287–307. (p. 340)

Nicol, S. E., & Gottesman, I. I. (1983). Clues to the genetics and neurobiology of schizophrenia. *American Scientist, 71*, 398–404. (p. 645)

Nicolas, S., & Levine, Z. (2012). Beyond intelligence testing: Remembering Alfred Binet after a century. *European Psychologist, 17*, 320–325. (p. 393)

Nicolaus, L. K., Cassel, J. F., Carlson, R. B., & Gustavson, C. R. (1983). Taste-aversion conditioning of crows to control predation on eggs. *Science, 220*, 212–214. (p. 302)

Nicolelis, M. A. L. (2011). *Beyond boundaries: The new neuroscience of connecting brains with machines—and how it will change our lives*. New York: Times Books. (p. 77)

NIDA. (2002). Methamphetamine abuse and addiction. *Research Report Series*. National Institute on Drug Abuse, NIH Publication Number 02–4210. (p. 123)

NIDA. (2005, May). Methamphetamine. *NIDA Info Facts*. National Institute on Drug Abuse. (p. 123)

NIDCD. (2013, accessed November 1). Cochlear implants. National Institute on Deafness and Other Communication Disorders (www.nidcd.nih.gov). (p. 259)

Nie, N. H. (2001). Sociability, interpersonal relations and the Internet: Reconciling conflicting findings. *American Behavioral Scientist, 45*, 420–435. (p. 452)

Nielsen, K. M., Faergeman, O., Larsen, M. L., & Foldspang, A. (2006). Danish singles have a twofold risk of acute coronary syndrome: Data from a cohort of 138,290 persons. *Journal of Epidemiology and Community Health, 60*, 721–728. (p. 505)

Nielsen, M., & Tomaseli, K. (2010). Overimitation in Kalahari Bushman children and the origins of human cultural cognition. *Psychological Science, 21*, 729–736. (p. 309)

Niemiec, C. P., Ryan, R. M., & Deci, E. L. (2009). The path taken: Consequences of attaining intrinsic and extrinsic aspirations in post-college life. *Journal of Research in Personality, 43*, 291–306. (p. 482)

NIH. (2001, July 20). *Workshop summary: Scientific evidence on condom effectiveness for sexually transmitted disease (STD) prevention*. Bethesda: National Institute of Allergy and Infectious Diseases, National Institutes of Health. (p. 436)

NIH. (2010). *Teacher's guide: Information about sleep*. National Institutes of Health (www.science.education.nih.gov). (p. 105)

NIH. (2013, January 24). *Prenatal inflammation linked to autism risk*. National Institutes of Health (www.nih.gov). (p. 193)

Niparko, J. K., Tobey, E. A., Thal, D. J., Eisenberg, L. S., Wang, N., Quittner, A. L., & Fink, N. E. (2010). Spoken language development in children following cochlear implantation. *JAMA: Journal of the American Medical Association, 303*, 1498–1506. (p. 375)

Nir, Y., & Tononi, G. (2010). Dreaming and the brain: From phenomenology to neurophysiology. *Trends in Cognitive Sciences, 14*, 88–100. (p. 115)

Nisbett, R. E. (1987). Lay personality theory: Its nature, origin, and utility. In N. E. Grunberg, R. E. Nisbett, et al. (Eds.), *A distinctive approach to psychological research: The influence of Stanley Schachter*. Hillsdale, NJ: Erlbaum. (p. A-5)

Nisbett, R. E. (2003). *The geography of thought: How Asians and Westerners think differently...and why*. New York: Free Press. (p. 518)

Nisbett, R. E. (2009). *Intelligence and how to get it: Why schools and culture count*. New York: Norton. (p. 412)

Nisbett, R. E., Aronson, J., Blair, C., Dickens, W., Flynn, J., Halpern, D. F., & Turkheimer, E. (2012). Intelligence: New findings and theoretical developments. *American Psychologist, 67*, 130–159. (pp. 406, 411)

Nisbett, R. E., & Cohen, D. (1996). *Culture of honor: The psychology of violence in the South*. Boulder, CO: Westview Press. (p. 548)

Nixon, G. M., Thompson, J. M. D., Han, D. Y., Becroft, D. M., Clark, P. M., Robinson, E., . . . & Mitchell, E. A. (2008). Short sleep duration in middle childhood: Risk factors and consequences. *Sleep, 31*, 71–78. (p. 108)

Nizzi, M. C., Demertzi, A., Gosseries, O., Bruno, M. A., Jouen, F., & Laureys, S. (2012). From armchair to wheelchair: How patients with a locked-in syndrome integrate bodily changes in experienced identity. *Consciousness and Cognition, 21*, 431–437. (p. 481)

Nocera, J. (2012, December 7.) It's hard to be a hero. *New York Times* (www.nytimes.com). (p. 561)

Nock, M. K. (2010). Self-injury. *Annual Review of Clinical Psychology, 6*, 339–363. (p. 638)

Nock, M. K., Borges, G., Bromet, E. J., Alonso, J., Angermeyer, M., Beautrais, A., . . . Williams, D. (2008). Cross-national prevalence and risk factors for suicidal ideation, plans, and attempts. *British Journal of Psychiatry, 192*, 98–105. (p. 638)

Nock, M. K., & Kessler, R. C. (2006). Prevalence of and risk factors for suicide attempts versus suicide gestures: Analysis of the National Comorbidity Survey. *Journal of Abnormal Psychology, 115*, 616–623. (p. 639)

Noel, J. G., Forsyth, D. R., & Kelley, K. N. (1987). Improving the performance of failing students by overcoming their self-serving attributional biases. *Basic and Applied Social Psychology, 8*, 151–162. (p. 504)

Noice, H., & Noice, T. (2006). What studies of actors and acting can tell us about memory and cognitive functioning. *Current Directions in Psychological Science, 15*, 14–18. (p. 327)

Nolen-Hoeksema, S. (2001). Gender differences in depression. *Current Directions in Psychological Science, 10*, 173–176. (p. 635)

Nolen-Hoeksema, S. (2003). *Women who think too much: How to break free of overthinking and reclaim your life*. New York: Holt. (p. 635)

Nolen-Hoeksema, S., & Larson, J. (1999). *Coping with loss*. Mahwah, NJ: Erlbaum. (p. 225)

Norberg, M. M., Krystal, J. H., & Tolin, D. F. (2008). A meta-analysis of d-cycloserine and the facilitation of fear extinction and exposure therapy. *Biological Psychiatry, 63*, 1118–1126. (p. 626)

NORC. (2010). National Opinion Research Center (University of Chicago) General Social Survey data, 1972 through 2008, accessed via sda.berkeley.edu. (p. 449)

Nordgren, L. F., McDonnell, M-H. M., & Loewenstein, G. (2011). What constitutes torture? Psychological impediments to an objective evaluation of enhanced interrogation tactics. *Psychological Science, 22*, 689–694. (p. 238)

Nordgren, L. F., van der Pligt, J., & van Harreveld, F. (2006). Visceral drives in retrospect: Explanations about the inaccessible past. *Psychological Science, 17*, 635–640. (p. 425)

Nordgren, L. F., van der Pligt, J., & van Harreveld, F. (2007). Evaluating Eve: Visceral states influence the evaluation of impulsive behavior. *Journal of Personality and Social Psychology, 93*, 75–84. (p. 425)

Nordgren, L. F., van Harreveld, F., & van der Pligt, J. (2009). The restraint bias: How the illusion of self-restraint promoted impulsive behavior. *Psychological Science, 20*, 1523–1528. (p. 600)

Norem, J. K. (2001). *The positive power of negative thinking: Using defensive pessimism to harness anxiety and perform at your peak.* New York: Basic Books. (p. 600)

Norenzayan, A., & Hansen, I. G. (2006). Belief in supernatural agents in the face of death. *Personality and Social Psychology Bulletin, 32,* 174–187. (p. 581)

Norman, D. A. (2001). The perils of home theater (www.jnd.org/dn.mss/ProblemsOfHomeTheater.html). (p. A-14)

Norman, E. (2010). "The unconscious" in current psychology. *European Psychologist, 15,* 193–201. (p. 580)

Noroozian, M., Lofti, J., Gassemzadeh, H., Emami, H., & Mehrabi, Y. (2003). Academic achievement and learning abilities in left-handers: Guilt or gift? *Cortex, 38,* 779–785. (p. 86)

Norton, K. L., Olds, T. S., Olive, S., & Dank, S. (1996). Ken and Barbie at life size. *Sex Roles, 34,* 287–294. (p. 653)

Norton, M. I., & Ariely, D. (2011). Building a better America—One wealth quintile at a time. *Perspectives on Psychological Science, 6,* 9–12. (p. 42)

NPR. (2009, July 11). Afraid to fly? Try living on a plane. www.npr.org. (p. 288)

NSF. (2001, October 24). Public bounces back after Sept. 11 attacks, national study shows. *NSF News,* National Science Foundation (www.nsf.gov/od/lpa/news/press/ol/pr0185.htm). (p. 489)

Nurmikko, A. V., Donoghue, J. P., Hochberg, L. R., Patterson, W. R., Song, Y-K., Bull, C. W., . . . & Aceros, J. (2010). Listening to brain microcircuits for interfacing with external world—Progress in wireless implantable microelectronic neuroengineering devices. *Proceedings of the IEEE, 98,* 375–388. (p. 77)

Nussinovitch, U., & Shoenfeld, Y. (2012). The role of gender and organ specific autoimmunity. *Autoimmunity Reviews, 11,* A377–A385. (p. 493)

Nutt, D. J., & Malizia, A. L. (2004). Structural and functional brain changes in posttraumatic stress disorder. *Journal of Clinical Psychology, 65,* 11–17. (p. 626)

Nuttin, J. M., Jr. (1987). Affective consequences of mere ownership: The name letter effect in twelve European languages. *European Journal of Social Psychology, 17,* 381–402. (p. 551)

Nye, C. D., Su, R., Rounds, J., & Drasgow, F. (2012). Vocational interests and performance: A quantitative summary of over 60 years of research. *Perspectives on Psychological Science, 7,* 384–403. (p. A-3)

Oakley, D. A., & Halligan, P. W. (2013). Hypnotic suggestion: Opportunities for cognitive neuroscience. *Nature Reviews Neuroscience, 14,* 565–576. (p. 265)

Oaten, M., & Cheng, K. (2006a). Longitudinal gains in self-regulation from regular physical exercise. *British Journal of Health Psychology, 11,* 717–733. (p. 504)

Oaten, M., & Cheng, K. (2006b). Improved self-control: The benefits of a regular program of academic study. *Basic and Applied Social Psychology, 28,* 1–16. (p. 504)

Oberlander, J., & Gill, A. J. (2006). Language with character: A stratified corpus comparison of individual differences in e-mail communication. *Discourse Processes, 42,* 239–270. (p. 593)

Oberman, L. M., & Ramachandran, V. S. (2007). The simulating social mind: The role of the mirror neuron system and simulation in the social and communicative deficits of autism spectrum disorders. *Psychological Bulletin, 133,* 310–327. (p. 194)

O'Boyle, E. H., Jr., Humphrey, R. H., Pollack, J. M., Hawver, T. H., & Story, P. A. (2011). The relation between emotional intelligence and job performance: A meta-analysis. *Journal of Organizational Behavior, 32,* 788–818. (p. 391)

O'Brien, E., & Ellsworth, P. C. (2012). Saving the last for best: A positivity bias for end experiences. *Psychological Science, 23,* 163–165. (p. 263)

O'Brien, L., Albert, D., Chein, J., & Steinberg, L. (2011). Adolescents prefer more immediate rewards when in the presence of their peers. *Journal of Research on Adolescence, 21,* 747–753. (p. 211)

Ochsner, K. N., Ray, R. R., Hughes, B., McRae, K., Cooper, J. C., Weber, J., Gabrieli, J. D. E., & Gross, J. J. (2009). Bottom-up and top-down processes in emotion generation: Common and distinct neural mechanisms. *Psychological Science, 20,* 1322–1331. (p. 462)

O'Connor, P., & Brown, G. W. (1984). Supportive relationships: Fact or fancy? *Journal of Social and Personal Relationships, 1,* 159–175. (p. 679)

Odgers, C. L., Caspi, A., Nagin, D. S., Piquero, A. R., Slutske, W. S., Milne, B. J., . . . Moffitt, T. E. (2008). Is it important to prevent early exposure to drugs and alcohol among adolescents? *Psychological Science, 19,* 1037–1044. (p. 129)

O'Donnell, L., Stueve, A., O'Donnell, C., Duran, R., San Doval, A., Wilson, R. F., . . . & Pleck, J. H. (2002). Long-term reduction in sexual initiation and sexual activity among urban middle schoolers in the reach for health service learning program. *Journal of Adolescent Health, 31,* 93–100. (p. 439)

O'Donovan, A., Neylan, T. C., Metzler, T., & Cohen, B. E. (2012). Lifetime exposure to traumatic psychological stress is associated with elevated inflammation in the heart and soul study. *Brain, Behavior, and Immunity, 26,* 642–649. (p. 496)

Oettingen, G., & Mayer, D. (2002). The motivating function of thinking about the future: Expectations versus fantasies. *Journal of Personality and Social Psychology, 83,* 1198–1212. (p. 504)

Offer, D., Kaiz, M., Howard, K. I., & Bennett, E. S. (2000). The altering of reported experiences. *Journal of the American Academy of Child and Adolescent Psychiatry, 39,* 735–742. (p. 347)

Offer, D., Ostrov, E., Howard, K. I., & Atkinson, R. (1988). *The teenage world: Adolescents' self-image in ten countries.* New York: Plenum. (p. 210)

Ogden, J. (2012, January 16). HM, the man with no memory. www.psychologytoday.com. (p. 338)

O'Hara, R. E., Gibbons, F. X., Gerrard, M., Li, Z., & Sargent, J. D. (2012). Greater exposure to sexual content in popular movies predicts earlier sexual debut and increased sexual risk taking. *Psychological Science, 23,* 984–993. (p. 439)

Ohgami, H., Terao, T., Shiotsuki, I., Ishii, N., & Iwata, N. (2009). Lithium levels in drinking water and risk of suicide. *British Journal of Psychiatry, 194,* 464–465. (p. 685)

Óhman, A. (2009). Of snakes and fears: An evolutionary perspective on the psychology of fear. *Scandinavian Journal of Psychology, 50,* 543–552. (p. 627)

Oishi, S., & Schimmack, U. (2010). Culture and well-being: A new inquiry into the psychological wealth of nations. *Perspectives in Psychological Science, 5,* 463–471. (p. 485)

Oishi, S., & Schimmack, U. (2010). Residential mobility, well-being, and mortality. *Journal of Personality and Social Psychology, 98,* 980–994. (p. 449)

Oishi, S., Diener, E. F., Lucas, R. E., & Suh, E. M. (1999). Cross-cultural variations in predictors of life satisfaction: Perspectives from needs and values. *Personality and Social Psychology Bulletin, 25,* 980–990. (p. 423)

Oishi, S., Kesebir, S., & Diener, E. (2011). Income inequality and happiness. *Psychological Science, 22,* 1095–1100. (pp. 484, 548)

Oishi, S., Kesebir, S., Miao, F., et. al. (2013). Residential mobility increases motivation to expand social network. But why? *Journal of Experimental Social Psychology, 49,* 217–223. (p. 449)

Okada, K., & Samreth, S. (2013). A study on the socio-economic determinants of suicide: Evidence from 13 European OECD countries. *Journal of Behavioral Economics, 45,* 78–85. (p. 637)

Okimoto, T. G., & Brescoll, V. L. (2010). The price of power: Power seeking and backlash against female politicians. *Personality and Social Psychology Bulletin, 36,* 923–936. (p. 163)

Olatunji, B. O., & Wolitzky-Taylor, K. B. (2009). Anxiety sensitivity and the anxiety disorders: A meta-analytic review and synthesis. *Psychological Bulletin, 135,* 974–999. (p. 621)

Olds, J. (1958). Self-stimulation of the brain. *Science, 127,* 315–324. (p. 72)

Olds, J. (1975). Mapping the mind onto the brain. In F. G. Worden, J. P. Swazey, & G. Adelman (Eds.), *The neurosciences: Paths of discovery.* Cambridge, MA: MIT Press. (p. 72)

Olds, J., & Milner, P. (1954). Positive reinforcement produced by electrical stimulation of the septal area and other regions of rat brain. *Journal of Comparative and Physiological Psychology, 47,* 419–427. (p. 72)

Olff, M., Langeland, W., Draijer, N., & Gersons, B. P. R. (2007). Gender differences in posttraumatic stress disorder. *Psychological Bulletin, 135,* 183–204. (p. 624)

Olfson, M., Marcus, S. C., Wan, G. J., & Geissler, E. C. (2004). National trends in the outpatient treatment of anxiety disorders. *Journal of Clinical Psychiatry, 65,* 1166–1173. (p. 683)

Oliner, S. P., & Oliner, P. M. (1988). *The altruistic personality: Rescuers of Jews in Nazi Europe.* New York: Free Press. (p. 310)

Olivola, C. Y., & Todorov, A. (2010). Elected in 100 milliseconds: Appearance-based trait inferences and voting. *Journal of Nonverbal Behavior, 54,* 83–110. (p. 469)

Olson, M. A., & Fazio, R. H. (2001). Implicit attitude formation through classical conditioning. *Psychological Science, 12,* 413–417. (p. 304)

Olsson, A., Nearing, K. I., & Phelps, E. A. (2007). Learning fears by observing others: The neural systems of social fear transmission. *Social Cognitive and Affective Neuroscience, 2,* 3–11. (p. 625)

Olweus, D., Mattsson, A., Schalling, D., & Low, H. (1988). Circulating testosterone levels and aggression in adolescent males: A causal analysis. *Psychosomatic Medicine, 50,* 261–272. (p. 546)

Oman, D., Kurata, J. H., Strawbridge, W. J., & Cohen, R. D. (2002). Religious attendance and cause of death over 31 years. *International Journal of Psychiatry in Medicine, 32,* 69–89. (p. 512)

O'Neill, M. J. (1993). *The relationship between privacy, control, and stress responses in office workers.* Paper presented to the Human Factors and Ergonomics Society convention. (p. 501)

Ong, A. D., Fuller-Rowell, T., & Burrow, A. L. (2009). Racial discrimination and the stress process. *Journal of Personality and Social Psychology, 96,* 1259–1271. (p. 490)

Open Source Collaboration. (2012). An open, large-scale, collaborative effort to estimate the reproducibility of psychological science. *Perspectives on Psychological Science, 7,* 657–660. (p. 27)

Oppenheimer, D. M., & Trail, T. E. (2010). Why leaning to the left makes you lean to the left: Effects of spatial orientation on political attitudes. *Social Cognition, 28,* 651–661. (p. 270)

Oppenheimer, D., Jerez-Fernandez, A., & Angulo, A. N. (2014). Show me the numbers. *Psychological Science, 25,* 633–635. (p. 43)

Opriş, D., Pintea, S., Garcia-Palacios, A., Botella, C., Szamosközi, Ş., & David, D. (2012). Virtual reality exposure therapy in anxiety disorders: A quantitative meta-analysis. *Depression and Anxiety, 29,* 85–93. (p. 665)

Oquendo, M. A., Galfalvy, H. C., Currier, D., Grunebaum, M. F., Sher, L., Sullivan, G. M., . . . Mann, J. J. (2011). Treatment of suicide attempters with bipolar disorder: A randomized clinical trial comparing lithium and valproate in the prevention of suicidal behavior. *The American Journal of Psychiatry, 168,* 1050–1056. (p. 685)

Oren, D. A., & Terman, M. (1998). Tweaking the human circadian clock with light. *Science, 279,* 333–334. (pp. 104, 105)

Organisation for Economic Co-operation and Development (2013). *OECD guidelines on measuring subjective well-being.* Paris, France: OECD (www.oecd.org/statistics/guidelines-on-measuring-subjective-well-being.htm). (p. 486)

Orth, U., Robins, R. W., & Meier, L. L. (2009). Disentangling the effects of low self-esteem and stressful events on depression: Findings from three longitudinal studies. *Personality Processes and Individual Differences, 97,* 307–321. (p. 599)

Orth, U., Robins, R. W., & Roberts, B. W. (2008). Low self-esteem prospectively predicts depression in adolescence and young adulthood. *Journal of Personality and Social Psychology, 95,* 695–708. (p. 599)

Orth, U., Robins, R. W., Trzesniewski, K. H., Maes, J., & Schmitt, M. (2009). Low self-esteem is a risk factor for depressive symptoms from young adulthood to old age. *Journal of Abnormal Psychology, 118,* 472–478. (p. 632)

Orth, U., Robins, R. W., & Widaman, K. F. (2012). Life-span development of self-esteem and its effects on important life outcomes. *Journal of Personality and Social Psychology, 102,* 1271–1288. (p. 180)

Osborne, C., Manning, W. D., & Smock, P. J. (2007). Married and cohabiting parents' relationship stability: A focus on race and ethnicity. *Journal of Marriage and Family, 69,* 1345–1366. (p. 221)

Osborne, J. W. (1997). Race and academic disidentification. *Journal of Educational Psychology, 89,* 728–735. (p. 415)

Osborne, L. (1999, October 27). A linguistic big bang. *New York Times Magazine* (www.nytimes.com). (p. 373)

Osgood, C. E. (1962). *An alternative to war or surrender.* Urbana: University of Illinois Press. (p. 567)

Osgood, C. E. (1980). *GRIT: A strategy for survival in mankind's nuclear age?* Paper presented at the Pugwash Conference on New Directions in Disarmament. (p. 567)

Oskarsson, A. T., Van Voven, L., McClelland, G. H., & Hastie, R. (2009). What's next? Judging sequences of binary events. *Psychological Bulletin, 135,* 262–285. (p. 22)

OSS Assessment Staff. (1948). *The assessment of men.* New York: Rinehart. (p. 596)

Ossher, L., Flegal, K. E., & Lustig, C. (2012). Everyday memory errors in older adults. *Aging, Neuropsychology, and Cognition, 20,* 220–242. (p. 218)

Ost, L. G., & Hugdahl, K. (1981). Acquisition of phobias and anxiety response patterns in clinical patients. *Behaviour Research and Therapy, 16,* 439–447. (p. 624)

Ostfeld, A. M., Kasl, S. V., D'Atri, D. A., & Fitzgerald, E. F. (1987). *Stress, crowding, and blood pressure in prison.* Hillsdale, NJ: Erlbaum. (p. 502)

O'Sullivan, M., Frank, M. G., Hurley, C. M., & Tiwana, J. (2009). Police lie detection accuracy: The effect of lie scenario. *Law and Human Behavior, 33,* 530–538. (p. 469)

Osvath, M., & Karvonen, E. (2012). Spontaneous innovation for future deception in a male chimpanzee. *PLoS ONE, 7*(5), e36782. (p. 368)

Oswald, A. J., & Wu, S. (2010). Objective confirmation of subjective measures of human well-being: Evidence from the U.S.A. *Science, 327,* 576–579. (p. 482)

Oswald, F. L., Mitchell, G., Blanton, H., Jaccard, J., & Tetlock, P. E. (2013). Predicting ethnic and racial discrimination: A meta-analysis of IAT criterion studies. *Journal of Personality and Social Psychology, 105,* 171–192. (p. 539)

Oswalt, S. B., & Wyatt, T. J. (2011). Sexual orientation and differences in mental health, stress, and academic performance in a national sample of U.S. college students. *Journal of Homosexuality, 58,* 1255–1280. (p. 441)

Ott, B. (2007, June 14). Investors, take note: Engagement boosts earnings. *Gallup Management Journal* (gmj.gallup.com). (p. A-10)

Ott, C. H., Lueger, R. J., Kelber, S. T., & Prigerson, H. G. (2007). Spousal bereavement in older adults: Common, resilient, and chronic grief with defining characteristics. *Journal of Nervous and Mental Disease, 195,* 332–341. (p. 225)

Ouellette, J. A., & Wood, W. (1998). Habit and intention in everyday life: The multiple processes by which past behavior predicts future behavior. *Psychological Bulletin, 124,* 54–74. (p. A-6)

Overgaard, M. (2012). Blindsight: Recent and historical controversies on the blindness of blindsight. *Wiley Interdisciplinary Reviews: Cognitive Science, 3,* 607–614. (p. 94)

Owen, A. M. (2014). Disorders of consciousness: Diagnostic accuracy of brain imaging in the vegetative state. *Nature Review: Neurology, 10,* 370–371. (p. 93)

Owen, A. M., Coleman, M. R., Boly, M., Davis, M. H., Laureys, S., & Pickard, J. D. (2006). Detecting awareness in the vegetative state. *Science, 313,* 1402. (p. 93)

Owen, A. M., Hampshire, A., Grahn, J. A., Stenton, R., Dajani, S., Burns, A. S., Howard, R. J., & Ballard, C. G. (2010). Putting brain training to the test. *Nature, 465,* 775–778. (p. 218)

Owen, D. J., Slep, A. M. S., & Heyman, R. E. (2012). The effect of praise, positive nonverbal response, reprimand, and negative nonverbal response on child compliance: A systematic review. *Clinical Child and Family Psychology Review, 15,* 364–385. (p. 295)

Owen, R. (1814). First essay in *New view of society or the formation of character.* Quoted in *The story of New Lamark.* New Lamark Mills, Lamark, Scotland: New Lamark Conservation Trust, 1993. (p. A-8)

Owens, J. A., Belon, K., & Moss, P. (2010). Impact of delaying school start time on adolescent sleep, mood, and behavior. *Archives of Pediatric Adolescent Medicine, 164,* 608–614. (p. 107)

Oxfam. (2005, March 26). *Three months on: New figures show tsunami may have killed up to four times as many women as men.* Oxfam Press Release (www.oxfam.org.uk). (p. 168)

Ozer, E. J., Best, S. R., Lipsey, T. L., & Weiss, D. S. (2003). Predictors of posttraumatic stress disorder and symptoms in adults: A meta-analysis. *Psychological Bulletin, 129,* 52–73. (p. 623)

Ozer, E. J., & Weiss, D. S. (2004). Who develops posttraumatic stress disorder? *Current Directions in Psychological Science, 13,* 169–172. (pp. 623, 624)

Özgen, E. (2004). Language, learning, and color perception. *Current Directions in Psychological Science, 13,* 95–98. (p. 381)

Pace-Schott, E. P., & Spencer, R. M. C. (2011). Age-related changes in the cognitive function of sleep. *Progress in Brain Research, 191,* 75–89. (p. 106)

Padgett, V. R. (1989). *Predicting organizational violence: An application of 11 powerful principles of obedience.* Paper presented at the American Psychological Association convention. (p. 530)

Pagani, L. S., Fitzpatrick, C., Barnett, T. A., & Dubow, E. (2010). Prospective associations between early childhood television exposure and academic, psychosocial, and physical well-being by middle childhood. *Archive of Pediatric and Adolescent Medicine, 164,* 425–431. (p. 432)

Page, S. E. (2007). *The difference: How the power of diversity creates better groups, firms, schools, and societies.* Princeton, NJ: Princeton University Press. (p. 536)

Palladino, J. J., & Carducci, B. J. (1983). *"Things that go bump in the night": Students' knowledge of sleep and dreams.* Paper presented at the meeting of the Southeastern Psychological Association. (p. 100)

Pallier, C., Colomé, A., & Sebastián-Gallés, N. (2001). The influence of native-language phonology on lexical access: Exemplar-based versus abstract lexical entries. *Psychological Science, 12,* 445–448. (p. 372)

Palmer, S., Schreiber, C., & Box, C. (1991). *Remembering the earthquake: "Flashbulb" memory for experienced vs. reported events.* Paper presented at the Psychonomic Society convention. (p. 331)

Palmese, L. B., DeGeorge, P. C., Ratliff, J. C., Srihari, V. H., Wexler, B. E., Krystal, A. D., & Tek, C. (2011). Insomnia is frequent in schizophrenia and associated with night eating and obesity. *Schizophrenia Research, 133,* 238–243. (p. 641)

Pandey, J., Sinha, Y., Prakash, A., & Tripathi, R. C. (1982). Right-left political ideologies and attribution of the causes of poverty. *European Journal of Social Psychology, 12,* 327–331. (p. 519)

Pandya, H. (2013, April 23). Shakuntala Devi, 'Human Computer' who bested the machines, dies at 83. *New York Times* (www.nytimes.com). (p. 411)

Panksepp, J. (2007). Neurologizing the psychology of affects: How appraisal-based constructivism and basic emotion theory can coexist. *Perspectives on Psychological Science, 2,* 281–295. (p. 466)

Pantev, C., Oostenveld, R., Engelien, A., Ross, B., Roberts, L. R., & Hoke, M. (1998). Increased auditory cortical representation in musicians. *Nature, 392,* 811–814. (p. 81)

Panzarella, C., Alloy, L. B., & Whitehouse, W. G. (2006). Expanded hopelessness theory of depression: On the mechanisms by which social support protects against depression. *Cognitive Theory and Research, 30,* 307–333. (p. 635)

Pardini, D. A., Erickson, K., Leober, R. & Raine, A. (2013). Lower amygdala volume in men is associated with childhood aggression, early psychopathic traits, and future violence. *Biological Psychiatry, 75*(1), 73–80. (p. 650)

Park, C. L. (2007). Religiousness/spirituality and health: A meaning systems perspective. *Journal of Behavioral Medicine, 30,* 319–328. (p. 512)

Park, C. L., Riley, K. E., & Snyder, L. B. (2012). Meaning making coping, making sense, and post-traumatic growth following the 9/11 terrorist attacks. *The Journal of Positive Psychology, 7,* 198–207. (p. 691)

Park, D. C., & McDonough, I. M. (2013). The dynamic aging mind: Revelations from functional neuroimaging research. *Perspectives on Psychological Science, 8,* 62–67. (p. 216)

Park, G., Lubinski, D., & Benbow, C. P. (2008). Ability differences among people who have commensurate degrees matter for scientific creativity. *Psychological Science, 19,* 957–961. (p. 365)

Park, R. L. (1999, July 12). Liars never break a sweat. *New York Times* (www.nytimes.com). (p. 467)

Parker, C. P., Baltes, B. B., Young, S. A., Huff, J. W., Altmann, R. A., LaCost, H. A., & Roberts, J. E. (2003). Relationships between psychological climate perceptions and work outcomes: A meta-analytic review. *Journal of Organizational Behavior, 24,* 389–416. (p. A-9)

Parker, E. S., Cahill, L., & McGaugh, J. L. (2006). A case of unusual autobiographical remembering. *Neurocase, 12,* 35–49. (p. 338)

Parkes, A., Wight, D., Hunt, K., Henderson, M., & Sargent, J. (2013). Are sexual media exposure, parental restrictions on media use and co-viewing TV and DVDs with parents and friends associated with teenagers' early sexual behaviour? *Journal of Adolescence, 36,* 1121–1133. (p. 439)

Parnia, S., Fenwick, P., Spearpoint K., & Devos, G. (2013). AWAreness during REsuscitation (AWARE). *Circulation 128,* A236. (p. 124)

Parsons, T. D., & Rizzo, A. A. (2008). Affective outcomes of virtual reality exposure therapy for anxiety and specific phobias: A meta-analysis. *Journal of Behavior Therapy and Experimental Psychiatry, 39,* 250–261. (p. 665)

Partanen, E., Kujala, T., Näätänen, R., Liitola, A., Sambeth, A., & Huotilainen, M. (2013). Learning-induced neural plasticity of speech processing before birth. *PNAS Proceedings of the National Academy of Sciences of the United States of America, 110,* 15145–15150. (p. 182)

Pasco, J. A., Williams, L. A., Jacks, F. N., Ng, F., Henry, M. J., Nicholson, G. C., Kotowicz, M. A., & Berk, M. (2008). Tobacco smoking as a risk factor for major depressive disorder: Population-based study. *British Journal of Psychiatry, 193,* 322–326. (p. 634)

Pascoe, E. A., & Richman, L. S. (2009). Perceived discrimination and health: A meta-analytic review. *Psychological Bulletin, 135,* 531–554. (p. 490)

Passell, P. (1993, March 9). Like a new drug, social programs are put to the test. *New York Times,* pp. C1, C10. (p. 38)

Patall, E. A., Cooper, H., & Robinson, J. C. (2008). The effects of choice on intrinsic motivation and related outcomes: A meta-analysis of research findings. *Psychological Bulletin, 134,* 270–300. (p. 305)

Pate, J. E., Pumariega, A. J., Hester, C., & Garner, D. M. (1992). Cross-cultural patterns in eating disorders: A review. *Journal of the American Academy of Child and Adolescent Psychiatry, 31,* 802–809. (p. 652)

Patel, S. R., Malhotra, A., White, D. P., Gottlieb, D. J., & Hu, F. B. (2006). Association between reduced sleep and weight gain in women. *American Journal of Epidemiology, 164,* 947–954. (p. 108)

Patihis, L., Ho, L. Y., Tingen, I. W., Lilienfeld, S. O., & Loftus, E. F. (2014). Are the "memory wars" over? A scientist-practitioner gap in beliefs about repressed memory. *Psychological Science, 25,* 519–530. (pp. 343, 348)

Patten, S. B., Wang, J. L., Williams, J. V. A., Currie, S., Beck, C. A., Maxwell, C. J., & el-Guebaly, N. (2006). Descriptive epidemiology of major depression in Canada. *Canadian Journal of Psychiatry, 51,* 84–90. (p. 631)

Patterson, F. (1978, October). Conversations with a gorilla. *National Geographic,* pp. 438–465. (p. 378)

Patterson, G. R., Chamberlain, P., & Reid, J. B. (1982). A comparative evaluation of parent training procedures. *Behavior Therapy, 13,* 638–650. (p. 296)

Patterson, M., Warr, P., & West, M. (2004). Organizational climate and company productivity: The role of employee affect and employee level. *Journal of Occupational and Organizational Psychology, 77,* 193–216. (p. A-9)

Patterson, R. (1951). *The riddle of Emily Dickinson.* Boston: Houghton Mifflin. (p. 637)

Pauker, K., Weisbuch, M., Ambady, N., Sommers, S. R., Adams, Jr., R. B., & Ivcevic, Z. (2009). Not so Black and White: Memory for ambiguous group members. *Journal of Personality and Social Psychology, 96,* 795–810. (p. 412)

Paulesu, E., Demonet, J-F., Fazio, F., McCrory, E., Chanoine, V., Brunswick, N., . . . & Frith, U. (2001). Dyslexia: Cultural diversity and biological unity. *Science, 291,* 2165–2167. (p. 7)

Pauly, K., Finkelmeyer, A., Schneider, F., & Habel, U. (2013). The neural correlates of positive self-evaluation and self-related memory. *Social Cognitive and Affective Neuroscience, 8,* 878–886. (p. 598)

Paus, T., Zijdenbos, A., Worsley, K., Collins, D. L., Blumenthal, J., Giedd, J. N., Rapoport, J. L., & Evans, A. C. (1999). Structural maturation of neural pathways in children and adolescents: In vivo study. *Science, 283,* 1908–1911. (p. 185)

Pavlov, I. (1927). Conditioned reflexes: An investigation of the physiological activity of the cerebral cortex. Oxford: Oxford University Press. (pp. 282, 286)

Payne, B. K. (2006). Weapon bias: Split-second decisions and unintended stereotyping. *Current Directions in Psychological Science, 15,* 287–291. (p. 539)

Payne, B. K., & Corrigan, E. (2007). Emotional constraints on intentional forgetting. *Journal of Experimental Social Psychology, 43,* 780–786. (p. 343)

Payne, B. K., Krosnick, J. A., Pasek, J., Lelkes, Y., Akhtar, O., & Tompson, T. (2010). Implicit and explicit prejudice in the 2008 American presidential election. *Journal of Experimental Social Psychology, 46,* 367–374. (p. 539)

Payne, J. W., Sagara, N., Shu, S., Appelt, K. C., & Johnson, E. J. (2013). Life expectancy as a constructed belief: Evidence of a live-to or die-by framing effect. *Journal of Risk and Uncertainty, 46,* 27–50. (p. 31)

Payne, J. W., Samper, A., Bettman, J. R., & Luce, M. F. (2008). Boundary conditions on unconscious thought in complex decision making. *Psychological Science, 19,* 1118–1123. (p. 365)

Pea, R., Nass, C., Meheula, L., Rance, M., Kumar, A., Bamford, H., . . . Zhou, M. (2012). Media use, face-to-face communication, media multitasking, and social well-being among 8- to 12-year-old girls. *Developmental Psychology, 48,* 327–336. (p. 452)

Peckham, A. D., McHugh, R. K., & Otto, M. W. (2010). A meta-analysis of the magnitude of biased attention in depression. *Depression and Anxiety, 27,* 1135–1142. (p. 631)

Pedersen, A., Zachariae, R., & Bovbjerg, D. H. (2010). Influence of psychological stress on upper respiratory infection—A meta-analysis of prospective studies. *Psychosomatic Medicine, 72,* 823–832. (p. 494)

Pedersen, N. L., Plomin, R., McClearn, G. E., & Friberg, L. (1988). Neuroticism, extraversion, and related traits in adult twins reared apart and reared together. *Journal of Personality and Social Psychology, 55,* 950–957. (p. 138)

Peigneux, P., Laurcys, S., Fuchs, S., Collette, F., Perrin, F., Reggers, J., . . . Maquet, P. (2004). Are spatial memories strengthened in the human hippocampus during slow wave sleep? *Neuron, 44,* 535–545. (p. 330)

Peikoff, K. (2013). I had my DNA picture taken, with varying results. Retrieved January 7, 2014 from http://www.nytimes.com/2013/12/31/science/i-had-my-dna-picture-taken-with-varying-results.html. (p. 143)

Pekkanen, J. (1982, June). Why do we sleep? *Science, 82,* p. 86. (p. 106)

Pelham, B., & Crabtree, S. (2008, October 8). Worldwide, highly religious more likely to help others. Gallup Poll (www.gallup.com). (p. 561)

Pelham, B. W. (1993). On the highly positive thoughts of the highly depressed. In R. F. Baumeister (Ed.), *Self-esteem: The puzzle of low self-regard.* New York: Plenum. (p. 599)

Pelham, B. W. (2009, October 22). About one in six Americans report history of depression. *Gallup* (www.gallup.com). (p. 631)

Pennebaker, J. (1990). *Opening up: The healing power of confiding in others.* New York: William Morrow. (p. 580)

Pennebaker, J. W. (1985). Traumatic experience and psychosomatic disease: Exploring the roles of behavioral inhibition, obsession, and confiding. *Canadian Psychology, 26,* 82–95. (p. 506)

Pennebaker, J. W. (1990). *Opening up: The healing power of confiding in others.* New York: William Morrow. (p. 507)

Pennebaker, J. W. (2002, January 28). Personal communication. (p. 565)

Pennebaker, J. W. (2011). *The secret life of pronouns: What our words say about us.* New York: Bloomsbury Press. (p. 593)

Pennebaker, J. W., Barger, S. D., & Tiebout, J. (1989). Disclosure of traumas and health among Holocaust survivors. *Psychosomatic Medicine, 51,* 577–589. (p. 506)

Pennebaker, J. W., & O'Heeron, R. C. (1984). Confiding in others and illness rate among spouses of suicide and accidental death victims. *Journal of Abnormal Psychology, 93,* 473–476. (p. 506)

Pennebaker, J. W., & Stone, L. D. (2003). Words of wisdom: Language use over the life span. *Journal of Personality and Social Psychology, 85,* 291–301. (p. 223)

Peplau, L. A., & Fingerhut, A. W. (2007). The close relationships of lesbians and gay men. *Annual Review of Psychology, 58,* 405–424. (pp. 148, 221)

Peppard, P. E., Szklo-Coxe, M., Hia, K. M., & Young, T. (2006). Longitudinal association of sleep-related breathing disorder and depression. *Archives of Internal Medicine, 166,* 1709–1715. (p. 111)

Pepperberg, I. M. (2009). *Alex & me: How a scientist and a parrot discovered a hidden world of animal intelligence—and formed a deep bond in the process.* New York: Harper. (p. 368)

Pepperberg, I. M. (2012). Further evidence for addition and numerical competence by a grey parrot (psittacus erithacus). *Animal Cognition, 15,* 711–717. (p. 368)

Pepperberg, I. M. (2013). Abstract concepts: Data from a grey parrot. *Behavioural Processes, 93,* 82–90. (p. 368)

Perani, D., & Abutalebi, J. (2005). The neural basis of first and second language processing. *Current Opinion in Neurobiology, 15,* 202–206. (p. 376)

Pereg, D., Gow, R., Mosseri, M., Lishner, M., Rieder, M., Van Uum, S., & Koren, G. (2011). Hair cortisol and the risk for acute myocardial infarction in adult men. *Stress, 14,* 73–81. (p. 496)

Pereira, A. C., Huddleston, D. E., Brickman, A. M., Sosunov, A. A., Hen, R., McKhann, G. M., . . . & Small, S. A. (2007). An *in vivo* correlate of exercise-induced neurogenesis in the adult dentate gyrus. *Proceedings of the National Academy of Sciences, 104,* 5638–5643. (pp. 82, 216)

Pereira, G. M., & Osburn, H. G. (2007). Effects of participation in decision making on performance and employee attitudes: A quality circles meta-analysis. *Journal of Business Psychology, 22,* 145–153. (p. A-12)

Pergadia, M. L., et al. (2011). A 3p26-3p25 genetic linkage finding for DSM-IV major depression in heavy smoking families. *American Journal of Psychiatry. 168,* 848–852. (p. 633)

Pergamin-Hight, L., Bakermans-Kranenburg, M. J., can IJzendoorn, M. H., & Bar-Haim, Y. (2012). Variations in the promoter region of the serotonin transporter gene and biased attention for emotional information: A meta-analysis. *Biological Psychiatry, 71,* 373–379. (p. 626)

Perilloux, C., Easton, J. A., & Buss, D. M. (2012). The misperception of sexual interest. *Psychological Science, 23,* 146–151. (p. 148)

Perilloux, H. K., Webster, G. D., & Gaulin, S. J. (2010). Signals of genetic quality and maternal investment capacity: The dynamic effects of fluctuating asymmetry and waist-to-hip ratio on men's ratings of women's attractiveness. *Social Psychology and Personality Science, 1,* 34–42. (pp. 149, 554)

Perkins, A., & Fitzgerald, J. A. (1997). Sexual orientation in domestic rams: Some biological and social correlates. In L. Ellis & L. Ebertz (Eds.), *Sexual orientation: Toward biological understanding.* Westport, CT: Praeger Publishers. (p. 443)

Perkins, A. M., Inchley-Mort, S. L., Pickering, A. D., Corr, P. J., & Burgess, A. P. (2012). A facial expression for anxiety. *Journal of Personality and Social Psychology, 102,* 910-924. (p. 468)

Perkinson-Gloor, N., Lemola, S., & Grob, A. (2013). Sleep duration, positive attitude toward life, and academic achievement: The role of daytime tiredness, behavioral persistence, and school start times. *Journal of Adolescence, 36,* 311–318. (p. 107)

Perra, O., Williams, J. H. G., Whiten, A., Fraser, L., Benzie, H., & Perrett, D. I. (2008). Imitation and 'theory of mind' competencies in discrimination of autism from other neurodevelopmental disorders. *Research in Autism Disorders, 2,* 456–468. (p. 194)

Perrachione, T. K., Del Tufo, S. N., & Gabrieli, J. D. E. (2011). Human voice recognition depends on language ability. *Science, 333,* 595. (p. 377)

Perrett, D. (2002, October 1). Perception laboratory, Department of Psychology, University of St. Andrews, Scotland (www.perception.st-and.ac.uk). (p. 555)

Perrett, D. (2010). *In your face: The new science of human attraction.* New York: Palgrave Macmillan. (p. 555)

Perrett, D. I., Harries, M., Misflin, A. J., & Chitty, A. J. (1988). Three stages in the classification of body movements by visual neurons. In H. B. Barlow, C. Blakemore, & M. Weston Smith (Eds.), *Images and understanding.* Cambridge: Cambridge University Press. (p. 245)

Perrett, D. I., Hietanen, J. K., Oram, M. W., & Benson, P. J. (1992). Organization and functions of cells responsive to faces in the temporal cortex. *Philosophical Transactions of the Royal Society of London: Series B, 335,* 23–30. (p. 245)

Perrett, D. I., Lee, K. J., Penton-Voak, I., Rowland, D., Yoshikawa, S., Burt, D. M., . . . Akamatsu, S. (1998, August). Effects of sexual dimorphism on facial attractiveness. *Nature, 394,* 884–887. (p. 540)

Perrett, D. I., May, K. A., & Yoshikawa, S. (1994). Facial shape and judgments of female attractiveness. *Nature, 368,* 239–242. (p. 245)

Perrin, J. S., Merz, S., Bennett, D. M., Currie, J., Steele, D. J., Reid, I. C., & Schwarzbauer, C. (2012). Electroconvulsive therapy reduced frontal cortical connectivity in severe depressive disorder. *PNAS, 109,* 5464–5468. (p. 685)

Perron, H., Mekaoui, L., Bernard, C., Veas, F., Stefas, I., & Leboyer, M. (2008). Endogenous retrovirus type W GAG and envelope protein antigenemia in serum of schizophrenic patients. *Biological Psychiatry, 64,* 1019–1023. (p. 643)

Perry, G. (2013). *Behind the shock machine: The untold story of the notorious Milgram psychology experiments.* New York: New Press. (p. 529)

Person, C., Tracy, M., & Galea, S. (2006). Risk factors for depression after a disaster. *Journal of Nervous and Mental Disease, 194,* 659–666. (p. 690)

Pert, C. B. (1986). Quoted in J. Hooper & D. Teresi, *The three-pound universe.* New York: Macmillan. (p. 73)

Pert, C. B., & Snyder, S. H. (1973). Opiate receptor: Demonstration in nervous tissue. *Science, 179,* 1011–1014. (p. 58)

Perugini, E. M., Kirsch, I., Allen, S. T., Coldwell, E., Meredith, J., Montgomery, G. H., & Sheehan, J. (1998). Surreptitious observation of responses to hypnotically suggested hallucinations: A test of the compliance hypothesis. *International Journal of Clinical and Experimental Hypnosis, 46,* 191–203. (p. 265)

Peschel, E. R., & Peschel, R. E. (1987). Medical insights into the castrati in opera. *American Scientist, 75,* 578–583. (p. 434)

Pescosolido, B. A., Martin, J. K., Long, J. S., Medina, T. R., Phelan, J. C., & Link, B. G. (2010). "A disease like any other"? A decade of change in public reactions to schizophrenia, depression, and alcohol dependence. *American Journal of Psychiatry, 167*(11), 1321–30. doi: 10.1176/appi.ajp.2010.09121743 (p. 645)

Pesko, M. F. (2014). Stress and smoking: Associations with terrorism and causal impact. *Contemporary Economic Policy, 32,* 351–371. (p. 122)

Peters, M., Reimers, S., & Manning, J. T. (2006). Hand preference for writing and associations with selected demographic and behavioral variables in 255,100 subjects: The BBC Internet study. *Brain and Cognition, 62,* 177–189. (p. 86)

Peters, M., Rhodes, G., & Simmons, L. W. (2007). Contributions of the face and body to overall attractiveness. *Animal Behaviour, 73,* 937–942. (p. 554)

Peters, T. J., & Waterman, R. H., Jr. (1982). *In search of excellence: Lessons from America's best-run companies.* New York: Harper & Row. (p. 298)

Petersen, J. L., & Hyde, J. S. (2010). A meta-analytic review of research on gender differences in sexuality, 1993–2007. *Psychological Bulletin, 136,* 21–38. (p. 147)

Petersen, J. L., & Hyde, J. S. (2011). Gender differences in sexual attitudes and behaviors: A review of meta-analytic results and large datasets. *Journal of Sex Research, 48,* 149–165. (p. 434)

Peterson, C., & Barrett, L. C. (1987). Explanatory style and academic performance among university freshmen. *Journal of Personality and Social Psychology, 53,* 603–607. (p. 504)

Peterson, C., Peterson, J., & Skevington, S. (1986). Heated argument and adolescent development. *Journal of Social and Personal Relationships, 3,* 229–240. (p. 206)

Peterson, C. C., & Siegal, M. (1999). Representing inner worlds: Theory of mind in autistic, deaf, and normal hearing children. *Psychological Science, 10,* 126–129. (p. 190)

Peterson, C. K., & Harmon-Jones, E. (2012). Anger and testosterone: Evidence that situationally-induced anger relates to situationally-induced testosterone. *Emotion, 12,* 899–902. (p. 477)

Peterson, L. R., & Peterson, M. J. (1959). Short-term retention of individual verbal items. *Journal of Experimental Psychology, 58,* 193–198. (p. 323)

Petitto, L. A., & Marentette, P. F. (1991). Babbling in the manual mode: Evidence for the ontogeny of language. *Science, 251,* 1493–1496. (p. 372)

Pettegrew, J. W., Keshavan, M. S., & Minshew, N. J. (1993). 31P nuclear magnetic resonance spectroscopy: Neurodevelopment and schizophrenia. *Schizophrenia Bulletin, 19,* 35–53. (p. 642)

Petticrew, M., Bell, R., & Hunter, D. (2002). Influence of psychological coping on survival and recurrence in people with cancer: Systematic review. *British Medical Journal, 325,* 1066. (p. 496)

Petticrew, M., Fraser, J. M., & Regan, M. F. (1999). Adverse life events and risk of breast cancer: A meta-analysis. *British Journal of Health Psychology, 4,* 1–17. (p. 496)

Pettigrew, T. F., & Tropp, L. R. (2011). *When groups meet: The dynamics of intergroup contact.* New York: Psychology Press. (p. 564)

Pettigrew, T. F., Christ, O., Wagner, U., & Stellmacher, J. (2007). Direct and indirect intergroup contact effects on prejudice: A normative interpretation. *International Journal of Intercultural Relations, 31,* 411–425. (p. 564)

Pew Research Center. (2007, July 18). Modern marriage: "I like hugs. I like kisses. But what I really love is help with the dishes." Pew Research Center (www.pewresearch.org). (p. 557)

Pew Research Center. (2009, November 4). Social isolation and new technology: How the Internet and mobile phones impact Americans' social networks. Pew Research Center (www.pewresearch.org). (p. 452)

Pew Research Center. (2010, July 1). Gender equality universally embraced, but inequalities acknowledged. Pew Research Center Publications (pewresearch.org). (p. 168)

Pew Research Center. (2011, December 15). 17% and 61%—Texting, talking on the phone and driving. Pew Research Center (www.pewresearch.org). (p. 96)

Pew Research Center. (2012, March 19). Teens, smartphones & texting. Pew Research Center (pewresearch.org). (p. 211)

Pew Research Center. (2012, June 4). Section 8: Values about immigration and race. Pew Research Center for the People & the Press (www.people-press.org). (p. 538)

Pew Research Center. (2013). Teens, social media, and privacy (by M. Madden, A. Lenhart, S. Cortesi, U. Gasser, M. Duggan, A. Smith, & M. Beaton). Pew Research Center's Internet & American Life Project (www.pewinternet.org). (p. 211)

Pew Research Center. (2013, June 4). The global divide on homosexuality. Pew Research Global Attitudes Project (www.pewglobal.org). (p. 440)

Pew Research Center. (2013, June 11). Gay Marriage: Key Data Points from Pew Research. Pew Research Center (www.PewResearch.org). (p. 564)

Pew Research Center. (2013, June 13). A survey of LGBT Americans. Pew Research Center (www.pewsocialtrends.org). (p. 540)

Pew Research Center. (2014, January 27). Climate change: Key data points from Pew Research. Pew Research Center (www.pewresearch.org). (p. 360)

Pew Research Center. (2014). Global views of morality. Pew Research Global Attitudes Project (www.pewglobal.org). (pp. 438, 540)

Pfaff, L. A., Boatwright, K. J., Potthoff, A. L., Finan, C., Ulrey, L. A., & Huber, D. M. (2013). Perceptions of women and men leaders following 360-degree feedback evaluations. *Performance Improvement Quarterly, 26,* 35–56. (p. A-12)

Phelps, J. A., Davis J. O., & Schartz, K. M. (1997). Nature, nurture, and twin research strategies. *Current Directions in Psychological Science, 6,* 117–120. (pp. 136, 644)

Philip Morris. (2003). Philip Morris USA youth smoking prevention. Teenage attitudes and behavior study, 2002. In *Raising kids who don't smoke,* vol. 1(2). (p. 128)

Philip Morris Companies, Inc. (1999, Oct. 13). Referenced in Myron Levin, Philip Morris' new campaign echoes medical experts, *Los Angeles Times.* (p. 121)

Phillips, A. C., Batty, G. D., Gale, C. R., Deary, I. J., Osborn, D., MacIntyre, K., & Carroll, D. (2009). Generalized anxiety disorder, major depressive disorder, and their comorbidity as predictors of all-cause and cardiovascular mortality: The Vietnam Experience Study. *Psychosomatic Medicine, 71,* 395–403. (p. 505)

Phillips, A. L. (2011). A walk in the woods. *American Scientist, 69,* 301–302. (p. 688)

Phillips, D. P. (1985). Natural experiments on the effects of mass media violence on fatal aggression: Strengths and weaknesses of a new approach. In L. Berkowitz (Ed.), *Advances in experimental social psychology* (Vol. 19). Orlando, FL: Academic Press. (p. 525)

Phillips, D. P., Carstensen, L. L., & Paight, D. J. (1989). Effects of mass media news stories on suicide, with new evidence on the role of story content. In D. R. Pfeffer (Ed.), *Suicide among youth: Perspectives on risk and prevention.* Washington, DC: American Psychiatric Press. (p. 525)

Phillips, J. L. (1969). *Origins of intellect: Piaget's theory.* San Francisco: Freeman. (p. 189)

Piaget, J. (1930). *The child's conception of physical causality.* London: Routledge & Kegan Paul. (p. 186)

Piaget, J. (1932). *The moral judgment of the child.* New York: Harcourt, Brace & World. (p. 206)

Pianta, R. C., Barnett, W. S., Burchinal, M., & Thornburg, K. R. (2009). The effects of preschool education: What we know, how public policy is or is not aligned with the evidence base, and what we need to know. *Psychological Science in the Public Interest, 10*(2), 49–88. (p. 409)

Picchioni, M. M., & Murray, R. M. (2007). Schizophrenia. *British Medical Journal, 335,* 91–95. (p. 641)

Pieters, G. L. M., de Bruijn, E. R. A., Maas, Y., Hultijn, W., Vandereycken, W., Peuskens, J., & Sabbe, B. G. (2007). Action monitoring and perfectionism in anorexia nervosa. *Brain and Cognition, 63,* 42–50. (p. 652)

Pike, K. M., & Rodin, J. (1991). Mothers, daughters, and disordered eating. *Journal of Abnormal Psychology, 100,* 198–204. (p. 652)

Piliavin, J. A. (2003). Doing well by doing good: Benefits for the benefactor. In C. L. M. Keyes & J. Haidt (Eds.), *Flourishing: Positive psychology and the life well-lived.* Washington, DC: American Psychological Association. (p. 208)

Pillemer, D. (1998). *Momentous events, vivid memories.* Cambridge, MA: Harvard University Press. (p. 217)

Pillemer, D. B. (1995). *What is remembered about early childhood events?* Invited paper presentation to the American Psychological Society convention. (p. 185)

Pillemer, D. B., Ivcevic, Z., Gooze, R. A., & Collins, K. A. (2007). Self-esteem memories: Feeling good about achievement success, feeling bad about relationship distress. *Personality and Social Psychology Bulletin, 33,* 1292–1305. (p. 450)

Pilley, J. W., & Reid, A. K. (2011). Border collie comprehends object names as verbal referents. *Behavioural Processes, 86,* 184–195. (p. 378)

Pinker, S. (1990, September-October). Quoted by J. de Cuevas, "No, she holded them loosely." *Harvard Magazine,* pp. 60–67. (p. 370)

Pinker, S. (1995). The language instinct. *The General Psychologist, 31,* 63–65. (p. 378)

Pinker, S. (1998). Words and rules. *Lingua, 106,* 219–242. (p. 370)

Pinker, S. (2002, September 9). A biological understanding of human nature: A talk with Steven Pinker. *The Edge Third Culture Mail List* (www.edge.org). (pp. 138, 145)

Pinker, S. (2005, April 22). The science of gender and science: A conversation with Elizabeth Spelke. Harvard University (www.edge.org). (p. 410)

Pinker, S. (2007). *The stuff of thought.* New York: Viking. (p. 381)

Pinker, S. (2008). *The sexual paradox: Men, women, and the real gender gap.* New York: Scribner. (p. 164)

Pinker, S. (2010, June 10). Mind over mass media. *New York Times,* A31. (p. 454)

Pinker, S. (2011, September 27). A history of violence. *Edge* (www.edge.org). (p. 550)

Pinkham, A. E., Griffin, M., Baron, R., Sasson, N. J., & Gur, R. C. (2010). The face in the crowd effect: Anger superiority when using real faces and multiple identities. *Emotion, 10,* 141–146. (p. 468)

Piore, A. (2011, April). Silent warrior. *Discover,* pp. 49–54, 76. (p. 77)

Pipe, M-E. (1996). Children's eyewitness memory. *New Zealand Journal of Psychology, 25,* 36–43. (p. 349)

Pipe, M-E., Lamb, M. E., Orbach, Y., & Esplin, P. W. (2004). Recent research on children's testimony about experienced and witnessed events. *Developmental Review, 24,* 440–468. (p. 349)

Pipher, M. (2002). *The middle of everywhere: The world's refugees come to our town.* New York: Harcourt Brace. (pp. 450, 490)

Pitcher, D., Walsh, V., Yovel, G., & Duchaine, B. (2007). TMS evidence for the involvement of the right occipital face area in early face processing. *Current Biology, 17,* 1568–1573. (p. 245)

Pitman, R. K., & Delahanty, D. L. (2005). Conceptually driven pharmacologic approaches to acute trauma. *CNS Spectrums, 10*(2), 99–106. (p. 333)

Pitman, R. K., Sanders, K. M., Zusman, R. M., Healy, A. R., Cheema, F., Lasko, N. B., Cahill, L., & Orr, S. P. (2002). Pilot study of secondary prevention of posttraumatic stress disorder with propranolol. *Biological Psychiatry, 51,* 189–192. (p. 333)

Pittenger, D. J. (1993). The utility of the Myers-Briggs Type Indicator. *Review of Educational Research, 63,* 467–488. (p. 586)

Place, S. S., Todd, P. M., Penke, L., & Asendorpf, J. B. (2009). The ability to judge the romantic interest of others. *Psychological Science, 20,* 22–26. (pp. 468, 553)

Plassmann, H., O'Doherty, J., Shiv, B., & Rangel, A. (2008). Marketing actions can modulate neural representations of experienced pleasantness. *Proceedings of the National Academy of Sciences, 105,* 1050–1054. (p. 266)

Platek, S. M., & Singh, D. (2010) Optimal waist-to-hip ratios in women activate neural reward centers in men. PLoS ONE, 5(2), e9042. doi:10.1371/journal.pone.0009042. (p. 554)

Pliner, P. (1982). The effects of mere exposure on liking for edible substances. *Appetite: Journal for Intake Research, 3*, 283–290. (p. 428)

Pliner, P., Pelchat, M., & Grabski, M. (1993). Reduction of neophobia in humans by exposure to novel foods. *Appetite, 20*, 111–123. (p. 428)

Plöderl, M., Wagenmakers, E., Tremblay, P., Ramsay, R., Kralovec, K., Fartacek, C., & Fartacek, R. (2013). Suicide risk and sexual orientation: A critical review. *Archives of Sexual Behavior, 42*, 715–727. (p. 441)

Plomin, R. (1999). Genetics and general cognitive ability. *Nature, 402* (Suppl), C25–C29. (p. 386)

Plomin, R. (2011). Why are children in the same family so different? Nonshared environment three decades later. *International Journal of Epidemiology, 40*, 582–592. (pp. 138, 154)

Plomin, R., & Bergeman, C. S. (1991). The nature of nurture: Genetic influence on "environmental" measures. *Behavioral and Brain Sciences, 14*, 373–427. (p. 152)

Plomin, R., & Daniels, D. (1987). Why are children in the same family so different from one another? *Behavioral and Brain Sciences, 10*, 1–60. (p. 154)

Plomin, R., & DeFries, J. C. (1998, May). The genetics of cognitive abilities and disabilities. *Scientific American*, pp. 62–69. (p. 407)

Plomin, R., DeFries, J. C., McClearn, G. E., & Rutter, M. (1997). *Behavioral genetics*. New York: Freeman. (pp. 145, 431, 644)

Plomin, R., Haworth, C. M. A., Meaburn, E. L., Price, T. S., & Davis, O. S. P. (2013). Common DNA markers can account for more than half of the genetic influence on cognitive abilities. *Psychological Science, 24*, 562–568. (p. 406)

Plomin, R., McClearn, G. E., Pedersen, N. L., Nesselroade, J. R., & Bergeman, C. S. (1988). Genetic influence on childhood family environment perceived retrospectively from the last half of the life span. *Developmental Psychology, 24*, 37–45. (p. 152)

Plomin, R., & McGuffin, P. (2003). Psychopathology in the postgenomic era. *Annual Review of Psychology, 54*, 205–228. (p. 633)

Plomin, R., Reiss, D., Hetherington, E. M., & Howe, G. W. (January, 1994). Nature and nurture: Genetic contributions to measures of the family environment. *Developmental Psychology, 30*(1), 32–43. (p. 152)

Plotkin, H. (1994). *Darwin machines and the nature of knowledge*. Cambridge, MA: Harvard University Press. (p. 632)

Plotnik, J. M., de Waal, F. B. M., & Reiss, D. (2006). Self-recognition in an Asian elephant. *Proceedings of the National Academy of Sciences, 103*, 17053–17057. (p. 201)

Plous, S., & Herzog, H. A. (2000). Poll shows researchers favor lab animal protection. *Science, 290*, 711. (p. 40)

Pluess, M., & Belsky, J. (2013). Vantage sensitivity: Individual differences in response to positive experiences. *Psychological Bulletin, 139*, 901–916. (pp. 626, 651)

Poelmans, G., Pauls, D. L., Buitelaar, J. K., & Franke, B. (2011). Integrated genome-wide association study findings: Identification of a neurodevelopmental network for attention deficit hyperactivity disorder. *American Journal of Psychiatry, 168*, 365–377. (p. 615)

Polanin, J. R., Espelage, D. L., & Pigott, T. D. (2012). A meta-analysis of school-based bully prevention programs' effects on bystander intervention behavior. *School Psychology Review, 41*, 47–65. (p. 12)

Poldrack, R. A., Halchenko, Y. O., & Hanson, S. J. (2009). Decoding the large-scale structure of brain function by classifying mental states across individuals. *Psychological Science, 20*, 1364–1372. (p. 68)

Polivy, J., & Herman, C. P. (2002). Causes of eating disorders. *Annual Review of Psychology, 53*, 187–213. (p. 652)

Polivy, J., Herman, C. P., & Coelho, J. S. (2008). Caloric restriction in the presence of attractive food cues: External cues, eating, and weight. *Physiology and Behavior, 94*, 729–733. (p. 429)

Pollak, S., Cicchetti, D., & Klorman, R. (1998). Stress, memory, and emotion: Developmental considerations from the study of child maltreatment. *Developmental Psychopathology, 10*, 811–828. (p. 286)

Pollak, S. D., & Kistler, D. J. (2002). Early experience is associated with the development of categorical representations for facial expressions of emotion. *Proceedings of the National Academy of Sciences, 99*, 9072–9076. (p. 469)

Pollak, S. D., & Tolley-Schell, S. A. (2003). Selective attention to facial emotion in physically abused children. *Journal of Abnormal Psychology, 112*, 323–328. (p. 469)

Pollard, R. (1992). *100 years in psychology and deafness: A centennial retrospective*. Invited address to the American Psychological Association convention, Washington, DC. (p. 378)

Pollatsek, A., Romoser, M. R. E., & Fisher, D. L. (2012). Identifying and remediating failures of selective attention in older drivers. *Current Directions in Psychological Science, 21*, 3–7. (p. 216)

Pollick, A. S., & de Waal, F. B. M. (2007). Ape gestures and language evolution. *Proceedings of the National Academy of Sciences, 104*, 8184–8189. (p. 378)

Poole, D. A., & Lindsay, D. S. (1995). Interviewing preschoolers: Effects of nonsuggestive techniques, parental coaching and leading questions on reports of nonexperienced events. *Journal of Experimental Child Psychology, 60*, 129–154. (p. 346)

Poole, D. A., & Lindsay, D. S. (2001). Children's eyewitness reports after exposure to misinformation from parents. *Journal of Experimental Psychology: Applied, 7*, 27–50. (p. 346)

Poole, D. A., & Lindsay, D. S. (2002). Reducing child witnesses' false reports of misinformation from parents. *Journal of Experimental Child Psychology, 81*, 117–140. (p. 346)

Poon, L. W. (1987). *Myths and truisms: Beyond extant analyses of speed of behavior and age*. Address to the Eastern Psychological Association convention. (p. 216)

Pope, D., & Simonsohn, U. (2011). Round numbers as goals: Evidence from baseball, SAT takers, and the lab. *Psychological Science, 22*, 71–79. (p. 43)

Popenoe, D. (1993). *The evolution of marriage and the problem of stepfamilies: A biosocial perspective*. Paper presented at the National Symposium on Stepfamilies, Pennsylvania State University. (p. 159)

Porter, D., & Neuringer, A. (1984). Music discriminations by pigeons. *Journal of Experimental Psychology: Animal Behavior Processes, 10*, 138–148. (p. 291)

Porter, S., Birt, A. R., Yuille, J. C., & Lehman, D. R. (2000, November). Negotiating false memories: Interviewer and rememberer characteristics relate to memory distortion. *Psychological Science, 11*, 507–510. (p. 345)

Porter, S., & Peace, K. A. (2007). The scars of memory: A prospective, longitudinal investigation of the consistency of traumatic and positive emotional memories in adulthood. *Psychological Science, 18*, 435–441. (p. 349)

Porter, S., & ten Brinke, L. (2008). Reading between the lies: Identifying concealed and falsified emotions in universal facial expressions. *Psychological Science, 19*, 508–514. (p. 469)

Posner, M. I., & Carr, T. H. (1992). Lexical access and the brain: Anatomical constraints on cognitive models of word recognition. *American Journal of Psychology, 105*, 1–26. (p. 377)

Poulton, R., & Milne, B. J. (2002). Low fear in childhood is associated with sporting prowess in adolescence and young adulthood. *Behaviour Research and Therapy, 40*, 1191–1197. (p. 650)

Powell, J. (1989). *Happiness is an inside job*. Valencia, CA: Tabor. (p. 602)

Powell, K. E., Thompson, P. D., Caspersen, C. J., & Kendrick, J. S. (1987). Physical activity and the incidence of coronary heart disease. *Annual Review of Public Health, 8*, 253–287. (p. 507)

Powell, R., Digdon, N. A., Harris, B., & Smithson, C. (2014). Correcting the record on Watson, Rayner and Little Albert: Albert Barger as 'Psychology's Lost Boy.' *American Psychologist, 69*, 600–611. (p. 288)

Powell, R. A., & Boer, D. P. (1994). Did Freud mislead patients to confabulate memories of abuse? *Psychological Reports, 74*, 1283–1298. (p. 579)

Powledge, T. (2011). Behavioral epigenetics: How nurture shapes nature. *BioScience, 61*, 588-592. (p. 612)

Preckel, F., Lipnevich, A., Boehme, K., Branderner, L., Georgi, K., Könen, T., Mursin, K., & Roberts, R. (2013). Morningness–eveningness and educational outcomes: The lark has an advantage over the owl at high school. *British Journal of Educational Psychology, 83*, 114–134. (p. 101)

Premack, D. G, (2007). Human and animal cognition: Continuity and discontinuity. *PNAS, 104*, 13861–13867. (p. 371)

Premack, D. G., & Woodruff, G. (1978). Does the chimpanzee have a theory of mind? *Behavioral and Brain Sciences, 1*, 515–526. (p. 190)

Prentice, D. A., & Miller, D. T. (1993). Pluralistic ignorance and alcohol use on campus: Some consequences of misperceiving the social norm. *Journal of Personality and Social Psychology, 64*, 243–256. (p. 129)

Presley, C. A., Meilman, P. W., & Lyerla, R. (1997). *Alcohol and drugs on American college campuses: Issues of violence and harassment*. Carbondale: Core Institute, Southern Illinois University. (p. 119)

Prince Charles. (2000). BBC Reith Lecture. (p. 20)

Principe, G. F., Kanaya, T., Ceci, S. J., & Singh, M. (2006). Believing is seeing: How rumors can engender false memories in preschoolers. *Psychological Science, 17*, 243–248. (p. 348)

Prioleau, L., Murdock, M., & Brody, N. (1983). An analysis of psychotherapy versus placebo studies. *The Behavioral and Brain Sciences, 6*, 275–310. (p. 679)

Prior, H., Schwarz, A., & Güntürkün, O. (2008). Mirror-induced behavior in the magpie (*Pica pica*): Evidence of self-recognition. *PloS Biology, 6*, 1642–1650. (p. 201)

Prior, M., Smart, D., Sanson, A., & Oberklaid, F. (2000). Does shy-inhibited temperament in childhood lead to anxiety problems in adolescence? *Journal of American Academy of Child and Adolescent Psychiatry, 39*, 461–468. (p. 140)

Profet, M. (1992). Pregnancy sickness as adaptation: A deterrent to maternal ingestion of teratogens. In J. H. Barkow, L. Cosmides, and J. Tooby (Eds). *The adapted mind: Evolutionary psychology and the generation of culture* (pp. 327–366). New York: Oxford University Press. (p. 146)

Proffitt, D. R. (2006a). Embodied perception and the economy of action. *Perspectives on Psychological Science, 1*, 110–122. (p. 237)

Proffitt, D. R. (2006b). Distance perception. *Current Directions in Psychological Research, 15*, 131–135. (p. 237)

Project Match Research Group. (1997). Matching alcoholism treatments to client heterogeneity: Project MATCH posttreatment drinking outcomes. *Journal of Studies on Alcohol, 58*, 7–29. (p. 671)

Pronin, E. (2007). Perception and misperception of bias in human judgment. *Trends in Cognitive Sciences, 11*, 37–43. (p. 602)

Pronin, E. (2013). When the mind races: Effects of thought speed on feeling and action. *Current Directions in Psychological Science, 22*, 283–288. (p. 630)

Pronin, E., Berger, J., & Molouki, S. (2007). Alone in a crowd of sheep: Asymmetric perceptions of conformity and their roots in an introspection illusion. *Journal of Personality and Social Psychology, 92*, 585–595. (p. 527)

Propper, R. E., Stickgold, R., Keeley, R., & Christman, S. D. (2007). Is television traumatic? Dreams, stress, and media exposure in the aftermath of September 11, 2001. *Psychological Science, 18*, 334–340. (p. 112)

Prot, S., et al. (2014). Long-term relations among prosocial-media use, empathy, and prosocial behavior. *Psychological Science, 25*, 358–368. (pp. 310, 549)

Protzko, J., Aronson, J., & Blair, C. (2013). How to make a young child smarter: Evidence from the database of raising intelligence. *Perspectives on Psychological Science, 8*, 25–40. (p. 409)

Provine, R. R. (2001). *Laughter: A scientific investigation.* New York: Penguin. (p. 29)

Provine, R. (2012). *Curious behavior: Yawning, laughing, hiccupping, and beyond.* Cambridge, MA: Harvard University Press. (pp. 28, 29, 524)

Provine, R. R., Krosnowski, K. A., & Brocato, N. W. (2009). Tearing: Breakthrough in human emotional signaling. *Evolutionary Psychology, 7*, 52–56. (p. 473)

Pryor, J. H., Hurtado, S., DeAngelo, L., Blake, L. P., & Tran, S. (2011). *The American Freshman: National norms fall 2010.* Los Angeles: UCLA Higher Education Research Institute. (pp. 163, 164, 452, 488)

Pryor, J. H., Hurtado, S., Saenz, V. B., Korn, J. S., Santos, J. L., & Korn, W. S. (2006). *The American freshman: National norms for fall 2006.* Los Angeles: UCLA Higher Education Research Institute. (p. 635)

Pryor, J. H., Hurtado, S., Saenz, V. B., Lindholm, J. A., Korn, W. S., & Mahoney, K. M. (2005). *The American freshman: National norms for fall 2005.* Los Angeles: UCLA Higher Education Research Institute. (p. 148)

Pryor, J. H., Hurtado, S., Sharkness, J., & Korn, W. S. (2007). *The American freshman: National norms for fall 2007.* Los Angeles: UCLA Higher Education Research Institute. (p. 163)

Psaltopoulou, T., Sergentanis, T. N., Panagiotakos, D. B., Sergentanis, I. N., Kosti, R., & Scarmeas, N. (2013). Mediterranean diet, stroke, cognitive impairment, and depression: A meta-analysis. *Annals of Neurology.* (p. 634)

Psychologist. (2003, April). Who's the greatest? *The Psychologist, 16*, p. 17. (p. 192)

PTC. (2007, January 10). *Dying to entertain: Violence on prime time broadcast TV, 1998 to 2006.* Parents Television Council (www.parentstv.org). (p. 311)

Puetz, T. W., O'Connor, P. J., & Dishman, R. K. (2006). Effects of chronic exercise on feelings of energy and fatigue: A quantitative synthesis. *Psychological Bulletin, 132*, 866–876. (p. 508)

Putnam, F. W. (1991). Recent research on multiple personality disorder. *Psychiatric Clinics of North America, 14*, 489–502. (p. 648)

Putnam, F. W. (1995). Rebuttal of Paul McHugh. *Journal of the American Academy of Child and Adolescent Psychiatry, 34*, 963. (p. 648)

Putnam, R. (2000). *Bowling alone.* New York: Simon and Schuster. (p. 157)

Pyszczynski, T. A., Hamilton, J. C., Greenberg, J., & Becker, S. E. (1991). Self-awareness and psychological dysfunction. In C. R. Snyder & D. O. Forsyth (Eds.), *Handbook of social and clinical psychology: The health perspective.* New York: Pergamon. (p. 635)

Pyszczynski, T. A., Motyl, M., Vail, K. E., I., II, Hirschberger, G., Arndt, J., & Kesebir, P. (2012). Drawing attention to global climate change decreases support for war. *Peace and Conflict: Journal of Peace Psychology, 18*, 354–368. (p. 566)

Pyszczynski, T. A., Rothschild, Z., & Abdollahi, A. (2008). Terrorism, violence, and hope for peace: A terror management perspective. *Current Directions in Psychological Science 17*, 318–322. (p. 543)

Pyszczynski, T. A., Solomon, S., & Greenberg, J. (2002). *In the wake of 9/11: The psychology of terror.* Washington, DC: American Psychological Association. (p. 543)

Qin, H-F., & Piao, T-J. (2011). Dispositional optimism and life satisfaction of Chinese and Japanese college students: Examining the mediating effects of affects and coping efficacy. *Chinese Journal of Clinical Psychology, 19*, 259–261. (p. 504)

Qirko, H. N. (2004). "Fictive kin" and suicide terrorism. *Science, 304*, 49–50. (p. 534)

Qiu, L., Lin, H., Ramsay, J., & Yang, F. (2012). You are what you tweet: Personality expression and perception on Twitter. *Journal of Research in Personality, 46*, 710–718. (p. 453)

Quasha, S. (1980). *Albert Einstein: An intimate portrait.* New York: Forest. (p. 401)

Quinn, P. C., Bhatt, R. S., Brush, D., Grimes, A., & Sharpnack, H. (2002). Development of form similarity as a Gestalt grouping principle in infancy. *Psychological Science, 13*, 320–328. (p., 248)

Quinn, P. J., Williams, G. M., Najman, J. M., Andersen, M. J., & Bor, W. (2001). The effect of breastfeeding on child development at 5 years: A cohort study. *Journal of Pediatrics & Child Health, 3*, 465–469. (p. 35)

Quiroga, R. Q., Fried, I., & Koch, C. (2013, February). Brain cells for grandmother. *Scientific American*, pp. 30–35. (p. 246)

Quoidbach, J., Dunn, E. W., Petrides, K. V., & Mikolajczak, M. (2010). Money giveth, money taketh away: The dual effect of wealth on happiness. *Psychological Science, 21*, 759–763. (p. 482)

Rabbitt, P. (2006). Tales of the unexpected: 25 years of cognitive gerontology. *The Psychologist, 19*, 674–676. (p. 217)

Rabinowicz, T., Dean, D. E., Petetot, J. M., & de Courten-Myers, G. M. (1999). Gender differences in the human cerebral cortex: More neurons in males; more processes in females. *Journal of Child Neurology, 14*, 98–107. (p. 184)

Rabinowicz, T., deCourten-Myers, G. M., Petetot, J. M., Xi, G., & de los Reyes, E. (1996). Human cortex development: Estimates of neuronal numbers indicate major loss late during gestation. *Journal of Neuropathology and Experimental Neurology, 55*, 320–328. (p. 184)

Rabins, P., et al. (2009). Scientific and ethical issues related to deep brain stimulation for disorders of mood, behavior, and thought. *Archives of General Psychiatry, 66*, 931–937. (p. 687)

Raby, K. L., Cicchetti, Carlson, E. A., Cutuli, J. J., Englund, M. M., & Egeland, B. (2012). Genetic and caregiving-based contributions to infant attachment: Unique associations with distress reactivity and attachment security. *Psychological Science, 23*, 1016–1023. (p. 140)

Racsmány, M., Conway, M. A., & Demeter, G. (2010). Consolidation of episodic memories during sleep: Long-term effects of retrieval practice. *Psychological Science, 21*, 80–85. (p. 106)

Radford, B. (2010, February 18). Tiger Woods and sex addiction: Real disease or easy excuse? LiveScience.com (accessed via news.yahoo.com). (p. 118)

Radford, B. (2010, March 5). Missing persons and abductions reveal psychics' failures. *DiscoveryNews* (news.discovery.com). (p. 272)

Radford, B. (2013, May 8). Psychic claimed Amanda Berry was dead. *DNews.* http://news.discovery.com/human/psychic-claimed-amanda-berry-dead-130508.htm. (p. 272)

Rahman, Q., & Koerting, J. (2008). Sexual orientation-related differences in allocentric spatial memory tasks. *Hippocampus, 18*, 55–63. (pp. 445, 446)

Rahman, Q., & Wilson, G. D. (2003). Born gay? The psychobiology of human sexual orientation. *Personality and Individual Differences, 34*, 1337–1382. (pp. 443, 446)

Rahman, Q., Wilson, G. D., & Abrahams, S. (2004). Biosocial factors, sexual orientation and neurocognitive functioning. *Psychoneuroendocrinology, 29*, 867–881. (pp. 446, 447)

Raichle, M. (2010, March). The brain's dark energy. *Scientific American*, pp. 44–49. (p. 95)

Raichlen, D. A., & Polk, J. D. (2013). Linking brains and brawn: Exercise and the evolution of human neurobiology. *Proceedings of the Royal Society Biology, 280,* 20122250. (p. 507)

Raine, A. (1999). Murderous minds: Can we see the mark of Cain? *Cerebrum: The Dana Forum on Brain Science 1*(1), 15–29. (p. 650)

Raine, A. (2005). The interaction of biological and social measures in the explanation of antisocial and violent behavior. In D. M. Stoff & E. J. Susman (Eds.) *Developmental psychobiology of aggression.* New York: Cambridge University Press. (p. 650)

Raine, A. (2013). *The anatomy of violence: The biological roots of crime.* New York: Pantheon. (p. 546)

Raine, A., Brennan, P., Mednick, B., & Mednick, S. A. (1996). High rates of violence, crime, academic problems, and behavioral problems in males with both early neuromotor deficits and unstable family environments. *Archives of General Psychiatry, 53,* 544–549. (pp. 650, 651)

Raine, A., Lencz, T., Bihrle, S., LaCasse, L., & Colletti, P. (2000). Reduced prefrontal gray matter volume and reduced autonomic activity in antisocial personality disorder. *Archives of General Psychiatry, 57,* 119–127. (p. 650)

Rainie, L., Purcell, K., Goulet, L. S., & Hampton, K. H. (2011, June 16). Social networking sites and our lives. *Pew Research Center* (pewresearch.org). (p. 452)

Rainville, P., Duncan, G. H., Price, D. D., Carrier, B., & Bushnell, M. C. (1997). Pain affect encoded in human anterior cingulate but not somatosensory cortex. *Science, 277,* 968–971. (p. 265)

Raison, C. L., Klein, H. M., & Steckler, M. (1999). The mood and madness reconsidered. *Journal of Affective Disorders, 53,* 99–106. (p. 650)

Rajendran, G., & Mitchell, P. (2007). Cognitive theories of autism. *Developmental Review, 27,* 224–260. (p. 193)

Ramachandran, V. S., & Blakeslee, S. (1998). *Phantoms in the brain: Probing the mysteries of the human mind.* New York: Morrow. (pp. 82, 262)

Ramirez-Esparza, N., Gosling, S. D., Benet-Martinez, V., Potter, J. P., & Pennebaker, J. W. (2006). Do bilinguals have two personalities? A special case of cultural frame switching. *Journal of Research in Personality, 40,* 99–120. (p. 380)

Ramos, M. R., Cassidy, C., Reicher, S., & Haslam, S. A. (2012). A longitudinal investigation of the rejection-identification hypothesis. *British Journal of Social Psychology, 51,* 642–660. (p. 565)

Randall, D. K. (2012, September 22). Rethinking sleep. *New York Times* (www.nytimes.com). (p. 104)

Randi, J. (1999, February 4). 2000 club mailing list e-mail letter. (p. 274)

Randler, C. (2008). Morningness–eveningness and satisfaction with life. *Social Indicators Research, 86,* 297–302. (p. 101)

Randler, C. (2009). Proactive people are morning people. *Journal of Applied Social Psychology, 39,* 2787–2797. (p. 101)

Randler, C., & Bausback, V. (2010). Morningness-eveningness in women around the transition through menopause and its relationship with climacteric complaints. *Biological Rhythm Research, 41,* 415–431. (p. 101)

Rapoport, J. L. (1989, March). The biology of obsessions and compulsions. *Scientific American,* pp. 83–89. (pp. 622, 627)

Räsänen, S., Pakaslahti, A., Syvalahti, E., Jones, P. B., & Isohanni, M. (2000). Sex differences in schizophrenia: A review. *Nordic Journal of Psychiatry, 54,* 37–45. (p. 641)

Rasmussen, H. N., Scheier, M. F., & Greenhouse, J. B. (2009). Optimism and physical health: A meta-analytic review. *Annals of Behavioral Medicine, 37,* 239–256. (p. 504)

Ratcliff, K. S. (2013). The power of poverty: Individual agency and structural constraints. In K. M. Fitzpatrick (Ed.), *Poverty and health: A crisis among America's most vulnerable* (vol. 1, pp. 5-30). Santa Barbara, CA: Praeger. (p. 484)

Rath, T., & Harter, J. K. (2010, August 19). Your friends and your social well-being: Close friendships are vital to health, happiness, and even workplace productivity. *Gallup Management Journal* (ww.gmj.gallup.com). (p. A-13)

Rattan, A., Savani, K., Naidu, N. V. R., & Dweck, C. S. (2012). Can everyone become highly intelligent? Cultural differences in and societal consequences of beliefs about the universal potential for intelligence. *Journal of Personality and Social Psychology, 103,* 787–803. (p. 409)

Rawn, C. D., & Vohs, K. D. (2011). People use self-control to risk personal harm: An intra-interpersonal dilemma. *Personality and Social Psychology Review, 15,* 267–289. (p. 505)

Ray, J. (2005, April 12). U.S. teens walk away from anger: Boys and girls manage anger differently. *The Gallup Organization* (www.gallup.com). (p. 477)

Ray, J., & Kafka, S. (2014, May 6). Life in college matters for life after college. Gallup (www.gallup.com/poll). (p. A-11)

Ray, O., & Ksir, C. (1990). *Drugs, society, and human behavior* (5th ed.). St. Louis: Times Mirror/Mosby. (p. 123)

Ray, R., Sanes, M., & Schmitt, J. (2013). *No-vacation nation revisited.* Center for Economic and Policy Research, 1–22. (p. 156)

Raynor, H. A., & Epstein, L. H. (2001). Dietary variety, energy regulation, and obesity. *Psychological Bulletin, 127,* 325–341. (p. 427)

Reason, J. (1987). The Chernobyl errors. *Bulletin of the British Psychological Society, 40,* 201–206. (p. 535)

Reason, J., & Mycielska, K. (1982). *Absent-minded? The psychology of mental lapses and everyday errors.* Englewood Cliffs, NJ: Prentice-Hall. (p. 236)

Redick, T. S., Shipstead, Z., Harrison, T. L., Hicks, K. L., Fried, D.E., Hambrick, D. Z., Kane, M. J., & Engle, R. W. (2013). No evidence of intelligence improvement after working memory training: A randomized, placebo-controlled study. *Journal of Experimental Psychology: General, 142,* 359–379. (p. 218)

Reece, M., Herbenick, D., Schick, V., Sanders, S.A., Dodge, B., & Fortenberry, J. D. (2010). Sexual behaviors, relationships, and perceived health among adult men in the United States: Results from a national probability sample. *Journal of Sexual Medicine, 7* (suppl 5), 291–304. (p. 214)

Reed, D. (2011). A thing or two about twins. Quoted by Miller, P. *National Geographic,* (January Issue), 39–65. (p. 143)

Reed, P. (2000). Serial position effects in recognition memory for odors. *Journal of Experimental Psychology: Learning, Memory, and Cognition, 26,* 411–422. (p. 337)

Rees, M. (1999). *Just six numbers: The deep forces that shape the universe.* New York: Basic Books. (p. 173)

Regan, P. C., & Atkins, L. (2007). Sex differences and similarities in frequency and intensity of sexual desire. *Social Behavior and Personality, 34,* 95–102. (p. 147)

Rehm, J., Shield, K. D., Joharchi, M., & Shuper, P. A. (2012). Alcohol consumption and the intention to engage in unprotected sex: Systematic review and meta-analysis of experimental studies. *Addiction, 107,* 51–59. (p. 119)

Reichenberg, A., Gross, R., Weiser, M., Bresnahan, M., Silverman, J., Harlap, S., . . . Susser, E. (2007). Advancing paternal age and autism. *Archives of General Psychiatry, 63,* 1026–1032. (p. 194)

Reichenberg, A., & Harvey, P. D. (2007). Neuropsychological impairments in schizophrenia: Integration of performance-based and brain imaging findings. *Psychological Bulletin, 133,* 833–858. (p. 640)

Reichert, R. A., Robb, M. B., Fender, J. G., & Wartella, E. (2010). Word learning from baby videos. *Archives of Pediatrics & Adolescent Medicine, 164,* 432–437. (p. 409)

Reifman, A., & Cleveland, H. H. (2007). *Shared environment: A quantitative review.* Paper presented to the Society for Research in Child Development, Boston, MA. (p. 139)

Reifman, A. S., Larrick, R. P., & Fein, S. (1991). Temper and temperature on the diamond: The heat-aggression relationship in major league baseball. *Personality and Social Psychology Bulletin, 17,* 580–585. (p. 547)

Reimann, F., et al. (2010). Pain perception is altered by a nucleotide polymorphism in SCN9A. *PNAS, 107,* 5148–5153. (p. 262)

Reiner, W. G., & Gearhart, J. P. (2004). Discordant sexual identity in some genetic males with cloacal exstrophy assigned to female sex at birth. *New England Journal of Medicine, 350,* 333–341. (p. 167)

Reinhard, M-A., Greifeneder, R., & Scharmach, M. (2013). Unconscious processes improve lie detection. *Journal of Personality and Social Psychology, 105,* 721–739. (p. 469)

Reis, D., & Marino, L. (2001). Mirror self-recognition in the bottlenose dolphin: A case of cognitive convergence. *PNAS, 98,* 5937–5942. (p. 201)

Reis, H. T., & Aron, A. (2008). Love: What is it, why does it matter, and how does it operate? *Perspectives on Psychological Science, 3,* 80–86. (p. 557)

Reis, H. T., Smith, S. M., Carmichael, C. L., Caprariello, P. A., Tsa, F-F., Rodrigues, A., & Maniaci, M. R. (2010). Are you happy for me? How sharing positive events with others provides personal and interpersonal benefits. *Journal of Personality and Social Psychology, 99,* 311–329. (p. 448)

Reis, S. M. (2001). Toward a theory of creativity in diverse creative women. In M. Bloom & T. Gullotta (Eds.), *Promoting creativity across the life span* (pp. 231–275). Washington, DC: CWLA Press. (p. 366)

Reisenzein, R. (1983). The Schachter theory of emotion: Two decades later. *Psychological Bulletin, 94,* 239–264. (p. 461)

Reiser, M. (1982). *Police psychology.* Los Angeles: LEHI. (p. 272)

Reitzle, M. (2006). The connections between adulthood transitions and the self-perception of being adult in the changing contexts of East and West Germany. *European Psychologist, 11,* 25–38. (p. 212)

Reivich, K., Gillham, J. E., Chaplin, T. M., & Seligman, M. E. P. (2013). *From helplessness to optimism: The role of resilience in treating and preventing depression in youth.* Springer Science + Business Media, New York, NY. (p. 668)

Remick, A. K., Polivy, J., & Pliner, P. (2009). Internal and external moderators of the effect of variety on food intake. *Psychological Bulletin, 135,* 434–451. (p. 429)

Remington, A., Swettenham, J., Campbell, R., & Coleman, M. (2009). Selective attention and perceptual load in autism spectrum disorder. *Psychological Science, 20,* 1388–1393. (p. 193)

Remley, A. (1988, October). From obedience to independence. *Psychology Today,* pp. 56–59. (p. 160)

Renner, M. J., & Renner, C. H. (1993). Expert and novice intuitive judgments about animal behavior. *Bulletin of the Psychonomic Society, 31,* 551–552. (p. 152)

Renner, M. J., & Rosenzweig, M. R. (1987). *Enriched and impoverished environments: Effects on brain and behavior.* New York: Springer-Verlag. (p. 152)

Renninger, K. A., & Granott, N. (2005). The process of scaffolding in learning and development. *New Ideas in Psychology, 23*(3), 111–114. (p. 191)

Rentfrow, P. J., & Gosling, S. D. (2003). The Do Re Mi's of everyday life: The structure and personality correlates of music preferences. *Journal of Personality and Social Psychology, 84,* 1236–1256. (p. 593)

Rentfrow, P. J., & Gosling, S. D. (2006). Message in a ballad: The role of music preferences in interpersonal perception. *Psychological Science, 17,* 236–242. (p. 593)

Rescorla, R. A., & Wagner, A. R. (1972). A theory of Pavlovian conditioning: Variations in the effectiveness of reinforcement and nonreinforcement. In A. H. Black & W. F. Perokasy (Eds.), *Classical conditioning II: Current theory.* New York: Appleton-Century-Crofts. (p. 304)

Resnick, M. D., Bearman, P. S., Blum, R. W., Bauman, K. E., Harris, K. M., Jones, J., . . . Udry, J. R. (1997). Protecting adolescents from harm: Findings from the National Longitudinal Study on Adolescent Health. *Journal of the American Medical Association, 278,* 823–832. (pp. 35, 98, 211)

Resnick, S. M. (1992). Positron emission tomography in psychiatric illness. *Current Directions in Psychological Science, 1,* 92–98. (p. 642)

Rethorst, C. D., Wipfli, B. M., & Landers, D. M. (2009). The antidepressive effects of exercise: A meta-analysis of randomized trials. *Sports Medicine, 39,* 491–511. (p. 508)

Reuters. (2000, July 5). Many teens regret decision to have sex (National Campaign to Prevent Teen Pregnancy survey). www.washingtonpost.com. (p. 438)

Reyna, V. F., Chick, C. F., Corbin, J. C., & Hsia, A. N. (2014). Developmental reversals in risky decision making: Intelligence agents show larger decision biases than college students. *Psychological Science, 25,* 76–84. (p. 364)

Reyna, V. F., & Farley, F. (2006). Risk and rationality in adolescent decision making: Implications for theory, practice, and public policy. *Psychological Science in the Public Interest, 7*(1), 1–44. (p. 205)

Reynolds, G. (2009, November 18). Phys ed: Why exercise makes you less anxious. *New York Times blog* (well.blogs.nytimes.com). (p. 509)

Rhodes, G., Sumich, A., & Byatt, G. (1999). Are average facial configurations attractive only because of their symmetry? *Psychological Science, 10,* 52–58. (p. 555)

Rhodes, M. G., & Anastasi, J. S. (2012). The own-age bias in face recognition: A meta-analytic and theoretical review. *Psychological Bulletin, 138,* 146–174. (p. 545)

Rholes, W. S., & Simpson, J. A. (Eds.). (2004). *Adult attachment: Theory, research, and clinical implications.* New York: Guilford. (p. 199)

Ribeiz, S. R. I., Duran, F., Oliveira, M. C., Bezerra, D., Castro, C. C., Steffens, D. C., Busatto, F. G., & Bottino, C. M. (2013). Structural brain changes as biomarkers and outcomes in patients with late-life depression: A cross-sectional and prospective study. *PLOS One, 8*(11), e80049. (p. 633)

Ricciardelli, L. A., & McCabe, M. P. (2004). A biopsychosocial model of disordered eating and the pursuit of muscularity in adolescent boys. *Psychological Bulletin, 130,* 179–205. (p. 652)

Rice, M. E., & Grusec, J. E. (1975). Saying and doing: Effects on observer performance. *Journal of Personality and Social Psychology, 32,* 584–593. (p. 311)

Rice, W. R., Friberg, U., & Gavrilets, S. (2012). Homosexuality as a consequence of epigenetically canalized sexual development. *Quarterly Review of Biology, 87,* 343–368. (p. 444)

Richardson, J. (1993). The curious case of coins: Remembering the appearance of familiar objects. *The Psychologist: Bulletin of the British Psychological Society, 6,* 360–366. (p. 340)

Richardson, J. T. E., & Zucco, G. M. (1989). Cognition and olfaction: A review. *Psychological Bulletin, 105,* 352–360. (p. 267)

Richardson, M., Abraham, C., & Bond, R. (2012). Psychological correlates of university students' academic performance: A systematic review and meta-analysis. *Psychological Bulletin, 138,* 353–387. (p. 409)

Richeson, J. A., & Shelton, J. N. (2007). Negotiating interracial interactions. *Current Directions in Psychological Science, 16,* 316–320. (p. 565)

Rickard, I. J., Frankenhuis, W. E., & Nettle, D. (2014). Why are childhood family factors associated with timing of maturation? A role for internal prediction. *Perspectives on Psychological Science, 9,* 3–15. (p. 166)

Rieff, P. (1979). *Freud: The mind of a moralist* (3rd ed.). Chicago: University of Chicago Press. (p. 580)

Rieger, G., Rosenthal, A. M., Cash, B. M., Linsenmeier, J. A. W., Bailey, J. M., & Savin-Williams, R. (2013). Male bisexual arousal: A matter of curiosity? *Biological Psychology, 94,* 479–489. (p. 440)

Rieger, G., & Savin-Williams, R. (2012). The eyes have it: Sex and sexual orientation differences in pupil dilation patterns. *PLoS ONE, 7*(8), e40256 (www.plosone.org). (p. 441)

Rietveld, C. A., et al. (2013). GWAS of 126,559 individuals identifies genetic variants associated with educational attainment. *Science, 340,* 1467–1471. (p. 406)

Riffkin, R. (2014, July 9). Obesity linked to lower social well-being. Gallup-Healthways Well-Being Index. www.gallup.com. (p. 429)

Riis, J., Loewenstein, G., Baron, J., Jepson, C., Fagerlin, A., & Ubel, P. A. (2005). Ignorance of hedonic adaptation to hemodialysis: A study using ecological momentary assessment. *Journal of Experimental Psychology: General, 134,* 3–9. (p. 481)

Riley, L. D., & Bowen, C. (2005). The sandwich generation: Challenges and coping strategies of multigenerational families. *The Family Journal, 13,* 52–58. (p. 220)

Rindermann, H., & Ceci, S. J. (2009). Educational policy and country outcomes in international cognitive competence studies. *Perspectives on Psychological Science, 4,* 551–577. (p. 412)

Riordan, M. (2013, March 19). Tobacco warning labels: Evidence of effectiveness. Washington, DC: The Campaign for Tobacco-Free Kids (www.tobaccofreekids.org). (p. 360)

Ripke, S., et al. (2011). Genome-wide association study identifies five new schizophrenia loci. *Nature Genetics, 43,* 969–976. (p. 644)

Ripley, A. (2013, January 28). Your brain under fire. *Time,* pp. 34ff. (p. 362)

Ritchie, S. J., Wiseman, R., & French, C. C. (2012). Failing the future: Three unsuccessful attempts to replicate Bem's 'retroactive facilitation of recall' effect. *PLoS One, 7,* e33r23 (www.plosone.org). (p. 274)

Ritter, S. M., Damian, R. I., Simonton, D. K., van Baaren, R. B., Strick, M., Derks, J., & Dijksterhuis, A. (2012). Diversifying experiences enhance cognitive flexibility. *Journal of Experimental Social Psychology, 48,* 961–964. (p. 367)

Rizzolatti, G., Fadiga, L., Fogassi, L., & Gallese, V. (2002). From mirror neurons to imitation: Facts and speculations. In A. N. Meltzoff & W. Prinz (Eds.), *The imitative mind: Development, evolution, and brain bases.* Cambridge: Cambridge University Press. (p. 307)

Rizzolatti, G., Fogassi, L., & Gallese, V. (2006, November). Mirrors in the mind. *Scientific American,* pp. 54–61. (p. 307)

Roan, S. (2010, August 15). Medical treatment carries possible side effect of limiting homosexuality. *Los Angeles Times* (www.latimes.com). (p. 446)

Roberson, D., Davidoff, J., Davies, I. R. L., & Shapiro, L. R. (2004). The development of color categories in two languages: A longitudinal study. *Journal of Experimental Psychology: General, 133,* 554–571. (p. 380)

Roberson, D., Davies, I. R. L., Corbett, G. G., & Vandervyver, M. (2005). Free-sorting of colors across cultures: Are there universal grounds for grouping? *Journal of Cognition and Culture, 5,* 349–386. (p. 380)

Roberti, J. W., Storch, E. A., & Bravata, E. A. (2004). Sensation seeking, exposure to psychosocial stressors, and body modifications in a college population. *Personality and Individual Differences, 37,* 1167–1177. (p. 422)

Roberts, A. L., Glymour, M. M., & Koenen, K. C. (2013). Does maltreatment in childhood affect sexual orientation in adulthood? *Archives of Sexual Behavior, 42,* 161–171. (p. 442)

Roberts, B. W., & DelVecchio, W. F. (2000). The rank-order consistency of personality traits from childhood to old age: A quantitative review of longitudinal studies. *Psychological Bulletin, 126,* 3–25. (p. 592)

Roberts, B. W., Donnellan, M. B., & Hill, P. L. (2013). Personality trait development in adulthood. In H. Tennen, J. Suls, & I. B. Weiner (Eds.), *Handbook of psychology, Vol. 5: Personality and social psychology* (2nd ed.). Hoboken, NJ: John Wiley. (p. 180)

Roberts, B. W., Kuncel, N. R., Shiner, R., Caspi, A., & Goldberg, L. R. (2007). The power of personality: The comparative validity of personality traits, socioeconomic status, and cognitive ability for predicting important life outcomes. *Perspectives on Psychological Science, 2*, 313–345. (p. 592)

Roberts, B. W., & Mroczek, D. K. (2008). Personality trait change in adulthood. *Current Directions in Psychological Science, 17*, 31–35. (p. 180)

Roberts, L. (1988). Beyond Noah's ark: What do we need to know? *Science, 242*, 1247. (p. 502)

Roberts, T-A. (1991). Determinants of gender differences in responsiveness to others' evaluations. *Dissertation Abstracts International, 51*(8–B). (p. 163)

Robertson, K. F., Smeets, S., Lubinski, D., & Benbow, C. P. (2010). Beyond the threshold hypothesis: Even among the gifted and top math/science graduate students, cognitive abilities, vocational interests, and lifestyle preferences matter for career choice, performance, and persistence. *Current Directions in Psychological Science, 19*, 346–351. (pp. 303, 365)

Robins, L., & Regier, D. (Eds.). (1991). *Psychiatric disorders in America.* New York: Free Press. (p. 619)

Robins, L. N., Davis, D. H., & Goodwin, D. W. (1974). Drug use by U.S. Army enlisted men in Vietnam: A follow-up on their return home. *American Journal of Epidemiology, 99*, 235–249. (p. 129)

Robins, R. W., & Trzesniewski, K. H. (2005). Self-esteem development across the lifespan. *Current Directions in Psychological Science, 14*(3), 158–162. (p. 223)

Robinson, F. P. (1970). *Effective study.* New York: Harper & Row. (p. 14)

Robinson, J. P., & Martin, S. (2008). What Do Happy People Do? *Social Indicators Research, 89*, 565–571. (p. A-1)

Robinson, J. P., & Martin, S. (2009). Changes in American daily life: 1965–2005. *Social Indicators Research, 93*, 47–56. (pp. 104, 311)

Robinson, O. J., Cools, R., Carlisi, C. O., & Drevets, W. C. (2012). Ventral striatum response during reward and punishment reversal learning in unmedicated major depressive disorder. *American Journal of Psychiatry, 169*, 152–159. (p. 633)

Robinson, T. E., & Berridge, K. C. (2003). Addiction. *Annual Review of Psychology, 54*, 25–53. (p. 118)

Robinson, T. N., Borzekowski, D. L. G., Matheson, D. M., & Kraemer, H. C. (2007). Effects of fast food branding on young children's taste preferences. *Archives of Pediatric and Adolescent Medicine, 161*, 792–797. (p. 236)

Robinson, V. M. (1983). Humor and health. In P. E. McGhee & J. H. Goldstein (Eds.), *Handbook of humor research: Vol. II. Applied studies.* New York: Springer-Verlag. (p. 506)

Robles, T. F., Slatcher, R. B., Trombello, J. M., McGinn, M. M. (2014). Marital quality and health: A meta-analytic review. *Psychological Bulletin, 140*, 140–187. (p. 505)

Rochat, F. (1993). *How did they resist authority? Protecting refugees in Le Chambon during World War II.* Paper presented at the American Psychological Association convention. (p. 530)

Rock, I., & Palmer, S. (1990, December). The legacy of Gestalt psychology. *Scientific American*, pp. 84–90. (p. 248)

Rodenburg, R., Benjamin, A., de Roos, C., Meijer, A. M., & Stams, G. J. (2009). Efficacy of EMDR in children: A meta-analysis. *Clinical Psychology Review, 29*, 599–606. (p. 677)

Rodin, J. (1986). Aging and health: Effects of the sense of control. *Science, 233*, 1271–1276. (pp. 501, 502)

Roediger, H. L., III. (2013). Applying cognitive psychology to education: Translational educational science. *Psychological Science in the Public Interest, 14*, 1–3. (p. 326)

Roediger, H. L., III, & Finn, B. (2010, March/April). The pluses of getting it wrong. *Scientific American Mind*, pp. 39–41. (p. 14)

Roediger, H. L., III, & Geraci, L. (2007). Aging and the misinformation effect: A neuropsychological analysis. *Journal of Experimental Psychology, 33*, 321–334. (p. 349)

Roediger, H. L., III, & Karpicke, J. D. (2006). Test-enhanced learning: Taking memory tests improves long-term retention. *Psychological Science, 17*, 249–255. (pp. 13, 326)

Roediger, H. L., III, & McDaniel, M. A. (2007). Illusory recollection in older adults: Testing Mark Twain's conjecture. In M. Garry H. Hayne (Ed.), *Do justice and let the sky fall: Elizabeth F. Loftus and her contributions to science, law, and academic freedom.* Mahwah, NJ: Erlbaum. (p. 349)

Roediger, H. L., III, & McDermott, K. B. (1995). Creating false memories: Remembering words not presented in lists. *Journal of Experimental Psychology: Learning, Memory, and Cognition, 21*, 803–814. (p. 347)

Roediger, H. L., III, Wheeler, M. A., & Rajaram, S. (1993). Remembering, knowing, and reconstructing the past. In D. L. Medin (Ed.), *The psychology of learning and motivation: Advances in research and theory* (Vol. 30). Orlando, FL: Academic Press. (p. 344)

Roehling, P. V., Roehling, M. V., & Moen, P. (2001). The relationship between work-life policies and practices and employee loyalty: A life course perspective. *Journal of Family and Economic Issues, 22*, 141–170. (p. A-13)

Roelfsema, M. T., Hoekstra, R. A., Allison, C., Wheelwright, S., Brayne, C., Matthews, F. E., & Baron-Cohen, S. (2012). Are autism spectrum conditions more prevalent in an information-technology region? A school-based study of three regions in the Netherlands. *Journal of Autism and Developmental Disorders, 42*, 734–739. (p. 193)

Roelofs, T. (2010, September 22). Somali refugee takes oath of U.S. citizenship year after his brother. *Grand Rapids Press* (www.mlive.com). (p. A-9)

Roenneberg, T., Kuehnle, T., Pramstaller, P. P., Ricken, J., Havel, M., Guth, A., Merrow, M. (2004). A marker for the end of adolescence. *Current Biology, 14*, R1038–R1039. (p. 101)

Roese, N. J., & Summerville, A. (2005). What we regret most . . . and why. *Personality and Social Psychology Bulletin, 31*, 1273–1285. (p. 223)

Roese, N. J., & Vohs, K. D. (2012). Hindsight bias. *Perspectives on Psychological Science, 7*, 411–426. (p. 21)

Roesser, R. (1998). What you should know about hearing conservation. *Better Hearing Institute* (www.betterhearing.org). (p. 257)

Roest, A. M., Martens, E. J., Denollet, J., & De Jonge, P. (2010). Prognostic association of anxiety post myocardial infarction with mortality and new cardiac events: A meta-analysis. *Psychosomatic Medicine, 72*, 563–569. (p. 498)

Rofé, Y. (2008). Does repression exist? Memory, pathogenic, unconscious and clinical evidence. *Review of General Psychology, 12*, 63–85. (p. 580)

Rogers, C. R. (1961). *On becoming a person: A therapist's view of psychotherapy.* Boston: Houghton Mifflin. (p. 661)

Rogers, C. R. (1980). *A way of being.* Boston: Houghton Mifflin. (pp. 583, 584, 661)

Rohan, K. J., Roecklein, K. A., Lindsey, K. T., Johnson, L. G., Lippy, R. D., Lacy, T. J., & Barton, F. B. (2007). A randomized controlled trial of cognitive-behavioral therapy, light therapy, and their combination for seasonal affective disorder. *Journal of Consulting and Clinical Psychology, 75*, 489–500. (p. 678)

Rohner, R. P. (1986). *The warmth dimension: Foundations of parental acceptance-rejection theory.* Newbury Park, CA: Sage. (p. 161)

Rohner, R. P., & Veneziano, R. A. (2001). The importance of father love: History and contemporary evidence. *Review of General Psychology, 5*, 382–405. (pp. 198, 202)

Roiser, J. P., Cook, L. J., Cooper, J. D., Rubinsztein, D. C., & Sahakian, B. J. (2005). Association of a functional polymorphism in the serotonin transporter gene with abnormal emotional processing in Ecstasy users. *American Journal of Psychiatry, 162*, 609–612. (p. 124)

Rokach, A., Orzeck, T., Moya, M., & Exposito, F. (2002). Causes of loneliness in North America and Spain. *European Psychologist, 7*, 70–79. (p. 7)

Ronald, A., & Hoekstra, R. A. (2011). Autism spectrum disorders and autistic traits: A decade of new twin studies. *American Journal of Medical Genetics Part B, 156*, 255–274. (p. 136)

Ronay, R., & von Hippel, W. (2010). The presence of an attractive woman elevates testosterone and physical risk taking in young men. *Social Psychology and Personality Science, 1*, 57–64. (p. 434)

Root, T. L., Thornton, L. M., Lindroos, A. K., Stunkard, A. J., Lichtenstein, P., Pedersen, N. L., Rasmussen, F., & Bulik, C. M. (2010). Shared and unique genetic and environmental influences on binge eating and night eating: A Swedish twin study. *Eating Behaviors, 11*, 92–98. (p. 652)

Roque, L., Verissimo, M., Oliveira, T. F., & Oliveira, R. F. (2012). Attachment security and HPA axis reactivity to positive and challenging emotional situations in child-mother dyads in naturalistic settings. *Developmental Psychobiology, 54*, 401–411. (p. 140)

Rosch, E. (1978). Principles of categorization. In E. Rosch & B. L. Lloyd (Eds.), *Cognition and categorization.* Hillsdale, NJ: Erlbaum. (p. 356)

Rose, A. J., & Rudolph, K. D. (2006). A review of sex differences in peer relationship processes: Potential trade-offs for the emotional and behavioral development of girls and boys. *Psychological Bulletin, 132*, 98–131. (p. 163)

Rose, J. S., Chassin, L., Presson, C. C., & Sherman, S. J. (1999). Peer influences on adolescent cigarette smoking: A prospective sibling analysis. *Merrill-Palmer Quarterly, 45*, 62–84. (pp. 128, 154)

Rose, R. J., Kaprio, J., Winter, T., Dick, D. M., Viken, R. J., Pulkkinen, L., & Koskenvuo, M. (2002). Femininity and fertility in sisters with twin brothers: Prenatal androgenization? Cross-sex socialization? *Psychological Science, 13,* 263–266. (p. 445)

Rose, R. J., Viken, R. J., Dick, D. M., Bates, J. E., Pulkkinen, L., & Kaprio, J. (2003). It *does* take a village: Nonfamiliar environments and children's behavior. *Psychological Science, 14,* 273–277. (p. 154)

Rose, S. A., Feldman, J. F., & Jankowski, J. J. (2012). Implications of infant cognition for executive functions at age 11. *Psychological Science, 23,* 1345–1355. (p. 401)

Roselli, C. E., Larkin, K., Schrunk, J. M., & Stormshak, F. (2004). Sexual partner preference, hypothalamic morphology and aromatase in rams. *Physiology and Behavior, 83,* 233–245. (p. 443)

Roselli, C. E., Resko, J. A., & Stormshak, F. (2002). Hormonal influences on sexual partner preference in rams. *Archives of Sexual Behavior, 31,* 43–49. (p. 443)

Rosenbaum, M. (1986). The repulsion hypothesis: On the nondevelopment of relationships. *Journal of Personality and Social Psychology, 51,* 1156–1166. (p. 555)

Rosenberg, N. A., Pritchard, J. K., Weber, J. L., Cann, H. M., Kidd, K. K., Zhivotosky, L. A., & Feldman, M. W. (2002). Genetic structure of human populations. *Science, 298,* 2381–2385. (pp. 146, 412)

Rosenberg, T. (2010, November 1). The opt-out solution. *New York Times* (www.nytimes.com). (p. 364)

Rosenblum, L. D. (2013, January). A confederacy of senses. *Scientific American,* pp. 73–78. (p. 269)

Rosenfeld, M. J. (2013, August 26). Personal communication. (p. 221)

Rosenfeld, M. J. (2014). Couple longevity in the era of same-sex marriage in the United States. *Journal of Marriage and family, 76*(5), 905–911. (pp. 220, 447)

Rosenfeld, M. J., & Thomas, R. J. (2012). Searching for a mate: The rise of the Internet as a social intermediary. *American Sociological Review, 77,* 523–547. (pp. 221, 552, 553)

Rosenhan, D. L. (1973). On being sane in insane places. *Science, 179,* 250–258. (p. 614)

Rosenthal, A. M., Sylva, D., Safron, A., & Bailey, J. M. (2012). The male bisexuality debate revisited: Some bisexual men have bisexual arousal patterns. *Archives of Sexual Behavior, 41,* 135–147. (p. 440)

Rosenthal, E. (2009, November 2). When texting kills, Britain offers path of prison. *New York Times* (www.nytimes.com). (p. 97)

Rosenthal, R., Hall, J. A., Archer, D., DiMatteo, M. R., & Rogers, P. L. (1979). The PONS test: Measuring sensitivity to nonverbal cues. In S. Weitz (Ed.), *Nonverbal communication* (2nd ed.). New York: Oxford University Press. (p. 469)

Rosenzweig, M. R. (1984). Experience, memory, and the brain. *American Psychologist, 39,* 365–376. (pp. 152, 408)

Rosenzweig, M. R., Krech, D., Bennett, E. L., & Diamond, M. C. (1962). Effects of environmental complexity and training on brain chemistry and anatomy: A replication and extension. *Journal of Comparative and Physiological Psychology, 55,* 429–437. (p. 152)

Roseth, C. J., Johnson, D. W., & Johnson, R. T. (2008). Promoting early adolescents' achievement and peer relationships: The effects of cooperative, competitive, and individualistic goal structures. *Psychological Bulletin, 134,* 223–246. (p. 566)

Rosin, H. (2010, July, August). The end of men. *The Atlantic* (www.theatlantic.com). (p. 168)

Ross, J. (2006, December). Sleep on a problem . . . it works like a dream. *The Psychologist, 19,* 738–740. (p. 106)

Ross, L. (1977). The intuitive psychologist and his shortcomings: Distortions in the attribution process. In L. Berkowitz (Ed.) *Advances in experimental social psychology* (Vol. 10). New York: Academic Press. (p. 518)

Ross, M., McFarland, C., & Fletcher, G. J. O. (1981). The effect of attitude on the recall of personal histories. *Journal of Personality and Social Psychology, 40,* 627–634. (p. 342)

Ross, M., Xun, W. Q. E., & Wilson, A. E. (2002). Language and the bicultural self. *Personality and Social Psychology Bulletin, 28,* 1040–1050. (p. 380)

Rossi, A. S., & Rossi, P. H. (1993). *Of human bonding: Parent-child relations across the life course.* Hawthorne, NY: Aldine de Gruyter. (p. 164)

Rossi, P. J. (1968). Adaptation and negative aftereffect to lateral optical displacement in newly hatched chicks. *Science, 160,* 430–432. (p. 254)

Rossion, B., & Boremanse, A. (2011). Robust sensitivity to facial identity in the right human occipito-temporal cortex as revealed by steady-state visual-evoked potentials. *Journal of Vision, 11*(2), 16, 1–21. (p. 229)

Rotge, J-Y., Langbour, N., Guehl, D., Bioulac, B., Jaafari, N., Allard, M., Aouizerate, B., & Burbaud, P. (2010). Gray matter alterations in obsessive-compulsive disorder: An anatomic likelihood estimation meta-analysis. *Neuropsychopharmacology, 35,* 686–691. (p. 626)

Roth, T., Roehrs, T., Zwyghuizen-Doorenbos, A., Stpeanski, E., & Witting, R. (1988). Sleep and memory. In I. Hindmarch & H. Ott (Eds.), *Benzodiazepine receptor ligans, memory and information processing.* New York: Springer-Verlag. (p. 113)

Rothbart, M., Fulero, S., Jensen, C., Howard, J., & Birrell, P. (1978). From individual to group impressions: Availability heuristics in stereotype formation. *Journal of Experimental Social Psychology, 14,* 237–255. (p. 544)

Rothbart, M. K. (2007). Temperament, development, and personality. *Current Directions in Psychological Science, 16,* 207–212. (p. 140)

Rothbaum, F., & Tsang, B. Y-P. (1998). Lovesongs in the United States and China: On the nature of romantic love. *Journal of Cross-Cultural Psychology, 29,* 306–319. (p. 159)

Rothblum, E. D. (2007). *Same-sex couples in legalized relationships: I do, or do I?* Unpublished manuscript, Women's Studies Department, San Diego State University. (p. 148)

Rothman, A. J., & Salovey, P. (1997). Shaping perceptions to motivate healthy behavior: The role of message framing. *Psychological Bulletin, 121,* 3–19. (p. 362)

Rotton, J., & Kelly, I. W. (1985). Much ado about the full moon: A metaanalysis of lunar-lunacy research. *Psychological Bulletin, 97,* 286–306. (p. 650)

Rounds, J., & Su, R. (2014). The nature and power of interests. *Current Directions in Psychological Science, 23,* 98–103. (p. A-3)

Rovee-Collier, C. (1989). The joy of kicking: Memories, motives, and mobiles. In P. R. Solomon, G. R. Goethals, C. M. Kelley, & B. R. Stephens (Eds.), *Memory: Interdisciplinary approaches.* New York: Springer-Verlag. (p. 186)

Rovee-Collier, C. (1993). The capacity for long-term memory in infancy. *Current Directions in Psychological Science, 2,* 130–135. (p. 336)

Rovee-Collier, C. (1997). Dissociations in infant memory: Rethinking the development of implicit and explicit memory. *Psychological Review, 104,* 467–498. (p. 186)

Rovee-Collier, C. (1999). The development of infant memory. *Current Directions in Psychological Science, 8,* 80–85. (p. 186)

Rowe, D. C. (1990). As the twig is bent? The myth of child-rearing influences on personality development. *Journal of Counseling and Development, 68,* 606–611. (p. 138)

Rowe, D. C., Almeida, D. M., & Jacobson, K. C. (1999). School context and genetic influences on aggression in adolescence. *Psychological Science, 10,* 277–280. (p. 545)

Rowe, D. C., Jacobson, K. C., & Van den Oord, E. J. C. G. (1999). Genetic and environmental influences on vocabulary IQ: Parental education level as moderator. *Child Development, 70*(5), 1151–1162. (p. 406)

Rowe, D. C., Vazsonyi, A. T., & Flannery, D. J. (1994). No more than skin deep: Ethnic and racial similarity in developmental process. *Psychological Review, 101*(3), 396. (p. 161)

Rowe, D. C., Vazsonyi, A. T., & Flannery, D. J. (1995). Ethnic and racial similarity in developmental process: A study of academic achievement. *Psychological Science, 6,* 33–38. (p. 161)

Rozin, P., Dow, S., Mosovitch, M., & Rajaram, S. (1998). What causes humans to begin and end a meal? A role for memory for what has been eaten, as evidenced by a study of multiple meal eating in amnesic patients. *Psychological Science, 9,* 392–396. (p. 427)

Rozin, P., Millman, L., & Nemeroff, C. (1986). Operation of the laws of sympathetic magic in disgust and other domains. *Journal of Personality and Social Psychology, 50,* 703–712. (p. 286)

Ruau, D., Liu, L. Y., Clark, J. D., Angst, M. S., & Butte, A. J. (2012). Sex differences in reported pain across 11,000 patients captured in electronic medical records. *Journal of Pain, 13,* 228–234. (p. 261)

Ruback, R. B., Carr, T. S., & Hopper, C. H. (1986). Perceived control in prison: Its relation to reported crowding, stress, and symptoms. *Journal of Applied Social Psychology, 16,* 375–386. (p. 502)

Rubenstein, J. S., Meyer, D. E., & Evans, J. E. (2001). Executive control of cognitive processes in task switching. *Journal of Experimental Psychology: Human Perception and Performance, 27,* 763–797. (p. 96)

Rubin, D. C., Rahhal, T. A., & Poon, L. W. (1998). Things learned in early adulthood are remembered best. *Memory and Cognition, 26,* 3–19. (p. 217)

Rubin, J. Z., Pruitt, D. G., & Kim, S. H. (1994). *Social conflict: Escalation, stalemate, and settlement.* New York: McGraw-Hill. (p. 566)

Rubin, L. B. (1985). *Just friends: The role of friendship in our lives.* New York: Harper & Row. (p. 164)

Rubin, Z. (1970). Measurement of romantic love. *Journal of Personality and Social Psychology, 16,* 265–273. (p. 468)

Rubio, G., & López-Ibor, J. J. (2007). Generalized anxiety disorder: A 40-year follow-up study. *Acta Psychiatrica Scandinavica, 115,* 372–379. (p. 620)

Rubio-Fernández, P., & Geurts, B. (2013). How to pass the false-belief task before your fourth birthday. *Psychological Science, 24,* 27–33. (p. 190)

Ruchlis, H. (1990). *Clear thinking: A practical introduction.* Buffalo, NY: Prometheus Books. (p. 357)

Rudman, L. A., & Goodwin, S. A. (2004). Gender differences in automatic in-group bias: Why do women like women more than men like men? *Journal of Personality and Social Psychology, 87,* 494–509. (p. 540)

Rudman, L. A., McLean, M. C., & Bunzl, M. (2013). When truth is personally inconvenient, attitudes change: The impact of extreme weather on implicit support for green politicians and explicit climate-change beliefs. *Psychological Science, 14,* 2290–2296. (p. 360)

Rueckert, L., Doan, T., & Branch, B. (2010). *Emotion and relationship effects on gender differences in empathy.* Presented at the annual meeting of the Association for Psychological Science, Boston, MA. (p. 471)

Ruffin, C. L. (1993). Stress and health—little hassles vs. major life events. *Australian Psychologist, 28,* 201–208. (p. 490)

Rule, B. G., & Ferguson, T. J. (1986). The effects of media violence on attitudes, emotions, and cognitions. *Journal of Social Issues, 42*(3), 29–50. (p. 312)

Rule, N. O., Ambady, N., & Hallett, K. C. (2009). Female sexual orientation is perceived accurately, rapidly, and automatically from the face and its features. *Journal of Experimental Social Psychology, 45,* 1245–1251. (p. 593)

Rumbaugh, D. M. (1977). *Language learning by a chimpanzee: The Lana project.* New York: Academic Press. (p. 378)

Rusanen, M., Kivipelto, M., Quesenberry, C. P., Jr., Zhou, J., & Whitmer, R. A. (2011). Heavy smoking in midlife and long-term risk of Alzheimer disease and vascular dementia. *Archives of Internal Medicine, 171,* 333–339. (p. 218)

Rushton, J. P. (1975). Generosity in children: Immediate and long-term effects of modeling, preaching, and moral judgment. *Journal of Personality and Social Psychology, 31,* 459–466. (p. 311)

Rushton, P., & Irwing, P. (2011). The general factor of personality: Normal and abnormal. In T. Chamorro-Premuzic, S. von Stumm, & A. Furnham (Eds.), *The Wiley-Blackwell Handbook of Individual Differences* (pp. 132–161). New York: Wiley-Blackwell. (p. 590)

Russell, B. (1930/1985). *The conquest of happiness.* London: Unwin Paperbacks. (p. 484)

Russell, J. A. (2009). Emotion, Core Affect, and Psychological Construction. *Cognition and Emotion, 23,* 1259–1283. (p. 476)

Russell, J. A., & Carroll, J. M. (1999a, January). On the bipolarity of positive and negative affect. *Psychological Bulletin, 125,* 3–30. (p. 476)

Russell, J. A., & Carroll, J. M. (1999b). The phoenix of bipolarity: Reply to Watson and Tellegen (1999). *Psychological Bulletin, 125,* 611–614. (p. 476)

Russell, J. A., Lewicka, M., & Niit, T. (1989). A cross-cultural study of a circumplex model of affect. *Journal of Personality and Social Psychology, 57,* 848–856. (p. 476)

Rutchick, A. M. (2010). Deus ex machina: The influence of polling place on voting behavior. *Political Psychology, 31,* 209–225. (p. 280)

Rutchick, A. M., Slepian, M. L., & Ferris, B. D. (2010). The pen is mightier than the word: Object priming of evaluative standards. *European Journal of Social Psychology, 40,* 704–708. (p. 280)

Ruthsatz, J., & Urbach, J. B. (2012). Child prodigy: A novel cognitive profile places elevated general intelligence, exceptional working memory and attention to detail at the root of prodigiousness. *Intelligence, 40,* 419–426. (p. 455)

Ryan, C., Huebner, D., Diaz, R. M., & Sanchez, J. (2009). Family rejection as a predictor of negative health outcomes in White and Latino lesbian, gay, and bisexual young adults. *Pediatrics, 123,* 346–352. (p. 441)

Ryan, R. (1999, February 2). Quoted by Alfie Kohn, In pursuit of affluence, at a high price. *New York Times* (www.nytimes.com). (pp. 482, 483)

Ryan, R. M., & Deci, E. L. (2004). Avoiding death or engaging life as accounts of meaning and culture: Comment on Pyszczynski et al. (2004). *Psychological Bulletin, 130,* 473–477. (p. 605)

Rydell, R. J., Rydell, M. T., & Boucher, K. L. (2010). The effect of negative performance stereotypes on learning. *Journal of Personality and Social Psychology, 99,* 883–896. (p. 414)

Saad, L. (2002, November 21). Most smokers wish they could quit. *Gallup News Service* (www.gallup.com). (p. 122)

Saad, L. (2006, August 10). Anti-Muslim sentiments fairly commonplace. *Gallup News Service* (poll.gallup.com). (p. 538)

Sabbagh, M. A., Xu, F., Carlson, S. M., Moses, L. J., & Lee, K. (2006). The development of executive functioning and theory of mind: A comparison of Chinese and U.S. preschoolers. *Psychological Science, 17,* 74–81. (p. 190)

Sabini, J. (1986). Stanley Milgram (1933–1984). *American Psychologist, 41,* 1378–1379. (p. 528)

Sachdev, P., & Sachdev, J. (1997). Sixty years of psychosurgery: Its present status and its future. *Australian and New Zealand Journal of Psychiatry, 31,* 457–464. (p. 688)

Sackett, P. R., Borneman, M. J., & Connelly, B. S. (2008). High-stakes testing in higher education and employment: Appraising the evidence for validity and fairness. *American Psychologist, 63,* 215–227. (p. 414)

Sackett, P. R., Hardison, C. M., & Cullen, M. J. (2004). On interpreting stereotype threat as accounting for African American-White differences on cognitive tests. *American Psychologist, 59,* 7–13. (p. 414)

Sackett, P. R., Kuncel, N. R., Beatty, A. S., Rigdon, J. L., Shen, W., & Kiger, T. B. (2012). The role of socioeconomic status in SAT-grade relationships and in college admissions decisions. *Psychological Science, 23,* 1000–1007. (p. 398)

Sackett, P. R., & Lievens, F. (2008). Personnel selection. *Annual Review of Psychology, 59,* 419–450. (p. A-4)

Sacks, O. (1985). *The man who mistook his wife for a hat.* New York: Summit Books. (pp. 269, 338)

Sadato, N., Pascual-Leone, A., Grafman, J., Ibanez, V., Deiber, M-P., Dold, G., & Hallett, M. (1996). Activation of the primary visual cortex by Braille reading in blind subjects. *Nature, 380,* 526–528. (p. 81)

Sadler, M. S., Correll, J., Park, B., & Judd, C. M. (2012). The world is not Black and White: Racial bias in the decision to shoot in a multiethnic context. *Journal of Social Issues, 68,* 286–313. (p. 539)

Sadler, M. S., Meagor, E. L., & Kaye, M. E. (2012). Stereotypes of mental disorders differ in competence and warmth. *Social Science and Medicine, 74,* 915–922. (p. 614)

Saffran, J. A. (2009). What can statistical learning tell us about infant learning? In A. Woodward & A. Needham (eds.), *Learning and the infant mind.* New York: Oxford University Press. (p. 373)

Saffran, J. R., Aslin, R. N., & Newport, E. L. (1996). Statistical learning by 8-month-old infants. *Science, 274,* 1926–1928. (p. 373)

Sagan, C. (1979). *Broca's brain.* New York: Random House. (pp. 24, 66)

Sagan, C. (1987, February 1). The fine art of baloney detection. *Parade.* (p. 273)

Salas-Wright, C. P., Vaughn, M. G., Hodge, D. R., & Perron, B. E. (2012). Religiosity profiles of American youth in relation to substance use, violence, and delinquency. *Journal of Youth and Adolescence, 41,* 1560–1575. (p. 129)

Salmela-Aro, K., Tolvanen, A., & Nurmi, J. (2009). Achievement strategies during university studies predict early career burnout and engagement. *Journal of Vocational Behavior, 75,* 162–172. (p. A-6)

Salmon, P. (2001). Effects of physical exercise on anxiety, depression, and sensitivity to stress: A unifying theory. *Clinical Psychology Review, 21,* 33–61. (pp. 508, 509)

Salovey, P. (1990, January/February). Interview. *American Scientist,* pp. 25–29. (p. 479)

Salthouse, T. A. (2004). What and when of cognitive aging. *Current Directions in Psychological Science, 13,* 140–144. (p. 400)

Salthouse, T. A. (2009). When does age-related cognitive decline begin? *Neurobiology of Aging, 30,* 507–514. (p. 401)

Salthouse, T. A. (2010). Selective review of cognitive aging. *Journal of the International Neuropsychological Society, 16,* 754–760. (pp. 218, 401)

Salthouse, T. A. (2013). Within-cohort age-related differences in cognitive functioning. *Psychological Science, 24,* 123–130. (p. 401)

Salthouse, T. A., & Mandell, A. R. (2013). Do age-related increases in tip-of-the-tongue experiences signify episodic memory impairments? *Psychological Science, 24,* 2489–2497. (p. 341)

Sampson, E. E. (2000). Reinterpreting individualism and collectivism: Their religious roots and monologic versus dialogic person–other relationship. *American Psychologist, 55,* 1425–1432. (p. 157)

Samuels, J., & Nestadt, G. (1997). Epidemiology and genetics of obsessive-compulsive disorder. *International Review of Psychiatry, 9,* 61–71. (p. 623)

Sánchez-Villegas, A., Delgado-Rodríguez, M., Alonson, A., Schlatter, J., Lahortiga, F., Majem, L. S., & Martínez-González, M. A. (2009). Association of the Mediterranean dietary pattern with the incidence of depression. *Archives of General Psychiatry, 66*, 1090–1098. (p. 634)

Sanders, A. R., Dawood, K. Rieger, G., J. A. Badner, J. A., Gershon, E. S., Krishnappa, R. S., . . . Bailey, J. M. (2012). Genome-wide linkage scan of male sexual orientation. *Psychological Medicine.* (p. 444)

Sanders, G., Sjodin, M., & de Chastelaine, M. (2002). On the elusive nature of sex differences in cognition: hormonal influences contributing to within-sex variation. *Archives of Sexual Behavior, 31*, 145–152. (p. 445)

Sanders, G., & Wright, M. (1997). Sexual orientation differences in cerebral asymmetry and in the performance of sexually dimorphic cognitive and motor tasks. *Archives of Sexual Behavior, 26*, 463–479. (p. 446)

Sanders, M. A., Shirk, S. D., Burgin, C. J., & Martin, L. L. (2012). The gargle effect: Rinsing the mouth with glucose enhances self-control. *Psychological Science, 23*, 1470–1472. (p. 504)

Sandfort, T. G. M., de Graaf, R., Bijl, R., & Schnabel, P. (2001). Same-sex sexual behavior and psychiatric disorders. *Archives of General Psychiatry, 58*, 85–91. (p. 440)

Sandkühler, S., & Bhattacharya, J. (2008). Deconstructing insight: EEG correlates of insightful problem solving. *PloS ONE, 3*, e1459 (www.plosone.org). (p. 357)

Sandler, W., Meir, I., Padden, C., & Aronoff, M. (2005). The emergence of grammar: Systematic structure in a new language. *Proceedings of the National Academy of Sciences, 102*, 2261–2265. (p. 373)

Santomauro, J., & French, C. C. (2009). Terror in the night. *The Psychologist, 22*, 672–675. (p. 103)

Santos, A., Meyer-Lindenberg, A., & Deruelle, C. (2010). Absence of racial, but not gender, stereotyping in Williams syndrome children. *Current Biology, 20*, R307–R308. (p. 543)

Sanz, C., Blicher, A., Dalke, K., Gratton-Fabri, L., McClure-Richards, T., & Fouts, R. (1998, Winter-Spring). Enrichment object use: Five chimpanzees' use of temporary and semi-permanent enrichment objects. *Friends of Washoe, 19*(1,2), 9–14. (p. 378)

Sanz, C., Morgan, D., & Gulick, S. (2004). New insights into chimpanzees, tools, and termites from the Congo Basin. *American Naturalist, 164*, 567–581. (p. 368)

Sapadin, L. A. (1988). Friendship and gender: Perspectives of professional men and women. *Journal of Social and Personal Relationships, 5*, 387–403. (p. 164)

Saphire-Bernstein, S., Way, B. M., Kim, H. S, Sherman, D. K., & Taylor, S. E. (2011). Oxytocin receptor gene (OXTR) is related to psychological resources. *Proceedings of the National Academy of Sciences, 108*, 15118–15122. (p. 505)

Sapolsky, B. S., & Tabarlet, J. O. (1991). Sex in primetime television: 1979 versus 1989. *Journal of Broadcasting and Electronic Media, 35*, 505–516. (p. 439)

Sapolsky, R. (2003, September). Taming stress. *Scientific American*, pp. 87–95. (pp. 491, 629)

Sapolsky, R. (2005). The influence of social hierarchy on primate health. *Science, 308*, 648–652. (pp. 501, 502)

Sapolsky, R. (2010, November 14). This is your brain on metaphors. *New York Times* (www.nytimes.com). (p. 466)

Sarsam, M., Parkes, L. M., Roberts, N., Reid, G. S., & Kinderman, P. (2013). The queen and I: Neural correlates of altered self-related cognitions in major depressive episode. *PLOS One, 8*, e78844. (p. 635)

Satel, S., & Lilienfeld, S. G. (2013). *Brainwashed: The seductive appeal of mindless neuroscience.* New York: Basic Books. (p. 68)

Sato, K. (1987). Distribution of the cost of maintaining common resources. *Journal of Experimental Social Psychology, 23*, 19–31. (p. 563)

Saulny, S. (2006, June 21). A legacy of the storm: Depression and suicide. *New York Times* (www.nytimes.com). (p. 489)

Saurat, M., Agbakou, M., Attigui, P., Golmard, J., & Arnulf, I. (2011). Walking dreams in congenital and acquired paraplegia. *Consciousness and Cognition, 20*, 1425–1432. (p. 112)

Savage-Rumbaugh, E. S., Murphy, J., Sevcik, R. A., Brakke, K. E., Williams, S. L., & Rumbaugh, D. M., with commentary by Bates, E. (1993). Language comprehension in ape and child. *Monographs of the Society for Research in Child Development, 58* (233), 1–254. (p. 378)

Savage-Rumbaugh, E. S., Rumbaugh, D., & Fields, W. M. (2009). Empirical Kanzi: The ape language controversy revisited. *Skeptic, 15*, 25–33. (p. 378)

Savani, K., & Rattan, A. (2012). A choice mind-set increases the acceptance and maintenance of wealth inequality. *Psychological Science, 23*, 796–804. (p. 519)

Savic, I., Berglund, H., & Lindstrom, P. (2005). Brain response to putative pheromones in homosexual men. *Proceedings of the National Academy of Sciences, 102*, 7356–7361. (p. 443)

Savic, I., & Lindström, P. (2008). PET and MRI show differences in cerebral asymmetry and functional connectivity between homo- and heterosexual subjects. *Proceedings of the National Academy of Sciences, 105*, 9403–9408. (p. 443)

Savin-Williams, R., Joyner, K., & Rieger, G. (2012). Prevalence and stability of self-reported sexual orientation identity during young adulthood. *Archives of Sexual Behavior, 41*, 103–110. (p. 440)

Savitsky, K., Epley, N., & Gilovich, T. D. (2001). Do others judge us as harshly as we think? Overestimating the impact of our failures, shortcomings, and mishaps. *Journal of Personality and Social Psychology, 81*, 44–56. (p. 599)

Savitsky, K., & Gilovich, T. D. (2003). The illusion of transparency and the alleviation of speech anxiety. Journal *of Experimental Social Psychology, 39*, 618–625. (p. 599)

Savoy, C., & Beitel, P. (1996). Mental imagery for basketball. *International Journal of Sport Psychology, 27*, 454–462. (p. 382)

Sawyer, M. G., Arney, F. M., Baghurst, P. A., Clark, J. J., Graetz, B. W., Kosky, R. J., Nurcombe, B., . . . Zubrick, S. R. (2000). *The mental health of young people in Australia.* Canberra: Mental Health and Special Programs Branch, Commonwealth Department of Health and Aged Care. (p. 632)

Sayal, K., Heron, J., Golding, J., Alati, R., Smith, G. D., Gray, R., & Emond, A. (2009). Binge pattern of alcohol consumption during pregnancy and childhood mental health outcomes: Longitudinal population-based study. *Pediatrics, 123*, e289. (p. 182)

Sayette, M. A., Creswell, K. G., Kimoff, J. D., Fairbairn, C. E., Cohn, J. F., Heckman, B. W., . . . & Moreland, R. L. (2012). Alcohol and group formation: A multimodal investigation of the effects of alcohol on emotion and social bonding. *Psychological Science, 23*, 869–878. (p. 119)

Sayette, M. A., Loewenstein, G., Griffin, K. M., & Black, J. J. (2008). Exploring the cold-to-hot empathy gap in smokers. *Psychological Science, 19*, 926–932. (p. 121)

Sayette, M. A., Reichle, E. D., & Schooler, J. W. (2009). Lost in the sauce: The effects of alcohol on mind wandering. *Psychological Science, 20*, 747–752. (p. 120)

Sayette, M. A., Schooler, J. W., & Reichle, E. D. (2010). Out for a smoke: The impact of cigarette craving on zoning out during reading. *Psychological Science, 21*, 26–30. (p. 121)

Sayre, R. F. (1979). The parents' last lessons. In D. D. Van Tassel (Ed.), *Aging, death, and the completion of being.* Philadelphia: University of Pennsylvania Press. (p. 218)

Sbarra, D. A., Law, R. W., & Portley, R. M. (2011). Divorce and death: A meta-analysis and research agenda for clinical, social, and health psychology. *Perspectives on Psychological Science, 6*, 454-474. (pp. 449, 505)

Scarborough, E., & Furumoto, L. (1987). *Untold lives: The first generation of American women psychologists.* New York: Columbia University Press. (p. 3)

Scarr, S. (1984, May). What's a parent to do? A conversation with E. Hall. *Psychology Today*, pp. 58–63. (p. 409)

Scarr, S. (1989). Protecting general intelligence: Constructs and consequences for interventions. In R. J. Linn (Ed.), *Intelligence: Measurement, theory, and public policy.* Champaign: University of Illinois Press. (p. 389)

Scarr, S. (1990). Back cover comments on J. Dunn & R. Plomin (1990), *Separate lives: Why siblings are so different.* New York: Basic Books. (p. 152)

Scarr, S. (1993, May/June). Quoted by *Psychology Today*, Nature's thumbprint: So long, superparents, p. 16. (p. 154)

Schab, F. R. (1991). Odor memory: Taking stock. *Psychological Bulletin, 109*, 242–251. (p. 268)

Schachter, S., & Singer, J. E. (1962). Cognitive, social and physiological determinants of emotional state. *Psychological Review, 69*, 379–399. (p. 461)

Schacter, D. L. (1992). Understanding implicit memory: A cognitive neuroscience approach. *American Psychologist, 47*, 559–569. (p. 339)

Schacter, D. L. (1996). *Searching for memory: The brain, the mind, and the past.* New York: Basic Books. (pp. 216, 329, 339, 580)

Schafer, G. (2005). Infants can learn decontextualized words before their first birthday. *Child Development, 76*, 87–96. (p. 372)

Schaie, K. W. (1994). The life course of adult intellectual abilities. *American Psychologist, 49*, 304–313. (p. 400)

Schaie, K. W., & Geiwitz, J. (1982). *Adult development and aging.* Boston: Little, Brown. (p. 400)

Schalock, R. L., Borthwick-Duffy, S., Bradley, V. J., Buntinx, W. H. E., Coulter, D. L., Craig, E. M. (2010). *Intellectual disability: Definition, classification, and systems of supports* (11th edition). Washington, DC: American Association on Intellectual and Developmental Disabilities. (p. 403)

Schauer, F. (2010). Neuroscience, lie-detection, and the law. *Trends in Cognitive Sciences, 14*, 101–103. (p. 467)

Scheibe, S., & Carstensen, L. L. (2010). Emotional aging: Recent findings and future trends. *Journal of Gerontology: Psychological Sciences, 65B*, 135–144. (p. 223)

Schein, E. H. (1956). The Chinese indoctrination program for prisoners of war: A study of attempted brainwashing. *Psychiatry, 19*, 149–172. (p. 521)

Schetter, C. D., Schafer, P., Lanzi, R. G., Clark-Kauffman, E., Raju, T. N. K., & Hillemeier, M. M. (2013). Shedding light on the mechanisms underlying health disparities through community participatory methods: The stress pathway. *Perspectives on Psychological Science, 8*, 613–633. (p. 490)

Schiavi, R. C., & Schreiner-Engel, P. (1988). Nocturnal penile tumescence in healthy aging men. *Journal of Gerontology: Medical Sciences, 43*, M146–M150. (p. 103)

Schick, V., Herbenick, D., Reece, M., Sanders, S. A., Dodge, B., Middlestadt, S. E., & Fortenberry, J. D. (2010). Sexual behaviors, condom use, and sexual health of Americans over 50: Implications for sexual health promotion for older adults. *Journal of Sexual Medicine, 7*(suppl 5), 315–329. (p. 214)

Schiffenbauer, A., & Schiavo, R. S. (1976). Physical distance and attraction: An intensification effect. *Journal of Experimental Social Psychology, 12*, 274–282. (p. 532)

Schiffman, J., Abrahamsom, A., Cannon, T., LaBrie, J., Parnas, J., Schulsinger, F., & Mednick, S. (2001). Early rearing factors in schizophrenia. *International Journal of Mental Health, 30*, 3–16. (p. 645)

Schilt, T., de Win, M. M. L, Koeter, M., Jager, G., Korf, D. J., van den Brink, W., & Schmand, B. (2007). Cognition in novice Ecstasy users with minimal exposure to other drugs. *Archives of General Psychiatry, 64*, 728–736. (p. 124)

Schimel, J., Arndt, J., Pyszczynski, T., & Greenberg, J. (2001). Being accepted for who we are: Evidence that social validation of the intrinsic self reduces general defensiveness. *Journal of Personality and Social Psychology, 80*, 35–52. (p. 585)

Schimmack, U., & Lucas, R. (2007). Marriage matters: Spousal similarity in life satisfaction. *Schmollers Jahrbuch, 127*, 1–7. (p. 485)

Schlaug, G., Jancke, L., Huang, Y., & Steinmetz, H. (1995). In vivo evidence of structural brain asymmetry in musicians. *Science, 267*, 699–701. (p. 67)

Schlomer, G. L., Del Giudice, M., & Ellis, B. J. (2011). Parent-offspring conflict theory: An evolutionary framework for understanding conflict within human families. *Psychological Review, 118*, 496–521. (p. 210)

Schloss, J. (2009). Does evolution explain human nature? Totally, for a Martian. In *Celebrating the bicentenary of the birth of Charles Darwin*. Philadelphia: John Templeton Foundation (www.templeton.org). (p. 146)

Schmader, T. (2010). Stereotype threat deconstructed. *Current Directions in Psychological Science, 19*, 14–18. (p. 414)

Schmidt, F. L. (2002). The role of general cognitive ability and job performance: Why there cannot be a debate. *Human Performance, 15*, 187–210. (p. A-5)

Schmidt, F. L., & Hunter, J. E. (1998). The validity and utility of selection methods in personnel psychology: Practical and theoretical implications of 85 years of research findings. *Psychological Bulletin, 124*, 262–274. (pp. 597, A-5, A-6)

Schmidt, F. L., & Zimmerman, R. D. (2004). A counterintuitive hypothesis about employment interview validity and some supporting evidence. *Journal of Applied Psychology, 89*, 553–561. (p. A-6)

Schmidt, M. F. H., & Tomasello, M. (2012). Young children enforce social norms. *Current Directions in Psychological Science, 21*, 232–236. (p. 206)

Schmitt, D. P. (2007). Sexual strategies across sexual orientations: How personality traits and culture relate to sociosexuality among gays, lesbians, bisexuals, and heterosexuals. *Journal of Psychology and Human Sexuality, 18*, 183–214. (p. 147)

Schmitt, D. P., & Allik, J. (2005). Simultaneous administration of the Rosenberg Self-esteem Scale in 53 nations: Exploring the universal and culture-specific features of global self-esteem. *Journal of Personality and Social Psychology, 89*, 623–642. (p. 602)

Schmitt, D. P., Allik, J., McCrae, R. R., Benet-Martinez, V., et al. (2007). The geographic distribution of Big Five personality traits: Patterns and profiles of human self-description across 56 nations. *Journal of Cross-Cultural Psychology, 38*, 173–212. (pp. 590, 591)

Schmitt, D. P., Jonason, P. K., Byerley, G. J., Flores, S. D., Illbeck, B. E., O'Leary, K. N., & Qudrat, A. (2012). A reexamination of sex differences in sexuality: New studies reveal old truths. *Current Directions in Psychological Science, 21*, 135–139. (p. 438)

Schmitt, D. P., & Pilcher, J. J. (2004). Evaluating evidence of psychological adaptation: How do we know one when we see one? *Psychological Science, 15*, 643–649. (p. 146)

Schnall, E., Wassertheil-Smoller, S., Swencionis, C., Zemon, V., Tinker, L., O'Sullivan. M. J., Van Horn, K., & Goodwin, M. (2010). The relationship between religion and cardiovascular outcomes and all-cause mortality in the women's health initiative observational study. *Psychology and Health, 25*, 249–263. (p. 512)

Schnall, S., Haidt, J., Clore, G. L., & Jordan, A. (2008). Disgust as embodied moral judgment. *Personality and Social Psychology Bulletin, 34*, 1096–1109. (pp. 237, 268)

Schnall, S., Roper, J., & Fessler, D. M. T. (2010). Elevation leads to altruistic behavior. *Psychological Science, 21*, 315–320. (p. 560)

Schneider, S. L. (2001). In search of realistic optimism: Meaning, knowledge, and warm fuzziness. *American Psychologist, 56*, 250–263. (p. 600)

Schneiderman, N. (1999). Behavioral medicine and the management of HIV/AIDS. *International Journal of Behavioral Medicine, 6*, 3–12. (p. 495)

Schneier, B. (2007, May 17). Virginia Tech lesson: Rare risks breed irrational responses. *Wired* (www.wired.com). (p. 363)

Schoeneman, T. J. (1994). Individualism. In V. S. Ramachandran (Ed.), *Encyclopedia of human behavior*. San Diego: Academic Press. (p. 158)

Schofield, J. W. (1986). Black-White contact in desegregated schools. In M. Hewstone & R. Brown (Eds.), *Contact and conflict in intergroup encounters*. Oxford: Basil Blackwell. (p. 565)

Schonfield, D., & Robertson, B. A. (1966). Memory storage and aging. *Canadian Journal of Psychology, 20*, 228–236. (p. 217)

Schooler, J. W., Gerhard, D., & Loftus, E. F. (1986). Qualities of the unreal. *Journal of Experimental Psychology: Learning, Memory, and Cognition, 12*, 171–181. (p. 344)

Schorr, E. A., Fox, N.A., van Wassenhove, V., & Knudsen, E.I. (2005). Auditory-visual fusion in speech perception in children with cochlear implants. *Proceedings of the National Academy of Sciences, 102*, 18748–18750. (p. 259)

Schrauzer, G. N., & Shrestha, K. P. (1990). Lithium in drinking water and the incidences of crimes, suicides, and arrests related to drug addictions. *Biological Trace Element Research, 25*(2), 105–113. (p. 685)

Schrauzer, G. N., & Shrestha, K. P. (2010). Lithium in drinking water. *British Journal of Psychiatry, 196*, 159. (p. 685)

Schreiber, F. R. (1973). *Sybil*. Chicago: Regnery. (p. 648)

Schueller, S. M. (2010). Preferences for positive psychology exercises. *Journal of Positive Psychology, 5*, 192–203. (p. 479)

Schultheiss, O., Wiemers, U. & Wolf, O. (2014). Implicit need for achievement predicts attenuated cortisol responses to difficult tasks. *Journal of Research in Personality, 48*, 84–92. (p. 578)

Schuman, H., & Scott, J. (June, 1989). Generations and collective memories. *American Sociological Review, 54*(3), 359–381. (p. 217)

Schumann, K., & Ross, M. (2010). Why women apologize more than men: Gender differences in thresholds for perceiving offensive behavior. *Psychological Science, 21*, 1649–1655. (p. 163)

Schurger, A., Pereira, F., Treisman, A., & Cohen, J. D. (2010, Jan.) Reproducibility distinguishes conscious from nonconscious neural representations. *Science, 327*, 97–99. (p. 93)

Schurger, A., Sitt, J. D., & Dehaene, S. (2012). An accumulator model for spontaneous neural activity prior to self-initiated movement. *PNAS, 109*, E2904–13. (p. 95)

Schwartz, B. (1984). *Psychology of learning and behavior* (2nd ed.). New York: Norton. (pp. 287, 624)

Schwartz, B. (2000). Self-determination: The tyranny of freedom. *American Psychologist, 55*, 79–88. (p. 502)

Schwartz, B. (2004). *The paradox of choice: Why more is less*. New York: Ecco/HarperCollins. (p. 502)

Schwartz, H. A., Eichstaedt, J. C., Kern, M. L., Dziurzynski, L., Ramones, S. M., Agrawal, M., . . . Ungar, L. H. (2013). Personality, gender, and age in the language of social media: The open-vocabulary approach. *PLOS One, 8*, e73791. (p. 163)

Schwartz, J. M., Stoessel, P. W., Baxter, L. R., Jr., Martin, K. M., & Phelps, M. E. (1996). Systematic changes in cerebral glucose metabolic rate after successful behavior modification treatment of obsessive-compulsive disorder. *Archives of General Psychiatry, 53*, 109–113. (pp. 669, 688)

Schwartz, P. J. (2011). Season of birth in schizophrenia: A maternal-fetal chronobiological hypothesis. *Medical Hypotheses, 76*, 785–793. (p. 643)

Schwartz, S. H., & Rubel-Lifschitz, T. (2009). Cross-national variation in the size of sex differences in values: Effects of gender equality. *Journal of Personality and Social Psychology, 97,* 171–185. (p. 162)

Schwartz, S. J., Unger, J. B., Zamboanga, B. L., & Szapocznik, J. (2010). Rethinking the concept of acculturation: Implications for theory and research. *American Psychologist, 65,* 237–251. (p. 618)

Schwartzman-Morris, J., & Putterman, C. (2012). Gender differences in the pathogenesis and outcome of lupus and of lupus nephritis. *Clinical and Developmental Immunology, 2012,* 604892. doi: 10.1155/2012/604892. (p. 493)

Schwarz, A. (2007, April 6). Throwing batters curves before throwing a pitch. *New York Times* (www.nytimes.com). (p. 86)

Schwarz, A. (2012, June 9). Risky rise of the good-grade pill. *New York Times* (www.nytimes.com). (p. 615)

Schwarz, A., & Cohen, S. (2013, March 31). A.D.H.D. seen in 11% of U.S. children as diagnoses rise. *New York Times* (www.nytimes.com). (p. 615)

Schwarz, N., Strack, F., Kommer, D., & Wagner, D. (1987). Soccer, rooms, and the quality of your life: Mood effects on judgments of satisfaction with life in general and with specific domains. *European Journal of Social Psychology, 17,* 69–79. (p. 336)

Schwarz, S., & Singer, M. (2013). Romantic red revisited: Red enhances men's attraction to young, but not menopausal women. *Journal of Experimental Social Psychology, 49,* 161–164. (p. 303)

Sclafani, A. (1995). How food preferences are learned: Laboratory animal models. *Proceedings of the Nutrition Society, 54,* 419–427. (p. 428)

Scott, D. J., et al. (2004, November 9). U-M team reports evidence that smoking affects human brain's natural "feel good" chemical system (press release by Kara Gavin). University of Michigan Medical School (www.med.umich.edu). (p. 122)

Scott, D. J., Stohler, C. S., Egnatuk, C. M., Wang, H., Koeppe, R. A., & Zubieta, J-K. (2007). Individual differences in reward responding explain placebo-induced expectations and effects. *Neuron, 55,* 325–336. (p. 264)

Scott, K. M., et al. (2010). Gender and the relationship between marital status and first onset of mood, anxiety and substance use disorders. *Psychological Medicine, 40,* 1495–1505. (p. 221)

Scott, W. A., Scott, R., & McCabe, M. (1991). Family relationships and children's personality: A cross-cultural, cross-source comparison. *British Journal of Social Psychology, 30,* 1–20. (p. 161)

Scott-Sheldon, L., Carey, K. B., Elliott, J. C., Garey, L., & Carey, M. P. (2014). Efficacy of alcohol interventions for first-year college students: A meta-analytic review of randomized controlled trials. *Journal of Consulting and Clinical Psychology, 82,* 177–188. (p. 120)

Scullin, M. K., & McDaniel, M. A. (2010). Remembering to execute a goal: Sleep on it! *Psychological Science, 21,* 1028–1035. (p. 342)

Sdorow, L. M. (2005). The people behind psychology. In B. Perlman, L. McCann, & W. Buskist (Eds.), *Voices of experience: Memorable talks from the National Institute on the Teaching of Psychology.* Washington, DC: American Psychological Society. (p. 578)

Seal, K. H., Bertenthal, D., Miner, C. R., Sen, S., & Marmar, C. (2007). Bringing the war back home: Mental health disorders among 103,788 U.S. veterans returning from Iraq and Afghanistan seen at Department of Veterans Affairs facilities. *Archives of Internal Medicine, 167,* 467–482. (p. 623)

Seamon, J., Punjabi, P., & Busch, E. (2010). Memorizing Milton's *Paradise Lost:* A study of a septuagenarian exceptional memoriser. *Memory, 18,* 498–503. (p. 217)

Sebat, J., et al. (2007). Strong association of de novo copy number mutations with autism. *Science, 316,* 445–449. (p. 193)

Sechrest, L., Stickle, T. R., & Stewart, M. (1998). The role of assessment in clinical psychology. In A. Bellack, M. Hersen (series eds.), & C. R. Reynolds (vol. ed.), *Comprehensive clinical psychology: Vol. 4. Assessment.* New York: Pergamon. (p. 578)

Sedlmeier, P. Eberth, J., Schwarz, M., Zimmermann, D., Haarig, F., Jaeger, S., & Kunze, S. (2012). The psychological effects of meditation: A meta-analysis. *Psychological Bulletin, 138,* 1139–1171. (p. 510)

Seeman, P. (2007). Dopamine and schizophrenia. *Scholarpedia, 2*(10), 3634 (www.scholarpedia.org). (p. 642)

Seeman, P., Guan, H-C., & Van Tol, H. H. M. (1993). Dopamine D4 receptors elevated in schizophrenia. *Nature, 365,* 441–445. (p. 642)

Seery, M. D. (2011). Resilience: A silver lining to experiencing adverse life events. *Current Directions in Psychological Science, 20,* 390–394. (pp. 200, 489)

Segal, N. L., McGuire, S. A., & Stohs, J. H. (2012). What virtual twins reveal about general intelligence and other behaviors. *Personality and Individual Differences, 53,* 405–410. (p. 406)

Segall, M. H., Dasen, P. R., Berry, J. W., & Poortinga, Y. H. (1990). *Human behavior in global perspective: An introduction to cross-cultural psychology.* New York: Pergamon. (pp. 147, 168, 192)

Segerstrom, S. C. (2007). Stress, energy, and immunity. *Current Directions in Psychological Science, 16,* 326–330. (p. 489)

Segerstrom, S. C., Hardy, J. K., Evans, D. R., & Greenberg, R. N. (2012). Vulnerability, distress, and immune response to vaccination in older adults. *Brain, Behavior, and Immunity, 26,* 747–753. (p. 494)

Segerstrom, S. C., Taylor, S. E., Kemeny, M. E., & Fahey, J. L. (1998). Optimism is associated with mood, coping, and immune change in response to stress. *Journal of Personality and Social Psychology, 74,* 1646–1655. (p. 504)

Seibert, S. E., Wang, G., & Courtright, S. H. (2011). Antecedents and consequences of psychological and team empowerment in organizations: A meta-analytic review. *Journal of Applied Psychology, 96,* 981–1003. (p. A-13)

Seidel, A., & Prinz, J. (2013). Sound morality: Irritating and icky noises amplify judgments in divergent moral domains. *Cognition, 127,* 1–5. (p. 237)

Seidler, G. H., & Wagner, F. E. (2006). Comparing the efficacy of EMDR and trauma-focused cognitive-behavioral therapy in the treatment of PTSD: A meta-analytic study. *Psychological Medicine, 36,* 1515–1522. (p. 677)

Self, C. E. (1994). *Moral culture and victimization in residence halls.* Unpublished master's thesis. Bowling Green University. (p. 129)

Seligman, M. E. P. (1975). *Helplessness: On depression, development and death.* San Francisco: Freeman. (p. 501)

Seligman, M. E. P. (1991). *Learned optimism.* New York: Knopf. (pp. 92, 636)

Seligman, M. E. P. (1994). *What you can change and what you can't.* New York: Knopf. (pp. 507, 599)

Seligman, M. E. P. (1995). The effectiveness of psychotherapy: The Consumer Reports study. *American Psychologist, 50,* 965–974. (pp. 636, 673, 675)

Seligman, M. E. P. (2002). *Authentic happiness: Using the new positive psychology to realize your potential for lasting fulfillment.* New York: Free Press. (pp. 9, 480, 599)

Seligman, M. E. P. (2004). Eudaemonia, the good life. A talk with Martin Seligman. www.edge.org. (p. 480)

Seligman, M. E. P. (2008). Positive health. *Applied Psychology, 17,* 3–18. (p. 479)

Seligman, M. E. P. (2011). *Flourish: A visionary new understanding of happiness and well-being.* New York: Free Press. (p. 480)

Seligman, M. E. P., Ernst, R. M., Gillham, J., Reivich, K., & Linkins, M. (2009). Positive education: Positive psychology and classroom interventions. *Oxford Review of Education, 35,* 293–311. (pp. 479, 668, 669)

Seligman, M. E. P., & Maier, S. F. (1967). Failure to escape traumatic shock. *Journal of Experimental Psychology, 74,* 1–9. (p. 501)

Seligman, M. E. P., Peterson, C., Barsky, A. J., Boehm, J. K., Kubzansky, L. D., & Park, N. (2011). *Positive health and health assets: Reanalysis of longitudinal datasets.* Unpublished manuscript, University of Pennsylvania. (pp. 9, 479)

Seligman, M. E. P., Steen, T. A., Park, N., & Peterson, C. (2005). Positive psychology progress: Empirical validation of interventions. *American Psychologist, 60,* 410–421. (pp. 9, 480, 487)

Seligman, M. E. P., & Yellen, A. (1987). What is a dream? *Behavior Research and Therapy, 25,* 1–24. (p. 101)

Selimbeyoglu, A., & Parvizi, J. (2010). Electrical stimulation of the human brain: Perceptual and behavioral phenomena reported in the old and new literature. *Frontiers in Human Neuroscience, 4,* 1–11. (p. 66)

Sellers, H. (2010). *You don't look like anyone I know.* New York: Riverhead Books. (p. 229)

Selye, H. (1936). A syndrome produced by diverse nocuous agents. *Nature, 138,* 32. (p. 491)

Selye, H. (1976). *The stress of life.* New York: McGraw-Hill. (p. 491)

Senate Intelligence Committee. (2004, July 9). *Report of the select committee on intelligence on the U.S. intelligence community's prewar intelligence assessments on Iraq.* Washington, DC: Author. (pp. 358, 535)

Senghas, A., & Coppola, M. (2001). Children creating language: How Nicaraguan Sign Language acquired a spatial grammar. *Psychological Science, 12,* 323–328. (p. 373)

Sengupta, S. (2001, October 10). Sept. 11 attack narrows the racial divide. *New York Times* (www.nytimes.com). (p. 566)

Senju, A., Maeda, M., Kikuchi, Y., Hasegawa, T., Tojo, Y., & Osanai, H. (2007). Absence of contagious yawning in children with autism spectrum disorder. *Biology Letters, 3*, 706–708. (p. 194)

Senju, A., Southgate, V., White, S., & Frith, U. (2009). Mindblind eyes: An absence of spontaneous theory of mind in Asperger syndrome. *Science, 325*, 883–885. (p. 193)

Sergeant, S., & Mongrain, M. (2014). An online optimism intervention reduces depression in pessimistic individuals. *Journal of Consulting and Clinical Psychology, 82*, 263–274. (p. 505)

Serruya, M. D., Hatsopoulos, N. G., Paninski, L., Fellow, M. R., & Donoghue, J. P. (2002). Instant neural control of a movement signal. *Nature, 416*, 141–142. (p. 77)

Service, R. F. (1994). Will a new type of drug make memory-making easier? *Science, 266*, 218–219. (p. 332)

Shadish, W. R., & Baldwin, S. A. (2005). Effects of behavioral marital therapy: A meta-analysis of randomized controlled trials. *Journal of Consulting and Clinical Psychology, 73*, 6–14. (p. 676)

Shadish, W. R., Montgomery, L. M., Wilson, P., Wilson, M. R., Bright, I., & Okwumabua, T. (1993). Effects of family and marital psychotherapies: A meta-analysis. *Journal of Consulting and Clinical Psychology, 61*, 992–1002. (p. 671)

Shaffer, R. (2013, September–October). The psychic: Years later, Sylvia Browne's accuracy remains dismal. *Skeptical Inquirer*, pp. 30–35. (p. 272)

Shafir, E. (Ed.) (2013). *The behavioral foundations of public policy.* Princeton, NJ: Princeton University Press. (p. 25)

Shafir, E., & LeBoeuf, R. A. (2002). Rationality. *Annual Review of Psychology, 53*, 491–517. (p. 364)

Shakeshaft, N. G., Trzaskowski, M., McMillan, A., Rimfeld, K., Krapohl, E., Haworth, C. M. A., Dale, P. S., & Plomin, R. (2013) Strong genetic influence on a UK nationwide test of educational achievement at the end of compulsory education at age 16. *PLoS ONE 8(12)*, e80341. (p. 406)

Shaki, S. (2013). What's in a kiss? Spatial experience shapes directional bias during kissing. *Journal of Nonverbal Behavior, 37*, 43–50. (p. 8)

Shalev, I., Moffitt, T. E., Sugden, K., Williams, B., Houts, R. M., Danese, A., . . . Caspi, A. (2013). Exposure to violence during childhood is associated with telomere erosion from 5 to 10 years of age: A longitudinal study. *Molecular Psychiatry, 18*, 576–581. (p. 215)

Shallcross, A. J., Ford, B. Q., Floerke, V. A., & Mauss, I. B. (2013). Getting better with age: The relationship between age, acceptance, and negative affect. *Journal of Personality and Social Psychology, 104*, 734–749. (p. 223)

Shamir, B., House, R. J., & Arthur, M. B. (1993). The motivational effects of charismatic leadership: A self-concept based theory. *Organizational Science, 4*(4), 577–594. (p. A-12)

Shan, W., Shengua, J., Davis, H., Hunter, M., Peng, K., Shao, X., . . . Wang, Y. (2012). Mating strategies in Chinese culture: Female risk-avoiding vs. male risk-taking. *Evolution and Human Behavior, 33*, 182–192. (p. 149)

Shanahan, L., McHale, S. M., Osgood, D. W., & Crouter, A. C. (2007). Conflict frequency with mothers and fathers from middle childhood to late adolescence: Within- and between-families comparisons. *Developmental Psychology, 43*, 539–550. (p. 210)

Shanks, D. R. (2010). Learning: From association to cognition. *Annual Review of Psychology, 61*, 273–301. (p. 304)

Shannon, B. J., et al. (2011). Premotor functional connectivity predicts impulsivity in juvenile offenders. *PNAS, 108*, 11241–11245. (p. 205)

Shapin, S. (2013, October 15). The man who forgot everything. *New Yorker* (www.newyorker.com). (p. 339)

Shapiro, D. (1999). *Psychotherapy of neurotic character.* New York: Basic Books. (p. 660)

Shapiro, F. (1989). Efficacy of the eye movement desensitization procedure in the treatment of traumatic memories. *Journal of Traumatic Stress, 2*, 199–223. (p. 677)

Shapiro, F. (1999). Eye movement desensitization and reprocessing (EMDR) and the anxiety disorders: Clinical and research implications of an integrated psychotherapy treatment. *Journal of Anxiety Disorders, 13*, 35–67. (p. 677)

Shapiro, F. (Ed.). (2002). *EMDR as an integrative psychotherapy approach: Experts of diverse orientations explore the paradigm prism.* Washington, DC: APA Books. (p. 677)

Shapiro, F. (2007). EMDR and case conceptualization from an adaptive information processing perspective. In F. Shapiro, F. W. Kaslow, & L. Maxfield (Eds.), *Handbook of EMDR and family therapy processes.* Hoboken, NJ: Wiley. (p. 677)

Shapiro, F. (2012, March 2). The evidence on E.M.D.R. *New York Times* (www.nytimes.com). (p. 677)

Shapiro, K. A., Moo, L. R., & Caramazza, A. (2006). Cortical signatures of noun and verb production. *Proceedings of the National Academic of Sciences, 103*, 1644–1649. (p. 376)

Shargorodsky, J., Curhan, S. G., Curhan, G. C., & Eavey, R. (2010). Changes of prevalence of hearing loss in US adolescents. *JAMA, 304*, 772–778. (p. 257)

Sharma, A. R., McGue, M. K., & Benson, P. L. (1998). The psychological adjustment of United States adopted adolescents and their nonadopted siblings. *Child Development, 69*, 791–802. (p. 139)

Shattuck, P. T. (2006). The contribution of diagnostic substitution to the growing administrative prevalence of autism in US special education. *Pediatrics, 117*, 1028–1037. (p. 193)

Shaver, P. R., & Mikulincer, M. (2007). Adult attachment strategies and the regulation of emotion. In J. J. Gross (Ed.), *Handbook of emotion regulation.* New York: Guilford Press. (p. 199)

Shaver, P. R., Morgan, H. J., & Wu, S. (1996). Is love a basic emotion? *Personal Relationships, 3*, 81–96. (p. 476)

Shaw, B. A., Liang, J., & Krause, N. (2010). Age and race differences in the trajectories of self-esteem. *Psychology and Aging, 25*, 84–94. (p. 180)

Shedler, J. (2010a, November/December). Getting to know me. *Scientific American Mind*, pp. 53–57. (p. 659)

Shedler, J. (2010b). The efficacy of psychodynamic psychotherapy. *American Psychologist, 65*, 98–109. (pp. 575, 676)

Sheehan, S. (1982). *Is there no place on earth for me?* Boston: Houghton Mifflin. (p. 640)

Sheikh, S., & Janoff-Bulman, R. (2013). Paradoxical consequences of prohibitions. *Journal of Personality and Social Psychology, 105*, 301–315. (p. 297)

Sheldon, K. M. (2011). Integrating behavioral-motive and experiential-requirement perspectives on psychological needs: A two process model. *Psychological Review, 118*, 552–569. (p. 448)

Sheldon, K. M., Abad, N., & Hinsch, C. (2011). A two-process view of Facebook use and relatedness need-satisfaction: Disconnection drives use, and connection rewards it. *Journal of Personality and Social Psychology, 100*, 766–775. (p. 452)

Sheldon, K. M., Elliot, A. J., Kim, Y., & Kasser, T. (2001). What is satisfying about satisfying events? Testing 10 candidate psychological needs. *Journal of Personality and Social Psychology, 80*, 325–339. (p. 449)

Sheldon, K. M., & Lyubomirsky, S. (2012). The challenge of staying happier: Testing the hedonic adaptation prevention model. *Personality and Social Psychology Bulletin, 38*, 670–680. (p. 487)

Shelton, L. T., Elliott, E. M., Matthews, R. A., Hill, B. H., & Gouvier, W. D. (2010). The relationships of working memory, secondary memory, and general fluid intelligence: working memory is special. *Journal of Experimental Psychology, 36*, 813–820. (p. 324)

Shenton, M. E. (1992). Abnormalities of the left temporal lobe and thought disorder in schizophrenia: A quantitative magnetic resonance imaging study. *New England Journal of Medicine, 327*, 604–612. (p. 642)

Shepard, R. N. (1990). *Mind sights.* New York: Freeman. (p. 41)

Shepherd, C. (1997, April). News of the weird. *Funny Times*, p. 15. (p. 137)

Shepherd, C. (1999, June). News of the weird. *Funny Times*, p. 21. (p. 432)

Shepherd, C., Kohut, J. J., & Sweet, R. (1990). *More news of the weird.* New York: Penguin/Plume Books. (p. 650)

Sher, L. (2006). Alcohol consumption and suicide. *QJM: An International Journal of Medicine, 99*, 57–61. (p. 638)

Shergill, S. S., Bays, P. M., Frith, C. D., & Wolpert, D. M. (2003). Two eyes for an eye: The neuroscience of force escalation. *Science, 301*, 187. (p. 563)

Sherif, M. (1966). *In common predicament: Social psychology of intergroup conflict and cooperation.* Boston: Houghton Mifflin. (p. 565)

Sherman, D. K., Hartson, K. A., Binning, K. R., Purdie-Vaughns, V., Garcia, J., Taborsky-Barba, S., . . . Cohen, G. L. (2013). Deflecting the trajectory and changing the narrative: How self-affirmation affects academic performance and motivation under identity threat. *Journal of Personality and Social Psychology, 104*, 591–618. (p. 415)

Sherman, G. D., Lee, J. J., Cuddy, A. J. C., Renshon, J., Oveis, C., Gross, J. J., & Lerner, J. S. (2012). Leadership is associated with lower levels of stress. *Proceedings of the National Academy of Science, 109*, 17903–17907. (p. 489)

Sherman, P. W., & Flaxman, S. M. (2001). Protecting ourselves from food. *American Scientist, 89*, 142–151. (p. 428)

Shermer, M. (1999). If that's true, what else would be true? *Skeptic, 7*(4), 192–193. (p. 164)

Sherry, D., & Vaccarino, A. L. (1989). Hippocampus and memory for food caches in black-capped chickadees. *Behavioral Neuroscience, 103*, 308–318. (p. 329)

Sherry, S. B., & Hall, P. A. (2009). The perfectionism model of binge eating: Tests of an integrative model. *Journal of Personality and Social Psychology, 96*, 690–709. (p. 652)

Shettleworth, S. J. (1973). Food reinforcement and the organization of behavior in golden hamsters. In R. A. Hinde & J. Stevenson-Hinde (Eds.), *Constraints on learning*. London: Academic Press. (p. 303)

Shettleworth, S. J. (1993). Where is the comparison in comparative cognition? Alternative research programs. *Psychological Science, 4*, 179–184. (p. 330)

Shiell, M. M., Champoux, F., & Zatorre, R. (2014). Enhancement of visual motion detection thresholds in early deaf people. *PLoS One, 9*(2), e90498. (p. 81)

Shifren, J. L., Monz, B. U., Russo, P. A., Segreti, A., Johannes, C. B. (2008). Sexual problems and distress in United States women: Prevalence and correlates. *Obstetrics & Gynecology, 112*, 970–978. (p. 435)

Shilsky, J. D., Hartman, T. J., Kris-Etherton, P. M., Rogers, C. J., Sharkey, N. A., & Nickols-Richardson, S. M. (2012). Partial sleep deprivation and energy balance in adults: An emerging issue for consideration by dietetics practitioners. *Journal of the Academy of Nutrition and Dietetics, 112*, 1785–1797. (p. 108)

Shimamura, A. P. (2010). Bridging psychological and biological science: The good, bad, and ugly. *Perspectives on Psychological Science, 5*, 772–775. (p. 81)

Shimizu, M., & Pelham, B. W. (2008). Postponing a date with the grim reaper. *Basic and Applied Social Psychology, 30*, 36–45. (p. 215)

Shinkareva, S. V., Mason, R. A., Malave, V. L., Wang, W., Mitchell, T. M., & Just, M. A. (2008, January 2). Using fMRI brain activation to identify cognitive states associated with perceptions of tools and dwellings. *PloS One* 3(1), 31394. (p. 93)

Shipstead, Z., Hicks, K. L., & Engle, R. W. (2012b). Cogmed working memory training: Does the evidence support the claims? *Journal of Applied Research in Memory and Cognition, 1*, 185–193. (p. 218)

Shipstead, Z., Redick, T. S., & Engle, R. W. (2012a). Is working memory training effective? *Psychological Bulletin, 138*, 628–654. (p. 218)

Shiromani, P. J., Horvath, T., Redline, S., & Van Cauter E. (Eds.) (2012). *Sleep loss and obesity: Intersecting epidemics*. New York: Springer Science. (p. 108)

Shockley, K. M., Ispas, D., Rossi, M. E., & Levine, E. L. (2012). A meta-analytic investigation of the relationship between state affect, discrete emotions, and job performance. *Human Performance, 25*, 377–411. (p. A-8)

Short, S. J., Lubach, G. R., Karasin, A. I., Olsen, C. W., Styner, M., Knickmeyer, R. C., Gilmore, J. H., & Coe, C. L. (2010). Maternal influenza infection during pregnancy impacts postnatal brain development in the rhesus monkey. *Biological Psychiatry, 67*, 965–973. (p. 643)

Shotland, R. L. (1984, March 12). Quoted in Maureen Dowd, 20 years after the murder of Kitty Genovese, the question remains: Why? *The New York Times*, p. B1. (p. 559)

Showers, C. (1992). The motivational and emotional consequences of considering positive or negative possibilities for an upcoming event. *Journal of Personality and Social Psychology, 63*, 474–484. (p. 600)

Shrestha, A., Nohr, E. A., Bech, B. H., Ramlau-Hansen, C. H., & Olsen, J. (2011). Smoking and alcohol during pregnancy and age of menarche in daughters. *Human Reproduction, 26*, 259–265. (p. 166)

Shuffler, M. L., Burke, C. S., Kramer, W. S., & Salas, E. (2013). Leading teams: Past, present, and future perspectives. In M. G. Rumsey (Ed.), *The Oxford Handbook of Leadership*. New York: Oxford University Press. (p. A-12)

Shuffler, M. L., DiazGranados, D., & Salas, E. (2011). There's a science for that: Team development interventions in organizations. *Current Directions in Psychological Science, 20*, 365–372. (p. A-12)

Shute, N. (2010, October). Desperate for an autism cure. *Scientific American*, pp. 80–85. (p. 193)

Siahpush, M., Spittal, M., & Singh, G. K. (2008). Happiness and life satisfaction prospectively predict self-rated health, physical health and the presence of limiting long-term health conditions. *American Journal of Health Promotion, 23*, 18–26. (p. 498)

Siegel, J. M. (1990). Stressful life events and use of physician services among the elderly: The moderating role of pet ownership. *Journal of Personality and Social Psychology, 58*, 1081–1086. (p. 506)

Siegel, J. M. (2000, Winter). Recent developments in narcolepsy research: An explanation for patients and the general public. *Narcolepsy Network Newsletter*, pp. 1–2. (p. 111)

Siegel, J. M. (2009). Sleep viewed as a state of adaptive inactivity. *Nature Reviews Neuroscience, 10*, 747–753. (p. 105)

Siegel, J. M. (2012). Suppression of sleep for mating. *Science, 337*, 1610–1611. (p. 105)

Siegel, R. K. (1977, October). Hallucinations. *Scientific American*, pp. 132–140. (p. 124)

Siegel, R. K. (1980). The psychology of life after death. *American Psychologist, 35*, 911–931. (p. 124)

Siegel, R. K. (1982, October). Quoted by J. Hooper, Mind tripping. *Omni*, pp. 72–82, 159–160. (p. 124)

Siegel, R. K. (1984, March 15). Personal communication. (p. 125)

Siegel, R. K. (1990). *Intoxication*. New York: Pocket Books. (p. 125)

Siegel, S. (2005). Drug tolerance, drug addiction, and drug anticipation. *Current Directions in Psychological Science, 14*, 296–300. (p. 288)

Silber, M. H. et al. (2008). The visual scoring of sleep in adults. *Journal of Clinical Sleep Medicine, 3*, 121–131. (p. 102)

Silbersweig, D. A., Stern, E., Frith, C., Cahill, C., Holmes, A., Grootoonk, S., Seaward, J., . . . Frackowiak, R. S. J. (1995). A functional neuroanatomy of hallucinations in schizophrenia. *Nature, 378*, 176–179. (p. 642)

Silk, J. B., Beehner, J. C., Bergman, T. J., Crockford, C., Engh, A. L., Moscovice, L. R., . . . Cheney, D. L. (2010). Strong and consistent social bonds enhance the longevity of female baboons. *Current Biology, 20*, 1359–1361. (p. 505)

Silva, A. J., Stevens, C. F., Tonegawa, S., & Wang, Y. (1992). Deficient hippocampal long-term potentiation in alpha-calcium-calmodulin kinase II mutant mice. *Science, 257*, 201–206. (p. 332)

Silva, C. E., & Kirsch, I. (1992). Interpretive sets, expectancy, fantasy proneness, and dissociation as predictors of hypnotic response. *Journal of Personality and Social Psychology, 63*, 847–856. (p. 265)

Silva, K., Bessa, J., & de Sousa, L. (2012). Auditory contagious yawning in domestic dogs (canis familiaris): First evidence for social modulation. *Animal Cognition, 15*, 721–724. (p. 524)

Silver, M., & Geller, D. (1978). On the irrelevance of evil: The organization and individual action. *Journal of Social Issues, 34*, 125–136. (p. 531)

Silver, N. (2012). *The signal and the noise. Why so many predictions fail—but some don't*. New York: Penguin. (p. 214)

Silver, R. C., Holman, E. A., Anderson, J. P., Poulin, M., McIntosh, D. N., & Gil-Rivas, V. (2013). Mental- and physical-health effects of acute exposure to media images of the September 11, 2001 attacks and Iraq War. *Psychological Science, 24*, 1623–1634. (p. 489)

Silver, R. C., Holman, E. A., McIntosh, D. N., Poulin, M., & Gil-Rivas, V. (2002). Nationwide longitudinal study of psychological responses to September 11. *Journal of the American Medical Association, 288*, 1235–1244. (p. 489)

Silveri, M. M., Rohan, M. L., Pimental, P. J., Gruber, S. A., Rosso, I. M., & Yurgelun-Todd, D. A. (2006). Sex differences in the relationship between white matter microstructure and impulsivity in adolescents. *Magnetic Resonance Imaging, 24*, 833–841. (p. 205)

Silverman, K., Evans, S. M., Strain, E. C., & Griffiths, R. R. (1992). Withdrawal syndrome after the double-blind cessation of caffeine consumption. *New England Journal of Medicine, 327*, 1109–1114. (p. 121)

Simek, T. C., & O'Brien, R. M. (1981). *Total golf: A behavioral approach to lowering your score and getting more out of your game*. Huntington, NY: B-MOD Associates. (p. 298)

Simek, T. C., & O'Brien, R. M. (1988). A chaining-mastery, discrimination training program to teach Little Leaguers to hit a baseball. *Human Performance, 1*, 73–84. (p. 298)

Simon, H. (2001, February). Quoted by A. M. Hayashi, When to trust your gut. *Harvard Business Review*, pp. 59–65. (p. 364)

Simon, H. A., & Chase, W. G. (1973) Skill in chess. *American Scientist, 61*, 394–403. (p. 390)

Simon, V., Czobor, P., Bálint, S., Mésáros, A., & Bitter, I. (2009). Prevalence and correlates of adult attention-deficit hyperactivity disorder: Meta-analysis. *British Journal of Psychiatry, 194*, 204–211. (p. 615)

Simons, D. J., & Chabris, C. F. (1999). Gorillas in our midst: Sustained inattentional blindness for dynamic events. *Perception, 28*, 1059–1074. (p. 97)

Simons, D. J., & Levin, D. T. (1998). Failure to detect changes to people during a real-world interaction. *Psychonomic Bulletin & Review, 5,* 644–649. (p. 98)

Simonsohn, U., & Gino, F. (2013). Daily horizons: Evidence of narrow bracketing in judgment from 10 years of M.B.A. admissions interviews. *Psychological Science, 24,* 219–224. (p A-6)

Simonton, D. K. (1988). Age and outstanding achievement: What do we know after a century of research? *Psychological Bulletin, 104,* 251–267. (p. 401)

Simonton, D. K. (1990). Creativity in the later years: Optimistic prospects for achievement. *The Gerontologist, 30,* 626–631. (p. 401)

Simonton, D. K. (1992). The social context of career success and course for 2,026 scientists and inventors. *Personality and Social Psychology Bulletin, 18,* 452–463. (p. 366)

Simonton, D. K. (2000). Methodological and theoretical orientation and the long-term disciplinary impact of 54 eminent psychologists. *Review of General Psychology, 4,* 13–24. (p. 312)

Simonton, D. K. (2012a). Teaching creativity: Current findings, trends, and controversies in the psychology of creativity. *Teaching of Psychology, 39,* 217–222. (p. 366)

Simonton, D. K. (2012b, November–December). The science of genius. *Scientific American Mind,* pp. 35–41. (p. 366)

Sin, N. L., & Lyubomirsky, S. (2009). Enhancing well-being and alleviating depressive symptoms with positive psychology interventions: A practice-friendly meta-analysis. *Journal of Clinical Psychology: In Session, 65,* 467–487. (p. 479)

Sinclair, R. C., Hoffman, C., Mark, M. M., Martin, L. L., & Pickering, T. L. (1994). Construct accessibility and the misattribution of arousal: Schachter and Singer revisited. *Psychological Science, 5,* 15–18. (p. 461)

Singer, J. L. (1981). Clinical intervention: New developments in methods and evaluation. In L. T. Benjamin, Jr. (Ed.), *The G. Stanley Hall Lecture Series* (Vol. 1). Washington, DC: American Psychological Association. (p. 676)

Singer, T., Seymour, B., O'Doherty, J., Kaube, H., Dolan, R. J., & Frith, C. (2004). Empathy for pain involves the affective but not sensory components of pain. *Science, 303,* 1157–1162. (pp. 263, 310)

Singh, D. (1993). Adaptive significance of female physical attractiveness: Role of waist-to-hip ratio. *Journal of Personality and Social Psychology, 65,* 293–307. (p. 149)

Singh, D. (1995). Female health, attractiveness, and desirability for relationships: Role of breast asymmetry and waist-to-hip ratio. *Ethology and Sociobiology, 16,* 465–481. (pp. 149, 555)

Singh, D., & Randall, P. K. (2007). Beauty is in the eye of the plastic surgeon: Waist-hip ration (WHR) and women's attractiveness. *Personality and Individual Differences, 43,* 329–340. (p. 149)

Singh, S. (1997). *Fermat's enigma: The epic quest to solve the world's greatest mathematical problem.* New York: Bantam Books. (p. 365)

Singh, S., & Riber, K. A. (1997, November). Fermat's last stand. *Scientific American,* pp. 68–73. (p. 366)

Sinha, P. (2013, July). Once blind and now they see. *Scientific American,* pp. 49–55. (p. 254)

Sio, U. N., Monahan, P., & Ormerod, T. (2013). Sleep on it, but only if it is difficult: Effects of sleep on problem solving. *Memory and Cognition, 41,* 159–166. (p. 106)

Sio, U. N., & Ormerod, T. C. (2009). Does incubation enhance problem solving? A meta-analtic review. *Psychological Bulletin, 135,* 94–120. (p. 365)

Sipski, M. L., & Alexander, C. J. (1999). Sexual response in women with spinal cord injuries: Implications for our understanding of the able bodied. *Journal of Sex and Marital Therapy, 25,* 11–22. (p. 63)

Sireteanu, R. (1999). Switching on the infant brain. *Science, 286,* 59, 61. (p. 259)

Skeem, J. L., & Cooke, D. J. (2010). Is criminal behavior a central component of psychopathy? Conceptual directions for resolving the debate. *Psychological Assessment, 22,* 433–445. (p. 649)

Skinner, B. F. (1953). *Science and human behavior.* New York: Macmillan. (p. 293)

Skinner, B. F. (1956). A case history in scientific method. *American Psychologist, 11,* 221–233. (p. 294)

Skinner, B. F. (1961, November). Teaching machines. *Scientific American,* pp. 91–102. (p. 294)

Skinner, B. F. (1983, September). Origins of a behaviorist. *Psychology Today,* pp. 22–33. (p. 297)

Skinner, B. F. (1986). What is wrong with daily life in the Western world? *American Psychologist, 41,* 568–574. (p. 298)

Skinner, B. F. (1988). *The school of the future.* Address to the American Psychological Association convention. (p. 298)

Skinner, B. F. (1989). Teaching machines. *Science, 243,* 1535. (p. 298)

Skitka, L. J., Bauman, C. W., & Mullen, E. (2004). Political tolerance and coming to psychological closure following the September 11, 2001, terrorist attacks: An integrative approach. *Personality and Social Psychology Bulletin, 30,* 743–756. (p. 478)

Sklar, L. S., & Anisman, H. (1981). Stress and cancer. *Psychological Bulletin, 89,* 369–406. (p. 496)

Skoog, G., & Skoog, I. (1999). A 40-year follow-up of patients with obsessive-compulsive disorder. *Archives of General Psychiatry, 56,* 121–127. (p. 623)

Skov, R. B., & Sherman, S. J. (1986). Information-gathering processes: Diagnosticity, hypothesis-confirmatory strategies, and perceived hypothesis confirmation. *Journal of Experimental Social Psychology, 22,* 93–121. (p. 357)

Slatcher, R. B., & Pennebaker, J. W. (2006) How do I love thee? Let me count the words: The social effects of expressive writing, *Psychological Science, 17,* 660–664. (p. 558)

Slater, E., & Meyer, A. (1959). *Confinia psychiatra.* Basel: S. Karger AG. (p. 630)

Slavin, R. E., & Braddock, J. H., III. (1993, Summer). Ability grouping: On the wrong track. *The College Board Review,* pp. 11–18. (p. 405)

Slepian, M. L., Rule, N. O., & Ambady, N. (2012). Proprioception and person perception: Politicians and professors. *Personality and Social Psychology Bulletin, 38,* 1621–1628. (p. 270)

Sloan, R. P. (2005). Field analysis of the literature on religion, spirituality, and health. Columbia University (available at www.metanexus.net/tarp). (p. 512)

Sloan, R. P., & Bagiella, E. (2002). Claims about religious involvement and health outcomes. *Annals of Behavioral Medicine, 24,* 14–21. (p. 512)

Sloan, R. P., Bagiella, E., & Powell, T. (1999). Religion, spirituality, and medicine. *Lancet, 353,* 664–667. (p. 512)

Sloan, R. P., Bagiella, E., VandeCreek, L., & Poulos, P. (2000). Should physicians prescribe religious activities? *New England Journal of Medicine, 342,* 1913–1917. (p. 512)

Slopen, N., Glynn, R. J., Buring, J., & Albert, M. A. (2010, November 23). Job strain, job insecurity, and incident cardiovascular disease in the Women's Health Study (Abstract 18520). *Circulation,* A18520 (circ.ahajournals.org). (p. 498)

Slovic, P. (2007). "If I look at the mass I will never act": Psychic numbing and genocide. *Judgment and Decision Making, 2,* 79–95. (p. 360)

Slovic, P. (2010, Winter). The more who die, the less we care: Confronting psychic numbing. *Trauma Psychology* (APA Division 56 Newsletter), pp. 4–8. (p. 360)

Slutske, W. S., Moffitt, T. E., Poulton, R., & Caspi A. (2012). Under-controlled temperament at age 3 predicts disordered gambling at age 32: A longitudinal study of a complete birth cohort. *Psychological Science, 23,* 510–516. (p. 179)

Small, D. A., Loewenstein, G., & Slovic, P. (2007). Sympathy and callousness: The impact of deliberative thought on donations to identifiable and statistical victims. *Organizational Behavior and Human Decision Processes, 102,* 143–153. (p. 360)

Small, M. F. (1997). Making connections. *American Scientist, 85,* 502–504. (p. 160)

Smart Richman, L., & Leary, M. (2009). Reactions to discrimination, stigmatization, ostracism, and other forms of interpersonal rejection: A dynamic, multi-motive model. *Psychological Review, 116,* 365–383. (p. 450)

Smedley, A., & Smedley, B. D. (2005). Race as biology is fiction, racism as a social problem is real: Anthropological and historical perspectives on the social construction of race. *American Psychologist, 60,* 16–26. (p. 412)

Smelser, N. J., & Mitchell, F. (Eds.). (2002). *Terrorism: Perspectives from the behavioral and social sciences.* Washington, DC: National Research Council, National Academies Press. (p. 544)

Smith, A. (1983). Personal correspondence. (p. 642)

Smith, B. C. (2011, January 16). The senses and the multi-sensory. *World Question Center* (www.edge.org). (p. 270)

Smith, C. (2006, January 7). Nearly 100, LSD's father ponders his "problem child." *New York Times* (www.nytimes.com). (p. 125)

Smith, D. M., Loewenstein, G., Jankovic, A., & Ubel, P. A. (2009). Happily hopeless: Adaptation to a permanent, but not to a temporary, disability. *Health Psychology, 28,* 787–791. (p. 481)

Smith, E., & Delargy, M. (2005). Locked-in syndrome. *British Medical Journal, 330,* 406–409. (p. 481)

Smith, M. B. (1978). Psychology and values. *Journal of Social Issues, 34,* 181–199. (p. 585)

Smith, M. L., & Glass, G. V. (1977). Meta-analysis of psychotherapy outcome studies. *American Psychologist, 32*, 752–760. (p. 675)

Smith, M. L., Glass, G. V., & Miller, R. L. (1980). *The benefits of psychotherapy.* Baltimore: Johns Hopkins Press. (p. 675)

Smith, P. B., & Tayeb, M. (1989). Organizational structure and processes. In M. Bond (Ed.), *The cross-cultural challenge to social psychology.* Newbury Park, CA: Sage. (p. A-13)

Smith, S. F., Lilienfeld, S. O., Coffey, K., & Dabbs, J. M. (2013). Are psychopaths and heroes twigs off the same branch? Evidence from college, community, and presidential samples. *Journal of Research in Personality, 47*, 634–646. (p. 650)

Smith, S. J., Axelton, A. M., & Saucier, D. A. (2009). The effects of contact on sexual prejudice: A meta-analysis. *Sex Roles, 61*, 178–191. (p. 564)

Smith, S. J., Zanotti, D. C., Axelton, A. M., & Saucier, D. A. (2011). Individuals' beliefs about the etiology of same-sex sexual orientation. *Journal of Homosexuality, 58*, 1110–1131. (p. 447)

Smith, T. B., Bartz, J., & Richards, P. S. (2007). Outcomes of religious and spiritual adaptations to psychotherapy: A meta-analytic review. *Psychotherapy Research, 17*, 643–655. (p. 680)

Smith, T. W. (1998, December). *American sexual behavior: Trends, sociodemographic differences, and risk behavior* (National Opinion Research Center GSS Topical Report No. 25). (p. 441)

Smits, I. A. M., Dolan, C. V., Vorst, H. C. M., Wicherts, J. M., & Timmerman, M. E. (2011). Cohort differences in big five personality traits over a period of 25 years. *Journal of Personality and Social Psychology, 100*, 1124–1138. (pp. 508, 591)

Smock, P. J., & Manning, W. D. (2004). Living together unmarried in the United States: Demographic perspectives and implications for family policy. *Law and Policy, 26*, 87–117. (p. 221)

Smolak, L., & Murnen, S. K. (2002). A meta-analytic examination of the relationship between child sexual abuse and eating disorders. *International Journal of Eating Disorders, 31*, 136–150. (p. 652)

Smoreda, Z., & Licoppe, C. (2000). Gender-specific use of the domestic telephone. *Social Psychology Quarterly, 63*, 238–252. (p. 163)

Snedeker, J., Geren, J., & Shafto, C. L. (2007). Starting over: International adoption as a natural experiment in language development. *Psychological Science, 18*, 79–86. (p. 373)

Snodgrass, S. E., Higgins, J. G., & Todisco, L. (1986). *The effects of walking behavior on mood.* Paper presented at the American Psychological Association convention. (pp. 474, 477)

Snowden, R. J., & Gray, N. S. (2013). Implicit sexual associations in heterosexual and homosexual women and men. *Archives of Sexual Behavior, 42*, 475–485. (p. 441)

Snowdon, D. A., Kemper, S. J., Mortimer, J. A., Greiner, L. H., Wekstein, D. R., & Markesbery, W. R. (1996). Linguistic ability in early life and cognitive function and Alzheimer's disease in late life: Finds from the Nun Study. *Journal of the American Medical Association, 275*, 528–532. (p. 402)

Snyder, F., & Scott, J. (1972). The psychophysiology of sleep. In N. S. Greenfield & R. A. Sterbach (Eds.), *Handbook of psychophysiology.* New York: Holt, Rinehart & Winston. (p. 115)

Snyder, S. H. (1984). Neurosciences: An integrative discipline. *Science, 225*, 1255–1257. (p. 614)

Snyder, S. H. (1986). *Drugs and the brain.* New York: Scientific American Library. (p. 684)

Social Watch. (2006, March 8). No country in the world treats its women as well as its men (www.socialwatch.org). (p. 168)

Society for Personality Assessment. (2005). The status of the Rorschach in clinical and forensic practice: An official statement by the Board of Trustees of the Society for Personality Assessment. *Journal of Personality Assessment, 85*, 219–237. (p. 578)

Sokol, D. K., Moore, C. A., Rose, R. J., Williams, C. J., Reed, T., & Christian, J. C. (1995). Intrapair differences in personality and cognitive ability among young monozygotic twins distinguished by chorion type. *Behavior Genetics, 25*, 457–466. (p. 136)

Solnick, S. J., & Hemenway, D. (1998). Is more always better?: A survey on positional concerns. *Journal of Economic Behavior & Organization, 37*, 373–383. (p. 484)

Solnick, S. J., & Hemenway, D. (2009). Do spending comparisons affect spending and satisfaction? *Journal of Socio-Economics, 38*, 568–573. (p. 484)

Solomon, D. A., Keitner, G. I., Miller, I. W., Shea, M. T., & Keller, M. B. (1995). Course of illness and maintenance treatments for patients with bipolar disorder. *Journal of Clinical Psychiatry, 56*, 5–13. (p. 684)

Solomon, J. (1996, May 20). Breaking the silence. *Newsweek*, pp. 20–22. (p. 616)

Solomon, M. (1987, December). Standard issue. *Psychology Today*, pp. 30–31. (p. 554)

Somerville, L. H., Jones, R. M., Ruberry, E. J., Dyke, J. P., Glover, G., & Casey, B. J. (2013). The medial prefrontal cortex and the emergence of self-conscious emotion in adolescence. *Psychological Science, 24*, 1554–1562. (p. 205)

Song, S. (2006, March 27). Mind over medicine. *Time*, p. 47. (p. 265)

Sontag, S. (1978). *Illness as metaphor.* New York: Farrar, Straus, & Giroux. (p. 496)

Soon, C. S., Brass, M., Heinze, H., & Haynes, J. (2008). Unconscious determinants of free decisions in the human brain. *Nature Neuroscience, 11*, 543–545. (p. 95)

Sorkhabi, N. (2005). Applicability of Baumrind's parent typology to collective cultures: Analysis of cultural explanations of parent socialization effects. *International Journal of Behavioral Development, 29*, 552–563. (p. 202)

Soto, C. J., John, O. P., & Gosling, S. D., & Potter, J. (2011). Age differences in personality traits from 10 to 65: Big five domains and facets in a large cross-sectional sample. *Journal of Personality and Social Psychology, 100*, 330–348. (p. 590)

Soussignan, R. (2001). Duchenne smile, emotional experience, and autonomic reactivity: A test of the facial feedback hypothesis. *Emotion, 2*, 52–74. (p. 474)

South, S. C., Krueger, R. F., Johnson, W., & Iacono, W. G. (2008). Adolescent personality moderates genetic and environmental influences on relationships with parents. *Journal of Personality and Social Psychology, 94*, 899–912. (p. 202)

Sowell, T. (1991, May/June). Cultural diversity: A world view. *American Enterprise*, pp. 44–55. (p. 567)

Sowislo, J. F., & Orth, U. (2012). Does low self-esteem predict depression and anxiety? A meta-analysis of longitudinal studies. *Psychological Bulletin, 139*, 213–240. (pp. 628, 634)

Spalding, K. L., et al. (2013). Dynamics of hippocampal neurogenesis in adult humans. *Cell, 153*, 1219–1227. (p. 82)

Spanos, N. P. (1986). Hypnosis, nonvolitional responding, and multiple personality: A social psychological perspective. *Progress in Experimental Personality Research, 14*, 1–62. (p. 647)

Spanos, N. P. (1994). Multiple identity enactments and multiple personality disorder: A sociocognitive perspective. *Psychological Bulletin, 116*, 143–165. (p. 647)

Spanos, N. P. (1996). *Multiple identities and false memories: A sociocognitive perspective.* Washington, DC: American Psychological Association Books. (p. 647)

Spanos, N. P., & Coe, W. C. (1992). A social-psychological approach to hypnosis. In E. Fromm & M. R. Nash (Eds.), *Contemporary hypnosis research.* New York: Guilford. (p. 265)

Sparrow, B., Liu, J., & Wegner, D. M. (2011). Google effects on memory: Cognitive consequences of having information at our fingertips. *Science, 333*, 776–778. (p. 321)

Spaulding, S. (2013). Mirror neurons and social cognition. *Mind and Language, 28*, 233–257. (p. 309)

Specht, J., Egloff, B., & Schmukle, S. C. (2011). Stability and change of personality across the life course: The impact of age and major life events on mean-level and rank-order stability of the Big Five. *Journal of Personality and Social Psychology, 101*, 862–882. (p. 180)

Spector, T. (2012). *Identically different: Why you can change your genes.* London, UK: Weidenfeld & Nicolson. (p. 143)

Speer, N. K., Reynolds, J. R., Swallow, K. M., & Zacks, J. M. (2009). Reading stories activates neural representations of visual and motor experiences. *Psychological Science, 20*, 989–999. (pp. 310, 376)

Spelke, E. S., Bernier, E. P., & Skerry, A. E. (2013). Core social cognition. In M. R. Banaji & S. A. Gelman (Eds.), *Navigating the social world: What infants, children, and other species can teach us.* Oxford University Press. (p. 188)

Spence, I., & Feng, J. (2010). Video games and spatial cognition. *Review of General Psychology, 14*, 92–104. (p. 254)

Spencer, K. M., Nestor, P. G., Perlmutter, R., Niznikiewicz, M. A., Klump, M. C., Frumin, M., Shenton, M. E., & McCarley, R. W. (2004). Neural synchrony indexes disordered perception and cognition in schizophrenia. *Proceedings of the National Academy of Sciences, 101*, 17288–17293. (p. 642)

Spencer, S. J., Steele, C. M., & Quinn, D. M. (1997). *Stereotype threat and women's math performance.* Unpublished manuscript, Hope College. (p. 414)

Sperling, G. (1960). The information available in brief visual presentations. *Psychological Monographs, 74* (Whole No. 498). (p. 322)

Sperry, R. W. (1964). *Problems outstanding in the evolution of brain function.* James Arthur Lecture, American Museum of Natural History, New York. Cited by R. Ornstein (1977), *The psychology of consciousness* (2nd ed.). New York: Harcourt Brace Jovanovich. (p. 84)

Sperry, R. W. (1985). Changed concepts of brain and consciousness: Some value implications. *Zygon, 20*, 41–57. (p. 246)

Sperry, R. W. (1992, Summer). Turnabout on consciousness: A mentalist view. *Journal of Mind & Behavior, 13*(3), 259–280. (p. 87)

Spiegel, A. (2010, July 12). 'Voice blind' man befuddled by mysterious callers. National Public Radio (npr.org). (p. 229)

Spiegel, D. (2007). The mind prepared: Hypnosis in surgery. *Journal of the National Cancer Institute, 99,* 1280–1281. (p. 265)

Spiegel, D. (2008, January 31). *Coming apart: Trauma and the fragmentation of the self.* Dana Foundation (www.dana.org). (p. 648)

Spiegel, K., Leproult, R., L'Hermite-Balériaux, M., Copinschi, G., Penev, P. D., & Van Cauter, E. (2004). Leptin levels are dependent on sleep duration: Relationships with sympathovagal balance, carbohydrate regulation, cortisol, and thyrotropin. *Journal of Clinical Endocrinology and Metabolism, 89,* 5762–5771. (p. 108)

Spielberger, C., & London, P. (1982). Rage boomerangs. *American Health, 1,* 52–56. (p. 497)

Sprecher, S., Treger, S., & Sakaluk, J. K. (2013). Premarital sexual standards and sociosexuality: Gender, ethnicity, and cohort differences. *Archives of Sexual Behavior, 42,* 1395–1405. (p. 147)

Spring, B., Pingitore, R., Bourgeois, M., Kessler, K. H., & Bruckner, E. (1992). *The effects and non-effects of skipping breakfast: Results of three studies.* Paper presented at the American Psychological Association convention. (p. 432)

Sproesser, G., Schupp, H. T., & Renner, B. (2014). The bright side of stress-induced eating: Eating more when stressed but less when pleased. *Psychological Science, 25,* 58–65. (pp. 428, 451)

Squire, L. R., & Wixted, J. T. (2011). The cognitive neuroscience of human memory since H. M. *Annual Review of Neuroscience, 34,* 259–288. (p. 329)

Squire, L. R., & Zola-Morgan, S. (1991, September 20). The medial temporal lobe memory system. *Science, 253,* 1380–1386. (p. 330)

Srivastava, A., Locke, E. A., & Bartol, K. M. (2001). Money and subject well-being: It's not the money, it's the motives. *Journal of Personality and Social Psychology, 80,* 959–971. (p. 482)

Srivastava, S., McGonigal, K. M., Richards, J. M., Butler, E. A., & Gross, J. J. (2006). Optimism in close relationships: How seeing things in a positive light makes them so. *Journal of Personality and Social Psychology, 91,* 143–153. (p. 504)

St. Clair, D., Xu, M., Wang, P., Yu, Y., Fang, Y., Zhang, F., Zheng, X., . . . & He, L. (2005). Rates of adult schizophrenia following prenatal exposure to the Chinese famine of 1959–1961. *Journal of the American Medical Association, 294,* 557–562. (p. 643)

Stacey, D., et al. (2012). *RASGRF2 regulates alcohol-induced reinforcement by influencing mesolimbic dopamine neuron activity and dopamine release. PNAS, 109,* 21128–21133. (p. 127)

Stack, S. (1992). Marriage, family, religion, and suicide. In R. Maris, A. Berman, J. Maltsberger, & R. Yufit (Eds.), *Assessment and prediction of suicide.* New York: Guilford Press. (p. 637)

Stafford, T., & Dewar, M. (2014). Tracing the trajectory of skill learning with a very large sample of online game players. *Psychological Science, 25,* 511–518. (p. 326)

Stager, C. L., & Werker, J. F. (1997). Infants listen for more phonetic detail in speech perception than in word-learning tasks. *Nature, 388,* 381–382. (p. 371)

Stanford University Center for Narcolepsy. (2002). Narcolepsy is a serious medical disorder and a key to understanding other sleep disorders. (www.med.stanford.edu/school/Psychiatry/narcolepsy). (p. 110)

Stanley, D., Phelps, E., & Banaji, M. (2008). The neural basis of implicit attitudes. *Current Directions in Psychological Science, 17,* 164–170. (p. 540)

Stanley, S. M., Rhoades, G. K., Amato, P. R., Markman, H. J., & Johnson, C. A. (2010). The timing of cohabitation and engagement: Impact on first and second marriages. *Journal of Marriage and Family, 72,* 906–918. (p. 221)

Stanovich, K. (1996). *How to think straight about psychology.* New York: HarperCollins. (p. 572)

Stanovich, K. E., & West, R. F. (2014). What intelligence tests miss. *Psychologist, 27,* 80–83. (p. 415)

Stanovich, K. E., West, R. F., & Toplak, M. E. (2013). My side bias, rational thinking, and intelligence. *Current Directions in Psychological Science, 22,* 259–264. (p. 364)

Stark, R. (2002). Physiology and faith: Addressing the "universal" gender difference in religious commitment. *Journal for the Scientific Study of Religion, 41,* 495–507. (p. 164)

Stark, R. (2003a). *For the glory of God: How monotheism led to reformations, science, witch-hunts, and the end of slavery.* Princeton, NJ: Princeton University Press. (p. 24)

Stark, R. (2003b, October-November). False conflict: Christianity is not only compatible with science—it created it. *American Enterprise,* pp. 27–33. (p. 24)

Starr, J. M., Deary, I. J., Lemmon, H., & Whalley, L. J. (2000). Mental ability age 11 years and health status age 77 years. *Age and Ageing, 29,* 523–528. (p. 402)

State, M. W., & Šestan, N. (2012). The emerging biology of autism spectrum disorders. *Science, 337,* 1301–1304. (p. 193)

Statistics Canada. (1999, September). *Statistical report on the health of Canadians.* Prepared by the Federal, Provincial and Territorial Advisory Committee on Population Health for the Meeting of Ministers of Health, Charlottetown, PEI. (pp. 211, 490)

Statistics Canada. (2013). Table A.5.1.Second language immersion program enrolments in public elementary and secondary schools, Canada, provinces and territories, 2005/2006 to 2009/2010 (http://www.statcan.gc.ca/pub/81-595-m/2011095/tbl/tbla.5.1-eng.htm). (p. 381)

Staub, E. (1989). *The roots of evil: The psychological and cultural sources of genocide.* New York: Cambridge University Press. (p. 522)

Steel, P., Schmidt, J., & Schultz, J. (2008). Refining the relationship between personality and subject well-being. *Psychological Bulletin, 134,* 138–161. (p. 485)

Steele, C. M. (1990, May). A conversation with Claude Steele. *APS Observer,* pp. 11–17. (p. 411)

Steele, C. M. (1995, August 31). Black students live down to expectations. *New York Times.* (p. 414)

Steele, C. M. (2010). *Whistling Vivaldi: And other clues to how stereotypes affect us.* New York: Norton. (p. 414)

Steele, C. M., & Josephs, R. A. (1990). Alcohol myopia: Its prized and dangerous effects. *American Psychologist, 45,* 921–933. (p. 120)

Steele, C. M., Spencer, S. J., & Aronson, J. (2002). Contending with group image: The psychology of stereotype and social identity threat. *Advances in Experimental Social Psychology, 34,* 379–440. (p. 414)

Steenhuysen, J. (2002, May 8). Bionic retina gives six patients partial sight. *Reuters News Service.* (See also www.optobionics.com/artificialretina.htm.). (p. 259)

Steger, M. F., Hicks, B. M., Krueger, R. F., & Bouchard, T. J. (2011). Genetic and environmental influences and covariance among meaning in life, religiousness, and spirituality. *The Journal of Positive Psychology, 6,* 181–191. (p. 139)

Stein, J. I., et al. (2012). Identification of common variants associated with human hippocampal and intracranial volumes. *Nature Genetics, 44,* 552–561. (p. 406)

Steinberg, L. (1987, September). Bound to bicker. *Psychology Today,* pp. 36–39 (p., 210)

Steinberg, L. (2007). Risk taking in adolescence: New perspectives from brain and behavioral science. *Current Directions in Psychological Science, 16,* 55–59. (p. 205)

Steinberg, L. (2010, March). Analyzing adolescence. Interview with Sara Martin. *Monitor on Psychology,* pp. 26–29. (p. 205)

Steinberg, L. (2012, Spring). Should the science of adolescent brain development inform public policy? *Issues in Science and Technology,* pp. 67–78 (p., 205)

Steinberg, L. (2013). The influence of neuroscience on U.S. Supreme Court decisions involving adolescents' criminal culpability. *Nature Reviews Neuroscience, 14,* 513–518. (p. 205)

Steinberg, L., Cauffman, E., Woolard, J., Graham, S., & Banich, M. (2009). Are adolescents less mature than adults? Minors' access to abortion, the juvenile death penalty, and the alleged APA "flip-flop." *American Psychologist, 64,* 583–594. (p. 205)

Steinberg, L., & Morris, A. S. (2001). Adolescent development. *Annual Review of Psychology, 52,* 83–110. (pp. 202, 210, 211)

Steinberg, L., & Scott, E. S. (2003). Less guilty by reason of adolescence: Developmental immaturity, diminished responsibility, and the juvenile death penalty. *American Psychologist, 58,* 1009–1018. (p. 205)

Steinberg, N. (1993, February). Astonishing love stories (from an earlier United Press International report). *Games,* p. 47. (p. 551)

Steiner, J. L., Murphy, E. A., McClellan, J. L., Carmichael, M. D., & Davis, J. M. (2011). Exercise training increases mitochondrial biogenesis in the brain. *Journal of Applied Physiology, 111,* 1066–1071. (p. 216)

Steingard, R. J., Renshaw, P. F., Hennen, J., Lenox, M., Cintron, C. B., Young, A. D., . . . Yurgelun-Todd, D. A. (2002). Smaller frontal lobe white matter volumes in depressed adolescents. *Biological Psychiatry, 52*(5), 413–417. (p. 633)

Steinhauer, J. (1999, November 29). Number of twins rises: So does parental stress. *New York Times* (www.nytimes.com). (p. 136)

Steinmetz, J. E. (1999). The localization of a simple type of learning and memory: The cerebellum and classical eyeblink conditioning. *Contemporary Psychology, 7,* 72–77. (p. 330)

Stender, J., et al. (2014). Diagnostic precision of PET imaging and functional MRI in disorders of consciousness: A clinical validation study. *The Lancet.* Published online at http://dx.doi.org/10.1016/S0140-6736(14)60042-8. (p. 93)

Stengel, E. (1981). Suicide. In *The new Encyclopaedia Britannica, macropaedia* (Vol. 17, pp. 777–782). Chicago: Encyclopaedia Britannica. (p. 637)

Stepanikova, I., Nie, N. H., & He, X. (2010). Time on the Internet at home, loneliness, and life satisfaction: Evidence from panel time-diary data. *Computers in Human Behavior, 26,* 329–338. (p. 452)

Stephens-Davidowitz, S. (2013, December 7). How many American men are gay? *New York Times* (www.nytimes.com). (p. 440)

Stephens-Davidowitz, S. (2014). The effects of racial animus on a black candidate: Evidence using Google search data. *Journal of Public Economics, 118,* 26–40. (pp. 539, 540)

Steptoe, A., Chida, Y., Hamer, M., & Wardle, J. (2010). Author reply: Meta-analysis of stress-related factors in cancer. *Nature Reviews: Clinical Oncology, 7,* doi:10.1038/ncponc1134-c2. (p. 496)

Steptoe, A., Shankar, A., Demakakos, P., & Wardle, J. (2013). Social isolation, loneliness, and all-cause mortality in older men and women. *Proceedings of the National Academy of Sciences, 110,* 5797–5801. (p. 505)

Stern, M., & Karraker, K. H. (1989). Sex stereotyping of infants: A review of gender labeling studies. *Sex Roles, 20,* 501–522. (p. 236)

Sternberg, R. J. (1985). *Beyond IQ: A triarchic theory of human intelligence.* New York: Cambridge University Press. (p. 388)

Sternberg, R. J. (1988). Applying cognitive theory to the testing and teaching of intelligence. *Applied Cognitive Psychology, 2,* 231–255. (p. 366)

Sternberg, R. J. (2003). Our research program validating the triarchic theory of successful intelligence: Reply to Gottfredson. *Intelligence, 31,* 399–413. (p. 366)

Sternberg, R. J. (2006). The Rainbow Project: Enhance the SAT through assessments of analytical, practical, and creative skills. *Intelligence, 34,* 321–350. (pp. 366, 389)

Sternberg, R. J. (2007, July 6). Finding students who are wise, practical, and creative. *The Chronicle Review* (www.chronicle.com). (p. 389)

Sternberg, R. J. (2010). Assessment of gifted students for identification purposes: New techniques for a new millennium. *Learning and Individual Differences, 20,* 327–336. (p. 389)

Sternberg, R. J. (2011). The theory of successful intelligence. In R. J. Sternberg & S. B. Kaufman (Eds.), *The Cambridge handbook of intelligence.* New York: Cambridge University Press. (p. 388)

Sternberg, R. J., & Grajek, S. (1984). The nature of love. *Journal of Personality and Social Psychology, 47,* 312–329. (p. 557)

Sternberg, R. J., & Kaufman, J. C. (1998). Human abilities. *Annual Review of Psychology, 49,* 479–502. (p. 386)

Sternberg, R. J., & Lubart, T. I. (1991). An investment theory of creativity and its development. *Human Development,* 1–31. (p. 366)

Sternberg, R. J., & Lubart, T. I. (1992). Buy low and sell high: An investment approach to creativity. *Psychological Science, 1,* 1–5. (p. 366)

Sternberg, R. J., & Wagner, R. K. (1993). The g-ocentric view of intelligence and job performance is wrong. *Current Directions in Psychological Science, 2,* 1–5. (p. 388)

Sternberg, R. J., Wagner, R. K., Williams, W. M., & Horvath, J. A. (1995). Testing common sense. *American Psychologist, 50,* 912–927. (p. 388)

Sterzing, P. R., Shattuck, P. T., Narendorf, S. C., Wagner, M., & Cooper, B. P. (2012). Bullying involvement and autism spectrum disorders: prevalence and correlates of bullying involvement among adolescents with an autism spectrum disorder. *Archives of Pediatric and Adolescent Medicine, 166,* 1058–1064. (p. 193)

Stetter, F., & Kupper, S. (2002). Autogenic training: A meta-analysis of clinical outcome studies. *Applied Psychophysiology and Biofeedback, 27,* 45–98. (p. 509)

Stevenson, H. W. (1992, December). Learning from Asian schools. *Scientific American,* pp. 70–76. (p. 412)

Stevenson, H. W., & Lee, S-Y. (1990). Contexts of achievement: A study of American, Chinese, and Japanese children. *Monographs of the Society for Research in Child Development, 55* (Serial No. 221, Nos. 1–2). (p. 405)

Stevenson, R. J. (2014). Flavor binding: Its nature and cause. *Psychological Bulletin, 140,* 487–510. (p. 270)

Stevenson, R. J., & Tomiczek, C. (2007). Olfactory-induced synesthesias: A review and model. *Psychological Bulletin, 133,* 294–309. (p. 271)

Stewart, R. E., & Chambless, D. L. (2009). Cognitive-behavioral therapy for adult anxiety disorders in clinical practice: A meta-analysis of effectiveness studies. *Journal of Consulting and Clinical Psychology, 77,* 595–606. (p. 676)

Stice, E. (2002). Risk and maintenance factors for eating pathology: A meta-analytic review. *Psychological Bulletin, 128,* 825–848. (p. 652)

Stice, E., Ng, J., & Shaw, H. (2010). Risk factors and prodromal eating pathology. *Journal of Child Psychology and Psychiatry, 51,* 518–525. (p. 652)

Stice, E., Shaw, H., & Marti, C. N. (2007). A meta-analytic review of eating disorder prevention programs: Encouraging findings. *Annual Review of Clinical Psychology, 3,* 233–257. (p. 653)

Stice, E., Spangler, D., & Agras, W. S. (2001). Exposure to media-portrayed thin-ideal images adversely affects vulnerable girls: A longitudinal experiment. *Journal of Social and Clinical Psychology, 20,* 270–288. (p. 652)

Stickgold, R. (2000, March 7). Quoted by S. Blakeslee, For better learning, researchers endorse "sleep on it" adage. *New York Times,* p. F2. (p. 114)

Stickgold, R. (2012). Sleep, memory and dreams: Putting it all together. In *Aquém e além do Cérebro (Behind and beyond the brain).* Bial: Fundação Bial Institution of Public Utility. (p. 113)

Stickgold, R., & Ellenbogen, J. M. (2008, August/September). Quiet! Sleeping brain at work. *Scientific American Mind,* pp. 23–29. (p. 106)

Stillman, T. F., Baumeister, R. F., Vohs, K. D., Lambert, N. M., Fincham, F. D., & Brewer, L. E. (2010). Personal philosophy and personnel achievement: Belief in free will predicts better job performance. *Social Psychological and Personality Science, 1,* 43–50. (p. 503)

Stillman, T. F., Lambet, N. M., Fincham, F. D., & Baumeister, R. F. (2011). Meaning as magnetic force: Evidence that meaning in life promotes interpersonal appeal. *Social Psychological and Personality Science, 2,* 13–20. (p. 690)

Stinson, D. A., Logel, C., Zanna, M. P., Holmes, J. G., Cameron, J. J., Wood, J. V., & Spencer, S. J. (2008). The cost of lower self-esteem: Testing a self- and social-bonds model of health. *Journal of Personality and Social Psychology, 94,* 412–428. (p. 507)

Stipek, D. (1992). The child at school. In M. H. Bornstein & M. E. Lamb (Eds.), *Developmental psychology: An advanced textbook.* Hillsdale, NJ: Erlbaum. (p. 201)

Stirrat, M., & Perrett, D. I. (2010). Valid facial cues to cooperation and trust: Male facial width and trustworthiness. *Psychological Science 21,* 349–354. (p. 546)

Stith, S. M., Rosen, K. H., Middleton, K. A., Busch, A. L., Lunderberg, K., & Carlton, R. P. (2000). The intergenerational transmission of spouse abuse: A meta-analysis. *Journal of Marriage and the Family, 62,* 640–654. (p. 311)

Stockton, M. C., & Murnen, S. K. (1992). *Gender and sexual arousal in response to sexual stimuli: A meta-analytic review.* Paper presented at the American Psychological Society convention. (p. 437)

Stoet, G., & Geary, D. C. (2012). Can stereotype threat explain the gender gap in mathematics performance and achievement? *Review of General Psychology, 16,* 93–102. (p. 414)

Stokoe, W. C. (1960). Sign language structure: An outline of the visual communication systems of the American Deaf. *Studies in Linguistics: Occasional papers* (No. 8). Buffalo: Dept. of Anthropology and Linguistics, University of Buffalo. (p. 375)

Stone, A. A., & Neale, J. M. (1984). Effects of severe daily events on mood. *Journal of Personality and Social Psychology, 46,* 137–144. (p. 481)

Stone, A. A., Schneider, S., & Harter, J. K. (2012). Day-of-week mood patterns in the United States: On the existence of 'Blue Monday,' 'Thank God it's Friday' and weekend effects. *Journal of Positive Psychology, 7,* 306–314. (p. 30)

Stone, A. A., Schwartz, J. E., Broderick, J. E., & Deaton, A. (2010). A snapshot of the age distribution of psychological well-being in the United States. *PNAS, 107,* 9985–9990. (p. 223)

Stone, A. A., Schwartz, J. E., Broderick, J. E., & Shiffman, S. S. (2005). Variability of momentary pain predicts recall of weekly pain: A consequences of the peak (or salience) memory heuristic. *Personality and Social Psychology Bulletin, 31,* 1340–1346. (p. 263)

Stone, G. (2006, February 17). Homeless man discovered to be lawyer with amnesia. *ABC News* (abcnews.go.com). (p. 647)

St-Onge, M-P., McReynolds, A., Trivedi, Z. B., Roberts, A. L., Sy, M., & Hirsch, J. (2012). Sleep restriction leads to increased activation of brain regions sensitive to food stimuli. *American Journal of Clinical Nutrition, 95,* 818–824. (p. 108)

Storbeck, J., Robinson, M. D., & McCourt, M. E. (2006). Semantic processing precedes affect retrieval: The neurological case for cognitive primary in visual processing. *Review of General Psychology, 10,* 41–55. (p. 463)

Storm, B. C., & Jobe, T. A. (2012). Retrieval-induced forgetting predicts failure to recall negative autobiographical memories. *Psychological Science, 23,* 1356–1363. (p. 332)

Storm, L., Tressoldi, P. E., & Di Risio, L. (2010a). A meta-analysis with nothing to hide: Reply to Hyman (2010). *Psychological Bulletin, 136,* 491–494. (pp. 272, 273)

Storm, L., Tressoldi, P. E., & Di Risio, L. (2010b). Meta-analysis of free-response studies, 1992–2008: Assessing the noise reduction model in parapsychology. *Psychological Bulletin, 136,* 471–485. (pp. 272, 273)

Storm, L., Tressoldi, P. E., & Utts, J. (2013). Testing the Storm et al. (2010) meta-analysis using Bayesian and frequentist approaches: Reply to Rouder et al. (2013). *Psychological Bulletin, 139,* 248–254. (p. 273)

Storms, M. D. (1973). Videotape and the attribution process: Reversing actors' and observers' points of view. *Journal of Personality and Social Psychology, 27,* 165–175. (p. 519)

Storms, M. D. (1981). A theory of erotic orientation development. *Psychological Review, 88,* 340–353. (p. 442)

Storms, M. D. (1983). *Development of sexual orientation.* Washington, DC: Office of Social and Ethical Responsibility, American Psychological Association. (p. 442)

Storms, M. D., & Thomas, G. C. (1977). Reactions to physical closeness. *Journal of Personality and Social Psychology, 35,* 412–418. (p. 532)

Stout, J. A., & Dasgupta, N. (2011). When *he* doesn't mean *you:* Gender-exclusive language as ostracism. *Personality and Social Psychology Bulletin, 37,* 75–769. (p. 450)

Stowell, J. R., Oldham, T., & Bennett, D. (2010). Using student response systems ("clickers") to combat conformity and shyness. *Teaching of Psychology, 37,* 135–140. (p. 527)

Strahan, E. J., Spencer, S. J., & Zanna, M. P. (2002). Subliminal priming and persuasion: Striking while the iron is hot. *Journal of Experimental Social Psychology, 38,* 556–568. (p. 233)

Stranahan, A. M., Khalil, D., & Gould, E. (2006). Social isolation delays the positive effects of running on adult neurogenesis. *Nature Neuroscience, 9,* 526–533. (p. 82)

Strang, S., Utikal, V., Fischbacher, U., Weber, B., & Falk, A. (2014). Neural correlates of receiving an apology and active forgiveness: An fMRI study. *PLoS One, 9,* e87654. (p. 478)

Strange, D., Hayne, H., & Garry, M. (2008). A photo, a suggestion, a false memory. *Applied Cognitive Psychology, 22,* 587–603. (p. 345)

Strasburger, V. C., Jordan, A. B., & Donnerstein, E. (2010). Health effects of media on children and adolescents. *Pediatrics, 125,* 756–767. (p. 311)

Stratton, G. M. (1896). Some preliminary experiments on vision without inversion of the retinal image. *Psychological Review, 3,* 611–617. (p. 255)

Straub, R. O., Seidenberg, M. S., Bever, T. G., & Terrace, H. S. (1979). Serial learning in the pigeon. *Journal of the Experimental Analysis of Behavior, 32,* 137–148. (p. 378)

Straus, M. A., & Gelles, R. J. (1980). *Behind closed doors: Violence in the American family.* New York: Anchor/Doubleday. (p. 296)

Straus, M. A., Sugarman, D. B., & Giles-Sims, J. (1997). Spanking by parents and subsequent antisocial behavior of children. *Archives of Pediatric Adolescent Medicine, 151,* 761–767. (p. 296)

Strawbridge, W. J. (1999). *Mortality and religious involvement: A review and critique of the results, the methods, and the measures.* Paper presented at a Harvard University conference on religion and health, sponsored by the National Institute for Health Research and the John Templeton Foundation. (p. 512)

Strawbridge, W. J., Cohen, R. D., & Shema, S. J. (1997). Frequent attendance at religious services and mortality over 28 years. *American Journal of Public Health, 87,* 957–961. (p. 512)

Strayer, D. L., & Drews, F. A. (2007). Cell-phone-induced driver distraction. *Current Directions in Psychological Science, 16,* 128–131. (p. 97)

Strayer, D. L., & Watson, J. M. (2012, March/April). Supertaskers and the multitasking brain. *Scientific American Mind,* pp. 22–29. (p. 97)

Strick, M., Dijksterhuis, A., Bos, M. W., Sjoerdsma, A., & van Baaren, R. B. (2011). A meta-analysis on unconscious thought effects. *Social Cognition, 29,* 738–762. (p. 364)

Strick, M., Dijksterhuis, A., & van Baaren, R. B. (2010). Unconscious-thought effects take place off-line, not on-line. *Psychological Science, 21,* 484–488. (p. 364)

Strickland, B. (1992, February 20). *Gender differences in health and illness.* Sigma Xi national lecture delivered at Hope College. (p. 215)

Stroebe, M., Finenauer, C., Wijngaards-de Meij, L., Schut, H., van den Bout, J., & Stroebe, W. (2013). Partner-oriented self-regulation among bereaved parents: The costs of holding in grief for the partner's sake. *Psychological Science, 24,* 395–402. (p. 225)

Stroebe, W. (2012). The truth about Triplett (1898), but nobody seems to care. *Perspectives on Psychological Science, 7,* 54–57. (p. 532)

Stroebe, W. (2013). Firearm possession and violent death: A critical review. *Aggression and Violent Behavior, 18,* 709–721. (p. 545)

Stroebe, W., Schut, H., & Stroebe, M. S. (2005). Grief work, disclosure and counseling: Do they help the bereaved? *Clinical Psychology Review, 25,* 395–414. (p. 225)

Stross, R. (2011, July 9). The therapist will see you now, via the web. *New York Times* (www.nytimes.com). (p. 670)

Strully, K. W. (2009). Job loss and health in the U.S. labor market. *Demography, 46,* 221–246. (p. 490)

Strupp, H. H. (1986). Psychotherapy: Research, practice, and public policy (How to avoid dead ends). *American Psychologist, 41,* 120–130. (p. 678)

Stutzer, A., & Frey, B. S. (2006). Does marriage make people happy, or do happy people get married? *Journal of Socio-Economics, 35,* 326–347. (p. 479)

Su, R., Rounds, J., & Armstrong, P. I. (2009). Men and things, women and people: A meta-analysis of sex differences in interests. *Psychological Bulletin, 135,* 859–884. (p. 164)

Subiaul, F., Cantlon, J. F., Holloway, R. L., & Terrace, H. S. (2004). Cognitive imitation in rhesus macaques. *Science, 305,* 407–410. (p. 308)

Subotnik, R. F., Olszewski-Kubilius, P., & Worrell, F. C. (2011). Rethinking giftedness and gifted education: A proposed direction forward based on psychological science. *Psychological Science in the Public Interest, 12*(1), 3–54. (pp. 405, 409)

Subrahmanyam, K., & Greenfield, P. (2008). Online communication and adolescent relationships. *The Future of Children, 18,* 119–146. (p. 211)

Suddath, R. L., Christison, G. W., Torrey, E. F., Casanova, M. F., & Weinberger, D. R. (1990). Anatomical abnormalities in the brains of monozygotic twins discordant for schizophrenia. *New England Journal of Medicine, 322,* 789–794. (p. 644)

Sue, S. (2006). Research to address racial and ethnic disparities in mental health: Some lessons learned. In S. I. Donaldson, D. E. Berger, & K. Pezdek (Eds.), *Applied psychology: New frontiers and rewarding careers.* Mahwah, NJ: Erlbaum. (p. 680)

Suedfeld, P., & Mocellin, J. S. P. (1987). The The "sensed presence" in unusual environments. *Environment and Behavior, 19,* 33–52. (p. 124)

Sugaya, L., Hasin, D. S., Olfson, M., Lin, K-H, Grant, B. F., & Blanco, C. (2012). Child physical abuse and adult mental health: A national study. *Journal of Traumatic Stress, 25,* 384–392. (p. 200)

Suinn, R. M. (1997). Mental practice in sports psychology: Where have we been, Where do we go? *Clinical Psychology: Science and Practice, 4,* 189–207. (p. 382)

Sullivan, K. T., Pasch, L. A., Johnson, M. D., & Bradbury, T. N. (2010). Social support, problem solving, and the longitudinal course of newlywed marriage. *Journal of Personality and Social Psychology, 98,* 631–644. (p. 558)

Sullivan, P. F., Neale, M. C., & Kendler, K. S. (2000). Genetic epidemiology of major depression: Review and meta-analysis. *American Journal of Psychiatry, 157,* 1552–1562. (p. 632)

Suls, J. M., & Tesch, F. (1978). Students' preferences for information about their test performance: A social comparison study. *Journal of Experimental Social Psychology, 8,* 189–197. (p. 484)

Summers, M. (1996, December 9). Mister clean. *People Weekly,* pp. 139–142. (p. 609)

Sun, Q. I., Townsend, M. K., Okereke, O., Franco, O. H., Hu, F. B., & Grodstein, F. (2009). Adiposity and weight change in mid-life in relation to healthy survival after age 70 in women: Prospective cohort study. *British Medical Journal, 339,* b3796. (p. 430)

Sundet, J. M., Borren, I., & Tambs, K. (2008). The Flynn effect is partly caused by changing fertility patterns. *Intelligence, 36,* 183–191. (p. 397)

Sundie, J. M., Kenrick, D. T., Griskevicius, V., Tybur, J. M., Vohs, K. D., & Beal, D. J. (2011). Peacocks, Porsches, and Thorsten Veblen: Conspicuous consumption as a sexual signaling system. *Journal of Personality and Social Psychology, 100,* 664–680. (p. 149)

Sundstrom, E., De Meuse, K. P., & Futrell, D. (1990). Work teams: Applications and effectiveness. *American Psychologist, 45,* 120–133. (p. A-13)

Sunstein, C. R. (2007). On the divergent American reactions to terrorism and climate change. *Columbia Law Review, 107,* 503–557. (p. 360)

Suomi, S. J. (1986). Anxiety-like disorders in young nonhuman primates. In R. Gettleman (Ed.), *Anxiety disorders of childhood.* New York: Guilford Press. (p. 626)

Suppes, P. (1982). Quoted by R. H. Ennis, Children's ability to handle Piaget's propositional logic: A conceptual critique. In S. Modgil & C. Modgil (Eds.), *Jean Piaget: Consensus and controversy.* New York: Praeger. (p. 191)

Surgeon General. (1986). *The surgeon general's workshop on pornography and public health,* June 22–24. Report prepared by E. P. Mulvey & J. L. Haugaard and released by Office of the Surgeon General on August 4, 1986. (p. 547)

Surgeon General. (1999). *Mental health: A report of the surgeon general.* Rockville, MD: U.S. Department of Health and Human Services. (p. 616)

Surgeon General. (2012). *Preventing tobacco use among youth and young adults: A report of the Surgeon General.* Rockville, MD: Department of Health and Human Services, Office of the Surgeon General. (p. 128)

Susser, E. S. (1999). Life course cohort studies of schizophrenia. *Psychiatric Annals, 29,* 161–165. (p. 645)

Susser, E. S., Neugenbauer, R., Hoek, H. W., Brown, A. S., Lin, S., Labovitz, D., & Gorman, J. M. (1996). Schizophrenia after prenatal famine. *Archives of General Psychiatry, 53(1),* 25–31. (p. 643)

Sutcliffe, J. S. (2008). Insights into the pathogenesis of autism. *Science, 321,* 208–209. (p. 193)

Sutherland, A. (2006a). *Bitten and scratched: Life and lessons at the premier school for exotic animal trainers.* New York: Viking. (p. 279)

Sutherland, A. (2006b, June 25). What Shamu taught me about a happy marriage. *New York Times* (www.nytimes.com). (p. 279)

Sutin, A. R., Ferrucci, L., Zonderman, A. B., & Terracciano, A. (2011). Personality and obesity across the adult life span. *Journal of Personality and Social Psychology, 101,* 579–592. (p. 592)

Swami, V., et al. (2010). The attractive female body weight and female body dissatisfaction in 26 countries across 10 world regions: Results of the international body project I. *Personality and Social Psychology Bulletin, 36,* 309–325. (p. 652)

Swami, V., Henderson, G., Custance, D., & Tovée, M. J. (2011). A cross-cultural investigation of men's judgments of female body weight in Britain and Indonesia. *Journal of Cross-Cultural Psychology, 42,* 140–145. (p. 430)

Swann, W. B., Jr., Chang-Schneider, C., & McClarty, K. L. (2007). Do people's self-views matter: Self-concept and self-esteem in everyday life. *American Psychologist, 62,* 84–94. (p. 599)

Swart, H., Hewstone, M., Christ, O., & Voci, A. (2011). Affective mediators of intergroup contact: A three-wave longitudinal study in South Africa. *Journal of Personality and Social Psychology, 101,* 1221–1238. (p. 564)

Sweat, J. A., & Durm, M. W. (1993). Psychics: Do police departments really use them? *Skeptical Inquirer, 17,* 148–158. (p. 272)

Sweeny, K., & Krizan, Z. (2013). Sobering up: A quantitative review of temporal declines in expectations. *Psychological Bulletin, 139,* 702–724. (p. 600)

Swerdlow, N. R., & Koob, G. F. (1987). Dopamine, schizophrenia, mania, and depression: Toward a unified hypothesis of cortico-stiato-pallido-thalamic function (with commentary). *Behavioral and Brain Sciences, 10,* 197–246. (p. 642)

Swim, J. K. (1994). Perceived versus meta-analytic effect sizes: An assessment of the accuracy of gender stereotypes. *Journal of Personality and Social Psychology, 66,* 21–36. (p. 540)

Symbaluk, D. G., Heth, C. D., Cameron, J., & Pierce, W. D. (1997). Social modeling, monetary incentives, and pain endurance: The role of self-efficacy and pain perception. *Personality and Social Psychology Bulletin, 23,* 258–269. (p. 263)

Symond, M. B., Harris, A. W. F., Gordon, E., & Williams, L. M. (2005). "Gamma synchrony" in first-episode schizophrenia: A disorder of temporal connectivity? *American Journal of Psychiatry, 162,* 459–465. (p. 642)

Symons, C. S., & Johnson, B. T. (1997). The self-reference effect in memory: A meta-analysis. *Psychological Bulletin, 121(3),* 371–394. (p. 327)

Tadmor, C. T., Galinsky, A. D., & Maddux, W. W. (2012). Getting the most out of living abroad: Biculturalism and integrative complexity as key drivers of creative and professional success. *Journal of Personality and Social Psychology, 103,* 520–542. (p. 367)

Taha, F. A. (1972). A comparative study of how sighted and blind perceive the manifest content of dreams. *National Review of Social Sciences, 9(3),* 28 (p. 112)

Taheri, S. (2004a, 20 December). Does the lack of sleep make you fat? *University of Bristol Research News* (www.bristol.ac.uk). (p. 431)

Taheri, S., Lin, L., Austin, D., Young, T., & Mignot, E. (2004b). Short sleep duration is associated with reduced leptin, elevated ghrelin, and increased body mass index. *PloS Medicine, 1(3),* e62. (p. 431)

Taheri, S., Zeitzer, J. M., & Mignot, E. (2002). The role of hypocretins (orexins) in sleep regulation and narcolepsy. *Annual Review of Neuroscience, 25,* 283–313. (p. 110)

Tajfel, H. (Ed.). (1982). *Social identity and intergroup relations.* New York: Cambridge University Press. (p. 542)

Talarico, J. M., & Moore, K. M. (2012). Memories of 'the rivalry': Differences in how fans of the winning and losing teams remember the same game. *Applied Cognitive Psychology, 26,* 746–756. (p. 332)

Talbot, M. (1999, October). The Rorschach Chronicles. *New York Times.* www.nytimes.com. (p. 578)

Talhelm, T., Zhang, X., Oishi, S., Shimin, C., Duan, D., Lan, X., & Kitayama, S. (2014). Large-scale psychological differences within China explained by rice versus wheat agriculture. *Science, 344,* 603–608. (p. 158)

Talwar, S. K., Xu, S., Hawley, E. S., Weiss, S. A., Moxon, K. A., & Chapin, J. K. (2002). Rat navigation guided by remote control. *Nature, 417,* 37–38. (p. 72)

Tamres, L. K., Janicki, D., & Helgeson, V. S. (2002). Sex differences in coping behavior: A meta-analytic review and an examination of relative coping. *Personality and Social Psychology Review, 6,* 2–30. (p. 164)

Tang, S-H., & Hall, V. C. (1995). The overjustification effect: A meta-analysis. *Applied Cognitive Psychology, 9,* 365–404. (p. 305)

Tangney, C. C., Kwasny, M. J., Li, H., Wilson, R. S., Evans, D. A., & Morris, M. C. (2011). Adherence to a Mediterranean-type dietary pattern and cognitive decline in a community population. *American Journal of Clinical Nutrition, 93,* 601–607. (p. 634)

Tannen, D. (1990). *You just don't understand: Women and men in conversation.* New York: Morrow. (p. 163)

Tannen, D. (2001). *You just don't understand: Women and men in conversation.* New York: Harper. (p. 8)

Tannenbaum, P. (2002, February). Quoted in R. Kubey & M. Csikszentmihalyi, Television addiction is no mere metaphor. *Scientific American,* pp. 74–80. (p. 234)

Tanner, J. M. (1978). *Fetus into man: Physical growth from conception to maturity.* Cambridge, MA: Harvard University Press. (p. 166)

Tardif, T., Fletcher, P., Liang, W., Zhang, Z., Kaciroti, N., & Marchman, V. A. (2008). Baby's first 10 words. *Developmental Psychology, 44,* 929–938. (p. 372)

Tarrant, M., Branscombe, N. R., Warner, R. H., & Weston, D. (2012). Social identity and perceptions of torture: It's moral when we do it. *Journal of Experimental Social Psychology, 48,* 513–518. (p. 563)

Tasbihsazan, R., Nettelbeck, T., & Kirby, N. (2003). Predictive validity of the Fagan test of infant intelligence. *British Journal of Developmental Psychology, 21,* 585–597. (p. 401)

Taub, E. (2004). Harnessing brain plasticity through behavioral techniques to produce new treatments in neurorehabilitation. *American Psychologist, 59,* 692–698. (p. 81)

Taubes, G. (2001). The soft science of dietary fat. *Science, 291,* 2536–2545. (p. 432)

Taubes, G. (2002, July 7). What if it's all been a big fat lie? *New York Times* (www.nytimes.com). (p. 432)

Tausch, N., Hewstone, M., Kenworthy, J. B., Psaltis, C., Schmid, K., Popan, J. R., Cairns, E., & Hughes, J. (2010). Secondary transfer effects of intergroup contact: Alternative accounts and underlying processes. *Journal of Personality and Social Psychology, 99,* 282–302. (p. 563)

Tavernier, R., & Willoughby, T. (2014). Bidirectional associations between sleep (quality and duration) and psychosocial functioning across the university years. *Developmental Psychology, 50,* 674–682. (p. 107)

Tavris, C. (1982, November). Anger defused. *Psychology Today,* pp. 25–35. (p. 478)

Tavris, C., & Aronson, E. (2007). *Mistakes were made (but not by me).* Orlando, FL: Harcourt. (p. 342)

Tay, L., & Diener, E. (2011). Needs and subjective well-being around the world. *Journal of Personality and Social Psychology, 101,* 354–365. (pp. 423, 482)

Taylor, C. A., Manganello, J. A., Lee, S. J., & Rice, J. C. (2010). Mothers' spanking of 3-year-old children and subsequent risk of children's aggressive behavior. *Pediatrics, 125,* 1057–1065. (p. 296)

Taylor, K., & Rohrer, D. (2010). The effects of interleaved practice. *Applied Cognitive Psychology, 24,* 837–848. (p. 15)

Taylor, P. J., Gooding, P., Wood, A. M., & Tarrier, N. (2011). The role of defeat and entrapment in depression, anxiety, and suicide. *Psychological Bulletin, 137,* 391–420. (p. 638)

Taylor, P. J., Russ-Eft, D. F., & Chan, D. W. L. (2005). A meta-analytic review of behavior modeling training. *Journal of Applied Psychology, 90,* 692–709. (p. 310)

Taylor, S. (2011). Etiology of obsessions and compulsions: A meta-analysis and narrative review of twin studies. *Clinical Psychology Review, 31,* 1361–1372. (p. 623)

Taylor, S. (2013). Molecular genetics of obsessive-compulsive disorder: A comprehensive meta-analysis of genetic association studies. *Molecular Psychiatry, 18,* 799–805. (p. 626)

Taylor, S., Kuch, K., Koch, W. J., Crockett, D. J., & Passey, G. (1998). The structure of posttraumatic stress symptoms. *Journal of Abnormal Psychology, 107,* 154–160. (p. 623)

Taylor, S. E. (1989). *Positive illusions*. New York: Basic Books. (p. 603)

Taylor, S. E. (2002). *The tending instinct: How nurturing is essential to who we are and how we live*. New York: Times Books. (p. 164)

Taylor, S. E. (2006). Tend and befriend: Biobehavioral bases of affiliation under stress. *Current Directions in Psychological Science, 15*, 273–277. (p. 492)

Taylor, S. E., Cousino, L. K., Lewis, B. P., Gruenewald, T. L., Gurung, R. A. R., & Updegraff, J. A. (2000). Biobehavioral responses to stress in females: Tend-and-befriend, not fight-or-flight. *Psychological Review, 107*, 411–430. (p. 492)

Taylor, S. E., Pham, L. B., Rivkin, I. D., & Armor, D. A. (1998). Harnessing the imagination: Mental simulation, self-regulation, and coping. *American Psychologist, 53*, 429–439. (p. 382)

Taylor, S. P., & Chermack, S. T. (1993). Alcohol, drugs and human physical aggression. *Journal of Studies on Alcohol,* Supplement No. 11, 78–88. (p. 546)

Taylor, V. J., & Walton, G. M. (2011). Stereotype threat undermines academic learning. *Personality and Social Psychology Bulletin, 37*, 1055–1067. (p. 414)

Teachman, B. A. (2014). No appointment necessary: Treating mental illness outside the therapist's office. *Perspectives on Psychological Science, 9*, 85–87. (p. 670)

Teasdale, T. W., & Owen, D. R. (2005). A long-term rise and recent decline in intelligence test performance: The Flynn effect in reverse. *Personality and Individual Differences, 39*, 837–843. (p. 396)

Teasdale, T. W., & Owen, D. R. (2008). Secular declines in cognitive test scores: A reversal of the Flynn effect. *Intelligence, 36*, 121–126. (p. 396)

Tedeschi, R. G., & Calhoun, L. G. (2004). Posttraumatic growth: Conceptual foundations and empirical evidence. *Psychological Inquiry, 15*, 1–18. (p. 691)

Teghtsoonian, R. (1971). On the exponents in Stevens' law and the constant in Ekinan's law. *Psychological Review, 78*, 71–80. (p. 233)

Teicher, M. H. (2002, March). The neurobiology of child abuse. *Scientific American*, pp. 68–75. (p. 200)

Teller. (2009, April 20). Quoted by J. Lehrer, Magic and the brain: Teller reveals the neuroscience of illusion. *Wired Magazine* (www.wired.com) (p. 98)

Telzer, E. H., Flannery, J., Shapiro, M., Humphreys, K. L., Goff, B., Gabard-Durman, L., Gee, D. D., & Tottenham, N. (2013). Early experience shapes amygdala sensitivity to race: An international adoption design. *The Journal of Neuroscience, 33*, 13484–13488. (p. 544)

Tenenbaum, H. R., & Leaper, C. (2002). Are parents' gender schemas related to their children's gender-related cognitions? A meta-analysis. *Developmental Psychology, 38*, 615–630. (p. 169)

Tenopyr, M. L. (1997). Improving the workplace: Industrial/organizational psychology as a career. In R. J. Sternberg (Ed.), *Career paths in psychology: Where your degree can take you*. Washington, DC: American Psychological Association. (p. A-3)

Tepper, S. J. (2000). Fiction reading in America: Explaining the gender gap. *Poetics, 27*, 255–275. (p. 471)

Terao, T., Ohgami, H., Shlotsuki, I., Ishil, N., & Iwata, N. (2010). Author's reply. *British Journal of Psychiatry, 196*, 160. (p. 685)

Terman, J. S., Terman, M., Lo, E-S., & Cooper, T. B. (2001). Circadian time of morning light administration and therapeutic response in winter depression. *Archives of General Psychiatry, 58*, 69–73. (p. 678)

Terman, L. M. (1916). *The measurement of intelligence*. Boston: Houghton Mifflin. (p. 394)

Terman, M., Terman, J. S., & Ross, D. C. (1998). A controlled trial of timed bright light and negative air ionization for treatment of winter depression. *Archives of General Psychiatry, 55*, 875–882. (p. 678)

Terracciano, A., Costa, P. T., Jr., & McCrae, R. R. (2006). Personality plasticity after age 30. *Personality and Social Psychology Bulletin, 32*, 999–1009. (p. 160)

Terrace, H. S. (1979, November). How Nim Chimpsky changed my mind. *Psychology Today*, pp. 65–76. (p. 378)

Terre, L., & Stoddart, R. (2000). Cutting edge specialties for graduate study in psychology. *Eye on Psi Chi, 23*–26. (p. B-1)

Tesser, A., Forehand, R., Brody, G., & Long, N. (1989). Conflict: The role of calm and angry parent-child discussion in adolescent development. *Journal of Social and Clinical Psychology, 8*, 317–330. (p. 210)

Tetlock, P. E. (1988). Monitoring the integrative complexity of American and Soviet policy rhetoric: What can be learned? *Journal of Social Issues, 44*, 101–131. (p. 567)

Tetlock, P. E. (1998). Close-call counterfactuals and belief-system defenses: I was not almost wrong but I was almost right. *Journal of Personality and Social Psychology, 75*, 639–652. (p. 21)

Tetlock, P. E. (2005). *Expert political judgement: How good is it? How can we know?* Princeton, NJ: Princeton University Press. (p. 21)

Thaler, R. H., & Sunstein, C. R. (2008). *Nudge: Improving decisions about health, wealth, and happiness*. New Haven, CT: Yale University Press. (p. 363)

Thannickal, T. C., Moore, R. Y., Nienhuis, R., Ramanathan, L., Gulyani, S., Aldrich, M., Cornford, M., & Siegel, J. M. (2000). Reduced number of hypocretin neurons in human narcolepsy. *Neuron, 27*, 469–474. (p. 110)

Thatcher, R. W., Walker, R. A., & Giudice, S. (1987). Human cerebral hemispheres develop at different rates and ages. *Science, 236*, 1110–1113. (pp. 178, 185)

Thayer, R. E. (1987). Energy, tiredness, and tension effects of a sugar snack versus moderate exercise. *Journal of Personality and Social Psychology, 52*, 119–125. (p. 509)

Thayer, R. E. (1993). Mood and behavior (smoking and sugar snacking) following moderate exercise: A partial test of self-regulation theory. *Personality and Individual Differences, 14*, 97–104. (p. 509)

Théoret, H., Halligan, H., Kobayashi, M., Fregni, F., Tager-Flusberg, H., & Pascual-Leone, A. (2005). Impaired motor facilitation during action observation in individuals with autism spectrum disorder. *Current Biology, 15*, R84–R85. (p. 194)

Thernstrom, M. (2006, May 14). My pain, my brain. *New York Times* (www.nytimes.com). (p. 264)

Thiel, A., Hadedank, B., Herholz, K., Kessler, J., Winhuisen, L., Haupt, W. F., & Heiss, W-D. (2006). From the left to the right: How the brain compensates progressive loss of language function. *Brain and Language, 98*, 57–65. (p. 82)

Thiele, T. E., Marsh, D. J., Ste. Marie, L., Bernstein, I. L., & Palmiter, R. D. (1998). Ethanol consumption and resistance are inversely related to neuropeptide Y levels. *Nature, 396*, 366–369. (p. 127)

Thomas, A., & Chess, S. (1977). *Temperament and development*. New York: Brunner/Mazel. (p. 140)

Thomas, A., & Chess, S. (1986). The New York Longitudinal Study: From infancy to early adult life. In R. Plomin & J. Dunn (Eds.), *The study of temperament: Changes, continuities, and challenges*. Hillsdale, NJ: Erlbaum. (p. 180)

Thomas, L. (1974). *The lives of a cell*. New York: Viking Press. (p. 268)

Thomas, L. (1983). *The youngest science: Notes of a medicine watcher*. New York: Viking Press. (p. 58)

Thomas, L. (1992). *The fragile species*. New York: Scribner's. (pp. 173, 374, 674)

Thompson, G. (2010). The $1 million dollar challenge. *Skeptic Magazine, 15*, 8–9. (p. 274)

Thompson, J. K., Jarvie, G. J., Lahey, B. B., & Cureton, K. J. (1982). Exercise and obesity: Etiology, physiology, and intervention. *Psychological Bulletin, 91*, 55–79. (p. 432)

Thompson, P. M., Cannon, T. D., Narr, K. L., van Erp, T., Poutanen, V-P., Huttunen, M., . . . Toga, A. W. (2001). Genetic influences on brain structure. *Nature Neuroscience, 4*, 1253–1258. (p. 406)

Thompson, P. M., Giedd, J. N., Woods, R. P., MacDonald, D., Evans, A. C., & Toga, A. W. (2000). Growth patterns in the developing brain detected by using continuum mechanical tensor maps. *Nature, 404*, 190–193. (p. 185)

Thompson, R., Emmorey, K., & Gollan, T. H. (2005). "Tip of the fingers" experiences by Deaf signers. *Psychological Science, 16*, 856–860. (p. 341)

Thomson, R., & Murachver, T. (2001). Predicting gender from electronic discourse. *British Journal of Social Psychology, 40*, 193–208 (and personal correspondence from T. Murachver, May 23, 2002). (p. 163)

Thorndike, E. L. (1898). Animal intelligence: An experimental study of the associative processes in animals. *Psychological Review Monograph Supplement 2*, 4–160. (p. 290)

Thorne, J., with Rothstein, L. (1993). *You are not alone: Words of experience and hope for the journey through depression*. New York: HarperPerennial. (p. 609)

Thornhill, R., & Gangestad, S. W. (1994). Human fluctuating asymmetry and sexual behavior. *Psychological Science, 5*, 297–302. (p. 555)

Thornton, B., & Moore, S. (1993). Physical attractiveness contrast effect: Implications for self-esteem and evaluations of the social self. *Personality and Social Psychology Bulletin, 19*, 474–480. (p. 554)

Thorpe, W. H. (1974). *Animal nature and human nature*. London: Metheun. (p. 379)

Tickle, J. J., Hull, J. G., Sargent, J. D., Dalton, M. A., & Heatherton, T. F. (2006). A structural equation model of social influences and exposure to media smoking on adolescent smoking. *Basic and Applied Social Psychology, 28*, 117–129. (p. 128)

Tiedens, L. Z. (2001). Anger and advancement versus sadness and subjugation: The effect of negative emotion expressions on social status conferral. *Journal of Personality and Social Psychology, 80*, 86–94. (p. 478)

Tiggemann, M., & Miller, J. (2010). The Internet and adolescent girls' weight satisfaction and drive for thinness. *Sex Roles, 63*, 79–90. (p. 652)

Tiihonen, J., Lönnqvist, J., Wahlbeck, K., Klaukka, T., Niskanen, L., Tanskanen, A., Haukka, J. (2009). 11-year follow-up of mortality in patients with schizophrenia: A population-based cohort study (FIN11 study). *Lancet, 374*, 260–267. (p. 682)

Time. (2009, Oct. 14). The state of the American woman. pp. 32–33. (p. 164)

Time/CNN Survey. (1994, December 19). Vox pop: Happy holidays, *Time.* (p. 630)

Timmerman, T. A. (2007). "It was a thought pitch": Personal, situational, and target influences on hit-by-pitch events across time. *Journal of Applied Psychology, 92*, 876–884. (p. 547)

Tinbergen, N. (1951). *The study of instinct.* Oxford: Clarendon. (p. 420)

Tirrell, M. E. (1990). Personal communication. (p. 285)

Tobin, D. D., Menon, M., Menon, M., Spatta, B. C., Hodges, E. V. E., & Perry, D. G. (2010). The intrapsychics of gender: A model of self-socialization. *Psychological Review, 117*, 601–622. (p. 168)

Toews, P. (2004, December 30). *Dirk Willems: A heart undivided.* Mennonite Brethren Historical Commission (www.mbhistory.org/profiles/dirk.en.html). (p. 517)

Tolin, D. F. (2010). Is cognitive-behavioral therapy more effective than other therapies? A meta-analytic review. *Clinical psychology Review, 30*, 710–720. (p. 676)

Tolin, D. F., Stevens, M. C., Villavicencio, A. L., et al. (2012). Neural mechanisms of decision making in hoarding disorder. *Archives of General Psychiatry, 69*, 832–841. (p. 626)

Tolman, E. C., & Honzik, C. H. (1930). Introduction and removal of reward, and maze performance in rats. *University of California Publications in Psychology, 4*, 257–275. (p. 305)

Tolstoy, L. (1904). *My confessions.* Boston: Dana Estes. (p. 13)

Toma, C., & Hancock, J. (2013). Self-affirmation underlies Facebook use. *Personality and Social Psychology Bulletin, 369*, 321–331. (p. 599)

Tomaka, J., Blascovich, J., & Kelsey, R. M. (1992). Effects of self-deception, social desirability, and repressive coping on psychophysiological reactivity to stress. *Personality and Social Psychology Bulletin, 18*, 616–624. (p. 602)

Toni, N., Buchs, P.-A., Nikonenko, I., Bron, C. R., & Muller, D. (1999). LTP promotes formation of multiple spine synapses between a single axon terminal and a dendrite. *Nature, 402*, 421–442. (p. 332)

Tononi, G., & Cirelli, C. (2013, August). Perchance to prune. *Scientific American*, pp. 34–39. (p. 105)

Topolinski, S., & Reber, R. (2010). Gaining insight into the "aha" experience. *Current Directions in Psychological Science, 19*, 401–405. (p. 357)

Torrey, E. F. (1986). *Witchdoctors and psychiatrists.* New York: Harper & Row. (p. 679)

Torrey, E. F., & Miller, J. (2002). *The invisible plague: The rise of mental illness from 1750 to the present.* New Brunswick, NJ: Rutgers University Press. (p. 643)

Torrey, E. F., Miller, J., Rawlings, R., & Yolken, R. H. (1997). Seasonality of births in schizophrenia and bipolar disorder: A review of the literature. *Schizophrenia Research, 28*, 1–38. (p. 643)

Totterdell, P., Kellett, S., Briner, R. B., & Teuchmann, K. (1998). Evidence of mood linkage in work groups. *Journal of Personality and Social Psychology, 74*, 1504–1515. (p. 525)

Tracy, J. L., Cheng, J. T., Robins, R. W., & Trzesniewski, K. H. (2009). Authentic and hubristic pride: The affective core of self-esteem and narcissism. *Self and Identity, 8*, 196–213. (p. 603)

Tracy, J. L., & Robins, R. W. (2004). Show your pride: Evidence for a discrete emotion expression. *Psychological Science, 15*, 194–197. (p. 476)

Tracy, J. L., Shariff, A. F., Zhao, W., & Henrich, J. (2013). Cross-cultural evidence that the nonverbal expression of pride is an automatic status signal. *Journal of Experimental Psychology: General, 142*, 163–180. (p. 469)

Trautwein, U., Lüdtke, O., Köller, O., & Baumert, J. (2006). Self-esteem, academic self-concept, and achievement: How the learning environment moderates the dynamics of self-concept. *Journal of Personality and Social Psychology, 90*, 334–349. (p. 599)

Treffert, D. A., & Christensen, D. D. (2005, December). Inside the mind of a savant. *Scientific American*, pp. 108–113. (p. 388)

Treffert, D. A., & Wallace, G. L. (2002). Island of genius—The artistic brilliance and dazzling memory that sometimes accompany autism and other disorders hint at how all brains work. *Scientific American, 286*, 76–86. (p. 387)

Treisman, A. (1987). Properties, parts, and objects. In K. R. Boff, L. Kaufman, & J. P. Thomas (Eds.), *Handbook of perception and human performance.* New York: Wiley. (p. 248)

Tremblay, R. E., Pihl, R. O., Vitaro, F., & Dobkin, P. L. (1994). Predicting early onset of male antisocial behavior from preschool behavior. *Archives of General Psychiatry, 51*, 732–739. (p. 650)

Triandis, H. C. (1981). *Some dimensions of intercultural variation and their implications for interpersonal behavior.* Paper presented at the American Psychological Association convention. (p. 156)

Triandis, H. C. (1994). *Culture and social behavior.* New York: McGraw-Hill. (pp. 158, 547)

Triandis, H. C., Bontempo, R., Villareal, M. J., Asai, M., & Lucca, N. (1988). Individualism and collectivism: Cross-cultural perspectives on self-ingroup relationships. *Journal of Personality and Social Psychology, 54*, 323–338. (p. 159)

Trickett, E. (2009). Community psychology: Individuals and interventions in community context. *Annual Review of Psychology, 60*, 395–419. (p. 12)

Trickett, P. K., Noll, J. G., & Putnam, F. W. (2011). The impact of sexual abuse on female development: Lessons from a multigenerational, longitudinal research study. *Development and Psychopathology, 23*, 453–476. (p. 200)

Trillin, C. (2006, March 27). Alice off the page. *The New Yorker*, p. 44. (p. 584)

Triplett, N. (1898). The dynamogenic factors in pacemaking and competition. *American Journal of Psychology, 9*, 507–533. (p. 532)

Trotter, J. (2014). The power of positive coaching. *Sports Illustrated* (www.mmqb.si.com). (p. A-11)

Trut, L. N. (1999). Early canid domestication: The farm-fox experiment. *American Scientist, 87*, 160–169. (p. 145)

Tsai, J. L., & Chentsova-Dutton, Y. (2003). Variation among European Americans in emotional facial expression. *Journal of Cross-Cultural Psychology, 34*, 650–657. (p. 474)

Tsai, J. L., Miao, F. F., Seppala, E., Fung, H. H., & Yeung, D. Y. (2007). Influence and adjustment goals: Sources of cultural differences in ideal affect. *Journal of Personality and Social Psychology, 92*, 1102–1117. (p. 474)

Tsang, Y. C. (1938). Hunger motivation in gastrectomized rats. *Journal of Comparative Psychology, 26*, 1–17. (p. 425)

Tsankova, N., Renthal, W., Kumar, A., & Nestler, E. J. (2007). Epigenetic regulation in psychiatric disorders. *Nature Reviews Neuroscience, 8*, 355–367. (p. 142)

Tse, D., Langston, R. F., Kakeyama, M., Bethus, I., Spooner P. A., Wood, E. R., Witter, M. P., & Morris, R. G. M. (2007). Schemas and memory consolidation. *Science, 316*, 76–82. (p. 330)

Tsuang, M. T., & Faraone, S. V. (1990). *The genetics of mood disorders.* Baltimore, MD: Johns Hopkins University Press. (p. 633)

Tsvetkova, M., & Macy, M. W. (2014). The social contagion of generosity. *PLoS ONE, 9*(2), e87275. (p. 561)

Tuber, D. S., Miller, D. D., Caris, K. A., Halter, R., Linden, F., & Hennessy, M. B. (1999). Dogs in animal shelters: Problems, suggestions, and needed expertise. *Psychological Science, 10*, 379–386. (p. 40)

Tucker-Drob, E. (2012). Preschools reduce early academic-achievement gaps: A longitudinal twin approach. *Psychological Science, 23*, 310–319. (p. 409)

Tucker-Drob, E. M., Rhemtulla, M., Harden, K. P., Turkheimer, E., & Fask, D. (2011). Emergence of a gene × socioeconomic status interaction on infant mental ability between 10 months and 2 years. *Psychological Science, 22*, 125–133. (p. 406)

Tucker, K. A. (2002). I believe you can fly. *Gallup Management Journal* (www.gallupjournal.com/CA/st/20020520.asp). (p. A-10)

Tuerk, P. W. (2005). Research in the high-stakes era: Achievement, resources, and No Child Left Behind. *Psychological Science, 16*, 419–425. (p. 408)

Tully, T. (2003). Reply: The myth of a myth. *Current Biology, 13*, R426. (p. 283)

Turkheimer, E., Haley, A., Waldron, M., D'Onofrio, B., & Gottesman, I. I. (2003). Socioeconomic status modifies heritability of IQ in young children. *Psychological Science, 14*, 623–628. (p. 406)

Turner, J. C. (1987). *Rediscovering the social group: A self-categorization theory.* New York: Basil Blackwell. (p. 542)

Turner, J. C. (2007) Self-categorization theory. In R. Baumeister & K. Vohs (Eds.), *Encyclopedia of social psychology.* Thousand Oaks, CA: Sage. (p. 542)

Turner, N., Barling, J., & Zacharatos, A. (2002). Positive psychology at work. In C. R. Snyder & S. J. Lopez (Eds.), *The handbook of positive psychology.* New York: Oxford University Press. (p. A-12)

Turpin, A. (2005, April 3). The science of psi. *FT Weekend*, pp. W1, W2. (p. 272)

Tuvblad, C., Narusyte, J., Grann, M., Sarnecki, J., & Lichtenstein, P. (2011). The genetic and environmental etiology of antisocial behavior from childhood to emerging adulthood. *Behavior Genetics, 41*, 629–640. (p. 649)

Tversky, A. (1985, June). Quoted in K. McKean, Decisions, decisions. *Discover*, pp. 22–31. (p. 359)

Tversky, A., & Kahneman, D. (1974). Judgment under uncertainty: Heuristics and biases. *Science, 185*, 1124–1131. (pp. 34, 359)

Tversky, B. (2008, June/July). Glimpses of Chinese psychology: Reflections on the APS trip to China. *Observer*, pp. 13–14 (also at psychologicalscience.org/observer). (p. 6)

Twenge, J. M. (2001). Birth cohort changes in extraversion: A cross-temporal meta-analysis, 1966–1993. *Personality and Individual Differences, 30*, 735–748. (p. 591)

Twenge, J. M. (2006). *Generation me*. New York: Free Press. (p. 604)

Twenge, J. M., Abebe, E. M., & Campbell, W. K. (2010). Fitting in or standing out: Trends in American parents' choices for children's names, 1880–2007. *Social Psychology and Personality Science, 1*, 19–25. (pp. 158, 159)

Twenge, J. M., Baumeister, R. F., DeWall, C. N., Ciarocco, N. J., & Bartels, J. M. (2007). Social exclusion decreases prosocial behavior. *Journal of Personality and Social Psychology, 92*, 56–66. (p. 451)

Twenge, J. M., Baumeister, R. F., Tice, D. M., & Stucke, T. S. (2001). If you can't join them, beat them: Effects of social exclusion on aggressive behavior. *Journal of Personality and Social Psychology, 81*, 1058–1069. (p. 451)

Twenge, J. M., & Campbell, W. K. (2008). Increases in positive self-views among high school students: Birth-cohort changes in anticipated performance, self-satisfaction, self-liking, and self-competence. *Psychological Science, 19*, 1082–1086. (p. 585)

Twenge, J. M., Campbell, W. K., & Freeman, E. C. (2012). Generational differences in young adults' life goals, concern for others, and civic orientation, 1966-2009. *Journal of Personality and Social Psychology, 102*, 1045–1062. (pp. 159, 604)

Twenge, J. M., Campbell, W. K., & Gentile, B. (2013). Changes in pronoun use in American books and the rise of individualism, 1960–2008. *Journal of Cross-Cultural Psychology, 44*, 406–415. (p. 604)

Twenge, J. M., Catanese, K. R., & Baumeister, R. F. (2002). Social exclusion causes self-defeating behavior. *Journal of Personality and Social Psychology, 83*, 606–615. (p. 451)

Twenge, J. M., & Foster, J. D. (2010). Birth cohort increases in narcissistic personality traits among American college students, 1982–2009. *Social Psychological and Personality Science, 1*, 99–106. (p. 604)

Twenge, J. M., Gentile, B., DeWall, C. D., Ma, D., & Lacefield, K. (2008). *A growing disturbance: Increasing psychopathology in young people 1938-2007 in a meta-analysis of the MMPI*. Unpublished manuscript, San Diego State University. (p. 632)

Twenge, J. M., Gentile, B., DeWall, C. N., Ma, D., Lacefield, K., & Schurtz, D. R. (2010). Birth cohort increases in psychopathology among young Americans, 1938–2007: A cross-temporal meta-analysis of the MMPI. *Clinical Psychology Review, 30*, 145–154. (p. 503)

Twenge, J. M., Zhang, L., & Im, C. (2004). It's beyond my control: A cross-temporal meta-analysis of increasing externality in locus of control, 1960-2002. *Personality and Social Psychology Review, 8*, 308–319. (p. 503)

Twiss, C., Tabb, S., & Crosby, F. (1989). Affirmative action and aggregate data: The importance of patterns in the perception of discrimination. In F. Blanchard & F. Crosby (Eds.), *Affirmative action: Social psychological perspectives*. New York: Springer-Verlag. (p. 32)

Uchida, Y., & Kitayama, S. (2009). Happiness and unhappiness in East and West: Themes and variations. *Emotion, 9*, 441–456. (p. 485)

Uchino, B. N. (2009). Understanding the links between social support and physical health. *Perspectives on Psychological Science, 4*, 236–255. (p. 505)

Uchino, B. N., Cacioppo, J. T., & Kiecolt-Glaser, J. K. (1996). The relationship between social support and physiological processes: A review with emphasis on underlying mechanisms and implications for health. *Psychological Bulletin, 119*, 488–531. (p. 506)

Uchino, B. N., Uno, D., & Holt-Lunstad, J. (1999). Social support, physiological processes, and health. *Current Directions in Psychological Science, 8*, 145–148. (p. 506)

Udry, J. R. (2000). Biological limits of gender construction. *American Sociological Review, 65*, 443–457. (p. 165)

Uga, V., Lemut, M. C., Zampi, C., Zilli, I., & Salzarulo, P. (2006). Music in dreams. *Consciousness and Cognition, 15*, 351–357. (p. 112)

Ugander, J., Backstrom, L., Marlow, C., & Kleinberg, J. (2012). Structural diversity in social contagion. *Proceedings of the National Academy of Sciences, 109*, 5962–5966. (p. 452)

Uher, R., & McGuffin, P. (2010). The moderation by the serotonin transporter gene of environmental adversity in the etiology of depression: 2009 update. *Molecular Psychiatry, 15*, 18–22. (p. 634)

Ulrich, R. E. (1991). Animal rights, animal wrongs and the question of balance. *Psychological Science, 2*, 197–201. (p. 40)

UNAIDS. (2005). *AIDS epidemic update, December 2005*. United Nations (www.unaids.org). (p. 495)

UNAIDS. (2010). *UNAIDS report on the global AIDS epidemic 2010*. www.unaids.org. (p. 495)

UNAIDS. (2013). *UNAIDS report on the global AIDS epidemic 2013*. www.UNAIDS.org. (pp. 436, 495)

Underwood, E. (2013). Short-circuiting depression. *Science, 342*, 548–551. (p. 687)

UNESCO. (2013, September). *Adult and youth literacy*. UIS Fact Sheet No. 26, UNESCO Institute for Statistics. United Nations Education, Scientific and Cultural Organization. (p. 540)

Ungerleider, S. (2005). *Mental training for peak performance, revised & updated edition*. New York: Rodale. (p. 382)

United Nations. (2001). *World population ageing: 1950–2050*. United Nations (www.un.org). (p. 215)

United Nations. (2010). Chapter 8, Poverty, in *The world's women: Trends and Statistics*. New York: United Nations. (p. 540)

United Nations. (2010). *The ageing of the world's population*. United Nations (www.un.org). (p. 215)

United Nations. (2011, November 17). *Discriminatory laws and practices and acts of violence against individuals based on their sexual orientation and gender identity*. Report of the United Nations High Commissioner for Human Rights. (p. 540)

Unsworth, N., & Engle, R. W. (2007). The nature of individual differences in working memory capacity: Active maintenance in primary memory and controlled search from secondary memory. *Psychological Review, 114*, 104–132. (p. 324)

Urbina, I. (2010, May 29). Documents show early worries about safety of rig. *New York Times* (www.nytimes.com). (p. 361)

Urry, H. L., & Gross, J. J. (2010). Emotion regulation in older age. *Current Directions in Psychological Science, 19*, 352–357. (p. 223)

Urry, H. L., Nitschke, J. B., Dolski, I., Jackson, D. C., Dalton, K. M., Mueller, C. J., . . . Davidson, R. J. (2004). Making a life worth living: Neural correlates of well-being. *Psychological Science, 15*, 367–372. (p. 467)

U.S. Senate Select Committee on Intelligence (2004, July 9). *Report of the U.S. intelligence community's prewar intelligence assessments on Iraq*. www.gpoaccess.gov/serialset/creports/iraq.html. (p. 26)

Uttal, W. R. (2001). *The new phrenology: The limits of localizing cognitive processes in the brain*. Cambridge, MA: MIT Press. (p. 81)

Vacic, V., et al. (2011). Duplications of the neuropeptide receptor gene VIPR2 confer significant risk for schizophrenia. *Nature, 471*, 499–503. (p. 644)

Vaillant, G. E. (1977). *Adaptation to life*. New York: Little, Brown. (p. 347)

Vaillant, G. E. (2002). *Aging well: Surprising guideposts to a happier life from the landmark Harvard study of adult development*. Boston: Little, Brown. (p. 505)

Vaillant, G. (2013, May). What makes us happy, revisited? *The Atlantic*, Washington, D.C. (p. 451)

Valenstein, E. S. (1986). *Great and desperate cures: The rise and decline of psychosurgery*. New York: Basic Books. (p. 687)

Valentine, K. A., Li, N. P., Penke, L., & Perrett, D. I. (2014). Judging a man by the width of his face: The role of facial ratios and dominance in mate choice at speed-dating events. *Psychological Science, 25*, 806–811. (p. 546)

Valkenburg, P. M., & Peter, J. (2009). Social consequences of the Internet for adolescents: A decade of research. *Current Directions in Psychological Science, 18*, 1–5 (pp. 211, 452, 453)

van Anders, S. M. (2012). Testosterone and sexual desire in healthy women and men. *Archives of Sexual Behavior, 41*, 1471–1484. (p. 434)

Van Baaren, R. B., Holland, R. W., Kawakami, K., & van Knippenberg, A. (2004). Mimicry and pro-social behavior. *Psychological Science, 15*, 71–74. (p. 525)

Van Baaren, R. B., Holland, R. W., Steenaert, B., & van Knippenberg, A. (2003). Mimicry for money: Behavioral consequences of imitation. *Journal of Experimental Social Psychology, 39*, 393–398. (p. 525)

van Boxtel, H. W., Orobio de Castro, B., & Goossens, F. A. (2004). High self-perceived social competence in rejected children is related to frequent fighting. *European Journal of Developmental Psychology, 1*, 205–214. (p. 603)

Van Cauter, E., Holmback, U., Knutson, K., Leproult, R., Miller, A., Nedeltcheva, A., . . . Spiegel, K. (2007). Impact of sleep and sleep loss on neuroendocrine and metabolic function. *Hormone Research, 67*(1), Supp. 1: 2–9. (p. 108)

Vance, E. B., & Wagner, N. N. (1976). Written descriptions of orgasm: A study of sex differences. *Archives of Sexual Behavior, 5,* 87–98. (p. 435)

vanDellen, M. R., Campbell, W. K., Hoyle, R. H., & Bradfield, E. K. (2011). Compensating, resisting, and breaking: A meta-analytic examination of reactions to self-esteem threat. *Personality and Social Psychological Review, 15,* 51–74. (p. 599)

Vandenberg, S. G., & Kuse, A. R. (1978). Mental rotations: A group test of three-dimensional spatial visualization. *Perceptual and Motor Skills, 47,* 599–604. (p. 410)

van den Bos, K., & Spruijt, N. (2002). Appropriateness of decisions as a moderator of the psychology of voice. *European Journal of Social Psychology, 32,* 57–72. (p. A-13)

Van den Bussche, E., Van Den Noortgate, W., & Reynvoet, B. (2009). Mechanisms of masked priming: A meta-analysis. *Psychological Bulletin, 135,* 452–477. (p. 231)

VanderLaan, D. P., & Vasey, P. L. (2011). Male sexual orientation in Independent Samoa: Evidence for fraternal birth order and maternal fecundity effects. *Archives of Sexual Behavior, 40,* 495–503. (p. 444)

VanderLaan, D. P., Forrester, D. L., Petterson, L. J., & Vasey, P. L. (2012). Offspring production among the extended relatives of Samoan men and fa'afafine. *PLoS One 7,* e36088. (p. 444)

van de Waal, E., Borgeaud, C., & Whiten, A. (2013). Potent social learning and conformity shape a wild primate's foraging decisions. *Science, 340,* 483–485. (p. 308)

Van Dijk, W. W., Van Koningsbruggen, G. M., Ouwerkerk, J. W., & Wesseling, Y. M. (2011). Self-esteem, self-affirmation, and schadenfreude. *Emotion, 11,* 1445–1449. (p. 599)

Van Dyke, C., & Byck, R. (1982, March). Cocaine. *Scientific American,* pp. 128–141. (p. 123)

van Emmerik, A. A. P., Reijntjes, A., & Kamphuis, J. H. (2013). Writing therapy for posttraumatic stress: A meta-analysis. *Psychotherapy and Psychosomatics, 82,* 82–88. (p. 507)

van Engen, M. L., & Willemsen, T. M. (2004). Sex and leadership styles: A meta-analysis of research published in the 1990s. *Psychological Reports, 94,* 3–18. (p. 163)

van Gelder, J., Hershfield, H. E., & Nordgren, L. F. (2013). Vividness of the future self predicts delinquency. *Psychological Science, 24,* 974–980. (p. 208)

van Goozen, S. H. M., Fairchild, G., Snoek, H., & Harold, G. T. (2007). The evidence for a neurobiological model of childhood antisocial behavior. *Psychological Bulletin, 133,* 149–182. (p. 649)

Van Haren, N. M., Rijsdijk, F., Schnack, H. G., Picchioni, M. M., Toulopoulou, T., Weisbrod, M., & ... Kahn, R. S. (2012). The genetic and environmental determinants of the association between brain abnormalities and schizophrenia: The schizophrenia twins and relatives consortium. *Biological Psychiatry, 71,* 915–921. (p. 642)

van Hemert, D. A., Poortinga, Y. H., & van de Vijver, F. J. R. (2007). Emotion and culture: A meta-analysis. *Cognition and Emotion, 21,* 913–943. (p. 473)

van Honk, J., Schutter, D. J., Bos, P. A., Kruijt, A-W., Lentje, E. G. & Baron-Cohen, S. (2011). Testosterone administration impairs cognitive empathy in women depending on second-to-fourth digit ratio. *Proceedings of the National Academy of Sciences, 108,* 3448–3452. (p. 193)

Van Horn, J., Irimia, A., Torgerson, C., Chambers, M., Kikinis, R., & Toga, A. (2012). Mapping connectivity damage in the case of Phineas Gage. *PLoS ONE, 7,* e37454. (p. 80)

Van Houtem, C. M. H. H., Lain, M. L., Boomsma, D. I., Ligthart, L., van Wijk, A. J., & De Jongh, A. (2013). A review and meta-analysis of the heritability of specific phobia subtypes and corresponding fears. *Journal of Anxiety Disorders,* 379–388. (p. 626)

Van IJzendoorn, M. H., & Juffer, F. (2005). Adoption is a successful natural intervention enhancing adopted children's IQ and school performance. *Current Directions in Psychological Science, 14,* 326–330. (p. 406)

Van IJzendoorn, M. H., & Juffer, F. (2006). The Emanual Miller Memorial Lecture 2006: Adoption as intervention. Meta-analytic evidence for massive catch-up and plasticity in physical, socio-emotional, and cognitive development. *Journal of Child Psychology and Psychiatry, 47,* 1228–1245. (pp. 139, 406)

Van IJzendoorn, M. H., & Kroonenberg, P. M. (1988). Cross-cultural patterns of attachment: A meta-analysis of the strange situation. *Child Development, 59,* 147–156. (p. 197)

Van IJzendoorn, M. H., Luijk, M. P. C. M., & Juffer, F. (2008). IQ of children growing up in children's homes: A meta-analysis on IQ delays in ophanages. *Merrill-Palmer Quarterly, 54,* 341–366. (pp. 199, 408)

Van Ittersum, K., & Wansink, B. (2012). Plate size and color suggestibility: The Delboeuf illusion's bias on serving and eating behavior. *Journal of Consumer Research, 39,* 215–228. (p. 429)

Van Kestern, P. J. M., Asscheman, H., Megens, J. A. J., & Gooren, J. G. (1997). Mortality and morbidity in transsexual subjects treated with cross-sex hormones. *Clinical Endocrinology, 47,* 337–342. (p. 170)

Van Leeuwen, M. S. (1978). A cross-cultural examination of psychological differentiation in males and females. *International Journal of Psychology, 13,* 87–122. (p. 168)

van Praag, H. (2009). Exercise and the brain: Something to chew on. *Trends in Neuroscience, 32,* 283–290. (p. 509)

Van Yperen, N. W., & Buunk, B. P. (1990). A longitudinal study of equity and satisfaction in intimate relationships. *European Journal of Social Psychology, 20,* 287–309. (p. 557)

Van Zeijl, J., Mesman, J., Van IJzendoorn, M. H., Bakermans-Kranenburg, M. J., Juffer, F., Stolk, M. N., Koot, H. M., & Alink, L. R. A. (2006). Attachment-based intervention for enhancing sensitive discipline in mothers of 1- to 3-year-old children at risk for externalizing behavior problems: A randomized controlled trial. *Journal of Consulting and Clinical Psychology, 74,* 994–1005. (p. 198)

Van Zuiden, M., (2012). Gluocorticoid receptor pathway components predict posttraumatic stress disorder symptom development: A prospective study. *Biological Psychiatry, 71,* 309–316. (p. 200)

Varese, F., Smeets, F., Drukker, M., Lieverse, R., Lataster, T., Viechtbauer, W., . . . Bentall, R. P. (2012). Childhood adversities increase the risk of psychosis: A meta-analysis of patient-control, prospective- and cross-sectional cohort studies. *Schizophrenia Bulletin, 38,* 661–671. (p. 641)

Varnum, M. E. W., Grossmann, I., Kitayama, S., & Nisbett, R. E. (2010). The origin of cultural differences in cognition: The social orientation hypothesis. *Current Directions in Psychological Science, 19,* 9–13. (p. 159)

Varnum, M. E. W., & Kitayama, S. (2011). What's in a name? Popular names are less common on frontiers. *Psychological Science, 22,* 176–183. (p. 159)

Vasey, P. L., & VanderLaan, D. P. (2010). An adaptive cognitive dissociation between willingness to help kin and nonkin in Samoan *Fa'afafine. Psychological Science, 21,* 292–297. (p. 444)

Vaughn, E. L., de Dios, M. A., Steinfeldt, J. A., & Kratz, L. M. (2011). Religiosity, alcohol use attitudes, and alcohol use in a national sample of adolescents. *Psychology of Addictive Behaviors, 25,* 547–553. (p. 129)

Vaughn, K. B., & Lanzetta, J. T. (1981). The effect of modification of expressive displays on vicarious emotional arousal. *Journal of Experimental Social Psychology, 17,* 16–30. (p. 475)

Vecera, S. P., Vogel, E. K., & Woodman, G. F. (2002). Lower region: A new cue for figure-ground assignment. *Journal of Experimental Psychology: General, 13,* 194–205. (p. 250)

Veenhoven, R. (2014, accessed March 17). World database of happiness. www.worlddatabaseofhappiness.eur.nl. (p. 485)

Veerman, J. L. Healy, G. N., Cobiac, L. J., Vos, T., Winkler, E. A. H., Owen, N., & Dunstan, D. W. (2012) Television viewing time and reduced life expectancy: A life table analysis. *British Journal of Sports Medicine, 46,* 927–930. (p. 507)

Vekassy, L. (1977). Dreams of the blind. *Magyar Pszichologiai Szemle, 34,* 478–491. (p. 112)

Velliste, M., Perel, S., Spalding, M. C., Whitford, A. S., & Schwartz, A. B. (2008). Cortical control of a prosthetic arm for self-feeding. *Nature, 453,* 1098–1101. (p. 77)

Veltkamp, M., Custers, R., & Aarts, H. (2011). Motivating consumer behavior by subliminal conditioning in the absence of basic needs: Striking even while the iron is cold. *Journal of Consumer Psychology, 21,* 49–56. (p. 233)

Verbeek, M. E. M., Drent, P. J., & Wiepkema, P. R. (1994). Consistent individual differences in early exploratory behaviour of male great tits. *Animal Behaviour, 48,* 1113–1121. (p. 589)

Verhaeghen, P., & Salthouse, T. A. (1997). Meta-analyses of age-cognition relations in adulthood: Estimates of linear and nonlinear age effects and structural models. *Psychological Bulletin, 122,* 231–249. (p. 216)

Vermetten, E., Schmahl, C., Lindner, S., Loewenstein, R. J., & Bremner, J. D. (2006). Hippocampal and amygdalar volumes in dissociative identity disorder. *American Journal of Psychiatry, 163,* 630–636. (p. 648)

Verona, E., & Sullivan, E. A. (2008). Emotional catharsis and aggression revisited: Heart rate reduction following aggressive responding. *Emotion, 8,* 331–340. (p. 477)

Verwijmeren, T., Karremans, J. C., Stroebe, W., & Wigboldus, D. H. J. (2011a). The workings and limits of subliminal advertising: The role of habits. *Journal of Consumer Psychology, 21,* 206–213. (p. 233)

Verwijmeren, T., Karremans, J. C., Stroebe, W., Wigboldus, D. H. J., & Ooigen, I. (2011b). *Vicary's victory: Subliminal ads in movies work!* Poster presented at the Society for Personality and Social Psychology meeting, San Antonio, TX. (p. 233)

Vigil, J. M. (2009). A socio-relational framework of sex differences in the expression of emotion. *Behavioral and Brain Sciences, 32,* 375–428. (p. 470)

Vigliocco, G., & Hartsuiker, R. J. (2002). The interplay of meaning, sound, and syntax in sentence production. *Psychological Bulletin, 128,* 442–472. (p. 371)

Vining, E. P. G., Freeman, J. M., Pillas, D. J., Uematsu, S., Carson, B. S., Brandt, J., . . . Zukerberg, A. (1997). Why would you remove half a brain? The outcome of 58 children after hemispherectomy—The Johns Hopkins Experience: 1968 to 1996. *Pediatrics, 100,* 163–171. (p. 81)

Vinkhuyzen, A. A. E., van der Sluis, S., Posthuma, D., & Boomsma, D. I. (2009). The heritability of aptitude and exceptional talent across different domains in adolescents and young adults. *Behavior Genetics, 39,* 380–392. (p. 406)

Visalberghi, E. Addessi, E., Truppa, V., Spagnoletti, N., Ottoni, E., Izar, P., & Fragaszy, D. (2009). Selection of effective stone tools by wild bearded capuchin monkeys. *Current Biology, 19,* 213–217. (p. 368)

Visich, P. S., & Fletcher, E. (2009). Myocardial infarction. In J. K. Ehrman, P. M., Gordon, P. S. Visich, & S. J. Keleyian (Eds.). *Clinical exercise physiology, 2nd Edition.* Champaign, IL: Human Kinetics. (p. 507)

Visser, B. A., Ashton, M. C., & Vernon, P. A. (2006). Beyond *g*: Putting multiple intelligences theory to the test. *Intelligence, 34*(5), 487–502. (p. 391)

Vita, A. J., Terry, R. B., Hubert, H. B., & Fries, J. F. (1998). Aging, health risks, and cumulative disability. *New England Journal of Medicine, 338,* 1035–1041. (p. 122)

Vitello, P. (2012, August 1). George A. Miller. A pioneer in cognitive psychology, is dead at 92. *New York Times* (www.nytimes.com). (p. 323)

Vitevitch, M. S. (2003). Change deafness: The inability to detect changes between two voices. *Journal of Experimental Psychology: Human Perception and Performance, 29,* 333–342. (p. 99)

Vitiello, M. V. (2009). Recent advances in understanding sleep and sleep disturbances in older adults: Growing older does not mean sleeping poorly. *Current Directions in Psychological Science, 18,* 316–320. (p. 110)

Vitória, P. D., Salgueiro, M. F., Silva, S. A., & De Vries, H. (2009). The impact of social influence on adolescent intention to smoke: Combining types and referents of influence. *British Journal of Health Psychology, 14,* 681–699. (p. 129)

Vittengl, J. R., Clark, L. A., Dunn, T. W., & Jarrett, R. B. (2007). Reducing relapse and recurrence in unipolar depression: A comparative meta-analysis of cognitive-behavioral therapy's effects. *Journal of Consulting and Clinical Psychology, 75,* 475–488. (p. 684)

Vocks, S., Tuschen-Caffier, B., Pietrowsky, R., Rustenbach, S. J., Kersting, A., & Herpertz, S. (2010). Meta-analysis of the effectiveness of psychological and pharmacological treatments for binge eating disorder. *International Journal of Eating Disorders, 43,* 205–217. (p. 653)

Vogel, G. (2010). Long-fought compromise reached on European animal rules. *Science, 329,* 1588–1589. (p. 40)

Vogel, N., Schilling, Wahl, H-W., Beekman, A. T. F., & Penninx, B. W. J. H. (2013). Time-to-death-related change in positive and negative affect among older adults approaching the end of life. *Psychology and Aging, 28,* 128–141. (p. 218)

Vogel, S. (1999). *The skinny on fat: Our obsession with weight control.* New York: W. H. Freeman. (p. 142)

Vohs, K. D., & Baumeister, R. F. (eds.) (2011). *Handbook of self-regulation, 2nd edition.* New York: Guilford. (p. 503)

Vohs, K. D., Baumeister, R. F., & Schmeichel, B. J. (2012). Motivation, personal beliefs, and limited resources all contribute to self-control. *Journal of Experimental Social Psychology, 48,* 943–947. (p. 503)

Vohs, K. D., Mead, N. L., & Goode, M. R. (2006). The psychological consequences of money. *Science, 314,* 1154–1156. (p. 335)

Volkow, N. D., et al. (2009). Evaluating dopamine reward pathway in ADHD: Clinical implications. *JAMA, 302,* 1084–1091. (p. 615)

von Békésy, G. (1957, August). The ear. *Scientific American,* pp. 66–78. (p. 260)

von Hippel, W. (2007). Aging, executive functioning, and social control. *Current Directions in Psychological Science, 16,* 240–244. (p. 216)

von Hippel, W. & Trivers, R. (2011). The evolution and psychology of self-deception. *Behavioral and Brain Sciences, 34,* 1–56. (p. 602)

Vonk, J., Jett, S. E., & Mosteller, K. W. (2012). Concept formation in American black bears, ursus americanus. *Animal Behaviour, 84,* 953–964. (p. 367)

von Senden, M. (1932). *The perception of space and shape in the congenitally blind before and after operation.* Glencoe, IL: Free Press. (p. 254)

Von Stumm, S., Hell, B., & Chamorro-Premuzic, T. (2011). The hungry mind: Intellectual curiosity is the third pillar of academic performance. *Perspectives on Psychological Science, 6,* 574–588. (p. 409)

Vorona, R. D., Szklo-Coxe, M., Wu, A., Dubik, M., Zhao, Y., & Ware, J. C. (2011). Dissimilar teen crash rates in two neighboring Southeastern Virginia cities with different high school start times. *Journal of Clinical Sleep Medicine, 7,* 145–151. (p. 108)

Voss, U., Tuin, I., Schermelleh-Engel, K., & Hobson, A. (2011). Waking and dreaming: Related but structurally independent. Dream reports of congenitally paraplegic and deaf-mute persons. *Consciousness and Cognition, 20,* 673–687. (p. 112)

VPC. (2013, February 7). States with higher gun ownership and weak gun laws lead nation in gun death. Violence Policy Center (www.vpc.org/press/1302gundeath.htm). (p. 545)

Vroom, V. H., & Jago, A. G. (2007). The role of the situation in leadership. *American Psychologist, 62,* 17–24. (p. A-12)

VTTI. (2009, September). *Driver distraction in commercial vehicle operations.* Virginia Tech Transportation Institute and U.S. Department of Transportation. (p. 96)

Vul, E., Harris, C., Winkielman, P., & Pashler, H. (2009a). Puzzlingly high correlations in fMRI studies of emotion, personality, and social cognition. *Perspectives on Psychological Science, 4,* 274–290. (p. 68)

Vul, E., Harris, C., Winkielman, P., & Pashler, H. (2009b). Reply to comments on "Puzzlingly high correlations in fMRI studies of emotion, personality, and social cognition." *Perspectives on Psychological Science, 4,* 319–324. (p. 68)

Vuoksimaa, E., Kaprio, J., Kremen, W. S., Hokkanen, L., Viken, R. J., Tuulio-Henriksson, A., & Rose, R. J. (2010). Having a male co-twin masculinizes mental rotation performance in females. *Psychological Science, 21,* 1069–1071. (p. 446)

Vuoksimaa, E., Koskenvuo, M., Rose, R. J., & Kaprio, J. (2009). Origins of handedness: A nationwide study of 30,161 adults. *Neuropsychologia, 47,* 1294–1301. (p. 86)

Waber, R. L., Shiv, B., Carmon, & Ariely, D. (2008). Commercial features of placebo and therapeutic efficacy. *Journal of the American Medical Association, 299,* 1016–1017. (p. 36)

Wacker, J., Chavanon, M.-L., & Stemmler, G. (2006). Investigating the dopaminergic basis of extraversion in humans: A multilevel approach. *Journal of Personality and Social Psychology, 91,* 177–187. (p. 587)

Wade, K. A., Garry, M., Read, J. D., & Lindsay, D. S. (2002). A picture is worth a thousand lies: Using false photographs to create false childhood memories. *Psychonomic Bulletin & Review, 9,* 597–603. (p. 345)

Wade, N. G., Worthington, E. L., Jr., & Vogel, D. L. (2006). Effectiveness of religiously tailored interventions in Christian therapy. *Psychotherapy Research, 17,* 91–105. (p. 680)

Wagar, B. M., & Cohen, D. (2003). Culture, memory, and the self: An analysis of the personal and collective self in long-term memory. *Journal of Experimental Social Psychology, 39,* 458–475. (p. 327)

Wagemans, J., Elder, J. H., Kubovy, M., Palmer, S. E., Peterson, M. A., Singh, M., & von der Heydt, R. (2012a). A century of Gestalt psychology in visual perception: I. Perceptual grouping and figure-ground organization. *Psychological Bulletin, 138,* 1172–1217. (p. 247)

Wagemans, J., Feldman, J., Gepshtein, S., Kimchi, R., Pomerantz, J. R, van der Helm, P., & van Leeuwen C. (2012b). A century of Gestalt psychology in visual perception: II. Conceptual and theoretical foundations. *Psychological Bulletin, 138,* 1218–1252. (p. 247)

Wagenmakers, E-J., Wetzels, R., Borsboom, D., & van der Maas, H. (2011). Why psychologists must change the way they analyze their data: The case of psi. *Journal of Personality and Social Psychology, 100,* 1–12. (p. 274)

Wager, R. D., & Atlas, L. Y. (2013). How is pain influenced by cognition? Neuroimaging weighs in. *Perspectives on Psychological Science, 8,* 91–97. (p. 264)

Wager, T., Atlas, L. Y., Lindquist, M. A., Roy, M., Woo, C. W. & Kross, E. (2013). An fMRI-based neurologic signature of physical pain. *The New England Journal of Medicine, 368,* 1388–1397. (p. 450)

Wagner, A. (2010). Can neuroscience identify lies? In F. E. Bloom et al., *A judge's guide to neuroscience: A concise introduction.* Santa Barbara, CA: University of California, Santa Barbara. (p. 467)

Wagner, B., Klinitzke, G., Brähler, E., & Kersting, A. (2013). Extreme obesity is associated with suicidal behavior and suicide attempts in adults: Results of a population-based representative sample. *Depression and Anxiety, 30,* 975–981. (p. 430)

Wagner, D., Becker, B., Koester, P., Gouzoulis-Mayfrank, E., & Daumann, J. (2012). A prospective study of learning, memory, and executive function in new MDMA users. *Addiction, 108,* 136–145. (p. 124)

Wagner, D. D., Altman, M., Boswell, R. G., Kelley, W. M., & Heatherton, T. F. (2013). Self-regulatory depletion enhances neural responses to rewards and impairs top-down control. *Psychological Science, 24,* 2262–2271. (p. 503)

Wagner, D. D., Cin, S. D., Sargent, J. C., Kelley, W. M., & Heatherton, T. F. (2011). Spontaneous action representation in smokers when watching movie characters smoke. *Journal of Neuroscience, 31,* 894–898. (p. 309)

Wagner, D. T., Barnes, C. M., Lim, V. K. G., & Ferris, D. L. (2012). Lost sleep and cyberloafing: Evidence from the laboratory and a daylight saving time quasi-experiment. *Journal of Applied Psychology, 97,* 1068–1076. (p. 108)

Wagner, J., Gerstorf, D., Hoppmann, C., & Luszcz, M. A. (2013). The nature and correlates of self-esteem trajectories in late life. *Journal of Personality and Social Psychology, 105,* 139–153. (pp. 210, 223)

Wagner, K., & Dobkins, K. R. (2011). Synaesthetic associations decrease during infancy. *Psychological Science, 22,* 1067–1072. (p. 271)

Wagner, R. K. (2011). Practical intelligence. In R. J. Sternberg & S. B. Kaufman (Eds.), *The Cambridge handbook of intelligence.* New York: Cambridge University Press. (p. 388)

Wagstaff, G. (1982). Attitudes to rape: The "just world" strikes again? *Bulletin of the British Psychological Society, 13,* 275–283. (p. 519)

Wai, J., Lubinski, D., & Benbow, C. P. (2005). Creativity and occupational accomplishments among intellectually precocious youths: An age 13 to age 33 longitudinal study. *Journal of Educational Psychology, 97,* 484–492. (p. 404)

Wakefield, J. C., Schmitz, M.F., First, M. B., & Horwitz, A. V. (2007). Extending the bereavement exclusion for major depression to other losses: Evidence from the National Comorbidity Survey. *Archives of General Psychiatry, 64,* 433–440. (p. 632)

Wakefield, J. C., & Spitzer, R. L. (2002). Lowered estimates—but of what? *Archives of General Psychiatry, 59,* 129–130. (p. 624)

Walker, E., Shapiro, D., Esterberg, M., & Trotman, H. (2010). Neurodevelopment and schizophrenia: Broadening the focus. *Current Directions in Psychological Science, 19,* 204–208. (pp. 642, 645)

Walker, M. P., & van der Helm, E. (2009). Overnight therapy? The role of sleep in emotional brain processing. *Psychological Bulletin, 135,* 731–748. (p. 107)

Walker, W. R., Skowronski, J. J., & Thompson, C. P. (2003). Life is pleasant—and memory helps to keep it that way! *Review of General Psychology, 7,* 203–210. (p. 224)

Walkup, J. T., et al. (2008). Cognitive behavioral therapy, sertraline, or a combination in childhood anxiety. *New England Journal of Medicine, 359,* 2753–2766. (p. 684)

Walkup, J. T., & Rubin, D. H. (2013). Social withdrawal and violence. Newtown, Connecticut. *The New England Journal of Medicine, 368,* 399–401. (p. 616)

Wall, P. D. (2000). *Pain: The science of suffering.* New York: Columbia University Press. (p. 262)

Wallace, D. S., Paulson, R. M., Lord, C. G., & Bond, C. F., Jr. (2005). Which behaviors do attitudes predict? Meta-analyzing the effects of social pressure and perceived difficulty. *Review of General Psychology, 9(3),* 214–227. (p. 520)

Wallach, M. A., & Wallach, L. (1983). *Psychology's sanction for selfishness: The error of egoism in theory and therapy.* New York: Freeman. (p. 585)

Wallach, M. A., & Wallach, L. (1985, February). How psychology sanctions the cult of the self. *Washington Monthly,* pp. 46–56. (p. 585)

Walsh, J. L., Fielder, R. L., Carey, K. B., & Carey, M. P. (2013). Female college students' media use and academic outcomes: Results from a longitudinal cohort study. *Emerging Adulthood, 1,* 219–232. (p. 453)

Walsh, R. (2011). Lifestyle and mental health. *American Psychologist, 66,* 579–592. (p. 688)

Walster, E., Aronson, V., Abrahams, D., & Rottman, L. (1966). Importance of physical attractiveness in dating behavior. *Journal of Personality and Social Psychology, 4,* 508–516. (p. 553)

Walton, G. M., & Spencer S. J. (2009). Latent ability: Grades and test scores systematically underestimate the intellectual ability of negatively stereotyped students. *Psychological Science, 20,* 1132–1139. (p. 414)

Wampold, B. E. (2001). *The great psychotherapy debate: Models, methods, and findings.* Mahwah, NJ: Erlbaum. (pp. 678, 679)

Wampold, B. E. (2007). Psychotherapy: The humanistic (and effective) treatment. *American Psychologist, 62,* 857–873. (pp. 675, 678)

Wampold, B. E., Mondin, G. W., Moody, M., & Ahn, H. (1997). The flat earth as a metaphor for the evidence for uniform efficacy of bona fide psychotherapies: Reply to Crits-Christoph (1997) and Howard et al. (1997). *Psychological Bulletin, 122,* 226–230. (p. 675)

Wang, F., DesMeules, M., Luo, W., Dai, S., Lagace, C. & Morrison, H. (2011). Leisure-time physical activity and marital status in relation to depression between men and women: A prospective study. *Health Psychology, 30,* 204–211. (pp. 507, 508)

Wang, J., Häusermann, M., Wydler, H., Mohler-Kuo, M., & Weiss, M. G. (2012). Suicidality and sexual orientation among men in Switzerland: Findings from 3 probability surveys. *Journal of Psychiatric Research, 46,* 980–986. (p. 441)

Wang, J., Leu, J., & Shoda, Y. (2011). When the seemingly innocuous "stings": Racial microaggressions and their emotional consequences. *Personality and Social Psychology Bulletin, 37,* 1666–1678. (p. 538)

Wang, S. (2014, March 29). How to think about the risk of autism. *New York Times* (www.nytimes.com). (p. 193)

Wang, S-H., Baillargeon, R., & Brueckner, L. (2004). Young infants' reasoning about hidden objects: Evidence from violation-of-expectation tasks with test trials only. *Cognition, 93,* 167–198. (p. 188)

Wang, X. T., & Dvorak, R. D. (2010). Sweet Future: Fluctuating blood glucose levels affect future discounting. *Psychological Science, 21,* 183–188. (p. 504)

Wann, J. P. Poulter, D. R., & Purcell, C. (2011). Reduced sensitivity to visual looming inflates the risk posed by speeding vehicles when children try to cross the road. *Psychological Science, 22,* 429–434. (p. 251)

Wansink, B. (2007). *Mindless eating: Why we eat more than we think.* New York: Bantam Dell. (p. 429)

Wansink, B., van Ittersum, K., & Painter, J. E. (2006). Ice cream illusions: Bowls, spoons, and self-served portion sizes. *American Journal of Preventive Medicine, 31,* 240–243. (p. 429)

Warburton, W. A., Williams, K. D., & Cairns, D. R. (2006). When ostracism leads to aggression: The moderating effects of control deprivation. *Journal of Experimental Social Psychology, 42,* 213–220. (p. 502)

Ward, A., & Mann, T. (2000). Don't mind if I do: Disinhibited eating under cognitive load. *Journal of Personality and Social Psychology, 78,* 753–763. (p. 432)

Ward, B. W., Dahlhamer, J. M., Galinsky, A. M., & Joestl, S. S. (2014, July 15). Sexual orientation and health among U.S. adults: National Health Interview Survey, 2013. Centers for Disease Control and Prevention: National Health Statistics Reports, Number 77. (p. 440)

Ward, C. (1994). Culture and altered states of consciousness. In W. J. Lonner & R. Malpass (Eds.), *Psychology and culture.* Boston: Allyn & Bacon. (p. 117)

Ward, C. A. (2000). Models and measurements of psychological androgyny: A cross-cultural extension of theory and research. *Sex Roles, 43,* 529–552. (p. 169)

Ward, J. (2003). State of the art synaesthesia. *The Psychologist, 16,* 196–199. (p. 271)

Ward, K. D., Klesges, R. C., & Halpern, M. T. (1997). Predictors of smoking cessation and state-of-the-art smoking interventions. *Journal of Socies Issues, 53,* 129–145. (p. 122)

Ward, L. M., Reed, L., Trinh, S. L., & Foust, M. (2014). Sexuality and entertainment media. In L. M. Ward, L. Reed, S. L. Trinh, & M. Foust (Eds.) APA *handbook of sexuality and psychology, Vol. 2: Contextual approaches.* Washington, DC: American Psychological Association. (p. 439)

Wardle, J., Cooke, L. J., Gibson, L., Sapochnik, M., Sheiham, A., & Lawson, M. (2003). Increasing children's acceptance of vegetables: A randomized trial of parent-led exposure. *Appetite, 40,* 155–162. (p. 266)

Wargo, E. (2007, December). Understanding the have-knots. *APS Observer,* pp. 18–21. (p. 510)

Wason, P. C. (1960). On the failure to eliminate hypotheses in a conceptual task. *Quarterly Journal of Experimental Psychology, 12,* 129–140. (p. 357)

Wason, P. C. (1981). The importance of cognitive illusions. *The Behavioral and Brain Sciences, 4,* 356, 358.

Wasserman, E. A. (1993). Comparative cognition: Toward a general understanding of cognition in behavior. *Psychological Science, 4,* 156–161. (p. 291)

Wasserman, E. A. (1995). The conceptual abilities of pigeons. *American Scientist, 83,* 246–255. (p. 367)

Wastell, C. A. (2002). Exposure to trauma: The long-term effects of suppressing emotional reactions. *Journal of Nervous and Mental Disorders, 190,* 839–845. (p. 507)

Waterhouse, R. (1993, July 19). Income for 62 percent is below average pay. *The Independent,* p. 4. (p. 44)

Waterman, A. S. (1988). Identity status theory and Erikson's theory: Commonalities and differences. *Developmental Review, 8,* 185–208. (p. 210)

Watkins, E. R. (2008). Constructive and unconstructive repetitive thought. *Psychological Bulletin, 134,* 163–206. (p. 628)

Watkins, J. G. (1984). The Bianchi (L. A. Hillside Strangler) case: Sociopath or multiple personality? *International Journal of Clinical and Experimental Hypnosis, 32,* 67–101. (p. 647)

Watson, D. (2000). *Mood and temperament.* New York: Guilford Press. (pp. 480, 481, 509, 638)

Watson, D., Wiese, D., Vaidya, J., & Tellegen, A. (1999). The two general activation systems of affect: Structured findings, evolutionary considerations, and psychobiological evidence. *Journal of Personality and Social Psychology, 76,* 820–838. (p. 476)

Watson, J. B. (1913). Psychology as the behaviorist views it. *Psychological Review, 20,* 158–177. (pp. 92, 282, 288)

Watson, J. B. (1924). The unverbalized in human behavior. *Psychological Review, 31,* 339–347. (p. 288)

Watson, J. B., & Rayner, R. (1920). Conditioned emotional reactions. *Journal of Experimental Psychology, 3,* 1–14. (p. 288)

Watson, R. I., Jr. (1973). Investigation into deindividuation using a cross-cultural survey technique. *Journal of Personality and Social Psychology, 25,* 342–345. (p. 533)

Watson, S. J., Benson, J. A., Jr., & Joy, J. E. (2000). NEWS AND VIEWS—Marijuana and medicine: Assessing the science base: A summary of the 1999 Institute of Medicine report. *Archives of General Psychiatry, 57,* 547–553. (p. 125)

Watters, E. (2010). *Crazy like us: The globalization of the American psyche.* New York: Free Press. (p. 612)

Way, B. M., Creswell, J. D., Eisenberger, N. I., & Lieberman, M. D. (2010). Dispositional mindfulness and depressive symptomatology: Correlations with limbic and self-referential neural activity during rest. *Emotion, 10,* 12–24. (p. 511)

Wayment, H. A., & Peplau, L. A. (1995). Social support and well-being among lesbian and heterosexual women: A structural modeling approach. *Personality and Social Psychology Bulletin, 21,* 1189–1199. (p. 221)

Weaver, J. B., Masland, J. L., & Zillmann, D. (1984). Effect of erotica on young men's aesthetic perception of their female sexual partners. *Perceptual and Motor Skills, 58,* 929–930. (p. 438)

Webb, W. B. (1992). *Sleep: The gentle tyrant.* Bolton, MA: Anker. (p. 110)

Webb, W. B., & Campbell, S. S. (1983). Relationships in sleep characteristics of identical and fraternal twins. *Archives of General Psychiatry, 40,* 1093–1095. (p. 104)

Webley, K. (2009, June 15). Behind the drop in Chinese adoptions. *Time,* p. 55. (p. 540)

Webster, G. D., Jonason, P. K., & Schember, T. O. (2009). Hot topics and popular papers in evolutionary psychology: Analyses of title words and citation counts in *Evolution and Human Behavior,* 1979–2008. *Evolutionary Psychology, 7,* 348–362. (p. 147)

Wechsler, D. (1972). "Hold" and "Don't Hold" tests. In S. M. Chown (Ed.), *Human aging.* New York: Penguin. (p. 400)

Wegner, D. M. (2002). *The illusion of conscious will.* Cambridge, MA: MIT Press (p. 91)

Wegner, D. M., & Ward, A. F. (2013, December). How Google is changing your brain. *Scientific American,* pp. 58–61. (p. 321)

Wei, Q., Fentress, H. M., Hoversten, M. T., Zhang, L., Hebda-Bauer, E. K., Watson, S. J., Seasholtz, A. F., & Akil, H. (2012). Early-life forebrain glucocorticoid receptor overexpression increases anxiety behavior and cocaine sensitization. *Biological Psychiatry, 71,* 224–231. (p. 200)

Wei, W., Lu, H., Zhao, H., Chen, C., Dong, Q., & Zhou, X. (2012). Gender differences in children's arithmetic performance are accounted for by gender differences in language abilities. *Psychological Science, 23,* 320–330. (p. 410)

Weingarden, H., & Renshaw, K. D. (2012). Early and late perceived pubertal timing as risk factors for anxiety disorders in adult women. *Journal of Psychiatric Research, 46,* 1524–1529. (p. 204)

Weingarten, G. (2002, March 10). Below the beltway. *Washington Post,* p. WO3. (p. A-1)

Weinstein, N. D. (1980). Unrealistic optimism about future life events. *Journal of Personality and Social Psychology, 39,* 806–820. (p. 600)

Weinstein, N. D. (1982). Unrealistic optimism about susceptibility to health problems. *Journal of Behavioral Medicine, 5,* 441–460. (p. 600)

Weinstein, N. D. (1996, October 4). 1996 optimistic bias bibliography. (weinstein_c@aesop.rutgers.edu). (p. 600)

Weinstein, N. D., Ryan, W. S., DeHaan, C. R., Przbylski, A. K., Legate, N., & Ryan, R. M. (2012). Parental autonomy support and discrepancies between implicit and explicit sexual identities: Dynamics of self-acceptance and defense. *Journal of Personality and Social Psychology, 102,* 815–832. (p. 581)

Weir, K. (2013, May). Captive audience. *Monitor on Psychology,* pp. 44–49. (p. 40)

Weir, W. (2010, May 17). Middletown man, age 76, has memorized epic poem "Paradise Lost." *Hartford Courant* (www.courant.com). (p. 217)

Weisbuch, M., Ivcevic, Z., & Ambady, N. (2009). On being liked on the web and in the "real world": Consistency in first impressions across personal webpages and spontaneous behavior. *Journal of Experimental Social Psychology, 45,* 573–576. (p. 453)

Weiskrantz, L. (2009). *Blindsight.* Oxford: Oxford University Press. (p. 94)

Weiskrantz, L. (2010). Blindsight in hindsight. *The Psychologist, 23,* 356–358. (p. 94)

Weiss, A., King, J. E., & Perkins, L. (2006). Personality and subjective well-being in orangutans (*Pongo pygmaeus* and *Pongo abelii*). *Journal of Personality and Social Psychology, 90,* 501–511. (p. 588)

Weiss, J. M. (1977). Psychological and behavioral influences on gastrointestinal lesions in animal models. In J. D. Maser & M. E. P. Seligman (Eds.), *Psychopathology: Experimental models.* San Francisco: Freeman. (p. 501)

Welch, J. M., Lu, J., Rodriquiz, R. M., Trotta, N. C., Peca, J., Ding, J.-D., Feliciano, C., . . . Feng, G. (2007). Cortico-striatal synaptic defects and OCD-like behaviours in *Sapap3*-mutant mice. *Nature, 448,* 894–900. (p. 626)

Welch, W. W. (2005, February 28). Trauma of Iraq war haunting thousands returning home. *USA Today* (www.usatoday.com). (p. 623)

Welham, J., Isohanni, M., Jones, P., & McGrath, J. (2009). The antecedents of schizophrenia: A review of birth cohort studies. *Schizophrenia Bulletin, 35,* 603–623. (p. 645)

Weller, S., & Davis-Beaty, K. (2002). The effectiveness of male condoms in prevention of sexually transmitted diseases (protocol). *Cochrane Database of Systematic Reviews,* Issue 4, Art. No. CD004090. (p. 436)

Wellman, H. M., & Gelman, S. A. (1992). Cognitive development: Foundational theories of core domains. *Annual Review of Psychology, 43,* 337–375. (p. 188)

Wells, G. L. (1981). Lay analyses of causal forces on behavior. In J. Harvey (Ed.), *Cognition, social behavior and the environment.* Hillsdale, NJ: Erlbaum. (p. 280)

Wenze, S. J., Gunthert, K. C., & German, R. E. (2012). Biases in affective forecasting and recall in individuals with depression and anxiety symptoms. *Personality and Social Psychology Bulletin, 38,* 895–906. (p. 634)

Werker, J. F., Yeung, H. H., & Yoshida, K. A. (2012). How do infants become experts at native-speech perception. *Current Directions in Psychological Science, 21,* 221–226. (p. 373)

Westen, D. (1996). *Is Freud really dead? Teaching psychodynamic theory to introductory psychology.* Presentation to the Annual Institute on the Teaching of Psychology, St. Petersburg Beach, FL. (p. 577)

Westen, D. (1998). The scientific legacy of Sigmund Freud: Toward a psychodynamically informed psychological science. *Psychological Bulletin, 124,* 333–371. (p. 579)

Westen, D. (2007). *The political brain: The role of emotion in deciding the fate of the nation.* New York: PublicAffairs. (p. 463)

Westen, D., & Morrison, K. (2001). A multidimensional meta-analysis of treatments for depression, panic, and generalized anxiety disorder: An empirical examination of the status of empirically supported therapies. *Journal of Consulting and Clinical Psychology, 69,* 875–899. (p. 676)

Wetherell, J. L., Petkus, A. J., White, K. S., Nguyen, H., Kornblith, S., Andreescu, C., Zisook, S., & Lenze, E. J. (2013). Antidepressant medication augmented with cognitive-behavioral therapy for generalized anxiety disorder in older adults. *The American Journal of Psychiatry, 170,* 782–789. (p. 683)

Whalen, P. J., Shin, L. M., McInerney, S. C., Fisher, H., Wright, C. I., & Rauch, S. L. (2001). A functional MRI study of human amygdala responses to facial expressions of fear versus anger. *Emotion, 1,* 70–83. (p. 466)

Whalley, L. J., & Deary, I. J. (2001). Longitudinal cohort study of childhood IQ and survival up to age 76. *British Medical Journal, 322,* 1–5. (p. 403)

Whalley, L. J., Starr, J. M., Athawes, R., Hunter, D., Pattie, A., & Deary, I. J. (2000). Childhood mental ability and dementia. *Neurology, 55,* 1455–1459. (p. 402)

Whang, W., Kubzansky, L, D., Kawachi, I., Rexrode, K. M., Kroenke, C. H., Glynn, R. J., Garan, H., & Albert, C. M. (2009). Depression and risk of sudden cardiac death and coronary heart disease in women. *Journal of the American College of Cardiology, 53,* 950–958. (p. 498)

Wheaton, A. G., Perry, G. S., Chapman, D. P., & Croft, J. B. (2012). Sleep disordered breathing and depression among U.S. adults: National Health and Nutrition Examination Survey, 2005–2008. *Sleep, 35,* 461–467. (p. 111)

Whelan, R., et al. (2012). Adolescent impulsivity phenotypes characterized by distinct brain networks. *Nature Neuroscience, 15,* 920–925. (p. 205)

White, G. L., & Kight, T. D. (1984). Misattribution of arousal and attraction: Effects of salience of explanations for arousal. *Journal of Experimental Social Psychology, 20,* 55–64. (p. 556)

White, H. R., Brick, J., & Hansell, S. (1993). A longitudinal investigation of alcohol use and aggression in adolescence. *Journal of Studies on Alcohol,* Supplement No. 11, 62–77. (p. 546)

White, L., & Edwards, J. (1990). Emptying the nest and parental well-being: An analysis of national panel data. *American Sociological Review, 55,* 235–242. (p. 222)

White, R. A. (1998). Intuition, heart knowledge, and parapsychology. *Journal of the American Society for Psychical Research, 92,* 158–171. (p. 273)

Whitelock, C. F., Lamb, M. E., & Rentfrow, P. J. (2013). Overcoming trauma: Psychological and demographic characteristics of child sexual abuse survivors in adulthood. *Clinical Psychological Science, 1,* 351–362. (p. 200)

Whiten, A., & Boesch, C. (2001, January). Cultures of chimpanzees. *Scientific American,* pp. 60–67. (p. 368)

Whiten, A., & Byrne, R. W. (1988). Tactical deception in primates. *Behavioral and Brain Sciences, 11,* 233–244, 267–273. (p. 29)

Whiten, A., Goodall, J., McGrew, W. C., Nishidas, T., Reynolds, V., Sugiyama, Y., . . . Boesch, C. (1999). Cultures in chimpanzees. *Nature, 399,* 682–685. (p. 155)

Whiten, A., Spiteri, A., Horner, V., Bonnie, K. E., Lambeth, S. P., Schapiro, S. J., & de Waal, F. B. M. (2007). Transmission of multiple traditions within and between chimpanzee groups. *Current Biology, 17,* 1038–1043. (p. 307)

Whiting, B. B., & Edwards, C. P. (1988). *Children of different worlds: The formation of social behavior.* Cambridge, MA: Harvard University Press. (p. 160)

Whitley, B. E., Jr. (1999). Right-wing authoritarianism, social dominance orientation, and prejudice. *Journal of Personality and Social Psychology, 77,* 126–134. (p. 542)

Whitlock, J. R., Heynen, A. L., Shuler, M. G., & Bear, M. F. (2006). Learning induces long-term potentiation in the hippocampus. *Science, 313,* 1093–1097. (p. 332)

Whitmer, R. A., Gustafson, D. R., Barrett-Connor, E. B., Haan, M. N., Gunderson, E. P., & Yaffe, K. (2008). Central obesity and increased risk of dementia more than three decades later. *Neurology, 71,* 1057–1064. (p. 430)

WHO. (1979). *Schizophrenia: An international followup study.* Chicester, England: Wiley. (p. 641)

WHO. (2000). *Effectiveness of male latex condoms in protecting against pregnancy and sexually transmitted infections.* World Health Organization (www.who.int). (p. 436)

WHO. (2003). *The male latex condom: Specification and guidelines for condom procurement.* Department of Reproductive Health and Research, Family and Community Health, World Health Organization. (p. 436)

WHO. (2004). *Women, girls, HIV, and AIDS.* World Health Organization, Western Pacific Regional Office. (p. 436)

WHO. (2004a). Prevalence, severity, and unmet need for treatment of mental disorders in the World Health Organization World Health Surveys. *Journal of the American Mental Medical Association, 291,* 2581–2590. (pp. 618, 636)

WHO. (2004b). *Prevention of mental disorders: Effective interventions and policy options. Summary report.* Geneva: World Health Organization, Department of Mental Health and Substance Abuse. (p. 618)

WHO. (2004c). *Promoting mental health: Concepts, emerging evidence, practice. Summary report.* Geneva: World Health Organization, Department of Mental Health and Substance Abuse. (p. 618)

WHO. (2008). *Mental health (nearly 1 million annual suicide deaths).* Geneva: World Health Organization (www.who.int/mental_health/en). (p. 637)

WHO. (2010, September). Mental health: Strengthening our response. Fact sheet No. 220. Retrieved online at www.who.int/mediacentre/factsheets/fs220/en/. (p. 609)

WHO. (2011). Country reports and charts available. Geneva: World Health Organization (int/mental_health/prevention/suicide/country_reports/en/index.html). (p. 637)

WHO. (2011). Schizophrenia. Geneva: World Health Organization (www.who.int). (p. 641)

WHO. (2012). WHO global estimates on prevalence of hearing loss: Mortality and burden of diseases and prevention of blindness and deafness. Geneva: World Health Organization (www.who.int). (p. 257)

WHO. (2012, May). Tobacco: Fact sheet N339. Geneva: World Health Organization (www.who.int) (p., 121)

WHO. (2012, August). Depression. Geneva: World Health Organization (www.who.int/mediacentre/factsheets/fs369/en/). (pp. 631, 637)

WHO. (2012, October). Depression. World Health Organization. http://www.who.int/mediacentre/factsheets/fs369/en. (p. 638)

WHO. (2013, February). Deafness and hearing loss. Geneva: World Health Organization Media Centre Fact Sheets (www.who.int/mediacentre/factsheets/fs300/en). (p. 375)

WHO. (2013, November). Sexually transmitted infections (STIs). Fact sheet No. 110. (www.who.int). (p. 436)

WHO. (2014). World Health Statistics 2014, Part II. *Highlighted topics.* pp. 42–44. (p. 214)

WHO. (2014a, accessed June 3). Global health improvement and WHO: Shaping the future. World Health Organization (www.who.int/whr/2003/media_centre/lee_article/en/index2.html). (p. 214)

WHO. (2014b, accessed March 3). Life expectancy. World Health Organization (www.who.int/gho/mortality_burden_disease/life_tables/en/). (pp. 214, 215)

WHO. (2014, accessed September 20). Chain-free initiative. Geneva: World Health Organization (www.emro.who.int/mental-health/chain-free-initiative). (p. 611)

Whooley, M. A., et al. (2008). Depressive symptoms, health behaviors, and risk of cardiovascular events in patients with coronary heart disease. *JAMA, 300,* 2379–2388. (p. 498)

Whorf, B. L. (1956). Science and linguistics. In J. B. Carroll (Ed.), *Language, thought, and reality: Selected writings of Benjamin Lee Whorf.* Cambridge, MA: MIT Press. (p. 379)

Wicherts, J. M., Dolan, C. V., Carlson, J. S., & van der Maas, H. L. J. (2010). Raven's test performance of sub-Saharan Africans: Mean level, psychometric properties, and the Flynn Effect. *Learning and Individual Differences, 20,* 135–151. (p. 412)

Wickelgren, I. (2009, September/October). I do not feel your pain. *Scientific American Mind,* pp. 51–57. (pp. 261, 267)

Wickelgren, W. A. (1977). *Learning and memory.* Englewood Cliffs, NJ: Prentice-Hall. (p. 327)

Widiger, T. A., & Costa, P. T., Jr. (2012). Integrating normal and abnormal personality structure: The five-factor model. *Journal of Personality, 80,* 1471–1505. (p. 592)

Wielkiewicz, R. M., & Stelzner, S. P. (2005). An ecological perspective on leadership theory, research, and practice. *Review of General Psychology, 9,* 326–341. (p. A-12)

Wiens, A. N., & Menustik, C. E. (1983). Treatment outcome and patient characteristics in an aversion therapy program for alcoholism. *American Psychologist, 38,* 1089–1096. (p. 665)

Wierson, M., & Forehand, R. (1994). Parent behavioral training for child noncompliance: Rationale, concepts, and effectiveness. *Current Directions in Psychological Science, 3,* 146–149. (p. 298)

Wierzbicki, M. (1993). Psychological adjustment of adoptees: A meta-analysis. *Journal of Clinical Child Psychology, 22,* 447–454. (p. 139)

Wiesel, T. N. (1982). Postnatal development of the visual cortex and the influence of environment. *Nature, 299,* 583–591. (pp. 153, 254)

Wiesner, W. H., & Cronshow, S. P. (1988). A meta-analytic investigation of the impact of interview format and degree of structure on the validity of the employment interview. *Journal of Occupational Psychology, 61,* 275–290. (p. A-6)

Wigdor, A. K., & Garner, W. R. (1982). *Ability testing: Uses, consequences, and controversies.* Washington, DC: National Academy Press. (p. 413)

Wike, R., & Grim, B. J. (2007, October 30). *Widespread negativity: Muslims distrust Westerners more than vice versa.* Pew Research Center (www.pewresearch.org). (p. 538)

Wilcox, A. J., Baird, D. D., Dunson, D. B., McConnaughey, D. R., Kesner, J. S., & Weinberg, C. R. (2004). On the frequency of intercourse around ovulation: Evidence for biological influences. *Human Reproduction, 19,* 1539–1543. (p. 434)

Wilcox, W. B., & Marquardt, E. (2011, December). *When baby makes three: How parenthood makes life meaningful and how marriage makes parenthood bearable.* Charlottesville, VA: National Marriage Project, University of Virginia. (p. 198)

Wilder, D. A. (1981). Perceiving persons as a group: Categorization and intergroup relations. In D. L. Hamilton (Ed.), *Cognitive processes in stereotyping and intergroup behavior.* Hillsdale, NJ: Erlbaum. (p. 542)

Wildman, D. E., Uddin, M., Liu, G., Grossman, L. I., & Goodman, M. (2003). Implications of natural selection in shaping 99.4% nonsynonymous DNA identity between humans and chimpanzees: Enlarging genus Homo. *Proceedings of the National Academy of Sciences, 100,* 7181–7188. (p. 135)

Wiley, J., & Jarosz, A. F. (2012). Working memory capacity, attentional focus, and problem solving. *Current Directions in Psychological Science, 21,* 258–262. (p. 324)

Wilford, J. N. (1999, February 9). New findings help balance the cosmological books. *New York Times* (www.nytimes.com). (p. 173)

Wilkinson, P., & Goodyer, I. (2011). Non-suicidal self-injury. *European Child & Adolescent Psychiatry, 20,* 103–108. (p. 639)

Wilkinson, R., & Pickett, K. (2009). *The spirit level: Why greater equality makes societies stronger.* London: Bloomsbury Press. (pp. 484, 547)

Wilkowski, B. M., Robinson, M. D., & Troop-Gordon, W. (2011). How does cognitive control reduce anger and aggression? The role of conflict monitoring and forgiveness processes. *Journal of Personality and Social Psychology, 98,* 830–840. (p. 545)

Williams, C. L., & Berry, J. W. (1991). Primary prevention of acculturative stress among refugees. *American Psychologist, 46,* 632–641. (p. 490)

Williams, E. F., Dunning, D., & Kruger, J. (2013). The hobgoblin of consistency: Algorithmic judgment strategies underlie inflated self-assessments of performance. *Journal of Personality and Social Psychology, 104,* 976–994. (p. 601)

Williams, J. E., & Best, D. L. (1990). *Measuring sex stereotypes: A multination study.* Newbury Park, CA: Sage. (p. 162)

Williams, J. E., Paton, C. C., Siegler, I. C., Eigenbrodt, M. L., Nieto, F. J., & Tyroler, H. A. (2000). Anger proneness predicts coronary heart disease risk: Prospective analysis from the artherosclerosis risk in communities (ARIC) study. *Circulation, 101*(17), 2034–2040. (p. 497)

Williams, K. D. (2007). Ostracism. *Annual Review of Psychology, 58,* 425–452. (pp. 450, 451)

Williams, K. D. (2009). Ostracism: A temporal need-threat model. *Advances in Experimental Social Psychology, 41,* 275–313. (p. 450)

Williams, L. A., & DeSteno, D. (2009). Adaptive social emotion or seventh sin? *Psychological Science, 20,* 284–288. (p. 603)

Williams, L. E., & Bargh, J. A. (2008). Experiencing physical warmth promotes interpersonal warmth. *Science, 322,* 606–607. (p. 270)

Williams, N. M., et al. (2010). Rare chromosomal deletions and duplications in attention-deficit hyperactivity disorder: A genome-wide analysis. *Lancet, 376,* 1401–1408. (p. 615)

Williams, S. L. (1987). *Self-efficacy and mastery-oriented treatment for severe phobias.* Paper presented to the American Psychological Association convention. (p. 664)

Willingham, D. T. (2010, Summer). Have technology and multitasking rewired how students learn? *American Educator,* pp. 23–28, 42. (pp. 324, 454)

Willingham, W. W., Lewis, C., Morgan, R., & Ramist, L. (1990). *Predicting college grades: An analysis of institutional trends over two decades.* Princeton, NJ: Educational Testing Service. (p. 398)

Willis, J., & Todorov, A. (2006). First impressions: Making up your mind after a 100-ms. exposure to a face. *Psychological Science, 17,* 592–598. (p. 469)

Willis, S. L., Tennstedt, S. L., Marsiske, M., Ball, K., Elias, J., Koepke, K. M., . . . Wright, E. (2006). Long-term effects of cognitive training on everyday functional outcomes in older adults. *JAMA, 296,* 2805–2814. (p. 218)

Willmuth, M. E. (1987). Sexuality after spinal cord injury: A critical review. *Clinical Psychology Review, 7,* 389–412. (p. 438)

Wilmot, E. G., Edwardson, C. L., Achana, F. A., Davies, M. J., Gorely, T., Gray, L. J., . . . Biddle, S. J. H. (2012). Sedentary time in adults and the association with diabetes, cardiovascular disease and death: Systematic review and meta-analysis. *Diabetologia, 55,* 2895–2905. (p. 507)

Wilson, A. E., & Ross, M. (2001). From chump to champ: People's appraisals of their earlier and present selves. *Journal of Personality and Social Psychology, 80,* 572–584. (p. 604)

Wilson, G. D., & Rahman, Q. (2005). *Born Gay: The biology of sex orientation.* London: Peter Owen Publishers. (p. 444)

Wilson, R. E., Gosling, S. D., & Graham, L. T. (2012). A review of Facebook research in the social sciences. *Perspectives on Psychological Science, 7,* 203–220. (p. 211)

Wilson, R. S. (1979). Analysis of longitudinal twin data: Basic model and applications to physical growth measures. *Acta Geneticae Medicae et Gemellologiae, 28,* 93–105. (p. 185)

Wilson, R. S., Arnold, S. E., Schneider, J. A., Tang, Y., & Bennett, D. A. (2007). The relationship between cerebral Alzheimer's disease pathology and odour identification in old age. *Journal of Neurology, Neurosurgery, and Psychiatry, 78,* 30–35. (p. 219)

Wilson, R. S., Beck, T. L., Bienias, J. L., & Bennett, D. A. (2007). Terminal cognitive decline: Accelerated loss of cognition in the last years of life. *Psychosomatic Medicine, 69,* 131–137. (p. 218)

Wilson, R. S., & Matheny, A. P., Jr. (1986). Behavior-genetics research in infant temperament: The Louisville twin study. In R. Plomin & J. Dunn (Eds.), *The study of temperament: Changes, continuities, and challenges.* Hillsdale, NJ: Erlbaum. (p. 140)

Wilson, S., Miller, G., & Horwitz, S. (2013, April 23). Boston bombing suspect cites U.S. wars as motivation, officials say. *Washington Post* (www.washingtonpost.com). (p. 535)

Wilson, T. D. (2002). *Strangers to ourselves: Discovering the adaptive unconscious.* Cambridge, MA: Harvard University Press. (p. 96)

Wilson, T. D. (2006). The power of social psychological interventions. *Science, 313,* 1251–1252. (p. 415)

Wilson, W. A., & Kuhn, C. M. (2005). How addiction hijacks our reward system. *Cerebrum, 7*(2), 53–66. (p. 127)

Windholz, G. (1989, April-June). The discovery of the principles of reinforcement, extinction, generalization, and differentiation of conditional reflexes in Pavlov's laboratories. *Pavlovian Journal of Biological Science, 26,* 64–74. (p. 286)

Windholz, G. (1997). Ivan P. Pavlov: An overview of his life and psychological work. *American Psychologist, 52,* 941–946. (p. 284)

Windle, G., Hughes, D., Linck, P., Russell, I., & Woods, B. (2010). Is exercise effective in promoting mental well-being in older age? A systematic review. *Aging and Mental Health, 14,* 652–669. (p. 508)

Wingfield, A., McCoy, S. L., Peelle, J. E., Tun, P. A., & Cox, L. C. (2005). Effects of adult aging and hearing loss on comprehension of rapid speech varying in syntactic complexity. *Journal of the American Academy of Audiology, 17,* 487–497. (p. 375)

Winkler, A., Dörsing, B., Rief, W., Shen, Y., & Glombiewski, J. A. (2013). Treatment of Internet addiction: A meta-analysis. *Clinical Psychology Review, 33,* 317–329. (p. 118)

Winner, E. (2000). The origins and ends of giftedness. *American Psychologist, 55,* 159–169. (p. 404)

Winter, W. C., Hammond, W. R., Green, N. H., Zhang, Z., & Bilwise, D. L. (2009). Measuring circadian advantage in major league baseball: A 10-year retrospective study. *International Journal of Sports Physiology and Performance, 4,* 394–401. (p. 104)

Wirth, J. H., Sacco, D. F., Hugenberg, K., & Williams, K. D. (2010). Eye gaze as relational evaluation: Averted eye gaze leads to feelings of ostracism and relational devaluation. *Personality and Social Psychology Bulletin, 36,* 869–882. (p. 450)

Wirz-Justice, A. (2009). From the basic neuroscience of circadian clock function to light therapy for depression: On the emergence of chronotherapeutics. *Journal of Affective Disorders, 116,* 159–160. (pp. 104, 678)

Wiseman, R., & Greening, E. (2002). The Mind Machine: A mass participation experiment into the possible existence of extra-sensory perception. *British Journal of Psychology, 93,* 487–499. (p. 274)

Witek-Janusek, L., Albuquerque, K., Chroniak, K. R., Chroniak, C., Durazo, R., & Mathews, H. L. (2008). Effect of mindfulness based stress reduction on immune function, quality of life and coping in women newly diagnosed with early stage breast cancer. *Brain Behavior and Immunity, 22*(6), 969–981. (p. 510)

Witelson, S. F., Kigar, D. L., & Harvey, T. (1999). The exceptional brain of Albert Einstein. *Lancet, 353,* 2149–2153. (p. 80)

Witt, J. K., & Brockmole, J. R. (2012). Action alters object identification: Wielding a gun increases the bias to see guns. *Journal of Experimental Psychology: Human Perception and Performance, 38,* 1159–1167. (p. 237)

Witt, J. K., Linkenauger, S. A., & Proffitt, D. R. (2012). Get me out of this slump! Visual illusions improve sports performance. *Psychological Science, 23,* 397–399. (p. 238)

Witt, J. K., & Proffitt, D. R. (2005). See the ball, hit the ball: Apparent ball size is correlated with batting average. *Psychological Science, 16,* 937–938. (p. 238)

Wittgenstein, L. (1922). *Tractatus logico-philosophicus.* New York: Harcourt, Brace. (p. 173)

Witvliet, C. V. O., & Vrana, S. R. (1995). Psychophysiological responses as indices of affective dimensions. *Psychophysiology, 32,* 436–443. (p. 466)

Wixted, J. T., & Ebbesen, E. B. (1991). On the form of forgetting. *Psychological Science, 2,* 409–415. (p. 340)

Wolff, J. J., et al. (2012). Differences in white matter fiber tract development present from 6 to 24 months in infants with autism. *American Journal of Psychiatry, 169,* 589–600. (p. 194)

Wolfson, A. R., & Carskadon, M. A. (1998). Sleep schedules and daytime functioning in adolescents. *Child Development, 69,* 875–887. (p. 114)

Wolke, D., Copeland, W. E., Angold, A., & Costello, E. J. (2013). Impact of bullying in childhood on adult health, wealth, crime, and social outcomes. *Psychological Science, 24,* 1958–1970. (p. 200)

Wollmer, M. A., et al. (2012). Facing depression with botulinum toxin: A randomized controlled trial. *Journal of Psychiatric Research, 46,* 574–581. (p. 474)

Wolpe, J. (1958). *Psychotherapy by reciprocal inhibition.* Stanford, CA: Stanford University Press. (p. 664)

Wolpe, J., & Plaud, J. J. (1997). Pavlov's contributions to behavior therapy: The obvious and the not so obvious. *American Psychologist, 52*, 966–972. (p. 664)

Wonderlich, S. A., Joiner, T. E., Jr., Keel, P. K., Williamson, D. A., & Crosby, R. D. (2007). Eating disorder diagnoses: Empirical approaches to classification. *American Psychologist, 62*, 167–180. (p. 652)

Wong, D. F., Wagner, H. N., Tune, L. E., Dannals, R. F., et al. (1986). Positron emission tomography reveals elevated D_2 dopamine receptors in drug-naive schizophrenics. *Science, 234*, 1588–1593. (p. 642)

Wong, M. M., & Csikszentmihalyi, M. (1991). Affiliation motivation and daily experience: Some issues on gender differences. *Journal of Personality and Social Psychology, 60*, 154–164. (p. 163)

Wood, C. J, & Aggleton, J. P. (1989). Handedness in 'fast ball' sports: Do left-handers have an innate advantage? *British Journal of Psychology, 80*, 227–240. (p. 86)

Wood, W. (1987). Meta-analytic review of sex differences in group performance. *Psychological Bulletin, 102*, 53–71. (p. 163)

Wood, W., & Eagly, A. H. (2002). A cross-cultural analysis of the behavior of women and men: Implications for the origins of sex differences. *Psychological Bulletin, 128*, 699–727. (p. 162)

Wood, W., & Eagly, A. H. (2007). Social structural origins of sex differences in human mating. In S. W. Gagestad & J. A. Simpson (Eds.), *The evolution of mind: Fundamental questions and controversies.* New York: Guilford Press. (p. 162)

Wood, W., Labrecque, J. S., Lin, P-T., & Rúnger, D. (2014). Habits in dual process models. In J. Sherman, B. Gawronski, & Y. Trope (Eds.), *Dual process theories of the social mind.* New York: Guilford Press. (p. 280)

Wood, W., Lundgren, S., Ouellette, J. A., Busceme, S., & Blackstone, T. (1994). Minority influence: A meta-analytic review of social influence processes. *Psychological Bulletin, 115*, 323–345. (p. 536)

Wood, J. M. (2003, May 19). Quoted by R. Mestel, Rorschach tested: Blot out the famous method? Some experts say it has no place in psychiatry. *Los Angeles Times* (www.latimes.com). (p. 579)

Wood, J. M. (2006, Spring). The controversy over Exner's Comprehensive System for the Rorschach: The critics speak. *Independent Practitioner* (works.bepress.com/james_wood/7). (p. 579)

Wood, J. M., Bootzin, R. R., Kihlstrom, J. F., & Schacter, D. L. (1992). Implicit and explicit memory for verbal information presented during sleep. *Psychological Science, 3*, 236–239. (p. 342)

Wood, J. M., Lilienfeld, S. O., Nezworski, M. T., Garb, H. N., Allen, K. H., & Wildermuth, J. L. (2010). Validity of Rorschach inkblot scores for discriminating psychopaths from nonpsychopaths in forensic populations: A meta-analysis. *Psychological Assessment, 22*, 336–349. (p. 579)

Wood, J. M., Nezworski, M. T., Garb, H. N., & Lilienfeld, S. O. (2006). The controversy over the Exner Comprehensive System and the Society for Personality Assessment's white paper on the Rorschach. *Independent Practitioner, 26.* (p. 579)

Wood, J. V., Heimpel, S. A., Manwell, L. A., & Whittington, E. J. (2009). This mood is familiar and I don't deserve to feel better anyway: Mechanisms underlying self-esteem differences in motivation to repair sad moods. *Journal of Personality and Social Psychology, 96*, 363–380. (p. 599)

Wood, J. V., Saltzberg, J. A., & Goldsamt, L. A. (1990a). Does affect induce self-focused attention? *Journal of Personality and Social Psychology, 58*, 899–908. (p. 635)

Wood, J. V., Saltzberg, J. A., Neale, J. M., Stone, A. A., & Rachmiel, T. B. (1990b). Self-focused attention, coping responses, and distressed mood in everyday life. *Journal of Personality and Social Psychology, 58*, 1027–1036. (p. 635)

Woods, N. F., Dery, G. K., & Most, A. (1983). Recollections of menarche, current menstrual attitudes, and premenstrual symptoms. In S. Golub (Ed.), *Menarche: The transition from girl to woman.* Lexington, MA: Lexington Books. (p. 167)

Woolcock, N. (2004, September 3). Driver thought everyone else was on wrong side. *The Times*, p. 22. (p. 527)

Woolett, K., & Maguire, E. A. (2011). Acquiring "the knowledge" of London's layout drives structural brain changes. *Current Biology, 21*, 2109–2114. (p. 329)

Woolley, A. W., Chabris, C. F., Pentland, A., Hasmi, N., & Malone, T. W. (2010). Evidence for a collective intelligence factor in the performance of human groups. *Science, 330*, 686–688. (p. A-12)

World Federation for Mental Health. (2005). ADHD: The hope behind the hype (www.wfmh.org). (p. 615)

World Health Organization. (2004a). Prevalence, severity, and unmet need for treatment of mental disorders in the World Health Organization World Mental Health Surveys. *Journal of the American Medical Association, 291*, 2581–2590. (p. 617)

World Health Organization. (2008). The numbers count: Mental disorders in America (www.nimh.nih.gov). (p. 118)

World Health Organization. (2013). The top 10 causes of death. Retrieved April 11, 2014 from http://www.who.int/mediacentre/factsheets/fs310/en/. (p. 495)

Worobey, J., & Blajda, V. M. (1989). Temperament ratings at 2 weeks, 2 months, and 1 year: Differential stability of activity and emotionality. *Developmental Psychology, 25*, 257–263. (p. 140)

Wortham, J. (2010, May 13). Cellphones now used more for data than for calls. *New York Times* (www.nytimes.com). (p. 452)

Worthington, E. L., Jr., Kurusu, T. A., McCulloh, M. E., & Sandage, S. J. (1996). Empirical research on religion and psychotherapeutic processes and outcomes: A 10-year review and research prospectus. *Psychological Bulletin, 119*, 448–487. (p. 680)

Wortman, C. B., & Silver, R. C. (1989). The myths of coping with loss. *Journal of Consulting and Clinical Psychology, 57*, 349–357. (p. 225)

Wren, C. S. (1999, April 8). Drug survey of children finds middle school a pivotal time. *New York Times* (www.nytimes.com). (p. 129)

Wrenn, J. M. (2012). NBA rookie Royce White battles anxiety disorder and fear of flying. CNN (www.cnn.com). (p. 623)

Wright, I. C., Rabe-Hesketh, S., Woodruff, P. W. R., David, A. S., Murray, R. M., & Bullmore, E. T. (2000). Meta-analysis of regional brain volumes in schizophrenia. *American Journal of Psychiatry, 157*, 16–25. (p. 642)

Wright, J. (2006, March 16). Boomers in the bedroom: Sexual attitudes and behaviours in the boomer generation. Ipsos Reid survey (www.ipsos-na.com). (p. 214)

Wright, P., Takei, N., Rifkin, L., & Murray, R. M. (1995). Maternal influenza, obstetric complications, and schizophrenia. *American Journal of Psychiatry, 152*, 1714–1720. (p. 643)

Wright, P. H. (1989). Gender differences in adults' same- and cross-gender friendships. In R. G. Adams & R. Blieszner (Eds.), *Older adult friendships: Structure and process.* Newbury Park, CA: Sage. (p. 163)

Wrosch, C., & Miller, G. E. (2009). Depressive symptoms can be useful: Self-regulatory and emotional benefits of dysphoric mood in adolescence. *Journal of Personality and Social Psychology, 96*, 1181–1190. (p. 628)

Wrzesniewski, A., McCauley, C. R., Rozin, P., & Schwartz, B. (1997). Jobs, careers, and callings: People's relations to their work. *Journal of Research in Personality, 31*, 21–33. (p. A-1)

Wrzesniewski, A., Schwartz, B., Cong, X., Kane, M., Omar, A., & Kolditz, T. (2014). Multiple types of motives don't multiply the motivation of West Point cadets. *PNAS, 111*, 10990–10995. (p. 305)

Wrzus, C., Hänel, M., Wagner, J., & Neyer, F. J. (2012). Social network changes and life events across the life span: A meta-analysis. *Psychological Bulletin, 139*, 53–80. (p. 223)

Wu, W., & Small, S. A. (2006). Imaging the earliest stages of Alzheimer's disease. *Current Alzheimer Research, 3*, 529–539. (p. 219)

Wuethrich, B. (2001, March). Features—GETTING STUPID—Surprising new neurological behavioral research reveals that teenagers who drink too much may permanently damage their brains and seriously compromise their ability to learn. *Discover, 56*, 56–64. (p. 120)

Wulsin, L. R., Vaillant, G. E., & Wells, V. E. (1999). A systematic review of the mortality of depression. *Psychosomatic Medicine, 61*, 6–17. (p. 498)

Wyatt, J. K., & Bootzin, R. R. (1994). Cognitive processing and sleep: Implications for enhancing job performance. *Human Performance, 7*, 119–139. (pp. 113, 342)

Wyatt, R. J., Henter, I., & Sherman-Elvy, E. (2001). Tantalizing clues to preventing schizophrenia. *Cerebrum: The Dana Forum on Brain Science, 3*, pp. 15–30. (p. 643)

Wynn, K. (1992). Addition and subtraction by human infants. *Nature, 358*, 749–759. (pp. 188, 189)

Wynn, K. (2000). Findings of addition and subtraction in infants are robust and consistent: Reply to Wakeley, Rivera, and Langer. *Child Development, 71*, 1535–1536. (p. 188)

Wynn, K. (2008). Some innate foundations of social and moral cognition. In K. Wynn (Ed.) *The innate mind. Volume 3: Foundations and the future*, pgs. 330–347. New York: Oxford University Press. (p. 188)

Wynne, C. D. L. (2004). *Do animals think?* Princeton, NJ: Princeton University Press. (p. 378)

Wynne, C. D. L. (2008). Aping language: A skeptical analysis of the evidence for nonhuman primate language. *Skeptic, 13*(4), 10–13. (p. 378)

Wysocki, C. J., & Gilbert, A. N. (1989). *National Geographic* Survey: Effects of age are heterogeneous. *Annals of the New York Academy of Sciences, 561*, 12–28. (pp. 267, 268)

Xie, L., et al. (2013). Sleep drives metabolite clearance from the adult brain. *Science, 342,* 373–377. (p. 105)

Xu, B., Ionita-Laza, I., Roos, J. L., Boone, B., Woodrick, S., Sun, S., Levy, S., . . . Karayiorgou, M. De novo gene mutations highlight patterns of genetic and neural complexity in schizophrenia. *Nature Genetics, 44,* 1365–1369. (p. 644)

Xu, Y., & Corkin, S. (2001). H.M. revisits the Tower of Hanoi puzzle. *Neuropsychology, 15,* 69–79. (p. 339)

Yalom, I. D. (1985). *The theory and practice of group psychotherapy* (3rd ed.). New York: Basic Books. (p. 671)

Yamagata, S., et al. (2006). Is the genetic structure of human personality universal? A cross-cultural twin study from North America, Europe, and Asia. *Journal of Personality and Social Psychology, 90,* 987–998. (p. 590)

Yang, Q., Wu, X., Zhou, X., Mead, N. L., Vohs, K. D., & Baumeister, R. F. (2013). Diverging effects of clean versus dirty money on attitudes, values, and interpersonal behavior. *Journal of Personality and Social Psychology, 104,* 473–489. (p. 280)

Yang, S., Markoczy, L., & Qi, M. (2006). Unrealistic optimism in consumer credit card adoption. *Journal of Economic Psychology, 28,* 170–185. (p. 600)

Yang, Y., Raine, A., Colletti, P., Toga, A. W., & Narr, K. L. (2010). Morphological alterations in the prefrontal cortex and the amygdala in unsuccessful psychopaths. *Journal of Abnormal Psychology, 119,* 546–554. (p. 650)

Yankelovich Partners. (1995, May/June). Growing old. *American Enterprise,* p. 108. (p. 213)

Yarkoni, T. (2010). Personality in 100,000 words: A large-scale analysis of personality and word use among bloggers. *Journal of Research in Personality, 44,* 363–373. (p. 593)

Yarnell, P. R., & Lynch, S. (1970, April 25). Retrograde memory immediately after concussion. *Lancet,* pp. 863–865. (p. 332)

Yates, A. (1989). Current perspectives on the eating disorders: I. History, psychological and biological aspects. *Journal of the American Academy of Child and Adolescent Psychiatry, 28,* 813–828. (p. 652)

Yates, A. (1990). Current perspectives on the eating disorders: II. Treatment, outcome, and research directions. *Journal of the American Academy of Child and Adolescent Psychiatry, 29,* 1–9. (p. 652)

Yates, W. R. (2000). Testosterone in psychiatry. *Archives of General Psychiatry, 57,* 155–156. (p. 434)

Ybarra, O. (1999). Misanthropic person memory when the need to self-enhance is absent. *Personality and Social Psychology Bulletin, 25,* 261–269. (p. 599)

Yeager, D. S., Johnson, R., Spitzer, B. J., Trzesniewski, K. H., Powers, J., & Dweck, C. S. (2014). The far-reaching effects of believing people can change: Implicit theories of personality shape stress, health, and achievement during adolescence. *Journal of Personality and Social Psychology, 106,* 867–884. (p. 409)

Yeager, D. S., Miu, A. S., Powers, J., & Dweck, C. S. (2013). Implicit theories of personality and attributions of hostile intent: A meta-analysis, an experiment, and a longitudinal intervention. *Child Development, 84,* 1651–1667. (p. 409)

Yerkes, R. M., & Dodson, J. D. (1908). The relation of strength of stimulus to rapidity of habit-formation. *Journal of Comparative Neurology and Psychology, 18,* 459–482. (pp. 422, 464)

Yeung, J. W. K., Chan, Y, & Lee, B. L. K. (2009). Youth religiosity and substance use: A meta-analysis from 1995 to 2007. *Psychological Reports, 105,* 255–266. (p. 129)

Yoshikawa, H., Aber, J. L., & Beardslee, W. R. (2012). The effects of poverty on the mental, emotional, and behavioral health of children and youth: Implications for prevention. *American Psychologist, 67,* 272–284. (p. 690)

YOU Magazine. (2009, September 10). Wow, look at Caster now! http://you.co.za/. (p. 167)

Young, C. B., Wu, S. S., & Menon, V. (2012). The neurodevelopmental basis of math anxiety. *Psychological Science, 23,* 492–501. (p. 71)

Young, S. G., Hugenberg, K., Bernstein, M. J., & Sacco, D. F. (2012). Perception and motivation in face recognition: A critical review of theories of the cross-race effect. *Personality and Social Psychology Review, 16,* 116–142. (p. 544)

Young, S. M., & Pinsky, D. (2006). Narcissism and celebrity. *Journal of Personality, 40,* 463–471. (p. 604)

Youngentob, S. L., & Glendinning, J. I. (2009). Fetal ethanol exposure increases ethanol intake by making it smell and taste better. *PNAS, 106,* 5359. (p. 182)

Youngentob, S. L., Kent, P. F., Sheehe, P. R., Molina, J. C., Spear, N. E., & Youngentob, L. M. (2007). Experience-induced fetal plasticity: The effect of gestational ethanol exposure on the behavioral and neurophysiologic olfactory response to ethanol odor in early postnatal and adult rats. *Behavioral Neuroscience, 121,* 1293–1305. (p. 182)

Younger, J., Aron, A., Parke, S., Chatterjee, N., & Mackey, S. (2010) Viewing Pictures of a Romantic Partner Reduces Experimental Pain: Involvement of Neural Reward Systems. *PLoS ONE* 5(10): e13309. doi:10.1371/journal.pone.0013309. (p. 449)

Yücel, M., Solowij, N., Respondek, C., Whittle, S., Fornito, A., Pantelis, C., & Lubman, D. I. (2008). Regional brain abnormalities associated with long-term cannabis use. *Archives of General Psychiatry, 65,* 694–701. (p. 125)

Yuki, M., Maddux, W. W., & Masuda. T. (2007). Are the windows to the soul the same in the East and West? Cultural differences in using the eyes and mouth as cues to recognize emotions in Japan and the United States. *Journal of Experimental Social Psychology, 43,* 303–311. (p. 474)

Zaccaro, S. J. (2007). Trait-based perspectives of leadership. *American Psychologist, 62,* 6–16. (p. A-12)

Zagorsky, J. L. (2007). Do you have to be smart to be rich? The impact of IQ on wealth, income and financial distress. *Intelligence, 35,* 489–501. (p. 389)

Zajonc, R. B. (1965). Social facilitation. *Science, 149,* 269–274. (p. 532)

Zajonc, R. B. (1980). Feeling and thinking: Preferences need no inferences. *American Psychologist, 35,* 151–175. (p. 462)

Zajonc, R. B. (1984a). On the primacy of affect. *American Psychologist, 39,* 117–123. (p. 462)

Zajonc, R. B. (1984b, July 22). Quoted by D. Goleman, Rethinking IQ tests and their value. *The New York Times,* p. D22. (p. 394)

Zajonc, R. B. (1998). Emotions. In D. Gilbert, S. T. Fiske, & G. Lindzey (Eds.), *Handbook of social psychology* (4th ed.). New York: McGraw-Hill. (p. 552)

Zajonc, R. B. (2001). Mere exposure: A gateway to the subliminal. *Current Directions in Psychological Science, 10,* 224–228. (p. 551)

Zajonc, R. B., & Markus, G. B. (1975). Birth order and intellectual development. *Psychological Review, 82,* 74–88. (p. 47)

Zak, P. J. (2012). *The moral molecule: The source of love and prosperity.* New York: Dutton. (p. 64)

Zalta, A. K. (2011). A meta-analysis of anxiety symptom prevention with cognitive-behavioral interventions. *Journal of Anxiety Disorders, 25*(5), 749–760. (p. 670)

Zatorre, R. J., & Salimpoor, V. N. (2013, June 7). Why music makes our brain sing. *New York Times* (www.nytimes.com). (p. 73)

Zauberman, G., & Lynch, J. G., Jr. (2005). Resource slack and propensity to discount delayed investments of time versus money. *Journal of Experimental Psychology: General, 134,* 23–37. (p. 361)

Zaval, L., Keenan, E. A., Johnson, E. J., & Weber, E. U. (2014). How warm days increase belief in global warming. *Nature Climate Change, 4,* 143–147. (p. 360)

Zeelenberg, R., Wagenmakers, E-J., & Rotteveel, M. (2006). The impact of emotion on perception. *Psychological Science, 17,* 287–291. (p. 462)

Zeidner, M. (1990). Perceptions of ethnic group modal intelligence: Reflections of cultural stereotypes or intelligence test scores? *Journal of Cross-Cultural Psychology, 21,* 214–231. (p. 411)

Zeineh, M. M., Engel, S. A., Thompson, P. M., & Bookheimer, S. Y. (2003). Dynamics of the hippocampus during encoding and retrieval of face-name pairs. *Science, 299,* 577–580. (p. 329)

Zelenski, J. M., & Nisbet, E. K. (2014). Happiness and feeling connected: The distinct role of nature relatedness. *Environmental Behavior, 46,* 3–23. (p. 454)

Zell, E., & Alicke, M. D. (2010). The local dominance effect in self-evaluation: Evidence and explanations. *Personality and Social Psychology Review, 14,* 368–384. (p. 484)

Zhang, J., Fang, L., Yow-Wu, B. W., & Wieczorek, W. F. (2013). Depression, anxiety, and suicidal ideation among Chinese Americans: A study of immigration-related factors. *The Journal of Nervous and Mental Disease, 201,* 17–22. (p. 632)

Zhong, C-B., Dijksterhuis, A., & Galinsky, A. D. (2008). The merits of unconscious thought in creativity. *Psychological Science, 19,* 912–918. (p. 366)

Zhong, C-B., & Leonardelli, G. J. (2008). Cold and lonely: Does social exclusion literally feel cold? *Psychological Science, 19,* 838–842. (p. 270)

Zhu, W. X., Lu, L., & Hesketh, T. (2009). China's excess males, sex selective abortion, and one child policy: Analysis of data from 2005 national intercensus survey. *British Medical Journal (BMJ), 338,* b1211. (p. 540)

Zilbergeld, B. (1983). *The shrinking of America: Myths of psychological change.* Boston: Little, Brown. (p. 673)

Zillmann, D. (1986). Effects of prolonged consumption of pornography. Background paper for *The surgeon general's workshop on pornography and public health,* June 22–24. Report prepared by E. P. Mulvey & J. L. Haugaard and released by Office of the Surgeon General on August 4, 1986. (p. 461)

Zillmann, D. (1989). Effects of prolonged consumption of pornography. In D. Zillmann & J. Bryant (Eds.), *Pornography: Research advances and policy considerations*. Hillsdale, NJ: Erlbaum. (p. 438)

Zillmann, D., & Bryant, J. (1984). Effects of massive exposure to pornography. In N. Malamuth & E. Donnerstein (Eds.), *Pornography and sexual aggression*. Orlando, FL: Academic Press. (p. 547)

Zimbardo, P. G. (1970). The human choice: Individuation, reason, and order versus deindividuation, impulse, and chaos. In W. J. Arnold & D. Levine (Eds.), *Nebraska Symposium on Motivation, 1969*. Lincoln, NE: University of Nebraska Press. (p. 533)

Zimbardo, P. G. (1972, April). Pathology of imprisonment. *Transaction/Society*, pp. 4–8. (p. 522)

Zimbardo, P. G. (2001, September 16). Fighting terrorism by understanding man's capacity for evil. Op-ed essay distributed by spsp-discuss@stolaf.edu. (p. 542)

Zimbardo, P. G. (2004, May 25). *Journalist interview re: Abu Ghraib prison abuses: Eleven answers to eleven questions*. Unpublished manuscript, Stanford University. (p. 522)

Zimbardo, P. G. (2007, September). Person × situation × system dynamics. *The Observer* (Association for Psychological Science), p. 43. (pp. 522, 523)

Zimmermann, T. D., & Meier, B. (2006). The rise and decline of prospective memory performance across the lifespan. *Quarterly Journal of Experimental Psychology, 59*, 2040–2046. (p. 217)

Zogby, J. (2006, March). Survey of teens and adults about the use of personal electronic devices and head phones. *Zogby International*. (p. 257)

Zou, Z., Li, F., & Buck, L. B. (2005). From the cover: Odor maps in the olfactory cortex. *Proceedings of the National Academy of Sciences, 102*, 7724–7729. (p. 267)

Zubieta, J-K., Bueller, J. A., Jackson, L. R., Scott, D. J., Xu, Y., Koeppe, R. A., Nichols, T E., & Stohler, C. S. (2005). Placebo effects mediated by endogenous opioid activity on μ-opioid receptors. *Journal of Neuroscience, 25*, 7754–7762. (p. 264)

Zubieta, J-K., Heitzeg, M. M., Smith, Y. R., Bueller, J. A., Xu, K., Xu, Y., . . . Goldman, D. (2003). COMT val158met genotype affects μ-opioid neurotransmitter responses to a pain stressor. *Science, 299*, 1240–1243. (p. 264)

Zucco, G. M. (2003). Anomalies in cognition: Olfactory memory. *European Psychologist, 8*, 77–86. (p. 267)

Zucker, G. S., & Weiner, B. (1993). Conservatism and perceptions of poverty: An attributional analysis. *Journal of Applied Social Psychology, 23*, 925–943. (p. 519)

Zuckerman, M. (1979). *Sensation seeking: Beyond the optimal level of arousal*. Hillsdale, NJ: Erlbaum. (p. 422)

Zuckerman, M. (2009). Sensation seeking. In M. Zuckerman (Ed.), *Handbook of individual differences in social behavior*. New York: Guilford Press. (p. 422)

Zuger, A. (2013, July 29). Guides to a journey into the brain. *New York Times* (www.nytimes.com). (p. 124)

Zvolensky, M. J., & Bernstein, A. (2005). Cigarette smoking and panic psychopathology. *Current Directions in Psychological Science, 14*, 301–305. (p. 621)

Name Index

Subject Index

The Story of Psychology: A Timeline (continued from inside front cover)

1949 In *The Organization of Behavior: A Neuropsychological Theory,* Canadian psychologist Donald O. Hebb outlines a new and influential conceptualization of how the nervous system functions.

1950 Solomon Asch publishes studies of effects of conformity on judgments of line length.

In *Childhood and Society,* Erik Erikson outlines his stages of psychosocial development.

1951 Carl Rogers publishes *Client-Centered Therapy.*

1952 The American Psychiatric Association publishes the *Diagnostic and Statistical Manual of Mental Disorders,* an influential book that will be updated periodically.

1953 Eugene Aserinski and Nathaniel Kleitman describe rapid eye movements (REM) that occur during sleep.

Janet Taylor's Manifest Anxiety Scale appears in the *Journal of Abnormal Psychology.*

1954 In *Motivation and Personality,* Abraham Maslow proposes a hierarchy of motives ranging from physiological needs to self-actualization. (Maslow later updates the hierarchy to include self-transcendence needs.)

James Olds and Peter Milner, McGill University neuropsychologists, describe rewarding effects of electrical stimulation of the hypothalamus in rats.

Gordon Allport publishes *The Nature of Prejudice.*

1956 In his *Psychological Review* article titled "The Magical Number Seven, Plus or Minus Two: Some Limits on Our Capacity for Processing Information," George Miller coins the term *chunk* for memory researchers.

1957 Robert Sears, Eleanor Maccoby, and Harry Levin publish *Patterns of Child Rearing.*

Charles Ferster and B. F. Skinner publish *Schedules of Reinforcement.*

1958 Harry Harlow outlines "The Nature of Love," his work on attachment in monkeys.

1959 Noam Chomsky's critical review of B. F. Skinner's *Verbal Behavior* appears in the journal *Language.*

Eleanor Gibson and Richard Walk report their research on infants' depth perception in "The Visual Cliff."

Lloyd Peterson and Margaret Peterson in the *Journal of Experimental Psychology* article, "Short-Term Retention of Individual Verbal Items," highlight the importance of rehearsal in memory.

John Thibaut and Harold Kelley publish *The Social Psychology of Groups.*

1969 In his APA presidential address, "Psychology as a Means of Promoting Human Welfare," George Miller emphasizes the importance of "giving psychology away."

1971 Kenneth B. Clark becomes the first African-American president of the American Psychological Association.

Albert Bandura publishes *Social Learning Theory.*

Allan Paivio publishes *Imagery and Verbal Processes.*

B. F. Skinner publishes *Beyond Freedom and Dignity.*

1972 Elliot Aronson publishes *The Social Animal.*

Fergus Craik and Robert Lockhart's "'Levels of Processing: A Framework for Memory Research" appears in the *Journal of Verbal Learning and Verbal Behavior.*

Robert Rescorla and Allan Wagner publish their associative model of Pavlovian conditioning.

Under the leadership of Derald Sue and Stanley Sue, the Asian American Psychological Association is founded.

1973 Ethologists Karl von Frisch, Konrad Lorenz, and Nikolaas Tinbergen receive the Nobel Prize for their research on animal behavior.

1974 APA's Division 2 first publishes its journal, *Teaching of Psychology,* with Robert S. Daniel as editor.

Eleanor Maccoby and Carol Jacklin publish *The Psychology of Sex Differences.*

1975 Biologist Edward O. Wilson's *Sociobiology* appears; it will be a controversial precursor to evolutionary psychology.

1976 Sandra Wood Scarr and Richard A. Weinberg publish "IQ Test Performance of Black Children Adopted by White Families" in *American Psychologist.*

1978 Psychologist Herbert A. Simon, Carnegie-Mellon University, wins a Nobel Prize for pioneering research on computer simulations of human thinking and problem solving.

1979 James J. Gibson publishes *The Ecological Approach to Visual Perception.*

Elizabeth Loftus publishes *Eyewitness Testimony.*

1981 David Hubel and Torsten Wiesel receive a Nobel Prize for research on single-cell recordings that identified feature detector cells in the visual cortex.

Roger Sperry receives a Nobel Prize for research on split-brain patients.

Paleontologist Stephen Jay Gould publishes *The Mismeasure of Man,* highlighting the debate concerning biological determination of intelligence.